GREAT BOOKS OF THE WESTERN WORLD

GREAT BOOKS
OF THE WESTERN WORLD

ROBERT MAYNARD HUTCHINS, *EDITOR IN CHIEF*

2.

THE GREAT IDEAS: I

GREAT BOOKS
OF THE WESTERN WORLD

ROBERT MAYNARD HUTCHINS, EDITOR IN CHIEF

2

THE GREAT IDEAS: I

MORTIMER J. ADLER, Associate Editor

Members of the Advisory Board: STRINGFELLOW BARR, SCOTT BUCHANAN, JOHN ERSKINE,
CLARENCE H. FAUST, ALEXANDER MEIKLEJOHN, JOSEPH J. SCHWAB, MARK VAN DOREN.
Editorial Consultants: A. F. B. CLARK, F. L. LUCAS, WALTER MURDOCH.
WALLACE BROCKWAY, Executive Editor

THE GREAT IDEAS

A Syntopicon of
Great Books of the Western World

MORTIMER J. ADLER, *Editor in Chief*

WILLIAM GORMAN, *General Editor*

VOLUME I

WILLIAM BENTON, *Publisher*

ENCYCLOPÆDIA BRITANNICA, INC.

CHICAGO · LONDON · TORONTO

GENERAL CONTENTS

VOLUME I

VOLUME II

GENERAL CONTENTS

VOLUME I

VOLUME II

CONTENTS

CONTENTS

PREFACE

I. THE NATURE OF THE SYNTOPICON

BY calling this work "a Syntopicon of *Great Books of the Western World*," the editors hope to characterize its nature, to indicate the function it performs in relation to the set as a whole, and to assert its originality as an intellectual instrument. The relation of these two volumes of *The Great Ideas* to the rest of the set is the key to the nature of the Syntopicon and its originality as an instrument. Apart from this relation, *The Great Ideas*, though to some extent readable in itself, does not perform the function for which it was created—to show that the 443 works which comprise Volumes 4 to 54 can be seen and used as something more than a collection of books.

The great books are pre-eminently those which have given the western tradition its life and light. The unity of this set of books does not consist merely in the fact that each member of it is a great book worth reading. A deeper unity exists in the relation of all the books to one tradition, a unity shown by the continuity of the discussion of common themes and problems. It is claimed for this set of great books that all the works in it are significantly related to one another and that, taken together, they adequately present the ideas and issues, the terms and topics, that have made the western tradition what it is. More than a collection of books, then, this set is a certain kind of whole that can and should be read as such.

The Great Ideas results from and records such a reading of the great books. The aim of this "syntopical reading" was to discover the unity and continuity of western thought in the discussion of common themes and problems from one end of the tradition to the other. The Syntopicon does not reproduce or present the results of this reading in a digest to save others the trouble of reading the great books for themselves. On the contrary, it only lays down the lines along which a syntopical reading of the great books can be done, and shows why and how it should be done. The various uses of the Syntopicon, described in Section III of this Preface, all derive from its primary purpose—to serve as a guide to the reading of *Great Books of the Western World* as a unified whole.

The lines along which a syntopical reading of the great books can and should be done are the main lines of the continuous discussion that runs through the thirty centuries of western civilization. This great conversation across the ages is a living organism whose structure the Syntopicon tries to articulate. It tries to show the many strands of this conversation between the greatest minds of western civilization on the themes which have concerned men in every epoch, and which cover the whole range of man's speculative inquiries and practical interests. To the extent that it succeeds, it reveals the unity and continuity of the western tradition.

It was with these considerations in mind that the editors called *The Great Ideas* a syntopicon of the great books—literally, a collection of the topics which are the main themes of the conversation to be found in the books. A topic is a subject of discussion. It is a place at which minds meet —to agree or disagree, but at least to communicate with one another about some common concern. Just as a number of minds, or what they have to say, can be related by their relevance to a common theme, so a number of topics can be related by their relevance to a common term—a single concept or category which generates a number of problems or themes for discussion. Hence the Syntopicon is organized, first, by a listing of the ideas that are the important common terms of discussion; and, then, by an enumeration of the topics that are the various particular points about which the discussion of each of these ideas revolves.

The full title of this work—*The Great Ideas, a Syntopicon of Great Books of the Western World*—thus indicates not only that its structure consists of terms and topics, but also that it functions as a guide to the great books from which its terms and topics are drawn. But the title may fail to indicate another equally important function which the Syntopicon performs when it is taken together with the great books. By serving as a guide to the syntopical reading of the great books, it does more than transform them from a mere collection of books into a unified whole; it transforms them into a new kind of encyclopaedic whole—a new kind of reference library. Without in any way interfering with all the values the great books have as books to be read individually, the Syntopicon gives them the further utility of a unified reference library in the realm of thought and opinion.

Because of the traditional and proved importance of the thought and opinion contained in the great books, the Syntopicon, in the editors' opinion, creates an intellectual instrument which is comparable to, though quite distinct from, the dictionary and the encyclopaedia. The dictionary is a basic reference work in the sphere of language. The general encyclopaedia is a basic reference work in the sphere of fact, concerned with all matters ascertainable in the present state of historical and scientific knowledge. The Syntopicon—these two volumes taken together with the rest of the set—is a basic reference work in the sphere of ideas, comprehending the wisdom and understanding accumulated thus far in all major fields of inquiry. As its utility is realized, it will, the editors hope, take its place beside the dictionary and the encyclopaedia in a triad of fundamental reference works.

II. THE STRUCTURE OF THE SYNTOPICON

The Great Ideas consists of 102 chapters, each of which provides a syntopical treatment of one of the basic terms or concepts in the great books. As the Table of Contents indicates, the chapters are arranged in the alphabetical order of these 102 terms or concepts: from ANGEL to LOVE in Volume I, and from MAN to WORLD in Volume II.

Following the chapter on WORLD, there are two appendices. Appendix I is a Bibliography of Additional Readings. Appendix II is an essay on the Principles and Methods of Syntopical Construction. These two appendices are in turn followed by an Inventory of Terms.

THE 102 CHAPTERS

Each of the 102 chapters is constructed according to the same pattern. Each consists of five parts—an Introduction, an Outline of Topics, References, Cross-References, and Additional Readings. The inner structure of the Syntopicon is constituted by the order and relation of these five parts, and by the integral relation of the Inventory of Terms to the 102 chapters as a whole.

(1) *INTRODUCTION.* Each chapter begins with an essay which comments on the various meanings of the idea under consideration, and takes note of the problems it has raised and the controversies it has occasioned in the tradition of western thought.

The Introduction to a great idea is designed to serve as a guide to its topics and, through them, to the content of the references. For certain of the most important topics, it frequently provides, in the words of the authors themselves, a foretaste of the great conversation contained in the passages referred to. The Introduction usually expands on the necessarily brief statement of the themes or issues in the Outline of Topics, and furnishes some comment on the structure of the Outline as a whole, and on the relation of particular topics to one another.

The Introduction serves one other purpose. It indicates some of the connections between the idea it discusses and other great ideas, thus functioning as a commentary on the Cross-References. In some cases, the Introduction also calls attention to the way in which certain works recommended in the Additional Readings supplement the references to the great books in the discussion of certain aspects of the idea under consideration.

(2) *OUTLINE OF TOPICS.* In each chapter, the Outline of Topics follows the Introduction. It states the major themes of the conversation to be found in the great books on the idea of that chapter. It exhibits the internal structure of the idea by presenting its topics in relation to one another. There are about 3000 topics in the Syntopicon as a whole, an average of 30 to a chapter, though the actual number varies from as few as six topics in a chapter to as many as 76.

The 3000 topics provide a statement of the scope and variety of subjects with which the great books deal in a substantial and significant fashion. Since the topics are divided among 102 chapters, according to the great ideas under which they fall, the user of the Syntopicon can find a particular topic by turning to the chapter on the idea which is a central term expressed in the statement of that topic or, if not actually present in the phrasing of the topic, is implied by it.

Almost all the topics involve one or more terms other than the name of the great idea under which they fall. Hence, by consulting the Inventory of Terms, the user of the Syntopicon can ascertain whether the particular subject in which he is interested is represented by one or more of the 3000 topics. As will be seen below, the prime function of the Inventory is to enable the user of the Syntopicon to find topics in which he is interested and which he could not otherwise find except by examining the Outlines of Topics, chapter by chapter.

Since the references to the great books are organized by topics, the individual topic, rather than a great idea, is the elementary unit of the Syntopicon. From the standpoint of the references, the great ideas are collections of topics. The same is true of all the other terms listed in the Inventory of Terms. For each of these, one or more topics are the headings under which the discussion of the subject can be found in the great books. The user of the Syntopicon must, therefore, always use a topic rather than a term to discover what the great books have to say on a particular subject. However, with the help of the Inventory of Terms, he can always use a term to find the topics which either state or approximately represent the subject of his interest.

For the convenience of the reader, the Outline of Topics in each chapter is keyed to the pages of the Reference section which immediately follows. In the Outline, the number to the right of a particular topic indicates on which page of the Reference section it begins.

(3) *REFERENCES*. The References are the heart of each chapter. As the Introduction and the Outline of Topics are designed to help the reader use the References, so the References, organized topically, are designed to enable him to turn to the great books for the discussion of a particular subject. For each topic they locate, by volume and page, the relevant works and passages in *Great Books of the Western World*. There are about 163,000 references in the Syntopicon as a whole, an average of 1500 to a chapter, though the actual number varies from as few as 284 references in a chapter to as many as 7065.

Under each topic, the references are arranged in the order in which the authors and their works appear in *Great Books of the Western World*. References to the Bible, when present, are always placed first. The order of references enables the user of the Syntopicon either to follow the discussion of some theme through the great books in the historical sequence, or to select particular authors or the authors of a particular period, according to his interest.

Ideally, a syntopical reading of the great books in relation to any single topic should cover all the works or passages cited under that topic. Ideally, such a reading should proceed, in the first instance at least, in the order in which the references are presented. Reading the materials in chronological order enables the reader to follow the actual development of thought on a topic. In many passages, later authors explicitly refer to earlier ones; and even more frequently, the expression of later views presupposes an understanding of earlier ones, on which they are based or with which they take issue.

But the individual reader may deviate from this ideal procedure in a number of ways, according to his particular interests. He may wish only to sample the materials referred to under a given topic; or he may wish to examine what a certain group of authors have to say on a particular topic. The reader may know sufficiently well the position of certain authors on the topic in question, and so may turn his attention to other authors whose works are cited there; or he may wish to examine thoroughly the thought of certain authors, while merely forming a general impression of what others have to say. The Reference section is so constructed that it permits the reader, almost at a glance, to follow any one of a wide variety of procedures.

A brief explanatory note, repeated at the beginning of every Reference section, gives the minimum necessary directions for going from the references to the passages to which they refer. For the sake of brevity, it offers only such information as is uniform for all of the works cited. If the reader wishes complete information concerning the way in which each particular work is cited, he will find this set forth, by authors and titles, in the Explanation of Reference Style, which immediately follows this Preface (see pg. xxxiii) and is also printed, for the reader's convenience, at the opening of Volume II. The Explanation of Reference Style contains a complete account of all the symbols and abbreviations used in the Reference section and gives examples of the usual typographical form of the references.

Only one further point requires comment here. In some chapters, a few topics contain no references. These topics serve in the Outline as headings for other topics grouped analytically under them. The user of the Syntopicon who wants to know what the great books have to say on a particular subject, and finds that subject represented by a topic without reference

content, will find in its subordinate topics references to the great books
on various aspects of the general subject he has in mind.

(4) *CROSS-REFERENCES*. The Cross-References follow the References in each chapter. They direct the reader to other chapters in which
similar or related matters are considered. By relating the topics of one
chapter to those of other chapters, the Cross-References show the interconnection of the great ideas.

In general, the order of the Cross-References follows that of the Outline
of Topics. Each entry in the Cross-References indicates, by its phrasing,
the subject of the topic in a given chapter to which topics in other chapters
are related or similar.

The phrasing of the Cross-References enables the reader to determine
whether the topics in the other chapters mentioned are *similar* or *related*
to the topic in this chapter. The *related* topics will usually offer a quite
different set of references.

The user of the Syntopicon will find that topics in different chapters
often resemble one another, both in their phrasing and in the references
set forth under them. In a few cases they are identical or almost identical.
But *similar* topics will usually differ in their reference content because the
meaning of a topic is partly determined by the idea under which it falls,
and by the surrounding topics which form its context. Hence, in most
cases, the reader who turns to similar topics in other chapters will find
some proportion of different references.

(5) *ADDITIONAL READINGS. Great Books of the Western World*
comprises 443 works by 74 authors; if we add the 77 books of the Bible,
which are syntopically treated along with these published works, the number is 520. But this large number does not represent all the books which
make signal contributions to the great conversation in the sphere of each
of the great ideas.

The list of Additional Readings which is the last part of each chapter is
a list of books recommended as companions to the works and passages
cited in the Reference section. For the ideas and topics of each chapter,
they supplement or amplify the discussion to be found in the great books.
They represent some of the works in the wider field of literature, in which
the great books occupy a central position.

In each list of Additional Readings, the recommended titles are divided into two groups: first, works written by authors represented in *Great Books of the Western World*; and second, works by other authors. Each group is listed chronologically. Whenever they are available, translations of foreign works are suggested. The existence of English translations is always indicated by the use of English titles; these are usually accompanied by the title in the original language.

The 102 lists of Additional Readings, each constructed for the idea and topics of a particular chapter, contain in all 2603 titles by 1181 authors. For the convenience of the reader, the authors and titles in the 102 separate lists of Additional Readings are compiled into a single list in the Bibliography of Additional Readings, which is Appendix I (see Volume II, pg. 1143).

In the Bibliography of Additional Readings, the authors' names are in alphabetical order and the works of each author are listed alphabetically under his name. In addition, the Bibliography provides useful information concerning authors and works, such as birth and death dates of authors, date and place of writing or publication, names of editors or translators, names of publishers, and names of standard collections in which individual works appear. A note, preceding the Bibliography, explains the principles of its construction.

THE INVENTORY OF TERMS

The Inventory of Terms is an integral part of the Syntopicon placed for convenience at the end of Volume II.

The Syntopicon is both a book to be read and a reference book. The Table of Contents sets forth its contents as a book to be read. But since this is limited to listing the 102 great ideas chapter by chapter, it cannot indicate the scope and range of the Syntopicon as a reference book. The Inventory of Terms performs that function; it serves as a table of contents for the Syntopicon as a reference book.

The person who wishes to use the Syntopicon as a reference book, in order to learn what the great books have to say on a particular subject, must be able to find that subject among the 3000 topics. The primary function of the Inventory of Terms is to enable him to find the topic or topics which either clearly express or approximately represent the subject of his inquiry. It does so by citing, for each term listed, the topics in which that term is a principal element. It cites these by giving the name of the chapter in which the topic appears, and the number of the topic in that chapter. The reader can find the topic in which he is interested by looking in the Inventory for the term or terms that would appear in a statement of the subject.

The user of the Syntopicon may have a broader interest than can be expressed in a particular topic. He may wish to examine the whole range of discussion of a basic concept, whether that be one of the great ideas or some other term. This may involve, not one or two topics, but a large number, as is certainly the case for the great ideas, and for many other important concepts as well. Since the Inventory of Terms cites all the topics in which each term is significantly involved, it enables the reader to investigate the whole range of the discussion in the great books relevant to that term.

Among the terms listed in the Inventory are the names of the 102 great ideas. This does not duplicate the information furnished by the Table of Contents. For each of the great ideas, the Table of Contents locates only the whole chapter which deals with that great idea; whereas the Inventory of Terms usually cites topics in many other chapters, in addition to the chapter on that idea itself. For the reader who wishes to explore the discussion of a great idea as thoroughly as possible, the Inventory of Terms supplements the topics to be found in the chapter on that idea, and even those mentioned in the Cross-References of that chapter.

The 1800 terms in the Inventory are listed alphabetically, and for each term the relevant topics are cited in the alphabetical order of the chapters in which the topics occur. Sometimes the topics are divided into two groups, of primary and secondary importance. Within each group, the chapters are alphabetically arranged.

The Inventory is likely to present only one difficulty to the person who consults it in order to find a particular topic. The first step in the location of a topic is accomplished when the reader turns in the Inventory to the term that he thinks is involved in a statement of the subject of his interest. But, finding a number of topics cited there, he must choose among them.

There are two ways for him to proceed: (1) he can examine the topics one after another, until he finds the one which satisfies him as a statement of the subject; or (2) he can use the names of the chapters in which the topics occur as a clue to finding the topic which states the subject of his inquiry. Since the content of particular topics is largely determined by the idea under which they fall, the chapter names will quite frequently prove a reliable guide.

A brief note, at the beginning of the Inventory of Terms, explains its construction and furnishes directions for its use. Nothing more need be said here of its structure, or of its utility in making the Syntopicon a reference book. But a word should be added about the significance of the Inventory in relation to the great ideas.

The division of the Syntopicon into 102 chapters may give rise to the notion that its editors think there are only 102 ideas worth discussing. The number of really great, that is, primary or pivotal ideas may be smaller or larger than 102. That number represents an editorial judgment which was made in the course of constructing the Syntopicon. How it was reached is explained elsewhere (see Appendix II, Section I); but here it should be said that it does not represent a judgment by the editors that the 102 terms selected by them are the only concepts or ideas which have notable significance in the tradition of western thought. The Inventory of Terms manifests exactly the opposite judgment. Its 1800 words or phrases express important concepts. Though many of these will immediately be seen to have much less comprehensive or critical meaning than the 102 major terms of the Syntopicon, they all have general currency or importance in some special field of inquiry. They also represent notions or topics which fall under one or more of the 102 great ideas.

THE PRINCIPLES AND METHODS OF SYNTOPICAL CONSTRUCTION

The essay on the Principles and Methods of Syntopical Construction is Appendix II (see Volume II, pg. 1219). It is intended as a supplement to this Preface. The foregoing brief descriptions of the parts of the Syntopicon indicate its structure, but they do not explain how it was constructed.

The work of creating each part of the Syntopicon raised many difficult intellectual and editorial problems. These problems, and especially the principles and methods by which they were solved, may be of interest to the reader after he has had some experience in using the Syntopicon, but probably not before. The editors decided to make the essay on the Syntopicon's construction an appendix to the work, rather than burden the Preface with an account of the methods employed and an exposition of the principles adopted. While freeing the Preface from the burden of fuller explanations, they nevertheless hoped to provide systematic answers to questions which might arise in the reader's mind as a result of using the Syntopicon.

III. THE USES OF THE SYNTOPICON

The foregoing discussion of the nature and structure of the Syntopicon has expressed the purpose for which it was designed, but it does not fully state all its possible uses. There are four basic types of usefulness which the editors hope the Syntopicon will have. Two of these have already been mentioned. It has been pointed out that the Syntopicon is both a reference book and a book to be read. But the Syntopicon is also intended to serve as an instrument of liberal education, through the aid it can give to a certain kind of study and teaching of the great books. It is not inconsistent with its primary function as a reference book that it should, in addition, prove to be an instrument of research and discovery.

(1) *The Syntopicon as a reference book.*

The description (in Section II of this Preface) of the parts of the Syntopicon, and their function in the structure of the whole, includes some indication of how it may be used as a reference book. Here we are concerned with its general character as a reference work, as evidenced by the types of questions it has been constructed to answer.

In contradistinction to books of other sorts, reference books are designed to help the reader who comes to them with inquiries on particular subjects. If, in addition to answering the questions he brings, they raise further questions in his mind and excite him to further inquiries, which, in turn, they are able to satisfy, they are more than answer-books. They are pedagogues, leading the mind from question to question in the pursuit of learning. Reference books at their best perform an educational function, not simply by answering questions, but by arousing and sustaining inquiry.

Nevertheless, the field of any reference book is defined, in the first instance, by the types of questions it is able to answer. The specific type of inquiry which the Syntopicon is able to satisfy, and which gives it its special character as a reference book, can be formulated by the question. *What do the great books have to say on this subject?* This is not the only question the Syntopicon is designed to answer, but it is the primary one.

The topics are the units through which the Syntopicon functions as a reference book, since it is under the topics that the references to the great books are assembled; and it is through reading the works or passages recommended by these references that the person who consults the Syntopicon finds the answer to his question, What do the great books have to say on this subject?

The range and variety of the particular subjects of inquiry on which the Syntopicon can be consulted, is indicated *quantitatively* by the number of topics and terms: 2987 topics are covered in the 102 chapters; 1798 terms are listed in the Inventory of Terms. *Qualitatively*, the range and variety of the inquiries the Syntopicon is able to satisfy, can be seen only through an examination of the topics, chapter by chapter, or by an examination of the chapter titles in the Table of Contents and the words or phrases listed in the Inventory of Terms.

To every question expressed in this way—What do the great books have to say on this subject?—the Syntopicon helps the reader to discover the answer *for himself* by a syntopical reading of the great books in the light of the topics and guided by the references assembled under them. This fact distinguishes the Syntopicon from all other familiar reference books, which contain *within themselves* the answers to the questions on which they are consulted. The Syntopicon does not contain the answers, but only a guide to where the answers can be found in the pages of the great books. The references which constitute this guide do not tell the reader *what* the great books have to say on a particular subject. They only tell him *where* to read in the great books in order to discover for himself the thought and opinion, the imagination and emotion, in which the authors of these books have expressed their minds on this or that particular subject. For this reason it was said earlier in this Preface that only when it is taken together with the great books themselves, does the Syntopicon create a reference library in the sphere of thought and opinion.

While this is true for the primary type of question which the Syntopicon is designed to answer through its system of references to the great books, it is not true, at least not to the same extent, for the subordinate types of questions now to be considered.

The question, *What themes have been discussed in the tradition of western thought under this idea?* is answered in the first instance by the Outline of Topics in the chapter on each of the great ideas. If the reader becomes interested in the actual content of the discussion under one or more of these topics, he will then be asking the primary sort of question, to which the references, assembled under these topics, provide the beginning of an answer, and the great books the fullness of it.

The question, *To which of the other great ideas is this idea related and how is it related?* is answered by the Cross-References in the chapter on each of the great ideas. The Cross-References enumerate the topics in other chapters which are related to the topics covered by the idea in question. The introductory essay on the idea also usually contains references to other Introductions in which related ideas are considered. By reading the Introduction and examining the Cross-References, a person can use the Syntopicon to discover, at least initially, the connections between one great idea and others.

The question, *What books other than those published in this set contain important discussions of this idea?* is answered, to some extent, by the Additional Readings listed in the chapter on each of the great ideas.

The question, *What is the history of the idea, its various meanings, and the problems or controversies it has raised?* is answered, at least initially, by the Introduction to the chapter on each of the great ideas. Here as before, if the reader's interest is aroused to further inquiry, the topics, the references under them, the passages in the great books referred to, and the books listed in the Additional Readings, provide the means for a fuller exploration of the idea, in varying degrees of thoroughness and ramification.

(2) *The Syntopicon as a book to be read.*

With respect to its 102 essays on the great ideas, the Syntopicon is first of all a book to be read. These essays are arranged in the alphabetical order of the ideas, but they need not be read in that order. Each is intended to be intelligible in itself, independently of the others.

The reader can therefore begin according to his interests with any one of the Introductions to the great ideas. No matter where he begins, he will find that the reading of no other Introduction is presupposed. But he will also find that each Introduction traces some of the connections between the particular idea which it treats and other great ideas.

With whatever idea he begins, the introductory essay will at least suggest other ideas as subjects of related interest. These in turn will turn his attention to, and may arouse his interest in, still others. Since each of the great ideas is directly or remotely related to many others—perhaps to all— through a network of connections radiating from each idea as a point of origin, the reader, starting at any point in the realm of thought, can explore the whole of it by going from any one idea to all the rest by circuits or pathways of his own choosing.

The reading of one or more Introductions should also turn attention to the Outlines of Topics in these same chapters; and, through them and the references organized under them, to the great books themselves. As integral parts of the Syntopicon, the Introductions to the great ideas are not intended to satisfy the reader's interest, but rather to arouse it, and then direct it to the great books. The name "Introduction" specifies the function these essays were designed to perform. When they function effectively as introductions to the Outlines of Topics and the References, they implement the use of the Syntopicon, not simply as a reference book, but as an instrument of liberal education.

(3) *The Syntopicon as an instrument of liberal education.*

The Syntopicon serves the end of liberal education to the extent that it facilitates the reading of the great books and, beyond that, the study and teaching of them. To make the nature of this educational contribution clear, it is necessary to distinguish between the *integral* and the *syntopical* reading of great books.

Integral reading consists simply in reading a whole book through. But syntopical reading does not consist simply in reading parts of a book rather than the whole. It involves the reading of one book in relation to others, all of them relevant to the consideration of the same topic.

In some cases, as the References show, whole works are cited along with passages from other works, which may be as short as a paragraph or as long as a chapter or a series of chapters. For the most part, a syntopical reading consists in reading passages of varying length rather than whole works; but the point remains that the essence of syntopical reading lies in the juxtaposition of many authors under the same topic and, in consequence, the *reading together* of their works, in whole or part.

Neither of these two types of reading can ever be a substitute for the other, nor can either be taken as sufficient in itself. On the contrary, each is incomplete without the other. Those who begin by reading *in* the great books and reading them syntopically must eventually read at least some of them integrally. Those who have already read some of the great books *through* must read them syntopically to discover what an integral reading of the great books seldom reveals, except, perhaps, to the most mature student or conscientious scholar. For each of these two sorts of persons— the beginning reader and the more advanced student or scholar—the Syntopicon functions differently and the syntopical reading of the great books serves a different purpose.

FOR THE BEGINNING READER—in the extreme case, a person who has read none of the great books—a syntopical reading, done in accordance with the references under even a few topics, works in three ways: initiatively, suggestively, and instructively.

It works *initiatively* by overcoming the initial difficulty that anyone faces when confronted by a collection of books as vast and, in a sense, as overpowering as *Great Books of the Western World.* The problem is where to begin and in what order to proceed. There are many solutions to this problem, usually in the form of courses of reading based on different principles of selection; but these usually require the reading of whole books or, at least, the integral reading of large parts of them.

It is a matter of general experience that this kind of solution seldom achieves the intended result. A syntopical reading of the great books provides a radically different sort of solution, which promises to be more effective. It initiates the reading of the great books by enabling persons to read in them on the subjects in which they are interested; and on those subjects, to read relatively short passages from a large number of authors. It assumes only that every educable mind has some interest in one or more of the themes, problems, or ideas on which the great books touch.

A syntopical reading may also work *suggestively.* Starting from a reader's existing interest in a particular topic, it may arouse or create an interest in other topics related to those which initiated his reading in the great books. The syntopical reading of a collection of authors under a particular topic may also impel the reader to look beyond the passages cited. Except when they cite whole works, the references cite passages which necessarily exist in a context, ultimately the context of the whole book. Few of these passages are absolutely self-contained. For few of them can it be said that it will be finally satisfactory to read them without looking further into the author's thought. Hence, proceeding along the natural lines of his own interests, the reader may be led from reading small parts of certain books to reading larger parts and, eventually, to reading whole books. If this process is repeated, each syntopical reading may occasion and stimulate a more and more extensive integral reading of the great books.

Working initiatively and suggestively, syntopical reading opens the great books at the pages of maximum interest to the individual and, by the force of the passages read and their dependence on context, carries him from reading parts to reading whole works. Syntopical reading works *instructively* when it guides the mind in interpreting and understanding the passages or works being read. It does this in three ways.

First, the topic in connection with which the passage is being read serves to give direction to the reader in interpreting the passage. But it does not tell him what the passage means, since the passage cited may be relevant to the topic in any one of a number of ways. Hence the reader is called upon to discover precisely what relevance the passage has to the topic. To learn to do this is to acquire a major skill in the art of reading.

Second, the collection of a number of passages on the same topic, but from different works and different authors, serves to sharpen the reader's interpretation of each passage read. Sometimes, when passages from the same book or author are read in sequence and in the context of one another, each becomes clearer. Sometimes the meaning of each of a series of contrasting or conflicting passages from different books or authors is accentuated when they are read against one another. And sometimes the passages from one author, by amplifying or commenting on the passages cited from another, materially help the reader's understanding of the second author.

Third, if the individual does a syntopical reading of the great books under a number of distinct topics, the fact that the same passage will often be found cited under two or more topics will have its instructive effect. As relevant to distinct topics, the passage must have an amplitude of meaning which the reader will come to perceive when he interprets it somewhat differently in relation to different topics. Such multiple interpretation not only is a basic exercise in the art of reading, but also tends to make the mind habitually alert to the many strains of meaning which any rich or complex passage can contain.

In this description of the ways in which a syntopical reading instructs in the art of reading the great books, we have emphasized only the influence of the topic under which the reading is done and the effect of reading one passage in relation to another or in relation to several distinct topics. But to assure or reinforce its instructive effect, two other factors may operate in the background of a syntopical reading. One is the whole Outline of Topics, which places a particular topic in the context of other topics under the same idea. The other is the Introduction to that idea, which may help the reader to interpret the particular topic, thereby increasing the effectiveness of that topic as a guide to the interpretation of the works or passages referred to under it.

IF WE TURN NOW FROM THE BEGINNING READER to the more mature student or scholar—in the extreme case, a person who has read through many, if not all, of the great books—we shall see that a syntopical reading works in a different way. It no longer need function initiatively or suggestively; nor, for the competent reader, need it serve instructively, to develop skill in the art of reading. But it does provide the occasion and the materials for a more intensive and critical reading of passages already read; and it supplements the reading of whole works independently of one another by requiring an examination of these works, or passages from them, in mutual relation, as relevant to the same topic.

It is the general experience of highly competent readers that a great book can be read through many times without the attainment of such complete mastery that the reader knows the relevance of every passage in it to every theme it touches. On the contrary, the integral reading of a great book, even when done more than once, seldom reveals even a large part of its meaning. Only the most intensive scholarly study of a particular book or author ever arrives at such mastery.

Short of that, reading a great book through one or more times will inevitably leave unnoticed or only partly recognized many passages of critical significance to a particular theme or problem. Only when the book is read with that particular subject in mind will these passages, hitherto unobserved, be found.

The truth of this can be verified by accomplished readers of the great books if they will examine, under particular topics, passages from books they have already read or even studied to some extent. Unless their previous reading of the books was done in the light of the particular intellectual interest represented by this topic, they are likely to find some passages that they never saw before, or at least never fully recognized as having the significance they take on when read syntopically—in the light of this topic and in relation to other works and passages relevant to the same theme.

The Syntopicon can thus serve those who have already done, to a greater or less extent, an integral reading of the great books. The method of syntopical reading not only provides a different and rewarding way of reading them, but also carries the study of them to deeper and deeper levels of understanding. It overcomes the defects of the ordinary integral reading in several ways. It involves reading the great books in relation to one another rather than in isolation. It supplements the knowledge of whole works by concentration on the significance of parts. Taking each of 3000 topics as the occasion for a purposeful reading in all the great books, it makes possible the close study of each work in relation to all the problems or issues on which it bears.

There is still another way in which the method of syntopical reading can advance the study of the great books, or rather a studious use of them. Here the aim is not to study the books themselves, but to consider a problem or an issue to the solution or clarification of which they contribute.

The particular problem may involve many topics in one or more chapters. It may involve a number of great ideas and many subordinate terms. The organization of the Syntopicon enables the student of such a problem to discover the range of the terms and topics traditionally involved in its consideration. The References enable him to examine systematically, in their chronological order or in any order he wishes, the record of western thought concerning this problem, so far as it is contained in the great books. The Additional Readings supplement these materials by citing other books which bear upon the problem more or less directly.

It does not seem an exaggeration to say that a person who has done all the syntopical reading suggested by the References and the Additional Readings on a particular problem, will have a fairly adequate knowledge of that problem and its proposed solutions in the development of western

thought. The Syntopicon should be able to save the person who is beginning his inquiry into a certain problem much of the preliminary labor of
research, and advance him rapidly to the point where he can begin to
think independently about it, because he knows what thinking has been
done. For the scholar, already advanced in his research on a given problem,
it may still be possible for the Syntopicon to serve some good purpose as
a reminder or a check; it may even uncover a neglected passage, or throw
new light upon one by placing it in the context of other passages.

WHAT HAS JUST BEEN SAID about the studious or scholarly use of the Syntopicon suggests how it may serve as an instrument in teaching the great
books, or in using them as teaching materials. For the most part, the great
books enter the curricula of schools and colleges engaged in liberal
education only by way of courses in which some of these books, or most
of them, are read integrally. Even when they are read in selections rather
than as wholes, they are, for the most part, used as materials in a general
course of study rather than as applicable to the study of particular subject
matters.

Without detracting from or competing with the unquestionable value
of such procedures, the Syntopicon offers another pedagogical use of the
great books. The method of syntopical reading makes them available in
the teaching of courses concerned with particular subject matters, or in
the conduct of seminars devoted to the study of particular problems. In
certain cases, it may encourage the reading of the great texts in place of
textbooks.

For a particular problem or subject matter, whose name is either one of
the great ideas or a major term in the Inventory of Terms, the Syntopicon
suggests some, if not all, of the topics which deserve to be studied, and
some, if not all, of the works which deserve to be read in whole or part.
It thus provides a set of materials organized so as to be adaptable to the
method and interest of the individual teacher. For example, at one extreme, the teacher can use the Syntopicon merely as a guide to supplementary reading; at the other extreme, he can use it to construct his own set
of textual materials, selected from the References and the Additional
Readings and organized in the framework of a sequence of topics.

(4) *The Syntopicon as an instrument of discovery and research.*

What has already been said about the use of the Syntopicon by the serious student, or even the advanced scholar, in the sphere of a particular problem or subject matter, obviously covers part of the Syntopicon's utility as an instrument of research or discovery. But there are three special types of inquiry for the pursuit of which the Syntopicon seems to be especially adapted.

The first of these is the study of the history of ideas. The chapter on each of the 102 great ideas presents the record of thought in the form of references to the great books, organized under each topic. Since the references are arranged in the order in which the authors and works appear in the set of great books, and since, with few exceptions, this is a strictly chronological order, the record of thought is presented in an order suited to the historian's interest. The Additional Readings, which supplement the great books in the record, are also arranged chronologically. Hence the Syntopicon provides an organization of materials eminently useful to the scholar engaged in the historical study of ideas.

The second type of special inquiry concerns the thought of a single author, in its historical relation to the thought of predecessors who influenced him and followers influenced by him. If that author happens to be one of the authors of the great books, the Syntopicon can facilitate such research, since, for hundreds of distinct topics, it places references to the work of the particular author in the context of references to other authors —earlier, later, or contemporary—whom he may have influenced or by whom he may have been influenced.

The third type of special inquiry is limited to the thought of a particular period rather than a particular author. Within this limitation, the historical interest may extend to all the great and near-great minds who formed the thought of this period, as well as to all the ideas with which they dealt. So far as the formative minds of the particular period are represented by authors of the great books and by other authors cited in the Additional Readings, the Syntopicon can assist such research. Instead of using its references vertically, from one end of the tradition to the other, as would the student of the history of an idea, the student of an epoch of thought would cut through the references horizontally. He would take all the authors and books which fell within the period under consideration; he would examine the materials referred to under every idea or topic which appeared to have been considered by the minds of that period.

In these three types of historical inquiry, the Syntopicon is at best an auxiliary instrument in the service of scholarship. If it proves to be more than that for the ordinary student, it will probably be less than that for the accomplished scholar whose documentary resources in a particular field are more extensive than those from which the Syntopicon is constructed. This is especially true of those problems in the history of ideas which have been investigated by prolonged research. But some problems have not been so investigated, and the Syntopicon may have something to contribute to the study of these. It is even possible that the Syntopicon may uncover or call attention to new problems, or may cause the re-formulation of old problems in a new way.

THE GRAND RESEARCH suggested by the existence of the Syntopicon is not historical, however, but philosophical. Stated simply, it is the project of creating in and for the twentieth century a synthesis or summation of western thought, past and present, which will serve the intellectual needs of our time, as analogous syntheses or summations have served antiquity, the Middle Ages, and the period of the enlightenment.

The 102 great ideas, the 1800 other terms, and the 3000 topics of the Syntopicon are a fair representation of the *objects*, as the materials to be found in the 443 works here published and the 2600 other works listed in the Additional Readings are a fair representation of the *content*, of western inquiry and discussion. The Syntopicon is, therefore, an instrument adapted to the sort of research which might produce a summation of western thought from the beginning to the present.

Because the existence of the Syntopicon makes it possible and suggests that it be undertaken, the project envisaged might be called a Program of Syntopical Research. Because the method of this research, like the method which produced the Syntopicon, would be thoroughly dialectical in character, the intellectual summation which would be its product could be called a Summa Dialectica.

MORTIMER J. ADLER, *Editor*

Chicago, 1952

tion; he would examine the materials referred to under every idea or topic which appeared to have been considered by the minds of that period.

In these three types of historical inquiry, the Syntopicon is at best an auxiliary instrument in the service of scholarship. If it proves to be more than that for the ordinary student it will probably be less than that for the accomplished scholar whose documentary resources in a particular field are more extensive than those from which the Syntopicon is constructed. This is especially true of those problems in the history of ideas which have been investigated by prolonged research. But some problems have not been so investigated, and the Syntopicon may have something to contribute to the study of these. It is even possible that the Syntopicon may uncover or call attention to new problems, or may cause the re-formulation of old problems in a new way.

THE GRAND RESEARCH suggested by the existence of the Syntopicon is not historical, however, but philosophical. Stated simply, it is the project of creating in and for the twentieth century a synthesis or summation of western thought, past and present, which will serve the intellectual needs of our time, as analogous syntheses or summations have served antiquity, the Middle Ages, and the period of the enlightenment.

The 102 great ideas, the 1800 other terms, and the 3000 topics of the Syntopicon are a fair representation of the objects, as the materials to be found in the 443 works here published and the 1800 other works listed in the Additional Readings are a fair representation of the content, of western inquiry and discussion. The Syntopicon is, therefore, an instrument adapted to the sort of research which might produce a summation of western thought from the beginning to the present.

Because the existence of the Syntopicon makes it possible and suggests that it be undertaken, the project envisaged might be called a Program of Syntopical Research. Because the method of this research, like the method which produced the Syntopicon, would be thoroughly dialectical in character, the intellectual summation which would be its product could be called a Summa Dialectica.

Mortimer J. Adler, Editor

Chicago, 1952

EXPLANATION OF REFERENCE STYLE

T HE references have a uniform typographical style, but the manner of referring to particular works varies in certain respects. The Explanation of Reference Style describes the typographical construction of the references, with some comment on the variations. It is divided into four parts:

    I. General Typographical Style

    II. Style of Bible References

    III. Punctuation, Symbols, Abbreviations

    IV. Table of Authors, Titles, and Author's Divisions Cited

I. GENERAL TYPOGRAPHICAL STYLE

The two examples below illustrate the general typographical pattern of the references to *Great Books of the Western World*; and the headings above the examples call attention to the five elements commonly present in the construction of the references.

Volume Number	Author's Name	Title of Work	Author's Divisions	Page Sections
35	LOCKE:	*Human Understanding*,	BK II, CH XXI	178a-200d
41	GIBBON:	*Decline and Fall*,		365b-378d

(1) Volume Number:

The volume number indicates in which volume of *Great Books of the Western World* the work or passage referred to can be found. Most volumes contain the work of one author. When a single volume contains the works of two or more authors, the volume number is given for each author. When the work of a single author is contained in two volumes, the volume number is assigned according to the contents of the volume.

(2) Author's Name:

The author's name immediately follows the volume number, except in the case of the American State Papers and the Federalist, which are included in Volume 43. Authors' names are usually given in shortened form.

(3) Title of Work:

The title follows the author's name, with the two exceptions above noted. Titles are also frequently abbreviated or shortened. When two or more works are cited for a single author, the titles are listed in the order in which the works appear in the volume.

(4) Author's Divisions:

By "author's divisions" is meant all such subdivisions of a work as book, part, section, chapter, paragraph, line number. The phrase "author's divisions" does not necessarily mean divisions made by the author; they may have been made by an editor of his work.

Author's divisions are given only for some works, according as, in the judgment of the editors, their inclusion would prove meaningful or helpful to the reader. References to Locke, for instance, as in the example, always cite author's divisions; whereas references to Gibbon, as in the example, do not.

For some works, author's divisions are completely given, as for Locke. For other works, only the most important or largest divisions are given. Thus for Rabelais only the book but not the chapter is given.

Line numbers, in brackets, are given for all works of poetry, including those published in prose translations. For Goethe's *Faust*, the line numbers cited refer to the lines of the English translation as well as to the lines of the original German. For other poetical works in translation—the works of Homer, the Greek dramatists, Lucretius, Virgil, and Dante—the line numbers cited refer to the lines of the works in their original languages; for these works, the line numbers printed on the pages of this edition furnish only an approximate indication of the location of the equivalent lines in the English translation. For all poetical works written in English, the line numbers are the numbers of the English lines. In the case of Chaucer's *Canterbury Tales*, the numbering of the lines is consecutive for all the tales written in verse.

In references to the works of Aristotle (in Volumes 8 and 9), the figures and letters enclosed in the brackets signify the page, column, and approximate line in the Berlin edition of the Greek text edited by Immanuel Bekker. In references to the American State Papers (in Volume 43), the bracketed line numbers refer to the lines on the pages of this edition only.

In references to the *Summa Theologica* of Thomas Aquinas (in Volumes 19 and 20), the author's division "Part I–II" stands for Part I of the Second Part, and "Part II–II" stands for Part II of the Second Part. In the case of the *Summa Theologica*, the author's divisions cited may include not only questions and articles, but the subdivisions of articles. In such cases the page sections correspond in extent to that of a whole article, to enable the reader to see the subdivision of an article, when it is cited, in the context of other parts to which it is related.

Author's divisions precede page sections except in the case of footnote and note numbers, which follow page sections. When more than one passage is cited within the same author's division, the author's division is not repeated; as, for example:

> 38 ROUSSEAU: *Social Contract*, BK II, 403a-404a; 405d-406a

(5) Page Sections:

The pages of *Great Books of the Western World* are printed in either one or two columns. The upper and lower halves of a one-column page are indicated by the letters **a** and **b**. When the text is printed in two columns, the letters **a** and **b** refer to the upper and lower halves of the left-hand column, the letters **c** and **d** to the upper and lower halves of the right-hand column. These half and quarter page sections are based on divisions of a full text page.

Page sections give the page numbers and locate the sections of the page in which the passage referred to begins and ends. For example, in the reference:

> 53 JAMES: *Psychology*, 116a-119b

the passage cited begins in the upper half of page 116 and ends in the lower half of page 119. In the reference:

> 7 PLATO: *Symposium*, 163b-164c

the passage cited begins in the lower half of the left-hand column of page 163 and ends in the upper half of the right-hand column of page 164.

In references to works printed in two columns, the format of the page sometimes places continuous reading matter in the a and c sections of the upper half of the page, or in the b and d sections of the lower half of the page. This occurs when a work or an author's division begins in the lower, or ends in the upper, half of the two-column page. Where continuous reading matter thus appears in discontinuous page sections, it is indicated by **a,c** or **b,d**. For example:

> 14 PLUTARCH: *Solon* 64b,d-77a,c

means that the work cited begins in the lower half of page 64 and ends in the upper half of page 77.

Footnotes or notes are sometimes specifically cited by themselves in the references, in which case the page sections given correspond to their location on the pages referred to. When a footnote or a note is not specifically cited, the page sections given mark the beginning and the end of the text referred to. The reader is expected to consult the footnotes or notes indicated in the body of that text.

Chaucer's works (in Volume 22) are printed in two columns; the inside column of each page contains the Middle English text, the outside column a Modern English version. Since both columns contain equivalent passages, the references to this volume employ page sections (a and b) which divide each page only into an upper and a lower half.

II. STYLE OF BIBLE REFERENCES

All Bible references are to book, chapter, and verse in both the King James and Douay versions of the Bible. When the King James and Douay versions differ in the title of books or in the numbering of chapters or verses, the King James version is cited first and the Douay, indicated by a (*D*), follows. For example:

> OLD TESTAMENT: *Nehemiah,* 7:45—(*D*) *II Esdras,* 7:46

In references to the Bible, a colon is used to separate chapter and verse numbers; and a comma separates the numbers of verses in the same chapter. For example:

> OLD TESTAMENT: *Exodus,* 6:1–4,16–18

III. PUNCTUATION, SYMBOLS, ABBREVIATIONS

(1) Punctuation

Diagonal line: When a series of references to one author includes two or more of his works published in the same volume, a diagonal line is used to separate references to one work from references to another. The diagonal line is used in the same way to separate references to different books of the Bible. For example:

> OLD TESTAMENT: *Exodus*, 33:12–23 / *Job*, 11:7–9
>
> 43 MILL: *Liberty*, 302d-303a / *Representative Government*, 327b,d-332d

Semi-Colon: When a series of references includes the citation of two or more passages in the same work, a semi-colon is used to separate the references to these passages. For example:

> OLD TESTAMENT: *Genesis*, 1:12–14; 9:1–11
>
> 38 ROUSSEAU: *Social Contract*, BK II, 403a-404a; 405d-406a
>
> 46 HEGEL: *Philosophy of History*, PART II, 265c-266a; PART IV, 346c-348a

Comma: When a comma separates the title of a work, or an author's division of a work, from the page sections which follow, passages cited are only a part of the whole work or of the author's division indicated. For example, in the references:

> 14 PLUTARCH: *Lycurgus*, 36a-b; 44d-45c
>
> 36 SWIFT: *Gulliver*, PART II, 73a-74b

the passages from Plutarch are only a part of *Lycurgus*, and the passage from Swift is only a few pages from Part II of *Gulliver's Travels*.

When the title of a work, or an author's division of a work, is *not* separated by a comma from the page sections which follow, the reference is to the whole work or to the whole of the indicated author's division. For example, in the references:

> 14 PLUTARCH: *Lycurgus* 32a-48d
>
> 36 SWIFT: *Gulliver*, PART II 45a-87b

the whole of *Lycurgus* and the whole of Part II of *Gulliver's Travels* are cited.

(2) Symbols

esp: The abbreviation "esp" precedes one or more especially relevant passages which are contained within the page boundaries of a larger passage or a whole work that has just been cited.

Whenever passages contained within a single reference are especially referred to, a comma after the page sections separates these passages. For example:

42 KANT: *Science of Right*, 435a-441d esp 435c-436b, 437c-d, 438d-441d

Whenever passages contained within a single reference to the Bible are especially referred to, a comma is also used to separate these passages. For example:

NEW TESTAMENT: *Romans*, 1–8 esp 2:11–16, 2:27–29, 7:21–25, 8:27

passim: The word "passim" following a reference signifies that the work or passage referred to discusses the topic under which it is cited, intermittently rather than continuously. For example:

9 ARISTOTLE: *Politics*, BK II, CH 7 461d-463c passim / *Athenian Constitution*, CH 1–41 553a-572d passim

(3) Abbreviations

The following is a list of the abbreviations used in the references. Unless an abbreviation for the plural is listed below, the singular abbreviation is used for both singular and plural words.

A	. . .	ARTICLE	[n]	. . .	note
AA	. . .	ARTICLES	OT	. . .	OLD TESTAMENT
ANS	. . .	ANSWER	par	. . .	paragraph
APH	. . .	APHORISM	PREF	. . .	PREFACE
BK	. . .	BOOK	PROP	. . .	PROPOSITION
CH	. . .	CHAPTER	Q	. . .	QUESTION
COROL	. . .	COROLLARY	QQ	. . .	QUESTIONS
(D)	. . .	DOUAY	REP	. . .	REPLY
DEF	. . .	DEFINITION	SC	. . .	SCENE
DEMONST	. . .	DEMONSTRATION	SCHOL	. . .	SCHOLIUM
DIV	. . .	DIVISION	SECT	. . .	SECTION
EXPL	. . .	EXPLANATION	SUPPL	. . .	SUPPLEMENT
[fn]	. . .	footnote	TR	. . .	TRACTATE
INTRO	. . .	INTRODUCTION			

IV. TABLE OF AUTHORS, TITLES, AND
AUTHOR'S DIVISIONS CITED

The following pages present a tabulation of the contents of *Great Books of the Western World*, Volumes 4–54. The authors are enumerated in the order in which they appear in the successive volumes of the set; and under each author's name the titles of his works are listed in the order of their appearance.

In the references, the name of the author is frequently given in shortened form. In this table, their full names are given, followed by their life dates when these are ascertainable. Because some volumes contain the works of two or more authors who may be separated by centuries, the order in which the authors are cited in the references sometimes departs from the strict chronological order. The life dates help the reader to place the authors and their works in the right chronological order.

In the references, the title of a work is frequently given in an abbreviated or shortened form. In this table, the titles are first given exactly as they appear in the references. Whenever this is an abbreviated or shortened title, the full title follows.

The table also includes a notation of the author's divisions that are used in references to particular works.

A dash in the column headed "Author's Divisions Cited" means that references to the work or works in question cite page sections only. Where the author's divisions cited are the same for several titles, they are named only once, either opposite the set of titles as a whole, or opposite the last title in the group.

Titles in brackets are collective titles which appear on the title page of the work, but do not appear in the references. The names of the authors of *The Federalist* (in Volume 43) are bracketed because they do not appear in the references.

Volume Number, Author, and Title		Author's Divisions Cited
4 HOMER		
The Iliad	*The Odyssey*	BOOK, Line
5 AESCHYLUS (*c.* 525–456 B.C.)		
The Suppliant Maidens	*Agamemnon*	
The Persians	*Choephoroe*	
The Seven Against Thebes	*Eumenides*	Line
Prometheus Bound		

Volume Number, Author, and Title	*Author's Divisions Cited*

Volume Number, Author, and Title   *Author's Divisions Cited*

32   MILTON, JOHN (1608–1674)

     [*English Minor Poems*]   Line, except *Sonnets* and *Psalms*

       Christs Nativity——*On the Morning*
         of Christs Nativity and *The Hymn*   *Death of a Fair Infant*——*On the Death of*
       A Paraphrase on Psalm 114   *a Fair Infant*
       Psalm 136   *Vacation Exercise*——*At a Vacation Exercise*
       The Passion   *The Fifth Ode of Horace*——*The Fifth Ode*
       On Time   *of Horace. Lib. I*
       Upon the Circumcision   *Sonnets,* I, VII–XIX
       At a Solemn Musick   *New Forcers of Conscience*——*On the New*
       An Epitaph on the Marchioness of   *Forcers of Conscience under the Long*
         Winchester   *Parliament*
       Song on May Morning   *Lord Gen. Fairfax*——*On the Lord Gen.*
       On Shakespear. 1630   *Fairfax at the siege of Colchester*
       On the University Carrier   *Lord Gen. Cromwell*——*To the Lord Generall*
       Another on the Same   *Cromwell May 1652*
       L'Allegro   *Sr Henry Vane*——*To Sr Henry Vane the*
       Il Penseroso   *Younger*
       Arcades   *Mr. Cyriack Skinner*——*To Mr. Cyriack*
       Lycidas   *Skinner upon his Blindness*
       Comus   *Psalms,* I–VIII, LXXX–LXXXVIII

       Paradise Lost   BOOK, Line
       Samson Agonistes   Line
       Areopagitica   ——

33   PASCAL, BLAISE (1623–1662)

     The Provincial Letters   ——
     Pensées   Number of Pensée
     Vacuum——*Preface to the Treatise on the Vacuum* and
       New Experiments Concerning the Vacuum
     Great Experiment——*Account of the Great Experiment*
       Concerning the Equilibrium of Fluids
     Equilibrium of Liquids and
     Weight of Air——*Treatises on the Equilibrium of*
       Liquids and on the Weight of the Mass of the Air
     Geometrical Demonstration——*On Geometrical*
       Demonstration
     Arithmetical Triangle——*Treatise on the Arithmetical*
       Triangle
     Correspondence with Fermat——*Correspondence with*
       Fermat on the Theory of Probabilities

34   NEWTON, SIR ISAAC (1642–1727)

     Principles——*Mathematical Principles*   DEFINITION, SCHOLIUM, LAW, COROLLARY, BOOK, RULE,
       of Natural Philosophy   LEMMA, PROPOSITION, PHENOMENON, HYPOTHESIS
     Optics   BOOK

THE GREAT IDEAS: I

Chapters 1–50: ANGEL *to* LOVE

THE GREAT IDEAS: I

Chapters 1-50: Angel to Love

Chapter 1: ANGEL

INTRODUCTION

INFLUENCED by a long tradition of religious symbolism in painting and poetry, our imagination responds to the word "angel" by picturing a winged figure robed in dazzling white and having the bodily aspect of a human being.

This image, common to believers and unbelievers, contains features which represent some of the elements of meaning in the abstract conception of angels as this is found in the writings of Jewish and Christian theologians and in related discussions by the philosophers. The human appearance suggests that angels, like men, are persons; that they are most essentially characterized by their intelligence. The wings suggest the function of angels—their service as messengers from God to man. The aura of light which surrounds them signifies, according to established conventions of symbolism, the spirituality of angels. It suggests that to imagine angels with bodies is to use a pictorial metaphor.

Another interpretation might be put upon this aura of light if one considers the role which the notion of angel has played in the history of thought. Wherever that notion has entered into discussions of God and man, of matter, mind, and soul, of knowledge and love, and even of time, space, and motion, it has cast light upon these other topics. The illumination which has been and can be derived from the idea of angels as a special kind of being or nature is in no way affected by doubts or denials of their existence.

Whether such beings exist or not, the fact that they are conceivable has significance for theory and analysis. Those who do not believe in the existence—or even the possible existence—of utopias nevertheless regard them as fictions useful analytically in appraising accepted realities. What an ideal society would be like can be considered apart from the question of its existence; and, so considered, it functions as an hypothesis in political and economic thought. What sort of being an angel would be if one existed can likewise serve as an hypothesis in the examination of a wide variety of theoretical problems.

The idea of angels does in fact serve in precisely this way as an analytical tool. It sharpens our understanding of what man is, how his mind operates, what the soul is, what manner of existence and action anything would have apart from matter. Hence it suggests how matter and its motions in time and space determine the characteristics of corporeal existence. Pascal's remark—that "man is neither angel nor brute, and the unfortunate thing is that he who would act the angel acts the brute"—points to the different conceptions of man which result from supposing him to be either angel or brute rather than neither. Such views of human nature, considered in the chapters on ANIMAL and MAN, cannot be fully explored without reference to theories of the human mind or soul in its relation to matter and to body. As the chapters on MIND and SOUL indicate, theories carrying the names of Plato and Descartes, which attribute to the human mind or soul the being and powers of a purely spiritual substance or entity, seem to place man in the company of the angels. In this tradition Locke applies the word "spirits" equally to human minds and to suprahuman intelligences.

IT WOULD BE misleading to suppose that the idea of angels is primarily a construction of the philosophers—a fiction invented for their analytical purposes; or that it is simply their conception of a supra-mundane reality, concerning the existence and nature of which they dispute. In the literature of western civilization, angels first appear by name or reference in the Old and the New Testaments. Readers of the Bible will remember many scenes in which an angel of the Lord performs the mission of acquainting man with God's will. Among the most memorable of such occasions are the visits of the angels to Abraham and Lot and the angelic ministry of Gabriel in the Annunciation to Mary.

In one book of the Bible, Tobias (Tobit, as it is called in the King James Apocrypha), one of the leading characters is the angel Raphael. Through most of the story he appears as a man, but at the end, after he has accomplished his mission, he reveals his identity. "I am the angel Raphael," he declares,

one of the seven, who stand before the Lord.

And when they had heard these things they were troubled; and being seized with fear they fell upon the ground on their face.

And the angel said to them: Peace be to you. Fear not.

For when I was with you, I was there by the will of God: bless ye him and sing praises to him.

I seemed to eat and to drink with you; but I use an invisible meat and drink, which cannot be seen by men.

It is time therefore that I return to him that sent me. . . .

And when he had said these things, he was taken from their sight; and they could see him no more.

As a result of scriptural exegesis and commentary, the angels become a fundamental topic for Jewish theologians from Philo to Maimonides, and for such Christian theologians as Augustine, Scotus Erigena, Gregory the Great, Aquinas, Luther, Calvin, Pascal, and Schleiermacher. They figure in the great poetry of the Judaeo-Christian tradition—in the *Divine Comedy* of Dante, in *Paradise Lost* of Milton, and in Chaucer's *Canterbury Tales* and Goethe's *Faust*.

The philosophers, especially in the 17th and 18th centuries, are motivated by Scripture or provoked by theology to consider the existence, the nature, and the activity of angels. Hobbes, for example, attacks the supposition that angels are immaterial on the ground that the notion of incorporeal substance is self-contradictory, and undertakes to re-interpret all the scriptural passages in which angels are described as spirits. After examining a great many, he says that "to mention all the places of the Old Testament where the name of Angel is found, would be too long. Therefore to comprehend them all at once, I say, there is no text in that part of the

Old Testament, which the Church of England holdeth for Canonical, from which we can conclude, there is, or hath been created, any permanent thing (understood by the name of *Spirit* or *Angel*) that hath not quantity . . . and, in sum, which is not (taking Body for that which is somewhat or somewhere) Corporeal."

All the passages can be interpreted, Hobbes thinks, simply in the sense in which "angel" means "messenger" and "most often, a messenger of God," which signifies "anything that makes known his extra-ordinary presence." If, instead of existing only when they carry God's word to men, the angels are supposed to have permanent being, then they must be corporeal. As "in the resurrection men shall be permanent and not incorporeal," Hobbes writes, "so therefore also are the angels . . . To men that understand the signification of these words, *substance* and *incorporeal*"—and mean by "incorporeal" having no body at all, not just a *subtle* body—the words taken together "imply a contradiction." Hence Hobbes argues that to say "an angel, or spirit, is (in that sense) an incorporeal substance, is to say in effect that there is no angel or spirit at all. Considering therefore the signification of the word *angel* in the Old Testament, and the nature of dreams and visions that happen to men by the ordinary way of nature," Hobbes concludes that the angels are "nothing but supernatural apparitions of the fancy, raised by the special and extraordinary operation of God, thereby to make his presence and commandments known to mankind, and chiefly to his own people."

Locke seems to take the exactly opposite position. Asserting that we have "no clear or distinct idea of substance in general," he does not think spirits any less intelligible than bodies. "The idea of *corporeal substance*," he writes, "is as remote from our conceptions and apprehensions, as that of *spiritual substance* or spirit; and therefore, from our not having any notion of the substance of spirit, we can no more conclude its non-existence, than we can, for the same reason, deny the existence of body." Just as we form the complex idea of bodies by supposing their qualities, such as figure and motion, or color and weight, to co-exist in some substratum; so by supposing the activities we find in ourselves—such as "thinking, understanding, willing, knowing, and the power of beginning motion, etc."—to co-exist in some substance, "we are able to frame the *complex idea of an immaterial spirit*."

Not only does Locke think that "we have as clear a perception and notion of immaterial substances as we have of material," but he also finds the traditional doctrine of a hierarchy of angels quite acceptable to reason. "It is not impossible to conceive, nor repugnant to reason, that there may be many species of spirits, as much separated and diversified one from another by distinct properties whereof we have no ideas, as the species of sensible things are distinguished one from another by qualities which we know and observe in them."

Locke goes even further—beyond the mere possibility of angels to the likelihood of their real existence. His reasoning resembles the traditional argument of the theologians on this difficult point. "When we consider the infinite power and wisdom of the Maker," he writes, "we have reason to think that it is suitable to the magnificent harmony of the Universe, and the great design and infinite goodness of the Architect, that the species of creatures should also, by gentle degrees, ascend upward from us toward his infinite perfection, as we see they gradually descend from us downwards."

Such speculations concerning the existence and the order of angels are usually thought to be the province of the theologian rather than the philosopher. But Bacon, like Locke, does not think it unfitting for the philosopher to inquire into such matters. In natural theology—for him a part of philosophy—Bacon thinks it is improper "from the contemplation of nature, and the principles of human reason, to dispute or urge anything with vehemence as to the mysteries of faith." But "it is otherwise," he declares, "as to the nature of spirits and angels; this being neither unsearchable nor forbid, but in a great part level to the human mind on account of their affinity."

He does not further instruct us concerning angels in the *Advancement of Learning*, but in the *Novum Organum* he throws light on their nature as well as ours by touching on one characteristic difference between the human and the angelic mind. Discussing there the theory of induction, he holds that "it is only for God

(the bestower and creator of forms), and perhaps for angels or intelligences at once to recognize forms affirmatively at the first glance of contemplation."

UNLIKE MOST of the great ideas with which we are concerned, the idea of angel seems to be limited in its historical scope. It is not merely that since the 18th century the discussion has dwindled, but also that the idea makes no appearance in the great books of pagan antiquity —certainly not in the strict sense of the term, whereby "angel" signifies a creature of God, spiritual in substance and nature, and playing a role in the divine government of the universe.

There are, nevertheless, analogous conceptions in the religion and philosophy of the ancients; and in philosophy at least, the points of resemblance between the analogous concepts are sufficiently strong to establish a continuity of discussion. Furthermore, elements in the thought of Plato, Aristotle, and Plotinus exercise a critical influence on Judaeo-Christian angelology.

Gibbon relates how the early Christians made the connection between the gods of polytheism and their doctrine about angels. "It was the universal sentiment both of the church and of heretics," he writes, "that the daemons were the authors, the patrons, and the objects of idolatry. Those rebellious spirits who had been degraded from the rank of angels, and cast down into the infernal pit, were still permitted to roam upon the earth, to torment the bodies and to seduce the minds of sinful men. The daemons soon discovered and abused the natural propensity of the human heart towards devotion, and, artfully withdrawing the adoration of mankind from their Creator, they usurped the place and honors of the Supreme Deity."

In the polytheistic religions of antiquity, the demi-gods or inferior deities are beings superior in nature and power to man. "The polytheist and the philosopher, the Greek and the barbarian," writes Gibbon, "were alike accustomed to conceive a long succession, an infinite chain of angels, or daemons, or deities, or aeons, or emanations, issuing from the throne of light." In Plato's *Symposium*, for example, Diotima tells Socrates that Love "is intermediate between the divine and the mortal . . . and interprets between gods and men, conveying and taking across to the gods the prayers and sacrifices of men, and to men the commands and replies of the gods; he is the mediator who spans the chasm which divides them." Love, Diotima explains, is only one of "these spirits and intermediate powers" which "are many and diverse."

Such demi-gods are intermediate by their very nature. Although superhuman in knowledge and action, they still are not completely divine. Occupying a place between men and gods, they are, according to Plato, "by nature neither mortal nor immortal." Their existence is necessary to fill out the hierarchy of natures. They are links in what has come to be called "the great chain of being."

The analogy with the angels arises primarily from this fact of hierarchy. Both pagan and Christian religions believe in an order of supernatural or at least superhuman beings graded in perfection and power. In both, these beings serve as messengers from the gods to men; they act sometimes as guardians or protectors, sometimes as traducers, deceivers, and enemies of man. But the analogy cannot be carried much further than this. The angels, according to Christian teaching, are not inferior gods, or even demi-gods. As compared with the "intermediate spirits" of pagan religion, they are less human in character, as well as less divine. Nevertheless, the reader of the great poems of antiquity will find a striking parallelism between the heavenly insurrection which underlies the action of *Prometheus Bound* and the angelic warfare in *Paradise Lost*.

IN THE WRITINGS of Plato, Aristotle, and Plotinus, philosophical inquiry turns from the sensible world of material things to consider the existence and nature of an order of purely intelligible beings. As there is an inherent connection between being perceptible to the senses and being material, so that which is purely intelligible must be completely immaterial. If ideas exist independently—in their own right and apart from knowing or thinking minds—then they constitute such an order of purely intelligible entities.

At this point a number of difficult questions arise. Are the intelligibles also intelligences, *i.e.*, are they an order of knowers as well as a realm of knowables? Can they be regarded as substances? And if so, do they have a mode of action appropriate to their mode of being—action which is other than knowing, action which in some way impinges on the course of events or the motions of the physical world?

Plotinus answers affirmatively that the purely intelligible beings are also pure intelligences, but he does not conceive them as having any power or action except that of knowledge. Another answer to these questions given in antiquity and the Middle Ages is that the intelligences are the celestial motors, the movers of the heavenly bodies. "Since we see," Aristotle writes, "that besides the simple spatial movement of the universe, which we say that the first and unmovable substance produces, there are other spatial movements—those of the planets—which are eternal (for a body which moves in a circle moves eternally), each of *these* movements also must be caused by a substance, both unmovable in itself and eternal." These secondary movers, Aristotle thinks, are "of the same number as the movements of the stars," and not only must they be eternal and unmovable, as is the prime mover, but also "without magnitude" or immaterial.

Plato offers an alternative hypothesis—that the celestial bodies are alive and have souls. This hypothesis, like Aristotle's, tends in the Middle Ages to be restated in terms of the theory of angels. Aquinas reports Augustine as thinking that "if the heavenly bodies are really living beings, their souls must be akin to the angelic nature." He himself holds that "spiritual substances are united to them as movers to things moved," the proof of which, he says, "lies in the fact that whereas nature moves to one fixed end, in which having attained it, it rests; this does not appear in the movement of the heavenly bodies. Hence it follows that they are moved by some intellectual substances."

The question whether intelligences govern the planets also occupies the attention of an astronomer like Kepler. Although he denies any need for such intelligences—among other reasons because planetary motion is not circular but elliptical—he argues that the celestial movements are the work either "of the natural power of the bodies, or else a work of the soul acting uniformly in accordance with those bodily powers." But whether or not they are to be regarded as *movers*, as well as *knowers* and *knowables*, the intelligences represent for ancient and mediaeval thought a mode of being exempt from the vicissitudes of physical change even as it is separate from matter.

WHEN MODERN philosophers consider spirits or spiritual being, they seldom deal with the ancient speculations about pure intelligibles or separate intelligences without being influenced by the theological doctrine of angels which developed in mediaeval thought.

The extent of this doctrine may be judged from the fact that the *Summa Theologica* of Aquinas contains a whole treatise on the angels, as well as additional questions on the speech of angels, their hierarchies and orders, the division between the good and the bad angels, and their action on men—the guardianship of the good angels and the assaults of the demons. That these additional questions are contained in the treatise on divine government throws some light on their theological significance.

The primary fact about the angelic nature is immateriality. An angel is immaterial both in its substantial being and in its characteristic activity which, says Aquinas, is "an altogether immaterial mode of operation." Being immaterial, they are also incorruptible. "Nothing is corrupted except by its form being separated from the matter ... Consequently," Aquinas writes, "a subject composed of matter and form ceases to be actually when the form is separated from the matter. But if the form subsists in its own being, as happens in the angels, it cannot lose its being." To signify that they are intelligences existing apart from matter, the angels are sometimes called "subsisting forms" and sometimes "separate substances."

Although they are imperishable in being and have immortal life, the angels are not, like God, truly eternal. "That *heaven of heavens* which Thou *createdst in the beginning* is some intellectual creature," Augustine writes, but it is in "no ways coeternal unto Thee." As created, the angels have a beginning. Yet, while not eternal, neither are they temporal creatures in continual flux, but, according to Augustine, they "partake of Thy eternity ... through the sweetness of that most happy contemplation of Thyself ... cleaving close unto Thee, placed beyond all the rolling vicissitudes of times." It is for this reason that the angels are spoken of as "aeviternal."

The familiar question concerning the number of angels able to stand on a needle's point—if it was ever asked by mediaeval theologians—merely poses the problem of how an incorporeal substance occupies space. The way in which Aquinas discusses "angels in relation to place" discloses how the question serves to raise generally significant issues concerning the nature of space and quantity, and their relation to causality. He points out that a body occupies place in a circumscribed fashion, *i.e.*, its dimensive quantity is contained within the space; whereas "an angel is said to be in a corporeal place by application of the angelic power in any manner whatever to the place. ... An incorporeal substance virtually contains the thing with which it comes into contact, and is not contained by it." To an objector who thinks that since, unlike bodies, angels do not fill a place, several can be in the same place at the same time, Aquinas replies that two angels cannot be in the same place because "it is impossible for two complete causes to be immediately the cause of one and the same thing." Since an angel is where he acts, and since by the power of his action he contains the place at which he acts, "there cannot be but one angel at one place."

Angels are also said to go from one place to another without traversing the intervening space and without the lapse of time. Considering their immateriality, such action is less remarkable for angels to perform than is the action of electrons, which, according to modern quantum mechanics, jump from outer to inner orbits of the atom without taking time or passing through inter-orbital space.

The immateriality of angels has other consequences which throw comparative light on the conditions of corporeal existence. In the world of physical things we ordinarily think of a species as including a number of individuals. While all men have the same specific nature, they differ numerically or individually. But because angels are immaterial substances, it is held that each angel *is* a distinct species. "Things which agree in species but differ in number," Aquinas explains, "agree in form but are distinguished materially. If, therefore, the angels are not composed of matter and form . . . it follows that it is impossible for two angels to be of one species."

Furthermore, as Aquinas states in another place, among "incorporeal substances there cannot be diversity of number without diversity of species and inequality of nature." Each species is necessarily higher or lower than another, so that the society of angels is a perfect hierarchy in which each member occupies a distinct rank. No two angels are equal as, on the supposition that they share in the same specific humanity, all men are. Yet such names as "seraphim" and "cherubim" and the distinction between archangels and angels indicate an organization of spiritual substances into various groups—according to the tradition, into nine orders or subordinate hierarchies.

The nine orders or ranks of angelic being are described by Dante in the *Paradiso* as distinct circles of love and light. Using these metaphors he thus reports his vision of the heavenly hierarchy. "I saw a Point which was raying out light so keen that the sight on which it blazes must needs close because of its intense brightness. . . . Perhaps as near as a halo seems to girdle the light which paints it, when the vapor that bears it is most dense, at such distance around the Point a circle of fire was whirling so rapidly that it would have surpassed that motion which most swiftly girds the world; and this was girt around by another, and that by the third, and the third then by the fourth, by the fifth the fourth, and then by the sixth the fifth. Thereon the seventh followed, so widespread now in compass that the messenger of Juno entire would be narrow to contain it. So the eighth and ninth."

Beatrice explains to him how the relation of the circles to one another and to the Point which is God depends upon their measure of love and truth, whereby there is "in each heaven a marvellous agreement with its Intelligence, of greater to more and of smaller to less." She then amplifies her meaning: "The first circles have shown to thee the Seraphim and the Cherubim. Thus swiftly they follow their own bonds, in order to liken themselves to the Point as most they can, and they can in proportion

as they are exalted to see. Those other loves, which go around them, are called Thrones of the divine aspect, because they terminated the first triad. . . . The next triad, that in like manner bourgeons in this sempiternal spring which the nightly Aries despoils not, perpetually sing Hosannah with three melodies, which sound in the three orders of joy . . . first Dominations, and then Virtues; the third order is of Powers. Then in the two penultimate dances, the Principalities and Archangels circle; the last is wholly of Angelic sports. These orders all gaze upward, and downward so prevail, that towards God all are drawn, and all draw."

THE THEORY of angels raises many questions regarding the similarity and difference between them and disembodied souls. But for comparison with men, perhaps the most striking consequences of the theory of angels as bodiless intelligences concern the manner of their knowledge and government. The comparison can be made on quite different views of the nature of man and the soul. In fact, diverse conceptions of man or the soul can themselves be compared by reference to the angelic properties which one conception attributes to human nature and another denies.

Lacking bodies, the angels are without sense-perception and imagination. Not being immersed in time and motion, they do not reason or think discursively as men do by reasoning from premises to conclusion. Whereas "human intellects," according to Aquinas, "obtain their perfection in the knowledge of truth by a kind of movement and discursive intellectual operation . . . as they advance from one known thing to another," the angels, "from the knowledge of a known principle . . . straightway perceive as known all its consequent conclusions . . . with no discursive process at all." Their knowledge is intuitive and immediate, not by means of concepts abstracted from experience or otherwise formed, but through the archetypal ideas infused in them at their creation by God. That is why, Aquinas goes on to say, angels "are called *intellectual* beings" as contrasted with such *rational* natures as "human souls which acquire knowledge of truth discursively." If men "possessed the fulness of intellectual light, like the angels, then in the first grasping of principles they would at once comprehend their whole range, by perceiving whatever could be reasoned out from them."

It would appear from this that conceptions of the human intellect which minimize its dependence on sense and imagination, and which emphasize the intuitive rather than the discursive character of human thought, attribute angelic power to man. The same may be said of theories of human knowledge which account for its origin in terms of innate ideas or implanted principles. Still another example of the attribution of angelic properties to man is to be found in the supposition that human beings can communicate with one another by telepathy. The angels are telepathic; one angel, it is said, can make its ideas known to another simply by an act of will and without any exterior means of communication.

Lacking bodies, the angels are without bodily emotions, free from the human conflict between reason and passion, and completely directed in their love—or the motion of their will—by what they know. In the Divine Comedy Beatrice speaks of the angelic society as one in which "the Eternal Love disclosed himself in new loves." Adverting to the division between the good and the bad angels, she tells Dante, "those whom thou seest here were modest in grateful recognition of the Goodness which had made them apt for intelligence so great, wherefore their vision was exalted with illuminant grace and by their merit, so that they have full and steadfast will." Yet their vision and love of God is not equal. In heaven "the Primal Light that irradiates it all is received in it by as many modes as are the splendors with which the Light pairs Itself. Wherefore, since the affection follows upon the act that conceives, in this nature the sweetness of love diversely glows and warms."

Such a society, governed by knowledge and love, has no need for the application of coercive force, for angels are ordered to one another in such a way that no misunderstandings or disagreements can occur among them. The philosophical anarchist who proposes the ideal of a human society without restraint or coercion seems, therefore, to be angelicizing men, or at least to be wishing for heaven on earth. Conceiving government on earth in other terms,

the writers of The Federalist remark that "if men were angels, no government would be necessary." If they had considered that the angelic society is governed by love alone and without force, they might have said, "if men were angels, no coercion would be necessary in their government."

ONE OF THE GREAT theological dogmas asserts that, from the beginning, the angels are divided into two hosts—the good and evil spirits. The sin of Lucifer, or Satan, and his followers is that of disobedience, or rebellion against God, motivated by a pride which refuses to be satisfied with being less than God. As Satan himself says, in Paradise Lost,

... pride and worse Ambition threw me down
Warring in Heav'n against Heav'ns matchless King.
... All his good prov'd ill in me,
And wrought but malice; lifted up so high
I 'sdeind subjection, and thought one step higher
Would set me highest, and in a moment quit
The debt immense of endless gratitude ...
.... And that word
Disdain forbids me, and my dread of shame
Among the spirits beneath, whom I seduc'd
Then to submit, boasting I could subdue
Th' Omnipotent.

The theologians try to define precisely the nature of Satan's pride in wishing to be God. "To be as God," Aquinas explains, "can be understood in two ways: first, by equality; secondly, by likeness. An angel could not seek to be as God in the first way, because by natural knowledge he knew that this was impossible ... And even supposing it were possible, it would be against natural desire, because there exists in everything the natural desire to preserve its own nature which would not be preserved were it to be changed into another nature. Consequently, no creature of a lower nature can ever covet the grade of a higher nature, just as an ass does not desire to be a horse."

It must be in the other way, then, Aquinas thinks, that Satan sinned by wishing to be like God. But this requires further explanation. "To desire to be as God according to likeness can happen in two ways. In one way, as to that likeness whereby everything is likened unto God. And so, if anyone desire in this way to be Godlike, he commits no sin; provided that he desires such likeness in proper order, that is to say, that he may obtain it from God. But he would sin were he to desire to be like God even in the right way, but of his own power, and not of God's. In another way, he may desire to be like God in some respect which is not natural to one; *e.g.*, if one were to desire to create heaven and earth, which is proper to God, in which desire there would be sin."

In this last way, Aquinas asserts, "the devil desired to be as God. Not that he desired to resemble God by being subject to no one else absolutely, for thus he would be desiring his own non-being, since no creature can exist except by participating under God." But he "desired as the last end of his beatitude something which he could attain by virtue of his own nature, turning his appetite away from the supernatural beatitude which is attained by God's grace."

In the original sin of Lucifer and the other fallen angels, as well as in all subsequent intervention by Satan or his demons in the affairs of men, lie the theological mysteries of the origin of evil in a world created by God's love and goodness, and of the liberty of those creatures who, while free, can only do God's will. As indicated in the chapter on SIN, the fall of Adam from grace and innocence involves the same mysteries. Man's destiny is connected with the career of Lucifer in traditional Christian teaching, not only on the side of sin, but also with regard to man's redemption—salvation replacing the fallen angels by the souls of the elect in the heavenly choir.

Among the most extraordinary moments in our literature are those in which Lucifer talks with God about mankind, as in *Paradise Lost*; or about a particular man, as in the Book of Job or in the Prologue in Heaven in *Faust*. Their pagan parallel is the speech of Prometheus to a silent Zeus, but Prometheus, unlike Satan, is man's benefactor and he can defy Zeus because the Fates, whose secret he knows, rule over the gods. Lucifer, on the contrary, seems always to be in the service of God. When he appears to Ivan in the *Brothers Karamazov*, he protests, "I love men genuinely . . . . and against the grain I serve to produce events and do what is irrational because I am

commanded to." If it were otherwise, the warfare between the powers of light and darkness would have to be construed as a battle between equals, which, according to Christian orthodoxy, is the Manichean heresy that regards the world as the battle ground of the forces of good and evil.

The word "angelic" usually has the connotation of perfect moral goodness, but that must not lead us to forget that the demons are angelic in their nature although of a diabolical or evil will. Nor should the fact of Satan's subservience to God cause us to forget that Christian theology tries not to underestimate the power of the devil in his goings and comings on earth. Satan tried to tempt even Christ, and throughout the New Testament the destruction of the diabolical influence over men occupies a prominent place. The intervention of the devil in man's life provides, if not the theme, the background of Goethe's *Faust*.

As the theory of demonic influences and diabolical possession is an integral part of the traditional doctrine of angels, so, in modern times, demonology has been a major focus of attack upon theological teaching concerning spirits. Moralists have thought it possible to explain human depravity without recourse to the seductions of the devil, and psychiatrists have thought it possible for men to go mad or to behave as if bewitched without the help of evil spirits. The idea of the devil, according to Freud, is a religious fiction—"the best way out in acquittal of God" for those who try "to reconcile the undeniable existence . . . . of evil with His omnipotence and supreme goodness."

The characteristic skepticism of our age has been directed against the belief in angels generally. It casts doubt by satire or denies by argument the existence of spirits both good and evil. Yet, all arguments considered, it may be wondered whether the existence of angels—or, in philosophical terms, the existence of pure intelligences—is or is not still a genuine issue. Or are there two issues here, one philosophical and the other theological, one to be resolved or left unresolved on the level of argument, the other to be answered dogmatically by the declarations of a religious faith?

OUTLINE OF TOPICS

REFERENCES

To find the passages cited, use the numbers in heavy type, which are the volume and page numbers of the passages referred to. For example, in 4 HOMER: *Iliad*, BK II [265–283] 12d, the number 4 is the number of the volume in the set; the number 12d indicates that the passage is in section d of page 12.

PAGE SECTIONS: When the text is printed in one column, the letters a and b refer to the upper and lower halves of the page. For example, in 53 JAMES: *Psychology*, 116a-119b, the passage begins in the upper half of page 116 and ends in the lower half of page 119. When the text is printed in two columns, the letters a and b refer to the upper and lower halves of the left-hand side of the page, the letters c and d to the upper and lower halves of the right-hand side of the page. For example, in 7 PLATO: *Symposium*, 163b-164c, the passage begins in the lower half of the left-hand side of page 163 and ends in the upper half of the right-hand side of page 164.

AUTHOR'S DIVISIONS: One or more of the main divisions of a work (such as PART, BK, CH, SECT) are sometimes included in the reference; line numbers, in brackets, are given in certain cases; *e.g.*, *Iliad*, BK II [265–283] 12d.

BIBLE REFERENCES: The references are to book, chapter, and verse. When the King James and Douay versions differ in title of books or in the numbering of chapters or verses, the King James version is cited first and the Douay, indicated by a (*D*), follows; *e.g.*, OLD TESTA-MENT: *Nehemiah*, 7:45—(*D*) *II Esdras*, 7:46.

SYMBOLS: The abbreviation "esp" calls the reader's attention to one or more especially relevant parts of a whole reference; "passim" signifies that the topic is discussed intermittently rather than continuously in the work or passage cited.

For additional information concerning the style of the references, see the Explanation of Reference Style; for general guidance in the use of *The Great Ideas*, consult the Preface.

1. Inferior deities or demi-gods in polytheistic religion

4 HOMER: *Iliad*, BK VIII 51a-56d esp [1–40] 51a-b; BK XIV [135–360] 99c-101d; BK XV [1–235] 104a-106c; BK XVIII [368–467] 133d-134d; BK XX 142a-147d; BK XXI [383–513] 152a-153c / *Odyssey*, BK V [1–147] 208a-209c; BK IX [231–280] 231c-232a; BK XIII [125–164] 256b-d

5 AESCHYLUS: *Prometheus Bound* 40a-51d / *Eumenides* 81a-91d

5 SOPHOCLES: *Trachiniae* 170a-181a,c / *Philoctetes* [1409–1471] 194d-195a,c

5 EURIPIDES: *Rhesus* [890–982] 210d-211d / *Hippolytus* 225a-236d esp [1–55] 225a-c, [1268–1440] 235b-236d / *Alcestis* 237a-247a,c / *Trojan Women* [1–97] 270a-271a / *Ion* 282a-297d / *Helen* 298a-314a,c / *Andromache* [1226–1288] 325c-326a,c / *Electra* [1233–1359] 338b-339a,c / *Bacchantes* 340a-352a,c / *Heracles Mad* 365a-377d esp [1–59] 365a-c / *Orestes* [1625–1693] 410b-d

5 ARISTOPHANES: *Clouds* [595–626] 496a-b / *Peace* 526a-541d / *Birds* 542a-563d esp [571–638] 549d-550d, [1199–1261] 557c-558b, [1494–1693] 560c-562d / *Frogs* 564a-582a,c / *Plutus* 629a-642d

6 HERODOTUS: *History*, BK I, 21d-22a; 31a-b; 48c; BK II, 58a-60d; 79d-80c; 82d-83b; BK IV, 155c-156a; BK VIII, 266c-d

7 PLATO: *Protagoras*, 44a-45a / *Euthydemus*, 81d-82b / *Cratylus*, 92b-97d / *Phaedrus*, 116b-d; 122c-125b passim, esp 124d-125a; 130d-131a; 141c / *Symposium*, 152b; 153b-d; 159d-161a; 163a-164c / *Euthyphro*, 193a-c / *Apology*, 204c-205c / *Republic*, BK II–III, 320d-328a / *Timaeus*, 452b / *Critias*, 481c-482a / *Statesman*, 588a-589c / *Laws*, BK II, 653a-c; 662c-d; BK IV, 680c-684a passim; BK VII, 730a-d; BK X 757d-771b

8 ARISTOTLE: *Metaphysics*, BK III, CH 4 [1000ᵃ8–18] 518d-519a; BK XII, CH 8 [1074ᵇ1–14] 604d-605a

9 ARISTOTLE: *Rhetoric*, BK III, CH 18 [1419ᵃ8–13] 673d-674a

12 LUCRETIUS: *Nature of Things*, BK I [1–41] 1a-c; BK II [581–660] 22b-23b; BK V [396–404] 66b

12 EPICTETUS: *Discourses*, BK I, CH 3 108b-c; CH 12 118d-120b; CH 14 120d-121c; BK II, CH 16, 158b-d; BK IV, CH 4, 226d-228a; CH 11, 240d-241a

12 AURELIUS: *Meditations*, BK II, SECT 11 258a-b

13 VIRGIL: *Aeneid* 103a-379a esp BK I [223–233] 109a, [297–304] 111a, [657–694] 121a-122a, BK IV [218–258] 173a-174a, BK X [1–117] 302a-305a

14 PLUTARCH: *Numa Pompilius*, 50d-51c; 57b-58a / *Coriolanus*, 189a-c / *Aemilius Paulus*, 220d-221b / *Pelopidas*, 238a-b; 239d-240c / *Aristides*, 268a-d / *Dion*, 781d-782a

15 TACITUS: *Annals*, BK II, 35d-36a; BK III, 59d-60c / *Histories*, BK II, 214d-215a; BK IV, 293b-294a; BK V, 294d-296a

17 PLOTINUS: *Second Ennead*, TR IX, CH 9 70d-72a passim / *Third Ennead*, TR V 100c-106b / *Fourth Ennead*, TR III, CH 14 149d-150a / *Fifth Ennead*, TR VIII, CH 3, 241a; CH 10 244c-245a

18 AUGUSTINE: *City of God*, BK I–X 129a-322a,c passim; BK XVIII, CH 8–19 475d-482c; CH 21 482d-483b; CH 24 485a-b; BK XIX, CH 9 516a-c / *Christian Doctrine*, BK II, CH 17 645d-646a

19 AQUINAS: *Summa Theologica*, PART I, Q 22, A 3, ANS 130d-131c; Q 63, A 7, ANS 331c-332b

21 DANTE: *Divine Comedy*, HELL, XXXI 46a-47c; PARADISE, VIII [1–15] 116d

22 CHAUCER: *Knight's Tale* [1902-2482] 191a-200b

23 HOBBES: *Leviathan*, PART I, 79d-82c

24 RABELAIS: *Gargantua and Pantagruel*, BK III, 132b-c

25 MONTAIGNE: *Essays*, 246d-248c; 256d-257d; 269a-b

26 SHAKESPEARE: *As You Like It*, ACT V, SC IV [114–152] 625a-b

27 SHAKESPEARE: *Tempest*, ACT IV, SC I 541c-544d

30 BACON: *Advancement of Learning*, 20b-c

32 MILTON: *Christs Nativity* 1a-7b / *L'Allegro* 17b-21a / *Il Penseroso* 21a-25a / *Arcades* 25a-27b / *Lycidas* 27b-32a / *Comus* 33a-56b / *Paradise Lost*, BK I [331–621] 100b-107a / *Samson Agonistes* [896–902] 359a

35 LOCKE: *Human Understanding*, BK I, CH III, SECT 15 116c-d

37 FIELDING: *Tom Jones*, 152b-c

40 GIBBON: *Decline and Fall*, 12b-d; 184c-185d; 345b-347d esp 346c-347a; 461b-c; 583d-584a

41 GIBBON: *Decline and Fall*, 135b; 226a-227c

46 HEGEL: *Philosophy of History*, INTRO, 196d-197c; PART I, 224a-b; 228a-c; 238d-239b; 252d-253c; PART II, 263d-265c; 268b-271c

47 GOETHE: *Faust*, PART II [5300–5392] 131a-133a; [7005–8487] 171b-206b esp [7005–7039] 171b-172a, [7080–7248] 173b-177b, [7263–7270] 178a, [7495–7820] 183b-190b

2. The philosophical consideration of pure intelligences, spiritual substances, suprahuman persons

17 PLOTINUS: *Second Ennead*, TR IX, CH 17 76b-77a / *Third Ennead*, TR II, CH 11 88b-c; TR V 100c-106b; TR VIII, CH 8–10 132d-136a / *Fifth Ennead*, TR I, CH 4 209d-210c; TR VIII, CH 3, 241a / *Sixth Ennead*, TR VIII, CH 3 344a-b

18 AUGUSTINE: *Confessions*, BK XII 99b-110d

19 AQUINAS: *Summa Theologica*, PART I, Q 22, A 3, ANS 130d-131c; Q 45, A 5, ANS 245c-247a; Q 47, A 1, ANS 256a-257b; Q 50, A 3, ANS 272a-

273b; Q 65, A 4, ANS 342b-343c; Q 79, A 4 417a-418c; A 10, ANS 423d-424d; Q 84, A 4, ANS and REP 1,3 444d-446b; Q 87, A 1, ANS and REP 3 465a-466c; Q 88, A 1, ANS 469a-471c; Q 110, A 1, REP 3 564c-565d; Q 115, A 1, ANS 585d-587c

20 AQUINAS: *Summa Theologica*, PART III SUPPL, Q 92, A 1, ANS and REP 9–10 1025c-1032b

21 DANTE: *Divine Comedy*, PARADISE, II [112–123] 109a; XXVIII [1–78] 148d-149c; XXIX [13–45] 150b-c

23 HOBBES: *Leviathan*, PART III, 174b-176d; PART IV, 258b-260c

24 RABELAIS: *Gargantua and Pantagruel*, BK III, 172d-173c

30 BACON: *Advancement of Learning*, 41d-42a / *Novum Organum*, BK II, APH 15 149a

31 DESCARTES: *Objections and Replies*, 225d-226a

32 MILTON: *Paradise Lost*, BK II [142–154] 114b; BK III [694–735] 150b-151b; BK V [388–450] 183b-185a; [469–505] 185b-186a; BK VI [316–353] 203a-204a

35 LOCKE: *Human Understanding*, BK II, CH XV, SECT 11 165a-b; CH XXI, SECT 2 178c; CH XXIII, SECT 5 205a-b; SECT 15–37 208c-214b passim, BK III, CH VI, SECT 11–12 271b-272b; BK IV, CH III, SECT 6, 315a-b; SECT 27 321d-322a; CH XVI, SECT 12 370b-371a; CH XVII, SECT 14 378c-d

35 BERKELEY: *Human Knowledge*, SECT 25–27 417d-418b; SECT 135–145 440a-442a

41 GIBBON: *Decline and Fall*, 136b; 136d

42 KANT: *Pure Reason*, 237c-d / *Fund. Prin. Metaphysic of Morals*, 253d-254a; 259c-d; 263a; 263d-264d; 266a-c; 271a-277b; 278a; 280b-281a; 282c; 286a-287b / *Practical Reason*, 296a-c; 300a-c; 303b-304a; 305c-d; 308c-309b; 321b-c; 325d-327a; 328b; 340c-d; 347d-348b / *Judgement*, 508b; 572d-574b

46 HEGEL: *Philosophy of History*, PART I, 238d-239a

2a. The celestial motors or secondary prime movers: the intelligences attached to the celestial bodies

7 PLATO: *Timaeus*, 452c-d / *Laws*, BK X, 765b

8 ARISTOTLE: *Heavens*, BK II, CH 1 [284ª27-ᵇ6] 376a; CH 12 383b-384c / *Metaphysics*, BK XII, CH 8 603b-605a / *Soul*, BK I, CH 3 [406ᵇ27-407ᵇ13] 636b-637b

12 LUCRETIUS: *Nature of Things*, BK V [110–145] 62c-63a

13 VIRGIL: *Aeneid*, BK VI [724–732] 230b

16 KEPLER: *Epitome*, BK IV, 890a-895b esp 890b-893b; 896a-897a; 914a-b; 930b; 932a-933a; 959a-960a / *Harmonies of the World*, 1080b-1085b esp 1083b-1085b

17 PLOTINUS: *Second Ennead*, TR II, CH 1 40a-41a; CH 3 41c-42a; TR III, CH 2 42c-d / *Third Ennead*, TR II, CH 3, 84b; TR IV, CH 6, 99d; TR V, CH 6 103b-104a / *Fourth Ennead*, TR IV, CH 8, 162b-d; CH 22–27 168d-172a; CH 30

(2. *The philosophical consideration of pure intelligences, spiritual substances, supra-
human persons.* 2a. *The celestial motors or
secondary prime movers: the intelligences
attached to the celestial bodies.*)

174b-c; CH 35, 177c; CH 42 180d-181b; TR
VIII, CH 2, 202a

19 AQUINAS: *Summa Theologica*, PART I, Q 47,
A 1, ANS 256a-257b; Q 50, A 3, ANS and REP 3
272a-273b; Q 51, A 3, REP 3 277a-278c; Q 52,
A 2 279b-280a; Q 66, A 2, ANS 345d-347b; Q 70,
A 3 365b-367a; Q 76, A 6, REP 3 396a-d; Q 110,
A 1, REP 2-3 564c-565d; A 3, ANS 566d-567b;
Q 115, A 4, REP 1 589d-590c; Q 117, A 4, REP 1
599b-d; PART I–II, Q 6, A 5, REP 2 648b-649a

20 AQUINAS: *Summa Theologica*, PART III SUPPL,
Q 91, A 2, REP 10 1017c-1020c

21 DANTE: *Divine Comedy*, HELL, VII [67–96]
10b-c; PARADISE, I [103–126] 107b-c; II [112–
138] 109a; VIII [16–39] 116d-117a; [97–114]
118a; XIII [52–72] 126a; XXVIII 148d-150b;
XXIX [37–45] 150c

28 GILBERT: *Loadstone*, BK V, 104b-105d

2b. Our knowledge of immaterial beings

17 PLOTINUS: *Third Ennead*, TR VIII, CH 8–10
132d-136a

18 AUGUSTINE: *Confessions*, BK XII, par 2–9 99c-
101c

19 AQUINAS: *Summa Theologica*, PART I, Q 50,
A 2, ANS 270a-272a; Q 84, A 7, REP 3 449b-
450b; Q 88, AA 1–2 469a-472c; Q 94, A 2 503a-
504a; Q 111, A 1, REP 3 568c-569b; PART I–II,
Q 3, A 6, ANS 627b-628a; A 7 628a-d

20 AQUINAS: *Summa Theologica*, PART III SUPPL,
Q 92, A 1, ANS and REP 9 1025c-1032b

30 BACON: *Advancement of Learning*, 41d-42a

31 DESCARTES: *Objections and Replies*, 122c

35 LOCKE: *Human Understanding*, BK II, CH XV,
SECT 11 165a-b; CH XXIII, SECT 5 205a-b;
SECT 13 207d-208b; SECT 15–37 208c-214b;
BK III, CH VI, SECT 11–12 271b-272b; CH XI,
SECT 23 305a-b; BK IV, CH III, SECT 17 317c;
SECT 27 321d-322a; CH VI, SECT 14, 336a-b;
CH XI, SECT 12 357c-d; CH XVI, SECT 12 370b-
371a

35 BERKELEY: *Human Knowledge*, SECT 27
418a-b; SECT 81 428c-d; SECT 89 430b-c;
SECT 135–145 440a-442a

3. The conception of angels in Judaeo-Christian doctrine

18 AUGUSTINE: *City of God*, BK VIII–XII 264b,d-
360a,c

19 AQUINAS: *Summa Theologica*, PART I, QQ 50–64
269a-338d

21 DANTE: *Divine Comedy*, PARADISE, XXVIII–
XXIX 148d-151d

23 HOBBES: *Leviathan*, PART III, 174b-176d

32 MILTON: *Paradise Lost*, BK I 93a-110b esp
[84–191] 95b-97b, [423–431] 102b; BK V [769–
904] 192a-195a; BK VI [320–353] 203a-204a

3a. The first creatures of God: their place in the order of creation

OLD TESTAMENT: *I Kings*, 8:27—(D) *III Kings*,
8:27 / *II Chronicles*, 2:6; 6:18—(D) *II Paralipomenon*, 2:6; 6:18 / *Psalms*, 8:4–5; 115:16;
148:4—(D) *Psalms*, 8:5-6; 113:16; 148:4 /
Isaiah, 6:1-3—(D) *Isaias*, 6:1-3 / *Ezekiel*,
1—(D) *Ezechiel*, 1 / *Daniel*, 7:10

NEW TESTAMENT: *Matthew*, 18:10 / *John*, 1:51 /
Acts, 23:8 / *Hebrews*, 1–2 esp 1:1-8, 2:1–9 /
I Peter, 3:22 / *Revelation*, 5:11–14—(D) *Apoc-
alypse*, 5:11–14

18 AUGUSTINE: *Confessions*, BK XII 99b-110d; BK
XIII, par 4 111c / *City of God*, BK XI 322b,d-
342a,c; BK XXII, CH 1 586b,d-587b

19 AQUINAS: *Summa Theologica*, PART I, Q 45,
A 5, ANS and REP 1 245c-247a; Q 47, A 1, ANS
256a-257b; A 2, ANS 257b-258c; Q 50, AA 1–3
269b-273b; Q 61 314d-317c; Q 62, A 1 317d-
318c; A 3 319c-320b; Q 65, AA 3–4 341c-343c;
Q 66, A 3, ANS and REP 3 347b-348d; A 4, ANS
and REP 1 348d-349d; Q 67, A 4, ANS and REP 4
352a-354a; Q 85, A 1, ANS 451c-453c; Q 90,
A 3 482c-483a

21 DANTE: *Divine Comedy*, PURGATORY, XII [25–
27] 70c; PARADISE, VII [121–148] 116b-c; XIX
[40–51] 135c; XXIX [1–48] 150b-d

23 HOBBES: *Leviathan*, PART III, 174d

24 RABELAIS: *Gargantua and Pantagruel*, BK III,
132b-c

30 BACON: *Advancement of Learning*, 17c-d

32 MILTON: *Paradise Lost*, BK III [86–102] 137a-b;
BK V [800–868] 192b-194a / *Samson Agonistes*
[667–673] 354a

33 PASCAL: *Pensées*, 140 199a-b

35 LOCKE: *Human Understanding*, BK III, CH VI,
SECT 11–12 271b-272b; BK IV, CH XVI, SECT 12
370b-371a

3b. The angelic nature

OLD TESTAMENT: *Psalms*, 103:20–22; 104:4—(D)
Psalms, 102:20–22; 103:4 / *Isaiah*, 6:1-3—(D)
Isaias, 6:1-3 / *Ezekiel*, 1; 10—(D) *Ezechiel*, 1;
10

NEW TESTAMENT: *Hebrews*, 1–2 esp 1:1-8 / *II
Peter*, 2:10-11 / *Revelation*, 18:1—(D) *Apocalypse*, 18:1

18 AUGUSTINE: *Confessions*, BK XII, par 7 100d-
101a; par 9 101b-c; par 12 101d-102a; par
18–22, 103b-104a / *City of God*, BK XXI, CH 1
560a-d

19 AQUINAS: *Summa Theologica*, PART I, QQ 50–
53 269a-284d; Q 79, A 1, REP 3 414a-d; Q 87,
A 1, ANS and REP 2–3 465a-466c

21 DANTE: *Divine Comedy*, PARADISE, XXIX [1–
48] 150b-d; [127–145] 151c-d

23 HOBBES: *Leviathan*, PART III, 174b-176d

31 DESCARTES: *Objections and Replies*, 218d;
225d-226a

32 MILTON: *Paradise Lost*, BK I [84–191] 95b-97b;
[423–431] 102b; BK V [800–868] 192b-194a;
BK VI [320–353] 203a-204a

33 PASCAL: *Provincial Letters*, 87a-88a

35 LOCKE: *Human Understanding*, BK II, CH X, SECT 9, 143a-b; BK III, CH VI, SECT 11-12 271b-272b

3c. The aeviternity and incorruptibility of angels

18 AUGUSTINE: *Confessions*, BK XII, par 9 101b-c; par 12 101d-102a; par 15-16 102b-103a; par 18-22, 103b-104a; par 28, 105c / *City of God*, BK XII, CH 15 351b-352d; BK XIII, CH I 360a-b

19 AQUINAS: *Summa Theologica*, PART I, Q 10, A 3, ANS and REP 1 42c-43b; AA 5-6 44b-46d; Q 50, A 5 274b-275a; Q 61, A 2 315c-316a; Q 97, A 1, ANS 513c-514c; Q 104, A 1, ANS and REP 1,3 534c-536c

21 DANTE: *Divine Comedy*, PARADISE, VII [64-69] 115d; [121-148] 116b-c

23 HOBBES: *Leviathan*, PART III, 175d-176d

24 RABELAIS: *Gargantua and Pantagruel*, BK III, 173a-c

32 MILTON: *Paradise Lost*, BK I [116-159] 96a-97a; BK II [81-105] 113a-b; BK V [846-860] 193b-194a; [889-892] 194b; BK VI [296-353] 202b-204a esp [320-353] 203a-204a; [430-436] 205b

3d. The angelic intellect and angelic knowledge

OLD TESTAMENT: *Genesis*, 16:7-12; 18:9-15; 22:15-18 / *Judges*, 6:11-16; 13:2-14 / *II Samuel*, 14:20—(D) *II Kings*, 14:20 / *Daniel*, 10-12

NEW TESTAMENT: *Matthew*, 24:35-36 / *Mark*, 13:28-32 / *I Timothy*, 3:16 / *I Peter*, 1:12 / *Revelation*, 17; 18:21-24; 21:9-22:7—(D) *Apocalypse*, 17; 18:21-24; 21:9-22:7

18 AUGUSTINE: *Confessions*, BK XII, par 12 101d-102a; par 16 102d-103a; par 20 103c-d / *City of God*, BK IX, CH 20-22 296a-297a; BK X, CH 2 299d-300a; BK XI, CH 11 328d-329b; CH 13-15 329c-331a; CH 29 339a-b; BK XVI, CH 6 426c-427a; BK XXII, CH I 586b,d-587b; CH 29, 614b-d

19 AQUINAS: *Summa Theologica*, PART I, Q 7, A 2, ANS and REP 2 31d-32c; Q 12, A 4, REP 2 53b-54c; QQ 54-58 284d-306b; Q 64, A 1 334a-335c; Q 75, A 7, REP 3 384d-385c; Q 79, A 1, REP 3 414a-d; A 2, ANS 414d-416a; A 8, ANS and REP 3 421c-422b; A 10, ANS 423d-424d; Q 84, A 2, ANS 442b-443c; A 3, REP 1 443d-444d; A 7, ANS 449b-450b; Q 85, A 1, ANS 451c-453c; A 5, ANS 457d-458d; Q 87, A 1, ANS and REP 2 465a-466c; A 3, ANS 467b-468a; Q 89, A 3, ANS 475d-476c; A 4, ANS 476c-477a; Q 117, A 2 597c-598c; PART I-II, Q 3, A 8, REP 2 628d-629c

20 AQUINAS: *Summa Theologica*, PART I-II, Q 50, A 6 11a-12a; Q 51, A 1, ANS and REP 2 12b-13c; PART II-II, Q 5, AA 1-2 410a-412a

21 DANTE: *Divine Comedy*, PARADISE, XIX [40-57] 135c; XXI [73-102] 139a-b; XXVIII [98-114] 149d-150a; XXIX [67-84] 151a; [127-145] 151c-d

30 BACON: *Novum Organum*, BK II, APH 15 149a

32 MILTON: *Paradise Lost*, BK I [242-255] 98b-99a; BK II [142-151] 114b; BK III [654-735] 149b-151b esp [681-693] 150a-b; BK V [388-505] 183b-186a esp [388-413] 183b-184a, [469-505] 185b-186a; BK VIII [66-79] 233b-234a

33 PASCAL: *Pensées*, 285 224a

35 LOCKE: *Human Understanding*, BK II, CH X, SECT 9 143a-c; CH XXIII, SECT 13 207d-208b; SECT 36 213c-d; BK III, CH VI, SECT 3 268d; CH XI, SECT 23 305a-b; BK IV, CH III, SECT 6, 315a-b; SECT 23 320a-c; CH XVII, SECT 14 378c-d

35 BERKELEY: *Human Knowledge*, SECT 8; 428c-d

36 STERNE: *Tristram Shandy*, 318b

3e. The angelic will and angelic love

18 AUGUSTINE: *Confessions*, BK XII, par 9 101b-c; par 12-13 101d-102b; par 15 102b-c; par 18, 103b-c; par 21-22, 103d-104a; par 28, 105c / *City of God*, BK IX, CH 20-22 296a-297a; BK X, CH 7 302d-303a; BK XII, CH 3 343d-344b; CH 6-9 345b-348b; BK XXII, CH I 586b,d-587b

19 AQUINAS: *Summa Theologica*, PART I, QQ 59-60 306b-314c; Q 62, A 2 318d-319c; Q 64, AA 2-3 335d-337c

20 AQUINAS: *Summa Theologica*, PART I-II, Q 50, A 6 11a-12a; PART II-II, Q 5, A 2 411b-412a

21 DANTE: *Divine Comedy*, PARADISE, VIII [31-39] 117a; XXIII [70-139] 142a-c; XXVIII 148d-150b esp [106-114] 150a; XXIX [55-66] 150d-151a; [127-145] 151c-d

32 MILTON: *Paradise Lost*, BK V [535-543] 187a; BK VIII [612-643] 245b-246a

35 LOCKE: *Human Understanding*, BK II, CH XXI, SECT 50-51 191b-c

47 GOETHE: *Faust*, PART II [11,676-824] 284a-287b; [11,854-12,111] 288b-294b

3f. Angelic action: its characteristics in general

19 AQUINAS: *Summa Theologica*, PART I, Q 45, A 5, ANS and REP 1 245c-247a; QQ 51-53 275a-284d; Q 91, A 2, REP 1 485b-486b; A 4, REP 2 487d-488c; QQ 106-107 545c-552b; QQ 110-111 564c-571d

23 HOBBES: *Leviathan*, PART III, 174c; 175c-d

32 MILTON: *Paradise Lost*, BK VIII [107-114] 234b

35 LOCKE: *Human Understanding*, BK II, CH XXIII, SECT 13 207d-208b

3g. The angelic hierarchy: the inequality, order, and number of the angels and their relation to one another

OLD TESTAMENT: *Psalms*, 80:1—(D) *Psalms*, 79:2 / *Isaiah*, 6:1-7; 37:16—(D) *Isaias*, 6:1-8; 37:16 / *Ezekiel*, 10; 11:22—(D) *Ezechiel*, 10; 11:22 / *Daniel*, 7:10

APOCRYPHA: *Tobit*, 12:15-21—(D) OT, *Tobias*, 12:15-21

(3. *The conception of angels in Judaeo-Christian doctrine. 3g. The angelic hierarchy: the inequality, order, and number of the angels and their relation to one another.*)

NEW TESTAMENT: *Colossians*, 1:16 / *I Thessalonians*, 4:16—(D) *I Thessalonians*, 4:15 / *Hebrews*, 12:22–23 / *Jude*, 9 / *Revelation*, 5:11—(D) *Apocalypse*, 5:11

18 AUGUSTINE: *Confessions*, BK XII, par 12, 102a; par 31, 106c-d / *City of God*, BK VIII, CH 24, 283b; BK XXII, CH 30, 617c

19 AQUINAS: *Summa Theologica*, PART I, Q 47, A 2, ANS 257b-258c; Q 50, AA 3–4 272a-274b; Q 63, A 7 331c-332b; A 9, REP 3 333b-d; QQ 106–109 545c-564b; PART I–II, Q 4, A 5, REP 6 632c-634b

20 AQUINAS: *Summa Theologica*, PART III, Q 8, A 4 759b-d

21 DANTE: *Divine Comedy*, PARADISE, II [112–138] 109a; XXVIII 148d-150b; XXIX [127–145] 151c-d

30 BACON: *Advancement of Learning*, 17d

32 MILTON: *Paradise Lost*, BK V [600–904] 188b-195a esp [769–799] 192a-b, [809–845] 193a-b

35 LOCKE: *Human Understanding*, BK IV, CH III, SECT 27 321d-322a; CH XVI, SECT 12, 370c-371a

35 BERKELEY: *Human Knowledge*, SECT 81 428c-d

47 GOETHE: *Faust*, PROLOGUE [243–270] 7a-b; PART II [11,844–12,111] 288a-294b

4. Comparison of angels with men and with disembodied souls: their relation to the blessed in the heavenly choir

OLD TESTAMENT: *Job*, 4:18–19 / *Psalms*, 8:4–5—(D) *Psalms*, 8:5–6

NEW TESTAMENT: *Matthew*, 22:23–33 / *Mark*, 12:18–27 / *Luke*, 20:27–38 / *I Corinthians*, 6:2–3 / *Hebrews*, 1:13–14; 2:7; 12:22–23 / *Revelation*, 22:8–9—(D) *Apocalypse*, 22:8–9

18 AUGUSTINE: *Confessions*, BK XII, par 23 104b-c / *City of God*, BK VII, CH 30, 261d; BK VIII, CH 14–18 273d-277a; CH 25 283b-c; BK IX, CH 5–13 288b-292d; CH 22 296d-297a; BK XI, CH 29 339a-b; BK XIII, CH 1 360a-b; BK XVI, CH 6 426c-427a; BK XXI, CH 10 569d-570b; BK XXII, CH 29, 614b-d / *Christian Doctrine*, BK I, CH 23 630a-c; CH 30 632c-633b; CH 33 633d-634b

19 AQUINAS: *Summa Theologica*, PART I, Q 7, A 2, REP 2 31d-32c; Q 23, A 1, REP 3 132c-133b; Q 47, A 2, ANS 257b-258c; Q 51, A 1, ANS and REP 2–3 275b-276b; QQ 54–60 284d-314c passim; Q 62 317c-325b passim; Q 66, A 3, ANS and REP 3 347b-348d; Q 75, A 7 384d-385c; Q 76, A 2, REP 1 388c-391a; A 5, ANS 394c-396a; Q 79, A 1, REP 3 414a-d; A 2, ANS 414d-416a; A 8, ANS and REP 3 421c-422b; Q 84, A 3, REP 1 443d-444d; A 7, ANS 449b-450b; Q 85, A 1, ANS 451c-453c; A 5, ANS 457d-458d; Q 87, A 1, ANS and REP 2–3 465a-466c; A 3, ANS 467b-468a; Q 89, A 3, ANS 475d-476c;

A 4, ANS 476c-477a; A 7, REP 2 478d-479c; Q 93, A 3 493d-494c; Q 97, A 1, ANS 513c-514c; Q 108, A 1, ANS 552c-553c; A 8 561a-562a; Q 117, A 2 597c-598c; PART I–II, Q 2, A 3, REP 1 617b-618a; Q 4, A 5, REP 6 632c-634b; Q 5, A 1, REP 1 636d-637c

20 AQUINAS: *Summa Theologica*, PART I–II, Q 50, A 6 11a-12a; Q 51, A 1, ANS and REP 2 12b-13c; PART II–II, Q 5, A 2 411b-412a; PART III, Q 6, A 3, REP 2 742a-743a; Q 8, A 4 759b-d; PART III SUPPL, Q 69, A 3, REP 5 887d-889c; Q 70, A 3, CONTRARY 897d-900d; Q 89, A 3 1007d-1008b; A 8 1011b-1012a; Q 95, A 4 1046d-1047d; Q 96, A 9 1062d-1063b; Q 99, A 3 1081d-1083a

21 DANTE: *Divine Comedy*, PARADISE, IV [28–48] 111a; VII [121–148] 116b-c; VIII [22–39] 116d-117c; XIX [40–66] 135c-d; XXI [73–102] 139a-b; XXIX [13–36] 150b-c; XXXI 153b-154c; XXXII [85–114] 155c-d

27 SHAKESPEARE: *Hamlet*, ACT II, SC II [314–322] 43d

30 BACON: *Advancement of Learning*, 80d-81a / *Novum Organum*, BK II, APH 15 149a

32 MILTON: *At a Solemn Musick* 13a-b / *Paradise Lost*, BK II [345–353] 118b-119a; BK III [654–735] 149b-151b esp [681–693] 150a-b; BK IV [358–365] 160a-b; BK V [388–450] 183b-185a; [469–505] 185b-186a; BK VI [316–353] 203a-204a; BK VIII [66–178] 233b-236a; BK X [888–908] 293b-294a

33 PASCAL: *Pensées*, 140 199a-b; 418 243a; 793, 326b

35 LOCKE: *Human Understanding*, BK II, CH X, SECT 9 143a-c; CH XXIII, SECT 13 207d-208b; BK IV, CH III, SECT 17 317c; CH XVII, SECT 14 378c-d

36 STERNE: *Tristram Shandy*, 318b-319a; 394a

43 FEDERALIST: NUMBER 51, 163b-c

44 BOSWELL: *Johnson*, 363a-b

47 GOETHE: *Faust*, PART II [11,894–12,111] 289b-294b

51 TOLSTOY: *War and Peace*, BK VII, 295b-c

52 DOSTOEVSKY: *Brothers Karamazov*, BK II, 22c-23a

5. The distinction and comparison of the good and the bad angels

OLD TESTAMENT: *Job*, 4:18

NEW TESTAMENT: *II Peter*, 2:4 / *Jude*, 6

18 AUGUSTINE: *Confessions*, BK X, par 67 88b-c / *City of God*, BK IX 285b,d-298a,c passim; BK XI 322b,d-342a,c passim, esp CH 11–13 328c-330b, CH 19–20 332b-333a; BK XII, CH 1–9 342b,d-348b; BK XXII, CH 1 586b,d-587b / *Christian Doctrine*, BK I, CH 33, 633d-634a

19 AQUINAS: *Summa Theologica*, PART I, Q 47, A 2, ANS 257b-258c; QQ 63–64 325b-338d

21 DANTE: *Divine Comedy*, PARADISE, XXIX [49–81] 150d-151a

23 HOBBES: *Leviathan*, PART III, 174d-175a; PART IV, 258d-259b

32 MILTON: *Paradise Lost*, BK I 93a-110b esp [27–282] 94a-99b, [587–615] 106a-b; BK II [229–283] 116a-117a; [477–485] 121b; BK III [613–742] 148b-151b; BK IV [1–130] 152b-155a; [788–1015] 169b-174b; BK V [577]–BK VI [912] 187b-216a passim

47 GOETHE: *Faust*, PROLOGUE [243–292] 7a-8a

48 MELVILLE: *Moby Dick*, 219b

5a. The origin of the division between angels and demons: the sin of Lucifer or Satan

OLD TESTAMENT: *Isaiah*, 14:4–27—(D) *Isaias*, 14:4–27

APOCRYPHA: *Wisdom of Solomon*, 2:24—(D) OT, *Book of Wisdom*, 2:24–25

NEW TESTAMENT: *II Peter*, 2:4 / *Jude*, 6 / *Revelation*, 12:7–10—(D) *Apocalypse*, 12:7–10

18 AUGUSTINE: *Confessions*, BK X, par 67 88b-c / *City of God*, BK XI, CH 9–20 326d-333a; BK XII, CH 3 343d-344b; CH 6–9 345d-348b; BK XXII, CH 1 586b,d-587b

19 AQUINAS: *Summa Theologica*, PART I, Q 47, A 2, ANS 257b-258c; Q 63 325b-333d

21 DANTE: *Divine Comedy*, HELL, III [22–51] 4b-c; XXXIV [28–36] 51c; PURGATORY, XII [25–27] 70c; PARADISE, XIX [40–51] 135c; XXIX [49–66] 150d-151a

22 CHAUCER: *Monk's Tale* [14,005–012] 434a

30 BACON: *Advancement of Learning*, 81a

32 MILTON: *Paradise Lost*, BK I 93a-110b esp [27–83] 94a-95a; BK IV [32–104] 153a-154b; BK V [600–904] 188b-195a

47 GOETHE: *Faust*, PART II [10,075–121] 246a-247a

52 DOSTOEVSKY: *Brothers Karamazov*, BK XI, 344c-d

5b. The society of the demons: the rule of Satan over the powers of darkness

APOCRYPHA: *Ecclesiasticus*, 39:28—(D) OT, *Ecclesiasticus*, 39:33–34

NEW TESTAMENT: *Matthew*, 9:34; 10:25; 12:22–30 / *Mark*, 3:22 / *Luke*, 11:14–23 / *John*, 8:31–59 / *Ephesians*, 2:1–3; 6:12 / *Hebrews*, 2:13–15 / *I John*, 3:8–12 / *Revelation*, 2:9,13; 9:1–11; 18:2—(D) *Apocalypse*, 2:9,13; 9:1–11; 18:2

18 AUGUSTINE: *City of God*, BK XX, CH 11 541a-c / *Christian Doctrine*, BK III, CH 37, 673d-674a

19 AQUINAS: *Summa Theologica*, PART I, Q 63, AA 8–9 332c-333d; Q 109 562a-564b

21 DANTE: *Divine Comedy*, HELL 1a-52d esp VIII [65]–IX [103] 11c-13b, XVIII [19–39] 25c-d, XXI–XXIII 30a-34c, XXVIII [1–42] 41b-c, XXXIV [16–31] 51c

22 CHAUCER: *Friar's Tale* [6957–7220] 279a-283b / *Summoner's Prologue* 284b-285a

23 HOBBES: *Leviathan*, PART III, 195a; PART IV, 247a-248a

32 MILTON: *Paradise Lost*, BK I [242–263] 98b-99a; BK II [1–520] 111a-122b esp [11–42] 111b-112a; BK IV [89–92] 154b; BK V [600–904] 188b-195a

33 PASCAL: *Provincial Letters*, 116a

47 GOETHE: *Faust*, PART I [2338–2604] 56b-63b esp [2465–2531] 60a-61b; [3835–4222] 93b-103a; PART II [11,636–675] 283a-284a

6. The role of the angels in the government of the universe

OLD TESTAMENT: *Genesis*, 3:24; 28:12 / *Psalms*, 103:20–22—(D) *Psalms*, 102:20–22 / *Daniel*, 7:10 / *Zechariah*, 1:7–21; 4:1–6:8—(D) *Zacharias*, 1:7–21; 4:1–6:8

NEW TESTAMENT: *Matthew*, 24:31 / *Mark*, 13:27 / *John*, 1:51 / *Revelation*, 5:2,11–14; 8–20 passim—(D) *Apocalypse*, 5:2,11–14; 8–20 passim

18 AUGUSTINE: *City of God*, BK VII, CH 30, 261d; BK VIII, CH 24, 283a-b; BK X, CH 15 308a-b; CH 21 311c-312a; BK XII, CH 27 359c-360a,c; BK XVI, CH 5–6, 426a-c; BK XXII, CH 1, 586b,d

19 AQUINAS: *Summa Theologica*, PART I, Q 45, A 5, ANS and REP 1 245c-247a; Q 63, A 7, ANS 331c-332b; Q 64, A 4, ANS 337d-338d; Q 66, A 3, REP 2 347b-348d; Q 89, A 8, REP 2 479c-480c; Q 91, A 2, REP 1,3 485b-486b; A 4, REP 2 487d-488c; QQ 106–114 545c-585c

21 DANTE: *Divine Comedy*, HELL, VII [67–96] 10b-c; PURGATORY, II [10–51] 54c-55a; VIII [22–36] 64c; XV [1–36] 75b-d; XVII [40–63] 78d-79a; XXIV [133–154] 91a-b; PARADISE, II [112–138] 109a; VIII [91–148] 117d-118c; XIII [52–72] 126a; XXVIII [120–129] 150a; XXIX [13–45] 150b-c

24 RABELAIS: *Gargantua and Pantagruel*, BK II, 117d

32 MILTON: *Paradise Lost*, BK II [119–134] 113b-114a; [237–249] 116b; [402–416] 120a; BK VII [550–601] 229a-230a / *Areopagitica*, 410a

6a. The ministry of the good angels in the affairs of men: guardianship

OLD TESTAMENT: *Genesis*, 16:7–12; 18:1–19:22; 21:9–21; 22:1–19; 24:7,40; 32:1–2,24–30; 48:15–16 / *Exodus*, 14:19–20; 23:20–23; 32:34; 33:2 / *Numbers*, 20:16; 22:22–35 / *Joshua*, 5:13–15—(D) *Josue*, 5:13–16 / *Judges*, 2:1–4; 6:11–24;13 / *II Samuel*, 24:15–17—(D) *II Kings*, 24:15–17 / *I Kings*, 19:5–8—(D) *III Kings*, 19:5–8 / *II Kings*, 19:32–35—(D) *IV Kings*, 19:32–35 / *I Chronicles*, 21:11–30—(D) *I Paralipomenon*, 21:11–30 / *II Chronicles*, 32:21—(D) *II Paralipomenon*, 32:21 / *Psalms*, 34:7; 35:5–6; 91:10–13—(D) *Psalms*, 33:8; 34:5–6; 90:10–13 / *Isaiah*, 6:6–7; 37:36—(D) *Isaias*, 6:6–7; 37:36 / *Daniel*, 3:28; 6:22; 8–12—(D) *Daniel*, 3:95; 6:22; 8–12 / *Hosea*, 12:2–4—(D) *Osee*, 12:2–4 / *Zechariah*, 1:7–21; 3—(D) *Zacharias*, 1:7–21; 3

APOCRYPHA: *Tobit*, 3:17; 5–12—(D) OT, *Tobias*, 3:25; 5–12 / *Baruch*, 6:7—(D) OT, *Baruch*, 6:6 / *Song of Three Children*, 25–26—(D) OT, *Daniel*, 3:49–50 / *Bel and Dragon*, 31–42—(D) OT, *Daniel*, 14:30–41

(6. The role of the angels in the government of the universe. 6a. The ministry of the good angels in the affairs of men: guardianship.)

New Testament: *Matthew*, 1:18–25; 2:13,19–20; 13:24–30,36–43,47–51; 18:10; 24:31; 28:1–7 / *Mark*, 1:13; 13:27 / *Luke*, 1:1–38; 2:8–15; 16:22 / *John*, 5:4; 12:28–29 / *Acts*, 5:17–20; 7:52–53; 8:26; 10:1–7,22,30–32; 12:5–11; 23:9; 27:21–24 / *Galatians*, 3:19 / *Hebrews*, 1:13–14 / *Revelation*, 1:1; 7–11; 14:6–20; 15–18; 19:17–18; 22:16 —(D) *Apocalypse*, 1:1; 7–11; 14:6–20; 15–18; 19:17–18; 22:16

18 Augustine: *Confessions*, BK XII, par 37, 108d / *City of God*, BK VIII, CH 25 283b-c; BK X, CH 8 303a-d; CH 12–13 306d-307c; BK XIX, CH 9 516a-c / *Christian Doctrine*, BK I, CH 30 632c-633b; CH 33 633d-634b

19 Aquinas: *Summa Theologica*, PART I, Q 64, A 4, ANS 337d-338d; Q 66, A 3, REP 2 347b-348d; Q 86, A 4, REP 2 463d-464d; Q 89, A 8, REP 2 479c-480c; Q 91, A 2, REP 1,3 485b-486b; QQ 111–113 568b-581d; PART I–II, Q 3, A 7, REP 2 628a-d; Q 5, A 6 641a-642a

20 Aquinas: *Summa Theologica*, PART I–II, Q 98, A 3 241c-242b; PART III SUPPL, Q 76, A 3 942b-d; Q 89, A 3 1007d-1008b

21 Dante: *Divine Comedy*, HELL, VIII [65]–IX [103] 11c-13b; PURGATORY, V [85–129] 59d-60c; VIII [1–108] 64a-65b; IX [70–145] 66c-67b; XII [73–136] 71a-d; XVII [40–63] 78d-79a; PARADISE, XXXII [85–114] 155c-d

22 Chaucer: *Second Nun's Tale* [15,588–825] 463b-467b

23 Hobbes: *Leviathan*, PART III, 174d-175a; 175c-d

24 Rabelais: *Gargantua and Pantagruel*, BK III, 132b-c; 158c-159b; 168c

27 Shakespeare: *King Lear*, ACT IV, SC II [38–50] 270d-271a

32 Milton: *Comus* 33a-56b esp [170–229] 37a-38b / *Paradise Lost*, BK II [1024–1033] 133b; BK IV [549–588] 164b-165a; [776–843] 169b-170b; BK V [224–247] 180a-b; BK VI [893–912] 215b-216a; BK VIII [630–643] 246a / *Areopagitica*, 410a-b

33 Pascal: *Provincial Letters*, 124a / *Pensées*, 722, 309b-312a; 846 339a-b

47 Goethe: *Faust*, PART II [11,676–12,111] 284a-294b

48 Melville: *Moby Dick*, 409b-410a

52 Dostoevsky: *Brothers Karamazov*, BK VII, 185a-c

6b. The intervention of the demons in the affairs of men: temptation, possession

Old Testament: *Genesis*, 3 / *I Samuel*, 16:14–23 —(D) *I Kings*, 16:14–23 / *I Kings*, 22:20–23— (D) *III Kings*, 22:20–23 / *I Chronicles*, 21:1— (D) *I Paralipomenon*, 21:1 / *II Chronicles*, 18:20–22—(D) *II Paralipomenon*, 18:20–22 / *Job*, 1–2

Apocrypha: *Tobit*, 3:8—(D) OT, *Tobias*, 3:8 / *Wisdom of Solomon*, 2:24—(D) OT, *Book of Wisdom*, 2:24-25

New Testament: *Matthew*, 4:1–11; 8:28–34; 9:32–34; 12:22–30,43–45; 13:19,24–30,36–43; 17:14–18 / *Mark*, 1:13; 4:15; 5:1–20 / *Luke*, 4:1–13; 8:2–3,12,26–36; 11:14–26; 22:3–6 / *John*, 8:31–59; 10:19–21; 13:2,21–27 / *Acts*, 5:1–11; 8:5–8; 10:37–38; 16:16–18 / *Romans*, 8:38–39 / *II Corinthians*, 2:10–11; 11:13–15 / *Galatians*, 1:8 / *Ephesians*, 2:2 / *I Thessalonians*, 2:18 / *I Peter*, 5:8–9 / *Revelation*, 2:10; 9; 12–13—(D) *Apocalypse*, 2:10; 9; 12–13

18 Augustine: *Confessions*, BK X, par 67 88b-c / *City of God*, BK II, CH 24–26, 164c-166d; BK VIII, CH 15–24 274d-283b; BK IX, CH 18 295c-d; BK X, CH 9–11 303d-306d; CH 21–22 311c-312b; BK XVIII, CH 18 480d-482a; BK XIX, CH 9 516a-c / *Christian Doctrine*, BK II, CH 23–24 648a-649a; BK III, CH 37, 673d-674a

19 Aquinas: *Summa Theologica*, PART I, Q 63, A 9, REP 3 333b-d; Q 64, A 4, ANS 337d-338d; Q 86, A 4, REP 2 463d-464d; Q 89, A 8, REP 2 479c-480c; Q 114 581d-585c

20 Aquinas: *Summa Theologica*, PART I–II, Q 80 159d-162d; PART III, Q 8, AA 7–8 761d-763b

21 Dante: *Divine Comedy*, HELL, VIII [65]–IX [103] 11c-13b; XXVII [55–136] 40a-41b; XXXIII [91–157] 50c-51b; PURGATORY, V [85–129] 59d-60c; VIII [1–108] 64a-65b

22 Chaucer: *Tale of Man of Law* [4778–4805] 240b-241a / *Friar's Tale* 278a-284a / *Physician's Tale* [12,055–072] 368a-b / *Pardoner's Tale* [12,778–828] 380b-381b / *Parson's Tale*, par 20 508b-509a

23 Hobbes: *Leviathan*, PART I, 69c-71a; PART III, 174d-175a; 195a; PART IV, 258c-261a

24 Rabelais: *Gargantua and Pantagruel*, BK II, 93d-94a; BK III, 169d-173d; BK IV, 261a-265a; 285c-288d; 300b-d

27 Shakespeare: *Othello*, ACT II, SC III [356–379] 220c-d

32 Milton: *Paradise Lost*, BK I [27–36] 94a; [331–621] 100b-107a; BK II [310–389] 118a-119b; [496–505] 122a; [1024–1033] 133b; BK IV [32–113] 153a-155a; [358–392] 160a-161a; [502–535] 163b-164a; [776–1015] 169b-174b; BK VI [893–912] 215b-216a; BK IX [404–794] 256a-264b

33 Pascal: *Provincial Letters*, 140a / *Pensées*, 784 325b; 843, 337b-338a; 850 340a

40 Gibbon: *Decline and Fall*, 184c-d

47 Goethe: *Faust*, PROLOGUE 7a-9b; PART I [482–517] 14a-b; [1178–2336] 29b-56a esp [1322–1384] 32b-34a, [1530–1867] 37a-44b; [3776–3834] 92a-93b; [4176–4205] 102a-103a; PART II [4941–4970] 122b-123a; [5357–5392] 132b-133a

52 Dostoevsky: *Brothers Karamazov*, BK II, 21d-22b; BK IV, 86b-c; BK V, 130b-132c; BK VI, 169c-170b; BK VII, 175b-176b; BK X, 295a-c

7. God and Satan

18 AUGUSTINE: *City of God*, BK XX 530a-560a,c passim

19 AQUINAS: *Summa Theologica*, PART I, Q 63 325b-333d esp A 3 327b-328b

20 AQUINAS: *Summa Theologica*, PART I-II, Q 80, A I, REP 2-3 159d-160c

21 DANTE: *Divine Comedy*, HELL, XXXIV 51b-52d

22 CHAUCER: *Friar's Tale* 278a-284a

23 HOBBES: *Leviathan*, PART III, 195a

32 MILTON: *Paradise Lost* 93a-333a esp BK I-II 93a-134a, BK III [56-134] 136b-138a, BK IV [1006-1015] 174b, BK V [224-245] 180a-b, BK V [563]-BK VI [892] 187b-215b, BK X [1-62] 274b-275b, [460-584] 284b-287a

33 PASCAL: *Pensées*, 784 325b; 820 331b; 826 332b-333a; 846 339a-b

52 DOSTOEVSKY: *Brothers Karamazov*, BK XI, 337a-346a

7a. Warfare between the powers of light and darkness: their struggle for dominion over man

OLD TESTAMENT: *I Samuel*, 16:14-23—(D) *I Kings*, 16:14-23 / *Job*, 1-2 / *Zechariah*, 3:1-7—(D) *Zacharias*, 3:1-7

APOCRYPHA: *Tobit*, 8:3—(D) OT, *Tobias*, 8:3

NEW TESTAMENT: *Matthew*, 4:1-11; 12:22-30; 13:19,24-30,36-43; 25:41 / *Mark*, 1:13; 5:1-20 / *Luke*, 4:1-13; 8:26-36; 10:17-20; 11:14-23; 22:31-34 / *John*, 12:31-32 / *Acts*, 8:5-8; 19:11-20; 26:9-29 / *Romans*, 16:17-20 / *I Corinthians*, 10:20-21 / *II Corinthians*, 2:10-11; 4:3-4; 10:2-5; 11:13-15 / *Ephesians*, 4:27; 6:10-18 / *II Thessalonians*, 2:8-9 / *I Timothy*, 4:1-5 / *II Timothy*, 2:24-26 / *Hebrews*, 2:13-15 / *James*, 4:7 / *I Peter*, 5:8-9 / *I John*, 3:8-12 / *Jude*, 9 / *Revelation*, 2:9-13; 3:9-13; 12-14; 16:13-14; 20:1-10—(D) *Apocalypse*, 2:9-13; 3:9-13; 12-14; 16:13-14; 20:1-10

18 AUGUSTINE: *Confessions*, BK IV, par 24-27 25b-26a; BK V, par 20 32d-33a; BK X, par 67 88b-c / *City of God*, BK II, CH 25 165c-166b; BK XII, CH 6 345b-346c; BK XX, CH 11-13 541a-542d / *Christian Doctrine*, BK II, CH 23 648a-c; BK III, CH 37, 673d-674a

19 AQUINAS: *Summa Theologica*, PART I, Q 8, A I, REP 4 34d-35c; A 3, ANS 36b-37c; Q 49, A 3 266d-268a,c; Q 63, A 2, ANS 326c-327b

20 AQUINAS: *Summa Theologica*, PART III SUPPL, Q 74, A I, REP I 925c-926c

21 DANTE: *Divine Comedy*, HELL, VIII [65]-IX [103] 11c-13b; XXVII [55-136] 40a-41b; PURGATORY, V [85-129] 59d-60c; VIII [1-108] 64a-65b; XI [1-30] 68d-69a; XIV [130-151] 75a-b

22 CHAUCER: *Friar's Tale* [7227-7246] 284a

23 HOBBES: *Leviathan*, PART IV, 247a-248a

32 MILTON: *Paradise Lost*, BK II [890-1009] 130b-133a; BK III [1-415] 135b-144b; BK IX [679-779] 262a-264a

33 PASCAL: *Provincial Letters*, 116a-b

40 GIBBON: *Decline and Fall*, 81b-c

41 GIBBON: *Decline and Fall*, 330b

47 GOETHE: *Faust*, PROLOGUE 7a-9b; PART I [1335-1378] 33a-34a; PART II [11,612-843] 282b-288a

48 MELVILLE: *Moby Dick* esp 4b-5a, 117a-122b, 131a-138a, 144a-b, 370b-372a, 418a-419b

52 DOSTOEVSKY: *Brothers Karamazov*, BK III, 50c-54b esp 54a-b; BK IV, 86b-c; BK V, 130b-136b; BK VI, 151b-d; 169c-170b; BK VII, 175b-176c; 185a-c; BK XI, 342d-343b

7b. Lucifer in the service of God

OLD TESTAMENT: *Job*, 1-2 / *Psalms*, 78:49—(D) *Psalms*, 77:49

APOCRYPHA: *Ecclesiasticus*, 39:28 — (D) OT, *Ecclesiasticus*, 39:33-34

18 AUGUSTINE: *City of God*, BK VIII, CH 24, 283a-b; BK X, CH 21 311c-312a; BK XII, CH 27 359c-360a,c; CH I 586b,d-587b

19 AQUINAS: *Summa Theologica*, PART I, Q 64, A 4, ANS 337d-338d; Q 114, A I 581d-582c

20 AQUINAS: *Summa Theologica*, PART III SUPPL, Q 89, A 4 1008b-1009b

21 DANTE: *Divine Comedy*, HELL, XVIII [19-39] 25c-d; XXI-XXIII 30a-34c; XXVII [55]-XXVIII [42] 40a-41c; XXXIV 51b-52d

22 CHAUCER: *Friar's Tale* [7055-7085] 281a-b

32 MILTON: *Paradise Lost*, BK I [157-168] 97a; [209-220] 98a; BK X [616-640] 288a-b

47 GOETHE: *Faust*, PROLOGUE [271-353] 7b-9b; PART II [7127-7137] 174b-175a

52 DOSTOEVSKY: *Brothers Karamazov*, BK VI, 151b-d; BK XI, 341a-344d

54 FREUD: *Civilization and Its Discontents*, 790d

8. Criticism and satire with respect to the belief in angels and demons

23 HOBBES: *Leviathan*, PART I, 51d-52b; 69c-71a; PART III, 174b-176d; 195a; PART IV, 258b-261a; 276c

24 RABELAIS: *Gargantua and Pantagruel*, BK III, 171a-173d; BK IV, 285c-288d; 300b-d

25 MONTAIGNE: *Essays*, 500a-501a

30 BACON: *Advancement of Learning*, 41d-42a / *Novum Organum*, BK I, APH 62, 113d

38 MONTESQUIEU: *Spirit of Laws*, BK XII, 86d-87b

40 GIBBON: *Decline and Fall*, 184c-d; 189c; 347a

41 GIBBON: *Decline and Fall*, 229d; 231b; 244c; 334c

42 KANT: *Judgement*, 592a-c; 599d-600a

46 HEGEL: *Philosophy of History*, PART IV, 354c-355b

50 MARX: *Capital*, 31d

52 DOSTOEVSKY: *Brothers Karamazov*, BK II, 21d-22b; BK XI, 337a-346a

53 JAMES: *Psychology*, 148b

54 FREUD: *New Introductory Lectures*, 876d-877a; 877c

CROSS-REFERENCES

For: Other discussions relevant to the theory of angels, see ETERNITY 4a; IDEA 1e; KNOWLEDGE
    7b; MIND 10c; SOUL 4d(2); and for the metaphysical consideration of immaterial substances,
    see BEING 7b(2).
  The theological doctrine of the fallen angels, see SIN 3, 3b; and for the related doctrines of
    Heaven and Hell, see ETERNITY 4d; GOOD AND EVIL 1d, 2b; IMMORTALITY 5e–5f; PUNISH-
    MENT 5e(1).
  The theory of the celestial motors, see ASTRONOMY 8b; CHANGE 14.

ADDITIONAL READINGS

Listed below are works not included in Great Books of the Western World, but relevant to the
idea and topics with which this chapter deals. These works are divided into two groups:

    I. Works by authors represented in this collection.
    II. Works by authors not represented in this collection.

For the date, place, and other facts concerning the publication of the works cited, consult
the Bibliography of Additional Readings which follows the last chapter of The Great Ideas.

I.

AUGUSTINE. De Genesi ad Litteram
AQUINAS. On Being and Essence, CH 4
——. Summa Contra Gentiles, BK II, CH 46–55, 91–
    101; BK III, CH 104–110
——. Quaestiones Disputatae, De Veritate, QQ 8–9; De
    Malo, Q 16; De Anima, A 7
——. On Spiritual Creatures, AA 1–3, 5–8
——. De Substantiis Separatis
DANTE. Convivio (The Banquet), SECOND TREATISE,
    CH 5–7
MACHIAVELLI. Belfagor

II.

PHILO JUDAEUS. On the Cherubim
PROCLUS. The Elements of Theology, (M)
"DIONYSIUS". On the Celestial Hierarchy
ERIGENA. De Divisione Naturae, BK I (4, 7–9), II (6,
    22), IV (7–9), V (13)
MAIMONIDES. The Guide for the Perplexed, PART I,
    CH 49; PART II, CH 2–7
BONAVENTURA. Breviloquium, PART II (6–8)
R. BACON. Opus Majus, PART VII
ALBO. The Book of Principles (Sefer ha-Ikkarim), BK
    II, CH 12
CALVIN. Institutes of the Christian Religion, BK I,
    CH 14 (3)
LUTHER. Table Talk
DONNE. Aire and Angells
SUÁREZ. Disputationes Metaphysicae, XII (14),
    XXXIV (3, 5), XXXV, XLI (2), LI (3–4)
MARLOWE. The Tragical History of Doctor Faustus

HEYWOOD. The Hierarchie of the Blessed Angells
H. LAWRENCE. Of Our Communion and Warre with
    Angels
CAMFIELD. A Theological Discourse of Angels and
    Their Ministries
LEIBNITZ. Discourse on Metaphysics, XXIII, XXXIV–
    XXXVI
JOHN REYNOLDS. Inquiries Concerning the State and
    Economy of the Angelical Worlds
SWEDENBORG. Angelic Wisdom Concerning the Divine
    Providence
VOLTAIRE. "Angels," in A Philosophical Dictionary
SCHLEIERMACHER. The Christian Faith, par 42–45
W. SCOTT. Letters on Demonology and Witchcraft
J. H. NEWMAN. "The Powers of Nature," in VOL II,
    Parochial and Plain Sermons
HEINE. Gods in Exile
LOTZE. Microcosmos, BK IX, CH 2
MICHELET. Satanism and Witchcraft
FRAZER. The Golden Bough, PART IV, BK I, CH 4;
    PART VI; PART VII, CH 4–7
WENDELL. "Were the Witches of Salem Guiltless?"
    in Stelligeri
LEA. Materials Toward a History of Witchcraft
FRANCE. The Revolt of the Angels
FARNELL. Greek Hero Cults and Ideas of Immortality
WILLIAMS. The Place of the Lion
GLOVER. "The Daemon Environment," in Greek
    Byways
ZILBOORG. The Medical Man and the Witch During
    the Renaissance
VONIER. The Angels
C. S. LEWIS. Out of the Silent Planet
——. The Screwtape Letters

Chapter 2: ANIMAL

INTRODUCTION

ALPHABETICAL ordering places ANIMAL after ANGEL in this list of ideas. There is a third term which belongs with these two and, but for the alphabet, might have come between them. That term is MAN.

These three terms—and a fourth, GOD, which rounds out the comparison—are conjoined in Shakespeare's statement of what is perhaps the most universal reflection of man upon himself. "What a piece of work is man!" says Hamlet, "How noble in reason! how infinite in faculty! in form and moving, how express and admirable! in action, how like an angel! in apprehension, how like a god! the beauty of the world! the paragon of animals!" Animal, angel, god—in each of these man has seen his image. And at different moments in the history of thought, he has tended to identify himself with one to the exclusion of the others.

Yet predominantly man has regarded himself as an animal, even when he has understood himself to be created in God's image, and to share with the angels, through the possession of intellect, the dignity of being a person. As his understanding of himself has varied, so has he altered his conception of what it is to be an animal.

In terms of a conception of personality which involves the attributes of reason and free will, man has legally, as well as morally and metaphysically, drawn a sharp line between persons and things, and placed brute animals in the class of things. According to the principle of this distinction, being alive or even being sensitive does not give animals, any more than plants and stones, the dignity or status of persons.

When man's animality—either in terms of his biological affinities or his evolutionary origins—has seemed an adequate definition of his nature, man has attributed to animals many of his own traits, his intelligence and freedom, even his moral qualities and political propensities. Nevertheless, he has seldom ceased to regard himself as the paragon of animals, possessing in a higher degree than other animals the characteristic properties of all.

There are exceptions to this, however. Animals have been glorified by man for skeptical or satiric purposes.

Montaigne, for example, doubts that man can lay claim to any special attributes or excellences, and further suggests that, in some particulars at least, men are less able and less noble than the beasts. Relying on legends found in Pliny and Plutarch which describe the marvelous exploits of animals, he argues that "it is not upon any true ground of reason, but by a foolish pride and vain opinion, that we prefer ourselves before other animals, and separate ourselves from their conditions and society."

Why, Montaigne asks, "should we attribute to I know not what natural and servile inclination the works that surpass all we can do by nature and art"? We have no grounds for believing that "beasts, by natural and compulsory tendency, do the same things that we do by our choice and industry." Rather "we ought," he continues, "from like effects, to conclude like faculties, and consequently confess that the same reason, the same method, by which we operate, are common with them, or that they have others that are better."

Nor can we excuse our presumption of superiority by the fact that we are compelled to look at animals from our human point of view. "When I play with my cat," Montaigne writes, "who knows whether I do not make her more sport than she makes me? We mutually divert one another with our monkey tricks; if I have my hour to begin or to refuse, she also has hers." Suppose animals were to tell us what they thought of us. "The defect that hinders communication betwixt them and us, why may it not be on our part as well as theirs? 'Tis yet to determine," Montaigne thinks, "where the fault lies that we understand not one another; for we understand them no more than they do us; by the same reason they may think us to be beasts as we think them."

If Montaigne's view were to prevail, no special significance could be given to "brute" as opposed to "rational" animal. For that matter, the same holds true whenever man is conceived as *just an animal*, paragon or not. Animals are brute only when man is not—only when to be human is to be somehow more than an animal, different in kind, not merely in degree.

Satirists like Swift idealize an animal nature to berate the folly and depravity of man. In his last voyage, Gulliver finds in the land of the Houyhnhnms a race of human-looking creatures, the Yahoos, who by contrast with their noble masters, the horses, are a miserable and sorry lot. Here it is the Yahoos who are brutes, bereft as they are of the intelligence and virtue which grace the splendid Houyhnhnms.

THE COMPARISON of men and animals takes still another direction in the allegories of fable and poetry. From Aesop to the mediaeval *Bestiaries*, there is the tradition of stories in which animals are personified in order to teach a moral lesson. In the *Divine Comedy* Dante uses specific animals to symbolize the epitome of certain passions, vices, and virtues. The intent of his allegory is, however, never derogatory to man as man. But when Machiavelli allegorizes the qualities required for political power, he advises the prince "knowingly to adopt the beast" and "to choose the fox and the lion." This tends to reduce human society to the jungle where strength and guile compete for supremacy.

The comparison of men and animals fails to touch the distinction, or lack of distinction, between animals and plants. This is basic to the definition or conception of animal nature. As in the case of men and animals, this problem can be approached in two ways: *either* from the side of plant life, and with respect to those functions which seem to be common to all living things; *or* from the side of animal life, and with respect to those functions which seem to belong only to

animals, never to plants. On either approach the issue remains whether plants and animals are different in kind, not merely in degree.

On the one hand, it may be argued that sensitivity, desire, and locomotion (even perhaps sleeping and waking) are, in some form or degree, to be found in all living things. On the other hand, it may be argued that such functions as nutrition, growth, and reproduction, though obviously common to plants and animals, are performed by animals in a distinctive manner. If plants manifest all the vital powers or activities present in animals; or if in functions common to both, animals differ only in degree, then the scale of life would seem to be a continuous gradation rather than a hierarchy.

The opposite position, which affirms a difference in kind and consequently a hierarchy, is taken by Aristotle. In his biological writings, as well as in his treatise *On the Soul*, he draws a sharp line between plant and animal life by reference to faculties or functions absent in the one and found in the other. Aristotle first points out that "living may mean thinking or perception or local movement and rest, or movement in the sense of nutrition, decay, and growth. Hence," he goes on, "we think of plants also as living, for they are observed to possess in themselves an originative power through which they increase or decrease in all spatial directions; they grow up and down, and everything that grows increases its bulk alike in both directions or indeed in all, and continues to live so long as it can absorb nutriment."

This leads him to assign to plants what he calls a nutritive or vegetative soul, whereby they have the three basic faculties common to all living things—nutrition, growth, and reproduction. But Aristotle does not find in plants any evidence of the functions performed by animals, such as sensation, appetite, and local motion. These are the characteristic powers of the animal soul, called by him the "sensitive soul" because sensation is the source both of animal desire and animal movement.

Galen follows Aristotle in this distinction. In his *Natural Faculties* he limits his investigations to the functions common to all living things. He uses the word "natural" for those effects, such as "growth and nutrition . . . common to plants as well as animals," which, in his view, are opposed to such activities as "feeling and voluntary motion ... peculiar to animals," that he calls "effects of the soul," or "psychic." It may seem surprising at first that Galen's study of nutrition, growth, and reproduction—not only of the functions themselves but of the bodily organs and processes involved in these functions—should be restricted to their manifestation in animals, and not in plants as well. The reason may be that for the naturalists of antiquity, the biological functions of vegetable matter did not yield their secrets readily enough to observation. A treatise on plants, not written by Aristotle but attributed to his school, begins with the remark that "life is found in animals and plants; but whereas in animals it is clearly manifest, in plants it is hidden and less evident."

This view of the world of living things as divided into the two great kingdoms of plant and animal life prevailed through centuries of speculation and research. But from the time that Aristotle began the work of classification, it has been realized that there exist numerous examples of what Bacon called "bordering instances ... such as exhibit those species of bodies which appear to be composed of two species, or to be the rudiments between the one and the other."

Within the last hundred years the difficulty of classifying such specimens, particularly those which seem to fall between plant and animal, has raised the question whether the traditional distinction can be maintained. "If we look even to the two main divisions, namely, to the animal and vegetable kingdoms," writes Darwin, "certain low forms are so far intermediate in character that naturalists have disputed to which kingdom they should belong." Yet Darwin does not find the evidence available to him sufficient to determine whether all living things have descended "from one primordial form" or whether the evolution of life is to be represented in two distinct lines of development.

Since Darwin's day the researches of scientists like Loeb and Jennings on the behavior of micro-organisms, and the phenomena of tropisms (e.g., the sunflower's turning toward the sun), and the study of what appears to be local motion in plants, have contributed additional evidence relevant to the issue. It is, however, still considered open and arguable.

The fact that organisms exist which do not readily fall into either classification may signify continuity rather than separation between plants and animals; but it may also be taken to mean that more acute observations are required to classify these so-called "intermediate forms." Plant tropisms may or may not require us to deny that sensitivity belongs to animals alone. The apparent local motion of plants may be a mode of growth or a random movement rather than a directed change from place to place; and the attachment to place of apparently stationary animals, such as barnacles and mussels, may be different from the immobility of rooted plants.

AGAINST THE BACKGROUND of these major issues concerning plants, animals, and men as continuous or radically distinct forms of life, the study of animal organisms—their anatomy and physiology—acquires much of its critical significance.

Anatomy is an ancient science. Several surgical treatises of Hippocrates display an extensive knowledge of the human skeletal structure and the disposition of some of the organs of the human body. The dissection of animals, as well as gross observation, provides Aristotle with a basis for the comparative anatomy of different species of animal. For Galen as well as Aristotle, much of this anatomical study was motivated by an interest in the structure and relation of the organs involved in the local motion of the body as a whole, and in local motions within the body, such as the motions of the alimentary or reproductive systems.

It remains for a later investigator, schooled in the tradition of ancient biology, to make the startling discovery of the circulation of the blood through the motions of the heart. Harvey not only does this, but he also suggests the functional interdependence of respiration and circulation, based on his observation of the intimate structural connections between heart, arteries, veins, and lungs. His contribution is at once a departure from and a product of the scientific tradition in which he worked, for though his conclusions are radically new, he reaches them by a method of research and reasoning which follows the general principles of Aristotle and Galen. His insistence, moreover, on the necessity of finding a functional purpose for an organic structure stands as the classic rejoinder to Francis Bacon's recommendation that formal and final causes be separated from material and efficient causes in the study of nature. Bacon assigns the first two types of cause to metaphysics, and limits physics to the last two.

Harvey's work on the generation of animals is another example of the continuity between ancient and modern biology. In some respects, Aristotle's researches on the reproductive organs and their functions are more general than Harvey's. They represent for him only part of the large field of comparative anatomy, and have significance for the study of mating habits in different classes of animals. Yet on the problem of the act of generation itself, its causes and consequences, especially the phenomena of embryonic development, Harvey's treatise reads partly as a conversation with Aristotle, and partly as the record of original observations undertaken experimentally.

"Respect for our predecessors and for antiquity at large," he writes, "inclines us to defend their conclusions to the extent that love of truth will allow. Nor do I think it becoming in us to neglect and make little of their labors and conclusions, who bore the torch that has lighted us to the shrine of philosophy." The ancients, in his opinion, "by their unwearied labor and variety of experiments, searching into the nature of things, have left us no doubtful light to guide us in our studies." Yet, Harvey adds, "no one of a surety will allow that all truth was engrossed by the ancients, unless he be utterly ignorant . . . of the many remarkable discoveries that have lately been made in anatomy." Referring to his own method of investigation, he proposes as a "safer way to the attainment of knowledge" that "in studying nature," we "question things themselves rather than by turning over books."

It is particularly with respect to animal generation that the great books exhibit continuity in the statement of basic problems in biology, as well as indicate the logical conditions of their solution. The issue of spontaneous generation as opposed to procreation runs through Aristotle, Lucretius, Aquinas, Harvey, and Darwin. The problem of sexual and asexual reproduction, with all the relevant considerations of sexual differentiation and sexual characteristics, is to be found in Aristotle, Darwin, and Freud. Questions of heredity, though they are raised with new significance by Darwin and William James, have a lineage as ancient as Plato.

Scientific learning has, of course, advanced in recent times with regard to the nature and behavior of animals. On such topics as heredity, the work of Mendel, Bateson, and Morgan is crucial; or, to take another example, our knowledge of the functioning of the respiratory and the nervous system has been greatly enlarged by the researches of Haldane, Sherrington, and Pavlov. Yet even in these areas, the background of recent scientific contributions is to be found in the great books—in the writings, for example, of Harvey, Darwin, and William James.

ANOTHER INTEREST which runs through the whole tradition of man's study of animals lies in the problem of their classification—both with respect to the principles of taxonomy itself, and also in the systematic effort to construct schemes whereby the extraordinary variety of animal types can be reduced to order. In this field Aristotle and Darwin are the two great masters. If the names of Buffon and Linnaeus also deserve to be mentioned, it must be with the double qualification that they are followers of Aristotle on the one hand, and precursors of Darwin on the other.

The Aristotelian classification is most fully set forth in the *History of Animals*. There one kind of animal is distinguished from another by many "properties": by locale or habitat; by shape and color and size; by manner of locomotion, nutrition, association, sensation; by organic parts and members; by temperament, instinct, or characteristic habits of action. With respect to some of these properties, Aristotle treats one kind of animal as differing from another by a degree—by more or less—of the same trait. With respect to other properties, he finds the difference to consist in the possession by one species of a trait totally lacking in another. He speaks of the lion as being more "ferocious" than the wolf, the crow as more "cunning" than the raven; but he also observes that the cow has an "organ of digestion" which the spider lacks, the lizard an "organ of locomotion" which the oyster lacks. The sponge lives in one manner so far as "locale" is concerned, and the viper in another; reptiles have one manner of locomotion, birds another. So ample were Aristotle's data and so expert were his classifications, that the major divisions and sub-divisions of his scheme remain intact in the taxonomy constructed by Linnaeus.

The radical character of Darwin's departure from the Linnaean classification stems from a difference in principle rather than a correction of observational errors or inadequacies. Where Aristotle and all taxonomists before Darwin classify animals by reference to their similarities and differences, Darwin makes inferred genealogy or descent the primary criterion in terms of which he groups animals into varieties, species, genera, and larger phyla.

Naturalists, according to Darwin, "try to arrange the species, genera, and families in each class, on what is called the Natural System. But what is meant by this system? Some authors look at it merely as a scheme for arranging together those living objects which are most alike, and for separating those which are most unlike. . . . The ingenuity and utility of this system are indisputable," but Darwin thinks that its rules cannot be explained or its difficulties overcome except "on the view that the Natural System is founded on descent with modification—that the characters which naturalists consider as showing true affinity between any two or more species, are those which have been inherited from a common parent, all true classification being genealogical—that community of descent is the hidden bond which naturalists have been unconsciously seeking, and not some unknown plan of creation, or the enunciation of general propositions, and the mere putting together and separating objects more or less alike."

In Darwin's opinion, classification "must be strictly genealogical in order to be natural." Only by the principle of descent—"the one certainly known cause of similarity in organic beings"—can we arrange "all organic beings throughout all time in groups under groups"; see "the nature of the relationships by which all living and extinct organisms are united by complex, radiating, and circuitous lines of affinities into a few grand classes"; and understand "the

wide opposition in value between analogical or adaptive characters, and characters of true affinity." Furthermore, "the importance of embryological characters and of rudimentary organs in classification" becomes "intelligible on the view that a natural arrangement must be genealogical." By reference to "this element of descent," not only shall we be able to "understand what is meant by the Natural System," but also, Darwin adds, "our classifications will come to be, as far as they can be so made, genealogies; and will then truly give what may be called the plan of creation."

Whereas the Aristotelian classification is static in principle, having no reference to temporal connections or the succession of generations, the Darwinian is dynamic—almost a moving picture of the ever-shifting arrangement of animals according to their affinities through common ancestry or their diversities through genetic variation. Connected with this opposition between static and dynamic principles of classification is a deeper conflict between two ways of understanding the nature of scientific classification itself.

The point at issue is whether the classes which the taxonomist constructs represent distinct natural forms. Do they exist independently as objects demanding scientific definition or are the scientist's groupings somewhat arbitrary and artificial? Do they divide and separate what in nature is more like a continuous distribution with accidental gaps and unevennesses? This issue, in turn, tends to raise the metaphysical question concerning the reality and fixity of species, which relates to the problem of the difference between real and nominal definitions, and the difference between natural and arbitrary systems of classification.

On these matters Aquinas and Locke have much to say, as well as Aristotle and Darwin. Fuller discussion of such questions is to be found in the chapters on DEFINITION and EVOLUTION. Insofar as problems of classification and the nature of species have a bearing on evolution, they are treated in that chapter, as are the related issues of *continuity* or *hierarchy* in the world of living things, and of difference in *degree* or *kind* as between plants and animals, animals and men. The last two problems also occur in the chapters on LIFE and MAN.

ON THE THEME of comparisons between animals and men, two further points should be noted.

The first concerns the soul of animals. When soul is conceived as the principle or source of life in whatever is alive, plants and animals can be said to have souls. Like Aristotle, Augustine distinguishes "three grades of soul in universal nature": one which has "only the power of life ... the second grade in which there is sensation ... the third grade ... where intelligence has its throne."

Though he also follows Aristotle in defining three kinds of soul, Aquinas distinguishes four grades of life, and in so doing differentiates between *perfect* and *imperfect* animals. "There are some living things," he writes, "in which there exists only vegetative power, as the plants. There are others in which with the vegetative there exists also the sensitive, but not the locomotive power; such are immovable animals, as shellfish. There are others which besides this have locomotive power, as perfect animals, which require many things for their life, and consequently movement to seek the necessaries of life from a distance. And there are some living things which with these have intellectual power—namely, men."

On this theory, man, viewed in terms of his animal nature, is a perfect animal. Viewed in terms of his reason or intellect, he stands above the highest animals. Yet having a soul is not peculiar to man, just as being alive, or sensitive, or mobile, is not. But when, as with Descartes, soul is identified with intellect—as "a thing which thinks, that is to say a mind ... or an understanding, or a reason"—and, in addition, soul is conceived as a spiritual and immortal substance, then the conclusion seems to follow that animals do not have souls.

For Descartes, the theory of the animal as a machine or automaton follows as a further corollary. "If there had been such machines, possessing the organs and outward form of a monkey or some other animal without reason," Descartes claims that "we should not have had any means of ascertaining that they were not of the same nature as those animals." Hobbes likewise would account for all the actions of animal life on mechanical principles. "For what is the heart, but a spring," he asks, "and the

nerves, but so many strings; and the joints, but so many wheels, giving motion to the whole body?" The animal is thus pictured as an elaborate system of moving parts, inflexibly determined to behave in certain ways under the impact of stimulation by external forces.

The doctrine of the animal automaton is sometimes generalized, as by La Mettrie, a follower of Descartes, to include the conception of man as a machine. The same conclusions which are reached from the denial of soul in animals seem to follow also from the theory that the soul, even in the case of man, is material or a function of matter. According to those who, like Lucretius, hold this view, the phenomena of life, sensation, and thought can be explained by the movement of atomic particles and their interaction.

The second point concerns the relation between instinct and intelligence in animals. The nature of animal instincts (or innate habits) is considered in the chapters on EMOTION and HABIT, as is the nature of animal intelligence in the chapters on MAN and REASONING. But here we face the issue whether instinct functions in animals, as reason does in man, to meet the exigencies of life; or whether in both, though varying in degree, intelligence cooperates with instinct to solve the problems of adjustment to environment.

Those who, like Aquinas, regard instinct and reason as the alternative and exclusive means which God provides for the ends of animal and human life, necessarily tend to interpret animal behavior in all its detail as pre-determined by elaborate instinctive endowments. Accordingly, animal behavior, even when voluntary rather than purely the action of physiological reflexes, is said not to be free, or an expression of free choice on the part of the animal; for, as is pointed out in the chapter on WILL, Aquinas calls behavior "voluntary" if it involves some knowledge or consciousness of the objects to which it is directed.

Instinctive behavior, such as an animal's flight from danger or its pursuit of food or a mate, involves sense-perception of the objects of these actions, as well as feelings or emotions about them. But though it is "voluntary" in the sense in which Aquinas uses that word, instinctive behavior is, according to him, the exact opposite of action based upon free will. It is completely determined by the inborn pattern of the instinct. It may vary in operation with the circumstances of the occasion, but it does not leave the animal the freedom to act or not to act, or to act this way rather than that. Such freedom of choice, Aquinas holds, depends on reason's ability to contemplate alternatives, to none of which is the human will bound by natural necessity.

Aquinas does not limit human reason and will to a role analogous to the one he ascribes to instinct and emotion in animal life. Their power enables man to engage in speculative thought and to seek remote ends. Nevertheless, on the level of his biological needs, man must resort to the use of his reason and will where other animals are guided by instinct. "Man has by nature," Aquinas writes, "his reason and his hands, which are *the organs of organs*, since by their means man can make for himself instruments of an infinite variety, and for any number of purposes." Just as the products of reason take the place of hair, hoofs, claws, teeth, and horns—"fixed means of defense or of clothing, as is the case with other animals"— so reason serves man's needs, in the view of Aquinas, as instinct serves other animals.

Others, like Darwin, James, and Freud, seem to take a different view. They attribute instinct to men as well as to animals. In their opinion instinctively determined behavior is influenced by intelligence, and affected by memory and imagination, in animals as well as in men. They recognize, however, that instinct predominates in some of the lower forms of animal life, and acknowledge that the contribution of intelligence is great only among the more highly developed organisms.

"Man has a far greater variety of *impulses* than any lower animal," writes James; "and any one of these impulses taken in itself, is as 'blind' as the lowest instinct can be; but, owing to man's memory, power of reflection, and power of inference, they come each one to be felt by him, after he has once yielded to them and experienced their results in connection with a *foresight* of those results." On the same grounds, James argues that "*every instinctive act, in an animal with memory, must cease to be 'blind' after being once repeated*, and must be accompanied

with foresight of its 'end' just so far as that end may have fallen under the animal's cognizance."

If instinct, in animals or men, were sufficient for solving the problems of survival, there would be no need for what James calls "sagacity" on the part of animals, or of learning from experience. Like Montaigne, James assembles anecdotes to show that animals exercise their wits and learn from experience. "No matter how well endowed an animal may originally be in the way of instincts," James declares, "his resultant actions will be much modified if the instincts combine with experience, if in addition to impulses he have memories, associations, inferences, and expectations, on any considerable scale."

In his consideration of "the intellectual contrast between brute and man," James places "the most elementary single difference between the human mind and that of brutes" in the "deficiency on the brute's part to associate ideas by similarity," so that "characters, the abstraction of which depends on this sort of association, must in the brute always remain drowned." Darwin similarly makes the difference in degree between human and animal intelligence a matter of greater or less power to associate ideas. In consequence, human instincts are much more modified by learning and experience than the instincts of other animals, as in turn the higher animals show much greater variability in their instinctive behavior than do lower organisms.

It is not necessary to deny that men alone have reason in order to affirm that, in addition to instinct, animals have intelligence in some proportion to the development of their sensitive powers, especially their memory and imagination. The position of Aristotle and Aquinas seems to involve both points. But if we attribute the extraordinary performances of animals to their intelligence *alone*, rather than primarily to instinct, then we are led to conclude with Montaigne that they possess not merely a sensitive intelligence, but a reasoning intellect.

"Why does the spider make her web tighter in one place and slacker in another?" Montaigne asks. "Why now one sort of knot and then another, if she has not deliberation, thought, and conclusion?" And in another place he asks, "What is there in our intelligence that we do not see in the operations of animals? Is there a polity better ordered, the offices better distributed, and more inviolably observed and maintained than that of bees? Can we imagine that such and so regular a distribution of employments can be carried on without reason and prudence?"

GREGARIOUSNESS in animals and the nature of animal communities are considered in the chapter on STATE, in connection with the formation of human society. But so far as human society itself is concerned, the domestication of animals signifies an advance from primitive to civilized life and an increase in the wealth and power of the tribe or city.

Aeschylus includes the taming of animals among the gifts of Prometheus, who "first brought under the yoke beasts of burden, who by draft and carrying relieved men of their hardest labors ... yoked the proud horse to the chariot, teaching him obedience to the reins, to be the adornment of wealth and luxury." The *Iliad* pays eloquent testimony to the change in the quality of human life which accompanied the training of animals to respond to human command. Homer's reference to Castor as "breaker of horses" indicates the sense of conquest or mastery which men felt when they subdued wild beasts; and the oft-repeated Homeric epithet "horse-taming," which is intended as a term of praise for both the Argives and the Trojans, implies the rise of a people from barbarous or primitive conditions—their emancipation from the discomforts and limitations of animal life.

Aristotle points out that one mark of wealthy men is "the number of horses which they keep, for they cannot afford to keep them unless they are rich." For the same reason, he explains, "in old times the cities whose strength lay in their cavalry were oligarchies."

Legend and history are full of stories of the loyalty and devotion of animals to their human masters, and of the reciprocal care and affection which men have given them. But, motivated as it is by their utility for economic or military purposes, the breaking of animals to human will also frequently involves a violent or wanton misuse.

The use, or even the exploitation, of animals by man seems to be justified by the inferiority of the brute to the rational nature. As plants exist for the sake of animals, so animals, according to Aristotle, "exist for the sake of man, the tame for use and food, the wild, if not all, at least the greater part of them, for food, and for the provision of clothing and various instruments." Aristotle's conception of the natural slave, discussed in the chapter on SLAVERY, uses the domesticated animal as a kind of model for the treatment of human beings as tools or instruments.

Though he does not share Aristotle's view that some men are by nature slaves, Spinoza takes a comparable position with regard to man's domination and use of animals. "The law against killing animals," he writes, "is based upon an empty superstition and womanish tenderness, rather than upon sound reason. A proper regard, indeed, to one's own profit teaches us to unite in friendship with men, and not with brutes, nor with things whose nature is different from human nature ... I by no means deny," he continues, "that brutes feel, but I do deny that on this account it is unlawful for us to consult our own profit by using them for our pleasure and treating them as is most convenient to us, inasmuch as they do not agree in nature with us."

But other moralists declare that men can befriend animals, and insist that charity, if not justice, should control man's treatment of beasts. Nor is such contrary teaching confined to Christianity, or to the maxims of St. Francis, who would persuade men to love not only their neighbors as themselves, but all of God's creatures. Plutarch, for instance, argues that although "law and justice we cannot, in the nature of things, employ on others than men," nevertheless, "we may extend our goodness and charity even to irrational creatures." In kindness to dumb animals he finds the mark of the "gentle nature"—the sign of a man's humaneness. "Towards human beings as they have reason, behave in a social spirit," says Marcus Aurelius; but he also writes: "As to animals which have no reason, and generally all things and objects, do thou, since thou hast reason and they have none, make use of them with a generous and liberal spirit."

OUTLINE OF TOPICS

REFERENCES

To find the passages cited, use the numbers in heavy type, which are the volume and page numbers of the passages referred to. For example, in 4 HOMER: *Iliad*, BK II [265–283] 12d, the number 4 is the number of the volume in the set; the number 12d indicates that the passage is in section d of page 12.

PAGE SECTIONS: When the text is printed in one column, the letters a and b refer to the upper and lower halves of the page. For example, in 53 JAMES: *Psychology*, 116a-119b, the passage begins in the upper half of page 116 and ends in the lower half of page 119. When the text is printed in two columns, the letters a and b refer to the upper and lower halves of the left-hand side of the page, the letters c and d to the upper and lower halves of the right-hand side of the page. For example, in 7 PLATO: *Symposium*, 163b-164c, the passage begins in the lower half of the left-hand side of page 163 and ends in the upper half of the right-hand side of page 164.

AUTHOR'S DIVISIONS: One or more of the main divisions of a work (such as PART, BK, CH, SECT) are sometimes included in the reference; line numbers, in brackets, are given in certain cases; *e.g.*, *Iliad*, BK II [265–283] 12d.

BIBLE REFERENCES: The references are to book, chapter, and verse. When the King James and Douay versions differ in title of books or in the numbering of chapters or verses, the King James version is cited first and the Douay, indicated by a (*D*), follows; *e.g.*, OLD TESTAMENT: *Nehemiah*, 7:45—(*D*) II *Esdras*, 7:46.

SYMBOLS: The abbreviation "esp" calls the reader's attention to one or more especially relevant parts of a whole reference; "passim" signifies that the topic is discussed intermittently rather than continuously in the work or passage cited.

For additional information concerning the style of the references, see the Explanation of Reference Style; for general guidance in the use of *The Great Ideas*, consult the Preface.

1. General theories about the animal nature

1a. Characteristics of animal life: the animal soul

7 PLATO: *Cratylus*, 93c-d / *Phaedo*, 233b-c / *Republic*, BK X, 440b-c / *Timaeus*, 476d-477a,c

8 ARISTOTLE: *Metaphysics*, BK V, CH 8 [1017^{b}10–17] 538b / *Soul* 631a-668d esp BK II, CH 2 [413^{a}20–^{b}4] 643b-c

9 ARISTOTLE: *History of Animals*, BK I, CH 1 [487^{a}10–488^{b}29] 7d-9d; BK VIII, CH 1 114b,d-115b / *Parts of Animals*, BK I, CH 1 [641^{a}33–^{b}10] 164b-c; CH 5 [645^{b}14–646^{a}5] 169c-d; BK III, CH 5 [667^{b}21–32] 196a / *Motion of Animals*, CH 6-11 235d-239d esp CH 10 238c-239a / *Generation of Animals*, BK I, CH 23 [731^{a}24–^{b}8] 271c-d; BK II, CH 3 [736^{a}24-737^{a}19] 276d-278a; CH 5 [741^{a}6-31] 282a-b

10 GALEN: *Natural Faculties*, BK I, CH 1 167a-b; CH 12 172d-173c

12 LUCRETIUS: *Nature of Things*, BK III [94–416] 31b-35c

12 AURELIUS: *Meditations*, BK III, SECT 16, 262d; BK IX, SECT 9 292b-d

16 KEPLER: *Epitome*, BK IV, 855a-b

17 PLOTINUS: *First Ennead*, TR I, CH 11 5b-c / *Fourth Ennead*, TR III, CH 23 153d-154b

18 AUGUSTINE: *Confessions*, BK X, PAR 11 74a-b / *City of God*, BK VII, CH 23, 256b-c

19 AQUINAS: *Summa Theologica*, PART I, Q 18, A 1 104c-105c; Q 72, A 1, REP 1 368b-369d; Q 75, A 3 380c-381b; A 6, REP 1 383c-384c; Q 78, A 1 407b-409a; Q 118, A 1 600a-601c; PART I–II, Q 17, A 2, REP 2 687d-688b

20 AQUINAS: *Summa Theologica*, PART III SUPPL, Q 79, A 1, ANS 951b-953b

21 DANTE: *Divine Comedy*, PURGATORY, XXV [34–78] 91d-92a

24 RABELAIS: *Gargantua and Pantagruel*, BK III, 138a-b; 192d

28 HARVEY: *Motion of the Heart*, 302d-303a / *On Animal Generation*, 369d-370b; 372b; 384d-390b passim; 403d-404b; 418b-419d; 431b-434a esp 433c-d; 456b-458a esp 457a-d; 488d-496d

30 BACON: *Novum Organum*, BK II, APH 48, 186a

31 DESCARTES: *Rules*, XII, 19d-20a / *Discourse*, PART V, 56a-b; 59a-60c / *Objections and Replies*, 156a-d; 208c; 226a-d

35 LOCKE: *Human Understanding*, BK II, CH IX, SECT 12 140c; CH XXVII, SECT 3–5 219d-220c passim; BK III, CH VI, SECT 33 278b-c

53 JAMES: *Psychology*, 4a-6b; 8a-14b passim, esp 11b-12a; 47b-52a passim

(1. *General theories about the animal nature.* 1a.
*Characteristics of animal life: the animal
soul.*)

54 FREUD: *Beyond the Pleasure Principle*, 651d-
657d esp 651d-652c, 655b-656a / *New Introductory Lectures*, 851a-c

1a(1) **Animal sensitivity: its degrees and differentiations**

7 PLATO: *Timaeus*, 453b-454a
8 ARISTOTLE: *Soul*, BK II, CH 2 [413^{b}1–13]
643c-d; [414^{a}1–3] 644a; BK II, CH 5–BK III,
CH 3 647b-661b; BK III, CH 8–13 664b-668d /
Sense and the Sensible 673a-689a,c
9 ARISTOTLE: *History of Animals*, BK I, CH 3
[489^{a}17–20] 10b; CH 4 [489^{a}23–27] 10c; CH
9–11 13b-15a; CH 15 [494^{b}11–18] 16d; BK II,
CH 10 25b-c; CH 12 [504^{a}19–29] 26c-d; CH 13
[505^{a}33–39] 27d-28a; BK IV, CH 6 [531^{a}27–^{b}4]
58b; CH 7 [532^{a}5–10] 58d-59a; CH 8 59d-62a;
BK V, CH 16 [548^{b}10–15] 75b-c; BK VIII, CH 1
[588^{b}17–31] 115a-b; BK IX, CH 34 [620^{a}1–5]
145c / *Parts of Animals*, BK II, CH 1 [647^{a}1–^{b}10]
171a-d; CH 8 [653^{b}22–29] 179b; CH 10–17 181d-
188a,c esp CH 10 [656^{a}14]–CH 12 [657^{a}25] 182b-
183d, CH 16–17 185d-188a,c; BK III, CH 4
[666^{a}34–^{b}1] 194b; [667^{a}10–15] 195b; BK IV, CH
5 [681^{b}14–682^{a}9] 212b-d; CH 11 [690^{b}17–691^{a}28]
222d-223c / *Gait of Animals*, CH 4 [705^{b}9–13]
244b / *Generation of Animals*, BK I, CH 23
[731^{a}24–^{b}8] 271c-d; BK II, CH 1 [732^{a}12–14]
272c; CH 3 [736^{a}25–^{b}14] 276d-277b; CH 5
[741^{a}6–30] 282a-b; CH 6 [743^{b}25–744^{b}11] 285a-
d; BK V, CH 1 [778^{b}20]–CH 2 [781^{b}30] 321a-324a
/ *Ethics*, BK I, CH 7 [1097^{b}33–1098^{a}2] 343b;
BK III, CH 10 [1118^{a}17–^{b}8] 364d-365a; BK VI,
CH 2 [1139^{a}17–21] 387d; BK IX, CH 9 [1170^{a}13–
19] 423d-424a; BK X, CH 4 [1174^{b}15–1175^{a}2]
429a-b
10 GALEN: *Natural Faculties*, BK I, CH 1 167a-b
12 LUCRETIUS: *Nature of Things*, BK II [398–477]
20a-21a; BK III [231–287] 33a-d; [323–416]
34b-35c; BK IV [216–268] 47a-d; [524–548]
51a-b; [615–721] 52b-53d
12 AURELIUS: *Meditations*, BK III, SECT 16, 262d
16 KEPLER: *Epitome*, BK IV, 855a
18 AUGUSTINE: *Confessions*, BK X, par 11 74a-b
19 AQUINAS: *Summa Theologica*, PART I, Q 18,
A 3, ANS 106b-107c; Q 75, A 3, ANS and REP 2
380c-381b; Q 78, AA 3–4 410a-413d; Q 91, A 3,
REP 1,3 486b-487d
23 HOBBES: *Leviathan*, PART I, 49a-d
25 MONTAIGNE: *Essays*, 286a-287b; 290c-291b
28 HARVEY: *On Animal Generation*, 369d-370b;
433c-435a; 456b-458a esp 457a-d
30 BACON: *Novum Organum*, BK II, APH 27,
157b-d; APH 40, 173c-d
31 DESCARTES: *Discourse*, PART V, 59a-c
35 LOCKE: *Human Understanding*, BK II, CH IX,
SECT 11–15 140b-141a
38 MONTESQUIEU: *Spirit of Laws*, BK XIV, 103a-c

38 ROUSSEAU: *Inequality*, 337c-d
48 MELVILLE: *Moby Dick*, 244a-245b
49 DARWIN: *Descent of Man*, 261c-262a; 301c-
302a; 397d-398a; 402b-c; 406c; 432c-434c
passim; 447b-d; 474a-b; 480a-482b passim;
529a-b; 553d-554a; 568d-569b; 595b-596a
esp 595d
53 JAMES: *Psychology*, 8a; 9b-13a passim, esp 13a;
27a-42b passim
54 FREUD: *Beyond the Pleasure Principle*, 647a-
648a

1a(2) **Animal memory, imagination, and intelligence**

4 HOMER: *Odyssey*, BK XVII [290–327] 280a-c
6 HERODOTUS: *History*, BK III, 112b-c
7 PLATO: *Republic*, BK II, 319c-320b
8 ARISTOTLE: *Metaphysics*, BK I, CH 1 [980^{a}28–
^{b}27] 499a-b / *Soul*, BK III, CH 3 [427^{b}14–429^{a}9]
660a-661b; CH 10 [433^{a}8–12] 665d; CH 10
[433^{b}27]–CH 11 [434^{a}9] 666c-d / *Memory and
Reminiscence* 690a-695d
9 ARISTOTLE: *History of Animals*, BK I, CH 1
[488^{b}25–27] 9d; BK VIII, CH 1 [588^{b}18–31]
114b,d; [589^{a}1–3] 115b; BK IX, CH 1 [608^{a}11–
32] 133b,d; CH 7 [612^{b}18–32] 138b-c; CH 46
[630^{b}17–23] 156a / *Ethics*, BK VII, CH 3
[1147^{b}3–5] 397d
12 LUCRETIUS: *Nature of Things*, BK IV [962–
1036] 56d-57c
18 AUGUSTINE: *Confessions*, BK X, par 26, 78b
19 AQUINAS: *Summa Theologica*, PART I, Q 78,
A 4, ANS and REP 3,5–6 411d-413d; PART I–II,
Q 13, A 2, REP 3 673c-674c
23 HOBBES: *Leviathan*, PART I, 50a-51b; 52b;
53d; 64b
25 MONTAIGNE: *Essays*, 218c-219b; 229d-230b
28 HARVEY: *On Animal Generation*, 454a
31 DESCARTES: *Rules*, XII, 19d-20a
32 MILTON: *Paradise Lost*, BK VIII [369–451]
240a-242a
35 LOCKE: *Human Understanding*, BK II, CH X,
SECT 10 143c-d
35 HUME: *Human Understanding*, SECT IX, DIV 83
487c-d
36 SWIFT: *Gulliver*, PART IV, 163b-164b
38 ROUSSEAU: *Inequality*, 337d-338a; 341d-342a
49 DARWIN: *Descent of Man*, 291d-294c; 296c-
297b; 400a-c; 412d; 447b-c; 480a-481b
53 JAMES: *Psychology*, 3b-6b esp 5b; 13a-14a;
49a-50a; 51a-52a; 679a-683a; 704a-706b

1a(3) **Animal appetite: desire and emotion in
animals**

4 HOMER: *Iliad*, BK XVII [426–455] 126c-d /
Odyssey, BK XVII [290–327] 280a-c
6 HERODOTUS: *History*, BK IV, 146c-d
7 PLATO: *Symposium*, 165c-166b / *Republic*, BK
II, 319c-320b / *Laws*, BK VI, 712b
8 ARISTOTLE: *Soul*, BK III, CH 9–11 664d-667a
9 ARISTOTLE: *History of Animals*, BK VI, CH 18
97b-99c; BK VIII, CH 1 [588^{b}24–589^{a}10] 115b;

BK IX, CH 4 [611ᵃ9–14] 136d; CH 37 [621ᵇ28–622ᵃ10] 147c / *Parts of Animals*, BK II, CH 4 [650ᵇ20–651ᵃ15] 175c-176a; BK III, CH 4 [667ᵃ10–22] 195b; BK IV, CH 5 [679ᵃ5–32] 209a-c; CH 11 [692ᵃ22–27] 224b-c / *Motion of Animals*, CH 6–11 235d-239d / *Ethics*, BK III, CH 8 [1116ᵇ23–1117ᵃ9] 363a-c; CH 10 [1118ᵃ17–ᵇ8] 364d-365a; BK VII, CH 6 [1149ᵇ30–36] 400c; CH 12 [1153ᵃ27–35] 404c-d

10 GALEN: *Natural Faculties*, BK III, CH 6 202d-203a; CH 8, 206b-c

12 LUCRETIUS: *Nature of Things*, BK III [136–160] 31d-32a; [288–322] 33d-34b; [741–753] 39c-d

13 VIRGIL: *Aeneid*, BK XI [745–760] 348b; BK XII [5–11] 354a

17 PLOTINUS: *Fourth Ennead*, TR III, CH 23, 154b

19 AQUINAS: *Summa Theologica*, PART I, Q 6, A 1, REP 2 28b-d; QQ 80–81 427a-431d; PART I–II, Q 6, A 2 646a-c; Q 11, A 2 667b-d; Q 12, A 5 672a-c; Q 13, A 2 673c-674c; Q 15, A 2 682a-c; Q 16, A 2 684d-685b; Q 17, A 2 687d-688b; Q 40, A 3 794c-795a; Q 46, A 4, ANS and REP 2 815b-d

22 CHAUCER: *Manciple's Tale* [17,104–135] 490a-b

23 HOBBES: *Leviathan*, PART I, 61a-d; 64a-c

25 MONTAIGNE: *Essays*, 224c-225b

27 SHAKESPEARE: *King Lear*, ACT IV, SC VI [109–125] 274c

28 HARVEY: *On Animal Generation*, 346a-347d; 349a-350a; 391a-c; 402a-d; 405c-406a; 476c-477a

31 SPINOZA: *Ethics*, PART III, PROP 57, SCHOL 415b

38 ROUSSEAU: *Inequality*, 343d-345a

44 BOSWELL: *Johnson*, 215d-216a

48 MELVILLE: *Moby Dick*, 289b-291a

49 DARWIN: *Descent of Man*, 289a-291a; 303c; 305c-309d; 371c-372c; 447b-c; 480a-481b; 543d-545d

51 TOLSTOY: *War and Peace*, BK XIII, 575b; BK XIV, 605d-606a

53 JAMES: *Psychology*, 14a-b; 49b-51a; 700b-711a passim, esp 702a-703a; 717b; 723b-725a; 729b

54 FREUD: *General Introduction*, 607d-609b esp 609b / *Inhibitions, Symptoms, and Anxiety*, 721b; 737c-d

1a(4) Locomotion: degrees of animal motility

8 ARISTOTLE: *Soul*, BK III, CH 9–11 664d-667a; CH 12 [434ᵃ30–ᵇ9] 667b-c

9 ARISTOTLE: *History of Animals*, BK I, CH 1 [487ᵇ5–34] 8b-d; BK II, CH 1 [497ᵇ18–498ᵇ10] 20a-d; BK IV, CH 1 [523ᵇ20–524ᵃ24] 48d-49d; CH 4 [528ᵃ30–ᵇ11] 55b; BK VIII, CH 1 [588ᵇ11–24] 115a; BK IX, CH 37 [621ᵇ2–13] 147a-b; CH 48 [631ᵃ20–30] 156c-d / *Parts of Animals*, BK IV, CH 6–9 213b-217b passim; CH 10 [686ᵃ25–ᵇ35] 217d-218c; CH 12 [693ᵃ25]–CH 13 [696ᵃ34] 225b-228a / *Motion of Animals*, CH 1–2 233a-234a; CH 8 [702ᵃ22]–CH 10 [703ᵇ1] 237c-239a / *Gait of Animals* 243a-252a,c / *Generation of Animals*, BK II, CH 1 [732ᵃ12–24] 272c

10 GALEN: *Natural Faculties*, BK II, CH 8, 193b-c

12 LUCRETIUS: *Nature of Things*, BK V [837–859] 72a-b

19 AQUINAS: *Summa Theologica*, PART I, Q 18, A 1, ANS 104c-105c; A 2, REP 1 105c-106b; A 3, ANS 106b-107c; Q 78, A 1, ANS and REP 4 407b-409a

24 RABELAIS: *Gargantua and Pantagruel*, BK III, 192d

31 DESCARTES: *Rules*, XII, 19d-20a

35 LOCKE: *Human Understanding*, BK II, CH IX, SECT 11 140b-c; SECT 13 140d

49 DARWIN: *Descent of Man*, 279a-280c; 371d-372c

53 JAMES: *Psychology*, 10a-12b esp 12a-b; 699a

1a(5) Sleeping and waking in animals

8 ARISTOTLE: *Sleep* 696a-701d

9 ARISTOTLE: *History of Animals*, BK III, CH 19 [521ᵃ15–17] 46a; BK IV, CH 10 63c-64b; BK VI, CH 12 [566ᵇ13–15] 92d; BK VIII, CH 14 [599ᵃ20]–CH 17 [600ᵇ15] 125b-126d / *Parts of Animals*, BK II, CH 7 [653ᵃ10–20] 178b-c / *Motion of Animals*, CH 11 [703ᵇ8–15] 239b / *Generation of Animals*, BK V, CH 1 [778ᵇ20–779ᵃ28] 321a-c

12 LUCRETIUS: *Nature of Things*, BK IV [907–961] 56a-d

20 AQUINAS: *Summa Theologica*, PART III SUPPL, Q 81, A 4, ANS 966d-967d; Q 82, A 3, ANS 971a-972d

38 ROUSSEAU: *Inequality*, 337c

1b. The distinction between plants and animals in faculty and function: cases difficult to classify

7 PLATO: *Timaeus*, 469d-470a

8 ARISTOTLE: *Topics*, BK VI, CH 10 [148ᵃ23–38] 202b-c / *Physics*, BK II, CH 8 [199ᵃ20–ᵇ13] 276c-d / *Heavens*, BK II, CH 12 [292ᵇ1–11] 384a / *Soul*, BK I, CH 5 [410ᵇ16–411ᵃ2] 640d-641a; BK II, CH 2 [413ᵃ20–ᵇ10] 643b-c; CH 3 644c-645b; BK III, CH 12 [434ᵃ22–ᵇ9] 667a-c / *Sleep*, CH 1 696a-697c

9 ARISTOTLE: *History of Animals*, BK IV, CH 6 [531ᵇ8–9] 58b; BK V, CH 1 [539ᵃ15–25] 65b-d; BK VIII, CH 1 [588ᵇ4–589ᵃ2] 114d-115b / *Parts of Animals*, BK II, CH 3 [650ᵃ1–37] 174c-175a; CH 10 [655ᵇ27–656ᵃ8] 181d-182a; BK IV, CH 4 [677ᵇ36–678ᵃ15] 207d-208a; CH 5 [681ᵃ10–ᵇ9] 211c-212b; CH 6 [682ᵇ26–28] 213d; CH 10 [686ᵇ23–687ᵃ1] 218b-c / *Gait of Animals*, CH 4 [705ᵃ26–ᵇ9] 244a-b / *Generation of Animals*, BK I, CH 1 [715ᵇ18–716ᵃ1] 255d-256a; CH 23 271b-d; BK II, CH 1 [732ᵃ12–14] 272c; [735ᵃ16–19] 275d; CH 3 [736ᵃ25–ᵇ14] 276d-277b; CH 4 [740ᵇ25]–CH 5 [741ᵃ30] 281d-282b; BK III, CH 7 [757ᵇ15–30] 298c-d; CH 11 302b-304d; BK V, CH 1 [778ᵇ30–779ᵃ4] 321a-b

10 GALEN: *Natural Faculties*, BK I, CH 1 167a-b

12 LUCRETIUS: *Nature of Things*, BK II [700–710] 23d-24a

12 AURELIUS: *Meditations*, BK VIII, SECT 7 286a; BK IX, SECT 9, 292c

8 221a-222a; SECT 12 223a-b; BK III, CH I,
SECT 1–3 251b,d-252a; CH VI, SECT 12 271d-
272b; SECT 22 273d-274a; SECT 26–27 274d-
276a; SECT 29 276b-d; SECT 33 278b-c; CH XI,
SECT 20 304c-d; BK IV, CH XVI, SECT 12,
370c-371a; CH XVII, SECT I 371c-d

35 BERKELEY: *Human Knowledge*, INTRO, SECT
II 407b-408a

35 HUME: *Human Understanding*, SECT IX 487b-
488c

38 MONTESQUIEU: *Spirit of Laws*, BK I, 1d-2a

38 ROUSSEAU: *Inequality*, 334d-335a; 337d-338d;
341d; 357c-d / *Social Contract*, BK I, 393b-c

39 SMITH: *Wealth of Nations*, BK I, 6d-8b

42 KANT: *Pure Reason*, 164a-c; 199c-200c / *Practical Reason*, 316c-317a / *Pref. Metaphysical
Elements of Ethics*, 372a-b / *Intro. Metaphysic
of Morals*, 385c-386d / *Judgement*, 479a-c;
584d-585c; 587a-588a; 602b;d [fn I]

43 MILL: *Utilitarianism*, 448a-449c passim;
469b-d

46 HEGEL: *Philosophy of Right*, PART I, par 47
24a-b; PART II, par 132 46b-47a; par 139 48d-
49b; PART III, par 190 66a-b; par 211, 70a-b;
ADDITIONS, 4–5, 116a-d; 8 117c-d; 10 117d-
118a; 28 121b; 62 126a; 118 136a-b; 121 136c-d
/ *Philosophy of History*, INTRO, 156c; 168d;
178a-b; 186a; PART I, 257d-258a; PART III,
304d-305a

49 DARWIN: *Descent of Man*, 255a-b; 278a-c;
287a-c; 294c-305c esp 294c-295a, 297a-298a,
304a; 311d-312c; 319b-d; 349d; 591d-593c

50 MARX: *Capital*, 85b-c; 86b-c

51 TOLSTOY: *War and Peace*, EPILOGUE II, 689c-
690a

52 DOSTOEVSKY: *Brothers Karamazov*, BK VI, 167c

53 JAMES: *Psychology*, 85a-b; 677a; 678b-686b
esp 678b, 683b-684a, 686a-b; 691a-b; 704a-
706b esp 704a-b; 721a; 873a

54 FREUD: *Sexual Enlightenment of Children*, 122c
/ *Interpretation of Dreams*, 385b-c / *General
Introduction*, 616b-c

1c(1) Comparison of brutes and men as animals

4 HOMER: *Iliad*, BK III [1–35] 19a-b; BK V [133–
143] 31c; [159–165] 31d; BK VI [503–516]
45b-c

8 ARISTOTLE: *Soul*, BK II, CH 9 [421ᵃ6-26] 652c-
d; [421ᵇ8–33] 653a-b / *Sense and the Sensible*,
CH I [436ᵇ17-437ᵃ17]673d-674a; CH 4 [440ᵇ25-
441ᵃ3] 678b-c; CH 5 [443ᵇ17-445ᵃ31] 681c-
683b

9 ARISTOTLE: *History of Animals* 7a-158d passim, esp BK I, CH I [488ᵃ5–10] 8d-9a, BK I, CH 6
[491ᵃ14]–BK III, CH 22 [523ᵃ27] 12d-48a,c, BK
VII 106b,d-114a,c, BK IX, CH I [608ᵃ10–ᵇ19]
133b,d-134a / *Parts of Animals*, BK II, CH 7
[653ᵃ29–ᵇ5] 178d; CH 9 [655ᵇ3-16] 181c; CH 10
[656ᵃ3-14] 182a-b; CH 14 184d-185c; CH 16
[659ᵇ28]–CH 17 [660ᵇ3] 186d-187c; BK III, CH I
[661ᵇ5-15] 188b,d; [662ᵇ17-23] 190a; CH 6

[669ᵇ4–8] 197d-198a; BK IV, CH 10 [686ᵃ25-
690ᵇ10] 217d-222c / *Gait of Animals* 243a-
252a,c esp CH 4 [705ᵇ30-706ᵃ25] 244c-245a,
CH 5 [706ᵇ7-16] 245b, CH 11-12 248d-249d /
Generation of Animals 255a-331a,c esp BK II,
CH 4 278b-282a, CH 6 [744ᵃ15-31] 285b-c /
Ethics, BK III, CH 10 [1118ᵃ18-ᵇ7] 364d-365a;
CH II [1119ᵃ5-11]365c; BK VIII, CH 12 [1162ᵃ16-
25] 414c / *Politics*, BK I, CH 2 [1253ᵃ29-39]446d

10 HIPPOCRATES: *Articulations*, par 8 93c-94b;
par 13 96b-c; par 46, 106a / *Instruments of
Reduction*, par 1, 122b

12 LUCRETIUS: *Nature of Things*, BK II [251–293]
18b-d; BK III [288–322] 33d-34b; BK IV [962–
1036] 56d-57c; [1192-1208] 59d-60a; [1251–
1267] 60c-d; BK V [878–900] 72c-d; [1028–1090]
74c-75b

19 AQUINAS: *Summa Theologica*, PART I, Q 75,
A 6, REP I 383c-384c; Q 76, A 5, ANS and REP
3–4 394c-396a; Q 78, A 4, ANS 411d-413d; QQ
80–81 427a-431d; Q 91, A 3, REP 1–3 486b-
487d; Q 98, A 2, ANS and REP 3 517d-519a;
Q 99, A 1, ANS and REP 2 519b-520a; PART I–II,
Q 2, A 5, CONTRARY 618d-619c; A 6, CONTRARY
619d-620d

20 AQUINAS: *Summa Theologica*, PART III, Q 2,
A 2, REP 2 711d-712d

22 CHAUCER: *Manciple's Tale* [17,104-144]
490a-b

25 MONTAIGNE: *Essays*, 215a-232c passim; 286a-
287b; 290c-291b; 424d-425c

27 SHAKESPEARE: *King Lear*, ACT IV, SC VI [109–
125] 274c

28 HARVEY: *Motion of the Heart*, 268d-304a,c esp
280c-283a / *On Animal Generation*, 338a-496d
esp 449a-454a, 463d-464a, 470c-472c

30 BACON: *Novum Organum*, BK II, APH 40,
173c-d

31 DESCARTES: *Rules*, XII, 19d-20a / *Discourse*,
PART V, 56a-b; 59a-60b / *Objections and
Replies*, 156a-d; 226a-d

31 SPINOZA: *Ethics*, PART III, PROP 57, SCHOL 415b

35 LOCKE: *Civil Government*, CH VII, SECT 78–80
42b-43a / *Human Understanding*, BK II, CH IX,
SECT 12–15 140c-141a

36 SWIFT: *Gulliver*, PART II, 58a-b; PART IV, 147b-
148b

38 ROUSSEAU: *Inequality*, 334b,d-337d; 338c;
346b-d; 348d-349c

47 GOETHE: *Faust*, PROLOGUE [281–292] 8a

48 MELVILLE: *Moby Dick*, 284a

49 DARWIN: *Descent of Man*, 255a-286d esp
265c-d, 273d-275c, 285c-286d; 287c-290c;
310a-312d; 331a-336a; 590a-593a

51 TOLSTOY: *War and Peace*, EPILOGUE II, 689c-
690a

52 DOSTOEVSKY: *Brothers Karamazov*, BK V,
122d-123a

53 JAMES: *Psychology*, 49a-50a; 702a-b; 704a-
706b

54 FREUD: *Civilization and Its Discontents*, 782a-d
[fn I]; 785a-b,d [fn I]

(1c. *The distinction between animal and human nature.*)

1c(2) Comparison of animal with human intelligence

7 PLATO: *Republic*, BK II, 319c-320c
8 ARISTOTLE: *Physics*, BK II, CH 8 [199ª20–23] 276c / *Metaphysics*, BK I, CH I [980ª28–981ª12] 499a-c
9 ARISTOTLE: *History of Animals*, BK I, CH I [488ᵇ20–27] 9d; BK VIII, CH I [588ª18–ᵇ4] 114b,d; BK IX, CH I [608ª10–ᵇ19] 133b,d-134a; CH 7 [612ᵇ18–32] 138b-c / *Parts of Animals*, BK I, CH I [641ᵇ5–10] 164b-c; BK IV, CH 10 [686ᵇ22–687ª23] 218b-d / *Generation of Animals*, BK I, CH 23 [731ª24–ᵇ8] 271c-d; BK II, CH 6 [744ª27–31] 285c / *Ethics*, BK VI, CH 7 [1141ª20–35] 390a-b; BK VII, CH 3 [1147ᵇ3–5] 397d / *Politics*, BK I, CH 5 [1254ᵇ20–25] 448b
10 GALEN: *Natural Faculties*, BK I, CH 12 172d-173c
12 AURELIUS: *Meditations*, BK IX, SECT 9 292b-d
19 AQUINAS: *Summa Theologica*, PART I, Q 59, A 3, ANS 308b-309a; Q 76, A 5, REP 4 394c-396a; Q 79, A 8, REP 3 421c-422b; Q 83, A I, ANS 436d-438a; Q 96, A I, ANS and REP 4 510b-511b; PART I–II, Q 12, A 5 672a-c; Q 17, A 2 687d-688b
20 AQUINAS: *Summa Theologica*, PART III SUPPL, Q 79, A I, ANS 951b-953b
23 HOBBES: *Leviathan*, PART I, 52b; 53a-b; 53d-54a; 59b-c; 63a; 64b-c; 79b-c; PART II, 100a-c; PART IV, 267b
25 MONTAIGNE: *Essays*, 215a-224a; 231d-232c
28 HARVEY: *On Animal Generation*, 428a-b; 454a
30 BACON: *Novum Organum*, BK I, APH 73 117d-118a; BK II, APH 35, 163d-164a
31 DESCARTES: *Rules*, XII, 19d-20a / *Discourse*, PART V, 59d-60b / *Objections and Replies*, 156a-d; 226a-d
32 MILTON: *Paradise Lost*, BK VIII [369–451] 240a-242a; BK IX [549–566] 259b
33 PASCAL: *Pensées*, 339–344 233a-b / *Vacuum*, 357a-358a
35 LOCKE: *Human Understanding*, BK II, CH IX, SECT 12–15 140c-141a; CH X, SECT 10 143c-d; CH XI, SECT 4–11 144d-146a passim; CH XXVII, SECT 8 221a-222a; SECT 12 223a-b; BK III, CH VI, SECT 12 271d-272b; BK IV, CH XVI, SECT 12, 370c-371a; CH XVII, SECT I 371c-d
35 BERKELEY: *Human Knowledge*, INTRO, SECT II 407b-408a
35 HUME: *Human Understanding*, SECT IX 487b-488c; SECT XII, DIV 118, 504c
36 SWIFT: *Gulliver*, PART IV 135a-184a esp 151b-152a, 159b-160a
38 ROUSSEAU: *Inequality*, 337d-338a; 341d-342a / *Social Contract*, BK I, 393b-c
39 SMITH: *Wealth of Nations*, BK I, 6d-8b
42 KANT: *Pure Reason*, 199c-200c; 235c-d / *Pref. Metaphysical Elements of Ethics*, 372a-b / *Judgement*, 479a-c; 584d-585c; 602b,d [fn 1]

43 MILL: *Utilitarianism*, 469c-d
46 HEGEL: *Philosophy of Right*, ADDITIONS, 25 121a; 121 136c-d
48 MELVILLE: *Moby Dick*, 134b-135a
49 DARWIN: *Descent of Man*, 287a-303d esp 291c-297b; 319b-d; 591d-592a
51 TOLSTOY: *War and Peace*, EPILOGUE II, 689c-690a
53 JAMES: *Psychology*, 5a-6b; 13a-15a passim; 49a-50a; 85a-b; 665a-666b; 677a; 678b-686b; 704a-706b; 873a
54 FREUD: *Interpretation of Dreams*, 385b-c

1d. The habits or instincts of animals: types of animal habit or instinct; the habits or instincts of different classes of animals

6 HERODOTUS: *History*, BK II, 62c-64c passim; 67b-c; BK III, 111d-112c; BK VII, 236c
7 PLATO: *Republic*, BK II, 320b
8 ARISTOTLE: *Physics*, BK II, CH 8 [199ª20–30] 276c
9 ARISTOTLE: *History of Animals*, BK I, CH I [487ª10–488ᵇ29] 7d-9d; BK IV, CH 9 62a-63c; BK V–VI 65a-106d esp BK V, CH 8 [542ª18–ᵇ2] 68d-69a; BK VIII–IX 114b,d-158d esp BK VIII, CH I [588ᵇ23–589ª9] 115b, CH 12 [596ᵇ20–28] 122d / *Parts of Animals*, BK II, CH 4 [650ᵇ19–651ª5] 175c-d; BK IV, CH 5 [679ª5–32] 209a-c / *Generation of Animals*, BK III, CH 2 [753ª8–17] 294a-b / *Politics*, BK I, CH 5 [1254ᵇ23–24] 448b; CH 8 [1256ª18–30] 450a; BK VII, CH 13 [1332ᵇ3–4] 537b
10 GALEN: *Natural Faculties*, BK I, CH 12, 173a-c
12 LUCRETIUS: *Nature of Things*, BK II [333–370] 19b-d; [661–668] 23b-c
19 AQUINAS: *Summa Theologica*, PART I, Q 19, A 10, ANS 117d-118b; Q 59, A 3, ANS 308b-309a; Q 78, A 4, ANS 411d-413d; Q 81, A 3, ANS and REP 2 430c-431d; Q 83, A I, ANS 436d-438a; Q 96, A I, ANS and REP 2,4 510b-511b; Q 115, A 4, ANS 589d-590c; PART I–II, Q 12, A 5, ANS and REP 3 672a-c; Q 13, A 2 esp REP 3 673c-674c; Q 15, A 2, ANS 682a-c; Q 16, A 2, REP 2 684d-685b; Q 17, A 2, REP 3 687d-688b; Q 40, A 3 794c-795a; Q 41, A I, REP 3 798b-d; Q 46, A 4, REP 2 815b-d
20 AQUINAS: *Summa Theologica*, PART I–II, Q 50, A 3, REP 2 8b-9a
22 CHAUCER: *Nun's Priest's Tale* [15,282–287] 457b / *Maniple's Tale* [17,104–144] 490a-b
23 HOBBES: *Leviathan*, PART II, 100a-c
24 RABELAIS: *Gargantua and Pantagruel*, BK IV, 247d-248b
25 MONTAIGNE: *Essays*, 184a-b; 216b-219a
26 SHAKESPEARE: *Henry V*, ACT I, SC II [187–204] 535d-536a
27 SHAKESPEARE: *Timon of Athens*, ACT IV, SC III [320–348] 414b-c
28 HARVEY: *On Animal Generation*, 339a-b; 346a-347d; 349a-350a; 361c-362a; 402a-d; 405c-406a; 428a-c; 476b-477b

30 BACON: *Advancement of Learning*, 72c / *Novum Organum*, BK I, APH 73 117d-118a

31 DESCARTES: *Discourse*, PART V, 60b / *Objections and Replies*, 156a-d

31 SPINOZA: *Ethics*, PART III, PROP 57, SCHOL 415b

33 PASCAL: *Pensées*, 342-344 233b

35 HUME: *Human Understanding*, SECT V, DIV 38, 466b; DIV 45 469c; SECT IX, DIV 85 488c; SECT XII, DIV 118, 504c

36 SWIFT: *Gulliver*, PART IV, 162a-b

38 ROUSSEAU: *Inequality*, 334d-335a; 337d-338a; 343d-344a

42 KANT: *Fund. Prin. Metaphysic of Morals*, 256d-257a / *Practical Reason*, 316c-317a

43 MILL: *Utilitarianism*, 469c-d

44 BOSWELL: *Johnson*, 221b-d

48 MELVILLE: *Moby Dick*, 144a-b; 146b-147a; 283b-284a; 289b-292a

49 DARWIN: *Origin of Species*, 66a-69c passim; 82d-85c; 108d-111b; 119a-135a,c esp 119a-122d, 134d-135a,c / *Descent of Man*, 287d-289a; 304b-310d esp 308a-310a; 312c-d; 369b-371b; 456b-457c; 463a-464b; 470d-475c passim, esp 475c; 504d-507a passim, esp 506c; 583a

51 TOLSTOY: *War and Peace*, BK XI, 499c-500c

53 JAMES: *Psychology*, 49b-50a; 68a-73b; 700a-711a; 724a-b; 730a-b; 890b-891b [fn 3]

54 FREUD: *Narcissism*, 401a-c / *Instincts*, 412b-415d / *General Introduction*, 615b-616c / *Beyond the Pleasure Principle*, 650c-662b esp 651d-654a / *Group Psychology*, 684d-686c esp 684d-685b / *Ego and Id*, 711c-712a / *New Introductory Lectures*, 846a-851d esp 846b-d, 849c-850a, 851a

1e. The conception of the animal as a machine or automaton

9 ARISTOTLE: *Parts of Animals*, BK I, CH I [640^b5-18] 163a-b / *Motion of Animals*, CH 7 [701^b1-13] 236d-237a / *Generation of Animals*, BK II, CH I [734^b3- 20] 275a-b; CH 5 [741^b5-10] 282c

10 GALEN: *Natural Faculties*, BK II, CH 3, 185a-b

23 HOBBES: *Leviathan*, INTRO, 47a

31 DESCARTES: *Discourse*, PART V, 56a-b; 59a-60c / *Objections and Replies*, 156a-d; 226a-d

33 PASCAL: *Pensées*, 340 233a

35 LOCKE: *Human Understanding*, BK II, CH X, SECT 10 143c-d; CH XI, SECT 11 145d-146a; CH XXVII, SECT 5 220b-c

38 ROUSSEAU: *Inequality*, 337d-338a

42 KANT: *Judgement*, 558b-559a; 575b-578a; 578d-582c

50 MARX: *Capital*, 190d [fn 2]

51 TOLSTOY: *War and Peace*, BK X, 449b-c; EPILOGUE II, 689c-690a

53 JAMES: *Psychology*, 3b-6b passim, esp 5b-6b; 11a-12a; 47b-52b esp 51a-52a; 84a-94b; 700a-706b esp 705a-706b

2. The classification of animals

2a. General schemes of classification: their principles and major divisions

OLD TESTAMENT: *Genesis*, 1:20-31; 2:19-20 / *Leviticus*, 11

8 ARISTOTLE: *Posterior Analytics*, BK II, CH 13 [96^b25-97^a6] 132a-b; CH 14 133c-134a / *Topics*, BK VI, CH 6 [144^a27-145^a2] 197d-198c passim / *Metaphysics*, BK V, CH 28 546b-c; BK VII, CH 12 [1037^b28-1038^a35] 561c-562a / *Soul*, BK II, CH 3 644c-645b

9 ARISTOTLE: *History of Animals*, BK I, CH I [486^a15]-CH 6 [491^a5] 7b-12c esp CH I [486^a15-487^a1] 7b-d; BK II, CH I [497^b4-18] 19b,d-20a; CH 15 [505^b25-32] 28b-c; BK IV, CH I [523^a30-^b20] 48b,d; BK V, CH I [539^a4-15] 65b; BK VIII, CH I [588^b4]-CH 2 [590^a18] 114d-116c / *Parts of Animals*, BK I, CH 2-4 165d-168c; CH 5 [645^b20-28] 169c-d; BK III, CH 6 [669^b7-14] 198a / *Generation of Animals*, BK I, CH I [715^a18-^b25] 255b-d; BK II, CH I [732^a13-733^b17] 272c-274a; BK III, CH II [761^b9-24] 302c-d / *Politics*, BK IV, CH 4 [1290^b25-36] 489d-490a

19 AQUINAS: *Summa Theologica*, PART I, Q 3, A 4, REP I 16d-17c; Q 50, A 4, REP I 273b-274b; QQ 71-72 367a-369d

28 HARVEY: *On Animal Generation*, 468b-469b

30 BACON: *Novum Organum*, BK II, APH 27, 158b-c; APH 30 159c-d

35 LOCKE: *Human Understanding*, BK III, CH VI 268b-283a passim, esp SECT 7 270b, SECT 36-37 279a-b; CH XI, SECT 19-20 304b-d

42 KANT: *Pure Reason*, 193a-200c / *Judgement*, 579b-c

48 MELVILLE: *Moby Dick*, 95b-105b

49 DARWIN: *Origin of Species*, 24a-b; 25d-29a esp 28c-29a; 30d-31d; 63d-64d; 207a-212c; 215b-217b; 224d-225b; 228c-229a,c; 238b-239a; 241d-242a / *Descent of Man*, 331a-341d esp 331b-333a, 337a-338c; 342a-350b passim, esp 342a-b

2b. Analogies of structure and function among different classes of animals

8 ARISTOTLE: *Posterior Analytics*, BK II, CH 14 [98^a20-23] 134a / *Youth, Life, and Breathing* 714a-726d passim

9 ARISTOTLE: *History of Animals* 7a-158d esp BK I, CH 1-6 7a-13a, BK II, CH I 19b,d-23d, BK IV, CH 8-BK V, CH I 59d-66a, BK VIII, CH I 114b,d-115b / *Parts of Animals* 161a-229d passim, esp BK I, CH 4 167d-168c, CH 5 [645^b1-646^a5] 169b-d / *Gait of Animals* 243a-252a,c / *Generation of Animals* 255a-331a,c esp BK II, CH I 272a-276a

10 GALEN: *Natural Faculties*, BK III, CH 2 199d-200a

28 HARVEY: *Motion of the Heart*, 274b-d; 277b-278d; 280c-283a; 299b-302c / *On Animal*

(2. *The classification of animals.* 2b. *Analogies of structure and function among different classes of animals.*)

Generation, 336b-d; 338a-496d esp 449a-454a, 463d-464a, 468b-472c

30 BACON: *Novum Organum*, BK II, APH 27, 157b-158c

35 LOCKE: *Human Understanding*, BK III, CH VI, SECT 12 271d-272b

35 HUME: *Human Understanding*, SECT IX, DIV 82 487b-c

42 KANT: *Judgement*, 579b-c

48 MELVILLE: *Moby Dick*, 273a-b; 279b

49 DARWIN: *Origin of Species*, 75b-78c; 82d-94c; 112b-113c; 212d-215a; 217b-219d; 225c-228c; 238c-239a / *Descent of Man*, 255a-265d; 271c-275c; 279a-284b; 331a-335a; 338d-340c passim; 348b-c

2c. Continuity and discontinuity in the scale of animal life: gradation from lower to higher forms

OLD TESTAMENT: *Genesis*, 1:20–25

8 ARISTOTLE: *Soul*, BK II, CH 2 [413^{b}4–10] 643c; [414^{a}1–3] 644a; BK III, CH 11 [433^{b}32–434^{a}9] 666d; CH 12 [434^{b}9–30] 667c-d / *Sense and the Sensible*, CH 1 [436^{b}12–437^{a}17] 673c-674a; CH 5 [443^{b}17–445^{a}3] 681c-682d

9 ARISTOTLE: *History of Animals*, BK VIII, CH 1 114b,d-115b / *Parts of Animals*, BK IV, CH 10 [686^{b}23–687^{a}1] 218b-c / *Generation of Animals*, BK II, CH 1 [732^{a}13–733^{b}17] 272c-274a

19 AQUINAS: *Summa Theologica*, PART I, Q 18, A 2, REP 1 105c-106b; A 3, ANS 106b-107c; Q 50, A 4, REP 1 273b-274b; Q 71, A 1, REP 4–5 367a-368b; Q 72, A 1, REP 1 368b-369d; Q 76, A 5, REP 3 394c-396a; Q 78, A 1, ANS and REP 4 407b-409a

28 HARVEY: *On Animal Generation*, 336b-d; 400d-401a; 412c-413a

30 BACON: *Novum Organum*, BK II, APH 30 159c-d

35 LOCKE: *Human Understanding*, BK II, CH IX, SECT 11–15 140b-141a passim, esp SECT 12 140c; BK III, CH VI, SECT 12 271d-272b; BK IV, CH XVI, SECT 12, 370c-371a

42 KANT: *Pure Reason*, 199c-200c / *Judgement*, 578d-580a esp 579b-c

49 DARWIN: *Origin of Species*, 3a-b; 55b-62a esp 60b-61a; 64a-d; 80a-82d; 117a-118d; 167a-180d esp 180a-d; 207a-208a; 224d-225b; 228c-229a,c; 238b-243d esp 241a-d, 243b-c / *Descent of Man*, 337a-338c; 340d-341c

53 JAMES: *Psychology*, 41b; 51a-52b; 95b-98a; 705b-706b

54 FREUD: *Civilization and Its Discontents*, 768d-769a

3. The anatomy of animals

6 HERODOTUS: *History*, BK II, 63b-64c passim

7 PLATO: *Timaeus*, 466a-469c

9 ARISTOTLE: *History of Animals*, BK I–IV 7a-65a,c esp BK I, CH 1–6 7a-13a / *Parts of Animals*, BK II–IV 170a-229d

19 AQUINAS: *Summa Theologica*, PART I, Q 91, A 3 486b-487d

24 RABELAIS: *Gargantua and Pantagruel*, BK IV, 271a-272d

28 HARVEY: *On Animal Generation*, 343b-345d; 377c-380c passim; 485a-d

30 BACON: *Advancement of Learning*, 52b-c / *Novum Organum*, BK II, APH 7 139c-140a

31 DESCARTES: *Discourse*, PART V, 56b-57a

42 KANT: *Judgement*, 579b-c

48 MELVILLE: *Moby Dick*, 243b-252a

49 DARWIN: *Origin of Species*, 14c-15b passim; 85d-87b; 89b-90c; 217b-219d / *Descent of Man*, 255a-265a passim; 266a-c; 271c-274d; 278c-284b

54 FREUD: *Beyond the Pleasure Principle*, 647a-648a

3a. Physical elements of the animal body: kinds of tissue

7 PLATO: *Timaeus*, 468a-469d

8 ARISTOTLE: *Meteorology*, BK IV, CH 10 [389^{a}19–23] 493b; CH 11 [389^{b}7–18] 493c-d; CH 12 493d-494d

9 ARISTOTLE: *History of Animals*, BK I, CH 1 [486^{a}5–15] 7a; [487^{a}1–10] 7d; BK III, CH 2 [511^{b}1–10] 35a; CH 5 [515^{a}27]–CH 20 [521^{b}17] 39c-46c / *Parts of Animals*, BK I, CH 1 [640^{b}11–24] 163a-b; BK II, CH 1 [646^{a}7]–CH 2 [648^{a}20] 170a-172c; CH 3 [649^{b}22]–CH 9 [655^{b}26] 174b-181d; BK III, CH 2 [663^{b}22–36] 191b-c / *Generation of Animals*, BK I, CH 1 [715^{a}8–11] 255a; CH 18 [722^{a}18–^{b}1] 262a-b; BK II, CH 6 [743^{a}1–^{b}18] 284b-d

10 GALEN: *Natural Faculties*, BK I, CH 6 169c-170c; BK II, CH 6 188c-191a; BK III, CH 11 207d-208b; CH 15, 215a-b

20 AQUINAS: *Summa Theologica*, PART III SUPPL, Q 79, A 3, ANS and REP 1 955c-956b

28 HARVEY: *Motion of the Heart*, 274d-275c; 302c-d / *Circulation of the Blood*, 316d / *On Animal Generation*, 414c-415b

45 LAVOISIER: *Elements of Chemistry*, PART I, 39a-41a

48 MELVILLE: *Moby Dick*, 226b-228b; 276b-277b

53 JAMES: *Psychology*, 53a-b; 118a

54 FREUD: *Beyond the Pleasure Principle*, 647a-d

3b. The skeletal structure

6 HERODOTUS: *History*, BK III, 91b-c; 112a; BK IX, 306b

7 PLATO: *Timaeus*, 468a-469d

9 ARISTOTLE: *History of Animals*, BK I, CH 7 13a-b; CH 13 [493^{a}21–24] 15b; CH 15 [493^{b}12–494^{a}18] 15d-16b; BK II, CH 1 [499^{a}18–500^{a}14] 21c-22b; [500^{b}20–25] 23a; CH 1 [501^{a}2]–CH 5 [502^{a}3] 23b-24b; CH 15 [506^{a}7–10] 28c; BK III, CH 7–9 40b-41d; CH 20 [521^{b}4–17] 46c; BK IV,

CH 1 [523ᵇ1–18] 48b,d; [524ᵇ21–30] 50c-d; CH 2 [525ᵇ11–14] 51d; CH 4 [528ᵃ1–30] 54d-55b; CH 7 [532ᵃ31–ᵇ5] 59b; BK VII, CH 10 [587ᵇ11–18] 113d-114a / *Parts of Animals*, BK II, CH 6 176d-177c; CH 7 [653ᵃ34–ᵇ2] 178d; CH 8 [653ᵇ30]–CH 9 [655ᵇ10] 179b-181c; BK III, CH 1–2 188b,d-191d; CH 4 [666ᵇ17–22] 194c-d; BK IV, CH 5 [679ᵇ13–35] 209d-210a; CH 10 [690ᵃ5–29] 221d-222b; CH 12 [695ᵃ1–26] 226c-227a; CH 13 [696ᵇ1–7] 228a-b / *Motion of Animals*, CH 1 [698ᵃ15–ᵇ9] 233b-c / *Gait of Animals*, CH 11 248d-249a / *Generation of Animals*, BK II, CH 6 [744ᵇ28–745ᵇ9] 286a-d

10 HIPPOCRATES: *Injuries of the Head*, par 1–2 63b,d-64c; par 18 69a-b / *Fractures* 74b,d-91d esp par 2–4 75a-76c, par 9–12 78c-80a, par 18 82b-c, par 20 83a, par 37 89a-b / *Articulations* 91b,d-121d passim / *Instruments of Reduction* 121b,d-130d passim, esp par 1 121b,d-122c

10 GALEN: *Natural Faculties*, BK III, CH 15, 215a-b

28 GALILEO: *Two New Sciences*, FIRST DAY, 132c; SECOND DAY, 187b-188c; 195c-d

28 HARVEY: *On Animal Generation*, 443d-444c

48 MELVILLE: *Moby Dick*, 333b-338a

49 DARWIN: *Origin of Species*, 15a-b; 94a; 107a-113c passim; 217b-219d / *Descent of Man*, 263c-264d; 273a; 280c-282c

3c. The visceral organs

7 PLATO: *Timaeus*, 466a-468a

8 ARISTOTLE: *Metaphysics*, BK VII, CH 10 [1035ᵇ26–28] 559b / *Soul*, BK II, CH 8 [420ᵇ23–27] 652a-b / *Sleep*, CH 3 [458ᵃ14–19] 701c / *Youth, Life, and Breathing*, CH 3 [468ᵇ28]–CH 4 [469ᵇ20] 715b-716b; CH 14 720d-721a

9 ARISTOTLE: *History of Animals*, BK I, CH 16–17 16d-19d; BK II, CH 15–BK III, CH 1 28b-35a; BK III, CH 3 [513ᵃ22–39] 36d-37a; CH 13–15 44a-c; BK IV, CH 1 [524ᵇ1–22] 50a-c; CH 2 [526ᵇ22–527ᵃ20] 53b-d; CH 3–7 54b-59d passim / *Parts of Animals*, BK III, CH 4 193a-195d; CH 6–14 197b-205c; BK IV, CH 1–5 205b,d-213b / *Generation of Animals*, BK I, CH 3–16 256c-261b passim

10 HIPPOCRATES: *Ancient Medicine*, par 22 8a-d / *Sacred Disease*, 156a

10 GALEN: *Natural Faculties*, BK I, CH 13 173d-177a; BK III, CH 8 205a-207b; CH 11 207d-208b

20 AQUINAS: *Summa Theologica*, PART III SUPPL, Q 80, A 2, ANS 957c-958b

24 RABELAIS: *Gargantua and Pantagruel*, BK I, 14a-b

28 HARVEY: *Motion of the Heart*, 271b-273a; 274d-275c; 278b-c; 299b-302d / *On Animal Generation*, 339c-343a; 344d-345a; 350a-352d; 375d-376c; 450d-451b; 452c-453b; 473b-476b; 485a-b

31 DESCARTES: *Discourse*, PART V, 56a

49 DARWIN: *Descent of Man*, 266c; 281a-c

53 JAMES: *Psychology*, 19a-42b; 118a

54 FREUD: *Beyond the Pleasure Principle*, 647a-b

3d. The utility or adaptation of bodily structures

9 ARISTOTLE: *History of Animals*, BK IV, CH 4 [528ᵇ29–529ᵃ1] 55d; CH 5 [530ᵇ19–24] 57c; BK IX, CH 37 [620ᵇ10–33] 146b-c; [622ᵇ9–15] 148a / *Parts of Animals*, BK II–IV 170a-229d passim / *Gait of Animals* 243a-252a,c esp CH 1 243a-b / *Generation of Animals*, BK I, CH 2 [716ᵃ18–ᵇ2] 256b-c; CH 4–13 257a-260b; BK IV, CH 1 [765ᵇ33–766ᵃ10] 307a-b; BK V, CH 8 330b-331a,c

10 GALEN: *Natural Faculties*, BK I, CH 6, 170b-c; CH 10 171b-172b; CH 13, 173d-174d; BK II, CH 4, 187c-d; BK III, CH 3 200a-201a; CH 8 205a-207b; CH 11 207d-208b

12 LUCRETIUS: *Nature of Things*, BK IV [823–857] 55a-b; BK V [837–877] 72a-c

18 AUGUSTINE: *City of God*, BK XXII, CH 24, 610c-611b

28 HARVEY: *Motion of the Heart*, 269a-b; 299b-304a,c / *On Animal Generation*, 390b-c; 401b; 402c; 418b-c; 453c-454c

34 NEWTON: *Optics*, BK III, 529a

48 MELVILLE: *Moby Dick*, 227b-228a; 277b-279b

49 DARWIN: *Origin of Species*, 1c; 10d-11b; 38c; 41c-44c esp 43a-b, 43d-44a; 66a-68b; 82d-98a,c esp 97b-98a,c; 103c-113c; 115c-116b; 225c-228c / *Descent of Man*, 258b-259a; 320b; 532d-543d

53 JAMES: *Psychology*, 701a

4. Animal movement

4a. Comparison of animal movement with other kinds of local motion

8 ARISTOTLE: *Physics*, BK VIII, CH 4 [254ᵇ12–33] 339a-b / *Heavens*, BK II, CH 2 376b-377c

9 ARISTOTLE: *Motion of Animals*, CH 1 233a-c; CH 4 [700ᵃ5–27] 235b-c; CH 6 235d-236b; CH 7 [701ᵇ1]–CH 8 [702ᵇ12] 236d-238a

19 AQUINAS: *Summa Theologica*, PART I, Q 18, A 1, REP 1–3 104c-105c; Q 70, A 3 365b-367a

31 DESCARTES: *Discourse*, PART V, 59a-d

35 LOCKE: *Human Understanding*, BK II, CH XXVII, SECT 4–5 220a-c

49 DARWIN: *Origin of Species*, 115b

53 JAMES: *Psychology*, 4a-6b

4b. The cause of animal movement: voluntary and involuntary movements

7 PLATO: *Phaedo*, 241d-242a

8 ARISTOTLE: *Physics*, BK VIII, CH 2 [252ᵇ16–28] 336c-d; [253ᵃ6–21] 337a-b; CH 4 [254ᵇ12–33] 339a-b / *Soul*, BK III, CH 9–11 664d-667a

9 ARISTOTLE: *Parts of Animals*, BK I, CH 1 [640ᵇ30–641ᵇ10] 163c-164c / *Motion of Animals*, CH 6–11 235d-239d / *Ethics*, BK III, CH 2 [1111ᵇ6–9] 357b

10 GALEN: *Natural Faculties*, BK I, CH 1 167a-b

(4. Animal movement. 4b. The cause of animal movement: voluntary and involuntary movements.)

12 LUCRETIUS: *Nature of Things*, BK II [251–293] 18b-d; BK III [161–167] 32b; BK IV [877–906] 55d-56a

19 AQUINAS: *Summa Theologica*, PART I, Q 18, A 3, ANS 106b-107c; Q 78, A 1, ANS and REP 4 407b-409a; Q 80, A 2, REP 3 428a-d; Q 115, A 4, ANS 589d-590c; PART I–II, Q 6, A 2 646a-c; Q 12, A 5 672a-c; Q 13, A 2 673c-674c; Q 15, A 2 682a-c; Q 16, A 2 684d-685b; Q 17, A 2 687d-688b

23 HOBBES: *Leviathan*, PART I, 61a-b

24 RABELAIS: *Gargantua and Pantagruel*, BK III, 192d-193a

28 HARVEY: *Motion of the Heart*, 267a-b; 285d-286a; 302d-303a / *Circulation of the Blood*, 316d; 325d-326d / *On Animal Generation*, 369d-370b; 415b-429c esp 417a-419b, 423b-424a, 427c-428c; 456b-458a; 488d-496d

31 DESCARTES: *Rules*, XII, 19d-20a / *Discourse*, PART V, 58d-59a; 60b / *Objections and Replies*, 156a-d

35 LOCKE: *Human Understanding*, BK II, CH XXI, SECT 5 179c-d; SECT 7–11 180a-d; CH XXXIII, SECT 6 249a-b; BK IV, CH X, SECT 19 354a-c

35 HUME: *Human Understanding*, SECT VII, DIV 51–52 472b-473c

42 KANT: *Pure Reason*, 164b-c / *Intro. Metaphysic of Morals*, 386b-d

49 DARWIN: *Origin of Species*, 115b

53 JAMES: *Psychology*, 3b; 5a; 8a-15a esp 12a-b, 15a; 71b [fn 1]; 694a-702a; 705a-706b; 761a-765b; 767b-768a; 827a-835a

54 FREUD: *Interpretation of Dreams*, 351d-352a; 363b-d / *Instincts*, 412b-414b passim

4c. The organs, mechanisms, and characteristics of locomotion

7 PLATO: *Timaeus*, 454b

8 ARISTOTLE: *Soul*, BK III, CH 10 [433^{b}13–27] 666b-c

9 ARISTOTLE: *History of Animals*, BK I, CH 1 [487^{b}14–34] 8c-d; CH 4 [489^{a}27–29] 10c; CH 5 [489^{b}20–490^{b}6] 11a-12a; CH 15 [493^{b}26–494^{a}18] 16a-b; BK II, CH 1 [497^{b}18–498^{b}10] 20a-d; CH 12 26b-27a passim; BK III, CH 5 39c-40a; BK IV, CH 1 [523^{b}21–524^{a}32] 48d-50a; CH 2 [525^{b}15–526^{b}18] 51d-53b; CH 4 [528^{a}29–^{b}11] 55b; CH 7 [532^{a}19–29] 59a-b / *Parts of Animals*, BK II, CH 9 [654^{a}31–^{b}35] 180a-d; BK IV, CH 6–9 213b-217b passim; CH 10 [690^{a}4–^{b}11] 221d-222c; CH 12 [693^{a}24]—CH 13 [696^{a}34] 225b-228a / *Motion of Animals*, CH 1–2 233a-234a; CH 7 [701^{b}1–13] 236d-237a; CH 8 [702^{a}22]—CH 10 [703^{b}1] 237c-239a / *Gait of Animals* 243a-252a,c

10 HIPPOCRATES: *Articulations*, par 60 113b-d

12 LUCRETIUS: *Nature of Things*, BK IV [877–897] 55d-56a

16 KEPLER: *Epitome*, BK IV, 855b

19 AQUINAS: *Summa Theologica*, PART I, Q 71, A 1, REP 2 367a-368b; Q 99, A 1, ANS 519b-520a

20 AQUINAS: *Summa Theologica*, PART III SUPPL, Q 84, A 1, REP 4 983c-984c

28 HARVEY: *Motion of the Heart*, 301d-302a / *Circulation of the Blood*, 319b / *On Animal Generation*, 450a-b

31 DESCARTES: *Rules*, XII, 19d-20a / *Discourse*, PART V, 58d-59a / *Objections and Replies*, 156a-d

34 NEWTON: *Principles*, COROL II 15a-16b esp 16b

48 MELVILLE: *Moby Dick*, 276b-278a

49 DARWIN: *Origin of Species*, 23a-b; 66a-67a; 83b-84b; 93b-c; 94d-95a; 105c-106a / *Descent of Man*, 278c-280c; 365b-c

53 JAMES: *Psychology*, 9a-12b; 19b-26b; 714a-715b passim

5. Local motion within the animal body

5a. The ducts, channels, and conduits involved in interior bodily motions

7 PLATO: *Timaeus*, 470a-471b

8 ARISTOTLE: *Youth, Life, and Breathing*, CH 14 [474^{b}2–9] 720d; CH 17 [476^{a}26–^{b}8] 722b-c; CH 22 724b-d passim

9 ARISTOTLE: *History of Animals*, BK I, CH 2 [488^{b}29]–CH 3 [489^{a}14] 9d-10b; CH 4 [489^{a}20–23] 10b-c; CH 12 15a; CH 16 [495^{a}18]–CH 17 [497^{a}29] 17b-19d; BK II, CH 15–BK III, CH 4 28b-39c; BK III, CH 20 [521^{b}4–8] 46c; BK V, CH 5 [540^{b}29–541^{a}12] 67b-c; BK VI, CH 11 [566^{a}2–14] 92a-b; BK VII, CH 8 [586^{b}12–24] 112d-113a / *Parts of Animals*, BK II, CH 9 [654^{a}31–^{b}12] 180a-b; BK III, CH 3 191d-193a; CH 4 [665^{b}10]–CH 5 [668^{b}31] 193d-197b; CH 7 [670^{a}7–18] 198c-d; CH 8 [670^{b}34]–CH 9 [671^{b}28] 199c-200c; CH 14 203b-205c; BK IV, CH 2 [676^{b}16–677^{a}24] 206b-207a; CH 4 [677^{b}36–678^{a}20] 207d-208a / *Generation of Animals*, BK I, CH 2 [716^{a}33]–CH 16 [721^{a}26] 256b-261a passim; BK II, CH 4 [738^{a}9–739^{a}2] 278d-279d; [740^{a}21–35] 281a-b; CH 6 [743^{a}1–11] 284b; CH 7 [745^{b}22–746^{a}19] 287a-c; BK IV, CH 4 [773^{a}13–29] 315a-b

10 HIPPOCRATES: *Ancient Medicine*, par 22 8a-d / *Sacred Disease*, 156a-b

10 GALEN: *Natural Faculties*, BK I, CH 10 171b-172b; CH 13 173d-177a; BK I, CH 15–BK II, CH 3, 179d-185b; BK II, CH 5–6 188b-191a; CH 9 195c-199a,c; BK III 199a-215d passim

28 HARVEY: *Motion of the Heart*, 268d-304a,c esp 295d-296a / *Circulation of the Blood* 305a-328a,c / *On Animal Generation*, 339c-340c; 342d-345a; 347d; 350a-353b; 368b-371c; 373b-374d; 378b-d; 379b-c; 388d-389a; 401c-402c; 430b-d; 438c-441a; 449c-d; 473d-476b; 485a-487b

31 DESCARTES: *Discourse*, PART V, 56b-59a

49 DARWIN: *Descent of Man*, 257c

5b. The circulatory system: the motions of the heart, blood, and lymph

7 PLATO: *Timaeus*, 466c-d; 471c-d

8 ARISTOTLE: *Youth, Life, and Breathing*, CH 26 725d-726b

9 ARISTOTLE: *History of Animals*, BK III, CH 19 [521ª6-31] 45d-46b; BK VI, CH 3 [561ª9-15] 87c / *Parts of Animals*, BK III, CH 4-5 193a-197b / *Generation of Animals*, BK II, CH 1 [735ª10-26] 275d-276a; CH 5 [741ᵇ15-24] 282d; CH 6 [742ᵇ33-743ª1] 284a; BK IV, CH 1 [766ª30-ᵇ2] 307c-d

10 HIPPOCRATES: *Sacred Disease*, 160a

10 GALEN: *Natural Faculties*, BK I, CH 15-BK II, CH 2 179d-185a; BK II, CH 4-6, 188a-d; BK III, CH 13-15, 213a-215d

17 PLOTINUS: *Fourth Ennead*, TR III, CH 23, 154b

19 AQUINAS: *Summa Theologica*, PART I-II, Q 17, A 9, REP 2 692d-693d

24 RABELAIS: *Gargantua and Pantagruel*, BK III, 138a-d

28 HARVEY: *Motion of the Heart*, 268d-304a,c esp 285b-296a / *Circulation of the Blood* 305a-328a,c esp 309b-d, 324a-326d / *On Animal Generation*, 368a-371b; 374a-d; 429c-441a; 449c-d; 456b-d; 488d-496d

30 BACON: *Novum Organum*, BK II, APH 48, 186d

31 DESCARTES: *Discourse*, PART V, 56b-59a / *Objections and Replies*, 156c-d

53 JAMES: *Psychology*, 64a-65a; 695a-696a

5c. The glandular system: the glands of internal and external secretion

7 PLATO: *Timaeus*, 472a-474b

9 ARISTOTLE: *History of Animals*, BK I, CH 12 [493ª10-16] 15a; BK II, CH 13 [504ᵇ22-27] 27a-b; BK III, CH 2 [511ᵇ1-10] 35a; CH 20 [521ᵇ21]-CH 21 [523ª13] 46d-48c; BK VI, CH 20 [574ᵇ7-13] 100b; CH 21 [575ᵇ9-12] 101b; CH 26 103d; CH 33 [580ª2-4] 105c-d; BK VII, CH 3 [583ª26-34] 108d-109a; CH 5 [585ª29-32] 111b; CH 11 114a,c / *Parts of Animals*, BK II, CH 7 [653ᵇ8-19] 179a; BK III, CH 5 [668ᵇ1-10] 196d; CH 15 205d; BK IV, CH 10 [688ª19-ᵇ34] 219d-220d / *Generation of Animals*, BK I, CH 20 [727ᵇ34-728ª9] 268a-b; BK III, CH 2 [752ᵇ23-24] 293d; BK IV, CH 8 318b-319c

10 HIPPOCRATES: *Ancient Medicine*, par 19 6d-7b / *Airs, Waters, Places*, par 8, 12a-b / *Prognostics*, par 6 20c

10 GALEN: *Natural Faculties*, BK I, CH 13, 175d-177a; BK II, CH 2 184b-185a; CH 4-5, 188a-c; CH 8-9 191b-199a,c; BK III, CH 5 202c-d; CH 12, 209a-b

28 HARVEY: *Motion of the Heart*, 288d / *Circulation of the Blood*, 320a-b / *On Animal Generation*, 396c-d; 435a-c; 451b; 461b; 464c-d; 487c-488a

31 SPINOZA: *Ethics*, PART V, PREF 451a-452c

34 NEWTON: *Optics*, BK III, 538a

49 DARWIN: *Origin of Species*, 110c-111a / *Descent of Man*, 339d-340c; 547c-548c

53 JAMES: *Psychology*, 66b-67a; 696b-697b

5d. The respiratory system: breathing, lungs, gills

7 PLATO: *Timaeus*, 470b-471b

8 ARISTOTLE: *Youth, Life, and Breathing*, CH 7-27 717a-726d

9 ARISTOTLE: *History of Animals*, BK I, CH 1 [487ª14-ᵇ3] 8a-b; CH 5 [489ª34-ᵇ6] 10d; CH 11 [492ᵇ5-12] 14b-c; CH 16 [495ª20-ᵇ19] 17b-d; CH 17 [496ª27-34] 18c; BK II, CH 13 [504ᵇ27-505ª19] 27b-c; CH 15 [505ᵇ32-506ª4] 28c; BK IV, CH 2 [526ᵇ18-22] 53b; BK VI, CH 12 [566ᵇ2-14] 92c-d; BK VIII, CH 2 [589ª10-ᵇ29] 115c-116b / *Parts of Animals*, BK II, CH 16 [658ᵇ26-659ᵇ19] 185d-186c; BK III, CH 1 [662ᵇ16-28] 189b-c; CH 3 191b-193a; CH 6 197b-198a; BK IV, CH 13 [696ª37-ᵇ24] 228a-c; [697ª16-ᵇ1] 229a-b / *Motion of Animals*, CH 11 [703ᵇ3-15] 239a-b

10 HIPPOCRATES: *Prognostics*, par 5 20b-c / *Articulations*, par 41 103c-104b

10 GALEN: *Natural Faculties*, BK III, CH 13, 211b-d

28 HARVEY: *Motion of the Heart*, 268d-273a passim; 282b-285b; 303d-304a,c / *Circulation of the Blood*, 309c; 317c-d; 324a; 325d / *On Animal Generation*, 339c-340c; 458a

30 BACON: *Novum Organum*, BK II, APH 12, 141d-142a

31 DESCARTES: *Discourse*, PART V, 58b-c

33 PASCAL: *Weight of Air*, 415a-b

48 MELVILLE: *Moby Dick*, 272b-276b

49 DARWIN: *Origin of Species*, 87d-88c; 90c-91a; 238d / *Descent of Man*, 339a

53 JAMES: *Psychology*, 696a-b; 740b [fn 1]

5e. The alimentary system: the motions of the digestive organs in the nutritive process

7 PLATO: *Timaeus*, 467d-468a

9 ARISTOTLE: *Parts of Animals*, BK II, CH 3 [650ª1-37] 174c-175a; BK III, CH 1 [661ª34-ᵇ12] 188b; CH 3 191d-193a; CH 14 203b-205c; BK IV, CH 11 [690ᵇ18-691ª1] 222d-223a; [691ª28-ᵇ27] 223c-d

10 HIPPOCRATES: *Ancient Medicine*, par 11 4b

10 GALEN: *Natural Faculties*, BK I, CH 9-10 171b-172b; CH 16, 180c-181b; BK III, CH 4-5 201b-202d; CH 7-8 203b-207b; CH 13, 211d-212d

28 HARVEY: *Motion of the Heart*, 279a-b / *On Animal Generation*, 350a-c; 451b; 452d-453a; 456d; 460a-461a

31 DESCARTES: *Discourse*, PART V, 58c-d

5f. The excretory system: the motions of elimination

9 ARISTOTLE: *History of Animals*, BK III, CH 15 44b-c; BK IV, CH 1 [524ª9-14] 49d; BK VI, CH 20 [574ᵇ19-25] 100b-c; BK VII, CH 10 [587ª27-33] 113c; BK VIII, CH 5 [594ᵇ21-26] 120d;

(5. *Local motion within the animal body.* 5f. *The excretory system: the motions of elimination.*)

BK IX, CH 45 [630[b]7-17] 155d-156a / *Parts of Animals*, BK III, CH 7 [670[b]23]-CH 9 [672[a]26] 199b-201a; CH 14 [675[a]31-[b]38] 204d-205c; BK IV, CH 1 [676[a]29-35] 206a; CH 2 206b-207b; CH 5 [679[a]5-32] 209a-c; CH 10 [689[a]3-34] 220d-221b / *Generation of Animals*, BK I, CH 13 [719[b]29-720[a]11] 259d-260a

10 HIPPOCRATES: *Airs, Waters, Places*, par 9 12d-13b / *Prognostics*, par 11-12 21c-22b

10 GALEN: *Natural Faculties*, BK I, CH 13, 173d-175d; CH 15-17 179d-183d; BK II, CH 2 184b-185a; BK III, CH 5 202c-d; CH 12-13 208b-213b

19 AQUINAS: *Summa Theologica*, PART I, Q 119, A 1, REP 1 604c-607b

20 AQUINAS: *Summa Theologica*, PART III SUPPL, Q 80, A 2, REP 1 957c-958b; A 3, ANS and REP 2 958b-959c

24 RABELAIS: *Gargantua and Pantagruel*, BK I, 16c-18b; BK III, 138b-c; BK IV, 293a-b; 310d-311d

28 HARVEY: *Motion of the Heart*, 273b-c; 283a-b / *On Animal Generation*, 344b-345a; 351a-b; 356c-d; 380c

36 SWIFT: *Gulliver*, PART I, 26a-b

45 LAVOISIER: *Elements of Chemistry*, PART I, 45c-d

49 DARWIN: *Origin of Species*, 111b-c; 120b-c

5g. **The brain and nervous system: the excitation and conduction of nervous impulses**

9 ARISTOTLE: *Parts of Animals*, BK II, CH 7 177c-179a; CH 10 [656[a]14-[b]28] 182b-183a

10 HIPPOCRATES: *Sacred Disease*, 156a-160b

10 GALEN: *Natural Faculties*, BK II, CH 6 188c-191a

16 KEPLER: *Epitome*, BK IV, 855a-b

17 PLOTINUS: *Fourth Ennead*, TR III, CH 23, 153d-154a

19 AQUINAS: *Summa Theologica*, PART I, Q 99, A 1, ANS 519b-520a

23 HOBBES: *Leviathan*, PART I, 49b-d

24 RABELAIS: *Gargantua and Pantagruel*, BK III, 190a-c

28 HARVEY: *On Animal Generation*, 456b-458a

31 DESCARTES: *Rules*, XII, 19d-20a / *Discourse*, PART V, 58d-59a / *Meditations*, VI, 102a-d / *Objections and Replies*, 156a-d

31 SPINOZA: *Ethics*, PART V, PREF 451a-452c

34 NEWTON: *Optics*, BK III, 518b-519b; 522a-b

45 FARADAY: *Researches in Electricity*, 540a-541a,c

53 JAMES: *Psychology*, 2b-3a; 8a-67b esp 9b-17a, 42a-b, 46b-47a; 70a-77b esp 70a-71a; 152a-153a; 497a-501b esp 500b-501b; 694a-695a; 698a-699a; 705a-b; 758a-759a; 827b-835a

54 FREUD: *Hysteria*, 87a / *Interpretation of Dreams*, 351c-352d; 363c-364b; 378a-b / *Instincts*, 413a-d / *Unconscious*, 431d / *Beyond the Pleasure Principle*, 646b-649d / *Ego and Id*, 700a-b

6. **Animal nutrition**

6a. **The nature of the nutriment**

OLD TESTAMENT: *Genesis*, 1:29-30

5 ARISTOPHANES: *Peace* [1-172] 526a-527d

7 PLATO: *Timaeus*, 469d-470a; 471d-472a

8 ARISTOTLE: *Generation and Corruption*, BK I, CH 5 [322[a]4-28] 419d-420b / *Metaphysics*, BK I, CH 3 [983[b]19-25] 501d-502a / *Soul*, BK II, CH 4 [416[a]18-[b]31] 646c-647b / *Sense and the Sensible*, CH 4 [441[b]24-442[a]12] 679b-d

9 ARISTOTLE: *History of Animals*, BK I, CH 1 [488[a]15-20] 9a; BK III, CH 20 [521[b]21]-CH 21 [523[a]13] 46d-48c; BK VIII, CH 2 [590[a]18]-CH 11 [596[b]19] 116d-122d; CH 21 [603[b]25-34] 129d; BK IX, CH 1 [608[b]19]-CH 2 [610[b]19] 134a-136b; CH 9 140a-b / *Parts of Animals*, BK II, CH 4 [651[a]12-19] 176a / *Generation of Animals*, BK IV, CH 8 [777[a]4-19] 319a-b / *Politics*, BK I, CH 8 [1256[a]18-30] 450a; [1256[b]11-20] 450b-c

10 HIPPOCRATES: *Ancient Medicine*, par 3-8 1d-3b; par 13-15 4c-5d / *Regimen in Acute Diseases*, par 4 27c-28a; par 14-17 32c-34c; APPENDIX, par 18 41a-d

10 GALEN: *Natural Faculties*, BK I, CH 2, 168a-b; CH 10-11 171b-172d; BK II, CH 8, 191b-193d esp 192d-193b

12 LUCRETIUS: *Nature of Things*, BK IV [633-672] 52c-53a

19 AQUINAS: *Summa Theologica*, PART I, Q 97, A 3, REP 2 515a-d; A 4 515d-516d; Q 119, A 1 604c-607b

24 RABELAIS: *Gargantua and Pantagruel*, BK III, 138b

28 HARVEY: *On Animal Generation*, 378b-d; 398d-399c; 408c-d; 409c-d; 414a-b; 435a-438b; 439a-440a; 448a-c; 461a-d; 463b-466b; 486c-d; 487c-488a; 494a-496d esp 494b, 495c-496a

30 BACON: *Novum Organum*, BK II, APH 50, 193b-c

38 ROUSSEAU: *Inequality*, 337d

6b. **The process of nutrition: ingestion, digestion, assimilation**

7 PLATO: *Timaeus*, 467d-468a; 471c-472a

8 ARISTOTLE: *Meteorology*, BK IV, CH 2 [379[b]10-24] 483d-484a / *Soul*, BK II, CH 4 [416[a]18-[b]29] 646c-647b / *Sleep*, CH 3 699b-701d passim

9 ARISTOTLE: *History of Animals*, BK VIII, CH 4 [594[a]11-21] 120a-b; CH 6 [595[a]6-13] 121a; CH 17 [600[b]7-12] 126c / *Parts of Animals*, BK II, CH 3 [650[a]1-[b]13] 174c-175b; BK III, CH 1 [661[a]36-[b]12] 188b; CH 3 191d-193a; CH 14 203b-205c; BK IV, CH 3 [677[b]30]-CH 4 [678[a]20] 207d-208a; CH 11 [690[b]20-691[a]1] 222d-223a; [691[a]28-[b]27] 223c-d

10 HIPPOCRATES: *Ancient Medicine*, par 11 4b / *Regimen in Acute Diseases*, APPENDIX, par 18 41a-d

10 GALEN: *Natural Faculties*, BK I, CH 2 167b-168c; CH 7-12 170c-173c esp CH 10-11 171b-

172d; CH 16, 180c-181b; BK II, CH 4, 187a-b;
CH 6-7 188c-191b; BK III, CH 1 199a-c; CH 4
201b-202c; CH 6-9 202d-207b; CH 13 209b-
213b esp 211d-213a

12 LUCRETIUS: *Nature of Things*, BK II [871–882]
26a; [1118–1147] 29b-c; BK IV [858–876] 55b-c

19 AQUINAS: *Summa Theologica*, PART I, Q 97,
A 3, REP 2 515a-d; A 4 515d-516d; Q 118, A 1,
ANS and REP 3–4 600a-601c; Q 119, A 1 604c-
607b

20 AQUINAS: *Summa Theologica*, PART III SUPPL,
Q 80, A 3, ANS 958b-959c; A 4 959c-963a

24 RABELAIS: *Gargantua and Pantagruel*, BK III,
134d-135a; 138a-139b

27 SHAKESPEARE: *Coriolanus*, ACT I, SC I [92–150]
352b-353a

28 HARVEY: *Motion of the Heart*, 279a-b; 296a-
297a esp 296d-297a; 297d-298b / *Circulation
of the Blood*, 307c-308c; 319b; 320a-b / *On
Animal Generation*, 350a-c; 408c-d; 413a-415a;
435a-438b; 441b-443b; 446c-447a; 455c-d;
460b-461d; 465b

30 BACON: *Novum Organum*, BK II, APH 48,
184a-c

31 DESCARTES: *Discourse*, PART V, 58c-d

7. Animal growth or augmentation: its nature, causes, and limits

6 HERODOTUS: *History*, BK II, 63b

7 PLATO: *Timaeus*, 471d-472a

8 ARISTOTLE: *Physics*, BK II, CH 1 [193^{b}13–19]
269d-270a; BK VI, CH 10 [241^{a}27–^{b}2] 325b-c;
BK VIII, CH 7 [260^{a}27–^{b}1] 346b-c / *Generation
and Corruption*, BK I, CH 5 417b-420b / *Metaphysics*, BK V, CH 4 [1014^{b}20–26] 535a

9 ARISTOTLE: *History of Animals*, BK V, CH 19
[550^{b}26–31] 77d; CH 33 [558^{a}18–24] 84d-85a /
Motion of Animals, BK 5 235c-d / *Generation
of Animals*, BK I, CH 18 [723^{a}9–23] 263a-b;
BK II, CH 1 [735^{a}13–23] 275d-276a; CH 3
[737^{a}35–^{b}7] 278b; CH 4 [739^{b}34–741^{a}2] 280d-
281d; CH 6 [744^{b}32–745^{b}9] 286a-d; BK IV, CH 4
[771^{b}33–772^{a}1] 313d / *Politics*, BK VII, CH 4
[1326^{a}35–40] 530c

10 HIPPOCRATES: *Ancient Medicine*, par 3 1d-2b

10 GALEN: *Natural Faculties*, BK I, CH 1-2, 167a-
d; CH 5 169b-c; CH 7 170c-171a; BK II, CH 3,
186c-d

12 LUCRETIUS: *Nature of Things*, BK I [184–214]
3b-d; BK II [1105–1147] 29a-c; BK V [783–820]
71b-d; [878–900] 72c-d

19 AQUINAS: *Summa Theologica*, PART I, Q 97,
A 4 515d-516d; Q 99, A 1 519b-520a; Q 119,
A 1, ANS and REP 4 604c-607b

20 AQUINAS: *Summa Theologica*, PART III SUPPL,
Q 80, A 4, ANS 959c-963a; A 5, REP 1 963a-964b

28 GALILEO: *Two New Sciences*, SECOND DAY,
187b-188c

28 HARVEY: *On Animal Generation*, 353b-354b;
374b-d; 388c-d; 408c-409b; 412b-415b esp
415a; 441a-443b; 450b-d; 494a-496d esp
495c-496a

48 MELVILLE: *Moby Dick*, 338a-339a

49 DARWIN: *Origin of Species*, 71a-d; 227c-228b /
Descent of Man, 402a-b; 405a-d; 540a-541c

54 FREUD: *Civilization and Its Discontents*, 770b

8. The generation of animals

8*a*. The origin of animals: creation or evolution

OLD TESTAMENT: *Genesis*, 1:11-12,20-28; 2:4-
9,19-23

7 PLATO: *Timaeus*, 452c-454a; 476b-477a,c

9 ARISTOTLE: *Generation of Animals*, BK III, CH
11 [762^{b}28–763^{a}8] 303d-304a

12 LUCRETIUS: *Nature of Things*, BK V [783–836]
71b-72a

18 AUGUSTINE: *City of God*, BK XII, CH 21 357a-
b; CH 27 359c-360a,c; BK XVI, CH 7 427a-b

19 AQUINAS: *Summa Theologica*, PART I, QQ 71–
72 367a-369d

32 MILTON: *Paradise Lost*, BK VII [387–550]
225b-229a

34 NEWTON: *Optics*, BK III, 542b

42 KANT: *Judgement*, 578d-580a esp 579b-c;
581b-582c

47 GOETHE: *Faust*, PART II [8245–8264] 201a

49 DARWIN: *Origin of Species* 1a-251a,c esp 1a-
7d, 63b-64d, 85b-c, 217d-219a, 230a-243d /
Descent of Man, 265a-d

8*b*. Diverse theories of animal generation: procreation and spontaneous generation

7 PLATO: *Timaeus*, 476b-477a,c

8 ARISTOTLE: *Meteorology*, BK IV, CH 1 [379^{b}6–
8] 483c; CH 3 [381^{b}9–13] 485d; CH 11 [389^{a}28–
^{b}7] 493c / *Metaphysics*, BK VII, CH 9 [1034^{a}32–
^{b}8] 557c-d; BK XII, CH 6 [1071^{b}29–31] 601c;
CH 7 [1072^{b}30–1073^{a}2] 603a

9 ARISTOTLE: *History of Animals*, BK V, CH 1
[539^{a}15–^{b}13] 65b-66a; CH 11 [543^{b}18–19] 70b;
CH 15 [546^{b}17–547^{a}1] 73c; CH 15 [547^{b}12]–CH
16 [548^{b}7] 74b-75b; CH 19 [550^{b}31–551^{a}13]
77d-78a; [551^{b}19–552^{b}27] 78c-79c; CH 21
[553^{a}16–^{b}2] 80a-b; CH 31 [556^{b}25]–CH 32
[557^{b}14] 83c-84b; BK VI, CH 15-16 95a-96a /
Generation of Animals, BK I, CH 1 [715^{a}18–
716^{a}2] 255b-256a; CH 16 [721^{a}3–11] 260d-261a;
BK II, CH 1 [732^{b}8–14] 272d-273a; CH 3 [737^{a}1–
5] 277d; BK III, CH 9 299b-300a; CH 11
[761^{b}24–763^{b}17] 302d-304d

12 LUCRETIUS: *Nature of Things*, BK II [865–943]
26a-27a; BK V [783–820] 71b-d

18 AUGUSTINE: *City of God*, BK XII, CH 11 349a-b;
BK XVI, CH 7 427a-b

19 AQUINAS: *Summa Theologica*, PART I, Q 25,
A 2, REP 2 144c-145b; Q 45, A 8, REP 3 249b-
250a; Q 71, A 1, REP 1 367a-368b; Q 72, A 1,
REP 5 368b-369d; Q 92, A 1, ANS and REP 1
488d-489d; Q 118, AA 1–2 600a-603b; Q 119,
A 2 607b-608d

20 AQUINAS: *Summa Theologica*, PART I-II, Q 60,
A 1, ANS 49d-50c

(8. *The generation of animals. 8b. Diverse theories of animal generation: procreation and spontaneous generation.*)

24 RABELAIS: *Gargantua and Pantagruel*, BK II, 114b-c

28 GILBERT: *Loadstone*, BK V, 105a-b

28 HARVEY: *On Animal Generation*, 338b-d; 390b-c; 400d-401a; 406c-d; 412c-413a; 428c-d; 449a-b; 454d-455a; 468b-472c

30 BACON: *Novum Organum*, BK II, APH 50, 192a-b

49 DARWIN: *Origin of Species*, 1c; 61a

8c. Modes of animal reproduction: sexual and asexual

7 PLATO: *Symposium*, 157d-158b / *Timaeus*, 476b-d / *Statesman*, 587a-588a

9 ARISTOTLE: *History of Animals*, BK IV, CH 11 [537^{b}22–538^{a}21] 64b-d; BK V–VII 65a-114a,c esp BK V, CH 1 65a-66a, BK VI, CH 18 97b-99c / *Generation of Animals* 255a-331a,c esp BK I, CH 1–2 255a-256c, BK I, CH 21–BK II, CH 1 269c-276a, BK II, CH 5 282a-d

10 GALEN: *Natural Faculties*, BK II, CH 3 185a-186d

19 AQUINAS: *Summa Theologica*, PART I, Q 119, A 2, ANS 607b-608d

28 HARVEY: *On Animal Generation*, 331a; 338a-496d esp 390b-429c

49 DARWIN: *Origin of Species*, 47c-49c; 220a-b / *Descent of Man*, 390c-391b; 395a-399c passim

54 FREUD: *Instincts*, 415b / *Beyond the Pleasure Principle*, 655b-657d; 659d-660c

8c(1) Sexual differentiation: its origins and determinations; primary and secondary characteristics

7 PLATO: *Symposium*, 157b-159b / *Timaeus*, 476b-d

9 ARISTOTLE: *History of Animals*, BK II, CH 3 [501^{b}20–25] 24a; BK III, CH 7 [516^{a}15–20] 40c; CH 11 [518^{a}30–^{b}4] 42d-43a; CH 19 [521^{a}21–31] 46b; CH 20 [522^{a}11–21] 47a-b; BK IV, CH 1 [524^{b}31–525^{a}13] 50d-51a; CH 2 [525^{b}34–526^{a}6] 52b; CH 3 [527^{b}30–34] 54c-d; CH 11 64b-65a,c; BK V, CH 5 [540^{b}14–28] 67b; CH 7 [541^{b}30]–CH 8 [542^{a}1] 68c; CH 14 [544^{b}32–545^{a}22] 71c-72a; CH 18 [550^{b}17–21] 77c-d; CH 28 [555^{b}18–23] 82c; CH 30 [556^{b}11–13] 83b; BK VI, CH 2 [559^{a}27–29] 86a; CH 10 [565^{b}13–15] 91d; CH 19 [573^{b}32–574^{a}1] 99d; BK VII, CH 1 [582^{a}27–32] 107d-108a; CH 3 [583^{b}14–29] 109b-c; CH 6 [585^{b}21–27] 111d; BK VIII, CH 2 [589^{b}29–590^{a}4] 116b-c; BK IX, CH 1 [608^{a}21–^{b}19] 133b,d-134a / *Parts of Animals*, BK III, CH 1 [661^{b}33–662^{a}5] 189a-b; BK IV, CH 10 [688^{a}20–26] 219d-220a; [688^{b}30–34] 220c-d / *Generation of Animals*, BK I, CH 2 256a-c; CH 18 [723^{a}23–^{b}3] 263b-c; CH 19–20 266c-269c; BK II, CH 1 [731^{b}18–732^{a}12] 272a-b; BK III, CH 10 [759^{b}1–7] 300c;

BK IV, CH 1–2 304b,d-308d esp CH 1 [766^{a}30–^{b}8] 307c-d; CH 3 [767^{b}5–14] 309a; BK V, CH 7 [786^{b}16–788^{a}13] 328c-330a

10 HIPPOCRATES: *Airs, Waters, Places*, par 9 12d-13b

12 LUCRETIUS: *Nature of Things*, BK IV [1225–1232] 60b

19 AQUINAS: *Summa Theologica*, PART I, Q 92, A 1, ANS and REP 1 488d-489d; Q 98, A 2, ANS 517d-519a; Q 99, A 2 520a-d; Q 115, A 3, REP 4 588c-589c; Q 118, A 1, REP 4 600a-601c

20 AQUINAS: *Summa Theologica*, PART III SUPPL, Q 81, A 3 966a-c; A 4, REP 2 966d-967d

28 HARVEY: *On Animal Generation*, 346b; 400c-401b; 402c-d; 454a-b; 462b; 481c

30 BACON: *Novum Organum*, BK II, APH 27, 158a

38 MONTESQUIEU: *Spirit of Laws*, BK XVI, 116d-117a

49 DARWIN: *Descent of Man*, 339b-340c; 364a-561d esp 364a-366b, 373b-374c, 384c-d; 586b-587d; 594a-595b

54 FREUD: *Beyond the Pleasure Principle*, 659d-661c / *Civilization and Its Discontents*, 785a [fn 1] / *New Introductory Lectures*, 853d-855b

8c(2) The reproductive organs: their differences in different classes of animals

7 PLATO: *Timaeus*, 476b-d

9 ARISTOTLE: *History of Animals*, BK I, CH 3 [489^{a}8–14] 10b; CH 13 [493^{a}24]–CH 14 [493^{b}6] 15b-c; CH 17 [497^{a}24–34] 19c-d; BK II, CH 1 [500^{a}32–^{b}25] 22c-23a; CH 10 [503^{a}4–7] 25b-c; CH 13 [504^{b}18–19] 27a; BK III, CH 1 32a-35a; BK IV, CH 1 [524^{a}2–9] 49a-c; [524^{b}31–525^{a}8] 50d; CH 2 [527^{a}11–30] 53c-d; BK V, CH 2 [540^{a}3]–CH 3 [540^{a}33] 66c-67a; CH 5 [540^{b}29–541^{a}12] 67b-c; CH 6 [541^{b}7–12] 68a-b; BK VI, CH 9 [564^{b}10]–CH 10 [564^{b}24] 90d-91a; CH 10 [565^{a}12–22] 91b-c; CH 11 [566^{a}2–14] 92a-b; CH 12 [567^{a}11]–CH 13 [567^{a}24] 93b; CH 32 105b-c; BK IX, CH 50 [631^{b}22–25] 157a; [632^{a}22–27] 157c / *Parts of Animals*, BK IV, CH 5 [680^{a}12–681^{a}5] 210b-211c; CH 10 [689^{a}3–34] 220d-221b; CH 12 [695^{a}26–27] 227a; CH 13 [697^{a}10–14] 228d-229a / *Generation of Animals*, BK I, CH 1–16 255a-261b; BK III, CH 5 [755^{b}5–756^{a}5] 296c-297a; CH 6 [756^{b}30–757^{a}13] 297d-298a; CH 8 [758^{a}7–15] 299a; BK IV, CH 1 [765^{b}35–766^{b}26] 307a-308a; CH 4 [772^{b}27–773^{a}25] 314d-315b

10 GALEN: *Natural Faculties*, BK III, CH 2–3 199d-201a

24 RABELAIS: *Gargantua and Pantagruel*, BK I, 10c-11a; 15a-c; BK II, 70b-c; 95a-97b; BK III, 131b,d; 143a-144c; 178b-185d; 192b-193b

28 HARVEY: *On Animal Generation*, 338d-352d; 401b-405c; 452c; 473b-476b; 477b-479c; 485a

30 BACON: *Novum Organum*, BK II, APH 27, 158a

48 MELVILLE: *Moby Dick*, 310a-b

49 DARWIN: *Origin of Species*, 136b / *Descent of Man*, 264d-265a; 272a-d; 339b-c; 364a-b

54 FREUD: *General Introduction*, 592a

8c(3) The reproductive cells and secretions: semen and catamenia, sperm and egg

8 ARISTOTLE: *Metaphysics*, BK VII, CH 9 [1034^{a}32–^{b}8] 557c-d; BK IX, CH 7 [1049^{a}12–19] 574d; BK XII, CH 6 [1071^{b}29–31] 601c; CH 7 [1072^{b}36–1073^{a}2] 603a

9 ARISTOTLE: *History of Animals*, BK I, CH 5 [489^{b}6–10] 10d; BK III, CH 22 48c; BK IV, CH I [525^{a}2–8] 50d; CH 2 [527^{a}31–33] 53d-54a; BK VI, CH 2 [559^{a}15–560^{b}2] 85d-87a; CH 10 [564^{b}24–26] 91a; CH 13 [567^{a}16–^{b}15] 93b-d; BK VII, CH I [582^{a}16]–CH 2 [583^{a}13] 107d-108c / *Generation of Animals*, BK I, CH 2 [716^{a}2–17] 256a; CH 17–23 261b-271d; BK II, CH I [733^{b}23]–CH 4 [739^{b}33] 274a-280d; CH 5 [741^{a}6–32] 282a-b; BK II, CH 7 [746^{b}25]–BK III, CH 2 [752^{b}15] 288a-293d; BK III, CH 3–5 295b-297c; CH 7–9 298a-300a; BK IV, CH I [764^{b}4–21] 305c-d; CH I [765^{b}10]–CH 2 [767^{a}8] 306d-308b; CH 3 [767^{b}16–769^{b}10] 309a-311b / *Politics*, BK VII, CH 16 [1335^{a}24–27] 540b

10 HIPPOCRATES: *Airs, Waters, Places*, par 14 15a-b / *Sacred Disease*, 155d

10 GALEN: *Natural Faculties*, BK II, CH 3 185a-186d

12 LUCRETIUS: *Nature of Things*, BK IV [1037–1051] 57d; [1209–1277] 60a-d

19 AQUINAS: *Summa Theologica*, PART I, Q 71, A I, REP I 367a-368b; Q 92, A 3, REP 2 490c-491b; A 4, ANS 491b-d; Q 97, A 2, REP 3 514c-515a; Q 118, AA 1–2 600a-603b; Q 119, A I, ANS 604c-607b; A 2 607b-608d

20 AQUINAS: *Summa Theologica*, PART III SUPPL, Q 80, A 2, REP 2 957c-958b; A 3, ANS 958b-959c; A 4, ANS and REP 2,4–5 959c-963a

21 DANTE: *Divine Comedy*, PURGATORY, XXV [37–51] 91d

24 RABELAIS: *Gargantua and Pantagruel*, BK III, 144b; 189b

25 MONTAIGNE: *Essays*, 269b-d

28 HARVEY: *On Animal Generation*, 338a-d; 340c-342d; 347d-348d; 353a-363d; 365a; 383d-407a esp 402d-405c; 417a-429c; 461d-472c; 473c-d

36 STERNE: *Tristram Shandy*, 192a-b

49 DARWIN: *Descent of Man*, 257c; 372b-c

54 FREUD: *Beyond the Pleasure Principle*, 653b-c; 655b-d / *New Introductory Lectures*, 853d-854c

8c(4) The mating of animals: pairing and copulation

6 HERODOTUS: *History*, BK II, 67b; BK III, 113a-b

7 PLATO: *Symposium*, 158a-b / *Republic*, BK V, 361c-d / *Laws*, BK VIII, 737d-738b

9 ARISTOTLE: *History of Animals*, BK II, CH I [500^{b}7–14] 22d; BK V, CH 2–14 66b-73b; CH 19 [550^{b}21–26] 77d; CH 28 [555^{b}18–23] 82c; CH 30 [556^{a}25–28] 83a; BK VI, CH 2 [560^{b}25–32] 87b; CH 4 [562^{b}26–29] 89a; CH 13 [567^{a}28–^{b}12] 93c; CH 17 [570^{a}27–29] 96b; CH 18–37 97b-106d; BK VII, CH 7 [586^{a}15–20] 112b; BK IX, CH I

[609^{b}21–26] 135b; CH 8 [613^{b}24–614^{a}30] 139b-140a; CH 37 [621^{b}22–28] 147b; CH 41 [628^{b}13–17] 153d; CH 47 156b / *Generation of Animals*, BK I, CH 4–7 257a-258b; CH 14–16 260b-261b; CH 18 [723^{b}9–724^{a}3] 263c-264a; CH 19 [727^{b}7]–CH 23 [731^{b}14] 267c-271d passim; BK II, CH 4 [737^{b}25–739^{b}20] 278c-280c; CH 7 [746^{a}29]–CH 8 [749^{a}5] 287c-290a,c; BK III, CH I [749^{b}7–750^{a}7] 290d-291b; CH 5–6 296c-298a; CH 8 298d-299b; CH 10 [760^{b}33–761^{a}12] 302a; BK IV, CH 5 [773^{b}23–774^{a}13] 315a-316a / *Politics*, BK I, CH 2 [1252^{a}26–31] 445c

10 HIPPOCRATES: *Airs, Waters, Places*, par 21 17b

12 LUCRETIUS: *Nature of Things*, BK IV [1037–1057] 57d; [1073–1120] 58a-d; [1192–1208] 59d-60a; [1263–1279] 60d

19 AQUINAS: *Summa Theologica*, PART I, Q 92, A 3, REP 2 490c-491b; Q 97, A 2, REP 3 514c-515a; Q 98, A 2 517d-519a

25 MONTAIGNE: *Essays*, 224a-225b; 399a-b

28 HARVEY: *On Animal Generation*, 343b-350a passim; 394b-398c; 401b-406a; 406d-407a; 417a-429c passim, esp 423b-c; 476b-477b

36 SWIFT: *Gulliver*, PART IV, 162b; 166a-b

36 STERNE: *Tristram Shandy*, 555a-556a

48 MELVILLE: *Moby Dick*, 287a-b; 289b-292a

49 DARWIN: *Origin of Species*, 43d-44a; 47c-d; 49b-c / *Descent of Man*, 366c-368b; 369b-372c; 387d; 395a-480a passim; 482b-486c; 532a-d; 543d-545d; 580c-581b

53 JAMES: *Psychology*, 14b

54 FREUD: *Ego and Id*, 711d-712a

8c(5) Factors affecting fertility and sterility

9 ARISTOTLE: *History of Animals*, BK III, CH II [518^{b}1–3] 43a; BK V, CH II [543^{b}21–31] 70c; CH 14 71b-73b; BK VII, CH I [581^{b}22]–CH 3 [583^{a}25] 107b-108d passim; CH 5 [585^{a}33]–CH 6 [585^{b}29] 111b-d; BK IX, CH 50 [631^{b}19–632^{a}32] 157a-c / *Generation of Animals*, BK I, CH 4 [717^{a}29–^{b}5] 257b; CH 7 258a-b; CH 18 [725^{a}4–726^{a}2] 265a-266a; CH 19 [727^{b}6–26] 267c-268a; BK II, CH 4 [739^{a}26–35] 280b; CH 7 [746^{b}12]–CH 8 [749^{a}5] 287d-290a,c; BK III, CH I [749^{b}26–750^{a}13] 291a-b; BK IV, CH 2 [767^{a}13–35] 308c-d; CH 5 [773^{b}29–33] 315d / *Politics*, BK VII, CH 16 [1335^{a}7–^{b}1] 540a-c

10 HIPPOCRATES: *Airs, Waters, Places*, par 3 9c-10a; par 19–23 16c-18c / *Aphorisms*, SECT V, par 46 139b; par 59 139d; par 62–63 139d-140a

12 LUCRETIUS: *Nature of Things*, BK IV [1233–1277] 60b-d

36 STERNE: *Tristram Shandy*, 474b-475a

38 MONTESQUIEU: *Spirit of Laws*, BK XXIII, 190c-d

38 ROUSSEAU: *Social Contract*, BK II, 404b-c

49 DARWIN: *Origin of Species*, 10a-b; 47d-48a; 132a-133a; 136a-151d esp 136a-b, 141a-c, 143b-145c; 230b-231b / *Descent of Man*, 354b-355a

(8. *The generation of animals.*)

8d. Comparison of human with animal reproduction

9 ARISTOTLE: *History of Animals*, BK I, CH 5 [489ª36–ᵇ18] 10d-11a; BK V–VII 65a-114a,c esp BK V, CH I 65a-66a, CH 8 [542ª17–ᵇ1] 68d-69a, BK VI, CH 18 97b-99c, BK VII 106b,d-114a,c / *Generation of Animals*, BK I, CH 9–11 258d-259b; BK II, CH I [732ª24–733ᵇ23] 272c-274a; CH 4–7 278b-288b esp CH 4 [737ᵇ25–739ᵇ33] 278c-280d / *Politics*, BK I, CH 2 [1252ª26–31] 445c; BK VII, CH 16 [1335ª11–18] 540a

18 AUGUSTINE: *City of God*, BK XXII, CH 24, 609b-610a

19 AQUINAS: *Summa Theologica*, PART I, Q 75, A 6, REP I 383c-384c; Q 92, A I, ANS 488d-489d; Q 98, A 2, ANS and REP 1,3 517d-519a; Q 118, AA 1–2 600a-603b

21 DANTE: *Divine Comedy*, PURGATORY, XXV [34–78] 91d-92a

25 MONTAIGNE: *Essays*, 399a-b; 424d-425c

28 HARVEY: *On Animal Generation*, 338a-496d esp 449a-454a, 463d-464a, 470c-472c

36 STERNE: *Tristram Shandy*, 555a-556a

38 ROUSSEAU: *Inequality*, 346b-d; 348d

47 GOETHE: *Faust*, PART II [6838–6847] 167b

49 DARWIN: *Descent of Man*, 256c-257a; 354b-355a

54 FREUD: *Sexual Enlightenment of Children*, 121d

9. The development of the embryo: birth and infancy

9a. Oviparous and viviparous development

9 ARISTOTLE: *History of Animals*, BK I, CH 5 [489ª34–ᵇ19] 10d-11a; BK V, CH 18 [549ᵇ30–550ª31] 76d-77b; BK VI, CH 3 87c-88d; CH 10 [564ᵇ26–565ª12] 91a-b; CH 13 [567ᵇ27–568ª4] 93d-94a; BK VII, CH 7 112b-c / *Parts of Animals*, BK IV, CH 12 [693ᵇ21–27] 225c / *Generation of Animals*, BK I, CH 8–13 258b-260b; BK II, CH I [732ª24–733ᵇ23] 272c-274a; CH 4 [737ᵇ7–25] 278b-c; [739ᵇ21–33] 280c-d; BK III, CH I [749ª12–33] 290b-d; CH I [751ª5]–CH 4 [755ª34] 292a-296c / *Politics*, BK I, CH 8 [1256ᵇ11–15] 450b-c

28 HARVEY: *Motion of the Heart*, 277c-d; 298b-c / *On Animal Generation*, 338a-496d esp 449a-454a, 463d-464a, 470c-472c

9b. The nourishment of the embryo or foetus

9 ARISTOTLE: *History of Animals*, BK V, CH 18 [550ª16–24] 77a; BK VI, CH 3 87c-88d; CH 10 [564ᵇ26–565ª12] 91a-b; [565ᵇ2–10] 91c-d; CH 13 [568ª1–4] 94a; BK VII, CH 8 112c-113a / *Generation of Animals*, BK I, CH 22 [730ª33–ᵇ9] 270d; BK II, CH 4 [740ª17–741ª2] 281a-d; CH 7 [745ᵇ22–746ª28] 287a-c; BK III, CH I [751ª6–7] 292a; CH 2 [752ª24–ᵇ28] 293b-294a; [753ª36–754ª15] 294c-295b; CH 3 [754ᵇ1–755ª6] 295c-

296a; BK IV, CH 6 [775ᵇ2–24] 317c-d; CH 8 318b-319c

19 AQUINAS: *Summa Theologica*, PART I, Q 118, A I, REP 4 600a-601c

20 AQUINAS: *Summa Theologica*, PART III SUPPL, Q 80, A 4, REP 5 959c-963a

28 HARVEY: *Motion of the Heart*, 298b-c / *On Animal Generation*, 366d-367b; 373b-c; 378b-d; 379b-381a; 396b; 398d-399c; 408b-415b; 438c-443b; 446c-447a; 458a-461d esp 461a-d; 463b-466b; 471d-472a; 481d-482b; 484c; 485c-488c

9c. The process of embryogeny: the stages of foetal growth

8 ARISTOTLE: *Metaphysics*, BK V, CH 4 [1014ᵇ20–22] 535a

9 ARISTOTLE: *History of Animals*, BK VI, CH 3 87c-88d; CH 10 [564ᵇ26–565ª12] 91a-b; CH 13 [567ᵇ27–568ª4] 93d-94a; BK VII, CH 3 [583ᵇ2–8] 109a; CH 7–8 112b-113a; BK VIII, CH 2 [589ª29–590ª11] 116b-c / *Parts of Animals*, BK III, CH 4 [665ª31–ᵇ1] 193a / *Generation of Animals*, BK I, CH 20 [729ª12]–CH 23 [731ª21] 269b-271c; BK II, CH I [733ᵇ22–735ª28] 274a-276a; CH 3 [737ª18–34] 278a-b; CH 4 [739ᵇ21–741ª5] 280c-282a; CH 5 [741ᵇ5]–CH 6 [745ᵇ22] 282c-287a; BK III, CH 2 [752ᵇ12]–CH 4 [755ª34] 293d-296c; CH 11 [762ª10–ᵇ19] 303a-d; BK IV, CH I 304b,d-308a; CH 4 [771ᵇ19–772ª39] 313c-314b

10 GALEN: *Natural Faculties*, BK I, CH 5–6 169b-170c; BK II, CH 3 185a-186d

19 AQUINAS: *Summa Theologica*, PART I, Q 118, A I, REP 4 600a-601c; A 2, REP 2 601c-603b

21 DANTE: *Divine Comedy*, PURGATORY, XXV [34–78] 91d-92a

28 HARVEY: *Motion of the Heart*, 277c-d; 298b-c; 302b-c / *On Animal Generation*, 359a-c; 363d-398c esp 394b-d; 402d-405c; 407c-431b esp 415a-b; 438c-456a esp 451c-453b; 478a-488d

36 STERNE: *Tristram Shandy*, 352b-353b

49 DARWIN: *Origin of Species*, 143d-144a; 219d-225b esp 219d-222a / *Descent of Man*, 257c-258b

54 FREUD: *General Introduction*, 509d-510a

9d. Multiple pregnancy: superfoetation

OLD TESTAMENT: *Genesis*, 25:24–26; 38:27–30

6 HERODOTUS: *History*, BK III, 112d-113a

9 ARISTOTLE: *History of Animals*, BK V, CH 9 [542ᵇ30–33] 69c; BK VI, CH 3 [562ª24–ᵇ2] 88c-d; CH 11 [566ª15–16] 92b; CH 12 [566ᵇ6–8] 92c-d; CH 19 [573ᵇ19–32] 99c-d; CH 20 [574ª25–26] 100c; CH 22 [575ᵇ34–576ª3] 101c; CH 30 [579ª20–21] 104d; CH 31 [579ª34–ᵇ12] 105a-b; CH 33–35 105c-106a; CH 37 [580ᵇ10–20] 106b-c; BK VII, CH 4 [584ᵇ26–585ª27] 110c-111b / *Parts of Animals*, BK IV, CH 10 [688ª28–ᵇ25] 220a-c / *Generation of Animals*, BK I, CH 18 [723ᵇ9–16] 263c-d; CH 20 [728ᵇ33–729ª20] 269a-b; BK IV, CH 4–5 311c-316c

(10. *Heredity and environment: the genetic determination of individual differences and similarities.*)

[724ᵃ13] 261c-264b; BK IV, CH 1 [766ᵇ7-12] 307d; CH 3-4 308d-315b / *Politics*, BK II, CH 3 [1262ᵃ14-24] 457a; BK VII, CH 16 [1335ᵇ17-19] 540c

10 HIPPOCRATES: *Airs, Waters, Places*, par 14 15a-b / *Sacred Disease*, 155d-156a

12 LUCRETIUS: *Nature of Things*, BK III [741-753] 39c-d; BK IV [1209-1232] 60a-b

19 AQUINAS: *Summa Theologica*, PART I, Q 119, A 2, REP 2 607b-608d

28 HARVEY: *On Animal Generation*, 363a-c; 386d-387b; 391c-393b; 395a-396a; 425b-d; 446b-c; 455d-456a

35 LOCKE: *Human Understanding*, BK III, CH VI, SECT 23 274b-c

36 STERNE: *Tristram Shandy*, 191b-192b

38 ROUSSEAU: *Inequality*, 335a-b; 337a; 347a-b

39 SMITH: *Wealth of Nations*, BK I, 7d-8a

42 KANT: *Judgement*, 580a; 581d-582a

49 DARWIN: *Origin of Species*, 9b-12a esp 9b-10d; 53b-55b; 62a-63a; 65a-71a; 98c; 132a-134c esp 134a-c; 144a; 149b-150c; 182d-183a; 220b-228a esp 222a-224b / *Descent of Man*, 268b-269a; 375a-382d esp 381c-382a; 413d [fn 61]; 429d-430c; 500a-525a passim, esp 500a-502a, 511a-b, 524d-525a; 529d-531a,c

53 JAMES: *Psychology*, 853a-858a esp 857b; 890b-897b esp 896a-897a

54 FREUD: *General Introduction*, 594d-595a

11. The habitat of animals

11*a*. The geographical distribution of animals: their natural habitats

OLD TESTAMENT: *Genesis*, 1:20-21,24-26

6 HERODOTUS: *History*, BK III, 113a-b; BK V, 161b-c; BK VII, 236d

9 ARISTOTLE: *History of Animals*, BK I, CH 1 [487ᵃ14-ᵇ5] 8a-b; BK IV, CH 1 [525ᵃ12-25] 51a-c; BK V, CH 15 [547ᵃ4-12] 73d; CH 15 [547ᵇ11]-CH 16 [548ᵃ28] 74b-75a; CH 16 [548ᵇ18-30] 75c-d; CH 17 [549ᵇ14-22] 76c; CH 22 [554ᵇ8-18] 81b-c; CH 28 [556ᵃ4-6] 82d; CH 30 [556ᵃ21-24] 83a; CH 31 [557ᵃ4-32] 83d-84a; BK VI, CH 5 [563ᵃ5-12] 89b; BK VIII, CH 2-20 115c-129b esp CH 2 [589ᵃ10-590ᵃ19] 115c-116c, CH 12-17 122d-127b; CH 28-29 131c-132d; BK IX, CH 11-27 140c-143c passim; CH 32 [618ᵇ18-619ᵃ8] 144b-c / *Generation of Animals*, BK III, CH 11 [761ᵇ9-24] 302c-d

12 LUCRETIUS: *Nature of Things*, BK II [532-540] 21d

19 AQUINAS: *Summa Theologica*, PART I, QQ 71-72 367a-369d

32 MILTON: *Paradise Lost*, BK VII [387-498] 225b-228a

41 GIBBON: *Decline and Fall*, 630b-c [n 43]

48 MELVILLE: *Moby Dick*, 146b-148a

49 DARWIN: *Origin of Species*, 181a-206a,c esp 181a-184d, 196a-199d, 204d-206a,c; 231b-c; 237c-238b

11*b*. The relation between animals and their environments

6 HERODOTUS: *History*, BK IV, 129a-b

8 ARISTOTLE: *Physics*, BK II, CH 8 [198ᵇ16-33] 275d-276a / *Longevity* 710a-713a,c passim

9 ARISTOTLE: *History of Animals*, BK I, CH 1 [487ᵃ14-ᵇ33] 8a-d; BK III, CH 12 [519ᵃ3-19] 43d-44a; CH 21 [522ᵇ12-523ᵃ1] 47d-48a; BK IV, CH 5 [530ᵇ19-24] 57c; BK V, CH 11 [543ᵇ19-31] 70b-c; CH 22 [553ᵇ20-24] 80c; BK VIII, CH 2-29 115c-132d; BK IX, CH 1 [608ᵇ18-610ᵃ34] 134a-136a; CH 37 [622ᵃ8-15] 147c / *Parts of Animals*, BK II, CH 16 [658ᵇ30-659ᵃ36] 185d-186b; BK IV, CH 5 [680ᵃ28-ᵇ3] 210d; CH 8 [684ᵃ1-14] 215b; CH 12 [693ᵃ10-24] 225a / *Gait of Animals*, CH 15 [713ᵃ4]-CH 18 [714ᵇ8] 250d-252a / *Generation of Animals*, BK II, CH 4 [738ᵃ9-27] 278d-279a; BK IV, CH 2 308b-d; BK V, CH 3 [782ᵇ23-783ᵇ22] 324d-325d

10 HIPPOCRATES: *Airs, Waters, Places*, par 12 14b-d; par 19 16c-17a

12 LUCRETIUS: *Nature of Things*, BK V [845-854] 72a-b

24 RABELAIS: *Gargantua and Pantagruel*, BK IV, 242a-b

25 MONTAIGNE: *Essays*, 223c

28 GALILEO: *Two New Sciences*, FIRST DAY, 160c-d; SECOND DAY, 187b-188c

30 BACON: *Novum Organum*, BK II, APH 13, 146c

33 PASCAL: *Equilibrium of Liquids*, 401a-403a

36 SWIFT: *Gulliver*, PART II, 79a-b

36 STERNE: *Tristram Shandy*, 224b; 295b-296b

38 MONTESQUIEU: *Spirit of Laws*, BK XIV, 102b,d-104a

42 KANT: *Judgement*, 553c-554b; 585b

43 FEDERALIST: NUMBER 11, 56a

45 LAVOISIER: *Elements of Chemistry*, PART II, 57b-c

45 FOURIER: *Theory of Heat*, 209b

45 FARADAY: *Researches in Electricity*, 534c-535b

49 DARWIN: *Origin of Species*, 9a-10d; 32a-39a,c passim, esp 34c-36a, 39a,c; 40d-42c; 53d-55b; 65a-69c esp 65b-66a; 106b-107a; 144a-145c; 182d-183a; 230d-231b / *Descent of Man*, 268b-269a; 320a-c; 341b,d [fn 32]; 354c-355a; 430d-432c; 442a-443b; 468d-469a; 525b-527c; 554d-555b

53 JAMES: *Psychology*, 857b

54 FREUD: *Civilization and Its Discontents*, 791d-792a

12. The treatment of animals by men

12*a*. The taming of animals

4 HOMER: *Odyssey*, BK IV [625-637] 205c

5 AESCHYLUS: *Prometheus Bound* [459-468] 44d

5 SOPHOCLES: *Antigone* [332-352] 134a

7 PLATO: *Phaedrus*, 128a-d

9 ARISTOTLE: *History of Animals*, BK I, CH I [488^{a}26–31] 9b; BK VI, CH 21 [575^{b}1–3] 101a; BK IX, CH I [608^{a}24–27] 133b,d; [608^{b}30–609^{a}3] 134b; [610^{a}24–34] 135d; CH 26 143b; CH 46 [630^{b}18–21] 156a / *Politics*, BK I, CH 5 [1254^{b}4–13] 448a

14 PLUTARCH: *Alexander*, 542d-543b

19 AQUINAS: *Summa Theologica*, PART I, Q 96, A I, REP 2 510b-511b

20 AQUINAS: *Summa Theologica*, PART I–II, Q 50, A 3, REP 2 8b-9a

25 MONTAIGNE: *Essays*, 220d-222c

36 SWIFT: *Gulliver*, PART IV, 146b-148b; 164b; 167b-168a

38 ROUSSEAU: *Inequality*, 337a; 356d-357a

41 GIBBON: *Decline and Fall*, 86d; 107a-b; 221d

46 HEGEL: *Philosophy of Right*, PART I, par 56 26b

49 DARWIN: *Origin of Species*, 13c-d; 121b-122c passim; 233c-d

50 MARX: *Capital*, 87b

53 JAMES: *Psychology*, 708a-709a

12*b*. The use and abuse of animals

OLD TESTAMENT: *Genesis*, 4:4; 8:6-12; 22:1-13 / *Exodus*, 20:8-11; 22:19; 23:12 / *Leviticus* passim, esp 11, 18:23, 20:15-16 / *Numbers*, 22:21-34 / *Deuteronomy*, 5:12-14; 22:6-7,10; 25:4; 27:21 / *Proverbs*, 12:10 / *Daniel*, 6:6-28

APOCRYPHA: *Bel and Dragon*, 23-28—(D) OT, *Daniel*, 14:22-27

NEW TESTAMENT: *Matthew*, 21:1-11 / *Mark*, 1:6; 6:34-44; 11:1-11 / *Luke*, 19:29-38 / *John*, 12:14-15 / *I Corinthians*, 9:9 / *I Timothy*, 5:18

4 HOMER: *Iliad* 3a-179d passim, esp BK I [428–471] 7c-8a, BK II [394–431] 14a-b, [760–779] 17c-d, BK IV [104–111] 25a, BK V [191–208] 32a-b, BK XXIII [262–611] 164a-167c / *Odyssey*, BK III [418–463] 197b-d; BK XI [23–50] 243b-c; BK XII [260–419] 252d-254c

5 AESCHYLUS: *Prometheus Bound* [459–468] 44d

5 ARISTOPHANES: *Peace* [1–181] 526a-528a / *Birds* [294–382] 545d-547b; [1076–1087] 556a-b

6 HERODOTUS: *History*, BK II, 57b-58b; 59b-c; 62c-64c; BK III, 95b-c; 111d-112c; 113c-d; BK IV, 127d-128a; 146d-147a; BK V, 183b-d

9 ARISTOTLE: *History of Animals*, BK III, CH 20 [522^{a}25]–CH 21 [523^{a}13] 47b-48c; BK V, CH 22 80b-81c; BK IX, CH I [610^{a}15–34] 135d / *Politics*, BK I, CH 8 [1256^{b}8–26] 450b-c; CH 11 [1258^{b}12–20] 452d-453a; BK IV, CH 3 [1289^{b}33–40] 488d-489a; BK VI, CH 7 [1321^{a}9–12] 524d; BK VII, CH 2 [1324^{b}36–41] 528d-529a

12 LUCRETIUS: *Nature of Things*, BK V [860–870] 72b-a

12 EPICTETUS: *Discourses*, BK I, CH 16, 121d-122a

12 AURELIUS: *Meditations*, BK VI, SECT 23 276b

13 VIRGIL: *Aeneid* 103a-379a esp BK III [218–257] 153a-154a, BK V [84–99] 189b, BK VIII [81–87] 261a

14 PLUTARCH: *Marcus Cato*, 278d-279c / *Alexander*, 541b-c

19 AQUINAS: *Summa Theologica*, PART I, Q 72, A I, REP 6 368b-369d; Q 96, A I 510b-511b

20 AQUINAS: *Summa Theologica*, PART I–II, Q 102, A 3 272b-276c; Q 105, A 2, REP 11–12 309d-316a

24 RABELAIS: *Gargantua and Pantagruel*, BK III, 143b-d; BK IV, 245d-248c

25 MONTAIGNE: *Essays*, 139c-143c; 206b-208a; 219b-d; 220d-222c

31 SPINOZA: *Ethics*, PART IV, PROP 37, SCHOL I, 435a-b

36 SWIFT: *Gulliver*, PART IV 135a-184a

36 STERNE: *Tristram Shandy*, 474b-477a; 483b-485a

38 ROUSSEAU: *Inequality*, 330d-331b

40 GIBBON: *Decline and Fall*, 38b-39a; 139c-140a; 411d-412c; 619d-620a

41 GIBBON: *Decline and Fall*, 107a-b; 221c-222a

44 BOSWELL: *Johnson*, 312b

48 MELVILLE: *Moby Dick*, 82b-83a; 307b-310b

49 DARWIN: *Origin of Species*, 13c-d; 233c-d

50 MARX: *Capital*, 86b; 183b-c

51 TOLSTOY: *War and Peace*, BK I, 19c-d; BK VII, 278a-287a; 296d-297d; BK VIII, 330d-332a; BK XII, 538a-d; BK XIV, 592a-c

53 JAMES: *Psychology*, 705a; 720a

54 FREUD: *War and Death*, 758b-c / *Civilization and Its Discontents*, 771d-772a

12*c*. Friendship or love between animals and men

4 HOMER: *Iliad*, BK XVII [426–455] 126c-d; BK XIX [399–424] 141a,c; BK XXIII [272–286] 164a / *Odyssey*, BK XVII [290–327] 280a-c

5 ARISTOPHANES: *Birds* [294–382] 545d-547b

6 HERODOTUS: *History*, BK I, 5b-d

9 ARISTOTLE: *History of Animals*, BK IX, CH 44 [630^{a}9–12] 155b; CH 48 [631^{a}7–10] 156b-c

14 PLUTARCH: *Pericles*, 121a-b / *Marcus Cato*, 278d-279c / *Alexander*, 562b; 570a-b

20 AQUINAS: *Summa Theologica*, PART II–II, Q 25, A 3 502c-503b

25 MONTAIGNE: *Essays*, 206b-208a; 224c-225b; 227b-228b

26 SHAKESPEARE: *Two Gentlemen of Verona*, ACT IV, SC IV [1–42] 248b-d

29 CERVANTES: *Don Quixote*, PART I, 2c-d; 112b-c

31 SPINOZA: *Ethics*, PART IV, PROP 37, SCHOL I, 435a-b

36 SWIFT: *Gulliver*, xixa; PART IV, 180a

36 STERNE: *Tristram Shandy*, 483b-485a

41 GIBBON: *Decline and Fall*, 221c-d passim

46 HEGEL: *Philosophy of History*, PART I, 229a

49 DARWIN: *Descent of Man*, 289c; 303c; 307a-c; 317d

51 TOLSTOY: *War and Peace*, BK VII, 278a-287a passim; BK XIII, 575b

52 DOSTOEVSKY: *Brothers Karamazov*, BK VI, 167c; BK X, 282a-288d

53 JAMES: *Psychology*, 722a-b

13. The attribution of human qualities or virtues to animals: personification in allegory and satire

  OLD TESTAMENT: *Genesis*, 3:1–5 / *Numbers*, 22:21–31

  4 HOMER: *Iliad*, BK XVII [426–455] 126c-d; BK XIX [399–424] 141a,c; BK XXIII [272–286] 164a

  5 ARISTOPHANES: *Knights* [591–610] 477b-d / *Wasps* 507a-525d / *Birds* 542a-563d / *Frogs* [205–270] 566d-567b

  6 HERODOTUS: *History*, BK I, 21d-22a; 33a-b; BK II, 61a-b; BK VI, 211a

  7 PLATO: *Phaedrus*, 128a-d / *Republic*, BK II, 319c-320c / *Statesman*, 583c-d; 588b-c

  9 ARISTOTLE: *History of Animals*, BK I, CH I [488^{b}3–25] 9c-d; BK VIII, CH I [588^{a}18–^{b}3] 114b,d; BK IX, CH I [608^{a}11–^{b}19] 133b,d-134a; CH 29 [618^{a}25–30] 143d; CH 38 148b; CH 48 [631^{a}8–20] 156b-c / *Politics*, BK III, CH 13 [1284^{a}11–18] 482b / *Rhetoric*, BK II, CH 20 [1393^{b}8–1394^{a}1] 641b-c

  14 PLUTARCH: *Lysander*, 357a / *Sulla*, 382c-d

  17 PLOTINUS: *Third Ennead*, TR IV, CH 2, 98a

  21 DANTE: *Divine Comedy*, HELL, I [1–111] 1a-2b; VI [1–33] 8b-d; XII [1–30] 16b-c; XVI [106]-XVII [36] 23c-24b; PURGATORY, XIV [16–66] 73d-74b; XXIX 97d-99b; XXXII [106–160] 103c-104a

  22 CHAUCER: *Nun's Priest's Tale* [14,853–15,452] 450b-460b

  23 MACHIAVELLI: *Prince*, CH XVIII, 25a-b

  24 RABELAIS: *Gargantua and Pantagruel*, BK I, 2b

  25 MONTAIGNE: *Essays*, 215a-232b passim

  27 SHAKESPEARE: *Timon of Athens*, ACT IV, SC III [320–348] 414b-c

  29 CERVANTES: *Don Quixote*, PART I, 39b-d; 40d-41a

  32 MILTON: *Paradise Lost*, BK IX [48–96] 248b-249b; [523–612] 258b-260b esp [549–566] 259b; BK X [209–590] 279a-287a

  36 SWIFT: *Gulliver*, PART IV 135a-184a

  44 BOSWELL: *Johnson*, 215b-c

  46 HEGEL: *Philosophy of History*, PART I, 253b-254d

  47 GOETHE: *Faust*, PART I [1202–1209] 30a

  48 MELVILLE: *Moby Dick* esp 131a-145a, 248b-249a, 289b-292a

  51 TOLSTOY: *War and Peace*, BK XII, 553d-554a

CROSS-REFERENCES

For: The general discussion of the grades of life and the kinds of soul, *see* LIFE AND DEATH 3, 3b; SOUL 2c–2c(3).

  Other considerations of the issue concerning continuity or discontinuity in the relation of plants, animals, and men, as well as between living and non-living things, *see* EVOLUTION 3e, 7a–7b; LIFE AND DEATH 2, 3a; MAN 1a–1c; NATURE 3b; SENSE 2a.

  The comparison of men and animals, or of different species of animals, with respect to sensitivity, memory, imagination, and intelligence, *see* MEMORY AND IMAGINATION 1; MIND 3a–3b; REASONING 1a; SENSE 2b–2c.

  The general theory of instinct, *see* HABIT 3–3e; and for the emotional aspect of instincts, *see* EMOTION 1c.

  Diverse theories of classification, *see* DEFINITION 2a–2e; EVOLUTION 1a–1b.

  Alternative theories of the origin and development of living organisms, *see* EVOLUTION 4a, 4c.

  Other discussions of heredity, *see* EVOLUTION 3–3e; FAMILY 6b.

  Other discussions of sexual attraction, mating, and reproduction, *see* CHANGE 10b; FAMILY 7a; LOVE 2a(1), 2d.

  The causes of animal movement, *see* CAUSE 2; DESIRE 2c; WILL 3a(1), 6c.

  Another consideration of sleeping and waking, *see* LIFE AND DEATH 5b.

  The comparison of human and animal societies, *see* STATE 1a.

ADDITIONAL READINGS

Listed below are works not included in *Great Books of the Western World*, but relevant to the idea and topics with which this chapter deals. These works are divided into two groups:

I. Works by authors represented in this collection.
II. Works by authors not represented in this collection.

For the date, place, and other facts concerning the publication of the works cited, consult the Bibliography of Additional Readings which follows the last chapter of *The Great Ideas*.

I.

GALEN. *On the Utility of Parts*
HOBBES. *Concerning Body*, PART IV, CH 25
GOETHE. *Metamorphose der Pflanzen*

II.

Aesop's Fables
THEOPHRASTUS. *Enquiry into Plants*
OVID. *Metamorphoses*
PLINY. *Natural History*
VESALIUS. *The Epitome*
SUÁREZ. *Disputationes Metaphysicae*, XLIV (3)
LA FONTAINE. *Fables*
LINNAEUS. *Systema Naturae*
LAMETTRIE. *Man a Machine*
CONDILLAC. *Traité des animaux*
BUFFON. *Natural History*
E. DARWIN. *The Loves of the Plants*
CUVIER. *The Animal Kingdom*
BALZAC. *A Passion in the Desert*
COMTE. *The Positive Philosophy*, BK V
SCHWANN. *Microscopical Researches into the Accordance in the Structure and Growth of Animals and Plants*
LOTZE. *Microcosmos*, BK I, CH 5

BERNARD. *Introduction to Experimental Medicine*
E. HARTMANN. *Philosophy of the Unconscious*, (C) II, IV
T. H. HUXLEY. *Methods and Results*, V
FRAZER. *The Golden Bough*, PART V, CH 9, 13-17
WUNDT. *Outlines of Psychology*, (19)
JENNINGS. *Behavior of the Lower Organisms*
SHERRINGTON. *The Integrative Action of the Nervous System*
DRIESCH. *The Science and Philosophy of the Organism*
HENDERSON. *The Fitness of the Environment*
KOEHLER. *The Mentality of Apes*
D. W. THOMPSON. *On Growth and Form*
LOEB. *The Organism as a Whole*
——. *Forced Movements, Tropisms and Animal Conduct*
J. S. HALDANE and J. G. PRIESTLEY. *Respiration*
PAVLOV. *Conditioned Reflexes*
ALVERDES. *Social Life in the Animal World*
WHEELER. *Foibles of Insects and Men*
BOSE. *Life Movements in Plants*
——. *Growth and Tropic Movements of Plants*
NEEDHAM. *Order and Life*
WHITEHEAD. *Modes of Thought*, LECT VII-VIII
LARGE. *The Advance of the Fungi*
WIENER. *Cybernetics*

Chapter 3: ARISTOCRACY

INTRODUCTION

THE forms of government have been variously enumerated, differently classified, and given quite contrary evaluations in the great books of political theory. In the actual history of political institutions, as well as in the tradition of political thought, the major practical issues with respect to the forms of government—the choices open, the ideals to be sought, or the evils to be remedied—have shifted with the times.

In an earlier day—not merely in ancient times, but as late as the 18th century—the form of government called "aristocracy" presented a genuine alternative to monarchy, and set a standard by which the defects and infirmities of democracy were usually measured. If aristocracy was not always regarded as *the* ideal form of government, the principle of aristocracy always entered into the definition of the political ideal.

Today, both in theory and practice, aristocracy is at the other end of the scale. For a large part of mankind, and for the political philosopher as well as in prevailing popular sentiment, aristocracy (together with monarchy) has become a subject of historical interest. It is a form of government with a past rather than a future. It no longer measures, but is measured by, democracy. If the aristocratic principle still signifies a factor of excellence in government or the state, it does so with a meaning now brought into harmony with democratic standards.

This change accounts for one ambiguity which the word "aristocracy" may have for contemporary readers. Formerly its primary, if not only, significance was to designate a form of government. It is currently used to name a special social class, separated from the masses by distinctions of birth, talent, property, power, or leisure. We speak of "the aristocracy" as we speak of "the elite" and "the four hundred"; or we follow Marx and Engels in thinking of the "feudal aristocracy" as the class "that was ruined by the bourgeoisie." The *Communist Manifesto* wastes little sympathy on the aristocrats who, while seeking an ally in the proletariat, forgot that "they [too] exploited under circumstances and conditions that were quite different." For Marx and Engels, the aristocracy and the bourgeoisie alike represent the propertied classes, but they differ in the manner in which they came by their property and power. The landed gentry and the feudal nobility got theirs largely by inheritance, the bourgeoisie by industry and trade.

Today, for the most part, we call a man an "aristocrat" if, justly or unjustly, he *claims* a right to certain social distinctions or privileges. We seldom use that word today to indicate a man who *deserves* special political status or preeminence, though we do sometimes use it to name the proponent of any form of government which rests upon the political inequality of men.

Since the discussion of aristocracy in the great books is largely political, we shall here be primarily concerned with aristocracy as a form of government. The general consideration of the forms of government will be found in the chapter on GOVERNMENT. Here and in the other chapters which are devoted to particular forms of government, we shall consider each of the several forms, both in itself and in relation to the others.

THERE IS ONE element in the conception of aristocracy which does not change with changing evaluations of aristocratic government. All of the writers of the great political books agree with Plato that aristocracy is a "government of the few," according as the few rather than the one or the many exercise political power and dominate the state. By this criterion of number, aristocracy is always differentiated from monarchy and democracy.

Though he uses the word "oligarchy" to name what others call "aristocracy," Locke defines the three forms of government by reference to numbers. When the majority themselves exercise the whole power of the community, Locke says, "then the form of the government is a perfect democracy." When they put "the power of making laws into the hands of a few select men . . . then it is an oligarchy; or else into the hands of one man, and then it is a monarchy." Kant proceeds similarly, though again in somewhat different language. "The relation of the supreme power to the people," he says, "is conceivable in three different forms: either *one* in the state rules over all; or *some*, united in relation of equality with each other, rule over all the others; or *all* together rule over each individually, including themselves. The form of the state is therefore either *autocratic*, or *aristocratic*, or *democratic*."

Hegel claims, however, that "purely quantitative distinctions like these are only superficial and do not afford the concept of the thing." The criterion of number does not seem to suffice when other forms of government are considered. It fails to distinguish monarchy from tyranny or despotism, which may consist of rule by one man, as has usually been the case historically. Number alone likewise fails to distinguish aristocracy from oligarchy. In the deliberations of the Medean conspirators, which Herodotus reports or invents, the rule of "a certain number of the worthiest" is set against both democracy and monarchy and identified as "oligarchy." How, then, shall aristocracy be distinguished from oligarchy?

There seem to be two answers to this question. In the *Statesman*, Plato adds to the characteristic of number the "criterion of law and the absence of law." The holders of political power, whatever their number, may govern either according to the established laws, or by arbitrary caprice in violation of them. "To go against the laws, which are based upon long experience, and the wisdom of counsellors who have graciously recommended them and persuaded the multitude to pass them, would be,"

the Eleatic Stranger declares in the *Statesman*, "a far greater and more ruinous error than any adherence to written law."

Taking the division of governments according to number, "the principle of law and the absence of law will bisect them all." Monarchy divides into "royalty and tyranny" depending on whether "an individual rules according to law . . . or governs neither by law nor by custom, but . . . pretends that he can only act for the best by violating the laws, while in reality appetite and ignorance are the motives." By the same criterion, the rule of the few divides "into aristocracy, which has an auspicious name, and oligarchy." While democracy is subject to the same division, Plato makes the same name apply to both its good and bad forms.

The second way in which aristocracy differs from oligarchy is also brought out in the *Statesman*. Since "the science of government," according to Plato, is "among the greatest of all sciences and most difficult to acquire . . . any true form of government can only be supposed to be the government of one, two, or, at any rate, of a few . . . really found to possess science." Because of this demand for "science," which presupposes virtue and competence in ruling, monarchy and aristocracy came to be defined as government by the single best man or by the few best men in the community.

A high degree of competence or virtue is, however, not the only mark by which the few may be distinguished from the many. The possession of wealth or property in any sizeable amount also seems to divide a small class in the community from the rest, and Plato at times refers to aristocracy simply as the government of the rich. Yet if wealth is the criterion by which the few are chosen to govern, then oligarchy results, at least in contrast to that sense of aristocracy in which the criterion is excellence of mind and character. Aristocracy is called aristocracy, writes Aristotle, "either because the rulers are the best men, or because they have at heart the best interests of the state and of the citizens."

By these additional criteria—never by numbers alone—the ancients conceive aristocracy. When it is so defined, it always appears to be a good form of government, but never the only good form, or even the best. The same criteria also place monarchy among the good forms, and—at least in Plato's *Statesman*—democracy is a third good form, when it is lawful government by the many, the many being competent or virtuous to some degree. In this triad of good forms, aristocracy ranks second-best, because government by one man is supposed to be more efficient, or because, in the hierarchy of excellence, the few may be superior, but only the one can be supreme. Aristotle, however, seems to rank aristocracy above monarchy. "If we call the rule of many men, who are all of them good, aristocracy, and the rule of one man royalty," he writes, "then aristocracy will be better for states than royalty."

THE INTRODUCTION of democracy into the comparison tends to complicate the discussion. Not only are the many usually the poor, but they are also seldom considered pre-eminent in virtue or competence. According to the way in which either wealth or human excellence is distributed, both oligarchy and aristocracy organize the political community in terms of inequalities in status, power, and privilege. This fact leads Rousseau, for example, to use the different kinds of inequality among men as a basis for distinguishing "three sorts of aristocracy—natural, elective, and hereditary."

Natural aristocracy, according to Rousseau, is based on that inequality among men which is due primarily to age and is found among simple peoples, where "the young bowed without question to the authority of experience." Elective aristocracy arose "in proportion as artificial inequality produced by institutions became predominant over natural inequality, and riches or power were put before age." This form, in Rousseau's opinion, is "the best, and is aristocracy properly so called." The third, which is characterized as "the worst of all governments," came about when "the transmission of the father's power along with his goods to his children, by creating patrician families, made government hereditary."

This emphasis upon inequality radically separates aristocracy from democracy. From Aristotle down to Montesquieu, Rousseau, and our own day, equality has been recognized as the distinctive element of democracy. Disregarding slaves who, for the ancients, were political

pariahs, Aristotle makes liberty the other mark of democracy—all freemen having, apart from wealth or virtue, an equal claim to political status. As "the principle of an aristocracy is virtue," Aristotle writes, so wealth is the principle "of an oligarchy, and freedom of a democracy."

To the defenders of democracy, ancient or modern, aristocracy and oligarchy stand together, at least negatively, in their denial of the principle of equality. To the defenders of aristocracy, oligarchy is as far removed as democracy, since both oligarchy and democracy neglect or underestimate the importance of virtue in organizing the state. Yet oligarchy more than democracy is the characteristic perversion of aristocracy. It also puts government in the hands of the few, but it substitutes wealth for virtue as the criterion. The democratic critic of aristocracy usually calls attention to the way in which oligarchy tries to wear the mask of aristocracy. However far apart aristocracy and oligarchy may be in definition, he insists that in actual practice they tend to become identical, in proportion as wealth, or noble birth, or social class is taken as the sign of intrinsic qualities which are thought to deserve special political recognition.

The defenders of aristocracy have admitted the tendency of aristocratic government to degenerate into oligarchy. Its critics are not satisfied with this admission. They deny that aristocracy has ever existed in purity of principle—they deny that the governing few have ever been chosen solely for their virtue. Machiavelli assumes it to be a generally accepted fact that "the nobles wish to rule and oppress the people . . . and give vent to their ambitions." Montesquieu, although more optimistic about the possibility of a truly virtuous aristocracy, recognizes its tendency to profit at the expense of the people. To overcome this he would have the laws make it "an essential point . . . that the nobles themselves should not levy the taxes . . . and should likewise forbid the nobles all kinds of commerce . . . and abolish the right of primogeniture among the nobles, to the end that by a continual division of the inheritances their fortunes may be always upon a level."

But perhaps the strongest attack upon aristocracy in all of the great political books is made by Mill in his *Representative Government*. He admits that "the governments which have been remarkable in history for sustained mental ability and vigour in the conduct of affairs have generally been aristocracies." But he claims that, whatever their abilities, such governments were "essentially bureaucracies," and the "dignity and estimation" of their ruling members were "quite different things from the prosperity or happiness of the general body of the citizens, and were often wholly incompatible with it." When their actions are dictated by "sinister interests," as frequently happens, the aristocratic class "assumes to themselves an endless variety of unjust privileges, sometimes benefiting their pockets at the expense of the people, sometimes merely tending to exalt them above others, or, what is the same thing in different words, to degrade others below themselves."

Yet except by those political thinkers who deny the distinction between good and bad government, and hence the relevance of virtue to institutions which are solely expressions of power, the aristocratic principle is seldom entirely rejected. Even when the notion of a pure aristocracy is dismissed as an ideal which can never be fully realized, the aristocratic principle reappears as a counsel of perfection in the improvement of other forms of government.

Even so, one difficulty remains, which tends to prevent aristocracy from being realized in practice, quite apart from any question of its soundness in principle. It lies in the reluctance of the best men to assume the burdens of public office. The parable told in the Book of Judges applies to aristocracy as much as to monarchy.

The trees went forth on a time to anoint a king over them; and they said unto the olive tree, Reign thou over us.

But the olive tree said unto them, Should I leave my fatness, wherewith by me they honor God and man, and go to be promoted over the trees?

And the trees said to the fig tree, Come thou, and reign over us.

But the fig tree said unto them, Should I forsake my sweetness, and my good fruit, and go to be promoted over the trees?

Then said the trees unto the vine, Come thou, and reign over us.

And the vine said unto them, Should I leave my wine, which cheereth God and man, and go to be promoted over the trees?

Then said all the trees unto the bramble, Come thou, and reign over us.

And the bramble said unto the trees, If in truth ye anoint me king over you, then come and put your trust in my shadow: and if not, let fire come out of the bramble, and devour the cedars of Lebanon.

Socrates thinks he has a solution for this problem. In the *Republic*, he proposes a new way to induce good men to rule. Since "money and honor have no attraction for them," necessity, Socrates says, "must be laid upon them, and they must be induced to serve from fear of punishment. . . . Now the worst part of the punishment is that he who refuses to rule is liable to be ruled by one who is worse than himself. And the fear of this, as I conceive, induces the good to take office . . . not under the idea that they are going to have any benefit or enjoyment themselves, but as a necessity, and because they are not able to commit the task of ruling to anyone who is better than themselves, or indeed as good."

THE POLITICAL ISSUES, in which monarchy, aristocracy, oligarchy, and democracy represent the major alternatives, cannot be clarified without recourse to the distinction between government by laws and government by men.

It has already been noted that in the *Statesman* Plato makes respect for the laws and violation of the laws the marks of good and bad government respectively. But he also proposes that "the best thing of all is not that the law should rule, but that a man should rule, supposing him to have wisdom and royal power." The imperfections of law could then be avoided, because one or a few men of almost superhuman wisdom would govern their inferiors even as the gods could direct the affairs of men without the aid of established laws. But if no man is a god in relation to other men, then, in Plato's opinion, it is better for laws or customs to be supreme, and for men to rule in accordance with them.

The larger issue concerning rule by law and rule by men is discussed in the chapters on CONSTITUTION and MONARCHY. But here we must observe how the difference between these two types of rule affects the understanding of all other forms of government. This can be seen in terms of Aristotle's distinction between royal and political government, which closely resembles the modern conception of the difference between absolute or despotic government on the one hand, and limited, constitutional, or republican government on the other.

There are passages in which Aristotle regards absolute rule by one or a few superior men as the divine or godlike form of government. When one man or a few excel "all the others together in virtue, and both rulers and subjects are fitted, the one to rule, the others to be ruled," it is right, in Aristotle's opinion, for the government to be royal or absolute rather than political or constitutional—whether one man rules or a few. "Royal rule is of the nature of an aristocracy," he says. "It is based upon merit, whether of the individual or of his family."

But in other passages Aristotle seems to regard absolute government as a despotic regime, appropriate to the family and the primitive tribe, but not to the state, in which it is better for equals to rule and be ruled in turn. In either case, it makes a difference to the meaning of aristocracy, as also to monarchy, whether it be conceived as absolute or constitutional government.

When it is conceived as absolute government, aristocracy differs from monarchy only on the point of numbers—the few as opposed to the one. Otherwise, aristocracy and monarchy are defended in the same way. The defense usually takes one of two directions. One line of argument which stems from Plato and Aristotle claims that inequality in wisdom or virtue between ruler and ruled justifies absolute rule by the superior. The other line is followed by those who, like Hobbes, maintain that since sovereignty is absolute, unlimited, and indivisible, the difference between kinds of government "consisteth not in the difference of Power, but in the difference of Convenience, or Aptitude to produce the Peace, and Security of the people." When they are conceived as forms of absolute government, aristocracy and monarchy are attacked for the same reason; to those who regard absolutism or despotism in government as unjust because it violates the basic equality of men, an absolute monarchy and a despotic aristocracy are both unjust.

Aristocracy, however, can also be conceived as a form or aspect of constitutional government. Montesquieu, for example, divides governments into "republican, monarchical, and despotic," and under "republican" places those "in which the body, or only a part, of the people is possessed of the supreme power," thus including both democracy and aristocracy. In both, laws, not men, are supreme, but the spirit of the laws is different. In democracy, the "spring," or principle, "by which it is made to act," is virtue resting on equality; in aristocracy, "moderation is the very soul . . . a moderation . . . founded on virtue, not that which proceeds from indolence and pusillanimity." Hegel's comment on this theory deserves mention. "The fact that 'moderation' is cited as the principle of aristocracy," he writes, "implies the beginning at this point of a divorce between public authority and private interest."

For Aristotle, in contrast to Montesquieu, the two major types of constitution are the democratic and the oligarchical, according as free-birth or wealth is made the chief qualification for citizenship and public office. Aristocracy enters the discussion of constitutional governments mainly in connection with the construction of the polity or mixed constitution. Although in most states "the fusion goes no further than the attempt to unite the freedom of the poor and the wealth of the rich," he points out that "there are three grounds on which men claim an equal share in the government, freedom, wealth, and virtue."

When the fusion goes no further than the attempt to unite the freedom of the poor and the wealth of the rich, "the admixture of the two elements," Aristotle says, is "to be called a polity." But sometimes the mixture of democracy with oligarchy may include an ingredient of aristocracy, as in "the distribution of offices according to merit." The union of these three elements "is to be called aristocracy or the government of the best," and "more than any other form of government, except the true and the ideal," it has, in Aristotle's judgment, "a right to this name." Polity and aristocracy, as mixed constitutions, are fusions of some of the same elements; hence, he says, it is "obvious that they are not very unlike."

BEGINNING IN the 18th century, and with the rise of representative government, the discussion of aristocracy as a distinct form of government is largely superceded by the consideration of the role which the aristocratic principle plays in the development of republican institutions.

The writers of *The Federalist*, for example, respond in several places to the charge that the constitution which they are defending shows tendencies toward aristocracy or oligarchy. Yet in their consideration and defense of the new instrument of government as essentially *republican*, they frequently appeal to principles that are aristocratic in nature.

In giving their own meanings to the terms "republic" and "pure democracy"—that is, government by elected representatives on the one hand, and by the direct participation of the whole people on the other—the Federalists also give an aristocratic bent to the very notion of representation. They seem to share the opinion of Montesquieu that "as most citizens have sufficient ability to choose, though unqualified to be chosen, so the people, though capable of calling others to account for their administration, are incapable of conducting administrations themselves."

Thus Madison praises "the delegation of the government . . . to a small number of citizens elected by the rest" as tending "to refine and enlarge the public views, by passing them through the medium of a chosen body of citizens, whose wisdom may best discern the true interest of their country." He further points out that "it may well happen that the public voice, pronounced by the representatives of the people, will be more consonant to the public good than if pronounced by the people themselves, convened for the purpose."

On such a view, the people's representatives in the legislature, or other branches of government, are supposed to be not their minions, but their betters. For the American constitutionalists, as for Edmund Burke, the representative serves his constituents by making independent decisions for the common good, not by doing their bidding. This theory of representation, to which Mill and other democratic thinkers agree in part, supposes that the representative knows better than his constituents what is for their good.

The effort to ensure leadership by superior men may involve the aristocratic principle, yet it is also claimed by Hamilton, Madison, and Jay to be a necessary safeguard for popular government. The senate, for instance, is not only to provide elder statesmen, but is also to serve as "a salutary check on the government . . . [which] doubles the security to the people, by requiring the concurrence of two distinct bodies in schemes of usurpation or perfidy, where the ambition or corruption of one would otherwise be sufficient." The electoral college aims directly at placing the immediate election of the president in the hands of "men most capable of analyzing the qualities adapted to the station . . . under circumstances favorable to deliberation." In addition it may serve as an "obstacle . . . opposed to cabal, intrigue, and corruption," which are the "most deadly adversaries of republican government."

In all these respects, as well as in the restrictions on suffrage which it permitted the states to impose, the unamended American constitution appears to have adopted an aristocratic principle in government. Whether the motivation of its proponents was in fact simply aristocratic, or whether it was partly or even largely oligarchical—leadership being the right of men of "good" family and substantial property—will always be a question to be decided in the light of the documents and the relevant historic evidence.

MORE DEMOCRATIC than the American constitutionalists of the 18th century, certainly so with regard to the extension of suffrage, John Stuart Mill appears to be no less concerned than they are to introduce aristocratic elements into the structure of representative government.

According to Mill, two grave dangers confront a democracy: "Danger of a low grade of intelligence in the representative body, and in the popular opinion which controls it; and danger of class legislation on the part of the numerical majority." Claiming that much of the blame for both dangers lies in the rule of the majority, Mill looks for means to overcome the situation in which "the numerical majority . . . alone possess practically any voice in the State."

His major remedy was a system of proportional representation. This would supposedly constitute a democratic improvement by securing representation for "every minority in the whole nation ... on principles of equal justice." But it may also serve to increase an aristocratic element, since it "affords the best security for the intellectual qualifications desirable in the representatives." This would be brought about by making possible the election of "hundreds of able men of independent thought, who would have no chance whatever of being chosen by the majority," with the result that Parliament would contain the "very *élite* of the country."

To make still more certain that men of superior political intelligence exert an effect upon government, Mill also proposes a plurality of votes for the educated and the establishment of an upper legislative chamber based on a specially qualified membership. Such proposals seem to indicate Mill's leanings toward aristocracy, not only because they aim at procuring a "government of the best," but also because they are designed to prevent a government based on a majority of "manual labourers" with the consequent danger of "too low a standard of political intelligence."

THE ISSUES RAISED by the theory of aristocracy, or by the aristocratic principle in government, seem to be basically the same in all centuries, however different the terms or the context in which they are expressed. Even when, as today, a purely aristocratic form of government does not present a genuine political alternative to peoples who have espoused democracy, there remains the sense that pure or unqualified democracy is an equally undesirable extreme. The qualifications proposed usually add an aristocratic leaven.

One issue concerns the equality and inequality of men. The affirmation that all men are created equal does not exclude a recognition of their individual inequalities—the wide diversity of human talents and the uneven distribution of intelligence and other abilities. Nor does it mean that all men use their native endowments to good purpose or in the same degree to acquire skill or knowledge or virtue.

To grasp the double truth—that no man is essentially more human than another, though one may have more of certain human abilities than another—is to see some necessity for the admixture of democratic and aristocratic principles in constructing a political constitution. But the issue is whether distributive justice requires, as a matter of right, that the best men should rule or hold public office.

Some political philosophers, like Plato and Aristotle, tend to take the aristocratic view that men of superior ability have a right to govern—that for them to be ruled by their inferiors would be unjust. This theory places greater emphasis on the inequality than on the equality of men. Their democratic opponents insist that the equality of men *as men* is the fundamental fact and the only fact having a bearing on the just distribution of suffrage. That certain individuals have superior aptitude for the exercise of political authority does not automatically confer that authority upon them. The inequality of men in merit or talent does not establish a political right, as does their equality in human nature. The selection of the best men for public office is, on this theory, not a matter of justice, but of expediency or prudence.

Another issue concerns the weight to be given the opinion of the majority as against the opinion of the wise or the expert when, as frequently happens, these opinions diverge or conflict. As the chapter on OPINION indicates, the experts themselves disagree about the soundness of the popular judgment.

Where Thucydides believes that "ordinary men usually manage public affairs better than their more gifted fellows," because "the latter are always wanting to appear wiser than the laws," Herodotus observes that "it seems easier to deceive the multitude than one man." Where Hegel holds it to be "a dangerous and a false prejudice, that the People alone have reason and insight, and know what justice is," John Jay declares that "the people of any country (if, like the Americans, intelligent and well-informed) seldom adopt and steadily persevere for many years in an erroneous opinion respecting their interests," and Hamilton adds that "the people commonly *intend* the public good."

Sometimes the same author seems to take both sides of the issue, as Aristotle does when, though he says that "a multitude is a better judge of many things than any individual," he yet prefers government by the one or few who are eminent in wisdom or virtue. Each side, perhaps, contributes only part of the truth. Certainly those who acknowledge a political wisdom in the preponderant voice of the many, but who also recognize another wisdom in the skilled judgment of the few, cannot wish to exclude either from exerting its due influence upon the course of government.

Still another issue has to do with education. Shall educational opportunity be as universal as the franchise? Shall those whose native endowments fit them for political leadership be trained differently or more extensively than their fellow citizens? Shall vocational education be given to the many, and liberal education be reserved for the few?

These questions provide some measure of the extent to which anyone's thinking is aristocratic or democratic—or involves some admixture of both strains. In the great discussion of these questions and issues, there is one ever-present ambiguity. We have already noted it in considering the reality of the line between aristocracy and oligarchy. The agreement or disagreement of Mill and Aristotle, of Burke and Plato, of Hamilton and Paine, of Veblen and Pareto, or John Dewey and Matthew Arnold cannot be judged without determining whether the distinction between the many and the few derives from nature or convention.

It is this distinction which Jefferson had in mind when, writing to Adams in 1813, he said, "There is a natural aristocracy among men. The grounds of this are virtue and talents . . . There is also an artificial aristocracy founded on wealth and birth, without either virtue or talents; for with these it would belong to the first class. The natural aristocracy I consider as the most precious gift of nature, for the instruction, the trusts, the government of society . . . The artificial aristocracy is a mischievous ingredient in government, and provision should be made to prevent its ascendancy."

OUTLINE OF TOPICS

REFERENCES

To find the passages cited, use the numbers in heavy type, which are the volume and page numbers of the passages referred to. For example, in 4 HOMER: *Iliad*, BK II [265-283] 12d, the number 4 is the number of the volume in the set; the number 12d indicates that the passage is in section d of page 12.

PAGE SECTIONS: When the text is printed in one column, the letters a and b refer to the upper and lower halves of the page. For example, in 53 JAMES: *Psychology*, 116a-119b, the passage begins in the upper half of page 116 and ends in the lower half of page 119. When the text is printed in two columns, the letters a and b refer to the upper and lower halves of the left-hand side of the page, the letters c and d to the upper and lower halves of the right-hand side of the page. For example, in 7 PLATO: *Symposium*, 163b-164c, the passage begins in the lower half of the left-hand side of page 163 and ends in the upper half of the right-hand side of page 164.

AUTHOR'S DIVISIONS: One or more of the main divisions of a work (such as PART, BK, CH, SECT) are sometimes included in the reference; line numbers, in brackets, are given in certain cases; *e.g.*, *Iliad*, BK II [265-283] 12d.

BIBLE REFERENCES: The references are to book, chapter, and verse. When the King James and Douay versions differ in title of books or in the numbering of chapters or verses, the King James version is cited first and the Douay, indicated by a (*D*), follows; *e.g.*, OLD TESTAMENT: *Nehemiah*, 7:45—(*D*) II *Esdras*, 7:46.

SYMBOLS: The abbreviation "esp" calls the reader's attention to one or more especially relevant parts of a whole reference; "passim" signifies that the topic is discussed intermittently rather than continuously in the work or passage cited.

For additional information concerning the style of the references, see the Explanation of Reference Style; for general guidance in the use of *The Great Ideas*, consult the Preface.

1. The general theory and evaluation of aristocracy

6 HERODOTUS: *History*, BK III, 107c-108c

7 PLATO: *Republic*, BK II-VII, 316a-401d / *Statesman*, 598b-604b / *Laws*, BK III, 665c-666c; 669d-672a

9 ARISTOTLE: *Ethics*, BK VIII, CH 10 [1160^{b}32-1161^{a}2] 413a-b; CH 11 [1161^{a}23-25] 413c / *Politics*, BK III, CH 7 [1279^{a}33-37] 476d; CH 9 [1281^{a}2-8] 478c-d; CH 15 [1286^{b}4-5] 484d; CH 17 [1288^{a}8-10] 486d; CH 18 487a,c; BK IV, CH 7 493a-b; CH 8 [1294^{a}9-24] 493d-494a; CH 14 [1298^{b}5-10] 499a / *Rhetoric*, BK I, CH 8 [1365^{b}32-39] 608a-b

20 AQUINAS: *Summa Theologica*, PART I-II, Q 95, A 4, ANS 229b-230c; Q 105, A 1, ANS 307d-309d

23 HOBBES: *Leviathan*, PART II, 104d-105a

33 PASCAL: *Pensées*, 319-324 229b-230c; 335 232b; 337-338 232b-233a

35 LOCKE: *Civil Government*, CH X, SECT 132 55a-b

38 MONTESQUIEU: *Spirit of Laws*, BK II, 6b-7c; BK III, 10c-11a; BK V, 23a-25a; BK VII, 45b-c

38 ROUSSEAU: *Inequality*, 359a-c / *Social Contract*, BK III, 410b-c; 411c-412c; 418c

42 KANT: *Science of Right*, 450a-d

1a. Aristocracy as a good form of government

OLD TESTAMENT: *Exodus*, 18:13-26 / *Deuteronomy*, 1:9-17 / *Proverbs*, 29:2

APOCRYPHA: *Ecclesiasticus*, 10:1-2—(*D*) OT, *Ecclesiasticus*, 10:1-2

6 HERODOTUS: *History*, BK III, 107d-108a

6 THUCYDIDES: *Peloponnesian War*, BK IV, 478d-479b

7 PLATO: *Republic*, BK III-IV, 339b-350a; BK VIII, 401d-402d / *Timaeus*, 442a-443b / *Statesman*, 598b-604b esp 603d-604b

9 ARISTOTLE: *Ethics*, BK VIII, CH 11 [1161^{a}23-24] 413c / *Politics*, BK III, CH 7 [1279^{a}28-38] 476d; CH 15 [1286^{b}3-7] 484d; CH 18 487a,c; BK IV, CH 7 493a-b; CH 8 [1294^{a}9-24] 493d-494a

14 PLUTARCH: *Lycurgus*, 47a-48d

15 TACITUS: *Annals*, BK XI, 106a-107b

18 AUGUSTINE: *City of God*, BK V, CH 12, 218d-219b

20 AQUINAS: *Summa Theologica*, PART I-II, Q 95, A 4, ANS 229b-230c; Q 105, A 1, ANS 307d-309d

27 SHAKESPEARE: *Coriolanus* 351a-392a,c esp ACT I, SC I [51-192] 351d-353c

38 MONTESQUIEU: *Spirit of Laws*, BK II, 7c

38 ROUSSEAU: *Social Contract*, BK III, 411c-412a

43 MILL: *Representative Government*, 340a-c; 353b-354b; 363d-364b

44 BOSWELL: *Johnson*, 125c-d; 141a; 211b-c; 220b

1b. Criticisms of aristocracy as unrealizable or unjust

6 HERODOTUS: *History*, BK III, 108b-c

6 THUCYDIDES: *Peloponnesian War*, BK VI, 520a-c

7 PLATO: *Republic*, BK V, 368c-369c; BK VI, 380b-383a; BK VII, 401c-d; BK IX, 426d-427b

9 ARISTOTLE: *Politics*, BK III, CH 10–13 478d-483a; BK IV, CH 8 [1293^{b}21–28] 493c

15 TACITUS: *Histories*, BK I, 193c-194a

23 HOBBES: *Leviathan*, PART II, 105a; PART IV, 273a-b

35 LOCKE: *Civil Government*, CH XI, SECT 138 57b-c

38 MONTESQUIEU: *Spirit of Laws*, BK II, 7c

38 ROUSSEAU: *Social Contract*, BK III, 411d

42 KANT: *Science of Right*, 442c-d; 445a-c

43 MILL: *Representative Government*, 366a-367b

46 HEGEL: *Philosophy of Right*, PART III, par 297 99b / *Philosophy of History*, PART IV, 356c-357 365a

50 MARX-ENGELS: *Communist Manifesto*, 420c

2. The relation of aristocracy to other forms of government

6 HERODOTUS: *History*, BK III, 107c-108c

6 THUCYDIDES: *Peloponnesian War*, BK VIII, 579c-590c passim

7 PLATO: *Republic*, BK I, 301c-d; BK VIII–IX, 401d-421a esp BK VIII, 401d-402d / *Statesman*, 598b-604b / *Laws*, BK III, 669d-672a

9 ARISTOTLE: *Ethics*, BK V, CH 3 [1131^{a}24–29] 378d; BK VIII, CH 10–11 412c-413d / *Politics*, BK III, CH 5 [1278^{a}15–34] 475b-c; CH 7 476c-477a; CH 13 [1284^{a}3–^{b}34] 482a-483a; CH 15 [1286^{b}8–22] 484d-485a; CH 17 [1287^{b}37]–CH 18 [1288^{a}37] 486c-487a,c; BK IV, CH 2 [1289^{a}26–^{b}4] 488b-c; CH 3 [1290^{a}13–29] 489b; CH 14 [1298^{a}34–^{b}10] 498d-499a; CH 15 [1299^{b}20-1300^{a}8] 500b-d; CH 16 [1301^{a}10–16] 502c / *Rhetoric*, BK I, CH 8 608a-c

14 PLUTARCH: *Lycurgus*, 34d-35d

20 AQUINAS: *Summa Theologica*, PART I–II, Q 95, A 4, ANS 229b-230c; Q 105, A I, ANS 307d-309d

23 HOBBES: *Leviathan*, PART I, 73b; PART II, 104d-108b passim; 154b-c

33 PASCAL: *Pensées*, 304 227b-228a

35 LOCKE: *Civil Government*, CH X, SECT 132 55a-b; CH XI, SECT 138 57b-c

38 MONTESQUIEU: *Spirit of Laws*, BK II–III 4a-13d esp BK II, 4a, 6b-7c, BK III, 10c-11a; BK VI, 34d-35a; BK VIII, 56b-57c; BK XII, 90b-c; BK XV, 109a-b; BK XVIII, 125a-b

38 ROUSSEAU: *Inequality*, 359a-c / *Social Contract*, BK III, 410b-c; 415d; 418c; BK IV, 427a-d

41 GIBBON: *Decline and Fall*, 81c-d

42 KANT: *Science of Right*, 450a-452a esp 450b-d

43 FEDERALIST: NUMBER 39, 125b-d

43 MILL: *Representative Government*, 363b-369b passim; 387c-d

46 HEGEL: *Philosophy of Right*, PART III, par 273, 90d-91c; par 279, 94b

2a. Aristocracy and monarchy

6 HERODOTUS: *History*, BK III, 107c-108c

7 PLATO: *Republic*, BK IV, 355d-356a / *Statesman*, 598b-604b

9 ARISTOTLE: *Politics*, BK III, CH 7 476c-477a; CH 13 [1284^{a}3–35] 482a-c; CH 15 [1286^{a}23–^{b}8] 484c-d esp [1286^{b}4–8] 484d; CH 16 [1287^{b}8–35] 486a-c; CH 17 [1288^{a}5–25] 486c-487a; CH 18 487a,c; BK IV, CH 2 [1289^{a}26–35] 488b; BK V, CH 10 [1310^{a}39–^{b}14] 512d-513a; [1310^{b}31–1311^{a}8] 513b / *Rhetoric*, BK I, CH 8 608a-c

15 TACITUS: *Annals*, BK VI, 97b

18 AUGUSTINE: *City of God*, BK V, CH 12, 218d-219b

20 AQUINAS: *Summa Theologica*, PART I–II, Q 95, A 4, ANS 229b-230c; Q 105, A I, ANS and REP 1–2 307d-309d

23 MACHIAVELLI: *Prince*, CH IV 7a-8a; CH IX 14c-16a passim; CH XIX, 27a-b

23 HOBBES: *Leviathan*, PART II, 104d-109a passim; PART III, 201a

38 MONTESQUIEU: *Spirit of Laws*, BK II, 6b-8c; BK III, 10c-11d; BK V, 23a-25d; 32b-c; BK VIII, 53d-54a; BK XI, 75b-d; 77b-c; BK XII, 90c; BK XX, 147a-d

38 ROUSSEAU: *Social Contract*, BK III, 418c

39 SMITH: *Wealth of Nations*, BK V, 308b-c

41 GIBBON: *Decline and Fall*, 81c-d

43 FEDERALIST: NUMBER 17, 70a-d

43 MILL: *Representative Government*, 351d-352b; 366a-c

46 HEGEL: *Philosophy of Right*, PART III, par 273, 90c-91d; par 279, 94b / *Philosophy of History*, PART IV, 356d-357a

51 TOLSTOY: *War and Peace*, BK VI, 241c-242b; BK IX, 384c-388a,c; EPILOGUE I, 668a-669c

2b. Aristocracy and constitutional government: the polity or mixed constitution

6 THUCYDIDES: *Peloponnesian War*, BK VIII, 579d-580d; 581b-c; 582a; 587a-b; 588a-589a; 590a-b

9 ARISTOTLE: *Politics*, BK III, CH 7 476c-477a; BK IV, CH 8 493c-494a; CH 11 [1295^{a}31–34] 495b-c; CH 14 [1298^{b}5–10] 499a; BK V, CH 7 [1307^{a}5–27] 509a-b / *Rhetoric*, BK I, CH 8 [1365^{b}22–1366^{a}2] 608a-b

14 PLUTARCH: *Lycurgus*, 34d / *Dion*, 800c

15 TACITUS: *Annals*, BK IV, 72a-b

20 AQUINAS: *Summa Theologica*, PART I–II, Q 95, A 4, ANS 229b-230c; Q 105, A I, ANS 307d-309d

38 MONTESQUIEU: *Spirit of Laws*, BK II, 4a; 6b-8c; BK V, 21d-22c; BK VIII, 52c; BK XI, 71d-72b; 75b-d; 76c-77c

41 GIBBON: *Decline and Fall*, 81c-d

42 KANT: *Science of Right*, 439c-440a; 450a-d

43 FEDERALIST: NUMBER 39, 125b-d; NUMBER 63, 194b-195b; NUMBER 71, 216a-b

(2. *The relation of aristocracy to other forms of government. 2b. Aristocracy and constitutional government: the polity or mixed constitution.*)

43 MILL: *Representative Government*, 353d-354b; 406a-409c; 419b-c

46 HEGEL: *Philosophy of Right*, PART III, par 279, 94b / *Philosophy of History*, PART II, 275b-276a; 277c-d; PART IV, 356d-357a

51 TOLSTOY: *War and Peace*, BK VI, 238c-243d passim, esp 241c-242b; BK IX, 384c-388a,c passim

2c. Aristocracy and democracy

6 HERODOTUS: *History*, BK III, 107c-108c

6 THUCYDIDES: *Peloponnesian War*, BK VI, 520a-c; 533a-c; BK VIII, 579c-581c; 582b-c; 590a-b

7 PLATO: *Republic*, BK VIII, 401d-402d; 408b-409d / *Statesman*, 598b-604b

9 ARISTOTLE: *Politics*, BK III, CH 11 [1281^{a}39-^{b}25] 479b-c; CH 13 [1284^{a}3-^{b}25] 482a-d; BK IV, CH 7 [1293^{b}12-18] 493b; BK V, CH 7 [1307^{a}5-27] 509a-b; CH 8 [1307^{b}39-1308^{a}24] 510a-b; [1308^{b}31-1309^{a}10] 511a-b / *Rhetoric*, BK I, CH 8 [1365^{b}22-1366^{a}2] 608a-b

14 PLUTARCH: *Lycurgus*, 34d / *Lycurgus-Numa*, 62b-c / *Dion*, 792d-802a,c esp 800c

15 TACITUS: *Annals*, BK VI, 97b

20 AQUINAS: *Summa Theologica*, PART I-II, Q 95, A 4, ANS 229b-230c; Q 105, A 1, ANS 307d-309d

23 MACHIAVELLI: *Prince*, CH IX 14c-16a passim

23 HOBBES: *Leviathan*, PART II, 104d-105a

27 SHAKESPEARE: *Coriolanus*, ACT I, SC 1 [1-47] 351a-d; ACT II, SC 1 [1-106] 361a-362a; ACT III, SC 1 [140-161] 370d-371a

33 PASCAL: *Pensées*, 294 225b-226b

38 MONTESQUIEU: *Spirit of Laws*, BK II, 4a-7c; BK III, 9b-11a; BK V, 23a-b; 23d; BK VII, 44d-45c; BK VIII, 51d; 53d-54a; BK IX, 58b; BK X, 64a-d; BK XII, 90b-c; BK XV, 109b

38 ROUSSEAU: *Political Economy*, 369c-d / *Social Contract*, BK IV, 427a-d

41 GIBBON: *Decline and Fall*, 81c-d

42 KANT: *Science of Right*, 450a-d

43 FEDERALIST: NUMBER 39, 125b-d; NUMBER 57 176d-179b passim; NUMBER 58, 181b-c; NUMBER 60, 185b-187a

43 MILL: *Liberty*, 298b-299a / *Representative Government*, 353b-354b; 364b-d; 366a-369b passim; 376b-c

44 BOSWELL: *Johnson*, 125c-d; 141a; 211b-c

46 HEGEL: *Philosophy of Right*, PART III, par 273, 91b-c; par 279, 94b / *Philosophy of History*, PART II, 275b-276a; 277c-d; PART III, 285b-d; 310a-c

2d. Aristocracy and oligarchy

7 PLATO: *Republic*, BK VIII, 401d-402d; 405c-407a / *Statesman*, 598b-604b

9 ARISTOTLE: *Ethics*, BK V, CH 3 [1131^{a}24-29] 378d; BK VIII, CH 10 [1160^{b}11-16] 412d;

[1160^{b}32-1161^{a}2] 413a-b / *Politics*, BK II, CH 10 [1272^{a}27-^{b}10] 468c-469a; CH 11 469a-470b; BK III, CH 5 [1278^{a}15-24] 475b-c; CH 7 476c-477a esp [1279^{b}4-10] 476d-477a; CH 13 [1283^{a}25-^{b}26] 481b-d; CH 15 [1286^{b}12-16] 485a; BK IV, CH 2 [1289^{a}26-^{b}4] 488b-c; CH 4 [1290^{b}17-20] 489d; CH 5 [1292^{a}39-^{b}6] 491d-492a; CH 7 [1293^{b}2-12] 493a-b; CH 8 [1293^{b}30-1294^{a}28] 493c-494a; CH 12 [1297^{a}6-9] 497b; BK V, CH 7 508c-509d; CH 12 [1316^{a}39-^{b}10] 519c / *Rhetoric*, BK I, CH 8 [1365^{b}22-1366^{a}6] 608a-b

14 PLUTARCH: *Lycurgus*, 36a-37b; 47a-48a

15 TACITUS: *Annals*, BK II, 35d

20 AQUINAS: *Summa Theologica*, PART I-II, Q 95, A 4, ANS 229b-230c

21 DANTE: *Divine Comedy*, HELL, XVI [64-78] 23a-b

23 HOBBES: *Leviathan*, PART II, 104d-105a; PART IV, 273a-b

38 MONTESQUIEU: *Spirit of Laws*, BK II, 7b-c; BK V, 23a-25a; BK XX, 151c-152a

38 ROUSSEAU: *Social Contract*, BK III, 419b

39 SMITH: *Wealth of Nations*, BK III, 165c-166a; BK V, 309c-310d

42 KANT: *Science of Right*, 450a-c

43 FEDERALIST: NUMBER 63, 194d

43 MILL: *Representative Government*, 363d-364d

46 HEGEL: *Philosophy of History*, PART II, 277c-d; PART III, 292d-293b

2e. Aristocracy and tyranny

6 THUCYDIDES: *Peloponnesian War*, BK VI, 533a-c

7 PLATO: *Republic*, BK VIII, 401d-402d; BK VIII-IX, 411d-421a / *Statesman*, 598b-604b passim, esp 603b-604b / *Laws*, BK IV, 679c-680b

9 ARISTOTLE: *Politics*, BK V, CH 10 [1310^{a}40-1311^{a}7] 512d-513b / *Rhetoric*, BK I, CH 8 [1365^{b}32-1366^{a}6] 608a-b

15 TACITUS: *Histories*, BK I, 193c-194a

20 AQUINAS: *Summa Theologica*, PART I-II, Q 95, A 4, ANS 229b-230c

23 HOBBES: *Leviathan*, PART IV, 273a-b

33 PASCAL: *Pensées*, 380 238a

35 LOCKE: *Civil Government*, CH XVIII, SECT 201 71c

38 MONTESQUIEU: *Spirit of Laws*, BK II, 4a; BK VI, 34d-35a; BK VIII, 52c-d; BK XI, 70c; 78d-79b; BK XV, 109a-b

43 FEDERALIST: NUMBER 47, 153d; NUMBER 48, 157b-c; NUMBER 70, 213d-214a

46 HEGEL: *Philosophy of Right*, PART III, par 273, 91c / *Philosophy of History*, PART II, 277c-d

51 TOLSTOY: *War and Peace*, BK I, 9b-c; EPILOGUE I, 668a-669d

3. The causes of degeneration or instability in aristocracies: aristocracy and revolution

OLD TESTAMENT: *I Samuel*, 7:15-8:5—(D) *I Kings*, 7:15-8:5

6 HERODOTUS: *History*, BK III, 108b-c

6 THUCYDIDES: *Peloponnesian War*, BK V, 482d-483a; BK VIII, 579c-583c; 587a-589a; 590a-c

7 PLATO: *Republic*, BK III-IV, 339b-350a; BK VIII, 403a-404a / *Critias*, 485a-c / *Seventh Letter*, 806d-807b

9 ARISTOTLE: *Politics*, BK II, CH 9 [1270^{b}7-34] 466d-467a; CH 12 [1273^{b}36-1274^{a}7] 470c; BK III, CH 15 [1286^{b}12-16] 485a; BK V, CH 3 [1303^{a}2-10] 504b-c; CH 4 [1304^{a}18-29] 505d-506a; CH 7 508c-509d; CH 8 [1307^{b}39-1308^{a}24] 510a-b; CH 12 [1316^{a}39-^{b}3] 519c

14 PLUTARCH: *Lycurgus*, 35c-d; 47a-48a / *Coriolanus*, 180a-184a / *Lysander*, 361a-368a,c / *Caius Gracchus*, 683b-c / *Cicero*, 708a-b

15 TACITUS: *Annals*, BK I, 1b-2a; 3a-b / *Histories*, BK I, 193c-194a

21 DANTE: *Divine Comedy*, HELL, XVI [64-78] 23a-b; PARADISE, XV-XVI 128b-132a

23 MACHIAVELLI: *Prince*, CH IV 7a-8a; CH IX 14c-16a

36 SWIFT: *Gulliver*, PART IV, 158a-b

38 MONTESQUIEU: *Spirit of Laws*, BK II, 6c-7b; BK III, 10c-11a; BK V, 23a-25a; BK VII, 45b; BK VIII, 52c-53a; BK X, 64a-d; BK XII, 91c-92b; BK XIII, 96d-97a; BK XX, 151c-152a

38 ROUSSEAU: *Social Contract*, BK III, 411c-d; 418c-419b

39 SMITH: *Wealth of Nations*, BK V, 420b-c

42 KANT: *Science of Right*, 451a

43 FEDERALIST: NUMBER 17, 70a-d

43 MILL: *Representative Government*, 366a-367b

46 HEGEL: *Philosophy of Right*, PART III, par 273, 91c / *Philosophy of History*, PART IV, 355d-357a esp 356c-357a; 364a-b

50 MARX-ENGELS: *Communist Manifesto*, 423d-424b; 429c-430b

51 TOLSTOY: *War and Peace*, EPILOGUE I, 666c-669d

4. Aristocracy and the issue of rule by men as opposed to rule by law

7 PLATO: *Republic*, BK VI, 380b-c / *Statesman*, 598b-604b / *Seventh Letter*, 806d-807b

9 ARISTOTLE: *Politics*, BK III, CH 10 [1281^{a}29-38] 479a; CH 13 [1284^{a}3-18] 482a-b; CH 15 [1286^{a}7-^{b}8] 484b-d; CH 17 486c-487a esp [1288^{a}5-14] 486c-d

23 HOBBES: *Leviathan*, PART IV, 273a-c

35 LOCKE: *Civil Government*, CH XVIII, SECT 199-202 71a-72a

38 MONTESQUIEU: *Spirit of Laws*, BK II, 4a; BK VIII, 52c; BK XI, 69a-c

42 KANT: *Science of Right*, 450d-451d

5. The training of those fitted for rule: aristocratic theories of education

OLD TESTAMENT: *Exodus*, 18:13-26 / *Deuteronomy*, 1:9-17

APOCRYPHA: *Ecclesiasticus*, 38:24-34—(D) OT, *Ecclesiasticus*, 38:25-39

7 PLATO: *Republic*, BK II-III, 320c-339a; BK VI-VII, 383b-401d esp BK VII, 389d-401d /

Timaeus, 442c-d / *Statesman*, 607b-608a / *Laws*, BK VII, 728b; BK XII, 794b-798b esp 796d-798b

9 ARISTOTLE: *Politics*, BK III, CH 4 [1277^{a}14-^{b}15] 474a-d; CH 18 487a,c; BK IV, CH 15 [1300^{a}3-8] 500d; BK VI, CH 8 [1322^{b}37-1323^{a}6] 526d; BK VII, CH 14 [1332^{b}13-1333^{a}16] 537b-538a / *Rhetoric*, BK I, CH 8 [1365^{b}32-39] 608a-b

14 PLUTARCH: *Lycurgus*, 38a-45c / *Alcibiades*, 156b-158b / *Marcus Cato*, 286c-287b / *Lysander*, 354b,d-355a / *Dion*, 781b,d-788b

15 TACITUS: *Annals*, BK II, 34c-d; BK XIII, 125d-126a / *Histories*, BK IV, 267c

21 DANTE: *Divine Comedy*, PARADISE, VIII [115-148] 118b-c

23 HOBBES: *Leviathan*, INTRO, 47b-d; PART I, 94b-c; PART II, 112d; 154a; 158c-d; 164a,c

24 RABELAIS: *Gargantua and Pantagruel*, BK I, 18b-19d; 24a-30c; BK II, 75a-77a; 78b-83b

25 MONTAIGNE: *Essays*, 60a-62a; 63d-64a; 71d-72b

26 SHAKESPEARE: *Taming of the Shrew*, ACT I, SC I [1-45] 202c-203a / *1st Henry IV*, ACT I, SC II [218-240] 437c-d / *Henry V*, ACT I, SC I [22-66] 533b-c / *As You Like It*, ACT I, SC I [1-28] 597a-b

29 CERVANTES: *Don Quixote*, PART II, 332c-336a; 362a-c

36 SWIFT: *Gulliver*, PART I, 29b-31a; PART IV, 158a-b; 166b-167a

38 MONTESQUIEU: *Spirit of Laws*, BK V, 18d

39 SMITH: *Wealth of Nations*, BK V, 347c-d

40 GIBBON: *Decline and Fall*, 86c

41 GIBBON: *Decline and Fall*, 508d-509d

43 MILL: *Liberty*, 298b-299a / *Representative Government*, 384a-387d; 415a-417c

46 HEGEL: *Philosophy of Right*, ADDITIONS, 169 145d / *Philosophy of History*, PART III, 310a-c; PART IV, 368a-b

51 TOLSTOY: *War and Peace*, BK VI, 244d-245c

6. The selection of the best men for public office: the aristocratic theory of representation in modern constitutional government

OLD TESTAMENT: *Genesis*, 41:33-40 / *Exodus*, 18:13-26 / *Deuteronomy*, 1:9-18 / *Judges* esp 9:8-15 / *I Samuel*, 1:1-25:1—(D) *I Kings*, 1:1-25:1 / *I Kings*, 3:5-15—(D) *III Kings*, 3:5-15 / *II Chronicles*, 1:7-12—(D) *II Paralipomenon*, 1:7-12 / *Proverbs*, 29:2 / *Daniel*, 6:1-4

APOCRYPHA: *Wisdom of Solomon*, 6; 9—(D) OT, *Book of Wisdom*, 6; 9 / *Ecclesiasticus*, 10:1-3—(D) OT, *Ecclesiasticus*, 10:1-3

5 EURIPIDES: *Electra* [367-400] 330c-d

6 HERODOTUS: *History*, BK III, 93c; 107d-108a

6 THUCYDIDES: *Peloponnesian War*, BK II, 396c-d; BK III, 425b-c; BK IV, 478d; BK VI, 520b-c

7 PLATO: *Protagoras*, 44d-45b / *Republic*, BK II, 319a-320c; BK III, 339b-341a; BK V, 369c-370a; BK VI, 373c-375b; 383b-d; BK VII,

(6. The selection of the best men for public office: the aristocratic theory of representation in modern constitutional government.)

390b-391b / *Statesman,* 598b-604b; 608c-d / *Laws,* BK VI, 697a-705c passim; BK XII, 786b-787b; 794b-799a,c esp 796d-798b / *Seventh Letter,* 807a-b

9 ARISTOTLE: *Politics,* BK II, CH 9 [1270^{b}7-1271^{a}17] 466d-467b; CH 11 [1272^{b}33-1273^{a}2] 469b-c; [1273^{a}22-^{b}7] 469d-470a; BK III, CH 4 [1277^{a}13-23] 474a-b; CH 5 [1278^{a}40-^{b}5] 475d; CH 7 [1279^{a}24-^{b}4] 476c-d; CH 10-13 478d-483a; CH 15 [1286^{a}22-^{b}14] 484c-485a; CH 16 [1287^{b}12-14] 486a; CH 18 487a,c; BK IV, CH 7 [1293^{b}2-21] 493a-b; CH 8 [1294^{a}9-24] 493d-494a; CH 14 [1298^{b}5-10] 499a; CH 15 [1300^{a}9-^{b}4] 500d-501b; BK V, CH 8 [1308^{b}31-1309^{a}10] 511a-b; CH 9 [1309^{a}33-^{b}13] 511c-d; BK VI, CH 4 [1318^{b}21-1319^{a}4] 522b-c; BK VII, CH 9 [1328^{b}33-1329^{a}17] 533b-c / *Rhetoric,* BK I, CH 8 [1365^{b}32-39] 608a-b

14 PLUTARCH: *Lycurgus,* 45c-d / *Lysander,* 365a-366a / *Lysander-Sulla,* 387d-388a

15 TACITUS: *Annals,* BK XI, 105d-107b

20 AQUINAS: *Summa Theologica,* PART I-II, Q 92, A I, REP 3 213c-214c; Q 105, A I, ANS and REP 1-2 307d-309d

23 HOBBES: *Leviathan,* PART II, 136b

25 MONTAIGNE: *Essays,* 364b-365a; 411a-d; 452a-d

27 SHAKESPEARE: *Coriolanus,* ACT I, SC I [90-166] 352b-353a; ACT II 361a-369a

35 LOCKE: *Civil Government,* CH VII, SECT 94, 46b; CH VIII, SECT 105-112 48c-51b passim

36 SWIFT: *Gulliver,* PART I, 28b-29a; PART II, 73a-b

38 MONTESQUIEU: *Spirit of Laws,* BK II, 4d-5a; BK III, 10c-11a; BK V, 21d-22c; BK XI, 71a-72b

38 ROUSSEAU: *Social Contract,* BK III, 412b-c; BK IV, 427a-d

39 SMITH: *Wealth of Nations,* BK IV, 269d-271d; BK V, 309c-311c

40 GIBBON: *Decline and Fall,* 61d-62a

43 CONSTITUTION OF THE U.S.: ARTICLE I, SECT 2 [11-16] 11b; SECT 3 [67-72] 12a; ARTICLE II, SECT I 14b-15a; SECT 2 [424-439] 15b; AMENDMENTS, XII 18a-c

43 FEDERALIST: NUMBER 3, 33d-34a; NUMBER 10, 51d-53a; NUMBER 28, 98a; NUMBER 35, 113a-114b; NUMBER 52-63 165a-195b passim, esp NUMBER 57, 176d-177a; NUMBER 68 205b-207a; NUMBER 76-77, 225a-229b

43 MILL: *Liberty,* 290d-291a; 320c-322a / *Representative Government,* 336b-337a; 338a-b; 341d-424c passim, esp 363b-366a, 384a-387d; 439d-442a

44 BOSWELL: *Johnson,* 125c-d; 141a; 178b-c; 191c

46 HEGEL: *Philosophy of Right,* PART III, par 279, 94b-c; par 291-295 97d-99a; par 308 102c-

103a; ADDITIONS, 169 145d; 182 148c-d / *Philosophy of History,* PART II, 277c-d; PART IV, 368b-d

51 TOLSTOY: *War and Peace,* BK VI, 241c-242b

7. Historic and poetic exemplifications of aristocracy

6 HERODOTUS: *History,* BK III, 107c-108d; BK V, 160d-161a

6 THUCYDIDES: *Peloponnesian War,* BK I, 355a-356a; BK II, 409a; BK III, 434c-438b passim; BK IV, 458d-459c; 463a-b; 465c; 478d-479b; BK V, 482d-483a; BK VI, 533a-c; BK VIII, 568d-569a; 579c-590c

9 ARISTOTLE: *Politics,* BK II, CH 9 [1270^{b}7-34] 466d-467a; BK V, CH 7 [1307^{a}27-^{b}24] 509b-d / *Athenian Constitution,* CH I-41 553a-572a passim, esp CH 23-26 563c-565a

14 PLUTARCH: *Theseus,* 9a-d / *Romulus,* 20c-21a / *Lycurgus* 32a-48d / *Pericles* 121a-141a,c esp 126d-127a / *Coriolanus,* 174b,d-184a / *Aristides,* 263c-266a

15 TACITUS: *Annals,* BK I, 1b-2a; 3a-b; BK II, 32b-d; 34a-c; BK IV, 65a-c; 72a-b; BK VI, 97b; BK XI, 105d-107b / *Histories,* BK I, 193c-194a; 212a-b

18 AUGUSTINE: *City of God,* BK V, CH 12, 218d-219b

21 DANTE: *Divine Comedy,* PURGATORY, VIII [112-139] 65c-d

22 CHAUCER: *Tale of Wife of Bath* [6701-6758] 274b-275b

25 MONTAIGNE: *Essays,* 181d-183c

27 SHAKESPEARE: *Troilus and Cressida,* ACT I, SC III [33-54] 108c / *All's Well That Ends Well,* ACT II, SC III [115-151] 152c-153a / *Coriolanus* 351a-392a,c esp ACT I, SC I [1-47] 351a-d, ACT II, SC I [1-106] 361a-362a

36 SWIFT: *Gulliver,* PART II, 73a-76b; PART IV, 157a-158b

38 MONTESQUIEU: *Spirit of Laws,* BK II, 6b-7c; BK V, 23a-25a; BK VII, 45b-c; BK XI, 76c-84c

38 ROUSSEAU: *Political Economy,* 369c-d / *Social Contract,* BK III, 418c-d [fn 2]

39 SMITH: *Wealth of Nations,* BK III, 165b-181a,c passim

40 GIBBON: *Decline and Fall,* 61d-62a

41 GIBBON: *Decline and Fall,* 71d-73c passim; 217d-219a; 387d-390b passim; 427d-428a; 452d-456a,c esp 452d-453a,c, 453a-b; 570d; 574b-582c; 588a-589a

43 FEDERALIST: NUMBER 17, 70a-d

43 MILL: *Representative Government,* 363d-364d

46 HEGEL: *Philosophy of History,* PART II, 277c-d; PART III, 285b-d; 310a-c; PART IV, 368b-d

50 MARX: *Capital,* 355d-364a esp 356a-357a, 359a-c

50 MARX-ENGELS: *Communist Manifesto,* 419b,d; 420b-c; 423d-424b; 429c-430b

51 TOLSTOY: *War and Peace,* BK IX, 384c-388a,c

CROSS-REFERENCES

For: The general theory of the forms of government, *see* GOVERNMENT 2–2e.

Other chapters on particular forms of government, *see* CONSTITUTION; DEMOCRACY; MONARCHY; OLIGARCHY; TYRANNY; and for the conception of the ideal state, *see* STATE 6–6b.

The comparison of aristocratic with democratic theories of education, *see* EDUCATION 8d.

Discussions of the role of virtue in political theory, in relation to citizenship and public office, *see* CITIZEN 5; VIRTUE AND VICE 7–7d.

Another discussion of the theory of representation, *see* CONSTITUTION 9–9b.

The role of honor in the organization of the state, and the theory of timocracy, *see* HONOR 4a.

ADDITIONAL READINGS

Listed below are works not included in *Great Books of the Western World*, but relevant to the idea and topics with which this chapter deals. These works are divided into two groups:

I. Works by authors represented in this collection.
II. Works by authors not represented in this collection.

For the date, place, and other facts concerning the publication of the works cited, consult the Bibliography of Additional Readings which follows the last chapter of *The Great Ideas*.

I.

DANTE. *Convivio(The Banquet),* FOURTH TREATISE, CH 10–14

SPINOZA. *Tractatus Politicus (Political Treatise),* CH 8–10

II.

Völsung Saga

SPENSER. *The Faerie Queene*

CAMPANELLA. *A Discourse Touching the Spanish Monarchy*

FILMER. *Patriarcha*

HARRINGTON. *Oceana*

SÉVIGNÉ. *Letters*

A. SIDNEY. *Discourses Concerning Government*

MILLAR. *Observations Concerning the Distinction of Ranks in Society*

PAINE. *Common Sense*

J. ADAMS. *A Defense of the Constitutions of Government of the United States of America*

JEFFERSON. *Notes on the State of Virginia*

SIEYÈS. *An Essay on Privileges*

GODWIN. *An Enquiry Concerning Political Justice,* BK V, CH 10–11, 13

BURKE. *An Appeal from the New to the Old Whigs*

——. *Letter to Sir Hercules Langrishe*

——. *Letter to a Noble Lord*

AUSTEN. *Pride and Prejudice*

J. MILL. *An Essay on Government,* III–V

STENDHAL. *The Red and the Black*

BALZAC. *Gobseck*

TOCQUEVILLE. *Democracy in America*

THACKERAY. *Vanity Fair*

GOBINEAU. *The Inequality of Human Races*

EMERSON. "Aristocracy," in *English Traits*

MONTALEMBERT. *On Constitutional Liberty*

ARNOLD. *Culture and Anarchy*

WHITMAN. *Democratic Vistas*

RENAN. *The Future of Science*

——. *Philosophical Dialogues*

H. JAMES. *The American*

T. H. HUXLEY. *Methods and Results,* VI–VII

IBSEN. *An Enemy of the People*

NIETZSCHE. *Thus Spake Zarathustra*

MOSCA. *The Ruling Class*

MALLOCK. *Social Equality*

——. *Aristocracy and Evolution*

T. VEBLEN. *The Theory of the Leisure Class*

SANTAYANA. *Reason in Society,* CH 4

BOUGLÉ. *Essais sur le régime des castes*

SOREL. *Reflexions on Violence*

WENDELL. *The Privileged Classes*

SHAW. *Socialism and Superior Brains*

WELLS. *The New Machiavelli*

WEBER. *Essays in Sociology,* PART IV

PONSONBY. *The Decline of Aristocracy*

P. E. MORE. *Aristocracy and Justice*

PARETO. *The Mind and Society*

BRYCE. *Modern Democracies,* PART I, CH 7; PART III, CH 75

DEWEY. *The Public and Its Problems*

MAIRET. *Aristocracy and the Meaning of Class Rule*

TAWNEY. *Equality*

BERGSON. *Two Sources of Morality and Religion,* CH 1, pp 62–82

J. B. S. HALDANE. *The Inequality of Man*

NOCK. *The Theory of Education in the United States*

MADARIAGA. *Anarchy or Hierarchy*

LANDTMAN. *The Origin of the Inequality of the Social Classes*

T.S. ELIOT. *Notes Towards the Definition of Culture*

Chapter 4: ART

INTRODUCTION

THE word "art" has a range of meanings which may be obscured by the current disposition to use the word in an extremely restricted sense. In contemporary thought, art is most readily associated with beauty; yet its historic connections with utility and knowledge are probably more intimate and pervasive.

The prevalent popular association reflects a tendency in the 19th century to annex the theory of art to aesthetics. This naturally led to the identification of art with one kind of art —the so-called "fine arts," "beaux arts" or "Schöne Künste" (arts of the beautiful). The contraction of meaning has gone so far that the word "art" sometimes signifies one group of the fine arts—painting and sculpture—as in the common phrase "literature, music, and the fine arts." This restricted usage has become so customary that we ordinarily refer to a museum of art or to an art exhibit in a manner which seems to assume that the word "art" is exclusively the name for something which can be hung on a wall or placed on a pedestal.

A moment's thought will, of course, correct the assumption. We are not unfamiliar with the conception of medicine and teaching as arts. We are acquainted with such phrases as "the industrial arts" and "arts and crafts" in which the reference is to the production of useful things. Our discussions of liberal education should require us to consider the liberal arts which, however defined or enumerated, are supposed to constitute skills of mind. We recognize that "art" is the root of "artisan" as well as "artist." We thus discern the presence of skill in even the lowest forms of productive labor. Seeing it also as the root of "artifice" and "artificial," we realize that art is distinguished from and sometimes even opposed to nature.

The ancient and traditional meanings are all present in our daily vocabulary. In our thought the first connotation of "art" is fine art; in the thought of all previous eras the useful arts came first. As late as the end of the 18th century, Adam Smith follows the traditional usage which begins with Plato when, in referring to the production of a woolen coat, he says: "The shepherd, the sorter of the wool, the wool-comber or carder, the dyer, the scribbler, the spinner, the weaver, the fuller, the dresser, with many others, must all join their different arts in order to complete even this homely production."

In the first great conversation on art—that presented in the Platonic dialogues—we find useful techniques and everyday skills typifying art, by reference to which all other skills are analyzed. Even when Socrates analyzes the art of the rhetorician, as in the *Gorgias*, he constantly turns to the productions of the cobbler and the weaver and to the procedures of the husbandman and the physician. If the liberal arts are praised as highest, because the logician or rhetorician works in the medium of the soul rather than in matter, they are called arts "only in a manner of speaking" and by comparison with the fundamental arts which handle physical material.

The Promethean gift of fire to men, which raised them from a brutish existence, carried with it various techniques for mastering matter —the basic useful arts. Lucretius, writing in a line that goes from Homer through Thucydides and Plato to Bacon, Adam Smith, and Rousseau, attributes the progress of civilization and the difference between civilized and primitive society to the development of the arts and sciences. "Ships and tillage, walls, laws, arms, roads, dress, and all such like things, all the prizes, all the elegancies too of life without exception, poems, pictures, and the chiselling of fine-wrought statues, all these things practiced together with the acquired knowledge of the untiring mind taught men by slow degrees as they advanced on the way step by step."

At the beginning of this progress Lucretius places man's discovery of the arts of metal-working, domesticating animals, and cultivating the soil. "Metallurgy and agriculture," says Rousseau, "were the two arts which produced this great revolution"—the advance from primitive to civilized life. The fine arts and the speculative sciences come last, not first, in the progress of civilization.

The fine arts and the speculative sciences complete human life. They are not necessary —except perhaps for the good life. They are the dedication of human leisure and its best fruit. The leisure without which they neither could come into being nor prosper is found for man and fostered by the work of the useful arts. Aristotle tells us that is "why the mathematical arts were founded in Egypt; for there the priestly caste was allowed to be at leisure."

THERE IS ANOTHER ambiguity in the reference of the word "art." Sometimes we use it to name the effects produced by human workmanship. We elliptically refer to *works of art* as art. Sometimes we use it to signify the cause of the things produced by human work—that skill of mind which directs the hand in its manipulation of matter. Art is both in the artist and in the work of art—in the one as *cause*, in the other as *effect*. What is effected is a certain ennoblement of matter, a transformation produced not merely by the hand of man, but by his thought or knowledge.

The more generic meaning of art seems to be that of art as cause rather than as effect. There are many spheres of art in which no tangible product results, as in navigation or military strategy. We might, of course, call a landfall or a victory a work of art, but we tend rather to speak of the art of the navigator or the general. So, too, in medicine and teaching, we look upon the health or knowledge which results from healing or teaching as natural. We do not find art in them, but rather in the skill of the healer or teacher who has helped

to produce that result. Hence even in the case of the shoe or the statue, art seems to be primarily in the mind and work of the cobbler or sculptor and only derivatively in the objects produced.

Aristotle, in defining art as a "capacity to make, involving a true course of reasoning," identifies it with making as distinct from doing and knowing. Though art, like science and moral action, belongs to the mind and involves experience and learning, imagination and thought, it is distinct from both in aiming at production, in being knowledge of *how* to make something or to obtain a desired effect. Science, on the other hand, is knowledge *that* something is the case, or that a thing has a certain nature. Knowledge is sometimes identified with science, to the exclusion of art or skill; but we depart from this narrow notion whenever we recognize that skill consists in *knowing how* to make something.

"Even in speculative matters," writes Aquinas, "there is something by way of work; *e.g.*, the making of a syllogism, or a fitting speech, or the work of counting or measuring. Hence whatever habits are ordained to suchlike works of the speculative reason, are, by a kind of comparison, called arts indeed, but *liberal* arts, in order to distinguish them from those arts which are ordained to works done by the body, which arts are, in a fashion, servile, inasmuch as the body is in servile subjection to the soul, and man as regards his soul is free. On the other hand, those sciences which are not ordained to any suchlike work, are called sciences simply, and not arts."

The discussion of medicine in the great books throws light on the relation of art and science, in their origin as well as their development. Hippocrates writes of medicine as both an art and a science. In his treatise on *Ancient Medicine*, he says, "It appears to me necessary to every physician to be skilled in nature, and strive to know—if he would wish to perform his duties —what man is in relation to the articles of food and drink, and to his other occupations, and what are the effects of each of them on every one. And it is not enough to know simply that cheese is a bad article of food, as disagreeing with whoever eats of it to satiety, but what sort of disturbance it creates, and wherefore,

and with what principle in man it disagrees. ...
Whoever does not know what effect these
things produce upon a man, cannot know the
consequences which result from them, nor how
to apply them." As a science, medicine involves knowledge of the causes of disease, the
different kinds of diseases, and their characteristic courses. Without such knowledge, diagnosis, prognosis, and therapy would be a
matter of guesswork—of *chance*, as Hippocrates
says—or at best the application of rule-of-
thumb in the light of past experience.

But the scientific knowledge does not by itself make a man a healer, a practitioner of medicine. The practice of medicine requires art in
addition to science—art based on science, but
going beyond science in formulating *general*
rules for the guidance of practice in *particular*
cases. The habit of proceeding according to
rules derived from science distinguishes for
Galen the artist in medicine from the mere
empiric. The antithesis of artist and empiric
—suggesting the contrast between operation
by tested rule and operation by trial and
error—parallels the antithesis between scientist
and man of opinion.

IT HAS SELDOM, if ever, been suggested that an
art can be originally discovered or developed
apart from some science of the subject matter
with which the art deals. This does not mean
that an individual cannot acquire the habit of
an art without being taught the relevant scientific knowledge. An art can be learned by practice; skill can be formed by repeated acts. But
the teacher of an art cannot direct the learning
without setting rules for his pupils to follow;
and if the truth or intelligibility of the rules
is questioned, the answers will come from the
science underlying the art.

According to Kant, "every art presupposes
rules which are laid down as the foundation
which first enables a product if it is to be called
one of art, to be represented as possible." In
the case of "fine art," which he distinguishes
from other kinds of art as being the product of
"genius," Kant claims that it arises only from
"a talent for producing that for which no definite
rule can be given." Yet he maintains that a
"rule" is still at its basis and may be "gathered
from the performance, *i.e.*, from the product,

which others may use to put their own talent
to the test."

Granting that there is no art without science,
is the reverse true, and is science possible without art? The question has two meanings. First,
are there arts peculiarly indispensable to the
development of science? Second, does every
science generate a correlative art and through
it work productively?

Traditionally, the liberal arts have been considered indispensable to science. This has been
held to be particularly true of logic. Because
they were intended to serve as the instrument
or *the art* for all the sciences, Aristotle's logical
treatises, which constitute the first systematic
treatment of the subject, deserve the title *Organon* which they traditionally carry. Bacon's
Novum Organum was in one sense an effort to
supply a new logic or art for science, and to
institute a renovation of the sciences by the
experimental method.

As an art, logic consists of rules for the conduct of the mind in the processes of inquiry,
inference, definition, and demonstration, by
which sciences are constructed. Scientific method is, in short, the art of getting scientific
knowledge. In the experimental sciences, there
are auxiliary arts—arts controlling the instruments or apparatus employed in experimentation. The experiment itself is a work of art,
combining many techniques and using many
products of art: the water-clock, the inclined
plane, and the pendulum of Galileo; the prisms,
mirrors, and lenses of Newton.

The second question—whether all sciences
have related arts and through them productive
power—raises one of the great issues about the
nature of scientific knowledge, discussed in the
chapters on PHILOSOPHY and SCIENCE.

For Francis Bacon, and to some extent Descartes, art is the necessary consequence of science. At the beginning of the *Novum Organum*,
Bacon declares that "knowledge and human
power are synonymous since the ignorance of
the cause frustrates the effect; for nature is only
subdued by submission, and that which in contemplative philosophy corresponds with the
cause, in practical science becomes the rule."
The distinction Bacon makes here between the
speculative and practical parts of knowledge
corresponds to the distinction between science

and art, or as we sometimes say, "pure and applied science." He opposes their divorce from one another. If science is the indispensable foundation of art and consists in a knowledge of causes, art in Bacon's view is the whole fruit of science, for it applies that knowledge to the production of effects.

His theory of science and his new method for its development are directed to the establishment of man's "empire over creation" which "is founded on the arts and sciences alone." Just as the present state of the arts accounts for "the immense difference between men's lives in the most polished countries of Europe, and in any wild and barbarous region of the new Indies," so further advances in science promise the untold power of new inventions and techniques.

On Bacon's view, not only the value, but even the validity, of scientific knowledge is to be measured by its productivity. A useless natural science—a science of nature which cannot be used to control nature—is unthinkable. With the exception of mathematics, every science has its appropriate magic or special productive power. Even metaphysics, in Bacon's conception of it, has its "true natural magic, which is that great liberty and latitude of operation which dependeth upon the knowledge of forms."

The opposite answer to the question about science and art is given by Plato, Aristotle, and others who distinguish between speculative and productive sciences. They differ from Bacon on the verbal level by using the word "practical" for those sciences which concern moral and political action rather than the production of effects. The sciences Bacon calls "practical" they call "productive," but under either name these are the sciences of making rather than doing—sciences which belong in the sphere of art rather than prudence. But the significant difference lies in the evaluation of the purely speculative sciences which consist in knowledge for its own sake, divorced from art and morals, or from the utilities of production and the necessities of action.

In tracing the history of the sciences, Aristotle notes that those men who first found the useful arts were thought wise and superior. "But as more arts were invented, and some were

directed to the necessities of life, others to recreation, the inventors of the latter were naturally always regarded as wiser than the inventors of the former, because their branches did not aim at utility. Hence, when all such inventions were already established, the sciences which do not aim at giving pleasure or at the necessities of life were discovered, and first in the places where men first began to have leisure. . . . So that the man of experience is thought to be wiser than the possessors of any sense-perception whatever, the artist wiser than the man of experience, the master-worker than the mechanic, and the theoretical kinds of knowledge to be more of the nature of Wisdom than the productive." That the theoretic sciences are useless, in the sense of not providing men with the necessities or pleasures of life, is a mark of their superiority. They give what is better than such utility—the insight and understanding which constitute wisdom.

The Baconian reply condemns the conception that there can be knowledge which is merely contemplation of the truth. It announces the revolution which, for John Dewey, ushered in the modern world. The pragmatic theory of knowledge had its origin in a conception of science at every point fused with art.

THE ANCIENTS, trying to understand the natural phenomena of change and generation, found that the processes of artistic production provided them with an analytic model. Through understanding how he himself worked in making things, man might come to know how nature worked.

When a man makes a house or a statue, he transforms matter. Changes in shape and position occur. The plan or idea in the artist's mind comes, through his manipulation of matter, to be embodied and realized objectively. To the ancients a number of different causes or factors seemed to be involved in every artistic production—material to be worked on; the activity of the artist at work; the form in his mind which he sought to impose on the matter, thus transforming it; and the purpose which motivated his effort.

In the medical tradition from Aristotle through Galen to Harvey, there is constant emphasis upon the artistic activity of nature.

Galen continually argues against those who do not conceive Nature as an artist. Harvey consciously compares the activity of nature in biological generation to that of an artist. "Like a potter she first divides her material, and then indicates the head and trunk and extremities; like a painter, she first sketches the parts in outline, and then fills them in with colours; or like the ship-builder, who first lays down his keel by way of foundation, and upon this raises the ribs and roof or deck: even as he builds his vessel does nature fashion the trunk of the body and add the extremities."

Of all natural changes, the one most closely resembling artistic production appears to be generation, especially the production of living things by living things. In both cases, a new individual seems to come into being. But upon further examination, artistic production and natural generation reveal significant differences —differences which divide nature from art.

Aquinas considers both and distinguishes them in his analysis of divine causation. In things not generated by chance, he points out that there are two different ways in which the form that is in the agent is passed on to another being. "In some agents the form of the thing to be made pre-exists according to its natural being, as in those that act by their nature; as a man generates a man, or fire generates fire. Whereas in other agents the form of the thing to be made pre-exists according to intelligible being, as in those that act by the intellect; and thus the likeness of a house pre-exists in the mind of the builder. And this may be called the idea of the house, since the builder intends to build his house like to the form conceived in his mind."

Thus in biological procreation the progeny have the form of their parents—a rabbit producing a rabbit, a horse, a horse. But in artistic production, the product has, not the form of the artist, but the form he has conceived in his mind and which he seeks to objectify. Furthermore, in generation, and in other natural changes as well, the matter which undergoes change seems to have in itself a tendency to become what it changes into, as for example the acorn naturally tends to become an oak, whereas the oaken wood does not have in itself any tendency to become a chair or a bed. The material the artist works on is entirely passive with respect to the change he wishes to produce. The artistic result is in this sense entirely of his making.

The realm of art, or of the artificial, is then opposed to the natural and differentiated from it. Kant, for whom art is distinguished from nature "as making is from acting or operating in general," claims that "by right, it is only production through freedom, i.e., through an act of will that places reason at the basis of its action, that should be termed art." Consequently, art is that which would not have come into being without human intervention. The man-made object is produced by man, not in any way, but specifically by his intelligence, by the reason which makes him free.

Animals other than man are apparently productive, but the question is whether they can be called "artists." "A spider conducts operations that resemble those of a weaver, and a bee puts to shame many an architect in the construction of her cells. But," according to Marx, "what distinguishes the worst architect from the best of bees is this, that the architect raises his structure in imagination before he erects it in reality. At the end of every labour-process, we get a result that already existed in the imagination of the labourer at its commencement. He not only effects a change of form in the material on which he works, but he also realizes a purpose of his own that gives the law to his modus operandi, and to which he must subordinate his will."

As indicated in the chapter on ANIMAL, some writers, like Montaigne, attribute the productivity of animals to reason rather than to instinct. Art then ceases to be one of man's distinctions from the brutes. But if man alone has reason, and if the productions of art are works of reason, then those who refer to animals as artists speak metaphorically, on the basis of what Kant calls "an analogy with art . . . As soon as we call to mind," he continues, "that no rational deliberation forms the basis of their labor, we see at once that it is a product of their nature (of instinct), and it is only to their Creator that we ascribe it as art."

This in turn leads to the question whether nature itself is a work of art. "Let me suppose," the Eleatic Stranger says in the Sophist, "that things which are said to be made by nature are the work of divine art, and that things which are made by man out of these are the work of human art. And so there are two kinds of making and production, the one human and the other divine."

If we suppose that the things of nature are originally made by a divine mind, how does their production differ from the work of human artists, or from biological generation? One answer, given in Plato's *Timaeus*, conceives the original production of things as a fashioning of primordial matter in the patterns set by the eternal archetypes or ideas. In consequence, the divine work would be more like human artistry than either would be like natural reproduction. The emanation of the world from the One, according to Plotinus, and the production of things out of the substance of God in Spinoza's theory, appear, on the other hand, to be more closely analogous to natural generation than to art.

Both analogies—of creation with art and with generation—are dismissed as false by Christian theologians. God's making is *absolutely* creative. It presupposes no matter to be formed; nor do things issue forth from God's own substance, but out of nothing.

Thus Augustine asks: "How didst Thou *make the heaven and the earth*?" And he answers: "It was not as a human artificer, forming one body from another, according to the discretion of his mind, which can in some way invest with such a form, as it seeth in itself by its inward eye ... Verily, neither in the heaven, nor in the earth, didst Thou *make heaven and earth*; nor in the air, or waters, seeing these also belong to the heaven and the earth; nor in the whole world didst Thou make the whole world; because there was no place where to make it, before it was made, that it might be . . . For what is, but because Thou art? Therefore *Thou spakest, and they were made, and in Thy Word Thou madest them*." According to this view, human art cannot be called creative, and God cannot be called an artist, except metaphorically.

The issue concerning various theories of creation, or of the origin of the universe, is discussed in the chapter on WORLD. But here we must observe that, according to the view we take of the similitude between human and divine workmanship, the line we are able to draw between the realms of art and nature becomes shadowy or sharp.

THE DISCUSSIONS OF ART in the great books afford materials from which a systematic classification of the arts might be constructed, but only fragments of such a classification are ever explicitly presented.

For example, the seven liberal arts are enumerated by various authors, but their distinction from other arts, and their ordered relation to one another, do not receive full explication. There is no treatment of grammar, rhetoric, and logic (or dialectic) to parallel Plato's consideration of arithmetic, geometry, music, and astronomy in the *Republic*; nor is there any analysis of the relation of the first three arts to the other four—traditionally organized as the *trivium* and the *quadrivium*.

However, in Augustine's work *On Christian Doctrine* we have a discussion of these arts as they are ordered to the study of theology. That orientation of the liberal arts is also the theme of Bonaventura's *Reduction of the Arts to Theology*. Quite apart from the problem of how they are ordered to one another, particular liberal arts receive so rich and varied a discussion in the tradition of the great books that the consideration of them must be distributed among a number of chapters, such as LOGIC, RHETORIC, LANGUAGE (for the discussion of grammar), and MATHEMATICS.

The principles of classification of the fine arts are laid down by Kant from "the analogy which art bears to the mode of expression of which men avail themselves in speech, with a view to communicating themselves to one another as completely as possible." Since such expression "consists in word, gesture, and tone," he finds three corresponding fine arts: "the art of speech, formative art, and the art of the play of sensations." In these terms he analyzes rhetoric and poetry, sculpture, architecture, painting and landscape gardening, and music.

A different principle of division is indicated in the opening chapters of Aristotle's *Poetics*. The principle that all art imitates nature suggests the possibility of distinguishing and relating the various arts according to their char-

acteristic differences *as imitations*—by reference to the *object* imitated and to the *medium*
and *manner* in which it is imitated by the poet,
sculptor or painter, and musician. "Color and
form," Aristotle writes, "are used as means by
some . . . who imitate and portray many things
by their aid, and the voice is used by others. . . .
Rhythm alone, without harmony, is the means
in the dancer's imitations. . . . There is, further,
an art which imitates by language alone, without harmony, in prose or in verse." Aristotle's
treatise deals mainly with this art—poetry; it
does not develop for the other fine arts the
analysis it suggests.

Aristotle's principle also suggests questions
about the useful arts. Are such arts as shoe-
making and house-building imitations of nature in the same sense as poetry and music?
Does the way in which the farmer, the physician, and the teacher imitate nature distinguish
these three arts from the way in which a statue
is an imitation, or poem, or a house?

The Aristotelian dictum about art imitating
nature has, of course, been as frequently challenged as approved. Apart from the issue of
its truth, the theory of art as imitation poses
many questions which Aristotle left unanswered.
If there are answers in the great books, they
are there by implication rather than by statement.

THE MOST FAMILIAR distinction between arts—
that between the useful and the fine—is also the
one most frequently made in modern discussion. The criterion of the distinction needs little
explanation. Some of man's productions are
intended to be used; others to be contemplated
or enjoyed. To describe them in terms of imitation, the products of the useful arts must be
said to imitate a natural function (the shoe, for
example, the protective function of calloused
skin). The imitation merely indicates the use,
and it is the use which counts. But in the products of the fine arts, the imitation of the form,
quality, or other aspect of a natural object is
considered to be the source of pleasure.

The least familiar distinction among the arts
is implied in any thorough discussion, yet its
divisions are seldom, if ever, named. Within
the sphere of useful art, some arts work toward
a result which can hardly be regarded as an
artificial product. Fruits and grains would grow
without the intervention of the farmer, yet
the farmer helps them to grow more abundantly
and regularly. Health and knowledge are
natural effects, even though the arts of medicine and teaching may aid in their production.

These arts, more fully discussed in the chapters on MEDICINE and EDUCATION, stand in
sharp contrast to those skills whereby man produces the useful things which, but for man's
work, would be totally lacking. In the one case,
it is the artist's activity itself which imitates
or cooperates with nature's manner of working;
in the other, the things which the artist makes
by operating on passive materials supplied by
nature imitate natural forms or functions.

For the most part, the industrial arts are of
the second sort. They transform dead matter
into commodities or tools. The arts which cooperate with nature usually work with living
matter, as in agriculture, medicine, and teaching. The distinction seems warranted and clear.
Yet it is cut across by Adam Smith's division
of labor into productive and non-productive.
The work of agriculture is associated with industry in the production of wealth, but whatever other use they may have, physicians and
teachers, according to Smith, do not directly
augment the wealth of nations.

If to the foregoing we add the division of the
arts into liberal and servile, the major traditional distinctions are covered. This last division had its origin in the recognition that
some arts, like sculpture and carpentry, could
not effect their products except by shaping
matter, whereas some arts, like poetry or logic,
were free from matter, at least in the sense that
they worked productively in symbolic mediums. But by other principles of classification,
poetry and sculpture are separated from logic
and carpentry, as fine from useful art. Logic,
along with grammar, rhetoric, and the mathematical arts, is separated from poetry and
sculpture, as liberal from fine art. When the
word "liberal" is used to state this last distinction, its meaning narrows. It signifies only the
speculative arts, or arts concerned with processes of thinking and knowing.

The adequacy of any classification, and the
intelligibility of its principles, must stand the
test of questions about particular arts. The

great books frequently discuss the arts of animal husbandry and navigation, the arts of cooking and hunting, the arts of war and government. Each raises a question about the nature of art in general, and challenges any analysis of the arts to classify them and explain their peculiarities.

THERE ARE TWO OTHER major issues which have been debated mainly with respect to the fine arts.

One, already mentioned, concerns the imitative character of art. The opponents of imitation do not deny that there may be some perceptible resemblance between a work of art and a natural object. A drama may remind us of human actions we have experienced; music may simulate the tonal qualities and rhythms of the human voice registering the course of the emotions. Nevertheless, the motivation of artistic creation lies deeper, it is said, than a desire to imitate nature, or to find some pleasure in such resemblances.

According to Tolstoy, the arts serve primarily as a medium of spiritual communication, helping to create the ties of human brotherhood. According to Freud, it is emotion or subconscious expression, rather than imitation or communication, which is the deepest spring of art; the poet or artist "forces us to become aware of our inner selves in which the same impulses are still extant even though they are suppressed." Freud's theory of sublimation of emotion or desire through art seems to connect with Aristotle's theory of emotional catharsis or purgation. But Freud is attempting to account for the origin of art, and Aristotle is trying to describe an effect proper to its enjoyment.

The theories of communication, expression, or imitation, attempt to explain art, or at least its motivation. But there is also a conception of art which, foregoing explanation, leaves it a mystery—the spontaneous product of inspiration, of a divine madness, the work of unfathomable genius. We encounter this notion first, but not last, in Plato's *Ion*.

THE OTHER MAJOR controversy concerns the regulation of the arts by the state for human welfare and the public good.

Here, as before, the fine arts (chiefly poetry and music) have been the focus of the debate. It is worth noting, however, that a parallel problem of political regulation occurs in the sphere of the industrial arts. On the question of state control over the production and distribution of wealth, Smith and Marx represent extreme opposites, as Milton and Plato are poles apart on the question of the state's right to censor the artist's work. In this debate, Aristotle stands on Plato's side in many particulars, and Mill with Milton.

The problem of censorship or political regulation of the fine arts presupposes some prior questions. Plato argues in the *Republic* that all poetry but "hymns to the gods and praises of famous men" must be banned from the State; "for if you go beyond this and allow the honeyed muse to enter, either in epic or lyric verse, not law and the reason of mankind, which by common consent have ever been deemed the best, but pleasure and pain will be the rulers in our State." Such a view presupposes a certain theory of the fine arts and of their influence on the citizens and the whole character of the community. Yet because both Plato and Aristotle judge that influence to be far from negligible, they do not see any reason in individual liberty for the state to refrain from interfering with the rights of the artist for the greater good of the community.

To Milton and Mill, the measure of the artist's influence does not affect the question of the freedom of the arts from political or ecclesiastical interference. While admitting the need for protecting the interests of peace and public safety, Milton demands: "Give me the liberty to know, to utter, and to argue freely according to conscience, above all liberties." The issue for them is entirely one of liberty. They espouse the cause of freedom—for the artist to express or communicate his work and for the community to receive from him whatever he has to offer.

OUTLINE OF TOPICS

REFERENCES

To find the passages cited, use the numbers in heavy type, which are the volume and page numbers of the passages referred to. For example, in 4 HOMER: *Iliad*, BK II [265-283] 12d, the number 4 is the number of the volume in the set; the number 12d indicates that the passage is in section d of page 12.

PAGE SECTIONS: When the text is printed in one column, the letters a and b refer to the upper and lower halves of the page. For example, in 53 JAMES: *Psychology*, 116a-119b, the passage begins in the upper half of page 116 and ends in the lower half of page 119. When the text is printed in two columns, the letters a and b refer to the upper and lower halves of the left-hand side of the page, the letters c and d to the upper and lower halves of the right-hand side of the page. For example, in 7 PLATO: *Symposium*, 163b-164c, the passage begins in the lower half of the left-hand side of page 163 and ends in the upper half of the right-hand side of page 164

AUTHOR'S DIVISIONS: One or more of the main divisions of a work (such as PART, BK, CH, SECT) are sometimes included in the reference; line numbers, in brackets, are given in certain cases; *e.g.*, *Iliad*, BK II [265-283] 12d.

BIBLE REFERENCES: The references are to book, chapter, and verse. When the King James and Douay versions differ in title of books or in the numbering of chapters or verses, the King James version is cited first and the Douay, indicated by a (*D*), follows; *e.g.*, OLD TESTAMENT: *Nehemiah*, 7:45—(*D*) II *Esdras*, 7:46.

SYMBOLS: The abbreviation "esp" calls the reader's attention to one or more especially relevant parts of a whole reference; "passim" signifies that the topic is discussed intermittently rather than continuously in the work or passage cited.

For additional information concerning the style of the references, see the Explanation of Reference Style; for general guidance in the use of *The Great Ideas*, consult the Preface.

1. The generic notion of art: skill of mind in making

7 PLATO: *Protagoras*, 44a-45b / *Phaedrus*, 136b; 138c-139a / *Ion*, 145d-146c / *Symposium*, 160c-d; 164d / *Gorgias*, 260a-262a; 280d-283c / *Republic*, BK I, 302c-306a; 307a-308a; BK III, 333b-d; BK X, 427c-434c / *Statesman*, 593d-595a / *Philebus*, 633a-c / *Laws*, BK IV, 679a-c

8 ARISTOTLE: *Physics*, BK II, CH I [192^{b}23-32] 268d-269a; [193^{b}12-16] 269d-270a; CH 8 [199^{b}26-31] 277a / *Metaphysics*, BK I, CH I [980^{b}25-981^{b}34] 499b-500b; BK VII, CH 7 [1032^{a}25-^{b}29] 555b-d; BK IX, CH 2 571c-572a; CH 5 573a-c; CH 7 [1048^{b}35-1049^{a}12] 574c-d

9 ARISTOTLE: *Parts of Animals*, BK I, CH I [640^{a}25-33] 162d / *Ethics*, BK I, CH 7 [1097^{b}23-1098^{a}18] 343a-c; BK VI, CH 4 388d-389a; BK IX, CH 7 [1167^{a}34-1168^{a}18] 421b-c / *Politics*, BK I, CH II [1258^{b}35-39] 453b; BK VII, CH 13 [1331^{b}30-38] 536c / *Rhetoric*, BK I, CH I [1354^{a}1-12] 593a; [1355^{b}9-14] 594d-595a; CH 2 [1355^{b}26-36] 595b; [1356^{b}26-1357^{a}7] 596b-c

12 AURELIUS: *Meditations*, BK VI, SECT 16, 275c

17 PLOTINUS: *Fifth Ennead*, TR VIII, CH I 239b-240a

18 AUGUSTINE: *City of God*, BK XXII, CH 24, 610a-c / *Christian Doctrine*, BK II, CH 30 651c-d

19 AQUINAS: *Summa Theologica*, PART I, Q 14, A 8 82c-83b; Q 15, A I, ANS 91b-92a; A 2, ANS and REP 2 92a-93b; Q 36, A 3, ANS 194c-195d; Q 117, A I, ANS and REP 2 595d-597c; PART I–II, Q 14, A 4, ANS 679b-d; Q 21, A 2, REP 2 718a-d; Q 34, A I, REP 3 768c-769d

20 AQUINAS: *Summa Theologica*, PART I-II, Q 57, AA 3-4 37b-39a; Q 58, A 2, REP I 42a-43a; A 5, REP 2 44d-45c; Q 65, A I, REP 4 70b-72a

25 MONTAIGNE: *Essays*, 437b

28 HARVEY: *On Animal Generation*, 333a

30 BACON: *Novum Organum*, BK I, APH 85, 121d-122b

31 DESCARTES: *Discourse*, PART VI, 61b-c

42 KANT: *Judgement*, 523c-524b; 525c-527b

46 HEGEL: *Philosophy of Right*, PART I, par 68 29d-30a / *Philosophy of History*, INTRO, 176a-c; PART II, 266a-274a; PART IV, 346c-d

47 GOETHE: *Faust*, PRELUDE [134-157] 4a-b

49 DARWIN: *Descent of Man*, 278b-c

50 MARX: *Capital*, 85b-d

53 JAMES: *Psychology*, 186b; 774a

2. Art and nature

2a. Causation in art and nature: artistic production compared with natural generation

7 PLATO: *Ion*, 144b / *Symposium*, 155d-157a / *Timaeus*, 447a-449c / *Laws*, BK X, 760a-761d

(2. Art and nature. 2a. Causation in art and nature: artistic production compared with natural generation.)

8 ARISTOTLE: *Posterior Analytics*, BK II, CH 11 [95^{a}3–9] 129d / *Physics*, BK I, CH 8 [191^{a}33–^{b}9] 267b; BK II, CH I [192^{b}8–32] 268b,d-269a; CH 2 [194^{a}33–^{b}8] 270d-271a; CH 8–9 275d-278a,c esp CH 8 [199^{a}8–^{b}7] 276b-d / *Generation and Corruption*, BK II, CH 9 [335^{b}18–336^{a}13] 437b-d / *Meteorology*, BK IV, CH 12 [390^{b}2–14] 494c / *Metaphysics*, BK I, CH 6 [988^{a}1–7] 506a; CH 9 [992^{a}29–34] 510c; BK VI, CH I [1025^{b}18–27] 547d; BK VII, CH 7–9 555a-558a; BK IX, CH 2 571c-572a; CH 5 573a-c; BK XI, CH 7 [1064^{a}10–16] 592b-c; BK XII, CH 3 [1070^{a}4–8] 599b

9 ARISTOTLE: *Parts of Animals*, BK I, CH I [639^{b}12–640^{a}35] 161d-162d; [641^{b}13–29] 164c-d / *Generation of Animals*, BK I, CH 21–22 269c-271a; BK II, CH I [734^{a}17–735^{a}5] 274c-275c; CH 4 [738^{b}18–28] 279c; [740^{a}13–18] 281a; [740^{a}25–741^{a}2] 281d; CH 6 [743^{b}20–25] 285a; BK III, CH 11 [762^{a}15–20] 303b; BK IV, CH 2 [767^{a}16–25] 308c; CH 6 [775^{a}20–23] 317b / *Ethics*, BK I, CH 9 [1099^{b}18–24] 345a-b; BK VI, CH 4 [1140^{a}11–16] 388d

10 GALEN: *Natural Faculties*, BK I, CH 7 170c-171a; CH 12 172d-173c; BK II, CH 3 185a-186d; CH 6, 189a-190a

12 LUCRETIUS: *Nature of Things*, BK IV [823–857] 55a-b

12 AURELIUS: *Meditations*, BK III, SECT 2 259d-260a; BK VI, SECT 40 277d

17 PLOTINUS: *Third Ennead*, TR VIII, CH 3–4 130a-131a / *Fourth Ennead*, TR III, CH 10 147c-148b; TR IV, CH 31, 174d-175a / *Fifth Ennead*, TR VIII, CH 1–2 239b-240c; CH 5, 242a; TR IX, CH 2, 247a / *Sixth Ennead*, TR II, CH 11, 275c

19 AQUINAS: *Summa Theologica*, PART I, Q 18, A 3, ANS 106b-107c; Q 36, A 3, ANS 194c-195d; Q 41, A 3, ANS 219d-221c; Q 45, A 2, ANS 242d-244a; Q 104, A I, ANS 534c-536c; Q 105, A 5, ANS 542a-543b; Q 117, A I, ANS and REP 1–2 595d-597c

20 AQUINAS: *Summa Theologica*, PART III SUPPL, Q 80, AA 1–2 956c-958b

21 DANTE: *Divine Comedy*, HELL, XI [91–111] 16a-b; PARADISE, I [94–142] 107b-d; II [112–138] 109a; VIII [91–111] 117d-118a; XIII [52–84] 126a-b

22 CHAUCER: *Physician's Tale* [11,941–972] 366b-367a

23 HOBBES: *Leviathan*, INTRO, 47a-b

25 MONTAIGNE: *Essays*, 93b-d

28 HARVEY: *On Animal Generation*, 385a-c; 400d-401a; 407c; 412b-415b; 427d-428c; 442d-443b; 443d-444c; 447d-448a; 450c; 492a-b

29 CERVANTES: *Don Quixote*, PART II, 251d-252a

30 BACON: *Novum Organum*, BK I, APH 4 107b

33 PASCAL: *Geometrical Demonstration*, 437a

35 LOCKE: *Human Understanding*, BK II, CH XXVI, SECT 2 217b-d

42 KANT: *Pure Reason*, 188c-189a / *Judgement*, 523c-d; 557c-558b; 564d-565b

43 MILL: *Representative Government*, 327b,d-328d passim

46 HEGEL: *Philosophy of History*, PART II, 266a-267b

50 MARX: *Capital*, 85b-d

53 JAMES: *Psychology*, 186b

2b. The role of matter and form in artistic and natural production

8 ARISTOTLE: *Physics*, BK I, CH 7 [191^{a}7–12] 266d; BK II, CH I [193^{a}9–^{b}19] 269b-270a; CH 2 [194^{a}21–^{b}13] 270c-271a; CH 3 271a-272c / *Metaphysics*, BK I, CH 6 [988^{a}1–7] 506a; BK VII, CH 7–9 555a-558a esp CH 8 556b-557b; BK VIII, CH 3 [1043^{b}5–24] 567d-568b / *Soul*, BK II, CH I [412^{b}10–18] 642c-d

9 ARISTOTLE: *Parts of Animals*, BK I, CH I [640^{a}10–641^{b}42] 162b-165a / *Generation of Animals*, BK I, CH 20 [729^{a}9]–CH 22 [730^{b}32] 269b-271a; BK II, CH I [734^{b}8–735^{a}10] 275a-d

10 GALEN: *Natural Faculties* 167a-215d esp BK II, CH 3 185a-186d

12 AURELIUS: *Meditations*, BK VII, SECT 23 281b

17 PLOTINUS: *First Ennead*, TR VI, CH 2–3 21d-23a / *Fifth Ennead*, TR VIII, CH 1–2 239b-240c; TR IX, CH 2, 247a

18 AUGUSTINE: *Confessions*, BK XI, par 7 90d-91a

19 AQUINAS: *Summa Theologica*, PART I, Q 41, A 3, ANS 219d-221c; Q 45, A 2, ANS 242d-244a; Q 47, A I, REP I 256a-257b; Q 91, A 3, ANS 486b-487d; Q 104, A I, ANS 534c-536c; Q 105, A 5, ANS 542a-543b

20 AQUINAS: *Summa Theologica*, PART III, Q 2, A I, ANS 710a-711c; PART III SUPPL, Q 79, A 2, REP 4 953b-955c; Q 80, AA 1–2 956c-958b

21 DANTE: *Divine Comedy*, PARADISE, I [127–142] 107c-d; XIII [52–84] 126a-b

28 HARVEY: *On Animal Generation*, 412b-415b

30 BACON: *Advancement of Learning*, 17b-d; 43c-45a

32 MILTON: *Paradise Lost*, BK V [468–505] 185b-186a

46 HEGEL: *Philosophy of Right*, PART I, par 56–57 26b-27a; ADDITIONS, 32 121d-122a / *Philosophy of History*, INTRO, 165a-166b; 185c-d; PART II, 266a-267b

50 MARX: *Capital*, 17a; 85b-c; 86d-87c

2c. The natural and the artificial as respectively the work of God and man

OLD TESTAMENT: *Genesis*, 1–2 / *Leviticus*, 26:1 / *Numbers*, 33:52 / *Deuteronomy*, 5:7–10; 16:21–22 / *Job*, 37:1–40:5—(D) *Job*, 37–39 / *Isaiah*, 40:18–26—(D) *Isaias*, 40:18–26

7 PLATO: *Republic*, BK X, 427c-428d / *Timaeus*, 447a-449c / *Sophist*, 577d-578d / *Laws*, BK X, 760a-761d

12 AURELIUS: *Meditations*, BK VI, SECT 40 277d

16 KEPLER: *Harmonies of the World*, 1048a

17 PLOTINUS: *Fourth Ennead*, TR IV, CH 31, 174d-175a / *Fifth Ennead*, TR VIII, CH 5, 242a

18 AUGUSTINE: *Confessions*, BK XI, par 7 90d-91a / *City of God*, BK XXII, CH 24, 610a-d / *Christian Doctrine*, BK II, CH 30 651c-d

19 AQUINAS: *Summa Theologica*, PART I, Q 2, A 3, ANS and REP 2 12c-14a; Q 14, A 8 82c-83b; A II, ANS 84c-85c; Q 15 91b-94a; Q 16, A I 94b-95c; Q 17, A I 100d-101d; Q 22, A 2, ANS and REP 3 128d-130d; Q 41, A 3, ANS 219d-221c; QQ 44-46 238a-255d passim; QQ 65-66 339a-349d passim; Q 74, A 3, REP I 375a-377a,c; Q 91, A 3, ANS 486b-487d; Q 93, A 2, REP 4 493a-d; Q 103, A I, REP I,3 528b-529a; Q 104, A I 534c-536c; PART I-II, Q I, A 2 610b-611b; Q 13, A 2, REP 3 673c-674c

20 AQUINAS: *Summa Theologica*, PART III, Q 3, A 8, ANS 729b-730b; PART III SUPPL, Q 75, A 3, REP 4 938a-939d

21 DANTE: *Divine Comedy*, HELL, XI [91-111] 16a-b; PARADISE, VIII [91-111] 117d-118a; IX [103-108] 119d; X [7-21] 120b-c; XIII [52-84] 126a-b; XVIII [70-117] 134b-d esp [109-111] 134d

22 CHAUCER: *Physician's Tale* [11,941-972] 366b-367a

23 HOBBES: *Leviathan*, INTRO, 47a-b

28 HARVEY: *On Animal Generation*, 427d-428c; 442d-443b; 492a-b

32 MILTON: *Paradise Lost*, BK III [694-735] 150b-151b

40 GIBBON: *Decline and Fall*, 663d-664a

42 KANT: *Pure Reason*, 188c-189a / *Judgement*, 521b-523d

49 DARWIN: *Origin of Species*, 87a-b

3. Art as imitation

4 HOMER: *Iliad*, BK XVIII [478-608] 135a-136c

7 PLATO: *Cratylus*, 104c-106c; 108c-110d / *Republic*, BK II-III, 320c-334b; BK VI, 382a-c; BK X, 427c-434c / *Timaeus*, 443b-d; 455b-c / *Critias*, 478c-d / *Sophist*, 552c-d; 560b-561d; 577c-579d / *Statesman*, 596c-d / *Laws*, BK II, 654a-c; 660a-662a; BK X, 760a-b

8 ARISTOTLE: *Physics*, BK II, CH 2 [194^{a}22-26] 270c

9 ARISTOTLE: *Politics*, BK III, CH 11 [1281^{b}10-15] 479b-c; BK VIII, CH 5 [1340^{a}14-^{b}19] 545c-546a / *Rhetoric*, BK II, CH 11 [1371^{b}4-10] 615a / *Poetics* 681a-699a,c esp CH 1-5 681a-684a

12 LUCRETIUS: *Nature of Things*, BK V [1379-1383] 79a

12 AURELIUS: *Meditations*, BK III, SECT 2 259d-260a; BK XI, SECT 10 303b-c

16 KEPLER: *Harmonies of the World*, 1048a

17 PLOTINUS: *First Ennead*, TR VI, CH 2-3 21d-23a / *Fourth Ennead*, TR III, CH 10 147c-148b / *Fifth Ennead*, TR VIII, CH 1-2 239b-240c; TR IX, CH 2, 247a; CH 11 250c-251a / *Sixth Ennead*, TR II, CH 11, 275c

18 AUGUSTINE: *Christian Doctrine*, BK II, CH 25 649b-d

19 AQUINAS: *Summa Theologica*, PART I, Q I, A 9, REP I 8d-9c; Q 93, A 2, REP 4 493a-d; Q 117, A I, ANS 595d-597c

21 DANTE: *Divine Comedy*, HELL, XI [91-111] 16a-b; PURGATORY, X [22-99] 67c-68b; XII [10-72] 70b-71a

22 CHAUCER: *Troilus and Cressida*, BK II, STANZA 149 41a / *Physician's Tale* [11,941-972] 366b-367a

23 HOBBES: *Leviathan*, INTRO, 47a-b; PART IV, 262c

27 SHAKESPEARE: *Hamlet*, ACT II, SC II [576-592] 46b; ACT III, SC II [1-39] 49a-b / *Timon of Athens*, ACT I, SC I [28-38] 393d-394a; [156-160] 395b-c / *Winter's Tale*, ACT IV, SC IV [77-108] 508c-509a / *Sonnets*, LXVII-LXVIII 596c-d

28 HARVEY: *On Animal Generation*, 332c-333c; 438c; 444b-c; 492b

29 CERVANTES: *Don Quixote*, PART I, 82c-d; 184a-185b; PART II, 237b-c; 251d-252a

30 BACON: *Advancement of Learning*, 33c-d / *Novum Organum*, BK II, APH 29 159b-c

31 DESCARTES: *Meditations*, I, 76a-b

32 MILTON: *Samson Agonistes*, 337a-338a

33 PASCAL: *Pensées*, 29 176a; 32-33 176a-b; 120 195a; 134 196a

35 HUME: *Human Understanding*, SECT I, DIV 5, 452d-453a

37 FIELDING: *Tom Jones*, 121b,d-123a; 243a-d

40 GIBBON: *Decline and Fall*, 158d

42 KANT: *Judgement*, 521b-524b; 525a-528c esp 527b-528c; 557a-558b

44 BOSWELL: *Johnson*, 196d-197a

46 HEGEL: *Philosophy of Right*, PART I, par 68 29d-30a / *Philosophy of History*, PART I, 219b-c

52 DOSTOEVSKY: *Brothers Karamazov*, BK X, 284b-d

53 JAMES: *Psychology*, 186b; 686b-688a

54 FREUD: *Interpretation of Dreams*, 265c / *Civilization and Its Discontents*, 779c-d

4. Diverse classifications of the arts: useful and fine, liberal and servile

7 PLATO: *Euthydemus*, 74b-76b / *Ion*, 145d-148a,c / *Gorgias*, 253c-255c; 260a-262a; 280d-282b / *Republic*, BK I, 305b-306a / *Sophist*, 552c-553a; 560b-561d; 577c-579d / *Statesman*, 592d-593a; 593d-595a / *Philebus*, 633a-635b / *Laws*, BK II, 662c-663b; BK X, 760a-b

8 ARISTOTLE: *Physics*, BK II, CH 2 [194^{a}33-^{b}9] 270d-271a / *Metaphysics*, BK I, CH 1 [981^{b}13-24] 500a

9 ARISTOTLE: *Ethics*, BK I, CH 1 339a-b; CH 7 [1097^{a}15-23] 342c / *Politics*, BK I, CH 11 [1258^{b}9-39] 452d-453b; BK VIII, CH 2 [1337^{b}3-23] 542c-d / *Rhetoric*, BK I, CH 2 [1355^{b}26-36] 595b / *Poetics*, CH 1-3 681a-682c

17 PLOTINUS: *Fourth Ennead*, TR IV, CH 31, 175a / *Fifth Ennead*, TR IX, CH 11 250c-251a

18 AUGUSTINE: *Christian Doctrine*, BK II, CH 30 651c-d

(4. *Diverse classifications of the arts: useful and fine, liberal and servile.*)

19 AQUINAS: *Summa Theologica*, PART I, Q 18, A 3, ANS 106b-107c; Q 103, A 2, REP 2 529a-530a; PART I-II, Q 8, A 2, REP 3 656a-d; Q 9, A 1, ANS 657d-658d

20 AQUINAS: *Summa Theologica*, PART I-II, Q 57, A 3, REP 3 37b-38a

24 RABELAIS: *Gargantua and Pantagruel*, BK II, 82c-d; BK III, 190d-191a

25 MONTAIGNE: *Essays*, 69d-70d

29 CERVANTES: *Don Quixote*, PART II, 251b-c

30 BACON: *Advancement of Learning*, 38c-39d; 56a-b / *Novum Organum*, BK I, APH 85, 121d-122b

42 KANT: *Judgement*, 524a-b; 526a-527b; 532a-536d

5. The sources of art in experience, imagination, and inspiration

OLD TESTAMENT: *Exodus*, 31:1-11; 35:30-36:8

4 HOMER: *Iliad*, BK I [1-7] 3a; BK II [484-493] 14d-15a / *Odyssey*, BK I [1-10] 183a

7 PLATO: *Phaedrus*, 124a / *Ion* 142a-148a,c / *Symposium*, 160c-d / *Apology*, 202b-d / *Gorgias*, 253a; 260a-262a / *Sophist*, 561b-d; 577d-579d / *Laws*, BK IV, 684b-c

8 ARISTOTLE: *Posterior Analytics*, BK II, CH 19 [100^{a}3-9] 136c / *Metaphysics*, BK I, CH 1 [980^{b}25-982^{a}1] 499b-500b

9 ARISTOTLE: *Ethics*, BK II, CH 1 [1103^{a}26-^{b}13] 348d-349a; BK X, CH 9 [1180^{b}29-1181^{b}23] 435d-436a,c / *Rhetoric*, BK I, CH 1 [1354^{a}1-12] 593a; BK III, CH 1 [1404^{a}13-19] 654b; CH 2 [1405^{a}3-9] 655b; CH 10 [1410^{b}5-8] 662c / *Poetics*, CH 17 [1455^{a}22-36] 690c

10 HIPPOCRATES: *Ancient Medicine* 1a-9a,c esp par 1-8 1a-3b / *Articulations*, par 10, 94d

13 VIRGIL: *Eclogues*, IV [1-3] 14a; VI [1-12] 19a / *Aeneid*, BK I [1-11] 103a; BK VII [37-44] 237a

14 PLUTARCH: *Demosthenes*, 692d-695d

17 PLOTINUS: *Fifth Ennead*, TR VIII, CH 1 239b-240a

20 AQUINAS: *Summa Theologica*, PART I-II, Q 68, A 4, REP 1 91b-92c

21 DANTE: *Divine Comedy*, HELL, II [7-9] 2c; XXXII [1-12] 47c; PURGATORY, I [1-12] 53a; XXIV [49-63] 90a-b; XXIX [37-42] 98a; PARADISE, I [1-36] 106a-b; II [1-18] 107d; [91-105] 108d; XVIII [70-117] 134b-d esp [109-111] 134d; XXII [112-123] 140d; XXIII [55-69] 141d-142a

23 HOBBES: *Leviathan*, PART IV, 262c

24 RABELAIS: *Gargantua and Pantagruel*, BK I, 2d-3a,c; BK III, 129c-d

25 MONTAIGNE: *Essays*, 52d-53a; 309c-310c; 450d-451a; 523c-524a; 532a-b

26 SHAKESPEARE: *Midsummer-Night's Dream*, ACT V, SC I [1-27] 370d-371a / *Henry V*, PROLOGUE 532b,d; ACT III, PROLOGUE 543c-d

27 SHAKESPEARE: *Sonnets*, XXXII 591a-b; LXXVIII-LXXXV 598b-599b; C-CVI 601c-602c

28 HARVEY: *On Animal Generation*, 332c-333c

29 CERVANTES: *Don Quixote*, PART II, 251d-252a; 340b

30 BACON: *Advancement of Learning*, 32d; 38c-39b

31 DESCARTES: *Discourse*, PART I, 43b / *Meditations*, I, 76a-b

32 MILTON: *On Shakespear. 1630* 16a / *Paradise Lost*, BK I [1-26] 93b-94a; BK III [1-55] 135b-136b; BK VII [1-39] 217a-218a; BK IX [1-47] 247a-248a

36 SWIFT: *Gulliver*, PART III, 97a-98a

36 STERNE: *Tristram Shandy*, 198a-b; 302a-b

37 FIELDING: *Tom Jones*, 152a-155b; 190b-191c; 273a-274c; 280a; 296b,d-298a

40 GIBBON: *Decline and Fall*, 185b; 627b-d

41 GIBBON: *Decline and Fall*, 528c

42 KANT: *Judgement*, 463a-464c; 473a-c; 482b-483d; 523d-524b; 525c-532a esp 526a-d, 528c-530c; 542b-543c

46 HEGEL: *Philosophy of History*, INTRO, 153a-c; 176a-c; PART II, 263d-268b

47 GOETHE: *Faust*, DEDICATION 1a-b; PART II [9945-9960] 242a

49 DARWIN: *Descent of Man*, 288d-289a; 292a-b

50 MARX: *Capital*, 85b-c

53 JAMES: *Psychology*, 165b [fn 1]; 686b-688a

54 FREUD: *Interpretation of Dreams*, 181a-b; 239c-240a; 246c-248c; 383d / *General Introduction*, 483c; 600d-601b / *Group Psychology*, 670a-b; 692c-693a

6. Art and science

6a. The comparison and distinction of art and science

7 PLATO: *Republic*, BK VI, 386d-388a; BK VII, 391b-398c; BK X, 427c-434c / *Laws*, BK IV, 684b-685a

8 ARISTOTLE: *Posterior Analytics*, BK II, CH 19 [100^{a}6-9] 136c / *Physics*, BK II, CH 2 [194^{a}21-^{b}13] 270c-271a / *Metaphysics*, BK I, CH 1 [980^{b}25-982^{a}1] 499b-500b; BK VI, CH 1 [1025^{b}18-28] 547d; BK XI, CH 7 [1064^{a}10-18] 592b-c

9 ARISTOTLE: *Ethics*, BK I, CH 1-2 339a-d; BK III, CH 3 [1112^{a}30-^{b}10] 358b-c; BK VI, CH 3 [1139^{b}14-18] 388b; CH 4 [1140^{a}10-16] 388d; CH 5 [1140^{a}33-^{b}2] 389b; CH 7 390a-d

10 HIPPOCRATES: *Regimen in Acute Diseases*, par 3 27a-c

17 PLOTINUS: *Third Ennead*, TR VIII, CH 3-4 130a-131a

19 AQUINAS: *Summa Theologica*, PART I, Q 16, A 1, ANS 94b-95c

20 AQUINAS: *Summa Theologica*, PART I-II, Q 57, A 3, ANS and REP 1,3 37b-38a; A 4, ANS and REP 2 38a-39a; Q 95, A 2, ANS 227c-228c

28 HARVEY: *On Animal Generation*, 333a-b

30 BACON: *Advancement of Learning*, 5b-6a; 48d-49b; 50c-51d; 53a-b

31 DESCARTES: *Rules*, I, 1a-b / *Discourse*, PART VI, 61b-d

34 NEWTON: *Principles*, 1a-b

42 KANT: *Intro. Metaphysic of Morals*, 388d / *Judgement*, 463a-464c; 515b-c; 523d-524a; 526a-527b esp 527a-b

43 MILL: *Utilitarianism*, 445c-d

46 HEGEL: *Philosophy of History*, PART IV, 346c-348a

53 JAMES: *Psychology*, 687a-688a; 863a-866a

54 FREUD: *New Introductory Lectures*, 874c-875a

6b. The liberal arts as productive of science: means and methods of achieving knowledge

7 PLATO: *Protagoras*, 50d-52d; 57a-c / *Phaedrus*, 134a-d; 139d-140b / *Meno*, 179d-183c / *Gorgias*, 252a-262a / *Republic*, BK VI, 386d-388a; BK VII, 391b-398c / *Parmenides*, 491a-d / *Theaetetus*, 525d-526b / *Sophist*, 571a-c / *Statesman*, 594d-595d / *Philebus*, 610d-613a; 633a-635a / *Seventh Letter*, 809c-810d

8 ARISTOTLE: *Prior Analytics*, BK I, CH 30 63d-64b / *Posterior Analytics* 97a-137a,c esp BK I, CH 1-3 97a-100a, BK II, CH 1-10 122b,d-128d / *Topics*, BK I, CH 1-3 143a-144b; CH 10-11 147b-148c; BK VIII, CH 1 [155^{b}1-16] 211a-b; CH 14 [163^{b}8-16] 222a / *Sophistical Refutations*, CH 9-11 234b-237c; CH 16 [175^{a}1-12] 241a; CH 34 252c-253d / *Physics*, BK I, CH 1 259a-b; CH 2 [184^{b}25-185^{a}19] 259c-260a / *Heavens*, BK I, CH 10 [279^{b}4-12] 370d; BK III, CH 7 [306^{a}1-18] 397b-c / *Generation and Corruption*, BK I, CH 2 [316^{a}5-14] 411c-d / *Metaphysics*, BK II, CH 3 513c-d; BK III, CH 1 [995^{a}23-^{b}4] 513b,d; BK IV, CH 3 [1005^{b}1-4] 524c; CH 4 [1005^{b}35-1006^{a}28] 525a-c; BK XI, CH 3 589a-d; CH 5 [1061^{b}34-1062^{a}19] 590a-c; BK XIII, CH 2 [1077^{b}1]-CH 3 [1078^{a}32] 608d-609d; CH 4 [1078^{b}18-32] 610b-c / *Soul*, BK I, CH 1 631a-632d; BK II, CH 4 [415^{a}14-22] 645b-c

9 ARISTOTLE: *Parts of Animals*, BK I, CH 1 161a-165d / *Ethics*, BK I, CH 3 339d-340b; CH 7 [1098^{a}20-^{b}8] 343c-344a; BK VI, CH 3 388b-c / *Politics*, BK I, CH 1 [1252^{a}18-24] 445b / *Rhetoric*, BK I, CH 2 [1358^{a}3-33] 597d-598b

11 ARCHIMEDES: *Method*, 569b-570a

12 EPICTETUS: *Discourses*, BK I, CH 7 112b-113d; CH 17 122d-124a; BK II, CH 25 174b-c

17 PLOTINUS: *First Ennead*, TR III 10a-12b

18 AUGUSTINE: *Confessions*, BK I, par 20-24 6a-7a / *City of God*, BK VIII, CH 3-4 266a-267c esp CH 4, 267b / *Christian Doctrine*, BK II, CH 31-37 651d-654b

19 AQUINAS: *Summa Theologica*, PART I, Q 117, A 1 595d-597c

20 AQUINAS: *Summa Theologica*, PART I-II, Q 57, A 3, REP 3 37b-38a; A 6, REP 3 40a-41a; PART III, Q 9, A 3, REP 2 765b-766b

23 HOBBES: *Leviathan*, PART I, 56b; 58a-61a; 65c-d

25 MONTAIGNE: *Essays*, 69d-77a passim; 240c-242a; 446d-450a

28 HARVEY: *On Animal Generation*, 331a-337a,c

30 BACON: *Advancement of Learning*, 56b-69c esp 56b-58c / *Novum Organum*, PREF 105a-106d; BK I 107a-136a,c esp APH 11-26 107d-108d, APH 39-69 109c-116b, APH 103-106 127d-128c / *New Atlantis*, 210d-214d

31 DESCARTES: *Rules* 1a-40a,c esp X 15d-17a / *Discourse* 41a-67a,c esp PART I, 41d-42b, PART II, 46c-48b, PART III, 50b-51a, PART IV, 52a, PART VI, 61d-62c / *Meditations*, I 75a-77c / *Objections and Replies*, 128a-129a / *Geometry*, BK I, 295a-298b; BK II, 304a-305a; BK III, 353a

33 PASCAL: *Pensées*, 1-4 171a-172d / *Vacuum*, 355a-358b passim; 365b-366a / *Great Experiment* 382a-389b / *Geometrical Demonstration*, 430a-434a; 442a-446b

34 NEWTON: *Principles*, BK III, RULES 270a-271b; LEMMA 5 338b-339a; GENERAL SCHOL, 371b-372a / *Optics*, BK III, 542a; 543a-544a

35 LOCKE: *Human Understanding*, INTRO, SECT 4-7 94a-95c; BK IV, CH III, SECT 18-20 317d-319c; CH VII, SECT 11 340a-342d; CH XII, SECT 1-8 358c-360c passim; SECT 14-15 362d-363b; CH XVII, SECT 11 378b

35 HUME: *Human Understanding*, SECT I, DIV 7-10 453c-455b passim; SECT VII, DIV 48 470d-471c

38 ROUSSEAU: *Inequality*, 339d-342b

39 SMITH: *Wealth of Nations*, BK V, 335d-336a

41 GIBBON: *Decline and Fall*, 299b

42 KANT: *Pure Reason*, 1a-13d; 15c-16c; 17d-19a; 36d-37d; 60a-c; 109d-112d; 119a-b; 146a-149d; 193d-194b; 211c-218d; 223a-d / *Fund. Prin. Metaphysic of Morals*, 253a-254d; 261c-d; 264b-d / *Practical Reason*, 291a-296d; 310a-b; 319c-321b; 329a-330c

43 FEDERALIST: NUMBER 31, 103c-104a

43 MILL: *Liberty*, 283d-284d; 287c-288c

45 LAVOISIER: *Elements of Chemistry*, PREF, 1c-2d

45 FOURIER: *Theory of Heat*, 172a-173b

45 FARADAY: *Researches in Electricity*, 659a; 774d-775a

46 HEGEL: *Philosophy of Right*, INTRO, par 31 19c-20a

50 MARX: *Capital*, 10a-11d

53 JAMES: *Psychology*, 175a-176a; 385a-b; 674a-675b; 677b; 687a; 862a-865a; 869a-878a

54 FREUD: *New Introductory Lectures*, 879c; 881b-c

6c. Art as the application of science: the productive powers of knowledge

7 PLATO: *Lysis*, 16c-18b / *Protagoras*, 43b-d / *Euthydemus*, 70a-c / *Ion* 142a-148a,c / *Gorgias*, 261a-262a / *Republic*, BK VII, 391b-397a esp 392b, 394b, 394d / *Statesman*, 580d-582a / *Laws*, BK IV, 684c-685a

8 ARISTOTLE: *Physics*, BK II, CH 2 [194^{a}21-^{b}13] 270c-271a / *Metaphysics*, BK I, CH 1 [980^{b}25-

(6. Art and science. 6c. Art as the application of science: the productive powers of knowledge.)

982[a]1] 499b-500b; BK VII, CH 7 [1032[a]25–1033[a]4] 555b-556a; CH 9 [1034[a]21–32] 557c; BK IX, CH 2 571c-572a; CH 5 573a-c; CH 7 [1049[a]5–12] 574c-d; BK XI, CH 7 [1064[a]10–14] 592b-c

9 ARISTOTLE: *Ethics*, BK I, CH I 339a-b; CH 7 [1098[a]28–32] 343d; BK II, CH 4 [1105[a]17–[b]4] 350d-351a; BK VI, CH 4 388d-389a

10 HIPPOCRATES: *Ancient Medicine* 1a-9a,c esp par 1–4 1a-2c, par 14 5a-c, par 20–22 7b-8d / *Epidemics*, BK III, SECT III, par 16 59b-c / *Surgery*, par 1 70b / *Articulations*, par 58, 112d / *The Law* 144a-d

10 GALEN: *Natural Faculties*, BK II, CH 9, 195c-197b

11 NICOMACHUS: *Arithmetic*, BK I, 812d-813a

12 EPICTETUS: *Discourses*, BK II, CH 17, 158d-159b

13 VIRGIL: *Georgics* 37a-99a passim, esp II [475–515] 65a-66a

14 PLUTARCH: *Marcellus*, 252a-255a

16 COPERNICUS: *Revolutions of the Heavenly Spheres*, BK I, 510b

18 AUGUSTINE: *City of God*, BK XXII, CH 24, 610a-c

19 AQUINAS: *Summa Theologica*, PART I, Q 14, A 8 82c-83b; Q 17, A 1, ANS 100d-101d; Q 19, A 4, REP 4 111c-112c; PART I–II, Q 14, A 4, ANS 679b-d

20 AQUINAS: *Summa Theologica*, PART I–II, Q 57, A 3, REP 3 37b-38a; A 4 38a-39a; Q 95, A 2, ANS 227c-228c

23 HOBBES: *Leviathan*, PART I, 60a-b; 73b; PART II, 158c-d; PART IV, 267a-b

25 MONTAIGNE: *Essays*, 450d-451a; 523c-524b

28 GILBERT: *Loadstone*, BK V, 100c-101c

28 HARVEY: *Motion of the Heart*, 289d-292a esp 289d, 291d-292a / *Circulation of the Blood*, 305a-d

29 CERVANTES: *Don Quixote*, PART I, 145c-d; PART II, 251b-252a

30 BACON: *Advancement of Learning*, 42a-c; 48d-49b; 50c-51d; 53a-b; 56b-58c / *Novum Organum* 105a-195d esp BK I, APH 1–3 107a-b, APH 11 107d, APH 19–21 108b-c, APH 81–82 120b-121b, APH 85 121d-122d, APH 92 125b-d, APH 103–105 127d-128c, APH 124 133c-d, APH 129–130 134d-136a,c, BK II, APH 1–9 137a-140c, APH 44–52 175d-195d / *New Atlantis*, 210d-214d

31 DESCARTES: *Discourse*, PART VI, 61b-c; 66d-67a,c

35 LOCKE: *Human Understanding*, BK IV, CH XII, SECT 11–12 361c-362c

35 HUME: *Human Understanding*, SECT I, DIV 5 452d-453b

36 SWIFT: *Gulliver*, PART III, 103b-115b

39 SMITH: *Wealth of Nations*, BK I, 5b-6a

40 GIBBON: *Decline and Fall*, 633c; 661c-663c

42 KANT: *Intro. Metaphysic of Morals*, 388d / *Judgement*, 523d-524a

43 MILL: *Representative Government*, 369a

45 FOURIER: *Theory of Heat*, 170a; 184a; 213a-b

46 HEGEL: *Philosophy of History*, PART I, 218d-219a; 251a-b; PART IV, 347b-348a

50 MARX: *Capital*, 170b-c; 177a; 183b-189a; 239c-241a; 299b-d

54 FREUD: *Psycho-Analytic Therapy*, 123a-125a / *General Introduction*, 484a / *Civilization and Its Discontents*, 777a-c; 778b-779a esp 778d

7. The enjoyment of the fine arts

7a. Art as a source of pleasure or delight

7 PLATO: *Gorgias*, 260a-262a / *Republic*, BK X, 433a-434c / *Timaeus*, 455b-c / *Statesman*, 596c-d / *Philebus*, 628d-630c / *Laws*, BK II, 654b-d; 658d-660d

8 ARISTOTLE: *Metaphysics*, BK I, CH I [981[b]13–19] 500a

9 ARISTOTLE: *Ethics*, BK VII, CH 11 [1152[b]18–19] 403d; CH 12 [1153[a]24–27] 404c; BK IX, CH 7 [1167[b]34–1168[a]18] 421b-c / *Politics*, BK VIII, CH 3 [1337[b]27–1338[a]29] 543a-c; CH 5 544c-546a / *Rhetoric*, BK I, CH 11 [1371[b]4–11] 615a; BK III, CH I [1403[b]15]–CH 12 [1414[a]13] 653b,d-667a esp CH 1 653b,d-654c / *Poetics*, CH 4 [1448[b]4–23] 682c-d; CH 14 688b-689a

12 LUCRETIUS: *Nature of Things*, BK V [1379–1411] 79a-b

13 VIRGIL: *Aeneid*, BK I [440–493] 115a-116b; BK VIII [608–731] 275a-278b

16 COPERNICUS: *Revolutions of the Heavenly Spheres*, BK I, 510a-b

18 AUGUSTINE: *Confessions*, BK I, par 20–27 6a-7d; BK III, par 2–4 13c-14b; BK X, par 49–53 83c-85a / *City of God*, BK I, CH 31–33 147d-149a; BK XXII, CH 24, 610a-c / *Christian Doctrine*, BK II, CH 6 638a-d

19 AQUINAS: *Summa Theologica*, PART I, Q 1, A 9, REP 1 8d-9c; PART I–II, Q 32, A 8, ANS 764c-765b; Q 34, A 1, REP 3 768c-769d

21 DANTE: *Divine Comedy*, PURGATORY, II [106–133] 55c-d

24 RABELAIS: *Gargantua and Pantagruel*, BK I, 1b,d-3a,c; BK III, 129d-130c; 190d-191a; BK IV, 232a-b

25 MONTAIGNE: *Essays*, 104d-105c; 191c-192d; 399d-401a

26 SHAKESPEARE: *Taming of the Shrew*, ACT III, SC I [10–12] 212d / *Merchant of Venice*, ACT V, SC I [66–88] 431b-c

29 CERVANTES: *Don Quixote*, PART I, 184a-185b; PART II, 251b-c

32 MILTON: *Samson Agonistes*, 337a-338a

37 FIELDING: *Tom Jones*, 1a-2a; 35a-d; 49a-50c

40 GIBBON: *Decline and Fall*, 502c-503a

42 KANT: *Judgement*, 471d-473a; 476a-483d; 516d-518d; 527b-528c; 532a-d; 534c-539d

43 MILL: *Utilitarianism*, 446d-447a; 451c

44 BOSWELL: *Johnson*, 254c-d

7b. The judgment of excellence in art

8. Art and emotion: expression, purgation, sublimation

49 Darwin: *Origin of Species,* 18a-22c esp 18b-c, 20d-21a; 41c-d

50 Marx: *Capital,* 16d-17a; 85a-88d esp 86a-b; 250a,c; 298c-d

50 Marx-Engels: *Communist Manifesto,* 421d

51 Tolstoy: *War and Peace,* bk ix, 372a-373b; bk x, 449b-c; epilogue i, 654a-655c

53 James: *Psychology,* 711b-712b

54 Freud: *Origin and Development of Psycho-Analysis,* 2a / *Civilization and Its Discontents,* 777a-b; 778b; 779a

9b. The production of wealth: the industrial arts

Old Testament: *Exodus,* 35-39 / *I Kings,* 5-7— (D) *III Kings,* 5-7 / *I Chronicles,* 22:15-16— (D) *I Paralipomenon,* 22:15-16 / *II Chronicles,* 2:11-5:14—(D) *II Paralipomenon,* 2:11-5:14 Apocrypha: *Ecclesiasticus,* 38:27-34—(D) OT, *Ecclesiasticus,* 38:28-39

7 Plato: *Republic,* bk ii, 316c-319a / *Statesman,* 591c-593d; 596a-597b

8 Aristotle: *Metaphysics,* bk i, ch 1 [981^{b}13-19] 500a

9 Aristotle: *Politics,* bk i, ch 4 447b-c; ch 8-11 449d-453d

12 Lucretius: *Nature of Things,* bk v [1241-1268] 77b-c; [1350-1360] 78c-d

18 Augustine: *Christian Doctrine,* bk ii, ch 30 651c-d

19 Aquinas: *Summa Theologica,* part i-ii, q 2, a 1 615d-616c

30 Bacon: *Novum Organum,* bk i, aph 85 121d-122d / *New Atlantis,* 210d-214d

31 Descartes: *Discourse,* part vi, 61b-c

36 Swift: *Gulliver,* part ii, 78a-b; part iii, 106a-112a

38 Montesquieu: *Spirit of Laws,* bk xxiii, 191a-c

38 Rousseau: *Inequality,* 349a; 352a-d; 365b-366b

39 Smith: *Wealth of Nations,* bk i, 6a-d; 27b-28a; 52d-53b; bk ii, 157a-b; bk iv, 288c-300d esp 288c-291c, 294d-295a

40 Gibbon: *Decline and Fall,* 88d-89d; 368a; 655d-656b; 658a-b

41 Gibbon: *Decline and Fall,* 314c-315b

42 Kant: *Judgement,* 524a-b

43 Federalist: number 8, 45d-46a

46 Hegel: *Philosophy of Right,* part i, par 56 26b; additions, 125 137a / *Philosophy of History,* part i, 243d-244c; part ii, 267a-b

48 Melville: *Moby Dick,* 79a-82a

50 Marx: *Capital,* 16d-17a; 31a-37c passim; 85a-89b; 96a-97a; 100a-147b passim; 157a-188c esp 158a-159a, 164a-166c, 180d-188c; 205a-207c; 251b-255a esp 254a-b; 279d-280a; 292d; 299b-c

50 Marx-Engels: *Communist Manifesto,* 420d-421a; 421d-422c

51 Tolstoy: *War and Peace,* epilogue i, 654a-655c

9c. The arts of war

Old Testament: *Genesis,* 14 / *Exodus,* 17:8-16 / *Numbers,* 31 / *Deuteronomy,* 2-3; 20 / *Joshua,* 1-12 esp 6, 8—(D) *Josue,* 1-12 esp 6, 8 / *Judges* esp 4, 7, 15 / *I Samuel* esp 17—(D) *I Kings* esp 17 / *II Samuel*—(D) *II Kings* Apocrypha: *Judith,* 7:8-31—(D) OT, *Judith,* 7:8-25 / *I Maccabees*—(D) OT, *I Machabees* / *II Maccabees*—(D) OT, *II Machabees*

4 Homer: *Iliad,* bk iv [292-309] 26d-27a; bk vii [433-463] 50b-c; bk viii [489-565] 56a-d; bk xiii [125-154] 89c-d; bk xviii [509-540] 135b-d / *Odyssey,* bk viii [491-520] 227a-b

5 Euripides: *Suppliants* [632-730] 264a-d / *Trojan Women* [1-14] 270a; [511-571] 274b-d / *Heracles Mad* [188-205] 366d

6 Herodotus: *History,* bk i, 41c-42b; bk iv, 141b-c; 144d-148d; 158d-159b; bk vi, 206d-208d; bk vii, 239a-241c; 247d-259a; bk viii 260a-287d passim; bk ix 288a-314a,c

6 Thucydides: *Peloponnesian War,* bk ii, 389d-391b; bk vi, 514d-516a; bk vii 538a-563a,c

7 Plato: *Euthydemus,* 75a-b / *Republic,* bk ii, 319a-c; bk iv, 343b-d; bk v, 366a-c / *Sophist,* 552d-554c / *Laws,* bk vii, 716c-717c

9 Aristotle: *Politics,* bk i, ch 7 [1255^{b}38-39] 449c; ch 8 [1256^{b}20-26] 450c

12 Lucretius: *Nature of Things,* bk v [1281-1349] 77d-78c

13 Virgil: *Aeneid,* bk ii [13-198] 124b-129b; bk vii [519-530] 250b; bk ix [25-76] 279b-281a; [590-620] 295a-b

14 Plutarch: *Themistocles,* 90b-95b / *Pericles,* 131b-139a / *Fabius-Pericles,* 154a-d / *Aemilius Paulus,* 216a-223a / *Marcellus,* 252a-255a; 257c-260c / *Aristides,* 266b-272c / *Philopoemen* 293a-302a,c / *Caius Marius,* 338c-344c / *Sulla,* 382c-d / *Lucullus* 400a-421a,c / *Nicias* 423a-438d / *Sertorius* 457b,d-470d esp 464c-d / *Agesilaus,* 498a-d / *Pompey,* 528c-534d / *Alexander,* 546b-550a; 555d-556b; 569b-d / *Caesar,* 583a-596a / *Antony,* 770a-773c / *Marcus Brutus,* 816d-824a,c

15 Tacitus: *Annals,* bk ii, 26c-28c esp 26c-27a; bk iii, 63a-b; bk xiii, 134a-136c / *Histories,* bk i, 210b-d; bk iii, 247a-c; bk iv, 275b-c

20 Aquinas: *Summa Theologica,* part i-ii, q 57, a 4, rep 3 38a-39a; part ii-ii, q 40, a 3 580d-581b

23 Machiavelli: *Prince,* ch iii-v 3c-8c; ch x 16a-d; ch xii-xiv 17d-22a; ch xviii, 25a-c; ch xx-xxi 30a-33a; ch xxv 35a-36b; ch xxvi, 37b-c

23 Hobbes: *Leviathan,* part i, 73b; part ii, 103b-c; 159a-b

24 Rabelais: *Gargantua and Pantagruel,* bk i, 28a-29b; 31d-35a; 39c-44a; 50c-52d; 55b-57c; bk ii, 95a-d; bk iii, 127d-128b; bk iv, 276a-282d; 304a-305a

25 Montaigne: *Essays,* 11b-13c; 21a-b; 133b-d; 136b-143c; 193a-194b; 327d-329d; 354b-358b

(10. *The moral and political significance of the arts.* 10b. *The political regulation of the arts for the common good: the problem of censorship.*)

29 CERVANTES: *Don Quixote*, PART I, 13b-16c; 117d-119d; 184a-187c

30 BACON: *New Atlantis*, 214a-b

32 MILTON: *Areopagitica* 381a-412b esp 384b-389a, 398a-b

37 FIELDING: *Tom Jones*, 253d-254d

38 MONTESQUIEU: *Spirit of Laws*, BK IV, 17b-18d; BK XII, 90b-c

39 SMITH: *Wealth of Nations*, BK V, 347c-d

40 GIBBON: *Decline and Fall*, 148a

42 KANT: *Pure Reason*, 220b-221b; 223a-c / *Science of Right*, 425c-426a

43 CONSTITUTION OF THE U.S.: ARTICLE I, SECT 8 [214–217] 13b; AMENDMENTS, I 17a

43 FEDERALIST: NUMBER 43, 139d-140a

43 MILL: *Representative Government*, 368d-369b

44 BOSWELL: *Johnson*, 259b-c; 300c-301a esp 301a-d [fn 1]

11. Myths and theories concerning the origin of the arts

OLD TESTAMENT: *Genesis*, 4:20–22; 10:8–9 / *I Chronicles*, 4:14—(D) *I Paralipomenon*, 4:14

5 AESCHYLUS: *Prometheus Bound* 40a-51d esp [109–113] 41b, [248–256] 42d, [459–461] 44d

7 PLATO: *Protagoras*, 44a-45a / *Phaedrus*, 138c-139a / *Symposium*, 160c-d / *Republic*, BK II, 316b-319c / *Statesman*, 589a-c / *Philebus*, 610d-613a esp 611d-613a / *Laws*, BK II, 653a-c; 662c-663b

9 ARISTOTLE: *Politics*, BK VIII, CH 6 [1341^{b}2–8] 547a / *Rhetoric*, BK III, CH 1 [1403^{b}15–1404^{a}39] 653b,d-654c / *Poetics*, CH 3 [1448^{a}25]–CH 5 [1449^{b}19] 682b-684a

10 HIPPOCRATES: *Ancient Medicine*, par 3 1d-2b; par 7 3a; par 12 4b-c; par 14, 5a

12 LUCRETIUS: *Nature of Things*, BK V [1028–1104] 74c-75c; [1241–1457] 77b-80a,c

13 VIRGIL: *Georgics*, I [121–146] 40b-41a

24 RABELAIS: *Gargantua and Pantagruel*, BK IV, 299a-300b

30 BACON: *Advancement of Learning*, 38d-39a / *Novum Organum*, BK I, APH 109 128d-129c

38 ROUSSEAU: *Inequality*, 352a-d

40 GIBBON: *Decline and Fall*, 655d-656a

46 HEGEL: *Philosophy of History*, PART I, 239a-b; 252a-c; PART II, 261b

49 DARWIN: *Descent of Man*, 278a-279c; 298a-301c; 329c; 348d-349d; 567c-571a esp 569d-570a, 570d

52 DOSTOEVSKY: *Brothers Karamazov*, BK X, 284b-d

53 JAMES: *Psychology*, 727b-728a

54 FREUD: *General Introduction*, 512d-513a / *Group Psychology*, 670a-b; 692a-693a / *Civilization and Its Discontents*, 778b,d [fn 2] / *New Introductory Lectures*, 862d

12. The history of the arts: progress in art as measuring stages of civilization

4 HOMER: *Iliad*, BK IV [104–111] 25a; BK IX [185–189] 59a; BK XI [15–46] 72b-c; BK XVIII [368–617] 133d-136d / *Odyssey*, BK IX [105–115] 230b

6 HERODOTUS: *History*, BK I, 5b; 5d-6a; BK II, 49d-50a; 75b-76a; BK III, 102c; BK VII, 220d-221b

6 THUCYDIDES: *Peloponnesian War*, BK I, 350b-d

7 PLATO: *Critias*, 479d / *Statesman*, 602b-c / *Laws*, BK II, 654c-655b; BK III, 675c-676b

8 ARISTOTLE: *Sophistical Refutations*, CH 34 [183^{b}16–184^{b}8] 253a-d / *Metaphysics*, BK I, CH 1 [981^{b}13–24] 500a; BK XII, CH 8 [1074^{b}11] 605a

9 ARISTOTLE: *Ethics*, BK I, CH 7 [1098^{a}21–25] 343c-d / *Politics*, BK II, CH 8 [1268^{b}23–1269^{a}29] 464d-465b / *Rhetoric*, BK III, CH 1 [1403^{b}15–1404^{a}39] 653b,d-654c / *Poetics*, CH 4–5 682c-684a

10 HIPPOCRATES: *Ancient Medicine*, par 1–4 1a-2c; par 12 4b-c

12 LUCRETIUS: *Nature of Things*, BK V [324–337] 65b-c; [925–1160] 73b-76b; [1241–1457] 77b-80a,c

13 VIRGIL: *Georgics*, I [121–146] 40b-41a

14 PLUTARCH: *Pericles*, 127a-129b / *Marcellus*, 252a-255a / *Aratus*, 830b-c

15 TACITUS: *Annals*, BK XV, 167c-168a

18 AUGUSTINE: *City of God*, BK XII, CH 10, 348b-c; BK XVIII, CH 13–14 478d-479d; BK XXII, CH 24, 610a-c

19 AQUINAS: *Summa Theologica*, PART I, Q 46, A 2, REP 4 253a-255a

21 DANTE: *Divine Comedy*, PURGATORY, XI [79–120] 69c-70a; XXIV [49–63] 90a-b

23 HOBBES: *Leviathan*, PART I, 85c; PART IV, 267c-269b passim

24 RABELAIS: *Gargantua and Pantagruel*, BK II, 81d-82c

30 BACON: *Advancement of Learning* 1a-101d esp 1a-15a, 18b, 20b-25c, 29a-32c, 33d-34a, 35b-36c, 38d-39a, 51d-54b / *Novum Organum*, BK I, APH 85 121d-122d; APH 129 134d-135d

31 DESCARTES: *Discourse*, PART VI, 61a-c

36 SWIFT: *Gulliver*, PART III, 103b-115b esp 106a-107a

38 ROUSSEAU: *Inequality*, 338d-340a; 346d-347a; 352a-d; 365b-366b

39 SMITH: *Wealth of Nations*, BK I, 6a-d; BK III, 173d-175b; BK IV, 191a; BK V, 308c-309a,c; 337d-338c

40 GIBBON: *Decline and Fall*, 18b-24a,c; 88d-89d; 157d-159a; 171c; 237c-239a; 502d-503a; 633b-634a,c; 641b-642b; 655d-658b; 661c-664d

41 GIBBON: *Decline and Fall*, 195d-197a; 225a-c; 291d-292c; 298a-300b; 327a-328a,c; 355a-d; 451c-452d; 509d-510a,c; 522b-528a,c esp 528a,c; 573a-574a; 590a-598a passim, esp 596d-598a

42 KANT: *Judgement*, 586a-587a
43 CONSTITUTION OF THE U.S.: ARTICLE I, SECT 8 [214-217] 13b
43 FEDERALIST: NUMBER 43, 139d-140a
43 MILL: *Representative Government*, 367b-c
44 BOSWELL: *Johnson*, 70d-71b; 307c-d; 380d-381a; 406c; 408d-409a; 446d
46 HEGEL: *Philosophy of Right*, PART I, par 69, 30b; PART III, par 356 113a-b / *Philosophy of History*, INTRO, 153a-b; 182b-c; 185a-186a; PART I, 219b-c; 229b-d; 243d-244c; 247c-248d; 251a-b; 253b-c; PART II, 259a-282d esp 261b, 267b-268b, 276a-d, 277d-278a; PART

III, 312c-d; PART IV, 323c-d; 335a-d; 346c-348a
49 DARWIN: *Origin of Species*, 13c; 19c-d / *Descent of Man*, 278a-279a; 320a-321a; 329a-330a,c; 349b-d; 569d
50 MARX: *Capital*, 86b-c esp 86d [fn 4]; 181d [fn 3]
50 MARX-ENGELS: *Communist Manifesto*, 420d-421a; 421d
53 JAMES: *Psychology*, 727b
54 FREUD: *Civilization and Its Discontents*, 776c-780b esp 779a-b / *New Introductory Lectures*, 882d-883b

CROSS-REFERENCES

For: The conception of art as a habit of mind or an intellectual virtue, *see* HABIT 5a, 5d; VIRTUE AND VICE 2a(2).

The applications of science in the useful arts, *see* KNOWLEDGE 8a; PHYSICS 5; SCIENCE 1b(1), 3b; and for the dependence of science on art, *see* PHYSICS 4a; SCIENCE 5b, 6a.

The distinction between art and prudence and the spheres of making and doing, *see* PRUDENCE 2b.

Other discussions of art and nature, *see* NATURE 2a; and for the comparison of artistic production, natural generation, and divine creation, *see* FORM 1d(1)–1d(2); WORLD 4e(1).

Experience as a source of art, *see* EXPERIENCE 3; for the distinction between artist and empiric, *see* EXPERIENCE 3a; and for the opposition between art and chance, *see* CHANCE 5.

The enjoyment of beauty in nature and in art, *see* BEAUTY 2; PLEASURE AND PAIN 4c(1); and for discussions of the aesthetic judgment or the judgment of taste, *see* BEAUTY 5.

Other considerations of the educational influence of the arts, *see* EDUCATION 4d; POETRY 9a; VIRTUE AND VICE 4d(4); and for the problem of political regulation or censorship of art, *see* EMOTION 5e; POETRY 9b.

More extended treatments of the liberal arts, *see* LANGUAGE 4-8; LOGIC; MATHEMATICS; RHETORIC; and for an analysis of one of the fine arts, *see* POETRY.

Discussions of the useful and industrial arts, *see* EDUCATION 5a-5b; LABOR 2b; MEDICINE; PROGRESS 3c, 4a, 6a; STATE 8d-8d(3); WAR AND PEACE 10-10f; WEALTH 3c-3d.

ADDITIONAL READINGS

Listed below are works not included in *Great Books of the Western World*, but relevant to the idea and topics with which this chapter deals. These works are divided into two groups:

I. Works by authors represented in this collection.
II. Works by authors not represented in this collection.

For the date, place, and other facts concerning the publication of the works cited, consult the Bibliography of Additional Readings which follows the last chapter of *The Great Ideas*.

I.

DANTE. *Convivio (The Banquet)*
HUME. *Of the Rise and Progress of the Arts and Sciences*
ROUSSEAU. *Discourse on the Arts and Sciences*
A. SMITH. "Of the Affinity Between Music, Dancing and Poetry," in *Essays Philosophical and Literary*

HEGEL. *The Phenomenology of Mind*, VII (B)
——. *The Philosophy of Mind*, SECT III, SUB-SECT A
——. *The Philosophy of Fine Art*
GOETHE. *Poetry and Truth*
——. *Travels in Italy*
——. *Conversations with Eckermann*
——. *Maxims and Reflections*
J. S. MILL. *A System of Logic*, BK VI, CH II

TOLSTOY. *What Is Art?*
FREUD. *Leonardo da Vinci*
——. *The Theme of the Three Caskets*
——. *The Moses of Michelangelo*
——. *A Childhood Memory from "Dichtung und Wahrheit"*

II.

EPICURUS. *Letter to Herodotus*
HORACE. *The Art of Poetry*
VITRUVIUS. *On Architecture*
QUINTILIAN. *Institutio Oratoria (Institutes of Oratory)*, BK XII
BONAVENTURA. *On the Reduction of the Arts to Theology*
LEONARDO DA VINCI. *Notebooks*
——. *A Treatise on Painting*
CELLINI. *Autobiography*
SUÁREZ. *Disputationes Metaphysicae*, XLIV (13)
CORNEILLE. *Trois discours sur l'art dramatique*
——. *Examens*
J. HARRIS. *Three Treatises. The First Concerning Art. The Second Concerning Music, Painting, and Poetry. The Third Concerning Happiness*
BURKE. *A Philosophical Enquiry into the Origin of Our Ideas of the Sublime and Beautiful*
VOLTAIRE. "Fine Arts," in *A Philosophical Dictionary*
LESSING. *Laocoön*
BEATTIE. *An Essay on Poetry and Music*
HERDER. *Plastik*
JOSHUA REYNOLDS. *Discourses on Art*
SCHILLER. *Letters upon the Esthetic Education of Man*
SCHELLING. *Philosophie der Kunst*
COLERIDGE. *Biographia Literaria*, CH 4
SCHOPENHAUER. *The World as Will and Idea*, VOL I, BK III; VOL III, SUP, CH 34–36
WHEWELL. *The Philosophy of the Inductive Sciences*, VOL II, BK XI, CH 8
EMERSON. "Art," in *Essays*, I
E. DELACROIX. *Journal*
BAUDELAIRE. *Curiosités esthétiques*
COMTE. *System of Positive Polity*, VOL I, *General View of Positivism*, CH 5

LOTZE. *Microcosmos*, BK VIII, CH 3
BURCKHARDT. *The Civilization of the Renaissance in Italy*
RUSKIN. *Modern Painters*
——. *The Stones of Venice*
——. *Sesame and Lilies*
TAINE. *The Philosophy of Art*
E. HARTMAN. *Philosophy of the Unconscious*, (B) V
ARNOLD. *Essays in Criticism*
VAN GOGH. *Letters*
MORRIS. *Hopes and Fears for Art*
——. *Art and Socialism*
——. *The Aims of Art*
GUYAU. *L'art au point de vue sociologique*
NIETZSCHE. *The Will to Power*, BK III (4)
BRUNETIÈRE. *An Apology for Rhetoric*
FRAZER. *The Golden Bough*, PART I, CH 17
GROSSE. *The Beginnings of Art*
SHAW. *The Sanity of Art*
HIRN. *The Origins of Art*
MANN. *Tonio Kröger*
SANTAYANA. *Reason in Art*
CROCE. *Aesthetic as Science of Expression*
——. *The Essence of Esthetics*
HARRISON. *Ancient Art and Ritual*
BOSANQUET. *Three Lectures on Aesthetic*, II
T. VEBLEN. *The Instinct of Workmanship, and the State of the Industrial Arts*, CH 2–4, 6–7
——. *The Vested Interests and the State of the Industrial Arts*, CH 3
ALAIN. *Système des beaux-arts*
MARITAIN. *Art and Scholasticism*
——. *An Introduction to Philosophy*, PART II (9)
ABERCROMBIE. *An Essay Towards a Theory of Art*
LALO. *L'art et la morale*
ORTEGA Y GASSET. *The Dehumanization of Art*
RANK. *Art and Artist*
H. DELACROIX. *Psychologie de l'art*
GILL. *Art-Nonsense*
COOMARASWAMY. *The Transformation of Nature in Art*
DEWEY. *Art as Experience*
MUMFORD. *Technics and Civilization*
ADLER. *Art and Prudence*

Chapter 5: ASTRONOMY

INTRODUCTION

ASTRONOMY could take its place in this catalog of ideas on the ground that several of the great books are monuments of astronomical science, exemplifying the imaginative and analytical powers which have made it one of the most remarkable triumphs of the human mind. Its claim might further be supported by the fact that other great books—of mathematics, physics, theology, and poetry—have a context of astronomical imagery and theory. But the inclusion of astronomy can be justified by what is perhaps an even more significant fact, namely, that astronomical speculation raises problems and suggests conclusions which have critical relevance for the whole range of the great ideas.

Man has used astronomy to measure, not only the passage of time or the course of a voyage, but also his position in the world, his power of knowing, his relation to God. When man first turns from himself and his immediate earthly surroundings to the larger universe of which he is a part, the object which presses on his vision is the overhanging firmament with its luminous bodies, moving with great basic regularity and, upon closer observation, with certain perplexing irregularities. Always abiding and always changing, the firmament, which provides man with the visible boundary of his universe, also becomes for him a basic, in fact an inescapable, object of contemplation.

Careful and precise astronomical observations antedate the birth of astronomy as a science. The early interest in the heavenly bodies and their motions is often attributed to the usefulness of the predictions which can be made from a knowledge of celestial phenomena.

Whether their motive was entirely utilitarian, or partly religious and speculative, the Egyptians and Babylonians, we learn from Herodotus, undertook patient study of the heavens. They observed and recorded with immense persistence. They calculated and predicted. They turned their predictions to use through the priestly office of prophecy to foretell eclipses, tides, and floods, and they employed their calculations in the mundane arts of navigation and surveying to guide travel and fix boundaries. But they did not, like the Greeks, develop elaborate theories which sought to organize all the observed facts systematically.

With the Greeks, the down-to-earth, everyday utility of astronomy seems to count for less than its speculative grandeur. The dignity which they confer upon astronomy among the disciplines reflects the scope and majesty of its subject matter. The Greek astronomer, concerned as he is with figuring motions that range through the whole of space and are as old as time or as interminable, takes for his object the structure of the cosmos.

Aristotle and Plato pay eloquent tribute to the special worth of astronomy. In the opening chapters of his *Metaphysics*, Aristotle associates astronomical inquiry with the birth of philosophy. "Apart from usefulness," he says, "men delight . . . in the sense of sight" and, he adds, "it is owing to their wonder that men both now begin and at first began to philosophise." They wondered first about "the obvious difficulties," but little by little they advanced to "greater matters," and "stated difficulties . . . about the phenomena of the moon and sun and stars, and about the genesis of the universe." In his own philosophical thought, Aristotle's treatise *On the Heavens* is not only one of the basic natural sciences, but certain of its principles have general significance for all the other parts of his physical science.

A wider view of the importance of astronomy is taken by Plato. In the *Timaeus*, he dwells on "the higher use and purpose for which God has given eyes to us. . . . Had we never seen the

stars, and the sun, and the heaven," Timaeus
says, "none of the words which we have spoken
about the universe would ever have been uttered. . . . God invented and gave us sight," he
continues, "to the end that we might behold
the courses of intelligence in the heaven, and
apply them to the courses of our own intelligence which are akin to them, the unperturbed
to the perturbed; and that we, learning them
and partaking of the natural truth of reason,
might imitate the absolutely unerring courses
of God and regulate our own vagaries."

For Plato, then, man's intellectual relation to
the heavens does more than initiate philosophy.
Man's self-rule, his purity and peace of soul, is
at stake in that relation. That is one reason why,
in both the *Republic* and the *Laws*, Plato makes
astronomy a required part of the curriculum
for the education of rulers. "He who has not
contemplated the mind of nature which is said
to exist in the stars . . . and seen the connection
of music with these things, and harmonized
them all with laws and institutions, is not able,"
the Athenian Stranger says in the *Laws*, "to
give a reason for such things as have a reason."

Plato considers the opposition to astronomy
on religious grounds by those who think that
men who approach celestial phenomena by the
methods of astronomy "may become godless
because they see . . . things happening by necessity, and not by an intelligent will accomplishing good." His answer points out that one
of the "two things which lead men to believe in
the gods . . . is the argument from the order of
the motion of the stars and of all things under
the dominion of the mind which ordered the
universe." It was a false understanding of these
matters which "gave rise to much atheism and
perplexity."

THE ISSUES RAISED by Plato concerning the importance of astronomy for purification and piety, for education and politics, run through the
tradition of western thought. Though they are
somewhat transformed in the context of Jewish
and Christian beliefs, and altered by later developments in the science of astronomy itself,
they remain as matters on which an author's
strong assent or dissent forcefully reflects his
whole intellectual position.

On the one hand, astronomers like Ptolemy,

Copernicus, and Kepler, for all their differences
on points of scientific theory, seem to concur in
reaffirming Plato's conception of the bearing of
their science on religion and morals. Lucretius
and Augustine, on the other hand, while not
agreeing with each other, seem to disagree with
Plato. In the tradition of western thought, they
represent different types of opposition to the
Platonic view.

Where Plato and his followers, including religious Christians like Copernicus and Kepler, hold that true piety profits from astronomical study, Lucretius hopes that astronomy may
help to free men from religious superstitions. If
when they "gaze on the heavenly quarters of the
great upper world" and direct their thoughts
"to the courses of the sun and moon," they do
so with "a mind at peace" because they see only
the workings of natural law and no evidences of
a controlling power in the will of the gods, then
men achieve the natural piety of the scientist
—different in the opinion of Lucretius from the
false worship which is based on fear.

From his own experiences in dealing with the
astronomy of the Manichean sect in relation to
their religious doctrine, Augustine insists that
the teachings of religion in no way depend upon
astronomy. He denies that such knowledge is in
any way essential to true piety. Though a man
does not know "even the circles of the Great
Bear, yet is it folly to doubt," he writes, "that
he is in a better state than one who can measure
the heavens and number the stars, and poise the
elements, yet neglecteth Thee 'Who hast made
all things in number, weight, and measure.' "

When Faustus, the leader of the Manicheans,
"was found out to have taught falsely of the
heaven and stars, and of the motions of the sun
and moon (although these things pertain not to
the doctrine of religion)," his religious teachings, according to Augustine, inevitably suffered
ridicule because of his pretension that they derived support from a science of the heavenly
bodies. Augustine would disengage theology
from astronomy. His position anticipates that
later taken by Cardinal Barberini who, during
the controversy over the Copernican hypothesis, is reported to have told Galileo that astronomy and religion have quite separate tasks,
the one teaching how the heavens go, the other
how to go to heaven.

Still another point of view on the importance of astronomy is represented in the skeptical and humanist attitude of Montaigne. "I am very well pleased with the Milesian girl," he remarks, "who . . . advised the philosopher Thales rather to look to himself than to gaze at heaven." In saying this, or in quoting with approval the question asked of Pythagoras by Anaximenes— "To what purpose should I trouble myself in searching out the secrets of the stars, having death or slavery continually before my eyes?" —Montaigne intends more than a preference for the moral over the natural sciences. He regards astronomical inquiry as a prime example of man's "natural and original disease—presumption." It is presumptuous to suppose that our minds can grasp and plot the course of the heavens when we fail to comprehend things much nearer at hand. Hence Montaigne advises everyone to say, in the spirit of Anaximenes: "Being assaulted as I am by ambition, avarice, temerity, superstition, and having so many other enemies of life, shall I go cudgel my brains about the world's revolutions?"

Kant can be as critical as Montaigne of the frailty of human knowledge. "The investigations and calculations of the astronomers," he writes, have shown us "the abyss of our ignorance in relation to the universe." But Kant—an astronomer himself as well as a moralist—does not, therefore, advise us to forsake the study of the heavens. On the contrary, he recommends it not only for its scientific value, but for its moral significance.

"Two things," Kant declares in a passage which has become famous, "fill the mind with ever new and increasing admiration and awe, the oftener and more steadily we reflect on them: the starry heavens above and the moral law within." The two fit together to produce a single effect. Astronomy with its view "of a countless multitude of worlds annihilates, as it were, my importance as an *animal* creature." Morality "elevates my worth as an *intelligence* by my personality, in which the moral law reveals to me a life independent of animality and even of the whole sensible world."

Kant's association of the starry heavens with the moral life is not so much an echo of, as a variant upon, Plato's precept that we apply "the courses of intelligence in heaven . . . to the courses of our own intelligence." But in one passage of Freud we find an almost complete return to the Platonic insight. "Order has been imitated from nature," he writes; "man's observations of the great astronomical periodicities not only furnished him with a model, but formed the ground plan of his first attempts to introduce order into his own life."

ASTRONOMY HAS connections with biology and psychology, as well as with mathematics and physics. The obvious fact that the sun supports terrestrial life—operating here as a unique and indispensable cause—occasions the inference by Aquinas that it may also operate as a cause in the production of new species by spontaneous generation from putrefying matter. This notion bears some resemblance to the theory in contemporary genetics of the effect of cosmic radiations upon gene mutations.

Unlike these notions in biology, speculations concerning celestial influences upon psychological phenomena seem to cross the line between astronomy and astrology. Sometimes the influence upon man and his actions is found in the constellations attending a nativity; sometimes it is a particular influence of the sort still signified by the meaning of the word "lunacy"; and sometimes omens and auguries are read in the aspect of the heavens.

The chapters on PROPHECY and SIGN AND SYMBOL deal with the issues raised by astrology. Problems more closely associated with astronomical science and speculation are treated in other chapters. The cosmological problem of the origin of the material universe is discussed in the chapters on ETERNITY, TIME, and WORLD; the question of its size in the chapter on SPACE; the question of whether the celestial spheres are themselves alive or are moved by intelligences or spirits in the chapters on ANGEL and SOUL; and the question of the nature of the heavenly bodies in the chapter on MATTER.

This last problem is of crucial significance in the history of astronomy itself. Opposed theories of the motions of the heavenly bodies become correlated with opposed theories concerning their matter—whether that is different in kind from terrestrial matter or the same. It is with reference to these related issues that what has come to be called "the Copernican revolution" represents one of the great crises, certainly one of the most dramatic turning points, in the development of astronomy, and of physics and natural science generally.

The Copernican revolution did not take place by the improvement and enlargement of astronomical observations alone, nor even by the effect of these on alternative mathematical formulations. If it had not been accompanied by the radical shift from ancient to modern physics —especially with regard to the diversity or uniformity of the world's matter—the Copernican hypothesis concerning the celestial motions would have been no more than a mathematical alternative to the Ptolemaic hypothesis. Copernicus seems to advance it only as such, but in the hands of Kepler, Galileo, and Newton it becomes much more than that. They, rather than Copernicus, seem to accomplish the revolution connected with his name.

When their contribution is neglected or inadequately grasped, the Copernican revolution appears to be, as is often popularly supposed, merely a shift in astronomical theory. The problem being to organize mathematically the *apparent* motions of the heavens, Copernicus offers an alternative solution to that of Ptolemy. Instead of treating the earth as stationary and central in the cosmic system, Copernicus attributes three motions to the earth by treating it as a planet which revolves around the sun, spins on its axis, and varies the inclination of its axis with reference to the sun.

What is usually supposed to be revolutionary about this hypothesis is its effect on man's estimate of himself and his place or rank in the universe. On either of the rival hypotheses, the apparent motions of the heavens remain unaltered, but not man's conception of himself, of his earth, or of the universe in which the earth's orbit cuts so small a figure. As Kant suggests, man's stature seems to shrink. He becomes "a mere speck in the universe" which has been enlarged to infinity, or at least to an unimaginable immensity. He is displaced from its center to become a wanderer with his planet. Humanity's self-esteem, according to Freud, was thus for the first time deeply wounded; he refers to the theory that "is associated in our minds with the name of Copernicus" as the "first great outrage"

which humanity "had to endure from the hands of science."

It has been questioned whether this interpretation of the Copernican revolution fits all the documents in the case. Freud may be accurately reporting a popular feeling which, since the 18th century, has become a widespread consequence of Copernican and post-Copernican astronomy. But in earlier centuries when the Ptolemaic system prevailed, or even after Copernicus, the appraisal of man's rank seems to depend more upon the position he occupies in the hierarchy of God's creatures—below the angels and above the brutes—than upon the place or motion of the earth, or the size of the world.

Boethius, for example, finds the Ptolemaic universe large enough to remind man of the infinitesimal space he occupies. Dante, too, comments on the smallness of the earth in the scheme of things. When in his visionary travel Dante reaches the Empyrean, he looks down upon the earth and "with my sight," he tells us, "I returned through all and each of the seven spheres, and saw this globe, such that I smiled at its mean semblance; and that counsel I approve as best which holds it of least account."

Kepler, a passionate Copernican deeply concerned with the human significance of astronomy, can be found arguing that the new hypothesis involves something more fitting for man than the old. In his last argument in defense of the Copernican view against that of Tycho Brahe as well as that of Ptolemy, he declares, "it was not fitting that man, who was going to be the dweller in this world and its contemplator, should reside in one place as in a closed cubicle. . . . It was his office to move around in this very spacious edifice by means of the transportation of the Earth his home." In order properly to view and measure the parts of his world, the astronomer "needed to have the Earth a ship and its annual voyage around the sun."

Yet the very fact that Kepler argues in this manner may be interpreted as indicating his sense of the drastic implications for man of the altered structure of the universe. Kepler may even be thought to announce the problem of the so-called "Copernican revolution" when, in denying that the earth can any longer "be reckoned among the primary parts of the great world," since it is only a part of a part, *i.e.*, the planetary region, he deliberately adds the qualification: "But I am speaking now of the Earth in so far as it is a part of the edifice of the world, and not of the dignity of the governing creatures which inhabit it."

Whether or not it was the traumatic blow to the human ego which Freud conjectures, there can be little doubt that the shift from Ptolemy to Copernicus involved a real shock to the imagination. The Ptolemaic system conforms to the look of the world, which is indeed the reason why it is still the one used in practical courses in navigation. Here again Kepler defends Copernicus by explaining why "our uncultivated eyesight" cannot be other than deceived and why it "should learn from reason" to understand that things are really different from the way they appear.

A certain disillusionment may result from this affirmation—repeated by every schoolboy who is taught the Copernican system—that, despite what we see, the sun does not move around the earth, and the earth both rotates and revolves. It undermines the trust men placed in their senses and the belief that science would describe the world as they saw it. In order to "save the appearances," that is, to account for the phenomena, science might henceforward be expected to destroy any naive acceptance of them as the reality.

Furthermore, though the Ptolemaic world was very large, the Copernican universe was much larger. Whereas in the former the radius of the earth was deemed negligible in relation to the radius of the sphere of the fixed stars, in the new universe the radius of the earth's orbit around the sun was negligible in relation to the same radius of the sphere of the fixed stars. It can hardly be doubted that this intensified some men's sense of almost being lost in an abyss of infinity. "I see those frightful spaces of the universe which surround me," Pascal writes, "and I find myself tied to one corner of this vast expanse, without knowing why I am put in this place rather than in another." When he regards the world's immensity as "the greatest sensible mark of the almighty power of God," Pascal experiences an awe which for him is qualified by reverence. Other men may experience the same feeling, but less with reverence than with a

gnawing loneliness, born of the doubt that so vast a cosmos—if cosmos it is rather than chaos —can have been beneficently designed as man's habitation.

WHATEVER THE TRUTH about the effect of the Copernican theory in the order of opinion, imagination, and feeling, it did produce a direct result on the intellectual plane. It, more than any other single factor, led to the overthrow of certain crucial doctrines which had been linked together in the physics and astronomy of Aristotle; it thus radically changed the fundamental principles in terms of which man had understood the order and unity of nature. That scientific event deserves not only the name but the fame of the "Copernican revolution."

The revolution in the realm of theory goes much deeper than the substitution of one mathematical construction for another to describe the motions of the world's great bodies. As Freud points out, the heliocentric hypothesis associated with the name of Copernicus was known to the Alexandrian astronomers of antiquity. It is, for example, attributed to Aristarchus by Archimedes in the *Sand-Reckoner*.

As far as the earth's rotation is concerned, Ptolemy admits it is quite "plausible" to suppose "the heavens immobile and the earth turning on the same axis from west to east very nearly one revolution a day. . . . As far as the appearances of the stars are concerned," he goes on, "nothing would perhaps keep things from being in accordance with this simpler conjecture."

Why, then, does Ptolemy reject a supposition which is not only plausible but also, in accounting for the appearances, *simpler*? In part the answer may be that he does so because the contrary supposition conforms to our ordinary sense-experience of the earth's immobility and the motions of the heavens from east to west. But that is far from being the most important part of the answer. Ptolemy indicates the crucial part when he tells us that the otherwise plausible supposition of a rotating earth becomes "altogether absurd" when we consider the speed and direction of the motions of bodies within the earth's own atmosphere. His strongest count against the supposition is that it does not conform to the Aristotelian physics which distinguishes between natural and violent motions, assigns certain fixed directions to the natural motions of each of the four elements of matter, and denies that these elementary kinds of terrestrial matter enter into the composition of the heavenly bodies.

That Aristotle's physics and cosmology lie at the very heart of the issue is confirmed by the way in which Kepler later argues for the Copernican theory against Ptolemy. He does not defend its truth on the ground that it accounts for observable facts which the Ptolemaic hypothesis cannot handle. Nor does he prefer it merely because it is mathematically the simpler hypothesis. On the contrary, he specifically notes that anything which can be claimed on mathematical grounds for Copernicus over Ptolemy can be equally claimed for Tycho Brahe over Ptolemy. (Brahe's theory was that while the other planets revolve around the sun, the sun, with its planets, revolves around a stationary earth.) According to Kepler, the truth of these competing theories must finally be judged *physically*, not *mathematically*, and when the question is put that way, as it is not by Copernicus himself, Copernicans like Kepler, Galileo, and Newton take issue with what had been associated with the Ptolemaic theory—the physics of Aristotle.

In order to examine this issue, it is necessary to state briefly here certain features of Aristotle's physics which are more fully discussed in the chapters on Change, Element, Mechanics, and Physics.

Just as Ptolemy's astronomy conforms to what we see as we look at the heavens, so Aristotle's physics represents a too simple conformity with everyday sense-experience. We observe fire rising and stones falling. Mix earth, air, and water in a closed container, and air bubbles will rise to the top, while the particles of earth will sink to the bottom. To cover a multitude of similar observations, Aristotle develops the theory of the natural motions and places of the four terrestrial elements—earth, air, fire, and water. Since bodies move naturally only to attain their proper places, the great body which is the earth, already at the bottom of all things, need not move at all. Being in its proper place, it is by nature stationary.

Two other observations exercise a decisive influence on Aristotle's theory. The naked eye sees no type of change in the heavenly bodies *other than* local motion or change of place. Unlike terrestrial bodies, they do not appear to come into being or perish; they do not change in size or quality. Furthermore, whereas the natural local motion of sub-lunary bodies appears to approximate the path of a straight line, the local motion of the celestial bodies appears to be circular rather than rectilinear.

To cover these observations, Aristotle's theory posits a different kind of matter for celestial and terrestrial bodies. An incorruptible matter must constitute the great orbs which are subject to local motion alone and have the most perfect kind of local motion—that of a circle. Since they are subject to generation and corruption, to change of quality and quantity, and are in local motion along straight lines, terrestrial bodies are of a corruptible matter.

The interconnection of all these points is marked by Aquinas when he summarizes Aristotle's doctrine. "Plato and all who preceded Aristotle," he writes, "held that all bodies are of the nature of the four elements" and consequently "that the matter of all bodies is the same. But the fact of the incorruptibility of some bodies was ascribed by Plato, not to the condition of matter, but to the will of the artificer, God. . . . This theory," Aquinas continues, "Aristotle disproves by the natural movements of bodies. For since he says that the heavenly bodies have a natural movement, different from that of the elements, it follows that they have a different nature from them. For movement in a circle, which is proper to the heavenly bodies, is not by contraries, whereas the movements of the elements are mutually opposite, one tending upwards, another downwards. . . . And as generation and corruption are from contraries, it follows that, whereas the elements are corruptible, the heavenly bodies are incorruptible."

The same points which Aquinas relates in his defense of the Aristotelian theory, Kepler also puts together when he expounds that theory in order to attack it and the Ptolemaic astronomy which tries to conform to it. "By what arguments did the ancients establish their opinion which is the opposite of yours?" he asks. "By four arguments in especial: (1) From the nature of moveable bodies. (2) From the nature of the motor virtue. (3) From the nature of the place in which the movement occurs. (4) From the perfection of the circle." He then states each of these arguments, and answers each in turn.

WHAT IS EXTRAORDINARY about Kepler's attack upon the Ptolemaic astronomy cannot be understood without examining Ptolemy's defense of his theory, a defense which Copernicus meets in Ptolemy's own terms rather than, as Kepler does, by going outside them.

Though his expressed intention was to construct a mathematical theory of the celestial motions which would also conform to Aristotle's physics, Ptolemy, when he finished, recognized that the complications he had been compelled to add in order "to save the appearances" left him with a theory that did not conform to Aristotle's doctrine of the perfect circular motion of the heavenly spheres. Instead of abandoning Aristotle's physics, he defended his theory on the ground that astronomy, being mathematical rather than physical, could admit such "unrealistic" complications if they served the purposes of calculation and of "saving the appearances."

In the thirteenth and last book of the *Almagest*, when he faces the fact that his mathematical devices have become exceedingly difficult —and strained from the point of view of the Aristotelian reality—Ptolemy writes: "Let no one, seeing the difficulty of our devices, find troublesome such hypotheses. . . . It is proper to try and fit as far as possible the simpler hypotheses to the movements of the heavens; and if this does not succeed, then any hypotheses possible. Once all the appearances are saved by the consequences of the hypotheses, why should it seem strange that such complications can come about in the movements of heavenly things?" We ought not to judge the simplicity of heavenly things by comparison with what seems to be simple in the explanation of earthly phenomena. "We should instead judge their simplicity from the unchangeableness of the natures in the heavens and their movements. For thus they would all appear simple, more than those things which seem so here with us."

Ignoring the supposition that simplicity must be judged differently in different spheres, Copernicus challenges Ptolemy on his own grounds when he proposes "simpler hypotheses" to fit "the movements of the heavens." But in doing so, he seems to adopt the traditional view of the mathematical character of astronomical hypotheses. Yet, as will appear, he does not adopt this view in the unqualified form in which Osiander states it in his Preface to the *Revolutions of the Heavenly Spheres*.

"It is the job of the astronomer," Osiander writes, "to use painstaking and skilled observation in gathering together the history of the celestial movements, and then—since he cannot by any line of reasoning reach the true causes of these movements—to think or construct whatever causes or hypotheses he pleases, such that, by the assumption of these causes, these same movements can be calculated from the principles of geometry, for the past and for the future too.

"It is not necessary," he adds, "that these hypotheses should be true, or even probable; it is enough if they provide a calculus which fits the observations. When for one and the same movement varying hypotheses are proposed, as eccentricity or epicycle for the movement of the sun, the astronomer much prefers to take the one which is easiest to grasp."

What distinguishes Kepler from both Ptolemy and Osiander is the way in which he is concerned with the *truth* of alternative hypotheses in astronomy. He looks upon the truth of an hypothesis as something to be judged not merely in mathematical terms according to the adequacy and simplicity of a calculating device, but to be measured by its conformity to *all* the physical realities. At the very beginning of his *Epitome of Copernican Astronomy*, he flatly declares that "astronomy is part of physics." And in the opening pages of the fourth book, he insists that astronomy has not one, but "two ends: to save the appearances and to contemplate the true form of the edifice of the World." He follows this immediately by observing that, if astronomy had only the first end, Tycho Brahe's theory would be as satisfactory as that of Copernicus.

Early in his scientific career, before writing the *Epitome*, Kepler asserts that "one cannot leave to the astronomer absolute license to feign no matter what hypotheses." He complains that astronomers "too often . . . constrain their thought from exceeding the limits of geometry."

It is necessary to go beyond geometry into physics to test the consequences of competing hypotheses which are equally good mathematically. "You must seek the foundations of your astronomy," he tells his fellow scientists, "in a more elevated science, I mean in physics or metaphysics."

Because Kepler thus conceives the task and truth of astronomy, Duhem in his great history of astronomy calls him a "realistic Copernican." Galileo also, Duhem thinks, was a realistic Copernican. "To confirm by physics the Copernican hypotheses," he writes, "is the center towards which converge Galileo's observations as an astronomer and his terrestrial mechanics."

Newton was the third member of this triumvirate. For him there remained the solution of the problem of deducing Kepler's formulation of the planetary orbits in a manner consistent with Galileo's laws of motion in the dynamics of bodies falling on the earth's surface. But the very posing of this problem itself depended on the insight that terrestrial and celestial mechanics can proceed according to the same principles and laws. That insight entailed the complete overthrow of the ancient physics, with its division of the universe into two distinct parts, having different kinds of matter and different laws of motion.

Copernicus, who, despite Osiander's apologetics, believed his theory to be true, did not himself face the great point at issue in the Copernican revolution—the material uniformity of the physical universe. We shall subsequently consider the question of the truth of astronomical hypotheses, but whether or not Copernicus and the Copernicans had *in their own day* a right to believe their theory true, it was the acceptance of the Copernican hypothesis as true which led Kepler and Galileo to deny the truth of Aristotelian physics.

If the earth is not at the center and stationary, then the basic doctrine of a natural direction in motion and a natural place of rest for the various elements is completely upset. If the earth is one of the planets, then anything true on the earth—or of the earth, such as Gilbert's theory of the magnetic fields generated by the earth's axial rotation—could be equally true of all the other planets.

"Read the philosophy of magnetism of the Englishman William Gilbert," writes Kepler; "for in that book, although the author did not believe that the Earth moved . . . nevertheless he attributes a magnetic nature to it by very many arguments. Therefore, it is by no means absurd or incredible that any one of the primary planets should be, what one of the primary planets, namely, the Earth, is." Such a statement plainly shows that when the earth becomes a planet, as it does in Copernican theory, no obstacle remains to the assertion of a homogeneity between the earth and the other planets both in matter and motion. The old physical dualism of a supralunar and a sublunar world is abandoned.

"Not the movement of the earth," Whitehead remarks, "but the glory of the heavens was the point at issue," for to assert the heavens to be of the same stuff and subject to the same laws as the rest of nature brings them down to the plane of earthly physics. That is precisely what Newton finally does when, in the enunciation of his Third Rule of reasoning in natural philosophy, he dryly but explicitly completes the Copernican Revolution. Those "qualities of bodies . . . which are found to belong to all bodies within the reach of our experiments, are," Newton maintains, "to be esteemed the universal qualities of all bodies whatsoever."

In the bifurcated world of ancient theory, astronomy had a very special place among the natural sciences, proportionate to the "glory of the heavens." But with Newton it could be completely merged into a general mechanics whose laws of motion have universal application. That merger, begun by Newton, has been perfected since his day. The last obstacle to the generalization lay in the apparent discrepancies between electrical phenomena on the subatomic scale and gravitational phenomena on the astronomic scale. But in our own time the unified field equations of Einstein's theory of relativity embrace the very large and the very small motions of matter within a single conceptual scheme, with radical consequences for the revision of the Newtonian or classical mechanics.

But the unification of nature which Kepler began and Newton completed, when set against Aristotle's physics, may be even more radical. Newton's theory, because of the amazing way in which it covered the widest variety of phenomena by the simplest, most universal formula, is considered by Kant to have "established the truth of that which Copernicus at first assumed only as an hypothesis." But the larger contribution, in Whitehead's opinion, is "the idea of the neutrality of situation and the universality of physical laws . . . holding indifferently in every part."

Whatever position we take today concerning the kind of truth which is possessed by hypotheses in mathematical physics, we now demand, in the spirit of the three Copernicans—Kepler, Galileo, and, above all, Newton—that physical hypotheses account at once for *all* the phenomena of the inanimate universe. Whatever the truth of modern as opposed to ancient physics, the Newtonian universe is so thoroughly established in our minds and feelings that, when we are reminded of the other universe in which men lived before the Copernican revolution, we tend to think it quaint, incredible, preposterous, superstitious, none of which it was.

Finally, from the point of view of our understanding of natural science itself, the astronomical controversy we have been considering is almost an archetypical model. It is necessary, of course, to appreciate the real achievement of Ptolemy as well as of Copernicus and Kepler in order to realize how genuine and difficult the issues were. Facts unknown to all of them may now have closed the dispute decisively, but issues in other spheres of modern science, almost identical in pattern with that great astronomical one, are not yet closed; and to the degree that we are able to re-enact in our minds the motion of thought on both sides of the Copernican controversy, we can confront comparable scientific issues—still open—with open minds.

Darwin, for example, finds in the astronomical controversy a precedent to which he can appeal in the defense of natural selection against its adversaries. "The belief in the revolution of the earth on its own axis," he writes, "was until lately not supported by any direct evidence." But the absence of direct evidence does not leave a scientific theory without foundation,

Darwin argues, if it has the power to explain several large classes of facts, which "it can hardly be supposed that a false theory would explain" in so satisfactory a manner. Darwin defends the theory of natural selection as having such power. To those who object that "this is an unsafe method of arguing," he replies—citing an example from astronomy—that "it has often been used by the greatest natural philosophers."

THE GREAT BOOKS of astronomy most lucidly exhibit the essential pattern of that kind of natural science which has, in modern times, come to be called "mathematical physics." Though that phrase may be modern, the ancients recognized the special character of the sciences which apply mathematics to nature and which consult experience to choose among hypotheses arising from different mathematical formulations.

Outlining a curriculum for liberal education, Plato, in the *Republic*, groups music and astronomy along with arithmetic and geometry as mathematical arts or sciences. In that context he treats them as pure mathematics. Astronomy is no more concerned with the visible heavens than music is with audible tones. Music is rather the arithmetic of harmonies, astronomy the geometry of motions. But in the *Timaeus* Plato turns mathematical formulae and calculations to use in telling what he calls "a likely story" concerning the formation and structure of the sensible world of becoming. Here rather than in the *Republic* we have, according to Whitehead, the initial conception of mathematical physics as well as deep insight into its nature and pattern.

Aristotle criticizes the notion of astronomy as a purely mathematical science. Just as "the things of which optics and mathematical harmonies treat" cannot be divorced from the sensible, so the objects of astronomy are also the visible heavens. "Astronomical experience," Aristotle writes, "supplies the principles of astronomical science." Yet, though its subject matter is physical and its method is in part empirical, astronomy like optics and harmonics takes the form of mathematical demonstration; and it is for this reason that Aquinas later calls such disciplines "mixed and intermediate sciences."

The development of astronomy from Plato and Aristotle through Ptolemy, Copernicus, and Kepler to Galileo and Newton thus constitutes an extraordinary set of "case histories" for the study of what J. B. Conant calls the "tactics and strategy" of science, and especially mathematical physics. But astronomy has one peculiar feature which distinguishes it from other branches of mathematical physics. It is empirical rather than experimental. The astronomer does not control the phenomena he observes. He does not, like the physicist, chemist, or physiologist, produce an isolated system of events by means of the laboratory arts.

Harvey comments on this aspect of astronomy when he proposes an experiment that will enable the physiologist to do what the astronomer cannot do, namely, deliberately prepare phenomena for examination by the senses. The astronomer must be content with the appearances as they are given. Defending psychoanalysis against attack "on the ground that it admits of no experimental proof," Freud points out that his critics "might have raised the same objection against astronomy; experimentation with the heavenly bodies is, after all, exceedingly difficult. There one has to rely on observation."

Since the invention of the telescope, the astronomer has had instruments of all sorts to increase the range and accuracy of his observations; but the fact that the place where he uses such apparatus is called an observatory rather than a laboratory indicates that these instruments do not make astronomy an experimental science. Nevertheless, as Bacon points out, the telescope enabled Galileo to do more than improve upon the accuracy of prior observations. It brought within the range of observation certain celestial phenomena, hitherto imperceptible to the naked eye, such as the phases of Venus, the satellites of Jupiter, and the constitution of the Milky Way.

Concerning the last of these, Pascal later remarks that the ancients can be excused for the idea they had of the cause of its color. "The weakness of their eyes not yet having been artificially helped, they attributed this color to the great solidity of this part of the sky"; but it would be inexcusable for us, he adds, "to retain the same thought now that, aided by the advantages of the telescope, we have discovered in the Milky Way an infinity of small stars whose more abundant splendor has made us recognize the real cause of this whiteness."

BECAUSE IT IS a mixed science, both empirical and mathematical, astronomy advances not only with the improvement and enlargement of observation, but also with new insights or developments in mathematics. Kant gives us striking examples of how the work of the pure mathematicians contributes to the advance of physics and astronomy. Their discoveries are often made without any knowledge of their application to natural phenomena. "They investigated the properties of the parabola," he writes, "in ignorance of the law of terrestrial gravitation which would have shown them its application to the trajectory of heavy bodies. . . . So again they investigated the properties of the ellipse without a suspicion that a gravitation was also discoverable in the celestial bodies, and without knowing the law that governs it as the distance from the point of attraction varies, and that makes the bodies describe this curve in free motion."

So amazing are such mathematical anticipations that Kant thinks Plato may be pardoned for supposing that pure mathematics "could dispense with all experience" in discovering the constitution of things. Whether or not Plato goes to this extreme, he does, in the *Republic*, seem to suggest the reverse of Kant's conception of the relationship between mathematics and astronomy. "The spangled heavens should be used as a pattern," he writes, "and with a view to that higher knowledge"—mathematics. Astronomy should be used to instigate discoveries in *pure* mathematics by suggesting good problems and by requiring formulations which transcend an interest in the truth about the heavens.

This twofold relation between mathematical discovery and empirical observation is present in the development of astronomy itself, and of all branches of mathematical physics. But there is another aspect of the relationship which must be taken into account if we are to consider the problem of truth in such sciences. The way in which mathematical formulations fit the phenomena measures the truth of rival hypotheses with respect to the same reality.

The logic of such verification has already been suggested in the discussion of the geocentric and heliocentric hypotheses. It is further considered in the chapter on HYPOTHESIS. To be satisfactory, an hypothesis must—in the language used ever since Simplicius—"save the appearances," that is, account for the relevant phenomena. But two hypotheses (as for example the geocentric and heliocentric) may, at a certain time, do an equally good job of saving the appearances. Then the choice between them becomes a matter of the greater mathematical elegance of one than the other.

That, however, does not give the mathematically superior theory a greater claim to truth. So far as reality is concerned, it is only, in Plato's words, "a likely story"; or as Aquinas points out with reference to the geocentric hypothesis, "the theory of eccentrics and epicycles is considered as established because thereby the sensible appearances of the heavenly movements can be explained; not however, as if this reason were sufficient, since some other theory might explain them."

Two hypotheses may be equally satisfactory for the range of phenomena they were both devised to fit. But only one of them may have the quite amazing virtue of fitting other sets of observations not originally thought to be related to the phenomena for which the hypothesis was devised. The word "consilience" has been used to name the property of an hypothesis which, in addition to saving a limited field of appearances, succeeds in fitting many other phenomena which seem to have become related —to have *jumped together* under its covering explanation. The heliocentric hypothesis, as developed by Newton's laws of motion and theory of gravitation, certainly has this property of consilience to a high degree, for it covers both celestial and terrestrial phenomena, and a wide variety of the latter.

Is the heliocentric hypothesis true then? If the truth of an hypothesis depends on the range of the phenomena it fits or saves, it might seem to be so, for by its consilience it accounts for phenomena that the Ptolemaic theory cannot handle. But though this may cause us to reject the unsuccessful hypothesis, does it establish beyond doubt the truth of the successful one? Or, to put the question another way, is not our judgment here a comparative one rather than absolute? Are we saying more than that one hypothesis is more successful than another in doing what an hypothesis should do? Are we logically entitled to regard that success as the sign of its exclusive truth, or must we restrict ourselves to the more modest statement that, as the better hypothesis, it simply tells a more likely story about reality?

OUTLINE OF TOPICS

REFERENCES

To find the passages cited, use the numbers in heavy type, which are the volume and page numbers of the passages referred to. For example, in 4 HOMER: *Iliad*, BK II [265–283] 12d, the number 4 is the number of the volume in the set; the number 12d indicates that the passage is in section d of page 12.

PAGE SECTIONS: When the text is printed in one column, the letters a and b refer to the upper and lower halves of the page. For example, in 53 JAMES: *Psychology*, 116a-119b, the passage begins in the upper half of page 116 and ends in the lower half of page 119. When the text is printed in two columns, the letters a and b refer to the upper and lower halves of the left-hand side of the page, the letters c and d to the upper and lower halves of the right-hand side of the page. For example, in 7 PLATO: *Symposium*, 163b-164c, the passage begins in the lower half of the left-hand side of page 163 and ends in the upper half of the right-hand side of page 164.

AUTHOR'S DIVISIONS: One or more of the main divisions of a work (such as PART, BK, CH, SECT) are sometimes included in the reference; line numbers, in brackets, are given in certain cases; *e.g.*, *Iliad*, BK II [265–283] 12d.

BIBLE REFERENCES: The references are to book, chapter, and verse. When the King James and Douay versions differ in title of books or in the numbering of chapters or verses, the King James version is cited first and the Douay, indicated by a (*D*), follows; *e.g.*, OLD TESTAMENT: *Nehemiah*, 7:45—(*D*) *II Esdras*, 7:46.

SYMBOLS: The abbreviation "esp" calls the reader's attention to one or more especially relevant parts of a whole reference; "passim" signifies that the topic is discussed intermittently rather than continuously in the work or passage cited.

For additional information concerning the style of the references, see the Explanation of Reference Style; for general guidance in the use of *The Great Ideas*, consult the Preface.

1. The end, dignity, and utility of astronomy

OLD TESTAMENT: *Job*, 38:4-38
7 PLATO: *Symposium*, 156d / *Gorgias*, 254c / *Republic*, BK VII, 394d-396b / *Timaeus*, 447a-452b; 455b-c / *Laws*, BK VII, 728b-c; 729d-730d; BK XII, 797c-798b
8 ARISTOTLE: *Metaphysics*, BK I, CH 2 [982^{b}11–17] 500d; BK XI, CH 6 [1063^{a}10–17] 591b; BK XII, CH 8 [1073^{b}1–7] 603d
9 ARISTOTLE: *Parts of Animals*, BK I, CH 5 [644^{b}21–645^{a}5] 168c-d
10 HIPPOCRATES: *Airs, Waters, Places*, par 2 9b-c
11 NICOMACHUS: *Arithmetic*, BK I, 812b-813a
12 LUCRETIUS: *Nature of Things*, BK V [509–771] 67d-71a
12 AURELIUS: *Meditations*, BK XI, SECT 27 306b
13 VIRGIL: *Aeneid*, BK VI [847–853] 233b-234a
14 PLUTARCH: *Nicias*, 435b-d
16 PTOLEMY: *Almagest*, BK I, 5a-6b; BK III, 83a; BK IV, 135b; BK IX, 270b-273a; BK XIII, 429a-b
16 COPERNICUS: *Revolutions of the Heavenly Spheres*, 505a-506a; 509a-b; BK I, 510a-511a
16 KEPLER: *Epitome*, BK IV, 846a-851a; 852a-853a; 888b-890a; 929a-b; BK V, 961a-965a / *Harmonies of the World*, 1080a-b
18 AUGUSTINE: *Confessions*, BK V, par 3–6 27c-28c / *Christian Doctrine*, BK II, CH 29 650d-651c

19 AQUINAS: *Summa Theologica*, PART I, Q 32, A I, REP 2 175d-178a
21 DANTE: *Divine Comedy*, PARADISE, II [46–148] 108b-109b; X [1-27] 120b-c
25 MONTAIGNE: *Essays*, 69d-70c; 213d-215a; 257d-259d
31 DESCARTES: *Meditations*, I, 76c
32 MILTON: *Paradise Lost*, BK VIII [1–202] 232a-236b
33 PASCAL: *Pensées*, 72 181a-184b; 242 217b-218a
34 NEWTON: *Principles*, 1a-2a
36 SWIFT: *Gulliver*, PART III, 94b-103a passim
36 STERNE: *Tristram Shandy*, 229a
41 GIBBON: *Decline and Fall*, 299b-c
42 KANT: *Pure Reason*, 175b [fn 1] / *Practical Reason*, 360d-361c
46 HEGEL: *Philosophy of Right*, ADDITIONS, 120, 136c
48 MELVILLE: *Moby Dick*, 365b-367a
54 FREUD: *General Introduction*, 562c / *Civilization and Its Discontents*, 779c / *New Introductory Lectures*, 832a; 876b-d

2. The method of astronomy

2a. Observation and measurement: instruments and tables

7 PLATO: *Republic*, BK VII, 394d-396b / *Timaeus*, 455a-b

(*2. The method of astronomy. 2a. Observation and measurement: instruments and tables.*)

8 ARISTOTLE: *Prior Analytics*, BK I, CH 30 [46ᵃ18–27] 64a / *Posterior Analytics*, BK I, CH 13 [78ᵇ31–79ᵃ7] 108b-c / *Heavens*, BK I, CH 3 [270ᵇ1–24] 361c-362a; BK II, CH 4 [287ᵃ31–ᵇ14] 379a; CH 11 383b; CH 12 [292ᵃ2–9] 383c / *Metaphysics*, BK XII, CH 8 [1073ᵇ17–1074ᵃ17] 604a-c

9 ARISTOTLE: *Parts of Animals*, BK I, CH I [639ᵇ7–12] 161c-d

16 PTOLEMY: *Almagest*, BK I, 24b-26a; BK I–III, 29a-86b; BK III–IV, 93a-119b; BK IV–VIII, 123a-269a; BK IX, 273a-290b; BK IX–XIII, 296a-465b

16 COPERNICUS: *Revolutions of the Heavenly Spheres*, BK II–III, 557b-626a; BK III, 631b-652b; 657b-674b; BK IV–V, 680a-739b; BK V, 744b-812a; BK VI, 818a-838a

16 KEPLER: *Epitome*, BK IV, 907b-908b

18 AUGUSTINE: *Confessions*, BK V, par 3–6 27c-28c / *Christian Doctrine*, BK II, CH 29, 651b-c

19 AQUINAS: *Summa Theologica*, PART I, Q 32, A I, REP 2 175d-178a

21 DANTE: *Divine Comedy*, PARADISE, II [46–105] 108b-d

22 CHAUCER: *Franklin's Tale* [11,582–605] 360b

23 HOBBES: *Leviathan*, PART IV, 267a-b

24 RABELAIS: *Gargantua and Pantagruel*, BK I, 29c

28 HARVEY: *Circulation of the Blood*, 320b

30 BACON: *Novum Organum*, BK I, APH 109, 129b; BK II, APH 39, 170b-c; APH 45, 176a; APH 46, 178a-b

32 MILTON: *Paradise Lost*, BK I [284–291] 99b; BK III [588–590] 148a; BK V [261–263] 181a

33 PASCAL: *Vacuum*, 358a

34 NEWTON: *Principles*, BK III, PHENOMENA 272a-275a; PROP 41–42 342a-368b / *Optics*, BK I, 412a-423b

35 BERKELEY: *Human Knowledge*, SECT 58–59 424a-b

36 SWIFT: *Gulliver*, PART III, 102a

41 GIBBON: *Decline and Fall*, 299b-c

48 MELVILLE: *Moby Dick*, 365b-367a

54 FREUD: *New Introductory Lectures*, 815a

2b. The use of hypotheses: the heliocentric and geocentric theories

7 PLATO: *Phaedo*, 241c-242b; 247c / *Republic*, BK VI, 386d-387d; BK VII, 395c-396b; BK X, 438c-439a / *Timaeus*, 447b-d; 452a-b / *Laws*, BK XII, 797d-798a

8 ARISTOTLE: *Heavens*, BK I, CH 3 [270ᵇ1–24] 361c-362a; BK II, CH I 375b,d-376a; CH 8 381a-382a; CH 11 [291ᵇ10]–CH 13 [293ᵇ33] 383b-385b; CH 14 [296ᵃ24–297ᵃ9] 387d-388c / *Meteorology*, BK I, CH 7 [344ᵃ5–9] 450b / *Metaphysics*, BK XII, CH 8 [1073ᵇ17–1074ᵃ17] 604a-c

9 ARISTOTLE: *Motion of Animals*, CH 3 234a-c

11 ARCHIMEDES: *Sand-Reckoner*, 520a-b

12 LUCRETIUS: *Nature of Things*, BK V [526–533] 67d-68a; [720–730] 70c

14 PLUTARCH: *Numa Pompilius*, 55a-b

16 PTOLEMY: *Almagest*, BK I, 7a-8b; 9a-12b; BK III, 83a; 86b-93a; BK IV, 120a-122b; BK IX, 270b-273a; 291a-296a; BK XIII, 429a-b

16 COPERNICUS: *Revolutions of the Heavenly Spheres*, 505a-506a; 507a-508b; BK I, 513b-515b; 517b-521a; BK III, 628b-629a; 653b-656b; BK IV, 675b-678a; BK V, 740a-b

16 KEPLER: *Epitome*, BK IV, 852a-853a; 857b-860b; 887a-890a; 907b-916a; BK V, 964b; 966a-967a / *Harmonies of the World*, 1014b-1016a

19 AQUINAS: *Summa Theologica*, PART I, Q 32, A I, REP 2 175d-178a

25 MONTAIGNE: *Essays*, 257d-261c; 276c

28 GILBERT: *Loadstone*, BK VI, 107c-116a

30 BACON: *Novum Organum*, BK II, APH 5, 139a; APH 36, 165c-166b; APH 46, 178b-c; APH 48, 186b-d

32 MILTON: *Paradise Lost*, BK III [552–587] 147b-148a; BK IV [589–597] 165a-b; BK VIII [66–178] 233b-236a esp [122–158] 234b-235b

33 PASCAL: *Provincial Letters*, 165a / *Vacuum*, 368b-369a

34 NEWTON: *Principles*, BK III, PHENOMENON III 273d-274a; GENERAL SCHOL, 371b-372a

36 STERNE: *Tristram Shandy*, 226b-227a

42 KANT: *Pure Reason*, 8d [fn 2]

43 MILL: *Liberty*, 284a-b

49 DARWIN: *Origin of Species*, 239c

51 TOLSTOY: *War and Peace*, BK XIII, 563a-b; EPILOGUE II, 694d-696d

2c. The relation of astronomy to mathematics: the use of mathematics by astronomy

7 PLATO: *Republic*, BK VII, 394d-396b / *Timaeus*, 451b-c; 455b

8 ARISTOTLE: *Posterior Analytics*, BK I, CH 13 [78ᵇ31–79ᵃ16] 108b-c / *Physics*, BK II, CH 2 [193ᵇ25–194ᵃ11] 270a-c / *Heavens*, BK II, CH 14 [297ᵃ3–9] 388c / *Metaphysics*, BK III, CH 2 [997ᵇ13–998ᵃ19] 516b-d; BK XII, CH 8 [1073ᵇ1–17] 603d-604a; BK XIII, CH 3 [1078ᵃ9–14] 609c

9 ARISTOTLE: *Parts of Animals*, BK I, CH I [639ᵇ6–12] 161c-d

11 NICOMACHUS: *Arithmetic*, BK I, 813d-814a

16 PTOLEMY: *Almagest*, BK I, 5a-6a; 14a-24b; 26a-28b

16 COPERNICUS: *Revolutions of the Heavenly Spheres*, 507a-508a; BK I, 510a-b; 532b-556b

16 KEPLER: *Epitome*, BK V, 964b-965a; 968a-986b passim

18 AUGUSTINE: *Confessions*, BK V, par 3–6 27c-28c / *Christian Doctrine*, BK II, CH 29, 651b-c

19 AQUINAS: *Summa Theologica*, PART I, Q 32, A I, REP 2 175d-178a; PART I–II, Q 35, A 8, ANS 779c-780c

20 AQUINAS: *Summa Theologica*, PART II–II, Q 9, A 2, REP 3 424b-425a

30 BACON: *Advancement of Learning*, 37b; 46b-c
31 DESCARTES: *Meditations*, I, 76c
34 NEWTON: *Principles*, 1a-2a; BK III 269a-372a
36 SWIFT: *Gulliver*, PART III, 94b-103a passim
42 KANT: *Practical Reason*, 361c / *Judgement*, 551a-552a

3. Causes in astronomy

3*a*. Formal archetypal causes: the number and the music of the spheres

7 PLATO: *Phaedo*, 241b-242b / *Republic*, BK VII, 395d-396b; BK X, 438c-439a / *Timaeus*, 447a-452b
8 ARISTOTLE: *Heavens*, BK I, CH 2-5 359d-364a; BK II, CH 1-12 375b,d-384c / *Metaphysics*, BK I, CH 5 [985^{b}22-986^{a}21] 503d-504b; CH 8 [989^{b}29-990^{a}12] 508a-b; BK XII, CH 8 603b-605a
11 NICOMACHUS: *Arithmetic*, BK I, 811a-814b
16 PTOLEMY: *Almagest*, BK I, 8a; BK IX, 270b
16 COPERNICUS: *Revolutions of the Heavenly Spheres*, BK I, 511b
16 KEPLER: *Epitome*, BK IV, 846a-847b; 857b-860b; 863b-887a passim; 913a-b; 915b-916a; 925b-928a; 932a-933a / *Harmonies of the World*, 1016b-1018a; 1023b-1085b esp 1049b-1050b
18 AUGUSTINE: *Confessions*, BK V, par 3-6 27c-28c
21 DANTE: *Divine Comedy*, PARADISE, I [76-126] 107a-c; XXVIII [1-78] 148d-149c
30 BACON: *Novum Organum*, BK II, APH 48, 185c-d
31 SPINOZA: *Ethics*, PART I, APPENDIX, 371d-372a
32 MILTON: *Christs Nativity* [117-140] 4b-5a / *At a Solemn Musick* 13a-b / *Arcades* [54-83] 26b-27a / *Comus* [238-243] 38b / *Paradise Lost*, BK IV [660-688] 166b-167b; BK V [153-184] 178b-179a; [616-627] 188b-189a; BK VIII [15-168] 232b-235b
34 NEWTON: *Principles*, BK III, GENERAL SCHOL, 369b-370a
35 HUME: *Human Understanding*, SECT I, DIV 9, 454c-d
36 SWIFT: *Gulliver*, PART III, 96b-97a
47 GOETHE: *Faust*, PROLOGUE [243-246] 7a

3*b*. Physical efficient causes: gravitation and action-at-a-distance

8 ARISTOTLE: *Heavens*, BK II, CH 8 381a-382a; CH 12 [292^{b}26-293^{a}12] 384b-c / *Meteorology*, BK I, CH 4-8 447d-452d / *Metaphysics*, BK XII, CH 8 603b-605a esp [1073^{b}17-1074^{a}17] 604a-c
12 LUCRETIUS: *Nature of Things*, BK V [509-533] 67d-68a
16 KEPLER: *Epitome*, BK IV, 895b-905a; 922a-b; 935a-952a passim; 959a-960a; BK V, 965a-967a
28 GILBERT: *Loadstone*, BK VI 106a-121a,c
30 BACON: *Novum Organum*, BK II, APH 35-37 162a-169c; APH 45 176a-177c; APH 48, 183b-c
31 DESCARTES: *Rules*, IX, 15c / *Discourse*, PART V, 55b-c

32 MILTON: *Paradise Lost*, BK III [573-587] 148a; BK VIII [122-158] 234b-235b
34 NEWTON: *Principles*, BK III, PROP 1-9 276a-284a esp PROP 7 281b-282b; PROP 35, SCHOL 320b-324a; GENERAL SCHOL, 371b-372a / *Optics*, BK III, 531b; 540a-541b
35 BERKELEY: *Human Knowledge*, SECT 102-108 432d-434a passim
35 HUME: *Human Understanding*, SECT I, DIV 9, 454c-d
36 SWIFT: *Gulliver*, PART III, 94b-103a; 118b-119a
42 KANT: *Pure Reason*, 8d [fn 2]
45 FARADAY: *Researches in Electricity*, 670a-673d; 817a-b; 824a-b; 832b [fn 1]
51 TOLSTOY: *War and Peace*, EPILOGUE II, 694c-695c

4. The relation of astronomy to the other liberal arts and sciences: the place of astronomy in the educational curriculum

7 PLATO: *Gorgias*, 254b-c / *Republic*, BK VII, 391b-398c esp 394d-396b / *Laws*, BK VII, 728b-730d; BK XII, 797b-798b
8 ARISTOTLE: *Physics*, BK II, CH 2 [193^{b}25-194^{a}11] 270a-c / *Metaphysics*, BK XI, CH 6 [1063^{a}10-17] 591b; BK XII, CH 8 [1073^{b}1-7] 603d
11 NICOMACHUS: *Arithmetic*, BK I, 812b-813d
13 VIRGIL: *Aeneid*, BK VI [847-853] 233b-234a
16 PTOLEMY: *Almagest*, BK I, 5a-6a
16 COPERNICUS: *Revolutions of the Heavenly Spheres*, BK I, 510a-b
18 AUGUSTINE: *Christian Doctrine*, BK II, CH 29, 651b-c
20 AQUINAS: *Summa Theologica*, PART II-II, Q 9, A 2, REP 3 424b-425a
23 HOBBES: *Leviathan*, PART I, 72a-d
24 RABELAIS: *Gargantua and Pantagruel*, BK I, 29c; BK II, 82c-d
25 MONTAIGNE: *Essays*, 69d-70c; 257d-259d
30 BACON: *Novum Organum*, BK I, APH 80 120a-b
31 DESCARTES: *Meditations*, I, 76c

5. Astronomy and cosmology: the theory of the world or universe as reflecting astronomical conceptions

7 PLATO: *Timaeus*, 447a-452b; 455a-b
8 ARISTOTLE: *Physics*, BK IV, CH 5 [212^{b}7-21] 291d-292a / *Heavens* 359a-405a,c / *Meteorology*, BK I, CH 1-3 445a-447d / *Metaphysics*, BK XII, CH 8 603b-605a
11 ARCHIMEDES: *Sand-Reckoner*, 520a-b
12 LUCRETIUS: *Nature of Things*, BK I [951-1113] 12d-14d; BK II [1048-1104] 28b-29a; BK VI [647-652] 89a
14 PLUTARCH: *Numa Pompilius*, 55a-b
16 PTOLEMY: *Almagest*, BK I, 10b
16 COPERNICUS: *Revolutions of the Heavenly Spheres*, BK I, 511b; 516a-529a esp 516a-517b
16 KEPLER: *Epitome*, BK IV, 853b-857b; 882a-886b

(5. Astronomy and cosmology: the theory of the world or universe as reflecting astronomical conceptions.)

17 PLOTINUS: *Second Ennead*, TR I 35a-39d
21 DANTE: *Divine Comedy*, PARADISE, X [7-21] 120b-c
25 MONTAIGNE: *Essays*, 213d-215a
31 DESCARTES: *Discourse*, PART V, 54d-56a
32 MILTON: *Paradise Lost*, BK II [890-920] 130b-131a; [1010-1055] 133a-134a; BK III [418-429] 144b; [501-539] 146b-147a; [552-587] 147b-148a; BK VII [261-273] 222b-223a; [551-557] 229a; [617-625] 230b; BK VIII [66-178] 233b-236a; BK X [282-329] 280b-281b
33 PASCAL: *Pensées*, 72 181a-184b
34 NEWTON: *Principles*, BK III, HYPOTHESIS I-PROP 12 285a-286a
35 LOCKE: *Human Understanding*, BK IV, CH III, SECT 24 320c-d
42 KANT: *Practical Reason*, 360d-361a
51 TOLSTOY: *War and Peace*, EPILOGUE II, 695c-d
54 FREUD: *General Introduction*, 562c

6. Astronomy and theology: astronomy as affecting views of God, creation, the divine plan, and the moral hierarchy

OLD TESTAMENT: *Genesis*, 1:1-19 / *Joshua*, 10:12-13—(D) *Josue*, 10:12-13 / *Job*, 9:6-9; 38:1-38 / *Psalms*, 19:1-6; 147:4—(D) *Psalms*, 18:1-7; 146:4 / *Jeremiah*, 33:22; 51:15—(D) *Jeremias*, 33:22; 51:15
APOCRYPHA: *Ecclesiasticus*, 43—(D) OT, *Ecclesiasticus*, 43 / *Song of Three Children*, 34-51—(D) OT, *Daniel*, 3:56-73
NEW TESTAMENT: *I Corinthians*, 15:40-41

7 PLATO: *Republic*, BK VII, 396a / *Timaeus*, 455b-c / *Statesman*, 586c-589c / *Laws*, BK VII, 729d-730d; BK XII, 797d-798b
8 ARISTOTLE: *Physics*, BK II, CH 4 [196^{a}25-^{b}4] 272d-273a; BK VIII 334a-355d esp CH 4-6 338d-346b, CH 10 353b-355d / *Heavens*, BK II, CH 1 375b,d-376a / *Metaphysics*, BK XII, CH 6-8 601b-605a
11 NICOMACHUS: *Arithmetic*, BK I, 811a-814b
12 LUCRETIUS: *Nature of Things*, BK V [55-771] 61d-71a esp [55-234] 61d-64a; [1161-1217] 76b-77a
12 AURELIUS: *Meditations*, BK XI, SECT 27 306b
14 PLUTARCH: *Nicias*, 435b-c
15 TACITUS: *Histories*, BK V, 295c
16 PTOLEMY: *Almagest*, BK I, 5a-6b passim
16 COPERNICUS: *Revolutions of the Heavenly Spheres*, BK I, 510a-511a
16 KEPLER: *Epitome*, BK IV, 853b-854a; 915b-916a; 933a / *Harmonies of the World*, 1017b-1018a; 1025a-b; 1048a; 1061a; 1071b; 1080b-1085b
17 PLOTINUS: *Second Ennead*, TR II, CH I 40a-41a; TR IX, CH 8-9 70a-72a / *Fourth Ennead*, TR III, CH 17 150d-151b

18 AUGUSTINE: *Confessions*, BK V, par 3-6 27c-28c; BK XIII, par 6-48 112a-124a / *Christian Doctrine*, BK II, CH 16, 644d-645a; CH 29 650d-651c
19 AQUINAS: *Summa Theologica*, PART I, Q 23, A 7, ANS and REP 2 138d-140a; Q 50, A 3, ANS and REP 3 272a-273b; Q 58, A I 300c-301a; Q 63, A I, REP 2 325c-326c; A 7, ANS 331c-332b; QQ 66-68 343d-359b; Q 70 362c-367a; Q 102, A 2, REP I 525a-526a; Q 110, A I, REP 2-3 564c-565d; Q 115, AA 3-6 588c-592d
20 AQUINAS: *Summa Theologica*, PART III, Q 5, A 2 736d-737c; PART III SUPPL, Q 77, AA 1-3 943a-947a; Q 91, AA 2-3 1017c-1022c
21 DANTE: *Divine Comedy*, HELL, VII [67-96] 10b-c; XXXIV [100-139] 52b-d; PARADISE, I [94-142] 107b-d; II [46-148] 108b-109b; IV [22-63] 110d-111b; VIII [16-39] 116d-117a; [91-148] 117d-118c; X [1-45] 120b-d; XIII [52-84] 126a-b; XXII [124-154] 140d-141b; XXVII [97-120] 148b-c; XXVIII 148d-150b
25 MONTAIGNE: *Essays*, 213d-215a
27 SHAKESPEARE: *Troilus and Cressida*, ACT I, SC III [85-101] 109a
30 BACON: *Novum Organum*, BK I, APH 89 124a-d
31 DESCARTES: *Discourse*, PART V, 54d-56a
32 MILTON: *Paradise Lost*, BK III [694-732] 150b-151b; BK V [153-184] 178b-179a; BK VIII [66-178] 233b-236a esp [66-84] 233b-234a
33 PASCAL: *Pensées*, 72 181a-184b; 194, 207b; 242 217b-218a
34 NEWTON: *Principles*, BK III, GENERAL SCHOL, 369b-371a / *Optics*, BK III, 542a-543a
41 GIBBON: *Decline and Fall*, 226a-b; 227b-c
42 KANT: *Practical Reason*, 360d-361a
47 GOETHE: *Faust*, PROLOGUE [243-266] 7a-b
49 DARWIN: *Origin of Species*, 239c-d
51 TOLSTOY: *War and Peace*, EPILOGUE II, 695d-696d
54 FREUD: *General Introduction*, 562c / *New Introductory Lectures*, 832a; 876b-d

7. Astronomy and the measurement of time: calendars and clocks; days and seasons

OLD TESTAMENT: *Genesis*, 1:4-5,14-18 / *Isaiah*, 38:7-8; 60:19-21—(D) *Isaias*, 38:7-8; 60:19-21 / *Jeremiah*, 33:20,25—(D) *Jeremias*, 33:20, 25
APOCRYPHA: *Ecclesiasticus*, 43:6-8—(D) OT, *Ecclesiasticus*, 43:6-8
NEW TESTAMENT: *Revelation*, 21:23-24; 22:5—(D) *Apocalypse*, 21:23-24; 22:5

5 AESCHYLUS: *Prometheus Bound* [454-461] 44c-d
5 ARISTOPHANES: *Clouds* [607-626] 496a-b
6 HERODOTUS: *History*, BK II, 49d-50a; 79c
6 THUCYDIDES: *Peloponnesian War*, BK V, 487d
7 PLATO: *Republic*, BK VII, 394d-396b / *Timaeus*, 451a-d
8 ARISTOTLE: *Physics*, BK IV, CH 14 [223^{b}12-224^{a}1] 303c-d / *Metaphysics*, BK X, CH 1 [1052^{b}34-1053^{a}12] 579b-c

9 Aristotle: *Generation of Animals*, bk iv, ch 10 [777^{b}16–778^{a}9] 319d-320a,c

12 Lucretius: *Nature of Things*, bk v [614–750] 69a-70d

14 Plutarch: *Numa Pompilius*, 58d-59c / *Solon*, 74a / *Caesar*, 599d-600a

16 Ptolemy: *Almagest*, bk ii, 34b-38a; bk iii, 77a-86b; 104b-107a

16 Copernicus: *Revolutions of the Heavenly Spheres*, bk i, 510b; bk ii, 568a-576a; bk iii, 646a-652b; 672a-674b

17 Plotinus: *Third Ennead*, tr vii, ch 7–8 122d-124c; ch 11–13 126a-129a

18 Augustine: *Confessions*, bk xi, par 29–30 95d-96c / *City of God*, bk xi, ch 6 325c-d; bk xii, ch 15 351b-352d

19 Aquinas: *Summa Theologica*, part i, q 10, a 6, ans 45c-46d; q 67, a 4, ans and rep 2–3 352a-354a; q 70, a 2, ans and rep 3,5 364b-365a

20 Aquinas: *Summa Theologica*, part iii suppl, q 77, a 2, ans 945a-946b; q 91, a 2, rep 1–3, 5,8 1017c-1020c

21 Dante: *Divine Comedy*, hell, i [37–45] 1b-c; purgatory, i [13–21] 53a-b; ii [1–9] 54c; iv [55–84] 58a-b; ix [1–12] 65d-66a; xv [1–15] 75b-c; xxv [1–9] 91b-c; xxvii [1–6] 94c; paradise, i [38–48] 106c; x [28–33] 120c; xxvii [97–120] 148b-c

23 Hobbes: *Leviathan*, part iv, 267b

24 Rabelais: *Gargantua and Pantagruel*, bk ii, 69b,d-70a

25 Montaigne: *Essays*, 497b-c

30 Bacon: *Novum Organum*, bk ii, aph 46, 177c-178b

32 Milton: *Paradise Lost*, bk iii [40–44] 136b; [555–623] 147b-149a; [726–732] 151a; bk v [166–179] 179a; bk viii [66–84] 233b-234a; bk x [651–679] 288b-289a

34 Newton: *Principles*, definitions, schol, 9b-10a; bk iii, prop 20 291b-294b

35 Locke: *Human Understanding*, bk ii, ch xiv, sect 17–31 158a-162a

36 Swift: *Gulliver*, part iv, 169a

36 Sterne: *Tristram Shandy*, 229a

41 Gibbon: *Decline and Fall*, 376a-b

46 Hegel: *Philosophy of History*, part i, 219a-b; 251a-b

8. The heavenly bodies in general

8a. The special character of matter in the supra-lunar spheres

New Testament: *I Corinthians*, 15:40–41

7 Plato: *Phaedo*, 247b-248c / *Timaeus*, 448a-449c; 451d-452a / *Laws*, bk xii, 797d-798a

8 Aristotle: *Heavens*, bk i, ch 3 [270^{a}12–^{b}26] 361b-362a; bk i, ch 9 [279^{a}12] 368a; ch i [284^{b}6] 370b-376a; bk ii, ch 7 380c-d / *Metaphysics*, bk viii, ch 4 [1044^{b}2–8] 569a-b; bk ix, ch 8 [1050^{b}6–27] 576b-d; bk xi, ch 6 [1063^{a}10–17] 591b; bk xii, ch 2 [1069^{b}24–27] 598d-599a

9 Aristotle: *Parts of Animals*, bk i, ch 5 [644^{b}21–645^{a}5] 168c-d

12 Lucretius: *Nature of Things*, bk i [418–448] 6b-c; [1052–1094] 14a-c; bk v [534–563] 68a-b

16 Ptolemy: *Almagest*, bk i, 5a-6a; 8b; 10b-11b; bk xiii, 429a-b

16 Copernicus: *Revolutions of the Heavenly Spheres*, bk i, 517b-518a; 519b-520a

16 Kepler: *Epitome*, bk iv, 853b-857b; 888b-890b; 894a-b; 904b-905a; 919b; 929b-930b; 931b-932a; 934b-935b

17 Plotinus: *Second Ennead*, tr i 35a-39d / *Third Ennead*, tr v, ch 6 103b-104a

19 Aquinas: *Summa Theologica*, part i, q 10, a 5, ans 44b-45c; a 6, rep 2 45c-46d; q 46, a 1, rep 2–3,5 250a-252d; q 55, a 2, ans 289d-290d; q 58, a 1, ans 300c-301a; a 3, ans 301d-302d; q 63, a 1, rep 2 325c-326c; q 66, a 2 345d-347b; q 68, a 1, ans 354a-355c; q 70, a 3, ans and rep 2 365b-367a; q 75, a 6, ans 383c-384c; q 84, a 3, rep 1 443d-444d; q 97, a 1, ans 513c-514c; q 104, a 1, rep 1,3 534c-536c; q 115, a 3, ans 588c-589c; q 119, a 1, ans 604c-607b

20 Aquinas: *Summa Theologica*, part i-ii, q 49, a 4, ans 5a-6a; part iii, q 5, a 2, ans and rep 3 736d-737c; part iii suppl, q 91, a 3, rep 3 1020d-1022c

21 Dante: *Divine Comedy*, purgatory, iii [28–30] 56a; paradise, ii [19–45] 108a; [112–148] 109a-b; xxviii [1–78] 148d-149c

25 Montaigne: *Essays*, 213d-215a; 257d-258b

28 Gilbert: *Loadstone*, bk vi, 110b-c

30 Bacon: *Novum Organum*, bk ii, aph 13, 146c-147a

33 Pascal: *Vacuum*, 358a

34 Newton: *Principles*, bk iii, rule iii 270b, 271a; prop 1–7 276a-282b esp prop 7 281b, 282b

41 Gibbon: *Decline and Fall*, 226b

8b. Soul and intellect in the heavenly bodies

7 Plato: *Phaedrus*, 124c-d / *Apology*, 204d-205a / *Timaeus*, 449b-450c; 451d-452b / *Philebus*, 618b-619c / *Laws*, bk x, 762b-765c esp 764a-765c; bk xii, 797c-798b

8 Aristotle: *Heavens*, bk ii, ch 1–2 375b,d-377c; ch 12 383b-384c / *Metaphysics*, bk xii, ch 8 603b-605a / *Soul*, bk i, ch 3 [406^{b}26–407^{b}13] 636b-637b

12 Lucretius: *Nature of Things*, bk v [76–90] 62a-b; [110–145] 62c-63a

13 Virgil: *Aeneid*, bk vi [724–738] 230b

16 Kepler: *Epitome*, bk iv, 854b-856a; 890a-895b; 896a-897a; 914a-b; 930b; 932a-933a; 959a-960a / *Harmonies of the World*, 1080b-1085b esp 1083b-1085b

17 Plotinus: *Second Ennead*, tr ii–iii 40a-50a / *Third Ennead*, tr ii, ch 3, 84b; tr iv, ch 6, 99d; tr v, ch 6 103b-104a / *Fourth Ennead*, tr iv, ch 6–8 161b-162d; ch 22–27 168d-172a;

8c(3) The laws of celestial motion: celestial mechanics

8d. The creation of the heavens

9. The particular heavenly bodies

9a. The sun: its position, distance, size, and mass

(9. The particular heavenly bodies. 9a. The sun: its position, distance, size, and mass.)

25 MONTAIGNE: *Essays*, 257d-258b
28 GILBERT: *Loadstone*, BK VI, 112d-113a
30 BACON: *Novum Organum*, BK II, APH 36, 165c-166b
31 DESCARTES: *Discourse*, PART V, 54d-56a passim / *Objections and Replies*, 231a; 233c
32 MILTON: *Paradise Lost*, BK III [555-623] 147b-149a; BK IV [539-543] 164a; BK VII [354-373] 224b-225a; BK VIII [66-168] 233b-235b
33 PASCAL: *Pensées*, 72, 181a
34 NEWTON: *Principles*, BK I, PROP 66 118a-128b; BK III, PHENOMENON III 273d-274a; PROP 2 276a-b; HYPOTHESIS I-PROP 12 285a-286a; PROP 25 299b-300b; PROP 36 324a-b; PROP 40 337b-338a / *Optics*, BK III, 518a-b
36 SWIFT: *Gulliver*, PART III, 98a-b
45 FARADAY: *Researches in Electricity*, 819d

9b. The moon: its irregularities

OLD TESTAMENT: *Genesis*, 1:14-18 / *Psalms*, 136:7-9—(D) *Psalms*, 135:7-9 / *Isaiah*, 13:9-11; 30:26; 60:19-20—(D) *Isaias*, 13:9-11; 30:26; 60:19-20 / *Joel*, 2:10,31; 3:15
APOCRYPHA: *Ecclesiasticus*, 43:6-8—(D) OT, *Ecclesiasticus*, 43:6-9
NEW TESTAMENT: *Matthew*, 24:29-30 / *Mark*, 13:24-25
7 PLATO: *Cratylus*, 98a-b / *Apology*, 204d-205a / *Timaeus*, 451b-d
8 ARISTOTLE: *Heavens*, BK II, CH 11 [291^{b}18-23] 383b; CH 12 [291^{b}29-292^{b}27] 383c-384b; CH 14 [297^{b}21-31] 389b-c
12 LUCRETIUS: *Nature of Things*, BK V [471-479] 67b; [575-584] 68c; [629-649] 69b-c; [705-771] 70b-71a
14 PLUTARCH: *Solon*, 74a / *Aemilius Paulus*, 220d-221b / *Nicias*, 435b-d / *Dion*, 789b-790a
16 PTOLEMY: *Almagest*, BK IV-VI 108a-222b
16 COPERNICUS: *Revolutions of the Heavenly Spheres*, BK IV 675a-731a
16 KEPLER: *Epitome*, BK IV, 876a-878a; 918a-928a; 952a-960a
17 PLOTINUS: *Second Ennead*, TR III, CH 5, 43d-44a
19 AQUINAS: *Summa Theologica*, PART I, Q 70, A 1, REP 5 362c-364b
21 DANTE: *Divine Comedy*, PARADISE, II [46-148] 108b-109b
24 RABELAIS: *Gargantua and Pantagruel*, BK III, 188c
26 SHAKESPEARE: *Romeo and Juliet*, ACT II, SC II [107-110] 295b / *Midsummer-Night's Dream*, ACT II, SC I [103-114] 357a-b
30 BACON: *Novum Organum*, BK II, APH 36, 167a-b
32 MILTON: *Paradise Lost*, BK II [662-666] 125b; BK III [708-735] 150b-151b; BK V [257-266] 180b-181a; BK VII [346-386] 224b-225b; BK

VIII [122-158] 234b-235b / *Samson Agonistes* [86-89] 341b
33 PASCAL: *Provincial Letters*, 164a / *Pensées*, 18 174b-175a; 817, 330b
34 NEWTON: *Principles*, BK I, PROP 43-45 92b-101a; PROP 66 118a-128b; BK III, PHENOMENON VI 275a; PROP 3-4 and SCHOL 276b-278b; PROP 22-38 294b-329a
34 HUYGENS: *Light*, CH I, 554b-555a

9c. The planets: their eccentricities, retrogradations, and stations

7 PLATO: *Republic*, BK X, 438c-439a / *Timaeus*, 451a-d
8 ARISTOTLE: *Heavens*, BK II, CH 2 [285^{b}28-33] 377b-c; CH 7-12 380c-384c / *Metaphysics*, BK XII, CH 8 603b-605a
16 PTOLEMY: *Almagest*, BK IX-XIII 270a-465b
16 COPERNICUS: *Revolutions of the Heavenly Spheres*, BK I, 521b-529a; BK V-VI 732a-838a
16 KEPLER: *Epitome*, BK IV, 860b-872b; 878b-882a; 888b-905a; 907b-910a; 928a-952a passim; BK V 961a-1004a / *Harmonies of the World*, 1015b-1080b
17 PLOTINUS: *Second Ennead*, TR III, CH 5, 44a
19 AQUINAS: *Summa Theologica*, PART I, Q 32, A 1, REP 2 175d-178a
21 DANTE: *Divine Comedy*, PARADISE, II [46-148] 108b-109b; X [1-27] 120b-c; XXII [124-154] 140d-141b
24 RABELAIS: *Gargantua and Pantagruel*, BK I, 29c
30 BACON: *Novum Organum*, BK II, APH 36, 165c-166b
31 DESCARTES: *Discourse*, PART V, 54d-56a passim
32 MILTON: *Paradise Lost*, BK III [481-483] 146a; [573-587] 148a; BK V [166-170] 179a; [618-627] 188b-189a; BK VII [557-564] 229a-b; BK VIII [122-152] 234b-235b; BK IX [48-51] 248b; BK X [657-661] 288b
33 PASCAL: *Vacuum*, 368b-369a
34 NEWTON: *Principles*, BK I, PROP 1-3 and SCHOL 32b-35b; PROP 4, COROL VI 36a; PROP 11 42b-43b; PROP 15 46b-47a; PROP 17 48b-50a; PROP 57-63 111b-115a; PROP 65-69 116b-130b; BK III, PHENOMENON I-V 272a-275a; PROP 1-2 276a-b; PROP 5-6 278b-281b; PROP 8-10 282b-285a; PROP 13-19 286a-291b
34 HUYGENS: *Light*, CH I, 556a-557b
36 SWIFT: *Gulliver*, PART III, 102a
36 STERNE: *Tristram Shandy*, 227a
45 FOURIER: *Theory of Heat*, 171b
45 FARADAY: *Researches in Electricity*, 632b
51 TOLSTOY: *War and Peace*, BK XIII, 563b

9d. The earth: its origin, position, shape, and motions

OLD TESTAMENT: *Genesis*, 1:1-10 / *Job*, 38:4-7 / *Psalms*, 90:2; 102:25; 119:90—(D) *Psalms*, 89:2; 101:26; 118:90 / *Proverbs*, 3:19; 8:23-29 /

(10. *The influence of the heavenly bodies upon terrestrial phenomena.*)

20 AQUINAS: *Summa Theologica*, PART III SUPPL, Q 76, A 1, REP 2 939d-941a; Q 77, A 1, ANS 943a-944d; Q 86, A 2, ANS and REP 1-2 993c-994d; Q 91, A 1, REP 1 1016b-1017c

21 DANTE: *Divine Comedy*, PARADISE, II [112-148] 109a-b; VII [121-141] 116b-c; VIII [97-114] 118a; X [1-27] 120b-c; XIII [52-78] 126a-b

22 CHAUCER: *Miller's Tale* [3187-3212] 212b-213a; [3513-3533] 218a

24 RABELAIS: *Gargantua and Pantagruel*, BK II, 72c

27 SHAKESPEARE: *Troilus and Cressida*, ACT I, SC III [85-101] 109a

28 GILBERT: *Loadstone*, BK I, 14a

32 MILTON: *Arcades* [61-73] 26b / *Paradise Lost*, BK III [606-612] 148b; BK IV [660-688] 166b-167b; BK VIII [85-106] 234a-b; BK X [641-719] 288b-290a

33 PASCAL: *Pensées*, 18 174b-175a

36 SWIFT: *Gulliver*, PART III, 98a-b

41 GIBBON: *Decline and Fall*, 226b

10a. The influence of the heavenly bodies on living matter: generation and corruption

7 PLATO: *Cratylus*, 98a / *Theaetetus*, 518b

8 ARISTOTLE: *Physics*, BK II, CH 2 [194^{b}13] 271a / *Heavens*, BK I, CH 9 [279^{a}22-30] 370c; BK II, CH 3 377c-378a / *Generation and Corruption*, BK II, CH 10 437d-439c / *Metaphysics*, BK XII, CH 5 [1071^{a}12-17] 600c; CH 6 [1072^{a}9-18] 602a

9 ARISTOTLE: *Parts of Animals*, BK IV, CH 5 [680^{a}30-35] 210d / *Generation of Animals*, BK I, CH 2 [716^{a}15-20] 256b; BK II, CH 3 [736^{b}30-737^{a}5] 277c-d; CH 4 [738^{a}9-25] 278d-279a; BK IV, CH 2 [767^{a}2-9] 308b; CH 10 [777^{b}15-778^{a}10] 319d-320a,c

12 LUCRETIUS: *Nature of Things*, BK V [76-81] 62a

19 AQUINAS: *Summa Theologica*, PART I, Q 25, A 2, REP 2 144c-145b; Q 70, A 1, REP 4 362c-364b; A 3, REP 3 365b-367a; Q 71, A 1, REP 1 367a-368b; Q 82, A 4, ANS 434c-435c; Q 86, A 4, REP 2-3 463d-464d; Q 91, A 2, REP 2 485b-486b; Q 92, A 1, ANS 488d-489d; Q 105, A 1, REP 1 538d-539c; Q 115, A 3 588c-589c; A 5, REP 1 590d-591c; Q 118, A 1, REP 3 600a-601c

20 AQUINAS: *Summa Theologica*, PART I-II, Q 60, A 1, ANS 49d-50c; PART III SUPPL, Q 76, A 1, REP 2 939d-941a; Q 84, A 2, REP 3 984c-985d; Q 86, A 2, ANS and REP 1-2 993c-994d; Q 91, A 1, REP 1 1016b-1017c; A 2, ANS and REP 1,4 1017c-1020c; A 3, REP 2 1020d-1022c

21 DANTE: *Divine Comedy*, PARADISE, VII [121-141] 116b-c; X [7-21] 120b-c; XIII [52-78] 126a-b

22 CHAUCER: *Franklin's Tale* [11,343-347] 356b

28 GILBERT: *Loadstone*, BK V, 105a-b

28 HARVEY: *On Animal Generation*, 416a; 427b-d; 428c-429a

29 CERVANTES: *Don Quixote*, PART II, 340b

30 BACON: *Novum Organum*, BK II, APH 11, 140d-141a; APH 12, 141d; APH 35, 162b-c

32 MILTON: *Paradise Lost*, BK IV [634-688] 166a-167b; BK VIII [66-178] 233b-236a esp [90-97] 234a; BK IX [99-113] 249b

33 PASCAL: *Pensées*, 18 174b-175a

49 DARWIN: *Descent of Man*, 256c

10b. The influence of the heavenly bodies on the tides

6 HERODOTUS: *History*, BK II, 53d-54b

16 KEPLER: *Epitome*, BK IV, 919b

19 AQUINAS: *Summa Theologica*, PART I, Q 105, A 6, REP 1 543b-544a; Q 110, A 3, REP 1 566d-567b

20 AQUINAS: *Summa Theologica*, PART II-II, Q 2, A 3, ANS 392d-393c

22 CHAUCER: *Franklin's Tale* [11,355-388] 356b-357a

28 GILBERT: *Loadstone*, BK II, 47a-b; BK VI, 113a

30 BACON: *Novum Organum*, BK II, APH 36, 164b-165c; APH 45, 176b; APH 46, 178c

31 DESCARTES: *Discourse*, PART V, 55c

33 PASCAL: *Pensées*, 817, 330b

34 NEWTON: *Principles*, BK I, PROP 66, COROL XVIII-XIX 126a-b; BK III, PROP 24 296a-299b; PROP 36-37 324a-328b

35 BERKELEY: *Human Knowledge*, SECT 104 433a-b

11. The influence of the stars and planets upon the character and actions of men

OLD TESTAMENT: *Isaiah*, 47:13—(D) *Isaias*, 47:13 / *Jeremiah*, 10:2—(D) *Jeremias*, 10:2

APOCRYPHA: *Baruch*, 6:60-69—(D) OT, *Baruch*, 6:60-68

6 HERODOTUS: *History*, BK II, 65b; BK VII, 223b-c; BK IX, 289d-290a

6 THUCYDIDES: *Peloponnesian War*, BK VII, 552a-c

14 PLUTARCH: *Romulus*, 20b-c / *Nicias*, 435b-d / *Dion*, 789b-790a

15 TACITUS: *Annals*, BK I, 9a-b; 9d; BK IV, 79b; BK VI, 91a-d / *Histories*, BK I, 195b-c; BK V, 295c

17 PLOTINUS: *Second Ennead*, TR III 42a-50a / *Third Ennead*, TR I, CH 2 78d-79b; CH 5-6 80a-81b; TR II, CH 10 88a-b / *Fourth Ennead*, TR IV, CH 30-45 174b-183a

18 AUGUSTINE: *Confessions*, BK IV, par 4-6 20a-d; BK VII, par 8-10 45d-47a / *City of God*, BK III, CH 15, 176d-177a; BK V, CH 1-7 207a-212c / *Christian Doctrine*, BK II, CH 21-23 647a-648d

19 AQUINAS: *Summa Theologica*, PART I, Q 70, A 2, REP 1 364b-365a; Q 86, A 4, REP 2-3 463d-464d; Q 96, A 3, ANS 512a-c; Q 115, A 4 589d-590c; A 5, REP 1 590d-591c; Q 116, A 1, ANS 592d-593d; PART I-II, Q 9, A 5 660d-662a

21 DANTE: *Divine Comedy*, HELL, VII [67-96] 10b-c; PURGATORY, XVI [52-84] 77b-d; PARA-

12. The worship of the earth, sun, moon, and stars

13. The history of astronomy

(13. *The history of astronomy*.)

25 MONTAIGNE: *Essays*, 257d-258b

28 GILBERT: *Loadstone*, BK VI, 107c-d; 117c-d; 118d-119c

30 BACON: *Advancement of Learning*, 24d / *Novum Organum*, BK I, APH 80 120a-b; APH 89 124a-d; BK II, APH 36, 165c-167b

32 MILTON: *Paradise Lost*, BK I [284-291] 99b; BK V [261-263] 181a; BK VIII [66-168] 233b-235b / *Areopagitica*, 400a

33 PASCAL: *Provincial Letters*, 165a / *Vacuum*, 358a; 368b-369a

35 BERKELEY: *Human Knowledge*, SECT 58 424a-b; SECT 104 433a-b

35 HUME: *Human Understanding*, SECT I, DIV 9, 454c-d

36 STERNE: *Tristram Shandy*, 227a

41 GIBBON: *Decline and Fall*, 68c-69a; 226b; 299b-c; 664d [n 55-56]

42 KANT: *Pure Reason*, 8d [fn 2]; 175b [fn 1] / *Practical Reason*, 361b-c

46 HEGEL: *Philosophy of History*, PART I, 219a-b; 251a-b

51 TOLSTOY: *War and Peace*, BK VIII, 340d-341a,c; BK XIII, 563b; EPILOGUE II, 694d-696d

CROSS-REFERENCES

For: The discussion of related disciplines, *see* MATHEMATICS; MECHANICS; PHYSICS.

The consideration of mathematical physics, *see* MATHEMATICS 5b; MECHANICS 3; PHYSICS 1b, 3; SCIENCE 5c.

Other treatments of observation and measurement in natural science, *see* EXPERIENCE 5-5c; MECHANICS 2a; PHYSICS 3, 4a, 4d; QUANTITY 6-6c; SCIENCE 5a-5b; SENSE 5.

The logic of hypotheses and their verification in scientific method, *see* HYPOTHESIS 4b-4d; PHYSICS 4b; PRINCIPLE 3c(2); SCIENCE 5e.

The general consideration of scientific method, *see* LOGIC 4b; REASONING 6c; SCIENCE 5-5e.

The distinction between formal and efficient causes, *see* CAUSE 1a; and for the role of causes and causal explanation in natural science, *see* CAUSE 5b; NATURE 3c; PHYSICS 2b; SCIENCE 4c.

The consideration of certain mathematical forms used in astronomy, *see* QUANTITY 3b(1)-3b(2), 3e(2).

Other discussions of celestial and terrestrial mechanics, *see* MECHANICS 4a, 5f-5f(2), 6c.

The theory of gravitation and the problem of action-at-a-distance, *see* MECHANICS 6d(1)-6d(2); SPACE 2c.

The issues concerning matter and soul or intellect in relation to the heavenly bodies, *see* ANGEL 2a; MATTER 1b; SOUL 1a; WORLD 6a.

Other discussions of the measurement of time, *see* QUANTITY 5b; TIME 4.

The interpretation of celestial phenomena in divination and augury, *see* LANGUAGE 10; PROPHECY 3b; SIGN AND SYMBOL 5b.

Criticisms of astrology, *see* RELIGION 6a.

The cosmological and theological implications of astronomy, *see* ANGEL 2a; CHANGE 13-14; ETERNITY 2; INFINITY 3d-3e; SPACE 3a; TIME 2b; WORLD 4a, 4e, 5, 7.

ADDITIONAL READINGS

Listed below are works not included in *Great Books of the Western World*, but relevant to the idea and topics with which this chapter deals. These works are divided into two groups:

I. Works by authors represented in this collection.
II. Works by authors not represented in this collection.

For the date, place, and other facts concerning the publication of the works cited, consult the Bibliography of Additional Readings which follows the last chapter of *The Great Ideas*.

I.

PTOLEMY. *Tetrabiblos*
AQUINAS. *Summa Contra Gentiles*, BK III, CH 84–87
——. *On the Trinity of Boethius*, Q 5
DANTE. *Convivio (The Banquet)*, SECOND TREATISE, CH 3–4
CHAUCER. *A Treatise on the Astrolabe*
COPERNICUS. *Commentariolus*
——. *Letter Against Werner*
KEPLER. *Mysterium Cosmographicum*
——. *De Motibus Stellae Martis*
——. *Harmonices Mundi*, BK I–IV
GALILEO. *The Sidereal Messenger*
——. *Dialogo dei massimi sistemi*
DESCARTES. *The Principles of Philosophy*, PART III, 5–47, 103–120, 126–157
HOBBES. *Concerning Body*, PART IV, CH 26
KANT. *Cosmogony*
A. SMITH. *The History of Astronomy*

II.

ARISTARCHUS. *On the Sizes and Distances of the Sun and Moon*
EPICURUS. *Letter to Pythocles*
——. *Letter to Herodotus*
IBN EZRA. *The Beginning of Wisdom*
MAIMONIDES. *The Guide for the Perplexed*, PART II, CH 8–12, 24
R. BACON. *Opus Majus*, PART IV
RHETICUS. *Narratio Prima*
SUÁREZ. *Disputationes Metaphysicae*, XIII (10–13), XV (3)
FONTENELLE. *Conversations on the Plurality of Worlds*
VOLTAIRE. "Astrology," "Astronomy," in *A Philosophical Dictionary*
LAGRANGE. *Mécanique analytique*

LAPLACE. *The System of the World*
——. *Mécanique céleste (Celestial Mechanics)*
GAUSS. *Inaugural Lecture on Astronomy*
WHEWELL. *Astronomy and General Physics Considered with Reference to Natural Theology*
COMTE. *The Positive Philosophy*, BK II
A. HUMBOLDT. *Cosmos*
HERSCHEL. *Familiar Lectures on Scientific Subjects*, II
FRAZER. *The Golden Bough*, PART IV, BK III, CH 7–9; PART V, NOTE (Pliades in Primitive Calendars)
G. H. DARWIN. *The Evolution of the Satellites*
——. *The Tides and Kindred Phenomena in the Solar System*
SANTAYANA. *Reason in Society*, CH 4
DREYER. *History of the Planetary Systems*
POINCARÉ. *The Value of Science*, PART II, CH 6
——. *Science and Method*, BK III, CH 3; BK IV
KAPTEYN. *Recent Researches in the Structure of the Universe*
DUHEM. *Le système du monde*
ARRHENIUS. *The Destinies of the Stars*
T. CHAMBERLIN. *The Origin of the Earth*
E. HUNTINGTON. *Earth and Sun*
DINGLE. *Modern Astrophysics*
SHAPLEY. *Starlight*
EDDINGTON. *The Internal Constitution of the Stars*
——. *Stars and Atoms*
JEANS. *Problems of Cosmogony and Stellar Dynamics*
——. *Astronomy and Cosmogony*
TOLMAN. *Relativity, Thermodynamics, and Cosmology*
H. N. RUSSELL. *The Solar System and Its Origin*
ABETTI. *The Sun: Its Phenomena and Physical Features*
HUBBLE. *The Realm of the Nebulae*
GAMOW. *The Birth and Death of the Sun*
B. RUSSELL. *Human Knowledge, Its Scope and Limits*, PART I, CH 2

Chapter 6: BEAUTY

INTRODUCTION

TRUTH, goodness, and beauty form a triad of terms which have been discussed together throughout the tradition of western thought.

They have been called "transcendental" on the ground that everything which *is* is in some measure or manner subject to denomination as true or false, good or evil, beautiful or ugly. But they have also been assigned to special spheres of being or subject matter—the true to thought and logic, the good to action and morals, the beautiful to enjoyment and aesthetics.

They have been called "the three fundamental values" with the implication that the worth of anything can be exhaustively judged by reference to these three standards—and no others. But other terms, such as pleasure or utility, have been proposed, either as additional values or as significant variants of the so-called fundamental three; or even sometimes as more fundamental. Pleasure or utility, for example, has been held by men like Spinoza or Mill to be the ultimate criterion of beauty or goodness.

Truth, goodness, and beauty, singly and together, have been the focus of the age-old controversy concerning the absolute and the relative, the objective and the subjective, the universal and the individual. At certain times it has been thought that the distinction of true from false, good from evil, beautiful from ugly, has its basis and warranty in the very nature of things, and that a man's judgment of these matters is measured for its soundness or accuracy by its conformity to fact. At other times the opposite position has been dominant. One meaning of the ancient saying that man is the measure of all things applies particularly to the true, good, and beautiful. Man measures truth, goodness, and beauty by the effect things have upon him, according to what they *seem* to him to be. What

seems good to one man may seem evil to another. What seems ugly or false may also seem beautiful or true to different men or to the same man at different times.

Yet it is not altogether true that these three terms have always suffered the same fortunes. For Spinoza goodness and beauty are subjective, but not truth. Because he "has persuaded himself that all things which exist are made for him," man, Spinoza says, judges that to be "of the greatest importance which is most useful to him, and he must esteem that to be of surpassing worth by which he is most beneficially affected." The notions of good and evil, beauty and ugliness, do not conform to anything in the nature of things. "The ignorant," says Spinoza, nevertheless, "call the nature of a thing good, evil, sound, putrid, or corrupt just as they are affected by it. For example, if the motion by which the nerves are affected by means of objects represented to the eye conduces to well-being, the objects by which it is caused are called *beautiful*; while those exciting a contrary motion are called *deformed*."

BEAUTY HAS BEEN most frequently regarded as subjective, or relative to the individual judgment. The familiar maxim, *de gustibus non disputandum*, has its original application in the sphere of beauty rather than truth and goodness. "Truth is disputable," Hume writes, "not taste . . . No man reasons concerning another's beauty; but frequently concerning the justice or injustice of his actions." Thus even when it was supposed that judgments of the true and the good could have a certain absoluteness or universality—or at least be considered as something about which men might reach agreement through argument—opinions about beauty were set apart as useless to dispute. Beauty being simply a matter of individual taste, it could afford no basis for argument or reasoning —no objective ground for settling differences of opinion.

From the ancient skeptics down to our own day, men have noted the great variety of traits, often sharply opposed, which have been considered beautiful at different times and places. "We fancy its forms," Montaigne says of beauty, "according to our appetite and liking . . . Indians paint it black and tawny, with great swollen lips, big flat noses, and load the cartilage betwixt the nostrils with great rings of gold to make it hang down to the mouth . . . In Peru, the greatest ears are the most beautiful, and they stretch them out as far as they can by art . . . There are, elsewhere, nations that take great care to blacken their teeth, and hate to see them white; elsewhere, people that paint them red . . . The Italians fashion beauty gross and massive; the Spaniards, gaunt and slender; among us one makes it white, another brown; one soft and delicate, another strong and vigorous . . . . Just as the preference in beauty is given by Plato to the spherical figure, the Epicureans give it to the pyramidal or the square, and cannot swallow a god in the form of a ball."

Like Montaigne, Darwin gives an extensive account of the things men have found beautiful, many of them so various and contradictory that it would seem there could be no objective basis for judgments of beauty. If any consensus is found among individuals about what is beautiful or ugly, the skeptics or relativists usually explain it by reference to the prevalence of certain prejudices, or customary standards, which in turn vary with different tribes and cultures, and at different times and places.

Beginning in the sphere of beauty, subjectivism or relativism spreads first to judgments of good and evil, and then to statements about truth, never in the opposite direction. It becomes complete when, as so frequently happens in our own time, what is good or true is held to be just as much a matter of private taste or customary opinion as what is beautiful.

The problem of the objectivity or subjectivity of beauty can, of course, be separated from similar problems with regard to truth and goodness, but any attempt to solve it will necessarily both draw on and bear on the discussion of these related problems. The degree to which the three problems must be considered interdependently is determined by the extent to which each of the three terms requires the context of the other two for its definition and analysis.

BEAUTY IS, PERHAPS, not definable in any strict sense of definition. But there have been, nevertheless, many attempts to state, with the brevity of definition, what beauty is. Usually notions of goodness, or correlative notions of desire and love, enter into the statement.

Aquinas, for example, declares that "the beautiful is the same as the good, and they differ in aspect only. . . . The notion of good is that which calms the desire, while the notion of the beautiful is that which calms the desire, by being seen or known." This, according to Aquinas, implies that "beauty adds to goodness a relation to the cognitive faculty; so that *good* means that which simply pleases the appetite, while the *beautiful* is something pleasant to apprehend."

Because of its relation to the cognitive power, Aquinas defines the beautiful as "that which pleases upon being seen" (*id quod visum placet*). Hence, he continues, "beauty consists in due proportion, for the senses delight in things duly proportioned . . . because the sense too is a sort of reason, as is every cognitive power."

The pleasure or delight involved in the perception of beauty belongs to the order of knowing rather than to desire or action. The knowing, furthermore, seems to be different from that which is proper to science, for it is concerned with the individual thing rather than with universal natures, and it occurs intuitively or contemplatively, rather than by judgment and reasoning. There is a mode of truth peculiar to the beautiful, as well as a special kind of goodness.

Fully to understand what Aquinas is saying about beauty we are required to understand his theory of goodness and truth. But enough is immediately clear to give meaning to Eric Gill's advice to those who are concerned with making things beautiful: "Look after goodness and truth," he says, "and beauty will take care of herself."

To define beauty in terms of pleasure would

seem to make it relative to the individual, for what gives pleasure—even contemplative pleasure—to one man, may not to another. It should be noted, however, that the pleasure in question is attributed· to the object as its cause. It may be asked, therefore, what in the object is the cause of the peculiar satisfaction which constitutes the experience of beauty? Can the same object just as readily arouse displeasure in another individual, and a consequent judgment of ugliness? Are these opposite reactions entirely the result of the way an individual feels?

Aquinas appears to meet this difficulty by specifying certain objective elements of beauty, or "conditions," as he calls them. "Beauty includes three conditions," he writes: "*integrity* or *perfection*, since those things which are impaired are by that very fact ugly; due *proportion* or *harmony*; and lastly, *brightness* or *clarity*, whence things are called beautiful which have a bright color." Quite apart from individual reactions, objects may differ in the degree to which they possess such properties— traits which are capable of pleasing or displeasing their beholder.

This does not mean that the individual reaction is invariably in accordance with the objective characteristics of the thing beheld. Men differ in the degree to which they possess good perception—and sound critical judgment— even as objects differ in the degree to which they possess the elements of beauty. Once again in the controversy concerning the objectivity or subjectivity of beauty, there seems to be a middle ground between the two extreme positions, which insists upon a beauty intrinsic to the object but does not deny the relevance of differences in individual sensibility.

William James would seem to be indicating such a position when, in his discussion of aesthetic principles, he declares: "We are once and for all so made that when certain impressions come before our mind, one of them will seem to call for or repel the others as its companions." As an example, he cites the fact that "a note sounds good with its third and fifth." Such an aesthetic judgment certainly depends upon individual sensibility, and, James adds, "to a certain extent the principle of habit will explain [it]." But he also points out that "to explain *all* aesthetic judgements in this way would be ab-

surd; for it is notorious how seldom natural experiences come up to our aesthetic demands." To the extent that aesthetic judgments "express inner harmonies and discords between objects of thought," the beautiful, according to James, has a certain objectivity; and good taste can be conceived as the capacity to be pleased by objects which *should* elicit that reaction.

KANT'S THEORY OF the beautiful, to take another conception, must also be understood in the general context of his theory of knowledge, and his analysis of such terms as good, pleasure, and desire. His definition, like that of Aquinas, calls an object beautiful if it satisfies the observer in a very special way—not merely pleasing his senses, or satisfying his desires, in the ways in which things good as means or ends fit a man's interests or purposes. The beautiful, according to Kant, "pleases *immediately ... apart from all interest*." The pleasure that results from its contemplation "may be said to be the one and only disinterested and *free* delight; for, with it, no interest, whether of sense or reason, extorts approval."

The aesthetic experience is for Kant also unique in that its judgment "is represented as *universal, i.e.* valid for every man," yet at the same time it is "incognizable by means of any universal concept." In other words, "all judgements of taste are singular judgements"; they are without concept in the sense that they do not apply to a class of objects. Nevertheless, they have a certain universality and are not merely the formulation of a private judgment. When "we call the object beautiful," Kant says, "we believe ourselves to be speaking with a universal voice, and lay claim to the concurrence of every one, whereas no private sensation would be decisive except for the observer alone and *his* liking."

In saying that aesthetic judgments have subjective, not objective, universality, and in holding that the beautiful is the object of a necessary satisfaction, Kant also seems to take the middle position which recognizes the subjectivity of the aesthetic judgment without denying that beauty is somehow an intrinsic property of objects. With regard to its subjective character, Kant cites Hume to the effect that "although critics are able to reason more plausibly than cooks, they must still share the same fate." The universal character of the aesthetic judgment, however, keeps it from being completely subjective and Kant goes to some length to refute the notion that in matters of the beautiful one can seek refuge in the adage that "every one has his own taste."

The fact that the aesthetic judgment requires universal assent, even though the universal rule on which it is based cannot be formulated, does not, of course, preclude the failure of the object to win such assent from many individuals. Not all men have good taste or, having it, have it to the same degree.

THE FOREGOING CONSIDERATIONS—selective rather than exhaustive—show the connection between definitions of beauty and the problem of aesthetic training. In the traditional discussion of the ends of education, there is the problem of how to cultivate good taste—the ability to discriminate critically between the beautiful and the ugly.

If beauty is entirely subjective, entirely a matter of individual feeling, then, except for conformity to standards set by the customs of the time and place, no criteria would seem to be available for measuring the taste of individuals. If beauty is simply objective—something immediately apparent to observation as are the simple sensible qualities—no special training would seem to be needed for sharpening our perception of it.

The genuineness of the educational problem in the sphere of beauty seems, therefore, to depend upon a theory of the beautiful which avoids both extremes, and which permits the educator to aim at a development of individual sensibilities in accordance with objective criteria of taste.

THE FOREGOING CONSIDERATIONS also provide background for the problem of beauty in nature and in art. As indicated in the chapter on ART, the consideration of art in recent times tends to become restricted to the theory of the fine arts. So too the consideration of beauty has become more and more an analysis of excellence in poetry, music, painting, and sculpture. In consequence, the meaning of the word "aesthetic" has progressively narrowed, until now it refers almost exclusively to the appreciation of works of fine art, where before it connoted any experience of the beautiful, in the things of nature as well as in the works of man.

The question is raised, then, whether natural beauty, or the perception of beauty in nature, involves the same elements and causes as beauty in art. Is the beauty of a flower or of a flowering field determined by the same factors as the beauty of a still life or a landscape painting?

The affirmative answer seems to be assumed in a large part of the tradition. In his discussion of the beautiful in the *Poetics*, Aristotle explicitly applies the same standard to both nature and art. "To be beautiful," he writes, "a living creature, and every whole made up of parts, must not only present a certain order in its arrangement of parts, but also be of a certain magnitude." Aristotle's notion that art imitates nature indicates a further relation between the beautiful in art and nature. Unity, proportion, and clarity would then be elements common to beauty in its every occurrence, though these elements may be embodied differently in things which have a difference in their mode of being, as do natural and artificial things.

With regard to the beauty of nature and of art, Kant tends to take the opposite position. He points out that "the mind cannot reflect on the beauty of nature without at the same time finding its interest engaged." Apart from any question of use that might be involved, he concludes that the "interest" aroused by the beautiful in nature is "akin to the moral," particularly from the fact that "nature ... in her beautiful products displays herself as art, not as a mere matter of chance, but, as it were, designedly, according to a law-directed arrangement."

The fact that natural things and works of art stand in a different relation to purpose or interest is for Kant an immediate indication that their beauty is different. Their susceptibility to disinterested enjoyment is not the same. Yet for Kant, as for his predecessors, nature provides the model or archetype which art follows, and he even speaks of art as an "imitation" of nature.

The Kantian discussion of nature and art moves into another dimension when it considers the distinction between the beautiful and the sublime. We must look for the sublime, Kant says, "not . . . in works of art . . . nor yet in things of nature, that in their very concept import a definite end, *e.g.* animals of a recognized natural order, but in rude nature merely as involving magnitude." In company with Longinus and Edmund Burke, Kant characterizes the sublime by reference to the limitations of human powers. Whereas the beautiful "consists in limitation," the sublime "immediately involves, or else by its presence provokes, a representation of limitlessness," which "may appear, indeed, in point of form to contravene the ends of our power of judgement, to be ill-adapted to our faculty of presentation, and to be, as it were, an outrage on the imagination."

Made aware of his own weakness, man is dwarfed by nature's magnificence, but at that very moment he is also elevated by realizing his ability to appreciate that which is so much greater than himself. This dual mood signalizes man's experience of the sublime. Unlike the enjoyment of beauty, it is neither disinterested nor devoid of moral tone.

TRUTH IS USUALLY connected with perception and thought, the good with desire and action. Both have been related to love and, in different ways, to pleasure and pain. All these terms naturally occur in the traditional discussion of beauty, partly by way of definition, but also partly in the course of considering the faculties engaged in the experience of beauty.

Basic here is the question whether beauty is an object of love or desire. The meaning of any answer will, of course, vary with different conceptions of desire and love.

Desire is sometimes thought of as fundamentally acquisitive, directed toward the appropriation of a good; whereas love, on the contrary, aims at no personal aggrandizement but rather, with complete generosity, wishes only the well-being of the beloved. In this context, beauty seems to be more closely associated with a good that is loved than with a good desired.

Love, moreover, is more akin to knowledge than is desire. The act of contemplation is sometimes understood as a union with the object through both knowledge and love. Here again the context of meaning favors the alignment of beauty with love, at least for theories which make beauty primarily an object of contemplation. In Plato and Plotinus, and on another level in the theologians, the two considerations—of love and beauty—fuse together inseparably.

It is the "privilege of beauty," Plato thinks, to offer man the readiest access to the world of ideas. According to the myth in the *Phaedrus*, the contemplation of beauty enables the soul to "grow wings." This experience, ultimately intellectual in its aim, is described by Plato as identical with love.

The observer of beauty "is amazed when he sees anyone having a godlike face or form, which is the expression of divine beauty; and at first a shudder runs through him, and again the old awe steals over him; then looking upon the face of his beloved as of a god, he reverences him, and if he were not afraid of being thought a downright madman, he would sacrifice to his beloved as to the image of a god." When the soul bathes herself "in the waters of beauty, her constraint is loosened, and she is refreshed, and has no more pangs and pains." This state of the soul enraptured by beauty, Plato goes on to say, "is by men called love."

Sharply opposed to Plato's intellectualization of beauty is that conception which connects it with sensual pleasure and sexual attraction. When Darwin, for instance, considers the sense of beauty, he confines his attention almost entirely to the colors and sounds used as "attractions of the opposite sex." Freud, likewise, while admitting that "psycho-analysis has less to say about beauty than about most things," claims that "its derivation from the realms of sexual sensation . . . seems certain."

Such considerations may not remove beauty from the sphere of love, but, as the chapter on LOVE makes clear, love has many meanings, and is of many sorts. The beautiful which is sexually attractive is the object of a love which is almost identical with desire—sometimes with lust—and certainly involves animal impulses and bodily pleasures. "The taste for the beautiful," writes Darwin, "at least as far as female beauty is concerned, is not of a special nature in the human mind."

On the other hand, Darwin attributes to man alone an aesthetic faculty for the appreciation of beauty apart from love or sex. No other animal, he thinks, is "capable of admiring such scenes as the heavens at night, a beautiful landscape, or refined music; but such high tastes are acquired through culture and depend on complex associations; they are not enjoyed by barbarians or by uneducated persons." For Freud, however, the appreciation of such beauties remains ultimately sexual in motivation, no matter how sublimated in effect. "The love of beauty," he says, "is the perfect example of a feeling with an inhibited aim. 'Beauty' and 'attraction' are first of all the attributes of a sexual object."

The theme of beauty's relation to desire and love is connected with another basic theme—the relation of beauty to sense and intellect, or to the realms of perception and thought. The two discussions naturally run parallel.

The main question here concerns the existence of beauty in the order of purely intelligible objects, and its relation to the sensible beauty of material things. Plotinus, holding that beauty of every kind comes from a "form" or "reason," traces the "beauty which is in bodies," as well as that "which is in the soul" to its source in the "eternal intelligence." This "intelligible beauty" lies outside the range of desire even as it is beyond the reach of sense-perception. Only the admiration or the adoration of love is proper to it.

THESE DISTINCTIONS in types of beauty—natural and artificial, sensible and intelligible, even, perhaps, material and spiritual—indicate the scope of the discussion, though not all writers on beauty deal with all its manifestations.

Primarily concerned with other subjects, many of the great books make only an indirect contribution to the theory of beauty: the moral treatises which consider the spiritual beauty of a noble man or of a virtuous character; the cosmologies of the philosophers or scientists which find beauty in the structure of the world—the intelligible, not sensible, order of the universe; the mathematical works which exhibit, and sometimes enunciate, an awareness of formal beauty in the necessary connection

of ideas; the great poems which crystallize beauty in a scene, in a face, in a deed; and, above all, the writings of the theologians which do not try to do more than suggest the ineffable splendor of God's infinite beauty, a beauty fused with truth and goodness, all absolute in the one absolute perfection of the divine being. "The Divine Goodness," observes Dante, "which from Itself spurns all envy, burning in Itself so sparkles that It displays the eternal beauties."

Some of the great books consider the various kinds of beauty, not so much with a view to classifying their variety, as in order to set forth the concordance of the grades of beauty with the grades of being, and with the levels of love and knowledge.

The ladder of love in Plato's *Symposium* describes an ascent from lower to higher forms of beauty. "He who has been instructed thus far in the things of love," Diotima tells Socrates, "and who has learned to see beauty in due order and succession, when he comes toward the end will suddenly perceive a nature of wondrous beauty ... beauty absolute, separate, simple, and everlasting, which without diminution and without increase, or any change, is imparted to the ever-growing and perishing beauties of all other things. He who from these, ascending under the influence of true love, begins to perceive that beauty, is not far from the end."

The order of ascent, according to Diotima, begins "with the beauties of earth and mounts upwards for the sake of that other beauty," going from one fair form to "all fair forms, and from fair forms to fair practises, and from fair practises to fair notions, until from fair notions" we come to "the notion of absolute beauty and at last know what the essence of beauty is. This, my dear Socrates," she concludes, "is the life above all others which man should live, in the contemplation of beauty absolute."

For Plotinus the degrees of beauty correspond to degrees of emancipation from matter. "The more it goes towards matter ... the feebler beauty becomes." A thing is ugly only because, "not dominated by a form and reason, the matter has not been completely informed by the idea." If a thing could be completely "without reason and form," it would be "absolute ugliness." But whatever exists possesses form and reason to some extent and has some share of the effulgent beauty of the One, even as it has some share through emanation in its overflowing being—the grades of beauty, as of being, signifying the remotion of each thing from its ultimate source.

Even separated from a continuous scale of beauty, the extreme terms—the beauty of God and the beauty of the least of finite things—have similitude for a theologian like Aquinas. The word *visum* in his definition of the beautiful (*id quod visum placet*, "that which pleases upon being seen") is the word used to signify

the type of supernatural knowledge promised to the souls of the blessed—the beatific *vision* in which God is beheld intuitively, not known discursively, and in which knowledge united with love is the principle of the soul's union with God.

An analogy is obviously implied. In this life and on the natural level, every experience of beauty—in nature or art, in sensible things or in ideas—occasions something *like* an act of vision, a moment of contemplation, of enjoyment detached from desire or action, and clear without the articulations of analysis or the demonstrations of reason.

OUTLINE OF TOPICS

REFERENCES

To find the passages cited, use the numbers in heavy type, which are the volume and page numbers of the passages referred to. For example, in 4 HOMER: *Iliad*, BK II [265–283] 12d, the number 4 is the number of the volume in the set; the number 12d indicates that the passage is in section d of page 12.

PAGE SECTIONS: When the text is printed in one column, the letters a and b refer to the upper and lower halves of the page. For example, in 53 JAMES: *Psychology*, 116a-119b, the passage begins in the upper half of page 116 and ends in the lower half of page 119. When the text is printed in two columns, the letters a and b refer to the upper and lower halves of the left-hand side of the page, the letters c and d to the upper and lower halves of the right-hand side of the page. For example, in 7 PLATO: *Symposium*, 163b-164c, the passage begins in the lower half of the left-hand side of page 163 and ends in the upper half of the right-hand side of page 164.

AUTHOR'S DIVISIONS: One or more of the main divisions of a work (such as PART, BK, CH, SECT) are sometimes included in the reference; line numbers, in brackets, are given in certain cases; *e.g.*, *Iliad*, BK II [265-283] 12d.

BIBLE REFERENCES: The references are to book, chapter, and verse. When the King James and Douay versions differ in title of books or in the numbering of chapters or verses, the King James version is cited first and the Douay, indicated by a (*D*), follows; *e.g.*, OLD TESTAMENT: *Nehemiah*, 7:45—(*D*) *II Esdras*, 7:46.

SYMBOLS: The abbreviation "esp" calls the reader's attention to one or more especially relevant parts of a whole reference; "passim" signifies that the topic is discussed intermittently rather than continuously in the work or passage cited.

For additional information concerning the style of the references, see the Explanation of Reference Style; for general guidance in the use of *The Great Ideas*, consult the Preface.

1. The general theory of the beautiful

7 PLATO: *Euthydemus*, 81a-b / *Cratylus*, 101c-102a; 113c-d / *Phaedrus*, 126b-d / *Symposium*, 167a-d / *Phaedo*, 242c-243a / *Gorgias*, 266d-267a / *Republic*, BK V, 370d-373c; BK VI, 385c / *Parmenides*, 490b-c / *Laws*, BK II, 654a-662a

8 ARISTOTLE: *Metaphysics*, BK V, CH I [1013^a 20–24] 533b; BK XII, CH 7 [1072^{a}23–^{b}4] 602b-c

9 ARISTOTLE: *Poetics*, CH 7 [1450^{b}23-1451^{a}15] 685b-c

12 AURELIUS: *Meditations*, BK III, SECT 2 259d-260a; BK IV, SECT 20 265a-b

17 PLOTINUS: *First Ennead*, TR III, CH 2 10d; TR VI 21a-26a / *Second Ennead*, TR IX, CH 17 76b-77a / *Fifth Ennead*, TR V, CH 12, 234a-c; TR VIII, CH I-TR IX, CH 2 239b-247b / *Sixth Ennead*, TR II, CH 18, 278a; TR III, CH II, 287b-c; TR VII, CH 22 332d-333b; CH 31–33 336d-338b

18 AUGUSTINE: *Confessions*, BK II, par 12 11c-d; BK IV, par 20 24b-c; par 24-27 25b-26a; BK X, par 53 84d-85a

19 AQUINAS: *Summa Theologica*, PART I, Q 5, A 4, REP 1 25d-26c; Q 91, A 3, REP 3 486b-487d; PART I-II, Q 27, A I, REP 3 737b-d

20 AQUINAS: *Summa Theologica*, PART I-II, Q 49, A 2, REP 1 2b-4a; PART II-II, Q 180, A 2, REP 3 608c-609c

31 SPINOZA: *Ethics*, PART I, APPENDIX, 371b-372d

33 PASCAL: *Pensées*, 32–33 176a-b

42 KANT: *Judgement*, 461a-549d esp 479c-d, 483d, 491c, 493b-495a,c; 550a; 560b-c; 564d-565b

44 BOSWELL: *Johnson*, 194b

49 DARWIN: *Origin of Species*, 95a-d

52 DOSTOEVSKY: *Brothers Karamazov*, BK III, 54a-b

53 JAMES: *Psychology*, 865a-b; 886b-888a

54 FREUD: *Civilization and Its Discontents*, 775a-c; 779b-d

1a. The beautiful and the good: beauty as a kind of fitness or order

7 PLATO: *Lysis*, 21b-c / *Symposium*, 162d-163a; 164c-d / *Gorgias*, 266c-267a / *Republic*, BK III, 333b-334b; BK V, 357d-358a / *Timaeus*, 474d-475a / *Statesman*, 594a-c / *Philebus*, 637d-638a / *Laws*, BK II, 654a-655b; 660a-662a

8 ARISTOTLE: *Topics*, BK III, CH 3 [118^{b}20-24] 165d / *Physics*, BK VII, CH 3 [246^{a}10-^{b}19] 329c-330a / *Metaphysics*, BK I, CH 3 [984^{b}8-22] 502d; BK V, CH I [1013^{a}20-24] 533b; BK XII, CH 7 [1072^{a}23-^{b}4] 602b-c; [1072^{b}30-1073^{a}2] 603a; BK XIII, CH 3 [1078^{a}31-^{b}6] 609d-610a

(1. *The general theory of the beautiful.* 1a. *The beautiful and the good: beauty as a kind of fitness or order.*)

9 ARISTOTLE: *Parts of Animals*, BK I, CH 5 [645ᵃ4–26] 168d-169a / *Ethics*, BK IV, CH 2 [1122ᵃ34–1123ᵃ33] 369a-370b passim / *Politics*, BK VII, CH 4 [1326ᵃ30–35] 530c / *Poetics*, CH 7 [1450ᵇ23–1451ᵃ15] 685b-c

12 EPICTETUS: *Discourses*, BK III, CH 1 175a-177c

12 AURELIUS: *Meditations*, BK II, SECT 1 256b,d

14 PLUTARCH: *Lycurgus*, 47a

16 KEPLER: *Epitome*, BK IV, 868b

17 PLOTINUS: *First Ennead*, TR VI 21a-26a / *Fifth Ennead*, TR V, CH 12, 234a-c; TR VIII 239b-246c / *Sixth Ennead*, TR VII, CH 22 332d-333b

18 AUGUSTINE: *Confessions*, BK II, par 12 11c-d; BK IV, par 20 24b-c; par 24–27 25b-26a; BK VII, par 23 50b-c / *City of God*, BK XXII, CH 24, 610c-611b

19 AQUINAS: *Summa Theologica*, PART I, Q 5, A 4, REP 1 25d-26c; Q 91, A 3 486b-487d; Q 96, A 3, REP 3 512a-c; PART I–II, Q 27, A 1, REP 3 737b-d

20 AQUINAS: *Summa Theologica*, PART I–II, Q 49, A 2, ANS and REP 1 2b-4a; A 4, ANS 5a-6a; Q 50, A 3, REP 2 8b-9a; Q 54, A 1, ANS 22d-23d; PART II–II, Q 180, A 2, REP 3 608c-609c

23 HOBBES: *Leviathan*, PART I, 62a

42 KANT: *Judgement*, 476a-482b; 486d-489a; 521b-523c; 540d-542a; 544c-545b; 546d-548c; 550a; 557c-558b

46 HEGEL: *Philosophy of History*, PART II, 266a-268b; 280b-281b

52 DOSTOEVSKY: *Brothers Karamazov*, BK VI, 153b-d

53 JAMES: *Psychology*, 755a; 865b

54 FREUD: *Civilization and Its Discontents*, 779b-d

1b. **Beauty and truth: the beautiful as an object of contemplation**

7 PLATO: *Cratylus*, 113c-d / *Phaedrus*, 124c-129d / *Symposium*, 167a-d / *Republic*, BK V, 370d-373c; BK VI, 383d-388a / *Theaetetus*, 525c-d / *Philebus*, 630d-631d / *Laws*, BK II, 660a-661b

8 ARISTOTLE: *Metaphysics*, BK XII, CH 7 [1072ᵃ23–ᵇ4] 602b-c; BK XIII, CH 3 [1078ᵃ32–ᵇ6] 609d-610a

12 AURELIUS: *Meditations*, BK IV, SECT 20 265a-b

17 PLOTINUS: *First Ennead*, TR III, CH 1–2 10a-d; TR VI 21a-26a / *Fifth Ennead*, TR VIII 239b-246c / *Sixth Ennead*, TR VII, CH 31–33 336d-338b

18 AUGUSTINE: *Confessions*, BK VII, par 23 50b-c

19 AQUINAS: *Summa Theologica*, PART I, Q 5, A 4, REP 1 25d-26c; Q 39, A 8, ANS 210a-213a; PART I–II, Q 27, A 1, REP 3 737b-d; A 2, ANS 737d-738c

20 AQUINAS: *Summa Theologica*, PART II–II, Q 180, A 2, REP 3 608c-609c; PART III SUPPL, Q 94, A 1, REP 2 1040d-1041b

27 SHAKESPEARE: *Sonnets*, XIV 588b; LIV 594c

29 CERVANTES: *Don Quixote*, PART I, 184b-d

35 HUME: *Human Understanding*, SECT I, DIV 5, 452d-453a

42 KANT: *Judgement*, 476a-479d esp 479a-d; 484d-485b; 496d; 501d-502a; 518a-d; 521b-523c; 525a-c

46 HEGEL: *Philosophy of History*, PART II, 266a-267a; 278a-c; PART IV, 346d-347a

52 DOSTOEVSKY: *Brothers Karamazov*, BK VI, 153b-d

53 JAMES: *Psychology*, 865b-866a; 886b-888a

54 FREUD: *New Introductory Lectures*, 880b

1c. **The elements of beauty: unity, proportion, clarity**

7 PLATO: *Republic*, BK III, 333b-334b; BK IV, 342b-c / *Timaeus*, 448a-c; 474d-475a / *Sophist*, 561b-d / *Statesman*, 594a-c / *Philebus*, 630d-631d; 637c-638a / *Laws*, BK II, 660a-661b

8 ARISTOTLE: *Physics*, BK VII, CH 3 [246ᵃ10–ᵇ19] 329c-330a / *Metaphysics*, BK I, CH 3 [984ᵇ8–22] 502d; BK XIII, CH 3 [1078ᵃ39–ᵇ5] 610a

9 ARISTOTLE: *Parts of Animals*, BK I, CH 5 [645ᵃ4–26] 168d-169a / *Ethics*, BK II, CH 6 [1106ᵇ6–14] 352a; BK IV, CH 2 [1122ᵃ34–1123ᵃ33] 369a-370b passim; CH 3 [1123ᵇ4–7] 370b / *Politics*, BK III, CH 11 [1281ᵇ10–15] 479b-c; CH 13 [1284ᵃ3–12] 482c-d; BK V, CH 9 [1309ᵇ23–30] 512a; BK VII, CH 4 [1326ᵃ30–35] 530c / *Poetics*, CH 7 [1450ᵇ23–1451ᵃ15] 685b-c

11 NICOMACHUS: *Arithmetic*, BK I, 814a; 820a; 826d-827a; BK II, 839d-840b

16 KEPLER: *Harmonies of the World*, 1079b

17 PLOTINUS: *First Ennead*, TR VI, CH 1–2 21a-22b / *Sixth Ennead*, TR VII, CH 22, 333b; TR IX, CH 1 353d-354b

18 AUGUSTINE: *Confessions*, BK IV, par 20 24b-c / *City of God*, BK II, CH 21, 161b-c; BK XI, CH 22, 334b; BK XVII, CH 14, 464d; BK XXII, CH 19, 604d-605a; CH 24, 610c-611b

19 AQUINAS: *Summa Theologica*, PART I, Q 5, A 4, REP 1 25d-26c; Q 39, A 8, ANS 210a-213a; Q 91, A 3 486b-487d

20 AQUINAS: *Summa Theologica*, PART I–II, Q 49, A 2, REP 1 2b-4a; Q 54, A 1, ANS 22d-23d; PART II–II, Q 180, A 2, REP 3 608c-609c

29 CERVANTES: *Don Quixote*, PART I, 184b

31 DESCARTES: *Discourse*, PART II, 44c-d

33 PASCAL: *Pensées*, 28 176a

35 LOCKE: *Human Understanding*, BK II, CH XII, SECT 5, 148b

42 KANT: *Judgement*, 471b-473a; 485c-491c; 493c-495a,c

46 HEGEL: *Philosophy of History*, INTRO, 185c-d; PART I, 219b-c

48 MELVILLE: *Moby Dick*, 277a-b

49 DARWIN: *Descent of Man*, 301d-302a

53 JAMES: *Psychology*, 186b; 755a

1d. The distinction between the beautiful and the sublime

42 KANT: *Judgement*, 473a; 480a-482b; 488a-489a; 495a-539d esp 495a-496d, 499b-c, 501d-502a, 502d-512a

2. Beauty in nature and in art

7 PLATO: *Symposium*, 167a-d / *Republic*, BK II-III, 320c-334b / *Timaeus*, 447a-448c / *Sophist*, 561b-d / *Statesman*, 594a-c / *Philebus*, 630d-631d

8 ARISTOTLE: *Physics*, BK VII, CH 3 [246^{a}10-^{b}19] 329c-330a / *Metaphysics*, BK XIII, CH 3 [1078^{a}31-^{b}6] 609d-610a

9 ARISTOTLE: *Parts of Animals*, BK I, CH 5 [645^{a}4-26] 168d-169a / *Politics*, BK III, CH 11 [1281^{b}10-15] 479b-c; BK VIII, CH 5 [1340^{a}24-29] 545d / *Poetics*, CH 7 685b-c

12 AURELIUS: *Meditations*, BK III, SECT 2 259d-260a; BK IV, SECT 20 265a-b

17 PLOTINUS: *Fifth Ennead*, TR VIII, CH 1-3 239b-241a

19 AQUINAS: *Summa Theologica*, PART I, Q 39, A 8, ANS 210a-213a; Q 91, A 3 486b-487d

20 AQUINAS: *Summa Theologica*, PART I-II, Q 49, A 2, REP 1 2b-4a; Q 50, A 3, REP 2 8b-9a; Q 54, A 1, ANS 22d-23d

22 CHAUCER: *Physician's Tale* [11,941-972] 366b-367a

25 MONTAIGNE: *Essays*, 93b-d; 230b-231c

32 MILTON: *Paradise Lost*, BK V [291-297] 181b

33 PASCAL: *Pensées*, 29 176a; 32 176a-b; 134 196a

42 KANT: *Judgement*, 473a-d; 488a-489a; 494c-496c; 501d-502a; 521b-524b esp 523c-d; 525a-528c; 544c-546d esp 546a-c; 557a-558b

46 HEGEL: *Philosophy of History*, PART I, 219b-c; 254b-d; PART II, 264a-268b

47 GOETHE: *Faust*, PRELUDE [134-157] 4a-b

48 MELVILLE: *Moby Dick*, 276b-277b

49 DARWIN: *Origin of Species*, 94c-95c; 235c-d / *Descent of Man*, 576b-577d

53 JAMES: *Psychology*, 186b

3. Beauty in relation to desire and love, as object or cause

OLD TESTAMENT: *Genesis*, 3:6; 6:1-2; 12:11-20; 26:7-11; 29:15-31; 39:6-20 / *Deuteronomy*, 21:10-13 / *I Samuel*, 16:7—(D) *I Kings*, 16:7 / *II Samuel*, 11; 13:1-19—(D) *II Kings*, 11; 13:1-19 / *Esther*, 2:15-17 / *Proverbs*, 6:24-26 / *Song of Solomon*—(D) *Canticle of Canticles* / *Isaiah*, 53:2—(D) *Isaias*, 53:2

APOCRYPHA: *Judith*, 11:20-23; 12:16-20; 16:7-9—(D) OT, *Judith*, 11:18-21; 12:16-20; 16:8-11 / *Ecclesiasticus*, 9:8; 25:21; 36:22—(D) OT, *Ecclesiasticus*, 9:8-9; 25:28; 36:24 / *Susanna*—(D) OT, *Daniel*, 13

4 HOMER: *Iliad*, BK III [121-160] 20b-c; BK XIV [153-351] 99d-101d

5 EURIPIDES: *Helen* [1-67] 298a-d; [229-305] 300b-d

5 ARISTOPHANES: *Ecclesiazusae* [611-634] 622a-b; [877-1111] 625b-628a

6 HERODOTUS: *History*, BK I, 2d-3d; BK V, 168d-169a; BK VI, 196d-197b

7 PLATO: *Charmides*, 1b-2a / *Phaedrus*, 120a-c; 126b-129d / *Symposium*, 159d-160c; 161b-167d / *Republic*, BK III, 333b-334b / *Timaeus*, 455a-c / *Laws*, BK V, 687b; BK VIII, 735c-736c; 738a-c

8 ARISTOTLE: *Metaphysics*, BK XII, CH 7 [1072^{a}23-^{b}4] 602b-c

12 LUCRETIUS: *Nature of Things*, BK IV [1141-1170] 59a-b

12 EPICTETUS: *Discourses*, BK II, CH 22, 169b

13 VIRGIL: *Aeneid*, BK I [657-722] 121a-123a; BK IV [1-30] 167a-b; BK VIII [369-393] 269a-b

17 PLOTINUS: *First Ennead*, TR III, CH 1-2 10a-d; TR VI 21a-26a / *Third Ennead*, TR V, CH 1 100c-101c / *Fifth Ennead*, TR V, CH 12 234a-d; TR VIII, CH 9, 244b-c / *Sixth Ennead*, TR VII, CH 22 332d-333b; CH 30-34 336b-338d

18 AUGUSTINE: *Confessions*, BK IV, par 15 23a-b; par 20 24b-c; par 24-27 25b-26a; BK VII, par 23 50b-c; BK X, par 8-38 73b-81a; par 51-53 84b-85a / *City of God*, BK XII, CH 6, 346a-b; BK XXII, CH 24, 610c-611b

19 AQUINAS: *Summa Theologica*, PART I, Q 5, A 4, REP 1 25d-26c; PART I-II, Q 27, A 1, REP 3 737b-d; A 2, ANS 737d-738c

20 AQUINAS: *Summa Theologica*, PART II-II, Q 180, A 2, REP 3 608c-609c; PART III, Q 6, A 1, REP 3 740b-741b

21 DANTE: *Divine Comedy*, HELL, V [73-142] 7d-8b; PURGATORY, XXVII 94c-96a; XXX-XXXI 99b-102b; PARADISE, XXVII [88-96] 148b; XXX [1-33] 151d-152a

22 CHAUCER: *Troilus and Cressida*, BK II, STANZA 48-50 27b-28a / *Physician's Tale* 366a-371a esp [12,055-191] 368a-370b

25 MONTAIGNE: *Essays*, 84b-85a; 230b-231c; 310d-312a; 398c-399d; 432d-434c; 513a-514a

26 SHAKESPEARE: *Love's Labour's Lost*, ACT IV, SC III [299-332] 271c-d / *Romeo and Juliet*, ACT I, SC I [214-244] 287d-288a; SC V [43-55] 292b; ACT II, SC II [1-32] 294b-c

27 SHAKESPEARE: *Troilus and Cressida*, ACT II, SC II [61-92] 114b-c / *Antony and Cleopatra*, ACT II, SC II [196-250] 320d-321b / *Sonnets*, XX 589b; XXIV 589d-590a; LIV 594c; CXXX 606a-b

29 CERVANTES: *Don Quixote*, PART II, 381d-382a

31 SPINOZA: *Ethics*, PART I, APPENDIX, 371d

32 MILTON: *Comus* [667-823] 48a-52a / *Paradise Lost*, BK VIII [500-560] 243a-244a / *Samson Agonistes* [1003-1007] 361b

37 FIELDING: *Tom Jones*, 15b-c; 17b-c; 50d-51a; 130b-c; 331b-332a

38 ROUSSEAU: *Inequality*, 345d-346a; 347b-c

42 KANT: *Judgement*, 476a-483d

44 BOSWELL: *Johnson*, 485a

46 HEGEL: *Philosophy of History*, PART I, 220b-c

47 GOETHE: *Faust*, PART II [6377-6565] 156a-160a esp [6483-6500] 158b; [8516-8523] 207b; [9192-9355] 223b-227a

(3. *Beauty in relation to desire and love, as object or cause.*)

49 DARWIN: *Origin of Species*, 95c / *Descent of Man*, 301c; 366b-c; 481c-482b; 571b-576b passim

51 TOLSTOY: *War and Peace*, BK I, 4a; 5d-6b; 49a-b; BK II, 80d-81a; BK III, 113a-115a; 120c-123a; 141b-d; BK VI, 235a-238a; BK VIII, 316d-317d; BK XI, 497d-498b; 530c-d; BK XII, 541b-542b; EPILOGUE I, 659a; 660b-c

52 DOSTOEVSKY: *Brothers Karamazov*, BK III, 53d-54b

53 JAMES: *Psychology*, 865b

54 FREUD: *Civilization and Its Discontents*, 775b-c

4. Beauty and ugliness in relation to pleasure and pain

7 PLATO: *Gorgias*, 266d-267a / *Philebus*, 630d-631d / *Laws*, BK II, 654a-656c; BK VII, 720c-d

8 ARISTOTLE: *Topics*, BK VI, CH 7 [146^{a}21–32] 200a-b

9 ARISTOTLE: *Parts of Animals*, BK I, CH 5 [645^{a}4–26] 168d-169a / *Ethics*, BK III, CH 10 [1118^{a}1–16] 364c / *Politics*, BK VIII, CH 3 [1337^{b}27–1338^{a}29] 543a-c; CH 5 [1340^{a}24–29] 545d / *Rhetoric*, BK I, CH 6 [1362^{b}5–9] 603b

12 AURELIUS: *Meditations*, BK III, SECT 2 259d-260a

17 PLOTINUS: *First Ennead*, TR VI, CH 1–7 21a-25a passim / *Fifth Ennead*, TR V, CH 12, 234a-c

18 AUGUSTINE: *Confessions*, BK X, par 51–53 84b-85a

19 AQUINAS: *Summa Theologica*, PART I, Q 5, A 4, REP 1 25d-26c; Q 91, A 3, REP 3 486b-487d; PART I–II, Q 11, A 1, REP 2 666b,d-667a; Q 27, A 1, REP 3 737b-d; Q 32, A 8, ANS 764c-765b

23 HOBBES: *Leviathan*, PART I, 62a-c

29 CERVANTES: *Don Quixote*, PART I, 184b-d

31 SPINOZA: *Ethics*, PART I, APPENDIX, 371d

33 PASCAL: *Pensées*, 32 176a-b

42 KANT: *Judgement*, 471d-473a; 476a-495a,c esp 488a-489a; 502d-503d; 516d-518d; 527b-528c esp 527d-528a; 537a-539d

46 HEGEL: *Philosophy of History*, PART I, 220b-c; PART II, 267b-268b

47 GOETHE: *Faust*, PART II [8697–8811] 211b-214a; [11,288–303] 274b-275a

49 DARWIN: *Origin of Species*, 95a-d / *Descent of Man*, 301d-302a; 568d-571b passim; 577b-d

51 TOLSTOY: *War and Peace*, BK IV, 190d-192b

53 JAMES: *Psychology*, 157a; 755a-757b esp 755a-b; 886b

54 FREUD: *Beyond the Pleasure Principle*, 643c / *Civilization and Its Discontents*, 775b

5. Judgments of beauty: the objective and the subjective in aesthetic judgments or judgments of taste

7 PLATO: *Ion* 142a-148a,c / *Symposium*, 167a-d / *Gorgias*, 261a-c / *Republic*, BK III, 333b-334b

/ *Statesman*, 593d-595a / *Laws*, BK II, 654a-656b; 660a-662a; BK III, 675c-676b; BK VII, 720c-d

9 ARISTOTLE: *Politics*, BK III, CH 11 [1281^{a}43–^{b}15] 479b-c

12 LUCRETIUS: *Nature of Things*, BK IV [1141–1170] 59a-b

12 EPICTETUS: *Discourses*, BK III, CH 1 175a-177c

12 AURELIUS: *Meditations*, BK III, SECT 2 259d-260a; BK IV, SECT 20 265a-b

17 PLOTINUS: *First Ennead*, TR VI, CH 2–3 21d-23a / *Sixth Ennead*, TR III, CH 11, 287b-c

18 AUGUSTINE: *Confessions*, BK IV, par 20 24b-c; BK VII, par 23 50b-c / *City of God*, BK VIII, CH 6, 269b-c

19 AQUINAS: *Summa Theologica*, PART I, Q 5, A 4, REP 1 25d-26c; PART I–II, Q 27, A 1, REP 3 737b-d

20 AQUINAS: *Summa Theologica*, PART II–II, Q 180, A 2, REP 3 608c-609c; PART III SUPPL, Q 94, A 1, REP 2 1040d-1041b

21 DANTE: *Divine Comedy*, PURGATORY, XI [79–120] 69c-70a; XXVI [91–126] 93d-94b

24 RABELAIS: *Gargantua and Pantagruel*, BK IV, 273d-274a

25 MONTAIGNE: *Essays*, 230b-231c

26 SHAKESPEARE: *Merchant of Venice*, ACT V, SC I [98–110] 431d

31 SPINOZA: *Ethics*, PART I, APPENDIX, 371b-372d

33 PASCAL: *Pensées*, 32–33 176a-b; 105 193a; 114 194b; 381 238b

35 LOCKE: *Human Understanding*, BK II, CH XII, SECT 5 148a-b

35 HUME: *Human Understanding*, SECT XII, DIV 132, 509c-d

42 KANT: *Pure Reason*, 23d [fn 1] / *Judgement*, 471b-473a; 476a-495a,c; 513b-516b; 516d-517c; 524d-525a; 540a-546d

44 BOSWELL: *Johnson*, 202b; 362b-c

46 HEGEL: *Philosophy of History*, INTRO, 185c-d; PART II, 264b-268c; 280b-c

49 DARWIN: *Origin of Species*, 95a-d / *Descent of Man*, 301c-302a; 462d-463a; 569c; 571c-577d esp 575d, 577b-c; 595c-596a

51 TOLSTOY: *War and Peace*, BK IV, 191b-192b; BK VIII, 318a-320b

53 JAMES: *Psychology*, 755b-757b; 886b-888a

6. The role of the beautiful in education

7 PLATO: *Symposium*, 167a-d / *Gorgias*, 261a-c / *Republic*, BK II–III, 320c-334b esp BK III, 333b-334b; BK VIII, 409d / *Laws*, BK II 653a-663d; BK III, 675c-676b; BK VII, 720c-d

9 ARISTOTLE: *Politics*, BK VIII, CH 3 542d-543d; CH 5–7 544c-548a,c

12 EPICTETUS: *Discourses*, BK IV, CH 11, 242a-d

17 PLOTINUS: *First Ennead*, TR III, CH 1–2 10a-d; TR VI 21a-26a / *Fifth Ennead*, TR IX, CH 2 246d-247b

18 AUGUSTINE: *Confessions*, BK VII, par 23 50b-c

33 PASCAL: *Pensées*, 381 238b

40 GIBBON: *Decline and Fall*, 24a

41 GIBBON: *Decline and Fall*, 300a-b

42 KANT: *Judgement*, 462b-d; 485b-491c; 493a-b; 513d-514b; 521b-523c; 528b-c; 548c-549d; 586d-587a

46 HEGEL: *Philosophy of History*, INTRO, 185c-d; PART II, 267a-268b; PART IV, 346d-347a

49 DARWIN: *Descent of Man*, 302a-b; 595c-596a

53 JAMES: *Psychology*, 288a; 757a-b

7. Intelligible beauty

7*a*. The beauty of God

OLD TESTAMENT: *Psalms*, 27:4; 90:17; 93; 97:6—(D) *Psalms*, 26:4; 89:17; 92; 96:6 / *Isaiah*, 28:5; 33:15-17—(D) *Isaias*, 28:5; 33:15-17 / *Zechariah*, 9:17—(D) *Zacharias*, 9:17

APOCRYPHA: *Wisdom of Solomon*, 13:1-5—(D) OT, *Book of Wisdom*, 13:1-5

7 PLATO: *Symposium*, 167a-d

8 ARISTOTLE: *Metaphysics*, BK XII, CH 7 602a-603b; BK XIV, CH 4 [1091^{a}29-1092^{a}9] 624a-d

17 PLOTINUS: *First Ennead*, TR VI, CH 6-9 24a-26a / *Fifth Ennead*, TR VIII, CH 1-TR IX, CH 2 239b-247b / *Sixth Ennead*, TR VII, CH 30-36 336b-339d

18 AUGUSTINE: *Confessions*, BK I, par 4 2a; BK II, par 12 11c-d; BK III, par 10, 15b; BK IV, par 29 26b; BK VII, par 23 50b-c; BK X, par 8-38 73b-81a; par 53 84d-85a; BK XI, par 6 90c-d / *City of God*, BK VIII, CH 6, 269b-c; BK XI, CH 4, 324b

19 AQUINAS: *Summa Theologica*, PART I, Q 39, A 8, ANS 210a-213a; PART I-II, Q 3, AA 4-5 625a-627a; A 8 628d-629c; Q 4, A 1 esp REP 2 629d-630b

21 DANTE: *Divine Comedy*, PARADISE, VII [64-66] 115d; XXX-XXXIII 151d-157d

31 DESCARTES: *Meditations*, III, 88d-89a

32 MILTON: *Paradise Lost*, BK III [372-389] 143b-144a

7*b*. The beauty of the universe

OLD TESTAMENT: *Psalms*, 8; 19:1-6; 104; 136:1-9—(D) *Psalms*, 8; 18:1-7; 103; 135:1-9

APOCRYPHA: *Wisdom of Solomon*, 13:1-9—(D) OT, *Book of Wisdom*, 13:1-9 / *Ecclesiasticus*, 16:26-27; 43—(D) OT, *Ecclesiasticus*, 16:26-27; 43

7 PLATO: *Timaeus*, 447a-448c

8 ARISTOTLE: *Metaphysics*, BK I, CH 3 [984^{b}8-22] 502d; BK XII, CH 7 [1072^{b}30-1073^{a}2] 603a; CH 10 [1075^{a}12-24] 605d-606a; BK XIV, CH 4 [1091^{a}29-1092^{a}9] 624a-d

9 ARISTOTLE: *Parts of Animals*, BK I, CH 5 [645^{a}4-26] 168d-169a

11 NICOMACHUS: *Arithmetic*, BK II, 839d-840b

12 AURELIUS: *Meditations*, BK III, SECT 2 259d-260a; BK VI, SECT 36-38 277c-d

16 PTOLEMY: *Almagest*, BK I, 5a

16 COPERNICUS: *Revolutions of the Heavenly Spheres*, BK I, 526a-529a

16 KEPLER: *Epitome*, BK IV, 853b-887a passim, esp 863b-872b / *Harmonies of the World*, 1023b-1085b esp 1049b-1050a, 1071b, 1077b-1080b

17 PLOTINUS: *Second Ennead*, TR IX, CH 17 76b-77a / *Third Ennead*, TR II, CH 3 83d-84c; CH 10-14 88a-89d / *Fifth Ennead*, TR VIII, CH 8-9 243c-244c; CH 12-13 245c-246c

18 AUGUSTINE: *Confessions*, BK VII, par 16-23 48c-50c; BK X, par 8-10 73b-74a / *City of God*, BK V, CH 11 216c-d; BK VIII, CH 6 268d-269c; BK X, CH 14 307c-308a; BK XI, CH 4, 324a-b; CH 18 331d-332a; CH 22-23 333d-335c; BK XII, CH 4-5 344b-345b; BK XXII, CH 24 609a-612a / *Christian Doctrine*, BK I, CH 4 625b-c

19 AQUINAS: *Summa Theologica*, PART I, Q 19, A 9, REP 2 116d-117d; Q 23, A 8, REP 2 140a-141a; Q 66, A 1 343d-345c; Q 74, A 3, REP 3 375a-377a,c

20 AQUINAS: *Summa Theologica*, PART III SUPPL, Q 91 1016a-1025b

21 DANTE: *Divine Comedy*, PARADISE, X [1-36] 120b-c; XXVIII 148d-150b

28 GILBERT: *Loadstone*, BK V, 104b-105d

28 HARVEY: *On Animal Generation*, 491d-492a

31 SPINOZA: *Ethics*, PART I, PROP 36-APPENDIX 369b-372d

32 MILTON: *Paradise Lost*, BK VII [548-568] 229a-b

34 NEWTON: *Principles*, BK III, GENERAL SCHOL, 369d-370a

35 BERKELEY: *Human Knowledge*, SECT 109 434b; SECT 146 442a-b; SECT 151-154 443b-444b

37 FIELDING: *Tom Jones*, 186c-d

42 KANT: *Pure Reason*, 187c-188c / *Judgement*, 544c-546d

52 DOSTOEVSKY: *Brothers Karamazov*, BK VI, 153b-d

7*c*. Beauty in the order of ideas

APOCRYPHA: *Wisdom of Solomon*, 7:24-29; 8:1-2—(D) OT, *Book of Wisdom*, 7:24-29; 8:1-2

7 PLATO: *Cratylus*, 113c-d / *Phaedrus*, 126b-d / *Symposium*, 167a-d / *Gorgias*, 266d / *Republic*, BK III, 333b-334b; BK V, 370d-373c; BK VI, 383d-388a

8 ARISTOTLE: *Metaphysics*, BK XIII, CH 3 [1078^{a}31-^{b}6] 609d-610a

17 PLOTINUS: *First Ennead*, TR III, CH 1-2 10a-d / *Fifth Ennead*, TR VIII 239b-246c; TR IX, CH 2, 246d; CH 11 250c-251a / *Sixth Ennead*, TR VII, CH 22 332d-333b; CH 30-33, 336d-338b

18 AUGUSTINE: *Confessions*, BK II, par 12 11c-d / *City of God*, BK XXII, CH 24, 611a

20 AQUINAS: *Summa Theologica*, PART II-II, Q 180, A 2, REP 3 608c-609c

21 DANTE: *Divine Comedy*, PURGATORY, XXVII 94c-96a; XXX-XXXI 99b-102b; PARADISE, XIV [67-139] 127c-128b; XXX [1-33] 151d-152a

29 CERVANTES: *Don Quixote*, PART II, 381d-382a

(7. *Intelligible beauty.* 7c. *Beauty in the order of ideas.*)

33 PASCAL: *Pensées*, 33 176b
42 KANT: *Judgement*, 508b-c; 553b-c
53 JAMES: *Psychology*, 755a; 757a-758a

7d. Beauty in the moral order

7 PLATO: *Charmides*, 1b-2a / *Symposium*, 164b-167b / *Republic*, BK II–III, 320c-334b esp BK III, 333b-334b; BK V, 357d-358a / *Theaetetus*, 513a-b; 535c / *Philebus*, 637c-638a / *Laws*, BK II, 654a-c

9 ARISTOTLE: *Ethics*, BK II, CH 6 351c-352d; BK IV, CH 2 368d-370b; CH 3 [1123^{b}4–7] 370b / *Politics*, BK III, CH 11 [1281^{b}10–15] 479b-c; CH 13 [1284^{b}3–12] 482c-d; BK V, CH 9 [1309^{b}18–1310^{a}2] 511d-512b; BK VII, CH 4 [1326^{a}30–35] 530c

12 EPICTETUS: *Discourses*, BK III, CH 1 175a-177c; BK IV, CH 11, 242a-d

14 PLUTARCH: *Lycurgus*, 47a

17 PLOTINUS: *First Ennead*, TR III, CH 1–2 10a-d; TR VI 21a-26a passim / *Second Ennead*, TR IX, CH 17, 76c / *Fifth Ennead*, TR IX, CH 2 246d-247b

18 AUGUSTINE: *Confessions*, BK II, par 12 11c-d / *City of God*, BK II, CH 21, 161b-c; BK XVII, CH 14, 464d; BK XXII, CH 19, 605b

19 AQUINAS: *Summa Theologica*, PART I, Q 93, A 8, REP 3 499b-500c; Q 96, A 3, REP 3 512a-c; PART I–II, Q 27, A 2, ANS 737d-738c

20 AQUINAS: *Summa Theologica*, PART I–II, Q 105, A 1, CONTRARY 307d-309d; PART II–II, Q 180, A 2, REP 3 608c-609c; PART III SUPPL, Q 82, A 1, REP 5 968a-970c

21 DANTE: *Divine Comedy*, PURGATORY, XXVII 94c-96a; XXX–XXXI 99b-102b; PARADISE, XIV [67–139] 127c-128b; XXVII [88–96] 148b; XXX [1–33] 151d-152a

25 MONTAIGNE: *Essays*, 84b-85a

26 SHAKESPEARE: *Merchant of Venice*, ACT III, SC II [73–107] 420d-421a

27 SHAKESPEARE: *Twelfth Night*, ACT I, SC II [47–51] 2b / *Hamlet*, ACT III, SC I [103–116] 48a / *Sonnets*, LIV 594c; LXVI–LXX 596b-597a; XCIII–XCVI 600b-601a

29 CERVANTES: *Don Quixote*, PART II, 381d-382a

32 MILTON: *Comus* [417–475] 42b-44a

42 KANT: *Judgement*, 488b-489a; 508b-c; 521b-523c; 546d-548c

46 HEGEL: *Philosophy of History*, PART II, 266a-267a; 276a-d; 278a-c; 280b-c; PART IV, 346d-347a

51 TOLSTOY: *War and Peace*, BK XII, 543b-544b; EPILOGUE I, 670c

53 JAMES: *Psychology*, 755a; 757a

CROSS-REFERENCES

For: Other discussions of the relation of beauty to goodness and truth, see GOOD AND EVIL 1c; TRUTH 1c; and for the relation of grades of beauty to degrees of perfection in being, see BEING 3a.

Unity, order, and proportion as elements of beauty, see RELATION 5c.

The consideration of beauty as an object of love or desire, see DESIRE 2b; LOVE 1d.

The theory of the aesthetic judgment or the judgment of taste, see SENSE 6; and for the controversy over the objectivity and universality of such judgments, see CUSTOM 9a; RELATION 6c; UNIVERSAL AND PARTICULAR 7c.

The problem of cultivating good taste and critical judgment in the field of the fine arts, see ART 7b; POETRY 8a–8b.

The context of the comparison of beauty in nature and in art, see ART 2a–3; NATURE 2a, 5d; PLEASURE AND PAIN 4c(1).

Consideration of the kind of knowledge which is involved in the apprehension of beauty, see KNOWLEDGE 6a(2), 6c(1).

Another discussion of sensible and intelligible beauty, see SENSE 6; and for the intelligible beauty of God and of the universe, see GOD 4h; WORLD 6d.

ADDITIONAL READINGS

Listed below are works not included in *Great Books of the Western World*, but relevant to the idea and topics with which this chapter deals. These works are divided into two groups:

I. Works by authors represented in this collection.
II. Works by authors not represented in this collection.

For the date, place, and other facts concerning the publication of the works cited, consult the Bibliography of Additional Readings which follows the last chapter of *The Great Ideas*.

I.

F. Bacon. "Of Beauty," "Of Deformity," in *Essays*

Hobbes. *Concerning Body*, part II, ch 10

Berkeley. *Alciphron*, III

A. Smith. *The Theory of Moral Sentiments*, part IV

Hegel. *The Philosophy of Fine Art*

C. R. Darwin. *The Different Forms of Flowers on Plants of the Same Species*

II.

Longinus. *On the Sublime*

Ebreo. *The Philosophy of Love*, dialogue III

Shaftesbury. *Characteristics of Men, Manners, Opinions, Times*

Leibnitz. *Monadology*, par 1-9

Hutcheson. *An Inquiry into the Original of Our Ideas of Beauty and Virtue*

Burke. *A Philosophical Enquiry into the Origin of Our Ideas of the Sublime and Beautiful*, part I-IV

Voltaire. "Beautiful," "Taste," in *A Philosophical Dictionary*

T. Reid. *Essays on the Intellectual Powers of Man*, VIII

Schiller. *Letters upon the Esthetic Education of Man*

Jean Paul. *Vorschule der Ästhetik*

D. Stewart. *Philosophical Essays*, part II

Cousin. *Lectures on the True, the Beautiful and the Good*

Hazlitt. *On Taste*

Schopenhauer. *The World as Will and Idea*, vol III, sup, ch 33

Stendhal. *On Love*

Chalmers. *On the Power, Wisdom, and Goodness of God*

Kierkegaard. *Either/Or*, part II

A. Humboldt. *Cosmos*

Lotze. *Microcosmos*, bk VIII, ch 3

Emerson. "Love," in *Essays*, I

———. "Beauty," in *The Conduct of Life*

Ruskin. *Sesame and Lilies*

Véron. *Aesthetics*

Lipps. *Ästhetik*

Santayana. *The Sense of Beauty*, part I-IV

———. *Reason in Art*, ch 10

Poincaré. *Science and Method*, bk I, ch 3

Croce. *Aesthetic as Science of Expression*

———. *The Essence of Esthetics*

Carritt. *The Theory of Beauty*

Bosanquet. *Science and Philosophy*, 22-24

———. *Three Lectures on Aesthetic*, I, III

Whitehead. *Process and Reality*, part III, ch 2(2), 3(3,5), 5(7,8)

Birkhoff. *Aesthetic Measure*

Gill. *Beauty Looks After Herself*

Mauron. *Aesthetics and Psychology*

Chapter 7: BEING

INTRODUCTION

THE words "is" and "(is) not" are probably the words most frequently used by anyone. They are unavoidable, by implication at least, in every statement. They have, in addition, a greater range of meaning than any other words.

Their manifold significance seems to be of a very special kind, for whatever is said *not to be* in one sense of being can always be said *to be* in another of its senses. Children and practiced liars know this. Playing on the meanings of being, or with "is" and "not," they move smoothly from fact to fiction, imagination to reality, or truth to falsehood.

Despite the obviousness and commonplaceness of the questions which arise with any consideration of the meanings of "is," the study of being is a highly technical inquiry which only philosophers have pursued at length. Berkeley gives one reason why they cannot avoid this task. "Nothing seems of more importance," he says, "towards erecting a firm system of sound and real knowledge . . . than to lay the beginning in a distinct explication of what is meant by *thing, reality, existence*; for in vain shall we dispute concerning the real existence of things, or pretend to any knowledge thereof, so long as we have not fixed the meaning of those words."

In the whole field of learning, philosophy is distinguished from other disciplines—from history, the sciences, and mathematics—by its concern with the problem of being. It alone asks about the nature of existence, the modes and properties of being, the difference between being and becoming, appearance and reality, the possible and the actual, being and non-being. Not all philosophers ask these questions; nor do all who ask such questions approach or formulate them in the same way. Nevertheless, the attempt to answer them is a task peculiar to philosophy. Though it often leads to subtleties, it also keeps the philosopher in deepest touch with common sense and the speculative wonder of all men.

As a TECHNICAL concept in philosophy, *being* has been called both the richest and the emptiest of all terms in the vocabulary of thought. Both remarks testify to the same fact, namely, that it is the highest abstraction, the most universal of predicates, and the most pervasive subject of discussion.

William James is in that long line of philosophers which began with the early Greeks when he points out that "in the strict and ultimate sense of the word 'existence,' everything which can be thought of at all exists as some *sort* of object, whether mythical object, individual thinker's object, or object in outer space and for intelligence at large." Even things which do not really exist have being insofar as they are objects of thought—things remembered which once existed, things conceivable which have the possibility of being, things imaginary which have being at least in the mind that thinks them. This leads to a paradox which the ancients delighted in pondering, that even nothing is something, even non-being has being, for before we can say "non-being is not" we must be able to say "non-being is." *Nothing* is at least an object of thought.

Any other word than "being" will tend to classify things. The application of any other name will divide the world into things of the sort denominated as distinct from everything else. "Chair," for example, divides the world into things which are chairs and all other objects; but "being" divides something or anything from nothing and, as we have seen, even applies to nothing.

"All other names," Aquinas writes, "are

either less universal, or, if convertible with it, add something above it at least in idea; hence in a certain way they inform and determine it." The concepts which such words express have, therefore, a restricted universality. They apply to *all things of a certain kind*, but not to *all things*, things of every kind or type. With the exception of a few terms inseparably associated with 'being' (or, as Aquinas says, convertible with it), only being is common to all kinds of things. When every other trait peculiar to a thing is removed, its being remains—the fact that it *is* in some sense.

If we start with a particular of any sort, classifying it progressively according to the characteristics which it shares with more and more things, we come at last to being. According to this method of abstraction, which Hegel follows in his *Science of Logic*, 'being' is the emptiest of terms precisely because it is the commonest. It signifies the very least that can be thought of anything. On this view, if all we are told of something is that it is—that it has being —we learn as little as possible about the thing. We have to be told that a thing is a material or a spiritual being, a real or an imaginary being, a living or a human being, in order to apprehend a determinate nature. Abstracted from everything else, 'being' has only the positive meaning of excluding 'non-being.'

There is an opposite procedure by which the term *being* has the maximal rather than the minimal significance. Since whatever else a thing is, it is a being, its being lies at the very heart of its nature and underlies all its other properties. Being is indeterminate only in the sense that it takes on every sort of determination. Wherever being is found by thought, it is understood as a determined mode of being. To conceive being in this way, we do not remove every difference or determination, but on the contrary, embrace all, since all are differences or determinations of being.

Aquinas, for example, conceives "being taken simply as including all perfections of being"; and in the Judaeo-Christian tradition, 'being' without qualification is taken as the most proper name for God. When Moses asked God His name, he received as answer: "I AM THAT I AM ... Thus shalt thou say unto the children of Israel, I AM hath sent me unto you." Used in this sense, 'being' becomes the richest of terms—the one which has the greatest amplitude of meaning.

BOTH WAYS OF thinking about being are relevant to the problem of the relations among the various meanings of 'being.' Both are also related to the problem of whether being is one or many—the problem first raised by the Eleatics, exhaustively explored in Plato's *Parmenides*, and recurrent in the thought of Plotinus, Spinoza, and Hegel.

The two problems are connected. If everything that is exists only as a part of being as a whole, or if the unity of being requires everything to be the same in being, then whatever diversities there are do not multiply the meanings of *being*. Although he speaks of substance rather than of being, Spinoza argues that "there cannot be any substance excepting God, and consequently none other can be conceived." From this it follows that "whatever is, is in God, and nothing can be or be conceived without God."

Since "there cannot be two or more substances of the same nature or attribute," and since God is defined as a "substance consisting of infinite attributes, each one of which expresses eternal and infinite essence," it is absurd, in Spinoza's opinion, to think of any other substance. "If there were any substance besides God, it would have to be explained," he says, "by some attribute of God, and thus two substances would exist possessing the same attribute," which is impossible.

Spinoza's definition of substance, attribute, and mode or affection, combined with his axiom that "everything which is, is either in itself or in another," enables him to embrace whatever multiplicity or diversity he finds in the world as aspects of one being. Everything which is not substance, existing in and of itself, exists in that one substance as an infinite attribute *or* a finite mode. "The thing extended (*rem extensam*) and the thinking thing (*rem cogitantem*)," he writes, "are either attributes of God or affections of the attributes of God."

If, on the contrary, there is no unitary whole of being, but only a plurality of beings which are alike in being and yet are diverse in being from one another, then our conception of being must involve a system of meanings, a stem of many branches. Descartes, for example, distinguishes between an infinite being, whose essence involves its existence, and finite beings, which do not necessarily exist of themselves but must be caused to exist. The infinite being which is God causes, but does not contain within itself, other finite substances; and among finite things, Descartes holds, "two substances are said to be really distinct, when each of them can exist apart from the other."

In addition to God—"that substance which we understand to be supremely perfect"—Descartes defines two kinds of finite substance. "That substance in which thought immediately resides, I call Mind," he writes; and "that substance, which is the immediate subject of extension in space, and of the accidents that presuppose extension, e.g., figure, situation, movement in space, etc., is called Body." All these substances, and even their accidents, have being, but not being of the same kind or to the same degree. "There are," according to Descartes, "diverse degrees of reality, or (the quality of being an) entity. For substance has more reality than accident or mode; and infinite substance has more than finite substance." Its being is independent, theirs dependent.

The issue between Spinoza and Descartes—a single substance or many—is only one of the ways in which the problem of the unity or diversity of being presents itself. Both Plato and Aristotle, for example, affirm a multiplicity of separate existences, but though both are, in this sense, pluralists, being seems to have one meaning for Plato, many for Aristotle.

According to Plato's distinction between being and becoming, only the immutable essences, the eternal ideas, are beings, and though they are many in number, they all belong to one realm and possess the same type of being. But for Aristotle, not only do perishable as well as imperishable substances exist; not only is there sensible and mutable as well as immaterial and eternal being; but the being which substances possess is not the same as that of accidents; essential is not the same as accidental being; potential being is not the same as being actual; and to be is not the same as to be conceived, that is, to exist in reality is not the same as to exist in mind.

Again and again Aristotle insists that "there are many senses in which a thing is said to be . . . Some things are said to be because they are substances, others because they are affections of substance, others because they are in process towards substance, or destructions or privations or qualities of substance, or productive or generative of substance, or of things which are relative to substance, or negations of one of these things or of substance itself. It is for this reason," he continues, "that we say even of non-being that it *is* non-being"; and, in another place, he adds that "besides all these there is that which 'is' potentially or actually."

All these senses of being, according to Aristotle, "refer to one starting point," namely, substance, or that which has being in and of itself. "That which is primarily, *i.e.*, not in a qualified sense," he writes, "must be a substance." But when he also says that "that which 'is' primarily is the 'what' which indicates the substance of a thing," he seems to be using the words "substance" and "essence" interchangeably. This, in turn, seems to be related to the fact that, although Aristotle distinguishes between actual and potential being, and between necessary or incorruptible and contingent or corruptible beings, he, like Plato and unlike Aquinas, Descartes, or Spinoza, does not consider whether the essence and existence of a being are identical or separate.

It may be held that this distinction is implied, since a contingent being is one which is able not to exist, whereas a necessary being cannot *not* exist. A contingent being is, therefore, one whose essence can be divorced from existence; a necessary being, one which *must be* precisely because its essence is identical with its existence. But the explicit recognition of a real distinction between essence and existence seems to be reserved for the later theologians and philosophers who conceive of an infinite being, as Aristotle does not.

The infinity of a being lies not only in its possession of all perfections, but even more fundamentally in its requiring no cause outside itself for its own existence. "That thing," says Aquinas, "whose being differs from its essence, must have its being caused by another. . . . That which has being, but is not being, is a being by participation." Where Aristotle makes substance the primary type of being, and the "starting-point" of all its other meanings, Aquinas makes the infinite being of God, whose very essence it is to be, the source of all finite and participated beings, in which there is a composition of existence and essence, or "of that *whereby they are* and that *which they are.*"

Since "being itself is that whereby a thing is," being belongs to God primarily and to all other things according to modes of derivation or participation. God and his creatures can be called "beings" but, Aquinas points out, not in the *identically same* sense, nor yet with *utter diversity* of meaning. A similarity—a sameness-in-diversity or analogy—obtains between the unqualified being of God and the being of all other things, which have being subject to various qualifications or limitations.

All other questions about being are affected by the solution of these basic problems concerning the unity of being, the kinds of being, and the order of the various kinds. If they are solved in one way—in favor of unity— certain questions are not even raised, for they are genuine only on the basis of the other solution which finds being diverse. The discussion, in the chapters on SAME AND OTHER, and on SIGN AND SYMBOL, of sameness, diversity, and analogy is, therefore, relevant to the problem of how things are at once alike and unlike in being.

THE GREEKS, NOTABLY Plato and Aristotle, began the inquiry about being. They realized that after all other questions are answered, there still remains the question, What does it mean to say of anything that it *is* or *is not*? After we understand what it means for a thing to be a man, or to be alive, or to be a body, we must still consider what it means for that thing simply to be in any way at all; or to be in one sense, and not to be in another.

The discussion of being, in itself and in relation to unity and truth, rest and motion, runs through many dialogues of Plato. It is central in the *Sophist* and *Parmenides*. The same terms and problems appear in Aristotle's scientific treatise which makes *being* its distinctive subject matter, and which he sometimes calls "first philosophy" and sometimes "theology." It belongs to this science, he declares, "to consider being *qua* being—both what it is and the properties which belong to it *qua* being."

As pointed out in the chapter on METAPHYSICS, it is an historical accident that this inquiry concerning being came to be called "metaphysics." That is the name which, according to legend, the ancient editors gave to a collection of writings in which Aristotle pursued this inquiry. Since they came after the books on physics, they were called "metaphysics" on the supposition that Aristotle intended the discussion of being to follow his treatise on change and motion.

If one were to invent a word to describe the science of being, it would be "ontology," not "metaphysics" or even "theology." Yet "metaphysics" has remained the traditionally accepted name for the inquiry or science which goes beyond physics—or all of natural science—in that it asks about the very existence of things, and their modes of being. The traditional connection of metaphysics with theology, discussed in the chapters on THEOLOGY and METAPHYSICS, seems to have its origin in the fact that Aristotle's treatise on being passes from a consideration of sensible and mutable substances to the problem of the existence of immaterial beings, and to the conception of a divine being, purely actual, absolutely immutable.

In a science intended to treat "of that which *is* primarily, and to which all the other categories of being are referred, namely, substance," Aristotle says, "we must first sketch the nature of substance." Hence he begins with what he calls "the generally recognized substances. These are the sensible substances." He postpones until later his critical discussion of "the Ideas and the objects of mathematics, for some say these are substances in addition to the sensible substances"; yet he directs his whole inquiry to the ultimate question "whether there are or are not any besides sensible substances." His attempt to answer this question in the twelfth book makes it the theological part of his *Metaphysics*.

THOUGH THEIR ORDER of discussion is different, the metaphysicians of the 17th century, like Descartes, Spinoza, and Leibnitz, deal with many, if not all, major points in the analysis of being which the Greek philosophers initiated and the mediaeval theologians developed. Later philosophers, whose main concern is with the origin and validity of human knowledge, come to the traditional metaphysical questions through an analysis, not of substance or essence, existence or power, but of our *ideas* of substance and power.

This transformation of the ancient problem of being is stated by Berkeley in almost epigrammatic form. Considering "what is meant by the term *exist*," he argues from the experience of sensible things that "their *esse* is *percipi*, nor is it possible they should have any existence, out of the minds or thinking things which perceive them." Locke, too, although he does not identify being with perception, makes the same shift on the ground that "the first step towards satisfying several inquiries the mind of man was apt to run into, was to make a survey of our own understandings, examine our own powers, and see to what things they were adapted."

Once the problems of being are viewed first in terms of the mind, the questions for the philosopher become primarily those of the relation of our definitions to real and nominal essences, the conditions of our knowledge of existence, and the identification of the real and ideal with perceptible matters of fact and intelligible relations between ideas.

For Kant the basic distinction is between the sensible and supra-sensible, or the phenomenal and noumenal, realms of being. From another point of view, Kant considers the being of things in themselves apart from human experience and the being of natural things or, what is the same for him, the things of experience. The former are unconditioned, the latter conditioned, by the knowing mind which is formative or constitutive of experience.

"The sole aim of pure reason," Kant writes, "is the absolute totality of the synthesis on the side of the conditions . . . in order to preposit the whole series of conditions, and thus present them to the understanding *a priori*." Having obtained these "conditions," we can ascend through them "until we reach the unconditioned, that is, the principles." It is with these ideas of pure reason that metaphysics, according to Kant, properly deals. Instead of *being*, its object consists in "three grand ideas: God,

Freedom, and Immortality, and it aims at showing that the second conception, conjoined with the first, must lead to the third as a necessary conclusion."

Hegel, on the other hand, does not approach the problem of being or reality through a critique of knowledge. For Hegel, as for Plotinus before him, the heart of metaphysics lies in understanding that "nothing is actual except the Idea" or the Absolute, "and the great thing is to apprehend in the show of the temporal and the transient, the substance which is immanent, and the eternal which is present." Plotinus calls the absolute, not the Idea, but the All-one, yet he tries to show that the One is the principle, the light, and the life of all things, just as Hegel reduces everything to a manifestation of the underlying reality of the Absolute Idea.

Despite all such changes in terminology, despite radical differences in philosophical principle or conclusion, and regardless of the attitude taken toward the possibility of metaphysics as a science, the central question which is faced by anyone who goes beyond physics, or natural philosophy, is a question about being or existence. It may or may not be asked explicitly, but it is always present by implication.

The question about God, for example, or free will or immortality, is first of all a question about whether such things *exist*, and *how* they exist. Do they have reality or are they only fictions of the mind? Similarly, questions about the infinite, the absolute, or the unconditioned are questions about that primary reality apart from whose existence nothing else could be or be conceived, and which therefore has an existence different from the things dependent on it for their being. Here again the first question is whether such a reality exists.

Enough has been said to indicate why this discussion cannot consider all topics which have some connection with the theory of being. To try to make this Introduction adequate even for the topics outlined here, under which the references to the great books are assembled, would be to make it almost co-extensive in scope with the sum of many other Introductions—all, in fact, which open chapters dealing with metaphysical concepts or problems.

It is to be expected, of course, that the special

problems of the existence of God, of an immortal soul, and of a free will should be treated in the chapters on GOD, IMMORTALITY, and WILL. But it may not be realized that such chapters as CAUSE, ETERNITY, FORM, INFINITY, IDEA, MATTER, ONE AND MANY, SAME AND OTHER, RELATION, UNIVERSAL AND PARTICULAR—all these and still others cited in the Cross-References below—include topics which would have to be discussed here if we were to try to cover all relevant considerations.

Reasons of economy and intelligibility dictate the opposite course. Limiting the scope of this Introduction to a few principal points in the theory of being, we can also exhibit, through the relation of this chapter to others, the interconnection of the great ideas. The various modes of being (such as essence and existence, substance and accident, potentiality and actuality, the real and the ideal) and the basic correlatives of being (such as unity, goodness, truth) are, therefore, left for fuller treatment in other contexts. But two topics deserve further attention here. One is the distinction between being and becoming, the other the relation of being to knowledge.

THE FACT OF CHANGE or motion—of coming to be and passing away—is so evident to the senses that it has never been denied, at least not as an experienced phenomenon. But it has been regarded as irrational and unreal, an illusion perpetrated by the senses. Galen, for instance, charges the Sophists with "allowing that bread in turning into blood becomes changed as regards sight, taste, and touch," but denying that "this change occurs in reality." They explain it away, he says, as "tricks and illusions of our senses . . . which are affected now in one way, now in another, whereas the underlying substance does not admit of any of these changes."

The familiar paradoxes of Zeno are *reductio ad absurdum* arguments to show that motion is unthinkable, full of self-contradiction. The way of truth, according to Parmenides, Zeno's master in the Eleatic school, lies in the insight that whatever is always was and will be, that nothing comes into being out of non-being, or passes out of being into nothingness.

The doctrine of Parmenides provoked many criticisms. Yet his opponents tried to preserve the reality of change, without having to accord it the fullness of being. The Greek atomists, for example, think that change cannot be explained except in terms of permanent beings—in fact eternal ones. Lucretius, who expounds their views, remarks that in any change "something unchangeable must remain over, that all things be not utterly reduced to nothing; for whenever a thing changes and quits its proper limits, at once this change of state is the death of that which was before." The "something unchangeable" is thought to be the atom, the absolutely indivisible, and hence imperishable, unit of matter. Change does not touch the being of the atoms, "but only breaks up the union amongst them, and then joins anew the different elements with others; and thus it comes to pass that all things change"—that is, all things composite, not the simple bodies of solid singleness —"when the clashings, motions, arrangement, position, and shapes of matter change about."

In a conversation with Cratylus, who favors the Heraclitean theory of a universal flux, Socrates asks, "How can that be a real thing which is never in the same state?" How "can we reasonably say, Cratylus," he goes on, "that there is any knowledge at all, if everything is in a state of transition and there is nothing abiding"?

When he gets Glaucon to admit in the *Republic* that "being is the sphere or subject matter of knowledge, and knowing is to know the nature of being," Socrates leads him to see the correlation of being, not-being, and becoming with knowledge, ignorance, and opinion. "If opinion and knowledge are distinct faculties then the sphere of knowledge and opinion cannot be the same . . . If being is the subject matter of knowledge, something else must be the subject matter of opinion." It cannot be not-being, for "of not-being ignorance was assumed to be the necessary correlative."

Since "opinion is not concerned either with being or with not-being" because it is obviously intermediate between knowledge and ignorance, Socrates concludes that "if anything appeared to be of a sort which is and is not at the same time, that sort of thing would appear also to lie in the interval between pure being and absolute not-being," and "the corresponding faculty is neither knowledge nor ignorance, but will be found in the interval between them." This "intermediate flux" or sphere of becoming, this "region of the many and the variable," can yield only opinion. Being, the realm of the "absolute and eternal and immutable [Ideas]," is the only object that one "may be said to know."

Aristotle would seem to agree with Plato that change "partakes equally of the nature of being and not-being, and cannot rightly be termed either, pure and simple." He points out that his predecessors, particularly the Eleatics, held change to be impossible, because they believed that "what comes to be must do so either from what is or from what is not, both of which are impossible." It is impossible, so they argued, since "what is cannot come to be (because it *is* already), and from what is not nothing could have come to be." Aristotle concedes the cogency of this argument on one condition, namely, that the terms 'being' and 'not-being' are taken "without qualification." But his whole point is that they need not be taken without qualification and should not be, if we wish to explain change rather than make a mystery of it.

The qualification Aristotle introduces rests on the distinction between two modes of being —the potentiality and actuality correlative with matter and form. This makes it possible for him to maintain that "a thing may come to be from what is not . . . in a qualified sense." He illustrates his meaning by the example of the bronze, which from a mere lump of metal comes to be a statue under the hands of the artist. The bronze, he says, was "potentially a statue," and the change whereby it came to be actually a statue is the process between potentiality and actuality. While the change is going on, the bronze is neither completely potential nor fully actual in respect of *being a statue*.

Like Plato, Aristotle recognizes that there is "something indefinite" about change. "The reason," he explains, "is that it cannot be classed simply as a potentiality or as an actuality—a thing that is merely *capable* of having a certain size is not undergoing change, nor yet a thing that is *actually* of a certain size." Change is "a sort of actuality, but incomplete . . . hard to grasp, but not incapable of existing."

If to exist is to be completely actual, then changing things and change itself do not fully exist. They exist only to the extent that they have actuality. Yet potentiality, no less than actuality, is a mode of being. That potentiality —power or capacity—belongs to being seems also to be affirmed by the Eleatic Stranger in Plato's *Sophist*. "Anything which possesses any sort of power to affect another, or to be affected by another," he says, "if only for a single moment, however trifling the cause and however slight the effect, has real existence . . . I hold," he adds, "that the definition of being is simply power."

The basic issue concerning being and becoming, and the issue concerning eternal as opposed to mutable existence, recur again and again in the tradition of western thought. They are involved in the distinction between corruptible and incorruptible substances (which is in turn connected with the division of substances into corporeal and spiritual), and with the nature of God as the only purely actual, or truly eternal, being. They are implicit in Spinoza's distinction between *natura naturans* and *natura naturata*, and in his distinction between God's knowledge of things under the aspect of eternity and man's temporal view of the world in process. They are relevant to Hegel's Absolute Idea which, while remaining fixed, progressively reveals itself in the ever-changing face of nature and history. In our own day these issues engage Dewey, Santayana, and Whitehead in controversy, as yesterday they engaged Bradley, William James, and Bergson.

As ALREADY NOTED, Plato's division of reality into the realms of being and becoming has a bearing on his analysis of knowledge and opinion. The division relates to the distinction between the intelligible and the sensible, and between the opposed qualities of certainty and probability, or necessity and contingency, in our judgments about things. The distinctions between essence and existence and between substance and accident separate aspects or modes of being which function differently as objects for the knowing mind.

Aristotle, for example, holds that "there can be no scientific treatment of the *accidental* . . . for the accidental is practically a mere name.

And," he adds, "Plato was in a sense not wrong in ranking sophistic as dealing with that which is not. For the arguments of the sophists deal, we may say, above all, with the accidental." That the accidental is "akin to non-being," Aristotle thinks may be seen in the fact that "things which are in another sense come into being and pass out of being by a process, but things which are accidentally do not." But though he rejects the accidental as an object of science, he does not, like Plato or Plotinus, exclude the whole realm of sensible, changing things from the sphere of scientific knowledge. For him, both metaphysics and physics treat of sensible substances, the one with regard to their mutable *being*, the other with regard to their being *mutable*—their becoming or changing.

For Plotinus, on the other hand, "the true sciences have an intelligible object and contain no notion of anything sensible." They are directed, not "to variable things, suffering from all sorts of changes, divided in space, to which the name of becoming and not being belongs," but to the "eternal being which is not divided, existing always in the same way, which is not born and does not perish, and has neither space, place, nor situation . . . but rests immovable in itself."

According to another view, represented by Locke, substance is as such unknowable, whether it be body or spirit. We use the word "substance" to name the "support of such qualities, which are capable of producing simple ideas in us; which qualities are commonly called accidents." The sensible accidents are all that we truly know and "we give the general name substance" to "the supposed, but unknown, support of those qualities we find existing." Some of these sensible accidents are what Locke calls "primary qualities"—the powers or potentialities by which things affect one another and also our senses.

But to the extent that our senses fail to discover "the bulk, texture, and figure of the minute parts of bodies, on which their constitutions and differences depend, we are fain to make use of their secondary qualities, as the characteristical notes and marks whereby to frame ideas of them in our mind." Nevertheless, powers—which are qualities or accidents, not substances—seem to be, for Locke, the

ultimate reality we can know. "The secondary sensible qualities," he writes, "are nothing but the powers" which corporeal substances have "to produce several ideas in us by our sense, which ideas"—unlike the primary qualities— "are not in the things themselves, otherwise than as anything is in its cause."

Hobbes exemplifies still another view. "A man can have no thought," he says, "representing anything not subject to sense." Hobbes does not object to calling bodies "substances," but thinks that when we speak of "an incorporeal body, or (which is all one) an incorporeal substance," we talk nonsense; "for none of these things ever have, or can be incident to sense; but are absurd speeches, taken upon credit (without any signification at all) from deceived Philosophers, and deceived, or deceiving, Schoolmen."

He enumerates other absurdities, such as "the giving of names of bodies to accidents, or of accidents to bodies," *e.g.*, by those who say that "extension is body." Criticism of the fallacy of reification—the fallacy first pointed out by Ockham and criticized so repeatedly in contemporary semantics—also appears in Hobbes' warning against making substances out of abstractions or universals "by giving the names of bodies to names or speeches."

WHENEVER A THEORY of knowledge is concerned with how we know reality, as opposed to mere appearances, it considers the manner in which existing beings can be known—by perception, intuition, or demonstration; and with respect to demonstration, it attempts to formulate the conditions of valid reasoning about matters of fact or real existence. But it has seldom been supposed that reality exhausts the objects of our thought or knowledge. We can conceive possibilities not realized in this world. We can imagine things which do not exist in nature.

The meaning of reality—of real as opposed to purely conceptual or ideal being—is derived from the notion of thinghood, of having being outside the mind, not merely in it. In traditional controversies about the existence of ideas— or of universals, the objects of mathematics, or relations—it is not the being of such things which is questioned, but their reality, their existence outside the mind. If, for example, ideas exist apart from minds, the minds of men and God, they have real, not ideal, existence. If the objects of mathematics, such as numbers and figures, have existence only as figments of the mind, they are ideal beings.

The judgment of the reality of a thing, James thinks, involves "a state of consciousness *sui generis*" about which not much can be said "in the way of internal analysis." The focus of this problem in modern times is indicated by James' phrasing of the question, "Under what circumstances do we think things real?" And James gives a typically modern answer to the question.

He begins by saying that "any object which remains uncontradicted is ipso facto believed and posited as absolute reality." He admits that "for most men . . . the 'things of sense' . . . are the absolutely real world's nucleus. Other things," James writes, "may be real for this man or that—things of science, abstract moral relations, things of the Christian theology, or what not. But even for the special man, these things are usually real with a less real reality than that of the things of sense." But his basic conviction is that "our own reality, that sense of our own life which we at every moment possess, is the ultimate of ultimates for our belief. 'As sure as I exist!'—this is our uttermost warrant for the being of all other things. As Descartes made the indubitable reality of the *cogito* go bail for the reality of all that the *cogito* involved, so all of us, feeling our own present reality with absolutely coercive force, ascribe an all but equal degree of reality, first to whatever things we lay hold on with a sense of personal need, and second, to whatever farther things continuously belong with these."

The self or ego is the ultimate criterion of being or reality. "The world of living realities as contrasted with unrealities," James writes, "is thus anchored in the Ego. . . . That is the hook from which the rest dangles, the absolute support. And as from a painted hook it has been said that one can only hang a painted chain, so conversely from a real hook only a real chain can properly be hung. *Whatever things have intimate and continuous connection with my life are things of whose reality I cannot doubt.* Whatever things fail to establish this connection are things which are practically no better for me than if they existed not at all." James would be the first to concede to any critic of his position, that its truth and good sense depend upon noting that word "practically," for it is "the world of 'practical realities'" with which he professes to be concerned.

WE CAN IN CONCLUSION observe one obvious measure of the importance of *being* in philosophical thought. The major *isms* by which the historians of philosophy have tried to classify its doctrines represent affirmations or denials with respect to being or the modes of being. They are such antitheses as realism and idealism; materialism and spiritualism; monism, dualism, and pluralism; even atheism and theism. Undoubtedly, no great philosopher can be so simply boxed. Yet the opposing *isms* do indicate the great speculative issues which no mind can avoid if it pursues the truth or seeks the ultimate principles of good and evil.

OUTLINE OF TOPICS

REFERENCES

To find the passages cited, use the numbers in heavy type, which are the volume and page numbers of the passages referred to. For example, in 4 HOMER: *Iliad*, BK II [265-283] 12d, the number 4 is the number of the volume in the set; the number 12d indicates that the passage is in section d of page 12.

PAGE SECTIONS: When the text is printed in one column, the letters a and b refer to the upper and lower halves of the page. For example, in 53 JAMES: *Psychology*, 116a-119b, the passage begins in the upper half of page 116 and ends in the lower half of page 119. When the text is printed in two columns, the letters a and b refer to the upper and lower halves of the left-hand side of the page, the letters c and d to the upper and lower halves of the right-hand side of the page. For example, in 7 PLATO: *Symposium*, 163b-164c, the passage begins in the lower half of the left-hand side of page 163 and ends in the upper half of the right-hand side of page 164.

AUTHOR'S DIVISIONS: One or more of the main divisions of a work (such as PART, BK, CH, SECT) are sometimes included in the reference; line numbers, in brackets, are given in certain cases; *e.g.*, *Iliad*, BK II [265-283] 12d.

BIBLE REFERENCES: The references are to book, chapter, and verse. When the King James and Douay versions differ in title of books or in the numbering of chapters or verses, the King James version is cited first and the Douay, indicated by a (*D*), follows; *e.g.*, OLD TESTAMENT: *Nehemiah*, 7:45—(*D*) *II Esdras*, 7:46.

SYMBOLS: The abbreviation "esp" calls the reader's attention to one or more especially relevant parts of a whole reference; "passim" signifies that the topic is discussed intermittently rather than continuously in the work or passage cited.

For additional information concerning the style of the references, see the Explanation of Reference Style; for general guidance in the use of *The Great Ideas*, consult the Preface.

1. Diverse conceptions of being and non-being: being as a term or concept; the meanings of *is* and *is not*

7 PLATO: *Republic*, BK V, 370d-373c / *Timaeus*, 447b-d; 455c-458b / *Parmenides* 486a-511d / *Theaetetus*, 517d-518b; 520b; 521d-522a / *Sophist*, 561d-563b esp 562a-563a; 565a-566b; 567a-569a; 571d-573b passim

8 ARISTOTLE: *Interpretation*, CH 3 [16^{b}19-26] 25d-26a; CH 13 [23^{a}18-26] 35b-c / *Prior Analytics*, BK I, CH 36 [48^{a}40-^{b}9] 66d / *Posterior Analytics*, BK II, CH 7 [92^{b}13] 126c / *Topics*, BK IV, CH 1 [121^{a}14-26] 169a-b; [121^{b}1-8] 169c; CH 6 [127^{a}26-40] 176d-177a; BK VI, CH 7 [146^{a}21-32] 200a-b / *Sophistical Refutations*, CH 5 [166^{b}37-167^{a}7] 229d; CH 7 [169^{a}22-24] 232d; CH 25 [180^{a}32-38] 248c / *Physics*, BK I, CH 2 [185^{a}20-^{b}4] 260a-b; CH 3 [186^{a}23-187^{a}10] 261b-262a; CH 5 [188^{a}18-23] 263c; BK III, CH 6 [206^{a}13-34] 284b-d; BK V, CH 1 [225^{a}20-29] 305b-c / *Generation and Corruption*, BK I, CH 3 413c-416c passim / *Metaphysics*, BK I, CH 3-10 501c-511d passim; BK III, CH 3 [998^{b}14-28] 517b-c; BK IV, CH 2 [1003^{a}33-^{b}10] 522b; CH 5 [1009^{a}22-38] 528d; BK V, CH 7 537c-538b; BK VII, CH 1 550b,d-551a; CH 4 [1030^{a}17-^{b}14] 552d-553b; BK IX, CH 10 [1051^{a}34-^{b}2] 577c;

BK XI, CH 2 [1060^{a}36-^{b}10] 588c; CH 3 [1060^{b}31] 1061^{a}10] 589a-b; BK XII, CH 2 [1069^{b}15-34-598d-599a; CH 4 [1070^{b}7-8] 599d-600a / *Soul*, BK II, CH 1 [412^{b}6-9] 642c

17 PLOTINUS: *First Ennead*, TR VIII, CH 3, 28a-b / *Third Ennead*, TR VI, CH 6-7 109d-111c; TR VII, CH 6 122a-d / *Fifth Ennead*, TR I, CH 4 209d-210c; TR II, CH 1 214c-215a; TR VI, CH 6 237b-d / *Sixth Ennead*, TR II, CH 7-8 272a-273c

18 AUGUSTINE: *Confessions*, BK VII, par 1-2 43b-44a / *City of God*, BK VIII, CH 11, 272c; BK XII, CH 2 343c-d / *Christian Doctrine*, BK I, CH 32 633c-d

19 AQUINAS: *Summa Theologica*, PART I, QQ 2-13 10c-75b passim, esp Q 3, A 4, REP 1 16d-17c, Q 11, A 1 46d-47d, Q 13, A 5, ANS and REP 1 66b-67d, A 10, ANS 72c-73c; Q 14, A 9, ANS 83b-d; Q 16, A 3, REP 2 96b-d; Q 22, A 4, REP 3 131c-132b; Q 29, A 1, REP 4 162a-163b; QQ 44-45 238a-250a; Q 48, A 2, REP 2 260c-261b; Q 54, A 2, ANS 285d-286c; Q 104 534c-538c; Q 105, A 5, ANS 542a-543b; PART I-II, Q 2, A 5 esp REP 2-3 618d-619c

20 AQUINAS: *Summa Theologica*, PART I-II, Q 61, A 1, REP 1 54d-55c

23 HOBBES: *Leviathan*, PART IV, 269d-270c

25 MONTAIGNE: *Essays*, 292d-294a

31 DESCARTES: *Discourse*, PART IV 51b-54b / *Meditations*, IV, 89c-d / *Objections and Replies*, 139b-c; 214d-215a

31 SPINOZA: *Ethics*, PART I, PROP II, DEMONST, 358d; SCHOL, 359a; PART II, PROP 40, SCHOL I 387b-388a

33 PASCAL: *Geometrical Demonstration*, 432b

35 LOCKE: *Human Understanding*, BK III, CH VII, SECT I 283a-b

35 BERKELEY: *Human Knowledge*, SECT 2-3 413b-d; SECT 17 416a-b; SECT 45-46 421b-c; SECT 48 422a; SECT 81 428c-d; SECT 88-91 430a-431a; SECT 139 440d

42 KANT: *Pure Reason*, 43d-44a; 52a-b; 107b-108a,c; 133c; 177b-187a esp 179c-182b, 185c-187a; 197b-198a / *Pref. Metaphysical Elements of Ethics*, 367d-368a / *Judgement*, 603b-c

46 HEGEL: *Philosophy of History*, INTRO, 156d-157b; PART I, 224a-b; 233b-235a; 237d-238d; 251d-252d; PART IV, 322a-b

53 JAMES: *Psychology*, 636a-661b esp 639a-640a, 641a-b, 643a-645b; 871b-872a

2. Being and the one and the many

7 PLATO: *Republic*, BK III, 333b-d; BK V, 370a-373c esp 372d-373c; BK VII, 392b-394b; BK X, 427c-429c / *Parmenides* 486a-511d / *Theaetetus*, 537a-c; 544d-547c esp 547a / *Sophist*, 564d-574c / *Statesman*, 594d-595a / *Philebus*, 610d-617d

8 ARISTOTLE: *Physics*, BK I, CH 2-3 259b-262a / *Metaphysics*, BK I, CH 7 [988ª34-ᵇ5] 506c; BK III, CH I [996ª4-8] 514c; CH 4 [1001ª4-ᵇ25] 519d-520c; BK VII, CH 16 [1040ᵇ16-27] 564d; BK X, CH 2 580b-d; BK XI, CH 2 [1060ª36-ᵇ19] 588c-d; BK XIV, CH 2 [1088ᵇ28-1090ª2] 621b-622c

12 EPICTETUS: *Discourses*, BK I, CH 14, 120d-121a

12 AURELIUS: *Meditations*, BK II, SECT 3 257a-b; BK IV, SECT 29 266a; SECT 40 267a-b; BK V, SECT 30 273a; BK VI, SECT 36-45 277c-278c; BK VII, SECT 9 280b-c; SECT 19 281a; BK IX, SECT 8-9 292b-d; BK X, SECT 6-7 297a-c; BK XII, SECT 30 310a-b

17 PLOTINUS: *Third Ennead*, TR I, CH 4 79d-80a; TR II, CH 1-2 82c-83d; TR VIII, CH 8-10 132d-136a; TR IX, CH 3 137b-138a,c / *Fifth Ennead*, TR I, CH 4-9 209d-213c; TR II, CH 1 214c-215a; TR III, CH 11-12 222b-223c; CH 15-16 224c-226a; TR IV 226d-228b; TR VI 6 237b-d / *Sixth Ennead*, TR II 268d-280d; TR IV, CH II 302c-d; TR V, CH I 305c-306a; CH 5-8 307a-308c; TR VI, CH 5-6 312c-313d; CH 8-16 314a-319d

18 AUGUSTINE: *Confessions*, BK IV, par 15-17 23a-c

19 AQUINAS: *Summa Theologica*, PART I, Q 3, A 3, ANS 16a-d; Q II 46d-50b; Q 30, A 3 169b-170c; Q 93, A 9, ANS 500c-501c

21 DANTE: *Divine Comedy*, PARADISE, II [112-123] 109a

31 DESCARTES: *Objections and Replies*, 123c-d

31 SPINOZA: *Ethics*, PART I, DEF 2 355a; DEF 6 355b; PROP 5-16 356b-362a

35 LOCKE: *Human Understanding*, BK III, CH III, SECT 19 259c-260a

42 KANT: *Pure Reason*, 43d-44a; 49c-51d esp 51c-d; 99a-101b; 107b-c; 173b-177b; 193a-200c

46 HEGEL: *Philosophy of History*, PART I, 218c; 224a-b; 232d; 237d-238a

51 TOLSTOY: *War and Peace*, BK XIV, 608a-b

2*a*. Infinite being and the plurality of finite beings

8 ARISTOTLE: *Physics*, BK I, CH 8 [191ª24-ᵇ12] 267a-c / *Metaphysics*, BK I, CH 5 [986ᵇ18-987ª1] 504d-505a

12 AURELIUS: *Meditations*, BK IV, SECT 29 266a; SECT 40 267a-b; BK XII, SECT 30 310a-b

17 PLOTINUS: *Third Ennead*, TR II, CH 1-2 82c-83d; TR VII, CH 6 122a-d; TR VIII, CH 8-10 132d-136a / *Fourth Ennead*, TR IX, CH 2 205c-206a; CH 5 206d-207a,c / *Fifth Ennead*, TR I, CH 4-7 209d-212c; TR III, CH 11-12 222b-223c; CH 15-16 224c-226a; TR IV 226d-228b

18 AUGUSTINE: *Confessions*, BK VII, par 20-21 49d-50a

19 AQUINAS: *Summa Theologica*, PART I, Q 3, A 3, ANS 16a-d; A 7, REP 2 19a-c; QQ 7-8 31a-38c; Q II, AA 3-4 49a-50b; Q 13, A II 73c-74b; QQ 44-45 238a-250a; Q 47 256a-259a; Q 50, A I, ANS and REP 3 269b-270a; Q 90, A I 480d-481d; QQ 103-105 528a-545b

31 DESCARTES: *Meditations*, III, 84a-b; 86a-88d / *Objections and Replies*, 121d-122c; 123c-d; 139b-c

31 SPINOZA: *Ethics*, PART I 355a-372d esp DEF 2 355a, DEF 6 355b, PROP 7-16 356c-362a, PROP 21-25 364a-365b, PROP 28 365c-366a, PROP 29, SCHOL 366b-c, PROP 30 366c-d; PART II, PROP 45, SCHOL 390b

33 PASCAL: *Pensées*, 121 195a

42 KANT: *Pure Reason*, 130b-133c / *Judgement*, 550a-551a,c; 564c-565d esp 565c-d; 566c-d; 580c-d

46 HEGEL: *Philosophy of History*, PART I, 227d-228a; 234d-235a

2*b*. The unity of a being

8 ARISTOTLE: *Categories*, CH 2 [1ᵇ3-9] 5c / *Topics*, BK IV, CH I [121ª14-19] 169a; [121ᵇ4-8] 169c; CH 6 [127ª26-40] 176d-177a; BK VI, CH 4 [141ª26-ᵇ2] 194c-d / *Sophistical Refutations*, CH 7 [169ª32-36] 233a / *Metaphysics*, BK IV, CH 2 [1003ᵇ23-34] 522d; BK V, CH 6 536a-537c; CH 9 [1018ª3-9] 538d; BK VIII, CH 6 569d-570d; BK X, CH 1-2 578b,d-580d; CH 3 [1054ª33-35] 581a; BK XII, CH 10 [1075ᵇ34-37] 606d; BK XIII, CH 2 [1077ª20-23] 608c / *Soul*, BK II, CH I [412ᵇ6-9] 642c

11 EUCLID: *Elements*, BK VII, DEFINITIONS, I 127a

11 NICOMACHUS: *Arithmetic*, BK II, 840a-b

(2. Being and the one and the many. 2b. The unity of a being.)

17 Plotinus: *Fourth Ennead*, TR II, CH I 139c-140c / *Sixth Ennead*, TR VI, CH 11-16 315d-319d; TR IX, CH 1-2 353d-355a

19 Aquinas: *Summa Theologica*, PART I, Q 6, A 3, REP 1 29c-30b; Q 11, AA 1-4 46d-50b passim; Q 39, A 3, ANS 204c-205c; Q 76 385c-399b passim; Q 103, A 3, ANS 530a-c; PART I-II, Q 12, A 3, REP 2-3 670d-671b; Q 17, A 4, ANS 688d-689c

20 Aquinas: *Summa Theologica*, PART III, Q 2, A 1, ANS and REP 2 710a-711c; A 9 719d-720c; Q 17 806d-809d; Q 19, A 1, REP 4 816a-818b; PART III SUPPL, Q 83, A 3, REP 4 978c-980d

31 Descartes: *Objections and Replies*, 153b-154a; 213d-214a; 224d-225d

31 Spinoza: *Ethics*, PART I, PROP 12-13 359b-d; PART II, DEF 7 373c

35 Locke: *Human Understanding*, BK II, CH XIII, SECT 26 154b-c; CH XVI, SECT 1 165c-d; CH XXIII, SECT 1-6 204a-205c; CH XXIII, SECT 37-CH XXIV, SECT 3 213d-214d; CH XXVII 218d-228c; BK III, CH VI, SECT 2-5 268c-269d; SECT 10 271b; SECT 49 282c

35 Berkeley: *Human Knowledge*, SECT 1 413a-b; SECT 12 415b-c; SECT 99 432b

42 Kant: *Pure Reason*, 120c-129c esp 121a-124d, 126a-128b / *Judgement*, 566c-d

53 James: *Psychology*, 104a-107b esp 104a-b; 215b-216a; 406b

3. Being and good

Old Testament: *Genesis*, I
New Testament: *I Timothy*, 4:4

7 Plato: *Phaedrus*, 124c-125b / *Republic*, BK VI-VII, 383d-398c / *Timaeus*, 447b-448b

8 Aristotle: *Topics*, BK VI, CH 5 [143^{a}9-12] 196c; CH 6 [145^{a}19-27] 198d-199a; CH 8 [146^{b}9-147^{a}11] 200c-201a; CH 12 [149^{b}31-39] 204b-c / *Generation and Corruption*, BK II, CH 10 [336^{b}28-30] 438d / *Metaphysics*, BK I, CH 6 [988^{a}8-16] 506a-b; CH 7 [988^{b}6-16] 506c-d; CH 9 [992^{a}29-34] 510c; BK XII, CH 7 602a-603b; CH 10 [1075^{a}11-24] 605d-606a; BK XIV, CH 4 [1091^{a}29]-CH 5 [1092^{a}17] 624a-625a

9 Aristotle: *Generation of Animals*, BK II, CH I [731^{b}26-29] 272a / *Ethics*, BK I, CH 6 [1096^{a}23-29] 341c

17 Plotinus: *First Ennead*, TR III 10a-12b; TR VII, CH 1, 26c; TR VIII, CH 3-12 28a-34a / *Fifth Ennead*, TR III, CH 15-16 224c-226a; TR IX, CH 10, 250c / *Sixth Ennead*, TR V, CH I 305c-306a; TR VII, CH 24-26 333d-334d; CH 28 335b-d

18 Augustine: *Confessions*, BK III, par 10 15b-d; par 12 16b; BK IV, par 24 25b-c; BK V, par 20 32d-33a; BK VII, par 3-7 44a-45d; par 16-23 48c-50c / *City of God*, BK XI, CH 22, 333d-334a; BK XII, CH 3 343d-344b

19 Aquinas: *Summa Theologica*, PART I, Q 3, A 2, ANS 15c-16a; QQ 4-6 20c-30d; Q 13, A 11, REP 2 73c-74b; Q 21, A 1, REP 4 124b-125b; Q 22, A 1, ANS 127d-128d; Q 25, A 6, ANS 149a-150a; Q 48, AA 1-3 259b-262a; Q 73, A 1 370a-371a; A 3, REP 3 371d-372c; Q 74, A 3, REP 3 375a-377a,c; PART I-II, Q 2, A 5 618d-619c; Q 18, AA 1-4 694a-696d esp A 1, ANS and REP 1 694a-d, A 2, ANS 694d-695c; Q 29, A 5, ANS 747c-748b

20 Aquinas: *Summa Theologica*, PART I-II, Q 54, A 3, REP 2 24c-25b; Q 55, A 4, REP 1-2 28c-29d

31 Spinoza: *Ethics*, PART I, APPENDIX 369b-372d; PART II, DEF 6 373c; PART IV, DEF 1-2 424a

42 Kant: *Fund. Prin. Metaphysic of Morals*, 278b-c / *Practical Reason*, 307b-c

3a. The hierarchy of being: grades of reality, degrees of intelligibility

7 Plato: *Phaedrus*, 124c-126a / *Symposium*, 167a-d / *Republic*, BK V, 370c-373c; BK VI-VII, 383d-398c; BK IX, 422c-425b esp 423b-424d / *Timaeus*, 447a-455c / *Philebus*, 637c-639a,c

8 Aristotle: *Interpretation*, CH 13 [23^{a}18-26] 35b-c / *Topics*, BK VI, CH 4 [141^{a}26-142^{a}22] 194c-195c / *Heavens*, BK I, CH 2 359d-360d; BK II, CH 12 383b-384c; BK IV, CH 3 [310^{b}32-311^{a}3] 402b-c / *Generation and Corruption*, BK I, CH 3 413c-416c; BK II, CH 10 [336^{b}25-34] 438d / *Meteorology*, BK IV, CH 12 [389^{b}23-390^{a}17] 493d-494b / *Metaphysics*, BK I, CH 6 505b-506b; CH 7 [988^{a}34-^{b}5] 506c; CH 8 [989^{b}21-990^{a}8] 507d-508a; CH 9 508c-511c; BK II, CH 1 [993^{b}19-31] 512a-b; BK IV, CH 4 [1008^{b}32-1009^{a}5] 528b; BK IX, CH 9 [1051^{a}4-22] 577a-b; BK XII, CH 5 [1071^{a}30-36] 601a; CH 7 602a-603b; CH 10 605d-606d; BK XIII, CH 2 [1077^{a}14-^{b}14] 608b-609a; BK XIV, CH 4 [1091^{a}29]-CH 5 [1092^{a}17] 624a-625a / *Soul*, BK III, CH 4 [429^{a}29-^{b}4] 661c-d

9 Aristotle: *Parts of Animals*, BK I, CH 5 [644^{b}20-645^{a}5] 168c-d / *Generation of Animals*, BK II, CH I [731^{b}24-33] 272a-b / *Ethics*, BK I, CH 6 [1096^{a}17-23] 341b-c

13 Virgil: *Aeneid*, BK VI [724-751] 230b-231a

17 Plotinus: *First Ennead*, TR VII, CH 1-2 26a-d; TR VIII, CH 3-10 28a-33a; CH 12 33d-34a / *Second Ennead*, TR III, CH 11-12 46b-c; CH 16-18 48b-50a; TR IX, CH 3 67b-c / *Third Ennead*, TR III, CH 1-2 82c-83d; TR VIII, CH 8-10 132d-136a / *Fourth Ennead*, TR VIII, CH 6 203d-204b / *Fifth Ennead*, TR II, CH 1 214c-215a; TR III, CH 11-12 222b-223c; TR IV 226c-228b / *Sixth Ennead*, TR VI, CH 18 320c-321b; TR VII, CH 28-29 335b-336b

18 Augustine: *City of God*, BK VIII, CH 11, 272c; BK XI, CH 16 331a-c; CH 22, 334b-c; BK XII, CH 2-5 343c-345b; BK XIV, CH 13, 387d / *Christian Doctrine*, BK I, CH 8 626c-627a; CH 32 633c-d

19 Aquinas: *Summa Theologica*, PART I, Q 2, A 1, REP 2 10d-11d; A 3, ANS 12c-14a; Q 3, A 1, ANS

14b-15b; A 2, ANS 15c-16a; A 7, REP 2 19a-c; QQ 4–6 20c-30d passim; Q 11, A 4 49d-50b; Q 16, A 6, REP 1 98b-d; Q 18, A 3 106b-107c; Q 19, A 8 116a-d; Q 22, A 4, ANS 131c-132b; Q 23, A 5, REP 3 135d-137d; Q 25, A 6, ANS and REP 1,3 149a-150a; Q 36, A 2, ANS 192a-194c; Q 42, A 1, REP 1–2 224b-225d; Q 44, A 1, ANS 238b-239a; Q 47, A 2 257b-258c; Q 48, A 2, ANS and REP 3 260c-261b; Q 50, A 1, ANS and REP 1 269b-270a; A 2, REP 1 270a-272a; A 3, ANS 272a-273b; Q 57, A 1, ANS 295a-d; Q 65, A 2, ANS and REP 3 340b-341b; Q 70, A 3, REP 2 365b-367a; Q 75, A 7 384d-385c; Q 76, A 3, ANS 391a-393a; A 4, REP 3 393a-394c; Q 77, A 2 401b-d; A 4, REP 1 403a-d; Q 79, A 9, REP 3 422b-423d; Q 82, A 3, ANS 433c-434c; Q 93, A 3 493d-494c; Q 106, A 4, ANS 548b-549a; Q 108, A 4 555b-d; Q 118, A 2, REP 2 601c-603b; PART I–II, Q 1, A 4, REP 1 612a-613a; Q 2, A 5, REP 2 618d-619c; A 8, REP 1 621c-622b; Q 3, A 7, ANS 628a-d; Q 18, AA 1–4 694a-696d passim

20 AQUINAS: *Summa Theologica*, PART I–II, Q 52, A 1, ANS 15d-18a; Q 71, A 3, REP 1 107c-108b; Q 85, A 4 181b-d; PART II–II, Q 23, A 3, REP 3 485a-d; PART III, Q 7, A 9, ANS 751d-752c; PART III SUPPL, Q 74, A 1, REP 3 925c-926c

21 DANTE: *Divine Comedy*, PARADISE, I [103–142] 107b-d; II [112–148] 109a-b; VII [64–75] 115d-116a; [121–148] 116b-c; XIII [52–87] 126a-b; XXVIII [64–72] 149b-c; XXIX [13–36] 150b-c

31 DESCARTES: *Discourse*, PART IV, 52d / *Meditations*, III, 84a-b / *Objections and Replies*, 111d-112a; 121d-122c; AXIOM VI 132a; 139b-c; 211b-d

31 SPINOZA: *Ethics*, PART I, APPENDIX, 372c-d; PART IV, PREF 422b,d-424a; PART V, PROP 40, DEMONST 462c

32 MILTON: *Paradise Lost*, BK V [468–490] 185b-186a

35 LOCKE: *Human Understanding*, BK II, CH XXI, SECT 2 178c; CH XXIII, SECT 28 211b-d; SECT 36 213c-d; BK III, CH VI, SECT 11–12 271b-272b; BK IV, CH XVI, SECT 12 370b-371a

42 KANT: *Pure Reason*, 206d-207c / *Judgement*, 556b-558b; 566d-567a

46 HEGEL: *Philosophy of History*, PART I, 224a-d; 233b-235a; 237d-238d

51 TOLSTOY: *War and Peace*, BK V, 217c

53 JAMES: *Psychology*, 639a-645b esp 641b-644a

3b. Being as the object of love and desire

7 PLATO: *Phaedrus*, 124c-126a / *Symposium*, 165b-167d / *Republic*, BK V–VI, 369c-375b; BK VI, 376d; BK IX, 422c-425b esp 423b-424d

8 ARISTOTLE: *Physics*, BK I, CH 9 [192^{a}16–24] 268b-c / *Metaphysics*, BK I, CH 3 [984^{b}8]–CH 4 [985^{a}28] 502d-503c; CH 7 [988^{b}5–16] 506c-d; BK XII, CH 7 602a-603b; CH 10 605d-606d

9 ARISTOTLE: *Ethics*, BK IX, CH 7 [1167^{b}34–1168^{a}18] 421b-c; CH 9 [1170^{a}14–^{b}19] 423d-424b

17 PLOTINUS: *First Ennead*, TR VI, CH 7 24c-25a / *Fifth Ennead*, TR VIII, CH 9, 244b-c; TR IX, CH 1 246c-d

18 AUGUSTINE: *Christian Doctrine*, BK I, CH 5 625d-626a

19 AQUINAS: *Summa Theologica*, PART I, Q 5 23b-28b; Q 16, A 4, ANS and REP 1–2 97a-c; Q 19, A 1, ANS 108d-109c; Q 20, A 2, ANS and REP 4 121b-122a; Q 48, A 1, ANS and REP 4 259b-260c; PART I–II, Q 1, A 8 615a-c; Q 2, A 5, ANS and REP 3 618d-619c; Q 8, A 1, ANS and REP 3 655b-656a; Q 22, A 2, ANS 721c-722c; Q 27, A 3 738c-739c; Q 29, A 1, REP 1 745a-c; A 5 747c-748b

21 DANTE: *Divine Comedy*, PARADISE, I [103–142] 107b-d

30 BACON: *Advancement of Learning*, 73a-c

31 SPINOZA: *Ethics*, PART III, PROP 4–9 398d-399c; PROP 12–13 400b-d; PART IV, PROP 19–22 429d-430c

46 HEGEL: *Philosophy of History*, PART I, 224a-225b; 233d-234b

4. Being and truth

7 PLATO: *Euthydemus*, 71c-74a / *Cratylus*, 86a; 113b-114a,c / *Phaedrus*, 124c-126c / *Republic*, BK VI, 386b-388a; BK IX, 423b-424a / *Timaeus*, 447a-d / *Parmenides*, 508d / *Theaetetus*, 534d-536a; 537a-c / *Sophist*, 561d-577b / *Philebus*, 634b-635b / *Seventh Letter*, 809c-810c

8 ARISTOTLE: *Interpretation*, CH 3 [16^{b}19–26] 25d-26a / *Prior Analytics*, BK I, CH 36 [48^{a}40–^{b}9] 66d / *Metaphysics*, BK II, CH 1 511b,d-512b; BK V, CH 7 [1017^{a}31–34] 538a; CH 29 [1024^{b}16–26] 546c-d; BK VI, CH 4 550a,c; BK IX, CH 10 577c-578a,c

17 PLOTINUS: *Third Ennead*, TR VIII, CH 8 132d-133c / *Fifth Ennead*, TR III, CH 5, 218b; TR V, CH 1–2 228b-229d; TR VI, CH 6 237b-d

18 AUGUSTINE: *Confessions*, BK III, par 10 15b-d; BK V, par 5 28b-c; BK VII, par 16–23 48c-50c / *City of God*, BK XI, CH 10, 328c-d / *Christian Doctrine*, BK I, CH 34 634b-c

19 AQUINAS: *Summa Theologica*, PART I, Q 3, A 4, REP 2 16d-17c; Q 14, A 9, REP 1 83b-d; Q 16 94b-100d; Q 17, A 1 100d-101d; A 4, REP 1–2 103c-104b; Q 18, A 4, REP 3 107d-108c; Q 44, A 1, ANS 238b-239a; Q 79, A 9, REP 3 422b-423d; Q 119, A 1, ANS 604c-607b; PART I–II, Q 3, A 7, ANS 628a-d; Q 22, A 2, ANS 721c-722c; Q 29, A 5, ANS 747c-748b

21 DANTE: *Divine Comedy*, PARADISE, IV [124–126] 112a; XXXIII [49–54] 156d

31 DESCARTES: *Discourse*, PART IV 51b-54b / *Objections and Replies*, 124c-125b; AXIOM X 132b; 226d; 229c-d

31 SPINOZA: *Ethics*, PART I, AXIOM 6 355d; PART II, PROP 10, SCHOL 376d-377a; PROP 20–21 382d-383a; PROP 32 385c; PROP 43 388c-389b; PROP 44, COROL 2 and DEMONST 390a

35 LOCKE: *Human Understanding*, BK IV, CH V, SECT 8 330d

(4. *Being and truth.*)

42 KANT: *Pure Reason*, 36a-37b; 91d-93b; 102c-103a

46 HEGEL: *Philosophy of Right*, INTRO, par 23 17d; PART III, par 280 94d-95a / *Philosophy of History*, INTRO, 156d-157b; PART I, 237d-238a

53 JAMES: *Psychology*, 141a-b; 636a; 852a

4a. Being as the pervasive object of mind, and the formal object of the first philosophy, metaphysics, or dialectic

7 PLATO: *Phaedrus*, 125a-b / *Republic*, BK V, 368c-373c; BK VI-VII, 383d-398c / *Parmenides*, 486a-491c esp 489a-c; 507c-509a / *Theaetetus*, 535b-536a / *Sophist*, 561d-574c esp 571a-c / *Philebus*, 633a-635a esp 634b-635a / *Seventh Letter*, 809c-810d

8 ARISTOTLE: *Topics*, BK VI, CH 12 [149^{b}3–23] 203d-204a / *Metaphysics*, BK I, CH 9 [992^{b}18–993^{a}10] 511a-c; BK II, CH I [993^{b}19–31] 512a-b; BK IV 522a-532d; BK VI, CH I-BK VII, CH I 547b,d-551a; BK XI, CH 3–6 589a-592b

17 PLOTINUS: *First Ennead*, TR III 10a-12b / *Fifth Ennead*, TR I, CH 4 209d-210c; TR V, CH I-2 228b-229d; TR IX, CH II 250c-251a

19 AQUINAS: *Summa Theologica*, PART I, Q I, A I, REP I-2 3b-4a; Q 3, A 4, REP I 16d-17c; Q 5, A 2 24b-25a; Q II, A 2, REP 4 47d-48d; Q 14, A 9, REP I 83b-d; Q 16, AA 3–4 96b-97c; Q 79, A 7, ANS 420d-421c; A 9, REP 3 422b-423d; Q 82, A 4, REP I 434c-435c; Q 87, A 3, REP I 467b-468a; PART I-II, Q 3, A 7, ANS 628a-d; Q 9, A I, ANS and REP 3 657d-658d; Q 10, A I, REP 3 662d-663d

20 AQUINAS: *Summa Theologica*, PART I-II, Q 94, A 2, ANS 221d-223a

23 HOBBES: *Leviathan*, PART IV, 269b-270c

30 BACON: *Advancement of Learning*, 40a-48d esp 40a-41b, 43a-c, 43d-45a

31 DESCARTES: *Discourse*, PART IV, 53b-d / *Objections and Replies*, 261a

31 SPINOZA: *Ethics*, PART II, PROP 44, COROL 2 and DEMONST 390a

35 LOCKE: *Human Understanding*, BK II, CH VII, SECT 7 132d

42 KANT: *Pure Reason*, 1a-4a,c; 119a-c; 120b [fn I] / *Judgement*, 551a-552c; 603d-607c esp 606d-607c

46 HEGEL: *Philosophy of Right*, PREF, 6a-7a; PART III, par 360 113d-114a,c / *Philosophy of History*, INTRO, 156d-157b; PART I, 234b-c; 245d-246c

4b. Being as the measure of truth in judgments of the mind: clarity and distinctness as criteria of the reality of an idea

7 PLATO: *Euthydemus*, 71c-74a esp 72b-c / *Cratylus*, 85a-89b / *Parmenides*, 507c-509a esp 508d-509a / *Sophist*, 558c-d; 575a-577b

8 ARISTOTLE: *Categories*, CH 5 [4^{a}10–^{b}12] 8b-9a; CH 10 [12^{b}6–15] 17d-18a; CH 12 [14^{b}10–21] 20b

/ *Interpretation*, CH 3 [16^{b}19–26] 25d-26a / *Prior Analytics*, BK II, CH 2 [53^{b}11–26] 72d-73a / *Posterior Analytics*, BK I, CH 19 [81^{b}17–24] 111c-d / *Physics*, BK I, CH I 259a-b / *Metaphysics*, BK IV, CH 3–8 524b-532d; BK V, CH 7 [1017^{a}31–34] 538a; CH 29 [1024^{b}22–39] 546c-547a; BK VI, CH 4 550a,c; BK IX, CH 10 577c-578a,c; BK XI, CH 4–6 589d-592b

19 AQUINAS: *Summa Theologica*, PART I, Q 3, A 4, REP 2 16d-17c; Q 14, A 8, REP 3 82c-83b; Q 16, AA 1–2 94b-96b; Q 16, A 8–Q 17, A I 99d-101d; Q 21, A 2, ANS 125c-d; PART I-II, Q 2, A 3, ANS 617b-618a

22 CHAUCER: *Troilus and Cressida*, BK IV, STANZA 154 108b

23 HOBBES: *Leviathan*, PART I, 56b

31 DESCARTES: *Discourse*, PART IV 51b-54b / *Meditations*, I-IV, 75a-89b; IV-V, 92d-96a; VI, 98c-d / *Objections and Replies*, 108a-115a,c; 121b-122c; 124c-125b; 126b-127c; DEF III-IV 130b; POSTULATE IV-VII 131a-c; AXIOM VI 132a; AXIOM X 132b; PROP II-III 132c-133a; 237c-238b; 257d

31 SPINOZA: *Ethics*, PART II, DEF 4 373b; PROP 32 385c; PROP 43 388c-389b

35 LOCKE: *Human Understanding*, BK I, CH III, SECT 24–25 120a-d; BK II, CH VIII, SECT 1–6 133b-134a; CH XIII, SECT 11 150d-151b; SECT 25–26 154a-c; CH XXIII, SECT 5 205a-b; SECT 15 208c-d; SECT 32 212c-d; CH XXXII 243c-248b passim, esp SECT 19 247a-b; BK III, CH VI, SECT 46–47 281d-282b; BK IV, CH V, SECT 7–9 330b-331a; CH X, SECT 7 350d-351a; CH X, SECT 19-CH XI, SECT I 354a-c; CH XI, SECT 12 357c-d

42 KANT: *Pure Reason*, 36b-c; 85d-88a; 179c-182b / *Pref. Metaphysical Elements of Ethics*, 367d-368a / *Judgement*, 603d-604b

53 JAMES: *Psychology*, 141a-142a; 636a; 638a-641a; 879b-882a esp 881a-b

5. Being and becoming: the reality of change; the nature of mutable being

7 PLATO: *Cratylus*, 94c-d; 99b-104b; 113c-114a,c / *Phaedrus*, 124c-126c / *Symposium*, 165c-166b; 167a-d / *Phaedo*, 231b-232b; 247b-248c / *Republic*, BK II, 322d-323a; BK V, 368c-373c; BK VI-VII, 383d-398c; BK VIII, 403a-b / *Timaeus* 442a-477a,c esp 447a-d, 455c-458b / *Parmenides* 486a-511d / *Theaetetus*, 517d-534b / *Sophist*, 561d-574c / *Statesman*, 587a-b / *Philebus*, 610d-617d; 631d-635a esp 634b-635a / *Laws*, BK X, 760a-765c

8 ARISTOTLE: *Physics*, BK I 259a-268d esp CH 8 267a-d; BK II, CH I 268b,d-270a; BK III, CH 1–3 278a-280c; CH 6 [206^{a}18–^{b}16] 284c-285a; BK IV, CH 11 [219^{b}23–31] 299c-d; BK VI, CH 6 319c-321a / *Heavens*, BK I, CH 3 360d-362a; CH 9 [277^{b}29–278^{b}9] 369a-d; BK IV, CH 3 [310^{b}22–311^{a}12] 402b-c; CH 4 [311^{b}29–33] 403c / *Generation and Corruption*, BK I, CH 3 413c-416c; BK II, CH 9–11 436d-441a,c / *Meta-*

physics, BK I, CH 3–10 501c-511d passim; BK II, CH 2 512b-513b; BK III, CH I [996ᵃ2–4] 514c; CH 2 [996ᵃ18–ᵇ26] 514d-515b; CH 4 [1000ᵃ5–1001ᵃ2] 518d-519d; BK IV, CH 5 528c-530c; CH 7 [1011ᵇ23–1012ᵃ9] 531c-532a; CH 8 [1012ᵇ 22–33] 532d; BK V, CH 4 534d-535c; BK VII, CH 7–9 555a-558a; BK IX, CH 3 [1047ᵃ10–29] 572b-c; CH 6 [1048ᵇ18–34] 574a-c; CH 8 [1049ᵇ29–1050ᵃ3] 575c-d; CH 10 [1051ᵇ26–30] 578a; BK X, CH 10 586c-d; BK XI, CH 6 590d-592b; CH 9 593d-594d; CH 11–12 596a-598a,c; BK XII 598a-606d esp CH 2–3 598c-599d, CH 6–8 601b-605a

9 ARISTOTLE: *Generation of Animals*, BK V, CH I [778ᵃ29–ᵇ7] 320a-d

10 GALEN: *Natural Faculties*, BK I, CH 2 167b-168c; CH 5 169b-c; BK II, CH 3, 186d

11 NICOMACHUS: *Arithmetic*, BK I, 811b-d

12 LUCRETIUS: *Nature of Things*, BK I [146–328] 2d-5a; BK II [294–307] 18d-19a; [749–754] 24c; [1002–1022] 27d-28a

12 AURELIUS: *Meditations*, BK II, SECT 17, 259c-d; BK IV, SECT 36 266d; SECT 42–43 267b; SECT 46 267c; BK V, SECT 23 272b; BK VI, SECT 15 275a-b; BK VII, SECT 18 281a; SECT 49–50 282d-283a; BK VIII, SECT 6 285d-286a; BK IX, SECT 19 293b; SECT 35–36 294d-295a; BK X, SECT 7 297b-c

16 KEPLER: *Harmonies of the World*, 1051b

17 PLOTINUS: *Second Ennead*, TR I, CH 3–4 36b-37b; TR IV, CH 6 51d-52a; TR V 57d-60c passim / *Third Ennead*, TR II, CH 1–2 82c-83d; TR VI, CH 7–19 110d-119a / *Fifth Ennead*, TR VIII, CH 12–13 245c-246c / *Sixth Ennead*, TR I, CH 17–22 261c-264c; CH 25–30 265b-268c; TR III 281a-297b esp CH 1–8 281a-285d, CH 21–27 293a-297a; TR V, CH 2 306a-b

18 AUGUSTINE: *Confessions*, BK III, par 10 15b-d; BK IV, par 15–19 23a-24b; BK VII, par 1–7 43b-45d; par 16–23 48c-50c; BK XI, par 6 90c-d; BK XII, par 3–6 99d-100c esp par 6, 100c; par 8, 101b; par 15 102b-c; par 24–26 104c-105b; par 28 105c-d; BK XIII, par 48 124a / *Christian Doctrine*, BK I, CH 9 627a; BK II, CH 38 654b-c

19 AQUINAS: *Summa Theologica*, PART I, Q 2, A 3, ANS 12c-14a; Q 4, A I, REP I 20d-21b; Q 9, A I, ANS 38c-39c; Q 10, A 4, REP 3 43b-44b; A 5, ANS 44b-45c; Q 26, A I, REP 2 150b-c; Q 29, A I, REP 4 162a-163b; Q 65, A 4 342b-343c; Q 86, A 3 463b-d; PART I–II, Q 10, A I, REP 2 662d-663d

20 AQUINAS: *Summa Theologica*, PART I–II, Q 110, A 2, REP 3 349a-d; PART III, Q 62, A 4, REP 2 861a-862a; PART III SUPPL, Q 91, A 3, REP 2 1020d-1022c

22 CHAUCER: *Knight's Tale* [2987–3040] 209a-210a

25 MONTAIGNE: *Essays*, 292a-294b

31 DESCARTES: *Discourse*, PART IV, 52d / *Objections and Replies*, 212a

31 SPINOZA: *Ethics*, PART I, DEF 2 355a; PART II, PROP 31 385b-c

35 LOCKE: *Human Understanding*, BK III, CH IV, SECT 8 260d-261a

35 BERKELEY: *Human Knowledge*, SECT 89 430b-c; SECT 102 432d-433a; SECT 141 441a-b

42 KANT: *Pure Reason*, 15a-b; 27a-33d esp 27a, 28b-c, 31d-32a; 43a-b; 74b-76c; 82a-83b; 91d-93c; 95a-d; 138b-139b [thesis]; 141b,d-145c; 200c-204c

46 HEGEL: *Philosophy of History*, INTRO, 178a-179d; 186d-190b

51 TOLSTOY: *War and Peace*, BK XIV, 608a-b

53 JAMES: *Psychology*, 882a-884b passim

6. The cause of existence

OLD TESTAMENT: *Genesis*, 1–2; 7:1–5 / *Nehemiah*, 9:6—(D) II *Esdras*, 9:6 / *Job*, 26:7; 38:1–42:2 / *Psalms*, 8 esp 8:3–6; 19:1; 89:11–12; 102:25; 136:5–9—(D) *Psalms*, 8 esp 8:4–6; 18:2; 88:12–13; 101:26; 135:5–9 / *Jeremiah*, 31:35—(D) *Jeremias*, 31:35 / *Amos*, 5:8

APOCRYPHA: *Ecclesiasticus*, 18:1—(D) OT, *Ecclesiasticus*, 18:1

NEW TESTAMENT: *Acts*, 14:15; 17:22–32—(D) *Acts*, 14:14; 17:22–32 / *Romans*, 11:36 / *Colossians*, 1:16–17 / *Hebrews*, 1:10 / *Revelation*, 4:11—(D) *Apocalypse*, 4:11

7 PLATO: *Timaeus*, 447b-448a / *Laws*, BK X, 760a-765d esp 763d-764a

8 ARISTOTLE: *Posterior Analytics*, BK II, CH 1–2 122b,d-123c; CH 7 [92ᵇ18–25] 126d; CH 8–12 127a-131b / *Metaphysics*, BK I, CH 7 [988ᵇ5–16] 506c-d; CH 9 [991ᵇ1–9] 509c-d; CH 10 511c-d; BK II, CH I [993ᵇ27–31] 512a-b; BK V, CH 8 [1017ᵇ10–17] 538b; BK VII, CH 17 565a-566a,c; BK XII, CH 6–7 601b-603b / *Soul*, BK II, CH 4 [415ᵇ11–14] 645d

9 ARISTOTLE: *Parts of Animals*, BK I, CH I [640ᵃ4–9] 162b

12 EPICTETUS: *Discourses*, BK I, CH 14, 120d-121a

18 AUGUSTINE: *Confessions*, BK I, par 10 3b-c / *Christian Doctrine*, BK I, CH 32 633c-d

19 AQUINAS: *Summa Theologica*, PART I, Q 2, A 3, ANS 12c-14a; Q 3, A 4, ANS 16d-17c; A 5, REP 2 17c-18b; Q 5, A 2, REP 1-2 24b-25a; Q 8, A I 34d-35c; A 2, ANS 35c-36b; A 3, ANS and REP 1 36b-37c; A 4, ANS 37c-38c; Q 9, A 2, ANS 39c-40d; Q 14, A 8 82c-83b; QQ 44–46 238a-255d; Q 57, A 2, ANS and REP 2 295d-297a; Q 61, A I 314d-315b; Q 65 339a-343c; Q 75, A 6, REP 2 383c-384c; Q 104 534c-538c; Q 105, A 3, ANS 540c-541b; A 5, ANS 542a-543b; PART I–II, Q 18, A 4, ANS 696b-d

28 HARVEY: *On Animal Generation*, 443b-c

31 DESCARTES: *Discourse*, PART V, 55d-56a / *Meditations*, III, 87c-d / *Objections and Replies*, AXIOM IX 132b; 213b-d

31 SPINOZA: *Ethics*, PART I, DEF I 355a; PROP 17, SCHOL 362c-363c; PROP 24–29 365a-366c; PROP 33 367b-369a; PART II, PROP 6–7 374d-375c; PROP 10, SCHOL 376d-377a; PROP 45, SCHOL 390b

(6. The cause of existence.)

32 MILTON: *Paradise Lost*, BK III [80–134] 137a-138a; BK VII 217a-231a esp [162–169] 220b, [601–640] 230a-231a

35 LOCKE: *Human Understanding*, BK II, CH XV, SECT 12 165b-c; CH XXVI, SECT 1–2, 217a-c

35 BERKELEY: *Human Knowledge*, SECT 2–4 413b-414a; SECT 25–33 417d-419a; SECT 36 419c-d; SECT 45–46 421b-c; SECT 48 422a; SECT 88–91 430a-431a; SECT 146–150 442a-443b

35 HUME: *Human Understanding*, SECT VIII, DIV 74, 484a

42 KANT: *Pure Reason*, 140b,d-145c; 177b-179b / *Practical Reason*, 334b-337a,c

46 HEGEL: *Philosophy of History*, PART I, 245d-246c

7. The divisions or modes of being

7a. The distinction between essence and existence: existence as the act of being

OLD TESTAMENT: *Exodus*, 3:14

8 ARISTOTLE: *Metaphysics*, BK IX, CH 3 [1047 ^{a}30–^{b}2] 572c

17 PLOTINUS: *Third Ennead*, TR VII, CH 6 122a-d / *Fifth Ennead*, TR V, CH 13, 234d-235a

18 AUGUSTINE: *City of God*, BK XI, CH 10, 328c-d

19 AQUINAS: *Summa Theologica*, PART I, Q 3, A 4 16d-17c; A 5, ANS and REP 1 17c-18b; A 6, ANS 18c-19a; A 7, ANS and REP 1 19a-c; Q 4, A 1, REP 3 20d-21b; A 2, ANS and REP 3 21b-22b; A 3, REP 3 22b-23b; Q 6, A 3 29c-30b; Q 7, A 1, ANS and REP 3 31a-d; A 2, ANS and REP 1 31d-32c; Q 8, A 1, ANS 34d-35c; Q 9, A 2, ANS 39c-40d; Q 10, A 2, ANS 41d-42c; Q 11, A 4, ANS 49d-50b; Q 12, A 2, ANS and REP 3 51c-52c; A 4, ANS and REP 3 53b-54c; Q 13, A 11, ANS 73c-74b; Q 25, A 1, REP 2 143d-144c; Q 29, A 1, REP 4 162a-163b; Q 34, A 1, REP 2 185b-187b; Q 39, A 2, REP 3 203b-204c; Q 44, A 1 238b-239a; Q 50, A 2, REP 3 270a-272a; Q 54, A 1, ANS and REP 2 285a-d; A 2, REP 2 285d-286c; A 3, ANS and REP 2 286c-287b; Q 75, A 5, REP 4 382a-383b; Q 88, A 2, REP 4 471c-472c; PART I–II, Q 3, A 7, ANS 628a-d

31 DESCARTES: *Discourse*, PART IV, 52d-53a / *Meditations*, V 93a-96a / *Objections and Replies*, 110a-112a; 112d-113b; 126b-127c; POSTULATE V 131b-c; AXIOM I 131d; AXIOM X–PROP I 132b-c; 158b-162a passim; 217d-218a

31 SPINOZA: *Ethics*, PART I, DEF 8 355c; AXIOM 7 355d; PROP 7 356c; PROP 8, SCHOL 2 356d-357d; PROP 11 358b-359b; PROP 17, SCHOL, 363b-c; PROP 20 363d-364a; PROP 24–25 365a-b; PROP 34 369a; PART II, DEF 2 373b; AXIOM I 373c; PART III, PROP 7 399a; PART IV, DEF 3 424a

35 LOCKE: *Human Understanding*, BK III, CH V, SECT 1–6 263d-265a; BK IV, CH IX, SECT 1 349a

42 KANT: *Pure Reason*, 179c-182b; 191d-192b

46 HEGEL: *Philosophy of Right*, PART III, par 280 94d-95a / *Philosophy of History*, INTRO, 165a-b; 178c-d; PART I, 233d-234b

53 JAMES: *Psychology*, 640b [fn 1]; 644b

7b. The distinction between substance and attribute, accident or modification: independent and dependent being

8 ARISTOTLE: *Categories*, CH 2 [1^{a}20–^{b}9] 5b-c; CH 5 6a-9a; CH 7 [8^{a}12–^{b}24] 13a-d / *Topics*, BK V, CH 4 [133^{b}15–134^{a}4] 184d-185b / *Sophistical Refutations*, CH 7 [169^{a}33–36] 233a; CH 22 [178^{b}37–179^{a}10] 246c / *Physics*, BK I, CH 2 [185^{a}20]–CH 3 [187^{a}10] 260a-262a / *Metaphysics*, BK I, CH 9 [990^{b}22–991^{a}2] 509a; [992^{b}18–24] 511a; BK IV, CH 4 [1007^{a}20–^{b}18] 526c-527a; BK V, CH 7 [1017^{a}23–31] 537d-538a; CH 11 [1019^{a}1–14] 540a; BK VII, CH 3 [1029^{a}7–26] 551c-d; CH 4–6 552b-555a; BK VIII, CH 3 [1043^{b}18–24] 568a-b; CH 4 [1044^{b}8–20] 569b; BK IX, CH 1 [1045^{b}28–32] 570b; CH 7 [1049^{a}19–^{b}1] 574a-575a; BK X, CH 2 580b-d; BK XII, CH 1 [1069^{a}18–25] 598a; CH 4–5 599d-601a; CH 7 [1072^{b}4–13] 602c-d

9 ARISTOTLE: *Parts of Animals*, BK II, CH 2 [648^{b}35]–CH 3 [649^{b}22] 173b-174b

12 AURELIUS: *Meditations*, BK XII, SECT 30, 310a

17 PLOTINUS: *Fourth Ennead*, TR VIII, CH 6 203d-204b / *Sixth Ennead*, TR I, CH 3 253a-b; CH 5, 254c-d; CH 15 260c-d; CH 25 265b-d; TR II, CH 14–15 276c-277b; TR III, CH 3 282a-c; CH 6 284a-c; CH 8, 285b-c

19 AQUINAS: *Summa Theologica*, PART I, Q 3, A 6 18c-19a; Q 6, A 3, ANS 29c-30b; Q 7, A 2, ANS 31d-32c; Q 9, A 2 39c-40d; Q 11, A 1, REP 1–2 46d-47d; A 2, REP 1 47d-48d; A 4, REP 2 49d-50b; Q 29, A 1, ANS and REP 3 162a-163b; Q 39, A 3, ANS 204c-205c; Q 40, A 1, REP 1 213b-214b; A 4, REP 4 214b-215b; Q 44, A 2, ANS and REP 1 239b-240a; Q 45, A 4 244d-245c; Q 54, A 1 285a-d; A 3 286c-287b; Q 67, A 3 351b-352a; Q 76, A 4 393a-394c; A 6 396a-d; Q 77, A 1 399c-401b; A 6 404c-405c; Q 85, A 5, REP 3 457d-458d; Q 90, A 2, ANS 481d-482c; Q 115, A 1, ANS and REP 5 585d-587c; PART I–II, Q 7, A 1, ANS and REP 2–3 651d-652c; A 4, REP 3 654b-655a; Q 17, A 4, ANS 688d-689c; Q 18, A 3, REP 3 695d-696b; Q 29, A 2, REP 1 745c-746b

20 AQUINAS: *Summa Theologica*, PART I–II, Q 49, A 2, ANS and REP 3 2b-4a; Q 50, A 2 7c-8a; Q 52, A 1, ANS 15d-18a; Q 53, A 2, REP 3 21a-d; Q 66, A 4, ANS 78c-79b; PART II–II, Q 23, A 3, REP 3 485a-d; PART III, Q 2, A 1, ANS 710a-711c; PART III SUPPL, Q 70, A 1, ANS 893d-895d; Q 79, A 1, REP 4 951b-953b; Q 83, A 3, ANS 978c-980d

30 BACON: *Novum Organum*, BK I, APH 66, 114d-115a

31 DESCARTES: *Discourse*, PART I, 41d; PART IV, 52d / *Meditations*, III 81d-89a passim, esp

87b-88c / *Objections and Replies*, DEF V 130b-c; DEF IX 130d; 135b-136b; 136c; 139b-c; 153d; 162d-165d; 170d; 211b-c; 228c-229c

31 SPINOZA: *Ethics*, PART I, DEF 3–5 355b; AXIOM 1–2 355c-d; PROP 1–9 355d-357d; PROP 10, SCHOL 358a-b; PROP 19 363c-d; PROP 20, COROL 2 364a; PROP 21–23 364a-365a

35 LOCKE: *Human Understanding*, BK I, CH III, SECT 19 117c-d; BK II, CH XII, SECT 3–6 147d-148c; CH XIII, SECT 17–20 152a-d; CH XXIII 204a-214b esp SECT 1–15 204a-208d; CH XXXII, SECT 24 247c-d; BK III, CH IX, SECT 12–13 287d-288d

35 BERKELEY: *Human Knowledge*, SECT 1–7 413a-414c; SECT 25–33 417d-419a passim; SECT 49 422b; SECT 73–78 427b-428b; SECT 88–91 430a-431a; SECT 101–102 432c-433a

42 KANT: *Pure Reason*, 33a-d; 74b-76c; 130b-133c esp 131c-d; 140b,d-143a / *Practical Reason*, 310d-311d / *Judgement*, 529c-530a; 550a-551a,c; 566b-d; 580c-d

46 HEGEL: *Philosophy of Right*, ADDITIONS, 26 121a-b; 39 122d / *Philosophy of History*, INTRO, 160c-161a; PART I, 211a-c

53 JAMES: *Psychology*, 572a-b

7b(1) The conceptions of substance

8 ARISTOTLE: *Categories*, CH 5 6a-9a; CH 7 [8^a12–$^b24$] 13a-d / *Metaphysics*, BK V, CH 8 538b-c; BK VII–VIII 550b,d-570d; BK X, CH 2 580b-d; BK XII, CH 1 598a-c; BK XIII, CH 2 [1077^a14–$^b11$] 608b-609a

12 AURELIUS: *Meditations*, BK VII, SECT 23 281b

17 PLOTINUS: *Sixth Ennead*, TR I, CH 2–3 252c-253b; CH 10 257b-258b; CH 25 265b-d; TR III, CH 2–10 281c-286d

19 AQUINAS: *Summa Theologica*, PART I, Q 3, A 5, REP 1–2 17c-18b; A 6 18c-19a; Q 11, A 3, ANS 49a-c; Q 13, A 9, ANS 71b-72c; QQ 29–43 161d-237a,c passim, esp Q 29, A 2 163b-164b; Q 45, A 4 244d-245c; QQ 75–76 378a-399b passim; Q 88, A 2, REP 4 471c-472c; PART I–II, Q 17, A 4, ANS 688d-689c

20 AQUINAS: *Summa Theologica*, PART II–II, Q 4, A 1, ANS and REP 1 402a-403d; PART III, QQ 1–3 701b,d-730b; Q 17 806d-809d passim; PART III SUPPL, Q 83 974d-983b passim

23 HOBBES: *Leviathan*, PART III, 172b

30 BACON: *Novum Organum*, BK II, APH 37 168d-169c

31 DESCARTES: *Objections and Replies*, DEF V–VIII 130b-d; 153c-155c

31 SPINOZA: *Ethics*, PART I, DEF 3,6 355b; PROP 1–9 355d-357d; PROP 11–14 358b-360a; PROP 15, SCHOL 360b-361d; PROP 19 363c-d; PART II, PROP 10 376c-377a

35 LOCKE: *Human Understanding*, BK I, CH III, SECT 19 117c-d; BK II, CH XII, SECT 6 148b-c; CH XIII, SECT 17–20 152a-d; CH XXIII 204a-214b; CH XXXI, SECT 6–13 240d-243b; CH XXXII, SECT 24 247c-d; BK III, CH VI, SECT 21 273c-d; SECT 42 280b-c; CH IX, SECT 11–17

287d-290a; BK IV, CH VI, SECT 4–16 331d-336d passim, esp SECT 11 334b-335b

35 BERKELEY: *Human Knowledge*, SECT 6–7 414b-c; SECT 26–27 418a-b; SECT 73 427b-c; SECT 88–91 430a-431a; SECT 135–136 440a-b; SECT 139 440d

42 KANT: *Pure Reason*, 15b-c; 63a; 63d-64a; 69c-72c; 74b-76c; 81b-83b; 86c-87b; 91d-93b; 95a-d; 100d-101b; 121a-128b; 131c-d; 137a-140c; 162b-163a; 186b-d / *Judgement*, 565b-d; 566d-567a

46 HEGEL: *Philosophy of Right*, PART III, par 146 55c-d / *Philosophy of History*, INTRO, 156d-157b; PART I, 211a-c; 227d-228a

53 JAMES: *Psychology*, 221b; 223a

7b(2) Corporeal and spiritual substances, composite and simple substances: the kinds of substance in relation to matter and form

8 ARISTOTLE: *Physics*, BK I, CH 7 265b-267a; BK II, CH 1 268b,d-270a; BK IV, CH 2 288b-289a / *Heavens*, BK I, CH 9 [277^b26–278^b9] 369a-d; BK IV, CH 4 [312^a12–17] 403d / *Generation and Corruption*, BK I, CH 3 413c-416c / *Meteorology*, BK IV, CH 12 493d-494d / *Metaphysics*, BK III, CH 1 [995^b13–18] 514a; [995^b31–39] 514b; [996^a13–15] 514c; CH 2 [997^a34–998^a19] 516a-d; CH 4 [999^a24–$^b23$] 518a-c; CH 5 520c-521b; CH 6 [1002^b11–32] 521b-d; BK V, CH 8 538b-c; BK VII–VIII 550b,d-570d; BK XI, CH 1 [1059^a33–$^b14$] 587b-c; CH 2 [1060^a3–27] 588a-b; [1060^b23–29] 588d-589a; BK XII–XIV 598a-626d / *Soul*, BK II, CH 1–2 642a-644c

12 EPICTETUS: *Discourses*, BK IV, CH 11, 240d-241a

12 AURELIUS: *Meditations*, BK IV, SECT 21 265b-c; BK VII, SECT 23 281b; BK VIII, SECT 11 286b; BK XII, SECT 30 310a-b

17 PLOTINUS: *Second Ennead*, TR IV, CH 2–4 50b-51a; CH 6 51d-52a; TR V, CH 2 58b-d / *Third Ennead*, TR VI, CH 7–19 110d-119a / *Fourth Ennead*, TR VIII, CH 6 203d-204b / *Fifth Ennead*, TR I, CH 2 208c-209b; TR IX, CH 3 247b-d / *Sixth Ennead*, TR I, CH 27–28 266c-267c; TR III, CH 2–10 281c-286d; TR V, CH 5–8 307a-308c

18 AUGUSTINE: *Confessions*, BK VII, par 1–2 43b-44a; par 7 45a-d; par 16 48c-49a; par 20 49d; par 26 51c-d; BK XII, par 5–6 100a-c; par 8 101a-b; par 16 102d-103a; par 18–22 103a-104b; par 24–26 104c-105b; par 28–30 105c-106c; par 38–40 108d-110a; BK XIII, par 48 124a / *City of God*, BK XI, CH 10 327d-328d

19 AQUINAS: *Summa Theologica*, PART I, Q 3 14a-20c; Q 6, A 3, REP 1 29c-30b; Q 7, A 1, ANS 31a-d; Q 8, A 1, REP 2 34d-35c; A 2 35c-36b; Q 9, A 2, REP 3 39c-40d; Q 11, A 4, REP 3 49d-50b; Q 14, A 2, REP 1,3 76d-77d; Q 18, A 4, REP 3 107d-108c; Q 29, A 1, REP 4 162a-163b; A 2, REP 3,5 163b-164b; Q 40, A 1, REP 1 213b-214b; Q 45, A 4 244d-245c; Q 50 269a-275a;

(7b. *The distinction between substance and attribute, accident or modification: independent and dependent being. 7b(2) Corporeal and spiritual substances, composite and simple substances: the kinds of substance in relation to matter and form.*)

Q 70, A 3, REP 2 365b-367a; QQ 75-76 378a-399b; Q 77, A 1, ANS and REP 2-3,6 399c-401b; Q 85, A 5, REP 3 457d-458d; Q 86, A 3 463b-d; Q 88, A 2, REP 4 471c-472c; Q 104, A 1, ANS and REP 1 534c-536c; Q 115, A 1 585d-587c; A 3, REP 2 588c-589c

20 AQUINAS: *Summa Theologica*, PART I-II, Q 52, A 1, ANS 15d-18a; PART II-II, Q 24, A II, ANS 498b-499c; PART III, Q 2, A 1, ANS and REP 2 710a-711c; PART III SUPPL, Q 69, A 1, ANS and REP 2 885c-886c; Q 79, A 2, REP 2 953b-955c; Q 92, A 1, ANS 1025c-1032b

21 DANTE: *Divine Comedy*, PARADISE, VII [121-148] 116b-c; XXIX [13-36] 150b-c

23 HOBBES: *Leviathan*, PART III, 172a-177c; PART IV, 258b-261a; 269d-271b

30 BACON: *Advancement of Learning*, 17b-d / *Novum Organum*, BK II, APH 37 168d-169c

31 DESCARTES: *Discourse*, PART IV, 51d-52a / *Meditations*, VI 96b-103d / *Objections and Replies*, DEF VI-VIII 130c-d; 153c-155c

31 SPINOZA: *Ethics*, PART I, PROP 15 360a-361d; PART II, PROP 1-2 373d-374a; PROP 6 374d-375a; PROP 7, SCHOL 375b-c

35 LOCKE: *Human Understanding*, BK II, CH XIII, SECT 16-18 151d-152c; CH XV, SECT 11 165a-b; CH XXI, SECT 2-4 178c-179c; CH XXIII, SECT 5 205a-b; SECT 15-37 208c-214b; CH XXVII, SECT 2 219b-c; BK III, CH X, SECT 15 295a-c; BK IV, CH III, SECT 6 313c-315b; CH X, SECT 9-19 351b-354c passim; CH XVI, SECT 12, 370c-371a

35 BERKELEY: *Human Knowledge*, SECT 1-29 413a-418c; SECT 35-38 419c-420a; SECT 47-50 421c-422c; SECT 67-81 426b-428d; SECT 86-91 429c-431a passim; SECT 133-142 439c-441c

42 KANT: *Pure Reason*, 100d-101b; 121a-128b; 186b-d; 203d-204c / *Judgement*, 557c-558b; 565b-d; 566d-567a

46 HEGEL: *Philosophy of History*, INTRO, 156d-157b; 160c-161a; 165a-b; PART I, 227d-228a

53 JAMES: *Psychology*, 118b-119b passim; 220b-226a esp 221a-223a

7b(3) Corruptible and incorruptible substances

8 ARISTOTLE: *Interpretation*, CH 13 [23ᵃ18-26] 35b-c / *Heavens*, BK I, CH 1-3 359a-362a; CH 9 [279ᵃ12-ᵇ4] 370b-d; BK I, CH 10-BK II, CH 1 370d-376a; BK III, CH 6 396a-c / *Metaphysics*, BK III, CH 2 [996ᵃ21-28] 514d; BK IV, CH 5 [1009ᵃ36-39] 528d; BK V, CH 5 [1015ᵇ9-16] 536a; BK IX, CH 8 [1050ᵇ5]-CH 9 [1051ᵃ21] 576b-577b; BK X, CH 10 586c-d; BK XI, CH 6 [1063ᵃ10-17] 591b; BK XII, CH 1 [1069ᵃ30-ᵇ2] 598b-c; CH 2 [1069ᵇ24-27] 598d-599a; CH 3 [1070ᵃ20-27] 599c; CH 6-8 601b-605a; CH 10

[1075ᵇ13-14] 606b / *Soul*, BK II, CH 2 [413ᵇ24-29] 643d-644a

9 ARISTOTLE: *Motion of Animals*, CH 4 [699ᵇ12-700ᵃ5] 234d-235a

12 LUCRETIUS: *Nature of Things*, BK I [215-250] 3d-4b; [483-634] 7a-8d

16 PTOLEMY: *Almagest*, BK I, 5a-6a; BK XIII, 429a-b

16 KEPLER: *Epitome*, BK IV, 929b-930b

17 PLOTINUS: *Second Ennead*, TR I, CH 1-4 35a-37b; CH 8 39c-d; TR IV, CH 6 51d-52a / *Fourth Ennead*, TR VII, CH 10-12 198d-200a

19 AQUINAS: *Summa Theologica*, PART I, Q 9, A 2 39c-40d; Q 10, A 2, REP 1-2 41d-42c; A 3, ANS and REP 1 42c-43b; AA 5-6 44b-46d; Q 18, A 3, REP 3 106b-107c; Q 22, A 2, ANS 128d-130d; Q 46, A 1, REP 2-3 250a-252d; Q 48, A 2, ANS and REP 3 260c-261b; Q 50, A 5 274b-275a; Q 63, A 1, REP 2 325c-326c; Q 66, A 2 345d-347b; Q 68, A 1, ANS 354a-355c; Q 75, A 6 383c-384c; Q 76, A 3, REP 1-2 391a-393a; Q 97, A 1 513c-514c; A 4 515d-516d; Q 104, A 1, REP 1,3 534c-536c; Q 113, A 2, ANS 576d-577d; PART I-II, Q 22, A 1, REP 3 720d-721c

20 AQUINAS: *Summa Theologica*, PART I-II, Q 49, A 4, ANS 5a-6a; Q 85, A 6 182d-184a; PART II-II, Q 24, A II, ANS 498b-499c; PART III SUPPL, Q 91, A 1 1016b-1017c; AA 4-5 1022d-1025b

21 DANTE: *Divine Comedy*, PARADISE, VII [64-84] 115d-116a; [121-148] 116b-c; XIII [52-87] 126a-b

31 DESCARTES: *Objections and Replies*, 127c-d

31 SPINOZA: *Ethics*, PART I, PROP 6-8 356b-357d; PROP 12-13 359b-d; PROP 15, SCHOL, 361d

32 MILTON: *Paradise Lost*, BK I [116-156] 96a-97a; BK II [94-105] 113a-b; BK VI [320-347] 203a-b; [430-436] 205b

33 PASCAL: *Vacuum*, 358a

34 NEWTON: *Optics*, BK III, 541b

35 LOCKE: *Human Understanding*, BK III, CH III, SECT 19, 259c

35 BERKELEY: *Human Knowledge*, SECT 141 441a-b

42 KANT: *Pure Reason*, 121a-128b; 203d-204c / *Practical Reason*, 348d-349a

53 JAMES: *Psychology*, 221b-222b; 224a-b

7b(4) Extension and thought as dependent substances or as attributes of infinite substance

31 DESCARTES: *Discourse*, PART IV, 51d-52a / *Meditations*, VI 96b-103d / *Objections and Replies*, DEF VI-VIII 130c-d; PROP IV 133c; 135d-136b; 152d-155d esp 153c-155c; 224d-225d; 231a-232d; 248b

31 SPINOZA: *Ethics*, PART I, PROP 14, COROL 2 360a; PART II, DEF 1-2 373a-b; PROP 1-2 373d-374a; PROP 5-6 374c-375a; PROP 7, SCHOL 375b-c

35 LOCKE: *Human Understanding*, BK II, CH XIII, SECT 18 152a-c

42 KANT: *Judgement*, 580c-d

7b(5) Substance as subject to change and to different kinds of change: the role of accidents or modifications

8 ARISTOTLE: *Categories*, CH 5 [4ª10–ᵇ19] 8b-9a / *Physics*, BK I, CH 6–BK II, CH I 264c-270a; BK III, CH 1–3 278a-280c; BK V–VIII 304a-355d / *Generation and Corruption*, BK I, CH 1–5 409a-420b; BK II, CH 9–10 436d-439c / *Metaphysics*, BK I, CH 3 [983ᵇ7–984ᵇ8] 501d-502c; BK III, CH 4 [999ª24–ᵇ24] 518a-c; BK VII, CH 7–9 555a-558a; BK VIII, CH I [1042ª24–ᵇ7] 566b-d; CH 3 [1043ᵇ15–23] 568a-b; CH 4–5 568d-569d; BK IX, CH I 570b,d-571b; CH 3 572a-c; CH 6–7 573c-575a; BK XI, CH 9 593d-594d; CH II 596a-d; CH 12 [1068ª7–ᵇ26] 596d-597d; BK XII, CH 1–5 598a-601a / *Soul*, BK II, CH 4 [416ᵇ8–17] 646d-647a

10 GALEN: *Natural Faculties*, BK I, CH 2 167b-168c; CH 5 169b-c; BK II, CH 4, 187a-b; BK III, CH 7 203b-205a; CH 15, 214d-215d

17 PLOTINUS: *Second Ennead*, TR I, CH 3–4 36b-37b; TR IV, CH 6 51d-52a; TR VI, CH 1–2 60c-62b / *Third Ennead*, TR VI, CH 7–19 110d-119a

19 AQUINAS: *Summa Theologica*, PART I, Q 3, A 6, ANS 18c-19a; Q 9, A 2 39c-40d; Q 41, A 3 219d-221c; A 5 222b-223b; Q 44, A 2 239b-240a; Q 45, AA 1–5 242a-247a passim; A 8 249b-250a; Q 50, A 5 274b-275a; Q 53 280d-284d; Q 65, A 4 342b-343c; Q 66, AA 1–2 343d-347b; Q 67, A 3, ANS and REP I 351b-352a; Q 73, A 3 371d-372c; Q 75, A 6 383c-384c; Q 76, A 4 393a-394c; Q 78, A 2, ANS and REP 4 409a-410a; Q 90, A 2, ANS and REP 2 481d-482c; Q 92, A 3, REP I 490c-491b; Q 98, A I 516d-517d; Q 104 534c-538c; Q 105, AA 1–2 538d-540c; A 5, ANS 542a-543b; Q 115, AA 1–3 585d-589c; A 6, ANS 591d-592d; Q 118, A I 600a-601c; Q 119 604c-608d; PART I–II, Q 22, A I 720d-721c

20 AQUINAS: *Summa Theologica*, PART I–II, Q 51, A 2, ANS and REP 1–2 13c-14b; Q 52, AA 1–2 15d-19a; Q 53, A I, REP I 19d-21a; A 2, REP 1–3 21a-d; Q 110, A 2, REP 3 349a-d; PART III SUPPL, Q 75, A 3, ANS 938a-939d; Q 80, A 4 959c-963a; Q 82, AA 1–2 968a-971a; Q 83, A I 974d-976b; A 5, ANS 981b-982c; Q 84 983c-989b; Q 86, AA 2–3 993c-996a,c

30 BACON: *Novum Organum*, BK I, APH 66, 115a-b

31 DESCARTES: *Objections and Replies*, 162d-165d

31 SPINOZA: *Ethics*, PART I, PROP 6 356b-c; PROP 12–13 359b-d; PROP 23 364d-365a; PROP 28 365c-366a; PART II, PROP 13 377d-378c

35 LOCKE: *Human Understanding*, BK II, CH XXII, SECT II 203c-d; CH XXVI, SECT 1–2 217a-d; BK III, CH VI, SECT 42 280b-c

42 KANT: *Pure Reason*, 74b-76c; 82a-83b; 86c-87b; 141b,d-143a passim

46 HEGEL: *Philosophy of History*, INTRO, 156d-157b; 178c-d

7b(6) The nature and kinds of accidents or modifications

8 ARISTOTLE: *Categories*, CH 2 [1ª20–ᵇ9] 5b-c; CH 4 5d-6a; CH 5 [2ª27–ᵇ6] 6b-c; [3ª6–21] 7b; CH 6–9 9a-16d / *Prior Analytics*, BK I, CH 13 [32ᵇ4–14] 48b-c / *Posterior Analytics*, BK I, CH 4 [73ª33–ᵇ16] 100b-d / *Topics*, BK I, CH 9 147a-b / *Physics*, BK I, CH 2 [185ª20–186ª4] 260a-d; CH 4 [188ª5–13] 263b; BK II, CH I [192ᵇ35–39] 269a; BK IV, CH 3 [210ᵇ1–8] 289b-c; BK VII, CH 3 329a-330d / *Metaphysics*, BK V, CH 6 [1015ᵇ16–34] 536a-b; CH 7 [1017ª23–30] 537d-538a; CH 9 [1017ᵇ27–1018ª3] 538c; CH 30 547a-d; BK VII, CH I [1028ª10–18] 550b; CH 4–6 552b-555a; BK VIII, CH 4 [1044ᵇ8–20] 569b; BK X, CH 9 586a-c; BK XII, CH I [1069ª18–25] 598a / *Sense and the Sensible*, CH 6 [445ᵇ4–446ª20] 683b-684c

12 LUCRETIUS: *Nature of Things*, BK I [449–482] 6c-7a

17 PLOTINUS: *Second Ennead*, TR VI 60c-62d / *Sixth Ennead*, TR I, CH 4–24 253b-265b; CH 30 268b-c

19 AQUINAS: *Summa Theologica*, PART I, Q 3, A 6 18c-19a; Q 8, A 2, REP 3 35c-36b; Q 9, A 2, ANS 39c-40d; Q 28, A 2 158d-160a; Q 29, A 2, ANS and REP 4–5 163b-164b; Q 44, A 2, ANS 239b-240a; Q 45, A 4, ANS 244d-245c; Q 54, A I 285a-d; A 3 286c-287b; Q 66, A I, REP 3 343d-345c; Q 67, A 3 351b-352a; Q 76, A 6 396a-d; A 8, 397d-399b; Q 77 399b-407a passim; Q 101, A I, REP I 522c-523a; Q 108, A 5, ANS 555d-558b; Q 115, A I, ANS and REP 3,5 585d-587c; A 6, ANS 591d-592d; Q 116, A I, ANS 592d-593d; PART I–II, Q 2, A 6, ANS 619d-620d; Q 7 651d-655a passim; Q 17, A 4, ANS 688d-689c; Q 18, A 3 695d-696b; Q 35, A 4, ANS and REP 2 774d-775d

20 AQUINAS: *Summa Theologica*, PART I–II, QQ 49–54 1a-25d passim, esp Q 49, AA 1–2 1b-4a; Q 56, A I, REP I,3 30a-c; PART II–II, Q 23, A 3, REP 3 485a-d; Q 24, A 5, ANS and REP I 492b-493d; PART III, Q 2, A 6 716b-718b; PART III SUPPL, Q 70, A I, ANS 893d-895d; Q 79, A I, REP 4 951b-953b; Q 83, A 3 978c-980d

23 HOBBES: *Leviathan*, PART I, 57a-b; 59c-d

30 BACON: *Novum Organum*, BK I, APH 66, 114d-115a

31 DESCARTES: *Discourse*, PART I, 41d / *Objections and Replies*, 135b-136b; 136c; 162d-165d; 228c-229c

31 SPINOZA: *Ethics*, PART I, DEF 4–5 355b; PROP 10 358a-b; PROP 19, DEMONST 363c-d; PROP 20, COROL 2 364a; PROP 21–23 364a-365a

35 LOCKE: *Human Understanding*, BK II, CH VIII 133b-138b esp SECT 8–10 134b-d; CH XII, SECT 3–6 147d-148c; CH XIII, SECT 17–20 152a-d; CH XXI, SECT 3 178d; SECT 75 200b-d; CH XXIII, SECT 7–10 205d-206d; SECT 37 213d-214b; CH XXX, SECT 2 238b-c; CH XXXI,

(7b. *The distinction between substance and attribute, accident or modification: independent and dependent being. 7b(6) The nature and kinds of accidents or modifications.*)

SECT 2 239b-d; BK III, CH IV, SECT 16 263b-c; CH IX, SECT 13 288a-d

35 BERKELEY: *Human Knowledge*, SECT 1–15 413a-416a; SECT 25 417d-418a; SECT 49 422b; SECT 73 427b-c; SECT 78 428a-b; SECT 102 432d-433a

35 HUME: *Human Understanding*, SECT XII, DIV 122 505c-d

53 JAMES: *Psychology*, 503a-b; 572a-b; 650b-651a

7c. The distinction between potentiality and actuality: possible and actual being

8 ARISTOTLE: *Interpretation*, CH 9 [19^{a}6–^{b}4] 29b-d; CH 13 [23^{a}18–26] 35b-c / *Topics*, BK V, CH 8 [138^{b}27–139^{a}9] 191c-d / *Physics*, BK III, CH 1–3 278a-280c; BK IV, CH 9 [217^{a}20–^{b}26] 297a-c / *Heavens*, BK III, CH 2 [301^{b}33–302^{a}9] 393b / *Metaphysics*, BK IV, CH 5 [1009^{a}22–39] 528d; BK V, CH 2 [1014^{a}7-9] 534b; [1014^{a}19–25] 534b-c; CH 7 [1017^{a}35–^{b}9] 538a-b; CH 12 540b-541b; BK IX 570b,d-578a,c; BK XII, CH 2 [1069^{b}15–34] 598d-599a; CH 5 600b-601a; BK XIII, CH 3 [1078^{a}21–31] 609d; CH 10 [1087^{a}10–25] 619c / *Soul*, BK II, CH 2 [414^{a}14–28] 644b-c; CH 5 [417^{a}2–418^{a}6] 647c-648d

17 PLOTINUS: *Second Ennead*, TR V 57d-60c / *Third Ennead*, TR VI, CH 8–19 111c-119a; TR IX, CH 3, 137d-138a / *Sixth Ennead*, TR I, CH 15–17 260c-261d; CH 25–30 265b-268c; TR III, CH 22, 293d-294a; CH 27 296b-297a

18 AUGUSTINE: *Christian Doctrine*, BK II, CH 35, 653c

19 AQUINAS: *Summa Theologica*, PART I, Q 2, A 3, ANS 12c-14a; Q 3, A 1, ANS 14b-15b; A 2, ANS 15c-16a; A 4, ANS 16d-17c; A 5, ANS 17c-18b; A 6, ANS 18c-19a; A 7, ANS 19a-c; A 8, ANS 19d-20c; Q 4, A 1 20d-21b; A 2, ANS 21b-22b; Q 5, A 1 23c-24a; A 2, REP 2 24b-25a; A 3, REP 3 25a-d; Q 6, A 3, REP 1 29c-30b; Q 7, A 2, REP 3 31d-32c; Q 9, A 1, ANS and REP 1 38c-39c; A 2, ANS 39c-40d; Q 11, A 1, REP 2 46d-47d; Q 14, A 2 76d-77d; A 3, ANS 77d-78b; A 4, ANS 78b-79a; Q 18, A 1, ANS 104c-105c; A 3, REP 1 106b-107c; A 4, REP 3 107d-108c; Q 25, A 1, REP 1 143d-144c; Q 45, A 5, REP 3 245c-247a; Q 46, A 1, REP 1 250a-252d; Q 54, A 1, ANS 285a-d; A 3, ANS and REP 2 286c-287b; Q 75, A 1, ANS and REP 2 378b-379c; Q 86, A 3 463b-d; Q 115, A 1, ANS and REP 1,4 585d-587c; PART I–II, Q 10, A 1, REP 2 662d-663d; Q 27, A 3 738c-739c

31 DESCARTES: *Meditations*, III, 86d-87a

31 SPINOZA: *Ethics*, PART IV, DEF 4 424a

42 KANT: *Pure Reason*, 90c-91a / *Practical Reason*, 291a-292a / *Judgement*, 570c-571c

46 HEGEL: *Philosophy of History*, INTRO, 156d-157b; 160d-161c; 178a-179d

7c(1) The order of potentiality and actuality

8 ARISTOTLE: *Interpretation*, CH 13 [23^{a}21–26] 35b-c / *Physics*, BK III, CH 1 [201^{a}19–27] 278d / *Heavens*, BK IV, CH 3 [310^{b}22–311^{a}12] 402b-c / *Metaphysics*, BK III, CH 6 [1002^{b}32–1003^{a}5] 521d; BK V, CH 11 [1019^{a}1–14] 540a; BK VII, CH 9 [1034^{b}16–19] 558a; BK IX, CH 8–9 575b-577c; BK XII, CH 5 [1071^{a}30–36] 601a; CH 6–7 601b-603b

17 PLOTINUS: *Second Ennead*, TR V 57d-60c / *Third Ennead*, TR VI, CH 7, 111a-b; CH 11, 113b-c; CH 14–15 115b-116c; TR IX, CH 3, 137d-138a / *Sixth Ennead*, TR I, CH 15–22 260c-264c

19 AQUINAS: *Summa Theologica*, PART I, Q 3, A 1, ANS 14b-15b; A 8, ANS 19d-20c; Q 4, A 1, REP 2 20d-21b; A 2, ANS 21b-22b; Q 9, A 1, ANS 38c-39c; Q 11, A 2, REP 1 47d-48d; Q 25, A 1, REP 2 143d-144c; Q 94, A 3, ANS 504a-505a; PART I–II, Q 2, A 7, ANS 620d-621c; Q 3, A 2, ANS 623a-624b; Q 9, A 1, ANS 657d-658d; Q 22, A 2, REP 1 721c-722c

20 AQUINAS: *Summa Theologica*, PART I–II, Q 50, A 2, REP 3 7c-8a; Q 71, A 3 107c-108b; PART III, Q 10, A 3, ANS 769d-771b

21 DANTE: *Divine Comedy*, PARADISE, I [103–142] 107b-d; XIII [52–87] 126a-b; XXIX [22–36] 150c

7c(2) Types of potency and degrees of actuality

8 ARISTOTLE: *Interpretation*, CH 13 [22^{b}35–23^{a}17] 34d-35b / *Physics*, BK III, CH 6 [206^{a}18–24] 284c; BK IV, CH 1 [208^{b}8–209^{a}1] 287b-c; BK VII, CH 3 [247^{b}1–248^{a}6] 330b-d; BK VIII, CH 4 [255^{a}30–^{b}31] 340a-c / *Heavens*, BK IV, CH 3 [310^{b}22–311^{a}12] 402b-c / *Metaphysics*, BK V, CH 12 540b-541b; BK IX, CH 1–9 570b,d-577c; BK XII, CH 5 600b-601a / *Soul*, BK II, CH 1 [412^{a}6–12] 642a; [412^{a}22–28] 642b; BK III, CH 4–5 661b-662d / *Sense and the Sensible*, CH 4 [441^{b}16–24] 679b

9 ARISTOTLE: *Ethics*, BK II, CH 1 [1103^{a}26–^{b}24] 348d-349b; CH 5 [1106^{a}7–10] 351c

17 PLOTINUS: *Second Ennead*, TR V 57d-60c

18 AUGUSTINE: *Confessions*, BK I, par 10 3b-c / *Christian Doctrine*, BK I, CH 8 626c-627a

19 AQUINAS: *Summa Theologica*, PART I, Q 4, A 2, ANS 21b-22b; Q 5, A 1, REP 1 23c-24a; Q 14, A 2, ANS and REP 2–3 76d-77d; Q 18, A 3, ANS and REP 1 106b-107c; Q 25 143c-150a; Q 48, A 4, ANS 262a-263a; Q 50, A 2 270a-272a; Q 52, AA 1–2 278d-280a; Q 58, A 1 300c-301a; Q 63, A 1, REP 1 325c-326c; Q 66, A 2 345d-347b; Q 75, A 5 382a-383b; A 6, REP 2 383c-384c; Q 77, A 1 399c-401b; A 3 401d-403a; A 6 404c-405c; Q 79, A 2 414a-416a; A 10 423d-424d; Q 87, A 2, ANS 466c-467b; Q 92, A 4, REP 3 491b-d; Q 104, A 4, REP 2 538a-c; Q 105, A 5, ANS 542a-543b; PART I–II, Q 3, A 2, ANS and REP 1 623a-624b; Q 10, A 1, REP 2 662d-663d; Q 22, A 1 720d-721c

20 AQUINAS: *Summa Theologica*, PART I–II, Q 49, A 3 4b-5a; Q 50, A 2 7c-8a; A 6 11a-12a; Q 51,

A 2 13c-14b; Q 55, A 2, ANS 27a-d; Q 71, A 4, REP 3 108b-109a

35 LOCKE: *Human Understanding*, BK II, CH VII, SECT 8 132d-133a; CH XXI, SECT 1-4 178b-179c; SECT 74, 199d-200b; CH XXIII, SECT 7 205d-206a; SECT 28 211b-d

7c(3) Potentiality and actuality in relation to matter and form

8 ARISTOTLE: *Physics*, BK I, CH 9 [192ª25-33] 268c; BK II, CH I [193ª9-b21] 269b-270a; BK III, CH 1-3 278a-280c / *Heavens*, BK IV, CH 3 [310b22-311ª12] 402b-c / *Generation and Corruption*, BK I, CH 3 413c-416c; CH 7 421d-423b; CH 9 425d-426c / *Metaphysics*, BK V, CH 4 534d-535c; BK VII, CH 16 [1040b5-16] 564c; BK VIII, CH 6 569d-570d; BK IX, CH 6-9 573c-577c; BK XI, CH 9 593d-594d; BK XII, CH 5 600b-601a; BK XIII, CH 3 [1078ª21-31] 609d / *Soul*, BK II, CH 1-2 642a-644c

17 PLOTINUS: *First Ennead*, TR VIII, CH 3-8 28a-31c; CH 10 32a-33a; CH 12 33d-34a / *Second Ennead*, TR IV, CH 6 51d-52a; TR V 57d-60c / *Third Ennead*, TR VI, CH 7-19 110d-119a; TR IX, CH 3, 137d-138a / *Fifth Ennead*, TR I, CH 2 208c-209b; TR IX, CH 3 247b-d / *Sixth Ennead*, TR I, CH 25-30 265b-268c; TR V, CH 5-8 307a-308c

18 AUGUSTINE: *Confessions*, BK XII, par 3-6 99d-100c; par 8, 101b; par 9, 101c; par 14-16 102b-103a; par 24-26 104c-105b; par 28-31 105c-107a; par 38-40 108d-110a

19 AQUINAS: *Summa Theologica*, PART I, Q 3, A 2, ANS and REP 3 15c-16a; A 4, ANS 16d-17c; Q 4, A 1 20d-21b; A 2, ANS 21b-22b; Q 7, A 1, ANS 31a-d; A 2, ANS and REP 3 31d-32c; Q 14, A 2, REP 3 76d-77d; Q 18, A 3, REP 1 106b-107c; Q 25, A 1, REP 1 143d-144c; Q 44, A 2, ANS and REP 3 239b-240a; Q 45, A 5, REP 2 245c-247a; Q 50, A 2, REP 3 270a-272a; A 5, ANS 274b-275a; Q 55, A 2, ANS 289d-290d; Q 62, A 7, REP 1 322d-323b; Q 66, A 2 345d-347b; Q 75, A 2, ANS 379c-380c; A 5 382a-383b; Q 77, A 1, REP 2 399c-401b; Q 86, A 3 463b-d; Q 90, A 2, REP 2 481d-482c; Q 92, A 3, REP 1 490c-491b; Q 104, A 1, ANS and REP 1 534c-536c; Q 105, A 1, ANS 538d-539c; PART I-II, Q 1, A 3, ANS 611b-612a; Q 10, A 1, ANS and REP 2 662d-663d; Q 22, A 1, ANS and REP 1 720d-721c

20 AQUINAS: *Summa Theologica*, PART I-II, Q 49, A 4, ANS and REP 1 5a-6a; Q 85, A 6 182d-184a; PART III, Q 2, A 1, ANS and REP 2 710a-711c; PART III SUPPL, Q 82, A 1, REP 2 968a-970c; Q 92, A 1, ANS 1025c-1032b

21 DANTE: *Divine Comedy*, PARADISE, I [121-141] 107c-d

28 HARVEY: *On Animal Generation*, 384c-d; 494a-b

31 DESCARTES: *Objections and Replies*, 212a

46 HEGEL: *Philosophy of History*, INTRO, 156d-157b

7d. The distinction between real and ideal being, or between natural being and being in mind

7 PLATO: *Parmenides*, 489a-b

8 ARISTOTLE: *Prior Analytics*, BK I, CH 36 [48ª40-b9] 66d / *Metaphysics*, BK V, CH 7 [1017ª31-34] 538a; BK VI, CH 4 550a,c; BK IX, CH 3 [1047ª30-b2] 572c; CH 10 577c-578a,c; BK XII, CH 7 [1072b18-24] 602d-603a; CH 9 [1074b35-1075ª11] 605c-d / *Soul*, BK III, CH 4 [429ª13-29] 661b-c; CH 8 [431b20-432ª9] 664b-c / *Memory and Reminiscence*, CH 1 [450b12-451ª14] 691c-692b

11 ARCHIMEDES: *Sphere and Cylinder*, BK I, 403b

17 PLOTINUS: *Third Ennead*, TR VIII, CH 8 132d-133c

19 AQUINAS: *Summa Theologica*, PART I, Q 2, A 1, REP 2 10d-11d; Q 3, A 4, REP 2 16d-17c; Q 11, A 1, ANS and REP 3 46d-47d; Q 12, A 2 51c-52c; Q 13, A 3, REP 3 64d-65c; A 7, ANS and REP 2,4-5 68d-70d; A 9, ANS and REP 2 71b-72c; A 12 74c-75b; Q 14, A 1, ANS and REP 3 75d-76c; A 2, ANS and REP 2-3 76d-77d; A 6, REP 1 80a-81c; A 8, ANS 82c-83b; A 9, ANS 83b-d; A 13, REP 2-3 86d-88c; Q 15, A 1, ANS and REP 1,3 91b-92a; A 3, REP 4 93b-94a; Q 16, A 2 95c-96b; A 7, REP 2 99a-d; Q 17, A 3, ANS 102d-103c; Q 18, A 4, REP 2-3 107d-108c; Q 19, A 3, REP 6 110b-111c; Q 29, A 1, REP 3 162a-163b; Q 30, A 1, REP 4 167a-168a; A 4 170c-171b; Q 34, A 1, REP 3 185b-187b; Q 50, A 2, ANS 270a-272a; Q 55, A 2, ANS and REP 1 289d-290d; A 3 esp REP 1 291a-d; Q 56, A 2, ANS and REP 3 292d-294a; A 3, ANS 294a-d; Q 57, A 2 295d-297a; Q 58, A 6, ANS and REP 1,3 304c-305b; A 7, ANS 305c-306b; Q 66, A 2, REP 2 345d-347b; Q 67, A 3, ANS 351b-352a; Q 74, A 3, REP 5 375a-377a,c; Q 76, A 3, REP 4 391a-393a; A 6, REP 2 396a-d; Q 84 440b-451b; Q 85, A 2 453d-455b; A 3, REP 1,4 455b-457a; A 5, REP 3 457d-458d; Q 88, A 2, REP 4 471c-472c; PART I-II, Q 5, A 6, REP 2 641a-642a; Q 6, A 6, ANS and REP 2 649a-650a; Q 8, A 1, ANS and REP 3 655b-656a; Q 12, A 3, REP 2-3 670d-671b; Q 17, A 4, ANS 688d-689c; Q 22, A 2, ANS and REP 3 721c-722c; Q 28, A 1, REP 3 740b-741a

20 AQUINAS: *Summa Theologica*, PART III, Q 2, A 5, REP 2 715a-716b; PART III SUPPL, Q 82, A 3, ANS and REP 2 971a-972d

23 HOBBES: *Leviathan*, PART I, 53c; PART III, 172a-d; PART IV, 262a-d; 270a-c

26 SHAKESPEARE: *Richard II*, ACT V, SC V [1-41] 349d-350a

29 CERVANTES: *Don Quixote* esp PART I, 1a-8c, 18d-22a, PART II, 285a-288c

31 DESCARTES: *Meditations*, 71d-72a; III, 83b-86a; V, 93a-94a / *Objections and Replies*, 108b-109d; 121a-c; DEF III-IV 130b; AXIOM V 131d-132a; 157b-158a; 212c-213a

(7. *The divisions or modes of being.* 7d. *The distinction between real and ideal being, or between natural being and being in mind.*)

31 SPINOZA: *Ethics*, PART I, APPENDIX 369b-372d esp 371c-372c; PART II, PROP 5-9 374c-376c

35 LOCKE: *Human Understanding*, BK II, CH XXII, SECT 2 201a-b; CH XXX, SECT 2 238b-c; CH XXXI, SECT 2 239b-d; CH XXXII, SECT 14-18 245c-247a passim; BK III, CH III, SECT 15-19 258b-260a; CH VI 268b-283a passim, esp SECT 2-3 268c-d, SECT 8 270b-c; BK IV, CH II, SECT 14 312b-d; CH IV, SECT 6-8 325a-c; CH IX, SECT I 349a; CH XI, SECT 4-9 355b-357a

35 BERKELEY: *Human Knowledge*, SECT 1-96 413a-431d esp SECT 1-24 413a-417d, SECT 29-44 418c-421a, SECT 48-49 422a-b, SECT 82-84 428d-429c, SECT 86-91 429c-431a

35 HUME: *Human Understanding*, SECT V, DIV 44 468d-469c esp 469b-c; SECT XII, DIV 117-123 504a-506a

42 KANT: *Pure Reason*, 24a-33d esp 25c-26a, 28a-b, 31d-32c; 85d-93c; 200c-209d; 211c-212a / *Practical Reason*, 295b-d / *Judgement*, 551a-553c; 604a-b

44 BOSWELL: *Johnson*, 134c-d

46 HEGEL: *Philosophy of History*, INTRO, 153a-c; 158a-160b; 188d-189a; PART I, 219d-220a; 236a-c; 257c-d; PART IV, 354b; 364b-c

48 MELVILLE: *Moby Dick*, 385b

50 MARX: *Capital*, 11b-c

53 JAMES: *Psychology*, 128a-b; 142a-b; 176a-177a; 191b-192a; 302a; 639a-645b esp 640a, 644b-645b; 659a-660b; 851b-852a; 865b-866a; 868b; 879b-886a esp 881a-882a; 889a-890a

54 FREUD: *General Introduction*, 597d-598a

7d(1) The being of the possible

7 PLATO: *Republic*, BK V-VI, 368c-383a

8 ARISTOTLE: *Metaphysics*, BK IX, CH 3 572a-c / *Soul*, BK III, CH 4 [429ᵃ18-23] 661c

17 PLOTINUS: *Second Ennead*, TR V, CH 4-5 59c-60c

19 AQUINAS: *Summa Theologica*, PART I, Q 7, A 2, ANS and REP 3 31d-32c; Q 9, A 2, ANS 39c-40d; Q 14, A 2, REP 3 76d-77d; A 9, REP I 83b-d; A 13, REP 2-3 86d-88c; Q 18, A 4, REP 3 107d-108c; Q 46, A I, REP 1-2 250a-252d

31 SPINOZA: *Ethics*, PART I, PROP 33, SCHOL I 367c-d; PART II, PROP 8 375c-376a

38 MONTESQUIEU: *Spirit of Laws*, BK I, 1c

42 KANT: *Pure Reason*, 85d-88a; 95a-d; 97a-b; 176d-177a; 179c-180c / *Judgement*, 550a-578a esp 550c-d, 552c-d, 555a-b, 564a-565b, 568a-c, 569a, 570c-575b

46 HEGEL: *Philosophy of History*, INTRO, 153a-c; 156d-157b; 178a-179d

53 JAMES: *Psychology*, 233b [fn I]; 301b-302a

7d(2) The being of ideas, universals, rights

7 PLATO: *Cratylus*, 87d-89a; 113c-114a,c / *Phaedo*, 224a-225a; 228d-230c; 231b-232b;

240b-246c esp 242c-244b / *Republic*, BK V-VI, 368c-388a; BK IX-X, 426d-429c / *Timaeus*, 447a-d; 457b-458a / *Parmenides*, 486c-491a esp 489a-c / *Sophist*, 567b; 570a-574c / *Philebus*, 610d-613a / *Seventh Letter*, 809c-810b

8 ARISTOTLE: *Posterior Analytics*, BK I, CH II [77ᵃ5-9] 105d-106a; CH 22 [83ᵃ23-35] 113c-d; CH 24 [85ᵃ31-ᵇ3] 116c; [85ᵇ17-22] 117a / *Topics*, BK II, CH 7 [113ᵃ24-33] 158d; BK VI, CH 8 [147ᵃ5-11] 201a / *Sophistical Refutations*, CH 22 [178ᵇ37-179ᵃ10] 246c / *Physics*, BK II, CH 2 [193ᵇ31-194ᵃ6] 270b; BK III, CH 4 [203ᵃ4-9] 280d / *Metaphysics*, BK I, CH 6 505b-506b; CH 9 508c-511c; BK III, CH I [995ᵇ13-18] 514a; [995ᵇ27-996ᵃ10] 514b-c; CH 2 [997ᵃ34-ᵇ12] 516a-b; [998ᵃ6-13] 516d; CH 4 [999ᵇ24-1000ᵃ4] 518c-d; [1001ᵃ4-ᵇ25] 519d-520c; CH 6 [1002ᵇ11-31] 521b-d; [1003ᵃ5-17] 521d-522a,c; BK VII, CH 8 [1033ᵇ19-1034ᵃ8] 556d-557b; CH 10 [1035ᵇ28-32] 559b; CH 13-16 562a-565a; BK VIII, CH 6 569d-570d; BK IX, CH 8 [1050ᵇ35-1051ᵃ2] 576d-577a; BK X, CH 2 [1053ᵇ9-23] 580b-c; CH 10 586c-d; BK XI, CH I [1059ᵇ34-ᵇ8] 587b-c; CH I [1059ᵇ21]-CH 2 [1060ᵃ27] 587d-588b; CH 2 [1060ᵃ36-ᵇ30] 588c-589a; BK XII, CH I [1069ᵃ27-37] 598b; CH 3 [1070ᵃ4]-CH 5 [1071ᵇ2] 599b-601a; BK XIII, CH I [1076ᵃ17-33] 607a-b; CH 4-5 610a-611d; CH 10 618c-619a,c / *Soul*, BK II, CH 5 [417ᵇ17-28] 648b-c

9 ARISTOTLE: *Ethics*, BK I, CH 6 341b-342c passim

17 PLOTINUS: *Second Ennead*, TR V, CH 3 58d-59c; TR VI, CH 3 62b-d / *Third Ennead*, TR VIII, CH 8 132d-133c / *Fifth Ennead*, TR V, CH I, 229a; TR VII 238a-239b; TR IX, CH 5-8 248a-250a / *Sixth Ennead*, TR V, CH 5-8 307a-308c

18 AUGUSTINE: *Confessions*, BK I, par 9, 3a / *City of God*, BK VIII, CH 6, 269b-c

19 AQUINAS: *Summa Theologica*, PART I, Q 8, A 4, REP I 37c-38c; Q 14, PREAMBLE 75c-d; Q 15 91b-94a; Q 16, A 7, REP 2 99a-d; Q 18, A 4 107d-108c; Q 29, A 2, REP 4 163b-164b; Q 44, A 3 240b-241a; Q 47, A I, REP 2 256a-257b; Q 55 288d-291d; Q 57, AA 1-2 295a-297a; Q 65, A 4 342b-343c; Q 76, A 2, REP 4 388c-391a; Q 79, A 3, ANS 416a-417a; Q 84, AA 1-7 440d-450b; Q 85, A I, ANS and REP 1-2 451c-453c; A 2, ANS and REP 2 453d-455b; A 3, REP 1,4 455b-457a; A 8, ANS 460b-461b; Q 86, A 4, REP 2 463d-464d; Q 87, A I, ANS 465a-466c; Q 88, A I, ANS 469a-471c; A 2, ANS 471c-472c; Q 105, A 3, ANS 540c-541b; Q 110, A I, REP 3 564c-565d; A 2, ANS 565d-566d; Q 115, A I, ANS 585d-587c; A 3, REP 2 588c-589c; PART I-II, Q 29, A 6, ANS 748b-749a

20 AQUINAS: *Summa Theologica*, PART III, Q 2, A 5, REP 2 715a-716b; Q 4, A 4, ANS and REP 2 733a-734a; PART III SUPPL, Q 92, A I, ANS 1025c-1032b

23 HOBBES: *Leviathan*, PART I, 55b-c; 59d; PART IV, 262a-b

30 BACON: *Advancement of Learning*, 43d-44c / *Novum Organum*, BK I, APH 51 111c; BK II, APH 2 137b-c; APH 17 149b-d

31 DESCARTES: *Meditations*, III, 84a-85a / *Objections and Replies*, 121a-c; DEF I–IV 130a-b; AXIOM VI 132a

31 SPINOZA: *Ethics*, PART II, PROP 37–40 386b-388b

35 LOCKE: *Human Understanding*, BK I, CH I, SECT 15 98d-99a; BK II, CH VIII 133b-138b passim; CH XI, SECT 8–9 145b-c; CH XXII, SECT 2 201a-b; CH XXX 238a-239b; CH XXXI, SECT 2 239b-d; CH XXXII, SECT 6-8 244b-d; SECT 14–18 245c-247a; BK III, CH III, SECT 11–20 257a-260a; CH V–VI 263d-283a passim, esp CH VI, SECT 32–33 277c-278c, SECT 36–37 279a-b; BK IV, CH IV, SECT 4–5 324c-d; SECT 11–12 326b-d; CH VI, SECT 4 331d-332b; CH IX, SECT 1 349a; CH XI, SECT 4–9 355b-357a

35 BERKELEY: *Human Knowledge*, INTRO, SECT 12–16 408a-409d; SECT 2–4 413b-414a; SECT 48–49 422a-b; SECT 86–91 429c-431a

35 HUME: *Human Understanding*, SECT XII, DIV 122 505c-d

42 KANT: *Pure Reason*, 93c-99a; 112d-209d esp 112d-120c, 121a-128b, 129c-145c, 173b-190a; 237b / *Fund. Prin. Metaphysic of Morals*, 281c-282d / *Science of Right*, 404d-408b; 416b-417b / *Judgement*, 461a-c; 489b-c; 504d-505a; 528d-530c; 542b-544c; 551a-552c; 570b-c

46 HEGEL: *Philosophy of Right*, PREF, 6a-7a; INTRO, par 1 9a; PART I, par 66–67 29a-c; par 71 31b-c; PART III, par 184 64b; par 280 94d-95a; ADDITIONS, 2 115d / *Philosophy of History*, INTRO, 156d-190b esp 156d-157b, 158a-160b, 165a-b; PART IV, 364b-c

53 JAMES: *Psychology*, 113a-115a esp 113b-114a; 128a-b; 300a-313a passim, esp 300a-301a, 304b, 307a-b, 309a-311a; 641b-643a passim; 659a-b; 865b; 881b-882a

7d(3) The being of mathematical objects

7 PLATO: *Phaedo*, 228b-229d / *Republic*, BK VI, 387b-c; BK VII, 392a-394c; 395c-397a / *Theaetetus*, 535b-c; 541b-d / *Sophist*, 562c-d / *Philebus*, 636b-c / *Seventh Letter*, 809c-810b

8 ARISTOTLE: *Posterior Analytics*, BK I, CH 13 [79^{a}6–10] 108c; CH 18 [81^{a}40–^{b}5] 111b-c / *Topics*, BK VI, CH 6 [143^{b}11–33] 197b-c / *Physics*, BK II, CH 2 [193^{b}23–194^{a}11] 270a-c; BK III, CH 4 [203^{a}4–9] 280d; CH 5 [204^{a}8–34] 282a-b; BK IV, CH 1 [208^{b}19–24] 287b-c; CH 11 [219^{b}5–8] 299b; CH 14 [223^{a}21–29] 303a / *Metaphysics*, BK I, CH 5 [985^{b}22–986^{a}21] 503d-504b; CH 6 [987^{b}10–34] 505c-506a; CH 8 [989^{b}29–990^{a}32] 508a-c; CH 9 [991^{b}9–992^{b}18] 509d-511a; BK III, CH 1 [995^{b}13–18] 514a; [996^{a}13–15] 514c; CH 2 [997^{b}12–998^{a}19] 516b-d; CH 5 [1001^{b}26]–CH 6 [1002^{b}25] 520c-521c; BK VII, CH 2 [1028^{b}18–28] 551a-b; CH 10 [1035^{b}32–1036^{a}12] 559b-c; CH 11 [1036^{b}32–1037^{a}4] 560b-c; BK XI, CH 2 [1060^{a}36–^{b}19] 588c-d; CH 3 [1061^{a}29–^{b}4]

589c; BK XII, CH 1 [1069^{a}30–37] 598b; CH 10 [1075^{b}25–1076^{a}4] 606c-d; BK XIII, CH 1–3 607a-610a; CH 6–9 611d-618c; BK XIV 619b,d-626d / *Soul*, BK III, CH 7 [431^{b}13–19] 664b

9 ARISTOTLE: *Ethics*, BK I, CH 6 [1096^{a}17–19] 341b; BK VI, CH 8 [1142^{a}16–19] 391b

11 NICOMACHUS: *Arithmetic*, BK I, 811a-812a; 813d-814b

17 PLOTINUS: *Sixth Ennead*, TR VI 310d-321b

18 AUGUSTINE: *Confessions*, BK X, par 19 76a-b / *Christian Doctrine*, BK II, CH 38 654b-c

19 AQUINAS: *Summa Theologica*, PART I, Q 5, A 3, REP 4 25a-d; Q 10, A 6, ANS 45c-46d; Q 11, A 1, REP 1 46d-47d; A 3, REP 2 49a-c; Q 30, A 1, REP 4 167a-168a; Q 44, A 1, REP 3 238b-239a; Q 85, A 1, REP 2 451c-453c

20 AQUINAS: *Summa Theologica*, PART III SUPPL, Q 83, A 2, ANS 976c-978c; A 3, REP 2 978c-980d

31 DESCARTES: *Rules*, XIV, 30b-32a / *Discourse*, PART IV, 52d-53a / *Meditations*, I, 76c; V, 93a-d; V–VI, 96a-b / *Objections and Replies*, 169c-170a; 216d-217c; 218c; 228c-229a

35 LOCKE: *Human Understanding*, BK II, CH XIII, SECT 5–6 149b-d; BK III, CH III, SECT 19, 259c-d; BK IV, CH IV, SECT 5–8 324d-325c

35 BERKELEY: *Human Knowledge*, INTRO, SECT 12–16 408a-409d; SECT 12–16 415b-416a; SECT 118–128 436b-438d passim, esp SECT 121–122 436d-437c, SECT 125–126 438a-c

35 HUME: *Human Understanding*, SECT IV, DIV 20 458a-b; SECT XII, DIV 122 505c-d

42 KANT: *Pure Reason*, 16a-b; 17d-18d; 24d-25b; 31b-d; 46a-c; 55c; 62a-d; 68a-69c; 86b-c; 87b-c; 91c-d; 94b-95a; 211c-213c; 217c-d / *Practical Reason*, 312c / *Judgement*, 551a-552c

53 JAMES: *Psychology*, 874a-878a passim; 880b-881a

7d(4) The being of relations

7 PLATO: *Phaedo*, 242c-245b / *Parmenides*, 489a-c / *Sophist*, 570a-574c

8 ARISTOTLE: *Metaphysics*, BK I, CH 9 [990^{b}9–17] 508d; BK XIV, CH 1 [1088^{a}15–^{b}4] 620b-d

9 ARISTOTLE: *Ethics*, BK I, CH 6 [1096^{a}18–22] 341b-c

17 PLOTINUS: *Sixth Ennead*, TR I, CH 6–9 254d-257a

19 AQUINAS: *Summa Theologica*, PART I, Q 13, A 7, ANS and REP 2,4–5 68d-70d; Q 28, AA 1–2 157c-160a; A 4, ANS and REP 1,3–4 160c-161d; Q 40, A 2, REP 4 214b-215b; Q 45, A 3, REP 1–3 244a-d

20 AQUINAS: *Summa Theologica*, PART III, Q 2, A 7, REP 2 718b-d

30 BACON: *Novum Organum*, BK I, APH 45 110b

35 LOCKE: *Human Understanding*, BK II, CH XXV, SECT 1 214d-215b; SECT 10 216d-217a; CH XXX, SECT 4 238d-239a

35 BERKELEY: *Human Knowledge*, SECT 11, 415a

42 KANT: *Pure Reason*, 24a-33d esp 31d-32c; 61a-64a esp 62d-63c; 72c-85d; 99a-108a,c; 119b

46 HEGEL: *Philosophy of History*, INTRO, 156b-c

(7d. The distinction between real and ideal being, or between natural being and being in mind. 7d(4) The being of relations.)

53 JAMES: Psychology, 157b-161a esp 158b-159b; 458a-459b; 865b; 873a-b; 879b-886a esp 884b-885a; 889a-890a

7d(5) The being of fictions and negations

7 PLATO: Sophist, 561d-564b; 571d-574c esp 573a-574c

8 ARISTOTLE: Metaphysics, BK I, CH 9 [990^{b}9-15] 508d; BK IV, CH 2 [1004^{a}9-15] 523a; BK V, CH 7 [1017^{a}18] 537d; [1017^{a}31-34] 538a; BK VII, CH 4 [1030^{a}24-27] 553a; CH 7 [1032^{b}1-6] 555b-c; BK IX, CH 3 [1047^{a}30-^{b}2] 572c; BK XII, CH I [1069^{a}18-24] 598a

9 ARISTOTLE: Rhetoric, BK II, CH 24 [1402^{a}3-6] 651b-c

12 LUCRETIUS: Nature of Things, BK IV [722-748] 53d-54a

18 AUGUSTINE: Confessions, BK III, par 12 16b / City of God, BK XI, CH 22 333d-334c; BK XII, CH 7 346c-d

19 AQUINAS: Summa Theologica, PART I, Q 13, A 7, ANS 68d-70d; Q 34, A 3, REP 5 188b-189a; Q 48, A 2 esp REP 2 260c-261b; Q 51, A 2, ANS 276b-277a; PART I-II, Q 8, A I, REP 3 655b-656a

23 HOBBES: Leviathan, PART I, 50d; 53c; 57b-c; PART IV, 262a-d

31 DESCARTES: Objections and Replies, 157b

35 LOCKE: Human Understanding, BK II, CH VIII, SECT I-6 133b-134a; BK III, CH III, SECT 19 259c-260a

40 GIBBON: Decline and Fall, 345c

42 KANT: Pure Reason, 62d-63a; 174d-175b

46 HEGEL: Philosophy of History, INTRO, 160a

53 JAMES: Psychology, 639a-644a esp 642b [fn 2]

54 FREUD: General Introduction, 597b-598a esp 598a

7e. The distinction between appearance and reality, between the sensible and suprasensible, between the phenomenal and noumenal orders

7 PLATO: Cratylus, 113c-114a,c / Phaedrus, 124d-127a / Symposium, 167a-d / Phaedo, 224a-225a; 228a-232a / Republic, BK V, 370d-373c; BK VI, 383d-388a; BK VII, 396d-398c / Timaeus, 447a-d; 450b-c; 455c-458a esp 457c-458a / Theaetetus, 534d-536a / Sophist, 567a-568c / Statesman, 595b-c / Philebus, 634b-635b / Seventh Letter, 809c-810d

8 ARISTOTLE: Physics, BK I, CH 4 [187^{a}27-^{b}7] 262b-c / Metaphysics, BK V, CH 29 [1024^{b}22-27] 546c-d

12 LUCRETIUS: Nature of Things, BK II [308-332] 19a-b

17 PLOTINUS: Second Ennead, TR VI, CH I, 60c-61b / Fourth Ennead, TR VIII, CH 6 203d-204b / Sixth Ennead, TR III, CH I-2 281a-282a

18 AUGUSTINE: Confessions, BK II, par 10 11a-b; BK III, par 10 15b-d; BK VII, par 23 50b-c; BK X, par 13 74c-d; par 16-19 75b-76b / Christian Doctrine, BK II, CH 38 654b-c

19 AQUINAS: Summa Theologica, PART I, Q 18, A 2, ANS 105c-106b

25 MONTAIGNE: Essays, 291b-294b

31 DESCARTES: Objections and Replies, 238a-b; 257d

31 SPINOZA: Ethics, PART I, APPENDIX, 372a-c

35 LOCKE: Human Understanding, BK II, CH VIII 133b-138b passim, esp SECT 7-10 134b-d, SECT 15-20 135c-136c; CH XXIII, SECT 5 205a-b; SECT 15 208c-d; SECT 29 211d-212a; SECT 32 212c-d; CH XXXI, SECT 6-13 240d-243b; BK III, CH III, SECT 15-18 258b-259c; CH VI 268b-283a passim, esp SECT 9 270d-271a; BK IV, CH XVI, SECT 12 370b-371a

35 BERKELEY: Human Knowledge, SECT 25-27 417d-418b; SECT 86-91 429c-431a passim; SECT 101-102 432c-433a; SECT 135-142 440a-441c; SECT 148 442b-d

35 HUME: Human Understanding, SECT IV, DIV 29 461a-d

42 KANT: Pure Reason, 15c-16c; 19a; 19d-20c; 27b-33d; 53b-59b esp 58a-b; 86c-88c; 93c-99a; 101b-108a,c; 112b-d; 113c-115a; 153a-c; 164a-165c; 172c-173a; 227a-228b / Fund. Prin. Metaphysic of Morals, 281c-282d / Practical Reason, 292a-c; 307d-314d; 319c-321b; 328a-329a; 331a-337c; 340a-342d esp 340c-341c; 348b-353d / Intro. Metaphysic of Morals, 383c-d / Science of Right, 416b-417b / Judgement, 465a-c; 474b-475d; 500c-d; 501d-502a; 506d-507a; 510b-c; 530a; 541a-542a; 543a; 543c-544c; 551a-552c; 558d; 560c; 564a-c; 570b-572b esp 571c-572a; 574b-577a; 579a; 581a-b; 584c-d; 587d-588a; 594d [fn 1]; 599d-600d; 603a-b; 604a-b; 606d-607c; 611c-613a,c

46 HEGEL: Philosophy of Right, PART I, par 82-83 34d-35a; ADDITIONS, 52-53 124d-125a / Philosophy of History, INTRO, 156d-157b; PART II, 270d-271c; PART IV, 349b-350a

48 MELVILLE: Moby Dick, 120a-121a; 385b

52 DOSTOEVSKY: Brothers Karamazov, BK VI, 168b-c

53 JAMES: Psychology, 185a-b; 234a-b; 503a-b; 569b-570a; 606b-608b esp 608a-b; 648a

54 FREUD: Unconscious, 430b-c

8. Being and knowledge

8a. Being and becoming in relation to sense: perception and imagination

7 PLATO: Phaedrus, 126b-d / Phaedo, 224a-225a; 231b-232a / Republic, BK III, 333b-334b; BK V, 368c-373c; BK VI-VII, 383d-398c / Timaeus, 447b-d; 450b-c; 453b-454a; 455c-458b esp 457b-458a / Theaetetus, 517b-536b / Sophist, 565a-569a esp 568a-569a / Philebus, 610d-613a

8 ARISTOTLE: Generation and Corruption, BK I, CH 3 [318^{b}18-319^{a}2] 415c-d; CH 4 [319^{b}5-24]

416c-d / *Metaphysics*, BK I, CH 5 [986^b25–987^a1] 504d-505a; CH 6 [987^a29–^b18] 505b-d; BK IV, CH 5–6 528c-531c; BK XI, CH 6 [1062^b33–1063^b8] 591a-d / *Soul*, BK I, CH 2 [404^b7–405^b29] 633d-635a; CH 5 [409^b18–411^a7] 639c-641a; BK II, CH 5 647b-648d; BK II, CH 12 [424^a16]–BK III, CH 2 [426^a25] 656a-658c

11 NICOMACHUS: *Arithmetic*, BK I, 811c-d

17 PLOTINUS: *Fifth Ennead*, TR V, CH I 228b-229c; TR IX, CH 5 248a-249a / *Sixth Ennead*, TR I, CH 27–28 266c-267c esp CH 28 267b-c

18 AUGUSTINE: *Confessions*, BK III, par 10 15b-d; BK IV, par 15–17 23a-c; BK VII, par 23 50b-c / *Christian Doctrine*, BK II, CH 38 654b-c

19 AQUINAS: *Summa Theologica*, PART I, Q 67, A 3, ANS 351b-352a; Q 78, A 3, ANS 410a-411d; Q 86, A 3 463b-d

25 MONTAIGNE: *Essays*, 292d-293d

31 DESCARTES: *Discourse*, PART IV, 51c-53b / *Meditations*, 74a,c; II, 81d

35 BERKELEY: *Human Knowledge*, SECT 2–3 413b-d; SECT 25–27 417d-418b; SECT 88–91 430a-431a; SECT 135–142 440a-441c

42 KANT: *Pure Reason*, 34a-72c esp 34a-c, 39a-c, 41c-42b, 45b-59b, 61a-64a, 65d-72c / *Fund. Prin. Metaphysic of Morals*, 281c-282d / *Judgement*, 603d-604b

8b. Being and becoming in relation to intellect: abstraction and intuition

7 PLATO: *Cratylus*, 113c-114a,c / *Phaedrus*, 125a-126c / *Symposium*, 167a-d / *Phaedo*, 224a-226c; 228a-232a / *Republic*, BK III, 333b-334b; BK V–VI, 368c-375b; BK VI, 376d; 382a-c; BK VI–VII, 383d-398c / *Timaeus*, 447b-d; 450b-c; 455c-458b / *Theaetetus*, 534d-536b/ *Sophist*, 565a-569a esp 568a-569a / *Philebus*, 610d-613a; 615c-619d esp 619a-d; 634b-635b / *Seventh Letter*, 809c-810d

8 ARISTOTLE: *Posterior Analytics*, BK I, CH 8 104a-b / *Topics*, BK IV, CH I [121^a20–26] 169a-b / *Physics*, BK IV, CH 11 [219^b23–31] 299c-d; BK VII, CH 3 [247^b1–248^a8] 330b-d / *Heavens*, BK III, CH I [298^b15–24] 390a-b / *Metaphysics*, BK I, CH 5 [986^b25–987^a1] 504d-505a; CH 6 [987^a29–^b18] 505b-d; BK III, CH I [995^b4–26] 513d-514b; CH 2 [996^a18–997^a34] 514d-516a; BK IV 522a-532d; BK VI 547b,d-550a,c; BK VII, CH 15 [1039^b20–1040^a8] 563c-564a; BK XI, CH I–8 587a-593d; BK XII, CH 7 602a-603b; CH 9 605a-d / *Soul*, BK I, CH 2 [404^b7–405^b29] 633d-635a; CH 5 [409^b18–411^a7] 639c-641a; BK II, CH 5 [417^a21–418^a3] 647d-648c; BK III, CH 4–8 661b-664d

11 NICOMACHUS: *Arithmetic*, BK I, 811a-d

17 PLOTINUS: *Fifth Ennead*, TR V, CH 1–2 228b-229d; TR IX, CH 5 248a-249a / *Sixth Ennead*, TR I, CH 27–28 266c-267c esp CH 28 267b-c

18 AUGUSTINE: *Confessions*, BK VII, par 23 50b-c / *City of God*, BK XI, CH 10, 328c-d / *Christian Doctrine*, BK II, CH 38 654b-c

19 AQUINAS: *Summa Theologica*, PART I, Q 5, A 2, ANS 24b-25a; Q 12, A 1 50c-51c; AA 3–4 52c-54c; Q 16, AA 2–3 95c-96d; Q 26, A 2, ANS 150c-151a; Q 34, A 1, REP 2 185b-187b; Q 50, A 2, ANS and REP I 270a-272a; Q 54, A 2 285d-286c; Q 78, A I, ANS 407b-409a; Q 79, AA I–10 413d-424d passim; Q 84, AA 1–2 440d-443c; AA 6–7 447c-450b; Q 85, A 1 451c-453c; A 5, REP 3 457d-458d; Q 86, A 1 461c-462a; A 3 463b-d; Q 88 468d-473a; Q 89, A 4 476c-477a; Q 105, A 3, ANS 540c-541b; PART I–II, Q 3, A 8, ANS 628d-629c; Q 10, A I, REP 3 662d-663d

20 AQUINAS: *Summa Theologica*, PART II–II, Q 2, A 3, ANS 392d-393c; PART III SUPPL, Q 92, A I 1025c-1032b

31 DESCARTES: *Discourse*, PART IV, 51c-53b / *Meditations*, II, 81b-d

35 BERKELEY: *Human Knowledge*, SECT 25–27 417d-418b; SECT 88–91 430a-431a; SECT 135–142 440a-441c

42 KANT: *Pure Reason*, 38a-108a,c esp 39a-c, 41c-93c / *Fund. Prin. Metaphysic of Morals*, 281c-282d; 285a-287d / *Judgement*, 465a-c

46 HEGEL: *Philosophy of Right*, PART III, par 343 110d-111a / *Philosophy of History*, INTRO, 160d-161c

8c. Essence or substance as the object of definition: real and nominal essences

7 PLATO: *Meno*, 174a-179b passim / *Euthyphro*, 196a-b / *Gorgias*, 252d-253b / *Republic*, BK VI, 384a-386c esp 385b-c / *Theaetetus*, 514b-515c; 547c-549c / *Sophist*, 551a-552c / *Laws*, BK X, 763c-d / *Seventh Letter*, 809a-810b

8 ARISTOTLE: *Categories*, CH 5 [2^a19–3^b24] 6b-8a / *Posterior Analytics*, BK I, CH 22 113b-115b; CH 33 [89^a17–^b5] 121d-122a,c; BK II, CH 3–10 123c-128d; CH 13 131b-133c / *Topics*, BK I, CH 4 [101^b17–23] 144b-c; CH 5 [101^b37–102^a5] 144d; CH 8 [103^b1–11] 146d; CH 18 [108^a38–^b9] 152d; [108^b19–32] 153a,c; BK VI, CH 1 [139^a24–34] 192a; BK VI, CH 4–BK VII, CH 5 194c-211a,c passim / *Physics*, BK I, CH 3 [186^b14–34] 261c-262a; BK II, CH I [193^a30–^b19] 269c-270a; CH 2 [194^a11–14] 270c / *Meteorology*, BK IV, CH 12 493d-494d / *Metaphysics*, BK I, CH 3 [983^a24–29] 501c; CH 5 [987^a19–27] 505b; CH 6 [987^a35–^b10] 505c; [987^b30–33] 506a; BK II, CH 2 [994^b16–27] 513a-b; BK III, CH 2 [996^b12–21] 515a-b; BK IV, CH 4 [1006^a29–^b18] 525c-d; [1007^a20–^b18] 526c-527a; BK V, CH 2 [1013^a27–28] 533b; BK VI, CH I [1025^b28–1026^a6] 547d-548a; BK VII, CH I [1028^a31–37] 550d; CH 4–6 552b-555a; CH 10–17 558a-566a,c; BK VIII, CH 2–3 566d-568d; CH 6 569d-570d; BK XI, CH 7 [1064^a19–28] 592c; BK XII, CH 9 [1074^b37–1075^a2] 605c; BK XIII, CH 2 [1077^b1–10] 608d-609a; CH 4 [1078^b18–32] 610b-c / *Soul*, BK I, CH I 631a-632d; BK II, CH I [412^a1–^b24] 642a-d; BK III, CH 6 [430^b26–31] 663b-c

9 ARISTOTLE: *Parts of Animals*, BK I, CH I [641^a14–31] 163d-164a; CH 2–3 165d-167d

(8. *Being and knowledge.* 8c. *Essence or substance as the object of definition: real and nominal essences.*)

19 AQUINAS: *Summa Theologica*, PART I, Q I, A 7, REP I 7a-c; Q 2, A I, REP 2 10d-11d; A 2, REP 2 11d-12c; Q 3, A 3, ANS 16a-d; A 5, ANS 17c-18b; Q 17, A 3 102d-103c; Q 18, A 2, ANS 105c-106b; Q 29, A I 162a-163b; A 2, REP 3 163b-164b; Q 44, A I, REP I 238b-239a; A 3, REP 3 240b-241a; Q 58, A 5 303c-304c; Q 75, A 4, ANS 381b-382a; Q 85, A 6 458d-459c; Q 116, A I, CONTRARY 592d-593d; PART I-II, Q 10, A I, REP 3 662d-663d

20 AQUINAS: *Summa Theologica*, PART III, Q 2, A I, ANS 710a-711c; A 2, ANS 711d-712d; Q 60, A 4, REP I 849c-850b

23 HOBBES: *Leviathan*, PART I, 55b-c; 56b; PART IV, 269b-271a

28 GALILEO: *Two New Sciences*, FIRST DAY, 142d-143a

30 BACON: *Advancement of Learning*, 43d-44c / *Novum Organum*, BK II, APH 4 137d-138b

31 DESCARTES: *Discourse*, PART IV, 51d-52a / *Objections and Replies*, POSTULATE IV 131a-b; 153d; 160d

31 SPINOZA: *Ethics*, PART I, DEF 4 355b; PROP 8, SCHOL 2, 357b-d; PROP 10 358a-b; PART II, DEF 2 373b; PROP 37 386b-c; PART III, PROP 4 398d

33 PASCAL: *Vacuum*, 372b-373b; 376b-377a / *Geometrical Demonstration*, 430b-431b

35 LOCKE: *Human Understanding*, BK II, CH XXIII, SECT I-16 204a-209a esp SECT 6 205b-c, SECT 14 208b-c; SECT 29-32 211d-212d; CH XXXI, SECT 3 240a-b; SECT 6-13 240d-243b; CH XXXII, SECT 18 246c-247a; SECT 24 247c-d; BK III, CH III, SECT 12-20 257b-260a; CH IV, SECT 3 260b; CH V, SECT 14 267b-c; CH VI 268b-283a; CH IX, SECT 11-17 287d-290a; CH X, SECT 17-21 295d-297b; CH XI, SECT 15-23 303b-305b; BK IV, CH IV, SECT 11-17 326b-328d; CH VI, SECT 4-16 331d-336d; CH XII, SECT 7-12 360b-362c passim, esp SECT 9 360d-361b

35 BERKELEY: *Human Knowledge*, INTRO, SECT 18 410a-c; SECT 101-102 432c-433a

42 KANT: *Pure Reason*, 179d-180a; 215d-216c / *Science of Right*, 404d; 423d-424b

46 HEGEL: *Philosophy of History*, INTRO, 176c

53 JAMES: *Psychology*, 185a-b; 668a-670b

8d. **The role of essence in demonstration: the use of essence, property, and accident in inference**

8 ARISTOTLE: *Prior Analytics*, BK II, CH 27 [70^{a}3-39] 92a-c / *Posterior Analytics* 97a-137a,c esp BK II 122b,d-137a,c / *Metaphysics*, BK I, CH 3 [983^{a}24-29] 501c; BK III, CH 2 [996^{b}12-21] 515a-b; [997^{a}25-34] 515d-516a; BK VI, CH I [1025^{b}1-18] 547b,d; BK XI, CH I [1059^{a}29-34] 587b; CH 7 [1063^{b}36-1064^{a}9] 592b / *Soul*, BK II, CH 2 [413^{a}10-^{b}13] 643a-d; CH 4 [415^{a}14-23] 645b-c

19 AQUINAS: *Summa Theologica*, PART I, Q 2, A 2, REP 2-3 11d-12c; Q 3, A 5, ANS 17c-18b; Q 17, A 3, REP 1-2 102d-103c; Q 18, A 2, ANS 105c-106b; Q 46, A 2, ANS 253a-255a; Q 77, A I, REP 7 399c-401b

23 HOBBES: *Leviathan*, PART IV, 269d-270c

31 DESCARTES: *Meditations*, V, 93b-c / *Objections and Replies*, 207b

35 LOCKE: *Human Understanding*, BK III, CH XI, SECT 15-17 303b-304a esp SECT 16 303c-d; BK IV, CH III, SECT 9-17 315c-317c passim, esp SECT 14 316b-d; CH VI, SECT 4-16 331d-336d passim; CH XII, SECT 6-9 360a-361b

42 KANT: *Pure Reason*, 180c-182b

53 JAMES: *Psychology*, 666b-673a esp 667b-671a

8e. **The accidental in relation to science and definition**

8 ARISTOTLE: *Prior Analytics*, BK I, CH 13 [32^{b}4-23] 48b-d / *Posterior Analytics*, BK I, CH 4 100a-101b; CH 6 [75^{a}18-38] 103a-c; CH 8 104a-b; CH 30 119d / *Topics*, BK II-III 153a-168a,c; BK IV, CH I [121^{a}6-9] 168d-169a; CH 2 [122^{b}12-18] 170d-171a; CH 4 [125^{a}33-^{b}10] 174b-c; CH 6 [127^{b}1-4] 177a; BK V 178b,d-192a,c; BK VI, CH 6 196d-199c; CH 14 [151^{a}32-^{b}2] 206b-c / *Metaphysics*, BK I, CH 9 [990^{b}22-991^{a}2] 509a; BK III, CH I [995^{b}18-27] 514a-b; CH 2 [997^{a}25-34] 515d-516a; BK IV, CH 2 522b-524b esp [1005^{a}13-17] 524b; BK VI, CH 2 548c-549c; BK VII, CH 4-6 552b-555a; BK VIII, CH 4 [1044^{b}8-20] 569b; BK XI, CH I [1059^{a}29-34] 587b; CH 3 589a-d; BK XIII, CH 2 [1077^{a}23-^{b}14] 608c-609a

11 NICOMACHUS: *Arithmetic*, BK I, 811b-812a

19 AQUINAS: *Summa Theologica*, PART I, Q 14, A 13, ANS and REP 3 86d-88c; Q 18, A 2, ANS 105c-106b; Q 57, A 3, ANS 297b-298a; Q 86, A 3 463b-d; PART I-II, Q 7, A 2 esp REP 2 652d-653c; Q 18, A 3, REP 2 695d-696b

31 DESCARTES: *Objections and Replies*, 135b-136b; 153d; 170d; 207b; 209c-210b

35 LOCKE: *Human Understanding*, BK II, CH XXIII, SECT 3-16 204c-209a esp SECT 6 205b-c, SECT 14 208b-c; SECT 29-32 211d-212d; SECT 37 213d-214b; CH XXXI, SECT 8-11 242a-243a; SECT 13 243a-b; BK VI, CH VI 268b-283a passim, esp SECT 2-5 268c-269d; CH IX, SECT 13-17 288a-290a; CH XI, SECT 19-22 304b-305a

35 BERKELEY: *Human Knowledge*, SECT I 413a-b; SECT 49 422b

35 HUME: *Human Understanding*, SECT VIII, DIV 67 480c-481a

8f. **Judgments and demonstrations of existence: their sources and validity**

7 PLATO: *Laws*, BK X, 757d-765d esp 758c-760a, 760d-762b, 765b-d

8 ARISTOTLE: *Metaphysics*, BK I, CH 9 [990^{b}9-22] 508d-509a; BK VI, CH I [1025^{b}1-18] 547b,d

9 ARISTOTLE: *Ethics*, BK IX, CH 9 [1170^{a}16-^{b}8] 423d-424b passim, esp [1170^{a}28-^{b}1] 424a

12 LUCRETIUS: *Nature of Things*, BK I [418-448] 6b-c

18 Augustine: *City of God*, bk xi, ch 26 336d-337b

19 Aquinas: *Summa Theologica*, part i, q 2, a i, rep 2 10d-11d; a 2 11d-12c; q 3, a 4, rep 2 16d-17c; a 5, ans 17c-18b; q 12, a 12, ans and rep 1 60d-61c; q 46, a 2, ans 253a-255a

23 Hobbes: *Leviathan*, part iv, 269d-270c

31 Descartes: *Discourse*, part iv, 51c-53b / *Meditations*, 71d-72a; ii, 78a-b; iii, 85a-86d; v-vi 93a-103d / *Objections and Replies*, 110b-c; 121b-c; 122c-123a; 126b-127c; postulate iv-vii 131a-c; 140b-c; 207b; 209d-210b; 224b,d; 261a

31 Spinoza: *Ethics*, part i, prop ii 358b-359b; prop 14 359d-360a

35 Locke: *Human Understanding*, bk ii, ch vii, sect 7 132d; ch xiv, sect 3 155c-d; ch xxiii, sect 5 205a-b; bk iv, ch ii, sect 14 312b-d;

ch iii, sect 21 319c; ch vii, sect 7 338c; ch ix-xi 349a-358c; ch xvii, sect 2, 371d

35 Berkeley: *Human Knowledge*, sect 18-20 416b-417a; sect 25-29 417d-418c; sect 88-89 430a-c

35 Hume: *Human Understanding*, sect iv, div 20-sect v, div 38 458a-466c passim, esp sect iv, div 30 461d-462b, sect v, div 35 464c-d, div 38, 466b; sect xi 497b-503c passim, esp div 115 503b-c; sect xii, div 117-123 504a-506a; div 132 509a-d

42 Kant: *Pure Reason*, 85d-88a; 179c-201c esp 193a-b; 228c-d

44 Boswell: *Johnson*, 134c-d

46 Hegel: *Philosophy of Right*, part iii, par 280 94d-95a

53 James: *Psychology*, 176a-177a; 640b [fn 1]; 643a-659a esp 643b-645b, 648a

CROSS-REFERENCES

For: 'Being' as a transcendental term or concept, *see* Idea 4b(4); Metaphysics 2b; Opposition 2c; for the analysis of the meaning of words like "being," and for the theory of 'being' as an analogical term or concept, *see* Relation 1d; Same and Other 4c; Sign and Symbol 3d.

The discussion of unity, goodness, and truth as properties of being, or as convertible with being, *see* Good and Evil 1b; One and Many 1; Same and Other 1a, 2e; Truth 1b.

Other treatments of the distinction between being and becoming, and of the problem of the reality of mutable as compared with immutable being, *see* Change 1, 10c; Eternity 4a-4b; Matter 1; Necessity and Contingency 2c.

Considerations relevant to the distinction between essence and existence, *see* Form 2a; God 2a-2b, 4a; Necessity and Contingency 2a-2b; Soul 4b; Universal and Particular 2a; for considerations relevant to the distinction between substance and accident, or between the essential and the accidental, *see* Form 2c(2); Matter 1b; Nature 1a(1); Necessity and Contingency 2d; Quality 1; Quantity 1; Same and Other 3a; Soul 2a; and for the problem of the being of qualities, quantities, and relations, *see* Quality 1; Quantity 1; Relation 1a.

Considerations relevant to the distinction between potentiality and actuality, or matter and form, *see* Change 2a; Desire 2a; Form 2c(1); Habit 1a; Infinity 1b, 4c; Matter 1-1a, 3b; Mind 2b, 4c; Necessity and Contingency 1; for considerations relevant to the distinction between the real and the ideal, *see* Idea 3c, 6a-6b; Knowledge 6a(3); and for the controversy over the real existence of ideas, forms, mathematical objects, universals, *see* Form 1a, 2a; Mathematics 2b; Space 5; Universal and Particular 2a-2c.

Considerations relevant to the distinction between sensible and supra-sensible being, *see* Knowledge 6a(1), 6a(4); Mind 1a(1).

Elaborations of the theory of substance and treatments of the distinction between material and immaterial, corruptible and incorruptible substances, *see* Angel 2; Change 10c; Element 5a; Form 2d; Man 3a-3a(1), 3b; Matter 2, 2d, 3a; Mind 1b, 2a, 10c-10d; Soul 3a-3c, 4b.

The relation of being and becoming as objects of knowledge to the faculties of sense and reason, *see* Change 11; Knowledge 6a(1); Opinion 1; Sense 1b.

Essence in relation to the natures of things and to their definitions, *see* Definition 1a; Form 3c; Knowledge 6a(2); Nature 1a, 1a(2), 4a.

The relation of the concept 'being' to the principle of contradiction, both as a principle of being and of thought, *see* Opposition 2a; Principle 1c.

Logical problems concerning judgments of existence and proofs of existence, *see* God 2c; Judgment 8c; Knowledge 6a(3); Necessity and Contingency 2b; Reasoning 6a.

ADDITIONAL READINGS

Listed below are works not included in *Great Books of the Western World*, but relevant to the idea and topics with which this chapter deals. These works are divided into two groups:

I. Works by authors represented in this collection.
II. Works by authors not represented in this collection.

For the date, place, and other facts concerning the publication of the works cited, consult the Bibliography of Additional Readings which follows the last chapter of *The Great Ideas*.

I.

AQUINAS. *On Being and Essence*
DESCARTES. *The Principles of Philosophy*, PART I, 51–54
HOBBES. *Concerning Body*, PART II, CH 8, 10
BERKELEY. *Three Dialogues Between Hylas and Philonous*
HUME. *A Treatise of Human Nature*, BK I, PART I, SECT VI; PART II, SECT VI
KANT. *Metaphysical Foundations of Natural Science*
HEGEL. *The Phenomenology of Mind*, VIII
——. *Science of Logic*, VOL I, BK I, SECT I; SECT III, CH I (C), 3; BK II, SECT I, CH I; SECT II, CH I; SECT III, CH 2, 3 (A)
——. *Logic*, CH 7–8
W. JAMES. *Some Problems of Philosophy*, CH 2–3

II.

SEXTUS EMPIRICUS. *Against the Physicists*, BK II, CH 5
PORPHYRY. *Introduction to Aristotle's Predicaments*
PROCLUS. *The Elements of Theology*, (C, J)
BOETHIUS. *In Isagogem Porphyrii Commenta*
——. *De Trinitate (On the Trinity)*
ERIGENA. *De Divisione Naturae*
BONAVENTURA. *Itinerarium Mentis in Deum (The Itinerary of the Mind to God)*
DUNS SCOTUS. *Tractatus de Primo Principio (A Tract Concerning the First Principle)*
CRESCAS. *Or Adonai*, PROPOSITIONS 18–25
ALBO. *The Book of Principles (Sefer ha-Ikkarim)*, BK II, CH I
G. PICO DELLA MIRANDOLA. *Of Being and Unity*
CAJETAN. *De Conceptu Entis*
SUÁREZ. *Disputationes Metaphysicae*
JOHN OF SAINT THOMAS. *Cursus Philosophicus Thomisticus, Ars Logica*, PART II, QQ 2, 13–19
MALEBRANCHE. *Dialogues on Metaphysics and Religion*
LEIBNITZ. *Discourse on Metaphysics*, VIII–XIII
——. *New Essays Concerning Human Understanding*, BK II, CH 23–24
——. *Monadology*, par 1–9
WOLFF. *Ontologia*
DIDEROT. *Le rêve de d'Alembert*

J. G. FICHTE. *The Science of Knowledge*
SCHOPENHAUER. *The World as Will and Idea*, VOL I, BK I, IV
I. H. FICHTE. *Ontologie*
KIERKEGAARD. *Concluding Unscientific Postscript*
CLIFFORD. "On the Nature of Things-In-Themselves," in VOL II, *Lectures and Essays*
LOTZE. *Microcosmos*, BK IX, CH 1–3
——. *Metaphysics*, BK I, CH 1–3
C. S. PEIRCE. *Collected Papers*, VOL I, par 545–567; VOL VI, par 327–372, 385
BRADLEY. *The Principles of Logic*, Terminal Essays, VII, XI
——. *Appearance and Reality*, BK I, CH 2, 7–8; BK II, CH 13–15, 24, 26
ROYCE. *The World and the Individual*, SERIES I (1–4, 8)
CASSIRER. *Substance and Function*, PART I; PART II, CH 6
HUSSERL. *Ideas: General Introduction to Pure Phenomenology*
GARRIGOU-LAGRANGE. *God, His Existence and Nature*, PART II, APPENDIX 2
BERGSON. *Creative Evolution*
——. *The Creative Mind*, CH 3, 6
McTAGGART. *The Nature of Existence*, BK I
MOORE. *Philosophical Studies*, CH 6
DEWEY. *Experience and Nature*, CH 2, 8, 10
HEIDEGGER. *Sein und Zeit*
B. RUSSELL. *The Analysis of Matter*, CH 23
SANTAYANA. *The Realm of Essence*, CH 1–11
WHITEHEAD. *Process and Reality*
LOVEJOY. *The Great Chain of Being*
A. E. TAYLOR. *Philosophical Studies*, CH III
BLONDEL. *L'être et les êtres*
WEISS. *Reality*
SARTRE. *L'être et le néant*
——. *Existentialism*
MARITAIN. *An Introduction to Philosophy*, PART II (5–7)
——. *The Degrees of Knowledge*, CH 4
——. *A Preface to Metaphysics*, LECT I–IV
——. *Existence and the Existent*
GILSON. *L'être et l'essence*
——. *Being and Some Philosophers*

Chapter 8: CAUSE

INTRODUCTION

EXPLANATION is an inveterate human tendency. Even philosophers who think that we cannot attain to knowledge of causes get involved in explaining why that is so. Nor will their disputes about the theory of causes ever remove the word "because" from the vocabulary of common speech. It is as unavoidable as the word "is." "The impulse to seek causes," says Tolstoy, "is innate in the soul of man."

The question "Why?" remains after all other questions are answered. It is sometimes the only unanswerable question—unanswerable either in the very nature of the case or because there are secrets men cannot fathom. Sometimes, as Dante says, man must be "content with the *quia*," the knowledge *that* something is without knowing *why*. "Why?" is the one question which it has been deemed the better part of wisdom not to ask; yet it has also been thought the one question which holds the key to wisdom. As Virgil writes, in one of his most famous lines, *Felix, qui potuit rerum cognoscere causas* (Happy the man who has been able to know the causes of things).

The question "Why?" takes many forms and can be answered in many ways. Other knowledge may prove useful in providing the answers. A definition, for example, which tells us what a thing is, may explain why it behaves as it does or why it has certain properties. A narrative, which tells us how something happened by describing a succession of events, may also be part of the total explanation of some event in question.

In other circumstances, a demonstration or a statement of grounds or reasons may be explanatory. "How do you know?" is often a concealed form of the "Why" question. To answer it we may have to give our reasons for thinking that something or other is the case; or perhaps give the genesis of our opinion. Things as different as a logical demonstration and a piece of autobiography seem to be relevant in accounting for our convictions; as, in accounting for our behavior, we may refer to our purposes and to our past.

THE GREEK WORD for cause, from which our English word "aetiology" is derived, came into the vocabulary of science and philosophy from the language of the law courts. In its legal sense it was used to point out where the responsibility lay. A suit at law is based upon a cause of action; he who demands redress for an injury suffered is expected to place the blame. The charge of responsibility for wrongdoing—the blame or fault which is the cause for legal redress or punishment—naturally calls for excuses, which may include a man's motives.

In the context of these legal considerations, two different meanings of cause begin to appear. One man's act is the cause of injury to another, in the sense of being responsible for its occurrence. If the act was intentional, it probably had a cause in the purpose which motivated it.

These two types of cause appear in the explanations of the historians as well as in trials at law. Herodotus and Thucydides, trying to account for the Persian or the Peloponnesian war, enumerate the incidents which led up to the outbreak of hostilities. They cite certain past events as the causes of war—the factors which predisposed the parties toward conflict, and even precipitated it. The historians do not think they can fully explain why the particular events become the occasions for war except by considering the hopes and ambitions, or, as Thucydides suggests, the fears of the contestants. For the ancient historians at least, finding the causes includes a search for the motives which underlie other causes and help to explain how other factors get their causal efficacy.

Thucydides explicitly distinguishes these two kinds of causes in the first chapter of his history. After noting that the "immediate cause" of the war was the breaking of a treaty, he adds that the "real cause" was one "which was formally most kept out of sight," namely, the "growth of the power of Athens, and the alarm which this inspired in Lacedaemon."

It is sometimes supposed that Thucydides owes his conception of causes to the early medical tradition. That might very well be the case, for Hippocrates constantly seeks the "natural causes" of disease; and in his analysis of the various factors involved in any particular disease, he tries to distinguish between the predisposing and the exciting causes.

But the classification of causes was not completed in the Athenian law courts, in the Greek interpretation of history, or in the early practice of medicine. Causes were also the preoccupation of the pre-Socratic physicists. Their study of nature was largely devoted to an analysis of the principles, elements, and causes of change. Concerned with the problem of change in general, not merely with human action, or particular phenomena such as crime, war, or disease, Greek scientists or philosophers, from Thales and Anaxagoras to Empedocles, Democritus, Plato, and Aristotle, tried to discover the causes involved in any change. Aristotle carried the analysis furthest and set a pattern for all later discussions of cause.

THE EXPLANATION OF a thing, according to Aristotle, must answer all of the queries "comprehended under the question 'why.'" This question can be answered, he thinks, in at least four different ways, and these four ways of saying why something is the case constitute his famous theory of the four causes.

"In one sense," he writes, "that out of which a thing comes to be and which persists, is called 'cause'"—the material cause. "In another sense, the form or the archetype" is a cause—the formal cause. "Again the primary source of the change or coming to rest" is a cause—the efficient cause. "Again the end or 'that for the sake of which' a thing is done" is a cause—the final cause. "This," he concludes, "perhaps exhausts the number of ways in which the term 'cause' is used."

The production of works of art, to which Aristotle himself frequently turns for examples, most readily illustrates these four different kinds of causes. In making a shoe, the material cause is that out of which the shoe is made—the leather or hide. The efficient cause is the shoemaker, or more precisely the shoemaker's acts which transform the raw material into the finished product. The formal cause is the pattern which directs the work; it is, in a sense, the definition or type of the thing to be made, which, beginning as a plan in the artist's mind, appears at the end of the work in the transformed material as its own intrinsic form. The protection of the foot is the final cause or end—that for the sake of which the shoe was made.

Two of the four causes seem to be less discernible in nature than in art. The material and efficient causes remain evident enough. The material cause can usually be identified as that which undergoes the change—the thing which grows, alters in color, or moves from place to place. The efficient cause is always that by which the change is produced. It is the moving cause working on that which is susceptible to change, e.g., the fire heating the water, the rolling stone setting another stone in motion.

But the formal cause is not as apparent in nature as in art. Whereas in art it can be identified by reference to the plan in the maker's mind, it must be discovered in nature in the change itself, as that which completes the process. For example, the redness which the apple takes on in ripening is the formal cause of its alteration in color. The trouble with the final cause is that it so often tends to be inseparable from the formal cause; for unless some extrinsic purpose can be found for a natural change—some end beyond itself which the change serves—the final cause, or that for the sake of which the change took place, is no other than the quality or form which the matter assumes as a result of its transformation.

THIS SUMMARY of Aristotle's doctrine of the four causes enables us to note some of the basic issues and shifts in the theory of causation.

The attack on final causes does not, at the beginning at least, reject them completely. Bacon, for example, divides natural philosophy into two parts, of which one part, "physics, inquireth and handleth the material and efficient causes; and the other, which is metaphysics, handleth the formal and final causes." The error of his predecessors, of which he complains, is their failure to separate these two types of inquiry. The study of final causes is inappropriate in physics, he thinks.

"This misplacing," Bacon comments, "hath caused a deficiency, or at least a great improficiency in the sciences themselves. For the handling of final causes, mixed with the rest in physical inquiries, hath intercepted the severe and diligent inquiry of all real and physical causes, and given men the occasion to stay upon these satisfactory and specious causes, to the great arrest and prejudice of further discovery." On this score, he charges Plato, Aristotle, and Galen with impeding the development of science, not because "final causes are not true, and worthy to be inquired, being kept within their own province; but because their excursions into the limits of physical causes hath bred a vastness and solitude in that tract."

Such statements as "the hairs of the eyelids are for a quickset and fence about the sight," or that "the leaves of trees are for protecting of the fruit," or that "the clouds are for watering of the earth," are, in Bacon's opinion, "impertinent" in physics. He therefore praises the mechanical philosophy of Democritus. It seems to him to inquire into the "particularities of physical causes" better "than that of Aristotle and Plato, whereof both intermingled final causes, the one as a part of theology, the other as a part of logic."

As Bacon's criticisms indicate, the attack on final causes in nature raises a whole series of questions. Does every natural change serve some purpose, either for the good of the changing thing or for the order of nature itself? Is there a plan, analogous to that of an artist, which orders the parts of nature, and their activities, to one another as means to ends? A natural teleology, which attributes final causes to everything, seems to imply that every natural thing is governed by an indwelling form working toward a definite end, and that the whole of nature exhibits the working out of a divine plan or design.

Spinoza answers such questions negatively. "Nature has set no end before herself," he declares, and "all final causes are nothing but human fictions." Furthermore, he insists, "this doctrine concerning an end altogether overturns nature. For that which is in truth the cause it considers as the effect, and *vice versa*." He deplores those who "will not cease from asking the causes of causes, until at last you fly to the will of God, the refuge of ignorance."

Spinoza denies that God acts for an end and that the universe expresses a divine purpose. He also thinks that final causes are illusory even in the sphere of human action. When we say that "having a house to live in was the final cause of this or that house," we do no more than indicate a "particular desire, which is really an efficient cause, and is considered as primary, because men are usually ignorant of the causes of their desires."

Though Descartes replies to Pierre Gassendi's arguments "on behalf of final causality," by saying that they should "be referred to the efficient cause," his position more closely resembles that of Bacon than of Spinoza. When we behold "the uses of the various parts in plants and animals," we may be led to admire "the God who brings these into existence," but "that does not imply," he adds, "that we can divine the purpose for which He made each thing. And although in Ethics, where it is often allowable to employ conjecture, it is at times pious to consider the end which we may conjecture God set before Himself in ruling the universe, certainly in Physics, where everything should rest upon the securest arguments, it is futile to do so."

The elimination of final causes from natural science leads Descartes to formulate Harvey's discoveries concerning the motion of the heart and blood in purely mechanical terms. But Harvey himself, as Boyle points out in his *Disquisition About the Final Causes of Natural Things*, interprets organic structures in terms of their functional utility; and Boyle defends the soundness of Harvey's method—employing final causes—against Descartes.

Guided as it is by the principle of utility or function, Harvey's reasoning about the circulation of the blood—especially its venal and arterial flow in relation to the action of the lungs —appeals to final causes. He remarks upon the need of arguing from the final cause in his work on animal generation. "It appears advisable to me," he writes, "to look back from the perfect animal, and to inquire by what process it has arisen and grown to maturity, to retrace our steps, as it were, from the goal to the starting place."

Kant generalizes this type of argument in his *Critique of Teleological Judgement*. "No one has ever questioned," he says, "the correctness of the principle that when judging certain things in nature, namely organisms and their possibility, we must look to the conception of final causes. Such a principle is admittedly necessary even where we require no more than a *guiding-thread* for the purpose of becoming acquainted with the character of these things by means of observation." Kant criticizes a mechanism which totally excludes the principle of finality —whether it is based on the doctrine of "blind chance" of Democritus and Epicurus, or the "system of fatality" he attributes to Spinoza. Physical science, he thinks, can be extended by the principle of final causes "without interfering with the principle of the mechanism of physical causality."

THE TENDENCY TO dispense with final causes seems to prevail, however, in the science of mechanics and especially in the domain of inanimate nature. Huygens, for example, defines light as "the motion of some sort of matter." He explicitly insists that conceiving natural things in this way is the only way proper to what he calls the "true Philosophy, in which one conceives the causes of all natural effects in terms of mechanical motions."

Mechanical explanation is distinguished by the fact that it appeals to no principles except matter and motion. The material and the moving (or efficient) causes suffice. The philosophical thought of the 17th century, influenced by that century's brilliant accomplishments in mechanics, tends to be mechanistic in its theory of causation. Yet, being also influenced by the model and method of mathematics, thinkers like Descartes and Spinoza retain the formal cause as a principle of demonstration, if not of

explanation. Spinoza, in fact, claims that the reliance upon final causes "would have been sufficient to keep the human race in darkness to all eternity, if mathematics, which does not deal with ends, but with the essences and properties of forms, had not placed before us another rule of truth."

Nevertheless, the tendency to restrict causality to efficiency—a motion producing a motion —gains headway. By the time Hume questions man's ability to know causes, the term *cause* signifies only *efficiency*, understood as the energy expended in producing an effect. Hume's doubt concerning our ability to know causes presupposes this conception of cause and effect, which asserts that "there is some connection between them, some power in the one by which it infallibly produces the other." The identification of cause with the efficient type of cause becomes a commonly accepted notion, even among those who do not agree with Hume that "we are ignorant . . . of the manner in which bodies operate on each other"; and that "their force and energy is entirely incomprehensible" to us.

The narrowing of causality to efficiency also appears in the doctrine, more prevalent today than ever before, that natural science describes, but does not explain—that it tells us *how* things happen, but not *why*. If it does not require the scientist to avoid all reference to causes, it does limit him to the one type of causality which can be expressed in terms of sequences and correlations. The exclusion of all causes except the efficient tends furthermore to reduce the causal order to nothing but the relation of cause and effect.

The four causes taken together as the sufficient reason for things or events do not as such stand in relation to an effect, in the sense in which an effect is something separable from and externally related to its cause. That way of conceiving causation—as a relation of cause to effect—is appropriate to the efficient cause alone. When the efficient cause is regarded as the only cause, having a power proportionate to the reality of its effect, the very meaning of *cause* involves relation to an *effect*.

In the other conception of causation, the causal order relates the four causes to one another. Of the four causes of any change or act, the first, says Aquinas, "is the final cause; the reason of which is that matter does not receive form, save in so far as it is moved by an agent, for nothing reduces itself from potentiality to act. But an agent does not move except from the intention of an end." Hence in operation the order of the four causes is final, efficient, material, and formal; or, as Aquinas states it, "first comes goodness and the end, moving the agent to act; secondly the action of the agent moving to the form; thirdly, comes the form."

THE THEORY OF causes, as developed by Aristotle and Aquinas, proposes other distinctions beyond that of the four causes, such as the difference between the essential cause or the cause *per se* and the accidental or coincidental cause. As indicated in the chapter on CHANCE, it is in terms of coincidental causes that Aristotle speaks of chance as a cause.

A given effect may be the result of a number of efficient causes. Sometimes these form a series, as when one body in motion sets another in motion, and that moves a third; or, to take another example, a man is the cause of his grandson only through having begotten a son who later begets a son. In such a succession of causes, the first cause may be indispensable, but it is not by itself sufficient to produce the effect. With respect to the effect which it fails to produce unless other causes intervene, it is an accidental cause. In contrast, an essential cause is one which, by its operation, immediately brings the effect into existence.

Sometimes, however, a number of efficient causes may be involved simultaneously rather than successively in the production of a single effect. They may be related to one another as cause and effect rather than by mere coincidence. One cause may be the essential cause of another which in turn is the essential cause of the effect. When two causes are thus simultaneously related to the same effect, Aquinas calls one the principal, the other the instrumental cause; and he gives as an example the action of a workman sawing wood. The action of the saw causes a shaping of the wood, but it is instrumental to the operation of the principal cause, which is the action of the workman using the saw.

These two distinctions—between essential and accidental causes and between principal and instrumental causes—become of great significance in arguments, metaphysical or theological, concerning the cause of causes—a first or ultimate cause. Aristotle's proof of a prime mover, for example, depends upon the proposition that there cannot be an infinite number of causes for a given effect. But since Aristotle also holds that the world is without beginning or end and that time is infinite, it may be wondered why the chain of causes cannot stretch back to infinity.

If time is infinite, a temporal sequence of causes reaching back to infinity would seem to present no difficulty. As Descartes points out, you cannot "prove that that regress to infinity is absurd, unless you at the same time show that the world has a definite beginning in time." Though it is a matter of their Jewish and Christian faith that the world had a beginning in time, theologians like Maimonides and Aquinas do not think the world's beginning can be proved by reason. They do, however, think that the necessity of a first cause can be demonstrated, and both adopt or perhaps adapt the argument of Aristotle which relies on the impossibility of an infinite regression in causes.

The argument is valid, Aquinas makes clear, only if we distinguish between essential and accidental causes. "It is not impossible," he says, "to proceed to infinity *accidentally* as regards efficient causes. . . . It is not impossible for man to be generated by man to infinity." But, he holds, "there cannot be an infinite number of causes that are *per se* required for a certain effect; for instance, that a stone be moved by a stick, the stick by the hand, and so on to infinity." In the latter case, it should be observed, the cooperating causes are simultaneous and so if there were an infinity of them, that would not require an infinite time. The crux of the argument, therefore, lies either in the impossibility of an infinite number of simultaneous causes, or in the impossibility of an infinite number of causes related to one another as instrumental to principal cause.

Among causes so related, Descartes, like Aquinas, argues that there must be one first or principal cause. "In the case of causes which are so connected and subordinated to one another, that no action on the part of the lower is possible without the activity of the higher; *e.g.*, in the case where something is moved by a stone, itself impelled by a stick, which the hand moves . . . we must go on until we come to one thing in motion which first moves." But for Descartes, unlike Aquinas, this method of proving God as the first cause of all observable effects has less elegance than the so-called "ontological argument" in which the conception of God as a necessary being, incapable of not existing, immediately implies his existence.

The argument from effect to cause is traditionally called *a posteriori* reasoning, in contrast to *a priori* reasoning from cause to effect. According to Aristotle and Aquinas, the latter mode of reasoning can only demonstrate the nature of a thing, not its existence. Aquinas, furthermore, does not regard the ontological argument as a form of reasoning at all, but rather as the assertion that God's existence is self-evident to us, which he denies.

The various forms which these arguments take and the issue concerning their validity are more fully discussed in the chapters on BEING, GOD, and NECESSITY AND CONTINGENCY. But here it is worth noting that Kant questions whether the *a posteriori* method of proving God's existence really differs from the ontological argument. It is, according to him, not only "illusory and inadequate," but also "possesses the additional blemish of an *ignoratio elenchi*— professing to conduct us by a new road to the desired goal, but bringing us back, after a short circuit, to the old path which we had deserted at its call." Hence the causal proof does not, in Kant's opinion, succeed in avoiding the fallacies which he, along with Maimonides and Aquinas, finds in the ontological argument.

THE ANALYSIS OF CAUSATION figures critically in the speculation of the theologians concerning creation, providence, and the government of the world.

The dogma of creation, for example, requires the conception of a unique type of cause. Even if the world always existed—a supposition which, as we have seen, is contrary to Jewish and Christian faith but not to reason—the religious belief in a Creator would remain a belief in that unique cause without whose action to preserve its being at every moment the world would cease to be.

On the assumption that God created the world in the beginning, it is, perhaps, easy enough to see with Augustine how "the creating and originating work which gave being to all natures, differs from all other types of causation which cause motions or changes, or even the generation of things, rather than their very existence." It may, however, be more difficult to understand the creative action of God in relation to a world already in existence.

But a theologian like Aquinas explains that "as long as a thing has being, so long must God be present to it" as the cause of its being—a doctrine which Berkeley later reports by saying that this makes "the divine conservation . . . to be a continual creation." Aquinas agrees that "the conservation of things by God is not by a new action, but by the continuation of that action whereby He gives being." But in the conservation of things Aquinas thinks that God acts through natural or created causes, whereas in their initiation, being is the proper effect of God alone.

The dogma of divine providence also requires a theory of the cooperation of the first cause with natural or secondary causes. Dante, in describing the direction which providence gives to the course of nature, uses the image of a bow. "Whatsoever this bow shoots falls disposed to its foreseen end, even as a thing directed to its aim." That God governs and cares for all things may be supposed to reduce nature to a puppet show in which every action takes place in obedience to the divine will alone. Natural causes would thus cease to be causes or to have any genuine efficacy in the production of their own effects.

Some theologians have tended toward this extreme position, but Aquinas argues contrariwise that natural causes retain their efficacy as instrumental causes, subordinate to God's will as the one principal cause. "Since God wills that effects be because of their causes," he writes, "all effects that presuppose some other effect do not depend solely on the will of God"; and, in another place, he says, "whatsoever causes He assigns to certain effects, He gives them the power to produce those effects . . . so that the dignity of causality is imparted even to creatures."

In addition to the role of divine causality in

the regular processes of nature, still another kind of divine causation is presupposed by the religious belief in supernatural events, such as the elevation of nature by grace and the deviations from the course of nature which are called "miracles." All these considerations, and especially the matter of God's miraculous intervention in the regular course of nature, have been subjects of dispute among theologians and philosophers (and sometime physicists and historians). Some of those who do not deny the existence of a Creator, or the divine government of the universe through natural law, nevertheless question the need for divine cooperation with the action of every natural cause, or God's intervention in the order of nature.

Throughout these controversies, the theory of causes defines the issues and determines the lines of opposing argument. But since other basic notions are also involved in the debate of these issues, the further consideration of them is reserved for other chapters, especially GOD, NATURE, and WORLD.

THE DISCUSSION OF CAUSE takes a new turn in modern times. The new issues arise, not from different interpretations of the principle of causality, but from the skeptic's doubts concerning our ability to know the causes of things, and from the tendency of the physical sciences to limit or even to abandon the investigation of causes.

According to the ancient conception of science, knowledge, to be scientific, must state the causes of things. The essence of scientific method, according to the *Posterior Analytics* of Aristotle, consists in using causes both to define and to demonstrate. Sometimes genus and differentia are translated into material and formal cause; sometimes a thing is defined genetically by reference to its efficient cause, and sometimes teleologically by reference to its final cause.

The degree to which this conception of science is realized in particular fields may be questioned. The treatises of the astronomers, for example, do not seem to exemplify it as much as do Aristotle's own physical treatises or Harvey's work on the circulation of the blood. Yet until modern developments in mathematical physics, the ascertainment of causes seems to be the dominant conception of the scientific task;

and until the separation widens between the experimental and the philosophical sciences, the possibility of knowing causes is not generally doubted.

Galileo's exposition of the new mechanics explicitly announces a departure from the traditional interest of the natural philosopher in the discovery of causes. The aim, he says in his *Two New Sciences*, is not "to investigate the cause of the acceleration of natural motion, concerning which various opinions have been expressed by various philosophers"; but rather "to investigate and to demonstrate some of the properties of accelerated motion." The "various opinions" about causes are referred to as "fantasies" which it is "not really worth while" for the scientist to examine.

This attitude toward causes, especially efficient causes, characterizes the aim of mathematical physics, both in astronomy and mechanics. For Newton it is enough—in fact, he says, it "would be a very great step in philosophy"—"to derive two or three general principles of motion from phenomena ... though the causes of those principles were not yet discovered. And, therefore, I scruple not to propose the principles of motion ... and leave their causes to be found out." In other passages, Newton disparages the search for "hidden or occult causes" as no part of the business of science.

Hume goes further. He insists that all causes are hidden. By the very nature of what causes are supposed to be and because of the manner in which the human mind knows, man can have no knowledge of how causes really produce their effects. "We never can, by our utmost scrutiny," he says, "discover anything but one event following another, without being able to comprehend any force or power by which the cause operates, or any connexion between it and its supposed effect."

All that men can be referring to when they use the words "cause" and "effect," Hume thinks, is the customary sequence of "one object followed by another, and where all objects similar to the first are followed by objects similar to the second." So far as any knowledge based upon reason or experience can go, the relation of cause and effect is simply one of succession, impressed upon the mind "by a customary transition." That one event leads to another becomes more and more probable—but never more than probable—as the sequence recurs more and more frequently in experience.

Hume's skepticism about causes, and his re-interpretation of the meaning of cause, gains wide acceptance in subsequent thought, especially among natural scientists. William James, for example, considering "the principle that 'nothing can happen without a cause,'" declares that "we have no definite idea of what we mean by cause, or of what causality consists in. But the principle expresses a demand for *some* deeper sort of inward connection between phenomena than their merely habitual time-sequence seems to be. The word 'cause' is, in short, an altar to an unknown god; an empty pedestal still marking the place for a hoped-for statue. Any really inward belonging-together of the sequent terms," he continues, "if dis-covered, would be accepted as what the word cause was meant to stand for."

Though Hume holds that we cannot pene-trate beyond experience to the operation of real causes imbedded in the nature of things, he does not deny the reality of causation as a principle of nature. On the contrary, he denies that anything happens by chance or that any natural occurrence can be uncaused. "It is uni-versally allowed," Hume says with approval, "that nothing exists without a cause of its exist-ence, and that chance, when strictly examined, is a mere negative word, and means not any real power which has anywhere a being in na-ture." But "though there is no such thing as *chance* in the world, our ignorance of the real cause of any event has the same influence on the understanding, and begets a like species of belief or opinion."

In other words, Hume's position seems to be that man's ignorance of real causes, and the mere probability of his opinions about custom-ary sequences of "cause" and "effect," indicate human limitations, not limits to causal deter-mination in the order of nature itself. Adversar-ies of Hume, coming before as well as after him in the tradition of the great books, take issue with him on both points.

Against Hume's determinism, which is no less complete than Spinoza's, Aristotle, for example, affirms the existence of chance or real contingency in the happenings of nature. Against Hume's reduction of statements about causes to probable opinion, Kant insists that, in the metaphysics of nature, such judgments can be made with absolute certainty. These related issues are discussed in the chapters on CHANCE, FATE, and NECESSITY AND CONTIN-GENCY.

In the development of the natural sciences since Hume's day, his translation of cause and effect into observed sequences or correlations reinforces the tendency, which first appears with Galileo and Newton, to *describe* rather than to *explain* natural phenomena. Yet to the extent that the findings of science bear fruit in technology, man's control over nature seems to confirm Bacon's view of science rather than Hume's—at least to the extent that the appli-cation of scientific knowledge to the production of effects implies a knowledge of their causes.

THE PRINCIPLE OF CAUSALITY—that nothing happens without a cause or sufficient reason, or, as Spinoza puts it, "nothing exists from whose nature an effect does not follow"—has been made the basis for denials of human free-dom as well as of chance or contingency in the order of nature. The problem of man's free will is discussed in the chapters on FATE, LIBERTY, and WILL, but we can here observe how the problem is stated in terms of cause, with re-spect to both divine providence and natural causation.

If God's will is the cause of everything which happens, if nothing can happen contrary to His will or escape the foresight of His providence, then how is man free from God's foreordination when he chooses between good and evil? If, as the theologians say, "the very act of free choice is traced to God as to a cause," in what sense can the act be called "free"? Is it not neces-sarily determined to conform to God's will and to His plan? But, on the other hand, if "every-thing happening from the exercise of free choice must be subject to divine providence," must not the evil that men do be attributed to God as cause?

The problem takes another form for the scien-tist who thinks only in terms of natural causes, especially if he affirms a reign of causality in nature from which nothing is exempt—just as, for the theologian, nothing is exempt from God's will. Since the realm of nature includes human nature, must not human acts be caused as are all other natural events? Are some human acts free in the sense of being totally uncaused, or only in the sense of being caused differently from the motions of matter? Are causality and freedom opposed principles within the order of nature, appropriate to physical and psychological action; or do they constitute distinct realms —as for Kant, the realms of phenomena and noumena, the sensible and the supra-sensible; or as for Hegel, the realms of nature and history?

The different answers which the great books give to these questions have profound consequences for man's view of himself, the universe, and his place in it. As the issue of necessity and chance is central in physics or the philosophy of nature, so the issue of determinism and freedom is central in psychology and ethics, in political theory and the philosophy of history, and above all in theology. It makes opponents of James and Freud, of Hegel and Marx, of Hume and Kant, of Spinoza and Descartes, of Lucretius and Marcus Aurelius. It raises one of the most perplexing of all theological questions for Augustine, Aquinas, Pascal, and for the two great poets of God's will and man's freedom—Dante and Milton.

OUTLINE OF TOPICS

REFERENCES

To find the passages cited, use the numbers in heavy type, which are the volume and page numbers of the passages referred to. For example, in 4 HOMER: *Iliad*, BK II [265–283] 12d, the number 4 is the number of the volume in the set; the number 12d indicates that the passage is in section d of page 12.

PAGE SECTIONS: When the text is printed in one column, the letters a and b refer to the upper and lower halves of the page. For example, in 53 JAMES: *Psychology*, 116a–119b, the passage begins in the upper half of page 116 and ends in the lower half of page 119. When the text is printed in two columns, the letters a and b refer to the upper and lower halves of the left-hand side of the page, the letters c and d to the upper and lower halves of the right-hand side of the page. For example, in 7 PLATO: *Symposium*, 163b–164c, the passage begins in the lower half of the left-hand side of page 163 and ends in the upper half of the right-hand side of page 164.

AUTHOR'S DIVISIONS: One or more of the main divisions of a work (such as PART, BK, CH, SECT) are sometimes included in the reference; line numbers, in brackets, are given in certain cases; *e.g.*, *Iliad*, BK II [265–283] 12d.

BIBLE REFERENCES: The references are to book, chapter, and verse. When the King James and Douay versions differ in title of books or in the numbering of chapters or verses, the King James version is cited first and the Douay, indicated by a (*D*), follows; *e.g.*, OLD TESTAMENT: *Nehemiah*, 7:45—(*D*) II *Esdras*, 7:46.

SYMBOLS: The abbreviation "esp" calls the reader's attention to one or more especially relevant parts of a whole reference; "passim" signifies that the topic is discussed intermittently rather than continuously in the work or passage cited.

For additional information concerning the style of the references, see the Explanation of Reference Style; for general guidance in the use of *The Great Ideas*, consult the Preface.

1. The general theory of causation

7 PLATO: *Euthyphro*, 195c–d / *Phaedo*, 226d–228a; 240b–246c / *Timaeus*, 447b–d / *Philebus*, 615c–619d / *Laws*, BK X, 760a–765c

8 ARISTOTLE: *Posterior Analytics*, BK II, CH 11–12 128d–131b / *Physics*, BK II, CH 3–9 271a–278a,c / *Metaphysics*, BK III, CH 2 [996ª18–997ª14] 514d–515d; BK V, CH 1–2 533a–534c; BK VI, CH 2 [1026ᵇ24–1027ª15] 549a–b; BK VII, CH 17 565a–566a,c; BK VIII, CH 3 [1043ᵇ5–14] 567d–568a; CH 4 568d–569b; CH 6 569d–570d; BK X, CH 1 [1052ᵇ8–14] 579a; BK XII, CH 4–5 599d–601a; BK XIV, CH 6 625d–626d

9 ARISTOTLE: *Rhetoric*, BK I, CH 5 [1361ᵇ39–1362ª11] 602c–d; CH 10 [1369ª5–ᵇ27] 612b–613a

12 LUCRETIUS: *Nature of Things*, BK VI [703–711] 89c–d

12 AURELIUS: *Meditations*, BK V, SECT 8 269d–270b

17 PLOTINUS: *Third Ennead*, TR I, CH 1 78a–c; CH 4 79d–80a; CH 10 82b / *Fourth Ennead*, TR IV, CH 31 174d–175c / *Sixth Ennead*, TR VII, CH 2 322b–323a

19 AQUINAS: *Summa Theologica*, PART I, Q 2, A 3 12c–14a; Q 3, A 4, ANS 16d–17c; Q 33, A 1, REP 1 180d–181c; Q 49 264d–268a,c passim; Q 52, A 3, ANS 280a–d; Q 65, A 1 339b–340b;

A 3 341c–342b; Q 82, A 3, REP 1 433c–434c; Q 87, A 2, REP 3 466c–467b; Q 103, A 7 533b–d; Q 104, AA 1–2 534c–537b; Q 105, AA 1–2 538d–540c; A 5 542a–543b; Q 106, A 3 547c–548b; Q 115, AA 1–2 585d–588c; Q 115, A 6–Q 116, A 4 591d–595c

20 AQUINAS: *Summa Theologica*, PART I–II, Q 51, AA 2–3 13c–15a; Q 75, A 1 137d–138c; A 4 140a–d; Q 76, A 1 141a–c; PART III SUPPL, Q 76, A 1 939d–941a

23 HOBBES: *Leviathan*, PART I, 80b–c

30 BACON: *Advancement of Learning*, 42a–46a

31 DESCARTES: *Meditations*, III, 84b–86b / *Objections and Replies*, 111d–112a; 121b–c; AXIOM I–IV 131d; 212a; 212c

31 SPINOZA: *Ethics*, PART I, DEF 1 355a; DEF 7 355b; AXIOM 3–5 355d; PROP 3 356a; PROP 8, SCHOL 2, 357b–d; PROP 36 369b; APPENDIX 369b–372d; PART II, PROP 7, COROL and SCHOL 375a–c

34 NEWTON: *Principles*, BK III, RULE I–II 270a

35 LOCKE: *Human Understanding*, BK II, CH XXI, SECT 1–5 178b–179d; SECT 19 182b–c; CH XXII, SECT 11 203c–d; CH XXVI, SECT 1–2 217a–d

35 BERKELEY: *Human Knowledge*, SECT 25–33 417d–419a passim; SECT 60–66 424b–426a

35 HUME: *Human Understanding*, SECT III, DIV 18–SECT VIII, DIV 75 457c–485a passim

42 KANT: *Pure Reason*, 15a-b; 17c-d; 46d-47c; 57c-d; 58d-59b; 63b; 67d-68b [fn 1]; 76c-83b; 95a-d; 133a; 140b,d-143a; 152a-153a; 164a-171a; 187c-189a; 214b,d [fn 1]; 225c-226b / *Fund. Prin. Metaphysic of Morals*, 279b,d-287d esp 285c-286a / *Practical Reason*, 291a-292a; 294c-295d; 311d-314d; 339a / *Judgement*, 550a-578a esp 550a-551a,c, 555a-558b, 564a-c, 566a-b, 568c-570a, 577c-578a; 587a-591b; 592a-d; 597a-599d; 611d-613a,c

53 JAMES: *Psychology*, 885b-886a

1a. The kinds of causes: their distinction and enumeration

7 PLATO: *Phaedo*, 240c-245c / *Timaeus*, 447b-c; 455a-458a; 465d-466a / *Sophist*, 577d-578b / *Statesman*, 592d-593a; 596a-b / *Philebus*, 615c-619d; 637c-d / *Laws*, BK X, 760a-765c esp 762b-763b

8 ARISTOTLE: *Posterior Analytics*, BK I, CH 2 [71^{b}33-72^{a}6] 98b-c; BK II, CH 11 128d-129d / *Physics*, BK II, CH 3-7 271a-275d esp CH 3 271a-272c; BK III, CH 7 [207^{b}35-208^{a}4] 286c; BK IV, CH 1 [209^{a}18-23] 288a / *Generation and Corruption*, BK II, CH 9-10 436d-439c / *Metaphysics*, BK I, CH 3-10 501c-511d; BK II, CH 2 [994^{b}28-31] 513b; BK III, CH 2 [996^{a}18-^{b}26] 514d-515b; BK V, CH 2 533b-534c; CH 18 543c-d; CH 30 547a-d; BK VI, CH 2-3 548c-549d; BK VII, CH 17 565a-566a,c; BK VIII, CH 2 566d-567d; CH 3 [1043^{b}5-24] 567d-568b; CH 4 568d-569b; BK XI, CH 8 [1065^{a}26-^{b}4] 593d; BK XII, CH 4-5 599d-601a

9 ARISTOTLE: *Parts of Animals*, BK I, CH 1 [639^{b}8-642^{b}4] 161d-165d / *Generation of Animals*, BK I, CH 1 [715^{a}1-18] 255a-b; CH 20 [729^{a}10]-CH 22 [730^{b}33] 269b-271a passim; BK V, CH 1 [778^{a}16-^{b}19] 320a-321a / *Ethics*, BK III, CH 3 [1112^{a}30-33] 358b / *Rhetoric*, BK I, CH 10 [1369^{a}31-^{b}5] 612c-d

19 AQUINAS: *Summa Theologica*, PART I, Q 2, A 3 12c-14a; Q 3, A 8, REP 1 19d-20c; Q 4, A 3, ANS 22b-23b; Q 5, A 2, REP 1-2 24b-25a; A 4 25d-26c; Q 11, A 3, ANS 49a-c; Q 13, A 5, ANS and REP 1 66b-67d; Q 14, A 8, ANS and REP 1 82c-83b; A 11, ANS 84c-85c; A 16, REP 1 90b-91b; Q 19, A 6, ANS 113c-114d; Q 25, A 2, REP 2-3 144c-145b; Q 36, A 3, ANS 194c-195d; Q 39, A 2, REP 5 203b-204c; Q 44 238a-241d; Q 46, A 2, REP 7 253a-255a; Q 48, A 1, REP 4 259b-260c; Q 49, A 1, ANS 264d-265d; Q 51, A 1, REP 3 275b-276b; Q 52, A 3, ANS 280a-d; Q 65 339a-343c; Q 75, A 5, REP 3 382a-383b; Q 82, A 4, ANS 434c-435c; Q 87, A 2, REP 3 466c-467b; Q 104 534c-538c; Q 105, A 5, ANS 542a-543b; PART I-II, Q 2, A 5, REP 3 618d-619c; Q 7, A 3, ANS 653c-654b

20 AQUINAS: *Summa Theologica*, PART I-II, Q 60, A 1, ANS 49d-50c; Q 72, A 3 113b-114a; Q 75, A 1, ANS and REP 2 137d-138c; Q 76, A 1, ANS and REP 1 141a-c; Q 85, A 1, REP 4 178b-179b; A 5, ANS and REP 1 181d-182d; PART III, Q 62,

A 1 858c-859d; A 4 861a-862a; PART III SUPPL, Q 76, A 1, ANS 939d-941a

22 CHAUCER: *Tale of Melibeus*, par 37 417b

23 HOBBES: *Leviathan*, PART I, 78c-d

28 GILBERT: *Loadstone*, BK II, 36d

28 HARVEY: *On Animal Generation*, 335d; 407c; 408b; 415b-417a; 425a-429b

30 BACON: *Advancement of Learning*, 43a-d; 45a-46a

31 DESCARTES: *Meditations*, III, 87c-88c; IV, 90a-b / *Objections and Replies*, 110c-111d; AXIOM VIII 132b; 158b-161d passim, esp 158c-161b; 212a; 213b-c; 214c; 229c-d

31 SPINOZA: *Ethics*, PART I, DEF 1 355a; PROP 11 358b-359b; PROP 17, SCHOL-PROP 18 362c-363c; PROP 28, SCHOL 366a; APPENDIX 369b-372d; PART II, PROP 45, SCHOL 390b; PART III, DEF 1-3 395d-396a; PROP 1-3 396a-398c; PART IV, PREF 422b,d-424a; DEF 7 424b

35 LOCKE: *Human Understanding*, BK II, CH XXVI, SECT 2 217b-d

35 BERKELEY: *Human Knowledge*, SECT 51-53 422d-423a

36 STERNE: *Tristram Shandy*, 229b-230a

42 KANT: *Pure Reason*, 133a; 164a-171a / *Judgement*, 550a-551a,c; 553c-555a; 556b-558b; 577c-578a; 584c-d; 594b-c

46 HEGEL: *Philosophy of History*, INTRO, 165a-166b

1b. The order of causes: the relation of cause and effect

7 PLATO: *Lysis*, 24b / *Phaedrus*, 124b-c / *Euthyphro*, 195c-d / *Gorgias*, 267c-268a / *Timaeus*, 455a-b; 460c; 465d-466a / *Theaetetus*, 521b-522b / *Philebus*, 617b-c / *Laws*, BK x, 760a-765c esp 762b-763b

8 ARISTOTLE: *Categories*, CH 12 [14^{b}10-22] 20b / *Posterior Analytics*, BK I, CH 2 [71^{b}33-72^{a}6] 98b-c; BK II, CH 12 129d-131b; CH 16-18 134b-136a / *Physics*, BK II, CH 6 [198^{a}5-13] 275a; CH 8-9 275d-278a,c; BK III, CH 2 [202^{a}2]-CH 3 [202^{b}22] 279c-280c; BK VII, CH 1-2 326a-329a; BK VIII 334a-355d / *Heavens*, BK I, CH 7 [275^{a}1-^{b}29] 366a-367a / *Generation and Corruption*, BK I, CH 7 421d-423b / *Metaphysics*, BK II, CH 1 [993^{b}23]-CH 2 [994^{b}30] 512a-513b; BK V, CH 2 [1013^{b}3-16] 533c-d; [1014^{a}20-25] 534b-c; BK XI, CH 8 [1065^{b}2-4] 593d; BK XII, CH 3 [1070^{a}20-24] 599c; CH 4 [1070^{b}22-35] 600b; CH 6-8 601b-605a / *Soul*, BK I, CH 3 [406^{a}2-12] 635b-c; [406^{b}5-9] 635d-636a; CH 4 [408^{a}29-33] 638a

9 ARISTOTLE: *Parts of Animals*, BK I, CH 1 [639^{b}13-642^{a}24] 161d-165b esp [639^{b}13-32] 161d-162a; BK II, CH 1 [646^{a}25-^{b}10] 170b-c / *Motion of Animals*, CH 5 235c-d / *Generation of Animals*, BK II, CH 6 [742^{a}16-^{b}17] 283b-d / *Rhetoric*, BK I, CH 7 [1364^{a}33-36] 606a; BK II, CH 23 [1400^{a}28-35] 649a-b

10 GALEN: *Natural Faculties*, BK I, CH 2, 168b-c; CH 4 169a

(1. *The general theory of causation.* 1b. *The order of causes: the relation of cause and effect.*)

16 KEPLER: *Epitome*, BK IV, 854b; 940b-941a

17 PLOTINUS: *Fifth Ennead*, TR II, CH I 214c-215a / *Sixth Ennead*, TR VII, CH 2 322b-323a

18 AUGUSTINE: *City of God*, BK XII, CH 24–25 358a-359a; BK XXII, CH 2 587b-588a; CH 24 609a-612a

19 AQUINAS: *Summa Theologica*, PART I, Q 2, A 3 12c-14a; Q 3, A 1, ANS 14b-15b; A 2, ANS 15c-16a; A 4, ANS 16d-17c; A 6, ANS 18c-19a; A 7, ANS and REP I 19a-c; A 8, ANS and REP 1–2 19d-20c; Q 4, A 2, ANS 21b-22b; A 3, ANS and REP 4 22b-23b; Q 5, A 2, REP I 24b-25a; A 4, ANS 25d-26c; Q 8, A I 34d-35c; Q 13, A 5, ANS and REP I 66b-67d; A II, REP 2 73c-74b; Q 18, A 3, ANS 106b-107c; Q 19, AA 4–5 111c-113c; A 6, ANS and REP 3 113c-114d; A 7, REP 2 114d-115d; A 8 116a-d; Q 22, AA 2–3 128d-131c; Q 23, A 5, ANS 135d-137d; Q 36, A 3, ANS and REP 4 194c-195d; Q 39, A 2, REP 5 203b-204c; Q 41, A I, REP 2 217d-218c; A 2, ANS 218c-219d; Q 42, A 2, ANS 225d-227a; A 3, ANS and REP 2 227a-d; Q 44, A I, REP I 238b-239a; A 2 239b-240a; Q 45, A 2, REP 2 242d-244a; A 3 244a-d; A 5, ANS 245c-247a; Q 46, A I, REP 6 250a-252d; A 2, REP I 253a-255a; Q 48, A I, REP 4 259b-260c; Q 50, A I, ANS 269b-270a; Q 52, A 3, ANS 280a-d; Q 63, A 8, REP I 332c-333b; Q 65, A 3 341c-342b; Q 75, A I, REP I 378b-379c; Q 82, A 3, REP I 433c-434c; A 4 434c-435c; Q 87, A 2, REP 3 466c-467b; Q 88, A 3, REP 2 472c-473a; Q 90, A 3 482c-483a; Q 103, AA 6–8 532b-534b; Q 104, A I, ANS 534c-536c; A 2 536c-537b; Q 105 538d-545b; Q 112, A I, ANS 571d-573a; Q 114, A 3, ANS 583b-d; QQ 115–116 585c-595c; Q 118, A 2, REP 3 601c-603b; PART I–II, Q I, A 2 610b-611b; Q 46, A I, ANS 813b-814a

20 AQUINAS: *Summa Theologica*, PART I–II, Q 66, A 6, REP 3 80c-81b; Q 75, A 4 140a-d; Q 112, AA 1–3 356c-358d; Q 113, A 8 367d-368c; PART II–II, Q I, A 7, REP 3 385c-387a; Q 9, A 2, ANS 424b-425a; PART III, Q 6, A I, ANS 740b-741b; A 5, ANS 744a-d; Q 18, A I, REP 2 810a-811c; Q 19, A I, ANS and REP 2 816a-818b; Q 62 858b-864c passim; Q 64, A I, ANS 870c-871b; A 8, REP I 876c-877c; PART III SUPPL, Q 70, A 3, ANS 897d-900d; Q 74, A 3, REP 2 927c-928d; Q 76, A I, REP I 939d-941a; A 2 941b-942b; Q 80, A I, REP I 956c-957c; Q 86, A 3, REP 2 994d-996a,c

21 DANTE: *Divine Comedy*, PARADISE, II [112–148] 109a-b

22 CHAUCER: *Tale of Melibeus*, par 37 417b

23 HOBBES: *Leviathan*, PART I, 78c-79a; 79d-80a

28 GALILEO: *Two New Sciences*, FIRST DAY, 135c-136b

28 HARVEY: *On Animal Generation*, 390c; 415b-416c; 426a-429b; 442c-443c; 445c; 447a-b

30 BACON: *Advancement of Learning*, 43a-d

31 DESCARTES: *Discourse*, PART V, 55d-56a / *Meditations*, III, 84b-86b; 87c-88c / *Objections and Replies*, 110a-112a esp 111d-112a; 120b-121c; AXIOM I–V 131d-132a; AXIOM VIII 132b; PROP II 132c; 158b-161d passim; 212a; 213b-d; 229c-d

31 SPINOZA: *Ethics*, PART I, DEF I 355a; AXIOM 3–5 355d; PROP 3 356a; PROP 8, SCHOL 2, 357b-d; PROP II 358b-359b; PROP 21–29 364a-366c esp PROP 28 365c-366a; PROP 33 367b-369a; PROP 36 369b; APPENDIX 369b-372d; PART II, DEF 5 373b-c; DEF 7 373c; PROP 7, COROL and SCHOL 375a-c; LEMMA 3 378d-379a; PROP 48, DEMONST 391a; PART III, DEF 2–3 395d-396a; PROP 1–3 396a-398c; PART V, AXIOM 2 452c

32 MILTON: *Paradise Lost*, BK V [469–490] 185b-186a

33 PASCAL: *Pensées*, 505 261a-b / *Vacuum*, 369a

34 NEWTON: *Principles*, BK III, RULE I–II 270a

35 LOCKE: *Human Understanding*, BK II, CH XXI, SECT 1–5 178b-179d; SECT 19 182b-c; CH XXII, SECT II 203c-d; CH XXVI, SECT 1–2 217a-d

35 BERKELEY: *Human Knowledge*, SECT 25–33 417d-419a passim; SECT 65–66 425d-426a

35 HUME: *Human Understanding*, SECT III, DIV 18–SECT VIII, DIV 75 457c-485a passim, esp SECT VII, DIV 60 477a-c; SECT XI 497b-503c passim, esp DIV 105 498d-499a

42 KANT: *Pure Reason*, 15a-b; 17c-d; 47b-c; 57c-d; 58d-59b; 63b; 67d-68b [fn I]; 76c-83b esp 81c-d; 95a-d; 140b,d-145c; 152a-153a; 187c-189c; 214b,d [fn I] / *Practical Reason*, 311d-314d; 339a / *Judgement*, 550a-551a,c; 553c-555a; 561c-562a,c; 577c-578a; 582c-583b

45 FARADAY: *Researches in Electricity*, 582b-584a passim

49 DARWIN: *Origin of Species*, 9b-c; 10d; 65a-66a / *Descent of Man*, 285b-c

51 TOLSTOY: *War and Peace*, BK X, 447c-448d; BK XI, 470a-c; EPILOGUE I, 650b-c; EPILOGUE II 675a-696d

53 JAMES: *Psychology*, 772b; 884b-885a

2. **Comparison of causes in animate and inanimate nature**

7 PLATO: *Phaedo*, 241d-242b / *Laws*, BK X, 763a-765d

8 ARISTOTLE: *Physics*, BK II, CH 8–9 275d-278a,c; BK VIII, CH 2 [252^{b}16–28] 336c-d; [253^{a}6–21] 337a-b; CH 4 [254^{b}12–33] 339a-b / *Heavens*, BK II, CH 12 383b-384c / *Meteorology*, BK IV, CH 12 493d-494d / *Metaphysics*, BK V, CH 2 [1014^{b}20–26] 535a; BK VII, CH 9 [1034^{a}32–^{b}8] 557c-d; CH 10 [1035^{b}14–28] 559a-b; CH 16 [1040^{b}5–16] 564c; BK IX, CH 2 571c-572a; CH 5 573a-c; CH 7 [1049^{a}12–19] 574d / *Soul*, BK II, CH 4 [415^{b}8–28] 645d-646a; BK III, CH 9–13 664d-668d / *Sleep*, CH 2 [455^{b}13–28] 698b-c

9 ARISTOTLE: *Parts of Animals*, BK I, CH I [639^{b}12–642^{a}14] 161d-165b / *Gait of Animals*, CH 2 [704^{b}12–18] 243c / *Generation of Animals*, BK I, CH I [715^{a}1–7] 255a; BK II, CH I [734^{a}17–735^{a}4] 274c-275c

10 GALEN: *Natural Faculties*, BK I, CH 12 172d-173c; CH 14–17 177a-183d; BK II, CH I–7 183b,d-191b passim; CH 9, 197b

12 LUCRETIUS: *Nature of Things*, BK II [700–729] 23d-24b

16 KEPLER: *Epitome*, BK IV, 930b-931b; 959a-960a

19 AQUINAS: *Summa Theologica*, PART I, Q 8, A I, REP 3 34d-35c; Q 14, A 8, ANS 82c-83b; Q 18, A 3, ANS 106b-107c; Q 22, A 2, ANS 128d-130d; Q 70, A 3 365b-367a; Q 98, A I, ANS 516c-517c; PART I–II, Q I, A 2 610b-611b

20 AQUINAS: *Summa Theologica*, PART III SUPPL, Q 75, A 3, REP 4 938a-939d

21 DANTE: *Divine Comedy*, PURGATORY, XVIII [19–39] 80a-b; PARADISE, I [94–142] 107b-d; II [112–148] 109a-b

23 HOBBES: *Leviathan*, PART I, 50a; PART IV, 271d

27 SHAKESPEARE: *Othello*, ACT V, SC II [7–14] 239a

28 HARVEY: *On Animal Generation*, 385a-c

31 DESCARTES: *Meditations*, IV, 90a-b / *Objections and Replies*, 215a-b

34 NEWTON: *Principles*, BK III, RULE I–II 270a

35 LOCKE: *Human Understanding*, BK II, CH XXIII, SECT 28–29 211b-212a

42 KANT: *Judgement*, 555a-558b esp 557c-558b; 564a-c; 566a-b; 578d-580a; 581a-582c

45 FARADAY: *Researches in Electricity*, 540a-541a,c

49 DARWIN: *Origin of Species*, 9b-10d

53 JAMES: *Psychology*, 4a-6b; 84a-94b esp 85a-87b, 88b-90b

3. Causality and freedom

8 ARISTOTLE: *Metaphysics*, BK IX, CH 5 573a-c

9 ARISTOTLE: *Ethics*, BK III, CH 3 [1112^{a}18–^{b}12] 358a-c / *Rhetoric*, BK I, CH 10 [1368^{b}7–1369^{b}27] 611d-613a

12 LUCRETIUS: *Nature of Things*, BK II [251–293] 18b-d; BK V [306–310] 65a

12 AURELIUS: *Meditations*, BK V, SECT 8 269d-270b

15 TACITUS: *Annals*, BK III, 49c; BK IV, 69a; BK VI, 91b-d

17 PLOTINUS: *Third Ennead*, TR I 78a-82b esp CH 4 79d-80a, CH 9–10 82a-b

18 AUGUSTINE: *City of God*, BK V, CH 9–10 213b-216c

19 AQUINAS: *Summa Theologica*, PART I, Q 19, AA 3–10 110b-118b passim; Q 41, A 2 218c-219d; Q 46, A I, REP 9–10 250a-252d; Q 47, A I, REP I 256a-257b; Q 59, A 3 308b-309a; Q 62, A 8, REP 2 323c-324a; Q 83, A I 436d-438a; Q 103, A I, REP I,3 528b-529a; Q 115, A 6, ANS 591d-592d; PART I–II, Q 10 662d-666a,c; Q 13, A 6 676c-677b

20 AQUINAS: *Summa Theologica*, PART I–II, Q 71, A 4, ANS and REP 3 108b-109a

21 DANTE: *Divine Comedy*, PURGATORY, XVI [52–84] 77b-d

22 CHAUCER: *Troilus and Cressida*, BK IV, STANZA 138–154 106b-108b / *Nun's Priest's Tale* [15,238–256] 456b-457a

23 HOBBES: *Leviathan*, PART II, 112d-113c

25 MONTAIGNE: *Essays*, 452a-d

26 SHAKESPEARE: *Julius Caesar*, ACT I, SC II [135–141] 570d

31 SPINOZA: *Ethics*, PART I, DEF 7 355b; PROP 16–17 362a-363c; PROP 26–36 365b-369b; APPENDIX 369b-372d; PART II, PROP 48–49 391a-394d; PART III, 395a-d; PART IV, PREF, 423b-c

33 PASCAL: *Provincial Letters*, 154b-159a / *Pensées*, 821 331b-332a

35 LOCKE: *Human Understanding*, BK I, CH II, SECT 14, 108d-109a; BK II, CH XXI, SECT 7–27 180a-184c; SECT 48–53 190c-192b

35 HUME: *Human Understanding*, SECT VIII 478b-487a

38 ROUSSEAU: *Inequality*, 337d-338a

42 KANT: *Pure Reason*, 113b-115a; 132d-133a; 140b,d-145c; 164a-171a; 234c-235a; 236d-237a; 238b / *Fund. Prin. Metaphysic of Morals*, 264d-265a; 275b; 279b,d-287d esp 282c, 286a-c / *Practical Reason*, 292a-293b; 296a-d; 301d-302d; 310b-321b esp 314b-d, 320c-321b; 327d-329a; 331c-337a,c / *Intro. Metaphysic of Morals*, 383c / 386b-387a,c; 390b; 392d-393c / *Judgement*, 463a-465c; 571c-572a; 587a-588a; 594d [fn 1]

44 BOSWELL: *Johnson*, 392d-393a

46 HEGEL: *Philosophy of Right*, PART I, par 39 21d; par 66, 29a; PART II, par 139 48d-49b; PART III, par 187 65a-c; par 352 112b; ADDITIONS, 90 130b-d / *Philosophy of History*, INTRO, 160c-164d; 170c-172b; 178a-d

48 MELVILLE: *Moby Dick*, 158b-159a

51 TOLSTOY: *War and Peace*, BK IX, 342a-344b; BK X, 389a-391c; BK XI, 469a-472b; BK XIII, 563a-572a; BK XV, 619d-621b; EPILOGUE I, 645a-650c; EPILOGUE II, 688a-696d

53 JAMES: *Psychology*, 84a-94b esp 85a-87b, 88b-90b; 291a-295b; 388a; 820b-826a esp 825b-826b [fn 2]

54 FREUD: *Origin and Development of Psycho-Analysis*, 13c / *General Introduction*, 454b-c; 486c-487a

4. The analysis of means and ends in the practical order

7 PLATO: *Lysis*, 23a-b / *Laches*, 29b-c / *Gorgias*, 262a-264b; 280b-d / *Republic*, BK II, 310c-d

8 ARISTOTLE: *Topics*, BK III, CH I [116^{b}22–36] 163b-c / *Heavens*, BK II, CH 12 [292^{a}14–^{b}26] 383d-384b / *Metaphysics*, BK II, CH 2 [994^{b}8–16] 512b-513a; BK V, CH 2 [1013^{a}32–^{b}3] 533c; [1013^{b}25–28] 533d-534a; BK IX, CH 8 [1050^{a}4–^{b}1] 575d-576b / *Soul*, BK III, CH 10 665d-666d

(4. The analysis of means and ends in the practical order.)

5. Cause in relation to knowledge

5a. Cause as the object of our inquiries

6. The existence and operation of final causes

7 PLATO: *Phaedo*, 241b-242b / *Timaeus*, 447d-448a; 465d-466a

8 ARISTOTLE: *Posterior Analytics*, BK II, CH 11 [94^{b}8-95^{a}9] 129b-d / *Physics*, BK I, CH 9 [192^{a}16-24] 268b-c; BK II, CH 1 [193^{b}12-19] 269d-270a; CH 2 [194^{a}27-^{b}8] 270d-271a; CH 3 [194^{b}33-195^{a}2] 271b-c; [195^{a}22-26] 271d; CH 8-9 275d-278a,c / *Heavens*, BK II, CH 12 [292^{a}14-^{b}26] 383d-384b / *Meteorology*, BK IV, CH 12 [389^{b}22-390^{b}2] 493d-494c / *Metaphysics*, BK I, CH 2 [982^{b}4-11] 500d; CH 7 [988^{b}6-15] 506c-d; CH 9 [992^{a}29-34] 510c; BK II, CH 2 [994^{b}8-16] 512d-513a; BK III, CH 2 [996^{a}22-36] 514d-515a; BK V, CH 2 [1013^{a}33-^{b}2] 533c; CH 4 [1014^{b}34-1015^{a}10] 535b; BK XII, CH 7 [1072^{b}1-4] 602c; CH 10 [1075^{a}12-^{b}16] 605d-606c / *Soul*, BK II, CH 4 [415^{b}15-22] 645d-646a; CH 8 [420^{b}16-23] 652a; BK III, CH 9 [432^{b}21-26] 665b-c; CH 12-13 667a-668d passim / *Sleep*, CH 2 [455^{b}13-28] 698b-c

9 ARISTOTLE: *Parts of Animals*, BK I, CH 1 [639^{b}8-640^{a}12] 161d-162b; [641^{b}10-642^{b}4] 164c-165d; CH 5 [645^{a}23-26] 169a; BK II-IV 170a-229d passim, esp BK II, CH 1 [646^{a}25-^{b}27] 170b-d, BK III, CH 2 [663^{b}22-23] 191b, BK IV, CH 2 [677^{a}15-19] 206d-207a / *Gait of Animals*, CH 2 [704^{b}12-18] 243c; CH 12 249b-d passim / *Generation of Animals*, BK I, CH 1 [715^{a}1-11] 255a; CH 4-13 257a-260b; BK II, CH 5 [741^{b}2-4] 282c; CH 6 [742^{a}16-^{b}17] 283b-d; [744^{a}36-^{b}28] 285c-286a; BK III, CH 4 296b-c; BK IV, CH 3 [767^{b}6-15] 309a; BK V, CH 1 [778^{a}15-^{b}19] 320a-321a; CH 8 [788^{b}22-789^{b}15] 330c-331a,c / *Politics*, BK I, CH 2 [1252^{b}30-1253^{a}1] 446a-b; CH 8 [1256^{b}8-26] 450b-c

10 GALEN: *Natural Faculties*, BK I, CH 6, 170b-c; CH 10 171b-172b; CH 12 172d-173c; CH 13, 174d-175c; BK II, CH 3 185a-186d; CH 4, 187c; BK III, CH 1 199a-c; CH 3 200a-201a

12 LUCRETIUS: *Nature of Things*, BK I [1022-1037] 13c-d; BK II [1052-1063] 28b-c; BK IV [823-857] 55a-b; BK V [76-90] 62a-b; [156-234] 63a-64a

12 AURELIUS: *Meditations*, BK V, SECT 8 269d-270b; BK VI, SECT 40 277d

16 COPERNICUS: *Revolutions of the Heavenly Spheres*, BK I, 511b

16 KEPLER: *Epitome*, BK IV, 846b-847a; 857b-860b; 863b-887a passim; 913a-b; 915b-916a; 925b-928a; 932a-933a / *Harmonies of the World*, 1023b-1080b esp 1049b-1050a

17 PLOTINUS: *Second Ennead*, TR II, CH 1 40a-41a / *Fifth Ennead*, TR VIII, CH 7 242d-243c

18 AUGUSTINE: *City of God*, BK XI, CH 22 333d-334c; BK XII, CH 4-5 344b-345b; BK XIX, CH 12-14, 518c-520c; BK XXII, CH 24, 610c-611c

19 AQUINAS: *Summa Theologica*, PART I, Q 2, A 3, ANS and REP 2 12c-14a; Q 5, A 2, REP 1-2 24b-25a; A 4 25d-26c; Q 6, A 1, REP 2 28b-d;

Q 18, A 3, ANS 106b-107c; Q 19, A 1, ANS 108d-109c; A 4, ANS 111c-112c; Q 22, A 2, ANS 128d-130d; Q 23, A 1, ANS and REP 1-2 132c-133b; Q 36, A 3, ANS 194c-195d; Q 44, A 4 241a-d; Q 48, A 1, REP 4 259b-260c; Q 59, A 1, ANS 306c-307b; Q 60, A 5, ANS 313b-314c; Q 65, A 2 340b-341b; Q 70, A 3, ANS 365b-367a; Q 76, A 5, ANS 394c-396a; Q 78, A 1, REP 3 407b-409a; Q 82, A 4, ANS 434c-435c; Q 85, A 3, REP 1 455b-457a; Q 91, A 3 486b-487d; Q 92, A 1, REP 1 488d-489d; Q 98, A 1, ANS 516d-517c; Q 103 528a-534b passim; Q 105, A 5, ANS 542a-543b; PART I-II, Q 1, A 2 610b-611b; A 3, ANS and REP 3 611b-612a; A 6, ANS 614a-c; A 8 615a-c; Q 2, A 5, REP 3 618d-619c; Q 8, A 1, ANS 655b-656a; Q 9, A 1, ANS 657d-658d; Q 12, A 5, ANS 672a-c; Q 21, A 1, ANS and REP 1-2 717a-d

20 AQUINAS: *Summa Theologica*, PART III SUPPL, Q 75, A 3, ANS and REP 4 938a-939d

21 DANTE: *Divine Comedy*, PURGATORY, XVIII [19-39] 80a-b; PARADISE, I [94-142] 107b-d

23 HOBBES: *Leviathan*, PART I, 50a; PART IV, 271d

28 HARVEY: *Motion of the Heart*, 302c / *Circulation of the Blood*, 309b-d / *On Animal Generation*, 349a-b; 355c-d; 390b-c; 402c; 418b-c; 439c-440a; 442d-443c; 447a-b; 453c; 454b-c; 461a-c; 462c-d

30 BACON: *Advancement of Learning*, 43a-d; 45a-46a / *Novum Organum*, BK I, APH 48 110d-111a

31 DESCARTES: *Discourse*, PART II, 44c-45a / *Meditations*, IV, 90a-b / *Objections and Replies*, 215a-b

31 SPINOZA: *Ethics*, PART I, APPENDIX 369b-372d; PART IV, PREF 422b,d-424a; DEF 7 424b

33 PASCAL: *Pensées*, 72, 184b; 75 185b-186a

34 NEWTON: *Principles*, BK III, GENERAL SCHOL, 371a / *Optics*, BK III, 528b-529a

35 LOCKE: *Human Understanding*, BK II, CH I, SECT 15, 125b

35 BERKELEY: *Human Knowledge*, SECT 60-66 424b-426a passim; SECT 107 433d-434a

35 HUME: *Human Understanding*, SECT V, DIV 44, 469b-c; SECT XI, DIV III 501b-c

36 STERNE: *Tristram Shandy*, 229b-230a

42 KANT: *Pure Reason*, 187a-190a; 205a-209b; 239a-240b / *Judgement*, 467d-470b; 473a-474b; 523c-d; 550a-613a,c esp 550a-562a,c, 568c-570b, 575b-578a, 587a-588a

46 HEGEL: *Philosophy of History*, INTRO, 157b-c; 161d-162a

49 DARWIN: *Origin of Species*, 40c-d; 41c-42a; 60b-61d passim; 95d-97a esp 96b; 217d-218a / *Descent of Man*, 593d

51 TOLSTOY: *War and Peace*, EPILOGUE I, 646c-647b; 650b-c; EPILOGUE II, 687d-688a

53 JAMES: *Psychology*, 4a-6b; 671b [fn 1]

54 FREUD: *Narcissism*, 401b / *Instincts*, 415b / *Beyond the Pleasure Principle*, 651d-654c passim, esp 654a-c

7. The causality of God or the gods

7a. Divine causality in the origin and existence of the world: creation and conservation

7b. Divine causality in the order of nature or change: the first cause in relation to all other causes

18 AUGUSTINE: *Confessions*, BK I, par 10 3b-c; BK VII, par 16–23 48c-50c / *City of God*, BK VII, CH 29–31 261a-262a; BK X, CH 14 307c-308a; BK XI, CH 22 333d-334c; BK XII, CH 25 358b-359a; BK XIX, CH 12–17 517b-523a; BK XXII, CH 24 609a-612a

19 AQUINAS: *Summa Theologica*, PART I, Q 2, A 3 12c-14a; Q 3, A I, ANS 14b-15b; A 2, ANS 15c-16a; A 4, ANS 16d-17c; A 6, ANS 18c-19a; A 7, ANS and REP 1 19a-c; A 8, ANS and REP 1–2 19d-20c; Q 4 20c-23b; Q 12, A I, ANS 50c-51c; Q 18, A 3, ANS 106b-107c; Q 19, A 5 112d-113c; Q 23, A I, ANS and REP 1–2 132c-133b; Q 46, A 2, REP 7 253a-255a; Q 47, AA 1–2 256a-258c; Q 49, A 2 266a-c; Q 51, A I, REP 3 275b-276b; A 3, REP 3 277a-278c; Q 52, A 2 279b-280a; Q 60, A I, REP 2–3 310b-311a; Q 75, A I, REP I 378b-379c; Q 76, A 5, REP I 394c-396a; Q 83, A I, REP 3 436d-438a; Q 84, A 2, ANS 442b-443c; A 4, REP I 444d-446b; A 5 446c-447c; Q 88, A 3, REP 2 472c-473a; Q 89, A I, REP 3 473b-475a; Q 92, A I, REP I 488d-489d; A 2, REP 2 489d-490c; A 4 491b-d; Q 94, A 3, ANS 504a-505a; QQ 104–105 534c-545b; Q 116 592d-595c; PART I–II, Q 2, A 3, ANS 617b-618a; A 5, REP 3 618d-619c; Q 6, A I, REP 3 644d-646a; Q 9, A 6 662a-d; Q 12, A 5, ANS 672a-c; Q 17, A 8, REP 2 692a-c

20 AQUINAS: *Summa Theologica*, PART I–II, Q 79, A 2, ANS 157b-158a; Q 85, A 6 182d-184a; Q 109, A I, ANS 338b-339c; Q 110, A I, REP 2 347d-349a; PART II–II, Q 9, A 2, ANS 424b-425a; Q 18, A 4, ANS 464c-465a; PART III, Q 6, A I, REP I 740b-741b; Q 13, A 3, CONTRARY 782b-783b; PART III SUPPL, Q 74, A 2, REP 3 926c-927c

21 DANTE: *Divine Comedy*, PARADISE, I [94–142] 107b-d; II [112–148] 109a-b; XIII [52–84] 126a-b; XXVII [97–120] 148b-c

22 CHAUCER: *Knight's Tale* [2987–3040] 209a-210a / *Tale of Melibeus*, par 37–38 417b-418a

23 HOBBES: *Leviathan*, PART I, 78d-79a; 79d-80a; PART III, 241c-242a; PART IV, 272b-c

28 HARVEY: *On Animal Generation*, 390d-391a; 406b-407b; 416b-c; 426a-429b; 443a-c; 490d-493a

30 BACON: *Advancement of Learning*, 2c-d; 4b-c / *New Atlantis*, 203a-b

31 DESCARTES: *Discourse*, PART V, 55d-56a / *Meditations*, III, 87c-88c; IV, 90a-b / *Objections and Replies*, 110a; 123b; AXIOM IX 132b; 158a-162a; 213b-d; 229c-d

31 SPINOZA: *Ethics*, PART I, PROP 16–18 362a-363c; PROP 24–29 365a-366c; PROP 33 367b-369a; APPENDIX 369b-372d; PART II, PROP 5–7 374c-375c; PROP 9–10 376a-377a; PROP 45 390a-b

32 MILTON: *Paradise Lost*, BK V [468–474] 185b

33 PASCAL: *Pensées*, 77 186a; 513, 262a

34 NEWTON: *Principles*, BK III, GENERAL SCHOL, 369b-371a / *Optics*, BK III, 528b-529a

35 LOCKE: *Human Understanding*, BK II, CH XXI, SECT 2 178c; CH XXIII, SECT 28 211b-d; BK IV, CH III, SECT 28–29 322a-323a

35 BERKELEY: *Human Knowledge*, SECT 25–33 417d-419a passim, esp SECT 29–33 418c-419a; SECT 51–53 422d-423a; SECT 57 423d-424a; SECT 60–66 424b-426a; SECT 105–109 433b-434b passim; SECT 146–153 442a-444a passim, esp SECT 150 442d-443b

35 HUME: *Human Understanding*, SECT VII, DIV 54–57 474b-475d

42 KANT: *Pure Reason*, 140b,d-145c; 164a-165c; 171a-172c; 177b-179b; 183b [fn 1]; 184b-c; 187a-189c esp 188c-189a; 190a-b; 191a-d; 205a-209a; 239a-240b / *Practical Reason*, 334b-335c; 345a-c / *Judgement*, 564a-567b; 572b-578a; 581b-582c; 587a-592d; 597a-599d

46 HEGEL: *Philosophy of History*, INTRO, 161d-162a; PART I, 245d-246c

48 MELVILLE: *Moby Dick*, 396b-397a

49 DARWIN: *Origin of Species*, 243b-d

7c. Divine causality in the government of the universe: providence and free will

OLD TESTAMENT: *Genesis*, 1–3; 4:5-7; 6–9 esp 8:21-22; 12–13 esp 12:1-3, 12:7, 13:14-18; 15 esp 15:13-21; 17–18; 21–22 esp 22:1-19; 26:1-6,22-25; 28:10-22; 35:9-15; 37–50 esp 45:7-8 / *Exodus*, 3; 4:21; 7–14 esp 7:3, 9:12, 10:1, 10:20, 10:27, 11:10, 12:1-51, 13:21-22, 14:4, 14:8, 14:17; 15:18; 19–20 esp 19:3-9; 23:20-33; 33:18-19; 40:34-38—(D) *Exodus*, 3; 4:21; 7–14 esp 7:3, 9:12, 10:1, 10:20, 10:27, 11:10, 12:1-51, 13:21-22, 14:4, 14:8, 14:17; 15:18; 19–20 esp 19:3-9; 23:20-33; 33:18-19; 40:32-36 / *Numbers*, 9:15-23; 12; 22–24 / *Deuteronomy*, 4:1-40; 5–11 esp 11:26-28; 29:1-31:8 esp 30:1-4, 30:19-20 / *Joshua*, 1–11; 23–24 esp 24:14-28—(D) *Josue*, 1–11; 23–24 esp 24:14-28 / *Judges*, 1–16 / *I Samuel*, 8–10; 15–16—(D) *I Kings*, 8–10; 15–16 / *II Samuel*, 7—(D) *II Kings*, 7 / *I Kings*, 11; 13–22 passim—(D) *III Kings*, 11; 13–22 passim / *II Kings* passim —(D) *IV Kings* passim / *I Chronicles*, 17:4-14; 29:11-12—(D) *I Paralipomenon*, 17:4-14; 29:11-12 / *II Chronicles*, 11–36 passim, esp 36— (D) *II Paralipomenon*, 11–36 passim, esp 36 / *Esther* esp 4:12-17—(D) *Esther*, 1:1-10:3 esp 4:12-17 / *Job* esp 1–2, 24, 27, 38–41 / *Psalms* passim, esp 3-4, 9-11, 13, 17-18, 20, 23, 65, 104—(D) *Psalms* passim, esp 3-4, 9-10, 12, 16-17, 19, 22, 64, 103 / *Proverbs*, 16:33 / *Ecclesiastes*, 3; 8–9; 11–12 / *Isaiah*, 36–37; 46; 51; 52:7—(D) *Isaias*, 36–37; 46; 51; 52:7 / *Jeremiah*, 17:5-8; 18–19; 31; 45—(D) *Jeremias*, 17:5-8; 18–19; 31; 45 / *Ezekiel*, 18—(D) *Ezechiel*, 18 / *Daniel* esp 3, 6—(D) *Daniel*, 1:1-3:23 esp 3:1-23; 3:91-12:13 esp 3:91-97, 6:1-28 / *Jonah*, 1–2—(D) *Jonas*, 1–2

APOCRYPHA: *Tobit*—(D) OT, *Tobias* / *Judith* esp 5–6, 8–16—(D) OT, *Judith* esp 5–6, 8–16 / *Rest of Esther*—(D) OT, *Esther*, 10:4-16:24 /

(7. *The causality of God or the gods. 7c. Divine causality in the government of the universe: providence and free will.*)

Ecclesiasticus, 15:11-20—(D) OT, *Ecclesiasticus*, 15:11-22 / *Song of Three Children*—(D) OT, *Daniel*, 3:24-90 / *Susanna*—(D) OT, *Daniel*, 13:1-64 / *Bel and Dragon*—(D) OT, *Daniel*, 13:65-14:42 / *I Maccabees*, 3:13-26—(D) OT, *I Maccabees*, 3:13-26 / *II Maccabees*, 6:1-16—(D) OT, *II Maccabees*, 6:1-16

NEW TESTAMENT: *Matthew*, 6:25-34; 10:29-33; 23:37 / *Luke*, 12:4-7,22-34; 21:12-19 esp 21:18 / *John*, 6:22-71 esp 6:40, 6:44-45, 6:64-65— (D) *John*, 6:22-72 esp 6:40, 6:44-45, 6:65-66 / *Acts*, 6:8-7:60 esp 7:51; 13:48—(D) *Acts*, 6:8-7:59 esp 7:51; 13:48 / *Romans*, 8:28-11:36 / *Ephesians*, 1:4-2:10; 4:1-7 / *Philippians*, 2:12-13 / *II Timothy*, 1:9 / *Hebrews*, 13:5-6 / *I Peter*, 1:1-5 / *Revelation*, 11:15-18—(D) *Apocalypse*, 11:15-18

4 HOMER: *Iliad*, BK VIII [130-144] 52c; BK XXIV [522-551] 176d-177a

5 EURIPIDES: *Helen* [703-733] 304d-305a

6 HERODOTUS: *History*, BK III, 112d-113b

7 PLATO: *Republic*, BK II, 321d-322d; BK X, 439b / *Critias*, 479c

8 ARISTOTLE: *Generation and Corruption*, BK II, CH 10 [336ᵇ25-34] 438d / *Metaphysics*, BK XII, CH 10 605d-606d

9 ARISTOTLE: *Ethics*, BK X, CH 8 [1179ᵃ23-32] 434a / *Politics*, BK VII, CH 4 [1326ᵃ29-32] 530b-c

12 LUCRETIUS: *Nature of Things*, BK II [167-183] 17a-b; [1090-1104] 29a; BK V [146-234] 63a-64a; [1161-1240] 76b-77b; BK VI [43-95] 80d-81c; [379-422] 85b-d

12 EPICTETUS: *Discourses*, BK I, CH 6 110c-112b; CH 12 118d-120b; CH 16 121d-122d; BK II, CH 14 153d-155b; BK III, CH 17 191d-192a; CH 22 195a-201a; BK IV, CH 3 224b-d; CH 5 228a-230b; CH 7 232c-235a

12 AURELIUS: *Meditations*, BK II, SECT 3 257a-b; SECT 11 258a-b; BK III, SECT 11 262a-b; BK V, SECT 8 269d-270b; BK VI, SECT 8 274b; SECT 11 274c; SECT 40-45 277d-278c; SECT 58 279d; BK VII, SECT 8 280b; SECT 58 283c-d; SECT 68 284c-d; BK VIII, SECT 17 286d; SECT 35 288b; SECT 46-47 289b-c; SECT 51 289d-290a; BK X, SECT 3 296d; SECT 6 297a-b; SECT 25 299c; SECT 35 301b; BK XII, SECT 3 307b-d; SECT 5 307d-308a; SECT 11-14 308b-c

13 VIRGIL: *Aeneid*, BK I [254-296] 110a-111a; BK IV [332-363] 176a-177a; BK IX [123-139] 282a-b

14 PLUTARCH: *Coriolanus*, 189a-c / *Nicias*, 435b-d

17 PLOTINUS: *Second Ennead*, TR III, CH 7 44c-45a / *Third Ennead*, TR II-III 82c-97b passim / *Fourth Ennead*, TR III, CH 13 149b-d; TR IV, CH 31, 175b-c

18 AUGUSTINE: *Confessions*, BK II, par 14 12a-b; BK IX, par 1 61c-d / *City of God*, BK I, CH 8-9 133a-135a; BK IV, CH 33 206c-d; BK V, CH 1-11 207d-216d; CH 21-22 226a-227a; BK VII, CH 30

261b-d; BK IX, CH 22 296d-297a; BK X, CH 14-15 307c-308b; BK XI, CH 17 331c-d; CH 22 333d-334c; BK XII, CH 1-9 342b,d-348b; CH 22 357c; CH 25 358b-359a; CH 27 359c-360a,c; BK XIV, CH 27 396c-397a; BK XIX, CH 12-17 517b-523a; BK XXII, CH 1-2 586b,d-588a

19 AQUINAS: *Summa Theologica*, PART I, Q 2, A 3, ANS 12c-14a; Q 3, A 1, REP 1 14b-15b; Q 8, A 3, ANS and REP 2-3 36b-37c; Q 13, A 8, ANS and REP 1 70d-71b; Q 15, A 3, REP 4 93b-94a; Q 19, A 3 110b-111c; QQ 22-24 127c-143c; Q 63, A 7, ANS 331c-332b; Q 96, A 1, ANS and REP 2 510b-511b; QQ 103-119 528a-608d esp QQ 103-105 528a-545b; PART I-II, Q 9, A 6 662a-d; Q 10, A 4 665d-666a,c; Q 19, A 4 705b-c; Q 21, A 4, REP 2 719d-720a,c

20 AQUINAS: *Summa Theologica*, PART I-II, Q 91, AA 1-2 208b-209d; Q 93 215b,d-220d passim; PART II-II, Q 1, A 7, ANS 385c-387a; Q 25, A 11, REP 3 508d-509c; PART III, Q 61, A 1, ANS 855a-d

21 DANTE: *Divine Comedy*, HELL, VII [61-96] 10b-c; PURGATORY, XVI [52-114] 77b-78a; XXI [40-72] 85b-d; PARADISE, I [94-142] 107b-d; II [112-148] 109a-b; VIII [85-148] 117c-118c; XI [28-39] 122b; XII [37-45] 124a; XX [118-138] 138a

22 CHAUCER: *Troilus and Cressida*, BK IV, STANZA 137-154 106b-108b / *Knight's Tale* [1251-1267] 180b; [1303-1333] 181b-182a; [1663-1672] 187b; [2987-3046] 209a-210a / *Friar's Tale* [7064-7085] 281a-b / *Franklin's Tale* [11,177-206] 353b-354a / *Monk's Tale* 434a-448b / *Nun's Priest's Tale* [15,236-256] 456b-457a

23 MACHIAVELLI: *Prince*, CH XXV, 35a-b

23 HOBBES: *Leviathan*, PART I, 53d; 96b; PART II, 113b-c; 160b-c; 163d-164a; PART IV, 254b; 271b; 272b-c

25 MONTAIGNE: *Essays*, 98b-99a

27 SHAKESPEARE: *Hamlet*, ACT V, SC II [7-11] 68a; [230-235] 70a

28 HARVEY: *On Animal Generation*, 491d-492a

29 CERVANTES: *Don Quixote*, PART II, 408c

30 BACON: *Advancement of Learning*, 38a; 94b-c / *Novum Organum*, BK I, APH 93 125d-126a

31 DESCARTES: *Meditations*, IV 89a-93a; VI, 99c / *Objections and Replies*, 229c-d

31 SPINOZA: *Ethics*, PART I, DEF 7 355b; PROP 17, COROL 1-2 and SCHOL 362b-363c; APPENDIX 369b-372d; PART II, PROP 3, SCHOL 374b-c

32 MILTON: *Sonnets*, XVI 66b-67a / *Paradise Lost*, BK II [310-328] 118a; BK III [80-134] 137a-138a; BK V [600-615] 188b; BK VI [171-188] 200a; BK VII [139-173] 220a-221a; BK X [1-62] 274b-275b / *Samson Agonistes* [667-709] 354a-355a / *Areopagitica*, 394b-395b

33 PASCAL: *Pensées*, 205 211a; 619-641 284b-290a; 876 345a

35 LOCKE: *Human Understanding*, BK II, CH XXVIII, SECT 8 230a

35 BERKELEY: *Human Knowledge*, INTRO, SECT 3 405b-c; SECT 29-33 418c-419a passim; SECT 57 423d-424a; SECT 60-66 424b-426a; SECT 93-

94 431b-c; SECT 105–109 433b-434b passim; SECT 146-155 442a-444c passim

35 HUME: *Human Understanding*, SECT VII, DIV 54–57 474b-475d; SECT VIII, DIV 78–81 485c-487a; SECT XI 497b-503c passim, esp DIV 108–109 500b-501a

37 FIELDING: *Tom Jones*, 75c-d

38 MONTESQUIEU: *Spirit of Laws*, BK I, 1a-2b

38 ROUSSEAU: *Social Contract*, BK III, 414d; BK IV, 437d-438b

40 GIBBON: *Decline and Fall*, 292d-293b

42 KANT: *Practical Reason*, 334a-335c / *Judgement*, 594d [fn 1]

46 HEGEL: *Philosophy of History*, INTRO, 156d-160b; 161d-168b; 168d-170b; 182d-184d; PART IV, 368d-369a,c

47 GOETHE: *Faust*, PROLOGUE [243–270] 7a-b

48 MELVILLE: *Moby Dick*, 85a; 237a; 396b-397a

51 TOLSTOY: *War and Peace*, BK VI, 272a-b; BK VIII, 303d-304b; BK IX, 342a-344b; 357b-358b; BK X, 389a-391c; 447c-448a; 465c-467a passim; BK XIII, 563a-b; BK XV, 619d-620a; 631a-c; EPILOGUE I, 645a-650c passim, esp 646c-647b, 650b-c; EPILOGUE II, 675a-676a; 680b-c; 684b-d

52 DOSTOEVSKY: *Brothers Karamazov*, BK V, 127b-137c passim; BK XI, 343b-c

54 FREUD: *Civilization and Its Discontents*, 771a-b / *New Introductory Lectures*, 878a-b

7d. Divine causality in the supernatural order: grace, miracles

OLD TESTAMENT: *Genesis*, 19:24-26; 21:1-8 / *Exodus*, 3–12 passim, esp 3:2, 3:20; 14; 16–17 / *Numbers*, 9:15-23; 11–12; 16–17; 20:1-13; 21:5-9; 22:21-34 / *Joshua*, 3:13-4:24; 6:1-20; 10:12-14; 24:6-7—(D) *Josue*, 3:13-4:25; 6:1-20; 10:12-14; 24:6-7 / *Judges*, 6:36-40 / *I Samuel*, 12:17-19—(D) *I Kings*, 12:17-19 / *I Kings*, 17; 18:30-39—(D) *III Kings*, 17; 18:30-39 / *II Kings*, 1-6; 13:20-21; 20:1-11— (D) *IV Kings*, 1-6; 13:20-21; 20:1-11 / *Nehemiah*, 9—(D) *II Esdras*, 9 / *Psalms*, 78; 84:11; 85:1-3; 86:5; 103:1-5; 105; 106:7-11; 130—(D) *Psalms*, 77; 83:12; 84:2-4; 85:5; 102:1-5; 104; 105:7-11; 129 / *Proverbs*, 3:1-4,21-26 / *Isaiah*, 38; 44:22; 55:7—(D) *Isaias*, 38; 44:22; 55:7 / *Jeremiah*, 33:1-14—(D) *Jeremias*, 33:1-14 / *Daniel*, 3:1-4:3; 5-6; 9:9—(D) *Daniel*, 3:1-23,91-100; 5-6; 9:9 / *Joel*, 2:30-31 / *Jonah*— (D) *Jonas* / *Micah*, 7:18-20—(D) *Micheas*, 7:18-20 / *Zechariah*, 12:10—(D) *Zacharias*, 12:10

APOCRYPHA: *Song of Three Children*—(D) OT, *Daniel*, 3:24-90 / *Bel and Dragon*, 28-42—(D) OT, *Daniel*, 14:27-42 / *II Maccabees*, 1:18-22; 2:10—(D) OT, *II Machabees*, 1:18-22; 2:10

NEW TESTAMENT: *Matthew*, 8–9; 12:22-29; 14:13-36; 15:22-39; 17:1-8; 20:29-34 / *Mark*, 1:29-34,40-44; 2:3-12; 4:34-41; 5; 6:34-56; 7:24-8:26; 9:2-10,17-30; 10:46-52; 13:24-26 —(D) *Mark*, 1:29-34,40-44; 2:3-12; 4:34-40; 5; 6:34-56; 7:24-8:26; 9:1-9,16-29; 10:46-52; 13:24-26 / *Luke*, 1:5-66; 4:31-5:26; 7:1-16; 8:22-56; 9:12-17,28-42; 11:14-26; 13:11-17; 14:1-6; 17:11-19; 18:35-43—(D) *Luke*, 1:5-66; 4:31-5:26; 7:1-16; 8:22-56; 9:12-17,28-43; 11:14-26; 13:11-17; 14:1-6; 17:11-19; 18:35-43 / *John*, 1:14-17; 2:1-11; 4:46-54; 11:1-45 / *Acts*, 2:1-22; 3:1-16; 4:33; 5:12-16; 9:36-43; 14:8-10; 19:11-12; 20:7-12; 28:1-10—(D) *Acts*, 2:1-22; 3:1-16; 4:33; 5:12-16; 9:36-43; 14:8-10; 19:11-12; 20:7-12; 28:1-10 / *Romans*, 1:3-5; 3:19-7:25; 11 / *I Corinthians*, 3:1-15; 15:9-10 / *II Corinthians*, 4:15; 8-9 passim; 12:1-10 / *Galatians*, 5:4 / *Ephesians*, 1:1-11 / *Philippians*, 2:12-13; 4:13 / *II Thessalonians*, 2:16-17—(D) *II Thessalonians*, 2:15-16 / *II Timothy*, 2:1 / *Titus*, 2:11-15; 3:3-9 / *Hebrews*, 2:9; 12:14-29 / *James*, 4:6 / *I Peter*, 5:5

14 PLUTARCH: *Coriolanus*, 191d-192b

18 AUGUSTINE: *Confessions*, BK I, par 5–6 2b-c; BK II, par 15 12b-c; BK VI, par 4 36a-b / *City of God*, BK X, CH 8 303a-d; CH 12–18 306d-310d; BK XIII, CH 3–5 361a-362c; CH 7 362d-363b; CH 14–15 366b-d; CH 20 370c-371a; BK XIII, CH 23–BK XIV, CH 1 372a-377a; BK XIV, CH 26–27, 396b-397a; BK XV, CH 1–3 397b,d-399c; BK XVI, CH 26 438c-439a; CH 37 444b-445a; BK XVIII, CH 11 477c-d; BK XXI, CH 5–8 563d-568d; CH 15–16 572c-574a; BK XXII, CH 5–10 589a-599b / *Christian Doctrine*, BK I, CH 1 624b,d

19 AQUINAS: *Summa Theologica*, PART I, Q 2, A 2, REP 1 11d-12c; Q 8, A 3, ANS and REP 4 36b-37c; Q 12, A 2 51c-52c; AA 4–5 53b-55b; A 13 61c-62b; Q 62 317c-325b; Q 89, A 1, REP 3 473b-475a; A 2, REP 3 475a-d; A 8, REP 2 479c-480c; Q 92, A 4, ANS 491b-d; Q 95 506b-510a; Q 104, A 4, ANS 538a-c; Q 105, AA 6–8 543b-545b; Q 106, A 3, ANS 547c-548b; Q 108, A 8, ANS and REP 1–2 561a-562a; Q 110, A 4 567c-568b; Q 113, A 1, REP 2 576a-d; Q 114, A 4 584a-585a; Q 119, A 1, ANS 604c-607b; PART I–II, Q 5, A 6, REP 2 641a-642a; Q 10, A 4, REP 2 665d-666a,c

20 AQUINAS: *Summa Theologica*, PART I–II, Q 51, A 4 15a-d; Q 55, A 4, ANS and REP 6 28c-29d; Q 58, A 3, REP 3 43b-44a; Q 62, A 1 60a-d; Q 63, A 2, ANS and REP 1–2 64b-65a; Q 65, A 3, ANS 72d-73d; Q 66, A 2, REP 1 76c-77c; Q 76, A 2, REP 2 141d-142c; Q 79, A 3, ANS 158a-d; Q 81, A 3, REP 3 165d-166b; A 4 166b-167a; Q 85, A 6, ANS 182d-184a; Q 98, A 1, ANS 239b-240c; Q 106, A 1, ANS and REP 1,3 321a-322a; QQ 109–114 338a-378a,c esp Q 113, A 10 369c-370b; PART II–II, Q 24, A 3, REP 1 491a-d; PART III, QQ 7–8 745c-763b; Q 61, A 1, REP 2 855a-d; Q 62 858b-864c; PART III SUPPL, Q 75, A 3 938a-939d; Q 83, A 3 978c-980d; Q 92, A 1 1025c-1032b

21 DANTE: *Divine Comedy*, PARADISE, VII [16–120] 115b-116b; XIII [52–87] 126a-b; XX [79–138] 137c-138a; XXIX [58–66] 150d-151a; XXXII [40–87] 155a-c; XXXII [139]–XXXIII [145] 156a-157d

(7. *The causality of God or the gods. 7d. Divine causality in the supernatural order: grace, miracles.*)

22 CHAUCER: *Tale of Man of Law* 236b-255b esp [4869-4924] 242b-243b, [5247-5253] 249b / *Prioress's Tale* [13,418-620] 392a-395b

23 HOBBES: *Leviathan*, PART I, 83c; 88c-89a; PART II, 137b-c; 149c-d; 160b-c; PART III, 165d-167b; 172a-177c passim; 183d-187a; 188a-191a; 241c-242a; PART IV, 249b-250a; 264a

25 MONTAIGNE: *Essays*, 212a-d; 267d-268a; 273a-b; 294a-b

30 BACON: *Advancement of Learning*, 19b-c; 33c-d; 41b-c / *New Atlantis*, 201d-203c

31 DESCARTES: *Objections and Replies*, 125d-126a

32 MILTON: *Paradise Lost*, BK II [1024-1033] 133b; BK III [56-415] 136b-144b esp [130-134] 138a, [167-184] 139a-b, [227-238] 140b; BK XI [1-21] 299a-b; [251-262] 304b-305a; BK XII [173-222] 323a-324a / *Samson Agonistes* [356-372] 347b; [652-666] 353b-354a

33 PASCAL: *Provincial Letters*, 1a-14a; 19a-26b; 29b; 154b-159a / *Pensées*, 202 211a; 430-435 245a-251a; 458 254a; 505 261a-b; 508-511 261b; 513-517 262a-263b; 520-524 263b-264a; 643-644 290b-291b; 803-856 328b-341b; 876 345a; 881 345b

35 LOCKE: *Human Understanding*, BK IV, CH XVI, SECT 13 371a-b

35 BERKELEY: *Human Knowledge*, SECT 62-63 425a-c; SECT 84 429b-c

35 HUME: *Human Understanding*, SECT VII, DIV 54 474b-c; SECT X 488d-497b

37 FIELDING: *Tom Jones*, 38d

40 GIBBON: *Decline and Fall*, 180b-c; 189b-191a; 206b-d; 295b-296b; 465d-467a; 605b-d

41 GIBBON: *Decline and Fall*, 227d-228a; 232a-c; 398b-399b

42 KANT: *Pure Reason*, 238b

44 BOSWELL: *Johnson*, 126b-c; 359a

46 HEGEL: *Philosophy of History*, PART III, 307a-b; PART IV, 338b-c; 348d-349a

51 TOLSTOY: *War and Peace*, BK V, 219b-220a

52 DOSTOEVSKY: *Brothers Karamazov*, BK I, 11a-b; BK V, 127b-137c passim; BK VII, 171a-177b; 189d-190a

8. The operation of causes in the process of history

6 HERODOTUS: *History*, BK I, 21d-22a; BK IX, 291b-c

6 THUCYDIDES: *Peloponnesian War*, BK I, 354d-355a; BK IV, 462a-b

7 PLATO: *Statesman*, 587a-589c / *Laws*, BK III, 663d-666d; BK IV, 679a-c

9 ARISTOTLE: *Politics*, BK V 502a-519d passim

12 LUCRETIUS: *Nature of Things*, BK I [449-482] 6c-7a

12 AURELIUS: *Meditations*, BK V, SECT 8 269d-

270b; BK VII, SECT 1 279b; SECT 49 282d; BK IX, SECT 28 293d-294a; BK X, SECT 27 299d

13 VIRGIL: *Aeneid* 103a-379a esp BK I [254-296] 110a-111a, BK VI [713-853] 230a-234a

14 PLUTARCH: *Camillus*, 107c / *Timoleon*, 201a-203b

15 TACITUS: *Annals*, BK III, 49c; BK VI, 91b-d / *Histories*, BK I, 190a-b

18 AUGUSTINE: *City of God*, BK I, PREF 129a-d; CH 36 149c-d; BK II, CH 2-3 150c-151c; BK IV, CH 33 206c-d; BK V, CH 1 207d-208c; CH 11-26 216c-230a,c; BK XI, CH 1 322b,d-323a; CH 18 331d-332a; BK XIV, CH 28-BK XV, CH 1 397a-398c; BK XV, CH 21-22 415b-416c; BK XVIII, CH 1-2 472b,d-473d

21 DANTE: *Divine Comedy*, HELL, VII [61-96] 10b-c; PURGATORY, XVI [52-114] 77b-78a; PARADISE, VI [28-111] 113d-114d

23 MACHIAVELLI: *Prince*, CH XIV, 21b; CH XXV 35a-36b

23 HOBBES: *Leviathan*, PART I, 76c-d

25 MONTAIGNE: *Essays*, 464b-465c passim

26 SHAKESPEARE: *Julius Caesar*, ACT IV, SC III [215-224] 590d

30 BACON: *Advancement of Learning*, 34c

33 PASCAL: *Pensées*, 505 261a-b; 619-641 284b-290a

36 SWIFT: *Gulliver*, PART III, 121a-b

38 MONTESQUIEU: *Spirit of Laws*, BK VIII, 56b-57c; BK XVII 122a-125a,c

38 ROUSSEAU: *Inequality*, 348a,c

40 GIBBON: *Decline and Fall*, 456d-457a,c; 609b-c; 630b,d-634a,c

41 GIBBON: *Decline and Fall*, 451c-453a,c; 590a-b

43 FEDERALIST: NUMBER 3, 33c

43 MILL: *Representative Government*, 327b,d-332a passim, esp 331b-332d

46 HEGEL: *Philosophy of Right*, PART II, par 115 42b-c; PART III, par 340-360 110b-114a,c par 342 110c-d, par 347 111b-c / *Philosophy of History*, INTRO, 155c; 156d-170b; 173a-175c; 190b-201a,c esp 190b-d, 194b-196a; 203a-206a,c; PART I, 235d-237a; 258b-d; PART II, 262c-263d; 274a-275a; 281d-282d; 283c-284a,c; PART III, 300a-301c; PART IV, 337d-342a

49 DARWIN: *Descent of Man*, 323a-b; 327a-328d

50 MARX: *Capital*, 7b; 8a-11d passim; 377c-378d

50 MARX-ENGELS: *Communist Manifesto*, 416c-417a,c; 419b,d-425b passim; 428b-d

51 TOLSTOY: *War and Peace*, BK IX, 342a-344b; BK X, 389a-391c; 430b-432c; 447c-448c; BK XI, 469a-472b; BK XIII, 563a-575a; BK XIV, 588a-590c; 609a-613d; BK XV, 618b-621b; EPILOGUE I, 645a-650c; EPILOGUE II 675a-696d

52 DOSTOEVSKY: *Brothers Karamazov*, BK V, 127b-137c

54 FREUD: *War and Death*, 761a-c / *Civilization and Its Discontents*, 781a-782d; 787a-788d; 791b-d; 799a-802a,c esp 801d-802a,c / *New Introductory Lectures*, 834b-c; 882b-884c

CROSS-REFERENCES

For: The consideration of cause in relation to principle and element, *see* ELEMENT 2; PRINCIPLE 1a.

The distinction between necessary and contingent causes, and for the conception of chance in relation to cause, *see* CHANCE 1a–1b; NATURE 3c–3c(1); NECESSITY AND CONTINGENCY 3a–3c.

The issue concerning determinism in nature or history, *see* FATE 5–6; HISTORY 4a(1); MECHANICS 4c(1); NATURE 2f, 3c(2).

Other discussions of the controversy concerning causality and free will, and of the problem of man's freedom in relation to God's will, *see* FATE 2, 4; HISTORY 4a(1); LIBERTY 4a–4b, 5a, 5d; WILL 5a(3)–5a(4), 5b(2), 5c, 7c.

The theory of divine causality in creation, providence, and the performance of miracles, *see* ASTRONOMY 8d; GOD 5a, 7a–7e; MATTER 3d; NATURE 3c(4); WORLD 4b, 4d–4e.

The role of ends or final causes in the order of nature and the structure of the universe, *see* DESIRE 1; GOD 5b; NATURE 3c(3); WORLD 1c, 6c; and for the general theory of means and ends, *see* GOOD AND EVIL 4b, 5c; JUDGMENT 3; PRUDENCE 3a, 4b; WILL 2c(2)–2c(3).

The discussion of cause as an object of knowledge and in relation to the methods and aims of philosophy, science, and history, *see* ASTRONOMY 3a–3b; DEFINITION 2d; HISTORY 3b; KNOWLEDGE 5a(3); MECHANICS 2c; PHYSICS 2b; REASONING 5b(4)–5b(5); SCIENCE 1b(1), 4c.

ADDITIONAL READINGS

Listed below are works not included in *Great Books of the Western World*, but relevant to the idea and topics with which this chapter deals. These works are divided into two groups:

I. Works by authors represented in this collection.
II. Works by authors not represented in this collection.

For the date, place, and other facts concerning the publication of the works cited, consult the Bibliography of Additional Readings which follows the last chapter of *The Great Ideas.*

I.

AQUINAS. *Summa Contra Gentiles,* BK III, CH 1–16, 64–83, 88–98

DESCARTES. *The Principles of Philosophy,* PART I, 28

HOBBES. *Concerning Body,* PART II, CH 9

HUME. *A Treatise of Human Nature,* BK I, PART III, SECT II–IV, XV

BERKELEY. *Siris*

KANT. *Metaphysical Foundations of Natural Science,* DIV III

GIBBON. *An Essay on the Study of Literature,* XLVIII–LV, LXXVIII–LXXXII

HEGEL. *Science of Logic,* VOL I, BK II, SECT I, CH 3; SECT III, CH 3(B); VOL II, SECT II, CH 3

J. S. MILL. *A System of Logic,* BK III, CH 4–6, 9–10, 15, 21

——. *An Examination of Sir William Hamilton's Philosophy,* CH 16

FREUD. *The Psychopathology of Everyday Life,* CH 12

W. JAMES. *Some Problems of Philosophy,* CH 12–13

II.

SEXTUS EMPIRICUS. *Outlines of Pyrrhonism,* BK III, CH 1–20

——. *Against the Physicists,* BK I (Concerning Cause and the Passive)

PROCLUS. *The Elements of Theology,* (B,G,I)

MAIMONIDES. *The Guide for the Perplexed,* PART I, CH 69; PART II, CH 48

DUNS SCOTUS. *Tractatus de Primo Principio (A Tract Concerning the First Principle)*

BRUNO. *De la causa, principio, e uno*

SUÁREZ. *Disputationes Metaphysicae,* XI (3), XII–XXVII,XXIX,XXXI (8–10), XXXIV(6–7),XLVIII(1)

JOHN OF SAINT THOMAS. *Cursus Philosophicus Thomisticus, Philosophia Naturalis* PART I, QQ 10–13, 25–26

BOYLE. *A Disquisition About the Final Causes of Natural Things*

MALEBRANCHE. *De la recherche de la vérité,* BK VI(II), CH 3; Eclaircissement 15

MALEBRANCHE. *Dialogues on Metaphysics and Religion*, VII

LEIBNITZ. *Discourse on Metaphysics*, XV–XXII

——. *New Essays Concerning Human Understanding*, BK II, CH 26

VOLTAIRE. *Candide*

——. "Change or Generation of Events," "Final Causes," in *A Philosophical Dictionary*

T. REID. *Essays on the Active Powers of the Human Mind*, I

SCHOPENHAUER. *On the Fourfold Root of the Principle of Sufficient Reason*

——. *The World as Will and Idea*, VOL III, SUP, CH 26; APPENDIX

BROWN. *An Inquiry into the Relation of Cause and Effect*

——. *Lectures on the Philosophy of the Human Mind*, VOL I, pp 189–220; VOL II, pp 128–134

COMTE. *The Positive Philosophy*, INTRO, CH I; BK III, CH I

W. HAMILTON. *Lectures on Metaphysics and Logic*, VOL I (38–40)

WHEWELL. *The Philosophy of the Inductive Sciences*, VOL I, BK III, CH 1–4; BK IX, CH 6; BK X, CH 5; VOL II, BK XI, CH 7

HELMHOLTZ. *Popular Lectures on Scientific Subjects*, VIII

WUNDT. *Die Prinzipien der mechanischen Naturlehre*

JEVONS. *The Principles of Science*, CH 11

LOTZE. *Logic*, BK I, CH 2 (B)

P. A. JANET. *Final Causes*

C. S. PEIRCE. *Collected Papers*, VOL VI, par 66–87, 393–394

DOMET DE VORGES. *Cause efficiente et cause finale*

WATTS. *The Reign of Causality*

VENN. *Principles of Empirical or Inductive Logic*, CH 2

FRAZER. *The Golden Bough*, PART I, CH 3

PEARSON. *The Grammar of Science*, CH 4

BRADLEY. *The Principles of Logic*, BK III, PART II, CH 2

——. *Appearance and Reality*, BK I, CH 6

BOSANQUET. *Science and Philosophy*, 8

BERGSON. *Creative Evolution*

BROAD. *Perception, Physics, and Reality*, CH 1–2

HENDERSON. *The Order of Nature*

W. E. JOHNSON. *Logic*, PART III, CH 3–11

MEYERSON. *Identity and Reality*, CH I

——. *De l'explication dans les sciences*

DUCASSE. *Causation and the Types of Necessity*

WHITEHEAD. *An Enquiry Concerning the Principles of Natural Knowledge*, CH 16

——. *Symbolism, Its Meaning and Effects*

EDDINGTON. *The Nature of the Physical World*, CH 14

McTAGGART. *The Nature of Existence*, CH 24–26

SANTAYANA. *The Realm of Matter*, CH 7

M. R. COHEN. *Reason and Nature*, BK I, CH 4(2); BK II, CH 2

LENZEN. *The Nature of Physical Theory*, PART IV, CH 16

WEYL. *The Open World*, LECT II

MARITAIN. *A Preface to Metaphysics*, LECT V–VII

A. J. TOYNBEE. *A Study of History*

PLANCK. *Where Is Science Going?*, CH 4–5

——. *The Philosophy of Physics*, CH 2

DEWEY. *Logic, the Theory of Inquiry*, CH 22

B. RUSSELL. *Principles of Mathematics*, CH 55

——. *Our Knowledge of the External World*, VIII

——. *Mysticism and Logic*, CH 9

——. *The Analysis of Matter*, CH 30–31, 35

——. *Human Knowledge, Its Scope and Limits*, PART IV, CH 9–10; PART VI, CH 5–6

Chapter 9: CHANCE

INTRODUCTION

ONE sense in which we use the word "chance" does not exclude the operation of causes. The chance event, in this sense, is not uncaused. But within this meaning of chance, there is the question of *how* the chance event is caused.

On one view, what happens by chance is distinguished from what happens by nature in terms of a difference in manner of causation—the difference between the contingent and the necessary. On another view, the chance event does not differ causally from that which happens regularly or uniformly. The difference lies not in the pattern of causes, but in our knowledge of them. The chance event is unpredictable or less predictable because of our ignorance of its causes, not because of any real contingency in the order of nature.

There is still a third sense of "chance" in which it means that which happens totally without cause—the absolutely spontaneous or fortuitous.

These three meanings of *chance* at once indicate the basic issues in which the concept is involved. The third meaning is the most radical. It stands in opposition to the other two. Their opposition to one another can be considered after we examine the sense in which chance excludes every type of cause.

THE DOCTRINE OF absolute fortuitousness is indeterminism in its most extreme form. The familiar phrase, "a fortuitous concourse of atoms," indicates the classical statement of this doctrine, and identifies it in the great books with the theory of atomism. It would be more precise to say "with Lucretius' version of that theory," because it is with regard to chance that he departs from the teachings of Democritus and Epicurus, and adds an hypothesis of his own.

The swerve of the atoms, according to Lucretius, accounts for the origin of the world, the motions of nature, and the free will of man. But nothing accounts for the swerve of the atoms. It is uncaused, spontaneous, fortuitous. "When the atoms are being carried downwards straight through the void by their own weight, they push a little from their path at times quite undetermined and at undetermined places, yet only just so much as you would call a change of trend. If they did not swerve, all things would fall downward through the deep void like drops of rain, nor could collision come to be, nor blows be brought to pass among the atoms; thus nature would never have brought anything to being."

Since the atoms differ in shape, size, and weight, it might be supposed that the heavier atoms, falling straight yet more rapidly, would overtake and hit the lighter atoms, thus bringing about their grouping or interlocking. But this supposition, says Lucretius, is contrary to reason. It may hold for things falling through water or thin air, but through the empty void "all things, even of unequal weight, move with an equal velocity through the unresisting void." Therefore heavier things will never be able to fall on the lighter from above nor of themselves bring about the blows sufficient to produce the varied motions by which nature carries things on. Wherefore, Lucretius concludes, the atoms "must swerve a little."

Once the atoms have collided, the way in which they are locked together in the patterns of composite things, and all the subsequent motions of these things, can be accounted for by reference to the natural properties of the atoms. The atomic sizes, shapes, and weights determine how they behave singly or in combination. But the swerve of the atoms is not so determined. It is completely spontaneous.

"If each motion is always due to another, and the new always springs from the old in a determined order, and if the atoms do not by swerving break through the decrees of fate, so that cause does not follow cause through infinite time"; whence, asks Lucretius, "is it wrested from fate, this will whereby we move forward where pleasure leads each one of us, and swerve likewise in our motions, neither at a fixed time nor at a fixed place, but only when and where the mind itself has prompted us?" The answer he gives is that there must be "in the atoms . . . another cause of motion besides blows and weights, whence comes this power born in us, since we see that nothing can come to be from nothing."

BEING ABSOLUTELY fortuitous, the swerve of the atoms is absolutely unintelligible. There is no answer to the question why they chance to swerve at undetermined times and places. This unintelligibility may not, however, make the fortuitous either unreal or impossible. It can be argued that chance may exist even though, for our limited understanding, it remains mysterious.

The same problem of intelligibility arises with respect to that meaning of chance wherein it is identified with coincidence or contingency. Here, as in the case of the absolutely fortuitous, chance belongs to reality or nature. "Some things always come to pass in the same way, and others for the most part," writes Aristotle as an observer of nature, but there is also "a third class of events besides these two—events which all say are 'by chance.'" Things of this last kind, he goes on to say, are those which "come to pass incidentally"—or accidentally.

According to this theory, a real or objective indeterminism exists. Chance or contingency is not just an expression of human uncertainty born of insufficient knowledge. Contingency, however, differs from the fortuitousness or spontaneity of the atom's swerve, in that it is a product of causes, not their total absence. Of the contingent event, "there is no definite cause," in Aristotle's opinion, but there is "a chance cause, i.e., an indefinite one."

In the chance happening, two lines of action coincide and thereby produce a single result. This is our ordinary understanding of the way accidents happen. The chance meeting of old friends who run across each other in a railroad station after a separation of many years is a coincidence—a coinciding of the two quite separate and independent lines of action which brought each of them to the same station at the same time, coming from different places, going to different places, and proceeding under the influence of different causes or purposes. That each is there can be explained by the operation of causes. That both are there together cannot be explained by the causes determining their independent paths.

So understood, the chance event exemplifies what Aquinas calls a "clashing of two causes." And what makes it a matter of chance is the fact that "the clashing of these two causes, inasmuch as it is accidental, has no cause." Precisely because it is accidental, "this clashing of causes is not to be reduced to a further pre-existing cause from which it follows of necessity."

The illustration is not affected by considerations of free will. Whether men have free will or not, whether free acts are caused or are, as Kant suggests, uncaused and spontaneous, the event we call a "chance meeting" remains accidental or, more precisely, a coincidence. Whatever the factors are which control the motions of each man, they operate entirely within that single man's line of action. Prior to the meeting, they do not influence the other man's conduct. If we could state the cause for the coincidence of the two lines of motion, it would have to be some factor which influenced both lines. Were there such a cause and were it known to us, we could not say that the meeting happened by chance. It would still be a coincidence in the merely physical sense of coming together, but it would not be a coincidence causally.

That free will is irrelevant to this meaning of chance can be seen from the fact that the collision of particles which produces atomic fission is regarded as resulting from chance or coincidence in a manner no different from the accidental meeting of friends. Causes control the speeds and directions of the colliding particles, but no cause determines their collision; or, in other words, there is no cause for the coincidence of two separate lines of causation. Contemporary physics affirms a real or objective indeterminism insofar as it does not merely say that the cause of the coincidence is unknown to us, but rather holds that no such cause exists to be known.

THE CONCEPTION OF THE chance event as an uncaused coincidence of causes is an ancient as well as a modern doctrine. In his *Physics*, Aristotle distinguishes between what happens by nature and what happens by chance in terms of different types of causality. "Chance," he writes, is "reckoned among causes; many things are said both to be and to come to be as a result of chance." But the fact that its effects cannot be "identified with any of the things that come to pass by necessity and always, or for the most part" at once distinguishes the causality of chance from that of nature.

"The early physicists," Aristotle observes, "found no place for chance among the causes which they recognized ... Others there are who, indeed, believe that chance is a cause, but that it is inscrutable to human intelligence, as being a divine thing and full of mystery." But to Aristotle himself "it is clear that chance is an incidental cause" and "that the causes of what comes to pass by chance are infinite." For this reason, he explains, "chance is supposed to belong to the class of the indefinite, and to be inscrutable to man." Though he distinguishes between spontaneity and chance, he says that both "are causes of effects which, though they might result from intelligence or nature, have in fact been caused by something *incidentally*."

What happens by nature happens regularly, or for the most part, through causal necessity. This necessity results from the operation of essential causes, causes in the very nature of the moving things. When the regularity fails, it is due to the intervention of some accidental cause. What happens by chance, then, or contingently, is always due to an accidental (or better, incidental) cause. As indicated in the chapter on CAUSE, an accidental as opposed to an essential cause is, in Aristotle's theory, one which does not *by itself* produce the given effect. It does so only through the conjunction of other causes. But since it does not determine these other causes to operate, the effect—*contingent on their combined activity*—is produced by chance, that is, by the contingency of several incidental causes working coincidentally.

A world in which chance really exists is remarkably different from a world in which necessity prevails, in which everything is determined by causes and there are no uncaused coincidences. William James vividly epitomizes their difference by calling the world of absolute necessity or determinism—the world of Spinoza or Hegel—a "block universe" in contrast to what he describes as a "concatenated universe." Voltaire before him, in his *Philosophical Dictionary*, had used the phrase "the concatenation of events" to express the meaning of chance.

The phrase evokes the right image, the picture of a world in which many concurrent lines of causality, exercising no influence upon one another, may nevertheless concatenate or be joined together to produce a chance result. The block universe presents the contrasting picture of a world in which each motion or act determines and is determined by every other in the fixed structure of the whole.

Spinoza claims, for example, that "in nature there is nothing contingent, but all things are determined from the necessity of the divine nature to exist and act in a certain manner." Chance, in other words, does not exist in nature. A thing is said to be contingent, Spinoza writes, only "with reference to a deficiency in our knowledge. For if we do not know that the essence of a thing involves a contradiction, or if we actually know that it involves no contradiction, and nevertheless we can affirm nothing with certainty about its existence because the order of causes is concealed from us, that thing can never appear to us either as necessary or impossible, and therefore we call it either contingent or possible." Hence, for Spinoza, contingency or chance is illusory rather than real—a projection of the mind's ignorance or of its inadequate knowledge of causes.

The issue between real indeterminism and absolute determinism—further discussed in the chapters on FATE and NECESSITY AND CONTINGENCY—inevitably raises theological questions. Just as the theologian must reconcile man's free will with God's predestination, so must he, if he accepts its reality, also reconcile chance with divine providence, apart from which nothing can happen either necessarily or contingently.

For Augustine it would seem that divine

providence leaves no room for chance among natural things. After noting that causes are sometimes divided into a "fortuitous cause, a natural cause, and a voluntary cause," he dismisses "those causes which are called fortuitous" by saying that they "are not a mere name for the absence of causes, but are only latent, and we attribute them either to the will of the true God, or to that of spirits of some kind or other."

In certain places Aquinas seems to talk in much the same fashion—as though chance existed only for our limited intellects and not for God. "Nothing," he declares, "hinders certain things from happening by luck or chance, if compared to their proximate causes; but not if compared to divine providence, according to which 'nothing happens at random in the world,' as Augustine says." The example he uses to illustrate his point is that of two servants who have been sent by their master to the same place: "the meeting of the two servants, although to them it appears a chance circumstance, has been fully foreseen by their master, who has purposely sent them to meet at one place, in such a way that one has no knowledge of the other." In such a way also "all things must of necessity come under God's ordering," from which it follows that God directly causes the action of even accidental causes, and their coincidence. The chance event would then be necessitated by God. It would be determined by His will, however indeterminate it might appear to us.

Yet in other places Aquinas writes that "God wills some things to be done necessarily, some contingently .... To some effects He has attached unfailing necessary causes, from which the effects follow necessarily; but to other defectible and contingent causes, from which effects arise contingently." For some minds this may only deepen the mystery rather than solve it. At least it leaves many questions unanswered.

Does Aquinas mean that a coincidence of causes is not itself uncaused? Does he mean that God causes the concatenation of events, and that a sufficient reason for every contingency exists in God's will? If so, is chance an illusion, a function of our ignorance of divine providence? May chance be quite real on the level of nature where no natural causes determine the coincidence, while not real—at least not in the same sense—for God? Or does the statement that what "divine providence plans to happen contingently, happens contingently" mean that chance remains a real feature of the universe even for God?

One thing is clear. In one sense of the word, the Christian theologians completely deny chance. If "chance" means something which God does not foresee, something unplanned by His providence, then according to their faith nothing happens by chance. It is in this sense also that what happens by chance is opposed to what happens on purpose, or has a final as well as an efficient cause. As the chapter on CAUSE indicates, those who deny final causes in nature sometimes use the word "chance" to signify not lack of cause, nor even contingency, but only the blindness of causality—working to no end.

The controversy discussed in the chapter on WORLD—between those who see in the structure of the universe the grand design of a divine plan and those who attribute whatever order there is in nature to blind chance—further indicates the sense in which theologians like Augustine and Aquinas deny chance. But if "chance" means no more than *contingency*, then to affirm chance excludes, not providence, but fate, at least that sense of "fate" according to which everything is blindly necessitated. Here it is Spinoza's statement that "in nature there is nothing contingent, but all things are determined from the necessity of the divine nature" which opposes the statement of Aquinas that "the mode both of necessity and contingency falls under the foresight of God."

THE THEORY OF chance has obvious bearings on the theory of knowledge, especially with regard to the distinction between knowledge and opinion and between certainty and probability.

On any view of chance—whether it is real or illusory—when men call a future event contingent they mean that they cannot predict it with certitude. So far as human prediction goes, it makes no difference whether the future event is necessarily determined and we lack adequate knowledge of its causes, or the event has a genuine indeterminacy in the way it is caused or uncaused. Regardless of what the objective situation is, the assurance with which we predict anything reflects the state of our knowledge about it.

The ancients who, for the most part, regard chance as real and objective, treat probability as subjective. For them, the different degrees of probability which men attach to their statements measure the inadequacy of their knowledge and the consequent uncertainty of their opinions about matters which cannot be known but only guessed. Holding different theories of the distinction between knowledge and opinion, both Plato and Aristotle exclude the accidental and the contingent, along with the particular, from the objects of science. Since in their view certitude belongs to the essence of science—or of knowledge as contrasted with opinion—science for them deals not only with the universal but with the necessary.

In the *Republic* Socrates assigns opinion to the realm of becoming—the realm of changing and contingent particulars. Unlike Plato, Aristotle does not restrict knowledge to the realm of eternal and immutable being, but he does insist that physics, as a science of changing things, preserve the certitude of science by concerning itself only with the essential and the necessary. "That a science of the accidental is not even possible," he writes, "will be evident if we try to see what the accidental really is." It is a matter of chance that cold weather occurs during the dog-days, for "this occurs neither always and of necessity, nor for the most part, though it might happen sometimes. The accidental, then, is what occurs, but not always nor of necessity, nor for the most part. Now ... it is obvious why there is no science of such a thing."

Though he disagrees with Aristotle and Aquinas about the reality of chance or contingency, Spinoza agrees with them that knowledge—at least adequate knowledge—has the necessary for its object. Of individual things, he says, "we can have no adequate knowledge ... and this is what is to be understood by us as their contingency." To be true to itself and to the nature of things, reason must "perceive things truly, that is to say, as they are in themselves, that is to say, not as contingent but as necessary."

The position of Aquinas is worth stating for comparison. To the question "whether our intellect can know contingent things," he replies that "the contingent, considered as such, is known directly by sense and indirectly by the intellect, while the universal and necessary principles of contingent things are known by the intellect. Hence," he goes on, "if we consider knowable things in their universal principles, then all science is of necessary things. But if we consider the things themselves, thus some sciences are of necessary things, some of contingent things."

Among the sciences of contingent things, Aquinas includes not only "the sciences of nature" but also "the moral sciences," because the latter, dealing with human action, must reach down to contingent particulars. In the sphere of morals as of nature, certainty can be achieved only on the level of universal principles. Deliberation about particular acts to be done moves on the level of probable opinion. In contrast to the moral scientist, the man of action must weigh chances and make decisions with regard to future contingencies. It would be as foolish, Aristotle says, to expect the certitude of scientific demonstration from an orator or a judge, as "to accept probable reasoning from a mathematician."

IT IS NOT SURPRISING that the modern theory of probability—or, as it was later called by Boole, Venn, and others, the "logic of chance"—should have its origin in the sphere of practical problems. Pascal's correspondence with Fermat illustrates the early mathematical speculations concerning formulae for predicting the outcome in games of pure chance. For Pascal the logic of chance also has moral implications. If we are willing to risk money at the gaming table on the basis of calculated probabilities, how much more willing should we be to act decisively in the face of life's uncertainties, even to risking life itself on the chance of eternal salvation.

When we act "on an uncertainty, we act reasonably," Pascal writes, "for we ought to work for an uncertainty according to the doctrine of chance." If the chance of there being an after-life is equal to the chance of there being none—if the equiprobability reflects our equal ignorance of either alternative—then,

Pascal argues, we ought to wager in favor of immortality and act accordingly. "There is here the infinity of an infinitely happy life to gain, a chance to gain against a finite number of chances of loss, and what you stake is finite."

Like Pascal, Hume thinks that we must be content with probability as a basis for action. "The great subverter of *Pyrrhonism* or the excessive principles of skepticism," he writes, "is action, and employment, and the occupations of common life." But unlike the ancients, Hume also thinks we should be content with probabilities in the sphere of the natural sciences. Certitude is attainable only by the mathematician who deals with the relations between ideas. Since the natural sciences deal with matters of fact or real existence, and since to know such things we must rely entirely upon our experience of cause and effect, we cannot reach better than probable conclusions.

The scientist, according to Hume, "weighs opposite experiments. He considers which side is supported by the greater number of experiments; to that side he inclines, with doubt and hesitation; and when at last he fixes his judgment, the evidence exceeds not what we properly call *probability*. All probability, then, supposes an opposition of experiments and observations ... A hundred instances or experiments on one side, and fifty on another, afford a doubtful expectation of any event; though a hundred uniform experiments, with only one that is contradictory, reasonably beget a pretty strong degree of assurance."

Hume applies the logic of chance to weighing the evidence against and the testimony in favor of miracles, as well as to contrary hypotheses in science. As much as Spinoza, he denies the existence of chance or contingency in the order of nature. Chance is entirely subjective. It is identical with the probability of our opinions. In the throw of dice, the mind, he says, "considers the turning up of each particular side as alike probable; and this is the very nature of chance, to render all the particular events, comprehended in it, entirely equal." But there may also be "a probability, which arises from a superiority of chances on any side; and according as this superiority increases, and surpasses the opposite chances, the probability receives a proportionate increase ... The case,"

Hume asserts, "is the same with the probability of causes, as with that of chance."

Since Hume's day, the theory of probability has become an essential ingredient of empirical science. The development of thermodynamics in the 19th century would have been impossible without it. This is also true of the quantum mechanics and atomic physics of our own time. But like the doctrine of chance, the theory of probability tends in one of two directions: *either* toward the subjective view that probability is only a quality of our judgments, measuring the degree of our ignorance of the real causes which leave nothing in nature undetermined; *or* toward the objective view that there is genuine indeterminism in nature and that mathematical calculations of probability estimate the real chance of an event's occurring.

THE ELEMENT OF chance also has a bearing on the general theory of art. The hypothesis of the melody which a kitten might compose by walking on the keyboard, is obviously intended to contrast a product of chance with a work of art. The competent musician knows with certainty that he can do what the meandering kitten has only one chance in many millions of ever accomplishing.

In proportion as an art is developed, and to the degree that its rules represent a mastery of the medium in which the artist works, chance is excluded from its productions. This point is strikingly exemplified in the history of medicine. "If there had been no such thing as medicine," Hippocrates suggests, "and if nothing had been investigated or found out in it," all practitioners "would have been equally unskilled and ignorant of it, and everything concerning the sick would have been directed by chance." On the same principle, Galen distinguishes the physician from the empiric, who, "without knowing the cause," pretends that he is "able to rectify the failures of function." The empiric works by trial and error—the very opposite of art and science, for trial and error can succeed only by chance. The physician, learned and skilled in medicine, works from a knowledge of causes and by rules of art which tend to eliminate chance.

Augustine reports a conversation with the proconsul concerning the relative merits of medicine and astrology. When the proconsul tells him that, as compared with medicine, astrology is a false art, Augustine, at this time himself "much given to the books of the horoscope-casters," asks how the fact that "many things were foretold truly by [astrology]" can be explained. The proconsul "answered, very reasonably, that it was due to the force of chance, which is always to be allowed for in the order of things." Thus, Augustine says later, "I saw it as obvious that such things as happened to be said truly from the casting of horoscopes were true not by skill but by chance; and such things as were false were not due to want of skill in the art but merely that luck had fallen the other way."

Neither art itself, nor skill in its practice, can ever be perfect enough to remove chance entirely, for the artist deals with particulars. Yet the measure of an art is the certainty which its rules have as directions for achieving the desired result; and the skill of the artist is measured by the extent to which he succeeds by rule and judgment rather than by chance.

When Aristotle quotes Agathon's remark that "art loves chance and chance loves art," he explains its sense to be that "chance and art are concerned with the same objects"—that which does not come to be by nature nor from necessity. Hence art sometimes fails, either from uncontrollable contingencies or from insufficient knowledge of causes. "All causes," says Hume, "are not conjoined to their usual effects with like uniformity. An artificer, who handles only dead matter, may be disappointed of his aim, as well as the politician, who directs the conduct of sensible and intelligent agents."

IN THE REALM OF human affairs—in morals, politics, and history—the factor of chance is usually discussed in terms of good and bad fortune. The word "fortune"—as may be seen in the root which it shares with "fortuitous"—has the same connotations as "chance." Aristotle treats fortune as the kind of chance that operates in the sphere of human action rather than natural change. Fortune, he thinks, can be attributed properly only to intelligent beings capable of deliberate choice. The sense of this distinction between chance and fortune seems to be borne out in history by the fact that fortune, unlike chance, receives personification in myth and legend. Fortune is a goddess or, like the Fates whom she combats, a power with which even the gods must reckon.

The doctrine of chance or fortune occupies an important place in moral theory. Aristotle's classification of goods tends to identify external goods with goods of fortune—the goods which, unlike knowledge and virtue, we cannot obtain merely by the exercise of our will and faculties. Considering the elements of happiness, Aquinas groups together wealth, honor, fame, and power as goods of the same sort because they are "due to external causes and in most cases to fortune."

The goods of fortune, as well as its ills, consist in things beyond man's power to command and, in consequence, to deserve. Recognizing the unpredictable operation of fortune, Epictetus, the Stoic, argues that "we must make the best of those things that are in our power, and take the rest as nature gives it." We have "the power to deal rightly with our own impressions." Hence the Stoics advise us to control our reactions to things even though we cannot control the things themselves. Yet men will always ask, as Hamlet does, "Whether 'tis nobler in the mind to suffer the slings and arrows of outrageous fortune, or to take arms against a sea of troubles, and by opposing end them?"

The fact that the goods and ills of fortune are beyond our power to control raises the further question of man's responsibility regarding them. We can hardly be held responsible for everything that happens to us, but only for those things which are subject to our will. This traditional moral distinction between the good or evil which befalls us by fortune and that which we willfully obtain or accomplish, parallels the legal distinction between accidental and intentional wrongdoing.

What is true of the individual life seems to apply to history— the life of states and the development of civilization generally. For the most part, the historians—Herodotus and Thucydides, Plutarch, Tacitus, and Gibbon— find fortune a useful principle of interpretation. To Machiavelli history seems to be so full of accidents and contingencies—"great changes in affairs ... beyond all human conjecture"— that he tries to advise the prince how to make use of fortune in order to avoid being ruined by it. Such advice can be followed because, in his opinion, "Fortune is the arbiter of one half of our actions, but still leaves us to direct the other half, or perhaps a little less."

Hegel, on the contrary, does not admit chance or fortune in his view of world history as a "necessary development out of the concept of the mind's freedom alone." For Tolstoy also, either necessity or freedom rules the affairs of men. Chance, he writes, does "not denote any really existing thing," but only "a certain stage of understanding of phenomena." Once we succeed in calculating the composition of forces involved in the mass movements of men, "we

shall not be obliged to have recourse to chance for an explanation of those small events which made these people what they were, but it will be clear that all those small events were inevitable."

As the contingent is opposed to the necessary, as that which happens by chance is opposed to that which is fully determined by causes, so fortune is opposed to fate or destiny. This opposition is most evident in the great poems, especially the tragedies, which depict man's efforts to direct his own destiny, now pitting his freedom against both fate and fortune, now courting fortune in his struggle against fate.

OUTLINE OF TOPICS

REFERENCES

To find the passages cited, use the numbers in heavy type, which are the volume and page numbers of the passages referred to. For example, in **4** HOMER: *Iliad*, BK II [265–283] **12d**, the number **4** is the number of the volume in the set; the number **12d** indicates that the passage is in section d of page 12.

PAGE SECTIONS: When the text is printed in one column, the letters a and b refer to the upper and lower halves of the page. For example, in **53** JAMES: *Psychology*, **116a-119b**, the passage begins in the upper half of page 116 and ends in the lower half of page 119. When the text is printed in two columns, the letters a and b refer to the upper and lower halves of the left-hand side of the page, the letters c and d to the upper and lower halves of the right-hand side of the page. For example, in **7** PLATO: *Symposium*, **163b-164c**, the passage begins in the lower half of the left-hand side of page 163 and ends in the upper half of the right-hand side of page 164.

AUTHOR'S DIVISIONS: One or more of the main divisions of a work (such as PART, BK, CH, SECT) are sometimes included in the reference; line numbers, in brackets, are given in certain cases; *e.g.*, *Iliad*, BK II [265–283] **12d**.

BIBLE REFERENCES: The references are to book, chapter, and verse. When the King James and Douay versions differ in title of books or in the numbering of chapters or verses, the King James version is cited first and the Douay, indicated by a (*D*), follows; *e.g.*, OLD TESTAMENT: *Nehemiah*, 7:45—(*D*) *II Esdras*, 7:46.

SYMBOLS: The abbreviation "esp" calls the reader's attention to one or more especially relevant parts of a whole reference; "passim" signifies that the topic is discussed intermittently rather than continuously in the work or passage cited.

For additional information concerning the style of the references, see the Explanation of Reference Style; for general guidance in the use of *The Great Ideas*, consult the Preface.

1. The conception of chance

1a. Chance as the coincidence of causes

7 PLATO: *Timaeus*, 455a-b

8 ARISTOTLE: *Interpretation*, CH 9 [18^{b}5–9] 28c / *Prior Analytics*, BK I, CH 13 [32^{b}4–14] 48b-c / *Posterior Analytics*, BK II, CH 11 [95^{a}3–9] 129d / *Topics*, BK II, CH 6 [112^{b}1–21] 157d-158a; BK III, CH 1 [116^{b}1–7] 162d-163a / *Physics*, BK II, CH 4–6 272c-275a; CH 8 275d-277b / *Heavens*, BK I, CH 12 [283^{a}30–^{b}6] 375a-c; BK II, CH 5 [287^{b}22–26] 379b; CH 8 [289^{b}22–28] 381b; BK IV, CH 3 [310^{a}23–31] 401d / *Metaphysics*, BK V, CH 30 [1025^{a}13–29] 547a-c; BK VI, CH 2–3 548c-549d; BK XI, CH 8 593a-d; BK XII, CH 3 [1070^{a}4–9] 599b / *Memory and Reminiscence*, CH 2 [452^{a}30–^{b}6] 694b

9 ARISTOTLE: *Parts of Animals*, BK I, CH 1 [640^{a}12–33] 162b-d / *Rhetoric*, BK I, CH 10 [1369^{a}31–^{b}5] 612c-d

12 AURELIUS: *Meditations*, BK II, SECT 3 257a-b

17 PLOTINUS: *Fourth Ennead*, TR III, CH 16, 150c / *Sixth Ennead*, TR VIII, CH 10, 347c-d

18 AUGUSTINE: *Confessions*, BK IV, par 4–6 20a-d; BK VII, par 8–10 45d-47a passim

19 AQUINAS: *Summa Theologica*, PART I, Q 22, A 2, REP 1 128d-130d; Q 47, A 1, ANS 256a-257b; Q 57, A 3, ANS 297b-298a; Q 103, A 5,

REP 1 531b-532b; A 7, REP 2 533b-d; Q 115, A 6, ANS and REP 3 591d-592d; Q 116, A 1 592d-593d

23 HOBBES: *Leviathan*, PART IV, 272b

31 SPINOZA: *Ethics*, PART III, DEF 1–3 395d-396a

35 HUME: *Human Understanding*, SECT VI 469d-470d passim; SECT VIII, DIV 67 480c-481a

42 KANT: *Judgement*, 566a-b

51 TOLSTOY: *War and Peace*, BK IX, 342a-344b; BK XIII, 584d-585b

53 JAMES: *Psychology*, 71a; 91a-92a; 765b; 857b-858a passim

1b. Chance as the absolutely fortuitous, the spontaneous or uncaused

8 ARISTOTLE: *Physics*, BK II, CH 4 [196^{a}25–^{b}4] 272d-273a; CH 6 [198^{a}5–14] 275a

12 LUCRETIUS: *Nature of Things*, BK I [1022–1029] 13c-d; BK II [184–293] 17b-18d esp [284–293] 18c-d; [1048–1066] 28b-c; BK V [181–194] 63b-c; [416–431] 66c-d

17 PLOTINUS: *Third Ennead*, TR I, CH 3 79b-c

18 AUGUSTINE: *City of God*, BK IV, CH 18 197c-198a

19 AQUINAS: *Summa Theologica*, PART I, Q 16, A 1, REP 2 94b-95c; Q 22, A 2, ANS 128d-130d; Q 47, A 1, ANS 256a-257b

(1. *The conception of chance.* 1*b. Chance as the absolutely fortuitous, the spontaneous or uncaused.*)

42 KANT: *Pure Reason*, 132d-133a; 140b,d-143a / *Practical Reason*, 331c-332a / *Judgement*, 566a-b

54 FREUD: *General Introduction*, 454b-c

2. The issue concerning the existence of chance or fortune

2*a.* The relation of chance to causality: philosophical or scientific determinism

7 PLATO: *Republic*, BK X, 438c-439a / *Timaeus*, 455c-456a; 465d-466a / *Statesman*, 587a-589c esp 587a-b / *Laws*, BK X, 759d-765d

8 ARISTOTLE: *Interpretation*, CH 9 28a-29d / *Posterior Analytics*, BK II, CH 11 [95^{a}3–9] 129d / *Physics*, BK II, CH 4–5 272c-274b; CH 8 [199^{a}33–^{b}26] 276c-277a / *Heavens*, BK II, CH 5 [287^{b}22–26] 379b; CH 8 [289^{b}22–28] 381b; BK IV, CH 3 [310^{a}23–31] 401d / *Generation and Corruption*, BK II, CH 6 [333^{a}35–^{b}20] 434b-c / *Metaphysics*, BK V, CH 30 547a-d; BK VI, CH 2 [1027^{a}8–18] 549b; CH 3 549c-d; BK XI, CH 8 [1065^{a}6–^{b}4] 593b-d; BK XII, CH 3 [1070^{a}4–9] 599b / *Memory and Reminiscence*, CH 2 [452^{a}30–^{b}6] 694b

9 ARISTOTLE: *Parts of Animals*, BK I, CH 1 [640^{a}12–^{b}4] 162b-163a / *Ethics*, BK III, CH 3 [1112^{a}30–33] 358b / *Rhetoric*, BK I, CH 10 [1369^{a}31–^{b}5] 612c-d

12 LUCRETIUS: *Nature of Things*, BK II [184–307] 17b-19a; [1048–1066] 28b-c; BK V [55–58] 61d; [181–194] 63b-c; [306–310] 65a; [416–431] 66c-d

12 AURELIUS: *Meditations*, BK VII, SECT 1 279b; SECT 49 282d; BK IX, SECT 28 293d-294a; SECT 35–36 294d-295a; SECT 39 295a; BK X, SECT 27 299d

17 PLOTINUS: *Third Ennead*, TR I, CH 2, 78d; CH 3 79b-c; TR II, CH 1, 82c / *Fourth Ennead*, TR III, CH 16 150c-d; TR IV, CH 33 176b-d / *Sixth Ennead*, TR VIII, CH 9–10 347a-348a

19 AQUINAS: *Summa Theologica*, PART I, Q 14, A 13, REP 1 86d-88c; Q 19, A 8 116a-d; Q 22, A 2, REP 1 128d-130d; A 4 131c-132b; Q 103, A 5, REP 1 531b-532b; A 7, REP 2 533b-d; Q 115, A 6 591d-592d; Q 116, A 1 592d-593d; A 3 594c-595a

23 HOBBES: *Leviathan*, PART II, 113b-c; PART IV, 272b

28 HARVEY: *On Animal Generation*, 412c-413a

30 BACON: *Advancement of Learning*, 45b-c

31 SPINOZA: *Ethics*, PART I, DEF 7 355b; AXIOM 3 355d; PROP 16 362a; PROP 21–23 364a-365a; PROP 26–29 365b-366c; PROP 33–36 367b-369b; PART II, PROP 31, COROL 385c; PROP 44 389b-390a; PART III, 395a-d; PROP 2, SCHOL 396d-398b; PART IV, PREF 422b,d-424a; DEF 3–4 424a; APPENDIX, VI 447c-d; PART V, PROP 6, DEMONST 454a

34 NEWTON: *Optics*, BK III, 542a-b

35 HUME: *Human Understanding*, SECT VI, DIV 46, 469d; DIV 47, 470b; SECT VIII 478b-487a passim, esp DIV 67 480c-481a, DIV 74 484a-c

38 ROUSSEAU: *Social Contract*, BK II, 397a

42 KANT: *Pure Reason*, 72c-85d esp 74b-76c; 91d-92c; 132d-133a; 140b,d-143a; 153a; 171a-172c; 184b-c / *Fund. Prin. Metaphysic of Morals*, 285c-d / *Practical Reason*, 331c-333a / *Judgement*, 558b-c; 564a-c; 566a-b; 587a-c

46 HEGEL: *Philosophy of Right*, PART III, par 342 110c-d / *Philosophy of History*, INTRO, 157b-158a

48 MELVILLE: *Moby Dick*, 159a

49 DARWIN: *Origin of Species*, 37c-d; 65a / *Descent of Man*, 593d

50 MARX: *Capital*, 10b-11b

51 TOLSTOY: *War and Peace*, BK IX, 342a-344b; BK X, 389a-391c; BK XI, 469a-472b; EPILOGUE I, 646c-650c esp 646c-647b; EPILOGUE II 675a-696d

53 JAMES: *Psychology*, 71a; 90b-93a esp 91a-92a; 377b; 387b-388a; 765b; 823a-825a passim

54 FREUD: *General Introduction*, 454b-c; 486c-487a / *Beyond the Pleasure Principle*, 660c

2*b.* The relation of chance to fate, providence, and predestination

OLD TESTAMENT: *Proverbs*, 16:33 / *Jonah*, 1:1–10 —(D) *Jonas*, 1:1–10

NEW TESTAMENT: *John*, 6:44–45,64–65—(D) *John*, 6:44–45,65–66 / *Acts*, 1:15–26; 13:48 / *Romans*, 8:28–11:36 esp 8:28–30, 9:15, 10:13–14, 11:5 / *Ephesians*, 1:4–2:10

4 HOMER: *Iliad*, BK XXIV [522–551] 176d-177a

5 AESCHYLUS: *Prometheus Bound* [507–520] 45a-b

5 SOPHOCLES: *Trachiniae* [95–140] 171a-b / *Philoctetes* [169–200] 183d-184a

5 EURIPIDES: *Helen* [712–720] 304d-305a / *Heracles Mad* [60–81] 365c-d

7 PLATO: *Laws*, BK IV, 679a-c

8 ARISTOTLE: *Physics*, BK II, CH 4 [196^{b}5–7] 273a / *Metaphysics*, BK XII, CH 10 [1075^{a}11–24] 605d-606a

9 ARISTOTLE: *Ethics*, BK I, CH 9 [1099^{b}8–24] 345a-b

12 EPICTETUS: *Discourses*, BK I, CH 6 110c-112b; CH 12 118d-120b; CH 16 121d-122d; BK III, CH 17 191d-192a; BK IV, CH 3 224b-d

12 AURELIUS: *Meditations*, BK II, SECT 3 257a-b; SECT 11 258a-b; BK III, SECT 11 262a-b; BK IV, SECT 3, 263c; BK IX, SECT 28 293d-294a; BK XII, SECT 14 308c

13 VIRGIL: *Aeneid*, BK I [194–209] 108a-b; [595–624] 119b-120a; BK XII [631–649] 370b-371a

14 PLUTARCH: *Camillus*, 107c

15 TACITUS: *Annals*, BK VI, 91b-d / *Histories*, BK I, 194a-c

17 PLOTINUS: *Third Ennead*, TR II, CH 1–2 82c-83d; TR III, CH 2 93d / *Fourth Ennead*, TR III, CH 16 150c-d

(5. *The control of chance or contingency by art.*)

8 ARISTOTLE: *Posterior Analytics*, BK II, CH 11 [95^{a}3–9] 129d / *Metaphysics*, BK I, CH 1 [980^b 25–981^{a}5] 499b; BK XII, CH 3 [1070^{a}4–9] 599b

9 ARISTOTLE: *Parts of Animals*, BK I, CH 1 [640^{a}25–33] 162d / *Ethics*, BK I, CH 9 [1099^{b}18–24] 345a-b; BK II, CH 4 [1105^{a}18–26] 350d; BK III, CH 3 [1112^{a}19–^{b}12] 358a-c; BK VI, CH 4 [1140^{a}10–23] 388d-389a / *Politics*, BK I, CH 11 [1258^{b}35–36] 453b; BK II, CH 11 [1273^{b}17–24] 470b; BK VII, CH 13 [1332^{a}28–32] 537a / *Rhetoric*, BK I, CH 1 [1354^{a}1–11] 593a; CH 5 [1361^b 39–1362^{a}4] 602c

10 HIPPOCRATES: *Ancient Medicine*, par 1 1a-b

13 VIRGIL: *Aeneid*, BK XII [391–440] 364b-365b

19 AQUINAS: *Summa Theologica*, PART I, Q 57, A 3, ANS 297b-298a; PART I–II, Q 14, A 4, ANS 679b-d

21 DANTE: *Divine Comedy*, PARADISE, XIII [52–84] 126a-b

25 MONTAIGNE: *Essays*, 52c-53c; 377a-d

26 SHAKESPEARE: *Richard II*, ACT III, SC IV [29–66] 340c-d

30 BACON: *Advancement of Learning*, 50c-51d; 56b-57b; 85c-86c; 90b-91a / *Novum Organum*, BK I, APH 8 107c-d; APH 82, 121a; APH 108–109 128d-129c; BK II, APH 31 159d-161a

35 HUME: *Human Understanding*, SECT VIII, DIV 67 480c-481a

43 MILL: *Utilitarianism*, 452a-b

47 GOETHE: *Faust*, PRELUDE [134–157] 4a-b

50 MARX: *Capital*, 183b-184a

51 TOLSTOY: *War and Peace*, BK IV, 188a-190c; BK IX, 359a-365c; BK X, 425b-426a; 441b-442c; 445d-448c; 456a-459d esp 458c-459d; BK XI, 471c-472b; 505a-507a esp 505d-506a, 507a; BK XIII, 563c-575a esp 563c-564d, 570d-572a, 573c-575a; 582a-587d esp 584c-585b; BK XIV, 609a-613d; BK XV, 618b-621b

53 JAMES: *Psychology*, 673a-b

6. Chance and fortune in human affairs: the mythology of Fortune

6a. Chance and fortune in the life of the individual

OLD TESTAMENT: *Ecclesiastes*, 9:11

4 HOMER: *Iliad* 3a-179d esp BK XXIV [522–551] 176d-177a

5 AESCHYLUS: *Persians* [909–1076] 24d-26d

5 SOPHOCLES: *Oedipus the King* 99a-113a,c esp [1522–1530] 113c / *Antigone* [1155–1171] 140d-141a / *Trachiniae* [1–48] 170a-c; [293–306] 172c-d; [932–946] 178b / *Philoctetes* [500–506] 186c

5 EURIPIDES: *Heracleidae* 248a-257a,c esp [853–866] 255d / *Suppliants* [263–270] 260c; [549–557] 263a / *Trojan Women* 270a-281a,c esp [1200–1206] 280a-b / *Heracles Mad* 365a-377d esp [474–496] 369a

6 HERODOTUS: *History*, BK I, 7b-8a; 46c; BK III, 91d-92b; 98a-99a; 116a-b; BK VII, 225b-d; 252b-c

6 THUCYDIDES: *Peloponnesian War*, BK II, 398c-d

7 PLATO: *Euthydemus*, 69a-71a / *Republic*, BK X, 439b-440c

8 ARISTOTLE: *Physics*, BK II, CH 5 [197^{a}25–32] 274a-b

9 ARISTOTLE: *Ethics*, BK I, CH 9–10 345a-346c; BK VII, CH 13 [1153^{b}14–24] 405a / *Politics*, BK VII, CH 1 [1323^{b}22–36] 527c-d / *Rhetoric*, BK I, CH 5 [1361^{b}39–1362^{a}11] 602c-d; CH 10 [1368^b 33–1369^{a}7] 612a-b; [1369^{a}31–^{b}5] 612c-d; BK II, CH 12 [1388^{b}31–1389^{a}1] 636a; CH 15–17 638a-639a

12 AURELIUS: *Meditations*, BK II, SECT 3 257a-b; SECT 17 259b-d; BK III, SECT 4 260b-261a; SECT 10–11 261d-262b; BK IV, SECT 26 265d; SECT 33–36 266c-d; SECT 44 267b; SECT 49 268a-c; BK V, SECT 8 269d-270b; SECT 24 272c; SECT 27 272d; BK VI, SECT 11 274c; SECT 20 276a; SECT 39 277d; SECT 58 279d; BK VII, SECT 8 280b; SECT 34 282a; SECT 54 283b; SECT 57–58 283c-d; SECT 68 284c-d; SECT 75 285c; BK VIII, SECT 17 286d; SECT 32 287d-288a; SECT 35 288b; SECT 44–47 289a-c; SECT 51 289d-290a; BK IX, SECT 28 293d-294a; BK X, SECT 3 296d; SECT 5–6 296d-297b; SECT 25 299c; SECT 33 300c-301a; SECT 35 301b; BK XII, SECT 3 307b-d; SECT 11–14 308b-c

13 VIRGIL: *Aeneid*, BK I [194–209] 108a-b; [595–624] 119b-120a; BK XII [391–440] 364b-365b; [631–649] 370b-371a

14 PLUTARCH: *Solon*, 66b-d; 74c-75c / *Sulla*, 370c-371b / *Sertorius*, 457b,d-458b / *Pompey*, 535c-d / *Demetrius*, 739c-740d; 744b-c

15 TACITUS: *Annals*, BK VI, 91b-d / *Histories*, BK IV, 281a-b

17 PLOTINUS: *Second Ennead*, TR III, CH 10 46a-b / *Third Ennead*, TR II–III 82c-97b passim / *Fourth Ennead*, TR III, CH 16 150c-d

18 AUGUSTINE: *Confessions*, BK IV, par 4–6 20a-d; BK VII, par 8–10 45d-47a / *City of God*, BK IV, CH 18–19 197c-198b

21 DANTE: *Divine Comedy*, HELL, VII [49–99] 10a-c; XV [22–99] 21b-22a; PARADISE, VIII [94–148] 118a-c

22 CHAUCER: *Troilus and Cressida*, BK I, STANZA 120–122 16b-17a; BK II, STANZA 40–42 26b-27a; BK III, STANZA 89 66a; BK IV, STANZA 41 94a; STANZA 55–56 95b-96a / *Words of the Host* [12,226–231] 371a / *Tale of Melibeus*, par 42 419a-b / *Monk's Tale* 434a-448b

23 MACHIAVELLI: *Prince*, CH XXV 35a-36b

23 HOBBES: *Leviathan*, PART I, 79b-80d; 81b-c

24 RABELAIS: *Gargantua and Pantagruel*, BK III, 144d-156c; 158b-178a; 204c-215c; BK IV, 258c-259d

25 MONTAIGNE: *Essays*, 26d-28a; 52c-53c; 100a-101c; 169c-170a; 302b-306a passim; 312d-

CROSS-REFERENCES

For: Other discussions of the issue of determinism and chance, *see* FATE 3, 5-6; HISTORY 4a(1);
NATURE 3c-3c(1); NECESSITY AND CONTINGENCY 3a-3c; and for the relation of chance to
free will, *see* LIBERTY 4a; WILL 5a(3), 5c.

The general theory of cause and its bearing on the concept of chance, *see* CAUSE 1-1b, 5d-6;
NATURE 3c(3).

The theological problems of chance in relation to fate, providence, and predestination, *see*
CAUSE 7b-7c; FATE 4; GOD 7b.

Other discussions of the theory of probability, *see* JUDGMENT 6c; KNOWLEDGE 4b, 6d(1)-
6d(3); NECESSITY AND CONTINGENCY 4a; OPINION 1, 3b; SCIENCE 4e; TRUTH 4d.

Discussions bearing on the relation of art to chance, *see* ART 1, 2a; and for the role of chance
in the sphere of prudence, *see* PRUDENCE 4a-4b, 5a.

The theory of the goods of fortune, *see* GOOD AND EVIL 4d; HAPPINESS 2b(1); VIRTUE AND
VICE 6c; WEALTH 10a.

ADDITIONAL READINGS

Listed below are works not included in *Great Books of the Western World*, but relevant to the
idea and topics with which this chapter deals. These works are divided into two groups:

I. Works by authors represented in this collection.
II. Works by authors not represented in this collection.

For the date, place, and other facts concerning the publication of the works cited, consult
the Bibliography of Additional Readings which follows the last chapter of *The Great Ideas*.

I.

PLUTARCH. "Of Fortune," "Of the Tranquillity of
the Mind," in *Moralia*
F. BACON. "Of Fortune," in *Essays*
HUME. *A Treatise of Human Nature*, BK I, PART III,
SECT XI–XIII
KANT. *Introduction to Logic*, X
J. S. MILL. *A System of Logic*, BK III, CH 17–18
FREUD. *The Psychopathology of Everyday Life*, CH 12
W. JAMES. "The Dilemma of Determinism," in
The Will to Believe
———. *Some Problems of Philosophy*, CH 9–13

II.

BOETHIUS. *The Consolation of Philosophy*, BK II,
IV–V
SUÁREZ. *Disputationes Metaphysicae*, XIX (12)
J. BUTLER. *The Analogy of Religion*, INTRO
VOLTAIRE. "Change or Generation of Events,"
"Necessary-Necessity," "Power-Omnipotence,"
in *A Philosophical Dictionary*
SCHOPENHAUER. *On the Fourfold Root of the Princi-
ple of Sufficient Reason*
LAPLACE. *A Philosophical Essay on Probabilities*
DE MORGAN. *An Essay on Probabilities*
COURNOT. *Exposition de la théorie des chances et des
probabilités*
BOOLE. *An Investigation of the Laws of Thought*, CH
16–18, 21
TODHUNTER. *History of the Mathematical Theory of
Probability*

VENN. *The Logic of Chance*
WHITWORTH. *Choice and Chance*
BOUTROUX. *The Contingency of the Laws of Nature*
JEVONS. *The Principles of Science*, CH 10–12
BRADLEY. *The Principles of Logic*, Terminal Essays,
VIII
C. S. PEIRCE. *Collected Papers*, VOL II, par 645–754;
VOL VI, par 35–65
T. HARDY. *Life's Little Ironies*
PEARSON. *The Chances of Death*
MEYERSON. *Identity and Reality*, CH 9
POINCARÉ. *Science and Hypothesis*, PART IV, CH 11
———. *Science and Method*, BK I, CH 4
HENDERSON. *The Fitness of the Environment*
N. R. CAMPBELL. *Physics; the Elements*, CH 7
W. E. JOHNSON. *Logic*, PART III, CH 2
J. M. KEYNES. *A Treatise on Probability*, PART I–II,
IV–V
G. N. LEWIS. *The Anatomy of Science*, ESSAY VI
DEWEY. *The Quest for Certainty*, CH 1
HEISENBERG. *The Physical Principles of the Quantum
Theory*
NAGEL. *On the Logic of Measurement*
M. R. COHEN. *Reason and Nature*, BK I, CH 3(4)
MARITAIN. *A Preface to Metaphysics*, LECT VII
REICHENBACH. *Theory of Probability*
SANTAYANA. *The Realm of Truth*, CH 11
VON NEUMANN and MORGENSTERN. *Theory of Games
and Economic Behavior*
JEFFREYS. *Theory of Probability*
B. RUSSELL. *Human Knowledge, Its Scope and
Limits*, PART V

Chapter 10: CHANGE

INTRODUCTION

FROM the pre-Socratic physicists and the ancient philosophers to Darwin, Marx, and James—and, in our own day, Dewey and Whitehead—the fact of change has been a major focus of speculative and scientific inquiry.

Except by Parmenides and his school, the existence of change has never been denied. Nor can it be without rejecting all sense-perception as illusory, which is precisely what Zeno's paradoxes seem to do, according to one interpretation of them. But if argument cannot refute the testimony of the senses, neither can reasoning support it. The fact of change, because it is evident to the senses, does not need proof.

That change is, is evident, but *what* change is, is neither evident nor easy to define. What principles or factors are common to every sort of change, how change or becoming is related to permanence or being, what sort of existence belongs to mutable things and to change itself—these are questions to which answers are not obtainable merely by observation. Nor will simple observation, without the aid of experiment, measurement, and mathematical calculation, discover the laws and properties of motion.

The analysis of change or motion has been a problem for the philosophers of nature. They have been concerned with the definition of change, its relation to being, the classification of the kinds of change. The measurement of motion, on the other hand, and the mathematical formulation of its laws have occupied the experimental natural scientists. Both natural philosophy and natural science share a common subject matter, though they approach it by different methods and with different interests. Both are entitled to use the name "physics" for their subject matter.

The Greek word *phüsis* from which "physics" comes has, as its Latin equivalent, the word *natura* from which "nature" comes. In their original significance, both words had reference to the sensible world of changing things, or to its underlying principle—to the ultimate source of change. The physics of the philosopher and the physics of the empirical scientist are alike inquiries concerning the nature of things, not in every respect but in regard to their change and motion. The conclusions of both inquiries have metaphysical implications for the nature of the physical world and for the character of physical existence.

The philosopher draws these implications for being from the study of becoming. The scientist, in turn, draws upon philosophical distinctions in order to define the objects of his study. Galileo, for example, in separating the problem of freely falling bodies from the motion of projectiles, employs the traditional philosophical distinction between natural and violent motion. The analysis of time and space (basic variables in Newtonian mechanics), the distinction between discontinuous and continuous change, and the problem of the divisibility of a continuous motion—these are philosophical considerations pre-supposed by the scientific measurement of motion.

WE HAVE SO FAR used the words "change" and "motion," as well as "becoming," as if all three were interchangeable in meaning. That is somewhat inaccurate, even for the ancients who regarded all kinds of change except one as motions; it is much less accurate for the moderns who have tended to restrict the meaning of "motion" to local motion or change of place. It is necessary, therefore, to examine briefly the kinds of change and to indicate the problems which arise with these distinctions.

In his physical treatises, Aristotle distinguishes four kinds of change. "When the change from contrary to contrary is *in quantity*," he writes, "it is 'growth and diminution'; when it is *in place*, it is 'motion'; when it is ... *in quality*, it is 'alteration'; but when nothing persists of which the resultant is a property (or an 'accident' in any sense of the term), it is 'coming to be,' and the converse change is 'passing away.'" Aristotle also uses other pairs of words—"generation" and "corruption," "becoming" and "perishing"—to name the last kind of change.

Of the four kinds of change, only the last is not called "motion." But in the context of saying that "becoming cannot be a motion," Aristotle also remarks that "every motion is a kind of change." He does not restrict the meaning of motion to change in place, which is usually called "local motion" or "locomotion." There are, then, according to Aristotle's vocabulary, three kinds of motion: (1) local motion, in which bodies change from place to place; (2) alteration or qualitative motion, in which bodies change with respect to such attributes as color, texture, or temperature; (3) increase and decrease, or quantitative motion, in which bodies change in size. And, in addition, there is the one kind of change which is not motion—generation and corruption. This consists in the coming to be or passing away of a body which, while it has being, exists as an individual substance of a certain sort.

Becoming and perishing are most readily exemplified by the birth and death of living things, but Aristotle also includes the transformation of water into ice or vapor as examples of generation and corruption. One distinctive characteristic of generation and corruption, in Aristotle's conception of this type of change, is their instantaneity. He thinks that the other three kinds of change are continuous processes, taking time, whereas things come into being or pass away instantaneously. Aristotle thus applies the word "motion" only to the continuous changes which time can measure. He never says that time is the measure of change, but only of motion.

But the contrast between the one mode of change which is not motion and the three kinds of motion involves more than this difference with regard to time and continuity. Aristotle's analysis considers the subject of change—that

which undergoes transformation—and the starting-point and goal of motion. "Every motion," he says, "proceeds from something and to something, that which is directly in motion being distinct from that to which it is in motion and that from which it is in motion; for instance, we may take the three things 'wood,' 'hot,' and 'cold,' of which the first is that which is in motion, the second is that which to which the motion proceeds, and the third is that from which it proceeds."

In the alteration which occurs when the wood changes quality, just as in the increase or decrease which occurs with a body's change in quantity and in the local motion which occurs with a body's change of place, *that which changes* persists throughout the change as the same kind of substance. The wood does not cease to be wood when it becomes hot or cold; the stone does not cease to be a stone when it rolls from here to there, or the organism an animal of a certain kind when it grows in size. In all these cases, "the substratum"—that which is the subject of change—"persists and changes in its own properties. ... The body, although persisting as the same body, is now healthy and now ill; and the bronze is now spherical and at another time angular, and yet remains the same bronze."

Because the substance of the changing thing remains the same while changing in its properties—*i.e.*, in such attributes or accidents as quality, quantity, and place—Aristotle groups the three kinds of motion together as *accidental change*. The changing thing does not come to be or pass away absolutely, but only in a certain respect. In contrast, generation and corruption involve a change in the very substance of a thing. "When nothing perceptible persists in its identity as a substratum, and the thing changes as a whole," then, according to Aristotle, "it is a coming-to-be of one substance, and the passing-away of another."

In such becoming or perishing, it is matter itself rather than a body or a substance which is transformed. Matter takes on or loses the form of a certain kind of substance. For example, when the nutriment is assimilated to the form of a living body, the bread or corn becomes the flesh and blood of a man. When an animal dies, its body decomposes into the elements of inorganic matter. Because it is a change of substance itself, Aristotle calls the one kind of change which is not motion *substantial change*, and speaks of it as "a coming-to-be or passing-away simply"—that is, not in a certain respect, but absolutely or "without qualification."

These distinctions are involved in a long tradition of discussion and controversy. They cannot be affirmed or denied without opposite sides being taken on the fundamental issues concerning substance and accident, matter and form, and the causes of change or motion. The adoption or rejection of these distinctions affects one's view of the difference between inorganic and organic change, and the difference between the motions of matter and the changes which take place in mind. The statement of certain problems is determined accordingly; as, for example, the problem of the transmutation of the elements, which persists in various forms from the physics of the ancients through mediaeval alchemy and the beginnings of modern chemistry to present considerations of radioactivity and atomic fission.

SINCE THE 17TH CENTURY, motion has been identified with local motion. "I can conceive no other kind" of motion, Descartes writes, "and do not consider that we ought to conceive any other in nature." As it is expressed "in common parlance," motion, he says, "is nothing more than the *action by which any body passes from one place to another.*"

This can hardly be taken to mean that change of place is the only observable type of change. That other kinds of change are observable cannot be denied. The science of mechanics or dynamics may be primarily or exclusively concerned with local motions, but other branches of natural science, certainly chemistry, deal with qualitative transformations; and the biological sciences study growth and decay, birth and death.

The emphasis on local motion as the only kind of motion, while it does not exclude apparent changes of other sorts, does raise a question about their reality. The question can be put in several ways. Are the various *apparently* different kinds of change *really* distinct, or can they all be reduced to aspects of one underlying

mode of change which is local motion? Even supposing that the kinds of change are not reducible to one another, is local motion primary in the sense that it is involved in all the others?

When mechanics dominates the physical sciences (as has been so largely the case in modern times), there is a tendency to reduce all the observable diversity of change to various appearances of local motion. Newton, for example, explicitly expresses this desire to formulate all natural phenomena in terms of the mechanics of moving particles. In the Preface to the first edition of his *Mathematical Principles*, after recounting his success in dealing with celestial phenomena, he says, "I wish we could derive the rest of the phenomena of Nature by the same kind of reasoning from mechanical principles, for I am induced by many reasons to suspect that they may all depend upon certain forces by which the particles of bodies, by some causes hitherto unknown, are either mutually impelled towards one another, and cohere in regular figures, or are repelled and recede from one another."

The notion that all change can be reduced to the results of local motion is not, however, of modern origin. Lucretius expounds the theory of the Greek atomists that all the phenomena of change can be explained by reference to the local motion of indivisible particles coming together and separating. Change of place is the only change which occurs on the level of the ultimate physical reality. The atoms neither come to be nor pass away, nor change in quality or size.

But though we find the notion in ancient atomism, it is only in modern physics that the emphasis upon local motion tends to exclude all other kinds of change. It is characteristic of what James calls "the modern mechanico-physical philosophy" to begin "by saying that the *only* facts are collocations and motions of primordial solids, and the only laws the changes of motion which changes in collocation bring." James quotes Helmholtz to the effect that "the ultimate goal of theoretic physics is to find the last *unchanging* causes of the processes of Nature." If, to this end, "we imagine the world composed of elements with unalterable qualities," then, Helmholtz continues, "the only changes that can remain in such a world are spatial changes, *i.e.*, movements, and the only outer relations which can modify the action of the forces are spatial too, or, in other words, the forces are motor forces dependent for their effect on spatial relations."

In the history of physics, Aristotle represents the opposite view. No one of the four kinds of change which he distinguishes has for him greater physical reality than the others. Just as quality cannot be reduced to quantity, or either of these to place, so in his judgment the motions associated with these terms are irreducible to one another. Yet Aristotle does assign to local motion a certain primacy. "Motion in its most general and primary sense," he writes, "is change of place, which we call locomotion." He does not mean merely that this is the primary sense of the word, but rather that no other kind of motion can occur without local motion being somehow involved in the process. Showing how increase and decrease depends on alteration, and how that in turn depends on change of place, he says that "of the three kinds of motion . . . it is this last, which we call locomotion, that must be primary."

THE SHIFT IN MEANING of the word "motion" would not by itself mark a radical departure in the theory of change, but it is accompanied by a shift in thought which has the most radical consequences. At the same time that motion is identified with local motion, Descartes conceives motion as something completely actual and thoroughly intelligible. For the ancients, becoming of any sort had both less reality and less intelligibility than being.

Aristotle had defined motion as the actuality of that which is potential in a respect in which it is still potential to some degree. According to what Descartes calls its strict as opposed to its popular meaning, motion is "the transference of one part of matter or one body from the vicinity of those bodies that are in immediate contact with it, and which we regard as in repose, into the vicinity of others." This definition—contrasted with the Aristotelian conception which it generally supersedes in the subsequent tradition of natural science—is as revolutionary as the Cartesian analytical geometry is by comparison with the Euclidean. Nor

is it an unconnected fact that the analytical geometry prepares the way for the differential calculus that is needed to measure variable motions, their velocities, and their accelerations.

The central point on which the two definitions are opposed constitutes one of the most fundamental issues in the philosophy of nature. Does motion involve a transition from potential to actual existence, or only the substitution of one actual state for another—only a "transportation," as Descartes says, from one place to another?

While motion is going on, the moving thing, according to Aristotle's definition, must be partly potential and partly actual in the same respect. The leaf turning red, *while it is altering*, has not yet fully reddened. When it becomes as red as it can get, it can no longer change in that respect. Before it began to change, it was actually green; and since it could become red, it was potentially red. But while the change is in process, the potentiality of the leaf to become red is being actualized. This actualization progresses until the change is completed.

The same analysis would apply to a ball in motion. Until it comes to rest in a given place, its potentiality for being there is undergoing progressive actualization. In short, motion involves some departure from pure potentiality in a given respect, and never complete attainment of full actuality in that same respect. When there is no departure from potentiality, motion has not yet begun; when the attainment of actuality is complete, the motion has terminated.

The Aristotelian definition of motion is the object of much ridicule in the 17th century. Repeating the phrasing which had become traditional in the schools—"the actualization of what exists in potentiality, in so far as it is potential"—Descartes asks: "Now who understands these words? And who at the same time does not know what motion is? Will not everyone admit that those philosophers have been trying to find a knot in a bulrush?" Locke also finds it meaningless. "What more exquisite jargon could the wit of man invent than this definition . . . which would puzzle any rational man to whom it was not already known by its famous absurdity, to guess what word it could ever be supposed to be the explication of. If

Tully, asking a Dutchman what *beweeginge* was," Locke continues, "should have received this explication in his own language, that it was *actus entis in potentia quatenus in potentia*; I ask whether any one can imagine he could thereby have guessed what the word *beweeginge* signified?"

Locke does not seem to be satisfied with any definition of motion. "The atomists, who define motion to be 'a passage from one place to another,' what do they more than put one synonymous word for another? For what is *passage* other than *motion*? . . . Nor will 'the successive application of the superficies of one body to those of another,' which the Cartesians give us, prove a much better definition of motion, when well examined." But though Locke rejects the definition of the atomists and the Cartesians on formal grounds, he accepts their idea of motion as simply change of place; whereas he dismisses the Aristotelian definition as sheer absurdity and rejects the idea that motion or change necessarily involves a potentiality capable of progressive fulfillment.

As we have already remarked, the omission of potentiality from the conception of motion is a theoretical shift of the deepest significance. It occurs not only in Descartes' *Principles of Philosophy* and in the atomism of Hobbes and Gassendi, but also in the mechanics of Galileo and Newton. According to these modern philosophers and scientists, a moving body is *always actually* somewhere. It occupies a different place at every moment in a continuous motion. The motion can be described as the successive occupation by the body of different places at different times. Though all the parts of the motion do not coexist, the moving particle is completely actual throughout. It loses no reality and gains none in the course of the motion, since the various positions the body occupies lie totally outside its material nature. It would, of course, be more difficult to analyze alteration in color or biological growth in these terms, but it must be remembered that efforts have been made to apply such an analysis through the reduction of all other modes of change to local motion.

The principle of inertia, first discerned by Galileo, is critically relevant to the issue between these two conceptions of motion. It is stated by Newton as the first of his "axioms or laws of motion." "Every body," he writes, "continues in its state of rest, or of uniform motion in a right line, unless it is compelled to change that state by forces impressed upon it." As applied to the motion of projectiles, the law declares that they "continue in their motions, so far as they are not retarded by the resistance of air, or impelled downwards by the force of gravity."

In his experimental reasoning concerning the acceleration of bodies moving down inclined planes, Galileo argues that a body which has achieved a certain velocity on the descent would, if it then proceeded along a horizontal plane, continue infinitely at the same velocity —except for the retardation of air resistance and friction. "Any velocity once imparted to a moving body," he maintains, "will be rigidly maintained as long as the external causes of acceleration or retardation are removed." So in the case of projectiles, they would retain the velocity and direction imparted to them by the cannon, were it not for the factors of gravity and air resistance. Bodies actually in motion possess their motion in themselves as a complete actuality. They need no causes acting on them to keep them in motion, but only to change their direction or bring them to rest.

The motion of projectiles presents a difficulty for the theory which describes all motion as a reduction of potency to act. "If everything that is in motion, with the exception of things that move themselves, is moved by something else, how is it," Aristotle asks, "that some things, *e.g.*, things thrown, continue to be in motion when their movent is no longer in contact with them?" This is a problem for Aristotle precisely because he supposes that the moving cause must act on the thing being moved throughout the period of the motion. For the potentiality to be progressively reduced to actuality, it must be continuously acted upon.

Aristotle's answer postulates a series of causes so that contact can be maintained between the projectile and the moving cause. "The original movent," he writes, "gives the power of being a movent either to air or to water or to something else of the kind, naturally adapted for imparting and undergoing motion. . . . The motion begins to cease when the motive force produced in one member of the consecutive series is at each stage less than that possessed by the preceding member, and it finally ceases when one member no longer causes the next member to be a movent but only causes it to be in motion." It follows that inertia must be denied by those who hold that a moving body *always* requires a mover; or even that a body cannot sustain itself in motion beyond a point proportionate to the quantity of the impressed force which originally set it in motion.

FOR THE ANCIENTS, the basic contrast between being and becoming (or between the permanent and the changing) is a contrast between the intelligible and the sensible. This is most sharply expressed in Plato's distinction between the sensible realm of material things and the intelligible realm of ideas. "What is that which always is and has no becoming," Timaeus asks; "and what is that which is always becoming and never is?" He answers his own question by saying that "that which is apprehended by intelligence and reason is always in the same state; but that which is conceived by opinion with the help of sensations and without reason, is always in a process of becoming and perishing, and never really is."

Even though Aristotle differs from Plato in thinking that change and the changing can be objects of scientific knowledge, he, too, holds becoming to be less intelligible than being, precisely because change necessarily involves potentiality. Yet becoming can be understood to the extent that we can discover the principles of its being—the unchanging principles of change. "In pursuing the truth," Aristotle remarks—and this applies to the truth about change as well as everything else—"one must start from the things that are always in the same state and suffer no change."

For Aristotle, change is intelligible through the three elements of permanence which are its principles: (1) the enduring substratum of change, and the contraries—(2) that to which, and (3) that from which, the change takes place. The same principles are sometimes stated to be (1) matter, (2) form, and (3) privation; the matter or substratum being that which both lacks a certain form and has a definite potentiality for possessing it. Change occurs when

the matter undergoes a transformation in which it comes to have the form of which it was deprived by the possession of a contrary form.

Neither of the contrary forms changes. Only the thing composite of matter and form changes with respect to the forms of its matter. Hence these principles of change are themselves unchanging. Change takes place *through*, not *in*, them. As constituents of the changing thing, they are the principles of its mutable being, principles of its *being* as well as of its being *mutable*.

The explanation of change by reference to what does not change seems to be common to all theories of becoming. Lucretius, as we have already seen, explains the coming to be and passing away of all other things by the motions of atoms which neither come to be nor pass away. The eternity of the atoms underlies the mutability of everything else.

Yet the atoms are not completely immutable. They move forever through the void which, according to Lucretius, is required for their motion. Their local motion is, moreover, an actual property of the atoms. For them, *to be* is *to be in motion*. Here then, as in the Cartesian theory, no potentiality is involved, and motion is completely real and completely intelligible.

THE NOTIONS OF time and eternity are inseparable from the theory of change or motion. As the chapters on TIME and SPACE indicate, local motion involves the dimensions of space as well as time, but all change requires time, and time itself is inconceivable apart from change or motion. Furthermore, as appears in the chapters on TIME and ETERNITY, the two fundamentally opposed meanings of eternity differ according to whether they imply endless change or absolute changelessness.

Eternity is sometimes identified with infinite time. It is in this sense that Plato, in the *Timaeus*, refers to time as "the moving image of eternity" and implies that time, which belongs to the realm of ever-changing things, resembles the eternal only through its perpetual endurance. The other sense of the eternal is also implied—the sense in which eternity belongs to the realm of immutable being. The eternal in this sense, as Montaigne points out, is not merely that "which never had beginning nor never shall have ending," but rather that "to which time can bring no mutation."

There are two great problems which use the word "eternity" in these opposite senses. One is the problem of the eternity of motion: the question whether motion has or can have either a beginning or an end. The other is the problem of the existence of eternal objects—immutable things which have their being apart from time and change.

The two problems are connected in ancient thought. Aristotle, for example, argues that "it is impossible that movement should either have come into being or cease to be, for it must always have existed." Since "nothing is moved at random, but there must always be something present to move it," a cause is required to sustain the endless motions of nature. This cause, which Aristotle calls "the prime mover," must be "something which moves without being moved, being eternal, substance, and actuality."

Aristotle's theory of a prime mover sets up a hierarchy of causes to account for the different kinds of motion observable in the universe. The perfect circular motion of the heavens serves to mediate between the prime mover which is totally unmoved and the less regular cycles of terrestrial change. The "constant cycle" of movement in the stars differs from the irregular cycle of "generation and destruction" on earth. For the first, Aristotle asserts the necessity of "something which is always moved with an unceasing motion, which is motion in a circle." He calls this motion of the first heavenly sphere "the simple spatial movement of the universe" as a whole. Besides this "there are other spatial movements—those of the planets —which are eternal" but are "always acting in different ways" and so are able to account for the other cycle in nature—the irregular cycle of generation and corruption.

In addition, a kind of changelessness is attributed to all the celestial bodies which Aristotle calls "eternal." Eternally in motion, they are also eternally in being. Though not immovable, they are supposed to be incorruptible substances. They never begin to be and never perish.

The theory of a world eternally in motion is challenged by Jewish and Christian theologians who affirm, as an article of their religious faith, that "in the beginning God created heaven and earth." The world's motions, like its existence, have a beginning in the act of creation. Creation itself, Aquinas insists, is not change or motion of any sort, "except according to our way of understanding. For change means that the same thing should be different now from what it was previously. . . . But in creation, by which the whole substance of a thing is produced, the same thing can be taken as different now and before, only according to our way of understanding, so that a thing is understood as first not existing at all, and afterwards as existing." Since creation is an absolute coming to be from non-being, no pre-existent matter is acted upon as in generation, in artistic production, or in any of the forms of motion.

THE PHILOSOPHICAL and theological issues concerning creation and change, eternity and time, are further discussed in the chapters on CAUSE, ETERNITY, and WORLD. Other problems arising from the analysis of change must at least be briefly mentioned here.

Though less radical than the difference between creation and change, the difference between the motions of inert or non-living things and the vital activities of plants and animals raises for any theory of change the question whether the same principles apply to both. The rolling stone and the running animal both move locally, but are both motions *locomotion* in the same sense? Augmentation occurs both in the growth of a crystal and the growth of a plant, but are both of them *growing* in the same sense? In addition, there seems to be one kind of change in living things which has no parallel in the movements of inert bodies. Animals and men learn. They acquire knowledge, form habits and change them. Can change of mind be explained in the same terms as change in matter?

The issues raised by questions of this sort are more fully discussed in the chapters on ANIMAL, HABIT, and LIFE. Certain other issues must be entirely reserved for discussion elsewhere. The special problems of local motion—such as the properties of rectilinear and circular motion, the distinction between uniform and variable motion, and the uniform or variable acceleration of the latter—are problems which belong to the chapters on Astronomy and Mechanics. Change, furthermore, is a basic fact not only for the natural scientist, but for the historian—the natural historian or the historian of man and society. The considerations relevant to this aspect of change receive treatment in the chapters on Evolution, History, and Progress.

Even these ramifications of discussion do not exhaust the significance of change. The cyclical course of the emotions and the alternation of pleasure and pain have been thought inexplicable without reference to change of state in regard to desire and aversion—the motion from want to satisfaction, or from possession to deprivation. Change is not only a factor in the analysis of emotion, but it is also itself an object of man's emotional attitudes. It is both loved and hated, sought and avoided.

According to Pascal, man tries desperately to avoid a state of rest. He does everything he can to keep things in flux. "Our nature consists in motion," he writes; "complete rest is death. . . . Nothing is so insufferable to man," he continues, "as to be completely at rest, without pas-sions, without business, without diversion, without study. He then feels his nothingness, his forlornness, his dependence, his weakness, his emptiness." Darwin does not think that the desire for change is peculiar to man. "The lower animals," he writes, "are . . . likewise capricious in their affections, aversions, and sense of beauty. There is also reason to suspect that they love novelty for its own sake."

But men also wish to avoid change. The old Prince Bolkonski, in *War and Peace*, "could not comprehend how anyone could wish to alter his life or introduce anything new into it." This is not merely an old man's view. For the most part, it is permanence rather than transiency, the enduring rather than the novel, which the poets celebrate when they express man's discontent with his own mutability. The withering and perishing of all mortal things, the assault of time and change upon all things familiar and loved, have moved them to elegy over the evanescent and the ephemeral. From Virgil's *Sunt lacrimae rerum et mentem mortalia tangunt* to Shakespeare's "Love is not love which alters when it alteration finds," the poets have mourned the inevitability of change.

OUTLINE OF TOPICS

REFERENCES

To find the passages cited, use the numbers in heavy type, which are the volume and page numbers of the passages referred to. For example, in 4 HOMER: *Iliad*, BK II [265–283] 12d, the number 4 is the number of the volume in the set; the number 12d indicates that the passage is in section d of page 12.

PAGE SECTIONS: When the text is printed in one column, the letters a and b refer to the upper and lower halves of the page. For example, in 53 JAMES: *Psychology*, 116a–119b, the passage begins in the upper half of page 116 and ends in the lower half of page 119. When the text is printed in two columns, the letters a and b refer to the upper and lower halves of the left-hand side of the page, the letters c and d to the upper and lower halves of the right-hand side of the page. For example, in 7 PLATO: *Symposium*, 163b–164c, the passage begins in the lower half of the left-hand side of page 163 and ends in the upper half of the right-hand side of page 164.

AUTHOR'S DIVISIONS: One or more of the main divisions of a work (such as PART, BK, CH, SECT) are sometimes included in the reference; line numbers, in brackets, are given in certain cases; *e.g.*, *Iliad*, BK II [265–283] 12d.

BIBLE REFERENCES: The references are to book, chapter, and verse. When the King James and Douay versions differ in title of books or in the numbering of chapters or verses, the King James version is cited first and the Douay, indicated by a (D), follows; *e.g.*, OLD TESTAMENT: *Nehemiah*, 7:45—(D) II Esdras, 7:46.

SYMBOLS: The abbreviation "esp" calls the reader's attention to one or more especially relevant parts of a whole reference; "passim" signifies that the topic is discussed intermittently rather than continuously in the work or passage cited.

For additional information concerning the style of the references, see the Explanation of Reference Style; for general guidance in the use of *The Great Ideas*, consult the Preface.

1. The nature and reality of change or motion

7 PLATO: *Cratylus*, 86b–89b; 94c–d; 99b–104b; 112a–114a,c / *Phaedrus*, 124c–126c / *Symposium*, 165c–166b / *Phaedo*, 231c–232b / *Republic*, BK II, 322d–323a; BK V, 370a–373c / *Timaeus*, 447b–d; 455c–458b passim; 460c–d / *Parmenides*, 504c–505c / *Theaetetus*, 517d–534b esp 517d–518b, 532a–534b / *Sophist*, 564d–574c / *Statesman*, 587a–b / *Philebus*, 632a–d / *Laws*, BK X, 760a–765d esp 762b–765d

8 ARISTOTLE: *Physics*, BK I, CH 2 [184^{b}15–185^{a}14] 259b–d; CH 4–9 262a–268d; BK III, CH 1–3 278a–280c; BK IV, CH 11 [219^{b}9–31] 299b–d; BK VI, CH 6 319c–321a / *Heavens*, BK IV, CH 3 [310^{b}22–311^{a}12] 402b–c; CH 4 [311^{b}29–33] 403c / *Generation and Corruption*, BK II, CH 10 [336^{b}25–34] 438d / *Metaphysics*, BK I, CH 3–10 501c–511d passim; BK IV, CH 2 [1004^{b}27–29] 523d; CH 5 [1010^{a}6–38] 529c–530a; CH 8 [1012^{b}22–33] 532d; BK IX, CH 3 [1047^{a}10–29] 572b–c; CH 6 573c–574c; CH 8 [1049^{b}29–1050^{a}3] 575c–d; CH 10 [1051^{b}28–30] 578a; BK XI, CH 6 590d–592b; CH 9 593d–594d; CH 11–12 596a–598a,c esp CH 11 [1067^{b}15–1068^{a}7] 596b–d, CH 12 [1068^{b}20–25] 597c–d; BK XII, CH 5 [1070^{b}36–1071^{a}4] 600b–c / *Soul*, BK I, CH 3 [406^{b}11–14] 636a; BK III, CH 7 [431^{a}1–8] 663c

9 ARISTOTLE: *Generation of Animals*, BK V, CH 1 [778^{b}2–7] 320c–d / *Ethics*, BK X, CH 4 [1174^{a}13–^{b}14] 428b–429a

10 GALEN: *Natural Faculties*, BK I, CH 2 167b–168c

11 NICOMACHUS: *Arithmetic*, BK I, 811b–d

12 LUCRETIUS: *Nature of Things*, BK I [146–448] 2d–6c; BK II [62–332] 15d–19b; [1105–1174] 29a–30a,c; BK V [235–415] 64a–66c

12 AURELIUS: *Meditations*, BK IV, SECT 35–36 266d; SECT 42–43 267b; SECT 46 267c; BK V, SECT 23 272b; BK VI, SECT 15 275a–b; BK VII, SECT 18 281a; SECT 50 283a; BK VIII, SECT 6 285d–286a; BK IX, SECT 19 293b; SECT 28 293d–294a

16 KEPLER: *Harmonies of the World*, 1051b

17 PLOTINUS: *Second Ennead*, TR I, CH 3–4 36b–37b; TR V 57d–60c / *Sixth Ennead*, TR I, CH 15–22 260c–264c; TR III, CH 21–28 293a–297b

18 AUGUSTINE: *Confessions*, BK IV, par 15–17 23a–c; BK VII, par 17–18 49a–b; BK XI, par 6 90c–d

19 AQUINAS: *Summa Theologica*, PART I, Q 2, A 3, ANS 12c–14a; Q 9, A 1, ANS and REP 1 38c–39c; Q 10, A 4, REP 3 43b–44b; A 5, ANS 44b–45c; Q 18, A 1, ANS 104c–105c; A 3, REP 1 106b–107c; Q 23, A 1, REP 3 132c–133b; Q 53, A 1, REP 2–3 280d–282a; A 3, ANS 283b–284d;

Q 65, A 4 342b-343c; Q 67, A 3, REP 1 351b-352a; A 4, ANS 352a-354a; Q 73, A 1, REP 2 370a-371a; A 2, ANS 371b-d; Q 79, A 9, ANS 422b-423d; Q 103, A 5, REP 2 531b-532b; PART I-II, Q 10, A 1, REP 2 662d-663d; Q 23, AA 3-4 725c-727a; Q 25, A 1, ANS and REP 2 730b-731b; Q 31, A 3, REP 2 754a-d; A 8 758b-759a

20 AQUINAS: *Summa Theologica*, PART III, Q 15, A 10, REP 1 795b-796a; Q 62, A 4 861a-862a; PART III SUPPL, Q 91, A 3, REP 2 1020d-1022c

22 CHAUCER: *Knight's Tale* [2987-3040] 209a-210a

25 MONTAIGNE: *Essays*, 292d-294b

28 GALILEO: *Two New Sciences*, THIRD DAY-FOURTH DAY 197a-260a,c esp THIRD DAY, 224d

30 BACON: *Novum Organum*, BK I, APH 66 114d-115c; BK II, APH 48 179d-188b

31 DESCARTES: *Rules*, XII, 24a

31 SPINOZA: *Ethics*, PART II, LEMMA 3 378d-379a

33 PASCAL: *Geometrical Demonstration*, 433b-434a

34 NEWTON: *Principles*, DEFINITIONS-BK II 5a-267a esp DEFINITIONS, SCHOL 8b-13a, LAW 1 14a

35 LOCKE: *Human Understanding*, BK III, CH IV, SECT 8-9 260d-261b

35 BERKELEY: *Human Knowledge*, SECT 102 432d-433a; SECT 110-115 434b-435c

42 KANT: *Pure Reason*, 27a; 28b-c; 29c-d; 31d-32a; 55c-56a; 72c-85d esp 74b-76c, 82a-83b; 91d-93c; 95a-d

46 HEGEL: *Philosophy of History*, INTRO, 178a-179d; 186d-190b

51 TOLSTOY: *War and Peace*, BK XIV, 608a-b

53 JAMES: *Psychology*, 882a-884b

2. The unchanging principles of change

7 PLATO: *Phaedrus*, 124b-c / *Timaeus*, 455c-458a / *Sophist*, 564d-574c / *Philebus*, 610d-619d / *Laws*, BK X, 760a-765d

8 ARISTOTLE: *Physics*, BK I 259a-268d / *Heavens*, BK I, CH 3 [270ª12-17] 361b / *Metaphysics*, BK III, CH 4 [999ª24-^{b}24] 518a-c; BK XII, CH 10 [1075ª25-34] 606a

10 GALEN: *Natural Faculties*, BK I, CH 2 167b-168c

12 LUCRETIUS: *Nature of Things*, BK I [146-920] 2d-12b

12 AURELIUS: *Meditations*, BK IV, SECT 4 264a; BK VI, SECT 15 275a-b; BK IX, SECT 28 293d-294a; BK X, SECT 7 297b-c

16 KEPLER: *Epitome*, BK IV, 854b

17 PLOTINUS: *Second Ennead*, TR I, CH 1-4 35a-37b; TR IV-V 50a-60c / *Third Ennead*, TR VI, CH 7-19 110d-119a

19 AQUINAS: *Summa Theologica*, PART I, Q 19, A 1, ANS 108d-109c; Q 84, A 1, REP 3 440d-442a; Q 86, A 3 463b-d; Q 113, A 1, ANS 576a-d; Q 115, A 3, ANS and REP 2 588c-589c

42 KANT: *Pure Reason*, 23a-33d esp 27a, 29c-d; 49c-51d esp 51c-d; 72c-76c; 82a-83b; 91d-

93c; 120c-129c esp 121a-124d, 126a-128b; 141b,d-145c; 200c-204c

2a. The constituents of the changing thing

7 PLATO: *Timaeus*, 458a-460d / *Philebus*, 610d-619d

8 ARISTOTLE: *Physics*, BK I, CH 1 259a-b; CH 6-9 264c-268d; BK III, CH 1-3 278a-280c; BK IV, CH 9 [217ª20-^{b}27] 297a-c; BK V, CH 1 [225ª12-29] 305b-c; BK VI, CH 10 [240^{b}8-241ª26] 324c-325b / *Heavens*, BK I, CH 3 [270ª12-17] 361b; BK IV, CH 4 [312ª3-22] 403c-d / *Generation and Corruption*, BK I, CH 1 [314^{b}26-315ª3] 410a-b; CH 3 413c-416c esp [318ª1-319^{b}4] 414b-416c; CH 4 [320ª2-6] 417a; BK II, CH 1 [329ª24-^{b}2] 429a-b / *Metaphysics*, BK I, CH 6 [987^{b}30-988ª8] 506a; CH 8 [988^{b}22-989^{b}24] 506d-508a; BK III, CH 4 [999ª24-^{b}24] 518a-c; BK IV, CH 5 [1009ª22-38] 528d; BK V, CH 1 [1013ª3-7] 533a; CH 2 [1013ª24-27] 533b; CH 4 534d-535c; BK VII, CH 8-10 556b-559d; CH 15 [1039^{b}20-1040ª8] 563c-564a; BK VIII-IX 566a-578a,c; BK XI, CH 9 [1065^{b}25-31] 594b; CH 12 [1068^{b}10-14] 597c; BK XII, CH 1-5 598a-601a; CH 10 [1075ª25-34] 606a

9 ARISTOTLE: *Generation of Animals*, BK I, CH 18 [724ª20-^{b}13] 264b-d; CH 20 [729ª6]-CH 22 [730^{b}33] 269b-271a

10 GALEN: *Natural Faculties*, BK I, CH 2-3 167b-169a

12 LUCRETIUS: *Nature of Things*, BK I [146-634] 2d-8d; BK II [62-1022] 15d-28a

12 AURELIUS: *Meditations*, BK XII, SECT 30 310a-b

17 PLOTINUS: *First Ennead*, TR VIII, CH 8 30d-31c / *Second Ennead*, TR I, CH 1-4 35a-37b; TR IV, CH 6-8 51d-53a; TR V, CH 1-TR VI, CH 2 57d-62b / *Third Ennead*, TR VI, CH 8-19 111c-119a / *Sixth Ennead*, TR III, CH 22 293d-294c; TR V, CH 8 307d-308c

18 AUGUSTINE: *Confessions*, BK XII, par 3-16 99d-103a

19 AQUINAS: *Summa Theologica*, PART I, Q 9, A 1, ANS 38c-39c; Q 19, A 1, ANS 108d-109c; Q 29, A 1, REP 4 162a-163b; Q 45, A 2, REP 2 242d-244a; Q 48, A 3, ANS 261b-262a; Q 58, A 7, REP 3 305c-306b; Q 62, A 7, REP 1 322d-323b; Q 66, A 2, ANS 345d-347b; Q 75, A 5, REP 2 382a-383b; Q 92, A 2, REP 2 489d-490c; A 3, REP 1 490c-491b; A 4, ANS and REP 1 491b-d; Q 104, A 1, ANS and REP 1-2 534c-536c; PART I-II, Q 1, A 3, ANS 611b-612a; Q 10, A 1, REP 2 662d-663d

20 AQUINAS: *Summa Theologica*, PART II-II, Q 24, A 11, ANS 498b-499c

23 HOBBES: *Leviathan*, PART III, 172b

28 HARVEY: *On Animal Generation*, 494a-496d esp 494b, 495c-496a

30 BACON: *Novum Organum*, BK II, APH 6 139b-c

34 NEWTON: *Optics*, BK III, 541b

42 KANT: *Pure Reason*, 74b-76c

(2. *The unchanging principles of change.*)

2b. The factor of opposites or contraries in change

7 PLATO: *Symposium*, 165c-166b / *Phaedo*, 226d-228a; 243c-246c / *Republic*, BK IV, 350d-351b / *Theaetetus*, 519d-520b / *Sophist*, 565a-c / *Laws*, BK X, 760a-c; 762b-764c

8 ARISTOTLE: *Categories*, CH 5 [4ᵃ10-ᵇ19] 8b-9a; CH 10 [13ᵃ17-37] 18d-19a; CH 14 [15ᵇ1-16] 21b-c / *Physics*, BK I, CH 5-9 263c-268d; BK II, CH 1 [193ᵇ19-22] 270a; BK III, CH 1 [201ᵃ4-8] 278c; BK IV, CH 9 [217ᵃ20-ᵇ26] 297a-c; BK V, CH 1 [224ᵇ27-225ᵃ12] 304d-305a; [225ᵃ34-ᵇ9] 305d; CH 2 [226ᵃ23-ᵇ9] 306d-307a; CH 3 [226ᵇ24-34] 307c; CH 5 310a-311a; CH 6 [230ᵇ27-231ᵃ2] 312b-c; BK VI, CH 4 [234ᵇ10-21] 316d-317a; BK VIII, CH 2 [252ᵇ9-11] 336b-c; CH 7 [260ᵃ29-ᵇ1] 346b-c / *Heavens*, BK I, CH 3 [270ᵃ13-23] 361b-c; CH 4 362a-c; CH 8 [277ᵃ13-34] 368b-c; CH 12 [283ᵇ17-23] 375c-d; BK IV, CH 3 401c-402c; CH 4 [311ᵇ29-312ᵃ22] 403c-d / *Generation and Corruption*, BK I, CH 4 416c-417a; CH 7 421d-423b; BK II, CH 1-5 428b,d-433d esp CH 4-5 431b-433d / *Metaphysics*, BK I, CH 8 [989ᵃ18-29] 507b-c; BK II, CH 2 [994ᵇ19-ᵇ6] 512c-d; BK IV, CH 7 [1011ᵇ29-38] 531d; BK VIII, CH 5 569b-d; BK IX, CH 9 [1051ᵃ4-13] 577a; BK X, CH 7 [1057ᵃ18-34] 584c-d; BK XI, CH 9 [1065ᵇ5-14] 593d-594a; CH 11 596a-d; BK XII, CH 2 598c-599a; CH 10 [1075ᵃ25-34] 606a / *Soul*, BK II, CH 4 [416ᵃ18-ᵇ8] 646c-d / *Longevity*, CH 3 710d-711b

9 ARISTOTLE: *Generation of Animals*, BK I, CH 18 [724ᵃ20-ᵇ13] 264b-d; BK IV, CH 3 [768ᵃ2-7] 309c / *Ethics*, BK VIII, CH 8 [1159ᵇ19-23] 411d

10 GALEN: *Natural Faculties*, BK I, CH 2, 167b-d

17 PLOTINUS: *Third Ennead*, TR VI, CH 8 111c-d / *Sixth Ennead*, TR III, CH 22 293d-294c; CH 27 296b-297a

19 AQUINAS: *Summa Theologica*, PART I, Q 19, A 1, ANS 108d-109c; Q 23, A 1, REP 3 132c-133b; Q 26, A 1, REP 2 150b-c; Q 58, A 7, REP 3 305c-306b; Q 62, A 7, REP 1 322d-323b; PART I-II, Q 18, A 8, REP 1 699d-700b; Q 23, A 2 724c-725c

28 HARVEY: *On Animal Generation*, 408c-d

31 SPINOZA: *Ethics*, PART III, PROP 4-6 398d-399a; PART IV, PROP 29-35 431d-434a; PART V, AXIOM 1 452c

42 KANT: *Pure Reason*, 27a; 76c-83b esp 76c-d; 91d-93c

46 HEGEL: *Philosophy of History*, INTRO, 160c-d; 165a-b; 178a-d; 179b-d

3. Cause and effect in motion: the relation of mover and moved, or action and passion

7 PLATO: *Phaedrus*, 124b-c / *Gorgias*, 267c-268a / *Timaeus*, 460c-d / *Laws*, BK X, 760a-765d esp 761b-765d

8 ARISTOTLE: *Categories*, CH 9 [11ᵇ1-7] 16c-d / *Physics*, BK III, CH 1 [200ᵇ29-32] 278b; CH 2

[202ᵃ2]-CH 3[202ᵇ29] 279c-280c; BK VII, CH 1-2 326a-329a; BK VIII, CH 10 [266ᵇ27-267ᵃ21] 354b-d / *Heavens*, BK I, CH 3 [270ᵃ12-17] 361b; CH 7 [275ᵃ1-ᵇ29] 366a-367a; CH 8 [277ᵇ1-8] 368c-d; BK III, CH 2 [300ᵇ8-301ᵃ12] 391d-392c; [301ᵇ2-32] 392d-393b; BK IV, CH 3 401c-402c / *Generation and Corruption*, BK I, CH 6 [323ᵃ12-34] 421b-c; CH 7-9 421d-426c; BK II, CH 9-10 436d-439c / *Metaphysics*, BK I, CH 6 [987ᵇ30-988ᵃ8] 506a; CH 7 [988ᵃ31-ᵇ16] 506c-d; BK V, CH 2 [1013ᵇ3-16] 533c-d; BK IX, CH 1-5 570b,d-573c; CH 7 [1048ᵇ35-1049ᵃ18] 574c-d; BK XI, CH 9 [1066ᵃ27-34] 594d; BK XII, CH 3 [1069ᵇ35-1070ᵃ9] 599a-b; [1070ᵃ21-30] 599c-d; CH 4 [1070ᵇ22]-CH 8 [1074ᵇ14] 600b-605a; CH 10 [1075ᵇ1-37] 606b-d / *Soul*, BK II, CH 5 647b-648d; BK III, CH 2 [426ᵃ2-6] 658a-b

9 ARISTOTLE: *Motion of Animals*, CH 8 [702ᵃ5-22] 237b-c / *Generation of Animals*, BK I, CH 20 [729ᵃ9]-CH 21 [729ᵇ21] 269b-270a; BK II, CH 4 [740ᵇ18-26] 281c-d; BK IV, CH 3 [768ᵇ16-24] 310b-c

10 GALEN: *Natural Faculties*, BK I, CH 2, 168b-c; BK III, CH 7, 203b-c

12 LUCRETIUS: *Nature of Things*, BK II [80-141] 16a-d; [184-293] 17b-18d

16 KEPLER: *Epitome*, BK IV, 854b; 855b; 940b-941a; 959a-960a

17 PLOTINUS: *Sixth Ennead*, TR I, CH 15-22 260c-264c; TR III, CH 23 294d-295a

19 AQUINAS: *Summa Theologica*, PART I, Q 8, A 1, ANS and REP 2 34d-35c; Q 41, A 1, REP 2 217d-218c; Q 44, A 2, REP 2 239b-240a; Q 48, A 1, REP 4 259b-260c; Q 60, A 1, REP 2 310b-311a; Q 75, A 1, REP 3 378b-379c; Q 80, A 2, ANS 428a-d; Q 115, A 1 585d-587c; PART I-II, Q 1, A 3, ANS and REP 1 611b-612a; A 6, ANS 614a-c; Q 9, A 4, ANS 660a-d; Q 22 720b,d-723b; Q 23, A 4 726a-727a

20 AQUINAS: *Summa Theologica*, PART I-II, Q 113, A 8 367d-368c

28 GILBERT: *Loadstone*, BK II, 26d-40b passim; BK VI, 109a-b; 112d

28 GALILEO: *Two New Sciences*, THIRD DAY, 202a-203a

28 HARVEY: *On Animal Generation*, 423d

31 DESCARTES: *Meditations*, III, 87c-88a / *Objections and Replies*, AXIOM II 131d; 212a

31 SPINOZA: *Ethics*, PART II, AXIOM 1-5 373c-d; LEMMA 3 378d-379a; PART III, DEF 1-3 395d-396a; PROP 1-4 396a-398d; PART IV, AXIOM-PROP 7 424c-426b; PART V, AXIOM 2 452c; PROP 3-4 453a-d

34 NEWTON: *Principles*, DEF III-IV 5b-6a; LAW I-III 14a-b

35 LOCKE: *Human Understanding*, BK II, CH XXI, SECT 1-5 178b-179d; SECT 74, 199d-200b; CH XXII, SECT 11 203c-d; CH XXIII, SECT 28-29 211b-212a

35 HUME: *Human Understanding*, SECT III, DIV 18-SECT VIII, DIV 74 457c-484c passim, esp SECT VII, DIV 60 477a-c

42 KANT: *Pure Reason*, 15a-b; 43a-b; 76c-83b; 91d-93c

4. Motion and rest: contrary motions

7 PLATO: *Cratylus*, 112b / *Republic*, BK IV, 350d-351b / *Timaeus*, 453b-c; 460c-d / *Sophist*, 567a-574c / *Statesman*, 587a-589c esp 587a-b
8 ARISTOTLE: *Categories*, CH 14 [15^{b}1–16] 21b-c / *Physics*, BK V, CH 5–6 310a-312d / *Heavens*, BK I, CH 4 362a-c / *Metaphysics*, BK IV, CH 2 [1004^{b}27–29] 523d; BK XI, CH 12 [1068^{b}20–25] 597c-d / *Soul*, BK I, CH 3 [406^{a}22–27] 635c
10 GALEN: *Natural Faculties*, BK I, CH 2, 167b-d
11 NICOMACHUS: *Arithmetic*, BK II, 832c
16 COPERNICUS: *Revolutions of the Heavenly Spheres*, BK I, 517b-518a; 519b-520b
16 KEPLER: *Epitome*, BK IV, 931b
17 PLOTINUS: *Sixth Ennead*, TR III, CH 24 295b-c; CH 27 296b-297a
19 AQUINAS: *Summa Theologica*, PART I, Q 10, A 4, REP 3 43b-44b; Q 18, A 1, REP 2 104c-105c; Q 53, A 3, ANS 283b-284d; Q 73, A 2, ANS 371b-d; PART I–II, Q 6, A 1 644d-646a; A 4 647b-648a; Q 9, A 4, REP 2 660a-d; Q 41, A 3 799c-800b
20 AQUINAS: *Summa Theologica*, PART III SUPPL, Q 75, A 3, ANS and REP 3–5 938a-939d; Q 84, A 3, REP 2 985d-989b
23 HOBBES: *Leviathan*, PART I, 50a
28 GILBERT: *Loadstone*, BK II, 26a-b; BK VI, 110b
30 BACON: *Novum Organum*, BK II, APH 35, 163a
31 SPINOZA: *Ethics*, PART II, AXIOM 1 378c; LEMMA 1–3 378c-379a
34 NEWTON: *Principles*, DEF III 5b; LAW I 14a

5. The measure of motion

5a. Time or duration as the measure of motion

7 PLATO: *Timaeus*, 450c-451d / *Parmenides*, 504c-505c
8 ARISTOTLE: *Physics*, BK IV, CH 10–14 297c-304a,c; BK VI 312b,d-325d esp CH 2 314a-315d / *Generation and Corruption*, BK II, CH 10 [337^{a}22–34] 439b-c / *Metaphysics*, BK V, CH 13 [1020^{a}25–33] 541c; BK X, CH 1 [1053^{a}9–12] 579c; BK XII, CH 6 [1071^{b}6–12] 601b
9 ARISTOTLE: *Ethics*, BK X, CH 4 [1174^{a}12–^{b}14] 428b-429a
12 AURELIUS: *Meditations*, BK VI, SECT 15 275a-b
17 PLOTINUS: *Third Ennead*, TR VII, CH 7–13 122d-129a / *Fourth Ennead*, TR IV, CH 15 165c-d / *Sixth Ennead*, TR I, CH 5, 254c-d; CH 16 260d-261c; TR III, CH 22, 294c
18 AUGUSTINE: *Confessions*, BK XI, par 12–40 92b-99a; BK XII, par 9 101b-c / *City of God*, BK XI, CH 6 325c-d; BK XII, CH 15 351b-352d
19 AQUINAS: *Summa Theologica*, PART I, Q 7, A 3, REP 4 32c-33c; Q 10, A 1, ANS 40d-41d; AA 4–6 43b-46d; Q 53, A 3 283b-284d; Q 57, A 3, REP 2 297b-298a; Q 63, A 5, ANS 329a-330c;

A 6, REP 4 330c-331c; Q 66, A 4, REP 4 348d-349d; PART I–II, Q 31, A 2, ANS and REP 1 753c-754a
20 AQUINAS: *Summa Theologica*, PART I–II, Q 113, A 7, REP 5 366a-367c; PART III SUPPL, Q 84, A 3 985d-989b
21 DANTE: *Divine Comedy*, PARADISE, XXVII [106–120] 148b-c
28 GALILEO: *Two New Sciences*, THIRD DAY, 201a-202a
30 BACON: *Novum Organum*, BK II, APH 46 177c-179a
31 SPINOZA: *Ethics*, PART II, DEF 5 373b-c
32 MILTON: *Paradise Lost*, BK V [580–582] 188a
33 PASCAL: *Geometrical Demonstration*, 432b-433b; 434a-439b passim
34 NEWTON: *Principles*, DEFINITIONS, SCHOL, 8b-10a; 12a-b
35 LOCKE: *Human Understanding*, BK II, CH XIV, SECT 22 159d; CH XVIII, SECT 2 174a-b
36 STERNE: *Tristram Shandy*, 292a-293a
42 KANT: *Pure Reason*, 27a; 29c-d; 72c-76c
45 FOURIER: *Theory of Heat*, 249a-251b

5b. The divisibility and continuity of motion

8 ARISTOTLE: *Physics*, BK IV, CH 11 [219^{a}10–13] 298d-299a; BK V, CH 4 308b-310a; BK VI 312b,d-325d; BK VII, CH 1 [242^{a}32–^{b}4] 326c-d; BK VIII, CH 7 [261^{a}28]–CH 8 [265^{a}12] 347c-352a / *Metaphysics*, BK V, CH 6 [1016^{a}4–7] 536b-c; CH 13 [1020^{a}25–33] 541c; BK X, CH 1 [1052^{a}15–21] 578b; BK XII, CH 6 [1071^{b}8–11] 601b
9 ARISTOTLE: *Ethics*, BK X, CH 4 [1174^{b}9–14] 428d-429a
17 PLOTINUS: *Third Ennead*, TR VII, CH 8–9 123b-125d
19 AQUINAS: *Summa Theologica*, PART I, Q 7, A 3, REP 4 32c-33c; Q 53 280d-284d
20 AQUINAS: *Summa Theologica*, PART I–II, Q 113, A 7 366a-367c
28 GALILEO: *Two New Sciences*, THIRD DAY, 201a-202a
30 BACON: *Novum Organum*, BK II, APH 6 139b-c; APH 41 173d-174b
31 DESCARTES: *Meditations*, III, 87c-d / *Objections and Replies*, 213b-c
33 PASCAL: *Geometrical Demonstration*, 434a-439b
34 NEWTON: *Principles*, BK I, LEMMA II, SCHOL, 31b-32a
42 KANT: *Pure Reason*, 26b-27a; 74b-76c
51 TOLSTOY: *War and Peace*, BK XI, 469a-d

6. The kinds of change

7 PLATO: *Timaeus*, 449b-450c esp 450a / *Parmenides*, 492a-493b esp 492d-493b; 504c-505a / *Theaetetus*, 533a-b / *Laws*, BK X, 762b-763b
8 ARISTOTLE: *Categories*, CH 14 20d-21c / *Physics*, BK III, CH 1 [200^{b}32–201^{a}14] 278b-c; BK V, CH 1–2 304a-307b; CH 5 310a-311a; BK VII, CH 4 330d-333a / *Heavens*, BK I, CH 2 [268^{b}15–269^{a}8] 359d-360a; BK IV, CH 3 401c-402c /

and REP 1 720d-721c; A 2, REP 3 721c-722c;
Q 35, A 6, REP 2 777b-778c; Q 36, A 1, ANS
780c-781b

20 AQUINAS: *Summa Theologica*, PART I–II, Q 52,
A 1, ANS and REP 3 15d-18a; Q 72, A 3, ANS and
REP 1–2 113b-114a; Q 113, A 7, ANS and REP 1,4
366a-367c; PART II–II, Q 180, A 6 613a-614d;
PART III SUPPL, Q 82, A 3, ANS and REP 2
971a-972d; Q 84, A 3, ANS and REP 1 985d-
989b

21 DANTE: *Divine Comedy*, PURGATORY, XVIII
[10–33] 80a

23 HOBBES: *Leviathan*, PART I, 49a-d; 61a-c

31 SPINOZA: *Ethics*, PART II, PROP 7 375a-c; PART
III, 395a-d; PROP 1–3 396a-398c; PART IV,
PROP 7 426a-b; PART V, PROP 1 452d

35 LOCKE: *Human Understanding*, BK II, CH XII,
SECT 1 147b-d; CH XXI, SECT 74 199c-200b

35 BERKELEY: *Human Knowledge*, SECT 144 441d

46 HEGEL: *Philosophy of History*, INTRO, 160c-
161a; 178a-179c; 186d-190b

53 JAMES: *Psychology*, 95b-97a

7. The analysis of local motion

7a. Space, place, and void

7 PLATO: *Timaeus*, 460c-d; 471b-c / *Laws*, BK
X, 762b-d

8 ARISTOTLE: *Physics*, BK III, CH 5 [205^{a}10–
206^{a}8] 283b-284b; BK IV, CH 1–9 287a-297c /
Heavens, BK I, CH 7 [274^{b}30–33] 366a; [275^{b}30–
276^{a}18] 367a-b; CH 8 [276^{a}22–27] 367b-c;
[277^{b}14–23] 368d-369a; BK II, CH 2 376b-377c;
BK III, CH 6 [305^{a}27–28] 396c; BK IV, CH 1–5
399a-404d / *Metaphysics*, BK V, CH 13 [1020^a
25–33] 541c; BK IX, CH 6 [1048^{b}9–17] 574a;
BK XI, CH 10 [1067^{a}8–33] 595c-596a / *Soul*,
BK I, CH 3 [406^{a}12–21] 635c

10 GALEN: *Natural Faculties*, BK I, CH 16, 181a-d;
BK II, CH 1–2, 183b,d-184c; CH 6 188c-191a;
BK III, CH 14–15, 213b-214c

11 NICOMACHUS: *Arithmetic*, BK II, 832c

12 LUCRETIUS: *Nature of Things*, BK I [329–448]
5b-6c; [958–1007] 12d-13b; [1052–1082] 14a-c;
BK II [80–250] 16a-18a; BK VI [830–839] 91b-c;
[998–1041] 93c-94a

16 PTOLEMY: *Almagest*, BK I, 10b-11b

16 COPERNICUS: *Revolutions of the Heavenly
Spheres*, BK I, 517b-518a; 519a-520b

16 KEPLER: *Epitome*, BK IV, 855b; 900b-903a;
922a-b; 931b-932a

17 PLOTINUS: *Third Ennead*, TR VII, CH 8, 123d-
124a

19 AQUINAS: *Summa Theologica*, PART I, Q 8,
A 1, REP 3 34d-35c; A 4 37c-38c; Q 52, AA 1–2
278d-280a; Q 53, AA 1–2 280d-283b

20 AQUINAS: *Summa Theologica*, PART III SUPPL,
Q 83, AA 2–5 976c-982c; Q 84, A 2, REP 1 984c-
985d; A 3 985d-989b

23 HOBBES: *Leviathan*, PART I, 50a; 61b; PART
III, 173a; PART IV, 271d

28 GILBERT: *Loadstone*, BK II, 32c; BK VI, 110b-c

28 GALILEO: *Two New Sciences*, FIRST DAY, 157b-
160a passim; THIRD DAY, 202d

30 BACON: *Novum Organum*, BK II, APH 37 168d-
169c; APH 45 176a-177c; APH 48, 180a

31 DESCARTES: *Rules*, IX, 15c

33 PASCAL: *Vacuum*, 366a-367a; 370a / *Weight
of Air*, 405b-415b passim

34 NEWTON: *Principles*, DEFINITIONS, SCHOL 8b-
13a; BK III, GENERAL SCHOL, 370a-372a /
Optics, BK III, 520a-522b; 542a-543a

35 LOCKE: *Human Understanding*, BK II, CH XIII,
SECT 23 153c-d; CH XVII, SECT 4 168b-d

35 BERKELEY: *Human Knowledge*, SECT 110–117
434b-436a

42 KANT: *Pure Reason*, 29c-d; 31d-32a; 55c-56a;
84b-c; 135d [fn 2]

45 FARADAY: *Researches in Electricity*, 513d-514c;
685d-686c; 816b,d-819a,c; 824a-b; 855a,c

7b. Natural and violent motion

7 PLATO: *Timaeus*, 463d-464b

8 ARISTOTLE: *Physics*, BK IV, CH 1 [208^{b}9–22]
287b; CH 8 [215^{a}1–13] 294c-d; BK V, CH 6
[230^{a}18–231^{a}19] 311c-312d; BK VIII, CH 4
338d-340d / *Heavens*, BK I, CH 2 [268^{b}12]–
CH 3 [270^{a}13] 359d-361b; CH 7 [274^{b}30–33]
366a; [275^{b}12–29] 366d-367a; CH 7 [276^{a}8]–
CH 8 [277^{b}25] 367b-369a; CH 9 [278^{b}22–
279^{a}8] 370a-b; BK II, CH 13 [294^{b}31–295^{a}29]
386b-d; BK III, CH 2 391c-393b; CH 5 [304^b
11–23] 395d-396a; CH 6 [305^{a}22–28] 396c /
Generation and Corruption, BK II, CH 6 [333^b
22–33] 434c-d / *Soul*, BK I, CH 3 [406^{a}12–29]
635c-d

12 LUCRETIUS: *Nature of Things*, BK I [1052–
1094] 14a-c; BK II [184–215] 17b-d

16 PTOLEMY: *Almagest*, BK I, 11a-b; BK III, 86b;
BK IX, 270b

16 COPERNICUS: *Revolutions of the Heavenly
Spheres*, BK I, 517b-520b passim

16 KEPLER: *Epitome*, BK IV, 929b-930b

17 PLOTINUS: *Second Ennead*, TR I, CH 8, 39d

19 AQUINAS: *Summa Theologica*, PART I, Q 18,
A 1, REP 2 104c-105c; Q 105, A 4, REP 1 541c-
542a; A 6, REP 1 543b-544a; PART I–II, Q 6,
A 1, ANS and REP 3 644d-646a; A 4 647b-648a;
A 5, ANS and REP 2–3 648b-649a; Q 41, A 3
799c-800b

20 AQUINAS: *Summa Theologica*, PART III SUPPL,
Q 75, A 3, ANS and REP 3–5 938a-939d; Q 91,
A 2, ANS and REP 6 1017c-1020c

21 DANTE: *Divine Comedy*, PARADISE, I [94–142]
107b-d

23 HOBBES: *Leviathan*, PART I, 50a; PART IV,
271d

28 GILBERT: *Loadstone*, BK VI, 109a-b; 110b-d

28 GALILEO: *Two New Sciences*, FIRST DAY, 157d-
158a; THIRD DAY, 200a-d; 203d; FOURTH DAY,
238a-b

30 BACON: *Novum Organum*, BK I, APH 66, 115b-
c; BK II, APH 36 164a-168d passim; APH 48
179d-188b

7c. Kinds of local motion

7c(1) Rectilinear and rotary or circular motion

7 PLATO: *Republic*, BK IV, 350d-351b / *Parmenides*, 492d-493b / *Laws*, BK X, 762b-d; 764b-765a

8 ARISTOTLE: *Physics*, BK IV, CH 5 [212ᵃ31–ᵇ2] 291d; BK VII, CH 4 [248ᵃ10–ᵇ6] 330d-331b; BK VIII, CH 8–9 348b-353b / *Heavens*, BK I, CH 2–6 359d-365c; CH 7 [274ᵇ22–29] 365d-366a; [275ᵇ12–18] 366d; CH 8 [277ᵃ12–26] 368b-c; [277ᵇ8–18] 368d / *Metaphysics*, BK XII, CH 6 [1071ᵇ10–11] 601b; CH 7 [1072ᵃ20–22] 602b / *Soul*, BK I, CH 3 [406ᵇ26–407ᵇ13] 636b-637b

16 PTOLEMY: *Almagest*, BK I, 6a; 7a-8b; BK III, 86b; BK IX, 270b

16 COPERNICUS: *Revolutions of the Heavenly Spheres*, BK I, 514a; 517b-518a; 519b-520b

16 KEPLER: *Epitome*, BK IV, 887a; 913a; 931b-933a

17 PLOTINUS: *Second Ennead*, TR I, CH 3, 36b-c; CH 8 39c-d; TR II, CH I, 40b-c; CH 2, 41b-c / *Sixth Ennead*, TR III, CH 24 295b-c

19 AQUINAS: *Summa Theologica*, PART I, Q 7, A 3, ANS 32c-33c; Q 66, A 2, ANS 345d-347b

28 GILBERT: *Loadstone*, BK VI, 110b-c

28 GALILEO: *Two New Sciences*, FOURTH DAY, 240d; 245b-c

30 BACON: *Novum Organum*, BK II, APH 35, 163a-d; APH 48, 186b-d

34 NEWTON: *Principles*, DEF III 5b; DEF V 6a-7a; DEFINITIONS, SCHOL, 11b-12a; LAW I 14a; LAWS OF MOTION, SCHOL, 19b-20a; BK I, PROP 1–3 and SCHOL 32b-35b; BK II, PROP 53, SCHOL 266a-267a

7c(2) Uniform or variable motion

8 ARISTOTLE: *Physics*, BK IV, CH 8 [215ᵃ24–216ᵃ21] 295a-d; BK V, CH 4 [228ᵇ15–229ᵃ7] 309d-310a

12 LUCRETIUS: *Nature of Things*, BK II [225–242] 17d-18a

28 GALILEO: *Two New Sciences*, FIRST DAY, 157b-160a; THIRD DAY, 197b-198b; 200a-d; 203d; 205b-d; 209a-c; 224d

30 BACON: *Novum Organum*, BK II, APH 48, 186b-d

34 NEWTON: *Principles*, DEF III–IV 5b-6a; LAW I–II 14a-b; COROL IV–VI 18a-19b

7c(3) Absolute or relative motion

12 LUCRETIUS: *Nature of Things*, BK IV [387–390] 49b

16 COPERNICUS: *Revolutions of the Heavenly Spheres*, BK I, 514b-515a; 519a; BK II, 557a-b

16 KEPLER: *Harmonies of the World*, 1015a-b

28 GILBERT: *Loadstone*, BK VI, 115a-d

30 BACON: *Novum Organum*, BK II, APH 36, 165c-166b

34 NEWTON: *Principles*, DEFINITIONS, SCHOL 8b-13a esp 9a-b; COROL V–VI 19a-b; BK I, PROP 57–61 111b-114b

35 LOCKE: *Human Understanding*, BK II, CH XIII, SECT 7–10 149d-150d passim

35 BERKELEY: *Human Knowledge*, SECT 110–115 434b-435c

53 JAMES: *Psychology*, 511b-512a

7c(4) Terrestrial and celestial motion

7 PLATO: *Statesman*, 587a-b / *Laws*, BK VII, 729d-730d; BK X, 763d-765c

8 ARISTOTLE: *Heavens* 359a-405a,c esp BK I, CH 2–3 359d-362a / *Metaphysics*, BK IX, CH 8 [1050ᵇ20–28] 576c-d; BK XII, CH 2 [1069ᵇ24–27] 599a; CH 6 [1071ᵇ32]–CH 7 [1072ᵃ22] 601d-602b / *Soul*, BK I, CH 3 [406ᵇ26–407ᵇ13] 636b-637b

9 ARISTOTLE: *Motion of Animals*, CH 3 234a-c

16 PTOLEMY: *Almagest*, BK I, 5a-6a; 7a-8b; 12a; BK III, 86b-87a; BK IX, 270b; BK XIII, 429a-b

16 COPERNICUS: *Revolutions of the Heavenly Spheres*, BK I, 513b-514b; 517b-518a; 519b-520b

16 KEPLER: *Epitome*, BK IV, 888b-895b; 897a-905a passim, esp 904b-905a; 929a-933a; 934b-935b; 940b-941a; 959a-960a

17 PLOTINUS: *Second Ennead*, TR I, CH 1–4 35a-37b; TR I, CH 8–TR II, CH 2 39c-41c

19 AQUINAS: *Summa Theologica*, PART I, Q 66, A 2, ANS 345d-347b; Q 70, A 3 365b-367a

20 AQUINAS: *Summa Theologica*, PART I–II, Q 49, A 4, ANS 5a-6a; PART III SUPPL, Q 84, A 3, REP 2 985d-989b

28 GILBERT: *Loadstone*, BK VI, 110b-c

28 GALILEO: *Two New Sciences*, FOURTH DAY, 245b-d

30 BACON: *Novum Organum*, BK II, APH 35, 163a-b; APH 36, 165d-166a; APH 48, 186b-d

34 NEWTON: *Principles*, 1a-2a; BK III 269a-372a passim, esp RULE I–III 270a-271a, PROP 1–7 276a-282b, PROP 35, SCHOL 320b-324a, GENERAL SCHOL, 371b-372a / *Optics*, BK III, 540a-541b

7d. The properties of variable motion: the laws of motion

8 ARISTOTLE: *Physics*, BK IV, CH 8 [215ᵃ24–216ᵃ21] 295a-d; BK VII, CH 4 330d-333a

9 ARISTOTLE: *Motion of Animals*, CH 1–4 233a-235c passim / *Gait of Animals*, CH 3 243d-244a / *Generation of Animals*, BK IV, CH 3 [768ᵇ16–24] 310b-c

12 LUCRETIUS: *Nature of Things*, BK II [80–99] 16a-b; [184–250] 17b-18b

16 KEPLER: *Epitome*, BK IV, 894a; 899a-900a; 905a-906b; 933b-934b; 936a-937a; 938b-939a

23 HOBBES: *Leviathan*, PART I, 50a; PART IV, 271d

28 GILBERT: *Loadstone*, BK II, 56b-c

28 GALILEO: *Two New Sciences*, FIRST DAY, 157b-172d passim; THIRD DAY–FOURTH DAY 197a-260a,c

30 BACON: *Novum Organum*, BK II, APH 35, 163c-d; APH 36, 166b-c; 167b-c; APH 48 179d-188b

31 SPINOZA: *Ethics*, PART II, AXIOM I–LEMMA 7 378c-380b

34 NEWTON: *Principles*, DEF III 5b; LAWS OF MOTION 14a-24a; BK I, PROP I–17 and SCHOL 32b-50a; PROP 30–69 and SCHOL 76a-131a; PROP 94–98 and SCHOL 152b-157b; BK II 159a-267a passim / *Optics*, BK III, 540a-542a

34 HUYGENS: *Light*, CH I, 558b-563b

35 LOCKE: *Human Understanding*, BK II, CH XXI, SECT 4 178d-179c; CH XXIII, SECT 17 209a; SECT 22 209d; SECT 28–29 211b-212a

35 BERKELEY: *Human Knowledge*, SECT 50 422c; SECT 102 432d-433a

35 HUME: *Human Understanding*, SECT IV, DIV 27, 460c; SECT VII, DIV 57, 475d-476b [fn 2]

38 MONTESQUIEU: *Spirit of Laws*, BK I, 1b

45 FOURIER: *Theory of Heat*, 169a-b

51 TOLSTOY: *War and Peace*, EPILOGUE II, 694d-695c

8. Change of size

8*a*. The increase and decrease of inanimate bodies

7 PLATO: *Timaeus*, 460c-d / *Laws*, BK X, 762b-c

8 ARISTOTLE: *Physics*, BK IV, CH I [209^{a}27–29] 288a; CH 6 [213^{b}19–22] 293b; CH 9 296b-297c; BK VII, CH 2 [245^{a}12–18] 328d-329a; BK VIII, CH 3 [253^{b}12–23] 337d / *Heavens*, BK I, CH 3 [270^{a}23–36] 361c / *Generation and Corruption*, BK II, CH 6 [333^{a}35–^{b}3] 434b / *Soul*, BK II, CH 4 [415^{b}28–416^{a}18] 646a-c

10 GALEN: *Natural Faculties*, BK I, CH 7 170c-171a; BK II, CH 3, 186c-d

12 LUCRETIUS: *Nature of Things*, BK I [311–328] 5a; BK II [62–79] 15d-16a; [1105–1174] 29a-30a,c; BK V [235–323] 64a-65b

19 AQUINAS: *Summa Theologica*, PART I, Q 119, A I, ANS 604c-607b

20 AQUINAS: *Summa Theologica*, PART I–II, Q 52, AA I–2 15d-19a; PART II–II, Q 24, A 5 492b-493d; A 6, ANS 493d-494b; PART III, Q 7, A I2, REP I 754c-755c

23 HOBBES: *Leviathan*, PART IV, 271d-272a

28 GALILEO: *Two New Sciences*, FIRST DAY, 139b-141d; 151c-154b

28 HARVEY: *On Animal Generation*, 412b

30 BACON: *Novum Organum*, BK II, APH 40, 171a-172d; APH 48, 180a-181a; 184a-c

34 NEWTON: *Principles*, BK III, PROP 6, COROL IV 281b / *Optics*, BK III, 539b

45 LAVOISIER: *Elements of Chemistry*, PART I, 9a-15c esp 9a-10b

45 FOURIER: *Theory of Heat*, 184a-185b; 192a-b

8*b*. Growth in living organisms

7 PLATO: *Timaeus*, 471d-472a

8 ARISTOTLE: *Physics*, BK II, CH I [193^{b}13–19] 269d-270a; BK VI, CH 10 [241^{a}32–^{b}2] 325c; BK

VIII, CH 7 [260^{a}29–^{b}1] 346b-c / *Generation and Corruption*, BK I, CH 2 [315^{a}26–^{b}3] 410d-411a; CH 5 417b-420b; BK II, CH 6 [333^{a}35–^{b}3] 434b; CH 8 [335^{a}10–14] 436c / *Metaphysics*, BK V, CH 4 [1014^{b}20–26] 535a / *Soul*, BK II, CH 4 [415^{b}28–416^{a}18] 646a-c

9 ARISTOTLE: *History of Animals*, BK V, CH 19 [550^{b}26–31] 77d; CH 33 [558^{a}17–24] 84d-85a; BK VII, CH I [582^{a}21–25] 107d / *Motion of Animals*, CH 5 235c-d / *Generation of Animals*, BK I, CH 18 [723^{a}9–23] 263a-b; CH 22 [730^{a}33–^{b}9] 270d; BK II, CH I [733^{b}1–4] 273d; [735^{a}13–26] 275d-276a; CH 4 [739^{b}34–741^{a}2] 280d-281d; CH 6 [744^{b}28–745^{b}9] 286a-d

10 GALEN: *Natural Faculties*, BK I, CH 2, 167b-d; CH 5 169b-c; CH 7 170c-171a; CH 11 172b-d; BK II, CH 3 185a-186d

12 LUCRETIUS: *Nature of Things*, BK I [146–264] 2d-4b; BK II [1105–1174] 29a-30a,c; BK IV [858–876] 55b-c

28 GALILEO: *Two New Sciences*, SECOND DAY, 187b-d

28 HARVEY: *Circulation of the Blood*, 320a-b / *On Animal Generation*, 353b-354a; 388c-d; 408c-409b; 412b-415b esp 415a; 441a-443b; 494a-d

49 DARWIN: *Origin of Species*, 71a-c

9. Change of quality

7 PLATO: *Parmenides*, 509a-510a / *Theaetetus*, 533a-534a

8 ARISTOTLE: *Categories*, CH 5 [4^{a}10–^{b}19] 8b-9a; CH 14 [15^{a}14–32] 20d-21a / *Topics*, BK VI, CH 6 [145^{a}2–13] 198c-d / *Physics*, BK I, CH 7 [190^{b}5–9] 266b; BK V, CH 2 [226^{a}26–29] 306d; [226^{b}1–9] 307a; BK VI, CH 10 [241^{a}26–32] 325b-c; BK VII, CH 2 [244^{b}1–245^{a}12] 328b-d; CH 3 329a-330d; BK VIII, CH 7 [260^{a}26–^{b}14] 346b-c / *Heavens*, BK I, CH 3 [270^{a}26–36] 361c; CH 12 [283^{b}17–23] 375c-d / *Generation and Corruption*, BK I, CH 1–4 409a-417a esp CH 4 416c-417a / *Metaphysics*, BK I, CH 8 [989^{a}18–29] 507b-c; BK V, CH 21 544a-b; BK XI, CH 12 [1068^{b}15–19] 597c / *Sense and the Sensible*, CH 6 [446^{b}27–447^{a}9] 685b-c

10 GALEN: *Natural Faculties*, BK I, CH 2, 167b-168b

17 PLOTINUS: *Third Ennead*, TR VI, CH 8–10 111c-113a

19 AQUINAS: *Summa Theologica*, PART I, Q 48, A 4, ANS and REP 3 262a-263a

20 AQUINAS: *Summa Theologica*, PART I–II, Q 50, A I, REP 3 6a-7b; Q 52, A I, ANS and REP 3 15d-18a; PART III SUPPL, Q 82, A 3, ANS and REP 2 971a-972d; Q 91, A I, REP 2,4 1016b-1017c

23 HOBBES: *Leviathan*, PART III, 172b

34 NEWTON: *Optics*, BK III, 541b

35 LOCKE: *Human Understanding*, BK II, CH XXVI, SECT 1–2 217a-d

35 BERKELEY: *Human Knowledge*, SECT 25–33 417d-419a passim, esp SECT 25–26 417d-418a

(9. *Change of quality.*)

9a. Physical and chemical change: compounds and mixtures

7 PLATO: *Timaeus*, 448b-d; 459d-462b

8 ARISTOTLE: *Topics*, BK VI, CH 14 [151^{a}20–32] 206a / *Heavens*, BK I, CH 3 [270^{a}26–36] 361c; CH 5 [271^{b}18–23] 362d-363a; BK III, CH 3 393c-d; CH 8 [306^{b}22–29] 398a / *Generation and Corruption*, BK I, CH 2 [315^{a}28–33] 410d; CH 10 426c-428d; BK II, CH 6–8 433d-436d / *Meteorology*, BK III, CH 6 [378^{a}13]–BK IV, CH 12 [390^{b}21] 482c-494d / *Metaphysics*, BK VII, CH 17 [1041^{b}12–33] 565d-566a,c / *Sense and the Sensible*, CH 3 [440^{a}33–^{b}13] 677d-678a

9 ARISTOTLE: *Parts of Animals*, BK II, CH 1 [646^{a}12–24] 170a-b

12 LUCRETIUS: *Nature of Things*, BK I [635–920] 8d-12b; BK II [730–864] 24b-26a

12 AURELIUS: *Meditations*, BK X, SECT 7 297b-c

17 PLOTINUS: *Second Ennead*, TR I, CH 6–8 37d-39d; TR VII, CH 1–2 62d-64b

19 AQUINAS: *Summa Theologica*, PART I, Q 71, A I, REP 1–2 367a-368b; Q 76, A 4, REP 4 393a-394c; Q 91, A I 484a-485b

20 AQUINAS: *Summa Theologica*, PART I-II, Q 50, A I, REP 3 6a-7b; PART III, Q 2, A I, ANS 710a-711c; PART III SUPPL, Q 74, A I, REP 3 925c-926c; A 5 929d-931b; Q 80, A 3, REP 3 958b-959c; Q 82, A I, ANS 968a-970c

28 GILBERT: *Loadstone*, BK I, 13b-14d; BK II, 29c-30a

28 GALILEO: *Two New Sciences*, FIRST DAY, 148c-d

28 HARVEY: *On Animal Generation*, 495c-496d

30 BACON: *Novum Organum*, BK I, APH 50 111b; BK II, APH 7 139c-140a; APH 48, 181a-183a

34 NEWTON: *Optics*, BK III, 517b-518a; 531b-542a esp 541b

35 LOCKE: *Human Understanding*, BK II, CH XXVI, SECT 1–2 217a-d

45 LAVOISIER: *Elements of Chemistry*, PART I-II, 22c-86a,c; PART III, 87c-d; 103b-c; 105d; 117a-128c esp 117a-118a

45 FOURIER: *Theory of Heat*, 169b

45 FARADAY: *Researches in Electricity*, 309a-312a; 312c-313d; 314a-b; 315a-b; 327a-422a,c passim; 541b,d-584a,c passim

53 JAMES: *Psychology*, 68a-b; 104a-105a; 876a

9b. Biological change: vital alterations

7 PLATO: *Laws*, BK II, 659c-d; BK VII, 713d

8 ARISTOTLE: *Physics*, BK VII, CH 3 [246^{a}10–^{b}19] 329c-330a

9 ARISTOTLE: *History of Animals*, BK V, CH 19 [551^{a}13–552^{b}5] 78a-79b; CH 30 [556^{b}5–9] 83b; BK VII, CH 1 106b,d-108a; BK IX, CH 50 [631^{b}19–632^{a}32] 157a-c; CH 49B [632^{b}14–633^{a}29] 157d-158c / *Motion of Animals*, CH 5 235c-d; CH 7 [701^{b}1]–CH 8 [702^{a}22] 236d-237c; CH 11 [703^{b}8–21] 239b-c / *Generation of Animals*, BK I, CH 18 [724^{a}20–^{b}13] 264b-d; BK II,

CH 1 [733^{b}1–17] 273d-274a; CH 5 [741^{b}5–15] 282c; CH 6 [742^{a}8–16] 283a; BK V, CH 1 [778^{a}15–20] 320a-b; CH 3 [782^{a}1–20] 324a-b

10 GALEN: *Natural Faculties*, BK I, CH 5, 169b; CH 8 171a; BK III, CH 7, 203c-204c

12 LUCRETIUS: *Nature of Things*, BK IV [1030–1057] 57c-d

25 MONTAIGNE: *Essays*, 292d-293d

28 HARVEY: *On Animal Generation*, 412a-415b; 450b-d

31 SPINOZA: *Ethics*, PART IV, PROP 38–39 436b-437a

49 DARWIN: *Origin of Species*, 10a-c; 61d-62a; 219d-222a esp 221b-222a; 224b-c / *Descent of Man*, 354c-355a

51 TOLSTOY: *War and Peace*, EPILOGUE I, 665a-d

53 JAMES: *Psychology*, 68b-73b

54 FREUD: *Beyond the Pleasure Principle*, 655a-657d esp 655b, 656b-657c / *Civilization and Its Discontents*, 770b

10. Substantial change: generation and corruption

7 PLATO: *Symposium*, 165c-166b / *Phaedo*, 226d-228a / *Republic*, BK VIII, 403a-b; BK X, 434c-436a / *Parmenides*, 504c-d; 509a-d / *Laws*, BK X, 761b-762c

8 ARISTOTLE: *Topics*, BK VII, CH 3 [153^{b}31–34] 209a / *Physics*, BK II, CH 1 [193^{b}19–22] 270a / *Generation and Corruption* 409a-441a,c / *Metaphysics*, BK I, CH 3 [983^{b}8–19] 501d; CH 8 [988^{b}22–989^{b}24] 506d-508a; BK II, CH 2 [994^{a}19–^{b}8] 512c-d; BK VII, CH 7–9 555a-558a; BK XI, CH 11 596a-d; BK XII, CH 2–3 598c-599d / *Soul*, BK II, CH 4 [416^{b}8–17] 646d-647a

10 GALEN: *Natural Faculties*, BK I, CH 2, 167d-168b; CH 5 169b-c; CH 12 172d-173c

12 LUCRETIUS: *Nature of Things*, BK II [569–580] 22b; [865–1022] 26a-28a; BK III [117–129] 31c-d; [203–230] 32c-33a; [323–349] 34b-c; [417–869] 35c-41a; BK V [783–836] 71b-72a

12 AURELIUS: *Meditations*, BK VII, SECT 23 281b; SECT 25 281c

18 AUGUSTINE: *Confessions*, BK VII, par 18 49a-b

19 AQUINAS: *Summa Theologica*, PART I, Q 15, A I, ANS 91b-92a; Q 19, A 9, ANS 116d-117d; Q 27, A 2 154c-155b; Q 33, A 2, REP 4 181c-182b; Q 41, A 5, ANS and REP 1 222b-223b; Q 44, A 2, ANS 239b-240a; Q 45, A 2, REP 2 242d-244a; Q 50, A 5, REP 3 274b-275a; Q 53, A 3, ANS 283b-284d; Q 65, A 4, ANS 342b-343c; Q 66, A I, ANS 343d-345c; A 2, ANS 345d-347b; Q 67, A 3, REP 1 351b-352a; Q 71, A I, REP 1 367a-368b; Q 72, A I, REP 5 368b-369d; Q 75, A 6, ANS 383c-384c; Q 90, A 2, ANS 481d-482c; Q 96, A I, ANS 510b-511b; Q 119 604c-608d; PART I-II, Q 22, A I, ANS and REP 3 720d-721c

20 AQUINAS: *Summa Theologica*, PART I-II, Q 53, A I 19d-21a; A 3 21d-22d; Q 85, A 6 182d-184a; Q 110, A 2, REP 3 349a-d; PART II-II, Q I, A 7, REP 3 385c-387a; PART III SUPPL, Q 75, A 3, ANS 938a-939d; Q 79, A I, REP 3–4 951b-953b;

(10. *Substantial change: generation and corruption. 10c. The incorruptibility of atoms, the heavenly bodies, and spiritual substances.*)

10 GALEN: *Natural Faculties*, BK I, CH 12, 173a-b; BK II, CH 6, 189c-190a

12 LUCRETIUS: *Nature of Things*, BK I [483-634] 7a-8d; BK II [842-864] 25c-26a

16 PTOLEMY: *Almagest*, BK I, 5a-6a; BK XIII, 429a-b

16 KEPLER: *Epitome*, BK IV, 929b-930b

17 PLOTINUS: *Second Ennead*, TR I, CH 1-4 35a-37b; CH 8 39c-d

19 AQUINAS: *Summa Theologica*, PART I, Q 9, A 2 39c-40d; Q 10, A 2, REP 1-2 41d-42c; A 3, ANS 42c-43b; A 5 44b-45c; Q 46, A 1, REP 2-3,5 250a-252d; Q 50, A 5 274b-275a; Q 58, A 3, ANS 301d-302d; Q 63, A 1, REP 2 325c-326c; Q 66, A 2 345d-347b; Q 68, A 1, ANS 354a-355c; Q 70, A 3 365b-367a; Q 97, A 1, ANS 513c-514c; Q 104, A 1, REP 1,3 534c-536c

20 AQUINAS: *Summa Theologica*, PART I-II, Q 49, A 4, ANS 5a-6a

21 DANTE: *Divine Comedy*, PARADISE, VII [121-148] 116b-c; XIII [52-60] 126a

31 SPINOZA: *Ethics*, PART I 355a-372d passim, esp DEF I 355a, DEF 3,6 355b, AXIOM 1-2 355c-d, PROP 1-15 355d-361d

32 MILTON: *Paradise Lost*, BK I [128-142] 96a-b; BK II [81-105] 113a-b; BK VI [296-353] 202b-204a esp [320-353] 203a-204a; [430-436] 205b

33 PASCAL: *Vacuum*, 358a

34 NEWTON: *Optics*, BK III, 541b

42 KANT: *Pure Reason*, 137a-140c

53 JAMES: *Psychology*, 68a-b

11. The apprehension of change: by sense, by reason

7 PLATO: *Cratylus*, 113c-114a,c / *Phaedo*, 231c-232a / *Timaeus*, 447b-d; 457c-d / *Sophist*, 565a-569a esp 568a-569a / *Laws*, BK X, 765a-b

8 ARISTOTLE: *Physics*, BK IV, CH 11 298c-300a / *Metaphysics*, BK I, CH 6 [987^{a}29-^{b}18] 505b-d; CH 9 [990^{b}9-15] 508d; BK III, CH 2 [996^{a}18-^{b}26] 514d-515b; BK IV, CH 5 528c-530c; CH 8 [1012^{b}23-32] 532d; BK XI, CH 6 [1063^{a}10-^{b}8] 591b-d / *Soul*, BK III, CH 1 [425^{a}14-^{b}10] 657b-d

12 LUCRETIUS: *Nature of Things*, BK I [311-328] 5a; BK II [62-141] 15d-16d; [308-332] 19a-b

18 AUGUSTINE: *Confessions*, BK VII, PAR 23 50b-c; BK XI, PAR 17-41 93b-99b / *Christian Doctrine*, BK I, CH 8-9 626c-627a; BK II, CH 38 654b-c

19 AQUINAS: *Summa Theologica*, PART I, Q 14, A 15, REP 2 89b-90b; Q 78, A 3, REP 2 410a-411d; Q 84, A 1 esp REP 3 440d-442a; Q 86, A 3 463b-d

23 HOBBES: *Leviathan*, PART III, 172b; PART IV, 249c-d

25 MONTAIGNE: *Essays*, 291b-294b

30 BACON: *Novum Organum*, BK II, APH 5-6 138b-139c; APH 23 153d-154c; APH 40-41 170c-174b

31 DESCARTES: *Rules*, XII, 24a

35 LOCKE: *Human Understanding*, BK II, CH V 131b; CH VII, SECT 8-9 132d-133a; CH VIII, SECT 18 136a-b; CH XIV, SECT 6-12 156b-157c; CH XXIII, SECT 28-29 211b-212a; CH XXVI, SECT 1-2 217a-d

42 KANT: *Pure Reason*, 27a-33d esp 28b-c, 29c-d; 43a-b; 55c-56a; 76c-83b esp 76c-d; 91d-93c

53 JAMES: *Psychology*, 405b-406b; 418b-419b; 510a-512a; 563a-567a; 612a-616b esp 616a; 634b-635a

12. Emotional aspects of change

12a. Rest and motion in relation to pleasure and pain

7 PLATO: *Gorgias*, 275c-277c / *Timaeus*, 463d-464b / *Philebus*, 619d-620b; 626a-c; 631d-632d / *Laws*, BK VII, 713c-715a

8 ARISTOTLE: *Topics*, BK IV, CH 1 [121^{a}27-39] 169b

9 ARISTOTLE: *Ethics*, BK VII, CH 11 [1152^{b}8]-CH 12 [1153^{a}17] 403c-404b; CH 14 [1154^{b}20-30] 406c; BK X, CH 3 [1173^{a}29-^{b}7] 427c-d; CH 4 [1174^{a}13-^{b}14] 428b-429a / *Politics*, BK VIII, CH 5 [1340^{a}1-^{b}19] 545c-546a / *Rhetoric*, BK I, CH 11 [1369^{b}33-1370^{a}17] 613a-c; [1371^{a}26-30] 614d

17 PLOTINUS: *Fourth Ennead*, TR IV, CH 18-21, 167a-168c

19 AQUINAS: *Summa Theologica*, PART I-II, Q 32, A 2 759d-760d

23 HOBBES: *Leviathan*, PART I, 50a

31 SPINOZA: *Ethics*, PART III 395a-422a,c

35 LOCKE: *Human Understanding*, BK II, CH XXI, SECT 29-48 184d-190d passim

50 MARX: *Capital*, 166b-c

53 JAMES: *Psychology*, 410a

54 FREUD: *Narcissism*, 403d-404a / *General Introduction*, 592c-593a / *Beyond the Pleasure Principle*, 639b-640a; 648d-649c / *Ego and Id*, 701a-b

12b. The love and hatred of change

5 SOPHOCLES: *Oedipus at Colonus* [1211-1248] 125b-c

6 HERODOTUS: *History*, BK VII, 224d-225a

7 PLATO: *Republic*, BK IV, 344b-d / *Laws*, BK VII, 717d-718d

9 ARISTOTLE: *Ethics*, BK VII, CH 14 [1154^{b}20-30] 406c

10 HIPPOCRATES: *Fractures*, PAR 1 74b,d-75a / *Aphorisms*, SECT II, PAR 50 133d

12 LUCRETIUS: *Nature of Things*, BK II [1105-1174] 29a-30a,c; BK III [912-977] 41d-42c; [1053-1084] 43c-44a; BK V [156-173] 63a-b; [1379-1435] 79a-d

12 AURELIUS: *Meditations*, BK II, SECT 14 258d; SECT 17 259b-d; BK IV, SECT 3 263b-264a; SECT 5 264b; SECT 12 264c; SECT 33 266c-d; SECT 35-36 266d; SECT 42-43 267b; BK V,

SECT 10 270c-d; SECT 13 271b; SECT 23 272b; SECT 33 273b-c; BK VI, SECT 15 275a-b; SECT 36 277c; BK VII, SECT 18–19 281a; SECT 35 282a; SECT 49 282d; BK VIII, SECT 6 285d-286a; SECT 16,18 286d; BK IX, SECT 21 293b-c; SECT 28 293d-294a; BK X, SECT 7 297b-c; SECT 31 300a-b; SECT 34 301a

13 VIRGIL: *Aeneid*, BK I [441–462] 115a-b esp [462] 115b

14 PLUTARCH: *Aemilius Paulus*, 225b-c; 229a-c

17 PLOTINUS: *First Ennead*, TR IV 12b-19b

18 AUGUSTINE: *Confessions*, BK VIII, par 18 57d-58a; par 25–26 60a-b / *Christian Doctrine*, BK I, CH 9 627a

21 DANTE: *Divine Comedy*, HELL, VII [61–96] 10b-c; XIV [94–120] 20c-d; XXVI [90–142] 39a-c; PURGATORY, XI [73–117] 69c-70a; XIV [91–126] 74c-75a; XXVIII [76–148] 96d-97c; PARADISE, XV–XVI 128b-132a

22 CHAUCER: *Wife of Bath's Prologue* [5583–6410] 256a-269b

23 MACHIAVELLI: *Prince*, CH VI, 9b-c

23 HOBBES: *Leviathan*, PART I, 79c-d; PART II, 150c; 154b-c; PART IV, 271d

25 MONTAIGNE: *Essays*, 33b-36a; 47a-51a; 131b-132a; 281a-282a; 292d-294b; 318c-319b; 458b-c; 462c-465c; 478c-479c; 540d-541c

26 SHAKESPEARE: *2nd Henry IV*, ACT III, SC I [45–56] 483b

27 SHAKESPEARE: *Hamlet*, ACT I, SC II [68–73] 32b; ACT V, SC I [202–240] 66c-d / *Troilus and Cressida*, ACT III, SC III [145–189] 124a-c; ACT IV, SC IV [26–50] 128c / *King Lear*, ACT IV, SC I [10–12] 269c / *Sonnets*, XV 588b-c; XXV 590a; XLIX 593d; LX 595b-c; LXIV–LXV 596a-b; CXVI 604a; CXXIII 605a

28 GILBERT: *Loadstone*, PREF, 2a

28 HARVEY: *Motion of the Heart*, 274a; 285b-c

30 BACON: *Advancement of Learning*, 14c-15c esp 15a-b; 16c-d; 61b; 65b-c; 90b-d / *Novum Organum*, BK I, APH 90 124d-125a

31 DESCARTES: *Discourse*, PART II, 45d

31 SPINOZA: *Ethics*, PART III, PROP 4–11 398d-400b; PART V, PROP 6, SCHOL 454a

33 PASCAL: *Pensées*, 129–131 195b; 135 196a; 139–143 196b-200a; 164–172 202b-203b; 181 204b / *Vacuum*, 355a-358b

35 LOCKE: *Civil Government*, CH XIX, SECT 223 76c-d / *Human Understanding*, 85a-c

36 SWIFT: *Gulliver*, PART III, 105a-106b

38 ROUSSEAU: *Inequality*, 335c

43 DECLARATION OF INDEPENDENCE: [15–20] 1b

43 FEDERALIST: NUMBER 14, 62a-d

43 MILL: *Liberty*, 293b-302c passim / *Representative Government*, 336b-c; 350c; 377d-378a

46 HEGEL: *Philosophy of History*, INTRO, 178a-c; PART I, 209b; 258b

47 GOETHE: *Faust*, DEDICATION 1a-b; PART II [11,573–586] 281b-282a; [11,612–622] 282b-283a

49 DARWIN: *Descent of Man*, 302b; 577c-d

51 TOLSTOY: *War and Peace*, BK V, 221b-d; BK VI, 238c-243d passim; 267c; BK VII, 275a-276b; 294a-b; BK VIII, 305b-d; 307d-309c; BK IX, 356b-d; BK X, 394d; 403a-405a; BK XII, 538a-539c; 556d-557a; BK XV, 639c; EPILOGUE I, 645a-646c; 668a-669c

53 JAMES: *Psychology*, 524a-525a; 707b-708a

54 FREUD: *Beyond the Pleasure Principle*, 651b-d

13. The problem of the eternity of motion or change

7 PLATO: *Phaedrus*, 124b-c / *Timaeus*, 450c-451a; 460c-d

8 ARISTOTLE: *Physics*, BK IV, CH 13 [222^{a}29–^{b}8] 302b; BK VIII, CH 1–4 334a-340d; CH 8 348b-352a / *Heavens*, BK I, CH 2 [269^{b}2–10] 360c-d; CH 3 [270^{b}1–24] 361c-362a; BK I, CH 9 [279^{a}12]–BK II, CH 1 [284^{b}6] 370b-376a; BK II, CH 6 379c-380c / *Generation and Corruption*, BK II, CH 10–11 437d-441a,c / *Meteorology*, BK I, CH 14 [352^{a}16–353^{a}27] 458b-459a,c passim; BK II, CH 3 [356^{b}2–357^{a}4] 462b-c / *Metaphysics*, BK IX, CH 8 [1050^{b}20–28] 576c-d; BK XII, CH 6 [1071^{b}3]–CH 7 [1072^{a}22] 601b-602b; CH 7 [1073^{a}2–34] 603a-c

12 LUCRETIUS: *Nature of Things*, BK I [951–1051] 12d-14a esp [988–1007] 13b; BK II [80–141] 16a-d; [294–302] 18d; [569–580] 22b

12 AURELIUS: *Meditations*, BK V, SECT 13 271b; SECT 23 272b; BK VI, SECT 15 275a-b; BK IX, SECT 28 293d-294a; BK XI, SECT 27 306b

16 PTOLEMY: *Almagest*, BK XIII, 429a-b

16 KEPLER: *Epitome*, BK IV, 888b-891a

17 PLOTINUS: *Third Ennead*, TR VII, CH 7–8 122d-124c; CH 11–13 126a-129a / *Fourth Ennead*, TR IV, CH 7–8 161d-162d

18 AUGUSTINE: *Confessions*, BK XI, par 10–17 91d-93c; BK XII, par 8–9 101a-c; par 12–16 101d-103a; par 29 105d-106a; par 33 107b-c; par 39–40 109a-110a / *City of God*, BK XI, CH 4–6 324a-325d; BK XII, CH 10–20 348b-357a

19 AQUINAS: *Summa Theologica*, PART I, Q 10, A 2, REP 2 41d-42c; A 4, ANS 43b-44b; Q 14, A 12, ANS 85d-86d; Q 46, AA 1–2 250a-255a; Q 75, A 1, REP 1 378b-379c

20 AQUINAS: *Summa Theologica*, PART III SUPPL, Q 77, A 2, ANS 945a-946b; Q 91, A 2 1017c-1020c

28 GILBERT: *Loadstone*, BK II, 56b-c

28 GALILEO: *Two New Sciences*, THIRD DAY, 224d

30 BACON: *Novum Organum*, BK II, APH 35, 163a; APH 48, 186b-c

31 DESCARTES: *Rules*, XIII, 27b-c

34 NEWTON: *Principles*, LAW I 14a; BK III, PROP 10 284a-285a / *Optics*, BK III, 540a-541b

35 LOCKE: *Human Understanding*, BK II, CH XIV, SECT 26 160c-d

42 KANT: *Pure Reason*, 135a-137a,c; 152a-d; 160b-161d

53 JAMES: *Psychology*, 882a

14. The theory of the prime mover: the order and hierarchy of movers and moved

7 PLATO: *Phaedrus*, 124b-c / *Statesman*, 587a-589c / *Laws*, BK X, 758d-765c

8 ARISTOTLE: *Physics*, BK VII, CH 1–2 326a-329a; BK VIII 334a-355d / *Heavens*, BK III, CH 2 [300^{b}8–301^{a}12] 391d-392c / *Generation and Corruption*, BK I, CH 7 421d-423b; BK II, CH 6 [334^{a}6–9] 435a / *Metaphysics*, BK IV, CH 8 [1012^{b}22–32] 532d; BK V, CH 11 [1018^{b}19–22] 539c-d; BK IX, CH 8 [1049^{b}17–28] 575b-c; [1050^{a}3–^{b}6] 575d-576b; BK XII, CH 4 [1070^{b}22–35] 600b; CH 5 [1071^{a}30–36] 601a; CH 6–8 601b-605a

9 ARISTOTLE: *Motion of Animals*, CH 1 [698^{a}10–15] 233a; CH 3–6 234a-236b

12 EPICTETUS: *Discourses*, BK I, CH 14, 120d-121a

16 PTOLEMY: *Almagest*, BK I, 5a-b

19 AQUINAS: *Summa Theologica*, PART I, Q 2, A 3, ANS 12c-14a; Q 3, A 1, ANS 14b-15b; Q 9, A 1, REP 1 38c-39c; Q 19, A 1, REP 3 108d-109c; Q 25, A 2, REP 3 144c-145b; Q 46, A 1, REP 5 250a-252d; Q 51, A 3, REP 3 277a-278c; Q 60, A 1, REP 2 310b-311a; Q 75, A 1, REP 1 378b-379c; QQ 105–119 538d-608d passim; PART I–II, Q 1, A 4, ANS 612a-613a; A 6, ANS 614a-c; Q 6, A 1, REP 3 644d-646a

20 AQUINAS: *Summa Theologica*, PART I–II, Q 109, A 1, ANS 338b-339c; PART III SUPPL, Q 91, A 1, REP 2 1016b-1017c

21 DANTE: *Divine Comedy*, PARADISE, I [103–142] 107b-d; XIII [52–84] 126a-b; XXVII [106–120] 148b-c; XXVIII [1–78] 148d-149c

23 HOBBES: *Leviathan*, PART I, 79d-80a

28 GILBERT: *Loadstone*, BK VI, 107c-110d

28 HARVEY: *On Animal Generation*, 415b-417a esp 416b-c; 426a-429b; 443a-c; 490d-493a esp 492b-c

32 MILTON: *Paradise Lost*, BK V [469–505] 185b-186a

33 PASCAL: *Pensées*, 77 186a

42 KANT: *Pure Reason*, 140b,d-145c; 177b-179b; 239a-240b / *Practical Reason*, 334a-337a,c / *Judgement*, 597d-599d; 610b-613a,c

15. The immutable

15a. The immutability of the objects of thought: the realm of truth

OLD TESTAMENT: *Psalms*, 100:5; 117:2; 119:160; 146:6—(D) *Psalms*, 99:5; 116:2; 118:160; 145:7 / *Proverbs*, 8:22–30

APOCRYPHA: *Ecclesiasticus*, 24:9—(D) OT, *Ecclesiasticus*, 24:14

NEW TESTAMENT: *II John*, 2

7 PLATO: *Cratylus*, 113c-114a,c / *Phaedrus*, 125a-b / *Symposium*, 167b-d / *Phaedo*, 231b-232b / *Republic*, BK V, 371a-373c / *Timaeus*, 447a-d; 457b-458a / *Parmenides*, 487c-491a / *Sophist*,

568a-b / *Philebus*, 634b-635b / *Seventh Letter*, 809c-810d

8 ARISTOTLE: *Categories*, CH 5 [4^{a}10–^{b}12] 8b-9a / *Posterior Analytics*, BK I, CH 8 104a-b / *Metaphysics*, BK I, CH 6 505b-506b; CH 9 508c-511c; BK III, CH 1 [995^{b}13–18] 514a; [995^{b}31–996^{a}1] 514b; [996^{a}4–9] [996^{a}13–15] 514c; CH 2 [997^{a}34–998^{a}19] 516a-d; CH 3 [998^{b}14]–CH 4 [999^{b}24] 517b-518c; CH 4 [1001^{a}4]–CH 6 [1002^{b}31] 519d-521d; BK VII, CH 8 [1033^{b}19–1034^{a}8] 556d-557b; CH 10 [1035^{b}32–1036^{a}12] 559b-c; CH 11 [1036^{b}32–1037^{a}4] 560b-c; CH 13–14 562a-563c; CH 15 [1040^{a}8–^{b}4] 564a-c; CH 16 [1040^{b}28–1041^{a}4] 564d-565a; BK IX, CH 8 [1050^{b}35–1051^{a}2] 576d-577a; BK X, CH 10 586c-d; BK XI, CH 1 [1059^{a}33–^{b}14] 587b-c; BK XII, CH 1 [1069^{a}30–^{b}2] 598b-c; CH 3 [1070^{a}4–30] 599b-d; BK XIII, CH 1–5 607a-611d

9 ARISTOTLE: *Ethics*, BK I, CH 6 341b-342c

11 NICOMACHUS: *Arithmetic*, BK I, 811b-d; 813d-814b

17 PLOTINUS: *Second Ennead*, TR V, CH 3 58d-59c / *Third Ennead*, TR IX 136a-138a,c / *Fifth Ennead*, TR VII, CH 1 238a-b; TR IX, CH 5–13 248a-251c

18 AUGUSTINE: *Confessions*, BK I, par 9, 3a; BK XI, par 9–11 91c-92b / *Christian Doctrine*, BK I, CH 8–10 626c-627b; BK II, CH 38 654b-c

19 AQUINAS: *Summa Theologica*, PART I, Q 5, A 3, REP 4 25a-d; Q 10, A 3, REP 3 42c-43b; Q 16, AA 7–8 99a-100d; Q 44, A 1, REP 3 238b-239a; Q 84, A 1, ANS and REP 3 440d-442a; Q 85, A 1, REP 2 451c-453c; Q 86, A 3 463b-d; Q 113, A 1, ANS 576a-d

20 AQUINAS: *Summa Theologica*, PART I–II, Q 53, A 1, ANS and REP 2–3 19d-21a; Q 94, AA 5–6 224d-226b

30 BACON: *Advancement of Learning*, 27d-28c; 43d-44c

31 DESCARTES: *Discourse*, PART IV, 52d-53a / *Meditations*, V 93a-96a / *Objections and Replies*, 123b; 216d-217d; 228a-c; 229c-d

31 SPINOZA: *Ethics*, PART I, DEF 8 355c; PROP 7 356c; PROP 8, SCHOL 2 356d-357d; PROP 17, SCHOL 362c-363c; PART II, PROP 32 385c; PROP 34 385d; PROP 37–39 386b-387a; PROP 40, DEMONST 387a; PROP 43–47 388c-391a

32 MILTON: *Areopagitica*, 384a-b

33 PASCAL: *Vacuum*, 358b

35 LOCKE: *Human Understanding*, BK II, CH II, SECT 2 128a-b; BK III, CH III, SECT 19 259c-260a; CH VI, SECT 6 269d-270a; BK IV, CH I, SECT 9 308c-309b; CH III, SECT 31 323c-d; CH XI, SECT 14 358b-c

42 KANT: *Judgement*, 551a-553c

46 HEGEL: *Philosophy of Right*, ADDITIONS, I, 115a / *Philosophy of History*, INTRO, 156d-157b

47 GOETHE: *Faust*, PRELUDE [73–74] 3a

50 MARX-ENGELS: *Communist Manifesto*, 428b-d

53 JAMES: *Psychology*, 299a-304b esp 301a, 302a-304b; 869a; 879b-882a

15*b*. The unalterability of the decrees of fate

4 HOMER: *Iliad*, BK XVIII [52-126] 130c-131c; BK XXII [131-223] 156c-157c

5 AESCHYLUS: *Prometheus Bound* [507-525] 45a-b / *Agamemnon* [1018-1033] 63a

5 EURIPIDES: *Heracles Mad* [1313-1353] 376c-d / *Iphigenia Among the Tauri* [1435-1499] 424a-d

6 HERODOTUS: *History*, BK I, 6c-10a; 20b-22a; BK II, 77a-b

12 LUCRETIUS: *Nature of Things*, BK II [251-293] 18b-d

12 EPICTETUS: *Discourses*, BK I, CH 12 118d-120b; BK II, CH 8 146a-147c

12 AURELIUS: *Meditations*, BK III, SECT 11 262a-b; BK X, SECT 5 296d

13 VIRGIL: *Aeneid*, BK X [606-632] 318b-319b

14 PLUTARCH: *Caesar*, 601c-604d

18 AUGUSTINE: *City of God*, BK V, CH 1-10 207d-216c

19 AQUINAS: *Summa Theologica*, PART I, Q 116, A 3 594c-595a

22 CHAUCER: *Troilus and Cressida*, BK IV, STANZA 136-154 106a-108b

32 MILTON: *Arcades* [54-83] 26b-27a / *Paradise Lost*, BK VII [170-173] 220b-221a

51 TOLSTOY: *War and Peace*, BK IX, 342a-344b; EPILOGUE I, 645a-650c; EPILOGUE II, 675a-c

15*c*. The immutability of God

OLD TESTAMENT: *Exodus*, 15:18 / *Deuteronomy*, 32:39-40 / *I Chronicles*, 16:34-36—(D) *I Paralipomenon*, 16:34-36 / *Psalms*, 9:5-8; 10:16; 29:10-11; 33:10-11; 45:6; 48 esp 48:8, 48:14; 66:7; 89-90 esp 89:30-35, 90:1-4; 93:2; 102 esp 102:11-12, 102:26-27; 103:17-18; 136; 145-146 esp 145:13, 146:10—(D) *Psalms*, 9:6-9; 9:16; 28:10; 32:10-11; 44:7; 47 esp 47:9, 47:15; 65:7; 88-89 esp 88:31-36, 89:1-4; 92:2; 101 esp 101:12-13, 101:27-28; 102:17-18; 135; 144-145 esp 144:13, 145:10 / *Ecclesiastes*, 3:14-15 / *Isaiah*, 40:8,28; 43:10-13; 57:15—(D) *Isaias*, 40:8,28; 43:10-13; 57:15 / *Jeremiah*, 10:10—(D) *Jeremias*, 10:10 / *Lamentations*, 5:19 / *Daniel*, 6:25-27 / *Malachi*, 3:6—(D) *Malachias*, 3:6

APOCRYPHA: *Ecclesiasticus*, 36:17; 39:20; 42:21—(D) OT, *Ecclesiasticus*, 36:18-19; 39:25;42:21-22

NEW TESTAMENT: *Matthew*, 24:35 / *John*, 1:1-5 / *Romans*, 1:21-25; 6:23 / *Colossians*, 1:16-17 / *I Timothy*, 1:17 / *Hebrews*, 1:10-12; 7:23-28; 13:7-8 / *James*, 1:17 / *I John*, 5:11-12 / *Revelation*, 1:17-18; 10:6; 11:15-18—(D) *Apocalypse*, 1:17-18; 10:6; 11:15-18

5 SOPHOCLES: *Oedipus at Colonus* [607-615] 120a

7 PLATO: *Republic*, BK II, 322d-323c; 324a-b

8 ARISTOTLE: *Physics*, BK VIII, CH 6 [258^{b}10-259^{b}31] 344b-345d / *Heavens*, BK I, CH 9 [279^{a}23-^{b}4] 370c-d; BK II, CH 3 [286^{a}8-13] 377c / *Generation and Corruption*, BK II, CH 10 [337^{a}15-23] 439a-b / *Metaphysics*, BK V, CH 5 [1015^{b}9-16] 536a; BK XII, CH 6-7 601b-603b; CH 9 605a-d

9 ARISTOTLE: *Ethics*, BK VII, CH 14 [1154^{b}20-30] 406c

15 TACITUS: *Histories*, BK V, 296a

17 PLOTINUS: *Third Ennead*, TR VII, CH 1-6 119b-122d / *Sixth Ennead*, TR VIII, CH 18-21 351d-353d

18 AUGUSTINE: *Confessions*, BK I, par 10 3b-c; BK IV, par 26 25c-d; par 29 26b; BK VII, par 1-6 43b-45a; par 17-18 49a-b; par 23 50b-c; par 26, 51c; BK XII, par 11 101d; par 18 103a-c; BK XIII, par 44 122d / *City of God*, BK VII, CH 30 261b-d; BK VIII, CH 11, 272c; BK X, CH 1, 298b,d; BK XI, CH 10 327d-328d; CH 21-22 333a-334c; BK XII, CH 1-3 342b,d-344b; CH 14 350d-351b; CH 17 353a-354a / *Christian Doctrine*, BK I, CH 5 625d-626a; CH 8 626c-627a; CH 10 627b; CH 22-23 629b-630c

19 AQUINAS: *Summa Theologica*, PART I, Q 2, A 3, ANS 12c-14a; Q 3, A 1, ANS and REP 4 14b-15b; QQ 9-10 38c-46d; Q 14, A 7 81d-82b; A 15 89b-90b; Q 18, A 3 106b-107c; Q 19, A 7 114d-115d; Q 26, A 1, REP 2 150b-c; Q 43, A 2, REP 2 230c-231c; Q 51, A 3, REP 3 277a-278c

20 AQUINAS: *Summa Theologica*, PART I-II, Q 61, A 5, ANS 58b-59d; PART III, Q 1, A 1, REP 3 701d-703a; Q 2, A 1, ANS 710a-711c

21 DANTE: *Divine Comedy*, PARADISE, XIII [52-84] 126a-b; XXIV [130-141] 144a; XXVIII [1-78] 148d-149c; XXIX [13-36] 150b-c

22 CHAUCER: *Knight's Tale* [2994-3015] 209a-b

23 HOBBES: *Leviathan*, PART III, 173a

25 MONTAIGNE: *Essays*, 292d-294b

31 DESCARTES: *Discourse*, PART IV, 52b-d / *Meditations*, III, 86a-87a; V 93a-96a esp 93d-95b / *Objections and Replies*, 228a-c; 229c-d

31 SPINOZA: *Ethics*, PART I 355a-372d esp DEF I 355a, DEF 3,6-7 355b, PROP 3 356a, PROP 5-8 356b-357d, PROP 11-15 358b-361d, PROP 17 362b-363c, PROP 19-20 363c-364a, PROP 33, SCHOL 1 367c-d, PROP 34 369a; PART V, PROP 17 456c-d

32 MILTON: *Paradise Lost*, BK III [372-389] 143b-144a

33 PASCAL: *Pensées*, 469 256a

34 NEWTON: *Principles*, BK III, GENERAL SCHOL, 370a-371a

35 LOCKE: *Human Understanding*, BK II, CH XVII, SECT 20 172d-173c; CH XXIII, SECT 21 209c

35 BERKELEY: *Human Knowledge*, SECT 117 436a

42 KANT: *Pure Reason*, 175d-176c; 177b-179b; 190c; 192d; 201b-c / *Practical Reason*, 352a-b

46 HEGEL: *Philosophy of Right*, PART III, par 270, 85c / *Philosophy of History*, PART III, 306a

CROSS-REFERENCES

For: The broad philosophical context of the theory of change, *see* BEING 5; DESIRE 1; FORM 1–1b; MATTER 1–1b, 2b.

The distinction between the mutable and the immutable, *see* ASTRONOMY 8a; BEING 7b(3); ELEMENT 5a; ETERNITY 4–4d; FORM 1a; TRUTH 5.

The issue concerning time and eternity in relation to change, *see* ASTRONOMY 8c(1); ETERNITY 1; TIME 2, 2b; WORLD 4a.

A discussion relevant to the theory of the prime mover, *see* ANGEL 2a.

The mathematical and experimental approach to the study of local motion and the formulation of its laws, *see* ASTRONOMY 8c–8c(3); MECHANICS 5–5f(2), 6c–6e; ONE AND MANY 3a(2); QUANTITY 5c; SPACE 2a.

The discussion of biological and psychological change, *see* ANIMAL 4a, 6b–7, 8b; CAUSE 2; DESIRE 2c–2d; EDUCATION 4, 5c, 6; EMOTION 1b, 2b; HABIT 4b; REASONING 1b; TIME 7; VIRTUE AND VICE 4b–4c.

Other discussions of the distinction between generation and other kinds of change, *see* ART 2a; FORM 1d(2); WORLD 4e(1); and for the problem of the transmutation of the elements, *see* ELEMENT 3c.

The theory of historical change in nature and society, *see* EVOLUTION 4d, 6a, 7c; HISTORY 4b; PROGRESS 1a, 1c–2; TIME 8a.

The consideration of economic, political, and cultural change, *see* CONSTITUTION 7–7a, 8–8b; PROGRESS 3–4c, 6–6b; REVOLUTION 2–2c, 4–4b; WEALTH 12.

The discussion of change or becoming as an object of knowledge, *see* BEING 8a–8b; KNOWLEDGE 6a(1); OPINION 1.

Other considerations of man's attitude toward change and mutability, *see* CUSTOM AND CONVENTION 8; PROGRESS 5; TIME 7.

ADDITIONAL READINGS

Listed below are works not included in *Great Books of the Western World*, but relevant to the idea and topics with which this chapter deals. These works are divided into two groups:

    I. Works by authors represented in this collection.
    II. Works by authors not represented in this collection.

For the date, place, and other facts concerning the publication of the works cited, consult the Bibliography of Additional Readings which follows the last chapter of *The Great Ideas.*

I.

AQUINAS. *De Principiis Naturae*
DESCARTES. *The Principles of Philosophy*, PART II, 24–53
HOBBES. *Concerning Body*, PART III, CH 15–16, 21–22
BERKELEY. *Siris*
KANT. *Metaphysical Foundations of Natural Science*
HEGEL. *The Phenomenology of Mind*, III
——. *Science of Logic*, VOL I, BK I, SECT I, CH 1(c)
——. *Logic*, CH 7
W. JAMES. *Some Problems of Philosophy*, CH 9–10, 12

II.

SEXTUS EMPIRICUS. *Against the Physicists*, BK II, CH 2, 5
——. *Outlines of Pyrrhonism*, BK III, CH 1–20
CRESCAS. *Or Adonai*, PROPOSITIONS 4–9, 13–14, 17, 25
SUÁREZ. *Disputationes Metaphysicae*, XVIII (11), XXX (8–9), LX (8), XLVI (3), XLVIII–L
JOHN OF SAINT THOMAS. *Cursus Philosophicus Thomisticus, Philosophia Naturalis*, PART I, QQ 14, 19, 22–24; PART III, QQ 1–2, 10–12
LEIBNITZ. *Discourse on Metaphysics*, XV–XXII
——. *Monadology*, par 10–18

VOLTAIRE. "Motion," in *A Philosophical Dictionary*
SCHOPENHAUER. *The World as Will and Idea*
WHEWELL. *The Philosophy of the Inductive Sciences*, VOL I, BK II, CH 13
HELMHOLTZ. *Popular Lectures on Scientific Subjects*, VII
MAXWELL. *Matter and Motion*
CLIFFORD. *The Common Sense of the Exact Sciences*, CH 5
LOTZE. *Metaphysics*, BK I, CH 4–5; BK II, CH 4
BRADLEY. *Appearance and Reality*, BK I, CH 5
CROCE. *History, Its Theory and Practice*
BERGSON. *Creative Evolution*
——. *The Creative Mind*, CH 5

G. N. LEWIS. *The Anatomy of Science*, ESSAY III–IV
HEIDEGGER. *Sein und Zeit*
B. RUSSELL. *Principles of Mathematics*, CH 54, 56–59
——. *The Analysis of Matter*, CH 27, 33–34
EDDINGTON. *The Nature of the Physical World*, CH 5
DEWEY. *Experience and Nature*, CH 2
——. *The Quest for Certainty*, CH 2
WHITEHEAD. *The Concept of Nature*, CH 5
——. *Process and Reality*, PART II, CH 10
SANTAYANA. *Scepticism and Animal Faith*, CH 5
——. *The Realm of Matter*, CH 5–6
RIEZLER. *Physics and Reality*

Chapter 11: CITIZEN

INTRODUCTION

"CITIZEN," like "comrade," has been and still is a revolutionary word. Both words have been titles proudly adopted by men to mark their liberation from the yoke of despotism or tyranny. Both titles are still sought by those who have not yet gained admission to the fraternity of the free and equal.

The rank and status of citizenship first appeared in the ancient world with the beginning of constitutional government in the city-states of Greece. The Greeks were conscious of this fact, and proud of it. In terms of it, they set themselves apart from the barbarians who were subjects of the Great King of Persia or the Egyptian Pharaoh. The Spartan heralds, according to Herodotus, thus address the Persian commander: "Thou hast experience of half the matter; but the other half is beyond thy knowledge. A slave's life thou understandest; but, never having tasted liberty, thou canst not tell whether it is sweet or no. Ah! hadst thou known what freedom is, thou wouldst have bidden us fight for it, not with the spear only, but with the battle-axe."

Not only Herodotus and Thucydides but also the great tragic poets, notably Aeschylus in the *Persians*, record this Hellenic sense of distinction from the surrounding peoples who still lived in childlike submission to absolute rule. But the Greeks were also conscious that their political maturity as self-governing citizens was, as Aristotle intimates in the *Politics*, a recent development from the primitive condition in which tribal chieftains ruled despotically.

The basic distinction between *subjection* and *citizenship* is inseparable from the equally basic distinction between absolute and limited, or between despotic and constitutional, government. The difference between these two modes of government is treated in the chapter on CONSTITUTION. It is sufficient here to note that the difference in the authority and power possessed by rulers—according as it is absolute or limited—corresponds with a difference in the status, the degree of freedom, and the rights and privileges of the people ruled.

IN ORDER TO UNDERSTAND citizenship it is necessary to understand the several ways in which men can belong to or be parts of a political community. There are two divisions among men within a community which help us to define citizenship.

According to one of these divisions, the native-born are separated from aliens or foreigners. In the Greek city-states it was almost impossible for aliens to become citizens. Plutarch notes that Solon's law of naturalization, which he qualifies as "of doubtful character," would not allow strangers to become citizens unless "they were in perpetual exile from their own country, or came with their whole family to trade there." The *metics*, or aliens, who were allowed in the city were usually a class apart.

In Rome the situation was different; it was possible for outsiders to receive the high honor of Roman citizenship. "The aspiring genius of Rome," Gibbon writes, "sacrificed vanity to ambition, and deemed it more prudent, as well as honourable, to adopt virtue and merit for her own wheresoever they were found, among slaves or strangers, enemies or barbarians."

Most modern republics set up naturalization proceedings for the regular admission of some, if not all, immigrants to membership in the state. Yet a difference always remains between a citizen and a denizen, or mere resident. Accordingly, Rousseau criticizes Bodin for confusing citizens with townsmen. "M. D'Alembert," he says, "has avoided this error, and in his article on Geneva, has clearly distinguished the four orders of men (or even five, counting mere foreigners) who dwell in our town, of which two only compose the Republic."

According to a second way in which men are divided within the political community, free men are separated from slaves. The latter, though they may be native-born, are not members of the political community, but merely part of its property. A slave, according to Aristotle, is one "who, being a human being, is also a possession." But, he says in another place, "property, even though living beings are included in it, is no part of a state; for a state is not a community of living beings only, but a community of equals."

On this principle, Aristotle excludes more than the chattel slave from the status and privilege of citizenship. "We cannot consider all those to be citizens," he writes, "who are necessary to the existence of the state; for example, children are not citizens equally with grown-up men. . . . In ancient times, and among some nations," he continues, "the artisan class *were* slaves or foreigners, and therefore the majority of them are so now. The best form of state will not admit them to citizenship."

The "slaves who minister to the wants of individuals," and the "mechanics or laborers who are the servants of the community" are to be counted as its "necessary people" but not as members of the state. When he discusses the size and character of the population for an ideal state, Aristotle says, "we ought not to include everybody, for there must always be in cities a multitude of slaves and sojourners and foreigners; but we should include only those who are members of the state, and who form an essential part of it."

The exclusion of slaves and resident aliens from membership in the political community has a profound bearing on the meaning of the political concept expressed by the words "the people." The *people* is not the same as the *population*—all those human beings who live within the state's borders. Even in societies which have abolished chattel slavery and in which suffrage tends to be unrestricted, infants and aliens remain outside the pale of political life. The *people* is always a part—the active political part—of the population.

THE DISTINCTION OF citizen from slave, infant, or alien does not complete the picture. The subjects of a king are not slaves, nor are they citizens of a republic. Yet like citizens, subjects have membership in the political community. They constitute the people the king serves as well as rules, unless he is a tyrant, for only if he is a tyrant does he treat them as if they were his property, to be used for his own pleasure or interest. Sometimes a distinction is made between first- and second-class citizens, and then the latter, who occupy an intermediate position between citizenship and slavery, are regarded as subjects. "Since there are many forms of government," Aristotle writes, "there must be many varieties of citizens, and especially of citizens who are subjects; so that under some governments the mechanic and the laborer will be citizens, but not in others." The whole meaning of citizenship changes for Aristotle when the working classes are admitted to it.

From a somewhat different point of view, Aquinas holds that a man can be "said to be a citizen in two ways: first, absolutely; secondly, in a restricted sense. A man is a citizen absolutely if he has all the rights of citizenship; for instance, the right of debating or voting in the popular assembly. On the other hand, any man may be called citizen only in a restricted sense if he dwells within the state, even lowly people, or children, or old men, who are not fit to enjoy power in matters pertaining to the common welfare." Those who are thus disfranchised, but are not slaves, are subjects rather than citizens in the full sense.

It is possible, of course, for men to have the dual status of subject and citizen, as is the case now in England and the self-governing dominions of the British commonwealth. This double status does not blur the distinction between citizen and subject; rather it signifies the mixed nature of a form of government which is both royal—at least in its vestiges of monarchy—and constitutional. In the time of Locke, when a great constitutional victory had been won against the despotism of the last Stuart, the English people did not yet regard themselves as citizens. Observing that the title of citizen has never been given "to the subjects of any prince, not even the ancient Macedonians," Rousseau finds himself compelled to add: "not even the English of today, though they are nearer liberty than anyone else."

Unlike citizens, the subjects of a king, especially of one claiming absolute power, have no voice in their own government, and no legal means for protecting their natural rights as men. So long as the absolute ruler does not tyrannize, he governs for the welfare of his people; and so, though a despot in the sense of wielding absolute power over political inferiors, he is benevolent in the sense of serving rather than using them. But if he ceases to be benevolent and turns tyrannical, his subjects have no recourse except rebellion. They must resort to violence in order to emancipate themselves from a condition which amounts to slavery.

A citizen, on the other hand, is safeguarded in his legal as well as in his natural rights and, in some modern republics at least, he is provided with juridical means for rectifying supposed injustices. For citizens, the right of rebellion is the *last*, not the *only*, resort.

THE DISTINCT CONDITIONS of slavery, subjection, and citizenship can be summarized by defining three ways in which rulers are related to the persons they rule. These three relations seem to have been first clearly differentiated by Aristotle.

He finds all three relationships in the structure of the household, as that is constituted in antiquity. Of household management, he writes, "there are three parts—one is the rule of a master over slaves . . . another of a father, and a third of a husband." In each case, "the kind of rule differs: the freeman rules over the slave after another manner from that in which the male rules over the female, or the man over the child."

As we have already seen, Aristotle conceives the slave as a piece of property. When he says that the slave "wholly belongs to his master" or that "he is a part of his master, a living but separated part of his bodily frame," he is obviously considering only the chattel slave. There are, as the chapter on SLAVERY indicates, other kinds or degrees of slavery less extreme than this.

But chattel slavery, more clearly than the attenuated forms of servitude, defines the nature of mastery. The master manages or uses the slave as he manages and uses other instruments—inanimate tools or domesticated animals. "The rule of a master," Aristotle declares, is "exercised primarily with a view to the interest of the master." Yet it "accidentally considers the slave, since, if the slave perish, the rule of the master perishes with him."

Thus conceived, the slave lacks every vestige of political liberty. He is treated as radically inferior to his master—almost as if he were something less than a man. He has no voice in his own government, nor is his welfare the paramount consideration of his ruler. In short, we have slavery when one man governs another in the way in which a man manages his property, using it for his own good.

When one man governs another in the way in which good parents administer the affairs of children as members of the household, we have the type of rule which also appears in the relation between absolute kings or benevolent despots and their subjects. "The rule of a father over his children is royal," Aristotle writes, "for he rules by virtue of both love and of the respect due to age, exercising a kind of royal power. . . . A king," Aristotle adds, "is the natural superior of his subjects, but he should be of the same kin or kind with them, and such is the relation of elder and younger, father and son."

From the analogous type of rule in the family, we see two differences between the condition of a slave and that of a subject under absolute or despotic rule in the state. The inferiority of children, unlike that of slaves, is not their permanent condition. It is an aspect of their immaturity. They are temporarily incapable of judging what is for their good, and so need the direction of their superiors in age, experience, and prudence. But children have some equality with their parents, to the extent that their humanity is recognized as the reason why they should not be ruled as slaves, but governed for their own welfare.

The government of children, Aristotle declares, "is exercised in the first instance for the good of the governed, or for the common good of both parties, but essentially for the good of the governed." In the same way, the subjects of a benevolent despot, or of any absolute monarch who rules paternalistically, are said to be governed for their own good. They are served, not used, by their rulers; and to this extent they have a degree of political liberty. But they do not have the complete liberty which exists only with self-government.

That occurs only under constitutional rule, which for Aristotle has an imperfect analogue in the family in the relation of husband and wife. In the state, however, it is perfectly represented by the relation between the holders of public office and *other* citizens. "In the constitutional state," Aristotle says, "the citizens rule and are ruled by turns; for the idea of a constitutional state implies that the natures of the citizens are equal, and do not differ at all." The citizen, in other words, is one "who has the power to take part in the deliberative or judicial administration of the state." Rousseau seems to have a similar conception of the citizen as both ruling and ruled, though he uses the word "subject" to designate the citizen *as ruled*. "The people," he writes, "are called *citizens*, as sharing in the sovereign power, and *subjects*, as being under the laws of the State."

Because the man who holds office in a constitutional government is first of all a citizen himself, and only secondly an official vested with the authority of a political office, the citizen is a man ruled by his equals and ruled as an equal. Observing these facts, Aristotle describes citizenship as the one *"indefinite* office" set up by a constitution. It is indefinite both in tenure and by comparison with the various magistracies or other offices which have more definitely assigned functions. Since a citizen is ruled only by other citizens, and since he has the opportunity of ruling others in turn, citizenship involves political liberty in the fullest sense. This does not mean freedom *from* government, but freedom through *self-government*—all the freedom a man can have in society, liberty under law and proportioned to justice.

Two of these three political conditions—slavery and subjection—naturally receive fuller treatment in the chapter on SLAVERY. The discussion of the third, citizenship, belongs not only to this chapter, but also to the chapter on CONSTITUTION, and to other chapters which deal with forms of constitutional government, such as ARISTOCRACY, DEMOCRACY, and OLIGARCHY.

FOR THE SAME REASON that the revolutionists against absolutism or despotism in the 18th century use the phrase "free government" for republican institutions, they also use "citizen" to designate a free man, a man who possesses the political liberty and equality which they regard as the natural right of men because they are men. In this respect they do not differ substantially from their Greek or Roman ancestors who prize constitutional government and citizenship as conditions of freedom and equality.

Furthermore, like the constitutionalists of antiquity, the republicans of the 18th century are, with few if any exceptions, *not* democrats in the sense of extending the rights and privileges of citizenship to *all* adults. In the 18th century slavery still exists; and a large part even of those who are not in economic bondage remains outside the pale of citizenship, disqualified by accidents of birth such as race or sex, and by the lack of sufficient wealth or property which makes it necessary for them to labor in order to live. It is not only an ancient oligarch like Aristotle who thinks that "the ruling class should be the owners of property, for they are citizens, and the citizens of a state should be in good circumstances; whereas mechanics" should have "no share in the state." In the 18th century, as well as in ancient Greece, extending the privileges of citizenship to indentured apprentices, day laborers, or journeymen, is a form of radicalism known as "extreme democracy."

Kant may be taken as representative of an enlightened point of view in the 18th century. He finds that there are "three juridical attributes" that belong by right to the citizens: "1. constitutional freedom, as the right of every citizen to have to obey no other law than that to which he has given his consent or approval; 2. civil equality, as the right of the citizen to recognize no one as a superior among the people in relation to himself . . . and 3. political independence, as the right to owe his existence and continuance in society not to the arbitrary will of another, but to his own rights and powers as a member of the commonwealth."

The last attribute leads Kant to distinguish between "active and passive citizenship." Although he admits that this "appears to stand in contradiction to the definition of a citizen as such," he concludes that there are some in the community not entitled to the full privileges of citizenship. It is his contention, widely shared in the 18th century, that suffrage, which "properly constitutes the political qualification of a citizen," presupposes the "independence or self-sufficiency of the individual citizen among the people."

Consequently he denies suffrage to "everyone who is compelled to maintain himself not according to his own industry, but as it is arranged by others." Such a restriction, he says, includes "the apprentice of a merchant or tradesman, a servant who is not in the employ of the state, a minor" and "all women." They are "passive parts" of the state and do not have "the right to deal with the state as active members of it, to reorganize it, or to take action by way of introducing certain laws." Kant insists, however, that "it must be made possible for them to raise themselves from this passive condition in the State, to the condition of active citizenship."

THE FOREGOING DISCUSSION shows the connection between the idea of citizenship and the two revolutionary movements which John Stuart Mill notes in the history of political thought and action. The first is the movement to obtain "recognition of certain immunities, called political liberties or rights, which it was to be regarded as a breach of duty in the ruler to infringe, and which if he did infringe, specific resistance, or general rebellion, was held to be justifiable." This is the revolutionary effort to overthrow despotism and to establish constitutional government, with the status of citizenship for at least some part of the population—frequently much less than half of the total.

The second revolutionary movement goes further. It presupposes the existence of government by law and aims to perfect it. It therefore seeks to obtain "the establishment of constitutional checks, by which the consent of the community, or of a body of some sort, supposed to represent its interests, is made a necessary condition to some of the more important acts of the governing power." Since, according to Mill, it aims to make the consent of the governed effective through an adequate representation of their wishes, this movement inevitably leads to

the fight *against* franchise restrictions and *for* universal suffrage, which would admit every normal, adult human being to the freedom and equality of citizenship.

The first revolution has a long history. It begins with the Greek city-states which, having won this victory against the Persians, lost it to the Macedonian conquerors. It happens again with the establishment of the Roman republic after the expulsion of the Tarquins, and again it is undone when the Caesars assume absolute power. This part of the story is told with varying emotions by Plutarch and Polybius, Tacitus and Gibbon. During the Middle Ages the same struggle appears in the various efforts to establish the supremacy of law, particularly through the development of customary and canon law. The revolution still continues in the 17th and 18th centuries and the new heights it reaches are reflected in the writings of a constitutionalist like Locke and republicans like Rousseau, Kant, and the American Federalists. The Declaration of Independence and the Constitution of the United States are perhaps the classic documents of this historical phase.

The second revolution, particularly as identified with the fight for universal suffrage, is a relatively recent event. Its roots may go back as far as Cromwell's time to the activity of the Levellers, and in the 18th century to the writings of John Cartwright. But what is, perhaps, its first full expression does not appear until Mill's *Representative Government*. In that book, Mill lays down the principles of the franchise reforms which began in the 19th century, but which, as in the case of woman suffrage or the repeal of the poll tax, were carried through only yesterday or are still in progress.

Yet the struggle for universal suffrage—or, as Mill would say, against treating any human being as a "political pariah"—does have an ancient parallel in the conflict between democratic and oligarchical constitutions in Greek political life and thought. These two types of constitution were opposed on the qualifications for citizenship and public office. The oligarchical constitution restricted both to men of considerable wealth. At the other extreme, as Aristotle observes, the most radical forms of Greek democracy granted citizenship to the working classes, and gave no advantage to the rich in filling the magistracies, for they selected officials from the whole citizenry by lot.

The parallelism goes no further than that. Greek democracy, even when it denied special privileges to the propertied classes, never contemplated the abolition of slavery or the political emancipation of women.

THERE ARE OTHER differences between ancient and modern institutions which affect the character of citizenship. The problem of who shall be admitted to citizenship is fundamental in both epochs. Insofar as it connotes the condition of political liberty and equality, the status of citizenship remains essentially the same. But the rights and duties, the privileges and immunities, which belong to citizenship vary with the difference between ancient and modern constitutionalism.

Even if they had been written, the constitutions of the ancient world would not have declared the rights of man and the citizen, nor would they have had bills of rights appended to them. The significance of these modern innovations (which begin, perhaps, with Magna Carta) lies, not in a new conception of citizenship, but in the invention of juridical means to endow the primary office of citizenship with sufficient legal power to protect it from invasion by government.

In *The Federalist*, Hamilton maintains that "bills of rights are, in their origin, stipulations between kings and their subjects, abridgments of prerogative in favour of privilege, reservations of rights not surrendered to the prince." Defending the absence of a special bill of rights in the original Constitution, he insists that "the Constitution is itself, in every rational sense, and to every useful purpose, a bill of rights." It declares and specifies "the political privileges of the citizens in the structure and administration of the government," and "defines certain immunities and modes of proceeding, which are relative to personal and private concerns."

Nevertheless, the right of free speech and free assembly and the right to trial by a jury of peers, along with the immunity from unwarranted searches and seizures or from *ex post facto* laws and bills of attainder, provided by the early amendments to the Constitution, do give the citizen additional protection against interference in the performance of his civic duties, such as independent political thought and action, or in the exercise of his human privileges, such as freedom of religious worship. The invention of these constitutional devices sprang from the bitter experience of coercion and intimidation under Star Chamber proceedings, royal censorship, and unlimited police power. A citizen who can be coerced or intimidated by his government differs only in name from the subject of an absolute despot.

In addition to having these legal safeguards, modern differs from ancient citizenship in the way in which its rights and privileges are exercised. The machinery of suffrage is not the same when citizens act through elected representatives and when they participate directly in the deliberations and decisions of government, by voting in the public forum.

THE PROBLEM OF EDUCATION for citizenship is in some respects stated in almost identical terms by such different political philosophers as Plato and John Stuart Mill.

In both the *Republic* and the *Laws*, Plato emphasizes that "education is the constraining and directing of youth towards that right reason which the law affirms." By this he means not only that education will affect the laws, but also that the laws themselves have an educational task to perform. The educational program is thus planned and conducted by the state. The guardians—the only citizens in the *Republic* in the full sense of the term—are trained for public life, first by the discipline of their passions, and second by the cultivation of their minds. Their passions are disciplined by music and gymnastics, their minds cultivated by the liberal arts and dialectic.

In the democracy which Mill contemplates as an ideal, "the most important point of excellence . . . is to promote the virtue and intelligence of the people themselves." He does not outline a specific curriculum for the training of citizens, but it is clear that he thinks their education cannot be accomplished in the schools alone. The superiority of democracy, according to Mill, lies in the fact that it calls upon the citizen "to weigh interests not his own; to be guided, in case of conflicting claims, by another rule than his private partialities; to apply at every turn, principles and maxims which have for their reason of existence the common good; and he usually finds associated with him in the same work minds more familiarized than his own with these ideas and operations, whose study it will be to supply reasons to his understanding, and stimulation to his feeling for the general interest." In this "school of public spirit" a man becomes a citizen by doing the work of a citizen and so learning to act like one.

If the future citizen is to act like a free man, must he not also be trained in youth to think like one? Vocational training prepares a man to be an artisan, not a citizen. Only liberal education is adequate to the task of creating the free and critical intelligence required for citizenship. Hence in a state which rests on universal suffrage, the educational problem becomes greatly enlarged in scope, if not in intrinsic difficulty.

With the advent of universal suffrage, which Mill advocates, the state must face the responsibility for making liberal education available to every future citizen. To say that all normal children have enough intelligence to become citizens, but to regard the native endowment of a large number of them as incapable of liberal education, makes a travesty of citizenship. Will the child who cannot profit by liberal education be able to discharge the duties of the office to which he will be admitted upon coming of age?

THE TRAINING OF CHARACTER is always more difficult than the training of mind. In education for citizenship, the problem of moral training involves the question—discussed in the chapter on VIRTUE—whether the good man and the good citizen are identical in virtue.

For Aristotle, and seemingly also for Mill, the virtue of the good man under an ideal constitution would be identical with that of the good citizen. As both ruling and being ruled, "the good citizen ought to be capable of both," Aristotle writes. "He should know how to govern like a freeman, and how to obey like a freeman—these are the virtues of a citizen. And although the temperance and justice of a ruler are distinct from those of a subject, the virtue of a good man will include both; for the virtue of the good man who is free and also a subject, e.g. his justice, will not be one but will comprise distinct kinds, the one qualifying him to rule, the other to obey."

The virtues of the citizen direct him primarily in the performance of his obligations to the state. But if the welfare of the state is not the ultimate end of man, if there are higher goods which command human loyalty, if man's common humanity takes precedence over his membership in a particular state, then civic virtue does not exhaust human excellence. More may be morally required of the good man than of the good citizen. The virtues of the saint and the patriot may be of a different order.

On this question, the great books reveal a fundamental disagreement among moralists and political philosophers, who differ as Plato and Hegel differ from Augustine and Aquinas, or from Locke and Mill, on the place of the state in human life.

The ancients frequently appeal to a law higher than that of the state. Socrates forever stands as the classic example of one who would rather die than disobey his inner voice—the command of his conscience. A Stoic like Marcus Aurelius is willing to give unqualified allegiance to the political community only when it is the ideal city of man, embracing the whole human brotherhood. "My city and my country, so far as I am Antoninus," he says, "is Rome, but so far as I am a man"—whose "nature is rational and social"—"it is the world."

For Christian theologians, membership in the city of God is a higher vocation than citizenship in any earthly community—even when that is the city of man at its best. The city of God demands a higher order of virtue than the city of man. Referring to the earthly city, Augustine says that "the things which this city desires cannot justly be said to be evil, for it is itself, in its own kind, better than all other human goods. For it desires earthly peace for the sake of enjoying earthly goods." It is all right for men to seek "these things" for they "are good things, and without doubt the gifts of God." But, Augustine goes on to say, "if they neglect the better things of the heavenly city, which are secured by eternal victory and peace never-ending, and so inordinately covet these present good things that they believe them to be the only desirable things," then, in Augustine's opinion, they are misdirected in their love.

In giving precedence to the commandments of God, the theologians do not deprecate the commands of the state or the obligations of citizenship. But those who belong to both cities may find themselves faced with a conflict between the law of the state and the divine law. In such circumstances, the faithful have no choice. They must obey God before man. "Laws that are contrary to the commandments of God," Aquinas holds, do not "bind a man in conscience" and "should not be obeyed."

THIS CONFLICT BETWEEN human and divine law finds expression in antiquity in the *Antigone* of Sophocles. "It was not Zeus who had published me that edict," Antigone says of the human law she disobeys; "nor deemed I that the decrees were of such force, that a mortal could override the unwritten and unfailing statutes of heaven. For their life is not of to-day or yesterday, but from all time, and no man knows when they were first put forth."

The problem which Antigone faces can occur in as many other ways as there are possibilities of tension between individual conscience or desire and political obligation. Whatever form this takes, the conflict confronts the political philosopher with all the questions that constitute the problem of the individual and society, or man and the state.

To what extent and in what respects is the individual's personality sacred and inviolable by the state? How much freedom from government has the individual a right to demand? How much individual sacrifice has the state a right to expect? Is the state merely a means in the individual's pursuit of happiness, or the end to which all other goods must be ordered? Is man made for the state, or the state for man?

To questions of this sort, the answers range from philosophical anarchism at one extreme to equally philosophical totalitarianism at the other, with all degrees of individualism and communism in between. The general problem of man and the state, with all its controversial issues, runs through many other chapters—such as CONSTITUTION, GOOD AND EVIL, LAW, LIBERTY, and STATE—but we have placed its principal formulation in this chapter because the concept of citizenship signifies the ideal condition of the human individual as a member of the political community.

OUTLINE OF TOPICS

REFERENCES

To find the passages cited, use the numbers in heavy type, which are the volume and page numbers of the passages referred to. For example, in **4** Homer: *Iliad*, BK II [265–283] **12d**, the number **4** is the number of the volume in the set; the number **12d** indicates that the passage is in section d of page 12.

PAGE SECTIONS: When the text is printed in one column, the letters a and b refer to the upper and lower halves of the page. For example, in **53** JAMES: *Psychology*, 116a–119b, the passage begins in the upper half of page 116 and ends in the lower half of page 119. When the text is printed in two columns, the letters a and b refer to the upper and lower halves of the left-hand side of the page, the letters c and d to the upper and lower halves of the right-hand side of the page. For example, in **7** PLATO: *Symposium*, 163b–164c, the passage begins in the lower half of the left-hand side of page 163 and ends in the upper half of the right-hand side of page 164.

AUTHOR'S DIVISIONS: One or more of the main divisions of a work (such as PART, BK, CH, SECT) are sometimes included in the reference; line numbers, in brackets, are given in certain cases; *e.g., Iliad*, BK II [265–283] **12d**.

BIBLE REFERENCES: The references are to book, chapter, and verse. When the King James and Douay versions differ in title of books or in the numbering of chapters or verses, the King James version is cited first and the Douay, indicated by a (*D*), follows; *e.g.*, OLD TESTAMENT: *Nehemiah*, 7:45—(*D*) *II Esdras*, 7:46.

SYMBOLS: The abbreviation "esp" calls the reader's attention to one or more especially relevant parts of a whole reference; "passim" signifies that the topic is discussed intermittently rather than continuously in the work or passage cited.

For additional information concerning the style of the references, see the Explanation of Reference Style; for general guidance in the use of *The Great Ideas*, consult the Preface.

1. The individual in relation to the state

5 AESCHYLUS: *Suppliant Maidens* [366–401] 5c–6a / *Seven Against Thebes* [1005–1078] 38b–39a,c

5 SOPHOCLES: *Antigone* 131a–142d / *Ajax* [1071–1090] 152b; [1226–1263] 153c–154a / *Philoctetes* 182a–195a,c

5 EURIPIDES: *Heracleidae* [500–534] 252c-d / *Suppliants* [338–364] 261b-c / *Phoenician Maidens* [991–1020] 387a-b; [1625–1682] 392b-d / *Iphigenia at Aulis* 425a–439d esp [1255–1275] 436c, [1368–1401] 437c-d

5 ARISTOPHANES: *Acharnians* 455a–469a,c

6 HERODOTUS: *History*, BK I, 6c–7a

6 THUCYDIDES: *Peloponnesian War*, BK II, 395d–399a; 402b–404a; BK VI, 511c-d

7 PLATO: *Apology* 200a–212a,c / *Crito* 213a–219a,c esp 216d–219a,c / *Republic*, BK IV, 342a-d; 350a-d; BK V, 365c-d; BK VI, 379d–380c; BK VII, 390b–391b; 401a-b; BK VIII 401d–416a esp 402b-c / *Laws*, BK III, 672d–676b; BK V, 692c–693c; BK VI, 707b–708a; BK VII, 721d; BK IX, 754a-b; BK XI, 775d–778a; BK XII, 791c

9 ARISTOTLE: *Ethics*, BK I, CH 2 [1094ᵇ5–10] 339c-d; BK V, CH 11 [1138ᵃ4–13] 386b-c / *Politics*, BK I, CH 2 [1253ᵃ19–39] 446c-d; BK II, CH 1 [1260ᵇ37–1261ᵃ7] 455b,d; CH 2 [1261ᵃ15–

30] 455d–456a; CH 5 [1264ᵇ16–25] 459d–460a; BK III, CH 6 [1278ᵇ15–29] 475d–476a; BK VII, CH 1–3 527a–530a; CH 9 [1329ᵃ22–24] 533c; CH 13 [1332ᵃ28–38] 537a; BK VIII, CH 1 [1337ᵃ 27–32] 542b

12 LUCRETIUS: *Nature of Things*, BK II [1–61] 15a-d; BK III [59–93] 30d–31b; [978–1002] 42d–43a; BK V [1105–1135] 75c-d

12 EPICTETUS: *Discourses*, BK I, CH 19 125b–126c; BK II, CH 10 148c–150a; BK III, CH 22 195a–201a

12 AURELIUS: *Meditations*, BK V, SECT 22 272b; BK VII, SECT 5 280a-b; BK XI, SECT 21 305d–306a

13 VIRGIL: *Aeneid*, BK I [418–465] 114b–115b

14 PLUTARCH: *Lycurgus*, 44d–45c / *Numa Pompilius*, 51c–52b / *Solon*, 71b; 71d / *Marcus Cato*, 284b / *Lysander*, 361a-d / *Cato the Younger*, 626d–627b; 632b-c / *Demosthenes*, 699c–700a

18 AUGUSTINE: *City of God*, BK XIX, CH 5 513d–514b; CH 17 522b–523a

19 AQUINAS: *Summa Theologica*, PART I–II, Q 21, A 3 718d–719c; A 4, REP 3 719d–720a,c

20 AQUINAS: *Summa Theologica*, PART I–II, Q 90, AA 2–3 206b–207c; Q 92, A 1, REP 2 213c–214c; Q 94, A 2, ANS 221d–223a

21 DANTE: *Divine Comedy*, PURGATORY, XVI [52–114] 77b–78a; PARADISE, VIII [115–148] 118b-c

(2. *The conception of citizenship. 2a. The status or office of citizenship in relation to the principle of constitutional government.*)

43 FEDERALIST: NUMBER 52, 165a-c; NUMBER 84, 251a-253d

43 MILL: *Liberty,* 267b,d-268c / *Representative Government,* 344d-350a

46 HEGEL: *Philosophy of History,* PART II, 272a-d

2*b*. The distinction between citizen and subject: the distinction between the subjects of a constitutional monarchy and of a despotism

5 EURIPIDES: *Suppliants* [338–456] 261b-262b

6 HERODOTUS: *History,* BK VII, 233a-d; 238b-c

7 PLATO: *Laws,* BK VIII, 733d-734a

9 ARISTOTLE: *Politics,* BK I, CH I [1252ª7–17] 445a-b; CH 7 [1255ᵇ16–20] 449b; BK III, CH 5 475a-d passim; CH 6 [1278ᵇ30–1279ª22] 476a-c; CH 14 [1285ª17–29] 483b-c; CH 15 [1286ᵇ8–14] 484d-485a; CH 17 486c-487a; BK VII, CH 14 [1332ᵇ14–27] 537b-c

15 TACITUS: *Annals,* BK XI, 106a-d

23 MACHIAVELLI: *Prince,* CH V 8a-c

23 HOBBES: *Leviathan,* PART II, 104d-106b; 113c-115a; 150c-151a; 154b-c

25 MONTAIGNE: *Essays,* 383c-d

35 LOCKE: *Civil Government,* CH VII, SECT 87–94 44a-46c; CH XI 55b-58b; CH XIV, SECT 163–164 63a-c

38 MONTESQUIEU: *Spirit of Laws,* BK III, 11a-13c; BK IV, 13b,d-15c; BK V, 25d-26d; BK V–VI, 30c-34d; BK VI, 36a-b; BK VII, 47d-48a; BK XII, 93c-96a,c; BK XIX, 142a-146a,c passim

38 ROUSSEAU: *Inequality,* 356b-d; 359a-b / *Social Contract,* BK I, 392a esp 392b [fn 1]; BK III, 417c; 420d; BK IV, 426b-c

40 GIBBON: *Decline and Fall,* 14a-15c passim; 16c-17b; 17d; 521a-523a,c

41 GIBBON: *Decline and Fall,* 81c-82a; 161c-162a

42 KANT: *Science of Right,* 436d-437c; 450b-d

43 FEDERALIST: NUMBER 42, 138d-139c; NUMBER 43, 142b-c; NUMBER 54, 171a-b

43 MILL: *Liberty,* 267b,d-268c / *Representative Government,* 339d-340c; 341d-344d passim; 348c-355b; 427a-b

46 HEGEL: *Philosophy of Right,* ADDITIONS, 155 142a-b / *Philosophy of History,* PART I, 213b; PART II, 271c-d; PART IV, 356d

51 TOLSTOY: *War and Peace,* BK IX, 384c-388a,c passim

2*c*. The character and extent of citizenship under different types of constitutions

6 HERODOTUS: *History,* BK III, 107c-108c

6 THUCYDIDES: *Peloponnesian War,* BK II, 395d-399a; BK VI, 520b-c

7 PLATO: *Republic,* BK VIII–IX, 401d-420d / *Laws,* BK VIII, 733d-734a

9 ARISTOTLE: *Ethics,* BK VIII, CH 11 413b-d passim / *Politics,* BK III, CH 1 471b,d-472c; CH 5 475a-d; CH 13 [1283ᵇ44–1284ª3] 482a; BK IV,

CH 3 488d-489b; CH 8–9 493c-494d; BK V, CH I [1301ª25–1302ª15] 502b-503b; BK VI, CH 4 [1319ᵇ2–32] 523a-b; CH 6 524b-c / *Rhetoric,* BK I, CH 8 [1365ᵇ29–1366ª3] 608a-b

12 AURELIUS: *Meditations,* BK I, SECT 14 254b-c

38 MONTESQUIEU: *Spirit of Laws,* xxiia-d; BK II, 4a-7c; BK III, 9a-11a; BK V, 18b,d-25a; 31b-33a,c passim; BK XI, 68b,d-75a; BK XII, 84b,d-85c; BK XIII, 99b-100c

39 SMITH: *Wealth of Nations,* BK IV, 271a-b

41 GIBBON: *Decline and Fall,* 223c-224a; 403b-404d

42 KANT: *Pure Reason,* 114b-d / *Science of Right,* 450b-d

43 FEDERALIST: NUMBER 10, 51c-52d passim; NUMBER 14, 60b-c

43 MILL: *Representative Government,* 350a; 370a

46 HEGEL: *Philosophy of History,* PART II, 273d-274a

3. The qualifications for citizenship: extent of suffrage

5 ARISTOPHANES: *Frogs* [686–705] 572a-b / *Lysistrata* [575–580] 590c-d

6 HERODOTUS: *History,* BK I, 39b-c

7 PLATO: *Republic,* BK VIII 401d-416a / *Statesman,* 605d-608d / *Laws,* BK V, 690d-691b

9 ARISTOTLE: *Politics,* BK II, CH 9 [1270ª33–39] 466c; BK III, CH 1–5 471b,d-475d; BK VI, CH 4 [1319ᵇ2–32] 523a-b; CH 6 524b-c; BK VII, CH 4 [1326ª5–ᵇ25] 530a-d; CH 9 533a-d passim, esp [1329ª18–30] 533c-d / *Athenian Constitution,* CH 21 562b-c; CH 26, par 3–4 565a; CH 42 572b-d / *Rhetoric,* BK I, CH 8 [1365ᵇ29–1366ª3] 608a-b

14 PLUTARCH: *Solon,* 73d / *Pericles,* 139c-140a

15 TACITUS: *Annals,* BK XI, 106a-d

20 AQUINAS: *Summa Theologica,* PART I–II, Q 105, A 3, ANS and REP 2 316a-318b

38 MONTESQUIEU: *Spirit of Laws,* BK II, 4a-6b; BK XV, 114c-115b; BK XXIII, 189a

38 ROUSSEAU: *Social Contract,* BK IV, 428a-432b passim

39 SMITH: *Wealth of Nations,* BK III, 168d-169a; BK IV, 269d-271d

40 GIBBON: *Decline and Fall,* 14a-d; 15c; 17a-b

41 GIBBON: *Decline and Fall,* 73b

42 KANT: *Science of Right,* 436d-437c; 450d-452a

43 CONSTITUTION OF THE U.S.: ARTICLE I, SECT 8 [204–205] 13b; AMENDMENTS, XIV, SECT 1–2 18d-19a; XV 19b; XIX 19d

43 FEDERALIST: NUMBER 42, 138d-139c passim; NUMBER 52, 165a-c; NUMBER 54, 171a-b; NUMBER 57, 177a; 178c-d

43 MILL: *Representative Government,* 380c-389b; 395b-c

4. The rights, duties, privileges, and immunities of citizenship

OLD TESTAMENT: *Exodus,* 12:48–49; 22:21; 23:9 / *Leviticus,* 19:33–34; 24:22 / *Numbers,* 35:30 / *Deuteronomy,* 10:18–19; 17:6; 19:15; 20:1–9

5. The virtues of the citizen and the virtues of the good man

(5. *The virtues of the citizen and the virtues of the good man.*)

14 PLUTARCH: *Lycurgus*, 45b; 48b-c / *Coriolanus*, 174b,d-175a / *Aristides*, 263d / *Lysander*, 361a-d / *Agesilaus*, 480b,d-481a / *Cleomenes*, 659d-660a / *Demosthenes*, 699c-700a

15 TACITUS: *Histories*, BK I, 191c-d; BK IV, 267c-d

17 PLOTINUS: *First Ennead*, TR II 6b-10a

18 AUGUSTINE: *City of God*, BK II, CH 21 161b-162d; BK XIX, CH 17 522b-523a; CH 21 524a-525a; CH 24-26 528b-529a

20 AQUINAS: *Summa Theologica*, PART I-II, Q 61, A 5 58b-59d; Q 92, A I esp REP 3 213c-214c

21 DANTE: *Divine Comedy*, HELL, VI [58-75] 9a; XI [1-66] 15a-d; XV [55-78] 21d; XVI [64-78] 23a-b; XXXII [70]-XXXIII [90] 48c-50c passim; PURGATORY, VI [58-151] 61b-62c; XVII [91-123] 79b-d; PARADISE, XV [97]-XVI [154] 129b-132a

23 HOBBES: *Leviathan*, CONCLUSION, 279a-c

25 MONTAIGNE: *Essays*, 48a-b; 381a-388c; 390c-391c; 480b-482b; 486b-489b; 490c-491d

26 SHAKESPEARE: *Julius Caesar*, ACT V, SC V [68-81] 596a,c

30 BACON: *Advancement of Learning*, 74b-c; 81d-82a; 94b-95b

31 DESCARTES: *Discourse*, PART III, 48b-49a

31 SPINOZA: *Ethics*, PART IV, PROP 73 446c-447a

32 MILTON: *Samson Agonistes* [843-870] 358a-b

33 PASCAL: *Pensées*, 6 173a

35 LOCKE: *Toleration*, 15d / *Human Understanding*, BK I, CH II, SECT 5-6 105a-c

36 SWIFT: *Gulliver*, PART III, 112a-115b

38 MONTESQUIEU: *Spirit of Laws*, XXIIa-d; BK III, 9b-12a; BK IV, 13b,d-15a; 15c-16a; BK V, 18d-19d; 21b-23a; 31b-c; BK VII, 44d-45c; BK VIII, 51a-52c; 55c-d; BK XIX, 137a-c

38 ROUSSEAU: *Inequality*, 323a-328a; 360b,d [fn 1]; 366b-d / *Political Economy*, 369b-370a; 372a-377b / *Social Contract*, BK II, 402b-403a; BK III, 411a-c; 412a-b; BK IV, 428a-432b passim; 434b-435a

39 SMITH: *Wealth of Nations*, BK V, 337d-338c; 340c-343d; 346c-347d

40 GIBBON: *Decline and Fall*, 630b,d-631a; 644b-645c

43 FEDERALIST: NUMBER 55, 174c-d

43 MILL: *Representative Government*, 329b-330a; 334b; 336c-341c passim, esp 337a-b; 346c-350a passim

44 BOSWELL: *Johnson*, 393a-c

46 HEGEL: *Philosophy of Right*, PART III, par 268 84c-d / *Philosophy of History*, INTRO, 171b-c; PART II, 272a-d; PART IV, 365b-c

49 DARWIN: *Descent of Man*, 314c-316a; 321b-c

51 TOLSTOY: *War and Peace*, BK VI, 244d-245d; BK XII, 537b-538a; BK XV, 634a-635a; EPILOGUE I, 668a-669c; EPILOGUE II, 686c-687a

6. Education for citizenship

5 EURIPIDES: *Suppliants* [857-917] 266a-b

5 ARISTOPHANES: *Frogs* [1008-1098] 576b-577c

6 THUCYDIDES: *Peloponnesian War*, BK I, 370a-c; BK II, 396c-397d

7 PLATO: *Protagoras*, 43a-47c / *Crito* 213a-219a,c / *Republic*, BK II-III, 320c-339a; BK IV, 344b-d; BK V, 366a-c; BK VI, 380d-381a / *Statesman*, 607b-608d / *Laws*, BK I-II 640a-663d esp BK I, 644b-645c; BK VII 713c-731d; BK VIII, 732b-735a

9 ARISTOTLE: *Ethics*, BK I, CH 2 [1094^{a}28-^{b}11] 339c-d; CH 9 [1099^{b}29-32] 345b; BK V, CH 2 [1130^{b}25-29] 378b; BK X, CH 9 434a-436a,c / *Politics*, BK II, CH 5 [1263^{b}36-1264^{a}1] 459a; [1264^{a}26-32] 459c; CH 7 [1266^{b}27-35] 462b-c; BK III, CH 4 [1277^{a}14-^{b}29] 474a-475a; BK IV, CH 9 [1294^{b}19-24] 494c; BK V, CH 9 [1310^{a}13-22] 512b-c; BK VII, CH 13 [1332^{a}28-^{b}10] 537a-b; CH 14 [1332^{b}42-1334^{a}11] 537d-538d; CH 15 [1334^{b}7-28] 539b-d; CH 17 541a-542a,c; BK VIII 542a-548a,c passim / *Athenian Constitution*, CH 42 572b-d

12 AURELIUS: *Meditations*, BK I 253a-256d

14 PLUTARCH: *Lycurgus*, 33c-34a; 39a-45b / *Lycurgus-Numa* 61b,d-64a,c / *Solon* 64b,d-77a,c passim / *Agesilaus*, 480b,d-481a

21 DANTE: *Divine Comedy*, PARADISE, VIII [115-148] 118b-c

23 HOBBES: *Leviathan*, PART II, 114b-115a; 150c-151a; PART IV, 273a-c; CONCLUSION, 282d-283a

25 MONTAIGNE: *Essays*, 60c-62a

30 BACON: *Advancement of Learning*, 23a; 79c-80a

32 MILTON: *Areopagitica* 381a-412b esp 384b-389a, 398a-b

38 MONTESQUIEU: *Spirit of Laws*, BK IV 13b,d-18d

38 ROUSSEAU: *Political Economy*, 373c-377b / *Social Contract*, BK II, 402b-403a

39 SMITH: *Wealth of Nations*, BK V, 303b-305c; 337d-343d; 347c-d

40 GIBBON: *Decline and Fall*, 6b; 669a-b

42 KANT: *Judgement*, 586a-587a

43 FEDERALIST: NUMBER 27, 95c-d

43 MILL: *Liberty*, 317d-319b; 320a-c; 322d-323a,c / *Representative Government*, 336c-341d passim, esp 339a-340c; 349a-350a; 381b-387d passim; 417c-418d; 424b-c

46 HEGEL: *Philosophy of Right*, PART III, par 187 65a-c; par 239 76d; par 315 104c; ADDITIONS, 98 133a; 147 140c; 166 145b-c; 183 148d-149a

51 TOLSTOY: *War and Peace*, BK VI, 244d-245c

54 FREUD: *Sexual Enlightenment of Children*, 122a,c

7. Political citizenship and membership in the city of God

OLD TESTAMENT: *I Samuel*, 8:9-18—(D) *I Kings*, 8:9-18 / *Jeremiah*, 29:4-7 esp 29:7—(D) *Jeremias*, 29:4-7 esp 29:7

APOCRYPHA: *I Maccabees*, 1:41-2:70—(D) OT, *I Machabees*, 1:43-2:70 / *II Maccabees*, 6:8-7:42—(D) OT, *II Machabees*, 6:8-7:42

NEW TESTAMENT: *Matthew*, 22:15–22 / *Mark*, 12:13–17 / *Luke*, 20:21–25 / *Romans*, 13:1–10 / *Ephesians*, 2:19–22 / *Titus*, 3:1 / *Hebrews*, 13:17

12 EPICTETUS: *Discourses*, BK I, CH 30 138a,c; BK II, CH 5, 143d-144a; BK IV, CH 3 224b-d

12 AURELIUS: *Meditations*, BK III, SECT 11 262a-b; SECT 13 262c; BK IV, SECT 23 265c

18 AQUINAS: *Confessions*, BK III, par 15 17a-b / *City of God*, BK I, PREF 129a-d; BK V, CH 15–16 220d-221b; BK XI, CH 1 322b,d-323a; BK XIV, CH 28–BK XV, CH 4 397a-400a; BK XVIII, CH 1–2 472b-473d; CH 47 500d-501b; BK XIX, CH 11 516d-517b; CH 14 520a-d; CH 17 522b-523a; CH 21 524a-525a; CH 24–26 528b-529a

19 AQUINAS: *Summa Theologica*, PART I–II, Q 21, A 4, ANS and REP 3 719d-720a,c

21 DANTE: *Divine Comedy*, PURGATORY, XIII [79–96] 72d; XVI [85–114] 77d-78a; XIX [127–141] 82d-83a

23 HOBBES: *Leviathan*, PART II, 151a-c; PART III, 198d-199a; 240a-246a,c; PART IV, 275a-277d

32 MILTON: *Paradise Lost*, BK XII [485–551] 329b-331a

35 LOCKE: *Toleration*, 15d; 16c-17b

38 MONTESQUIEU: *Spirit of Laws*, BK XXIV–XXVI, 200a-215a; BK XXVI, 218a-219d

38 ROUSSEAU: *Inequality*, 327a-c; 358d-359a / *Social Contract*, BK II, 401c-402a; BK IV, 435a-439c esp 437d-438c

40 GIBBON: *Decline and Fall*, 193c-194a; 226a-b; 291d-292d; 299b-300d passim

42 KANT: *Science of Right*, 444a-c

43 CONSTITUTION OF THE U.S.: ARTICLE VI [591–599] 16d; AMENDMENTS, I [615–617] 17a

43 MILL: *Liberty*, 279a-d

46 HEGEL: *Philosophy of Right*, PART III, par 270 84d-89c; ADDITIONS, 162 143b-144c / *Philosophy of History*, INTRO, 205d-206a,c; PART I, 216b-217c; 245d-247b; PART III, 308b-c; 309d-310a; 310d-311a; PART IV, 316a-d; 321b-322a; 325d-326b; 331b-d; 333b-c; 336c-337d; 345c-346c; 350b-c; 351b-354a; 365b-c

52 DOSTOEVSKY: *Brothers Karamazov*, BK II, 28d-32a; BK V, 127b-137c passim

8. The idea of world citizenship: the political brotherhood of man

12 EPICTETUS: *Discourses*, BK I, CH 9 114c-116b; CH 13 120b-c; BK II, CH 10 148c-150a; CH 20, 164d-165c; BK III, CH 11 187a-b; CH 22, 199c-d; CH 24 203c-210a

12 AURELIUS: *Meditations*, BK III, SECT 4 260b-261a; SECT 11 262a-b; BK IV, SECT 3–4 263b-264a; BK VI, SECT 44 278b-c

13 VIRGIL: *Aeneid*, BK I [254–296] 110a-111a; BK VI [845–853] 233b-234a

18 AUGUSTINE: *City of God*, BK XIX, CH 7 515a-c; CH 17, 522d

25 MONTAIGNE: *Essays*, 471a-c

30 BACON: *Advancement of Learning*, 31d-32a

38 ROUSSEAU: *Inequality*, 355b-c / *Political Economy*, 369a-b; 373c / *Social Contract*, BK IV, 437c

42 KANT: *Science of Right*, 452c-d; 455a-458a,c / *Judgement*, 586a-587a

43 MILL: *Representative Government*, 424c-428a passim, esp 426a-b

49 DARWIN: *Descent of Man*, 317c-d

51 TOLSTOY: *War and Peace*, BK VI, 244d-245d; BK X, 466b-c

52 DOSTOEVSKY: *Brothers Karamazov*, BK VI, 166c-167b

54 FREUD: *War and Death*, 755a-761c esp 755b-757c / *Civilization and Its Discontents*, 785d-788d

9. Historical episodes and stages in the struggle for citizenship

6 HERODOTUS: *History*, BK III, 104b-108d esp 107c-108c; BK IV, 152d-153b; BK V, 171c-175b; BK VI, 193b-c; BK VII, 245b

6 THUCYDIDES: *Peloponnesian War*, BK IV, 468a-469a; BK VI, 520a-d; 534b-c

7 PLATO: *Laws*, BK III, 672d-676b

9 ARISTOTLE: *Politics*, BK II, CH 12 470b-471d; BK III, CH 15 [1286^{b}8–21] 484d-485a; BK IV, CH 13 [1297^{b}16–28] 498a; BK V, CH 4 [1304^{a}18–38] 505d-506a / *Athenian Constitution*, CH 1–41 553a-572a passim, esp CH 41 571c-572a

13 VIRGIL: *Aeneid*, BK VI [756–853] 231a-234a; BK VIII [626–731] 275b-278b

14 PLUTARCH: *Theseus*, 9c-d / *Romulus*, 21a-27c esp 22c / *Poplicola*, 79d-80a / *Coriolanus* 174b,d-193a,c esp 176b-184c / *Tiberius Gracchus* 671b,d-681a,c / *Caius Gracchus* 681b,d-689a,c

15 TACITUS: *Annals*, BK III, 51b-52a; BK XI, 106a-d

26 SHAKESPEARE: *Julius Caesar* 568a-596a,c

27 SHAKESPEARE: *Coriolanus* 351a-392a,c

32 MILTON: *New Forcers of Conscience* 68a-b / *Lord Gen. Cromwell* 69a-b

35 LOCKE: *Civil Government*, CH VI, SECT 74–76 41b-42a; CH VII, SECT 94 46a-c; CH VIII, SECT 100–111 47c-51a; CH XIV, SECT 162–166 63a-64a

38 ROUSSEAU: *Social Contract*, BK III, 413b [fn 1]

39 SMITH: *Wealth of Nations*, BK I, 58d-61b esp 61b; BK III, 170c-173b; 176a-179a; BK IV, 269d-271d

40 GIBBON: *Decline and Fall*, 14a-d; 15c; 29c-d; 90d-92a; 521a-523a,c

41 GIBBON: *Decline and Fall*, 202a-d; 215c-219a; 403b-404d esp 404c; 452d-453a,c; 562b-564b; 574b-582b; 586c-589a

42 KANT: *Science of Right*, 451d-452a

43 DECLARATION OF INDEPENDENCE: 1a-3b

43 CONSTITUTION OF THE U.S.: 11a-20a,c

43 FEDERALIST: NUMBER 14, 62b-d

43 MILL: *Liberty*, 267b,d-268c

46 HEGEL: *Philosophy of History*, PART II, 263a-d; 275b-276a; PART III, 288c; 295d-296c; 299c-300a

50 MARX-ENGELS: *Communist Manifesto*, 415b-416c; 423d-425b; 431c-433d

51 TOLSTOY: *War and Peace*, BK I, 10a-b; BK VI, 238c-243b

CROSS-REFERENCES

For: Other considerations of the issues involved in the relation between the individual and the state, *see* GOOD AND EVIL 5d; HAPPINESS 5b; JUSTICE 10b; STATE 2f, 3c, 3e, 8e.

The context of the concept of citizenship in the theory of constitutional government or government by law rather than by men, *see* CONSTITUTION; LAW 7a–7b; LIBERTY 1d, 1f–1g; MONARCHY 1a(1); TYRANNY 5–5d.

Other comparisons of citizens with subjects or slaves, *see* JUSTICE 9d; SLAVERY 6a–6c.

The bearing of different types of constitution on the character of citizenship and especially on the extent of the franchise, *see* CONSTITUTION 5–5b; DEMOCRACY 4–4a(2), 5b(2); OLIGARCHY 5–5a.

The political machinery, such as elections and representation, by which the citizen exercises his suffrage, *see* CONSTITUTION 9–9b; DEMOCRACY 5b–5b(4); GOVERNMENT 1h.

The consideration of civic virtue in relation to virtue generally, *see* VIRTUE AND VICE 7b; and for the problem of education for citizenship, *see* ARISTOCRACY 5; DEMOCRACY 6; EDUCATION 8d; STATE 7d; VIRTUE AND VICE 7a.

Another discussion of the distinction between the city of man and the city of God, *see* STATE 2g; and for matters relevant to the ideal of world citizenship, *see* LOVE 4c; STATE 10f; WAR AND PEACE 11d.

Descriptions of the historical struggle for citizenship, and for the extension of the franchise, *see* LABOR 7d; LIBERTY 6b; SLAVERY 6c; TYRANNY 8.

ADDITIONAL READINGS

Listed below are works not included in *Great Books of the Western World,* but relevant to the idea and topics with which this chapter deals. These works are divided into two groups:

I. Works by authors represented in this collection.
II. Works by authors not represented in this collection.

For the date, place, and other facts concerning the publication of the works cited, consult the Bibliography of Additional Readings which follows the last chapter of *The Great Ideas.*

I.

MACHIAVELLI. *The Discourses,* BK I
MONTESQUIEU. *Considerations on the Causes of the Grandeur and Decadence of the Romans*
J. S. MILL. *The Subjection of Women*

II.

CICERO. *De Officiis (On Duties),* I
BODIN. *The Six Bookes of a Commonweale,* BK I, CH 6–7; BK III, CH 8
HOOKER. *Of the Laws of Ecclesiastical Polity*
PUFENDORF. *De Officio Hominis et Civis Juxta Legem Naturalem (Of the Duties of Man and of the Citizen According to Natural Law)*
DIDEROT. *Citoyen*
MABLY. *Des droits et devoirs du citoyen*
CARTWRIGHT. *Take Your Choice!*
BURKE. *Letter to the Sheriffs of Bristol*
——. *On the Reform of the Representation in the House of Commons*

PAINE. *Rights of Man*
GODWIN. *An Enquiry Concerning Political Justice,* BK IV, CH 2, SECT I
TOCQUEVILLE. *Democracy in America*
THOREAU. *Civil Disobedience*
FUSTEL DE COULANGES. *The Ancient City*
T. H. GREEN. *Principles of Political Obligation,* (H)
SPENCER. *The Man Versus the State*
JELLINEK. *The Declaration of the Rights of Man and Citizens*
BOSANQUET. *Science and Philosophy,* 16
HOBHOUSE. *The Metaphysical Theory of the State*
BRYCE. *The Hindrances to Good Citizenship*
——. *Modern Democracies*
G. NEWMAN. *Citizenship and the Survival of Civilization*
MERRIAM. *The Making of Citizens*
TAWNEY. *Equality*
MARITAIN. *The Rights of Man and Natural Law*
EWING. *The Individual, the State and World Government*

Chapter 12: CONSTITUTION

INTRODUCTION

THE idea of a constitution as establishing and organizing a political community; the principle of constitutionality as determining a generic form of government having many varieties; and the nature of constitutional government—these three problems are so intimately connected that they must be treated together. We have used the word "constitution" to express the root notion from which all other matters considered in this chapter are derived.

It is impossible to say precisely what a constitution is in a way that will fit the political reality of the Greek city-states, the Roman republic and its transformation into the empire, mediaeval kingdoms and communes and their gradual metamorphosis into the limited monarchies and republics of modern times. No definition can adequately comprehend all the variations of meaning to be found in the great works of political theory and history. But there are a number of related points in the various meanings of "constitution" which indicate what is common to the understanding of such diverse thinkers as Plato and Locke, Aristotle and Rousseau, Kant and Mill, Montesquieu and Hegel, Aquinas, Hobbes, and the American Federalists.

IT HAS BEEN SAID that the constitution is the form of the state. This can be interpreted to mean that the political, as opposed to the domestic, community requires a constitution in order to exist; just as a work of art has the very principle of its being in the form which the artist imposes upon matter. In the context of his general theory of political association, Aristotle's remark that "the man who first founded the state was the greatest of benefactors," may imply that the idea of a constitution is the creative principle by which the state was originally formed—or at least differentiated from the tribe and family.

Kant gives explicit expression to the notion that the invention of constitutions is coeval with the formation of states. "The act by which a People is represented as constituting itself into a State," he writes, "is termed the Original Contract" and this in turn signifies "the rightfulness of the process of organizing the Constitution."

In this sense, the constitution appears to be identical with the organization of a state. It would then seem to follow that every state, no matter what its form of government, is constitutional in character. But this would leave no basis for the fundamental distinction between constitutional and non-constitutional—or what is usually called "absolute," "royal," or "despotic"—government.

That basic distinction among forms of government is as old as Plato and Aristotle. It is first made by Plato in the *Statesman* in terms of the role of law in government. It occurs at the very opening of Aristotle's *Politics* with his insistence on the difference between the king and the statesman, and between royal and political government. But Locke seems to go further than the ancients when he says that "absolute monarchy . . . is inconsistent with civil society, and so can be no form of civil government at all."

In addition to affirming the gravity of the distinction between constitutional and non-constitutional government, he seems to be denying that the latter can constitute the form of a truly *civil* society, as opposed to a domestic society or the primitive patriarchate of a tribe. Yet Locke obviously does not deny the historic fact that there have been communities, which otherwise appear to be states, that have their character or form determined by absolute government. His point, therefore, seems to be that among types of government, absolute monarchy does not fit the nature of civil society.

If "constitution" is used merely as a synonym for "form" or "type," then even a state under absolute monarchy or despotic government can be said to have a constitution. Since every state is of some type, it can be said that it has a certain constitution, or that it is constituted in a certain way. If, however, we use the word "constitution" to conform to the distinction between constitutional and non-constitutional government, we are compelled to say that there are states which do not have constitutions.

With this distinction in mind, the statement that "the constitution is the form of the state" takes on a different and more radical meaning. It signifies that there are communities, larger than and distinct from the family or the tribe, which cannot be called "states" in the strict sense because they do not have constitutions. Hegel, for instance, points out that "it would be contrary even to commonplace ideas to call patriarchal conditions a 'constitution' or a people under patriarchal government a 'state' or its independence 'sovereignty.'" In such conditions, what is lacking, he writes, is "the objectivity of possessing in its own eyes and in the eyes of others, a universal and universally valid embodiment in laws." Without such an "objective law and an explicitly established rational constitution, its autonomy is . . . not sovereignty."

From this it would appear that a despotically governed community, such as ancient Persia, is a political anomaly. It is intermediate between the family and the state, for it is like a state in its extent and in the size and character of its population, yet it is not a state in its political form. The truly political community is constitutionally organized and governed. In this sense, the English words "political" and "constitutional" become almost interchangeable, and we can understand how these two English words translate a single word in Greek political discourse.

As THE FORM of the state, the constitution is the principle of its organization. Whether written or unwritten, whether a product of custom or explicit enactment, a constitution, Aristotle writes, "is the organization of offices in a state, and determines what is to be the governing body, and what is the end of each community."

The idea of political office—of officials and official status—is inseparable from the idea of constitution. That is why the concept of citizenship is also inseparable from constitution. As the chapter on CITIZEN indicates, citizenship is the primary or *indefinite* office set up by a constitution. Citizenship is always the prerequisite for holding any other *more definite* office in a constitutional government, from juryman to chief magistrate. In specifying the qualifications for citizenship, a constitution sets the minimum qualifications for all other offices which usually, though not always, demand more than citizenship of the man who is to fill them.

A political office represents a share of political power and authority. "Those are to be called offices," Aristotle explains, "to which the duties are assigned of deliberating about certain measures and of judging and commanding, especially the last; for to command is the especial duty of a magistrate." As representing a share of political power and authority, a political office can be said to constitute a share of sovereignty. That would not seem to be true, however, for those who, like Rousseau, maintain that "sovereignty is indivisible." Yet Rousseau also admits that "each magistrate is almost always charged with some governmental function" and exercises a "function of sovereignty."

Since it is an arrangement of offices, a constitution is, therefore, also a division or partition of the whole sovereignty of government—or at least of the exercise of sovereignty—into units which have certain functions to perform, and which must be given the requisite power and authority to perform them. These units are political offices, defined according to their functions, and vested with a certain power and authority depending on their place and purpose within the whole.

Hamilton's maxim that "every power ought to be in proportion to its object" formulates the equation by which the function of an office, or its duties, determines its rights and powers, privileges and immunities. And except for the provision of a temporary dictatorship in the early Roman constitution, or its modern constitutional equivalent in emergency grants of power, political offices under constitutional government always represent limited amounts of power and authority—limited in that each is always only a part of the whole.

A CONSTITUTION defines and relates the various political offices. It determines the qualifications of office-holders. But it does not name the individuals who, from all those qualified, shall be selected for any office. Because its provisions have this sort of generality, a constitution has the character of law. This is equally true of written and unwritten constitutions, of those shaped by custom and those enacted by constituent assemblies.

Unlike all other man-made laws, a constitution is the law which creates and regulates government itself, rather than the law which a government creates and by which it regulates the conduct of men, their relation to one another and to the state. This is perhaps the basic distinction with regard to the laws of the state. "The fundamental law in every commonwealth," says Hobbes, "is that which being taken away the commonwealth faileth and is utterly dissolved." Montesquieu distinguishes what he calls "the law politic," which constitutes the state, from ordinary legislation; and Rousseau likewise divides the laws into the "political" or "fundamental" laws and the "civil laws"—those "which determine the form of the government" and those which the government, once it is constituted, enacts and enforces.

In addition to being the source of all other positive laws of the state—for it sets up the very machinery of lawmaking—a constitution is fundamental law in that it establishes the standard of legality by which all subsequent laws are measured. Aristotle observes that "the justice or injustice of laws varies of necessity with constitutions." What may be a just enactment in one state may be unjust in another according to the difference of their constitutions.

In American practice and that modeled upon it, a law which violates the letter or spirit of the constitution is judged to be unconstitutional and is deprived thereby of the authority of law. "Every act of a delegated authority," Hamilton writes in The Federalist, "contrary to the tenor of the commission under which it is exercised, is void. No legislative act, therefore, contrary to the Constitution can be valid. To deny this would be to affirm that the deputy is greater than his principal; that the servant is above his master; that the representatives of the people are superior to the people themselves; that men acting by virtue of powers may do not only what their powers do not authorize, but what they forbid."

THE CONCEPTION of a constitution as a law or set of laws antecedent to all acts of government inevitably raises the question of how or by whom constitutions are made. If the provisions of a constitution were precepts of natural law, they would, according to the theory of natural law, be discovered by reason, not positively instituted. But though constitutions have the character of positive law, they cannot be made as other positive laws are made—by legislators, i.e., men holding that office under the constitution.

The generally accepted answer is that a constitution is made by the people who form the political community. But, as Madison observes, some evidence exists to the contrary. "It is not a little remarkable," he writes, "that in every case reported by ancient history, in which government has been established with deliberation and consent, the task of framing it has not been committed to an assembly of men, but has been performed by some individual citizen of pre-eminent wisdom and approved integrity." He cites many examples from Plutarch to support this observation, but he adds the comment that it cannot be ascertained to what extent these lawgivers were "clothed with the legitimate authority of the people." In some cases, however, he claims that "the proceeding was strictly regular."

The writers of The Federalist are, of course, primarily concerned with a constitution that is not the work of one man but the enactment of a constituent assembly or constitutional convention. From their knowledge of British law, they are also well aware that a constitution may sometimes be the product of custom, growing and altering with change of custom. But however it is exercised, the constitutive power is held by them to reside in the constituents of the state, the sovereign people. This power may be exercised through force of custom to produce an unwritten constitution, or through deliberative processes to draft a written one; but it can never be exercised by a government *except with popular consent*, since all the powers of a duly constituted government derive from its constitution. In the American if not the British practice, the amendment of the constitution also involves, at least indirectly, an appeal to the people.

Rousseau assigns the constitutive power to a mythical figure he calls "the legislator" or "the law-giver," describing him as the man who "sets up the Republic." Yet Rousseau says of this special office that it "nowhere enters into the constitution." He thus reaffirms the essential point that a constitution cannot create the office of constitution-making.

These remarks in the *Social Contract* have another significance. Rousseau tries to distinguish the formation of a government by the constitution (the political or fundamental law made by *the* legislator) from the formation of the state by the social contract entered into by the people in their original act of association. But is not the constitution also a formative contract or convention? If it is popular in origin, either through custom or enactment, is there more than a verbal difference between these two contracts—the one which establishes a political society and the one which establishes its government?

For Hobbes, and seemingly also for Locke, the compact by which men abandon the state of nature and establish a civil society results at the same time in the establishment of a government. It is, Hobbes writes, "as if every man should say to every man, I authorize and give up my right of governing my self, to this Man or to this Assembly of men, on this condition, that thou give up thy right to him, and authorize all his actions in like manner." According to Rousseau, "there is only one contract in the State, and that is the [original] act of association." For him, "the institution of government is not a contract."

The reality and significance of the difference between these three political philosophers would seem to depend on the precise historical meaning each gives to the hypothesis of men living in a state of nature prior to political association. If, prior to the state, men live in non-political societies, and if the state, as opposed to the family or the despotically ruled community, begins to exist only when it is constituted, then the formation of the state and the formation of its government would seem to be the product of a single convention.

THE PRINCIPLE OF constitutionality is also necessary in order to understand the familiar distinction between government by laws and government by men. Except for the divine sort of government which is above both law and lawlessness, Plato employs "the distinction of ruling with law or without law" to divide the various forms of government into two groups. "The principle of law and the absence of law will bisect them all," the Eleatic Stranger says in the *Statesman*.

In the ordinary meaning of law as an instrument of government, it is difficult to conceive government by laws without men to make and administer them, or government by men who do not issue general directives which have the character of law. Government always involves both laws and men. But not all government rests upon the supremacy of law, a supremacy which consists in the equality of all before the law and the predominance of regular law as opposed to arbitrary decision. Nor is all government based upon a law that regulates the officials of government as well as the citizens, and determines the legality of official acts, legislative, judicial, or executive. That law is, of course, the constitution.

Locke makes a distinction between governing by "absolute arbitrary power" and governing by "settled standing laws." It is his contention that "whatever form the commonwealth is under, the ruling power ought to govern by declared and received laws, and not by extemporary dictates and undetermined resolutions, for then mankind will be in a far worse condition than in a state of Nature. . . . All the power the government has, being only for the good of the society, as it ought not to be arbitrary and at pleasure, so it ought to be exercised by established and promulgated laws, that both the people may know their duty, and be safe and secure within the limits of the law, and the rulers, too, kept within their due bounds."

As Locke states the distinction between government by laws and government by men, it seems to be identical with the distinction between constitutional and non-constitutional government. In the latter, an individual man invests himself with sovereignty and, as sovereign, puts himself above all human law, being both its source and the arbiter of its legality. Such government is absolute, for nothing limits the power the sovereign man exercises as a prerogative vested in his person. In constitutional government, men are not sovereigns but office-holders, having only a share of the sovereignty. They rule not through *de facto* power, but through the juridical power which is vested in the office they hold. That power is both created and limited by the law of the constitution which defines the various offices of government.

ALTHOUGH ABSTRACTLY or in theory absolute and constitutional government are clearly distinct—more than that, opposed—political history contains the record of intermediate types. These can be regarded as imperfect embodiments of the principle of constitutionality, or as attenuations of absolute rule by constitutional encroachments. Despite their incompatibility in principle, historic circumstances have managed to combine absolute with constitutional government. It is this combination which mediaeval jurists and philosophers call "the mixed regime" or the *regimen regale et politicum,* "royal and political government."

It may be thought that a foreshadowing of the mediaeval mixed regime can be found in Plato's *Laws,* in the passage in which the Athenian Stranger says that monarchy and democracy are the "two mother forms of states from which the rest may be truly derived." He then asserts that, to combine liberty with wisdom, "you must have both these forms of government in a measure." Since the Persian despotism is cited as the "highest form" of monarchy and the Athenian constitution as the archetype of democracy, the combination proposed would seem to be a mixture of absolute with constitutional government. But the Athenian Stranger also says that "there ought to be no great and unmixed powers" if the arbitrary is to be avoided; and since the whole tenor of the book, as indicated by its title, is to uphold the supremacy of law, it is doubtful that a truly mixed regime is intended—a government which is *partly* absolute and *partly* constitutional.

Aristotle, furthermore, gives us reason to think that such a mixture would be unthinkable to a Greek. At least in his own vocabulary, the terms *royal* and *political* are as contradictory as *round* and *square.* Royal, or kingly, government for Aristotle is "absolute monarchy, or the arbitrary rule of a sovereign over all." In royal government, there are no political offices, and no citizens. The ruler is sovereign in his own person and the ruled are subject to his will, which is both the source of law and exempt from all legal limitations.

To Aristotle, political government means pure constitutionalism. It exists only where "the citizens rule and are ruled in turn," for "when the state is framed upon the principle of equality and likeness, the citizens think they ought to hold office by turns." To the generic form of constitutional government, Aristotle sometimes gives the name of "polity," though he also uses this name for the mixed constitution which combines democratic with oligarchical criteria for citizenship and public office. The mixed constitution is not to be confused with the mixed regime, for it is a mixture of different constitutional principles, not of constitutionalism itself with absolute government. When the word "polity" signifies constitutional government generally, it has the meaning which the Romans express by the word "republic" and which the constitutionalists of the 18th century call "free government."

The distinctive characteristics of such government—whether it is called political, republican, constitutional, or free—lie in the fact that the citizens are both rulers and ruled; that no man, not even the chief magistrate, is above the law; that all political power or authority is derived from and limited by the constitution which, being popular in origin, cannot be changed except by the people as a whole.

It is perhaps only in the Middle Ages that we find the mixed regime in actual existence. "That rule is called politic and royal," Aquinas writes, "by which a man rules over free subjects who, though subject to the government of the ruler, have nevertheless something of their own, by reason of which they can resist the orders of him who commands." These words seem to present an accurate picture of the peculiarly mediaeval political formation which resulted from the adaptation of Roman law (itself partly republican and partly imperial) to feudal conditions under the influence of local customs and the Christian religion.

The mediaeval mixed regime is not to be confused with modern forms of constitutional monarchy any more than with the mixed constitution or polity of the Greeks. "The so-called limited monarchy, or kingship according to law," Aristotle remarks, "is not a distinct form of government." The chapter on MONARCHY deals with the nature of constitutional monarchy and its difference from the mixed regime as well as its relation to purely republican government. The mediaeval king was not a constitutional monarch, but a sovereign person, in one sense above the law and in another limited by it.

To the extent that he had powers and prerogatives unlimited by law, the mediaeval king was an absolute ruler. He was, as Aquinas says, quoting the phrase of the Roman jurists, *legibus solutus*—exempt from the force of all man-made law. Aquinas also describes him as "above the law" insofar as "when it is expedient, he can change the law, and rule without it according to time and place." Yet he was also bound by his coronation oath to perform the duties of his office, first among which was the maintenance of the laws of the realm—the immemorial customs of the people which define their rights and liberties. The king's subjects could be released from their oath of allegiance by his malfeasance or dereliction in office.

To this extent, then, the mediaeval king was a responsible ruler, and the mixed regime was constitutional. Furthermore, the king did not have jurisdiction over customary law; yet where custom was silent, the king was free to govern absolutely, to decree what he willed, and even to innovate laws.

MEDIAEVAL IN ORIGIN, the institution of a government both royal and political, or what Fortescue, describing England in the 15th century, called a "political kingdom," exerted great influence on modern constitutional developments. As late as the end of the 17th century, Locke's conception of the relation of king and parliament, royal prerogative and legal limitations, may emphasize the primacy of law, but it does not entirely divest the king of personal sovereignty. Locke quotes with approval the speech from the throne in 1609, in which James I said that "the king binds himself by a double oath, to the observation of the fundamental laws of his kingdom. Tacitly, as by being a king, and so bound to protect as well the people, as the laws of his kingdom, and expressly by his oath at his coronation." To this extent the British kingdom is, as Fortescue had said, "political." But the king also retains the prerogative to dispense with law and to govern in particular matters by decree apart from law, and to this extent the government still remains royal.

Locke recognizes the difficulty of combining the absolute power of the king in administration with the limitations on that power represented by Parliament's jurisdiction over the laws which bind the king. To the question, Who shall be judge of the right use of the royal prerogative? he replies that "between an executive power in being, with such prerogative, and a legislative that depends upon his will for their convening, there can be no judge on earth . . . The people have no other remedy . . . but to appeal to heaven."

Montesquieu as well as Locke can conceive monarchy, as distinct from despotism, in no other terms than those of the mixed regime. He separates despotism as lawless, or arbitrary and absolute, government from all forms of government by law, and divides the latter into monarchies and republics. Montesquieu insists that the ancients had no notion of the kind of monarchy which, while it is legal government, is not purely constitutional in the sense of being republican. He calls this kind of monarchy "Gothic government," and, as Hegel later points out, it is clear that "by 'monarchy' he understands, not the patriarchal or any ancient type, nor on the other hand, the type organized into an objective constitution, but only feudal monarchy."

It is not until the 18th century that the slightest vestige of royal power comes to be regarded as inimical to law. For Rousseau "every legitimate government is republican"; for Kant, "the only rightful Constitution . . . is that of a Pure Republic," which, in his view, "can only be constituted by a *representative system* of the people." The writers of *The Federalist* take the same stand. They interpret the "aversion of the people to monarchy" as signifying their espousal of purely constitutional or republican government. In the tradition of the great books, only Hegel speaks thereafter in a contrary vein. Constitutional monarchy represents for him the essence of constitutionalism and the only perfect expression of the idea of the state.

Because modern republics, and even modern constitutional or limited monarchies, have developed gradually or by revolution out of mixed regimes; and because this development came as a reaction against the increasing absolutism or despotism of kings, the principle of constitutionality has been made more effective in modern practice than it was in the ancient world. In addition to asserting limitations upon governments, constitutions have also provided means of controlling them. They have been given the *force*, as well as the authority, of positive law. They have made office-holders accountable for their acts; and through such juridical processes as impeachment and such political devices as frequent elections and short terms of office, they have brought the administration of government within the purview of the law.

Following Montesquieu, the Federalists recommend the separation of powers, with checks and balances, as the essential means of enforcing constitutional limitations of office and of preventing one department of government from usurping the power of another. The citizens are further protected from the misuse of power by constitutional declarations of their rights and immunities; and constitutional government is itself safeguarded from revolutionary violence by such institutions as judicial review and by the availability of the amending power as a means of changing the constitution through due process of law.

IN THE HISTORY of political change, it is necessary to distinguish *change from* or *to* constitutional government and, within the sphere of constitutional government, the *change of* constitutions.

Republics are set up and constitutions established by the overthrow of despots or with their abdication. Republics are destroyed and constitutions overthrown by dictators who usurp the powers of government. Violence, or the threat of violence, usually attends these changes.

The other sort of change may take place in two ways: either when one constitution replaces another, as frequently occurs in the revolutions of the Greek city-states; or when an enduring constitution is modified by amendment, as is customary in modern republics. Every constitutional change is in a sense revolutionary, but if it can be accomplished by due process of law, violence can be avoided.

All the changes in which constitutional government or constitutions are involved raise fundamental questions of justice. Is republican government always better than absolute monarchy and the mixed regime—better in the sense of being more just, better because it gives men the liberty and equality they justly deserve? Is it better relative to the nature and condition of certain peoples but not all, or of a people at a certain stage of their development, but not always? In what respects does one constitution embody more justice than another? What sorts of amendment or reform can rectify the injustice of a constitution? Without answering such questions, we cannot discriminate between progress and decline in the history of constitutionalism.

Divergent answers will, of course, be found in the great books. Among the political philosophers, there are the defenders of absolutism and those who think that royal government is most like the divine; the exponents of the supremacy of the mixed regime; the republicans who insist that nothing less than constitutional government is fit for free men and equals. And there are those who argue that the justice of any form of government must be considered relative to the condition of the people, so that republican government may be better only in some circumstances, not in all.

The issue arising from these conflicting views

concerning constitutional and absolute government is treated in the chapters on CITIZEN, MONARCHY, and TYRANNY. But one other issue remains to be discussed here. It concerns the comparative justice of diverse constitutions. Constitutions can differ from one another in the way in which they plan the operations of government, or in the qualifications they set for citizenship and public office. Usually only the second mode of difference seriously affects their justice.

In Greek political life, the issue of justice as between the democratic and the oligarchical constitution is a conflict between those who think that all free men deserve the equality of citizenship and the opportunity to hold office, and those who think it is unjust to treat the rich and the poor as equals. The latter insist that citizenship should be restricted to the wealthy and that the magistracies should be reserved for men of considerable means.

Finding justice and injustice on both sides, Aristotle favors what he calls "the mixed constitution." This unites the justice of treating free men alike so far as citizenship goes, with the justice of discriminating between rich and poor with respect to public office. Such a mixture, he writes, "may be described generally as a fusion of oligarchy and democracy," since it attempts "to unite the freedom of the poor and the wealth of the rich." The mixed constitution, especially if accompanied by a numerical predominance of the middle class, seems to him to have greater stability, as well as more justice, than either of the pure types of constitution which, oppressive to either poor or rich, provoke revolution.

In modern political life, the issue between oligarchy and democracy tends toward a different resolution. The last defenders of the oligarchical constitution were men like Burke, Hamilton, and John Adams in the 18th century. Since then, the great constitutional reforms have progressively extended the franchise almost to the point of universal suffrage. These matters are, of course, further treated in the chapters on DEMOCRACY and OLIGARCHY.

POLITICAL REPRESENTATION, with a system of periodic elections, seems to be indispensable to constitutional government under modern conditions. The territorial extent and populousness of the nation-state as compared with the ancient city-state makes impossible direct participation by the whole body of citizens in the major functions of government.

Considering the ancient republics of Sparta, Rome, and Carthage, the writers of *The Federalist* try to explain the sense in which the principle of representation differentiates the American republic from these ancient constitutional governments. "The principle of representation," they say, "was neither unknown to the ancients nor wholly overlooked in their political constitutions. The true distinction between these and the American government lies *in the total exclusion of the people, in their collective capacity*, from any share in the *latter*, and not in the *total exclusion of the representatives of the people* from the administration of the *former*."

The Federalists then go on to say that "the distinction . . . thus qualified must be admitted to leave a most advantageous superiority in favor of the United States. But to insure to this advantage its full effect, we must be careful not to separate it from the other advantage of an extensive territory. For it cannot be believed that any form of representative government could have succeeded within the narrow limits occupied by the democracies of Greece."

In their opinion, representative government is not merely necessitated by the conditions of modern society, but also has the political advantage of safeguarding constitutional government from the masses. As pointed out in the chapter on ARISTOCRACY, where the theory of representation is discussed, the officers of government chosen by the whole body of citizens are supposed—at least on one conception of representatives—to be more competent in the business of government than their constituents. It is in these terms that the Federalists advocate what they call "republican government" as opposed to "pure democracy."

Like the idea of political offices, the principle of representation seems to be inseparable from constitutionalism and constitutional government. Though the principle appears to a certain extent in ancient republics—whether oligarchies or democracies—ancient political writing does not contain a formal discussion of the theory of representation. That begins in mediaeval treatises which recognize the consultative or advisory function of those who represent the nobles and the commons at the king's court. But it is only in recent centuries—when legislation has become the exclusive function of representative assemblies—that the idea of representation and the theory of its practice assume a place of such importance that a political philosopher like Mill does not hesitate to identify representative with constitutional government.

OUTLINE OF TOPICS

REFERENCES

To find the passages cited, use the numbers in heavy type, which are the volume and page numbers of the passages referred to. For example, in 4 HOMER: *Iliad*, BK II [265–283] 12d, the number 4 is the number of the volume in the set; the number 12d indicates that the passage is in section d of page 12.

PAGE SECTIONS: When the text is printed in one column, the letters a and b refer to the upper and lower halves of the page. For example, in 53 JAMES: *Psychology*, 116a-119b, the passage begins in the upper half of page 116 and ends in the lower half of page 119. When the text is printed in two columns, the letters a and b refer to the upper and lower halves of the left-hand side of the page, the letters c and d to the upper and lower halves of the right-hand side of the page. For example, in 7 PLATO: *Symposium*, 163b-164c, the passage begins in the lower half of the left-hand side of page 163 and ends in the upper half of the right-hand side of page 164.

AUTHOR'S DIVISIONS: One or more of the main divisions of a work (such as PART, BK, CH, SECT) are sometimes included in the reference; line numbers, in brackets, are given in certain cases; *e.g.*, *Iliad*, BK II [265–283] 12d.

BIBLE REFERENCES: The references are to book, chapter, and verse. When the King James and Douay versions differ in title of books or in the numbering of chapters or verses, the King James version is cited first and the Douay, indicated by a (D), follows; *e.g.*, OLD TESTAMENT: *Nehemiah*, 7:45—(D) II *Esdras*, 7:46.

SYMBOLS: The abbreviation "esp" calls the reader's attention to one or more especially relevant parts of a whole reference; "passim" signifies that the topic is discussed intermittently rather than continuously in the work or passage cited.

For additional information concerning the style of the references, see the Explanation of Reference Style; for general guidance in the use of *The Great Ideas*, consult the Preface.

1. **The difference between government by law and government by men: the nature of constitutional government**

5 AESCHYLUS: *Eumenides* [681–710] 88b-c

5 SOPHOCLES: *Oedipus at Colonus* [904–931] 122d-123a

5 EURIPIDES: *Suppliants* [399–462] 261d-262b

5 ARISTOPHANES: *Wasps* [463–507] 512d-513c

6 HERODOTUS: *History*, BK III, 107c-108c; BK VII, 233a-d

6 THUCYDIDES: *Peloponnesian War*, BK I, 368c-d; BK III, 425a-c; 438a-b

7 PLATO: *Republic*, BK V, 369c-d; BK VI, 380b-c / *Statesman*, 598b-604b / *Laws*, BK III, 667c-676b esp 671c; BK IV, 681b-682c; BK VIII, 733d-734a; BK IX, 745c-746a; 754a-b / *Seventh Letter*, 805d; 807a-b

9 ARISTOTLE: *Ethics*, BK V, CH 6 [1134^{a}24–^{b}17] 382a-c esp [1134^{a}35–37] 382b; BK X, CH 9 [1180^{a}14–24] 434d-435a / *Politics*, BK I, CH I [1252^{a}13–17] 445a-b; CH 5 [1254^{a}34–^{b}9] 448a; CH 7 [1255^{b}15–20] 449b; CH 12 453d-454a; BK II, CH 10 [1272^{a}35–^{b}10] 468d-469a; BK III, CH 10 [1281^{a}29–39] 479a; CH 11 [1282^{b}1–13] 480b-c; CH 15-17 484b-487a; BK IV, CH 4 [1291^{b}30–1292^{a}37] 491a-d; CH 6 492b-493a; BK V, CH 9 [1310^{a}25–36] 512c; BK VII, CH 2 [1324^{b}32–40] 528d-529a

12 AURELIUS: *Meditations*, BK I, SECT 14 254b-c

14 PLUTARCH: *Caesar*, 591d / *Cato the Younger*, 635a-b; 638b-639a / *Tiberius Gracchus*, 678b-b

15 TACITUS: *Annals*, BK I, 1a-2b; BK III, 51b-c; 61c-62a

18 AUGUSTINE: *Confessions*, BK III, par 15 17a-b

20 AQUINAS: *Summa Theologica*, PART I-II, Q 90, A I, REP 3 205b-206b; A 3 207a-c; Q 95, A I esp REP 2 226c-227c; Q 96, A 5, REP 3 233d-234d

23 HOBBES: *Leviathan*, PART II, 104d-106d; 114b-115a; 131d-132a; 138b-c; 149b-151a; PART IV, 272c; 273a-c

26 SHAKESPEARE: *2nd Henry VI*, ACT II, SC III [1–15] 44c-d; ACT III, SC I [223–242] 49c

27 SHAKESPEARE: *Henry VIII*, ACT I, SC II [91–101] 553d

31 SPINOZA: *Ethics*, PART IV, PROP 37, SCHOL 2 435b-436a

32 MILTON: *Paradise Lost*, BK XII [63–110] 320b-321b

35 LOCKE: *Civil Government* 25a-81d esp CH IV, SECT 21 29d, CH VI, SECT 57 36d-37b, CH VII, SECT 87-94 44a-46c, CH XI 55b-58b, CH XIV 62b-64c, CH XVIII, SECT 199-202 71a-72a

37 FIELDING: *Tom Jones*, 268c-269b

38 MONTESQUIEU: *Spirit of Laws*, BK II, 4a; 7c-9a,c; BK III, 12a-13c; BK IV, 15a-c; BK V, 25d-31a; BK VI, 33a-35a; 36a-b; BK VIII, 54a-b;

57c-58d; BK XI, 69a-c; BK XIX, 137c-d; BK XXV, 211c-d; BK XXVI, 223c-d

38 ROUSSEAU: *Inequality*, 323d-324a; 357b-c; 358b-d; 361c-362a / *Political Economy*, 370b-371a / *Social Contract*, BK I, 387b,d-391b; BK II, 400a; 406a-b; BK III, 408c; 419a-c; BK IV, 433a-434b

40 GIBBON: *Decline and Fall*, 24b,d-28b passim; 51b-d; 154a-c; 342a-c; 592a

41 GIBBON: *Decline and Fall*, 73d-75a; 96d; 125a; 161c-162a

42 KANT: *Pure Reason*, 113b-115a / *Science of Right*, 435c-437c; 450d-452a / *Judgement*, 586a-587a

43 DECLARATION OF INDEPENDENCE: 1a-3b passim

43 FEDERALIST: NUMBER 16, 68b-c; NUMBER 33 107b-109b passim; NUMBER 44, 146d-147a; NUMBER 47, 153c-154d; NUMBER 53, 167d-168b; NUMBER 55, 174c-d; NUMBER 57, 176d-178a; NUMBER 75, 223c-d passim; NUMBER 78, 230d-232a; NUMBER 81, 237d-238b

43 MILL: *Liberty*, 267d-268b / *Representative Government*, 327b,d-355b passim

44 BOSWELL: *Johnson*, 203d-205d

46 HEGEL: *Philosophy of Right*, PART III, par 260-265 82a-84b; par 278 92c-93a; par 286 96c-97a; par 298-299 99c-100b; ADDITIONS, 132 137d-138b; 171 146b-c / *Philosophy of History*, INTRO, 198b-199c; PART I, 207d-208c; 213b-214d; PART II, 261d-262c; 271d-272a; PART III, 301c-302d; PART IV, 327a-328a; 342a-d; 363c-365c

54 FREUD: *Civilization and Its Discontents*, 780b-d

2. The notion of a constitution

2a. The constitution as the form or organization of a political community: arrangement of offices; division of functions

7 PLATO: *Laws*, BK VI, 697a-705c esp 697a

9 ARISTOTLE: *Politics*, BK III, CH I [1274^{b}36-37] 471b; CH 3 [1276^{a}35-^{b}14] 473b-c; CH 6 [1278^b 10-14] 475d; CH 7 476c-477a passim, esp [1279^{a}25-27] 476c; BK IV, CH I [1289^{a}15-17] 488a; CH 3 [1290^{a}8-12] 489a

20 AQUINAS: *Summa Theologica*, PART I-II, Q 105, A 1, ANS 307d-309d

35 LOCKE: *Civil Government*, CH X-XIV 55a-64c passim; CH XVII, SECT 198 70d-71a; CH XIX, SECT 212-220 74a-75d

38 MONTESQUIEU: *Spirit of Laws*, BK XI, 69d-75a

38 ROUSSEAU: *Social Contract*, BK III, 406b,d-410a

40 GIBBON: *Decline and Fall*, 1a; 521c

41 GIBBON: *Decline and Fall*, 562b-c

42 KANT: *Science of Right*, 435a-439a; 450d-452a / *Judgement*, 557d [fn 2]

43 CONSTITUTION OF THE U.S.: 11a-20a,c esp ARTICLE I-III 11a-16a

43 FEDERALIST: NUMBER 39 125a-128b passim; NUMBER 47-83 153c-251a passim

43 MILL: *Liberty*, 321b-c / *Representative Government*, 327b,d-332d passim; 355b-356a; 401d-402a

46 HEGEL: *Philosophy of Right*, PART III, par 267 84b; par 269 84d; par 271-273 89c-92a; par 290 97d; ADDITIONS, 161 143a-b; 164 144c-145a / *Philosophy of History*, INTRO, 173a-175c

2b. The constitution as the fundamental law: its relation to other laws, as a source or measure of legality or justice

7 PLATO: *Republic*, BK VI, 380b-c / *Laws*, BK IV, 681b-682c

9 ARISTOTLE: *Politics*, BK III, CH 3 [1276^{b}1-15] 473b-c; CH II [1282^{b}1-13] 480b-c; BK IV, CH I [1289^{a}13-25] 488a-b; CH II [1295^{a}40-^{b}1] 495c; BK V, CH 9 [1310^{a}12-35] 512b-c; BK VIII, CH I [1337^{a}7-19] 542a

23 HOBBES: *Leviathan*, PART II, 101a-104d; 138b-c

35 LOCKE: *Civil Government*, CH XIX, SECT 212 74a-b

38 MONTESQUIEU: *Spirit of Laws*, BK I-II, 2d-6b; BK V, 18b,d-25c; BK XXVI, 214b,d; BK XXIX, 265d

38 ROUSSEAU: *Inequality*, 358b-d / *Social Contract*, BK II, 405d-406d

42 KANT: *Pure Reason*, 113b-115a esp 114b-d / *Science of Right*, 435a-441d esp 435c-436b, 437c-d, 438d-441d; 450d-452a

43 ARTICLES OF CONFEDERATION: XIII-CONCLUSION 9c-d

43 CONSTITUTION OF THE U.S.: ARTICLE I, SECT 8 13a-d esp [254-259] 13c-d; ARTICLE VI [583-590] 16d

43 FEDERALIST: NUMBER 33 107b-109b; NUMBER 44, 146d-147a; NUMBER 53, 167d-168b; NUMBER 78 229d-233c; NUMBER 80, 236d-237a; NUMBER 81, 237d-238b

43 MILL: *Representative Government*, 430a-431a

46 HEGEL: *Philosophy of Right*, PART III, par 260-269 82a-84d; par 274 92a; par 298 99c; par 349 111d-112a; ADDITIONS, 166 145b-c / *Philosophy of History*, INTRO, 173a-175c; PART IV, 364b

3. The relation of constitutional government to other forms of government

3a. The combination of constitutional with absolute government: the mixed regime; constitutional or limited monarchy

5 AESCHYLUS: *Suppliant Maidens* [359-422] 5b-6b; [600-624] 8d-9a

5 EURIPIDES: *Suppliants* [339-358] 261b-c

6 HERODOTUS: *History*, BK IV, 152d-153b

7 PLATO: *Statesman*, 598b-604b / *Laws*, BK III, 667a-676b

9 ARISTOTLE: *Politics*, BK III, CH 14 483a-484a; CH 15-16 484b-486c esp CH 15 [1286^{b}31]-CH 16 [1287^{a}8] 485b-c; BK V, CH II [1313^{a}18-33]

(3. *The relation of constitutional government to other forms of government. 3a. The combination of constitutional with absolute government: the mixed regime; constitutional or limited monarchy.*)

515d-516a / *Rhetoric*, BK I, CH 8 [1365ᵇ39-1366ᵃ2] 608b

14 PLUTARCH: *Lycurgus*, 34b-35d / *Dion*, 800c

15 TACITUS: *Annals*, BK III, 59d

23 MACHIAVELLI: *Prince*, CH IV 7a-8a; CH XIX, 27a-b; 29c-d

23 HOBBES: *Leviathan*, PART II, 103d-104b; 106d-107c; 151c-152a; PART III, 228a-b

35 LOCKE: *Civil Government*, CH VII, SECT 94 46a-c; CH X, SECT 132 55a-b; CH XI 55b-58b; CH XIII 59b-62b passim; CH XIV 62b-64c; CH XVIII, SECT 199-206 71a-72c; CH XIX 73d-81d passim, esp SECT 213 74b-c

36 STERNE: *Tristram Shandy*, 216b

37 FIELDING: *Tom Jones*, 266d

38 MONTESQUIEU: *Spirit of Laws*, BK II, 7c-8c; BK III, 11c-12b; 13c; BK VI, 36a-b; BK IX, 58b,d-60a; BK XI, 69a-77b esp 69d-75a; BK XIX, 142a-146a,c

38 ROUSSEAU: *Inequality*, 357b-c / *Social Contract*, BK III, 414d-415b

40 GIBBON: *Decline and Fall*, 26d-28b; 622d-623a

42 KANT: *Science of Right*, 439c-440a; 441b-c; 450a-452a

43 FEDERALIST: NUMBER 39, 125c; NUMBER 43, 141a-d; NUMBER 47, 154a-c; NUMBER 69 207a-210c passim; NUMBER 70, 213b-c; NUMBER 71, 216a-b; NUMBER 84, 252b-c

43 MILL: *Liberty*, 267d-268c / *Representative Government*, 343c-344a; 351a-c; 353d-354b; 401d-402b

44 BOSWELL: *Johnson*, 178a-b; 255a-d; 390a-b

46 HEGEL: *Philosophy of Right*, PART III, par 273 90c-92a; par 275-286 92a-97a; ADDITIONS, 170-172 145d-146d / *Philosophy of History*, PART I, 208b-c; PART IV, 342b-d; 368c-d

51 TOLSTOY: *War and Peace*, BK VI, 238c-243d; BK IX, 384c-388a,c passim

3b. The merits of constitutional government compared with royal government and the mixed regime

5 EURIPIDES: *Suppliants* [391-460] 261d-262b

6 HERODOTUS: *History*, BK III, 107c-108c

7 PLATO: *Statesman*, 598b-604b / *Laws*, BK III, 672c-676c; BK IV, 681d-682c; BK IX, 754a-b

9 ARISTOTLE: *Ethics*, BK V, CH 6 [1134ᵃ24-ᵇ17] 382a-c / *Politics*, BK I, CH 5 [1254ᵃ24-ᵇ24] 447d-448b; CH 7 [1255ᵇ16-20] 449b; CH 13 [1259ᵇ32-1260ᵇ7] 454b-455a,c; BK III, CH 7 476c-477a; CH 15-17 484b-487a; BK IV, CH 2 [1289ᵃ26-ᵇ10] 488b-c; CH 10-11 495a-496d; BK V, CH 8 [1308ᵇ10-30] 510d-511a

15 TACITUS: *Annals*, BK III, 51b-c

23 HOBBES: *Leviathan*, PART II, 151c-152a

35 LOCKE: *Civil Government*, CH II, SECT 13 28a-b; CH VII, SECT 87-94 44a-46c; CH XI 55b-58b; CH XIV, SECT 162-163 63a-b

36 STERNE: *Tristram Shandy*, 216b

38 MONTESQUIEU: *Spirit of Laws*, BK II, 7c-9a,c; BK III, 12a-13c; BK IV, 13b,d-15c; BK V, 25d-31b; BK VI, 33a-35a; 36a-b; 37d-38c; BK VII, 45c-46a; 47d-48a; BK XI, 69a-75d

38 ROUSSEAU: *Inequality*, 356b-359c / *Social Contract*, BK I, 387b,d-391b; BK III, 408b-c; 412c-414d

40 GIBBON: *Decline and Fall*, 24b; 32b-34a,c; 68b,d-69b; 521d; 522c-523a,c; 523d-524a

42 KANT: *Science of Right*, 439c-440a; 450a-452a / *Judgement*, 586a-587a

43 FEDERALIST: NUMBER 6, 40a-41a; NUMBER 69 207a-210c passim

43 MILL: *Liberty*, 267d-269a / *Representative Government*, 338d-340d; 341d-350a; 351a-354a; 363b-366a; 436b-437a

46 HEGEL: *Philosophy of Right*, PART III, par 301, 101a; ADDITIONS, 180 148b / *Philosophy of History*, PART I, 213b-214d; PART IV, 359b

4. The constitutional conception of political office: the qualifications and duties of public officials

7 PLATO: *Laws*, BK VI, 697a-705c

9 ARISTOTLE: *Politics*, BK I, CH 12 [1259ᵇ4-9] 454a; BK II, CH 9 [1270ᵇ7-1271ᵃ18] 466d-467b; CH 10 [1272ᵃ35-ᵇ10] 468d-469a; BK III, CH 6 [1278ᵇ30-1279ᵃ22] 476a-c; CH 11 479b-480c passim; CH 12 [1282ᵇ15]-CH 13 [1284ᵃ2] 480c-482a; BK IV, CH 3 [1290ᵃ5-13] 489a; CH 14-16 498b-502a,c; BK V, CH 9 [1309ᵃ33-ᵇ14] 511c-d; BK VI, CH 4 [1318ᵇ21-1319ᵃ4] 522b-c / *Rhetoric*, BK I, CH 8 [1365ᵇ31-36] 608a

14 PLUTARCH: *Lycurgus*, 45c / *Cato the Younger*, 625b-627b / *Tiberius Gracchus*, 678b-d

15 TACITUS: *Annals*, BK XI, 105d-107b

20 AQUINAS: *Summa Theologica*, PART I-II, Q 90, A 3 207a-c

23 HOBBES: *Leviathan*, PART II, 122b-124b

27 SHAKESPEARE: *Coriolanus*, ACT II, SC II-III 364a-369a

35 LOCKE: *Civil Government*, CH VII, SECT 94 46a-c; CH IX, SECT 131 54d; CH XII, SECT 143 58c-d; CH XIII 59b-62b; CH XVII, SECT 198 70d-71a; CH XIX, SECT 221-222 75d-76c

36 SWIFT: *Gulliver*, PART I, 28b-29b

38 MONTESQUIEU: *Spirit of Laws*, BK XI, 71a-72a

38 ROUSSEAU: *Inequality*, 324d-325b; 356a-c; 358b-d / *Social Contract*, BK III, 423c-424d; BK IV, 427a-428a

40 GIBBON: *Decline and Fall*, 26d-27a; 27d-28a

41 GIBBON: *Decline and Fall*, 73d; 94c-95c; 563d-564b; 586c-587a

43 ARTICLES OF CONFEDERATION: V 5d-6a; IX [299-310] 8b

43 CONSTITUTION OF THE U.S.: ARTICLE I, SECT 2-6 11b-12d; ARTICLE II-III, SECT I 14b-15c;

ARTICLE VI [583–599] 16d; AMENDMENTS, XII 18a-c; XIV, SECT 2–3 18d-19a; XX–XXI 19d-20a,c

43 FEDERALIST: NUMBER 39, 125c-126b; NUMBER 52–80 165a-237d passim, esp NUMBER 57, 176d-177a

43 MILL: *Liberty*, 268b-c; 320c-323a,c / *Representative Government*, 354b-362c; 363a-b; 365b-366a; 398d-406a; 409d-417c passim

46 HEGEL: *Philosophy of Right*, PART III, par 277 92b-c; par 293–297 98b-99b; ADDITIONS, 169 145d

51 TOLSTOY: *War and Peace*, BK VI, 241c-242b

5. The diversity of constitutions among the forms of government

6 HERODOTUS: *History*, BK III, 107c-108c

7 PLATO: *Republic*, BK VIII–IX, 401d-421a / *Statesman*, 598b-604b / *Laws*, BK IV, 679c-682c

9 ARISTOTLE: *Ethics*, BK VIII, CH 10 [1160ª31–ᵇ22] 412c-413a / *Politics*, BK II, CH 7–11 461d-470b; BK III, CH 5 [1278ª3–33] 475a-c; CH 6–9 475d-478d esp CH 8 [1279ᵇ17]–CH 9 [1280ª33] 477a-d; BK IV, CH 2 [1289ᵇ13]–CH 9 [1294ᵇ11] 488c-494c; CH 11–12 495b-497b; CH 14 [1297ᵇ 37–1298ᵇ40] 498b-499c; BK V, CH 1 [1301ª25–35] 502b; BK VI 520a-526d; BK VII, CH 8–10 532c-534d / *Athenian Constitution*, CH 41 571c-572a / *Rhetoric*, BK I, CH 8 608a-c

20 AQUINAS: *Summa Theologica*, PART I–II, Q 105, A 1, ANS 307c-309d

23 HOBBES: *Leviathan*, PART II, 104d-108a

35 LOCKE: *Civil Government*, CH X, SECT 132 55a-b

38 MONTESQUIEU: *Spirit of Laws*, BK II, 4a-8c; BK III, 9a-12a; BK V, 18d-19d; 23a-c; BK XI, 75d

38 ROUSSEAU: *Inequality*, 359a-d / *Social Contract*, BK III, 419b-c; BK IV, 427a-428a

42 KANT: *Science of Right*, 450b-d

43 FEDERALIST: NUMBER 10, 51c-52d passim; NUMBER 14, 60b-d; NUMBER 39, 125b-c

43 MILL: *Representative Government*, 355b-356b

46 HEGEL: *Philosophy of Right*, PART III, par 273–274, 90d-92a; ADDITIONS, 166 145b-c / *Philosophy of History*, INTRO, 173a-175c; PART IV, 367c-368b

5a. The justice of different constitutions: the extent and character of citizenship under each

6 HERODOTUS: *History*, BK III, 107c-108c

6 THUCYDIDES: *Peloponnesian War*, BK II, 395d-399a; BK VI, 520b-c

7 PLATO: *Republic*, BK VIII–IX, 401d-421a / *Statesman*, 598b-604b / *Laws*, BK III, 667c-676b; BK IV, 679c-680d; BK VIII, 733d-734a

9 ARISTOTLE: *Ethics*, BK V, CH 3 [1131ª24–29] 378d; CH 7 [1135ª2–4] 382d; BK VIII, CH 10–11 412c-413d / *Politics*, BK III, CH 1–2 471b,d-472d; CH 5 475a-d; CH 9 477c-478d; CH 13 [1283ᵇ44–

1284ª3] 482a; BK IV, CH 3 488d-489b; CH 8–9 493c-494d; BK V, CH 1 [1301ª25–1302ª15] 502b-503b; CH 3 [1303ᵇ5–8] 505a; BK VI, CH 3 521c-522a; CH 4 [1319ᵇ2–32] 523a-b; CH 6 524b-c / *Athenian Constitution*, CH 2 553a-c; CH 12 557b-558a / *Rhetoric*, BK I, CH 8 [1365ᵇ 31–1366ª6] 608a-b

12 AURELIUS: *Meditations*, BK I, SECT 14 254b-c

20 AQUINAS: *Summa Theologica*, PART I–II, Q 105, A 1, ANS 307d-309d

38 MONTESQUIEU: *Spirit of Laws*, BK II, 4a-8c; BK III, 9a-11a; BK V, 18b,d-25a; 31b-33a,c passim; BK VI 33a-43d; BK XI, 68b,d-75a; BK XII, 84b,d-85c; BK XIII, 99b-100c

38 ROUSSEAU: *Social Contract*, BK II, 405a-406a

39 SMITH: *Wealth of Nations*, BK IV, 271a-b

40 GIBBON: *Decline and Fall*, 616d-617d

41 GIBBON: *Decline and Fall*, 81d-82a; 223c-224a; 403b-404d

42 KANT: *Pure Reason*, 114b-d / *Science of Right*, 401b-402a; 436d-437c; 450b-451d

43 FEDERALIST: NUMBER 10, 51c-52d; NUMBER 57 176d-179b

43 MILL: *Representative Government*, 350a; 370a-372b

46 HEGEL: *Philosophy of Right*, PART III, par 274 92a; ADDITIONS, 166 145b-c / *Philosophy of History*, INTRO, 173a-175c; PART II, 272a-d; 273d-274a; 275b-276a; PART IV, 367c-368b

5b. The mixed constitution: its advantages

6 THUCYDIDES: *Peloponnesian War*, BK VIII, 590a-b

7 PLATO: *Laws*, BK III, 667a-676b; BK IV, 680d-681a; BK VI, 699d-700b

9 ARISTOTLE: *Politics*, BK II, CH 6 [1265ᵇ25–1266ª30] 461b-d esp [1265ᵇ33–39] 461b; CH 11 [1272ᵇ24]–CH 12 [1274ª13] 469b-470d; BK IV, CH 8–9 493c-494d; CH 11–12 495b-497b; BK V, CH 7 [1307ª5–28] 509a-b; CH 8 [1308ᵇ10–1309ª32] 510d-511c

14 PLUTARCH: *Lycurgus*, 34d-35d / *Dion*, 800c

15 TACITUS: *Annals*, BK IV, 72a; BK VI, 97b

20 AQUINAS: *Summa Theologica*, PART I–II, Q 95, A 4, ANS 229b-230c; Q 105, A 1, ANS 307d-309d

23 MACHIAVELLI: *Prince*, CH XIX, 27a-b

23 HOBBES: *Leviathan*, PART III, 228a-b

35 LOCKE: *Civil Government*, CH X, SECT 132 55a-b

36 STERNE: *Tristram Shandy*, 216b

38 MONTESQUIEU: *Spirit of Laws*, BK IX, 58b,d-60a; BK XI 68b,d-84d esp 69d-75a

38 ROUSSEAU: *Social Contract*, BK III, 410c; 414d-415b; BK IV, 427a-c

40 GIBBON: *Decline and Fall*, 24b; 630b,d-631a

41 GIBBON: *Decline and Fall*, 71d; 81c-d; 218c-219a; 403c-d; 404c-d; 428a

43 FEDERALIST: NUMBER 39, 125c

43 MILL: *Representative Government*, 355b-356b; 401d-402b

6. The origin of constitutions: the lawgiver, the social contract, the constituent assembly

6 HERODOTUS: *History*, BK I, 14a-c; BK IV, 152d-153b

7 PLATO: *Republic*, BK II, 311b-c / *Statesman*, 603c / *Laws*, BK III, 664a-667d / *Seventh Letter*, 807a-b

9 ARISTOTLE: *Politics*, BK I, CH 2 445b-446d esp [1253ᵃ30] 446d; BK II, CH 12 470b-471d; BK III, CH 15 [1286ᵇ8–22] 484d-485a; BK IV, CH 13 [1297ᵇ16–28] 498a / *Athenian Constitution* 553a-584a,c esp CH 5–12 554d-558a, CH 29–31 566b-567d, CH 41 571c-572a

12 LUCRETIUS: *Nature of Things*, BK V [1011–1027] 74b-c

14 PLUTARCH: *Theseus*, 9a-d / *Romulus*, 20c-28a / *Lycurgus* 32a-48d esp 33c-35d, 47a-c / *Solon*, 68a-74b / *Poplicola-Solon*, 86a-87b

15 TACITUS: *Annals*, BK III, 51b-c

23 HOBBES: *Leviathan*, PART I, 84c-90d; 97c-d; PART II, 99a-104d; 109b-c; 133b; PART III, 200a-b

25 MONTAIGNE: *Essays*, 462d-463b

31 SPINOZA: *Ethics*, PART IV, PROP 37, SCHOL 2 435b-436a

35 LOCKE: *Toleration*, 16a-c / *Civil Government*, CH VI, SECT 76 42a; CH VII, SECT 87 44a-b; CH VIII 46c-53c esp SECT 96–97 47a-b; CH X, SECT 132 55a-b; CH XI, SECT 141 58a-b; CH XV, SECT 171 65a-b; CH XVI, SECT 175 65d; CH XIX, SECT 220 75c-d; SECT 243 81d

36 STERNE: *Tristram Shandy*, 216b; 262a

38 MONTESQUIEU: *Spirit of Laws*, BK IX, 58b,d-60a

38 ROUSSEAU: *Inequality*, 353c-355b; 358b-d / *Political Economy*, 370b-d / *Social Contract*, BK I, 391a-393c; BK II, 400a-402a; BK III, 423a-424d

41 GIBBON: *Decline and Fall*, 71d-72d; 403b-c; 562b-c

42 KANT: *Science of Right*, 434b-c; 435a-436c; 437c-d; 439a-441d; 450d-452a esp 450d-451c

43 DECLARATION OF INDEPENDENCE: [7–28] 1a-b

43 CONSTITUTION OF THE U.S.: PREAMBLE 11a,c; ARTICLE VII [604–610] 17a,c

43 FEDERALIST: NUMBER 1, 29a-b; NUMBER 2, 32a-33b; NUMBER 22, 84d-85a; NUMBER 37-38, 117d-124a; NUMBER 40 128b-132a; NUMBER 49, 159b-c; NUMBER 53, 167d-168b; NUMBER 78, 232a-c

43 MILL: *Liberty*, 302d-303a / *Representative Government*, 327b,d-332d passim

46 HEGEL: *Philosophy of Right*, PART III, par 258, 80d-81b; par 273, 91d-92a; ADDITIONS, 116 135c-d / *Philosophy of History*, INTRO, 173a-175c; PART IV, 365c-366b

51 TOLSTOY: *War and Peace*, EPILOGUE II, 680b-684a

7. The preservation of constitutions: factors tending toward their dissolution

6 THUCYDIDES: *Peloponnesian War*, BK II, 396c-d

7 PLATO: *Republic*, BK VI, 380b-c; BK VIII-IX, 401d-421a esp BK VIII, 403a-404a, 405c-406a, 408b-409b, 411d-414b / *Laws*, BK III, 667c-676b; BK XII, 786c-787d; 794a-799a,c / *Seventh Letter*, 801b-c; 806d-807b

9 ARISTOTLE: *Politics*, BK II, CH 9 [1270ᵇ7–26] 466d-467a; CH 10 [1272ᵃ35–ᵇ11] 468d-469a; BK IV, CH 11–12 495b-497b; BK V 502a-519d passim, esp CH 7–9 508c-512d, CH 11 515d-518c; BK VI, CH 5 [1319ᵇ33–1320ᵃ4] 523b-c; BK VII, CH 9 [1329ᵃ3–12] 533b-c / *Rhetoric*, BK I, CH 4 [1360ᵃ20–29] 600c

14 PLUTARCH: *Lycurgus*, 35c-d; 47a-48a / *Coriolanus*, 180b-d / *Lysander*, 361a-d / *Agesilaus*, 482a-c; 495c-d / *Agis*, 649b-c

15 TACITUS: *Histories*, BK I, 210d-212d

20 AQUINAS: *Summa Theologica*, PART I-II, Q 97, AA 2–3 236d-238b

23 HOBBES: *Leviathan*, PART II, 148c-153a; 154b-c

25 MONTAIGNE: *Essays*, 47a-51a; 318c-319b; 462c-465c; 504c-506a

26 SHAKESPEARE: *Julius Caesar* 568a-596a,c

30 BACON: *Novum Organum*, BK I, APH 90, 125a / *New Atlantis*, 205d-207b

35 LOCKE: *Civil Government*, CH VIII, SECT 97-98 47a-c; CH XIII, SECT 155 60d-61a; CH XIV, SECT 162–168 63a-64c; CH XVIII, SECT 203–210 72a-73c; CH XIX, SECT 223–225 76c-77a

38 MONTESQUIEU: *Spirit of Laws*, BK III, 9b-10c; BK IV, 15d-16a; BK V, 21d-22b; BK VII, 44d-45b; BK VIII, 51a-57a; BK X, 63b-c; BK XI, 74c-d

38 ROUSSEAU: *Inequality*, 361b-362a / *Social Contract*, BK II, 403a-404a; 405d-406a; BK III, 408b-c; 418a-421c; BK IV, 432b-435a

40 GIBBON: *Decline and Fall*, 622d-623a

42 KANT: *Science of Right*, 441b-c; 450d-452a esp 450d-451a

43 DECLARATION OF INDEPENDENCE: 1a-3b

43 FEDERALIST: NUMBER 8, 45a-47a; NUMBER 10 49c-53a; NUMBER 15–16, 64b-68d; NUMBER 18–22 71a-85a esp NUMBER 20, 77c; NUMBER 25, 91b-d; NUMBER 27–28 94d-98b passim; NUMBER 41, 133a-134c; NUMBER 43, 141a-142d; NUMBER 44, 147a-b; NUMBER 71, 215b-c; NUMBER 78 229d-233c

43 MILL: *Liberty*, 320a-c / *Representative Government*, 327b,d-332d; 350b-356b; 401d-402b; 413c-414d; 425b-d

44 BOSWELL: *Johnson*, 120a-c

46 HEGEL: *Philosophy of Right*, PART III, par 273, 91d-92a / *Philosophy of History*, PART II, 272c-273a; PART IV, 365c-d; 367c-d

51 TOLSTOY: *War and Peace*, EPILOGUE I, 668a-669c

7a. The relative stability of different types of constitutions

6 HERODOTUS: *History*, BK III, 107c-108c

6 THUCYDIDES: *Peloponnesian War*, BK VIII, 587a-b

7 PLATO: *Republic*, BK VIII–IX, 401d-421a esp BK VIII, 403a-404a, 405c-406a, 408b-409b, 411d-414b / *Laws*, BK III, 667c-676b / *Seventh Letter*, 801b-c

9 ARISTOTLE: *Politics*, BK II, CH 9–11 465b-470b passim; BK III, CH 13 [1284^{a}3–^{b}34] 482a-483a; BK IV, CH 11 [1295^{b}35-1296^{b}2] 496a-c; CH 12 496d-497b; BK V 502a-519d esp CH 1 [1301^{b}5–1302^{a}16] 502d-503b, CH 3 [1302^{b}34-1303^{b}18] 504b-505a, CH 4 [1304^{a}18–^{b}18] 505d-506b, CH 7 [1307^{a}5-27] 509a-b, CH 12 [1315^{b}11–39] 518c-d; BK VI, CH 5 [1319^{b}33-1320^{a}3] 523b-c

15 TACITUS: *Annals*, BK IV, 72a-b / *Histories*, BK II, 224d-225a

20 AQUINAS: *Summa Theologica*, PART I–II, Q 105, A I, ANS 307d-309d

23 HOBBES: *Leviathan*, PART II, 105c-106d

38 MONTESQUIEU: *Spirit of Laws*, BK III, 10c-d; BK VIII, 51a-54b; 57b-c; BK XV, 112c-114a; BK XIX, 142a-143c; 145d

38 ROUSSEAU: *Social Contract*, BK III, 411b-c; 413d-414c

40 GIBBON: *Decline and Fall*, 48d-49a; 522d-523a,c

43 FEDERALIST: NUMBER 10, 51c-53a; NUMBER 27, 96b; NUMBER 48, 157b-c

43 MILL: *Liberty*, 321b-c / *Representative Government*, 355b-356b; 401d-402b

44 BOSWELL: *Johnson*, 195c-d; 390a-b

7b. The safeguards of constitutional government: bills of rights; separation of powers; impeachment

14 PLUTARCH: *Lycurgus*, 34d-35d / *Solon*, 70c-71c / *Coriolanus*, 179c-184c / *Tiberius Gracchus*, 678b-d

15 TACITUS: *Annals*, BK III, 51b-c

23 HOBBES: *Leviathan*, PART II, 103d-104a; 150b; 151d-152a

35 LOCKE: *Civil Government*, CH VIII, SECT 107 49b-d; CH XI, SECT 134–CH XII, SECT 143 55b-58d; CH XIII 59b-62b; CH XVII, SECT 198 70d-71a; CH XIX 73d-81d passim

38 MONTESQUIEU: *Spirit of Laws*, BK II, 7c-8c; BK V, 29a; 31d; BK VI, 33a-35a; BK VIII, 54b-c; BK XI, 68b,d-75a; 82c-83a; BK XII, 84b,d-85c; BK XIX, 142a-143c

38 ROUSSEAU: *Political Economy*, 370b-377b / *Social Contract*, BK III, 407d-408a; 410d-411a; 414d-415b; 423a; 424a-d; BK IV, 432b-433a

40 GIBBON: *Decline and Fall*, 24b; 25a; 27a-b

41 GIBBON: *Decline and Fall*, 81c-d; 93a-c; 94c-95c; 96c-d

42 KANT: *Science of Right*, 435c-441d passim; 450d-452a esp 451d-452a

43 DECLARATION OF INDEPENDENCE: [7–28] 1a-b; [52–55] 2a; [66–67] [70–71] 2b; [95–105] 3a

43 ARTICLES OF CONFEDERATION: V [74]–VI [93] 6a-b

43 CONSTITUTION OF THE U.S.: PREAMBLE 11a,c; ARTICLE I, SECT 2 [45–47] 11d; SECT 3 [81–95] 12a-b; SECT 6 [143]–SECT 7 [169] 12c-d; SECT 9 [267–275] 13d; [283–295] 13d-14a; SECT 10 [300–303] 14a; ARTICLE II, SECT 1 [331–334] 14b; SECT 4 15c; ARTICLE III, SECT 2 [493]–SECT 3 [511] 15d-16a; ARTICLE IV, SECT 4 16b-c; ARTICLE VI [583–599] 16d; AMENDMENTS, I–X 17a-18a; XIII, SECT I–XIV, SECT I 18c-d; XV 19b; XIX 19d

43 FEDERALIST: NUMBER 8, 46c-d; NUMBER 9–10 47a-53a; NUMBER 21, 78d-79b; NUMBER 25, 90a-b; NUMBER 26–28 92a-98b passim; NUMBER 41, 133a-134c; NUMBER 43, 140c-142d; NUMBER 44, 144d-145a; 146c-d; NUMBER 46–51, 151a-165a; NUMBER 53, 167b-168b; NUMBER 55, 173b-174c; NUMBER 57, 176d-178b passim; NUMBER 58, 180d; NUMBER 62, 189d-191c; NUMBER 63, 192c-193c; NUMBER 65–66 198a-203a; NUMBER 68, 205d-206a; NUMBER 69, 207b-d; NUMBER 73 218d-221c; NUMBER 76, 226a-227b; NUMBER 78 229d-233c; NUMBER 80, 236a-b; NUMBER 81, 237d-239c; NUMBER 83–84 244b-256a

43 MILL: *Liberty*, 267d-268b; 269a-c / *Representative Government*, 355b-356b; 361b; 365b-366a; 369b-389b; 392b-401a; 401d-402b; 406c-407d; 412b-c

44 BOSWELL: *Johnson*, 195c-d

46 HEGEL: *Philosophy of Right*, PART III, PAR 272 89d-90c; PAR 286 96c-97a; ADDITIONS, 164 144c-145a; 184 149a / *Philosophy of History*, PART IV, 368c-d

8. The change of constitutions

8a. Methods of changing a constitution: revolution, amendment

6 THUCYDIDES: *Peloponnesian War*, BK VIII, 575c-577d

7 PLATO: *Republic*, BK VII, 401c-d; BK VIII–IX, 401d-421a esp BK VIII, 403a-404a, 405c-406a, 408b-409b, 411d-414b / *Seventh Letter*, 800b-801b; 804a-b

9 ARISTOTLE: *Ethics*, BK VIII, CH 10 [1160^{a}31–^{b}22] 412c-413a / *Politics*, BK II, CH 12 [1273^{b}36–1274^{a}22] 470c-d; BK III, CH 3 [1276^{a}35–^{b}15] 473b-c; BK IV, CH 1 [1288^{b}43–1289^{a}8] 487d-488a; CH 5 [1292^{b}12–22] 492a; BK V, CH 1–2 502a-503d; CH 3 [1303^{a}14–24] 504c-d; CH 4 [1304^{b}8]–CH 7 [1307^{b}25] 506b-509d / *Athenian Constitution*, CH 5 554d-555a; CH 29 566b-d; CH 33–34 568b-569a; CH 38 570a-c

15 TACITUS: *Annals*, BK I, 6a-b

20 AQUINAS: *Summa Theologica*, PART I–II, Q 97, A 3 237b-238b

(8. The change of constitutions. 8a. Methods of changing a constitution: revolution, amendment.)

23 HOBBES: *Leviathan*, PART II, 150c-151a; CONCLUSION, 280c-281a

25 MONTAIGNE: *Essays*, 47a-51a; 462c-465c

35 LOCKE: *Civil Government*, CH XIX 73d-81d passim

38 MONTESQUIEU: *Spirit of Laws*, BK XI, 77a; 77d

38 ROUSSEAU: *Social Contract*, BK III, 424a-d

42 KANT: *Science of Right*, 441b-c; 450d-451a

43 DECLARATION OF INDEPENDENCE: [7-28] 1a-b; [95-108] 3a

43 ARTICLES OF CONFEDERATION: XIII 9c

43 CONSTITUTION OF THE U.S.: ARTICLE V 16c; AMENDMENTS, XVIII, SECT 3 19d; XX, SECT 6, XXI, SECT 3 20c

43 FEDERALIST: NUMBER 14, 62a-d; NUMBER 21, 78d-79b; NUMBER 39-40, 127d-132a; NUMBER 43, 143a-b; NUMBER 49-50 159b-162c; NUMBER 53, 167d-168b; NUMBER 78, 232a-c; NUMBER 85, 257a-259a

43 MILL: *Liberty*, 321a-b / *Representative Government*, 327b,d-332d

46 HEGEL: *Philosophy of Right*, PART III, par 273-274, 91d-92a; ADDITIONS, 161 143a-b; 166 145b-c; 176 147c-d / *Philosophy of History*, PART IV, 364a-c

50 MARX-ENGELS: *Communist Manifesto*, 424c-d; 425b-c; 432b-c

8b. The violation and overthrow of constitutional government

6 THUCYDIDES: *Peloponnesian War*, BK III, 438a-b; BK VIII, 579c-583c; 585d-586b; 587a-589a; 590a-c

9 ARISTOTLE: *Politics*, BK IV, CH 4 [1292ª5-37] 491b-d; CH 5 [1292ᵇ6-11] 492a; CH 6 [1293ª1-10] 492c; [1293ª27-34] 492d-493a; BK V, CH 5-7 506b-509d; BK VI, CH 4 [1319ᵇ2-31] 523a-b; CH 6 [1320ᵇ29-37] 524c / *Athenian Constitution*, CH 14-19 558d-561d / *Rhetoric*, BK I, CH 4 [1360ª17-29] 600c

14 PLUTARCH: *Coriolanus*, 180b-d / *Lysander*, 361a-362a / *Agesilaus*, 482a-c; 495c-d / *Pompey* 499a-538a,c / *Caesar* 577a-604d esp 578b-c / *Cato the Younger*, 629d-639c

15 TACITUS: *Annals*, BK I, 1a-2a; 3a-b; 23c / *Histories*, BK I, 210d-212d

25 MONTAIGNE: *Essays*, 47a-51a; 318c-319b; 462c-465c; 504c-506a

35 LOCKE: *Civil Government*, CH XIII, SECT 149 59b-d; SECT 155 60d-61a; CH XVI-XIX 65d-81d passim

38 MONTESQUIEU: *Spirit of Laws*, BK VIII, 51a-52c; 53c-d; BK XI, 82c-83a

38 ROUSSEAU: *Inequality*, 358b-359d / *Social Contract*, BK III, 407c; 408b-c; 418a-419c

40 GIBBON: *Decline and Fall*, 24b,d-28b; 51c-d; 153c-154b; 592a

41 GIBBON: *Decline and Fall*, 74b-d

42 KANT: *Science of Right*, 450d-451a

43 DECLARATION OF INDEPENDENCE: 1a-3b

43 FEDERALIST: NUMBER 16, 68a-c; NUMBER 20, 77c; NUMBER 21, 78d-79b; NUMBER 25, 91b-d; NUMBER 26, 93c-94d; NUMBER 28 96c-98b; NUMBER 44, 146c-d; NUMBER 47-48 153c-159a

43 MILL: *Representative Government*, 350c-351c

44 BOSWELL: *Johnson*, 176a-b

46 HEGEL: *Philosophy of History*, PART III, 300b-301c

51 TOLSTOY: *War and Peace*, BK I, 8d-10d

9. The theory of representation

9 ARISTOTLE: *Politics*, BK IV, CH 8 [1294ª9-15] 493d-494a; CH 14 498b-499c passim, esp [1298ᵇ21-22] 499b

20 AQUINAS: *Summa Theologica*, PART I-II, Q 90, A 3, ANS and REP 2 207a-c; Q 97, A 3, REP 3 237b-238b

23 HOBBES: *Leviathan*, PART I, 96c-98a,c; PART II, 101a-b; 105a-c; 117b-121a; 153a-159c

35 LOCKE: *Civil Government*, CH VII, SECT 88-89 44c-d; CH XI, SECT 140 58a; CH XIX, SECT 222 75d-76c; SECT 240 81b

38 MONTESQUIEU: *Spirit of Laws*, BK II, 4c-5a

38 ROUSSEAU: *Social Contract*, BK II, 396b-d; BK III, 421c-423a

39 SMITH: *Wealth of Nations*, BK IV, 269d-271d

42 KANT: *Science of Right*, 451c-452a

43 DECLARATION OF INDEPENDENCE: [41-47] 2a

43 CONSTITUTION OF THE U.S.: ARTICLE I 11a-14b passim

43 FEDERALIST: NUMBER 10, 51d-53a esp 51d-52a; NUMBER 14, 60a-61b; NUMBER 35, 113a-114b; NUMBER 52-66 165a-203a passim, esp NUMBER 57, 176d-178b, NUMBER 63, 193c-194a; NUMBER 76, 227a; NUMBER 78, 231a-c

43 MILL: *Liberty*, 268b-c / *Representative Government* 327a-442d passim, esp 338a-b, 355b-362c, 370a-372b, 401a-406a

46 HEGEL: *Philosophy of Right*, PART III, par 301-303 100b-102a; par 308-311 102c-104a; ADDITIONS, 182 148c-d / *Philosophy of History*, INTRO, 175b-c

9a. The functions and duties of representatives: their relation to their constituents

23 HOBBES: *Leviathan*, PART I, 97c-98a,c; PART II, 105a-c

35 LOCKE: *Civil Government*, CH XII, SECT 143 58c-d

36 SWIFT: *Gulliver*, PART II, 73a-74b

38 MONTESQUIEU: *Spirit of Laws*, BK XI, 71a-c

38 ROUSSEAU: *Social Contract*, BK III, 421c-423a

40 GIBBON: *Decline and Fall*, 522c-d

42 KANT: *Science of Right*, 438d-439a; 441b-c; 450a-b; 451d-452a

43 DECLARATION OF INDEPENDENCE: [35-47] 1b-2a; [109-121] 3a-b

43 ARTICLES OF CONFEDERATION: V [49-58] 5d; IX-X 7a-9a; CONCLUSION 9c-d

43 CONSTITUTION OF THE U.S.: ARTICLE I 11a-14b

43 FEDERALIST: NUMBER 10, 51d-52c; NUMBER 28, 97b-d; NUMBER 35-36, 113a-115a; NUMBER 44, 146c-d; NUMBER 48, 157c; NUMBER 49, 160c-d; NUMBER 52-66 165a-203a passim, esp NUMBER 53, 168b-169d, NUMBER 62, 190a-b, NUMBER 63, 192b-193a; NUMBER 78, 231a-c

43 MILL: *Representative Government*, 351a-c; 353b; 355b-362c; 400a-406a

44 BOSWELL: *Johnson*, 86a-b; 176a-b

9*b*. Types of representation: diverse methods of selecting representatives

7 PLATO: *Laws*, BK VI, 697a-705c; BK XII, 786b-787b

9 ARISTOTLE: *Politics*, BK III, CH 10 478d-479a; CH 13 [1283^{a}21-^{b}34] 481b-d; BK IV, CH 9 [1294^{b}6-13] 494c; CH 14 498b-499c; CH 15 [1300^{a}9-^{b}4] 500d-501b; BK VI, CH 2 [1317^{b}2-16] 520d; CH 3 [1318^{a}19-^{b}5] 521c-522a; CH 4 [1318^{b}21-26] 522b

14 PLUTARCH: *Lycurgus*, 45c-46a

27 SHAKESPEARE: *Coriolanus*, ACT II 361a-369a

35 LOCKE: *Civil Government*, CH VIII, SECT 95-99 46c-47c; CH XIII, SECT 154-158 60c-62b; CH XIX, SECT 216 74d

36 SWIFT: *Gulliver*, PART II, 73a-74b

38 MONTESQUIEU: *Spirit of Laws*, BK II, 4a-6d; BK XI, 71a-d

38 ROUSSEAU: *Inequality*, 324c-325b / *Social Contract*, BK I, 391b; BK IV, 425d-428a esp 426d-427a

43 ARTICLES OF CONFEDERATION: V [49-73] 5d-6a

43 CONSTITUTION OF THE U.S.: ARTICLE I, SECT 2 [5]-SECT 4 [102] 11b-12b; SECT 5 [107-115] 12b; AMENDMENTS, XII 18a-c; XIV, SECT 2 18d-19a; XVII 19b-c

43 FEDERALIST: NUMBER 22, 82a-c; NUMBER 35, 113a-114b; NUMBER 52-63 165a-195b passim, esp NUMBER 54 170a-172b, NUMBER 62 188d-191c; NUMBER 68 205b-207a

43 MILL: *Representative Government*, 369b-399d; 407d-409c; 412a-414d

44 BOSWELL: *Johnson*, 176a-b; 251a; 261c-d

46 HEGEL: *Philosophy of Right*, PART III, par 311-313 103d-104b / *Philosophy of History*, INTRO, 172d-173c; PART II, 277c-d; PART IV, 365a; 368a-b

10. The origin, growth, and vicissitudes of constitutional government

6 HERODOTUS: *History*, BK IV, 152d-153b

6 THUCYDIDES: *Peloponnesian War*, BK II, 396b-397d; BK III, 432b-c; 438a-b; BK VIII, 575c-576c; 579c-583c; 585d-586b; 587a-589a; 590a-c

7 PLATO: *Laws*, BK III, 667c-676b

9 ARISTOTLE: *Ethics*, BK X, CH 9 [1181^{b}13-24] 436c / *Politics*, BK II, CH 12 470b-471d; BK III, CH 15 [1286^{b}8-21] 484d-485a; BK IV, CH 13 [1297^{b}16-28] 498a; BK V, CH 4 [1304^{a}18-38] 505d-506a; CH 5-7 506b-509d / *Athenian Constitution*, CH 1-41 553a-572a passim, esp CH 41 571c-572a

14 PLUTARCH: *Theseus*, 9a-d / *Romulus*, 20c-28a / *Lycurgus* 32a-48d / *Solon* 64b,d-77a,c / *Poplicola*, 77a-82a / *Poplicola-Solon*, 86a-87b / *Coriolanus* 174b,d-193a,c esp 176b-184c / *Lysander*, 365a-368a,c / *Cato the Younger* 620a-648a,c / *Agis* 648b,d-656d / *Cleomenes*, 657a-663c / *Tiberius Gracchus* 671b,d-681a,c / *Caius Gracchus* 681b,d-689a,c

15 TACITUS: *Annals*, BK I, 1a-2a; 3a-b; 21b-22d; BK III, 51b-c; BK IV, 72a-b; BK VI, 97b / *Histories*, BK I, 210d-212d

20 AQUINAS: *Summa Theologica*, PART I-II, Q 105, A I, ANS 307d-309d

27 SHAKESPEARE: *Coriolanus* 351a-392a,c

32 MILTON: *Sonnets*, XII 65a-b / *Lord Gen. Fairfax* 68b-69a

35 LOCKE: *Civil Government*, CH VII, SECT 94 46a-c; CH VIII, SECT 100-111 47c-51a passim; CH XIV, SECT 162-166 63a-64a

36 SWIFT: *Gulliver*, PART II, 74a-76b; PART III, 120a

38 MONTESQUIEU: *Spirit of Laws*, BK XI 68b,d-84d

38 ROUSSEAU: *Inequality*, 356a-b; 357b-c / *Social Contract*, BK III, 420a-c; BK IV, 428a-434b

39 SMITH: *Wealth of Nations*, BK IV, 269d-271d

40 GIBBON: *Decline and Fall*, 1a; 24b,d-28a; 51a-d; 153c-154b; 241b-244a passim; 521a-523a,c; 622d-623c

41 GIBBON: *Decline and Fall*, 71d-75b esp 71d-72a, 73b-c; 202a-d; 217a-b; 403b-404d; 562b-565a; 574b-582b; 586c-589a esp 587a

42 KANT: *Science of Right*, 451d-452a

43 DECLARATION OF INDEPENDENCE: 1a-3b

43 ARTICLES OF CONFEDERATION: 5a-9d

43 CONSTITUTION OF THE U.S.: 11a-20a,c

43 FEDERALIST: NUMBER 2 31a-33b; NUMBER 9, 47a-d; NUMBER 18-20 71a-78b passim; NUMBER 37-38 117d-125a; NUMBER 40 128b-132a; NUMBER 48 156d-159a; NUMBER 52, 165d-167b; NUMBER 63 191d-195b passim; NUMBER 85 256a-259a,c

43 MILL: *Liberty*, 267b,d-268c

44 BOSWELL: *Johnson*, 176a-b

46 HEGEL: *Philosophy of Right*, ADDITIONS, 176 147c-d / *Philosophy of History*, INTRO, 192d-193a; PART II, 275b-276a; PART III, 295d-296c; PART IV, 335a-336c; 362b-368d

51 TOLSTOY: *War and Peace*, BK VI, 238c-243d; 260b-c; EPILOGUE I, 668a-669c

CROSS-REFERENCES

For: Other considerations of the distinction between government by law and government by men, and for the comparison of constitutional government with other forms of government, *see* ARISTOCRACY 4; LAW 6b, 7a–7b; LIBERTY 1d, 1f; MONARCHY 1a–1a(2), 4c–4e(4); TYRANNY 5–5d.

The exposition of different types of constitutions and different forms of constitutional government in themselves and in relation to one another, *see* ARISTOCRACY 1–2e; CITIZEN 2c–3; DEMOCRACY 3–3c, 4a(1)–4a(2), 4d; OLIGARCHY 1–2, 4, 5a.

Other discussions of the mixed regime and the mixed constitution, *see* ARISTOCRACY 2b; DEMOCRACY 3a–3b; GOVERNMENT 2b; MONARCHY 1b(1)–1b(2).

The idea of citizenship in relation to constitutional government, *see* CITIZEN 2a–2b; and for the conception of the statesman as a constitutional office-holder, *see* STATE 8.

The conception of constitutional law and its relation to other bodies of law and legal justice, *see* JUSTICE 9c, 10a; LAW 7a.

Matters relevant to the conventional character of constitutions and the relation of the idea of a constitution to the theory of the social contract, *see* CUSTOM AND CONVENTION 6a; LAW 7c; NATURE 2b; STATE 3d.

Constitutional government in relation to the theory of sovereignty, *see* DEMOCRACY 4b; GOVERNMENT 1g(1)–1g(3); LAW 6b; MONARCHY 4e(3); STATE 2c; TYRANNY 5c.

Other discussions of the safeguards of constitutional government and of the theory and machinery of representation, *see* ARISTOCRACY 6; DEMOCRACY 4b, 5–5c; GOVERNMENT 1h; LIBERTY 1g.

The problem of constitutional change and the stability of different types of constitution, *see* ARISTOCRACY 3; DEMOCRACY 7–7a; REVOLUTION 2a, 3c(2); STATE 3g.

The issues involved in the development of constitutional government and the establishment of liberty under law, *see* GOVERNMENT 6; LIBERTY 6b; MONARCHY 4e(2); PROGRESS 4a; REVOLUTION 3a; TYRANNY 4b, 8.

ADDITIONAL READINGS

Listed below are works not included in *Great Books of the Western World*, but relevant to the idea and topics with which this chapter deals. These works are divided into two groups:

I. Works by authors represented in this collection.
II. Works by authors not represented in this collection.

For the date, place, and other facts concerning the publication of the works cited, consult the Bibliography of Additional Readings which follows the last chapter of *The Great Ideas.*

I.

MACHIAVELLI. *The Discourses*, BK I
MILTON. *The Tenure of Kings and Magistrates*
HUME. *Idea of a Perfect Commonwealth*

II.

POLYBIUS. *Histories*, VOL I, BK VI
CICERO. *De Republica (The Republic)*
MARSILIUS OF PADUA. *Defensor Pacis*

FORTESCUE. *Governance of England.*
GUICCIARDINI. *Dialogo e discorsi del reggimento di Firenze*
BODIN. *The Six Bookes of a Commonweale*
BELLARMINE. *The Treatise on Civil Government (De Laicis)*
HOOKER. *Of the Laws of Ecclesiastical Polity*
BOLINGBROKE. *Dissertation upon Parties*, LETTER 18
VATTEL. *The Law of Nations*, BK I, CH 3
J. WILSON. *Works*, PART I, CH II, V, X–XI; PART II

BENTHAM. *Fragment on Government*, CH 1 (36–48), 3

J. ADAMS. *A Defense of the Constitutions of Government of the United States of America*

PAINE. *Rights of Man*

BURKE. *Letter to the Sheriffs of Bristol*

——. *On the Reform of the Representation in the House of Commons*

——. *An Appeal from the New to the Old Whigs*

——. *Letter to Sir Hercules Langrishe*

GODWIN. *An Enquiry Concerning Political Justice*, BK VI, CH 7

SIEYÈS. *Discours dans les débats constitutionels de l'an III*

JEFFERSON. *Notes on the State of Virginia*

——. *Democracy*, CH 3

WHEWELL. *The Elements of Morality*, BK V, CH 4–5

CALHOUN. *A Disquisition on Government*

——. *A Discourse on the Constitution and Government of the United States*

TOCQUEVILLE. *Democracy in America*

——. *L'ancien régime (Ancient Regime)*

BAGEHOT. *The English Constitution*

DICEY. *Introduction to the Study of the Law of the Constitution*

MOSCA. *The Ruling Class*

JELLINEK. *Allgemeine Staatslehre*

BRYCE. *The American Commonwealth*

——. *Studies in History and Jurisprudence*

BEARD. *The Supreme Court and the Constitution*

DUGUIT. *Law in the Modern State*

FARRAND. *The Framing of the Constitution of the United States*

J. DICKINSON. *Administrative Justice and the Supremacy of Law in the United States*

MERRIAM. *The Written Constitution and the Unwritten Attitude*

MCILWAIN. *The Fundamental Law Behind the Constitution*

——. *Constitutionalism and the Changing World*

——. *Constitutionalism, Ancient and Modern*

KELSEN. *General Theory of Law and State*

ROSSITER. *Constitutional Dictatorship*

BORGESE et al. *Preliminary Draft of a World Constitution*

Chapter 13: COURAGE

INTRODUCTION

THE heroes of history and poetry may be cruel, violent, self-seeking, ruthless, intemperate, and unjust, but they are never cowards. They do not falter or give way. They do not despair in the face of almost hopeless odds. They have the strength and stamina to achieve whatever they set their minds and wills to do. They would not be heroes if they were not men of courage.

This is the very meaning of heroism which gives the legendary heroes almost the stature of gods. In the Homeric age they do in fact contend with gods as well as men. The two Homeric epics, especially the *Iliad*, are peopled with men who cannot be dared or daunted. In Tennyson's poem, Ulysses, now restive in Ithaca, remembering the years at Troy and the long voyage home, says to his companions,

Some work of noble note may yet be done
Not unbecoming men that strove with Gods
......................and though
We are not now that strength which in old days
Moved earth and heaven; that which we are, we are:
One equal temper of heroic hearts,
Made weak by time and fate, but strong in will
To strive, to seek, to find, and not to yield.

In the *Iliad*, courage is the quality above all others which characterizes the great figures of Achilles and Hector, Ajax, Patroclus, and Diomedes, Agamemnon and Menelaus. The only other quality which seems to be equally prized, and made the subject of rivalry and boast, is cunning—the craft of Odysseus, that man of many devices, and the cleverness in speech of Nestor. Yet the best speech is only the prelude to action, and except for the night expedition of Odysseus and Diomedes into the Trojan camp, the great actions of the *Iliad* are unplanned deeds of prowess—stark, not stealthy.

The heroes have boundless passions, and fear is among them. When they are called fearless,

it is not because nothing affrights them or turns their blood cold. Fear seizes them, as does anger, with all its bodily force. They are fearless only in the sense that they do not act afraid or fail to act. Their courage is always equal to the peril sensed or felt, so that they can perform what must be done as if they had no fear of pain or death.

Yet brave men often speak of courage as if it were fearlessness and mark the coward as one who is undone by fear. An ambush, Indomeneus says in the *Iliad*, will show "who is cowardly and who is brave; the coward will change color at every touch and turn; he is full of fears, and keeps shifting his weight first on one knee and then on the other; his heart beats fast as he thinks of death, and one can hear the chattering of his teeth." The brave man, mastering fear, will appear to be fearless.

This is the courage of men of action, men in war, found not only in the heroes of Troy's siege, but in the stalwarts of all other battles—Leonidas at Thermopylae, Aeneas and Turnus engaged in single combat, the conquerors in Plutarch, the warrior-nobility in Shakespeare, the civilized Prince Andrew and young Rostov in *War and Peace*. It is the sort of courage which goes with physical strength, with feats of endurance; and, as signified by the root-meaning of "fortitude," which is a synonym for courage, it is a reservoir of moral or spiritual strength to sustain action even when flesh and blood can carry on no further. Such courage is a virtue in the primary sense of the Latin word *virtus*—manliness, the spirit, or strength of spirit, required to be a man.

THERE ARE OTHER sorts of courage. The courage of the tragic hero, of Oedipus and Antigone, goes with strength of mind, not body. This, perhaps even more than being lion-hearted, is a specifically human strength. Courage does not consist only in conquering fear and in withholding the body from flight no matter what the risk of pain. It consists at least as much in steeling the will, reinforcing its resolutions, and turning the mind relentlessly to seek or face the truth.

Civil no less than martial action requires courage. Weary of empire, Marcus Aurelius summons courage each day for the performance of an endless round of duties. "In the morning when thou risest unwilling," he reminds himself, "let this thought be present—I am rising to the work of a human being." How he conceives the work of an emperor, he makes plain. "Let the deity which is in thee be the guardian of a living being, manly and of ripe age, and engaged in matter political, and a Roman, and a ruler, who has taken his post like a man waiting for the signal which summons him from life, and ready to go, having need neither of oath nor of any man's testimony." The burdens are heavy, the task difficult but not impossible, for a man "can live well even in a palace."

Civil courage is as necessary for the citizen as for the ruler. This virtue, in Mill's opinion, is especially necessary for citizens of a free government. "A people may prefer a free government," he writes, "but if, from indolence, or carelessness, or cowardice, or want of public spirit, they are unequal to the exertions necessary for preserving it; if they will not fight for it when it is directly attacked; if they can be deluded by the artifices used to cheat them out of it; if by momentary discouragement, or temporary panic, or a fit of enthusiasm for an individual, they can be induced to lay their liberties at the feet even of a great man, or trust him with powers which enable him to subvert their institutions; in all these cases they are more or less unfit for liberty: and though it may be for their good to have had it even for a short time, they are unlikely long to enjoy it."

The courage or pusillanimity of a people is sometimes regarded as the cause, and sometimes as the effect, of their political institutions. "The inhabitants of Europe," Hippocrates writes, are "more courageous than those of Asia; for a climate which is always the same induces indolence, but a changeable climate, laborious exertions, both of body and mind; and from rest

and indolence cowardice is engendered, and from laborious exertions and pains, courage." This, according to Hippocrates, partly explains why the Asiatics readily submit to despotism and why the Europeans fight for political liberty. But the character of the Europeans, he adds, is also the result of "their institutions, because they are not governed by kings . . . for where men are governed by kings, there they must be very cowardly . . . and they will not readily undergo dangers in order to promote the power of another; but those that are free undertake dangers on their own account . . . and thus their institutions contribute not a little to their courage."

For Hegel, on the contrary, civic courage consists in undertaking dangers, even to the point of sacrifice, for the state. Moreover, for him true courage is entirely a civic virtue. "The intrinsic worth of courage as a disposition of the mind," he writes, "is to be found in the genuine, absolute, final end, the sovereignty of the state. The work of courage is to actualize this final end, and the means to this end is the sacrifice of personal actuality." Though he admits that courage "is multiform," he insists that "the mettle of an animal or a brigand, courage for the sake of honor, the courage of a knight, these are not true forms of courage. The true courage of civilized nations is readiness for sacrifice in the service of the state, so that the individual counts as only one amongst many."

THE WORK OF MAN IS learning as well as action. Man has a duty to the truth as well as to the state. The ability to face without flinching the hard questions reality can put constitutes the temper of a courageous mind. "The huge world that girdles us about," William James writes, "puts all sorts of questions to us, and tests us in all sorts of ways. Some of the tests we meet by actions that are easy, and some of the questions we answer in articulately formulated words. But the deepest question that is ever asked admits of no reply but the dumb turning of the will and tightening of our heart-strings as we say, 'Yes, I will even have it so!' When a dreadful object is presented, or when life as a whole turns up its dark abysses to our view, then the worthless ones among us lose their hold on the situation altogether . . . But the heroic mind does differently . . . It can face them if necessary, without for that losing its hold upon the rest of life. The world thus finds in the heroic man its worthy match and mate . . . He can *stand* this Universe."

Not only in answering questions, but in asking them, courage is required. The story which St. Augustine tells in the *Confessions*, of his persistent questioning of doctrines and dogmas, his refusal to rest in any creed which did not wholly satisfy his mind, is a story of speculative courage, capped by the fortitude with which he bore the agony of irresolution and doubt.

Learning is never an easy enterprise, nor truth an easy master. The great scientists and philosophers have shown the patience and perseverance of courage in surmounting the social hardships of opposition and distrust, as well as the intellectual difficulties which might discourage men less resolved to seek and find the truth. The great religious martyrs, as indomitable in their humility as soldiers are in daring, have been as resolute—never yielding to a despair which would have dishonored their faith.

In all these types of fortitude, different motivations are apparent, as diverse as the forms which courage takes under the various demands of life. Not all the forms of courage may be equally admirable, partly because they are unequal in degree, but also partly because the courageous acts themselves, or the purposes for which fortitude is needed, are not of equal moral worth. Yet the essence of courage seems to be the same throughout. It sustains the honor of Don Quixote and in some sense even of Sir John Falstaff; it burnishes the fame of Alexander and Caesar; it fortifies Socrates and Galileo to withstand their trials. Whether in the discharge of duty or in the pursuit of happiness, courage confirms a man in the hard choices he has been forced to make.

As THE CHAPTER on VIRTUE indicates, the traditional theory of the moral qualities places courage or fortitude among the four principal virtues. The other three are temperance, justice, and either wisdom or prudence, according to the enumeration of different writers.

Plato names these virtues when, in the *Republic*, he compares the parts of the state with the parts of the soul. "The same principles which exist in the State exist also in the individual," Socrates says, and "they are three in number." There is one "with which a man reasons . . . the rational part of the soul, another with which he loves and hungers and thirsts and feels the flutterings of any other desire—the irrational or appetitive, the ally of sundry pleasures and satisfactions." The third part is "passion or spirit" which "when not corrupted by bad education is the natural auxiliary of reason."

Corresponding to these three parts of the soul, there are, or should be, according to Plato, three classes in the state: the guardians or rulers, the husbandmen and artisans, or the workers, and the auxiliaries or the soldiers.

The virtues which belong to the several parts of the soul also belong to the corresponding parts of the state. Wise is the man, Socrates declares, "who has in him that little part which rules, and which proclaims commands, that part too being supposed to have a knowledge of what is for the interest of each of the three parts and of the whole." Courageous is he "whose spirit retains in pleasure and in pain the commands of reason about what he ought or ought not to fear."

Temperance, however, instead of being exclusively the perfection of one part, pervades the whole, and is found, according to Socrates, in the man "who has these same elements in friendly harmony, in which the one ruling principle of reason, and the two subject ones of spirit and desire are equally agreed that reason ought to rule." Justice—"the only virtue which remains . . . when the other virtues of temperance and courage and wisdom are abstracted"—"is the ultimate cause and condition of the existence of all of them, and while remaining in them is also their preservative." It is the virtue which "does not permit the several elements within a man to interfere with one another, or any of them to do the work of others."

The political analogy finds justice in the well-ordered state, where wisdom rules, courage defends the laws and peace, and temperance balances the economy. Wisdom would belong most properly to the guardians, courage to the auxiliaries, while all three classes would need temperance. Hegel also associates courage with "the military class"—"that universal class which is charged with the defence of the state" and whose duty it is "to make real the ideality implicit within itself, *i.e.*, to sacrifice itself." But whereas for Hegel courage seems to be the foremost political virtue, Plato puts it last in the order of goods. "Wisdom is chief," the Athenian Stranger says in the *Laws*; "next follows temperance; and from the union of these two with courage springs justice, and fourth in the scale of virtue is courage."

In the context of a different psychological analysis, and a theory of the virtues which considers them primarily as habits, Aristotle's conception of courage differs from Plato's in a number of respects. It is most closely allied with temperance. These two virtues together belong to the irrational part of the soul—the passions or appetites—and are concerned with our attitude toward pleasure and pain. They discipline us, both in feeling and action, with regard to the pleasurable objects of desire and the painful objects of fear or aversion. Aristotle seems to think courage more praiseworthy than temperance, "for it is harder to face what is painful than to abstain from what is pleasant."

Just as the temperate man is one who habitually forgoes certain pleasures and seeks other pleasures moderately for the sake of achieving some greater good, so the courageous man is one who can at any time endure pain and hardship, or overcome fear of danger and death, in order to achieve a paramount end. Since death is "the most terrible of all things," Aristotle declares that "properly, he will be called brave who is fearless in face of a noble death, and of all emergencies that involve death." But it must be "for a noble end that the brave man endures and acts as courage directs."

The paramount end, the greatest good, which the moderation of temperance and the endurance of courage serve, is for Aristotle happiness. Yet through their relation to justice, which concerns the good of others and the welfare of the state, temperance and courage help a man to perform his social duties, whether as ruler or citizen, in peace or war. The man who acts lawfully will not only be just, but also courageous and temperate, for, in Aristotle's view, "the law bids us do both the acts of a brave man, *e.g.*, not to desert our post nor take to flight nor throw away our arms, and those of a temperate man, *e.g.*, not to commit adultery nor to gratify one's lust." Not only may the law-abiding man be called upon to be courageous in the respects which Aristotle indicates, but it may sometimes take great courage to uphold the law itself against many temptations to the contrary. "After the death of Moses . . . the Lord spake unto Joshua," and said unto him: "Be thou strong and very courageous, that thou mayest observe to do according to all the law which Moses my servant commanded thee: turn not from it to the right hand or to the left."

The fourth virtue with which courage, temperance, and justice are associated in the conduct of private or public life is prudence, or "practical wisdom." Though Aristotle classifies prudence as an intellectual virtue, consisting in the capacity for making a right judgment about things to be done, he also regards prudence as inseparable in origin and exercise from these other three virtues which he calls "moral" rather than "intellectual." Later writers call the four virtues taken together—courage, temperance, justice, and prudence—the "cardinal" virtues in order to signify, as Aquinas explains, that the whole of moral life "hinges" upon them.

The theory of the cardinal virtues, and of their connection with one another in such wise that none can be perfect in the absence of the others, is treated in the chapter on VIRTUE. The chapters on JUSTICE, TEMPERANCE, and PRUDENCE discuss the doctrine that each of these virtues is only a part of virtue, which must be integrated with the other parts. The special role which prudence plays in relation to virtues like courage and temperance—at least according to Aristotle's view that "it is not possible to be good in the strict sense without practical wisdom, nor practically wise without moral virtue"—must be reserved for the chapter dealing with that virtue. Nevertheless, it is necessary to consider here how its dependence on prudence may qualify the meaning or nature of courage.

THE CONNECTION which some writers see between courage and prudence affects the definition of courage in two ways. The first involves the doctrine of the mean which enters into the consideration of all the moral virtues, but especially courage and temperance.

Aristotle originates the analysis of virtue as "a mean between two vices . . . because the vices respectively fall short of or exceed what is right in both passions and actions." It requires prudence to decide what things should be feared, when they should be feared, and how much; and so a prudent judgment is involved in fearing the right things at the right time and in the right manner—neither too much nor too little. "The coward, the rash man, and the brave man," Aristotle writes, "are concerned with the same objects but are differently disposed to them; for the first two exceed and fall short, while the third holds the middle, which is the right, position; and rash men are precipitate and wish for dangers beforehand but draw back when they are in them, while brave men are keen in the moment of action, but quiet beforehand."

Aristotle is not the only one to define courage as a middleground between contrary extremes. Most writers who devote any attention to the nature of courage come to somewhat the same conclusion. Epictetus, for example, in declaring that we should "combine confidence with caution in everything we do," seems also to make courage a mean. He points out that such a combination at first "may appear a paradox" since "caution seems to be contrary to confidence, and contraries are by no means compatible." But this, he says, is only due to "confusion." There would be a paradox "if we really called upon a man to use caution and confidence in regard to the same things . . . as uniting qualities which cannot be united." But, as Epictetus explains, caution and confidence can be united because they concern different objects.

The difference in objects which he has in mind becomes clear in the light of the Stoic maxim, "Be confident in all that lies beyond the will's control, be cautious in all that is dependent on the will." Sharply distinguishing between what does and does not lie within our control, Epictetus tells us to look with care and caution only to those things in which we can do evil by making an evil choice. "In such matters of will it is right to use caution." But in other matters, "in things outside the will's control, which do not depend on us . . . we should use confidence."

By uniting caution and confidence, we avoid the extremes of foolhardiness and cowardice and achieve the mean in which Aristotle says courage consists. Both are necessary. Cowardice is not the only vice opposed to courage. The man who acts without caution in the face of danger, recklessly disregarding what might be reasonably feared, is foolhardy rather than courageous; even as the coward is held back by fears which his reason tells him should be overcome.

Because he agrees that courage consists in avoiding both extremes, Spinoza writes that "flight at the proper time, just as well as fighting, is to be reckoned as showing strength of mind." These two acts are allied, since it is by "the same virtue of the mind" that a man "avoids danger . . . and seeks to overcome it."

To determine at a given moment whether to flee or to fight, so as to avoid either foolhardiness or cowardice, obviously involves a decision of reason. Such a decision, according to Spinoza, demands "strength of mind," by which he means "the desire by which each person endeavours from the dictates of reason alone to preserve his own being." Without rational direction or, as Aristotle would say, without prudence, one may be fearless but not courageous.

Those who, like Hobbes, do not include reason or prudence as an essential element in their conception of courage, treat courage as an emotion rather than a virtue, and tend to identify it with fearlessness, making its opposite the condition of being over-fearful. "Amongst the passions," writes Hobbes, "*courage* (by which I mean the contempt of wounds and violent death) inclines men to private revenges, and sometimes to endeavor the unsettling of the public peace; and *timorousness* many times disposes to the desertion of the public defense." As Hobbes describes courage, it may be of doubtful value to the individual or to the state. Melville seems to have this meaning of courage in mind when he says that "the most reliable and useful courage is that which arises from the fair estimation of the encountered peril"—the lack of which makes "an utterly fearless man . . . a far more dangerous companion than a coward."

If apparent fearlessness were courage, then certain animals might be called "courageous," and men of sanguine temperament, extremely self-confident or at least free from fear, would be as courageous as those who succeed in mastering their fears in order to do what is expected of them. But, as Aristotle observes, drunken men often behave fearlessly and we do not praise them for their courage. Plato likewise presents a view of courage which requires forethought and a genuine concern for danger.

"I do not call animals . . . which have no fear of dangers, because they are ignorant of them, courageous," says Nicias in the *Laches*. They are "only fearless and senseless . . . There is a difference to my way of thinking," he goes on, "between fearlessness and courage. I am of the opinion that thoughtful courage is a quality possessed by very few, but that rashness and boldness, and fearlessness, which has no forethought, are very common qualities possessed by many men, many women, many children, and many animals." According to this conception of courage, "courageous actions," Nicias says, "are wise actions."

IN LINE WITH these considerations, the definition of courage would involve a reasonable, a wise or prudent, discrimination between what should be feared and what should be undertaken in spite of peril or pain. As the Parson declares, in his discourse on the Seven Deadly Sins in the *Canterbury Tales*, "this virtue is so mighty and so vigorous that it dares to withstand sturdily, and wisely to keep itself from dangers that are wicked, and to wrestle against the assaults of the Devil. For it enhances and strengthens the soul . . . It can endure, by long suffering, the toils that are fitting."

To be able to make decisions of this sort in particular cases, a man must have some view of the order of goods and the end of life. For a man to act habitually in a courageous manner, he must be generally disposed to value certain things as more important than others, so that he is willing to take risks and endure hardships for their sake.

Freud seems to be skeptical of what he calls "the rational explanation for heroism," according to which "it consists in the decision that the personal life cannot be so precious as certain abstract general ideals." More frequent, in his opinion, "is that instinctive and impulsive hero-

ism which knows no such motivation and flouts danger in the spirit of Anzengruber's Hans the Road-Mender: 'Nothing can happen to *me*.'" But Aquinas, who emphasizes rational motivation as much as Freud discounts it, insists that courageous men "face the danger on account of the good of virtue, which is the abiding object of their will, however great the danger be."

Courage as Aquinas conceives it, though only a part of virtue in the sense of being one virtue among many, nevertheless represents the whole moral life from one point of view. The quality of courage, he points out, "overflows into the rest" of the virtues, as these in turn enter into courage. "Whoever can curb his desires for the pleasures of touch," Aquinas writes, "so that they keep within bounds, which is a very hard thing to do, for this very reason is more able to check his daring in dangers of death, so as not to go too far, which is much easier; and in this sense fortitude is said to be temperate.

"Again," he continues, "temperance is said to be brave because fortitude overflows into temperance. This is true in so far as he whose soul is strengthened by fortitude against dangers of death, which is a matter of very great difficulty, is more able to remain firm against the onslaught of pleasures; for, as Cicero says, *it would be inconsistent for a man to be unbroken by fear, and yet vanquished by cupidity, or that he should be conquered by lust, after showing himself to be unconquered by toil.*"

As the man who is temperate because he has rationally ordered his actions to a certain end can be expected to be courageous for the same reason, so, according to Aquinas, he will also be prudent, since both his temperance and his courage result from a prudent or rational choice of means to the end he pursues.

Writing as a theologian, Aquinas distinguishes what he calls "the perfecting virtues" of the religious life from "the social virtues" of the political life—the virtues with which the moral philosopher is concerned. He holds courage to be inseparable from the other virtues on either plane—whether directed to a natural or supernatural end—because it is the sameness of the end in each case which binds the virtues together. "Thus prudence by contemplating the things of God," he explains, "counts as nothing all the things of this world" and "temperance, so far as nature allows, neglects the needs of the body; fortitude prevents the soul from being afraid of neglecting the body and rising to heavenly things; and justice consists in the soul's giving a whole-hearted consent to follow the way thus proposed."

WE ARE THUS brought to the second qualification upon courage which arises from its connection with prudence, and through prudence with the other virtues. Does it make any difference whether the end for which a man strives valiantly is itself something commendable rather than despicable? If not, then the thief can have courage just as truly as the man who fears dishonor more than death; the tyrant can be courageous no less and no differently than the law-abiding citizen.

In his advice to the prince, Machiavelli seems to consider only the utility of courage. Referring to the end which he says "every man has before him, namely glory and riches," he points out that men proceed in various ways: "one with caution, another with haste; one by force, another by skill; one by patience, another by its opposite; and each one succeeds in reaching the goal by a different method." Fortune, he thinks, plays a large part in their success, and for that reason he holds no method certain. Any method requires us to use fortune to the best advantage. This demands courage and even audacity.

"It is better to be adventurous than cautious," he writes, "because fortune is a woman, and if you wish to keep her under it is necessary to beat and ill-use her; and it is seen that she allows herself to be mastered by the adventurous rather than by those who go to work more coldly. She is, therefore, always woman-like, a lover of young men, because they are less cautious, more violent, and with more audacity command her."

It would appear that Machiavelli recommends courage, or at least daring, to those who wish to succeed in great undertakings, whether the end in view is commendable or not. In either case, courage may improve the chances of success, and it is success that counts. According to their notions of courage as a virtue, Plato, Aristotle, and Aquinas sharply disagree with this, as we have already seen. So do Kant and Hegel.

"It is the positive aspect, the end and content," Hegel writes, which "gives significance to the spiritedness" of courageous actions. "Robbers and murderers bent on crime as their end, adventurers pursuing ends planned to suit their own whims, etc., these too have spirit enough to risk their lives." Because their ends are either malicious or unworthy, the mettle of a brigand and even the courage of a knight do not seem to Hegel to be true forms of courage.

According to Kant, "intelligence, wit, judgement, and other talents of the mind, however they be named, or courage, resolution, perseverance, as qualities of temperament, are undoubtedly good and desirable in many respects; but these gifts of nature may also become extremely bad and mischievous if the will which is to make use of them, and which, therefore, constitutes what is called *character*, is not good." If a good will is necessary to make courage virtuous, then the behavior of a scoundrel may look courageous, but it can only be a counterfeit. "Without the principles of a good will," such things as the ability to face dangers or to bear hardships, Kant thinks, "may become extremely bad . . . The coolness of a villain," he adds, "not only makes him far more dangerous, but also makes him more abominable in our eyes than he would have been without it."

It may still remain true that courage can take many forms according to the variety of objects which inspire fear, or according to the types of action which men find burdensome or painful. But if the truly courageous man must always be generally virtuous as well, then many of the appearances of courage do not spring from genuine virtue. The conception of virtue as a habit adds the criterion of a settled disposition: even the habitual coward may perform a single courageous act. Nor should courage be attributed to those who by freak of temperament are utterly fearless. The merit of virtue—overcoming fear—cannot be claimed by them.

IN THE GREAT political books, especially those of antiquity, the place of courage in the state and in the training of citizens receives particular attention. The constitutions of Crete and Sparta seem to make courage the only essential virtue for the citizen.

Plutarch, in his life of Lycurgus, shows how "the city was a sort of camp." The training and education of all was directed to military valor. "Their very songs had a life and spirit in them that inflamed and possessed men's minds with an enthusiasm and ardour for action ... The subject always serious and moral; most usually, it was in praise of such men as had died in defence of their country, or in derision of those that had been cowards; the former they declared happy and glorified; the life of the latter they described as most miserable and abject." The result was, according to Plutarch, that "they were the only people in the world to whom war gave repose."

Both Plato and Aristotle criticize the constitutions of Crete and Sparta for making war the end of the state and exalting courage, which is only a part, above "the whole of virtue." Courage must be joined with the other virtues to make a man good, not only as a citizen but as a man. "Justice, temperance, and wisdom," says the Athenian Stranger in the *Laws*, "when united with courage are better than courage only."

Furthermore, military courage is not even the whole of courage. While recognizing the need for it, Plato thinks that a wise statesman would put it in its proper place, if men are to be trained to be good citizens, not merely good soldiers. Arguing that no sound legislator would order "peace for the sake of war, and not war for the sake of peace," the Athenian Stranger suggests that a broader conception of courage than the Cretans and Spartans seem to have would recognize its use, not only in external warfare, but in the tasks of peace—in the struggle to lead a good life and build a good society. "What is there," he asks Megillus the Spartan and Cleinias the Cretan, "which makes your citizens equally brave against pleasure and pain, conquering what they ought to conquer, and superior to the enemies who are most dangerous and nearest home?"

Nevertheless, through the centuries the type of courage which the poets and historians celebrate has been the bravery of men who put their very lives in jeopardy for their fellow men—the courage of the citizen doing his duty, or, what is still more spectacular, of the soldier confronting the enemy. This fact among others is one reason why many writers, from the Greeks to Hegel, have found a moral stimulus in war; or, like William James, have sought for its moral equivalent. On this point they are answered not merely by those who see only degradation in war, but also by the many expressions of the insight that peace can have its heroes too.

OUTLINE OF TOPICS

REFERENCES

To find the passages cited, use the numbers in heavy type, which are the volume and page numbers of the passages referred to. For example, in 4 HOMER: *Iliad*, BK II [265–283] 12d, the number 4 is the number of the volume in the set; the number 12d indicates that the passage is in section d of page 12.

PAGE SECTIONS: When the text is printed in one column, the letters a and b refer to the upper and lower halves of the page. For example, in 53 JAMES: *Psychology*, 116a-119b, the passage begins in the upper half of page 116 and ends in the lower half of page 119. When the text is printed in two columns, the letters a and b refer to the upper and lower halves of the left-hand side of the page, the letters c and d to the upper and lower halves of the right-hand side of the page. For example, in 7 PLATO: *Symposium*, 163b-164c, the passage begins in the lower half of the left-hand side of page 163 and ends in the upper half of the right-hand side of page 164.

AUTHOR'S DIVISIONS: One or more of the main divisions of a work (such as PART, BK, CH, SECT) are sometimes included in the reference; line numbers, in brackets, are given in certain cases; *e.g.*, *Iliad*, BK II [265–283] 12d.

BIBLE REFERENCES: The references are to book, chapter, and verse. When the King James and Douay versions differ in title of books or in the numbering of chapters or verses, the King James version is cited first and the Douay, indicated by a (D), follows; *e.g.*, OLD TESTAMENT: *Nehemiah*, 7:45—(D) II Esdras, 7:46.

SYMBOLS: The abbreviation "esp" calls the reader's attention to one or more especially relevant parts of a whole reference; "passim" signifies that the topic is discussed intermittently rather than continuously in the work or passage cited.

For additional information concerning the style of the references, see the Explanation of Reference Style; for general guidance in the use of *The Great Ideas*, consult the Preface.

1. The nature of courage

4 HOMER: *Iliad*, BK XII [310–328] 85b-c; BK XIII [266–294] 91a-b; BK XVI [493–501] 117c

5 EURIPIDES: *Heracles Mad* [140–160] 366b-c

6 THUCYDIDES: *Peloponnesian War*, BK II, 396d-398c passim

7 PLATO: *Laches* 26a-37d esp 32a-37d / *Protagoras*, 57d-64d / *Cratylus*, 100c / *Apology*, 205d-206d / *Phaedo*, 225b-226c / *Republic*, BK IV, 346a-355a esp 347a-d / *Statesman*, 605d-608d / *Laws*, BK I, 644c-d

8 ARISTOTLE: *Topics*, BK IV, CH 5 [125^{b}20–27] 174d-175a; BK VI, CH 13 [151^{a}3–13] 205d

9 ARISTOTLE: *Ethics*, BK II, CH 3 [1104^{b}4–8] 350a; CH 6 [1107^{a}9]–CH 7 [1107^{b}3] 352c-353a; BK III, CH 6–9 361a-364b / *Rhetoric*, BK I, CH 9 [1366^{a}33–^{b}14] 608d-609a

12 EPICTETUS: *Discourses*, BK II, CH 1 138b,d-140c

12 AURELIUS: *Meditations*, BK XI, SECT 18 304b-305b

13 VIRGIL: *Aeneid*, BK X [466–472] 315a

14 PLUTARCH: *Numa Pompilius*, 50c / *Pelopidas*, 232a-233a / *Cleomenes*, 659d-660a

15 TACITUS: *Histories*, BK II, 227a

19 AQUINAS: *Summa Theologica*, PART I, Q 59, A 4, REP 3 309a-310a; PART I-II, Q 45, A 4, ANS 812b-813a

20 AQUINAS: *Summa Theologica*, PART I-II, Q 61, AA 2–4 55c-58b; Q 66, A 4, ANS and REP 2 78c-79b

21 DANTE: *Divine Comedy*, PARADISE, XIV [67]–XVIII [51] 127c-134a

22 CHAUCER: *Parson's Tale*, par 60–61 529b-530a

23 HOBBES: *Leviathan*, PART I, 62d; 75b; CONCLUSION, 279b

25 MONTAIGNE: *Essays*, 20d-22a; 96b-c; 115b-121c esp 117d-119d; 167a-170a

26 SHAKESPEARE: *Julius Caesar*, ACT II, SC II [32–37] 578c

27 SHAKESPEARE: *Troilus and Cressida*, ACT I, SC III [45–54] 108c / *Coriolanus*, ACT IV, SC I [1–11] 377a / *Timon of Athens*, ACT III, SC V [24–58] 407a-c

29 CERVANTES: *Don Quixote*, PART II, 256c-d; 291d

31 SPINOZA: *Ethics*, PART III, PROP 59, SCHOL 415d-416b; PART IV, PROP 69, COROL and SCHOL 445c; PROP 72–73 446b-447a

32 MILTON: *Samson Agonistes* [652–666] 353b-354a

37 FIELDING: *Tom Jones*, 70a-b

40 GIBBON: *Decline and Fall*, 93a-b

41 GIBBON: *Decline and Fall*, 159a

42 KANT: *Fund. Prin. Metaphysic of Morals*, 256a-b

46 HEGEL: *Philosophy of Right*, PART III, par 327–328 108a-c; ADDITIONS, 189 149d / *Philosophy of History*, INTRO, 195c-d; PART I, 243d-244c; PART IV, 343d-344a

48 MELVILLE: *Moby Dick*, 83a-86b

51 TOLSTOY: *War and Peace*, BK II, 77d-78a; BK IX, 369c-d; BK XI, 480a-482b esp 481d-482a; BK XIII, 577a-578b; BK XIV, 589c-590c esp 590a; 605b-d

53 JAMES: *Psychology*, 826a-827a

2. The vices opposed to courage: cowardice, foolhardiness

OLD TESTAMENT: *Exodus*, 14:9-14 / *Leviticus*, 26:32-40 / *Deuteronomy*, 20:8 / *I Samuel*, 17 esp 17:11, 17:24—(D) *I Kings*, 17 esp 17:11, 17:24 / *Proverbs*, 28:1 / *Isaiah*, 30:15-18—(D) *Isaias*, 30:15-18

APOCRYPHA: *Ecclesiasticus*, 3:26—(D) OT, *Ecclesiasticus*, 3:27

NEW TESTAMENT: *Matthew*, 26:56,69-75 / *Mark*, 14:50,66-72 / *Luke*, 22:55-61 / *John*, 7:13; 18:15-18,25-27

4 HOMER: *Iliad*, BK III 19a-23d; BK XIII [266–294] 91a-b; BK XXII [1–366] 155a-159a / *Odyssey*, BK IX [461–542] 234a-d; BK XII [111–126] 251b

5 AESCHYLUS: *Seven Against Thebes* [631–723] 34a-35a

5 SOPHOCLES: *Ajax* [733–783] 149b-d / *Electra* [947–1057] 163d-164d

5 EURIPIDES: *Suppliants* [473–510] 262c-d

5 ARISTOPHANES: *Frogs* [277–311] 567c-d; [460–674] 569c-571d

6 HERODOTUS: *History*, BK III, 120d-121b; BK VII, 216b-218b; 225c-d; BK IX, 303c-304a

6 THUCYDIDES: *Peloponnesian War*, BK I, 370a-c; BK II, 389d-390b; BK IV, 462d-463a; BK V, 484a-c

7 PLATO: *Laches*, 35c-d / *Protagoras*, 58a-59a; 63a-d / *Phaedo*, 225d-226b / *Republic*, BK V, 366c-d / *Timaeus*, 474b-d / *Theaetetus*, 513b / *Sophist*, 557b-d

9 ARISTOTLE: *Ethics*, BK II, CH 2 [1104^{a}19]–CH 3 [1104^{b}13] 349c-350a; CH 7 [1107^{a}32–^{b}3] 353a; CH 8 354a-d; BK III, CH 6 [1115^{a}10–24] 361a-b; CH 7 361c-362b; CH 8 [1116^{b}15–22] 363a; CH 12 [1119^{a}21–34] 365d-366a; BK V, CH 2 [1130^{a}13–^{b}8] 377c-378a passim; BK VII, CH 5 [1149^{a}5–8] 399c / *Politics*, BK VIII, CH 4 [1338^{b}8–38] 544a-b / *Rhetoric*, BK I, CH 9 [1366^{b}11–14] 609a; BK II, CH 13 [1389^{b}29–1390^{a}6] 637b; CH 14 [1390^{a}28–^{b}9] 637d-638a

12 EPICTETUS: *Discourses*, BK II, CH 1 138b,d-140c; CH 7 145b-146a; BK IV, CH 7 232c-235a

13 VIRGIL: *Aeneid*, BK XI [336–444] 337a-340a

14 PLUTARCH: *Aemilius Paulus*, 219d-229c / *Pelopidas*, 232a-233a; 244c-245d / *Marcellus-Pelopidas* 261a-262d / *Nicias* 423a-438d / *Demosthenes*, 695d-703b

17 PLOTINUS: *Third Ennead*, TR II, CH 8, 86d-87b

19 AQUINAS: *Summa Theologica*, PART I-II, Q 44, A 4, ANS 809c-810a; Q 45, A 4, ANS 812b-813a

20 AQUINAS: *Summa Theologica*, PART I-II, Q 105, A 3, REP 5-6 316a-318b

21 DANTE: *Divine Comedy*, HELL, I–II 1a-4a; III [22–69] 4b-d; VIII [67]–IX [105] 11c-13b

23 MACHIAVELLI: *Prince*, CH XII–XIII 17d-21a

23 HOBBES: *Leviathan*, PART II, 115d

24 RABELAIS: *Gargantua and Pantagruel*, BK IV, 264c-265a

25 MONTAIGNE: *Essays*, 22d-24a; 25c-26d; 115b-119d; 167a-170a; 334b-335a; 337b-c

26 SHAKESPEARE: *1st Henry VI*, ACT IV, SC I [9–47] 20a-b / *1st Henry IV*, ACT II, SC IV [126–312] 445c-447b; ACT IV, SC III [1–29] 459b-c / *Julius Caesar*, ACT II, SC II [32–37] 578c

27 SHAKESPEARE: *Hamlet*, ACT II, SC II [575–633] 46b-d; ACT IV, SC IV [31–66] 59a-c / *Macbeth*, ACT I, SC VII [29–82] 289c-290b

29 CERVANTES: *Don Quixote*, PART II, 256c-d; 291c-d

32 MILTON: *Paradise Lost*, BK II [204–208] 115b

37 FIELDING: *Tom Jones*, 272b

38 MONTESQUIEU: *Spirit of Laws*, BK XXVIII, 239d-240a

43 MILL: *Representative Government*, 392b-c

47 GOETHE: *Faust*, PART II [9711–9904] 235b-240b

48 MELVILLE: *Moby Dick*, 305a-307a

51 TOLSTOY: *War and Peace*, BK I, 16a-18b; BK II, 80d-81b; 102a-c; BK V, 203c-d; BK VIII, 330d-332a; BK IX, 344b-346a; 366c-367b; BK X, 419b-420d; 426b; BK XI, 475b-476c; 480a-482b; BK XIII, 569d-570a; BK XIV, 596c-d; 603a-604b; 610c-611c; BK XV, 618d-619d; EPILOGUE I, 648b-c

52 DOSTOEVSKY: *Brothers Karamazov*, BK X, 273a-d

3. The passions in the sphere of courage: fear, daring, anger, hope, despair

OLD TESTAMENT: *Exodus*, 23:27 / *Leviticus*, 26:36-38 / *Numbers*, 13:16-14:10—(D) *Numbers*, 13:17-14:10 / *Deuteronomy*, 11:23-25; 20:1-9 / *Joshua*, 2:8-11,23-24—(D) *Josue*, 2:8-11,23-24 / *Judges*, 14:19 / *Psalms*, 31:24—(D) *Psalms*, 30:25 / *Proverbs*, 29:25

APOCRYPHA: *Wisdom of Solomon*, 17—(D) OT, *Book of Wisdom*, 17 / *Ecclesiasticus*, 22:16-18; 40:1-7—(D) OT, *Ecclesiasticus*, 22:19-23; 40:1-7

NEW TESTAMENT: *Romans*, 5:1-5 / *II Corinthians*, 1:8-10 / *II Timothy*, 1:7 / *I John*, 4:18

4 HOMER: *Iliad*, BK III 19a-23d; BK XXII [1–366] 155a-159a / *Odyssey*, BK IX [461–542] 234a-d

5 AESCHYLUS: *Prometheus Bound* 40a-51d esp [944–1093] 50b-51d

5 SOPHOCLES: *Electra* [949–1195] 163d-166a

5 EURIPIDES: *Suppliants* [473–510] 262c-d

5 ARISTOPHANES: *Frogs* [277–311] 567c-d; [460–674] 569c-571d

6 HERODOTUS: *History*, BK IX, 303c-304a; 309d-310a

(3. The passions in the sphere of courage: fear, daring, anger, hope, despair.)

6 THUCYDIDES: *Peloponnesian War*, BK II, 402c-404a; BK IV, 460c-d; BK VII, 555b-557b; 559b-560b

7 PLATO: *Laches*, 36b-c / *Phaedo*, 225d-226b / *Republic*, BK IV, 346a-355a esp 347a-d / *Timaeus*, 466a-c / *Laws*, BK I, 651a-c; BK III, 675a-c

8 ARISTOTLE: *Topics*, BK IV, CH 5 [125^{b}20–27] 174d-175a

9 ARISTOTLE: *Ethics*, BK III, CH 6-9 361a-364b / *Politics*, BK VIII, CH 4 [1338^{b}8–38] 544a-b / *Rhetoric*, BK II, CH 5 628b-629d; CH 13 [1389^{b}29–1390^{a}11] 637b-c

12 LUCRETIUS: *Nature of Things*, BK I [62–158] 1d-3a; BK II [1–61] 15a-d; BK III [1–93] 30a-31b; [830–1094] 40c-44a,c; BK V [1194–1240] 76d-77b; BK VI [1–42] 80a-d

12 AURELIUS: *Meditations*, BK XI, SECT 18 304b-305b

13 VIRGIL: *Aeneid*, BK I [194–209] 108a-b; [450–465] 115b; BK VII [445–474] 248b-249a; BK IX [123–158] 282a-283a; BK XII [593–611] 370a; [650–696] 371b-372b

14 PLUTARCH: *Aemilius Paulus*, 224d-229c / *Pelopidas*, 232a-233a; 244c-245d / *Caesar*, 583b-585d / *Cleomenes*, 659d-660a

15 TACITUS: *Annals*, BK III, 49d-50a / *Histories*, BK II, 226b-227a; 235a; BK III, 249a; 265b-d

18 AUGUSTINE: *Confessions*, BK VI, par 13 39a-c / *City of God*, BK IX, CH 4-5 287a-289a; BK XIX, CH 4 511a-513c esp 512b-513c

19 AQUINAS: *Summa Theologica*, PART I, Q 59, A 4, REP 3 309a-310a; PART I-II, Q 35, A 6, REP 3 777b-778c; QQ 40–48 792d-826a,c

20 AQUINAS: *Summa Theologica*, PART I-II, Q 60, A 4, ANS 52b-53a; A 5, ANS and REP 4 53a-54d; Q 61, AA 2-3 55c-57a; A 4, ANS and REP 1-2 57a-58b; A 5, ANS and REP 1-2 58b-59d; Q 66, A 4, ANS and REP 2 78c-79b; PART III SUPPL, Q 96, A 6 1058a-1061b

21 DANTE: *Divine Comedy*, HELL, I-II 1a-4a; VIII [67]-IX [105] 11c-13b

22 CHAUCER: *Troilus and Cressida*, BK I, STANZA 68–70 10a; STANZA 80–81 11b; BK III, STANZA 129 71a-b; BK IV, STANZA 89 100a; BK V, STANZA 258 154a / *Nun's Priest's Tale* [14,914–928] 451b / *Parson's Tale*, par 60–61 529b-530a

23 MACHIAVELLI: *Prince*, CH XVII, 24a-b; CH XIX, 26c-d

23 HOBBES: *Leviathan*, PART I, 62c-63a esp 62d; 68d; 77d; 79b-d; 96b

24 RABELAIS: *Gargantua and Pantagruel*, BK IV, 261a-266c; 297b-d

25 MONTAIGNE: *Essays*, 20d-22a; 25c-26d; 53c-55d; 115b-119d; 167a-170a; 334b-335a; 337b-c; 342a-d; 435a-d

26 SHAKESPEARE: *1st Henry IV*, ACT I, SC III 437d-440d; ACT II, SC III 443b-444b; ACT IV, SC III [1–29] 459b-c / *Julius Caesar*, ACT II, SC

II [34–37] 578c; ACT IV, SC III [145–195] 589d-590c

27 SHAKESPEARE: *Macbeth*, ACT I, SC VII 289b-290b / *Coriolanus*, ACT IV, SC I [1–33] 377a-b / *Timon of Athens*, ACT III, SC V [24–58] 407a-c / *Henry VIII*, ACT I, SC II [68–88] 553c-d

31 SPINOZA: *Ethics*, PART III, PROP 51, SCHOL 411d-412a; THE AFFECTS, DEF 39–41 420d; PART IV, PROP 69, COROL and SCHOL 445c

33 PASCAL: *Pensées*, 215 212a

35 LOCKE: *Human Understanding*, BK II, CH XX, SECT 9-12 177b-c

37 FIELDING: *Tom Jones*, 52a-53b; 69a-70c; 111d-112b; 234a-b

38 MONTESQUIEU: *Spirit of Laws*, BK I, 2b-d

38 ROUSSEAU: *Inequality*, 335c-d

42 KANT: *Judgement*, 502d-503d

44 BOSWELL: *Johnson*, 394a-c

47 GOETHE: *Faust*, PART II [5407–5456] 133b-134b; [9711–9904] 235b-240b

48 MELVILLE: *Moby Dick*, 83a-85a; 90b; 118a-131a; 417b-418a

51 TOLSTOY: *War and Peace*, BK I, 17b-18a; 48c; BK II, 77c-81b; 95a-c; 97c-106d; BK III, 134a-135c; 150a-164a,c; BK IV, 173d-177a; 188a-190c; BK V, 203c-d; BK IX, 369a-372a; BK X, 419b-420c; 451c-456a; 457a-c; 461d-463c; 467a-468a,c; BK XI, 480a-482b; 513d-515a esp 514c-d; 527b-532a,c; BK XII, 549d-551c; 560a-562d; BK XIII, 569d-570a; 586d-587c; BK XV, 614a-618b; 627a-c; EPILOGUE I, 648b-c

52 DOSTOEVSKY: *Brothers Karamazov*, BK VI, 155d-157b

53 JAMES: *Psychology*, 826a-b

54 FREUD: *General Introduction*, 607d-608c; 613d-614a / *War and Death*, 762b-c; 765a-b

4. The relation and comparison of courage with other virtues

5 SOPHOCLES: *Electra* [947–1057] 163d-164d

5 EURIPIDES: *Phoenician Maidens* [697–747] 384a-d

6 THUCYDIDES: *Peloponnesian War*, BK I, 370a-c; BK II, 402d-403b; 411b-c; BK VII, 555b-557b

7 PLATO: *Laches*, 31d-37d / *Protagoras*, 57d-64d esp 58a-c, 63a-64a / *Cratylus*, 100c / *Meno*, 183d-184c / *Phaedo*, 225d-226b / *Gorgias*, 284a-c / *Republic*, BK IV, 346a-350a; BK VIII, 404a-405c / *Timaeus*, 466a-c / *Sophist*, 557b-d / *Statesman*, 605d-608d / *Laws*, BK I, 643a-d; 644b-645c; 651a-c; BK III, 673d-674a; 675a-c; BK XII, 795c-796b

8 ARISTOTLE: *Topics*, BK III, CH 2 [117^{a}35–^{b}2] 164a; [118^{a}16–17] 165a

9 ARISTOTLE: *Ethics*, BK II, CH 2 [1104^{a}19]-CH 3 [1104^{b}13] 349c-350a; CH 8 354a-d; BK III, CH 11 [1118^{b}28–34] 365b-c; CH 12 [1119^{a}21–34] 365d-366a; BK V, CH 2 [1130^{a}13–^{b}8] 377c-378a passim; BK VI, CH 13 [1144^{b}1–1145^{a}5] 394a-d; BK IX, CH 4 [1166^{b}8–12] 419d; BK X, CH 7 [1177^{a}28–^{b}25] 432a-c / *Politics*, BK VII, CH 1 [1323^{a}22–34] 527a-b; CH 2 [1324^{a}23–1325^{a}15] 528b-529a passim; CH 7 531d-532c; CH 15 [1334^{a}11–^{b}8]

539a-c; BK VIII, CH 4 [1338ᵇ8–38] 544a-b /
Rhetoric, BK I, CH 9 [1366ᵃ33–ᵇ14] 608d-609a;
BK II, CH 14 637d-638a

12 EPICTETUS: *Discourses*, BK II, CH I 138b,d-
140c

12 AURELIUS: *Meditations*, BK XI, SECT 18 304b-
305b

14 PLUTARCH: *Coriolanus*, 175b / *Cato the
Younger*, 637b-c

15 TACITUS: *Histories*, BK I, 211c-212b

17 PLOTINUS: *Third Ennead*, TR II, CH 8, 86d-87b

18 AUGUSTINE: *City of God*, BK XIX, CH 4, 511d-
513c; CH 20 523d-524a

19 AQUINAS: *Summa Theologica*, PART I-II, Q 35,
A 6, REP 3 777b-778a

20 AQUINAS: *Summa Theologica*, PART I-II, Q 60,
A 4-Q 61, A 5 52b-59d; Q 65, AA 1-3 70b-73d;
Q 66, AA 1-4 75b-79b; PART III SUPPL, Q 96,
A 6, ANS and REP 3-4,8-9 1058a-1061b; A 12
1064d-1065b

22 CHAUCER: *Parson's Tale*, par 60–61 529b-530a

23 HOBBES: *Leviathan*, PART I, 62c-63a; CONCLU-
SION, 279c

24 RABELAIS: *Gargantua and Pantagruel*, BK III,
133b-134d

25 MONTAIGNE: *Essays*, 183a-c

26 SHAKESPEARE: *Julius Caesar*, ACT IV, SC III
[145–195] 589d-590c

27 SHAKESPEARE: *Coriolanus*, ACT II, SC II [86–
91] 365a / *Timon of Athens*, ACT III, SC V [24–
58] 407a-c

29 CERVANTES: *Don Quixote*, PART II, 256c-d;
291d

30 BACON: *Advancement of Learning*, 80a-81a

31 SPINOZA: *Ethics*, PART III, PROP 51, SCHOL
411d-412a; PART IV, PROP 73, SCHOL 446d-
447a

32 MILTON: *Samson Agonistes* [38–59] 340b;
[652–666] 353b-354a

42 KANT: *Fund. Prin. Metaphysic of Morals*, 256a-
b / *Pref. Metaphysical Elements of Ethics*, 377d

44 BOSWELL: *Johnson*, 251a; 539b

46 HEGEL: *Philosophy of History*, PART IV, 343d-
344a

48 MELVILLE: *Moby Dick*, 45a-46a; 83a-85a

49 DARWIN: *Descent of Man*, 315b-d

51 TOLSTOY: *War and Peace*, BK X, 440d-442a; BK
XI, 481a-482a

52 DOSTOEVSKY: *Brothers Karamazov*, BK VI,
155d-157b

5. The motivations of courage: fame or honor, happiness, love, duty, religious faith

OLD TESTAMENT: *Genesis*, 22:1-14 / *Numbers*,
13:16-14:10—(D) *Numbers*, 13:17-14:10 /
Deuteronomy, 7:16-24; 20:1-9; 31:6-8 / *Joshua*,
1:5-9; 23:6-11—(D) *Josue*, 1:5-9; 23:6-11 /
Judges, 7 / *I Samuel*, 17; 20—(D) *I Kings*,
17; 20 / *I Chronicles*, 22:12-13; 28:20—(D)
I Paralipomenon, 22:12-13; 28:20 / *Esther*, 4:1-
5:8 / *Psalms*, 27; 46; 56:4; 91; 118—(D)
Psalms, 26; 45; 55:5; 90; 117 / *Proverbs*, 28:1;
29:25 / *Isaiah*, 12:2; 35:4; 41:10-16; 43:1-7;

51:7-13—(D) *Isaias*, 12:2; 35:4; 41:10-16;
43:1-7; 51:7-13 / *Daniel*, 1; 3:1-4:3; 6:1-22—
(D) *Daniel*, 1; 3:1-23,91-100; 6:1-22

APOCRYPHA: *Judith*, 8-13—(D) OT, *Judith*, 8:1-
13:26 / *Song of Three Children*—(D) OT,
Daniel, 3:24-90 / *Susanna*—(D) OT, *Daniel*,
13:1-64 / *I Maccabees*, 2:49-64; 6:43-46; 9:7-
10; 13:1-6—(D) OT, *I Machabees*, 2:49-64;
6:43-46; 9:7-10; 13:1-6 / *II Maccabees*, 6:18-
7:42; 8:12-22; 11:7-11; 13:10-15; 14:37-46;
15:7-27—(D) OT, *II Machabees*, 6:18-7:42;
8:12-22; 11:7-11; 13:10-15; 14:37-46; 15:7-27

NEW TESTAMENT: *Matthew*, 5:10-12; 10:26-31 /
Luke, 1:70-75; 12:32 / *John*, 15:13 / *Acts* esp
4:1-30, 5:40-41, 6:8-7:60, 16:1-40, 19:1-41,
20:22-24—(D) *Acts* esp 4:1-30, 5:40-41,
6:8-7:59, 16:1-40, 19:1-40, 20:22-24 / *Romans*,
8:31-39 / *II Corinthians*, 1:1-12; 6:4-10; 11:23-
30 / *Philippians*, 1:27-28; 2:29-30 / *II Thessalonians*, 1:4-5 / *Hebrews*, 11; 13:6 / *I Peter*,
3:8-22

4 HOMER: *Iliad*, BK V [520–532] 35c; BK VI
[369–502] 43d-45a; BK VIII [130–156] 52c; BK
XII [310–328] 85b-c; BK XIII [206–294] 90b-
91b; BK XVI [493–501] 117c; BK XXII [77–130]
156a-c; [289–305] 158b

5 AESCHYLUS: *Seven Against Thebes* [630–723]
34a-35a / *Prometheus Bound* 40a-51d

5 SOPHOCLES: *Antigone* 131a-142d / *Ajax* [430–
480] 146d-147b / *Electra* [949–1195] 163d-166a

5 EURIPIDES: *Heracleidae* [484–573] 252c-253a /
Suppliants [297–356] 261a-c / *Hecuba* [343–
383] 355d-356a; [482–603] 357a-358a / *Heracles Mad* [275–311] 367c-d / *Phoenician
Maidens* [991–1030] 387a-b / *Iphigenia at Aulis*
[1375–1565] 437c-439b

5 ARISTOPHANES: *Knights* [565–580] 477a-b

6 HERODOTUS: *History*, BK IV, 126a-b; BK VII,
216b-220b; 226b-c; 233a-234b; 255c-d; BK
VIII, 264c; 274d; BK IX, 291c-292a; 303c-304a;
309d-310a

6 THUCYDIDES: *Peloponnesian War*, BK I, 370a-
c; BK II, 396b-399a esp 397d-398c; 402c-404a;
BK V, 484a-c; 501a-b; BK VI, 527b-d; BK VII,
542b-c; 555b-557b; 559d-560b

7 PLATO: *Symposium*, 152b-153b; 160c / *Phaedo*,
225b-226c / *Republic*, BK V, 366c-367b / *Laws*,
BK I, 651a-652a; BK III, 675a-c / *Seventh Letter*,
800c-d

9 ARISTOTLE: *Ethics*, BK III, CH 6-9 361a-364b;
BK IV, CH 3 [1124ᵇ7-9] 371b-c / *Politics*, BK V,
CH 10 [1312ᵃ24-39] 514d; BK VII, CH 2 [1324ᵇ
10-23] 528c-d / *Rhetoric*, BK I, CH 9 [1366ᵇ11-
14] 609a

10 HIPPOCRATES: *Airs, Waters, Places*, par 16 15d-
16a; par 23 18a-c

12 EPICTETUS: *Discourses*, BK III, CH 22 195a-
201a; CH 24 203c-210a

13 VIRGIL: *Aeneid*, BK I [441–493] 115a-116b; BK
VIII [520–540] 273a-b; BK X [276–286] 309b-
310a; [466–472] 315a; BK XI [376–444] 338b-
340a; BK XII [53–80] 355b-356a; [650–696]
371b-372b

6. The formation or training of the courageous man

13 VIRGIL: *Aeneid*, BK VIII [494–520] 272a-273a; BK IX [590–620] 295a-b; BK XII [425–440] 365b

14 PLUTARCH: *Lycurgus*, 39a-45c / *Coriolanus*, 175b / *Pelopidas*, 238b-239c / *Cleomenes*, 661a-663c

24 RABELAIS: *Gargantua and Pantagruel*, BK I, 28a-29b

25 MONTAIGNE: *Essays*, 331a-332a; 336c-337b

30 BACON: *Advancement of Learning*, 23a

39 SMITH: *Wealth of Nations*, BK V, 303b-305c; 337d-338a

40 GIBBON: *Decline and Fall*, 93d-94b; 644b-645d esp 645a

41 GIBBON: *Decline and Fall*, 223a; 224a

42 KANT: *Practical Reason*, 325d-327d / *Judgement*, 504a-b

43 MILL: *Liberty*, 282b-283a

51 TOLSTOY: *War and Peace*, BK IV, 175a-b; BK IX, 369c-d; BK XI, 481a-482a; BK XIV, 605b-d

53 JAMES: *Psychology*, 82b-83a

7. The political or civic significance of courage

7*a*. The courage required of citizens and statesmen: the political recognition of courage

4 HOMER: *Iliad*, BK XII [310–328] 85b-c

5 SOPHOCLES: *Ajax* [1264–1363] 154a-d / *Philoctetes* [1418–1433] 195a

5 EURIPIDES: *Rhesus* [150–202] 204c-205a / *Heracleidae* [489–573] 252c-253a / *Suppliants* [297–356] 261a-c / *Hecuba* [300–330] 355b-c / *Phoenician Maidens* [991–1018] 387a-b / *Iphigenia at Aulis* [1368–1562] 437c-439b

5 ARISTOPHANES: *Knights* [565–580] 477a-b / *Wasps* [1060–1121] 520c-521b

6 HERODOTUS: *History*, BK VII, 225c-d; 226b-c; 233a-234b; 239a-c; 256c-257c; BK VIII, 282c-283a; BK IX, 291c-292a; 293c-294d

6 THUCYDIDES: *Peloponnesian War*, BK II, 396b-399a; 402c-404a; BK VII, 555b-557b; 559d-560b

7 PLATO: *Apology*, 207b-d / *Crito*, 217b-c / *Republic*, BK II, 319c-320c; BK IV, 347a-d; BK V, 366c-367b / *Statesman*, 605e-608d / *Laws*, BK I, 644a-645c; BK XII, 784d-786b

9 ARISTOTLE: *Ethics*, BK III, CH 8 [1116^{a}15–^{b}3] 362b-d; BK V, CH I [1129^{b}19–24] 377a / *Politics*, BK III, CH 4 [1277^{a}8–25] 474a-b; CH 12 [1283^{a}18–20] 481b; BK VII, CH 2 [1324^{b}5–23] 528c-d; CH 7 531d-532c; CH 15 [1334^{a}11–^{b}6] 539a-b; BK VIII, CH 4 [1338^{b}8–38] 544a-b

12 EPICTETUS: *Discourses*, BK II, CH 10 148c-150a; BK III, CH 24 203c-210a

12 AURELIUS: *Meditations*, BK III, SECT 5 261a; BK V, SECT I 268b,d

13 VIRGIL: *Aeneid*, BK VI [781–807] 232a-b; BK XI [225–444] 334a-340a

14 PLUTARCH: *Lycurgus*, 40c-45c / *Poplicola*, 83b-84a / *Coriolanus*, 177b-179a; 180d-181b / *Aemilius Paulus*, 226c-229c / *Pyrrhus*, 328c-330a / *Nicias*, 423a-430d / *Cato the Younger* 620a-648a,c / *Cleomenes*, 659d-660a / *Demosthenes*, 695d-703b / *Aratus*, 835b-c

15 TACITUS: *Annals*, BK I, 16d-17a; BK XII, 117a

17 PLOTINUS: *Third Ennead*, TR II, CH 8, 86d-87b

20 AQUINAS: *Summa Theologica*, PART I–II, Q 105, A 3, ANS and REP 5–6 316a-318b

23 MACHIAVELLI: *Prince*, CH III, 5c; CH VI, 9b-c; CH VIII, 14b-c; CH IX, 15a-b; CH X, 16b-c; CH XVII 23d-24d; CH XIX 26a-30a; CH XXI, 32a-d; CH XXIV–XXVI, 34d-37d

23 HOBBES: *Leviathan*, PART II, 115d; CONCLUSION, 279b-c

25 MONTAIGNE: *Essays*, 53c-55d; 181d-183c; 327d-329d; 331a-332a

26 SHAKESPEARE: *Richard III*, ACT V, SC III [237–341] 146b-147c / *Henry V*, ACT III, SC I 543d-544b; ACT IV, SC III [1–78] 555c-556c; SC V 558a-b / *Julius Caesar* 568a-596a,c esp ACT I, SC II [84–96] 570b, ACT V, SC V [68–81] 596a,c

27 SHAKESPEARE: *Troilus and Cressida*, ACT I, SC III [33–54] 108c / *Coriolanus*, ACT II, SC II [86–138] 365a-c; ACT IV, SC I [1–11] 377a / *Timon of Athens*, ACT IV, SC V 406d-408a / *Cymbeline*, ACT V, SC III 479d-480d / *Henry VIII*, ACT I, SC II [68–88] 553c-d

29 CERVANTES: *Don Quixote*, PART I, 40d

30 BACON: *Advancement of Learning*, 23a

31 SPINOZA: *Ethics*, PART IV, PROP 72–73 446b-447a

32 MILTON: *Lord Gen. Cromwell* 69a-b / *Sr Henry Vane* 69b / *Paradise Lost*, BK II [430–456] 120b-121a

38 MONTESQUIEU: *Spirit of Laws*, BK III, 12b-c; BK IV, 15a-c; BK XIV, 107b-d; BK XXX, 281a

38 ROUSSEAU: *Political Economy*, 375a / *Social Contract*, BK III, 411b-c; BK IV, 437d-438c

40 GIBBON: *Decline and Fall*, 23c; 369d-370c; 427a-c; 630b,d-631a; 644d-645c

43 MILL: *Representative Government*, 329b-c; 334b-c; 392b-c

46 HEGEL: *Philosophy of Right*, PART III, par 325 107d; par 328 108b-c; ADDITIONS, 189 149d / *Philosophy of History*, PART I, 213d-214a

49 DARWIN: *Descent of Man*, 315b-c; 321b-c

51 TOLSTOY: *War and Peace*, BK I, 9c-10d; BK III, 149d-150a; BK X, 445c; BK XI, 475b-476c; 513d-515a; BK XII, 537b-538a; BK XIV, 610c-611c; EPILOGUE I, 648b-c; 668a-669c

7*b*. Courage in relation to law and liberty

6 HERODOTUS: *History*, BK V, 175b; BK VII, 232c-233d; 238a-c; 239a-c

6 THUCYDIDES: *Peloponnesian War*, BK II, 396b-399a; 402c-404a; BK IV, 469d-470b; 478d-479b; BK V, 484a-c; BK VII, 555b-557b

7 PLATO: *Apology* 200a-212a,c / *Crito* 213a-219a,c / *Laws*, BK I, 644a-645c; BK III, 675a-c; BK XII, 784d-786b

9 ARISTOTLE: *Ethics*, BK III, CH 8 [1116^{a}15–^{b}24] 362b-363a / *Politics*, BK V, CH 10 [1312^{a}18–39] 514d; CH 11 [1313^{a}34–^{b}10] 516a-b; BK VII, CH 7 531d-532c; CH 15 [1334^{a}19–22] 539a / *Rhetoric*, BK I, CH 9 [1366^{b}1–14] 608d-609a

10 HIPPOCRATES: *Airs, Waters, Places*, par 16 15d-16a; par 23 18a-c

(7. The political or civic significance of courage.
7b. Courage in relation to law and liberty.)

14 PLUTARCH: *Cato the Younger* 620a-648a,c esp 643a-644b / *Cleomenes*, 659d-660a / *Aratus*, 826c-836d

15 TACITUS: *Annals*, BK XII, 117a; BK XVI, 180d-184a / *Histories*, BK IV, 271b

17 PLOTINUS: *Third Ennead*, TR II, CH 8, 86d-87b

20 AQUINAS: *Summa Theologica*, PART I-II, Q 105, A 3, ANS and REP 5-6 316a-318b

23 MACHIAVELLI: *Prince*, CH V 8a-c; CH X, 16b-d; CH XXVI 36b-37d

23 HOBBES: *Leviathan*, PART II, 113b

25 MONTAIGNE: *Essays*, 23b-24a

31 SPINOZA: *Ethics*, PART IV, PROP 72-73 446b-447a

32 MILTON: *Lord Gen. Fairfax* 68b-69a / *Samson Agonistes* [888–902] 359a

38 MONTESQUIEU: *Spirit of Laws*, BK III, 12b-c; BK IV, 15a-c; BK XIV, 107b-d; BK XVII, 122a-b

38 ROUSSEAU: *Inequality*, 324c / *Social Contract*, BK I, 388c; BK III, 411b-c; BK IV, 437d-438c

40 GIBBON: *Decline and Fall*, 23c; 523d-524a

41 GIBBON: *Decline and Fall*, 223a; 224a; 324c-325a

42 KANT: *Science of Right*, 448d-449c

43 MILL: *Liberty*, 282b-283a / *Representative Government*, 329b-c

46 HEGEL: *Philosophy of Right*, PART III, par 324, 107c-d

47 GOETHE: *Faust*, PART II [9855–9862] 239b

51 TOLSTOY: *War and Peace*, BK XI, 513d-515a; EPILOGUE I, 668a-669c

7c. Courage in war

OLD TESTAMENT: *Deuteronomy*, 20:1-4,8 / *Judges*, 14-16 / *I Samuel*, 14:4-13; 17—(D) *I Kings*, 14:4-13; 17

APOCRYPHA: *Judith*, 8-13—(D) OT, *Judith*, 8:1-13:26 / *I Maccabees*, 6:43-46; 9:1-22—(D) OT, *I Machabees*, 6:43-46; 9:1-22

4 HOMER: *Iliad* 3a-179d esp BK III 19a-23d, BK VI [369–502] 43d-45a, BK XII [310–328] 85b-c, BK XIII [206–294] 90b-91b, BK XVI [493–501] 117c, BK XXII [77–130] 156a-c, BK XXIII [1–367] 161a-165a

5 AESCHYLUS: *Persians* 15a-26d esp [331–432] 18d-19d / *Seven Against Thebes* [630–723] 34a-35a

5 EURIPIDES: *Suppliants* [857–917] 266a-b / *Phoenician Maidens* [697–747] 384a-d; [991–1030] 387a-b

5 ARISTOPHANES: *Knights* [565–580] 477a-b / *Wasps* [1060–1121] 520c-521b

6 HERODOTUS: *History*, BK VII, 233a-d; 239a-c; 252a-259a esp 256d-257c; BK IX, 291c-292a; 298c-304c; 309d-310a

6 THUCYDIDES: *Peloponnesian War*, BK I, 367c-368a; 370a-c; BK II, 389d-390b; 396b-399a; 402c-404a; 411b-412c; BK IV, 457b-c; 460c-d; 469d-470b; 478d-479b; BK V, 484a-c; 491b-c;

501a-b; BK VI, 522b-c; 527b-c; BK VII, 555b-557b; 559b-560b; 561a-b

7 PLATO: *Laches*, 32a-c / *Symposium*, 172a-b / *Apology*, 205d-206a / *Crito*, 217b-c / *Republic*, BK III, 324c-325b; BK IV, 347a-d; BK V, 366c-367b / *Timaeus*, 445d-446b / *Laws*, BK I, 642b-643a; BK XII, 784d-786b

8 ARISTOTLE: *Topics*, BK VI, CH 13 [151ª3-13] 205d

9 ARISTOTLE: *Ethics*, BK III, CH 6 [1115ª24-35] 361b-c; CH 8 [1116ª15-b24] 362b-363a; BK V, CH 1 [1129b19-24] 377a / *Politics*, BK II, CH 9 [1269b34-39] 466a; BK III, CH 7 [1279ª40-b3] 476d; BK V, CH 10 [1312ª25-39] 514d; BK VII, CH 11 [1330b32-1331ª8] 535c; BK VIII, CH 4 [1338b8-38] 544a-b / *Rhetoric*, BK I, CH 9 [1366b1-14] 608d-609a

10 HIPPOCRATES: *Airs, Waters, Places*, par 16 15d-16a; par 23 18a-c

13 VIRGIL: *Aeneid*, BK II 124a-146b; BK IX-XII 279a-379b

14 PLUTARCH: *Lycurgus*, 40c-45c / *Poplicola*, 83b-84a / *Coriolanus*, 177b-179a / *Aemilius Paulus*, 219d-229c / *Pelopidas*, 232a-233a; 238b-239c / *Marcellus* 246b,d-261a,c / *Marcellus-Pelopidas* 261a-262d / *Philopoemen* 293a-302a,c / *Pyrrhus*, 328c-330a / *Nicias* 423a-438d / *Caesar*, 583b-585d / *Cleomenes*, 659d-660a; 661a-663c / *Demosthenes*, 695d-703b / *Aratus*, 826c-836d

15 TACITUS: *Annals*, BK II, 44d-45a; BK III, 49d-50a; BK XII, 117a-b / *Histories*, BK I, 210c; 211c-212b; BK II, 226d-227a; 232d-233a; BK III, 246b-c; 248b-c; 249a

20 AQUINAS: *Summa Theologica*, PART I-II, Q 105, A 3, ANS and REP 5-6 316a-318b

22 CHAUCER: *Troilus and Cressida*, BK I, STANZA 68–70 10a; BK II, STANZA 88–93 33a-b; BK V, STANZA 258 154a

23 MACHIAVELLI: *Prince*, CH X, 16c-d; CH XII-XIII 17d-21a

23 HOBBES: *Leviathan*, PART II, 115d

24 RABELAIS: *Gargantua and Pantagruel*, BK I, 32c-35a; BK IV, 297b-d

25 MONTAIGNE: *Essays*, 3a-5a; 20d-22a; 22d-24a; 25c-26d; 53c-55d; 95d-97b; 302b-306a; 327d-329d; 336c-337a; 532d-533a

26 SHAKESPEARE: *1st Henry VI*, ACT IV, SC V-VI 23d-25a / *3rd Henry VI*, ACT V, SC IV [1–59] 101a-c / *Richard III*, ACT V, SC III [237–341] 146b-147c / *King John*, ACT V, SC I [44–79] 399d-400a / *1st Henry IV*, ACT I, SC III 437d-440d; ACT II, SC III 443b-444b; ACT IV, SC III [1–29] 459b-c / *Henry V*, ACT III, SC I 543b-544b; ACT IV, SC III [1–78] 555c-556c; SC V 558a-b

27 SHAKESPEARE: *Hamlet*, ACT IV, SC IV [46–66] 59b-c / *Troilus and Cressida*, ACT II, SC II 113c-115d / *Coriolanus*, ACT I, SC IV [8–63] 356c-357c; SC VI [55–87] 358d-359a; ACT II, SC II [86–135] 365a-c / *Timon of Athens*, ACT III, SC V 406d-408a / *Cymbeline*, ACT V, SC III 479d-480d

29 CERVANTES: *Don Quixote*, PART I, 147b-d; PART II, 203a-b; 280b-c

32 MILTON: *Lord Gen. Fairfax* 68b-69a / *Paradise Lost*, BK II [430-466] 120b-121a

38 MONTESQUIEU: *Spirit of Laws*, BK XIV, 102b,d-103a; BK XXVIII, 239d-240a

38 ROUSSEAU: *Social Contract*, BK IV, 437d-438c

40 GIBBON: *Decline and Fall*, 93d-94b; 94d; 369d-376a esp 370a-c, 375b-c; 427a-c

41 GIBBON: *Decline and Fall*, 19d-20a; 238c; 324c-325a; 357c-359c; 534b-536d passim; 543a-551a passim, esp 543d-544a, 549c-550c

42 KANT: *Judgement*, 504a-b

44 BOSWELL: *Johnson*, 384b-c

46 HEGEL: *Philosophy of Right*, ADDITIONS, 189 149d / *Philosophy of History*, PART I, 242d-243b; PART II, 274a-275a; PART IV, 343d-344a

47 GOETHE: *Faust*, PART II [9435-9505] 228b-230b

49 DARWIN: *Descent of Man*, 321c

51 TOLSTOY: *War and Peace*, BK II, 77c-81b; 95a-c; 97c-106d; BK III, 134a-135c; 149a-164a,c; BK IX, 344b-346a; 366d-367b; 369a-372a; BK X, 426b; 441d-442c; 445c; 451c-456a; 457a-c; 461d-463c; 467a-468a,c; BK XI, 475b-476c; 480a-482b; 517d-518a; BK XII, 537b-538a; BK XIII, 569d-570a; 586d-587c; BK XIV, 589c-590c; 590d-604b passim; 610c-611c; 613a-c; BK XV, 627a-c

CROSS-REFERENCES

For: The general theory of virtue and the virtues, *see* VIRTUE AND VICE.

The virtues most closely related to courage, *see* JUSTICE; PRUDENCE; TEMPERANCE.

The relation of these other virtues to courage, *see* PRUDENCE 3a-3b, 3e; TEMPERANCE 1a; VIRTUE AND VICE 2-3b.

Courage and other virtues in relation to happiness and duty, *see* HAPPINESS 2b(3); VIRTUE AND VICE 1d, 6a.

Matters relevant to the emotional aspects of courage, *see* EMOTION 4b(1); PLEASURE AND PAIN 8a; VIRTUE AND VICE 5a.

The general consideration of moral training, *see* EDUCATION 4-4d; VIRTUE AND VICE 4-4e(3).

The general consideration of civic virtue, *see* CITIZEN 5; STATE 8b-8c; VIRTUE AND VICE 7-7d; and for courage as a military virtue, *see* WAR AND PEACE 10c.

The analysis of the heroic and the conception of the hero, *see* HONOR 5-5a, 5c.

ADDITIONAL READINGS

Listed below are works not included in *Great Books of the Western World*, but relevant to the idea and topics with which this chapter deals. These works are divided into two groups:

> I. Works by authors represented in this collection.
> II. Works by authors not represented in this collection.

For the date, place, and other facts concerning the publication of the works cited, consult the Bibliography of Additional Readings which follows the last chapter of *The Great Ideas*.

I.

AQUINAS. *Summa Theologica*, PART II-II, QQ 123-140

F. BACON. "Of Boldness," in *Essays*

MILTON. *The Readie and Easie Way to Establish a Free Commonwealth*

DOSTOEVSKY. *The Idiot*

II.

THEOPHRASTUS. *The Characters*

CICERO. *De Officiis* (*On Duties*), III

SENECA. *De Constantia Sapientis* (*On the Firmness of the Wise Man*)

Sir Gawain and the Green Knight

P. SIDNEY. *The Countess of Pembroke's Arcadia*

CORNEILLE. *Polyeucte*

VAUVENARGUES. *Introduction à la connaissance de l'esprit humain*, PART I, CH I

MORGANN. *Essay on the Dramatic Character of Sir John Falstaff*

LEOPARDI. *Essays, Dialogues, and Thoughts*

STENDHAL. *The Charterhouse of Parma*

T. CARLYLE. *On Heroes, Hero-Worship and the Heroic in History*

EMERSON. "Courage," in *Society and Solitude*

T. H. GREEN. *Prolegomena to Ethics*, IV

CRANE. *The Red Badge of Courage*

ROSTAND. *Cyrano de Bergerac*

RANK. *The Myth of the Birth of the Hero*

G. W. RUSSELL. *The Hero in Man*

ROUTH. *God, Man, and Epic Poetry*

RAGLAN. *The Hero*

Chapter 14: CUSTOM AND CONVENTION

INTRODUCTION

THE contrast between the artificial and the natural is generally understood in terms of the contribution which man does or does not make to the origin or character of a thing. Works of art are man-made. The artificial is somehow humanly caused or contrived. The contrast between the natural and the conventional or customary involves the same point of difference. Though customs are not, in the strict sense, *made* by man, as are works of art, they do grow only as the result of the kind of acts which men perform voluntarily rather than instinctively. Similarly, conventions, like contracts, are social arrangements or agreements into which men enter voluntarily.

The fundamental notions with which this chapter deals are thus seen to be closely related to ideas and distinctions treated in the chapters on ART and NATURE. For example, the distinction between human action and production, or doing and making, helps us to understand how the conventional and the artificial differ from one another as opposites of the natural. Art involves voluntary making. Customs result from voluntary doing. In both cases, the distinction between the voluntary and the instinctive—the latter representing the natural—seems to be presupposed.

A third term—habit—is traditionally associated with the consideration of the voluntary and the instinctive. Like these others, it seems to have a critical bearing on the discussion of custom and art. Aristotle, for example, conceives art as an intellectual virtue, that is, a habit of mind, an acquired skill. For Hume the customary and the habitual are almost the same. Whether they are to be identified or are only connected causally, the relation of habit to custom not only throws some light on the nature of custom, but also calls our attention to the fact that the words "custom" and "convention" cannot be treated simply as synonyms.

In the tradition of the great books, the word "convention" has at least two meanings, in only one of which is it synonymous with "custom." When "convention" is used to signify habitual social practices it is, for the most part, interchangeable with "custom." In this significance, the notion of convention, like that of custom, is an extension of the idea of habit. What habit is in the behavior of the individual, customary or conventional conduct is in the behavior of the social group.

The other meaning of "convention" does not connote the habitual in social behavior, but stresses rather the voluntary as opposed to the instinctive origin of social institutions, arrangements, or practices. For example, different sorts of family organization are conventional in the sense that at different times or in different communities men have set up their domestic arrangements in different ways. In each case they tend to perpetuate the particular institutions which they or their ancestors originated. Whatever is conventional about social institutions might have been otherwise, if men had seen fit to invent and adopt different schemes for the organization of their social life. This indicates the connection between the two senses of the word "convention," for all customs are conventional in origin, and all conventions become customary when perpetuated.

THE FACT THAT men can depart from, as well as abide by, their conventions—that they can transgress as well as conform to custom—seems to indicate that custom and convention belong to the sphere of human freedom. Yet there is also a sense in which custom is a constraining force, which reduces the tendency of individuals to differ from one another, and which has the effect of moulding them alike and regimenting their lives.

The repressive effect of custom can be seen, according to Freud, in the neurotic disorders from which men suffer when their instinctive impulses come into conflict with "accepted custom." Discussing the influence of custom upon the developing individual, he says that "its ordinances, frequently too stringent, exact a great deal from him, much self-restraint, much renunciation of instinctual gratification." It becomes, therefore, one of the aims of psychoanalytic therapy to release the individual from his bondage to custom, or at least to make him conscious of the way in which certain desires have been submerged or distorted, and his whole personality shaped, by the constraints which the mores and taboos of the tribe have imposed upon him.

Considered in relation to society, custom also seems to exercise a conservative, if not repressive effect. Established customs tend to resist change. They are sometimes thought to impede progress. But to the extent that they conserve the achievements of the past, they may be indispensable to progress because they provide the substance of what we call "tradition." A passage in Bacon's *Advancement of Learning* illustrates these apparently contrary effects of custom.

Over-emphasis upon either antiquity or novelty seems to Bacon a disease of learning, or an obstacle to its advancement. "Antiquity envieth there should be new additions," he writes, "and novelty cannot be content to add but it must deface." If custom tends to support antiquity against novelty, it may also encourage inventions or discoveries which genuinely enhance the tradition without defacing it. "Antiquity deserveth that reverence," Bacon says, "that men should make a stand thereupon and discover what is the best way; but when the discovery is well taken, then to make progression." As the preserver of antiquity, custom thus appears to afford a basis for progress.

One other fact about customs which most commentators from Herodotus to Montaigne and Freud have observed is their variety and variability. Customs differ from time to time, and from place to place. But this diversity and variation in custom does not necessarily mean that no uniformity at all exists in the actions of men. "Were there no uniformity in human actions," Hume points out, it would be impossible "to collect any general observations concerning mankind." At least enough uniformity is found, in his opinion, for it to be "universally acknowledged that human nature remains still the same." To whatever extent human behavior is purely natural or instinctive, it is common to all members of the species, and does not, like customary conduct, vary remarkably from one part of the human race to another, or from generation to generation.

The diversity and variation of customs seems therefore to be of their essence and to show that they are both man-made and voluntary in origin. "If they were not devices of men," Augustine writes, "they would not be different in different nations, and could not be changed among particular nations." The distinction between nature and convention can be formulated, therefore, partly in terms of the contrast between the constant and the variable, and partly in terms of the difference between the instinctive and the voluntary.

The early Greeks had an apt way of expressing this. As Aristotle phrases their insight, they referred to the natural as "that which everywhere has the same force and does not exist by people's thinking this or that," as, for example, "fire burns both here and in Persia." The conventional and those things which are "not by nature but by human enactment are not everywhere the same." The laws of Persia differ from the laws of Greece, and in Greece or in Persia, they change from time to time.

THE VARIABILITY of custom in contrast to the constancy or uniformity of nature puts the distinction between nature and convention at the service of the skeptic. One form of the skeptical attack upon natural law, universal moral standards, and the objectivity of truth or beauty consists in making custom the only measure of the acceptability of human actions or judgments. To say, for example, as Hume does, that the connection which the mind seems to make between cause and effect is based on custom rather than reason, has the skeptical effect which Hume intends. It substitutes the arbitrary for the rational. It dispossesses reason as a source of either the validity or the intelligibility of our conclusions concerning cause and effect.

As the chapters on KNOWLEDGE and OPINION indicate, the skeptical argument takes other forms. The reduction of all human judgments to opinion makes the differences between men, in either action or thought, unresolvable by argument or debate. One opinion can predominate over another only by force or by the weight of numbers. When it predominates by weight of numbers, it prevails by custom or convention. It is the opinion which the majority have agreed upon at a given time or place. To settle every controversy about what men should think or do by counting heads is to hold that everything is a matter of opinion and purely conventional.

Whether the skeptic reduces everything to opinion or to convention, he achieves the same effect. What he means by calling everything an "opinion" or a "convention" is equally inimical to reason. In either case, the willful or arbitrary is enthroned in reason's place and only force can be finally decisive. The two ideas—opinion and convention—seem to be corollaries of one another. Both imply a kind of relativity. Opinion normally suggests relativity to the individual, custom or convention relativity to the social group. Either may be involved in the origin of the other. The individual may form his opinions under the pressure of prevailing customs of thought or action; the customary beliefs or practices of a society or culture may, and usually do, result from opinions which have come to prevail.

The Greek sophists, we learn from the dialogues of Plato, appealed to the distinction between nature and convention and to the distinction between knowledge and opinion in exactly the same way. They used the notions of opinion and convention with equal force in their efforts to question absolute standards of conduct and the objectivity or universality of truth. The most familiar of all the sophistical sayings—the remark attributed to Protagoras that "man is the measure of all things"—is interpreted by both Plato and Aristotle to mean that what men wish to think or do determines *for them* what is true or right. Man's will governs his reason, and convention, or the agreement of individual wills, decides what is acceptable to the group.

In the *Gorgias*, which is named after another of the leading sophists of the day, Plato puts into the mouth of Callicles the sophistic position that there is no law or standard of justice except the rule of the stronger. Insisting that "convention and nature are generally at variance with one another," Callicles attempts to show that all of Socrates' efforts to discover an absolute standard of justice come to naught, because he cannot help but resort "to the popular and vulgar notions of right, which are not natural, but conventional."

As they appear in Plato's dialogues, the sophists are obviously impressed by the kind of information which fills the *History* of Herodotus —information about the great diversity of human beliefs and practices which anyone could discover for himself if he traveled, as Herodotus did, from people to people, observing their institutions and collecting their legends. Herodotus himself does not explicitly draw the skeptical conclusion, yet his own suspended judgment on many matters betokens a turn of mind made cautious by the impact of contrary opinions and conflicting customs.

In the Hellenistic period when the main stream of Greek philosophy divides into a number of Roman schools of thought, the skeptical position receives what is perhaps its fullest and most explicit statement. But in the writings of Lucian and Pyrrho, to take two examples, it is not so much the conflict of customs as it is what Lucian calls "the warfare of creeds," which occasions universal doubt. Yet whatever the source of doubt, Pyrrhonism states the traditional denials of the skeptic in their most extreme form. The senses are entirely untrustworthy. Reason is both impotent and self-deceiving. Men possess no knowledge or science. No truth is self-evident; none can be demonstrated.

THE CRITICAL TEMPER of the Greek sophists, and of an observer of men and manners like Herodotus, reappears later in the questionings of Montaigne—sharpened somewhat, perhaps, by his acquaintance with the Roman skeptics. In his case, perhaps more than any other, it is the implications of custom which, everywhere expatiated on in his *Essays*, give them their skeptical tone. Not himself a traveler in distant parts, Montaigne traverses the world of time and space by reading. He becomes conversant with the strange customs of the aborigines and of the Orient through the reports of returned explorers. He culls from the historians and geographers of antiquity every difference in custom which their books set forth as fact or fable.

Montaigne's insatiable appetite for collecting and comparing customs is not an aimless fascination on his part with the spectacle of human variety. It steadfastly leads him to the conclusion which is for him the only one possible. Since every belief or practice can be paired with its opposite in the customs of some other time or place, no belief or practice can demand unqualified or universal assent. "There is nothing," he writes, "which custom does not, or may not do; and therefore, with every good reason it is that Pindar calls her the ruler of the world."

To say, as Montaigne does, that "the taste for good and evil depends in good part upon the opinion we have of them" and that "everyone is well or ill at ease, according as he so finds himself," amounts to saying that all moral judgments are matters of opinion, either individual or customary in origin. Beauty, too, is a matter of taste. "We fancy its forms," Montaigne thinks, "according to our own appetite and liking." As may be seen in the chapter on BEAUTY, Montaigne assembles an abundance of evidence to show that standards of beauty vary with different peoples. The tastes or preferences of one group are as unaccountable as they are frequently revolting to another.

Even in the field of speculative thought about the nature of things, Montaigne regards the things men hold to be true as nothing more than prevailing opinions—the cultural conventions of a time or place. "We have no other level of truth and reason," he declares, "than the example and idea of the opinions and customs of the place wherein we live: there is always the perfect religion, there the most perfect government, there the most exact and accomplished usage of all things."

Of all human deceptions or impostures, none is worse than that which flows from a man's unwillingness to qualify every remark with the admission that *this is the way it seems to me*. In Montaigne's eyes, "there is no greater folly in the world" than the failure to recognize that we reduce truth and falsity "to the measure of our capacity and the bounds of our sufficiency." When new ideas or the strange beliefs of others at first seem incredible simply because they are not our own, "we shall find that it is rather custom than knowledge that takes away their strangeness." For his own part, Montaigne makes his "emblem" the question, "What do I know?" This, he says, sums up his Pyrrhonian philosophy.

ACCORDING TO the modern social scientist who claims that custom is the ultimate standard of conduct and that it provides the only criterion of moral judgment, no questions can be raised about the goodness or evil of particular customs. The customs of one people cannot be judged by another, at least not objectively or impartially, for those who judge must do so on the basis of their own customs. Since there is no arbiter above conflicting customs to say which is right, a particular custom has validity only for the group in which it prevails. Within that social group the character or conduct of its individual members is measured by conformity to the prevailing customs.

The *descriptive* science of sociology or comparative ethnology thus tends to replace the *normative* science of ethics—or moral philosophy. The only scientifically answerable questions about human conduct take the form of "How *do* men behave?" or "How *have* they acted individually or in groups?" but not "How *should* they?" The study of morality, as in Sumner's *Folkways*, becomes a study of the mores—how the customs which measure conduct develop and dominate; or, as in the writings of Freud, it becomes a study of how the individual is psychologically formed or deformed by the mores of his tribe and culture, according to the way in which the growing child reacts to the pressures which the community imposes through parental discipline.

With these views, many philosophers and theologians, both ancient and modern, take issue. But their opposing doctrine seldom goes so far as to deny that morality has certain conventional aspects. In arguing that there are "no innate practical principles," Locke, for example, like Montaigne, cites instances of contradictory customs to show that "there is scarce that principle of morality to be named, or rule of virtue to be thought on . . . which is not, somewhere or other, slighted and condemned by the general fashion of whole societies of men, governed by practical opinions and rules of living quite opposite to others."

But Locke does not leave this observation of the diversity of customs unqualified. He goes on to assert that "though perhaps, by the different temper, education, fashion, maxims, or interest of different sorts of men, it fell out, that what was thought praiseworthy in one place, escaped not censure in another; and so in different societies, virtues and vices were changed: yet, as to the main, they for the most part kept the same everywhere. For, since nothing can be more natural than to encourage with esteem and reputation that wherein every one finds his advantage, and to blame and discountenance the contrary; it is no wonder that esteem and discredit, virtue and vice, should, in a great measure, everywhere correspond with the unchangeable rule of right and wrong, which the law of God hath established. . . . Even in the corruption of manners, the true boundaries of the law of nature, which ought to be the rule of virtue and vice, were pretty well preferred."

For Locke, then, as for many others, there appear to be, underlying the variety of customs, moral principles of universal validity that draw their truth from the nature of man which represents a constant and common factor throughout the diversity of cultures. Accordingly, it would seem to follow that just as habits are modifications of instinct or developments of the individual's native capacities for action, so customs are conventional elaborations of what is natural to man as a social animal. On this theory, the conventional cannot be understood except by reference to the natural, *i.e.*, the nature of man or society.

THE VIEW THAT conventions have a natural basis is most readily exemplified by Aristotle's theory of natural and legal (or conventional) justice, and by the teaching of Aquinas concerning natural and positive law. For the Greeks the legal and the conventional are almost identical, so that it is a kind of justice rather than a kind of law which Aristotle calls "natural." Roman philosophers like Cicero, and Roman jurists like Gaius and Ulpian, make what seems to be an equivalent distinction in terms of law rather than justice. In his analysis, Aquinas follows the Latin, not the Greek vocabulary.

The Roman system of jurisprudence, Gibbon tells us, distinguished between those laws which are "positive institutions" and those which "reason prescribes, the laws of nature and nations." The former are man-made—the "result of custom and prejudice." This holds true of both written and unwritten laws, although only the unwritten precepts are now usually called "customary laws." These customary laws are *positive* in the sense that they are humanly instituted or enacted—posited by the will of the legislator rather than merely discovered by the reason of the philosopher. They are *conventional* in the sense that they represent some voluntary agreement on the part of the members of the community they govern, whether that consist in obeying the edicts of the emperor or in giving consent to the enactments of the senate.

So far as it is conventional, the law of one community differs from another; and within the history of a single community, the positive law changes from time to time. But such bodies of law, "however modified by accident or custom," the Roman jurists, Gibbon says, conceived as "drawn from the rule of right." The fact that "reason prescribes" this rule was their explanation of certain common elements which all bodies of positive law seem to contain.

The principles underlying all codes of civil law, whether discovered directly by reason or drawn inductively, as Grotius later suggests, from the comparative study of diverse legal systems, comprise the precepts of what the Romans, and later Aquinas, call "natural law." Thus these writers seem to re-affirm, though in somewhat different language, Aristotle's point that what is naturally just is the same for all men everywhere and always, while the laws of Greece and Persia represent diverse conventional determinations of the universal principles of justice.

The theory of natural right and natural law, as expressed in the writings of Hobbes, Locke, and Kant, as well as in the ancient and mediaeval tradition, is, of course, more fully treated in the chapters on JUSTICE and LAW. But one example of the distinction between natural and conventional justice may be instructive here.

Aquinas conceives positive rules as "determinations" of, rather than "deductions" from, natural law. He treats such precepts as "Thou shalt not kill" and "Thou shalt not steal" as conclusions that reason can draw deductively from the first principle of natural law, which is sometimes stated in the form of the command: *Do good, harm no one, and render to each his own.* Because these precepts are the prescriptions of reason rather than enactments of the state, they can be interpreted as declaring that murder and larceny are always and everywhere unjust. But what sort of killing and taking of what is not one's own shall be defined as murder and theft; and how offenders shall be tried, judged, and punished—these are matters which natural justice or the precepts of natural law leave open for determination by the positive laws of each community, according to its own constitution and its local customs.

The theory thus exemplified, of the relation between conventional and natural justice, or between positive and natural law, applies to moral rules and ethical standards generally. For the same reason that a positive law which violates natural justice cannot be called "just" even though it is harmonious with the customs of the community, so no rule of conduct, however much it represents prevailing custom, can be approved as morally right if it violates the right as reason sees it. The defenders of natural law, which is also sometimes called "the law of reason," proclaim the existence of an absolute standard, above the diversity and conflict of customs, by which their soundness is measured.

Conflicting ethical doctrines raise many issues concerning what it is right for men to do or good for them to seek; but the moralists at least agree that morality is based on reason or nature. For them the facts of human nature or the intuitions of reason will ultimately decide the points in issue. However far apart Plato and Aristotle, Aquinas and Hegel, Kant and Mill may be in their conceptions or analyses of the right and the good, they stand together, at least negatively, on the question of how their disputes can be resolved: *not* by appealing to the mores of the tribe, *not* by looking to the conventions of the community as a measure, *not* by letting the customs of the majority decide.

The deepest of all moral issues therefore exists between those who think that morality somehow derives from nature or reason and those who, like the ancient sophists or Montaigne or Freud, find its source in custom and convention. According to the side a man takes on this issue, he does or does not believe it possible to discover standards independent of custom, thereby to judge whether customs are good, bad, or indifferent. On one belief, public manners are conventional determinations of moral principles or they are sometimes violations of them, just as positive laws are either determinations or violations of natural law. On the other belief, the individual may be approved or condemned for conforming to or transgressing the manners or mores of his group; but those manners or mores, whether they are liked or disliked by the individual, are above any tenable, objective criticism.

The controversy in jurisprudence and morality between the naturalists or rationalists who appeal to man's nature or reason, and the positivists who hold that human customs cannot be appealed from, parallels a controversy in the theory of knowledge or science. The parallel issue, considered at greater length in the chapters on HYPOTHESIS and PRINCIPLE, can be stated by the question whether the foundation of science —even of such sciences as logic and mathematics—consists of postulates or axioms.

Axioms, like the precepts of natural law, are supposed to have a universality derived from the nature of human reason. They are self-evident truths, compelling assent. Postulates, on the contrary, are like rules of positive law—voluntarily accepted assumptions which, when agreed upon by the experts in a certain science, become its conventional basis. In science as in law, the positivists recognize nothing beyond the agreement of men to determine what shall be *taken for granted* as true or just.

THE DIFFERENCE between nature and convention also enters into the traditional discussion of two of the most characteristic activities of man: speech and political association.

No one disputes whether the faculty of speech is natural to man. It is as natural for man to speak as for dogs to bark or birds to sing. But the question is whether any human language, having a certain vocabulary and syntax, is natural or conventional. The answer seems to be dictated at once by the facts of the matter.

Human languages exist or have existed in great number and diversity, and those which still endure have gradually developed and are undoubtedly subject to further change. Hence, according to the traditional understanding of the natural and the conventional, these various tongues must represent conventional languages —originally invented by this human group or that, perpetuated by custom, altered by the conventions of usage. In contrast, the expressive sounds instinctively made by other animals show themselves to be natural by the fact that they are common to all members of a species and do not change as long as the species endures.

Nevertheless, as the chapter on LANGUAGE indicates, the writers of the great books consider the hypothesis of a natural human language. The Old Testament story of the Tower of Babel is sometimes interpreted as implying the existence of one language for all men before God confounded their speech and diversified their tongues. The story of Adam's giving names to the various species of plants and animals in the Garden of Eden is also cited by those who think there can be natural as well as conventional signs. In Plato's *Cratylus* the attempt is made to discover the natural names for things, or at least to discern some natural basis for the words of a conventional language like Greek.

These who reject the hypothesis of a single human language from which all others have developed by diversification, or who regard a purely natural language as impossible in the very nature of the case, sometimes acknowledge the possibility of certain common elements—principles of syntax, if not words—present in all human languages. The discovery of the common rules of speech was the object of the speculative grammarians in the Middle Ages, and of those who, like Arnauld and others, later tried to formulate a "universal grammar." On their view, all languages, even if they are conventional as written or spoken, may have the same natural basis in the fact that they are all used to express what men can naturally perceive or think.

As in the case of language, so in the case of society, the question is whether the family and the state are wholly natural, wholly conventional, or partly one and partly the other—their institutions being erected by choice and custom upon a natural basis. And as in the case of language, here too the great books do not, for the most part, give either of the extreme answers. They do not say that the state is entirely natural, that it is the expression of human instinct as the bee-hive and the ant-mound are instinctive formations. Nor do they say that the state is completely conventional, that it comes into existence *only* as the result of voluntary association on the part of men contracting to live together in a political community.

While Aristotle says that "man is by nature a political animal," and that the state is, therefore, "a creation of nature," he also distinguishes between the ways in which men and other animals are gregarious. Unlike the association of animals, which he attributes to instinct, the society of men rests on reason and speech. "Man is the only animal," he writes, "endowed with the gift of speech . . . intended to set forth the expedient and the inexpedient, and therefore likewise the just and the unjust." Because of these things, cities differ from one another, as bee-hives or ant-mounds do not.

The diversity of states represents for Aristotle a deliberate inventiveness on the part of reason and an exercise of free choice—certainly insofar as states are politically constituted, each with its own constitution. Aristotle's remark that while "a social impulse is implanted in all men by nature," yet "he who first founded the state was the greatest of benefactors," may look self-contradictory; but its two parts can be read as quite consistent with one another, if the first is taken as signifying the natural basis of the state (in a social impulse), and the second as saying that a certain convention (a constitution) is required to shape that impulse before any state is actually established.

As Aristotle is sometimes interpreted to uphold the theory that the state is entirely natural, so Hobbes, Locke, and Rousseau are often read as maintaining the opposite extreme—that it is entirely conventional. The extreme interpretation is based on the sharpness with which each of them distinguishes between men living in a state of nature and in a state of civil society.

Though they differ among themselves in their exposition of these two conditions of man, they seem to agree that for men to pass from a state of nature, whether hypothetical or historical, in which men live in anarchy or at least in isolation, it is necessary for them to enter into a contract or compact with one another. Since this social contract is the original, or originating, convention by which the commonwealth or civil society is established, it would seem to follow that, on their view, the state is entirely a product of convention, and in no way natural.

Yet Hobbes, Locke, and Rousseau, each in his own way, add a qualification in favor of the naturalness of the state, just as Aristotle qualifies his remark that "the state is a creation of nature" by praising the man "who first founded the state." The exponents of the social contract theory of the state's origin find in the nature of man or in his reason an instinct, a need, or a law which impels or bids him to seek association with others for the sake of advantages which he cannot enjoy apart from civil society. This suffices to affirm the existence of a natural basis for the convention or contract which establishes the state.

These apparently opposed theories of what is natural and what conventional about the state thus appear to approach each other, though one starts from an emphasis on the state's naturalness, the other from its conventional origin. The whole problem is, of course, further treated in the chapters on FAMILY and STATE; but one point which the foregoing discussion suggests receives special consideration in still another chapter. The point concerns the relation between the idea of a constitution and the idea of a social contract. Both are conceived as the basic or primary convention which establishes the state. The question whether the two ideas are interchangeable or only analogous is examined in the chapter on CONSTITUTION.

CUSTOM IS BOTH a cause and an effect of habit. The habits of the individual certainly reflect the customs of the community in which he lives; and in turn, the living customs of any social group get their vitality from the habits of its members. A custom which does not command general compliance is as dead as a language no longer spoken or a law no longer observed. This general compliance consists in nothing more than a certain conformity among the habits of individuals.

The continuity between custom and statute as parts or phases of the positive law rests upon the relation of both to habit. "Custom," according to Aquinas, "has the force of a law, abolishes law, and is the interpreter of law" precisely because it operates through the habits of the people. "By repeated external actions," such as produce a custom, "the inward movement of the will and the conceptions of the reason are most revealingly declared," and, according to Aquinas, "all law proceeds from the reason and will of the lawgiver." The law which a prince or a people enacts, to become effective as social regulation, must develop a particular habit of conduct in many individuals. Then and only then does a new enactment obtain the full force of law. To remain effective it must continue to have the support of "the customs of the country."

Without that support it may be a law on the books but not in practice, for the authority of a law cannot long prevail against a contrary custom, except through a degree of coercion so oppressive as to produce rebellion. That is also why the customary or unwritten rule—usually the primitive form of positive law—is less flexible, less amenable to change or modification. Custom is a conservative factor. "There is nothing more difficult to take in hand," writes Machiavelli, nothing "more perilous to conduct, or more uncertain in its success, than to take the lead in the introduction of a new order of things. The innovator has for enemies all those who have done well under the old conditions, and lukewarm defenders in those who may do well under the new."

Just as custom may either support the written law or render it ineffective, so custom works in opposite directions as a social force. It is both a factor of cohesion and of division among men— a cause of what is called "social solidarity" and a barrier separating peoples from one another. When the Athenians refuse to ally themselves with the Persians, they chide the Spartans, according to Herodotus, for fearing that they "might make terms with the barbarian." For all the gold on earth, they tell the Spartan envoys, they could not "take part with the Medes." To do so would betray "our common brotherhood with the Greeks, our common language, the altars and sacrifices of which we all partake, and the common character which we bear."

The barbarians or the gentiles—to use the traditional names for aliens or foreigners— are excluded by a social, not a geographic, boundary line, the line drawn between those who share a set of customs and all outsiders. When the stranger is assimilated, the group does not adopt him; he adopts the customs of the community. The very word "community" implies a multitude having much in common. More important than the land they occupy are the customs they share.

The Federalists, advocating the political union of the thirteen American states, could urge its feasibility on the ground that a social union already existed. "Providence has been pleased to give this one connected country," Jay writes, "to one united people—a people descended from the same ancestors, speaking the same language, professing the same religion, attached to the same principles of government, very similar in their manners and customs."

Those who today advocate world federal union cannot similarly point to a world society already in existence. They can only hope that if the separate states were to unite politically, the social cohesion of the world's people might subsequently develop as a result of the fostering of universal customs by universal law.

OUTLINE OF TOPICS

REFERENCES

To find the passages cited, use the numbers in heavy type, which are the volume and page numbers of the passages referred to. For example, in 4 HOMER: *Iliad*, BK II [265–283] 12d, the number 4 is the number of the volume in the set; the number 12d indicates that the passage is in section d of page 12.

PAGE SECTIONS: When the text is printed in one column, the letters a and b refer to the upper and lower halves of the page. For example, in 53 JAMES: *Psychology*, 116a-119b, the passage begins in the upper half of page 116 and ends in the lower half of page 119. When the text is printed in two columns, the letters a and b refer to the upper and lower halves of the left-hand side of the page, the letters c and d to the upper and lower halves of the right-hand side of the page. For example, in 7 PLATO: *Symposium*, 163b-164c, the passage begins in the lower half of the left-hand side of page 163 and ends in the upper half of the right-hand side of page 164.

AUTHOR'S DIVISIONS: One or more of the main divisions of a work (such as PART, BK, CH, SECT) are sometimes included in the reference; line numbers, in brackets, are given in certain cases; *e.g.*, *Iliad*, BK II [265–283] 12d.

BIBLE REFERENCES: The references are to book, chapter, and verse. When the King James and Douay versions differ in title of books or in the numbering of chapters or verses, the King James version is cited first and the Douay, indicated by a (*D*), follows; *e.g.*, OLD TESTAMENT: *Nehemiah*, 7:45—(*D*) II *Esdras*, 7:46.

SYMBOLS: The abbreviation "esp" calls the reader's attention to one or more especially relevant parts of a whole reference; "passim" signifies that the topic is discussed intermittently rather than continuously in the work or passage cited.

For additional information concerning the style of the references, see the Explanation of Reference Style; for general guidance in the use of *The Great Ideas*, consult the Preface.

1. The distinction between nature and convention: its application to the origin of the state and of language

6 HERODOTUS: *History*, BK II, 49a-c

7 PLATO: *Protagoras*, 52b / *Cratylus* 85a-114a,c esp 104d-105a, 106b-c, 110c-111c / *Gorgias*, 271b-272b / *Republic*, BK II, 311b-c / *Theaetetus*, 528b-c / *Laws*, BK III, 663d-666c; BK X, 760a-b

8 ARISTOTLE: *Sophistical Refutations*, CH 12 [173ᵃ7–30] 238b-c

9 ARISTOTLE: *Ethics*, BK V, CH 7 [1134ᵇ18–1135ᵃ7] 382c-383a / *Politics*, BK I, CH 2 445b-446d esp [1253ᵃ2–31] 446b-d; CH 6 448c-449b / *Rhetoric*, BK I, CH 13 [1373ᵇ1–17] 617c-d; CH 15 [1375ᵃ25–ᵇ3] 619d-620a

10 HIPPOCRATES: *Airs, Waters, Places*, par 14 15a-b

12 LUCRETIUS: *Nature of Things*, BK IV [823–857] 55a-b; BK V [925–1090] 73b-75b

18 AUGUSTINE: *City of God*, BK XIX, CH 7 515a-c / *Christian Doctrine*, BK II, CH 19–27 646b-650a passim, esp CH 24 648d-649a

20 AQUINAS: *Summa Theologica*, PART I-II, Q 95, A 2 227c-228c; A 4, ANS 229b-230c; Q 96, A 2, ANS 231c-232b; Q 97, A 3, REP 1 237b-238b

21 DANTE: *Divine Comedy*, PARADISE, XXVI [70–142] 146c-147b esp [124–138] 147a-b

23 HOBBES: *Leviathan*, INTRO, 47a-b; PART I, 84c-87b; 91a-b; 94b-c; 95a; PART II, 99a-101a esp 100c; 113c; 131a-c; 136d-137a

24 RABELAIS: *Gargantua and Pantagruel*, BK I, 11d-14b

25 MONTAIGNE: *Essays*, 46b-47c; 63d-64b; 93b-94a; 102a-103a; 218a-c; 278a-279a; 424d-426b; 489b-490c

27 SHAKESPEARE: *King Lear*, ACT I, SC II [1–22] 247d-248a; ACT II, SC IV [267–274] 261c

30 BACON: *Advancement of Learning*, 20c-d; 94d

31 SPINOZA: *Ethics*, PART IV, PROP 37, SCHOL 2 435b-436a

33 PASCAL: *Pensées*, 89–98 189b-190b; 294 225b-226b; 306 228a

35 LOCKE: *Toleration*, 16a-c / *Civil Government*, CH I-IX 25a-54d passim; CH XIX, SECT 211, 73d / *Human Understanding*, BK II, CH XXVIII, SECT 2–3 228c-229b; BK III, CH I, SECT 5 252b-c; CH II, SECT 1 252d-253a

38 MONTESQUIEU: *Spirit of Laws*, BK I, 1c-d; 2b-3a; BK VIII, 52a; BK XVI, 119d-120a; BK XXVI, 215b-217b passim; 219d-221c

38 ROUSSEAU: *Inequality*, 329a-331d; 340a-342c; 348b,d-363a,c / *Political Economy*, 367b; 369a-b / *Social Contract*, BK I 387b,d-394d; BK II, 399b-c; 405d-406a

39 SMITH: *Wealth of Nations*, BK V, 397a-c

40 GIBBON: *Decline and Fall*, 409d-410a

(1. The distinction between nature and convention: its application to the origin of the state and of language.)

42 KANT: *Science of Right*, 402c; 405d-406c; 433c-434d esp 433d-434a; 435a-436b; 437c-d

43 MILL: *Liberty*, 294b-295b / *Representative Government*, 327b,d-332d

44 BOSWELL: *Johnson*, 363c-364a

46 HEGEL: *Philosophy of Right*, PART I, par 75 31d-32b; PART III, par 168 60b-c; ADDITIONS, 47 124a-b; 97 132c-133a; 108 134b-c / *Philosophy of History*, INTRO, 170d-171d; PART II, 260b

49 DARWIN: *Descent of Man*, 298a-b; 349d

53 JAMES: *Psychology*, 733b-734b

54 FREUD: *Origin and Development of Psycho-Analysis*, 20c-d / *General Introduction*, 452c-d; 573c / *War and Death*, 757d-759d / *Civilization and Its Discontents*, 776b-802a,c esp 776b-777a, 778a, 780b-781d, 783c-784b, 787a-c, 788d-789b, 791b-792a, 799b-802a,c / *New Introductory Lectures*, 853a-b

2. The origin, development, and transmission of customs

6 HERODOTUS: *History*, BK I, 31a-b; 38a-b; BK II, 58a-b; 59d-60a; 62b-c; 66c-d; 69b-d; 87a-b; BK III, 107b-c; BK IV, 125d-126a; 129c-130a; BK V, 177a-b; 183d-184a; BK VI, 201b-c

6 THUCYDIDES: *Peloponnesian War*, BK II, 395c-d; BK III, 442c-443a

7 PLATO: *Laws*, BK III, 663d-666c esp 666a-b

13 VIRGIL: *Aeneid*, BK V [42–83] 188a-189a; BK VII [601–615] 252b-253a; BK VIII [152–279] 263a-266b

14 PLUTARCH: *Theseus* 1a-15a,c passim / *Romulus* 15a-30a,c passim / *Lycurgus*, 36a-47c passim / *Numa Pompilius* 49a-61d passim / *Solon*, 70c-74b / *Poplicola*, 80d; 84d-85a / *Camillus*, 116a-c / *Coriolanus*, 175c-d / *Marcellus*, 254c-256b

15 TACITUS: *Histories*, BK II, 214d-215a

18 AUGUSTINE: *Christian Doctrine*, BK II, CH 24–25 648d-649d; BK III, CH 12 662c-663c

20 AQUINAS: *Summa Theologica*, PART I-II, Q 97, A 3 237b-238b

25 MONTAIGNE: *Essays*, 278a-279a

31 SPINOZA: *Ethics*, PART III, THE AFFECTS, DEF 27, EXPL 419a-b

36 SWIFT: *Gulliver*, PART II, 80a-b

36 STERNE: *Tristram Shandy*, 309b-310a

38 MONTESQUIEU: *Spirit of Laws*, BK XIV, 107a-b; BK XVI, 116a-117c; 118a-119c; BK XVIII, 132a-b; BK XX, 146a-b; BK XXI, 169a-170b; BK XXIII, 187b,d-189d; BK XXIV, 205d-206a; BK XXV, 209a-b

38 ROUSSEAU: *Social Contract*, BK III, 416c-417a

40 GIBBON: *Decline and Fall*, 154b-155a; 583d-584b; 704d [n 79]

41 GIBBON: *Decline and Fall*, 227b; 389b-d

43 MILL: *Liberty*, 308b [fn 1]

46 HEGEL: *Philosophy of History*, PART II, 259c-d; 265c-266a; PART IV, 315d-316b; 347b-d; 351d-353a; 367a-b

48 MELVILLE: *Moby Dick*, 228b-229b

49 DARWIN: *Descent of Man*, 317a-c; 318b-c

54 FREUD: *Civilization and Its Discontents*, 799a-800c / *New Introductory Lectures*, 834b-c

3. The conflict of customs: their variation from place to place

4 HOMER: *Odyssey*, BK I [1–5] 183a; BK VIII [234–255] 224c-d; BK IX [82–115] 230a-b

5 AESCHYLUS: *Suppliant Maidens* [234–245] 3d

5 EURIPIDES: *Andromache* [147–245] 316c-317b

6 HERODOTUS: *History*, BK I, 22d-23a; 31a-33a; 35b-c; 39a-c; 44b-45b; 48a,c; BK II, 56c-68a; 80a-c; BK III, 93d-94a; 97d-98a; 111b-113d; BK IV, 128c-d; 129c-130b; 132a-b; 134a; 137a-138c; 142b-144b; 154b-158d passim; BK V, 160b-161c; BK VI, 195d-196c; BK VII, 238c; 253b-d

6 THUCYDIDES: *Peloponnesian War*, BK I, 350b-d

7 PLATO: *Symposium*, 154a-155c / *Laws*, BK IV, 678c-679a

8 ARISTOTLE: *Metaphysics*, BK II, CH 3 [994^{b}32–995^{a}5] 513c

9 ARISTOTLE: *Ethics*, BK V, CH 7 [1134^{b}18–1135^{a}4] 382c-d

10 HIPPOCRATES: *Airs, Waters, Places*, par 1 9a-b; par 14–18 15a-16c

13 VIRGIL: *Aeneid*, BK I [520–543] 117b-118a; BK IX [590–620] 295a-b; BK XII [791–842] 375a-376b

14 PLUTARCH: *Themistocles*, 99b-c / *Marcellus*, 254c-256b esp 256a-b

15 TACITUS: *Annals*, BK II, 23d-24a

18 AUGUSTINE: *Christian Doctrine*, BK II, CH 25 649b-d

20 AQUINAS: *Summa Theologica*, PART I-II, Q 96, A 2, ANS 231c-232b

22 CHAUCER: *Troilus and Cressida*, BK I, STANZA 22–23 3b-4a; BK II, STANZA 6–7 22a-b

25 MONTAIGNE: *Essays*, 44a-47a; 91d-98b esp 93b-94a; 102a-103a; 230b-231a; 246b-257d passim; 278a-279c; 281a-284c; 415a-416b; 524b-d

26 SHAKESPEARE: *Henry V*, ACT V, SC I [1–84] 562c-563b

31 DESCARTES: *Discourse*, PART II, 46b-c

33 PASCAL: *Pensées*, 294 225b-226b

35 LOCKE: *Human Understanding*, BK I, CH II, SECT 8–12 105d-107d

35 HUME: *Human Understanding*, SECT VIII, DIV 66, 480b

36 SWIFT: *Gulliver*, PART II, 76b-78b; PART III, 98b-99a; 105a

38 MONTESQUIEU: *Spirit of Laws*, BK VI, 38b; BK XV, 110a-b; BK XVI, 116a-119c; BK XIX, 139c-140a; BK XXI, 153a-c; BK XXV, 209a-b

38 ROUSSEAU: *Social Contract*, BK III, 416c-417a

40 GIBBON: *Decline and Fall*, 89d-94b passim; 99c; 260d-261a; 409d-415a passim; 670d-671a

41 GIBBON: *Decline and Fall*, 33d-36c passim; 85c-d; 223c-227b passim; 337c-339b passim

43 FEDERALIST: NUMBER 60, 184d

43 MILL: *Liberty*, 269c-d; 301b-302c; 307b-312a

46 HEGEL: *Philosophy of History*, PART I, 250c-d; PART IV, 347b-d; 351d-353a

48 MELVILLE: *Moby Dick*, 43b-44a; 60b-65a; 351b-352a

49 DARWIN: *Descent of Man*, 571b-577d

52 DOSTOEVSKY: *Brothers Karamazov*, BK V, 122d-125c

4. The change of customs: their variation from time to time

5 ARISTOPHANES: *Clouds* [957–1002] 500a-d

6 HERODOTUS: *History*, BK I, 31a-b; 39a-b

6 THUCYDIDES: *Peloponnesian War*, BK I, 350b-d

7 PLATO: *Republic*, BK IV, 344b-d; BK V, 357d-358a / *Laws*, BK IV, 678c-679a; BK VII, 717d-718c

9 ARISTOTLE: *Politics*, BK II, CH 8 [1268ᵇ23–1269ᵃ28] 464d-465b

10 HIPPOCRATES: *Airs, Waters, Places*, par 14, 15b

12 LUCRETIUS: *Nature of Things*, BK V [925–1027] 73b-74c

13 VIRGIL: *Aeneid*, BK XII [791–842] 375a-376b

14 PLUTARCH: *Lysander*, 361a-d

15 TACITUS: *Annals*, BK III, 58b-d; BK IV, 67d-68a; BK XI, 105d-107b; BK XII, 111b-c

18 AUGUSTINE: *Confessions*, BK III, par 13 16c-d / *City of God*, BK XV, CH 16 410b-411d / *Christian Doctrine*, BK II, CH 25 649b-d esp 649d; BK III, CH 12 662c-663c; CH 18–22 664d-666c

20 AQUINAS: *Summa Theologica*, PART I–II, Q 97, A 2 236d-237b; A 3, REP 1–2 237b-238b

21 DANTE: *Divine Comedy*, HELL, XVI [64–78] 23a-b; PURGATORY, VI [58–151] 61b-62c; XI [73–117] 69c-70a; PARADISE, XV [97]–XVI [154] 129b-132a; XXVI [124–138] 147a-b

22 CHAUCER: *Troilus and Cressida*, BK II, STANZA 4 22a

25 MONTAIGNE: *Essays*, 131b-132a; 143c-145c

33 PASCAL: *Pensées*, 294 225b-226b

35 LOCKE: *Civil Government*, CH XIII, SECT 157 61c-d

35 HUME: *Human Understanding*, SECT VIII, DIV 66, 480b

36 SWIFT: *Gulliver*, PART III, 105a-106b; 128a

38 MONTESQUIEU: *Spirit of Laws*, BK XIV, 104c; BK XIX 135a-146a,c esp 136c; BK XX, 146a-b

38 ROUSSEAU: *Social Contract*, BK II, 402b-c

40 GIBBON: *Decline and Fall*, 545c-d; 638c-639a

41 GIBBON: *Decline and Fall*, 6b; 107b; 485b-486b

43 MILL: *Liberty*, 269c-d; 300d-302c / *Representative Government*, 377d-378a

44 BOSWELL: *Johnson*, 204c-205b

49 DARWIN: *Descent of Man*, 528c-529a; 579b-582a passim

51 TOLSTOY: *War and Peace*, BK X, 403a-c; BK XI, 498a-499a; EPILOGUE I, 647b-c

5. Custom and convention in the moral order

5*a*. The conventional determination of moral judgments: the moral evaluation of conventions

5 EURIPIDES: *Hecuba* [798–805] 359d / *Phoenician Maidens* [499–522] 382b-c

5 ARISTOPHANES: *Clouds* [1031–1114] 501a-502b

6 HERODOTUS: *History*, BK I, 32a; BK III, 92c-93a; 97d-98a

6 THUCYDIDES: *Peloponnesian War*, BK I, 368b-c

7 PLATO: *Symposium*, 154a-155c / *Gorgias*, 271b-284b / *Republic*, BK V, 357d-358a / *Theaetetus*, 525c-526a; 527b-528c esp 528b-c / *Laws*, BK X, 759d-760c

9 ARISTOTLE: *Ethics*, BK I, CH 3 [1094ᵇ12–28] 339d-340a; CH 8 [1098ᵇ9–29] 344a-b; BK V, CH 7 [1134ᵇ18–1135ᵃ4] 382c-d / *Politics*, BK I, CH 6 448c-449b

12 LUCRETIUS: *Nature of Things*, BK V [1412–1435] 79b-d

12 EPICTETUS: *Discourses*, BK I, CH 2, 107a-b; CH 11, 117b-c; BK II, CH 11, 150a-151a

12 AURELIUS: *Meditations*, BK IV, SECT 18 264d

14 PLUTARCH: *Themistocles*, 99b-c / *Marcus Cato*, 285c-d

15 TACITUS: *Annals*, BK II, 24a; BK III, 58b-d

18 AUGUSTINE: *Confessions*, BK I, par 14–16 4c-5b; par 19–30 5d-8d esp par 25–27 7a-d; BK III, par 13 16c-d; par 15 17a-b; BK VI, par 2 35a-c; par 11–13 38b-39c / *City of God*, BK XV, CH 16 410b-411d / *Christian Doctrine*, BK II, CH 19–26 646b-650a; CH 39–40 654c-656a; BK III, CH 10, 661b-662a; CH 12–14 662c-663d; CH 18–22 664d-666c

23 HOBBES: *Leviathan*, PART I, 61d-62a; 75a-b; 78b-c; 96a; PART II, 140b

24 RABELAIS: *Gargantua and Pantagruel*, BK III, 141d-142b

25 MONTAIGNE: *Essays*, 46b-47c; 93b-c; 102a-103a; 143c-144a; 281a-284c; 307b; 424d-426b

27 SHAKESPEARE: *Hamlet*, ACT II, SC II [249–259] 43b / *Troilus and Cressida*, ACT II, SC II [1–206] 113c-115c / *King Lear*, ACT I, SC II [1–22] 247d-248a / *Henry VIII*, ACT I, SC III [3–5] 555b

29 CERVANTES: *Don Quixote*, PART I, 32c-33a

31 DESCARTES: *Discourse*, PART II, 46b-c; PART III, 48b-49d

31 SPINOZA: *Ethics*, PART III, THE AFFECTS, DEF 27 419a-b

33 PASCAL: *Pensées*, 309 228b; 312 229a; 325 230b-231a; 381–385 238b-239a

35 LOCKE: *Human Understanding*, 90a-d; BK I, CH II, SECT 8–12 105d-107d passim; SECT 21–26 111a-112b; BK II, CH XXI, SECT 71, 197d; CH XXVIII, SECT 10–13 230b-231c

35 HUME: *Human Understanding*, SECT XII, DIV 132, 509c-d

36 SWIFT: *Gulliver*, PART I, 21b-23a; PART II, 76b-77a

[1287^{b}5–7] 486a / *Rhetoric*, BK I, CH 13 [1373^{b}1–17] 617c-d

14 PLUTARCH: *Lycurgus*, 33d-34b / *Themistocles*, 99b-c

18 AUGUSTINE: *Confessions*, BK III, par 15 17a-b / *City of God*, BK IV, CH 4 190d; BK XIX, CH 17, 522d-523a; CH 24 528b-c

20 AQUINAS: *Summa Theologica*, PART I–II, Q 95, AA 2–3 227c-229b; A 4, ANS 229b-230c

23 HOBBES: *Leviathan*, PART I, 78b-c; PART II, 99a-101b esp 100c, 101a-b; 140b

25 MONTAIGNE: *Essays*, 46b-48b; 93b-94a; 102a-b; 281a-283c; 426a-b; 462d-463b; 519a-520b

27 SHAKESPEARE: *King Lear*, ACT I, SC II [1–22] 247d-248a

30 BACON: *Advancement of Learning*, 94d-95b

31 DESCARTES: *Discourse*, PART II, 45b-d

33 PASCAL: *Pensées*, 291–338 225a-233a esp 294 225b-226b, 312 229a, 325–326 230b-231a

35 LOCKE: *Civil Government*, CH II, SECT 12 27d-28a; SECT 14–15 28b-c; CH VII, SECT 94–CH VIII, SECT 122 46a-53c esp CH VIII, SECT 95–99 46c-47c; CH X, SECT 132 55a-b; CH XIII, SECT 157–158 61c-62b; CH XV, SECT 171 65a-b; CH XIX, SECT 243 81d

36 SWIFT: *Gulliver*, PART I, 22a-23a; 28a-b

38 MONTESQUIEU: *Spirit of Laws*, BK I, 1c-d; 2d-3d; BK XIX, 140c-142b; BK XXVI, 214d-215a; BK XXVIII, 240b; 261a-262a,c

38 ROUSSEAU: *Social Contract*, BK I 387b,d-394d esp 391a-d

40 GIBBON: *Decline and Fall*, 616d-617a

41 GIBBON: *Decline and Fall*, 71d-73a passim; 75b-d; 86d-89c esp 87a, 87d

42 KANT: *Science of Right*, 419a-420b; 435a-436c; 437c-d; 450d-451c

43 DECLARATION OF INDEPENDENCE: [7–28] 1a-b

43 MILL: *Liberty*, 269c-d; 270c-271b; 305b-312a passim, esp 307b-d / *Representative Government*, 327b,d-332d passim

44 BOSWELL: *Johnson*, 276a-b

46 HEGEL: *Philosophy of Right*, PART III, par 211 70a-c; par 217 72b-c; par 234 75d-76a / *Philosophy of History*, PART II, 271c-273c; PART IV, 365b-c

47 GOETHE: *Faust*, PART I [1972–1979] 46b-47a

48 MELVILLE: *Moby Dick*, 292a-297a esp 294a

50 MARX-ENGELS: *Communist Manifesto*, 427a-b

51 TOLSTOY: *War and Peace*, EPILOGUE II, 680b-684a

6b. The force of custom with respect to law

5 EURIPIDES: *Bacchantes* [877–911] 347b-c / *Hecuba* [798–805] 359d

6 HERODOTUS: *History*, BK III, 97d-98a

7 PLATO: *Republic*, BK IV, 344b-d; BK VII, 401c-d / *Laws*, BK III, 665c-666c; BK IV, 678d-679a; BK V, 692b-c; BK VII, 713c-714c; 716a-b; 718b-c; BK VIII, 736c-737a

8 ARISTOTLE: *Metaphysics*, BK II, CH 3 [995^{a}4–6] 513c

9 ARISTOTLE: *Politics*, BK I, CH 6 448c-449b; BK II, CH 8 [1269^{a}14–23] 465b; BK III, CH 16

[1287^{b}5–8] 486a; BK V, CH 8 [1307^{b}30–38] 509d-510a; CH 9 [1310^{a}12–19] 512b-c

14 PLUTARCH: *Lycurgus*, 36b-37b; 38b-d; 46b-c; 47a-48a / *Lycurgus-Numa*, 63d-64a / *Solon*, 73d-74b

15 TACITUS: *Annals*, BK III, 57d-58b; BK IV, 67d-68a; BK XI, 106a-107b; BK XII, 111b-c; BK XIV, 151d-152c

18 AUGUSTINE: *Confessions*, BK III, par 15 17a-b; BK V, par 14 30c-31a / *City of God*, BK XV, CH 16 410b-411d

20 AQUINAS: *Summa Theologica*, PART I–II, Q 95, A 3 228c-229b; Q 96, A 2, ANS 231c-232b; Q 97, AA 2–3 236d-238b

23 HOBBES: *Leviathan*, PART I, 78b-c; PART II, 108c; 130d-131a; 131c; 136d

25 MONTAIGNE: *Essays*, 47a-51a; 131b-132a; 283c; 462c-465c

27 SHAKESPEARE: *Measure for Measure*, ACT II, SC I [1–4] 178d-179a

30 BACON: *New Atlantis*, 205d-206b

31 DESCARTES: *Discourse*, PART II, 45b-d

33 PASCAL: *Pensées*, 308 228b; 312 229a; 325–326 230b-231a

35 LOCKE: *Human Understanding*, BK II, CH XXVIII, SECT 10–13 230b-231c

36 SWIFT: *Gulliver*, PART I, 22a-23a

38 MONTESQUIEU: *Spirit of Laws*, BK I, 3c-d; BK X, 65b; BK XIV, 106b; BK XVIII, 127c; BK XIX, 135b-136b; 137c-140c; BK XXI, 168d-169a; BK XXIII, 188b-189a; 189d; 197c-198a; BK XXV, 212a; BK XXVI, 218d; 221a-c; 223a-c; BK XXVIII, 237a-d

38 ROUSSEAU: *Inequality*, 324d / *Social Contract*, BK II, 402b-c; 406c-d; BK III, 419d-420a; BK IV, 434b-435a

40 GIBBON: *Decline and Fall*, 464c-d

41 GIBBON: *Decline and Fall*, 77c-d; 80a; 96b-c

42 KANT: *Science of Right*, 448d-449c

43 DECLARATION OF INDEPENDENCE: [15–22] 1b

43 FEDERALIST: NUMBER 27, 95c-d; NUMBER 49, 159d-160a

43 MILL: *Liberty*, 270c-271b; 308b [fn 1] / *Representative Government*, 329d-330a; 330d-331a

44 BOSWELL: *Johnson*, 204c-205b; 276a-b; 277b

46 HEGEL: *Philosophy of Right*, PART III, par 257 80b; par 274 92a; par 339 110b; par 355 112d-113a; ADDITIONS, 132 137d-138b / *Philosophy of History*, PART II, 271c-273c; 277c-d; PART III, 294c-d

47 GOETHE: *Faust*, PART I [1972–1979] 46b-47a

48 MELVILLE: *Moby Dick*, 292a-297a esp 294a

49 DARWIN: *Descent of Man*, 317a-b

51 TOLSTOY: *War and Peace*, BK III, 137c-139a

7. Custom in social life

7a. Custom as unifying a community

6 HERODOTUS: *History*, BK VIII, 287c-d

7 PLATO: *Laws*, BK IV, 678c-679a; BK VII, 716a-b

13 VIRGIL: *Aeneid*, BK XII [791–842] 375a-376b

(7. *Custom in social life. 7a. Custom as unifying a community.*)

14 PLUTARCH: *Lycurgus*, 46b-c / *Alexander*, 562b-563c

18 AUGUSTINE: *Confessions*, BK III, par 15 17a-b / *City of God*, BK XIX, CH 7 515a-c; CH 17, 522d-523a; CH 24 528b-c / *Christian Doctrine*, BK II, CH 25–26 649b-650a; CH 39–40 654c-656a

20 AQUINAS: *Summa Theologica*, PART I–II, Q 95, A 3 228c-229b; Q 97, AA 2–3 236d-238b

21 DANTE: *Divine Comedy*, PURGATORY, VI [58–151] 61b-62c; PARADISE, XV [97]–XVI [154] 129b-132a passim

23 HOBBES: *Leviathan*, PART I, 54c

25 MONTAIGNE: *Essays*, 46b-47a; 131b-132a

30 BACON: *New Atlantis*, 205d-206b

31 DESCARTES: *Discourse*, PART II, 45b-d

31 SPINOZA: *Ethics*, PART IV, APPENDIX, XV 448c

33 PASCAL: *Pensées*, 294 225b-226b

38 MONTESQUIEU: *Spirit of Laws*, BK XIX, 137c-d; 138c-140c

40 GIBBON: *Decline and Fall*, 1a; 15d-16c

41 GIBBON: *Decline and Fall*, 389c-d

43 FEDERALIST: NUMBER 2, 31c-d; NUMBER 27, 95c-d

43 MILL: *Representative Government*, 424c-425b; 428b-c

46 HEGEL: *Philosophy of Right*, PART III, par 274 92a / *Philosophy of History*, INTRO, 176b; PART I, 240d-241a; PART II, 260b-c; 277c; 280b-281b

50 MARX-ENGELS: *Communist Manifesto*, 421a-b

51 TOLSTOY: *War and Peace*, BK VI, 254c-260a; 263a-265d; BK VII, 288c-290b; BK X, 403a-405a; BK XI, 499c-500c; BK XII, 533a-534d; 538d-539c; 556c-557b; EPILOGUE I, 647b-c

52 DOSTOEVSKY: *Brothers Karamazov*, EPILOGUE, 406a-c

54 FREUD: *War and Death*, 756a-d

7b. Custom as a barrier between communities

4 HOMER: *Odyssey*, BK VII [27–36] 218b

5 AESCHYLUS: *Suppliant Maidens* [825–965] 11d-13b

6 HERODOTUS: *History*, BK I, 2a; 31d-32a; BK IV, 137a-138c; 143b-144b; BK VIII, 287c-d

7 PLATO: *Laws*, BK IV, 678c-679a

13 VIRGIL: *Aeneid*, BK I [520–543] 117b-118a; BK IX [590–620] 295a-b

14 PLUTARCH: *Lycurgus*, 46b-c / *Themistocles*, 99b-c / *Marcus Cato*, 287c-288c / *Alexander*, 562b-563c

15 TACITUS: *Histories*, BK V, 295b-296a

18 AUGUSTINE: *City of God*, BK XIX, CH 7 515a-c / *Christian Doctrine*, BK III, CH 14 663c-d

22 CHAUCER: *Tale of Man of Law* [4638–4644] 238a

23 HOBBES: *Leviathan*, PART I, 96a

25 MONTAIGNE: *Essays*, 44b-c; 46b-47a; 91d-98b esp 93b-94a; 477d-478a; 524b-d

26 SHAKESPEARE: *Richard II*, ACT I, SC III [154–173] 325b / *Merchant of Venice*, ACT I, SC III

[41–53] 410a; [106–138] 410c-411a; ACT IV, SC I [35–62] 425d-426a

30 BACON: *New Atlantis*, 205d-207b

32 MILTON: *Areopagitica*, 385b

36 SWIFT: *Gulliver*, PART I, 21b-23a; 25b-26a; PART IV, 149b-150b

38 MONTESQUIEU: *Spirit of Laws*, BK XV, 110a-b; BK XIX, 139c-140a; BK XX, 146a-b; BK XXIV, 206c; 207c-208a,c; BK XXV, 209a-b

38 ROUSSEAU: *Inequality*, 355b-c

40 GIBBON: *Decline and Fall*, 15d-16b; 179d-183a esp 179d, 180d-181a; 207b-211c esp 208b-d; 638d-639a

41 GIBBON: *Decline and Fall*, 224b-225a; 423d

43 MILL: *Liberty*, 300a-302c passim / *Representative Government*, 424c-428a passim, esp 427d; 437b-c

48 MELVILLE: *Moby Dick*, 60b-65a

51 TOLSTOY: *War and Peace*, BK VIII, 309b-c; BK IX, 362d-363a; BK XI, 515c-521c passim

52 DOSTOEVSKY: *Brothers Karamazov*, EPILOGUE, 406a-c

54 FREUD: *War and Death*, 755c-757a passim / *Civilization and Its Discontents*, 788b-c

7c. Custom as determining economic needs or standards

7 PLATO: *Republic*, BK II, 318a-d

14 PLUTARCH: *Marcus Cato*, 285c-d / *Lysander*, 361a-d

15 TACITUS: *Annals*, BK III, 58b-d

25 MONTAIGNE: *Essays*, 131b-132a; 489b-490c

35 LOCKE: *Civil Government*, CH V, SECT 46–49 35a-d; CH XVI, SECT 184 68b-d

38 MONTESQUIEU: *Spirit of Laws*, BK XVIII, 128b-c; BK XIX, 136c-137b; BK XXI, 153a-c

39 SMITH: *Wealth of Nations*, BK I, 10b-12c; BK V, 383c-d

50 MARX: *Capital*, 17d-18a; 28d-29b; 44d-45c; 66c-67a; 81b-c; 112a-c

7d. The influence of custom on the liberty of the individual

6 THUCYDIDES: *Peloponnesian War*, BK II, 396c-d

25 MONTAIGNE: *Essays*, 22a-c; 42b-c; 46b-47c; 143c-144a; 307b; 424d-426b esp 426a-b

27 SHAKESPEARE: *Coriolanus*, ACT II, SC II [136–164] 365a-366a; SC III [119–131] 367b

38 MONTESQUIEU: *Spirit of Laws*, BK XII, 84b,d; BK XIX, 138a-c; 142a; 145b-c

38 ROUSSEAU: *Inequality*, 324a-b

39 SMITH: *Wealth of Nations*, BK I, 41a

43 MILL: *Liberty*, 269b-271d; 293b-302c; 307b-312a passim

46 HEGEL: *Philosophy of Right*, PART III, par 355 112d-113a; ADDITIONS, 123 136d-137a / *Philosophy of History*, PART II, 279c-281b; PART III, 310d-311b; PART IV, 333b-c

51 TOLSTOY: *War and Peace*, BK VIII, 303a-305b

54 FREUD: *Origin and Development of Psycho-Analysis*, 20c-d / *General Introduction*, 452c-d; 573c / *War and Death*, 755d; 757c-759d / *Civilization and Its Discontents*, 776b-802a,c

CROSS-REFERENCES

For: Other discussions of the distinction between nature and convention, and for the examination of related distinctions, *see* ART 2c; HABIT 1, 7; NATURE 2a–2c.

The consideration of the natural and the conventional in language and society, *see* FAMILY 1; LANGUAGE 2–2b; NATURE 2b, 5c; SIGN AND SYMBOL 1a–1f; STATE 3b–3d.

Applications of the distinction between nature and convention in law and jurisprudence, *see* JUSTICE 6a–6b, 9a, 10a; LAW 4–4h, 5c, 7c; and for the relation of law to custom and habit, *see* HABIT 7; LAW 5f.

The discussion of custom as a conservative force in relation to progress, *see* CHANGE 12b; HISTORY 4b; PROGRESS 4a, 5.

The bearing of custom and convention on the issues of morality, *see* GOOD AND EVIL 3a, 6d; NATURE 5a; OPINION 6a; RELATION 6c; UNIVERSAL AND PARTICULAR 7b.

The relativity of truth to the customs of the time and place, and for the theory that the foundations of science are conventional, *see* HYPOTHESIS 3; KNOWLEDGE 4b, 5c; OPINION 3c; PRINCIPLE 3c(2), 5; RELATION 6b; TRUTH 7–7b; UNIVERSAL AND PARTICULAR 7a.

Matters relevant to the influence of custom on taste or judgments of beauty, *see* BEAUTY 5; NATURE 5d; RELATION 6c; UNIVERSAL AND PARTICULAR 7c.

The significance of nature and custom in the sphere of economic activity, *see* NATURE 5b; WEALTH 1, 10b.

ADDITIONAL READINGS

Listed below are works not included in *Great Books of the Western World*, but relevant to the idea and topics with which this chapter deals. These works are divided into two groups:

I. Works by authors represented in this collection.
II. Works by authors not represented in this collection.

For the date, place, and other facts concerning the publication of the works cited, consult the Bibliography of Additional Readings, which follows the last chapter of *The Great Ideas*.

I.

F. BACON. "Of Custom and Education," in *Essays*

MONTESQUIEU. *Persian Letters*

HUME. *Of Some Remarkable Customs*

A. SMITH. *The Theory of Moral Sentiments*, PART V

STERNE. *A Sentimental Journey*

HEGEL. *The Phenomenology of Mind*, V (B)

MELVILLE. *Typee*

——. *Omoo*

DOSTOEVSKY. *A Raw Youth*

FREUD. *"Civilized" Sexual Morality and Modern Nervousness*

——. *Totem and Taboo*

II.

HORACE. *Satires*

JUVENAL. *Satires*

Beowulf

Völsung Saga

SPENSER. *The Faerie Queene*

GRACIÁN Y MORALES. *The Art of Worldly Wisdom*

BROWNE. *Hydriotaphia*

PEPYS. *Diary*

LE SAGE. *The Adventures of Gil Blas*

DEFOE. *Moll Flanders*

RICHARDSON. *Pamela*

CHESTERFIELD. *Letters to His Son*

VOLTAIRE. "Customs . . . Usages," in *A Philosophical Dictionary*

SMOLLETT. *The Expedition of Humphry Clinker*

GOLDSMITH. *The Citizen of the World*

——. *She Stoops to Conquer*

BENTHAM. *A Comment on the Commentaries*, SECT 13–20

SHERIDAN. *The School for Scandal*

LAMB. *On the Custom of Hissing at the Theatres*

AUSTEN. *Pride and Prejudice*

MANZONI. *The Betrothed*

T. CARLYLE. *Sartor Resartus*, BK I

LERMONTOV. *A Hero of Our Own Times*

SAVIGNY. *Vom Beruf unserer Zeit für Gesetzgebung und Rechtswissenschaft*

——. *Jural Relations*

GOGOL. *Taras Bulba*

——. *Dead Souls*

DICKENS. *Bleak House*

THACKERAY. *The History of Henry Esmond, Esq.*

LOTZE. *Microcosmos*, BK VI, CH 3

FLAUBERT. *Madame Bovary*

TROLLOPE. *Barchester Towers*

DAUDET. *Letters from My Mill*

BAGEHOT. *Physics and Politics*

TYLOR. *Primitive Culture*

H. JAMES. *Daisy Miller*

MEREDITH. *The Egoist*

L. STEPHEN. *The Science of Ethics*

MAINE. *Ancient Law*

——. *Lectures on the Early History of Institutions*

——. *Dissertations on Early Law and Customs*

LANG. *Custom and Myth*

WUNDT. *Ethics*, PART I, CH 3

FRAZER. *The Golden Bough*

TARDE. *The Laws of Imitation*

KOVALEVSKY. *Modern Customs and Ancient Laws of Russia*

DUGUIT. *L'état, le droit objectif et la loi positive*

MANN. *Buddenbrooks*

WESTERMARCK. *The Origin and Development of the Moral Ideas*

SUMNER. *Folkways*

T. VEBLEN. *The Vested Interests and the State of the Industrial Arts*, CH 2

T. S. ELIOT. "Tradition and the Individual Talent," in *The Sacred Wood*

DEWEY. *Reconstruction in Philosophy*, CH 1, 5

——. *Human Conduct and Conduct*, PART I–II

S. LEWIS. *Babbitt*

UNDSET. *Kristin Lavransdatter*

VINOGRADOFF. *Custom and Right*

MALINOWSKI. *Crime and Custom in Savage Society*

——. *The Sexual Life of Savages*

DIAMOND. *Primitive Law*

Chapter 15: DEFINITION

INTRODUCTION

DEFINITION has been variously defined in the tradition of the great books. These diverse conceptions of what a definition is raise many issues.

At one extreme, writers like Hobbes look upon definition as nothing more than an attempt to say what a word means—how it has been or is being used. At the other, writers like Aquinas regard definition as that act of the mind by which it expresses the nature of a thing or formulates its essence.

In one technical view associated with the name of Aristotle, to define is to state the genus and differentia by which the species of a thing is constituted. In another theory of definition advanced by Locke and others, any combination of traits which distinguishes one class or kind of thing from another defines the character common to all members of that class. In still another view, to be found in Spinoza, definition consists in giving the cause or genesis of a thing, in saying how the thing originated or was produced.

Sometimes definition through causes employs the final rather than the efficient or productive cause, and characterizes the thing by the end it naturally serves. And sometimes, as with William James, definitions simply express the purposes or interests which we have in mind when we classify things to suit ourselves.

In the tradition of the liberal arts of grammar, rhetoric, and logic, these various conceptions of definition are connected with controversies concerning the power and activity of the human mind, the relation of language to thought, the structure of science or, more generally, the nature of knowledge, and the constitution of reality, with particular reference to the existence of universals and individuals and their relation to one another.

These connections appear in the thought of Aristotle and Spinoza, Hobbes and Locke, Aquinas and William James. Their views of the way in which definitions should be constructed or their conceptions of the function of definitions determine and reflect lines of agreement and opposition on many other matters. The use of definitions in the great works of mathematics and natural science—by Euclid, Descartes, Galileo, Newton, Lavoisier, and Darwin—tends to exemplify now one, now another, theory of definition. Modern discussions of the nature of science and mathematics, especially discussions influenced by the development of mathematical logic—from Whewell, Mill, and Poincaré to Whitehead, Russell, and Dewey—focus critical attention on the nature and role of definitions.

MANY OTHER chapters provide an illuminating context for topics discussed in this one, especially the chapters on LANGUAGE and LOGIC, IDEA, PRINCIPLE and REASONING, PHILOSOPHY and SCIENCE, and TRUTH. Though the issues concerning definition cannot be resolved apart from this larger context of controversy about the mind, reality, and knowledge, we can nevertheless formulate these issues in isolation. But in doing so we ought to bear in mind that they can be more readily understood in proportion as they are seen in the light of other relevant considerations.

There is, first of all, the question about the object of definition. What is being defined when men make or defend definitions? This question broadens into the problem of nominal as opposed to real definitions. That is a complex problem which raises a number of further questions. Are all definitions arbitrary, expressing the conventions of our speech or the particular purpose we have in mind when we classify things? Or do some, if not all, definitions express the real natures of the things defined? Do they classify things according to natural kinds which have reality apart from our mind and its interests?

These issues are in turn related to the issue concerning the limits of definition and its ultimate principles—whether all things, or only some, are definable, and whether the indefinable terms, without which definition is itself impossible, can be arbitrarily chosen or must always be terms of a certain sort. The sense in which definitions may be true or false and the sense in which they cannot be either, have a bearing on all these issues; and through them all run the divergent conceptions of how definitions can or should be constructed.

WHEN IN THE course of argument one man dismisses the opinion of another by saying, "That is just a matter of definition," the usual implication is that the rejected opinion has no truth apart from the way in which the man who proposed it uses words. He may even be accused of begging the question, of framing definitions which implicitly contain the conclusion he subsequently draws from them.

The underlying supposition here seems to be expressed by Pascal when, in his essay *On Geometrical Demonstration*, he asserts that "there is great freedom of definition and definitions are never subject to contradiction, for nothing is more permissible than to give whatever name we please to a thing we have clearly pointed out." He calls "true definitions" those which are "arbitrary, permissible, and geometrical." The only restriction he would place upon our freedom to make definitions is that "we must be careful not to take advantage of our freedom to impose names by giving the same name to two different things." And even this case, he claims, is permissible "if we avoid confusion by not extending the consequences of one to the other."

If we are free to make whatever definitions we please, it would seem to follow that definitions cannot be matters of argument; and differences of opinion which result from differences in definition would seem to be irreconcilable by any appeal to reason or to fact.

Such a conception of definition as verbal does not seem to prevent Hobbes from holding

that definitions are first principles or foundations of science. "In Geometry (which is the only science that it hath pleased God hitherto to bestow on mankind), men begin," he writes, "at settling the signification of their words; which settling of significations, they call *Definitions*; and place them in the beginning of their reckoning." This shows, Hobbes thinks, "how necessary it is for any man that aspires to true knowledge to examine the definitions of former authors; and either to correct them, where they are negligently set down; or to make them himself. For the errors of definitions multiply themselves, according as the reckoning proceeds."

For Hobbes, then, definition is verbal; yet definitions can also be true or false, and on the truth of definitions depends the distinction between knowledge and opinion. "In the right definition of names," he says, "lies the first use of speech; which is the acquisition of science." Only when discourse "begins with the definitions of words" can it reach conclusions that have the character of knowledge. "If the first ground of such discourse be not definitions ... then the end or conclusion is opinion."

Hobbes accurately reports the nature of geometry when he says that in that science definitions serve as principles in reasoning or proof. The words "by definition" mark one of the steps in many Euclidean proofs. Descartes and Spinoza, proceeding in the geometrical manner, place definitions at the head of their works as ultimate principles to be used in validating their conclusions. But, unlike Hobbes, these writers do not seem to regard their definitions as merely verbal. Euclid goes further, as we shall presently see, and offers what amounts to proofs of his definitions, or at least of their geometrical reality. Aristotle and Aquinas certainly take the position not only that definitions are principles, but also that definitions themselves are capable of being demonstrated. But they complicate the matter by insisting that definitions are neither true nor false, since, as Aristotle says, they do not involve "the assertion of something concerning something."

At least two questions seem to be involved in this familiar dispute about the arguability of definitions and their role in argumentation. To avoid confusion, they should be kept distinct. One is the question of the truth and falsity of definitions. It should be separated from, even though it is related to, the other question about whether all definitions are nominal, *i.e.*, concerned only with assigning meanings to the words by which we name things. To understand what is involved in this second question, it may be helpful to consider the relation of words, thoughts, and things in the process of definition.

A DICTIONARY IS supposed to contain definitions. It does in part—insofar as the meaning of any word is expressed in a phrase containing other words which are not synonyms for the word in question. The combined meanings of these other words determine the meaning of the word being defined.

For example, one definition of the word "brother" is "a male relative, the son of the same parents or parent." Another is "a male member of a religious order." These two definitions give different meanings for the same word. The dictionary is here recording two ways in which, as a matter of historical fact, the word has been used. It has been and can be used in still other ways. No one of these definitions can be called "right" and the others "wrong."

Dictionary definitions seem to be verbal and arbitrary in a number of ways. That the word "brother" should carry any of the meanings which the dictionary records is an accident of English usage. It is arbitrary that that particular sound or mark should be the name for a male relative who is the son of the same parents. It would be equally arbitrary to restrict the meaning of the word "brother" to any one of its definitions.

Nothing about a word limits the number of distinct meanings with which it can be used. As Locke says, "every man has so inviolable a liberty to make words stand for what ideas he pleases, that no one hath the power to make others have the same ideas in their minds that he has, when they use the same words that he does." A word is thus a conventional sound or mark, which can be given any meaning convention assigns to it. When that meaning is expressed *in other words*, we have a verbal definition, and such definitions are certainly nominal in this sense—that they state the meaning of a *name*.

But are they merely nominal? Are they entirely arbitrary? That this word should be used to name this thing is arbitrary, but that when it is so used a certain definition also applies may not be arbitrary. Among the several verbal definitions of a word, the one which applies in any particular case will depend upon the character of the thing which the word is used to name.

For example, if John and James are sons of the same parents, the name "brother" applies, but not with the same definition which is required for the application of the name to Mark and Matthew who, unrelated by blood, are members of the same monastic order. What the word "brother" is used to mean may be arbitrary, but when it is used now of John and James, and now of Mark and Matthew, it would be misapplied if it did not carry the appropriate definition. Which definition is appropriate in each case does not seem to be arbitrary, since that appropriateness depends not on our will but on the objective facts of the case—the actual relation of the persons called "brothers."

Precisely because the word is used to name a thing, the definition of the word *as so used* does more than state the meaning of the word. It states something about the character of the thing named. Definitions remain merely verbal only so long as the words they define are not actually used to name or to signify things in some way. Whenever a thing is named or signified, the definition which gives the meaning of the word must also signify something about the nature of the thing.

"In the natural order of ideas," writes Lavoisier, "the name of the class or genus is that which expresses a quality common to a great number of individuals; the name of the species, on the contrary, expresses a quality peculiar to certain individuals only. These distinctions are not, as some may imagine, merely metaphysical, but are established by Nature."

YET IT MAY BE said that the definition is still nominal, for it depends entirely on the meanings of the words which express it. For example, one definition of "brother" involves the meanings of such words as "male" and "relative," "son," "parent," and "same." If we were to look these words up in a dictionary, the definitions we found would involve the meanings of still other words, and so on in an endlessly circular fashion. Furthermore, we would find the account of certain words, such as "relative" and "same," somewhat unsatisfactory as definitions because the meaning of the defining words would immediately involve the meaning of the word to be defined. To say that "same" means "not other" or "not different" seems the same as saying "same" means "same." Yet we must know the meaning of "same," for otherwise we could not understand the meaning of "brother," in the definition of which the word "same" appears.

That some words seem to have indefinable meanings suggests that not all meanings are merely verbal or nominal, and that the meaning of every word cannot be found in the meanings of other words. In the Preface to his dictionary, Dr. Johnson observes that "as nothing can be proved but by supposing something intuitively known, and evident without proof, so nothing can be defined but by the use of words too plain to admit of definition." The circularity of the dictionary is thus avoided. When we trace meanings from one word to another, we finally come to words whose meanings we seem to understand immediately, or at least without reference to the meanings of other words.

Just as the arbitrary character of verbal definitions seems to be removed by the consideration of the things which words name or signify, so the purely nominal character of definitions seem to be removed by recourse to meanings which are understood without further verbal explanation—meanings which may in fact be incapable of such explanation.

NOT ALL WRITERS agree with Dr. Johnson. All of them would admit that some words must be left undefined in order to define others, but which shall be used as indefinable and which shall be defined is, in the opinion of some, a matter of choice. It is not something which can be determined by the order intrinsic to our ideas or meanings. The issue between the mathematical logicians who think that we are free to choose our primitive or indefinable terms, and those who, like Aquinas, think that certain terms, such as *being, same, one,* and *rela-*

tion, impose themselves upon our minds as principles, leaving us no choice, parallels the issue between the view that the principles of a science consist of postulates voluntarily assumed and the view that they are axiomatic or unavoidable.

Far from regarding such basic indefinable terms as clearest and most indisputable in meaning, Spinoza thinks that "these terms signify ideas in the highest degree confused." For him "the true definition of any one thing . . . expresses nothing but the nature of the thing defined." But to arrive at the true definition, it is necessary to discover the cause of the thing. For "every existing thing," he writes, "there is some certain cause by reason of which it exists." This cause "must either be contained in the nature itself and definition of the existing thing . . . or it must exist outside the thing." In the latter case, the definition of the thing always involves a statement of the external cause of its existence.

Accordingly, Spinoza rejects the traditional type of Aristotelian definition as purely subjective—a matter of individual memory and imagination. "Those who have more frequently looked with admiration upon the stature of men," he writes, "by the name *man* will understand an animal of erect stature, while those who have been in the habit of fixing their thoughts on something else will form another common image of men, describing man, for instance, as an animal capable of laughter, a biped without feathers, a rational animal, and so on; each person forming universal images of things according to the temperament of his own body."

However the issue between Spinoza and Aristotle is resolved, both seem to agree that more is involved in the process of definition than the statement of verbal equivalences. "We have a definition," Aristotle says, "not where we have a word and formula identical in meaning (for in that case all formulae or sets of words would be definitions)." The formula which is expressed in a phrase or combination of words must state the nature or essence of a thing, not just the meaning of a word. "The formula . . . in which the term itself is not present but its meaning is expressed, this," according to Aristotle, "is the formula of the essence of each thing" and, he adds, "there is an essence only of those things whose formula is a definition."

Even supposing the truth of these statements, which Hobbes or Locke certainly would question, the problem of real as opposed to nominal definition requires further examination. To explore the matter further, let us take two of the most famous definitions to be found in the great books. Both are definitions of man —"featherless biped" and "rational animal." As we have seen, these definitions must remain purely nominal—only stating the meaning of the word "man"—until that word is used to name some kind of thing. If, however, we apply the word "man" to existing entities which combine the characteristics of having two legs and lacking feathers, then "featherless biped" defines, not the word "man," but a class of real, that is, existing things. In addition to being nominal, the definition is now also real in the sense that the class or kind which it determines has existing members.

That animals exist may similarly be a fact of observation. But "animal" is only one of the two terms in the other nominal definition of "man." In order to make "rational animal" more than a nominal definition, it is necessary to verify the existence of animals which possess a certain characteristic, *rationality*, not possessed by all animals. If rationality in some degree belonged to all animals, then the word "man" (nominally defined by "rational animal") would be synonymous with "animal." But, unlike feathers, the presence or absence of which seems readily observable, the possession or lack of rationality is difficult to ascertain.

Here we face two possibilities. One is that we can never be sure that some existing animals are and some are not rational. Then the definition "rational animal" will never become real. It will always remain merely nominal, the statement of a possible meaning for "man," but one which we cannot employ when we apply the word to name any existing thing. The other possibility is that we can infer the existence of a special class of animals (distinguished by the possession of reason) from such evident facts as the activities of reading and writing, activities not performed by all animals. Then, members of the class defined having been found to exist, "rational animal" becomes a real definition of

the beings to which we also arbitrarily assign the name "man."

THE PROCESS of verification by which a nominal is converted into a real definition can be regarded as the demonstration of a definition. Strictly speaking, it is not the definition which is thereby proved. It is rather a proposition in which the subject of the definition is affirmed to exist, or in which a subject already known to exist is said to have a certain definition. For example, it is not the definition "rational animal" which is proved, but the proposition "there exists an animal which differs from other animals in being rational," or the proposition "the real being which we call 'man' is both an animal and rational, and he alone is rational." If these propositions cannot be proved, "rational animal" remains a purely nominal definition.

That definitions are not as such either true or false is unaffected by the distinction between real and nominal definitions. The point is simply that a definition, which is always linguistically expressed by a phrase, never a sentence, neither affirms nor denies anything, and so cannot be either true or false. "Featherless biped" or "son of the same parents" makes no assertion about reality or existence.

Yet there is a special sense in which definitions can be true or false, which does have a bearing on the distinction between real and nominal definitions. Pascal suggests three alternatives with regard to the truth or falsity of definitions. "If we find it impossible," he writes, "it passes for false; if we demonstrate that it is true, it passes for a truth; and as long as it cannot be proved to be either possible or impossible, it is considered a fancy."

According to Aquinas, there are two ways in which a definition can be false. In one way, when the intellect applies "to one thing the definition proper to another; as that of a circle to a man. In another way, by composing a definition of parts which are mutually repugnant. A definition such as 'a four-footed rational animal' would be of this kind . . . for such a statement as 'some rational animals are four-footed' is false in itself."

But the truth or falsity of that statement can conceivably be argued, and therefore it is not so clear an example of a false definition as one which, in Pascal's terms, plainly represents an impossibility. Suppose someone offered "round square" as the nominal definition of "rectacycle." The phrase "round square" expresses a self-contradiction, and in consequence the definition is false. Its falsity is tantamount to the *impossibility* of there being any such figure as a *rectacycle* which has the definition proposed.

The truth of a definition—which is nothing more than its freedom from self-contradiction—is equivalent to the *possibility*, as opposed to the impossibility, of the thing defined. To call the definition "son of the same parents" or "featherless biped" *true* is to say that the words defined—"brother" or "man"—signify possible existences. In short, only those nominal definitions which are true can ever become real, and they become real only when the possibility they signify is actually known to be realized in existence.

THE METHOD OF Euclid's *Elements* illustrates the foregoing points. Euclid defines certain geometrical figures, such as triangle, parallelogram, square. These definitions may appear to be free from contradiction, but that does not tell us whether they are more than nominal. The defined figures are possible, but the question is whether they exist in the space determined by Euclid's postulates.

To show that they do exist, Euclid undertakes to construct them according to his postulates which permit him the use of a straight edge and a compass for purposes of construction. When in Proposition 1 Euclid proves that he can construct an equilateral triangle, he establishes the geometrical reality of the figure defined in Definition 20. A geometrical construction is thus seen to be what is called an "existence proof." It converts a nominal into a real definition. Figures which cannot be constructed must be postulated; as, for example, the straight line and the circle. Postulates 1 and 3 ask us to assume that a straight line can be drawn between any two points and that a circle can be described with any center and radius. These postulates give Definitions 4 and 15 their geometrical reality.

Though the method of construction is peculiar to geometry, the relation of definitions to proofs or postulates of existence is the same for all sciences. Until a definition ceases to be nominal and becomes real, it cannot be used scientifically in the demonstration of other conclusions; to use a merely nominal definition in the proof begs the question.

If the existence of the thing defined is either directly observable or self-evident, no proof or postulation of existence is required. In theology, for example, there are those who think that the existence of God is immediately seen in the definition of God. Descartes and Spinoza seem to be of this opinion.

Descartes argues that "eternal existence" is necessarily included in the idea of God as "a supremely perfect Being." This is so evident, he declares, that "existence can no more be separated from the essence of God than can its having its three angles equal to two right angles be separated from the essence of a triangle, or the idea of a mountain from the idea of a valley." Concerning substance or God, Spinoza holds that, since it pertains to its nature to exist, "its definition must involve necessary existence, and consequently from its definition alone its existence must be concluded."

On the other hand, there are those who think that the existence of God must be proved by inference from effect to cause. Supposing that a man understands the meaning of the word "God," Aquinas maintains that it "does not therefore follow that he understands that what the name signifies exists actually, but only that it exists mentally." Hence, he declares, it is necessary to prove the existence of God, "accepting as a middle term the meaning of the name," but using an effect in "place of the definition of the cause in proving the cause's existence."

The difference between these two positions might be summed up by saying that Descartes and Spinoza, like Anselm before them, think the definition of God is intrinsically real, whereas Aquinas thinks we must begin with a nominal definition of God, which becomes real only with proof of God's existence. For some confirmed atheists, any definition of God is not only nominal, but false—the definition of an impossible being, incapable of existing.

THERE IS STILL another issue about nominal and real definitions. The point involved is the one raised by Locke's discussion of nominal and real essences. It is also raised by Aristotle's discrimination between essential and accidental unities, *i.e.*, the difference between the unity signified by the phrase "featherless biped" and by the phrase "black man." Both phrases look like definitions. Each designates a possible class of individuals and sets up the conditions for membership in that class or exclusion from it.

The distinction between them does not rest, according to Aristotle, on the criterion of existence. Both of the objects defined may exist, but whereas the first is truly a species, the second is only, in Aristotle's opinion, an accidental variety within the species *man*. *Man*, being a species, can have a real essence, and so any definition of man—whether "featherless biped" or "rational animal"—can be a real definition, constituted by genus and differentia. But *negro* or *aryan*, not being a species, but only a race or variety, has no essence as such. The definitions —"black man" and "white man"—indicate this in that they are constituted by two terms which are related as substance and accident, not as genus and differentia.

Though Aristotle distinguishes these two types of formulae as essential and accidental definitions rather than as real and nominal definitions, the one principle of distinction is closely related to the other, for only essential definitions can have real essences for their objects. Accidental definitions do little more than state the meanings of words, or express what Locke calls the "nominal essences" of things. He doubts that the definition of anything except a mathematical object can ever grasp the real essence of a thing. For him all definitions are nominal, which is equivalent to saying that we never define by means of the true genus and differentia, but always by accidental and external signs, or by stating the component parts of a complex whole.

"Speaking of a man, or gold," Locke explains, "or any other species of natural substance, as supposed constituted by a precise and real essence which nature regularly imparts to every individual of that kind, whereby it is made to be of that species, we cannot be certain of the truth of any affirmation or negation made of it. For man or gold, taken in this sense, and used for species of things constituted by real essences, different from the complex idea

in the mind of the speaker, stand for we know not what; and the extent of these species, with such boundaries, are so unknown and undetermined, that it is impossible with any certainty to affirm, that all men are rational, or that all gold is yellow."

THIS ISSUE HAS MANY ramifications. In one direction it leads into Aristotle's quarrel with Plato over the method of definition by division or dichotomy. In the *Sophist* and the *Statesman*, the search for definitions proceeds by the division of a class of things into two sub-classes, one of which is then further subdivided, and so on until a class is reached which has the characteristics of the object to be defined. The attempt to define a sophist, for example, starts with the notion that he is a man of art, and proceeds by dividing and subdividing the various kinds of art. At one point in the course of doing this, the Athenian Stranger summarizes the process to that point.

"You and I," he says to Theaetetus, "have come to an understanding not only about the name of the angler's art, but about the definition of the thing itself. One half of all art was acquisitive—half of the acquisitive art was conquest or taking by force, half of this was hunting, and half of hunting was hunting animals, half of this was hunting water animals—of this again, the under half was fishing, half of fishing was striking; a part of striking was fishing with a barb, and one half of this again, being the kind which strikes with a hook and draws the fish from below upwards, is the art which we have been seeking, and which from the nature of the operation is denoted angling or drawing up . . . And now, following this pattern," he continues, "let us endeavor to find out what a Sophist is."

The pattern as illustrated indicates that, in the course of division, one of the two classes is discarded while the other is subject to further subdivision. Aristotle's criticism of this procedure turns partly on the fact that the division is always dichotomous, or into *two* sub-classes, and partly on the fact that the terms which Plato uses in a succession of subdivisions do not seem to have any systematic relation to one another. If the class of animals, for example, is divided into those with and those without feet, it makes a difference, according to Aristotle, what terms are then used to differentiate footed animals into their proper sub-classes.

"It is necessary," he insists, "that the division be by the differentia *of the differentia*; *e.g.*, 'endowed with feet' is a differentia of 'animal'; again the differentia of 'animal endowed with feet' must be of it *qua* endowed with feet. Therefore we must not say, if we are to speak rightly, that of that which is endowed with feet one part has feathers and one is featherless (if we do this we do it through incapacity); we must divide it only into cloven-footed and not-cloven; for these are differentiae in the foot; cloven-footedness is a form of footedness. And the process wants always to go on so till it reaches the species that contains no difference. And then there will be as many kinds of foot as there are differentiae; and the kinds of animals endowed with feet will be equal in number to the differentiae. If then this is so, clearly the *last* differentia will be the essence of the thing and its definition."

As Aristotle quarrels with Plato's method of division, so William James takes issue with Aristotle's theory that a real essence is defined when the right differentia is properly chosen within a certain genus of things. He tends to follow Locke's notion that definitions indicate no more than the nominal essences of things, but he gives this theory a special twist by adding the notion that all our definitions merely group things according to the interest or purpose, whether theoretical or practical, which motivates our classification of them. This has come to be known as the pragmatic theory of definition.

"My thinking," writes James, "is first and last and always for the sake of my doing." After pointing out that Locke "undermined the fallacy" of supposing that we can define the real essences of things, he goes on to say that "none of his successors, as far as I know, have radically escaped it, or seen that *the only meaning of essence is teleological, and that classification and conception are purely teleological weapons of the mind*. The essence of a thing is that one of its properties which is so *important for my interests* that in comparison with it I may neglect the rest. ... The properties which are important

vary from man to man and from hour to hour."

In a footnote James adds: "A substance like oil has as many different essences as it has uses to different individuals." The classification of natural as well as artificial objects should therefore proceed according to the advice Mephistopheles gives to the student in Goethe's *Faust*. "You will have more success," he says, "if you will learn to reduce all, and to classify each according to its use." But if this is so, then no one scheme of classification, more than any other, represents the real structure or order of nature. Nature indifferently submits to any and all divisions which we wish to make among existing things. Some classifications may be more significant than others, but only by reference to our interests, not because they represent reality more accurately or adequately. It does not matter, therefore, whether we define by genus and differentia, by other characteristics in combination, or by reference to origins or functions.

Darwin's scheme of classification provides evidence relevant to this whole issue. As indicated in the chapters on ANIMAL and EVOLUTION, Darwin thinks that his genealogical classification of plants and animals comes nearer to the natural system of living organisms than the classifications proposed by his predecessors. "The Natural System," he writes, "is a genealogical arrangement, with the acquired grades of difference, marked by the terms, varieties, species, genera, families, etc.; and we have to discover the lines of descent by the most permanent characters whatever they may be and of however slight vital importance." Henceforth, following his method, "systematists will have only to decide ... whether any form be sufficiently constant and distinct from other forms, to be capable of definition; and if definable, whether the differences be sufficiently important to deserve a specific name."

But Darwin's statement re-opens rather than resolves the great traditional questions. Are the various groupings made in classification divisions which the classifier finds useful to impose on nature, or do they represent lines of real distinction in the very nature of things? If the latter is the case, either wholly or in part, are we able to do more than approximate real distinction by whatever method of definition we employ? Can we discover real species, essentially distinct from one another, and can our definitions formulate the essence of each?

THE SEARCH FOR definitions basically belongs to the activity of the human mind in all its scientific or dialectical efforts to clarify discourse, to achieve precision of thought, to focus issues and to resolve them.

Men have no other way of coming to terms with one another than by defining the words they use to express their concepts or meanings. They make terms out of words by endowing words with exactness or precision of meaning. Definition does this and makes possible the meeting of minds either in agreement or in dispute. Definition also makes it possible for any

mind to submit itself to the test of agreement with reality. Definition helps man to ask nature or experience the only sort of question to which answers can be found.

The search for definitions has, perhaps, its most dramatic exemplification in the dialogues of Plato. Socrates usually leads the conversation in quest of them; though it is only in certain dialogues, such as the *Sophist* and the *Statesman*, that the making of definitions is practiced in detail. Two other books in this set are largely concerned with ways of reaching and defending definitions—Aristotle's *Topics* (which should be considered together with the opening chapters of his *Parts of Animals*) and Bacon's *Novum Organum*.

OUTLINE OF TOPICS

REFERENCES

To find the passages cited, use the numbers in heavy type, which are the volume and page numbers of the passages referred to. For example, in **4** Homer: *Iliad*, bk ii [265–283] 12d, the number **4** is the number of the volume in the set; the number 12d indicates that the passage is in section d of page 12.

Page Sections: When the text is printed in one column, the letters a and b refer to the upper and lower halves of the page. For example, in **53** James: *Psychology*, 116a-119b, the passage begins in the upper half of page 116 and ends in the lower half of page 119. When the text is printed in two columns, the letters a and b refer to the upper and lower halves of the left-hand side of the page, the letters c and d to the upper and lower halves of the right-hand side of the page. For example, in **7** Plato: *Symposium*, 163b-164c, the passage begins in the lower half of the left-hand side of page 163 and ends in the upper half of the right-hand side of page 164.

Author's Divisions: One or more of the main divisions of a work (such as part, bk, ch, sect) are sometimes included in the reference; line numbers, in brackets, are given in certain cases; *e.g., Iliad*, bk ii [265–283] 12d.

Bible References: The references are to book, chapter, and verse. When the King James and Douay versions differ in title of books or in the numbering of chapters or verses, the King James version is cited first and the Douay, indicated by a (D), follows; *e.g.*, Old Testament: *Nehemiah*, 7:45—(D) *II Esdras*, 7:46.

Symbols: The abbreviation "esp" calls the reader's attention to one or more especially relevant parts of a whole reference; "passim" signifies that the topic is discussed intermittently rather than continuously in the work or passage cited.

For additional information concerning the style of the references, see the Explanation of Reference Style; for general guidance in the use of *The Great Ideas*, consult the Preface.

1. The theory of definition

7 Plato: *Meno*, 174a-177d / *Theaetetus*, 544d-549d / *Sophist* 551a-579d / *Statesman* 580a-608d / *Laws*, bk x, 763c-d / *Seventh Letter*, 809c-810d

8 Aristotle: *Posterior Analytics*, bk ii, ch 3–10 123c-128d; ch 13 131b-133c / *Topics*, bk vi-vii 192a-211a,c / *Metaphysics*, bk vii, ch 4–6 552b-555a; ch 10–17 558a-566a,c; bk viii, ch 2–3 566d-568d; ch 6 569d-570d

9 Aristotle: *Parts of Animals*, bk i, ch 2–4 165d-168c

12 Aurelius: *Meditations*, bk iii, sect 11 262a-b

18 Augustine: *Christian Doctrine*, bk ii, ch 35 653b-c

23 Hobbes: *Leviathan*, part i, 56b-d

30 Bacon: *Novum Organum*, bk ii 137a-195d esp aph 17 149b-d, aph 22–51 153b-194c

31 Descartes: *Rules*, xii, 23c-24a

31 Spinoza: *Ethics*, part i, prop 8, schol 2 356d-357d; part ii, prop 40, schol 1 387b-388a

33 Pascal: *Geometrical Demonstration*, 430b-434b; 442a-443b

35 Locke: *Human Understanding*, bk iii, ch iii–vi 254d-283a passim

35 Hume: *Human Understanding*, sect vii, div 48–49 470d-471d

42 Kant: *Pure Reason*, 44c-45b; 215d-217a

44 Boswell: *Johnson*, 82a-c

53 James: *Psychology*, 314a-b; 668a-673b

1a. The object of definition: definitions as arbitrary and nominal or real and concerned with essence

7 Plato: *Cratylus*, 104d-105b; 113a-114a,c / *Gorgias*, 252d-253b / *Republic*, bk vi, 384a-387d; bk ix, 426d-427b / *Timaeus*, 457b-458b / *Theaetetus*, 514b-515c; 547c-549c / *Sophist*, 551a-d / *Philebus*, 610d-613a / *Laws*, bk x, 763c-d / *Seventh Letter*, 809a-810b

8 Aristotle: *Categories*, ch 5 [2^{a}19–3^{b}24] 6b-8a / *Posterior Analytics*, bk i, ch 22 113b-115b; ch 33 [88^{b}30–89^{a}1] 121b-c; bk ii, ch 3–10 123c-128d; ch 13 131b-133c / *Topics*, bk i, ch 4 [101^{b}17–23] 144b-c; ch 5 [101^{b}37–102^{a}5] 144d; ch 8 [103^{b}1–11] 146d; ch 18 [108^{a}38–^{b}9] 152d;[108^{b}19–32]153a,c; bk vi, ch i [139^{a}24–34] 192a; bk vi, ch 4–bk vii, ch 5 194c-211a,c passim / *Physics*, bk ii, ch i [193^{a}30–^{b}19] 269c-270a / *Generation and Corruption*, bk i, ch 2 [317^{a}17–27] 413b / *Meteorology*, bk iv, ch 12 493d-494d / *Metaphysics*, bk i, ch 5 [986^{b}8–987^{a}1] 504c-505a; [987^{a}19–27] 505b; ch 6 [987^{b}1–10] 505c; [987^{b}30–33] 506a; bk ii, ch 2 [994^{b}16–27] 513a-b; bk iii, ch 2 [996^{b}12–21] 515a-b; bk iv, ch 4 525a-528b; bk vi,

(1. *The theory of definition.* 1a. *The object of definition: definitions as arbitrary and nominal or real and concerned with essence.*)

CH 1 [1025^{b}28–1026^{a}6] 547d-548a; BK VII, CH 1 [1028^{a}31–37] 550d; CH 4–6 552b-555a; CH 10–17 558a-566a,c; BK VIII, CH 2–3 566d-568d; CH 6 569d-570d; BK X, CH 1 [1052^{b}1–15] 578d-579a; BK XI, CH 5 590a-d; BK XIII, CH 4 [1078^{b}18–32] 610b-c / *Soul*, BK I, CH 1 631a-632d; BK III, CH 6 [430^{b}26–31] 663b-c

9 ARISTOTLE: *Parts of Animals*, BK I, CH 1 [641^{a}14–31] 163d-164a; CH 2–4 165d-168c

19 AQUINAS: *Summa Theologica*, PART I, Q 1, A 7, REP 1 7a-c; Q 2, A 1, REP 2 10d-11d; A 2, REP 2 11d-12c; Q 3, A 3, ANS 16a-d; A 5, ANS 17c-18b; Q 17, A 3 102d-103c; Q 29, A 1, REP 1,3–4 162a-163b; A 2, REP 3 163b-164b; Q 44, A 1, REP 1 238b-239a; A 3, REP 3 240b-241a; Q 58, A 5 303c-304c; Q 75, A 4, ANS 381b-382a; Q 85, A 6 458d-459c; Q 116, A 1, CONTRARY 592d-593d

20 AQUINAS: *Summa Theologica*, PART II-II, Q 4, A 1, ANS 402a-403d; PART III, Q 2, A 2, ANS 711d-712d; Q 60, A 4, REP 1 849c-850b

23 HOBBES: *Leviathan*, PART I, 55b-c; 56b; 59c-d; PART IV, 270a-c

25 MONTAIGNE: *Essays*, 518d-519a

28 GALILEO: *Two New Sciences*, FIRST DAY, 142d-143a

30 BACON: *Novum Organum*, BK II, APH 4 137d-138b

31 DESCARTES: *Rules*, XIII, 26b-c / *Objections and Replies*, POSTULATE IV 131a-b

31 SPINOZA: *Ethics*, PART I, PROP 8, SCHOL 2 356d-357d; PART II, PROP 40, SCHOL 1 387b-388a; PART III, PROP 4 398d

33 PASCAL: *Vacuum*, 372b-373b; 376b-377a / *Geometrical Demonstration*, 430b-431b

35 LOCKE: *Human Understanding*, BK II, CH XXXI, SECT 6–13 240d-243b; CH XXXII, SECT 18 246c-247a; SECT 24 247c-d; BK III, CH III, SECT 11–20 257a-260a esp SECT 18–20 259b-260a; CH V, SECT 14 267b-c; CH VI 268b-283a; CH X, SECT 17–21 295d-297b; CH XI, SECT 15–24 303b-305d; BK IV, CH IV, SECT 11–17 326b-328d passim; CH VI, SECT 4–16 331d-336d passim; CH XII, SECT 9 360d-361b

35 BERKELEY: *Human Knowledge*, INTRO, SECT 18 410a-c

42 KANT: *Pure Reason*, 179d-182b; 215d-216c / *Science of Right*, 404d; 423d-424b

45 LAVOISIER: *Elements of Chemistry*, PART I, 10a-b

46 HEGEL: *Philosophy of History*, INTRO, 176c; 184d-185a

49 DARWIN: *Origin of Species*, 27b-29a esp 29a

51 TOLSTOY: *War and Peace*, EPILOGUE II, 694b-d

53 JAMES: *Psychology*, 106a; 185a-b; 668a-671a; 882b-883a

1b. The purpose of definition: the clarification of ideas

7 PLATO: *Phaedrus*, 120a-b / *Meno*, 174a-179b / *Euthyphro*, 193c / *Seventh Letter*, 809c-810b

8 ARISTOTLE: *Posterior Analytics*, BK II, CH 14 [98^{a}1–2] 133c-d / *Topics*, BK I, CH 18 [108^{a}17–37] 152b-d; BK VI, CH 1 [139^{b}11–15] 192b-c; CH 4 [141^{a}26–32] 194c; BK VIII, CH 3 [158^{a}31–159^{a}2] 214d-215c / *Metaphysics*, BK IV, CH 4 525a-528b; BK XI, CH 5 590a-d / *Soul*, BK I, CH 1 [402^{b}15–403^{a}2] 631d-632a

9 ARISTOTLE: *Parts of Animals*, BK II, CH 2 [648^{b}1–5] 172d / *Rhetoric*, BK II, CH 23 [1398^{a}15–27] 646c

12 AURELIUS: *Meditations*, BK III, SECT 11 262a-b

19 AQUINAS: *Summa Theologica*, PART I, Q 85, A 3, REP 3 455b-457a

23 HOBBES: *Leviathan*, PART I, 56b; 58d-59a; PART IV, 269b-c

28 GALILEO: *Two New Sciences*, FIRST DAY, 142d-143a

30 BACON: *Advancement of Learning*, 60b-c; 61b-c / *Novum Organum*, BK I, APH 59 112b-c

31 DESCARTES: *Rules*, XII, 23c-24a; XIII, 26b-c

33 PASCAL: *Geometrical Demonstration*, 430b-434b passim

34 NEWTON: *Principles*, DEFINITIONS, SCHOL, 8b

35 LOCKE: *Human Understanding*, BK III, CH IV, SECT 6–14 260d-263a

35 HUME: *Human Understanding*, SECT VIII, DIV 62 478b-c; DIV 74 484a-c

42 KANT: *Pure Reason*, 113b-c / *Practical Reason*, 293c-294b

44 BOSWELL: *Johnson*, 377d

45 LAVOISIER: *Elements of Chemistry*, PREF, 4a-5c; PART I, 10a-b; 21a-22c

45 FARADAY: *Researches in Electricity*, 361a-b

46 HEGEL: *Philosophy of Right*, INTRO, par 2 9b-10a

49 DARWIN: *Origin of Species*, 207d-208a

51 TOLSTOY: *War and Peace*, EPILOGUE II, 694b-d

53 JAMES: *Psychology*, 314a-b; 669a-671a; 871a-b

1c. The limits of definition: the definable and the indefinable

7 PLATO: *Republic*, BK VI, 384a-388a / *Theaetetus*, 544c-547c / *Seventh Letter*, 809c-810b

8 ARISTOTLE: *Metaphysics*, BK I, CH 9 [992^{b}24–993^{a}1] 511a-b; BK II, CH 2 [994^{b}16–27] 513a-b; BK V, CH 3 [1014^{b}3–13] 534d; BK VII, CH 4–5 552b-554a; CH 10–11 558a-561a; CH 13 [1039^{a}15–23] 563a; CH 15 563c-564c; BK VIII, CH 3 [1043^{b}23–33] 568b; BK X, CH 8–9 585b-586c

17 PLOTINUS: *Fifth Ennead*, TR V, CH 6 231b-d

19 AQUINAS: *Summa Theologica*, PART I, Q 1, A 7, REP 1 7a-c; Q 2, A 1, REP 2 10d-11d; A 2, REP 2 11d-12c; Q 3, A 3, ANS 16a-d; A 5, ANS 17c-18b; Q 29, A 1, REP 1 162a-163b; A 2, REP 3 163b-164b; Q 44, A 3, REP 3 240b-241a; Q 85, A 1, REP 2 451c-453c

30 Bacon: *Novum Organum*, bk i, aph 59 112b-c
31 Descartes: *Rules*, xii, 23c-24a
31 Spinoza: *Ethics*, part i, axiom 2 355d
33 Pascal: *Geometrical Demonstration*, 431b-434b; 442a-443b
35 Locke: *Human Understanding*, bk ii, ch ii, sect i 127d-128a; ch iv, sect 6 131a; ch xx, sect i 176b-c; bk iii, ch iv, sect 4–17 260b-263c; ch vi 268b-283a passim, esp sect 7–10 270b-271b; ch xi, sect 13–25 302d-306c
35 Hume: *Human Understanding*, sect vii, div 49 471c-d
42 Kant: *Pure Reason*, 29d-33d; 53b-54b; 179d-182b; 215d-216c / *Judgement*, 603a-604b
43 Federalist: number 37, 119b-120b
44 Boswell: *Johnson*, 82b
49 Darwin: *Origin of Species*, 242a / *Descent of Man*, 346d-347b
51 Tolstoy: *War and Peace*, epilogue ii, 694b-d
53 James: *Psychology*, 314a

1d. The unity of a definition in relation to the unity of the thing defined

7 Plato: *Laches*, 32a-33a / *Cratylus* 85a-114a,c esp 85a-89a, 104b-114a,c / *Meno*, 174a-179b / *Theaetetus*, 514b-515d / *Sophist*, 559a-c
8 Aristotle: *Posterior Analytics*, bk ii, ch 6 [92^{a}28–33] 126b; ch 10 [93^{b}28–94^{a}7] 128b-c; ch 13 [97^{b}6–25] 133a-b / *Topics*, bk vi, ch 4 [141^{a}26–^{b}2] 194c-d; ch 5 [142^{b}30–143^{a}12] 196b-c; ch 13–14 204c-206d; bk vii, ch 3 [153^{a}6–22] 208a-b; [154^{a}3–11] 209b / *Physics*, bk i, ch 3 [186^{b}14–30] 261c-d / *Metaphysics*, bk i, ch 5 [986^{b}8–987^{a}1] 504c-505a; bk v, ch 6 [1016^{a}33–^{b}11] 536d-537a; bk vii, ch 4–6 552b-555a; ch 10–17 558a-566a,c; bk viii, ch 2–3 566d-568d; ch 6 569d-570d; bk x, ch i [1052^{a}28–37] 578d / *Soul*, bk ii, ch 3 [414^{b}20–415^{a}14] 644d-645b
30 Bacon: *Novum Organum*, bk ii, aph 35 162a-164a
35 Locke: *Human Understanding*, bk ii, ch xxii, sect 4 201c-d; ch xxiii, sect 1–2 204a-c; bk iii, ch v, sect 4 264b; ch vi, sect 21 273c-d; sect 28–30 276a-277b
35 Berkeley: *Human Knowledge*, sect i 413a-b
53 James: *Psychology*, 503a-b

1e. The truth and falsity of definitions

7 Plato: *Cratylus* 85a-114a,c esp 85a-89a, 104b-114a,c / *Seventh Letter*, 809c-810b
8 Aristotle: *Topics*, bk vi-vii 192a-211a,c passim, esp bk vi, ch 4–14 194c-206d / *Metaphysics*, bk v, ch 29 [1024^{b}27–38] 546d-547a; bk vi, ch 4 [1027^{b}17–28] 550a,c; bk ix, ch 10 [1051^{b}18–33] 577d-578a / *Soul*, bk iii, ch 6 [430^{b}26–30] 663b-c
19 Aquinas: *Summa Theologica*, part i, q 2, a i, rep 2 10d-11d; q 17, a 3 102d-103c; q 58, a 5 303c-304c; q 85, a 6 458d-459c
23 Hobbes: *Leviathan*, part i, 56b-d

28 Galileo: *Two New Sciences*, third day, 200a-b
30 Bacon: *Novum Organum*, bk i, aph 59 112b-c; bk ii, aph 35 162a-164a
31 Descartes: *Rules*, xiii, 26b-c
31 Spinoza: *Ethics*, part i, prop 8, schol 2, 357b-d; part ii, prop 40, schol 1–2 387b-388b
33 Pascal: *Geometrical Demonstration*, 430b-431b
35 Locke: *Human Understanding*, bk ii, ch xxxii 243c-248b passim
42 Kant: *Pure Reason*, 179d-182b
43 Mill: *Utilitarianism*, 469a-b
44 Boswell: *Johnson*, 82a-c
46 Hegel: *Philosophy of Right*, intro, par 2 9b-10a
53 James: *Psychology*, 669a-671a

2. The various methods of definition or classification

2a. The use of division or dichotomy in definition

7 Plato: *Phaedrus*, 134a-c / *Sophist*, 552b-561d; 577c-579d / *Statesman* 580a-608d / *Philebus*, 610d-613a
8 Aristotle: *Prior Analytics*, bk i, ch 31 64b-65a / *Posterior Analytics*, bk ii, ch 5 125b-d; ch 13 [96^{b}25–97^{b}6] 132a-133a / *Topics*, bk vi, ch 6 [143^{b}11–144^{a}4] 197b-c / *Metaphysics*, bk vii, ch 12 [1037^{b}28–1038^{a}35] 561c-562a
9 Aristotle: *Parts of Animals*, bk i, ch 2–4 165d-168c
17 Plotinus: *First Ennead*, tr iii, ch 4 11a-c / *Sixth Ennead*, tr iii, ch 8–10 285a-286d; ch 16–18 289c-291d
18 Augustine: *Christian Doctrine*, bk ii, ch 35 653b-c

2b. Definition by genus and differentia: properties

7 Plato: *Theaetetus*, 548c-549d
8 Aristotle: *Categories*, ch 3 [1^{b}16–24] 5d; ch 5 [2^{a}11–3^{b}24] 6a-8a; ch 13 [14^{b}32–15^{a}8] 20c-d / *Prior Analytics*, bk i, ch 27 [43^{a}25–44] 60c-d / *Posterior Analytics*, bk i, ch 22 113b-115b; bk ii, ch 13–14 131b-134a / *Topics*, bk i, ch 4–9 144b-147b; ch 18 [108^{a}38–^{b}9] 152d; [108^{b}19–32] 153a,c; bk iv-vii 168b,d-211a,c / *Physics*, bk i, ch 3 [186^{b}14–34] 261c-262a / *Metaphysics*, bk iii, ch i [995^{b}27–31] 514b; ch 3 517a-518a; bk v, ch 3 [1014^{b}3–13] 534d; ch 25 [1023^{b}22–25] 545c; ch 28 [1024^{a}37–^{b}9] 546b-c; bk vii, ch 4 [1030^{a}7–14] 552d; ch 12–14 561b-563c; bk viii, ch 3 [1043^{b}24–1044^{a}14] 568b-d; ch 6 569d-570d; bk x, ch 8–9 585b-586c; bk xi, ch i [1059^{b}21–1060^{a}1] 587d-588a / *Soul*, bk i, ch i [402^{b}15–403^{a}2] 631d-632a
9 Aristotle: *History of Animals*, bk i, ch i [486^{a}15–487^{a}1] 7b-d / *Parts of Animals*, bk i,

(2. The various methods of definition or classification. 2b. Definition by genus and differentia: properties.)

CH I [641ᵃ14-31] 163d-164a; CH 2-4 165d-168c / *Ethics*, BK II, CH 5 [1105ᵇ19]-CH 6 [1107ᵃ9] 351b-352c

17 PLOTINUS: *Sixth Ennead*, TR III, CH I, 281a-b; CH 8-10 285a-286d; CH 16-18 289c-291d

19 AQUINAS: *Summa Theologica*, PART I, Q 3, A 4, REP I 16d-17c; A 5, ANS 17c-18b; Q 29, A I, REP 3-4 162a-163b; Q 50, A 2, REP I 270a-272a; A 4, REP I 273b-274b; Q 66, A 2, REP 2 345d-347b; Q 75, A 3, REP I 380c-381b; Q 76, A 3, ANS and REP 2,4 391a-393a; Q 77, A I, REP 7 399c-401b; Q 85, A 3 455b-457a; Q 88, A 2, REP 4 471c-472c; PART I-II, Q I, A 3 611b-612a; Q 18, AA 5-11 697a-703a passim, esp A 7 698c-699c; Q 23 723c-727a passim, esp A I 723c-724c; Q 35, A 4 774d-775d; A 8, ANS and REP 3 779c-780c

20 AQUINAS: *Summa Theologica*, PART I-II, Q 49, AA 1-2 1b-4a; Q 52, A I, ANS and REP 2 15d-18a; Q 53, A 2, REP 3 21a-d; Q 54 22d-25d passim; Q 55, A 4, ANS and REP 1-2 28c-29d; QQ 60-61 49d-59d passim; Q 71, A 6 110b-111b; Q 72 111b-119b passim; Q 95, A 4, ANS 229b-230c; PART II-II, Q 4, A I 402a-403d; PART III, Q 2, A I, ANS 710a-711c

30 BACON: *Novum Organum*, BK II 137a-195d passim, esp APH 20-52 150d-195d

31 DESCARTES: *Objections and Replies*, 154a-b

35 LOCKE: *Human Understanding*, BK III, CH III 254d-260a passim, esp SECT 6-10 255c-257a; CH VI 268b-283a passim, esp SECT 6 269d-270a, SECT 30-32 276d-278b

42 KANT: *Pure Reason*, 193a-200c; 215d-216c

45 LAVOISIER: *Elements of Chemistry*, PREF, 4a-5c; PART I, 21d; 25c-d

46 HEGEL: *Philosophy of History*, INTRO, 176c

48 MELVILLE: *Moby Dick*, 98a-b; 104a

49 DARWIN: *Origin of Species*, 12c-13a; 25d-29a esp 28b-29a; 30d-31d; 207d-210b esp 207d-208a / *Descent of Man*, 331b-332a; 346d-347c

53 JAMES: *Psychology*, 344b-345b; 669a-671a; 869a-871a esp 870a-871a

2c. Definition by accidental or extrinsic signs or by component parts

8 ARISTOTLE: *Topics*, BK VI, CH 6 [144ᵃ23-27] 197d; [144ᵇ3-145ᵇ33] 198a-199c; CH 13 [150ᵃ1]-CH 14 [151ᵃ32] 204c-206a / *Metaphysics*, BK VII, CH 12 [1038ᵃ8-30] 561d-562a

9 ARISTOTLE: *Politics*, BK IV, CH 4 [1290ᵇ25-36] 489d-490a

19 AQUINAS: *Summa Theologica*, PART I, Q 29, A I, REP 3 162a-163b; Q 77, A I, REP 7 399c-401b; PART I-II, Q 35, A 8, ANS and REP 3 779c-780c

31 SPINOZA: *Ethics*, PART II, PROP 40, SCHOL 1-2, 387b-388a

35 LOCKE: *Human Understanding*, BK II, CH XXII, SECT 3 201b-c; SECT 9 202c-203a; CH XXIII, SECT 3-10 204c-206d; SECT 14-18 208b-209a; SECT 37 213d-214b; BK III, CH III, SECT 10 256c-257a; CH IV, SECT 12-14 262b-263a; CH VI 268b-283a passim, esp SECT 2-3 268c-d, SECT 29 276b-d; CH XI, SECT 19-22 304b-305a; SECT 25 305d-306c

35 HUME: *Human Understanding*, SECT VII, DIV 49 471c-d

45 LAVOISIER: *Elements of Chemistry*, PART I, 21a-22c; 25c-29d

48 MELVILLE: *Moby Dick*, 95b-105b

49 DARWIN: *Origin of Species*, 207a-210b esp 207a, 208b, 210b; 212d-215a / *Descent of Man*, 332b-c

53 JAMES: *Psychology*, 503a-b; 742a-b

2d. The appeal to genesis, origin, cause, or end in definition

7 PLATO: *Theaetetus*, 544c-548d

8 ARISTOTLE: *Topics*, BK VI, CH 5 [143ᵃ9-12] 196c; CH 6 [145ᵃ19-27] 198d-199a; [145ᵃ32-ᵇ20] 199a-b; CH 8 [146ᵇ9-147ᵃ11] 200c-201a; CH 12 [149ᵇ31-39] 204b-c / *Meteorology*, BK IV, CH 12 493d-494d / *Metaphysics*, BK I, CH 3 [983ᵃ24-29] 501c; BK V, CH 28 [1024ᵃ29-ᵇ9] 546b-c; BK VIII, CH 2 [1043ᵃ2-17] 567b-c; CH 4 [1044ᵇ12-15] 569b; BK XII, CH 3 [1070ᵃ21-24] 599c / *Soul*, BK I, CH I [403ᵃ25-ᵇ7] 632b-c; BK II, CH 2 [413ᵃ11-19] 643a-b

9 ARISTOTLE: *Politics*, BK I, CH 1-2 445a-446d; BK III, CH 9 [1280ᵃ25-1281ᵃ2] 477d-478c

19 AQUINAS: *Summa Theologica*, PART I, Q 44, A I, REP I 238b-239a; PART I-II, Q I, A 3 611b-612a

20 AQUINAS: *Summa Theologica*, PART I-II, Q 55, A 4 28c-29d

30 BACON: *Advancement of Learning*, 43a-d / *Novum Organum*, BK I, APH 63 113d-114a

31 SPINOZA: *Ethics*, PART I, PROP 8, SCHOL 2 356d-357d; APPENDIX 369b-372d

35 LOCKE: *Human Understanding*, BK III, CH IV, SECT 10 261b-d; SECT 16 263b-c; CH VI, SECT 23 274b-c

42 KANT: *Judgement*, 574a-b; 579b-c

49 DARWIN: *Origin of Species*, 207a-229a,c esp 207d-208a, 211b-c, 217d-218a, 228c-d; 238b-239a / *Descent of Man*, 331b-333a esp 332b-c; 337a-341d passim

53 JAMES: *Psychology*, 742a-b

2e. Definition by reference to purpose or interest

31 SPINOZA: *Ethics*, PART I, APPENDIX 369b-372d; PART II, PROP 40, SCHOL I 387b-388a

35 LOCKE: *Human Understanding*, BK II, CH XVIII, SECT 7 174d-175a; CH XXII, SECT 5-7 201d-202b; BK III, CH V 263d-268a passim, esp SECT 6 264c-265a; CH VI, SECT 30 276d-277b esp 277a-b

47 GOETHE: *Faust*, PART I [1942-1945] 46a

49 DARWIN: *Origin of Species*, 27c-29a passim, esp 29a

53 JAMES: *Psychology*, 184a-186a; 314a-b; 668a-671a

3. The grammatical or verbal aspects of definition

7 PLATO: *Charmides*, 6b-d / *Cratylus* 85a-114a,c / *Theaetetus*, 544d-545b / *Laws*, BK X, 763c-d / *Seventh Letter*, 809c-810b

8 ARISTOTLE: *Categories*, CH I 5a-b; CH 5 [3ª 32-ᵇ9] 7c-d / *Posterior Analytics*, BK II, CH 13 [97ᵇ27-39] 133b-c; CH 14 [98ª13-23] 133d-134a / *Topics*, BK I, CH 5 [101ᵇ37-102ª11] 144d; CH 15 149d-152a; CH 18 [108ª17-37] 152b-d; BK IV, CH 3 [123ª27-29] 171d; CH 6 [127ᵇ5-6] 177a; BK VI, CH I [139ᵇ12-18] 192b-c; CH 2-14 192c-206d passim, esp CH 10-11 202b-203d; BK VII 206b,d-211a,c passim; BK VIII, CH 3 [158ᵇ8-159ª2] 215b-c / *Metaphysics*, BK IV, CH 4 525a-528b; CH 7 [1012ª22-24] 532b; BK VII, CH 4-5 552b-554a; CH 15 [1040ª9-14] 564a; BK X, CH I [1052ᵇ1-15] 578d-579a; BK XI, CH 5 590a-d / *Soul*, BK I, CH I [402ᵇ5-8] 631c-d

20 AQUINAS: *Summa Theologica*, PART II-II, Q 4, A I, ANS 402a-403d

23 HOBBES: *Leviathan*, PART I, 56b-57c; PART IV, 269b-c; 270a-c

31 DESCARTES: *Rules*, XII, 23c-24a; XIII, 26b-c

35 LOCKE: *Human Understanding*, BK II, CH XXII, SECT 3-10 201b-203c passim; BK III, CH III, SECT 10 256c-257a; CH IV, SECT 6-7 260d; CH V, SECT 4 264b; SECT 10-11 266b-d; CH VI, SECT 32 277c-278b

43 FEDERALIST: NUMBER 37, 119b-120b

44 BOSWELL: *Johnson*, 82a-c

45 LAVOISIER: *Elements of Chemistry*, PREF, 4a-5d; PART I, 10a; 21a-22c; 25c-29d

45 FARADAY: *Researches in Electricity*, 361a-362c

53 JAMES: *Psychology*, 171b-172a

4. The search for definitions and the methods of defending them

7 PLATO: *Charmides*, 4a-13d / *Laches*, 31c-37c / *Meno* 174a-190a,c esp 174a-179b / *Republic*, BK I-IV 295a-356a esp BK IV, 346a-355a / *Theaetetus* 512a-550a,c / *Sophist*, 552b-579d / *Statesman* 580a-608d

8 ARISTOTLE: *Posterior Analytics*, BK II, CH I-10 122b,d-128d; CH 13-14 131b-134a / *Topics*, BK I-VII 143a-211a,c esp BK I, CH 4-9 144b-147b / *Metaphysics*, BK I, CH 5 [987ª19-27] 505b; CH 6 [987ᵇ1-10] 505c; [987ᵇ30-33] 506a; BK IX, CH 6 [1048ª25-ᵇ9] 573c-574a; BK XIII, CH 4 [1078ᵇ18-32] 610b-c / *Soul*, BK I 631a-641d esp CH I 631a-632d; BK II, CH I [412ª1]-CH 4 [415ª23] 642a-645c

9 ARISTOTLE: *Parts of Animals*, BK I, CH 2-4 165d-168c

12 AURELIUS: *Meditations*, BK III, SECT II 262a-b

17 PLOTINUS: *First Ennead*, TR III, CH 4 11a-c / *Fifth Ennead*, TR V, CH 6 231b-d / *Sixth Ennead*, TR III, CH 6-10 284a-286d

19 AQUINAS: *Summa Theologica*, PART I, Q 10, A I 40d-41d; Q 29, A I 162a-163b

20 AQUINAS: *Summa Theologica*, PART I-II, Q 49, AA 1-2 1b-4a; Q 55, A 4 28c-29d; Q 71, A 6 110b-111b; Q 90 205a-208b; PART II-II, Q 4, A I 402a-403d

25 MONTAIGNE: *Essays*, 518d-519a

28 GALILEO: *Two New Sciences*, THIRD DAY, 200a-203d esp 200a-b

30 BACON: *Advancement of Learning*, 61b-c / *Novum Organum*, BK I, APH 59 112b-c; APH 105 128b-c; BK II, APH 10-20 140c-153a; APH 24-25 154c-155d

31 DESCARTES: *Rules*, XII, 23c-24a

31 SPINOZA: *Ethics*, PART II, PROP 40, SCHOL 1-2 387b-388b

35 LOCKE: *Human Understanding*, BK III, CH XI, SECT 24 305b-d

35 HUME: *Human Understanding*, SECT VII 470d-478a

38 ROUSSEAU: *Inequality*, 330a-d

42 KANT: *Pure Reason*, 215d-216d / *Practical Reason*, 293c-294b

43 FEDERALIST: NUMBER 37, 119b-120b

49 DARWIN: *Origin of Species*, 241d-242a

51 TOLSTOY: *War and Peace*, EPILOGUE II, 683d-684c; 690b

5. Definition and demonstration: definitions as principles and as conclusions

8 ARISTOTLE: *Prior Analytics*, BK I, CH 31 64b-65a; CH 43 68d / *Posterior Analytics*, BK I, CH 2 [72ª19-24] 98d; CH 8 [75ᵇ21-32] 104a; CH 10 [76ᵇ35-77ª4] 105c-d; CH 22 113b-115b; CH 33 [88ᵇ30-89ª1] 121b-c; [89ª17-ᵇ5] 121d-122a,c; BK II, CH 3-10 123c-128d / *Topics*, BK VI, CH 4 [141ª26-32] 194c; BK VII, CH 3 208a-209b; CH 5 [154ª23-ᵇ13] 209d-210a; [155ª17-23] 210d; BK VIII, CH 3 [158ª31-159ª2] 214d-215c / *Metaphysics*, BK I, CH 9 [992ᵇ30-993ª1] 511b; BK III, CH 2 [996ᵇ8-21] 515a-b; BK IV, CH 4 525a-528b; CH 7 [1012ª18-24] 532a-b; CH 8 [1012ᵇ5-8] 532c; BK XI, CH 5 590a-d; BK XIII, CH 4 [1078ᵇ17-30] 610b-c / *Soul*, BK I, CH I [402ª10-23] 631b; [402ᵇ15-403ª2] 631d-632a; CH 3 [407ª22-30] 636d-637a; CH 5 [409ª31-ᵇ18] 639b-c; BK II, CH 2 [413ª11-19] 643a-b

9 ARISTOTLE: *Parts of Animals*, BK I, CH I [639ᵇ7-642ᵇ5] 161d-165c

17 PLOTINUS: *Sixth Ennead*, TR V, CH 2 306a-b

19 AQUINAS: *Summa Theologica*, PART I, Q I, A 7, REP I 7a-c; Q 2, A I, REP 2 10d-11d; A 2, REP 2 11d-12c; Q 3, A 5, ANS 17c-18b; Q 17, A 3, REP 1-2 102d-103c; Q 58, A 5 303c-304c; Q 85, A 6 458d-459c

23 HOBBES: *Leviathan*, PART I, 56b-60c; 65c-d

31 DESCARTES: *Objections and Replies*, 128c-129a

(5. *Definition and demonstration: definitions as principles and as conclusions.*)

33 PASCAL: *Pensées*, I 171a-172a / *Geometrical Demonstration*, 430b-434b passim, esp 430b, 431b-432a; 442a-443b

35 LOCKE: *Human Understanding*, BK III, CH IX, SECT 15-16 288d-289c; CH XI, SECT 15-17 303b-304a; BK IV, CH III, SECT 20, 319b

35 HUME: *Human Understanding*, SECT XII, DIV 131 508d-509a

42 KANT: *Pure Reason*, 179d-182b; 211c-218d esp 215d-216d / *Practical Reason*, 293c-294b

46 HEGEL: *Philosophy of Right*, INTRO, par 2 9b-10a

51 TOLSTOY: *War and Peace*, EPILOGUE II, 690b

54 FREUD: *Instincts*, 412a-b

6. The character of definitions in diverse disciplines

6a. The formulation of definitions in physics, mathematics, and metaphysics

7 PLATO: *Seventh Letter*, 809c-810b

8 ARISTOTLE: *Topics*, BK VI, CH 4 [141^{a}26-^{b}24] 194c-195a; BK VII, CH 3 [153^{a}6-11] 208a-b / *Physics*, BK I, CH 9 [192^{a}25-^{b}2] 268c-d; BK II, CH 2 270a-271a; BK III, CH 1-2 278a-279c; CH 6 [206^{b}33-207^{a}14] 285b-c; BK IV, CH 1-5 287a-292c; CH 11 298c-300a / *Meteorology*, BK IV, CH 12 493d-494d / *Metaphysics*, BK IV, CH 4 525a-528b; BK V, CH 1-BK VI, CH 1 533a-548c; BK IX, CH 6 [1048^{a}25-^{b}9] 573c-574a; BK XI, CH 5 590a-d; CH 7 592b-593a; BK XIII, CH 2 [1077^{b}1]-CH 3 [1078^{a}32] 608d-609d / *Soul*, BK I, CH 1-BK II, CH 3 631a-645b esp BK I, CH 1 631a-632d

9 ARISTOTLE: *Parts of Animals*, BK I, CH 2-4 165d-168c / *Ethics*, BK I, CH 7 [1098^{a}20-^{b}8] 343c-344a

11 EUCLID: *Elements*, BK I, DEFINITIONS 1a-2a esp 1-2,4,10 1a, 15 1b, 23 2a; BK II, DEFINITIONS 30a; BK III, DEFINITIONS 41a-b esp 2-3 41a; BK IV, DEFINITIONS 67a-b; BK V, DEFINITIONS 81a-82a esp 3-7 81a-b; BK VI, DEFINITIONS 99a; BK VII, DEFINITIONS 127a-128a esp 1-2 127a, 11-12,20 127b; BK X, DEFINITIONS I 191a-b esp 1,3 191a; DEFINITIONS II 229a; DEFINITIONS III 264b; BK XI, DEFINITIONS 301a-302b esp 14 301b, 18,21 302a

11 ARCHIMEDES: *Sphere and Cylinder*, BK I, DEFINITIONS 404a / *Conoids and Spheroids*, 452a-454a passim; DEFINITIONS 455a-b / *Spirals*, DEFINITIONS 490a / *Equilibrium of Planes*, BK II, 511a / *Sand-Reckoner*, 524a-b / *Quadrature of the Parabola*, DEF 534b-535a

11 APOLLONIUS: *Conics*, BK I, FIRST DEFINITIONS 604a-b esp 1 604a; SECOND DEFINITIONS 626a

11 NICOMACHUS: *Arithmetic*, BK I, 814b-c

16 KEPLER: *Epitome*, BK V, 986b-1004a passim

17 PLOTINUS: *Sixth Ennead*, TR III, CH 1, 281a-b

19 AQUINAS: *Summa Theologica*, PART I, Q 1, A 7, REP 1 7a-c; Q 2, A 2, REP 2 11d-12c; Q 3, A 5, ANS 17c-18b; Q 10, A 1 40d-41d; Q 29, A 1 162a-163b; Q 75, A 4, ANS 381b-382a; Q 85, A 1, REP 2 451c-453c; A 8, REP 2 460b-461b

23 HOBBES: *Leviathan*, PART I, 56b; PART IV, 269b-c

28 GALILEO: *Two New Sciences*, FIRST DAY, 142d-143a; THIRD DAY, 197b-c; 200a-203d

30 BACON: *Advancement of Learning*, 43a-d

31 DESCARTES: *Rules*, XII, 23c-24a; XIII, 26b-c / *Objections and Replies*, 128c-129a

31 SPINOZA: *Ethics*, PART I, APPENDIX 369b-372d; PART II, PROP 40, SCHOL 1-2 387b-388b

33 PASCAL: *Pensées*, I 171a-172a / *Vacuum*, 372b-373b; 376b-377a / *Geometrical Demonstration*, 430b-434b passim, esp 430b-431b

34 NEWTON: *Principles*, DEFINITIONS 5a-13a / *Optics*, BK I, 379a-380b

35 HUME: *Human Understanding*, SECT VII, DIV 48-49 470d-471d

42 KANT: *Pure Reason*, 15c-16c; 17d-19a; 68a-69c; 215d-217a; 245c-248d

6b. The use of definition in speculative philosophy and empirical science

7 PLATO: *Theaetetus*, 544c-549d / *Statesman*, 595b-c / *Seventh Letter*, 809c-810b

8 ARISTOTLE: *Posterior Analytics*, BK II, CH 13-14 131b-134a / *Soul*, BK I 631a-641d esp CH 1 631a-632d; BK II, CH 1-3 642a-645b

9 ARISTOTLE: *Parts of Animals*, BK I, CH 1-4 161a-168c passim / *Politics*, BK IV, CH 4 [1290^{b}25-40] 489d-490a

28 GILBERT: *Loadstone*, BK II, 43c-44d

28 GALILEO: *Two New Sciences*, THIRD DAY, 200a-203d

30 BACON: *Novum Organum*, BK I, APH 63 113d-114a; BK II, APH 10-20 140c-153a; APH 48 179d-188b

31 DESCARTES: *Rules*, XII, 23c-24a; XIII, 26b-c

31 SPINOZA: *Ethics*, PART II, PROP 40, SCHOL 1-2 387b-388b

33 PASCAL: *Vacuum*, 372b-373b; 376b-377a

34 NEWTON: *Principles*, DEFINITIONS 5a-13a / *Optics*, BK I, 379a-380b

35 LOCKE: *Human Understanding*, BK II, CH XXIII, SECT 3-10 204c-206d; SECT 14-18 208b-209a; SECT 37 213d-214b; BK III, CH IX, SECT 15-17 288d-290a; CH XI, SECT 10 302b; SECT 19-25 304b-306c

35 HUME: *Human Understanding*, SECT II, DIV 17, 457b,d [fn 1]; SECT VII, DIV 48-49 470d-471d; SECT VIII, DIV 74 484a-c

42 KANT: *Pure Reason*, 15c-16c; 215d-216d; 243c-244c / *Practical Reason*, 293c-294b / *Intro. Metaphysic of Morals*, 388a-c / *Judgement*, 603b-d

43 FEDERALIST: NUMBER 37, 119b-120b

45 LAVOISIER: *Elements of Chemistry*, PART I, 10a-b; 21a-22c; 25c-29d

CROSS-REFERENCES

For: The linguistic aspects of definition and the general theory of the meaning of words, *see* LANGUAGE 1a; SIGN AND SYMBOL 4a.

The logical aspects of definition, *see* IDEA 4a.

Other discussions of the object of definition and the problem of essences or universals, *see* BEING 8c; NATURE 4a; UNIVERSAL AND PARTICULAR 2a–2c.

The notions of genus and differentia, species and property, *see* BEING 8d; IDEA 4b(3); NATURE 1a(1); RELATION 5a(4); UNIVERSAL AND PARTICULAR 5b.

Other considerations of indefinable terms, *see* INFINITY 2c; PRINCIPLE 2a(3); and for the indefinability of individuals, *see* UNIVERSAL AND PARTICULAR 4e.

The use of definitions as principles in reasoning or proof, and for the problem of demonstrating definitions, *see* PRINCIPLE 2a(2); REASONING 5b(2).

The discussion of matters related to the truth or falsity of definitions, *see* IDEA 6f; TRUTH 3b(1).

The role of definitions in dialectic and science, and in the various sciences, *see* DIALECTIC 2a(2), 2b(1); MATHEMATICS 3a; MATTER 4b; METAPHYSICS 2b; PHILOSOPHY 3b–3c; PHYSICS 2a; SCIENCE 4a.

ADDITIONAL READINGS

Listed below are works not included in *Great Books of the Western World*, but relevant to the idea and topics with which this chapter deals. These works are divided into two groups:

I. Works by authors represented in this collection.
II. Works by authors not represented in this collection.

For the date, place, and other facts concerning the publication of the works cited, consult the Bibliography of Additional Readings which follows the last chapter of *The Great Ideas*.

I.

AQUINAS. *On Being and Essence*, CH 2–3
HOBBES. *Concerning Body*, PART I, CH 2
SPINOZA. *Correspondence*, IX
LOCKE. *Conduct of the Understanding*
KANT. *Introduction to Logic*, VIII
HEGEL. *Science of Logic*, VOL I, BK II, SECT I, CH I
J. S. MILL. *A System of Logic*, BK I, CH 7–8; BK 4, CH 7–8

II.

QUINTILIAN. *Institutio Oratoria (Institutes of Oratory)*, BK VII, CH 3
SEXTUS EMPIRICUS. *Outlines of Pyrrhonism*, BK II
JOHN OF SAINT THOMAS. *Cursus Philosophicus Thomisticus, Ars Logica*, PART II, QQ 6–12
ARNAULD. *Logic or the Art of Thinking*, PART I, CH 12–14; PART IV, CH 4–5
LEIBNITZ. *New Essays Concerning Human Understanding*, BK III, CH 3
T. REID. *Essays on the Intellectual Powers of Man*, I
J. MILL. *Analysis of the Phenomena of the Human Mind*, CH 8
W. HAMILTON. *Lectures on Metaphysics and Logic*, VOL II (24)

WHEWELL. *The Philosophy of the Inductive Sciences*, VOL I, BK VIII
SIGWART. *Logic*, PART I, CH I, SECT 44; PART III, CH I, SECT 74
JEVONS. *The Principles of Science*, CH 30
——. *Studies in Deductive Logic*, CH 1–2, 7
VENN. *Principles of Empirical or Inductive Logic*, CH 11–13
POINCARÉ. *Science and Method*, BK II, CH 2
WHITEHEAD and RUSSELL. *Principia Mathematica*, INTRO, CH I, esp pp 11–19; PART I, SECT A, esp pp 91–94
B. RUSSELL. *Principles of Mathematics*, PART I
——. *Introduction to Mathematical Philosophy*, CH 13, 16–17
WHITEHEAD. *An Enquiry Concerning the Principles of Natural Knowledge*, CH 8–13
——. *The Concept of Nature*, CH 4
W. E. JOHNSON. *Logic*, PART I, CH 7–8
OGDEN and RICHARDS. *The Meaning of Meaning*
DUBISLAV. *Die Definition*
MARITAIN. *The Degrees of Knowledge*, CH 3
CARNAP. *The Logical Syntax of Language*, PART I, SECT 8; PART II, SECT 22; PART III, SECT 29
DEWEY. *Logic, the Theory of Inquiry*, CH 13–14, 16–18, 20.
DEWEY and BENTLEY. *Knowing and the Known*, CH 7

Chapter 16: DEMOCRACY

INTRODUCTION

OF all the traditional names for forms of government, "democracy" has the liveliest currency today. Yet like all the others, it has a long history in the literature of political thought and a career of shifting meanings. How radically the various conceptions of democracy differ may be judged from the fact that, in one of its meanings, democracy flourished in the Greek city-states as early as the fifth century B.C.; while in another, democracy only began to exist in recent times or perhaps does not yet exist anywhere in the world.

In our minds democracy is inseparably connected with constitutional government. We tend to think of despotism or dictatorship as its only opposites or enemies. That is how the major political issue of our day is understood. But as recently as the 18th century, some of the American constitutionalists prefer a republican form of government to democracy; and at other times, both ancient and modern, oligarchy or aristocracy, rather than monarchy or despotism, is the major alternative. "Democracy" has even stood for the lawless rule of the mob—either itself a kind of tyranny or the immediate precursor of tyranny.

Throughout all these shifts in meaning and value, the word "democracy" preserves certain constant political connotations. Democracy exists, according to Montesquieu, "when the body of the people is possessed of the supreme power." As the root meaning of the word indicates, democracy is the "rule of the people." While there may be, and in fact often has been, a difference of opinion with respect to the meaning of "the people," this notion has been traditionally associated with the doctrine of popular sovereignty, which makes the political community as such the origin and basis of political authority. In the development of the democratic tradition, particularly in modern times, this has been accompanied by the elaboration of safeguards for the rights of man to assure that government actually functions for the people, and not merely for one group of them.

Although they are essential parts of democracy, neither popular sovereignty nor the safeguarding of natural rights provides the specific characteristic of democracy, since both are compatible with any other just form of government. The specifically democratic element is apparent from the fact that throughout the many shifts of meaning which democracy has undergone, the common thread is the notion of political power in the hands of the many rather than the few or the one. Thus at the very beginning of democratic government, we find Pericles calling Athens a democracy because "its administration favours the many instead of the few." Close to our own day, Mill likewise holds that democracy is "the government of the whole people by the whole people" in which "the majority . . . will outvote and prevail."

According as the many exercise *legal* power as citizens or merely *actual* power as a mob, democracy is aligned with or against constitutional government. The quantitative meaning of "many" can vary from *more than the few* to *all* or something approximating all, and with this variance the same constitution may be at one time regarded as oligarchical or aristocratic, and at another as democratic. The way in which the many who are citizens exercise their power—either directly or through representatives—occasions the 18th century distinction between a democracy and a republic, though this verbal ambiguity can be easily avoided by using the phrases "direct democracy" and "representative democracy," as was sometimes done by the writers of *The Federalist* and their American contemporaries.

These last two points—the extension of the

franchise and a system of representation—mark the chief differences between ancient and contemporary institutions of democracy. Today constitutional democracy tends to be representative, and the grant of citizenship under a democratic constitution tends toward universal suffrage. That is why we no longer contrast democracy and republic. That is why even the most democratic Greek constitutions may seem undemocratic—oligarchical or aristocratic—to us.

To the extent that democracy, ancient or modern, is conceived as a lawful form of government, it has elements in common with other forms of lawful government which, for one reason or another, may not be democratic. The significance of these common elements—the principle of constitutionality and the status of citizenship—will be assumed here. They are discussed in the chapters on CONSTITUTION and CITIZEN. The general theory of the forms of government is treated in the chapter on GOVERNMENT, and the two forms most closely related to democracy, in the chapters on ARISTOCRACY and OLIGARCHY.

THE EVALUATIONS of democracy are even more various than its meanings. It has been denounced as an extreme perversion of government. It has been grouped with other good, or other bad, forms of government, and accorded the faint praise of being called either the most tolerable of bad governments or the least efficient among acceptable forms. It has been held up as the political ideal, the only perfectly just state—that paragon of justice which has always been, whether recognized or not, the goal of political progress.

Sometimes the same writer will express divergent views. Plato, for example, in the *Statesman*, claims that democracy has "a twofold meaning" according as it involves "ruling with law or without law." Finding it "in every respect weak and unable to do either any great good or any great evil," he concludes that it is "the worst of all lawful governments, and the best of all lawless ones." The rule of the many is least efficient for either good or evil. But in the *Republic*, he places democracy at only one remove from tyranny. On the ground that "the excessive increase of anything often causes a reaction in the opposite direction," tyranny is

said to "arise naturally out of democracy, and the most aggravated form of tyranny and slavery out of the most extreme form of liberty."

Similarly, Aristotle, in the *Politics*, calls democracy "the most tolerable" of the three perverted forms of government, in contrast to oligarchy, which he thinks is only "a little better" than tyranny, "the worst of governments." Yet he also notes that, among existing governments, "there are generally thought to be two principal forms—democracy and oligarchy, . . . and the rest are only variations of these." His own treatment conforms with this observation. He devotes the central portion of his *Politics* to the analysis of oligarchy and democracy. In his view they are equal and opposite in their injustice, and to him both seem capable of degenerating into despotism and tyranny.

Among the political philosophers of modern times a certain uniformity of treatment seems to prevail in the context of otherwise divergent theories. Writers like Hobbes, Locke, and Rousseau, or Machiavelli, Montesquieu, and Kant differ in many and profound respects. But they classify the forms of government in much the same fashion. As Hobbes expresses it, "when the representative is one man, then is the commonwealth a monarchy; when an assembly of all that will come together, then it is a democracy, or popular commonwealth; when an assembly of a part only, then it is called an aristocracy." Though Hobbes favors monarchy and Montesquieu either aristocracy or democracy, these writers do not make the choice among the three traditional forms a significant expression of their own political theories. For them the more important choice is presented by other alternatives: for Hobbes between absolute and limited government; for Montesquieu and Locke, between government by law and despotism; for Rousseau and Kant, between a republic and a monarchy.

The authors of *The Federalist* definitely show their preference for "popular government" as opposed to monarchy, aristocracy, or oligarchy. They usually refer to it as a "republic," by which they mean "a government which derives all its powers directly or indirectly from the great body of the people, and is administered by persons holding their offices during pleasure, for a limited period, or during good behavior."

Alexander Hamilton and others involved in the American constitutional debates, as for example James Wilson, occasionally call this system a "representative democracy," but in *The Federalist* a republic is sharply differentiated from a democracy. The "great points of difference," however, turn out to be only "the delegation of the government (in a republic) to a small number of citizens elected by the rest," and the "greater number of citizens, and greater sphere of country" to which a republic may extend. The difference, as already noted, is best expressed in the words "representative" and "direct" democracy.

In Mill's *Representative Government* we find democracy identified with the ideal state. "The ideally best form of government," he writes, "is that in which the sovereignty, or supreme controlling power in the last resort, is vested in the entire aggregate of the community, every citizen not only having a voice in the exercise of that ultimate sovereignty, but being, at least occasionally, called on to take an actual part in the government, by the personal discharge of some public function, local or general." Though Mill recognizes the infirmities of democracy and though he readily concedes that it may not be the best government for all peoples under all circumstances, his argument for its superiority to all other forms of government remains substantially unqualified.

IN MILL'S CONSTRUCTION of the democratic ideal as providing liberty and equality for all, the essential distinction from previous conceptions lies in the meaning of the word *all*. The republicans of the 18th century, in their doctrines of popular sovereignty and natural rights, understood citizenship in terms of equality of status and conceived liberty in terms of a man's having a voice in his own government. The ancients, seeing that men could be free and equal members of a political community only when they lived as citizens under the rule of law, recognized that the democratic constitution alone bestowed such equality upon all men not born slaves. But generally neither the ancients nor the 18th century republicans understood liberty and equality *for all men* to require the abolition of slavery, the emancipation of women from political subjection, or the eradication of all constitutional discriminations based on wealth, race, or previous condition of servitude.

With Mill, *all* means every human person without regard to the accidents of birth or fortune. "There ought to be no pariahs in a full-grown and civilized nation," he writes, "no persons disqualified, except through their own default." Under the latter condition, he would withhold the franchise from infants, idiots, or criminals (including the criminally indigent), but with these exceptions he would make suffrage universal. He sums up his argument by claiming that "it is a personal injustice to withhold from any one, unless for the prevention of greater evils, the ordinary privilege of having his voice reckoned in the disposal of affairs in which he has the same interest as other people," and whoever "has no vote, and no prospect of obtaining it, will either be a permanent malcontent, or will feel as one whom the general affairs of society do not concern." But it should be added that for Mill the franchise is not merely a privilege or even a right; "it is," he says, "strictly a matter of duty." How the voter uses the ballot "has no more to do with his personal wishes than the verdict of a juryman. . . . He is bound to give it according to his best and most conscientious opinion of the public good. Whoever has any other idea of it is unfit to have the suffrage."

The notion of universal suffrage raises at once the question of the economic conditions prerequisite to the perfection of political democracy. Can men exercise the political freedom of citizenship without freedom from economic dependence on the will of other men? It was commonly thought by 18th century republicans that they could not. "A power over a man's subsistence," Hamilton declares, "amounts to a power over his will." On that basis it was urged by many during the Philadelphia convention that a property qualification was necessary for suffrage.

Kant also argues that suffrage "presupposes the independence or self-sufficiency of the individual citizen." Because apprentices, servants, minors, women, and the like do not maintain themselves, each "according to his own industry, but as it is arranged by others," he claims that they are "mere subsidiaries of the Commonwealth and not active independent members of it," being "of necessity commanded and protected by others." For this reason, he concludes, they are "passive," not "active," citizens and can be rightfully deprived of the franchise.

For political democracy to be realized in practice, more may be required than the abolition of poll taxes and other discriminations based on wealth. In the opinion of Karl Marx, the "battle for democracy" will not be won, nor even the "first step" taken towards it, until "the working class raises the proletariat to the position of ruling class." Quite apart from the merits of the revolutionary political philosophy which Marx erects, his views, and those of other social reformers of the 19th century, have made it a central issue that democracy be conceived in social and economic terms as well as political. Otherwise, they insist, what is called "democracy" will permit, and may even try to condone, social inequalities and economic injustices which vitiate political liberty.

THERE IS ONE other condition of equality which the status of citizenship demands. This is equality of educational opportunity. According to Mill, it is "almost a self-evident axiom that the State should require and compel the education, up to a certain standard, of every human being who is born its citizen." All men may not be endowed with the same native abilities or talents, but all born with enough intelligence to become citizens deserve the sort of education which fits them for the life of political freedom. Quantitatively, this means a system of education as universal as the franchise; and as much for every individual as he can take, both in youth and adult life. Qualitatively, this means liberal education rather than vocational training, though in contemporary controversy this point is still disputed.

The way in which it recognizes and discharges its educational responsibility tests the sincerity of modern democracy. No other form of government has a comparable burden, for no other calls *all* men to citizenship. In such a government, Montesquieu declares, "the whole power of education is required." Whereas despotism may be preserved by fear and a monarchy by a system of honor, a democracy depends on civic virtue. For where "government is intrusted to private citizens," it requires "love of the laws and of the country," and this, according to Montesquieu, is generally "conducive to purity of morals."

Universal schooling by itself is not sufficient for this purpose. Democracy also needs what Mill calls the "school of public spirit." It is only by participating in the functions of government that men can become competent as citizens. By engaging in civic activities, a man "is made to feel himself one of the public, and whatever is for their benefit to be for his benefit." The "moral part of the instruction afforded by the participation of the private citizen, if even rarely, in public functions," results, according to Mill, in a man's being able "to weigh interests not his own; to be guided, in case of conflicting claims, by another rule than his private partialities; to apply, at every turn, principles and maxims which have for their reason of existence the common good." If national affairs cannot afford an opportunity for every citizen to take an active part in government, then that must be achieved through local government, and it is for this reason that Mill advocates the revitalization of the latter.

THERE ARE OTHER problems peculiar to modern democracy. Because of the size of the territory and population of the national state, democratic government has necessarily become representative. Representation, according to *The Federalist*, becomes almost indispensable when *the people* is too large and too dispersed for assembly or for continuous, as well as direct, participation in national affairs. The pure democracy which the Federalists attribute to the Greek city-states may still be appropriate for local government of the town-meeting variety, but for the operations of federal or national government, the Federalists think the republican institutions of Rome a better model to follow.

The Federalists have another reason for espousing representative government. The "mortal disease" of popular government, in their view, is the "violence of faction" which decides measures "not according to the rules of justice and the rights of the minor party, but by the superior force of an interested and overbearing majority." Believing the spirit of faction to be rooted in the nature of man in society, the American statesmen seek to cure its evil not by "removing its causes," but by "controlling its effects." The principle of representation, Madison claims, "promises the cure."

Representation, by delegating government to a small number of citizens elected by the rest, is said "to refine and enlarge the public views by passing them through the medium of a chosen body of citizens, whose wisdom may best discern the true interest of their country." From this it appears that representation provides a way of combining popular government with the aristocratic principle of government by the best men.

The assumption that representation would normally secure the advantages of aristocratic government is not unmixed with oligarchical prejudices. If, as the Federalists frankly suppose, the best men are also likely to be men of breeding and property, representative government would safeguard the interests of the gentry, as well as the safety of the republic, against the *demos*—in Hamilton's words, "that great beast." Their concern with the evil of factions seems to be colored by the fear of the dominant faction in any democracy—the always more numerous poor.

The leavening of popular government by representative institutions in the formation of modern democracies raises the whole problem of the nature and function of representatives. To what extent does representation merely provide an instrument which the people employs to express its will in the process of self-government? To what extent is it a device whereby the great mass of the people select their betters to decide for them what is beyond their competence to decide for themselves?

According to the way these questions are answered, the conception of the representative's function—especially in legislative matters—will vary from that of serving as the mere messenger of his constituents to that of acting independently, exercising his own judgment, and representing his constituents not in the sense of doing their bidding, but only in the sense that he has been chosen by them to decide what is to be done for the common good.

At one extreme, the representative seems to be reduced to the ignominious role of a mouthpiece, a convenience required by the exigencies of time and space. Far from being a leader, or one of the best men, he need not even be a better man than his constituents. At the other extreme, it is not clear why the completely independent representative need even be popularly elected. In Edmund Burke's theory of *virtual* representation, occasioned by his argument against the extension of the franchise, even those who do not vote are adequately represented by men who have the welfare of the state at heart. They, no less than voting constituents, can expect the representative to consider what is for their interest, and to oppose their wishes if he thinks their local or special interest is inimical to the general welfare.

Between these two extremes, Mill tries to find a middle course, in order to achieve the "two great requisites of government: responsibility to those for whose benefit political power ought to be, and always professes to be, employed; and jointly therewith to obtain, in the greatest measure possible, for the function of government the benefits of superior intellect, trained by long meditation and practical discipline to that special task." Accordingly, Mill would preserve some measure of independent judgment for the representative and make him both responsive and responsible to his constituents, yet without directing or restraining him by the checks of initiative, referendum, and recall.

Mill's discussion of representation leaves few crucial questions unasked, though it may not provide clearly satisfactory answers to all of them. It goes beyond the nature and function of the representative to the problem of securing representation for minorities by the now familiar method of proportional voting. It is concerned with the details of electoral procedure—the nomination of candidates, public and secret balloting, plural voting—as well as the more general question of the differences among the executive, judicial, and legislative departments of government with respect to representation, especially the difference of representatives in the upper and lower houses of a bicameral legislature. Like the writers of *The Federalist*, Mill seeks a leaven for the democratic mass in the leadership of men of talent or training. He would qualify the common sense of the many by the expertness or wisdom of the few.

THE ANCIENT ISSUE between the democratic and the oligarchical constitution turns primarily on a question of justice, not on the relative competence of the many and the few to rule. Either form of government may take on a more or less aristocratic cast according as men of eminent virtue or ability assume public office, but in neither case does the constitution itself guarantee their choice, except possibly on the oligarchical assumption that the possession of wealth signifies superior intelligence and virtue.

The justice peculiar to the democratic constitution, Aristotle thinks, "arises out of the notion that those who are equal in any respect are equal in all respects; because men are equally free, they claim to be absolutely equal." It does not seem to him inconsistent with democratic justice that slaves, women, and resident aliens should be excluded from citizenship and public office.

In the extreme form of Greek democracy, the qualifications for public office are no different from the qualifications for citizenship. Since they are equally eligible for almost every governmental post, the citizens can be chosen by lot rather than elected by vote. Rousseau agrees with Montesquieu's opinion of the Greek practice, that "election by lot is democratic in nature." He thinks it "would have few disadvantages in a real democracy, but," he adds, "I have already said that a real democracy is only an ideal."

The justice peculiar to the oligarchical constitution is, according to Aristotle, "based on the notion that those who are unequal in one respect are in all respects unequal; being unequal, that is, in property, they suppose themselves to be unequal absolutely." The oligarchical constitution consequently does not grant citizenship or open public office to all the freeborn, but in varying degrees sets a substantial property qualification for both.

Though he admits that the opposite claims of the oligarch and the democrat "have a kind of justice," Aristotle also points out the injustice of each. The democratic constitution, he thinks, does injustice to the rich by treating them as equal with the poor simply because both are freeborn, while the oligarchical constitution does injustice to the poor by failing to treat all free men, regardless of wealth, as equals. "Tried by an absolute standard," Aristotle goes on to say, "they are faulty, and, therefore, both parties, whenever their share in the government does not accord with their preconceived ideas, stir up a revolution."

Plato, Thucydides, and Plutarch, as well as Aristotle, observe that this unstable situation permits demagogue or dynast to encourage lawless rule by the mob or by a coterie of the rich. Either paves the way to tyranny.

To stabilize the state and to remove injustice, Aristotle proposes a mixed constitution which, by a number of different methods, "attempts to unite the freedom of the poor and the wealth of the rich." In this way he hopes to satisfy the two requirements of good government. "One is the actual obedience of citizens to the laws, the other is the goodness of the laws which they obey." By participating in the making of laws, all free men, the poor included, would be more inclined to obey them. But since the rich are also given a special function, there is, according to Aristotle, the possibility of also getting good laws passed, since "birth and education are commonly the accompaniments of wealth."

To Aristotle the mixed constitution is perfectly just, and with an aristocratic aspect added to the blend, it approaches the ideal polity. Relative to certain circumstances it has "a greater right than any other form of government, except the true and ideal, to the name of the government of the best."

Yet the true and the ideal, or what he sometimes calls the "divine form of government," seems to be monarchy for Aristotle, or rule by the one superior man; and in his own sketch of the best constitution at the end of the *Politics*—the best practicable, if not the ideal—Aristotle clearly opposes admitting all the laboring classes to citizenship.

As INDICATED IN the chapter on CONSTITUTION, Aristotle's mixed constitution should be distinguished from the mediaeval mixed regime, which was a combination of constitutional with non-constitutional or absolute government, rather than a mixture of different constitutional principles. The mixed regime—or "royal and political government"—seems to have come into being not as an attempt to reconcile conflicting principles of justice, but as the inevitable product of a decaying feudalism and a rising nationalism. Yet Aquinas claims that a mixed regime was established by divine law for the people of Israel; for it was "partly kingdom, since there is one at the head of all; partly aristocracy, in so far as a number of persons are set in authority; partly democracy, *i.e.*, government by the people, in so far as the rulers can be chosen from the people, and the people have the right to choose their rulers." In such a system, the monarchical principle is blended with aristocratic and democratic elements to whatever extent the nobles and the commons play a part in the government. But neither group functions politically as citizens do under purely constitutional government.

The question of constitutional justice can, however, be carried over from ancient to modern times. Modern democracy answers it differently, granting equality to all men on the basis of their being born human. It recognizes in wealth or breeding no basis for special political preferment or privilege. By these standards, the mixed constitution and even the most extreme form of Greek democracy must be regarded as oligarchical in character by a writer like Mill.

Yet Mill, no less than Aristotle, would agree with Montesquieu's theory that the rightness of any form of government must be considered with reference to the "humor and disposition of the people in whose favor it is established." The constitution and laws, Montesquieu writes, "should be adapted in such a manner to the people for whom they are framed that it would be a great chance if those of one nation suit another."

Mill makes the same point somewhat differently when he says, "the ideally best form of government . . . does not mean one which is practicable or eligible in all states of civilization." But although he is willing to consider the forms of government in relation to the historic conditions of a people, not simply by absolute standards, Mill differs sharply from Montesquieu and Aristotle in one very important respect. For him, as we have seen, representative democracy founded on universal suffrage is, absolutely speaking, the only truly just government—the only one perfectly suited to the nature of man. Peoples whose accidental circumstances temporarily justify less just or even unjust forms of government, such as oligarchy or despotism, must not be forever condemned to subjection or disfranchisement, but should rather be raised by education, experience, and economic reforms to a condition in which the ideal polity becomes appropriate for them.

THE BASIC PROBLEMS of democratic government—seen from the point of view of those who either attack or defend it—remain constant despite the altered conception of democracy in various epochs.

At all times, there is the question of leadership and the need for obtaining the political services of the best men without infringing on the political prerogatives of all men. The difference between the many and the few, between the equality of men as free or human and their individual inequality in virtue or talent, must always be given political recognition, if not by superiority in status, then by allocation of the technically difficult problems of statecraft to the expert or specially competent, with only certain broad general policies left to the determination of a majority vote. Jefferson and Mill alike hope that popular government may abolish privileged classes without losing the benefits of leadership by peculiarly gifted individuals. The realization of that hope, Jefferson writes Adams, depends on leaving "to the citizens the free election and separation of the *aristoi* from the *pseudo-aristoi*, of the wheat from the chaff."

At all times there is the danger of tyranny by the majority and, under the threat of revolution, the rise of a demagogue who uses mob rule to establish a dictatorship. Hobbes phrases this peculiar susceptibility of democracy to the mischief of demagogues by saying of popular assemblies that they "are as subject to evil counsel, and to be seduced by orators, as a monarch by flatterers," with the result that democracy tends to degenerate into government by the most powerful orator.

The democratic state has seldom been tempted to undertake the burdens of empire without suffering from a discordance between its domestic and its foreign policy. Again and again,

Thucydides describes the efforts of the Athenians to reconcile their imperialism abroad with democracy at home.

In his oration at the end of the first year of the Peloponnesian war, Pericles praises the democracy of Athens and at the same time celebrates the might of her empire. "It is only the Athenians," he says, "who, fearless of consequences, confer their benefits not from calculations of expediency, but in the confidence of liberality." But four years later, after the revolt of Mitylene, Cleon speaks in a different vein. Thucydides describes him as being "at that time by far the most powerful with the commons." He tells his fellow citizens of democratic Athens that he has "often before now been convinced that a democracy is incapable of empire," but "never more so than by your present change of mind in the matter of Mitylene." He urges them to return to their earlier decision to punish the Mitylenians, for, he says, if they reverse that decision they will be "giving way to the three failings most fatal to empire —pity, sentiment, and indulgence."

Diodotus, who in this debate recommends a policy of leniency, does not do so in the "confidence of liberality" which Pericles had said was the attitude of a democratic state toward its dependencies. "The question is not of justice," Diodotus declares, "but how to make the Mitylenians useful to Athens. . . . We must not," he continues, "sit as strict judges of the offenders to our own prejudice, but rather see how by moderate chastisements we may be enabled to benefit in the future by the revenue-producing powers of our dependencies. . . . It is far more useful for the preservation of our empire," he concludes, "voluntarily to put up with injustice, than to put to death, however justly, those whom it is our interest to keep alive."

Twelve years later, Alcibiades, no democrat himself, urges the Athenians to undertake the Sicilian expedition by saying, "we cannot fix the exact point at which our empire shall stop; we have reached a position in which we must not be content with retaining but must scheme to extend it, for, if we cease to rule others, we are in danger of being ruled ourselves." In the diplomatic skirmishes which precede the invasion of Sicily, Hermocrates of Syracuse tries to unite the Sicilian cities so that they may escape "disgraceful submission to an Athenian master." The Athenian ambassador, Euphemus, finds himself compelled to speak at first of "our empire and of the good right we have to it"; but he soon finds himself frankly confessing that "for tyrants and imperial cities nothing is unreasonable if expedient."

The denouement of the Peloponnesian war, and especially of the Syracusan expedition, is the collapse of democracy, not through the loss of empire but as a result of the moral sacrifices involved in trying to maintain or increase it. Tacitus, commenting on the decay of republican institutions with the extension of Rome's conquests, underlines the same theme. It is still the same theme when the problems of British imperialism appear in Mill's discussion of how a democracy should govern its colonies or dependencies.

The incompatibility of empire with democracy is one side of the picture of the democratic state in external affairs. The other side is the tension between democratic institutions and military power or policy—in the form of standing armies and warlike maneuvers. The inefficiency traditionally attributed to democracy under peaceful conditions does not, from all the evidences of history, seem to render democracy weak or pusillanimous in the face of aggression.

The deeper peril for democracy seems to lie in the effect of war upon its institutions and on the morality of its people As Hamilton writes in *The Federalist:* "The violent destruction of life and property incident to war, the continual effort and alarm attendant on a state of continual danger, will compel nations the most attached to liberty to resort for repose and security to institutions which have a tendency to destroy their civil and political rights. To be more safe, they at length become willing to run the risk of being less free."

OUTLINE OF TOPICS

REFERENCES

To find the passages cited, use the numbers in heavy type, which are the volume and page numbers of the passages referred to. For example, in **4** Homer: *Iliad*, BK II [265–283] 12d, the number **4** is the number of the volume in the set; the number 12d indicates that the passage is in section d of page 12.

Page Sections: When the text is printed in one column, the letters a and b refer to the upper and lower halves of the page. For example, in **53** James: *Psychology*, 116a-119b, the passage begins in the upper half of page 116 and ends in the lower half of page 119. When the text is printed in two columns, the letters a and b refer to the upper and lower halves of the left-hand side of the page, the letters c and d to the upper and lower halves of the right-hand side of the page. For example, in **7** Plato: *Symposium*, 163b-164c, the passage begins in the lower half of the left-hand side of page 163 and ends in the upper half of the right-hand side of page 164.

Author's Divisions: One or more of the main divisions of a work (such as part, bk, ch, sect) are sometimes included in the reference; line numbers, in brackets, are given in certain cases; *e.g.*, *Iliad*, BK II [265–283] 12d.

Bible References: The references are to book, chapter, and verse. When the King James and Douay versions differ in title of books or in the numbering of chapters or verses, the King James version is cited first and the Douay, indicated by a (*D*), follows; *e.g.*, Old Testament: *Nehemiah*, 7:45—(*D*) II Esdras, 7:46.

Symbols: The abbreviation "esp" calls the reader's attention to one or more especially relevant parts of a whole reference; "passim" signifies that the topic is discussed intermittently rather than continuously in the work or passage cited.

For additional information concerning the style of the references, see the Explanation of Reference Style; for general guidance in the use of *The Great Ideas*, consult the Preface.

1. Conceptions of democracy: the comparison of democracy with other forms of government

5 Euripides: *Suppliants* [399–462] 261d-262b

6 Herodotus: *History*, BK III, 107c-108c

6 Thucydides: *Peloponnesian War*, BK II, 395d-399a esp 396c-d

7 Plato: *Republic*, BK I, 301c-d; BK VIII, 408b-413d / *Statesman*, 598b-604b esp 603d-604b / *Laws*, BK III, 667c-676b esp 672d-676b; BK IV, 679c-682c; BK VI, 699d-700c; BK VIII, 733d-734a

9 Aristotle: *Politics*, BK III, CH 1 471b,d-472c; CH 6 [1278^{b}7–14] 475d; CH 7–8 476c-477c; BK IV, CH 2–6 488b-493a; CH 11–12 495b-497b; CH 16 [1301^{a}10–15] 502c; BK V, CH 1 502a-503b; BK VI, CH 1–6 520a-524c / *Rhetoric*, BK I, CH 8 608a-c

14 Plutarch: *Lycurgus-Numa*, 62b-c / *Solon*, 70d-71c

20 Aquinas: *Summa Theologica*, PART I-II, Q 95, A 4, ANS 229b-230c; Q 105, A 1, ANS 307d-309d

23 Hobbes: *Leviathan*, PART II, 104b-106d; 114b-115a; 150c-151a; 154b-c; PART III, 228b; PART IV, 273a-b

35 Locke: *Civil Government*, CH II 25d-28c; CH IV, SECT 21 29d; CH VII, SECT 87–89 44a-d;

CH VIII 46c-53c passim; CH X, SECT 132 55a-b; CH XI 55b-58b passim; CH XIII, SECT 149 59b-d

38 Montesquieu: *Spirit of Laws*, BK II-III 4a-13d esp BK II, 4a-6b, BK III, 9b-10c; BK V, 18d-25a; 31b-33a,c; BK VI, 34d-35c; BK VII, 44d-45b; 47c-48a; BK VIII, 51a-52c; BK IX, 59c; BK XI, 68b,d-69c

38 Rousseau: *Inequality*, 359a-b / *Social Contract*, BK I, 391a-393c; BK II, 395a-398b; BK III, 410b-411c; 413c; 420a-424d

41 Gibbon: *Decline and Fall*, 81d

42 Kant: *Pure Reason*, 114b-d / *Science of Right*, 436c-d; 445a-c; 450a-452a esp 450a-d

43 Federalist: NUMBER 9, 47a-48d; NUMBER 10, 51c-53a; NUMBER 14, 60a-61b; NUMBER 39, 125b-126b; NUMBER 48, 157c; NUMBER 63, 193d-194a

43 Mill: *Liberty*, 267d-268c / *Representative Government* 327a-442d passim, esp 341d-350a, 355b-356a, 366c-367a, 370a-372b

46 Hegel: *Philosophy of Right*, PART III, par 273 90c-92a; par 279, 93d-94c / *Philosophy of History*, INTRO, 172d-175c; PART II, 271c-274a esp 271d-272d, 273d-274a; 275b-276d

48 Melville: *Moby Dick*, 84b-85a

50 Marx-Engels: *Communist Manifesto*, 428d-429c

2. The derogation of democracy: the anarchic tendency of freedom and equality

5 Euripides: *Suppliants* [399–425] 261d-262a

6 Herodotus: *History*, BK III, 107c-108c

6 Thucydides: *Peloponnesian War*, BK VI, 533a-c

7 Plato: *Republic*, BK VIII, 408b-414b / *Laws*, BK III, 674c-676b; BK IV, 681b-682c; BK VIII, 733d-734a

9 Aristotle: *Ethics*, BK VIII, CH 10 [1161^{a}7–9] 413b / *Politics*, BK IV, CH 2 [1289^{a}35–^{b}11] 488b-c; CH 4 [1292^{a}4–37] 491b-d; CH 6 [1292^{b}40–1293^{a}9] 492c; BK V, CH 9 [1310^{a}25–36] 512c; CH 11 [1313^{b}33–1314^{a}1] 516c; BK VI, CH 4 [1319^{b}2–32] 523a-b / *Athenian Constitution*, CH 28 565c-566b

14 Plutarch: *Dion*, 800c

23 Hobbes: *Leviathan*, PART II, 114b-115a; 150c-151a; PART IV, 273a-b

35 Locke: *Civil Government*, CH IV, SECT 21 29d; CH VI, SECT 57, 37a-b

38 Montesquieu: *Spirit of Laws*, BK III, 10a; BK VIII, 51a-52c; BK XI, 68b,d-69c

38 Rousseau: *Social Contract*, BK III, 424b

43 Federalist: NUMBER 10, 51c-d

43 Mill: *Liberty*, 298b-299a / *Representative Government*, 354b-355b; 387b-c; 403d

44 Boswell: *Johnson*, 125c-d; 127b-c; 211b-c

46 Hegel: *Philosophy of Right*, PART III, par 301 100b-101a; par 308 102c-103a / *Philosophy of History*, INTRO, 175b-c; PART IV, 366c-367a

50 Marx-Engels: *Communist Manifesto*, 431c

2a. Lawless mob-rule: the tyranny of the majority

5 Euripides: *Suppliants* [409–427] 261d-262a

6 Herodotus: *History*, BK III, 108a

6 Thucydides: *Peloponnesian War*, BK VI, 525a-b; 533a-c

7 Plato: *Republic*, BK VIII, 411d-412d / *Statesman*, 598b-604b esp 603d-604b / *Laws*, BK III, 675c-676b; BK IV, 681b-682c

9 Aristotle: *Politics*, BK II, CH 12 [1274^{a}5–14] 470c-d; BK III, CH 10 [1281^{a}11–28] 478d-479a; CH 11 [1281^{b}39–1282^{a}41] 479d-480b; BK IV, CH 4 [1292^{a}4–37] 491b-d; CH 6 [1292^{b}40–1293^{a}9] 492c; BK V, CH 9 [1310^{a}25–36] 512c; CH 10 [1312^{a}40–^{b}8] 514d-515a; BK VI, CH 4 [1319^{b}2–32] 523a-b

14 Plutarch: *Agis*, 648b,d-649b

23 Hobbes: *Leviathan*, PART II, 114d-115a; PART IV, 273b

26 Shakespeare: *2nd Henry VI*, ACT IV, SC VI-VIII 61a-63b

27 Shakespeare: *Coriolanus*, ACT I, SC I [1–225] 351a-353d; ACT III, SC I [140–161] 370d-371a

33 Pascal: *Pensées*, 878 345a-b

38 Montesquieu: *Spirit of Laws*, BK III, 10a; BK VI, 35c-36a; BK VIII, 51a-52c

38 Rousseau: *Social Contract*, BK III, 419b

40 Gibbon: *Decline and Fall*, 14b

41 Gibbon: *Decline and Fall*, 73b-c; 94d

43 Federalist: NUMBER 9, 47a-c; NUMBER 10, 50b-d; NUMBER 22, 84c-d; NUMBER 51, 164a-165a; NUMBER 58, 181b-c; NUMBER 63, 192c-193a

43 Mill: *Liberty*, 268d-271c; 298b-299a; 302b-c / *Representative Government*, 366c-380b passim, esp 376b-c; 406c-d

44 Boswell: *Johnson*, 260b; 422c

46 Hegel: *Philosophy of Right*, PART III, par 303 101c-102a; ADDITIONS, 180 148b / *Philosophy of History*, INTRO, 172d-173a; PART III, 300a-b; PART IV, 365a

2b. The incompetence of the people and the need for leadership: the superiority of monarchy and aristocracy

5 Euripides: *Suppliants* [399–462] 261d-262b

5 Aristophanes: *Knights* 470a-487a,c

6 Herodotus: *History*, BK III, 107c-108c

6 Thucydides: *Peloponnesian War*, BK III, 425a-d; BK V, 504c-505a; BK VI, 520b-c; 533a-c

7 Plato: *Republic*, BK IV, 346c-347a; BK VI, 375d-376c; BK VIII, 409a-d; 411d-414b / *Statesman*, 598b-604b / *Laws*, BK III, 674d-676b

9 Aristotle: *Politics*, BK II, CH 9 [1270^{b}7–17] 466d; BK III, CH 10–13 478d-483a; CH 15 [1286^{a}22–^{b}8] 484c-d / *Athenian Constitution*, CH 28 565c-566b

12 Aurelius: *Meditations*, BK XI, SECT 23 306a

14 Plutarch: *Lycurgus*, 34d / *Lycurgus-Numa*, 62b-64a,c / *Agis*, 648b,d-649b / *Dion*, 792d-802a,c esp 800c

23 Hobbes: *Leviathan*, PART I, 94b-c; PART II, 104d-106d; 129d-130a; 152b-c; PART IV, 273a-b

25 Montaigne: *Essays*, 147b-148a

26 Shakespeare: *Julius Caesar*, ACT I, SC I-II 568b,d-572c

27 Shakespeare: *Coriolanus*, ACT I, SC I [1–225] 351a-353d; ACT II, SC I [1–106] 361a-362a; ACT III, SC I [140–161] 370d-371a; ACT IV, SC VI [74–156] 383a-384a

31 Descartes: *Discourse*, PART II, 44d-45a

33 Pascal: *Pensées*, 878 345a-b

35 Locke: *Civil Government*, CH XIX, SECT 223 76c-d

38 Montesquieu: *Spirit of Laws*, BK II, 4d-5a; BK III, 10c-d; BK V, 25c-d; BK VIII, 51a-52c; BK XI, 71a-c; 72b; BK XIX, 142c-143a

38 Rousseau: *Social Contract*, BK II, 401c-d; BK III, 411a; 412a

40 Gibbon: *Decline and Fall*, 68b,d-69a

42 Kant: *Science of Right*, 450a-d

43 Federalist: NUMBER 55, 172b-173a; NUMBER 58, 181b-c; NUMBER 63, 192c-d

43 Mill: *Liberty*, 298b-299a; 319d-323a,c passim / *Representative Government*, 353b-354b; 363b-366a; 375a-377a

(2. *The derogation of democracy: the anarchic tendency of freedom and equality. 2b. The incompetence of the people and the need for leadership: the superiority of monarchy and aristocracy.*)

44 BOSWELL: *Johnson*, 86a-b; 172d-173a; 178a-c; 220a-d; 414c; 422c

46 HEGEL: *Philosophy of Right*, PART III, par 281 95b-d; par 308 102c-103a; par 317–318 104d-105b; ADDITIONS, 186 149b / *Philosophy of History*, INTRO, 173a-175c; PART II, 272c-273a; PART III, 300a-301c

3. The acceptance of democracy as one of several good forms of government

6 HERODOTUS: *History*, BK III, 107c-108c

7 PLATO: *Statesman*, 600c-604b esp 603d-604b

9 ARISTOTLE: *Politics*, BK III, CH I 471b,d-472c; CH 6 [1278^{b}6-14] 475d; CH 7-8 476c-477c; CH II 479b-480c; BK IV, CH II-12 495b-497b / *Rhetoric*, BK I, CH 8 608a-c

20 AQUINAS: *Summa Theologica*, PART I-II, Q 95, A 4, ANS 229b-230c; Q 105, A I, ANS 307d-309d

23 HOBBES: *Leviathan*, PART II, 154b-c; PART III, 228b; PART IV, 273a-b

35 LOCKE: *Civil Government*, CH X, SECT 132 55a-b

38 MONTESQUIEU: *Spirit of Laws*, BK II, 4a-6b; BK III, 9b-10c

38 ROUSSEAU: *Inequality*, 359a-b / *Social Contract*, BK III, 410b-411c

42 KANT: *Science of Right*, 450a-d

43 FEDERALIST: NUMBER 10, 51c-53a; NUMBER 14, 60a-d; NUMBER 39, 125b-126b

46 HEGEL: *Philosophy of Right*, PART III, par 273 90c-92a / *Philosophy of History*, INTRO, 173a-175c; PART II, 271c-274a passim

3a. Comparison of democratic and oligarchic justice: the mixed constitution as a compromise between the interests of the poor and rich

5 EURIPIDES: *Suppliants* [399-462] 261d-262b

6 THUCYDIDES: *Peloponnesian War*, BK II, 396b-c; BK VI, 520a-d; BK VIII, 575d-576b; 590a-b

7 PLATO: *Laws*, BK IV, 681b-682c; BK VI, 699d-700b

9 ARISTOTLE: *Politics*, BK II, CH 6 [1265^{b}26-1266^{a}30] 461b-d; BK III, CH 8-13 477a-483a; BK IV, CH 3 [1289^{b}26]-CH 4 [1290^{b}21] 488d-489d; CH 8-9 493c-494d; CH II-12 495b-497b; BK IV, CH 14-BK V, CH I 498b-503b; BK VI, CH 2 [1318^{a}4]-CH 3 [1318^{b}5] 521b-522a

14 PLUTARCH: *Lycurgus*, 34d-35d / *Solon*, 70d-71c / *Dion*, 800c

23 HOBBES: *Leviathan*, PART II, 156b-c

38 MONTESQUIEU: *Spirit of Laws*, BK II, 5b-c; BK XI, 71d-72b

38 ROUSSEAU: *Social Contract*, BK III, 412b-c

40 GIBBON: *Decline and Fall*, 90d-91a

41 GIBBON: *Decline and Fall*, 81d; 94c-95b; 96b-d; 403b-404d

43 FEDERALIST: NUMBER 54, 171b-172b; NUMBER 57 176d-179b passim

43 MILL: *Representative Government*, 384a-387d

46 HEGEL: *Philosophy of History*, PART II, 275b-276a

50 MARX-ENGELS: *Communist Manifesto*, 432b-d

3b. Comparison of the political wisdom of the many and the few: the mixed regime as including both

5 EURIPIDES: *Suppliants* [399-462] 261d-262b

6 HERODOTUS: *History*, BK III, 107c-108c; BK V, 180c-d

6 THUCYDIDES: *Peloponnesian War*, BK III, 425a-d; BK VI, 520a-d

7 PLATO: *Crito* 213a-219a,c esp 213a-215d / *Republic*, BK IV, 346c-347a; BK VI, 375d-376c; 377a-379c / *Statesman*, 598b-604b / *Laws*, BK III, 674d-676b

9 ARISTOTLE: *Politics*, BK III, CH 10-13 478d-483a; CH 15 [1286^{a}7-^{b}8] 484b-d; CH 16 [1287^{b}8-36] 486a-c

14 PLUTARCH: *Lycurgus*, 34d-35d / *Agis*, 648b,d-649a / *Dion*, 800c

20 AQUINAS: *Summa Theologica*, PART I-II, Q 95, A 4, ANS 229b-230c; Q 105, A I, ANS and REP I-2 307d-309d

23 HOBBES: *Leviathan*, PART II, 105d-106b; 129b-130a

25 MONTAIGNE: *Essays*, 303c-304a

27 SHAKESPEARE: *Coriolanus* 351a-392a,c

31 DESCARTES: *Discourse*, PART II, 44d-45a

35 LOCKE: *Civil Government*, CH XIX, SECT 223 76c-d; SECT 240-242 81b-d

38 MONTESQUIEU: *Spirit of Laws*, BK II, 4d-5a; BK XI, 71a-c; BK XIX, 145c-d

38 ROUSSEAU: *Political Economy*, 369c-d / *Social Contract*, BK III, 411d-412a; 413c; 414d-415b; BK IV, 427a-428a passim

41 GIBBON: *Decline and Fall*, 94c-95b

43 FEDERALIST: NUMBER 3, 33b; NUMBER 10, 51d-52a; NUMBER 40, 130d-132a; NUMBER 49-50 159b-162c passim; NUMBER 55, 172d-173a; NUMBER 57 176d-179b passim; NUMBER 58, 181b-c; NUMBER 63, 192c-193a; NUMBER 68, 205b-d; NUMBER 71, 214d-215a; NUMBER 76, 227a

43 MILL: *Liberty*, 298b-299a; 319d-323a,c passim / *Representative Government*, 353b-354b; 356b-362c passim; 363b-366a; 374c-377a; 384a-387d; 401a-406a passim, esp 402b-c; 407d-409c; 410d-412a

44 BOSWELL: *Johnson*, 86a-b

46 HEGEL: *Philosophy of Right*, PART III, par 281 95b-d; par 297 99b; par 301 100b-101a; par 308 102c-103a; par 317-318 104d-105b; ADDITIONS, 186 149b

3c. Comparison of democracy, aristocracy, and monarchy with respect to efficiency

6 HERODOTUS: *History*, BK III, 107c-108c

7 PLATO: *Statesman*, 603d-604b / *Laws*, BK IV, 679b-680c; BK VI, 699d-700c

9 ARISTOTLE: *Politics*, BK III, CH 11–13 479b-483a; CH 15–18 484b-487a,c; BK IV, CH 11 495b-496d

15 TACITUS: *Annals*, BK I, 4d-5b

23 HOBBES: *Leviathan*, PART II, 104d-106d; 107d-108a; 129b-130a

38 MONTESQUIEU: *Spirit of Laws*, BK III, 10c-d; BK V, 25c-d; BK XI, 72b

38 ROUSSEAU: *Social Contract*, BK III, 411d-412a

42 KANT: *Science of Right*, 450b-c

43 FEDERALIST: NUMBER 37, 118d-119b; NUMBER 70, 210c-211a

43 MILL: *Representative Government*, 344a-d; 363b-366a

4. The praise of democracy: the ideal state

5 EURIPIDES: *Suppliants* [399–462] 261d-262b

6 HERODOTUS: *History*, BK III, 107c-d; BK V, 175b; BK VII, 238b-c

6 THUCYDIDES: *Peloponnesian War*, BK II, 395d-399a esp 396c-397c; BK VI, 520a-d

7 PLATO: *Republic*, BK VIII, 408b-413d

9 ARISTOTLE: *Politics*, BK III, CH 11–12 479b-481b; BK IV, CH 11–12 495b-497b

14 PLUTARCH: *Lycurgus-Numa*, 62b-c

23 HOBBES: *Leviathan*, PART II, 114b-115a; 150c-151a

35 LOCKE: *Civil Government*, CH XIX, SECT 223 76c-d; SECT 240–242 81b-d

38 MONTESQUIEU: *Spirit of Laws*, BK II, 4c-5a; BK III, 9b-10c

38 ROUSSEAU: *Inequality*, 323a-328a,c passim / *Social Contract*, BK III, 411a-c; BK IV, 427d

42 KANT: *Pure Reason*, 114b-d / *Science of Right*, 450d-452a / *Judgement*, 586a-587a

43 FEDERALIST: NUMBER 10 49c-53a; NUMBER 14, 60c-d; NUMBER 39, 125b-126b; NUMBER 46, 150c; NUMBER 55, 174c-d

43 MILL: *Representative Government*, 341d-350a esp 344d, 350a

46 HEGEL: *Philosophy of History*, PART II, 276a-d

48 MELVILLE: *Moby Dick*, 84b-85a

4a. Liberty and equality for all under law

5 EURIPIDES: *Suppliants* [399–462] 261d-262b

6 HERODOTUS: *History*, BK III, 107c-108d; BK VII, 232d-233d

6 THUCYDIDES: *Peloponnesian War*, BK II, 396c-d; BK VI, 520a-d

7 PLATO: *Laws*, BK III, 674c-676c; BK IV, 681b-682c; BK VI, 699d-700c

9 ARISTOTLE: *Ethics*, BK V, CH 6 [1134ª24–ᵇ17] 382a-c / *Politics*, BK III, CH 1 471b,d-472c; CH 6 [1278ᵇ30-1279ª22] 476a-c; CH 8–13 477a-483a passim; CH 16–17 485b-487a passim; BK IV, CH 4 [1291ᵇ30-38] 491a-b; CH 14

[1298ª4–34] 498b-d; BK V, CH 1 502a-503b; CH 8 [1308ª10–25] 510a-b; CH 9 [1310ª25–36] 512c; BK VI, CH 2 520d-521b

12 AURELIUS: *Meditations*, BK I, SECT 14 254b-c

14 PLUTARCH: *Lycurgus*, 36a-37b

15 TACITUS: *Annals*, BK XIII, 132a-c

23 MACHIAVELLI: *Prince*, CH V 8a-c

23 HOBBES: *Leviathan*, PART I, 94b-d; PART II, 113c-116b; 150c-151a; 156b-c; PART IV, 273a-c

35 LOCKE: *Civil Government*, CH IV, SECT 21 29d; CH VI, SECT 54–57 36c-37b; CH VII, SECT 87–94 44a-46c; CH XI, SECT 136–139 56c-58a; SECT 142 58b

38 MONTESQUIEU: *Spirit of Laws*, BK V, 19a-21a; BK VI, 34d; BK VIII, 51a-52c; BK XI, 68b,d-69c

38 ROUSSEAU: *Inequality*, 359a-b / *Social Contract*, BK II, 396d-398b; 405a-c; BK IV, 427d

40 GIBBON: *Decline and Fall*, 14b

41 GIBBON: *Decline and Fall*, 81d

42 KANT: *Pure Reason*, 114b-d / *Science of Right*, 398c-399c; 400b,d-402a,c; 408c-409c; 436c-d; 438d-439a; 450d-452a esp 451b-c / *Judgement*, 586a-587a

43 DECLARATION OF INDEPENDENCE: [7–28] 1a-b passim

43 ARTICLES OF CONFEDERATION: IV [17–36] 5b-c

43 CONSTITUTION OF THE U.S.: PREAMBLE 11a,c; ARTICLE IV, SECT 2 [519–521] 16a; AMENDMENTS, I–X 17a-18a; XIII, SECT I–XIV, SECT 2 18c-19a; XV 19b; XIX 19d

43 FEDERALIST: NUMBER 26 92a-94d; NUMBER 37, 118d-119b; NUMBER 57, 177d-178a; NUMBER 84, 251b-254b

43 MILL: *Liberty*, 267a-274a / *Representative Government*, 346a-c; 365b-366a; 370a-372b; 387b-d; 403d / *Utilitarianism*, 460a-c; 467a-b; 474d-476a

44 BOSWELL: *Johnson*, 125c-d; 127b-c; 211b-c

46 HEGEL: *Philosophy of History*, PART I, 213b; PART II, 271d-272d; 275b-276d; PART IV, 362d-363a

48 MELVILLE: *Moby Dick*, 84b-85a

50 MARX-ENGELS: *Communist Manifesto*, 429b-c

51 TOLSTOY: *War and Peace*, BK I, 10a-b

4a(1) Universal suffrage: the abolition of privileged classes

5 ARISTOPHANES: *Ecclesiazusae* 615a-628d

6 THUCYDIDES: *Peloponnesian War*, BK VI, 520b-c

7 PLATO: *Republic*, BK VIII, 406a-407a / *Laws*, BK VI, 705b

9 ARISTOTLE: *Politics*, BK III, CH 9–12 477c-481b passim; BK IV, CH 6 492b-493a; BK VI, CH 4 [1319ᵇ2-32] 523a-b

38 MONTESQUIEU: *Spirit of Laws*, BK II, 4a-5c; BK XI, 71d-72b

38 ROUSSEAU: *Social Contract*, BK IV, 427d

40 GIBBON: *Decline and Fall*, 14b

41 GIBBON: *Decline and Fall*, 73b-c; 81d-82b

42 KANT: *Science of Right*, 436d-437c; 445a-c

(4a. Liberty and equality for all under law.
4a(1) Universal suffrage: the abolition of
privileged classes.)

43 ARTICLES OF CONFEDERATION: VI [87-93]
6b

43 CONSTITUTION OF THE U.S.: ARTICLE I, SECT
9 [289-295] 14a; ARTICLE VI [597-599] 16d;
AMENDMENTS, XIV, SECT 1-3 18d-19a; XV
19b; XVII 19b-c; XIX 19d

43 FEDERALIST: NUMBER 39, 125c-126b; NUM-
BER 57, 177a-b; NUMBER 84, 252a

43 MILL: Representative Government, 344d-346c;
350a; 369b-370a; 380c-389b; 394a-396d;
403d

50 MARX-ENGELS: Communist Manifesto, 416c-
d; 425b-c; 428d-429c

4a(2) The problem of economic justice: the
choice between capitalism and socialism

5 EURIPIDES: Suppliants [399-462] 261d-262b

5 ARISTOPHANES: Ecclesiazusae 615a-628d

7 PLATO: Republic, BK III, 341c-d; BK V, 363b-
365d / Laws, BK V, 691b-697a

9 ARISTOTLE: Ethics, BK V, CH 2 [1130^{b}30]-CH
4 [1132^{b}20] 378b-380b / Politics, BK II, CH 5
458a-460a; CH 6 [1265^{a}27-37] 460c-d; CH 7
461d-463c; BK V, CH 1 502a-503b; BK VI, CH
3 521c-522a; CH 5 [1320^{a}17-^{b}11] 523d-524b

14 PLUTARCH: Lycurgus, 36a

20 AQUINAS: Summa Theologica, PART I-II, Q
105, A 2, ANS and REP 1-6 309d-316a

23 HOBBES: Leviathan, PART II, 156b-157a

27 SHAKESPEARE: Coriolanus, ACT I, SC I [1-226]
351a-353d

35 LOCKE: Civil Government, CH V 30b-36a

38 MONTESQUIEU: Spirit of Laws, BK IV, 16a-17b;
BK V, 19d-21d; BK VII, 44d-45b; BK XIII,
96a-102a,c

38 ROUSSEAU: Political Economy, 375b-d; 377b-
d / Social Contract, BK I, 393d-394d; BK II,
405a-d

39 SMITH: Wealth of Nations, BK I, 28a-d;
61c-d; 109d-110d; BK IV, 201b-d; 239c-240a;
287c-d

43 CONSTITUTION OF THE U.S.: AMENDMENTS,
V [645-648] 17c; XIII 18c; XVI 19b

43 FEDERALIST: NUMBER 10, 50b-53a; NUMBER
35, 113a-114b; NUMBER 60, 184d-186b; NUM-
BER 79, 233c

43 MILL: Liberty, 309a-c / Representative Government, 345d-346a; 369b-370a / Utilitarianism,
467a-b; 472d-473c

44 BOSWELL: Johnson, 304c

46 HEGEL: Philosophy of History, PART IV,
356d

50 MARX: Capital, 33b-37a; 104b-105a; 113c-
115c; 377c-378d

50 MARX-ENGELS: Communist Manifesto, 419a-
434d esp 428d-429c, 432b-c, 433b, 434c-d

54 FREUD: Civilization and Its Discontents, 787d-
788b

4b. The democratic realization of popular sovereignty: the safeguarding of natural
rights

5 EURIPIDES: Suppliants [334-358] 261b-c;
[399-462] 261d-262b

6 HERODOTUS: History, BK III, 107c-d; BK VII,
245b

6 THUCYDIDES: Peloponnesian War, BK II,
396b-397c

7 PLATO: Laws, BK IV, 681d-682c

9 ARISTOTLE: Politics, BK III, CH 1 471b,d-472c;
CH 6 [1278^{b}7-14] 475d / Rhetoric, BK I, CH 8
[1365^{b}22-31] 608a

14 PLUTARCH: Tiberius Gracchus, 678b-d

23 HOBBES: Leviathan, PART II, 101a-104d;
PART III, 228b-c; PART IV, 273a-c

31 SPINOZA: Ethics, PART IV, PROP 37, SCHOL 2
435b-436a

35 LOCKE: Civil Government, CH IV, SECT 21 29d;
CH VII, SECT 87-CH VIII, SECT 99 44a-47c;
CH IX, SECT 127-CH X, SECT 132 54a-55b;
CH XI 55b-58b; CH XIII, SECT 149 59b-d; CH
XIX 73d-81d passim, esp SECT 212 74a-b,
SECT 243 81d

38 MONTESQUIEU: Spirit of Laws, BK II, 4a-6b

38 ROUSSEAU: Inequality, 323d; 356b-359a /
Political Economy, 369b-c / Social Contract,
BK I, 387b,d-392a; BK II, 395a-396a; BK III,
420a-424d

40 GIBBON: Decline and Fall, 14b; 91a-d

41 GIBBON: Decline and Fall, 94d

42 KANT: Science of Right, 429a-c; 434a; 435a-
458a,c esp 436c, 437c-d, 450a-b, 451c-d

43 DECLARATION OF INDEPENDENCE: [1-28] 1a-
b; [41-47] 2a; [109-121] 3a-b

43 CONSTITUTION OF THE U.S.: PREAMBLE 11a,c;
AMENDMENTS, I-X 17a-18a; XIII-XV 18c-19b;
XIX 19d

43 FEDERALIST: NUMBER 10 49c-53a; NUMBER
14, 60c-d; NUMBER 22, 84d-85a; NUMBER 39
125a-128b; NUMBER 40, 131b; NUMBER 44,
144d-145a; 146c-d; NUMBER 46, 150b-c; NUM-
BER 51, 164a-165a; NUMBER 78, 231a-232c;
NUMBER 83, 246a-b; NUMBER 84, 251b-254b

43 MILL: Liberty, 267a-274a / Representative
Government, 344d; 350a; 382b-c

46 HEGEL: Philosophy of Right, PART III, par
279, 93d-94d; par 308 102c-103a / Philosophy
of History, INTRO, 175b-c; PART II, 272a-d

4c. The infirmities of democracy in practice
and the reforms or remedies for these
defects

5 EURIPIDES: Suppliants [399-462] 261d-262b

5 ARISTOPHANES: Acharnians 455a-469a,c /
Knights 470a-487a,c esp [1111-1150] 483d-
484b / Wasps 507a-525d / Peace 526a-541d
esp [601-692] 532d-534a / Birds 542a-563d /
Frogs [686-705] 572a-b / Lysistrata [486-586]
589a-590d / Ecclesiazusae [169-188] 617a

6 HERODOTUS: History, BK III, 108a-c; BK V,
180c-d

6 THUCYDIDES: *Peloponnesian War*, BK III, 425a-d; BK V, 504c-505a; BK VI, 533a-c

7 PLATO: *Republic*, BK VIII, 411d-413d / *Laws*, BK III, 674c-676b; BK VI, 699d-700c

9 ARISTOTLE: *Politics*, BK IV, CH 4 [1292^{a}4-37] 491b-d; CH 6 [1292^{b}40-1293^{a}9] 492c; BK V, CH 9 [1310^{a}25-36] 512c; BK VI, CH 4 [1318^{b}6-1319^{b}32] 522a-523b / *Athenian Constitution*, CH 28 565c-566b

14 PLUTARCH: *Lycurgus*, 34d-35c / *Lycurgus-Numa*, 62b-64a,c / *Agis*, 648b,d-649b

23 HOBBES: *Leviathan*, PART II, 148d-149b; 150c-d

35 LOCKE: *Civil Government*, CH XIII, SECT 157-158 61c-62b

38 MONTESQUIEU: *Spirit of Laws*, BK II, 5a; BK III, 10a-c; BK VI, 35c-36a; BK VIII, 51a-52c; BK IX, 58b,d-59b; BK XI, 69a-c; BK XIX, 142c-143a

38 ROUSSEAU: *Social Contract*, BK III, 418a-420a; BK IV, 433a-434b

40 GIBBON: *Decline and Fall*, 14b

41 GIBBON: *Decline and Fall*, 94d-95c; 562c-565a esp 563d-564a

43 FEDERALIST: NUMBER 10 49c-53a passim; NUMBER 22, 83b-d; NUMBER 44, 146c-d; NUMBER 48, 157c; NUMBER 49-50 159b-162c; NUMBER 55, 172b-173b; NUMBER 58, 181b-c; NUMBER 62, 189d-191c; NUMBER 63, 192b-195b; NUMBER 75, 223c-d

43 MILL: *Liberty*, 268d-271a; 298b-299b; 309a-b / *Representative Government*, 354b-355b; 362c-389b passim, esp 380c-381a, 387b-d; 392b-399d; 403b-d; 406a-409c passim

44 BOSWELL: *Johnson*, 178a-c; 374b-c

46 HEGEL: *Philosophy of Right*, PART III, par 303 101c-102a / *Philosophy of History*, INTRO, 172d-173a

4d. The suitability of democratic constitutions to all men under all circumstances: conditions favorable to democracy; progress toward democracy

6 HERODOTUS: *History*, BK VI, 193b-c; BK IX, 314a,c

7 PLATO: *Republic*, BK IX, 425c-427b

9 ARISTOTLE: *Politics*, BK III, CH 15 [1286^{b}8-22] 484d-485a; BK IV, CH 2 [1289^{b}13-20] 488c-d; CH 11-12 495b-497b; BK VI, CH 4 522a-523b

38 MONTESQUIEU: *Spirit of Laws*, BK I, 3b-d; BK VIII, 56b-c; 57b-c; BK XIV, 107b-d; BK XVI, 118b-c; BK XVII-XVIII, 122a-126c; BK XIX, 139c-140a

38 ROUSSEAU: *Inequality*, 324a-b / *Social Contract*, BK II, 402b-405a; 405c-406a; BK III, 410c; 411a-c; 415d; 421c-423a

41 GIBBON: *Decline and Fall*, 562c-565a esp 562c-d, 563d-564a

42 KANT: *Pure Reason*, 114b-115a / *Science of Right*, 436d-437c; 451a-b

43 FEDERALIST: NUMBER 14, 60a-61b; NUMBER 39, 125b; NUMBER 55, 174c-d

43 MILL: *Liberty*, 267d-268c; 272a / *Representative Government*, 328d-332d; 338b-340d; 344d-345a; 350b-355b; 387c-d; 395b-c; 413d-414d; 424c-428a passim, esp 427a-b; 433b-442d passim

46 HEGEL: *Philosophy of History*, INTRO, 161a-c; 172d-175c; PART II, 271c-274a; PART III, 300c-d

5. Democracy and representative government

5a. The distinction between direct democracy and representative, or republican, government: the territorial limits of democracy

9 ARISTOTLE: *Politics*, BK VI, CH 4 [1318^{b}21-27] 522b

35 LOCKE: *Civil Government*, CH X, SECT 132 55a-b

38 MONTESQUIEU: *Spirit of Laws*, BK VIII, 56c-d; BK IX, 58b,d-60a; BK XI, 71a-c; BK XIX, 142c-143a

38 ROUSSEAU: *Social Contract*, BK III, 410c; 420a-423a

42 KANT: *Science of Right*, 451c-452a

43 FEDERALIST: NUMBER 10, 51c-53a; NUMBER 14, 60a-61b; NUMBER 48, 157c; NUMBER 63, 192c-194a

43 MILL: *Representative Government*, 330a-b; 350a

46 HEGEL: *Philosophy of History*, INTRO, 175b-c; PART II, 273d-274a

5b. The theory of representation

7 PLATO: *Laws*, BK VI, 697a-705c

9 ARISTOTLE: *Politics*, BK IV, CH 14 498b-499c passim; CH 15 499c-501c; BK VI, CH 3-4 521c-523b

14 PLUTARCH: *Lycurgus*, 34d-35d / *Solon*, 70d-71c

20 AQUINAS: *Summa Theologica*, PART I-II, Q 90, A 3, ANS and REP 2 207a-c; Q 97, A 3, REP 3 237b-238b

23 HOBBES: *Leviathan*, PART I, 96c-98a,c; PART II, 101a-b; 104d-105c; 117b-121a; 153a-159c

35 LOCKE: *Civil Government*, CH VII, SECT 87-89 44a-d; CH XI, SECT 140 58a; CH XII, SECT 143 58c-d; CH XIII, SECT 154-158 60c-62b; CH XIX, SECT 240 81b

38 MONTESQUIEU: *Spirit of Laws*, BK XI, 71a-d

38 ROUSSEAU: *Social Contract*, BK III, 421c-423a

39 SMITH: *Wealth of Nations*, BK IV, 269d-271d

40 GIBBON: *Decline and Fall*, 522c-523a

42 KANT: *Science of Right*, 436c; 450a-b; 451c-452a

43 DECLARATION OF INDEPENDENCE: [35-47] 1b-2a; [109-121] 3a-b passim

43 CONSTITUTION OF THE U.S.: ARTICLE I 11a-14b passim

43 FEDERALIST: NUMBER 10 49c-53a; NUMBER 14, 60a-61b; NUMBER 22, 82a-83a; NUMBER 28, 97b-d; NUMBER 35, 113a-114b;

(5. Democracy and representative government.
5b. The theory of representation.)

NUMBER 52–66 165a-203a passim, esp NUM-
BER 57, 176d-178b, NUMBER 63, 192b-194a;
NUMBER 76, 227a; NUMBER 78, 231a-232c

43 MILL: *Liberty*, 268b-c / *Representative Government* 327a-442d passim, esp 329d-330b,
338a-b, 350a, 355b-356b, 370a-372b, 389c-
392b, 401a-406a

46 HEGEL: *Philosophy of Right*, PART III, par 301–
303 100b-102a; par 308–311 102c-104a; ADDI-
TIONS, 182 148c-d / *Philosophy of History*,
INTRO, 175b-c

5b(1) Majority rule and minority or propor-
tional representation

9 ARISTOTLE: *Politics*, BK III, CH 10 478d-479a;
CH 13 [1283ᵃ21–ᵇ34] 481b-d; CH 15 [1286ᵃ22–
ᵇ22] 484c-485a; BK IV, CH 8 [1294ᵃ12–15]
493d-494a; BK V, CH 9 [1310ᵃ25-35] 512c;
BK VI, CH 2 [1317ᵇ2–16] 520d; CH 3 [1318ᵃ19–
ᵇ5] 521c-522a; CH 4 [1318ᵇ21–26] 522b

33 PASCAL: *Pensées*, 301–303 227b; 878 345a-b

35 LOCKE: *Civil Government*, CH VIII, SECT 95–99
46c-47c; CH X, SECT 132 55a-b; CH XI, SECT
140 58a

38 MONTESQUIEU: *Spirit of Laws*, BK II, 4b-6d

38 ROUSSEAU: *Social Contract*, BK I, 391b; BK
IV, 425d-427a esp 426d-427a

39 SMITH: *Wealth of Nations*, BK IV, 269d-271d

40 GIBBON: *Decline and Fall*, 91b

43 ARTICLES OF CONFEDERATION: V [49–73]
5d-6a

43 CONSTITUTION OF THE U.S.: AMENDMENTS,
XIV, SECT 2 18d-19a

43 FEDERALIST: NUMBER 10 49c-53a; NUMBER
22, 82a-83a; NUMBER 35, 113a-114b; NUM-
BER 37, 120b-c; NUMBER 43, 141d-142d;
NUMBER 51, 164a-165a passim; NUMBER 54
170a-172b; NUMBER 58, 181d-182a; NUMBER
62, 189b-d

43 MILL: *Liberty*, 268d-271c; 298b-302c; 307b-
312a / *Representative Government*, 366a-380b;
386a-387d; 406d-407d; 410b-c

44 BOSWELL: *Johnson*, 261c-d

46 HEGEL: *Philosophy of Right*, PART III, par
311–313 103d-104b / *Philosophy of History*,
INTRO, 172d-173a; PART IV, 365a

5b(2) Ultimate limitations on the franchise

7 PLATO: *Laws*, BK VI, 697d-700b; BK VIII,
740d-741a

9 ARISTOTLE: *Politics*, BK IV, CH 6 492b-493a;
BK VI, CH 3 521c-522a; CH 4 [1319ᵇ2–32]
523a-b; BK VII, CH 9 533a-d / *Athenian Constitution*, CH 4 554b-d; CH 42 572b-d

14 PLUTARCH: *Lycurgus-Numa*, 62b-d

38 MONTESQUIEU: *Spirit of Laws*, BK II, 4a-5c

38 ROUSSEAU: *Social Contract*, BK IV, 427c-432b

42 KANT: *Science of Right*, 436d-437c

43 CONSTITUTION OF THE U.S.: ARTICLE I, SECT
2 [5–10] 11b

43 FEDERALIST: NUMBER 52, 165a-c; NUMBER 54
170a-172b; NUMBER 57, 177a

43 MILL: *Representative Government*, 375a-b;
380c-389b passim, esp 382c-383c; 394b-
396d

46 HEGEL: *Philosophy of Right*, PART III, par 311
103d-104a

5b(3) Methods of election and voting

7 PLATO: *Laws*, BK VI, 697a-705c; BK XII,
786b-787b

9 ARISTOTLE: *Politics*, BK IV, CH 9 [1294ᵇ6–13]
494c; CH 14 [1298ᵇ13–1299ᵃ1] 499a-c; CH 15
[1300ᵃ9–ᵇ4] 500d-501b

14 PLUTARCH: *Lycurgus*, 45d

15 TACITUS: *Annals*, BK I, 6a-b / *Histories*, BK
IV, 267d-268c

35 LOCKE: *Civil Government*, CH XIII, SECT 154–
158 60d-62b; CH XIX, SECT 216 74d

38 MONTESQUIEU: *Spirit of Laws*, BK II, 5b-
6a

38 ROUSSEAU: *Inequality*, 324c-325b / *Social
Contract*, BK IV, 426c-428a

43 CONSTITUTION OF THE U.S.: ARTICLE I,
SECT 2 [5–10] 11b; SECT 2 [17]–SECT 3 [66]
11b-12a; SECT 4 [96–102], SECT 5 [107–109]
12b; ARTICLE II, SECT 1 [321–374] 14b-d;
AMENDMENTS, XII 18a-c; XVII 19b-c

43 FEDERALIST: NUMBER 52–61 165a-188d passim; NUMBER 62, 189a-b; NUMBER 68 205b-
207a

43 MILL: *Representative Government*, 370a-406a;
412a-414d

44 BOSWELL: *Johnson*, 176a-b; 251a

46 HEGEL: *Philosophy of Right*, PART III, par
309–311 103b-104a / *Philosophy of History*,
PART II, 277c-d

5b(4) The role of political parties: factions

5 ARISTOPHANES: *Lysistrata* [577–580] 590c

6 THUCYDIDES: *Peloponnesian War*, BK III,
434c-438b; BK IV, 458d-459c; 463a-465c; BK
V, 502d-504a; BK VIII 564a-593a,c esp 568d-
569a, 575c-576c, 577b-d, 579c-583c, 584b-
585a, 585d-586b, 587a-590c

7 PLATO: *Laws*, BK V, 695a-c; BK IX, 744c-d

9 ARISTOTLE: *Ethics*, BK IX, CH 6 420c-421a /
Politics, BK V, CH 9 [1309ᵇ14–1310ᵃ12] 511d-
512b / *Athenian Constitution*, CH 5 554d-555a;
CH 8, par 5 556c

14 PLUTARCH: *Solon*, 68d; 75c-d / *Pericles*,
126c-d / *Pompey*, 521d

15 TACITUS: *Annals*, BK VI, 97b-c / *Histories*,
BK II, 224d-225a

23 MACHIAVELLI: *Prince*, CH IX, 14c-d

23 HOBBES: *Leviathan*, PART II, 121c-d; 148d-
149b; 150b

38 MONTESQUIEU: *Spirit of Laws*, BK III, 9d; BK
XIX, 142b-143a

38 ROUSSEAU: *Social Contract*, BK II, 396b-d;
BK III, 424b

39 SMITH: *Wealth of Nations*, BK IV, 269d-271a;
BK V, 420c-421a

40 GIBBON: *Decline and Fall*, 652b-655c

43 FEDERALIST: NUMBER 10 49c-53a; NUMBER 43, 141d-142d; NUMBER 50, 161d-162c passim; NUMBER 51, 164a-165a; NUMBER 60, 185b-187a

43 MILL: *Liberty*, 289c-d / *Representative Government*, 366a-370a; 371c-372a; 376a-377a; 412b-413a

44 BOSWELL: *Johnson*, 261c-d; 374b-c

46 HEGEL: *Philosophy of History*, PART II, 275b-d; 279b; PART III, 285d; PART IV, 336a-c; 366d-367a

50 MARX-ENGELS: *Communist Manifesto*, 423d-425b

5c. The distribution of functions and powers: checks and balances in representative democracy

7 PLATO: *Laws*, BK VI, 697a-705c

9 ARISTOTLE: *Politics*, BK IV, CH 14-16 498b-502a,c; BK VI, CH 8 525b-526d / *Athenian Constitution*, CH 42-69 572b-584a,c passim

14 PLUTARCH: *Lycurgus*, 34d-35d / *Solon*, 70d-71c

23 HOBBES: *Leviathan*, PART II, 103d-104b; 150b; 151c-152a

35 LOCKE: *Civil Government*, CH VIII, SECT 107 49b-d; CH XII-XIII 58c-62b

38 MONTESQUIEU: *Spirit of Laws*, BK XI, 69d-75a

38 ROUSSEAU: *Social Contract*, BK IV, 428a-435a

40 GIBBON: *Decline and Fall*, 26d-27b

42 KANT: *Science of Right*, 436b-c; 438a-439a; 451d-452a

43 ARTICLES OF CONFEDERATION: IX 7a-9a

43 CONSTITUTION OF THE U.S.: ARTICLE I, SECT 1 11a-b; SECT 2 [41-47] 11d; SECT 3 [73-87] 12a; SECT 4 [96-102] 12b; SECT 5 12b-c; ARTICLE I, SECT 7 [152]-ARTICLE II, SECT 1 [326] 12d-14b; ARTICLE II, SECT 2 [409]-ARTICLE III, SECT 2 [492] 15a-d

43 FEDERALIST: NUMBER 47-48 153c-159a esp NUMBER 48, 157c; NUMBER 51 162d-165a; NUMBER 52, 167a-b; NUMBER 57 176d-179b; NUMBER 58, 180d; NUMBER 60, 184d-185b; NUMBER 62, 189d-191c; NUMBER 63, 192c-193c; NUMBER 66, 200c-201d; NUMBER 69 207a-210c passim; NUMBER 73, 219b-221c; NUMBER 76, 226a-227b; NUMBER 78, 230a-233a; NUMBER 81, 237d-239c

43 MILL: *Representative Government*, 355b-356b; 365b-366a; 369b-370a; 401d-402b; 406a-409c; 412b-c

46 HEGEL: *Philosophy of Right*, PART III, par 272 89d-90c; ADDITIONS, 178 147d-148a / *Philosophy of History*, INTRO, 192d-193a

6. The educational task of democracy: the training of all citizens

5 EURIPIDES: *Suppliants* [399-462] 261d-262b

6 THUCYDIDES: *Peloponnesian War*, BK II, 395d-399a

7 PLATO: *Laws*, BK III, 675c-676b

9 ARISTOTLE: *Politics*, BK IV, CH 9 [1294^{b}19-24] 494c; BK V, CH 9 [1310^{a}12-35] 512b-c; BK VII, CH 14 537b-538d; BK VIII, CH I 542a-b

23 HOBBES: *Leviathan*, PART II, 114d-115a; 153a-155c

32 MILTON: *Areopagitica* 381a-412b esp 384b-389a

38 MONTESQUIEU: *Spirit of Laws*, BK IV, 15c-18d

38 ROUSSEAU: *Political Economy*, 375d-377b

39 SMITH: *Wealth of Nations*, BK V, 340c-343d

43 FEDERALIST: NUMBER 27, 95c-d; NUMBER 84, 253d-254b

43 MILL: *Liberty*, 317d-323a,c / *Representative Government*, 330a-b; 339a-341c; 349a-350a; 351a-c; 381b-382b; 386b-387d; 401a-406a passim; 418b-d; 420b-d; 424b-c

50 MARX: *Capital*, 237d-240d esp 238b-c

50 MARX-ENGELS: *Communist Manifesto*, 427c; 429b

7. The growth and vicissitudes of democracy

5 ARISTOPHANES: *Ecclesiazusae* [169-188] 617a

6 HERODOTUS: *History*, BK III, 120b-c

6 THUCYDIDES: *Peloponnesian War*, BK III, 434c-438b; BK VIII, 579d-580a

7 PLATO: *Republic*, BK VIII, 408b-414b / *Laws*, BK III, 674d-676b

9 ARISTOTLE: *Politics*, BK II, CH 12 [1273^{b}27-1274^{a}22] 470b-d / *Athenian Constitution*, CH 1-41 553a-572a esp CH 41 571c-572a / *Rhetoric*, BK I, CH 4 [1360^{a}17-29] 600c

14 PLUTARCH: *Theseus*, 9a-d / *Themistocles*, 96b-c / *Pericles* 121a-141a,c / *Alcibiades*, 166a-174d / *Phocion* 604b,d-619d / *Tiberius Gracchus*, 675b-d; 678b-d / *Caius Gracchus* 681b,d-689a,c esp 683b-c

15 TACITUS: *Annals*, BK I, 1a-2a

23 MACHIAVELLI: *Prince*, CH V 8a-c

23 HOBBES: *Leviathan*, PART II, 114b-115a; 150c-151a; PART IV, 273a-b

26 SHAKESPEARE: *Julius Caesar* 568a-596a,c

27 SHAKESPEARE: *Coriolanus* 351a-392a,c

38 MONTESQUIEU: *Spirit of Laws*, BK III, 9b-10c

38 ROUSSEAU: *Social Contract*, BK III, 418a-419b

41 GIBBON: *Decline and Fall*, 71d-73d passim; 217a-b; 218c-219a; 427b-428b; 562b-565a esp 562c-d; 574b-582b esp 574b-577d; 587b-588b

43 FEDERALIST: NUMBER I 29a-31a passim; NUMBER 6 38d-41c passim; NUMBER 9-10 47a-53a; NUMBER 22, 82d-83d; NUMBER 43, 141a-142d; NUMBER 44, 146c-d; NUMBER 51, 164a-165a; NUMBER 58 179c-182a passim; NUMBER 63, 192c-194a

43 MILL: *Liberty*, 267d-269c / *Representative Government*, 376b-c

46 HEGEL: *Philosophy of History*, PART II, 271c-274a; 275b-276a

(7. *The growth and vicissitudes of democracy.*)

7a. Demagoguery and the danger of revolution

5 EURIPIDES: *Suppliants* [399–462] 261d-262b

5 ARISTOPHANES: *Knights* 470a-487a,c esp [1111–1150] 483d-484b / *Wasps* [655–724] 515c-516d / *Peace* [601–692] 532d-534a

6 HERODOTUS: *History*, BK III, 108a-c

6 THUCYDIDES: *Peloponnesian War*, BK III, 434c-438b; BK IV, 463a-465c; 466a-469b; BK VI, 519c-d; 520a-d; 533a-c; BK VIII, 575c-582c esp 575c-576c, 577b-d, 579c-581c, 582a-c

7 PLATO: *Republic*, BK VIII, 411d-414b / *Laws*, BK IX, 744c-d

9 ARISTOTLE: *Politics*, BK II, CH 12 [1273^{b}36–1274^{a}14] 470c-d; BK V, CH I [1302^{a}8–16] 503b; CH 5 506b-507a; CH 8 [1308^{a}11–24] 510a-b; CH 9 [1309^{b}14–1310^{a}12] 511d-512b; BK VI, CH 4 [1319^{b}2]–CH 5 [1320^{b}17] 523a-524b / *Athenian Constitution*, CH 14–15 558d-559c; CH 28–29 565c-566d; CH 34 568c-569a

14 PLUTARCH: *Theseus*, 13a-14c / *Solon*, 75c-76d / *Camillus*, 117c-121a,c / *Coriolanus*, 180b-d / *Pompey*, 521c-d / *Caesar* 577a-604d esp 577d-583a / *Phocion* 604b,d-619d / *Cato the Younger*, 628b-d / *Caius Gracchus* 681b,d-689a,c esp 684c-685c / *Dion*, 792d-802a,c

15 TACITUS: *Annals*, BK I, 1a-2a / *Histories*, BK II, 224d-225a

23 HOBBES: *Leviathan*, PART II, 105c-106d; 127d-129d; 152a-d

30 BACON: *Advancement of Learning*, 23a-26a

35 LOCKE: *Civil Government*, CH XIX, SECT 224–228 76d-78a

38 MONTESQUIEU: *Spirit of Laws*, BK VIII, 52b-c; BK XIX, 142d-143a

38 ROUSSEAU: *Social Contract*, BK III, 419b

42 KANT: *Science of Right*, 439c-441d

43 FEDERALIST: NUMBER 1, 30b; NUMBER 9, 47a-b; NUMBER 21, 78d-79a; NUMBER 48, 157c; NUMBER 58, 181b-c

43 MILL: *Representative Government*, 329b-330c

46 HEGEL: *Philosophy of History*, PART III, 300a-301c

7b. The dangers of imperialism: the treatment of dependencies

5 ARISTOPHANES: *Lysistrata* [572–586] 590c-d

6 THUCYDIDES: *Peloponnesian War*, BK II, 403b-c; BK III, 425a-429a

7 PLATO: *Laws*, BK VI, 698c-d

14 PLUTARCH: *Romulus*, 21a-27c esp 22c / *Pericles*, 129a-141a,c passim

15 TACITUS: *Histories*, BK II, 224d-225a

23 HOBBES: *Leviathan*, PART II, 107a; 107c

35 LOCKE: *Civil Government*, CH XVI 65d-70c

36 SWIFT: *Gulliver*, PART IV, 182b-183a

38 MONTESQUIEU: *Spirit of Laws*, BK X, 64a-d

39 SMITH: *Wealth of Nations*, BK IV, 252d-253a; 267c-271d

40 GIBBON: *Decline and Fall*, 79b-d; 630b,d-631b

42 KANT: *Science of Right*, 413d; 454a-455a

43 DECLARATION OF INDEPENDENCE: 1a-3b

43 MILL: *Representative Government*, 427a-b; 433b-442d

7c. The challenge of war and peace: the citizen army

5 EURIPIDES: *Suppliants* [399–462] 261d-262b

5 ARISTOPHANES: *Acharnians* 455a-469a,c / *Knights* 470a-487a,c / *Peace* 526a-541d esp [601–692] 532d-534a / *Lysistrata* 583a-599a,c esp [486–586] 589a-590d

6 HERODOTUS: *History*, BK V, 175b; 177d-178a; 180c-d; BK VII, 232d-233d

6 THUCYDIDES: *Peloponnesian War*, BK II, 402b-404d; BK III, 425a-d; 434c-438b; BK VI, 513d-514d; 515d-516a; BK VIII, 564a-c

7 PLATO: *Laws*, BK I, 640b-642b; BK III, 674d-675c; BK VIII, 732b-735a

9 ARISTOTLE: *Politics*, BK VI, CH 7 [1321^{a}5–26] 524d-525a; BK VII, CH 9 [1329^{a}3–17] 533b-c; CH 14 [1333^{b}1–1334^{a}10] 538b-d / *Athenian Constitution*, CH 8, par 5 556c; CH 15 559b-c; CH 27, par 1–2 565a-b

23 MACHIAVELLI: *Prince*, CH V 8a-c; CH XII–XIII 17d-21a; CH XXVI 36b-37d

35 LOCKE: *Civil Government*, CH XIX, SECT 224–230 76d-78c

36 SWIFT: *Gulliver*, PART II, 80a-b

38 MONTESQUIEU: *Spirit of Laws*, BK III, 10a-c; BK IX, 58b,d-60a

38 ROUSSEAU: *Inequality*, 324c / *Political Economy*, 380b-d

40 GIBBON: *Decline and Fall*, 4b-5c

42 KANT: *Science of Right*, 452d-458a,c esp 454d-455a, 457a-458a,c / *Judgement*, 586a-587a

43 FEDERALIST: NUMBER 6, 40a-41a; NUMBER 8 44c-47a; NUMBER 22, 83a-b; NUMBER 29 98c-101a passim; NUMBER 46, 152b-153a

46 HEGEL: *Philosophy of History*, PART II, 274b-275b; 278c-279b

CROSS-REFERENCES

For: The general theory of government and the forms of government, *see* GOVERNMENT; and for the forms of government most closely related to democracy, *see* ARISTOCRACY; OLIGARCHY.

The theory of constitutional or representative government, in itself and in contrast to monarchy or absolute government, *see* CONSTITUTION; MONARCHY.

Other discussions of the mixed constitution and the mixed regime, *see* ARISTOCRACY 2b; CONSTITUTION 3a, 5b; GOVERNMENT 2b; MONARCHY 1b(1).

Other expositions of the theory of the conditions relative to which democracy is a suitable form of government, *see* MONARCHY 4e(2); SLAVERY 6c; TYRANNY 4b.

The general discussion of political liberty and equality in relation to the rights of citizenship, *see* JUSTICE 9e; LIBERTY 1f.

The problem of suffrage and the debate concerning the extension of the franchise, *see* CITIZEN 2c–3; LABOR 7d; OLIGARCHY 4, 5a; SLAVERY 5b.

The relation between economic and political democracy, and the problems of economic as well as political justice, *see* LABOR 7f; LIBERTY 2d; SLAVERY 5a–5b.

The theory of popular sovereignty and natural rights, *see* GOVERNMENT 1g(3); JUSTICE 6–6e; LAW 7b–7c; STATE 2c; TYRANNY 5c.

The consideration of majority rule and the tyranny of the majority, *see* OPINION 7–7b; TYRANNY 2c.

Other discussions of the theory of representation, *see* ARISTOCRACY 6; CONSTITUTION 9–9b.

Matters relevant to the educational problems of democracy, *see* ARISTOCRACY 5; EDUCATION 8d; STATE 7d.

ADDITIONAL READINGS

Listed below are works not included in *Great Books of the Western World*, but relevant to the idea and topics with which this chapter deals. These works are divided into two groups:

I. Works by authors represented in this collection.
II. Works by authors not represented in this collection.

For the date, place, and other facts concerning the publication of the works cited, consult the Bibliography of Additional Readings which follows the last chapter of *The Great Ideas*.

I.

PLUTARCH. "Of the Three Sorts of Government— Monarchy, Democracy and Oligarchy," in *Moralia*

SPINOZA. *Tractatus Politicus (Political Treatise)*, CH 11

J. S. MILL. "M. De Tocqueville on Democracy in America," "Enfranchisement of Women," in VOL II, *Dissertations and Discussions*

——. *Socialism*

MARX. *The Civil War in France*

——. *Critique of the Gotha Programme*

II.

Clarke Papers, The Putney Debates

VOLTAIRE. "Democracy," in *A Philosophical Dictionary*

J. WILSON. *Works*, PART I, CH VI–IX; PART II, CH XII

CARTWRIGHT. *Take Your Choice!*

BURKE. *An Appeal from the New to the Old Whigs*

——. *Letter to Sir Hercules Langrishe*

PAINE. *Rights of Man*, PART II, CH I

——. *Dissertation on First Principles of Government*

JEFFERSON. *Democracy*, CH 1–2

TOCQUEVILLE. *Democracy in America*

T. CARLYLE. *Chartism*

MICHELET. *The People*

CALHOUN. *A Disquisition on Government*

——. *A Discourse on the Constitution and Government of the United States*

MAZZINI. *The Duties of Man*

THOREAU. *A Plea for Captain John Brown*

WHITMAN. *Democratic Vistas*

J. F. STEPHEN. *Liberty, Equality, Fraternity*

ACTON. *Essays on Freedom and Power*, CH 5, 7–8

ARNOLD. "Democracy," "Equality," in *Mixed Essays*.

MAINE. *Popular Government*

LECKY. *Democracy and Liberty*

GIDDINGS. *Democracy and Empire*

M. HIRSCH. *Democracy Versus Socialism*

H. ADAMS. *The Degradation of the Democratic Dogma*

OSTROGORSKI. *Democracy and the Organization of Political Parties*

DICEY. *The Relation Between Law and Public Opinion in England During the Nineteenth Century*

SANTAYANA. *Reason in Society*, CH 5

SOREL. *Reflexions on Violence*

MICHELS. *Political Parties*

MORLEY. *Notes on Politics and History*

BEARD. *Economic Origins of Jeffersonian Democracy*

CROLY. *Progressive Democracy*

PARETO. *The Mind and Society*, VOL IV

T. VEBLEN. *The Vested Interests and the State of the Industrial Arts*

LENIN. *The State and Revolution*, CH 5

——. *"Left-Wing" Communism, an Infantile Disorder*

TROTSKY. *The Defense of Terrorism*

BRYCE. *The American Commonwealth*

——. *Modern Democracies*

TAWNEY. *Equality*

NOCK. *The Theory of Education in the United States*

KELSEN. *Vom Wesen und Wert der Demokratie*

——. *Staatsform und Weltanschauung*

LASKI. *Democracy in Crisis*

J. A. HOBSON. *Democracy and a Changing Civilisation*

FRIEDRICH. *Constitutional Government and Democracy*

BENES. *Democracy Today and Tomorrow*

DEWEY. *Characters and Events*, VOL II, BK V (17)

——. *The Public and Its Problems*, CH 3

——. *Freedom and Culture*, CH 4–7

MACIVER. *Leviathan and the People*

HOOK. *Reason, Social Myths and Democracy*

BECKER. *Modern Democracy*

MERRIAM. *The New Democracy and the New Despotism*

——. *What Is Democracy?*

AGARD. *What Democracy Meant to the Greeks*

BARKER. *Reflections on Government*

LINDSAY. *The Modern Democratic State*

MARITAIN. *Scholasticism and Politics*, CH III–IV

——. *Ransoming the Time*, CH 2

——. *Christianity and Democracy*

——. *Principes d'une politique humaniste*

PERRY. *Puritanism and Democracy*

SIMON. *Community of the Free*, CH 4

Chapter 17: DESIRE

INTRODUCTION

IN Darwin, Mill, James, and Freud, at the modern end of the great tradition, the word "desire" primarily signifies a cause of animal and human behavior. It is one of the basic terms in psychological analysis, covering that whole range of phenomena which are also referred to by such terms as *wanting, needing, craving, wishing, willing*, all of which are discussed in connection with theories of instinct and emotion, *libido* and love, motivation and purpose.

If we turn to traditional beginnings, to the writings of Plato, Aristotle, Galen, and Plotinus, we find that the psychological consideration of desire is part of a much larger context. The ancients are, of course, concerned with the role of desire in causing animal or human behavior, and with the causes of such desire, but they are also interested in cravings which seem to be present in plants as well as animals. Plato, for example, attributes to plants "feelings of pleasure and pain and the desires which accompany them." The vegetative activities of nutrition, growth, and reproduction seem to spring from basic appetites—or, in modern phraseology, "biological needs"—inherent in all living matter.

Because hunger and thirst so readily symbolize the essence of desire (or certainly represent its most general manifestation in living things), the words "appetite" and "desire" are frequently used as synonyms in the earlier phase of the tradition. As Hobbes observes, when he proposes to use "appetite" and "desire" as synonyms, desire is "the general name," and appetite is "oftentimes restrained to signify the desire for food, namely hunger and thirst." So, too, Spinoza says that "there is no difference between appetite and desire," yet he adds, "unless in this particular, that desire is generally related to men in so far as they are conscious of their appetites, and it may therefore be defined as appetite of which we are conscious."

Spinoza here seems to be reflecting the distinction made by earlier writers between natural appetite and conscious desire, which we today would, perhaps, express in terms of "need" and "wish." The ancient conception of tendencies inherent in all things—inanimate as well as living—which seek a natural fulfillment broadens the meaning of appetite or desire. When Aristotle says that "each thing seeks its own perfection" and that "nature does nothing in vain," he is thinking of non-living as well as living bodies. Wherever in the physical world things seem to have a natural tendency to move in a certain direction or to change in a certain way, there appetite, belonging to the very nature of the moving thing, operates as a cause. Adopting this view, Dante declares that "neither Creator nor creature was ever without love, either natural or of the mind"; and in his *Convivio* he shows how each thing has its "specific love." The love, or desire, of the elements is their "innate affinity to their proper place"; minerals desire "the place where their generation is ordained" with the result that "the magnet ever receives power from the direction of its generation."

According to this view it is possible to speak of the natural desire of raindrops to fall or of smoke to rise. Such a manner of speaking may at first seem metaphorical—an expression of primitive animism or anthropomorphism—but the ancients, observing different natural tendencies in heavy and light bodies, mean this literally.

The sense of such statements is no different from what is meant when it is said that the sunflower, without consciousness, naturally tends to turn toward the sun, or that all men by nature desire to know.

FROM ITS NARROWEST meaning with reference to the behavior of animals and men, desire gains a wider connotation when it is conceived as covering the appetites found in living organisms. But in its broadest significance, it refers to the innate tendency inherent in matter itself. As we shall presently see, appetite, desire, or tendency is seated in matter according to that conception of matter which identifies it with potentiality or potential being. These considerations are more fully treated in the chapters on BEING, CHANGE, and MATTER, but their significance for the notion of desire can be briefly indicated here.

Plotinus suggests the basic insight when he describes matter as "in beggardom, striving as it were by violence to acquire, and always disappointed." Matter is that in natural things which is the reason for their motion and change. Considering natural change, Aristotle names what he thinks are its three principles. In addition to "something divine, good, and desirable," he writes, "we hold that there are two other principles, the one contrary to it, the other such as of its own nature to desire and yearn for it." These are respectively form, privation, and matter. The relation between matter and form is expressed by Aristotle in terms of desire. "The form cannot desire itself," he says, "for it is not defective; nor can the contrary desire it, for contraries are mutually destructive. The truth is that what desires the form is matter, as the female desires the male."

Conceived most generally as natural appetite or tendency, desire becomes a physical or metaphysical term. "Natural appetite," says Aquinas, "is that inclination which each thing has of its own nature." The significance of desire in this sense extends, far beyond psychological phenomena, to all things in motion under the impetus or inclination of their own natures, rather than moved violently by forces impressed on them from without.

In ancient physics every natural tendency has an end or fulfillment in which the motion governed by that tendency comes to rest. *Eros* and *telos*—desire and end—are complementary concepts, each implying the other as principles of physics, *i.e.*, as factors operating together throughout nature in the order of change. The *telos* of each thing is the perfection which satis- fies the tendency of its nature. That nature does nothing in vain means simply that no natural desire—need or appetite—exists without the possibility of fulfillment.

CONSIDERING THE DESIGN of the universe and the relation of creatures to God, theologians like Augustine and Aquinas use the concept of desire in both its psychological and its metaphysical sense.

Considered metaphysically, desire can be present only in finite beings, for to be finite is to be in want of some perfection. Hence desire can in no way enter into the immutable, infinite, and perfect being of God. In desire, Aquinas points out, "a certain imperfection is implied," namely, the lack "of the good which we have not." Since God is perfect, desire cannot be attributed to Him, "except metaphorically." Love, however, implies perfection rather than imperfection, since it flows from the act of the will "to diffuse its own goodness among others." For that reason, although the infinite perfection of God precludes desire, it does not preclude love.

The theologian goes beyond the metaphysician or physicist when he carries the analysis of desire to the supernatural plane. As God is the supernatural efficient cause of all created things, so God is also the supernatural final cause—the end or ultimate good toward which all creatures tend. The metaphysical maxim that each thing seeks its own perfection is then transformed. "All things," Aquinas writes, "by desiring their own perfection, desire God Himself, inasmuch as the perfections of all things are so many similitudes of the divine being. . . . Of those things which desire God, some know Him as He is Himself, and this is proper to the rational creature; others know some participation of His goodness, and this belongs also to sensible knowledge; others have a natural desire without knowledge, as being directed to their ends by a higher intelligence."

The existence in the creature of a desire for God raises difficult questions concerning the manner in which this desire is fulfilled. A supernatural end cannot be attained by purely natural means, *i.e.*, without God's help. The vision of God in which the souls of the blessed come to rest is, according to the theologian, the ultimate gift of grace. Hence, in man's case at least, it becomes necessary to ask whether he can have a purely natural desire to see God if the goal of such desire cannot be achieved by purely natural means.

The question is not whether men to whom God has revealed the promise of ultimate glory can *consciously* desire the beatific vision. Clearly that is possible, though to sustain such desire the theological virtue of hope, inseparable from faith and charity, may be required. Rather the question is whether the beatific vision which is man's supernatural end can be the object of natural desire. On this the theologians appear to be less clearly decided.

Aquinas holds that "neither man, nor any creature, can attain final happiness by his natural powers." Yet he also seems to maintain that man has a natural desire for the perfect happiness of eternal life. "The object of the will, *i.e.*, of man's appetite," he writes, "is the universal good, just as the object of the intellect is the universal truth." Man's natural desire to know the truth—not just some truths but the whole truth, the infinite truth—would seem to require the vision of God for its fulfillment. Aquinas argues similarly from the will's natural desire for the infinite good. "Naught can lull man's will," he writes, "save the universal good . . . to be found not in any creature, but in God alone." Some writers find this confirmed in the fact that whatever good a man sets his heart upon he pursues to infinity. No finite amount of pleasure or power or wealth seems to satisfy him. He always wants more. But there is no end to wanting more of such things. The infinity of such desires must result in frustration. Only God, says the theologian, only an infinite being, can satisfy man's infinite craving for all the good there is.

Seeing man's restlessness, no matter where he turns to find rest, Augustine declares: "Thou madest us for Thyself, and our heart is restless, until it repose in Thee." Pascal reaches the same conclusion when he considers the ennui of men which results from the desperation of their unending search. "Their error," he writes, "does not lie in seeking excitement, if they seek it only as a diversion; the evil is that they seek it as if the possession of the objects of their quest would make them really happy."

With regard to the frantic pursuit of diversions, he claims that "both the censurers and the censured do not understand man's true nature" and the "misery of man without God." In such restlessness and vain seeking, the theologian sees evidence of man's natural desire to be *with* God.

Admitting the same facts, the skeptics interpret the infinity of man's desire as a craving to *be* God. If this is not every man's desire, it is certainly Satan's in *Paradise Lost*. Skeptic or believer, every man understands the question which Goethe and Dante among the great poets make their central theme. At what moment, amid man's striving and restlessness, will the soul gladly cry, "Ah, linger on, thou art so fair?" Confident that there can be no such moment, Faust makes that the basis of his wager with Mephistopheles.

The two poets appear to give opposite answers to the question. Faust finds surcease in an earthly vision of progressive endeavor. Heavenly rest comes to the soul of Dante at the very moment it relinquishes its quest, winning peace through surrender.

IN THE BROADEST OR theological sense of the word, God alone does not desire. In the narrowest or psychological sense, only animals and men do. The contrast of meanings is useful. Natural appetite or tendency throws light on the nature of conscious desire.

In order to "determine the nature and seat of desire," Socrates in the *Philebus* considers such things as "hunger, thirst, and the like" as "in the class of desires." He points out that "when we say 'a man thirsts,' we mean to say that he 'is empty.'" It is not drink he desires, but replenishment by drink, which is a change of state. This insight Socrates generalizes by saying that "he who is empty desires . . . the opposite of what he experiences; for he is empty and desires to be full." In the *Symposium*, using the words "love" and "desire" as if they were interchangeable, Socrates declares that "he who desires something is in want of something" and "love is of something which a man wants and has not."

In the psychological sphere, desire and love are often identified—at least verbally. The one word is frequently substituted for the other. Here the fact already noted, that God loves but does not desire, suggests the root of the distinction between desire and love. Desire always involves some lack or privation to be remedied by a change; whereas love, certainly requited love, implies the kind of satisfaction which abhors change. Love and desire are, of course, frequently mixed, but this does not affect their essential difference as tendencies. They are as different as giving and getting. Love aims at the well-being of the beloved, while desire seeks to enjoy a pleasure or possess a good.

Not all writers, however, contrast the generosity of love with the acquisitiveness of desire. Locke, for example, finds self-interest and self-seeking in both. The meaning of love, he observes, is known to anyone who reflects "upon the thought he has of the delight which any present or absent thing is apt to produce in him. . . . For when a man declares in autumn when he is eating them, or in spring when there are none, that he loves grapes, it is no more but that the taste of grapes delights him." The meaning of desire is, in Locke's opinion, closely related. It consists in "the uneasiness a man finds in himself upon the absence of anything whose present enjoyment carries the idea of delight with it." We desire, in short, the things we love but do not possess.

The distinction between love and desire, the question whether they are distinct in animals as well as in men, and their relation to one another when they are distinct, are matters more fully discussed in the chapter on LOVE. It is enough to observe here that when writers use the two words interchangeably, they use both words to signify wanting and seeking.

In the case of animals and men, the thing wanted is an object of conscious desire only if it is something known. In addition to being known as an object of science is known, it must also be deemed good or pleasant—in other words, worth having. For Locke, desire, as we have seen, is no more than "an uneasiness of the mind for want of some absent good," which is measured in terms of pleasure and pain. "What has an aptness to produce pleasure in us is that we call *good*, and what is apt to produce pain in us we call *evil*." That which we consciously desire, that which we judge to be desirable, would thus be something we regard as good for us, while the "bad" or "evil" would be that

which we seek to avoid as somehow injurious rather than beneficial to us.

There is no question that desire and aversion are psychologically connected with estimations of good and evil or pleasure and pain. This is the case no matter how we answer the moralist's question, Do we desire something because it is good, or do we call it "good" simply because we desire it? The ethical significance of the question, and of the opposite answers to it, is discussed in the chapter on GOOD AND EVIL.

THE METAPHYSICAL conception of natural desire provides terms for the psychological analysis of conscious desire and its object. Viewed as belonging to the very nature of a thing, appetite, according to Aristotle, consists in the tendency toward "something we do not have" and "which we need." Both factors are essential—the privation and the capacity, or potentiality, for having what is lacked. Privation in the strict sense is always correlative to potentiality.

The writers who use these terms would not speak of the sunflower being deprived of wisdom, even as they would not call a stone blind. Blindness is the deprivation of sight in things which have by nature a capacity to see. So when it is said that man by nature desires to know, or that certain animals, instinctively gregarious, naturally tend to associate with one another in herds or societies, the potentiality of knowledge or social life is indicated; and precisely because of these potentialities, ignorance and solitariness are considered privations.

We observe here two different conditions of appetite or desire. As the opposite of privation is possession—or of lacking, having—so the opposite states of appetite are the drive toward the unpossessed and satisfaction in possession. We do not strive for that which we have, unless it be to retain our possession of it against loss; and we do not feel satisfied until we get that which we have been seeking.

"If a man being strong desired to be strong," says Socrates in the *Symposium*, "or being swift desired to be swift, or being healthy desired to be healthy, he might be thought to desire something which he already has or is." This would be a misconception which we must avoid. To anyone who says "I desire to have simply what I have," Socrates thinks we should reply: "You, my friend, having wealth and health and strength, want to have the continuance of them. . . . When you say, 'I desire that which I have and nothing else,' is not your meaning that you want to have in the future what you now have?" This "is equivalent to saying that a man desires something which is for him non-existent, and which he has not got"; from which Socrates draws the conclusion that everyone "desires that which he has not already, which is future and not present . . . and of which he is in want."

The object of desire—natural or conscious—thus seems to be an altered condition in the desirer, the result of union with the object desired. Man's natural desire to know impels him to learn. Every act of learning which satisfies this natural desire consists in a changed condition of his mind, a change which both Plato and Aristotle describe as a motion from ignorance to knowledge.

When we consciously desire food, it is not the edible thing as such we seek, but rather the eating of it. Only the eating of it will quiet our desire, with that change in our condition we call "nourishment." That the edible thing is only incidentally the object of our desire may be seen in the fact that no way in which we can possess food, *other than eating it*, satisfies hunger.

THE DISTINCTION between natural and conscious desire is complicated by other closely related distinctions which psychologists have made. Freud, for example, distinguishes between conscious and unconscious desire; Darwin separates instinctive from learned desires; and James observes how a conscious desire may become habitual and operate almost automatically, without our awareness of either its object or its action.

Part of the complication is verbal and can be removed by referring to natural desires as *non*-conscious rather than *un*-conscious. The word "conscious" literally means *with knowledge*. Creatures which lack the faculty of knowing cannot desire consciously. It does not follow, however, that sentient or conscious beings cannot have natural appetites. Man's natural desire to know is a case in point. That natural human tendency is not excluded by the fact that many men also consciously seek knowledge, knowing what knowledge is and considering it something worth having.

The instinctive desires of animals are not generally thought to operate apart from the perception of the object toward which the animal is emotionally impelled. The instinctive desire works consciously, both on the side of perception and on the side of the emotionally felt impulse. If, because it is innate rather than learned, or acquired through experience, we call the instinctive desire "natural," it is well to remember that we are not here using the word to signify lack of consciousness. Yet both instinctive and acquired desires may operate unconsciously.

What Freud means by a repressed desire illustrates this point. The repressed desire, whether instinctual in origin or the result of some acquired fixation of the libido on object or ego, would be a conscious tendency *if it were not repressed*. Freud compares the process of repression to the efforts of a man to get from one room to another past the guard of a doorkeeper. "The excitations in the unconscious . . . to begin with, remain unconscious. When they have pressed forward to the threshold and been turned back by the door-keeper, they are 'incapable of becoming conscious'; we call them then repressed. . . . Being repressed, when applied to any single impulse, means being unable to pass out of the unconscious system because of the door-keeper's refusal of admittance into the preconscious."

The repressed desire is made to operate unconsciously by being repressed, which does not prevent it from influencing our conduct or thought, but only from intruding its driving force and its goal upon our attention. In contrast, the desire which works habitually and therefore to some extent unconsciously, is not repressed, but merely one which no longer demands our full attention.

DESIRE AND EMOTION are often identified in our description of the behavior of animals and men. Sometimes, however, desire along with aversion is treated as just one of the emotions, and sometimes all the emotions are treated as manifestations of just one type of conscious appetite, namely, animal as opposed to rational desire.

The appetitive or driving aspect of emotions is indicated by William James in his analysis of instinctive behavior. The functioning of an instinct may be viewed, according to James, as a train of psychological events of "general reflex type . . . called forth by determinate sensory stimuli in contact with the animal's body, or at a distance in his environment," arousing "emotional excitements which go with them." The emotional part of the instinctive behavior is at once an impulse to perform certain acts and the feeling which accompanies the acts performed. The sheep, instinctively recognizing the wolf as dangerous, fears and flees. It runs away because it is afraid and feels fear in the act of flight. When, in his theory of the emotions, James goes so far as to say that the feeling of fear results from running away, he does not mean to deny that the emotion of fear involves the impulse to flee.

In its aspect as impulse—or tendency to act —an emotion is a desire, consciously aroused by sense-perceptions and accompanied by conscious feelings. This conception of emotion has been variously expressed in the tradition of the great books. Aquinas, for example, calls all the emotions or passions "movements of the sensitive appetite." But he also uses the words "desire" and "aversion" along with "love" and "hate," "anger" and "fear" to name specific emotions.

Hobbes recognizes the appetitive tendency which is common to all the emotions when he finds at their root what he calls "endeavor"— "those small beginnings of motion, within the body of man, before they appear in walking, speaking, striking, and other visible actions. . . . This endeavor," he goes on to say, "when it is toward something which causes it, is called appetite or desire." Spinoza makes the same point in somewhat different terms. "Desire," he writes, "is the essence itself or nature of a person in so far as this nature is conceived from its given constitution as determined towards any action. . . . As his nature is constituted in this or that way, so must his desire vary and the nature of one desire differ from another, just as the affects from which each desire arises differ. There are as many kinds of desire, therefore, as there are kinds of joy, sorrow, love, etc., and in consequence . . . as there are kinds of objects by which we are affected."

Those psychologists who find in man two distinct faculties of knowledge—the senses and the reason or intellect—also find in him two distinct faculties of appetite or desire. The distinction is perhaps most sharply made by Aristotle and Aquinas, who claim that "there must be one appetite tending towards the universal good, which belongs to reason, and another with a tendency towards the particular good, which appetite belongs to sense." The traditional name for the intellectual appetite, or the faculty of rational desire, is "will." In Spinoza's vocabulary, the effort of desire, "when it is related to the mind alone, is called *will*, but when it is related at the same time both to the mind and the body, is called *appetite*."

Psychologists who attribute these diverse modes of desire, as they attribute sensation and thought, to a single faculty called "mind" or "understanding," nevertheless deal with the whole range of appetitive phenomena, including both the animal passions and acts of will. James, for example, treats the instinctive acts associated with the emotions as "automatic and reflex" movements, and separates them from "voluntary movements which, being desired and intended beforehand, are done with full prevision of what they are to be." In so doing, he draws a line between emotional impulses and acts of will, even though he does not distinguish two appetitive faculties.

With or without the distinction in faculties, almost all observers of human experience and conduct seem to agree upon a distinction in types of conscious desire, at least insofar as they recognize the ever-present conflict between the passions and the will. These matters are more fully considered in the chapters on EMOTION and WILL.

THE ROLE OF DESIRE in human life—especially emotional desire—is so intimately connected with problems of good and evil, virtue, duty, and happiness, that until quite recently the subject was discussed mainly in books on ethics, politics, or rhetoric rather than psychology. Even Freud, who tries to separate psychological description and explanation from moral principles or conclusions, cannot avoid treating the effects of morality upon the dynamics of desire and the life of the passions. Many of the fundamental terms of psychoanalysis—conflict, repression, rationalization, sublimation, to name only some—carry the connotation of moral issues, even though they imply a purely psychological resolution of them.

Contrary to a popular misconception, Freud expressly declares that "it is out of the question that part of the analytic treatment should consist of advice to 'live freely.'" The conflict "between libidinal desires and sexual repression," he explains, is "not resolved by helping one side to win a victory over the other." Although Freud thinks that "what the world calls its code of morals demands more sacrifices than it is worth," he also declares that "we must beware of overestimating the importance of abstinence in effecting neurosis."

What Freud calls emotional infantilism resembles to some degree what a moralist like Aristotle calls self-indulgence or incontinence. To give vent to all the promptings of desire, without regard to the demands of society or reality is to revert to infancy—a state characterized, according to Freud, by "the irreconcilability of its wishes with reality." Because children "live at the beck and call of appetite, and it is in them that the desire for what is pleasant is strongest," Aristotle thinks it fitting that we should speak of self-indulgence when it occurs in an adult as a "childish fault."

Aristotle and Freud seem to be looking at the same facts of human nature and seeing them in the same light. What Freud describes as the conflict between the "pleasure-principle" and the "reality-principle," Aristotle—and with him Spinoza—treats as a conflict between the passions and the reason, and Kant conceives in terms of the opposition between desire and duty. What Freud says of the reality-principle —that it "demands and enforces the postponement of satisfaction, the renunciation of manifold possibilities, and the temporary endurance of pain"—parallels traditional statements concerning the role of reason or of duty in the moral life. Where the moralists speak of the necessity for regulating or moderating emotional desires, Freud refers to the need of "domesticating" them, as one would train a beast to serve the ends of human life.

The implication, in Aristotle and Spinoza as well as in Freud, does not seem to be that man's animal appetites are in themselves bad, but that, if they are undisciplined or uncontrolled, they cause disorder in the individual life and in society. Some moralists, however, take an opposite view. For them desire is intrinsically evil, a factor of discontent, and fraught with pain.

"While what we crave is wanting," Lucretius writes, "it seems to transcend all the rest; then, when it has been gotten, we crave something else"; yet as often as a man gains something new, he discovers afresh that "he is not better off." Either our desires are unsatisfied, and then we suffer the agony of frustration; or they are satiated and so are we—desperate with ennui. Hence, freedom from all desires, not just their moderation, seems to be recommended for peace of mind; as centuries later Schopenhauer recommended the negation of the will to live in order to avoid frustration or boredom.

Marcus Aurelius and the Stoics, and later Kant, similarly urge us "not to yield to the persuasions of the body . . . and never to be over-powered either by the motion of the senses or of the appetites." But whereas the Stoics would restrain desire "because it is animal" and in order to avoid pain, Kant argues that the renunciation of desire should be undertaken "not merely in accordance with duty . . . but from duty, which must be the true end of all moral cultivation."

The opposition between these two views of desire in the moral life represents one of the major issues in ethical theory, further discussed in the chapters on DUTY and VIRTUE. The doctrine of natural appetite is crucially relevant to the issue. If the naturalist in ethics is right, he is so by virtue of the truth that natural tendencies are everywhere the measure of good and evil. If, however, there is no truth in the doctrine of natural desire, then the impulses which spring from man's animal passions can claim no authority in the court of reason.

OUTLINE OF TOPICS

REFERENCES

To find the passages cited, use the numbers in heavy type, which are the volume and page numbers of the passages referred to. For example, in 4 HOMER: *Iliad*, BK II [265-283] 12d, the number 4 is the number of the volume in the set; the number 12d indicates that the passage is in section d of page 12.

PAGE SECTIONS: When the text is printed in one column, the letters a and b refer to the upper and lower halves of the page. For example, in 53 JAMES: *Psychology*, 116a-119b, the passage begins in the upper half of page 116 and ends in the lower half of page 119. When the text is printed in two columns, the letters a and b refer to the upper and lower halves of the left-hand side of the page, the letters c and d to the upper and lower halves of the right-hand side of the page. For example, in 7 PLATO: *Symposium*, 163b-164c, the passage begins in the lower half of the left-hand side of page 163 and ends in the upper half of the right-hand side of page 164.

AUTHOR'S DIVISIONS: One or more of the main divisions of a work (such as PART, BK, CH, SECT) are sometimes included in the reference; line numbers, in brackets, are given in certain cases; *e.g., Iliad*, BK II [265-283] 12d.

BIBLE REFERENCES: The references are to book, chapter, and verse. When the King James and Douay versions differ in title of books or in the numbering of chapters or verses, the King James version is cited first and the Douay, indicated by a (D), follows; *e.g.*, OLD TESTAMENT: *Nehemiah*, 7:45—(D) *II Esdras*, 7:46.

SYMBOLS: The abbreviation "esp" calls the reader's attention to one or more especially relevant parts of a whole reference; "passim" signifies that the topic is discussed intermittently rather than continuously in the work or passage cited.

For additional information concerning the style of the references, see the Explanation of Reference Style; for general guidance in the use of *The Great Ideas*, consult the Preface.

1. Desire and the order of change: *eros* and *telos*

7 PLATO: *Cratylus*, 103c-d / *Symposium*, 165c-166b / *Phaedo*, 241b-242b

8 ARISTOTLE: *Physics*, BK I, CH 9 [192^{a}16-24] 268b-c; BK II, CH 8-9 275d-278a,c; BK VIII, CH 4 [255^{a}30-^{b}31] 340a-c / *Generation and Corruption*, BK II, CH 6 [333^{a}35-334^{a}9] 434b-435a / *Metaphysics*, BK I, CH 3 [984^{b}8]-CH 4 [985^{a}28] 502d-503c; CH 7 [988^{b}6-16] 506c-d; BK IX, CH 8 [1050^{a}3-^{b}6] 575d-576b; BK XII, CH 5 [1070^{b}36-1071^{a}4] 600b-c; CH 7 [1072^{a}20-^{b}13] 602b-d; CH 10 [1075^{b}1-10] 606b

10 GALEN: *Natural Faculties*, BK III, CH 6 202d-203a

12 LUCRETIUS: *Nature of Things*, BK I [1-61] 1a-d; [1022-1037] 13c-d; [1052-1082] 14a-c; BK II [167-183] 17a-b; [1048-1066] 28b-c; BK IV [823-857] 55a-b; BK V [156-194] 63a-c; [416-431] 66c-d; [509-533] 67d-68a

17 PLOTINUS: *Third Ennead*, TR V 100c-106b / *Fourth Ennead*, TR IV, CH 18-21 166d-168c

18 AUGUSTINE: *Confessions*, BK I, par 1, 1a; BK IV, par 15-17 23a-c / *City of God*, BK XII, CH 4-5 344b-345b; BK XIX, CH 12-14 517b-520d

19 AQUINAS: *Summa Theologica*, PART I, QQ 5-6 23b-30d passim; QQ 19-20 108d-124a passim; Q 26, A 2, ANS 150c-151a; Q 48, A 1,

ANS and REP 4 259b-260c; QQ 59-60 306b-314c passim; Q 62, A 1, ANS 317d-318c; Q 104, A 3, REP 1 537b-d; Q 105, A 4, ANS 541c-542a; PART I-II, Q I, A 2 610b-611b; A 8 615a-c; Q 2, A 5, REP 3 618d-619c; Q 26, A 1, ANS and REP 3 734a-d; Q 27, A 3, ANS and REP 3-4 738c-739c

21 DANTE: *Divine Comedy*, PURGATORY, XVII [91]-XVIII [75] 79b-80c; PARADISE, I [94-142] 107b-d

23 HOBBES: *Leviathan*, PART I, 50a; 61a-c; PART IV, 271d

28 GILBERT: *Loadstone*, BK II, 38a-d

28 HARVEY: *On Animal Generation*, 426d-427a

30 BACON: *Advancement of Learning*, 73a-c

31 SPINOZA: *Ethics*, PART IV, PREF 422b,d-424a

33 PASCAL: *Pensées*, 72, 184b; 75 185b-186a

35 LOCKE: *Human Understanding*, BK II, CH XXI, SECT 29-41 184d-188c

42 KANT: *Practical Reason*, 293d [fn 3]; 304b-d; 315b-c / *Intro. Metaphysic of Morals*, 385a-386d / *Judgement*, 465c-466c esp 466b,d [fn 1]; 483d-484b; 577c-578a

46 HEGEL: *Philosophy of History*, INTRO, 161d-168b esp 162a-163d, 164c, 165b-c

49 DARWIN: *Origin of Species*, 40c-42a; 96b-98a,c

53 JAMES: *Psychology*, 4a-7a esp 4b-5a

(1. *Desire and the order of change:* eros *and* telos.)

54 FREUD: *Beyond the Pleasure Principle* 639a-663d esp 651d-654c, 662c-663d / *Ego and Id,* 708d-712a esp 711c-712a / *Civilization and Its Discontents,* 790a-791d; 799a-800a / *New Introductory Lectures,* 849c-851d

2. The analysis of desire or appetite

2a. The roots of desire in need, privation, or potency: the instinctual sources of the libido

7 PLATO: *Lysis,* 24a-c / *Symposium,* 162a-166b / *Republic,* BK IV, 352b-d / *Philebus,* 621c-622b

8 ARISTOTLE: *Physics,* BK I, CH 9 [192ª16-24] 268b-c

9 ARISTOTLE: *History of Animals,* BK VII, CH I [581ª21-ᵇ22] 107a-b / *Parts of Animals,* BK III, CH 14 [675ᵇ25-30] 205b / *Ethics,* BK III, CH 11 [1118ᵇ8-18] 365a-b / *Rhetoric,* BK II, CH 13 [1389ᵇ32-35] 637b

10 GALEN: *Natural Faculties,* BK III, CH 6 202d-203a; CH 8 205a-207b; CH 13, 211d-212d

12 LUCRETIUS: *Nature of Things,* BK IV [858-876] 55b-c; BK V [156-173] 63a-b

17 PLOTINUS: *Third Ennead,* TR V, CH I 100c-101c; CH 10 105d-106b / *Fourth Ennead,* TR IV, CH 18-21 166d-168c

18 AUGUSTINE: *Confessions,* BK I, par 1-6 1a-2c; BK III, par 1 13b-c; par 10 15b-d; BK IV, par 15-19 23a-24b; BK V, par 1-2 27a-c; BK VII, par 16-23 48c-50c

19 AQUINAS: *Summa Theologica,* PART I, Q 5, A 3, REP 3 25a-d; Q 19, A 1, REP 2 108d-109c; Q 59, A 2, ANS 307c-308b; Q 81, A 2 429c-430c; PART I-II, Q 27, A 3, ANS and REP 3-4 738c-739c

21 DANTE: *Divine Comedy,* PURGATORY, XVII [91]-XVIII [75] 79b-80c; XX [124]-XXI [75] 84c-85d passim; PARADISE, I [103-120] 107b-c

23 HOBBES: *Leviathan,* PART I, 61a-d

27 SHAKESPEARE: *King Lear,* ACT II, SC IV [263-274] 261c

28 HARVEY: *On Animal Generation,* 347c; 349a-350a; 402a-d

31 DESCARTES: *Meditations,* VI, 97d-98a; 99d-102d

31 SPINOZA: *Ethics,* PART IV, PROP 2-7 425a-426b

33 PASCAL: *Pensées,* 100 191a-192b

35 LOCKE: *Human Understanding,* BK II, CH XX, SECT 6 177a-b; CH XXI, SECT 30-35 185a-186d esp SECT 31 185c-d

38 ROUSSEAU: *Inequality,* 346b

43 MILL: *Liberty,* 295b-d

46 HEGEL: *Philosophy of Right,* PART III, par 190-195 66a-67a

51 TOLSTOY: *War and Peace,* BK XIII, 577a-578b esp 577d-578a; BK XIV, 605b-d; BK XV, 630c-631c; EPILOGUE I, 665a-d

53 JAMES: *Psychology,* 51a-b; 767a

54 FREUD: *Interpretation of Dreams,* 363c-d / *Narcissism,* 400c-402c / *Instincts,* 412c-413a; 414a-d / *General Introduction,* 574a; 580a-d; 591d-592b; 615b-616b; 618d-619a / *Beyond the Pleasure Principle,* 654a-c; 657d-659a / *Group Psychology,* 673b-c / *Ego and Id,* 710c-711b / *Civilization and Its Discontents,* 789c-791c esp 791a / *New Introductory Lectures,* 846a-851d esp 846a-847b, 849b-851c

2b. The objects of desire: the good and the pleasant

7 PLATO: *Euthydemus,* 69a-71a / *Phaedrus,* 120a-122a / *Symposium,* 161d-166b / *Meno,* 177d-178b / *Gorgias,* 262a-264b; 275b-280d / *Republic,* BK II, 310c-d; BK IV, 351b-352d; BK IX, 422c-425b esp 423b-424d / *Philebus,* 614a / *Laws,* BK V, 689c-690c; BK VI, 712b; BK VIII, 735c-736c

8 ARISTOTLE: *Topics,* BK II, CH 3 [110ᵇ38-111ª6] 155d; BK III, CH 1-4 162a-166b; BK VI, CH 8 [146ª37-ᵇ19] 200b-c; [146ᵇ36-147ª11] 200d-201a / *Physics,* BK I, CH 9 [192ª16-24] 268b-c / *Metaphysics,* BK I, CH 2 [982ᵇ12-27] 500d-501a; [983ª14-21] 501b-c; BK XII, CH 7 [1072ª23-ᵇ13] 602b-d / *Soul,* BK II, CH 3 [414ª28-ᵇ5] 644c; BK III, CH 7 [431ª1-ᵇ12] 663c-664b; CH 10 [433ª13-ᵇ19] 665d-666c

9 ARISTOTLE: *History of Animals,* BK VIII, CH I [589ª3-10] 115b / *Parts of Animals,* BK II, CH 17 [661ª6-8] 188a / *Motion of Animals,* CH 6 [700ᵇ23-30] 236a / *Ethics,* BK I, CH I [1094ª1-3] 339a; CH 2 [1094ª17-22] 339b; BK VI, CH 2 387d-388b; BK VII, CH 11-14 403c-406a,c; BK X, CH 2 426c-427b; CH 3 [1174ª4-11] 428b; CH 4 [1175ª10-22] 429c; CH 5 [1175ᵇ24-33] 430b / *Rhetoric,* BK I, CH 6-7 602d-607d; CH 10 [1369ª1-4] 612b; CH 11 [1370ª17-28] 613c

12 LUCRETIUS: *Nature of Things,* BK II [1-61] 15a-d

12 EPICTETUS: *Discourses,* BK I, CH 4 108d-110a

17 PLOTINUS: *First Ennead,* TR VI 21a-26a passim / *Third Ennead,* TR V 100c-106b / *Fourth Ennead,* TR IV, CH 35, 177d-178a / *Fifth Ennead,* TR V, CH 12 234a-d / *Sixth Ennead,* TR VII, CH 30 336b-d

18 AUGUSTINE: *Confessions,* BK II, par 9-18 10d-13a; BK X, par 29-33 78d-80b / *City of God,* BK XII, CH 6 345b-346c; BK XIX, CH 1 507a-509a / *Christian Doctrine,* BK I, CH 3-4 625b-c; CH 22-30 629b-633b

19 AQUINAS: *Summa Theologica,* PART I, QQ 5-6 23b-30d passim; Q 16, A 1, ANS 94b-95c; A 4 97a-c; QQ 19-20 108d-124a passim; Q 26, A 2, ANS 150c-151a; Q 48, A 1, ANS and REP 4 259b-260c; QQ 59-60 306b-314c passim, esp Q 60, AA 3-5 311d-314c; Q 62, A 1, ANS 317d-318c; Q 63, A 4 328c-329a; QQ 80-83 427a-440b passim; Q 104, A 3, REP 1 537b-d; Q 105, A 4, ANS 541c-542a; Q 106, A 2, ANS 546d-547c;

PART I–II, QQ 1–5 609a-643d passim; Q 8 655a-657c; Q 22, A 2, ANS 721c-722c; A 3, REP 2 722d-723b; Q 23 723c-727a; Q 26, A 1, ANS and REP 3 734a-d; Q 27 737a-740a; Q 30 749a-752b passim; Q 33, A 2 766a-767a

20 AQUINAS: *Summa Theologica*, PART I–II, Q 94, A 2, ANS 221d-223a; PART III SUPPL, Q 98, A 3 1074a-c

21 DANTE: *Divine Comedy*, PURGATORY, XVII [91]–XVIII [75] 79b-80c; PARADISE, V [1–12] 112a-b

23 HOBBES: *Leviathan*, PART I, 61a-62c; 76c-77b; 96a; PART IV, 272c

29 CERVANTES: *Don Quixote*, PART II, 381d-382a

30 BACON: *Advancement of Learning*, 73a-74a

31 DESCARTES: *Discourse*, PART III, 50b

31 SPINOZA: *Ethics*, PART III, PROP 4–13 398d-400d; PROP 39, SCHOL 408b-d; PROP 56 414a-d; THE AFFECTS, DEF 1–3 416b-417a; PART IV, DEF 1–2 424a; PROP 9–13 426d-428a; PROP 19–28 429d-431c; PROP 63 443d-444a; PROP 65–66 444b-d

33 PASCAL: *Pensées*, 81 186b

35 LOCKE: *Human Understanding*, BK I, CH II, SECT 3 104b-d; BK II, CH VII, SECT 3 131d-132a; CH XX, SECT 6 177a-b; CH XXI, SECT 29–48 184d-190d passim, esp SECT 31 185c-d, SECT 42 188c; SECT 55–56 192c-193b; SECT 61–62 194b-d; SECT 70 197a-b; SECT 73 198c-199c

42 KANT: *Fund. Prin. Metaphysic of Morals*, 264d-265b / *Practical Reason*, 298a-300d; 315c-317b; 330c-331a; 341c-342a / *Judgement*, 605d-606b [fn 2]

43 MILL: *Utilitarianism*, 448a-450b; 461c-464d

46 HEGEL: *Philosophy of Right*, PART II, par 123–124 44a-d / *Philosophy of History*, PART IV, 319b-320a

47 GOETHE: *Faust*, PART I [1194–1216] 29b-30a; PART II [11,559–586] 281b-282a

49 DARWIN: *Descent of Man*, 308a-b; 316a-317a; 592d

51 TOLSTOY: *War and Peace*, BK XI, 524c-527a; BK XII, 560a-561c; BK XIII, 577a-578b esp 577d-578a; BK XIV, 605b-d; BK XV, 630c-631c

53 JAMES: *Psychology*, 198b-211a; 808b-814b esp 812b-813a

54 FREUD: *Instincts*, 414a-b; 418d-420b esp 420a-b / *General Introduction*, 592c-593a / *Beyond the Pleasure Principle*, 639a-640c / *Civilization and Its Discontents*, 772a-b

2c. Desire as a cause of action: motivation or purpose; voluntariness

7 PLATO: *Cratylus*, 95a-b / *Symposium*, 163a-166b / *Republic*, BK IV, 352d-353b / *Timaeus*, 474b-d / *Laws*, BK VI, 712b; BK IX, 751b-d

8 ARISTOTLE: *Metaphysics*, BK II, CH 2 [994^{b}9–16] 512d-513a; BK VI, CH 1 [1025^{b}23–25] 547d; BK IX, CH 5 [1047^{b}35–1048^{a}24] 573b-c; CH 7

[1049^{a}5–12] 574c-d / *Soul*, BK III, CH 7 [431^{a}8–^{b}12] 663c-664b; CH 9–11 664d-667a

9 ARISTOTLE: *Motion of An'mals*, CH 6–11 235d-239d esp CH 6 235d-236b, CH 10 238c-239a / *Ethics*, BK III, CH 1 355b,d-357b esp [1111^{a}21–^{b}3] 357a-b; CH 12 365d-366a,c; BK VI, CH 2 387d-388b / *Politics*, BK II, CH 7 [1267^{a}3–8] 462c-d / *Rhetoric*, BK I, CH 10 611c-613a

12 LUCRETIUS: *Nature of Things*, BK II [251–293] 18b-d; BK IV [877–906] 55d-56a

17 PLOTINUS: *Third Ennead*, TR V, CH 10 105d-106b / *Fourth Ennead*, TR IV, CH 18–21 166d-168c / *Sixth Ennead*, TR VIII, CH 4 344b-d

18 AUGUSTINE: *Confessions*, BK IV, par 25 25c; BK VIII, par 19–27 58b-60c / *City of God*, BK XII, CH 6 345b-346c

19 AQUINAS: *Summa Theologica*, PART I, Q 14, A 8, ANS and REP 1 82c-83b; Q 18, A 3, ANS 106b-107c; Q 19, A 4 111c-112c; Q 41, A 2 218c-219d; Q 57, A 4, REP 3 298a-299a; Q 59, A 1, REP 3 306c-307b; Q 75, A 3, REP 3 380c-381b; Q 78, A 1, ANS and REP 4 407b-409a; Q 80, A 2, REP 3 428a-d; Q 81, A 3, ANS and REP 2 430c-431d; PART I–II, Q 1, AA 1–6 609b-614c; Q 6 644a-651c; QQ 16–17 684a-693d; Q 22, A 2, REP 2 721c-722c; Q 28, A 6 744b-d

21 DANTE: *Divine Comedy*, PURGATORY, XVIII [19–75] 80a-c

23 HOBBES: *Leviathan*, PART I, 53a; 61a-c; 64a-c; 76c; PART II, 112d-113c

31 DESCARTES: *Discourse*, PART V, 60b

31 SPINOZA: *Ethics*, PART III, THE AFFECTS, DEF I 416b-d; PART IV, DEF 7 424b; PROP 19 429d; PROP 59 442b-d

33 PASCAL: *Provincial Letters*, 24b-26b

35 LOCKE: *Human Understanding*, BK I, CH II, SECT 13 107d-108c; BK II, CH XX, SECT 6 177a-b; CH XXI, SECT 29–48 184d-190d passim, esp SECT 33 186a; SECT 73 198c-199c

38 ROUSSEAU: *Inequality*, 338c-339b

42 KANT: *Fund. Prin. Metaphysic of Morals*, 262a-c; 271c-d; 279b; 282d-283d / *Practical Reason*, 293d [fn 3]; 298d-300a; 303b-304b; 341c-342a / *Intro. Metaphysic of Morals*, 385a-386d

43 MILL: *Representative Government*, 346c-348c / *Utilitarianism*, 461c-464d

46 HEGEL: *Philosophy of Right*, INTRO, par 11 15a-b; par 17 16c; PART II, par 123 44a-b / *Philosophy of History*, INTRO, 162a-c; 164b-166b

49 DARWIN: *Descent of Man*, 308a-314c passim; 316a-317a

53 JAMES: *Psychology*, 4a-7a; 8a-9a; 13a-15a; 51a-b; 767a-768a; 788a-799b

54 FREUD: *Interpretation of Dreams*, 363b-364d; 377c-378b / *Instincts*, 412c-413a; 418d-419a / *General Introduction*, 453b-476a,c passim, esp 469a-470c, 473b-d / *Civilization and Its Discontents*, 768b-c

(2. *The analysis of desire or appetite.*)

2d. **The satisfaction of desire: possession and enjoyment**

7 PLATO: *Symposium*, 162b-c / *Gorgias*, 275b-276b / *Republic*, BK IX, 421a-425b / *Philebus*, 620a-b

8 ARISTOTLE: *Topics*, BK VI, CH 8 [146^{b}13-19] 200c

9 ARISTOTLE: *Ethics*, BK III, CH 10-11 364b-365d; BK X, CH 4-5 428b-430d esp CH 4 [1175^{a}10-22] 429c

12 LUCRETIUS: *Nature of Things*, BK III [1003-1010] 43a; BK IV [1073-1120] 58a-d

18 AUGUSTINE: *Confessions*, BK II, par 2-4 9b-d; BK IV, par 15 23a-b; BK VI, par 9-10 37c-38b; par 26 42d-43a; BK VIII, par 6-8 54c-55a / *Christian Doctrine*, BK I, CH 3-4 625b-c

19 AQUINAS: *Summa Theologica*, PART I, Q 5, A 6, ANS and REP 2 27c-28b; PART I-II, Q 1, AA 7-8 614c-615c; Q 2, A 6 619d-620d; Q 3, A 4 625a-626b; Q 4, AA 1-2 629d-631a; Q 5, A 8, REP 3 642d-643d; Q 11 666b,d-669b; Q 27, A 3, ANS 738c-739c; Q 30, A 4, REP 3 751c-752b; QQ 31-34 752b-772b

20 AQUINAS: *Summa Theologica*, PART II-II, QQ 28-29 527b-533a; PART III SUPPL, Q 69, A 4, ANS 889c-890c

21 DANTE: *Divine Comedy*, PURGATORY, XVIII [19-39] 80a-b; PARADISE, III [34-90] 109d-110b; XXXII [52-72] 155b-c; XXXIII [46-48] 156c

23 HOBBES: *Leviathan*, PART I, 76c-d

31 SPINOZA: *Ethics*, PART III, PROP 32 406b-c; PROP 35-36 406d-407c; PROP 39, SCHOL 408b-d

33 PASCAL: *Pensées*, 109 193b-194a

38 ROUSSEAU: *Inequality*, 346b

42 KANT: *Practical Reason*, 298a-300a; 341c-342a / *Judgement*, 470a-471b

43 MILL: *Representative Government*, 347b-348b / *Utilitarianism*, 448d-449c

46 HEGEL: *Philosophy of Right*, PART I, par 45 23c-d; par 59 27a-b; PART II, par 124 44b-d; PART III, par 154 57c; par 182 64a / *Philosophy of History*, INTRO, 165b-166a

47 GOETHE: *Faust* esp PART I [2605-3216] 63b-79a, PART II [9192-9573] 223b-232a

49 DARWIN: *Descent of Man*, 308a-309d passim; 312b

53 JAMES: *Psychology*, 725b-726a; 812a-813b

54 FREUD: *Interpretation of Dreams*, 363c-d; 377c-d / *Instincts*, 412d-413a / *Beyond the Pleasure Principle*, 663a / *Ego and Id*, 711d-712a / *Civilization and Its Discontents*, 773b-d

3. **The modes of desire or appetite**

7 PLATO: *Phaedrus*, 120b-c

8 ARISTOTLE: *Soul*, BK III, CH 9 [432^{b}5-7] 665a

9 ARISTOTLE: *Rhetoric*, BK I, CH 11 [1370^{a}17-27] 613c

17 PLOTINUS: *Third Ennead*, TR VI, CH 4-5 108c-109d

18 AUGUSTINE: *Confessions*, BK X, par 29-33 78d-80b

19 AQUINAS: *Summa Theologica*, PART I, Q 6, A 1, REP 2 28b-d; Q 19, A 1, ANS 108d-109c; Q 59, A 1, ANS 306c-307b; Q 78, A 1, REP 3 407b-409a; Q 80 427a-428d; PART I-II, Q 5, A 8, REP 3 642d-643d; Q 8, A 1, ANS 655b-656a; Q 26, A 1 734a-d

21 DANTE: *Divine Comedy*, PURGATORY, XVII [91]-XVIII [75] 79b-80c esp XVII [91-96] 79b

23 HOBBES: *Leviathan*, PART I, 61a-62a

31 SPINOZA: *Ethics*, PART III, PROP 9 399b-c; PROP 56-57 414a-415b; THE AFFECTS, DEF I 416b-d; PART IV, PROP 59 442b-d; APPENDIX, I-III 447a-b; PART V, PROP 4, SCHOL 453b-d

49 DARWIN: *Origin of Species*, 119a-b / *Descent of Man*, 287d-289a

53 JAMES: *Psychology*, 8a-17b esp 8a-9a, 13a-15a; 47b-52b esp 49b-50a, 51a-52a

54 FREUD: *General Introduction*, 591d-593b / *War and Death*, 757d-759d esp 758d-759a

3a. **Natural appetite: desires determined by nature or instinct**

7 PLATO: *Phaedrus*, 120b-c / *Symposium*, 165b-c / *Republic*, BK II, 311b-312b / *Timaeus*, 474b-d / *Philebus*, 621c-622b / *Laws*, BK VI, 712b

8 ARISTOTLE: *Physics*, BK I, CH 9 [192^{a}16-24] 268b-c; BK VIII, CH 4 [255^{a}30-^{b}31] 340a-c / *Metaphysics*, BK I, CH 1 [980^{a}22-28] 499a

9 ARISTOTLE: *History of Animals*, BK V, CH 8 [542^{a}17-^{b}4] 68d-69a; BK VI, CH 18-BK VII, CH 2 97b-108c passim, esp BK VI, CH 18 97b-99c, BK VII, CH 1 106b,d-108a; BK VIII, CH 1 [589^{a}4-9] 115b / *Ethics*, BK III, CH 11 [1118^{b}8-18] 365a-b / *Rhetoric*, BK I, CH 11 [1370^{a}18-25] 613c; BK II, CH 7 [1385^{a}21-25] 631d

10 GALEN: *Natural Faculties*, BK III, CH 6 202d-203a; CH 8 205a-207b; CH 13, 211d-212d

12 LUCRETIUS: *Nature of Things*, BK II [1-61] 15a-d; BK IV [858-876] 55b-c; [1037-1057] 57d

15 TACITUS: *Histories*, BK II, 224d-225a

17 PLOTINUS: *Third Ennead*, TR V 100c-106b / *Fourth Ennead*, TR III, CH 28, 157a-b

19 AQUINAS: *Summa Theologica*, PART I, Q 6, A 1, REP 2 28b-d; Q 12, A 1, ANS 50c-51c; A 8, REP 4 57b-58b; Q 19, A 1, ANS 108d-109c; A 4 111c-112c; Q 26, A 2, ANS 150c-151a; Q 59, A 1, ANS 306c-307b; Q 60 310a-314c; Q 62, A 1, ANS 317d-318c; Q 63, A 3 327b-328b; Q 75, A 6, ANS 383c-384c; Q 78, A 1, REP 3 407b-409a; Q 80, A 1, ANS and REP 1,3 427b-428a; Q 82, A 1 431d-432c; PART I-II, Q 5, A 8 642d-643d; Q 8, A 1, ANS 655b-656a; Q 10, A 2 663d-664d; Q 12, A 5 672a-c; Q 13, A 2 673c-674c; Q 26, A 1, ANS and REP 3 734a-d; A 2, ANS 734d-735c; Q 27, A 2, REP 3 737d-738c; Q 30, AA 3-4 750d-752b; Q 34, A 1, REP 2 768c-769d; Q 36, AA 1-2 780c-782b; Q 40, A 3 794c-795a

20 AQUINAS: *Summa Theologica*, PART I–II, Q 94, A 2, ANS and REP 2 221d-223a; Q 109, A 3 340c-341b; PART III SUPPL, Q 93, A 1, ANS 1037d-1039a

21 DANTE: *Divine Comedy*, PURGATORY, XVII [91]–XVIII [75] 79b-80c; XX [124]–XXI [75] 84c-85d passim; PARADISE, I [103–120] 107b-c

22 CHAUCER: *Maniciple's Tale* [17,104–144] 490a-b

23 HOBBES: *Leviathan*, PART I, 50a; 61a-d; 76c-d; PART IV, 271d

25 MONTAIGNE: *Essays*, 224d-225a; 489b-d

28 HARVEY: *On Animal Generation*, 347c; 349a-350a; 402a-d; 405c-406a; 476c-477a

31 DESCARTES: *Discourse*, PART V, 60b / *Meditations*, VI, 97d-98a; 99d-103d / *Objections and Replies*, 124b; 156a-d

31 SPINOZA: *Ethics*, PART III, 395a-d; PROP 7 399a; PART IV, PROP 19 429d

33 PASCAL: *Pensées*, 81 186b / *Geometrical Demonstration*, 440b

35 LOCKE: *Human Understanding*, BK I, CH II, SECT 3 104b-d

35 BERKELEY: *Human Knowledge*, INTRO, SECT 3 405b-c

38 ROUSSEAU: *Inequality*, 338c-339b; 346b

44 BOSWELL: *Johnson*, 130b

46 HEGEL: *Philosophy of Right*, INTRO, par 11 15a-b; ADDITIONS, 121 136c-d

49 DARWIN: *Origin of Species*, 119a / *Descent of Man*, 287d-289a; 304a-313a passim, esp 304b,d [fn 5], 307d-309d, 310c-311b; 371c-372c

53 JAMES: *Psychology*, 49b-50a; 198b-199a; 204b-211a esp 205b-206a, 209a-b; 700a-737a esp 700a-701a, 712b-737a; 799a-b; 890b-892a esp 891b [fn 1]

54 FREUD: *Origin and Development of Psycho-Analysis*, 15d-18a / *Interpretation of Dreams*, 363c-d / *Narcissism*, 400c-402c esp 401b-c / *Instincts*, 414b-421c passim, esp 414c-415d / *General Introduction*, 569c-576d esp 574a-d / *Beyond the Pleasure Principle*, 651d-654c; 658b-659d / *War and Death*, 758a-759a; 764d-765a / *Civilization and Its Discontents*, 787a-788d esp 787a-c; 789b-791d / *New Introductory Lectures*, 837b-d; 846a-851d esp 846a-847b; 883b-c

3b. Desires determined by knowledge or judgment

7 PLATO: *Protagoras*, 59a-62d / *Phaedrus*, 120b-c / *Philebus*, 621c-622b

8 ARISTOTLE: *Topics*, BK VI, CH 8 [146ᵇ36–147ᵃ11] 200d-201a / *Metaphysics*, BK XII, CH 7 [1072ᵃ26–30] 602b / *Soul*, BK II, CH 2 [413ᵇ19–24] 643d; CH 3 [414ᵃ28–ᵇ16] 644c-d; BK III, CH 3 [427ᵇ21–24] 660a; CH 7 [431ᵃ8–ᵇ12] 663c-664b

9 ARISTOTLE: *Ethics*, BK III, CH 3 [1113ᵃ3–13] 359a / *Rhetoric*, BK I, CH 11 [1370ᵃ17–28] 613c

17 PLOTINUS: *Fourth Ennead*, TR III, CH 28, 157a-b; TR IV, CH 20, 168a-b / *Sixth Ennead*, TR VIII, CH 2–4 343c-344d

18 AUGUSTINE: *Confessions*, BK X, par 29–33 78d-80b / *City of God*, BK XIV, CH 6 380b-c

19 AQUINAS: *Summa Theologica*, PART I, Q 78, A 1, REP 3 407b-409a; QQ 80–83 427a-440b; PART I–II, Q 27, A 2 737d-738c; Q 40, A 2 793d-794c

21 DANTE: *Divine Comedy*, PURGATORY, XVII [91]–XVIII [75] 79b-80c

23 HOBBES: *Leviathan*, PART I, 61c-d

31 DESCARTES: *Discourse*, PART III, 50b / *Meditations*, III, 82d-83a

31 SPINOZA: *Ethics*, PART II, AXIOM 3 373d; PART IV, PROP 59 442b-d; PROP 61–62 443a-d; APPENDIX, III 447b; PART V, PROP 4, SCHOL 453b-d

38 ROUSSEAU: *Inequality*, 338c-339b

42 KANT: *Fund. Prin. Metaphysic of Morals*, 264d-265b esp 265b,d [fn 1]

49 DARWIN: *Descent of Man*, 310c-313a passim, esp 312a-c

53 JAMES: *Psychology*, 13a-15a; 51a-52a; 729b-730a

54 FREUD: *General Introduction*, 501d-504b; 593a / *War and Death*, 758a-759a

3b(1) The distinction between sensitive and rational desire: emotional tendencies and acts of the will

7 PLATO: *Republic*, BK IX, 421a-425b

8 ARISTOTLE: *Metaphysics*, BK IX, CH 5 573a-c; BK XII, CH 7 [1072ᵃ27–29] 602b / *Soul*, BK III, CH 7 [431ᵃ8–ᵇ12] 663c-664b; CH 9 [432ᵇ5–7] 665a; CH 10 [433ᵇ5–13] 666b; CH 10 [433ᵇ27]–CH 11 [434ᵃ22] 666c-667a / *Memory and Reminiscence*, CH 2 [453ᵃ15–31] 695b-d

9 ARISTOTLE: *Rhetoric*, BK I, CH 10 [1368ᵇ28–1369ᵃ4] 612a-b; CH 11 [1370ᵃ17–28] 613c

17 PLOTINUS: *First Ennead*, TR VI 21a-26a passim / *Third Ennead*, TR V, CH 1 100c-101c; TR VI, CH 4–5 108c-109d / *Fourth Ennead*, TR IV, CH 28 172a-173b / *Sixth Ennead*, TR VIII, CH 2–4 343c-344d

19 AQUINAS: *Summa Theologica*, PART I, Q 19, A 1, ANS 108d-109c; Q 59, A 1, ANS and REP 1 306c-307b; Q 79, A 1, REP 2 414a-d; Q 80, A 2 428a-d; Q 82, A 2, REP 3 432d-433c; A 5 435c-436c; Q 106, A 2, REP 3 546d-547c; PART I–II, Q 1, A 2, REP 3 610b-611b; Q 6, A 2 646a-c; Q 11, A 2 667b-d; Q 12, A 5 672a-c; Q 13, A 2 673c-674c; Q 15, A 2 682a-c; Q 16, A 2 684d-685b; Q 17, A 2 687d-688b; Q 22, A 3 722d-723b; Q 24, A 2, ANS 727d-728c; Q 26, A 1, ANS 734a-d; Q 30, A 1 749a-d; A 3 750d-751c; Q 31, AA 3–4 754a-755c

20 AQUINAS: *Summa Theologica*, PART III, Q 18, A 2 811d-812b

21 DANTE: *Divine Comedy*, PURGATORY, XVIII [19–75] 80a-c

23 HOBBES: *Leviathan*, PART I, 63a; 64a-c; PART II, 162c

31 DESCARTES: *Discourse*, PART III, 50b

(3b. Desires determined by knowledge or judgment. 3b(1) The distinction between sensitive and rational desire: emotional tendencies and acts of the will.)

31 SPINOZA: Ethics, PART II, PROP 48, SCHOL 391b-c; PART III, PROP 9, SCHOL 399c; PROP 58–59 415c-416b; THE AFFECTS, DEF I, EXPL 416c-d; PART V, PROP 32 460b

35 LOCKE: Human Understanding, BK II, CH XXI, SECT 30 185a-c

42 KANT: Fund. Prin. Metaphysic of Morals, 264d-265b esp 265b,d [fn 1]; 271c-d; 279b; 282d-283b; 284d-285a / Practical Reason, 301a-c; 303b-304b; 314d-317c; 330c-331a / Intro. Metaphysic of Morals, 385c-386b / Judgement, 483d-484b; 605d-606b [fn 2]

43 MILL: Utilitarianism, 463c-464d

46 HEGEL: Philosophy of Right, INTRO, par 19 16d-17a; par 25–26 18a-c; PART II, par 139 48d-49b; PART III, par 194 66c-d; ADDITIONS, 121 136c-d; 131 137d / Philosophy of History, INTRO, 163a-164a; PART IV, 362b-c

49 DARWIN: Descent of Man, 310c-314c; 592d-593a

53 JAMES: Psychology, 8a-9a; 13a-15a; 767b-768a; 790a-799b passim, esp 794a-798b

54 FREUD: Hysteria, 110c / Interpretation of Dreams, 377c-380d esp 377c-378b, 379d-380b / General Introduction, 501d-504b; 590a-593b; 607d-608c; 615b-616c / Ego and Id, 702c / New Introductory Lectures, 837b-838d; 843d-844b

3b(2) Conscious and unconscious desires: habitual desire

7 PLATO: Republic, BK IX, 416a-c

9 ARISTOTLE: Ethics, BK II, CH I 348b,d-349b; CH 5 351b-c

18 AUGUSTINE: Confessions, BK VIII, par 10–11 55c-56b

19 AQUINAS: Summa Theologica, PART I, Q 87, A 2 466c-467b; PART I–II, Q 1, A 6, REP 3 614a-c

20 AQUINAS: Summa Theologica, PART I–II, Q 50, A 3 8b-9a; A 5 10b-d; Q 56, A 4 32b-33c; A 6 34b-35a

31 SPINOZA: Ethics, PART III, PROP 9, SCHOL 399c; THE AFFECTS, DEF I, EXPL 416c-d

42 KANT: Fund. Prin. Metaphysic of Morals, 262a-c / Intro. Metaphysic of Morals, 385c-386b

43 MILL: Utilitarianism, 463d-464d

49 DARWIN: Origin of Species, 119a-b

51 TOLSTOY: War and Peace, BK X, 407c-d

53 JAMES: Psychology, 8b-9a; 90b-93a passim; 788a-792a

54 FREUD: Hysteria, 110b-c / Interpretation of Dreams, 357b-358c; 363b-365c esp 364c; 369a-b; 377b-387a,c passim, esp 386d-387a / Unconscious, 428a-443d esp 428a, 429d-430b, 432c-433d, 436b-437c / General Introduction,

452a-c; 453b-476a,c esp 468a-469c, 473c-d; 501d-503d esp 503b-c; 531d-532b; 599d / Beyond the Pleasure Principle, 643d-646a / Inhibitions, Symptoms, and Anxiety, 720a

3c. Desire and love: their distinction and connection

5 EURIPIDES: Iphigenia at Aulis [543–589] 429d-430a

7 PLATO: Lysis, 20c-d; 23d-24d / Phaedrus, 115a-129d esp 120b-c, 123b-124a / Symposium, 164c-165b / Laws, BK VIII, 735c-736c

8 ARISTOTLE: Prior Analytics, BK II, CH 22 [68ᵃ25–ᵇ7] 89d-90a / Topics, BK VI, CH 7 [146ᵃ9–12] 199d; BK VII, CH I [152ᵇ6–9] 207c

9 ARISTOTLE: Ethics, BK III, CH II [1118ᵇ8–18] 365a-b; BK VIII, CH I–8 406b,d-411d passim; CH 13–14 414d-416d; BK IX, CH I 416b,d-417c passim; CH 5 420a-c; CH 8 421d-423a

12 LUCRETIUS: Nature of Things, BK IV [1037–1062] 57d-58a

12 EPICTETUS: Discourses, BK III, CH 24 203c-210a

17 PLOTINUS: First Ennead, TR V, CH 7–TR VI, CH 9 20a-26a

18 AUGUSTINE: Confessions, BK II, par I–BK III, par I 9a-13c / City of God, BK XIV, CH 7 380c-381c / Christian Doctrine, BK III, CH 10, 661d-662a

19 AQUINAS: Summa Theologica, PART I, Q 19, A I, REP 2 108d-109c; A 2, ANS 109c-110b; Q 20, A I, ANS and REP 2 120a-121b; A 2, REP 3 121b-122a; Q 60, A 3, ANS 311d-312b; PART I–II, Q 2, A I, REP 3 615d-616c; Q 23, A 2 724c-725c; A 4 726a-727a; Q 25, A 2 731b-732a; A 3, ANS 732a-733a; Q 26 733d-737a; Q 27, AA 3–4 738c-740a; Q 28, A I, ANS and REP I–2 740b-741a; A 2, ANS 741a-742a; A 3, ANS and REP 2–3 742a-d; A 4 742d-743c; Q 30, A 2 749d-750d; Q 32, A 3, REP 3 760d-761c; A 8, ANS 764c-765b

20 AQUINAS: Summa Theologica, PART I–II, Q 62, A 3, ANS and REP 3 61c-62b

21 DANTE: Divine Comedy, PURGATORY, XV [40–81] 75d-76a; XVII [91]–XVIII [75] 79b-80c

23 HOBBES: Leviathan, PART I, 61c; 63a

25 MONTAIGNE: Essays, 83d-84a; 398c-399d; 424d-425a; 473a-b

27 SHAKESPEARE: Troilus and Cressida, ACT I, SC II [308–321] 107d-108a

29 CERVANTES: Don Quixote, PART I, 79d

31 SPINOZA: Ethics, PART III, THE AFFECTS, DEF 6 417b-c; PART IV, APPENDIX, I–II 447a-b; XIX–XX 449a

32 MILTON: Paradise Lost, BK VIII [500–617] 243a-245b

35 LOCKE: Human Understanding, BK II, CH XX, SECT 4–6 176d-177b

38 ROUSSEAU: Inequality, 345c-346b

53 JAMES: Psychology, 204b-209b passim

54 FREUD: Narcissism, 404d-406b; 409b-411a,c / Instincts, 420a-421a / General Introduction,

581b; 617c-618a / *Group Psychology*, 673b-674a; 679a-b; 681c-683a; 693a-694b / *Civilization and Its Discontents*, 783b-c / *New Introductory Lectures*, 847d-848a

3d. Desire and aversion as emotional opposites

7 PLATO: *Republic*, BK IV, 352d-353a

8 ARISTOTLE: *Soul*, BK III, CH 7 [431^{a}8-^{b}9] 663c-664a

9 ARISTOTLE: *Ethics*, BK VI, CH 2 [1139^{a}21-31] 387d-388a; BK X, CH 2 [1173^{a}5-13] 427a-b

18 AUGUSTINE: *City of God*, BK XIV, CH 6 380b-c

19 AQUINAS: *Summa Theologica*, PART I-II, Q 23, A 2 724c-725c; A 4 726a-727a; Q 25, AA 1-2 730b-732a; A 3, REP 3 732a-733a; Q 30 749a-752b; Q 35, A 6 777b-778c

23 HOBBES: *Leviathan*, PART I, 61a-d

31 SPINOZA: *Ethics*, PART III 395a-422a,c esp PROP 12-13 400b-d, PROP 15-48 401a-411a, PROP 51 411c-412a, THE AFFECTS, DEF 2-3 416d-417a, DEF 6-7 417b-d; PART IV, DEF 5 424b

35 LOCKE: *Human Understanding*, BK II, CH XX, SECT 4-5 176d-177a

42 KANT: *Intro. Metaphysic of Morals*, 385a-c

53 JAMES: *Psychology*, 708a-709a

54 FREUD: *Instincts*, 418c-421a,c esp 418c / *Beyond the Pleasure Principle*, 659b-d / *Group Psychology*, 677c-678c / *Ego and Id*, 708d-710c esp 709d-710c / *War and Death*, 766a-b / *Civilization and Its Discontents*, 790a-791b

4. The economy of desire in human life

4a. The conflict of desires with one another

APOCRYPHA: *Susanna*, 22-24—(D) OT, *Daniel*, 13:22-24

NEW TESTAMENT: *Matthew*, 6:24; 8:21-22; 26:36-45 / *Romans*, 7:14-25 / *Philippians*, 1:21-26 / *James*, 4:1-10

7 PLATO: *Phaedrus*, 128a-d

8 ARISTOTLE: *Metaphysics*, BK IX, CH 5 [1048^{a}21-24] 573c / *Soul*, BK III, CH 10 [433^{b}5-13] 666b; CH 11 [434^{a}10-15] 666d-667a / *Memory and Reminiscence*, CH 2 [453^{a}15-31] 695b-d

9 ARISTOTLE: *Ethics*, BK VII 395a-406a,c

12 LUCRETIUS: *Nature of Things*, BK IV [1073-1085] 58a-b

13 VIRGIL: *Aeneid*, BK IV [332-360] 176a-177a

18 AUGUSTINE: *Confessions*, BK IV, par 11-12 21d-22b; BK X, par 39 81b-c; par 41-64 81c-87d

19 AQUINAS: *Summa Theologica*, PART I-II, Q 6, AA 6-7 649a-650d; Q 9, A 2, REP 3 658d-659c; Q 10, A 3 664d-665c

20 AQUINAS: *Summa Theologica*, PART I-II, Q 77, A 1 145a-d; PART II-II, Q 29, A 1 530b-531a; PART III, Q 18, A 6 814d-815d; PART III SUPPL, Q 96, AA 11-12 1063d-1065b

21 DANTE: *Divine Comedy*, PARADISE, IV [1-27] 110d-111a

25 MONTAIGNE: *Essays*, 297b-d; 350d-354b

31 SPINOZA: *Ethics*, PART III-IV 395a-450d passim,

esp PART III, PROP 31 405d-406a, PART IV, DEF 5 424b, PROP 7, COROL 426b, PROP 15-18 428a-429d, PROP 60-61 442d-443b

46 HEGEL: *Philosophy of Right*, INTRO, par 17 16c; ADDITIONS, 13 118c

47 GOETHE: *Faust* esp PART I [354-513] 11a-14b, [614-685] 17a-18a, [1110-1117] 27b-28a

48 MELVILLE: *Moby Dick*, 394a-397a

49 DARWIN: *Descent of Man*, 309c-313a; 318d-319a

50 MARX: *Capital*, 293c-294a

52 DOSTOEVSKY: *Brothers Karamazov*, BK III, 53d-54b

53 JAMES: *Psychology*, 199b-204b; 705a-706b; 717a-718a; 720b; 734b-735a; 791a-798b passim, esp 794a-795a

54 FREUD: *Origin and Development of Psycho-Analysis*, 7a-8a / *Hysteria*, 65c-66a; 82c-83a; 117a / *Interpretation of Dreams*, 370b / *Narcissism*, 407a-c / *Unconscious*, 433d-436c esp 436b-c / *General Introduction*, 467b-476a,c esp 469c-470c, 474d-475a; 501d-504b; 589c-593b esp 589c-591d; 599d-600d; 615b-616c; 624b-d; 633d-635d / *Beyond the Pleasure Principle*, 640c-d / *Ego and Id*, 699a-c; 704d; 712a-717a,c passim / *Inhibitions, Symptoms, and Anxiety*, 720a-733c passim, esp 722b-d, 724a-725a, 731c-d / *Civilization and Its Discontents*, 783d-784a; 789b-791d passim / *New Introductory Lectures*, 843d-845a

4b. The attachment of desires: fixations, projections, identifications, transferences

12 LUCRETIUS: *Nature of Things*, BK IV [1058-1072] 57d-58a

12 EPICTETUS: *Discourses*, BK II, CH 15 155c-156b

14 PLUTARCH: *Solon*, 66c-d

25 MONTAIGNE: *Essays*, 10b-11b

26 SHAKESPEARE: *3rd Henry VI*, ACT III, SC II [123-195] 87c-88a

31 SPINOZA: *Ethics*, PART III, PROP 13-17 400c-402a; PROP 46 410c; PART IV, PROP 6 426a; PROP 44, SCHOL 437d-438a

33 PASCAL: *Pensées*, 81 186b

46 HEGEL: *Philosophy of History*, INTRO, 196d-197c

47 GOETHE: *Faust*, PART I [1583-1606] 38b-39a

48 MELVILLE: *Moby Dick* esp 135a-136b, 156b-158b

53 JAMES: *Psychology*, 648b-650b; 707a-712b esp 707b-708a; 734b-735b

54 FREUD: *Origin and Development of Psycho-Analysis*, 16b-18a; 19a-c / *Narcissism* 399a-411a,c esp 404d-406c, 409d-410d / *Instincts*, 414b / *General Introduction*, 557b-558d esp 558a-b; 569c-589c esp 574c-d, 580a-581c, 585b-586d, 589a-c; 593d-597c; 599d-600d; 616d-622b; 623c-631b esp 628d-630d; 634b-d / *Beyond the Pleasure Principle*, 644d-645d; 648c / *Group Psychology*, 678d-684a esp 678d-681a, 681b,d [fn 4] / *Ego and Id*, 703c-706c esp 704d-705c; 711b-c; 712b-c / *New Intro-*

(*4. The economy of desire in human life. 4b. The attachment of desires: fixations, projections, identifications, transferences.*)

ductory *Lectures*, 832b-834b esp 832d-833b; 847b-849b; 855d-856d; 862d-863c

4c. The focusing of desires: emotional complexes

54 FREUD: *Origin and Development of Psycho-Analysis*, 10c; 16b-17d / *Interpretation of Dreams*, 246a-248c / *Instincts*, 415d-418c / *General Introduction*, 529d-531d; 557b-558d; 569c-585a esp 574a-576d; 580a-584c; 593d-600d; 607b-623c / *Beyond the Pleasure Principle*, 644d-646a / *Group Psychology*, 680c-d / *Ego and Id*, 704d-706d / *Inhibitions, Symptoms, and Anxiety*, 724a-742a esp 724a-727c, 733c-734d, 739a-740b / *Civilization and Its Discontents*, 774c-d; 792b-796c esp 794c-796c / *New Introductory Lectures*, 833c-834a; 847b-849b; 855d-863c esp 856b-860a

4d. The discharge of desires: catharsis and sublimation

9 ARISTOTLE: *Poetics*, CH 6 [1449^{b}28] 684a
24 RABELAIS: *Gargantua and Pantagruel*, BK III, 190a-c
32 MILTON: *Samson Agonistes*, 337a
42 KANT: *Judgement*, 509b-d
44 BOSWELL: *Johnson*, 308b-c
53 JAMES: *Psychology*, 718a-719a
54 FREUD: *Origin and Development of Psycho-Analysis*, 2b-6c esp 4c-5a; 8d-9a; 11c-17b; 20a-d / *Hysteria*, 26c-31a esp 27a-c; 62c-64a / *Interpretation of Dreams*, 189b-193b; 356d-373a esp 363c-d, 364d-365c, 369a-370a / *Narcissism*, 407c-408a / *General Introduction*, 452c-d; 495a-499b esp 496a-497b; 527c-539c esp 532d-535d; 587d-588b; 592c-593a / *Beyond the Pleasure Principle*, 641d-643c / *Group Psychology*, 693b-694b / *Ego and Id*, 704b-c; 710c-712a / *Inhibitions, Symptoms, and |Anxiety*, 739a-c; 745a; 751b-d / *Civilization and Its Discontents*, 773d-774c; 781a-c / *New Introductory Lectures*, 847a-b

5. Desire as ruler

5a. Desire ruling imagination: daydreaming and fantasy

7 PLATO: *Republic*, BK V, 361a
8 ARISTOTLE: *Dreams*, CH 2 [460^{a}33–^{b}27] 704b-d
18 AUGUSTINE: *Confessions*, BK X, par 42 82a
20 AQUINAS: *Summa Theologica*, PART I–II, Q 77, A I, ANS 145a-d
23 HOBBES: *Leviathan*, PART I, 52d-53a; PART II, 138d-139a
25 MONTAIGNE: *Essays*, 37a-b; 405d-406a
26 SHAKESPEARE: *3rd Henry VI*, ACT III, SC II [123-195] 87c-88a / *Richard II*, ACT V, SC V [1-41] 349d-350a

29 CERVANTES: *Don Quixote* esp PART I, 1b-2b, 18d-19b, 50b-52d, 134b-135d
32 MILTON: *Paradise Lost*, BK V [95-128] 177b-178a / *Samson Agonistes* [599-605] 352b
46 HEGEL: *Philosophy of History*, PART I, 220c-221a
47 GOETHE: *Faust*, PART II [7271-7312] 178b-179a; [10,039-066] 245a-b
51 TOLSTOY: *War and Peace*, BK II, 82a-d; BK III, 125b-c; 146d-148c; BK VI, 254b-c; BK X, 394d; 443c-444a; BK XI, 497c-499c; BK XII, 542d-543a; 544a-b; BK XIV, 601c-602d; BK XV, 615a-617a
53 JAMES: *Psychology*, 374a-375a
54 FREUD: *Origin and Development of Psycho-Analysis*, 18c-d / *Hysteria*, 115a-116a / *Interpretation of Dreams*, 333c-336a esp 333c-d; 347d-349c / *General Introduction*, 483b-c; 486b-489c esp 486d-487a, 487d-488a; 597b-601b esp 599b-600b, 600d-601b / *Civilization and Its Discontents*, 774a-c

5b. Desire ruling thought: rationalization and wishful thinking

6 HERODOTUS: *History*, BK I, 11b-d; 21d-22a
6 THUCYDIDES: *Peloponnesian War*, BK III, 427d-428a; BK IV, 474a-c; BK V, 506b; 507a-c
9 ARISTOTLE: *Politics*, BK III, CH 16 [1287^{a}20–^{b}5] 485c-486a
12 LUCRETIUS: *Nature of Things*, BK IV [1141-1191] 59a-d
12 EPICTETUS: *Discourses*, BK II, CH 18 161a-162b
19 AQUINAS: *Summa Theologica*, PART I–II, Q 9, A 2, ANS and REP 2 658d-659c
20 AQUINAS: *Summa Theologica*, PART I–II, Q 74, AA 5-10 131d-137c; Q 77, A I, ANS 145a-d
23 HOBBES: *Leviathan*, PART I, 52d-53a
24 RABELAIS: *Gargantua and Pantagruel*, BK III, 148d-150d; 154a-156c; 159d-163c; 166a-168a
25 MONTAIGNE: *Essays*, 210b-212a; 273b-276a; 490d-491d
26 SHAKESPEARE: *3rd Henry VI*, ACT III, SC II [123-195] 87c-88a
27 SHAKESPEARE: *Troilus and Cressida*, ACT V, SC II [106-114] 136a
28 GILBERT: *Loadstone*, BK III, 60d-61a
28 HARVEY: *Circulation of the Blood*, 306a-c; 309d
30 BACON: *Novum Organum*, BK I, APH 49 111a
31 DESCARTES: *Meditations*, IV 89a-93a / *Objections and Replies*, 215d-216a
31 SPINOZA: *Ethics*, PART III, PROP 39, SCHOL 408b-d
33 PASCAL: *Pensées*, 82-87 186b-189a; 99-100 191a-192b / *Geometrical Demonstration*, 439b-442a
35 LOCKE: *Human Understanding*, BK II, CH XXI, SECT 12 180d-181a; SECT 65-67 195b-196c; BK IV, CH XX, SECT 12 392c
43 FEDERALIST: NUMBER I, 29b-30a; NUMBER 31, 103c-104a; NUMBER 50, 162a-b

43 Mill: *Liberty*, 269d-270a

44 Boswell: *Johnson*, 103b-c; 106d

51 Tolstoy: *War and Peace*, bk i, 15b-16a; bk ii, 82d-83a; bk iii, 134a-c; bk iv, 170d-171c; bk vi, 238a-c; bk ix, 366d-367b; bk x, 426b; bk xi, 505a-511b esp 509d-510a; bk xiii, 585b

53 James: *Psychology*, 314b; 381b-385b; 643a-646a; 652a-657b; 668a-671a

54 Freud: *Interpretation of Dreams*, 363d-364b; 379a-380d / *Narcissism*, 400a / *Group Psychology*, 682b-d / *Ego and Id*, 716a / *War and Death*, 760d-761a; 765a-766b / *Civilization and Its Discontents*, 774c-d / *New Introductory Lectures*, 873d-879c passim, esp 874a-d, 876d-877b, 878b-c

5c. Desire ruling action: the unchecked expression of desires; incontinence

Old Testament: *Genesis*, 4:1-16; 25:29-34; 34; 39:7-20 / *Exodus*, 16:1-3 / *Numbers*, 11:4-35; 16:1-35—(D) *Numbers*, 11:4-34; 16:1-35 / *I Samuel*, 18:5-12; 19:8-10—(D) *I Kings*, 18:5-12; 19:8-10 / *II Samuel*, 11; 13—(D) *II Kings*, 11; 13

Apocrypha: *Wisdom of Solomon*, 2:6-9—(D) OT, *Book of Wisdom*, 2:6-9

New Testament: *Romans*, 1:18-32 / *Philippians*, 3:18-19 / *I Timothy*, 6:9-10 / *James*, 4:1-4 / *I John*, 2:15-17

5 Aeschylus: *Seven Against Thebes* [653-719] 34b-35a

5 Sophocles: *Ajax* [1047-1090] 152a-b / *Trachiniae* [431-492] 174a-c

5 Euripides: *Medea* [623-641] 217c

5 Aristophanes: *Clouds* [882-1104] 499b-502a

6 Herodotus: *History*, bk iii, 95d-98b; bk vii, 222c-d

6 Thucydides: *Peloponnesian War*, bk iii, 436d-438b

7 Plato: *Phaedrus*, 120a-122a; 128a-129c / *Republic*, bk ii, 311b-312b; bk iii, 326c-327b; bk iv, 352b-354d; bk ix, 416a-418c; 425c-427b / *Timaeus*, 474b-d / *Seventh Letter*, 801b-c

8 Aristotle: *Soul*, bk iii, ch 9 [433^{a}1]–ch 11 [435^{a}21] 665c-667a

9 Aristotle: *History of Animals*, bk vii, ch 1 [581^{a}21–^{b}22] 107a-b / *Motion of Animals*, ch 7 [701^{a}6]–ch 8 [702^{a}22] 236b-237c / *Ethics*, bk i, ch 13 [1102^{b}13-26] 348a-b; bk iii, ch 11 [1118^{b}8-19] 365a-b; ch 12 [1119^{a}34-^{b}19] 366a,c; bk vii, ch 1-10 395a-403c; ch 14 [1154^{b}2-15] 405d-406a / *Politics*, bk ii, ch 7 [1267^{a}3-8] 462c-d / *Rhetoric*, bk i, ch 10 [1369^{a}5-22] 612b-c; bk ii, ch 12 [1389^{a}3-^{b}11] 636b-d

12 Epictetus: *Discourses*, bk ii, ch 18 161a-162b

12 Aurelius: *Meditations*, bk ii, sect 10 257d-258a

14 Plutarch: *Antony* 748a-779d

15 Tacitus: *Annals*, bk iii, 57b-58d

18 Augustine: *Confessions*, bk iv, par 25 25c; bk vi, par 11-13 38b-39c; bk viii, par 25-27 60a-c; bk x, par 40-70 81c-89a / *Christian Doctrine*, bk iii, ch 18-21 664d-666b

19 Aquinas: *Summa Theologica*, part i, q 81, a 3, rep 1-2 430c-431d; q 83, a 1, rep 1 436d-438a; part i-ii, q 6, a 7 650a-d; q 9, a 2 658d-659c; q 10, a 3 664d-665c

20 Aquinas: *Summa Theologica*, part i-ii, q 75, aa 2-3 138c-139d; q 77 144d-152a

21 Dante: *Divine Comedy*, hell, v [1]-viii [64] 7a-11c; xi [67-90] 15d-16a; purgatory, xvii [91-139] 79b-d; xix-xxvi 81c-94c

22 Chaucer: *Manciple's Tale* [17,104-144] 490a-b

24 Rabelais: *Gargantua and Pantagruel*, bk i, 65c-66b

25 Montaigne: *Essays*, 107a-112d; 159a-167a; 232b-238d; 350d-354b; 413a-416c; 486b-495a; 527b-528a; 538a-543a,c

26 Shakespeare: *3rd Henry VI*, act iii, sc ii [123-195] 87c-88a; act v, sc vi [61-93] 103d-104a / *Richard III* 105a-148a,c / *Romeo and Juliet*, act ii, sc vi [1-15] 300c

27 Shakespeare: *Hamlet*, act iii, sc ii [61-79] 49c-d; sc iv [65-81] 55b-c / *Troilus and Cressida*, act i, sc iii [101-124] 109b; act ii, sc ii 113c-115d / *Othello* 205a-243a,c esp act iv, sc i 229d-233a, act v, sc ii [291-356] 242b-243a / *King Lear*, act iv, sc vi [109-134] 274c-d / *Antony and Cleopatra* 311a-350d

31 Spinoza: *Ethics*, part iv, prop 1-18 424c-429d; prop 44 437c-438a; prop 60-61 442d-443b

32 Milton: *Paradise Lost*, bk viii [521-594] 243b-245a; bk ix [990-1066] 269a-270b; bk xii [79-90] 321a / *Samson Agonistes* [521-540] 351a-b

35 Locke: *Human Understanding*, bk i, ch ii, sect 3 104b-d; bk ii, ch xxi, sect 29-48 184d-190d passim; sect 65-67 195b-196c

36 Sterne: *Tristram Shandy*, 239b-243a

37 Fielding: *Tom Jones*, 109c; 122d-123a

40 Gibbon: *Decline and Fall*, 34d-39d passim, esp 35a-b, 38a-b; 60a-c

41 Gibbon: *Decline and Fall*, 174c-175a; 559a-c

42 Kant: *Judgement*, 586a-587a

44 Boswell: *Johnson*, 135c-136a; 301c-d

46 Hegel: *Philosophy of History*, intro, 162b-c; 171c-172b

47 Goethe: *Faust*, part i [2605-2677] 63b-65a; part ii [9695-9944] 235a-241b

51 Tolstoy: *War and Peace*, bk i, 15b-16a; bk v, 201a-c; bk vi, 248b-250a; 251d-252d; bk viii, 321d-322d; 329c-333a; 334d-335a; 336b-337d

52 Dostoevsky: *Brothers Karamazov*, bk i, 4a-d; bk ii, 39b-40a; bk vi, 164b-d

53 James: *Psychology*, 718a-720a; 799a-807a

54 Freud: *Group Psychology*, 690b-c / *Ego and Id*, 702c-d / *New Introductory Lectures*, 837b-839b

6. Desire as subject to rule

6a. The regulation of desire by reason: the discipline of moral virtue or duty

OLD TESTAMENT: *Exodus*, 20:14,17 / *Numbers*, 15:38–41 / *Deuteronomy*, 5:18,21 / *Psalms*, 37:1–13 esp 37:7–8—(D) *Psalms*, 36:1–13 esp 36:7–8 / *Proverbs*, 7; 23:1–8; 25:16; 30:7–9

APOCRYPHA: *Ecclesiasticus*, 18:30–31; 23:5–6; 31:1–17—(D) OT, *Ecclesiasticus*, 18:30–31; 23:5–6; 31:1–17

NEW TESTAMENT: *Romans*, 8:1–13 / *I Corinthians*, 13:4–8 / *Galatians*, 5:16–24 / *Colossians*, 3:5–15 / *I Thessalonians*, 4:3–8 / *I Timothy*, 6:3–12 / *Titus*, 2:11–14; 3:3–7 / *James*, 4:1–7 / *I Peter*, 2:11

5 AESCHYLUS: *Eumenides* [490–565] 86b–87a

5 EURIPIDES: *Iphigenia at Aulis* [543–589] 429d–430a

5 ARISTOPHANES: *Clouds* [882–1104] 499b–502a / *Lysistrata* 583a–599a,c

7 PLATO: *Phaedrus*, 128a–d / *Phaedo*, 225d–226c / *Gorgias*, 275b–280d / *Republic*, BK III, 326c–327b; BK IV, 346a–356a; BK IX, 416a–c; 425c–427b / *Laws*, BK VI, 712b; BK VIII, 735c–738c

8 ARISTOTLE: *Topics*, BK V, CH 1 [129ª10–16] 179a / *Soul*, BK III, CH 9 [433ª5–8] 665c; CH 11 [434ª10–15] 666d–667a

9 ARISTOTLE: *Ethics*, BK I, CH 13 [1102ᵇ13–1103ª3] 348a–c; BK III, CH 10–12 364b–366a,c; BK VI, CH 2 387d–388b; BK VII, CH 1–10 395a–403c passim / *Politics*, BK II, CH 7 [1266ᵇ26–1267ª17] 462b–d

11 NICOMACHUS: *Arithmetic*, BK I, 826d–827a

12 AURELIUS: *Meditations* 253a–310d esp BK II, SECT 16 259a, BK IV, SECT 24 265c–d, BK VII, SECT 55 283b–c

13 VIRGIL: *Aeneid*, BK IV 167a–186b

14 PLUTARCH: *Coriolanus*, 174b,d–175a / *Caius Marius*, 353d–354a,c

15 TACITUS: *Annals*, BK III, 57b–58d

17 PLOTINUS: *Fifth Ennead*, TR IX, CH 1–2 246c–247b

18 AUGUSTINE: *Confessions*, BK II, par 2–4 9b–d; BK III, par 1 13b–c; BK VI, par 18–26 40d–43a; BK VIII, par 1–2 52c–53b; par 10–11 55c–56b; par 25–27 60a–c; BK X, par 40–70 81c–89a / *City of God*, BK XIV, CH 4–5 287a–289a; BK XIV, CH 8–9 381c–385b; BK XIX, CH 4, 511d–512a / *Christian Doctrine*, BK I, CH 24 630c–631a; CH 27 631d; BK III, CH 18–21 664d–666b

19 AQUINAS: *Summa Theologica*, PART I, Q 81, A 3 430c–431d; Q 95, A 2 507c–508a; Q 98, A 2 517d–519a; PART I–II, Q 10, A 3 664d–665c; Q 17, A 7 690d–692a; Q 24 727a–730a; Q 45, A 4, ANS 812b–813a

20 AQUINAS: *Summa Theologica*, PART I–II, Q 50, A 3 8b–9a; Q 56, A 4 32b–33c; A 5, REP 1 33c–34b; QQ 59–60 45d–54d; PART III, Q 15, A 4 790d–791c

21 DANTE: *Divine Comedy*, PURGATORY 53a–105d esp XV [40]–XVIII [75] 75d–80c

22 CHAUCER: *Troilus and Cressida*, BK IV, STANZA 82 99a / *Parson's Tale*, par 80 541b–542a

23 HOBBES: *Leviathan*, PART I, 95d–96b

25 MONTAIGNE: *Essays*, 89b–90c; 159a–167a; 184a–d; 200d–205b; 232b–238d; 431c–432d; 486b–495a; 538a–543a,c

26 SHAKESPEARE: *Henry V*, ACT I, SC I [24–69] 533b–c

27 SHAKESPEARE: *Hamlet*, ACT I, SC III [5–51] 34b–d; ACT III, SC II [61–79] 49c–d / *Troilus and Cressida*, ACT I, SC III [101–124] 109b; ACT II, SC II 113c–115d / *Othello*, ACT I, SC III [322–337] 212b–c

30 BACON: *Advancement of Learning*, 26a–c; 78a–d

31 DESCARTES: *Discourse*, PART III, 49b–d

31 SPINOZA: *Ethics*, PART III, PROP 1 396a–c; PROP 9, SCHOL 399c; PART IV, PREF 422b,d–424a; PROP 14–18 428a–429d; PROP 44–73 437c–447a; APPENDIX, I–III 447a–b; XXXII 450c–d; PART V, PREF 451a–452c; PROP 1–16 452d–456c; PROP 42 463b–d

32 MILTON: *Areopagitica*, 390b–391a

33 PASCAL: *Pensées*, 104 193a; 502 260b–261a

35 LOCKE: *Human Understanding*, BK I, CH II, SECT 13 107d–108c; BK II, CH XXI, SECT 46–54 189d–192c; SECT 71 197b–198a; SECT 73 198c–199c

42 KANT: *Fund. Prin. Metaphysic of Morals*, 256b; 258b–c; 259a–c; 264d–265b / *Pref. Metaphysical Elements of Ethics*, 378b–c / *Judgement*, 586a–587a

43 MILL: *Liberty*, 295a–d / *Representative Government*, 348a–b / *Utilitarianism*, 463d–464d

44 BOSWELL: *Johnson*, 135c–136a; 176d

46 HEGEL: *Philosophy of Right*, INTRO, par 19 16d–17a; PART III, par 149 56b; par 187 65a–c; ADDITIONS, 13–14 118c–d / *Philosophy of History*, INTRO, 162a–172b; PART III, 312d–313a

49 DARWIN: *Descent of Man*, 304a–305a; 310c–319a esp 310c–312c, 313d–314b, 318d–319a; 592b–593b

51 TOLSTOY: *War and Peace*, BK VI, 245b–c; 248b–250a; EPILOGUE I, 655c–656b

53 JAMES: *Psychology*, 80a–83b passim; 202a–204b; 797b–798a; 807a–808a; 816a–819a

54 FREUD: *Origin and Development of Psycho-Analysis*, 9a; 16c / *Hysteria*, 110b–c / *Interpretation of Dreams*, 386d–387a / *Narcissism*, 407b–c / *General Introduction*, 452c–d; 501d–504b esp 504b; 590a–593b; 624a–625b esp 625a–b / *Ego and Id*, 701d–702d; 704a–707d esp 706d–707c; 715a–716c esp 715c–d / *Inhibitions, Symptoms, and Anxiety*, 721d–722c; 744a / *War and Death*, 757c–759d / *Civilization and Its Discontents*, 773b–774a esp 773c; 780b–781d; 783c–785a; 785d–789a esp 787b–c; 792a–796c esp 792a–b, 793a–b, 793d–794b; 800c–801b / *New Introductory Lectures*, 837d–840a

6b. The restraint or renunciation of desire: abstention, inhibition, repression

5 ARISTOPHANES: *Lysistrata* 583a-599a,c
12 EPICTETUS: *Discourses* 105a-245a,c esp BK I, CH I 105a-106c, CH 3-4 108b-110a, BK II, CH 2 140c-141c, CH 17-18 158d-162b, BK III, CH 24 203c-210a, BK IV, CH 4 225a-228a
12 AURELIUS: *Meditations*, BK II, SECT 5 257b-c; BK VII, SECT 2 279b,d; SECT 55-57 283b-c; BK IX, SECT 7 292b
13 VIRGIL: *Aeneid*, BK IV [393-449] 178a-179b
18 AUGUSTINE: *City of God*, BK IX, CH 4-5 287a-289a; BK XIV, CH 8-9 381c-385b
19 AQUINAS: *Summa Theologica*, PART I-II, Q 10, A 3 664d-665c; Q 24 727a-730a esp A 2 727d-728c
20 AQUINAS: *Summa Theologica*, PART II-II, Q 186 650b-663b; PART III SUPPL, Q 96 1049d-1066a
22 CHAUCER: *Wife of Bath's Prologue* [5587-5743] 256a-258b
24 RABELAIS: *Gargantua and Pantagruel*, BK III, 188d-191c
25 MONTAIGNE: *Essays*, 89b-91b; 99b-c; 107a-112d; 166a-d; 200d-205b; 232b-238d; 297d-300c; 353c-354b; 432b-d; 538a-543a,c
30 BACON: *Advancement of Learning*, 71d-72b
31 DESCARTES: *Discourse*, PART III, 49b-d
31 SPINOZA: *Ethics*, PART IV, PROP 9-18 426d-429d; PART V, PROP 2 452d-453a; PROP 6 453d-454a; PROP 42 463b-d
32 MILTON: *Comus* [420-475] 42b-44a; [716-765] 49a-50a / *Areopagitica*, 390b-391a
33 PASCAL: *Provincial Letters*, 64b-65b
40 GIBBON: *Decline and Fall*, 192a-193c; 596c-d
42 KANT: *Practical Reason*, 346a-d / *Pref. Metaphysical Elements of Ethics*, 378d-379a
44 BOSWELL: *Johnson*, 283a
46 HEGEL: *Philosophy of History*, PART I, 224a-225a
47 GOETHE: *Faust*, PART I [1544-1571] 37b-38a
51 TOLSTOY: *War and Peace*, BK III, 122b-c; BK V, 201a-c; BK VI, 248b-250a; BK IX, 373b-374a; BK XIII, 577a-578b esp 577d-578a; BK XIV, 605b-d; BK XV, 630c-631a
52 DOSTOEVSKY: *Brothers Karamazov*, BK VI, 164d-165a
53 JAMES: *Psychology*, 80b-83b esp 81a; 199b-202a esp 200b-201a; 720a; 725a; 734b-735b; 799a-800a
54 FREUD: *Origin and Development of Psycho-Analysis*, 6d-8b esp 7a-c; 16c / *Interpretation of Dreams*, 377d-378d esp 378b-d / *Repression* 422a-427a,c esp 422c-d / *Unconscious*, 432d-436b / *General Introduction*, 566a-568a; 573c-d; 585b-586d esp 586d / *Beyond the Pleasure Principle*, 640c / *Ego and Id*, 699a; 706b-c / *Inhibitions, Symptoms, and Anxiety*, 718a-722b esp 719b-c, 720a-d; 726a-728b; 741d [fn 1]; 747b-c; 750a-d / *Civilization and Its Discontents*, 773b-d; 781a-d; 782a-b,d [fn 1]; 793a-

795c esp 793d-794b / *New Introductory Lectures*, 834d-835b; 842a-845b esp 842b-d, 843d-844c

6c. The results of repression: dreaming, symbolic over-reactions, neuroses

18 AUGUSTINE: *City of God*, BK XIV, CH 8-9 381c-385b esp CH 9, 384b, 385b
32 MILTON: *Paradise Lost*, BK V [28-128] 176a-178a
40 GIBBON: *Decline and Fall*, 598a-b
51 TOLSTOY: *War and Peace*, BK V, 220b-c; 233b-234a; BK VI, 238a-c; 248b-250a; BK VII, 292b-296a; BK VIII, 338b-339c esp 338d
53 JAMES: *Psychology*, 753b-754b
54 FREUD: *Origin and Development of Psycho-Analysis* 1a-20d esp 4c-5a, 6d-9a, 11c-12b, 13a-b, 14b-15a, 20c-d / *Hysteria* 25a-118a,c esp 27a-28c, 35b-c, 38a-b, 52c-53c, 65c-66a, 75a-d, 82c-87a, 90d-96a, 97b-102a, 111a-115a, 116d-118a,c / *Interpretation of Dreams*, 164d-168d esp 167d-168a; 176a-b; 189b-205c passim; 216b-219a; 234d-235d; 240d-249b esp 240d-241a, 248c-249a; 294d-295b; 323b-c; 328a-d; 331d-332a; 352d-382a esp 356d-365c, 375c-376a, 380d-382a; 386b-387a / *Repression*, 423b-427a,c esp 423b-424b, 425c-426a / *Unconscious*, 434c-436b / *General Introduction*, 469c-470b; 476a-544d esp 489c-491b, 495a-504d, 532d-539b; 557b-631b esp 563a-569c, 586b-590a, 593b-600d, 614b-615a; 633d-635d / *Group Psychology*, 690a-c / *Ego and Id*, 712c-715c esp 713c-714b, 715a-b / *Inhibitions, Symptoms, and Anxiety* 718a-754a,c esp 720a, 721c-d, 722c-723d, 728b-733c, 741d [fn 1]; 745d-747b / *War and Death*, 759c-d / *Civilization and Its Discontents*, 781c-d; 793a-794a; 796a-c; 798c-799a; 800d-801c / *New Introductory Lectures*, 810d-813c esp 811b-812b; 817a-818b; 840a-846a

7. Desire and infinity

7a. The infinite tendency of desires

OLD TESTAMENT: *Proverbs*, 27:20 / *Ecclesiastes*, 6:7 / *Habakkuk*, 2:5—(D) *Habacuc*, 2:5
APOCRYPHA: *Ecclesiasticus*, 14:9—(D) OT, *Ecclesiasticus*, 14:9
NEW TESTAMENT: *John*, 4:13-14
7 PLATO: *Gorgias*, 275b-277c / *Republic*, BK V, 370a-c; BK IX, 416a-418c
12 LUCRETIUS: *Nature of Things*, BK III [1003-1010] 43a; [1076-1094] 44a,c; BK VI [1-42] 80a-c
12 EPICTETUS: *Discourses*, BK III, CH 9, 185d; BK IV, CH 9, 237d-238a
14 PLUTARCH: *Caius Marius*, 353d-354a,c
18 AUGUSTINE: *Confessions*, BK I, par 19 5d
19 AQUINAS: *Summa Theologica*, PART I-II, Q I A 4 612a-613a; Q 2, A I, REP 3 615d-616c; Q 30, A 4 751c-752b
25 MONTAIGNE: *Essays*, 149b-d; 297d-299c; 429a-b; 489b-d; 503b-d

(7. Desire and infinity. 7a. The infinite tendency of desires.)

27 SHAKESPEARE: *Troilus and Cressida*, ACT III, SC II [82–90] 121a / *Macbeth*, ACT IV, SC III [57–99] 304a-c
31 SPINOZA: *Ethics*, PART III, PROP 6–9 398d-399c
33 PASCAL: *Pensées*, 109 193b-194a; 125–183 195b-204b
36 STERNE: *Tristram Shandy*, 236b-238a
42 KANT: *Judgement*, 584d-585c
46 HEGEL: *Philosophy of Right*, PART III, par 185 64b-d; ADDITIONS, 118 136a-b
47 GOETHE: *Faust* esp PART I [354–481] 11a-14a, [602–784] 16b-20b, [1671–1706] 40a-41a, PART II [11,433–466] 278a-279a, [11,559–586] 281b-282a
52 DOSTOEVSKY: *Brothers Karamazov*, BK VI, 164b-d

7a(1) The pursuit of pleasure

APOCRYPHA: *Ecclesiasticus*, 23:16–17—(D) OT, *Ecclesiasticus*, 23:21–24
NEW TESTAMENT: *John*, 4:13–14
7 PLATO: *Gorgias*, 275b-277c / *Philebus*, 628a-d
9 ARISTOTLE: *Ethics*, BK III, CH 12 [1119^{b}6–12] 366c / *Politics*, BK I, CH 9 [1257^{b}38–1258^{a}14] 452a-b
12 LUCRETIUS: *Nature of Things*, BK III [1003–1010] 43a; [1076–1094] 44a,c; BK IV [1073–1120] 58a-d; BK V [1405–1435] 79b-d
12 EPICTETUS: *Discourses*, BK IV, CH 9, 237d-238a
18 AUGUSTINE: *Confessions*, BK II, par 2–4 9b-d
19 AQUINAS: *Summa Theologica*, PART I–II, Q 30, A 4 751c-752b
21 DANTE: *Divine Comedy*, HELL, V [25–45] 7b-c
22 CHAUCER: *Troilus and Cressida*, BK I, STANZA 58–66 8b-9b / *Wife of Bath's Prologue* [5953–5960] 262a
25 MONTAIGNE: *Essays*, 429a-b
27 SHAKESPEARE: *Antony and Cleopatra*, ACT I, SC I [1–55] 311b-312a
35 LOCKE: *Human Understanding*, BK II, CH XXI, SECT 42–45 188c-189d
37 FIELDING: *Tom Jones*, 283a-b
38 ROUSSEAU: *Inequality*, 364a-b
42 KANT: *Judgement*, 584d-585b; 586d
46 HEGEL: *Philosophy of Right*, PART III, par 185 64b-d
47 GOETHE: *Faust*, PART I [3217–3250] 79a-b
52 DOSTOEVSKY: *Brothers Karamazov*, BK III, 53b-54b

7a(2) The lust for power

OLD TESTAMENT: *Isaiah*, 14:12–14—(D) *Isaias*, 14:12–14 / *Habakkuk*, 2:5—(D) *Habacuc*, 2:5
6 HERODOTUS: *History*, BK VII, 215c-216b
6 THUCYDIDES: *Peloponnesian War*, BK V, 506b-c
7 PLATO: *Gorgias*, 275b-277c
12 LUCRETIUS: *Nature of Things*, BK III [59–86] 30d-31b; [995–1002] 42d-43a

12 EPICTETUS: *Discourses*, BK IV, CH 9, 237d-238a
14 PLUTARCH: *Pyrrhus*, 319b-321a / *Pompey*, 525a-b; 533a-c / *Caesar*, 599b-d / *Cicero*, 706b-c
18 AUGUSTINE: *City of God*, BK XIV, CH 13 387c-388c
19 AQUINAS: *Summa Theologica*, PART I, Q 63, A 3 327b-328b
23 HOBBES: *Leviathan*, PART I, 76c-d
25 MONTAIGNE: *Essays*, 350d-354b
26 SHAKESPEARE: *Richard III* 105a-148a,c / *Julius Caesar*, ACT II, SC I [10–34] 574c-d
32 MILTON: *Paradise Lost*, BK I [242–270] 98b-99a
35 LOCKE: *Civil Government*, CH XIX, SECT 229 78a
38 ROUSSEAU: *Inequality*, 364a-b

7a(3) The accumulation of wealth

OLD TESTAMENT: *Ecclesiastes*, 5:10; 6:7—(D) *Ecclesiastes*, 5:9; 6:7 / *Habakkuk*, 2:5–11—(D) *Habacuc*, 2:5–11
APOCRYPHA: *Ecclesiasticus*, 11:10; 14:9—(D) OT, *Ecclesiasticus*, 11:10; 14:9 / *Baruch*, 3:16–19—(D) OT, *Baruch*, 3:16–19
NEW TESTAMENT: *Luke*, 12:16–21
5 ARISTOPHANES: *Plutus* [143–197] 630d-631b
7 PLATO: *Gorgias*, 275b-277c / *Republic*, BK VIII, 405c-408a; 412a / *Laws*, BK VIII, 733b-d; BK IX, 751b-d
9 ARISTOTLE: *Politics*, BK I, CH 9 [1257^{b}38–1258^{a}14] 452a-b; BK II, CH 7 [1266^{b}27–1267^{b}5] 462b-463b
12 LUCRETIUS: *Nature of Things*, BK III [59–93] 30d-31b; BK VI [1–42] 80a-c
12 EPICTETUS: *Discourses*, BK IV, CH 9, 237d-238a
18 AUGUSTINE: *Confessions*, BK I, par 19 5d
19 AQUINAS: *Summa Theologica*, PART I–II, Q 2, A 1, REP 3 615d-616c; Q 30, A 4, ANS 751c-752b
20 AQUINAS: *Summa Theologica*, PART I–II, Q 84, A 1 174b-175a
21 DANTE: *Divine Comedy*, HELL, VII [52–66] 10a-b
22 CHAUCER: *Tale of Melibeus*, par 18, 408a
25 MONTAIGNE: *Essays*, 122a-124c
31 SPINOZA: *Ethics*, PART IV, APPENDIX, XXVIII–XXIX 450a
36 STERNE: *Tristram Shandy*, 237a
38 ROUSSEAU: *Inequality*, 364a-b
39 SMITH: *Wealth of Nations*, BK I, 71b-d
40 GIBBON: *Decline and Fall*, 510b
43 MILL: *Utilitarianism*, 462c-463a
44 BOSWELL: *Johnson*, 125a-b
46 HEGEL: *Philosophy of Right*, PART III, par 185 64b-d; par 195 66d-67a
47 GOETHE: *Faust*, PART II [5505–6172] 136a-151a; [11,151–287] 271b-274b esp [11,151–162] 271b, [11,239–258] 273b-274a
50 MARX: *Capital*, 60d-62d esp 62a-b; 71d-72c esp 72a-c; 292c-295a esp 293c-294a

7b. The restless search for the infinite: the desire for the vision of God

OLD TESTAMENT: *Exodus*, 33:11-23 / *Psalms*, 27 esp 27:4, 27:8; 42-43; 63; 73:25-28; 84—(D) *Psalms*, 26 esp 26:4, 26:8; 41-42; 62; 72:25-28; 83 / *Isaiah*, 26:8-9—(D) *Isaias*, 26:8-9

NEW TESTAMENT: *John*, 4:13-14; 6:35 / *Philippians*, 3:7-21 / *I John*, 3:1-3

7 PLATO: *Symposium*, 163a-167d

17 PLOTINUS: *First Ennead*, TR VI 21a-26a passim / *Sixth Ennead*, TR IX 353d-360d

18 AUGUSTINE: *Confessions* 1a-125a,c esp BK I, par 1-6 1a-2c, BK II, par 15 12b-c, BK III, par 1 13b-c, par 8 14d-15a, BK IV, par 15-19 23a-24b, BK V, par 1-2 27a-c, BK VII, par 16-23 48c-50c, BK VIII, par 17-18 57d-58a, BK IX, par 3 62a-b, BK X, par 1-40 71c-81c, BK XI, par 1-4 89b-90b, BK XII, par 10 101c, par 23 104b-c, BK XIII 110d-125a,c / *Christian Doctrine*, BK I, CH 38 635c-d

19 AQUINAS: *Summa Theologica*, PART I, Q 6, A 1, REP 2 28b-d; Q 12, A 1, ANS 50c-51c; A 8, REP 4 57b-58b; Q 26, A 2, ANS 150c-151a; Q 54, A 2, ANS 285d-286c; Q 60, A 5 313b-314c; Q 62, A 1, ANS 317d-318c; PART I-II, Q 2, A 1, REP 3 615d-616c; Q 5, A 1, ANS 636d-637c; Q 8 655a-657c

20 AQUINAS: *Summa Theologica*, PART I-II, Q 109, A 3 340c-341b; PART II-II, Q 27, A 6 524c-525c; Q 28, A 3 528d-529c; PART III SUPPL, Q 69, A 4 889c-890c

21 DANTE: *Divine Comedy*, PURGATORY, XV [40-81] 75d-76a; XVII [91]-XVIII [75] 79b-80c; PARADISE, IV [115]-V [12] 111d-112b; XXII [52-72] 140b; XXVI [1-78] 145d-146c; XXXIII 156b-157d esp [46-48] 156c

30 BACON: *Advancement of Learning*, 80b-81a

31 DESCARTES: *Meditations*, III, 88c-d

31 SPINOZA: *Ethics*, PART IV, APPENDIX, IV 447b-c; PART V, PROP 36 461a-c

32 MILTON: *Sonnets*, XIV 66a

33 PASCAL: *Pensées*, 72, 183a-b; 125-183 195b-204b; 463 255a; 468-492 255b-259b

35 LOCKE: *Human Understanding*, BK II, CH XXI, SECT 45-47 189b-190b

46 HEGEL: *Philosophy of History*, PART I, 224a-225a; PART III, 304c-306a

47 GOETHE: *Faust* esp PART I [354-481] 11a-14a, [602-784] 16b-20b, [1671-1706] 40a-41a, PART II [11,433-466] 278a-279a, [11,559-586] 281b-282a

48 MELVILLE: *Moby Dick*, 78a-b

51 TOLSTOY: *War and Peace*, BK XII, 560a-561d; BK XIV, 608a-b; BK XV, 631a-c

52 DOSTOEVSKY: *Brothers Karamazov*, BK III, 53b-54b

CROSS-REFERENCES

For: Matters relevant to the metaphysical conception of desire, *see* BEING 7c–7c(3); CHANGE 1; MATTER 1a, 3b.

Discussions bearing on the theory of natural appetite or desire, *see* HABIT 3a; HAPPINESS 1; NATURE 1a, 2d, 3c(3).

Other discussions of the distinction between conscious and natural desire, and of animal appetite in contrast to the human will, *see* ANIMAL 1a(3); MAN 4b; SENSE 3e; WILL 1, 2b(2).

The consideration of voluntary acts or movements, *see* ANIMAL 4b; NATURE 3c(2); WILL 3a(1)–3a(2).

Other treatments of the objects of desire in general, *see* BEING 3b; GOOD AND EVIL 1a, 3c; HAPPINESS 1, 4–4b; PLEASURE AND PAIN 6a–6b; and for particular objects of desire, *see* HONOR 2b; LIFE AND DEATH 8b; WEALTH 10a–10b, 10e(3).

The conception of pleasure as the satisfaction of desire, *see* PLEASURE AND PAIN 6d.

Another comparison of desire and love, *see* LOVE 1c, 2a–2a(4).

Further psychological analysis of emotional desires and impulses, *see* EMOTION 3–3c(4); LOVE 2a(3)–2a(4); MEDICINE 6c(2).

Other discussions of the influence of emotional desires on imagination and thought, *see* EMOTION 3b; MEMORY AND IMAGINATION 8c, 8e; OPINION 2a; WILL 3b(1).

The psychological or ethical consideration of problems arising from the conflict between desire and reason or duty, *see* DUTY 8; EMOTION 4–4b(2); LIBERTY 3a–3b; MIND 1e(3), 9b; VIRTUE AND VICE 5a; WILL 2b(2), 9b.

The discussion of man's relation to the infinite, *see* INFINITY 6a; MAN 10d; and for the theological conception of man's ultimate rest in the vision of God, *see* GOD 5b, 6c(4); HAPPINESS 7c–7c(1); LOVE 5a(2); WILL 7d.

ADDITIONAL READINGS

Listed below are works not included in *Great Books of the Western World*, but relevant to the idea and topics with which this chapter deals. These works are divided into two groups:

I. Works by authors represented in this collection.
II. Works by authors not represented in this collection.

For the date, place, and other facts concerning the publication of the works cited, consult the Bibliography of Additional Readings which follows the last chapter of *The Great Ideas*.

I.

EPICTETUS. *The Manual*

GOETHE. *Sorrows of Young Werther*

HEGEL. *The Phenomenology of Mind*, IV (3)

FREUD. *Three Contributions to the Theory of Sex*, CH I

II.

EPICURUS. *Letter to Menoeceus*

BOCCACCIO. *Decameron*

VILLON. *The Debate of the Heart and Body of Villon*

EBREO. *The Philosophy of Love*, DIALOGUE I

P. SIDNEY. *Astrophel and Stella*

MARLOWE. *Tamburlaine the Great*

SUÁREZ. *Disputationes Metaphysicae*, X (1), XXIII–XXIV, XXX (16), XLVII (14)

JOHN OF SAINT THOMAS. *Cursus Philosophicus Thomisticus, Philosophia Naturalis*, PART IV, Q 12

MOLIÈRE. *L'avare* (*The Miser*)

MALEBRANCHE. *De la recherche de la vérité*, BK IV

RACINE. *Phèdre*

——. *Athalie*

BOSSUET. *Traité de la concupiscence*

LEIBNITZ. *New Essays Concerning Human Understanding*, BK II, CH 21

J. BUTLER. *Fifteen Sermons upon Human Nature*, I–II

HUTCHESON. *A System of Moral Philosophy*, BK I, CH 2–3; BK II, CH 2

——. *An Essay on the Nature and Conduct of the Passions and Affections*

HELVÉTIUS. *Traité de l'esprit*, III, CH 9–11

T. REID. *Essays on the Active Powers of the Human Mind*, III, PART II, CH 1–2

J. G. FICHTE. *The Vocation of Man*

SCHOPENHAUER. *The World as Will and Idea*

BROWN. *Lectures on the Philosophy of the Human Mind*, VOL II, pp 153–179

D. STEWART. *Outlines of Moral Philosophy*, PART II, CH I (1–4)

——. *Philosophy of the Active and Moral Powers of Man*, BK I, CH 1–3

J. MILL. *Analysis of the Phenomena of the Human Mind*, CH I

STENDHAL. *The Red and the Black*

BENTHAM. *An Introduction to the Principles of Morals and Legislation*, CH 10

——. *Deontology*

PUSHKIN. *The Queen of Spades*

WHEWELL. *The Elements of Morality*, BK I, CH 2

BALZAC. *Cousin Bette*

SPENCER. *The Principles of Psychology*, VOL I, PART I, CH 6 (50); PART IV, CH 8

BAIN. *The Emotions and the Will*

E. HARTMANN. *Philosophy of the Unconscious*

H. SIDGWICK. *The Methods of Ethics*, BK I, CH 4

ZOLA. *Nana*

FRANCE. *The Crime of Sylvestre Bonnard*

T. H. GREEN. *Prolegomena to Ethics*, BK II, CH 2

L. STEPHEN. *The Science of Ethics*, CH 2

IBSEN. *The Master Builder*

CHEKHOV. *The Sea-Gull*

RIBOT. *The Psychology of the Emotions*

BRADLEY. *Collected Essays*, VOL I (14)

MOORE. *Principia Ethica*, CH 2 (39–47)

SCHELER. *Der Formalismus in der Ethik und die materiale Wertethik*

B. RUSSELL. *The Analysis of Mind*, LECT 3

DEWEY. *Human Nature and Conduct*, PART III (8)

FITZGERALD. *The Great Gatsby*

O'NEILL. *Desire Under the Elms*

F. ALEXANDER. *Psychoanalysis of the Total Personality*

BEEBE-CENTER. *The Psychology of Pleasantness and Unpleasantness*

NYGREN. *Agape and Eros*

ROUGEMONT. *Love in the Western World*

MARITAIN. *Scholasticism and Politics*, CH VI

D'ARCY. *The Mind and Heart of Love*

Chapter 18: DIALECTIC

INTRODUCTION

THE words "dialectical" and "dialectician" are currently used more often in a derogatory than in a descriptive sense. The person who criticizes an argument by saying, "It's just a matter of definition" is also apt to say, "That may be true dialectically, but ..." or "You're just being dialectical." Implied in such remarks is dispraise of reasoning which, however excellent or skillful it may be as reasoning, stands condemned for being out of touch with fact or experience.

Still other complaints against dialectic are that it plays with words, begs the question, makes sport of contradictions. When the theologian Hippothadeus almost convinces Panurge that he "should rather choose to marry once, than to burn still in fires of concupiscence," Rabelais has Panurge raise one last doubt against the proposal. "Shall I be a cuckold, father," he asks, "yea or no?" Hippothadeus answers: "By no means ... will you be a cuckold, if it please God." On receiving this reply Panurge cries out, "O the Lord help us now; whither are we driven to, good folks? To the conditionals, which, according to the rules and precepts of the dialectic faculty, admit of all contradictions and impossibilities. If my Transalpine mule had wings, my Transalpine mule would fly. If it please God, I shall not be a cuckold, but I shall be a cuckold if it please him."

As a term of disapproval, "dialectical" has been used by scientists against philosophers, by philosophers against theologians and, with equal invective, by religious men against those who resort to argument concerning matters of faith.

The early Middle Ages witnessed a conflict between the mystical and the rational approaches to the truths of religion. Those for whom religious experience and revelation were the only avenue to God condemned the dialecticians—the philosophers or theologians who tried to use reason discursively rather than proceed by intuition and vision. With the Reformation and with the Renaissance, men like Martin Luther and Francis Bacon regarded dialectic as the bane of mediaeval learning. Because of its dialectical character, Luther dismissed all theological speculation as sophistry. Bacon, for the same reason, stigmatized scholastic philosophy as consisting in "no great quantity of matter and infinite agitation of wit."

On grounds which were common as well as opposite, both mystics and experimentalists attacked dialectic as a futile, if not vicious, use of the mind—as "hair-splitting" and "logic-chopping." Even when they admitted that it might have some virtue, they approved of it as a method of argument or proof, proper enough perhaps in forensic oratory or political debate, but entirely out of place in the pursuit of truth or in approaching reality.

A CERTAIN CONCEPTION of dialectic is implicit in all such criticisms. The dialectician is a man who argues rather than observes, who appeals to reason rather than experience, who draws implications from whatever is said or can be said, pushing a premise to its logical conclusion or reducing it to absurdity. This aspect of dialectic appears to be the object of Rabelais' satire in the famous dispute between Panurge and Thaumast, which is carried on "by signs only, without speaking, for the matters are so abstruse, hard, and arduous, that words proceeding from the mouth of man will never be sufficient for the unfolding of them."

In view of those who think that truth can be learned only by observation, by induction from particulars, or generalization from experience, the technique of dialectic, far from being a

345

method of inquiry, seems to have virtue only for the purpose of disputation or criticism. "The human faculties," writes Gibbon, "are fortified by the art and practice of dialectics." It is "the keenest weapon of dispute," he adds, but "more effectual for the detection of error than for the investigation of truth."

Mill describes "the Socratic dialectics, so magnificently exemplified in the dialogues of Plato," as a "contrivance for making the difficulties of the question ... present to the learner's consciousness ... They were essentially a negative discussion of the great questions of philosophy and life," he continues, "directed with consummate skill to the purpose of convincing anyone who has merely adopted the commonplaces of received opinion that he did not understand the subject ... The school disputations of the Middle Ages had a somewhat similar object." In Mill's opinion, "as a discipline to the mind, they were in every respect inferior to the powerful dialectics which formed the intellects of the 'Socratic viri'; but the modern mind," he says, "owes far more to both than it is generally willing to admit, and the present modes of education contain nothing which in the smallest degree supplies the place either of the one or of the other."

Disparaging comment on dialectic comes not only from those who contrast it unfavorably with the methods of experiment or empirical research. It is made also by writers who trust reason's power to grasp truths intuitively and to develop their consequences deductively. Sensitive to what may seem to be a paradox here, Descartes writes in his *Rules for the Direction of the Mind:* "It may perhaps strike some with surprise that here, where we are discussing how to improve our power of deducing one truth from another, we have omitted all the precepts of the dialecticians." The dialectician can proceed only after he has been given premises to work from. Since, in Descartes' view, dialectic provides no method for establishing premises or for discovering first principles, it can "contribute nothing at all to the discovery of the truth ... Its only possible use is to serve to explain at times more easily to others the truths we have already ascertained; hence it should be transferred from Philosophy to Rhetoric."

THE CONNECTION of dialectic with disputation and rhetoric has some foundation in the historical fact that many of the techniques of dialectic originated with the Greek sophists who had primarily a rhetorical or forensic aim. Comparable to the Roman rhetoricians and to the law teachers of a later age, the sophists taught young men how to plead a case, how to defend themselves against attack, how to persuade an audience. Skill in argument had for them a practical, not a theoretical, purpose; not truth or knowledge, but success in litigation or in political controversy. The familiar charge that the method they taught enabled men "to make the worse appear the better reason," probably exaggerates, but none the less reflects, the difference between the standards of probability in disputation and the standards of truth in scientific inquiry. This has some bearing on the disrepute of sophistry and the derogatory light cast on the *dialectical* when it is identified with the *sophistical*.

But there is another historical fact which places dialectic in a different light. In the tradition of the liberal arts, especially in their Roman and mediaeval development, "dialectic" and "logic" are interchangeable names for the discipline which, together with grammar and rhetoric, comprises the three liberal arts known as the "trivium." In his treatise *On Christian Doctrine* Augustine uses the word "dialectic" in this way. Whatever else it means, the identification of dialectic with logic implies its distinction from rhetoric, and certainly from sophistry.

Yet Augustine does not fail to observe the misuse of dialectic which debases it to the level of sophistry. "In the use of it," he declares, "we must guard against the love of wrangling, and the childish vanity of entrapping an adversary. For there are many of what are called *sophisms*," he continues, "inferences in reasoning that are false, and yet so close an imitation of the true, as to deceive not only dull people, but clever men too, when they are not on their guard." He gives as an example the case of one man saying to another, "What I am, you are not." The other man may assent to this, thinking, as Augustine points out, that "the proposition is in part true, the one man being cunning, the other simple." But when "the first speaker adds: 'I am a man' " and "the other has given his assent to this also, the first draws his conclusion: 'Then you are not a man.' "

According to Augustine, "this sort of ensnaring argument" should not be called dialectical, but sophistical. He makes the same sort of observation about the abuse of rhetoric in speech which "only aims at verbal ornamentation more than is consistent with seriousness of purpose." That, too, he thinks, should be "called sophistical" in order to avoid attaching the name of rhetoric to misapplications of the art.

Dialectic for Augustine is the art which "deals with inferences, and definitions, and divisions" and "is of the greatest assistance in the discovery of meaning." Rhetoric, on the other hand, "is not to be used so much for ascertaining the meaning as for setting forth the meaning when it is ascertained." Dialectic, in other words, is divorced from the practical purpose of stating and winning an argument, and given theoretical status as a method of inquiry.

THIS CONCEPTION of dialectic originates in the dialogues of Plato. Not himself a sophist, either by profession or in aim, Socrates found other uses for the analytical and argumentative devices invented by the sophists. The same skills of mind which were practically useful in the public assembly and in the law courts could be used or adapted for clarification and precision in speculative discussions. They could also be used to find the truth implicit in the commonly expressed convictions of men and to lay bare errors caused by lack of definition in discourse or lack of rigor in reasoning.

In the *Sophist* Plato separates the philosopher from the sophist, not by any distinction in method, but by the difference in the use each makes of the same technique. And in the *Republic*, one of the reasons Socrates gives for postponing the study of dialectic until the age of thirty is that youngsters, "when they first get the taste in their mouths, argue for amusement" and "like puppy-dogs, they rejoice in pulling and tearing at all who come near them." As a result of being vainly disputatious, they "get into the way of not believing anything which they believed before, and hence, not only they, but philosophy and all that relates

to it is apt to have a bad name with the rest of the world ... But when a man begins to get older, he will no longer be guilty of such insanity; he will imitate the dialectician who is seeking for truth, and not the sophist, who is contradicting for the sake of amusement."

In the hands of the philosopher dialectic is an instrument of science. "There is," according to Socrates, "no other method of comprehending by any regular process all true existence or of ascertaining what each thing is in its own nature." It passes beyond the arts at the lowest level, "which are concerned with the desires or opinions of men, or are cultivated with a view to production and constructions." It likewise transcends the mathematical sciences, which, while they "have some apprehension of true being ... leave the hypotheses which they use unexamined, and are unable to give an account of them." Using these as "handmaids and helpers," dialectic "goes directly to the first principle and is the only science which does away with hypotheses in order to make her ground secure."

The dialectic of Plato has an upward and a downward path which somewhat resemble the inductive process of the mind from facts to principles, and the deductive process from principles to the conclusions they validate. Dialectic, says Socrates, ascends by using hypotheses "as steps and points of departure into a world which is above hypotheses, in order that she may soar beyond them to the first principle of the whole ... By successive steps she descends again without the aid of any sensible object, from ideas, through ideas, and in ideas she ends."

As the disciplined search for truth, dialectic includes all of logic. It is concerned with every phase of thought: with the establishment of definitions; the examination of hypotheses in the light of their presuppositions or consequences; the formulation of inferences and proofs; the resolution of dilemmas arising from opposition in thought.

WHEREAS FOR PLATO dialectic is more than the whole of logic, for Aristotle it is less. Dialectic is more than the process by which the mind goes from myth and fantasy, perception and opinion, to the highest truth. For Plato it is the ultimate fruit of intellectual labor—knowledge itself, and in its supreme form as a vision of being and unity. That is why Socrates makes it the ultimate study in the curriculum proposed for training the guardians to become philosopher kings. "Dialectic," he says, "is the copingstone of the sciences, and is set over them; no other science can be placed higher—the nature of knowledge can go no further."

For Aristotle, dialectic, far from being at the summit of science and philosophy, lies at their base, and must be carefully distinguished from sophistry, which it resembles in method. "Dialecticians and sophists assume the same guise as the philosopher," Aristotle writes, "for sophistic is wisdom which exists only in semblance, and dialecticians embrace all things in their dialectic, and being is common to all things; but evidently their dialectic embraces these subjects because these are proper to philosophy. Sophistic and dialectic," he continues, "turn on the same class of things as philosophy, but philosophy differs from dialectic in the nature of the faculty required and from sophistic in respect of the purpose of the philosophic life. Dialectic is merely critical where philosophy claims to know, and sophistic is what appears to be philosophy but is not."

ACCORDING TO ARISTOTLE, dialectic is neither itself a science nor the method of science. It is that part of logic or method which he treats in the *Topics*, and it differs from the scientific method expounded in the *Posterior Analytics* as argument in the sphere of opinion and probabilities differs from scientific demonstration. Unlike the conclusions of science, the conclusions of dialectical reasoning are only probable, because they are based on assumptions rather than self-evident truths. Since other and opposite assumptions cannot be excluded, one dialectical conclusion is usually opposed by another in an issue of competing probabilities.

Intermediate between science and rhetoric, dialectic can serve both. In addition to its practical employment in forensics, it is useful in the philosophical sciences because it develops skill in making and criticizing definitions, and in asking or answering questions. "The ability to raise searching difficulties on both sides of a subject," Aristotle says, "will make us detect

more easily the truth and error about the several points that arise."

Though it is primarily a method of arguing from assumptions and of dealing with disputes arising from contrary assumptions, dialectic is also concerned with the starting points of argument. The *Topics* considers how assumptions are chosen, what makes them acceptable, what determines their probability. Here again Aristotle shows how the philosopher can make use of dialectic—as that "process of criticism wherein lies the path to the principles of all inquiries."

THERE ARE FOUR major expositions of dialectic in the tradition of the great books. It is as pivotal a conception in the thought of Kant and Hegel as it is in the philosophies of Plato and Aristotle. With differences which may be more important than the similarities, the Kantian treatment resembles the Aristotelian, the Hegelian the Platonic.

Like the division between the *Posterior Analytics* and the *Topics* in Aristotle's *Organon*, the transcendental logic of Kant's *Critique of Pure Reason* falls into two parts—the analytic and the dialectic. The distinction between his transcendental logic and what Kant calls "general logic" is discussed in the chapter on LOGIC, but here it must be observed that for Kant "general logic, considered as an organon, must always be a logic of illusion, that is, be dialectical." He thinks that the ancients used the word "dialectic" in this sense, to signify "a sophistical art for giving ignorance, nay, even intentional sophistries, the coloring of truth, in which the thoroughness of procedure which logic requires was imitated." For his own purposes, however, he wishes "dialectic" to be understood "in the sense of a critique of dialectical illusion."

When he comes to his own transcendental logic, therefore, he divides it into two parts. The first part deals with "the elements of pure cognition of the understanding, and the principles without which no object at all can be thought." This is the "Transcendental Analytic, and at the same time a logic of truth"— a logic of science. Since in his view "it ought properly to be only a canon for judging of the empirical use of the understanding, this kind of logic is misused when we seek to employ it as an organon of the universal and unlimited exercise of the understanding."

When it is thus misused, "the exercise of the pure understanding becomes dialectical. The second part of our transcendental logic," Kant writes, "must therefore be a critique of dialectical illusion, and this critique we shall term Transcendental Dialectic—not meaning it as an art of producing dogmatically such illusion (an art which is unfortunately too current among the practitioners of metaphysical juggling), but as a critique of understanding and reason in regard to their hyperphysical use."

Kant goes further than Aristotle in separating dialectic from science. With regard to the sensible or phenomenal world of experience, science is possible; with regard to the mind's own structure, the supreme sort of science is possible. But when reason tries to use its ideas for other objects, and then regards them "as conceptions of actual things, their mode of application is *transcendent* and delusive." Kant explains that "an idea is employed transcendentally, when it is applied to an object falsely believed . . . to correspond to it; immanently, when it is applied solely to the employment of the *understanding* in the sphere of experience"; and he maintains that when ideas are used transcendentally, they do not give rise to science, but "assume a fallacious and dialectical character."

A conclusion of dialectical reasoning, according to Kant, is either opposed by a conclusion equally acceptable to reason—"a perfectly natural antithetic"—as in the antinomies of pure reason; or, as in the paralogisms, the reasoning has specious cogency which can be shown to "conclude falsely, while the form is correct and unexceptionable." In this balance of reason against itself lies the illusory character of the transcendental dialectic.

Where Aristotle recognizes that reason can be employed on both sides of a question because it involves competing probabilities, Kant in calling dialectic "a logic of appearance" explicitly remarks that "this does not signify a doctrine of probability." He further distinguishes what he calls "transcendental illusory appearance" from "empirical illusory appearance" and ordinary "logical illusion." The latter two can be corrected and totally removed.

But "transcendental illusion, on the contrary," he writes, "does not cease to exist even after it has been exposed and its nothingness has been clearly perceived by means of transcendental criticism."

The reason for this, Kant explains, is that "here we have to do with a *natural* and unavoidable illusion, which rests upon subjective principles, and imposes these upon us as objective. . . . There is, therefore," he continues, "a natural and unavoidable dialectic of pure reason" which arises because the mind seeks to answer questions "well nigh impossible to answer," such as "how objects exist as things in themselves" or "how the nature of things is to be subordinated to principles." In its effort to transcend experience—"in disregard of all the warnings of criticism"—the mind cannot escape the frustration, the dialectical illusion, "which is an inseparable adjunct of human reason." It is not, Kant repeatedly insists, that "the ideas of pure reason" are "in their own nature dialectical; it is from their misemployment alone that fallacies and illusions arise."

FOR HEGEL AS for Plato dialectic moves in the realm of truth and ideas, not probabilities and illusions. But for Hegel dialectic is always the process of mind, or of the Idea, in interminable motion toward absolute truth—never resting in the intuition of that truth. The Idea, he writes, "is self-determined, it assumes successive forms which it successively transcends; and by this very process of transcending its earlier stages, gains an affirmative, and, in fact, a richer and more concrete shape."

The dialectical process is a motion in which contrary and defective truths are harmonized. The synthesis of *thesis and antithesis* results in a more complete truth. To illustrate his meaning, Hegel uses the example of building a house. For such a purpose, we must have "in the first instance, a subjective aim and design" and as means, "the several substances required for the work—iron, wood, stones." In rendering these materials suitable for our purpose, we make use of the elements: "fire to melt the iron, wind to blow the fire, water to set the wheels in motion, in order to cut the wood, etc."

Yet the house that we build is, according to

Hegel, an opposite or antithesis of these elements. "The wind, which has helped to build the house, is shut out by the house; so also are the violence of rains and floods, and the destructive powers of fire, so far as the house is made fire-proof. The stones and beams obey the law of gravity—press downward—and so high walls are carried up." The result is that "the elements are made use of in accordance with their nature, and yet to cooperate for a product, by which their operation is limited." The initial opposition between the idea of a house and the elements is reconciled in the higher synthesis, which is the house itself.

While it shows the opposing theses and the resulting synthesis, this example does not fully exhibit the dynamic character of the Hegelian dialectic. If the resulting synthesis is not the whole truth, it too must be defective and require supplementation by a contrary which is defective in an opposite way. These two together then become the material for a higher synthesis, another step in that continuing dialectical process which is the life of mind—both the subjective dialectic of the human mind and the objective dialectic of the Absolute Mind or the Idea.

THE THREAD OF common meaning which runs through these four conceptions of dialectic is to be found in the principle of opposition. In each of them dialectic either begins or ends with some sort of intellectual conflict, or develops and then resolves such oppositions.

For Kant dialectical opposition takes the extreme form of irreducible contradictions from which the mind cannot escape. "It is a melancholy reflection," he declares, "that reason in its highest exercise, falls into an antithetic." This comes about because "all statements enunciated by pure reason transcend the conditions of possible experience, beyond the sphere of which we can discover no criterion of truth, while they are at the same time framed in accordance with the laws of the understanding, which are applicable only to experience; and thus it is the fate of all such speculative discussions, that while the one party attacks the weaker side of his opponent, he infallibly lays open his own weaknesses."

For Hegel the opposition takes the milder form of contrary theses and antitheses. They can be dialectically overcome by a synthesis which remedies the incompleteness of each half truth. "It is one of the most important discoveries of logic," Hegel says, "that a specific moment which, by standing in an opposition, has the position of an extreme, ceases to be such and is a moment in an organic whole by being at the same time a mean." The Hegelian opposition is thus also "mediation."

Dialectical opposition for Aristotle originates in the disagreements which occur in ordinary human discourse. But just as disagreement is reasonable only if there are two sides to the question in dispute, so reason can operate dialectically only with regard to genuinely arguable matters. The familiar topics concerning which men disagree represent the commonplace issues of dialectic, since for the most part they are formed from debatable propositions or questions. "Nobody in his senses," Aristotle believes, "would make a proposition of what no one holds; nor would he make a problem of what is obvious to everybody or to most people." Each of the conflicting opinions will therefore have some claim to probability. Here the dialectical process ends neither in a synthesis of incomplete opposites nor in a rejection of both as illusory; but, having "an eye to general opinion," it seeks to ascertain the more reasonable view—the more tenable or probable of the two.

In the Platonic theory of dialectic, the element of opposition appears in the tension between being and becoming, the one and many, or the intelligible and the sensible, which is found present in every stage of the mind's dialectical ascent to the contemplation of ideas. So fundamental is this tension that Socrates uses it to define the dialectician as one who is "able to see 'a One and Many' in Nature"—by comprehending "scattered particulars in one idea" and dividing it "into species according to their natural formation." Here as in the Hegelian theory the oppositions—*apparent* contradictions in discourse—can be resolved by dialectic, and through their resolution the mind then rises to a higher level.

IT IS ONLY IN the writings of Hegel or his followers that the meaning of dialectic is not limited to the activity of human thought. Hegel expressly warns that "the loftier dialectic ... is not an activity of subjective thinking applied to some matter externally, but is rather the matter's very soul putting forth its branches and fruit organically." It is the "development of the Idea," which is "the proper activity of its rationality." If the whole world in its existence and development is the thought and thinking of an Absolute Mind, or the Idea, then the events of nature and of history are moments in a dialectical process of cosmic proportions. The principles of dialectic become the principles of change, and change itself is conceived as a progress or evolution from lower to higher, from part to whole, from the indeterminate to the determinate.

The dialectical pattern of history, conceived by Hegel as the progressive objectification of spirit, is reconstructed by Karl Marx in terms of the conflict of material forces. Marx himself explicitly contrasts his dialectic with that of Hegel. "My dialectic method," he writes, "is not only different from the Hegelian, but is its direct opposite." Hegel, he claims, thinks that "the real world is only the external, phenomenal form of 'the Idea,'" whereas his own view is that "the ideal is nothing else than the material world reflected by the human mind, and translated into forms of thought."

Nevertheless, with respect to dialectic, Marx praises Hegel for being "the first to present its general form of working in a comprehensive and conscious manner." The only trouble is that with Hegel, dialectic "is standing on its head." It must therefore "be turned right side up again," a revolution which Marx thinks he accomplishes in his dialectical materialism.

Having put dialectic on its proper basis, Marx constructs the whole of history in terms of a conflict of material forces, or of social classes in economic strife, according to a dialectical pattern which provides "recognition of the existing state of things, at the same time also the recognition of the negation of that state, of its inevitable breaking up." History is thus viewed dialectically "as in fluid movement," yet it is also conceived as working towards a definite end—the revolution which has as its result the peace of the classless society. Bourgeois industry, by bringing about the concentration and association of the proletariat, produces "its own grave diggers; its fall and the victory of the proletariat" are "equally inevitable."

In Marx's vocabulary the phrases "historical materialism" and "dialectical materialism" are strictly synonymous. But Marx's protest to the contrary notwithstanding, a comparison of Marx and Hegel seems to show that a dialectic of history is equally capable of being conceived in terms of spirit or of matter.

The question whether there is a dialectic of nature as well as a dialectic of history remains a point of controversy in Marxist thought, despite the bearing which Hegel's *Science of Logic* and *Phenomenology of Mind* might have upon the question. Engels tries in his *Dialectics of Nature* to give a fuller rendering of the Hegelian dialectic in strictly materialistic terms. Its universal scope, including all of nature as well as all of history, is also reflected in certain post-Darwinian doctrines of cosmic evolution.

CONSIDERATIONS RELEVANT to the Hegelian or Marxist dialectic will be found in the chapters on HISTORY and PROGRESS. Without judging the issues which Hegel and Marx have raised in the thought of the last century, it may be permissible to report the almost violent intellectual aversion they have produced in certain quarters. Freud, for example, is as unsympathetic in his criticism of Marx and as uncompromising in his rejection of dialectical materialism, as James before him is extreme in the expression of his distaste for Hegel. Mocking "the Hegelizers" who think that "the glory and beauty of the psychic life is that in it all contradictions find their reconciliation," James declares: "With this intellectual temper I confess I cannot contend."

The Hegelian dialectic and what James calls "the pantomime-state of mind" are, in his opinion, "emotionally considered, one and the same thing. In the pantomime all common things are represented to happen in impossible ways, people jump down each other's throats, houses turn inside out, old women become young men, everything 'passes into its opposite' with inconceivable celerity and skill. . . . And so in the Hegelian logic," James continues, "relations elsewhere recognized under the insipid name of distinctions (such as that between knower and object, many and one) must first be translated into impossibilities and contradictions, then 'transcended' and identified by miracle, ere the proper temper is induced for thoroughly enjoying the spectacle they show."

OUTLINE OF TOPICS

REFERENCES

To find the passages cited, use the numbers in heavy type, which are the volume and page numbers of the passages referred to. For example, in **4** HOMER: *Iliad*, BK II [265–283] **12d**, the number **4** is the number of the volume in the set; the number **12d** indicates that the passage is in section d of page 12.

PAGE SECTIONS: When the text is printed in one column, the letters a and b refer to the upper and lower halves of the page. For example, in **53** JAMES: *Psychology*, 116a-119b, the passage begins in the upper half of page 116 and ends in the lower half of page 119. When the text is printed in two columns, the letters a and b refer to the upper and lower halves of the left-hand side of the page, the letters c and d to the upper and lower halves of the right-hand side of the page. For example, in **7** PLATO: *Symposium*, 163b-164c, the passage begins in the lower half of the left-hand side of page 163 and ends in the upper half of the right-hand side of page 164.

AUTHOR'S DIVISIONS: One or more of the main divisions of a work (such as PART, BK, CH, SECT) are sometimes included in the reference; line numbers, in brackets, are given in certain cases; *e.g.*, *Iliad*, BK II [265-283] **12d**.

BIBLE REFERENCES: The references are to book, chapter, and verse. When the King James and Douay versions differ in title of books or in the numbering of chapters or verses, the King James version is cited first and the Douay, indicated by a (*D*), follows; *e.g.*, OLD TESTAMENT: *Nehemiah*, 7:45—(*D*) II *Esdras*, 7:46.

SYMBOLS: The abbreviation "esp" calls the reader's attention to one or more especially relevant parts of a whole reference; "passim" signifies that the topic is discussed intermittently rather than continuously in the work or passage cited.

For additional information concerning the style of the references, see the Explanation of Reference Style; for general guidance in the use of *The Great Ideas*, consult the Preface.

1. Definitions of dialectic

7 PLATO: *Cratylus*, 88d-89a / *Phaedrus*, 139d-140a / *Republic*, BK VI, 387c-d; BK VII, 396d-398c / *Parmenides*, 491a-c / *Sophist*, 557a-b; 571a-c / *Philebus*, 611d-612b; 634b-c / *Seventh Letter*, 809c-810c

8 ARISTOTLE: *Prior Analytics*, BK I, CH I [24^a 21–^{b}15] 39a-c / *Posterior Analytics*, BK I, CH II [77^{a}25–35] 106b / *Topics*, BK I, CH I [100^{a}18–^{b}31] 143a-c; CH 2 [101^{b}3–4] 144a / *Sophistical Refutations*, CH 2 [165^{b}3–4] 228a; CH II [171^b 3–8] 236a-b; [172^{a}15–^{b}4] 237a-c / *Generation and Corruption*, BK I, CH 2 [316^{a}5–14] 411c-d / *Metaphysics*, BK IV, CH 2 [1004^{b}15–27] 523d; BK XI, CH 3 [1061^{a}29–^{b}10] 589c-d / *Soul*, BK I, CH I [403^{a}29–^{b}8] 632c-d

9 ARISTOTLE: *Rhetoric*, BK I, CH I [1354^{a}1–5] 593a; [1355^{a}7–10] 594b; CH 2 [1356^{a}31–33] 595d-596a

17 PLOTINUS: *First Ennead*, TR III, CH 4–6 11a-12b

20 AQUINAS: *Summa Theologica*, PART I–II, Q 57, A 6, REP 3 40a-41a

31 DESCARTES: *Rules*, X, 16d-17a

42 KANT: *Pure Reason*, 36d-37d; 59c-d; 108a-111c esp 108a-d; 227a-235a esp 229b-c, 231c-232a / *Practical Reason*, 337a-c / *Judgement*, 562a-564c esp 562d

43 MILL: *Liberty*, 287d-288a

46 HEGEL: *Philosophy of Right*, INTRO, par 31 19c-20a / *Philosophy of History*, INTRO, 179b-c; 182d

2. Diverse theories of dialectic

2a. Dialectic as the pursuit of truth and the contemplation of being

7 PLATO: *Protagoras*, 57a-c / *Phaedrus*, 139b-140b / *Phaedo*, 242b-c / *Republic*, BK VI, 383d-388a; BK VII, 396d-398c / *Parmenides*, 491a-d / *Sophist*, 556c-557b; 571a-c / *Statesman*, 585c / *Philebus*, 611d-612b; 634b-635a / *Seventh Letter*, 809c-810d

17 PLOTINUS: *First Ennead*, TR III 10a-12b esp CH 4–6 11a-12b

42 KANT: *Practical Reason*, 337a-338c / *Judgement*, 551a-552c

43 MILL: *Liberty*, 287c-288c

2a(1) The ascent from appearance to reality, or from opinion to knowledge: the upward and downward paths of dialectic

7 PLATO: *Republic*, BK VI, 385b-388a; BK VII, 391b-401d / *Sophist* 551a-579d esp 552b-c, 561d-579d / *Statesman* 580a-608d esp 585d, 586c, 589c-d, 591a-c, 594d-596a, 599a-c, 608d / *Seventh Letter*, 810a-d

(2a. Dialectic as the pursuit of truth and the con-
templation of being. 2a(1) The ascent
from appearance to reality, or from opinion
to knowledge: the upward and downward
paths of dialectic.)

17 PLOTINUS: *First Ennead*, TR III, CH 4–6 11a-12b
42 KANT: *Pure Reason*, 113b-115c; 173b-174a /
Judgement, 551a-552c
43 MILL: *Liberty*, 288a

**2a(2) Definition, division, hypothesis, and
myth in the service of dialectic**

7 PLATO: *Charmides*, 4a-13d esp 4b, 5a-b, 6d,
7c, 10a / *Laches*, 31c-37d / *Protagoras*, 43d-
45a; 49a / *Phaedrus*, 124b-129d; 134a-c; 139d-
140b / *Meno* 174a-190a,c esp 175d, 179d-180b,
183b-c / *Euthyphro*, 192c-199a,c esp 193a,
193d, 195b / *Phaedo*, 242b-243c / *Republic*,
BK I–II, 297b-316b; BK IV, 346a-356a; BK
VI–VII, 386d-398c / *Timaeus*, 462b-c / *Parmenides* 486a-511d esp 491a-d / *Sophist* 551a-579d
esp 552b-c, 553d-554a, 561b, 570c-571d /
Statesman 580a-608d esp 580d, 582d-583c,
586c-589c, 591a-d, 594d-596a / *Philebus*
609a-639a,c esp 610d-613a, 615c-617d /
Seventh Letter, 809c-810d
8 ARISTOTLE: *Generation and Corruption*, BK I,
CH 2 [316ᵃ5–14] 411c-d / *Metaphysics*, BK I, CH
6 [987ᵃ29–ᵇ7] 505b-c; [987ᵇ30–33] 506a; BK
XIII, CH 4 [1078ᵇ18–32] 610b-c / *Soul*, BK I,
CH 1 [403ᵃ29–ᵇ8] 632c-d
9 ARISTOTLE: *Parts of Animals*, BK I, CH 2–3
165d-167d
12 EPICTETUS: *Discourses*, BK I, CH 7 112b-113d
17 PLOTINUS: *First Ennead*, TR III, CH 4 11a-c

**2b. Dialectic as the method of inquiry, argu-
ment, and criticism in the sphere of
opinion**

8 ARISTOTLE: *Prior Analytics*, BK I, CH 1 [24ᵃ
21–ᵇ15] 39a-c / *Posterior Analytics*, BK I, CH
11 [77ᵃ25–35] 106b; CH 19 [81ᵇ17–22] 111c-d /
Topics 143a-223a,c / *Sophistical Refutations*
227a-253d esp CH 1–2 227a-228a, CH 9–11
234b-237c, CH 34 252c-253d / *Generation and
Corruption*, BK I, CH 2 [316ᵃ5–14] 411c-d /
Metaphysics, BK IV, CH 2 [1004ᵇ15–27] 523d
9 ARISTOTLE: *Rhetoric*, BK I, CH 1–2 593a-598b;
CH 4 [1359ᵃ30–ᵇ19] 599c-d
20 AQUINAS: *Summa Theologica*, PART I–II, Q 57,
A 6, REP 3 40a-41a; PART III, Q 9, A 3, REP 2
765b-766b
30 BACON: *Advancement of Learning*, 60a-c; 65a-c
31 DESCARTES: *Rules*, II, 2c-3a; IV, 5b-c; X,
16d-17a; XIII, 25b
41 GIBBON: *Decline and Fall*, 299b
42 KANT: *Pure Reason*, 36d-37d; 109b-c / *Judgement*, 600d-603d
43 MILL: *Liberty*, 287c-288c
46 HEGEL: *Philosophy of Right*, INTRO, par 31
19c-20a; PART II, par 140, 53a-b / *Philosophy
of History*, PART IV, 360c-d

**2b(1) Divisions of dialectic: the theory of the
predicables**

8 ARISTOTLE: *Topics*, BK I–VII 143a-211a,c esp
BK I, CH 2 143d-144a, CH 4–6 144b-146a, CH
12 148d / *Sophistical Refutations*, CH 11 [171ᵇ
3–8] 236a-b; [172ᵃ22–ᵇ4] 237b-c
9 ARISTOTLE: *Rhetoric*, BK I, CH 2 [1356ᵃ36–
1358ᵃ33] 596a-598b
20 AQUINAS: *Summa Theologica*, PART I–II, Q 57,
A 6, REP 3 40a-41a

2b(2) The technique of question and answer

7 PLATO: *Protagoras*, 50d-51b / *Euthydemus*,
78a-d / *Cratylus*, 88d-89a / *Republic*, BK VI,
375b-c / *Sophist*, 551d
8 ARISTOTLE: *Prior Analytics*, BK I, CH 1 [24ᵃ
21–ᵇ15] 39a-c / *Posterior Analytics*, BK I, CH
11 [77ᵃ25–35] 106b; BK II, CH 5 [91ᵇ11–17]
125b / *Topics*, BK VIII 211a-223a,c / *Sophistical Refutations*, CH 10 [171ᵃ27]–CH 11 [171ᵇ6]
235d-236a; CH 11 [172ᵃ15–21] 237a
12 EPICTETUS: *Discourses*, BK III, CH 2, 178a-b
30 BACON: *Advancement of Learning*, 65a
42 KANT: *Pure Reason*, 36a-b
46 HEGEL: *Philosophy of Right*, PART II, par 140,
53a-b

**2c. Dialectic as the logic of semblance and as
the critique of the illusory employment
of reason beyond experience**

42 KANT: *Pure Reason*, 1a-4a,c esp 1a-b; 7a-8b;
15c-16c; 20a; 36d-37b; 53b-54b; 59c-d; 93c-
99a; 101b-107b; 108a-209d esp 108a-112d,
120c-121c, 129c-130b, 133d, 157d, 173b-174a,
175c-d, 185b-c, 190a-209d; 217d-218a; 219a-
223d; 227a-235a esp 229b-c, 231c-232a /
Fund. Prin. Metaphysic of Morals, 260d-261c;
283d-284d / *Practical Reason*, 291a-292a;
296a-d; 309b; 310d-311d; 313b-314d; 320c-
321b; 335c-337a,c / *Judgement*, 461a-c; 540a-
542a; 543c-544c; 551a-552c; 562a-564c; 570b-
572b; 606d-607c

**2c(1) The division of logic into analytic and
dialectic: the distinction between general and transcendental dialectic**

42 KANT: *Pure Reason*, 34a-37d esp 36a-37d;
108a-111c

2c(2) The natural dialectic of human reason

42 KANT: *Pure Reason*, 1a-3b; 7a-8b; 20a; 120c-
121c; 133d; 192c-193b; 217d-218a; 227a-235a
esp 229b-c / *Practical Reason*, 335c-337d;
352b-c / *Judgement*, 570b-572b

2d. Dialectic as the evolution of spirit or matter

46 HEGEL: *Philosophy of Right*, INTRO, par 32–33
20a-d; PART III, par 342–344 110c-111a; par
353–360 112b-114a,c / *Philosophy of History*,
INTRO, 153a-206a,c esp 178a-179c, 182d-183a,
203a-206a,c; PART I, 208b-d; 236a-c; 257a-c;
PART II, 278a-c; PART IV, 315a

50 MARX: *Capital*, 10a-11d esp 11b-d
54 FREUD: *New Introductory Lectures*, 882c

2d(1) The distinction between subjective and objective dialectic: the realization of the moral will

46 HEGEL: *Philosophy of Right*, INTRO, par 26 18b-c; par 31 19c-20a; PART II, par 105-114 40a-42b esp par 109 41a-b; par 140 49b-54a; ADDITIONS, 67-72 126d-127c / *Philosophy of History*, PART IV, 360c-361a

2d(2) The dialectic of nature and of history: the actualization of freedom

46 HEGEL: *Philosophy of Right*, INTRO, par 4 12d-13a; PART III, par 194 66c-d; par 340-344 110b-111a; par 353-360 112b-114a,c / *Philosophy of History* 153a-369a,c esp INTRO, 156c-190b, 203d-206a,c, PART IV, 368d-369a,c

3. Types of dialectical opposition

3a. The opposition between being and becoming, the one and the many, the same and the other

7 PLATO: *Phaedrus*, 126a-c; 134b-c / *Symposium*, 167a-d / *Republic*, BK III, 333b-d; BK V, 370d-373c; BK VI-VII, 383d-398c / *Parmenides* 486a-511d / *Sophist*, 564d-574c / *Statesman*, 594d-595a / *Philebus*, 610d-613a; 615c-617d; 633a-635a esp 634b-635a / *Seventh Letter*, 809c-810d
8 ARISTOTLE: *Metaphysics*, BK I, CH 6 505b-506b; BK III, CH 1 [995^{b}20–25] 514a-b; BK IV, CH 2 522b-524b esp [1004^{b}15–26] 523d
11 NICOMACHUS: *Arithmetic*, BK II, 839d-840b
17 PLOTINUS: *First Ennead*, TR III, CH 4 11a-c / *Second Ennead*, TR IV, CH 5 51b-d / *Third Ennead*, TR III, CH 1 93b-c; TR VII 119b-129a; TR IX 136a-138a,c / *Fourth Ennead*, TR II, CH 1 139c-140c / *Fifth Ennead*, TR I, CH 4-7 209d-212c; TR II 214c-215c; TR VI 235b-237d / *Sixth Ennead*, TR VI, CH 1-3 310d-312b; TR IX, CH 1-2 353d-355a
53 JAMES: *Psychology*, 107a-b

3b. The opposed premises of dialectical argument: dialectical problems and theses; the conflict of probabilities

8 ARISTOTLE: *Prior Analytics*, BK I, CH 1 [24^a 21–^{b}15] 39a-c / *Posterior Analytics*, BK I, CH 11 [77^{a}25–35] 106b / *Topics*, BK I, CH 11 148a-c; BK VIII, CH 2 [157^{a}34–^{b}33] 213d-214b / *Sophistical Refutations*, CH 2 [165^{b}3–4] 228a / *Heavens*, BK I, CH 10 [279^{b}4-12] 370d
12 EPICTETUS: *Discourses*, BK II, CH 11, 150d-151a
19 AQUINAS: *Summa Theologica*, PART I, Q 83, A 1, ANS 436d-438a
30 BACON: *Advancement of Learning*, 47d-48d
31 DESCARTES: *Discourse*, PART I, 43d
35 LOCKE: *Human Understanding*, BK IV, CH XVI, SECT 9 369b-c

35 HUME: *Human Understanding*, SECT X, DIV 86-91 488d-491c
42 KANT: *Pure Reason*, 108a-d

3c. The opposed conclusions of dialectical reasoning: the antinomies and paralogisms of a transcendental dialectic

9 ARISTOTLE: *Rhetoric*, BK I, CH 1 [1355^{a}28-40] 594c-d
42 KANT: *Pure Reason*, 1a-4a,c; 7a-8b; 120c-173a esp 129c-130b, 133c; 174b-177b; 187a-192d; 200c-209d; 219a-220b; 229b-c / *Fund. Prin. Metaphysic of Morals*, 260d-261b; 283d-284d / *Practical Reason*, 291a-292a; 302a-d; 331c-337a,c; 340a-342d; 348d-349a / *Science of Right*, 407a-408b / *Judgement*, 540a-546d esp 543c-544c; 562a-578a esp 562d-564c, 575b-578a; 584c-d
46 HEGEL: *Philosophy of Right*, PART II, par 135 47b-d

3d. Thesis and antithesis as moments in the advance toward a dialectical synthesis

42 KANT: *Pure Reason*, 7a-8b; 43d-44a; 133c
46 HEGEL: *Philosophy of Right*, INTRO, par 17 16c; par 26 18b-c; par 31-33 19c-20d; PART I, par 104 39b-d; PART II, par 105-114 40a-42b esp par 109 41a-b; PART III, par 256 79d-80a; par 302 101a-c; par 353-360 112b-114a,c / *Philosophy of History* 153a-369a,c esp INTRO, 153a-190b, 203a-206a,c, PART I, 208b-d, 235d-236c, 238b, 245b-d, 257a-c, PART II, 279c-d, PART III, 286c-287a, 303c-311d, PART IV, 316a-b, 321d-322c, 326d-327a, 333d-334d
53 JAMES: *Psychology*, 117b; 238b [fn 2]

4. Dialectic in relation to philosophy and science

7 PLATO: *Republic*, BK VI-VII, 383d-398c esp BK VI, 386d-388a, BK VII, 396d-398c / *Parmenides*, 490d-491a / *Sophist*, 570a-574c esp 571a-c / *Philebus*, 610d-613a; 633a-635a esp 634b-635a / *Seventh Letter*, 809c-810d
8 ARISTOTLE: *Prior Analytics*, BK I, CH 1 [24^a 21-^{b}15] 39a-c / *Posterior Analytics*, BK I, CH 6 [74^{b}18-25] 102c; [75^{a}18-28] 103a-b; CH 11 [77^{a}22-35] 106b; CH 19 [81^{b}17-24] 111c-d; BK II, CH 5 [91^{b}11-17] 125b / *Topics*, BK I, CH 1-2 143a-144a; CH 10-11 147b-148c; CH 14 [105^{b}30-31] 149c; BK VIII, CH 3 [159^{a}2-14] 215c-d / *Sophistical Refutations*, CH 9-11 234b-237c / *Heavens*, BK I, CH 10 [279^{b}4-12] 370d / *Generation and Corruption*, BK I, CH 2 [316^a 5-14] 411c-d / *Metaphysics*, BK I, CH 1 [980^a 20]-BK II, CH 1 [993^{b}18] 499a-512a esp BK I, CH 3 [983^{a}24-^{b}7] 501c-d, CH 7 506b-d, BK I, CH 10 [993^{a}11]-BK II, CH 1 [993^{b}18] 511c-512a; BK III 513b,d-522a,c esp CH 1 [995^{a}23-^{b}4] 513b,d; BK IV, CH 2 [1004^{b}15-27] 523d; BK XI, CH 3 [1061^{a}29-^{b}12] 589c-d; BK XIII, CH 4 [1078^{b}18-32] 610b-c / *Soul*, BK I, CH 1 [403^a 25-^{b}19] 632b-d

(4. Dialectic in relation to philosophy and science.)

9 ARISTOTLE: *Rhetoric*, BK I, CH 2 [1358ª3–33] 597d-598b; CH 4 [1359ᵇ12–18] 599d

17 PLOTINUS: *First Ennead*, TR III 10a-12b

18 AUGUSTINE: *City of God*, BK VIII, CH 3–4, 266b-267b

20 AQUINAS: *Summa Theologica*, PART I–II, Q 57, A 6, REP 3 40a-41a; PART III, Q 9, A 3, REP 2 765b-766b

31 DESCARTES: *Rules*, II, 2c-3a; IV, 5b-c; X 15d-17a; XIII, 25b-26a

42 KANT: *Pure Reason*, 37a-b / *Fund. Prin. Metaphysic of Morals*, 261c-d / *Judgement*, 551a-552c

43 MILL: *Liberty*, 287c-288c

46 HEGEL: *Philosophy of Right*, INTRO, par 31 19c-20a

54 FREUD: *General Introduction*, 545d-546a

5. The spheres of dialectic and rhetoric: proof and persuasion

7 PLATO: *Protagoras*, 39d-42c / *Euthydemus*, 83a-b / *Phaedrus*, 131b-141a,c / *Apology*, 200a-201b; 203a-205c / *Gorgias* 252a-294d esp 253b-256c, 258b-259a, 265a-267c, 280d-285a / *Statesman*, 595a-d / *Philebus*, 610d-613a; 634b-635a

9 ARISTOTLE: *Rhetoric*, BK I, CH 1–2 593a-598b; CH 4 [1359ª30–ᵇ19] 599c-d

18 AUGUSTINE: *Christian Doctrine*, BK II, CH 37 653d-654b

19 AQUINAS: *Summa Theologica*, PART I, Q 83, A 1, ANS 436d-438a

25 MONTAIGNE: *Essays*, 446d-450a; 453c-455a

30 BACON: *Advancement of Learning*, 60a-c; 66c-67c

31 DESCARTES: *Rules*, X, 16d-17a

6. The evaluation of dialectic: the line between dialectic and sophistry

5 ARISTOPHANES: *Clouds* 488a-506d esp [889–1104] 499b-502a

7 PLATO: *Protagoras*, 52a-b / *Euthydemus* 65a-84a,c esp 72b-73c / *Meno*, 176d-177a / *Phaedo*, 243b-c / *Republic*, BK VII, 388a-398c esp 396d-398c / *Theaetetus*, 522a-523a; 525d-526b / *Sophist* 551a-579d esp 559c-562a, 577c-579d / *Philebus*, 611d-612b; 633a-635a esp 634b-635a

8 ARISTOTLE: *Topics*, BK I, CH 1–2 143a-144a; CH 18 [108ª17–37] 152b-d; BK VI, CH 2 [139ᵇ 32–140ª2] 192d-193a / *Sophistical Refutations*, CH 2 227d-228a; CH 8–11 233c-237c / *Generation and Corruption*, BK I, CH 2 [316ª5–14] 411c-d / *Metaphysics*, BK IV, CH 2 [1004ᵇ15–27] 523d; BK XI, CH 3 [1061ª29–ᵇ12] 589c-d / *Soul*, BK I, CH 1 [402ᵇ15–403ª2] 631d-632a

9 ARISTOTLE: *Rhetoric*, BK I, CH 1 [1355ᵇ14–22] 595a

12 EPICTETUS: *Discourses*, BK I, CH 8 113d-114c; BK III, CH 2 177c-178d; CH 21 193d-195a; CH 24, 207d-208a

17 PLOTINUS: *First Ennead*, TR III, CH 4–6 11a-12b

18 AUGUSTINE: *Christian Doctrine*, BK II, CH 31 651d-652b; CH 37 653d-654b

24 RABELAIS: *Gargantua and Pantagruel*, BK II, 101b-106a; BK III, 187b-c; 197b-200d

25 MONTAIGNE: *Essays*, 75a-77a; 260a-261a; 446d-450a

30 BACON: *Advancement of Learning*, 60a-c / 66c-67c / *Novum Organum*, BK I, APH 62–63 113b-114a; APH 65 114b-c

31 DESCARTES: *Rules*, II, 2c-3a; IV, 5b-c; X, 16d-17a; XIV, 28b-c / *Discourse*, PART VI, 63d

36 STERNE: *Tristram Shandy*, 227a-228a; 234b-236b; 329b-336a; 421b-422b

41 GIBBON: *Decline and Fall*, 299b

42 KANT: *Pure Reason*, 36a-b; 36d-37d; 109b-c; 120c-121c; 133d; 157d; 187c-188b; 221c-222b / *Judgement*, 600d-601c; 607d-608c esp 608b-c

43 MILL: *Liberty*, 287c-288c passim

46 HEGEL: *Philosophy of History*, PART IV, 360c-361a

53 JAMES: *Psychology*, 107a-b; 117b; 238b [fn 2]

54 FREUD: *General Introduction*, 545d

CROSS-REFERENCES

For: The consideration of dialectic as logic or a part of logic, and of its relation to the other liberal arts, see LANGUAGE 7; LOGIC 1, 1b, 3–3b; RHETORIC 1a.

Other discussions of the conception of dialectic as the highest science, the supreme form of knowledge or wisdom, see METAPHYSICS 1; PHILOSOPHY 2b; SCIENCE 1a(2); WISDOM 1a.

Other discussions of dialectic as a method of argument in the sphere of opinion, see OPINION 2c; REASONING 5c; RHETORIC 4c–4c(3); and for matters relevant to the use of dialectic as a method of inquiry, see DEFINITION 4; HYPOTHESIS 1; PRINCIPLE 3c(2).

The role of dialectic in the philosophy of history, see HISTORY 4a(2)–4a(3); PROGRESS 1a.

The discussion of the types of opposition which have significance for dialectic, see OPPOSITION 1e, 2b, 2e; REASONING 5c.

Dialectic in relation to philosophy and theology, see METAPHYSICS 3c; PHILOSOPHY 3c; THEOLOGY 5.

Discussions of sophistry, and for the condemnation of dialectic as sophistry, see LOGIC 5; METAPHYSICS 4a; PHILOSOPHY 6b; THEOLOGY 5; TRUTH 8e; WISDOM 3.

ADDITIONAL READINGS

Listed below are works not included in *Great Books of the Western World*, but relevant to the idea and topics with which this chapter deals. These works are divided into two groups:

I. Works by authors represented in this collection.
II. Works by authors not represented in this collection.

For the date, place, and other facts concerning the publication of the works cited, consult the Bibliography of Additional Readings which follows the last chapter of *The Great Ideas*.

I.

AUGUSTINE. *Divine Providence and the Problem of Evil*, BK II, CH 11–16
——. *Concerning the Teacher*
HOBBES. *The Art of Sophistry*
HEGEL. *The Phenomenology of Mind*
——. *Science of Logic*
ENGELS. *Dialectics of Nature*
——. *Herr Eugen Dühring's Revolution in Science*, PART I (12–13)

II.

SEXTUS EMPIRICUS. *Outlines of Pyrrhonism*, BK I–II
PHILOSTRATUS. *Lives of the Sophists*
ERIGENA. *De Divisione Naturae*, BK V (4)
ABAILARD. *Sic et Non*
——. *Dialectica*
JOHN OF SALISBURY. *Metalogicon*
NICOLAS OF CUSA. *De Docta Ignorantia*
MELANCHTHON. *Dialectica*
RAMUS. *Dialecticae Institutiones*

J. G. FICHTE. *The Science of Knowledge*, PART III, A–D
SCHLEIERMACHER. *Dialektik*
WHEWELL. *On the Philosophy of Discovery*, APPENDIX C
LOTZE. *Logic*, BK I, CH 3 (C)
C. S. PEIRCE, *Collected Papers*, VOL I, par 284–572; VOL V, par 41–119; VOL VI, par 7–34
BRUNETIÈRE. *An Apology for Rhetoric*
BRADLEY. *Appearance and Reality*
McTAGGART. *Studies in the Hegelian Dialectic*
PLEKHANOV. *Fundamental Problems of Marxism*
TROELTSCH. *Gesammelte Schriften*, VOL III, CH 3 (4)
LENIN. *Selected Works*, VOL XI (On Dialectics)
BUKHARIN. *Historical Materialism*
ADLER. *Dialectic*
BUCHANAN. *Possibility*
SANTAYANA. *Reason in Science*, CH 7
——. *The Realm of Essence*, CH 7
WHITEHEAD. *Process and Reality*, PART I
JACKSON. *Dialectics*
B. RUSSELL. *An Inquiry into Meaning and Truth*, CH 24

Chapter 19: DUTY

INTRODUCTION

LOCKE, discussing in the course of his essay on *Human Understanding* "why a man must keep his word," notes that we meet with three different answers to this question. "If a Christian be asked, he will give as reason: Because God, who has the power of eternal life and death, requires it of us. But if a Hobbist be asked why? he will answer: Because the public requires it, and the Leviathan will punish you if you do not. And if one of the old philosophers had been asked, he would have answered: Because it was dishonest, below the dignity of a man, and opposite to virtue, the highest perfection of human nature, to do otherwise."

With these three answers Locke introduces us to some of the alternative views on what is perhaps the central problem concerning duty. All three acknowledge the existence of duty and the force of obligation. By accepting the question they affirm the proposition that a man *must* or *ought to* keep his word. But why? What creates the *ought* or obligation?

Two of the answers Locke cites—that of the Christian and that of the Hobbist—seem to derive duty from the commands of law, the law of God or of the state, in either case a law to be enforced by the sanctions of a superior power. Accordingly, the citizen has duties to the state, the religious man to God. Yet it does not seem to be entirely the case that such duties rest exclusively on the *superior power* of God or the state. Men who obey either divine or civil law from fear of punishment alone, are said to act not from duty but from expediency—in terms of a calculation of risks and consequences.

Obedience to law would appear to be acknowledged as a duty only by those who recognize the authority of the law or the right of the lawmaker to command. They would be willing to obey the law even if no external sanction could be enforced against them by a superior power. Those whom the law binds in conscience rather than by its coercive force obey the law because it is morally right to do so. The sense of the law's moral authority is for them the sense of duty from which the dictates of conscience flow.

Locke's third answer—that of the ancient philosophers—shows that duty is sometimes understood without reference to law, divine or human. We share this understanding whenever, having made a promise or contracted a debt, we feel an obligation to discharge it even if no superior commands the act. Here, furthermore, the obligation seems to be to another individual—to a person who may be our equal —rather than to the state or God.

As indicated by Locke's statement of this ancient view, it is the honest or just man who acknowledges such obligations apart from the law or his relation to any superior. Virtue may, of course, also direct a man to act for the common welfare and to obey the laws of the state or the commandments of God. But the immediate source of the obligation to act in a certain way toward one's fellow men is placed by the ancients, according to Locke, in "virtue, the highest perfection of human nature." On this view, virtue alone provides the motivation. Without it men would act lawfully only because of the law's coercive force. Without it men would recognize no obligations to their fellow men or to the state.

THESE TWO conceptions of duty—for the moment grouping the Christian and Hobbist answers together against the ancient view—may seem at first to be only verbally different. It seems certain that dutiful conduct would frequently be the same on either view. Yet they do conflict with one another, and each, if examined further, presents difficulties.

The theory that duty arises from a man's own virtue receives its classic expression, as Locke intimates, in the ancient philosophers, particularly Plato and Aristotle. It appears in the *Republic*, for example, when Socrates has to meet Glaucon's argument that men abide by moral rules, not simply because they ought to, but in order to avoid the pain of censure and punishment. Glaucon claims that, given the possession of Gyges' ring which can render a man invisible to others, "no man would keep his hands off what was not his own when he could safely take what he liked." He could "in all respects be like a God among men."

Against this Socrates sets his conception of the "just man" who does what he ought to do because it is just, and because justice is essential to the very life and health of the soul. According to Socrates' way of thinking, it is ridiculous to ask "which is the more profitable, to be just and act justly and practise virtue, whether seen or unseen of gods and men, or to be unjust. . . . We know that, when the bodily constitution is gone, life is no longer endurable, though pampered with all kinds of meat and drinks, and having all wealth and all power; and shall we be told that when the very essence of the vital principle is undermined and corrupted, life is still worth having to a man, if only he be allowed to do whatever he likes with the single exception that he is not to acquire justice and virtue, or to escape from injustice and vice?"

On this view, it seems to be the virtue of justice which lies at the root of duty or obligation. But for Plato justice, though only one of the virtues, is inseparable from the other three —temperance, courage, and wisdom. It is almost indifferent therefore whether one attributes moral obligation to the particular virtue of justice or to virtue in general. As the chapters on JUSTICE and VIRTUE indicate, Aristotle differs from Plato, both with respect to the virtues in general and to justice in particular. For Aristotle it is justice alone, not virtue in general or any other particular virtue, which gives rise to duty or obligation.

Justice differs from the other virtues, according to Aristotle, in that it "alone of the virtues is thought to consider 'another's good' because it concerns the relation of a man to his neighbor." The other virtues, such as temperance and courage, do not give rise to obligations, *unless* they are somehow annexed to or united with justice. Whenever Aristotle speaks of duties he does so with reference to the obligations that follow from justice—"the duties of parents to children and those of brothers to each other . . . those of comrades and those of fellow-citizens."

Whereas for Aristotle justice always refers to the good of another, or to the common good of all, such virtues as temperance and courage, when they are isolated from justice, concern the well-being of the individual himself. That is why only justice entails duties, which are obligations to act in a certain way for the welfare of others. If the good of no other individual is involved, it seems that a man has no duty to be temperate or courageous, even when he possesses these virtues.

Precisely because of the essentially social character of justice, Aristotle raises the question "whether a man can treat himself unjustly or not." He is willing to admit that a man can do justice or injustice to himself only in a metaphorical sense. What he calls "metaphorical justice" is not a relation between a man and himself, but a relation between one part of himself and another.

Aquinas seems to follow Aristotle in connecting duty with justice and with no other virtue. "Justice alone of all the virtues," he writes, "implies the notion of duty." If he also intimates that duty may somehow enter into the acts of other virtues—as when he says that "it is not so patent in the other virtues as it is in justice"—his position still remains fundamentally Aristotelian. Referring to that "kind of metaphorical justice" to which Aristotle appeals in stating the sense in which a man can treat himself unjustly, Aquinas explains how "all the other virtues" can be said to "involve the duty of the lower powers to reason." Apart from this metaphorical duty of the passions to obey reason, duty in the strict sense comes, in the opinion of Aquinas, only from the precepts of justice, which concern the relation of one person to another.

ON THIS THEORY, duty is not co-extensive with morality, the sense of duty is not identical with the moral sense, and specific duties obligate a man to other men even when no general law exists to be obeyed. Difficulty is found with this theory by those critics who think that the whole of morality, not simply one part of it, involves duties. Does not the sense of duty operate, they ask, in matters which do not affect any other individual or even the common good? Does a man, for example, have a duty to tell the truth only to others, but not to seek it for himself? Kant, as we shall see, holds that there are private as well as public duties, or, in his language, internal duties in the realm of ethics as well as external duties in the realm of jurisprudence.

The Hobbist theory of duty seems to face similar difficulties. The specific duties which are determined by the precepts of justice may, as we have seen, not always be the same as the specific duties imposed by civil law, though they will be identical whenever the law of the state is itself an expression or determination of justice. But when law rather than justice is the principle, duty seems to consist primarily in obedience to the law or rather to the lawgiver who has superior power and authority. Only secondarily, or in consequence, does it involve obligations to other men who are one's equals.

With Hobbes, for example, justice, and obligation as well, begin only with the establishment of a constituted authority with the power of making laws. "Where there is no Commonwealth," he writes, "there is nothing unjust. So that the nature of justice consisteth in keeping of valid covenants; but the validity of covenants begins not but with the constitution of a civil power, sufficient to compel men to keep them." Duty and justice are both said to be "laws of nature," but, Hobbes adds, they "are not properly laws, but qualities that dispose men to peace, and to obedience," until "a Commonwealth is once settled," and then they become "the commands of the Commonwealth." In other words, "it is the Sovereign power that obliges men to obey them," and obedience, which is said to be "part also of the law of nature," is its proper expression.

So far the two conceptions conflict or at least diverge. But if the legal theory of duty goes no further than the enactments of the state, the same question arises here as before. Does a man have no duties apart from his relation to the state? Can duty be co-extensive with morality if the only rules of conduct to be obeyed are laws imposed from without—regulations which have authority simply because they come from one who has the right to command? Again, as we shall see, Kant would say No.

WE HAVE now stated the questions about duty which raise difficulties for Aristotle and Hobbes. Though they differ in their theories of law and justice, as well as in their conceptions of duty, they seem to concur in thinking that doing one's duty does not exhaustively solve all moral problems.

The same questions do not, however, seem to present difficulties to other moralists—to Kant and to the Stoics of antiquity, such as Marcus Aurelius and Epictetus. On the contrary, their moral philosophy, by making the sphere of duty co-extensive with the whole of the moral life, seems to prevent such questions from being raised.

As we turn to examine their conception of duty, we must observe that, in two respects, it alters Locke's threefold division of the answers to the question, Why must a man keep his word? In the first place, Locke's statement of the answer given by "the ancient philosophers" seems to have only Plato and Aristotle in mind, certainly not the Stoics. In the second place, Locke's statement of the Christian position seems to associate it with the Hobbist answer, against that of Plato and Aristotle. That association may be justified on the ground that duty to God, like duty to the state, involves obligation to a superior. But Aquinas, as we have seen, seems to agree with Aristotle about justice as a source of duty; and, as we shall see, he also seems to agree with Kant and the Stoics about the pervasiveness of duty in the realm of morals. Locke's statement of the Christian position, which selects one aspect of it only, may therefore be inadequate.

The point which unites Kant, the Stoics, and Aquinas is their agreement concerning the existence of a law which is neither enacted by the state nor proclaimed by God in his revealed commandments. This law the Stoics speak of as "the law of reason," Aquinas calls "the natural law," and Kant conceives to be "the moral law within." The common conception thus variously expressed is more fully treated in the chapter on LAW; but that ampler discussion is not needed to perceive that the law of reason or of nature is a moral law, in that its general principles and detailed precepts govern the entire range of moral acts.

"Morality," according to Kant, "consists in the reference of all action to the legislation which alone can render a kingdom of ends possible." By this he means that "the will is never to act on any maxim which could not without contradiction be also a universal law." This law is also moral in the sense that it exercises only moral authority and should prevail even without the support of the external sanctions which accompany the positive commands of a superior. "The idea of duty," Kant declares, "would alone be sufficient as a spring [of action] even if the spring were absent which is connected by forensic legislation . . . namely external compulsion."

Making the natural or moral law the principle of duty introduces the element of obligation into every moral act. Whatever is right to do we are obliged to do in conformity to the law of nature or in obedience to the commands of the moral law. We need no external promulgation of this law—i.e., no express formulation in words by a lawgiver—for this law is inherent in reason itself. Its various maxims or precepts can be deduced from what Aquinas calls the "first principle . . . of the practical reason" and Kant "the categorical imperative." Or, as the Stoics say, since reason is the "ruling principle" in man, man's duty consists in "holding fast" to it and "going straight on" so that it has "what is its own."

On this theory, we are obliged in conscience to do whatever reason declares right, whether or not others are directly involved. The distinction between public and private morality—between the spheres of justice and the other virtues—is irrelevant to conscience. Conscience, according to Kant, functions equally in the spheres of internal and external duty. In both the realm of ethics and the realm of jurisprudence, conscience, applying the moral law, dictates our duty in the particular case. We stand in no different relation to ourselves and others, since the moral law is universally and equally binding on all persons. The obligation is in every case to obey the law. It is not a duty to persons, *except* as the moral law commands us to respect the dignity of the human person, ourselves and others alike.

The element of a superior commanding an inferior seems to be present in this conception of duty through the relation of reason to the will and appetites of man. Acting dutifully consists in the submission of the will to reason, and in overcoming all contrary inclinations or desires. But though Kant sometimes speaks in these terms, he also conceives duty as carrying with it an obligation to God. "The subjective principle of a responsibility for one's deeds before God," he says, is "contained, though it be only obscurely, in every moral self-consciousness."

Nevertheless, Kant insists that "the Christian principle of *morality* itself is not theological." It rests, in his opinion, on the "autonomy of pure practical reason, since it does not make the knowledge of God and his will the foundation of these laws, but only of the attainment of the *summum bonum*, on the condition of following these laws, and it does not even place the proper *spring* of this obedience in the desired results, but solely in the conception of duty, as that of which the faithful observance alone constitutes the worthiness to obtain those happy consequences."

It is "through the *summum bonum* as the object and final end of pure practical reason" that, in Kant's view of Christian morality, we pass from moral philosophy to "*religion*, that is, to the *recognition of all duties as divine commands.*" A Christian theologian like Aquinas, however, seems to go further than Kant in equating conformity to the moral law—or the natural law of reason—with religious obedience to God. Nor does he explain this equivalence by reference to the fact that God has made man's attainment of the *summum bonum*—or eternal happiness—depend on his free compliance with the moral law. Rather, for Aquinas, the natural law is "nothing else than the rational creature's participation in the eternal law" of God—the "imprint on us of the divine light." As God is the author of man's nature and reason, so is He the ultimate authority behind the commands of the natural law which He implanted in man's reason at creation.

For a Christian theologian like Aquinas, duty to God involves obedience to the moral law which reason can discover by itself, no less than obedience to those positive commandments which God has revealed to man. Aquinas seems to think that violation of the natural law is as much a sin as violation of the divine law. Both involve a rupture of that order laid down by God, the one "in relation to the rule of reason, in so far as all our actions and passions should be commensurate with the rule of reason," the other "in relation to the rule of the divine law." Thus, in all moral matters, it would appear that duty is, in Wordsworth's phrase, "stern daughter of the voice of God." If the natural law commands us to use our faculties to the ends for which they were created, then the possession of a mind imposes upon us what Socrates in the *Apology* calls man's "duty to inquire." If we fail to seek the truth, we sin against God by sinning against our nature, even though "Thou shalt seek the truth" is nowhere explicitly prescribed in Holy Writ.

ETHICAL DOCTRINES can be classified according to the role which they assign to duty as a moral principle. There is perhaps no more fundamental issue in moral philosophy than that between the ethics of duty and the ethics of pleasure or happiness. This issue obviously belongs to the chapters on HAPPINESS and PLEASURE as well as the present one. All three must be read together—and perhaps also the chapters on DESIRE, LAW, and VIRTUE—to complete the picture.

According to the morality of duty, every act is to be judged for its obedience or disobedience to law, and the basic moral distinction is between right and wrong. But where pleasure or happiness are central, the basic distinction is between good and evil, and desire rather than law sets the standard of appraisal. An analysis of means and ends and a theory of the virtues are usually found in the ethics of happiness, as a theory of conscience and sanctions is usually prominent in the ethics of duty.

At one extreme, there is the position which totally excludes the concept of duty. This fact more than any other characterizes the Epicureanism of Lucretius. The good life for him is one where "nature craves for herself no more than this, that pain hold aloof from the body, and she in mind enjoy a feeling of pleasure exempt from care and fear." The life he describes—so disciplined and moderated that all but the simplest pleasures are relinquished in the effort to avoid pain—seems to leave no place for obligation or social responsibility.

In the much more elaborate moral philosophy of Aristotle, virtue entails moderation in the avoidance of pain as well as in the pursuit of pleasure. Though he admits that "most pleasures might perhaps be bad without qualification," Aristotle claims that "the chief good," which is happiness, "would involve some pleasure." But even as a good, pleasure is not the only good, for there are other objects of desire.

The happy man, according to Aristotle, is one who somehow succeeds in satisfying all his desires by seeking the various kinds of goods in some order and relation to one another. Happiness itself is something that "we choose always for itself and never for the sake of something else." Although we may also choose other things in some sense for themselves, such as "honor, pleasure, reason, and every virtue," still they are chosen "for the sake of happiness," since we judge them as "the means by which we shall be happy."

In Aristotle's ethics of happiness, duty is not entirely excluded, but neither is it given any independent significance. As we have seen, it is merely an aspect of the virtue of justice, and amounts to no more than the just man's acknowledgment of the debt he owes to others; or his recognition that he is under some obligation to avoid injuring other men and to serve the common good.

At the other extreme, there is the position which identifies the sense of duty with the moral sense. In the Stoicism of Marcus Aurelius and Epictetus, to live well is to do one's duty, and to set aside all contrary desires. "It is thy duty," the Emperor writes, "to order thy life well in every single act; and if every act does its duty, as far as is possible, be content; and no one is able to hinder thee so that each act shall not do its duty." Man is not destined to be happy; his happiness consists rather in doing what is required of him at his post of duty in the order of the universe. The only good is a good will, a dutiful will, a will which conforms itself to the law of nature.

Kant's much more elaborate moral philosophy presents the same fundamental teachings. This is indicated by the fact that he associates what he calls *eudaemonism* (*i.e.*, the ethics of happiness) with *hedonism* (*i.e.*, the ethics of pleasure). Happiness, he writes, is "a rational being's consciousness of the pleasantness of life uninterruptedly accompanying his whole existence," and its basis is "the principle of self-love." Therefore, according to Kant, both eudaemonism and hedonism commit the same error. Both "undermine morality and destroy its sublimity, since they put the motives to virtue and to vice in the same class, and only teach us to make a better calculation." Both admit desire as a moral criterion of good and evil. Both are utilitarian in that they are concerned with consequences, with means and ends. Both measure the moral act by reference to the end it serves.

For Kant, "an action done from duty derives its moral worth, not from the purpose which is to be attained by it, but from the maxim by which it is determined, and therefore does not depend on the realization of the object of the action, but merely on the principle of volition by which the action has taken place, without any regard to any object of desire. . . . Duty," he goes on to say, "is the necessity of acting from respect for the law." From this he argues that duty, and consequently all moral action, must be done because it is right, because the law commands it, and for no other reason. The recommendation of any action solely on the ground that it will contribute to happiness as satisfying the inclination of the person and achieving the object of the will, is completely ruled out. That would be a judgment of pure expediency. Worse than *not* moral, it is, in the opinion of Kant, *immoral*.

"An action done from duty," Kant writes, "must wholly exclude the influence of inclination, and with it every object of the will, so that nothing remains which can determine the will except objectively the law, and subjectively pure respect for this practical law, and consequently the maxim that I should follow this law even to the thwarting of all my inclinations. . . . The pre-eminent good which we call

moral can therefore consist in nothing else than the conception of law in itself, which certainly is only possible in a rational being in so far as this conception, and not the expected effect, determines the will."

This law, which is the source of duty and of all moral action, is Kant's famous "categorical imperative"—or, in other words, reason's unconditional command. According to its decree, Kant declares, "I am never to act otherwise than so that I could also will that my maxim should become a universal law." By obeying the categorical imperative, we can know and do our duty and rest assured that our will is morally good. "I do not, therefore, need any far-reaching penetration to discern what I have to do," Kant writes, "in order that my will may be morally good. Inexperienced in the course of the world, incapable of being prepared for all its contingencies, I only ask myself: Canst thou also will that thy maxim should be a universal law? If not, then it must be rejected, and that not because of a disadvantage accruing from it to myself, or even to others, but because it cannot enter as a principle into a possible universal legislation."

To say that a man *ought to* do this or refrain from doing that *in order to* achieve happiness is, for Kant, at best a conditional obligation, ultimately a specious one since he is not unconditionally obliged to be happy. Kant does not totally exclude happiness or the *summum bonum*. In fact he says that there is no need to maintain "an opposition" between them and morality. But he claims that "the moment duty is in question we should take no account of happiness." Just as Aristotle treats duty only in terms of justice, so Kant considers happiness to have a moral quality only insofar as to be worthy of it is an end set by the moral law.

Two OTHER voices join in this great argument concerning duty and happiness. One is that of John Stuart Mill, whose *Utilitarianism* recognizes Kant as the chief opponent of an ethics of happiness. Though Mill differs from Aristotle on many points, particularly in regard to the virtues as means to happiness, Mill's answer to Kant can be read as a defense of Aristotle as well as of his own theory.

From Kant's point of view, they are both

utilitarians. They both argue in terms of means and ends. They both make purely pragmatic, not moral, judgments—judgments of expediency instead of judgments of right and wrong.

From Mill's point of view, Aristotle like himself needs no other principle of morality than happiness, an ultimate end which justifies every means that tends towards its realization. "The ultimate sanction of all morality, external motives apart," Mill writes, "is a subjective feeling in our own minds." He asserts that "when once the general happiness is recognized as the ethical standard," it will appeal to "a powerful natural sentiment." Man's nature as a social being, he holds, "tends to make him feel it one of his natural wants that there should be harmony between his feelings and aims and those of his fellow-creatures."

This conviction, in persons who have it, "does not present itself to their minds as a superstition of education, or a law despotically imposed by the power of society, but as an attribute which it would not be well for them to be without." This conviction, rather than an internal sense of obligation or fear of external sanctions imposed by a superior power, is for Mill "the ultimate sanction of the greatest happiness morality"—which aims at the greatest happiness for the greatest number.

Where Mill answers Kant by excluding duty —even from considerations of justice—Aquinas seems to develop an analysis in which every moral act can be regarded as obeying or disobeying the natural law and yet, at the same time, be judged as a means which serves or fails to serve the ultimate end of man's natural desire. "The order of the precepts of the natural law is," in the words of Aquinas, "according to the order of natural inclinations." The dilemma set up by the opposition between duty and happiness seems to be denied, or at least avoided, by a theory which finds a perfect parallelism between the precepts of natural law and the objects of natural desire, a parallelism resulting from their common source in the creation of human nature by God.

THE TENSION between duty and desire—between obedience to rules of conduct and unrestrained indulgence—is one of the burdens which no other animal except man must bear. It

is a constant theme in the great poems. It is pivotal to the plot of most of the great love stories. It is a theme of tragedy, for in whichever direction the tension is resolved—whether in the line of duty (as by Aeneas forsaking Dido) or in disobedience to law (as by Adam yielding to Eve in *Paradise Lost*)—ruin results.

The tragedy of being both rational and animal seems to consist in *having to choose* between duty and desire rather than in making any particular choice. It may be significant, however, that the tragic heroes of poetry more frequently abandon duty than desire or love, though seldom without mortal punishment, preceded by a deep sense of their transgression. Sometimes, however, they are self-deceived, and cloak desire in the guise of duty.

There is another source of tragic conflict in the sphere of duty. Men are torn by competing loyalties, obligations which pull them in opposite directions. In the basic relationships of the family, the duty a man owes to his parents often cannot be discharged without violating or neglecting obligations to his wife. When the moral law and the law of the state command contrary actions, duty is weighed against duty in an ordeal of conscience. Sometimes, however, one obligation seems to take clear precedence over another, as in the mind of Sophocles' Antigone, for whom the king's edict loses its authority when it runs counter to the law of God. Creon the king, not Antigone his subject, may be the play's more tragic personage. He sacrifices a dearly beloved son to uphold the authority he considers it his duty as a ruler to maintain.

If man is not a rational animal or if, whatever his nature, reason is not its ruling principle, then the sense of duty would appear to be an imposture that draws its driving force from the emotional energies with which certain manmade rules of conduct are invested. Rather than acting as a counterweight to desire, duty is itself the shape which certain desires take to combat others.

Conscience, or the *super-ego*, according to Freud, is born of the struggle between the *ego* and the *id*. Translated into "popular language," Freud tells us, "the ego stands for reason and circumspection, while the id stands for the untamed passions." What may originally have had a necessary function to perform in the psychic economy can grow to play too dominant a part. For the psychoanalyst, not tragedy but neurosis results from an overdeveloped sense of duty. When "the ego [is] forced to acknowledge its weakness," Freud explains, it "breaks out into anxiety: reality anxiety in face of the external world, normal anxiety in face of the super-ego, and neurotic anxiety in face of the strength of the passions in the id."

THE RELATION of ruler and ruled in the domestic or the political community may seem at first to impose duties or obligations only on the ruled. The ruler commands. His subjects are obliged to obey. Does the ruler in turn have no duties, no obligations to those whom he governs? If he has none, then neither have the persons he rules rights which he must respect. Such absolute rule—defined by a correlative absence of duties in the ruler and rights in the ruled—has been one conception of the relation between master and slave.

In the state rulers who are merely office-holders are obligated by the duties of their office as well as vested with its authority and power. The office-holder, duty-bound by the constitution, is not an absolute ruler. He is, in fact, a servant of the state, not its master. The mediaeval king who pledged himself in his coronation oath to discharge the duties of his office may not have been bound by human law, but so long as his conscience kept him loyal to his pledge, he recognized the supremacy of the natural law or of the law of God. The self-governing citizen of a republic is similarly duty-bound only when he recognizes the supremacy of the common good.

According to the theory of constitutional government, rights and duties are correlative. The acknowledgment of duties signifies that the holder of rights recognizes their limited or conditional character. To consider oneself entirely exempt from duties or obligations is to regard one's rights as absolute. Can anyone have absolute rights except on condition of being without a superior of any sort? One implied answer to this question is that neither despot nor state, but only God, is autonomous or without duty.

OUTLINE OF TOPICS

REFERENCES

To find the passages cited, use the numbers in heavy type, which are the volume and page numbers of the passages referred to. For example, in 4 HOMER: *Iliad*, BK II [265–283] 12d, the number 4 is the number of the volume in the set; the number 12d indicates that the passage is in section d of page 12.

PAGE SECTIONS: When the text is printed in one column, the letters a and b refer to the upper and lower halves of the page. For example, in 53 JAMES: *Psychology*, 116a–119b, the passage begins in the upper half of page 116 and ends in the lower half of page 119. When the text is printed in two columns, the letters a and b refer to the upper and lower halves of the left-hand side of the page, the letters c and d to the upper and lower halves of the right-hand side of the page. For example, in 7 PLATO: *Symposium*, 163b–164c, the passage begins in the lower half of the left-hand side of page 163 and ends in the upper half of the right-hand side of page 164.

AUTHOR'S DIVISIONS: One or more of the main divisions of a work (such as PART, BK, CH, SECT) are sometimes included in the reference; line numbers, in brackets, are given in certain cases; *e.g.*, *Iliad*, BK II [265–283] 12d.

BIBLE REFERENCES: The references are to book, chapter, and verse. When the King James and Douay versions differ in title of books or in the numbering of chapters or verses, the King James version is cited first and the Douay, indicated by a (*D*), follows; *e.g.*, OLD TESTAMENT: *Nehemiah*, 7:45—(*D*) *II Esdras*, 7:46.

SYMBOLS: The abbreviation "esp" calls the reader's attention to one or more especially relevant parts of a whole reference; "passim" signifies that the topic is discussed intermittently rather than continuously in the work or passage cited.

For additional information concerning the style of the references, see the Explanation of Reference Style; for general guidance in the use of *The Great Ideas*, consult the Preface.

1. The concept of duty or obligation: its moral significance

7 PLATO: *Gorgias*, 269d–270c
12 EPICTETUS: *Discourses*, BK II, CH 5, 143d–144a
12 AURELIUS: *Meditations*, BK III, SECT 1 259b,d; SECT 6 261a-c; BK IV, SECT 4 264a; BK V, SECT 6 269b-d; BK VI, SECT 22–23 276a-b; SECT 26 276b-c; BK VII, SECT 5 280a-b; BK VIII, SECT 26 287c; SECT 32 287d–288a
18 AUGUSTINE: *City of God*, BK IX, CH 4, 287d; BK XIX, CH 14–16, 520c-522a; CH 19 523b-d / *Christian Doctrine*, BK I, CH 22–30 629b-633b
20 AQUINAS: *Summa Theologica*, PART I–II, Q 99, A 5 249a-250a; PART II–II, Q 4, A 7, REP 3 407d-409a; QQ 183–189 625a-700d passim, esp Q 183, A 1, REP 3 625a-626a, A 3 627a-d
23 HOBBES: *Leviathan*, PART I, 86c-87c; PART II, 115a-b
25 MONTAIGNE: *Essays*, 7a-d; 24c-25c; 233a-b; 319b; 383c-385a; 467b-470a
30 BACON: *Advancement of Learning*, 74b-76a
38 ROUSSEAU: *Social Contract*, BK I, 388d-389a
42 KANT: *Pure Reason*, 114d-115a; 149d-150a; 190c-d; 236d-237a / *Fund. Prin. Metaphysic of Morals*, 253d-254d; 256a-279d esp 276b-277a; 282d-283d / *Practical Reason*, 305d-307d; 325a-d; 327d-329a / *Pref. Metaphysical Elements of Ethics*, 366d-367a; 368a-d; 373b-d / *Intro. Metaphysic of Morals*, 383a-390a,c esp 383a-384d, 389a-390a,c; 391a-c; 392b-393a / *Science of Right*, 397c-398a; 416b-417b / *Judgement*, 571c-572a; 594c-596c esp 595a-d; 605d-606b [fn 2]
43 MILL: *Liberty*, 304c-306b passim / *Utilitarianism*, 453c-454a; 468b-469b
46 HEGEL: *Philosophy of Right*, PART II, par 133–135 47a-d; PART III, par 148–150 56a-57a; ADDITIONS, 84 129b; 95 132b / *Philosophy of History*, INTRO, 170d-171c; PART I, 224a; PART IV, 362c-d
49 DARWIN: *Descent of Man*, 304a; 310d-314c esp 313d-314a; 592b-c

2. Comparison of the ethics of duty with the ethics of happiness, pleasure, or utility

12 EPICTETUS: *Discourses*, BK II, CH 11 150a-151b; CH 19 162c-164b; BK III, CH 24 203c-210a
12 AURELIUS: *Meditations*, BK II, SECT 11–12 258a-c; BK VIII, SECT 10 286b; SECT 28 287c; SECT 39 288c; BK IX, SECT 1 291a-c; SECT 7 292b
18 AUGUSTINE: *City of God*, BK IX, CH 4–5 287a-289a; BK XIV, CH 8–9 381c-385b

19 Aquinas: *Summa Theologica*, part i–ii, q 24, a 2 727d-728c

24 Rabelais: *Gargantua and Pantagruel*, bk i, 65c-66b

30 Bacon: *Advancement of Learning*, 69d-76a

33 Pascal: *Provincial Letters*, 62b-68b

39 Smith: *Wealth of Nations*, bk v, 336c-d

42 Kant: *Pure Reason*, 235a-b; 236b-239a / *Fund. Prin. Metaphysic of Morals*, 256a-257d; 258d-264a; 265b; 267b-d; 280d-281a; 282b-283d; 286a-c / *Practical Reason*, 297a-319b esp 298a-300a, 304d-307d; 325a-331a; 338c-355d esp 345d-347a / *Pref. Metaphysical Elements of Ethics*, 365b-366d; 369c-373b / *Intro. Metaphysic of Morals*, 387b-388a; 389a-390a,c / *Science of Right*, 446b-c / *Judgement*, 478a-479c; 584d-587a; 588b [fn 2]; 591b-592a; 594c-596c; 605d-606b [fn 2]

43 Mill: *Liberty*, 296a-297b / *Utilitarianism* 445a-476a,c esp 457c-461c, 464d-476a,c

46 Hegel: *Philosophy of Right*, part ii, par 124 44b-d; par 134–135 47b-d; additions, 85–87 129b-d

53 James: *Psychology*, 813a-814a

54 Freud: *Civilization and Its Discontents*, 800c-801b

3. The divisions of duty: internal and external duty; the realms of ethics and jurisprudence

7 Plato: *Gorgias*, 269d-270c

19 Aquinas: *Summa Theologica*, part i, q 16, a 4, rep 3 97a-c

20 Aquinas: *Summa Theologica*, part i–ii, q 99, a 5, ans 249a-250a; q 100, a 2, rep 2 252b-253a

23 Hobbes: *Leviathan*, part i, 95d-96a

25 Montaigne: *Essays*, 7a

30 Bacon: *Advancement of Learning*, 74b-c

32 Milton: *Samson Agonistes* [1334–1379] 368b-369b

41 Gibbon: *Decline and Fall*, 89d-91a; 96a-b

42 Kant: *Fund. Prin. Metaphysic of Morals*, 268d-270c; 272b-273a / *Pref. Metaphysical Elements of Ethics* 365a-379d esp 366d, 367b-368a, 370d-372a, 374a-c, 378a / *Intro. Metaphysic of Morals*, 383a-384a,c; 386d-387a,c; 389a-390a,c; 391a-394a,c / *Science of Right*, 398a-399c; 400b,d-401b

43 Mill: *Utilitarianism*, 458a-d; 468b-469b

46 Hegel: *Philosophy of Right*, part i, par 79 33a-c; part ii, par 137–141 48a-54d / *Philosophy of History*, intro, 170d-171c; 186b-c; part i, 207b-c; 211a-c; 214d-216b; part iii, 290a-b

51 Tolstoy: *War and Peace*, epilogue ii, 689b

4. The sense of duty

5 Aeschylus: *Choephoroe* 70a-80d esp [1010–1047] 80a-c / *Eumenides* 81a-91d esp [436–666] 86a-88a

5 Sophocles: *Oedipus at Colonus* [1–509] 114a-118d / *Antigone* 131a-142d / *Electra* 156a-169a,c / *Philoctetes* 182a-195a,c

5 Euripides: *Hippolytus* 225a-236d esp [373–430] 228b-d / *Alcestis* 237a-247a,c / *Heracleidae* 248a-257a,c esp [748–783] 254d-255a / *Suppliants* 258a-269a,c esp [87–597] 258d-263c / *Electra* 327a-339a,c / *Phoenician Maidens* [1625–1766] 392b-393d

6 Thucydides: *Peloponnesian War*, bk ii, 397d-398c

7 Plato: *Euthydemus*, 70d-71b / *Meno*, 183a-b / *Apology*, 206b-d / *Crito* 213a-219a,c / *Republic*, bk vii, 390b-391b

12 Epictetus: *Discourses*, bk i, ch 5 110b-c

12 Aurelius: *Meditations*, bk viii, sect 32 287d-288a

14 Plutarch: *Marcus Cato* 276b,d-290d esp 282a / *Cato the Younger* 620a-648a,c esp 626d-627b, 632b-c

22 Chaucer: *Knight's Tale* [859–1004] 174a-176b

25 Montaigne: *Essays*, 301d-303c; 467d-468b

26 Shakespeare: *As You Like It*, act ii, sc iii [56–65] 605a

29 Cervantes: *Don Quixote*, part i, 81b-88b

32 Milton: *Comus* [170–229] 37a-38b / *Paradise Lost*, bk iii [194–197] 139b

42 Kant: *Fund. Prin. Metaphysic of Morals*, 253d-254b / *Practical Reason*, 325c-327d; 333a-334a / *Pref. Metaphysical Elements of Ethics*, 375a-b / *Judgement*, 593a-d; 599b-d

43 Mill: *Utilitarianism*, 458b-461c esp 458b-c

49 Darwin: *Descent of Man*, 310a-314a esp 310c-d, 314a; 592b-c

51 Tolstoy: *War and Peace*, bk vii, 275a; bk x, 465c-467a; bk xi, 513d-514d; 527b-528b

53 James: *Psychology*, 807a-808a

4a. The moral and social development of conscience: its dictates

Old Testament: *Proverbs*, 28:1 / *Ecclesiastes*, 7:21–22—(D) *Ecclesiastes*, 7:22–23

Apocrypha: *Wisdom of Solomon*, 17:11—(D) OT, *Book of Wisdom*, 17:10 / *Ecclesiasticus*, 14:2—(D) OT, *Ecclesiasticus*, 14:2

New Testament: *Romans*, 2:14-15 / *I Corinthians*, 8 / *I Timothy*, 4:1–2 / *Titus*, 1:15

5 Aeschylus: *Choephoroe* 70a-80d esp [1010–1076] 80a-d

12 Aurelius: *Meditations*, bk ii, sect 5 257b-c; bk iii, sect 4 260b-261a; bk iv, sect 18 264d; bk viii, sect 32 287d-288a

18 Augustine: *Confessions*, bk ii, par 9, 10d; bk iv, par 14 22d-23a

19 Aquinas: *Summa Theologica*, part i, q 79, aa 12–13 425c-427a; part i–ii, q 19, aa 5–6 705d-708a

20 Aquinas: *Summa Theologica*, part i–ii, q 96, a 4 233a-d

21 Dante: *Divine Comedy*, purgatory, xxvii [124–142] 95d-96a

25 MONTAIGNE: *Essays*, 46b-d; 233a-b

31 SPINOZA: *Ethics*, PART IV, PROP 37, SCHOL 2 435b-436a

32 MILTON: *Paradise Lost*, BK IX [647-654] 261b

35 LOCKE: *Civil Government*, CH II, SECT 4-6 25d-26c; CH XVI, SECT 186 68d-69a; SECT 195 70a-b / *Human Understanding*, BK I, CH II, SECT 5-6 105a-c; SECT 12-13 107b-108c

38 MONTESQUIEU: *Spirit of Laws*, BK I, 2a-b; BK XXIII, 187d-188a

38 ROUSSEAU: *Inequality*, 330a-331c; 356b-359a / *Social Contract*, BK I, 388d-389a; 392b-393c; BK II, 397d-398a; 399b-c

42 KANT: *Pure Reason*, 114d-115a; 236d-237a / *Fund. Prin. Metaphysic of Morals*, 253d-254d; 260a-261d; 268c-270c; 272a-b; 273d-287d esp 275b-d, 277d-279d, 281c-283d / *Practical Reason*, 297a-314d esp 307d-314d; 321b-329a / *Pref. Metaphysical Elements of Ethics*, 366a-d; 369a-c; 373d / *Intro. Metaphysic of Morals*, 386b-d; 388b-c; 390b,d-391c; 392b-393a / *Judgement*, 571c-572a; 605d-606b [fn 2]

43 MILL: *Utilitarianism*, 445d-446d; 470a-b

46 HEGEL: *Philosophy of Right*, PART II, par 135 47b-d; ADDITIONS, 86 129c / *Philosophy of History*, INTRO, 170d-171c; 186b-c; PART IV, 362b-d

6. Conflicts between duties of diverse origins

OLD TESTAMENT: *Genesis*, 2:18-25 esp 2:24 / *Deuteronomy*, 21:18-21

NEW TESTAMENT: *Matthew*, 8:21-22; 12:46-50; 22:17-21 / *Mark*, 12:14-17 / *Luke*, 20:20-26

5 AESCHYLUS: *Suppliant Maidens* [333-489] 5a-7a / *Seven Against Thebes* 27a-39a,c / *Agamemnon* [184-247] 54a-c / *Choephoroe* [885-930] 78d-79b / *Eumenides* 81a-91d

5 SOPHOCLES: *Antigone* 131a-142d esp [1-99] 131a-132a / *Philoctetes* 182a-195a,c esp [50-122] 182d-183b

5 EURIPIDES: *Electra* 327a-339a,c esp [962-987] 335d-336a / *Phoenician Maidens* 378a-393d / *Iphigenia at Aulis* 425a-439d

6 HERODOTUS: *History*, BK II, 71d-72a; BK V, 171d-172a

7 PLATO: *Crito*, 213d-219a,c

13 VIRGIL: *Aeneid*, BK IV [331-361] 176a-177a

14 PLUTARCH: *Fabius*, 152b-d / *Coriolanus*, 189d-191c / *Timoleon*, 196b-198b / *Agis*, 654c-655a

18 AUGUSTINE: *City of God*, BK XIX, CH 19 523b-d

23 HOBBES: *Leviathan*, PART II, 101c; 151a-c; PART III, 198d-199a; 240a-246a,c

25 MONTAIGNE: *Essays*, 381a-388c esp 386a-d; 467b-470a; 486b-488b

26 SHAKESPEARE: *Richard II*, ACT I, SC II [1-43] 322d-323a

32 MILTON: *Samson Agonistes* [843-902] 358a-359a

35 LOCKE: *Toleration*, 16c-17b; 18a-b

38 ROUSSEAU: *Political Economy*, 369c / *Social Contract*, BK IV, 435a-439c passim

40 GIBBON: *Decline and Fall*, 193c-194a; 226a-b

41 GIBBON: *Decline and Fall*, 89b-c

42 KANT: *Intro. Metaphysic of Morals*, 392a

43 MILL: *Liberty*, 304c-d / *Utilitarianism*, 456d-457b

44 BOSWELL: *Johnson*, 145b; 221d-224a; 542a-c

46 HEGEL: *Philosophy of Right*, PART III, par 150 56c-57a

51 TOLSTOY: *War and Peace*, BK VII, 275a-276b; EPILOGUE I, 668a-669c; 670d-671a

7. The relation of duty to justice and to rights: oaths and promises

OLD TESTAMENT: *Genesis*, 28:18-22; 29:15-30 / *Leviticus*, 5:4-13; 27 / *Numbers*, 6; 30 / *Deuteronomy*, 23:21-23 / *Joshua*, 2; 6:22-25; 24:1-28—(D) *Josue*, 2; 6:22-25; 24:1-28 / *Judges*, 1-2; 11:28-40 / *I Samuel*, 1:11-28—(D) *I Kings*, 1:11-28 / *Psalms*, 50:14; 66:13-14—(D) *Psalms*, 49:14; 65:13-14 / *Ecclesiastes*, 5:4 —(D) *Ecclesiastes*, 5:3 / *Zechariah*, 8:17—(D) *Zacharias*, 8:17

APOCRYPHA: *Ecclesiasticus*, 29:3—(D) OT, *Ecclesiasticus*, 29:3

NEW TESTAMENT: *Matthew*, 5:33-37 / *James*, 5:12

4 HOMER: *Iliad*, BK IV [153-239] 25c-26b

5 AESCHYLUS: *Choephoroe* 70a-80d

5 SOPHOCLES: *Philoctetes* 182a-195a,c esp [895-1292] 190a-193c

5 EURIPIDES: *Hecuba* [218-331] 354d-355c / *Iphigenia at Aulis* [16-140] 425b-426b

6 HERODOTUS: *History*, BK III, 90c-d; BK IV, 151a-b; 159a-b; BK VI, 197a-b; 201d-202c; BK IX, 311b-312d

6 THUCYDIDES: *Peloponnesian War*, BK II, 406a-407b; BK III, 429c-434c; BK V, 490a-b

7 PLATO: *Apology*, 209a-b / *Crito*, 216d-219a,c / *Gorgias*, 284a-285a / *Republic*, BK I, 297a-300b / *Laws*, BK XII, 787d-788c

9 ARISTOTLE: *Ethics*, BK VIII, CH 9 [1159^{b}25-1160^{a}9] 411d-412b / *Rhetoric*, BK I, CH 14 [1375^{a}8-11] 619c

12 AURELIUS: *Meditations*, BK III, SECT 7 261c

13 VIRGIL: *Aeneid*, BK XII [175-215] 358b-360a

14 PLUTARCH: *Lysander*, 357a-b / *Agesilaus*, 484a-b

19 AQUINAS: *Summa Theologica*, PART I, Q 16, A 4, REP 3 97a-c; Q 21, A 1, REP 3 124b-125b

20 AQUINAS: *Summa Theologica*, PART I-II, Q 60, A 3 51c-52b; Q 99, A 5 249a-250a; Q 100, A 2, REP 2 252b-253a; A 3, REP 3 253a-d; PART II-II, Q 4, A 7, REP 3 407d-409a; Q 23, A 3, REP 1 485a-d

22 CHAUCER: *Knight's Tale* [1128-1176] 178b-179a / *Franklin's Tale* [11,770-844] 363b-36[?]b

23 HOBBES: *Leviathan*, PART I, 77b-c; 86c-92b; PART II, 115a-116a; 127b; 138c; 142a-d; 145a-b

25 MONTAIGNE: *Essays*, 13d-14c; 381a-388c esp 383c-d, 387b-c; 467b-470a

26 SHAKESPEARE: *2nd Henry VI*, ACT V, SC I [175-190] 66d-67a / *3rd Henry VI*, ACT I, SC II [1-34] 72d-73b / *Titus Andronicus*, ACT V,

(7. The relation of duty to justice and to rights: oaths and promises.)

8. The tension between duty and instinct, desire, or love

52 DOSTOEVSKY: *Brothers Karamazov*, BK IV, 95b-100c

53 JAMES: *Psychology*, 807a-808a

54 FREUD: *General Introduction*, 452c-d; 573c; 624a-625b / *War and Death*, 758c-759d esp 759c-d; 764c-765a / *Civilization and Its Discontents*, 780b-802a,c esp 781a-d, 783c-789b, 791b-d, 793d-794a, 800c-801b / *New Introductory Lectures*, 853a-b

9. The duties of command and obedience in family life

OLD TESTAMENT: *Genesis*, 2:18-25; 9:18-29 / *Exodus*, 20:12; 21:1-21,26-27 / *Leviticus*, 19:3 / *Deuteronomy*, 5:16; 15:12-18; 21:15-23; 22:13-30; 24:1-4,14-15; 25:5-10; 27:16,20,22-23 / *Ruth* / *Proverbs*, 20:20; 30:17

APOCRYPHA: *Ecclesiasticus*, 3:1-18; 4:30; 7:19-28; 30:1-13; 33:24-31—(D) OT, *Ecclesiasticus*, 3:1-20; 4:35; 7:21-30; 30:1-13; 33:25-33

NEW TESTAMENT: *Matthew*, 15:3-6 / *II Corinthians*, 12:14 / *Ephesians*, 5:22-25; 6:1-9 / *Colossians*, 3:18-4:1 / *I Timothy*, 5:8 / *Titus*, 2:9-11 / *Philemon* / *I Peter*, 3:1-7

4 HOMER: *Odyssey*, BK I-II 183a-192d

5 SOPHOCLES: *Oedipus at Colonus* [421-460] 118a-b / *Antigone* 131a-142d esp [631-680] 136c-137a / *Trachiniae* 170a-181a,c esp [1157-1258] 180a-181a,c

5 ARISTOPHANES: *Clouds* [791-885] 498b-499b; [1321-1451] 504c-506b

6 HERODOTUS: *History*, BK II, 56c; BK III, 104c-105a; BK VIII, 281c

7 PLATO: *Laws*, BK IV, 683b-c; BK XI, 779b-781c / *Seventh Letter*, 803d-804a

9 ARISTOTLE: *Ethics*, BK VIII, CH 9 [1159^{b}25-1160^{a}9] 411d-412b; CH 10 [1160^{b}23]-CH 11 [1161^{a}29] 413a-c / *Politics*, BK I, CH 12-13 453d-455a,c

14 PLUTARCH: *Agis*, 654c-655a

18 AUGUSTINE: *Confessions*, BK II, par 3-8 9b-10d; BK XIII, par 47, 123d / *City of God*, BK XIX, CH 14-16, 520c-522a

20 AQUINAS: *Summa Theologica*, PART I-II, Q 105, A 4 318b-321a

22 CHAUCER: *Tale of Man of Law* [4701-4707] 239a / *Wife of Bath's Prologue* [5583-6410] 256a-269b esp [5893-5914] 261a-b, [6385-6410] 269a-b / *Tale of Wife of Bath* [6619-6627] 273a-b / *Clerk's Tale* 296a-318a esp [9053-9088] 317a-318a / *Merchant's Tale* 319a-338a esp [9249-9266] 321a / *Franklin's Tale* [11,041-110] 351b-352b / *Tale of Melibeus*, par 13-16 404b-407b / *Parson's Tale*, par 79-80, 541a-b

23 HOBBES: *Leviathan*, PART II, 109c-110b; 121a; 155b

24 RABELAIS: *Gargantua and Pantagruel*, BK III, 219b-222b

25 MONTAIGNE: *Essays*, 184a-191c; 410a-422b; 427d-430a

26 SHAKESPEARE: *Comedy of Errors*, ACT II, SC

I [7-43] 152a-c / *Taming of the Shrew* 199a-228a,c esp ACT V, SC II [136-179] 227d-228a,c / *Romeo and Juliet*, ACT III, SC V [127-197] 308c-309b / *Midsummer-Night's Dream*, ACT I, SC I [1-121] 352a-353c / *Merchant of Venice*, ACT I, SC II 408b-409c / *1st Henry IV*, ACT II, SC III 443b-444b

27 SHAKESPEARE: *Othello*, ACT I, SC III [175-189] 210d-211a / *King Lear* 244a-283a,c

30 BACON: *Advancement of Learning*, 75c / *New Atlantis*, 207b-209d

32 MILTON: *Paradise Lost*, BK IV [288-301] 158b-159a; [440-502] 162a-163a; [634-638] 166a; BK VIII [452-594] 242a-245a; BK X [144-156] 277b; [867-936] 293b-294b / *Samson Agonistes*[871-902]358b-359a;[997-1060]361b-362b

35 LOCKE: *Civil Government*, CH VI, SECT 52-CH VII, SECT 86 36a-44a; CH XV, SECT 169-170 64c-65a; SECT 173-174 65c-d

36 SWIFT: *Gulliver*, PART I, 29b

37 FIELDING: *Tom Jones*, 6b-c; 21a-22d; 100b-102a; 105a-107b; 108c-110c; 120c-121a,c; 124a-125c; 126d-127b; 136b-c; 283c-d; 312c-313a; 321b-324b; 340c-341d; 359b-362c

38 MONTESQUIEU: *Spirit of Laws*, BK V, 22d-23a; BK XXIII, 187b,d-189d; BK XXVI, 216a-b

38 ROUSSEAU: *Inequality*, 357a-b; 364d-365b / *Political Economy*, 367a-368c / *Social Contract*, BK I, 387d-388a

41 GIBBON: *Decline and Fall*, 82b-84a; 86b-d

42 KANT: *Science of Right*, 404d; 419a-422d esp 419b-c, 420a-d; 445c-446a

43 MILL: *Liberty*, 317c-318a

46 HEGEL: *Philosophy of Right*, PART III, par 174 61b; ADDITIONS, 111 134d-135a / *Philosophy of History*, PART I, 211c-213a

51 TOLSTOY: *War and Peace*, BK VI, 249b-d; 267c-d; BK VI-VII, 271c-276b; BK VII, 291a-292b; 301b-302d; BK VIII, 305b-307a

54 FREUD: *Interpretation of Dreams*, 244a-c / *New Introductory Lectures*, 876c

10. Political obligation: cares, functions, loyalties

OLD TESTAMENT: *Exodus*, 20:13-17 / *Leviticus*, 19:9-20,32-37; 25:14-55 / *Numbers*, 35 / *Deuteronomy*, 5:17-21; 15; 17:8-20; 19; 22:1-4; 23:15-25; 24:10-13; 27:17-19,24-25 / *Proverbs*, 3:27-28; 16:10-15; 28:15-18; 29:2,4,12, 14 / *Jeremiah*, 29:7—(D) *Jeremias*, 29:7 / *Zechariah*, 8:16-17—(D) *Zacharias*, 8:16-17

NEW TESTAMENT: *Matthew*, 5:21-24; 22:17-21 / *Mark*, 12:14-17 / *Luke*, 20:20-26 / *Romans*, 13:1-7 / *Titus*, 3:1 / *I Peter*, 2:13-19

4 HOMER: *Iliad*, BK IX [1-172] 57a-58d

5 AESCHYLUS: *Seven Against Thebes* [1-77] 27a-28a

5 SOPHOCLES: *Oedipus the King* [1-77] 99a-d / *Antigone* [631-680] 136c-137a / *Philoctetes* 182a-195a,c

5 EURIPIDES: *Suppliants* [297-331] 261a-b / *Iphigenia at Aulis* [1368-1401] 437c-d

11. Duty to God: piety and worship

OLD TESTAMENT: *Genesis*, 4:2–5; 8:18–22; 12:7–8; 13:1–4; 22:1–19 esp 22:18; 28:18–22 / *Exodus*, 12–13; 35–40 / *Leviticus* passim, esp 1–7, 16, 23 / *Numbers*, 9:1–14; 19 / *Deuteronomy*, 6; 8; 10–12; 23:21–23 / *Joshua*, 22:1–6; 24:14–28—(D) *Josue*, 22:1–6; 24:14–28 / *Judges*, 11:28–40 / *I Samuel*, 15:10–35—(D) *I Kings*, 15:10–35 / *II Kings*, 12:1–16—(D) *IV Kings*, 12:1–16 / *I Chronicles*, 16:29—(D) *I Paralipomenon*, 16:29 / *II Chronicles*, 1–7; 29–31—(D) *II Paralipomenon*, 1–7; 29–31 / *Ezra*—(D) *I Esdras* / *Nehemiah*—(D) *II Esdras* / *Psalms* passim / *Ecclesiastes*, 5:2–7; 12:13—(D) *Ecclesiastes*, 5:1–6; 12:13 / *Isaiah*, 1:11–20—(D) *Isaias*, 1:11–20 / *Daniel*, 9 / *Micah*, 6:8—(D) *Micheas*, 6:8

APOCRYPHA: *Tobit*, 4:5–11,19; 12:8–10—(D) OT, *Tobias*, 4:6–12,20; 12:8–10 / *Judith*, 4; 8–9—(D) OT, *Judith*, 4; 8–9 / *Ecclesiasticus*, 18:22–24; 35:4–12—(D) OT, *Ecclesiasticus*, 18:22–24; 35:6–15 / *Baruch*, 1; 4:1–3—(D) OT, *Baruch*, 1; 4:1–3 / *Bel and Dragon*, 2–28—(D) OT, *Daniel*, 14:1–27 / *I Maccabees*, 4:38–61—(D) OT, *I Machabees*, 4:38–61

NEW TESTAMENT: *Matthew*, 4:1–11; 5:33–36; 6:1–8,16–18; 7:21; 18:23–35; 22:21,34–40 / *Mark*, 12:28–34 / *Luke*, 2:21–24; 4:1–13; 9:23–26,57–62; 10:25–42; 17:7–10; 18:1–14; 20:25 / *Acts*, 5:17–32; 20:22–24 / *Romans*, 12–13 / *Ephesians*, 4 esp 4:17–32 / *Colossians*, 3 / *I Timothy*, 2:1–8 / *II Timothy* / *James*, 5:13–18 / *I John* esp 2:3–11, 2:15, 3:23, 4:7–5:5 / *II John*

4 HOMER: *Iliad*, BK I [206–222] 5b; BK IX [485–514] 62a-b; BK XXIV [424–431] 175d / *Odyssey*, BK XIII [125–184] 256b-257a

5 AESCHYLUS: *Suppliant Maidens* 1a-14a,c esp [600–709] 8d-10b / *Agamemnon* [369–398] 56a-b / *Eumenides* [490–565] 86b-87a

5 SOPHOCLES: *Oedipus the King* [863–910] 107b-c / *Oedipus at Colonus* [461–509] 118b-d / *Antigone* 131a-142d esp [441–470] 134d-135a, [1347–1353] 142d / *Ajax* [748–779] 149c-d; [1316–1421] 154b-155a,c / *Electra* [1058–1097] 164d-165a / *Philoctetes* [1440–1444] 195a,c

5 EURIPIDES: *Suppliants* 258a-269a,c esp [1–41] 258a-b, [513–563] 262d-263b / *Electra* [167–212] 328c-d / *Bacchantes* 340a-352a,c / *Hecuba* [799–805] 359d

5 ARISTOPHANES: *Birds* 542a-563d esp [1170–1266] 557b-558b

6 HERODOTUS: *History*, BK V, 171d-172a; BK VI, 201d-202c; BK VIII, 282b-c; BK IX, 308a-c

7 PLATO: *Euthyphro* 191a-199a,c / *Apology*, 206b-d / *Timaeus*, 447a / *Laws*, BK IV, 682d-683b; BK X, 769c-771b

8 ARISTOTLE: *Topics*, BK I, CH 11 [105^{a}2–6] 148c

9 ARISTOTLE: *Politics*, BK VII, CH 9 [1329^{a}26–34] 533d

12 LUCRETIUS: *Nature of Things*, BK VI [56–79] 81a-b

12 EPICTETUS: *Discourses*, BK I, CH 16 121d-122d; CH 27, 132c-133a; BK II, CH 16, 158b-d; BK III, CH 24 203c-210a; BK IV, CH 3 224b-d; CH 12 242d-244a

12 AURELIUS: *Meditations*, BK I, SECT 17 255d-256d; BK II, SECT 13 258c; BK V, SECT 7 269d; BK IX, SECT 1 291a-c; SECT 40 295b

13 VIRGIL: *Aeneid*, BK V [42–103] 188a-190a

14 PLUTARCH: *Aemilius Paulus*, 214b-d

15 TACITUS: *Histories*, BK IV, 282d-283b

16 KEPLER: *Harmonies of the World*, 1011a

18 AUGUSTINE: *Confessions*, BK I, par 4 2a; BK III, par 15 17a-b / *City of God*, BK VII, CH 27–31 259c-262a; BK X, CH 1–7 298b,d-303a; CH 16 308b-309c; CH 19 310d-311b; BK XIX, CH 14–16, 520c-522a; CH 19 523b-d / *Christian Doctrine*, BK I, CH 10 627b; CH 22–30 629b-633b

19 AQUINAS: *Summa Theologica*, PART I, Q 63, A 1, ANS 325c-326c; PART I-II, Q 19, A 5, REP 1–2 705d-707a; A 6, ANS and REP 2 707a-708a; Q 21, A 4 719d-720a,c

20 AQUINAS: *Summa Theologica*, PART I-II, Q 91, AA 4–5 210c-212c; Q 96, A 4 233a-d; QQ 98–108 239b-337d; PART II-II, Q 4, A 7, REP 3 407d-409a; Q 16 454c-456d; Q 22 480d-482c; Q 44 592d-598c; QQ 183–189 625a-700d; PART III, Q 25 839c-845a

21 DANTE: *Divine Comedy*, PURGATORY, XIII [103–129] 73a-b; XVII [82]–XVIII [75] 79b-80c; XXX–XXXI 99b-102b; PARADISE, III [1]–V [87] 109b-113a passim; VII [25–33] 115c; [64–102] 115d-116a; XXVI [115–117] 147a

22 CHAUCER: *Second Nun's Tale* [15,829–16,021] 468a-471b

23 HOBBES: *Leviathan*, PART I, 80c; PART II, 137b-138b; PART II-III, 159d-167b; PART III, 177c-180d; 198a-207b; 240a-246a,c; PART IV, 261d-262a

25 MONTAIGNE: *Essays*, 152b-156d; 233a-b

26 SHAKESPEARE: *Richard II*, ACT I, SC II [1–41] 322d-323a

27 SHAKESPEARE: *Henry VIII*, ACT III, SC II [435–457] 573c-d

30 BACON: *Advancement of Learning*, 80b-81a; 100d-101a

31 DESCARTES: *Meditations*, 69b

31 SPINOZA: *Ethics*, PART V, PROP 41 462d-463b

32 MILTON: *Sonnets*, XVI 66b-67a / *Paradise Lost* 93a-333a esp BK I [242–283] 98b-99b, BK IV [411–439] 161b-162a, [720–739] 168a-b, BK V [136–210] 178a-179b, [506–543] 186a-187a, BK VII [449–518] 227a-228b, BK VIII [311–333] 239a-b, [630–643] 246a, BK IX [647–654] 261b, BK XI [133–161] 302a-b, BK XII [386–410] 327b-328a / *Samson Agonistes* [1334–1409] 368b-370a / *Areopagitica*, 402a-b

33 PASCAL: *Provincial Letters*, 78b-80b / *Pensées*, 476 256b-257a; 482 258a; 489,491 259a; 539 265b

(11. *Duty to God: piety and worship.*)

35 LOCKE: *Toleration*, 2a-b; 3b-4a; 10d-11a; 15d-16a; 16c-17b / *Civil Government*, CH II, SECT 6 26b-c; CH VI, SECT 56 36d

36 STERNE: *Tristram Shandy*, 255a-268a

37 FIELDING: *Tom Jones*, 187d-188a

38 ROUSSEAU: *Social Contract*, BK IV, 435a-439c passim

40 GIBBON: *Decline and Fall*, 81d-82b; 180c-182c esp 181b-c; 184d-185d; 191a-194a passim; 226a-b; 291d-292d; 350b-d; 533b-d; 593b,d-599a passim, esp 593b,d

41 GIBBON: *Decline and Fall*, 226c-227b; 232c-233c; 259b-260a

42 KANT: *Practical Reason*, 325a-327d; 345c-d / *Intro. Metaphysic of Morals*, 383b,d-384a,c / *Judgement*, 502d-503a; 504b-505a; 509a-c; 593a-d; 611a-c

43 MILL: *Liberty*, 296b-d; 310d-311a

44 BOSWELL: *Johnson*, 84b-c; 262b

46 HEGEL: *Philosophy of History*, PART I, 225b

48 MELVILLE: *Moby Dick*, 30a-36b; 39a-b

51 TOLSTOY: *War and Peace*, BK I, 50b-c; BK III, 122b-c; BK V, 218b-220a; BK VI, 271c-d; 273c-274a,c; BK XI, 476c-480a

52 DOSTOEVSKY: *Brothers Karamazov*, BK IV, 83c-84a; BK V, 127b-137c; BK VI, 164a-165a; 167b-170b

CROSS-REFERENCES

For: Other discussions of the issue between the ethics of duty and the ethics of happiness or pleasure, *see* HAPPINESS 3; PLEASURE AND PAIN 6–6a, 8b.

Matters relevant to this issue, *see* DESIRE 2b, 3a; GOOD AND EVIL 3a–3b(2); JUSTICE 1e–1f, 4; LAW 3a(1), 4–4a, 4c–4d; TEMPERANCE 3; VIRTUE AND VICE 1d, 6a; WILL 8b(2), 8c–8d.

Other treatments of conscience, both psychological and ethical, *see* HONOR 2a; PUNISHMENT 5c; SIN 5; TEMPERANCE 3.

The consideration of duty in relation to law, justice, and rights, *see* GOD 3d; JUSTICE 1e, 3, 11b; LAW 2, 4a, 4c–4d, 6a; RELIGION 2; WILL 8d.

The conflict between duty and desire or love, *see* DESIRE 6a–6b; LOVE 3c.

The treatment of specific duties, domestic, political, and religious, *see* CITIZEN 4; FAMILY 6d; GOD 3d; JUSTICE 11b; RELIGION 2; STATE 8a; TRUTH 8e.

ADDITIONAL READINGS

Listed below are works not included in *Great Books of the Western World*, but relevant to the idea and topics with which this chapter deals. These works are divided into two groups:

I. Works by authors represented in this collection.
II. Works by authors not represented in this collection.

For the date, place, and other facts concerning the publication of the works cited, consult the Bibliography of Additional Readings which follows the last chapter of *The Great Ideas*.

I.

EPICTETUS. *The Manual*

HOBBES. *Philosophical Rudiments Concerning Government and Society*, CH 13

HUME. *A Treatise of Human Nature*, BK III, PART II, SECT VII–X

FIELDING. *Amelia*

A. SMITH. *The Theory of Moral Sentiments*, PART III

KANT. *Lectures on Ethics*, pp 11–47, 116–253

——. *Religion Within the Limits of Reason Alone*

DOSTOEVSKY. *Crime and Punishment*

II.

CICERO. *De Finibus (On the Supreme Good)*
——. *De Officiis (On Duties)*

SENECA. *Moral Essays*

MAIMONIDES. *Eight Chapters on Ethics*

BOCCACCIO. *Patient Griselda*

BEAUMONT and FLETCHER. *The Maid's Tragedy*

SANDERSON. *De Obligatione Conscientiae (On the Obligations of Conscience)*

CORNEILLE. *Le Cid*
——. *Horace*
——. *Polyeucte*

J. TAYLOR. *Of Holy Living*
——. *Ductor Dubitantium*

RACINE. *Andromaque*

BAXTER. *Chapters from A Christian Directory*

PUFENDORF. *De Officio Hominis et Civis Juxta Legem Naturalem (Of the Duties of Man and of the Citizen According to Natural Law)*

J. BUTLER. *Fifteen Sermons upon Human Nature*, III, X, XIII

T. REID. *Essays on the Active Powers of the Human Mind*, III, PART III, CH 5–8

D. STEWART. *Outlines of Moral Philosophy*, PART II, CH 2

J. G. FICHTE. *The Vocation of Man*, PART III

WORDSWORTH. *Ode to Duty*

BENTHAM. *Deontology*

WHEWELL. *The Elements of Morality*, BK II, CH 5–12; BK V, CH 2, 10–17

MAZZINI. *The Duties of Man*

MAURICE. *The Conscience*

P. A. JANET. *The Theory of Morals*, BK II, CH 2

H. SIDGWICK. *The Methods of Ethics*, BK II, CH 5; BK III, CH 2

BRADLEY. *Ethical Studies*, IV–V

T. H. GREEN. *The Principles of Political Obligation*, (A)

GUYAU. *Esquisse d'une morale sans obligation ni sanction*

NIETZSCHE. *The Genealogy of Morals*, II

BRENTANO. *The Origin of the Knowledge of Right and Wrong*, par 1–13

SPENCER. *The Principles of Ethics*, VOL II, PART IV, CH 9–29; PART V–VI

DEWEY. "The Idea of Obligation," in *Outlines of a Critical Theory of Ethics*

——. *The Study of Ethics*, CH 7–8

BOSANQUET. *Science and Philosophy*, 16

CROCE. *The Philosophy of the Practical*, PART I, SECT II; PART II, SECT I (IV); SECT II (I); PART III (IV)

ROYCE. *The Philosophy of Loyalty*

MOORE. *Principia Ethica*, CH 4

——. *Ethics*, CH 4–5

PRICHARD. *Duty and Interest*

N. HARTMANN. *Ethics*, VOL I, *Moral Phenomena*, SECT 4–6

KIRK. *Conscience and Its Problems*

ROSS. *The Right and the Good*, I–II, VII

BERGSON. *Two Sources of Morality and Religion*, CH I

MUIRHEAD. *Rule and End in Morals*

Chapter 20: EDUCATION

INTRODUCTION

THE great books assembled in this set are offered as means to a liberal or general education. The authors of these books were educated men; more than that, they typified the ideal of education in their various epochs. As their writings reveal, their minds were largely formed, or at least deeply impressed, by reading the works of their predecessors. Many of them were related as teacher and student, sometimes through personal contact, sometimes only through the written word. Many of them were related as divergent disciples of the same master, yet they often differed with him as well as with one another. There is scarcely one among them—except Homer—who was not acquainted with the minds of the others who came before him and, more often than not, profoundly conversant with their thought.

Yet not one of the writings in this set is specifically a treatise on education, except Montaigne's essay *Of the Education of Children.* Some of these authors speak more or less fully of their own education, as does Marcus Aurelius in the opening book of his *Meditations*, Augustine in his *Confessions*, Descartes in his *Discourse*, and Boswell. Others refer to their educational experience in fictional guise, as does Aristophanes in the argument in the *Clouds* between the Just and Unjust Discourses; or Rabelais when he tells of Gargantua's schooling in Gargantua's letter to Pantagruel. Sometimes they report the way in which other men were trained to greatness, as does Plutarch; or, like Gibbon, Hegel, and Mill, they describe and comment on the historic systems of education.

In still other instances the great books contain sections or chapters devoted to the ends and means of education, the order of studies, the nature of learning and teaching, the training of statesmen and citizens; as for example,

Plato's *Republic*, Aristotle's *Politics*, Augustine's *Christian Doctrine*, Bacon's *Advancement of Learning*, Adam Smith's *Wealth of Nations*, Hegel's *Philosophy of Right*, and the psychological writings of James and Freud. But in no case is education the principal theme of these books, as it is for most of the works cited in the list of Additional Readings, among which will be found treatises on education by authors in this set.

EDUCATION IS not itself so much an idea or a subject matter as it is a theme to which the great ideas and the basic subject matters are relevant. It is one of the perennial practical problems which men cannot discuss without engaging in the deepest speculative considerations. It is a problem which carries discussion into and across a great many subject matters—the liberal arts of grammar, rhetoric, and logic; psychology, medicine, metaphysics, and theology; ethics, politics, and economics. It is a problem which draws into focus many of the great ideas—virtue and truth, knowledge and opinion, art and science; desire, will, sense, memory, mind, habit; change and progress; family and state; man, nature, and God.

This can be verified by noting the diverse contexts in which education is discussed in the great books. In each connection we shall find some of the special questions which together make up the complex problem of education. For example, the nature of teaching and learning is examined in the wider context of psychological considerations concerning man's abilities, the way in which knowledge is acquired, and how it is communicated by means of language or other symbols. Different conceptions of the nature of man and of the relation of his several capacities surround the question of the ends of education. In this context questions also arise concerning the parts of education—the training of man's body, the formation of his character, the cultivation of his mind—and how these are related to one another.

The whole theory of the virtues and of habit formation is involved in the question whether virtue can be taught or must be acquired in some other way, and in related questions about the influence of the family and the state on the growth of character. These questions are also asked in terms of general political theory. Different views of the state are involved in questions about the division of responsibility for education among various agencies. Questions about the purpose of education, and what sort of education shall be given to the diverse classes in the state, are differently raised and differently answered in the context of discussions of different forms of government.

Though they are far from exhaustive, these examples should nevertheless suffice to make the point that there can be no philosophy of education apart from philosophy as a whole. It may therefore not be a disadvantage to find the discussion of education in the great books almost always imbedded in the context of some more general theory or problem.

ONE OPINION FROM which there is hardly a dissenting voice in the great books is that education should aim to make men good as men and as citizens. "If you ask what is the good of education," Plato writes, "the answer is easy— that education makes good men, and that good men act nobly, and conquer their enemies in battle, because they are good." Men should enter upon learning, Bacon declares, in order "to give a true account of their gift of reason, to the benefit and use of men"; while William James stresses the need for "a perfectly-rounded development." Thus it would seem to be a common opinion in all ages that education should seek to develop the characteristic excellences of which men are capable and that its ultimate ends are human happiness and the welfare of society.

Within this area of general agreement there are, of course, differences which result from the different views that are taken of man's relation to the state or to God. If the good of the state takes precedence over individual happiness, then education must be directed to training men for the role they play as parts of a larger organism. Education then serves the purpose of preserving the state. Of all things, Aristotle says, "that which contributes most to the permanence of constitutions is the adaptation of education to the form of government. . . . The best laws," he continues, "though sanctioned by every citizen of the state, will be of no avail unless the young are trained by habit and education in the spirit of the constitution."

Rousseau seems to take a similar view when he calls for a system of public education run by the state. Its object is to assure that the citizens are "early accustomed to regard their individuality only in its relation to the body of the state, and to be aware, so to speak, of their own existence merely as a part of that of the state." Taught in this way, the citizens, Rousseau claims, "might at length come to identify themselves in some degree with this greater whole, to feel themselves members of their country, and to love it with that exquisite feeling which no isolated person has save for himself."

If happiness cannot be fully achieved on earth, then whatever temporal ends education serves must themselves be ordered to eternal salvation, and the whole process of human development must be a direction of the soul to God. "What did it profit me," Augustine asks in his *Confessions*, "that all the books I could procure of the so-called liberal arts, I, the vile slave of vile affections, read by myself and understood? . . . For I had my back to the light, and my face to the things enlightened; whence my face, with which I discerned the things enlightened, was not itself enlightened. Whatever was written, either on rhetoric, or logic, geometry, music and arithmetic, by myself without much difficulty or any instructor, I understood, Thou knowest, O Lord my God; because both quickness of understanding and acuteness in discerning, is Thy gift; yet did I not thence sacrifice to Thee." Wherefore, Augustine concludes concerning this stage of his learning, "it served not to my use but to my perdition." But Augustine does not therefore conclude that, under no circumstances, can liberal education be put to good use. In his treatise *On Christian Doctrine*, he considers in detail how the liberal arts, which serve so well in the study of Sacred Scripture, may also serve to bring the soul to God.

SUCH DIFFERENCES DO NOT, however, annul one consequence of the general agreement, namely, the conception that education is concerned with the vocation of man, and prepares him in thought and action for his purpose and station in life. In these terms Adam Smith argues for a minimum general education. He claims that "a man without the proper use of the intellectual faculties of a man, is, if possible, more contemptible than even a coward, and seems to be mutilated and deformed in a still more essential part of the character of human nature." He explicitly points out that this is the condition of "the great body of the people," who, by the division of labor, are confined in their employment "to a few very simple operations," in which the worker "has no occasion to exert his understanding, or to exercise his invention in finding out expedients for removing difficulties which never occur." The result, according to Smith, is that "the torpor of his mind renders him, not only incapable of relishing or bearing a part in any rational conversation, but of conceiving any generous, noble, or tender sentiment, and consequently of forming any just judgment concerning many even of the ordinary duties of private life."

When the vocation of man is thus understood, a general or liberal education is vocational in that it prepares each man for the common conditions and callings of human life. In this sense specialized training, which by implication at least seems to be the object of Smith's criticism, is not vocational. It fits a man only for some specialized function, according to which he or his social class is differentiated from some other man or class.

In our day, the word "vocational" is used in the opposite sense to mean specialized training, whether it is preparation for the least skilled of trades or for the most learned of professions. Since all men are not called to the practice of law or medicine—any more than all are called to productive work in the various arts and crafts, or the tasks of commerce and industry—the training they may need to perform these functions does not fully develop their common humanity. It is not adequate to make them good as men, as citizens, or as children of God.

The traditional meaning of the word "liberal" as applied to education entails a distinction between free men and slaves. Slaves, like domesticated animals, are trained to perform special functions. They are not treated as ends, but as means, and so they are not educated for their own good, but for the use to which they are put. This is true not only of slaves in the strict sense of household chattel; it is also true of all the servile classes in any society which divides its human beings into those who work in order to live and those who live off the work of others and who therefore have the leisure in which to strive to live well.

In accordance with these distinctions, Aristotle divides education into "liberal" and "illiberal." Certain subjects are illiberal by nature, namely, "any occupation, art, or science, which makes the body or soul of the freeman less fit for the practice or exercise of virtue." In this category Aristotle includes "those arts which tend to deform the body, and likewise all paid employments, for they absorb and degrade the mind."

It is not only the nature of the subject, but also the end which education serves, that determines whether its character is liberal or illiberal. Even a liberal art becomes, in Aristotle's opinion, "menial and servile . . . if done for the sake of others." A man's education "will not appear illiberal" only so long as "he does or learns anything for his own sake or for the sake of his friends, or with a view to excellence." In other words, to be liberal, education must serve the use of leisure in the pursuit of excellence. It must treat man as an end, not as a means to be used by other men or by the state.

It follows that any society which abolishes the distinction of social classes and which calls all men to freedom, should conceive education as essentially liberal and for all men. It should, furthermore, direct education, in *all* its parts and phases, to the end of each man's living well rather than to the end of his earning a living for himself or others.

IN THE CLASSIFICATION of the kinds of education, the word "liberal" is frequently used in a more restricted sense to signify not all education designed for free men, but only the improvement of the mind through the acquisition of knowledge and skill. In this sense liberal education is set apart from physical education which concerns bodily health and proficiency, and moral education which concerns excellence in action rather than in thought.

These divisions are clearly made, perhaps for the first time, in Plato's *Republic*. The education described there begins in the early years with music and gymnastic. Gymnastic "presides over the growth and decay of the body." Music, which includes literature as well as the arts of harmony and rhythm, is said to educate its students "by the influence of habit, by harmony making them harmonious, by rhythm rhythmical," and its function is to develop moral as well as aesthetic sensibilities.

The second part of Plato's curriculum, "which leads naturally to reflection" and draws "the soul towards being," consists in the mathematical arts and sciences of arithmetic, geometry, music, and astronomy. The program is capped by the study of dialectic, to which all the rest is but "a prelude"; for "when a person starts on the discovery of the absolute by the light of reason only, and without any assistance of sense, and perseveres until by pure intelligence he arrives at the perception of the absolute good, he at last finds himself at the end of the intellectual world."

Up to this point, the program can be taken as liberal education in the narrow sense of learning how and what to think. The fifteen years of experience in civic affairs and the tasks of government, which Plato interposes at the age of thirty-five, seem to function as another phase of moral training. This period provides "an opportunity of trying whether, when they are drawn all manner of ways by temptation, they will stand firm or flinch."

To the extent that physical training aims, beyond health, at the acquirement of skill in a coordinated use of one's body, it can be annexed to liberal rather than moral education. Plato notes, for example, that gymnastic should not be too sharply distinguished from music as "the training of the body" from the "training of the soul." Gymnastic as well as music, he claims, has "in view chiefly the improvement of the soul," and he considers the two as balancing and tempering one another.

Whether they produce competence in gymnastic or athletic feats, or, like the manual arts, proficiency in productive work, all bodily skills, even the simplest, involve the senses and the mind as well as bones and muscles. They are arts no less than music or logic. Apart from their utility, they represent a certain type of human excellence, which will be denied only by those who can see no difference between the quality of a racehorse and the skill of his rider. Whether these skills as well as other useful arts are part of liberal education in the broader sense depends, as we have seen, on the end for which they are taught or learned. Even the arts which are traditionally called liberal, such as rhetoric or logic, can be degraded to servility if the sole motive for becoming skilled in them is wealth won by success in the law courts.

IN THE TWO traditional distinctions so far discussed, "liberal education" seems to have a somewhat different meaning when it signifies the opposite of servile training and when it signifies the opposite of moral cultivation. In the first case, the distinction is based upon the purpose of the education; in the second, it refers to the faculties or functions being cultivated. When the second is stated in terms of the distinction between the intellectual and the moral virtues, liberal (*i.e.*, intellectual) education is conceived as aiming at good habits of thinking and knowing, and moral education is thought of as aiming at good habits of will, desire, or emotion, along with their consequences in action.

Although he does not use these terms, Montaigne seems to have the contrast between moral and intellectual training in mind when he criticizes the education of his day for aiming "at nothing but to furnish our heads with knowledge, but not a word of judgment and virtue." It is, to him, a "pedantic education," which not only fails to achieve the highest educational purpose, but also results in a great evil, in that "all knowledge is hurtful to him who has not the science of goodness."

A too sharp separation of the intellectual

and the moral may be questioned, or at least qualified, by those who, like Socrates, tend to identify knowledge and virtue. Yet they seldom go to the opposite extreme of supposing that no distinction can be made between the task of imparting knowledge to the mind and that of forming character. Socrates, for example, in the *Meno*, recognizes that a man cannot be made temperate, courageous, or just in the same way that he can be taught geometry.

From another point of view, the notion of moral training is questioned by those who, like Freud, think that the patterns of human desire or emotion can be beneficially changed apart from moral discipline. It is the object of psychoanalysis, he writes, "to strengthen the ego, to make it more independent of the super-ego, to widen its field of vision, and so to extend its organization that it can take over new portions of the id." To do this is radically to alter the individual's behavior-pattern. "It is reclamation work," Freud says, "like the draining of the Zuyder Zee." Emotional education, so conceived, is therapeutic—more like preventive and remedial medicine than moral training.

Religious education is usually regarded as both intellectual and moral, even as the science of theology is said to be both speculative and practical. Citing the admonition of St. James, "Be ye doers of the word, and not hearers only," Aquinas holds that religious education is concerned with the knowledge not only of "divine things" but also of the "human acts" by which man comes to God. Since man is infinitely removed from God, he needs for this purpose the grace of God, which, according to Aquinas, "is nothing short of a partaking of the divine nature."

Both on the side of man's knowledge of God and on the side of his love and worship of God, religious education involves the operation of supernatural factors—revelation, grace, sacraments. Hence God is Himself the primary source of religious education. But as the dispenser of the sacraments whereby "grace is instrumentally caused," the church, according to Aquinas, functions instrumentally in the service of the divine teacher.

THE CONCEPTION OF THE means and ends of moral education will differ with different ethical theories of the good man and the good life, and according to differing enumerations and definitions of the virtues. It will differ even more fundamentally according to whether the primary emphasis is placed on pleasure and happiness or duty. The parties to this basic issue in moral philosophy, which is discussed in the chapters on DUTY and HAPPINESS, inevitably propose different ways of forming good character—by strengthening the will in obedience to law, or by habituating the appetites to be moderate or reasonable in their inclinations.

On either theory, the basic problem of moral education is whether morality can be taught and how. The Greeks formulated this question in terms of virtue, by asking whether such things as courage and temperance are *at all* teachable, as geometry and horsemanship plainly are. The problem remains essentially the same if the question is how the will can be trained. Can it be trained by the same methods as those which work in the improvement of the understanding?

The answer to the question, whichever way it is formulated, depends on the view that is taken of the relation between moral knowledge and moral conduct. Do those who understand the principles of ethics or who know the moral law necessarily act in accordance with their knowledge? Can a man know what is good or right to do in a particular case, and yet do the opposite? St. Paul seems to suggest this when he says, "For the good that I would I do not: but the evil which I would not, that I do." If something more than knowledge or straight thinking is needed for good conduct, how is it acquired and how can one man help another to acquire it? Certainly not by learning and teaching in the ordinary sense which applies to the arts and sciences. Then how—by practice, by guidance or advice, by example, by rewards and punishments; or if by none of these, then by a gift of nature or by the grace of God?

These questions are necessarily prior to any discussion of the role of the family, the state, and the church in the process of moral training. They also provide the general background for the consideration of particular influences on character formation in men and children, such things as poetry and music, or laws and customs. All of these related problems of moral education have a political aspect, which appears in the issue concerning the state's right to censor or regulate the arts for morality's sake; in the question of the primacy of the family or the state in the moral guidance of the young; in the distinction between the good man and the good citizen or ruler, and the possible difference between the training appropriate for the one and for the other.

THE MAIN PROBLEM of intellectual education seems to be the curriculum or course of study. The traditional attempts to construct an ideal curriculum turn on such questions as what studies shall be included, what shall be their order, and how shall they be taught or learned. A variety of answers results from a variety of views of man's faculties or capacities, the nature of knowledge itself, the classification and order of the arts and sciences. Especially important are the various conceptions of the nature and function of the liberal arts. Subordinate questions concern the place of the fine and useful arts in liberal education, and the role of experience and experiment—both in contrast to and in cooperation with the role of books and teachers.

In addition to the problem of the curriculum and its materials, the theory of intellectual education necessarily considers methods of teaching and learning. Here the various proposals derive from different views of the learning process—of the causes or factors at work in any acquisition of skill or knowledge.

The contribution of the teacher cannot be understood apart from a psychological analysis of learning, for the teacher is obviously only one among its many causes. It makes the greatest difference to the whole enterprise of learning whether the teacher is regarded as the principal cause of understanding on the part of the student; or whether the teacher is, as Socrates describes himself, merely "a midwife" assisting the labor of the mind in bringing knowledge and wisdom to birth, and "thoroughly examining whether the thought which the mind ... brings forth is a false idol or a noble and true birth."

This Socratic insight is later reformulated in the comparison which Aquinas makes, in his tract *Concerning the Teacher*, between the art of teaching and the art of healing. Both are co-operative arts, arts which succeed only as "ministers of nature which is the principal actor," and not by acting, like the art of the cobbler or sculptor, to produce a result by shaping plastic but dead materials.

The comparison which Hippocrates makes of instruction in medicine with "the culture of the productions of the earth" exhibits the same conception of teaching. "Our natural disposition," he writes, "is, as it were, the soil; the tenets of our teacher are, as it were, the seed; instruction in youth is like the planting of the seed in the ground at the proper season; the place where the instruction is communicated is like the food imparted to vegetables by the atmosphere; diligent study is like the cultivation of the fields; and it is time which imparts strength to all things and brings them to maturity."

This conception of teaching as a cooperative art, analogous to medicine or to agriculture, underlies the principles of pedagogy in the *Great Didactic* of Comenius. It gives significance to the distinction that Aquinas makes between learning by discovery, or from experience, and learning by instruction, or from a teacher—even as a person is healed "in one way by the operation of nature alone, and in another by nature with the administration of medicine."

In addition to the technical considerations raised by the nature of the learning process, the discussion of teaching deals with the moral or emotional aspect of the relation between teacher and student. Without interest, learning seldom takes place, or if it does, it cannot rise above the level of rote memory. It is one thing to lay down a course of study; another to motivate the student. Though he does not hesitate to prescribe what is to be learned by the student, Plato adds the caution that there must be no "notion of forcing our system of education."

More than interest is required. Teaching, Augustine declares, is the greatest act of charity. Learning is facilitated by love. The courtesies between Dante and Virgil in the *Divine Comedy* present an eloquent picture of love between student and teacher, master and dis-ciple. Not only love, but docility, is required on the part of the student; and respect for the student's mind on the part of the teacher. Intellectual education may not be directly concerned with the formation of character, yet the moral virtues seem to be factors in the pursuit of truth and in the discipline of the learning process.

WE HAVE ALREADY noted some of the political problems of education. Of these probably the chief question is whether the organization and institution of education shall be private or public. Any answer which assigns the control of education largely or wholly to the state must lead to a number of other determinations.

Who shall be educated, all or only some? Should the education of leaders be different from the education of others? If educational opportunity is to be equal for all, must the same kind as well as the same quantity of education be offered to all? And, in every case, to what end shall the state direct the education of its members—to its own welfare and security, or to the happiness of men and the greater glory of God? Should education always serve the status quo by preserving extant customs and perpetuating existing forms of government; or can and should it aim at a better society and a higher culture?

These are some of the questions with which statesmen and political philosophers have dealt, answering them differently according to the institutions of their time and in accordance with one or another theory of the state and its government. There are still other questions. Is freedom of expression, in teaching and discussion, indispensable to the pursuit of truth and the dissemination of knowledge? To what extent shall the state control the content and methods of education or leave such determination to the teaching profession? How shall public education be supported? Should it be carried beyond childhood and youth to all the ages of adult life; and if so, how should such education be organized outside of schools?

Mill, for example, holds it to be "almost a self-evident axiom that the State should require and compel the education, up to a certain standard, of every human being who is born

its citizen." Yet he deprecates the idea of a "general state education" as a "mere contrivance for moulding people to be exactly like one another."

Discussing the pro's and con's of this issue, Mill touches upon most, if not all, of the questions just raised. He believes that the difficulties could be avoided if the government would leave it "to parents to obtain the education where and how they pleased, and content itself with helping to pay the school fees of the poorer classes of children, and defraying the entire school expenses of those who have no one else to pay for them." Schools completely established and controlled by the state, he maintains, "should only exist, if they exist at all, as one among many competing experiments, carried on for the purpose of example and stimulus, to keep the others up to a certain standard of excellence."

So far as the problem of adult education concerns citizenship, Mill's answer, like Montesquieu's and Plato's before him, is that nothing can take the place of active participation in political life. Men become citizens by living and acting as citizens, under the tutelage of good laws and in an atmosphere of civic virtue. So far as the problem of adult education concerns the continued growth of the mind throughout the life of mature men and women, the answer is not to be found in the great books in the words of their authors. Yet the great books as a whole may constitute a solution to that problem.

The authors of these books, from Homer to Freud, are the great original teachers in the tradition of our culture. They taught one another. They wrote for adults, not children, and in the main they wrote for the mass of men, not for scholars in this or that specialized field of learning.

The books exhibit these teachers at work in the process of teaching. They contain, moreover, expositions or exemplifications of the liberal arts as the arts of teaching and learning in every field of subject matter. To make these books and their authors work for us by working with them is, it seems to the editors and publishers of this set of books, a feasible and desirable program of adult education.

OUTLINE OF TOPICS

REFERENCES

To find the passages cited, use the numbers in heavy type, which are the volume and page numbers of the passages referred to. For example, in 4 HOMER: *Iliad*, BK II [265–283] 12d, the number 4 is the number of the volume in the set; the number 12d indicates that the passage is in section d of page 12.

PAGE SECTIONS: When the text is printed in one column, the letters a and b refer to the upper and lower halves of the page. For example, in 53 JAMES: *Psychology*, 116a-119b, the passage begins in the upper half of page 116 and ends in the lower half of page 119. When the text is printed in two columns, the letters a and b refer to the upper and lower halves of the left-hand side of the page, the letters c and d to the upper and lower halves of the right-hand side of the page. For example, in 7 PLATO: *Symposium*, 163b-164c, the passage begins in the lower half of the left-hand side of page 163 and ends in the upper half of the right-hand side of page 164.

AUTHOR'S DIVISIONS: One or more of the main divisions of a work (such as PART, BK, CH, SECT) are sometimes included in the reference; line numbers, in brackets, are given in certain cases; *e.g.*, *Iliad*, BK II [265–283] 12d.

BIBLE REFERENCES: The references are to book, chapter, and verse. When the King James and Douay versions differ in title of books or in the numbering of chapters or verses, the King James version is cited first and the Douay, indicated by a (*D*), follows; *e.g.*, OLD TESTAMENT: *Nehemiah*, 7:45—(*D*) II *Esdras*, 7:46.

SYMBOLS: The abbreviation "esp" calls the reader's attention to one or more especially relevant parts of a whole reference; "passim" signifies that the topic is discussed intermittently rather than continuously in the work or passage cited.

For additional information concerning the style of the references, see the Explanation of Reference Style; for general guidance in the use of *The Great Ideas*, consult the Preface.

1. The ends of education

4 HOMER: *Iliad*, BK IX [430–441] 61c

5 ARISTOPHANES: *Clouds* 488a-506d esp [866–1114] 499a-502b

7 PLATO: *Protagoras*, 45d-46d / *Apology*, 201b-c / *Republic*, BK II–III, 320c-339a passim, esp BK III, 333b-c, 338a-339a; 341b-c; BK VI–VII, 383d-398c / *Timaeus*, 474b-d / *Laws*, BK I, 648b-649d; BK II, 653a-c; 656b-c; BK VII 713c-731d passim; BK XII, 796b-799a,c

8 ARISTOTLE: *Topics*, BK I, CH 2 143d-144a / *Metaphysics*, BK I, CH 1–2 499a-501c

9 ARISTOTLE: *Parts of Animals*, BK I, CH 1 [639ᵃ1–15] 161a-b / *Ethics*, BK I, CH 2 339b-d; CH 13 [1102ᵃ5–25] 347b-c / *Politics*, BK II, CH 5 [1263ᵇ36–1264ᵃ1] 459a; BK VII, CH 13–BK VIII, CH 7 536b-548a,c

12 LUCRETIUS: *Nature of Things*, BK II [1–61] 15a-d; BK III [1053–1075] 43c-d; BK V [1–54] 61a-d; BK VI [1–42] 80a-d

12 EPICTETUS: *Discourses*, BK I, CH 22 127c-128c; BK III, CH 15 190a-191a; CH 21 193d-195a; CH 24 203c-210a esp 208d-210a

12 AURELIUS: *Meditations*, BK IV, SECT 3 263b-264a; SECT 16 264d; BK X, SECT 11–12 298b-d

13 VIRGIL: *Aeneid*, BK VIII [508–519] 272b-273a

14 PLUTARCH: *Lycurgus-Numa*, 63d-64a / *Coriolanus*, 174b,d-175a

17 PLOTINUS: *First Ennead*, TR III 10a-12b

18 AUGUSTINE: *Confessions*, BK I, par 14 4c-d; par 16 5a-b; par 19 5d; par 24 7a

19 AQUINAS: *Summa Theologica*, PART I, Q 1, A 1 3b-4a; Q 94, A 3, ANS 504a-505a

23 HOBBES: *Leviathan*, PART II, 153a-156b

24 RABELAIS: *Gargantua and Pantagruel*, BK II, 81a-83b

25 MONTAIGNE: *Essays*, 55d-62a esp 60c-61c; 64c-66b; 69d-72a

26 SHAKESPEARE: *Taming of the Shrew*, ACT I, SC I [1–40] 202c-203a

29 CERVANTES: *Don Quixote*, PART I, 145d

30 BACON: *Advancement of Learning*, 1a-28d esp 9c-d, 16d-17a

31 DESCARTES: *Rules*, I 1a-2a; III, 3c-d / *Discourse*, PART I, 42d-43a; 44a-b

31 SPINOZA: *Ethics*, PART IV, APPENDIX, IV 447b-c; IX 448a

32 MILTON: *Areopagitica*, 385b; 390b-391a; 394b-395b; 397a

35 LOCKE: *Human Understanding*, BK II, CH XXXIII, SECT 8 249c-d

36 SWIFT: *Gulliver*, PART IV, 165a-167a

36 STERNE: *Tristram Shandy*, 417b-419b

38 MONTESQUIEU: *Spirit of Laws*, BK IV, 13b,d-16a

38 ROUSSEAU: *Inequality*, 346d-347a

39 SMITH: *Wealth of Nations*, BK V, 340b-343d

42 KANT: *Pure Reason*, 223a-d / *Fund. Prin. Metaphysic of Morals*, 266a-b

43 MILL: *Liberty*, 303b-d / *Representative Government*, 344b-c; 424b-c

46 HEGEL: *Philosophy of Right*, INTRO, par 20 17a; PART III, par 187 65a-c; ADDITIONS, 97 132c-133a

50 MARX: *Capital*, 238b-c

51 TOLSTOY: *War and Peace*, BK I, 47b-c; BK VI, 244d-245d

53 JAMES: *Psychology*, 274b-275a; 711b-712b

54 FREUD: *New Introductory Lectures*, 868d-871a esp 870a-871a

1a. The ideal of the educated man

7 PLATO: *Lysis*, 16c-18b / *Laches*, 37c-d / *Republic*, BK II, 319c-320c; BK III, 338a-339a; BK VII 388a-401d esp 390b-391b / *Timaeus*, 454a / *Laws*, BK I, 649b-d; BK II, 653a-654a; BK VI, 704a-b; BK XII, 796b-799a,c

8 ARISTOTLE: *Topics*, BK I, CH 3 144a-b / *Metaphysics*, BK I, CH 1-2 499a-501c esp CH 2 [982^{a}5-20] 500b-c

9 ARISTOTLE: *Parts of Animals*, BK I, CH 1 [639^{a}1-15] 161a-b / *Politics*, BK VII, CH 13-BK VIII, CH 7 536b-548a,c passim / *Rhetoric*, BK I, CH 8 [1365^{b}32-39] 608a-b; BK II, CH 6 [1384^{a}33-35] 630d; CH 8 [1385^{b}24-28] 632c; CH 23 [1399^{a}12-17] 647c

12 EPICTETUS: *Discourses*, BK I, CH 27 132b-133b; BK III, CH 10 185d-187a; CH 15 190a-191a; CH 21 193d-195a; BK IV, CH 6 230b-232c

12 AURELIUS: *Meditations*, BK I 253a-256d; BK II, SECT 17 259b-d; BK IV, SECT 3 263b-264a; SECT 16 264d; BK X, SECT 11-12 298b-d

24 RABELAIS: *Gargantua and Pantagruel*, BK II, 81a-83b

25 MONTAIGNE: *Essays*, 59b-61c; 63d-80b esp 70d-72b, 74b-75a

26 SHAKESPEARE: *Taming of the Shrew*, ACT I, SC I [1-40] 202c-203a / *Love's Labour's Lost*, ACT IV, SC II [22-34] 266c

30 BACON: *Advancement of Learning*, 1a-28d esp 17b-27c; 86b-c

31 DESCARTES: *Rules*, III, 3c-d

32 MILTON: *Areopagitica*, 397a

33 PASCAL: *Pensées*, 34-37 177a-b

35 HUME: *Human Understanding*, SECT I, DIV 1-4 451a-452c

37 FIELDING: *Tom Jones*, 99d-100a; 274b-c

38 ROUSSEAU: *Inequality*, 346d-347b

39 SMITH: *Wealth of Nations*, BK V, 340b-343d esp 343c-d

40 GIBBON: *Decline and Fall*, 88c-d; 644b-645d esp 644d-645a

42 KANT: *Pure Reason*, 223a-d / *Fund. Prin. Metaphysic of Morals*, 260d-261d / *Practical Reason*, 337a-338c / *Judgement*, 508c-509a

43 MILL: *Liberty*, 294b-296d / *Utilitarianism*, 451c-452b

44 BOSWELL: *Johnson*, 130b; 283c

46 HEGEL: *Philosophy of Right*, ADDITIONS, 15 118d; 68 126d-127a; 98 133a; 119 136b

47 GOETHE: *Faust*, PART I [1765-1775] 42b

50 MARX: *Capital*, 176d-178a; 238b-c

52 DOSTOEVSKY: *Brothers Karamazov*, EPILOGUE, 411b-412d

53 JAMES: *Psychology*, 736b-737a

1b. The disadvantages of being educated

5 EURIPIDES: *Medea* [276-305] 214c-d

5 ARISTOPHANES: *Clouds* 488a-506d

6 THUCYDIDES: *Peloponnesian War*, BK I, 370a-c

7 PLATO: *Protagoras*, 47a-b / *Gorgias*, 272b

9 ARISTOTLE: *Rhetoric*, BK II, CH 21 [1394^{a}29-34] 642a; [1394^{b}25-32] 642c; CH 22 [1395^{b}27-32] 643d; CH 23 [1399^{a}12-17] 647c

12 EPICTETUS: *Discourses*, BK III, CH 21 193d-195a; CH 24, 205c-206a; 207d-208a; BK IV, CH 1, 221b-c; CH 8 235b-237d

12 AURELIUS: *Meditations*, BK II, SECT 3 257a-b

18 AUGUSTINE: *Confessions*, BK I, par 25-26 7a-c; BK IV, par 28-31 26a-27a

22 CHAUCER: *Miller's Tale* [3448-3464] 217a

23 HOBBES: *Leviathan*, PART I, 56d; PART II, 150c-d

24 RABELAIS: *Gargantua and Pantagruel*, BK II, 77b-78b

25 MONTAIGNE: *Essays*, 55d-62a; 75a-77d; 150d-151a; 232d-240a; 321a-c; 397a-398c; 448b-449a; 502c-504c; 508a-512a; 520b-d

26 SHAKESPEARE: *2nd Henry VI*, ACT IV, SC II [92-117] 58d-59a / *Love's Labour's Lost*, ACT I, SC I [55-94] 254d-255b; [143-147] 255d; ACT V, SC II [69-72] 274d

30 BACON: *Advancement of Learning*, 1a-28d esp 2c-17b; 30b-c; 73d-74c

31 DESCARTES: *Rules*, II, 2a-b / *Discourse*, PART I, 42b-c

35 LOCKE: *Human Understanding*, BK I, CH II, SECT 20 110c-111a; BK II, CH XXXIII, SECT 3 248c

36 SWIFT: *Gulliver*, PART II, 58a-b; PART III, 94b-95a

37 FIELDING: *Tom Jones*, 99d-100a; 158a-161d esp 158c-159a

38 ROUSSEAU: *Inequality*, 344d-345c; 346d-348a; 362a-d; 363a-366d

39 SMITH: *Wealth of Nations*, BK V, 337a-d; 340b-c

42 KANT: *Practical Reason*, 304d-305a; 358a / *Judgement*, 608b-c

44 BOSWELL: *Johnson*, 201b-c

47 GOETHE: *Faust*, PART I [354-417] 11a-12b; [614-807] 17a-21a; [1583-1606] 38b-39a; [1803-1815] 43a; PART II [4917-4922] 122a; [6228-6238] 152a-b

51 TOLSTOY: *War and Peace*, BK I, 19c-20b; BK V, 215b-c

2. The kinds of education: physical, moral, liberal, professional, religious

7 PLATO: *Protagoras*, 46b-d / *Republic*, BK II-III, 320c-339a esp BK III, 333b-339a; BK VI, 380d-381a; BK VII, 391b-401a / *Sophist*, 555b-c / *Laws*, BK I, 649b-d; BK II, 653a-663b esp 662d-663b; BK VII, 717b-d; 728b-730d; BK XII, 797b-798b

9 ARISTOTLE: *Politics*, BK VII, CH 15 [1334^{b}7-28] 539b-d; BK VIII, CH 2-3 542b-543d

12 EPICTETUS: *Discourses*, BK III, CH 15 190a-191a

13 VIRGIL: *Aeneid*, BK IX [590-620] 295a-b

17 PLOTINUS: *First Ennead*, TR III 10a-12b

18 AUGUSTINE: *Confessions*, BK III, par 7-9 14c-15b; BK IV, par 28-31 26a-27a / *Christian Doctrine*, BK II, CH 8-42 639d-656d; BK IV 675a-698a,c

20 AQUINAS: *Summa Theologica*, PART I-II, Q 105, A 4, ANS 318b-321a

25 MONTAIGNE: *Essays*, 57b-61c esp 60b-61c; 63d-75a passim

30 BACON: *Advancement of Learning*, 30b-c; 53d-54b

31 DESCARTES: *Discourse*, PART I, 42d-43a

33 PASCAL: *Pensées*, 34-37 177a-b

36 SWIFT: *Gulliver*, PART IV, 166b-167a

38 MONTESQUIEU: *Spirit of Laws*, BK IV, 15c

46 HEGEL: *Philosophy of Right*, PART III, par 197 67a-b

50 MARX: *Capital*, 237d-238c

51 TOLSTOY: *War and Peace*, BK I, 47b-c; BK VI, 244d-245d

3. The training of the body and the cultivation of bodily skills: gymnastics, manual work

5 ARISTOPHANES: *Clouds* [866-1114] 499a-502b esp [1002-1024] 500d-501a

7 PLATO: *Protagoras*, 46c / *Gorgias*, 261a-262a; 289d-290a / *Republic*, BK II, 310c-d; 320c-321a; BK III, 334b-335b; BK VI, 380d-381a; BK VII, 391c-d; 398c-399d / *Timaeus*, 475b-d / *Statesman*, 599d-600a / *Laws*, BK I, 644b-646a; BK II, 653b-654a; 663a-b; BK VII, 717b-d; 721d-722c; 726a-727c; BK VIII, 734a-735a

8 ARISTOTLE: *Physics*, BK VII, CH 3 [246^{a}10-^{b}19] 329c-330a / *Heavens*, BK II, CH 12 [292^{a}14-^{b}18] 383d-384b

9 ARISTOTLE: *Ethics*, BK II, CH 6 [1106^{a}35-^{b}8] 352a / *Politics*, BK IV, CH 1 [1288^{b}10-20] 487a-b; BK VII, CH 15 [1334^{b}7-28] 539b-d; CH 17 [1336^{a}4-39] 541a-c; BK VIII, CH 3-4 542d-544c

10 HIPPOCRATES: *Articulations*, par 52 109b-110a; par 55, 111c; par 58 112b-113a / *Aphorisms*, SECT I, par 3 131a-b; SECT II, par 49-50 133d

12 EPICTETUS: *Discourses*, BK III, CH 15, 190a-c

13 VIRGIL: *Aeneid*, BK IX [590-620] 295a-b

14 PLUTARCH: *Lycurgus*, 40c-42a / *Coriolanus*, 175b / *Philopoemen*, 293d-294a

17 PLOTINUS: *Third Ennead*, TR II, CH 8, 86d-87b

20 AQUINAS: *Summa Theologica*, PART I-II, Q 50, A I, ANS 6a-7b

24 RABELAIS: *Gargantua and Pantagruel*, BK I, 28a-29b

25 MONTAIGNE: *Essays*, 43d; 66c-67a; 73b-c

30 BACON: *Advancement of Learning*, 53d-54a

36 SWIFT: *Gulliver*, PART IV, 166b-167a

38 ROUSSEAU: *Inequality*, 335a-b; 348d-349a

39 SMITH: *Wealth of Nations*, BK I, 42d-43c; 53a; BK V, 337d-338a

40 GIBBON: *Decline and Fall*, 5a-b

46 HEGEL: *Philosophy of Right*, PART I, par 52, 25c / *Philosophy of History*, PART II, 267b-268b

49 DARWIN: *Descent of Man*, 269b-271a; 278c-d

50 MARX: *Capital*, 164b-166a; 170c-171b; 237d-240c

53 JAMES: *Psychology*, 74a-75a; 332a; 774a

4. The formation of a good character, virtue, a right will

5 EURIPIDES: *Suppliants* [857-917] 266a-b / *Hecuba* [592-602] 357d-358a

5 ARISTOPHANES: *Clouds* [866-1114] 499a-502b

7 PLATO: *Laches*, 30a-b / *Protagoras*, 45d-46d / *Euthydemus*, 66b-67b / *Phaedrus*, 128a-d / *Meno* 174a-190a,c / *Republic*, BK II, 314b-c; BK II-III, 320c-339a / *Timaeus*, 474c-d / *Laws* 640a-799a,c esp BK I, 644b-645c, 649b-650b, 651a-c, BK II, 653a-b, 656b-c, BK VI, 706c, BK VII 713c-731d / *Seventh Letter*, 801b-c

9 ARISTOTLE: *Ethics*, BK I, CH 13 [1102^{b}28-1103^{a}3] 348c; BK II, CH 3 [1104^{b}4-14] 350a; III, CH 12 [1119^{a}35-^{b}19] 366a,c / *Politics*, BK II, CH 7 461d-463c; BK VII, CH 13-BK VIII, CH 7 536b-548a,c

12 LUCRETIUS: *Nature of Things*, BK III [1-30] 30a-b; BK V [1-54] 61a-d; BK VI [1-42] 80a-d

12 EPICTETUS: *Discourses* 105a-245a,c esp BK I, CH 1-5 105a-110c, CH 18 124a-125a, BK I, CH 24-BK II, CH 2 129a-141c, BK II, CH 21-24 166c-174b, BK III, CH 3 178d-180a, CH 8-11 184b-187b, CH 13 188b-189c, CH 23-26 201a-213a,c, BK IV, CH 3-7 224b-235a, CH 9-13 237d-245a,c

12 AURELIUS: *Meditations* 253a-310d esp BK I, SECT 7-9 253b-254a, SECT 11 254b, SECT 14-16 254b-255d, BK II, SECT 17 259b-d, BK IV, SECT 18 264d, BK V, SECT 14 271b, SECT 16 271c-d, BK VI, SECT 12 274c, BK VII, SECT 69 284d, BK VIII, SECT I 285a-b, SECT 13 286c, BK IX, SECT 41 295c

13 VIRGIL: *Aeneid*, BK IX [590-620] 295a-b

14 PLUTARCH: *Lycurgus-Numa*, 63d-64a / *Pericles*, 121a-122b / *Coriolanus*, 174b,d-175a

15 TACITUS: *Annals*, BK XIII, 125d-126a

17 PLOTINUS: *First Ennead*, TR III, CH 2 10d; CH 6 11d-12b

18 AUGUSTINE: *Confessions*, BK I, par 13-31 4b-9a

20 AQUINAS: *Summa Theologica*, PART I-II, Q 96, A 2, ANS 231c-232b; Q 99, A 6, ANS 250a-251a; Q 100, A 9 261b-262b; Q 105, A 4, ANS 318b-321a; Q 108, A 3 334a-336b

4a. The possibility and limits of moral education: knowledge and virtue

(4. *The formation of a good character, virtue, a right will. 4a. The possibility and limits of moral education: knowledge and virtue.*)

49 DARWIN: *Descent of Man*, 313d-314b; 317c-319a

51 TOLSTOY: *War and Peace*, BK VI, 244d-245d

52 DOSTOEVSKY: *Brothers Karamazov*, EPILOGUE, 411b-412d

53 JAMES: *Psychology*, 806a-808a

54 FREUD: *General Introduction*, 573c-d; 592b-c; 596b-c; 624d-625b / *Civilization and Its Discontents*, 781a-d; 784a-789b; 796d [fn 2]; 800c-801a / *New Introductory Lectures*, 870a-c

4b. The influence of the family in moral training

OLD TESTAMENT: *Exodus*, 20:12 / *Deuteronomy*, 5:16; 6:6-7; 11:18-19; 27:16 / *Proverbs*, 1:8-9; 3:12; 6:20-24; 13:1,24; 15:5; 19:18; 22:6,15; 23:13-26; 29:15,17

APOCRYPHA: *Tobit*, 4—(D) OT, *Tobias*, 4 / *Ecclesiasticus*, 7:23-24; 30:1-13—(D) OT, *Ecclesiasticus*, 7:25-26; 30:1-13

NEW TESTAMENT: *Ephesians*, 6:1-4 / *Colossians*, 3:20-21

7 PLATO: *Protagoras*, 45d-47a / *Meno*, 186a-187b / *Republic*, BK V, 366a-c / *Laws*, BK V, 687d-688a; BK VII, 713c-716d

9 ARISTOTLE: *Ethics*, BK X, CH 9 [1180^{a}25-^{b}14] 435a-c / *Politics*, BK IV, CH 11 [1295^{b}14-18] 495d; BK VII, CH 17 [1336^{a}23-^{b}3] 541b-c

12 AURELIUS: *Meditations*, BK I 253a-256d esp SECT 1-4 253a, SECT 14 254b-c, SECT 16 254d-255d

14 PLUTARCH: *Marcus Cato*, 286c-287b

18 AUGUSTINE: *Confessions*, BK I, par 14-15 4c-5a; BK II, par 2-8 9b-10d esp par 7 10b-c; BK III, par 19-20 18b-19a; BK IX, par 19-22 67a-d

20 AQUINAS: *Summa Theologica*, PART I-II, Q 95, A 1, ANS 226c-227c; Q 105, A 4, ANS 318b-321a

22 CHAUCER: *Physician's Tale* [12,006-037] 367b-368a

24 RABELAIS: *Gargantua and Pantagruel*, BK II, 83a-b

25 MONTAIGNE: *Essays*, 16c; 43a-c; 63d-64b; 66c-67a; 184a-187d; 344a-c; 414a-d; 534c-d

29 CERVANTES: *Don Quixote*, PART II, 251b

31 SPINOZA: *Ethics*, PART III, PROP 55, SCHOL, 413d; THE AFFECTS, DEF 27 419a-b; PART IV, APPENDIX, XX 449a

35 LOCKE: *Civil Government*, CH VI, SECT 55-69 36c-40b; CH XV, SECT 170 64d-65a

36 SWIFT: *Gulliver*, PART I, 29b-30a; PART IV, 166b

36 STERNE: *Tristram Shandy*, 250b-251a

37 FIELDING: *Tom Jones*, 108c-110c; 136a-c; 217d-219c; 283c-d; 310b-313b; 359b-362c

38 MONTESQUIEU: *Spirit of Laws*, BK IV, 15c

38 ROUSSEAU: *Inequality*, 326c-327a; 327c-328a / *Political Economy*, 376b-377a

39 SMITH: *Wealth of Nations*, BK V, 337c-d

42 KANT: *Science of Right*, 420b-421c

44 BOSWELL: *Johnson*, 372c

46 HEGEL: *Philosophy of Right*, PART III, par 173-175 61a-d; par 239 76d; ADDITIONS, 111 134d-135a; 147 140c

52 DOSTOEVSKY: *Brothers Karamazov*, BK XII, 395b-d

54 FREUD: *Origin and Development of Psycho-Analysis*, 17d-18a / *Sexual Enlightenment of Children* 119a-122a,c passim / *Narcissism*, 408b / *Ego and Id*, 704d-707d / *Civilization and Its Discontents*, 794c-795a esp 795b [fn 2] / *New Introductory Lectures*, 834b-c; 844b-c; 876b-c

4c. The role of the state in moral education: law, custom, public opinion

5 ARISTOPHANES: *Clouds* 488a-506d

6 HERODOTUS: *History*, BK I, 35c-d

6 THUCYDIDES: *Peloponnesian War*, BK I, 370a-c; BK II, 396d-397a

7 PLATO: *Protagoras*, 45b-47c / *Apology*, 203c-204b / *Gorgias*, 287c-291b / *Republic*, BK II-III, 320c-339a; BK VI, 377a-379c / *Timaeus*, 474c-d / *Statesman*, 607a-608a / *Laws* 640a-799a,c esp BK I, 643a-644a, 645c-646d, BK III, 676b-c, BK IV, 683d-685a, BK V-VI, 696c-697d, BK VI, 704a-c, 710d-711c, BK VII 713c-731d, BK VIII, 735c-738c, BK IX, 757a, BK XII, 792c-d / *Seventh Letter*, 800b-c

9 ARISTOTLE: *Ethics*, BK I, CH 9 [1099^{b}29-32] 345b; CH 13 [1102^{a}8-25] 347c; BK II, CH 1 [1103^{b}3-7] 349a; BK V, CH 1 [1129^{b}12-24] 377a; CH 2 [1130^{b}20-30] 378b; BK X, CH 9 [1179^{b}31-1180^{b}28] 434c-435c / *Politics*, BK II, CH 5 [1263^{b}36-1264^{a}1] 459a; CH 7 461d-463c; BK VII, CH 13-17 536b-542a,c; BK VIII, CH 1 542a-b

12 AURELIUS: *Meditations*, BK IV, SECT 18 264d

13 VIRGIL: *Aeneid*, BK VI [845-853] 233b-234a

14 PLUTARCH: *Lycurgus* 32a-48d / *Lycurgus-Numa*, 63d-64a / *Solon* 64b,d-77a,c passim / *Marcus Cato*, 284b-286b / *Lysander*, 361b-d / *Agesilaus*, 480b,d-481a

18 AUGUSTINE: *Confessions*, BK I, par 14-16 4c-5b; par 19-30 5d-8d; BK VI, par 2 35a-c; par 11-13 38b-39c / *Christian Doctrine*, BK III, CH 12-13 662c-663c; CH 18-22 664d-666c

20 AQUINAS: *Summa Theologica*, PART I-II, Q 92, A 1 213c-214c; A 2, REP 4 214d-215a,c; Q 95, A 1 226c-227c; A 3 228c-229b; Q 96, AA 2-3 231c-233a; Q 98, A 6, ANS 244c-245b; Q 100, A 9 261b-262b; Q 105, A 4, ANS 318b-321a

21 DANTE: *Divine Comedy*, PURGATORY, XVI [52-105] 77b-d

23 HOBBES: *Leviathan*, PART II, 149b-c; 154a-156b; PART IV, 272c

25 MONTAIGNE: *Essays*, 42b-43c; 46b-48b; 60c-61d; 63d-64b; 131b-132a

27 SHAKESPEARE: *Measure for Measure*, ACT II, SC I [225-270] 181a-c; ACT III, SC II [91-128] 190c-d

30 BACON: *Advancement of Learning*, 78d-80a

4*d*. The effect upon character of poetry, music,
and other arts: the role of history and
examples

(4. *The formation of a good character, virtue, a right will. 4d. The effect upon character of poetry, music, and other arts: the role of history and examples.*)

42 KANT: *Fund. Prin. Metaphysic of Morals*, 263a-b; 264b [fn 1]; 266d [fn 2] / *Practical Reason*, 325d-327d esp 327b-d; 356a-360d / *Judgement*, 504a-b; 513d-514b; 521b-523c; 586d-587a

44 BOSWELL: *Johnson*, 308b-d; 347c-d

46 HEGEL: *Philosophy of History*, PART II, 267a-268b; 276a-b; PART IV, 347b-d

53 JAMES: *Psychology*, 826b-827a

5. The improvement of the mind by teaching and learning

5a. The profession of teaching: the relation of teacher and student

4 HOMER: *Iliad*, BK IX [430–605] 61c-63b

5 ARISTOPHANES: *Clouds* 488a-506d

7 PLATO: *Laches*, 29d-31b / *Protagoras*, 38a-47c esp 39d-41a, 42a-c / *Euthydemus* 65a-84a,c / *Symposium*, 169c-170a / *Meno* 174a-190a,c esp 179b-183a / *Apology*, 203a-204c; 206b-208c / *Crito*, 215a-c / *Gorgias*, 252a-259c; 290b-291b / *Theaetetus*, 515d-517b; 544a-c / *Sophist*, 556b-559a ; *Laws*, BK VII, 723c-d / *Seventh Letter*, 801c-802d; 808b-c

8 ARISTOTLE: *Sophistical Refutations*, CH 1 [165ᵃ19–24] 227c; CH 2 [165ᵃ38–ᵇ3] 227d-228a; CH 11 [171ᵇ18–35] 236b-d / *Metaphysics*, BK I, CH 1 [981ᵇ7–9] 499d; CH 2 [982ᵃ13–14] 500b; [982ᵃ28–30] 500c; BK IV, CH 2 [1004ᵇ18–27] 523d

9 ARISTOTLE: *Ethics*, BK IX, CH 1 [1164ᵃ22–ᵇ6] 417a-b; BK X, CH 9 [1180ᵇ28–1181ᵇ19] 435d-436a,c

10 HIPPOCRATES: *The Oath*, xiiia

12 LUCRETIUS: *Nature of Things*, BK III [1–30] 30a-b; BK V [1–54] 61a-d; BK VI [1–42] 80a-d

12 EPICTETUS: *Discourses*, BK II, CH 17 158d-161a esp 160b-161a; CH 24 172d-174b; BK III, CH 2 177c-178d; CH 9, 185b-d; CH 21–23 193d-203b; BK IV, CH 8 235b-237d

14 PLUTARCH: *Pericles*, 122d-123d / *Alcibiades*, 155b,d-158b / *Alexander*, 542d-544a / *Cato the Younger*, 623a-b / *Dion*, 782c-788b

15 TACITUS: *Annals*, BK XIII, 125d-126a; BK XIV, 153d-155a

18 AUGUSTINE: *Confessions*, BK I, par 22 6b-c; BK IV, par 2 19d; BK V, par 22 33b-c; BK VI, par 11 38b-c / *Christian Doctrine*, BK IV, CH 4 676d-677a; CH 27 696a-c

19 AQUINAS: *Summa Theologica*, PROLOGUE 1a-b; PART I, Q 76, A 2, REP 5 388c-391a; Q 106 545c-549a; Q 107, A 3, ANS and REP 1 551a-c; Q 111, A 1 568c-569b; Q 117, AA 1–2 595d-598c

20 AQUINAS: *Summa Theologica*, PART II–II, Q 1, A 7, REP 2 385c-387a; Q 2, A 3, ANS 392d-393c; Q 181, A 3 618c-619b; Q 188, A 6, ANS 681b-

682c; PART III SUPPL, Q 96, A 7 1061b-1062a; A 11, ANS and REP 1,5 1063d-1064d; A 12 1064d-1065b

21 DANTE: *Divine Comedy*, HELL 1a-52d passim, esp I–II 1a-4a, VII [64]–IX [105] 10b-13b, XV 21a-22c, XXIV [1–78] 34d-35b; PURGATORY 53a-105d passim, esp V [1–21] 59a, XVIII [1–96] 79d-80d, XXVII 94c-96a, XXX [22–81] 99c-100b; PARADISE, IV [115–142] 111d-112a

22 CHAUCER: *Prologue* [285–308] 164a-b

24 RABELAIS: *Gargantua and Pantagruel*, BK I, 1b,d; 18b-25a passim; BK II, 101b-106a

25 MONTAIGNE: *Essays*, 57b-60c; 64c-79c passim, esp 70c-72a

30 BACON: *Advancement of Learning*, 7d-11a; 14c-15a; 16c; 29c-32c; 68b-69b

31 DESCARTES: *Discourse*, PART I, 42b

31 SPINOZA: *Ethics*, PART IV, APPENDIX, IX 448a

32 MILTON: *Areopagitica*, 398a-b

36 STERNE: *Tristram Shandy*, 423b-424b

37 FIELDING: *Tom Jones*, 41a-43b; 45d-46a; 94d-95a

38 ROUSSEAU: *Inequality*, 326c-d / *Political Economy*, 376d-377a

39 SMITH: *Wealth of Nations*, BK I, 57b-58b; BK V, 331b,d-334c; 338c-340b; 354d-355d esp 355c-d

40 GIBBON: *Decline and Fall*, 669a-671b

43 MILL: *Representative Government*, 420b-d; 424b-c

44 BOSWELL: *Johnson*, 23b-c; 191b-c; 199d-200b; 300a-c

47 GOETHE: *Faust*, PART II [6689–6818] 164a-166b

51 TOLSTOY: *War and Peace*, BK I, 47b-48d; BK VIII, 306b

54 FREUD: *New Introductory Lectures*, 870b-c

5b. The means and methods of teaching

5 ARISTOPHANES: *Clouds* 488a-506d

7 PLATO: *Protagoras*, 50c-52d / *Cratylus*, 85d-88a esp 87c-d; 112d-113d / *Phaedrus*, 131b-141a,c esp 139b-140b / *Meno*, 179b-183a / *Apology*, 206b-d / *Republic*, BK VII, 388a-398c esp 389d-390b; 399c / *Theaetetus*, 515d-517b; 549c-550a,c / *Sophist*, 551d; 556b-559a / *Statesman*, 590d-591c / *Philebus*, 610d-613a / *Laws*, BK II, 656b-c; BK IV, 684c-685a / *Seventh Letter*, 809a-811a esp 809a-c

8 ARISTOTLE: *Posterior Analytics*, BK I, CH 1 [71ᵃ1–10] 97a / *Sophistical Refutations*, CH 2 [165ᵃ38–ᵇ3] 227d-228a; CH 10 [171ᵃ27–ᵇ2] 235d-236a; CH 11 [172ᵃ15–21] 237a / *Heavens*, BK I, CH 10 [279ᵇ32–280ᵃ11] 371b-c / *Metaphysics*, BK II, CH 3 513c-d / *Sense and the Sensible*, CH 1 [436ᵇ18–437ᵃ17] 673d-674a

9 ARISTOTLE: *Parts of Animals*, BK I, CH 1 [639ᵃ1–ᵇ12] 161a-d / *Ethics*, BK VI, CH 3 [1139ᵇ18–34] 388b-c

12 LUCRETIUS: *Nature of Things*, BK I [921–950] 12b-c; BK IV [1–25] 44a-b

12 EPICTETUS: *Discourses*, BK II, CH 24, 172d-173c; BK III, CH 9, 185b; CH 23, 203a-b

(5. *The improvement of the mind by teaching and learning.*)

5d. The order of learning: the organization of the curriculum

7 PLATO: *Protagoras*, 46b-c / *Meno*, 179b-183a / *Gorgias*, 272b-273b / *Republic*, BK II, 320c-321a; BK III, 333b-334b; BK VI, 380d-381a; BK VI-VII, 383d-401d / *Timaeus*, 465d-466a / *Sophist*, 552b-c / *Philebus*, 610d-613a / *Laws*, BK II, 653a-654a; BK V, 696b-d; BK VII, 728b-730c; BK XII, 798a-799a,c / *Seventh Letter*, 809c-810d

8 ARISTOTLE: *Physics*, BK I, CH I 259a-b; CH 7 [189^{b}30–33] 265b-c / *Metaphysics*, BK II, CH 3 [995^{a}12–14] 513c; BK IV, CH 3 [1005^{b}2–5] 524c; CH 4 [1006^{a}5–12] 525a-b; BK V, CH I [1013^{a}1–3] 533a; BK VII, CH 3 [1029^{a}35–^{b}12] 552a; BK IX, CH 8 [1049^{b}29–1050^{a}3] 575c-d / *Soul*, BK I, CH I [402^{b}15–403^{a}2] 631d-632a; BK II, CH 2 [413^{a}11–13] 643a

9 ARISTOTLE: *Parts of Animals*, BK I, CH I [639^{a}12–^{b}12] 161b-d / *Ethics*, BK I, CH 3 [1094^{b}28–1095^{a}3] 340a; BK VI, CH 3 [1139^{b}25–29] 388c / *Politics*, BK VII, CH 15 [1334^{b}20–28] 539c-d; BK VIII, CH 3 542d-543d

11 NICOMACHUS: *Arithmetic*, BK I, 812b-813d

12 EPICTETUS: *Discourses*, BK I, CH 26 131b-132b; BK II, CH 25 174b-c

16 PTOLEMY: *Almagest*, BK I, 5a-6b passim

16 KEPLER: *Epitome*, BK IV, 847b-848a

17 PLOTINUS: *First Ennead*, TR III, CH I–4 10a-11c

18 AUGUSTINE: *Confessions*, BK I, par 13–31 4b-9a; BK IV, par 30 26b-c / *Christian Doctrine*, BK II, CH 8–42 639d-656d

19 AQUINAS: *Summa Theologica*, PROLOGUE 1a-b; PART I, Q I, A 9 8d-9c; Q 2, AA 1–2 10d-12c; Q 10, A 1, ANS and REP 1 40d-41d; A 2, REP 1 41d-42c; A 6, ANS 45c-46d; Q 11, A 2, REP 4 47d-48d; Q 14, A 6, REP 2 80a-81c; Q 18, A 2, ANS 105c-106b; Q 84, A 3, REP 3 443d-444d; A 6 447c-449a; Q 85, A 1 451c-453c; A 3 455b-457a; A 8 460b-461b; Q 117, A 1, ANS 595d-597c

20 AQUINAS: *Summa Theologica*, PART I-II, Q 100, A 6, ANS and REP 2 257c-258c

23 HOBBES: *Leviathan*, PART I, 56b; 59b-c; 71c-d; 72a-d; PART IV, 268c-269b

24 RABELAIS: *Gargantua and Pantagruel*, BK I, 18b-19d; 25a-30c; BK II, 75c-77a; 78b-80d; 82c-83b

25 MONTAIGNE: *Essays*, 63d-80b passim, esp 69d-70c

28 HARVEY: *On Animal Generation*, 332a-336a esp 334c-d, 335c-336a

30 BACON: *Advancement of Learning*, 4c-5b; 14c-15a; 30b-c; 31a-d; 44c; 56b-66a; 68c-69c; 79c-80a; 85a-c / *Novum Organum*, PREF 105a-106d; BK I, APH 19–36 108b-109b; APH 90 124d-125a

31 DESCARTES: *Rules*, IV–VI 5a-10a; VIII–X 12a-17a; XIII 25b-27d / *Discourse*, PART I, 42b-

44a; PART II, 47a-b; PART VI, 61d-62c / *Geometry*, BK I, 297a-b; 298b; BK III, 341b

35 LOCKE: *Human Understanding*, BK I, CH I, SECT 15 98d-99a; SECT 20 100c-d; SECT 23 101b-102a; CH III, SECT 13 116a-b; BK II, CH I, SECT 6–8 122b-123a; SECT 22 127a; CH XI, SECT 8–9 145b-c; BK III, CH II, SECT 7 254a-b; CH III, SECT 7–9 255d-256c; CH V, SECT 15 267c-d; CH IX, SECT 9 286d-287b; BK IV, CH VII, SECT 9 338d-339b; SECT 11 340a-342d passim, esp 340d-341a; CH XII, SECT 3 358d-359c

36 SWIFT: *Gulliver*, PART II, 78b

36 STERNE: *Tristram Shandy*, 421b-422b

39 SMITH: *Wealth of Nations*, BK V, 334c-337b; 338c-d; 342b

42 KANT: *Practical Reason*, 294a-b / *Judgement*, 551a-552c; 572a-b

44 BOSWELL: *Johnson*, 11b-d; 15a-c; 23d-24b; 121d; 128c; 135b-c; 273a-b; 309c-d; 448a-b

46 HEGEL: *Philosophy of History*, PART I, 213c

47 GOETHE: *Faust*, PART I [1868–2045] 44b-48a

52 DOSTOEVSKY: *Brothers Karamazov*, BK X, 291d-292b

53 JAMES: *Psychology*, 317b-319a; 323a-b; 360a; 406a-b; 453a-457a esp 453b, 456b-457a; 503b; 524b-525a; 711b-712b

54 FREUD: *Civilization and Its Discontents*, 768b-c

5e. The emotional aspect of learning: pleasure, desire, interest

7 PLATO: *Republic*, BK VI, 374a-375a; BK VII, 388a-389c; 399b-401a esp 399c; BK IX, 421a-422b / *Laws*, BK II, 660b / *Seventh Letter*, 808b-809a

8 ARISTOTLE: *Metaphysics*, BK I, CH I [980^{a}22–27] 499a

9 ARISTOTLE: *Parts of Animals*, BK I, CH 5 [644^{b}22–645^{a}37] 168c-169b / *Ethics*, BK VII, CH 12 [1153^{a}22–24] 404c; BK X, CH I [1172^{a}16–21] 426a / *Politics*, BK VIII, CH 5 [1339^{a}25–31] 544d; [1339^{b}10–20] 545a; CH 6 [1340^{b}25–30] 546b / *Rhetoric*, BK I, CH II [1371^{a}30–33] 614d; BK III, CH 10 [1410^{b}9–12] 662c / *Poetics*, CH 4 [1448^{b}4–19] 682c-d

10 HIPPOCRATES: *The Law*, par 2 144b

10 GALEN: *Natural Faculties*, BK III, CH 10, 207d

12 LUCRETIUS: *Nature of Things*, BK I [41–53] 1c-d; BK II [1023–1047] 28a-b; BK III [1–30] 30a-b; BK IV [1–25] 44a-b

12 EPICTETUS: *Discourses*, BK IV, CH 4 225a-228a

17 PLOTINUS: *First Ennead*, TR III, CH 1–3 10a-11a

18 AUGUSTINE: *Confessions*, BK I, par 14–16 4c-5b; par 19–27 5d-7d

19 AQUINAS: *Summa Theologica*, PART I, Q 12, A 1, ANS 50c-51c; A 8, REP 4 57b-58b; PART I-II, Q 3, A 8, ANS 628d-629c; Q 30, A 1, REP 1 749a-d; Q 37, A 1 783d-784c

21 DANTE: *Divine Comedy*, HELL, XXVI [112–142] 39b-c; PURGATORY, XX [124]–XXI [75] 84c-85d; PARADISE, IV [115–142] 111d-112a

22 CHAUCER: *Prologue* [285–308] 164a-b

23 HOBBES: *Leviathan*, PART I, 52d-53b; PART II, 154a

24 RABELAIS: *Gargantua and Pantagruel*, BK III, 190a-191a

25 MONTAIGNE: *Essays*, 70d-74a; 244d-246a

26 SHAKESPEARE: *Taming of the Shrew*, ACT I, SC I [1-40] 202c-203a

28 HARVEY: *On Animal Generation*, 331c-332a

30 BACON: *Advancement of Learning*, 79b-c

31 DESCARTES: *Geometry*, BK I, 297a-b

31 SPINOZA: *Ethics*, PART III, PROP 55, SCHOL 413b-d; THE AFFECTS, DEF 27 419a-b

33 PASCAL: *Geometrical Demonstration*, 440b-442a

35 LOCKE: *Human Understanding*, BK II, CH XXXIII, SECT 15 250c

37 FIELDING: *Tom Jones*, 7b-c

38 ROUSSEAU: *Inequality*, 326c-d; 338c-339a

42 KANT: *Judgement*, 551d

44 BOSWELL: *Johnson*, 7d-8a; 11b-d; 14b; 15a-c; 130b; 135b-136a; 151d; 199d-200b; 273a; 309c-d; 360d; 423c; 448a-b

45 LAVOISIER: *Elements of Chemistry*, PREF, 1d-2a

46 HEGEL: *Philosophy of Right*, PART III, par 175, 61c-d; par 197 67a-b

47 GOETHE: *Faust*, PART I [354-736] 11a-19b

51 TOLSTOY: *War and Peace*, BK I, 47b-48d; BK VIII, 306b

53 JAMES: *Psychology*, 271b-275a esp 274b-275a; 290a-291a; 433a-434a; 448b-449b; 524a-525a; 711b-712b

5f. Learning apart from teachers and books: the role of experience

APOCRYPHA: *Ecclesiasticus*, 25:3-6—(D) OT, *Ecclesiasticus*, 25:5-8

4 HOMER: *Odyssey* 183a-322d

5 AESCHYLUS: *Agamemnon* [160-257] 53d-54d

7 PLATO: *Laches*, 29d-30b; 37c-d / *Gorgias*, 253a / *Republic*, BK III, 333b-d; 337b-d; BK V, 366a-c; BK VI, 377a-379c; BK VII, 401a / *Theaetetus*, 535d

8 ARISTOTLE: *Prior Analytics*, BK I, CH 30 63d-64b / *Posterior Analytics*, BK I, CH I 97a-d; BK II, CH 19 136a-137a,c / *Physics*, BK I, CH I 259a-b / *Generation and Corruption*, BK I, CH 2 [316ᵃ5-14] 411c-d / *Metaphysics*, BK I, CH I [980ᵃ22-981ᵃ13] 499a-c; BK IX, CH 8 [1050ᵃ10-15] 575d / *Soul*, BK I, CH I [402ᵇ11-403ᵃ2] 631d-632a; BK III, CH 8 [432ᵃ3-9] 664c

9 ARISTOTLE: *Ethics*, BK I, CH 3 [1094ᵇ28-1095ᵃ3] 340a; CH 4 [1095ᵃ30-ᵇ13] 340c-d; BK II, CH I [1103ᵃ14-17] 348b; BK VI, CH 8 [1142ᵃ12-19] 391b; CH II [1143ᵃ25-ᵇ13] 392d-393a; BK X, CH 9 [1180ᵇ13-23] 435b-c; [1181ᵃ18-ᵇ6] 436a / *Politics*, BK III, CH 16 [1287ᵃ32-33] 485d; BK VIII, CH 6 546b-547b

10 HIPPOCRATES: *Articulations*, par 10 94d-95a / *The Law*, par 3-4 144c-d

12 LUCRETIUS: *Nature of Things*, BK V [925-1457] 73b-80a,c passim, esp [1448-1457] 79d-80a,c

13 VIRGIL: *Aeneid*, BK VIII [508-519] 272b-273a

14 PLUTARCH: *Demosthenes*, 691b,d-692b; 692d-695d

18 AUGUSTINE: *Confessions*, BK I, par 13 4b-c / *Christian Doctrine*, BK IV, CH 3 676a-d

19 AQUINAS: *Summa Theologica*, PART I, Q 84, A 6 447c-449a; Q 85, A I 451c-453c; Q 87, AA 1-3 465a-468a passim; Q 94, A 3, REP 3 504a-505a; Q 117, A I, ANS and REP 4 595d-597c

20 AQUINAS: *Summa Theologica*, PART III, Q 9, A 4, REP I 766b-767b; Q 12, A I, REP I 776c-777b; A 2 777b-778b; A 3, REP 2 778b-779a

21 DANTE: *Divine Comedy*, HELL, XXVI [49-142] 38c-39c

23 HOBBES: *Leviathan*, INTRO, 47b-d; PART I, 60a-61a; 66c-68b

24 RABELAIS: *Gargantua and Pantagruel*, BK I, 29d-30c

25 MONTAIGNE: *Essays*, 24a-c; 66b-69d; 74d-75a; 395b-398c; 520d-522d

26 SHAKESPEARE: *Love's Labour's Lost*, ACT IV, SC III [296-365] 271c-272a / *Henry V*, ACT I, SC I [22-66] 533b-c / *As You Like It*, ACT IV, SC I [1-26] 617a-b

28 GILBERT: *Loadstone*, PREF, 1a-b

28 HARVEY: *Motion of the Heart*, 268c / *On Animal Generation*, 331b-332a; 333b-d; 411c-d

30 BACON: *Advancement of Learning*, 16a; 16c; 30d-31a; 82c-d / *Novum Organum*, BK I, APH 97-98 126c-127b

31 DESCARTES: *Rules*, II, 2d-3b; XII, 22c-23a / *Discourse*, PART I, 43a; 44a-c; PART III, 50b-51a; PART VI, 61d-62c / *Geometry*, BK I, 297a-b; BK III, 341b

31 SPINOZA: *Ethics*, PART II, PROP 40, SCHOL 1-2 387b-388b

33 PASCAL: *Pensées*, 6 173a / *Vacuum*, 355a-358b

35 LOCKE: *Human Understanding*, BK II, CH I-XII 121a-148d passim; CH XXIII, SECT 3 204c-d; BK III, CH III, SECT 7-8 255d-256a; BK IV, CH XII, SECT 9-13 360d-362d

35 BERKELEY: *Human Knowledge*, SECT 30-31 418c-d

35 HUME: *Human Understanding*, SECT VIII, DIV 65, 479d-480a

37 FIELDING: *Tom Jones*, 12d; 99d-100a; 142c-d; 274c; 296b,d-297c

38 MONTESQUIEU: *Spirit of Laws*, BK IV, 15c

38 ROUSSEAU: *Inequality*, 334c

39 SMITH: *Wealth of Nations*, BK V, 337c-d

42 KANT: *Pure Reason*, 14a-15c; 146a-149d esp 148b-c

43 MILL: *Liberty*, 287b-c; 288a-b; 294c-295a / *Representative Government*, 341d-343a passim; 418b-d / *Utilitarianism*, 456a-d

44 BOSWELL: *Johnson*, 257c; 378b-c

45 LAVOISIER: *Elements of Chemistry*, PREF, 1d-2b; PART III, 87b-c

46 HEGEL: *Philosophy of Right*, PART III, par 197 67a-b / *Philosophy of History*, PART I, 230c-231b

47 GOETHE: *Faust*, PART I [522-601] 15a-16b

(5. *The improvement of the mind by teaching and learning. 5f. Learning apart from teachers and books: the role of experience.*)

48 MELVILLE: *Moby Dick*, 82a; 243a

51 TOLSTOY: *War and Peace*, BK X, 424a-b; BK XIII, 584c-585b

53 JAMES: *Psychology*, 362b-364a passim; 453b-454a; 767b-768a; 852b-862a esp 852b-853a, 856b-857a, 859b-860a

6. The acquisition of techniques: preparation for the vocations, arts, and professions

5 ARISTOPHANES: *Clouds* 488a-506d esp [461–509] 494b-d, [723–812] 497b-498c

7 PLATO: *Phaedrus*, 136a-b / *Gorgias*, 258d-262a esp 260a-d / *Republic*, BK II, 319a-c; BK III, 337b-338a; BK V, 366a-c; BK VI, 377d-378c / *Philebus*, 633a-d / *Laws*, BK I, 649b-c; BK IV, 684d-685a

8 ARISTOTLE: *Topics*, BK I, CH 3 144a-b

9 ARISTOTLE: *Ethics*, BK I, CH 13 [1102^{a}17–22] 347c; BK II, CH 1 348b,d-349b; CH 4 350d-351b; BK X, CH 9 [1180^{b}13–1181^{b}13] 435b-436a,c passim / *Politics*, BK IV, CH 1 [1288^{b}10–20] 487a-b; BK VIII, CH 6 546b-547b / *Athenian Constitution*, CH 42, par 3 572c

10 HIPPOCRATES: *Ancient Medicine*, par 1–4 1a-2c; par 9 3b-d / *Epidemics*, BK III, SECT III, par 16 59b-c / *Articulations*, par 10, 94d / *The Law*, par 2–5 144b-d

12 LUCRETIUS: *Nature of Things*, BK V [1091–1104] 75b-c; [1241–1408] 77b-79b

13 VIRGIL: *Aeneid*, BK VIII [512–517] 272b

14 PLUTARCH: *Demosthenes*, 692c-695d

18 AUGUSTINE: *Christian Doctrine*, BK IV, CH 3 676a-d

20 AQUINAS: *Summa Theologica*, PART II–II, Q I, A 7, REP 2 385c-387a

24 RABELAIS: *Gargantua and Pantagruel*, BK I, 27d-30c; BK II, 76b-77a; 85c-87c esp 87a; BK IV, 232a-233b

29 CERVANTES: *Don Quixote*, PART I, 82b-83c

30 BACON: *Advancement of Learning*, 30b-c; 53d-54b; 82c-d

31 DESCARTES: *Discourse*, PART VI, 66c

36 SWIFT: *Gulliver*, PART I, 29b-31a

39 SMITH: *Wealth of Nations*, BK I, 42d-43c; 51c-58b esp 51c-53b, 54c-55a; BK V, 301a-305c; 339b-c; 342d-343c

40 GIBBON: *Decline and Fall*, 5a-c; 245b-d; 411d-412c

41 GIBBON: *Decline and Fall*, 75d-78b passim; 298a-300a esp 299c-300a; 311d-312a; 355a-c; 508d-509d

42 KANT: *Fund. Prin. Metaphysic of Morals*, 253c-d

43 MILL: *Representative Government*, 415a-417c passim

46 HEGEL: *Philosophy of Right*, PART III, par 197 67a-b; par 252 78d-79a; par 296 99a-b; ADDITIONS, 126 137a-b

47 GOETHE: *Faust*, PART I [1868–2050] 44b-48b

49 DARWIN: *Descent of Man*, 278c-d

50 MARX: *Capital*, 81d; 165c-166a; 170c-171c; 237d-241a esp 240c-d

53 JAMES: *Psychology*, 774a

54 FREUD: *"Wild" Psycho-Analysis*, 130b-c / *General Introduction*, 449a-452a passim

7. Religious education

OLD TESTAMENT: *Exodus*, 12:24–27; 18:19–20; 24:12 / *Deuteronomy*, 4:9–10,14; 5:31; 6:1,6–9; 11:18–21; 31:9–13 / *Joshua*, 8:30–35—(D) *Josue*, 8:30–35 / *II Kings*, 23:1–2—(D) IV *Kings*, 23:1–2 / *II Chronicles*, 34:29–30—(D) II *Paralipomenon*, 34:29–30 / *Nehemiah*, 8—(D) II *Esdras*, 8 / *Psalms*, 78:1–4—(D) *Psalms*, 77:1–4

NEW TESTAMENT: *Ephesians*, 6:4

7 PLATO: *Laws*, BK X 757d-771b; BK XII, 797b-798b

12 EPICTETUS: *Discourses*, BK III, CH 22 195a-201a

18 AUGUSTINE: *Christian Doctrine* 621a-698a,c

19 AQUINAS: *Summa Theologica*, PROLOGUE 1a-b

20 AQUINAS: *Summa Theologica*, PART I–II, Q 105, A 4, ANS 318b-321a; Q III, A I, ANS 351d-352d; A 4 354c-355d; PART II–II, Q 2, A 6, ANS 395b-396a; Q 16, A 2, ANS and REP 2 455c-456d; Q 188, A 5 679d-681a; A 6, ANS 681b-682c; PART III SUPPL, Q 96, A 7 1061b-1062a

23 HOBBES: *Leviathan*, PART II, 123a-b; 153a-156b passim, esp 154d-155a; PART III, 208d-209a; 211b-c; 241c-242a; PART IV, 269a

24 RABELAIS: *Gargantua and Pantagruel*, BK I, 24c-d; 27a; BK II, 82c-83b

33 PASCAL: *Pensées*, 185–194 205a-209b; 285 224a

35 LOCKE: *Toleration*, 3c-4a; 7a-b

38 MONTESQUIEU: *Spirit of Laws*, BK XXIV, 202b-c

39 SMITH: *Wealth of Nations*, BK V, 343b,d-356d passim; 357c

40 GIBBON: *Decline and Fall*, 82d; 601b-c

42 KANT: *Practical Reason*, 325a-327d esp 326b-327a

43 MILL: *Liberty*, 285b; 290a-292a passim / *Representative Government*, 437d-438b

44 BOSWELL: *Johnson*, 151b-d

52 DOSTOEVSKY: *Brothers Karamazov*, BK VI, 150d-153d

7a. God as teacher: divine revelation and inspiration

OLD TESTAMENT: *Genesis*, 9:1–17 / *Exodus*, 4:10–17; 20:1–20 / *Deuteronomy*, 4:1–5,10–13; 5:1–20 esp 5:4–11 / *I Kings*, 8:35–36—(D) III *Kings*, 8:35–36 / *Job*, 33:14–17; 34:31–32; 38–41 / *Psalms*, 25:4–5,8–9,12; 32:8–9; 94:10–13; 143—(D) *Psalms*, 24:4–5,8–9,12; 31:8–9; 93:10–13; 142 / *Proverbs*, 6:23 / *Isaiah*, 28:9–13—(D) *Isaias*, 28:9–13 / *Daniel*, 2:19–23

APOCRYPHA: *Ecclesiasticus*, 17:6–14—(D) OT, *Ecclesiasticus*, 17:5–12

7b. The teaching function of the church, of priests and prophets

(7. Religious education. 7b. The teaching function of the church, of priests and prophets.)

40 GIBBON: *Decline and Fall*, 194d; 302d-304a passim, esp 303d; 307d-308a; 355b-d; 601b-c

41 GIBBON: *Decline and Fall*, 230c-231d; 522d-523a

43 MILL: *Liberty*, 285b / *Representative Government*, 341a-c

44 BOSWELL: *Johnson*, 313d-316d

46 HEGEL: *Philosophy of History*, PART III, 308b-c

51 TOLSTOY: *War and Peace*, BK VI, 245a-b

52 DOSTOEVSKY: *Brothers Karamazov*, BK VI, 152a-153a; 164a-165a

54 FREUD: *Civilization and Its Discontents*, 793c

8. Education and the state

8*a*. The educational responsibility of the family and the state

7 PLATO: *Crito*, 217a-b / *Laws*, BK VII, 721d-722c; BK VIII, 723c-d; BK XI, 778d

9 ARISTOTLE: *Ethics*, BK X, CH 9 [1179^{b}31-1180^{b}13] 434c-435b / *Politics*, BK I, CH 13 [1260^{b}9-19] 455c; BK VIII, CH I 542a-b

12 AURELIUS: *Meditations*, BK I, SECT 4 253a

14 PLUTARCH: *Lycurgus*, 39a-45b esp 40c-41a / *Lycurgus-Numa*, 63d-64a,c

20 AQUINAS: *Summa Theologica*, PART I-II, Q 95, A I, ANS 226c-227c; Q 105, A 4, ANS and REP 5 318b-321a

23 HOBBES: *Leviathan*, PART II, 155b

25 MONTAIGNE: *Essays*, 344a-c

30 BACON: *New Atlantis*, 207c-d

35 LOCKE: *Civil Government*, CH VI, SECT 58-59 37b-d

36 SWIFT: *Gulliver*, PART I, 29b-31a; PART IV, 166b

38 ROUSSEAU: *Political Economy*, 376b-377a

39 SMITH: *Wealth of Nations*, BK V, 338c-339a; 340c-343d

41 GIBBON: *Decline and Fall*, 86b-c; 92c

42 KANT: *Science of Right*, 420b-421c

43 MILL: *Liberty*, 317d-319b passim

46 HEGEL: *Philosophy of Right*, PART III, par 174 61b; par 239 76d; ADDITIONS, 111-112 134d-135a; 147 140c

50 MARX: *Capital*, 176d-178a; 195b-196d; 237d-241d; 245a-d

50 MARX-ENGELS: *Communist Manifesto*, 427b-c

54 FREUD: *Origin and Development of Psycho-Analysis*, 17d-18a

8*b*. The economic support of educational institutions

7 PLATO: *Apology*, 209b-d

30 BACON: *Advancement of Learning*, 30c-31a

36 SWIFT: *Gulliver*, PART I, 29b-31a; PART III, 106a-b

39 SMITH: *Wealth of Nations*, BK I, 56b-58b; BK V, 331b,d-356d

40 GIBBON: *Decline and Fall*, 669d-670d

41 GIBBON: *Decline and Fall*, 298c

43 MILL: *Liberty*, 317d-319b passim / *Representative Government*, 382c-383b

44 BOSWELL: *Johnson*, 300a-c

46 HEGEL: *Philosophy of History*, PART IV, 325d

8*c*. The political regulation and censorship of education

5 ARISTOPHANES: *Acharnians* [366-384] 459c-d; [497-508] 460d-461a

7 PLATO: *Republic*, BK II-III, 320c-339a; BK IV, 344b-d; BK V, 365d-366c; BK X, 427c-434c esp 432d-434c / *Statesman*, 601c-602c / *Laws*, BK II, 654c-655b; BK III, 675c-676b; BK VII, 713c-731d; BK VIII, 732c-d; BK XI, 782d-783b

9 ARISTOTLE: *Politics*, BK I, CH 13 [1260^{b}9-19] 455c; BK V, CH 11 [1313^{a}38-^{b}5] 516a; BK VII, CH 17 [1336^{a}30-^{b}24] 541b-d; BK VIII, CH I [1337^{a}10-19] 542a

14 PLUTARCH: *Lycurgus-Numa* 61b,d-64a,c passim / *Solon*, 76a

15 TACITUS: *Annals*, BK III, 56d-57b; BK IV, 67c; 72b-73a; BK XIV, 152d-153c

18 AUGUSTINE: *City of God*, BK II, CH 9 154a-c; CH 12-14 155c-157c; BK VIII, CH 13 273b-d

23 HOBBES: *Leviathan*, PART II, 102a-103a; 114d-115a; 123a-b; 150c-151a; PART III, 224d-225d; CONCLUSION, 282d-283a

29 CERVANTES: *Don Quixote*, PART I, 117d-119d; 184a-187c

30 BACON: *Advancement of Learning*, 7a / *New Atlantis*, 210d-214d esp 213d, 214b

32 MILTON: *Areopagitica* 381a-412b esp 384b-389a, 398a-b

36 SWIFT: *Gulliver*, PART I, 29b-31a

38 MONTESQUIEU: *Spirit of Laws*, BK IV 13b,d-18d; BK XII, 90b-c

38 ROUSSEAU: *Social Contract*, BK IV, 434b-435a

39 SMITH: *Wealth of Nations*, BK V, 347c-d

40 GIBBON: *Decline and Fall*, 148a-b; 355b-d

42 KANT: *Pure Reason*, 220b-221b; 223a-c

43 CONSTITUTION OF THE U.S.: AMENDMENTS, I 17a

43 MILL: *Liberty*, 274b-293b passim; 317d-319b passim / *Representative Government*, 343b; 344b-c; 368c-369a; 387b-c; 437d-438b

44 BOSWELL: *Johnson*, 222d-223b; 512c-d

46 HEGEL: *Philosophy of Right*, PART III, par 270, 89a-b / *Philosophy of History*, PART I, 213b-214a; 217c-218a

8*d*. The training of the prince, the statesman, the citizen: aristocratic and democratic theories of education

APOCRYPHA: *Ecclesiasticus*, 38:24-34—(D) OT, *Ecclesiasticus*, 38:25-39

5 ARISTOPHANES: *Knights* 470a-487a,c / *Clouds* 488a-506d

6 THUCYDIDES: *Peloponnesian War*, BK I, 370a-c; BK II, 396d-397a

7 PLATO: *Protagoras*, 43a-47c / *Republic*, BK II-III, 320c-339a; BK III, 340b-341a; BK V, 366a-c; BK VI-VII, 383b-401d esp BK VII, 389d-401d / *Timaeus*, 442c-d / *Statesman*, 607b-

608d / *Laws* 640a-799a,c esp BK I, 640d-641a, 644b-645c, BK III, 672d-676b, BK IV, 683d-685a, BK V–VI, 696c-697d, BK VI, 704a-c, 706c, BK VII–VIII, 713c-735b, BK XII, 784d-785b, 796b-799a / *Seventh Letter*, 801c-802d

9 ARISTOTLE: *Politics*, BK I, CH 13 [1260ᵇ9–19] 455c; BK II, CH 5 [1264ᵃ12–40] 459b-c; CH 7 [1266ᵇ26–1267ᵃ2] 462b-c; BK III, CH 4 [1277ᵃ 14–ᵇ13] 474a-c; CH 18 [1288ᵃ34–ᵇ3] 487a,c; BK IV, CH 9 [1294ᵇ18–28] 494c-d; CH 15 [1300ᵃ3–8] 500d; BK V, CH 9 [1310ᵃ12–36] 512b-c; BK VII, CH 14 537b-538d; BK VIII 542a-548a,c / *Athenian Constitution*, CH 42 572b-d / *Rhetoric*, BK I, CH 8 [1365ᵇ32–39] 608a-b

12 AURELIUS: *Meditations*, BK III, SECT 5 261a

13 VIRGIL: *Aeneid*, BK VIII [508–519] 272b-273a

14 PLUTARCH: *Lycurgus* 32a-48d / *Lycurgus-Numa*, 63d-64a / *Solon* 64b,d-77a,c passim, esp 64b,d-65c, 74b-75b / *Pericles*, 122d-123d / *Alcibiades*, 156b-158b passim / *Lysander*, 354b,d-355a / *Agesilaus*, 480b,d-481a / *Alexander*, 542d-544a / *Dion*, 781b,d-788b

15 TACITUS: *Annals*, BK XII, 111d; BK XIII, 125d-126a; BK XIV, 153d-155a / *Histories*, BK IV, 267c

21 DANTE: *Divine Comedy*, PARADISE, VIII [115–148] 118b-c

23 MACHIAVELLI: *Prince* 1a-37d esp CH VI, 8c-d, CH XIV–XIX 21b-30a

23 HOBBES: *Leviathan*, INTRO, 47b-d; PART I, 94b-c; PART II, 114d-115a; 128c-130a; 150c-151a; 153a-156b; 158b-d; 164a,c; PART IV, 273a-c; CONCLUSION, 282d-283a

24 RABELAIS: *Gargantua and Pantagruel*, BK I, 18b-19d; 24a-30c; BK II, 75a-77a; 78b-83b

25 MONTAIGNE: *Essays*, 60a-62a; 63d-64d; 71d-72b

26 SHAKESPEARE: *1st Henry IV*, ACT I, SC II [218–240] 437c-d / *Henry V*, ACT I, SC I [22–66] 533b-c / *As You Like It*, ACT I, SC I [1–28] 597a-b

29 CERVANTES: *Don Quixote*, PART II, 332c-336a; 362a-c

30 BACON: *Advancement of Learning*, 20b-28d; 94b-95a

32 MILTON: *Areopagitica*, 384b-389a

36 SWIFT: *Gulliver*, PART I, 29b-31a; PART IV, 166b-167a

38 MONTESQUIEU: *Spirit of Laws*, BK IV 13b,d-18d

38 ROUSSEAU: *Political Economy*, 372a-377b esp 375d-377b / *Social Contract*, BK III, 414b

39 SMITH: *Wealth of Nations*, BK V, 303b-304c; 337d-338c; 340c-343d; 346c-347d

40 GIBBON: *Decline and Fall*, 62a-c; 86c; 260a-b; 275c-276b; 284a-c; 435b-c; 534a-c; 633b; 669b

41 GIBBON: *Decline and Fall*, 15b-c; 298c; 508c-509d

43 FEDERALIST: NUMBER 27, 95c-d; NUMBER 35, 113b-c; NUMBER 53, 168b-169b; NUMBER 56 174d-176d esp 175d-176a; NUMBER 62, 190b-d; NUMBER 84, 253d-254b

43 MILL: *Liberty*, 284d-285b; 298b-299a; 302a-c; 317d-323a,c / *Representative Government*, 336c-341d; 344b-c; 349a-350a; 351b-c; 357c; 362c-366a; 375a-377a; 380c-389b passim, esp 382c-383b; 401a-406a passim, esp 405d-406a; 407d-408b; 415a-417c; 418b-d; 420b-d; 424b-c

44 BOSWELL: *Johnson*, 201b-c; 307d

46 HEGEL: *Philosophy of Right*, PART III, par 151-153 57a-c; par 209 69d; par 296-297 99a-b; ADDITIONS, 98 133a; 169 145d; 171 146b-c / *Philosophy of History*, PART I, 212d-214d; 243b-c; PART II, 281d; PART IV, 368b

50 MARX: *Capital*, 237d-241d esp 238b-c, 240c-241a

50 MARX-ENGELS: *Communist Manifesto*, 427c; 429b

51 TOLSTOY: *War and Peace*, BK VI, 244d-245d

54 FREUD: *Sexual Enlightenment of Children*, 122a,c

9. Historical and biographical observations concerning the institutions and practices of education

5 ARISTOPHANES: *Clouds* 488a-506d

6 HERODOTUS: *History*, BK I, 32a-b

6 THUCYDIDES: *Peloponnesian War*, BK I, 370a-c; BK II, 396d-397a

7 PLATO: *Gorgias*, 290b-291b / *Laws*, BK I, 644b-646b; BK III, 672d-673d

9 ARISTOTLE: *Politics*, BK IV, CH 9 [1294ᵇ18–28] 494c-d; BK VII, CH 14[1333ᵃ41–1334ᵃ10]538b-d; BK VIII, CH I [1337ᵃ19–33] 542b; CH 4 544a-c

10 HIPPOCRATES: *The Oath*, xiiia

12 AURELIUS: *Meditations*, BK I 253a-256d

14 PLUTARCH: *Lycurgus*, 38a-45b passim / *Alcibiades*, 155b,d-158b / *Marcus Cato*, 286c-287b / *Alexander*, 542d-544a / *Demosthenes*, 691b,d-692b / *Dion*, 782c-788b

18 AUGUSTINE: *Confessions*, BK I, par 14–31 4c-9a; BK III, par 6–7 14b-d

23 HOBBES: *Leviathan*, PART II, 155d-156b; PART IV, 267c-269c

24 RABELAIS: *Gargantua and Pantagruel*, BK I, 18b-19d; 24a-30c; BK II, 75c-83b

25 MONTAIGNE: *Essays*, 57b-63d; 68b-69a; 77d-80b; 194c-199c; 395b-401a

29 CERVANTES: *Don Quixote*, PART I, xia-xvid

30 BACON: *Advancement of Learning* 1a-101d passim, esp 8c-d, 29c-32c / *Novum Organum*, BK I, APH 78 119b-c; APH 80–81 120a-c; APH 90 124d-125a

31 DESCARTES: *Discourse* 41a-67a,c / *Meditations*, I 75a-77c / *Objections and Replies*, 278a-293a,c passim

32 MILTON: *Areopagitica*, 384b-389a

33 PASCAL: *Pensées*, 626 286b

35 LOCKE: *Human Understanding*, BK I, CH III, SECT 25 120c-d

36 SWIFT: *Gulliver*, PART I, 3a-b

38 MONTESQUIEU: *Spirit of Laws*, BK IV, 15c; 16a-18d

38 ROUSSEAU: *Inequality*, 335a-b / *Political Economy*, 377a

(9. *Historical and biographical observations concerning the institutions and practices of education.*)

39 SMITH: *Wealth of Nations*, BK I, 57b-58b; BK V, 303b-304c; 334c-340c; 354d-355d

40 GIBBON: *Decline and Fall*, 23d-24a; 245b-d; 260a; 344c-347b passim; 355b-d; 364a-c; 543d; 644b-c; 668d-671b

41 GIBBON: *Decline and Fall*, 40a-41a; 210c-d; 298a-300c; 325d-328a,c; 452a-b; 522b-528a,c

43 MILL: *Liberty*, 288a-b

44 BOSWELL: *Johnson*, 7b-9b; 11b-12c; 15a-17b

46 HEGEL: *Philosophy of Right*, ADDITIONS, 98 133a / *Philosophy of History*, PART I, 213b-c; PART IV, 325d

47 GOETHE: *Faust*, PART I [354-685] 11a-18a passim

CROSS-REFERENCES

For: Matters relevant to physical education or the training of bodily skills, *see* ART 9b; HABIT 5a; LABOR 2b.

Matters relevant to moral education, *see* ART 10a; CUSTOM AND CONVENTION 5b; GOOD AND EVIL 6a; HABIT 5b; HISTORY 2; KNOWLEDGE 8b(1); PLEASURE AND PAIN 10a; POETRY 9a; PUNISHMENT 3a; VIRTUE AND VICE 1a, 4-4c, 4d(2), 4d(4), 8b; and for the training of specific virtues, *see* COURAGE 6; TEMPERANCE 4.

Matters relevant to liberal education or intellectual training, *see* ART 6b; HABIT 4a-4b, 5d; HISTORY 2; KNOWLEDGE 9a; MAN 6a; MIND 4a-4c; PLEASURE AND PAIN 10a; POETRY 5a, 9a; TRUTH 3d(3); VIRTUE AND VICE 4b-4c; and for discussions of the liberal arts, *see* LANGUAGE 1a, 7-8; LOGIC 3-3b; MATHEMATICS 1b; RHETORIC 1b, 2c-2d, 6.

Matters relevant to professional education or training in the useful arts and crafts, *see* LAW 9; MEDICINE 1, 2c; PHILOSOPHY 5; RHETORIC 6; STATE 8c.

Matters relevant to religious education, *see* GOD 6c(1)-6c(3); KNOWLEDGE 6c(5); PROPHECY 1c-1d; RELIGION 1a-1b(3), 5c; THEOLOGY 2, 4a-4c; VIRTUE AND VICE 8b, 8e; WISDOM 1c.

The consideration of factors involved in learning and teaching, *see* EMOTION 5d; EXPERIENCE 2-3b; HABIT 4a-4b; KNOWLEDGE 4a-4b, 9a; LANGUAGE 8; LOGIC 4; MIND 4c; PLEASURE AND PAIN 4c(2); TRUTH 3d(3), 8e; VIRTUE AND VICE 4b-4c.

The role of the family in education, *see* FAMILY 2c, 6d; VIRTUE AND VICE 4d(1).

The role of the state in education, *see* LAW 6d; VIRTUE AND VICE 4d(3), 7a; and for the problem of education in relation to different forms of government, *see* ARISTOCRACY 5; CITIZEN 6; DEMOCRACY 6; MONARCHY 3a; STATE 8c.

The discussion of freedom in the communication of knowledge and art, *see* ART 10b; KNOWLEDGE 9b; LIBERTY 2a; OPINION 5b; POETRY 9b; TRUTH 8d.

ADDITIONAL READINGS

Listed below are works not included in *Great Books of the Western World*, but relevant to the idea and topics with which this chapter deals. These works are divided into two groups:

I. Works by authors represented in this collection.
II. Works by authors not represented in this collection.

For the date, place, and other facts concerning the publication of the works cited, consult the Bibliography of Additional Readings which follows the last chapter of *The Great Ideas*.

I.

PLUTARCH. "A Discourse Touching the Training of Children," in *Moralia*

AUGUSTINE. *Concerning the Teacher*

AQUINAS. *Concerning the Teacher*

———. *Summa Theologica*, PART II-II, QQ 166-167

F. BACON. "Of Custom and Education," "Of Studies," in *Essays*

MILTON. *Of Education*

LOCKE. *Some Thoughts Concerning Education*

SWIFT. *An Essay on Modern Education*

ROUSSEAU. *Émile*

GOETHE. *William Meister*

Chapter 21: ELEMENT

INTRODUCTION

THE words "atom" and "element" express basic notions in the analysis of matter. To some extent their meaning seems to be the same. Atoms or elements are usually understood to be ultimate units, the parts out of which other things are formed by combination. But as soon as further questions are asked—about the divisibility or indivisibility of these units, or about their number and variety—we are confronted with differing conceptions of the atom, and with a theory of the elements which is opposed to the atomic analysis of matter.

Even when the two notions are not opposed to one another, they are not interchangeable. "Atom" has a much narrower meaning. It usually designates a small particle of matter, whereas "element" signifies the least part into which anything at all can be divided. It is this broader meaning of "element" which permits Euclid to call his collection of the theorems in terms of which all geometric problems can be solved, the "elements" of geometry. According to Aristotle, this is true, not only of geometrical proofs, but also "in general of the elements of demonstration; for the primary demonstrations, each of which is implied in many demonstrations," he says, "are called elements of demonstration." From this it follows that elements will be found in any subject matter or science in which analysis occurs, and not only in physics.

"An element," writes Nicomachus in his *Introduction to Arithmetic*, "is the smallest thing which enters into the composition of an object, and the least thing into which it can be analyzed. Letters, for example, are called the elements of literate speech, for out of them all articulate speech is composed and into them finally it is resolved. Sounds are the elements of all melody; for they are the beginning of its composition and into them it is resolved. The so-called four elements of the universe in general are simple bodies, fire, water, air, and earth; for out of them in the first instance we account for the constitution of the universe, and into them finally we conceive of it as being resolved."

This explains why books in so many different fields have the word "element" in their titles. There are the elements of grammar or logic, the elements of language or music, the elements of psychology or economics. Elements in one subject matter or science are analogous to elements in another because in each sphere they stand to everything else as the simple to the complex, the pure to the mixed, the parts to the whole. Thus the factors of price may be said to function in economic analysis as do the parts of speech in grammatical analysis.

Another illustration comes from the theory of the four bodily humors in ancient physiology. In the traditional enumeration, which goes back to Hippocrates, they are blood, phlegm, yellow bile, and black bile, and they function analytically as do fire, water, air, and earth in ancient physics. They "make up the nature of the body of man," according to a Hippocratic treatise on the nature of man, "and through them he feels pain or enjoys health." Perfect health is enjoyed by a man "when these elements are duly proportioned to one another in respect of compounding, power, and bulk, and when they are perfectly mingled." Galen, in an analysis of temperaments, explains all varieties of temperament and all complexions of physique in terms of these humors, either by their mixture or by the predominance of one or another. Thus the sanguine, phlegmatic, choleric, or melancholic temperament is accounted for by the excess of one and a deficiency of the other humors.

Still another physiological application of the notion of element is to be found in the ancient division of tissue into flesh and bone, or in the more elaborate modern analysis of the types of cells which comprise all living matter.

THESE ILLUSTRATIONS indicate that the irreducibility of elements to anything simpler than themselves does not necessarily mean that they are absolutely indivisible. Cells can be further divided into nucleus, protoplasm, and membrane without ceasing to be the elements of tissue. The parts of speech—nouns, verbs, adjectives—can be further divided into syllables and letters without ceasing to be the elements of significant utterance. Letters, treated as the elements of language, can be physically divided. The fact that terms are sometimes regarded as the logical elements out of which propositions and syllogisms are formed does not prevent a distinction from being made between simple and complex terms. Nicomachus calls the triangle elementary among all plane figures, "for everything else is resolved into it, but it into nothing else"; yet the triangle is divisible into the lines which compose it and these lines in turn are divisible into points.

When Nicomachus says that the triangle is the element of all other figures "and has itself no element," he does not mean that the triangle is absolutely indivisible, but only relatively so. Relative to the analysis of plane figures, there is no simpler figure out of which the triangle can be formed. Similarly, relative to the analysis of significant speech, there is no simpler part than the word. Relative to the analysis of melody, there is no simpler part than the tone. Musical tones may be physically, but they are not musically, complex.

THE DEFINITION OF element can also be approached by comparing its meaning with that of principle and cause. All three terms are brought together by Aristotle in the beginning of his *Physics*, when he declares that we attain "scientific knowledge" through acquaintance with the "principles, causes, and elements" of things.

The word "principle" occurs almost as frequently as "element" in the titles of books which claim to be basic expositions or analyses.

The two words are often used as synonyms. Lavoisier, for example, says that we can use "the term *elements*, or *principles of bodies*, to express our idea of the last point which analysis is capable of reaching."

To discover any difference in the meaning of "element" and "principle," it is necessary to specify their correlatives precisely. Out of elements, *compounds* or *mixtures* are formed. From principles, *consequences* are derived. In logic, for example, we say that terms are the elements of propositions (the proposition 'Socrates is a man' comprising the terms 'Socrates' and 'man'), but we say that axioms are the principles from which conclusions are derived. This does not prevent the same thing from being viewed in different connections as both element and principle—as an element because it is the simple part out of which a more complex whole is composed, and as a principle because it is the source from which something else is derived. The parts of speech in grammar are the elementary components of phrases and sentences; they are also the principles from which the rules of syntax are derived.

The third notion which belongs with element and principle is cause. Its correlative is *effect*. Again it can be said that that which is an element in one connection and a principle in another can be regarded as a cause from still a third point of view. In Aristotle's physical treatises, for example, matter is regarded in all three ways: it is an element of all bodies, for they are substances composed of matter and form; it is a principle of change, since from matter, form, and privation change is derived; it is a cause (*i.e.*, the material cause) of certain results.

But it must also be observed that everything which is any one of these three is not necessarily both of the others also. Since an element, according to Aristotle, is a "component immanent in a thing," anything that is an extrinsic principle or cause cannot be an element. Thus the action of one body upon another is a cause and a principle, but not an element. Referring to these distinctions, Aquinas declares that "*principle* is a wider term than *cause*, just as *cause* is more common than *element*." The chapters on CAUSE and PRINCIPLE tend to substantiate this observation about the scope of these ideas in the tradition of western thought.

THE BASIC ISSUES concerning elements occur in the analysis of matter. Before Plato and Aristotle, the early Greek physicists had asked such questions as, From what do all things come? Of what are all things made? A number of answers were given, ranging from one kind of ultimate, such as earth or fire, through a small set of ultimate kinds, to an infinite variety. The classical theory of the four elements is the middle answer, avoiding the extremes of unity and infinity.

According to Galen, it was Hippocrates who "first took in hand to demonstrate that there are, in all, four mutually interacting qualities" and who provided "at least the beginnings of the proofs to which Aristotle later set his hand" in developing the theory of the four elements. Galen also indicates that it was a subject of controversy among the ancients whether the "substances as well as the qualities" of the four elements "undergo this intimate mingling" from which results "the genesis and destruction of all things that come into and pass out of being."

Aristotle, in his treatise On Generation and Corruption, enumerates the various senses in which the physicist considers elements. "We have to recognize three 'originative sources' (or elements)," he writes: "firstly, that which is potentially perceptible body; secondly, the contrarieties (e.g., heat and cold); and thirdly, Fire, Water, and the like." The "potentially perceptible body" is identified with prime matter, and, since this "has no separate existence, but is always bound up with a contrariety," it can be ruled out from the usual notion of element. The elementary qualities, the "contrarieties" named secondly, are the hot and cold and dry and moist. The so-called elements, Fire, Air, Water, and Earth, are left to the last, and are mentioned "only thirdly," Aristotle says, because they "change into one another . . . whereas the contrarieties do not change."

The elementary qualities "attach themselves" by couples to the "apparently 'simple' bodies." In consequence, Aristotle writes, "Fire is hot and dry, whereas Air is hot and moist . . . and Water is cold and moist, while Earth is cold and dry." Each of them, however, "is characterized par excellence by a single quality."

In terms of these simple bodies and the elementary qualities all other material things can be explained.

In contrast to the elements stand the mixed, or compound, bodies, in the constitution of which two or more elements combine. There may be many kinds of mixed bodies, but none is irreducible in kind, as are the four elements; any mixed body can be divided into the different kinds of elementary bodies which compose it, whereas the elementary bodies cannot be divided into parts which are different in kind from themselves. A living body, for example, may contain parts of earth and water, but the parts of earth are earth, the parts of water, water.

It is precisely the mode of divisibility that Aristotle declares is "the fundamental question." In answering this question he opposes the theory of the four elements to another Greek account of the constitution of matter—the atomic theory, developed by Leucippus and Democritus, and expounded for us in Lucretius' poem On the Nature of Things.

ACCORDING TO the Greek atomists, matter is not infinitely divisible. "If nature had set no limit to the breaking of things," Lucretius writes, "by this time the bodies of matter could have been so far reduced . . . that nothing could within a fixed time be conceived out of them and reach its utmost growth of being." There must then be "a fixed limit to their breaking"—a limit in physical division which ultimately reaches units of matter that are absolutely indivisible. Lucretius calls them "first beginnings . . . of solid singleness, . . . not compounded out of a union of parts, but, rather, strong in everlasting singleness"—the "seeds of things," or atoms. The Greek word from which "atom" comes literally means uncuttable.

From this it is evident that Aristotle can deny the existence of atoms while at the same time he affirms the existence of elementary bodies. The elements, unlike the atoms, are not conceived as indivisible in quantity, but only as incapable of division into diverse kinds of matter.

In the Greek conception of atom and element, the difference between them lies in this distinction between quantitative and qualitative indivisibility. The atom is the least quantity of matter. It cannot be broken into quantitative parts. The elementary body is not atomic. It is always capable of division into *smaller* units, but all of these units must be of the same kind as the elementary body undergoing division.

The element is indivisible only in the sense that it cannot be decomposed into other *kinds* of matter, as a mixed body can be decomposed into its diverse elements. The atom cannot be divided in any way. Only compound bodies can be divided into their constituent atoms, all of which are alike in kind, differing only quantitatively—in size, shape, or weight. Different kinds of matter occur only on the level of compounds and as the result of diverse combinations of atoms.

This last point indicates another contrast between atoms and elements in ancient physical theory. The elements are defined, as we have seen, by their qualitative differences from one another; or, more strictly, according to combinations of elementary sensible qualities—hot and cold, moist and dry. By virtue of the qualities peculiar to them, the four elements stand in a certain order to one another. Water and air, according to Plato, are "in the mean between fire and earth" and have "the same proportion so far as possible; as fire is to air so is air to water, and as air is to water so is water to earth." The quality which two of the elements have in common provides the mean. Thus fire and air are joined by the common quality of hot; air and water by moist; and water and earth by cold.

When their analysis reached its greatest refinement, the ancients recognized that the earth, air, fire, and water of common experience do not actually have the purity requisite for elements. They are "not simple, but blended," Aristotle writes, and while the elements "are indeed similar in nature to them, [they] are not identical with them." The element "corresponding to fire is 'such-as-fire,' not fire; that which corresponds to air is 'such-as-air,' and so on with the rest of them." Thus the four elements are only analogous to, for they are purer than, ordinary earth, air, fire, and water; yet their names continued to be used as symbols for the true elements, a connotation which is

still retained when we speak of men struggling against or battling with "the elements."

"IT WILL NO DOUBT be a matter of surprise," Lavoisier writes in the Preface to his *Elements of Chemistry*, "that in a treatise upon the elements of chemistry, there should be no chapter on the constituent and elementary parts of matter; but I shall take occasion, in this place, to remark that the fondness for reducing all the bodies in nature to three or four elements, proceeds from a prejudice which has descended to us from the Greek philosophers. The notion of four elements, which, by the variety of their proportions, compose all the known substances in nature, is a mere hypothesis, assumed long before the first principles of experimental philosophy or of chemistry had any existence."

This does not mean that Lavoisier entirely rejects the notion of elements in chemical analysis. On the contrary, he says that "we must admit, as elements, all the substances into which we are capable, by any means, to reduce bodies by decomposition." His quarrel with the ancients chiefly concerns two points. The first is on the number of the elements, which he thinks experiment has shown to be much greater than the four of classical theory. The second is on the simplicity of the experimentally discovered elements. They can be called atoms or simple bodies only if we do not thereby imply that we know them to be absolutely indivisible—either qualitatively or quantitatively. We are not entitled "to affirm that these substances we consider as simple may not be compounded of two, or even of a greater number of principles" merely because we have not yet discovered "the means of separating them."

In modern physics and chemistry, the distinction between element and atom seems to be abolished. The same unit of matter is at once both an atom and an element. The table of atomic weights is also a chart of the elements. The classification of atoms is both quantitative and qualitative—qualitative in the sense that the atoms of different elementary kinds of matter differ in their active properties.

According to the ancient meaning of the terms, the molecule would seem to be both a mixture and a compound—*mixed*, in that it can be broken up into other *kinds* of matter; *compound*, in that it can be divided into *smaller* units of matter. But in modern theory the meanings of "compound" and "mixture" have also changed, the molecule being classified as a compound rather than a mixture. The combination of the elements to form molecular compounds is determined by the proportion of their weights or valences rather than by a fusion of their qualities.

The most radical change in theory is not this, however; nor is it the increase in the number of the elements from four to more than ninety-four; nor the ordering of the elements by reference to their atomic weights rather than by the contrariety of their qualities. It results from the discovery that an atom is not uncuttable and that new elements can be produced by atomic fission. Faraday's experimental work in ionization and in electro-chemical decomposition lies at the beginning of the physical researches which have penetrated the interior structure of the atom and isolated smaller units of matter. Even before atoms were experimentally exploded, analysis had pictured them as constituted by positive and negative charges.

As the result of his researches, Faraday, for example, conceives of atoms as "mere centres of forces or powers, not particles of matter, in which the powers themselves reside." The atom thus ceases to be "a little unchangeable, impenetrable piece of matter," and "consists of the powers" it exercises. What was ordinarily referred to "under the term *shape*" becomes the "disposition and relative intensity of the forces" that are observed.

With Faraday it is evident that the meaning of "atom" has departed far from the sense in which Lucretius speaks of "units of solid singleness" or Newton of "solid, massy, hard, impenetrable, movable particles ... incomparably harder than any porous bodies compounded of them; even so very hard as never to wear or break in pieces; no ordinary power being able to divide what God himself made one in the first creation." With the conception of the elements as different kinds of atoms; then, with the discovery of radio-active elements undergoing slow disintegration; finally, with the production of isotopes and new elements through

atomic change; the meaning of "element" has moved equally far from its original sense.

Do THESE ALTERED meanings change the basic issues in the philosophy of nature? Are these issues resolved or rendered meaningless by experimental science?

The central point in the theory of elements is an irreducible qualitative diversity in kinds of matter. The elements of modern chemistry may no longer be *elementary* types of matter in the strict sense of the word; but the kind of difference which would be strictly elemental may be found in the distinction of the positive, the negative, and the neutral with respect to the electrical charge of sub-atomic particles.

Similarly, the central point in atomism as a philosophy of nature is the existence of absolutely indivisible units or quanta of matter; in other words, the denial that matter is infinitely divisible, that any particle, no matter how small, is capable of being broken into smaller parts. The strict conception of the atom is, therefore, not invalidated by the experimental discovery that the particles called "atoms" are not *atomic*, that they are themselves complex structures of moving particles, and that they can be physically divided.

It makes no difference to the philosophical atomist whether the particles which constitute molecules or the particles—the electrons and protons, the neutrons and mesons—which constitute "atoms," are *atomic*. Even if further experimental work should succeed in dividing these "sub-atomic" particles, the question could still be asked: Is matter infinitely divisible, regardless of our actual power to continue making divisions *ad infinitum*? Since the question, when thus formulated, cannot be put to experimental test, the issue concerning atoms would remain.

That issue would not refer to any particle of matter defined at a certain stage of physical analysis or experimental discovery. It would consist in the opposition of two views of the nature of matter and the constitution of the material universe: the affirmation, on the one hand, that truly atomic particles must exist; and the denial, on the other, that no particle of matter can be atomic. The affirmative arguments of Lucretius and Newton make the constancy of nature and the indestructibility of matter depend on the absolute solidity and impenetrability of matter's ultimate parts. The negative arguments of Aristotle and Descartes proceed from the divisibility of whatever is continuous to the conclusion that any unit of matter must have parts.

The philosophical doctrine of atomism, in the form in which Lucretius adopts it from Epicurus, insists upon void as the other basic principle of the universe. "Nature," he writes, "is founded on two things: there are bodies and there is void in which these bodies are placed and through which they move about." Compound bodies are divisible because the atoms of which they are composed are not absolutely continuous with one another, but are separated by void or empty space. That is why they are not solid or impenetrable, as are the atomic particles which are composed of matter entirely without void. In Newton's language hardness must be "reckoned the property of all uncompounded matter," for if "compound bodies are so very hard as we find some of them to be, and yet are very porous," how much harder must be "simple particles which are void of pores."

The opponents of atomism tend to deny the existence not only of atoms, but of the void as well. Descartes, for example, denies that there can be "any atoms or parts of matter which are indivisible of their own nature. . . . For however small the parts are supposed to be, yet because they are necessarily extended we are always able in thought to divide any one of them into two or more parts." For the same reason, he maintains, there cannot be "a space in which there is no substance . . . because the extension of space or internal place is not different from that of body." The physical world, on this view, is conceived as what the ancients called a plenum, continuously filled with matter. This controversy over void and plenum is elaborated in the chapter on SPACE.

Although he uses the language of the atomists, Faraday seems to agree with Descartes rather than with Newton. He pictures matter as "continuous throughout," with no distinction between "its atoms and any intervening space." Atoms, he thinks, instead of being absolutely hard, are "highly elastic," and they are all "mutually penetrable." He compares the combination and separation of two atoms with "the conjunction of two sea waves of different velocities into one, their perfect union for a time, and final separation into the constituent waves." Such a view of the constitution of matter, Faraday writes, leads to "the conclusion that matter fills all space, or at least all space to which gravitation extends."

The very continuity—the voidlessness or lack of pores—which the opponents of atomism insist is the source of matter's infinite divisibility, the atomists seem to give as the reason why the ultimate particles are without parts, hence simple, solid, and indivisible.

ON STILL OTHER POINTS, there is disagreement among the atomists themselves. Not all of them go to the extreme of denying existence or reality to anything immaterial; nor do all insist that whatever exists is either an atom or made up of atoms and void. In the tradition of the great books, the extreme doctrine is found in Lucretius alone. Though it is shared by Hobbes, and is reflected in the *Leviathan*, it is not expounded there. It is developed in his treatise *Concerning Body*.

For Lucretius, the atoms are eternal as well as indestructible. The "first beginnings" of all other things are themselves without beginning. "In time gone by," Lucretius writes, "they moved in the same way in which now they move, and will ever hereafter be borne along in like manner" through an endless succession of worlds, each of which comes to be through a concourse of atoms, each in turn perishing as with decay that concourse is dissolved. Newton writes in what seems to be a contrary vein. "It seems probable to me," he says, "that God in the beginning formed matter in solid, massy, hard, impenetrable, movable particles." "All material things," he continues, "seem to have been composed of the hard and solid particles above mentioned, variously associated in the first Creation by the counsel of an intelligent Agent."

Nor does Newton appeal to the properties and motions of the ultimate particles except to explain the characteristics and laws of the physical world. Unlike Lucretius and Hobbes, he does not—and there seems to be some evidence in the *Optics* that he would not—reduce the soul of man to a flow of extremely mobile atoms, or attempt to account for all psychological phenomena (thought as well as sensation and memory) in terms of atom buffeting atom.

The atomic theory of the cause of sensation is not limited to the materialists. Writers like Locke, who conceive man as having a spiritual nature as well as a body, adopt an atomistic view of the material world. "The different motions and figures, bulk and number of such particles," he writes, "affecting the several organs of our senses, produce in us those different sensations which we have from the colours and smells of bodies." Furthermore, the distinction which is here implicit—between primary and secondary sense qualities—is not peculiar to atomism. It can also be found in a critic of atomism like Descartes.

The atomistic account of sensation is, nevertheless, of critical significance in the controversy concerning this type of materialism. Critics of atomism have contended that the truth of atomism as a materialistic philosophy can be no greater than the measure of its success in explaining sensation—the source upon which the atomist himself relies for his knowledge of nature—in terms of the properties and motions of particles themselves imperceptible.

OUTLINE OF TOPICS

REFERENCES

To find the passages cited, use the numbers in heavy type, which are the volume and page numbers of the passages referred to. For example, in 4 HOMER: *Iliad*, BK II [265–283] 12d, the number 4 is the number of the volume in the set; the number 12d indicates that the passage is in section d of page 12.

PAGE SECTIONS: When the text is printed in one column, the letters a and b refer to the upper and lower halves of the page. For example, in 53 JAMES: *Psychology*, 116a-119b, the passage begins in the upper half of page 116 and ends in the lower half of page 119. When the text is printed in two columns, the letters a and b refer to the upper and lower halves of the left-hand side of the page, the letters c and d to the upper and lower halves of the right-hand side of the page. For example, in 7 PLATO: *Symposium*, 163b-164c, the passage begins in the lower half of the left-hand side of page 163 and ends in the upper half of the right-hand side of page 164.

AUTHOR'S DIVISIONS: One or more of the main divisions of a work (such as PART, BK, CH, SECT) are sometimes included in the reference; line numbers, in brackets, are given in certain cases; *e.g.*, *Iliad*, BK II [265–283] 12d.

BIBLE REFERENCES: The references are to book, chapter, and verse. When the King James and Douay versions differ in title of books or in the numbering of chapters or verses, the King James version is cited first and the Douay, indicated by a (*D*), follows; *e.g.*, OLD TESTAMENT: *Nehemiah*, 7:45—(D) *II Esdras*, 7:46.

SYMBOLS: The abbreviation "esp" calls the reader's attention to one or more especially relevant parts of a whole reference; "passim" signifies that the topic is discussed intermittently rather than continuously in the work or passage cited.

For additional information concerning the style of the references, see the Explanation of Reference Style; for general guidance in the use of *The Great Ideas*, consult the Preface.

1. The concept of element

7 PLATO: *Timaeus*, 455d-456a / *Theaetetus*, 544d-547c esp 544d-545a, 547a / *Laws*, BK X, 761b-d

8 ARISTOTLE: *Topics*, BK VI, CH 13 204c-206a esp [150^{b}18–26] 205b-c / *Physics*, BK I, CH I 259a-b / *Heavens*, BK III, CH 3 [302^{a}10]–CH 4 [302^{b}20] 393c-394a / *Metaphysics*, BK I, CH 3 [983^{a}24]–CH 5 [986^{b}8] 501c-504c; CH 6 [987^{b}19]–CH 7 [988^{a}31] 505d-506c; CH 8 506d-508c; CH 9 [992^{a}1–9] 510b; [992^{a}18–993^{a}10] 510b-511c esp [992^{b}18–993^{a}10] 511a-c; BK III, CH I [995^{b}27–29] 514b; CH 3 [998^{a}20–^{b}14] 517a-b; BK V, CH 3 534c-d; CH 4 [1014^{b}27–34] 535a-b; CH 25 [1023^{b}17–25] 545b-c; BK VII, CH 7 555a-556b; CH 10 558a-559d; CH 17 [1041^{b}11–33] 565d-566a,c; BK X, CH I [1052^{b}8–14] 579a; BK XII, CH 4–5 599d-601a; BK XIV, CH 2 [1088^{b}14–28] 620d-621a / *Soul*, BK I, CH 5 [410^{a}12–23] 640a-b

9 ARISTOTLE: *Politics*, BK I, CH I [1252^{a}18–24] 445b

11 NICOMACHUS: *Arithmetic*, BK II, 829a; 833a-b

17 PLOTINUS: *Third Ennead*, TR I, CH 3 79b-c

18 AUGUSTINE: *City of God*, BK XIX, CH 16, 522a

19 AQUINAS: *Summa Theologica*, PART I, Q 66, A 2 345d-347b; Q 91, A I, ANS and REP 3 484a-485b

20 AQUINAS: *Summa Theologica*, PART III SUPPL, Q 74, A I, REP 3 925c-926c; Q 91, A 5, ANS and REP 4 1024a-1025b

31 DESCARTES: *Rules*, VIII, 14b-c; XII, 22b-c

42 KANT: *Pure Reason*, 100c-d; 103a; 105b-106a; 137a-140c

45 LAVOISIER: *Elements of Chemistry*, PREF, 3b-4a esp 3d-4a

53 JAMES: *Psychology*, 327a-331b passim

2. The comparison of element, principle, and cause

7 PLATO: *Timaeus*, 455d

8 ARISTOTLE: *Physics*, BK I, CH I 259a-b; CH 4–9 262a-268d passim / *Generation and Corruption*, BK II, CH I [329^{a}24–^{b}2] 429a-b / *Metaphysics*, BK I, CH 6 [987^{b}19–23] 505d; [988^{a}7–16] 506a-b; BK III, CH 3 [998^{a}20–^{b}13] 517a-b; BK V, CH 1–3 533a-534d; CH 24 545a-b; BK VII, CH 16 [1040^{b}16–23] 564d; CH 17 [1041^{b}11–33] 565d-566a,c; BK VIII, CH 3 [1043^{b}5–14] 567d-568a; BK X, CH I [1052^{b}8–14] 579a; BK XII, CH I 598a-c; CH 4–5 599d-601a esp CH 4 [1070^{b}22–35] 600b

17 PLOTINUS: *Third Ennead*, TR I, CH 3, 79c

19 AQUINAS: *Summa Theologica*, PART I, Q 33, A I, REP I 180d-181c

45 LAVOISIER: *Elements of Chemistry*, PREF, 3d-4a

3. The theory of the elements in natural philosophy, physics, and chemistry

7 PLATO: *Phaedo*, 240d-242b / *Timaeus*, 448b-d; 455c-462b / *Philebus*, 618c-619a / *Laws*, BK X, 760a-761d

8 ARISTOTLE: *Physics*, BK I, CH I [184^{a}10]–CH 2 [184^{b}24] 259a-c; CH 4–9 262a-268d / *Heavens*, BK III–IV 389b,d-405a,c / *Generation and Corruption* 409a-441a,c esp BK II, CH 1–3 428b,d-431a / *Meteorology* 445a-494d

10 GALEN: *Natural Faculties*, BK I, CH 2–3 167b-169a; CH 6 169c-170c; BK II, CH 4, 186d-187b

12 LUCRETIUS: *Nature of Things*, BK I [635-920] 8d-12b

17 PLOTINUS: *Second Ennead*, TR I, CH I, 35a

20 AQUINAS: *Summa Theologica*, PART I-II, Q 49, A 4, ANS 5a-6a; PART III SUPPL, Q 74 925b-935a,c passim; Q 91, A 4 1022d-1023d; A 5, ANS and REP 4 1024a-1025b

28 GILBERT: *Loadstone*, BK III, 60c-d

45 LAVOISIER: *Elements of Chemistry* 1a-159d passim

45 FARADAY: *Researches in Electricity*, 383b-386c

53 JAMES: *Psychology*, 876a

3a. Element and atom: qualitative and quantitative indivisibility

8 ARISTOTLE: *Physics*, BK I, CH 2 [184^{b}15–22] 259b-c / *Heavens*, BK III, CH 4 [303^{a}3]–CH 5 [304^{b}23] 394b-396a; CH 7 [305^{b}27–306^{b}2] 397a-d; BK IV, CH 2 [308^{a}29–310^{a}13] 400b-401c / *Metaphysics*, BK I, CH 4 [985^{b}3–19] 503c-d; BK V, CH 3 [1014^{b}3–6] 534d; CH 25 545b-c / *Soul*, BK I, CH 2 [403^{b}28–404^{a}5] 633a-b

12 LUCRETIUS: *Nature of Things*, BK I [599-920] 8b-12b esp [705-920] 9c-12b

17 PLOTINUS: *Third Ennead*, TR I, CH 3 79b-c

30 BACON: *Novum Organum*, BK I, APH 45 110b; APH 66, 114d-115a

42 KANT: *Pure Reason*, 161d-163a

45 LAVOISIER: *Elements of Chemistry*, PREF, 3b-4a; PART III, 87c-d; 103b-c; 105d

3b. The enumeration of the elements: their properties and order

7 PLATO: *Cratylus*, 98d / *Phaedo*, 247b-248c / *Timaeus*, 448b-d; 458b-460b / *Philebus*, 618c-619a / *Laws*, BK X, 760a-761d

8 ARISTOTLE: *Physics*, BK III, CH 5 [204^{b}10–205^{a}6] 282c-283a; BK IV, CH I [208^{b}8–22] 287b / *Heavens*, BK I, CH 1–8 359a-369a; CH 9 [278^{b}22–35] 370a; BK II, CH 3 377c-378a; BK III, CH I 389b,d-391c; CH 3–5 393c-396a; BK III, CH 7 [306^{a}1]–BK IV, CH 6 [313^{b}24] 397b-405a,c esp BK IV, CH 3–5 401c-404d / *Generation and Corruption*, BK I, CH I 409a-410c; BK II, CH 1–3 428b,d-431a / *Meteorology*, BK I, CH 2–3 445b-447d; BK IV, CH I [378^{b}10–26] 482b,d-483a / *Metaphysics*, BK I, CH 3 [983^{a}24]–CH 5 [986^{b}8] 501c-504c; CH 7 [988^{a}17–31] 506b-c; CH 8 506d-508c; BK V, CH 4 [1014^{b}27–35] 535a-b / *Soul*, BK I, CH 2 [404^{b}7–31] 633d-

634a; CH 5 [409^{b}18–411^{a}7] 639c-641a; BK III, CH I [424^{b}20–425^{a}13] 656b,d-657a / *Sense and the Sensible*, CH 2–5 674a-683b passim

9 ARISTOTLE: *Parts of Animals*, BK II, CH I [646^{a}12–^{b}20] 170a-d; CH 2 [648^{a}20]–CH 3 [649^{b}22] 172c-174b / *Generation of Animals*, BK III, CH 11 [761^{b}7–24] 302c-d

10 GALEN: *Natural Faculties*, BK I, CH 2–3, 167d-169a; CH 6 169c-170c; BK II, CH 4, 186d-187a; CH 8, 193b-d

11 NICOMACHUS: *Arithmetic*, BK II, 829a

12 LUCRETIUS: *Nature of Things*, BK I [705-715] 9d; [763–788] 10b-c

12 EPICTETUS: *Discourses*, BK III, CH 13, 188d-189a

13 VIRGIL: *Aeneid*, BK VI [724-731] 230b

17 PLOTINUS: *Second Ennead*, TR I, CH 3 36b-d; CH 6–7 37d-39c / *Fourth Ennead*, TR VII, CH 2 192a-b / *Sixth Ennead*, TR III, CH 9, 285d-286a; TR VII, CH 11 326d-327d

18 AUGUSTINE: *City of God*, BK VIII, CH 2 265b-266a

19 AQUINAS: *Summa Theologica*, PART I, Q 66, A 1, CONTRARY and REP to CONTRARY 343d-345c; A 2 345d-347b; Q 71, A 1, REP 2 367a-368b; Q 91, A 1, ANS and REP 3 484a-485b; Q 115, A 3, REP 2 588c-589c

20 AQUINAS: *Summa Theologica*, PART III SUPPL, Q 74 925b-935a,c passim, esp A 5 929d-931b; Q 79, A 1, REP 4 951b-953b; Q 91, A 4 1022d-1023d

28 GILBERT: *Loadstone*, BK I, 13b-d; BK III, 60c-d

28 HARVEY: *On Animal Generation*, 491a-b; 496a-c

30 BACON: *Novum Organum*, BK I, APH 45 110b; APH 66, 114d-115a; BK II, APH 40, 171a-173a

32 MILTON: *Paradise Lost*, BK III [708-721] 150b-151a

45 LAVOISIER: *Elements of Chemistry*, PREF, 3b-4a; PART I, 29d-33b; PART II, 53a-55a; 57c-65a,c

45 FARADAY: *Researches in Electricity*, 383b-386c

51 TOLSTOY: *War and Peace*, BK VI, 248d-249a

3c. The mutability of the elements: their transmutation

7 PLATO: *Timaeus*, 456b-c; 458d-460b

8 ARISTOTLE: *Heavens*, BK I, CH 3 360d-362a; BK III, CH I [298^{a}24–299^{a}1] 389b,d-390b; CH 2 [301^{b}33–302^{a}9] 393b; CH 6 [304^{b}23]–CH 8 [306^{b}29] 396a-398a / *Generation and Corruption*, BK I, CH I 409a-410c; CH 6 [322^{b}1–21] 420b-d; BK II, CH 4–6 431b-435a / *Meteorology*, BK I, CH 3 [339^{a}36–^{b}3] 445d / *Metaphysics*, BK I, CH 8 [989^{a}18–29] 507b-c

10 GALEN: *Natural Faculties*, BK I, CH 2, 167d-168b; BK II, CH 3, 185c-d

12 LUCRETIUS: *Nature of Things*, BK I [635-829] 8d-11a; BK V [235-305] 64a-65a; [380-415] 66a-c

12 AURELIUS: *Meditations*, BK II, SECT 3 257a-b; BK IV, SECT 46 267c; BK V, SECT 13 271b; BK VII, SECT 18 281a; SECT 23 281b; SECT 25 281c; SECT 50 283a; BK X, SECT 7 297b-c

19 AQUINAS: *Summa Theologica*, PART I, Q 66, A 2, ANS 345d-347b

20 AQUINAS: *Summa Theologica*, PART III SUPPL, Q 74, AA 1–6 925c-932b passim; Q 91, A 5, ANS and REP 4 1024a-1025b

21 DANTE: *Divine Comedy*, PARADISE, VII [121–148] 116b-c

22 CHAUCER: *Canon's Yeoman's Prologue* 471b-474a / *Canon's Yeoman's Tale* 474b-487a

30 BACON: *Advancement of Learning*, 14b-c

34 NEWTON: *Optics*, BK III, 531a-b

40 GIBBON: *Decline and Fall*, 148a-b

41 GIBBON: *Decline and Fall*, 299d-300a

44 BOSWELL: *Johnson*, 262c

45 LAVOISIER: *Elements of Chemistry*, PART I, 41b-c

3d. Combinations of the elements: compounds and mixtures

7 PLATO: *Timaeus*, 448b-d; 449c-450a; 452d-454a; 460b-462c

8 ARISTOTLE: *Topics*, BK VI, CH 14 [151ª20–32] 206a / *Physics*, BK III, CH 5 [204ᵇ10–22] 282c-d; BK VII, CH 3 [246ᵇ2–19] 329c-330a / *Heavens*, BK I, CH 2 [268ᵇ27–269ª30] 360a-c; CH 5 [271ᵇ18–23] 362d-363a; BK III, CH 3 [302ª10]–CH 4 [302ᵇ28] 393c-394a; CH 8 [306ᵇ22–29] 398a; BK IV, CH 4 [311ª30–ᵇ14] 402d-403a / *Generation and Corruption*, BK I, CH 1 [314ª25–ᵇ2] 409c; CH 2 [315ª28–33] 410d; CH 10 426c-428d; BK II, CH 6–8 433d-436d / *Meteorology*, BK III, CH 6 [378ª13]–BK IV, CH 12 [390ᵇ21] 482c-494d / *Metaphysics*, BK VII, CH 17 [1041ᵇ 12–33] 565d-566a,c / *Soul*, BK I, CH 2 [404ᵇ7–29] 633d-634a; [405ᵇ8–31] 634d-635a; CH 5 [409ᵇ18–411ª7] 639c-641a; BK III, CH 13 [435ª11–ᵇ4] 668a-c / *Sense and the Sensible*, CH 2–3 674a-678b

9 ARISTOTLE: *Parts of Animals*, BK I, CH 1 [640ᵇ5–18] 163a-b; BK II, CH 1 [646ª12–ᵇ20] 170a-d

10 HIPPOCRATES: *Ancient Medicine*, par 15 5c-d

10 GALEN: *Natural Faculties*, BK I, CH 2–3 167b-169a; CH 6 169c-170c; BK II, CH 8, 193b-d

12 LUCRETIUS: *Nature of Things*, BK I [635–920] 8d-12b

12 EPICTETUS: *Discourses*, BK III, CH 13, 189a

12 AURELIUS: *Meditations*, BK X, SECT 7, 297b

16 KEPLER: *Epitome*, BK IV, 929b-930a

17 PLOTINUS: *Second Ennead*, TR I, CH 6–8 37d-39d; TR VII, CH 1–2 62d-64b

18 AUGUSTINE: *City of God*, BK VIII, CH 2 265b-266a

19 AQUINAS: *Summa Theologica*, PART I, Q 71, A 1 367a-368b; Q 76, A 4, REP 4 393a-394c; Q 91, A 1 484a-485b

20 AQUINAS: *Summa Theologica*, PART III, Q 2, A 1, ANS 710a-711c; PART III SUPPL, Q 74, A 1, REP 3 925c-926c; A 4, ANS 928d-929d; A 5 929d-931b; Q 79, A 1, REP 4 951b-953b; Q 80, A 3, REP 3 958b-959c; Q 82, A 1, ANS 968a-970c; Q 91, A 5 1024a-1025b

21 DANTE: *Divine Comedy*, PARADISE, VII [121–148] 116b-c

28 GILBERT: *Loadstone*, BK I, 13b-14d; BK II, 29c-30a

28 HARVEY: *On Animal Generation*, 495c-496d

30 BACON: *Novum Organum*, BK I, APH 66 114d-115c; BK II, APH 7 139c-140a; APH 40, 171a-173a; APH 48, 181a-184a

33 PASCAL: *Vacuum*, 367a-b

35 BERKELEY: *Human Knowledge*, SECT 65 425d-426a

45 LAVOISIER: *Elements of Chemistry*, PART I, 22c-52a,c; PART II, 54b,d-55d; 57c-86a,c; PART III, 87c-d; 103b-c; 105d; 117a-128c esp 117a-118a

45 FARADAY: *Researches in Electricity*, 309a-312a; 312c-313d; 314a-b; 315a-b; 327a-422a,c passim; 541b,d-584a,c passim

51 TOLSTOY: *War and Peace*, BK VI, 248d-249a

53 JAMES: *Psychology*, 104a-105a; 876a

4. The discovery of elements in other arts and sciences

7 PLATO: *Cratylus*, 104c-110d esp 106a-107b / *Republic*, BK III, 333c-d / *Theaetetus*, 544c-548c / *Philebus*, 615c-617d; 618d-619b; 635b-639a,c

8 ARISTOTLE: *Categories*, CH 2 [1ª17–19] 5b / *Interpretation*, CH 4 [16ᵇ27–35] 26a / *Prior Analytics*, BK I, CH 1 [24ᵇ17–22] 39c; CH 23 [40ᵇ18–22] 57b; [41ª4–7] 57d / *Posterior Analytics*, BK I, CH 4 [73ª3–ᵇ2] 100b-c; CH 7 [75ª38–ᵇ7] 103c; CH 23 [84ᵇ19–85ª1] 115c-116a; CH 27 119b / *Topics*, BK I, CH 4–9 144b-147b esp CH 4 [101ᵇ11–25] 144b-c; BK VI, CH 1 [139ª24–32] 192a; CH 13 204c-206a / *Metaphysics*, BK I, CH 5 [985ᵇ22–986ª21] 503d-504b; CH 6 [987ᵇ 19–23] 505d; [988ª7–16] 506a-b; CH 9 [992ᵇ 18–993ª10] 511a-c; BK III, CH 3 [998ª20–ᵇ11] 517a-b; CH 6 [1002ᵇ11–25] 521b-c; BK V, CH 3 534c-d; BK XII, CH 4–5 599d-601a / *Soul*, BK I, CH 2 [404ᵇ7–29] 633d-634a; CH 5 [409ᵇ23–411ª 23] 639d-641b; BK III, CH 5 [430ª10–14] 662c

9 ARISTOTLE: *Parts of Animals*, BK II, CH 1 [646ª10]–CH 2 [647ᵇ30] 170a-172a / *Politics*, BK I, CH 1 [1252ª18–24] 445b; BK III, CH 1 [1274ᵇ 31–1275ª2] 471b; CH 3 [1276ᵇ34–ᵇ15] 473b-c / *Rhetoric*, BK III, CH 13 667b-d / *Poetics*, CH 6 684a-685a; CH 20 692b-693a

10 GALEN: *Natural Faculties*, BK I, CH 6 169c-170c; BK II, CH 6 188c-191a; BK III, CH 15, 215a-b

11 EUCLID: *Elements* 1a-396b

11 NICOMACHUS: *Arithmetic*, BK II, 829b-d

12 LUCRETIUS: *Nature of Things*, BK I [823–829] 11a; BK II [688–699] 23d

16 KEPLER: *Harmonies of the World*, 1016b-1017a

18 AUGUSTINE: *City of God*, BK XIX, CH 16, 522a

19 AQUINAS: *Summa Theologica*, PART I, Q 119, A 1, REP 3 604c-607b

20 AQUINAS: *Summa Theologica*, PART II-II, Q 179, A 2, REP 2 607a-c; PART III SUPPL, Q 80, A 3 958b-959c

24 RABELAIS: *Gargantua and Pantagruel*, BK III, 138a-d

(4. *The discovery of elements in other arts and sciences.*)

28 HARVEY: *Circulation of the Blood*, 316d / *On Animal Generation*, 429c-438c esp 432d-433b; 488d-496d esp 490d-491c, 494a-b

30 BACON: *Advancement of Learning*, 52b-d; 76d-77c

31 DESCARTES: *Rules*, VI, 8b-9a; VIII, 14b-c; XII, 21b-24c / *Discourse*, PART VI, 62a / *Objections and Replies*, 128a-129a

35 LOCKE: *Human Understanding*, BK II, CH II, SECT 1-2 127d-128b; CH VII, SECT 10 133a-b; CH XII, SECT 1-2 147b-d; SECT 8 148c-d; CH XV, SECT 9 164b-d; CH XVI, SECT 1 165c-d; CH XXI, SECT 75 200b-d; BK III, CH IV, SECT 15-16 263a-c

39 SMITH: *Wealth of Nations*, BK I, 20b-23b esp 20b-21c, 22b-c

46 HEGEL: *Philosophy of Right*, PART III, par 341 110c

50 MARX: *Capital*, 6b-c; 19c-26d passim, esp 20b-22a, 25d-26d; 62a; 85d-88d esp 85d, 88c

51 TOLSTOY: *War and Peace*, BK XI, 469a-470c; BK XIV, 589c-590c; EPILOGUE II, 694d-695c

53 JAMES: *Psychology*, xiiib; 18b-19b; 116b-117a; 126a; 150a

54 FREUD: *War and Death*, 758a

5. The theory of atomism: critiques of atomism

7 PLATO: *Sophist*, 567a-568a

8 ARISTOTLE: *Physics*, BK I, CH 2 [184^{b}15-22] 259b-c / *Heavens*, BK I, CH 7 [275^{b}30-276^{a}18] 367a-b; BK III, CH 4 [303^{a}3-^{b}8] 394b-d; BK IV, CH 2 [308^{b}29-310^{a}14] 400b-401c / *Generation and Corruption*, BK I, CH 2 410d-413c; CH 8 [325^{a}23-^{b}11] 423d-424b / *Metaphysics*, BK I, CH 4 [985^{b}3-19] 503c-d

10 GALEN: *Natural Faculties*, BK I, CH 12-14 172d-179d; BK II, CH 6 188c-191a

12 LUCRETIUS: *Nature of Things* 1a-97a,c

12 AURELIUS: *Meditations*, BK IV, SECT 3, 263b-c; BK IX, SECT 39 295a; BK X, SECT 6 297a-b

17 PLOTINUS: *Second Ennead*, TR IV, CH 7, 52c / *Third Ennead*, TR I, CH 2, 78d; CH 3 79b-c / *Fourth Ennead*, TR VII, CH 2-4 192a-193c

19 AQUINAS: *Summa Theologica*, PART I, Q 115, A I, ANS and REP 3,5 585d-587c

25 MONTAIGNE: *Essays*, 263a

28 HARVEY: *On Animal Generation*, 355b-d; 495c-496d

30 BACON: *Novum Organum*, BK II, APH 8 140b

34 NEWTON: *Principles*, BK III, RULE III 270b-271a / *Optics*, BK III, 531b-542a

35 LOCKE: *Human Understanding*, BK IV, CH III, SECT 25-26 321a-c

42 KANT: *Pure Reason*, 161d-163a

45 FARADAY: *Researches in Electricity*, 850b,d-855a,c

52 DOSTOEVSKY: *Brothers Karamazov*, BK XI, 341d

53 JAMES: *Psychology*, 876a; 882a-884b

5a. The conception of atomic bodies: imperceptible, indestructible, and indivisible

8 ARISTOTLE: *Generation and Corruption*, BK I, CH 1 [314^{a}22-24] 409b-c / *Metaphysics*, BK VII, CH 13 [1039^{a}2-11] 562d

10 GALEN: *Natural Faculties*, BK I, CH 12 172d-173c; BK II, CH 6 188c-191a

12 LUCRETIUS: *Nature of Things*, BK I [146-328] 2d-5a; [483-634] 7a-8d

17 PLOTINUS: *Second Ennead*, TR IV, CH 7, 52c

34 NEWTON: *Principles*, BK I, PROP 73, SCHOL 133b-134a; BK III, RULE III 270b-271a / *Optics*, BK III, 537a-b; 541b; 543a

35 LOCKE: *Human Understanding*, BK IV, CH III, SECT 25 321a-b

45 FARADAY: *Researches in Electricity*, 386c-d; 850b,d-855a,c

53 JAMES: *Psychology*, 68a

5b. Arguments for and against the existence of atoms: the issue concerning the infinite divisibility of matter

8 ARISTOTLE: *Physics*, BK III, CH 6-7 284b-286c / *Heavens*, BK III, CH 6 [304^{b}23-305^{a}10] 396a-b; BK IV, CH 4 [311^{a}30-^{b}1] 402d-403a / *Generation and Corruption*, BK I, CH 2 [315^{b}25-317^{a}17] 411b-413a; CH 8 423b-425d / *Sense and the Sensible*, CH 6 [445^{b}4-446^{a}20] 683b-684c

12 LUCRETIUS: *Nature of Things*, BK I [146-328] 2d-5a; [483-920] 7a-12b; BK II [62-141] 15d-16d

12 AURELIUS: *Meditations*, BK X, SECT 6 297a-b

17 PLOTINUS: *Second Ennead*, TR IV, CH 7 52a-c / *Third Ennead*, TR I, CH 3 79b-c / *Fourth Ennead*, TR II, CH 1, 139d

19 AQUINAS: *Summa Theologica*, PART I, Q 7, A 3, REP 3 32c-33c; A 4, ANS 33d-34c

28 GALILEO: *Two New Sciences*, FIRST DAY, 139c-141d; 147d-148b; 151d-153a

30 BACON: *Novum Organum*, BK I, APH 66, 115c

31 SPINOZA: *Ethics*, PART I, PROP 15, SCHOL 360b-361d

34 NEWTON: *Principles*, BK III, RULE III 270b-271a / *Optics*, BK II, 478b-485b; BK III, 537a-541b esp 541b

35 LOCKE: *Human Understanding*, BK II, CH XVII, SECT 12 170d; CH XXIX, SECT 16 237b-238a; BK IV, CH X, SECT 10, 351c-352a

35 BERKELEY: *Human Knowledge*, SECT 47 421c-422a

42 KANT: *Pure Reason*, 131c; 137a-140c; 152d; 161d-163a

43 FEDERALIST: NUMBER 31, 103d

45 LAVOISIER: *Elements of Chemistry*, PART I, 9a-d

45 FARADAY: *Researches in Electricity*, 386c-d; 850b,d-855a,c

5c. Atoms and the void as the ultimate constituents of reality

7 PLATO: *Sophist*, 567a-b

8 ARISTOTLE: *Physics*, BK I, CH 5 [188^{a}18-23] 263c; BK IV, CH 6-9 292c-297c / *Heavens*, BK

I, CH 7 [275^{b}30–276^{a}18] 367a-b; CH 9 [279^{a}12–18] 370b-c; BK III, CH 6 [305^{a}14–22] 396b-c; BK IV, CH 2 [308^{b}29–310^{a}14] 400b-401c; CH 5 [312^{b}20–313^{a}14] 404b-d / *Generation and Corruption*, BK I, CH 8 423b-425d / *Metaphysics*, BK I, CH 4 [985^{b}3–19] 503c-d; BK IV, CH 5 [1009^{a}22–37] 528d; BK VII, CH 13 [1039^{a}2–11] 562d

10 GALEN: *Natural Faculties*, BK I, CH 12, 173a; BK II, CH 6 188c-191a esp 189a-b

12 LUCRETIUS: *Nature of Things*, BK I [265–634] 4b-8d esp [418–448] 6b-c

28 GALILEO: *Two New Sciences*, FIRST DAY, 141c-d

30 BACON: *Novum Organum*, BK II, APH 8 140b

34 NEWTON: *Principles*, BK III, PROP 6, COROL III–IV 281b / *Optics*, BK III, 528b

45 FARADAY: *Researches in Electricity*, 850b,d-855a,c

53 JAMES: *Psychology*, 106a; 882a-883a

5d. The number, variety, and properties of atoms: the production of sensible things by their collocation

8 ARISTOTLE: *Physics*, BK I, CH 2 [184^{b}15–22] 259b-c; CH 5 [188^{a}18–25] 263c; BK III, CH 4 [203^{a}33–^{b}2] 281b / *Heavens*, BK I, CH 7 [275^{b}30–276^{a}18] 367a-b; BK III, CH 4 [303^{a}3–^{b}8] 394b-d; CH 7 [305^{b}27–306^{a}1] 397a-b; BK IV, CH 2 [308^{b}29–310^{a}14] 400b-401c / *Generation and Corruption*, BK I, CH 1 [314^{a}22–24] 409b-c; CH 2 [315^{a}34–316^{a}4] 410d-411c; CH 10 [327^{b}34–328^{a}18] 427b-c / *Metaphysics*, BK I, CH 4 [985^{b}3–19] 503c-d

10 GALEN: *Natural Faculties*, BK I, CH 12, 173a-b; BK II, CH 6, 189a-190a

12 LUCRETIUS: *Nature of Things*, BK II [62–141] 15d-16d; [184–250] 17b-18b; [333–599] 19b-22c; [730–1022] 24b-28a

17 PLOTINUS: *Third Ennead*, TR I, CH 3, 79b

28 HARVEY: *On Animal Generation*, 495c-496a

34 NEWTON: *Optics*, BK III, 536b-537b; 539a-b

34 HUYGENS: *Light*, CH III, 566b-569b

35 LOCKE: *Human Understanding*, BK II, CH XXVI, SECT 2 217b-d; BK IV, CH XX, SECT 15, 393b

35 HUME: *Human Understanding*, SECT XI, DIV 104, 498c

45 LAVOISIER: *Elements of Chemistry*, PART I, 13a-d

45 FARADAY: *Researches in Electricity*, 850b,d-855a,c

53 JAMES: *Psychology*, 104a-b; 876a

5e. The atomistic account of sensation and thought: the *idola*

7 PLATO: *Meno*, 177b-c

12 LUCRETIUS: *Nature of Things*, BK II [398–443] 20a-c; [865–990] 26a-27c; BK III [231–395] 33a-35a; BK IV [26–906] 44b-56a esp [26–268] 44b-47d, [722–817] 53d-54d

17 PLOTINUS: *Third Ennead*, TR I, CH 2, 78d; CH 3 79b-c / *Fourth Ennead*, TR VII, CH 6–8, 194b-196c

19 AQUINAS: *Summa Theologica*, PART I, Q 84, A 6, ANS 447c-449a

34 NEWTON: *Optics*, BK III, 518b-519b; 522a

35 LOCKE: *Human Understanding*, BK III, CH IV, SECT 10 261b-d; BK IV, CH X, SECT 5 350a-b

53 JAMES: *Psychology*, 98a-117b esp 98b-103b, 115a

5f. The atomic constitution of mind and soul: its bearing on immortality

8 ARISTOTLE: *Soul*, BK I, CH 2 [403^{b}28–404^{a}15] 633a-b; [405^{a}8–13] 634b; CH 3 [406^{b}15–26] 636a-b; CH 4 [409^{a}10]–CH 5 [409^{b}18] 639a-c

10 GALEN: *Natural Faculties*, BK I, CH 12 172d-173c

12 LUCRETIUS: *Nature of Things*, BK III [94–869] 31b-41a esp [161–322] 32b-34b; BK IV [916–961] 56b-d

17 PLOTINUS: *Second Ennead*, TR IV, CH 7, 52c; TR IX, CH 5, 68b / *Third Ennead*, TR I, CH 3 79b-c / *Fourth Ennead*, TR VII, CH 2–4 192a-193c

35 BERKELEY: *Human Knowledge*, SECT 93 431b; SECT 141 441a-b

42 KANT: *Pure Reason*, 126c-d

53 JAMES: *Psychology*, 95a-118b esp 95b-98a, 103a-106b, 117a-118b

5g. The explanation of natural phenomena by reference to the properties and motions of atoms

8 ARISTOTLE: *Heavens*, BK IV, CH 2 [308^{b}29–310^{a}14] 400b-401c; CH 4 [311^{a}30–^{b}1] 402d-403a; CH 5 [312^{b}20]–CH 6 [313^{b}25] 404b-405a,c / *Generation and Corruption*, BK I, CH 2 410d-413c; CH 8 423b-425d

10 GALEN: *Natural Faculties*, BK I, CH 12, 172d-173b; CH 14, 177a-178d; BK II, CH 6 188c-191a

12 LUCRETIUS: *Nature of Things*, BK I [265–328] 4b-5a; BK II [184–215] 17b-d; [333–477] 19b-21a; [522–540] 21c-d; [757–771] 24c-d; BK IV [524–614] 51a-52b; BK VI 80a-97a,c

17 PLOTINUS: *Third Ennead*, TR I, CH 2, 78d; CH 3 79b-c

19 AQUINAS: *Summa Theologica*, PART I, Q 115, A 1, ANS and REP 3,5 585d-587c

28 GILBERT: *Loadstone*, BK II, 34c-35a

28 GALILEO: *Two New Sciences*, FIRST DAY, 139c-141d; 151d-153a

28 HARVEY: *On Animal Generation*, 355b-d; 495c-496a

30 BACON: *Advancement of Learning*, 45b-c

34 NEWTON: *Principles*, 1b-2a / *Optics*, BK III, 531b-542a

34 HUYGENS: *Light*, CH III, 566b-569b

35 LOCKE: *Human Understanding*, BK IV, CH III, SECT 25–26 321a-c

45 FARADAY: *Researches in Electricity*, 850b,d-855a,c

53 JAMES: *Psychology*, 882a-884b

(5. *The theory of atomism: critiques of atomism.*)

5h. The atomistic account of the origin and decay of the world, its evolution and order

12 LUCRETIUS: *Nature of Things*, BK I [1008–1037] 13c-d; BK II [1023–1174] 28a-30a,c; BK V [55–508] 61d-67c

12 AURELIUS: *Meditations*, BK VI, SECT 10 274b-c

17 PLOTINUS: *Third Ennead*, TR I, CH 3 79b-c

19 AQUINAS: *Summa Theologica*, PART I, Q 47, A I, ANS 256a-257b; A 3, ANS 258c-259a

34 NEWTON: *Optics*, BK III, 541b

53 JAMES: *Psychology*, 95b

CROSS-REFERENCES

For: The discussion of the ideas most closely associated with element, *see* CAUSE; PRINCIPLE.

Matters relevant to the conception of elements or atoms as simple parts of a whole, *see* ONE AND MANY 2b–2c; and for another discussion of the distinction between elements or atoms and compounds or mixtures, *see* CHANGE 9a; MATTER 2.

The problem of the transmutation of the elements, *see* CHANGE 10a.

The issue concerning the divisibility of matter and the existence of a void, *see* INFINITY 4b; ONE AND MANY 3a(3); SPACE 2b(1)–2b(3); and for the question of the number of the elements or of the atoms, *see* INFINITY 5–5b; QUANTITY 7.

Other considerations of atomistic materialism, *see* MATTER 3a, 6; MECHANICS 4c; MIND 2e; SOUL 3d; WORLD 1b, 4c.

ADDITIONAL READINGS

Listed below are works not included in *Great Books of the Western World*, but relevant to the idea and topics with which this chapter deals. These works are divided into two groups:

I. Works by authors represented in this collection.
II. Works by authors not represented in this collection.

For the date, place, and other facts concerning the publication of the works cited, consult the Bibliography of Additional Readings which follows the last chapter of *The Great Ideas*.

I.

AUGUSTINE. *De Genesi ad Litteram*
AQUINAS. *De Mixtione Elementorum*
DESCARTES. *The Principles of Philosophy*, PART II, 20; PART III, 48–102; PART IV, 1–19, 31–48, 61–132, 201–203
HOBBES. *Concerning Body*
KANT. *Metaphysical Foundations of Natural Science*, DIV II
MARX. *Über die Differenz der demokritischen und epikureischen Naturphilosophie*

II.

EPICURUS. *Letter to Herodotus*
SEXTUS EMPIRICUS. *Against the Physicists*
MAIMONIDES. *The Guide for the Perplexed*, PART II, CH 10
JOHN OF SAINT THOMAS. *Cursus Philosophicus Thomisticus, Philosophia Naturalis*, PART III, Q 10
BOYLE. *The Sceptical Chymist*
LEIBNITZ. *New Essays Concerning Human Understanding*, APPENDIX, CH 3
——. *Monadology*, par 1–9
VOLTAIRE. "Atoms," in *A Philosophical Dictionary*
DALTON. *A New System of Chemical Philosophy*
WHEWELL. *The Philosophy of the Inductive Sciences*, VOL I, BK VI

MAXWELL. *Scientific Papers*, LXXIII
HERSCHEL. *Familiar Lectures on Scientific Subjects*, XI
LANGE. *The History of Materialism*
MENDELEYEV. *The Principles of Chemistry*
CLIFFORD. "Atoms," in VOL I, *Lectures and Essays*
STALLO. *Concepts and Theories of Modern Physics*, CH 7–8, 13
WHITEHEAD. *An Enquiry Concerning the Principles of Natural Knowledge*, CH 5
PLANCK. *The Origin and Development of the Quantum Theory*
EDDINGTON. *Stars and Atoms*
B. RUSSELL. *The Analysis of Matter*, CH 3
BOHR. *The Theory of Spectra and Atomic Constitution*
——. *On the Application of the Quantum Theory to Atomic Structure*
——. *Atomic Theory and the Description of Nature*
JEANS. *The Universe Around Us*, CH 2
C. G. DARWIN. *The New Conceptions of Matter*
SODDY. *The Interpretation of the Atom*
STRANATHAN. *The "Particles" of Modern Physics*
SMYTH. *Atomic Energy for Military Purposes*
GAMOW. *Atomic Energy in Cosmic and Human Life*
ANDRADE. *The Atom and Its Energy*
HECHT. *Explaining the Atom*
G. THOMSON. *The Atom*

Chapter 22: EMOTION

INTRODUCTION

THE emotions claim our attention in two ways. We experience them, sometimes in a manner which overwhelms us; and we analyze them by defining and classifying the several passions, and by studying their role in human life and society. We seldom do both at once, for analysis requires emotional detachment, and moments of passion do not permit study or reflection.

With regard to the emotions the great books are similarly divided into two sorts—those which are theoretical discussions and those which concretely describe the passions of particular men, exhibit their vigor, and induce in us a vicarious experience. Books of the first sort are scientific, philosophical, or theological treatises. Books of the second sort are the great epic and dramatic poems, the novels and plays, the literature of biography and history.

We customarily think of the emotions as belonging to the subject matter of psychology —proper to the science of animal and human behavior. It is worth noting therefore that this is largely a recent development, which appears in the works of Darwin, James, and Freud. In earlier centuries, the analysis of the passions occurs in other contexts: in treatments of rhetoric, as in certain dialogues of Plato and in Aristotle's *Rhetoric*; in the Greek discussions of virtue and vice; in the moral theology of Aquinas and in Spinoza's *Ethics*; and in books of political theory, such as Machiavelli's *Prince* and Hobbes' *Leviathan*.

Descartes' treatise on *The Passions of the Soul* is probably one of the first discourses on the subject to be separated from the practical considerations of oratory, morals, and politics. Only subsequently do the emotions become an object of purely theoretic interest in psychology. But even then the interest of the psychiatrist or psychoanalyst—to the extent that it is medical or therapeutic—has a strong practical bent.

In the great works of poetry and history no similar shift takes place as one goes from Homer and Virgil to Tolstoy and Dostoevsky, from Greek to Shakespearean tragedy, from Plutarch and Tacitus to Gibbon. What Wordsworth said of the lyric poem—that it is "emotion recollected in tranquillity"—may not apply to the narratives in an identical sense. Yet they too re-enact the passions in all their vitality. Their pages are filled with the emotions of men in conflict with one another or suffering conflict within themselves.

This is no less true of historical narrative than of fiction. The memorable actions of men on the stage of history did not occur in calm and quiet. We would certainly not remember them as well if the historian failed to re-create for us the turbulence of crisis and catastrophe, or the biographer the storm and stress which accompanies the inward resolution of heroic lives.

It is impossible, of course, to cite *all* the relevant passages of poetry and history. In many instances, nothing less than a whole book would suffice. The particular references given in this chapter, which are far from exhaustive, have been selected for their peculiar exemplary significance in relation to a particular topic; but for the whole range of topics connected with emotion, the reader should certainly seek further in the realms of history and poetry for the raw materials which the scientists and philosophers have tried to analyze and understand.

To the student of the emotions, Bacon recommends "the poets and writers of histories" as "the best doctors of this knowledge; where we may find painted forth with great life, how affections are kindled and incited; and how pacified and refrained; and how again contained from act and further degree; how they disclose themselves; how they work; how they vary; how they gather and fortify; how they are enwrapped one within another; and how they do fight and encounter one with another; and other like particularities."

FOUR WORDS—"passion," "affection" or "affect," and "emotion"—have been traditionally used to designate the same psychological fact. Of these, "affection" and "affect" have ceased to be generally current, although we do find them in Freud; and "passion" is now usually restricted to mean one of the emotions, or the more violent aspect of any emotional experience. But if we are to connect discussions collected from widely separated centuries, we must be able to use all these words interchangeably.

The psychological fact to which they all refer is one every human being has experienced in moments of great excitement, especially during intense seizure by rage or fear. In his treatise *On the Circulation of the Blood*, Harvey calls attention to "the fact that in almost every affection, appetite, hope, or fear, our body suffers, the countenance changes, and the blood appears to course hither and thither. In anger the eyes are fiery and the pupils contracted; in modesty the cheeks are suffused with blushes; in fear, and under a sense of infamy and of shame, the face is pale" and "in lust how quickly is the member distended with blood and erected!"

Emotional experience seems to involve an awareness of widespread bodily commotion, which includes changes in the tension of the blood vessels and the muscles, changes in heartbeat and breathing, changes in the condition of the skin and other tissues. Though some degree of bodily disturbance would seem to be an essential ingredient in all emotional experience, the intensity and extent of the physiological reverberation, or bodily commotion, is not the same or equal in all the emotions. Some emotions are much more violent than others. This leads William James to distinguish what he calls the "coarser emotions . . . in which every one recognizes a strong organic reverberation" from the "subtler emotions" in which the "organic reverberation is less obvious and strong."

This fact is sometimes used to draw the line between what are truly emotions and what are only mild feelings of pleasure and pain or enduring sentiments. Nevertheless, sentiments may be emotional residues—stable attitudes which pervade a life even during moments of emotional detachment and calm—and pleasure and pain may color all the emotions. "Pleasure and pain," Locke suggests, are "the hinges on which our passions turn." Even though they may not be passions in the strict sense, they are obviously closely connected with them.

THAT THE EMOTIONS are organic disturbances, upsetting the normal course of the body's functioning, is sometimes thought to be a modern discovery, connected with the James-Lange theory that the emotional experience is nothing but the "feeling of . . . the bodily changes" which "follow directly the perception of the exciting fact." On this view, the explanation of emotion seems to be the very opposite of "common sense," which says, "we meet a bear, are frightened, and run." According to James, "this order of sequence is incorrect," and "the more rational statement is that we feel . . . afraid because we tremble." In other words, we do not run away because we are afraid, but are afraid because we run away.

This fact about the emotions was known to antiquity and the Middle Ages. Aristotle, for example, holds that mere awareness of an object does not induce flight unless "the heart is moved," and Aquinas declares that "passion is properly to be found where there is corporeal transmutation." He describes at some length the bodily changes which take place in anger and fear. Only very recently, however, have apparatus and techniques been devised for recording and, in some cases, measuring the physiological changes accompanying experimentally produced emotions—in both animals and men.

Modern theory also tries to throw some light on these organic changes by pointing out their adaptive utility in the struggle for existence. This type of explanation is advanced by Darwin in *The Expression of Emotions in Man and Animals*, and is adopted by other evolutionists. "The snarl or sneer, the one-sided uncovering of the upper teeth," James writes, "is accounted for by Darwin as a survival from the time when our ancestors had large canines, and unfleshed them (as dogs now do) for attack. . . .

The distention of the nostrils in anger is interpreted by Spencer as an echo of the way in which our ancestors had to breathe when, during combat, their 'mouth was filled up by a part of the antagonist's body that had been seized' ... The redding of the face and neck is called by Wundt a compensatory arrangement for relieving the brain of the blood-pressure which the simultaneous excitement of the heart brings with it. The effusion of tears is explained both by this author and by Darwin to be a blood-withdrawing agency of a similar sort."

Reviewing statements of this sort, James is willing to concede that "some movements of expression can be accounted for as *weakened repetitions of movements which formerly* (when they were stronger) *were of utility to the subject*"; but though we may thus "see the reason for a few emotional reactions," he thinks "others remain for which no plausible reason can even be conceived." The latter, James suggests, "may be reactions which are purely mechanical results of the way in which our nervous centres are framed, reactions which, although permanent in us now, may be called accidental as far as their origin goes."

Whether or not *all* the bodily changes which occur in such emotions as anger or fear serve the purpose of increasing the animal's efficiency in combat or flight—as, for example, the increase of sugar in the blood and the greater supply of blood to arms and legs seem to do—the basic emotions are generally thought to be connected with the instinctively determined patterns of behavior by which animals struggle to survive. "The actions we call instinctive," James writes, "are expressions or manifestations of the emotions"; or, as other writers suggest, an emotion, whether in outward expression or in inner experience, is the central phase of an instinct in operation.

The observation of the close relation between instinct and emotion does not belong exclusively to modern, or post-Darwinian, thought. The ancients also recognize it, though in different terms. Following Aristotle's analysis of the various "interior senses," Aquinas, for example, speaks of the "estimative power" by which animals seem to be innately prepared to react to things useful or harmful.

"If an animal were moved by pleasing and disagreeable things only as affecting the sense" —that is, the exterior senses—"there would be no need to suppose," Aquinas writes, "that an animal has a power besides the apprehension of those forms which the senses perceive, and in which the animal takes pleasure, or from which it shrinks with horror." But animals need to seek or avoid certain things on account of their advantages or disadvantages, and such emotional reactions of approach or avoidance require, in his opinion, a sense of the useful and the dangerous, which is innate rather than learned. The estimative power thus seems to play a role which later writers assign to instinct. The relation of instinct to the emotions and to fundamental biological needs is further considered, from other points of view, in the chapters on DESIRE and HABIT.

LIKE DESIRE, emotion is neither knowledge nor action, but something intermediate between the one and the other. The various passions are usually aroused by objects perceived, imagined, or remembered, and once aroused they in turn originate impulses to act in certain ways. For example, fear arises with the perception of a threatening danger or with the imagination of some fancied peril. The thing feared is somehow recognized as capable of inflicting injury with consequent pain. The thing feared is also something from which one naturally tends to flee in order to avoid harm. Once the danger is known and until it is avoided by flight or in some other way, the characteristic feeling of fear pervades the whole experience. It is partly a result of what is known and what is done, and partly the cause of how things seem and how one behaves.

Analytically isolated from its causes and effects, the emotion itself seems to be the feeling rather than the knowing or the doing. But it is not simply an awareness of a certain bodily condition. It also involves the felt impulse to do something about the object of the passion.

Those writers who, like Aquinas, identify emotion with the impulse by which "the soul is drawn to a thing," define the several passions as specifically different acts of appetite or desire—specific tendencies to action. Aquinas, for instance, adopts the definition given by Damascene: "Passion is a movement of the sensitive appetite when we imagine good or evil."

Other writers who, like Spinoza, find that "the order of the actions and passions of our body is coincident in nature with the order of the actions and passions of the mind," stress the cognitive rather than the impulsive aspect of emotion. They accordingly define the passions in terms of the characteristic feelings, pleasant and unpleasant, which flow from the estimation of certain objects as beneficial or harmful. Spinoza goes furthest in this direction when he says that "an affect or passion of the mind *is a confused idea . . . by which the mind affirms of its body, or any part of it, a greater or less power of existence than before.*"

There seems to be no serious issue here, for writers of both sorts acknowledge, though with different emphasis, the two sides of an emotion —the cognitive and the impulsive, that which faces toward the object and that which leads into action. On either view, the human passions are regarded as part of man's animal nature. It is generally admitted that disembodied spirits, if such exist, cannot have emotions. The angels, Augustine writes, "feel no anger while they punish those whom the eternal law of God consigns to punishment, no fellow-feeling with misery while they relieve the miserable, no fear while they aid those who are in danger." When we do ascribe emotions to spirits, it is, Augustine claims, because, "though they have none of our weakness, their acts resemble the actions to which these emotions move us."

In connection with the objects which arouse them, the emotions necessarily depend upon the senses and the imagination; and their perturbations and impulses require bodily organs for expression. That is why, as indicated in the chapter on DESIRE, some writers separate the passions from acts of the will, as belonging to the sensitive or animal appetite rather than to the rational or specifically human appetite. Even those writers who do not place so high an estimate on the role of reason, refer the emotions to the animal aspect of human behavior, or to what is sometimes called "man's lower nature." When this phrase is used, it usually signifies the passions as opposed to the reason, not the purely vegetative functions which man shares with plants as well as animals.

There seems to be no doubt that emotions are common to men and animals and that they are more closely related to instinct than to reason or intelligence. Darwin presents many instances which, he claims, prove that "the senses and intuitions, the various emotions and faculties, such as love, memory, attention, curiosity, imitation, reason, etc., of which man boasts, may be found in an incipient, or even sometimes in a well-developed, condition in the lower animals." Where Darwin remarks upon "the fewness and the comparative simplicity of the instincts in the higher animals . . . in contrast with those of the lower animals," James takes the position that man "is the animal richest in instinctive impulses." However that issue is decided, the emotions seem to be more elaborately developed in the higher animals, and man's emotional life would seem to be the most complex and varied of all.

The question then arises whether particular passions are identical—or are only analogous —when they occur in men and animals. For example, is human anger, no matter how closely it resembles brute rage in its physiology and impulses, nevertheless peculiarly human? Do men alone experience righteous indignation because of some admixture in them of reason and passion? When similar questions are asked about the sexual passions of men and animals, the answers will determine the view one takes of the characteristically human aspects of love and hate. It may even be asked whether hate, as men suffer it, is ever experienced by brutes, or whether certain passions, such as hope and despair, are known to brutes at all?

IN THE TRADITIONAL theory of the emotions, the chief problem, after the definition of emotion, is the classification or grouping of the passions, and the ordering of particular passions. The vocabulary of common speech in all ages and cultures includes a large number of words for naming emotions, and it has been the task of analysts to decide which of these words designate distinct affects or affections. The precise character of the object and the direction of the impulse have been, for the most part, the criteria of definition. As previously noted, it is but recently that the experimental observation of bodily changes has contributed to the differentiation of emotions from one another.

Spinoza offers the longest listing of the passions. For him, the emotions, which are all "compounded of the three primary affects, desire, joy, and sorrow," develop into the following forms: astonishment, contempt, love, hatred, inclination, aversion, devotion, derision, hope, fear, confidence, despair, gladness, remorse, commiseration, favor, indignation, overestimation, envy, compassion, self-satisfaction, humility, repentance, pride, despondency, self-exaltation, shame, regret, emulation, gratitude, benevolence, anger, vengeance, ferocity, audacity, consternation, courtesy, ambition, luxuriousness, drunkenness, avarice, lust.

Many of the foregoing are, for Hobbes, derived from what he calls "the simple passions," which include "appetite, desire, love, aversion, hate, joy, and grief." There are more emotions in Spinoza's list than either Aristotle or Locke or James mentions, but none which they include is omitted. Some of the items in Spinoza's enumeration are treated by other writers as virtues and vices rather than as passions.

The passions have been classified by reference to various criteria. As we have seen, James distinguishes emotions as "coarse" or "subtle" in terms of the violence or mildness of the accompanying physiological changes; and Spinoza distinguishes them according as "the mind passes to a greater perfection" or "to a less perfection." Spinoza's division would also seem to imply a distinction between the beneficial and the harmful in the objects causing these two types of emotion, or at least to involve the opposite components of pleasure and pain, for in his view the emotions which correspond to "a greater or less power of existence than before" are attended in the one case by "pleasurable excitement" and in the other by "pain."

Hobbes uses another principle of division. The passions differ basically according to the direction of their impulses—according as each is "a motion or endeavor . . . to or from the object moving." Aquinas adds still another criterion—"the difficulty or struggle . . . in acquiring certain goods or in avoiding certain evils" which, in contrast to those we "can easily acquire or avoid," makes them, therefore, "of an arduous or difficult nature." In these terms, he divides all the passions into the "concupiscible," which regard "good or evil simply" (i.e., love, hate, desire, aversion, joy, sorrow), and the "irascible," which "regard good or evil as arduous through being difficult to obtain or avoid" (i.e., fear, daring, hope, despair, anger).

Within each of these groups, Aquinas pairs particular passions as opposites, such as joy and sorrow, or hope and despair, either according to the "contrariety of object, i.e., of good and evil . . . or according to approach and withdrawal." Anger seems to be the only passion for which no opposite can be given, other than that "cessation from its movement" which Aristotle calls "calmness" and which Aquinas says is an opposite not by way of "contrariety but of negation or privation."

Using these distinctions, Aquinas also describes the order in which one passion leads to or generates another, beginning with love and hate, passing through hope, desire, and fear, with their opposites, and, after anger, ending in joy or despair. On one point, all observers and theorists from Plato to Freud seem to agree, namely, that love and hate lie at the root of all the other passions and generate hope or despair, fear and anger, according as the aspirations of love prosper or fail. Nor is the insight that even hate derives from love peculiarly modern, though Freud's theory of what he calls the "ambivalence" of love and hate toward the same object, seems to be part of his own special contribution to our understanding of the passions.

THE ROLE OF THE emotions or passions in human behavior has always raised two questions, one concerning the effect of conflict between diverse emotions, the other concerning the conflict between the passions and the reason or will. It is the latter question which has been of the greatest interest to moralists and statesmen.

Even though human emotions may have instinctive origin and be innately determined, man's emotional responses seem to be subject to voluntary control, so that men are able to form or change their emotional habits. If this were not so, there could be no moral problem of the regulation of the passions; nor, for that matter, could there be a medical problem of therapy for emotional disorders. The psychoanalytic treatment of neuroses seems, moreover, to assume the possibility of a voluntary, or even a rational, resolution of emotional conflicts—not perhaps without the aid of therapeutic efforts to uncover the sources of conflict and to remove the barriers between repressed emotion and rational decision.

The relation of the passions to the will, especially their antagonism, is relevant to the question whether the actions of men always conform to their judgments of good and evil, or right and wrong. As Socrates discusses the problem of knowledge and virtue, it would seem to be his view that a man who knows what is good for him will act accordingly. Men may "desire things which they imagine to be good," he says, "but which in reality are evil." Hence their misconduct will be due to a mistaken judgment, not to a discrepancy between action and thought. Eliminating the case of erroneous judgment, Socrates gets Meno to admit that "no man wills or chooses anything evil."

Aristotle criticizes the Socratic position which he summarizes in the statement that "no one . . . when he judges acts against what he judges best—people act badly only by reason of ignorance." According to Aristotle, "this view plainly contradicts the observed facts." Yet he admits that whatever a man does must at least *seem* good to him *at the moment*; and to that extent the judgment that something is good or bad would seem to determine action accordingly. In his analysis of incontinence, Aristotle tries to explain how a man may act against what is his better judgment and yet, at the moment of action, seek what he holds to be good.

Action may be caused either by a rational judgment concerning what is good or by an emotional estimate of the desirable. If these two factors are independent of one another—more than that, if they can tend in opposite directions—then a man may act under emotional persuasion at one moment in a manner contrary to his rational predilection at another. That a man may act either emotionally or rationally, Aristotle thinks, explains how, under strong emotional influences, a man can do the very opposite of what his reason would tell him is right or good. The point is that, while the emotions dominate his mind and action, he does not listen to reason.

These matters are further discussed in the chapter on TEMPERANCE. But it should be noted here that the passions and the reason, or the "lower" and the "higher" natures of man, are not always in conflict. Sometimes emotions or emotional attitudes serve reason by supporting voluntary decisions. They reinforce and make effective moral resolutions which might otherwise be too difficult to execute.

THE ANCIENTS DID not underestimate the force of the passions, nor were they too confident of the strength of reason in its struggle to control them, or to be free of them. They were acquainted with the violence of emotional excess which they called "madness" or "frenzy." So, too, were the theologians of the Middle Ages and modern philosophers like Spinoza and Hobbes. But not until Freud—and perhaps also William James, though to a lesser extent—do we find in the tradition of the great books insight into the pathology of the passions, the origin of emotional disorders, and the general theory of the neuroses and neurotic character as the consequence of emotional repression.

For Freud, the primary fact is not the conflict between reason and emotion, or, in his language, between the *ego* and the *id*. It is rather the repression which results from such conflict. On the one side is the ego, which "stands for reason and circumspection" and has "the task of representing the external world," or expressing what Freud calls "the reality-principle." Associated with the ego is the super-ego—"the vehicle of the ego-ideal, by which the ego measures itself, towards which it strives, and whose demands for ever-increasing perfection it is always striving to fulfill." On the other side is the id, which "stands for the untamed passions" and is the source of instinctual life.

The ego, according to Freud, is constantly attempting "to mediate between the id and reality" and to measure up to the ideal set by the super-ego, so as to dethrone "the pleasure-principle, which exerts undisputed sway over the processes in the id, and substitute for it the reality-principle, which promises greater security and greater success." But sometimes it fails in this task. Sometimes, when no socially acceptable channels of behavior are available for expressing emotional drives in action, the ego, supported by the super-ego, represses the emotional or instinctual impulses, that is, prevents them from expressing themselves overtly.

Freud's great insight is that emotions repressed do not atrophy and disappear. On the contrary, their dammed-up energies accumulate and, like a sore, they fester inwardly. Together with related ideas, memories, and wishes, the repressed emotions form what Freud calls a "complex," which is not only the active nucleus of emotional disorder, but also the cause of neurotic symptoms and behavior—phobias and anxieties, obsessions or compulsions, and the various physical manifestations of hysteria, such as a blindness or a paralysis that has no organic basis.

The line between the neurotic and the normal is shadowy, for repressed emotional complexes are, according to Freud, also responsible for the hidden or latent psychological significance of slips of speech, forgetting, the content of dreams, occupational or marital choices, and a wide variety of other phenomena usually regarded as accidental or as rationally determined. In fact, Freud sometimes goes to the extreme of insisting that all apparently rational processes—both of thought and decision—are themselves emotionally determined; and that most, or all, reasoning is nothing but the rationalization of emotionally fixed prejudices or beliefs. "The ego," he writes, "is after all only a part of the id, a part purposively modified by its proximity to the dangers of reality."

The ancient distinction between knowledge and opinion seems to be in essential agreement with the insight that emotions can control the course of thinking. But at the same time it denies that all thinking is necessarily dominated by the passions. The sort of thinking which is free from emotional bias or domination may result in knowledge, if reason itself is not defective in its processes. But the sort of thinking which is directed and determined by the passions *must* result in opinion. The former is reasoning; the latter what Freud calls "rationalization" or sometimes "wishful thinking."

BECAUSE THEY CAN be ordered when they get out of order, the emotions raise problems for both medicine and morals. Whether or not there is a fundamental opposition between the medical and the moral approaches to the problem, whether psychotherapy is needed only when morality has failed, whether morality is itself partly responsible for the disorders which psychotherapy must cure, the difference between the medical and the moral approaches is clear. Medically, emotional disorders call for diagnosis and therapy. Morally, they call for criticism and correction.

Human bondage, according to Spinoza, consists in "the impotence of man to govern or restrain the affects . . . for a man who is under their control is not his own master." A free man he describes as one "who lives according to the dictates of reason alone," and he tries to show "how much reason itself can control the affects" to achieve what he calls "freedom of mind or blessedness." While moralists tend to agree on this point, they do not all offer the same prescription for establishing the right relation between man's higher and lower natures.

The issue which arises here is also discussed in the chapters on DESIRE and DUTY. It exists between those who think that the passions are intrinsically evil, the natural enemies of a good will, lawless elements always in rebellion against duty; and those who think that the passions represent a natural desire for certain goods which belong to the happy life, or a natural aversion for certain evils.

Those who, like the Stoics and Kant, tend to adopt the former view recommend a policy of attrition toward the passions. Their force must be attenuated in order to emancipate reason from their influence and to protect the will from their seductions. Nothing is lost, according to this theory, if the passions atrophy and die. But if, according to the opposite doctrine, the passions have a natural place in the moral life, then the aim should be, not to dispossess them entirely, but to keep them in their place. Aristotle therefore recommends a policy of moderation. The passions can be made to serve reason's purposes by restraining them from excesses and by directing their energies to ends which reason approves.

As Aristotle conceives them, certain of the virtues—especially temperance and courage—are stable emotional attitudes, or *habits* of emotional response, which conform to reason and carry out its rule. The moral virtues require more than a momentary control or moderation of the passions; they require a discipline of them which has become habitual. What Aristotle calls continence, as opposed to virtue, consists in reason's effort to check emotions which are still unruly because they have not yet become habituated to reason's rule.

The fact of individual differences in temperament is of the utmost importance to the moralist who is willing to recognize that universal moral rules apply to individuals differently according to their temperaments. Both psychologists and moralists have classified men into temperamental types by reference to the dominance or deficiency of certain emotional predispositions in their inherited makeup. These temperamental differences also have a medical or physiological aspect insofar as certain elements in human physique—the four bodily humors of the ancients or the hormones of modern endocrinology—seem to be correlated with types of personality.

ONE OF THE GREAT issues in political theory concerns the role of the passions in human association. Have men banded together to form states because they feared the insecurity and the hazards of natural anarchy and universal war, or because they sought the benefits which only political life could provide? In the political community, once it is formed, do love and friendship or distrust and fear determine the relation of fellow citizens, or of rulers and ruled? Should the prince, or any other man who wishes to get and hold political power, try to inspire love or to instill fear in those whom he seeks to dominate? Or are each of these emotions useful for different political purposes and in the handling of different kinds of men?

Considering whether for the success of the prince it is "better to be loved than feared or feared than loved," Machiavelli says that "one should wish to be both, but, because it is difficult to unite them in one person, it is much safer to be feared than loved, when, of the two, either must be dispensed with. . . . Nevertheless," he continues, "a prince ought to inspire fear in such a way that, if he does not win love, he avoids hatred; because he can endure very well being feared whilst he is not hated."

According to Hobbes, when men enter into a commonwealth so that they can live peacefully with one another, they are moved partly by reason and partly by their passions. "The passions that incline men to peace," he writes, "are fear of death; desire of such things as are necessary to commodious living; and a hope by their industry to obtain them." But once a commonwealth is formed, the one passion which seems to be the mainspring of all political activity is "a perpetual and restless desire of power after power, that ceaseth only in death"; for a man "cannot assure the power and means to live well, which he has present, without the acquisition of more."

Not all political thinkers agree with the answers which Machiavelli and Hobbes give on such matters; nor do all make such questions the pivots of their political theory. But there is general agreement that the passions are a force to be reckoned with in the government of men; that the ruler, whether he is despotic prince or constitutional officeholder, must move men through their emotions as well as by appeals to reason.

The two political instruments through which an influence over the emotions is exercised are oratory (now sometimes called "propaganda") and law. Both may work persuasively. Laws, like other discourses, according to Plato, may have preludes or preambles, intended by the legislator "to create good-will in the persons whom he addresses, in order that, by reason of this good-will, they will more intelligently receive his command." But the law also carries with it the threat of coercive force. The threat of punishment for disobedience addresses itself entirely to fear, whereas the devices of the orator—or even of the legislator in his preamble—are not so restricted. The orator can play upon the whole scale of the emotions to obtain the actions or decisions at which he aims.

Finally, there is the problem of whether the statesman should exercise political control over other influences which affect the emotional life of a people, especially the arts and public spectacles. The earliest and perhaps the classic statement of this problem is to be found in Plato's *Republic* and in his *Laws*. Considerations relevant to the question he raises, and the implications of diverse solutions of the problem, are discussed in the chapters on ART, LIBERTY, and POETRY.

OUTLINE OF TOPICS

REFERENCES

To find the passages cited, use the numbers in heavy type, which are the volume and page numbers of the passages referred to. For example, in **4** HOMER: *Iliad*, BK II [265–283] **12d**, the number **4** is the number of the volume in the set; the number **12d** indicates that the passage is in section d of page 12.

PAGE SECTIONS: When the text is printed in one column, the letters a and b reier to the upper and lower halves of the page. For example, in **53** JAMES: *Psychology*, 116a–119b, the passage begins in the upper half of page 116 and ends in the lower half of page 119. When the text is printed in two columns, the letters a and b refer to the upper and lower halves of the left-hand side of the page, the letters c and d to the upper and lower halves of the right-hand side of the page. For example, in **7** PLATO: *Symposium*, 163b–164c, the passage begins in the lower half of the left-hand side of page 163 and ends in the upper half of the right-hand side of page 164.

AUTHOR'S DIVISIONS: One or more of the main divisions of a work (such as PART, BK, CH, SECT) are sometimes included in the reference; line numbers, in brackets, are given in certain cases; *e.g.*, *Iliad*, BK II [265–283] **12d**.

BIBLE REFERENCES: The references are to book, chapter, and verse. When the King James and Douay versions differ in title of books or in the numbering of chapters or verses, the King James version is cited first and the Douay, indicated by a *(D)*, follows; *e.g.*, OLD TESTA-MENT: *Nehemiah*, 7:45—(D) II Esdras, 7:46.

SYMBOLS: The abbreviation "esp" calls the reader's attention to one or more especially relevant parts of a whole reference; "passim" signifies that the topic is discussed intermittently rather than continuously in the work or passage cited.

For additional information concerning the style of the references, see the Explanation of Reference Style; for general guidance in the use of *The Great Ideas*, consult the Preface.

1. **The nature and causes of the emotions or passions**

   7 PLATO: *Republic*, BK IV, 350c–353d; BK IX, 416b–c; 421a–b / *Timaeus*, 466b–d / *Philebus*, 621c–622b; 627c–628a; 628d–630c / *Laws*, BK IX, 748a
   8 ARISTOTLE: *Soul*, BK I, CH I [403ª2–b3] 632a–c; CH 4 [408ª34–b31] 638b–d; BK III, CH 3 [427b21–24] 660a; CH 9 [432b26–433ª2] 665c
   9 ARISTOTLE: *Parts of Animals*, BK IV, CH II [692ª22–27] 224b–c / *Ethics*, BK II, CH 5 [1105b19–1106ª6] 351b–c / *Politics*, BK VII, CH 7 [1327b40–1328ª18] 532a–c / *Rhetoric*, BK II, CH I [1378ª20]–CH II [1388b30] 623b–636a
   12 LUCRETIUS: *Nature of Things*, BK III [136–160] 31d–32a; [231–322] 33a–34b
   13 VIRGIL: *Aeneid*, BK VI [724–734] 230b
   17 PLOTINUS: *First Ennead*, TR I, CH I 1a–b; CH 5 2d–3c; CH 9–11 4c–5c / *Third Ennead*, TR VI, CH 3–4 108a–109b / *Fourth Ennead*, TR IV, CH 18 166d–167b; CH 20–21 167d–168c; CH 28 172a–173b / *Sixth Ennead*, TR I, CH 19–22 262a–264c
   18 AUGUSTINE: *City of God*, BK IX, CH 4–5 287a–289a
   19 AQUINAS: *Summa Theologica*, PART I, Q 81, AA 2–3 429c–431d; PART I–II, QQ 22–48 720b,d–826a,c

   20 AQUINAS: *Summa Theologica*, PART III SUPPL, Q 82, A I, ANS 968a–970c; Q 86, A 3, ANS and REP 3–4 994d–996a,c
   23 HOBBES: *Leviathan*, INTRO, 47c–d; PART I, 61a–65b esp 61a–c; 68b–c; 77b–c; PART II, 162c
   30 BACON: *Advancement of Learning*, 55b–c
   31 DESCARTES: *Meditations*, III, 82d–83a
   31 SPINOZA: *Ethics*, PART II, AXIOM 3 373d; PART III 395a–422a,c esp 395a–d, DEF 1–3 395d–396a, PROP I 396a–c, PROP 3 398b–c, PROP 56 414a–d, THE AFFECTS 416b–422a,c; PART IV, DEF 7 424b; PROP 1–4 424c–425d; PROP 9–13 426d–428a; APPENDIX, I–II 447a–b; PART V, AXIOM 2 452c; PROP 34 460c–d
   35 LOCKE: *Human Understanding*, BK II, CH XX 176b–178a esp SECT 3 176d; CH XXXIII, SECT 5–15 248d–250c
   38 ROUSSEAU: *Inequality*, 338c–d
   42 KANT: *Pref. Metaphysical Elements of Ethics*, 378b–c / *Intro. Metaphysic of Morals*, 385a–d; 386b–d / *Judgement*, 483d–484b; 508d [fn I]
   43 FEDERALIST: NUMBER 17, 69c
   53 JAMES: *Psychology*, 49b–50a; 87b; 209a–b; 327b–328a; 738a–766a esp 738a–b, 742a–746a, 758a–759a, 761a–765b
   54 FREUD: *Origin and Development of Psycho-Analysis*, 4d–5a / *Interpretation of Dreams*, 363c–d / *Repression*, 424d–425b / *Uncon-*

(1. *The nature and causes of the emotions or passions.*)

1c. Instinctive emotional reactions in animals and men

6 HERODOTUS: *History*, BK III, 111d-112c esp 112c; BK VII, 236c

7 PLATO: *Symposium*, 157b-159b esp 158a-159a; 165b-166b / *Republic*, BK II, 320b-c / *Laws*, BK VI, 712b

8 ARISTOTLE: *Prior Analytics*, BK II, CH 27 [70ᵇ6-39] 92c-93a,c

9 ARISTOTLE: *History of Animals*, BK IV, CH 1 [524ᵇ17-19] 50c; BK V, CH 8 [542ᵃ17-ᵇ4] 68d-69a; CH 18 [550ᵃ29-31] 77b; BK VI, CH 18-BK VII, CH 2 97b-108c passim, esp BK VI, CH 18 97b-99c, BK VII, CH 1 106b,d-108a; BK IX, CH 1 [608ᵃ21-ᵇ20] 133b,d-134a; CH 37 [621ᵇ28-622ᵃ10] 147c / *Parts of Animals*, BK IV, CH 5 [679ᵃ5-32] 209a-c; CH 11 [692ᵃ22-27] 224b-c / *Generation of Animals*, BK III, CH 2 [753ᵃ6-17] 294a-b / *Ethics*, BK III, CH 8 [1116ᵇ24-1117ᵃ3] 363a-b; BK VII, CH 6 [1149ᵇ24-1150ᵃ8] 400b-c

10 GALEN: *Natural Faculties*, BK I, CH 12, 173a-c

12 EPICTETUS: *Discourses*, BK I, CH 23 128c-d; BK III, CH 7, 183c-d

12 AURELIUS: *Meditations*, BK IX, SECT 9 292b-d

19 AQUINAS: *Summa Theologica*, PART I, Q 78, A 4, ANS 411d-413d; Q 82, AA 2-3 429c-431c; Q 96, A 1, REP 2 510b-511b; PART I-II, Q 17, A 2, REP 3 687d-688b; Q 40, AA 2-3 793d-795a; Q 41, A 1, REP 3 798b-d; Q 46, A 4, REP 2 815b-d; A 5, REP 1 815d-816d

21 DANTE: *Divine Comedy*, PURGATORY, XVIII [19-75] 80a-c

22 CHAUCER: *Nun's Priest's Tale* [15,282-287] 457b / *Manciple's Tale* [17,104-144] 490a-b

25 MONTAIGNE: *Essays*, 184a-b

28 HARVEY: *On Animal Generation*, 346a-347d; 349a-350a; 361b-362a; 381b-c; 402a-d; 405c-406a; 476c-477a

31 DESCARTES: *Meditations*, VI, 99d-100a; 102b-103a / *Objections and Replies*, 156a-d

31 SPINOZA: *Ethics*, PART III, PROP 57, SCHOL 415b

35 HUME: *Human Understanding*, SECT VIII, DIV 80 486c-d

38 ROUSSEAU: *Inequality*, 343d-346d

43 MILL: *Utilitarianism*, 469c-d

44 BOSWELL: *Johnson*, 124b; 174b; 347a-c; 386a

48 MELVILLE: *Moby Dick*, 144a-b

49 DARWIN: *Descent of Man*, 287d-291a esp 289a-291a; 304b-313a esp 305c-309a, 312b,d [fn 27]; 371c-372c

51 TOLSTOY: *War and Peace*, BK XI, 499c-500c

53 JAMES: *Psychology*, 49b-51a; 198a-199a; 204b-211a passim, esp 206a, 208a-209b; 700a-738b esp 717a-731b, 734b-735a, 738a-b

54 FREUD: *General Introduction*, 591d-592c; 607d-609b esp 608d-609b; 613a; 615b-616c; 623b-c / *Inhibitions, Symptoms, and Anxiety*,

721a-b; 737c-739c; 752a-c / *Civilization and Its Discontents*, 782a-b,d [fn 1]; 787a-b; 789b-791d esp 789c-790b / *New Introductory Lectures*, 840a-853b esp 840b-c, 846b-849b, 851a-c

2. The classification and enumeration of the emotions

7 PLATO: *Philebus*, 628d-630c

9 ARISTOTLE: *Ethics*, BK II, CH 5 351b-c / *Rhetoric*, BK I, CH II, [1378ᵃ20-30] 623b

19 AQUINAS: *Summa Theologica*, PART I, Q 81, A 2 429c-430c; PART I-II, Q 23 723c-727a; Q 24, A 4 729c-730a; Q 30, A 2, ANS and REP 1 749d-750d

23 HOBBES: *Leviathan*, PART I, 62c-64a

31 SPINOZA: *Ethics*, PART III, THE AFFECTS 416b-422a,c

35 LOCKE: *Human Understanding*, BK II, CH XX, SECT 1-3 176b-d; SECT 18 178a

53 JAMES: *Psychology*, 127b; 656a; 742a-743a; 745b-746a; 766a

2a. Definitions of particular passions

7 PLATO: *Cratylus*, 103b-d / *Phaedrus*, 120a-c / *Symposium* 149a-173a,c esp 161d-168a / *Euthyphro*, 193d-194b / *Apology*, 202a / *Philebus*, 628d-630c / *Laws*, BK I, 650a; 651a-c

8 ARISTOTLE: *Topics*, BK II, CH 7 [113ᵃ33-ᵇ3] 158d-159a; BK IV, CH 5 [125ᵇ28-34] 175a; CH 6 [127ᵇ26-32] 177b; CH 13 [151ᵃ14-19] 205d-206a; BK VIII, CH 1 [156ᵃ26-ᵇ3] 212b-c / *Soul*, BK I, CH 1 [403ᵃ25-33] 632b-c

9 ARISTOTLE: *Parts of Animals*, BK IV, CH II [692ᵃ22-27] 224b-c / *Ethics*, BK III, CH 6 [1115ᵃ7-14] 361a-b; CH 8 [1116ᵇ24-1117ᵃ3] 363a-b; BK IV, CH 9 [1128ᵇ10-14] 375d-376a; BK VIII, CH 6 [1158ᵃ10-14] 409d-410a; BK IX, CH 10 [1171ᵃ11-13] 424d; CH 12 [1171ᵇ29-33] 425d / *Politics*, BK V, CH 10 [1312ᵇ24-33] 515b / *Rhetoric*, BK II, CH 1 [1378ᵃ20]-CH 11 [1388ᵇ30] 623b-636a

17 PLOTINUS: *Fourth Ennead*, TR IV, CH 28 172a-173b

18 AUGUSTINE: *Confessions*, BK II, par 13 11d-12a; BK III, par 2 13c-d; BK IV, par 7-14 20d-23a esp par 11 21d-22a

19 AQUINAS: *Summa Theologica*, PART I-II, QQ 26-48 733d-826a,c

23 HOBBES: *Leviathan*, PART I, 61a-65b esp 61a-62c

25 MONTAIGNE: *Essays*, 5a-6c; 25c-26d; 344a-347c; 409d-434d passim, esp 424d-425a

27 SHAKESPEARE: *Othello*, ACT III, SC III [165-192] 223d-224a; [322-357] 225c-226a; SC IV [155-162] 229a

31 SPINOZA: *Ethics*, PART III, PROP 11-59 399d-416b; THE AFFECTS 416b-422a,c; PART IV, APPENDIX, XXI-XXV 449a-c

33 PASCAL: *Pensées*, 262 221a

35 LOCKE: *Human Understanding*, BK II, CH XX, SECT 3-18 176d-178a

(3. *The disorder or pathology of the passions.* 3*a*. *Madness or frenzy due to emotional excess: excessively emotional or emotionally over-determined behavior.*)

22 CHAUCER: *Troilus and Cressida* 1a-155a esp BK IV, STANZA 32–49 92b-95a, BK V, STANZA 33–39 124b-125b

23 HOBBES: *Leviathan*, PART I, 63b; 68b-71a

24 RABELAIS: *Gargantua and Pantagruel*, BK III, 192b-d

25 MONTAIGNE: *Essays*, 5a-6c; 10b-11b; 25c-26d; 166a-167a; 275c-d; 289b-290a; 344a-347c; 418c-d; 420d-421d

26 SHAKESPEARE: *3rd Henry VI*, ACT III, SC II [104–195] 87b-88a; ACT V, SC VI [61–93] 103d-104a / *Richard III* 105a-148a,c / *Romeo and Juliet* 285a-319a,c esp ACT III, SC III [1–115] 304d-306a / *Merchant of Venice*, ACT IV, SC I [40–62] 426a

27 SHAKESPEARE: *Hamlet* 29a-72a,c esp ACT IV, SC V 59c-62a / *Othello* 205a-243a,c esp ACT IV, SC I 229d-233a / *King Lear* 244a-283a,c esp ACT I 244a-254c, ACT II, SC IV [274–289] 261c-d, ACT III, SC IV 264a-266b, ACT IV, SC VI [80–207] 274b-275c / *Macbeth*, ACT V, SC I 306b-307a; SC III [37–46] 308a / *Antony and Cleopatra*, ACT II, SC V 322a-323d / *Timon of Athens*, ACT IV, SC III–ACT V, SC IV 410c-420d

29 CERVANTES: *Don Quixote*, PART I, 83a-c; 88c-89a

35 LOCKE: *Toleration*, 7d-8c / *Human Understanding*, BK II, CH XXI, SECT 12 180d-181a; SECT 69 196d-197a

37 FIELDING: *Tom Jones*, 231c-232b; 234a-b

40 GIBBON: *Decline and Fall*, 216a-c; 509d-510c esp 509d

44 BOSWELL: *Johnson*, 481d

46 HEGEL: *Philosophy of History*, PART IV, 323a-c

47 GOETHE: *Faust*, PART I [3374–3413] 82b-83a; [4405–4612] 110a-114b

48 MELVILLE: *Moby Dick* esp 135a-136b, 148b-150a

51 TOLSTOY: *War and Peace*, BK I, 51d; BK III, 119a-120c; 159b-162b esp 160d; BK IV, 178b-179a; BK V, 207b-208a; 233b-234a; BK VI, 238a-c; 245d-246a; 266c-d; 271b-273c; BK VII, 277a-278a; 292b-296a; BK VIII, 305b-307d; BK IX, 350d-354a; BK XI, 505a-511b; 531a-532a,c; BK XII, 549d-551c; BK XIII, 567d-568c; BK XV, 616a-617a; 642d-643b

52 DOSTOEVSKY: *Brothers Karamazov*, BK I, 4a-d; BK II, 17b-21b; 21d-22b; 41c-45d; BK III 46a-82a,c esp 50c-62a; BK VIII, 200c-201c; 206a-207d; 228d-235d; BK IX, 259c-265a; BK XII, 395a-396a; 397c-398d

53 JAMES: *Psychology*, 204b; 653a-b; 716b; 718a-719a; 750a-b; 754a; 797a-b

54 FREUD: *Hysteria*, 27a-c / *Interpretation of Dreams*, 210c-d; 328a-b / *General Introduc-*

tion, 547b-549d / *Group Psychology*, 670d-671c; 675b-676b / *Inhibitions, Symptoms, and Anxiety*, 743b-744a / *Civilization and Its Discontents*, 787a-b

3*b*. Rationalization or the emotional determination of thought

6 THUCYDIDES: *Peloponnesian War*, BK III, 427d-428a; BK IV, 474a-c; BK V, 506b; 507a-c

7 PLATO: *Phaedrus*, 118d

9 ARISTOTLE: *Politics*, BK III, CH 16 [1287[a]20–[b]5] 485c-486a / *Rhetoric*, BK I, CH 2 [1356[a]11–18] 595c; BK II, CH 1 [1377[b]28–1378[a]5] 622d-623a

12 LUCRETIUS: *Nature of Things*, BK IV [1141–1191] 59a-d

23 HOBBES: *Leviathan*, PART I, 52d-53a; 58a; 68c; 78a-b; PART II, 154a

24 RABELAIS: *Gargantua and Pantagruel*, BK III, 148d-150d; 154a-156c; 159d-163c; 166a-168a

25 MONTAIGNE: *Essays*, 210b-212a; 273b-276a; 447c-448c; 490d-491d

28 HARVEY: *Circulation of the Blood*, 306a-c; 309d

30 BACON: *Advancement of Learning*, 38d-39a; 66c-d / *Novum Organum*, BK I, APH 49 111a

31 SPINOZA: *Ethics*, PART III, PROP 39, SCHOL 408b-d

33 PASCAL: *Pensées*, 82–87 186b-189a; 99–100 191a-192b / *Geometrical Demonstration*, 439b-442a

35 LOCKE: *Toleration*, 2d-3a / *Civil Government*, CH II, SECT 13 28a-b / *Human Understanding*, BK II, CH XXXIII, SECT 1–9 248b-249d; BK IV, CH XX, SECT 12 392c

35 HUME: *Human Understanding*, SECT I, DIV 6, 453c

43 FEDERALIST: NUMBER 1, 29c-30b; NUMBER 31, 103c-104a; NUMBER 50, 162a-b

43 MILL: *Liberty*, 270a

51 TOLSTOY: *War and Peace*, BK II, 82d-83a; BK III, 134a-c; BK IV, 170d-171c; BK V, 233b-234a; BK VI, 238a-b; BK X, 426b; BK XI, 497c-499c; 505a-511b esp 509c-510d; BK XIII, 585b, EPILOGUE II, 686c-687a

53 JAMES: *Psychology*, 371b; 374a-377a passim, esp 376b-377a; 439a; 643a-646a; 652a-657b

54 FREUD: *Origin and Development of Psycho-Analysis*, 13d-14a / *Interpretation of Dreams*, 210c-d; 379a-380d / *General Introduction*, 486b-488b esp 487d-488a / *Group Psychology*, 682b-c / *War and Death*, 760d-761a / *New Introductory Lectures*, 874a-879b esp 874a-d, 878b-879b

3*c*. Particular emotional disorders: psychoneuroses due to repression

28 HARVEY: *On Animal Generation*, 347c-d

53 JAMES: *Psychology*, 244b-253b esp 248a; 645b-646a; 746b-748a; 749a-750b; 753b-754b; 759b-760a; 799b-807a; 838a-839b

54 FREUD: *Origin and Development of Psycho-Analysis* 1a-20d esp 4d-5a, 7a-9a, 14b-19a /

Hysteria 25a-118a,c esp 35b-c, 37d-38d, 52c-53c, 65a-72b, 81c-87a, 111b-115a / *Interpretation of Dreams*, 320b-c; 328c; 380d-382a / *Narcissism*, 402c-404d / *Repression* 422a-427a,c / *Unconscious*, 432d-436b / *General Introduction*, 545a-638a,c esp 557b-569c; 585b-600d, 604c-606a, 611a-615a, 632b-635d / *Group Psychology*, 690a-691c esp 690c-d; 695b-696a,c / *Ego and Id*, 712c-715c / *Inhibitions, Symptoms, and Anxiety* 718a-754a,c esp 720a-723d, 728b-731d, 741d [fn 1], 745d-747b, 750a-d / *Civilization and Its Discontents*, 792b-799a esp 797a-b, 798d-799a / *New Introductory Lectures*, 840a-846a; 851d-852d; 859c-860c

3c(1) Hysterias

10 HIPPOCRATES: *Regimen in Acute Diseases*, APPENDIX, par 35 43d

53 JAMES: *Psychology*, 131b-137b esp 135a, 137a; 248a-252a; 747b [fn 3]; 768b-770a esp 770b [fn 3]; 789b-790b [fn 2]; 802b-803a

54 FREUD: *Origin and Development of Psycho-Analysis*, 1a-5d esp 4c-5d / *Hysteria*, 25a-62b esp 35b-c, 37d-38d, 53b-c; 72d-73b; 76c-d; 81d-83c; 97b-99c; 111b-118a,c / *Interpretation of Dreams*, 200a-d / *Repression*, 426b-c / *Unconscious*, 434c-436a esp 435d-436a / *General Introduction*, 572a-b; 586d-587b; 610d-612b passim / *Ego and Id*, 713d-714a / *Inhibitions, Symptoms, and Anxiety*, 718c-719c; 728b-729a; 741c-742a; 747c-748a; 750b

3c(2) Obsessions and compulsions

12 LUCRETIUS: *Nature of Things*, BK III [59-93] 30d-31b; [1053-1075] 43c-d

27 SHAKESPEARE: *Macbeth*, ACT V, SC I 306b-307a; SC III [37-46] 308a

29 CERVANTES: *Don Quixote*, PART I, 2b

31 SPINOZA: *Ethics*, PART IV, PROP 44, SCHOL 437d-438a

33 PASCAL: *Pensées*, 139 196b-199a; 142-143 199b-200a

44 BOSWELL: *Johnson*, 138c-139a

48 MELVILLE: *Moby Dick* esp 135a-136b

51 TOLSTOY: *War and Peace*, BK XI, 513d-515a

53 JAMES: *Psychology*, 733b [fn 1]; 801a-805b

54 FREUD: *Hysteria*, 83d-86a; 90a-b; 99c-102a / *Repression*, 426d-427a,c / *Unconscious*, 436b / *General Introduction*, 550d-557b esp 551b-552c; 561c-562c; 568a-569a; 572b-c; 587b-c; 600d; 612a-b / *Ego and Id*, 713c-715c passim / *Inhibitions, Symptoms, and Anxiety*, 718b-719b passim; 721c; 723c-d; 729a-733c; 735c-d; 747c-d; 750b-d / *New Introductory Lectures*, 841b-c

3c(3) Phobias and anxieties

12 LUCRETIUS: *Nature of Things*, BK I [102-158] 2b-3a; BK III [59-93] 30d-31b

19 AQUINAS: *Summa Theologica*, PART I-II, Q 35, A 8, ANS 779c-780c

23 HOBBES: *Leviathan*, PART I, 68d

35 LOCKE: *Human Understanding*, BK II, CH XXXIII, SECT 10 249d

51 TOLSTOY: *War and Peace*, BK V, 210b-211a; BK XV, 618a

52 DOSTOEVSKY: *Brothers Karamazov*, BK IX, 260d-262a; BK XI, 318a-348d; BK XII, 376b-d

53 JAMES: *Psychology*, 722a-725a passim, esp 723a, 724b; 733b [fn 1]

54 FREUD: *Hysteria*, 83d-86a passim, esp 84d-85a; 87a-97b / *Interpretation of Dreams*, 205a-c; 235b-d; 276c; 370b-373a / *Repression*, 425d-426b / *Unconscious*, 434c-435d / *General Introduction*, 607b-615b esp 610d-612a; 623b-c / *Ego and Id*, 715d-717a,c / *Inhibitions, Symptoms, and Anxiety*, 720a-754a esp 724a-728b, 733c-742a, 744b-748b / *New Introductory Lectures*, 840a-846a

3c(4) Traumas and traumatic neuroses

54 FREUD: *Origin and Development of Psycho-Analysis*, 3a-5a esp 4b-c; 14d-15a / *Hysteria*, 25a-30a esp 26a-c, 27c-d / *General Introduction*, 558a-d; 603a-b / *Beyond the Pleasure Principle*, 641a-d; 648d-650c / *Inhibitions, Symptoms, and Anxiety*, 735d-736c; 741a-b; 744b-745d; 749b-c; 751b-752b / *New Introductory Lectures*, 817c-818b; 845b-846a

3d. The alleviation and cure of emotional disorders

12 LUCRETIUS: *Nature of Things*, BK III [31-93] 30b-31b esp [87-93] 31b; BK VI [1-42] 80a-c

19 AQUINAS: *Summa Theologica*, PART I-II, Q 38 786d-789d

25 MONTAIGNE: *Essays*, 37c-39a; 401b-406a

27 SHAKESPEARE: *Macbeth*, ACT V, SC I 306b-307a; SC III [37-46] 308a

35 LOCKE: *Human Understanding*, BK II, CH XXXIII, SECT 13 250a-b

44 BOSWELL: *Johnson*, 13b-c; 127a-b; 284c-d; 297d-298a

48 MELVILLE: *Moby Dick*, 357b-358b

51 TOLSTOY: *War and Peace*, BK VI, 271b-c; BK XII, 551c-554a; BK XV, 614a-d; 616a-618b esp 617a-b

52 DOSTOEVSKY: *Brothers Karamazov*, BK II, 21d-23c

53 JAMES: *Psychology*, 132b; 135a-b

54 FREUD: *Origin and Development of Psycho-Analysis*, 1a-4d; 6c-7a; 10c-13d; 14d-15a; 18a-20d / *Hysteria*, 25a-81c passim, esp 30d-31a, 59d-60a, 62c-72d, 75d-81c; 106c-111b / *Psycho-Analytic Therapy* 123a-127a,c / *"Wild" Psycho-Analysis* 128a-130d / *General Introduction*, 546b-c; 550a-c; 560b-561b; 603b-604c; 623c-638a,c / *Beyond the Pleasure Principle*, 643d-644d; 651c-d / *Ego and Id*, 712c-713a / *Inhibitions, Symptoms, and Anxiety*, 748b-d / *New Introductory Lectures*, 840a; 851d-852d; 864a-873d esp 871a-873d

4. The moral consideration of the passions

4a. The conflict between reason and emotion

(4a. *The conflict between reason and emotion.*
4a(1) *The force of the passions.*)

52 DOSTOEVSKY: *Brothers Karamazov*, BK I,
4a-d; BK II, 39b-40a; BK III, 50c-62a; BK VII,
177c; BK XII, 397c-398d

53 JAMES: *Psychology*, 799a-b

54 FREUD: *Hysteria*, 110c / *General Introduction*,
502a-504b esp 503d-504a / *Group Psychology*,
690a-c / *Ego and Id*, 701d-702d; 715d-716a /
Inhibitions, Symptoms, and Anxiety, 745d-
747b / *War and Death*, 760d-761a / *Civilization and Its Discontents*, 787b-c / *New Introductory Lectures*, 837b-839b esp 838c-839b

4a(2) The strength of reason or will

4 HOMER: *Odyssey*, BK IV [265–295] 201d-202a;
BK IX [82–104] 230a; BK XIX [203–219] 291b

7 PLATO: *Symposium*, 168a-173a,c / *Apology*,
205d-206d / *Crito*, 214d-215d / *Phaedo*, 220b-
221a; 225b-226c; 232b-234c; 250b-251d /
Laws, BK I, 649d-650b

9 ARISTOTLE: *Ethics*, BK IX, CH 8 [1168^{b}28–
1169^{a}11] 422b-d / *Politics*, BK I, CH 5 [1254^a
18–^{b}8] 447d-448a

12 LUCRETIUS: *Nature of Things*, BK III [307–
322] 34a-b

12 EPICTETUS: *Discourses*, BK I, CH 3 108b-c;
BK II, CH 23 170a-172d

12 AURELIUS: *Meditations*, BK VII, SECT 55
283b-c; BK VIII, SECT 39 288c; BK IX, SECT 7
292b; BK XI, SECT 18 304b-305b

14 PLUTARCH: *Pericles*, 139a-140d

18 AUGUSTINE: *Confessions*, BK VI, par 11–13
38b-39c; par 16 40a-c; BK VIII, par 10–11 55c-
56b; par 19–27 58b-60c / *City of God*, BK IX,
CH 4-5 287a-289a; BK XIV, CH 8–9 381c-
385b

19 AQUINAS: *Summa Theologica*, PART I, Q 81,
A 3 430c-431d; Q 111, A 2, ANS 569c-570b;
PART I-II, Q 10, A 3 664d-665c; Q 17, A 7 690d-
692a

23 HOBBES: *Leviathan*, PART II, 141a-b

25 MONTAIGNE: *Essays*, 20d-22a; 36c-41a esp
39b-40a; 159a-167a; 184a-d; 200d-205b;
273b-276a

27 SHAKESPEARE: *Othello*, ACT I, SC III [322–
337] 212b-c

30 BACON: *Advancement of Learning*, 27a-c

31 SPINOZA: *Ethics*, PART IV, PROP 15–17 428a-d;
PROP 59–73 442b-447a; APPENDIX, I–III
447a-b; XXXII 450c-d; PART V 451a-463d

32 MILTON: *Comus* [414–475] 42b-44a / *Paradise
Lost*, BK VIII [500–617] 243a-245b

33 PASCAL: *Pensées*, 350 234a

35 LOCKE: *Human Understanding*, BK II, CH
XXI, SECT 54 192b-c

38 ROUSSEAU: *Inequality*, 344d-345c

42 KANT: *Pure Reason*, 164a-165c; 235c-d /
Fund. Prin. Metaphysic of Morals, 259a-c;
264d-265b; 271c-d; 279b; 282d-283d; 284d-
285a / *Practical Reason*, 303b-304b; 314a-d;

315b-c; 346b,d [fn 1] / *Pref. Metaphysical
Elements of Ethics*, 365b-366a / *Intro. Metaphysic of Morals*, 386b-d / *Judgement*, 483d-
484b; 586a-587a; 605d-606b [fn 2]

43 MILL: *Representative Government*, 332c-d /
Utilitarianism, 463d-464c

49 DARWIN: *Descent of Man*, 312a-c; 313d-314a;
318d-319a

53 JAMES: *Psychology*, 798b-800a; 807a-808a

54 FREUD: *Hysteria*, 110c / *Interpretation of
Dreams*, 384c-385c; 386d-387a / *Unconscious*, 433b-c / *Group Psychology*, 690a-c / *Ego
and Id*, 702c-d; 715c-716c / *Inhibitions, Symptoms, and Anxiety*, 721d-722c; 744a / *War and
Death*, 760d-761a / *Civilization and Its Discontents*, 800d-801a / *New Introductory Lectures*, 837d-839b; 845b; 880a

4b. The treatment of the emotions by or for the sake of reason

4b(1) Moderation of the passions by reason: virtue, continence, avoidance of sin

OLD TESTAMENT: *Exodus*, 20:14,17; 23:4–5 /
Leviticus, 19:17–18 / *Numbers*, 15:37–41 / *Deu-
teronomy*, 5:18,21 / *Psalms*, 32:8–10; 37:1–8—
(D) *Psalms*, 31:8–10; 36:1–8 / *Proverbs*, 7;
15:1; 23; 30:7–9 / *Ecclesiastes*, 7:8–9—(D)
Ecclesiastes, 7:9–10

APOCRYPHA: *Ecclesiasticus*, 18:30–33; 31; 38:16–
23—(D) OT, *Ecclesiasticus*, 18:30–33; 31;
38:16–24

NEW TESTAMENT: *Matthew*, 5:21–26,43–48 /
I Corinthians, 13:4–8 / *Ephesians*, 4:31–32 /
Colossians, 3:5–15 / *I Thessalonians*, 4:3–8 /
I Timothy, 6:3–12 / *Titus*, 2:11–14; 3:1–7 /
James, 4:1–7 / *I Peter*, 2:11–12

5 ARISTOPHANES: *Clouds* [866–1114] 499a-502b

7 PLATO: *Charmides*, 5a-b / *Laches*, 31d-37a /
Protagoras, 59b-64a / *Phaedrus*, 120b-c / *Symposium*, 153b-157a; 168a-173a,c / *Phaedo*,
225b-226c; 233c-234c / *Republic*, BK III,
325b-326b; BK IV, 346a-356a; BK IX, 416a-c;
BK X, 431b-434a / *Timaeus*, 466a-467a / *Laws*,
BK I, 649d-650b; BK VII, 713c-716a esp 715d-
716a; BK VIII, 735c-738c

8 ARISTOTLE: *Topics*, BK IV, CH 5 [125^{b}20–28]
174d-175a

9 ARISTOTLE: *Ethics*, BK I, CH 13 347b-348d;
BK II, CH I–BK III, CH I 348b,d-357b; BK III,
CH 6–BK IV, CH 9 361a-376a,c; BK VII 395a-
406a,c; BK IX, CH 8 [1168^{b}28–1169^{a}11] 422b-d /
Politics, BK I, CH 5 [1254^{a}18–^{b}8] 447d-448a /
Rhetoric, BK II, CH 14 637d-638a

11 NICOMACHUS: *Arithmetic*, BK I, 826d-827a

12 LUCRETIUS: *Nature of Things*, BK II [1–61]
15a-d; BK III [307–322] 34a-b; [1053–1094]
43c-44a,c; BK V [1–54] 61a-d; [1117–1135] 75d;
BK VI [1–42] 80a-d

12 EPICTETUS: *Discourses*, BK I, CH I 105a-106c;
CH 3 108b-c; BK II, CH 2 140c-141c; CH 11,
151a-b; CH 18 161a-162b

12 AURELIUS: *Meditations*, BK II, SECT 5 257b-c; BK IV, SECT 24 265c-d; BK VII, SECT 55 283b-c; BK VIII, SECT 39 288c; BK IX, SECT 7 292b

14 PLUTARCH: *Dion*, 798b-d

18 AUGUSTINE: *Confessions*, BK II, par 2–4 9b-d; BK III, par 1 13b-c; BK IV, par 25 25c; BK VI, par 18–26 40d-43a; BK VIII, par 1–2 52c-53b; par 10–11 55c-56b; par 25–27 60a-c / *City of God*, BK IV, CH 3 190a-c; BK IX, CH 5–6 288b-289b; BK XIV, CH 6–9 380b-385b; BK XIX, CH 15 521a-c / *Christian Doctrine*, BK I, CH 24 630c-631a

19 AQUINAS: *Summa Theologica*, PART I, Q 95, AA 2–3 507c-509b; Q 98, A 2 esp REP 3 517d-519a; PART I–II, Q 20, A 4, ANS 714c-715b; Q 24 727a-730a

20 AQUINAS: *Summa Theologica*, PART I–II, Q 56, A 4 32b-33c; Q 59 45d-49d; Q 60, A 4–Q 61, A 5 52b-59d; Q 64, AA 1–2 66d-68b; Q 65, A 1 70b-72a; PART III, Q 15, AA 4–9 790d-795b

21 DANTE: *Divine Comedy*, PURGATORY, XVIII [19–75] 80a-c

22 CHAUCER: *Tale of Melibeus*, par 4–7 401b-402b / *Parson's Tale*, par 12, 503b-504a

23 HOBBES: *Leviathan*, PART I, 93d-94a; 95d-96b

24 RABELAIS: *Gargantua and Pantagruel*, BK IV, 234a-240a

25 MONTAIGNE: *Essays*, 20d-22a; 89b-91b; 159a-167a; 184a-d; 200d-205b; 232b-238d; 251a-c; 346b-347c; 353c-354b; 402c-404b; 431c-432d; 486b-495a

26 SHAKESPEARE: *Romeo and Juliet*, ACT II, SC VI [1–15] 300c / *Henry V*, ACT I, SC I [24–69] 533b-c

27 SHAKESPEARE: *Hamlet*, ACT I, SC III [5–51] 34c-d; ACT III, SC II [68–79] 49c-d

30 BACON: *Advancement of Learning*, 27b-c; 67a-b; 71d-72b; 78a-d

31 SPINOZA: *Ethics*, PART IV, PROP 1–18 424c-429d esp PROP 18, SCHOL 429a-d; PROP 59–73 442b-447a; APPENDIX 447a-450d; PART V 451a-463d esp PROP 1–20 452d-458a, PROP 38–42 461d-463d

32 MILTON: *Paradise Lost*, BK VIII [500–617] 243a-245b; BK XI [334–369] 306b-307a; [527–551] 310b-311a / *Samson Agonistes* [541–576] 351b-352a / *Areopagitica*, 390a-391a

33 PASCAL: *Pensées*, 104 193a; 203 211a; 413 242a; 423 243b; 502–503 260b-261a

35 LOCKE: *Human Understanding*, BK II, CH XXI, SECT 46–54 189d-192c esp SECT 54 192b-c; SECT 69 196d-197a

40 GIBBON: *Decline and Fall*, 32a-b

42 KANT: *Fund. Prin. Metaphysic of Morals*, 256b / *Pref. Metaphysical Elements of Ethics*, 368d-369a / *Judgement*, 586d-587a

44 BOSWELL: *Johnson*, 92b-c

46 HEGEL: *Philosophy of Right*, ADDITIONS, 105 133d-134a / *Philosophy of History*, PART III, 312d-313a; PART IV, 365d-366a

49 DARWIN: *Descent of Man*, 310c-319a esp 313d-314b, 318d-319a; 322c-d; 592b-c; 593a-b

51 TOLSTOY: *War and Peace*, BK III, 122b-c; BK V, 201a-c; BK VI, 245b-c; 247d-250a; EPILOGUE I, 655c-656b

52 DOSTOEVSKY: *Brothers Karamazov*, BK VI, 164a-167a

53 JAMES: *Psychology*, 807a-808a; 816a-819a esp 817a-818a

54 FREUD: *Origin and Development of Psycho-Analysis*, 9a; 20a-c / *Hysteria*, 110c / *Narcissism*, 407b-408a / *Ego and Id*, 702c; 706d-707d; 715a-716a / *War and Death*, 757d-759c / *Civilization and Its Discontents*, 773b-c / *New Introductory Lectures*, 838c-839b; 844b-c

4b(2) Attenuation and atrophy of the passions: the liberation of reason

7 PLATO: *Phaedo*, 233c-234c / *Republic*, BK I, 295d-296c

9 ARISTOTLE: *Rhetoric*, BK II, CH 13 [1389^{b}12–1390^{a}24] 637a-c

12 LUCRETIUS: *Nature of Things*, BK V [1–54] 61a-d

12 EPICTETUS: *Discourses*, BK I, CH 1 105a-106c; CH 4 108d-110a; BK II, CH 2 140c-141c; CH 17–18 158d-162b; BK III, CH 8 184b-c; CH 22 195a-201a; BK IV, CH 4 225a-228a; CH 12 242d-244a

12 AURELIUS: *Meditations*, BK II, SECT 2 257a; SECT 5 257b-c; SECT 10 257d-258a; SECT 16–17 259a-d; BK III, SECT 4 260b-261a; SECT 6 261a-c; SECT 12 262b-c; BK IV, SECT 39 267a; BK V, SECT 8 269d-270b; SECT 26 272c; BK VI, SECT 40–46 277d-278d; BK VII, SECT 55 283b-c; SECT 68–69 284c-d; BK IX, SECT 7 292b

17 PLOTINUS: *Third Ennead*, TR VI, CH 4–5 108c-109d esp CH 5, 109c-d

18 AUGUSTINE: *City of God*, BK IX, CH 4–5 287a-289a; BK XIV, CH 8–10 381d-385d / *Christian Doctrine*, BK I, CH 24 630c-631a

19 AQUINAS: *Summa Theologica*, PART I–II, Q 24, A 2 727b-728c

24 RABELAIS: *Gargantua and Pantagruel*, BK III, 152a-d; 188d-191c

25 MONTAIGNE: *Essays*, 89b-91b; 99b-100a; 107a-112d; 165d-167a; 200d-205b; 232b-238d esp 235c-236a; 251a-c; 402c-404b; 432b-d; 486b-495a esp 491d-495a

30 BACON: *Advancement of Learning*, 26b-c; 71d-72b

32 MILTON: *Comus* [414–475] 42b-44a; [706–755] 49a-50a / *Areopagitica*, 390a-391a

33 PASCAL: *Pensées*, 413 242a

38 MONTESQUIEU: *Spirit of Laws*, BK V, 19a

38 ROUSSEAU: *Inequality*, 344d-345c

40 GIBBON: *Decline and Fall*, 32a-b

42 KANT: *Fund. Prin. Metaphysic of Morals*, 256b / *Practical Reason*, 346b,d [fn 1] / *Pref. Metaphysical Elements of Ethics*, 378d-379a / *Judgement*, 586a-587a

(4b. The treatment of the emotions by or for the sake of reason. 4b(2) Attenuation and atrophy of the passions: the liberation of reason.)

51 TOLSTOY: *War and Peace*, BK XIII, 577a-578b; BK XIV, 605b-d; BK XV, 630c-631a

53 JAMES: *Psychology*, 751a-752a; 753b-754b; 760a-b

54 FREUD: *Origin and Development of Psycho-Analysis*, 20b-c / *Hysteria*, 110c / *Inhibitions, Symptoms, and Anxiety*, 745d-746c / *Civilization and Its Discontents*, 773b-c / *New Introductory Lectures*, 839d-840a

4c. The moral significance of temperamental type or emotional disposition

7 PLATO: *Charmides*, 3b-d / *Republic*, BK I, 296b-c; BK II, 319c-320c; BK III, 338a-339a / *Timaeus*, 474b-d / *Statesman*, 607a-608d

8 ARISTOTLE: *Categories*, CH 8 [9^{b}34-10^{a}6] 15a

9 ARISTOTLE: *Ethics*, BK IV, CH 9 [1128^{b}10-20] 375d-376a; BK VI, CH 13 [1144^{b}1-17] 394b; BK VII, CH 4 [1148^{a}18-22] 398c; CH 5 399a-d / *Rhetoric*, BK I, CH 10 [1369^{a}5-29] 612b-c; BK II, CH 12-14 636a-638a

12 LUCRETIUS: *Nature of Things*, BK III [288-322] 33d-34b

12 EPICTETUS: *Discourses*, BK I, CH 5 110b-c; BK II, CH 15 155c-156b

17 PLOTINUS: *First Ennead*, TR III, CH 1-3 10a-11a / *Fifth Ennead*, TR IX, CH 1-2 246c-247b

19 AQUINAS: *Summa Theologica*, PART I-II, Q 46, A 5, ANS and REP 1 815d-816d

20 AQUINAS: *Summa Theologica*, PART I-II, Q 51, A 1, ANS 12b-13c; Q 63, A 1 63a-64a; Q 65, A 1, ANS 70b-72a

21 DANTE: *Divine Comedy*, PURGATORY, XXX [100-145] 100b-d

22 CHAUCER: *Troilus and Cressida*, BK III, STANZA 129 71a-b / *Wife of Bath's Prologue* [6191-6208] 266a

23 HOBBES: *Leviathan*, PART I, 68b-c; 77c-78a

25 MONTAIGNE: *Essays*, 200d-205b esp 203a-204a; 434d-435d; 491d-495a esp 494d-495a

26 SHAKESPEARE: *Richard II*, ACT III, SC II 335b-337d / *1st Henry IV*, ACT III, SC I [146-189] 451c-452a / *2nd Henry IV*, ACT IV, SC V 494b-496d

27 SHAKESPEARE: *Hamlet*, ACT IV, SC IV [32-66] 59a-c

30 BACON: *Advancement of Learning*, 49b-50b; 76d-77c

38 MONTESQUIEU: *Spirit of Laws*, BK XIV 102b,d-108d

40 GIBBON: *Decline and Fall*, 435b-d

42 KANT: *Fund. Prin. Metaphysic of Morals*, 256a; 258b-c / *Practical Reason*, 356a-360d

43 MILL: *Liberty*, 303d-304d / *Representative Government*, 346c-348c

46 HEGEL: *Philosophy of Right*, PART III, par 150 56c-57a / *Philosophy of History*, PART IV, 323b-c; 357b-c

49 DARWIN: *Descent of Man*, 311c

51 TOLSTOY: *War and Peace*, BK VIII, 321d-322d; 336b-337d; BK IX, 362d-363a; BK XI, 514c-d; 519a-c; 527b-528b; EPILOGUE I, 655c-656b

52 DOSTOEVSKY: *Brothers Karamazov*, BK II, 38a-40c; BK III, 48b-50b; 53a-60a esp 54a-b, 57b-c; 69c-71c

53 JAMES: *Psychology*, 799b-808a passim, esp 802b-803a, 806b-807a

5. The political consideration of the passions

5 SOPHOCLES: *Antigone* [162-210] 132c-d

5 ARISTOPHANES: *Lysistrata* 583a-599a,c

6 THUCYDIDES: *Peloponnesian War*, BK III, 436d-438b

7 PLATO: *Republic*, BK VIII-IX, 404a-418a passim, esp BK VIII, 404d-405c, 407a-408a, 409d-411a, BK IX, 416a-418a / *Laws*, BK I-II, 643c-663d esp BK I, 651a-652d; BK III, 665a-c; 668a-670c; 671a-672c; 674c-675c; BK IV, 681b-d; 682b; BK V, 686d-691b esp 689c-690c; BK VI, 707c-708a; BK VII, 718c-719d; 726d-728b; BK VIII, 732d-738c esp 735c-736c, 738a-c; BK IX, 747d-748d

9 ARISTOTLE: *Ethics*, BK IV, CH 1 [1121^{b}28-30] 368c / *Politics*, BK II, CH 9 [1271^{a}9-17] 467b; BK III, CH 15 [1286^{a}17-20] 484b-c; [1286^{a}33-37] 484d; CH 16 [1287^{a}28-39] 485d; BK V 502a-519d passim, esp CH 2-3 503b-505b, CH 10-11 512d-518c; BK VII, CH 7 [1327^{b}40-1328^{a}18] 532a-c

14 PLUTARCH: *Cleomenes*, 659d-660a / *Dion*, 784d-785a

15 TACITUS: *Histories*, BK III, 257c-d

23 MACHIAVELLI: *Prince*, 3a-37d passim

23 HOBBES: *Leviathan*, INTRO, 47b-d; PART I, 85c-d; 90b-d; 93d-94a; 95d-96b; PART II, 104b-d; 105c-106b; 113b; 140c-142a; 151b-c; PART IV, 272c; CONCLUSION, 279a-c

27 SHAKESPEARE: *Timon of Athens*, ACT III, SC V 406d-408a

30 BACON: *Advancement of Learning*, 20c-d; 78a-d

31 SPINOZA: *Ethics*, PART III, PROP 46 410c; PART IV, PROP 35, SCHOL 433d-434a; APPENDIX, VIII-XVII 447d-448d

33 PASCAL: *Pensées*, 291-338 225a-233a

35 LOCKE: *Civil Government*, CH XI, SECT 136-137 56c-57b

36 SWIFT: *Gulliver*, PART I, 28b-29a; 37a-b; PART III, 112a-114b; 119b-121a

38 MONTESQUIEU: *Spirit of Laws*, BK II, 6a-b; BK III, 9a; 10a; 10c-11a; 12b-d; BK V, 18d-19d; BK VII, 47c-48a; BK XIII, 96a; BK XIX, 135d-139c passim; BK XXVIII, 259b; BK XXIX, 269a,c

38 ROUSSEAU: *Political Economy*, 368a-b; 375d-376b

40 GIBBON: *Decline and Fall*, 4d-5a

43 FEDERALIST: NUMBER 1 29a-31a passim; NUMBER 5-6 37a-41c passim, esp NUMBER 6, 40a-b; NUMBER 10 49c-53a esp 50a-d; NUMBER 15, 65b-d; NUMBER 17 69a-70d; NUMBER 27, 95c-d; NUMBER 31, 103d-104a; NUMBER 34, 119c-d; NUMBER 46, 150b-152a; NUMBER 49, 160b-161a; NUMBER 50, 162a-b; NUMBER 55, 173a-b; NUMBER 63, 192c-193a; NUMBER 70, 211d-212a; NUMBER 76, 225d-226a

43 MILL: *Representative Government*, 329b-c; 336c-337a; 346c-348c

46 HEGEL: *Philosophy of History*, INTRO, 166b-167c; PART I, 241d-242a; PART III, 300c-d; PART IV, 323b-c

53 JAMES: *Psychology*, 201a

54 FREUD: *Civilization and Its Discontents*, 780b-802a,c esp 780c-d, 781c, 783c-784b, 785d-787c, 792a-b, 800c-802a,c

5a. The causes of political association: fear or need

6 HERODOTUS: *History*, BK I, 23b-d

6 THUCYDIDES: *Peloponnesian War*, BK II, 402b-404a

7 PLATO: *Protagoras*, 44a-45b / *Republic*, BK II, 311b-c; 316c-319a

9 ARISTOTLE: *Politics*, BK III, CH 6 [1278^{b}15-30] 475d-476a; CH 9 [1280^{a}32-1281^{a}2] 477d-478c; BK V, CH 8 [1308^{a}25-30] 510b-c

12 LUCRETIUS: *Nature of Things*, BK V [1011-1027] 74b-c

15 TACITUS: *Annals*, BK III, 51b

18 AUGUSTINE: *City of God*, BK I, CH 30 147b-d

23 HOBBES: *Leviathan*, PART I, 77a; 77c; 84c-87b esp 86b; 90b-91b; PART II, 99a-101a; 109b-c; 116c-d

31 SPINOZA: *Ethics*, PART IV, PROP 37, SCHOL 1-2 434d-436a

35 LOCKE: *Toleration*, 16a-c / *Civil Government*, CH II, SECT 13-15 28a-c; CH VIII, SECT 95 46c-d; CH IX 53c-54d

38 MONTESQUIEU: *Spirit of Laws*, BK I, 2b-d

38 ROUSSEAU: *Inequality*, 354c-355a / *Political Economy*, 370b; 374a-b / *Social Contract*, BK I, 393b-c

39 SMITH: *Wealth of Nations*, BK V, 309a-c; 311b-c

40 GIBBON: *Decline and Fall*, 91b-c

42 KANT: *Science of Right*, 435c-d

43 FEDERALIST: NUMBER 10, 50a-d; NUMBER 15, 65b-d; NUMBER 17 69a-70d passim; NUMBER 27, 95c-d; NUMBER 29, 101a; NUMBER 46, 150b-152a; NUMBER 51, 163b-c

43 MILL: *Representative Government*, 424c-425b / *Utilitarianism*, 471a-b

46 HEGEL: *Philosophy of Right*, PART III, par 183 64a; par 261, 83c-d / *Philosophy of History*, PART II, 262a; 283b-c; PART III, 289b-d; PART IV, 328b-c

49 DARWIN: *Descent of Man*, 308a-310d; 321b-c

52 DOSTOEVSKY: *Brothers Karamazov*, BK V, 133c-d passim; BK VI, 158b-159a

54 FREUD: *Group Psychology* 664a-696a,c esp 665c, 672a-676b, 687b-c / *Civilization and Its Discontents*, 781d-782d; 783b-c; 785c-788d; 796a-b / *New Introductory Lectures*, 884a

5b. The acquisition and retention of power: love or fear

6 HERODOTUS: *History*, BK III, 95d-96b; 103d-104a; 107c-d

6 THUCYDIDES: *Peloponnesian War*, BK I, 368b-d; BK II, 402a-404a; BK III, 425d-426d; BK VI, 519a-520d; 523c-524c; BK VIII, 580b-c

7 PLATO: *Republic*, BK II, 311c-312b / *Laws*, BK III, 671a-c; 674c-d; BK IV, 682b / *Seventh Letter*, 806d-807a

9 ARISTOTLE: *Politics*, BK V, CH 2 [1302^{a}16]-CH 3 [1302^{b}34] 503b-504b; CH 8 [1308^{a}25-34] 510b-c; CH 10 512d-515d; CH 11 [1313^{a}34-1315^{b}11] 516a-518c

12 EPICTETUS: *Discourses*, BK IV, CH 4, 225a-226c; CH 9 237d-238d

14 PLUTARCH: *Coriolanus*, 180d-181b / *Pyrrhus* 314b,d-332d esp 319b-321a / *Lysander*, 362b-365a / *Sulla*, 384a-c / *Crassus* 438b,d-455a,c / *Sertorius*, 462a-c; 466d-467a / *Agesilaus*, 482d-484a / *Pompey*, 517d-518a; 533a-c / *Caesar*, 577d-583a / *Cleomenes*, 659d-660a / *Cicero*, 717a-b / *Demetrius*, 737b-d / *Dion*, 784d-785a / *Artaxerxes*, 856b-c

15 TACITUS: *Histories*, BK II, 224d-225a

23 MACHIAVELLI: *Prince*, CH VI, 9b-d; CH VII, 11b-c; 12b-d; CH XVII 23d-24d; CH XIX 26a-30a; CH XX, 31b-c

23 HOBBES: *Leviathan*, INTRO, 47b-d; PART I, 76d; PART II, 100d; 109b-c; 156c

24 RABELAIS: *Gargantua and Pantagruel*, BK III, 132a-d

25 MONTAIGNE: *Essays*, 51a-55d passim

26 SHAKESPEARE: *Richard III*, ACT V, SC III [238-270] 146b-c / *1st Henry IV*, ACT III, SC II [39-84] 453b-d

27 SHAKESPEARE: *Macbeth*, ACT IV, SC III [37-114] 303d-304c

29 CERVANTES: *Don Quixote*, PART I, 40d

30 BACON: *Advancement of Learning*, 78a-d

38 MONTESQUIEU: *Spirit of Laws*, BK III, 12b-13c; BK IV, 15a-c; BK V, 26d-27d; BK VI, 43c-d; BK XII, 93d-94a; 94c-95a

38 ROUSSEAU: *Inequality*, 364a-b / *Social Contract*, BK III, 412d-413a

39 SMITH: *Wealth of Nations*, BK V, 348a-349c

40 GIBBON: *Decline and Fall*, 263a-b; 436a-b

41 GIBBON: *Decline and Fall*, 549a

43 FEDERALIST: NUMBER 6, 39a-b; NUMBER 15, 65b-d; NUMBER 17, 69a-d; NUMBER 72, 217a-c

43 MILL: *Representative Government*, 354b-355b / *Utilitarianism*, 462d

46 HEGEL: *Philosophy of History*, PART III, 287a-d; PART IV, 365d-366b

54 FREUD: *Group Psychology*, 669a-c; 686c-689b esp 687a-b

CROSS-REFERENCES

For: The general theory of instinct, *see* HABIT 3–3e; and for the consideration of instinctual drives, *see* DESIRE 2a, 3a.

The relation of pleasure and pain to the emotions, *see* PLEASURE AND PAIN 4a.

The conception of the emotions as forms of animal appetite or sensitive desire, *see* DESIRE 3b(1); WILL 2b(2).

The analysis of the one emotion which is held to be the root of all the others, *see* LOVE 2a–2a(3).

Other discussions of the conflict between the passions and reason, or between one emotion and another, *see* DESIRE 3d, 4a, 6c; DUTY 8; MIND 9b–9c; OPPOSITION 4a–4b, 4d.

Other discussions of emotional disorder from a psychological or medical point of view, *see* DESIRE 4a–4d; MEDICINE 6c(2); MIND 8b; ONE AND MANY 3b(5); OPPOSITION 4c.

The influence of the emotions upon imagination or thought, *see* DESIRE 5a–5b, 6c; MEMORY AND IMAGINATION 8c, 8d(1); OPINION 2a; TRUTH 3d(2).

The moral problems raised by the conflict between reason and emotion, *see* DESIRE 6a–6b; DUTY 4–4b; LIBERTY 3a–3b; MIND 9c–9d; SIN 5; SLAVERY 7; TYRANNY 5d; VIRTUE AND VICE 5a.

The significance of the passions in relation to law, government, and the state, *see* LAW 5, 6a; PUNISHMENT 1c–1d; STATE 3e–3f; and for the problem of political censorship or regulation of the arts because of their emotional influence, *see* ART 10b; LIBERTY 2a; POETRY 9b.

The consideration of emotion by the orator, *see* RHETORIC 4b.

Emotion in relation to artistic inspiration or expression, *see* ART 8; POETRY 3.

ADDITIONAL READINGS

Listed below are works not included in *Great Books of the Western World*, but relevant to the idea and topics with which this chapter deals. These works are divided into two groups:

I. Works by authors represented in this collection.
II. Works by authors not represented in this collection.

For the date, place, and other facts concerning the publication of the works cited, consult the Bibliography of Additional Readings which follows the last chapter of *The Great Ideas*.

I.

PLUTARCH. "Whether the Passions of the Soul or Diseases of the Body Are Worse," in *Moralia*
EPICTETUS. *The Manual*
AUGUSTINE. *Of Continence*
AQUINAS. *Quaestiones Disputatae, De Veritate*, QQ 25–26
F. BACON. "Of Anger," in *Essays*
DESCARTES. *The Passions of the Soul*
PASCAL. *Discours sur les passions de l'amour*
HOBBES. *The Elements of Law, Natural and Politic*, PART I, CH 12
——. *The Whole Art of Rhetoric*, BK II, CH 1–13
HUME. *A Treatise of Human Nature*, BK II, PART III
——. *A Dissertation on the Passions*
A. SMITH. *The Theory of Moral Sentiments*, PART I, SECT II
STERNE. *A Sentimental Journey*

GOETHE. *Sorrows of Young Werther*
HEGEL. *The Phenomenology of Mind*, IV, B (3)
DOSTOEVSKY. *Notes from Underground*
C. R. DARWIN. *The Expression of Emotions in Man and Animals*
W. JAMES. *Collected Essays and Reviews*, XV, XXV
FREUD. *The Predisposition to Obsessional Neurosis*

II.

CICERO. *Tusculan Disputations*, III–IV
BEN JONSON. *Every Man in His Humour*
BURTON. *The Anatomy of Melancholy*
MALEBRANCHE. *De la recherche de la vérité*, BK V
SHAFTESBURY. *Characteristics of Men, Manners, Opinions, Times*
HUTCHESON. *An Essay on the Nature and Conduct of the Passions and Affections*
COLLINS. *The Passions*

Voltaire. "Passions," in *A Philosophical Dictionary*

T. Reid. *Essays on the Active Powers of the Human Mind*, iii, part ii, ch 3–7

Brown. *Lectures on the Philosophy of the Human Mind*, vol iii, pp 26–473

D. Stewart. *Philosophy of the Active and Moral Powers of Man*

W. Hamilton. *Lectures on Metaphysics and Logic*, vol i (41–46)

Comte. *System of Positive Polity*, vol iv, *Theory of the Future of Man*, ch 2

Lotze. *Microcosmos*, bk ii, ch 5

Bain. *The Emotions and the Will*

E. Hartmann. *Philosophy of the Unconscious*, (b) ii–iii

Frazer. *The Golden Bough*, part vi, ch 8

Wundt. *Outlines of Psychology*, (12–13)

Bradley. *Collected Essays*, vol ii (23)

Strindberg. *The Dance of Death*

Titchener. *Lectures on the Elementary Psychology of Feeling and Attention*

Cannon. *Bodily Changes in Pain, Hunger, Fear and Rage*

Crile. *The Origin and Nature of the Emotions*

Carlson. *The Control of Hunger in Health and Disease*

Pareto. *The Mind and Society*, vol iii, ch 9

Proust. *Remembrance of Things Past*

Jung. *Psychological Types*

McTaggart. *The Nature of Existence*, ch 41, 57

B. Russell. *The Analysis of Mind*, lect 3, 14

——. *Skeptical Essays*, vi

Chapter 23: ETERNITY

INTRODUCTION

THE notion of eternity, like that of infinity, has two meanings. One meaning may refer to something positive, yet both seem to be formulated by the human mind in a negative way. We grasp one meaning of eternity by saying that there is *no* beginning or end to time's process. The other sense of eternity we conceive by *denying* time itself and, with it, change or mutability.

Considering eternity as infinite duration, Locke says that we form this notion "by the same means and from the same original that we come to have the idea of time . . . *viz.*, having got the idea of succession and duration . . . we can in our thoughts add such lengths of duration to one another, as often as we please, and apply them, so added, to durations past or to come. And this we can continue to do, without bounds or limits, and proceed *in infinitum.*"

The unimaginability of the infinite is no different in the sphere of time than in that of space or number. The difficulty, Locke points out, is the same in all three cases. "The idea of *so much* is positive and clear. The idea of *greater* is also clear." But these do not yet give us the idea of the infinite. That only comes with "the idea of *so much greater as cannot be comprehended*, and this is plainly negative, not positive . . . What lies beyond our positive idea *towards* infinity," Locke continues, "lies in obscurity, and has the indeterminate confusion of a negative idea, wherein I know I neither do nor can comprehend all I would, it being too large for a finite and narrow capacity."

In insisting that we can have no positive idea of infinity—whether of space, time, or number—Locke's point seems to be that it is beyond our finite capacity to form an image of an infinite object. But though our imaginations may be limited in this way, we do seem able to construct—in a negative manner—conceptions that go beyond experience, and have some meaning even if they lack imaginative content. Locke indicates this other aspect of the matter when he criticizes those who assert dogmatically that "the world is neither eternal nor infinite." It seems to him that the world's eternity or the world's infinity is "at least as conceivable as the contrary."

It may not be inconsistent, therefore, to say that infinite time, while unimaginable, remains quite conceivable; for to say that eternity is conceivable is simply to say that endless time is neither more nor less possible than time with a beginning and an end. The first conception is as meaningful as the second. It is in fact formed from the second by negation—by substituting the word "without" for "with" with respect to "a beginning and an end." But unlike our conceptions, our images cannot be formed by negation. When we imagine, as when we perceive, the object before us is positive and definite. We cannot imagine, as we cannot experience, a duration, or a span of time, without a beginning and an end.

WITH REGARD TO the other traditional meaning of "eternity," Locke takes a different position. It too might be defended as a negative conception, so far as human comprehension is concerned, since it involves the denial of time itself, *i.e.*, of a duration comprising a succession of moments. But here Locke says that there is "nothing more inconceivable to me than duration without succession. . . . If our weak apprehensions," he continues, "cannot separate succession from any duration whatsoever, our idea of eternity can be nothing but of an infinite succession of moments of duration, wherein anything does exist."

Nevertheless, Locke affirms that "we can easily conceive in God infinite duration, and we cannot avoid doing so." Whether he means by this that God's eternity involves temporal succession, must be determined by an interpretation of the passage in which he maintains that "God's infinite duration being accompanied with infinite knowledge and infinite power, he sees all things past and to come; and they are no more distant from his knowledge, no farther removed from his sight, than the present; they all lie under the same view."

If this passage means that time stands still for God in a single moment in which all things are co-present, then Locke may not be as resolute as Hobbes in rejecting the theologian's conception of God's eternity. Criticizing the Scholastics, Hobbes says that "for the meaning of *Eternity*, they will not have it be an endless succession of time." Instead, "they will teach us that eternity is the standing still of the present time, a *Nunc-stans* (as the Schools call it)." This, Hobbes thinks, "neither they nor anyone else understands, no more than they would a *Hic-stans* for an infinite greatness of place."

A theologian like Aquinas tries to avoid the difficulty which Hobbes finds in this conception by distinguishing between the *now* of eternity and the *now* of time. "The *now* of time is the same," he writes, "as regards its subject in the whole course of time, but it differs in aspect." Furthermore, "the flow of the *now*, as altering in aspect, is time. But eternity remains the same according to both subject and aspect; and hence eternity is not the same as the *now* of time."

The notion of the eternal as the timeless and the immutable does not belong exclusively to Christian theology. In the tradition of the great books it is found, for example, in Plato and Plotinus. Eternity, according to Plotinus, is "a Life changelessly motionless and ever holding the Universal content in actual presence; not this now and now that other, but always all; not existing now in one mode and now in another, but a consummation without part or interval. All its content is in immediate concentration as at one point; nothing in it ever knows development: all remains identical within itself, knowing nothing of change, for ever in a Now since nothing of it has passed away or will come into being; but what it is now, that it is ever."

Eternity so conceived is perhaps even more unimaginable than the eternity which is infinite time. We may feel that we have some sense of an infinite duration when we talk, as Ivan does in the *Brothers Karamazov*, about a billion years or "a quadrillion of a quadrillion raised to the quadrillionth power." Infinite time is *like* that, *only longer*. But because all our experience is temporal through and through, it is more difficult to get any sense of that which is both absolutely timeless and endlessly enduring.

Poets, and sometimes philosophers turned poets, have struggled to give this concept imaginative content by contrasting "the white radiance of eternity" with a "many-colored glass," or by speaking of time itself as "the moving image of eternity." When Dimmler in *War and Peace* tells Natasha that "it is hard for us to imagine eternity," she replies that it does not seem hard to her—that eternity "is now today, and it will be tomorrow, and always, and was there yesterday and the day before. . . ."

These and similar attempts may not succeed as much as the insight that if we could hold the present moment still, or fix the fleeting instant, we could draw an experience of the eternal from the heart of time. "The *now* that stands still," Aquinas writes, "is said to make eternity according to our apprehension. For just as the apprehension of time is caused in us by the fact that we apprehend the flow of the *now*, so the apprehension of eternity is caused in us by our apprehending the *now* standing still."

To UNDERSTAND the opposed views that constitute the major issues with regard to eternity, it is necessary to hold quite separate the two meanings of the word which have run side by side in the tradition of western thought. The first of these two senses, signifying interminable time, is the meaning of "eternity" which has greatest currency in popular speech. This is the meaning which appears in the chapters on INFINITY and TIME. It is also the sense in which philosophers and theologians debate the problem of the eternity of the world—whether the world ever began or will ever end.

Since that which exists interminably is imperishable, the word "eternal" is also applied to substances which are thought to be everlasting. Thus Ptolemy, and the ancients generally, think of the heavenly bodies as "beings which are sensible and both moving and moved, but eternal and impassible." Aristotle calls the heavenly bodies "eternal and incorruptible." For Lucretius and the atomists, the atoms and the atoms alone are eternal. They are, he says, "everlasting, though all things else are dissolved." Unless they were eternal, "all things before this would have utterly returned to nothing." If the atomic particles "were to wear away, or break in pieces," Newton argues, "the nature of things depending on them, would be changed. . . . And therefore, that nature may be lasting, the changes of corporeal things are to be placed only in the various separations and new associations and motions of these permanent particles."

The heavenly bodies and the atoms may be thought everlasting, but they are not immutable in all respects, for local motion is of their very essence. Imperishable in existence, they are also endlessly in motion. In Aristotle's view, local motion can be perpetual or eternal *only* if it is circular. Circular motion alone has neither beginning nor end.

The eternal circular motion of the heavens, according to Aristotle, in turn communicates an eternal cyclical movement to the rest of reality. "Since the sun revolves thus, the seasons in consequence come-to-be in a cycle . . . . and since they come-to-be cyclically, so in their turn do the things whose coming-to-be the seasons initiate." Such an eternal return, it would seem, is also applied by Aristotle to human things, for he writes that "probably each art and each science has often been developed as far as possible and has again perished."

SINCE THE HEAVENS and the atoms are in motion, even though their motion is everlasting or eternal, they cannot be eternal in the second meaning of "eternity," which is the very opposite of the first, not a variation or extension of it. In this meaning, the eternal is an existence absolutely immutable—a being which neither comes to be nor passes away, nor changes, nor moves in any respect whatsoever. Aquinas uses the word in this sense when he says that "the nature of eternity" consists in "the uniformity of what is absolutely outside of movement."

He also includes in this meaning of "eternity" the notion of interminability; for, he writes, "as whatever is wholly immutable can have no succession, so it has no beginning, and no end." Yet Aquinas preserves the sharp distinction between the two meanings when he differentiates the sense in which the world might be called eternal and the sense in which he would attribute eternity to God alone. "Even supposing that the world always was, it would not be equal to God in eternity," he writes; for "the divine being is all being simultaneously without succession, but with the world it is otherwise."

The conception of eternity as absolutely immutable existence is found in the ancient pagan writers. Plotinus, as we have already seen, makes immutability the mark of eternity. The unmoved prime mover of Aristotle and the Platonic Ideas or Forms also possess this characteristic. But it is the Jewish and Christian theologians who make eternity in this sense one of the prime attributes of God.

Augustine, for example, invokes God as "that everfixed Eternity" in whom "nothing passeth, but the whole is present." Since time is for him inconceivable apart from change or motion, that which exists immutably does not exist in time. Referring to God's eternity, he says, "Compare it with the times which are never fixed, and see that it cannot be compared. . . . Thy years neither come nor go; whereas ours both come and go, that they all may come. . . . Thy years are one day; and Thy day is not daily, but To-day. . . . Thy To-day is Eternity."

Time and eternity are here conceived as two distinct orders of reality. The temporal order is the order of things in change or motion, the eternal the realm of the fixed or permanent, the immobile and immutable. "As eternity is the proper measure of being," Aquinas writes, "so time is the proper measure of movement."

The eternal and the temporal are similarly distinguished by Plato in terms of the realms of being and becoming—"the world of immutable being" and "the world of generation." In the one we find "the parts of time, and the past and the future," which do not apply to the other. "We unconsciously but wrongly transfer them," Plato declares, "to the eternal essence

... but the truth is that 'is' alone is properly attributed to it, and 'was' and 'will be' are only to be spoken of becoming in time, for they are motions, but that which is immovably the same cannot become older or younger by time ... nor is it subject at all to any of those states which affect moving and sensible things of which generation is the cause."

For Spinoza, the distinction consists in two ways of viewing the order of nature. "Things are conceived by us as actual in two ways," he writes; "either in so far as we conceive them to exist with relation to a fixed time and place, or in so far as we conceive them to be contained in God, and to follow from the necessity of the divine nature." Only in the second way do "we conceive things under the form of eternity." We can view things under the aspect of eternity only insofar as we know God and, through knowing God, are able to know all things according as "their ideas involve the eternal and infinite essence of God."

The separation of time and eternity into distinct spheres of reality, or even into distinct ways of conceiving the whole of being, is challenged by thinkers who find the eternal within the process of time. For both Jew and Christian, the eternal God intervenes directly in the temporal order. The most radical form which this fusion takes is perhaps exemplified in the doctrine of the Incarnation of Christ, when "the Word was made flesh, and dwelt among us."

Whitehead challenges the sharpness of the separation from another point of view. He not only makes "eternal objects" ingredients in actual occasions or temporal events; but since the events which constitute the process of change are themselves unchangeable, they are for him eternal—even though they have their being within the sphere of change.

A similar point seems to be made in Aristotle's theory of change. When change is conceived as consisting in a transformation of matter, it is the thing composed of matter and form which changes, and neither the matter nor the form. Matter as matter, Aristotle writes, "does not cease to be in its own nature, but is necessarily outside the sphere of becoming and ceasing to be." The remark would seem to hold true as well of the form as form.

As indicated in the chapter on CHANGE, the Aristotelian analysis of motion finds in matter or the substratum of change, and in the contrary forms *from which* and *to which* a motion takes place, the elements of permanence underlying change. When a green leaf turns red, for instance, green has not changed into red; the leaf has changed from one color to another. The changing leaf is not eternal, but *red* and *green* are, since they are incapable of change. This is the sense of eternity in which the unchanging instant is eternal, or the past is eternal, even though both are somehow elements or aspects of time and the process of change.

The past may be eternal but it no longer exists. The passing moment may be eternal, but it has no duration. Lack of existence and lack of duration together distinguish that meaning of "eternal" in which it merely signifies the unchanging, from the meaning in which it signifies that which exists or endures forever without changing. It is only in the second of these two meanings that the eternal can be conceived as that which exists entirely outside the realm of time.

As WE HAVE ALREADY observed, the basic philosophical and theological issues concerning eternity cannot be intelligibly stated unless these meanings of "eternity" and "the eternal" are kept distinct.

The traditional problem of the eternity of the world asks, for example, not whether the order of nature is free from change or succession, but whether the changing physical universe ever had a beginning or ever will end. As indicated in the chapters on CHANGE, TIME, and WORLD, it is a question of the infinity of time; or, in another formulation, a question of the interminability of change or motion.

Aristotle appears to answer these questions affirmatively, especially in the last book of his *Physics* where he claims to demonstrate the impossibility of there having been a beginning to motion. Aquinas, on the other hand, does not think that the eternity of the world can be demonstrated; and of Aristotle's arguments he says that they are not "absolutely demonstrative, but only relatively so—*viz.*, as against the arguments of some of the ancients who asserted that the world began to be in some actually impossible ways." In support of this contention, he cites a remark made by Aristotle in the *Topics*, that among "dialectical problems which we cannot solve demonstratively," one is "*whether the world is eternal.*"

For Kant the problem is typically dialectical. It occurs as part of the first antinomy in the Transcendental Dialectic, the thesis of which asserts that "the world has a beginning in time" and the antithesis that "the world has no beginning, but is infinite in respect both to time and space." The fact that *apparently* cogent arguments can be marshalled for both of these contradictory propositions shows, in Kant's opinion, that the reasoning on either side is not demonstrative, but only dialectical and, as he says, "illusory."

The Jewish and Christian doctrine of the world's creation by God might seem to require the denial of the world's eternity. But in fact the theologians find either alternative compatible with divine creation, which they conceive as the cause of the world's *being*, not necessarily of its *beginning*. Augustine, for example, examines the sense in which the world is held by some to be co-eternal with God, even though made or created by God. "It is as if a foot," he interprets them to say, "had been always from eternity in the dust; there would always have been a print underneath it; and yet no one would doubt that this print was made by the pressure of the foot, nor that, though the one was made by the other, neither was prior to the other." So, he goes on, it might also be said that the world has always existed and yet is always, throughout eternity, created, *i.e., caused to exist,* by God.

Commenting on this passage, Aquinas adds the observation that if an "action is instantaneous and not successive, it is not necessary for the maker to be prior in duration to the thing made." Hence it does not follow necessarily, he writes, "that if God is the active cause of the world, He must be prior to the world in duration; because creation, by which He produced the world, is not a successive change" —but an instantaneous act.

Writing both as a philosopher and as a theologian, Maimonides—many centuries before Kant stated his antinomy—thinks he is able to show that the question of infinite time and endless motion "cannot be decided by proof, neither in the affirmative nor in the negative." Just as for Augustine and Aquinas, so for him it is indifferent—from a *philosophical* point of view—whether the created world and its Creator are co-eternal or whether, as Genesis says, "in the beginning God created heaven and earth."

But both alternatives are not equally acceptable to the theologian. Since there is no proof on either side "sufficient to convince us," Maimonides writes, "we take the text of the Bible literally, and say that it teaches us a truth which we cannot prove"—namely, that the world had a beginning in time. Aquinas comes to the same conclusion. "That the world did not always exist," he writes, "we hold by faith alone." It is not "an object . . . of demonstration or science." For Christian and Jew alike, the religious dogma that the world is not only created by God, in the sense of depending for its existence upon God as cause, but was also initiated by God, or caused to begin to exist and move, is based on the revealed word of God in Holy Writ.

Those who, on philosophical grounds, deny creation *ex nihilo* also deny the world's beginning. Pursuant to his theory of the world as a necessary and perpetual emanation from the One, Plotinus, for example, declares that "the Kosmos has had no beginning . . . and this is warrant for its continued existence. Why should there be in the future a change that has not yet occurred?" For Spinoza likewise, "all things which follow from the absolute nature of any attribute of God must for ever exist"; and to this extent at least, the world is eternal and uncreated.

The man of faith, however, believes in a God who is free to create or not to create, not one from whom the world emanates as a necessary effect from its source. When, therefore, he affirms that God freely chose to produce the world out of nothing, he seems to meet the question, "What was God doing before He made heaven and earth?" To the questioner Augustine does not wish to give "the jesting answer—said to have been given by one who sought to evade the force of the question—'He was getting Hell ready for people who pry too deep.' "

Instead he points out that the question itself

is illicit for it assumes a time before time began. "If before heaven and earth were made,"
he writes, "there was no time, then what is
meant by the question 'What were You doing
then?' If there was not any time, there was not
any 'then.' " In the phrase "before creation"
the word "before" has no temporal significance.
It signifies a different kind of priority—the
sense in which eternity precedes time, the sense
in which Augustine says of God that "it is not
in time that You are before all time. . . . You
are before all the past by the eminence of Your
ever-present eternity."

TURNING FROM eternity in the sense of infinite
time to the eternal in the sense of the timeless
and unchanging, the great question is whether
anything eternal exists. The atoms of Lucretius
are not eternal in this sense, nor are the supposedly imperishable heavenly bodies. Nor is
it sufficient to point out that change itself involves aspects or elements of permanence; for
the question, strictly interpreted, asks whether
anything exists in and of itself which, having no
beginning or end, also has no past, present, or
future—no temporal phases in its continued
endurance. Only such a thing would be utterly
non-temporal or changeless.

Since nothing made of matter is exempt from
motion, it is generally supposed that no material thing is eternal in this sense. Not even
God is eternal unless God is absolutely immutable as well as spiritual. The angels are spiritual
beings, yet, according to Christian theology,
they cannot be called "eternal" because, in
the first place, they are creatures and had an
origin; and, in the second place, they are subject to spiritual change even if they are not
involved in the sorts of motion to which bodies
are susceptible. The theologians, therefore, use
the word "aeviternal" to signify the mode of
angelic existence in that it is "a mean between
eternity and time." Aeviternity, Aquinas explains, has "a beginning but no end," while
"eternity has neither beginning nor end . . .
and time both beginning and end."

THE QUESTION ABOUT the eternal as timeless
and immutable existence has two parts: Does
an immutable God exist? Does anything else
exist which is immutable?

To the first question, it does not suffice to
reply by affirming the existence of God. Some
modern theologians deny God's absolute immutability, and so deny the eternality of His
being in the precise sense under consideration.

With regard to the second question, we must
observe that, in the tradition of the great books,
eternality has been claimed for two things other
than God, namely, for truth and ideas. Whatever "is produced by reasoning aright," Hobbes
says, is "general, eternal, and immutable
truth." On somewhat different grounds James
declares, "there is no denying the fact that
the mind is filled with necessary and eternal
relations which it finds between certain of
its ideal conceptions, and which form a determinate system, independent of the order of
frequency in which experience may have associated the conception's originals in time and
space." He quotes Locke to the effect that
"truths belonging to the essences of things . . .
are eternal, and are to be found out only by the
contemplation of those essences."

The common phrase—"the eternal verities"
—which James uses testifies to the prevalence
of the notion that truth itself cannot change,
and that when men speak of a new truth or
the growth of truth, the change they refer to
is only a change of mind with respect to what
men think is true or false, not a change in the
truth itself. Whatever is true now, always was
true and always will be. Time and change make
no difference to the truth of *two plus two equals
four.*

But even so it can still be asked how the
truth exists, for the attribution of eternity to
anything also requires us to consider its mode
of being. If, for example, the truth exists only
in the mind, then it exists unchangingly only
in the mind of an absolutely infallible knower,
a mind which neither learns nor forgets, nor
changes in any respect with regard to what it
knows. If God is such a knower, eternal truth
can have existence in God's mind.

The theologians sometimes go further and
identify absolute truth, as they identify absolute goodness, with God. Aquinas writes, for
example, that "if we speak of truth as it is in
things, then all things are true by one primary
truth; to which each one is assimilated according to its entity, and thus, although the es-

sences or forms of things are many, yet the truth of the divine intellect is one, in conformity to which all things are said to be true." On this view, it would appear that there are not two eternal beings, but only one.

William James finds immutability not only in the truth, but also in the concepts of the human mind. "Each conception," he writes, "eternally remains what it is, and never can become another. The mind may change its states, and its meanings, at different times; may drop one conception and take up another, but the dropped conception can in no intelligible sense be said to *change into* its successor. . . . Thus, amid the flux of opinions and of physical things, the world of conceptions, or things intended to be thought about, stands stiff and immutable, like Plato's Realm of Ideas."

In the case of ideas, however, the problem is complicated by the question whether ideas exist in and by themselves, outside the mind of God or man. If, according to a doctrine attributed to Plato and the Platonists, the Ideas or Forms exist separately, then they constitute a realm of eternal beings, for their immutability is unquestionable. If, from an opposite point of view, the realm of unchanging ideas is identical with the divine intellect, then no eternal being or beings exist apart from God.

THE PROPOSITION that God is the only eternal being, the only uncreated and immutable existence, is inextricably connected with the proposition that God is the only actually infinite being, the *ens realissimum* having all perfections. "Eternity is the very essence of God," Spinoza writes, "in so far as that essence involves necessary existence." In saying this he appeals to his definition of eternity, by which we are to understand "existence itself, so far as it is conceived necessarily to follow from the definition alone of the eternal thing." For Spinoza, as well as for Aquinas, the same fact which makes God eternal—namely, the identity of his essence and existence—also constitutes his infinity and uniqueness. It is impossible, Spinoza argues, for there to be two infinite substances. For the same reason, there cannot be two eternal beings.

As indicated in the chapter on INFINITY, when the word "infinite" is applied to God, the theologians give it a positive rather than a negative significance. They mean by it the actual infinity of perfect being and absolute power, in sharp distinction from the potential infinity by which the mathematicians signify the *lack* of a limit in addition or division.

These two meanings of "infinity" seem to parallel the two meanings of "eternity" which we have dealt with throughout this chapter—one the negative sense in which it means the *lack* of a beginning or an end to time, the other the positive sense in which God's eternity consists in that fullness of being which can exist apart from time and change. Because our intellects are finite, we may apprehend eternal being in a negative manner by calling it "timeless" or by conceiving it as infinite duration, but Spinoza cautions us against supposing that it can be "explained by duration or time, even if the duration be conceived without beginning or end."

One other theological discussion raises issues which involve in a unique way the two meanings of eternity. It deals with the revealed doctrine of perdition and salvation as eternal death and eternal life. Is the eternality of Hell and Heaven equivalent to a period of *endless* duration or does it mean—more fundamentally— the *unchanging* state of souls after the Last Judgment?

According to Augustine and Aquinas, the eternity of Heaven and Hell means the moral immutability of the immortal soul as well as the interminability of the beatitude it enjoys or the punishment it suffers. Only in Purgatory does a change of moral state occur, but the process of purification which takes place there is always limited in period. Purgatory is, therefore, not eternal in either sense.

As Kant sees it, however, the after-life must not only be interminable, or of infinite duration, but it must also permit a progressive moral development without end. Man is justified, according to Kant, "in hoping for an endless duration of his existence" only on the ground that "the holiness which the Christian law requires . . . leaves the creature nothing but a progress *in infinitum*." From still another point of view, Dr. Johnson questions the traditional Christian dogma that the souls of the blessed are secure in a perpetual state of rectitude—in this respect like the good angels who are confirmed in their goodness from the first instant of creation.

Boswell had "ventured to ask him whether, although the words of some texts of Scripture seemed strong in support of the dreadful doctrine of an eternity of punishment, we might not hope that the denunciation was figurative, and would not be literally executed." To this, Dr. Johnson replied: "Sir, you are to consider the intention of punishment in a future state. We have no reason to be sure that we shall then be no longer able to offend against God. We do not know that even the angels are quite in a state of security. . . . It may, therefore, perhaps be necessary, in order to preserve both men and angels in a state of rectitude, that they should have continually before them the punishment of those who have deviated from it."

On Dr. Johnson's theory, the moral condition of the damned seems to be immutable. It is irremediable even by the punishments which, according to him, may exercise some deterrent effect upon the blessed who, he seems to think, are not as unalterably set in the path of righteousness as the wicked are in their iniquity.

On any of these conceptions of Heaven and Hell, and of the state of the soul in the afterlife, the meaning of "eternity" is somewhat altered; for eternal life or eternal death is conceived as having a beginning, if not an end, for the individual soul. As in the case of all fundamental religious dogmas, the truth asserted remains obscure and mysterious. It is not only beyond imagination, but also beyond any adequate rational conception, analysis, or demonstration.

OUTLINE OF TOPICS

REFERENCES

To find the passages cited, use the numbers in heavy type, which are the volume and page numbers of the passages referred to. For example, in 4 HOMER: *Iliad*, BK II [265–283] 12d, the number 4 is the number of the volume in the set; the number 12d indicates that the passage is in section d of page 12.

PAGE SECTIONS: When the text is printed in one column, the letters a and b refer to the upper and lower halves of the page. For example, in 53 JAMES: *Psychology*, 116a–119b, the passage begins in the upper half of page 116 and ends in the lower half of page 119. When the text is printed in two columns, the letters a and b refer to the upper and lower halves of the left-hand side of the page, the letters c and d to the upper and lower halves of the right-hand side of the page. For example, in 7 PLATO: *Symposium*, 163b–164c, the passage begins in the lower half of the left-hand side of page 163 and ends in the upper half of the right-hand side of page 164.

AUTHOR'S DIVISIONS: One or more of the main divisions of a work (such as PART, BK, CH, SECT) are sometimes included in the reference; line numbers, in brackets, are given in certain cases; *e.g.*, *Iliad*, BK II [265–283] 12d.

BIBLE REFERENCES: The references are to book, chapter, and verse. When the King James and Douay versions differ in title of books or in the numbering of chapters or verses, the King James version is cited first and the Douay, indicated by a (*D*), follows; *e.g.*, OLD TESTAMENT: *Nehemiah*, 7:45—(*D*) II *Esdras*, 7:46.

SYMBOLS: The abbreviation "esp" calls the reader's attention to one or more especially relevant parts of a whole reference; "passim" signifies that the topic is discussed intermittently rather than continuously in the work or passage cited.

For additional information concerning the style of the references, see the Explanation of Reference Style; for general guidance in the use of *The Great Ideas*, consult the Preface.

1. Eternity as timelessness and immutability or as endless and infinite time: the distinction between eternity and time

APOCRYPHA: *Ecclesiasticus*, 18:10—(*D*) OT, *Ecclesiasticus*, 18:8

7 PLATO: *Timaeus*, 450b-451d

8 ARISTOTLE: *Interpretation*, CH 13 [23ª18–26] 35b-c / *Physics*, BK IV, CH 12 [221ª19]–CH 13 [222ᵇ29] 301a-302c; BK VI, CH 2 [233ª13–ᵇ16] 315a-c; CH 7 [237ᵇ23–238ª19] 321a-c; CH 10 [241ᵇ11–20] 325d; BK VIII, CH 1–2 334a-337b; CH 6 344b-346b; CH 8 348b-352a / *Heavens*, BK I, CH 12 372d-375d esp [282ª22–283ª2] 373d-374c, [283ᵇ7–22] 375c-d; BK II, CH 3 [286ª8–13] 377c / *Generation and Corruption*, BK II, CH 9 [335ª33–ᵇ2] 436d-437a / *Metaphysics*, BK V, CH 5 [1015ᵇ9–16] 536a; BK IX, CH 8 [1050ᵇ6–20] 576b-c; BK XI, CH 10 [1067ª 33–38] 596a; BK XII, CH 6 [1071ᵇ2–11] 601b; CH 7 [1072ª18–23] 602a-b; [1073ª3–11] 603a-b; BK XIV, CH 2 [1088ᵇ14–28] 620d-621a

12 AURELIUS: *Meditations*, BK VI, SECT 15 275a-b

17 PLOTINUS: *First Ennead*, TR V, CH 7 20a-c / *Third Ennead*, TR VII 119b-129a / *Fourth Ennead*, TR IV, CH 6–8 161b-162d; CH 15–16 165c-166b

18 AUGUSTINE: *Confessions*, BK VII, par 21 49d-50a; BK XI 89b-99b esp par 8–17 91b-93c, par 39–41 98c-99b; BK XII, par 13–20 102a-103d; par 40 109b-110a; BK XIII, par 44 122d / *City of God*, BK XI, CH 5–6 324d-325d; CH 21 333a-d; BK XII, CH 12–19 349b-355a

19 AQUINAS: *Summa Theologica*, PART I, Q 10, AA 1–5 40d-45c esp A 4 43b-44b; Q 14, A 9, ANS 83b-d; A 13, ANS and REP 3 86d-88c; Q 42, A 2, REP 2–4 225d-227a; Q 46, A 2, REP 5 253a-255a; Q 79, A 8, REP 2 421c-422b

21 DANTE: *Divine Comedy*, PURGATORY, XI [106–108] 69d; PARADISE, XXIX [10–45] 150b-c

23 HOBBES: *Leviathan*, PART IV, 271b

25 MONTAIGNE: *Essays*, 292d-294a

29 CERVANTES: *Don Quixote*, PART II, 366d-367a

30 BACON: *Novum Organum*, BK I, APH 48, 110d

31 DESCARTES: *Objections and Replies*, 216d-217c

31 SPINOZA: *Ethics*, PART I, DEF 8 355c; PROP 20, COROL 2 364a; PART II, PROP 44, COROL 2 and DEMONST 390a; PART V, PROP 23 458b-d; PROP 29, DEMONST 459c; PROP 34, SCHOL 460d

32 MILTON: *On Time* 12a-b / *Paradise Lost*, BK XII [553–556] 331a

33 PASCAL: *Pensées*, 121 195a; 205–206 211a

35 LOCKE: *Human Understanding*, BK II, CH XIV, SECT 26–27 160c-161a; SECT 30–31 161c-162a; CH XV, SECT 3–8 162d-164b; SECT 11–12 165a-c;

(1. *Eternity as timelessness and immutability or as endless and infinite time: the distinction between eternity and time.*)

CH XVII 167d-174a passim, esp SECT 5 168d-169a, SECT 10 170b-c, SECT 16 172a-b; CH XXIX, SECT 15 237a

42 KANT: *Pure Reason*, 26d; 130b-133c; 135a-137a,c; 152c; 160b-161d; 185a-b

46 HEGEL: *Philosophy of History*, INTRO, 206c

51 TOLSTOY: *War and Peace*, BK VII, 295b-c; EPILOGUE II, 681a

1a. The priority of eternity to time

7 PLATO: *Timaeus*, 450c-451a

8 ARISTOTLE: *Metaphysics*, BK IX, CH 8 [1050b 2-28] 576b-d

17 PLOTINUS: *Third Ennead*, TR VII, CH 1 119b-c; CH 6, 122c-d; CH 11, 126a; CH 13, 128c / *Fourth Ennead*, TR IV, CH 15-16 165c-166b

18 AUGUSTINE: *Confessions*, BK VII, par 21 49d-50a; BK XI, par 12-16 92b-93a; BK XII, par 40 109b-110a / *City of God*, BK XI, CH 4-6 324a-325d; BK XII, CH 12 349b-350a; CH 15-17 351b-354a

19 AQUINAS: *Summa Theologica*, PART I, Q 22, A 1, REP 2 127d-128d; Q 46 250a-255d; Q 61, A 2 315c-316a

21 DANTE: *Divine Comedy*, PARADISE, XXIX [10-45] 150b-c

32 MILTON: *Paradise Lost*, BK V [577-599] 187b-188a; BK VII [70-108] 218b-219b

42 KANT: *Pure Reason*, 135a-137a,c; 160b-161d esp 161d

1b. Aeviternity as intermediate between eternity and time

18 AUGUSTINE: *Confessions*, BK XII, par 9 101b-c; par 12-15 101d-102c; par 18-22, 103b-104a / *City of God*, BK XII, CH 15 351b-352d

19 AQUINAS: *Summa Theologica*, PART I, Q 10, A 2, REP 1-2 41d-42c; A 3, ANS 42c-43b; AA 5-6 44b-46d

2. The issue concerning the infinity of time and the eternity of the world or of motion

OLD TESTAMENT: *Genesis*, 1:1-2 / *Nehemiah*, 9:6 —(D) *II Esdras*, 9:6 / *Job*, 38:1-13 / *Psalms*, 90:2; 95:4-5; 102:25-26; 104:5-6; 119:90-91; 136:5-9; 148:1-6—(D) *Psalms*, 89:2; 94:4-5; 101:26-27; 103:5-6; 118:90-91; 135:5-9;148:1-6 / *Proverbs*, 3:19; 8:22-29 / *Isaiah*, 45:12,18; 48:13; 65:17-25—(D) *Isaias*, 45:12,18; 48:13; 65:17-25 / *Jeremiah*, 51:15—(D) *Jeremias*, 51:15

APOCRYPHA: *Wisdom of Solomon*, 7:17-18—(D) OT, *Book of Wisdom*, 7:17-18 / *Ecclesiasticus*, 23:19-20; 24:9—(D) OT, *Ecclesiasticus*, 23:28-29; 24:14 / *II Maccabees*, 7:23—(D) OT, *II Machabees*, 7:23

NEW TESTAMENT: *Matthew*, 13:24-30,36-43,49-50; 24:3-35 / *Mark*, 13:3-33 / *Luke*, 21:5-33 /

John, 1:1-3 / *Colossians*, 1:16-17 / *Hebrews*, 1:10-12 / *II Peter*, 3:3-13 / *Revelation*, 10:5-6—(D) *Apocalypse*, 10:5-6

7 PLATO: *Phaedrus*, 124b-c / *Timaeus*, 447b-c; 450b-451a

8 ARISTOTLE: *Topics*, BK I, CH 11 [104b13-18] 148a-b / *Physics*, BK IV, CH 13 [222a29-b8] 302b; BK VIII, CH 1-2 334a-337b; CH 6 344b-346b; CH 8 348b-352a / *Heavens*, BK I, CH 2 [269b2-10] 360c-d; CH 3 [270b1-26] 361c-362a; CH 9 [279a12]-CH 12 [283b22] 370b-375d / *Generation and Corruption*, BK II, CH 10-11 437d-441a,c / *Meteorology*, BK I, CH 14 [352a 16-353a27] 458b-459a,c; BK II, CH 3 [356b2-357a4] 462b-c / *Metaphysics*, BK IX, CH 8 [1050b20-28] 576c-d; BK XI, CH 6 [1063a13-16] 591b; CH 10 [1067a33-38] 596a; BK XII, CH 6-8 601b-605a esp CH 7 [1072a19-b14] 602b-d, [1073a5-11] 603b

9 ARISTOTLE: *Motion of Animals*, CH 4 [699b14-700a6] 234d-235a; CH 6 [700b29-701a7] 236a-b

12 LUCRETIUS: *Nature of Things*, BK I [146-264] 2d-4b; [483-634] 7a-8d; [951-1051] 12d-14a; BK II [89-141] 16a-d; [294-307] 18d-19a; [569-580] 22b; [1048-1063] 28b-c; [1105-1174] 29a-30a,c; BK V [1-431] 61a-66d esp [55-70] 61d-62a, [235-246] 64a-b, [351-379] 65c-66a; BK VI [535-607] 87c-88b

12 AURELIUS: *Meditations*, BK V, SECT 13 271b; BK VI, SECT 15 275a-b; BK IX, SECT 28 293d-294a

16 KEPLER: *Epitome*, BK IV, 847b-848b

17 PLOTINUS: *Second Ennead*, TR I 35a-39d esp CH 1-5 35a-37c

18 AUGUSTINE: *Confessions*, BK XI 89b-99b esp par 12-17, 92b-93b, par 40 98d-99a / *City of God*, BK XI, CH 4-6 324a-325d; BK XII, CH 10-20 348b-357a

19 AQUINAS: *Summa Theologica*, PART I, Q 14, A 12, ANS 85d-86d; Q 46 250a-255d esp A 1 250a-252d; Q 61, A 2 315c-316a; Q 66, A 4 348d-349d; Q 75, A 1, REP 1 378b-379c

20 AQUINAS: *Summa Theologica*, PART III SUPPL, Q 91, A 2 1017c-1020c

23 HOBBES: *Leviathan*, PART I, 50a; PART II, 162b

30 BACON: *Novum Organum*, BK I, APH 48, 110d

31 DESCARTES: *Rules*, XIII, 27b-c / *Objections and Replies*, 228a-b

32 MILTON: *Paradise Lost*, BK I [6-10] 93b; BK II [850-1009] 129b-133a esp [890-969] 130b-132a; BK V [577-599] 187b-188a; BK VII [70-108] 218b-219b

33 PASCAL: *Pensées*, 121 195a

34 NEWTON: *Optics*, BK III, 540a-541b

35 LOCKE: *Human Understanding*, BK II, CH XIV, SECT 26 160c-d

42 KANT: *Pure Reason*, 20a; 26d; 130b-133c esp 130b-131c, 132d-133a; 135a-137a,c; 152a-d; 160b-161d; 239b-c / *Practical Reason*, 334b-335c esp 335a-b

51 TOLSTOY: *War and Peace*, EPILOGUE II, 693c-694a passim

3. The eternity of God

OLD TESTAMENT: *Exodus*, 15:18 / *Deuteronomy*, 32:39-40 / *Psalms*, 9:5-8; 29:10-11; 33:10-11; 48 esp 48:8, 48:14; 90 esp 90:1-6; 93; 102:12-28; 103:14-18; 136; 145:10-13; 146:5-10—(D) *Psalms*, 9:6-9; 28:10; 32:10-11; 47 esp 47:9, 47:15; 89 esp 89:1-6; 92; 101:13-29; 102:14-18; 135; 144:10-13; 145:5-10 / *Isaiah*, 40:28-29; 43:10-13; 57:15—(D) *Isaias*, 40:28-29; 43:10-13; 57:15 / *Jeremiah*, 10:10—(D) *Jeremias*, 10:10 / *Lamentations*, 5:19 / *Daniel*, 6:25-27 / *Malachi*, 3:6—(D) *Malachias*, 3:6

APOCRYPHA: *Ecclesiasticus*, 39:20; 42:21—(D) OT, *Ecclesiasticus*, 39:25; 42:21-22

NEW TESTAMENT: *Matthew*, 24:35 / *Colossians*, 1:16-17 / *I Timothy*, 1:17 / *Hebrews*, 1:10-12; 13:7-8 / *Revelation*, 1:17-18; 10:6—(D) *Apocalypse*, 1:17-18; 10:6

5 SOPHOCLES: *Oedipus at Colonus* [607-615] 120a

8 ARISTOTLE: *Physics*, BK VIII, CH 6 [258^{b}10-259^{b}31] 344b-345d / *Heavens*, BK II, CH 3 [286^{a}3-13] 377c / *Metaphysics*, BK V, CH 5 [1015^{b}9-16] 536a; BK IX, CH 8 [1050^{b}6-20] 576b-c; BK XII, CH 1 [1069^{a}30-^{b}2] 598b-c; CH 6-7 601b-603b; CH 9 605a-d esp [1075^{a}5-11] 605c-d; BK XIV, CH 2 [1088^{b}14-28] 620d-621a / *Soul*, BK II, CH 4 [415^{a}22-^{b}8] 645c-d

16 KEPLER: *Harmonies of the World*, 1071b

17 PLOTINUS: *Third Ennead*, TR VII, CH 5 121c-122a / *Sixth Ennead*, TR VIII, CH 11 348b-c

18 AUGUSTINE: *Confessions*, BK VII, par 1-4 43b-44c; par 6 44d-45a; par 16-18 48c-49b; par 21 49d-50a; par 23-24 50b-51a; BK XI, par 12-16 92b-93a; BK XI, par 11 101c-d; par 18 103a-c; par 40 109b-110a; BK XIII, par 44 122d / *City of God*, BK XI, CH 21 333a-d; BK XII, CH 14-17 350d-354a / *Christian Doctrine*, BK I, CH 5-6 625d-626b; CH 22 629b-630a

19 AQUINAS: *Summa Theologica*, PART I, Q 10 40d-46d; Q 14, A 9, ANS 83b-d; A 13, ANS and REP 3 86d-88c; Q 18, A 3 106b-107c; Q 22, A 1, REP 2 127d-128d; Q 42, A 2 225d-227a; Q 43, A 2 230d-231c; Q 61, A 2, ANS 315c-316a

21 DANTE: *Divine Comedy*, PARADISE, VII [64-72] 115d; XIII [52-60] 126a; XXIV [130-141] 144a; XXIX [10-45] 150b-c; XXXIII 156b-157d esp [124-141] 157c-d

22 CHAUCER: *Knight's Tale* [2987-3040] 209a-210a

25 MONTAIGNE: *Essays*, 293d-294a

31 DESCARTES: *Discourse*, PART IV, 52b-c / *Meditations*, III, 84a-87a esp 86a; V, 94a-95a esp 95a / *Objections and Replies*, 228a-b

31 SPINOZA: *Ethics*, PART I, DEF 1 355a; DEF 3,6 355b; DEF 8 355c; PROP 6-8 356b-357d; PROP 10-11 358a-359b; PROP 19-20 363c-364a; PROP 33, SCHOL 2, 367d-368c; PART II, PROP 44, COROL 2-PROP 47 390a-391a

32 MILTON: *Paradise Lost*, BK III [1-12] 135b; [372-382] 143b

34 NEWTON: *Principles*, BK III, GENERAL SCHOL, 370a-371a

35 LOCKE: *Human Understanding*, BK II, CH XV, SECT 3-4 162d-163b; CH XVII, SECT 16-17 172a-c; SECT 20 172d-173c; BK IV, CH X 349c-354c passim, esp SECT 3-5 349d-350b, SECT 8-11 351a-352a

40 GIBBON: *Decline and Fall*, 81b-c

42 KANT: *Pure Reason*, 175d-176c; 190c; 201b-c / *Practical Reason*, 334b-335c; 344b-c / *Judgement*, 592a-c

46 HEGEL: *Philosophy of History*, INTRO, 156d-157b; 206c

51 TOLSTOY: *War and Peace*, BK XV, 631a-c

4. The things which partake of eternity

4a. The imperishability of angels, spiritual substances, souls

7 PLATO: *Phaedrus*, 124b-c / *Meno*, 179d-183a esp 180a / *Phaedo*, 223c-246c esp 226c-228b, 230c-232c, 245d-246c / *Republic*, BK X, 434d-436a / *Timaeus*, 452c-d

8 ARISTOTLE: *Interpretation*, CH 13 [23^{a}18-26] 35b-c / *Metaphysics*, BK XII, CH 3 [1070^{a}21-27] 599c; CH 8 603b-605a / *Soul*, BK II, CH 2 [413^{b}24-29] 643d-644a; BK III, CH 5 [430^{a}20-25] 662d

12 LUCRETIUS: *Nature of Things*, BK III [417-869] 35c-41a

16 KEPLER: *Epitome*, BK IV, 890b-891a

17 PLOTINUS: *Fourth Ennead*, TR IV, CH 6 161b-c; TR VII 191c-200c esp CH 8, 195d-196a, CH 9-15 198b-200c

18 AUGUSTINE: *Confessions*, BK XII, par 9 101b-c; par 12 101d-102a; par 15-16 102b-103a; par 18-22, 103b-104a; par 28, 105c / *City of God*, BK X, CH 31 319b-d; BK XII, CH 15 351b-352d; BK XIII, CH 1 360a-b; CH 16-17 367a-368d

19 AQUINAS: *Summa Theologica*, PART I, Q 10, A 2, REP 1-2 41d-42c; A 3, ANS and REP 1 42c-43b; AA 5-6 44b-46d; Q 50, A 5 274b-275a; Q 61, A 2 315c-316a; Q 75, A 6 383c-384c; Q 104, A 1, ANS and REP 1,3 534c-536c

21 DANTE: *Divine Comedy*, PARADISE, VII [64-75] 115d-116a; [121-148] 116b-c; XIII [52-72] 126a

23 HOBBES: *Leviathan*, PART III, 192c-193c; PART IV, 250c-251b; 253b-254a

31 DESCARTES: *Meditations*, 73b-c / *Objections and Replies*, 127c-d; 216d-217a; 228b

31 SPINOZA: *Ethics*, PART II, PROP 11 377b-c; PART V, PROP 23 458b-d; PROP 25 458d-459a; PROP 29-33 459b-460c; PROP 38-40 461d-462d

32 MILTON: *Paradise Lost*, BK I [116-159] 96a-97a; BK II [81-105] 113a-b; BK V [889-892] 194b; BK VI [296-353] 202b-204a; [430-436] 205b; [853-855] 215a

33 PASCAL: *Pensées*, 194-195, 206b-210b

35 BERKELEY: *Human Knowledge*, SECT 141 441a-b

40 GIBBON: *Decline and Fall*, 186a-b

(*4. The things which partake of eternity. 4a. The imperishability of angels, spiritual substances, souls.*)

42 KANT: *Pure Reason*, 121a-128b esp 124d-126c; 203d-204c / *Practical Reason*, 348d

51 TOLSTOY: *War and Peace*, BK V, 216d-218b; BK VII, 295b-c; BK XIV, 608a-b

4b. The imperishable in the physical order: matter, atoms, celestial bodies

7 PLATO: *Timaeus*, 450c-451a; 457a-b

8 ARISTOTLE: *Physics*, BK II, CH 1 [193^{a}9–28] 269b-c / *Heavens*, BK I, CH 3 360d-362a; BK I, CH 9 [279^{a}12]–BK II, CH 1 [284^{b}6] 370b-376a; BK II, CH 6 379c-380c; BK III, CH 6 396a-c / *Generation and Corruption*, BK II, CH 10–11 437d-441a,c esp CH 10 [336^{b}25–34] 438d / *Metaphysics*, BK I, CH 3 [983^{b}7–984^{a}17] 501d-502b; BK III, CH 2 [997^{a}34–^{b}12] 516a-b; CH 4 [999^{b}1–16] 518b-c; [1000^{a}5–1001^{a}3] 518d-519d; BK IX, CH 8 [1050^{b}16–28] 576c-d; BK XI, CH 2 [1060^{a}3–36] 588a-c; CH 6 [1063^{a}10–16] 591b; BK XII, CH 3 599a-d; CH 6–8 601b-605a / *Soul*, BK II, CH 4 [415^{a}23–^{b}8] 645c-d

9 ARISTOTLE: *Motion of Animals*, CH 4 [699^{b}14–700^{a}6] 234d-235a

12 LUCRETIUS: *Nature of Things*, BK I [146–264] 2d-4b; [483–634] 7a-8d; BK II [294–307] 18d-19a; BK V [110–145] 62c-63a

12 EPICTETUS: *Discourses*, BK III, CH 13, 188d-189a

12 AURELIUS: *Meditations*, BK II, SECT 3 257a-b; BK IV, SECT 46 267c; BK VI, SECT 15 275a-b; BK VII, SECT 18 281a; SECT 23 281b; SECT 25 281c; SECT 50 283a; BK X, SECT 7 297b-c

16 PTOLEMY: *Almagest*, BK I, 5a-6a; BK XIII, 429a-b

16 KEPLER: *Epitome*, BK IV, 888b-889b; 929b-930b

17 PLOTINUS: *Second Ennead*, TR I 35a-39d / *Fourth Ennead*, TR IV, CH 7–8 161d-162d

18 AUGUSTINE: *Confessions*, BK XII, par 8–9 101a-c; par 14–16 102b-103a; par 22 104a-b; par 28, 105c; par 40 109b-110a / *City of God*, BK XIII, CH 17, 367d-368b

19 AQUINAS: *Summa Theologica*, PART I, Q 10, A 2, REP 2 41d-42c; A 3, ANS 42c-43b; A 4, ANS 43b-44b; A 5, ANS 44b-45c; Q 46, A 1, REP 2–3 250a-252d; Q 58, A 3, ANS 301d-302d; Q 63, A 1, REP 2 325c-326c; Q 65, A 1, REP 1 339b-340b; Q 66, A 2 345d-347b; Q 75, A 6, ANS 383c-384c; Q 84, A 1, REP 3 440d-442a; Q 104, A 1, REP 1,3 534c-536c; Q 113, A 1, ANS 576a-d; Q 115, A 3, ANS 588c-589c

20 AQUINAS: *Summa Theologica*, PART III SUPPL, Q 77, A 2, ANS and REP 1 945a-946b; Q 91 1016a-1025b

21 DANTE: *Divine Comedy*, PARADISE, I [64–81] 106d-107a

28 HARVEY: *On Animal Generation*, 390b-d

30 BACON: *Novum Organum*, BK II, APH 48, 186b-d

31 SPINOZA: *Ethics*, PART I, PROP 15, SCHOL 360b-361d

33 PASCAL: *Vacuum*, 358a

34 NEWTON: *Optics*, BK III, 541b

35 LOCKE: *Human Understanding*, BK IV, CH X, SECT 10–19 351b-354c passim

40 GIBBON: *Decline and Fall*, 346d

41 GIBBON: *Decline and Fall*, 226b

42 KANT: *Pure Reason*, 18d-19a; 74b-76c

45 LAVOISIER: *Elements of Chemistry*, PART I, 41b-c

4c. The immutability of truth and ideas

OLD TESTAMENT: *Psalms*, 100:5; 117:2; 119:160; 146:5–6—(D) *Psalms*, 99:5; 116:2; 118:160; 145:5–6 / *Proverbs*, 8:22–30

APOCRYPHA: *Wisdom of Solomon*, 7:24–26—(D) OT, *Book of Wisdom*, 7:24–26 / *Ecclesiasticus*, 24:9—(D) OT, *Ecclesiasticus*, 24:14

NEW TESTAMENT: *II John*, 1–2

7 PLATO: *Phaedrus*, 125a-b / *Symposium*, 167b-d / *Meno*, 184d / *Phaedo*, 231b-232b / *Timaeus*, 447b-d; 457b-458b

8 ARISTOTLE: *Posterior Analytics*, BK I, CH 8 104a-b / *Metaphysics*, BK I, CH 6 [987^{a}29–^{b}18] 505b-d; BK II, CH 1 [993^{b}19–31] 512a-b; BK III, CH 2 [997^{a}34–^{b}12] 516a-b; BK IX, CH 10 [1051^{b}33–1052^{a}12] 578a,c

9 ARISTOTLE: *Ethics*, BK I, CH 6 [1096^{a}29–^{b}5] 341c-d; BK VI, CH 3 [1139^{b}18–24] 388b-c

11 NICOMACHUS: *Arithmetic*, BK I, 811a-812a; 813d-814a

17 PLOTINUS: *Fifth Ennead*, TR IX, CH 5–8 248a-250a

18 AUGUSTINE: *Confessions*, BK I, par 9, 3a / *Christian Doctrine*, BK I, CH 8–10 626c-627b; BK II, CH 38–39, 654b-d

19 AQUINAS: *Summa Theologica*, PART I, Q 10, A 3, REP 3 42c-43b; Q 14, A 13, ANS and REP 3 86d-88c; A 15 89b-90b; Q 16, AA 7–8 99a-100d; Q 18, A 4 107d-108c; Q 22, A 1, REP 2 127d-128d; Q 44, A 3 240b-241a; Q 84, A 1, REP 3 440d-442a; A 2, ANS and REP 3 442b-443c; A 5 446c-447c; Q 86, A 3 463b-d

20 AQUINAS: *Summa Theologica*, PART I-II, Q 91, A 1 208b-d; Q 93 215b,d-220d; Q 94, A 4, ANS 223d-224d; AA 5–6 224d-226b; PART II-II, Q 1, A 1, CONTRARY 380b-381a

23 HOBBES: *Leviathan*, PART IV, 267b

25 MONTAIGNE: *Essays*, 276b-285c passim, esp 279b-282a

30 BACON: *Novum Organum*, BK I, APH 56 112a

31 DESCARTES: *Objections and Replies*, 216d-217c; 228a-b; 229c-d

31 SPINOZA: *Ethics*, PART I, DEF 8 355c; PROP 8, SCHOL 2 356d-357d; PROP 17, SCHOL 362c-363c; PROP 19, SCHOL 363d; PROP 20, COROL 1 364a; PROP 33, SCHOL 2 367d-369a; PART II, PROP 44, COROL 2–PROP 47 390a-391a

32 MILTON: *Paradise Lost*, BK II [142–151] 114b

33 PASCAL: *Vacuum*, 358b

35 LOCKE: *Human Understanding*, BK IV, CH III, SECT 31 323c-d; CH XI, SECT 14 358b-c

42 KANT: *Pure Reason*, 113c-118a esp 113c-114b, 117b-118a; 173b-174a

46 HEGEL: *Philosophy of Right*, PREF, 6a-7a; PART III, par 270, 85c / *Philosophy of History*, INTRO, 156d-157b; 168b-d; PART III, 310d

53 JAMES: *Psychology*, 301a; 879b-882a

4d. The eternity of Heaven and Hell: everlasting life and death

OLD TESTAMENT: *Psalms*, 16 esp 16:10-11; 73 esp 73:24-28; 145:10-13—(D) *Psalms*, 15 esp 15:10-11; 72 esp 72:24-28; 144:10-13 / *Daniel*, 7:13-18 esp 7:18

APOCRYPHA: *Wisdom of Solomon*, 1-5 esp 3-5—(D) OT, *Book of Wisdom*, 1-5 esp 3-5

NEW TESTAMENT: *Matthew*, 6:19-21; 18:8-9; 25:31-46 / *Mark*, 9:43-50; 10:17-31—(D) *Mark*, 9:42-49; 10:17-31 / *Luke*, 10:25-37 / *John*, 6:37-40; 8:51; 10:24-30; 11:23-27; 17:1-3 / *Romans*, 6 esp 6:23 / *I Corinthians*, 15:34-58 / *II Corinthians*, 4:12-5:10 / *Galatians*, 6:8 / *I Peter*, 1:3-7,22-25 / *I John*, 2:16-17; 5:11-12 / *Jude*, 5-8 / *Revelation*, 2:7-11; 3:5; 20-22 esp 20:10-15, 21:4-6, 22:1-5—(D) *Apocalypse*, 2:7-11; 3:5; 20-22 esp 20:9-15, 21:4-6, 22:1-5

18 AUGUSTINE: *Confessions*, BK XIII, par 50-53 124c-125a,c / *City of God*, BK XIII, CH 2 360b-361a; CH 12 365d-366a; CH 14-20 366b-371a; BK XIII, CH 22–BK XIV, CH 1 371c-377a; BK XIV, CH 15 388d-390a; BK XV, CH 1-3 397b,d-399c; CH 6 400c-401b; BK XIX, CH 4 511a-513c; CH 10-11 516c-517b; CH 27-28 529a-530a,c; BK XXI–XXII 560a-618d / *Christian Doctrine*, BK I, CH 4 625b-c; CH 21 629b; CH 24, 630d; CH 38-39 635c-636a

19 AQUINAS: *Summa Theologica*, PART I, Q 10, A 3, ANS and REP 2 42c-43b; Q 18, A 2, REP 2 105c-106b; Q 23, A I, ANS and REP 3 132c-133b; Q 66, A 3 347b-348d; Q 75, A 7, REP 1 384d-385c; PART I-II, Q 4, A 7, REP 3 635b-636a; Q 5, A 4 639a-640b

20 AQUINAS: *Summa Theologica*, PART I-II, Q 67 81b-87c; Q 68, A 6 93c-94c; Q 87, AA 3-5 187b-189c; PART I-II, Q 18, AA 2-3 462d-464c; Q 19, A 11 472d-473d; Q 26, A 13 519d-520d

21 DANTE: *Divine Comedy*, HELL, I [112–129] 2b-c; III [1–18] 4a-b; [82–129] 5a-b; IV [13–45] 5c-d; VI [1–57] 8b-9a; VII [16–59] 9d-10a esp [55–59] 10a; XII [49–51] 16d-17a; XIV [28–42] 19d-20a; XV [22–42] 21b-c; PARADISE, III [34–90] 109d-110b; VII [64–78] 115d-116a; [121–148] 116b-c; XIV [1–66] 126d-127c; XV [1–12] 128b-c; XXX-XXXIII 151d-157d esp XXXI [31–93] 153c-154a

22 CHAUCER: *Second Nun's Tale* [15,787–800] 467a

23 HOBBES: *Leviathan*, PART III, 191b-198a; PART IV, 250c-251b; 253b-255b

25 MONTAIGNE: *Essays*, 265b-c

26 SHAKESPEARE: *Richard III*, ACT I, SC IV [42–63] 115a-b

29 CERVANTES: *Don Quixote*, PART II, 366d-367a

31 DESCARTES: *Objections and Replies*, 228b

32 MILTON: *Paradise Lost*, BK I [84–191] 95b-97b; [242–330] 98b-100b; BK II [85–92] 113a; [142–188] 114b-115a; BK III [274–343] 141b-143a; BK X [782–844] 291b-292b; BK XII [537–556] 331a

33 PASCAL: *Pensées*, 194-195, 206b-210b; 233, 214b-215a

35 LOCKE: *Toleration*, 5b-c; 15d-16a / *Human Understanding*, BK II, CH XXI, SECT 38 187b-c; SECT 62 194c-d

41 GIBBON: *Decline and Fall*, 233d-234d

42 KANT: *Practical Reason*, 346b-347c

44 BOSWELL: *Johnson*, 363a-b

46 HEGEL: *Philosophy of History*, PART IV, 315d

48 MELVILLE: *Moby Dick*, 347a

5. The knowledge and imagery of eternity

7 PLATO: *Apology*, 211b-c / *Timaeus*, 450b-451a

8 ARISTOTLE: *Topics*, BK I, CH 11 [104^{b}13–18] 148a-b / *Memory and Reminiscence*, CH I [449^{b}30–450^{a}10] 690c-d

16 KEPLER: *Harmonies of the World*, 1048a

17 PLOTINUS: *First Ennead*, TR V, CH 7 20a-c / *Third Ennead*, TR VII, CH 3 120a-d

18 AUGUSTINE: *Confessions*, BK XI, par 13-17 92b-93c; BK XII, par 40 109b-110a; BK XIII, par 44 122d / *City of God*, BK XI, CH 5-6 324d-325d; CH 21 333a-d

19 AQUINAS: *Summa Theologica*, PART I, Q 10, A I 40d-41d; A 2, REP 1 41d-42c; Q 13, A I, REP 3 62c-63c; Q 42, A 2, REP 1,4 225d-227a; Q 46, A I, ANS 250a-252d; A 2 253a-255a; Q 79, A 9, ANS and REP 3 422b-423d

21 DANTE: *Divine Comedy*, PURGATORY, XI [100–108] 69d; PARADISE, XXX-XXXIII 151d-157d esp XXXI [31–93] 153c-154a

23 HOBBES: *Leviathan*, PART IV, 271b

30 BACON: *Novum Organum*, BK I, APH 48 110d-111a

32 MILTON: *On Time* 12a-b / *At a Solemn Musick* 13a-b / *Sonnets*, XIV 66a / *Paradise Lost*, BK XII [537–556] 331a

35 LOCKE: *Human Understanding*, BK II, CH XIV, SECT 26-27 160c-161a; SECT 30-31 161c-162a; CH XV, SECT 3-5 162d-163c; SECT 11-12 165a-c; CH XVII 167d-174a passim, esp SECT 5 168d-169a, SECT 10 170b-c, SECT 16 172a-b; CH XXIX, SECT 15 237a; SECT 16, 237d-238a

42 KANT: *Pure Reason*, 185a-b

49 DARWIN: *Origin of Species*, 154c

51 TOLSTOY: *War and Peace*, BK III, 156d; BK V, 216d-218b esp 217a-c; BK VII, 295b-c; BK IX, 355d-356a

CROSS-REFERENCES

For: Other discussions of the distinction between eternity as infinite time and eternity as time-lessness, *see* TIME 2; and for the relation of eternity to time, *see* TIME 2c.

Another consideration of infinite time, *see* INFINITY 3e.

The controversy concerning the infinity of time and the eternity of the world or motion, *see* ASTRONOMY 8c(1), 8d; CHANGE 13; TIME 2b; WORLD 4a; and for the relation of creation to eternity and time, *see* GOD 7a; TIME 2c; WORLD 4e(2).

The notion of permanent elements or principles of change, *see* CHANGE 2.

Other discussions of the eternity of God, *see* CHANGE 15c; GOD 4d.

The conception of the angels as aeviternal, *see* ANGEL 3c; TIME 2a.

The discussion of imperishable or incorruptible bodies, *see* ASTRONOMY 8a; BEING 7b(3); CHANGE 10c; ELEMENT 5a.

The consideration of the eternality of truth and of ideas, *see* CHANGE 15a; FORM 2b; IDEA 1e; IMMORTALITY 6c; TRUTH 5.

The conception of the eternity of Heaven and Hell or of eternal salvation and damnation, *see* HAPPINESS 7c; IMMORTALITY 5e–5f; PUNISHMENT 5e(1); SIN 6d.

The problem of the knowability of the infinite, *see* INFINITY 6b; KNOWLEDGE 5a(4).

ADDITIONAL READINGS

Listed below are works not included in *Great Books of the Western World*, but relevant to the idea and topics with which this chapter deals. These works are divided into two groups:

I. Works by authors represented in this collection.
II. Works by authors not represented in this collection.

For the date, place, and other facts concerning the publication of the works cited, consult the Bibliography of Additional Readings which follows the last chapter of *The Great Ideas*.

I.

AUGUSTINE. *On the Immortality of the Soul*, CH 1
AQUINAS. *Summa Contra Gentiles*, BK II, CH 32–38
——. *On the Power of God*, Q 8
——. *De Aeternitate Mundi*
SPINOZA. *Correspondence*, XII

II.

PROCLUS. *The Elements of Theology*, (F)
BOETHIUS. *The Consolation of Philosophy*, BK V, PROSA 6
ANSELM OF CANTERBURY. *Monologium*
MAIMONIDES. *The Guide for the Perplexed*, PART II, CH 13–16, 18, 22–23
BONAVENTURA. *Breviloquium*, PART VII
DUNS SCOTUS. *Opus Oxoniense*, BK II, DIST 2, Q 2
——. *Tractatus de Primo Principio (A Tract Concerning the First Principle)*
ECKHART. *Sermons and Collations*, XXV
SUÁREZ. *Disputationes Metaphysicae*, XXX (7–9), L (3–6)

LEIBNITZ. *New Essays Concerning Human Understanding*, BK II, CH 14
——. *Monadology*, par 6
VOLTAIRE. "Eternity," in *A Philosophical Dictionary*
——. *The Ignorant Philosopher*, CH 14, 16, 20
KIERKEGAARD. "The Expectation of an Eternal Happiness," in VOL III, *Edifying Discourses*
——. *Philosophical Fragments*
——. *Concluding Unscientific Postscript*, pp 345–385, 468–492, 508–513
WHEWELL. *On the Philosophy of Discovery*, CH 26
BRADLEY. *Appearance and Reality*, BK I, CH 4–5; BK II, CH 18, 26
ROYCE. *The World and the Individual*, SERIES II (3)
POHLE. *Eschatology*
HÜGEL. *The Mystical Element of Religion*
BERGSON. *The Creative Mind*, CH 1, 5
A. E. TAYLOR. *The Faith of a Moralist*, SERIES I (3, 6)
DEWEY. *The Quest for Certainty*, CH 2
WHITEHEAD. *Process and Reality*, PART I, CH 2; PART II, CH 1; PART IV, CH 1 (5–6); PART V, CH 2
——. *Adventures of Ideas*, CH 11–15

Chapter 24: EVOLUTION

INTRODUCTION

THIS chapter belongs to Darwin. Not that his writings, which are cited under almost all headings, stand alone in the various places they appear. The point is rather that many of the topics are dictated by and draw their meaning from his thought, and that he figures in all the major issues connected with the origin of species, the theory of evolution, and the place of man in the order of nature. With respect to the matters under consideration in this chapter, the other writers in the tradition of the great books cannot escape from being classified as coming before or after Darwin, or as being with or against him.

Darwin's influence on later writers may be variously estimated, but it is plainly marked by their use of his language and their reference to his fundamental notions. James' *Principles of Psychology*, especially in its chapters on instinct and emotion, views the behavior of men and animals and the phenomena of intelligence or mind in evolutionary terms. The writings of Freud are similarly dominated by the genetic approach and by an appeal to man's animal ancestry in order to explain the inherited constitution of his psyche in conformity with the doctrine of evolution.

Outside psychology the concept of evolution is reflected in theories of progress or of a dialectical development in history; as, for example, in the dialectical or historical materialism of Marx and Engels, which is set forth in the latter's *Dialectics of Nature*. An even more general re-orientation of philosophy, which stems from an evolutionary way of thinking, is to be found in the writings of Bergson and Dewey, such as *Creative Evolution* and *The Influence of Darwin on Philosophy*. These, along with many of the specifically biological works cited in the list of Additional Readings, give some measure of the influence of Darwin not only on philosophical thought, but also on the direction of research in all the biological sciences.

WITH REGARD TO Darwin's predecessors the question is not so much one of their influence upon him as of their anticipation, in one way or another, of his discoveries, his conceptions, and his theory.

The observation made in antiquity concerning a hillside deposit of marine fossils is sometimes taken as implying an early recognition of the evolution of terrestrial life. More apposite perhaps is the statement by Lucretius that "the new earth first put forth grass and bushes, and next gave birth to the races of mortal creatures springing up many in number in many ways after divers fashions." Lucretius also speaks of strange monsters which nature did not permit to survive. "Nature set a ban on their increase and they could not reach the coveted flower of age nor find food nor be united in marriage ... And many races of living things must then have died out and been unable to beget and continue their breed." Those which survived, he adds, had qualities which "protected and preserved each particular race."

Apparently susceptible to similar interpretation are Aristotle's statements that "nature proceeds little by little from things lifeless to animal life"; that "there is observed in plants a continuous scale of ascent toward the animal"; and that "throughout the entire animal scale there is a graduated differentiation in amount of vitality and in capacity for motion." Augustine's commentary on the first chapter of Genesis seems even more explicitly to contemplate the successive appearance of the various forms of life. Plants and animals did not actually exist when the world began. Though their causes were created by God and existed from the beginning, the actual production of plants

451

and animals in their various kinds is, as Aquinas tells us while summarizing Augustine's view, "the work of propagation"—not of creation.

Like Aristotle, both Aquinas and Locke represent the world of living organisms as a graduated scale ascending from less to more perfect forms of life. But where Aquinas tends to conceive that graduated scale as a hierarchy involving essential differences, Locke sees an almost perfect continuity involving only differences in degree. "In all the visible world," he writes, "we see no chasms or gaps." To illustrate this, he points out that "there are fishes that have wings, and are not strangers to the airy region; and there are some birds that are inhabitants of the water, whose blood is cold as fishes . . . There are animals so near of kin to both birds and beasts that they are in the middle between both: amphibious animals link the terrestrial and aquatic together . . . and the animal and vegetable kingdoms are so nearly joined, that, if you will take the lowest of one and the highest of the other, there will scarce be perceived any great difference between them: and so on, till we come to the lowest and the most inorganical parts of matter, we shall find everywhere that the several species are linked together, and differ but in almost insensible degrees."

But for the theory of evolution the observation of a hierarchy in nature, or even of a continuity in which the species differ by "almost insensible degrees," constitutes only background. What the theory of evolution brings to the fore is the notion of a developmental or genetic relation among the various forms of life. Because it seems to contain this insight, the anticipation of Darwin to be found in Kant's *Critique of Judgement* is perhaps the most remarkable; even though, in a closely related passage in which Kant discusses epigenesis, he uses the word "evolution" in a sense quite contrary to Darwin's conception.

"It is praiseworthy," Kant writes, "to employ a comparative anatomy and go through the vast creation of organized beings in order to see if there is not discoverable in it some trace of a system, and indeed of a system following a genetic principle . . . When we consider the agreement of so many genera of animals in a certain common schema, which apparently underlies not only the structure of their bones,

but also the disposition of their remaining parts, and when we find here the wonderful simplicity of the original plan, which has been able to produce such an immense variety of species by the shortening of one member and the lengthening of another, by the involution of this part and the evolution of that, there gleams upon the mind a ray of hope, however faint, that the principle of the mechanism of nature, apart from which there can be no natural science at all, may yet enable us to arrive at some explanation in the case of organic life. This analogy of forms, which in all their differences seem to be produced in accordance with a common type, strengthens the suspicion that they have an actual kinship due to descent from a common parent. This we might trace in the gradual approximation of one animal species to another, from that in which the principle of ends seems best authenticated, namely from man, back to the polyp, and from this back even to mosses and lichens, and finally to the lowest perceivable stage of nature."

FINDING ANTICIPATIONS of Darwin involves judgments much more subject to controversy than tracing his influences. It is questionable, for example, whether the suggestive passages in Lucretius and Locke bear more than a superficial resemblance to Darwin's thought. The matter is further complicated by Darwin's own sense of his divergence from and disagreement with his predecessors—both immediate precursors like Buffon and Linnaeus and earlier philosophers and theologians.

Darwin tells us himself of his quarrel with the theologians. His followers elaborate on the opposition between his conception of species and that of Aristotle, an opposition which Darwin intimates by the great stress he lays on the difference between a static taxonomy and a dynamic or genealogical classification of living things.

We must therefore try to locate the central points of Darwin's theory in order to judge comparable views for their agreement or disagreement.

As the title of his major work indicates, it is not evolution as a grand scheme of biological, or cosmic, history, but the origin of species with which Darwin seems to be principally concerned. He is concerned with establishing the fact that new species do originate in the course of time, against those who suppose the species of living things to be fixed in number and immutable in type throughout the ages. He is concerned with describing the circumstances under which new species arise and other forms cease to have the status of species or become extinct. He is concerned with formulating the various factors in the differentiation of species, and with showing, against those who think a new species requires a special act of creation, that the origin of species, like their extinction, is entirely a natural process which requires no factors other than those at work every day in the life, death, and breeding of plants and animals. Only as a consequence of these primary considerations does he engage in speculations about the moving panorama of life on earth from its beginnings to its present and its future.

Darwin looks upon the term "species" as "arbitrarily given," and for that reason does not attempt any strict definition of it. He uses it, moreover, like his predecessors in systematic biological classification, to signify "a set of individuals closely resembling each other"—a class of plants or animals having certain common characteristics. Darwin would probably agree with Locke's criticism of those who suppose that our definitions of species grasp the real essences or relate to the substantial forms inherent in things. As indicated in the chapter on DEFINITION, Locke insists that our notion of a species expresses only what he calls the "nominal essence"—a set of characteristics we attach to the name we give things of a sort when we group them and separate them in our classifications. "The boundaries of species, whereby man sorts [things], are made by men," he writes; "the essences of the species, distinguished by different names, are . . . of man's making."

Species is not the only term of classification. A *genus*, for example, is a more inclusive group than a *species*. Groups which differ specifically belong to the same genus if their difference is accompanied by the possession of common traits. As species differ from one another within a generic group, so genera are in turn subclasses of more inclusive groupings, such as

phyla, families, and orders. But there are also smaller groupings within a species. There are races or varieties and sub-varieties, the members of which share the characteristics of the species but differ from one another in other respects. Ultimately, of course, within the smallest class the systematist bothers to define, each individual differs from every other in the same group with whom, at the same time, it shares certain characteristics of the race, the species, the genus, and all the larger classes to which they belong.

This general plan of botanical or zoological classification does not seem to give *species* peculiar status in the hierarchy of classes or groupings or to distinguish it from other classes except as these are more or less inclusive than itself. Why then should attention be focused on the origin of species, rather than of varieties or of genera?

One part of the answer comes from the facts of generation or reproduction. Offspring tend to differ from their parents, as well as from each other, but they also tend to resemble one another. "A given germ," Aristotle writes, "does not give rise to any chance living being, nor spring from any chance one; but each germ springs from a definite parent and gives rise to a definite progeny." This is an early formulation of the insight that in the process of reproduction, the law of like generating like always holds for those characteristics which identify the species of ancestors and progeny.

In other words, a species always breeds true; its members always generate organisms which can be classified as belonging to the *same* species, however much they vary among themselves as individuals within the group. Furthermore, the sub-groups—the races or varieties—of a species are able to breed with one another, but diverse species cannot interbreed. Organisms different in species either cannot mate productively at all, or if crossbred, like the horse and the ass, they produce a sterile hybrid like the mule.

In the hierarchy of classes, then, species would seem to be distinguished from all smaller groupings by their *stability* from generation to generation. If species are thus self-perpetuating, they in turn give stability to all the larger groupings—the genera, phyla, families—which remain as fixed from generation to generation as the species which constitute them. Hence the question of origin applies peculiarly to species rather than to varieties or to genera.

On the supposition stated, no origin of species would seem to be possible except by a special act of creation. Either all the existing species of organisms have always existed from the beginning of life on earth; or, if in the course of ages new species have arisen, their appearance cannot be accounted for by natural generation. By the law of natural generation, offspring will always be of the same species as the parent organisms.

Spontaneous generation, of course, remains a possibility. A new species of organism might come to be without being generated by other living organisms. But apart from the question of fact (i.e., whether spontaneous generation ever does occur), such origin of a form of life seems to lie outside the operation of natural causes and to imply the intervention of supernatural power.

The possibility of spontaneous generation was entertained in antiquity and the Middle Ages, and was even thought to be supported by observation, such as that of maggots emerging from putrefying matter. But modern science tends to affirm the biogenetic law that living organisms are generated only by living organisms. To Kant, the notion that "life could have sprung up from the nature of what is void of life," seems not only contrary to fact, but absurd or unreasonable. Yet, while affirming the principle that like produces like by insisting upon "the generation of something organic from something else that is also organic," Kant does not carry that principle to the point where it would make the generation of a *new* species impossible. "Within the class of organic beings," he writes, it is possible for one organism to generate another "differing specifically from it."

AGAINST THE BACKGROUND of these various suppositions, Darwin is moved to a new insight by the conjunction of certain types of fact: the results of breeding under domestication which exhibit the great range of variation within a species and the tendency of *inbred* varieties to breed true; his own observations of the geographical distribution of species of flora and fauna, especially those separated from one another by impassable barriers; the facts of comparative anatomy and embryology which reveal affinities in organic structure and development between organisms distinct in species; and the geological record which indicates the great antiquity of life upon the earth, which gives evidence of the cataclysmic changes in the earth's surface (with consequences for the survival of life), and which above all contains the fossil remains of forms of life now extinct but not dissimilar from species alive in the present age.

Briefly stated, Darwin's insight is that new species arise when, among the varieties of an existing species, certain intermediate forms become extinct, and the other circumstances are such that the surviving varieties, now become more sharply separated from one another in type, are able to reproduce their kind, and, in the course of many generations of inbreeding, also tend to breed true. They thus perpetuate their type until each in turn ceases to be a species and becomes a genus when its own extreme varieties, separated by the extinction of intermediates, become new species, as they themselves did at an earlier stage of history. For the very same reason that Darwin says "a well-marked variety may be called an incipient species," a species may be called an incipient genus.

The point is misunderstood if it is supposed that when new species originate from old, both the new and the old continue to survive as species. On the contrary, when in the course of thousands of generations some of the varieties of a species achieve the status of species, the species from which they originated by variation ceases to be a species and becomes a genus.

"The only distinction between species and well-marked varieties," Darwin writes, "is that the latter are known, or believed, to be connected at the present day with intermediate gradations, whereas species were formerly thus connected ... It is quite possible that forms now generally acknowledged to be merely varieties may hereafter be thought worthy of specific names; and in this case scientific and common language will come into accordance. In short, we shall have to treat species in the same manner as those naturalists treat genera who admit that genera are merely artificial combinations made for convenience ... Our classifications will come to be, as far as they can be so made, genealogies."

The *origin of species* thus seems to be identical with the *extinction of intermediate varieties*, combined with the survival of one or more of the extreme varieties. These seem to be simply two ways of looking at the same thing. Still another way of seeing the point may be achieved by supposing, contrary to fact, the survival of all the varieties ever produced through the breeding of organisms.

"If my theory be true," Darwin writes, "numberless intermediate varieties, linking closely together all the species of the same group, must assuredly have existed; but the very process of natural selection constantly tends, as has been so often remarked, to exterminate the parent-forms and the intermediate links." If one were to suppose the simultaneous co-existence of *all* intermediate varieties in the present day, the groups now called "species" would be continuously connected by slight differences among their members and would not, therefore, be divided into distinct species, as they now are because certain links are missing.

In the *Critique of Pure Reason*, Kant states the principle of continuity in the following manner. "This principle," he writes, "indicates that all differences of species limit each other, and do not admit of transition from one to another by a *saltus*, but only through smaller degrees of the difference between the one species and the other. In one word, there are no species or sub-species which ... are the nearest possible to each other; intermediate species or sub-species being always possible, the difference of which from each of the former is always smaller than the difference existing between these." But, Kant adds, "it is plain that this continuity of forms is a mere idea, to which no adequate object can be discovered in experience," partly because "the species in nature are really divided ... and if the gradual progression through their affinity were continuous, the intermediate members lying be-

tween two given species must be infinite in number, which is impossible."

The Russian geneticist, Theodore Dobzhansky, gives an interpretation of continuity in nature which differs from Kant's in that it follows and applies Darwin's conception of species and their origin. According to him, if we suppose the extreme case of all possible genetic variations being alive on earth together, the result would be not an infinite number of species, but no species and genera at all. The array of plants and animals would approach a perfectly continuous series in which there would only be individual differences. There would be no specific or generic groupings of the sort now made in our classification of the forms of life.

ON DARWIN's conception of the origin of species its causes divide into two sets of factors: first, those which determine the extinction or survival of organisms and, with their survival, their opportunities for mating and reproduction; second, those which determine the transmission of characteristics from one generation to another and the variation of offspring from their ancestors and from each other. Without genetic variation there would be no range of differences within a group on which the factors of selection could operate. Without the inheritance of ancestral traits there would be no perpetuation of group characteristics in the organisms which manage to survive and reproduce.

For Darwin the operation of the first set of factors constitutes the process of natural selection. This may take place in many ways: through geological catastrophes which make certain areas of the earth's surface uninhabitable for all organisms, or for those types which cannot adapt themselves to the radically changed environment; through the competition among organisms for the limited food supply available in their habitat; through the struggle for existence in which organisms not only compete for food but also prey upon one another; through the sexual selection which operates within a group when some organisms are prevented by others from mating and reproducing; and through all the obstacles which isolate groups from interbreeding, including geographical and physiological in-accessibility.

The struggle for existence is not only a struggle to survive, but also a struggle to re-produce. Natural selection operates with re-spect to reproduction as well as survival. Whether the survival is of the fittest alone, or whether the multiplication of inferior organisms also gives evolution another direction, has been disputed since Darwin's day; but according to his theory, "natural selection works solely by and for the good of each being; all corporeal and mental endowments will tend to progress toward perfection . . . Thus, from the war of nature, from famine and death . . . the production of the higher animals directly follows."

With respect to the factors of heredity and variation, tremendous advances since Darwin in the experimental science of genetics require revisions in this part of his theory of evolution. This is particularly true of the researches of Mendel, Bateson, and Morgan concerning the ways in which genetic factors operate. But on one major point in the theory of heredity Darwin holds a view which later investigations have tended to confirm. Antedating Weismann, he nevertheless opposes Lamarck's theory of the inheritance of acquired characteristics. As William James expresses it, where Lamarck supposes that environmental influences cause changes in the structure or functioning of the organism which then become hereditary, Darwin regards the environment merely as a selective agency, acting upon variations produced entirely by causes operating in the breeding process. James thinks "the evidence for Mr. Darwin's view . . . [was] . . . quite convincing," even before it received the support of Weismann's theory, according to which it is "*a priori* impossible that any peculiarity acquired during the lifetime by the parent should be transmitted to the germ."

The situation is not the same with regard to Darwin's views on the mechanism of heredity. Writing before Mendel's classic experiments in hybridization, Darwin seems to suppose a blending of hereditary factors; whereas, according to Mendel, inheritance is particulate. Distinct genetic factors combine to produce a certain somatic result without losing their separate identities. They can therefore be re-assorted and enter into new genetic combinations in the next generation. Most important of all, Darwin thinks that new forms of life arise gradually as the result of a continuous accumulation of slight and imperceptible variations. The opposite view is now taken. The discovery of abrupt mutations in a single generation discountenances Darwin's maxim *natura non facit saltum*—"nature does nothing by jumps."

These advances in genetics since Darwin's day do not alter the main outlines of his theory. The mechanisms of heredity may be much more complicated than Darwin knew, and involve much of which he was ignorant, such as mutation-rates, or the various types, causes, and effects of hybridization. But that merely leads to a more elaborate or different explanation of genetic variation in offspring and the transmission of ancestral traits. No matter how these are explained, their occurrence is all that is needed to permit new species to originate through natural processes of heredity and selection. "If Darwin were alive today," Julian Huxley writes, "the title of his book would have to be not the 'origin' but the 'Origins of Species.' For perhaps the most salient single fact that has emerged from recent studies is that species may arise in a number of quite distinct ways."

THE READER MUST judge for himself to what extent Darwin's theory of evolution was anticipated by those who, like Augustine, affirm the appearance of new species of life on earth at various stages in its history, or even by a writer like Kant, who seems to possess the germ of its insight.

The critical test in every case is whether those who affirm the occurrence of *new* species by natural processes rather than by special creation, think of them as simply *added* to the organic forms already in existence without any change in the status as species of the pre-existing forms. Those who think in this way do not have Darwin's idea of the origin of species; for in conceiving an increase in the number of species as merely a matter of addition, they necessarily attribute stability to each species, new as well as old. By this test, not even Kant seems to be near the center of Darwin's hypothesis of the origin of species by the extinction of intermediate varieties.

In comparing Darwin with certain of his predecessors, notably Aristotle and Aquinas, it seems necessary to apply another kind of test. Here the problem is not so much one of discovering affinities or disagreements, as one of determining whether they are talking about the same thing and therefore, when they appear to disagree, whether the issue between them is genuine. They do not seem to conceive a species in the same way. Certainly they use the word differently. This affects the way in which the whole problem of origins is understood. The controversies concerning the fixity or mutability of species, concerning evolution and creation, and concerning the origin of man involve genuine issues only if those who seem to disagree do not use the word "species" in widely different senses.

It is *possible* that certain forms of life do not originate by descent from a common ancestor and do not derive their status as quite distinct types from the mere absence of intermediate varieties—varieties which once must have existed but are now extinct. If such forms were to be called "species," the word would have a different meaning from the meaning it has when applied to types of pigeons, beetles, or rats.

The first of these two meanings may express the philosophical conception of a living species as a class of organisms having the same essential nature, according to which conception there never could have been intermediate varieties. The second meaning may be that of the scientific taxonomist in botany or zoology who constructs a system of classification, genealogical or otherwise. On this meaning, one million and a half would be a conservative estimate of the number of plant and animal types classified by the systematist as "species." In contrast, the number of species, in the philosophical sense of distinct essences, would be extremely small.

Darwin, for example, says, "I cannot doubt that the theory of descent with modification embraces all the members of the same great class or kingdom. I believe that animals are descended from at most only four or five progenitors, and plants from an equal or lesser number. Analogy would lead me one step farther, namely, to the belief that all animals and plants are descended from some one prototype. But analogy may be a deceitful guide." It is immaterial to the theory of evolution, he adds, whether this inference, "chiefly grounded on analogy . . . be accepted."

The issue between Darwin and the theologians may or may not be genuine according to the interpretation of this passage, and according to the possibility of a double use of the word "species"—for both the small number of progenitors from which all the extant types of plants and animals have evolved, *and* for a very large number of those extant types. If the theologians use the word "species" in the first sense, and Darwin in the second, they need not be in disagreement. The "view of life" which Darwin attributes to certain eminent authorities, he himself does not flatly reject, namely, that life, "with its several powers [has] been originally breathed by the Creator into a few forms or into one."

Is there common ground here in the admitted possibility that life may have been originally created in a small number of distinct forms and that these are to be regarded as species in one conception, though not in another? If so, the affirmation of a certain fixity to species would apply only to a few primordial forms. Concerning forms which have appeared with the passage of time, two questions would have to be answered. First, are they species in the philosopher's sense of distinct and immutable essences, or species in the scheme of systematic biological classification? Second, is their first appearance at an historical moment due to a special act of creation, to spontaneous generation, or to evolution from already existing organic forms by "descent with modification"?

To join issue with Darwin, it would seem to be necessary for the person answering these questions to use the word "species" in the biologist's sense and at the same time to account for the historical origin of the new species by special creation or spontaneous generation. But in the tradition of the great books, theologians like Augustine and Aquinas do not attribute to God any special acts of creation after the original production of the world, except to explain the origin of individual human souls.

"Nothing entirely new was afterwards made by God," Aquinas writes, "but all things subsequently made had in a sense been made before in the work of the six days ... Some existed not only in matter, but also in their causes, as those individual creatures that are now generated existed in the first of their kind. Species also that are new, if any such appear, existed beforehand in various active powers; so that animals, and perhaps even new species of animals, are produced by putrefaction by the power which the stars and elements received at the beginning. Again, animals of new kinds arise occasionally from the connection of individuals belonging to different species, as the mule is the offspring of an ass and a mare, but even these existed previously in their causes, in the work of the six days."

WHETHER OR NOT the theologian's conception of an historical development of the forms of life conforms to the evolutionist's hypothesis, even though it does not offer the same type of explanation, is a matter which the reader of the texts must decide. But one issue, which still remains to be discussed, can leave little doubt of a basic controversy between Darwin and some of his predecessors, especially the theologians.

It concerns the origin and nature of man. It can be stated in terms of two views of human nature. One is that man is a species in the philosophical sense, essentially and abruptly distinct from brute animals; the other, that man is a species in the biologist's sense, and differs from other animals only by continuous variation.

On the first view, *either* man would have to be created, in body as well as soul; *or* if the human species has an origin which in part or whole involves the operation of natural causes, it must be conceived as *emerging* from a lower form of life. The rational soul, Aquinas maintains, "cannot come to be except by creation." But it is not only man's soul which, according to Aquinas, "cannot be produced save immediately by God." He also insists that "the first formation of the human body could not be by the instrumentality of any created power, but was im-

mediately from God." He does not reject the suggestion of Augustine that the human body may have preexisted in other creatures *as an effect preexists in its causes*. But he adds the qualification that it preexists in its causes only in the manner of a "passive potentiality," so that "it can be produced out of pre-existing matter only by God." A Christian theologian like Aquinas might entertain the hypothesis of emergent evolution as applied to the human organism, but only with the qualification that natural causes by themselves do not suffice for the production of man.

On the second view, which is Darwin's, man and the anthropoid apes have descended from a common ancestral form which is now extinct, as are also many of the intermediate varieties in the chain of development—unless, as it is sometimes thought, certain fossil remains supply some of the missing links. "The great break in the organic chain between man and his nearest allies, which cannot be bridged over by any extinct or living species, has often been advanced," Darwin admits, "as a grave objection to the belief that man is descended from some lower form; but this objection," he continues, "will not appear of much weight to those who, from general reasons, believe in the general principle of evolution. Breaks often occur in all parts of the series, some being wide, sharp and defined, others less so in various degrees, as between the orang and its nearest allies—between the Tarsius and the other Lemuridae—between the elephant, and in a more striking manner between the Ornithorhynchus or Echidna, and all other mammals." Furthermore, Darwin insists, no one who has read Lyell's *Antiquity of Man* "will lay much stress ... on the absence of fossil remains"; for Lyell has shown "that in all the vertebrate classes the discovery of fossil remains has been a very slow and fortuitous process. Nor should it be forgotten that those regions which are the most likely to afford remains connecting man with some extinct ape-like creature, have not as yet been searched by geologists."

On either of these two conflicting views, the organic affinities between man and the most highly developed mammals would be equally intelligible, though they would be differently interpreted by Aquinas and Darwin. But according to the doctrine of man's creation by God, or even on the hypothesis of emergent evolution, there need not be—strictly speaking, there *cannot* be—a missing link between ape and man, for the emergent species is a whole step upward in the scale of life. Man is thus not one of several organic types which have become species through the extinction of intermediate varieties, and hence he differs from other animals not in an accidental, but rather in an essential manner—that is, he differs in kind rather than degree.

This issue concerning human nature is discussed from other points of view in the chapters on ANIMAL and MAN. Here the issue, stated in terms of man's origin, seems to involve three possibilities: special creation, evolution by descent from a common ancestor, and emergent evolution. But these three possibilities apply not only to man, but to the origin of every species which did not exist at the first moment of life on earth.

The hypothesis of special creation does not seem to be held by the theologians, at least not in the tradition of the great books. The hypothesis of emergent evolution raises questions concerning the factors—natural or supernatural—which must be operative to cause the emergence of higher from lower forms of organic matter. Whether or not Aristotle and Aquinas can supply an answer to these questions in terms of their theory of matter's

potentiality for a variety of forms, Darwin's theory of descent with modification seems to be definitely opposed to the hypothesis of emergent evolution. Speaking as a Darwinian, James says that "the point which as evolutionists we are bound to hold fast to is that all the new forms of being that make their appearance are really nothing more than results of the redistribution of the original and unchanging materials ... No new *natures*, no factors not present at the beginning, are introduced at any later stage."

In this dispute between two theories of evolution, does not the solution depend in every case upon a prior question concerning the relation of the species under consideration—whether or not it is possible for them to be or to have been developmentally connected by intermediate varieties? If, for example, the evidence were to prove that man and ape, as they now exist in the world, are essentially distinct—different in kind—then no intermediate varieties could ever have existed to account for their descent from a common ancestor. If, on the other hand, the evidence were to prove that they differ only in degree, then no difficulty stands in the way of the Darwinian hypothesis. The ultimate issue concerning the origin of species would thus seem to reduce to the problem of which meaning of "species" applies to the organic types in question.

OUTLINE OF TOPICS

REFERENCES

To find the passages cited, use the numbers in heavy type, which are the volume and page numbers of the passages referred to. For example, in 4 HOMER: *Iliad*, BK II [265–283] 12d, the number 4 is the number of the volume in the set; the number 12d indicates that the passage is in section d of page 12.

PAGE SECTIONS: When the text is printed in one column, the letters a and b refer to the upper and lower halves of the page. For example, in 53 JAMES: *Psychology*, 116a-119b, the passage begins in the upper half of page 116 and ends in the lower half of page 119. When the text is printed in two columns, the letters a and b refer to the upper and lower halves of the left-hand side of the page, the letters c and d to the upper and lower halves of the right-hand side of the page. For example, in 7 PLATO: *Symposium*, 163b-164c, the passage begins in the lower half of the left-hand side of page 163 and ends in the upper half of the right-hand side of page 164.

AUTHOR'S DIVISIONS: One or more of the main divisions of a work (such as PART, BK, CH, SECT) are sometimes included in the reference; line numbers, in brackets, are given in certain cases; *e.g., Iliad*, BK II [265–283] 12d.

BIBLE REFERENCES: The references are to book, chapter, and verse. When the King James and Douay versions differ in title of books or in the numbering of chapters or verses, the King James version is cited first and the Douay, indicated by a (D), follows; *e.g.*, OLD TESTAMENT: *Nehemiah*, 7:45—(D) II Esdras, 7:46.

SYMBOLS: The abbreviation "esp" calls the reader's attention to one or more especially relevant parts of a whole reference; "passim" signifies that the topic is discussed intermittently rather than continuously in the work or passage cited.

For additional information concerning the style of the references, see the Explanation of Reference Style; for general guidance in the use of *The Great Ideas*, consult the Preface.

1. The classification of animals

1a. Comparison of genealogical classification with other types of taxonomy: the phylogenetic series

8 ARISTOTLE: *Metaphysics*, BK V, CH 28 546b-c
9 ARISTOTLE: *History of Animals*, BK I, CH I [486ª15]–CH 6 [491ª5] 7b-12c esp CH I [486ª15-487ª1] 7b-d; BK V, CH I [539ª4-15] 65b; BK VIII, CH I [588ᵇ4]–CH 2 [590ª19] 114d-116c / *Parts of Animals*, BK I, CH 2-4 165d-168c / *Generation of Animals*, BK II, CH I [732ª13-733ᵇ17] 272c-274a; BK III, CH II [761ᵇ14-24] 302c-d
30 BACON: *Novum Organum*, BK II, APH 27, 158b-c
35 LOCKE: *Human Understanding*, BK III, CH VI, SECT 23 274b-c
49 DARWIN: *Origin of Species*, 31d; 63d-64d; 207a-229a,c esp 207a-212c, 215b-217b, 228c-229a,c; 238b-239a / *Descent of Man*, 331a-341d esp 332b-c, 337a-338c, 340d-341d

1b. The criteria for distinguishing races or varieties, species, genera, and all higher taxonomic groupings

8 ARISTOTLE: *Categories*, CH 13 [14ᵇ32-15ª8] 20c-d / *Topics*, BK VI, CH 6 [144ª27-145ª2] 197d-198c passim / *Metaphysics*, BK V, CH 28 546b-c

9 ARISTOTLE: *History of Animals*, BK I, CH I [486ª15]–CH 6 [491ª5] 7b-12c esp CH I [486ª15-487ª1] 7b-d; BK II, CH I [497ᵇ4-18] 19b,d-20a; BK IV, CH I [523ª30-ᵇ20] 48b,d / *Parts of Animals*, BK I, CH 4 [644ª12-ᵇ15] 167d-168a; CH 5 [645ᵇ20-28] 169c-d / *Politics*, BK IV, CH 4 [1290ᵇ25-36] 489d-490a
11 NICOMACHUS: *Arithmetic*, BK I, 813a-b
19 AQUINAS: *Summa Theologica*, PART I, Q 50, A 4, REP I 273b-274b; Q 76, A 5, REP 3 394c-396a
35 LOCKE: *Human Understanding*, BK III, CH VI 268b-283a passim, esp SECT 7 270b, SECT 36-37 279a-b; CH X, SECT 21 297a-b; CH XI, SECT 19-20 304b-d
42 KANT: *Pure Reason*, 193a-200c esp 195d-200c / *Judgement*, 579b-c
46 HEGEL: *Philosophy of History*, INTRO, 183c-d
49 DARWIN: *Origin of Species*, 12c-13a; 24a-b; 25d-29a; 30d-31d; 55c-60a passim; 64a; 136b-137a; 145c-151a passim, esp 146c-d, 147b-149a, 150c-d; 159c-160a; 207d-229a,c passim, esp 207d-210b; 234d; 241d-242a / *Descent of Man*, 331b-333a passim; 342a-350b passim, esp 342a-b, 346d-347d

2. Genetic variation in the course of generations

7 PLATO: *Republic*, BK VIII, 403b-d
9 ARISTOTLE: *Rhetoric*, BK II, CH 15 [1390ᵇ24-31] 638a-b

(2. *Genetic variation in the course of generations*.)

30 BACON: *Novum Organum*, BK II, APH 29 159b-c

36 SWIFT: *Gulliver*, PART II, 79b

42 KANT: *Judgement*, 579b-c

49 DARWIN: *Origin of Species*, 6d-7a; 9a-31d esp 9a-12a, 23c-d, 29a-31d; 53b-59d passim; 65a-79d; 99a-103c esp 100d; 149b-150c; 182d-183a; 234a-c / *Descent of Man*, 266a-271a esp 266a-268a; 275c-d; 284c-285d esp 285b-c; 347d-348c

53 JAMES: *Psychology*, 857b-858a

2a. Comparison of variation under conditions of natural and artificial breeding

30 BACON: *Novum Organum*, BK II, APH 29 159b-c / *New Atlantis*, 211c-212a

49 DARWIN: *Origin of Species*, 7a-b; 9a-31d esp 9a-b, 12a-c, 24a-c; 40a-42d; 53b-55a; 65a-66a; 117a-c; 149b-d; 233b-d / *Descent of Man*, 377a; 486d

2b. Characteristics which are more and less variable genetically: their bearing on the distinction of races, species, and genera

9 ARISTOTLE: *Parts of Animals*, BK I, CH 4 167d-168c

35 LOCKE: *Human Understanding*, BK III, CH VI, SECT 14-17 272d-273a; SECT 23-27 274b-276a passim

49 DARWIN: *Origin of Species*, 24c-25b; 71d-75b; 78c-79d; 236b-d / *Descent of Man*, 342a; 372d-375a; 486d-488b

3. The process of heredity

9 ARISTOTLE: *History of Animals*, BK VII, CH 6 [585^{b}29–586^{a}14] 111d-112b / *Parts of Animals*, BK I, CH I [640^{a}15–28] 162c-d; [641^{b}27–42] 164d-165a / *Generation of Animals*, BK I, CH 17 [721^{b}6]–CH 18 [724^{a}13] 261b-264b; BK IV, CH 3 [767^{a}36]–CH 4 [770^{b}27] 308d-312c

10 HIPPOCRATES: *Airs, Waters, Places*, par 14 15a-b / *Sacred Disease*, 155d-156a

12 LUCRETIUS: *Nature of Things*, BK I [159–191] 3a-c; [592–598] 8b; BK IV [1209–1232] 60a-b

25 MONTAIGNE: *Essays*, 367b-368a

28 HARVEY: *On Animal Generation*, 386d-387b; 391c-393b; 395a-396a; 425b-d; 446b-c; 455d-456a

36 STERNE: *Tristram Shandy*, 191b-192b

42 KANT: *Judgement*, 578d-580a esp 579b-c

49 DARWIN: *Origin of Species*, 10d-12c esp 11a-b, 11d-12a; 69c-71a passim; 222a-224b / *Descent of Man*, 375a-383a; 413d [fn 61]; 429d-430c; 500a-525a esp 500a-502a, 511a-b; 529d-531a,c; 590c-d

54 FREUD: *Beyond the Pleasure Principle*, 653b-c

3a. The inheritance of acquired characteristics: the use and disuse of parts

7 PLATO: *Laws*, BK VI, 708d-709a

9 ARISTOTLE: *History of Animals*, BK VII, CH 6 [585^{b}29–37] 111d-112a / *Generation of Animals*.

BK I, CH 17 [721^{b}18–722^{a}1] 261c-d; CH 18 [724^{a}3–7] 264a

10 HIPPOCRATES: *Airs, Waters, Places*, par 14 15a-b

20 AQUINAS: *Summa Theologica*, PART I-II, Q 81, A 2 164d-165c

25 MONTAIGNE: *Essays*, 367c

28 HARVEY: *On Animal Generation*, 455d-456a

42 KANT: *Judgement*, 580a

49 DARWIN: *Origin of Species*, 1c; 10d-12c; 66a-69c esp 66a-c, 69c; 82d-85c; 103c-116d passim, esp 115d; 119c-120a; 223c; 227c-228b / *Descent of Man*, 258d-259a; 269b-271a; 283a-284b; 299a-c; 318a-c; 319a; 320b-321b; 358d-359a; 587d-588a

53 JAMES: *Psychology*, 52a; 691a-b; 890b-897a

54 FREUD: *General Introduction*, 594d-595a / *Ego and Id*, 707d-708b

3b. The inheritance and variability of instincts

12 LUCRETIUS: *Nature of Things*, BK III [741–753] 39c-d

42 KANT: *Judgement*, 580a

49 DARWIN: *Origin of Species*, 111a; 119a-135a,c esp 121b-122d, 131c-134d; 236d-237a / *Descent of Man*, 288a-d; 292c-d; 304b,d [fn 5]; 318a-319a passim; 506d-507a

53 JAMES: *Psychology*, 691a-b; 718a-720b esp 718b; 722b-725a passim; 851b; 890b-897a

54 FREUD: *General Introduction*, 591d-592b; 594d-595b; 613a / *Beyond the Pleasure Principle*, 651d-654a / *Ego and Id*, 707c-708b esp 708b / *War and Death*, 758a-d esp 758d

3c. Interbreeding and crossbreeding: hybridism and sterility

6 HERODOTUS: *History*, BK III, 121d-122a

8 ARISTOTLE: *Metaphysics*, BK VII, CH 8 [1033^{b}29–1034^{a}1] 557a

9 ARISTOTLE: *History of Animals*, BK VI, CH 11 [566^{a}26–30] 92c; CH 23 [577^{b}5]–CH 24 [577^{b}29] 103a-c; BK VIII, CH 28 [606^{b}20–607^{a}9] 132b-c; BK IX, CH I [608^{a}31–34] 133d; CH 32 [619^{a}7–11] 144c / *Parts of Animals*, BK I, CH I [641^{b}27–39] 164d-165a / *Generation of Animals*, BK II, CH 4 [738^{b}26–35] 279c-d; CH 7 [746^{a}29–^{b}20] 287c-288a; CH 8 288c-290a,c

12 LUCRETIUS: *Nature of Things*, BK II [700–710] 23d-24a; [920–924] 26d; BK V [878–924] 72c-73a

19 AQUINAS: *Summa Theologica*, PART I, Q 73, A I, REP 3 370a-371a

28 HARVEY: *On Animal Generation*, 386d-387b; 392b-c; 395b-d; 425c

30 BACON: *Novum Organum*, BK II, APH 30 159c-d / *New Atlantis*, 211c-212a

42 KANT: *Judgement*, 581d-582a

43 MILL: *Representative Government*, 426d-427a

49 DARWIN: *Origin of Species*, 14a-c; 16b-d; 23c-d; 47c-50c; 136a-151d; 230b-231b / *Descent of Man*, 342a-b; 344b-345c esp 345b,d [fn 14]; 356a-b; 482b-483b

CROSS-REFERENCES

For: Other discussions of the classification of animals, *see* ANIMAL 2a–2c; LIFE AND DEATH 3–3b; and for the distinction between species and genera in relation to definition and classification, *see* DEFINITION 1a, 2b, 2d; RELATION 5a(4); SAME AND OTHER 3a(1).

Other considerations of the problem of heredity, *see* ANIMAL 10; FAMILY 6b; HABIT 3e.

Matters relevant to the origin of life, and of the major forms of life, *see* ANIMAL 1b, 8a–8b; LIFE AND DEATH 2, 3a.

Another treatment of the conflict of organisms in the struggle for existence, *see* OPPOSITION 3e.

Matters relevant to the origin of man and to his affinity with other animals, *see* ANIMAL 1c–1c(2); MAN 1a–1c, 4b–4c, 8–8c; MIND 3a–3b; SOUL 2c(2)–2c(3).

Evolution in relation to the idea of progress, *see* PROGRESS 2; and for matters bearing on social and mental evolution in human history, *see* HISTORY 4b; MAN 9c; MIND 3c; PROGRESS 1b, 6; TIME 8a.

ADDITIONAL READINGS

Listed below are works not included in *Great Books of the Western World*, but relevant to the idea and topics with which this chapter deals. These works are divided into two groups:

I. Works by authors represented in this collection.
II. Works by authors not represented in this collection.

For the date, place, and other facts concerning the publication of the works cited, consult the Bibliography of Additional Readings which follows the last chapter of *The Great Ideas*.

I.

AUGUSTINE. *De Genesi ad Litteram*
GOETHE. *Metamorphose der Pflanzen*
C. R. DARWIN. *Foundations of the Origin of Species*
——. *A Posthumous Essay on Instinct*
——. *The Variation of Animals and Plants Under Domestication*
ENGELS. *Dialectics of Nature*

II

LINNAEUS. *Systema Naturae*
E. DARWIN. *Zoonomia*
BUFFON. "Epochs of Nature," in *Natural History*
LAMARCK. *Zoological Philosophy*
CUVIER. *The Animal Kingdom*
CHAMBERS. *Vestiges of the Natural History of Creation*
TENNYSON. *Locksley Hall*
——. *In Memoriam*
SPENCER. *Progress: Its Law and Cause*
WALLACE. *Contributions to the Theory of Natural Selection*
LYELL. *Principles of Geology*
——. *The Geological Evidences of the Antiquity of Man*
MENDEL. *Experiments in Plant Hybridization*
BAGEHOT. *Physics and Politics*

E. HARTMANN. *Philosophy of the Unconscious*, (c) x
LEWES. *Problems of Life and Mind*
ROMANES. *Mental Evolution in Animals*
S. BUTLER. *Darwin Among the Machines*
——. *Evolution, Old and New*
——. *Note-Books*
C. S. PEIRCE. *Collected Papers*, VOL VI, par 13–17, 287–317
FRAZER. *The Golden Bough*, PART II, CH 7; PART VII
WEISMANN. *Studies in the Theory of Descent*
——. *Essays upon Heredity and Kindred Biological Problems*
——. *The Germ-Plasm*
T. H. HUXLEY. *Man's Place in Nature*
——. *Darwiniana*
——. *Evolution and Ethics*
COPE. *The Primary Factors of Organic Evolution*
FISKE. *Essays: Historical and Literary*, VOL II (9)
VRIES. *The Mutation Theory*
DEWEY. *The Influence of Darwin on Philosophy*, Title Essay
HOBHOUSE. *Mind in Evolution*
——. *Morals in Evolution*
BERGSON. *Matter and Memory*
——. *Creative Evolution*
DRIESCH. *The Science and Philosophy of the Organism*
POULTON. *Essays on Evolution*

GALTON. *Natural Inheritance*
——. *Essays in Eugenics*
D. H. SCOTT. *The Evolution of Plants*
BATESON. *Problems of Genetics*
HENDERSON. *The Fitness of the Environment*
D. W. THOMPSON. *On Growth and Form*
SHAW. *Man and Superman*
——. *Back to Methuselah*
C. L. MORGAN. *Emergent Evolution*
L. T. MORE. *The Dogma of Evolution*
SMUTS. *Holism and Evolution*
MCDOUGALL. *Modern Materialism and Emergent Evolution*
H. G. WELLS, J. HUXLEY, and G. P. WELLS. *Reproduction, Genetics and the Development of Sex*
M. R. COHEN. *Reason and Nature*, BK II, CH 3

T. H. MORGAN. *Evolution and Genetics*
——. *The Physical Basis of Heredity*
——. *The Theory of the Gene*
——. *The Scientific Basis of Evolution*
MARETT. *Head, Heart and Hands in Human Evolution*
DOBZHANSKY. *Genetics and the Origin of Species*
ADLER. *Problems for Thomists: The Problem of Species*
MAYR. *Systematics and the Origin of Species from the Viewpoint of a Zoologist*
J. S. HUXLEY. *Evolution, the Modern Synthesis*, CH 10
——. *Evolutionary Ethics*
B. RUSSELL. *Religion and Science*, CH 3
——. *Human Knowledge, Its Scope and Limits*, PART I, CH 4
KEITH. *A New Theory of Human Evolution*

Chapter 25: EXPERIENCE

INTRODUCTION

EXPERIENCE is regarded as a source of knowledge. It is also spoken of as containing what is known.

Sometimes it is identified with sense-perception; sometimes it involves more—memory and the activity of the imagination. Sometimes it includes thoughts, feelings, and desires as well, all the contents of consciousness, every phase of mental or psychic life. The temporal flow of experience is then identified with the stream of consciousness.

Experience may connote something which is private or public, subjective or objective—something which no man can share with another or something which is common to all men who live in the same world and who are acquainted with the same objects.

There are still other divisions of experience: intuitive or aesthetic experience, religious experience, and mystical experience.

Experience is said to be that which makes a man expert in an art or in a sphere of practical activity. A man is better able to do or make that which he has much experience in doing or making. He is also better able to judge what should be undertaken or what has been accomplished by others as well as by himself. In this connection experience is called practical, both because it is the result of practice and because it is a means to be used in directing action. But it is also praised for the opposite reason—as something to be enjoyed for its own sake, serving no end beyond itself unless it be the enrichment of life by the widest variety of experiences.

THESE ARE SOME of the myriad meanings of "experience"—not all, but those which occur with major emphasis in the tradition of the great books. No author uses the word in all these senses. Some of these senses are contradictory. According to the context of the discussion or the subject matter under consideration, the same author will shift from one meaning to another.

For example, in his account of the origin of science, Aristotle says that "out of sense-perception comes to be what we call memory, and out of frequently repeated memories of the same thing develops experience; for a number of memories constitute a single experience." The further product of experience—"the universal stabilized in its entirety within the soul" —is obtained by abstraction and the related act of induction or generalization. Art or science arises, Aristotle writes, "when from many notions gained by experience, one universal judgment about a class of objects is produced." Hence it can be said, he thinks, that from experience "originate the skill of the craftsman, the knowledge of the man of science, skill in the sphere of coming to be and science in the sphere of being."

In the study of nature, experience, according to Aristotle, is essential for "taking a comprehensive view of the admitted facts" which can come only from dwelling "in intimate association with nature and its phenomena." In the context of ethical or political problems, he treats experience as the basis for a prudent judgment, which is not "concerned with universals only," but "must also recognize the particulars." This fact, Aristotle writes, explains "why some who do not know," but who "have experience, are more practical than others who know." In the field of poetry, as in moral matters, it is the man of experience, according to Aristotle, who can best judge what is good or bad; he can "judge rightly the works produced . . . and understand by what means or how they are achieved, and what harmonizes with what," whereas "the inexperienced must be content if they do not fail to see whether the work has been well or ill made."

Hobbes and William James also use the word for the possession of expertness or sound judgment in practical affairs, as well as in connection with the origin or nature of knowledge. Hobbes, like Aristotle, says that "much memory, or memory of many things, is called *Experience*." He connects it with prudence. It is that knowledge, he writes, which "is not attained by reasoning, but found as well in brute beasts as in man; and is but a memory of successions of events in times past, wherein the omission of every little circumstance altering the effect, frustrates the expectation of the most prudent."

For James, however, experience is usually identified with the stream of consciousness. "Experience moulds us every hour," he writes, "and makes of our minds a mirror of the time-and-space-connections between the things in the world." He distinguishes it from conception, reasoning, or thought, and associates it with sensation and feeling. "The way of 'experience' proper is the front door," he writes, "the door of the five senses."

For the most part, experience is a term in psychological analysis, with implications for the development of theoretic knowledge or practical wisdom. That is the way it is chiefly used by Aquinas, Bacon, Descartes, Spinoza, Locke, and Hume, as well as the authors already mentioned. It is still a term in the dimension of psychology when it is used by Plotinus and by the theologians to discuss the mystical union of the soul with God.

But with Hume experience also is reality or, in his phrase, the realm of "matters of fact and existence," as opposed to "relations of ideas." He tends to identify the order of nature with the succession of events in experience, though he also seems to conceive a "pre-established harmony between the course of nature and the succession of our ideas." Nature, he goes on to say, "has implanted in us an instinct, which carries forward the thought in a correspondent course to that which she has established among external objects."

Hume's difficulty or indecision with regard to the objectivity of experience does not appear in Kant, for whom experience ceases to be psychological in any subjective sense of that word.

The order of nature—the object of the theoretic sciences—*is* the order of experience. In Kant's technical sense of *mögliche erfahrung*, nature is the realm of all possible experience. His distinction between judgments of perception and judgments of experience differentiates what for other writers is subjective sense-experience, from knowledge of reality or of objects shared by many minds.

Experience is the domain of such public objects precisely because its sense-materials are formed and ordered by the structure of the mind itself—by the forms of intuition and the categories of the understanding in a synthesis which Kant calls the "transcendental unity of apperception." Without this synthesis, experience "would be merely a rhapsody of perceptions, never fitting together into any connected text, according to rules of a thoroughly united (possible) consciousness, and therefore never subjected to the transcendental and necessary unity of apperception."

Though it may not seem possible, William James goes further than Kant in the conception of experience as a realm of being. Kant does not think that *all possible experience* circumscribes reality. "That which is not phenomenon," he writes, "cannot be an object of experience; it can never overstep the limits of sensibility, within which alone objects are presented to us." In contrast to this phenomenal reality with which he identifies experience, Kant posits a noumenal world—a world of intelligible or supra-sensible beings. To this realm, Kant writes, belong those "possible things which are not objects of our senses, but are cogitated by the understanding alone." Since the things Kant calls *ding-an-sich* are unconditioned, that is, not subject as they are in themselves to the forms of intuition or the categories of the understanding, they cannot have an empirical or sensible reality, but only an intelligible existence.

William James goes further in his *Essays in Radical Empiricism*, when he takes experience as equivalent to the whole of reality, including the actual and the possible or imaginary, the concrete and the abstract, the objective and the subjective. All differentiations must be made within experience, and experience itself is neutral with respect to all distinctions—receptive of all. There can be no meaningful distinction between experience and some other realm of existence. It is in this all-inclusive sense that experience is said to be the central term in the philosophy of John Dewey when it functions as *mind* does for Hegel, *substance* for Spinoza, or *being* for Aquinas and Aristotle.

WE HAVE GONE from one extreme to another in passing from a purely psychological to something like a metaphysical conception of experience. These are opposite in a way which suggests the contrast between the practical and the aesthetic values of experience—the actively useful and the intrinsically enjoyable. At least the metaphysical identification of experience with all existence seems analogous to the aesthetic ideal of a life which embraces every variety of experience.

There is some intimation of this ideal in the lust for adventure which motivates Odysseus and his men. Dante, in fact, finds the secret of his character in the ardor of Odysseus "to become experienced of the world, and of the vices of men, and of their virtue," which leads him "to pursue virtue and knowledge," even to the point of his "mad flight."

There is some suggestion of this ideal of experience in the unbounded vitality of Gargantua and Pantagruel, and in the enterprise of the Wife of Bath, in Chaucer's tale. But the great poetic expression of this ideal is written in *Faust*—in the worlds of experience Mephistopheles opens to the man who has wagered his soul for one ultimately satisfying moment.

Whatever to all mankind is assured,
I, in my inmost being, will enjoy and know,
Seize with my soul the highest and most deep;
Men's weal and woe upon my bosom heap;
And thus this self of mine to all their selves
    expanded,
Like them I too at last be stranded.

THE BASIC ISSUE concerning the role of experience in the origin of knowledge, especially the organized knowledge of the arts and sciences, turns on whether it is *the* source or only *a* source. It is rarely if ever supposed that nothing can be learned from experience, or that everything worth learning can come to be known entirely apart from experience. During the early centuries of Christianity, devoutly religious men preached that God has revealed to man all he needs to know in order to live well and be saved. But this extreme position rejects the constructions of reason as well as the materials of experience.

Among philosophers and scientists, concerned with what man can learn by the exercise of his own powers, the controversy over experience usually involves a distinction between the senses and the reason or intellect. As indicated in the chapters on IDEA, MIND, and SENSE, whether this distinction can be validly made is itself a major issue in the tradition of the great books. Those who make it, however, tend to regard experience as something which results from the activity of the senses. For them the problem is whether our ideas—the general notions or concepts that enter into our scientific judgments and reasoning—come from sense-experience, which either is or originates from the perception of particulars. The contrast between the particular and the universal, between percept, sense-impression, or concrete image on the one hand, and concept or abstract idea, on the other, lies at the heart of the problem.

One possibility is that the mind, by processes of abstraction or induction, somehow draws all its concepts and generalizations from experience. Aquinas is representative of this view. He adopts Aristotle's notion that the intellect is "like a tablet on which nothing is written." This *tabula rasa* depends upon the senses and the imagination for the materials out of which concepts are formed. "For the intellect to understand actually," Aquinas writes, "not only when it acquires new knowledge, but also when it uses knowledge already acquired, there is need for the act of the imagination and of the other powers."

Without experience the mind would remain empty, but experience itself does not fill the intellect with ideas. The activity of the sensitive faculty is not by itself the cause of knowledge. The perceptions and images furnished by sense-experience, Aquinas writes, "need to be made actually intelligible," and this requires the activity of the intellect, not merely its passivity in receiving impressions from experience. For this reason, he concludes, "it cannot be said that sensitive knowledge is the total and perfect cause of intellectual knowledge, but rather that it is in a way the material cause." Although experience is the indispensable source of the materials on which the intellect actively works, knowledge worthy of the name of science or of art does not come from experience alone.

Thus we see that those who, like Aquinas, affirm that there is nothing in the intellect which was not previously in the senses do not mean to imply that the materials of sense-experience reach the intellect untransformed. On the contrary, the primary contribution of the intellect is the translation of experienced particulars into universal notions. Nor do those who, like Bacon, affirm that the principles of knowledge are obtained by induction from experience necessarily imply that all knowledge is *directly* drawn from experience. To the extent that deductive reasoning is a way of learning new truths, the truths thus learned derive from experience only indirectly. Their direct source is truths already known, which must in turn have come from experience by induction.

Harvey criticizes those who misconceive the part which reason should play in relation to the senses. In the field of his own inquiries, "some weak and inexperienced persons," he writes, "vainly seek by dialectics and far-fetched arguments, either to upset or establish things that are only to be founded on anatomical demonstration, and believed on the evidence of the senses. . . . How difficult it is," he continues, "to teach those who have no experience, the things of which they have not any knowledge by their senses!"

As in geometry, so in all the sciences, according to Harvey, it is the business of reason "from things sensible to make rational demonstration of the things that are not sensible; to render credible or certain things abstruse and beyond sense from things more manifest and better known." Science depends upon both reason and sense; but sense, not reason, is the ultimate arbiter of what can be accepted as true. "To test whether anything has been well or ill advanced, to ascertain whether some falsehood does not lurk under a proposition, it is imperative on us," Harvey declares, "to bring it to the proof of sense, and to admit or reject it on the decision of sense."

THE FOREGOING views are not a necessary consequence of the distinction between the faculties of sense and reason. The theory of innate ideas presents another possibility. As expressed by Descartes, for example, this theory holds that there are "purely intellectual [ideas] which our understanding apprehends by means of a certain inborn light." Hence it would seem that experience can be dispensed with, except for its value in dealing with particulars. But for most of the writers who take this view, experience, in addition to providing acquaintance with particulars, acts as the stimulus or the occasion for the development of the seeds of knowledge implanted in the mind at birth. Although he rests his metaphysics on the innate ideas of self and God, Descartes also appeals to experimental knowledge in the sphere of natural science. To answer such a question as, "what is the nature of the magnet?" the inquirer must "first collect all the observations with which experience can supply him about this stone, and from these he will next try to deduce its character."

The extreme position which denies any role to experience can be taken only by those who think that the growth of actual knowledge from innate ideas requires no outside impetus; and perhaps also by those who make ideas the objects of the mind's intuitive apprehension. It is questionable whether anyone goes to this extreme without the qualification that, for particulars at least, sense-experience is knowledge.

The other extreme—that experience is the *only* source of knowledge—is approached by those who deny the distinction in faculties, and substitute for the duality of sense and reason, each with its characteristic contribution to human knowledge, a distinction between the function of perceiving and that of reworking the received materials. Though in different ways. Hobbes, Locke, Berkeley, and Hume all appear to take this position.

They represent, according to James, "the empirical school in psychology." He tries to summarize their view by saying that "if *all* the connections among ideas in the mind could be interpreted as so many combinations of sense-data wrought into fixity . . . then experience in the common and legitimate sense of the word would be the sole fashioner of the mind." If, in other words, all that is done with the sensations, impressions, or ideas—whatever term is used for the original data of experience—consists in their reproduction by memory and imagination, and their comparison, combination, and connection in various ways to produce complex ideas, judgments, and trains of reasoning, then the entire content of human knowledge can be reduced to elements derived exclusively from experience.

Whether this position is taken *with* or *without* qualification depends on the disposition that is made of the problem of universals or abstractions, which is more fully discussed in the chapters on IDEA, SENSE, and UNIVERSAL. Locke's treatment of abstract ideas and the special consideration given by Hume to the concepts of mathematics suggest that there are kinds or aspects of knowledge which cannot be accounted for by reduction to experience. Both men introduce a certain qualification upon their empiricism. However slight that may be, it does not appear in Hobbes and Berkeley, for they completely deny the existence of abstract or universal notions in the mind. If "abstract," "universal," or "general" applies to names alone, then the mind or understanding adds nothing to, and does not radically transform, the materials of experience.

THE CONTROVERSY concerning experience and knowledge can also be stated in terms of the opposition between the *a priori* and the *a posteriori*. These terms are sometimes used to signify what is possessed before and what comes after or from experience, and sometimes they are used to indicate, without reference to the time order, what is independent of and what is dependent upon experience.

The distinction between the *a priori* and the *a posteriori* is not made in the same way with respect to propositions or judgments and with respect to reasoning or inference. The distinction and its significance for science and philosophy are discussed in the chapters on JUDGMENT and REASONING. It is sufficient here to point out that an *a priori* judgment is not determined by experience nor does it need empirical verification.

It might at first be supposed that those who agree in thinking that experience is just one—

not the only—source of knowledge would also agree that some judgments, especially the basic propositions of science, are *a priori*. But this does not appear to be the case. Bacon, for example, like Aristotle, holds that the principles of the various sciences are derived by induction from experience. "There are and can exist," he writes, "but two ways of investigating and discovering truth. The one hurries on rapidly from the senses and particulars to the most general axioms, and from them, as principles and their supposed indisputable truth, derives and discovers the intermediate axioms. . . . The other constructs its axioms from the senses and particulars, by ascending continually and gradually, till it finally arrives at the most general axioms." All axioms, on this view, are *a posteriori* propositions.

Descartes and Kant, while differing in the terms of their analysis, think, as we have seen, that the mind itself provides the ground for certain judgments which are therefore *a priori*. It does not even seem to be the case that those who make experience the only source of knowledge regard all propositions as *a posteriori*. Hume's treatment of mathematical propositions and James' treatment of axioms or necessary truths seem to be the exceptions here.

There is still another way in which the issue can be stated. The question is whether human knowledge extends to objects beyond experience, to things or beings which are not sensible and which transcend all possible experience.

Again it might be supposed that those who take an *a posteriori* view of the origin of knowledge would also limit apprehension to things experienceable. But Aristotle and Aquinas seem to say that the origin of knowledge from experience does not restrict the knowable to things capable of being experienced. Aquinas cites Aristotle's work on the heavens to show that "we may have a scientific knowledge" of things we cannot experience, "by way of negation and by their relation to material things." He would hold what is true of astronomy to be even more the case in metaphysics and theology. Even though all our concepts are abstracted from experience, we can by means of them reach beyond the sensible world to purely intelligible realities—to immaterial and non-sensible beings or aspects of being. Locke, who may be thought even more emphatic than Aristotle or Aquinas in his insistence on the empirical origin of knowledge, goes as far as they do in affirming man's knowledge of God and the soul.

Hume, in contrast, holds that knowledge may go beyond experience only if it is knowledge of the relation of our ideas, as exemplified in the science of mathematics. Precisely because mathematics is not knowledge of matters of fact or real existence, its propositions are, according to Hume, "discoverable by the mere operation of thought, without dependence on what is anywhere existent in the universe." But with regard to "matters of fact," Hume thinks that "experience is our only guide."

Any science which claims to be knowledge of reality or existence rather than of the relations between ideas, is thus limited to the realm of experienceable objects. According as the objects of a science fall within experience, so also must its conclusions be verified by reference to experience. Experience is the ultimate test of what truth there is in the propositions of natural science. Only the propositions of mathematics can have a validity which does not require empirical verification.

By these criteria Hume challenges the validity of metaphysics or natural theology. Such disciplines claim to be knowledge of real existences, but their objects are not experienceable and their conclusions cannot be empirically verified. The existence of God and the immortality of the soul may be objects of faith, but they are not verifiable conclusions of science; nor for that matter can metaphysics give us scientific knowledge of the ultimate constitution of the physical world if that involves knowledge of substances and causes which lie behind the phenomena and outside of experience. "All the philosophy in the world," Hume writes, "and all the religion . . . will never be able to carry us beyond the usual course of experience."

Kant, like Hume, limits theoretic knowledge to mathematics and the study of nature. A metaphysics which pretends to know objects outside the phenomenal order cannot be defended. "The understanding has no power to decide," he writes, "whether other perceptions besides those which belong to the total of our possible experience [exist], and consequently whether some other sphere of matter exists." What transcends all possible experience, in other words, cannot be known, at least not in the manner of the speculative sciences; only the moral sciences, proceeding in a different fashion, have access to the realm of the supra-sensible.

Kant's position seems to resemble Hume's. But it involves a quite different conception of mathematics and natural science, especially the latter, which Kant divides into pure and empirical physics. Kant identifies "pure physic" with the "metaphysic of nature" in distinction from the "metaphysic of morals," the one a theoretic, the other a practical science. For Kant the principles of both mathematics and pure physics are *a priori* rather than *a posteriori*; the objects of both are objects of actual or possible experience.

IN THE CLASSIFICATION of sciences, the natural sciences are usually set apart from mathematics, as well as from metaphysics, by being called "empirical" or "experimental." These names signify not merely the inductive method by which the knowledge is obtained from experience; they also imply that hypotheses, however formulated, and conclusions, however reached, must be verified by the facts of experience. Newton states it as a rule of reasoning "in experimental philosophy [that] we are to look upon propositions inferred by general induction from phenomena as accurately or very nearly true, notwithstanding any contrary hypotheses that may be imagined, till such time as other phenomena occur, by which they may either be made more accurate, or liable to exceptions." In similar tenor, Lavoisier says that "we ought, in every instance, to submit our reasoning to the test of experiment, and never to search for truth but by the natural road of experiment and observation."

The two words "empirical" and "experimental" should not, however, be used interchangeably. No science can be experimental without being empirical, but, as the chapter on ASTRONOMY indicates, the converse does not appear to be true.

There seem to be three different types of experience from which knowledge can be derived: (1) the ordinary everyday experiences which men accumulate without making any special effort to investigate, explore, or test; (2) the special data of experience which men collect by undertaking methodical research and making systematic observations, with or without apparatus; and (3) experiences artificially produced by men who exercise control over the phenomena and with respect to which the observer himself determines the conditions of his experience. "Those experiences which are used to prove a scientific truth," James writes, "are for the most part artificial experiences of the laboratory, gained after the truth itself has been conjectured."

Of these three only the last is an experimental experience. The first type of experience may be employed by the scientist, but it is seldom sufficient or reliable enough for his purposes. The distinction between the empirical sciences which are and those which are not experimental turns on the difference between the second and third types.

It is not always possible for the scientist to perform experiments, as, for example, in astronomy, where the phenomena can be methodically observed and exactly recorded, but cannot be manipulated or controlled. Among the great books of natural science, the biological writings of Hippocrates, Aristotle, Galen, and Darwin, the astronomical works of Ptolemy, Copernicus, Kepler, and Newton, and the clinical studies of Freud are examples of scientific works which are more or less empirical, but not experimental. In contrast, Galileo's *Two New Sciences*, Newton's *Optics*, Harvey's *Motion of the Heart and Blood*, Lavoisier's *Elements of Chemistry*, and Faraday's *Experimental Researches in Electricity* represent empirical science which has recourse to experimentation at crucial points.

ON THE SIDE OF their production, experiments are like inventions. They do not happen by chance or without the intervention of art. They are usually performed under carefully controlled conditions and by means of apparatus artfully contrived. This explains the interplay between technology and experimental science. Progress in each occasions progress in the other.

On the side of their utility, experiments seem to serve three different though related purposes in scientific work. In those branches of physics which are both mathematical and experimental, the experiment enables the scientist to make exact measurements of the phenomena and so to determine whether one or another mathematical formulation fits the observable facts of nature. Investigating accelerated motion, Galileo seeks not only to demonstrate its definition and its properties, but also to show that "experimental results . . . agree with and exactly correspond with those properties which have been, one after another, demonstrated by us."

The experiment of the inclined plane yields measurements which exemplify those ratios between space and time that are determined by one rather than by another mathematical definition of the acceleration of a freely falling body. The experiment is thus used to decide between two competing mathematical theories, choosing that one "best fitting natural phenomena." In those sciences, Galileo writes, "in which mathematical demonstrations are applied to natural phenomena . . . the principles, once established by well-chosen experiments, become the foundation of the entire super-structure."

Concerned with the phenomena of heat, Fourier makes the same point concerning the relation of mathematics and experiments. "Mathematical analysis," he says, "can deduce from general and simple phenomena the expression of the laws of nature; but the special application of these laws to very complex effects demands a long series of exact observations" for which experiments are needed.

In addition to testing hypotheses and providing measurements whereby mathematical formulations can be applied to nature, experiments function as the source of inductions. A crucial experiment constitutes a single clear case from which a generalization can be drawn that is applicable to all cases. Newton's optical experiments are of this sort. He calls this use of experiments "the method of analysis." It consists in "making experiments and observations, and in drawing general conclusions from them by induction. . . . And although the arguing from experiments and observations by induction be no demonstration of general conclusions, yet it is the best way of arguing which the nature of things admits of."

A third use for experiments is in the exploration of new fields of phenomena, for purposes of discovery rather than of induction or verification. Hypotheses may result from such explorations, but in the first instance, the experimentation may be undertaken without the guidance of hypotheses. This employment of experimental technique is illustrated by Faraday's remark that "the science of electricity is in that state in which every part of it requires experimental investigation, not merely for the discovery of new effects, but what is just now of far more importance, the development of the means by which the old effects are produced."

Experimental exploration, apart from the direction of hypotheses, seems to be a procedure of trial and error. Experimentation in this sense reflects what Hippocrates had in mind when he spoke of "the experiment perilous." In the work of Hippocrates at the very beginning of empirical science, recourse to experiment, far from being the most prized technique, signified a lack of scientific knowledge. Only the physician who could not cure the patient by art based on science took the risk of experimenting —of proceeding by trial and error.

OUTLINE OF TOPICS

THE GREAT IDEAS

REFERENCES

To find the passages cited, use the numbers in heavy type, which are the volume and page numbers of the passages referred to. For example, in 4 HOMER: *Iliad*, BK II [265–283] 12d, the number 4 is the number of the volume in the set; the number 12d indicates that the passage is in section d of page 12.

PAGE SECTIONS: When the text is printed in one column, the letters a and b refer to the upper and lower halves of the page. For example, in 53 JAMES: *Psychology*, 116a-119b, the passage begins in the upper half of page 116 and ends in the lower half of page 119. When the text is printed in two columns, the letters a and b refer to the upper and lower halves of the left-hand side of the page, the letters c and d to the upper and lower halves of the right-hand side of the page. For example, in 7 PLATO: *Symposium*, 163b-164c, the passage begins in the lower half of the left-hand side of page 163 and ends in the upper half of the right-hand side of page 164.

AUTHOR'S DIVISIONS: One or more of the main divisions of a work (such as PART, BK, CH, SECT) are sometimes included in the reference; line numbers, in brackets, are given in certain cases; *e.g.*, *Iliad*, BK II [265–283] 12d.

BIBLE REFERENCES: The references are to book, chapter, and verse. When the King James and Douay versions differ in title of books or in the numbering of chapters or verses, the King James version is cited first and the Douay, indicated by a (D), follows; *e.g.*, OLD TESTAMENT: *Nehemiah*, 7:45—(D) II *Esdras*, 7:46.

SYMBOLS: The abbreviation "esp" calls the reader's attention to one or more especially relevant parts of a whole reference; "passim" signifies that the topic is discussed intermittently rather than continuously in the work or passage cited.

For additional information concerning the style of the references, see the Explanation of Reference Style; for general guidance in the use of *The Great Ideas*, consult the Preface.

1. Various conceptions of experience

8 ARISTOTLE: *Interpretation*, CH 1 [16^{a}3–8] 25a / *Posterior Analytics*, BK II, CH 19 [99^{b}34–100^{a}9] 136b-c / *Metaphysics*, BK I, CH 1 [980^{b}25–981^{b}9] 499b-d

19 AQUINAS: *Summa Theologica*, PART I, Q 54, A 5 288a-d; Q 58, A 3, REP 3 301d-302d; Q 64, A I, REP 5 334a-335c

20 AQUINAS: *Summa Theologica*, PART I-II, Q 112, A 5, ANS and REP 1,5 359c-360c

23 HOBBES: *Leviathan*, PART I, 50d; PART II, 128c; PART IV, 267b

25 MONTAIGNE: *Essays*, 516b-524a

28 HARVEY: *On Animal Generation*, 334a-335a

31 DESCARTES: *Rules*, XII, 22c / *Discourse*, PART I, 44a-c

31 SPINOZA: *Ethics*, PART II, AXIOM 5 373d

35 LOCKE: *Human Understanding*, BK II, CH I, SECT 1–8 121a-123a esp SECT 2 121b-c

35 BERKELEY: *Human Knowledge*, SECT 30 418c

35 HUME: *Human Understanding*, SECT IV, DIV 20–SECT VIII, DIV 74 458a-484c passim, esp SECT IV, DIV 28–SECT V, DIV 38 460d-466c, SECT VII, DIV 58–61 476a-478a

42 KANT: *Pure Reason*, 14a-15c; 45d-46a; 47d-48a; 53b-54b; 56d-57b; 58c-59b; 65d-66d; 72c-73a; 176d-177a; 225c-226b / *Practical Reason*, 308a-b

53 JAMES: *Psychology*, 185b-187b; 232b-238b esp 235a-236a; 260a-261a; 317b-318a; 852b-858b

2. Experience in relation to the acts of the mind

7 PLATO: *Meno*, 179d-183a / *Phaedo*, 224a-225a; 228a-230c / *Republic*, BK VII, 392c-393c / *Theaetetus*, 534d-536b

8 ARISTOTLE: *Posterior Analytics*, BK II, CH 19 136a-137a,c / *Metaphysics*, BK I, CH 1 499a-500b

12 LUCRETIUS: *Nature of Things*, BK IV [379–521] 49a-51a esp [469–521] 50b-51a

18 AUGUSTINE: *Confessions*, BK X, par 12–36 74b-80d esp par 14 74d-75a, par 26 78a-b, par 31 79c-d

19 AQUINAS: *Summa Theologica*, PART I, Q 54, A 5 288a-d; Q 58, A 3, REP 3 301d-302d; Q 64, A I, REP 5 334a-335c; Q 84, AA 5–8 446c-451b; PART I-II, Q 40, A 5 795d-796c; A 6, ANS and REP 3 796c-797a

20 AQUINAS: *Summa Theologica*, PART I-II, Q 112, A 5, ANS and REP 1,5 359c-360c

28 HARVEY: *On Animal Generation*, 332a-335c esp 334c-d

31 DESCARTES: *Rules*, XII, 22c-23a / *Discourse*, PART III, 50b-d / *Meditations*, I 75a-77c esp 75d-76c / *Objections and Replies*, 229d-230d

31 SPINOZA: *Ethics*, PART II, PROP 40–42 387a-388c

2a. Memory and imagination as factors in or products of experience

2b. The empirical sources of induction, abstraction, generalization

2c. The transcendental or innate structure of the mind as a condition of experience

(2. *Experience in relation to the acts of the mind.*)

2d. The *a priori* and *a posteriori* in judgment and reasoning

8 ARISTOTLE: *Posterior Analytics*, BK I, CH 3 [72^{b}25–33] 99c; BK II, CH 19 136a-137a,c / *Physics*, BK I, CH I 259a-b / *Metaphysics*, BK I, CH I 499a-500b; BK VII, CH 3 [1029^{a}33–^{b}12] 552a

19 AQUINAS: *Summa Theologica*, PART I, Q 2, A I, REP 2 10d-11d; A 2 11d-12c; Q 3, A 5, ANS 17c-18b

20 AQUINAS: *Summa Theologica*, PART I–II, Q 112, A 5, ANS and REP 1,5 359c-360c

28 HARVEY: *On Animal Generation*, 332a-335c

31 DESCARTES: *Rules*, II, 2d-3a / *Meditations*, III 81d-89a esp 88c-d / *Objections and Replies*, PROP I–II 132b-c; 215b-c; 224b,d

31 SPINOZA: *Ethics*, PART I, PROP II 358b-359b; PART II, PROP 40, SCHOL 2 388a-b

35 LOCKE: *Human Understanding*, BK I, CH I, SECT 15–16 98d-99c; SECT 23 101b-102a; BK IV, CH IX, SECT I 349a; CH XI, SECT 13–14 357d-358c

35 HUME: *Human Understanding*, SECT IV, DIV 20–SECT V, DIV 38 458a-466c esp SECT IV, DIV 30, 462a; SECT X, DIV 89 490b-c; SECT XI 497b-503c passim; SECT XII, DIV 131–132 508d-509d passim

42 KANT: *Pure Reason*, 14a-108a,c esp 14a-20c, 23a-24a, 25b-26b, 27b-28b, 29d-33d, 35b-36a, 41c-42b, 46a-48d, 57d-59b, 64b-66d; 108b-d; 110a-113b; 115d-120c; 123d-124b; 134c-d; 141d-142c [antithesis]; 146a; 170d-171a; 172c-173a; 174a; 177d; 179c-182b; 190c-191a; 192a-b; 199a; 209b-d; 211c-218d; 224a-227a; 228b-d; 230c-231c; 236d-237a; 244d-245a / *Fund. Prin. Metaphysic of Morals*, 253a-254d esp 253b, 254c-d; 268b-d; 283b / *Practical Reason*, 307d-308b; 309b-d; 329d-330c / *Science of Right*, 405b-d / *Judgement*, 461a-475d esp 465c-467d, 474b-475d; 570b-572b; 600d-603d esp 603a-b

43 MILL: *Utilitarianism*, 445d-447a passim; 475b,d [fn 1]

46 HEGEL: *Philosophy of History*, INTRO, 182d-183c

53 JAMES: *Psychology*, 851a-890a esp 851a-b, 859a-861b, 889a-890a

3. Experience in relation to organized knowledge: art and science

7 PLATO: *Gorgias*, 253a

8 ARISTOTLE: *Prior Analytics*, BK I, CH 30 [46^a 18–28] 64a / *Posterior Analytics*, BK II, CH 19 136a-137a,c / *Heavens*, BK III, CH 7 [306^{a}6–18] 397b-c / *Generation and Corruption*, BK I, CH 2 [316^{a}5–14] 411c-d / *Metaphysics*, BK I, CH I 499a-500b

9 ARISTOTLE: *Ethics*, BK X, CH 9 [1180^{b}13–1181^b 12] 435b-436a,c

10 HIPPOCRATES: *Ancient Medicine*, par 1–8 1a-3b / *Aphorisms*, SECT I, par I 131a

21 DANTE: *Divine Comedy*, PARADISE, II [46–105] 108b-d

23 HOBBES: *Leviathan*, PART I, 60c-61a; PART II, 128d-129b

28 HARVEY: *Circulation of the Blood*, 322d-323d; 324c-d / *On Animal Generation*, 331b-335c esp 334c-d

30 BACON: *Advancement of Learning*, 16a / *Novum Organum*, BK I, APH 98 126d-127b

31 DESCARTES: *Rules*, II, 2d-3a / *Discourse*, PART I, 44a-c; PART VI, 61b-d / *Meditations*, I 75a-77c esp 75d-76c

31 SPINOZA: *Ethics*, PART II, PROP 40, SCHOL 2 388a-b

35 PASCAL: *Pensées*, 396 240b

35 LOCKE: *Human Understanding*, BK II, CH I, SECT 1–8 121a-123a esp SECT 2 121b-c; CH XI, SECT 15 146d-147a

35 BERKELEY: *Human Knowledge*, SECT 30–32 418c-419a; SECT 43 420d

35 HUME: *Human Understanding*, SECT IV, DIV 20–SECT V, DIV 38 458a-466c passim, esp SECT V, DIV 36, 465a-d [fn 1]; 465c; SECT VII, DIV 60 477a-c; SECT VIII, DIV 65 479b-480a

42 KANT: *Pure Reason*, 14a-15c; 72c-85d esp 72c-74b, 82a-b / *Judgement*, 562d-563b

44 BOSWELL: *Johnson*, 281b-c

47 GOETHE: *Faust*, PART I [522–601] 15a-16b

54 FREUD: *General Introduction*, 449c-451b

3a. Particular experiences and general rules as conditions of expertness or skill: the contrast between the empiric and the artist

7 PLATO: *Charmides*, 6d-7b / *Phaedrus*, 136b-c / *Gorgias*, 253a; 261a-262a; 280d-282b; 287d-288b / *Republic*, BK I, 303a-304a / *Theaetetus*, 516a / *Philebus*, 633a-c / *Laws*, BK IV, 684c-685a; BK IX, 745a-b

8 ARISTOTLE: *Prior Analytics*, BK I, CH 30 [46^a 18–28] 64a / *Posterior Analytics*, BK II, CH 19 136c / *Metaphysics*, BK I, CH I [100^{a}3–9] 136c / *Metaphysics*, BK I, CH I [980^{b}25–982^{a}1] 499b-500b

9 ARISTOTLE: *Ethics*, BK I, CH 13 [1102^{a}15–26] 347c; BK II, CH I 348b,d-349b passim; BK III, CH 8 [1116^{b}3–15] 362d-363a; BK VI, CH I [1138^{b}25–34] 387b; BK X, CH 9 [1180^{b}13–1181^{b}12] 435b-436a,c / *Politics*, BK III, CH II [1281^{b}40–1282^{a}6] 479d

10 HIPPOCRATES: *Ancient Medicine*, par 1–8 1a-3b; par 20 7b-d / *Epidemics*, BK III, SECT III, par 16 59b-c / *Surgery*, par I 70b / *Articulations*, par 10, 94d / *The Law* 144a-d

10 GALEN: *Natural Faculties*, BK II, CH 9, 195c-196a

18 AUGUSTINE: *Christian Doctrine*, BK IV, CH 3 676a-d

23 HOBBES: *Leviathan*, PART I, 60c-d

25 MONTAIGNE: *Essays*, 66a-b; 368a-377d passim, esp 377a-d; 450d-451a; 523c-524a

(*4. Experience as measuring the scope of human knowledge. 4a. The knowability of that which is outside experience: the suprasensible, the noumenal or transcendent.*)

19 AQUINAS: *Summa Theologica*, PART I, Q 2, AA 1–2 10d-12c; QQ 12–13 50b-75b; Q 32 175d-180d; Q 77, A 1, REP 7 399c-401b; Q 84, A 5 446c-447c; A 6, REP 3 447c-449a; QQ 87–88 464d-473a; Q 89, A 2 475a-d; Q 94, AA 1–2 501d-504a

20 AQUINAS: *Summa Theologica*, PART I–II, Q 112, A 5 359c-360c; PART III SUPPL, Q 75, A 3, REP 2 938a-939c

21 DANTE: *Divine Comedy*, PARADISE, IV [28–48] 111a

23 HOBBES: *Leviathan*, PART I, 54b-c; 78d-79a; PART II, 163a-b

25 MONTAIGNE: *Essays*, 291b-294b

30 BACON: *Advancement of Learning*, 39d-40a; 41b-d; 96d-97b

31 DESCARTES: *Discourse*, PART IV, 53b-54b / *Objections and Replies*, 215b-c

32 MILTON: *Paradise Lost*, BK XII [552–587] 331a-332a

35 LOCKE: *Human Understanding*, BK II, CH I, SECT 2–10 121b-123d; SECT 19–24 126a-127c; CH XII, SECT 1–2 147b-d; CH XXIII, SECT 2–3 204b-d; SECT 6–7 205b-206a; SECT 29 211d-212a; SECT 32–37 212c-214b; BK III, CH VI 268b-283a passim, esp SECT 9–11 270d-271d; BK IV, CH III, SECT 14 316b-d; SECT 16 317a-c; SECT 25–29 321a-323a passim; CH XII, SECT 9–12 360d-362c passim; CH XVI, SECT 12 370b-371a

35 BERKELEY: *Human Knowledge*, SECT 27 418a-b; SECT 135–142 440a-441c

35 HUME: *Human Understanding*, SECT II 455b-457b; SECT IV, DIV 20–SECT V, DIV 38 458a-466c passim; SECT VIII, DIV 81 487a; SECT XI 497b-503c passim; SECT XII, DIV 119, 505a-b; DIV 127 507b-c

40 GIBBON: *Decline and Fall*, 308c-d

42 KANT: *Pure Reason*, 1a-4a,c; 15c-16c; 19a; 19d-20c esp 20a; 25b-26b; 27b-33d; 49c-59b esp 53b-54b; 86c-88c; 89c-91d; 93c-99a; 101b-108a,c; 112b-d; 113c-115a; 117b-118a; 119a-209d esp 121a-128b, 130b-145c, 153a-c, 164a-165c, 173b-192d, 200c-209d; 218d-223d; 227a-235a esp 231c-232b; 247a-b / *Fund. Prin. Metaphysic of Morals*, 260d-261b; 281c-282d; 283d-287d / *Practical Reason*, 291a-293b esp 292a-c; 296a-d; 307d-314d esp 307d-308b, 309b, 310d-311d; 320c-321b; 327d-329a; 335c-337a,c; 337a-c; 349b-353d / *Intro. Metaphysic of Morals*, 383c-d; 383b,d-384a,c / *Judgement*, 461a-c; 465a-c; 474b-475d; 500c-d; 506d-507a; 510b-c; 543a; 543d-544a; 547b-d; 551a-552c; 560c; 562a-564c; 570b-572b esp 570c-571c; 574b-577a; 579a; 581a-b; 584c-d; 588d-589c; 594d [fn 1]; 599d-600d; 603a-604b; 606d-607c; 609b-610a; 611c-613a,c

4b. Verification by experience: experience as the ultimate test of truth

7 PLATO: *Republic*, BK VII, 395c-396d; BK IX, 421a-422b

8 ARISTOTLE: *Heavens*, BK I, CH 3 [270^{b}1–13] 361c-d; BK III, CH 7 [306^{a}6–18] 397b-c / *Soul*, BK I, CH I [402^{b}15–403^{a}2] 631d-632a

9 ARISTOTLE: *Parts of Animals*, BK III, CH 4 [666^{a}7–10] 193d / *Motion of Animals*, CH I [698^{a}10–15] 233a / *Generation of Animals*, BK III, CH 10 [760^{b}27–35] 301d-302a / *Ethics*, BK II, CH 7 [1107^{a}27–32] 352d-353a; BK X, CH I [1172^{a}34–^{b}7] 426b; CH 8 [1179^{a}17–22] 433d-434a / *Politics*, BK II, CH 5 [1264^{a}1–11] 459a-b; BK VII, CH I [1323^{a}33–^{b}7] 527b

12 LUCRETIUS: *Nature of Things*, BK I [418–426] 6b; [693–701] 9c; BK IV [469–521] 50b-51a

23 HOBBES: *Leviathan*, PART III, 165a

25 MONTAIGNE: *Essays*, 260c-261c; 285c-288a; 291b-292d

28 GALILEO: *Two New Sciences*, THIRD DAY, 200a-b

28 HARVEY: *Motion of the Heart*, 268d / *Circulation of the Blood*, 322d-323d; 324c-d / *On Animal Generation*, 331b-332a; 357b

30 BACON: *Advancement of Learning*, 43d-44c / *Novum Organum* 105a-195d esp BK II 137a-195d

31 DESCARTES: *Rules*, II, 2d-3a; XII, 22c-23a / *Discourse*, PART VI, 66a-b / *Meditations*, I 75a-77c / *Objections and Replies*, 229d-230d

33 PASCAL: *Pensées*, 9 173b

34 NEWTON: *Principles*, BK III, RULE III 270b-271a

35 HUME: *Human Understanding*, SECT II, DIV 14 456b; SECT X 488d-497b passim, esp DIV 86–91 488d-491c; SECT XI, DIV 110 501a-b

42 KANT: *Pure Reason*, 36a-37a esp 36b-c; 77b-d; 85b-d; 86b-87c; 91d-93b; 114d-115a; 146a-149d; 153a-c; 231b-c

43 FEDERALIST: NUMBER 6, 40a-b; NUMBER 20, 78a-b

43 MILL: *Utilitarianism*, 450b-c; 461c-462a; 463c-d

44 BOSWELL: *Johnson*, 129a

45 FARADAY: *Researches in Electricity*, 774d

51 TOLSTOY: *War and Peace*, EPILOGUE II, 684a

53 JAMES: *Psychology*, 647b-648b; 863a-865a; 879b-880b [fn 2]; 881a-b

54 FREUD: *New Introductory Lectures*, 819d-820a; 879c

5. The theory of experimentation in scientific method

10 GALEN: *Natural Faculties*, BK III, CH 2 199d-200a

25 MONTAIGNE: *Essays*, 377a-d

28 HARVEY: *Motion of the Heart*, 267b,d-268d / *On Animal Generation*, 331b-337a,c

30 BACON: *Advancement of Learning*, 34b; 42a-c / *Novum Organum* 105a-195d / *New Atlantis*, 210d-214d

31 DESCARTES: *Discourse*, PART VI, 61c-62c

34 NEWTON: *Optics*, BK III, 543a-b

42 KANT: *Pure Reason*, 5d-6c

45 LAVOISIER: *Elements of Chemistry*, PART I, 22c

45 FOURIER: *Theory of Heat*, 175b

45 FARADAY: *Researches in Electricity*, 774d

50 MARX: *Capital*, 6c-d

53 JAMES: *Psychology*, 385a-b; 677b

54 FREUD: *New Introductory Lectures*, 879c

5a. Experimental exploration and discovery: the formulation of hypotheses

28 GILBERT: *Loadstone*, PREF, 1a-b; BK I, 6a-7a; BK II, 27c-d

28 GALILEO: *Two New Sciences*, FIRST DAY, 131a-138b; 157b-171b passim; THIRD DAY, 203d-205b; 207d-208a

28 HARVEY: *Motion of the Heart*, 273c-d; 280c-d; 285c-d / *On Animal Generation*, 331b-333d; 336b-d

30 BACON: *Advancement of Learning*, 16a; 30d-31a; 34b; 42a-c / *Novum Organum*, PREF 105a-106d; BK I 107a-136a,c esp APH 8 107c-d, APH 50 111b, APH 64 114b, APH 70 116b-117a, APH 82 120d-121b, APH 99–100 127b-c, APH 121 132b-d; BK II 137a-195d passim / *New Atlantis*, 214a-b

31 DESCARTES: *Discourse*, PART VI, 61d-62c; 66a-b

33 PASCAL: *Vacuum*, 359a-365b / *Equilibrium of Liquids* 390a-403a passim, esp 390a-392a

34 NEWTON: *Principles*, BK III, RULE III–IV 270b-271b; GENERAL SCHOL, 371b-372a / *Optics*, BK I, 379a; 386b-455a; BK II, 457a-470a; BK II–III, 496a-516a; BK III, 543a-b

35 LOCKE: *Human Understanding*, BK III, CH VI, SECT 46–47 281d-282b; BK IV, CH XII, SECT 9–13 360d-362d

38 ROUSSEAU: *Inequality*, 329d-330a

42 KANT: *Intro. Metaphysic of Morals*, 387a-b

45 LAVOISIER: *Elements of Chemistry*, PREF, 2a-b; PART I, 10d-12d; 17a-20d esp 17a; 22c-24a esp 23c; 29d-33b

45 FOURIER: *Theory of Heat*, 169a; 172a; 175b; 184a

45 FARADAY: *Researches in Electricity*, 440b,d; 607a,c; 659a; 774d

49 DARWIN: *Origin of Species*, 136b-139a passim

53 JAMES: *Psychology*, 126a-127a; 348a-357b passim; 385a-b; 677b

54 FREUD: *Instincts*, 412a-b

5b. Experimental verification: the testing of hypotheses

6 HERODOTUS: *History*, BK II, 49a-c

10 GALEN: *Natural Faculties*, BK I, CH 13 173d-177a passim; BK III, CH 2 199d-200a; CH 4 201b-202c; CH 8 205a-207b

21 DANTE: *Divine Comedy*, PARADISE, II [46–105] 108b-d

28 GALILEO: *Two New Sciences*, FIRST DAY, 148c-149c; 166d-168a; THIRD DAY, 203d-205b esp 205b; 207d-208c

28 HARVEY: *Motion of the Heart*, 268d-273c esp 268d, 273c; 286b-304a,c esp 286b-c, 295d-296a / *Circulation of the Blood*, 311c-312c; 324c-d

30 BACON: *Advancement of Learning*, 34b / *Novum Organum*, BK II, APH 36 164a-168d

31 DESCARTES: *Discourse*, PART VI, 61d-62c; 66a-b

33 PASCAL: *Vacuum*, 368b-370a / *Great Experiment* 382a-389b passim / *Weight of Air*, 404a-405b; 425a-429a

34 NEWTON: *Principles*, LAWS OF MOTION, SCHOL, 19b-22a; BK II, GENERAL SCHOL 211b-219a; PROP 40, SCHOL 239a-246b / *Optics*, BK I, 392a-396b; 408a-410b; 412a-416b; 453a-455a; BK III, 543a-b

34 HUYGENS: *Light*, PREF, 551b-552a

35 LOCKE: *Human Understanding*, BK IV, CH XII, SECT 13 362c-d

45 LAVOISIER: *Elements of Chemistry*, PREF, 2a-b; PART I, 32a-33a

45 FOURIER: *Theory of Heat*, 181b

45 FARADAY: *Researches in Electricity*, 385b-c; 440b,d; 467a-b

49 DARWIN: *Origin of Species*, 12b-c; 149d-150a

53 JAMES: *Psychology*, 865a

54 FREUD: *Interpretation of Dreams*, 291d-292a / *New Introductory Lectures*, 815a-b

5c. Experimental measurement: the application of mathematics

7 PLATO: *Republic*, BK VII, 396c-d

16 PTOLEMY: *Almagest*, BK I, 24b-26a; BK II, 38b-39b; BK V, 143a-144a; 166a-167b

16 COPERNICUS: *Revolutions of the Heavenly Spheres*, BK II, 558b-559b; 567b; 586b-589a; BK IV, 705b-706a

28 GILBERT: *Loadstone*, BK IV, 85c-89c; BK V, 92a-93b

28 GALILEO: *Two New Sciences*, FIRST DAY, 136d-137c; 148d-149c; 164a-166c; THIRD DAY, 207d-208c

28 HARVEY: *Motion of the Heart*, 286c-288c

30 BACON: *Advancement of Learning*, 46b-c / *Novum Organum*, BK II, APH 44–47 175d-179c

34 NEWTON: *Principles*, LAWS OF MOTION, SCHOL, 20a-22a; BK I, PROP 69, SCHOL, 131a; BK II, GENERAL SCHOL 211b-219a; PROP 40 and SCHOL 237b-246b

34 HUYGENS: *Light*, CH I, 554b-557b

35 HUME: *Human Understanding*, SECT IV, DIV 27 460c-d

45 LAVOISIER: *Elements of Chemistry*, PART I, 14b-c; 17a-20b; 22d-24a; 30a-32d; 33b-36a; 41a-44d; PART III, 87d-90a; 91a-95a; 96b-103b

45 FOURIER: *Theory of Heat*, 175b; 184b-185b

45 FARADAY: *Researches in Electricity*, 277d-279a; 316b-318c; 366d-371d; 444a-451a; 465d-467a,c; 768d-773d; 778b,d-793c

53 JAMES: *Psychology*, 56a-66a esp 61b-64a; 126a; 265a-268b; 341a-344b; 348a-359a

6. The man of experience in practical affairs

6a. Experience as indispensable to sound judgment and prudence

APOCRYPHA: *Ecclesiasticus*, 25:3-6; 34:9-11—(D) OT, *Ecclesiasticus*, 25:5-8; 34:9-12

4 HOMER: *Iliad*, BK IX [430-605] 61c-63b

5 SOPHOCLES: *Philoctetes* [50-122] 182d-183b

6 HERODOTUS: *History*, BK VII, 238b-c

6 THUCYDIDES: *Peloponnesian War*, BK I, 383d-384a; BK VII, 555b

7 PLATO: *Republic*, BK III, 337b-338a; BK V, 366a-c; BK VII, 400d-401c; BK IX, 421a-422b / *Laws*, BK I, 645b-652d

9 ARISTOTLE: *Ethics*, BK I, CH 3 [1094^{b}29-1095^{a}12] 340a-b; CH 4 [1095^{a}30-^{b}12] 340c-d; BK III, CH 8 [1116^{b}3-15] 362d-363a; BK VI, CH 7 [1141^{b}14-23] 390c-d; CH 8 [1142^{a}12-19] 391b; CH 11 392c-393b passim; BK X, CH 9 [1180^{b}13-1181^{b}12] 435b-436a,c / *Rhetoric*, BK II, CH 12 [1389^{a}3]-CH 14 [1390^{b}11] 636b-638a passim

10 HIPPOCRATES: *Articulations*, par 10, 94d

12 EPICTETUS: *Discourses*, BK I, CH 8, 114a-b

14 PLUTARCH: *Fabius-Pericles*, 154a-d

20 AQUINAS: *Summa Theologica*, PART I-II, Q 95, A 1, REP 2 226c-227c

22 CHAUCER: *Troilus and Cressida*, BK I, STANZA 90-93 12b-13a / *Knight's Tale* [2438-2452] 200a

23 HOBBES: *Leviathan*, PART I, 53c-54a; 60c-d; 66d-67b; 67d-68a

25 MONTAIGNE: *Essays*, 24a-c; 55d-62a esp 61a-62a; 63d-75a esp 66b-69d; 176c-180b; 450d-451a; 520b-522d

27 SHAKESPEARE: *Troilus and Cressida*, ACT II, SC II [163-173] 115b

29 CERVANTES: *Don Quixote*, PART II, 340b-343a; 345a-348c; 352b-356d; 360d-364a

30 BACON: *Advancement of Learning*, 5b-6a; 79c-80a; 86b-89b

31 DESCARTES: *Discourse*, PART I, 43a; 44a-c; PART III, 50b-d

35 BERKELEY: *Human Knowledge*, SECT 30-31 418c-d

35 HUME: *Human Understanding*, SECT V, DIV 36, 465a-d [fn 1]; 465c; SECT VIII, DIV 65, 479d-480a

37 FIELDING: *Tom Jones*, 99d-100a; 274c

42 KANT: *Practical Reason*, 305d / *Intro. Metaphysic of Morals*, 387b

43 FEDERALIST: NUMBER 2, 32b-d; NUMBER 72, 217d

43 MILL: *Liberty*, 287b-c / *Utilitarianism*, 448d; 450a-c; 456a-d

44 BOSWELL: *Johnson*, 106d

49 DARWIN: *Descent of Man*, 592d-593a

51 TOLSTOY: *War and Peace*, BK V, 211a-213a; BK VII, 277a-278a; BK X, 424a-b; BK XII, 559d; BK XIII, 584c-585b

53 JAMES: *Psychology*, 13a-15a; 886b-888a

6b. The role of experience in politics: the lessons of history

6 HERODOTUS: *History*, BK V, 178a-180a; BK VII, 225c-d

6 THUCYDIDES: *Peloponnesian War*, BK I, 354b-c; BK IV, 451a-b

7 PLATO: *Gorgias*, 288b-289b / *Republic*, BK VII, 400d-401b

9 ARISTOTLE: *Ethics*, BK I, CH 3 [1094^{b}27-1095^{a}11] 340a; BK VI, CH 8 390d-391c; BK X, CH 9 [1180^{b}13-1181^{b}24] 435b-436a,c / *Politics*, BK I, CH 5 [1264^{a}1-11] 459a-b; BK VII, CH 10 [1329^{a}40-^{b}35] 533d-534b / *Rhetoric*, BK I, CH 4 [1359^{b}19-1360^{a}37] 599d-600d

13 VIRGIL: *Aeneid*, BK I [441-493] 115a-116b; BK XI [243-295] 334b-336a

14 PLUTARCH: *Pericles*, 121a-122b / *Fabius* 141a-154a,c / *Timoleon*, 195a-b / *Flamininus*, 302d-303a / *Alexander*, 540b,d-549c / *Demosthenes*, 692d-695d / *Demetrius*, 726a-d

15 TACITUS: *Annals*, BK IV, 71d-72b / *Histories*, BK I, 189a-190b

23 MACHIAVELLI: *Prince* 1a-37d

23 HOBBES: *Leviathan*, PART I, 67d-68a; PART II, 112c-d; 128c-129b; PART III, 165a

25 MONTAIGNE: *Essays*, 24a-25c; 68b-69d; 198c-200d; 450d-451a; 455d-456c

30 BACON: *Advancement of Learning*, 4c-7c; 85a-c; 94b-d

35 LOCKE: *Civil Government*, CH VIII, SECT 107 49b-d

35 HUME: *Human Understanding*, SECT V, DIV 36, 465a-d [fn 1]; 465c

38 ROUSSEAU: *Social Contract*, BK III, 411c

40 GIBBON: *Decline and Fall*, 284a-c; 449a; 632a-634a,c passim

41 GIBBON: *Decline and Fall*, 13d; 194b; 326d

42 KANT: *Fund. Prin. Metaphysic of Morals*, 266d [fn 2]

43 FEDERALIST: NUMBER 6, 39a; NUMBER 28, 96c; NUMBER 38, 121b-122b; NUMBER 53, 168b-169b; NUMBER 72, 217d-218a; NUMBER 85, 258d-259a

43 MILL: *Liberty*, 320a-323a,c passim / *Representative Government*, 357b-d

46 HEGEL: *Philosophy of History*, INTRO, 155b-d; PART IV, 367d-368b

50 MARX: *Capital*, 7b

7. Mystical or religious experience: experience of the supernatural

OLD TESTAMENT: *Genesis*, 15; 17:1-19:23; 22:1-18; 26:1-6; 28:10-22; 32:34-32; 46:1-4 / *Exodus*, 3-4; 7-11; 19; 24 / *Numbers*, 12; 22:22-35 / *Joshua*, 3:7-8; 5:13-6:5—(D) *Josue*, 3:7-8; 5:13-6:5 / *Judges*, 6:11-40; 13 / *I Samuel*, 3; 16—(D) *I Kings*, 3; 16 / *I Kings*, 3:5-15; 9:1-9; 19—(D) *III Kings*, 3:5-15; 9:1-9; 19 / *I Chronicles*, 17—(D) *I Paralipomenon*, 17 / *Job*, 38:1-42:8 / *Isaiah*, 6—(D) *Isaias*, 6 / *Jeremiah*, 1—(D) *Jeremias*, 1 / *Ezekiel*, 1-4 esp 1; 8-12 esp 10; 40–48 passim—(D) *Ezechiel*, 1–4 esp 1; 8–12 esp 10; 40–48 passim / *Daniel*, 7–12 / *Hosea*, 1–3—(D) *Osee*, 1–3 / *Amos*, 7–8 / *Zechariah*, 1–6—(D) *Zacharias*, 1–6

NEW TESTAMENT: *Matthew*, 1:20–25; 3:16–17; 17:1–9; 28 / *Luke*, 1:1–38; 2:8–15,25–35 / *Acts*, 2:2–4; 7:55–56; 9:3–8; 10; 11:5–10; 12:7–11; 16:9; 18:9–11; 22:6–11; 23:11; 26:13–18; 27:21–25—(D) *Acts*, 2:2–4; 7:55; 9:3–8; 10; 11:5–10; 12:7–11; 16:9; 18:9–11; 22:6–11; 23:11; 26:13–18; 27:21–25 / *II Corinthians*, 12:1–9 / *Revelation*—(D) *Apocalypse*

4 HOMER: *Odyssey*, BK XI 243a-249d

5 AESCHYLUS: *Prometheus Bound* [640–886] 46d-49c

5 SOPHOCLES: *Oedipus at Colonus* [1500–1666] 127d-129b

5 EURIPIDES: *Iphigenia Among the Tauri* [1–41] 411a-b / *Bacchantes* 340a-352a,c

5 ARISTOPHANES: *Clouds* [250–365] 490d-492c / *Frogs* 564a-582a,c / *Plutus* [620–747] 636d-637d

6 HERODOTUS: *History*, BK VII, 218d-220a

13 VIRGIL: *Aeneid*, BK VI 211a-235a

17 PLOTINUS: *First Ennead*, TR VI, CH 4 23a-b / *Fifth Ennead*, TR III, CH 17 226a-c; TR V, CH 10–12 233b-234d; TR VIII, CH 10–12 244c-246a / *Sixth Ennead*, TR VII, CH 34–36 338b-339d; TR IX, CH 4 356a-b; CH 8–11 358b-360d

18 AUGUSTINE: *Confessions*, BK VIII, par 28–30 60d-61c; BK IX, par 23–25 68a-c; BK X, par 65 87d-88a / *City of God*, BK IX, CH 16 294a-295a; BK X, CH 13 307b-c; BK XVI, CH 6 426c-427a esp 426d; BK XXII, CH 29 614b-616d

19 AQUINAS: *Summa Theologica*, PART I, Q 12, A 9 58b-59a; A 11, REP 2 59d-60d; PART I–II, Q 28, A 3, ANS 742a-d

20 AQUINAS: *Summa Theologica*, PART I–II, Q 112, A 5, ANS and REP 1,5 359c-360c; PART III, Q 9, A 2 764c-765a; Q 10 767b-772a; PART III SUPPL, Q 92, A 1 1025c-1032b

21 DANTE: *Divine Comedy* esp PARADISE, XXX-XXXIII 151d-157d

22 CHAUCER: *Prioress's Tale* [13,418–620] 392a-395b esp [13,577–592] 394b-395a

23 HOBBES: *Leviathan*, PART II, 160b; PART III, 165d-166a; 174d-176d; 183d-185c

27 SHAKESPEARE: *Hamlet*, ACT I, SC I 29a-31c; SC II [160–258] 33b-34b; SC IV–V 35d-39a / *Macbeth*, ACT I, SC III [1–88] 285b-286b; ACT IV, SC I 300b-302b / *Tempest* 524a-548d

30 BACON: *Advancement of Learning*, 95d-96c

33 PASCAL: *Pensées*, 277–288 222b-224b

40 GIBBON: *Decline and Fall*, 81a; 189b-191a; 294d-296b; 605b-d

41 GIBBON: *Decline and Fall*, 476b-477a

42 KANT: *Practical Reason*, 320c-321b

47 GOETHE: *Faust*, PART I [354–514] 11a-14b; [1238–1321] 30b-32b; [2337–2604] 56b-63b; [3835–4398] 93b-108b; PART II [7005–8487] 171b-206b

51 TOLSTOY: *War and Peace*, BK III, 156d; 162b-164a,c; BK V, 219b-220a; BK XI, 525c-526b; BK XV, 631a-c

52 DOSTOEVSKY: *Brothers Karamazov*, BK V, 127b-137c; BK VII, 189a-191a,c

53 JAMES: *Psychology*, 847b-848a

54 FREUD: *Group Psychology*, 688a-b

8. Variety of experience as an ideal of human life

APOCRYPHA: *Ecclesiasticus*, 34:9–11—(D) OT, *Ecclesiasticus*, 34:9–12

4 HOMER: *Odyssey* 183a-322d esp BK I [1–10] 183a

7 PLATO: *Republic*, BK VIII, 409b-411d

12 EPICTETUS: *Discourses*, BK I, CH 6, 111c-112a

12 AURELIUS: *Meditations*, BK VIII, SECT I 285a-b

18 AUGUSTINE: *Confessions*, BK X, par 54–57 85a-86a

21 DANTE: *Divine Comedy*, HELL, XXVI [49–142] 38c-39c

22 CHAUCER: *Wife of Bath's Prologue* [5583–6410] 256a-269b

24 RABELAIS: *Gargantua and Pantagruel*

25 MONTAIGNE: *Essays*, 66b-69d; 74b-75a; 107a-112d; 458b-462c; 471a-472a; 478c-479c

26 SHAKESPEARE: *Two Gentlemen of Verona*, ACT I, SC III [1–44] 232c-233a / *1st Henry IV* 434a-466d / *2nd Henry IV* 467a-502d / *Henry V*, ACT I, SC I [22–66] 533b-c / *As You Like It*, ACT IV, SC I [21–41] 617b-c

31 DESCARTES: *Discourse*, PART I, 43a; 44a-c

33 PASCAL: *Pensées*, 34–38 177a-b

35 HUME: *Human Understanding*, SECT VIII, DIV 65, 479d-480a

37 FIELDING: *Tom Jones*, 164a-b; 274c

40 GIBBON: *Decline and Fall*, 88d

43 MILL: *Liberty*, 293b-302c passim, esp 294c-295a; 320a-c

44 BOSWELL: *Johnson*, 302c-303b

47 GOETHE: *Faust* esp PART I [1765–1775] 42b, [3217–3250] 79a-b

52 DOSTOEVSKY: *Brothers Karamazov*, BK II, 37c-38a

53 JAMES: *Psychology*, 736b-737a

CROSS-REFERENCES

For: The discussion of the faculties or the acts of the mind which are related to experience, *see* IDEA 1c, 2b, 2e–2g; INDUCTION 1a, 2; JUDGMENT 8c; KNOWLEDGE 6b(1), 6c(4); MEMORY AND IMAGINATION 1a, 3c, 5a–5b, 6c(1)–6c(2); MIND 1a(1)–1a(2), 1e(1); REASONING 1c, 4c, 5b(3); SENSE 1a, 1c–1d, 3c(5), 4b, 5a; UNIVERSAL AND PARTICULAR 4c.

The consideration of the empirical foundations or sources of science and art, *see* ART 5; DIALECTIC 2a(1); MEDICINE 2a; METAPHYSICS 2c; PHILOSOPHY 3a; PHYSICS 2; SCIENCE 1b, 1c, 5a; SENSE 5b–5c.

The discussion of experience in relation to the conditions or limits of human knowledge, *see* INDUCTION 2; KNOWLEDGE 5a–5a(6); MEMORY AND IMAGINATION 6d; METAPHYSICS 4b; MIND 5b.

Other treatments of the empirical verification of hypotheses or theories, *see* HYPOTHESIS 4d; PHYSICS 4c; SCIENCE 5e; SENSE 5c; TRUTH 1a.

Other discussions of the role of experimentation in scientific inquiry, *see* INDUCTION 5; LOGIC 4b; MECHANICS 2a; PHYSICS 4–4d; SCIENCE 5a.

Experience as a factor in education, *see* EDUCATION 5f.

The treatment of religious or mystical experience or of related matters, *see* GOD 6c(3); PROPHECY 1b; RELIGION 1b(2)–1b(3); SIGN AND SYMBOL 5b.

ADDITIONAL READINGS

Listed below are works not included in *Great Books of the Western World*, but relevant to the idea and topics with which this chapter deals. These works are divided into two groups:

I. Works by authors represented in this collection.
II. Works by authors not represented in this collection.

For the date, place, and other facts concerning the publication of the works cited, consult the Bibliography of Additional Readings which follows the last chapter of *The Great Ideas*.

I.

AUGUSTINE. *De Genesi ad Litteram*, BK XII
DESCARTES. *The Principles of Philosophy*, PART III, 4
HUME. *A Treatise of Human Nature*
KANT. *Prolegomena to Any Future Metaphysic*
HEGEL. *The Phenomenology of Mind*
———. *Science of Logic*, VOL I, BK II, SECT II; SECT III, CH I; VOL II, SECT III, CH 3
J. S. MILL. *A System of Logic*, BK III, CH 7–8
W. JAMES. *Essays in Radical Empiricism*
———. *The Varieties of Religious Experience*
———. *Pragmatism*
———. *The Meaning of Truth*

II.

R. BACON. *Opus Majus*, PART VI
DUNS SCOTUS. *Oxford Commentary*, BK I, DIST 3, Q 4 (9)
LEIBNITZ. *New Essays Concerning Human Understanding*
VOLTAIRE. *The Ignorant Philosopher*, CH 7
WORDSWORTH. *The Prelude*

J. MILL. *Analysis of the Phenomena of the Human Mind*
WHEWELL. *The Philosophy of the Inductive Sciences*, VOL I, BK I, CH 5, 7
TENNYSON. *Ulysses*
EMERSON. "Experience," in *Essays*, II
BERNARD. *Introduction to Experimental Medicine*
CLIFFORD. "On the Nature of Things-In-Themselves," in VOL II, *Lectures and Essays*
AVENARIUS. *Kritik der reinen Erfahrung*
HODGSON. *The Metaphysic of Experience*
ROYCE. *The World and the Individual*, SERIES I (6)
H. JAMES. *The Beast in the Jungle*
MACH. *The Analysis of Sensations*
———. *Erkenntnis und Irrtum*
PÉGUY. *Basic Verities* (Innocence and Experience)
———. *Men and Saints* (The Holy Innocents)
HÜGEL. *The Mystical Element of Religion*
LENIN. *Materialism and Empiriocriticism*
BRADLEY. *Appearance and Reality*, BK I, CH 11
———. *Essays on Truth and Reality*, CH 6
BROAD. *Perception, Physics, and Reality*, CH 3
PROUST. *Remembrance of Things Past*

JOYCE. *Ulysses*

SANTAYANA. *Scepticism and Animal Faith*, CH 15

BRIDGMAN. *The Logic of Modern Physics*

HOOK. *The Metaphysics of Pragmatism*

J. S. HALDANE. *The Sciences and Philosophy*, LECT XVI

C. I. LEWIS. *Mind and the World Order*

WHITEHEAD. *Science and the Modern World*

——. *Process and Reality*, PART III

HUSSERL. *Ideas: General Introduction to Pure Phenomenology*

——. *Méditations Cartésiennes*

BERGSON. *Time and Free Will*

——. *Two Sources of Morality and Religion*, CH 4

GILBY. *Poetic Experience*

FISHER. *The Design of Experiments*

DEWEY. "Experience and Objective Idealism," "The Postulate of Immediate Empiricism," "'Consciousness' and Experience," in *The Influence of Darwin on Philosophy*

——. *Reconstruction in Philosophy*, CH 4

——. *Experience and Nature*, CH 1, 9

——. *Experience and Education*, CH 2–3, 8

BLANSHARD. *The Nature of Thought*

MARITAIN. *The Degrees of Knowledge*, CH 1, 5

——. *Ransoming the Time*, CH 10

B. RUSSELL. *The Problems of Philosophy*, CH 1

——. *An Inquiry into Meaning and Truth*, CH 8–11, 16–18, 21–23

——. *Human Knowledge, Its Scope and Limits*, PART III, CH 1–5; PART VI, CH 4, 10

Chapter 26: FAMILY

INTRODUCTION

THE human family, according to Rousseau, is "the most ancient of all societies and the only one that is natural." On the naturalness of the family there seems to be general agreement in the great books, although not all would claim, like Rousseau, that it is the *only* natural society. The state is sometimes also regarded as a natural community, but its naturalness is not as obvious and has often been disputed.

The word "natural" applied to a community or association of men can mean either that men *instinctively* associate with one another as do bees and buffaloes; or that the association in question, while voluntary and to that extent conventional, is also *necessary* for human welfare. It is in this sense of necessity or need that Rousseau speaks of family ties as natural. "The children remain attached to the father only so long as they need him for their preservation," he writes. "As soon as this need ceases, the natural bond is dissolved." If after that "they remain united, they continue so no longer naturally, but voluntarily; and the family itself is then maintained only by convention."

Locke appears to attribute the existence of the human family to the same sort of instinctive determination which establishes familial ties among other animals, though he recognizes that the protracted infancy of human offspring make "the conjugal bonds ... more firm and lasting in man than the other species of animals." Since with other animals as well as in the human species, "the end of conjunction between male and female [is] not barely procreation, but the continuation of the species," it ought to last, in Locke's opinion, "even after procreation, so long as is necessary to the nourishment and support of the young ones, who are to be sustained by those who got them till they are able to shift and support for themselves. This rule," he adds, "which the infinite wise Maker hath set to the works of His hands, we find the inferior creatures steadily obey."

Yet Locke does not reduce the association of father, mother, and children entirely to a divinely implanted instinct for the perpetuation of the species. "Conjugal society," he writes, "is made by a voluntary compact between man and woman, and though it consists chiefly in such a communion and right in one another's bodies as is necessary to its chief end, procreation, yet it draws with it mutual support and assistance, and a communion of interests, too."

If the human family were *entirely* an instinctively formed society, we should expect to find the pattern or structure of the domestic community the same at all times and everywhere. But since the time of Herodotus, historians and, later, anthropologists have observed the great diversity in the institutions of the family in different tribes or cultures, or even at different times in the same culture. From his own travels among different peoples, Herodotus reports a wide variety of customs with respect to marriage and the family. From the travels of other men, Montaigne culls a similar collection of stories about the diversity of the mores with respect to sex, especially in relation to the rules or customs which hedge the community of man and wife.

Such facts raise the question whether the pattern of monogamy pictured by Locke represents anything more than one type of human family—the type which predominates in western civilization or, even more narrowly, in Christendom. Marx, for instance, holds that the structure of the family depends on the character of its "economical foundation," and insists that "it is of course just as absurd to hold the Teutonic-Christian form of the family to be absolute and final as it would be to apply that character to the ancient Roman, the ancient

Greek, or the Eastern forms which, moreover, taken together form a series in historic development."

Though the observation of the various forms which the human family takes has led some writers to deny the naturalness of the family—at least so far as its "naturalness" would mean a purely instinctive formation—it has seldom been disputed that the family fulfills a natural human need. Conventional in structure, the family remains natural as a means indispensable to an end which all men *naturally* desire. "There must be a union of those who cannot exist without each other," Aristotle writes, "namely, of male and female, that the race may continue"; and he goes on to say that this union is formed "not of deliberate purpose, but because, in common with other animals and with plants, mankind have a natural desire to leave behind them an image of themselves."

The human infant, as Locke observes, requires years of care in order to survive. If the family did not exist as a relatively stable organization to serve this purpose, some other social agency would have to provide sustained care for children. But wherever we find any other social units, such as tribes or cities, there we also find some form of the family in existence, not only performing the function of rearing children, but also being the primitive social group out of which all larger groupings seem to grow or to be formed. Aristotle, for example, describes the village or tribe as growing out of an association of families, just as later the city or state comes from a union of villages.

We have seen that the naturalness of the family—as answering a natural need—is not incompatible with its also being a product of custom or convention. The facts reported by Herodotus, Montaigne, and Darwin, which show the variability of families in size and membership, in form and government, do not exclude, but on the contrary emphasize, the further fact that wherever men live together at all, they also live in families.

Whether or not the political community is also a natural society, and if so, whether it is natural in the same way as the family, are questions reserved for the chapter on STATE. But it should be noted here that for some writers, for Aristotle particularly and to a lesser extent

for Locke, the naturalness of the family not only points to a natural development of the state, but also helps to explain how, in the transition from the family to the state, paternal government gives rise to royal rule or absolute monarchy. Even Rousseau, who thinks that the family is the *only* natural society, finds, in the correspondence between a political ruler and a father, reason for saying that "the family ... may be called the first model of political societies."

IN WESTERN CIVILIZATION, a family normally consists of a husband and wife and their offspring. If the procreation and rearing of offspring is *the* function, or even *a* function, which the family naturally exists to perform, then a childless family cannot be considered normal. Hegel suggests another reason for offspring. He sees in children the bond of union which makes the family a community.

"The relation of love between husband and wife," he writes, "is in itself not objective, because even if their feeling is their substantial unity, still this unity has no objectivity. Such an objectivity parents first acquire in their children, in whom they can see objectified the entirety of their union. In the child, a mother loves its father and he its mother. Both have their love objectified for them in the child. While in their goods their unity is embodied only in an external thing, in their children it is embodied in a spiritual one in which the parents are loved and which they love."

Until recent times when it has been affected by urban, industrial conditions, the family tended to be a much larger unit, not only with regard to the number of children, but also with respect to other members and relationships. The household included servants, if not slaves; it included blood-relatives in various degrees of consanguinity; its range extended over three or even four generations. Sancho Panza's wife, for instance, pictures the ideal marriage for her daughter as one in which "we shall have her always under our eyes, and be all one family, parents and children, grandchildren and sons-in-law, and the peace and blessing of God will dwell among us." Even though they belong to the nineteenth century, the families in *War and Peace* indicate how different is the domestic establishment under agrarian and semi-feudal conditions.

But even when it comprised a larger and more varied membership, the family differed from other social units, such as tribe or state, in both size and function. Its membership, determined by consanguinity, was usually more restricted than that of other groups, although blood-relationships, often more remote, may also operate to limit the membership of the tribe or the state. Its function, according to Aristotle, at least in origin, was to "supply men's everyday wants," whereas the state went beyond this in aiming at other conditions "of a good life."

In an agricultural society of the sort we find among the ancients, the household rather than the city is occupied with the problems of wealth. In addition to the breeding and rearing of children, and probably because of this in part, the family as a unit seems to have been concerned with the means of subsistence, on the side of both production and consumption. Its members shared in a division of labor and in a division of the fruits thereof.

Apart from those industries manned solely by slave labor in the service of the state, the production of goods largely depended on the industry of the family. In modern times this system of production came to be called the "domestic" as opposed to the "factory" system. It seems to persist even after the industrial revolution. But, according to Marx, "this modern so-called domestic industry has nothing, except the name, in common with the old-fashioned domestic industry, the existence of which presupposes independent urban handicrafts, independent peasant farming, and above all, a dwelling house for the laborer and his family."

In effect, the industrial revolution produced an economy in which not only agriculture but the family ceased to be central. The problem shifts from the wealth of families to the wealth of nations, even as production shifts from the family to the factory. "Modern industry," according to Marx, "by assigning an important part in the process of production, outside the domestic sphere, to women, to young persons, and to children of both sexes, creates a new economical foundation."

The family was for centuries what the factory and the storehouse have only recently become in an era of industrialism. For the ancients, the problems of wealth—its acquisition, accumulation, and use—were domestic, not political. "The so-called art of getting wealth," Aristotle writes, is "according to some . . . identical with household management, according to others, a principal part of it." In his own judgment, "property is a part of the household, and the art of acquiring property is a part of the art of managing the household"—but a *part only*, because the household includes human beings as well as property, and is concerned with the government of persons as well as the management of things.

The foregoing throws light on the extraordinary shift in the meaning of the word "economics" from ancient to modern times. In the significance of their Greek roots, the word "polity" signifies a state, the word "economy" a family; and as "politics" referred to the art of governing the political community, so "economics" referred to the art of governing the domestic community. Only in part was it concerned with the art of getting wealth. As the chapter on WEALTH indicates, Rousseau tries to preserve the broader meaning when he uses the phrase "political economy" for the general problems of government; but for the most part in modern usage "economics" refers to a science or art concerned with wealth, and it is "political" in the sense that the management of wealth, and of men with respect to wealth, has become the problem of the state rather than the family. Not only has the industrial economy become more and more a political affair, but the character of the family as a social institution has also changed with its altered economic status and function.

THE CHIEF QUESTION about the family in relation to the state has been, in ancient as well as in modern times, whether the family has natural rights which the state cannot justly invade or transgress.

The proposal in Plato's *Republic*—"that the wives of our guardians are to be common, and their children are to be common, and no parent is to know his own child, nor any child his parent"—was as radical in the fifth century

B.C. as its counterpart would be today. When Socrates proposes this, Glaucon suggests that "the possibility as well as the utility of such a law" may be subject to "a good many doubts." But Socrates does not think that "there can be any dispute about the very great utility of having wives and children in common; the possibility," he adds, "is quite another matter, and will be very much disputed."

Aristotle questions both the desirability and possibility. "The premise from which the argument of Socrates proceeds," he says, is "'the greater the unity of the state the better.'" He denies this premise. "Is it not obvious," he asks, "that a state may at length attain such a degree of unity as to be no longer a state?— since the nature of a state is to be a plurality, and in tending to a greater unity, from being a state, it becomes a family, and from being a family, an individual." Hence "we ought not to attain this greatest unity even if we could, for it would be the destruction of the state." In addition, "the scheme, taken literally, is impracticable."

It is significant that Aristotle's main argument against Plato's "communism" (which includes the community of property as well as the community of women and children) is based upon the nature of the state rather than on the rights of the family. It seems to have been a prevalent view in antiquity, at least among philosophers, that the children should be "regarded as belonging to the state rather than to their parents." Antigone's example shows, however, that this view was by no means without exception. Her defiance of Creon, based on "the unwritten and unfailing statutes of heaven," is also undertaken for "the majesty of kindred blood." In this sense, it constitutes an affirmation of the rights and duties of the family.

In the Christian tradition the rights of the family as against the state are also defended by reference to divine law. The point is not that the state is less a natural community than the family in the eyes of a theologian like Aquinas; but in addition to having a certain priority in the order of nature, the family, more directly than the state, is of divine origin. Not only is it founded on the sacrament of matrimony, but the express commandments of God dictate the duties of care and obedience which bind its members together. For the state to interfere in those relationships between parents and children or between husband and wife which fall under the regulation of divine law would be to exceed its authority, and hence to act without right and in violation of rights founded upon a higher authority.

In the Christian tradition philosophers like Hobbes and Kant state the rights of the family in terms of natural law or defend them as natural rights. "Because the first instruction of children," writes Hobbes, "depends on the care of their parents, it is necessary that they should be obedient to them while they are under their tuition.... Originally the father of every man was also his sovereign lord, with power over him of life and death." When the fathers of families relinquished such absolute power in order to form a commonwealth or state, they did not lose, nor did they have to give up, according to Hobbes, all control of their children. "Nor would there be any reason," he goes on, "why any man should desire to have children, or take the care to nourish and instruct them, if they were afterwards to have no other benefit from them than from other men. And this," he says, "accords with the Fifth Commandment."

In the section of his *Science of Right* devoted to the "rights of the family as a domestic society," Kant argues that "from the fact of procreation there follows the duty of preserving and rearing children." From this duty he derives "the right of parents to the management and training of the child, so long as it is itself incapable of making proper use of its body as an organism, and of its mind as an understanding. This includes its nourishment and the care of its education." It also "includes, in general, the function of forming and developing it practically, that it may be able in the future to maintain and advance itself, and also its moral culture and development, the guilt of neglecting it falling upon the parents."

As is evident from Hobbes and Kant, the rights of the family can be vindicated without denying that the family, like the individual, owes obedience to the state. In modern terms, at least, the problem is partly stated by the question, To what extent can parents justly claim exemption from political interference in the control of their own children? But this is only part of the problem. It must also be asked whether, in addition to regulating the family for the general welfare of the whole community, the state is also entitled to interfere in the affairs of the household in order to protect children from parental mismanagement or neglect. Both questions call for a consideration of the form and principles of domestic government.

THE KINDS OF RULE and the relation between ruler and ruled in the domestic community have a profound bearing on the theory of government in the larger community of the state. Many of the chapters on the forms of government—especially CONSTITUTION, MONARCHY, and TYRANNY—indicate that the great books of political theory, from Plato and Aristotle to Locke and Rousseau, derive critical points from the comparison of domestic and political government.

We shall pass over the master-slave relationship, both because that is considered in the chapter on SLAVERY, and because not all households include human chattel. Omitting this, two fundamental relationships which domestic government involves remain to be examined: the relation of husband and wife, and of parents and children.

With regard to the first, there are questions of equality and administrative supremacy. Even when the wife is regarded as the complete equal of her husband, the administrative question remains, for there must either be a division of authority, or unanimity must prevail, or one —either the husband or the wife—must have the last word when disagreement must be overcome to get any practical matter decided. So far as husband and wife are concerned, should the family be an absolute monarchy, or a kind of constitutional government?

Both an ancient and a modern writer appear to answer this question in the same way. "A husband and father," Aristotle says, "rules over wife and children, both free, but the rule differs, the rule over his children being a royal, over his wife a constitutional rule." Yet the relation between husband and wife, in Aristotle's view, is not perfectly constitutional. In the state "the citizens rule and are ruled in turn" on the supposition that their "natures . . . are equal and do not differ at all." In the family, however, Aristotle thinks that "although there may be exceptions to the order of nature, the male is by nature fitter for command than the female."

According to Locke, "the husband and wife, though they have but one common concern, yet having different understandings, will unavoidably sometimes have different wills too. It therefore being necessary that the last determination (i.e., the rule) should be placed somewhere, it naturally falls to the man's share as the abler and the stronger." But this, Locke thinks, "leaves the wife in the full and true possession of what by contract is her peculiar right, and at least gives the husband no more power over her than she has over his life; the power of the husband being so far from that of an absolute monarch that the wife has, in many cases, a liberty to separate from him where natural right or their contract allows it."

In the so-called Marriage Group of the *Canterbury Tales*, Chaucer gives voice to all of the possible positions that have ever been taken concerning the relation of husband and wife. The Wife of Bath, for example, argues for the rule of the wife. She claims that nothing will satisfy women until they "have the sovereignty as well upon their husband as their love, and to have mastery their man above." The Clerk of Oxford, in his tale of patient Griselda, presents the wife who freely admits to her husband, "When first I came to you, just so left I my will and all my liberty." The Franklin in his tale allows the mastery to neither wife nor husband, "save that the name and show of sovereignty" would belong to the latter. He dares to say

That friends each one the other must obey
If they'd be friends and long keep company.
Love will not be constrained by mastery; . . .
Women by nature love their liberty,
And not to be constrained like any thrall,
And so do men, if say the truth I shall. . . .
Thus did she take her servant and her lord,
Servant in love and lord in their marriage;
So was he both in lordship and bondage.

WHILE THERE MAY be disagreement regarding the relation between husband and wife, there is none regarding the inequality between parents and children during the offspring's immaturity. Although every man may enjoy "equal right . . . to his natural freedom, without being subjected to the will or authority of any other men," children, according to Locke, "are not born in this full state of equality, though they are born to it."

Paternal power, even absolute rule, over children arises from this fact. So long as the child "is in an estate wherein he has no understanding of his own to direct his will," Locke thinks he "is not to have any will of his own to follow. He that understands for him must will for him too; he must prescribe to his will, and regulate his actions." But Locke adds the important qualification that when the son "comes to the estate which made his father a free man, the son is a free man too."

Because children are truly inferior in competence, there would seem to be no injustice in their being ruled by their parents; or in the rule being absolute in the sense that children are precluded from exercising a decisive voice in the conduct of their own or their family's affairs. Those who think that kings cannot claim the absolute authority of parental rule frequently use the word "despotic" to signify unjustified paternalism—a transference to the state of a type of dominion which can be justified only in the family.

The nature of despotism as absolute rule is discussed in the chapters on MONARCHY and TYRANNY, but its relevance here makes it worth repeating that the Greek word from which "despot" comes, like its Latin equivalent *paterfamilias*, signifies the ruler of a household and carries the connotation of absolute rule— the complete mastery of the father over the children and the servants, if not over the wife. Accordingly there would seem to be nothing invidious in referring to domestic government as despotic, at least not to the extent that, in the case of the children, absolute rule is justified by their immaturity. The problem arises only with respect to despotism in the state, when one man rules another mature man as absolutely as a parent rules a child.

The great defender of the doctrine that the sovereign must be absolute, "or else there is no sovereignty at all," sees no difference between the rights of the ruler of a state—the "sovereign by institution"—and those of a father as the natural master of his family. "The rights and consequences of both paternal and despotical dominion," Hobbes maintains, "are the very same with those of a sovereign by institution." On the other hand, Rousseau, an equally staunch opponent of absolute rule, uses the word "despotism" only in an invidious sense for what he regards as illegitimate government —absolute monarchy. "Even if there were as close an analogy as many authors maintain between the State and the family," he writes, "it would not follow that the rules of conduct proper for one of these societies would be also proper for the other."

Rousseau even goes so far as to deny that parental rule is despotic in his sense of that term. "With regard to paternal authority, from which some writers have derived absolute government," he remarks that "nothing can be further from the ferocious spirit of despotism than the mildness of that authority which looks more to the advantage of him who obeys than to that of him who commands." He agrees with Locke in the observation that, unlike the political despot, "the father is the child's master no longer than his help is necessary." When both are equal, the son is perfectly independent of the father, and owes him "only respect and not obedience."

Misrule in the family, then, would seem to occur when these conditions or limits are violated. Parents may try to continue their absolute control past the point at which the children have become mature and are competent to take care of their own affairs. A parent who does not relinquish his absolutism at this point can be called "despotic" in the derogatory sense of that word.

Applying a distinction made by some political writers, the parent is tyrannical rather than despotic when he uses the children for his own good, treats them as property to exploit, even at a time when his absolute direction of their affairs would be justified if it were for the children's welfare. The existence of parental tyranny raises in its sharpest form the question of the state's right to intervene in the family for the good of its members.

THE CENTRAL ELEMENT in the domestic establishment is, of course, the institution of marriage. The discussion of marriage in the great books deals with most of the moral and psychological, if not all of the sociological and economic, aspects of the institution. The most profound question, perhaps, is whether marriage is merely a human institution to be regulated solely by custom and civil law, *or* a contract under the sanctions of natural law, *or* a religious sacrament signifying and imparting God's grace. The last two of these alternatives may not exclude one another, but those who insist upon the first usually reject the other two.

Some, like the Parson in the *Canterbury Tales*, consider marriage not only a natural but also a divine institution—a "sacrament ... ordained by God Himself in Paradise, and confirmed by Jesus Christ, as witness St. Matthew in the gospel: 'For this cause shall a man leave father and mother, and shall cleave to his wife; and they twain shall be one flesh,' which betokens the knitting together of Christ and of Holy Church."

Others, like Kant, seem to stress the character of marriage as an institution sanctioned by natural law. The "natural union of the sexes," he writes, "proceeds either according to the mere animal nature (*vaga libido, venus vulgivaga, fornicatio*), or according to law. The latter is marriage (*matrimonium*), which is the union of two persons of different sex for life-long reciprocal possession of their sexual faculties." Kant considers offspring as a natural end of marriage, but not the exclusive end, for then "the marriage would be dissolved of itself when the production of children ceased. ... Even assuming," he declares, "that enjoyment in the reciprocal use of the sexual endowments is an end of marriage, yet the contract of marriage is not on that account a matter of arbitrary will, but is a contract necessary in its nature by the Law of Humanity. In other words, if a man and a woman have the will to enter on reciprocal enjoyment in accordance with their sexual natures, they *must* necessarily marry each other."

Still others see marriage primarily as a civil contract. Freud, for example, considers the view that "sexual relations are permitted only on the basis of a final, indissoluble bond between a man and woman" as purely a convention of "present-day civilization." Marriage, as a set of taboos restricting the sexual life, varies from culture to culture; but in Freud's opinion the "high-water mark in this type of development has been reached in our Western European civilization."

The conception of marriage—whether it is merely a civil, or a natural, and even a divine institution—obviously affects the position to be taken on monogamy, on divorce, on chastity and adultery, and on the comparative merits of the married and the celibate condition. The pagans, for the most part, regard celibacy as a misfortune, especially for women, as witness the tragedy of the unwedded Electra. Christianity, on the other hand, celebrates the heroism of virginity and encourages the formation of monastic communities for celibates. Within the Judaeo-Christian tradition there are striking differences. Not only were the patriarchs of the Old Testament polygamous, but orthodox Judaism and orthodox Christianity also differ on divorce.

Augustine explains how a Christian should interpret those passages in the Old Testament which describe the polygamous practices of the patriarchs. "The saints of ancient times," he writes, "were under the form of an earthly kingdom, foreshadowing and foretelling the kingdom of heaven. And on account of the necessity for a numerous offspring, the custom of one man having several wives was at that time blameless; and for the same reason it was not proper for one woman to have several husbands, because a woman does not in that way become more fruitful ... In regard to matters of this sort," he concludes, "whatever the holy men of those times did without lust, Scripture passes over without blame, although they did things which could not be done at the present time except through lust."

On similar grounds Aquinas holds that "it was allowable to give a bill of divorce," under the law of the Old Testament, but it is not allowable under the Christian dispensation because divorce "is contrary to the nature of a sacrament." The greatest familiarity between man and wife requires the staunchest fidelity which "is impossible if the marriage bond can be sundered." Within the Christian tradition Locke takes an opposite view of divorce. He can see good reason why "the society of man and wife should be more lasting than that of male and female amongst other creatures," but he does not see "why this compact, where procreation and education are secured, and inheritance taken care for, may not be made determinable either by consent, or at a certain time, or upon certain conditions, as well as any other voluntary compact, there being no necessity in the nature of the thing . . . that it should always be for life." Against Locke, Dr. Johnson would argue that "to the contract of marriage, besides the man and wife, there is a third party—Society; and if it be considered as a vow—God; and therefore it cannot be dissolved by their consent alone."

Laws and customs, however, represent only the external or social aspect of marriage. The discussion of these externals cannot give any impression of the inwardness and depth of the problem which marriage is for the individual person. Only the great poems, the great novels and plays, the great books of history and biography can adequately present the psychological and emotional aspects of marriage in the life of individuals. Heightened in narration, they give more eloquent testimony than the case histories of Freud to support the proposition that marriage is at all times—in every culture and under the widest variety of circumstances—one of the supreme tests of human character.

The relation between men and women in and out of marriage, the relation of husband and wife before and after marriage, the relation of parents and children—these create crises and tensions, conflicts between love and duty, between reason and the passions, from which no individual can entirely escape. Marriage is not only a typically human problem, but it is the one problem which, both psychologically and morally, touches every man, woman, and child. Sometimes the resolution is tragic, sometimes the outcome seems to be happy, almost blessed; but whether a human life is built on this foundation or broken against these rocks, it is violently shaken in the process and forever shaped.

To some degree each reader of the great books has, in imagination if not in action, participated in the trials of Odysseus, Penelope, and Telemachus; in the affections of Hector and Andromache, Alcestis and Admetus, Tom Jones and Sophia, Natasha and Pierre Bezúkhov, in the jealousy of Othello, the anguish of Lear,

the decision of Aeneas or the indecision of Hamlet; and certainly in the reasoning of Panurge about whether to marry or not. In each of these cases, everyone finds some aspect of love in relation to marriage, some phase of parenthood or childhood which has colored his own life or that of his family; and he can find somewhere in his own experience the grounds for sympathetic understanding of the extraordinary relation between Electra and her mother Clytemnestra, between Augustine and Monica his mother, between Oedipus and Jocasta, Prince Hamlet and Queen Gertrude, Pierre Bezúkhov and his wife, or what is perhaps the most extraordinary case of all—Adam and Eve in *Paradise Lost*.

On one point the universality of the problem of marriage and family life seems to require qualification. The conflict between conjugal and illicit love exists in all ages. The entanglement of the bond between man and wife with the ties—of both love and blood—which unite parents and children, is equally universal. But the difficulties which arise in marriage as a result of the ideals or the illusions of romantic love seem to constitute a peculiarly modern problem. The ancients distinguished between sexual love and the love of friendship and they understood the necessity for both in the conjugal relationship if marriage is to prosper. But not until the later Middle Ages did men think of matrimony as a way to perpetuate throughout all the years the ardor of that moment in a romantic attachment when the lovers find each other without flaw and beyond reproach.

Matters relevant to this modern problem are discussed in the chapter on Love. As is there indicated, romantic love, though it seems to be of Christian origin, may also be a distortion—even an heretical perversion—of the kind of Christian love which is pledged in the reciprocal vows of holy matrimony.

We have already considered some of the problems of the family which relate to children and youth—the immature members of the human race—such as whether the child *belongs* to the family or the state, and whether the family is solely responsible for the care and training of children, or a share of this responsibility falls to the state or the church.

There are other problems. Why do men and women want offspring and what satisfactions do they get from rearing children? For the most part in Christendom, and certainly in antiquity, the lot of the childless is looked upon as a grievous frustration. To be childless is not merely contrary to nature, but for pagan as well as Christian it constitutes the deprivation of a blessing which should grace the declining years of married life. The opposite view, so rarely taken, is voiced by the chorus of women in the *Medea* of Euripides.

"Those who are wholly without experience and have never had children far surpass in happiness those who are parents," the women chant in response to Medea's tragic leave-taking from her own babes. "The childless, because they have never proved whether children grow up to be a blessing or a curse to men, are removed from all share in many troubles; whilst those who have a sweet race of children growing up in their houses do wear away ... their whole life through; first with the thought how they may train them up in virtue, next how they shall leave their sons the means to live; and after all this 'tis far from clear whether on good or bad children they bestow their toil."

Still other questions arise concerning children, quite apart from the attitude of parents toward having and rearing them. What is the economic position of the child, both with respect to ownership of property and with respect to a part in the division of labor? How has the economic status of children been affected by industrialism? What are the mental and moral characteristics of the immature which exclude them from participation in political life, and which require adult regulation of their affairs? What are the criteria—emotional and mental as well as chronological—which determine the classification of individuals as children or adults, and how is the transition from childhood to manhood effected economically, politically, and above all emotionally?

The authors of the great books discuss most of these questions, but among them only Freud sees in the relation of children to their parents the basic emotional determination of human life. The fundamental triangle of love and hate, devotion and rivalry, consists of father, mother, and child. For Freud all the intricacies and per-

versions of love, the qualitative distinctions of romantic, conjugal, and illicit love, the factors which determine the choice of a mate and success or failure in marriage, and the conditions which determine the emergence from emotional infantilism—all these can be understood only by reference to the emotional life of the child in the vortex of the family.

The child's "great task," according to Freud, is that of "freeing himself from the parents," for "only after this detachment is accomplished can he cease to be a child and so become a member of the social community. ... These tasks are laid down for every man" but, Freud writes, "it is noteworthy how seldom they are carried through ideally, that is, how seldom they are solved in a manner psychologically as well as socially satisfactory. In neurotics, however," he adds, "this detachment from the parents is not accomplished at all."

In one sense, it is never fully accomplished by anyone. What Freud calls the "ego-ideal"— which represents our higher nature and which, in the name of the reality-principle, resists instinctual compliance with the pleasure-principle—is said to have its origin in "the identification with the father, which takes place in the prehistory of every person." Even after an individual has achieved detachment from the family, this ego-ideal acts as "a substitute for the longing for a father"; and in the form of conscience it "continues ... to exercise the censorship of morals."

ONE OTHER GROUP of questions which involve the family—at least as background—concerns the position or role of women. We have already considered their relation to their husbands in the government of the family itself. The way in which that relation is conceived affects the status and activity of women in the larger community of the state, in relation to citizenship and the opportunities for education, to the possession of property and the production of wealth (for example, the role of female labor in an industrial economy).

Again it is Euripides who gives voice to the plight of women in a man's world, in two of his great tragedies, the *Trojan Women* and *Medea*. In the one, they cry out under the brunt of the suffering which men leave them to bear in the backwash of war. In the other, Medea passionately berates the ignominy and bondage which women must accept in being wives. "Of all things that have life and sense," she says, "we women are the most hapless creatures; first must we buy a husband at great price, and then o'er ourselves a tyrant set, which is an evil worse than the first."

The ancient world contains another feminist who goes further than Euripides in speaking for the right of women to be educated like men, to share in property with them, and to enjoy the privileges as well as to discharge the tasks of citizenship. In the tradition of the great books, the striking fact is that after Plato the next great declaration of the rights of women should be written by one who is as far removed from him in time and temper as John Stuart Mill.

In Plato's *Republic*, Socrates argues that if the difference between men and women "consists only in women bearing and men begetting children, this does not amount to proof that a woman differs from a man in respect to the sort of education she should receive." For the same reason, he says, "the guardians and their wives ought to have the same pursuits." Since he thinks that "the gifts of nature are alike diffused in both," Socrates insists that "there is no special faculty of administration in a state which a woman has because she is a woman, or which a man has by virtue of his sex. All the pursuits of men are the pursuits of women also." Yet he adds that "in all of them a woman is inferior to a man." Therefore when he proposes to let women "share in the toils of war and the defence of their country," Socrates suggests that "in the distribution of labors the lighter are to be assigned to the women, who are the weaker natures."

Mill's tract on *The Subjection of Women* is his fullest statement of the case for social, economic, and political equality between the sexes. In *Representative Government*, his defense of women's rights deals primarily with the question of extending the franchise to them. Difference of sex, he contends, is "as entirely irrelevant to political rights, as difference in height, or in the color of the hair. All human beings have the same interest in good government . . . Mankind have long since abandoned the only premises which will support the conclusion that women ought not to have votes. No one now holds that women should be in personal servitude; that they should have no thought, wish, or occupation, but to be the domestic drudges of husbands, fathers, or brothers. It is allowed to unmarried, and wants but little of being conceded to married women to hold property, and have pecuniary and business interests, in the same manner as men. It is considered suitable and proper that women should think, and write, and be teachers. As soon as these things are admitted," Mill concludes, "the political disqualification has no principle to rest on."

Though no other of the great books speaks so directly for the emancipation of women from domestic and political subjection, many of them do consider the differences between men and women in relation to war and love, pleasure and pain, virtue and vice, duty and honor. Some are concerned explicitly with the pivotal question—whether men and women are more alike than different, whether they are essentially equal in their humanity or unequal. Since these are matters pertinent to human nature itself, as it is affected by gender, the relevant passages are collected in the chapter on MAN.

OUTLINE OF TOPICS

REFERENCES

To find the passages cited, use the numbers in heavy type, which are the volume and page numbers of the passages referred to. For example, in 4 HOMER: *Iliad*, BK II [265–283] 12d, the number 4 is the number of the volume in the set; the number 12d indicates that the passage is in section d of page 12.

PAGE SECTIONS: When the text is printed in one column, the letters a and b refer to the upper and lower halves of the page. For example, in 53 JAMES: *Psychology*, 116a-119b, the passage begins in the upper half of page 116 and ends in the lower half of page 119. When the text is printed in two columns, the letters a and b refer to the upper and lower halves of the left-hand side of the page, the letters c and d to the upper and lower halves of the right-hand side of the page. For example, in 7 PLATO: *Symposium*, 163b-164c, the passage begins in the lower half of the left-hand side of page 163 and ends in the upper half of the right-hand side of page 164.

AUTHOR'S DIVISIONS: One or more of the main divisions of a work (such as PART, BK, CH, SECT) are sometimes included in the reference; line numbers, in brackets, are given in certain cases; *e.g.*, *Iliad*, BK II [265–283] 12d.

BIBLE REFERENCES: The references are to book, chapter, and verse. When the King James and Douay versions differ in title of books or in the numbering of chapters or verses, the King James version is cited first and the Douay, indicated by a (*D*), follows; *e.g.*, OLD TESTAMENT: *Nehemiah*, 7:45—(*D*) *II Esdras*, 7:46.

SYMBOLS: The abbreviation "esp" calls the reader's attention to one or more especially relevant parts of a whole reference; "passim" signifies that the topic is discussed intermittently rather than continuously in the work or passage cited.

For additional information concerning the style of the references, see the Explanation of Reference Style; for general guidance in the use of *The Great Ideas*, consult the Preface.

1. The nature and necessity of the family

OLD TESTAMENT: *Genesis*, 2:18–25
- 7 PLATO: *Republic*, BK V, 361b-365d / *Laws*, BK IV, 685a-c; BK VI, 707c-709a
- 9 ARISTOTLE: *Politics*, BK I 445a-455a,c; BK II, CH 1–4 455b,d-458a passim
- 12 LUCRETIUS: *Nature of Things*, BK V [1011–1027] 74b-c
- 12 EPICTETUS: *Discourses*, BK III, CH 22, 198c-199c
- 14 PLUTARCH: *Lycurgus*, 39a-41a / *Lycurgus-Numa*, 62d-64a
- 18 AUGUSTINE: *City of God*, BK XIX, CH 14–17 520a-523a
- 19 AQUINAS: *Summa Theologica*, PART I, Q 92, AA 1–2 488d-490c; Q 98 516d-519a
- 20 AQUINAS: *Summa Theologica*, PART I-II, Q 94, A 2, ANS 221d-223a; Q 105, A 4, ANS 318b-321a
- 23 HOBBES: *Leviathan*, PART II, 121a
- 31 SPINOZA: *Ethics*, PART IV, APPENDIX, XX 449a
- 32 MILTON: *Paradise Lost*, BK VIII [357–451] 240a-242a
- 35 LOCKE: *Civil Government*, CH VI, SECT 56–63 36d-38c; CH VII, SECT 77–86 42b-44a
- 36 SWIFT: *Gulliver*, PART I, 29b-30a
- 36 STERNE: *Tristram Shandy*, 410a-411a
- 38 MONTESQUIEU: *Spirit of Laws*, BK XXIII, 187d-188a
- 38 ROUSSEAU: *Inequality*, 350a-c / *Social Contract*, BK I, 387d-388a
- 42 KANT: *Science of Right*, 418c-422d; 433c-434a
- 46 HEGEL: *Philosophy of Right*, PART III, par 158–181 58a-63d; ADDITIONS, 47 124a-b / *Philosophy of History*, INTRO, 172b-d; PART IV, 353a-b
- 50 MARX: *Capital*, 241c-d
- 50 MARX-ENGELS: *Communist Manifesto*, 427b-c
- 51 TOLSTOY: *War and Peace*, EPILOGUE I, 659d-662a
- 53 JAMES: *Psychology*, 189a
- 54 FREUD: *Group Psychology*, 686c-687d esp 687d / *Civilization and Its Discontents*, 781d-782c; 788a-b

2. The family and the state

2a. Comparison of the domestic and political community in origin, structure, and function

- 7 PLATO: *Crito*, 216d-217d / *Republic*, BK V, 356b-365d / *Laws*, BK I, 641a-642b; BK III, 664a-666c
- 9 ARISTOTLE: *Ethics*, BK VIII, CH 12 [1162^{a}16-18] 414c / *Politics*, BK I, CH 1–2 445a-446d; BK II, CH 2 455d-456c; CH 5 [1263^{b}30–35] 459a

(2. The family and the state. 2a. Comparison of the domestic and political community in origin, structure, and function.)

13 VIRGIL: *Aeneid*, BK V [35–103] 188a-190a; BK VI [679–702] 229a-b; [756–789] 231a-232a; BK VIII [66–80] 260b-261a; BK X [1–117] 302a-305a

14 PLUTARCH: *Lycurgus*, 36a-b

18 AUGUSTINE: *City of God*, BK XIX, CH 12, 517c-d; CH 13–17 519a-523a

20 AQUINAS: *Summa Theologica*, PART I–II, Q 90, A 3, REP 3 207a-c

23 HOBBES: *Leviathan*, PART II, 99b-c; 111a-b

30 BACON: *Advancement of Learning*, 34a

35 LOCKE: *Civil Government*, CH VI–VII 36a-46c; CH XV 64c-65d

36 STERNE: *Tristram Shandy*, 214b-217b esp 216b; 410a-411a

38 MONTESQUIEU: *Spirit of Laws*, BK IV, 13b

38 ROUSSEAU: *Inequality*, 359b-c / *Political Economy*, 367a-368c / *Social Contract*, BK I, 387d-388a

46 HEGEL: *Philosophy of Right*, PART I, par 75 31d-32b; PART III, par 157 57d; par 181 63c-d; par 203 68a-c; par 255–256 79d-80a; par 303 101c-102a; par 349 111d-112a; ADDITIONS, 47 124a-b; 115–116 135c-d; 157 142b-c / *Philosophy of History*, INTRO, 172b-d; 180c-182c; PART I, 211a-212c; 246d-247a; PART III, 288c-289d

49 DARWIN: *Descent of Man*, 308b-d; 310a-c; 579b-581c esp 581a-b

54 FREUD: *Group Psychology*, 664b-d; 685b-687d esp 686c-687d; 692a-b / *Civilization and Its Discontents*, 781d-783d esp 781d-782d; 796b-c

2b. Comparison of the domestic and political community in manner of government

OLD TESTAMENT: *Isaiah*, 22:20–22—(D) *Isaias*, 22:20–22

6 HERODOTUS: *History*, BK I, 35c-d

7 PLATO: *Statesman*, 581a-b / *Laws*, BK I, 641a-642b; BK III, 664a-666c esp 666b-c

9 ARISTOTLE: *Ethics*, BK V, CH 6 [1134^{b}8–17] 382b-c; CH 11 [1138^{b}5–14] 387a,c; BK VI, CH 5 [1140^{b}7–10] 389b; CH 8 [1141^{b}28–1142^{a}11] 390d-391a; BK VIII, CH 10–11 412c-413d; BK X, CH 9 [1180^{b}3–7] 435b / *Politics*, BK I, CH 1–2 445a-446d; CH 5 447d-448c; CH 7 [1255^{b}15–20] 449b; CH 12 453d-454a; CH 13 [1259^{b}30–1260^{a}33] 454b-455a; BK III, CH 6 [1278^{b}30–1279^{a}2] 476a-b; CH 14 [1285^{b}29–33] 484a

13 VIRGIL: *Aeneid*, BK V [35–103] 188a-190a; BK VI [756–789] 231a-232a; BK VIII [66–80] 260b-261a; BK X [1–117] 302a-305a

18 AUGUSTINE: *City of God*, BK XIX, CH 12, 517c-d; CH 13–17 519a-523a

19 AQUINAS: *Summa Theologica*, PART I, Q 92, A 1, REP 2 488d-489d

20 AQUINAS: *Summa Theologica*, PART I–II, Q 90, A 3, REP 3 207a-c; Q 105, A 4, REP 5 318b-321a

23 HOBBES: *Leviathan*, PART I, 67d-68a; 86a; PART II, 109b-111b; 121a; 155b; PART III, 228b-c

30 BACON: *New Atlantis*, 207b-209d

32 MILTON: *Samson Agonistes* [1010–1060] 361b-362b

35 LOCKE: *Civil Government*, CH I, SECT 1–2 25a-c; CH VI–VII 36a-46c esp CH VI, SECT 66–75 39b-42a; CH VIII, SECT 105–112 48c-51b; CH XIV, SECT 162 63a; CH XV 64c-65d

36 STERNE: *Tristram Shandy*, 214b-217b esp 216b; 410a-411a

37 FIELDING: *Tom Jones*, 21a-22d; 120c-121a,c

38 MONTESQUIEU: *Spirit of Laws*, BK I, 3b; BK IV, 13b; BK V, 28b-29a; BK XVI, 118b-c; BK XIX, 140a-c

38 ROUSSEAU: *Inequality*, 357a-b / *Political Economy*, 367a-368c / *Social Contract*, BK I, 387d-388a; BK III, 411c-d; 414c

40 GIBBON: *Decline and Fall*, 412c-413b

41 GIBBON: *Decline and Fall*, 82b-83c

42 KANT: *Science of Right*, 421c-422d

46 HEGEL: *Philosophy of Right*, ADDITIONS, 47 124a-b; 111 134d-135a; 157 142b-c / *Philosophy of History*, INTRO, 172b-d; PART I, 211a-213a

54 FREUD: *Group Psychology*, 687a-d; 688d-689a

2c. The place and rights of the family in the state: the control and education of children

OLD TESTAMENT: *Deuteronomy*, 20:5–7; 24:5

5 AESCHYLUS: *Seven Against Thebes* 27a-39a,c esp [1011–1084] 38b-39a,c

5 SOPHOCLES: *Antigone* 131a-142d

5 EURIPIDES: *Iphigenia at Aulis* 425a-439d esp [1255–1275] 436c, [1368–1401] 437c-d

5 ARISTOPHANES: *Ecclesiazusae* [611–650] 622a-c

6 HERODOTUS: *History*, BK IV, 139a-b; BK VII, 223c-d

6 THUCYDIDES: *Peloponnesian War*, BK II, 398c-d

7 PLATO: *Crito*, 216d-217d / *Republic*, BK V, 360d-365d / *Statesman*, 606d-608d / *Laws*, BK III, 665d-666c; BK VI, 707b-708a; BK VII, 721d-723d; BK XI, 775d-780c

9 ARISTOTLE: *Ethics*, BK X, CH 9 [1179^{b}31–1180^{b}13] 434c-435b / *Politics*, BK I, CH 13 [1260^{b}8–19] 455c; BK II, CH 2–3 455d-457a; CH 6 [1265^{a}38–^{b}17] 460d-461a; CH 9 [1269^{b}13–1270^{b}6] 465d-466c; BK III, CH 9 [1280^{b}30–1281^{a}2] 478c; BK IV, CH 15 [1300^{a}4–8] 500d; BK VI, CH 8 [1322^{b}38–1323^{a}6] 526d; BK VII, CH 16 [1334^{b}28]–BK VIII, CH 2 [1337^{a}34] 539d-542b

14 PLUTARCH: *Romulus*, 21a-26b / *Lycurgus*, 36a-45c / *Numa Pompilius*, 58d / *Lycurgus-Numa*, 62d-64a / *Cato the Younger*, 629a-c

15 TACITUS: *Annals*, BK II, 32b-d; BK III, 51a; 51d-52a; BK XV, 162b-c / *Histories*, BK III, 248c-d

18 AUGUSTINE: *City of God*, BK XIX, CH 16 521d-522a

3. The economics of the family

3a. The wealth of families: the maintenance of the domestic economy

3b. The effects of political economy: the family in the industrial system

4. The institution of marriage: its nature and purpose

(4. The institution of marriage: its nature and purpose.)

13 VIRGIL: Aeneid, BK IV [1–172] 167a-171b; BK VII [81–106] 238a-239a; [248–434] 242b-248a; BK XI [336–375] 337a-338a

14 PLUTARCH: Lycurgus, 39a-40c / Lycurgus-Numa, 62d-64a / Solon, 71d-72a

18 AUGUSTINE: Confessions, BK II, par 3 9b-c; BK IV, par 2 19d; BK VI, par 22–25 41d-42d / City of God, BK XIV, CH 21–26 392b-396c; BK XV, CH 16 410b-411d / Christian Doctrine, BK III, CH 12, 663a-c; CH 18–20 664d-665d

19 AQUINAS: Summa Theologica, PART I, Q 92, AA 1–2 488d-490c; Q 98 516d-519a

22 CHAUCER: Wife of Bath's Prologue [5583–6410] 256a-269b / Merchant's Tale [9121–9562] 319a-326a / Franklin's Tale 351b-366a esp [11,041–117] 351b-352b / Parson's Tale, par 77–80 540b-542a

25 MONTAIGNE: Essays, 410d-413a

26 SHAKESPEARE: As You Like It, ACT V, SC IV [114–156] 625a-b

29 CERVANTES: Don Quixote, PART II, 261c-262a

31 SPINOZA: Ethics, PART IV, APPENDIX, XX 449a

32 MILTON: Paradise Lost, BK VIII [357–451] 240a-242a; BK IX [952–959] 268a

35 LOCKE: Civil Government, CH VII, SECT 77–83 42b-43c

36 SWIFT: Gulliver, PART I, 29b

38 MONTESQUIEU: Spirit of Laws, BK XXIII, 187d-188a

38 ROUSSEAU: Inequality, 364d-365b

42 KANT: Science of Right, 418c-420b; 433d-434a

43 MILL: Liberty, 316d-317c

44 BOSWELL: Johnson, 194a; 289d-290a

46 HEGEL: Philosophy of Right, PART I, par 75 31d-32b; PART III, par 161–169 58b-60c; ADDITIONS, 47 124a-b; 103–108 133c-134c

49 DARWIN: Descent of Man, 579b-581c

51 TOLSTOY: War and Peace, BK I, 14b-15a; 55c-59d; BK III, 111a-128d; BK VI, 245d-274a,c; BK VII, 301b-302d; EPILOGUE I, 659d-662a

54 FREUD: Civilization and Its Discontents, 784c / New Introductory Lectures, 862d-863b

4a. Monogamy and polygamy

OLD TESTAMENT: Genesis, 16; 29:1–30:24 / Deuteronomy, 17:16–17; 21:15–17 / I Samuel, 25:39–44—(D) I Kings, 25:39–44 / II Samuel, 3:1–5; 11–12—(D) II Kings, 3:1–5; 11–12 / I Kings, 11:1–13—(D) III Kings, 11:1–13

NEW TESTAMENT: I Timothy, 3:2,12

5 SOPHOCLES: Trachiniae [307–489] 172d-174b

5 EURIPIDES: Andromache 315a-326a,c esp [147–244] 316c-317b / Electra [1030–1040] 336c

6 HERODOTUS: History, BK I, 32a; 48c; BK IV, 155c-156a; BK V, 160d

14 PLUTARCH: Lycurgus, 39d-40c / Demetrius, 731a-b / Antony-Demetrius, 780d

18 AUGUSTINE: Christian Doctrine, BK III, CH 12, 663a-c; CH 18–22 664d-666c

22 CHAUCER: Wife of Bath's Prologue [5583–5640] 256a-257a

30 BACON: New Atlantis, 209b-d

36 SWIFT: Gulliver, PART IV, 162b-166b esp 162b, 166a-b

38 MONTESQUIEU: Spirit of Laws, BK V, 28d; BK XV, 112a-b; BK XVI, 116a-120a; BK XXIII 188c-d; BK XXVI, 218d

40 GIBBON: Decline and Fall, 92c

41 GIBBON: Decline and Fall, 86a; 245b-246c

42 KANT: Science of Right, 419c-420a

43 MILL: Liberty, 311a-312a

46 HEGEL: Philosophy of Right, PART III, par 167–168 60b-c; ADDITIONS, 105 133d-134a / Philosophy of History, PART III, 294c-d

49 DARWIN: Descent of Man, 579b-583a esp 581b-c

51 TOLSTOY: War and Peace, EPILOGUE I, 660d-661b

53 JAMES: Psychology, 735a-b

54 FREUD: Civilization and Its Discontents, 784b-c

4b. The religious view of marriage: the sacrament of matrimony

OLD TESTAMENT: Genesis, 2:23–24 / Proverbs, 18:22

APOCRYPHA: Tobit passim, esp 6:10–17, 8:1–17, 9:6, 10:1–12—(D) OT, Tobias passim, esp 6:10–22, 8:1–19, 9:12, 10:1–13

NEW TESTAMENT: Matthew, 19:3–12 / Mark, 10:1–12 / John, 2:1–12 / I Corinthians, 7 / Ephesians, 5:22–33 / I Timothy, 4:1–5 / Hebrews, 13:4

5 AESCHYLUS: Eumenides [210–224] 83b

5 EURIPIDES: Hippolytus 225a-236d

13 VIRGIL: Aeneid, BK VII [81–106] 238a-239a; [248–434] 242b-248a

18 AUGUSTINE: Confessions, BK II, par 3 9b-c; BK IV, par 2 19d / City of God, BK XIV, CH 22 392d-393b / Christian Doctrine, BK III, CH 18–22 664d-666c

19 AQUINAS: Summa Theologica, PART I, Q 92, AA 2–3 489d-491b; Q 98 516d-519a

20 AQUINAS: Summa Theologica, PART I-II, Q 102, A 5, REP 3 283c-292c; Q 105, A 4, ANS and REP 6–9 318b-321a; PART III, Q 65, A 1, ANS and REP 5 879c-881d; A 2, ANS and REP 1 881d-882c; A 3, ANS and REP 1,4 882d-883d; A 4, ANS and REP 3 883d-884a,c; PART III SUPPL, Q 95 1042c-1049d passim

22 CHAUCER: Wife of Bath's Prologue [5583–5749] 256a-258b / Merchant's Tale [9193–9210] 320a-b / Parson's Tale, par 75, 536a; par 77–80 540b-542a

23 HOBBES: Leviathan, PART IV, 250c; 272d-273a; 276a-b

24 RABELAIS: Gargantua and Pantagruel, BK III, 219b-222b

29 CERVANTES: Don Quixote, PART I, 124b-c

32 MILTON: Paradise Lost, BK VIII [379–560] 240b-244a

(4. *The institution of marriage: its nature and purpose. 4d. The laws and customs regulating marriage: adultery, incest.*)

23 HOBBES: *Leviathan*, PART II, 155b-c
24 RABELAIS: *Gargantua and Pantagruel*, BK I, 5c-6b; BK III, 140c-141c; 144d-146a; 148d-150d; 154a-156c; 159d-163c; 166a-169d; 173d-200d; BK IV, 248d-250a
25 MONTAIGNE: *Essays*, 44c-46b passim; 47a-c; 89d-90c; 185d-186c; 409d-434d passim
26 SHAKESPEARE: *1st Henry VI*, ACT V, SC V 31b-32a,c / *2nd Henry VI*, ACT I, SC I [1–74] 33b,d-34c / *Comedy of Errors*, ACT II, SC II [112–148] 154c-d; ACT III, SC II [1–70] 157c-158b / *Taming of the Shrew*, ACT I, SC I [48–101] 203a-c; ACT II, SC I [37–413] 208c-212c / *Romeo and Juliet*, ACT II, SC II [142–158] 295d-296a; SC III [55–94] 297a-b; SC VI 300c-d; ACT III, SC IV–V 306d-309d / *Much Ado About Nothing* 503a-531a,c esp ACT IV, SC I [1–256] 520b-523a / *As You Like It*, ACT III, SC III 613d-614d; ACT IV, SC I [127–180] 618b-c
27 SHAKESPEARE: *Hamlet*, ACT I, SC II [138–159] 33a; SC V [42–91] 37b-d; ACT III, SC IV [39–170] 55a-56b / *Merry Wives of Windsor* 73a-102d / *Troilus and Cressida*, ACT II, SC II [173–206] 115b-c / *Othello*, ACT I, SC III [52–209] 209c-211a; ACT IV, SC III [60–108] 236c-237a / *King Lear*, ACT IV, SC VI [109–135] 274c-d / *Pericles* 421a-448a,c esp ACT I, PROLOGUE–SC II 421b-425a / *Cymbeline* 449a-488d esp ACT II, SC IV–V 461b-463c, ACT III, SC IV 466d-468d / *Winter's Tale*, ACT I, SC II [186–228] 492a-c; ACT III, SC II [1–117] 501b-502c
29 CERVANTES: *Don Quixote*, PART I, 124a-c; PART II, 270c-271a
30 BACON: *New Atlantis*, 209a-d
32 MILTON: *Paradise Lost*, BK XI [708–721] 314b-315a / *Samson Agonistes* [30–1060] 340a-362b esp [292–325] 346a-b, [1010–1060] 361b-362b
35 LOCKE: *Civil Government*, CH VII, SECT 81–83 43a-c
36 SWIFT: *Gulliver*, PART III, 98b-99a; 127b; PART IV, 166a-b
36 STERNE: *Tristram Shandy*, 210b-213a; 258b-261a; 374b-376a
37 FIELDING: *Tom Jones*, 297d-298a; 375b-d; 388c-d
38 MONTESQUIEU: *Spirit of Laws*, BK VII, 48a-50a; BK X, 67a-b; BK XIV, 108a-b; BK XV–XVI, 115c-122a,c; BK XVIII, 132b-c; BK XIX, 141c-142a; BK XXIII, 187d-189d; 193a-197c; BK XXVI, 215b-c; 217c-218d; 219b-221c; 223a-c
38 ROUSSEAU: *Social Contract*, BK IV, 439b,d [fn 2]
40 GIBBON: *Decline and Fall*, 92c-d; 579a-b; 650c-d; 742b [n 93]; 750d [n 52]
41 GIBBON: *Decline and Fall*, 83d-86a; 93c-94a; 174b; 177d-178b; 245b-246a; 319b-d; 759b [n 30]

42 KANT: *Science of Right*, 419a-420b
43 MILL: *Liberty*, 311b-312a; 316d-317c; 319b-d
44 BOSWELL: *Johnson*, 160a-b; 304a-b; 411d; 429d-430b
46 HEGEL: *Philosophy of Right*, PART III, par 163–164 58d-59d; par 168 60b-c; ADDITIONS, 108 134b-c; 113 135a-b / *Philosophy of History*, PART III, 288c-289a; 294c-d
48 MELVILLE: *Moby Dick*, 289a-292a
49 DARWIN: *Descent of Man*, 276c; 313c-d; 315c-d; 565a-b; 578b-580c passim; 581d-582c; 584d-585d
50 MARX-ENGELS: *Communist Manifesto*, 427d-428a
51 TOLSTOY: *War and Peace*, BK III, 119a-128d; BK IV, 177a-179a; BK VI, 250a-251c; BK VII, 291a-292b; BK XI, 476c-479d; BK XII, 540d-541a; 545d
54 FREUD: *General Introduction*, 531c-d; 555a-b; 583c-d / *Civilization and Its Discontents*, 784a-d

4e. Divorce

OLD TESTAMENT: *Deuteronomy*, 24:1-4 / *Malachi*, 2:11-17—(D) *Malachias*, 2:11-17
APOCRYPHA: *Ecclesiasticus*, 7:19—(D) OT, *Ecclesiasticus*, 7:21
NEW TESTAMENT: *Matthew*, 5:31-32; 19:3-9 / *Mark*, 10:2-12 / *Luke*, 16:18 / *Romans*, 7:1-3 / *I Corinthians*, 7:10-16,39
5 EURIPIDES: *Medea* [131–268] 213b-214b
7 PLATO: *Laws*, BK VI, 712c-713c; BK XI, 780a-c
14 PLUTARCH: *Romulus*, 26a-b / *Lycurgus-Numa*, 62d-63c / *Alcibiades*, 158b-d / *Aemilius Paulus*, 215a-b / *Pompey*, 502d-503a / *Cato the Younger*, 629a-c
20 AQUINAS: *Summa Theologica*, PART I-II, Q 102, A 5, REP 3 283c-292c; Q 105, A 4, ANS and REP 8 318b-321a
25 MONTAIGNE: *Essays*, 299c
29 CERVANTES: *Don Quixote*, PART II, 261c-262a
30 BACON: *Advancement of Learning*, 84b
32 MILTON: *Paradise Lost*, BK IX [952–959] 268a
35 LOCKE: *Civil Government*, CH VII, SECT 81–82 43a-b
36 SWIFT: *Gulliver*, PART III, 127b
38 MONTESQUIEU: *Spirit of Laws*, BK XVI, 120b-122a,c; BK XXVI, 215c; 217c-218d
40 GIBBON: *Decline and Fall*, 92c
41 GIBBON: *Decline and Fall*, 84c-85c; 759b [n 30]
42 KANT: *Science of Right*, 419c-420a; 421c-d
43 MILL: *Liberty*, 316d-317c
44 BOSWELL: *Johnson*, 220d-221a; 304a-b; 411d
46 HEGEL: *Philosophy of Right*, PART III, par 176 61d-62a; ADDITIONS, 105 133d-134a; 113 135a-b / *Philosophy of History*, PART III, 288c-289a
49 DARWIN: *Descent of Man*, 584d-585c
51 TOLSTOY: *War and Peace*, BK IV, 177a-179a; BK V, 203a-d; BK XI, 476c-479d

5. The position of women

5*a*. The role of women in the family: the relation of husband and wife in domestic government

(5. The position of women. 5a. The role of women in the family: the relation of husband and wife in domestic government.)

52 DOSTOEVSKY: *Brothers Karamazov*, BK III, 46a-48b; BK V, 112a-113b

54 FREUD: *Group Psychology*, 692b / *Civilization and Its Discontents*, 783d-784a

5b. The status of women in the state: the right to citizenship, property, education

OLD TESTAMENT: *Numbers*, 27:1-11

4 HOMER: *Odyssey*, BK XI [385-461] 247a-c

5 AESCHYLUS: *Seven Against Thebes* [181-202] 29a-b

5 EURIPIDES: *Medea* [410-445] 215d

5 ARISTOPHANES: *Thesmophoriazusae* 600a-614d / *Ecclesiazusae* 615a-628d

6 HERODOTUS: *History*, BK I, 39b-c; BK II, 56c; BK IV, 128c-d; 143b-144b; 154b

7 PLATO: *Republic*, BK V, 356b-365d; BK VII, 401b-c / *Timaeus*, 442d / *Laws*, BK VI, 710d-711d; BK VII, 716b-717a; 721d-722c

9 ARISTOTLE: *Politics*, BK II, CH 1-4 455b,d-458a; CH 9 [1269^{b}13-1270^{a}33] 465d-466c; BK IV, CH 15 [1300^{a}4-8] 500d; BK V, CH 11 [1313^{b}33-42] 516c; BK VI, CH 4 [1319^{b}26-33] 523b; CH 8 [1322^{b}38-1323^{a}6] 526d; BK VII, CH 16 539d-541a / *Rhetoric*, BK I, CH 5 [1361^{a}6-12] 601c

13 VIRGIL: *Aeneid*, BK V [604-699] 202b-205b

14 PLUTARCH: *Lycurgus*, 39a-41a / *Numa Pompilius*, 54a-55a / *Lycurgus-Numa*, 62d-63c / *Solon*, 72c / *Pericles*, 133a-d / *Coriolanus*, 189d-191c / *Agis*, 650d-651b / *Marcus Brutus*, 811c-d

15 TACITUS: *Annals*, BK II, 44b-c; BK III, 53a-d; BK XII, 117d / *Histories*, BK IV, 285d-286a

20 AQUINAS: *Summa Theologica*, PART I-II, Q 105, A 2, REP 2 309d-316a

23 HOBBES: *Leviathan*, PART II, 109c-110b

24 RABELAIS: *Gargantua and Pantagruel*, BK I, 60c-66b

25 MONTAIGNE: *Essays*, 59d-60a; 399c-d

27 SHAKESPEARE: *Coriolanus*, ACT V, SC III 387a-389b

32 MILTON: *Samson Agonistes* [871-902] 358b-359a

35 LOCKE: *Civil Government*, CH VII, SECT 82 43b; CH XVI, SECT 183 67d-68b

36 SWIFT: *Gulliver*, PART III, 98b-99a; PART IV, 166b

36 STERNE: *Tristram Shandy*, 210b-213a

37 FIELDING: *Tom Jones*, 7b-c; 283b-c

38 MONTESQUIEU: *Spirit of Laws*, BK VII, 47c-50d; BK XII, 90c-d; BK XIV, 107d-108c; BK XVI 116a-122a,c; BK XIX, 137a; 137c-138c; 145c; BK XXVI, 215b-216a

38 ROUSSEAU: *Inequality*, 327c-d

39 SMITH: *Wealth of Nations*, BK III, 165b-166a; BK V, 340b-c

40 GIBBON: *Decline and Fall*, 61b-c; 122c-125b esp 122c; 533b-535d esp 533b-534a; 557c-d; 649c-652a

41 GIBBON: *Decline and Fall*, 14d-16a; 84a-b; 87d-88c passim; 89c; 164a-b; 170b-171c; 174b-c; 182a-183b

42 KANT: *Science of Right*, 419c-420a; 436d-437c

43 CONSTITUTION OF THE U.S.: AMENDMENTS, XIX 19d

43 MILL: *Liberty*, 317c-d / *Representative Government*, 387d-389b

44 BOSWELL: *Johnson*, 257d; 259d-260a; 274d-277d; 289c; 312a; 391c-392a

46 HEGEL: *Philosophy of Right*, PART III, par 166 59d-60a; ADDITIONS, 107 134a-b

50 MARX-ENGELS: *Communist Manifesto*, 423a; 427c-428a

5c. Women in relation to war

OLD TESTAMENT: *Deuteronomy*, 21:10-14 / *Judges*, 4-5

APOCRYPHA: *Judith*, 8-16—(D) OT, *Judith*, 8-16

4 HOMER: *Iliad*, BK II [155-162] 11c; BK III [146-160] 20c; BK XXII [405-515] 159c-160d; BK XXIV [707-804] 178d-179d / *Odyssey*, BK II 188a-192d

5 AESCHYLUS: *Persians* [1-139] 15a-16d / *Seven Against Thebes* [79-263] 28a-30a / *Agamemnon* [399-455] 56b-57a; [855-922] 61b-d

5 EURIPIDES: *Medea* [247-268] 214b / *Trojan Women* 270a-281a,c / *Helen* 298a-314a,c / *Andromache* [91-116] 316a-b / *Iphigenia at Aulis* 425a-439d

5 ARISTOPHANES: *Lysistrata* 583a-599a,c

6 HERODOTUS: *History*, BK I, 2a; BK III, 121c-d; 123c; BK IV, 143b-144b; 153a-b; BK VII, 232b

7 PLATO: *Republic*, BK V, 356b-368c / *Critias*, 479c-480a / *Laws*, BK VI, 713b-c; BK VII, 721d-722c; 726a-c; BK VIII, 734a-735a

9 ARISTOTLE: *Politics*, BK II, CH 9 [1269^{b}13-1270^{a}14] 465d-466b

10 HIPPOCRATES: *Airs, Waters, Places*, par 17 16a-b

13 VIRGIL: *Aeneid*, BK I [490-493] 116b; BK II [567-623] 140a-141b; BK V [605-699] 202b-205b; BK XI [486-915] 341b-353a

14 PLUTARCH: *Theseus*, 10b-11c / *Romulus*, 21a-24d / *Coriolanus*, 189d-191c / *Pyrrhus*, 328c-330a / *Antony*, 756c-779c esp 760c-d, 767c-774a / *Marcus Brutus*, 811c-d

15 TACITUS: *Annals*, BK I, 12b-d; 20b-c; BK II, 26b-c; BK III, 53a-d; BK XIV, 150a-b / *Histories*, BK IV, 271c-d

22 CHAUCER: *Knight's Tale* [859-1004] 174a-176b

24 RABELAIS: *Gargantua and Pantagruel*, BK III, 140c-141c; 144b-c

26 SHAKESPEARE: *King John*, ACT III, SC I [299-338] 389b-c / *1st Henry IV*, ACT II, SC III [77-120] 444a-b / *2nd Henry IV*, ACT II, SC III 477d-478c

27 SHAKESPEARE: *Troilus and Cressida*, ACT II, SC II [163–206] 115b-c / *Coriolanus*, ACT V, SC III 387a-389b

35 LOCKE: *Civil Government*, CH XVI, SECT 182–183 67c-68b

39 SMITH: *Wealth of Nations*, BK V, 301b-c

40 GIBBON: *Decline and Fall*, 93a-b; 509d-510b

41 GIBBON: *Decline and Fall*, 437b-c; 551d-552c

49 DARWIN: *Descent of Man*, 565a-b

51 TOLSTOY: *War and Peace*, BK I, 13a-14b; 55c-59d; BK II, 76a-b; 90c-91a; BK V, 222d-223a; BK IX, 367c-369a; BK X, 392a-b; 397a-398c; 410c-421c; BK XI, 485a-488c; 518b-c; 528b-531d; BK XII, 538a-539c; BK XIII, 580c-d

6. Parents and children: fatherhood, motherhood

OLD TESTAMENT: *Exodus*, 20:5-6,12 / *Proverbs*, 20:20 / *Jeremiah*, 31:29-30—(D) *Jeremias*, 31:29-30 / *Ezekiel*, 18—(D) *Ezechiel*, 18

APOCRYPHA: *Tobit*—(D) OT, *Tobias* / *Ecclesiasticus*, 3:1-16—(D) OT, *Ecclesiasticus*, 3:1-16

4 HOMER: *Iliad*, BK XXII [429–515] 159d-160d / *Odyssey*, BK II 188a-192d; BK XI [458–540] 247c-248b; BK XV–XVI 266a-276d

5 EURIPIDES: *Medea* [1081–1115] 221b-c

6 HERODOTUS: *History*, BK VI, 212c-213a

6 THUCYDIDES: *Peloponnesian War*, BK II, 398c-d

7 PLATO: *Laches*, 29b / *Symposium*, 165b-167a / *Crito*, 214c

9 ARISTOTLE: *Ethics*, BK VIII, CH 12 [1161^{b}16–32] 414a-b / *Politics*, BK I, CH 12 453d-454a; BK II, CH 3 [1262^{a}14–24] 457a; BK VII, CH 16–17 539d-542a,c / *Rhetoric*, BK I, CH 5 [1360^{b}9–1361^{a}11] 601a-c

10 GALEN: *Natural Faculties*, BK I, CH 12, 173b-c

12 EPICTETUS: *Discourses*, BK III, CH 22, 198c-199c

13 VIRGIL: *Aeneid*, BK VI [679–698] 229a-b; BK VIII [508–519] 272b-273a; BK IX [224–313] 285a-287a

18 AUGUSTINE: *Confessions*, BK V, par 15 31a-c

19 AQUINAS: *Summa Theologica*, PART I, Q 27, A 2 154c-155b; Q 28, A 4, ANS and REP 5 160c-161d; Q 30, A 2, ANS and REP 1-2 168a-169b; Q 31, A 2 172b-173c; Q 32, A 2, ANS and REP 2 178a-179b; A 3, ANS and REP 4-5 179b-180b; Q 33 180d-185a; Q 39, A 8 210a-213a; QQ 40–42 213a-230a passim; Q 43, A 4 232c-233a; Q 93, A 6, REP 2 496b-498a; Q 119, A 2, REP 2 607b-608d

20 AQUINAS: *Summa Theologica*, PART I–II, Q 81 162d-167d passim

25 MONTAIGNE: *Essays*, 184a-b; 191c-192d

26 SHAKESPEARE: *1st Henry VI*, ACT IV, SC V–VII 23d-26a / *3rd Henry VI*, ACT II, SC V [55–122] 82b-d

27 SHAKESPEARE: *King Lear*, ACT I, SC II [1–22] 247d-248a

30 BACON: *New Atlantis*, 207c-208d

32 MILTON: *Paradise Lost*, BK V [388–403] 183b-184a; BK X [182–196] 278b

35 LOCKE: *Civil Government*, CH VI 36a-42a

36 SWIFT: *Gulliver*, PART I, 29b-31a; PART IV, 165b-167a

36 STERNE: *Tristram Shandy*, 191b-192a; 210b-213a; 352a-353b; 400a-402a

37 FIELDING: *Tom Jones*, 44b-d; 305b

38 ROUSSEAU: *Inequality*, 364d-365b / *Political Economy*, 367a-368c / *Social Contract*, BK I, 387d-388a

42 KANT: *Science of Right*, 420b-421c

44 BOSWELL: *Johnson*, 510b-c

46 HEGEL: *Philosophy of Right*, PART III, par 173 61a-b

49 DARWIN: *Descent of Man*, 579d-580a

51 TOLSTOY: *War and Peace*

52 DOSTOEVSKY: *Brothers Karamazov*, BK XII, 395a-398d

53 JAMES: *Psychology*, 189a; 717b

54 FREUD: *Narcissism*, 406b-c / *New Introductory Lectures*, 863a-c; 876a-d

6a. The desire for offspring

OLD TESTAMENT: *Genesis*, 15:1-6; 19:30-38; 25:19-26; 30:1-24 / *I Samuel*, 1:1-2:11—(D) *I Kings*, 1:1-2:11

APOCRYPHA: *Tobit*, 8:4-8—(D) OT, *Tobias*, 8:4-10

NEW TESTAMENT: *Luke*, 1:5-25

5 EURIPIDES: *Medea* [1081–1115] 221b-c / *Ion* 282a-297a,c / *Andromache* 315a-326a,c esp [309–420] 318a-d

6 HERODOTUS: *History*, BK I, 32a-b

7 PLATO: *Symposium*, 165b-167a / *Laws*, BK IV, 685a-c; BK VI, 708a-b

9 ARISTOTLE: *Politics*, BK I, CH 2 [1252^{a}27–30] 445c

12 EPICTETUS: *Discourses*, BK III, CH 22, 198c-199c

13 VIRGIL: *Aeneid*, BK I [657–722] 121a-123a; BK IV [296–330] 175a-176a

14 PLUTARCH: *Cato the Younger*, 629a-c

15 TACITUS: *Annals*, BK III, 51a; BK XV, 162b-c

18 AUGUSTINE: *Confessions*, BK II, par 6 10a-b; BK IV, par 2 19d / *City of God*, BK XIV, CH 21–22 392b-393b / *Christian Doctrine*, BK III, CH 12, 663a-c

19 AQUINAS: *Summa Theologica*, PART I, Q 98, A 2 517d-519a

20 AQUINAS: *Summa Theologica*, PART I–II, Q 84, A 4, ANS 176d-178a; PART III, Q 65, A 1 879c-881d

23 HOBBES: *Leviathan*, PART II, 155b

25 MONTAIGNE: *Essays*, 484c

27 SHAKESPEARE: *Sonnets*, I–XVII 586a-588d

30 BACON: *Advancement of Learning*, 72c-73a

31 SPINOZA: *Ethics*, PART IV, APPENDIX, XX 449a

32 MILTON: *Paradise Lost*, BK IV [720–775] 168a-169a; BK X [966–1053] 295b-297a

36 SWIFT: *Gulliver*, PART IV, 165b-166b

36 STERNE: *Tristram Shandy*, 522a-523a; 549a

37 FIELDING: *Tom Jones*, 21c-d

38 ROUSSEAU: *Inequality*, 364d-365b

(6. Parents and children: fatherhood, motherhood. 6a. The desire for offspring.)

39 SMITH: *Wealth of Nations*, BK I, 29d-30d

44 BOSWELL: *Johnson*, 293d

46 HEGEL: *Philosophy of Right*, PART III, par 161 58b

54 FREUD: *Instincts*, 415a-b / *New Introductory Lectures*, 860d-861a; 863a-b

6b. Eugenics: control of breeding; birth control

6 HERODOTUS: *History*, BK IV, 143b-c

7 PLATO: *Republic*, BK V, 361c-363b; BK VIII, 403a-d / *Timaeus*, 443a / *Statesman*, 605d-608d esp 608a-c / *Laws*, BK V, 693a-c; BK VI, 707b-709a; 712b-713c

9 ARISTOTLE: *History of Animals*, BK VII, CH 3 [583ᵃ14-25] 108d / *Politics*, BK II, CH 6 [1265ᵃ38-ᵇ18] 460d-461a; CH 9 [1270ᵃ39-ᵇ6] 466c; CH 10 [1272ᵃ23-24] 468c; BK VII, CH 16 539d-541a

14 PLUTARCH: *Lycurgus*, 39a-40c / *Solon*, 71d-72a / *Cato the Younger*, 629a-c

15 TACITUS: *Annals*, BK III, 51a

19 AQUINAS: *Summa Theologica*, PART I, Q 99, A 2, REP 2 520a-d

22 CHAUCER: *Parson's Tale*, par 35, 520b

30 BACON: *New Atlantis*, 207b-209d

36 SWIFT: *Gulliver*, PART IV, 166a-b; 168a-b

36 STERNE: *Tristram Shandy*, 193b-194b; 271b

38 MONTESQUIEU: *Spirit of Laws*, BK XXIII, 187d; 190a-b; 191c-d; 192a-b; 192d-199b

38 ROUSSEAU: *Inequality*, 335a-b; 364d-365a

40 GIBBON: *Decline and Fall*, 175c

41 GIBBON: *Decline and Fall*, 83c

43 MILL: *Liberty*, 319b-d / *Representative Government*, 426d-427a

49 DARWIN: *Descent of Man*, 267b-c; 275d-277c esp 276d-277a; 323b-328a; 391d-394a,c; 578a-579a; 581c-d; 583a; 596b-d

6c. The condition of immaturity

NEW TESTAMENT: *I Corinthians*, 13:10-11

7 PLATO: *Lysis*, 16c-17c / *Protagoras*, 46b-d / *Euthydemus*, 67a / *Republic*, BK II, 320c-321d; BK IV, 353b-d; BK V, 366a-c; BK VII, 399c-401a / *Philebus*, 611c-d / *Laws*, BK II, 653a-c; BK VII, 723c-d

8 ARISTOTLE: *Physics*, BK VII, CH 3 [247ᵇ13-248ᵃ6] 330c-d

9 ARISTOTLE: *History of Animals*, BK VIII, CH 1 [588ᵃ25-ᵇ5] 114b,d / *Parts of Animals*, BK IV, CH 10 [686ᵇ5-30] 218a-c / *Ethics*, BK I, CH 3 [1094ᵇ27-1095ᵃ11] 340a; CH 9 [1099ᵇ32-1100ᵃ9] 345b-c; BK III, CH 12 [1119ᵃ35-ᵇ19] 366a,c; BK IV, CH 9 [1128ᵇ15-20] 376a; BK V, CH 6 [1134ᵇ8-17] 382b-c; BK VI, CH 8 [1142ᵃ12-19] 391b; BK VII, CH 13 [1153ᵃ27-35] 404c-d; BK VIII, CH 3 [1156ᵃ22-ᵇ5] 407d-408a; BK X, CH 3 [1174ᵃ1-4] 428b / *Politics*, BK I, CH 12 453d-454a; BK III, CH 5 [1278ᵃ3-6] 475a-b; BK VII, CH 9 [1329ᵃ2-17] 533b-c; CH 14 [1332ᵇ36-41]

537c-d; CH 15 [1334ᵇ8-28] 539b-d; CH 17 541a-542a,c / *Rhetoric*, BK II, CH 12 636a-d

12 LUCRETIUS: *Nature of Things*, BK V [222-234] 64a

12 EPICTETUS: *Discourses*, BK III, CH 6, 182b

12 AURELIUS: *Meditations*, BK I, SECT 17 255d-256d

14 PLUTARCH: *Alexander*, 540b,d-549c

18 AUGUSTINE: *Confessions*, BK I, par 7-31 2c-9a; BK II, par 3-9 9b-11a / *City of God*, BK XXI, CH 16 573b-574a

19 AQUINAS: *Summa Theologica*, PART I, QQ 100-101 520d-523d; PART I-II, Q 34, A 1, REP 2 768c-769d; Q 40, A 6 796c-797a

20 AQUINAS: *Summa Theologica*, PART I-II, Q 94, A 1, REP to CONTRARY 221a-d; Q 95, A 1 226c-227c

21 DANTE: *Divine Comedy*, PURGATORY, XVI [85-96] 77d

23 HOBBES: *Leviathan*, PART I, 60b; 78b; PART II, 132b-c

24 RABELAIS: *Gargantua and Pantagruel*, BK I, 9c-11d; 14c-18b; 24a-30c; BK II, 74b-75c

25 MONTAIGNE: *Essays*, 43a-c; 63d-79c passim, esp 72b-75a; 414a-d

27 SHAKESPEARE: *Troilus and Cressida*, ACT II, SC II [163-173] 115b

35 LOCKE: *Civil Government*, CH VI, SECT 54-75 36c-42a passim; CH VII, SECT 79-81 42c-43a; CH XV, SECT 170 64d-65a / *Human Understanding*, BK II, CH XXXIII, SECT 8-10 249c-d

37 FIELDING: *Tom Jones*, 36a-54c esp 36a-38b, 53b-54c

38 MONTESQUIEU: *Spirit of Laws*, BK XXIII, 189b

38 ROUSSEAU: *Social Contract*, BK I, 387d-388a; 389c

43 MILL: *Liberty*, 271d-272a

46 HEGEL: *Philosophy of Right*, PART III, par 159 58a; par 173-175 61a-d; ADDITIONS, 68 126d-127a; 111-112 134d-135a

51 TOLSTOY: *War and Peace*, BK I, 20c-26a; 35b-37d; BK III, 132b-c; BK IV, 192d-193c; BK VI, 252d-254c; 269c-270a; BK IX, 381b-c; 382a-384b; BK XII, 559d; BK XIV, 592d-604b

52 DOSTOEVSKY: *Brothers Karamazov*, BK IV, 90b-92b; 100c-109a,c; BK X 272a-297d; EPILOGUE, 408a-412d

53 JAMES: *Psychology*, 206b-207a

54 FREUD: *Origin and Development of Psycho-Analysis*, 15a-18a / *Sexual Enlightenment of Children* 119a-122a,c / *Interpretation of Dreams*, 191b-193a; 238c-239a; 241b-243c / *Narcissism*, 400a / *General Introduction*, 495a-496b passim; 526d-532a esp 526d-527c, 530d-532a; 572d-576d; 579b-584d esp 579b-580d; 591a-d; 592c; 594d-599b; 612d-614b / *Beyond the Pleasure Principle*, 641d-643c; 644d-645a; 651b-c / *Group Psychology*, 685b-d; 693a-c / *Inhibitions, Symptoms, and Anxiety*, 724a-727c; 737c-740c; 741b; 743a-d; 746c-747a; 751d-753c / *Civilization and Its Discontents*, 768b-c / *New Introductory Lectures*, 855b-861c passim; 868d-870c

CHAPTER 26: FAMILY

6d. The care and government of children: the rights and duties of the child; parental despotism and tyranny

OLD TESTAMENT: *Genesis*, 9:21-26 / *Exodus*, 12:26-27; 20:12; 21:15,17 / *Leviticus*, 19:3 / *Deuteronomy*, 5:16; 6:6-7; 21:15-23 / *Proverbs*, 1:8-9; 3:12; 6:20-23; 13:1,24; 15:5; 19:18; 20:20; 22:6,15; 23:13-24; 28:24; 29:15,17; 30:17 / *Zechariah*, 13:3—(D) *Zacharias*, 13:3

APOCRYPHA: *Tobit*, 4:1-5—(D) OT, *Tobias*, 4:1-6 / *Ecclesiasticus*, 3:1-18; 4:30; 7:23-28; 30:1-13; 42:9-11—(D) OT, *Ecclesiasticus*, 3:1-20; 4:35; 7:25-30; 30:1-13; 42:9-11

NEW TESTAMENT: *Matthew*, 10:35-37; 15:3-6 / *Luke*, 2:51-52; 12:51-53 / *II Corinthians*, 12:14 / *Galatians*, 4:1-2 / *Ephesians*, 6:1-4 / *Colossians*, 3:20-21 / *I Timothy*, 5:8

5 AESCHYLUS: *Eumenides* 81a-91d

5 SOPHOCLES: *Oedipus the King* [1458-1530] 112c-113a,c / *Oedipus at Colonus* 114a-130a,c / *Antigone* [626-767] 136c-137d / *Electra* 156a-169a,c / *Trachiniae* [1157-1278] 180a-181a,c

5 EURIPIDES: *Alcestis* [280-325] 239c-240a; [611-738] 242c-243c / *Heracles Mad* [562-584] 369d-370a; [622-636] 370c / *Phoenician Maidens* 378a-393d esp [1485-1766] 391a-393d / *Orestes* 394a-410d

5 ARISTOPHANES: *Clouds* [791-888] 498b-499b; [1321-1451] 504c-506b / *Birds* [1337-1371] 558d-559b; [1640-1675] 562b-c

6 HERODOTUS: *History*, BK II, 76a; BK IV, 155c-156a; BK V, 160d-161a; BK VIII, 281c

7 PLATO: *Lysis*, 16c-17c / *Laches*, 26a-27d / *Protagoras*, 42d-43d; 45d-47c / *Symposium*, 165c-166b / *Meno*, 186a-187b / *Euthyphro*, 192a-c / *Crito*, 214c; 216d-217d / *Republic*, BK II, 321b-c; BK V, 360d-365d / *Timaeus*, 442d-443a / *Laws*, BK III, 672d-673d; BK IV, 683b-c; BK V, 686d-688b esp 687d-688a; BK VII, 713c-716c; 723c-d; BK IX, 750d-751b; 755a-757c; BK XI, 779b-781c / *Seventh Letter*, 804a

9 ARISTOTLE: *History of Animals*, BK VII, CH I [581^{b}11-22] 107b / *Ethics*, BK III, CH 12 [1119^{a}33-^{b}18] 366a,c; BK V, CH 6 [1134^{b}8-17] 382b-c; BK VIII, CH 10 [1160^{b}23-32] 413a; BK IX, CH 2 417c-418b; BK X, CH 9 [1180^{a}14-^{b}14] 434d-435c / *Politics*, BK I, CH 12-13 453d-455a,c passim; BK III, CH 6 [1278^{b}30-1279^{a}2] 476a-b; BK IV, CH 11 [1295^{b}14-20] 495d; BK VII, CH 15 [1334^{b}8-28] 539b-d; CH 17 541a-542a,c; BK VIII, CH 3 [1338^{a}30-^{b}8] 543c-d

12 EPICTETUS: *Discourses*, BK I, CH 11 116d-118d; CH 23 128c-d; BK III, CH 22, 198c-199c

12 AURELIUS: *Meditations*, BK I 253a-256d

13 VIRGIL: *Eclogues*, IV [60-64] 15b / *Aeneid*, BK VIII [508-519] 272b-273a; BK IX [224-313] 285a-287a

14 PLUTARCH: *Lycurgus*, 40c-41a / *Fabius*, 152b-d / *Coriolanus*, 174b,d-175a; 189d-191d / *Marcus Cato*, 286c-287b

18 AUGUSTINE: *Confessions*, BK I, par 18 5c-d; BK II, par 3-8 9b-10d / *City of God*, BK XIX, CH 14 520a-d

20 AQUINAS: *Summa Theologica*, PART I-II, Q 94, A 2, ANS 221d-223a; Q 95, A I, ANS 226c-227c; Q 105, A 4, ANS 318b-321a; PART II-II, Q 26, AA 9-11 517a-519a

22 CHAUCER: *Physician's Tale* [12,006-038] 367b-368a

23 HOBBES: *Leviathan*, PART II, 109c-110b; 121a; 137d; 155b

24 RABELAIS: *Gargantua and Pantagruel*, BK I, 14c-18b; BK II, 74b-75c; 81a-83b; BK III, 219b-222b

25 MONTAIGNE: *Essays*, 43a-c; 63d-79c passim, esp 63d-64b, 66c-67a; 83a-c; 183c-192d esp 183d-185d; 344a-c; 534a-d

26 SHAKESPEARE: *3rd Henry VI*, ACT II, SC II [1-55] 78d-79b / *Titus Andronicus*, ACT V, SC III [35-64] 196d-197a / *Romeo and Juliet* 285a-319a,c esp ACT III, SC V [127-215] 308c-309c / *Midsummer-Night's Dream*, ACT I, SC I [1-121] 352c-353c / *1st Henry IV*, ACT III, SC II 452d-454d

27 SHAKESPEARE: *Othello*, ACT I, SC III [175-189] 210d-211a / *King Lear* 244a-283a,c esp ACT I 244a-254c / *Cymbeline*, ACT I, SC I [125-158] 451a-c

29 CERVANTES: *Don Quixote*, PART II, 218c-220c; 251b; 261c-262a

30 BACON: *New Atlantis*, 207b-209d

31 SPINOZA: *Ethics*, PART IV, APPENDIX, XX 449a

35 LOCKE: *Civil Government*, CH VI, SECT 52-CH VII, SECT 81 36a-43a; CH XV, SECT 170 64d-65a; SECT 173-174 65c-d / *Human Understanding*, BK I, CH II, SECT 9, 106a-b; SECT 12 107b-d; BK II, CH XXXIII, SECT 7-10 249b-d

36 SWIFT: *Gulliver*, PART I, 29b; PART IV, 166a-167a

36 STERNE: *Tristram Shandy*, 191b-192a; 250b-251a; 400a-402a; 410a-411a; 423b-424b

37 FIELDING: *Tom Jones*, 35a-49a,c; 65b-c; 108c-110c; 120c-121a,c; 124a-126c; 136a-c; 217d-219c; 283c-d; 310b-313b; 321b-324b; 338d-345d; 359b-364d

38 MONTESQUIEU: *Spirit of Laws*, BK V, 22d-23a; BK XXIII, 187d-188a; 189b-d; BK XXVI, 216a-217b; 220a-b

38 ROUSSEAU: *Inequality*, 326c-d; 357a-b; 365a-b / *Political Economy*, 367a-368c; 377a / *Social Contract*, BK I, 387d-388a; 389c

39 SMITH: *Wealth of Nations*, BK I, 29d-30d; BK V, 338c-d

41 GIBBON: *Decline and Fall*, 45b-c; 82b-83c

42 KANT: *Science of Right*, 404d; 420b-422d

43 MILL: *Liberty*, 316d-319d passim, esp 317d

44 BOSWELL: *Johnson*, 199d-200d; 247c-d; 301d-302a; 424d-425a

46 HEGEL: *Philosophy of Right*, PART III, par 159 58a; par 173-175 61a-d; ADDITIONS, 111 134d-135a / *Philosophy of History*, PART I, 211d-212c; PART III, 288c-289b

(6. *Parents and children: fatherhood, motherhood. 6d. The care and government of children: the rights and duties of the child;
parental despotism and tyranny.*)

50 MARX: *Capital*, 193a-194b; 241a-d

50 MARX-ENGELS: *Communist Manifesto*, 427c

51 TOLSTOY: *War and Peace*, BK I, 2c-3a; 22b-
23a; 34d-35b; 47b-48d; BK III, 119a-128d; BK
IV, 192b-193d; BK V, 207b-208a; 210b-211a;
BK VI, 252d-254c; 271c-274a,c; BK VII, 291a-
292b; BK VIII, 305b-307d; 324b-325c; 335d-
336a; BK IX, 356b-358b; 381b-c; 382a-384b;
BK X, 406c-410c; EPILOGUE I, 659d-674a,c
passim

52 DOSTOEVSKY: *Brothers Karamazov*, BK I, 2d-
11a; BK XII, 370b-d; 395a-398d

54 FREUD: *Origin and Development of Psycho-
Analysis*, 17d-18a / *Sexual Enlightenment of
Children* 119a-122a,c passim / *Interpretation of
Dreams*, 244a-c / *Narcissism*, 406b-c / *General
Introduction*, 573b-d / *Inhibitions, Symptoms,
and Anxiety*, 751d / *Civilization and Its Discontents*, 794c-795a esp 795b [fn 2] / *New Introductory Lectures*, 832b-c; 834b-c; 868d-
871a esp 869b-c, 870a-c; 876c

6e. The initiation of children into adult life

NEW TESTAMENT: *Luke*, 2:41-52

4 HOMER: *Odyssey*, BK I-II 183a-192d; BK XI
[487-540] 247d-248b

6 HERODOTUS: *History*, BK IV, 125c-126a; 155c-
156a

9 ARISTOTLE: *Ethics*, BK III, CH 12 [1119ª33-
ᵇ18] 366a,c

12 AURELIUS: *Meditations*, BK I 253a-256d

14 PLUTARCH: *Lycurgus*, 41b-42b

18 AUGUSTINE: *Confessions*, BK II, par 3-8 9b-10d

25 MONTAIGNE: *Essays*, 63d-79c passim, esp 72b-
75a; 156d-158a,c; 184a-191c esp 187a-c

26 SHAKESPEARE: *Two Gentlemen of Verona*, ACT
I, SC III [1-42] 232c-d / *2nd Henry IV*, ACT V,
SC II 497d-499b

27 SHAKESPEARE: *Hamlet*, ACT I, SC III [52-136]
34d-35d / *Cymbeline*, ACT IV, SC IV 478b-d

30 BACON: *New Atlantis*, 207b-209a

35 LOCKE: *Civil Government*, CH VI, SECT 59-69
37b-40b passim

38 MONTESQUIEU: *Spirit of Laws*, BK XVIII,
133a-b

38 ROUSSEAU: *Political Economy*, 376b-d /
Social Contract, BK I, 387d-388a

40 GIBBON: *Decline and Fall*, 82a; 91b

41 GIBBON: *Decline and Fall*, 86b-c

46 HEGEL: *Philosophy of Right*, PART III, par 159
58a; par 174 61b; par 177 62a; ADDITIONS,
III-II2 134d-135a

48 MELVILLE: *Moby Dick*, 387b

51 TOLSTOY: *War and Peace*, BK I, 36d-37a; BK
III, 128d-131c esp 130d-131b; BK IV, 192d-
193c; BK VI, 254c-260a; 267c-270a; BK IX,
381b-c; 382a-384b; BK XIV, 592d-604b

54 FREUD: *Origin and Development of Psycho-
Analysis*, 17d-18a / *Sexual Enlightenment of
Children* 119a-122a,c passim / *General Introduction*, 512a; 583c-d; 584b-c / *Group Psychology*, 682a-b / *Civilization and Its Discontents*, 783d

7. The life of the family

7a. Marriage and love: romantic, conjugal,
and illicit love

OLD TESTAMENT: *Genesis*, 2:23-24; 24:67; 29:16-
30 / *Ruth* / *I Samuel*, 1:1-8—(D) *I Kings*,
1:1-8 / *II Samuel*, 11; 13:1-20—(D) *II Kings*,
11; 13:1-20 / *Proverbs*, 5; 6:20-7:27 / *Ecclesiastes*, 9:9 / *Song of Solomon—(D) Canticle of
Canticles*

APOCRYPHA: *Tobit*, 6:10-17—(D) OT, *Tobias*,
6:11-22 / *Ecclesiasticus*, 7:26; 25:1; 40:23—
(D) OT, *Ecclesiasticus*, 7:28; 25:1-2; 40:23

NEW TESTAMENT: *Matthew*, 19:4-6 / *Mark*,
10:6-9 / *I Corinthians*, 7:1-15,32-34 / *Ephesians*, 5:22-33 / *Colossians*, 3:18-19 / *I Peter*,
3:1-7

4 HOMER: *Iliad*, BK IX [334-347] 60c-d; BK XIV
[229-360] 100c-101d / *Odyssey*, BK XXIII [152-
365] 313d-316a; BK XXIV [191-202] 319a

5 AESCHYLUS: *Agamemnon* [681-781] 59b-60b
/ *Choephoroe* [585-651] 75d-76b; [892-930]
78d-79b

5 SOPHOCLES: *Trachiniae* 170a-181a,c

5 EURIPIDES: *Medea* 212a-224a,c esp [446-662]
215d-217c / *Hippolytus* 225a-236d esp [373-
481] 228b-229b / *Alcestis* 237a-247a,c esp
[152-198] 238c-239a, [329-368] 240a-b / *Suppliants* [990-1071] 267a-c / *Trojan Women* [634-
683] 275c-d / *Helen* 298a-314a,c / *Andromache*
315a-326a,c esp [147-244] 316c-317b / *Electra*
[988-1122] 336a-337b

5 ARISTOPHANES: *Lysistrata* 583a-599a,c / *Thesmophoriazusae* 600a-614d esp [383-532] 604d-
606a

6 HERODOTUS: *History*, BK VI, 197a-c; BK IX,
311b-312d

7 PLATO: *Symposium*, 152d-153a / *Republic*, BK
V, 361b-363b

9 ARISTOTLE: *Ethics*, BK VIII, CH 12 [1162ª15-34]
414c-d

12 LUCRETIUS: *Nature of Things*, BK IV [1192-
1287] 59d-61a,c

13 VIRGIL: *Aeneid*, BK II [730-794] 144b-146b; BK
IV [1-361] 167a-177a

14 PLUTARCH: *Lycurgus*, 39d-40b / *Lycurgus-
Numa*, 62d-63c / *Solon*, 71d-72a / *Demetrius*,
731a-b / *Antony*, 756c-779d / *Marcus Brutus*,
807b-d; 811c-d

15 TACITUS: *Annals*, BK IV, 64b-c; BK XI, 107b-
110a; BK XII, 121c

17 PLOTINUS: *Third Ennead*, TR V, CH I 100c-
101c

18 AUGUSTINE: *Confessions*, BK II, par 2-8 9b-
10d; BK IV, par 2 19d; BK VI, par 21-25 41c-

42d / *City of God*, BK XIV, CH 16–26 390a-396c; BK XV, CH 16, 411b-c / *Christian Doctrine*, BK III, CH 12, 663a-c; CH 18–22 664d-666c

19 AQUINAS: *Summa Theologica*, PART I, Q 92, A 2, ANS 489d-490c; Q 98, A 2, ANS and REP 3 517d-519a; PART I–II, Q 28, A 4, ANS 742d-743c

20 AQUINAS: *Summa Theologica*, PART I–II, Q 105, A 4, ANS 318b-321a; PART II–II, Q 26, A 11 518b-519a; PART III, Q 6, A 1, REP 3 740b-741b

21 DANTE: *Divine Comedy*, HELL, V [25–142] 7b-8b; PURGATORY, VIII [67–84] 65a; XXV [109–139] 92c-d

22 CHAUCER: *Troilus and Cressida* 1a-155a / *Miller's Tale* 212b-223b / *Wife of Bath's Prologue* [5583–6410] 256a-269b / *Tale of Wife of Bath* 270a-277a esp [6619–6623] 273a / *Clerk's Tale* 296a-318a / *Merchant's Tale* 319a-338a / *Franklin's Tale* 351b-366a esp [11,041–125] 351b-352b, [11,754–766b] 363a / *Manciple's Tale* [17,088–103] 490a / *Parson's Tale*, par 79–80 541a-542a

23 HOBBES: *Leviathan*, PART II, 155b-c; PART IV, 272d

24 RABELAIS: *Gargantua and Pantagruel*, BK I, 8c-d; BK II, 73b-74b; 106a-108d; 109c-126d; BK III, 144d-146a; 148d-150d; 154a-156c; 159d-163c; 166a-169d; 186d-188c; 196b-d

25 MONTAIGNE: *Essays*, 37c-40a; 84a-b; 89d-90c; 306d-307a; 358b-362a; 409d-434d esp 410a-422b; 472a-473a

26 SHAKESPEARE: *Ist Henry VI*, ACT V, SC III [80–195] 28a-29b; SC V [48–78] 31d-32a / *Comedy of Errors*, ACT II, SC I 152a-153b; SC II [112–148] 154c-d; ACT III, SC II [1–70] 157c-158b; ACT V, SC I [38–122] 165c-166b / *Taming of the Shrew* 199a-228a,c / *Two Gentlemen of Verona*, ACT I, SC II [1–34] 230d-231b / *Romeo and Juliet* 285a-319a,c / *Richard II*, ACT V, SC I [71–102] 345d-346b / *Much Ado About Nothing* 503a-531a,c / *Henry V*, ACT V, SC II [98–306] 564b-566a / *Julius Caesar*, ACT II, SC I [261–309] 577b-c / *As You Like It*, ACT IV, SC I [127–180] 618b-c; ACT V, SC IV [114–156] 625a-b

27 SHAKESPEARE: *Hamlet*, ACT I, SC II [137–159] 33a; SC III [5–51] 34c-d; SC V [34–91] 37b-d; ACT III, SC I [120–157] 48b-c / *Merry Wives of Windsor* 73a-102d / *Troilus and Cressida* 103a-141a,c / *Othello* 205a-243a,c / *Antony and Cleopatra* 311a-350d / *Cymbeline* 449a-488d esp ACT II, SC V 463a-c, ACT III, SC IV 466d-468d, ACT V, SC V [25–68] 483c-484a, [129–227] 484d-485d / *Tempest*, ACT IV, SC I [1–133] 542b-543a

29 CERVANTES: *Don Quixote*, PART I, 120b-137d; PART II, 261c-262a; 270c-271a

31 SPINOZA: *Ethics*, PART IV, APPENDIX, XIX–XX 449a

32 MILTON: *Paradise Lost*, BK IV [172–340] 156a-159b; [440–504] 162a-163b; [736–775] 168b-169a; BK V [443–450] 185a; BK VIII [39–65] 233a-b; [491–520] 243a-b; BK IX [226–269] 252a-253a; [952–959] 268a; BK X [888–908] 293b-294a

36 STERNE: *Tristram Shandy*, 193b-194a; 522a-523a

37 FIELDING: *Tom Jones*, 2b-c; 14b-16b; 17a-b; 30a-32d; 108c-111c; 118d; 124a-125b; 130b-c; 199b-200a; 230a-231c; 283b-c; 289b-291a; 321b-322a; 332a-333a; 349b-350b; 352d-353a; 360b-d; 400a-402d; 405a,c

38 ROUSSEAU: *Inequality*, 364d-365b

40 GIBBON: *Decline and Fall*, 92c-93a; 649c-652a

42 KANT: *Science of Right*, 419a-420b

44 BOSWELL: *Johnson*, 22a; 57a; 64a; 107a; 160b; 194a; 294d-295a

46 HEGEL: *Philosophy of Right*, PART III, par 158 58a; par 161–168 58b-60c; ADDITIONS, 101–108 133b-134c

47 GOETHE: *Faust*, PART I [4243–4250] 104a; PART II [6479–9944] 158a-241b esp [6487–6500] 158b, [7070–7079] 173a-b, [9182–9272] 223a-225a, [9356–9573] 227a-232a, [9695–9754] 235a-236b, [9939–9944] 241b

51 TOLSTOY: *War and Peace* esp BK I, 3a-c, BK III, 122b-c, BK IV, 173d-179a, BK VI, 245d-250a, 269c-d, BK VII, 291a-292b, 301b-302d, BK VIII, 311a-313a, BK XII, 539c-547a, BK XV, 635a-644a,c, EPILOGUE I, 650d-674a,c

52 DOSTOEVSKY: *Brothers Karamazov*, BK I, 4a-5b; BK II, 21b-24d; 39a

53 JAMES: *Psychology*, 735a-b

54 FREUD: *Narcissism*, 404d-406b / *Group Psychology*, 694b-695b / *New Introductory Lectures*, 862d-863c

7b. The continuity of the family: the veneration of ancestors; family pride, feuds, curses

OLD TESTAMENT: *Genesis*, 9:21–27; 12:1–3; 13:14–17; 15:2–5; 17; 22:16–18; 25:20–34; 26:24; 27:1–28:5; 28:13–15; 30:1–24; 48–49 / *Exodus*, 3:15–16; 20:5–6 / *Numbers*, 36:3–10 / *Deuteronomy*, 5:9–10; 25:5–10 / *Ruth* / *II Samuel*, 21:1–9—(D) *II Kings*, 21:1–9 / *I Chronicles*, 28:1–8—(D) *I Paralipomenon*, 28:1–8 / *II Chronicles*, 25:3–4—(D) *II Paralipomenon*, 25:3–4 / *Proverbs*, 17:6 / *Jeremiah*, 31:29–30—(D) *Jeremias*, 31:29–30 / *Ezekiel*, 18—(D) *Ezechiel*, 18

APOCRYPHA: *Ecclesiasticus*, 3:1–16—(D) OT, *Ecclesiasticus*, 3:1–16

4 HOMER: *Odyssey*, BK XI [458–540] 247c-248b

5 AESCHYLUS: *Seven Against Thebes* 27a-39a,c esp [720–791] 35a-d / *Prometheus Bound* [887–893] 49c / *Agamemnon* 52a-69d

5 SOPHOCLES: *Oedipus the King* 99a-113a,c / *Ajax* [1290–1315] 154a-b / *Electra* 156a-169a,c

5 EURIPIDES: *Electra* 327a-339a,c / *Phoenician Maidens* 378a-393d

(7. The life of the family. 7b. The continuity of the family: the veneration of ancestors; family pride, feuds, curses.)

6 HERODOTUS: *History*, BK I, 13b-c; BK III, 96c-d; BK IV, 146a-b; 149b-c; BK V, 167b-168a

7 PLATO: *Charmides*, 3c-d / *Laws*, BK IV, 683b-c; BK IX, 752d-753a

9 ARISTOTLE: *Ethics*, BK VII, CH 6 [1149^{b}4–13] 400a; BK VIII, CH 11 [1161^{a}15–21] 413b-c / *Rhetoric*, BK I, CH 5 [1360^{b}19–38] 601a-b

12 AURELIUS: *Meditations*, BK I 253a-256d

13 VIRGIL: *Aeneid*, BK II [671–804] 143a-146b; BK V [42–103] 188a-190a; BK VI [679–702] 229a-b; [756–901] 231a-235a; BK VIII [609–731] 275a-278b; BK X [276–286] 309b-310a

14 PLUTARCH: *Aratus*, 826a-c

15 TACITUS: *Histories*, BK II, 227b-c

18 AUGUSTINE: *Confessions*, BK II, par 6 10a-b

21 DANTE: *Divine Comedy*, PURGATORY, XI [46–72] 69b-c; PARADISE, XV–XVI 128b-132a

22 CHAUCER: *Tale of Wife of Bath* [6691–6788] 274b-276a / *Parson's Tale*, par 27, 514b

23 HOBBES: *Leviathan*, PART II, 121d

24 RABELAIS: *Gargantua and Pantagruel*, BK III, 140c-d

25 MONTAIGNE: *Essays*, 411a-d

26 SHAKESPEARE: *1st Henry VI*, ACT IV, SC V–VII 23d-26a / *Romeo and Juliet* 285a-319a,c / *Julius Caesar*, ACT I, SC II [132–161] 570d-571a

27 SHAKESPEARE: *All's Well That Ends Well*, ACT II, SC III [110–151] 152c-153a

33 PASCAL: *Pensées*, 626 286b

36 STERNE: *Tristram Shandy*, 225b-227b; 307b-310a

37 FIELDING: *Tom Jones*, 15c-17d; 106b-c; 125b; 275a; 362c-364d

38 MONTESQUIEU: *Spirit of Laws*, BK XIX, 140a; BK XXIII, 188b-c; 189b-c

40 GIBBON: *Decline and Fall*, 242a-b; 412c-413a passim; 497a-498a

41 GIBBON: *Decline and Fall*, 81d; 389b-c; 453a-456a,c esp 453a-b; 571a-572d

44 BOSWELL: *Johnson*, 274b-278a; 280c-281a; 282a-b; 289c-d; 293d

46 HEGEL: *Philosophy of Right*, PART III, par 173 61a-b; par 180 62c-63c / *Philosophy of History*, INTRO, 197c-d; PART I, 211d-212c; PART IV, 320c

51 TOLSTOY: *War and Peace*, BK X, 399d-401d

52 DOSTOEVSKY: *Brothers Karamazov*, BK II, 41a-b

7c. Patterns of friendship in the family: man and wife; parents and children; brothers and sisters

OLD TESTAMENT: *Genesis*, 4:1–16; 9:18–29; 22:1–19; 24; 25:21–34; 27; 29:21–30; 32–34; 37; 42–45; 50:15–23 / *Exodus*, 2:1–8 / *Judges*, 11:30–40 / *Ruth*, 1:3–18 / *I Samuel*, 18:1–4; 20 —(D) *I Kings*, 18:1–4; 20 / *II Samuel*, 13–14; 18:33—(D) *II Kings*, 13–14; 18:33 / *Proverbs*, 10:1; 15:20/ *Micah*, 7:5–6—(D) *Micheas*, 7:5–6

APOCRYPHA: *Tobit*, 4:1–4—(D) OT, *Tobias*, 4:1–5 / *Ecclesiasticus*, 25:1; 40:23–24—(D) OT, *Ecclesiasticus*, 25:1–2; 40:23–24

NEW TESTAMENT: *Matthew*, 10:21,35–37; 12:46–50; 19:29 / *Mark*, 3:31–35; 13:12 / *Luke*, 8:19–21; 12:51–53; 14:26; 15:11–32; 18:29–30

4 HOMER: *Iliad*, BK XXII [1–98] 155a-156a; [405–515] 159c-160d; BK XXIV [159–804] 172d-179d / *Odyssey*, BK II 188a-192d; BK XI [458–540] 247c-248b; BK XIV–XV 260a-271d; BK XVI [167–225] 273d-274b; BK XVII [31–60] 277b-c; BK XXIII [1–245] 312a-314d; BK XXIV [290–361] 320a-d

5 AESCHYLUS: *Seven Against Thebes* [956–1078] 37d-39a,c / *Choephoroe* 70a-80d esp [212–305] 72b-73a, [892–930] 78d-79b

5 SOPHOCLES: *Oedipus at Colonus* 114a-130a,c esp [324–460] 117a-118b, [1150–1446] 124d-127b / *Antigone* 131a-142d / *Ajax* [1290–1315] 154a-b / *Electra* 156a-169a,c / *Trachiniae* 170a-181a,c

5 EURIPIDES: *Medea* 212a-224a,c esp [976–1270] 220b-222d / *Alcestis* 237a-247a,c esp [614–740] 242c-243c / *Suppliants* 258a-269a,c esp [990–1113] 267a-268a / *Trojan Women* [740–798] 276c-d; [1156–1255] 279d-280c / *Andromache* [309–420] 318a-d / *Electra* [988–1122] 336a-337b / *Hecuba* [383–443] 356a-d / *Heracles Mad* [562–584] 369d-370a; [622–645] 370c / *Phoenician Maidens* 378a-393d / *Orestes* 394a-410d esp [211–315] 396a-397a, [1012–1055] 404a-c / *Iphigenia Among the Tauri* 411a-424d esp [769–849] 417d-418c / *Iphigenia at Aulis* 425a-439d

6 HERODOTUS: *History*, BK I, 7a-b; 8a-10a; 32a-c; BK II, 73b-74d; 76b-d; BK III, 89d; 95d-96c; 100b-101b; 114d-115a; 116a; BK IV, 143b-144b; BK VI, 194d-195b; 212c-213a; BK IX, 311b-312d

6 THUCYDIDES: *Peloponnesian War*, BK II, 398c-d

7 PLATO: *Republic*, BK I, 296d-297a; BK V 360d-365d / *Laws*, BK IV, 683b-c

9 ARISTOTLE: *Generation of Animals*, BK III, CH 2 [753^{a}7–15] 294a-b / *Ethics*, BK VII, CH 4 [1148^{a}26–^{b}4] 398d; BK VIII, CH I [1155^{a}16–21] 406b,d; CH 7 [1158^{b}12–24] 410c-d; CH 8 [1159^{a}24–33] 411b-c; CH 9 [1159^{b}25–1160^{a}9] 411d-412b; CH 10 [1160^{b}23]–CH 11 [1161^{a}29] 413a-c; CH 12 413d-414d; CH 14 [1163^{b}13–27] 416c-d; BK IX, CH 2 417c-418b; CH 4 [1166^{a}1–9] 419a-b; CH 7 [1168^{a}21–27] 421d / *Politics*, BK I, CH 12–13 453d-455a,c; BK II, CH 3–4 456c-458a

12 LUCRETIUS: *Nature of Things*, BK V [1011–1018] 74b

12 EPICTETUS: *Discourses*, BK I, CH 23 128c-d

13 VIRGIL: *Eclogues*, IV [60–64] 15b / *Aeneid*, BK III [692–715] 166a-b; BK V [42–103] 188a-190a; BK VI [679–702] 229a-b; BK VIII [554–584] 273b-274b; BK IX [280–302] 286b-287a; BK X [822–828] 324b-325a; BK XI [29–71] 328b-

7d. The emotional impact of family life upon the child: the domestic triangle; the symbolic roles of father and mother

(*7. The life of the family. 7d. The emotional impact of family life upon the child: the domestic triangle; the symbolic roles of father and mother.*)

52 DOSTOEVSKY: *Brothers Karamazov*, BK II, 34b-36c; 38b-39b; BK III, 59d-62a; 69d-70c; BK IV, 104b-109a,c; BK VIII, 207a-d; BK IX, 244b-245b; BK XII, 365a-b; 395a-398d

54 FREUD: *Origin and Development of Psycho-Analysis*, 14b-19a esp 17b-18a / *Interpretation of Dreams*, 240d-249a / *General Introduction*, 528d-531d; 573d-574d; 580d-585a; 591a-d; 594d-599b passim / *Beyond the Pleasure Principle*, 644d-645a / *Group Psychology*, 678d-681b; 685b-687d; 692a-694b esp 693a-b / *Ego and Id*, 703c-708c esp 704d-707d / *Inhibitions, Symptoms, and Anxiety*, 724a-727c; 738d-742a; 743a-b; 751d; 752c-753c / *Civilization and Its Discontents*, 792b-796c esp 794c-795a / *New Introductory Lectures*, 832b-834d; 855a-863b esp 856b-860a; 876a-d

8. Historical observations on the institution of marriage and the family

4 HOMER: *Odyssey*, BK II 188a-192d; BK XIV-XV 260a-271d

6 HERODOTUS: *History*, BK I, 34a-b; 39b-c; 44b-d; 48c; BK III, 104d-105a; BK IV, 143b-144b; 155c-156a; BK V, 160d-161a; 167b-168a

9 ARISTOTLE: *Politics*, BK II, CH 9 [1269^{b}13-1270^{b}7] 465d-466c

12 LUCRETIUS: *Nature of Things*, BK V [953-965] 73c; [1011-1027] 74b-c

14 PLUTARCH: *Romulus*, 26a-b / *Lycurgus*, 39a-41a / *Numa Pompilius*, 54a-55a; 58d / *Lycur-*gus-Numa, 62d-64a / *Solon*, 72b-73a / *Themistocles*, 99a-b / *Alcibiades*, 158b-d / *Lysander*, 368a,c / *Cato the Younger*, 629a-c / *Agis*, 650d-651b / *Antony-Demetrius*, 780d

15 TACITUS: *Annals*, BK II, 44b-c; BK III, 53a-d; BK IV, 67d-68a; 73d-74c; BK XII, 111a-c; 121d-122a; BK XV, 162b-c

18 AUGUSTINE: *Christian Doctrine*, BK III, CH 12, 663a-c; CH 18-22 664d-666c

20 AQUINAS: *Summa Theologica*, PART I-II, Q 105, A 4 318b-321a

30 BACON: *New Atlantis*, 207b-209d

38 MONTESQUIEU: *Spirit of Laws*, BK VII, 47c-50d; BK XVI 116a-122a,c; BK XVIII, 129d-134a; BK XIX, 141c-142a; BK XXIII, 192c-198a; BK XXVI, 214b,d-221c; 223a-c; BK XXVII 225a-230d

38 ROUSSEAU: *Inequality*, 340b-c; 348b,d; 350a-c; 364d-365b

39 SMITH: *Wealth of Nations*, BK I, 29d-30d; BK III, 165b-166a; BK V, 338c-d

40 GIBBON: *Decline and Fall*, 92c-93a

41 GIBBON: *Decline and Fall*, 39a; 39d; 82b-89d esp 82b-86b; 319b-d

44 BOSWELL: *Johnson*, 197d; 289c-d; 301d-302a

46 HEGEL: *Philosophy of History*, INTRO, 194c-195a; PART I, 211a-212c; 246c-247b; PART III, 288c-289b; 294c-d

49 DARWIN: *Descent of Man*, 579b-583b

50 MARX: *Capital*, 241a-d

50 MARX ENGELS: *Communist Manifesto*, 427b-428a

54 FREUD: *Group Psychology*, 686c-687c; 692a-b; 694d-695a / *Civilization and Its Discontents*, 781d-782c

CROSS-REFERENCES

For: The general problem of the naturalness of human association in the family or in the state, *see* NATURE 2b; NECESSITY AND CONTINGENCY 5b; STATE 1a, 3b-3d.

The political significance of the domestic community, and for comparisons of government in the family and in the state, *see* EDUCATION 8a; GOVERNMENT 1b; MONARCHY 4a, 4e(1); SLAVERY 6b; STATE 1b, 5b; TYRANNY 4b.

The economic aspects of the family, *see* LABOR 5a, 5c; SLAVERY 4a; WEALTH 2, 3d.

Religious considerations relevant to matrimony and celibacy, *see* RELIGION 2c, 3d; VIRTUE AND VICE 8f-8g.

Other discussions of women in relation to men, and of the difference between the sexes, *see* HAPPINESS 4a; MAN 6b; WAR AND PEACE 5a.

Other discussions of childhood as a stage of human life, *see* LIFE AND DEATH 6c; MAN 6c; and for the problem of the care and training of the young, *see* DUTY 9; EDUCATION 4b, 8a; RELIGION 5c.

A more general consideration of the problems of heredity, *see* EVOLUTION 2-3e.

The distinction of the several kinds of love and friendship which may enter into marriage, *see* LOVE 2-2d; and for matters relevant to the emotional pattern of family relationships, *see* DESIRE 4a-4d; EMOTION 3c-3c(4); LOVE 2b(4), 2d.

ADDITIONAL READINGS

Listed below are works not included in *Great Books of the Western World*, but relevant to the idea and topics with which this chapter deals. These works are divided into two groups:

I. Works by authors represented in this collection.

II. Works by authors not represented in this collection.

For the date, place, and other facts concerning the publication of the works cited, consult the Bibliography of Additional Readings which follows the last chapter of *The Great Ideas*.

I.

PLUTARCH. "A Discourse Touching the Training of Children," "Concerning the Virtues of Women," "Conjugal Precepts," "Of Natural Affection Towards One's Offspring," in *Moralia*

AUGUSTINE. *On the Good of Marriage*
——. *On the Good of Widowhood*
——. *Of Marriage and Concupiscence*

AQUINAS. *Summa Contra Gentiles*, BK III, CH 122–126
——. *Summa Theologica*, PART II–II, QQ 151–154; PART III, SUPPL, QQ 41–68

F. BACON. "Of Parents and Children," "Of Marriage and Single Life," "Of Youth and Age," in *Essays*

MILTON. *The Doctrine and Discipline of Divorce*

HOBBES. *Philosophical Rudiments Concerning Government and Society*, CH 9
——. *The Elements of Law, Natural and Politic*, PART II, CH 4

SWIFT. *A Modest Proposal*

FIELDING. *Amelia*

J. S. MILL. *The Subjection of Women*

ENGELS. *The Origin of the Family, Private Property and the State*

FREUD. *Three Contributions to the Theory of Sex*, CH 2–3

II.

XENOPHON. *The Oeconomicus*

CICERO. *De Domo Sua*

Völsung Saga

Njalssaga

BOCCACCIO. *Patient Griselda*

ALBERTI. *Della Famiglia*

BODIN. *The Six Bookes of a Commonweale*, BK I, CH 2–4

SPENSER. *The Faerie Queene*, BK III
——. *Epithalamion*

HEYWOOD. *A Woman Killed with Kindness*

CALDERÓN. *Life Is a Dream*

MOLIÈRE. *L'école des maris* (*School for Husbands*)
——. *L'école des femmes* (*School for Wives*)

CHESTERFIELD. *Letters to His Son*

VOLTAIRE. "Marriage," "Women," in *A Philosophical Dictionary*

R. BURNS. *The Cotter's Saturday Night*

FRANKLIN. *On Marriage*

WOLLSTONECRAFT. *The Rights of Woman*

F. SCHLEGEL. *Lucinde*

FOURIER. *Traité de l'association domestique-agricole*

LAMB. "A Bachelor's Complaint," in *The Essays of Elia*

BALZAC. *The Physiology of Marriage*
——. *Eugénie Grandet*
——. *Old Goriot*
——. *The Petty Annoyances of Married Life*
——. *Cousin Bette*

WHEWELL. *The Elements of Morality*, BK IV, CH 5

E. J. BRONTË. *Wuthering Heights*

THACKERAY. *Vanity Fair*

SCHOPENHAUER. "On Women," in *Studies in Pessimism*

COMTE. *The Catechism of Positive Religion* (Preface to the first edition)
——. *System of Positive Polity*, VOL I, *General View of Positivism*, CH 4; VOL II, *Social Statics*, CH 3

FLAUBERT. *Madame Bovary*

BACHOFEN. *Das Mutterrecht*

MAINE. *Ancient Law*, CH 5

TURGENEV. *Fathers and Sons*

DICKENS. *Our Mutual Friend*

FUSTEL DE COULANGES. *The Ancient City*

TYLOR. *Primitive Culture*

ZOLA. *Les Rougon Macquart*

L. H. MORGAN. *Systems of Consanguinity and Affinity of the Human Family*
——. *Ancient Society*, PART III, CH I

S. BUTLER. *The Way of All Flesh*

T. H. GREEN. *Principles of Political Obligation*, (N)

IBSEN. *A Doll's House*
——. *Ghosts*

STEVENSON. *Virginibus Puerisque*

MARK TWAIN. *The Adventures of Tom Sawyer*
——. *The Adventures of Huckleberry Finn*

NIETZSCHE. *Human, All-Too-Human*, VII
——. *Beyond Good and Evil*, CH VII (232–238)

STRINDBERG. *The Father*

TÖNNIES. *Fundamental Concepts of Sociology*, PART I

FRAZER. *The Golden Bough*, PART I, CH 11–12; PART III, CH 6

WESTERMARCK. *The History of Human Marriage*

MASON. *Woman's Share in Primitive Culture*

MEREDITH. *The Ordeal of Richard Feverel*
——. *Modern Love*
——. *Diana of the Crossways*
——. *The Amazing Marriage*

SHAW. *Candida*

BRYCE. *Marriage and Divorce*
MANN. *Buddenbrooks*
SYNGE. *Riders to the Sea*
WEININGER. *Sex and Character*
SANTAYANA. *Reason in Society*, CH 2
GOSSE. *Father and Son*
SERTILLANGES. *La famille et l'état dans l'éducation*
DEWEY and TUFTS. *Ethics*, PART III, CH 26
GALTON. *Natural Inheritance*
——. *Essays in Eugenics*
CHESTERTON. *What's Wrong with the World*
BATESON. *Problems of Genetics*
ELLIS. *Man and Woman*
——. *Studies in the Psychology of Sex*
D. H. LAWRENCE. *Sons and Lovers*
H. JAMES. *A Small Boy and Others*
——. *Notes of a Son and Brother*
JOYCE. *A Portrait of the Artist as a Young Man*
PROUST. *Remembrance of Things Past*

FLÜGEL. *The Psycho-Analytic Study of the Family*
HARTLAND. *Primitive Society, the Beginnings of the Family and the Reckoning of Descent*
GALSWORTHY. *The Forsyte Saga*
MARTIN DU GARD. *The Thibaults*
UNDSET. *Kristin Lavransdatter*
J. B. S. HALDANE. *Daedalus*
GORKY. *Decadence*
JUNG. *Marriage as a Psychological Relationship*
BRIFFAULT. *The Mothers*
DAWSON. "Christianity and Sex," in *Enquiries into Religion and Culture*
PIUS XI. *Casti Connubii* (Encyclical on Christian Marriage)
O'NEILL. *Desire Under the Elms*
——. *Strange Interlude*
——. *Mourning Becomes Electra*
L. STURZO. *The Inner Laws of Society*, CH II
T. S. ELIOT. *The Family Reunion*

Chapter 27: FATE

INTRODUCTION

FATE—sometimes personified, sometimes abstractly conceived—is the antagonist of freedom in the drama of human life and history. So at least it seems to the poets of antiquity. In many of the Greek tragedies, fate sets the stage. Some curse must be fulfilled. A doom impends and is inexorable. But the actors on the stage are far from puppets. Within the framework of the inevitable the tragic hero works out his own destiny, making the choices from which his personal catastrophe ensues. Oedipus, doomed to kill his father and marry his mother, is not fated to inquire into his past and to discover the sins which, when he sees, he wills to see no more. The curse on the house of Atreus does not require Agamemnon to bring Cassandra back from Troy or to step on the purple carpet. The furies which pursue Orestes he has himself awakened by murdering his mother, Clytemnestra, a deed not fated but freely undertaken to avenge his father's death.

The ancients did not doubt that men could choose and, through choice, exercise some control over the disposition of their lives. Tacitus, for example, while admitting that "most men . . . cannot part with the belief that each person's future is fixed from his very birth," claims that "the wisest of the ancients . . . leave us the capacity of choosing our life." At the same time he recognizes an order of events beyond man's power to control, although he finds no agreement regarding its cause—whether it depends "on wandering stars" or "primary elements, and on a combination of natural causes." For his own part, Tacitus declares, "I suspend my judgment" on the question "whether it is fate and unchangeable necessity or chance which governs the revolutions of human affairs." In so doing, he grants the possibility that not everything which lies beyond man's control is fated. Some of the things which happen without man's willing them may happen by chance or fortune.

It is sometimes supposed that "fate" and "fortune" are synonyms, or that one has a tragic and the other a happy connotation. It is as if fortune were always good and fate always malevolent. But either may be good or evil from the point of view of man's desires. Although fate and fortune are hardly the same, there is some reason for associating them. Each imposes a limitation on man's freedom. A man cannot compel fortune to smile upon him any more than he can avoid his fate. Though alike in this respect, fate and fortune are also opposed to one another. Fate represents the inexorable march of events. There is no room for fortune unless some things are exempt from necessity. Only that which can happen by chance is in the lap of fortune.

It would seem that fate stands to fortune as the necessary to the contingent. If everything were necessitated, fate alone would reign. Contingency would be excluded from nature. Chance or the fortuitous in the order of nature and freedom in human life would be reduced to illusions men cherish only through ignorance of the inevitable.

In a sense fortune is the ally of freedom in the struggle against fate. Good fortune seems to aid and abet human desires. But even misfortune signifies the element of chance which is more congenial than fate, if not more amenable, to man's conceit that he can freely plan his life.

THE TERMS *necessity* and *contingency* cannot be substituted for *fate* and *fortune* without loss of significance. As the chapter on NECESSITY AND CONTINGENCY indicates, they are terms in the philosophical analysis of the order of nature and causality. They may have, but they need not have, theological implications. Necessity and contingency can be explained without any reference to the supernatural, as is evident from the discussion of these matters in the chapter on CHANCE. But fate and fortune, in their origin at least, are theological terms.

In ancient poetry and mythology, both inevitability and chance were personified as deities or supernatural forces. There were the goddess of Fortune and the three Fates, as well as their three evil sisters or counterparts, the Furies. The Latin word from which "fate" comes means an oracle, and so signifies what is divinely ordained. What happens by fate is *fated*—something destined and decreed in the councils of the gods on Olympus; or it may be the decision of Zeus, to whose rule all the other divinities are subject; or, as we shall see presently, it may be a supernatural destiny which even Zeus cannot set aside.

In any case, the notion of fate implies a supernatural will, even as destiny implies predestination by an intelligence able not only to plan the future but also to carry out that plan. The inevitability of fate and destiny is thus distinguished from that of merely natural necessity which determines the future only insofar as it may be the inevitable consequence of causes working naturally.

But the ancients do not seem to be fatalists in the extreme sense of the term. To the extent that men can propitiate the gods or provoke divine jealousy and anger, the attitudes and deeds of men seem to be a determining factor in the actions of the gods. To the extent that the gods align themselves on opposite sides of a human conflict (as in the *Iliad*), or oppose each other (as in the *Odyssey*), it may be thought that what happens on earth merely reflects the shifting balance of power among the gods.

But human planning and willing do not seem to be excluded by the divine will and plan which are forged out of the quarrels of the gods. On the contrary, polytheism seems to make fortune itself contingent on the outcome of the Olympian conflict, and so permits men a certain latitude of self-determination. Men can struggle against the gods precisely because the gods may be with them as well as against them.

The ultimate power of Zeus to decide the issue may, however, place the accent on fate rather than on freedom. This is certainly so if Zeus is not the master of even his own fate, much less the omnipotent ruler among the gods or the arbiter of human destiny. In *Prometheus Bound*, the Chorus asks, "Who is the pilot of Necessity?" Prometheus answers, "The Fates triform and the unforgetting Furies." The Chorus then asks, "Is Zeus of lesser might than these?" To which Prometheus replies, "He shall not shun the lot apportioned." When they ask what this doom is, Prometheus tells them to inquire no more, for they verge on mysteries. Later Zeus himself sends Hermes to wrest from Prometheus the secret of what has been ordained for him by "all consummating Fate" or "Fate's resistless law." Prometheus refuses, saying that "none shall bend my will or force me to disclose by whom 'tis fated he shall fall from power."

The question Aeschylus leaves unanswered is whether Zeus would be able to escape his doom if he could foresee what Fate holds in store for him. The suggestion seems to be that without omniscience the omnipotence of Zeus cannot break the chains of Fate.

IN THE TRADITION of Judaeo-Christian theology the problem of fate is in part verbal and in part real. The verbal aspect of the problem concerns the meaning of the word "fate" in relation to the divine will, providence, and predestination. With the verbal matter settled, there remains the real problem of God's will and human freedom. The strictly monotheistic conception of an omnipotent and omniscient God deepens the mystery, and makes it more difficult than the problem of fate and freedom in pagan thought.

If anyone "calls the will or the power of God itself by the name of fate," Augustine says, "let him keep his opinion, but correct his language.... For when men hear that word, according to the ordinary use of language, they simply understand by it the virtue of that particular position of the stars which may exist at the time when anyone is born or conceived, which some separate altogether from the will of God, whilst others affirm that this also is dependent on that will. But those who are of the opinion that, apart from the will of God, the stars determine what we shall do, or what good things we shall possess, or what evils we shall suffer, must be refused a hearing by all, not only by those who hold the true religion, but by those who wish to be the worshippers of any gods whatsoever, even false gods. For what does this opinion really amount to but this, that no god whatsoever is to be worshipped or prayed to?"

Since the word "fate" has been used for those things which are determined apart from the will of God or man, Augustine thinks it would be better for Christians not to use it, but to substitute "providence" or "predestination" when they wish to refer to what God wills. Aquinas, however, retains the word "fate" but restricts its meaning to the "ordering . . . of mediate causes" by which God wills "the production of certain effects."

According to the definition given by Boethius which Aquinas quotes, "Fate is a disposition inherent to changeable things, by which providence connects each one with its proper order." Thus fate is not identified with providence, but made subordinate to it. The distinction, Aquinas explains, depends on the way we consider "the ordering of effects" by God. "As being in God Himself . . . the ordering of the effects is called Providence." But "as being in the mediate causes ordered by God," it is called fate. While admitting that "the divine power or will can be called fate, as being the cause of fate," he declares that "essentially fate is the very disposition or *series*, *i.e.*, order, of second causes."

The position Lucretius takes seems to be exactly opposite to that of Augustine and Aquinas. Lucretius condemns the fatalism of those who believe that the gods control the order of nature and who therefore attribute whatever befalls them to divine ordination. For him, "nature free at once and rid of her haughty lords is seen to do all things spontaneously of herself without the meddling of the gods." He tries to teach men that everything happens according to the laws of nature, *other than which there is no fate*. The "decrees of fate" lie in the laws by which "all motion is ever linked together and a new motion ever springs from another in a fixed order." If man by his "power of free action" can "make some commencement of motion to break through the decrees

of fate, in order that cause follow not cause from everlasting," it is because in the atoms of his makeup "there is another cause of motions . . . caused by a minute swerving of first-beginnings at no fixed part of space and no fixed time."

Nevertheless, according to Augustine, Lucretius is a fatalist who disbelieves in providence, *other than which there is no fate*. Each of them uses the word "fate," the one to deny, the other to affirm, the power of God.

But even if a Christian avoids the superstitions of astrology, or some similar belief in a natural necessity which does not depend on God, he may still commit the sin of fatalism which follows from the denial of man's free will. Understanding fate as identical with providence, the Christian is a fatalist if, in the belief that every human act is foreordained by God, he resigns himself to his fate, making no moral effort and taking no moral responsibility for his soul's welfare. To do that is to argue like Chaucer's Troilus:

I am, he said, but done for, so to say;
For all that comes, comes by necessity,
Thus to be done for is my destiny.
I must believe and cannot other choose,
That Providence, in its divine foresight,
Hath known that Cressida I once must lose,
Since God sees everything from heaven's height
And plans things as he thinks both best and right,
As was arranged for by predestination.

Troilus sees no way of avoiding the conclusion that "free choice is an idle dream."

THE THEOLOGIANS recognize the difficulty of reconciling providence and free will. The truth must lie somewhere between two heresies. If it is heresy to deny God's omnipotence and omniscience, then nothing remains outside the all-encompassing scope of divine providence, nothing happens contrary to the divine will, no future contingency is or can be unforeseen by God. If, on the other hand, to deny that man sins freely means that God must be responsible for the evil that man does, then it is a heresy to deny free will, for that imputes evil to God.

This is the problem with which Milton deals in *Paradise Lost*, announcing that he will try "to justify the ways of God to man." In a conversation in heaven, the Father tells the

Son that though He knows Adam will disobey his rule, Adam remains quite free to sin or not to sin, and the fault is his own, just as the rebellious angels acted on their own free will. The angels, God says,

So were created, nor can justly accuse
Thir maker, or thir making, or thir Fate;
As if Predestination over-rul'd
Thir will, dispos'd by absolute Decree
Or high foreknowledge; they themselves decreed
Thir own revolt, not I: if I foreknew,
Foreknowledge had no influence on their fault,
Which had no less prov'd certain unforeknown.
So without least impulse or shadow of Fate,
Or aught by me immutablie foreseen,
They trespass, Authors to themselves in all,
Both what they judge and what they choose; for so
I formed them free, and free they must remain,
Till they enthrall themselves: I else must change
Thir nature, and revoke the high Decree
Unchangeable, Eternal, which ordain'd
Thir freedom, they themselves ordain'd their fall.

A solution of the problem is sometimes developed from the distinction between God's foreknowledge and God's foreordination. God foreordained the freedom of man, but only foreknew his fall; man ordained that himself. Strictly speaking, however, the word "foreknowledge" would seem to carry a false connotation, since nothing is future to God. Everything that has ever happened or ever will is simultaneously together in the eternal present of the divine vision.

During his ascent through Paradise, Dante, wishing to learn about his immediate future, asks his ancestor Cacciaguida to foretell his fortune, for he, "gazing upon the Point to which all times are present, can see contingent things, ere in themselves they are." Cacciaguida prefaces his prediction of Dante's exile from Florence by telling him that the contingency of material things "is all depicted in the Eternal Vision; yet thence it does not take necessity, more than does a ship which is going down the stream from the eye in which it is mirrored." The difference between time and eternity is conceived as permitting the temporal future to be contingent even though God knows its content with certitude.

But, it may still be asked, does not God's knowledge imply the absolute predestination of future events by providence, since what God knows with certitude cannot happen otherwise than as He knows it? In a discussion of divine grace and man's free will, Dr. Johnson remarks, "I can judge with great probability how a man will act in any case, without his being restrained by my judging. God may have this probability increased to certainty." To which Boswell replies that "when it is increased to *certainty*, freedom ceases, because that cannot be certainly foreknown, which is not certain at the time; but if it be certain at the time, it is a contradiction to maintain that there can be afterwards any contingency dependent upon the exercise of will or anything else."

Against such difficulties Aquinas insists that divine providence is compatible, not only with natural necessity, but also with contingency in nature and free will in human acts. Providence, he writes, "has prepared for some things necessary causes so that they happen of necessity; for others contingent causes, that they may happen by contingency." Human liberty does not imply that the will's acts are not caused by God who, being the first cause, "moves causes both natural and voluntary. Just as by moving natural causes, He does not prevent their acts being natural, so by moving voluntary causes, He does not deprive their actions of being voluntary." God causes man to choose freely and freely to execute his choice.

THE UNCOMPROMISING conception of fate is that which leaves no place for chance or freedom anywhere in the universe, neither in the acts of God, nor in the order of nature, nor in the course of history. The doctrine of absolute determinism, whether in theology, science, or history, is thus fatalism unqualified.

The ancient historians are not fatalists in this sense. Herodotus, for example, finds much that can be explained by the contingencies of fortune or by the choices of men. The crucial decision, for example, in the defense of Athens is presented as an act of man's choice. Upon receiving the prophecy that "safe shall the wooden wall continue for thee and thy children," the Athenians exercise their freedom by disagreeing about its meaning. "Certain of the old men," Herodotus writes, "were of the opinion that the god meant to tell them the citadel would escape; for this was anciently defended by a palisade. . . . Others maintained that the fleet was what the god pointed at; and their advice was that nothing should be thought of except the ships." The eloquence of Themistocles carried the latter view. To stress its importance, the historian observes that "the saving of Greece" lay in the decision that led Athens to "become a maritime power."

In presenting a comparable decision by the Persians, Herodotus seems to be contrasting their fatalism with the freedom of the Greeks. At first Xerxes accepts the council of Artabanus not to go to war against the Greeks. But after a series of visions, which appear to both the king and his councillor, that decision is reversed, for, according to the dream, the war "is fated to happen."

The conception of fate and freedom in the *Aeneid* seems closer to the Greek than to the Persian view. Even though the consummation of history, which will come with the founding of the Roman empire, is projected as a divinely appointed destiny, the hero who brings that great event to pass acts as if he were free to accept or evade his responsibilities.

The Christian understanding of historical destiny in terms of providence permits—more than that, requires—men to exercise free choice at every turn. "The cause of the greatness of the Roman empire," writes Augustine, "is neither fortuitous nor fatal, according to the judgment or opinion of those who call those things *fortuitous* which either have no causes or such causes as do not proceed from some intelligible order, and those things *fatal* which happen independently of the will of God and man, by the necessity of a certain *order*. . . . Human kingdoms are established by divine providence." The fatalism which Augustine here condemns involves independence not only of the will of God, but of man's will also.

It is only in modern times, with Hegel and Marx, that necessity reigns supreme in the philosophy of history. Hegel spurns the notion that history is "a superficial play of casual, so-called 'merely human' strivings and passions." He also condemns those who "speak of Providence and the plan of Providence" in a way that is "empty" of ideas since "for them the plan of Providence is inscrutable and incomprehensible." For Hegel, history is "the necessary development, out of the concept of the

mind's freedom alone." But this development and this freedom are entirely matters of necessity as far as individuals and their works are concerned. "They are all the time the unconscious tools and organs of the world mind at work within them."

For Marx, history seems likewise to have the same necessity. He deals with individuals, he writes in the preface to *Capital*, "only in so far as they are the personifications of economic categories, embodiments of particular class-relations and class-interests. My stand-point," he says, is one from which "the evolution of the economic formation of society is viewed as a process of natural history," and within which the individual cannot be "responsible for relations whose creature he socially remains, however much he may subjectively raise himself above them." Here it is a question only "of these laws themselves, of these tendencies working with iron necessity towards inevitable results."

According to the historical determinism of Hegel and Marx, which is further considered in the chapter on HISTORY, men play a part which is already written for them in the scroll of history. Human liberty apparently depends on man's knowledge of and acquiescence in the unfolding necessities.

HISTORICAL DETERMINISM is merely a part of the doctrine of a causal necessity which governs all things. Causality seems to be understood by moderns like Spinoza, Hume, and Freud as excluding the possibility of chance or free will. Among the ancients, Plotinus alone seems to go as far as Spinoza in affirming the universal reign of natural necessity. What Spinoza says of God or Nature, Plotinus says of the All-One, namely, that for the first principle which is the cause of everything else, freedom consists in being *causa sui*, or cause of itself—self-determined rather than determined by external causes.

"God does not act from freedom of the will," Spinoza writes. Yet "God alone is a free cause, for God alone exists . . . and acts from the necessity of his own nature." As for everything else in the universe, Spinoza maintains that "there is nothing contingent, but all things are determined from the necessity of the divine nature to exist and act in a certain manner." This applies to man, who, according to Spinoza, does "everything by the will of God alone."

From quite different premises, Hume seems to reach much the same conclusion concerning chance and liberty. "Chance," he writes, "when strictly examined, is a mere negative word, and means not any real power which has anywhere a being in nature." But he also thinks that liberty, "when opposed to necessity, not to constraint, is the same thing with chance."

Hume embraces the consequences of such a position. "If voluntary action be subjected to the same laws of necessity with the operations of matter, there is a continued chain of necessary causes, pre-ordained and pre-determined, reaching from the original cause of all to every single volition of every human creature. No contingency anywhere in the universe; no indifference; no liberty."

When confronted with the objection that it then becomes impossible "to explain distinctly, how the Deity can be the mediate cause of all the actions of men, without being the author of sin and moral turpitude," Hume replies that "these are mysteries, which natural and unassisted reason is very unfit to handle. . . . To defend absolute decrees, and yet free the Deity from being the author of sin, has been found hitherto to exceed all the power of philosophy."

Unlike Spinoza and Hume, Freud does not deal with the theological implications or presuppositions of determinism. For him, determinism is an essential postulate of science and even to some extent a scientifically discoverable fact. The "deeply rooted belief in psychic freedom and choice," he writes, is "quite unscientific, and it must give ground before the claims of a determinism which governs even mental life." He thinks it can be shown on the basis of clinical experience that every psychic association "will be strictly determined by important inner attitudes of mind, which are unknown to us at the moment when they operate, just as much unknown as are the disturbing tendencies which cause errors, and those tendencies which bring about so-called 'chance' actions."

The fatalism of what is often called "scientific determinism" is that of blind necessity. It not only eliminates liberty and chance, but also purpose and the operation of final causes. Every future event, in nature, history, or human behavior, is completely predetermined by efficient causes—predetermined, but not predestined, for there is no guiding intelligence at work, no purpose to be fulfilled. "The system of *fatality*, of which Spinoza is the accredited author," Kant writes, is one which "eliminates all *trace of design*, and leaves the original ground of the things of nature divested of all intelligence."

Whether such complete fatalism is the only doctrine compatible with the principles and findings of natural science has been questioned by philosophers like William James. It is certainly not the only doctrine compatible with the view that nothing happens without a cause. As the chapters on CHANCE and WILL show, ancient and mediaeval thinkers who affirm contingency in nature or freedom in human acts do so without denying the universal reign of causation.

OUTLINE OF TOPICS

REFERENCES

To find the passages cited, use the numbers in heavy type, which are the volume and page numbers of the passages referred to. For example, in 4 HOMER: *Iliad*, BK II [265–283] 12d, the number 4 is the number of the volume in the set; the number 12d indicates that the passage is in section d of page 12.

PAGE SECTIONS: When the text is printed in one column, the letters a and b refer to the upper and lower halves of the page. For example, in 53 JAMES: *Psychology*, 116a-119b, the passage begins in the upper half of page 116 and ends in the lower half of page 119. When the text is printed in two columns, the letters a and b refer to the upper and lower halves of the left-hand side of the page, the letters c and d to the upper and lower halves of the right-hand side of the page. For example, in 7 PLATO: *Symposium*, 163b-164c, the passage begins in the lower half of the left-hand side of page 163 and ends in the upper half of the right-hand side of page 164.

AUTHOR'S DIVISIONS: One or more of the main divisions of a work (such as PART, BK, CH, SECT) are sometimes included in the reference; line numbers, in brackets, are given in certain cases; *e.g.*, *Iliad*, BK II [265–283] 12d.

BIBLE REFERENCES: The references are to book, chapter, and verse. When the King James and Douay versions differ in title of books or in the numbering of chapters or verses, the King James version is cited first and the Douay, indicated by a (*D*), follows; *e.g.*, OLD TESTAMENT: *Nehemiah*, 7:45—(*D*) II *Esdras*, 7:46.

SYMBOLS: The abbreviation "esp" calls the reader's attention to one or more especially relevant parts of a whole reference; "passim" signifies that the topic is discussed intermittently rather than continuously in the work or passage cited.

For additional information concerning the style of the references, see the Explanation of Reference Style; for general guidance in the use of *The Great Ideas*, consult the Preface.

1. The decrees of fate and the decisions of the gods

4 HOMER: *Iliad*, BK I [503–531] 8b-c; BK VIII [66–77] 51d; BK XIII [631–632] 94d; BK XIV [52–53] 98c; BK XVI [431–461] 117a-b; [657–658] 119b; [843–861] 121c; BK XVIII [97–126] 131a-c; BK XIX [74–94] 137d-138a; BK XXI [81–84] 149a; BK XXII [131–223] 156c-157c / *Odyssey*, BK III [225–239] 195b-c; BK XX [75] 296d

5 AESCHYLUS: *Suppliant Maidens* [1032–1073] 14a,c / *Prometheus Bound* 40a-51d esp [507–521] 45a-b / *Agamemnon* [1018–1034] 63a

5 EURIPIDES: *Alcestis* 237a-247a,c esp [1–76] 237a-238a, [213–243] 239a-b, [962–990] 245c / *Heracles Mad* [1313–1357] 376c-d / *Iphigenia Among the Tauri* [1435–1499] 424a-d

6 HERODOTUS: *History*, BK I, 20a-22a

12 EPICTETUS: *Discourses*, BK I, CH 12 118d-120b

12 AURELIUS: *Meditations*, BK II, SECT 3 257a-b; SECT 11 258a-b; BK III, SECT 11 262a-b; BK V, SECT 8 269d-270b

13 VIRGIL: *Aeneid*, BK I [1–33] 103a-104a; [261–262] 110a; BK II [428–433] 136a; BK III [1–12] 147a; BK IV [440] 179a; [651] 185a; BK VII [286–322] 243b-245a; BK X [100–117] 304b-305a; BK XI [108–119] 331a; BK XII [725–842] 373b-376b

31 DESCARTES: *Objections and Replies*, 216d-217a

32 MILTON: *Arcades* [54–83] 26b-27a

46 HEGEL: *Philosophy of History*, PART II, 271b

47 GOETHE: *Faust*, PART II [5305–5344] 131b-132a

2. The fated or inevitable in human life

4 HOMER: *Iliad* 3a-179d esp BK XV [47–77] 104c-d, BK XVI [843–861] 121c, BK XVIII [52–137] 130c-131c, BK XXII [355–366] 159a, BK XXIV [522–532] 176d-177a / *Odyssey*, BK XVIII [124–150] 285b-c; BK XXII [412] 310a

5 AESCHYLUS: *Suppliant Maidens* [1032–1073] 14a,c / *Seven Against Thebes* 27a-39a,c esp [631–956] 34a-37d / *Prometheus Bound* [640–886] 46d-49c / *Agamemnon* 52a-69d / *Choephoroe* 70a-80d / *Eumenides* 81a-91d

5 SOPHOCLES: *Oedipus the King* 99a-113a,c / *Oedipus at Colonus* 114a-130a,c esp [939–999] 123a-c / *Antigone* [944–987] 139a-c / *Ajax* [736–783] 149b-d; [925–935] 151a / *Electra* 156a-169a,c / *Philoctetes* [1316–1347] 193-d 194a

5 EURIPIDES: *Rhesus* [595–641] 208b-c / *Alcestis* 237a-247a,c esp [1–76] 237a-238a, [213–243] 239a-b, [962–990] 245c / *Trojan Women* [686–705] 275d-276a / *Electra* 327a-339a,c / *Bacchantes* [1327–1392] 351b-352a,c / *Heracles Mad* [1311–1358] 376c-d / *Phoenician Maidens* 378a-393d esp [1–87] 378a-379a, [867–928]

(2: The fated or inevitable in human life.)

385d-386b, [1595-1614] 392a, [1758-1766] 393d / *Orestes* [1-70] 394a-d; [807-843] 402c-d / *Iphigenia Among the Tauri* [482-489] 414d-415a; [1435-1499] 424a-d

6 HERODOTUS: *History*, BK I, 8a-10a; 20a-22a; 46c; BK II, 65b; 77a-b; BK III, 98b-99a; 102d-104b; BK IV, 153b-d; 155b-c; BK IX, 291b-c

7 PLATO: *Apology*, 210d / *Republic*, BK X, 437b-441a,c esp 439a-441a,c / *Statesman*, 587a-589c

12 AURELIUS: *Meditations* 253a-310d esp BK II, SECT 3 257a-b, SECT 7 257c, BK III, SECT 11 262a-b, BK IV, SECT 33-35 266c-d, SECT 44 267b, BK V, SECT 8 269d-270b, SECT 19-20 272a, SECT 36 273d, BK VI, SECT 8 274b, SECT 11 274c, SECT 20 276a, SECT 39-40 277d, SECT 50 279a-b, SECT 58 279d, BK VII, SECT 8 280b, SECT 46 282c, SECT 54 283b, SECT 58 283c-d, BK VIII, SECT 17 286d, SECT 32 287d-288a, SECT 35 288b, SECT 45-47 289a-c, SECT 51 289d-290a, BK IX, SECT 41 295c, BK X, SECT 3 296d, SECT 5-6 296d-297b, SECT 25 299c, SECT 33 300c-301a, SECT 35 301b, BK XII, SECT 3 307b-d, SECT 11-14 308b-c

13 VIRGIL: *Eclogues*, IV 14a-15b / *Aeneid*, BK I [1-33] 103a-104a; [204-207] 108b; [223-304] 109a-111a; BK III [356-462] 157a-160a; BK IV [218-396] 173a-178a; BK VI [752-901] 231a-235a; BK VIII [520-540] 273a-b; BK IX [77-122] 281a-282a; BK X [100-117] 304b-305a; [621-632] 319a-b; BK XI [108-119] 331a; BK XII [133-150] 357b-358a

14 PLUTARCH: *Romulus*, 20b-c / *Camillus*, 107b-d / *Aemilius Paulus*, 225a-c; 228c-229c / *Sulla*, 370c-371b / *Caesar*, 600a-604d / *Marcus Brutus*, 814d-815c; 822a-b

15 TACITUS: *Annals*, BK III, 49c; BK VI, 91b-d / *Histories*, BK I, 191d; 194b

17 PLOTINUS: *Third Ennead*, TR I 78a-82b

22 CHAUCER: *Troilus and Cressida*, BK III, STANZA 89 66a; BK IV, STANZA 137-155 106b-108b / *Knight's Tale* 174a-211a esp [1081-1111] 177b-178a, [1251-1267] 180b, [1663-1672] 187b, [3027-3066] 209b-210a / *Tale of Man of Law* [4610-4623] 237b; [4701-4735] 239a-240a / *Monk's Prologue* 432a-434a / *Monk's Tale* 434a-448b

24 RABELAIS: *Gargantua and Pantagruel*, BK IV, 258c-259d

25 MONTAIGNE: *Essays*, 214a-c; 342a-d

26 SHAKESPEARE: *Romeo and Juliet*, PROLOGUE 285a-b; ACT I, SC IV [106-113] 291d / *Julius Caesar*, ACT II, SC II [1-107] 578a-579b

27 SHAKESPEARE: *Hamlet*, ACT V, SC II [4-48] 68a-b / *King Lear*, ACT I, SC II [112-166] 249a-c; ACT IV, SC III [34-37] 272a / *Macbeth* 284a-310d esp ACT I, SC III 285b-287b / *Cymbeline*, ACT V, SC IV [30-122] 481c-482b

36 STERNE: *Tristram Shandy*, 194b-195a; 202b-208b; 502b-503a

37 FIELDING: *Tom Jones*, 275d-276a; 310b

43 MILL: *Representative Government*, 347b-c

47 GOETHE: *Faust*, PART II [9695-9944] 235a-241b esp [9908-9938] 241a-b

48 MELVILLE: *Moby Dick*, 4a-b; 120a-b; 396b-397a; 398a; 409b-410b

51 TOLSTOY: *War and Peace*, BK VIII, 303d-304b; BK XII, 542d; 547a-549d; 553c-d; BK XIII, 578b-582a esp 578d-579a

54 FREUD: *Interpretation of Dreams*, 246b-247c / *General Introduction*, 581d-582a / *Civilization and Its Discontents*, 796a-c

3. The antitheses of fate: fortune, freedom, natural necessity, chance or contingency

7 PLATO: *Republic*, BK X, 437b-441a,c esp 439a-441a,c / *Statesman*, 586c-589c

8 ARISTOTLE: *Interpretation*, CH 9 28a-29d / *Physics*, BK II, CH 4-6 272c-275a / *Metaphysics*, BK VI, CH 3 549c-d; BK IX, CH 5 573a-c

9 ARISTOTLE: *Ethics*, BK I, CH 9 345a-c; BK III, CH 3 [1112^{a}18-33] 358a-b

12 LUCRETIUS: *Nature of Things*, BK II [251-293] 18b-d

12 AURELIUS: *Meditations*, BK II, SECT 3-4 257a-b; BK III, SECT 11 262a-b; BK V, SECT 8 269d-270b; SECT 36 273d; BK VI, SECT 40 277d; BK XII, SECT 14 308c

15 TACITUS: *Annals*, BK IV, 68a; BK VI, 91b-d

17 PLOTINUS: *Third Ennead*, TR I 78a-82b / *Fourth Ennead*, TR III, CH 16 150c-d

18 AUGUSTINE: *City of God*, BK V, CH I 207d-208c; CH 8-10 212c-216c

19 AQUINAS: *Summa Theologica*, PART I, Q 116 592d-595c

21 DANTE: *Divine Comedy*, PURGATORY, XVI [52-84] 77b-c

23 HOBBES: *Leviathan*, PART II, 163d-164a

26 SHAKESPEARE: *Julius Caesar*, ACT I, SC II [135-141] 570d; ACT IV, SC III [215-224] 590d

27 SHAKESPEARE: *Hamlet*, ACT III, SC II [220-223] 51b

31 DESCARTES: *Discourse*, PART III, 49b-d

31 SPINOZA: *Ethics*, PART II, PROP 49, SCHOL, 394c

32 MILTON: *Paradise Lost*, BK VII [170-173] 220b-221a

34 NEWTON: *Optics*, BK III, 542b

38 MONTESQUIEU: *Spirit of Laws*, BK I, 1a-b

42 KANT: *Pure Reason*, 45b-c; 133a; 140b,d-143a; 146a-c; 147b; 164a-171a; 205b-209b / *Fund. Prin. Metaphysic of Morals*, 264d-265a; 275b; 279b,d-287d esp 281c-283d / *Practical Reason*, 291a-293b; 296a-d; 301d-302d; 304a-d; 307d-314d; 319c-321b; 331c-337a,c / *Intro. Metaphysic of Morals*, 386d-387a,c; 390b / *Judgement*, 463a-467a; 571c-572a; 587a-588a

44 BOSWELL: *Johnson*, 549c

46 HEGEL: *Philosophy of Right*, PART III, par 340 110b-c; par 342-344 110c-111a / *Philosophy of History*, INTRO, 160c-165b; 166b-168a; PART IV, 368d-369a,c

48 MELVILLE: *Moby Dick*, 158b-159a

51 Tolstoy: *War and Peace*, bk ix, 342a-344b; bk x, 389a-391c; bk xi, 469a-472b; bk xiii-xiv, 563a-590c; bk xiv, 609a-613d; bk xv, 618b-621b; 626d-630a; epilogue i, 645a-650c; epilogue ii 675a-696d

53 James: *Psychology*, 291a-295b; 657a-b; 820b-824a

54 Freud: *General Introduction*, 486c-487a

4. Fatalism in relation to the will of God: the doctrine of predestination

Old Testament: *Genesis*, 45 esp 45:4-8 / *Exodus*, 4:21; 7-14 esp 7:3, 9:12, 10:1, 10:20, 10:27, 11:10, 14:4, 14:8, 14:17; 33:19 / *Deuteronomy*, 7:6-8; 14:2 / *Psalms*, 147:12-20 esp 147:20—(D) *Psalms*, 147 esp 147:20 / *Proverbs*, 16:33 / *Ecclesiastes*, 9:11-12 / *Isaiah*, 41:8-14—(D) *Isaias*, 41:8-14

Apocrypha: *Rest of Esther*, 13:8-18—(D) OT, *Esther*, 13:8-18 / *Wisdom of Solomon*, 19:4-5—(D) OT, *Book of Wisdom*, 19:4-5 / *Ecclesiasticus*, 33:10-13—(D) OT, *Ecclesiasticus*, 33:10-13

New Testament: *Matthew*, 22:1-14 / *John*, 6:22-71 esp 6:40, 6:44-45, 6:64-65—(D) *John*, 6:22-72 esp 6:40, 6:44-45, 6:65-66 / *Acts*, 17:24-27 / *Romans*, 8:28-11:36 / *II Corinthians*, 3-4 / *Galatians*, 4:4-6 / *Ephesians*, 1:4-2:10; 4:1-16 esp 4:7, 4:11 / *Philippians*, 2:12-15 / *James*, 4:13-15 / *I Peter*, 1:1-5

12 Epictetus: *Discourses*, bk i, ch 12 118d-120b; ch 17 122d-124a; bk ii, ch 16 156b-158d; bk iii, ch 22 195a-201a; bk iv, ch 1 213a-223d; ch 3 224b-d; ch 7 232c-235a

12 Aurelius: *Meditations*, bk iii, sect 11 262a-b; bk vi, sect 44 278b-c

17 Plotinus: *Fourth Ennead*, tr iii, ch 16 150c-d

18 Augustine: *City of God*, bk v, ch 1 207d-208c; ch 8-10 212c-216c; ch 15-16 220d-221b; bk xv, ch 1 397b,d-398c; bk xxi, ch 12 571a-c; bk xxii, ch 1-2 586b,d-588a

19 Aquinas: *Summa Theologica*, part i, qq 23-24 132b-143c; q 116 592d-595c

21 Dante: *Divine Comedy*, hell, vii [61-96] 10b-c; purgatory, xvi [52-84] 77b-c; paradise, i [94-142] 107b-d; iv [49-63] 111b; viii [91-148] 117d-118c; xvii [13-45] 132b-c; xx [31-141] 137a-138a

22 Chaucer: *Troilus and Cressida*, bk iv, stanza 137-154 106b-108b

23 Hobbes: *Leviathan*, part ii, 113b-c

25 Montaigne: *Essays*, 254b-d; 342a-c

29 Cervantes: *Don Quixote*, part ii, 408b-c

30 Bacon: *Novum Organum*, bk i, aph 93 125d-126a

31 Descartes: *Objections and Replies*, 141b

32 Milton: *Paradise Lost* 93a-333a esp bk i [1-26] 93b-94a, bk iii [80-134] 137a-138a, bk v [224-245] 180a-b, [506-543] 186a-187a, bk vii [139-173] 220a-221a / *Samson Agonistes* [373-419] 347b-348b; [667-709] 354a-355a / *Areopagitica*, 394b-395b

35 Hume: *Human Understanding*, sect viii, div 78-81 485c-487a

37 Fielding: *Tom Jones*, 32c-33b

38 Montesquieu: *Spirit of Laws*, bk xiv, 107a

38 Rousseau: *Social Contract*, bk iv, 437d-438b

41 Gibbon: *Decline and Fall*, 230b; 239c

42 Kant: *Practical Reason*, 334a-335b / *Judgement*, 594d [fn 1]

44 Boswell: *Johnson*, 13b; 173c

46 Hegel: *Philosophy of Right*, part iii, par 343 110d-111a / *Philosophy of History*, intro, 153a-190b esp 158c-162a; part iii, 305c-d; part iv, 368d-369a,c

47 Goethe: *Faust*, part ii [5305-5344] 131b-132a

48 Melville: *Moby Dick*, 396b-397a

51 Tolstoy: *War and Peace*, bk vi, 272a-b; bk ix, 357b-358b; bk xv, 631a-c; epilogue ii, 675b-677b; 680b-c; 684b-d

52 Dostoevsky: *Brothers Karamazov*, bk v, 127b-137c passim

54 Freud: *Interpretation of Dreams*, 246c-247d / *Civilization and Its Discontents*, 776b; 793c

5. The secularization of fate: scientific or philosophical determinism

7 Plato: bk x, 437b-441a,c esp 439a-441a,c

12 Lucretius: *Nature of Things*, bk ii [184-307] 17b-19a esp [251-293] 18b-d; bk v [55-58] 61d

12 Aurelius: *Meditations*, bk v, sect 8 269d-270b

17 Plotinus: *Third Ennead*, tr i 78a-82b / *Fourth Ennead*, tr iii, ch 16 150c-d

31 Spinoza: *Ethics*, part i, def 6-7 355b; axiom 3 355d; prop 17, schol 362c-363c; prop 25-29 365b-366c; prop 32-appendix 367a-372d; part ii, prop 48 391a-c; prop 49, schol, 394b-d

34 Newton: *Optics*, bk iii, 542b

35 Berkeley: *Human Knowledge*, sect 93 431b

35 Hume: *Human Understanding*, sect viii 478b-487a passim

42 Kant: *Pure Reason*, 140b,d-143a; 164a-171a / *Judgement*, 463a-467a; 575b-578a

46 Hegel: *Philosophy of Right*, part iii, par 342-348 110c-111d / *Philosophy of History*, intro, 156d-190b esp 156d-158a, 161d-162a; 203a-206a,c

50 Marx: *Capital*, 6d; 7c; 10b-11d; 35b-c; 36c-d [fn 2]; 378b-d esp 378d

50 Marx-Engels: *Communist Manifesto*, 416c-d

51 Tolstoy: *War and Peace*, epilogue ii 675a-696d

53 James: *Psychology*, 291a-295b; 820b-825a esp 823a-825a

54 Freud: *Origin and Development of Psycho-Analysis*, 13c / *Interpretation of Dreams*, 246b-247c / *General Introduction*, 454b-c; 486d-487a; 581d-582a / *Beyond the Pleasure Principle*, 645b-646a / *Civilization and Its Discontents*, 772b-c; 796a-c; 801c-802a,c / *New Introductory Lectures*, 882c-883d

6. The historian's recognition of fate: the destiny of cities, nations, empires

6 Herodotus: *History*, BK VII, 214d-220b esp 218b-220b; 239a-240d; BK VIII, 262b-c

7 Plato: *Republic*, BK VIII, 403a-d

13 Virgil: *Eclogues*, IV 14a-15b / *Aeneid*, BK I [441-493] 115a-116b; BK VI [752-901] 231a-235a; BK VIII [608-731] 275a-278b; BK X [100-117] 304b-305a; BK XII [725-842] 373b-376b

14 Plutarch: *Romulus*, 18d; 20b-c / *Camillus*, 107b-d; 109c-110a / *Philopoemen*, 300b / *Alexander*, 555c / *Demosthenes*, 698b-c / *Marcus Brutus*, 815c

15 Tacitus: *Annals*, BK III, 58b-d; BK VI, 91b-d / *Histories*, BK I, 189b-190a; BK II, 232d

18 Augustine: *City of God*, BK V 207b,d-230a,c esp CH 1 207d-208c, CH 12 216d-219b, CH 15 220d-221a

25 Montaigne: *Essays*, 214a-d; 462c-465c passim

43 Federalist: NUMBER 2, 31c-d

46 Hegel: *Philosophy of Right*, PART III, par 340-360 110b-114a,c esp par 342-343 110c-111a, par 347 111b-c / *Philosophy of History*, INTRO, 156d-190b esp 158c-162a; 203a-206a,c; PART I, 241d-242b; 258b-d; PART II, 278a-c; 280b-281b; 283-284a,c; PART III, 285b-d; 300a-301c; 303c-306a; PART IV, 315a; 368d-369a,c

50 Marx: *Capital*, 6c-7d passim; 377c-378d

50 Marx-Engels: *Communist Manifesto*, 416c-d; 421d-422c; 424d-425b

51 Tolstoy: *War and Peace*, BK IX, 342a-344b; BK X, 389a-391c; BK XI, 469a-472b; BK XIII-XIV, 563a-590c; BK XIV, 609a-613d; BK XV, 618b-621b; 626d-630a; EPILOGUE I, 645a-650c; EPILOGUE II 675a-696d

54 Freud: *New Introductory Lectures*, 882c-883c

CROSS-REFERENCES

For: The basic opposites of fate, *see* Chance 1a-1b, 2a; History 4a(1); Will 5-5a(4), 5c; and for other terms in which the opposition between fate and chance is expressed, *see* Necessity and Contingency 3.

The problem of human liberty in relation to fate, *see* Liberty 4b; Necessity and Contingency 5a(3); Will 5c.

The implications of fate in theology, or for the relation of human liberty to divine providence, *see* Cause 7c; God 1c, 7b; History 5a; Liberty 5a-5c; Will 7c.

The foretelling of fate or providence, *see* Prophecy 1a-1b; and for the condemnation of astrology and divination, *see* Prophecy 5.

Fatalism or determinism in the philosophy of nature, *see* Chance 2a; Nature 3c-3c(3); Will 5c; World 1b.

The same doctrine in the philosophy of history, *see* History 4a(1)-4a(4); Necessity and Contingency 5f; Will 7b.

ADDITIONAL READINGS

Listed below are works not included in *Great Books of the Western World*, but relevant to the idea and topics with which this chapter deals. These works are divided into two groups:

I. Works by authors represented in this collection.
II. Works by authors not represented in this collection.

For the date, place, and other facts concerning the publication of the works cited, consult the Bibliography of Additional Readings which follows the last chapter of *The Great Ideas*.

I.

Plutarch. "Of Fate," in *Moralia*
Augustine. *On the Predestination of the Saints*
Aquinas. *Summa Contra Gentiles*, BK III, CH 64-83, 88-98, 163
Descartes. *The Principles of Philosophy*, PART I, 40-41
Hobbes. *A Treatise of Liberty and Necessity*

J. S. Mill. *A System of Logic*, BK VI, CH 2
W. James. "The Dilemma of Determinism," in *The Will to Believe*

II.

Cicero. *De Fato* (On Fate)
———. *De Divinatione* (On Divination)
Maimonides. *The Guide for the Perplexed*, PART III, CH 17-19

Chapter 28: FORM

INTRODUCTION

THE great philosophical issues concerning form and matter have never been resolved. But the terms in which these issues were stated, from their first formulation in antiquity to the 17th or 18th centuries, have disappeared or at least do not have general currency in contemporary discourse. Kant is perhaps the last great philosopher to include these terms in his basic vocabulary. The conceptions of matter and form, he writes, "lie at the foundation of all other reflection, so inseparably are they connected with every mode of exercising the understanding. The former denotes the determinable in general, the second its determination."

The word "form" is no longer a pivotal term in the analysis of change or motion, nor in the distinction between being and becoming, nor in the consideration of the modes of being and the conditions of knowledge. The word "matter" is now used without reference to form, where earlier in the tradition all of its principal meanings involved "form" as a correlative or an opposite. Other words, such as "participation" and "imitation," have also fallen into disuse or lost the meanings which derived from their relation to form and matter.

The problems which these words were used to state and discuss remain active in contemporary thought. There is, for instance, the problem of the universal and the particular, the problem of the immutable and the mutable, the problem of the one and the many, or of sameness and diversity. These problems appear in the writings of William James and Bergson, Dewey and Santayana, Whitehead and Russell. Sometimes there is even a verbal approximation to the traditional formulation, as in Whitehead's doctrine of "eternal objects" or in Santayana's consideration of the "realm of essence" and the "realm of matter." Whatever expressions they use, these thinkers find themselves opposed on issues which represent part, if not the whole, of the great traditional controversy between Plato and Aristotle concerning form.

THERE IS A TENDENCY AMONG the historians of thought to use the names of Plato and Aristotle to symbolize a basic opposition in philosophical perspectives and methods, or even in what William James calls "intellectual temperaments." Later writers are called "Platonists" or "Aristotelians" and doctrines or theories are classified as Platonic or Aristotelian. It almost seems to be assumed at times that these names exhaust the typical possibilities: that minds or theories must be one or the other, or some sort of mixture or confusion of the two.

If this tendency is ever justified, it seems to be warranted with regard to the problems of form. Here, if anywhere, there may be poetic truth in Whitehead's remark that the history of western thought can be read as a series of footnotes to Plato; though perhaps the observation should be added that Aristotle, the first to comment on Plato, wrote many of the principal footnotes. In Plotinus the two strains seem to be intermingled. The issue between Plato and Aristotle concerning form dominates the great metaphysical and theological controversies of the later Middle Ages, and, with some alterations in language and thought, it appears in the writings of Hobbes, Bacon, Descartes, Spinoza, and Locke, where it is partly a continuation of, and partly a reaction against, the mediaeval versions of Platonic and Aristotelian doctrine.

The most extreme reaction is, of course, to be found in those who completely reject the term *form* or its equivalents as being without significance for the problems of motion, existence, or knowledge. Bacon retains the term, but radically changes its meaning. "None should suppose from the great part assigned by us to forms," Bacon writes, "that we mean such forms as the meditations and thoughts of men have hitherto been accustomed to." He does not mean either "the concrete forms" or "any abstract forms of ideas," but rather "the laws and regulations of simple action. . . . The form of heat or form of light, therefore, means no more than the law of heat or the law of light." But Hobbes and Locke tend to reject the term itself—especially when it occurs in the notion of substantial form—as meaningless or misleading.

"We are told," says Hobbes, "there be in the world certain essences, separated from bodies, which they call *abstract essences, and substantial forms.* . . . Being once fallen into this error of *separated essences,* [men] are thereby necessarily involved in many other absurdities that follow it. For seeing they will have these forms to be real, they are obliged to assign them *some place*"; which they cannot succeed in doing, according to Hobbes, "because they hold them incorporeal, without all dimension of quantity, and all men know that place is dimension, and not to be filled but by that which is corporeal."

With regard to *substantial form,* Locke declares, "I confess I have no idea at all, but only of the sound 'form.'" Those "who have been taught . . . that it was those *forms* which made the distinction of substances into their true species and genera, were led yet further out of the way by having their minds set upon fruitless inquiries after 'substantial forms' "—a subject which Locke regards as "wholly unintelligible." The general skepticism about this notion (or the distrust of its hollowness) in the 17th and 18th centuries is reflected in a bantering remark by Tristram Shandy's father. In a discussion of infant prodigies, he refers to some boy-wonders who "left off their substantial forms at nine years old, or sooner, and went on reasoning without them."

Since form and matter are supposed to be correlative, the denial to form of meaning or reality leads to materialism, as in the case of Hobbes—the affirmation of matter alone as a principle or cause. Materialists of one sort or another are the opponents of both Plato and Aristotle, and of Platonists and Aristotelians. That part of the controversy is discussed in the chapter on MATTER. Here we are concerned with the issues arising from different views of form and its relation to matter.

THE POPULAR meaning of "form" affords an approach to the subtleties of the subject. As ordinarily used, "form" connotes figure or shape. That connotation expresses one aspect of the technical significance of "form." A great variety of things, differing materially and in other respects, can have the *same* figure or shape. The same form can be embodied in an indefinite number of otherwise different individuals. But figures or shapes are sensible forms, forms perceptible to vision and touch. To identify form with figure or shape would put an improper limitation on the meaning of form. This is popularly recognized in the consideration of the form of a work of art—the structure of an epic poem or a symphony—which seems to be more a matter of understanding than of direct sense-perception.

Bertrand Russell's definition of the form of a proposition effectively illustrates the point involved. The form of a proposition, he says, is that which remains the same in a statement when everything else is changed. For example, these two statements have the same grammatical and logical form: (1) *John followed James,* and (2) *Paul accompanied Peter.* What might be called the matter or subject matter of the two statements is completely different, but both have the same form, as may an indefinite number of other statements.

This illustration helps us to grasp the meaning of form, and the distinction between form and matter, or the formal and the material aspects of anything. It is thus that we understand the phrase "formal logic" to signify a study of the forms of thought or discourse, separated from the subject matter being thought about or discussed. Similarly, abstractionism or surrealism is a kind of formalism in painting which tries to separate visible patterns or structures from their representative significance or their reference to familiar objects.

Kant's doctrine of space and time as transcendental forms of intuition exemplifies the meaning of form as pure order or structure divorced from sensuous content. "That which in the phenomenon corresponds to the sensation,

I term its *matter*," he writes; "that which effects that the content of the phenomenon can be arranged under certain relations, I call its *form*." Sometimes the consideration of form emphasizes not its separation from, but its union with matter. The form dwells in the thing, constituting its nature. The sensible or intelligible characteristics of a thing result from the various ways in which its matter has been formed.

It is impossible to say more about the meaning of *form* without facing at once the great controversy between Plato and Aristotle and the difficulties which their theories confront.

PLATO DOES NOT deny that things—the sensible, material, changing things of experience—have something like form. Nor does he deny that the ideas by which we understand the natures of things are like forms. Rather he asks us to consider that which they are *like*.

In the *Phaedo*—only one of the many dialogues in which the doctrine of forms is discussed—Socrates argues that "there is such a thing as equality, not of one piece of wood or stone with another, but that, over and above this, there is absolute equality." Socrates gets Simmias to admit that "we know the nature of this absolute essence," and then asks, "Whence did we obtain our knowledge?" It could not have been obtained from the pieces of wood or stone, Socrates tries to show, because they "appear at one time equal, and at another time unequal," whereas the idea of equality is never the same as that of inequality. Hence he thinks "we must have known equality previously to the time when we first saw the material equals. . . . Before we began to see or hear or perceive in any way, we must have had a knowledge of absolute equality, or we could not have referred to that standard the equals which are derived from the senses." The equality which supplies the "standard" by which material equals are measured is the Form or Idea of equality.

What is true in this one case Socrates thinks is true in every other. Whether we consider the "essence of equality, beauty, or anything else," Socrates holds, the "Ideas or essences, which in the dialectical process we define as . . . true existences . . . are each of them always

what they are, having the same simple self-existent and unchanging forms, not admitting of variation at all, or in any way or at any time." Apart from the perishable things of the sensible world, and apart from the ideas which are involved in our process of learning and thinking, there exist the Forms or the Ideas themselves—the immutable objects of our highest knowledge.

Because the same English words are employed in these quite distinct senses, it is useful to follow the convention of translators who capitalize the initial letter when "Form" or "Idea" refers to that which is separate from the characteristics of material things and from the ideas in our mind. The words "Form" and "Idea" are interchangeable, but the words "Idea" and "idea" are not. The latter refers to a notion in the human mind, by which it knows; whereas "Idea"—as Plato uses the word—signifies the object of knowledge, *i.e.* that which is known. These differences are further discussed in the chapter on IDEA.

By imitating the Forms, sensible things, according to Plato, have the characteristics we apprehend in them. The ideas we have when we apprehend the resemblance between sensible things and their Forms (which sensible things exhibit), would seem to be indirect apprehensions of the Forms themselves. When in the *Republic* Socrates discusses knowledge and opinion, he distinguishes them from one another according to a division of their objects—the realm of intelligible being on the one hand, and the realm of sensible becoming on the other. The latter stands to the former as image or copy to reality, and Socrates finds this relationship repeating itself when he further divides each of the two parts. The realm of becoming divides into images or shadows and into that "of which this is only the resemblance," namely, "the animals which we see, and everything that grows or is made." The realm of intelligible being he also subdivides into two parts, of which the first is as an image or reflection of the second, namely, the hypotheses we form in our minds and the Ideas or Forms themselves.

From this it appears that just as we should regard the form of the thing as an imitation of, or participation in, the separate Form, so should we regard the idea we have (that is, our understanding of the thing) as an approximation of the Idea. The Ideas are outside the human mind even as the Forms are separate from their sensible, material imitations. When we apprehend things by reason we know the Forms they imitate; when we apprehend them by our senses we know them as imitations, or as images of the Ideas.

THE PLATONIC THEORY changes the ordinary meaning of the word "imitation." We ordinarily think of imitation as involving a relation of resemblance between two sensible things, both of which we are able to perceive; for example, we say that a child imitates his father's manner, or that a portrait resembles the person who posed for it. The painter, according to Socrates in the *Republic*, is not the only "creator of appearances." He compares the painter who pictures a bed with the carpenter who makes one.

Like the bed in the painting, the bed made by the carpenter is not the real bed. It is not, says Socrates, the Idea "which, according to our view, is the essence of the bed." The carpenter "cannot make true existence, but only some semblance of existence." As the bed in the picture is an imitation of the particular bed made by the carpenter, so the latter is an imitation of the Idea—the essential *bed-ness* which is the model or archetype of all particular beds.

Shifting to another example, we can say that a statue, which resembles a particular man, is the imitation of an imitation, for the primary imitation lies in the resemblance between the particular man portrayed and the Form or Idea, Man. Just as the statue derives its distinctive character from the particular man it imitates, so that particular man, or any other, derives his manhood or humanity from Man. Just as the particular man imitates Man, so our idea of Man is also an imitation of that Idea. Knowledge, according to Plato, consists in the imitation of Ideas, even as sensible, material things have whatever being they have by imitation of the true beings, the Forms.

Another name for the primary type of imitation is "participation." To participate in is to partake of. In the dialogue in which Plato has the young Socrates inquiring into the relation between sensible particulars and the Ideas or Forms, Parmenides tells him that "there are certain ideas of which all other things partake, and from which they derive their names; that similars, for example, become similar, because they partake of similarity; and great things become great, because they partake of greatness; and that just and beautiful things become just and beautiful, because they partake of justice and beauty." The Forms or Ideas are, Parmenides suggests, "patterns fixed in nature, and other things are like them, and resemblances of them—what is meant by the participation of other things in the ideas, is really assimilation to them."

The fact of particularity and multiplicity seems to be inseparable from the fact of participation. That in which the many particulars participate must, on the other hand, have universality and unity. The Forms or Ideas are universals in the sense that each is a one which is somehow capable of being in a many—by resemblance or participation. Parmenides asks Socrates whether he thinks that "the whole idea is one, and yet, being one, is in each one of the many." When Socrates unhesitatingly says Yes, Parmenides points out to him that we then confront the difficulty that "one and the same thing will exist as a whole at the same time in many separate individuals" and that "the ideas themselves will be divisible, and things which participate in them will have a part of them only and not the whole idea existing in each of them." Nor can we say, Socrates is made to realize, that "the one idea is really divisible and yet remains one."

THIS DIFFICULTY concerning the relation of particulars to the Ideas they participate in, is discussed in the chapter on UNIVERSAL AND PARTICULAR. It is not the only difficulty which Plato himself finds in the theory of Ideas. Another concerns the individuality of each of the indefinite number of particulars which copy a single model or archetype. What makes the various copies of the same model different from one another?

Plato meets this problem by adding a third principle. To the intelligible patterns or archetypes and their sensible imitations, he adds, in the *Timaeus*, the principle which is variously named, sometimes "the receptacle," sometimes "space," sometimes "matter." However named, it is the absolutely formless, for "that which is to receive all Forms should have no form. . . . The mother and receptacle of all visible and in any way sensible things . . . is an invisible and formless being which receives all things and in some mysterious way partakes of the intelligible, and is most incomprehensible."

It is this material or receiving principle which somehow accounts for the numerical plurality and the particularization of the many copies of the one absolute model. When a number of replicas of the same pattern are produced by impressing a die on a sheet of plastic material at different places, it is the difference in the material at the several places which accounts for the plurality and particularity of the replicas. Yet the one die is responsible for the character common to them all.

The sensible things of any one sort are not only *particular* because the Form they imitate is somehow received in matter; they are also *perishable* because of that fact. The receptacle is the principle of generation or of change. It is, Timaeus says, "the natural recipient of all impressions," which is "stirred and informed by them, and appears different from time to time by reason of them, but the forms which enter into and go out of her are the likenesses of real existences modelled after their patterns in a wonderful and inexplicable manner."

Matter, as Plato here suggests, is the mother of changing things, things which, between coming to be and passing away, are what they are because of the unchanging Forms. The Form which is received in matter for a time makes the changing thing an *imitation*, as the matter in which the Form is received makes the changing thing a *participation*.

The admittedly mysterious partaking of the Forms by the formless receptacle constitutes the realm of becoming, in which being and non-being are mixed. But the Forms or Ideas themselves, existing apart from their sensible imitations, are "uncreated and indestructible, never receiving anything from without, nor going out to any other, but invisible and imperceptible by any sense." They constitute the realm of pure being. They are the intelligible reality.

THE CRITICISM OF the Forms or Ideas which we find in the writings of Aristotle is primarily directed against their separate existence. "Plato was not far wrong," Aristotle says, "when he said that there are as many Forms as there are kinds of natural object"; but he immediately adds the qualification: "if there *are* Forms distinct from the things of this earth." It is precisely that supposition which Aristotle challenges.

Aristotle's criticism of Plato stems from his own notion of substance, and especially from his conception of sensible substances as composed of matter and form. He uses the word "substance" to signify that which exists in and of itself; or, in other words, that which exists separately from other things. Hence, when he says that, in addition to sensible substances, "Plato posited two kinds of substances—the Forms and the objects of mathematics," he is translating the affirmation that the Forms have being separately from the sensible world of changing things, into an assertion that they are substances.

"Socrates did not make the universals or the definitions exist apart," Aristotle writes; but referring to the Platonists, he says, "*they*, however, gave them separate existence, and this was the kind of thing they called Ideas." What proof is there, he repeatedly asks, for the separate existence of the Forms, or universals, or the objects of mathematics? "Of the various ways in which it is proved that the Forms exist," he declares, "none is convincing." Furthermore, he objects to the statement that "all other things come from the Forms"; for "to say that they are patterns and the other things share in them is to use empty words and poetical metaphors." There is the additional difficulty, he thinks, that "there will be several patterns of the same thing, and therefore several Forms; *e.g.*, 'animal' and 'two-footed' and also 'man himself' will be Forms of man."

Aristotle's denial of separate existence, or substantiality, to the Ideas or universals stands side by side with his affirmation of the place of forms in the being of substances and the role of universals in the order of knowledge. Furthermore, he limits his denial of the substantiality of Ideas to those Forms which seem to be the archetypes or models of sensible things. Particular physical things—familiar sensible substances, such as the stone, the tree, or the man —are not, in his opinion, imitations of or participations in universal models which exist apart from these things. He leaves it an open question whether there are self-subsistent Forms or Ideas —that is, purely intelligible substances—which do not function as the models for sensible things to imitate.

Stated positively, the Aristotelian theory consists in two affirmations. The first is that the characteristics of things are determined by "indwelling forms," which have their being not apart from but in the things themselves. To illustrate his meaning he turns to the realm of art. When we make a brass sphere, he writes, "we bring the form," which is a sphere, "into this particular matter," the brass, and "the result is a brazen sphere." There is no "sphere apart from the individual spheres," and no brass apart from the particular lumps of metal that are brass. "The 'form' means the 'such,' and is not a 'this'—a definite thing," such as this individual brazen sphere.

Aristotle analyzes natural things in the same manner. It is from "the indwelling form and the matter," he says, that "the concrete substance is derived." Men such as Callias or Socrates, for example, consist of "such and such a form in this flesh and in these bones," and "they are different in virtue of their matter (for that is different) but the same in form." The flesh and bones of Callias are not the flesh and bones of Socrates; but though different as individual men, they are the same as men because they have the same form.

The second point is that our understanding of things involves the forms of things, but now somehow in the intellect rather than in the things themselves. In order to know things, Aristotle says, we must have within us "either the things themselves or their forms. The former alternative is of course impossible: it is not the stone which is present in the soul," he maintains, "but its form."

The form in the thing is as individual as the thing itself. But in the mind, as the result of the intellect's power to abstract this form from its matter, the form becomes a universal; it is then called by Aristotle an "idea," "abstraction," or "concept." Forms are universals in the mind

alone. If there were a form existing apart from both matter and mind, it would be neither an individual form nor an abstract universal.

The indwelling forms, according to Aristotle, are not universals. Except for the possibility of Forms which dwell apart and bear *no resemblance at all* to sensible things, all forms are either in matter or, abstracted from matter, in the human mind. These are often called "material forms" because they are the forms which matter takes or can take, and which the mind abstracts from matter. Their being consists in informing or determining matter, just as the being of matter consists in the capacity to receive these forms and to be determined by them.

THE FOREGOING helps to explain Aristotle's use of the word "composite" as a synonym for "substance" when he is considering particular sensible things. The independently existing, individual physical things which Aristotle calls "substances" are all composite of form and matter. He sometimes also calls form and matter "substances," but when he uses the word "substance" strictly and in its primary sense, he applies it only to the concrete individual. Form and matter are only principles or constituents of the concrete thing—the composite substance.

The union of form and matter to constitute physical substances also explains the Aristotelian identification of form with actuality and of matter with potentiality; and the relation of form and matter to a third term in the analysis of change, namely, *privation*. As a physical thing changes, its matter gives up one form to take on another. Its matter thus represents its capacity or *potentiality* for form. Matter is the *formable* aspect of changing things. What things are *actually* at any moment is due to the forms they possess. But they may have the potentiality for acquiring other forms, with respect to which they are in *privation*.

"The mutability of mutable things," Augustine writes, "is simply their capacity for all the forms into which mutable things can be changed." Change consists in a *transformation* of *matter*, which is another way of saying that it consists in the *actualization* of a thing's *potentialities*. The Aristotelian theory of form and matter is a theory of becoming as well as an analysis of the being of changing things. Illustrative applications of this theory will be found in the chapters on ART, CAUSE, and CHANGE.

Some forms are sensible. Some are shapes, some are qualities, some are quantities. But not all forms are perceptible by the senses; as, for example, the form which matter takes when a plant or animal is generated and which gives the generated thing its specific nature. This type of form came to be called a "substantial form" because it determines the kind of substance which the thing is. In contrast, the forms which determine the properties or attributes of a thing are called its "accidents" or "accidental forms." For example, size and shape, color and weight, are accidental forms of a man; whereas that by virtue of which this thing (having a certain size, shape, and color) is a *man*, is its substantial form.

Aristotle's distinction between substantial and accidental form affects his analysis of change and his conception of matter. Generation and corruption are for him substantial change, change in which matter undergoes transformation with respect to its substantial form. The various types of motion—alteration, increase or decrease, and local motion—are changes which take place in enduring substances, and with respect to their accidental forms.

The substratum of accidental change is not formless matter, but matter having a certain substantial form; whereas in the coming to be or passing away of substances, the substratum would seem to be a primary sort of matter, devoid of all form. As indicated in the chapter on MATTER, this, according to Aristotle, is "the primary substratum of each thing, from which it comes to be without qualification, and which persists in the result." He tries to help us grasp prime matter by using an analogy. "As the bronze is to the statue, the wood to the bed," he writes, "so is the underlying nature to substance"—matter absolutely formless to substantial form.

Aristotle sometimes speaks of the substantial form as a first act or actuality, and of accidental forms as second actualities. Accordingly he also distinguishes between a primary and secondary kind of matter—the one absolutely potential, and underlying substantial change; the other partly actualized and partly potential, and involved in accidental change. "Primary matter," Aquinas explains, "has substantial being through its form. . . . But when once it exists under one form it is in potentiality to others."

Perhaps one more distinction should be mentioned because of its significance for later discussions of form. Regarding living and nonliving things as essentially distinct, Aristotle differentiates between the forms constituting these two kinds of substances. As appears in the chapter on SOUL, he uses the word "soul" to name the substantial form of plants, animals, and men.

BOTH THE PLATONIC theory of the separate Forms and the Aristotelian theory of the composition of form and matter raise difficulties which their authors consider and which become the subject of intense controversy among Platonists and Aristotelians in the Hellenistic and mediaeval periods.

The Platonic theory faces a question which arises from supposing the existence of an eternal and immutable Form for every appearance in the sensible world of becoming. If the Idea and the individual are alike, then "some further idea of likeness will always be coming to light," Parmenides says to Socrates; "and if that be like anything else, then another; and new ideas will be always arising, if the idea resembles that which partakes of it." Because of this difficulty with the doctrine of participation, Parmenides suggests that it may be necessary to conclude that "the Idea cannot be like the individual or the individual like the Idea." In addition, the relationships of the Forms to one another presents a difficulty. Is the relation of one Form to another, Parmenides asks, determined by the essence of each Form, or by the relationships among the sensible particulars that imitate the Forms in question? Either solution seems to be unsatisfactory because of the further difficulties which both raise.

Yet, after propounding questions of this sort, and multiplying difficulties, Parmenides concludes by telling Socrates why the theory of Ideas cannot be given up. "If a man, fixing his attention on these and like difficulties," he says, "does away with the Forms of things and will not admit that every individual thing has its own determinate Idea which is always one and the same, he will have nothing on which his mind can rest; and so he will utterly destroy the power of reasoning."

The Aristotelian theory has difficulties of its own with respect to the ultimate character of matter apart from all forms. Completely form-less matter would be pure potentiality and would therefore have no actual being. It would be completely unintelligible, since form is the principle of anything's intelligibility. Never-theless, something like formless matter seems to be involved in substantial change, in contrast to the substantially formed matter which is the substratum of accidental change.

The problem of prime matter is related in later speculations to the problem of the number and order of the various forms which matter can take. The question is whether matter must have a substantial form before it can have any accidental form; and whether it can have a second substantial form in addition to a first, or is limited to having a single substantial form, all subsequent forms necessarily being acci-dental.

Aquinas plainly argues in favor of the unity of substantial form. "Nothing is absolutely one," he maintains, "except by one form, by which a thing has being; because a thing has both being and unity from the same source, and therefore things which are denominated by various forms are not absolutely one; as, for instance, a white man. If, therefore," Aquinas continues, "man were *living* by one form, the vegetative soul, and *animal* by another form, the sensitive soul, and *man* by another form, the intellectual soul, it would follow that man is not absolutely one. . . . We must, therefore, conclude," he says, "that the intellectual soul, the sensitive soul, and the nutritive soul are in man numerically one and the same soul." In other words, "of one thing there is but one sub-stantial form." It is not only "impossible that there be in man another substantial form be-sides the intellectual soul," but there is also no need of any other, because "the intellectual soul contains virtually whatever belongs to the sensitive soul of brute animals and the nutritive soul of plants."

The Aristotelian theory also has difficulties with respect to substantial forms as objects of knowledge and definition. The definition which the mind formulates attempts to state the es-sence of the thing defined. The formulable es-sence of a thing would seem to be identical with its form. But Aristotle raises the question and his followers debate at length whether the es-sence of a composite substance is identical with its substantial form or includes its matter as well.

Among his followers Aquinas maintains that, in defining the essence or species of a composite substance, the genus is used to signify the mat-ter and the differentia the form. "Some held," he writes, "that the form alone belongs to the species, while the matter is part of the individ-ual, and not of the species. This cannot be true, for to the nature of the species belongs what the definition signifies, and in natural things the definition does not signify the form only, but the form and the matter. Hence in natural things the matter is part of the species; not, indeed, signate matter, which is the prin-ciple of individuation, but common matter." He explains in another place that "matter is twofold; common and *signate*, or individual: common, such as flesh and bone; individual, such as this flesh and these bones." In forming the universal concept *man*, for example, the intellect abstracts the notion of the species "from *this flesh and these bones*, which do not belong to the species as such, but to the indi-vidual. . . . But the species of *man* cannot be ab-stracted by the intellect from *flesh and bones*."

As will be seen in the chapters on ONE AND MANY and UNIVERSAL AND PARTICULAR, the Platonic and the Aristotelian theories of form are equally involved in the great prob-lem of the universal and the individual. Even though they seem to be diametrically opposed on the existence of universals—whether apart from or only in minds—both Plato and Aris-totle face the necessity of explaining individu-ality. What makes the particular that imitates a universal Form the unique individual it is? What makes the indwelling form of a composite substance an individual form, as unique as the individual substance of which it is the form?

We have already noted that both Platonists and Aristotelians appeal to matter as somehow responsible for individuation or individuality, but that only raises further questions. The

Platonists conceive matter as the receptacle of all Forms, and so in itself absolutely formless. How, then, can it cause the particularizations which must be accounted for? Since prime matter, like the receptacle, is formless, the Aristotelians resort to what they call "signate matter" or "individual matter" to explain the individuality of forms and substances; but it has been argued that this only begs the question rather than solves it.

THE CORRELATIVE terms *form* and *matter* seem to occur in modern thought under the guise of certain equivalents; as, for example, the distinct substances which Descartes calls "thought" and "extension"—*res cogitans* and *res extensa*—or the infinite attributes of substance which Spinoza calls "mind" and "body." They appear more explicitly in Kant's analysis of knowledge, related as the *a priori* and the *a posteriori* elements of experience. But it is in the great theological speculations of the Middle Ages that the most explicit and extended use of these terms is made, often with new interpretations placed on ancient theories.

The doctrine of spiritual substances, for example, has a bearing on the theory of self-subsistent Forms. The angels are sometimes called "separate forms" by the theologians. They are conceived as immaterial substances, and hence as simple rather than composite. But though Plotinus identifies the order of purely intelligible beings with the pure intelligences, the Christian theologian does not identify the Platonic Ideas with the angels. He regards the angels as intelligences. They exist as pure forms, and therefore are intelligible as well as intellectual substances. But they are in no sense the archetypes or models which sensible things resemble.

Nevertheless, Christian theology does include that aspect of the Platonic theory which looks upon the Ideas as the eternal models or patterns. But, as Aquinas points out, the separately existing Forms are replaced by what Augustine calls "the exemplars existing in the divine mind."

Aquinas remarks on the fact that "whenever Augustine, who was imbued with the doctrines of the Platonists, found in their teaching anything consistent with faith, he adopted it; and

those things which he found contrary to faith he amended." He then goes on to say that Augustine could not adopt, but had to amend, the teaching of the Platonists that "the forms of things subsist of themselves apart from matter." He did this, not by denying the ideas, "according to which all things are formed," but by denying that they could exist outside the divine mind. The divine ideas are the eternal exemplars and the eternal types—*types*, Aquinas explains, insofar as they are the likenesses of things and so the principles of God's knowledge; *exemplars* insofar as they are "the principles of the making of things" in God's act of creation.

The profound mystery of the creative act which projects the divine ideas into substantial or material being replaces the older problem of how physical things derive their natures by participation in the Forms. According to the Aristotelian theory, both natural generation and artistic production involve the transformation of a pre-existent matter. According to the Platonic myth of the world's origin, only changing things are created, neither the receptacle nor the Ideas. But the Christian dogma of creation excludes everything from eternity except God.

Ideas are eternal only as inseparable from the divine mind. Being spiritual *creatures*, the angels, or self-subsistent forms, are not eternal. And in the world of corporeal creatures, matter as well as its forms must begin to be with the creation of things. Since matter and its forms cannot exist in separation from one another, the theologians hold that God cannot create them separately. God cannot be supposed, Augustine says, "first to have made formless matter, and after an interval of time, formed what He had first made formless; but," he goes on, "as intelligible sounds are made by a speaker, wherein the sound issues not formless at first and afterwards receives a form, but is uttered already formed; so must God be understood to have made the world of formless matter, but contemporaneously to have created the world." God "concreates" form and matter, Augustine holds, "giving form to matter's formlessness without any interval of time."

Defending Augustine's interpretation of the passage in Genesis which says that the earth, which God in the beginning created, "was un-formed and void," Aquinas argues that "if formless matter preceded in duration, it already existed; for this is implied by duration. . . . To say, then, that matter preceded, but without form, is to say that being existed actually, yet without actuality, which is a contradiction in terms. . . . Hence we must assert that primary matter was not created altogether formless." But neither, according to Aquinas, can the form of any material thing be created apart from its matter. "Forms and other non-sub-sisting things, which are said to co-exist rather than to exist," he declares, "ought to be called *concreated* rather than *created* things."

Aristotle's theory of physical substances as composite of form and matter raises certain special difficulties for Christian theology. Those who, like Aquinas, adopt his theory must also adapt it to supernatural conditions when they deal with the problems of substance involved in the mystery of the Incarnation of the second person of the Trinity and the mystery of tran-substantiation in the Eucharist.

Furthermore, Aristotle's identification of soul with the substantial form of a living thing makes it difficult to conceive the separate exist-ence of the individual human soul. Again an adaptation is required. As indicated in the chapters on IMMORTALITY and SOUL, the Chris-tian doctrine of personal survival is given an Aristotelian rendering by regarding the human soul as a form which is not completely material. Hence it is conceived as capable of self-subsist-ence when, with death and the dissolution of the composite nature, it is separated from the body.

OUTLINE OF TOPICS

REFERENCES

To find the passages cited, use the numbers in heavy type, which are the volume and page numbers of the passages referred to. For example, in 4 HOMER: *Iliad*, BK II [265-283] 12d, the number 4 is the number of the volume in the set; the number 12d indicates that the passage is in section d of page 12.

PAGE SECTIONS: When the text is printed in one column, the letters a and b refer to the upper and lower halves of the page. For example, in 53 JAMES: *Psychology*, 116a-119b, the passage begins in the upper half of page 116 and ends in the lower half of page 119. When the text is printed in two columns, the letters a and b refer to the upper and lower halves of the left-hand side of the page, the letters c and d to the upper and lower halves of the right-hand side of the page. For example, in 7 PLATO: *Symposium*, 163b-164c, the passage begins in the lower half of the left-hand side of page 163 and ends in the upper half of the right-hand side of page 164.

AUTHOR'S DIVISIONS: One or more of the main divisions of a work (such as PART, BK, CH, SECT) are sometimes included in the reference; line numbers, in brackets, are given in certain cases; *e.g.*, *Iliad*, BK II [265-283] 12d.

BIBLE REFERENCES: The references are to book, chapter, and verse. When the King James and Douay versions differ in title of books or in the numbering of chapters or verses, the King James version is cited first and the Douay, indicated by a (*D*), follows; *e.g.*, OLD TESTAMENT: *Nehemiah*, 7:45—(*D*) II *Esdras*, 7:46.

SYMBOLS: The abbreviation "esp" calls the reader's attention to one or more especially relevant parts of a whole reference; "passim" signifies that the topic is discussed intermittently rather than continuously in the work or passage cited.

For additional information concerning the style of the references, see the Explanation of Reference Style; for general guidance in the use of *The Great Ideas*, consult the Preface.

1. Form in relation to becoming or change

1a. Forms as immutable models or archetypes: the exemplar ideas

7 PLATO: *Cratylus*, 88a-89a; 113c-114a,c / *Phaedrus*, 125a-b / *Symposium*, 167b-d / *Phaedo*, 231b-232b; 247c-248c / *Republic*, BK III, 333b-334b; BK V, 368c-369c; BK VI, 382a-c; BK VI-VII, 386c-389c; BK IX-X, 426d-429b / *Timaeus*, 447a-458b passim, esp 447b-448b / *Parmenides*, 487c-491a / *Philebus*, 610d-613a / *Seventh Letter*, 809c-810b

8 ARISTOTLE: *Topics*, BK II, CH 7 [113ᵃ24-33] 158d; BK VI, CH 8 [147ᵃ5-11] 201a / *Generation and Corruption*, BK II, CH 9 [335ᵇ8-24] 437a-b / *Metaphysics*, BK I, CH 6 [987ᵃ29-ᵇ13] 505b-c; CH 7 [988ᵃ34-ᵇ5] 506c; CH 9 [991ᵃ19-32] 509c; BK VII, CH 8 [1033ᵇ19-1034ᵃ7] 556d-557b; BK XIII, CH 4-5 610a-611d

9 ARISTOTLE: *Ethics*, BK I, CH 6 [1096ᵇ32-1097ᵃ14] 342b-c

11 NICOMACHUS: *Arithmetic*, BK I, 811a-d

12 LUCRETIUS: *Nature of Things*, BK V [181-194] 63b-c

17 PLOTINUS: *Second Ennead*, TR III, CH 11 46b-c; TR III, CH 17-TR IV, CH 5 49b-51d; TR IV, CH 15 56c-57a / *Third Ennead*, TR IX, CH 1 136a-d / *Fourth Ennead*, TR II, CH 1 139c-140c; TR IX 205a-207a,c / *Fifth Ennead*, TR II, CH 1 214c-

215a; TR V, CH 4-TR IX, CH 14 230b-251d / *Sixth Ennead*, TR II, CH 20-22 278d-280d; TR VII, CH 4-17 323c-331a

18 AUGUSTINE: *Confessions*, BK I, par 9, 3a; BK XII, par 38 108d-109a / *City of God*, BK VIII, CH 3, 266a-b; CH 6, 269b-c; BK IX, CH 22 296d-297a; BK XI, CH 7 326a-c; CH 10, 328c-d; CH 29 339a-b / *Christian Doctrine*, BK I, CH 9-10 627a-b; BK II, CH 38 654b-c

19 AQUINAS: *Summa Theologica*, PART I, Q 15 91b-94a passim; Q 18, A 4, REP 2 107d-108c; Q 44, A 3 240b-241a; Q 47, A 1, REP 2 256a-257b; Q 50, A 3, ANS 272a-273b; Q 65, A 4, ANS 342b-343c; Q 108, A 1, ANS and REP 2 552c-553c

30 BACON: *Advancement of Learning*, 43d-44c

35 LOCKE: *Human Understanding*, BK III, CH III, SECT 17 258d-259b; SECT 19 259c-260a

42 KANT: *Pure Reason*, 113b-115a; 173b-174a / *Practical Reason*, 352c-353a / *Judgement*, 551a-552c

1b. Forms as indwelling causes or principles

8 ARISTOTLE: *Physics*, BK I 259a-268d; BK II, CH 1 [193ᵃ30-ᵇ19] 269c-270a; CH 2 [194ᵃ12-ᵇ15] 270c-271a; BK III, CH 2 [202ᵃ9-11] 279c / *Heavens*, BK I, CH 8 [277ᵃ12-27] 368b-c; BK IV, CH 4 [312ᵃ3-22] 403c-d / *Generation and Corruption*, BK I, CH 3 [318ᵇ13-18] 415b-c / *Meta-*

physics, BK V, CH 4 534d-535c; BK VII, CH 7-9 555a-558a esp CH 8 556b-557b; BK XII, CH 2-5 598c-601a

9 ARISTOTLE: *Parts of Animals*, BK I, CH I [640^{a}12–642^{a}24] 162b-165b / *Generation of Animals*, BK I, CH 20 [729^{a}6]–CH 22 [730^{b}33] 269b-271a

19 AQUINAS: *Summa Theologica*, PART I, Q 7, A I, ANS 31a-d; Q 9, A 2, REP 3 39c-40d; Q 14, A 8, ANS 82c-83b; Q 15, A I, ANS 91b-92a; Q 18, A 3, ANS 106b-107c; Q 19, A I, ANS 108d-109c; Q 42, A I, REP I 224b-225d; Q 51, A I, REP 3 275b-276b; Q 65, A 4, ANS 342b-343c; Q 85, A 2, ANS 453d-455b; Q 104, A I, ANS and REP I-2 534c-536c; Q 105, A 2, ANS 539c-540c; Q 115, AA I-2 585d-588c; PART I-II, Q 5, A 6, REP 2 641a-642a

20 AQUINAS: *Summa Theologica*, PART I-II, Q 49, A 4, ANS and REP I 5a-6a; Q 52, A I, ANS 15d-18a; Q 109, A I, ANS 338b-339c; PART II-II, Q 23, A 2, REP 3 483d-484d; Q 24, A II, ANS 498b-499c; PART III, Q 13, A I, ANS 780a-781b

21 DANTE: *Divine Comedy*, PURGATORY, XVIII [19–33] 80a; PARADISE, II [46–148] 108b-109b

28 GILBERT: *Loadstone*, BK II, 36d-37a

28 HARVEY: *On Animal Generation*, 386d-387a

30 BACON: *Advancement of Learning*, 43d-44c / *Novum Organum*, BK I, APH 51 111c; BK II, APH I-2 137a-c; APH 17 149b-d

35 LOCKE: *Human Understanding*, BK II, CH XXXI, SECT 6 240d-241d; SECT 13 243a-b; CH XXXII, SECT 24 247c-d; BK III, CH III, SECT 15-18 258b-259c; CH VI, SECT 2-3 268c-d; CH IX, SECT 12 287d-288a

42 KANT: *Judgement*, 550a-551a,c; 553c-562a,c; 565b-569a; 581c; 584c-d

46 HEGEL: *Philosophy of History*, INTRO, 156d-160b

1c. The transcendental or *a priori* forms as constitutive of order in experience

42 KANT: *Pure Reason*, 14a-108a,c esp 14a-15c, 23a-33d, 41c-42b, 48d-51d, 53b-55a, 56d-59b, 63d-64a, 66d-93c, 94d-96d, 100d-101b; 112d-113a; 115d; 129c-137a,c; 153c-155a; 162b-163a; 173b; 176d-177a; 186d-187a; 207c-d; 213d-215a / *Fund. Prin. Metaphysic of Morals*, 253a-c; 282b-c; 283b / *Practical Reason*, 308a-b; 319d; 335c-336a; 350b-c / *Judgement*, 461a-c; 471b-c; 482d; 492c-d; 515d-516b; 517b-c; 542c-d; 551a-553c; 562a-563b; 570b-572d; 612c-d

53 JAMES: *Psychology*, 627a-631a; 852a; 859a-882a

1d. The realization of forms in the sensible order

1d(1) Imitation or participation: the role of the receptacle

7 PLATO: *Euthydemus*, 81a-b / *Phaedrus*, 126b-c / *Symposium*, 167b-d / *Phaedo*, 242c-243c / *Republic*, BK III, 333b-334b; BK V, 368c-371b; BK VI, 382a-c; BK X, 427c-429b / *Timaeus*,

455c-477a,c esp 455c-458b / *Parmenides*, 487c-491a / *Seventh Letter*, 809c-810b

8 ARISTOTLE: *Physics*, BK IV, CH 2 [209^{b}5-17] 288b-c / *Generation and Corruption*, BK II, CH 9 [335^{b}8–24] 437a-b / *Metaphysics*, BK I, CH 6 505b-506b; CH 9 [990^{b}22–991^{a}8] 509a-b; BK VIII, CH 6 [1045^{a}14–19] 569d-570a; BK XII, CH 10 [1075^{b}16–20] 606c; BK XIII, CH 4 [1079^{a}19–^{b}3] 610d-611a

17 PLOTINUS: *First Ennead*, TR VI, CH 2-3 21d-23a; TR VII, CH 2 26c-d; TR VIII, CH 8 30d-31c; CH 10–11 32a-33d / *Second Ennead*, TR III, CH 11 46b-c; CH 18 49c-50a; TR IV, CH 5 51b-d; TR IX, CH 8 70a-d; CH 10–12 72a-73d; CH 16, 76a-b / *Third Ennead*, TR II, CH 1-3 82c-84c; CH 14 89b-d; TR V, CH 1, 100d-101b; CH 6, 104a; TR VI, CH 8–19 111c-119a; TR VII, CH 11 126a-d; TR VIII 129a-136a / *Fourth Ennead*, TR II, CH 1, 140a-c; TR III, CH 4–5 143d-144c; CH 15, 150a-b; TR IV, CH 13 164d-165b; TR VIII, 3-TR IX, CH 5 202a-207a,c esp TR IX, CH 2 205c-206a / *Fifth Ennead*, TR V, CH 4-13 230b-235b; TR VII, CH 1 238a-b; TR VIII, CH 1-3 239b-241a; CH 7, 243a-b; TR IX, CH 3 247b-d; CH 11–14 250c-251d / *Sixth Ennead*, TR II, CH 20–22 278d-280d; TR IV, CH 9–10 301c-302c; TR V, CH 6 307b-c; TR VI 310b-321b; TR VII, CH 4–9 323c-326c; CH 18–23 331b-333c

19 AQUINAS: *Summa Theologica*, PART I, Q 65, A 4, ANS 342b-343c; Q 115, A 3, REP 2 588c-589c

20 AQUINAS: *Summa Theologica*, PART I-II, Q 52, A I, ANS 15d-18a; A 2 18a-19a

30 BACON: *Advancement of Learning*, 43d-44c

42 KANT: *Pure Reason*, 113c-115a

1d(2) Creation, generation, production: embodiment in matter or substratum

7 PLATO: *Cratylus*, 88a-c

8 ARISTOTLE: *Physics*, BK I, CH 6-9 264c-268d; BK II, CH I [193^{a}9-^{b}19] 269b-270a; BK III, CH 6 [206^{b}33]–CH 7 [208^{a}4] 285b-286c; BK IV, CH 2 288b-289a; CH 9 [217^{a}20–^{b}26] 297a-c / *Heavens*, BK I, CH 9 [277^{b}26–278^{b}9] 369a-d; BK IV, CH 3 401c-402c; CH 4 [312^{a}3–22] 403c-d / *Generation and Corruption*, BK I, CH 7 [324^{b}5–24] 422d-423b / *Metaphysics*, BK I, CH 6 [987^{b}30–988^{a}8] 506a; BK III, CH 4 [999^{a}24–^{b}24] 518a-c; BK V, CH 4 534d-535c; BK XII, CH 10 [1075^{b}34–37] 606d

9 ARISTOTLE: *Parts of Animals*, BK I, CH I [640^{a}12–641^{b}39] 162b-165a / *Generation of Animals*, BK I, CH 20 [729^{a}6]–CH 22 [730^{b}33] 269b-271a

12 AURELIUS: *Meditations*, BK V, SECT 13 271b; BK VII, SECT 23 281b; BK XII, SECT 30 310a-b

17 PLOTINUS: *Second Ennead*, TR IV, CH 6-9 51d-53b; TR V 57d-60c

18 AUGUSTINE: *Confessions*, BK XI, par 7 90d-91a

19 AQUINAS: *Summa Theologica*, PART I, Q 3, A 2, REP 3 15c-16a; Q 7, A I, ANS 31a-d; Q 46, A I, REP 6 250a-252d; Q 65, A 4, ANS 342b-

(1d. The realization of forms in the sensible order. 1d(2) Creation, generation, production: embodiment in matter or substratum.)

343c; Q 66, A 1, ANS 343d-345c; Q 84, A 3, REP 2 443d-444d; Q 90, A 2 481d-482c; Q 104, A 1, ANS and REP 1-2 534c-536c; Q 105, A 1 538d-539c; Q 110, A 2 565d-566d; PART I-II, Q 20, A 1, REP 3 712a-d

20 AQUINAS: *Summa Theologica*, PART I-II, Q 52, A 1, ANS 15d-18a; PART II-II, Q 24, A 11, ANS 498b-499c

21 DANTE: *Divine Comedy*, PARADISE, II [46-148] 108b-109b; VII [121-148] 116b-c; XIII [52-84] 126a-b

42 KANT: *Pure Reason*, 100d-101b; 186b-d / *Judgement*, 556d-558a; 559b-d; 561c-562a; 565b-d; 566d-567a; 575c-576a; 577c-d

2. The being of forms

2a. The existence of forms: separately, in matter, in mind

7 PLATO: *Cratylus*, 113c-114a,c / *Symposium*, 167a-d / *Republic*, BK V, 368c-373c; BK VI, 385c-386c; BK IX-X, 426d-429b / *Timaeus*, 457b-458a / *Parmenides*, 487c-491a / *Sophist*, 570a-574c / *Philebus*, 610d-613a / *Seventh Letter*, 809c-810b

8 ARISTOTLE: *Posterior Analytics*, BK I, CH 11 [77ᵃ5-9] 105d-106a; CH 13 [79ᵃ6-10] 108c; CH 18 [81ᵃ40-ᵇ5] 111b-c; CH 22 [83ᵃ23-35] 113c-d; CH 24 [85ᵇ17-22] 117a / *Topics*, BK II, CH 7 [113ᵃ24-33] 158d; BK VI, CH 6 [143ᵇ11-33] 197b-c; CH 10 [148ᵃ13-22] 202b / *Physics*, BK II, CH 1 [193ᵇ2-5] 269d; CH 2 [193ᵇ23-194ᵃ6] 270a-b; BK IV, CH 1 [208ᵇ19-24] 287b-c / *Metaphysics*, BK I, CH 6 505b-506b; CH 9 508c-511c; BK III, CH 2 [997ᵃ34-998ᵃ19] 516a-d; CH 4 [999ᵃ24-ᵇ24] 518a-c; CH 4 [1001ᵃ4]-CH 6 [1002ᵇ31] 519d-521d; BK VII, CH 2 [1028ᵇ18-28] 551a-b; CH 8 [1033ᵇ19-1034ᵃ8] 556d-557b; CH 13-14 562a-563c; CH 15 [1040ᵃ8-ᵇ4] 564a-c; CH 16 [1040ᵇ28-1041ᵃ4] 564d-565a; BK VIII, CH 6 [1045ᵃ14-19] 569d-570a; BK IX, CH 8 [1050ᵇ 35-1051ᵃ2] 576d-577a; BK X, CH 10 586c-d; BK XI, CH 1 [1059ᵃ39-ᵇ21] 587b-c; CH 2 588a-589a; CH 3 [1061ᵃ29-ᵇ4] 589c; BK XII, CH 1 [1069ᵃ27-37] 598b; CH 3 [1070ᵃ4-30] 599b-d; CH 6 [1071ᵇ12-23] 601b-c; CH 10 [1075ᵇ25-33] 606c-d; BK XIII-XIV 607a-626d / *Soul*, BK III, CH 4 [429ᵃ10-29] 661b-c; CH 7 [431ᵇ13-19] 664b

11 NICOMACHUS: *Arithmetic*, BK I, 811a-d

17 PLOTINUS: *First Ennead*, TR VII, CH 1-2 26a-d; TR VIII, CH 2-3 27c-28c / *Third Ennead*, TR VIII, CH 8-10 132d-136a / *Fourth Ennead*, TR III, CH 4-5 143d-144c; CH 17 150d-151b / *Fifth Ennead*, TR IV 226d-228b; TR VII, CH 1-TR VIII, CH 3 238a-241a; TR IX, CH 4-14 247d-251d / *Sixth Ennead*, TR II, CH 20-22 278d-280d; TR V, CH 8 307d-308c; TR VI 310d-321b esp CH 4-10 312b-315d, CH 15-17 318b-320c; TR VII, CH 8-17 325b-331a

18 AUGUSTINE: *Confessions*, BK I, par 9, 3a; BK X, par 19 76a-b; BK XI, par 7, 90d / *City of God*, BK VIII, CH 6, 269b-c; BK XI, CH 27, 337d-338a

19 AQUINAS: *Summa Theologica*, PART I, Q 3, A 4, ANS 16d-17c; Q 4, A 1, REP 3 20d-21b; Q 5, A 3, REP 4 25a-d; Q 9, A 2, REP 3 39c-40d; Q 13, A 1, REP 2 62c-63c; Q 14, A 1, ANS 75d-76c; A 2, ANS 76d-77d; Q 15, A 1, ANS and REP 1 91b-92a; Q 18, A 4, REP 3 107d-108c; Q 44, A 1, REP 3 238b-239a; A 3 240b-241a; Q 65, A 4 342b-343c; Q 84, AA 1-4 440d-446b; Q 85, A 1, REP 2 451c-453c; Q 110, A 2, ANS 565d-566d; Q 115, A 1, ANS 585c-587c; A 3, REP 2 588c-589c

20 AQUINAS: *Summa Theologica*, PART I-II, Q 52, A 1, ANS 15d-18a; PART III, Q 4, A 4, ANS and REP 2 733a-734a

23 HOBBES: *Leviathan*, PART IV, 269d-271b

30 BACON: *Advancement of Learning*, 43d-44a

31 DESCARTES: *Meditations*, V, 93b-c

35 LOCKE: *Human Understanding*, BK III, CH III, SECT 11-20 257a-260a; CH V-VI 263d-283a passim, esp CH V, SECT 9 266a-b, SECT 12 266d-267a, CH VI, SECT 2-3 268c-d; BK IV, CH IV, SECT 6 325a-b; CH VI, SECT 4 331d-332b; CH IX, SECT 1 349a

35 BERKELEY: *Human Knowledge*, SECT 12 415b-c

42 KANT: *Pure Reason*, 23b-d; 34a-b; 36b-c; 45d-46a; 48d-49a; 100d-101b; 176d-177a; 186b-187a; 211c-213a / *Judgement*, 461a-c; 551a-553c; 556d-558a; 559b-d; 575c-576a; 577c-d; 580b-d

46 HEGEL: *Philosophy of History*, INTRO, 156d-157b

53 JAMES: *Psychology*, 881b

2b. The eternity of forms, the perpetuity of species: the divine ideas

7 PLATO: *Cratylus*, 113a-114a,c / *Phaedrus*, 125a-b / *Symposium*, 167b-d / *Phaedo*, 231c-232b / *Timaeus*, 447a-d; 457c-d / *Laws*, BK IV, 685b-c

8 ARISTOTLE: *Generation and Corruption*, BK II, CH 10 [336ᵇ25-34] 438d / *Metaphysics*, BK I, CH 6 [987ᵃ29-ᵇ18] 505b-d; BK III, CH 2 [997ᵃ34-ᵇ12] 516a-b; BK VI, CH 1 [1026ᵃ7-18] 548a-b; BK VII, CH 8 [1033ᵇ19-1034ᵃ8] 556d-557b; BK XI, CH 2 588a-589a; BK VII, CH 6 [1071ᵇ12-23] 601b-c; BK XIII, CH 4 [1078ᵇ7-1079ᵃ4] 610a-c / *Soul*, BK II, CH 4 [415ᵃ23-ᵇ8] 645c-d

9 ARISTOTLE: *Ethics*, BK I, CH 6 [1096ᵃ33-ᵇ5] 341c-d

11 NICOMACHUS: *Arithmetic*, BK I, 841a-d

17 PLOTINUS: *Sixth Ennead*, TR VII, CH 2-17 322b-331a

18 AUGUSTINE: *Confessions*, BK I, par 9, 3a; BK XII, par 38 108d-109a / *City of God*, BK VIII, CH 3, 266a-b; CH 6, 269b-c; BK IX, CH 22 296d-297a; BK XI, CH 7 326a-c; CH 10, 328c-d; CH 29 339a-b / *Christian Doctrine*, BK II, CH 38 654b-c

19 AQUINAS: *Summa Theologica*, PART I, Q 14, A 8 82c-83b; Q 15 91b-94a; Q 16, A 7, REP 2

99a-d; Q 18, A 4, REP 3 107d-108c; Q 44, A 3 240b-241a; Q 47, A 1, REP 2 256a-257b; Q 57, A 1, ANS 295a-d; Q 58, AA 6–7 304c-306b; Q 65, A 4 342b-343c; Q 84, A 2, ANS and REP 3 442b-443c; A 4, REP 1 444d-446b; A 5 446c-447c; Q 87, A 1, ANS 465a-466c; Q 98, A 1 516d-517d; Q 108, A 1, ANS and REP 2 552c-553c

20 AQUINAS: *Summa Theologica*, PART III SUPPL, Q 92, A 1, ANS 1025c-1032b

31 DESCARTES: *Meditations*, V, 93b-d / *Objections and Replies*, 216d-217c

31 SPINOZA: *Ethics*, PART I, PROP 17, SCHOL 362c-363c; PROP 21–23 364a-365a

42 KANT: *Pure Reason*, 113c-115a; 173b-174a / *Judgement*, 551a-552c

46 HEGEL: *Philosophy of History*, INTRO, 156d-157b

2c. Form in the composite being of the individual thing

2c(1) The union of matter and form: potentiality and actuality

8 ARISTOTLE: *Physics*, BK II, CH 1 [193^{a}9–^{b}19] 269b-270a / *Metaphysics*, BK V, CH 4 [1014^{b}26–1015^{a}11] 535a-b; CH 6 [1016^{b}12–18] 537a-b; CH 8 538b-c; CH 24 [1023^{a}32–^{b}1] 545a; BK VII, CH 17 565a-566a,c; BK VIII, CH 6 569d-570d; BK IX, CH 6–9 573c-577c; BK XII, CH 4–5 599d-601a; CH 10 [1075^{b}34-37] 606d / *Soul*, BK II, CH 1–2 642a-644c

9 ARISTOTLE: *Parts of Animals*, BK I, CH 1 [640^{a}12–641^{b}39] 162b-165a / *Generation of Animals*, BK I, CH 20 [729^{a}9]–CH 21 [729^{b}21] 269b-270a; CH 21 [730^{a}24]–CH 22 [730^{b}32] 270c-271a; BK II, CH 3 [737^{a}6–27] 277d-278a; CH 4 [738^{b}1–28] 279b-c

12 AURELIUS: *Meditations*, BK V, SECT 13 271b

16 KEPLER: *Harmonies of the World*, 1078a-b

17 PLOTINUS: *First Ennead*, TR VIII, CH 8 30d-31c; CH 10–11 32a-33d / *Second Ennead*, TR IV, CH 6 51d-52a; CH 8–9 52c-53b; TR V 57d-60c / *Third Ennead*, TR VI, CH 8–19 111c-119a / *Sixth Ennead*, TR V, CH 8 307d-308c

18 AUGUSTINE: *Confessions*, BK XI, PAR 7 90d-91a; BK XII, PAR 3–6 99d-100c; PAR 8, 101b; PAR 9, 101c; PAR 14–16 102b-103a; PAR 24–26 104c-105b; PAR 28–31 105c-107a; PAR 38–40 108d-110a; BK XIII, PAR 48 124a

19 AQUINAS: *Summa Theologica*, PART I, Q 3, A 2, ANS and REP 3 15c-16a; A 8 19d-20c; Q 7, A 1, ANS and REP 2 31a-d; A 2, ANS and REP 3 31d-32c; Q 9, A 2, REP 3 39c-40d; Q 14, A 1 75d-76c; A 2, REP 1,3 76d-77d; Q 18, A 4, REP 2–3 107d-108c; Q 29, A 1, REP 4 162a-163b; A 2, ANS and REP 4–5 163b-164b; Q 50, A 2 270a-272a; A 5, ANS 274b-275a; Q 55, A 2, ANS 289d-290d; Q 62, A 7, REP 1 322d-323b; Q 66, A 1 343d-345c; A 2, ANS 345d-347b; Q 70, A 3, REP 2 365b-367a; Q 76 385c-399b; Q 86, A 3 463b-d; Q 104, A 1, ANS 534c-536c; PART I–II, Q 10, A 1, REP 2 662d-663d

20 AQUINAS: *Summa Theologica*, PART I–II, Q 49, A 4, ANS and REP 1 5a-6a; PART II–II, Q 24, A 11, ANS 498b-499c; PART III, Q 2, A 1, ANS and REP 2 710a-711c; A 2, ANS 711d-712d; PART III SUPPL, Q 82, A 1, REP 2 968a-970c; Q 92, A 1, ANS 1025c-1032b

21 DANTE: *Divine Comedy*, PARADISE, I [127–142] 107c-d; II [46–148] 108b-109b; VII [121–148] 116b-c; XIII [52–84] 126a-b; XXIX [13–36] 150b-c

28 GILBERT: *Loadstone*, BK II, 30b

33 PASCAL: *Pensées*, 512 262a

42 KANT: *Pure Reason*, 23b; 34a-b; 36b-c; 45d-46a; 48d-49a; 100d-101b; 186b-187a; 188d-189a

2c(2) The distinction between substantial and accidental forms

19 AQUINAS: *Summa Theologica*, PART I, Q 7, A 2, ANS 31d-32c; Q 8, A 2, REP 3 35c-36b; Q 29, A 2, ANS and REP 4–5 163b-164b; Q 45, A 4, ANS 244d-245c; Q 54, AA 1–3 285a-287b; Q 66, A 1, REP 3 343d-345c; Q 67, A 3 351b-352a; Q 76, A 4 393a-394c; A 6 396a-d; Q 77, A 1 399c-401b; A 6, ANS 404c-405c; PART I–II, Q 7, A 4, REP 3 654b-655a

20 AQUINAS: *Summa Theologica*, PART I–II, Q 49, A 2, ANS 2b-4a; A 4, ANS and REP 1 5a-6a; Q 50, A 2 7c-8a; Q 52, A 1, ANS 15d-18a; Q 85, A 1, REP 4 178b-179b; PART III, Q 2, A 1, ANS 710a-711c; A 2, ANS 711d-712d; PART III SUPPL, Q 70, A 1, ANS 893d-895d; Q 79, A 1, REP 4 951b-953b

31 DESCARTES: *Discourse*, PART I, 41d

35 LOCKE: *Human Understanding*, BK II, CH XII, SECT 3–6 147d-148c; CH XXIII, SECT 3 204c-d; CH XXXI, SECT 6–13 240d-243b; CH XXXII, SECT 24 247c-d; BK III, CH III, SECT 15–19 258b-260a; CH VI 268b-283a passim, esp SECT 1–10 268b-271b, SECT 21, 273c, SECT 24 274c; CH IX, SECT 12–13 287d-288d; CH X, SECT 20 296d-297a

42 KANT: *Pure Reason*, 131c-d / *Judgement*, 580c-d

2c(3) The unity of substantial form: prime matter in relation to substantial form

8 ARISTOTLE: *Physics*, BK I, CH 9 [192^{a}3-33] 268a-c / *Generation and Corruption*, BK I, CH 3 [319^{a}29–^{b}4] 416b-c / *Meteorology*, BK IV, CH 12 [389^{b}22–390^{a}7] 493d-494a / *Metaphysics*, BK I, CH 9 [991^{a}26–32] 509c; BK II, CH 2 [994^{a}1–6] 512b; BK V, CH 4 [1015^{a}5–11] 535b; BK VII, CH 3 [1029^{a}11–26] 551c-d; CH 8 [1033^{b}1–5] 556c; CH 13 [1039^{a}2–23] 562d-563a; CH 16 [1040^{b}5–16] 564c; [1041^{a}5] 565a; BK VIII, CH 4 [1044^{a}15–32] 568d-569a; BK IX, CH 7 [1049^{a}24–^{b}1] 575a; BK XII, CH 3 [1069^{b}35–1070^{a}4] 599a-b; [1070^{a}9–11] 599b; BK XIII, CH 5 [1079^{b}31–34] 611c

17 PLOTINUS: *Second Ennead*, TR IV, CH 7–9 52a-53b; TR V 57d-60c / *Third Ennead*, TR VI, CH 7–19 110d-119a / *Fourth Ennead*, TR IX 205a-207a,c

(2c. Form in the composite being of the individual thing. 2c(3) The unity of substantial form: prime matter in relation to substantial form.)

19 AQUINAS: *Summa Theologica*, PART I, Q 3, A 8, REP 3 19d-20c; Q 5, A 3, REP 3 25a-d; Q 7, A 2, ANS and REP 3 31d-32c; Q 8, A 4, REP I 37c-38c; Q 14, A 2, REP 3 76d-77d; Q 15, A 3, REP 3 93b-94a; Q 16, A 7, REP 2 99a-d; Q 47, A I, ANS 256a-257b; Q 66, AA 1-2 343d-347b; Q 76, AA 3-4 391a-394c; Q 77, A I, REP 2 399c-401b; A 2, REP 3 401b-d; Q 84, A 3, REP 2 443d-444d; Q 115, A I, REP 1-2,4 585d-587c

20 AQUINAS: *Summa Theologica*, PART III SUPPL, Q 79, A I, REP 4 951b-953b

35 BERKELEY: *Human Knowledge*, SECT II 415a-b

2d. Angels and human souls as self-subsistent forms: the substantiality of thought or mind in separation from extension or body

17 PLOTINUS: *First Ennead*, TR VIII, CH 2 27c-d / *Fourth Ennead*, TR I, CH I, 139b; TR III, CH 9-12 146d-149b; CH 18 151b-c; TR IX 205a-207a,c / *Sixth Ennead*, TR IX, CH 5, 356d-357a

18 AUGUSTINE: *City of God*, BK XXII, CH I 586b,d-587b

19 AQUINAS: *Summa Theologica*, PART I, Q 7, A 2, ANS and REP 2 31d-32c; Q 8, A 2, REP 2-3 35c-36b; Q 50 269a-275a esp A 2 270a-272a; Q 75 378a-385c esp A 5 382a-383b

21 DANTE: *Divine Comedy*, PARADISE, VII [121-148] 116b-c; XXIX [13-36] 150b-c

23 HOBBES: *Leviathan*, PART I, 80a-b; PART III, 174b-176d; PART IV, 250c-251c; 258b-261a; 270c-271b

31 DESCARTES: *Discourse*, PART IV, 51d-52a; PART V, 60b-c / *Meditations*, II 77d-81d; VI 96b-103d / *Objections and Replies*, DEF X 130d; PROP IV 133c; 152b,d-156a; 224d-225b; 225d-226a; 231a-232d

31 SPINOZA: *Ethics*, PART I, PROP 10 358a-b; PROP 14, COROL 2 360a; PART II, PROP 1-2 373d-374a; PROP 7 375a-c; PROP 13 377d-378c; PART III, PROP 2 396c-398b

32 MILTON: *Paradise Lost*, BK I [423-431] 102b; BK V [388-443] 183b-185a; [469-505] 185b-186a; BK VI [320-353] 203a-204a

35 LOCKE: *Human Understanding*, BK II, CH XXIII, SECT 5 205a-b; SECT 15-37 208c-214b passim

35 BERKELEY: *Human Knowledge*, SECT 2 413b; SECT 26-27 418a-b; SECT 89 430b-c; SECT 135-142 440a-441c

40 GIBBON: *Decline and Fall*, 186b

41 GIBBON: *Decline and Fall*, 136b

42 KANT: *Pure Reason*, 121a-128b; 201b-c; 203d-204c

46 HEGEL: *Philosophy of History*, PART I, 257c-258a; PART IV, 360c-d

53 JAMES: *Psychology*, 221a-226a

3. Form in relation to knowledge

7 PLATO: *Cratylus*, 113c-114a,c / *Phaedrus*, 125a-c / *Republic*, BK V, 368c-373c; BK VI, 385c-388a / *Timaeus*, 457b-458a

8 ARISTOTLE: *Posterior Analytics*, BK I, CH II [77ª5-9] 105d-106a; CH 22 [83ª23-35] 113c-d / *Metaphysics*, BK I, CH 6 505b-506b; CH 9 [990ª 33-991ª18] 508c-509c; BK XIII, CH 4 [1078ᵇ6]-CH 5 [1079ᵇ24] 610a-611c / *Soul*, BK III, CH 4 [429ª13-28] 661b-c

11 NICOMACHUS: *Arithmetic*, BK I, 811a-d

18 AUGUSTINE: *City of God*, BK XI, CH 7 326a-c; CH 29 339a-b

19 AQUINAS: *Summa Theologica*, PART I, Q 7, A 2, REP 2 31d-32c; Q 13, A I, REP 2 62c-63c; Q 14, A I, ANS 75d-76c; A 2 76d-77d; Q 15, A I, ANS and REP 1,3 91b-92a; Q 19, A I, ANS 108d-109c; Q 34, A I, REP 3 185b-187b; Q 86, A 3 463b-d

21 DANTE: *Divine Comedy*, PURGATORY, XVIII [49-60] 80b-c

35 LOCKE: *Human Understanding*, BK II, CH XXXI, SECT 6-13 240d-243b; BK III, CH VI 268b-283a passim; CH IX, SECT 12 287d-288a; BK IV, CH IV, SECT 5-8 324d-325c

42 KANT: *Pure Reason*, 14a-108a,c; 173b / *Fund. Prin. Metaphysic of Morals*, 282b-c / *Practical Reason*, 308a-b

46 HEGEL: *Philosophy of Right*, PREF, 7a

51 TOLSTOY: *War and Peace*, EPILOGUE II, 693d-694c

53 JAMES: *Psychology*, 859a-860b

3a. Sensible forms, intelligible forms: the forms of intuition and understanding

7 PLATO: *Cratylus*, 113c-114a,c / *Phaedrus*, 125a-126c / *Symposium*, 167a-d / *Phaedo*, 228a-232b / *Republic*, BK III, 333b-334b; BK V, 370d-373c; BK VI, 383d-388a / *Timaeus*, 447a-d; 455c-458a / *Theaetetus*, 534c-536a

8 ARISTOTLE: *Posterior Analytics*, BK I, CH 13 [79ª6-10] 108c / *Topics*, BK II, CH 7 [113ª23-33] 158d / *Soul*, BK III, CH 2 [425ᵇ17-26] 657d-658a; CH 4 661b-662c; CH 8 664b-d / *Memory and Reminiscence*, CH I [450ª26-451ª19] 691a-692b

18 AUGUSTINE: *Confessions*, BK X, par 19 76a-b; BK XII, par 5 100a-b / *City of God*, BK VIII, CH 6, 269b-c; BK XI, CH 27, 337d-338a; BK XII, CH 7 346c-d

19 AQUINAS: *Summa Theologica*, PART I, Q 7, A 2, REP 2 31d-32c; Q 13, A 9, ANS 71b-72c; Q 14, A I, ANS 75d-76c; A 8, ANS 82c-83b; Q 15, A I, ANS and REP 1,3 91b-92a; Q 17, A 3, ANS 102d-103c; Q 18, A 3, ANS 106b-107c; Q 19, A I, ANS 108d-109c; Q 34, A I, REP 3 185b-187b; Q 50, A 2, REP 2 270a-272a; Q 84 440b-451b; Q 85, AA 1-2 451c-455b; A 5 457d-458d

20 AQUINAS: *Summa Theologica*, PART I-II, Q 62, A 3, REP I 61c-62b; PART III SUPPL, Q 92, A I, ANS 1025c-1032b

23 HOBBES: *Leviathan*, PART I, 49d

35 LOCKE: *Human Understanding*, BK III, CH VI, SECT 9-10 270d-271b

42 KANT: *Pure Reason*, 14a-108a,c esp 14a-15c, 23a-33d, 41c-42b, 48d-55a, 56d-59b, 61a-64a, 65d-66d, 68a-93c, 94d-96d, 100d-101b; 112d-113a; 115d; 135a-137a,c; 153c-155a; 173b; 207c-d; 213d-215a / *Fund. Prin. Metaphysic of Morals*, 282b-c; 283b / *Practical Reason*, 308a-b; 319d; 335c-336a; 350b-c / *Judgement*, 461a-c; 471b-c; 517b-c; 542c-d; 552b-c; 562a-b; 603d-604c; 612c-d

53 JAMES: *Psychology*, 420a-b; 628b-631a

3b. The problem of the universal: knowledge of the individual

7 PLATO: *Cratylus*, 113c-114a,c / *Phaedo*, 228a-232b / *Republic*, BK V, 370d-373c / *Parmenides*, 487c-491a / *Philebus*, 610d-613a

8 ARISTOTLE: *Categories*, CH 5 [2^{b}6-37] 6c-7a / *Posterior Analytics*, BK I, CH 11 [77^{a}5-9] 105d-106a; CH 24 [85^{a}31-^{b}22] 116c-117a / *Topics*, BK II, CH 7 [113^{a}23-33] 158d / *Sophistical Refutations*, CH 22 [178^{b}37-179^{a}10] 246c / *Physics*, BK VII, CH 3 [247^{b}1-7] 330b / *Metaphysics*, BK I, CH 6 505b-506b; CH 9 508c-511c; BK III, CH 3 [999^{a}6-14] 517d; CH 4 [999^{a}24-^{b}24] 518a-c; BK VII, CH 8 [1033^{b}19-1034^{a}8] 556d-557b; CH 10 [1035^{b}28-32] 559b; CH 11 [1037^{a}5-9] 560c; CH 13-15 562a-564c; BK XIII, CH 4-5 610a-611d; CH 10 618c-619a,c / *Soul*, BK III, CH 4 [429^{a}18-29] 661c

9 ARISTOTLE: *Ethics*, BK I, CH 6 341b-342c

19 AQUINAS: *Summa Theologica*, PART I, Q 3, A 2, REP 3 15c-16a; A 3, ANS 16a-d; Q 4, A 3, ANS 22b-23b; Q 11, A 3, ANS 49a-c; Q 13, A 9, ANS and REP 2 71b-72c; Q 14, A 11 84c-85c; Q 16, A 7, REP 2 99a-d; Q 39, A 3, ANS 204c-205c; Q 50, A 2, ANS 270a-272a; A 4, ANS 273b-274b; Q 57, A 2 295d-297a; Q 76, A 2, ANS 388c-391a; Q 85, A 7, REP 3 459c-460b; Q 86, A 1 461c-462a; A 3 463b-d

20 AQUINAS: *Summa Theologica*, PART III, Q 2, A 2, ANS 711d-712d

28 HARVEY: *On Animal Generation*, 332a-333b esp 333a-b

35 LOCKE: *Human Understanding*, BK III, CH III, SECT 6-20 255c-260a; CH V-VI 263d-283a passim, esp CH V, SECT 9 266a-b, CH VI, SECT 32 277c-278b, SECT 36-37 279a-b; BK IV, CH IV, SECT 5-8 324d-325c; CH VI, SECT 4 331d-332b; CH VII, SECT 9 338d-339b

35 BERKELEY: *Human Knowledge*, INTRO, SECT 6-19 405d-410c esp SECT 15-16 409a-d

38 ROUSSEAU: *Inequality*, 341b-342b

42 KANT: *Pure Reason*, 211c-218d / *Judgement*, 573a-c

46 HEGEL: *Philosophy of History*, INTRO, 158b-c; PART IV, 360c-361a

53 JAMES: *Psychology*, 308a-312a

3c. Form and definition: the formulable essence; the problem of matter in relation to definition

7 PLATO: *Phaedrus*, 134b-c / *Meno*, 174b-179b / *Seventh Letter*, 809c-810b

8 ARISTOTLE: *Posterior Analytics*, BK II, CH 3-10 123c-128d; CH 13 131b-133c / *Physics*, BK II, CH 1 [193^{a}30-^{b}19] 269c-270a / *Generation and Corruption*, BK I, CH 2 [317^{a}17-27] 413b / *Meteorology*, BK IV, CH 12 493d-494d / *Metaphysics*, BK I, CH 6 505b-506b; CH 7 [988^{a}34-^{b}5] 506c; BK II, CH 2 [994^{b}16-27] 513a-b; BK V, CH 2 [1013^{a}27-28] 533b; BK VI, CH 1 [1025^{b}28-1026^{a}6] 547d-548a; BK VII, CH 4-6 552b-555a; CH 10-15 558a-564c; BK VIII, CH 1-3 566a-568d; CH 6 569d-570d; BK XII, CH 9 [1074^{b}37-1075^{a}2] 605c; BK XIII, CH 4-5 610a-611d / *Soul*, BK I, CH 1 631a-632d; BK II, CH 1-3 642a-645b passim; BK III, CH 4 [429^{b}10-23] 661d-662a; CH 6 [430^{b}26-31] 663b-c

9 ARISTOTLE: *Parts of Animals*, BK I, CH 1 [641^{a}14-31] 163d-164a; CH 2-4 165d-168c esp CH 3 166a-167d

19 AQUINAS: *Summa Theologica*, PART I, Q 3, A 3, ANS 16a-d; A 5, ANS 17c-18b; Q 13, A 12, REP 2 74c-75b; Q 17, A 3, ANS 102d-103c; Q 18, A 4, REP 3 107d-108c; Q 29, A 1, REP 4 162a-163b; Q 50, A 4 273b-274b; Q 75, A 4, ANS 381c-382a; Q 85, A 1, REP 2 451c-453c; PART I-II, Q 1, A 3, ANS 611b-612a

20 AQUINAS: *Summa Theologica*, PART I-II, Q 55, A 4, ANS and REP 1-2 28c-29d; PART II-II, Q 4, A 1, ANS 402a-403d; PART III, Q 2, A 5, ANS 715a-716b

31 SPINOZA: *Ethics*, PART I, DEF 4 355b; PROP 8, SCHOL 2, 357a-d; PART II, PROP 37 386b-c

35 LOCKE: *Human Understanding*, BK II, CH XXIII 204a-214b; CH XXXI, SECT 6-13 240d-243b; CH XXXII, SECT 24 247c-d; BK III, CH III, SECT 12-20 257b-260a; CH V-VI 263d-283a passim; CH IX, SECT 11-17 287d-290a; CH X, SECT 17-21 295d-297b; CH XI, SECT 19-20 304b-d; BK IV, CH IV, SECT 5-8 324d-325c; CH VI, SECT 4-16 331d-336d passim

35 BERKELEY: *Human Knowledge*, SECT 1 413a-b

38 ROUSSEAU: *Inequality*, 342a

46 HEGEL: *Philosophy of History*, INTRO, 176c; 184d-185a

4. The denial of form as a principle of being, becoming, or knowledge

7 PLATO: *Cratylus*, 113c-114a,c / *Sophist*, 567a-568a

8 ARISTOTLE: *Metaphysics*, BK IV, CH 4 [1007^{a}20-^{b}18] 526c-527a; CH 5 528c-530c passim; BK XI, CH 6 590d-592b

23 HOBBES: *Leviathan*, PART I, 49d; PART IV, 269b-271a

30 BACON: *Novum Organum*, BK I, APH 51 111c; BK II, APH 1-2 137a-c; APH 17 149b-d

35 LOCKE: *Human Understanding*, BK II, CH VIII, SECT 2 133c; CH XXXI, SECT 6-13 240d-243b passim, esp SECT 6 240d-241d; BK III, CH VI, SECT 10 271b; SECT 24 274c; CH X, SECT 20 296d-297a

36 STERNE: *Tristram Shandy*, 422a-b

CROSS-REFERENCES

For: Other discussions of the Forms or Ideas as immutable models or archetypes, *see* CHANGE 15a; ETERNITY 4c; IDEA 1a, 6b.

Other discussions of forms as indwelling causes or principles in mutable things, *see* CAUSE 1a; CHANGE 2a; MATTER 1a; and for the consideration of form and matter as co-principles of composite substances, *see* BEING 7b(2).

Discussions of matter or the receptacle in relation to form, *see* CHANGE 2–2b; MATTER 1–1b; SPACE 1a; WORLD 4b; and for the consideration of matter apart from form, *see* MATTER 2, 3a.

The controversy over the separate existence of the Forms, the objects of mathematics, and universals, *see* BEING 7d(2)–7d(3); MATHEMATICS 2b; SAME AND OTHER 2a; UNIVERSAL AND PARTICULAR 2a–2c; and for the problem of the cause of individuality, *see* MATTER 1c; UNIVERSAL AND PARTICULAR 3.

The existence of forms in the mind as concepts abstracted from matter, *see* IDEA 2g; MATTER 4d; MEMORY AND IMAGINATION 6c(1); SENSE 5a; UNIVERSAL AND PARTICULAR 4c.

Other considerations of the *a priori* or transcendental forms of intuition, *see* SENSE 1c; SPACE 4a; TIME 6c.

Comparisons of creation, generation, and production as each relates to form and matter, *see* ART 2b–2c; MATTER 3d; WORLD 4e(1).

Other terms related to the distinction of form and matter or to the kinds of form, *see* BEING 7b, 7c(1)–7c(3); NATURE 1a(2); UNIVERSAL AND PARTICULAR 6a.

The theological doctrine of the angels as self-subsistent forms or simple substances, *see* ANGEL 2, 3b–3c; BEING 7b(2); for the theological doctrine of the forms as eternal exemplars or types in the mind of God, *see* GOD 5f; IDEA 1e; and for the theory of the soul as the substantial form of a living thing, *see* LIFE AND DEATH 1; MAN 3a; SOUL 1b.

Form and matter in relation to definition, *see* BEING 8c; DEFINITION 6a; MATTER 4b; NATURE 1a(2).

ADDITIONAL READINGS

Listed below are works not included in *Great Books of the Western World*, but relevant to the idea and topics with which this chapter deals. These works are divided into two groups:

I. Works by authors represented in this collection.
II. Works by authors not represented in this collection.

For the date, place, and other facts concerning the publication of the works cited, consult the Bibliography of Additional Readings, which follows the last chapter of *The Great Ideas*.

I.

AQUINAS. *On Being and Essence*
——. *Quaestiones Disputatae, De Anima*
——. *On Spiritual Creatures*
KANT. *De Mundi Sensibilis (Inaugural Dissertation),* SECT IV

II.

DUNS SCOTUS. *Opus Oxoniense,* BK I, DIST 7 (24)
CRESCAS. *Or Adonai,* PROPOSITIONS 10–11, 16
BRUNO. *De la causa, principio, e uno*
SUÁREZ. *Disputationes Metaphysicae,* V (4), XII (3), XIII (1–9), XIV–XVI, XVIII (2–6), XXVI (2), XXVII, XXX (4), XXXI (8, 10, 13), XXXIV (5–6), XXXV–XXXVI, XLII (2–3), XLV (4), XLVI

JOHN OF SAINT THOMAS. *Cursus Philosophicus Thomisticus, Philosophia Naturalis,* PART I, QQ 3–4, 6, 9, 11
MALEBRANCHE. *De la recherche de la vérité*
SCHOPENHAUER. *The World as Will and Idea,* VOL I, BK I–III
LOTZE. *Metaphysics*
C. S. PEIRCE. *Collected Papers,* VOL VI, par 353–363
BRADLEY. *Appearance and Reality*
DESCOQS. *Essai critique sur l'hylémorphisme*
SANTAYANA. *The Realm of Essence*
WHITEHEAD. *Process and Reality,* PART II, CH 1
FOREST. *La structure métaphysique du concret*
A. E. TAYLOR. *Philosophical Studies,* CH 3
KONINCK. *Le problème de l'indéterminisme*
BLANSHARD. *The Nature of Thought*

Chapter 29: GOD

INTRODUCTION

WITH the exception of certain mathematicians and physicists, all the authors of the great books are represented in this chapter. In sheer quantity of references, as well as in variety, it is the largest chapter. The reason is obvious. More consequences for thought and action follow from the affirmation or denial of God than from answering any other basic question. They follow for those who regard the question as answerable only by faith or only by reason, and even for those who insist upon suspending judgment entirely.

In addition to the primary question of God's existence, there are all the problems of the divine nature and of the relation of the world and man to the gods or God. The solutions of these problems cannot help influencing man's conception of the world in which he lives, the position that he occupies in it, and the life to which he is called.

The whole tenor of human life is certainly affected by whether men regard themselves as the supreme beings in the universe or acknowledge a superior—a superhuman being whom they conceive as an object of fear or love, a force to be defied or a Lord to be obeyed. Among those who acknowledge a divinity, it matters greatly whether the divine is represented merely by the concept of God—the object of philosophical speculation—or by the living God whom men worship in all the acts of piety which comprise the rituals of religion.

The most radical differences in man's conception of his own nature follow from the exclusion of divinity as its source or model on the one hand, and from the various ways in which man is seen as participating in divinity on the other. Many fundamental themes and issues are therefore common to this chapter and to the chapter on MAN.

SOME OF THE TOPICS IN this chapter are primarily philosophical. They belong to the subject matter of rational speculation or poetic imagination in all the great epochs of our culture, regardless of differences in religious belief. Other topics, however, are peculiarly restricted to matters of faith or religion. With respect to such matters, dogmatic differences, or differences in articles of faith, must be explicitly recognized.

The materials here assembled must therefore, in some instances, be divided according to their origin from pagan or from Jewish and Christian sources. Though no great books from the Mohammedan tradition are included in this set, the fact that Gibbon discusses the Moslem faith and compares its teachings with those of Judaism and Christianity explains the inclusion of Mohammedanism in one group of topics. That is the group which deals with the doctrines common to these three religions, as distinguished from the tenets on which Judaism and Christianity differ dogmatically. The existence of certain common beliefs in the western tradition enables us to begin, as it seems advisable to do, with the conception of God that is shared by the living religions of western culture today.

In our civilization, what is denied by an atheist who says there is no God? Not idols or images which men may seek to placate. Not philosophical constructions or mythological figures. Certainly not the universe itself, either as an infinite and everlasting whole, or as finite and temporal, but equally mysterious in its ultimate incomprehensibility to the human mind. In our civilization, the atheist denies the existence of a supernatural being, the object of religious belief and worship among Jews, Christians, and Mohammedans. He denies the single, personal God Who created the world out of nothing, Who transcends this created universe and sustains it by His immanent power, Who has made laws for the government of all things and cares for each particular by His providence, and Who created man in His own image, revealed Himself and His will to men, and metes out eternal rewards and punishments to the children of Adam, whom He also helps by His grace.

In this religious conception of God, one term must be saved from misinterpretation. The word "personal" should not be read with anthropomorphic imagery, though its meaning does entitle man as well as God to be called a person rather than a thing. "Although the term *person* is not found applied to God in Scripture, either in the Old or New Testament," Aquinas writes, "nevertheless what the term signifies is found to be affirmed of God in many places of Scripture; as that He is the supreme self-subsisting being, and the most perfectly intelligent being."

Boethius had defined a person as "an individual substance of a rational nature," or, as Locke later said, "a thinking intelligent being." In applying the term *person* to God, in the meaning which Boethius had given it, Aquinas comments on the difference in its meaning when it is applied to men. God can be said to have a *rational nature*, he writes, only "if reason be taken to mean, not discursive thought, but, in a general sense, an intelligent nature . . . God cannot be called an *individual*" in the sense in which physical things are, but only in the sense of uniqueness. "*Substance* can be applied to God [only] in the sense of signifying self-subsistence." Aquinas does not conclude from this that "person" is said improperly of God, but rather that when God is called "personal" the meaning is applied "in a more excellent way," for God does not *possess*, God *is*, an intelligence.

We shall use this idea of a personal God, the reality of which the contemporary atheist denies; in order to distinguish divergent conceptions in other doctrines. Then we shall examine more closely what is involved in this idea itself.

IN THE WESTERN tradition, the various pagan religions—reflected especially in the poems and histories of Greek and Roman antiquity—were all polytheistic. The number of their gods, Montaigne estimates, "amounts to six-and-thirty thousand." Augustine offers one explanation of why there were so many. "The ancients," he writes, "being deceived either by their own conjectures or by demons, supposed that many gods must be invited to take an interest in human affairs, and assigned to each a separate function and a separate department—to one the body, to another the soul; and in the body itself, to one the head, to another the neck, and each of the other members to one of the gods; and in like manner, in the soul, to one god the natural capacity was assigned, to another education, to another anger, to another lust; and so the various affairs of life were assigned—cattle to one, corn to another, wine to another, oil to another, the woods to another, money to another, navigation to another, wars and victories to another, marriages to another, births and fecundity to another, and other things to other gods."

That polytheism, no less than monotheism, conceives the divine as personal, appears in Plato's *Apology*. When Socrates is accused of atheism, he asks whether the indictment means that he does not "acknowledge the gods which the state acknowledges, but some other new divinities or spiritual agencies in their stead." Meletus answers that he thinks Socrates is a complete atheist who recognizes no gods at all. To this Socrates replies by suggesting that his enemies must be confusing him with Anaxagoras, who had blasphemed against Apollo by calling the sun "a red hot stone." As for himself, he offers evidence to show that he believes in divine or spiritual agencies "new or old, no matter"; and "if I believe in divine beings," he asks, "how can I help believing in spirits or demigods?"

Like the one God of Judaism and Christianity, the many gods of pagan antiquity have immortal life, but they are not without origin. Zeus is the son of Kronos, and he has many offspring, both gods and demigods, who perform different functions and are not of equal station in the Olympian hierarchy. The realm of the divine includes such figures as the Titans and the Cyclops, who are neither gods nor men; and demigods, like Heracles, who are offspring of divine and human mating. These deities exercise superhuman powers, but none is completely omnipotent or omniscient, not even Kronos or Zeus who cannot escape the decrees of Fate. Moreover, with the exception, perhaps, of that of Zeus, the power of one divinity is often challenged and thwarted by another. This aspect of polytheism and its bearing on the intervention of the gods in the affairs of men are discussed in the chapter on FATE.

The extent to which we think of the pagans as idolatrous because they made graven images of their gods in human form, or regard the pagan conceptions of the gods as anthropomorphic, depends on our interpretation of religious symbolism. Plato for one thinks that many of the poets' descriptions of the gods and their activities should be dismissed as unworthy, precisely because they debase the gods to the human level.

According to Gibbon, a Greek or Roman philosopher "who considered the system of polytheism as a composition of human fraud and error, could disguise a smile of contempt under the mask of devotion, without apprehending that either the mockery or the compliance would expose him to the resentment of any invisible, or, as he conceived them, imaginary powers." But the early Christians, he points out, saw the many gods of antiquity "in a much more odious and formidable light" and held them to be "the authors, the patrons, and the objects of idolatry."

Those who take symbols with flat literalism might also attack Christianity as anthropomorphic and idolatrous; in fact they have. The defense of Christianity against this charge does not avail in the case of Roman emperor-worship, which consisted not in the humanization of the divine for the sake of symbolic representation, but in the deification of the merely human for political purposes.

Although there are radical differences, there are also certain fundamental agreements between paganism and Judaeo-Christianity regarding the nature of the divine. As we have already noted, the deities are conceived personally, not in terms of impersonal, brute forces. Conceived as beings with intelligence and will, the gods concern themselves with earthly society; they aid or oppose man's plans

and efforts; they reward men for fidelity and virtue or punish them for impiety and sin.

Despite all other differences between paganism and Christianity, these agreements are substantial enough to provide many common threads of theological speculation throughout our tradition, especially with regard to the abiding practical problems of how man shall view himself and his destiny in relation to the divine or the supernatural. We have therefore attempted to place passages from the great books of pagan antiquity under every heading except those which are specifically restricted to the dogmas of Judaism and Christianity—even under headings which are worded monotheistically, since even here there is continuity of thought and expression from Homer and Virgil to Dante and Milton; from Plato, Aristotle, and Plotinus to Augustine, Aquinas, Descartes, and Kant; from Lucretius to Newton and Darwin.

THE DOCTRINES known as deism and pantheism, like unqualified atheism, are as much opposed to the religious beliefs of polytheism as to the faith of Judaism and Christianity.

Of these two, pantheism is much nearer atheism, for it denies the existence of a transcendent supernatural being or beings. God is Nature. God is immanent in the world and, in the extreme form of pantheism, not transcendent in any way. Certain historic doctrines which are often regarded as forms or kinds of pantheism seem to be less extreme than this, for they do not conceive the physical universe as exhausting the infinite being of God. The world, for all its vastness and variety, may only represent an aspect of the divine nature.

According to Spinoza, the attributes of extension and thought, in terms of which we understand the world or nature as being of the divine substance, are merely those aspects of God which are known to us, for the divine substance consists "of infinite attributes, each one of which expresses eternal and infinite essence." In the conception of Plotinus, the whole world represents only a partial emanation from the divine source. Yet thinkers like Plotinus and Spinoza so conceive the relation of the world to God that—as in the strictest pantheism—the religious doctrines of creation, providence, and salvation are either rejected or profoundly altered.

In the ancient world, the teaching of the Stoic philosophers expresses a kind of pantheism. "There is one universe made up of all things," Marcus Aurelius writes, "and one God who pervades all things, and one substance, and one law, one common reason in all intelligent animals, and one truth." He speaks of the "common nature," which is apparently divine, and of which "every particular nature is a part, as the nature of the leaf is a part of the nature of the plant." But, although he stresses the oneness and divinity of all things, Aurelius also at times uses language which seems to refer to a god who dwells apart from as well as in the world, as, for example, when he debates whether the gods have any concern with human affairs.

Another type of ancient pantheism appears in the thought of Plotinus, for whom all things have being only insofar as they participate in, even as they emanate from, the power of The One, or Primal Source. "God is sovranly present through all," he writes. "We cannot think of something of God here and something else there, nor of all of God gathered at some one spot: there is an instantaneous presence everywhere, nothing containing and nothing left void, everything therefore fully held by the divine." The relation between The One and every other thing is compared to the number series. "Just as there is, primarily or secondarily, some form or idea from the monad in each of the successive numbers—the latter still participating, though unequally, in the unit—so the series of beings following upon The First bear, each, some form or idea derived from that source. In Number the participation establishes Quantity; in the realm of Being, the trace of The One establishes reality: existence is a trace of The One."

But although The One is in all things, and all things depend upon it for their very existence, The One itself has no need of them. It is in this sense that Plotinus says that "The One is all things and no one of them . . . Holding all—though itself nowhere held—it is omnipresent, for where its presence failed something would elude its hold. At the same time, in the sense that it is nowhere held, it is not present: thus

it is both present and not present; not present as not being circumscribed by anything; yet as being utterly unattached, not inhibited from presence at any point." Thus all things partake of The One in absolute dependence. But The One, *considered in itself*, is absolutely transcendent. Plotinus even denies it the name of God or Good or Being, saying it is beyond these.

Whether or not Spinoza is a pantheist, has long been debated by his commentators. An explicit, even an extreme form of pantheism would seem to be expressed in the proposition that "whatever is, is in God, and nothing can be or be conceived without God." But while the one and only substance which exists is at once nature and God, Spinoza identifies God only with the nature he calls "*natura naturans*." God is not reduced to the nature that falls within man's limited experience or understanding— the nature he calls "*natura naturata*."

"By *natura naturans*," he explains, "we are to understand that which is in itself and is conceived through itself, or those attributes of substance which express eternal and infinite essence, that is to say, God in so far as He is considered as a free cause. But by *natura naturata* I understand everything which follows from the necessity of the nature of God, or of any one of God's attributes, that is to say, all the modes of God's attributes in so far as they are considered as things which are in God and which without God can neither be nor can be conceived."

God is the infinite and eternal substance of all finite existences, an absolute and unchanging *one* underlying the finite modes in which it variably manifests itself. Though God for Spinoza is transcendent in the sense of vastly exceeding the world known to man, in no sense does God exist apart from the whole of nature. Spinoza's view thus sharply departs from that of an orthodox Jewish or Christian theologian. When the latter says that God is transcendent, he means that God exists apart, infinitely removed from the whole created universe. When the latter speaks of God as being immanent in that universe, he carefully specifies that it is not by His substance, but by the power of His action and knowledge. But Spinoza calls God "the immanent, and not the transitive, cause of all things," for the reason that "outside God there can be no substance, that is to say, outside Him nothing can exist which is in itself."

These divergent conceptions of God's immanence and transcendence—so relevant to the question of who is or is not a pantheist—are further discussed in the chapters on NATURE and WORLD.

UNLIKE PANTHEISM, deism affirms gods or a God, personal intelligences existing apart from this world; but, as in the teaching of Lucretius, deism sometimes goes to the extreme of believing in absentee gods who neither intervene in the order of nature nor concern themselves with human affairs.

"The nature of the gods," Lucretius writes, "must ever in itself of necessity enjoy immortality together with supreme repose, far removed and withdrawn from our concerns; since exempt from every pain, exempt from all dangers, strong in its own resources, not wanting aught of us, it is neither gained by favors nor moved by anger."

Such gods neither create the world nor govern it; above all they do not reward or punish man, and so they do not have to be feared or propitiated. "To say that for the sake of men they have willed to set in order the glorious nature of the world and therefore it is meet to praise the work of the gods immortal, and that it is an unholy thing ever to shake by any force from its fixed seats that which by the forethought of the gods in ancient days has been established on everlasting foundations for mankind, or to assail it by speech and utterly overturn it from top to bottom; and to invent and add other figments of the kind . . . is all sheer folly. For what advantage can our gratitude bestow on immortal and blessed beings that for our sakes they should take in hand to administer aught?"

Divinity seems to have moral significance to Lucretius only insofar as the gods exemplify the happy life; and religion is immoral because its superstitions concerning divine motives and meddling make men servile and miserable.

When the deism of Lucretius is contrasted with the more familiar modern forms of that doctrine, the influence of Christianity is seen. The modern deist affirms the supremacy of one God, the infinite and eternal Creator of this world, Whose laws are the laws of nature which are laid down from the beginning and which govern all created things. Rousseau speaks of this as "the religion of man" and even identifies it with Christianity—"not the Christianity of today, but that of the Gospel, which is entirely different." He describes this religion as that "which has neither temples, nor altars, nor rites, and is confined to the purely internal cult of the supreme God and the eternal obligations of morality."

Not all deists, certainly not those of the 17th and early 18th centuries, go to the Lucretian extreme of picturing an uninterested and morally neutral God. Many of them believe in an after-life. But modern deism did tend toward this extreme. By Kant's time it had even ceased to look upon God as a personal intelligence. Kant therefore takes great pains to distinguish deism from theism.

The deist, according to Kant, "admits that we can cognize by pure reason alone the existence of a supreme being, but at the same time maintains that our conception of this being is purely transcendental, and that all we can say of it is, that it possesses all reality, without being able to define it more closely." The theist, on the other hand, "asserts that reason is capable of presenting us, from the analogy with nature, with a more definite conception of this being, and that its operations, as the cause of all things, are the results of intelligence and free will."

Kant even maintains that "we might, in strict rigor, deny to the deist any belief in God at all, and regard him merely as a maintainer of the existence of a primal being or thing —the supreme cause of all other things." In any case, deism seems to be an essentially un-Jewish and un-Christian or anti-Jewish and anti-Christian doctrine, for it denies God's supernatural revelation of Himself; it denies miracles and every other manifestation of supernatural agency in the course of nature or the life of man; it denies the efficacy of prayer and sacrament. In short, it rejects the institutions and practices, as well as the faith and hope, of any religion which claims supernatural foundation and supernatural warrant for its dogmas and rituals. Deism, which "consists simply in the worship of a God considered as great, powerful, and eternal," is, in Pascal's opinion, "almost as far removed from the Christian religion as atheism, which is its exact opposite."

What Pascal and Kant call "deism" and Rousseau "the religion of man," others like Hume call "natural religion." His *Dialogues Concerning Natural Religion* provide a classic statement of rationalism, which is the same as naturalism, in religion; though, as the chapter on RELIGION indicates, it may be questioned whether the word "religion" can be meaningfully used for a doctrine which claims no knowledge beyond that of the philosopher, and no guidance for human life beyond the precepts of the moralist.

THE SYSTEMATIC exposition of man's knowledge of God is the science of theology. In addition to considering all things—the whole world and human life—in relation to God, theology treats especially of God's existence, essence, and attributes. Throughout the range of its subject matter and problems, theology may be of two sorts: it may be either natural knowledge, obtained by ordinary processes of observation and reasoning; or knowledge which is supernatural in the sense of being based on divine revelation. This is the traditional distinction between natural and sacred or, as it is sometimes called, dogmatic theology. The one belongs to the domain of reason; it is the work of the philosopher. The other belongs to the domain of faith, and is the work of the theologian who seeks to understand his faith.

These distinctions are discussed in the chapters on THEOLOGY, METAPHYSICS, and WISDOM. Here we are concerned with different attitudes toward the problem of man's knowledge of God. The deist, as we have seen, rejects supernatural revelation and faith; theology, like religion, is held to be entirely natural, a work of reason. The agnostic makes the opposite denial. He denies that anything supernatural can be known by reason. It cannot be proved or, for that matter, disproved. The evidences of nature and the light of reason do not permit valid inferences or arguments concerning God or creation, providence or immortality.

It is usually with respect to God's existence that the agnostic most emphatically declares reason's incompetence to demonstrate. He often accompanies the declaration with elaborate criticisms of the arguments which may be offered by others. This is not always the case, however. For example, the great Jewish theologian, Moses Maimonides, thinks that God's existence can be proved by reason entirely apart from faith; but with regard to the essence or attributes of God, his position seems to be one which might be called agnostic.

When men "ascribe essential attributes to God," Maimonides declares, "these so-called essential attributes should not have any similarity to the attributes of other things, just as there is no similarity between the essence of God and that of other beings." Since the meaning of such positive attributes as *good* or *wise* is derived from our knowledge of things, they do not provide us with any knowledge of God's essence, for no comparison obtains between things and God. Hence Maimonides asserts that "the negative attributes of God are the true attributes." They tell us not what God is, but what God is not.

Even though Maimonides holds that "existence and essence are perfectly identical" in God, he also insists that "we comprehend only the fact that He exists, not His essence. . . . All we understand," he goes on to say, in addition to "the fact that He exists," is the fact that "He is a Being to whom none of his creatures is similar." This fact is confirmed in all the negative attributes such as eternal (meaning nontemporal), infinite, or incorporeal; even as it is falsified by all the positive attributes, expressed by such names as "good" or "living" or "knowing," insofar as they imply a comparison between God and creatures. When they cannot be interpreted negatively, they can be tolerated as metaphors, but they must not be taken as expressing an understanding "of the true essence of God," concerning which Maimonides maintains, "there is no possibility of obtaining a knowledge."

Aquinas takes issue with such agnosticism about the divine nature in his discussion of the names of God. Although he says that "we cannot know what God is, but rather what He is not," Aquinas disagrees with Maimonides that all names which express some knowledge of God's essence must be interpreted negatively or treated as metaphors. He denies that "when we say God lives, we mean merely that God is not like an inanimate thing" as "was taught by Rabbi Moses." On the contrary, he holds that "these names signify the divine substance . . . although they fall short of representing Him. . . . For these names express God, so far as our intellects know Him. Now since our intellect knows God from creatures, it knows Him as far as creatures represent Him." Therefore, Aquinas concludes, "when we say, *God is good*, the meaning is not, *God is the cause of goodness*, or, *God is not evil*: but the meaning is, *Whatever good we attribute to creatures pre-exists in God*, and in a higher way."

IF MAIMONIDES were right that the names which are said positively of both God and creatures are "applied . . . in a purely equivocal sense" (*e.g.*, having literal meaning when said of creatures but being only metaphorical when said of God), then, according to Aquinas, it would follow that "from creatures nothing at all could be known or demonstrated about God." Those who say, on the other hand, that "the things attributed to God and creatures are univocal" (*i.e.*, are said in exactly the same sense), claim to comprehend more than man can know of the divine essence. When the term *wise* "is applied to God," Aquinas writes, "it leaves the thing signified as uncomprehended and as exceeding the signification of the name. Hence it is evident that this term *wise* is not applied in the same way to God and to man. The same applies to other terms. Hence no name is predicated univocally of God and creatures" but rather all positives names "are said of God and creatures in an analogous sense."

A further discussion of the names of God will be found in the chapter on SIGN AND SYMBOL; and the consideration of the analogical, the univocal, and the equivocal will also be found there as well as in the chapter on SAME AND OTHER. We have dealt with these matters here only for the sake of describing that degree of agnosticism, according to which Maimonides, by contrast with Aquinas, is an agnostic. But agnosticism usually goes further and denies that man can have any natural knowledge of God—either of His existence or of His essence.

So understood, agnosticism need not be incompatible with religion, unless a given religion holds, as an article of faith itself, that the existence of God can be *proved by reason*. In fact, the agnostic may be a religious man who accepts divine revelation and regards faith as divinely inspired.

Montaigne's *Apology for Raimond de Sebonde* illustrates this position. Sebonde had written a treatise on natural theology, which to Montaigne seems "hardy and bold; for he undertakes, by human and natural reasons to establish and make good against the atheists all the articles of the Christian religion." Though Montaigne says of his work, "I do not think it possible to do better upon that subject," and though he entertains the conjecture that it may have been "drawn from St. Thomas Aquinas, for, in truth, that mind full of infinite learning and admirable subtlety, was alone capable of such imaginations"; nevertheless, Montaigne does "not believe that means purely human are, in any sort, capable of doing it."

According to Montaigne, "it is faith alone that vividly and certainly comprehends the deep mysteries of our religion." In his view, reason by itself is incapable of proving *anything*, much less *anything about God*. "Our human reasons," he writes, "are but sterile and undigested matter; the grace of God is its form; it is that which gives it fashion and value." The light and value in Sebonde's arguments come from the fact that faith supervenes "to tint and illustrate" them, and "renders them firm and solid."

Such arguments, Montaigne says, may serve as "direction and first guide to a learner" and may even "render him capable of the grace of God"; but for himself, skeptical of all arguments, the way of faith alone can provide "a certain constancy of opinion. . . . Thus have I, by the grace of God, preserved myself entire, without anxiety or trouble of conscience, in the ancient belief of our religion, amidst so many sects and divisions as our age has produced."

Far from being religious as Montaigne was, the agnostic may be a skeptic about faith as well as reason. He may look upon faith either as superstition or as the exercise of the will to believe with regard to the unknowable and the unintelligible—almost wishful thinking. He may even go so far as to treat religion as if it were pathological.

Freud, for example, regards religion as an illusion to be explained in terms of man's need to create gods in his own image—to find a surrogate for the father, on whom his infantile dependence can be projected. Freud finds confirmation for this in the fact that in the religions of the west, God "is openly called Father. Psychoanalysis," he goes on, "concludes that he really is the father, clothed in the grandeur in which he once appeared to the small child."

Though the grown man "has long ago realized that his father is a being with strictly limited powers and by no means endowed with every desirable attribute," Freud thinks that he nevertheless "looks back to the memory-image of the overrated father of his childhood, exalts it into a Deity, and brings it into the present and into reality. The emotional strength of this memory-image and the lasting nature of his need for protection"—for, as Freud explains, "in relation to the external world he is still a child"—"are the two supports of his belief in God."

AT THE OTHER extreme from agnosticism is, as the name implies, gnosticism. Like deism, it dispenses with faith, but it exceeds traditional deism in the claims it makes for reason's power to penetrate the divine mysteries. Between exclusive reliance on faith and an exaltation of reason to the point where there is no need for God to reveal anything, a middle ground is held by those who acknowledge the contributions of both faith and reason. Those who try to harmonize the two usually distinguish between the spheres proper to each, and formulate some principle according to which they are related to each other in an orderly fashion.

Whatever is purely a matter of faith, Aquinas says, is assented to solely because "it is revealed by God." The articles of Christian faith are typified by "the Trinity of Persons in Almighty God, the mystery of Christ's Incarnation, and the like." With regard to such matters, which Aquinas thinks belong primarily to faith, some auxiliary use can be made of reason, "not, indeed, to prove faith," he explains, but to make clear the things that follow from it. Certain

matters, such as God's existence and attributes, he classifies as belonging to "the preambles to faith" because they fall, in his view, within reason's power to demonstrate, unaided by faith. Yet even here he does not assign the affirmation of the truth to reason alone.

Just as "it was necessary for the salvation of man that certain truths which exceed human reason should be made known to him by divine revelation," so even with regard to "those truths about God which human reason can investigate," Aquinas thinks it was also necessary that "man be taught by a divine revelation. For the truth about God, such as reason can know it, would only be known by a few, and that after a long time, and with the admixture of many errors." Because "human reason is very deficient in things concerning God"—"a sign of which is that philosophers . . . have fallen into many errors and have disagreed among themselves"—men would have no knowledge of God "free from doubt and uncertainty" unless all divine truths were "delivered to them by the way of faith, being told to them, as it were, by God Himself Who cannot lie."

In different ways faith supports reason and reason helps faith. On matters which belong to both reason and faith, faith provides a greater certitude. On matters strictly of faith, reason provides some understanding, however remote and inadequate, of the mysteries of religion. "The use of human reason in religion," Bacon writes, "is of two sorts: the former, in the conception and apprehension of the mysteries of God to us revealed; the other, in the inferring and deriving of doctrine and direction thereupon. . . . In the former we see God vouchsafeth to descend to our capacity, in the expressing of his mysteries in sort as may be sensible unto us; and doth grift his revelations and holy doctrine upon the notions of our reason and applieth his inspiration to open our understanding, as the form of the key to the ward of the lock. For the latter, there is allowed us an use of reason and argument, secondary and respective, although not original and absolute. For after the articles and principles of religion are placed and exempted from examination of reason, it is then permitted unto us to make derivations and inferences from and according to the analogy of them, for our better direction."

In addition to all discursive knowledge of God, whether it be by faith or by reason, there is the totally incommunicable and intimate acquaintance with the supernatural which the mystic claims for his vision in moments of religious ecstasy or which is promised to the blessed as their heavenly beatitude. When, at the culmination of *Paradise*, Dante sees God, "my vision," he declares, "was greater than our speech."

Knowing that his "speech will fall more short . . . than that of an infant who still bathes his tongue at the breast," he tries nevertheless to communicate in words "one single spark of Thy glory for the folk to come." In the presence of God, he writes, his mind, "wholly rapt, was gazing fixed, motionless, and intent, and ever with gazing grew enkindled. In that Light one becomes such that it is impossible he should ever consent to turn himself from it for other sight; because the Good which is the object of the will is all collected in it, and outside of it that is defective which is perfect there."

THE ARGUMENTS FOR the existence of the gods or of one God constitute one of the greatest attempts of the human mind to go beyond the sensible or phenomenal world of experience. The attempt has been made in every age and by minds of quite different persuasions in religious belief or philosophical outlook. It is possible, nevertheless, to classify the arguments into two or three main types.

Within the domain of pure or speculative reason there seem to be two ways of approaching the problem of God's existence.

One is in terms of the conception of God as an infinite, perfect, and necessary being, whose non-existence is therefore inconceivable. According to Anselm, God cannot be conceived in any other way than as "a being than which nothing greater can be conceived." But since "the fool hath said in his heart, there is no God," how shall he be made to know that the God, which exists in his understanding at the moment when he denies His real existence, also really exists outside his understanding? "For it is one thing for an object to be in the understanding, and another to understand that the

object exists." Hence Anselm considers the consequence of supposing that God exists in the understanding alone.

"If that, than which nothing greater can be conceived," he argues, "exists in the understanding alone, the very being, than which nothing greater can be conceived, is one than which a greater can be conceived"—for to exist in reality as well as in the understanding is to have *more* being. But this leads to "an irreconcilable contradiction," since "if that, than which nothing greater can be conceived, can be conceived not to exist, it is not that than which nothing greater can be conceived." Therefore Anselm concludes that a being "than which nothing greater can be conceived" must exist "both in the understanding and reality."

Anselm summarizes his argument by saying that "no one who understands what God is, can conceive that God does not exist." Since the non-existence of God is inconceivable, God must exist. Descartes gives the same argument a slightly different statement in terms of the inseparability of God's essence from God's existence.

"Being accustomed," he writes, "in all other things to make a distinction between existence and essence, I easily persuade myself that the existence can be separated from the essence of God, and that we can thus conceive God as not actually existing. But, nevertheless, when I think of it with more attention, I clearly see that existence can no more be separated from the essence of God than can its having its three angles equal to two right angles be separated from the essence of a rectilinear triangle, or the idea of a mountain from the idea of a valley; and so there is not any less repugnance to our conceiving a God (that is, a Being supremely perfect) to whom existence is lacking (that is to say, to whom a certain perfection is lacking), than to conceive of a mountain which has no valley."

Spinoza defines a "cause of itself" as "that whose essence involves existence; or that whose nature cannot be conceived unless existing." Since in his conception of substance, substance is necessarily infinite, it is also cause of itself. Hence he concludes that "God or substance . . . necessarily exists"; for "if this be denied, conceive if it be possible that God does not exist. Then it follows that His essence does not involve existence. But this is absurd. Therefore God necessarily exists."

This mode of argument, which takes still other forms, is traditionally called the "ontological argument" or the "*a priori* proof" of God's existence. Its critics sometimes deny that it is an argument or proof in any sense at all. Aquinas, for example, interprets Anselm not as proving God's existence, but rather as asserting that God's existence is self-evident. Those who say that the proposition "God does not exist" is self-contradictory, are saying that the opposite proposition "God exists" must be self-evident.

Aquinas does not deny that the proposition "God exists" is intrinsically self-evident. On this point he goes further than Anselm, Descartes, and Spinoza. Where they say God's essence *involves* His existence, Aquinas asserts that in God essence and existence are *identical*. When Moses asks God, "If they should say to me, What is His name? what shall I say to them?" the Lord says unto Moses, "I AM THAT I AM," and adds, "Say to the children of Israel: HE WHO IS hath sent me to you." This name—HE WHO IS—Aquinas holds to be "the most proper name of God" because it signifies that "the being of God is His very essence."

For this reason he thinks that the proposition "God exists" is self-evident in itself. Its subject and predicate are immediately related. Nevertheless, Aquinas holds that the proposition is not self-evident to us "because we do not know the essence of God." Even supposing, he writes, "that everyone understands this name *God* as signifying something than which nothing greater can be thought, nevertheless, it does not therefore follow that he understands that what the name signifies exists actually, but only that it exists mentally. Nor can it be argued that it actually exists, unless it be admitted that there actually exists something than which nothing greater can be thought; and this precisely is not admitted by those who hold that God does not exist."

The writer of the First Set of Objections to Descartes' *Meditations* maintains that the criticism advanced by Aquinas applies to Descartes as well as to Anselm. Whether stated in terms of the conception of an absolutely perfect being or in terms of essence and existence, the argument is invalid, he thinks, which asserts that God actually exists because His non-existence is inconceivable. Kant's later criticism of the ontological argument takes a similar course. A proposition may be logically necessary without being true in fact.

"The conception of an absolutely necessary being," he writes, "is a mere idea, the objective reality of which is far from being established by the mere fact that it is a need of reason. . . . The unconditioned necessity of a judgment does not form the absolute necessity of a thing." From the fact that "existence belongs necessarily to the object of the conception," we cannot conclude that "the existence of the thing . . . is therefore absolutely necessary—merely," Kant says, "because its existence has been cogitated in the conception. . . . Whatever be the content of our conception of an object, it is necessary to go beyond it, if we wish to predicate existence of the object. . . . The celebrated ontological or Cartesian argument for the existence of a supreme being is therefore insufficient."

THE SECOND MAIN approach to the problem of God's existence lies in the sort of proof which, Locke thinks, "our own existence and the sensible parts of the universe offer so clearly and cogently to our thoughts." He refrains from criticizing the argument from "the *idea* of a most perfect being," but he does insist that we should not "take some men's having that idea of God in their minds . . . for the only proof of a Deity." He for one prefers to follow the counsel of St. Paul, that "the invisible things of God are clearly seen from the creation of the world, being understood by the things that are made, even his eternal power and Godhead."

We have, according to Locke, an intuitive knowledge of our own existence. We know, he says, that "nonentity cannot produce any real being"; and so "from the consideration of ourselves, and what we infallibly find in our constitution, our reason leads us to the knowledge of this certain and evident truth—*That there is an eternal, most powerful, and most knowing Being.*"

Without labelling it a proof of God's existence, Augustine in his *Confessions* presents a similar argument—from the visible creation. "Behold," he says, "the heavens and the earth are; they proclaim that they were created; for they change and vary. . . . They proclaim also that they made not themselves: 'therefore we are, because we have been made; we were not therefore, before we were, so as to make ourselves'. . . . Thou therefore, Lord, madest them."

This second approach to the existence of God by reasoning from the facts of experience or the evidences of nature is called the "*a posteriori* proof." In the tradition of the great books, it has been formulated in many different ways. What is common to all of them is the principle of causality, in terms of which the known existence of certain effects is made the basis for inferring the existence of a unique cause—a first cause, a highest cause, an uncaused cause.

Aristotle, for example, in the last book of his *Physics*, argues from the fact of motion or change to the existence of an unmoved mover. He sums up his elaborate reasoning on this point in the following statement. "We established the fact that everything that is in motion is moved by something, and that the movent is either unmoved or in motion, and that, if it is in motion, it is moved either by itself or by something else and so on throughout the series: and so we proceeded to the position that the first principle that directly causes things that are in motion to be moved is that which moves itself, and the first principle of the whole series is the unmoved."

Aristotle's argument, unlike that of Augustine or Locke, does not presuppose the creation of the world, at least not in the sense of the world's having a beginning. On the contrary, he holds the world and its motions to be as eternal as their unmoved mover. "It is impossible," he writes in the *Metaphysics*, "that movement should either have come into being or cease to be." Precisely because he thinks the world's motions are eternal, Aristotle holds that the prime mover, in addition to being everlasting, must be immutable. This for him means "a principle whose very essence is actuality." Only a substance without any potency, only one which is *purely actual*, can be an absolutely immutable, eternal being.

Whatever has any potentiality in its nature is capable of not existing. If everything were of this sort, nothing that now is "need be, for it is possible for all things to be capable of existing, but not yet to exist." Hence, in still another way, Aristotle seems to reach the conclusion that a purely actual being must exist; and, furthermore, he seems to identify this being with a living and thinking God. "Life also belongs to God," he writes; "for the actuality of thought is life, and God is that actuality; and God's self-dependent actuality is life most good and eternal."

Where Aristotle argues from motion and potentiality to a prime mover and a pure actuality, Newton gives the *a posteriori* proof another statement by arguing from the design of the universe to God as its designer or architect. "The most wise and excellent contrivances of things, and final causes" seem to him the best way of knowing God. "Blind metaphysical necessity, which is certainly the same always and everywhere, could produce no variety in things. All that diversity of natural things which we find suited to different times and places could arise from nothing but the ideas and will of a Being necessarily existing."

In similar fashion Berkeley maintains that "if we attentively consider the constant regularity, order, and concatenation of natural things, the surprising magnificence, beauty, and perfection of the larger, and the exquisite contrivance of the smaller parts of the creation, together with the exact harmony and correspondence of the whole, but, above all, the never enough admired laws of pain and pleasure, and the instincts or natural inclinations, appetites, and passions of animals; I say if we consider all these things, and at the same time attend to the meaning and import of the attributes, one, eternal, infinitely wise, good, and perfect, we shall clearly perceive that they belong to the . . . Spirit, who 'works all in all,' and 'by whom all things consist.'" This seems to him so certain that he adds, "we may even assert that the existence of God is far more evidently perceived than the existence of men."

But, according to Berkeley, all the visible things of nature exist only as ideas in our minds, ideas which, unlike our own memories or imaginations, we do not ourselves produce. "Everything we see, hear, feel, or anywise perceive by sense," he writes, must have some other cause than our own will, and is therefore "a sign or effect of the power of God." To the "unthinking herd" who claim that "they cannot *see* God," Berkeley replies that "God . . . is intimately present to our minds, producing in them all that variety of ideas or sensations which continually affect us."

The existence of any idea in us is for Berkeley ground for asserting God's existence and power as its cause. But for Descartes *one* idea alone becomes the basis of such an inference. He supplements his *a priori* or ontological argument with what he calls an "*a posteriori* demonstration of God's existence from the mere fact that the idea of God exists in us."

That he is himself imperfect, Descartes knows from the fact that he doubts. Even when doubting leads to knowledge, his knowledge is imperfect, "an infallible token" of which, he says, is the fact that "my knowledge increases little by little." But the idea which he has of God, he declares, is that of an absolutely perfect being, "in whom there is nothing merely potential, but in whom all is present really and actually." On the principle that there cannot be more reality or perfection in the effect than in the cause, Descartes concludes that his own imperfect mind cannot be the cause of the idea of a perfect being. "The idea that I possess of a being more perfect than I," he writes, "must necessarily have been placed in me by a being which is really more perfect."

The radical imperfection of man, and indeed of all creation, offers Augustine still another proof for God's existence, which he attributes to the "Platonists." "They have seen," he writes, "that whatever is changeable is not the most high God, and therefore they have transcended every soul and all changeable spirits in seeking the supreme. They have seen also that, in every changeable thing, the form which makes it that which it is, whatever be its mode or nature, can only *be* through Him who truly *is*, because He is unchangeable. And therefore, whether we consider the whole body of the world, its figure, qualities, and orderly movement, and also all the bodies which are in it; or whether we consider all life, either that

which nourishes and maintains, as the life of trees; or that which, besides this, has also sensation, as the life of beasts; or that which adds to all these intelligence, as the life of man; or that which does not need the support of nutriment, but only maintains, feels, understands, as the life of angels—all can only *be* through Him who absolutely *is*. For to Him it is not one thing to *be*, and another to live, as though He could *be*, not living; nor is it to Him one thing to live, and another to understand, as though He could live, not understanding; nor is it to Him one thing to understand, another to be blessed, as though He could understand and not be blessed. But to Him to live, to understand, to be blessed, are to *be*. They have understood, from this unchangeableness and this simplicity, that all things must have been made by Him, and that He could Himself have been made by none."

The variety of arguments we have so far examined seems to fit the "five ways" in which, according to Aquinas, the existence of God can be proved *a posteriori*. "The first and most manifest way is the argument from motion," which Aquinas attributes to Aristotle. "The second way is from the nature of an efficient cause." Berkeley's argument or Locke's would seem, in some respects, to offer a version of this mode of reasoning. "The third way is taken from possibility and necessity," and seems to develop the argument from potentiality in Aristotle's *Metaphysics*, and to contain the inference from mutability and contingency which is implicit in the argument attributed to the Platonists by Augustine. "The fourth way is taken from the gradation to be found in things." Proceeding from the existence of the imperfect to absolute perfection, it resembles in principle the reasoning of Descartes concerning the perfection in the cause relative to the perfection in the effect. "The fifth way is taken from the governance of the world"—from the fact that everything acts for an end—and so is like the argument which Newton offers from final causes and the existence of order in the universe.

These "five ways" may or may not be regarded as an exhaustive list of the *a posteriori* proofs. It may even be questioned whether the five ways are logically distinct and independent. Aquinas himself says that "in speculative matters the medium of demonstration, which demonstrates the conclusion perfectly, is only one; whereas probable means of proof are many." Since he considers the argument for God's existence to be a certain, not a probable proof, it would seem to follow that, in strict logic, only one principle can be involved in that proof.

As already suggested, the principle—common to all the various ways in which such *a posteriori* reasoning is expressed—seems to be the principal of causality. This appears in the argument from the existence of contingent beings, which cannot cause their own being, to the existence of a being which needs no cause of its being, because its very essence is to exist. This may be the one argument for God's existence or, if one among many, it may be the core of all the others. It has the distinction at least of conceiving God as the cause of being, rather than of motion or of hierarchy and order in the world.

According to the statement of Aquinas that "being is the proper effect of God," it establishes God as the *unique* and *direct* cause of the being possessed by every finite thing. This formulation of the proof is more fully examined in the chapter on NECESSITY AND CONTINGENCY; and its relation to the question of whether the world had a beginning or is eternal, and if eternal, whether it is created or uncreated, will be seen in the chapters on CAUSE, ETERNITY, and WORLD.

THE VALIDITY OF the *a posteriori* argument for God's existence—in one form or another—is questioned by those who think that the causal principle cannot be applied beyond experience, or who think that our knowledge of cause and effect is not sufficient to warrant such inferences.

"The existence of any being can only be proved by arguments from its cause or its effect," Hume writes; "and these arguments are founded entirely on experience. ... It is only experience which teaches us the nature and bounds of cause and effect, and enables us to infer the existence of one object from that of another." But Hume doubts "whether it be possible for a cause to be known only by its

effect ... or to be of so singular and particular a nature as to have no parallel and no similarity with any other cause or object, that has ever fallen under our observation. ... If experience and observation and analogy be, indeed, the only guides which we can reasonably follow in inferences of this nature," as Hume thinks is the case, then it follows that "both the effect and the cause must bear a similarity and resemblance to other effects and causes which we know.

"I leave it to your own reflection," he adds, "to pursue the consequences of this principle." One seems obvious enough; namely, that God —a unique and unparalleled cause—cannot be proved by reasoning from our experience of effects and their causes. Hume himself draws this conclusion when he declares that theology, insofar as it is concerned with the existence of a Deity, has "its best and most solid foundation," not in reason or experience, but in "*faith and divine revelation.*"

Like Hume, Kant thinks that our notions of cause and effect cannot be applied outside experience or to anything beyond the realm of sensible nature. But he offers an additional reason for denying validity to all *a posteriori* reasoning concerning God's existence. "It imposes upon us," he says, "an old argument in a new dress, and appeals to the agreement of two witnesses, the one with the credentials of pure reason, and the other with those of empiricism; while, in fact, it is only the former who has changed his dress and voice."

The principle of the argument from the contingency of the world or its parts Kant states as follows: "If something exists, an absolutely necessary being must likewise exist." One premise in the argument, namely, that contingent things exist, has its foundation in experience and therefore Kant admits that the reasoning "is not completely *a priori* or ontological." But in order to complete the proof, he thinks it must be shown that an *ens realissimum*, or most perfect being, is the same as an absolutely necessary being, in order for the obtained conclusion (*a necessary being exists*) to be translated into the conclusion desired (*God exists*).

That "an *ens realissimum* must possess the additional attribute of absolute necessity"—or, in other words, that a perfect being is identical with one which necessarily exists—is, according to Kant, "exactly what was maintained in the ontological argument." Hence he maintains that the argument from contingency is invalid because it cannot avoid including what is for Kant the invalid premise of the ontological argument as "the real ground of its disguised and illusory reasoning."

THE CONTROVERSY concerning the proof of God's existence raises issues in logic, in metaphysics and physics, and in the theory of knowledge. Philosophers are opposed on the question whether a valid demonstration is possible. Those who think it possible differ from one another on the way in which the proof should be constructed. Those who think it impossible do not always go to the opposite extreme of making the affirmation of God's existence a matter of faith; or of denying with the skeptic that we can have any light on the question at all. Pascal and Kant, for example, reject the theoretic arguments as inconclusive or untenable, but they do not think the problem is totally insoluble. They offer instead *practical* grounds or reasons for accepting God's existence.

"The metaphysical proofs of God are so remote from the reasoning of men," Pascal asserts, "and so complicated, that they make little impression." He will "not undertake," he tells us in his *Pensées*, "to prove by natural reasons . . . the existence of God." In his view "there are only three kinds of persons: those who serve God, having found Him; others who are occupied in seeking Him, not having found Him; while the remainder live without seeking Him, and without having found Him." Since he regards the first as "reasonable and happy," the last as "foolish and unhappy," he addresses himself to the middle group whom he regards as "unhappy and reasonable."

He asks them to consider whether God is or is not. "Reason can decide nothing here," he says. If a choice is to be made by reason, it must be in the form of a wager. "Which will you choose then? Let us see. Since you must choose, let us see which interests you least. You have two things to lose, the true and the good; and two things to stake, your reason and your will, your knowledge and your happiness; and your

nature has two things to shun, error and misery. Your reason is no more shocked in choosing one rather than another, since you must of necessity choose. This is one point settled. But your happiness? Let us weigh the gain and the loss in wagering that God is. Let us estimate these two chances. If you gain, you gain all, if you lose, you lose nothing. Wager then, without hesitation, that He is."

We are incapable of knowing either that God is or what God is, according to Pascal, because "if there is a God, He is infinitely incomprehensible" and "has no affinity to us." Nevertheless, proceeding on the practical level of the wager, reason may lead to Christian faith, yet not in such a way as to give adequate reasons for that belief, since Christians "profess a religion for which they cannot give a reason."

Kant also makes the affirmation of God a matter of faith, but for him it is a "purely rational faith, since pure reason . . . is the sole source from which it springs." He defines a *matter of faith* as any object which cannot be known through the speculative use of reason, but which "must be thought *a priori*, either as consequences or as grounds, if pure practical reason is to be used as duty commands . . . Such is the *summum bonum*," he says, "which has to be realized in the world through freedom . . . This effect which is commanded, *together with the only conditions on which its possibility is conceivable by us*, namely, the existence of God and the immortality of the soul, are *matters of faith* and are of all objects the only ones that can be so called."

For Kant, then, the existence of God is a "postulate of pure practical reason . . . as the necessary condition of the possibility of the *summum bonum*." The moral law commands us to seek the highest good, with perfect happiness as its concomitant; but Kant thinks that "there is not the slightest ground in the moral law for a necessary connexion between morality and proportionate happiness in a being that belongs to the world as a part of it." Since man is a part of the world or nature, and dependent on it, "he cannot by his will be a cause of this nature, nor by his own power make it thoroughly harmonize, as far as his happiness is concerned, with his practical principles." The only possible solution lies in "the existence of a cause of all nature, distinct from nature itself, and containing the principle of this connexion, namely, of the exact harmony of happiness with morality." That is why, Kant explains, "it is morally necessary to assume the existence of God."

IN THE TRADITION of the great books, the common ground shared by reason and faith is marked by the convergence of the contributions made by pagan, Jew, and Christian—and by poets, philosophers, and theologians—to the problem of God's existence and the understanding of the divine nature, the essence of God and His attributes.

Certain attributes of God, such as simplicity, immateriality, eternity, infinity, perfection, and glory, are usually regarded as so many different ways in which the human understanding apprehends the divine nature in itself. Other attributes, such as the divine causality, omnipotence, omnipresence, omniscience, love, justice, and mercy, are usually taken as ways of considering God's nature in relation to the world or to creatures. But to divide the attributes in this way, as is done in the Outline of Topics, is to make a division which cannot be fully justified except in terms of convenience for our understanding. God's will, for example, no less than God's intellect, can be considered in relation to Himself. God's intellect, no less than God's will, can have the world for its object. So, too, the divine goodness can be considered with reference to things, even as God's love can be considered with reference to Himself.

The difficulties we meet in classifying or ordering the attributes of God confirm the opinion of almost all theologians, that our understanding is inadequate to comprehend the essence of God. The fact that we employ a multiplicity of attributes to represent to ourselves what in itself is an absolute unity is another indication of the same point. The one attribute of *simplicity* would seem to deny us the right to name others, unless we take the plurality of attributes to signify something about man's understanding of God rather than a real complexity in the divine nature.

"He that will attribute to God," Hobbes writes, "nothing but what is warranted by natural reason, must either use such negative attributes, as *infinite, eternal, incomprehensible*; or superlatives, as *most high, most great*, and the like; or indefinite, as *good, just, holy, creator*; and in such sense, as if he meant not to declare what He is (for that were to circumscribe Him within the limits of our fancy), but how much we admire Him, and how ready we would be to obey Him; which is a sign of humility and of a will to honor Him as much as we can: for there is but one name to signify our conception of His nature, and that is, I AM: and but one name of His relation to us, and that is GOD; in which is contained Father, King, and Lord."

Even when they are discussed by the philosophers and reflected on by the poets, certain matters belong especially to theology because they constitute the dogmas of religion—articles of religious faith based solely on divine revelation, not discovered by human inquiry or speculation. That God created the world out of nothing and of His free will; that the world had a beginning and will have an end are, for example, dogmas of traditional Judaism and Christianity. Philosophers may argue about the freedom or necessity of the creative act, or about the possibility of a beginning or an end to time and the world, but Jewish and Christian theologians find in Sacred Scripture the warrant for believing that which may not be thoroughly intelligible to reason, much less demonstrable by it. What is true of creation applies generally to the religious belief in divine providence and the positive commandments of God, to the gift of grace which God bestows upon men, and to the performance of miracles.

Judaism and Christianity share certain dogmas, though the degree to which Jewish and Christian theologians commonly understand what is apparently the same dogma varies from great similarity of interpretation (as in the case of creation and providence) to differences so great (as, for example, with regard to grace) that there may be some doubt whether the dogma in question is really the same. The line of demarcation between these faiths would seem to be more easily determined than their common ground; yet even here such matters as the resurrection of the body—even when we take differences of interpretation into account —may be regarded as a dogma shared by both.

The basic differences between Jewish and Christian theology center, of course, on the issue between a unitarian and a trinitarian conception of the Godhead, with immediate consequences for disbelief or belief in Christ as the incarnate second person of the Trinity—the Word become flesh. This in turn has consequences for doctrines of salvation, and of the nature and mission of the church, its rituals and its sacraments. Even within Christianity, however, there have been and still are serious doctrinal differences on all these matters. The most fundamental heresies and schisms of early Christianity concerned the understanding of the Trinity and the Incarnation. The great modern schism which divided Christendom arose from issues about the sacraments, the organization and practices of the church, and the conditions of salvation.

It would seem to be just as easy to say what beliefs are common to religious Jews and Christians, as to articulate the faith common to all sects of Christianity. If all varieties of Protestant doctrine are included, little remains in common except belief in the God of Abraham, Isaac, and Jacob—creator and provider, governor and judge, dispenser of rewards and punishments.

ONE BOOK STANDS OUT from all the rest because, in our tradition, it is—as the use of "Bible" for its proper name implies—*the* book about God and man. For those who have faith, Holy Writ or Sacred Scripture is the revealed Word of God. Its division into Old and New Testaments represents the historic relation of the Jewish and Christian religions.

Without prejudice to the issue between belief and unbelief, or between Jewish and Christian faith, we have attempted to organize the references to specifically religious doctrines concerning God and His creatures according to their origin and foundation in either the Old or in the New Testament, or in both. On certain points, as we have already seen, the line of distinction can be clearly drawn. For example, the doctrines of God's covenant with Israel, of the Chosen People, of the Temple and the Torah, are indisputably drawn from the Old Testament; and from the New Testament come such dogmas as those concerning Christ's divinity and humanity, the Virgin Birth, the Church as the mystical body of Christ, and the seven sacraments.

Under all these topics we have assembled passages from the Bible, interpretations of them by the theologians, and materials from the great books of poetry and history, philosophy and science. Since the criterion of relevance here is the reflection of sacred or religious doctrine in secular literature, the writings of pagan antiquity are necessarily excluded, though they are included in the more philosophical topics of theology, such as the existence and nature of one God.

Despite its length, this chapter by no means exhausts the discussion of God in the great books. The long list of Cross-References, which follows the seventy-three topics comprising the Reference section of this chapter, indicates the various ways in which the idea of God occurs in the topics of other chapters. The reader will find that list useful not only as an indication of the topics in other chapters which elaborate on or extend the discussion of matters treated here, but also as a guide to other Introductions in which he is likely to find the conception of God a relevant part of the examination of some other great idea.

OUTLINE OF TOPICS

REFERENCES

To find the passages cited, use the numbers in heavy type, which are the volume and page numbers of the passages referred to. For example, in **4** Homer: *Iliad*, BK II [265–283] **12d**, the number **4** is the number of the volume in the set; the number **12d** indicates that the passage is in section d of page 12.

Page Sections: When the text is printed in one column, the letters a and b refer to the upper and lower halves of the page. For example, in **53** James: *Psychology*, **116a–119b**, the passage begins in the upper half of page 116 and ends in the lower half of page 119. When the text is printed in two columns, the letters a and b refer to the upper and lower halves of the left-hand side of the page, the letters c and d to the upper and lower halves of the right-hand side of the page. For example, in **7** Plato: *Symposium*, **163b–164c**, the passage begins in the lower half of the left-hand side of page 163 and ends in the upper half of the right-hand side of page 164.

Author's Divisions: One or more of the main divisions of a work (such as PART, BK, CH, SECT) are sometimes included in the reference; line numbers, in brackets, are given in certain cases; *e.g.*, *Iliad*, BK II [265–283] **12d**.

Bible References: The references are to book, chapter, and verse. When the King James and Douay versions differ in title of books or in the numbering of chapters or verses, the King James version is cited first and the Douay, indicated by a *(D)*, follows; *e.g.*, Old Testament: *Nehemiah*, 7:45—*(D)* II *Esdras*, 7:46.

Symbols: The abbreviation "esp" calls the reader's attention to one or more especially relevant parts of a whole reference; "passim" signifies that the topic is discussed intermittently rather than continuously in the work or passage cited.

For additional information concerning the style of the references, see the Explanation of Reference Style; for general guidance in the use of *The Great Ideas*, consult the Preface.

1. The polytheistic conception of the supernatural order

1a. The nature and existence of the gods

4 Homer: *Iliad*, BK V [330–351] **33c-d**; [814–909] **38b-39a,c** / *Odyssey*, BK VIII [266–366] **224d-225d**

5 Aeschylus: *Prometheus Bound* **40a-51d** / *Agamemnon* [158–183] **53d-54a**

5 Sophocles: *Oedipus at Colonus* [607–614] **120a** / *Antigone* [780–792] **138a**

5 Euripides: *Helen* [1137–1150] **309a** / *Bacchantes* **340a-352a,c** esp [272–327] **342b-c** / *Heracles Mad* [815–874] **371d-372c**; [1302–1353] **376c-d** / *Iphigenia Among the Tauri* [354–391] **414a-b**; [570–575] **416a**

5 Aristophanes: *Clouds* **488a-506d** esp [263–428] **491a-493d**, [813–833] **498c-d**, [1462–1477] **506c** / *Birds* **542a-563d** esp [684–736] **551b-552a**, [1492–1765] **560c-563d** / *Plutus* [87–93] **630a**

6 Herodotus: *History*, BK I, **10a-11d**; **31a-b**; **48c**; BK II, **58b-60d**; **75a-b**; **79d-80c**; **86c**; BK III, **95a-c**; BK IV, **134a**; **140c-d**

7 Plato: *Cratylus*, **91c-d** / *Phaedrus*, **124c-125b** / *Symposium*, **152b**; **153b-c**; **159d-161a**; **163a-164c** / *Euthyphro*, **193a-c** / *Apology*, **204c-205c**; **209a-b** / *Republic*, BK II, **313d-314d**;

BK II–III, **320c-328a** / *Timaeus*, **451d-452b**; **465d** / *Statesman*, **587a-589c** / *Laws*, BK VII, **730a-d**; BK X, **757d-769d**; BK XII, **787d-788a**

8 Aristotle: *Heavens*, BK I, CH 3 [270^{b}1–26] **361c-362a**; BK II, CH 1 **375b,d-376a** / *Metaphysics*, BK III, CH 4 [1000^{a}8–18] **518d-519a**; BK XII, CH 8 [1074^{b}1–14] **604d-605a**

9 Aristotle: *Ethics*, BK X, CH 8 [1178^{b}8–23] **433b-c** / *Rhetoric*, BK II, CH 23 [1397^{b}12–14] **645d**; [1398^{a}15–17] **646c**; [1398^{b}27–28] **647b**; [1399^{b}5–8] **648a-b**; BK III, CH 18 [1419^{a}6–13] **673d-674a**

12 Lucretius: *Nature of Things*, BK II [646–651] **23b**; [1090–1104] **29a**; BK III [14–24] **30b**; BK V [146–173] **63a-b**; [306–310] **65a**; [1161–1193] **76b-c**; BK VI [56–78] **81a-b**

12 Epictetus: *Discourses*, BK I, CH 3 **108b-c**; CH 12, **118d-119b**; BK III, CH 13, **188b-189a**; BK IV, CH 4, **227d-228a**; CH 11, **240d-241a**

12 Aurelius: *Meditations*, BK II, SECT 11 **258a-b**

14 Plutarch: *Pericles*, **140d** / *Coriolanus*, **191d-192b** / *Pelopidas*, **239d-240c**

15 Tacitus: *Annals*, BK III, **59d-60a**

17 Plotinus: *Third Ennead*, TR V, CH 2–3 **101c-102c**; CH 6 **103b-104a**; CH 8–10 **105a-106b** / *Fifth Ennead*, TR I, CH 7, **212b-c**; TR VIII, CH 3, **241a**; CH 10 **244c-245a** / *Sixth Ennead*, TR VIII, CH 1 **342d-343c**; CH 3 **344a-b**

(1. _The polytheistic conception of the supernatural order. 1a. The nature and existence of the gods._)

18 AUGUSTINE: _City of God_, BK I–X 129a-322a,c passim, esp BK VI, CH 5–9 234d-241b

19 AQUINAS: _Summa Theologica_, PART I, Q II, A 3, REP I 49a-c; Q 63, A 7, ANS 331c-332b; Q 115, A 3, REP I 588c-589c

23 HOBBES: _Leviathan_, PART I, 79a-b; 79d-80a; 81a-b

32 MILTON: _Christs Nativity_ 1a-7b / _Lycidas_ 27b-32a / _Comus_ 33a-56b / _Paradise Lost_, BK I [331–621] 100b-107a / _Samson Agonistes_ [896–902] 359a / _Areopagitica_, 384b

35 LOCKE: _Human Understanding_, BK I, CH III, SECT 15 116c-d

35 HUME: _Human Understanding_, SECT XI, DIV 103–110, 498b-501b

37 FIELDING: _Tom Jones_, 152a-c

40 GIBBON: _Decline and Fall_, 12b-c; 98a-c; 345b-347a; 461b-c; 584a; 600d-601a

41 GIBBON: _Decline and Fall_, 226a-227a

46 HEGEL: _Philosophy of History_, PART I, 224a-b; 237a-239c; 244c-245a; 251b-257c; PART II, 263d-265c; 268b-271c; PART III, 290b-292a

1b. The hierarchy of the gods: their relation to one another

4 HOMER: _Iliad_, BK I [493–611] 8a-9a,c; BK VIII [1–52] 51a-c; BK XV [184–217] 105d-106b; BK XVIII [356–367] 133d; BK XIX [74–144] 137d-138c; BK XX [1–160] 142a-143d / _Odyssey_, BK I [11–79] 183a-d; BK V [1–147] 208a-209c; BK XIII [125–158] 256b-d

5 AESCHYLUS: _Suppliant Maidens_ [22–28] 1b; [524–600] 7c-8d; [882–894] 12b; [1008–1073] 13d-14a,c / _Prometheus Bound_ 40a-51d / _Agamemnon_ [158–183] 53d-54a / _Eumenides_ 81a-91d

5 EURIPIDES: _Heracles Mad_ [1302–1353] 376c-d / _Iphigenia Among the Tauri_ [1234–1283] 422b-c

5 ARISTOPHANES: _Peace_ [403–426] 530d / _Birds_ 542a-563d esp [684–736] 551b-552a, [1195–1266] 557c-558b, [1494–1693] 560c-562d / _Plutus_ [111–146] 630b-d

6 HERODOTUS: _History_, BK I, 21d-22a; BK II, 58a-60d; 79d-80c; 82d-83b; BK IV, 134a; 155c-156a; BK VIII, 269a

7 PLATO: _Cratylus_, 91c-d / _Phaedrus_, 124d-125a / _Symposium_, 152b; 153b-c; 159d-161a; 163a-164c / _Euthyphro_, 193a-c / _Timaeus_, 452b / _Laws_, BK IV, 683b; BK VIII, 731d-732a

8 ARISTOTLE: _Metaphysics_, BK III, CH 4 [1000^{a}8–18] 518d-519a

9 ARISTOTLE: _Politics_, BK I, CH 2 [1252^{b}19–27] 446a

12 EPICTETUS: _Discourses_, BK I, CH 3, 108b; CH 14, 121a-b

13 VIRGIL: _Aeneid_, BK I [1–156] 103a-107a; BK X [1–117] 302a-305a; [606–632] 318b-319b

14 PLUTARCH: _Pelopidas_, 239d-240b / _Pompey_, 525b

15 TACITUS: _Histories_, BK IV, 293b-294a

17 PLOTINUS: _Second Ennead_, TR IX, CH 9, 71b-c / _Third Ennead_, TR V, CH 6 103b-104a / _Fifth Ennead_, TR I, CH 7, 212b-c

18 AUGUSTINE: _Christian Doctrine_, BK II, CH 17 645d-646a

19 AQUINAS: _Summa Theologica_, PART I, Q 22, A 3, ANS 130d-131c; Q 63, A 7, ANS 331c-332b

21 DANTE: _Divine Comedy_, HELL, XXXI 46a-47c

22 CHAUCER: _Troilus and Cressida_, BK III, STANZA 1–7 54b-55b

27 SHAKESPEARE: _Tempest_, ACT IV, SC I [60–133] 542b-543a

30 BACON: _Advancement of Learning_, 20b-c

32 MILTON: _Paradise Lost_, BK I [331–621] 100b-107a

38 ROUSSEAU: _Social Contract_, BK IV, 435b-c

40 GIBBON: _Decline and Fall_, 12b-d; 59c-60a; 346b-d; 461b-c

46 HEGEL: _Philosophy of History_, PART I, 224a-b; 228a-b; 252a-253c; PART II, 262b-c

1c. The intervention of the gods in the affairs of men: their judgment of the deserts of men

4 HOMER: _Iliad_ 3a-179d esp BK I [33–317] 3b-6b, [493–611] 8a-9a,c, BK IV [1–140] 24a-25b, BK V [311–519] 33b-35c, [711–909] 37b-39a,c, BK VIII 51a-56d, BK XIV–XV 98a-111d, BK XVI [431–461] 117a-b, [843–867] 121c-d, BK XVIII [356–367] 133d, BK XIX [74–144] 137d-138c, BK XX–XXI 142a-154d, BK XXIV [507–551] 176c-177a / _Odyssey_ 183a-322d esp BK II 188a-192d, BK IX [16–38] 229a-b, [67–81] 229d-230a, BK XVIII [124–150] 285b-c, BK XX 296a-300a,c, BK XXIV [438–548] 321c-322d

5 AESCHYLUS: _Suppliant Maidens_ [79–175] 2a-3a; [1008–1073] 13d-14a,c / _Persians_ [535–547] 20d; [738–842] 23a-24b / _Seven Against Thebes_ 27a-39a,c esp [790–801] 35d-36a / _Prometheus Bound_ 40a-51d esp [227–243] 42c, [436–502] 44c-45a, [564–891] 45d-49c / _Agamemnon_ 52a-69d esp [355–475] 55d-57b, [1200–1222] 64d-65a, [1485–1488] 67d, [1559–1570] 68c / _Choephoroe_ 70a-80d esp [269–314] 72d-73a, [1021–1076] 80a-d / _Eumenides_ 81a-91d

5 SOPHOCLES: _Oedipus the King_ 99a-113a,c esp [1297–1415] 111b-112b / _Oedipus at Colonus_ 114a-130a,c esp [229–253] 116b-c, [939–1015] 123a-d, [1448–1666] 127b-129b / _Antigone_ 131a-142d esp [100–162] 132a-c, [1348–1353] 142d / _Ajax_ 143a-155a,c esp [394–459] 146c-147a, [733–783] 149b-d / _Electra_ 156a-169a,c esp [516–576] 160a-c / _Trachiniae_ 170a-181a,c esp [94–140] 171a-b, [247–306] 172b-d, [1275–1278] 181c / _Philoctetes_ 182a-195a,c esp [169–200] 183d-184a, [446–452] 186a, [1408–1471] 194d-195a,c

5 EURIPIDES: _Rhesus_ 203a-211d esp [594–674] 208b-209a, [890–996] 210d-211d / _Medea_ [1415–1419] 224c / _Hippolytus_ 225a-236d esp

[1–55] 225a-c, [520–568] 229c-d, [1202–1466] 234d-236d / *Alcestis* 237a-247a,c esp [1–76] 237a-238a, [1159–1163] 247c / *Heracleidae* [750–1055] 254d-257a,c / *Suppliants* 258a-269a,c esp [113–283] 259a-260d, [1183–1234] 268c-269a,c / *Trojan Women* 270a-281a,c esp [1–97] 270a-271a, [914–1032] 277d-278d / *Ion* 282a-297d esp [1–81] 282a-d,[429–451]286b-c, [1470–1622] 296a-297d / *Helen* 298a-314a,c esp [1–67] 298a-d, [711–715] 304d-305a, [1644–1692] 313d-314a,c / *Andromache* [1225–1288] 325c-326a,c / *Electra* 327a-339a,c esp [1233–1359] 338b-339a,c / *Bacchantes* 340a-352a,c / *Hecuba* [488–500] 357a / *Heracles Mad* 365a-377d esp [1260–1390] 376a-377b / *Phoenician Maidens* 378a-393d esp [1–87] 378a-379a, [930–959] 386c, [1758–1763] 393d / *Orestes* 394a-410d esp [317–357] 397a-b, [1625–1693] 410b-d / *Iphigenia Among the Tauri* 411a-424d esp [1–41] 411a-b, [939–986] 419b-d, [1435–1499] 424a-d / *Iphigenia at Aulis* 425a-439d esp [1185–1194] 435d-436a, [1526–1629] 439a-d

5 Aristophanes: *Peace* 526a-541d esp [195–220] 528b-c / *Thesmophoriazusae* [655–687] 607c-608a / *Plutus* 629a-642d esp [86–92] 630a, [489–498] 634c-d, [653–747] 637a-d

6 Herodotus: *History*, bk i, 7b-10a esp 9d-10a; 20b-22a; bk ii, 54d-55a; 77a-b; 78d-79c; bk iii, 98b-c; bk iv, 124d-125a; 144c-d; 150b-d; 151b-153d; 155b-c; 158d-159a esp 159d; bk vi, 190c-d; 198b-d; 199d-200a; 200c-201a; 201d-202c; 205c-d; 211b-d; bk vii, 216d-217c esp 217c; 218b-220a; 224d-225a; 226d-227a; 239c-240d; 246b-247a; 250a-d; bk viii, 262b-c; 266a-d; 269c-270a; 270c-271a; 274b-c; 276b-d; 279d-280a; 283d; 284d-285a; bk ix, 302c; 308a-c; 309d-310a

6 Thucydides: *Peloponnesian War*, bk i,355b-c; 378a-b; bk ii, 407a-b; 415d-416c; bk v, 506b-c; bk vii, 559d-560a

7 Plato: *Protagoras*, 44a-45a / *Symposium*, 152d-153b / *Apology*, 211d / *Republic*, bk ii, 313b-314d; 322a-324c; bk vi, 378a-b; bk x, 436c-437a; 437c-438c / *Critias* 478a-485d / *Statesman*, 587a-589c / *Laws*, bk iv, 679a-b; 681b-683b; bk ix, 757a; bk x, 765d-768d; bk xii, 787d-788a

9 Aristotle: *Ethics*, bk i, ch 9 [1099^{b}9–18] 345a; bk x, ch 8 [1179^{a}23–33] 434a / *Rhetoric*, bk ii, ch 5 [1383^{b}3–8] 629d; ch 17 [1391^{a}30–^{b}3] 638d

10 Hippocrates: *Sacred Disease*, 154a-155d

12 Lucretius: *Nature of Things*, bk ii [1090–1104] 29a; bk v [1194–1240] 76d-77b; bk vi [43–79] 80d-81b; [379–422] 85b-d

12 Epictetus: *Discourses*, bk i, ch 12 118d-120b; ch 22, 128a-b; bk ii, ch 8 146a-147c

12 Aurelius: *Meditations*, bk i, sect 17 255d-256d; bk ii, sect 3 257a-b; bk iii, sect 11 262a-b; bk v, sect 8 269d-270b; bk vi, sect 40–46 277d-278d; bk x, sect 5 296d; bk xii, sect 5 307d-308a

13 Virgil: *Aeneid* 103a-379a esp bk i [223–417] 109a-114b, [657–722] 121a-123a, bk ii [162–200] 128b-129b, [588–633] 140b-142a, bk iii [84–120] 149b-150b, bk iv [90–128] 169b-170b, [173–278] 171b-174b, bk v [604–699] 202b-205b, [779–871] 207b-210a, bk vi [42–101] 212a-213b, bk vii [286–600] 243b-252b, bk viii [369–453] 269a-271a, [608–731] 275a-278b, bk ix [1–24] 279a-b, [77–122] 281a-282a, [638–663] 296a-297a, bk x [1–117] 302a-305a, [606–688] 318b-321a, bk xi [532–596] 342b-344b, [762–867] 349a-351b, bk xii [134–160] 357b-358a, [405–440] 365a-b, [766–886] 374b-377b

14 Plutarch: *Romulus*, 27d-29c / *Numa Pompilius*, 50d-51c; 57b-58a / *Solon*, 68a / *Camillus*, 104b-d; 107b-d / *Fabius*, 142d-143b / *Coriolanus*, 185b-186a; 188d-191b / *Aristides*, 268a-273c / *Lysander*, 365a-366a / *Sulla*, 370c-371b / *Lucullus*, 404d-405a / *Alexander*, 553b-554b / *Caesar*, 602c-604d esp 604b-d / *Phocion*, 615b-d / *Cato the Younger*, 639d / *Demosthenes*, 698a-699a / *Dion*, 781d-782a

15 Tacitus: *Annals*, bk iii, 59d-60a; bk vi, 91b-d; bk xvi, 179d; 183d / *Histories*, bk i, 189d-190a; bk ii, 235a-c; bk iv, 284b; 292c-294a

17 Plotinus: *Second Ennead*, tr ix, ch 9, 71a / *Third Ennead*, tr ii–iii 82c-97b

19 Aquinas: *Summa Theologica*, part i, q 22, a 3, ans 130d-131c

21 Dante: *Divine Comedy*, hell, xiv [43–72] 20a-b; paradise, iv [49–63] 111b; viii [1–12] 116d

22 Chaucer: *Troilus and Cressida*, bk i, stanza 30–35 5a-b; bk iii, stanza 89 66a / *Knight's Tale* 174a-211a esp [1303–1333] 181b-182a, [2663–2699] 203b-204a, [3099–3108] 211a / *Merchant's Tale* [10,093–230] 335a-337a

23 Hobbes: *Leviathan*, part i, 81b-c

27 Shakespeare: *King Lear*, act iv, sc i [33–39] 269d; [69–74] 270b; sc ii [38–50] 270d-271a; sc vi [35–40] 273d; act v, sc iii [166–174] 281a / *Antony and Cleopatra*, act ii, sc i [1–8] 317d / *Cymbeline*, act v, sc iv [1–151] 481a-482c; sc v [425–485] 488b-d

38 Rousseau: *Social Contract*, bk iv, 435a-436a

47 Goethe: *Faust*, part ii [8582–8590] 209a; [8610–8637] 209b-210a

2. The existence of one God

2a. The revelation of one God

Old Testament: *Genesis*, 17:1–14 / *Exodus*, 3 esp 3:6, 3:14–16; 6:1–8; 19:9-20:6 esp 20:1–6; 20:18–22 / *Deuteronomy*, 4:39; 5:1–10; 6 esp 6:4–5; 32:1–47 esp 32:36–43 / *I Kings*, 8:22-62 esp 8:23, 8:60—(D) *III Kings*, 8:22-62 esp 8:23, 8:60 / *I Chronicles*, 16:7–36—(D) *I Paralipomenon*, 16:7–36 / *Psalms*, 18 esp 18:30–32 —(D) *Psalms*, 17 esp 17:31–33 / *Isaiah*, 37:15–20; 43–45 passim, esp 43:3, 43:10–13, 44:6,

(2. The existence of one God. 2a. The revelation of one God.)

44:8, 44:24, 45:5-7, 45:18, 45:21-22; 48:12 —(D) Isaias, 37:15-20; 43-45 passim, esp 43:3, 43:10-13, 44:6, 44:8, 44:24, 45:5-7, 45:18, 45:21-22; 48:12 / Jeremiah, 10 esp 10:6, 10:10—(D) Jeremias, 10 esp 10:6, 10:10 / Daniel, 6 esp 6:20, 6:26-27 / Hosea, 13:4— (D) Osee, 13:4 / Joel, 2:27 / Zechariah, 14:9 —(D) Zacharias, 14:9 / Malachi, 2:10—(D) Malachias, 2:10

APOCRYPHA: Wisdom of Solomon, 12:13—(D) OT, Book of Wisdom, 12:13 / Ecclesiasticus, 1:8—(D) OT, Ecclesiasticus, 1:8 / II Maccabees, 1:24-29—(D) OT, II Machabees, 1:24-29

NEW TESTAMENT: Matthew, 23:9 / Mark, 12:28-34 / John, 1:1-2; 10:30; 17:3 / Acts, 17:22-29 / Romans, 1:14-32 / I Corinthians, 8:4-6; 12:4-6 / Ephesians, 4:5-6 / I Timothy, 2:5-6; 4:10; 6:14-16 / I John, 5:5-9

18 AUGUSTINE: Confessions, BK VII, par 16 48c-49a / City of God, BK VIII, CH 11, 272c / Christian Doctrine, BK I, CH 12 627c-d; CH 32 633c-d

19 AQUINAS: Summa Theologica, PART I, Q 2, A 2, REP 1 11d-12c; Q 11, A 3, CONTRARY and REP 1 49a-c; Q 13, A 11, CONTRARY 73c-74b

20 AQUINAS: Summa Theologica, PART I-II, Q 74, A 10, REP 3 136c-137c; Q 102, A 5, REP 1 283c-292c; PART II-II, Q 1, A 5, REP 3 383b-384b; A 8, ANS and REP 1 387a-388c

21 DANTE: Divine Comedy, PARADISE, XXIV [115-147] 143d-144a

30 BACON: Advancement of Learning, 38a; 41b-d

32 MILTON: Paradise Lost, BK VIII [267-318] 238a-239a; BK XII [106-151] 321b-322b; [223-248] 324a-b / Samson Agonistes [472-478] 350a

33 PASCAL: Pensées, 242-290 217b-225a; 428 244b; 557 272b

46 HEGEL: Philosophy of History, PART I, 245d-247b passim

2b. The evidences and proofs of God's existence

NEW TESTAMENT: Romans, 1:14-32 esp 1:18-21

7 PLATO: Laws, BK X, 758b-765c

8 ARISTOTLE: Physics, BK VII, CH 1 326a-327b; BK VIII, CH 1-6 334a-346b; CH 10 [267^{a}21-^{b}27] 354d-355d / Metaphysics, BK II, CH 2 512b-513b; BK IX, CH 8 575b-577a; BK XII, CH 6-7 601b-603b; CH 8 [1074^{a}33-^{b}1] 604d; CH 10 [1075^{b}35-1076^{a}5] 606d

12 EPICTETUS: Discourses, BK I, CH 6 110c-112b; CH 12 118d-120b; CH 16 121d-122d

18 AUGUSTINE: Confessions, BK I, par 10 3b-c; BK V, par 1 27a-b; BK VII, par 16-23 48c-50c; BK X, par 8-38 73b-81a; BK XI, par 6 90c-d / City of God, BK VIII, CH 6 268d-269c; BK X, CH 14 307c-308a / Christian Doctrine, BK I, CH 8 626c-627a

19 AQUINAS: Summa Theologica, PART I, Q 2 10c-14a esp A 3 12c-14a; Q 3, A 4, REP 2 16d-17c; Q 8 34c-38c; Q 11, A 3 49a-c; Q 19, A 5, REP 3 112d-113c; Q 44, A 1, REP 1 238b-239a; Q 65 339a-343c esp A 1, REP 3 339b-340b; Q 75, A 1, REP 1 378b-379c; Q 79, A 4, ANS 417a-418c; Q 104, AA 1-2 534c-537b; PART I-II, Q 1, A 2 610b-611b

22 CHAUCER: Knight's Tale [3003-3016] 209a-b

23 HOBBES: Leviathan, PART I, 78d-79a; 79d-80a

30 BACON: Advancement of Learning, 38a; 41b-d

31 DESCARTES: Discourse, PART IV 51b-54b / Meditations, 71d-72a; III 81d-89a; V 93a-96a / Objections and Replies, 108a-115a,c passim; 120c-123a; 126b-127c; DEF VIII 130d; POSTULATE V 131b-c; AXIOM I 131d; AXIOM IX-X 132b; PROP I-III 132b-133a; 137d-138a; 158b-162a; 168d-169a; 211c-212a; 213a-d; 217d-218a

31 SPINOZA: Ethics, PART I, DEF I 355a; DEF 3,6 355b; PROP 7 356c; PROP 11 358b-359b; PROP 14, DEMONST and COROL 1 359d-360a; PROP 20, DEMONST and COROL 1 363d-364a

32 MILTON: Psalm 136 8a-10a

33 PASCAL: Pensées, 242-244 217b-218a; 469 256a; 557 272b

34 NEWTON: Principles, BK III, GENERAL SCHOL, 369b-370a / Optics, BK III, 528b-529a; 542a-543a passim

35 LOCKE: Human Understanding, BK II, CH XVII, SECT 17 172b-c; SECT 20, 173a; BK IV, CH X, SECT I-II 349c-352a

35 BERKELEY: Human Knowledge, PREF, 404a; SECT 6-7 414b-c; SECT 25-33 417d-419a esp SECT 29-33 418c-419a; SECT 146-156 442a-444d passim

35 HUME: Human Understanding, SECT XI 497b-503c passim

37 FIELDING: Tom Jones, 187d-188a

42 KANT: Pure Reason, 143a-b [thesis]; 177b-192d; 236b-240b esp 239a-240b / Practical Reason, 353a-354d / Judgement, 593c-d; 607d-609b

44 BOSWELL: Johnson, 401a-b

46 HEGEL: Philosophy of Right, PART III, par 280 94d-95a

47 GOETHE: Faust, PART I [3431-3468] 84a-b

51 TOLSTOY: War and Peace, BK V, 196b-d; 217c-d

2c. Criticisms of the proofs of God's existence: agnosticism

19 AQUINAS: Summa Theologica, PART I, Q 2, A 1, REP 2 10d-11d; A 2 11d-12c

31 DESCARTES: Objections and Replies, 110a-111a; 112d-114c; 137d-138a

33 PASCAL: Pensées, 242 217b-218a; 428 244b; 543 266a; 547-549 266b-267a

35 HUME: Human Understanding, SECT XI 497b-503c passim, esp DIV 115 503b-c

42 KANT: Pure Reason, 33a-d; 143a-145c; 152a-153c; 177b-192d esp 177b-179c, 190a-192d;

200c-203d esp 202a-203b; 205a-208d esp
208a-b; 218d-223d; 234c-240b esp 239a-c;
241d-242c / *Practical Reason*, 291a-292c; 348b-
349b; 351b-352c / *Intro. Metaphysic of Morals*,
384a,c / *Judgement*, 567b; 568c-570a; 588a-
613a,c esp 588a-593d, 596c-599b, 600d-603d,
607d-613a,c

46 HEGEL: *Philosophy of Right*, PART III, par 280
94d-95a

49 DARWIN: *Descent of Man*, 593c

52 DOSTOEVSKY: *Brothers Karamazov*, BK V,
120d-121c; BK X, 292d-293a; BK XI, 337a-
346a esp 341c-342c

2d. The postulation of God: practical grounds for belief

33 PASCAL: *Pensées*, 184-241 205a-217b esp 233,
214b-216a; 425-427 243b-244b; 430 245a-
247b; 436-438 251a

42 KANT: *Pure Reason*, 236b-243c esp 239a-240b,
241d-242c / *Practical Reason*, 291a-292a;
314c-d; 344c-349b esp 345a-c; 351b-352c;
353a-354d / *Science of Right*, 432c-433a /
Judgement, 588a-607c esp 593d-596c, 606d-
607c; 608c-611d

52 DOSTOEVSKY: *Brothers Karamazov*, BK V,
120b-121c; BK XI, 313c-314a

53 JAMES: *Psychology*, 653a

3. Man's relation to God or the gods

3a. The fear of God or the gods

OLD TESTAMENT: *Leviticus*, 19:14,32; 25:17 /
Deuteronomy, 6:1-2,12-15; 8:6; 10:12-13,20-
22; 31:10-13 / *Joshua*, 24:14-16—(D) *Josue*,
24:14-16 / *II Samuel*, 23:3—(D) *II Kings*,
23:3 / *Nehemiah*, 5:7-13—(D) *II Esdras*,
5:7-13 / *Job*, 28:12-28 / *Psalms*, 2:10-12; 19:9;
25:12-14; 34 esp 34:9-11; 111:5,10; 112; 128—
(D) *Psalms*, 2:10-13; 18:10; 24:12-14; 33 esp
33:10-12; 110:5,10; 111; 127 / *Proverbs*, 1:7,
22-33; 2:3-5; 8:13; 9:10; 10:27; 14:26-27;
15:16,33; 16:6; 19:23; 22:4; 23:17-18; 24:21 /
Ecclesiastes, 5:2-7; 8:10-13; 12:13-14 / *Isaiah*,
8:11-14; 11:1-5; 33:6—(D) *Isaias*, 8:11-14;
11:1-5; 33:6 / *Jeremiah*, 2:19; 5:19-31—(D)
Jeremias, 2:19; 5:19-31 / *Jonah*, 1:1-16—(D)
Jonas, 1

APOCRYPHA: *Ecclesiasticus*, 1-2; 10:19-24; 15:1,
13; 19:20-24; 23:18-28; 25:10-12; 34:13-17;
40:26-27—(D) OT, *Ecclesiasticus*, 1-2; 10:23-
27; 15:1,13; 19:18-21; 23:25-38; 25:13-16;
34:14-20; 40:26-28

NEW TESTAMENT: *Acts*, 10:34-35 / *Colossians*,
3:22 / *I Peter*, 2:17 / *Revelation*, 14:6-7—(D)
Apocalypse, 14:6-7

4 HOMER: *Odyssey*, BK V [282-312] 210d-211a;
BK XVIII [124-150] 285b-c

5 AESCHYLUS: *Suppliant Maidens* [419-500] 6a-
7b / *Agamemnon* [901-954] 61c-62b / *Choephoroe* [269-301] 72d-73a; [885-1076] 78d-
80d / *Eumenides* [490-565] 86b-87a

5 SOPHOCLES: *Oedipus the King* [863-910] 107b-c
/ *Oedipus at Colonus* [258-291] 116c-d; [1448-
1485] 127b-c / *Electra* [221-250] 157d-158a

5 EURIPIDES: *Orestes* [251-316] 396c-397a

6 HERODOTUS: *History*, BK II, 78d; BK VI, 211b-c;
BK VII, 216d-218a; 218c-220a

6 THUCYDIDES: *Peloponnesian War*, BK II, 400d-
401a

7 PLATO: *Laws*, BK IX, 757a

12 LUCRETIUS: *Nature of Things*, BK I [62-158]
1d-3a; BK III [1-93] 30a-31b; [978-1023] 42d-
43b; BK V [1161-1240] 76b-77b; BK VI [43-95]
80d-81c

13 VIRGIL: *Aeneid*, BK IV [259-282] 174a-b; BK
VII [445-459] 248b-249a

14 PLUTARCH: *Pericles*, 123c-124a / *Nicias*,
435b-d / *Crassus*, 445d-446b / *Alexander*,
575a-576a / *Phocion*, 615b-d

15 TACITUS: *Histories*, BK IV, 292c-294a

18 AUGUSTINE: *Confessions*, BK V, par 2 27b-c /
Christian Doctrine, BK I, CH 15 628b-c; BK II,
CH 7 638d-639c

19 AQUINAS: *Summa Theologica*, PART I-II, Q 42,
A I, ANS 801c-802a; A 3, REP 1 802d-803c

20 AQUINAS: *Summa Theologica*, PART I-II, Q 67,
A 4, REP 2 84d-85d; Q 68, A 4, REP 4 91b-92c;
Q 69, A 3, REP 3 98c-100c; Q 99, A 6 250a-251a;
PART II-II, Q 7, A I 415c-416b; Q 19 465a-474d;
Q 22, A 2 481d-482c; Q 25, A I, REP 1 501b-502a

21 DANTE: *Divine Comedy*, HELL, III [100-136]
5a-b; PURGATORY, XIII [103-129] 73a-b

23 HOBBES: *Leviathan*, PART I, 79d-80a; 82b-c;
90b-d

29 CERVANTES: *Don Quixote*, PART II, 267b-c

32 MILTON: *Paradise Lost*, BK XII [561-566] 331b

33 PASCAL: *Pensées*, 262 221a

35 BERKELEY: *Human Knowledge*, SECT 155-156
444b-d

42 KANT: *Fund. Prin. Metaphysic of Morals*,
278b-c / *Science of Right*, 432c-433a / *Judgement*, 502d-503a; 504b-505a

43 MILL: *Utilitarianism*, 458a-b

46 HEGEL: *Philosophy of History*, PART II, 264c;
PART III, 304b

54 FREUD: *Group Psychology*, 688a-b

3b. The reproach or defiance of God or the gods

OLD TESTAMENT: *Genesis*, 4:4-9; 11:1-9 / *Exodus*,
5; 7-12; 14:10-15; 16:1-30 / *Numbers*, 11; 14;
20:1-13; 21:4-9 / *Deuteronomy*, 1:26-46; 9 /
Joshua, 22—(D) *Josue*, 22 / *I Samuel*, 12:14-
15; 15:22-23—(D) *I Kings*, 12:14-15; 15:22-
23 / *II Kings*, 19:22-23—(D) *IV Kings*, 19:22-
23 / *Job* / *Psalms*, 2; 5:8-10; 22:1-2; 44; 74;
79:12; 107:10-12—(D) *Psalms*, 2; 5:9-11;
21:2-3; 43; 73; 78:12; 106:10-12 / *Proverbs*,
14:31; 17:5 / *Isaiah*, 1:2-4; 3:8-9; 30-31; 36-
37; 45:9; 48:1-9; 59:1-15; 63:10; 65:2-7—
(D) *Isaias*, 1:2-4; 3:8-9; 30-31; 36-37; 45:9;
48:1-9; 59:1-15; 63:10; 65:2-7 / *Jeremiah* passim—(D) *Jeremias* passim / *Lamentations*,

19 Aquinas: *Summa Theologica*, PART I, Q 3, A I, REP 5 14b-15b; Q 8, A 3, ANS and REP 4 36b-37c; Q 60, A 5 313b-314c; Q 82, A 3, ANS and REP 3 433c-434c; Q 95, A 4, ANS 509b-510a; PART I-II, Q I, A 8 615a-c; Q 2, A I, REP 3 615d-616c; Q 26, A 3, REP 4 735c-736b; Q 28, A 2, CONTRARY 741a-742a; A 4, ANS 742d-743c; Q 35, A 5, REP I 775d-777a

20 Aquinas: *Summa Theologica*, PART I-II, Q 65, A 5, ANS and REP I 74c-75a; Q 66, A 6 80c-81b; Q 68, A 2, ANS 89c-90c; A 8, REP 2 95c-96c; Q 69, A 4, ANS 100c-101c; Q 70, A 3, ANS 103b-104d; Q 73, A 4, REP 3 122b-123a; A 5, ANS 123a-d; Q 77, A 4, CONTRARY and REP I 148b-149a; Q 78, A 2, REP I 153b-154a; Q 84, A I, REP I 174b-175a; Q 88, A 2, REP I 194b-195b; A 6, REP 2 198a-d; Q 89, A I, REP 3 199a-c; A 2, ANS 199c-200d; Q 99, A I, REP 2 245c-246b; Q 100, A 6, REP I 257c-258c; A 10 262b-263b; A 11, REP I 263c-264d; Q 102, A I, REP I 270c-271b; Q 109, A 3 340c-341b; PART I-II, Q I, A I, REP 3 380b-381a; A 3, REP I 381d-382c; Q 3, A 2, REP I 401a-d; Q 7, A 2 416b-d; Q 19, A 4, REP 3 467c-468b; A 12, ANS 473d-474d; Q 22, A 2, ANS 481d-482c; QQ 23-27 482c-527b; Q 180, A I, ANS and REP 2 607d-608c; A 2, REP I 608c-609c; A 7, ANS 614d-616a; Q 182, A 2, ANS 621d-623a; A 4, REP I 623d-624d; Q 184, A 2, ANS 629d-630d; A 3, ANS and REP 3 630d-632c; A 7, REP 2 636a-637a; Q 185, A 2, REP I 641c-643a; A 4, ANS 644a-645c; Q 186, A 2, REP 2 651d-652d; A 7, REP 2 658a-660a; Q 187, A 2, ANS 665a-666a; Q 188, A 2, ANS 675d-677a

21 Dante: *Divine Comedy*, PURGATORY, XV [40-81] 75d-76a; XVII [91]-XVIII [75] 79b-80c; PARADISE, I [94-142] 107b-d; III 109b-110c; v [1-12] 112a-b; VI [112-126] 114d-115a; XX [94-138] 137d-138a; XXI [52-102] 138d-139b; XXVI [1-81] 145d-146c; XXXII [139]-XXXIII [145] 156a-157d

22 Chaucer: *Troilus and Cressida*, BK V, STANZA 263-267 154b-155a / *Second Nun's Tale* 463b-471b / *Parson's Tale*, par 6, 497a; par 21 509a-b; par 31 517b-518b

23 Hobbes: *Leviathan*, PART III, 240d

25 Montaigne: *Essays*, 210d-211a

27 Shakespeare: *Henry VIII*, ACT III, SC II [435-457] 573c-d

30 Bacon: *Advancement of Learning*, 80b-81a

31 Descartes: *Meditations*, III, 88d-89a / *Objections and Replies*, 227b-228a

31 Spinoza: *Ethics*, PART V, PROP 14-16 456b-c; PROP 18-20 456d-458a; PROP 32-34 460b-d; PROP 36-37 461a-c

32 Milton: *Paradise Lost*, BK XII [561-566] 331b

33 Pascal: *Provincial Letters*, 78b-80b / *Pensées*, 430 245a-247b; 463 255a; 468 255b-256a; 471 256a-b; 476 256b-257a; 479 257b; 482-483 258a-b; 485 258b; 487-489 258b-259a; 491 259a; 544 266a; 821 331b-332a

35 Locke: *Human Understanding*, BK II, CH VII, SECT 5-6 132c-d

42 Kant: *Fund. Prin. Metaphysic of Morals*, 278b-279d / *Practical Reason*, 321b-329a esp 326b-327a

43 Mill: *Utilitarianism*, 458a-b

47 Goethe: *Faust*, PART I [1178-1185] 29b

48 Melville: *Moby Dick*, 318b

51 Tolstoy: *War and Peace*, BK XV, 631a-c

52 Dostoevsky: *Brothers Karamazov*, BK III, 54a-b; BK V, 127b-137c passim; BK VI, 164d-165a; BK XI, 313c-314d

3d. Obedience to God or the gods

Old Testament: *Genesis*, 2:15-17; 3; 22:1-18 esp 22:18; 26:4-5 / *Exodus*, 3:4-4:17; 24:1-8 / *Deuteronomy*, 4-11 passim; 27-30 passim / *Joshua*, 22; 24:1-28—(D) *Josue*, 22; 24:1-28 / *I Samuel*, 12:14-15; 15 esp 15:22-23—(D) *I Kings*, 12:14-15; 15 esp 15:22-23 / *I Kings*, 8:54-62—(D) *III Kings*, 8:54-62 / *I Chronicles*, 28:9—(D) *I Paralipomenon*, 28:9 / *Ezra*, 7:23 —(D) *I Esdras*, 7:23 / *Job* / *Ecclesiastes*, 5:1; 12:13—(D) *Ecclesiastes*, 4:17; 12:13 / *Isaiah*, 1:19-20—(D) *Isaias*, 1:19-20 / *Jeremiah* passim, esp 3, 7, 11, 35, 42-44—(D) *Jeremias* passim, esp 3, 7, 11, 35, 42-44 / *Daniel*, 7:27 / *Micah*, 6:8—(D) *Micheas*, 6:8

New Testament: *Matthew*, 6:10; 7:21; 12:46-50; 26:36-39 / *Mark*, 14:32-36 / *Luke*, 22:40-45 / *John*, 5:30; 18:10-11 / *Acts*, 5:29-32; 21:8-15 / *Romans*, 5:19 / *II Corinthians*, 10:5-6 / *Philippians*, 2:1-18 esp 2:7-8 / *II Thessalonians*, 1:7-9 / *Hebrews*, 5:8-9; 11:8

4 Homer: *Iliad*, BK I [188-222] 5a-b

5 Aeschylus: *Suppliant Maidens* [410-434] 6a-b / *Choephoroe* [269-301] 72d-73a; [885-1076] 78d-80d / *Eumenides* [490-565] 86b-87a

5 Sophocles: *Oedipus the King* [863-910] 107b-c / *Antigone* 131a-142d esp [374-378] 134b, [443-465] 134d-135a, [1351-1353] 142d / *Ajax* [666-676] 148d / *Electra* 156a-169a,c esp [23-37] 156b

5 Euripides: *Suppliants* [513-563] 262d-263b / *Helen* [1644-1692] 313d-314a,c / *Iphigenia Among the Tauri* [67-122] 411d-412b

6 Herodotus: *History*, BK I, 39c-d; BK II, 55a; BK IV, 124d-125a; 126d-127a; 150b-d; 151b-152a; BK VI, 201d-202c; BK VII, 218c-220a; BK IX, 308a-c

6 Thucydides: *Peloponnesian War*, BK I, 355b-c; 382c-d

7 Plato: *Apology*, 206b-d / *Laws*, BK IV, 681b-683b

12 Epictetus: *Discourses*, BK II, CH 16-17, 158a-161a; BK III, CH 24, 204c-d; 208d-210a; BK IV, CH I 213a-223d passim, esp 218b-219a; CH 3 224b-d; CH 7, 234b; CH 12, 242d-243c

12 Aurelius: *Meditations*, BK III, SECT 13 262c; BK V, SECT 27 272d; BK VI, SECT 10 274b-c; BK IX, SECT I 291a-c

13 Virgil: *Aeneid*, BK III [84-120] 149b-150b; BK IV [259-282] 174a-b; [356-361] 176b-177a

15 Tacitus: *Histories*, BK IV, 292c-294a

(3. Man's relation to God or the gods. 3d. Obedience to God or the gods.)

18 AUGUSTINE: *Confessions*, BK III, par 15 17a-b / *Christian Doctrine*, BK I, CH 15 628b-c
19 AQUINAS: *Summa Theologica*, PART I-II, Q 19, A 5, REP 2 705d-707a; A 6, ANS and REP 2 707a-708a
20 AQUINAS: *Summa Theologica*, PART I-II, Q 88, A 1, REP 2 193a-194b; Q 96, A 4 233a-d; Q 97, A 3, REP 1 237b-238b; PART II-II, Q 2, A 9, ANS 398c-399b; Q 4, A 7, REP 3 407d-409a; Q 33, A 7, REP 5 556a-557d; Q 186, A 7, REP 3 658d-660a; PART III, Q 7, A 3, REP 2 747b-748a
21 DANTE: *Divine Comedy*, PARADISE, III [1]-V [87] 109b-113a; VII [19-120] 115b-116b
22 CHAUCER: *Tale of Man of Law* [5240-5253] 249b / *Clerk's Tale* 296a-318a esp [9018-9038] 316b-317a / *Tale of Melibeus*, par 17 407b-408a / *Parson's Tale*, par 24 511a-b
23 HOBBES: *Leviathan*, PART I, 82b-d; PART II, 137b-138b; 154b-155c; 159d-160a; 162a; PART III, 199b-204a; 240a-241a; 244d-246a
25 MONTAIGNE: *Essays*, 213a-215a; 233a-234a; 238c-239c
26 SHAKESPEARE: *Richard III*, ACT II, SC II [77-95] 120b-c
32 MILTON: *Paradise Lost* 93a-333a esp BK IV [411-439] 161b-162a, [720-749] 168a-b, BK V [506-543] 186a-187a, BK VI [164-188] 199b-200a, BK VII [449-518] 227a-228b, BK VIII [311-333] 239a-b, [630-643] 246a, BK IX [366-375] 255b, [647-654] 261b, BK X [1013]-BK XI [44] 296b-300a, BK XI [133-161] 302a-b, BK XII [386-410] 327b-328a, [561-566] 331b / *Samson Agonistes* [373-419] 347b-348b / *Areopagitica*, 394b-395b
33 PASCAL: *Pensées*, 460 254b; 476 256b-257a; 482 258a; 489,491 259a; 531 264b; 539 265b
35 LOCKE: *Toleration*, 15d-16a; 16c / *Civil Government*, CH II, SECT 6 26b-c / *Human Understanding*, BK I, CH II, SECT 5-6 105a-c
38 MONTESQUIEU: *Spirit of Laws*, BK I, 2a-b; BK XII, 85d-86a
41 GIBBON: *Decline and Fall*, 259b-260a
42 KANT: *Practical Reason*, 321b-329a; 345c-d / *Intro. Metaphysic of Morals*, 383b,d-384a,c / *Judgement*, 504b-505a; 509a-c; 593a-d; 611a-c
43 MILL: *Liberty*, 296b-d
44 BOSWELL: *Johnson*, 394a
48 MELVILLE: *Moby Dick*, 30a-36b
52 DOSTOEVSKY: *Brothers Karamazov*, BK III, 64c-67a; BK V, 127b-137c passim; BK VII, 177b-180a
54 FREUD: *General Introduction*, 582a / *Civilization and Its Discontents*, 776b

3e. The worship of God or the gods: prayer, propitiation, sacrifice

OLD TESTAMENT: *Genesis*, 4:3-7; 15:7-21; 22:1-18 / *Exodus* passim, esp 12, 13:11-16, 15:1-21, 23:18-19 / *Leviticus* passim, esp 2, 4-7, 16-17, 22:1-24:9, 27:1-34 / *Numbers*, 5-8; 15; 18-19;

28-30 / *Deuteronomy*, 10-12; 14:22-17:1 / *Joshua*, 22:10-34—(D) *Josue*, 22:10-34 / *I Samuel*, 15 esp 15:22-23—(D) *I Kings*, 15 esp 15:22-23 / *I Kings*, 8; 18:21-39—(D) *III Kings*, 8; 18:21-39 / *II Chronicles*, 5-8; 29-31—(D) *II Paralipomenon*, 5-8; 29-31 / *Nehemiah*, 10:29-39—(D) *II Esdras*, 10:29-39 / *Psalms* / *Proverbs*, 15:8; 21:3 / *Isaiah*, 1:11-20; 58—(D) *Isaias*, 1:11-20; 58 / *Lamentations*, 5 / *Ezekiel*, 43:18-27; 45:13-46:24—(D) *Ezechiel*, 43:18-27; 45:13-46:24 / *Hosea*, 6 esp 6:6; 8—(D) *Osee*, 6 esp 6:6; 8 / *Joel*, 2:12-18 / *Amos*, 4 / *Micah*, 6:6-8—(D) *Micheas*, 6:6-8 / *Malachi*, 1:6-14—(D) *Malachias*, 1:6-14
APOCRYPHA: *Tobit*, 13—(D) OT, *Tobias*, 13 / *Rest of Esther*, 13:12-14—(D) OT, *Esther*, 13:12-14 / *Ecclesiasticus*, 18:22-23; 35—(D) OT, *Ecclesiasticus*, 18:22-23; 35
NEW TESTAMENT: *Matthew*, 6:1-18; 9:9-13; 26:36-44 / *Mark*, 9:14-29 esp 9:29; 12:32-33—(D) *Mark*, 9:13-28 esp 9:28; 12:32-33 / *Luke*, 11:1-13; 18:1-14 / *John*, 17 / *Colossians*, 4:2-4 / *I Thessalonians*, 5:17 / *Hebrews*, 10:1-22; 13:15-16 / *Revelation*, 5—(D) *Apocalypse*, 5
4 HOMER: *Iliad*, BK I [428-487] 7c-8a; BK II [394-431] 14a-b; BK IX [485-526] 62a-b / *Odyssey*, BK III [1-68] 193a-d
5 AESCHYLUS: *Suppliant Maidens* [1-175] 1a-3a; [525-600] 7c-8d; [1018-1073] 13d-14a,c / *Seven Against Thebes* [80-320] 28a-30d
5 SOPHOCLES: *Oedipus the King* [151-215] 100c-101a; [863-910] 107b-c / *Oedipus at Colonus* [465-509] 118b-d / *Electra* [516-576] 160a-c / *Philoctetes* [1440-1444] 195a,c
5 EURIPIDES: *Trojan Women* [1277-1283] 280d / *Bacchantes* 340a-352a,c esp [200-209] 341c, [337-433] 342c-343b / *Iphigenia at Aulis* 425a-439d
5 ARISTOPHANES: *Peace* [173-195] 528a; [922-1126] 536c-539a / *Birds* 542a-563d
6 HERODOTUS: *History*, BK I, 6a; 10a-11d; 20d-22a; 31a-c; 40d-41b; 48c; BK II, 57b-60a; 79a-c; 86c; BK III, 95a-c; BK IV, 126d-127a; 134a; 140c-d; 142b-c; 155c-156a; 156d-157a; BK V, 175d-176a; BK VI, 196d-197a; 199d-200a; 200d; 205c-d; BK VII, 226c; 235a; 248b-c; 250b-d; BK VIII, 267a; 270b-c; 282b-c
6 THUCYDIDES: *Peloponnesian War*, BK II, 407a-b; BK VI, 517d-518a
7 PLATO: *Phaedrus*, 127c-128a / *Symposium*, 156d-157a / *Euthyphro*, 197d-198c / *Phaedo*, 251d / *Republic*, BK I, 295a-d; 297a-b; BK II, 313d-314d; BK IV, 345d-346a / *Timaeus*, 447a / *Laws*, BK IV, 683a-b; BK VII, 721a-c; BK VIII, 731d-732d; BK X, 768d-769c; BK XII, 791d-792a
8 ARISTOTLE: *Topics*, BK I, CH 11 [105^{a}2-6] 148c / *Heavens*, BK I, CH 1 [268^{a}12-15] 359a-b
9 ARISTOTLE: *Ethics*, BK I, CH 12 347a-b; BK IV, CH 2 [1122^{b}18-23] 369c; BK VIII, CH 9 [1160^{a}19-29] 412b-c / *Politics*, BK VII, CH 9 [1329^{a}26-34] 533d

12 LUCRETIUS: *Nature of Things*, BK I [1–43] 1a-d; [80–101] 2a-b; BK II [589–660] 22c-23b; BK III [41–58] 30c-d; BK V [1194–1240] 76d-77b; BK VI [68–79] 81a-b

12 EPICTETUS: *Discourses*, BK I, CH 16 121d-122d

12 AURELIUS: *Meditations*, BK V, SECT 7 269d; BK IX, SECT 40 295b; BK XII, SECT 14 308c

13 VIRGIL: *Eclogues*, V [62–80] 18a-b / *Aeneid* 103a-379a passim, esp BK II [108–125] 127a-b, BK III [84–120] 149b-150b, [543–550] 162a, BK IV [54–67] 168b-169a, [198–221] 172b-173a, BK VI [42–76] 212a-213a, BK VIII [558–584] 274a-b, BK IX [621–631] 295b-296a, BK XI [783–798] 349b

14 PLUTARCH: *Theseus* 1a-15a,c passim / *Numa Pompilius* 49a-61d esp 56d-57b / *Camillus*, 104b-d; 107b-d / *Fabius*, 142d-143b / *Coriolanus*, 185b-186a / *Aemilius Paulus*, 214b-d / *Pelopidas*, 239d-240c / *Marcellus*, 247c-249d / *Lucullus*, 404d-405a / *Agesilaus*, 483a-b / *Alexander*, 541a-d

15 TACITUS: *Annals*, BK III, 59d-60c; BK XII, 112d-113a / *Histories*, BK II, 214d-215a; BK IV, 282d-283b; 292c-294a; BK V, 296a

16 KEPLER: *Harmonies of the World*, 1009a; 1011a; 1050b; 1080a-b; 1085b

18 AUGUSTINE: *Confessions*, BK I, par 1 1a-b; BK XIII, par 1 110d-111a / *City of God*, BK VII, CH 27–31 259c-262a; BK X 298b,d-322a,c / *Christian Doctrine*, BK I, CH 6 626a-b

19 AQUINAS: *Summa Theologica*, PART I–II, Q 30, A 1, REP 1 749a-d

20 AQUINAS: *Summa Theologica*, PART I–II, Q 99, A 3 247a-248a; A 4, REP 2 248a-d; QQ 101–103 265d-304a; PART I–II, Q 30, A 4, REP 1 536a-d; Q 32, A 2, ANS 541a-542c; QQ 179–189 606a-700d esp Q 181, A 3, REP 3 618c-619b, Q 182, A 2, REP 3 621d-623a, Q 186, A 4, ANS 655c-656b, A 5, REP 5 656c-657d, A 6, REP 2 657d-658d, Q 188, A 1, REP 1 674d-675d; PART III, QQ 21–22 823d-833a; Q 25 839c-845a; Q 60, A 5, ANS 850b-851b; Q 62, A 5, ANS 862b-863a; Q 63, A 2, ANS 865c-866c; A 4, REP 1,3 867d-868b; A 5, ANS 868c-869b; A 6, ANS 869b-870b; PART III SUPPL, QQ 71–72 900d-922b; Q 99, A 3, REP 2 1081d-1083a

21 DANTE: *Divine Comedy*, PURGATORY, III [133–145] 57b-c; IV [127–135] 58d; VI [25–48] 61a-b; XI [1–36] 68d-69a; PARADISE, V [13–84] 112b-113a; XIV [67–108] 127c-128a; XX [31–138] 137a-138a passim; XXXIII [1–45] 156b-c

22 CHAUCER: *Troilus and Cressida*, BK V, STANZA 263–267 154b-155a / *Knight's Tale* [2209–2437] 196b-200a / *Summoner's Tale* [7455–7529] 288a-289a / *Franklin's Tale* [11,176–206] 353b-354a; [11,340–398] 356b-357a / *Prioress's Tale* 391a-395b / *Parson's Tale*, par 93–94 547b-548a

23 HOBBES: *Leviathan*, PART I, 80c; 81c-d; PART II, 154d-155a; 161b-163d; PART III, 182d-183b; PART IV, 261a-c

24 RABELAIS: *Gargantua and Pantagruel*, BK II, 117c-118a; BK IV, 265b-c

25 MONTAIGNE: *Essays*, 91b-c; 152b-156d; 246b-d; 300c-d

26 SHAKESPEARE: *Henry V*, ACT IV, SC VIII [96–131] 561c-d

27 SHAKESPEARE: *Hamlet*, ACT III, SC III [36–96] 53d-54b

31 SPINOZA: *Ethics*, PART I, APPENDIX, 369b-371d passim

32 MILTON: *Paradise Lost*, BK III [185–197] 139b; BK IV [720–735] 168a-b; BK V [136–208] 178a-179b; BK VII [550–640] 229a-231a; BK X [1086]–BK XI [71] 298a-300b / *Areopagitica*, 402a-b

33 PASCAL: *Pensées*, 431 247b; 476 256b-257a; 487–489 258b-259a; 491 259a; 499 260b; 504 261a; 513–514 262a-263a

35 LOCKE: *Toleration*, 3b-5c; 10c-15a

35 HUME: *Human Understanding*, SECT V, DIV 41, 468a-b

37 FIELDING: *Tom Jones*, 187d-188a

38 MONTESQUIEU: *Spirit of Laws*, BK XXV, 209a-b; 209d-210a; 211a-c

38 ROUSSEAU: *Social Contract*, BK IV, 437a-c

40 GIBBON: *Decline and Fall*, 59c-60a; 81d-82a; 93b-c; 98a; 121a-b; 180d-182c esp 181b-c; 184d-185d; 208a-211a passim, esp 209a; 327d-328b; 349c-350b; 356d-358a; 457b,d-467d passim; 547a-b; 583d-584b

41 GIBBON: *Decline and Fall*, 110b-c; 195a-198d; 207a-208c; 226a-228a; 232c-233c

42 KANT: *Judgement*, 504b-505a; 509a-c

43 MILL: *Liberty*, 307d-309a

44 BOSWELL: *Johnson*, 52c-53a; 394a; 481d-482d

46 HEGEL: *Philosophy of History*, PART I, 224a-225a; 227c-228a; 234d-235c; 245b-247b; 253c-254b; PART III, 291d-292b; PART IV, 322a-c

47 GOETHE: *Faust*, PART I [3587–3619] 87b-88a; PART II [8568–8603] 208b-209b

48 MELVILLE: *Moby Dick*, 30a-36b; 39a-b; 130b-131a; 370b-371b

51 TOLSTOY: *War and Peace*, BK III, 122b-c; BK VII, 281d-282a; BK VIII, 323b; BK IX, 373b-377b; BK X, 435c-436c; BK XII, 544b-545a; 553c-554a; BK XIII, 585b-d

52 DOSTOEVSKY: *Brothers Karamazov*, BK V, 127b-137c passim; BK VI, 164d-165a; 167b-c

53 JAMES: *Psychology*, 203a-204b

3f. The imitation of God or the gods: the divine element in human nature; the deification of men; man as the image of God

OLD TESTAMENT: *Genesis*, 1:26–27; 3 esp 3:4–5, 3:22; 5:1–2; 9:6 / *Exodus*, 7:1 / *Leviticus*, 11:44–45; 19:2; 20:7–8 / *Psalms*, 82:6–7—(D) *Psalms*, 81:6–7 / *Isaiah*, 40:10–31; 42:8; 46—(D) *Isaias*, 40:10–31; 42:8; 46 / *Ezekiel*, 16:17–19; 28:1–19—(D) *Ezechiel*, 16:17–19; 28:1–19 / *Daniel*, 6:7–9

APOCRYPHA: *Judith*, 3:8; 5:23–6:4—(D) OT, *Judith*, 3:12–13; 5:27–6:4 / *Wisdom of Solomon*,

(3. *Man's relation to God or the gods. 3f. The imitation of God or the gods: the divine element in human nature; the deification of men; man as the image of God.*)

2:23; 13-15—(D) OT, *Book of Wisdom*, 2:23; 13-15 / *Ecclesiasticus*, 17:1-3—(D) OT, *Ecclesiasticus*, 17:1-3

NEW TESTAMENT: *John*, 10:34-35 / *Acts*, 12:21-23; 14:7-18; 17:27-29; 28:3-6 / *Romans*, 1:14-32 / *I Corinthians*, 11:7; 15:49 / *II Corinthians*, 3:18 / *Colossians*, 3:8-10 / *II Thessalonians*, 2:3-4 / *James*, 3:9 / *I Peter*, 1:15-16 / *II Peter*, 1:3-4

6 HERODOTUS: *History*, BK I, 7a-b; 12d-13b; 14a-d; BK II, 79d-80a; BK IV, 140c-141a; BK V, 168d-169a; 183d-184a; BK VII, 217c; 235b-c

7 PLATO: *Phaedrus*, 127c-128a / *Ion*, 144b-145c / *Republic*, BK II-III, 320c-328a / *Timaeus*, 452c-d; 466a-b; 476a-b / *Theaetetus*, 530b-531a / *Laws*, BK IV, 681b-683b; BK V, 686d-687c

8 ARISTOTLE: *Metaphysics*, BK I, CH 2 [982ᵇ28-983ᵃ11] 501a-b; BK XII, CH 7 [1072ᵇ14-29] 602d-603a; CH 9 605a-d / *Soul*, BK II, CH 4 [415ᵃ22-ᵇ8] 645c-d

9 ARISTOTLE: *Ethics*, BK I, CH 9 [1099ᵇ9-18] 345a; CH 12 347a-b; BK VII, CH I [1145ᵃ15-33] 395a-b; BK X, CH 8 [1178ᵇ8-27] 433b-c

12 LUCRETIUS: *Nature of Things*, BK V [1-54] 61a-d

12 EPICTETUS: *Discourses*, BK I, CH 3 108b-c; CH 6 110c-112b; CH 9 114c-116b; CH 13-14 120b-121c; CH 17 122d-124a esp 123d; BK II, CH 7-8 145b-147c; CH 14, 153d-154c; BK III, CH 13, 188b-d; BK IV, CH 11, 240d-241a

12 AURELIUS: *Meditations*, BK II, SECT I 256b,d; SECT 13 258c; BK III, SECT 12-13 262b-c; BK V, SECT 27 272d; BK XII, SECT 2-3 307b-d

13 VIRGIL: *Aeneid*, BK I [283-290] 110b-111a; [586-593] 119a-b

14 PLUTARCH: *Romulus*, 27d-29c / *Numa Pompilius*, 50d-51c; 52b-53c / *Alexander*, 541a-542a; 553b-554b / *Dion*, 784d-785a

15 TACITUS: *Annals*, BK I, 4c-d; BK IV, 73b-d; 80c-d / *Histories*, BK IV, 285d-286a; 287b

16 KEPLER: *Epitome*, BK IV, 849a-b / *Harmonies of the World*, 1038a; 1048a

17 PLOTINUS: *First Ennead*, TR II 6b-10a / *Second Ennead*, TR IX, CH 15 74d-75b / *Fourth Ennead*, TR III, CH 12, 148d

18 AUGUSTINE: *Confessions*, BK II, par 14 12a-b; BK IV, par 26 25c-d; par 31 26c-27a; BK VI, par 4 36a-b; BK XIII, par 32 119a-b / *City of God*, BK VIII, CH 8 270a-d; BK XI, CH 26-28 336d-338d; BK XII, CH 23 357d-358a / *Christian Doctrine*, BK I, CH 22 629b-630a

19 AQUINAS: *Summa Theologica*, PART I, Q 3, A I, REP 2 14b-15b; Q 14, A 2, REP 3 76d-77d; Q 26, A 4 151c-152a,c; Q 27, A I, ANS 153b-154b; Q 59, A I, CONTRARY 306c-307b; Q 72, A I, REP 3 368b-369d; Q 77, A 2, ANS and REP 1 401b-d; Q 88, A 3, REP 3 472c-473a; Q 91, A

4, REP 1-2 487d-488c; Q 92, A 2, ANS 489d-490c; Q 93 492a-501c; Q 106, A I, REP 3 545d-546d; PART I-II, Q I, A 8, 615a-c; Q 2, A 4, REP I 618a-d; Q 3, A 5, REP I 626b-627a

20 AQUINAS: *Summa Theologica*, PART I-II, Q 55, A 2, REP 3 27a-d; Q 87, A 8, REP 2 191d-192d; Q 93, A 3 217b-218a; A 6, ANS 219d-220d; Q 110, A 4, ANS 350d-351d; PART II-II, Q 2, A 9, REP 3 398c-399b; Q 10, A 11, ANS 435d-436b; Q 19, A 3, REP I 466d-467c; Q 31, A 3, REP 2 538b-539c; PART III, Q 4, A I, REP 2 730d-731d; PART III SUPPL, Q 71, A 12, CONTRARY 914c-915c; Q 75, A I, REP 4 935b-937a; Q 91, A 2, CONTRARY 1017c-1020c; Q 92, A 3, REP 9 1034b-1037c; Q 93, A I, REP I 1037d-1039a

21 DANTE: *Divine Comedy*, PURGATORY, XVI [85-90] 77d; XXV [58-78] 92a; PARADISE, V [19-24] 112b; VII [64-84] 115d-116a; XIII [52-78] 126a-b

22 CHAUCER: *Franklin's Tale* [11,189-192] 353b-354a

23 HOBBES: *Leviathan*, PART I, 82b-c; PART IV, 263a-d

25 MONTAIGNE: *Essays*, 215a; 233b-234a; 248a-c; 256c-d; 294a-b; 541d-543a,c

27 SHAKESPEARE: *Hamlet*, ACT II, SC II [314-322] 43d; ACT IV, SC IV [33-66] 59a-c

28 HARVEY: *On Animal Generation*, 428b-c

30 BACON: *Advancement of Learning*, 41b-d; 80b-81a

31 DESCARTES: *Objections and Replies*, 214a-d

32 MILTON: *Paradise Lost*, BK II [345-353] 118b-119a; BK VII [150-173] 220b-221a; [519-528] 228b; BK XI [466-522] 309b-310b / *Areopagitica*, 384a

33 PASCAL: *Pensées*, 430-431 245a-247b; 434-435 248a-251a; 485 258b; 537 265b; 555 270a

35 LOCKE: *Civil Government*, CH II, SECT 6 26b-c

37 FIELDING: *Tom Jones*, 187d-188a

40 GIBBON: *Decline and Fall*, 12b-c; 28b-d; 547a-c

41 GIBBON: *Decline and Fall*, 136b; 379b-d

46 HEGEL: *Philosophy of Right*, ADDITIONS, 90, 130d / *Philosophy of History*, INTRO, 168b-d; PART I, 224a-228a; 234d-235c; 245a; PART II, 266d-267a; 268b-271c esp 270c-271c; PART III, 306a-d; 308a-b; PART IV, 339b-d; 349c-350c

47 GOETHE: *Faust*, PART I [614-736] 17a-19b; [1566-1569] 38a

48 MELVILLE: *Moby Dick*, 84b-85a

51 TOLSTOY: *War and Peace*, BK XI, 525c-526b

52 DOSTOEVSKY: *Brothers Karamazov*, BK V, 121d-122c; BK XI, 313c-314d; 345a-c

54 FREUD: *Group Psychology*, 692a-693a esp 693a / *Civilization and Its Discontents*, 778d-779a; 790d

4. The divine nature in itself: the divine attributes

7 PLATO: *Phaedrus*, 126a / *Symposium*, 167b-d

9 ARISTOTLE: *Ethics*, BK X, CH 8 [1178ᵇ8-23] 433b-c

12 Epictetus: *Discourses*, bk II, ch 8, 146a; bk III, ch 13, 188b-c

17 Plotinus: *Fifth Ennead*, tr i–vi 208a-237d passim / *Sixth Ennead*, tr vii–ix 321b-360d passim

18 Augustine: *Confessions*, bk I, par 4 2a; bk IV, par 29 26b; bk VII, par 1–8, 43b-45d / *City of God*, bk VIII, ch 6 268d-269c

19 Aquinas: *Summa Theologica*, part I, QQ 3–11 14a-50b; Q 84, A 2, ans 442b-443c

21 Dante: *Divine Comedy*, paradise, xxxiii [76–145] 157a-d

23 Hobbes: *Leviathan*, part II, 162a-163b; part IV, 271b-c

31 Descartes: *Discourse*, part IV, 52b-d / *Meditations*, iii 81d-89a / *Objections and Replies*, prop iii 132d-133a; 211c-212a; 232b

31 Spinoza: *Ethics*, part I 355a-372d esp def 4,6 355b, prop 5 356b, prop 8–13 356d-359d, prop 14, corol 2–prop 15 360a-361d, prop 19–20 363c-364a; part II, prop 1–2 373d-374a

34 Newton: *Principles*, bk III, general schol, 369b-371a / *Optics*, bk III, 542a-543a

35 Locke: *Human Understanding*, bk I, ch III, sect 15 116c-d; bk II, ch XVII, sect 1 167d-168a; ch XXIII, sect 33–35 212d-213c; bk III, ch VI, sect 11–12 271b-272b

35 Berkeley: *Human Knowledge*, sect 146 442a-b

41 Gibbon: *Decline and Fall*, 229c-230b

42 Kant: *Pure Reason*, 187a-c; 190c; 236b-240b esp 239a-c / *Practical Reason*, 303b-304a; 325d-326a; 344b-c; 345a-c; 347d-348b; 350c-351a; 352a-c / *Judgement*, 592a-c; 608c-611d

46 Hegel: *Philosophy of Right*, additions, 161 143a-b

51 Tolstoy: *War and Peace*, bk v, 196b-d

4a. The identity of essence and existence in God: the necessity of a being whose essence involves its existence

Old Testament: *Exodus*, 3:13–14

8 Aristotle: *Metaphysics*, bk XII, ch 7 [1072b 4–14] 602c-d

17 Plotinus: *Sixth Ennead*, tr VIII, ch 14 349d-350c; ch 18–21 351d-353d

18 Augustine: *Confessions*, bk VII, par 23, 50c / *City of God*, bk VIII, ch II, 272c / *Christian Doctrine*, bk I, ch 32 633c-d

19 Aquinas: *Summa Theologica*, part I, Q 2, A 3, ans 12c-14a; Q 3, A 4 16d-17c; A 7, ans and rep 1 19a-c; Q 4, A 1, rep 3 20d-21b; A 2, ans and rep 3 21b-22b; A 3, rep 3 22b-23b; Q 6, A 3 29c-30b; Q 8, A 1, ans 34d-35c; Q 10, A 2, ans and rep 3 41d-42c; Q 11, A 4, ans 49d-50b; Q 13, A 11, ans 73c-74b; Q 14, A 13, rep 1 86d-88c; Q 19, A 3, rep 6 110b-111c; Q 44, A 1, ans 238b-239a; Q 50, A 2, rep 3 270a-272a; Q 54, A 1, ans 285a-d; A 3, rep 2 286c-287b; Q 75, A 5, rep 4 382a-383b; part I–II, Q 3, A 7, ans 628a-d

20 Aquinas: *Summa Theologica*, part III, Q 3, A 2, rep 3 724a-c

31 Descartes: *Meditations*, iii 81d-89a; v 93a-96a / *Objections and Replies*, 110a-112a; 112d-114c; 126b-127c; postulate v 131b-c; axiom I 131d; axiom x 132b; prop I 132b-c; 158b-162a; 217d-218a

31 Spinoza: *Ethics*, part I, def I 355a; def 6–8 355b-c; prop 6–8 356b-357d; prop II 358b-359b; prop 20 363d-364a; prop 24 365a; prop 34 369a

33 Pascal: *Pensées*, 469 256a

42 Kant: *Pure Reason*, 143a-145c; 153a; 177b-192d esp 177b-179c, 187a-c, 192c-d; 205a-b; 239a-c / *Practical Reason*, 344c-355d esp 353a-354d / *Judgement*, 570b-571c; 606d-609b esp 608b-609a

46 Hegel: *Philosophy of Right*, part III, par 280, 95a / *Philosophy of History*, part III, 305c-306c

4b. The unity and simplicity of the divine nature

8 Aristotle: *Physics*, bk VIII, ch 10 353b-355d / *Metaphysics*, bk XII, ch 7 [1073ᵃ2–11] 603a-b; ch 8 [1074ᵃ32–39] 604d; ch 9 [1075ᵃ5–11] 605c-d

9 Aristotle: *Ethics*, bk VII, ch 14 [1154ᵇ20–31] 406c

17 Plotinus: *Sixth Ennead*, tr IX 353d-360d

18 Augustine: *Confessions*, bk I, par 10 3b-c; par 12 4a; bk IV, par 24 25b-c; par 29 26b; bk VII, par 2 43c-44a; par 16 48c-49a; par 21 49d-50a; bk XIII, par 4 111c; par 19 115c-d / *City of God*, bk VIII, ch 6 268d-269c; ch II, 272c; bk XI, ch 10 327d-328d / *Christian Doctrine*, bk I, ch 5 625d-626a; ch 32 633c-d

19 Aquinas: *Summa Theologica*, part I, Q 3 14a-20c; Q 4, A 2, rep 1–2 21b-22b; A 3 22b-23b; Q 6, A 3 29c-30b; Q 7, A 2 31d-32c; Q 8, A 2, rep 2–3 35c-36b; A 4 37c-38c; Q 11 46d-50b; Q 13, A 1, rep 2–3 62c-63c; A 4, rep 3 65c-66b; Q 14, A 1, rep 2 75d-76c; A 4 78b-79a; Q 26, A 1, rep 1 150b-c; Q 27, A 1, rep 2 153b-154b; Q 28, A 2, rep 1 158d-160a; Q 30, A 1, rep 3–4 167a-168a; A 3 169b-170c; Q 40, A 1, rep 1 213b-214b; Q 44, A 1, ans 238b-239a; Q 47, A 1 256a-257b; Q 50, A 2, rep 3 270a-272a; A 3, rep 2 272a-273b; Q 54, A 1, ans 285a-d; A 3, rep 2 286c-287b; Q 57, A 1, ans 295a-d; Q 84, A 2, ans and rep 3 442b-443c; Q 88, A 2, rep 4 471c-472c; part I–II, Q 18, A 1, ans 694a-d

20 Aquinas: *Summa Theologica*, part I–II, Q 49, A 4, ans 5a-6a; Q 50, A 6, ans 11a-12a; Q 73, A 1, rep 3 119c-120c; part III, Q 2, A 2, ans and rep 1 711d-712d; Q 3, A 2, rep 3 724a-c; A 3 724c-725b; Q 6, A 5, rep 2 744a-d

21 Dante: *Divine Comedy*, paradise, XIII [52–66] 126a; xxiv [115–154] 143d-144b; xxix [127–145] 151c-d; xxxiii [76–145] 157a-d

23 Hobbes: *Leviathan*, part II, 151d

31 Descartes: *Discourse*, part IV, 52a-d / *Meditations*, iii, 86a-88b esp 88b / *Objections and Replies*, 122b-c; 232b

4e. The infinity of God: the freedom of an infinite being

4f. The perfection or goodness of God

42 KANT: *Practical Reason*, 347d-348b / *Judgement*, 594d [fn 1]

5. The divine nature in relation to the world or creatures

7 PLATO: *Republic*, BK II, 321d-322d / *Timaeus*, 447b-458b; 465d-466a

8 ARISTOTLE: *Physics*, BK VII, CH I 326a-327b; BK VIII, CH I-6 334a-346b

9 ARISTOTLE: *Ethics*, BK VII, CH 14 [1154^{b}20–31] 406c; BK X, CH 8 [1178^{b}8–27] 433b-c

12 EPICTETUS: *Discourses*, BK III, CH 22, 195a-b; BK IV, CH 11, 240d-241a

12 AURELIUS: *Meditations*, BK II, SECT 4 257b; BK V, SECT 8 269d-270b; BK VI, SECT 40–46 277d-278d

16 KEPLER: *Harmonies of the World*, 1017b-1018a; 1071b

17 PLOTINUS: *Fourth Ennead*, TR III, CH 13 149b-d

18 AUGUSTINE: *Confessions*, BK I, par 4 2a; par 10 3b-c; BK IV, par 25 25c; BK IV, par 31–BK V, par 1 26c-27b; BK VII, par 1–8, 43b-45d; par 16–23 48c-50c; BK X, par 38 81a; BK XI, par 6 90c-d; BK XIII, par 19 115c-d / *City of God*, BK VII, CH 29–31 261a-262a; BK VIII, CH 1–10 264b,d-271d; BK X, CH 1–2 298b,d-300a; BK XI, CH 24 335c-336a / *Christian Doctrine*, BK I, CH 9–10 627a-b

19 AQUINAS: *Summa Theologica*, PART I, QQ 14–25 75c-150a; Q 84, A 2, ANS 442b-443c

21 DANTE: *Divine Comedy*, PARADISE, I [1–3] 106a; [97–142] 107b-d; II [112–148] 109a-b; X [1–27] 120b-c; XIII [52–87] 126a-b; XIX [40–90] 135c-136a; XXVII [100–120] 148b-c; XXVIII 148d-150b; XXXIII [76–145] 157a-d

28 HARVEY: *On Animal Generation*, 428c-d

30 BACON: *Advancement of Learning*, 38a

31 DESCARTES: *Discourse*, PART IV, 52a-d / *Objections and Replies*, 123c-d; 214a-d; 229c-d

32 MILTON: *Paradise Lost*, BK VIII [412–436] 241a-b

34 NEWTON: *Principles*, BK III, GENERAL SCHOL, 369b-371a / *Optics*, BK III, 542a-543a

35 LOCKE: *Human Understanding*, BK II, CH XVII, SECT 1 167d-168a; BK III, CH VI, SECT 11–12 271b-272b

35 BERKELEY: *Human Knowledge*, SECT 57 423d-424a

35 HUME: *Human Understanding*, SECT XI, DIV 106 499b-c; DIV 113 502a-d

37 FIELDING: *Tom Jones*, 186c-d; 187d-188a

38 ROUSSEAU: *Social Contract*, BK IV, 439a

40 GIBBON: *Decline and Fall*, 81b-c; 183c;307b-c; 346b-347a

42 KANT: *Practical Reason*, 303b-304a; 321b-c; 325d-326a; 327d-328b; 342c; 344b-c; 345a-c; 347d-348b; 350c-351a; 352a-c / *Judgement*, 592a-c

52 DOSTOEVSKY: *Brothers Karamazov*, BK V, 120d-121c

5a. God as first and as exemplar cause: the relation of divine to natural causation

OLD TESTAMENT: *Genesis*, 1–2; 7:4 / *Nehemiah*, 9:6—(D) II *Esdras*, 9:6 / *Job*, 9:1–9; 12; 26:7–14; 28:24–27; 36:24-42:2 / *Psalms*, 8:3; 33:6–9; 65:5–13; 74:16–17; 89:11–12; 95:4-5; 96:5; 102:25–27; 104; 107:23–30; 115:3; 119:73; 121:2; 136:5–9; 146:5-6; 147–148—(D) *Psalms*, 8:4; 32:6-9; 64:6–14; 73:16–17; 88:12-13; 94:4-5; 95:5; 101:26–28; 103; 106:23–30; 113:3; 118:73; 120:2; 135:5–9; 145:5-6; 146-148 / *Proverbs*, 3:19 / *Isaiah*, 40:26–28; 42:5; 44:24; 45:7–12,18; 48:13; 51:13; 65:17—(D) *Isaias*, 40:26–28; 42:5; 44:24; 45:7–12,18; 48:13; 51:13; 65:17 / *Jeremiah*, 10:12; 27:5; 31:35; 51:15-16—(D) *Jeremias*, 10:12; 27:5; 31:35; 51:15-16 / *Amos*, 5:8 / *Zechariah*, 12:1 —(D) *Zacharias*, 12:1 / *Malachi*, 2:10—(D) *Malachias*, 2:10

APOCRYPHA: *Judith*, 16:14—(D) OT, *Judith*, 16:17 / *Rest of Esther*, 13:10—(D) OT, *Esther*, 13:10 / *Wisdom of Solomon*, 1:14; 2:23; 9:1–2; 11:17 —(D) OT, *Book of Wisdom*, 1:14; 2:23; 9:1–2; 11:18 / *Ecclesiasticus*, 18:1; 24:8-9; 33:10–13; 39:16–35; 43—(D) OT, *Ecclesiasticus*, 18:1; 24:12–14; 33:10–14; 39:21–41; 43 / *Bel and Dragon*, 5—(D) OT, *Daniel*, 14:4 / II *Maccabees*, 7:23,28—(D) OT, II *Machabees*, 7:23,28

NEW TESTAMENT: *John*, 1:1–3 / *Acts*, 7:49-50; 14:14–17; 17:22–28 / *Colossians*, 1:16–17 / *Hebrews*, 1:10–11; 2:10; 3:4; 11:3 / II *Peter*, 3:5–7 / *Revelation*, 4:11; 10:6; 14:7—(D) *Apocalypse*, 4:11; 10:6; 14:7

7 PLATO: *Republic*, BK X, 427c-429c / *Timaeus*, 447a-448b / *Sophist*, 577d-578b / *Statesman*, 587a-589c / *Laws*, BK X, 758b-765c esp 762b-765c

8 ARISTOTLE: *Physics*, BK VIII, CH 1–6 334a-346b / *Generation and Corruption*, BK II, CH 10 [336^{b}25–34] 438d; [337^{a}15–23] 439a-b / *Metaphysics*, BK I, CH 2 [983^{a}7–9] 501b; BK XII, CH 4 [1070^{b}22–35] 600b; CH 5 [1071^{a}30–36] 601a

9 ARISTOTLE: *Motion of Animals*, CH 3 [699^{a}11]-CH 4 [700^{a}5] 234a-235a

12 LUCRETIUS: *Nature of Things*, BK V [146–194] 63a-c

12 EPICTETUS: *Discourses*, BK I, CH 14 120d-121c

16 PTOLEMY: *Almagest*, BK I, 5a-b

16 KEPLER: *Epitome*, BK IV, 853b-854a / *Harmonies of the World*, 1017b-1018a; 1025a-b; 1049b-1050a; 1061a

18 AUGUSTINE: *Confessions*, BK I, par 10 3b-c; par 12 4a; BK VII, par 16–23 48c-50c; BK XI, par 4–11 90a-92b; BK XII, par 2–9 99c-101c; par 14–40 102b-110a esp par 38 108d-109a; BK XIII, par 6–48 112a-124a / *City of God*, BK VII, CH 29–31 261a-262a; BK VIII, CH 1 264b,d-265b; CH 4–6 266d-269c; CH 9 270d-271a; BK XI, CH 4–24 324a-336a; BK XII 342b,d-360a,c; BK XIX, CH 13 519a-520a; BK XXI, CH 4 562a-

(5. *The divine nature in relation to the world or creatures. 5a. God as first and as exemplar cause: the relation of divine to natural causation.*)

563c; CH 7-8 565d-568d; BK XXII, CH 2 587b-588a / *Christian Doctrine*, BK I, CH 32 633c-d; CH 34 634b-c

19 AQUINAS: *Summa Theologica*, PART I, Q 2, A 3, ANS and REP 2 12c-14a; Q 3, A 1, ANS 14b-15b; A 2, ANS 15c-16a; A 4, ANS 16d-17c; A 5, REP 2 17c-18b; A 6, ANS 18c-19a; A 7, ANS and REP 1 19a-c; A 8, ANS and REP 1-2 19d-20c; Q 4 20c-23b esp A 3 22b-23b; Q 18, AA 3-4 106b-108c; Q 26, A 4 151c-152a,c; Q 51, A 1, REP 3 275b-276b; Q 52, A 2 279b-280a; Q 56, A 2, ANS 292d-294a; Q 60, A 1, REP 2-3 310b-311a; Q 65 339a-343c; Q 74, A 3, REP 1 375a-377a,c; Q 75, A 1, REP 1 378b-379c; Q 76, A 5, REP 1 394c-396a; Q 83, A 1, REP 3 436d-438a; Q 84, A 2, ANS and REP 3 442b-443c; A 4, REP 1 444d-446b; Q 88, A 3, REP 2 472c-473a; Q 89, A 1, REP 3 473b-475a; Q 92, A 1, REP 1 488d-489d; A 2, REP 2 489d-490c; A 4, ANS 491b-d; Q 93 492a-501c; Q 94, A 3, ANS 504a-505a; QQ 103-105 528a-545b; Q 116 592d-595c; PART I-II, Q 1, A 2 610b-611b; Q 2, A 3, ANS 617b-618a; Q 6, A 1, REP 3 644d-646a; Q 9, A 6 662a-d; Q 10, A 4 665d-666a,c; Q 12, A 5, ANS 672a-c; Q 17, A 8, REP 2 692a-c

20 AQUINAS: *Summa Theologica*, PART I-II, Q 65, A 3, ANS 72d-73d; Q 66, A 1, REP 3 75b-76b; Q 68, A 1, ANS 87c-89c; Q 79, A 1, REP 3 156b-157b; A 2, ANS and REP 1 157b-158a; Q 80, A 1, ANS and REP 2-3 159d-160c; Q 85, A 6 182d-184a; Q 93, A 1 215b,d-216c; Q 100, A 6, REP 2 257c-258c; Q 102, A 3, ANS 272b-276c; Q 109, A 1, ANS 338b-339c; Q 110, A 1, REP 2 347d-349a; Q 111, A 2, ANS 352d-353d; PART II-II, Q 18, A 4, ANS 464c-465a; PART III, Q 2, A 5, REP 3 715a-716b; Q 5, A 3, REP 2 737d-739a; Q 13, A 3, CONTRARY 782b-783b; PART III SUPPL, Q 74, A 2, REP 3 926c-927c; Q 75, A 3 938a-939d; Q 88, A 1, ANS 1000d-1001d

21 DANTE: *Divine Comedy*, PARADISE, I [103-108] 107b; II [112-148] 109a-b; XXVII [100-120] 148b-c; XXIX [10-36] 150b-c

22 CHAUCER: *Knight's Tale* [2987-3040] 209a-210a

23 HOBBES: *Leviathan*, PART I, 78d-79a; 79d-80a; PART II, 113b-c; 149d; PART III, 185d; 241c-242a; PART IV, 272b-c

28 GALILEO: *Two New Sciences*, FOURTH DAY, 245b-c

28 HARVEY: *On Animal Generation*, 390d-391a; 406b-407b; 415b-417a esp 416b-c; 426a-429b; 443a-c; 490d-493a

30 BACON: *Advancement of Learning*, 2c-d; 4b-c

31 DESCARTES: *Discourse*, PART V, 55d-56a / *Meditations*, III 81d-89a esp 84b-85a, 87b-88c / *Objections and Replies*, 110b-112a; 158b-161d; 213b-214d; 229c-d

31 SPINOZA: *Ethics*, PART I, PROP 16-18 362a-363c; PROP 24-29 365a-366c; PROP 33, SCHOL 2 367d-369a; PART II, PROP 7 375a-c; PROP 10, SCHOL 376d-377a

32 MILTON: *Paradise Lost*, BK III [80-134] 137a-138a; [630-735] 149a-151b; BK V [468-474] 185b; BK VII 217a-231a esp [162-169] 220b, [601-640] 230a-231a

33 PASCAL: *Pensées*, 77 186a

34 NEWTON: *Principles*, BK III, GENERAL SCHOL, 369b-370a / *Optics*, BK III, 528b-529a

35 LOCKE: *Human Understanding*, BK II, CH XXI, SECT 2 178c; CH XXIII, SECT 28 211b-d; BK IV, CH III, SECT 28-29 322a-323a

35 BERKELEY: *Human Knowledge*, SECT 25-33 417d-419a esp SECT 32 418d-419a; SECT 36 419c-d; SECT 51-53 422d-423a; SECT 57 423d-424a; SECT 60-75 424b-427d; SECT 105-109 433b-434b; SECT 141 441a-b; SECT 146-153 442a-444a esp SECT 150 442d-443b

35 HUME: *Human Understanding*, SECT VII, DIV 54-57 474b-475d

42 KANT: *Pure Reason*, 140b,d-145c; 177b-179b; 187a-191d; 205a-209a; 236b-240b esp 239a-c / *Practical Reason*, 332d-337a,c esp 334b-335c / *Judgement*, 569a-570a; 581b-582c; 592c-596c; 597d-599d; 600d-601c; 608b-609a; 610b-613a,c

46 HEGEL: *Philosophy of History*, INTRO, 156d-157b; PART I, 245d-246c; PART IV, 368d-369a,c

49 DARWIN: *Origin of Species*, 239d; 243c-d

5b. God as final cause: the motion of all things toward God

OLD TESTAMENT: *Exodus*, 33:13-23 / *Deuteronomy*, 4:29 / *I Chronicles*, 28:9—(D) *I Paralipomenon*, 28:9 / *II Chronicles*, 15:2-4,12-15—(D) *II Paralipomenon*, 15:2-4,12-15 / *Psalms*, 24:6; 27:4-9; 42; 63; 70:4; 73:25-28; 84; 119:10—(D) *Psalms*, 23:6; 26:4-9; 41; 62; 69:5; 72:25-28; 83; 118:10 / *Proverbs*, 16:4 / *Isaiah*, 26:8-9; 43:7; 58:2—(D) *Isaias*, 26:8-9; 43:7; 58:2

APOCRYPHA: *Wisdom of Solomon*, 1:1; 13:1-7—(D) OT, *Book of Wisdom*, 1:1; 13:1-7

NEW TESTAMENT: *Romans*, 3:10-11 / *Colossians*, 1:16-17 / *Hebrews*, 2:10 / *Revelation*, 4:11—(D) *Apocalypse*, 4:11

8 ARISTOTLE: *Metaphysics*, BK XII, CH 7 [1072^{a}23-^{b}4] 602b-c

17 PLOTINUS: *Second Ennead*, TR II, CH 2 41a-c / *Fifth Ennead*, TR VIII, CH 7, 243b-c

18 AUGUSTINE: *Confessions*, BK I, par 1, 1a; par 5, 2b; BK IV, par 15-19 23a-24b; BK V, par 1-2 27a-c; BK X, par 29-33 78d-80b; BK XIII, par 3 111b-c / *City of God*, BK VIII, CH 4 266d-267c; CH 8-9 270a-271a; BK X, CH 1-3 298b,d-301a; BK XII, CH 1 342b,d-343c; BK XIX, CH 13 519a-520a / *Christian Doctrine*, BK I 624a-636a,c esp CH 3-5 625b-626a, CH 9-11 627a-c, CH 22-23 629b-630c, CH 34 634b-c

19 AQUINAS: *Summa Theologica*, PART I, Q 1, A 4, ANS 5a-b; Q 2, A 1, REP 1 10d-11d; A 3, ANS

5c. The power of God: the divine omnipotence

(5. *The divine nature in relation to the world or creatures. 5c. The power of God: the divine omnipotence.*)

23 HOBBES: *Leviathan*, PART II, 160c-161a; 162c
28 HARVEY: *On Animal Generation*, 428c
30 BACON: *Advancement of Learning*, 17c; 81a
31 DESCARTES: *Objections and Replies*, 110b-112a; 158b-159a; 229a-d
31 SPINOZA: *Ethics*, PART I, PROP 17 362b-363c; PROP 33, SCHOL 2–PROP 35 367d-369a
32 MILTON: *Paradise Lost*, BK II [106-225] 113b-116a; BK III [372-415] 143b-144b; BK VII [139-173] 220a-221a
33 PASCAL: *Pensées*, 654 292b
35 LOCKE: *Human Understanding*, BK II, CH XV, SECT 12 165b-c; CH XXI, SECT 2 178c; CH XXIII, SECT 28 211b-d; BK III, CH VI, SECT 11–12 271b-272b; BK IV, CH X, SECT 4 350a
35 BERKELEY: *Human Knowledge*, SECT 33 419a; SECT 36 419c-d; SECT 152 443c-d
35 HUME: *Human Understanding*, SECT VII, DIV 56 475a-b
36 STERNE: *Tristram Shandy*, 334a-b
37 FIELDING: *Tom Jones*, 186c-d
42 KANT: *Pure Reason*, 180b-c; 181b; 192c-d / *Practical Reason*, 351b-352c / *Judgement*, 504b-d; 592a-c; 594d [fn 1]; 600d-601c
46 HEGEL: *Philosophy of History*, INTRO, 156d-157b
54 FREUD: *Civilization and Its Discontents*, 790d

5d. The immanence of God: the divine omnipresence

OLD TESTAMENT: *Genesis*, 28:15 / *Exodus*, 20:24; 25:8; 29:45-46 / *Leviticus*, 26:11-12 / *Numbers*, 5:1-3 / *Joshua*, 3:10-11—(D) *Josue*, 3:10-11 / *II Samuel*, 7:1-13—(D) *II Kings*, 7:1-13 / *I Kings*, 6:11-13;8:12-13,26-30—(D) *III Kings*, 6:11-13; 8:12-13,26-30 / *I Chronicles*, 17:1-12 —(D) *I Paralipomenon*, 17:1-12 / *Psalms*, 68:7-8,16-18; 119:151; 139 esp 139:7-12; 145:18-19 —(D) *Psalms*, 67:8-9,17-19; 118:151; 138 esp 138:7-12; 144:18-19 / *Proverbs*, 15:3 / *Isaiah*, 50:7-9—(D) *Isaias*, 50:7-9 / *Jeremiah*, 23:24— (D) *Jeremias*, 23:24 / *Amos*, 9:1-4 / *Zechariah*, 8:3—(D) *Zachariah*, 8:3
APOCRYPHA: *Wisdom of Solomon*, 1:7; 12:1—(D) OT, *Book of Wisdom*, 1:7; 12:1
NEW TESTAMENT: *John*, 1:10 / *Acts*, 7:49; 17:22-29 / *Romans*, 11:36 / *I Corinthians*, 6:15-20 / *II Corinthians*, 6:14-18 / *Ephesians*, 4:6 / *Colossians*, 1:16-19; 2:8-13 / *II Timothy*, 1:14 / *Hebrews*, 13:5 / *I John*, 4:4-16
12 EPICTETUS: *Discourses*, BK I, CH 14 120d-121c
12 AURELIUS: *Meditations*, BK II, SECT 1 256b,d; BK VII, SECT 9 280b-c
17 PLOTINUS: *Second Ennead*, TR IX, CH 16, 75c-d / *Fifth Ennead*, TR VIII, CH 7 242d-243c
18 AUGUSTINE: *Confessions*, BK I, par 2-3 1b-2a; BK III, par 10 15b-d; par 18 18b; BK IV, par 26 25c-d; par 31 26c-27a; BK VI, par 4 36a-b; BK

VII, par 1-2 43b-44a; par 7 45a-d; par 21 49d-50a; BK X, par 8-10 73b-74a; BK XII, par 7 100d-101a; par 21 103d-104a / *City of God*, BK VII, CH 6, 248a; CH 30 261b-d; BK X, CH 14 307c-308a; BK XII, CH 25 358b-359a / *Christian Doctrine*, BK I, CH 12 627c-d
19 AQUINAS: *Summa Theologica*, PART I, Q 8 34c-38c; Q 51, A 3, REP 3 277a-278c; Q 52, A 2 279b-280a; Q 90, A 1 480d-481d; PART I-II, Q 17, A 8, REP 2 692a-c
20 AQUINAS: *Summa Theologica*, PART II-II, Q 26, A 2, REP 3 511a-d; PART III SUPPL, Q 84, A 2 REP 1 984c-985d
21 DANTE: *Divine Comedy*, PARADISE, XXXIII [76-93] 157a
28 HARVEY: *On Animal Generation*, 428c-d
31 DESCARTES: *Meditations*, VI, 99c
31 SPINOZA: *Ethics*, PART I 355a-372d esp DEF 3-5 355b, AXIOM 1-2 355c-d, PROP 2-8 355d-357d, PROP 10, SCHOL 358a-b, PROP 13, COROL–PROP 18 359d-363c, PROP 22-23 364d-365a, PROP 25 365b, PROP 28-31 365c-367a, PROP 33 367b-369a; PART II, PROP 1-11 373d-377c
32 MILTON: *Paradise Lost*, BK XI [334-346] 306b
34 NEWTON: *Principles*, BK III, GENERAL SCHOL, 370a-371a
35 LOCKE: *Human Understanding*, BK II, CH XIII, SECT 18 152a-c; CH XV, SECT 2-4 162c-163b
35 BERKELEY: *Human Knowledge*, SECT 149-150 442d-443b; SECT 155 444b-c
42 KANT: *Pure Reason*, 192c-d / *Practical Reason*, 334b-335b; 351b-352c / *Judgement*, 580c-d; 592a-c
46 HEGEL: *Philosophy of History*, INTRO, 156d-157b; PART I, 224a-b; 227d-228a
51 TOLSTOY: *War and Peace*, BK V, 217c-218a; BK XIV, 608a-b; BK XV, 631a-c
52 DOSTOEVSKY: *Brothers Karamazov*, BK VI, 153b-d

5e. The transcendence of God: the divine aseity

OLD TESTAMENT: *Exodus*, 15:11 / *I Samuel*, 2:2— (D) *I Kings*, 2:2 / *I Chronicles*, 17:20—(D) *I Paralipomenon*, 17:20 / *Job*, 11:7-9; 33:12; 35:6-7; 36:22-42:3 / *Psalms*, 89:6-8; 97:9; 99:2; 113:4-5—(D) *Psalms*, 88:7-9; 96:9; 98:2; 112:4-5 / *Isaiah*, 29:16; 40:12-26; 45:9; 46:5,9; 55:8-9—(D) *Isaias*, 29:16; 40:12-26; 45:9; 46:5,9; 55:8-9 / *Daniel*, 4:35—(D) *Daniel*, 4:32
APOCRYPHA: *Wisdom of Solomon*, 11:22; 12:12— (D) OT, *Book of Wisdom*, 11:23; 12:12 / *Ecclesiasticus*, 16:20-21; 18:4-7—(D) OT, *Ecclesiasticus*, 16:20-21; 18:2-6
NEW TESTAMENT: *John*, 3:31 / *Acts*, 7:47-50 / *Romans*, 9:19-21 / *Ephesians*, 1:19-23; 4:6 / *I Timothy*, 6:15-16
8 ARISTOTLE: *Metaphysics*, BK XII, CH 10 [1075ᵃ12-16] 605d
9 ARISTOTLE: *Motion of Animals*, CH 3 [699ᵃ11]– CH 4 [700ᵃ5] 234a-235a

5f. God's knowledge: the divine omniscience; the divine ideas

(5. The divine nature in relation to the world or creatures. 5f. God's knowledge: the divine omniscience; the divine ideas.)

31 Descartes: *Meditations*, III, 86a / *Objections and Replies*, 122a-b

31 Spinoza: *Ethics*, PART I, PROP 17 362b-363c; PROP 21, DEMONST 364a-c; PROP 33, SCHOL 2 367d-369a; PART II, PROP 1 373d-374a; PROP 3-4 374a-c; PROP 7, SCHOL–PROP 8 375b-376a; PROP 32 385c

32 Milton: *Paradise Lost*, BK II [188-193] 115b; BK III [56-134] 136b-138a; BK X [1-16] 274b

35 Locke: *Human Understanding*, BK II, CH X, SECT 9 143a-c; CH XV, SECT 12 165b-c; BK III, CH VI, SECT 3 268d; SECT 11 271b-d; BK IV, CH X, SECT 5-6 350a-c

35 Hume: *Human Understanding*, SECT VIII, DIV 78, 485d-486a

42 Kant: *Practical Reason*, 344a-c; 351b-352c / *Judgement*, 592a-c

44 Boswell: *Johnson*, 173c; 392d-393a

5g. God's will: divine choice

Old Testament: *Genesis*, 1-2 / *Psalms*, 135:6— (D) *Psalms*, 134:6 / *Isaiah*, 14:24-27; 46:9-11 —(D) *Isaias*, 14:24-27; 46:9-11 / *Jeremiah*, 4:28; 51:29—(D) *Jeremias*, 4:28; 51:29

New Testament: *Matthew*, 18:14; 20:1-16 / *John*, 5:21; 6:38-40 / *Romans*, 8:27-29; 9:11-19; 12:1-2 / *I Corinthians*, 12 / *Ephesians*, 1:8-12; 3:10-11 / *I Thessalonians*, 4:3-6; 5:18 / *II Timothy*, 1:8-10 / *James*, 1:18

5 Aeschylus: *Suppliant Maidens* [86-103] 2a-b

5 Euripides: *Bacchantes* [1388-1391] 352a,c

7 Plato: *Timaeus*, 452c

12 Epictetus: *Discourses*, BK IV, CH 3, 224d; CH 7, 232d-233a

12 Aurelius: *Meditations*, BK III, SECT 11 262a-b

17 Plotinus: *Sixth Ennead*, TR VIII 342d-353d

18 Augustine: *Confessions*, BK VII, par 6-7 44d-45d; BK XI, par 12 92b; BK XII, par 18, 103a-b; BK XIII, par 5 111d; par 19 115c-d / *City of God*, BK V, CH 9-10 213b-216c; BK X, CH 7 302d-303a; BK XII, CH 14 350d-351b; CH 17 353a-354a; BK XXI, CH 7-8 565d-568d; BK XXII, CH 2 587b-588a

19 Aquinas: *Summa Theologica*, PART I, Q 14, A 8, ANS 82c-83b; Q 19 108d-119d; Q 20, A 1, REP 3 120a-121b; A 4, ANS 122c-124a; Q 23, A 4 135a-d; Q 25, A 5, ANS and REP 1 147d-149a; Q 26, A 2, REP 2 150c-151a; Q 50, A 1, ANS 269b-270a; Q 54, A 2, ANS 285d-286c; Q 57, A 5, ANS 299b-300b; Q 59, A 2, ANS 307c-308b; Q 60, A 1, REP 2 310b-311a; Q 61, A 2, REP 1,3 315c-316a; Q 62, A 6, REP 1 322a-d; Q 63, A 1, ANS 325c-326c; Q 104, AA 3-4 537b-538c; Q 105, A 1, REP 2 538d-539c; PART I-II, Q 1, A 2, REP 3 610b-611b; Q 10, A 1, REP 2 662d-663d; Q 19, AA 9-10 709d-711d; Q 39, A 2, REP 3 790d-791b

20 Aquinas: *Summa Theologica*, PART I-II, Q 93, A 4, REP 1 218b-d; Q 97, A 3, REP 1 237b-238b;

PART III, Q 18, A 1, REP 1,4 810a-811c; Q 21, A 1, ANS 823d-824d; A 4, ANS 826b-827c; Q 61, A 4, REP 3 857c-858b; Q 64, A 7, ANS 875d-876c; PART III SUPPL, Q 72, A 3, ANS and REP 5 920c-922b; Q 74, A 4, ANS 928d-929d; Q 91, A 1, REP 2 1016b-1017c; A 2, ANS 1017c-1020c; Q 92, A 3, REP 6 1034b-1037c

21 Dante: *Divine Comedy*, PARADISE, III [64-90] 110a-b; XIX [85-90] 135d-136a

23 Hobbes: *Leviathan*, PART II, 113b-c; 162c; PART IV, 271b

24 Rabelais: *Gargantua and Pantagruel*, BK IV, 265b

30 Bacon: *Advancement of Learning*, 38a

31 Descartes: *Objections and Replies*, 228a-c; 229c

31 Spinoza: *Ethics*, PART I, PROP 17 362b-363c; PROP 32 367a-b; PROP 33, SCHOL 2 367d-369a; APPENDIX, 370c-371a

32 Milton: *Paradise Lost*, BK III [80-134] 137a-138a; BK VII [139-173] 220a-221a / *Samson Agonistes* [300-329] 346a-b

35 Locke: *Human Understanding*, BK II, CH XXI, SECT 50-51 191b-c

35 Berkeley: *Human Knowledge*, SECT 25-33 417d-419a esp SECT 29-30 418c

41 Gibbon: *Decline and Fall*, 150c-151b

42 Kant: *Fund. Prin. Metaphysic of Morals*, 265b-c esp 265b,d [fn 1]; 276b-277a; 278b-c / *Practical Reason*, 303b-304a; 321b-c; 324b-325a; 325d-326a; 328b / *Intro. Metaphysic of Morals*, 393c-d

51 Tolstoy: *War and Peace*, BK VI, 272a-b; BK XII, 553b; BK XIII, 563a-b; BK XV, 631c; EPILOGUE II, 675a-677b; 680b-c; 684b-d

5h. God's love: the diffusion of the divine goodness

Old Testament: *Exodus*, 33:19; 34:6 / *Deuteronomy*, 4:37-38; 7:7-8; 10:15,18; 32:4 / *I Chronicles*, 16:7-34—(D) *I Paralipomenon*, 16:7-34 / *Job* passim, esp 2:10 / *Psalms* / *Proverbs*, 3:12 / *Song of Solomon*—(D) *Canticle of Canticles* / *Isaiah*, 43; 45:7; 63:7-9— (D) *Isaias*, 43; 45:7; 63:7-9 / *Jeremiah*, 31:1-6; 32:17-44; 33:1-16—(D) *Jeremias*, 31:1-6; 32:17-44; 33:1-16 / *Lamentations*, 3:25,38 / *Ezekiel*, 16:1-15—(D) *Ezechiel*, 16:1-15 / *Hosea*, 1-3; 11—(D) *Osee*, 1-3; 11 / *Joel*, 2:12-3:21 / *Micah*, 1:12—(D) *Micheas*, 1:12 / *Zechariah*, 9:17—(D) *Zacharias*, 9:17 / *Malachi*, 1:1-3—(D) *Malachias*, 1:1-3

Apocrypha: *Tobit*, 13:10—(D) OT, *Tobias*, 13:12 / *Wisdom of Solomon*, 7:28; 11:22-26; 12:13-16; 16:20-29—(D) OT, *Book of Wisdom*, 7:28; 11:23-27; 12:13-16; 16:20-29 / *Ecclesiasticus*, 4:14; 11:14-17; 16:29-30; 17:8-18,29; 33:10-15; 39:16,25-34—(D) OT, *Ecclesiasticus*, 4:15; 11:14-17; 16:30-31; 17:8-18,28; 33:10-15; 39:21,30-40

New Testament: *Matthew*, 6:25-34; 7:7-11; 10:29-31 / *Luke*, 11:1-13; 12:6-7,16-33 / *John*,

3:16-21; 13:31-35; 14:21; 15:9-16; 17:21-26 /
Romans, 2:4; 5:5; 8:28-39 / *II Corinthians,*
13:11 / *Galatians,* 2:20 / *Ephesians,* 3:14-21;
5:1-2 / *I Timothy,* 1:14 / *Titus,* 3:3-7 / *Hebrews,* 12:6 / *I John,* 3-4 / *Revelation,* 3:19-21
—(D) *Apocalypse,* 3:19-21

7 PLATO: *Republic,* BK II, 321d-322d / *Timaeus,*
447c-448a

8 ARISTOTLE: *Generation and Corruption,* BK II,
CH 10 [336^{b}25-34] 438d

12 EPICTETUS: *Discourses,* BK II, CH 8 146a-147c

14 PLUTARCH: *Numa Pompilius,* 50d-51c

16 KEPLER: *Harmonies of the World,* 1049b-
1050b; 1071b

17 PLOTINUS: *Sixth Ennead,* TR IX, CH 9 358d-
359c

18 AUGUSTINE: *Confessions,* BK I, par 7 2c-d; par
31 8d-9a; BK V, par 2 27b-c; BK VII, par 16-23
48c-50c; BK XI, par 6 90c-d; BK XII, par 18,
103a-b; BK XIII, par 1-5 110d-111d / *City of
God,* BK VII, CH 31 261d-262a; BK XI, CH 21-24
333a-336a; BK XII, CH 1, 343b-c; CH 9 347b-
348b; BK XIX, CH 13 519a-520a; BK XXI, CH
15-16 572c-574a; BK XXII, CH 1 586b,d-587b;
CH 24 609a-612a / *Christian Doctrine,* BK I,
CH 31-32 633b-d

19 AQUINAS: *Summa Theologica,* PART I, Q 2, A 3,
REP 1 12c-14a; Q 3, A 1, REP 1 14b-15b; Q 6,
A 4 30b-d; Q 13, A 2, ANS 63c-64d; Q 19, A 2,
ANS and REP 2-4 109c-110b; A 4, ANS and REP 1
111c-112c; Q 20 119d-124a; Q 21, A 3, ANS
126a-c; Q 27, AA 3-4 155c-156d; Q 37 197c-
200c; Q 44, A 4, ANS and REP 1 241a-d; Q 49
264d-268a,c; Q 50, A 1, ANS 269b-270a; A 3,
ANS 272a-273b; Q 51, A 1, REP 3 275b-276b;
Q 59, A 1, ANS 306c-307b; A 2, ANS 307c-308b;
Q 60, A 5 313b-314c; Q 74, A 3, REP 3-4 375a-
377a,c; Q 75, A 5, REP 1 382a-383b; Q 82, A 5,
REP 1 435c-436c; Q 89, A 1, REP 3 473b-475a;
Q 91, A 1, ANS 484a-485b; Q 93, A 4, ANS 494c-
495b; A 8, ANS 499b-500c; Q 103 528a-534b
passim; Q 104, A 3, REP 2 537b-d; A 4, ANS
538a-c; Q 105, A 4, ANS 541c-542a; Q 106, A 4,
ANS 548b-549a; PART I-II, Q I, A 4, REP 1
612a-613a; Q 2, A 4, REP 1 618a-d; A 5, REP 3
618d-619c; Q 22, A 3, REP 3 722d-723b; Q 28,
A 3, CONTRARY 742a-d

20 AQUINAS: *Summa Theologica,* PART I-II, Q 64,
A 4, ANS 69b-70a; Q 65, A 5, ANS and REP 3
74c-75a; Q 73, A 10, ANS 128a-d; Q 75, A 3,
ANS 139b-d; Q 79, A 1 156b-157b; A 3, REP 1
158a-d; A 4, REP 1 158d-159c; Q 90, PREAMBLE,
205a; Q 92, A 1, REP 1 213c-214c; Q 93, A 6,
REP 1 219d-220d; Q 96, A 5, REP 2 233d-234d;
Q 110, A 1 347d-349a; A 4, ANS 350d-351d;
Q 111, A 3, REP 1 353d-354b; PART II-II, Q 6,
A 2, REP 2 414c-415c; Q 19, A 1, REP 3 465a-d;
A 5, REP 3 468b-469a; Q 23, A 2, REP 1-2
483d-484d; Q 24, A 2, ANS 490b-d; A 3, ANS
491a-d; A 8, ANS 495b-496a; A 11, REP 1 498b-
499c; A 12, ANS 499c-500d; Q 26, A 3, ANS
511d-512c; Q 30, A 2, REP 1 534b-535a; Q 189,

A 10, REP 1 699a-700d; PART III, Q 1, A 3, REP 3
704d-706a; Q 4, A 5, REP 2 734b-d; Q 23, A 1,
REP 2 833a-d; Q 62, A 2, CONTRARY 859d-860c;
PART III SUPPL, Q 71, A 3, REP 1 903c-904d;
Q 80, A 3, REP 3 958b-959c

21 DANTE: *Divine Comedy,* HELL, I [37-40] 1b-c;
PURGATORY, III [103-145] 57a-c; XI [1-30] 68d-
69a; XV [40-81] 75d-76a; XXVIII [91-96] 97a;
PARADISE, II [112-148] 109a-b; VII [64-75]
115b-116a; X [1-27]120b-c; XIII [52-87]126a-b;
XIX [86-90] 135d-136a; XXVI [1-81] 145d-146c;
XXVII [97-120] 148b-c; XXIX [13-36] 150b-c;
[127-145] 151c-d; XXXII [139]-XXXIII [145]
156a-157d

22 CHAUCER: *Troilus and Cressida,* BK III, STANZA
1-7 54b-55b; STANZA 250-253 87a-b; BK V,
STANZA 263-267 154b-155a

30 BACON: *Advancement of Learning,* 80b-81a

31 DESCARTES: *Objections and Replies,* 229c

31 SPINOZA: *Ethics,* PART V, PROP 17, COROL 456d;
PROP 19 457a; PROP 35-36 460d-461c

32 MILTON: *Paradise Lost,* BK III [80-343] 137a-
143a esp [135-166] 138b-139a; BK IV [411-439]
161b-162a; BK VII [499-518] 228a-b

35 LOCKE: *Human Understanding,* BK I, CH III,
SECT 12 115b-116a

35 BERKELEY: *Human Knowledge,* INTRO, SECT 3
405b-c; SECT 154 444a-b

37 FIELDING: *Tom Jones,* 186c-d

42 KANT: *Practical Reason,* 345a-c / *Judgement,*
592a-c

44 BOSWELL: *Johnson,* 539d-540a

48 MELVILLE: *Moby Dick,* 318b

51 TOLSTOY: *War and Peace,* BK VI, 272a-b

52 DOSTOEVSKY: *Brothers Karamazov,* BK II,
24a-c; BK V, 120d-137c; BK VI, 153a-d; BK VII,
189a-191a,c; BK XI, 313c-314d

5i. Divine justice and mercy: divine rewards and punishments

OLD TESTAMENT: *Genesis,* 3:1-4:16; 6-9; 11:1-9;
18:17-19:29; 22:1-19 esp 22:15-18 / *Exodus,*
7-12; 20:3-7; 32 esp 32:9-14; 33:19; 34:5-10 /
Leviticus, 26 / *Numbers,* 11-14; 16; 21:5-9; 25 /
Deuteronomy, 1-11 passim; 28-32 passim / *I
Samuel,* 15—(D) *I Kings,* 15 / *II Samuel,* 6:6-
8; 24—(D) *II Kings,* 6:6-8; 24 / *I Kings,* 8;
13; 14:2-16—(D) *III Kings,* 8; 13; 14:2-16 /
II Kings, 9:1-10:11—(D) *IV Kings,* 9:1-10:11 /
I Chronicles, 10:13-14; 21—(D) *I Paralipomenon,* 10:13-14; 21 / *II Chronicles,* 6; 12; 19:6-7;
21:11-20; 26:16-21—(D) *II Paralipomenon,* 6;
12; 19:6-7; 21:12-20; 26:16-21 / *Nehemiah,*
9:5-38—(D) *II Esdras,* 9:5-38 / *Job* / *Psalms* /
Proverbs, 11:1,20-21; 20:22; 22:22-23 / *Ecclesiastes,* 12:14 / *Isaiah* passim, esp 1, 3-4, 10, 13-
27, 30, 34-35, 40, 42, 47, 52-53, 59, 65-66—
(D) *Isaias* passim, esp 1, 3-4, 10, 13-27, 30,
34-35, 40, 42, 47, 52-53, 59, 65-66 / *Jeremiah*
passim, esp 3-8, 15, 19, 24-25, 29-31, 33, 46-52
—(D) *Jeremias* passim, esp 3-8, 15, 19, 24-25,
29-31, 33, 46-52 / *Lamentations* / *Ezekiel*

(5. _The divine nature in relation to the world or creatures. 5i. Divine justice and mercy: divine rewards and punishments._)

passim, esp 4-9, 11, 14-18, 25-33, 35-39—(D) _Ezechiel_ passim, esp 4-9, 11, 14-18, 25-33, 35-39 / _Daniel_, 4:4-5:31—(D) _Daniel_, 4-5 / _Joel_ / _Amos_ / _Obadiah_—(D) _Abdias_ / _Jonah_ —(D) _Jonas_ / _Micah_—(D) _Micheas_ / _Nahum_ / _Habakkuk_—(D) _Habacuc_ / _Zephaniah_—(D) _Sophonias_ / _Zechariah_—(D) _Zacharias_ / _Malachi_—(D) _Malachias_

APOCRYPHA: _Tobit_, 2-3; 13—(D) OT, _Tobias_, 2-3; 13 / _Judith_, 5—(D) OT, _Judith_, 5 / _Wisdom of Solomon_, 1-5; 11:23; 12—(D) OT, _Book of Wisdom_, 1-5; 11:24; 12 / _Ecclesiasticus_, 16; 17:19-29; 18:1-14; 23:18-21; 35; 39:25-31 —(D) OT, _Ecclesiasticus_, 16; 17:16-28; 18:1-14; 23:25-31; 35; 39:30-37 / _Susanna_—(D) OT, _Daniel_, 13 / _Bel and Dragon_, 23-42—(D) OT, _Daniel_, 14:22-42 / _II Maccabees_, 6:12-17 —(D) OT, _II Machabees_, 6:12-17

NEW TESTAMENT: _Matthew_, 5:1-22,29-30,45; 9:9-13; 11:20-24; 12:36-37; 13:24-30,36-43; 18:7-14; 19:16-20:16; 23 / _Mark_, 9:37-47; 10:17-31; 16:16 / _Luke_, 1:46-55;6:36-38; 7:36-50; 10:25-28; 14:7-14; 15; 16:19-31; 18:1-8; 19:1-10; 23:34,39-43 / _John_, 5:30; 8:1-11 / _Acts_, 12:18-23; 13:1-12 / _Romans_, 1:16-2:16; 6:23; 9:14-18 / _II Corinthians_, 4 / _Galatians_, 6:7-8 / _Ephesians_, 2 / _II Thessalonians_, 1:3-10; 2:10-12 / _II Timothy_, 4:8 / _Titus_, 3:4-6 / _Hebrews_, 10:26-31 / _I Peter_, 3:18 / _II Peter_ / _I John_, 1:5-10 / _Jude_ / _Revelation_ passim, esp 17-20—(D) _Apocalypse_ passim, esp 17-20

5 AESCHYLUS: _Suppliant Maidens_ [1-175] 1a-3a / _Agamemnon_ [636-781] 58d-60b; [1560-1566] 68c / _Eumenides_ 81a-91d

5 SOPHOCLES: _Oedipus the King_ 99a-113a,c esp [1-275] 99a-101c, [703-738] 105d-106a, [863-910] 107b-c, [1187-1285] 110b-111a / _Antigone_ [279-289] 133c / _Oedipus at Colonus_ 114a-130a,c esp [521-545] 119a-b, [939-1014]123a-d, [1254-1396] 125d-126d / _Ajax_ 143a-155a,c esp [430-459] 146d-147a, [748-783] 149c-d / _Electra_ [173-179] 157c / _Trachiniae_ [1264-1278] 181c / _Philoctetes_ [446-452] 186a

5 EURIPIDES: _Suppliants_ [598-617] 263c-d / _Hecuba_ [1023-1033] 361c-d / _Heracles Mad_ [772-780] 371c-d

6 HERODOTUS: _History_, BK I, 20b-22a; BK II, 77a-b; BK IV, 158d-159d esp 159d; BK VI, 199c-d; 201d-202c; 203a-b; BK VIII, 278d-279a; 283d; BK IX, 308a-c

6 THUCYDIDES: _Peloponnesian War_, BK V, 506b-c; BK VII, 560a

7 PLATO: _Republic_, BK X, 437c-441a,c / _Laws_, BK IV, 682d-683a; BK IX, 757a; BK X, 765d-769d esp 767c-768c / _Seventh Letter_, 806a

12 LUCRETIUS: _Nature of Things_, BK III [978-1023] 42d-43b; BK VI [43-79] 80d-81b; [379-422] 85b-d

14 PLUTARCH: _Romulus_, 26b-27a / _Camillus_, 107b-d / _Aristides_, 265c-d / _Cato the Younger_, 639d

15 TACITUS: _Histories_, BK I, 189d-190a

18 AUGUSTINE: _Confessions_, BK II, par 15 12b-c; BK V, par 2 27b-c; BK VII, par 5 44c-d; BK IX, par 34-36 70c-71a / _City of God_, BK V, CH 10-11 215c-216d; CH 14-26 220a-230a,c; BK IX, CH 10 291a; BK XI, CH 23 334c-335c; BK XIII, CH 1-8 360a-363c; CH 12-16 365d-367d; BK XIII, CH 21-BK XIV, CH 28 371a-397d esp BK XIV, CH 15 388d-390a, CH 26 395d-396c; BK XV, CH 24-25 418d-419b; BK XVI, CH 4 425b-426a; BK XIX, CH 10-13 516c-520a; CH 15 521a-c; BK XX 530a-560a,c; BK XXI 560a-586a,c esp CH 11-12 570b-571c, CH 18 574c-575b, CH 24 577b-579d; BK XXII 586b,d-618d / _Christian Doctrine_, BK I, CH 15 628b-c; CH 32 633c-d; BK II, CH 23 648a-c

19 AQUINAS: _Summa Theologica_, PART I, Q 19, A 6 113c-114d; A 9, ANS 116d-117d; Q 21 124b-127c; Q 23, A 5 135d-137d; Q 62 317c-325b; Q 63, A 8, ANS 332c-333b; Q 64, A 2, REP 2 335d-336d; Q 65, A 2, REP 3 340b-341b; Q 66, A 3, ANS 347b-348d; Q 95, A 4 509b-510a; Q 96, A 3, REP 3 512a-c; Q 103, A 5, REP 2 531b-532b; Q 105, A 6, REP 2 543b-544a; Q 113, A 7, ANS 580b-581a; Q 114, A 1, REP 1 581d-582c; PART I-II, Q 5, A 1 636d-637c; A 4, ANS 639a-640b; A 7 642a-d; Q 17, A 9, REP 3 692d-693d; Q 21, A 4 719d-720a,c; Q 39, A 2, REP 3 790d-791b; Q 47, A 1, REP 1 819c-820b

20 AQUINAS: _Summa Theologica_, PART I-II, Q 61, A 5, ANS 58b-59d; Q 62, A 1 60a-d; Q 63, A 3 65a-d; Q 68, A 2 89c-90c; Q 72, A 5 115a-116b; Q 73, A 9, REP 3 126d-128a; A 10, REP 2 128a-d; Q 79, AA 3-4 158a-159c; Q 81, A 2, REP 1 164d-165c; Q 85, A 5, ANS 181d-182d; A 6 182d-184a; QQ 87-88 185c-198d; Q 91, A 6 212c-213c; Q 94, A 5, REP 2 224d-225d; Q 98, A 2, REP 3 240c-241b; A 4 242b-243c; Q 100, A 7, REP 3 258c-259c; A 8, REP 2-3 259d-261a; A 12 264d-265d; Q 103, A 2 299b-300d; Q 106, A 2 322b-323a; Q 112, A 4, REP 1 358d-359c; QQ 113-114 360d-378a,c; PART II-II, Q 13, A 4, ANS 446c-447a; Q 14, A 2, ANS 448d-449d; Q 18, A 4, REP 2 464c-465a; Q 19, A 1, REP 2 465a-d; Q 20, A 1, ANS 474d-475d; Q 21, A 2, ANS 479a-c; Q 24, A 10, ANS 496c-498a; Q 28, A 3 528d-529c; Q 182, A 2 621d-623a; Q 184, A 4, ANS and REP 1 632c-633c; PART III, Q 2, A 11 721c-722b; Q 9, A 2 764c-765a; Q 64 870b-879c; PART III SUPPL, Q 69, A 2 886c-887d; Q 70, A 3 897d-900d; Q 71 900d-917b passim; Q 72, A 3, REP 4 920c-922b; QQ 73-74 922b-935a,c passim; Q 75, A 1 935b-937a; Q 78, A 1, ANS 947d-949b; A 3, REP 3 950b-951a; QQ 82-99 968a-1085a,c

21 DANTE: _Divine Comedy_ esp HELL, III [1-18] 4a-b, XI 15a-16b, PURGATORY, III [103-145] 57a-c, VI [25-48] 61a-b, XIX [97-126] 82c-d, PARADISE, III [1]-V [87] 109b-113a, VII [19-120]

6. Man's knowledge of God

7 PLATO: *Timaeus*, 465d-466a / *Laws*, BK VII, 728b-730c; BK X, 758b-759a

8 ARISTOTLE: *Heavens*, BK II, CH 1 375b,d-376a / *Metaphysics*, BK I, CH 2 [982^{b}28-983^{a}11] 501a-b; BK VI, CH 1 547b,d-548c esp [1026^{a}23-33] 548b-c; BK XI, CH 7 [1064^{b}13-13] 592d-593a

12 EPICTETUS: *Discourses*, BK I, CH 6 110c-112b; CH 9, 114c-115a; CH 16-17 121d-124a

12 AURELIUS: *Meditations*, BK XII, SECT 28 310a

14 PLUTARCH: *Pericles*, 123c-124a / *Coriolanus*, 191d-192b / *Nicias*, 435b-d

18 AUGUSTINE: *Confessions*, BK V, par 1 27a-b; BK VI, par 8 37b-c; BK VII, par 16-23 48c-50c; BK X, par 8-10 73b-74a; BK XI, par 6 90c-d / *City of God*, BK VIII, CH 3 266a-d; BK X, CH 14 307c-308a / *Christian Doctrine*, BK I, CH 4 625b-c

19 AQUINAS: *Summa Theologica*, PART I, Q 2, AA 1-2 10d-12c; Q 3, A 1, REP 1-5 14b-15b; A 3, REP 1 16a-d; A 4, REP 2 16d-17c; A 6, REP 1 18c-19a; Q 12, A 4 53b-54c; AA 12-13 60d-62b; Q 32, A 1 175d-178a; Q 50, A 2, ANS 270a-272a; Q 65, A 1, REP 3 339b-340b; Q 79, A 9, ANS 422b-423d; Q 86, A 2, REP 1 462a-463a; Q 88, A 2, REP 4 471c-472c; A 3 472c-473a; Q 94, A 1 501d-503a; Q 103, A 1, ANS 528b-529a; PART I-II, Q 5, A 5, ANS 640b-641a; Q 14, A 1, REP 2 677b-678a; Q 17, A 8, REP 2 692a-c

20 AQUINAS: *Summa Theologica*, PART I-II, Q 61, A 5, ANS 58b-59d; Q 66, A 5 79b-80c; Q 68, A 1, ANS and REP 2 87c-89c; Q 90, A 4, REP 1 207d-208b; Q 93, A 2 216c-217b; Q 94, A 2, ANS 221d-223a; Q 99, A 3, REP 3 247a-248a; Q 100, A 1 251b-252a; Q 109, A 1, REP 1 338b-339c; PART II-II, Q 1, A 5, REP 4 383b-384b; Q 4, A 7, ANS 407d-409a; Q 10, A 12, REP 4 436b-437d; Q 27, A 3, REP 2 522c-523b; A 4, REP 3 523c-524a; A 6, REP 3 524c-525c; PART III, Q 3, A 3, ANS 724c-725b; Q 12, A 3, REP 2 778b-779a; PART III SUPPL, Q 91, A 1, ANS 1016b-1017c

21 DANTE: *Divine Comedy*, PURGATORY, III [34-45] 56b; PARADISE, IV [28-48] 111a; X [1-27] 120b-c

23 HOBBES: *Leviathan*, PART I, 54b-c; 66a-c; 78d-79a; 79d-80b; 83a-b; PART II, 137b-c; 149c-d; 160b; 163a-b; PART III, 165a-167b; 172d-173a; 183d-184a; 241a-242a

25 MONTAIGNE: *Essays*, 98b-99a; 209a-d; 212a-d; 238c-239c; 246a-d; 251c-252b; 267c-268a

28 HARVEY: *On Animal Generation*, 421d; 429b

30 BACON: *Advancement of Learning*, 2c-4c; 17b-20a; 38a; 39d-40a; 41b-d; 55b-c; 96c-97c esp 96d-97a / *New Atlantis*, 203a-b

31 DESCARTES: *Discourse*, PART I, 43c; PART IV, 52a-d / *Meditations*, 69a-71a,c passim; 71d-72b; III-IV, 81d-89b; V 93a-96a / *Objections and Replies*, 110c-114c; 120c-122b; 127a-c; PROP I-III 132b-133a; 140b; 158b-161d; 168d-169a; 211c-212a; 212c-213a; 213d-214a; 215b-c; 232b; 283d-284a; 284d

31 SPINOZA: *Ethics*, PART II, DEF 1 373a; PROP 45-47 390a-391a; PART IV, PROP 28 431c; PROP

36-37, DEMONST 434a-d; APPENDIX, IV 447b-c; PART V, PROP 21-42 458a-463d esp PROP 24-25 458d-459a, PROP 30-33 459d-460c, PROP 36 461a-c

32 MILTON: *Paradise Lost*, BK VII [109-130] 219b-220a; BK VIII [114-130] 234b-235a

33 PASCAL: *Provincial Letters*, 163a-164b / *Pensées*, 229 213a-b; 242-253 217b-220a; 265-290 221b-225a; 557-567 272b-273b

34 NEWTON: *Principles*, BK III, GENERAL SCHOL, 371a

35 LOCKE: *Human Understanding*, BK I, CH II, SECT 12, 107c-d; CH III, SECT 7-18 113d-117c; BK II, CH VII, SECT 6 132d; CH XVII, SECT 1 167d-168a; SECT 17 172b-c; SECT 20, 173a; CH XXIII, SECT 33-37 212d-214b; BK III, CH VI, SECT 11 271b-d; BK IV, CH X 349c-354c

35 BERKELEY: *Human Knowledge*, SECT 29-33 418c-419a; SECT 146-156 442a-444d

35 HUME: *Human Understanding*, SECT II, DIV 14 456b; SECT XI 497b-503c passim; SECT XII, DIV 132, 509c

37 FIELDING: *Tom Jones*, 186c-d

38 ROUSSEAU: *Social Contract*, BK IV, 437a

40 GIBBON: *Decline and Fall*, 12d-13a; 200d; 308b-309c

42 KANT: *Pure Reason*, 33a-d; 173b-192d / *Practical Reason*, 320c-321b; 346b-347a; 349b-352c; 354d-355d / *Intro. Metaphysic of Morals*, 384a,c / *Judgement*, 547b-d; 598b-599b; 602b-603a; 603b-d; 607d-609b

46 HEGEL: *Philosophy of History*, INTRO, 159b-160a; PART III, 304d-305b

47 GOETHE: *Faust*, PART I [3432-3468] 84a-b

51 TOLSTOY: *War and Peace*, BK V, 217c-d; BK VI, 248d-249a

52 DOSTOEVSKY: *Brothers Karamazov*, BK V, 120d-121c

6c. Supernatural knowledge

6c(1) God as teacher: inspiration and revelation

OLD TESTAMENT: *Genesis*, 2:15-17; 3:8-24; 9:1-17; 17:1; 26:24; 35:11; 46:2-3 / *Exodus*, 3:4-6,13-15; 4:10-12; 6:2-8; 20:1-7; 24:12; 29:45-46; 33:11-34:8 / *Leviticus*, 11:44-45; 18:1-2 / *Numbers*, 12:1-8; 15:41 / *Deuteronomy*, 4:1-5,10-13,32-36; 5:4-11; 18:18-22; 29:29 / *I Kings*, 3:5-15; 8:35-36—(D) *III Kings*, 3:5-15; 8:35-36 / *Job*, 33; 34:31-32; 35:10-11; 38-42 / *Psalms*, 25:3-5,8-12; 32:8-9; 94:10-13; 119; 143 esp 143:8-10—(D) *Psalms*, 24:4-5,8-12; 31:8-9; 93:10-13; 118; 142 esp 142:8-10 / *Proverbs*, 2:5-6; 6:23 / *Isaiah*, 6:1-9; 11:1-3; 28:9-13; 48:3-8—(D) *Isaias*, 6:1-9; 11:1-3; 28:9-13; 48:3-8 / *Daniel*, 2; 4—(D) *Daniel*, 2; 3:98-4:34 / *Joel*, 2:28-29

APOCRYPHA: *Ecclesiasticus*, 17:5-14—(D) OT, *Ecclesiasticus*, 17:5-12

(*6c. Supernatural knowledge. 6c*(1) *God as teacher: inspiration and revelation.*)

NEW TESTAMENT: *Matthew* passim, esp 4:23, 7:28–29, 10:1–20, 11:25–27, 13:1–23, 17:5, 28:18–20 / *Mark* passim, esp 1:1–11, 4:1–2 / *Luke* passim, esp 2:41–50, 3:21–22, 8:4–15, 9:34–35, 10:21–22 / *John* passim, esp 3:2, 5:31–47, 10:26–27, 12:23–30, 15:15, 16:25–29, 17:6–8 / *Acts*, 22:6–14 / *Romans*, 1:16–20; 10:17 / *I Corinthians*, 2; 12:1–8 / *Galatians*, 1:11–12 / *Ephesians*, 1:9,17; 3:1–5 / *II Timothy*, 3:15–16 / *Hebrews*, 1:1–3; 2:3–4 / *I Peter*, 1:10–12,22–25 / *II Peter*, 1:19–21 / *I John*, 2:20–27

18 AUGUSTINE: *Confessions*, BK II, par 7 10b-c; BK IV, par 30–31 26b-27a; BK VI, par 8 37b-c; BK IX, par 23–25 68a-c; BK XI, par 2–5 89c-90c; BK XIII, par 16–18 114d-115c / *City of God*, BK VII, CH 30 261b-d; BK X, CH 13 307b-c; BK XI, CH 2–4 323a-324d; BK XIX, CH 18 523a-b; CH 22 525b-c; BK XX, CH 28 556c-557a / *Christian Doctrine*, BK II, CH 15 643c-644a

19 AQUINAS: *Summa Theologica*, PART I, Q 1 3a-10c; Q 3, A 1, REP 1–5 14b-15b; Q 8, A 3, REP 4 36b-37c; Q 12, A 13 61c-62b; Q 32 175d-180d; Q 46, A 2 253a-255a; Q 57, A 3, REP 1 297b-298a; Q 68, A 1, ANS 354a-355c; Q 89, A 1, REP 3 473b-475a; A 2, REP 3 475a-d; Q 94, A 3 504a-505a; Q 104, A 4, ANS 538a-c; Q 105, A 3 540c-541b; Q 106, A 3, ANS and REP 2 547c-548b; Q 113, A 1, REP 2 576a-d; Q 117, A 1, REP 1 595d-597c; A 2, REP 2 597c-598c

20 AQUINAS: *Summa Theologica*, PART I-II, Q 63, A 3 65a-d; Q 68 87c-96c; Q 91, AA 4–5 210c-212c; Q 98, AA 2–6 240c-245b; Q 100, A 3, ANS 253a-d; Q 101, A 2, REP 1 267a-268a; QQ 106–107 321a-330d; Q 111, A 4 354c-355d; Q 112, A 5, ANS 359c-360c; PART II-II, Q 1, A 7, REP 3 385c-387a; Q 2, A 10, ANS 399b-400b; Q 4, A 4, REP 3 405a-406a; Q 6, A 1, ANS 413d-414c; PART III, Q 1, A 3, ANS 704d-706a; Q 3, A 8 729b-730b; Q 7, A 7 750a-d; Q 11, A 6, REP 2 775d-776b; Q 12, A 3, ANS and REP 1–2 778b-779a

21 DANTE: *Divine Comedy*, PURGATORY, XXX-XXXIII 99b-105d passim; PARADISE, XIX [1–99] 135a-136a; XXIV [52–147] 143b-144a; XXV [64–96] 145a-b; XXVI [25–45] 146a-b

22 CHAUCER: *Second Nun's Tale* [15,787–816] 467a-b

23 HOBBES: *Leviathan*, PART I, 83a-b; PART II, 137b-138b; 160b; PART III, 165a-167b; 176d-177c; 181a-186c; 205b-d; CONCLUSION, 281d-282a

25 MONTAIGNE: *Essays*, 212a; 238c-239c; 267c-268a; 273a-b

30 BACON: *Advancement of Learning*, 19b-c; 38a; 54b-c; 95d-101d esp 95d-96c / *New Atlantis*, 203a-c

31 DESCARTES: *Discourse*, PART I, 43c

32 MILTON: *Paradise Lost*, BK V [308]–BK VIII

[653] 182a-246a esp BK VIII [283–477] 238b-242a; BK XI [99]–BK XII [649] 301b-333a

33 PASCAL: *Pensées*, 185 205a; 585–588 277a-b; 642–692 290b-301a; 881 345b / *Vacuum*, 355b / *Geometrical Demonstration*, 440a-b

35 LOCKE: *Human Understanding*, BK III, CH IX, SECT 23 291b-c; BK IV, CH VII, SECT 11, 340b-c; CH XVI, SECT 14 371b-c; CH XVIII–XIX 380d-388d

35 HUME: *Human Understanding*, SECT XII, DIV 132, 509c

38 ROUSSEAU: *Inequality*, 333d; 366c-d

40 GIBBON: *Decline and Fall*, 201a; 307d-308a; 346b-c

41 GIBBON: *Decline and Fall*, 227d-228a; 231a-d

43 MILL: *Utilitarianism*, 455a-c

44 BOSWELL: *Johnson*, 394a-b; 481d-482a

46 HEGEL: *Philosophy of History*, INTRO, 157c-d; 159b-160a; PART III, 306c-d

51 TOLSTOY: *War and Peace*, BK I, 50b-c

52 DOSTOEVSKY: *Brothers Karamazov*, BK V, 127b-137c; BK VI, 150d-153d

6c(2) The light of faith

APOCRYPHA: *Ecclesiasticus*, 44–50 esp 44:20, 45:4, 46:15, 49:10, 50:28–29—(D) OT, *Ecclesiasticus*, 44–50 esp 44:21, 45:4, 46:17–18, 49:12, 50:30–31

NEW TESTAMENT: *Luke*, 8:4–17 / *John*, 6:28–40; 10:37–38; 12:44–46; 14:1,7–11; 16:27–31; 20:24–29 / *Romans*, 3:21–5:2; 10:14–17 / *II Corinthians*, 4:3–6 / *I Thessalonians*, 2:13 / *Hebrews*, 4:2; 11 / *I Peter*, 1:7–9,21–23 / *I John*, 2:20–29; 5:4–10

18 AUGUSTINE: *Confessions*, BK I, par 1 1a-b; BK IV, par 25 25c; BK VI, par 6–8 36c-37c; BK VII, par 16 48c-49a; BK XIII, par 19 115c-d / *City of God*, BK X, CH 1–2 298b,d-300a; BK XI, CH 2 323a-c; BK XIX, CH 18 523a-b; BK XXI, CH 5 563d-564d; BK XXII, CH 4–5 588b-590a; CH 7 591c-d / *Christian Doctrine*, BK I, CH 15 628b-c

19 AQUINAS: *Summa Theologica*, PART I, Q 2, A 2, REP 1 11d-12c; Q 32, A 1, ANS 175d-178a; Q 46, A 2, ANS 253a-255a

20 AQUINAS: *Summa Theologica*, PART I-II, Q 62, AA 3–4 61c-63a; Q 65, AA 4–5 73d-75a; Q 66, A 6 80c-81b; Q 67, A 3 83b-84d; A 5 85d-86d; Q 100, A 4, REP 1 253d-255a; Q 108, A 2, REP 1 332b-333d; Q 110, A 3, REP 1 350a-d; A 4, ANS 350d-351d; PART II-II, QQ 1–16 380a-456d; Q 45, A 1, REP 2 598d-599d; PART III, Q 14, A 1, ANS 784b-785c

21 DANTE: *Divine Comedy*, PARADISE, II [34–45] 108a; XXIV 142d-144b

22 CHAUCER: *Second Nun's Tale* 463b-471b

23 HOBBES: *Leviathan*, PART I, 66a-c; PART II, 137b-d; 149c-d; 160b; PART III, 165b-c; 172d-173a; 209b; 209d; 241a-242a

25 MONTAIGNE: *Essays*, 98b-99a; 209a-d; 212a-d; 238c-239c; 267c-268a; 294a-b

30 BACON: *Advancement of Learning*, 19b-c; 95d-96c / *Novum Organum*, BK I, APH 65 114b-c

6c(3) Mystical experience

6c(4) The beatific vision

**7. Doctrines common to the Jewish, Moham-
medan, and Christian conceptions of God
and His relation to the world and man**

7a. Creation

OLD TESTAMENT: *Genesis*, 1–2; 5:1–2 / *Exodus*,
20:11 / *I Samuel*, 2:8—(D) *I Kings*, 2:8 /
Nehemiah, 9:6—(D) *II Esdras*, 9:6 / *Job*, 9:1–
13; 10:8–13; 12:7–10; 26:7–14; 28:24–27;
37:14–38:41 esp 38:4–11 / *Psalms*, 8 esp 8:5;
19:1–6; 24:1–2; 33; 74:16–17; 89:11–12; 90:2;
95:1–7; 96:5; 102:25–28; 104; 119:73,90;
121:2; 136:5–9; 139:14–16; 146:5–6; 148—
(D) *Psalms*, 8 esp 8:6–7; 18:1–7; 23:1–2; 32;
73:16–17; 88:12–13; 89:2; 94:1–7; 95:5; 101:26–
29; 103; 118:73,90; 120:2; 135:5–9; 138:14–16;
145:5–6; 148 / *Proverbs*, 3:19–20; 8:22–31 /
Ecclesiastes, 3:11 / *Isaiah*, 40:26–28; 42:5–8;
44:24–28; 45:5–13; 48:12–16; 51:12–16; 64:8;
65:17—(D) *Isaias*, 40:26–28; 42:5–8; 44:24–
28; 45:5–13; 48:12–16; 51:12–16; 64:8; 65:17
/ *Jeremiah*, 10:11–13; 27:5; 31:35; 51:15–16—
(D) *Jeremias*, 10:11–13; 27:5; 31:35; 51:15–16
/ *Amos*, 4:13; 5:8 / *Jonah*, 1:9—(D) *Jonas*,
1:9 / *Zechariah*, 12:1—(D) *Zacharias*, 12:1

APOCRYPHA: *Judith*, 16:14—(D) OT, *Judith*,
16:17 / *Rest of Esther*, 13:10—(D) OT, *Esther*,
13:10 / *Wisdom of Solomon*, 1:14; 2:23; 6:7;
9:1,9; 11:17,24—(D) OT, *Book of Wisdom*,
1:14; 2:23; 6:8; 9:1,9; 11:18,25 / *Ecclesiasticus*, 17:1–9; 18:1–5; 23:19–20; 24:8–9;
33:9–13; 39:16–35; 42:15–43:33—(D) OT,
Ecclesiasticus, 17:1–8; 18:1–5; 23:27–29;
24:12–14; 33:10–14; 39:21–41; 42:15–43:37 /
Song of Three Children, 34–60—(D) OT,
Daniel, 3:56–82 / *Bel and Dragon*, 5—(D)
OT, *Daniel*, 14:4 / *II Maccabees*, 7:23,28—
(D) OT, *II Machabees*, 7:23,28

NEW TESTAMENT: *John*, 1:1–10 / *Acts*, 14:14–15;
17:23–27 / *Romans*, 1:19–20 / *Colossians*, 1:12–
17 / *Hebrews*, 1:10; 3:4; 11:3 / *II Peter*, 3:5 /
Revelation, 4:11; 10:6; 14:7—(D) *Apocalypse*,
4:11; 10:6; 14:7

18 AUGUSTINE: *Confessions*, BK VII, par 7 45a-d;
BK XI, par 5–11 90b-92b; BK XII–XIII 99b-
125a,c / *City of God*, BK VII, CH 29 261a-b; BK
VIII, CH 9–12 270d-273a; BK X, CH 31 319b-d;
BK XI, CH 4–34 324a-342a,c; BK XII 342b,d-
360a,c esp CH 1–2 342b,d-343d, CH 4–5 344b-
345b, CH 9–27 347b-360a,c; BK XIII, CH 24
373d-376a,c; BK XXII, CH 1 586b,d-587b;
CH 24, 609c-610a

19 AQUINAS: *Summa Theologica*, PART I, Q 7,
A 2, REP 3 31d-32c; Q 8, A 1 34d-35c; A 2, ANS
35c-36b; A 3, ANS and REP 1 36b-37c; Q 9, A 2,
ANS 39c-40d; Q 21, A 4, ANS and REP 4 126c-
127c; QQ 44–46 238a-255d; Q 50, A 1, ANS 269b-
270a; A 3, ANS 272a-273b; Q 56, A 2, ANS and
REP 4 292d-294a; Q 57, A 2, ANS and REP 2
295d-297a; Q 61 314d-317c; QQ 65–74 339a-
377a,c; Q 75, A 6, REP 1–2 383c-384c; Q 84,
A 3, REP 2 443d-444d; QQ 90–93 480c-501c;

Q 94, A 3, ANS 504a-505a; Q 104, A 1 esp REP 4
534c-536c; AA 3–4 537b-538c; Q 118, AA 2–3
601c-604b; Q 119, A 1, ANS 604c-607b

20 AQUINAS: *Summa Theologica*, PART II–II, Q 24,
A 5, ANS 492b-493d; PART III, Q 2, A 7 718b-d;
Q 3, A 8, REP 2 729b-730b; Q 6, A 3, REP 2
742a-743a

21 DANTE: *Divine Comedy*, PURGATORY, XXV [58–
78] 92a; XXVIII [91–96] 97a; PARADISE, VII
[64–75] 115d-116a; [121–148] 116b-c; X [1–27]
120b-c; XIII [52–87] 126a-b; XIX [40–51] 135c;
XXIX [1–48] 150b-d

23 HOBBES: *Leviathan*, PART II, 162b; PART III,
188d

30 BACON: *Advancement of Learning*, 17b-d /
Novum Organum, BK II, APH 15 149a

31 DESCARTES: *Discourse*, PART V, 54d-56a /
Meditations, III–IV, 87a-90b / *Objections and
Replies*, PROP III 132d-133a; 137d-138a;
140b-c; 214a-c; 229c-d

31 SPINOZA: *Ethics*, PART I, PROP 17, SCHOL 362c-
363c; APPENDIX, 370c-372d passim; PART IV,
PROP 68, SCHOL 445a-b

32 MILTON: *Paradise Lost*, BK I [6–10] 93b; [650–
659] 107b; BK II [345–353] 118b-119a; BK III
[56–134] 136b-138a; [708–735] 150b-151b; BK
IV [720–735] 168a-b; BK V [468–505] 185b-
186a; [577–599] 187b-188a; [800–863] 192b-
194a; BK VII [59–640] 218b-231a esp [139–161]
220a-b, [216–550] 221b-229a; BK VIII [452–
499] 242a-243a

33 PASCAL: *Pensées*, 482 258a

35 LOCKE: *Civil Government*, CH VI, SECT 56–57
36d-37b / *Human Understanding*, BK II,
CH XV, SECT 12, 165c; BK IV, CH X, SECT 15
352d-353a; SECT 18–19 353c-354c

35 BERKELEY: *Human Knowledge*, SECT 46
421b-c

35 HUME: *Human Understanding*, SECT XII, DIV
132, 509d [fn 1]

38 MONTESQUIEU: *Spirit of Laws*, BK I, 1a-b

41 GIBBON: *Decline and Fall*, 228a

42 KANT: *Pure Reason*, 81d-82a / *Judgement*, 594d
[fn 1]

46 HEGEL: *Philosophy of History*, PART I, 245d-
246a; PART IV, 361a

47 GOETHE: *Faust*, PROLOGUE [243–270] 7a-b

49 DARWIN: *Origin of Species*, 239c-243d

54 FREUD: *New Introductory Lectures*, 875d-876a

7b. Providence

OLD TESTAMENT: *Genesis*, 1–3; 6–9 esp 8:21–22;
12–13 esp 12:1–3, 12:7, 13:14–18; 15 esp 15:13–
21; 17–18; 21–22 esp 22:15–18; 26:1–6,22–25;
28:10–22; 35:9–15; 37–50 esp 45:7–8 / *Exodus*,
3; 12; 13:21–17:7; 19–20; 40:34–38—(D)
Exodus, 3; 12; 13:21–17:7; 19–20; 40:32–36 /
Numbers, 9:15–23; 12; 22–24 / *Deuteronomy*,
4:1–40; 6–11; 29–33 / *Joshua*, 1–11; 23–24—(D)
Josue, 1–11; 23–24 / *Judges*, 1–16 / *I Samuel*,
8–10; 15–16—(D) *I Kings*, 8–10; 15–16 / *II
Samuel*, 7—(D) *II Kings*, 7 / *I Kings*, 11; 13–22

passim—(D) *III Kings,* 11; 13-22 passim / *II Kings* passim—(D) *IV Kings* passim / *I Chronicles,* 17:3-15—(D) *I Paralipomenon,* 17:3-15 / *II Chronicles,* 11-36 passim—(D) *II Paralipomenon,* 11-36 passim / *Esther* esp 4:13-14—(D) *Esther,* 1:1-10:3 esp 4:13-14 / *Job* esp 1-2, 24, 27, 38-41 / *Psalms* passim, esp 3-4, 9-11, 13, 17-18, 65, 77, 104—(D) *Psalms* passim, esp 3-4, 9-10, 12, 16-17, 64, 76, 103 / *Proverbs,* 16:33 / *Ecclesiastes,* 3; 7:13-15; 8-9; 11-12 / *Isaiah,* 36-37; 46; 51—(D) *Isaias,* 36-37; 46; 51 / *Jeremiah,* 17:5-8; 18-19; 31; 45— (D) *Jeremias,* 17:5-8; 18-19; 31; 45 / *Daniel* passim, esp 3:1-4:3, 6:1-28—(D) *Daniel,* 1:1-3:23 passim, esp 3:1-23; 3:91-12:13 passim, esp 3:91-100, 6:1-28 / *Jonah* esp 1, 4—(D) *Jonas* esp 1, 4 / *Malachi,* 1:2-3—(D) *Malachias,* 1:2-3

APOCRYPHA: *Tobit*—(D) OT, *Tobias* / *Judith* esp 5-6, 8-16—(D) OT, *Judith* esp 5-6, 8-16 / *Rest of Esther*—(D) OT, *Esther,* 10:4-16:24 / *Wisdom of Solomon,* 14:1-3—(D) OT, *Book of Wisdom,* 14:1-3 / *Ecclesiasticus,* 15:11-20—(D) OT, *Ecclesiasticus,* 15:11-22 / *Song of Three Children*—(D) OT, *Daniel,* 3:24-90 / *Susanna* —(D) OT, *Daniel,* 13:1-64 / *Bel and Dragon* —(D) OT, *Daniel,* 13:65-14:42 / *I Maccabees,* 3:13-26—(D) OT, *I Machabees,* 3:13-26 / *II Maccabees,* 6:1-16—(D) OT, *II Machabees,* 6:1-16

NEW TESTAMENT: *Matthew,* 6:25-34; 7:7-11; 10 esp 10:17-20, 10:29-33; 23:37 / *Luke,* 11:1-13; 12:1-34; 21:12-19 / *John,* 6:22-71 esp 6:40, 6:44-45, 6:64-65—(D) *John,* 6:22-72 esp 6:40, 6:44-45, 6:65-66 / *Acts,* 1:15-26; 6:8-7:60; 13:48—(D) *Acts,* 1:15-26; 6:8-7:59; 13:48 / *Romans,* 8:28-11:36; 13:1-2 / *Ephesians,* 1:4-2:10; 4:1-7 / *Philippians,* 2:12-13 / *II Timothy,* 1:9 / *Hebrews,* 1:1-3; 13:5-6 / *I Peter,* 1:1-5

18 AUGUSTINE: *Confessions,* BK IX, par 1 61c-d / *City of God,* BK I, CH 8-9 133a-135a; BK IV, CH 33 206c-d; BK V, CH I 207d-208c; CH 8-11 212c-216d; CH 19 224b-225b; CH 21-22 226a-227a; BK X, CH 14-17 307c-310b; BK XI, CH 22 333d-334c; BK XII, CH 27 359c-360a,c; BK XIV, CH 27 396c-397a; BK XXII, CH 1 586b,d-587b / *Christian Doctrine,* BK II, CH 27 650a

19 AQUINAS: *Summa Theologica,* PART I, Q 3, A 1, REP 1 14b-15b; Q 8, A 3, ANS 36b-37c; Q 13, A 8, ANS and REP 1 70d-71b; Q 15, A 3, REP 4 93b-94a; QQ 22-24 127c-143c; Q 96, A 1, ANS and REP 2 510b-511b; PART I-II, Q 9, A 6, REP 3 662a-d

20 AQUINAS: *Summa Theologica,* PART I-II, Q 93, A 5, REP 3 219a-d; PART II-II, Q 1, A 7, ANS 385c-387a; Q 25, A 11, REP 3 508d-509c; PART III, Q 61, A 1, ANS 855a-d; PART III SUPPL, Q 69, A 3, ANS 887d-889c; Q 71, A 5, ANS 905c-908b; Q 77, A 1, ANS 943a-944d; Q 78, A 3, ANS 950b-951a

21 DANTE: *Divine Comedy,* HELL, VII [61-96] 10b-c; PARADISE, I [94-142] 107b-d; VI [1-111]

113c-114d; VIII [85-148] 117c-118c; XI-XII 122a-125a esp XI [28-39] 122b, XII [37-45] 124a; XX [31-138] 137a-138a

22 CHAUCER: *Troilus and Cressida,* BK IV, STANZA 138-154 106b-108b / *Knight's Tale* [1251-1267] 180b; [1663-1672] 187b / *Tale of Man of Law* 236b-255b esp [4869-4924] 242b-243b, [5247-5253] 249b / *Friar's Tale* [7064-7085] 281a-b / *Franklin's Tale* [11,177-206] 353b-354a / *Monk's Tale* [14,021-052] 434b-435a; [14,149-252] 437a-438b

23 HOBBES: *Leviathan,* PART I, 53d; PART II, 113b-c; 160a; 162b; PART IV, 254b; 271b

25 MONTAIGNE: *Essays,* 98b-99a

26 SHAKESPEARE: *Richard III,* ACT II, SC II [77-95] 120b-c

27 SHAKESPEARE: *Hamlet,* ACT V, SC II [1-11] 67d-68a; [47-53] 68b-c; [230-235] 70a

29 CERVANTES: *Don Quixote,* PART II, 408c

30 BACON: *Advancement of Learning,* 19d; 38a / *Novum Organum,* BK I, APH 93 125d-126a

32 MILTON: *Sonnets,* XVI 66b-67a / *Paradise Lost,* BK III [80-134] 137a-138a / *Samson Agonistes* [210-214] 344a; [373-380] 347b-348a; [667-709] 354a-355a / *Areopagitica,* 394b-395b

33 PASCAL: *Pensées,* 619-641 284b-290a

35 BERKELEY: *Human Knowledge,* INTRO, SECT 3 405b-c; SECT 60-66 424b-426a; SECT 93-94 431b-c; SECT 105-107 433b-434a; SECT 146-155 442a-444c

35 HUME: *Human Understanding,* SECT VII, DIV 54-57 474b-475d; SECT XI, DIV 108 500b-d

37 FIELDING: *Tom Jones,* 75c-d; 377c-378a

38 ROUSSEAU: *Inequality,* 331c-d / *Social Contract,* BK III, 414d; BK IV, 437d-438b

40 GIBBON: *Decline and Fall,* 292d-294a

41 GIBBON: *Decline and Fall,* 542a-b

44 BOSWELL: *Johnson,* 95c-d

46 HEGEL: *Philosophy of History,* INTRO, 158c-160b; 168d-170b; PART IV, 321b-c; 368d-369a,c

48 MELVILLE: *Moby Dick,* 85a; 237a; 396b-397a

51 TOLSTOY: *War and Peace,* BK VI, 272a-b; BK IX, 342a-344b; 357b-358b; BK X, 447c-448a; 465c-467c passim; BK XII, 553b; BK XIII, 563a-b; BK XV, 619d-620a; 631a-c; EPILOGUE I, 650b-c; EPILOGUE II, 675a-677b; 680b-c; 684b-d

52 DOSTOEVSKY: *Brothers Karamazov,* BK V, 127b-137c passim; BK XI, 343b-c

54 FREUD: *Civilization and Its Discontents,* 771a-b

7c. Divine government and law

OLD TESTAMENT: *Genesis,* 9:1-7 / *Exodus,* 12-13; 15:18; 19-31 esp 20:1-17; 34-35 / *Leviticus* passim / *Numbers* passim, esp 5-10, 15, 18-19, 27-30, 35-36 / *Deuteronomy* passim, esp 5:6-21 / *I Chronicles,* 29:11-12—(D) *I Paralipomenon,* 29:11-12 / *Job,* 9:1-13; 34:12-18; 37-41 / *Psalms,* 1; 10:16; 19:7-14; 37:30-31; 40:8; 47; 59:13; 66:7; 72:8; 78:1-8; 89:30-32; 93;

7e. Miracles

**(7. Doctrines common to the Jewish, Mohamme-
dan, and Christian conceptions of God and
His relation to the world and man. 7e.
Miracles.)**

22 CHAUCER: *Tale of Man of Law* 236b-255b
esp [4869-4924] 242b-243b / *Prioress's Tale*
[13,418-620] 392a-395b / *Second Nun's Tale*
[16,001-021] 471a-b

23 HOBBES: *Leviathan*, PART I, 83c; PART II,
137b-c; 160b; PART III, 166a-167b; 188a-191a;
PART IV, 249b-250a

30 BACON: *Advancement of Learning*, 19b-c;
33c-d; 41b-d / *New Atlantis*, 201d-203c esp
203a-b

32 MILTON: *Paradise Lost*, BK XII [173-222] 323a-
324a

33 PASCAL: *Pensées*, 643-644 290b-291b; 803-856
328b-341b; 876 345a

35 LOCKE: *Human Understanding*, BK IV, CH XVI,
SECT 13 371a-b

35 BERKELEY: *Human Knowledge*, SECT 62-63
425a-c; SECT 84 429b-c

35 HUME: *Human Understanding*, SECT VII, DIV
54 474b-c; SECT X 488d-497b

40 GIBBON: *Decline and Fall*, 180b-c; 189b-191a;
206b-d; 295c-296b; 465d-466c; 605b-d

41 GIBBON: *Decline and Fall*, 227d-228a; 232a-c;
398b-399b

44 BOSWELL: *Johnson*, 126b-c; 359a

46 HEGEL: *Philosophy of History*, PART I, 247a;
PART III, 307a-b; PART IV, 338b-c; 348d-
349a

47 GOETHE: *Faust*, PART I [762-770] 20a

51 TOLSTOY: *War and Peace*, BK V, 219b-220a

52 DOSTOEVSKY: *Brothers Karamazov*, BK I,
11a-b; BK II, 21d-22b; BK V, 127b-137c passim;
BK VII, 171a-177b; 189d-190a

7f. The Book of Life

OLD TESTAMENT: *Exodus*, 32:31-33; 33:19 /
Psalms, 69:28—(D) *Psalms*, 68:29 / *Isaiah*,
4:3—(D) *Isaias*, 4:3

APOCRYPHA: *Ecclesiasticus*, 33:10-13—(D) OT,
Ecclesiasticus, 33:10-14

NEW TESTAMENT: *Matthew*, 20:1-16; 22:1-14 /
Luke, 10:20 / *John*, 5:21; 6:44; 10:26-29 / *Acts*,
13:48 / *Romans*, 8:28-9:23 / *Ephesians*, 1-3 /
II Thessalonians, 2:12-14 / *II Timothy*, 1:8-9;
2:19-20 / *Hebrews*, 12:22-23 / *I Peter*, 1:1-5;
2:1-9 / *II Peter*, 1:10 / *Revelation*, 3:4-5; 13:4-8;
17:7-8; 20:11-21:27 esp 20:15, 21:27; 22:18-
19—(D) *Apocalypse*, 3:4-5; 13:4-8; 17:7-8;
20:11-21:27 esp 20:15, 21:27; 22:18-19

18 AUGUSTINE: *City of God*, BK XV, CH 1 397b,d-
398c; BK XX, CH 8 536d-538c; CH 14-16 542d-
544d

19 AQUINAS: *Summa Theologica*, PART I, Q 24
141b-143c

20 AQUINAS: *Summa Theologica*, PART III, Q 63,
A I, REP I 864c-865b; PART III SUPPL, Q 87, A I
997b-998c

---

21 DANTE: *Divine Comedy*, PARADISE, XIX [103-
148] 136a-c; XX [94-138] 137d-138a; XXI [52-
102] 138d-139b; XXXII [40-84] 155a-c

32 MILTON: *Paradise Lost*, BK I [356-363] 101a

33 PASCAL: *Pensées*, 884 346a

41 GIBBON: *Decline and Fall*, 238c; 334b-c

7g. The resurrection of the body

OLD TESTAMENT: *Job*, 14:13-15; 19:25-27 /
Isaiah, 26:19; 66:14—(D) *Isaias*, 26:19; 66:14
/ *Ezekiel*, 37:1-14—(D) *Ezechiel*, 37:1-14 /
Daniel, 12:1-3

APOCRYPHA: *II Maccabees*, 12:41-45—(D) OT,
II Machabees, 12:42-46

NEW TESTAMENT: *Matthew*, 22:23-33; 27:52-53;
28 / *Mark*, 12:18-27; 16:1-9 / *Luke*, 20:27-38;
24:1-12 / *John*, 2:18-22 / *Acts*, 23:1-10; 24:15;
26:8 / *Romans*, 4:17; 6:3-11; 8:10-11 / *I Corinthians*, 6:14; 15 / *II Corinthians*, 1:9-10;
4:14 / *I Thessalonians*, 4:13-17 / *Hebrews*, 6:1-2

18 AUGUSTINE: *City of God*, BK X, CH 29, 317b-
318a; BK XIII, CH 1-2 360a-361a; CH 16-20
367a-371a; CH 22-24 371c-376a,c; BK XX, CH
6-7 534a-536d; CH 9-10 538c-541a; CH 12-17
541c-545c; CH 20-23 547c-552c; CH 26, 555d-
556a; BK XX, CH 30-BK XXI, CH 10, 559d-
570b; BK XXII 586b,d-618d esp CH 4-5 588b-
590a, CH 7 591c-d, CH 11-21 599c-606d, CH
25-30 612a-618d / *Christian Doctrine*, BK I,
CH 19-21 629a-b; CH 23-24 630a-631a

20 AQUINAS: *Summa Theologica*, PART III SUPPL,
QQ 75-86 935a-996a,c; Q 93, A I 1037d-1039a

21 DANTE: *Divine Comedy*, HELL, VI [94-111]
9b-c; X [1-15] 13d; XIII [85-108] 18d-19a;
PARADISE, VII [121-148] 116b-c; XIV [1-66]
126d-127c; XXV [64-129] 145a-c

23 HOBBES: *Leviathan*, PART III, 191b-193c;
195b-d; PART IV, 253b-255b; 259b-c

25 MONTAIGNE: *Essays*, 248c-249c; 311a

32 MILTON: *Paradise Lost*, BK III [227-343] 140b-
143a esp [294-329] 141b-142b; BK XII [386-
445] 327b-329a esp [411-429] 328a-b

35 BERKELEY: *Human Knowledge*, SECT 95 431c

38 MONTESQUIEU: *Spirit of Laws*, BK XXIV, 205d-
206a

41 GIBBON: *Decline and Fall*, 233d; 234d

44 BOSWELL: *Johnson*, 472a-b

7h. The Last Judgment and the end of the world

OLD TESTAMENT: *Job*, 19:25-27; 21:27-34 /
Psalms, 50; 96:10-13—(D) *Psalms*, 49; 95:10-
13 / *Ecclesiastes*, 3:16-17; 11:9-10; 12:14 /
Isaiah, 2-4; 11:11-16; 13:6-22; 24; 26-27;
30; 34-35; 65:17-25; 66—(D) *Isaias*, 2-4;
11:11-16; 13:6-22; 24; 26-27; 30; 34-35;
65:17-25; 66 / *Daniel*, 7:21-27; 12 / *Joel* /
Micah, 4—(D) *Micheas*, 4 / *Zephaniah*—(D)
Sophonias / *Zechariah*, 14—(D) *Zacharias*,
14 / *Malachi*, 3-4—(D) *Malachias*, 3-4

APOCRYPHA: *Judith*, 16:17—(D) OT, *Judith*,
16:20-21 / *Rest of Esther*, 10:4-11:12—(D)
OT, *Esther*, 10:4-11:12

NEW TESTAMENT: *Matthew,* 7:1-2; 10:14-15; 11:20-24; 12:36; 13:36-43,47-50; 24-25 / *Mark,* 13:4-37 / *Luke,* 17:20-37; 21:5-36 / *John,* 12:48 / *Acts,* 2:17-21; 17:31 / *Romans,* 2:5-11 / *I Corinthians,* 4:15-5:4; 15:23-28 / *I Thessalonians,* 1:9-10; 2:19; 4:14-5:4 / *II Thessalonians,* 1-2 / *II Timothy,* 3:1-4:9 / *Hebrews,* 9:26-27 / *James,* 5:7-9 / *I Peter,* 4:5-6 / *II Peter,* 2:9; 3:7-13 / *I John,* 2:18-29; 4:17 / *Jude* / *Revelation* passim, esp 14:15-16:21, 20:1-22:21—(D) *Apocalypse* passim, esp 14:15-16:21, 20:1-22:21

18 AUGUSTINE: *City of God,* BK XVIII, CH 53 504d-505c; BK XX 530a-560a,c; BK XXI, CH 11-27 570b-586a,c / *Christian Doctrine,* BK III, CH 37, 673d-674a

20 AQUINAS: *Summa Theologica,* PART III SUPPL, QQ 73-74 922b-935a,c; Q 77, A 2 945a-946b; QQ 87-99 997a-1085a,c

21 DANTE: *Divine Comedy,* HELL, VI [94-115] 9b-c; X [1-15] 13d; PARADISE, XIX [100-148] 136a-c

22 CHAUCER: *Parson's Tale,* par 10 498b-502a

23 HOBBES: *Leviathan,* PART III, 230a; 244b-c

32 MILTON: *Christs Nativity* [133-172] 4b-5b / *Paradise Lost,* BK III [274-343] 141b-143a esp [326-341] 142b; BK VII [139-173] 220a-221a; BK XI [45-83] 300a-301a; BK XII [451-465] 329a; [537-551] 331a / *Areopagitica,* 410a-b

35 LOCKE: *Toleration,* 17a-b

40 GIBBON: *Decline and Fall,* 187c-189a

41 GIBBON: *Decline and Fall,* 233c-234d

52 DOSTOEVSKY: *Brothers Karamazov,* BK V, 127b-137c passim, esp 134d-135a; BK XI, 337a-346a passim

8. Specifically Jewish doctrines concerning God and His people

8*a*. The Chosen People: Jew and gentile

OLD TESTAMENT: *Genesis,* 12:1-4; 13:14-17; 15; 17:1-18:19; 22:1-18 esp 22:15-17; 26:1-6,23-25; 27-28; 35:9-13; 46:1-7; 48-49 / *Exodus,* 3-17; 19-20; 33:1-34:18 / *Leviticus,* 26 / *Deuteronomy,* 1; 4-12 passim, esp 4:37-38, 7:6-8, 10:15; 14:1-2; 15:6; 23:1-8; 26-32 passim, esp 26:17-19, 28:1-68, 31:16-21, 32:9-14 / *Joshua,* 10:12-14; 23:1-13—(D) *Josue,* 10:12-14; 23:1-13 / *I Samuel,* 12—(D) *I Kings,* 12 / *I Kings,* 8:51-53—(D) *III Kings,* 8:51-53 / *II Kings,* 11:17—(D) *IV Kings,* 11:17 / *I Chronicles,* 17—(D) *I Paralipomenon,* 17 / *Nehemiah,* 9—(D) *II Esdras,* 9 / *Psalms* passim, esp 33:12, 50:7, 78:1-72, 81:1-16, 89:1-52, 105:1-106:48, 132:1-18, 135:4-14, 136:1-26—(D) *Psalms* passim, esp 32:12, 49:7, 77:1-72, 80:2-17, 88:2-53, 104:1-105:48, 131:1-18, 134:4-14, 135:1-27 / *Isaiah* passim, esp 40:1; 42:1-6, 43:1-7, 44:1-5, 46:3-4, 49:1-26, 63:7-8—(D) *Isaias* passim, esp 40:1, 42:1-6, 43:1-7, 44:1-5, 46:3-4, 49:1-26, 63:7-8 / *Jeremiah* passim, esp 3, 7:23, 11:4, 24:7, 30:22, 31:1, 31:33,

32:38—(D) *Jeremias* passim, esp 3, 7:23, 11:4, 24:7, 30:22, 31:1, 31:33, 32:38 / *Ezekiel,* 11:15-20; 14:11; 16-17; 20; 34; 36-37—(D) *Ezechiel,* 11:15-20; 14:11; 16-17; 20; 34; 36-37 / *Amos,* 3:1-2 / *Obadiah*—(D) *Abdias* / *Micah,* 5:7-15—(D) *Micheas,* 5:7-11 / *Zechariah,* 1:12-2:13; 8-10 esp 8:8—(D) *Zacharias,* 1:12-2:13; 8-10 esp 8:8 / *Malachi,* 1:1-3—(D) *Malachias,* 1:1-3

APOCRYPHA: *Rest of Esther,* 14:5—(D) OT, *Esther,* 14:5 / *Wisdom of Solomon,* 16:20-26—(D) OT, *Book of Wisdom,* 16:20-26 / *Ecclesiasticus,* 17:17-21; 47:22—(D) OT, *Ecclesiasticus,* 17:14-17; 47:24-25

NEW TESTAMENT: *Matthew,* 10:5-6 / *Acts,* 15:1-29; 21:19-25 / *Romans,* 1:13-16; 2-4; 9; 10:11-13; 11 / *I Corinthians,* 12:13 / *Galatians,* 2:6-16; 3:13-29; 4:21-31; 5:6; 6:15 / *Ephesians,* 2:11-3:8 / *Colossians,* 3:9-11

15 TACITUS: *Histories,* BK V, 295d

18 AUGUSTINE: *City of God,* BK IV, CH 34 206d-207a,c; BK XVI, CH 16 433c-434a; CH 18 434c; CH 21-28 435a-440b; CH 32 441c-442c; BK XVII, CH 7 458c-459d; BK XIX, CH 22 525b-c

19 AQUINAS: *Summa Theologica,* PART I, Q 21, A 4, REP 2 126c-127c

20 AQUINAS: *Summa Theologica,* PART I-II, Q 98, AA 4-5 242b-244b; QQ 102-105 270b-321a passim, esp Q 102, A 6 292c-298a

23 HOBBES: *Leviathan,* PART I, 82d-83a; PART II, 160b-c; PART III, 177c-180d

32 MILTON: *Paradise Lost,* BK XII [101-269] 321b-325a / *Samson Agonistes* 339a-378a esp [210-292] 344a-346a, [420-471] 348b-350a, [843-902] 358a-359a, [1156-1223] 364b-366a

33 PASCAL: *Pensées,* 603 279b; 610-612 280b-282b; 619-641 284b-290a; 713-718 304b-308b

38 ROUSSEAU: *Social Contract,* BK IV, 435b-c

40 GIBBON: *Decline and Fall,* 179d-183a

46 HEGEL: *Philosophy of History,* PART I, 245d-247b; PART III, 305b-c; PART IV, 322a-b

8*b*. God's Covenant with Israel: circumcision as sign of the Covenant

OLD TESTAMENT: *Genesis,* 12:1-3,7; 15:17-21; 17; 22:16-18; 26:2-3 / *Exodus,* 2:23-4:31 esp 2:24; 6:1-9; 19:3-8; 24:7-8; 31:16-17; 32:11-13; 34 esp 34:10, 34:27-28 / *Leviticus,* 2:13; 26 / *Deuteronomy,* 1:8; 4-11 passim, esp 4:23, 5:2-3, 7:12-13, 8:18-20, 10:16; 29-31; 34:4 / *Joshua,* 5:1-9; 7:10-12; 23:16-24:28—(D) *Josue,* 5:1-9; 7:10-12; 23:16-24:28 / *Judges,* 2:1-5 / *I Kings,* 8:56; 19:9-18—(D) *III Kings,* 8:56; 19:9-18 / *II Kings,* 11:17; 13:22-23; 17 esp 17:14-16, 17:34-40; 22-23 esp 23:2-3—(D) *IV Kings,* 11:17; 13:22-23; 17 esp 17:14-16, 17:34-40; 22-23 esp 23:2-3 / *I Chronicles,* 16:13-22—(D) *I Paralipomenon,* 16:13-22 / *II Chronicles,* 6:14-15—(D) *II Paralipomenon,* 6:14-15 / *Nehemiah,* 1:5; 9—(D) *II Esdras,* 1:5; 9 / *Psalms,* 25:14; 44:17; 74:19-20; 78; 105 esp 105:7-8; 111—(D) *Psalms,* 24:14; 43:18;

(8. *Specifically Jewish doctrines concerning God and His people. 8b. God's Covenant with Israel: circumcision as sign of the Covenant.*)

73:19-20; 77; 104 esp 104:7-8; 110 / *Isaiah*, 24:1-5; 33:1-8; 54 esp 54:10; 56 esp 56:4-6; 59:20-21; 61 esp 61:8—(D) *Isaias*, 24:1-5; 33:1-8; 54 esp 54:10; 56 esp 56:4-6; 59:20-21; 61 esp 61:8 / *Jeremiah*, 4:4; 11; 14:19-22; 22:5-9; 31-33 esp 31:31-33, 32:40, 33:20-26; 34:13-20; 50:4-5—(D) *Jeremias*, 4:4; 11; 14:19-22; 22:5-9; 31-33 esp 31:31-33, 32:40, 33:20-26; 34:13-20; 50:4-5 / *Ezekiel*, 16-17; 20:33-38; 37:21-28; 44:6-9—(D) *Ezechiel*, 16-17; 20:33-38; 37:21-28; 44:6-9 / *Hosea*, 2:16-20; 6 esp 6:7; 8—(D) *Osee*, 2:16-20; 6 esp 6:7; 8 / *Haggai*, 2:4-5—(D) *Aggeus*, 2:5-6

APOCRYPHA: *Ecclesiasticus*, 44:19-45:5—(D) OT, *Ecclesiasticus*, 44:20-45:6 / *I Maccabees*, 1:44-63; 2:19-6:8 esp 4:7-14—(D) OT, *I Machabees*, 1:46-66; 2:19-6:8 esp 4:7-14

NEW TESTAMENT: *Luke*, 1:70-75; 2:21 / *John*, 7:22-23 / *Acts*, 3:25; 7:1-8,51-53; 15:1-29; 21:20-21 / *Romans*, 2:25-4:16; 11:25-27 / *I Corinthians*, 7:18-19 / *Galatians*, 3:13-5:11; 6:12-15 / *Ephesians*, 2:11-13 / *Colossians*, 2:10-14; 3:9-11 / *Hebrews*, 8:6-10:17

18 AUGUSTINE: *City of God*, BK XVI, CH 16 433c-434a; CH 18 434c; CH 21-28 435a-440b; CH 32 441c-442c; CH 36-38 443d-446a; BK XIX, CH 22 525b-c

20 AQUINAS: *Summa Theologica*, PART I-II, Q 98, AA 4-6 242b-245b

23 HOBBES: *Leviathan*, PART I, 82d-83a; PART III, 177c-180a; 199b-201b; 206c

32 MILTON: *Upon the Circumcision* 12b-13a

33 PASCAL: *Pensées*, 610-612 280b-282b; 637-639 289b-290a; 675 296b-297a

46 HEGEL: *Philosophy of History*, PART IV, 322a-b

8c. The Law: its observance as a condition of righteousness and blessedness

OLD TESTAMENT: *Genesis*, 26:4-5 / *Exodus*, 12-13; 19-40 esp 20:1-17 / *Leviticus* passim, esp 26 / *Numbers* passim / *Deuteronomy* passim, esp 4:1-15, 5:6-21, 6:1-9, 6:17-25, 7:9-26, 10:12-13, 11:1-32, 12:32, 28:1-68, 30:11-20 / *Joshua*, 1:7-8; 8:30-35; 22:1-6—(D) *Josue*, 1:7-8; 8:30-35; 22:1-6 / *I Kings*, 8:54-62—(D) *III Kings*, 8:54-62 / *II Kings*, 17; 21:8—(D) *IV Kings*, 17; 21:8 / *I Chronicles*, 22:12-13—(D) *I Paralipomenon*, 22:12-13 / *II Chronicles*, 31; 33:8; 35:1-19—(D) *II Paralipomenon*, 31; 33:8; 35:1-19 / *Ezra*, 9-10—(D) *I Esdras*, 9-10 / *Nehemiah*, 1:5-9; 9:16-38—(D) *II Esdras*, 1:5-9; 9:16-38 / *Psalms*, 1; 19:7-14; 37:30-31; 40:8; 78; 89:20-36 esp 89:30-32; 94:12; 105:43-45; 119—(D) *Psalms*, 1; 18:8-15; 36:30-31; 39:9; 77; 88:21-37 esp 88:31-33; 93:12; 104:43-45; 118 / *Proverbs* passim, esp 6:20-23, 28:7, 29:18 / *Isaiah* passim, esp

5:24-25, 30:9, 42:21-25, 51:7-8—(D) *Isaias* passim, esp 5:24-25, 30:9, 42:21-25, 51:7-8 / *Jeremiah* passim, esp 2:5-8, 6:19, 9:13-16, 16:10-13, 26:4-6, 31:33, 44:10-14, 44:23—(D) *Jeremias* passim, esp 2:5-8, 6:19, 9:13-16, 16:10-13, 26:4-6, 31:33, 44:10-14, 44:23 / *Ezekiel*, 5:5-9; 11:17-20; 18; 22:26; 36:25-27; 43-48—(D) *Ezechiel*, 5:5-9; 11:17-20; 18; 22:26; 36:25-27; 43-48 / *Daniel*, 9:1-15 / *Hosea*, 4:6; 8:1—(D) *Osee*, 4:6; 8:1 / *Amos* 2:4-6 / *Zephaniah*, 3:1-7—(D) *Sophonias* 3:1-7 / *Zechariah*, 7:12-14—(D) *Zacharias* 7:12-14 / *Malachi*, 2:1-10; 3:7; 4:4—(D) *Malachias*, 2:1-10; 3:7; 4:4

APOCRYPHA: *Tobit*, 14:8-9—(D) OT, *Tobias*, 14:10-11 / *Ecclesiasticus* passim, esp 2:16, 9:15, 10:19, 11:15, 17:11-14, 19:17-20, 19:24, 24:23, 32:15, 33:2, 34:8, 39:1-11, 41:8, 42:1-2, 45:1-5—(D) OT, *Ecclesiasticus* passim, esp 2:19, 9:22-23, 10:23, 11:15, 17:9-12, 19:17-18, 19:21, 24:32-33, 32:19, 33:2, 34:8, 39:1-15, 41:11, 42:1-2, 45:1-6 / *Baruch*—(D) OT, *Baruch* / *I Maccabees*, 1:38-63; 2:19-68—(D) OT, *I Machabees*, 1:40-66; 2:19-68 / *II Maccabees*, 2:2-3; 6-7; 11:22-26—(D) OT, *II Machabees*, 2:2-3; 6-7; 11:22-26

NEW TESTAMENT: *Matthew*, 5:17-20; 12:1-13; 15:1-20; 19:3-9 / *Mark*, 7:1-23; 10:2-12 / *Luke*, 6:1-9; 11:37-41; 14:2-5; 16:16-17 / *John*, 1:17; 5:1-18,45-47; 7:19-23 / *Acts*, 10:9-15,25-28; 13:38-39; 15:1-10; 21:20-21 / *Romans* passim / *Galatians* passim / *Ephesians*, 2:14-15 / *I Timothy*, 1:5-11 / *Hebrews*, 7-10

18 AUGUSTINE: *City of God*, BK X, CH 17 309c-310b; BK XX, CH 28 556c-557a

20 AQUINAS: *Summa Theologica*, PART I-II, Q 91, AA 4-5 210c-212c; QQ 98-105 239b-321a

21 DANTE: *Divine Comedy*, PARADISE, V [13-84] 112b-113a passim

23 HOBBES: *Leviathan*, PART III, 177d-178a; 180a-d; 206c-207a; 216b-218a; 223a-c; PART IV, 269a

30 BACON: *Advancement of Learning*, 18b-c

32 MILTON: *Paradise Lost*, BK XII [223-260] 324a-325a; [285-314] 325b-326a

33 PASCAL: *Pensées*, 610 280b-282a; 619-620 284b-286a; 628-634 287a-289a; 678 297a-b; 680 298a

35 LOCKE: *Toleration*, 14b-15a

40 GIBBON: *Decline and Fall*, 179d-182c esp 181a-182a; 208a-c

46 HEGEL: *Philosophy of History*, PART I, 246c-d

8d. The Temple: the Ark of the Torah

OLD TESTAMENT: *Exodus*, 25-27; 30:1-6; 35:10-38:31; 39:32-40:36 / *Leviticus*, 26:11 / *Numbers*, 9:15-22 / *Deuteronomy*, 10:1-5; 12:5-6; 16:5-6; 31:24-26 / *Joshua*, 3-4; 6:1-16—(D) *Josue*, 3-4; 6:1-16 / *I Samuel*, 4:3-7:2—(D) *I Kings*, 4:3-7:2 / *II Samuel*, 6:1-17; 7:1-13—(D) *II Kings*, 6:1-17; 7:1-13 / *I Kings*, 5-8—(D) *III Kings*, 5-8 / *II Kings*, 12:4-16;

25:1–17—(D) *IV Kings*, 12:4–16; 25:1–17 /
I Chronicles, 13; 15:1–17:12; 22:1–29:10—(D)
I Paralipomenon, 13; 15:1–17:12; 22:1–29:10
/ *II Chronicles*, 2–7 esp 7:12–16; 8:11;
24:4–14; 29; 34; 36—(D) *II Paralipomenon*,
2–7 esp 7:12–16; 8:11; 24:4–14; 29; 34; 36 /
Ezra, 3–6—(D) *I Esdras*, 3–6 / *Psalms*, 5:7;
11:4; 27:4–6; 65:4; 68:29; 138:2—(D) *Psalms*,
5:8; 10:5; 26:4–6; 64:5; 67:30; 137:2 / *Isaiah*,
2:2–3; 56:6–7—(D) *Isaias*, 2:2–3; 56:6–7 /
Jeremiah, 7:1–4,29–30; 26:1–7—(D) *Jeremias*,
7:1–4,29–30; 26:1–7 / *Ezekiel*, 40–42—(D)
Ezechiel, 40–42 / *Jonah*, 2:4—(D) *Jonas*, 2:5 /
Micah, 4:1–2—(D) *Micheas*, 4:1–2 / *Habakkuk*, 2:20—(D) *Habacuc*, 2:20 / *Haggai*—
(D) *Aggeus* / *Zechariah*, 8:9—(D) *Zacharias*,
8:9 / *Malachi*, 3:1—(D) *Malachias*, 3:1

APOCRYPHA: *Tobit*, 14:4–7—(D) OT, *Tobias*,
14:6–9 / *Wisdom of Solomon*, 9:8—(D) OT,
Book of Wisdom, 9:8 / *Baruch*, 2:26—(D)
OT, *Baruch*, 2:26

NEW TESTAMENT: *John*, 2:13–17 / *Hebrews*,
9:1–10

15 TACITUS: *Histories*, BK V, 296a; 297d–298a

18 AUGUSTINE: *City of God*, BK X, CH 17 309c–
310b

20 AQUINAS: *Summa Theologica*, PART I–II, Q 101,
A 4, ANS and REP 1,4 269a–270b; Q 102, A 4
276d–283c

23 HOBBES: *Leviathan*, PART III, 178c; 180a–c;
184c; 198a–b

32 MILTON: *Paradise Lost*, BK XII [244–256] 324b;
[284–371] 325b–327a esp [331–343] 326b

40 GIBBON: *Decline and Fall*, 180a; 180d–181a;
352c–354d esp 354a–b

8e. The messianic hope

OLD TESTAMENT: *Genesis*, 49:10–12 / *Numbers*,
24:15–25 / *Deuteronomy*, 30:1–10 / *Psalms*,
22:27–31; 44; 46–48; 60; 67–69 passim; 74;
102; 106:40–48; 126; 132; 147:1–11—(D)
Psalms, 21:28–32; 43; 45–47; 59; 66–68 passim; 73; 101; 105:40–48; 125; 131; 146 /
Isaiah, 2–4; 7:10–16; 9:1–7; 11–12; 25–27;
30:18–33; 32; 40–46 esp 41:25–42:4; 49;
51–56 esp 52:13–53:12; 59:20–62:12; 65:17–
66:24—(D) *Isaias*, 2–4; 7:10–16; 9:1–7; 11–12;
25–27; 30:18–33; 32; 40–46 esp 41:25–42:4;
49; 51–56 esp 52:13–53:12; 59:20–62:12;
65:17–66:24 / *Jeremiah*, 23:3–6; 30–33—(D)
Jeremias, 23:3–6; 30–33 / *Ezekiel*, 17:22–
24; 34; 36–37—(D) *Ezechiel*, 17:22–24; 34;
36–37 / *Daniel*, 9:20–27 / *Hosea*, 1:10–11;
2:16–23; 3:3–5; 13–14—(D) *Osee*, 1:10–11;
2:16–24; 3:3–5; 13–14 / *Joel*, 2–3 / *Amos*,
9:9–15—(D) *Amos*, 9:9–14 / *Micah*, 2:12–13;
4–5; 7:7–20—(D) *Micheas*, 2:12–13; 4–5; 7:7–
20 / *Zephaniah*, 3—(D) *Sophonias*, 3 / *Zechariah*, 2; 8–10; 12–14—(D) *Zacharias*, 2; 8–10;
12–14 / *Malachi*, 3–4—(D) *Malachias*, 3–4

NEW TESTAMENT: *Matthew*, 1 esp 1:20–23; 3:1–
3,13–17; 12:14–21; 16:13–16; 17:1–13; 26:63–

64 / *Mark*, 8:27–29; 9:2–13; 14:61–62 / *Luke*,
1:30–35; 3:1–6,15–16; 7:24–28; 9:18–20,28–
36; 22:66–70 / *John*, 1:15–41 esp 1:41; 4:4–30
esp 4:25–26; 7:26–53; 10:24–38

20 AQUINAS: *Summa Theologica*, PART III, Q 1,
A 6 708c–709c

23 HOBBES: *Leviathan*, PART III, 229c

32 MILTON: *Paradise Lost*, BK XII [235–244]
324b; [284–330] 325b–326b

33 PASCAL: *Pensées*, 607 280a; 609 280b; 613
282b–283a; 616–619 283b–285a; 642 290b;
662 293b; 673 296a; 675 296b–297a; 692
300b–301a; 719 308b–309a; 727 315b–316b;
729–730 316b–317a

40 GIBBON: *Decline and Fall*, 181b; 207d–208a;
308a

41 GIBBON: *Decline and Fall*, 134b–135a

9. Specifically Christian dogmas concerning the divine nature and human destiny

9a. The Trinity

OLD TESTAMENT: *Genesis*, 1:26

NEW TESTAMENT: *Matthew*, 1:18–20; 3:11,16–
17; 10:19–20; 12:31–32; 28:19 / *Mark*, 1:8–12;
3:28–30; 13:11 / *Luke*, 1:15,26–35; 2:25–27;
3:16,21–22; 11:13; 12:10–12 / *John*, 1:1–8,14,
18,32–34; 3 esp 3:16–17, 3:35–36; 14–16;
20:22–23 / *Acts*, 1:2,5–8; 2:1–41 esp 2:32–39;
4:23–31; 5:32; 8:17–22; 9:31; 10:38,44–48;
11:15–17; 13:2–4; 15:7–9; 19:1–6; 20:28;
28:25–27 / *Romans*, 5 esp 5:5–10; 8:1–9:1;
14:17; 15:13,16 / *I Corinthians*, 2:9–14;
3:16–23; 6:19; 12:2–13 / *II Corinthians*,
1:18–22; 4:4; 13:14—(D) *II Corinthians*,
1:18–22; 4:4; 13:13 / *Ephesians*, 1–3 passim
/ *Colossians*, 1:13–15 / *I Thessalonians*,
1:5–6 / *II Timothy*, 1:14 / *Titus*, 3:4–7 /
Hebrews, 1:2–3; 6:4–6; 10:14–17 / *I Peter*,
1:1–12 / *II Peter*, 1:21 / *I John*, 4–5 esp
4:9–10, 4:14–15, 5:1–2, 5:5–7, 5:10–12 / *Jude*,
17–21

18 AUGUSTINE: *Confessions*, BK XIII, par 6–12
112a–113d; par 32, 119b / *City of God*, BK X,
CH 23–24 312c–313c; BK XI, CH 10 327d–328d;
CH 23–29 334c–339b; CH 32 340b–d; BK XIII,
CH 24 373d–376a,c; BK XVI, CH 6, 426c /
Christian Doctrine, BK I, CH 5 625d–626a;
CH 34 634b–c; BK III, CH 2, 657b–658a

19 AQUINAS: *Summa Theologica*, PART I, QQ 27–43
153a–237a,c; Q 59, A 1, CONTRARY 306c–307b;
Q 61, A 2, ANS 315c–316a; Q 88, A 3, REP 3 472c–
473a; Q 91, A 4, REP 2 487d–488c; Q 93, A 1,
REP 2 492a–d; AA 5–8 495b–500c; Q 108, A 1,
ANS 552c–553c

20 AQUINAS: *Summa Theologica*, PART I–II, Q 93,
A 1, REP 2 215b,d–216c; Q 106, A 4, REP 3 324a–
325c; PART II–II, Q 1, A 8, REP 3 387a–388c; Q 2,
A 8 397d–398b; PART III, Q 2, A 3, REP 3 713a–
714c; Q 8, A 1, REP 1 756d–757c; Q 16, A 1, REP 2
796b–797d; A 2, REP 2 797d–798b; A 5, REP 1
800c–801b; Q 17, A 1, REP 5 807a–808d; A 2,

(9. *Specifically Christian dogmas concerning the divine nature and human destiny. 9a. The Trinity.*)

REP 3 808d-809d; Q 19, A I, REP I 816a-818b; QQ 20-24 821a-839c; Q 25, A I, ANS and REP 1,3 839d-840d; Q 26, A 2, ANS and REP 2 846b-d; Q 63, A 3, REP I 866c-867c; A 4, CONTRARY 867d-868b; PART III SUPPL, Q 95, A I, REP 2 1042c-1044c; A 3, ANS 1045b-1046d

21 DANTE: *Divine Comedy*, PURGATORY, III [34–45] 56b; PARADISE, X [1–6] 120b; XIV [28–33] 127b; XXIV [124–147] 144a; XXXIII [76–145] 157a-d

22 CHAUCER: *Troilus and Cressida*, BK V, STANZA 267 155a / *Second Nun's Tale* [15,794–808] 467a-b

23 HOBBES: *Leviathan*, PART I, 97c; PART III, 182a-c; 207b; 207d-208c; 227b; PART IV, 259d

30 BACON: *Advancement of Learning*, 100c

31 DESCARTES: *Objections and Replies*, 159a; 232b

32 MILTON: *Christs Nativity* [1–14] 1a-b / *Paradise Lost*, BK III [56–415] 136b-144b esp [167–172] 139a, [372–389] 143b-144a; BK V [600–615] 188b; BK VI [719–733] 212a; BK XII [469–551] 329b-331a

40 GIBBON: *Decline and Fall*, 307a-314a esp 310b-311a; 438b-441d esp 438b-c, 441a-b; 605a-b; 607a

41 GIBBON: *Decline and Fall*, 422a-c; 520b-521c esp 521c

46 HEGEL: *Philosophy of History*, PART III, 303d-304a; 306a-c

9b. The Incarnation: the God-man

NEW TESTAMENT: *John*, 1:1–14

18 AUGUSTINE: *Confessions*, BK V, par 20 32d-33a; BK VII, par 13–14 47c-48b; par 24–25 50d-51c; BK X, par 67–70 88b-89a; BK XI, par 4 90a-b / *City of God*, BK IX, CH 15 293a-294a; CH 17 295a-c; CH 21 296b-d; BK X, CH 20 311b-c; CH 22 312a-b; CH 24 312d-313c; CH 27–29 315b-318b; BK XI, CH 2 323a-c; BK XXI, CH 15–16 572c-574a / *Christian Doctrine*, BK I, CH 11–14 627b-628b; CH 34 634b-c

19 AQUINAS: *Summa Theologica*, PART I, Q 62, A 9, REP 3 324a-325b; Q 64, A I, REP 4 334a-335c; Q 73, A I, REP I 370a-371a; Q 95, A I, REP I 506b-507c; PART I–II, Q 5, A 7, REP 2 642a-d

20 AQUINAS: *Summa Theologica*, PART III, QQ 1–26 701b,d-846d esp Q 26, A I, REP 3 845b-846a; PART III SUPPL, Q 76, A I 939d-941a; Q 95, A 3, ANS 1045b-1046d; A 4 1046d-1047d

21 DANTE: *Divine Comedy*, PURGATORY, XXIX [106–120] 98d-99a; XXXI [76–126] 101c-102a; XXXII [19–63] 102c-103a; PARADISE, II [31–45] 108a; VI [10–21] 113d; VII [16–120] 115b-116b; XIII [37–87] 125d-126b; XXXII [139]–XXXIII [145] 156a-157d

23 HOBBES: *Leviathan*, PART III, 182a-c

32 MILTON: *Christs Nativity* 1a-7b / *The Passion* 10b-12a / *Upon the Circumcision* 12b-13a / *Paradise Lost*, BK III [56–415] 136b-144b esp [315–341] 142a-b, [383–389] 143b-144a; BK XII [307–385] 326a-327b

33 PASCAL: *Pensées*, 512 262a; 763–765 322a; 785 325b; 862 342b-343a

40 GIBBON: *Decline and Fall*, 307d-308b

41 GIBBON: *Decline and Fall*, 134a-161a,c esp 134a-138a, 150c-151b; 230d-231a

46 HEGEL: *Philosophy of History*, PART III, 306b-c; 308a-b

52 DOSTOEVSKY: *Brothers Karamazov*, BK V, 127b-137c

9b(1) The divinity of Christ

OLD TESTAMENT: *Isaiah*, 9:6-7—(D) *Isaias*, 9:6-7

NEW TESTAMENT: *Matthew* passim, esp 1:18–25, 3:16–4:11, 7:21, 8:29–32, 10:32–33, 11:25–30, 14:22–33, 16:13–20, 17:1–8, 26:63–68, 27:38–54 / *Mark* passim, esp 1:1, 1:10–11, 1:21–28, 2:3–12, 3:11–12, 5:2–7, 9:1–8, 14:60–65, 15:39, 16:19 / *Luke* passim, esp 2:49, 4:41, 9:28–36, 10:21–22, 22:29, 24:49 / *John* passim, esp 1:1–14, 1:49, 5:17–27, 8:16, 10:30, 10:38, 11:27, 14:10–11, 14:20, 14:28, 17:1–3, 20:17 / *Acts*, 8:37 / *Romans*, 1:3–4; 8:3,29–33 / *I Corinthians*, 1:24; 15:28 / *II Corinthians*, 1:19; 5:18–21 / *Philippians*, 2:5–6 / *Colossians*, 1:15–17; 2:8–9 / *I Timothy*, 3:16 / *Hebrews*, 1:1–8; 4:14; 5:5,8; 13:8 / *I John*, 2:22–24; 3:8; 4:9–10,13–15; 5:1–13,20 / *II John*, 7–11 / *Jude*

18 AUGUSTINE: *Confessions*, BK VII, par 25 51a-c / *City of God*, BK IX, CH 15 293a-294a; CH 17 295a-c; BK X, CH 20 311b-c; CH 22 312a-b; CH 24 312d-313c; CH 27–29 315b-318b; BK XI, CH 2 323a-c; BK XXI, CH 15–16 572c-574a; BK XXII, CH 6 590a-591c

20 AQUINAS: *Summa Theologica*, PART III, Q 3 723a-730b; QQ 16–24 796a-839c; Q 25, A I 839d-840d; PART III SUPPL, Q 95, A 3, ANS 1045b-1046d

21 DANTE: *Divine Comedy*, PARADISE, VII [16–120] 115b-116b

22 CHAUCER: *Prioress's Tale* 391a-395b

32 MILTON: *Christs Nativity* 1a-7b / *The Passion* 10b-12a / *Upon the Circumcision* 12b-13a / *Paradise Lost*, BK III [56–415] 136b-144b esp [135–142] 138b, [167–172] 139a, [281–314] 141b-142a, [383–389] 143b-144a; BK V [600–615] 188b; BK VI [719–733] 212a; BK XII [307–385] 326a-327b

33 PASCAL: *Pensées*, 734 317a; 763–765 322a; 785 325b; 841–842 336a-337a

40 GIBBON: *Decline and Fall*, 308a-b

41 GIBBON: *Decline and Fall*, 134b-138a esp 135b-136b

46 HEGEL: *Philosophy of History*, PART II, 270d-271c; PART III, 306d-307b

52 DOSTOEVSKY: *Brothers Karamazov*, BK V, 127b-137c passim; BK VII, 189c-190c

9b(2) The humanity of Christ

NEW TESTAMENT: *Matthew*, 1:18–25; 2:11; 11:19; 13:54–56; 25:37–45; 26:1–28:8 / *Mark*, 6:2–3; 15:37–16:6 / *Luke*, 1–2; 7:33–34; 11:27–28; 22–23; 24:2–7,36–43 / *John*, 1:1–18 esp 1:14; 5:27; 6:42; 19:28–20:29 / *Romans*, 1:3–4; 8:3 / *II Corinthians*, 5:16 / *Galatians*, 4:4 / *Ephesians*, 2:14–16 / *Philippians*, 2:5–8 / *Colossians*, 1:20–22 / *I Timothy*, 3:16 / *Hebrews*, 2:14–18; 4:15; 5:7; 7:20–24 / *I John*, 4:2–3

18 AUGUSTINE: *Confessions*, BK VII, par 25 51a-c / *City of God*, BK IX, CH 15 293a-294a; CH 17 295a-c; BK X, CH 20 311b-c; CH 22 312a-b; CH 24 312d-313c; CH 27–29 315b-318b; BK XI, CH 2 323a-c; BK XXI, CH 15–16 572c-574a / *Christian Doctrine*, BK I, CH 14 627d-628b

19 AQUINAS: *Summa Theologica*, PART I, Q 51, A 2, REP I 276b-277a; A 3, REP 5 277a-278c; Q 113, A 4, REP I 578b-579a; Q 119, A 2, REP 4 607b-608d

20 AQUINAS: *Summa Theologica*, PART II–II, Q 1, A 1, REP I 380b-381a; Q 18, A 2, REP I 462d-463d; PART III, QQ 4–24 730c-839c; Q 25, AA 1–2 839d-841c; PART III SUPPL, Q 76, A 1 939d-941a; Q 90, AA 1–2 1012b-1014d; Q 92, A 3, REP 12 1034b-1037c

21 DANTE: *Divine Comedy*, PARADISE, VII [16–120] 115b-116b; XIII [37–45] 125d; [73–87] 126b

22 CHAUCER: *Parson's Tale*, par 12 503b-504b

32 MILTON: *Christs Nativity* 1a-7b / *The Passion* 10b-12a esp [15–21] 10b-11a / *Upon the Circumcision* 12b-13a / *Paradise Lost*, BK III [56–415] 136b-144b esp [238–241] 140b, [281–294] 141b; BK XI [22–44] 299b-300a; BK XII [307–385] 326a-327b

33 PASCAL: *Pensées*, 553 268a-270a; 763–765 322a; 785 325b

40 GIBBON: *Decline and Fall*, 308a

41 GIBBON: *Decline and Fall*, 134b-138a esp 134b-135b, 137a-d; 330a

46 HEGEL: *Philosophy of History*, PART II, 270d-271c; PART III, 306b-307a

52 DOSTOEVSKY: *Brothers Karamazov*, BK V, 127b-137c passim; BK VII, 189c-190c

9b(3) Mary, the Mother of God

OLD TESTAMENT: *Isaiah*, 7:14—(D) *Isaias*, 7:14

NEW TESTAMENT: *Matthew*, 1:18–25; 12:46–50 / *Mark*, 3:31–35 / *Luke*, 1–2; 8:19–21; 11:27–28 / *John*, 2:1–12; 19:25–27

18 AUGUSTINE: *City of God*, BK XVII, CH 16 465c-466d esp 466c-d; CH 24 471d-472a,c; BK XVIII, CH 35, 491d / *Christian Doctrine*, BK I, CH 14 627d-628b

20 AQUINAS: *Summa Theologica*, PART III, Q 7, A 10, REP I 752c-753c; Q 25, A 5 843d-844b; PART III SUPPL, Q 83, A 3, CONTRARY 978c-980d; Q 96, A 5, REP 2 1055c-1058a

21 DANTE: *Divine Comedy*, HELL, II [43–126] 3a-4a esp [94–99] 3c; PURGATORY, X [34–45] 67d; PARADISE, XIII [79–87] 126b; XXIII 141b-

142c; XXX–XXXI 151d-154c esp XXXI [94–142] 154b-c; XXXII [85]–XXXIII [45] 155c-156c

22 CHAUCER: *Prioress's Tale* 391a-395b

32 MILTON: *Christs Nativity* 1a-7b / *Paradise Lost*, BK III [274–285] 141b; BK XII [307–385] 326a-327b esp [375–382] 327b

33 PASCAL: *Provincial Letters*, 62b-64b / *Pensées*, 742 319a

41 GIBBON: *Decline and Fall*, 134d-137c passim; 140a; 154d

46 HEGEL: *Philosophy of History*, PART IV, 338b-c

47 GOETHE: *Faust*, PART I [3587–3619] 87b-88a; PART II [11,989–12,111] 291b-294b

9c. Christ the Saviour and Redeemer: the doctrines of original sin and salvation

OLD TESTAMENT: *I Samuel*, 2:1–10—(D) *I Kings*, 2:1–10 / *Isaiah*, 53—(D) *Isaias*, 53 / *Lamentations*, 4:20

NEW TESTAMENT: *Matthew*, 1:21; 9:2–8; 10:32–33; 16:24–27; 18:11–14; 26:26–28 / *Mark*, 2:1–12; 8:34–38; 14:22–24 / *Luke*, 1:67–79; 2:11; 5:17–26; 7:37–50; 9:23–26,56; 15; 19:1–10; 22:19–20; 24:46–47 / *John* esp 1:29, 3:16–18, 4:42, 6:31–59, 10:9–18, 14:6–7, 14:18–19, 15:1–4 / *Acts*, 3:12–26; 4:10–12; 5:30–31; 13:15–50 esp 13:38–39; 16:30–31 / *Romans* esp 3:20–26, 5:1–6:23, 8:1–4 / *I Corinthians*, 15:3,12–23 / *II Corinthians* esp 2:10, 4:13–14, 5:14–21, 8:9, 13:4–5 / *Galatians* passim, esp 2:20–3:14, 4:1–5 / *Ephesians* esp 1:5–7, 1:12–14, 2:1–22 / *Colossians* esp 1:12–14, 1:19–22, 2:13–14 / *I Timothy*, 1:12–17; 2:5–6 / *Titus* esp 2:11–3:7 / *Hebrews* esp 2:1–18, 5:9, 7:25–27, 9:1–10:39 / *I Peter* esp 1:3–11, 3:17–4:6 / *I John* esp 3:16, 4:9–10, 4:14 / *Revelation* passim, esp 5–7—(D) *Apocalypse* passim, esp 5–7

18 AUGUSTINE: *Confessions*, BK II, par 15 12b-c; BK IV, par 18–19 23d-24b; BK VII, par 24–27 50d-52c; BK X, par 67–70 88b-89a / *City of God*, BK VII, CH 31–32 261d-262b; BK IX, CH 15 293a-294a; CH 17 295a-c; BK X, CH 4–6 301a-302d; CH 19–20 310d-311c; CH 22–25 312a-314c; CH 27–32 315b-322a,c; BK XI, CH 2 323a-c; BK XIII, CH 2–4 360b-362a; CH 12–15 365d-366d; CH 23–24 372a-376a,c; BK XVII 449a-472a,c passim; BK XVIII, CH 23 483d-485a; CH 31–35 488a-493a; BK XX, CH 26 555a-556b; CH 30 557c-560a,c; BK XXI, CH 15–16 572c-574a; BK XXII, CH 1 586b,d-587b; CH 3 588a-b; CH 22–24 606d-612a; CH 29–30 614b-618d / *Christian Doctrine*, BK I, CH 11–12 627b-d; CH 14–18 627d-629a; CH 34 634b-c; BK II, CH 41 656a-c

19 AQUINAS: *Summa Theologica*, PART I, Q 97, A 1, REP 3 513c-514c; PART I–II, Q 5, A 7, REP 2 642a-d

20 AQUINAS: *Summa Theologica*, PART I–II, Q 85, A 5, REP 2 181d-182d; Q 87, A 7, REP 3 190c-191d; Q 89, A 5, REP I 202c-203b; Q 91, A 5, REP 2 211c-212c; Q 98, A I, ANS and REP 3 239b-240c; A 2 240c-241b; A 4, ANS and REP I

(9. *Specifically Christian dogmas concerning the divine nature and human destiny. 9c. Christ the Saviour and Redeemer: the doctrines of original sin and salvation.*)

242b-243c; A 6, REP 2 244c-245b; Q 100, A 12 264d-265d; Q 101, A 3, ANS and REP 1 268a-269a; Q 102, A 2, ANS 271b-272a; A 4, REP 2,5-6 esp REP 6 276d-283c; A 5, REP 5 283c-292c; Q 103, A 1, ANS 298b-299b; A 2 299b-300d; A 3, REP 2 300d-302a; Q 104, A 3, ANS 305d-306d; QQ 106-108 321a-337d; PART II, Q 1, A 7, REP 1,4 385c-387a; A 8, REP 4 387a-388c; Q 2, A 7 396a-397c; Q 14, A 2, REP 3 448d-449d; PART III, Q 1 701b,d-709c; Q 26 845a-846d; Q 60, A 3, ANS 848d-849c; A 5, REP 3 850b-851b; Q 61, A 1, REP 3 855a-d; A 3 856c-857c; Q 62, A 5, REP 2 862b-863a; A 6, ANS and REP 1-2 863a-864c; PART III SUPPL, Q 69, A 4 889c-890c; Q 71, A 14, REP 2 916c-917b; Q 75, A 2, REP 3-4 937a-938a; Q 76, A 1 939d-941a; Q 78, A 1, REP 3 947d-949b; Q 89, A 2, ANS and REP 4 1006b-1007c; A 5, ANS 1009b-d; Q 90 1012a-1016a; Q 95 1042c-1049d; Q 99, A 3, REP 1 1081d-1083a

21 DANTE: *Divine Comedy*, HELL, IV [46-63] 5d-6a; PURGATORY, XXXII [28-63] 102c-103a; XXXIII [52-72] 104d-105a; PARADISE, VII [16-120] 115b-116b; XIII [37-87] 125d-126b; XIX [103-111] 136a; XXIII 141b-142c; XXXII [1-138] 154d-156a

22 CHAUCER: *Troilus and Cressida*, BK V, STANZA 263-267 154b-155a / *Second Nun's Tale* [15,788-822] 467a-b / *Parson's Tale*, par 8 497b-498a; par 13 504b-505a; par 68-69 533b-534b

23 HOBBES: *Leviathan*, PART III, 191b-192c; 195d-196a; 197c-198a; 204a-207b; 240c; 242b-245a; PART IV, 260b-c

24 RABELAIS: *Gargantua and Pantagruel*, BK IV, 269c-270b

27 SHAKESPEARE: *Measure for Measure*, ACT II, SC II [71-79] 182d

31 SPINOZA: *Ethics*, PART IV, PROP 68, SCHOL 445a-b

32 MILTON: *Christs Nativity* 1a-7b passim / *The Passion* 10b-12a / *Upon the Circumcision* 12b-13a / *Lycidas* [165-185] 31b / *Paradise Lost* 93a-333a esp BK I [1-26] 93b-94a, BK III [56-415] 136b-144b, BK X [615-640] 287b-288b, BK XI [22-44] 299b-300a, BK XII [285-484] 325b-329b

33 PASCAL: *Pensées*, 425-856 243b-341b passim, esp 556-588 270b-277b

40 GIBBON: *Decline and Fall*, 181b

41 GIBBON: *Decline and Fall*, 334b-c

44 BOSWELL: *Johnson*, 482a-d

46 HEGEL: *Philosophy of History*, PART III, 306b-c; PART IV, 331d-332a; 354a-c

48 MELVILLE: *Moby Dick*, 318b

52 DOSTOEVSKY: *Brothers Karamazov*, BK V, 127b-137c passim

54 FREUD: *War and Death*, 763b-c

9d. The Church: the mystical body of Christ; the Apostolate

OLD TESTAMENT: *Song of Solomon*—(D) *Canticle of Canticles*

NEW TESTAMENT: *Matthew*, 3; 4:18-22; 8:18-23; 9:35-10:42; 11:1-15; 13:1-53; 16:17-24; 18:15-20; 20:25-28; 24:14; 25; 28:16-20 / *Mark*, 1:1-9,16-20; 3:13-19; 10:42-45; 13:10; 16:14-20 / *Luke*, 3:1-20; 4:43-44; 5:1-11; 6:13-16; 8:16-17; 9:1-6; 11:48-50; 12:11-12; 22:24-30; 24:47 / *John*, 1:6-8,15-42; 4:34-38; 10; 13:31-17:26; 20:19-21:24 esp 20:20-23, 21:15-17 / *Acts* esp 1:8, 1:13-26, 2:1-47, 5:1-42, 13:47, 16:1-40, 22:14-15 / *Romans* / *I Corinthians* passim, esp 3:1-23, 4:9-13, 6:1-20, 10:16-17, 12:12-31, 15:1-11 / *II Corinthians* esp 1:12-21, 2:10-11, 3:1-4:18, 5:20-21, 7:8-13, 10:1-13:10 / *Galatians* passim, esp 1-2, 3:28, 4:1-31 / *Ephesians* esp 1:22-23, 3:8-12, 4:1-12, 5:23-33 / *Philippians*, 1:27-2:4 / *Colossians* passim, esp 1:15-29, 2:13-19, 3:6-11 / *Hebrews*, 3:5-6 / *I Peter*, 2:4-10 / *I John*

18 AUGUSTINE: *Confessions*, BK VI, par 4 36a-b / *City of God*, BK I, CH 35 149b-c; BK X, CH 20 311b-c; BK XIII, CH 21 371a-c; BK XVII, CH 9 461b-d; CH 11 462c-463a; CH 15-16 465b-466d; CH 20 469a-470c; BK XVIII, CH 48-52 501b-504d; BK XIX, CH 22 525b-c; BK XX, CH 7-12 535b-541d; BK XXII, CH 17-18 603a-604b / *Christian Doctrine*, BK I, CH 16 628c-d; CH 18 628d-629a; BK III, CH 31-32 669c-670a

19 AQUINAS: *Summa Theologica*, PART I, Q 95, A 1, REP 1 506b-507c

20 AQUINAS: *Summa Theologica*, PART II-II, Q 1, A 9, CONTRARY and REP 3,5 388d-389d; A 10, ANS 389d-390d; Q 2, AA 6-8 395b-398b; Q 5 410a-413c; QQ 183-189 625a-700d; PART III, Q 8 756c-763b; PART III SUPPL, Q 71, A 9 910d-912b; Q 95, A 3, ANS and REP 4 1045b-1046d; A 4, REP 1,5 1046d-1047d

21 DANTE: *Divine Comedy*, PURGATORY, IX [73-145] 66c-67b; XIX [127-141] 82d-83a; XXIX [1]-XXX [21] 97d-99c; XXXII [1]-XXXIII [78] 102b-105a; PARADISE, XI 122a-123c esp [28-39] 122b; XII 123c-125a; XXIII [1]-XXVI [81] 141b-146c passim; XXVII [1-66] 147b-148a; XXIX [109-114] 151b; XXX-XXXII 151d-156a

23 HOBBES: *Leviathan*, PART II, 151a-c; PART III, 198a-199a; 207b-224c; PART IV, 247a-249b; 275a-278d

32 MILTON: *Paradise Lost*, BK XII [436-514] 328b-330b

33 PASCAL: *Pensées*, 473-484 256b-258b; 646 291b; 801-802 328b; 832 334a; 849 339b-340a; 852 341a-b; 857-861 342a; 867-905 343b-349a

35 LOCKE: *Toleration*, 4b-5d

46 HEGEL: *Philosophy of History*, PART III, 307b-310c; PART IV, 315d; 331d-332c; 338a-d

52 DOSTOEVSKY: *Brothers Karamazov*, BK V, 127b-137c passim

54 FREUD: *Group Psychology*, 674c-d; 691d-692a

9e. The sacraments

NEW TESTAMENT: *Matthew*, 3; 18:18; 19:4–6,10–12; 20:20–23; 26:26–29; 28:19 / *Mark*, 1:4,8–10; 10:2–12,35–40; 14:22–24; 16:16 / *Luke*, 3:3,16; 22:14–20 / *John*, 1:25–27,33; 3:1–8; 6 esp 6:32–35, 6:47–59; 19:33–34; 20:21–23 / *Acts*, 2:40–42; 8:12–17,26–40; 11:16; 19:1–7; 22:16 / *Romans*, 6:3–4 / *I Corinthians*, 1:12–17; 6:11; 7:8–14,34–39; 10:16–17; 11:23–30; 12:13; 15:28–29 / *Galatians*, 3:27 / *Ephesians*, 4:5; 5:21–33 esp 5:31–32 / *Colossians*, 2:11–12 / *Hebrews*, 5:1–6 / *James*, 5:14–16 / *I Peter*, 3:20–22

18 AUGUSTINE: *Confessions*, BK IX, par 12 64d–65a; BK XIII, par 26–29 117c–118c / *City of God*, BK X, CH 5–6 301b–302d; CH 19–20 310d–311c; BK XIII, CH 3–4 361a–362a; CH 7 362d–363b; BK XX, CH 26 555a–556b; BK XXI, CH 16 573b–574a; CH 20 575c–d; CH 25 579d–581a / *Christian Doctrine*, BK II, CH 3 637c–d; CH 41 656a–c; BK III, CH 9 661a–c; BK IV, CH 21, 690d–691b

19 AQUINAS: *Summa Theologica*, PART I, Q 92, A 3, ANS 490c–491b; Q 113, A 5, ANS and REP 3 579a–d

20 AQUINAS: *Summa Theologica*, PART I–II, Q 102, A 5 283c–292c; Q 103, A 4, ANS 302a–304a; Q 108, A 2, ANS and REP 2 332b–333d; PART II–II, Q 1, A 1, REP 1 380b–381a; A 3, REP 4 381d–382c; A 8, REP 6 387a–388c; Q 3, A 1, REP 1 400c–401a; Q 10, A 12, REP 5 436b–437d; PART III, QQ 60–65 847a–884a,c; PART III SUPPL, Q 83, A 3, ANS and REP 4 978c–980d; Q 99, A 4 1083a–1084a

21 DANTE: *Divine Comedy*, HELL, XXVII [67–132] 40c–41a

22 CHAUCER: *Pardoner's Tale* [12,829–849] 381b / *Parson's Tale*, par 12–22, 504b–510b esp par 22, 510b

23 HOBBES: *Leviathan*, PART I, 71b; PART III, 180c–d; 206c–207a; 208b; 211c–212c; PART IV, 249b–250c; 263d–264a

30 BACON: *Advancement of Learning*, 101a

31 DESCARTES: *Objections and Replies*, 162d–165d

32 MILTON: *Paradise Lost*, BK XII [436–445] 328b–329a

33 PASCAL: *Provincial Letters*, 71b–80b; 128b–137b / *Pensées*, 554 270a; 862, 343a; 870 344a–b; 904–905 348b–349a; 923 351b

35 LOCKE: *Toleration*, 12a / *Human Understanding*, BK II, CH XXIII, SECT 17 250d–251a; BK IV, CH XX, SECT 10 391c–392a

36 STERNE: *Tristram Shandy*, 221a–224a; 260b–261a; 373b–376a

40 GIBBON: *Decline and Fall*, 193a–b; 297c–d

41 GIBBON: *Decline and Fall*, 329d; 334b–c

44 BOSWELL: *Johnson*, 173d

46 HEGEL: *Philosophy of History*, PART IV, 331d–332c; 338a–d; 349d–350a

52 DOSTOEVSKY: *Brothers Karamazov*, BK III, 80c–81a

9f. The second coming of Christ

NEW TESTAMENT: *Matthew*, 10:14–15; 11:20–24; 12:36–37; 13:36–43,47–50; 24–25 / *Mark*, 13:4–37 / *Luke*, 10:11–15; 17:20–37; 19:11–28; 21:5–36 / *John*, 14:1–4 / *Acts*, 1:9–11; 2:17–21; 17:31 / *Romans*, 2:5–11 / *I Corinthians*, 15:23–28 / *Philippians*, 3:20–21 / *I Thessalonians*, 1:9–10; 2:19; 4:14–5:4 / *II Thessalonians*, 1–2 / *II Timothy*, 3:1–4:8 / *James*, 5:7–9 / *II Peter*, 2:9; 3:7–13 / *I John*, 2:18–29 / *Jude*, 17–25 / *Revelation* esp 1:4–20—(D) *Apocalypse* esp 1:4–20

18 AUGUSTINE: *City of God*, BK XIII, CH 2 360b–361a; CH 6 362c–d; CH 23–24 372a–376a,c; BK XVIII, CH 53 504d–505c; BK XX 530a–560a,c; BK XXI, CH 11–27 570b–586a,c / *Christian Doctrine*, BK I, CH 15 628b–c

20 AQUINAS: *Summa Theologica*, PART III SUPPL, Q 73, A 1 922b–923c; A 3 924b–925b; Q 77, A 2, ANS 945a–946b; QQ 87–90 997a–1016a

23 HOBBES: *Leviathan*, PART III, 179d; 191b–192c; 197c; 229c–230a; 244b–c; PART IV, 248a–b; 251c–252b; 254b–255b

32 MILTON: *Christs Nativity* 1a–7b esp [133–172] 4b–5b / *At a Solemn Musick* 13a–b / *Paradise Lost*, BK III [274–343] 141b–143a; BK VII [139–173] 220a–221a; BK XI [72–83] 300b–301a / *Areopagitica*, 404a–b

33 PASCAL: *Pensées*, 757 321a

40 GIBBON: *Decline and Fall*, 187b–188a

52 DOSTOEVSKY: *Brothers Karamazov*, BK I, 13c–d; BK V, 127a–137c

10. The denial of God or the gods, or of a supernatural order: the position of the atheist

OLD TESTAMENT: *Psalms*, 14:1–3; 53:1–3—(D) *Psalms*, 13:1–3; 52:1–4

5 ARISTOPHANES: *Thesmophoriazusae* [443–458] 605b

7 PLATO: *Apology*, 204c–205c / *Laws*, BK X, 758b–765d esp 758b–759a, 759d–760c, 761b–c

12 AURELIUS: *Meditations*, BK IV, SECT 3, 263c; BK IX, SECT 39 295a

18 AUGUSTINE: *City of God*, BK V, CH 9, 213c

19 AQUINAS: *Summa Theologica*, PART I, Q 2, A 3, REP 1–2 12c–14a

23 HOBBES: *Leviathan*, PART II, 160a

25 MONTAIGNE: *Essays*, 211b–212a

30 BACON: *Advancement of Learning*, 4b–c

31 DESCARTES: *Meditations*, 72a–b

32 MILTON: *Paradise Lost*, BK XI [569–723] 311b–315a esp [617–623] 312b / *Samson Agonistes* [293–299] 346a

33 PASCAL: *Pensées*, 184–241 205a–217b

35 LOCKE: *Toleration*, 18b / *Human Understanding*, BK I, CH III, SECT 8 114a–c

35 BERKELEY: *Human Knowledge*, SECT 92–96 431a–d; SECT 133, 439d–440a; SECT 154–155 444a–c

35 HUME: *Human Understanding*, SECT XII, DIV 116, 503c–d

36 SWIFT: *Gulliver*, PART I, 29a

(10. *The denial of God or the gods, or of a super-*
natural order: the position of the atheist.)

37 FIELDING: *Tom Jones*, 379c-380c

38 MONTESQUIEU: *Spirit of Laws*, BK XXIV, 200b-201a; BK XXV, 208a

40 GIBBON: *Decline and Fall*, 13a-b

42 KANT: *Pure Reason*, 11b-c; 192c-d / *Judgement*, 595d-596c

43 MILL: *Liberty*, 280d-281c

50 MARX: *Capital*, 31c-d; 35b-c; 305d [fn 2]

51 TOLSTOY: *War and Peace*, BK V, 196b-d

52 DOSTOEVSKY: *Brothers Karamazov*, BK I, 11a-c; BK V, 135b-136b; BK XI, 312b-314d; 345a-c

11. The denial of God as completely tran-
scending the world or nature: the posi-
tion of the pantheist

12 EPICTETUS: *Discourses*, BK I, CH 14 120d-121c

12 AURELIUS: *Meditations*, BK II, SECT 1 256b,d; SECT 13 258c; BK VII, SECT 9 280b-c; BK XII, SECT 30 310a-b

17 PLOTINUS: *Second Ennead*, TR IX, CH 16, 75c-76a / *Third Ennead*, TR VIII 129a-136a / *Fourth Ennead*, TR IX 205a-207a,c / *Fifth Ennead*, TR I, CH 1-2 208a-209b; TR II 214c-215c; TR III, CH 15-17 224c-226c; TR VIII, CH 7-10, 242d-244d

18 AUGUSTINE: *Confessions*, BK I, par 2-3 1b-2a; BK III, par 10 15b-d; par 18 18b; BK IV, par 26 25c-d; par 31 26c-27a; BK VII, par 1-3 43b-44b; BK X, par 8-10 73b-74a; BK XII, par 7 100d-101a; par 21 103d-104a / *City of God*, BK IV, CH 12-13 195d-196b; BK VII, CH 6 248a-b

19 AQUINAS: *Summa Theologica*, PART I, Q 3, A 8 19d-20c; Q 6, A 4 30b-d; Q 8, A 1, ANS 34d-35c; A 3, REP 1 36b-37c; Q 16, A 6 98b-d; Q 90, A 1 480d-481d; Q 105, A 5 542a-543b

23 HOBBES: *Leviathan*, PART II, 162b

31 DESCARTES: *Meditations*, VI, 99c

31 SPINOZA: *Ethics*, PART I 355a-372d esp DEF 3-6 355b, PROP 1-15 355d-361d, PROP 18 363c, PROP 25 365b, PROP 28-29 365c-366c; PART II, PROP 1-11 373d-377c; PART IV, PREF, 422b,d-423b; PROP 4 425b-d

35 LOCKE: *Human Understanding*, BK II, CH XIII, SECT 18 152a-c

42 KANT: *Judgement*, 564c-565d esp 565c-d; 566c-d; 580c-d

46 HEGEL: *Philosophy of History*, INTRO, 176b-c; PART I, 220c-221a

48 MELVILLE: *Moby Dick*, 115b-117a

51 TOLSTOY: *War and Peace*, BK V, 216b-218b; BK XIII, 581c-582a; BK XIV, 608a-b; BK XV, 631a-c

12. The denial of a revealed and providential
God: the position of the deist

7 PLATO: *Parmenides*, 489d-490d / *Laws*, BK X, 765d-768c

12 LUCRETIUS: *Nature of Things*, BK I [62-158] 1d-3a; BK II [167-183] 17a-b; [589-660] 22c-

23b; [1090-1104] 29a; BK V [55-90] 61d-62b; [146-234] 63a-64a; [306-310] 65a; [1161-1240] 76b-77b; BK VI [43-95] 80d-81c

15 TACITUS: *Annals*, BK VI, 91b-d

17 PLOTINUS: *Second Ennead*, TR IX, CH 16, 75c-76a

18 AUGUSTINE: *Confessions*, BK V, par 19 32b-c

23 HOBBES: *Leviathan*, PART II, 162a-b

33 PASCAL: *Provincial Letters*, 137a-b / *Pensées*, 242-290 217b-225a passim; 430-434 245a-250a; 543-549 266a-267a; 556-588 270b-277b

37 FIELDING: *Tom Jones*, 38c-39c; 53c; 75c-76a

42 KANT: *Pure Reason*, 190a-c / *Judgement*, 547d

52 DOSTOEVSKY: *Brothers Karamazov*, BK V, 120d-121c; 127b-137c passim; BK X, 292d-294a

13. God as a conception invented by man: its
emotional basis

APOCRYPHA: *Wisdom of Solomon*, 14:12-21—(D) OT, *Book of Wisdom*, 14:12-21

23 HOBBES: *Leviathan*, PART I, 79a-b; 79d-80a

25 MONTAIGNE: *Essays*, 256c-d

42 KANT: *Judgement*, 593c-d

49 DARWIN: *Descent of Man*, 302b-303d; 593b-c

50 MARX: *Capital*, 31c-d

52 DOSTOEVSKY: *Brothers Karamazov*, BK III, 67d-68c; BK V, 120d-121a; BK X, 293a

54 FREUD: *Group Psychology*, 692a-693a / *War and Death*, 763b-c / *Civilization and Its Discontents*, 771a-b; 778d / *New Introductory Lectures*, 875d-878c

14. The worship of false gods: deification and
idolatry

OLD TESTAMENT: *Genesis*, 31:19-35 / *Exodus*, 20:1-6,22-23; 22:20; 23:13; 32; 34:11-17 / *Leviticus*, 17:7; 19:4; 20:1-6; 26:1,28-30 / *Numbers*, 25:2-5; 33:51-52 / *Deuteronomy* passim, esp 4:1-3, 4:15-19, 4:23-28, 5:7-9, 6:14-16, 7:1-6, 7:25-26, 8:19-20, 9:15-21, 11:16-17; 11:28, 12:2-3, 12:29-13:18, 16:21-22, 17:2-7, 18:9-14, 20:16-18, 27:15, 28:14-68, 29:16-29, 30:15-20, 31:16-21, 32:15-39 / *Joshua*, 22-23; 24:14-25—(D) *Josue*, 22-23; 24:14-25 / *Judges*, 2:10-23; 3:5-8; 6:24-32; 8:33-34; 10; 17-18 / *I Samuel*, 7:3-4; 15:22-23—(D) *I Kings*, 7:3-4; 15:22-23 / *I Kings*, 3:1-4; 9:6-9; 11-16; 18:17-29; 20:22-28; 21:25-29; 22:51-53—(D) *III Kings*, 3:1-4; 9:6-9; 11-16; 18:17-29; 20:22-28; 21:25-29; 22:51-54 / *II Kings* passim, esp 1:1-18, 8:16-9:10, 10:1-36, 11:17-18, 14:1-18:37, 19:16-19, 21:1-23:37—(D) *IV Kings* passim, esp 1:1-18, 8:16-9:10, 10:1-36, 11:17-18, 14:1-18:37, 19:16-19, 21:1-23:37 / *II Chronicles*, 13:8-9; 28; 33—(D) *II Paralipomenon*, 13:8-9; 28; 33 / *Psalms*, 81:8-16; 97:7; 106; 115:1-8; 135:15-18—(D) *Psalms*, 80:9-17; 96:7; 105; 113:1-8; 134:15-18 / *Isaiah*, 1-2 esp 1:29, 2:8-9, 2:18-21; 10:10-11; 19 esp 19:1-3; 30-31 esp 30:22, 31:7; 36 esp 36:18-20; 40:18-20; 41 esp 41:29; 42:8,17; 44 esp

CROSS-REFERENCES

For: Other treatments of polytheism, and for discussions of the gods in relation to fate and human life, *see* ANGEL 1; FATE 1; MAN 10a.

Man's duty and piety toward God or the gods, and for man's worship of God or the gods, *see* DUTY 5, 11; JUSTICE 11b; RELIGION 2–2g.

Man's love of God and desire to be with God, *see* DESIRE 7b; LOVE 5a–5b(2); VIRTUE AND VICE 8d(3).

Matters relevant to proving God's existence and to other ways of affirming God's existence, *see* BEING 7a, 8f; CHANGE 14; METAPHYSICS 2d; NECESSITY AND CONTINGENCY 2a–2b; REASONING 5b(3), 5b(5); THEOLOGY 4c.

The problem of God's immanence and transcendence, and for the doctrine of pantheism, *see* NATURE 1b; ONE AND MANY 1b; WORLD 3–3b.

Matters relevant to the consideration of God as a necessary being, *see* BEING 7a; NECESSITY AND CONTINGENCY 2a–2b.

The consideration of the unity and simplicity of God, *see* ONE AND MANY 6a.

The consideration of God's eternity and immutability, *see* CHANGE 15c; ETERNITY 3.

The consideration of God's infinity and omnipresence, *see* INFINITY 7–7d.

The consideration of God's perfection and goodness, *see* GOOD AND EVIL 2–2a; and for the discussion of God in relation to Satan and to the problem of evil, *see* ANGEL 7–7b; GOOD AND EVIL 1d, 2b; OPPOSITION 2d.

The consideration of God's intellect, his knowledge and wisdom, the divine ideas and the divine truth, *see* IDEA 1e; INFINITY 7d; KNOWLEDGE 7a; MIND 10e–10f; TRUTH 2d; WISDOM 1d.

The consideration of God's will and love, *see* LOVE 5c; WILL 4–4a.

The consideration of God's beauty, happiness, and glory, *see* BEAUTY 7a; HAPPINESS 7d; HONOR 6–6b.

The consideration of the divine independence and God's free will, *see* LIBERTY 5d; WILL 4b.

The consideration of divine causality in relation to nature, the origin of the universe by creation or emanation, and the eternity of the world, *see* ART 2c; CAUSE 7–7a; CHANGE 14; MATTER 3d; NATURE 3c(4); TIME 2c; WORLD 4–4e(3); and for the special problem of the creation of life and of man, *see* EVOLUTION 4a, 7a; MAN 8b; SOUL 4c.

The consideration of God's foreknowledge and providence in relation to man's freedom and to the course of history, *see* CAUSE 7c; CHANCE 2b; FATE 4; HISTORY 5a; LIBERTY 5a–5c; PROPHECY 1b–1c; SIN 6a; WILL 7c.

The consideration of divine causality as expressed in divine law and in the government of the universe, *see* ASTRONOMY 6; CAUSE 7c; LAW 3–3b(2); MONARCHY 2b; SIN 1; VIRTUE AND VICE 8c; WORLD 1c.

The consideration of divine causality in the dispensation of grace and the performance of miracles, *see* CAUSE 7d; LIBERTY 5c; NATURE 3c(4), 6b; RELIGION 1b(2); SIN 7; VIRTUE AND VICE 8b, 8e; WILL 7e(2).

The consideration of God's justice and mercy, and of divine rewards and punishments, *see* HAPPINESS 7c–7c(3); IMMORTALITY 5e–5f; JUSTICE 11–11a; PUNISHMENT 5e; SIN 6c–6e.

Other discussions of the doctrine of the Messiah, the Trinity, the Incarnation, and the second coming of Christ, *see* MAN 11c; ONE AND MANY 6b–6c; PROPHECY 4c–4d; RELATION 2.

Other discussions of the doctrine of original sin and man's redemption and salvation, *see* HAPPINESS 7a; SIN 3–3e, 7; VIRTUE AND VICE 8a; WILL 7e(1).

Other discussions of the Last Judgment and the end of the world, *see* IMMORTALITY 5c; PROPHECY 4d; WORLD 8.

For: Other discussions of the church as the Mystical Body of Christ, and of the theory of the sacraments, *see* RELIGION 2c, 3a–3b; SIGN AND SYMBOL 5c.

The general theory of the relation of reason and faith in man's knowledge of God, *see* KNOWLEDGE 6c(5); LOGIC 4f; METAPHYSICS 3a; RELIGION 1b–1b(3); THEOLOGY 2, 4b–4c; VIRTUE AND VICE 8d(1); WISDOM 1c.

The distinction between man's natural and supernatural knowledge of God, and for the discussion of mystical experience and the beatific vision, *see* EXPERIENCE 7; HAPPINESS 7c(1); KNOWLEDGE 6c(5); RELIGION 6f; WILL 7d; WISDOM 1c.

Other discussions of God's revelation of Himself, of Sacred Scripture, and of man's interpretation of the Word of God, *see* EDUCATION 7a; LANGUAGE 12; PROPHECY 3d; SIGN AND SYMBOL 5e.

Other discussions of the relation of creatures to God, and especially of the problem of the resemblance between creatures and God, *see* MAN 10a, 11a; RELATION 3; SAME AND OTHER 6.

Other discussions of the names of God, and for the bearing thereon of the distinction between the univocal, the equivocal, and the analogical, *see* IDEA 4b(4); SAME AND OTHER 3a(3)–3b, 6; SIGN AND SYMBOL 3d, 5f.

Sciences peculiarly concerned with God, *see* ASTRONOMY 6; METAPHYSICS 2a, 2d, 3a; THEOLOGY.

ADDITIONAL READINGS

Listed below are works not included in *Great Books of the Western World*, but relevant to the idea and topics with which this chapter deals. These works are divided into two groups:

I. Works by authors represented in this collection.
II. Works by authors not represented in this collection.

For the date, place, and other facts concerning the publication of the works cited, consult the Bibliography of Additional Readings which follows the last chapter of *The Great Ideas*.

I.

PLUTARCH. "Of Isis and Osiris, or the Ancient Religion and Philosophy of Egypt," in *Moralia*
EPICTETUS. *The Manual*
AUGUSTINE. *Answer to Skeptics*
——. *De Genesi ad Litteram*, BK XII
——. *On the Trinity*
——. *On Grace and Free Will*
——. *The Enchiridion on Faith, Hope and Love*
AQUINAS. *On the Trinity of Boethius*, QQ 1–3
——. *Summa Contra Gentiles*, BK I; BK II, CH 1–28; BK III, CH 64–83, 146–162; BK IV, CH 1–49, 53–55
——. *Quaestiones Disputatae, De Veritate*, QQ 2, 5–7, 14, 23, 27–29; *De Unione Verbi Incarnati*
——. *On the Power of God*, QQ 1–3, 5–7, 9–10
——. *Summa Theologica*, PART III, QQ 27–59
——. *Compendium of Theology*
F. BACON. "Of Atheism," in *Essays*
DESCARTES. *The Principles of Philosophy*, PART I, 13–25, 29–31, 40, 51, 54; PART III, 1–3
HOBBES. *Philosophical Rudiments Concerning Government and Society*, CH 15–18
HUME. *Dialogues Concerning Natural Religion*
——. *The Natural History of Religion*

KANT. *Prolegomena to Any Future Metaphysic*, PAR 55
——. *Religion Within the Limits of Reason Alone*
HEGEL. *Science of Logic*, VOL I, BK II, SECT III, CH 1; VOL II, SECT III, CH 3
——. *On the Proofs of the Existence of God*
J. S. MILL. "Theism," in *Three Essays on Religion*
W. JAMES. *The Will to Believe*
——. *Pragmatism*, LECT III, VIII
——. *A Pluralistic Universe*

II.

HESIOD. *Theogony*
CLEANTHES. *Hymn to Zeus*
CICERO. *De Natura Deorum (On the Nature of the Gods)*
SEXTUS EMPIRICUS. *Against the Physicists*, BK I (Concerning Gods, Do Gods Exist?)
PROCLUS. *The Elements of Theology*, (E,L)
"DIONYSIUS". *On Mystical Theology*
——. *On the Divine Names*
BOETHIUS. *Contra Eutychen (A Treatise Against Eutyches and Nestorius)*
——. *De Trinitate (On the Trinity)*
——. *The Consolation of Philosophy*, BK IV–V
ERIGENA. *De Divisione Naturae*, BK I

Chapter 30: GOOD AND EVIL

INTRODUCTION

THE theory of good and evil crosses the boundaries of many sciences or subject matters. It occupies a place in metaphysics. It is of fundamental importance in all the moral sciences—ethics, economics, politics, jurisprudence. It appears in all the descriptive sciences of human behavior, such as psychology and sociology, though there it is of less importance and is differently treated.

The relation of good and evil to truth and falsity, beauty and ugliness, carries the discussion into logic, aesthetics, and the philosophy of art. The true, it has been said, is the good in the sphere of our thinking. So it may be said of the beautiful that it is a quality which things have when they are good as objects of contemplation and love, or good as productions. It is no less possible to understand goodness and beauty in terms of truth, or truth and goodness in terms of beauty.

One aim of analysis, with respect to the true, the good, and the beautiful, is to preserve their distinctness without rendering each less universal. This has been attempted by writers who treat these three terms as having a kind of parallelism in their application to everything, but who also insist that each of the three notions conceives things under a different aspect or in a different relation. "As good adds to being the notion of the desirable," Aquinas writes, "so the true adds a relation to the intellect"; and it is also said that the end "of the appetite, namely good, is in the desirable thing," whereas the end "of the intellect, namely the true, is in the intellect itself."

In that part of theology which goes beyond metaphysics and moral philosophy, we meet with the concept of infinite goodness—the goodness of an infinite being—and we then face the problem of how God's goodness is to be understood by man. The basic terms of moral

theology—righteousness and sin, salvation and damnation—are, like virtue and vice, happiness and misery, conceptions of good and evil in the condition of man. (Their special theological significance comes from the fact that they consider the goodness or evil of man in terms of his relation to God.) But the theological problem which is traditionally called "the problem of evil" concerns the whole universe in its relation to the divine perfection.

That problem, which is further discussed in the chapter on WORLD, can be formulated in a number of ways. How are we to understand the existence of evil in a world created by a God who is omnipotent and perfectly good? Since God is good and since everything which happens is within God's power, how can we account for the sin of Satan or the fall of man, with all the evil consequent thereupon, without limiting God's power or absolving the erring creature from responsibility? Can it be said that this is the best of all possible worlds, if it is also true that this world is far from perfectly good, and if, as certain theologians hold, "God could make other things, or add something to the present creation, and then there would be another and a better universe"?

THE CONTEMPORARY discussion of good and evil draws its terminology from economics rather than theology. The word "value" has almost replaced "good" and "evil." What in other centuries were the various moral sciences are now treated as parts of the general theory of value. The substitution of "value" for "good" or of "value judgment" for "moral judgment" reflects the influence of economics.

According to Marx, Aristotle "was the first to analyse . . . the form of value." As indicated in the chapter on WEALTH, economics at its origin was treated by Aristotle, along with ethics and politics, as a moral discipline. But he made it subordinate to them because it dealt not with the whole of human welfare, but only with wealth—one of the goods.

In the modern development of economics, the word "goods" comes to have a special significance. It refers to commodities or utilities, as in the phrase "goods and services." More generally, anything which is useful or exchangeable has the character of an economic good. This general sense is usually conveyed by the economist's use of the word "value." According to Adam Smith, "the word *value* . . . has two different meanings, and sometimes expresses the utility of some particular object, and sometimes the power of purchasing other goods which the possessor of that object conveys." These two meanings are distinguished as "value in use" and "value in exchange." Marx accepts this distinction, but thinks that there is a more fundamental notion of value. He thinks it is possible to abstract from both use-value and exchange-value, and to discover the underlying property which gives value to all exchangeable things, namely, that they are products of labor.

With Smith and Marx, as with Aristotle, the theory of value does not deal with every type of good, but only with that type which earlier moralists called "external goods" or "goods of fortune." But more recently the concept of value has been extended, by economists and others, to the evaluation of everything which men think of as desirable in any way. In consequence, the age-old controversy about the objectivity or subjectivity of good and evil is now stated in terms of the difference between facts and values, or between judgments of fact and judgments of value.

The issue, as currently stated, is whether questions of value can be answered in the same way as questions of fact. One position maintains that, unlike questions of fact which can be answered by scientific investigation and can be objectively solved, questions of value elicit no more than expressions of opinion, relative to the individual's subjective response or to the conventions of his society at a given time. The other side of the issue is held by those who insist that the norms of value are as objective and as scientifically determinable as the criteria of fact or existence.

THE WORD "VALUE" does not change the problem in any way; for what does evaluating anything mean except judging it as good or bad, better or worse? The problem, which has a history as long as the tradition of the great books, is the problem of how we can defend such judgments and what they signify about the things judged. Are good and evil determined by nature or convention? Are they objects of knowledge or opinion?

The title of an essay by Montaigne—"that the taste for good and evil depends in good part upon the opinion we have of them"— indicates one set of answers to these questions. "If evils have no admission into us," he writes, "but by the judgment we ourselves make of them, it should seem that it is, then, in our power to despise them or to turn them to good. . . . If what we call evil and torment is neither evil nor torment of itself, but only that our fancy gives it that quality, it is in us to change it." Echoing Montaigne, Hamlet remarks that "there is nothing either good or bad but thinking makes it so." The Greek sophists, centuries earlier, appear to take the same view. The statement of Protagoras that "man is the measure of all things," Plato thinks, does not significantly apply to *all* things, but only to such things as the good or the right, the true or the beautiful. In the *Theaetetus*, Protagoras is made to say that as "to the sick man his food appears to be bitter, and to the healthy man the opposite of bitter," so in general men estimate or judge all things according to their own condition and the way things affect them. This theory of good and evil necessarily denies the possibility of moral science. Socrates calls it "a high argument in which all things are said to be relative."

Plato and Aristotle respond to the sophists by arguing in the opposite vein. For Plato, the good is not a matter of opinion, but an object of knowledge. Knowledge of good and evil is the best fruit of the tree of knowledge. "Let each one of us leave every other kind of knowledge," Socrates says at the end of the *Republic*, "and seek and follow one thing only," that is, "to learn and discern between good and evil."

Aristotle does not think that ethics, or any science which deals with good and evil, can have as much precision as mathematics. "Our discussion will be adequate," he writes, "if it has as much clearness as the subject matter admits of, for precision is not to be sought for alike in all discussions." This, however, does not exclude the possibility of our knowing with great exactitude the first principles of moral science, such as the nature of happiness and virtue. Indefiniteness and even a certain kind of relativity occur only when these principles are applied to particular cases. Hence, in Aristotle's view, the moral sciences, such as ethics and politics, can have objective and universal validity no less than physics or mathematics, at least on the level of principles.

In modern times, Locke and Kant also affirm the scientific character of ethics, but without the qualification which Aristotle insists upon when we go from principles to practice. Locke explains the grounds on which he is "bold to think that morality is capable of demonstration, as well as mathematics"; for, he says, "the precise real essence of the things moral words stand for may be perfectly known, and so the congruity and incongruity of the things themselves may be certainly discovered; in which consists perfect knowledge." He is confident that "from self-evident propositions, by necessary consequences, as incontestible as those in mathematics, the measures of right and wrong might be made out, to any one that will apply himself with the same indifference and attention to the one as he does to the other of these sciences." But Locke adds, "this is not to be expected, whilst the desire of esteem, riches, or power makes men espouse the well-endowed opinions in fashion." He himself seems to tend in the opposite direction when he identifies the good with the pleasant and makes it relative to individual desires.

For Kant the two major parts of philosophy —physics and ethics—are on equal footing, the one concerned with the "laws of *nature*," the other with the "laws of *freedom*." In each case there is both empirical and *a priori* knowledge. Kant calls the latter in each case "metaphysics" and speaks of "a *metaphysic of nature* and a *metaphysic of morals*." The nature of science, he thinks, requires us to "separate the empirical from the rational part, and prefix to physics proper (or empirical physics) a metaphysic of nature, and to practical anthropology a meta-physic of morals, which must be carefully cleared of everything empirical."

This partial inventory of thinkers who stand against skepticism or relativism in the field of morals indicates that agreement on this point is accompanied by some disagreement about the reasons for holding what appears to be the same view. The opposite view seems also to be shared by thinkers of quite different cast, such as Spinoza and Mill, who differ from each other as well as from Montaigne and the ancient sophists.

The terms "good and evil," Spinoza writes, "indicate nothing positive in things considered in themselves, nor are they anything else than modes of thought . . . One and the same thing may at the same time be both good and evil or indifferent"—according to the person who makes the judgment of it. Spinoza therefore defines "good" as "that which we certainly know is useful to us." Apart from society, he says, "there is nothing which by universal consent is good or evil, since everyone in a natural state consults only his own profit." Only when men live together in a civil society under law can it be "decided by universal consent what is good and what is evil."

Holding that all men seek happiness and that they determine what is good and evil in particular cases by reference to this end, Mill seems to offer the standard of utility as an objective principle of morality. But insofar as he identifies happiness with a sum total of pleasures or satisfactions, it tends to become relative to the individual or the group. If competent judges disagree concerning which of two pleasures is the greater or higher, there can be no appeal, Mill says, except to the verdict of the majority. To this extent at least, judgments of value are expressions of opinion, not determinations of science. Nor does Mill hesitate to say that "the ultimate sanction of all morality" is "a subjective feeling in our minds."

IN ORDER to clarify this basic issue it is necessary to take note of other terms which are usually involved in the discussion of good and evil—such terms as pleasure and pain, desire and aversion, being, nature, and reason. In the course of doing this, we will perceive the relevance of the chapters which deal with those ideas.

It has been said, for example, that the good is identical with the pleasant; that the good is what men desire; that the good is a property of being or existence; that the good is that which conforms to the nature of a thing; that the good is that which is approved by reason. It is possible to see some truth in each of these statements. But each, taken by itself, may be too great a simplification. Searching questions can be asked by those who refuse to equate the good with the pleasant or the desirable, the real, the natural, or the reasonable. Are there no pleasures in any way bad, no pains in any way good? Are all desires themselves good, or are all equally good? How does calling a thing "good" add anything to its being or existence? Does not evil exist or qualify existence? By what standards can the natural and the rational be judged good, if the good is that which conforms to nature and reason?

These questions call for more analysis of each of these factors in the discussion of good and evil and suggest that no one of these factors *by itself* is sufficient to solve the problem of defining good and evil or formulating their criteria. Of the five things mentioned, two particularly —pleasure and desire—seem to leave open the question whether good and evil are objective or subjective. They require us to decide whether things please us *because they are good* or are good *because they please us*; whether we desire things because they are good or simply call them "good" when we desire them. On this issue Spinoza flatly declares that "we do not desire a thing because we adjudge it good, but, on the contrary, we call it good because we desire it." In saying that "a thing is good so far as it is desirable," Aquinas takes the opposite position, for according to him "a thing is desirable only in so far as it is perfect." It can be desirable, therefore, without being actually desired by this or that individual.

The other three terms—unlike pleasure and desire—seem to favor the objectivity of good and evil, at least for those who regard the order of existence, the nature of things, and the laws of reason as independent of our desires or preferences. Thus for Spinoza the *nature* of man and his *reason* seem to provide an objective standard for determining what is good alike for all men. Nothing, he writes, "can be good except in so far as it agrees with our nature, and therefore the more an object agrees with our nature the more profitable it will be." And in another place he says, "By *good* I understand . . . everything which we are certain is a means by which we may approach nearer and nearer to the model of human nature we set before us." That model, he tells us, is the man of reason, the man who always acts "according to the dictates of reason," for "those desires which are determined by man's power or reason are always good."

Nevertheless, if desire and pleasure cannot be eliminated from the consideration of good and evil—at least not the good and evil which enter into human life—then the problem of finding a purely objective foundation for our moral judgments is not solved simply by an appeal to being, nature, and reason.

Some help toward a solution may be found in one often reiterated fact about the relation between the good and human desire. The ancients insist that no man desires anything but what at the time *seems* good to him in some way. "No man," Socrates observes, "voluntarily pursues evil, or that which he thinks to be evil. To prefer evil to good is not in human nature; and when a man is compelled to choose one of two evils, no one will choose the greater when he may have the less." This, however, does not prevent men from desiring "what they suppose to be goods although they are really evils." Since they are mistaken in their judgment "and suppose the evils to be goods, they really desire goods."

The object consciously desired is always at least *apparently* good. When men are mistaken in their estimate of things as beneficial or injurious to themselves, the apparent good—the good actually desired—will be really an evil, that is, something actually undesirable. An object which is really good may not appear to be so, and so it will not be desired although it is desirable. The deception of appearances, Socrates says, tricks us into taking "at one time the things of which we repent at another, both in our actions and in our choice of things great and small."

THE DISTINCTION between the *real* and the *apparent* good is, of course, connected with the problem of the objective and the subjective good. The apparent good varies from individual to individual and from time to time. If there were a real good, it would be free from such relativity and variability. Unless there are real, as distinct from merely apparent, goods, moralists cannot distinguish between what men *should* desire and what in fact they *do* desire.

Since moral science deals with human behavior, its province can be separated from that of other sciences which treat the same subject matter—such as psychology and sociology—only in terms of a different treatment of that subject matter. Moral science must be normative or prescriptive rather than descriptive. It must determine what men *should* seek, not what they *do* seek. The very existence of normative sciences, as well as their validity, would thus seem to depend on the establishment of a real, as opposed to a merely apparent, good.

This creates no special difficulty for moralists who think that man knows what is really good for him, both in general and in particular, by intuition or rational deduction, through the commandments of the divine law, or through the precepts of the law of reason. But for those who insist that the good is always somehow relative to desire and always involves pleasure, the distinction between the real and the apparent good raises an extremely difficult problem.

To say that an apparent good is not really good suggests, as we have seen, that what is called "good" may not be in itself desirable. That something which is really good may not in fact appear to be so, seems to imply that the word "good" can be significantly applied to something which is not actually desired—at least not consciously. How, then, is the good always relative to desire? The traditional answer to this question must appeal to the distinction between natural and conscious desire, which is discussed in the chapter on DESIRE. It is by reference to natural desire that the good is said to be in itself always desirable—even when the really good thing is not consciously desired.

The relation of good and evil to pleasure and pain can also be clarified by a basic distinction between the pleasure which is an object of de-

sire and pleasure conceived as the satisfaction of desire. This is discussed in the chapter on PLEASURE AND PAIN. If obtaining a desired good is satisfying, then there is certainly a sense in which the good and the pleasant (or the satisfying) are always associated; but it may also be true that pleasure is only one kind of good among various objects of desire and that certain pleasures which men desire appear to be, but are not really good.

THE FOREGOING considerations apply to the good in the sphere of human conduct. But the human good, the practicable good, the good for man, does not exhaust the meaning of the term *good*. The idea of the good is, for Plato, the measure of perfection in all things; it is "not only the author of knowledge to all things known, but of their being and essence, and yet the good is not essence, but far exceeds essence in dignity and power."

The absolute good is also, as in the *Divine Comedy*, the final cause or ultimate end of the motions of the universe. It is "the Alpha and Omega," Dante says, "of every scripture that Love reads to me . . . the Essence wherein is such supremacy that every good which is found outside of It is naught else than a beam of Its own radiance . . . the Love which moves the sun and the other stars."

So too, in Aristotle's cosmology, the circular motions of the celestial spheres, and through them all other cycles of natural change, are sustained eternally by the prime mover, which moves all things by the attraction of its perfect being. It therefore "moves without being moved," for it "produces motion through being loved."

Though desire and love enter into the conception of the good as a cosmic final cause, they are not *human* desire or love. Though the goodness which inheres in things according to the degree of their perfection may make them desirable, it is not dependent on their being consciously desired by men.

In Jewish and Christian theology, for example, the goodness of God is in no way measured by human desires, purposes, or pleasures; nor is the goodness of created things which, according to Genesis, God surveyed and found "very good." The order of creation, moreover, involves a hierarchy of inequalities in being and goodness. Even when each thing is perfect in its kind, all things are not equally good, for according to the differences in their natures, diverse kinds are capable of greater or less perfection.

In the metaphysical conception of goodness, that which has more actuality either in existence or power has more perfection. God's infinite goodness is therefore said to follow from the fact that he is completely actual—infinite in being and power. Things "which have life," Augustine writes, "are ranked above those which have none ... And among those that have life, the sentient are higher than those which have no sensation ... and among the sentient, the intelligent above those that have no intelligence."

Augustine contrasts these gradations of perfection which are "according to the order of nature" with the "standards of value" which are "according to the utility each man finds in a thing." That which is less good in a metaphysical sense may be preferred on moral grounds as being better for man. "Who," he asks, "would not rather have bread in his house than mice, gold than fleas?" Is it not true that "more is often given for a horse than for a slave, for a jewel than for a maid"?

According to Augustine, as well as to Aquinas later, metaphysical goodness consists in "the value a thing has in itself in the scale of creation," while moral goodness depends upon the relation in which a thing stands to human need or desire, and according to the estimation placed upon it by human reason. It is in the moral, not the metaphysical sense that we speak of a good man, a good will, a good life, and a good society; or of all the things, such as health, wealth, pleasure, virtue, or knowledge, which it may be good for man to seek and possess. Only in the metaphysical sense can things be thought of as good entirely apart from man; only then can we find a hierarchy of perfections in the world which accords with a hierarchy of beings. Thus Spinoza declares that "the perfection of things is to be judged by their nature and power alone; nor are they more or less perfect because they delight or offend the human senses, or because they are beneficial or prejudicial to human nature."

THE METAPHYSICAL conception of goodness raises peculiarly difficult problems. Are there as many meanings of "good" as there are of "being"? When we say God is good, are we making a moral or a metaphysical judgement? Are we attributing perfection of being or goodness of will to God? If goodness is a property of being, then must not all evil become a privation of being? Conceiving evil in this way, Augustine points out that if things "be deprived of all good, they shall cease to be," so that there is "nothing whatsoever evil" in itself; and Aquinas maintains that "no being is said to be evil, considered as being, but only so far as it lacks being."

If to understand what the notion of goodness adds to the notion of being it is necessary to say that being has goodness in relation to appetite, the question inevitably arises, "Whose appetite?" Not man's certainly, for then the moral and the metaphysical good become identical. If God's, then not appetite in the form of desire, but in the form of love, for the divine perfection is usually thought to preclude desire.

Problems of this sort confront those who, conceiving the good both *apart from* and also *relative to* man, are obligated to connect the metaphysical and the moral meanings of good and to say whether they have a common thread. Some writers, however, limit their consideration to the strictly moral good, and deny, as do the Stoics, goodness or evil to anything but man's free acts of will.

We should, says Marcus Aurelius, "judge only those things which are in our power, to be good or bad." In this we are entirely free, for "things themselves have no natural power to form our judgments ... If thou art pained by any external thing, it is not this thing which disturbs thee, but thy own judgment about it. And it is in thy power to wipe out this judgment now ... Suppose that men kill thee, cut thee in pieces, curse thee. What then can these things do to prevent thy mind from remaining pure, wise, sober, just?"

Though Kant develops what he calls a "metaphysic of ethics," he does not seem to have a metaphysical as opposed to a moral conception of the good; unless in some analogous form it lies in his distinction between "value" and "dignity," according to which "whatever has reference to the general inclinations and wants of mankind has a *market value*," whereas "whatever . . . is above all value, and therefore admits of no equivalent, has a dignity"—"not a merely relative worth, but an intrinsic worth."

But since Kant thinks that only men, or rational beings, can have intrinsic worth, he finds goodness only in the moral order. He agrees with the Stoics that good and evil occur only in the realm of freedom, not at all in the realm of existence or nature. "Good or evil," he writes, "always implies a reference to the *will*, as determined by the *law of reason*" which is the law of freedom. According to Kant, "nothing can possibly be conceived in the world, or even out of it, which can be called good without qualification, except a Good Will"; and in another place he says, "If anything is to be good or evil absolutely . . . it can only be the manner of acting, the maxim of the will." In this sense, the free will complying with or resisting the imperatives of duty is either the seat or the source of all the goodness or evil that there is. "Men may laugh," Kant says, "at the Stoic, who in the severest paroxysms of gout cried out: Pain, however thou tormentest me, I will never admit that thou art an evil: he was right . . . for pain did not in the least diminish the worth of his person, but only that of his condition."

IN THE SPHERE of moral conduct, and especially for those who make desire or pleasure rather than duty the principle, there seems to be a plurality of goods which require classification and order.

Some things, it would appear, are not desired for themselves, but for the sake of something else. They are good only as means to be used. Some things are desired for their own sake, and are good as ends, to be possessed or enjoyed. This division of goods into means and ends—the useful and the enjoyable or pleasant—permits a third type of good which is an end in one respect, and a means in another. Analysis of this sort leads to the concept of a *summum bonum*—that good which is not a means in any respect, but entirely an end, the supreme or highest good for which all else is sought.

The chief question with respect to the *summum bonum* is whether it is *a* good or *the* good —whether it is merely one type of good, more

desirable than any other, or the sum of all good things which, when possessed, leaves nothing to be desired. Aristotle and Mill seem to take the latter view in their conception of happiness as the *summum bonum*. "Human nature," Mill says, "is so constituted as to desire nothing which is not either a part of happiness or a means of happiness." Happiness, he insists, is "not an abstract idea, but a concrete whole" including all other goods within itself. It is the only good which is desired entirely for its own sake. Aristotle treats virtue and knowledge as intrinsic goods, but he also regards them as means to happiness. In Mill's terms, their goodness remains subject to the criterion of utility, from which happiness alone is exempt since it measures the utility of all other goods.

If the evaluation of all things by reference to their contribution to happiness as the ultimate good constitutes utilitarianism in ethics, then Aristotle no less than Mill is a utilitarian, even though Aristotle does not refer to the principle of utility, does not identify the good with pleasure, and conceives the virtues as intrinsically good, not merely as means. Kant would regard them as in fundamental agreement despite all their differences—or at least he would regard them as committing the same fundamental error.

To Kant any discussion of human conduct which involves the calculation of means to ends is pragmatic or utilitarian, even when the controlling end is the *summum bonum* or happiness. Kant makes a sharp distinction between what he calls "pragmatical rules" of conduct which consider what should be done by one who wishes to be happy, and what he regards as the strictly "moral or ethical law" which "has no other motive than the *worthiness of being happy*." Morality, he says in another place, "is not properly the doctrine of how we should *make* ourselves happy, but how we should become *worthy* of happiness"—through doing our duty.

Kant's criticism of Aristotle's ethics of happiness is therefore applicable to the utilitarianism of Mill; and Mill's rejoinder to Kant serves as a defense of Aristotle. This basic issue concerning the primacy of happiness or duty—of desire or law—is discussed in the chapters on DUTY and HAPPINESS, where it is suggested that in an ethics of duty, right and wrong supplant good and evil as the fundamental terms, and the *summum bonum* becomes a derivative notion rather than the first principle of morality.

At the other extreme are those who deny duty entirely, and with it any meaning to right and wrong as distinct from good and evil. A middle ground is held by those who employ right and wrong as subordinate terms in the analysis of good and evil, finding their special significance in the consideration of the good of others or the social good. To do right is to do good to others; to do wrong is to injure them. The question which Plato so insistently raises, whether it is better to do injustice or to suffer it, can also be stated in terms of good and evil, or right and wrong. Is it better to suffer evil or to do it? Is it better to be wronged by others or to wrong them? As justice for Aristotle is that one among the virtues which concerns the good of others and the common good, and as it is the one virtue which is thought to involve duty or obligation, so the criteria of right and wrong measure the goodness or evil of human acts by reference to law and society.

THE DIVISION of goods into means and ends is not the only distinction made by moralists who recognize the plurality and inequality of goods.

Goods have been divided into the limited and the unlimited with respect to quantity; the pure and the mixed with respect to quality; sensible and intelligible goods or particular goods and the good in general; external goods, goods of the body, and goods of the soul; the pleasant, the useful, and the virtuous. More specific enumerations of the variety of goods list wealth, health, strength, beauty, longevity, pleasure, honor (or fame), virtue, knowledge, friendship.

All of the foregoing classifications can be combined with one another, but there is one distinction which stands by itself, although it affects all the others. That is the distinction between the individual and the common good, or between private and public good, the good for this one man and the good of all others and of the whole community. In the language of modern utilitarianism, it is the distinction between individual happiness and what Bentham called "the greatest good for the greatest number."

The phrase "common good" has several meanings in the tradition of the great books. One sense, which some think is the least significant, refers to that which can be shared or used by many, as, for example, land held in common and worked by a number of persons or families. Thus we speak of the "commons" of a town or village. This meaning applies particularly to economic goods which may either belong to the community as a whole or be divided into parcels of private property.

Another sense of common good is that in which the welfare of a community is a common good participated in by its members. The welfare of the family or the state is a good which belongs to a multitude organized for some common purpose. If the individual members of the group derive some benefit from their association with one another, then the prosperity of the community is not only a common good viewed collectively, but also a common good viewed distributively, for it is the good of each member of the group as well as of the whole.

With this in mind, perhaps, Mill speaks of "an indissoluble association between [the individual's] happiness and the practice of such mode of conduct, negative and positive, as regard for the universal happiness prescribes; so that not only he may be unable to conceive the possibility of happiness to himself, consistently with conduct opposed to the general good, but also that a direct impulse to promote the general good may be in every individual one of the habitual modes of action." If this statement by Mill is used to interpret Bentham's phrase— "the greatest good for the greatest number"— then the greatest number cannot be taken to mean a majority, for the good of nothing less than the whole collectively or of all distributively can be taken as the common or general good.

Still another conception of the common good is possible. A good may be common in the sense in which a specific nature is common to the members of the species—not as organized socially in any way, but simply as so many *like* individuals. If all men seek happiness, for example, then happiness is a common good, even though each individual seeks his own happiness. In a deeper sense it is a common good if the happiness each seeks is the same for all men because they are all of the same nature; but, most strictly, it is a common good if the happiness of each individual cannot be separated from the happiness of all.

Aquinas seems to be using this meaning of *common good* when, in defining law as a rule of conduct "directed to the common good," he refers not merely to the good of the community or body politic, but beyond that to "the last end of human life," which is "happiness or beatitude." Law, he says, "must needs concern itself properly with the order directed to universal happiness." Mill also seems to conceive happiness as a common good in this sense. "What the assailants of utilitarianism seldom have the justice to acknowledge," he writes, is "that the happiness which forms the utilitarian standard of what is right in conduct, is not the agent's own happiness, but that of all concerned."

The several meanings of the common good create a fundamental issue. Some writers use it in one sense only, rejecting the others. Some not only use the term in all its meanings, but also develop a hierarchy of common goods. They regard universal happiness, for example, as a common good of a higher order than the welfare of the political community. Yet in every order they insist upon the primacy of the common over the individual good. In the political order, for example, they think the welfare of the community takes precedence over individual happiness. They would regard Adam Smith's statement of the way in which individuals accidentally serve the common good while seeking their private interests, as a perversion of the relationship. To say that an individual considering only his own gain is "led by an invisible hand to promote an end which was no part of his intention" (*i.e.*, the general prosperity of society) does not excuse the individual's failure to aim at the common good.

The several meanings of the common good also complicate the statement of the issue between those who seem to say that the welfare of the community always takes precedence over individual well-being or happiness—that the good of the whole is always greater than the good of its parts—and those who seem to say that the state is made for man, not man for the state, or that the prosperity of the society in which men live is good primarily because it enables each of them to live well. This issue, which runs through all the great books of political theory from Plato and Aristotle to Hegel and Mill, is discussed in the chapters on CITIZEN and STATE.

The opposition between collectivism and individualism in economics and politics does not exhaust the issue which, stated in its broadest moral terms, is a conflict between self-interest and altruism. The primary problem to consider here is whether the issue is itself genuine, or only an opposition between false extremes which needlessly exclude the half-truth that each contains.

The collective aspect of the common good may not need to be emphasized at the expense of its distributive aspect. The good of each man and the good of mankind may be inseparable. It may be the same good which, in different respects, is individual and common. It may be that no good can be supreme which is not both immanent and transcendent—at once the highest perfection of the individual and a good greater than his whole being and his life.

OUTLINE OF TOPICS

REFERENCES

To find the passages cited, use the numbers in heavy type, which are the volume and page numbers of the passages referred to. For example, in **4** HOMER: *Iliad*, BK II [265-283] **12d**, the number **4** is the number of the volume in the set; the number **12d** indicates that the passage is in section d of page 12.

PAGE SECTIONS: When the text is printed in one column, the letters a and b refer to the upper and lower halves of the page. For example, in **53** JAMES: *Psychology*, 116a-119b, the passage begins in the upper half of page 116 and ends in the lower half of page 119. When the text is printed in two columns, the letters a and b refer to the upper and lower halves of the left-hand side of the page, the letters c and d to the upper and lower halves of the right-hand side of the page. For example, in **7** PLATO: *Symposium*, 163b-164c, the passage begins in the lower half of the left-hand side of page 163 and ends in the upper half of the right-hand side of page 164.

AUTHOR'S DIVISIONS: One or more of the main divisions of a work (such as PART, BK, CH, SECT) are sometimes included in the reference; line numbers, in brackets, are given in certain cases; *e.g.*, *Iliad*, BK II [265-283] **12d**.

BIBLE REFERENCES: The references are to book, chapter, and verse. When the King James and Douay versions differ in title of books or in the numbering of chapters or verses, the King James version is cited first and the Douay, indicated by a (D), follows; *e.g.*, OLD TESTAMENT: *Nehemiah*, 7:45—(D) II *Esdras*, 7:46.

SYMBOLS: The abbreviation "esp" calls the reader's attention to one or more especially relevant parts of a whole reference; "passim" signifies that the topic is discussed intermittently rather than continuously in the work or passage cited.

For additional information concerning the style of the references, see the Explanation of Reference Style; for general guidance in the use of *The Great Ideas*, consult the Preface.

1. The general theory of good and evil

OLD TESTAMENT: *Isaiah*, 45:7—(D) *Isaias*, 45:7 / *Lamentations*, 3:38

APOCRYPHA: *Ecclesiasticus*, 33:14-15; 39:25—(D) OT, *Ecclesiasticus*, 33:15; 39:30

7 PLATO: *Euthydemus*, 83b-84a / *Gorgias*, 282c-284b / *Republic*, BK II, 322d-323a; BK VII, 389b-c / *Theaetetus*, 518a-b

8 ARISTOTLE: *Heavens*, BK II, CH 12 383b-384c / *Metaphysics*, BK I, CH 6 [988^{a}8-16] 506a-b; CH 7 [988^{b}6-16] 506c-d; BK V, CH I [1013^{a}20-24] 533b; BK XII, CH 7 602a-603b

9 ARISTOTLE: *Ethics*, BK I, CH I 339a-b; CH 6-7 341b-344a

12 EPICTETUS: *Discourses*, BK I, CH 29, 134d-135b; BK II, CH 8 146a-147c

12 AURELIUS: *Meditations*, BK V, SECT 8 269d-270b; BK VI, SECT 40-45 277d-278c; BK VIII, SECT 19 286d-287a

17 PLOTINUS: *First Ennead*, TR VIII 27b-34a / *Third Ennead*, TR IX, CH 3, 138a,c / *Fifth Ennead*, TR I-VI 208a-237d passim; TR IX, CH 10, 250c / *Sixth Ennead*, TR V, CH 10 309a-d; TR VII, CH 24-26 333d-334d; CH 28 335b-d; TR IX 353d-360d

18 AUGUSTINE: *Confessions*, BK V, par 20 32d-33a / *City of God*, BK XII, CH 1-5 342b,d-345b

19 AQUINAS: *Summa Theologica*, PART I, QQ 4-6 20c-30d; Q 21, A I, REP 4 124b-125b; A 3, ANS 126a-c; QQ 48-49 259b-268a,c; PART I-II, Q I, A 4, REP I 612a-613a; A 8 615a-c; Q 2, A 5 618d-619c; Q 18, A I, ANS 694a-d; A 2, ANS 694d-695c; A 3, ANS 695d-696b

23 HOBBES: *Leviathan*, PART I, 61d-62a

26 SHAKESPEARE: *Romeo and Juliet*, ACT II, SC III [1-30] 296b-c

31 SPINOZA: *Ethics*, PART I, APPENDIX 369b-372d; PART III, PROP 9, SCHOL 399c; PROP 39, SCHOL 408b-d; PART IV, PREF-DEF 2 422b,d-424a; PROP 8 426b-c; PROP 27-28 431b-c

32 MILTON: *Areopagitica*, 390b-391a

42 KANT: *Fund. Prin. Metaphysic of Morals*, 256a-b / *Practical Reason*, 314d-321b esp 316a-317d, 318c-321b; 338c-355d

1a. The idea of the good: the notion of finality

7 PLATO: *Protagoras*, 50c-d / *Symposium*, 164c-165b / *Phaedo*, 240d-242b / *Gorgias*, 282c-284b / *Republic*, BK I, 309b-310a; BK VI-VII, 384b-401d / *Timaeus*, 447d-448a / *Theaetetus*, 535b-d / *Philebus* 609a-639a,c esp 609a-c, 614a, 635b-639a,c

8 ARISTOTLE: *Posterior Analytics*, BK II, CH 11 [94^{b}8-95^{a}9] 129b-d / *Topics*, BK I, CH 15 [107^{a}3-11] 151a; BK VI, CH 5 [143^{a}9-12] 196c;

1c. The good, the true, and the beautiful

1d. The origin, nature, and existence of evil

34 NEWTON: *Principles*, BK III, GENERAL SCHOL, 370a-371a

35 LOCKE: *Human Understanding*, BK II, CH XXIII, SECT 34-35 213a-c; BK III, CH VI, SECT 11-12 271b-272b passim

35 HUME: *Human Understanding*, SECT XI, DIV 106-107, 499c-500a passim; DIV 113, 502a-b

41 GIBBON: *Decline and Fall*, 230a-b

42 KANT: *Pure Reason*, 205a-b; 237d-239a / *Fund. Prin. Metaphysic of Morals*, 263a-b; 278b-d / *Practical Reason*, 307a-d; 325d-326a; 342c; 345a-c; 351b-352c / *Judgement*, 592a-c

2a. God's goodness as diffusive, causing the goodness of things: God's love

OLD TESTAMENT: *Genesis*, 1 / *Exodus*, 20:4-6 esp 20:6; 33:19; 34:5-10 / *Deuteronomy*, 4:1-40 esp 4:6-8, 4:31, 4:37; 5:7-10 esp 5:10; 7:6-11 / *Job*, 33:13-33 / *Psalms* passim, esp 8-10, 16-18, 20, 22-23, 25, 68, 97:10, 114:1-115:18, 118:1-119:176—(D) *Psalms* passim, esp 8-9, 15-17, 19, 21-22, 24, 67, 96:10, 113:1-18, 117:1-118:176 / *Proverbs*, 3:11-12 / *Song of Solomon*—(D) *Canticle of Canticles* / *Isaiah*, 40-66 passim, esp 42-44, 46:3-4, 49:1-26, 52:1-15, 56:1-8, 63:8-9—(D) *Isaias*, 40-66 passim, esp 42-44, 46:3-4, 49:1-26, 52:1-15, 56:1-8, 63:8-9 / *Jeremiah*, 31-33—(D) *Jeremias*, 31-33 / *Lamentations*, 3:22-39 esp 3:25, 3:38 / *Ezekiel*, 16 esp 16:6-14, 16:59-63—(D) *Ezechiel*, 16 esp 16:6-14, 16:59-63 / *Hosea* esp 2:14-23, 3:1, 3:5, 6:1-3, 11:1-4, 13:16-14:9—(D) *Osee* esp 2:14-23, 3:1, 3:5, 6:1-3, 11:1-4, 14:1-10 / *Joel*, 2 esp 2:18-32 / *Zechariah*, 9:17—(D) *Zacharias*, 9:17 / *Malachi*, 1:1-3—(D) *Malachias*, 1:1-3

APOCRYPHA: *Tobit*, 13:10—(D) OT, *Tobias*, 13:12 / *Wisdom of Solomon*, 11:22-26; 16:20-29—(D) OT, *Book of Wisdom*, 11:23-27; 16:20-29 / *Ecclesiasticus*, 11:14-17; 16:26-18:14 esp 16:29-30; 39:16,25-34—(D) OT, *Ecclesiasticus*, 11:14-17; 16:26-18:14 esp 16:30-31; 39:21,30-40

NEW TESTAMENT: *Matthew*, 6:25-34; 7:7-11 / *Luke*, 11:1-13; 12:6-7,16-33 / *John*, 1:1-5; 3:16-21; 13:31-35; 14:21; 15:9-16; 17:21-26 / *Romans*, 2:4; 8:31-39 / *Galatians*, 2:20 / *Ephesians*, 3:14-21; 5:1-2 / *I John*, 3-4 esp 3:1, 3:16, 4:7-12 / *Revelation*, 3:19—(D) *Apocalypse*, 3:19

7 PLATO: *Republic*, BK II, 321d-322d; BK VI-VII, 384a-389c / *Timaeus*, 447a-448a

8 ARISTOTLE: *Generation and Corruption*, BK II, CH 10 [336^{b}25-34] 438d / *Metaphysics*, BK XII, CH 7 602a-603b; CH 10 [1075^{a}11-24] 605d-606a

12 EPICTETUS: *Discourses*, BK II, CH 8 146a-147c

16 KEPLER: *Harmonies of the World*, 1049b-1050b; 1071b

17 PLOTINUS: *First Ennead*, TR VII, CH 1-2 26a-d / *Fifth Ennead*, TR V 228b-235b / *Sixth Ennead*, TR IX, CH 9 358d-359c

18 AUGUSTINE: *Confessions*, BK I, par 7 2c-d; BK II, par 10 11a-b; BK VII, par 4 44b-c; par 16-23 48c-50c; BK XI, par 6 90c-d; BK XIII, par 1-5 110d-111d / *City of God*, BK VII, CH 31 261d-262a; BK XI, CH 21-24 333a-336a; BK XII, CH 1 342b,d-343c; CH 9 347b-348b; BK XIV, CH 13 387c-388c; BK XXII, CH 24 609a-612a / *Christian Doctrine*, BK I, CH 31-32 633b-d

19 AQUINAS: *Summa Theologica*, PART I, Q 2, A 3, ANS and REP 1 12c-14a; Q 3, A 1, REP 1 14b-15b; A 2, ANS 15c-16a; Q 6 28b-30d; Q 13, A 2, ANS 63c-64d; Q 19, A 2, ANS and REP 2-4 109c-110b; A 4, ANS and REP 1 111c-112c; Q 20 119d-124a; Q 21, A 3, ANS 126a-c; Q 25, A 6 149a-150a; Q 50, A 1, ANS 269b-270a; A 3, ANS 272a-273b; Q 51, A 1, REP 3 275b-276b; Q 59, A 1, ANS 306c-307b; A 2, ANS 307c-308b; Q 60, A 5 313b-314c; Q 91, A 1, ANS 484a-485b; Q 103 528a-534b; Q 104, A 3, REP 2 537b-d; A 4, ANS 538a-c; Q 105, A 4, ANS 541c-542a; Q 106, A 4, ANS 548b-549a; PART I-II, Q 1, A 4, REP 1 612a-613a; Q 2, A 5, REP 3 618d-619c; Q 9, A 6, ANS 662a-d; Q 19, A 4, ANS 705b-c; Q 28, A 3, CONTRARY 742a-d

21 DANTE: *Divine Comedy*, PURGATORY, XV [40-81] 75d-76a; PARADISE, II [112-148] 109a-b; VII [16-148] 115b-116c esp [64-75] 115d-116a; XIII [52-87] 126a-b; XIX [40-90] 135c-136a; XXVI [1-69] 145d-146c; XXVIII [13-36] 150b-c; [127-145] 151c-d

23 HOBBES: *Leviathan*, PART III, 185d

31 DESCARTES: *Objections and Replies*, 229c-d

32 MILTON: *Paradise Lost*, BK III [135-143] 138b; BK V [153-208] 178b-179b; BK VII [170-173] 220b-221a

35 BERKELEY: *Human Knowledge*, INTRO, SECT 3 405b-c; SECT 154 444a-b

37 FIELDING: *Tom Jones*, 186c-d

46 HEGEL: *Philosophy of History*, INTRO, 169d-170a

52 DOSTOEVSKY: *Brothers Karamazov*, BK V, 127b-137c; BK VI, 167b-168c; BK VII, 189a-191a,c

2b. The divine goodness and the problem of evil

OLD TESTAMENT: *Deuteronomy*, 30:15-20 esp 30:15 / *I Samuel*, 16:14-23—(D) *I Kings*, 16:14-23 / *Job* / *Psalms*, 5 esp 5:4-6; 9-10; 13; 22 esp 22:7-8; 37; 39 esp 39:8-12; 44; 73; 88—(D) *Psalms*, 5 esp 5:5-7; 9; 12; 21 esp 21:8-9; 36; 38 esp 38:9-13; 43; 72; 87 / *Proverbs*, 8:13 / *Ecclesiastes*, 8:1-9:12 esp 8:10-14, 9:1-3 / *Isaiah*, 45:7—(D) *Isaias*, 45:7 / *Jeremiah*, 12 esp 12:1-2—(D) *Jeremias*, 12 esp 12:1-2 / *Lamentations*, 3:38 / *Amos*, 3:6 / *Micah*, 1:12—(D) *Micheas*, 1:12

APOCRYPHA: *Wisdom of Solomon*, 1:13-16; 2:23-24; 11:24—(D) OT, *Book of Wisdom*, 1:13-16; 2:23-25; 11:25 / *Ecclesiasticus*, 11:14-16; 15:11-20; 33:10-15; 39:25-31—(D) OT, *Ecclesiasticus*, 11:14-16; 15:11-22; 33:10-15; 39:30-37

(2. *The goodness or perfection of God: the pleni-*
tude of the divine being. 2b. The divine
goodness and the problem of evil.)

New Testament: *Matthew,* 13:24–30,36–43 esp
13:38–39 / *John,* 3:16–21 / *Romans,* 3:1–10;
5 / *James,* 1:12–15 / *I John,* 1 esp 1:5–6

5 Aeschylus: *Eumenides* 81a-91d

7 Plato: *Republic,* bk ii, 321d-322d / *Timaeus,*
452c-453b

8 Aristotle: *Metaphysics,* bk ix, ch 9 [1051ª
17–22] 577a-b

12 Epictetus: *Discourses,* bk i, ch 12 118d-120b

14 Plutarch: *Pericles,* 140d

17 Plotinus: *First Ennead,* tr viii 27b-34a

18 Augustine: *Confessions,* bk iii, par 11 15d-
16a; bk iv, par 24 25b-c; bk v, par 20 32d-
33a; bk vii, par 3–7 44a-45d; par 11–23 47a-
50d; bk xiii, par 45 123a / *City of God,* bk
viii, ch 24, 283a-b; bk x, ch 21 311c-312a;
bk xi, ch 9 326d-327d; ch 13–15 329c-331a;
ch 22 333d-334c; bk xii, ch 1–9 342b,d-348b;
ch 21–22 357a-c; ch 27 359c-360a,c; bk xiii,
ch 13–15 366a-d; bk xiv, ch 10–15 385b-
390a; bk xix, ch 13 519a-520a; bk xxii,
ch 1 586b,d-587b / *Christian Doctrine,* bk ii,
ch 23 648a-c; bk iii, ch 37, 673d-674a

19 Aquinas: *Summa Theologica,* part i, q 2, a
3, rep 1 12c-14a; q 8, a 1, rep 4 34d-35c; a
3, ans 36b-37c; q 14, a 10 83d-84c; q 15, a 3,
rep 1 93b-94a; q 17, a 1 100d-101d; q 18, a 4,
rep 4 107d-108c; q 19, a 9 116d-117d; a 12,
ans and rep 4 118d-119d; q 20, a 2, rep 4
121b-122a; q 22, a 2, rep 2 128d-130d; a 3,
rep 3 130d-131c; q 23, a 5, rep 3 135d-137d;
a 7, rep 3 138d-140a; q 25, a 3, rep 2 145b-
147a; q 48, a 2, rep 3 260c-261b; q 49, aa 2–3
266a-268a,c; q 63, a 4 328b-329a; a 5, ans
329a-330c; a 7, rep 2 331c-332b; q 64, a 4
337d-338d; q 65, a 1, rep 2–3 339b-340b; q
66, a 3, ans 347b-348d; q 72, a 1, rep 6 368b-
369d; q 92, a 1, rep 3 488d-489d; q 103, a 3,
rep 2 530a-c; a 7, rep 1 533b-d; a 8 533d-
534b; q 114, a 1, ans 581d-582c; part i-ii, q
39, a 2, rep 3 790d-791b

20 Aquinas: *Summa Theologica,* part i-ii, q 79
156a-159c; part iii suppl, q 74, a 1, rep 1
925c-926c

21 Dante: *Divine Comedy,* hell, xxxiv [28–36]
51c; paradise, i [103–142] 107b-d; vii [19–
148] 115b-116c; viii [91–148] 117d-118c; xiii
[52–87] 126a-b; xix [40–90] 135c-136a; xxix
[49–66] 150d-151a

22 Chaucer: *Friar's Tale* [7056–7085] 281a-b

23 Hobbes: *Leviathan,* part ii, 160d-161a

30 Bacon: *Advancement of Learning,* 17d-18a;
80b-81a

31 Descartes: *Meditations,* iv 89a-93a

31 Spinoza: *Ethics,* part i, prop 33, schol 2
367d-369a; appendix 369b-372d

32 Milton: *Paradise Lost* 93a-333a esp bk i [128–
168] 96a-97a, [209–220] 98a, bk iii [56–343]

136b-143a, bk iv [32–113] 153a-155a, bk vi
[262–295] 202a-b, bk vii [519–549] 228b-229a,
bk viii [316–337] 239a-b, bk ix [679–779]
262a-264a, bk x [585–640] 287a-288b, bk xi
[84–98] 301a / *Samson Agonistes* [1156–1177]
364b-365a / *Areopagitica,* 394b-395b

33 Pascal: *Provincial Letters,* 116a-b / *Pensées,*
735–736 317b; 820 331b

35 Berkeley: *Human Knowledge,* sect 154
444a-b

35 Hume: *Human Understanding,* sect viii, div
78–81 485c-487a; sect xi, div 106–107, 499c-
500a passim

40 Gibbon: *Decline and Fall,* 81b-c

41 Gibbon: *Decline and Fall,* 230b; 330a-b

44 Boswell: *Johnson,* 401a-b; 482a-d; 539d-
540a; 549c

46 Hegel: *Philosophy of Right,* additions, 90
130b-d / *Philosophy of History,* intro, 160a;
part iii, 304d-306a

47 Goethe: *Faust,* prologue 7a-9b

48 Melville: *Moby Dick,* 381a

51 Tolstoy: *War and Peace,* bk vi, 272a-b

52 Dostoevsky: *Brothers Karamazov,* bk v,
120d-121c; 122c-123b; 132a-135d; bk xi,
337a-346a

54 Freud: *Civilization and Its Discontents,* 790d /
New Introductory Lectures, 877d-878b

3. The moral theory of the good: the distinction between the moral and the metaphysical good

7 Plato: *Protagoras,* 58b-62d / *Gorgias,* 262a-
263c; 280d-285a / *Theaetetus,* 530b-531a /
Philebus 609a-639a,c

9 Aristotle: *Ethics,* bk i 339a-348d esp ch 6
341b-342c / *Rhetoric,* bk i, ch 6 [1362ᵇ2–6]
603b; ch 9 [1366ª23–1367ᵇ27] 608c-610c

12 Epictetus: *Discourses* 105a-245a,c esp bk i,
ch 1 105a-106c, ch 6 110c-112b, ch 11 116d-
118d, ch 15 121c-d, ch 18 124a-125a, ch 22
127c-128c, ch 25 129d-131b, ch 27–29 132b-
138a, bk ii, ch 5 142a-144a, ch 10–11 148c-
151b, bk iii, ch 1 175a-177c, ch 3 178d-180a,
ch 10 185d-187a, ch 24 203c-210a, bk iv, ch
1 213a-223d, ch 6 230b-232c

12 Aurelius: *Meditations* 253a-310d esp bk ii,
sect 1 256b,d, sect 9 257d, sect 11–12
258a-c, bk iv, sect 10 264c, sect 24 265c-d,
sect 32 266b-c, sect 37 266d-267a, sect 39
267a, bk v, sect 2 269a, sect 6 269b-d, sect
10 270c-d, sect 12 271a, sect 15–16 271b-d,
bk vi, sect 2 274a, sect 51 279b-c, bk vii,
sect 36 282b, sect 44 282b-c, sect 55 283b-c,
bk viii, sect 1 285a-b, sect 10 286b, sect
19 286d-287a, sect 32 287d-288a, sect 39
288c, sect 41 288d, sect 51 289d-290a,
bk ix, sect 1 291a-c, sect 16 293a, sect 42
295c-296a,c

18 Augustine: *City of God,* bk xi, ch 16 331a-c

19 Aquinas: *Summa Theologica,* part i-ii, qq
1–5 609a-643d; qq 18–21 693b,d-720a,c

21 DANTE: *Divine Comedy*, PURGATORY, XVI [52–114] 77b-78a; XVII [82]–XVIII [75] 79b-80c

30 BACON: *Advancement of Learning*, 69d-76a; 80a-81a

35 LOCKE: *Human Understanding*, BK II, CH XXVIII, SECT 4–17 229b-232d

42 KANT: *Pure Reason*, 114d-115a; 149d-150a; 169b [fn 1]; 173b-174a / *Fund. Prin. Metaphysic of Morals* 253a-287d esp 256a-261d, 263d-264a, 282d-287d / *Practical Reason* 291a-361d esp 297a-307d, 314d-321b, 325c, 337a-353a / *Pref. Metaphysical Elements of Ethics* 365a-379d esp 366d-373d / *Intro. Metaphysic of Morals*, 387b / *Judgement*, 594d [fn 1]; 595a-d

43 MILL: *Utilitarianism* 445a-476a,c

46 HEGEL: *Philosophy of Right*, PART II, par 129–140 45d-54a

49 DARWIN: *Descent of Man*, 304a-319a esp 304a-305a, 310a-319a

54 FREUD: *War and Death*, 757b-760a esp 757d-758c, 759d-760a

3a. Human nature and the determination of the good for man: the real and the apparent good; particular goods and the good in general

NEW TESTAMENT: *Romans*, 7:15–25

5 SOPHOCLES: *Antigone* [587–631] 136b-c / *Philoctetes* [895–903] 190a

7 PLATO: *Charmides*, 2d-3b esp 3a / *Protagoras*, 57d-62d / *Euthydemus*, 69a-71a; 74b-76b / *Meno*, 177d-178b / *Gorgias*, 261a-270c; 282b-284b / *Republic*, BK I–IV 295a-356a; BK VIII, 410a-c; BK IX, 421a-425b; BK X, 439b-441a,c / *Timaeus*, 474b-476b / *Theaetetus*, 528c-531a / *Sophist*, 557b-d / *Philebus*, 619d-620b / *Seventh Letter*, 805d-806a

8 ARISTOTLE: *Physics*, BK VII, CH 3 [246ª10–248ª6] 329c-330d / *Metaphysics*, BK I, CH 1 [980ª22–28] 499a; BK XII, CH 7 [1072ª26–29] 602b

9 ARISTOTLE: *Motion of Animals*, CH 6 [700ᵇ15–29] 235d-236a / *Ethics*, BK I, CH 6 341b-342c; CH 7 [1097ᵇ22–1098ª19] 343a-c; BK I, CH 13–BK II, CH 6 347b-352d; BK III, CH 4 359a-c; CH 5 [1114ª22–1115ª3] 360b-361a; BK V, CH 1 [1129ᵇ1–10] 376d-377a; BK VI, CH 5 389a-c; BK X, CH 6–8 430d-434a / *Politics*, BK I, CH 2 [1253ª2–38] 446b-d; CH 5–6 447d-449b; BK III, CH 6 [1278ᵇ15–29] 475d-476a; BK VII, CH 13 [1332ª39–ᵇ10] 537a-b; CH 14 [1333ª17–37] 538a-b / *Rhetoric*, BK I, CH 6–7 602b-607d; CH 10 [1369ᵇ19–27] 613a

12 LUCRETIUS: *Nature of Things*, BK II [1–61] 15a-d; BK V [1113–1135] 75c-d; [1412–1435] 79b-d; BK VI [1–42] 80a-d

12 EPICTETUS: *Discourses*, BK I, CH 6 110c-112b; CH 11 116d-118d; CH 15 121c-d; CH 27 132b-133b; BK III, CH 1 175a-177c; CH 3 178d-180a; BK IV, CH 6 230b-232c

12 AURELIUS: *Meditations*, BK II, SECT 9 257d; SECT 11 258a-b; BK IV, SECT 24 265c-d; SECT 32 266b-c; SECT 39 267a; BK V, SECT 15–16

271b-d; BK VI, SECT 13 274d; BK VII, SECT 20 281b; SECT 55 283b-c; BK VIII, SECT 1 285a-b; BK IX, SECT 1 291a-c; SECT 42 295c-296a,c

14 PLUTARCH: *Pericles*, 121a-122b

15 TACITUS: *Histories*, BK IV, 267c

17 PLOTINUS: *Fourth Ennead*, TR IV, CH 43–44 181b-182b / *Sixth Ennead*, TR VII, CH 26 334c-d

18 AUGUSTINE: *Confessions*, BK X, par 29–34 78d-80c / *City of God*, BK XII, CH 3 343d-344b; BK XIX, CH 1–9 507a-516c / *Christian Doctrine*, BK I, CH 38 635c-d

19 AQUINAS: *Summa Theologica*, PART I, Q 12, A 1, ANS 50c-51c; Q 26, A 2, ANS 150c-151a; A 4, ANS and REP 1 151c-152a,c; Q 59, A 1, ANS 306c-307b; A 3, ANS 308b-309a; A 4, ANS 309a-310a; Q 60, A 5 313b-314c; Q 62, A 1, ANS 317d-318c; Q 80, A 2, REP 2 428a-d; Q 82, A 4, REP 1 434c-435c; A 5, ANS 435c-436c; Q 92, A 1, ANS 488c-489d; Q 105, A 4, ANS 541c-542a; PART I–II, QQ 1–5 609a-643d; Q 9, A 6, REP 3 662a-d; Q 18 693b,d-703a; Q 19, A 1, REP 1 703b-d; Q 22, A 3, REP 2 722d-723b; Q 34, A 4 771c-772b

20 AQUINAS: *Summa Theologica*, PART I–II, Q 54, A 3 24c-25b; QQ 55–56 26a-35a; Q 63, A 1 63a-64a; Q 71, A 2 106d-107c; Q 91, A 2 208d-209d; Q 94 220d-226b; PART II–II, Q 29, A 2, REP 3 531a-d; A 3, REP 1 531d-532c

21 DANTE: *Divine Comedy*, PURGATORY, XVI [85–114] 77d-78a; XVII [82]–XVIII [75] 79b-80c

23 HOBBES: *Leviathan*, PART I, 61a-62c; 65a; 96a-b

24 RABELAIS: *Gargantua and Pantagruel*, BK I, 65c-d

25 MONTAIGNE: *Essays*, 149b-d; 231d-233a; 489b-490c

27 SHAKESPEARE: *Hamlet*, ACT III, SC I [103–134] 48a-b / *Measure for Measure*, ACT II, SC IV [1–17] 184c-d / *Othello*, ACT II, SC III [342–368] 220c-d

30 BACON: *Advancement of Learning*, 70d-71b

31 SPINOZA: *Ethics*, PART IV, PREF, 423c-d; PROP 18–28 428d-431c; PROP 31 432a-b; PROP 35, COROL 1–2 433c-d; APPENDIX, V 447c

33 PASCAL: *Pensées*, 425–426 243b-244b; 430 245a-247b; 438 251a; 463–468 255a-256a

35 LOCKE: *Human Understanding*, 90a-d; BK I, CH II, SECT 5–6 105a-c; SECT 13, 108b-c; BK II, CH XXI, SECT 52–53 191d-192b; SECT 55–56 192c-193b; SECT 60–70 194a-197b passim; CH XXVIII, SECT 11 230c-231a

36 STERNE: *Tristram Shandy*, 257a-268a

37 FIELDING: *Tom Jones*, 38c-40a; 41a-43b; 53b-54d; 82c-83b; 88b-89c

38 ROUSSEAU: *Inequality*, 343a-346d; 351c-352a

42 KANT: *Pure Reason*, 169b [fn 1] / *Fund. Prin. Metaphysic of Morals*, 253d-254b; 263d-264a; 270c-d / *Intro. Metaphysic of Morals*, 387d-388a / *Judgement*, 584d-587a

43 MILL: *Liberty*, 295d-296d / *Representative Government*, 367a-369a / *Utilitarianism*, 448a-455a; 456d-457b; 458b-464d

(3. *The moral theory of the good: the distinction between the moral and the metaphysical good. 3a. Human nature and the determination of the good for man: the real and the apparent good; particular goods and the good in general.*)

44 BOSWELL: *Johnson*, 130b

46 HEGEL: *Philosophy of Right*, ADDITIONS, 78 128c-d / *Philosophy of History*, INTRO, 166b; 182d-184d; PART I, 236a-c; PART II, 280b-c

48 MELVILLE: *Moby Dick*, 36a-b

49 DARWIN: *Descent of Man*, 310a-317d passim, esp 311d-313a; 592d

50 MARX: *Capital*, 301d [fn 3]

51 TOLSTOY: *War and Peace*, EPILOGUE II, 689b

52 DOSTOEVSKY: *Brothers Karamazov*, BK V, 127b-137c; BK VI, 164b-d

53 JAMES: *Psychology*, 198b-209b esp 198b-200a, 202a-204b, 208b-209b

54 FREUD: *Origin and Development of Psycho-Analysis*, 20c-d / *General Introduction*, 624a-625b / *Civilization and Its Discontents*, 767a; 785c-802a,c esp 786d-787a, 788d-789b, 792b-c, 800c-801b

3b. Goodness in the order of freedom and will

NEW TESTAMENT: *Romans*, 7:15-25

9 ARISTOTLE: *Ethics*, BK III, CH 1-5 355b,d-361a; BK IV, CH 9 [1128^{b}20-30] 376a,c

12 EPICTETUS: *Discourses* 105a-245a,c esp BK I, CH 1 105a-106c, CH 11 116d-118d, CH 18 124a-125a, CH 22 127c-128c, CH 25 129d-131b, CH 29 134d-138a, BK II, CH 5 142c-144a, BK III, CH 2 177c-178d, CH 10 185d-187a, CH 18 192a-c, CH 26 210d-213a,c, BK IV, CH 1 213a-223d

12 AURELIUS: *Meditations* 253a-310d esp BK IV, SECT 37 266d-267a, SECT 39 267a, BK V, SECT 2 269a, SECT 10 270c-d, BK VI, SECT 2 274a, BK VII, SECT 44 282b-c, BK VIII, SECT 32 287d-288a, SECT 41 288d, SECT 51 289d-290a

18 AUGUSTINE: *Confessions*, BK VIII, par 19-24 58b-60a / *City of God*, BK XII, CH 1-9 342b,d-348b

19 AQUINAS: *Summa Theologica*, PART I, Q 48, A 6, ANS 264a-d; Q 49, A 1, REP 1 264d-265d; Q 82, AA 1-2 431d-433c; Q 83, A 1 436d-438a; Q 87, A 4, REP 2 468b-d; Q 105, A 4, ANS 541c-542a; PART I-II, Q 10, AA 2-4 663d-666a,c

20 AQUINAS: *Summa Theologica*, PART I-II, Q 79, AA 1-2 156b-158a; Q 80, AA 1-3 159d-162b

21 DANTE: *Divine Comedy*, PURGATORY, XVI [58-129] 77c-78a; XVIII [19-75] 80a-c; XXI [40-72] 85b-d; PARADISE, IV [64-114] 111b-d

23 HOBBES: *Leviathan*, PART I, 87c; 93c

24 RABELAIS: *Gargantua and Pantagruel*, BK I, 65c-66b

30 BACON: *Advancement of Learning*, 69d-81c

31 DESCARTES: *Discourse*, PART III, 50b / *Objections and Replies*, AXIOM VII 132a; 228a-c

32 MILTON: *Paradise Lost*, BK III [80-134] 137a-

138a; BK V [224-245] 180a-b; [506-543] 186a-187a; BK IX [342-375] 254b-255b / *Areopagitica*, 390b-391a; 394b-395b

38 ROUSSEAU: *Inequality*, 337d-338a

42 KANT: *Pure Reason*, 164a-171a; 236d-237a / *Fund. Prin. Metaphysic of Morals*, 253d-254d; 256a-261d; 265b; 271d-287d / *Practical Reason*, 298a-300a; 304a-d; 310b-311d; 315b-c; 318c-d; 331c-337a,c / *Pref. Metaphysical Elements of Ethics*, 378a-b / *Intro. Metaphysic of Morals*, 391a-c; 393d / *Science of Right*, 397b-398a; 400b,d-402a; 403b-404a / *Judgement*, 571c-572a; 605d-606b [fn 2]

44 BOSWELL: *Johnson*, 112a-b

46 HEGEL: *Philosophy of Right*, INTRO, par 8 14c; PART II, par 114 42a-b; PART III, par 142-157 55a-57d; ADDITIONS, 68 126d-127a; 82-86 129a-c; 92-100 131d-133a

49 DARWIN: *Descent of Man*, 311a-d

52 DOSTOEVSKY: *Brothers Karamazov*, BK V, 127b-137c

53 JAMES: *Psychology*, 794a-808a esp 797b-798a, 799a-b, 807a-808a; 816a-819a esp 817a-818a; 825a-827a esp 827a

54 FREUD: *Interpretation of Dreams*, 164d-168d; 386c-387a

3b(1) The prescriptions of duty

5 EURIPIDES: *Hippolytus* [373-430] 228b-d

12 EPICTETUS: *Discourses*, BK III, CH 10 185d-187a

12 AURELIUS: *Meditations*, BK VI, SECT 2 274a; BK VII, SECT 44 282b-c; BK VIII, SECT 32 287d-288a

14 PLUTARCH: *Pericles*, 121a-122b

18 AUGUSTINE: *City of God*, BK XIX, CH 14-16 520a-522a; CH 19 523b-d

30 BACON: *Advancement of Learning*, 71a-76a esp 74b-76a

31 DESCARTES: *Discourse*, PART III, 48b-49d; PART VI, 62d-63a

38 ROUSSEAU: *Political Economy*, 372b-373b / *Social Contract*, BK I, 393b-c

42 KANT: *Pure Reason*, 114d-115a; 149d-150a; 190c-d; 236d-237a / *Fund. Prin. Metaphysic of Morals*, 253d-254d; 256a-b; 260a-261d; 265c-266d; 268c-270c; 272a-b; 273d-287d esp 277d-279d, 281c-282d / *Practical Reason*, 297a-314d esp 307d-314d; 321b-329a esp 325c; 330d-331a; 338c-355d / *Pref. Metaphysical Elements of Ethics*, 366d-367a; 368b-369a; 373d / *Intro. Metaphysic of Morals*, 383a-390a,c esp 383a-384d, 388b-c, 389a-390a,c; 391a-c; 392b-393a / *Science of Right*, 397c-398a; 416b-417b / *Judgement*, 571c-572a; 593a-d; 595a-d; 599b-d; 605d-606b [fn 2]

43 MILL: *Liberty*, 296b-c / *Utilitarianism*, 446a-d; 453c-d; 458b-459b; 468b-469b; 469d-470b; 475a-476a,c

46 HEGEL: *Philosophy of Right*, PART I, par 36 21b-c; par 79 33a-c; PART II, par 129-135 45d-47d esp par 133 47a; PART III, par 148-149

56a-b; ADDITIONS, 84 129b; 86 129c / *Philosophy of History*, PART IV, 362c-d

49 DARWIN: *Descent of Man*, 304a; 310d; 313d-314a; 592b-c

3b(2) The good will: its conditions and consequences

7 PLATO: *Gorgias*, 262a-263c / *Timaeus*, 474b-d / *Laws*, BK V, 688d-689a

8 ARISTOTLE: *Topics*, BK IV, CH 5 [126ª30–37] 175c-d

9 ARISTOTLE: *Ethics*, BK III, CH 1–5 355b,d-361a; BK IV, CH 9 [1128ᵇ20–30] 376a,c

12 EPICTETUS: *Discourses*, BK I, CH 1 105a-106c; CH 11 116d-118d; CH 18 124a-125a; CH 22 127c-128c; CH 25 129d-131b; CH 29 134d-138a; BK II, CH 5 142c-144a; CH 13 152c-153d; CH 16 156b-158d; CH 23 170a-172d; BK III, CH 10 185d-187a; BK IV, CH 10 238d-240d

17 PLOTINUS: *Fourth Ennead*, TR IV, CH 35, 177d-178a

18 AUGUSTINE: *City of God*, BK XII, CH 3–9 343d-348b; BK XIV, CH 11 385d-387a

19 AQUINAS: *Summa Theologica*, PART I, Q 5, A 4, REP 3 25d-26c; Q 48, AA 5–6 263a-264d; Q 49, A 1, REP 1 264d-265d; PART I-II, Q 3, A 4, REP 5 625a-626b; Q 4, A 4 631d-632c; Q 9, A 6, REP 3 662a-d; QQ 18–21 693b,d-720a,c esp Q 19 703a-711d

21 DANTE: *Divine Comedy*, PARADISE, XV [1–12] 128b-c

23 HOBBES: *Leviathan*, PART I, 62d

25 MONTAIGNE: *Essays*, 13d-14c; 115b-119d; 124c-125a; 146b-d

30 BACON: *Advancement of Learning*, 72a

32 MILTON: *Paradise Lost*, BK IX [342–375] 254b-255b / *Samson Agonistes* [1334–1379] 368b-369b

38 ROUSSEAU: *Political Economy*, 372a-373b / *Social Contract*, BK II, 396b-d; 400a-c

42 KANT: *Pure Reason*, 169b [fn 1] / *Fund. Prin. Metaphysic of Morals*, 253d-254d; 256a-257d esp 256a-b, 257c-d; 260a-261d; 265c; 268c-270c; 272a-b; 279b,d-287d esp 281c-282d / *Practical Reason*, 297a-319b esp 307d-314d, 316a-317d; 321b-329a; 330c-331a / *Intro. Metaphysic of Morals*, 386b-387a,c; 388b-c; 392b-393a / *Judgement*, 595a-d; 605d-606b [fn 2]

43 MILL: *Utilitarianism*, 453c-d

44 BOSWELL: *Johnson*, 112a-b; 145c-d

46 HEGEL: *Philosophy of Right*, PART II, par 105 40a; par 114 42a-b; ADDITIONS, 90 130b-d

3c. The good and desire: goodness causing movements of desire and desire causing estimations of goodness

NEW TESTAMENT: *Romans*, 7:15-25

6 HERODOTUS: *History*, BK III, 105c-d

7 PLATO: *Lysis*, 21b-25a / *Phaedrus*, 120b-c; 128a-d / *Symposium*, 164c-165c / *Meno*, 177d-178b / *Philebus*, 614a / *Laws*, BK V, 689b

8 ARISTOTLE: *Metaphysics*, BK XII, CH 7 [1072ª 26–29] 602b / *Soul*, BK III, CH 10–11 665d-667a

9 ARISTOTLE: *Motion of Animals*, CH 6 235d-236b / *Ethics*, BK I, CH 1 [1094ª1–3] 339a; CH 2 [1094ª17–22] 339b; BK III, CH 4 359a-c; BK V, CH 1 [1129ᵇ1–10] 376d-377a; BK VI, CH 2 387d-388b; BK IX, CH 9 [1170ª13–25] 423d-424a; BK X, CH 2 426c-427b esp [1172ᵇ35–1173ª4] 427a; CH 6 [1176ᵇ30–ᵇ8] 430d-431a / *Rhetoric*, BK I, CH 6–7 602d-607d; CH 10 [1369ª3–4] 612b; [1369ᵇ7–12] 612d; [1369ᵇ19–27] 613a

12 EPICTETUS: *Discourses*, BK II, CH 22 167d-170a

14 PLUTARCH: *Pericles*, 121a-122b

17 PLOTINUS: *Third Ennead*, TR V, CH 3 102a-c; CH 10 105d-106b / *Sixth Ennead*, TR VII, CH 19 332a-b; TR VIII, CH 7, 345d; CH 13, 349b-c

19 AQUINAS: *Summa Theologica*, PART I, Q 5, A 1, ANS 23c-24a; A 2, REP 4 24b-25a; A 4, ANS 25d-26c; A 6, ANS 27c-28b; Q 6, A 1, REP 2 28b-d; Q 20, A 2, ANS 121b-122a; PART I-II, Q 5, A 8 642d-643d; Q 8 655a-657c; Q 11, A 3 667d-668d; Q 12, AA 2–4 670b-672a; Q 22, A 3, REP 2 722d-723b; Q 23 723c-727a; Q 27, A 1 737b-d; Q 41, A 3 799c-800b

20 AQUINAS: *Summa Theologica*, PART I-II, Q 58, A 4 esp REP 3 44a-d

21 DANTE: *Divine Comedy*, PURGATORY, XV [40–81] 75d-76a; XVI [85–114] 77d-78a; XVII [82]–XVIII [75] 79b-80c esp XVIII [19–39] 80a-b; PARADISE, I [103–142] 107b-d; IV [115]–V [12] 111d-112b; VII [139–144] 116c; XXVI [1–69] 145d-146c

23 HOBBES: *Leviathan*, PART I, 61d-62a; 96a-b; PART IV, 272c

25 MONTAIGNE: *Essays*, 149b-d; 297d-300c

30 BACON: *Advancement of Learning*, 67a-b

31 DESCARTES: *Discourse*, PART III, 50b / *Objections and Replies*, AXIOM VII 132a

31 SPINOZA: *Ethics*, PART I, APPENDIX 369b-372d; PART III, PROP 6–9 398d-399c esp PROP 9, SCHOL 399c; PROP 12–13 400b-d; PROP 39, SCHOL 408b-d; PROP 54 413a-b; PART IV, PREF–DEF 2 422b,d-424a; PROP 8–13 426b-428a; PROP 19 429d; PROP 27–28 431b-c; PROP 63 443d-444a

35 LOCKE: *Human Understanding*, BK II, CH XX, SECT 6 177a-b; CH XXI, SECT 29–54 184d-192c passim; SECT 61–62 194b-d; SECT 70 197a-b

38 ROUSSEAU: *Inequality*, 338c-339a

42 KANT: *Fund. Prin. Metaphysic of Morals*, 259a-c; 264d-265b / *Practical Reason*, 293c-d [fn 3]; 298a-300a; 301a; 304a-d; 330c-331a; 341c-342a / *Intro. Metaphysic of Morals*, 385a-c / *Judgement*, 605d-606b [fn 2]

43 MILL: *Utilitarianism*, 461c-464d

46 HEGEL: *Philosophy of Right*, PART II, par 123 44a-b; ADDITIONS, 78 128c-d / *Philosophy of History*, INTRO, 166b

53 JAMES: *Psychology*, 810b-811a

54 FREUD: *Civilization and Its Discontents*, 792b-c; 801d

(3. *The moral theory of the good: the distinction between the moral and the metaphysical good.***)**

3d. Pleasure as *the* good, *a* good, or *feeling* good

7 PLATO: *Protagoras*, 59a-62d / *Gorgias*, 275b-280d / *Republic*, BK VI, 384b-d; BK IX, 421a-425b / *Philebus* 609a-639a,c / *Laws*, BK II, 656d-658b; 660a-d; BK V, 689c-690c

8 ARISTOTLE: *Prior Analytics*, BK I, CH 40 68b / *Topics*, BK III, CH 2 [117ᵃ23-25] 163d; CH 3 [118ᵇ27-36] 165d-166a; CH 6 [119ᵃ37-ᵇ1] 166d; BK IV, CH 4 [124ᵃ15-20] 172d; [124ᵇ7-14] 173b; BK VI, CH 8 [146ᵇ13-19] 200c; BK VIII, CH 9 [160ᵇ16-23] 218a-b / *Physics*, BK VII, CH 3 [246ᵇ20-247ᵃ19] 330a-b / *Metaphysics*, BK XII, CH 7 [1072ᵇ13-29] 602d-603a / *Soul*, BK III, CH 7 [431ᵃ8-ᵇ9] 663c-664a

9 ARISTOTLE: *Motion of Animals*, CH 6 [700ᵇ23-29] 236a / *Ethics*, BK I, CH 5 [1095ᵇ14-22] 340d; CH 8 [1099ᵃ7-30] 344c-d; BK II, CH 3 350a-c; BK III, CH 4 359a-c; BK VII, CH 4 398a-399a esp [1148ᵃ22-ᵇ4] 398c-d; CH 11-14 403c-406a,c; BK X, CH 1-5 426a-430d / *Politics*, BK VIII, CH 5 [1339ᵇ11-38] 545a-c / *Rhetoric*, BK I, CH 6 [1362ᵇ5-9] 603b; CH 7 [1364ᵇ23-27] 606c; [1365ᵇ11-13] 607d

12 LUCRETIUS: *Nature of Things*, BK II [14-21] 15a-b; BK V [1412-1436] 79b-d

12 EPICTETUS: *Discourses*, BK II, CH 11 150a-151b; BK III, CH 24 203c-210a

12 AURELIUS: *Meditations*, BK II, SECT 11-12 258a-c; BK VI, SECT 51 279b-c; BK VII, SECT 27 281d; SECT 64 284a-b; BK VIII, SECT 10 286b; SECT 19 286d-287a; SECT 39 288c; SECT 47 289b-c; BK IX, SECT 1 291a-c; BK X, SECT 34-35 301a-b

17 PLOTINUS: *First Ennead*, TR IV, CH 12 17d / *Second Ennead*, TR IX, CH 15, 74d-75a / *Sixth Ennead*, TR VII, CH 26 334c-d; CH 29-30 335d-336d

18 AUGUSTINE: *City of God*, BK V, CH 20 225b-226a; BK X, CH 18 310b-d; BK XIX, CH 1-3 507a-511a

19 AQUINAS: *Summa Theologica*, PART I, Q 5, A 6, ANS and REP 2 27c-28b; PART I-II, Q 1, A 6, REP 1 614a-c; A 7, ANS 614c-615a; Q 2, A 6 619d-620d; Q 3, A 4 625a-626b; Q 4, AA 1-2 629d-631a; Q 11 666b,d-669b; Q 27, A 3, ANS 738c-739c; Q 30, A 4, REP 3 751c-752b; QQ 31-34 752b-772b; Q 39 790a-792d

20 AQUINAS: *Summa Theologica*, PART II-II, QQ 28-29 527b-533a

21 DANTE: *Divine Comedy*, PURGATORY, XVII [127-139] 79d; XVIII [19-39] 80a-b

23 HOBBES: *Leviathan*, PART I, 61d-62c

24 RABELAIS: *Gargantua and Pantagruel*, BK I, 65c-66b

25 MONTAIGNE: *Essays*, 28a-d; 70d-72a; 235d-237d

30 BACON: *Advancement of Learning*, 71a-74a

31 SPINOZA: *Ethics*, PART III, PROP 39, SCHOL 408b-d; PART IV, PROP 8 426b-c; PROP 41-43 437a-c

32 MILTON: *Paradise Lost*, BK IV [877-945] 171b-173a

35 LOCKE: *Human Understanding*, BK II, CH XX, SECT 1-2 176b-c; CH XXI, SECT 43 188d; SECT 55-56 192c-193b; SECT 63 194d-195a; CH XXVIII, SECT 5 229c-d

42 KANT: *Pure Reason*, 173b-174a / *Fund. Prin. Metaphysic of Morals*, 259a-b; 265b / *Practical Reason*, 298a-300a; 304a-307d; 314d-319b esp 315c; 330c-331a; 338c-355d esp 341c-342a / *Intro. Metaphysic of Morals*, 387b-388a / *Judgement*, 478a-479d; 584d-587a; 588b [fn 2]; 591b-592a; 594c-596c

43 MILL: *Utilitarianism* 445a-476a,c passim, esp 447b-457b, 461c-464d

44 BOSWELL: *Johnson*, 216c; 378a-b

49 DARWIN: *Descent of Man*, 316b-c

52 DOSTOEVSKY: *Brothers Karamazov*, BK IV, 88d; BK XI, 343d-344a

53 JAMES: *Psychology*, 94a-b; 808b-814b esp 810a, 812b-814b

54 FREUD: *Instincts*, 418d-420b / *Civilization and Its Discontents*, 772a-c; 792b-c

3e. Right and wrong: the social incidence of the good; doing or suffering good and evil

OLD TESTAMENT: *Genesis*, 18:17-33 / *Exodus*, 20:12-17; 22:21-28; 23:1-9 / *Leviticus*, 19:9-18,33-36 / *Numbers*, 15:15 / *Deuteronomy*, 5:16-21; 10:17-19 / *I Samuel*, 24:26—(D) *I Kings*, 24:26 / *Proverbs*, 3:27-35; 12:21; 15:1; 17:13 / *Isaiah*, 3:13-15; 10:1-3—(D) *Isaias*, 3:13-15; 10:1-3 / *Ezekiel*, 18:5-22—(D) *Ezechiel*, 18:5-22 / *Hosea*, 4:1-3; 7:1-7—(D) *Osee*, 4:1-3; 7:1-7 / *Amos*, 2:6-8; 4:1-2; 8:4-7 / *Micah*, 6:8—(D) *Micheas*, 6:8 / *Zechariah*, 7:9-10—(D) *Zacharias*, 7:9-10

APOCRYPHA: *Tobit*, 1:1-2:9; 4:1-20—(D) OT, *Tobias*, 1:1-2:9; 4:1-20 / *Ecclesiasticus*, 7-8; 12-14 esp 12:3, 14:5-7; 28; 34:21-22—(D) OT, *Ecclesiasticus*, 7-8; 12-14 esp 12:3, 14:5-7; 28; 34:25-27 / *Susanna*—(D) OT, *Daniel*, 13

NEW TESTAMENT: *Matthew*, 5-7 passim, esp 7:12 / *Luke*, 6:27-38 / *Romans*, 12:17-21 / *I Corinthians*, 6:1-11 / *I Peter*, 2:13-21; 3:8-18

5 AESCHYLUS: *Prometheus Bound* 40a-51d esp [941-1093] 50b-51d / *Agamemnon* 52a-69d esp [1331-1673] 66b-69d / *Choephoroe* 70a-80d esp [235-651] 72c-76b / *Eumenides* 81a-91d

5 SOPHOCLES: *Oedipus the King* 99a-113a,c / *Oedipus at Colonus* [255-291] 116c-d; [1152-1207] 124d-125b / *Antigone* 131a-142d / *Ajax* 143a-155a-c esp [1045-1421] 152a-155a,c / *Electra* 156a-169a,c / *Philoctetes* 182a-195a,c

5 EURIPIDES: *Alcestis* 237a-247a,c / *Suppliants* [195-250] 260a-c / *Electra* 327a-339a,c esp [880-1359] 335a-339a,c / *Phoenician Maidens* 378a-393d esp [260-645] 380b-383d, [1628-

1684] 392b-d / *Orestes* [491–715] 399a-401a / *Iphigenia at Aulis* 425a-439d

6 HERODOTUS: *History*, BK III, 93c-d; BK VI, 201d-202c; BK VII, 217d

6 THUCYDIDES: *Peloponnesian War*, BK V, 505b-c

7 PLATO: *Apology*, 203c-204c; 206d / *Crito*, 213d-214a; 215d-216c / *Gorgias*, 262a-267c / *Republic* 295a-441a,c esp BK I–II, 300b-315a, BK X, 436c-437c / *Laws*, BK II, 656d-658b; BK V, 687c-689a; BK IX, 747b-d / *Seventh Letter*, 805d-806a

9 ARISTOTLE: *Ethics*, BK V 376a-387a,c / *Poetics*, CH 25 [1461ᵃ4–9] 697b-c

12 EPICTETUS: *Discourses*, BK I, CH 28 133b-134d; BK II, CH 10 148c-150a; BK III, CH 3 178d-180a; CH 18 192a-c; CH 24 203c-210a; BK IV, CH 1 213a-223d; CH 5 228a-230b

12 AURELIUS: *Meditations*, BK II, SECT 1 256b,d; SECT 16 259a; BK IV, SECT 10 264c; BK V, SECT 6 269b-d; BK VII, SECT 36 282b; BK VIII, SECT 55 290b; BK IX, SECT 4 292a; SECT 16 293a; SECT 38 295a

18 AUGUSTINE: *Confessions*, BK I, par 19 5d / *Christian Doctrine*, BK I, CH 36 634d-635b

19 AQUINAS: *Summa Theologica*, PART I, Q 21, A 1 124b-125b; PART I–II, Q 21, AA 3–4 718d-720a,c

20 AQUINAS: *Summa Theologica*, PART I–II, Q 59, AA 4–5 48c-49d; Q 60, A 2 50d-51b; Q 97, A 1, REP 3 236a-d

21 DANTE: *Divine Comedy*, HELL, XI 15a-16b; PURGATORY, XVI [58–129] 77c-78a; XVII [91–139] 79b-d

22 CHAUCER: *Tale of Melibeus*, par 30–31, 413b-414a

23 HOBBES: *Leviathan*, PART I, 78b-c; 86b; PART II, 149b-c; PART IV, 272c

26 SHAKESPEARE: *1st Henry VI*, ACT II, SC V 12d-14a / *2nd Henry VI*, ACT III, SC I [223–281] 49c-50a / *Richard II*, ACT II, SC III [140–147] 334b

27 SHAKESPEARE: *Troilus and Cressida*, ACT II, SC II [163–188] 115b-c; ACT V, SC III [16–24] 137b / *King Lear*, ACT IV, SC II [2–68] 270b-271b / *Henry VIII*, ACT III, SC II [428–450] 573c-d

29 CERVANTES: *Don Quixote*, PART I, 68b-73a

30 BACON: *Advancement of Learning*, 74b-c; 81d-82a; 93c-94a

32 MILTON: *Comus* 33a-56b

35 LOCKE: *Human Understanding*, BK I, CH II, SECT 5–6 105a-c; BK II, CH XXVIII, SECT 9–13 230b-231c

38 MONTESQUIEU: *Spirit of Laws*, BK III, 11c-d

38 ROUSSEAU: *Inequality*, 351b-c

42 KANT: *Pure Reason*, 149d-150a / *Practical Reason*, 306b-c / *Intro. Metaphysic of Morals*, 391d-392a / *Science of Right*, 397a-399c; 400b,d-401b

43 FEDERALIST: NUMBER 41, 132b-c

43 MILL: *Liberty*, 302d-323a,c passim / *Utilitarianism*, 448a; 452b-455a; 455c-456a; 465c-471b passim

44 BOSWELL: *Johnson*, 315b-c

46 HEGEL: *Philosophy of Right*, PART I, par 81 34c-d; par 89 35c-d; par 92 35d-36a; PART II, par 112 41c-d; par 129–132 45d-47a; par 138 48c-d; par 140 49b-54a; PART III, par 218 72c-d; par 223 73c-d; par 233 75d; ADDITIONS, 59 125c-d; 71 127b-c; 89 129d-130a; 92–100 131d-133a; 138 139a-b / *Philosophy of History*, INTRO, 165c-166b

48 MELVILLE: *Moby Dick*, 292a-297a; 375a-376b

49 DARWIN: *Descent of Man*, 310a-316a; 317c-d; 319d; 322c; 592d-593a

51 TOLSTOY: *War and Peace*, BK V, 194a-195a; 214c-216d; BK VIII, 304b-305a; BK XIV, 611a-c

52 DOSTOEVSKY: *Brothers Karamazov*, BK II, 33c-34b; BK III, 73a-b; BK V, 123b-127b; BK VI, 153d-157b; 165c; 168c-169c; BK XII, 398a-d

54 FREUD: *Civilization and Its Discontents*, 792a-793a

3f. The sources of evil in human life

OLD TESTAMENT: *Genesis*, 3 / *Exodus*, 23:8 / *Deuteronomy*, 16:19; 30:15-20 esp 30:15 / *Job* / *Ecclesiastes*, 9:3 / *Isaiah*, 45:7—(D) *Isaias*, 45:7 / *Lamentations*, 3:38 / *Amos*, 3:6

APOCRYPHA: *Wisdom of Solomon*, 1:12–16; 2 esp 2:23–24; 14:27—(D) OT, *Book of Wisdom*, 1:12–16; 2 esp 2:23–25; 14:27 / *Ecclesiasticus*, 8:2; 10:9; 11:16; 14:1–10; 15:10–20; 20:29; 27:1-2; 31:5-11—(D) OT, *Ecclesiasticus*, 8:2–3; 10:9-10; 11:16; 14:1-10; 15:10-21; 20:31; 27:1-2; 31:5-11

NEW TESTAMENT: *Matthew*, 6:13,19-24; 13:24-30,36-43,47-51; 15:10-20; 16:26; 19:16-30 / *Mark*, 1:13; 4:1-20; 7:14-23; 8:36; 10:21-30 / *Luke*, 4:1-13; 8:1-15; 9:25; 12:13-21; 16:1-13; 18:22-30 / *Romans*, 5:12-19; 7:15-25 / *I Corinthians*, 6:10 / *Ephesians*, 5:5 / *II Thessalonians*, 2:1-12—(D) *II Thessalonians*, 2:1-11 / *I Timothy*, 6:9-10 / *James*, 1:12-15 / *I Peter*, 5:8-9 / *I John*, 2:7-23 esp 2:15-17 / *Revelation*, 12—(D) *Apocalypse*, 12

5 SOPHOCLES: *Antigone* [284–308] 133c-d

5 ARISTOPHANES: *Plutus* [77–185] 630a-631a

7 PLATO: *Euthydemus*, 69a-71a / *Republic*, BK II, 318c-319a; BK IV, 354d-355c; BK VI, 377a-379c; BK VII, 389d-390b; BK X, 431b-434a / *Timaeus*, 466a-b / *Theaetetus*, 530b-531a / *Laws*, BK III, 669a-670c; BK VIII, 733a-734a; BK IX, 751b-d

12 LUCRETIUS: *Nature of Things*, BK III [31-93] 30b-31b; BK V [1412-1435] 79b-d; BK VI [1-42] 80a-d

12 EPICTETUS: *Discourses*, BK I, CH 25 129d-131b; BK II, CH 22 167d-170a; CH 26 174c-d

12 AURELIUS: *Meditations*, BK II, SECT 1 256b,d; BK VII, SECT 22 281b; BK IX, SECT 42 295c-296a,c; BK XII, SECT 12 308b-c

15 TACITUS: *Annals*, BK III, 51b

17 PLOTINUS: *First Ennead*, TR VIII, CH 5, 29a-c / *Second Ennead*, TR IX, CH 13 73d-74b / *Third*

(3. *The moral theory of the good: the distinction between the moral and the metaphysical good. 3f. The sources of evil in human life.*)

Ennead, TR II, CH 4–10 84c-88b; CH 14–18 89b-93a / *Fourth Ennead*, TR III, CH 16 150c-d; TR IV, CH 18, 167b

18 AUGUSTINE: *Confessions*, BK II, par 9–18 10d-13a; BK VII, par 4 44b-c; BK VIII, par 22–24 59a-60a / *City of God*, BK VIII, CH 24, 283a-b; BK X, CH 21 311c-312a; BK XII, CH 21–22 357a-c; BK XIII, CH 13–15 366a-d; BK XIV, CH 10–15 385b-390a; BK XIX, CH 13 519a-520a

19 AQUINAS: *Summa Theologica*, PART I, Q 17, A 1, ANS 100d-101d; Q 48, A 6, ANS 264a-d; Q 49, A 1, REP 3 264d-265d; Q 63, A 9, REP 1 333b-d; Q 114, A 3 583b-d; PART I–II, Q 20, A 1 712a-d; Q 21, A 2 718a-d

20 AQUINAS: *Summa Theologica*, PART I–II, QQ 75–84 137c-178a

21 DANTE: *Divine Comedy*, HELL, VIII [65]–IX [103] 11c-13b; XXIII [139–144] 34c; XXVII [55–136] 40a-41b; XXXIV [28–36] 51c; PURGATORY, V [85–129] 59d-60c; VIII [1–108] 64a-65b; XVI [58–129] 77c-78a; XVII [82]–XVIII [75] 79b-80c; XXVIII [91–96] 97a; PARADISE, VII 115a-116c; VIII [91–148] 117d-118c; IX [127–142] 120a; XIII [52–87] 126a-b; XVIII [115–136] 134d-135a; XXIX [49–66] 150d-151a

22 CHAUCER: *Knight's Tale* [2453–2469] 200a-b / *Prologue of Pardoner's Tale* [12,263–268] 372a / *Pardoner's Tale* [12,778–828] 380b-381b / *Tale of Melibeus*, par 18, 408a; par 76–77, 430b-431a / *Parson's Tale*, par 20 508b-509a; par 57–59 528b-529a; par 62–64 530a-531a

23 HOBBES: *Leviathan*, PART II, 153b

25 MONTAIGNE: *Essays*, 218c-219a; 231d-238d; 326b-327b; 381b-c

26 SHAKESPEARE: *Romeo and Juliet*, ACT II, SC III [15–30] 296c

27 SHAKESPEARE: *Timon of Athens*, ACT IV, SC III [1–44] 410c-411a

30 BACON: *Advancement of Learning*, 17d-18a; 80b-81a

31 SPINOZA: *Ethics*, PART I, APPENDIX 369b-372d; PART IV, APPENDIX, VI 447c-d

32 MILTON: *Comus* 33a-56b esp [331–489] 40b-44a / *Paradise Lost*, BK I [157–168] 97a; [209–220] 98a; BK II [496–505] 122a; [629–870] 125a-130a; [890–1009] 130b-133a; BK III [56–134] 136b-138a; BK IV [505–535] 163b-164a; BK VII [519–549] 228b-229a; BK VIII [316–337] 239a-b; BK IX [679–784] 262a-264b; BK XI [84–98] 301a; BK XI [334]–BK XII [649] 306b-333a / *Samson Agonistes* [38–59] 340b; [521–540] 351a-b / *Areopagitica*, 394b-395b; 409b-410a

33 PASCAL: *Provincial Letters*, 116a-b; 140a; 162a / *Pensées*, 850 340a

35 LOCKE: *Human Understanding*, BK II, CH XXI, SECT 58–70 193d-197b

35 HUME: *Human Understanding*, SECT VIII, DIV 76–81 485a-487a

38 ROUSSEAU: *Inequality*, 338b-c; 347d-348a; 350c; 351c-352a; 360c-361c; 363a-366d

40 GIBBON: *Decline and Fall*, 81b-c

43 MILL: *Utilitarianism*, 451b-452b

46 HEGEL: *Philosophy of Right*, INTRO, par 18 16c-d; PART II, par 139–140 48d-54a; ADDITIONS, 14 118c-d; 90 130b-d / *Philosophy of History*, PART I, 237d-238c; PART IV, 346a-c; 354a-c

48 MELVILLE: *Moby Dick*, 3b-4a; 204a-205a; 209b

51 TOLSTOY: *War and Peace*, BK V, 214c-215a esp 215a

52 DOSTOEVSKY: *Brothers Karamazov*, BK III, 53b-54b; BK V, 122c-123b; 130b-135d; BK VI, 164b-166a; BK XI, 307c-310c; 344a-d

54 FREUD: *General Introduction*, 531d-532a / *Civilization and Its Discontents* 767a-802a,c esp 787a-788b

4. Divisions of the human good

4a. Sensible and intelligible goods

7 PLATO: *Euthydemus*, 69a-71a / *Phaedrus*, 120a-122a / *Symposium*, 162d-167d / *Phaedo*, 224a-c; 230c; 242c-243a / *Republic*, BK VI, 386b-d; BK VII, 397c-398b; BK IX, 423b-424d / *Laws*, BK V, 689c-690c; BK VIII, 735c-736c

17 PLOTINUS: *First Ennead*, TR VI, CH 6–9 24a-26a passim; TR VIII, CH 2 27c-d / *Second Ennead*, TR IX, CH 15–18 74d-77d / *Third Ennead*, TR V, CH 7 104a-105a / *Fifth Ennead*, TR V, CH 12–13 234a-235b

18 AUGUSTINE: *Confessions*, BK IV, par 20 24b-c; par 24 25b-c; BK VI, par 26 42d-43a; BK VII, par 23 50b-c; BK X, par 43–66 82a-88b

19 AQUINAS: *Summa Theologica*, PART I, Q 63, A 4, ANS 328b-329a; Q 80, A 2, REP 2 428a-d; Q 82, A 5, ANS 435c-436c; PART I–II, Q 2, A 6, ANS 619d-620d; Q 3, A 4, ANS 625a-626b; Q 4, A 2, REP 2 630b-631a; Q 11, A 2, ANS 667b-d; Q 13, A 2, ANS 673c-674c; Q 30, A 1, ANS 749a-d; Q 31, A 5 755c-756c; A 6, ANS 756d-757c

46 HEGEL: *Philosophy of History*, PART IV, 362b-c

4b. Useful and enjoyable goods: good for an end and good in itself

5 AESCHYLUS: *Persians* [153–171] 16d-17a

7 PLATO: *Lysis*, 22c-24a / *Protagoras*, 60d-62d / *Euthydemus*, 69a-71a; 74b-76b / *Meno*, 183d-184b / *Gorgias*, 262a-264b; 266d-267a / *Republic*, BK I, 298a-299a; BK II, 310c-d

8 ARISTOTLE: *Topics*, BK I, CH 15 [106^{a}1–9] 149d; BK III, CH 1 [116^{a}28–^{b}7] 162d-163a; [116^{b}37–117^{a}4] 163c; CH 2 [118^{a}6–16] 164d-165a; CH 3 [118^{b}27–36] 165d-166a; BK IV, CH 4 [124^{a}15–20] 172d; BK VI, CH 9 [147^{a}33–^{b}1] 201b-c; CH 12 [149^{b}31–39] 204b-c; BK VII, CH 3 [153^{b}36–154^{a}2] 209b / *Metaphysics*, BK V, CH 2 [1013^{a}32–^{b}3] 533c; [1013^{b}25–28] 533d-534a

9 ARISTOTLE: *Ethics*, BK I, CH 1–2 339a-d; CH 5 [1096ᵃ5–10] 341a-b; CH 6 [1096ᵇ8–26] 341d-342a; CH 7 [1097ᵃ15–ᵇ22] 342c-343a; CH 9 [1099ᵇ25–32] 345b; BK VIII, CH 2 [1155ᵇ16–22] 407a-b; BK X, CH 6 [1176ᵃ30–ᵇ8] 430d-431a / *Politics*, BK VII, CH 1 [1323ᵃ23–ᵇ13] 527a-c; CH 13 [1332ᵃ10–25] 536d; CH 15 [1334ᵃ12–ᵇ7] 539a-b; BK VIII, CH 2–3 542b-543d passim / *Rhetoric*, BK I, CH 1 [1355ᵃ39–ᵇ8] 594d; CH 5 [1361ᵃ12–24] 601c-d; CH 6–7 602d-607d

12 EPICTETUS: *Discourses*, BK III, CH 14, 189c-d; CH 24 203c-210a

17 PLOTINUS: *First Ennead*, TR II, CH 3–4 7c-8c

18 AUGUSTINE: *Confessions*, BK II, par 9–18 10d-13a / *City of God*, BK VIII, CH 4 266d-267c; CH 8–9 270a-271a; BK XIX, CH 1–5 507a-514b; CH 17–20 522b-524a / *Christian Doctrine*, BK I, CH 35 634c-d

19 AQUINAS: *Summa Theologica*, PART I, Q 5, A 6 27c-28b; Q 62, A 9, REP 2 324a-325b; PART I–II, Q 2, A 1 615c-616c; Q 3, A 1, ANS 622c-623a; Q 7, A 2, REP 1 652d-653c; Q 8, AA 2–3 656a-657c

23 HOBBES: *Leviathan*, PART I, 62a

30 BACON: *Advancement of Learning*, 27c-d; 71a-b

31 SPINOZA: *Ethics*, PART IV, APPENDIX, V 447c

35 LOCKE: *Human Understanding*, BK II, CH XXI, SECT 63 194d-195a

36 STERNE: *Tristram Shandy*, 538a-539a

42 KANT: *Pure Reason*, 236d-237a / *Fund. Prin. Metaphysic of Morals*, 256a-b; 257c-d; 266a-267d; 268b; 271c-279d esp 273d-277b / *Practical Reason*, 314d-315c; 327d-329a / *Pref. Metaphysical Elements of Ethics*, 367c / *Intro. Metaphysic of Morals*, 387b-388a / *Judgement*, 477b-c; 478a-479d; 586a-b; 591b-592d; 595a-d

43 MILL: *Utilitarianism*, 446d-448a; 461c-464d

46 HEGEL: *Philosophy of Right*, PART III, par 183 64a / *Philosophy of History*, PART II, 267a-268b

53 JAMES: *Psychology*, 725b-726a

54 FREUD: *Civilization and Its Discontents*, 779d-780b

4c. Goods of the body and goods of the soul

7 PLATO: *Protagoras*, 40b-41a / *Symposium*, 162d-167d / *Meno*, 178c-d / *Apology*, 205d-206d; 209b-212a,c / *Crito*, 215a-d / *Phaedo*, 224a-c / *Gorgias*, 260a-270c / *Republic*, BK I, 295d-296c; 309b-310b; BK III, 334b-339a; BK IX, 421a-425b / *Timaeus*, 474b-476b / *Sophist*, 556d-558d / *Laws*, BK I, 643c-d; BK II, 656d-658b

8 ARISTOTLE: *Physics*, BK VII, CH 3 [246ᵃ10–248ᵃ6] 329c-330d

9 ARISTOTLE: *Ethics*, BK I, CH 7 [1097ᵇ23–1098ᵃ17] 343a-c / *Politics*, BK VII, CH 1 [1323ᵃ22–ᵇ21] 527a-c / *Rhetoric*, BK I, CH 5 [1360ᵇ19–1361ᵃ12] 601a-c; [1361ᵇ3–27] 602a-b

12 LUCRETIUS: *Nature of Things*, BK II [1–61] 15a-d

12 EPICTETUS: *Discourses*, BK I, CH 20 126c-127b; BK IV, CH 1 213a-223d

17 PLOTINUS: *First Ennead*, TR IV 12b-19b esp CH 2–7 12d-16a, CH 14–16 18a-19b; TR VII, CH 3 26d-27a

18 AUGUSTINE: *Confessions*, BK X, par 43–66 82a-88b / *City of God*, BK I, CH 11–19 136d-142a; BK VIII, CH 8 270a-d; BK XV, CH 22 416a-c; BK XIX, CH 1–3 507a-511a

19 AQUINAS: *Summa Theologica*, PART I–II, Q 2, AA 5–7 618d-621c; Q 3, A 3 624b-625a; Q 31, A 5 755c-756c

21 DANTE: *Divine Comedy*, PURGATORY, XVI [85–114] 77d-78a; XXX [55]–XXXI [90] 100a-101d

23 HOBBES: *Leviathan*, PART I, 62c

24 RABELAIS: *Gargantua and Pantagruel*, BK IV, 234a-235a

25 MONTAIGNE: *Essays*, 538a-d

31 DESCARTES: *Discourses*, PART I, 41d-42a

37 FIELDING: *Tom Jones*, 263c-d

38 ROUSSEAU: *Inequality*, 338c-d

43 MILL: *Utilitarianism*, 448a-450a; 471a-b

44 BOSWELL: *Johnson*, 378a-b

52 DOSTOEVSKY: *Brothers Karamazov*, BK V, 130b-132b; BK VI, 164b-165a

53 JAMES: *Psychology*, 198b-199b

4d. Intrinsic and external goods: intrinsic worth and extrinsic value

7 PLATO: *Apology*, 206a-d

9 ARISTOTLE: *Ethics*, BK I, CH 8 [1098ᵇ12–19] 344a; BK VII, CH 13 [1153ᵇ13–24] 405a; BK IX, CH 1 [1163ᵇ31–1164ᵃ13] 416b,d; CH 9 423a-424b; BK X, CH 8 432d-434a esp [1178ᵇ33–1179ᵃ16] 433c-d / *Politics*, BK IV, CH 11 [1295ᵇ2–34] 495c-496a; BK VII, CH 1 527a-d; CH 13 [1332ᵃ18–27] 536d-537a / *Rhetoric*, BK I, CH 5 600d-602d

12 LUCRETIUS: *Nature of Things*, BK II [1–61] 15a-d; BK V [1113–1135] 75c-d

12 EPICTETUS: *Discourses*, BK II, CH 16 156b-158d; BK III, CH 20 192d-193d; CH 24 203c-210a; BK IV, CH 4 225a-228a; CH 10 238d-240d

12 AURELIUS: *Meditations*, BK VI, SECT 51 279b-c; BK VII, SECT 3 279d-280a

14 PLUTARCH: *Solon*, 74c-75c / *Pericles*, 121a-122b

18 AUGUSTINE: *Confessions*, BK II, par 10 11a-b / *City of God*, BK I, CH 10 135b-136c; BK VIII, CH 8 270a-d; BK XV, CH 22 416a-c; BK XIX, CH 3, 510c; CH 20 523d-524a

19 AQUINAS: *Summa Theologica*, PART I, Q 103, A 2, REP 1–2 529a-530a; PART I–II, Q 2, AA 1–4 615d-618d esp A 4, ANS 618a-d; Q 4, AA 5–7 632c-636a esp A 7, ANS 635b-636a

21 DANTE: *Divine Comedy*, HELL, VII [1–66] 9c-10b

23 HOBBES: *Leviathan*, PART I, 73b-c; 93b-c

25 MONTAIGNE: *Essays*, 107a-112d esp 108c-109c; 126b-128c; 300c-306a

30 BACON: *Advancement of Learning*, 74b-c; 81d-82a

(4. *Divisions of the human good. 4d. Intrinsic and external goods: intrinsic worth and extrinsic value.*)

33 PASCAL: *Pensées*, 462 255a

35 LOCKE: *Civil Government*, CH V, SECT 37 33a-b

36 STERNE: *Tristram Shandy*, 538a-539a

37 FIELDING: *Tom Jones*, 263c-d

42 KANT: *Fund. Prin. Metaphysic of Morals*, 256b; 274d-275b / *Intro. Metaphysic of Morals*, 387d-388a / *Judgement*, 591b-592a

43 MILL: *Utilitarianism*, 462c-d

44 BOSWELL: *Johnson*, 349a-c

46 HEGEL: *Philosophy of Right*, PART I, par 45 23c-d; par 49 24c-25a; par 63–65 28b-29a; par 67–69 29c-31a; ADDITIONS, 29 121c

51 TOLSTOY: *War and Peace*, BK V, 194d

53 JAMES: *Psychology*, 826a

4e. Individual and common goods

7 PLATO: *Crito* 213a-219a,c / *Republic*, BK IV, 342a-d; BK V, 364c-365d / *Critias*, 480a / *Statesman*, 588a-b

8 ARISTOTLE: *Metaphysics*, BK XII, CH 10 [1075^a 11–24] 605d-606a

9 ARISTOTLE: *Ethics*, BK VI, CH 8 [1141^{b}28–1142^a 11] 390d-391a / *Politics*, BK I, CH 1 [1252^{a}1–6] 445a; BK II, CH 1–5 455b,d-460a; BK III, CH 6–7 475d-477a; BK IV, CH 11 [1295^{a}25–^{b}1] 495b-c

12 EPICTETUS: *Discourses*, BK I, CH 19 125b-126c

12 AURELIUS: *Meditations*, BK III, SECT 4 260b-261a; BK VII, SECT 5 280a-b

19 AQUINAS: *Summa Theologica*, PART I, Q 60, A 5, ANS 313b-314c; Q 65, A 2, ANS 340b-341b; Q 92, A 1, REP 1,3 488d-489d; Q 96, A 4 512d-513c; PART I–II, Q 1, A 5, ANS 613a-614a; AA 7–8 614c-615c; Q 19, A 10, ANS 710b-711d; Q 21, AA 3–4 718d-720a,c

20 AQUINAS: *Summa Theologica*, PART I–II, Q 90, A 2 206b-207a; A 3, ANS and REP 3 207a-c; A 4, ANS 207d-208b; Q 91, A 5, ANS 211c-212c; A 6, REP 3 212c-213c; Q 93, A 1, REP 1 215b,d-216c; Q 94, A 2, ANS 221d-223a; A 3, REP 1 223a-c; Q 95, A 4, ANS 229b-230c; Q 96, A 3, ANS and REP 3 232b-233a; A 4, ANS 233a-d; Q 97, A 4 238b-239b; Q 100, A 2, ANS 252b-253a; A 8, ANS and REP 3 259d-261a; Q 111, A 5, REP 1 355d-356c; PART II–III, Q 39, A 2, REP 3 575b-576b; Q 187, A 3, REP 1,3 666a-669b; PART III SUPPL, Q 96, A 6, REP 11 1058a-1061b

21 DANTE: *Divine Comedy*, PURGATORY, XV [40–81] 75d-76a

23 HOBBES: *Leviathan*, PART I, 87c-d

30 BACON: *Advancement of Learning*, 71a-b

31 SPINOZA: *Ethics*, PART IV, PROP 36 434a-b

35 LOCKE: *Toleration*, 15d / *Civil Government*, CH V 30b-36a passim

36 SWIFT: *Gulliver*, PART III, 112a-113a

42 KANT: *Pure Reason*, 114a-d / *Pref. Metaphysical Elements of Ethics*, 369c-373b / *Science of Right*, 438d-439a

43 FEDERALIST: NUMBER 64, 197d

43 MILL: *Liberty*, 297a / *Utilitarianism*, 461d

44 BOSWELL: *Johnson*, 393a-c

46 HEGEL: *Philosophy of Right*, PART I, par 46 23d-24a; PART III, par 170 60d; par 199 67c; par 249 78c; par 287 97a; ADDITIONS, 27 121b; 127 137b; 145 140b

47 GOETHE: *Faust*, PART II [11,559–572] 281b

49 DARWIN: *Descent of Man*, 316c-317a; 592d

52 DOSTOEVSKY: *Brothers Karamazov*, BK VI, 158b-159a

5. The order of human goods

5a. The supreme good or *summum bonum*: its existence and nature

7 PLATO: *Symposium*, 164c-167d / *Gorgias*, 254d-255c / *Republic*, BK VI–VII, 383d-401d esp BK VI, 383d-386c / *Philebus*, 635b-639a,c

8 ARISTOTLE: *Metaphysics*, BK V, CH 16 543a-b; BK XII, CH 7 [1072^{b}13–29] 602d-603a

9 ARISTOTLE: *Ethics*, BK I, CH 1–12 339a-347b esp CH 7 342c-344a; BK VII, CH 11–13 403c-405b passim, esp CH 13 404d-405b; BK X, CH 1–8 426a-434a esp CH 6–8 430d-434a / *Politics*, BK I, CH 1 [1252^{a}1–6] 445a; BK III, CH 12 [1282^b 15–18] 480c; BK VII, CH 1–3 527a-530a passim

12 LUCRETIUS: *Nature of Things*, BK II [1–61] 15a-d; BK VI [1–42] 80a-d

12 EPICTETUS: *Discourses*, BK I, CH 3 108b-c; BK II, CH 11 150a-151b; CH 19 162c-164b; BK III, CH 2 177c-178d; CH 10 185d-187a; CH 24 203c-210a

12 AURELIUS: *Meditations*, BK V, SECT 34 273c; BK VI, SECT 14 274d-275a

17 PLOTINUS: *First Ennead*, TR II, CH 4, 8a-b; TR VIII, CH 2 27c-d / *Sixth Ennead*, TR IX 353d-360d esp CH 6–11 357a-360d

18 AUGUSTINE: *Confessions*, BK IV, par 7 45a-d; BK X, par 29–34 78d-80c / *City of God*, BK VIII, CH 8–10 270a-271d; BK X, CH 1–3 298b,d-301a; CH 18 310b-d; BK XII, CH 1 342b,d-343c; BK XIX 507a-530a,c

19 AQUINAS: *Summa Theologica*, PART I, Q 12, A 1, ANS 50c-51c; Q 26 150a-152a,c; Q 62, A 1, ANS 317d-318c; PART I–II, QQ 1–5 609a-643d; Q 34, A 3 770c-771c

21 DANTE: *Divine Comedy*, PURGATORY, XVII [127–139] 79d; PARADISE, I [103–142] 107b-d; III [82–90] 110a-b; XXVI [1–69] 145d-146c; XXXII [139]–XXXIII [145] 156a-157d

22 CHAUCER: *Troilus and Cressida*, BK III, STANZA 1–7 54b-55b; STANZA 250–253 87a-b

23 HOBBES: *Leviathan*, PART I, 76c-d

24 RABELAIS: *Gargantua and Pantagruel*, BK I, 65c-66b

25 MONTAIGNE: *Essays*, 28a-d; 149b-d; 279c-281a

30 BACON: *Advancement of Learning*, 70b-d

31 SPINOZA: *Ethics*, PART IV, PROP 28 431c; PROP 36 434a-b; APPENDIX, IV 447b-c; XXXII 450c-d; PART V, PROP 42 463b-d

33 PASCAL: *Pensées*, 73 185a-b; 462 255a

5b. The judgment of diverse types of good: their subordination to one another

(5. The order of human goods. 5b. The judgment of diverse types of good: their subordination to one another.)

43 MILL: *Utilitarianism*, 448a-450c; 455c-456a; 461c-464d; 471a-b

44 BOSWELL: *Johnson*, 378a-b

46 HEGEL: *Philosophy of History*, PART III, 307b-308a; PART IV, 365b-c

51 TOLSTOY: *War and Peace*, BK V, 194d

52 DOSTOEVSKY: *Brothers Karamazov*, BK VI, 164b-165a

53 JAMES: *Psychology*, 198b-204b esp 199b-203a

5c. The dialectic of means and ends: mere means and ultimate ends

5 SOPHOCLES: *Philoctetes* 182a-195a,c esp [50–127] 182d-183c

6 THUCYDIDES: *Peloponnesian War*, BK V, 504c-507c

7 PLATO: *Lysis*, 22c-24a / *Laches*, 29c / *Euthydemus*, 69a-71a / *Crito* 213a-219a,c / *Gorgias*, 262a-264b; 280b-d / *Republic*, BK I–II, 300d-315d esp BK II, 310c-d / *Philebus*, 632a-d / *Laws*, BK V, 694d-695a; BK IX, 751c

8 ARISTOTLE: *Topics*, BK III, CH 1 [116^{b}22–36] 163b-c / *Heavens*, BK II, CH 12 [292^{a}14–^{b}26] 383d-384b / *Metaphysics*, BK II, CH 2 [994^{b}8–16] 512d-513a; BK V, CH 2 [1013^{a}32–^{b}3] 533c; [1013^{b}25–28] 533d-534a / *Soul*, BK III, CH 10 [433^{a}12–17] 665d

9 ARISTOTLE: *Ethics*, BK I, CH 1–2 339a-d; CH 5 340d-341b esp [1096^{a}5–10] 341a-b; CH 6 [1096^{b}8–26] 341d-342a; CH 7 [1097^{a}15–^{b}22] 342c-343a; CH 9 [1099^{b}25–32] 345b; BK III, CH 3 [1112^{b}12–1113^{a}2] 358c-359a; BK VI, CH 2 [1139^{a}17–^{b}5] 387d-388a; CH 5 389a-c passim; CH 9 [1142^{b}17–35] 391d-392b / *Politics*, BK VII, CH 1 [1323^{a}22–^{b}21] 527a-c; CH 13 [1331^{b}26–1332^{a}27] 536b-537a / *Rhetoric*, BK I, CH 6–7 602d-607d; CH 8 [1366^{a}3–16] 608b-c

12 EPICTETUS: *Discourses*, BK III, CH 10 185d-187a; CH 13–14 188b-190a; CH 24 203c-210a; BK IV, CH 4 225a-228a

12 AURELIUS: *Meditations*, BK V, SECT 16 271c-d; BK VI, SECT 40–45 277d-278c; BK VII, SECT 44 282b-c; BK VIII, SECT 19–20 286d-287a

14 PLUTARCH: *Alcibiades*, 160b-161b / *Lysander*, 357a-b / *Crassus-Nicias*, 456d-457c / *Agesilaus*, 491a-b / *Cleomenes*, 660b-661a

17 PLOTINUS: *First Ennead*, TR II, CH 3–4 7c-8c; TR IV, CH 6 15a-b / *Second Ennead*, TR IX, CH 15 74d-75b

18 AUGUSTINE: *City of God*, BK VIII, CH 4 266d-267c; CH 8–9 270a-271a; BK XIX, CH 1–3 507a-511a; CH 11–17 516d-523a; CH 20 523d-524a / *Christian Doctrine*, BK I, CH 3–4 625b-c; CH 22 629b-630a; CH 31–33 633b-634b; CH 35 634c-d

19 AQUINAS: *Summa Theologica*, PART I, Q 18, A 3, ANS 106b-107c; Q 19, A 2, REP 2 109c-110b; A 5, ANS and REP 1,3 112d-113c; Q 22, A 1, REP 3 127d-128d; Q 23, A 7, ANS 138d-140a; Q 65,

A 2, ANS and REP 1–2 340b-341b; Q 82, AA 1–4 431d-435c; Q 83, A 4, ANS 439c-440b; PART I–II, Q 1 609a-615c; Q 4 629c-636c; Q 5, A 6, REP 1 641a-642a; Q 8, AA 2–3 656a-657c; Q 11, A 3 667d-668d; Q 12, AA 2–4 670b-672a; Q 13, A 3 674c-675a; Q 14, A 2 678b-c; Q 15, A 3 682c-683b; Q 16, A 3 685b-686a; Q 20, AA 1–4 712a-715b

20 AQUINAS: *Summa Theologica*, PART I–II, Q 54, A 2, REP 3 23d-24c; Q 107, A 1, ANS 325c-327b; Q 114, A 4, REP 1 373a-d; PART II–II, Q 27, A 6, ANS 524c-525c

22 CHAUCER: *Tale of Melibeus* 401a-432a

23 MACHIAVELLI: *Prince*, CH XVIII, 25d-26a

23 HOBBES: *Leviathan*, PART I, 53a-b; 76c-d; 90a; PART III, 237d

25 MONTAIGNE: *Essays*, 28a-d; 52c-53c; 330b-332a; 368d; 381a-388c passim, esp 381c-d, 388a-c

26 SHAKESPEARE: *Richard II*, ACT II, SC III [140–147] 334b

30 BACON: *Advancement of Learning*, 75d-76a; 91d-92a

31 SPINOZA: *Ethics*, PART I, APPENDIX, 371b-c; PART IV, PREF 422b,d-424a passim; DEF 7 424b; PROP 65–66 444b-d; APPENDIX, V 447c

33 PASCAL: *Provincial Letters*, 94a-97a / *Pensées*, 98 190b; 505 261a-b

35 LOCKE: *Human Understanding*, BK II, CH XXI, SECT 52–53 191d-192b; SECT 62 194c-d

36 STERNE: *Tristram Shandy*, 538a-539a

41 GIBBON: *Decline and Fall*, 245a

42 KANT: *Pure Reason*, 234c-240b esp 235a-b, 236c-d, 238c-239a / *Fund. Prin. Metaphysic of Morals*, 256a-b; 257c-d; 260a-c; 265c-267d; 268b; 271c-279d esp 273d-277b; 282b-283d / *Practical Reason*, 307a-d; 315b-317b; 318c-321b esp 320c-321b; 327d-329a; 337a-355d; 357c-360d / *Pref. Metaphysical Elements of Ethics*, 367c / *Intro. Metaphysic of Morals*, 387d-388a / *Science of Right*, 397b-398a / *Judgement*, 477b-c; 478a-b; 557d [fn 2]; 586a-b; 588b [fn 2]; 591b-592d; 594b-595d; 605d-606b [fn 2]

43 FEDERALIST: NUMBER 23 85a-87a passim, esp 85b-c; NUMBER 31, 103c-d; 104b-c; NUMBER 40, 129a-b; NUMBER 41, 132b-c

43 MILL: *Utilitarianism*, 445c-d; 446d-447a; 461c-464d

46 HEGEL: *Philosophy of Right*, PART I, par 45 23c-d; par 61 27b-c; PART II, par 119–128 43b-45d esp par 122 44a; par 140 49b-54a; PART III, par 182 64a; par 191 66b; par 223 73c-d; par 328 108b-c; par 340 110b-c; par 348 111d; ADDITIONS, 38–39 122c-d; 76–81 128a-129a; 116 135c-d / *Philosophy of History*, INTRO, 162a-164c; 166b-168d; PART II, 267a-268b

51 TOLSTOY: *War and Peace*, BK XIII, 586d-587d

52 DOSTOEVSKY: *Brothers Karamazov*, BK V, 127b-137c

53 JAMES: *Psychology*, 4a-6b passim; 14b-15a; 199b-201b; 203a; 381b-382a; 788a-789a

(5. The order of human goods. 5d. The supremacy of the individual or the common good: the relation of the good of the individual person to the good of other persons and to the good of the state.)

42 KANT: *Pure Reason*, 114b-d / *Fund. Prin. Metaphysic of Morals*, 272d-273a / *Practical Reason*, 304b-305c / *Pref. Metaphysical Elements of Ethics*, 369c-373b; 373d; 375d-376b / *Science of Right*, 438d-439b

43 CONSTITUTION OF THE U.S.: AMENDMENTS, I-X 17a-18a

43 FEDERALIST: NUMBER 45, 147c-148a; NUMBER 64, 197d; NUMBER 85, 256d-257a

43 MILL: *Liberty*, 267b,d-274a; 293b-323a,c esp 322d-323a,c / *Representative Government*, 392b-396d / *Utilitarianism*, 450b-455a; 455c-456a; 460a-461c; 463a-b; 469b-470c; 473c-476a,c passim

44 BOSWELL: *Johnson*, 221d-224a; 261c-d; 304c; 393a-c

46 HEGEL: *Philosophy of Right*, PART I, par 46 23d-24a; PART II, par 125-126 44d-45b; par 134 47b; PART III, par 155 57c; par 170 60d; par 183 64a; par 192 66b-c; par 199 67c; par 240 76d; par 249 78c; par 254 79c; par 261 83a-d; par 277 92b-c; par 294 98b-d; par 308 102c-103a; par 323 107a; ADDITIONS, 27 121b; 47 124a-b; 117 135d-136a; 127 137b; 141 139c; 145 140b; 148 140c-d; 151 141b-c; 158 142d / *Philosophy of History*, INTRO, 164b; 192d-193a; PART I, 236a-c; PART II, 271c-d; 276a; PART III, 298c-299a; PART IV, 320c-321a; 363c-d; 365b-c; 367d-368a

47 GOETHE: *Faust*, PART II [11,559-572] 281b

49 DARWIN: *Descent of Man*, 310a-319a esp 312a-313a, 314b-315d, 316c-317c; 321b-322d esp 322c-d; 592d

50 MARX: *Capital*, 237a

50 MARX-ENGELS: *Communist Manifesto*, 429b-c

51 TOLSTOY: *War and Peace*, BK II, 67d-68c; 72d-74a; BK V, 214c-216d; BK VI, 260a-262a; BK XI, 475b-476c; 505a-511b passim, esp 509d-510a; 514b-515a; BK XII, 537b-538a; BK XIII, 577b-c; BK XV, 634a-635a; EPILOGUE I, 670d-671c

52 DOSTOEVSKY: *Brothers Karamazov*, BK VI, 158b-159a; 164a-167b; BK XII, 370b-d

54 FREUD: *General Introduction*, 452c-d; 573b-c / *War and Death*, 757b-759d esp 759c-d / *Civilization and Its Discontents*, 780b-781d; 799a-800a / *New Introductory Lectures*, 853a-b

6. Knowledge and the good

6a. Knowledge, wisdom, and virtue: the relation of being good and knowing what is good

OLD TESTAMENT: *Genesis*, 3 / *Proverbs*, 1-2; 7-8; 9:9; 10:8,31; 11:12; 14:16-18,22,29; 15:21; 28:7; 29:8

APOCRYPHA: *Wisdom of Solomon*, 1:1-7 esp 1:4; 6; 8-10—(D) OT, *Book of Wisdom*, 1:1-7 esp 1:4; 6; 8-10 / *Ecclesiasticus*, 19:22-24; 39:1-11; 43:33; 50:28-29—(D) OT, *Ecclesiasticus*, 19:19-21; 39:1-15; 43:37; 50:30-31

NEW TESTAMENT: *John*, 3:17-21 / *Romans*, 7:15-25 / *James*, 4:17

5 EURIPIDES: *Hippolytus* [375-430] 228b-d

7 PLATO: *Charmides*, 7b-c; 12a-13c / *Laches* 26a-37d / *Protagoras* 38a-64d / *Euthydemus*, 69a-71a / *Cratylus*, 86c-d / *Meno* 174a-190a,c esp 183b-190a,c / *Phaedo*, 225d-226c; 230d-234c / *Republic*, BK I, 306c-308a; BK II, 314d-315a; BK III, 333b-334b; 337b-d; BK IV, 354c-355a; BK VI-VII, 383d-401d esp BK VII, 389d-398c; BK X, 439b-441a,c / *Critias*, 485b-c / *Laws*, BK I, 643c-d; BK III, 669a-670c; BK IX, 754a-b; BK XII, 788d-789a / *Seventh Letter*, 806a-c

8 ARISTOTLE: *Topics*, BK III, CH 6 [120ª26-31] 168a; BK IV, CH 2 [121ᵇ24-122ª2] 169d-170a; CH 3 [124ª10-14] 172d

9 ARISTOTLE: *Ethics*, BK I, CH 3 339d-340b; BK II, CH 4 350d-351b; BK VI, CH 8 390d-391c; CH 12-13 393b-394d; BK VII, CH 2-3 395c-398a; CH 10 [1152ª7-24] 403a-b; BK X, CH 5 [1176ª15-29] 430c-d; CH 8 [1178ª16-18] 432d; CH 9 [1179ᵇ4-1180ª13] 434b-d / *Politics*, BK VII, CH 1 [1323ᵇ21-36] 527c-d

12 EPICTETUS: *Discourses*, BK I, CH 5 110b-c; CH 17 122d-124a; CH 26 131b-132b; CH 28 133b-134d; BK II, CH 22 167d-170a; CH 26 174c-d; BK IV, CH 1 213a-223d

12 AURELIUS: *Meditations*, BK II, SECT 1 256b,d; SECT 17 259b-d; BK VII, SECT 22 281b; SECT 26 281c; SECT 62-63 283d-284a; BK VIII, SECT 14 286c; BK IX, SECT 42 295c-296a,c; BK XII, SECT 12 308b-c

14 PLUTARCH: *Pericles*, 121a-122b / *Aristides*, 265c-d / *Agesilaus*, 490d-491b / *Demetrius*, 726a-d

17 PLOTINUS: *First Ennead*, TR II, CH 6-7 9a-10a; TR III, CH 6 11d-12b

18 AUGUSTINE: *Confessions*, BK VII, par 27 51d-52c; BK VIII, par 10-11 55c-56b / *City of God*, BK VIII, CH 3 266a-d; CH 8 270a-d; BK IX, CH 20 296a-b; BK XI, CH 28 338a-d

19 AQUINAS: *Summa Theologica*, PART I, Q 1, A 6, REP 3 6b-7a; PART I-II, Q 2, A 1, REP 1 615d-616c; A 2, REP 3 616d-617b

20 AQUINAS: *Summa Theologica*, PART I-II, Q 57, A 4, ANS 38a-39a; A 5, ANS 39a-40a; Q 58, A 2 42a-43a; AA 4-5 44a-45d; Q 65, A 1, REP 3-4 70b-72a; PART II-II, Q 18, A 4, ANS 464c-465a; Q 24, A 11, ANS 498b-499c

21 DANTE: *Divine Comedy*, PARADISE, XIX [40-66] 135c-d; XXVI [1-69] 145d-146c; XXVIII [106-114] 150a

25 MONTAIGNE: *Essays*, 59c-60a; 69d-75a esp 70d-72a; 208a; 478c-480c; 514a-b

26 SHAKESPEARE: *Merchant of Venice*, ACT I, SC II [13-23] 408b-c

27 SHAKESPEARE: *Measure for Measure*, ACT I, SC 1 [33–41] 174d; ACT II, SC IV [2–17] 184d

30 BACON: *Advancement of Learning*, 26c-27a

31 DESCARTES: *Discourse*, PART I, 43c; PART III, 49d-50b

31 SPINOZA: *Ethics*, PART IV, PROP 14–17 428a-d; PROP 18, SCHOL 429a-d; PROP 23–24 430c-d

32 MILTON: *Paradise Lost*, BK VII [519–549] 228b-229a; BK VIII [316–337] 239a-b; BK IX [679–779] 262a-264a; BK XI [84–98] 301a / *Samson Agonistes* [38–59] 340b

35 LOCKE: *Human Understanding*, BK I, CH III, SECT 16, 117a; BK II, CH XXI, SECT 35 186b-d; SECT 64 195a-b

35 BERKELEY: *Human Knowledge*, SECT 100 432b-c

36 SWIFT: *Gulliver*, PART I, 28b-29a; PART IV, 159b-160a

37 FIELDING: *Tom Jones*, 182a-c

38 ROUSSEAU: *Inequality*, 343b-345c esp 345a-c / *Social Contract*, BK IV, 434c

42 KANT: *Pure Reason*, 149d / *Fund. Prin. Metaphysic of Morals*, 265b; 282b-283d / *Practical Reason*, 326b-327a

43 MILL: *Utilitarianism*, 458b-459b

46 HEGEL: *Philosophy of Right*, PART II, par 139–140 48d-54a / *Philosophy of History*, INTRO, 168b-d; PART II, 280b-c

53 JAMES: *Psychology*, 82a-b; 806a-808a

54 FREUD: *General Introduction*, 560c-d; 625a-b

6b. The need for experience of evil

7 PLATO: *Republic*, BK III, 337b-d / *Laws*, BK VII, 727c-d

14 PLUTARCH: *Demetrius*, 726a-d

17 PLOTINUS: *Fourth Ennead*, TR VIII, CH 7, 204b-c

18 AUGUSTINE: *Confessions*, BK X, par 54–57 85a-86a

19 AQUINAS: *Summa Theologica*, PART I, Q 22, A 3, REP 3 130d-131c

21 DANTE: *Divine Comedy*, HELL 1a-52d esp I [112–136] 2b-c, XXVIII [43–51] 41d; PURGATORY, I 53a-54c

25 MONTAIGNE: *Essays*, 167a-169a passim; 200d-203b; 235c-236a; 509b-d

30 BACON: *Advancement of Learning*, 75b-c

32 MILTON: *Paradise Lost*, BK IV [505–535] 163b-164a; BK VII [519–549] 228b-229a; BK VIII [316–337] 239a-b; BK IX [679–779] 262a-264a; BK XI [84–98] 301a / *Areopagitica*, 389a-396a esp 390b-391a, 394b-395a

46 HEGEL: *Philosophy of History*, PART I, 237d-238c; PART IV, 354a-c

47 GOETHE: *Faust*, PROLOGUE [340–343] 9a

48 MELVILLE: *Moby Dick*, 4b-5a

51 TOLSTOY: *War and Peace*, BK XI, 481a-482a

52 DOSTOEVSKY: *Brothers Karamazov*, BK III, 53b-54b; BK V, 122c-125a; 132a-135a; BK XI, 344a-d

6c. The goodness of knowledge or wisdom: the use of knowledge

OLD TESTAMENT: *I Kings*, 3:5-15; 10—(D) *III Kings*, 3:5-15; 10 / *II Chronicles*, 1:7-12; 9:1-7—(D) *II Paralipomenon*, 1:7-12; 9:1-7 / *Job*, 28:12-20 / *Proverbs*, 1-4; 8; 9:10-12; 10:1; 12:8; 14:24; 15:24; 16:16; 17:16; 19:2,8; 20:15; 23:15-16,23-25; 24:1-14; 27:11; 28:2 / *Ecclesiastes*, 1:17-18; 2:12-26; 6:8; 7:11-12,16-19; 9:11,13-18—(D) *Ecclesiastes*, 1:17-18; 2:12-26; 6:8; 7:12-13,17-20; 9:11, 13-18 / *Ezekiel*, 28:2-7—(D) *Ezechiel*, 28:2-7

APOCRYPHA: *Wisdom of Solomon*, 6-10—(D) OT, *Book of Wisdom*, 6-10 / *Ecclesiasticus*, 1:16-19; 4:11-19; 6:18-37; 11:1; 14:20-15:8; 21:12-13,21; 24:1-22; 25:10; 34:8; 37:24,26; 40:25; 41:14-15; 51:13-28—(D) OT, *Ecclesiasticus*, 1:20-24; 4:12-22; 6:18-37; 11:1; 14:22-15:8; 21:14-16,24; 24:1-30; 25:13; 34:8; 37:27,29; 40:25; 41:17-18; 51:18-36

NEW TESTAMENT: *I Corinthians*, 1:17-31

5 SOPHOCLES: *Oedipus the King* [300–462] 102a-103c / *Antigone* [632–765] 136c-137d; [1348–1353] 142d

7 PLATO: *Charmides*, 8b / *Lysis*, 16c-18b / *Laches*, 28a-b / *Protagoras*, 40a-41a; 61d-62b / *Euthydemus*, 69a-71a; 74b-76b / *Meno*, 183d-184c / *Phaedo*, 226a-b / *Gorgias*, 272b-273b; 291c-292b / *Republic*, BK VII 388a-401d esp 389d-398c; BK IX, 421a-425b / *Timaeus*, 476a-b / *Theaetetus*, 525c-526a; 528c-531a / *Philebus* 609a-639a,c esp 635c-639a,c / *Laws*, BK I, 643c; BK III, 669d-670c; BK XII, 792c-d; 794c-799a,c / *Seventh Letter*, 801b

8 ARISTOTLE: *Topics*, BK III, CH 1 [116^{a}13-23] 162b-c / *Metaphysics*, BK I, CH 1 [980^{a}22-28] 499a; CH 2 500b-501c esp [982^{b}4-983^{a}11] 500d-501b; BK XII, CH 7 [1072^{b}13-29] 602d-603a / *Soul*, BK I, CH 1 [402^{a}1-7] 631a

9 ARISTOTLE: *Ethics*, BK VI, CH 12 [1143^{b}17-1144^{a}6] 393b-c; BK X, CH 2 [1172^{b}28-32] 426d-427a; CH 7–8 431d-434a / *Rhetoric*, BK I, CH 6 [1362^{b}10-26] 603b-c

12 LUCRETIUS: *Nature of Things*, BK I [62–79] 1d-2a; BK II [48–61] 15c-d; BK V [1–54] 61a-d; BK VI [1–42] 80a-d

12 EPICTETUS: *Discourses*, BK III, CH 20, 192d-193a

12 AURELIUS: *Meditations*, BK V, SECT 9 270b-c; BK X, SECT 12 298c-d

14 PLUTARCH: *Pericles*, 121a-122b

18 AUGUSTINE: *Confessions*, BK X, par 54–57 85a-86a / *City of God*, BK VIII, CH 8 270a-d

19 AQUINAS: *Summa Theologica*, PART I, Q 5, A 4, REP 3 25d-26c; PART I–II, Q 1, A 6, REP 1–2 614a-c; Q 2, A 1, REP 2 615d-616c

20 AQUINAS: *Summa Theologica*, PART II–II, Q 45, A 3, REP 3 600c-601a; PART III SUPPL, Q 96, A 7 1061b-1062a; A 11, ANS and REP 5 1063d-1064d; A 12 1064d-1065b

(6. Knowledge and the good. 6c. The goodness of knowledge or wisdom: the use of knowledge.)

6d. The possibility of moral knowledge: the subjectivity or conventionality of judgments of good and evil

377c-d / *Intro. Metaphysic of Morals*, 387a-388a / *Science of Right*, 397b-398a

43 MILL: *Liberty*, 269b-271c / *Utilitarianism*, 445a-447b; 448a-450a; 456c-462a; 463c-d; 471b-476a,c

44 BOSWELL: *Johnson*, 197a-b; 198b-d

46 HEGEL: *Philosophy of Right*, PREF, 2b-c; INTRO, par 18 16c-d; PART II, par 131-132 46a-47a; par 138 48c-d; par 140 49b-54a; PART III, par 150-152 56c-57b; par 339 110b; ADDITIONS, 1 115a-d; 86 129c; 89 129d-130a; 91 131a-d; 96-97 132c-133a / *Philosophy of History*, INTRO, 166a-b; PART II, 280b-281b

49 DARWIN: *Descent of Man*, 305a; 313b-d; 314c-315d; 317a-d; 592d-593b passim

50 MARX-ENGELS: *Communist Manifesto*, 427a-b; 428b-d

51 TOLSTOY: *War and Peace*, BK I, 15d-16a; BK V, 194a-195a; 214c-d; BK VIII, 304b-305a; BK XI, 514c-d; BK XII, 542d; BK XIV, 611a-c; EPILOGUE I, 645a-646c; EPILOGUE II, 689b

52 DOSTOEVSKY: *Brothers Karamazov*, BK II, 33c-34b; BK XI, 314b-c

53 JAMES: *Psychology*, 190a-191a; 886b-888a

54 FREUD: *War and Death*, 758a-c; 759a / *Civilization and Its Discontents*, 792b-c

CROSS-REFERENCES

For: Other statements of the metaphysical theory of good and evil, *see* BEING 3–3b; CAUSE 6; CHANGE 14; DESIRE 1; GOD 5b; WORLD 6b, 6d; for the relation of the good to the true and the beautiful, *see* BEAUTY 1a; TRUTH 1c; and for the theological consideration of the divine goodness and of the problem of evil, *see* GOD 4f, 5h; JUSTICE 11a; LOVE 5a, 5c; PUNISHMENT 5e–5e(2); SIN 3–3e, 6–6e; WILL 7d; WORLD 6d.

The consideration of the factors which enter into the moral theory of good and evil, *see* DESIRE 2b–2d; DUTY 1; MIND 9c; NATURE 5a; PLEASURE AND PAIN 6–6e; WILL 8b–8b(2).

Other discussions of right and wrong, *see* DUTY 3; JUSTICE 1–2, 4.

The theory of the *summum bonum* or of happiness, *see* DUTY 2; HAPPINESS 1, 3.

Particular human goods in themselves and in relation to the *summum bonum* or happiness, *see* HAPPINESS 2b–2b(7); HONOR 2b; KNOWLEDGE 8b(4); LOVE 3a; PLEASURE AND PAIN 6a–6b, 7; VIRTUE AND VICE 1d; WEALTH 1, 10a; WISDOM 2c.

The discussion of evil and its sources in human life, *see* LABOR 1a; SIN 3–3e; WEALTH 10e(3).

The general problem of the individual and the common good, or the good of the person and the good of the state, *see* CITIZEN 1; HAPPINESS 5–5b; STATE 2f.

General discussions of means and ends, *see* CAUSE 4; RELATION 5a(2).

The controversy over the objectivity or subjectivity of judgments of good and evil, *see* CUSTOM AND CONVENTION 5a; OPINION 6a–6b; RELATION 6c; UNIVERSAL AND PARTICULAR 7b.

The consideration of our knowledge of good and evil, and of the nature and method of the moral sciences, *see* KNOWLEDGE 8b(1); PHILOSOPHY 2c; SCIENCE 3a; WISDOM 2b.

A fuller treatment of the goodness and use of knowledge, *see* ART 6c; KNOWLEDGE 8a–8c; PHILOSOPHY 4b–4c; SCIENCE 1b(1).

ADDITIONAL READINGS

Listed below are works not included in *Great Books of the Western World*, but relevant to the idea and topics with which this chapter deals. These works are divided into two groups:

I. Works by authors represented in this collection.
II. Works by authors not represented in this collection.

For the date, place, and other facts concerning the publication of the works cited, consult the Bibliography of Additional Readings which follows the last chapter of *The Great Ideas*.

I.

EPICTETUS. *The Manual*

AUGUSTINE. *Divine Providence and the Problem of Evil*

———. *Concerning the Nature of Good*

AQUINAS. *Summa Contra Gentiles*, BK III, CH 1–16

———. *Quaestiones Disputatae, De Veritate*, Q 21; *De Malo*, Q 1

F. BACON. "Of Goodness, and Goodness of Nature," in *Essays*

HOBBES. *The Whole Art of Rhetoric*, BK I, CH 7

ing what he is, "any form of government," in Darwin's opinion, "is better than none." Some, like Hobbes and Kant, identify anarchy with the state of nature which is for them a state of war. Some, like Locke, think that the state of nature is not a state of war, yet find great advantages to living in civil society precisely because government remedies the inconveniences and ills which anarchy breeds. But though they often write as if men could choose between living in a state of nature or in a civil society, they do not think man has any option with respect to government if he wishes the benefits of the civilized life. They cannot conceive civil society as existing for a moment without government.

THE GENERAL AGREEMENT about the necessity of government tends to include an agreement about the two basic elements of government—authority and power. No government at all is possible, not even the most attenuated, unless men obey its directions or regulations. But one man may obey another either *voluntarily* or *involuntarily*—either because he recognizes the right vested in that other to give him commands or because he fears the consequences which he may suffer if he disobeys.

These two modes of obedience correspond to the authority and power of government. Authority elicits voluntary compliance. Power either actually coerces or, by threatening coercion, compels involuntary obedience. Authority and power are the right and might of government. Either can exist and may operate apart from the other; but, as Rousseau points out, when right is lacking, government is illegitimate; and as Hamilton points out, when might is lacking, it is ineffective.

In a famous passage, the Federalists explain that rule by authority alone might work in a society of angels. But since men are men, not angels, their obedience must be assured by the threat of force. In any society in which some men are good, some bad, and all may be either at one time or another, force is the only expedient to get the unwilling to do what they should do for the common good. Even when the institutions of government have their authority from the consent of the governed, they cannot function effectively without the use of power or force. For this reason Hamilton dismisses "the idea of governing at all times by the simple force of law" as having "no place but in the reveries of those political doctors whose sagacity disdains the admonitions of experimental instruction."

If authority without force is ineffective for the purposes of government, might without right is tyrannical. "Wherever law ends, tyranny begins," Locke writes, "and whosoever in authority exceeds the power given him by the law, and makes use of the force he has under his command to compass that upon the subject which the law allows not, ceases in that to be a magistrate." The use of unauthorized force may take the form of either usurpation or tyranny. If it is "the exercise of power which another hath a right to," Locke declares it is usurpation; if it is "the exercise of power beyond right, which nobody can have a right to," it is tyranny.

The distinction between legitimate rule and all dominations by force rests not on the use of power, but on whether the power which must be employed is or is not legally authorized.

THE NOTION OF sovereignty involves considerations of authority and power. The word itself is mediaeval and feudal in origin. It signifies the supremacy of an overlord who owes allegiance to no one and to whom fealty is due from all who hold fiefdoms under him. Since the supremacy of the sovereign lord is clothed with legal rights, according to the customs of feudal tenure, sovereignty seems to imply the union of power with authority, not the use of naked force.

The political philosophers of antiquity do not use the term *sovereignty*. But their discussion of the distribution of political power is certainly concerned with the possession of authority as well as the control of force. Aristotle's question, for example, about "what is to be the supreme power in the state—the multitude? or the wealthy? or the good? or the one best man?" deals with the same problem which modern writers express by asking where sovereignty resides. As Aristotle sees the conflict between the oligarchical and the democratic constitutions, the issue concerns the legal definition of the ruling class: whether the constitution puts all the political power in the hands of the rich or in the hands of the freeborn, rich and poor alike. It does not seem to be too violent an interpretation for modern translators to use the word "sovereignty" here, for sovereignty can be said to belong to whatever person or class holds the supreme power by law.

Within this meaning of sovereignty the basic difference between absolute and limited government, or between the despotic and the constitutional regime, leads to a distinction between the sovereign man and the sovereign office.

The ruler who holds sovereignty in his person is an absolute sovereign if his power and authority are in no way limited by positive law. According to some political philosophers, sovereignty must be absolute. In the opinion of Hobbes, for example, the notion of a limited sovereignty seems to be as self-contradictory as that of a supremacy which is not supreme.

After discussing the absolute rights which constitute sovereignty, Hobbes goes on to say that "this great authority being indivisible . . . there is little ground for the opinion of them that say of sovereign kings, though they be *singulis majores*, of greater power than every one of their subjects, yet they be *universis minores*, of less power than them all together. For if by *all together* they mean not the collective body as one person, then *all together* and *every one* signify the same, and the speech is absurd. But if by *all together* they understand them as one person (which person the sovereign bears), then the power of all together is the same as the sovereign's power, and so again the speech is absurd."

It makes no difference, Hobbes argues, whether the sovereignty is held by one man or by an assembly. In either case "the sovereign of a commonwealth . . . is not subject to the civil laws. For having the power to make and repeal laws, he may when he pleases, free himself from that subjection by repealing those laws that trouble him." The sovereign therefore has absolute power, which consists in the absolute right or liberty to do as he pleases, for "he that is bound to himself only is not bound" at all.

Aquinas seems to be taking the same view when he admits that "the sovereign is . . .

exempt from the law as to its coercive power, since, properly speaking, no man is coerced by himself, and law has no coercive power save from the authority of the sovereign." But Aquinas differs from Hobbes in thinking that the authority, if not the power, of the prince is limited by the constitutional character of the kingly office. In the mediaeval conception of monarchy, the king is bound not to himself alone, as Hobbes insists, but to his subjects. Their oath of allegiance to him is reciprocated by his coronation oath, in which he assumes the obligation to uphold the customs of the realm.

WHERE AQUINAS CONCEIVES the sovereign prince as one element—the other being established law—in a government which is therefore both absolute and constitutional, Hobbes conceives the sovereign as identical with a government which is wholly absolute. The distinction here implied—between a mixed regime and one that is purely absolute—is more fully discussed in the chapters on CONSTITUTION and MONARCHY. In contrast to both, a republic, or purely constitutional government, substitutes the sovereign office for the sovereign man. It denies the possession of sovereignty to men *except* in their capacity as office-holders.

According to the republican notions of Rousseau, not even government itself has sovereignty except as representing the political community as a whole, which is the sovereign. Sovereignty, he writes, is vested in the government "simply and solely as a commission, an employment in which the rulers, mere officials of the Sovereign, exercise in their own name the power of which it makes them depositaries." Since this power is not theirs except by delegation, it can be limited, modified, or recovered at pleasure, "for the alienation of such a right is incompatible with the nature of the social body, and contrary to the end of association."

The unity of sovereignty is not impaired by the fact that a number of men may share in the exercise of sovereign power, any more than the unity of government is destroyed by its division into separate departments or branches, such as the legislative, executive, and judicial. Since in a republic the government (in all its branches or offices) derives its power and authority from the constitution (or what Rousseau calls "the fundamental law"), and since it is the people as a whole, not the officials of government, who have the constitutive power, the people are in a sense supreme or sovereign.

Popular sovereignty may mean that the people as a whole govern themselves without the services of magistrates of any sort; but this would be possible only in a very small community. It is questionable whether a people has ever exercised sovereignty in this way in any state of historic importance. Popular sovereignty more usually means what is implied by Aquinas when he conceives the magistrate or ruler as merely the vicegerent of the people. "To order anything to the common good," he writes, "belongs either to the whole people, or to someone who is the vicegerent of the whole people. Hence the making of a law belongs either to the whole people or to a public personage who has the care of the whole people." Similarly, the exercise of coercive force "is vested in the whole people or in some public personage, to whom it belongs to inflict penalties."

The notion of a *public personage*, as Aquinas uses it in these passages, is clearly that of a surrogate for or representative of the whole people. The people as a whole have, in the first instance, the authority and power to perform all the functions of government. Only if for convenience or some other reason they constitute one or more public personages to act in their stead, do individual men exercise sovereignty, and then only as representatives.

Locke's fundamental principle—that "men being... by nature all free, equal, and independent, no one can be put out of this estate and subjected to the political power of another without his own consent"—is another expression of the idea of popular sovereignty. It reappears in the Declaration of Independence in the statement that since governments are instituted by men to secure their fundamental rights, they must derive "their just powers from the consent of the governed."

Hegel objects to the sense "in which men have recently begun to speak of the 'sovereignty of the people'" as "something opposed to the sovereignty existent in the monarch. So op-

posed to the sovereignty of the monarch," he writes, "the sovereignty of the people is one of the confused notions based on the wild idea of the 'people.'" If the sovereignty of the people means nothing more than the sovereignty of the whole state, then, he says, the sovereignty which "is there as the personality of the whole ... is there, in the real existence adequate to its concept, as the person of the monarch."

But republican writers would reply that the sense in which they speak of the sovereignty of the people cannot be opposed to the sovereignty of government, so long as that government is constitutional, not absolute. When the sovereignty of the people is conceived as the source or basis, not as the actual exercise, of the legitimate powers of government, there is no conflict between these two locations of sovereignty in the state. Yet the supremacy of the government always remains limited by the fact that all its powers are delegated and can be withdrawn or changed at the people's will.

THE QUESTION OF absolute or limited sovereignty and the connected question of unified or divided sovereignty have a different meaning in the case of the relation of governments to one another.

The theory of federal government, discussed in *The Federalist* and in Mill's *Representative Government*, contemplates a division of sovereignty, not as between the people and their government, but as between two distinct governments, to each of which the people grant certain powers. Distinguishing between the government of a national state and the government of a federal union, Madison writes: "Among a people consolidated into one nation ... supremacy is completely vested in the national legislature. Among communities united for particular purposes, it is vested partly in the general and partly in the municipal legislatures. In the former case, all local authorities are subordinate to the supreme; and may be controlled, directed, or abolished by it at pleasure. In the latter, the local or municipal authorities form distinct and independent portions of the supremacy, no more subject, within their respective spheres, to the general authority than the general authority is subject to them within its own sphere." The federal or general and the state or local governments draw on the same reservoir of popular sovereignty, but the sovereignty which each derives from that source is limited by the definition of matters reserved to the jurisdiction of the other.

The fundamental difference between the condition of states in a federation and the condition of colonial dependencies or subject peoples is that imperial government, unlike federal government, claims an unlimited sovereignty. The issues of imperialism which arise from the exercise of such power are discussed in the chapters on TYRANNY and SLAVERY.

The one remaining situation is that of independent governments, the governments of separate states associated with one another only by treaties or alliances, or at most in the kind of loose hegemony or league represented by the Greek confederacies or the American *Articles of Confederation*. In this situation, the word "sovereignty" applied to independent governments signifies supremacy, not in the sense of their having the authority and power to command, but in the opposite sense of *not being subject to any political superior*.

This radical difference in meaning is explicitly formulated in Hegel's distinction between internal and external sovereignty.

After stating the conditions of the sovereignty of the state in relation to its own people, Hegel says, "This is the sovereignty of the state at home. Sovereignty has another side, *i.e.*, sovereignty *vis-à-vis* foreign states." The state's individuality resides in its awareness of its own existence "as a unit in sharp distinction from others"; and in this individuality Hegel finds the state's autonomy, which he thinks is "the most fundamental freedom which a people possesses as well as its highest dignity."

But from the fact that "every state is sovereign and autonomous against its neighbors," it also follows, according to Hegel, that such sovereigns "are in a state of nature in relation to each other." It is this state of nature which Hobbes had earlier described as a state of war. Precisely because independent states have absolute sovereignty in relation to one another, "they live in the condition of perpetual war, and upon the confines of battle, with their frontiers armed, and cannons planted against their neighbors round about."

In their relation to one another they are, writes Kant, like "lawless savages." Following Rousseau, he thinks it is fitting that the state "viewed in relation to other peoples" should be called "a power." Unlike sovereign governments which unite authority with power in their domestic jurisdiction, sovereign states in their external relations can exert force alone upon each other. When their interests conflict, each yields only to superior force or to the threat of it. A fuller discussion of these matters will be found in the chapters on LAW, STATE, and WAR AND PEACE.

AS ALREADY INDICATED in several places, the materials covered in this chapter necessarily demand a study of many related chapters dealing with political topics. This is peculiarly true of the problems concerning the forms of government. Separate chapters are devoted to each of the traditionally recognized forms, *viz.*, ARISTOCRACY, DEMOCRACY, MONARCHY, OLIGARCHY, TYRANNY. Each of these chapters defines a particular form, distinguishes it from others, and compares their merits. In addition, the chapter on CONSTITUTION deals with what is perhaps the most fundamental of all distinctions in forms of government, that between a republic and a despotism, or between government by laws and government by men.

Here, then, it is necessary only to treat generally of the issues raised by the classification and comparison of diverse forms of government. They can be summarized in the following questions.

What are the criteria or marks of good government? Is the goodness of government determined by the end it serves, by the way in which it is instituted, by its efficiency in promoting whatever end it serves? Are such criteria of good government as justice, legitimacy, and efficiency, independent or interchangeable?

What is the nature of bad government? Can a distinction be made between the abuses or weakness to which good government is subject in actual operation, and government which is essentially bad because perverse or corrupt in principle as well as practice?

Are there several forms of good government? Of bad government? How are they differentiated from one another? Are all good forms equally good, all bad forms equally bad? If not, what is the principle in terms of which some order of desirability or undesirability is established? For example, is one good form of government better than another, one bad form worse than another, in terms of degrees of justice and injustice, or in terms of efficiency and inefficiency? To put this question in another way, is one form of good government better than another because it achieves a better result or merely because it achieves the same result more completely?

If there are several distinct forms of good government, are there one or more ways in which these can be combined to effect a composite or mixed form? If a mixed form is comparable with the pure forms it unites, is it superior to all, to some, to none of them? On what grounds? In what circumstances?

While proposing what they consider to be the ideal form of government, some political philosophers admit that the ideal may not be realizable under existing circumstances or with men as they are. Plato, for example, recognizes that the state he outlines in the *Republic* may not be practicable; and in the *Laws* he proposes institutions of government which represent for him something less than the ideal but which may be more achievable. The Athenian Stranger says of the state described in the *Republic* that, "whether it is possible or not, no man, acting upon any other principle, will ever constitute a state which will be truer or better or more exalted in virtue." The state which he is discussing in the *Laws* "takes the second place." He refers to "a third best" which, far from being even the practicable ideal, may be merely the best form of government which now actually exists.

Aristotle also sets down the various ways in which forms of government can be judged and compared. We may consider, he writes, "of what sort a government must be to be most in accordance with our aspirations, if there were no external impediment," but we must also consider "what kind of government is adapted to particular states." In addition, Aristotle thinks it is necessary "to know the form of government which is best suited to states in general" as well as "to say how a state may be constituted under any given conditions."

Most important of all, it is necessary to know "not only what form of government is best, but also what is possible." Though "political writers have excellent ideas," Aristotle thinks they "are often impractical." Since "the best is often unattainable," the true legislator "ought to be acquainted not only with what is best in the abstract, but also with what is best relative to circumstances."

Both Montesquieu and Mill later apply this basic distinction between the best form of government considered absolutely or in the abstract, and the best form relative to particular historic circumstances. Among these are a people's economic condition, level of culture, political experience, geography, climate, and racial characteristics. Montesquieu, for example, thinks that government by law, absolutely considered, is better than despotic government, yet he also holds that despotic government is better for certain peoples. Mill thinks that the institutions of a representative democracy represent the ideal form of government, but he acknowledges that absolute monarchy may be better for a rude or uncivilized people who have not yet advanced far from barbarism.

The great question here is whether the circumstances themselves can be improved so that a people may become fit or ready for a better form of government, and ultimately for the best that is attainable, that is, the form relative to the best possible conditions. Since Montesquieu emphasizes what he considers to be fixed racial characteristics, such as the servility of the Asiatics, whereas Mill stresses conditions which are remediable by education, economic progress, and social reforms, these two writers tend to give opposite answers. The issue is more fully discussed in the chapters on DEMOCRACY, MONARCHY, and PROGRESS.

Still other questions remain and should be mentioned here. Are the ideal state and the ideal form of government inseparable, or can one be conceived apart from the other? How shall the ideal government be conceived—in terms of the best that is practicably attainable, given man as he is or can be; or in terms of a perfection which exceeds human attainment and which men can imitate only remotely or imperfectly, if at all? Does divine government, for example, set a model which human government should aim to approximate? Is that human government ideal which is most like the divine; or, on the contrary, is the perfection of human government measured by standards drawn from the nature of man and the difficulties involved in the rule of men over men?

THE TRADITIONAL enumeration of the functions of government is threefold: the legislative, the judicial, and the executive. Locke adds what he calls "the federative power," the power of making treaties or alliances, and in general of conducting foreign affairs. It may be questioned whether this function is strictly coordinate with the other three, since foreign, like domestic, affairs may fall within the province of the executive or the legislature, or both, as in the case of the Constitution of the United States.

In our own day, the multiplication of administrative agencies and the development of planning boards have been thought to add a new dimension to the activities of government, but again it may be questioned whether these are not merely supplemental to the functions of making law, applying law to particular cases, and regulating by administrative decree those matters which fall outside the domain of enforceable law. The executive branch of government seems the most difficult to define, because it involves both law enforcement and the administration of matters not covered by legislative enactment or judicial decision.

If the threefold division of the functions of government is exhaustive, the question remains how these distinct activities shall be related to one another, and by whom they shall be performed. In an absolute monarchy, in which the king *is* the government, all powers are in the hands of one man. Though he may delegate his powers to others, they act only as his deputies or agents, not as independent officials. This does not obliterate the theoretical distinction between legislation, adjudication, and execution, but in this situation there can be no practical separation of the three powers, certainly no legal system of checks and balances.

It is the separation of powers, according to Montesquieu, that is the basis of political liberty. "Power should be a check to power," he writes. In a system of separated powers, "the legislative body being composed of two parts, they check one another by the mutual privilege of rejecting. They are both restrained by the executive power, as the executive is by the legislative."

Whether or not Montesquieu is right in attributing this aspect of constitutionalism to the limited monarchy of England in his own day, his argument can be examined apart from history, for it raises the general question whether government by law can be preserved from degenerating into despotic government except by the separation of powers.

For the American Federalists, the system of checks and balances, written into the Constitution, so contrives "the interior structure of the government that its several constituent parts may, by their mutual relations, be the means of keeping each other in their proper places." This they consider the prime advantage to be gained from Montesquieu's principle of the separation of powers. The principle itself they hold to be "the sacred maxim of free government."

OUTLINE OF TOPICS

REFERENCES

To find the passages cited, use the numbers in heavy type, which are the volume and page numbers of the passages referred to. For example, in 4 HOMER: *Iliad*, BK II [265–283] 12d, the number 4 is the number of the volume in the set; the number 12d indicates that the passage is in section d of page 12.

PAGE SECTIONS: When the text is printed in one column, the letters a and b refer to the upper and lower halves of the page. For example, in 53 JAMES: *Psychology*, 116a-119b, the passage begins in the upper half of page 116 and ends in the lower half of page 119. When the text is printed in two columns, the letters a and b refer to the upper and lower halves of the left-hand side of the page, the letters c and d to the upper and lower halves of the right-hand side of the page. For example, in 7 PLATO: *Symposium*, 163b-164c, the passage begins in the lower half of the left-hand side of page 163 and ends in the upper half of the right-hand side of page 164.

AUTHOR'S DIVISIONS: One or more of the main divisions of a work (such as PART, BK, CH, SECT) are sometimes included in the reference; line numbers, in brackets, are given in certain cases; *e.g.*, *Iliad*, BK II [265–283] 12d.

BIBLE REFERENCES: The references are to book, chapter, and verse. When the King James and Douay versions differ in title of books or in the numbering of chapters or verses, the King James version is cited first and the Douay, indicated by a (D), follows; *e.g.*, OLD TESTAMENT: *Nehemiah*, 7:45—(D) II Esdras, 7:46.

SYMBOLS: The abbreviation "esp" calls the reader's attention to one or more especially relevant parts of a whole reference; "passim" signifies that the topic is discussed intermittently rather than continuously in the work or passage cited.

For additional information concerning the style of the references, see the Explanation of Reference Style; for general guidance in the use of *The Great Ideas*, consult the Preface.

1. The general theory of government

7 PLATO: *Republic* 295a-441a,c esp BK II–VIII 310c-416a / *Statesman*, 598b-604b / *Laws*, BK III 663d-677a; BK IV, 679a-c

9 ARISTOTLE: *Ethics*, BK VI, CH 8 [1141^{b}24–1142^{a}12] 390d-391a / *Politics* 445a-548a,c esp BK I, CH 5 447d-448c, BK III, CH I 471b,d-472c, CH 6–13 475d-483a, BK IV, CH 14–16 498b-502a,c

12 LUCRETIUS: *Nature of Things*, BK V [1136–1160] 76a-b

12 AURELIUS: *Meditations*, BK I, SECT 14 254b-c

18 AUGUSTINE: *City of God*, BK II, CH 21 161b-162d; BK IV, CH 4 190d; BK XIX, CH 13–17 519a-523a; CH 21 524a-525a; CH 23–24, 528a-c; CH 26 528d-529a

19 AQUINAS: *Summa Theologica*, PART I, Q 96, A 4 512d-513c

23 HOBBES: *Leviathan*, PART I–II, 84c-104d

30 BACON: *Advancement of Learning*, 94b-95a

31 SPINOZA: *Ethics*, PART IV, PROP 37, SCHOL 2 435b-436a

33 PASCAL: *Pensées*, 291–338 225a-233a passim

35 LOCKE: *Toleration*, 16a-c / *Civil Government* 25a-81d esp CH VII, SECT 87–89 44a-d, CH VIII–IX 46c-54d, CH XI, SECT 136 56c-d, CH XV, SECT 171 65a-b, CH XIX, SECT 211 73d-74a

36 SWIFT: *Gulliver*, PART II, 78a-b; PART III, 112a-115b; PART IV, 157a-158a

38 MONTESQUIEU: *Spirit of Laws*, BK I 1a-3d

38 ROUSSEAU: *Political Economy* 367a-385a,c / *Social Contract*, BK III, 406b,d-410a; 423a-424d

39 SMITH: *Wealth of Nations*, BK V, 309a-311c

42 KANT: *Science of Right*, 435a-437c; 450a-452a

43 DECLARATION OF INDEPENDENCE: [7–25] 1a-b

43 CONSTITUTION OF THE U.S.: PREAMBLE 11a,c

43 FEDERALIST: NUMBER 31, 104b; NUMBER 45, 147d-148a

43 MILL: *Representative Government*, 327b,d-341d

46 HEGEL: *Philosophy of History*, PART IV, 364d-365a

54 FREUD: *Civilization and Its Discontents*, 780b-781a

1a. The origin and necessity of government: the issue concerning anarchy

NEW TESTAMENT: *Romans*, 13:1–8 / *I Peter*, 2:13–15

5 AESCHYLUS: *Eumenides* [681–710] 88b-c

5 SOPHOCLES: *Antigone* [332–372] 134a-b

6 HERODOTUS: *History*, BK I, 23b-d

6 THUCYDIDES: *Peloponnesian War*, BK III, 436d-438b

7 PLATO: *Protagoras*, 44c-d / *Crito*, 216b-217d / *Gorgias*, 271b-272b / *Republic*, BK II, 316c-319a / *Laws*, BK III, 663d-667b

9 ARISTOTLE: *History of Animals*, BK I, CH I [487^{b}32–488^{a}15] 8d-9a / *Ethics*, BK VIII, CH 12 [1162^{a}16–25] 414c; BK IX, CH 9 [1169^{b}18–22] 423b / *Politics*, BK I, CH 2 445b-446d esp [1253^{a}29–39] 446d; BK III, CH 6 [1278^{b}15–29] 475d-476a

12 LUCRETIUS: *Nature of Things*, BK V [1011–1027] 74b-c; [1136–1160] 76a-b

12 EPICTETUS: *Discourses*, BK I, CH 23 128c-d

12 AURELIUS: *Meditations*, BK IV, SECT 4 264a

14 PLUTARCH: *Cato the Younger*, 638b-d

15 TACITUS: *Annals*, BK III, 51b-c / *Histories*, BK I, 211c-212d

18 AUGUSTINE: *City of God*, BK IV, CH 4 190d; BK XII, CH 27 359c-360a,c; BK XIX, CH 14–17 520a-523a; CH 21 524a-525a; CH 23–24, 528a-c

19 AQUINAS: *Summa Theologica*, PART I, Q 96, A 4 512d-513c

20 AQUINAS: *Summa Theologica*, PART I–II, Q 95, A 1 226c-227c

21 DANTE: *Divine Comedy*, PURGATORY, VI [76–151] 61c-62c; XVI [85–105] 77d; PARADISE, VIII [115–117] 118a

23 HOBBES: *Leviathan*, PART I, 58c-d; 77a; 77c; 84c-87b; 91a-b; 96a-b; PART II, 99a-102a; 104b-d; 109b; 112b-d; 113c; 124c-125a; 131a-c; 159d

25 MONTAIGNE: *Essays*, 462c-465c

26 SHAKESPEARE: *Henry V*, ACT I, SC II [183–220] 535d-536b

27 SHAKESPEARE: *Troilus and Cressida*, ACT I, SC III [78–134] 109a-c

28 HARVEY: *On Animal Generation*, 454a

30 BACON: *Advancement of Learning*, 20c-d

31 SPINOZA: *Ethics*, PART IV, PROP 37, SCHOL 2 435b-436a

32 MILTON: *Paradise Lost*, BK VI [169–188] 200a

33 PASCAL: *Pensées*, 304 227b-228a; 306 228a; 330 231b-232a

35 LOCKE: *Toleration*, 4c-d; 16a-c / *Civil Government*, CH I, SECT I 25a-c; CH II, SECT 13–CH III, SECT 20 28a-29d; CH VI, SECT 57 36d-37b; SECT 74–76 41b-42a; CH VII, SECT 87–CH X, SECT 132 44a-55b; CH XI, SECT 136 56c-d; CH XV, SECT 171 65a-b; CH XVI, SECT 175 65d; CH XIX, SECT 212 74a-b; SECT 219 75b-c

36 SWIFT: *Gulliver*, PART IV 135a-184a

36 STERNE: *Tristram Shandy*, 214b-217b esp 216b; 261b-262a; 410a-411a

38 MONTESQUIEU: *Spirit of Laws*, BK I 1a-3d; BK VIII, 52a

38 ROUSSEAU: *Inequality*, 333b-d / *Political Economy*, 370b / *Social Contract*, BK I, 391b-393c; BK III, 406b,d-407a; 419b; 423a-424a

39 SMITH: *Wealth of Nations*, BK V, 309a-311c

40 GIBBON: *Decline and Fall*, 91b

41 GIBBON: *Decline and Fall*, 87a-b

42 KANT: *Pure Reason*, 222b-c / *Science of Right*, 433c-434d; 435c-436b; 437c-d; 450d-451c

43 DECLARATION OF INDEPENDENCE: [7–25] 1a-b

43 CONSTITUTION OF THE U.S.: PREAMBLE 11a,c

43 FEDERALIST: NUMBER 2, 31a-b; NUMBER 4, 36a; NUMBER 15, 63a-d; 65b-c; NUMBER 16 66c-68d passim; NUMBER 18–20 71a-78b passim; NUMBER 38, 121b-122a; NUMBER 51, 163b-c; 164c-d; NUMBER 85, 258d-259a,c

43 MILL: *Liberty*, 267d-268a; 269c; 302d-303a / *Utilitarianism*, 472b-c

44 BOSWELL: *Johnson*, 172d-173a

46 HEGEL: *Philosophy of Right*, ADDITIONS, 47 124a-b / *Philosophy of History*, INTRO, 173a-175c; PART II, 262a-c; PART IV, 342c-d

49 DARWIN: *Descent of Man*, 310a-c; 321b-c

51 TOLSTOY: *War and Peace*, EPILOGUE II, 680b-684a

54 FREUD: *Civilization and Its Discontents*, 780b-d

1b. Comparison of political or civil government with ecclesiastical government and with paternal or despotic rule

5 SOPHOCLES: *Antigone* [631–680] 136c-137a

5 EURIPIDES: *Andromache* [464–492] 319b-c

6 HERODOTUS: *History*, BK III, 107c-108d; BK V, 178a-180a

7 PLATO: *Crito*, 217a-c / *Statesman*, 581a-c / *Laws*, BK III 663d-677a

9 ARISTOTLE: *Ethics*, BK VIII, CH 10 [1160^{b}23–1161^{a}9] 413a-b / *Politics*, BK I, CH 1–2 445a-446d; CH 3 [1253^{b}15–22] 447a; CH 5 447d-448c; CH 7 [1255^{b}16–22] 449b-c; CH 12–13 453d-455a,c; BK III, CH 4 [1277^{a}33–^{b}24] 474c-d; CH 6 [1278^{b}30–1279^{a}22] 476a-c; BK VII, CH 2 [1324^{b}23–41] 528d-529a; CH 3 [1325^{a}18–^{b}13] 529b-d; CH 14 537b-538d

15 TACITUS: *Annals*, BK I, 1a-2a; 3a-b; BK III, 51b-c; 61c-62a

18 AUGUSTINE: *City of God*, BK XIX, CH 13–17 519a-523a

19 AQUINAS: *Summa Theologica*, PART I, Q 92, A 1, REP 2 488d-489d; Q 96, A 4 512d-513c

23 HOBBES: *Leviathan*, PART II, 109c-111b; 121a; 155b; PART III, 198a-199a; PART IV, 249a; 266a-c

30 BACON: *Advancement of Learning*, 34a; 101a

32 MILTON: *New Forcers of Conscience* 68a-b

35 LOCKE: *Toleration*, 3a-5d; 14b-15a / *Civil Government*, CH I, SECT 2 25c; CH II, SECT 13 28a-b; CH IV 29d-30b; CH VI–VII 36a-46c; CH XIV–XVIII 62b-73c

36 STERNE: *Tristram Shandy*, 214b-217b; 410a-411a

38 MONTESQUIEU: *Spirit of Laws*, BK I, 3b; BK II, 4a; 7c-9a,c; BK III, 12a-13c; BK IV, 15a-c; BK V, 25d-31b; BK VI, 33a-35a; 36a-37a; BK VII, 50d; BK VIII, 54a-b; BK XIX, 137c-d; BK XXIV, 202b-c; BK XXVI, 214b,d-215a; 218a-b; 218d-219a

38 ROUSSEAU: *Inequality*, 357a-c / *Political Economy*, 367a-368c; 370a-379b / *Social Contract*, BK I, 387a-388a; 391a; BK III, 415d; 418a-419c; BK IV, 436d [fn 1]

9 ARISTOTLE: *Politics*, BK I, CH 2 [1253ª29–39] 446d; CH 6 [1255ª7–25] 448c-d; BK III, CH 3 [1276ª7–16] 473a; CH 15 [[1286ᵇ28–40] 485b; BK V, CH 11 [1314ª35–1315ᵇ11] 517a-518c; BK VI, CH 8 [1321ᵇ40–1322ª28] 525d-526a; BK VII, CH 2 [1324ᵇ24–39] 528d

13 VIRGIL: *Aeneid*, BK VI [851–853] 234a

14 PLUTARCH: *Cleomenes*, 659d-660a

18 AUGUSTINE: *City of God*, BK II, CH 21 161b-162d; BK IV, CH 4 190d; BK XIX, CH 21 524a-525a; CH 23–24, 528a-c

20 AQUINAS: *Summa Theologica*, PART I–II, Q 90, A I, REP 3 205b-206b; A 3 207a-c; Q 95, A 5 233d-234d

23 HOBBES: *Leviathan*, PART I, 71d-73a; 89b; 91a-b; PART I–II, 96c-105c esp PART II, 99a-b; 109b-c; 112b-d; 117d; 122b-124b; 131d-132a; 145a-b; 148d-149b; 159d; PART III, 191b; 225c-d; PART IV, 273a-c

26 SHAKESPEARE: *Henry V*, ACT I, SC II [183–220] 535d-536b

27 SHAKESPEARE: *Troilus and Cressida*, ACT I, SC III [78–134] 109a-c / *Measure for Measure*, ACT I, SC II [120–127] 176b-c

31 SPINOZA: *Ethics*, PART IV, PROP 37, SCHOL 2 435b-436a; PROP 51, SCHOL 439d

33 PASCAL: *Pensées*, 294–308 225b-228b; 311 228b; 878 345a-b

35 LOCKE: *Toleration*, 3a-4a; 16a-c / *Civil Government*, CH I, SECT 2–3 25c-d; CH II 25d-28c passim; CH IV, SECT 21 29d; CH VI, SECT 69–71 40a-c; CH VII, SECT 87–89 44a-d; CH VIII, SECT 95–99 46c-47c; CH IX 53c-54d; CH XII, SECT 143–CH XIII, SECT 149 58c-59d; CH XIV 62b-64c passim; CH XV, SECT 171 65a-b; CH XVI–XIX 65d-81d passim, esp CH XIX, SECT 219 75b-c / *Human Understanding*, BK II, CH XXVIII, SECT 4–17 229b-232d passim, esp SECT 6 229d, SECT 9 230b

36 STERNE: *Tristram Shandy*, 261b-262a

38 MONTESQUIEU: *Spirit of Laws*, BK XII, 84b

38 ROUSSEAU: *Political Economy*, 367b; 370b-372b / *Social Contract*, BK I, 389a-393b; BK II, 396d-397a; BK III, 406b,d-409a; 418a-419c; BK IV, 433a-434b

39 SMITH: *Wealth of Nations*, BK V, 309c-311c; 349a-c

42 KANT: *Intro. Metaphysic of Morals*, 389a-b; 392b; 393c

43 FEDERALIST: NUMBER 2, 31a-b; NUMBER 15, 64b-65d; NUMBER 16 66c-68d passim, esp 67d-68c; NUMBER 20–21, 78a-d; NUMBER 23, 85d-87a passim; NUMBER 27–28, 94d-96c; NUMBER 29, 98c-99b; NUMBER 31, 104b; NUMBER 33, 108d-109a; NUMBER 37, 118d-119a; NUMBER 39, 127a-d; NUMBER 41, 132b-c; NUMBER 43, 141a-142d; NUMBER 44, 145c-147a; NUMBER 59, 182a-b

43 MILL: *Liberty*, 267d-269c / *Representative Government*, 327b,d-332d; 333c-334a; 350b-355b; 362c-363a; 429a-c / *Utilitarianism*, 472b-c

46 HEGEL: *Philosophy of Right*, PART III, par 209–213 69d-71a; par 230–237 75c-76c; par 278 92c-93a

51 TOLSTOY: *War and Peace*, EPILOGUE II, 680b-688a

52 DOSTOEVSKY: *Brothers Karamazov*, BK V, 127b-137c passim

1e. The attributes of good government

5 EURIPIDES: *Suppliants* [399–456] 261d-262b

6 HERODOTUS: *History*, BK III, 107c-108d

7 PLATO: *Republic*, BK IV, 342a-350a / *Statesman*, 598b-604b / *Laws*, BK IV, 681b-682c; BK VIII, 733b-734a esp 733d-734a

9 ARISTOTLE: *Ethics*, BK II, CH I [1103ᵇ2–6] 349a; BK VIII, CH 10–11 412c-413d / *Politics*, BK II, CH 2 [1261ª23–ᵇ6] 456a-b; CH 9 [1269ª29–33] 465b-c; BK III, CH 6 [1279ª17]–CH 7 [1279ᵇ10] 476c-477a; BK VI, CH 4 [1318ᵇ21–1319ª3] 522b-c; BK VII, CH 2 [1324ª24–25] 528b; CH 14 [1332ᵇ12–41] 537b-d

12 AURELIUS: *Meditations*, BK I, SECT 14 254b-c

18 AUGUSTINE: *City of God*, BK II, CH 21 161b-162d; BK IV, CH 3–4 190a-d; BK XIX, CH 24 528b-c

20 AQUINAS: *Summa Theologica*, PART I–II, Q 95, A 4, ANS 229b-230c; Q 105, A I, ANS 307d-309d

23 MACHIAVELLI: *Prince*, CH XII, 18a

23 HOBBES: *Leviathan*, PART II, 101a-104d; 112b-d; 153a-159c

29 CERVANTES: *Don Quixote*, PART I, 193a; PART II, 331a-336a; 352d-353a

35 LOCKE: *Civil Government*, CH IX, SECT 131 54d; CH XI, SECT 134–CH XII, SECT 143 55b-58d; CH XIII, SECT 158–CH XIV, SECT 168 61d-64c; CH XVIII, SECT 205 72a-c

36 SWIFT: *Gulliver*, PART II, 74a-76b; 78a-b

36 STERNE: *Tristram Shandy*, 216b

37 FIELDING: *Tom Jones*, 268c-269b

38 MONTESQUIEU: *Spirit of Laws*, BK I, 3b-d; BK VI, 39b; BK XI, 69a-75a; BK XII, 84b,d-85c; BK XIII, 96a-b; BK XIX, 135d-136a; 138a-c; BK XXIII, 199b-c; BK XXVI, 214b,d; BK XXIX, 262a

38 ROUSSEAU: *Inequality*, 323a-328a,c; 360b-c / *Political Economy*, 368c-372b; 375b-c / *Social Contract*, BK III, 411c-412c; 417c-418a; 424a-d

40 GIBBON: *Decline and Fall*, 50a-b

42 KANT: *Pure Reason*, 114b-d / *Science of Right*, 408c-409c; 438d-439a; 450b-452a / *Judgement*, 586a-587a

43 DECLARATION OF INDEPENDENCE: [7–23] 1a-b

43 FEDERALIST: NUMBER I, 30a-b; NUMBER 22, 84c-d; NUMBER 23 85a-87a; NUMBER 30, 101b-c; NUMBER 31, 104b; NUMBER 37, 118d-119b; NUMBER 39, 125a-126b; NUMBER 41, 132b-c; NUMBER 45, 147d-148a; NUMBER 47 153c-156d; NUMBER 57, 176d-177a; 177d-178a; NUMBER 62, 190c; NUMBER 68, 206b-c; NUMBER 70, 210c-d; NUMBER 71, 215b; NUMBER 78, 232d-233c; NUMBER 83, 250d-251a

(1. The general theory of government. 1e. The attributes of good government.)

43 MILL: *Liberty*, 272d-273d; 322a-323a,c / *Representative Government*, 332d-350a; 356d-357a; 362c-370a; 380c-382c; 387c-d; 436b-437a; 439b-c

44 BOSWELL: *Johnson*, 182c-d; 204b-c

46 HEGEL: *Philosophy of Right*, ADDITIONS, 165 145a-b / *Philosophy of History*, INTRO, 174a-175c; PART I, 208b-c; PART II, 275a-b; 276a; PART IV, 342a-343a

47 GOETHE: *Faust*, PART II [10,252–259] 249b-250a

1*f*. The abuses and corruptions to which government is subject

OLD TESTAMENT: *I Samuel*, 8:3–20—(*D*) *I Kings*, 8:3–20

6 THUCYDIDES: *Peloponnesian War*, BK III, 436d-437d

7 PLATO: *Republic*, BK VIII–IX 401d-427b / *Laws*, BK IV, 681d-682c

9 ARISTOTLE: *Politics*, BK II, CH 7 [1266^{b}36–1267^{b}10] 462c-463b; BK III, CH 15 [1286^{a}31–^{b}8] 484c-d; CH 16 [1287^{a}1–^{b}8] 485b-486a; BK V, CH 2–3 503b-505b; CH 8 [1308^{b}31–1309^{a}32] 511a-c passim; CH 12 [1316^{a}1–^{b}27] 518d-519d / *Rhetoric*, BK I, CH 4 [1360^{a}17–29] 600c

15 TACITUS: *Histories*, BK II, 224d-225a

18 AUGUSTINE: *City of God*, BK XIX, CH 6 514b-515a

21 DANTE: *Divine Comedy*, HELL, VI [58–75] 9a; XXVII [19–54] 39d-40a; PURGATORY, VI [76–151] 61c-62c; XVI [58–126] 77c-78a; PARADISE, XVI 130a-132a

23 HOBBES: *Leviathan*, PART I, 78b-d; PART II, 100a-c; 104b-d; 116c-d; 148c-153a; 164a,c; PART IV, 273a-b; CONCLUSION, 279a-c

25 MONTAIGNE: *Essays*, 381b-d; 384b-c

27 SHAKESPEARE: *Measure for Measure* 174a-204d

32 MILTON: *Lord Gen. Fairfax* 68b-69a / *Samson Agonistes* [237–276] 344b-345b / *Areopagitica*, 412b

35 LOCKE: *Civil Government*, CH XI, SECT 138 57b-c; CH XIII, SECT 149 59b-d; CH XVIII, SECT 199-201 71a-c

36 SWIFT: *Gulliver*, PART I, 11b; 15b-16b; 28b-29a; PART II, 74a-76b; PART III, 120a; PART IV, 152b-154a; 157a-158a

37 FIELDING: *Tom Jones*, 100d-101a; 268c-269b

38 MONTESQUIEU: *Spirit of Laws*, BK VI, 39c; BK VIII, 51a-55c; BK XI, 69a-c; BK XXVIII, 259b

38 ROUSSEAU: *Inequality*, 360b-361c / *Political Economy*, 372b-373a / *Social Contract*, BK III, 433a-434b

39 SMITH: *Wealth of Nations*, BK II, 148b-c; 149d-150a

40 GIBBON: *Decline and Fall*, 35a; 521d; 622d-623a

41 GIBBON: *Decline and Fall*, 307a-c; 586c-587b

42 KANT: *Science of Right*, 435a-441d esp 435c-436b, 437c-d, 438d-441d; 450a-c

43 FEDERALIST: NUMBER 10 49c-53a passim; NUMBER 15, 65c-66a; NUMBER 16, 68c-d; NUMBER 22, 82c-83d; NUMBER 28 96c-98b passim; NUMBER 37, 120d-121a; NUMBER 41, 132b-c; NUMBER 51 162d-165a passim; NUMBER 62, 190a-b; NUMBER 66, 201d-202a

43 MILL: *Liberty*, 267d-269c / *Representative Government*, 328d-330c; 350d-351a; 362c-370a; 376a-c; 387c-d

44 BOSWELL: *Johnson*, 120a-c; 178b-c; 195c-d; 261c-d; 374b-c

47 GOETHE: *Faust*, PART II [4772–4811] 118b-119b; [10,242–284] 249b-250b

52 DOSTOEVSKY: *Brothers Karamazov*, BK V, 127b-137c passim

1*g*. The sovereignty of government: the unity and disposition of sovereignty

9 ARISTOTLE: *Politics*, BK III, CH 6 [1278^{b}9–14] 475d; CH 7 476c-477a; CH 10 478d-479a / *Rhetoric*, BK I, CH 8 [1365^{b}27–1366^{a}2] 608a-b

20 AQUINAS: *Summa Theologica*, PART I-II, Q 90, A 3 207a-c

23 HOBBES: *Leviathan*, PART I, 97c-98a,c; PART II, 100c-105c; 112b-c; 114b-c; 116c-d; 117b-d; 122b-124b; 130d; 131d-132a; 148b; 150b; 151a-152a; 153b; 159c; PART III, 228b

32 MILTON: *Paradise Lost*, BK V [769–799] 192a-b

38 MONTESQUIEU: *Spirit of Laws*, BK IX, 58b,d-60a

38 ROUSSEAU: *Inequality*, 323d / *Political Economy*, 368c-369a / *Social Contract*, BK I, 392a-393b; BK II, 395a-398b; BK III, 406b,d-409a; 420d; BK IV, 423a-424b

40 GIBBON: *Decline and Fall*, 24b,d-28b passim, esp 28a-b; 521b

42 KANT: *Science of Right*, 435a-b; 437c-d; 438b-c; 439a-441d; 450d-451b; 452a-d

43 ARTICLES OF CONFEDERATION: II 5a-b

43 FEDERALIST: NUMBER 9, 48b-49c esp 49b; NUMBER 15, 63d-66b; NUMBER 16–20 66c-78b esp NUMBER 20, 78a-b; NUMBER 32 105c-107b passim, esp 105d; NUMBER 33, 108d-109a; NUMBER 39, 126b-128b; NUMBER 42, 138c; NUMBER 44, 146d-147a; NUMBER 62, 189c-d; NUMBER 81, 240d-241a; NUMBER 82, 242b-c

43 MILL: *Representative Government*, 331c-332d; 355b-356b

46 HEGEL: *Philosophy of Right*, PART III, par 276 92b; par 279 93a-94d; par 285 96b; par 321–322 106c-107a; ADDITIONS, 168 145c-d; 178 147d-148a; 187 149b / *Philosophy of History*, PART IV, 355c-d; 365a

51 TOLSTOY: *War and Peace*, EPILOGUE II, 680b-684a

1*g*(1) The sovereign person: sovereignty vested in the individual ruler

OLD TESTAMENT: *I Samuel*, 8:4–20—(*D*) *I Kings*, 8:4–20

1g(2) The sovereign office: the partition of sovereignty among the offices created by a constitution

1g(3) The sovereign people: the community as the source of governmental sovereignty

(1g. *The sovereignty of government: the unity and disposition of sovereignty.* 1g(3) *The sovereign people: the community as the source of governmental sovereignty.*)

42 KANT: *Science of Right*, 436c; 437c-d; 439a-441d; 450a-b; 450d-452a esp 451c-452a

43 DECLARATION OF INDEPENDENCE: [1–25]1a-b; [43–47] 2a

43 CONSTITUTION OF THE U.S.: PREAMBLE 11a,c; AMENDMENTS, IX–X 17d-18a

43 FEDERALIST: NUMBER 22, 84d-85a; NUMBER 33, 108b-c; NUMBER 39 125a-128b; NUMBER 46, 150b-c; NUMBER 49, 159c; NUMBER 53, 167d-168b; NUMBER 84, 252b-c

43 MILL: *Liberty*, 267d-269c / *Representative Government*, 341d-350a passim, esp 344d; 355b-356b; 380c-382c; 386d-393a esp 387c-d

46 HEGEL: *Philosophy of Right*, PART III, par 279 93a-94d; par 308 102c-103a / *Philosophy of History*, PART II, 272b-273a; PART III, 300a-301c; PART IV, 365c-366b

51 TOLSTOY: *War and Peace*, EPILOGUE II, 680b-684a

1h. Self-government: expressions of the popular will; elections; voting

OLD TESTAMENT: *Judges*, 21:24

9 ARISTOTLE: *Politics*, BK II, CH 6 [1266ᵃ5-30] 461c-d; CH 9 [1270ᵇ7-34] 466d-467a; [1271ᵃ9-17] 467b; CH 12 [1273ᵇ36-1274ᵃ22] 470c-d; BK III, CH 11 479b-480c; BK IV, CH 14 498b-499c; BK VI, CH 2-3 520d-522a / *Rhetoric*, BK I, CH 8 [1365ᵇ32-33] 608a

14 PLUTARCH: *Lycurgus*, 34d-35c / *Coriolanus*, 180b-d / *Tiberius Gracchus*, 676b-681a,c

20 AQUINAS: *Summa Theologica*, PART I-II, Q 90, A 3, ANS 207a-c

27 SHAKESPEARE: *Coriolanus* 351a-392a,c esp ACT II, SC II–III 364a-369a

32 MILTON: *Sonnets*, XII 65a-b

35 LOCKE: *Civil Government*, CH VIII, SECT 95-99 46c-47c; CH XIII, SECT 154 60c-d; CH XIX, SECT 216 74d; SECT 222 75d-76c

36 SWIFT: *Gulliver*, PART II, 73b-74b

38 MONTESQUIEU: *Spirit of Laws*, BK II, 4a-6b; BK XI, 71a-c; BK XIX, 142a-d

38 ROUSSEAU: *Inequality*, 324c-325b / *Social Contract*, BK I, 393a-b; BK II, 396b-d; BK IV, 425a-432b

40 GIBBON: *Decline and Fall*, 241b-c; 521a-523a,c passim

41 GIBBON: *Decline and Fall*, 73b; 562c-564b; 587a

42 KANT: *Science of Right*, 436d-437c; 451c-452a

43 CONSTITUTION OF THE U.S.: PREAMBLE 11a,c; ARTICLE I, SECT 2 [5-10] 11b; SECT 2 [17]-SECT 3 [66] 11b-12a; SECT 4 [96-102], SECT 5 [107-109] 12b; ARTICLE II, SECT I [321-374] 14b-d; AMENDMENTS, XII 18a-c; XVII 19b-c

43 FEDERALIST: NUMBER 39, 125a-b; NUMBER 49-50 159b-162c; NUMBER 51, 164d-165a; NUMBER 52-61 165a-188d passim; NUMBER 68 205b-207a; NUMBER 84, 252b-c

43 MILL: *Liberty*, 268d-269a / *Representative Government*, 370a-406a

46 HEGEL: *Philosophy of Right*, PART III, par 308-311 102c-104a / *Philosophy of History*, INTRO, 172d-173a

2. The forms of government: their evaluation and order

2a. The distinction and comparison of good and bad forms of government

5 EURIPIDES: *Suppliants* [399-456] 261d-262b

6 HERODOTUS: *History*, BK III, 107c-108c

6 THUCYDIDES: *Peloponnesian War*, BK II, 396c-d; BK III, 432b-c; BK VI, 520b-c; BK VIII, 587a-b

7 PLATO: *Republic*, BK I, 301c-d; BK VIII–IX, 401d-421a / *Statesman*, 598b-604b / *Laws*, BK III 663d-677a esp 669d-672a, 672c; BK IV, 679c-682c; BK V, 692c-693a

9 ARISTOTLE: *Ethics*, BK VIII, CH 10-11 412c-413d / *Politics*, BK III, CH I [1275ᵃ35-ᵇ2] 472b; CH 6-7 475d-477a; CH 11 [1282ᵇ8-14] 480c; CH 15 [1286ᵇ5-7] 484d; BK IV, CH 1-10 487a-495b / *Rhetoric*, BK I, CH 8 608a-c

14 PLUTARCH: *Lycurgus-Numa* 61b,d-64a,c / *Dion*, 800c

15 TACITUS: *Annals*, BK III, 51b; BK IV, 72a-b

20 AQUINAS: *Summa Theologica*, PART I-II, Q 95, A 4, ANS 229b-230c; Q 105, A I, ANS 307d-309d

23 MACHIAVELLI: *Prince*, CH I 3a-b

23 HOBBES: *Leviathan*, PART II, 104b-109a esp 104d-105a; 114b-115a; 129b-130a; 150c-151a; 154b-c; 158b-c; PART III, 228b; PART IV, 273a-b

35 LOCKE: *Civil Government*, CH VII, SECT 90-91 44d-45c; CH X, SECT 132 55a-b

36 SWIFT: *Gulliver*, PART II, 78a-b

36 STERNE: *Tristram Shandy*, 216b

37 FIELDING: *Tom Jones*, 268c-269b

38 MONTESQUIEU: *Spirit of Laws*, BK II-III 4a-13d; BK IV, 15a-c; BK V, 25d-31b; BK VI, 33a-35a; 37d-38b; BK VIII, 54a-b; BK XI, 69a-c; BK XV, 109a-b; BK XIX, 145d

38 ROUSSEAU: *Inequality*, 359a-b / *Social Contract*, BK III, 410b-415b

42 KANT: *Pure Reason*, 113b-115a / *Science of Right*, 439c-440a; 441b-c; 450a-452a / *Judgement*, 586a-587a

43 FEDERALIST: NUMBER 10, 51c-52d; NUMBER 14, 60b-61a; NUMBER 22, 83b-d; NUMBER 39, 125a-126b; NUMBER 48, 157c

43 MILL: *Representative Government*, 332d-355b

44 BOSWELL: *Johnson*, 195c-d; 260b; 390a-b

46 HEGEL: *Philosophy of Right*, PART III, par 273 90c-92a / *Philosophy of History*, INTRO, 203b-206a,c

2b. The combination of different forms of government: the mixed constitution, the mixed regime

5 Aeschylus: *Suppliant Maidens* [359–422] 5b-6b; [600–624] 8d-9a

5 Euripides: *Suppliants* [339–358] 261b-c

6 Herodotus: *History*, bk iv, 152d-153b

6 Thucydides: *Peloponnesian War*, bk viii, 590a-b

7 Plato: *Statesman*, 598b-604b / *Laws*, bk iii, 667a-676b; bk iv, 680d-681a; bk vi, 699d-700b

9 Aristotle: *Politics*, bk ii, ch 6 [1265^{b}26–1266^{a}4] 461b-c; ch 11 [1272^{b}23]–ch 12 [1274^{a}13] 469b-470d; bk iii, ch 15–16 484b-486c esp ch 15 [1286^{b}31]–ch 16 [1287^{a}8] 485b-c; bk iv, ch 8–9 493c-494d; ch 11–12 495b-497b; bk v, ch 7 [1307^{a}5–28] 509a-b; ch 8 [1308^{b}10–1309^{a}32] 510d-511c; ch 11 [1313^{a}18–33] 515d-516a / *Rhetoric*, bk i, ch 8 [1365^{b}39–1366^{a}2] 608b

14 Plutarch: *Lycurgus*, 34b-35d / *Dion*, 800c-d

15 Tacitus: *Annals*, bk iii, 59d; bk iv, 72a; bk vi, 97b

20 Aquinas: *Summa Theologica*, part i-ii, q 95, a 4, ans 229b-230c; q 105, a 1, ans 307d-309d

23 Machiavelli: *Prince*, ch iv 7a-8a; ch xix, 27a-b; 29c-d

23 Hobbes: *Leviathan*, part ii, 103d-104b; 106d-107c; 151c-152a; part iii, 228a-b

35 Locke: *Civil Government*, ch vii, sect 94 46a-c; ch x, sect 132 55a-b; ch xi 55b-58b; ch xiii-xiv 59b-64c passim; ch xviii, sect 199-206 71a-72c; ch xix 73d-81d passim, esp sect 213 74b-c

36 Sterne: *Tristram Shandy*, 216b

37 Fielding: *Tom Jones*, 266d

38 Montesquieu: *Spirit of Laws*, bk ii, 7c-8c; bk iii, 11c-12b; 13c; bk vi, 36a-b; bk ix, 58b,d-60a; bk xi 68b,d-84d; bk xix, 142a-146a,c

38 Rousseau: *Inequality*, 357b-c / *Social Contract*, bk iii, 410c; 414d-415b; bk iv, 427a-428a

40 Gibbon: *Decline and Fall*, 24b; 26d-28b; 622d-623a; 630b,d-631a

41 Gibbon: *Decline and Fall*, 71d; 81c-d; 218c-219a; 403b-d esp 403c; 404c-d; 428a

42 Kant: *Science of Right*, 439c-440a; 441b-c; 450a-452a

43 Federalist: number 39, 125c; number 43, 141a-d; number 47, 154a-c; number 69 207a-210c passim; number 70, 213b-c; number 71, 216a-b; number 84, 252b-c

43 Mill: *Liberty*, 267d-268c / *Representative Government*, 343c-344a; 351a-c; 353d-354b; 355b-356b; 401d-402b

44 Boswell: *Johnson*, 178a-b; 255a-d; 390a-b

46 Hegel: *Philosophy of Right*, part iii, par 273 90c-92a; par 275-286 92a-97a; additions, 170-172 145d-146d / *Philosophy of History*, part iv, 368c-d

51 Tolstoy: *War and Peace*, bk vi, 238c-243d

2c. The absolute and relative evaluation of forms of government: by reference to the nature of man or to historic circumstances

Old Testament: *I Samuel*, 8—(D) *I Kings*, 8

6 Herodotus: *History*, bk iii, 107c-108d; 120b-c; bk v, 178a-180a; bk vii, 233a-c

6 Thucydides: *Peloponnesian War*, bk viii, 587a-b; 590a-b

7 Plato: *Republic*, bk iii-iv, 339b-356a; bk viii-ix 401d-427b / *Laws*, bk iii 663d-677a; bk ix, 754a-b

9 Aristotle: *Politics*, bk i, ch 12 453d-454a; bk iii, ch 15 [1286^{b}8–22] 484d-485a; ch 17 486c-487a; bk iv, ch 1 487a-488b; ch 2 [1289^{b}13–20] 488c-d; ch 12 496d-497b

14 Plutarch: *Phocion*, 605a-d

15 Tacitus: *Histories*, bk i, 193c

23 Hobbes: *Leviathan*, part ii, 104b-d; 105c-106b; 129b-130a

25 Montaigne: *Essays*, 46d

26 Shakespeare: *Julius Caesar*, act i, sc i-ii 568b,d-572c

27 Shakespeare: *Coriolanus*, act iii, sc i [131-161] 370d-371a

32 Milton: *Samson Agonistes* [241-276] 344b-345b

35 Locke: *Civil Government*, ch ii, sect 13 28a-b; ch vii, sect 90-94 44d-46c; ch viii, sect 105-112 48c-51b

36 Swift: *Gulliver*, part iii, 112a-113a; 118a-121b

38 Montesquieu: *Spirit of Laws*, bk i, 3b-c; bk iv, 15c; bk v, 29a-b; bk xiv, 107a-d; bk xvi, 118b-c; bk xvii, 122a-124d; bk xviii, 125a-c; 126b-c; bk xix, 135a-b; 135d; 140d-141a

38 Rousseau: *Inequality*, 359a-b / *Political Economy*, 371c / *Social Contract*, bk ii, 405c-d; bk iii, 407c; 409a; 410c; 415b-417c

40 Gibbon: *Decline and Fall*, 32b-34a,c esp 33c; 68b,d-69a; 90d-91d; 513b-c

41 Gibbon: *Decline and Fall*, 222d-224a; 320d-321b

42 Kant: *Pure Reason*, 114b-d / *Science of Right*, 438d-439a; 450b-d

43 Declaration of Independence: [7–23] 1a-b

43 Federalist: number 6, 40a-41a; number 10, 51c-52d; number 15, 65b-66b; number 55, 174c-d; number 85, 257a-c

43 Mill: *Liberty*, 272a / *Representative Government*, 327b,d-355b passim; 366a-369b; 436b-437a

44 Boswell: *Johnson*, 195c-d

46 Hegel: *Philosophy of Right*, part iii, par 273-274 90c-92a; additions, 165-166 145a-c / *Philosophy of History*, intro, 173c-175c; 203b-206a,c; part i, 207d-209a; 243b-c; part ii, 271c-d; 273d-274a; part iii, 285b-d; 300a-301c; part iv, 344a-c

48 Melville: *Moby Dick*, 107a-b

52 Dostoevsky: *Brothers Karamazov*, bk v, 127b-137c passim

54 Freud: *New Introductory Lectures*, 883d-884c

43 MILL: *Representative Government*, 355b-424c passim

46 HEGEL: *Philosophy of Right*, PART III, par 272–273 89d-92a; ADDITIONS, 164 144c-145a / *Philosophy of History*, PART IV, 364d-365a; 365c-d

3a. The separation and coordination of the several powers: usurpations and infringements by one branch of government upon another

7 PLATO: *Laws*, BK III, 671a-672a; BK IX, 754c-d

9 ARISTOTLE: *Politics*, BK IV, CH 14–16 498b-502a,c / *Athenian Constitution*, CH 45, par 1 573d

14 PLUTARCH: *Solon*, 70d-71c / *Poplicola-Solon*, 86d-87a / *Agesilaus*, 482a-c / *Agis*, 650b-656d / *Cleomenes*, 660b-661a

15 TACITUS: *Annals*, BK I, 1a-2a; 3a-b; BK IV, 65a-c; BK XI, 101c; BK XIII, 126c-d

20 AQUINAS: *Summa Theologica*, PART I-II, Q 95, A 1, REP 2–3 226c-227c

23 HOBBES: *Leviathan*, PART II, 103d-104a; 150b; 151c-152a

35 LOCKE: *Civil Government*, CH II–III 25d-29d passim; CH VII, SECT 90–94 44d-46c; CH VIII, SECT 107 49b-d; CH XII–XIV 58c-64c; CH XVII–XVIII 70c-73c; CH XIX, SECT 212–219 74a-75c

38 MONTESQUIEU: *Spirit of Laws*, BK II, 6b-8c; BK V, 29a; BK VI, 36a-37b; BK XI 68b,d-84d esp 69d-75a; BK XIX, 142b-143a; BK XXVIII, 259b

38 ROUSSEAU: *Social Contract*, BK II, 397b-c; BK III, 406d-407a; 410d-411a; 415a-b; 422b-c; 423a; 423d; BK IV, 432b-433a

39 SMITH: *Wealth of Nations*, BK V, 311c-315a,c esp 314c-315a,c

40 GIBBON: *Decline and Fall*, 24b,d-28b esp 25a-26a, 27a-b; 154a-b; 343c

41 GIBBON: *Decline and Fall*, 74b-75a; 75d-78b esp 76a; 586c-587a

42 KANT: *Science of Right*, 436b; 437d-439a; 440a-441b; 450d-452a esp 451d-452a

43 DECLARATION OF INDEPENDENCE: [7–79] 1a-2b passim

43 ARTICLES OF CONFEDERATION: IX [192–197] 7b

43 CONSTITUTION OF THE U.S.: ARTICLE I, SECT 2 [45–47] 11d; SECT 3 [81–95] 12a-b; SECT 7 [156–191] 12d-13a; ARTICLE II, SECT 1 [335–374] 14b-d; [383–393] 14d-15a; SECT 2 [421]–SECT 4 [458] 15b-c

43 FEDERALIST: NUMBER 16, 68b-c; NUMBER 22, 83d-84b; NUMBER 27, 96a-b; NUMBER 47–49 153c-161b; NUMBER 51 162d-165a; NUMBER 52, 165c-167b; NUMBER 62, 189d-191c passim; NUMBER 64–67 195b-205b esp NUMBER 65–66 198a-203a; NUMBER 71, 215a-216b; NUMBER 73 218d-221c; NUMBER 75–77 222d-229d; NUMBER 78, 230a-232a; NUMBER 81, 237d-239c; NUMBER 82, 242d-243a

43 MILL: *Liberty*, 322a-d / *Representative Government*, 350d-351a; 353b-d; 355b-363a; 365b-366a; 401d-402b

44 BOSWELL: *Johnson*, 178b-c; 255d; 411a-b

46 HEGEL: *Philosophy of Right*, PART III, par 272–273 89d-92a; par 297 90b; par 300 100b; par 302 101a-c; par 312–313 104a-b; ADDITIONS, 163–164 144c-145a; 174 146d-147b; 178–179 147d-148a / *Philosophy of History*, PART IV, 365c-d

3b. The relation of the civil to the military power

6 HERODOTUS: *History*, BK II, 79a-c

6 THUCYDIDES: *Peloponnesian War*, BK VII, 551b-d; BK VIII, 582a-583c; 585d-586b; 587a-589a; 590a-c passim

7 PLATO: *Republic*, BK III–V, 340b-368d

9 ARISTOTLE: *Politics*, BK III, CH 7 [1279^{a}37–^{b}3] 476d; BK IV, CH 13 [1297^{b}10–28] 497d-498a; BK VI, CH 8 [1322^{a}29–^{b}6] 526a-b; BK VII, CH 9 [1329^{a}2–17] 533b-c

15 TACITUS: *Annals*, BK I, 6b-15a; BK IV, 64a-b / *Histories*, BK I, 190b-c; 194a-c; 195c-197d esp 197c-d; 210d-212d; BK II, 239c-240a

23 MACHIAVELLI: *Prince*, CH XII, 18a; CH XIV 21b-22a

23 HOBBES: *Leviathan*, PART II, 103b; 159a-c

35 LOCKE: *Civil Government*, CH XII, SECT 145–148 58d-59b; CH XVI 65d-70c

36 SWIFT: *Gulliver*, PART II, 80a-b

38 MONTESQUIEU: *Spirit of Laws*, BK V, 30b; 31c-32b; BK XI, 74b-d; BK XIX, 143c

38 ROUSSEAU: *Inequality*, 361a-b / *Social Contract*, BK III, 424b

39 SMITH: *Wealth of Nations*, BK V, 301a-309a,c esp 307d-308c

40 GIBBON: *Decline and Fall*, 25d-26d; 30a-b; 42b,d-43b; 50b-51a; 63a-64d; 68c; 76b-77b; 245d-246d esp 246c

43 DECLARATION OF INDEPENDENCE: [60–61] 2a; [65–67] 2b; [80–94] 2b-3a

43 ARTICLES OF CONFEDERATION: VI [107–123] 6b-c; VII 6d; IX [290–298] 8a; [318–365] 8b-d passim

43 CONSTITUTION OF THE U.S.: ARTICLE I, SECT 8 [226–242] 13b-c; ARTICLE II, SECT 2 [409–413] 15a; AMENDMENTS, III 17b

43 FEDERALIST: NUMBER 8, 45b-c; 46a-47a; NUMBER 24–29 87b-101a passim; NUMBER 46, 152b-153a; NUMBER 74, 221c-d

43 MILL: *Representative Government*, 409d; 425c-d

44 BOSWELL: *Johnson*, 281d-282a

46 HEGEL: *Philosophy of Right*, PART III, par 326 107d-108a; par 329 108c; ADDITIONS, 163 144c / *Philosophy of History*, PART IV, 325a-b

51 TOLSTOY: *War and Peace*, BK III, 138d; 144c; 146d; 153d-155a; BK V, 209a-c; BK IX, 346a-365c passim, esp 353a, 355b, 361b-d; BK X, 404c-405a; BK XII, 533a-537b esp 535d-537b; BK XIII, 565c-566d; BK XIV, 610d-611a; BK XV, 627d-630a

(3. The powers, branches, or departments of government: enumerations, definitions, and orderings of these several powers.)

3c. The legislative department of government: the making of law

7 PLATO: *Republic*, BK IV, 344a-346a / *Theaetetus*, 531a-b / *Statesman*, 599c-600d / *Laws*, BK III, 666b-c; BK IV, 679c-680d; 684b-686c; BK VI, 705d-706c; BK IX, 745c-746a; 754a-d; BK XI, 782a-b / *Seventh Letter*, 807a-b

9 ARISTOTLE: *Ethics*, BK X, CH 9 434a-436a,c / *Politics*, BK IV, CH 14 498b-499c

15 TACITUS: *Annals*, BK III, 51b

20 AQUINAS: *Summa Theologica*, PART I-II, Q 90 205a-208b; Q 91, A 3 209d-210c; Q 92 213c-215a,c; QQ 95-97 226b-239b

23 HOBBES: *Leviathan*, PART II, 103a; 130d-131a; 131d-132a; 133d-134a; 151c-152a; PART IV, 273d

29 CERVANTES: *Don Quixote*, PART II, 363d-364a

30 BACON: *Advancement of Learning*, 94d-95b

33 PASCAL: *Pensées*, 294 225b-226b

35 LOCKE: *Toleration*, 11b; 16a-c / *Civil Government*, CH VII, SECT 88-89 44c-d; CH IX, SECT 127-CH X, SECT 132 54a-55b; CH XI, SECT 134-CH XII, SECT 143 55b-58d; CH XIII, SECT 150 59d; CH XIX, SECT 212-217 74a-75a

36 SWIFT: *Gulliver*, PART II, 73a-74b; 78b

38 MONTESQUIEU: *Spirit of Laws*, BK II, 6b; BK XI, 69d; 71a-72b passim; BK XXIX 262a-269a,c

38 ROUSSEAU: *Inequality*, 324c-d / *Political Economy*, 368c-369a; 372a-b / *Social Contract*, BK II, 399b-402a; BK III, 419d-420a

40 GIBBON: *Decline and Fall*, 151b-156a; 616d-617b; 624b-c

41 GIBBON: *Decline and Fall*, 79d-80b; 96a-d; 108a-c

42 KANT: *Intro. Metaphysic of Morals*, 393c / *Science of Right*, 397a-b; 436b-c; 438b-c; 450d-452a esp 451c-452a

43 DECLARATION OF INDEPENDENCE: [29-47] 1b-2a; [62-64] [72-79] 2b

43 CONSTITUTION OF THE U.S.: ARTICLE I, SECT 1-9 11a-14a

43 FEDERALIST: NUMBER 10, 50d-51b; NUMBER 15, 64b; NUMBER 33, 107d-109b; NUMBER 44, 145c-146d; NUMBER 51, 163c-d; NUMBER 52-66 165a-203a esp NUMBER 53, 167d-168b, NUMBER 64, 197a-b; NUMBER 70, 212b; NUMBER 75, 223a-c; NUMBER 81, 239a-b

43 MILL: *Representative Government*, 355b-409c passim

44 BOSWELL: *Johnson*, 255d

46 HEGEL: *Philosophy of Right*, PART III, par 211 70a-c; par 298-314 99c-104b / *Philosophy of History*, PART II, 271d-272a; PART IV, 364d-365a; 365c-d

3c(1) The powers and duties of the legislature

7 PLATO: *Republic*, BK IV, 344a-346a / *Theaetetus*, 531a-b

9 ARISTOTLE: *Politics*, BK IV, CH 14 [1298ᵃ4-ᵇ11] 498b-499a

35 LOCKE: *Toleration*, 16a-c / *Civil Government*, CH IV, SECT 21 29d; CH XI, SECT 134-CH XII, SECT 143 55b-58d; CH XIII SECT 150-153 59d-60c; CH XIX, SECT 212-217 74a-75a; SECT 221-222 75d-76c

36 SWIFT: *Gulliver*, PART IV, 167a-b

38 MONTESQUIEU: *Spirit of Laws*, BK II, 6b; BK V, 21d-22c; BK XI, 69d-75a

40 GIBBON: *Decline and Fall*, 25d; 27d-28a; 130c-131a

42 KANT: *Science of Right*, 451c-452a

43 DECLARATION OF INDEPENDENCE: [29-47] 1b-2a

43 ARTICLES OF CONFEDERATION: IX 7a-9a passim

43 CONSTITUTION OF THE U.S.: ARTICLE I, SECT 1-9 11a-14a; ARTICLE II, SECT 2 [421-435] 15b; ARTICLE III, SECT 3 [507]-ARTICLE IV, SECT I [518] 16a; ARTICLE IV, SECT 3-ARTICLE V 16b-c; ARTICLE VI [591-599] 16d; AMENDMENTS, I 17a; XII-XX 18a-20a,c passim

43 FEDERALIST: NUMBER 23-36 85a-117d passim; NUMBER 41-46 132a-153b passim; NUMBER 52-66 165a-203a passim, esp NUMBER 53, 167d-168b; NUMBER 75, 223a-224a; NUMBER 77, 227b-229b; NUMBER 78, 230d-231c; NUMBER 81, 237d-240b; NUMBER 82 242b-244a passim; NUMBER 83, 244c-245c

43 MILL: *Representative Government*, 355b-363a; 365c-366a; 401a-409c passim; 417c-424c; 431a-c

44 BOSWELL: *Johnson*, 255d; 364c-365a; 370a

46 HEGEL: *Philosophy of Right*, PART III, par 298 99c; par 309-311 103b-104a

3c(2) Legislative institutions and procedures

9 ARISTOTLE: *Politics*, BK IV, CH 14 [1298ᵇ12-1299ᵃ2] 499a-c / *Athenian Constitution*, CH 43-44 572d-573d

14 PLUTARCH: *Lycurgus*, 34d-35c; 45c-46a / *Solon*, 71b-c

15 TACITUS: *Histories*, BK IV, 267d-268c

35 LOCKE: *Civil Government*, CH XI, SECT 138 57b-c; CH XII, SECT 147 59a-b; CH XIII, SECT 153-158 60b-62b; CH XIV, SECT 167-168 64a-c; CH XIX, SECT 215 74d

36 SWIFT: *Gulliver*, PART II, 73a-74b; PART IV, 167a-b

36 STERNE: *Tristram Shandy*, 435b-436a

38 MONTESQUIEU: *Spirit of Laws*, BK II, 4a-6b; BK V, 22a-c; BK XI, 71a-d; 72b-d

38 ROUSSEAU: *Social Contract*, BK III, 423d

40 GIBBON: *Decline and Fall*, 27d-28a

41 GIBBON: *Decline and Fall*, 71d-74b passim, esp 71d-72a, 73a-b; 587a

43 DECLARATION OF INDEPENDENCE: [29-47] 1b-2a; [62-64] [72-79] 2b

43 CONSTITUTION OF THE U.S.: ARTICLE I, SECT 1-9 11a-14a; ARTICLE IV, SECT I 16a; ARTICLE V 16c; ARTICLE VI [591-599] 16d; AMEND-

MENTS, XIV, SECT 2 18d-19a; XVII 19b-c; XX, SECT 1-2 19d-20a

43 FEDERALIST: NUMBER 15, 66a; NUMBER 22, 82a-83a; 84c-d; NUMBER 37, 120d-121a; NUMBER 51, 163c-d; NUMBER 52-66 165a-203a passim

43 MILL: *Representative Government*, 355b-362c; 370a-409c passim; 417c-424c; 431c-d

44 BOSWELL: *Johnson*, 176a-b

46 HEGEL: *Philosophy of Right*, PART III, par 312-314 104a-b

51 TOLSTOY: *War and Peace*, BK VI, 238c-243d; 260a-262a

3d. The judicial department of government: the application of law

5 ARISTOPHANES: *Wasps* 507a-525d

7 PLATO: *Statesman*, 605b-c

9 ARISTOTLE: *Politics*, BK III, CH 16 485b-486c; BK IV, CH 16 501c-502a,c / *Rhetoric*, BK I, CH 15 619d-622d

20 AQUINAS: *Summa Theologica*, PART I-II, Q 105, A 2, REP 7 309d-316a

23 HOBBES: *Leviathan*, PART II, 103a-b; 123b-d; 132a-136b; 148a

27 SHAKESPEARE: *Measure for Measure* 174a-204d

29 CERVANTES: *Don Quixote*, PART II, 332d-333b; 340d-343a; 353b-356d; 361a-d

30 BACON: *Advancement of Learning*, 94d-95b

35 LOCKE: *Civil Government*, CH II, SECT 13 28a-b; CH III, SECT 19-20 29b-d; CH VII, SECT 87-94 44a-46c; CH IX, SECT 125 54a; CH XI, SECT 136 56c-d

36 SWIFT: *Gulliver*, PART II, 73b-75a; PART IV, 152b-154a

36 STERNE: *Tristram Shandy*, 266a-b

38 MONTESQUIEU: *Spirit of Laws*, BK II, 8b-c; BK VI, 33a-35c; BK XI, 69d-70a; 80c-83c; BK XX, 151d

39 SMITH: *Wealth of Nations*, BK V, 309a-315a,c

40 GIBBON: *Decline and Fall*, 27d-28a

42 KANT: *Science of Right*, 438c-d

43 CONSTITUTION OF THE U.S.: ARTICLE III 15c-16a

43 FEDERALIST: NUMBER 17, 69d-70a; NUMBER 22, 83d-84b; NUMBER 78-83 229d-251a esp NUMBER 82, 243b, NUMBER 83, 244c-245d

43 MILL: *Utilitarianism*, 474d

46 HEGEL: *Philosophy of Right*, PART III, par 209-228 69d-75b; ADDITIONS, 141-142 139c-d / *Philosophy of History*, PART I, 250d-251a

3d(1) The powers and duties of the judiciary

OLD TESTAMENT: *Exodus*, 18:13-26 / *Deuteronomy*, 1:16-17; 16:18-20 / *Ezra*, 7:25-26—(D) *I Esdras*, 7:25-26

7 PLATO: *Apology*, 200a-c; 208c-209b / *Statesman*, 605b-c

9 ARISTOTLE: *Rhetoric*, BK I, CH 1 [1354^{a}13-1355^{a}3] 593b-594a; CH 15 619d-622d

14 PLUTARCH: *Solon*, 70d-71b

18 AUGUSTINE: *City of God*, BK XIX, CH 6 514b-515a

20 AQUINAS: *Summa Theologica*, PART I-II, Q 105, A 2, REP 7 309d-316a; PART III SUPPL, Q 89, A 2 esp REP 3 1006b-1007c

35 LOCKE: *Civil Government*, CH IX, SECT 125 54a; CH XI, SECT 136 56c-d

36 SWIFT: *Gulliver*, PART II, 73b-75a; PART IV, 152b-154a

37 FIELDING: *Tom Jones*, 65c-66a; 135c-d

38 MONTESQUIEU: *Spirit of Laws*, BK II, 8b-c; BK XI, 73b-d

40 GIBBON: *Decline and Fall*, 91d; 243b; 343a-c

41 GIBBON: *Decline and Fall*, 94c-95c; 403c-d

43 ARTICLES OF CONFEDERATION: IX [192-197] 7b

43 CONSTITUTION OF THE U.S.: ARTICLE III, SECT 2 15c-d; ARTICLE VI [583-590] 16d; AMENDMENTS, IV-VIII 17b-d; XI 18a

43 FEDERALIST: NUMBER 17, 69d-70a; NUMBER 22, 83d-84b; NUMBER 51, 162d-163a; NUMBER 65, 199a-d; NUMBER 73, 221b-c; NUMBER 78-83 229d-251a esp NUMBER 78, 231b, NUMBER 83, 245b

43 MILL: *Representative Government*, 413d-414d; 421d-422c; 430a-431a / *Utilitarianism*, 466d-467a

44 BOSWELL: *Johnson*, 251d-252b

46 HEGEL: *Philosophy of Right*, PART III, par 219 72d-73a; par 221 73b; par 225-226 73d-74b; ADDITIONS, 139 139b; 141-142 139c-d

3d(2) Judicial institutions and procedures

OLD TESTAMENT: *Exodus*, 18:13-26; 23:1-3,6-9 / *Numbers*, 35:9-34 / *Deuteronomy*, 1:12-17; 17:2-13; 19; 25:1-3 / *I Samuel*, 8:5-6,19-22; 9:15-17—(D) *I Kings*, 8:5-6,19-22; 9:15-17

NEW TESTAMENT: *Matthew*, 26:46-27:26 / *Acts*, 5:16-40; 21:26-23:24

5 AESCHYLUS: *Eumenides* 81a-91d

6 HERODOTUS: *History*, BK III, 95d-96b

7 PLATO: *Apology*, 209b-210b / *Laws*, BK VI, 704c-705c; BK XII, 786b-788c; 792a-793a

9 ARISTOTLE: *Politics*, BK II, CH 8 [1267^{b}36-1268^{a}6] 463d; [1268^{b}5-23] 464c; CH 12 [1273^{b}36-1274^{a}21] 470c-d; BK IV, CH 16 501c-502a,c / *Athenian Constitution*, CH 45 573d-574a; CH 48 574d-575b; CH 52-53 576b-577b; CH 57-59 579b-580c; CH 63-69 581b-584a,c / *Rhetoric*, BK I, CH 15 619d-622d

15 TACITUS: *Annals*, BK II, 30b-c; BK XII, 123b-c; BK XIII, 132c-d

20 AQUINAS: *Summa Theologica*, PART I-II, Q 105, A 2, REP 7 309d-316a

22 CHAUCER: *Physician's Tale* [12,055-146] 368a-369b

23 HOBBES: *Leviathan*, PART II, 123b-d

24 RABELAIS: *Gargantua and Pantagruel*, BK III, 204c-215c

26 SHAKESPEARE: *Merchant of Venice*, ACT IV, SC I 425c-430b

30 BACON: *Advancement of Learning*, 94d-95b

(3d. *The judicial department of government: the application of law.* 3d(2) *Judicial institutions and procedures.*)

36 SWIFT: *Gulliver*, PART I, 37a-b; PART II, 73b-75a; PART IV, 152b-154a

36 STERNE: *Tristram Shandy*, 266a-b

37 FIELDING:*Tom Jones*, 8c-10c; 65c-66a; 135c-d; 176d-177d; 217a-c; 267d-268b

38 MONTESQUIEU: *Spirit of Laws*, BK II, 8b-c; BK VI, 33a-37d; BK XI, 70c-71a; 73b-d

39 SMITH: *Wealth of Nations*, BK V, 311c-315a,c

40 GIBBON: *Decline and Fall*, 243a-245d passim, esp 244d-245b; 251b-d; 617a-618d

41 GIBBON: *Decline and Fall*, 73d-74b; 94c-95c; 403c-404d; 458c-d; 586c-d

43 DECLARATION OF INDEPENDENCE: [52-55] 2a; [70-71] 2b

43 ARTICLES OF CONFEDERATION: IX [198-274] 7b-8a

43 CONSTITUTION OF THE U.S.: ARTICLE III, SECT 1 15c; SECT 2 [485-499] 15d; ARTICLE III, SECT 3 [507]-ARTICLE IV, SECT 1 [518] 16a; ARTICLE IV, SECT 2 [522-528] 16a-b; AMENDMENTS, IV-VIII 17b-d

43 FEDERALIST: NUMBER 22, 83d-84b; NUMBER 51, 162d-163a; NUMBER 65, 199a-c; NUMBER 78-83 229d-251a passim

43 MILL: *Representative Government*, 336c-d; 337b-c; 413d-414d; 421d-422c

44 BOSWELL: *Johnson*, 255a-b

46 HEGEL: *Philosophy of Right*, PART III, par 223 73c-d / *Philosophy of History*, PART IV, 326b-c

51 TOLSTOY: *War and Peace*, BK XII, 547b-d

52 DOSTOEVSKY: *Brothers Karamazov*, BK IX 235b,d-271d passim; BK XII 348b,d-401d

3e. The executive department of government: the enforcement of law; administrative decrees

9 ARISTOTLE: *Politics*, BK IV, CH 15 499c-501c

35 LOCKE: *Toleration*, 3a / *Civil Government*, CH II, SECT 7-13 26c-28b; CH VII, SECT 88-89 44c-d; CH IX, SECT 126-131 54a-d; CH XII, SECT 144-CH XIV, SECT 168 58d-64c; CH XVIII, SECT 203-210 72a-73c; CH XIX, SECT 218-219 75a-c

36 SWIFT: *Gulliver*, PART IV, 157b-158a

38 MONTESQUIEU: *Spirit of Laws*, BK XI, 69d-70a; 72b; 80a-c

38 ROUSSEAU: *Social Contract*, BK III, 414d-415a; 423a; 424a-b

42 KANT: *Science of Right*, 438a-b

43 CONSTITUTION OF THE U.S.: ARTICLE II 14b-15c

43 FEDERALIST: NUMBER 15, 64b-66b; NUMBER 16 66c-68d passim; NUMBER 21, 78b-d; NUMBER 27-29, 94d-99b; NUMBER 48, 157c; NUMBER 67-77 203b-229d passim

43 MILL: *Representative Government*, 350d-351a; 356b-359a; 409d-417c

44 BOSWELL: *Johnson*, 178b-c

46 HEGEL: *Philosophy of Right*, PART III, par 287-

297 97a-99b; ADDITIONS, 174 146d-147b / *Philosophy of History*, PART IV, 325c-d; 364d-365a

3e(1) The powers and duties of the executive

23 HOBBES: *Leviathan*, PART II, 101a-104d; 122b-124b; 130d; 153a-159c

29 CERVANTES: *Don Quixote*, PART I, 193a; PART II, 331a-336a

35 LOCKE: *Civil Government*, CH II, SECT 10-11 27b-d; CH XII, SECT 144-148 58d-59b; CH XIII, SECT 154-CH XIV, SECT 168 60c-64c; CH XIX, SECT 218-219 75a-c; SECT 221-222 75d-76c

36 SWIFT: *Gulliver*, PART IV, 157b-158a

38 MONTESQUIEU: *Spirit of Laws*, BK VI, 36a-37a; 43c-d; BK XI, 72b-73b; 73d-74c

38 ROUSSEAU: *Social Contract*, BK IV, 433a-434b

39 SMITH: *Wealth of Nations*, BK V, 319b-320a

40 GIBBON: *Decline and Fall*, 25d-26a; 26d-27c; 243b

41 GIBBON: *Decline and Fall*, 586d

42 KANT: *Science of Right*, 448a-b

43 DECLARATION OF INDEPENDENCE: [28-61] 1b-2a

43 ARTICLES OF CONFEDERATION: IX [299-310] 8b; X 9a

43 CONSTITUTION OF THE U.S.: ARTICLE I, SECT 7 [156-191] 12d-13a; ARTICLE II 14b-15c

43 FEDERALIST: NUMBER 8, 45b-c; NUMBER 48, 157c; NUMBER 51, 163d; NUMBER 66, 201a-203a; NUMBER 67-77 203b-229d passim

43 MILL: *Liberty*, 319d-323a,c / *Representative Government*, 356b-359a; 409d-417c; 421c-422c

46 HEGEL: *Philosophy of Right*, PART III, par 290-296 97d-99b / *Philosophy of History*, PART IV, 365c-d

3e(2) Administrative institutions and procedures

OLD TESTAMENT: *Daniel*, 6:1-2

7 PLATO: *Laws*, BK VI, 700d-704c

9 ARISTOTLE: *Politics*, BK IV, CH 15 [1299ᵃ31-1300ᵇ4] 500a-501b; BK VI, CH 8 525b-526d / *Athenian Constitution*, CH 43-52 572d-576d; CH 54-61 577c-581b

15 TACITUS: *Annals*, BK I, 22b; BK VI, 88d-89a

23 MACHIAVELLI: *Prince*, CH XXII-XXIII 33a-34b

23 HOBBES: *Leviathan*, PART II, 122b-123a; 123d

38 MONTESQUIEU: *Spirit of Laws*, BK V, 31b-33a,c; BK XXVI, 224d-225a

38 ROUSSEAU: *Social Contract*, BK II, 403a-404a

40 GIBBON: *Decline and Fall*, 25d-27c passim; 240b-246d; 248d-251a

41 GIBBON: *Decline and Fall*, 317d-318b; 563d-564b; 586c-587a

43 ARTICLES OF CONFEDERATION: IV [37-44] 5d; IX [299-310] 8b; IX [368]-X [395] 8d-9a

43 CONSTITUTION OF THE U.S.: ARTICLE II 14b-15c; AMENDMENTS, XII 18a-c; XX 19d-20a,c

43 FEDERALIST: NUMBER 13, 59b-c; NUMBER 66, 201a-203a; NUMBER 67-77 203b-229d passim; NUMBER 84, 255a-b

(5. *The relation of governments to one another: sovereign princes or states as in a condition of anarchy.*)

5a. Foreign policy: the making of treaties; the conduct of war and peace

OLD TESTAMENT: *Numbers*, 31 / *Deuteronomy*, 2:26–37; 9:1–4; 20 / *Joshua*, 9—(D) *Josue*, 9 / *II Samuel*, 3:12–21—(D) *II Kings*, 3:12–21 / *I Kings*, 5:1–12—(D) *III Kings*, 5:1–12

APOCRYPHA: *I Maccabees*, 8; 10; 12:1–23; 13:34–41; 14:16–24; 15:1–9,15–27—(D) OT, *I Machabees*, 8; 10; 12:1–23; 13:34–41; 14:16–24; 15:1–9,15–27 / *II Maccabees*, 11:16–38—(D) OT, *II Machabees*, 11:16–38

5 EURIPIDES: *Suppliants* 258a–269a,c esp [399–598] 261d–263c

5 ARISTOPHANES: *Acharnians* [61–173] 455d–457b; [497–556] 460d–461c / *Peace* [601–692] 532d–534a / *Lysistrata* 583a–599a,c esp [486–613] 589a–591a, [1072–1321] 596d–599a,c / *Ecclesiazusae* [193–203] 617b

6 HERODOTUS: *History*, BK I, 6a-b; 15d-16a; BK IV, 144b-d; BK V, 175b-c; BK VI, 193b; 206b-d; BK VII, 239a-247c passim; BK VIII, 286b-287d; BK IX, 289a-290b; 310d-311a

6 THUCYDIDES: *Peloponnesian War*, BK I, 353d; 360c-d; 368c-d; 371b-372d; 378a-380d; BK III, 418d-420c; 425a-428d; 430c; 432b-c; BK IV, 450d-452d; 457c-d; 461b-463a; 468a-469b; 476a-477a; BK V, 486c-500c; 502d-508a,c esp 504c-508a,c; BK VI, 529b-533a; BK VIII, 568a-c; 572c-573a; 578b-579a

7 PLATO: *Republic*, BK II, 318c-319a / *Critias*, 485a-b / *Laws*, BK III, 667c-668d

9 ARISTOTLE: *Politics*, BK II, CH 6 [1265ª18–27] 460c; CH 7 [1267ª18–21] 462d-463a; BK III, CH 9 [1280ª35–ᵇ12] 478a-b; CH 13 [1284ª38–ᵇ3] 482c; BK VII, CH 2 [1324ª35–1325ª15] 528b-529a; CH 6 531b-d; CH 14 [1333ᵇ10–1334ª10] 538c-d / *Rhetoric*, BK I, CH 4 [1359ᵇ33–1360ª 18] 600a-c

13 VIRGIL: *Aeneid*, BK XII [172–211] 358b-359b

14 PLUTARCH: *Romulus*, 21a-27c / *Numa Pompilius*, 55c-56a / *Pericles* 121a-141a,c / *Nicias*, 427a-428c / *Aratus*, 834d

15 TACITUS: *Annals*, BK II, 34d-35c / *Histories*, BK IV, 286c-287c

18 AUGUSTINE: *City of God*, BK XIX, CH 7 515a-c

20 AQUINAS: *Summa Theologica*, PART I-II, Q 105, A 3 316a-318b

23 MACHIAVELLI: *Prince*, CH XXI, 32a-d

23 HOBBES: *Leviathan*, PART II, 121b-c; 159c

24 RABELAIS: *Gargantua and Pantagruel*, BK I, 36d-38a; BK IV, 276a-d

26 SHAKESPEARE: *1st Henry VI*, ACT V, SC IV [94–175] 30c-31b / *2nd Henry VI*, ACT I, SC I [1–74] 33b,d-34c / *King John*, ACT II, SC I [416–560] 384a-385c / *2nd Henry IV*, ACT IV, SC II 489d-491b / *Henry V*, ACT V, SC II 563b-567a,c

30 BACON: *New Atlantis*, 204d-205a

35 LOCKE: *Civil Government*, CH V, SECT 45 34d-

35a; CH XII, SECT 145–148 58d-59b; CH XVI 65d-70c passim; CH XIX, SECT 211 73d-74a

36 SWIFT: *Gulliver*, PART I, 21b-25b; PART II, 75a-b; 77b-78b

36 STERNE: *Tristram Shandy*, 354a-355a; 449b-453a

38 MONTESQUIEU: *Spirit of Laws*, BK I, 2d-3b; BK IX-X, 58b,d-62b; BK X, 63d-64a; BK XXVI, 223c-224a

38 ROUSSEAU: *Inequality*, 325c-d; 355c / *Political Economy*, 380a-b / *Social Contract*, BK I, 390a-c; BK II, 403c-404a

39 SMITH: *Wealth of Nations*, BK V, 319b-c

40 GIBBON: *Decline and Fall*, 4a-b; 83b-85a esp 84d-85a; 95b-96a; 103c-d; 119a-c; 150d-152c; 174d-175b; 378b-d; 402b-404b; 431d-432d; 433d-435a,c; 491d-492b; 495d-496b; 503d-507c esp 504d-506a; 535d-537a,c; 543a-c

41 GIBBON: *Decline and Fall*, 48d-49c; 283d-284a; 428a-d; 503a-c

42 KANT: *Science of Right*, 452c-d; 454a-455b

43 ARTICLES OF CONFEDERATION: 5a-9d

43 CONSTITUTION OF THE U.S.: ARTICLE I, SECT 8 [201–203] [223–225] 13b; SECT 10 [296–298] 14a; [314–320] 14b; ARTICLE II, SECT 2 [421–435] 15b

43 FEDERALIST: NUMBER 4–8 35a-47a; NUMBER 9, 47c-49c; NUMBER 11 53b-56b; NUMBER 15, 64c-65a; NUMBER 16, 66c-68a; NUMBER 22, 80d-81c; 83b-d; NUMBER 24, 88d-89b; NUMBER 25, 89c-91b; NUMBER 34, 110a-111b; NUMBER 41, 132d-133b; NUMBER 42, 136b-138c; NUMBER 43, 142d; 143b-d; NUMBER 44, 144a-145c; NUMBER 62, 190d-191a; NUMBER 63, 191d-192a; NUMBER 64 195b-198a; NUMBER 75 222d-225a passim; NUMBER 80, 235b-236c; NUMBER 81, 240b-c; NUMBER 83, 248b-c; NUMBER 84, 254b-c

43 MILL: *Representative Government*, 428b-433b passim; 434a-436b

46 HEGEL: *Philosophy of Right*, PART III, par 321–329 106c-108c; par 332–337 109a-110a; ADDITIONS, 153 141d; 188 149b-c / *Philosophy of History*, PART II, 278c-279b; PART III, 297a-d; 299a-c; PART IV, 343b-c; 357c-358b; 359c-360a

48 MELVILLE: *Moby Dick*, 292a-295a

51 TOLSTOY: *War and Peace*, BK II, 83d-86a; BK V, 204a-206c; 208d-209a; 232a-234a,c; BK VIII, 307d-309c; BK IX, 344b-355c; BK XIII, 565a-b; 572b; 573d-574a; 582a; BK XV, 629b-630a; EPILOGUE I, 645a-646c; 649c-650b

5b. The government of dependencies: colonial government; the government of conquered peoples

OLD TESTAMENT: *Joshua*, 9 esp 9:18–27—(D) *Josue*, 9 esp 9:18–27 / *I Kings*, 9:20–23—(D) *III Kings*, 9:20–23 / *II Kings*, 23:30–35; 24:12–16; 25:5–30—(D) *IV Kings*, 23:30–35; 24:12–16; 25:5–30 / *II Chronicles*, 8:7–8—(D) *II Paralipomenon*, 8:7–8

APOCRYPHA: *I Maccabees*, 8:1–13—(*D*) OT, *I Machabees*, 8:1–13 / *II Maccabees*, 5:11–7:42 —(*D*) OT, *II Machabees*, 5:11–7:42

NEW TESTAMENT: *Acts*, 16:19–40; 21–28 passim

5 AESCHYLUS: *Persians* [852–908] 24b-d

5 ARISTOPHANES: *Lysistrata* [565–586] 590b-d

6 HERODOTUS: *History*, BK I, 31d-32a; 35c-36a; BK III, 109d-111b

6 THUCYDIDES: *Peloponnesian War*, BK I, 353d; 368b-369a; BK II, 403c-404a; BK III, 425a-428d; BK V, 504c-507c; BK VIII, 579d-580b

7 PLATO: *Laws*, BK VI, 698c-d

9 ARISTOTLE: *Politics*, BK III, CH 13 [1284ª36–ᵇ3] 482c; BK V, CH 7 [1307ᵇ19–24] 509d; BK VII, CH 2 [1324ª35–1325ª15] 528b-529a; CH 14 [1333ᵇ10–1334ª10] 538c-d

13 VIRGIL: *Aeneid*, BK I [254–296] 110a-111a; BK VI [845–853] 233b-234a; BK VIII [714–731] 278a-b

14 PLUTARCH: *Lycurgus*, 47d-48c / *Lucullus*, 409b-410d

15 TACITUS: *Annals*, BK II, 39d-40c; BK XI, 104a-c; 106a-d; BK XII, 122a-c; BK XIII, 139c-140d; BK XV, 162c-163a / *Histories*, BK I, 191d-192a; BK IV, 290a-d

18 AUGUSTINE: *City of God*, BK I, PREF 129a-d; BK IV, CH 14–15 196b-197a; BK V, CH 12 216d-219b; CH 17 221b-222a; BK XIX, CH 21, 524c-d

23 MACHIAVELLI: *Prince*, CH III–VIII 3c-14c; CH XX 30a-31c

23 HOBBES: *Leviathan*, PART II, 106d-107c; 108d-109c; 110b-111a; 119a-c; 126d-127a; 131c; CONCLUSION, 280b-281a

24 RABELAIS: *Gargantua and Pantagruel*, BK III, 131b,d-133b

29 CERVANTES: *Don Quixote*, PART I, 40d

32 MILTON: *Samson Agonistes* [241–276] 344b-345b

35 LOCKE: *Toleration*, 13c-d; 14c-15a / *Civil Government*, CH IV, SECT 22–23 30a-b; CH VII, SECT 85 43c-d; CH XV, SECT 172 65b-c; CH XVI 65d-70c passim; CH XIX, SECT 211 73d-74a

36 SWIFT: *Gulliver*, PART I, 24b-25a; PART IV, 182b-183a

38 MONTESQUIEU: *Spirit of Laws*, BK X 61b,d-68d; BK XI, 83c-84c; BK XV, 109b-c; 110a-d; BK XXI, 170c-171d

38 ROUSSEAU: *Political Economy*, 380a-b

39 SMITH: *Wealth of Nations*, BK IV, 239a-279b

40 GIBBON: *Decline and Fall*, 14d-15c; 18a; 26a-c; 134a-b; 245d-246d; 420b-d; 518b-519a; 522c-523a,c; 550b-551b; 608b,d; 624b-c; 632d-633a; 638a-639a

41 GIBBON: *Decline and Fall*, 65a-c; 216c-d; 285a-c; 505b-c

42 KANT: *Science of Right*, 413d; 454a-455a; 456c-457a

43 DECLARATION OF INDEPENDENCE: 1a-3b passim

43 CONSTITUTION OF THE U.S.: ARTICLE IV, SECT 3 [544–550] 16b

43 FEDERALIST: NUMBER 43, 140d-141a

43 MILL: *Liberty*, 272a; 281d-282b [fn 3] / *Representative Government*, 339a-341a; 353c; 411b-412a; 427a-428a passim; 433b-442d

44 BOSWELL: *Johnson*, 179c; 364c-365a; 370a; 511c-d

46 HEGEL: *Philosophy of History*, PART I, 242d-243d; PART III, 299a-c

5c. The relation of local to national government: the centralization and decentralization of governmental functions

6 THUCYDIDES: *Peloponnesian War*, BK II, 391c-392a

9 ARISTOTLE: *Politics*, BK IV, CH 15 [1299ᵇ15–18] 500b

14 PLUTARCH: *Theseus*, 9a-d

23 HOBBES: *Leviathan*, PART II, 120d-121a

38 MONTESQUIEU: *Spirit of Laws*, BK V, 30a-c

38 ROUSSEAU: *Social Contract*, BK II, 403a-c; BK III, 412a-b; 420d-421a

39 SMITH: *Wealth of Nations*, BK V, 318d-319a; 420b-d

40 GIBBON: *Decline and Fall*, 14c; 578b-c

43 CONSTITUTION OF THE U.S.: ARTICLE I, SECT 4 12b; ARTICLE IV, SECT 1–2 16a-b

43 FEDERALIST: NUMBER 1, 30d-31a; NUMBER 3, 33d-35a; NUMBER 14, 61b-d; NUMBER 17 69a-70d; NUMBER 28 96c-98b passim; NUMBER 31, 105b-c; NUMBER 32 105c-107b passim; NUMBER 34 109b-111d passim; NUMBER 36 114c-117d passim; NUMBER 39, 126b-128b; NUMBER 43, 141a-d; NUMBER 44, 144a-145c passim; NUMBER 45, 148b-150b; NUMBER 46 150b-153b passim; NUMBER 84, 253d-254b

43 MILL: *Liberty*, 322a-d / *Representative Government*, 417c-424c

46 HEGEL: *Philosophy of Right*, PART III, par 290 97d; ADDITIONS, 174 146d-147b

50 MARX-ENGELS: *Communist Manifesto*, 421c-d

5d. Confederation and federal union: the division of jurisdiction between state and federal governments

6 THUCYDIDES: *Peloponnesian War*, BK I, 365a-371b

7 PLATO: *Laws*, BK III, 667c-670a

9 ARISTOTLE: *Politics*, BK III, CH 9 [1280ª34–ᵇ32] 478a-c

14 PLUTARCH: *Philopoemen*, 296a-b / *Aratus*, 834c-d

38 MONTESQUIEU: *Spirit of Laws*, BK IX, 58b,d-60a

39 SMITH: *Wealth of Nations*, BK V, 420b-d

40 GIBBON: *Decline and Fall*, 103c-d

41 GIBBON: *Decline and Fall*, 218c-219a; 577b-c

43 ARTICLES OF CONFEDERATION: 5a-9d

43 CONSTITUTION OF THE U.S.: 11a-20a,c esp ARTICLE VI [583–599] 16d

43 FEDERALIST: NUMBER 1–30 29a-103c passim, esp NUMBER 10, 52b-c, NUMBER 14, 61b-c, NUMBER 15, 65c-d; NUMBER 31–34, 104c-111d; NUMBER 36, 115a-117b; NUMBER 37, 119b-

(5. *The relation of governments to one another: sovereign princes or states as in a condition of anarchy. 5d. Confederation and federal union: the division of jurisdiction between state and federal governments.*)

120d; NUMBER 39, 126b-128b; NUMBER 41–46 132a-153b esp NUMBER 46, 150b-c; NUMBER 51, 164a-165a passim; NUMBER 52, 167a-b; NUMBER 59–61 182a-188d passim; NUMBER 62, 189b-d; NUMBER 80, 235a; NUMBER 81, 239c-241a; NUMBER 82 242b-244a; NUMBER 84, 253d-254b; NUMBER 85, 258d-259a,c

43 MILL: *Representative Government*, 427d-433b

46 HEGEL: *Philosophy of History*, PART II, 278c-279b

6. Historical developments in government: revolution and progress

OLD TESTAMENT: *Exodus*, 18:13–26 / *I Samuel*, 8—(D) *I Kings*, 8 / *I Kings*, 12:1–25—(D) *III Kings*, 12:1–25 / *II Chronicles*, 10—(D) *II Paralipomenon*, 10

6 HERODOTUS: *History*, BK I, 12b-14c; 23b-24b; BK III, 107c-108d; BK V, 164d-165a

6 THUCYDIDES: *Peloponnesian War*, BK I, 352c-d; 353c-d; 366d-367a; BK II, 391b-392a; BK III, 434c-438b passim; BK IV, 458d-459c; 463a-465c; BK VI, 523b-525d; BK VIII, 568d-569a; 575c-576c; 577b-d; 579c-583c; 585d-586b; 587a-589a; 590b-c

7 PLATO: *Laws*, BK III 663d-677a

9 ARISTOTLE: *Ethics*, BK X, CH 9 [1181^{b}12–24] 436c / *Politics*, BK II, CH 8 [1268^{b}23]–CH 12 [1274^{b}28] 464d-471d; BK III, CH 14 483a-484a; CH 15 [1286^{b}8–22] 484d-485a; BK V 502a-519d passim; BK VII, CH 10 [1329^{a}40–^{b}36] 533d-534b / *Athenian Constitution*, CH 1–41 553a-572a

12 AURELIUS: *Meditations*, BK I, SECT 14 254b-c

13 VIRGIL: *Aeneid*, BK VI [851–853] 234a

14 PLUTARCH: *Theseus*, 9a-10a; 13a-14c / *Lycurgus* 32a-48d / *Lycurgus-Numa*, 63d-64a,c / *Solon* 64b,d-77a,c / *Poplicola*, 80d-82a / *Poplicola-Solon*, 86d-87b / *Agis*, 650b-656d / *Cleomenes*, 659b-660d / *Tiberius Gracchus* 671b,d-681a,c / *Caius Gracchus* 681b,d-689a,c / *Caius and Tiberius Gracchus-Agis and Cleomenes* 689b,d-691a,c / *Dion* 781b,d-802a,c

15 TACITUS: *Annals*, BK I, 1a-2a; 3a-b; BK III, 51b-c; BK IV, 72a-b; BK XII, 123b-c; BK XIII, 126c-d; 132c-133a / *Histories*, BK I, 190b-c; BK II, 224d-225a

18 AUGUSTINE: *City of God*, BK II, CH 21 161b-162d; BK V, CH 12 216d-219b; CH 21–26 226a-230a,c

20 AQUINAS: *Summa Theologica*, PART I–II, Q 104, A 3 305d-306d

21 DANTE: *Divine Comedy*, PARADISE, VI [28–111] 113d-114d

23 HOBBES: *Leviathan*, PART IV, 275a-278d

26 SHAKESPEARE: *Julius Caesar* 568a-596a,c

27 SHAKESPEARE: *Coriolanus* 351a-392a,c / *Henry VIII* 549a-585a,c

30 BACON: *Advancement of Learning*, 94d-95b

32 MILTON: *New Forcers of Conscience* 68a-b / *Lord Gen. Cromwell* 69a-b

35 LOCKE: *Civil Government*, CH VIII, SECT 100–112 47c-51b

35 HUME: *Human Understanding*, SECT I, DIV 5, 453a-b

36 SWIFT: *Gulliver*, PART III, 117b-121b

38 MONTESQUIEU: *Spirit of Laws*, BK III, 9b-d; BK IV, 15c; BK XI 68b,d-84d

38 ROUSSEAU: *Inequality*, 359a-362a passim / *Social Contract*, BK II, 402b-403a; BK III, 418c-d [fn 2]

39 SMITH: *Wealth of Nations*, BK III, 165b-181a,c; BK V, 348a-352a

40 GIBBON: *Decline and Fall*, 24b,d-34a,c esp 24b,d-28b; 50b-51d esp 51c-d; 153c-156a; 240b-255d; 521a-523a,c; 622d-623c

41 GIBBON: *Decline and Fall*, 71d-79d; 199c-202d esp 202a-c; 215c-220a,c esp 217a-b, 218c-219a; 403b-404d; 427b-428a esp 428a; 452d-453a,c; 562b-566c; 574b-582b; 586c-589a

42 KANT: *Science of Right*, 450d-451a; 451d-452a

43 DECLARATION OF INDEPENDENCE: 1a-3b

43 CONSTITUTION OF THE U.S.: 11a-20a,c

43 FEDERALIST: NUMBER 1, 29a-b; NUMBER 9 47a-49c passim; NUMBER 14, 62a-d; NUMBER 18–20 71a-78b; NUMBER 25, 91b-d; NUMBER 37, 120d-121b; NUMBER 41, 133a-d; NUMBER 52, 165d-167b; NUMBER 70, 211b-d; NUMBER 84, 252b-c

43 MILL: *Liberty*, 267d-272a / *Representative Government*, 367b-c; 434a-436b

46 HEGEL: *Philosophy of Right*, ADDITIONS, 176 147c-d / *Philosophy of History*, INTRO, 174a-175c; 198b-199c; 203b-206a,c; PART I, 207d-208c; PART II, 263a-d; 275b-276a; PART III, 295d-296c; PART IV, 316c-d; 328b-331d; 342a-343a; 355d-357a

50 MARX: *Capital*, 355d-364a esp 356a-357a, 359a-c

50 MARX-ENGELS: *Communist Manifesto*, 420b-d

51 TOLSTOY: *War and Peace*, BK I, 10a-b; BK VI, 238c-243d

CROSS-REFERENCES

For: The basic context of the problems discussed in this chapter, *see* STATE; for the discussion of domestic government, *see* FAMILY 2b, 5a; for the discussion of ecclesiastical government, *see* RELIGION 3c(2); for the discussion of divine government, *see* GOD 7c; WORLD 1c; and for the discussion of government in relation to economic affairs, *see* WEALTH 9d.

Other considerations of the issues concerning anarchy, *see* LIBERTY 1b; TYRANNY 3; WAR AND PEACE 1.

Other discussions of the notion of sovereignty in its various forms or meanings, *see* DEMOCRACY 4b; LAW 6b; LIBERTY 1b, 6c; STATE 2c, 9d; TYRANNY 5c; and for the problems of foreign policy as between sovereign states, *see* JUSTICE 9f; STATE 9e(1)–9e(2); WAR AND PEACE 11c.

Sovereignty in relation to federal government, and for the idea of world government, *see* STATE 10e–10f; WAR AND PEACE 11d.

Justice, liberty, and property in relation to government, *see* JUSTICE 1a, 6–6e, 9–9e, 10–10e; LIBERTY 1d, 1f, 1h; WEALTH 7a.

The relation of the ideal form of government to the ideal state, *see* STATE 2e, 6–6b.

The abuses or corruption of government, *see* LAW 7d; MONARCHY 4e(3)–4e(4); TYRANNY 1–1c.

The issues of imperialism in the government of colonies or subject peoples, *see* DEMOCRACY 7b; LIBERTY 6c; MONARCHY 5–5b; REVOLUTION 7; SLAVERY 6d; STATE 10b; TYRANNY 6.

The analysis of particular forms of government, *see* ARISTOCRACY 1–2e; CONSTITUTION 1–3b, 5–5b; DEMOCRACY 1–4c; MONARCHY 1–1a(2), 4–4e(1), 4e(3)–4e(4); OLIGARCHY 1–2, 4–5; TYRANNY 1–5d; and for the discussion of mixed forms of government, *see* CONSTITUTION 3a–3b; MONARCHY 1b–1b(2).

The condition of the ruled under diverse forms of government, *see* CITIZEN 2b; LIBERTY 1f; SLAVERY 6a–6b.

The institutions of self-government, such as representation, elections, voting, *see* ARISTOCRACY 6; CONSTITUTION 9–9b; DEMOCRACY 5a–5b(4).

The problem of the relativity of the forms of government to the character and circumstances of particular peoples, *see* DEMOCRACY 4d; MONARCHY 4e(2); TYRANNY 4b.

The general discussion of political revolution and progress, *see* LIBERTY 6b; PROGRESS 4a–4c; REVOLUTION 2a–2c, 3a, 3c–3c(3); and for the consideration of revolution with respect to particular forms of government, *see* ARISTOCRACY 3; CONSTITUTION 8–8b; DEMOCRACY 7a; OLIGARCHY 3–3b; TYRANNY 8.

Matters relevant to the legislative branch of government, *see* LAW 5d.

Matters relevant to the judicial branch of government, *see* JUSTICE 10d; LAW 5g; PRUDENCE 6b.

Matters relevant to the executive branch of government, especially problems of law enforcement and administration, *see* LAW 5a, 6a, 7e; MONARCHY 1b(3).

Other discussions of the separation of powers and the system of checks and balances, *see* CONSTITUTION 7b; DEMOCRACY 5c; LIBERTY 1g.

Other discussions of the relation between the civil and military powers, *see* STATE 8d(1), 9e(1); WAR AND PEACE 10–10a.

The problem of the economic support of government, *see* WEALTH 9e–9e(2).

The consideration of the art and science of government, *see* EDUCATION 8d; KNOWLEDGE 8c; PRUDENCE 6a; RHETORIC 1c; STATE 8c–8d(3); and for the relation of politics to ethics and economics, *see* PHILOSOPHY 2c; SCIENCE 3a; STATE 8d; WEALTH 9.

ADDITIONAL READINGS

Listed below are works not included in *Great Books of the Western World*, but relevant to the idea and topics with which this chapter deals. These works are divided into two groups:

I. Works by authors represented in this collection.
II. Works by authors not represented in this collection.

For the date, place, and other facts concerning the publication of the works cited, consult the Bibliography of Additional Readings which follows the last chapter of *The Great Ideas*.

I.

PLUTARCH. "Political Precepts," "Of the Three Sorts of Government—Monarchy, Democracy and Oligarchy," in *Moralia*

AQUINAS. *On the Governance of Rulers*

DANTE. *Convivio (The Banquet)*, FOURTH TREATISE, CH 4-5

——. *On World-Government or De Monarchia*

MACHIAVELLI. *The Discourses*

——. *Florentine History*

F. BACON. "Of Faction," in *Essays*

MILTON. *Defence of the People of England*

HOBBES. *Philosophical Rudiments Concerning Government and Society*, CH 6-7, 10-11

——. *The Elements of Law, Natural and Politic*, PART I, CH 19; PART II, CH 1

——. *A Dialogue Between a Philosopher and a Student of the Common Laws of England*

SPINOZA. *Tractatus Theologico-Politicus (Theological-Political Treatise)*, CH 16-19

——. *Tractatus Politicus (Political Treatise)*, CH 3-5

HUME. *A Treatise of Human Nature*, BK III, PART II, SECT VII-X

A. SMITH. *Lectures on Justice, Police, Revenue and Arms*

MARX. *A Criticism of the Hegelian Philosophy of Right*

DOSTOEVSKY. *The Possessed*

II.

POLYBIUS. *Histories*, VOL I, BK VI

CICERO. *De Republica (The Republic)*

JOHN OF SALISBURY. *The Statesman's Book*

MARSILIUS OF PADUA. *Defensor Pacis*

FORTESCUE. *Governance of England*

ERASMUS. *The Education of a Christian Prince*

T. MORE. *Utopia*

CALVIN. *Institutes of the Christian Religion*, BK IV, CH 20

BODIN. *The Six Bookes of a Commonweale*

BELLARMINE. *The Treatise on Civil Government (De Laicis)*

HOOKER. *Of the Laws of Ecclesiastical Polity*

A. SIDNEY. *Discourses Concerning Government*

BURLAMAQUI. *Principles of Natural and Politic Law*

VATTEL. *The Law of Nations*, BK I, CH 1-13

VOLTAIRE. *Letters on the English*, VIII-IX

——. "Government," in *A Philosophical Dictionary*

J. WILSON. *Works*, PART I, CH II, V, X

BENTHAM. *A Fragment on Government*, CH 2, 4-5

J. ADAMS. *A Defense of the Constitutions of Government of the United States of America*

JEFFERSON. *The Commonplace Book*

——. *Notes on the State of Virginia*

BURKE. *An Appeal from the New to the Old Whigs*

W. HUMBOLDT. *The Sphere and Duties of Government*

PAINE. *Rights of Man*

——. *The Age of Reason*

——. *Dissertation on First Principles of Government*

J. MILL. *An Essay on Government*

GOGOL. *The Government Inspector*

——. *The Nose*

WHEWELL. *The Elements of Morality*, BK IV, CH 6; BK V, CH 7-9

CALHOUN. *A Disquisition on Government*

——. *A Discourse on the Constitution and Government of the United States*

DICKENS. *Little Dorritt*

LOTZE. *Microcosmos*, BK VIII, CH 5

J. H. NEWMAN. *A Letter to the Duke of Norfolk*

TURGENEV. *Fathers and Sons*

——. *Virgin Soil*

T. H. HUXLEY. *Methods and Results*, IX

T. H. GREEN. *The Principles of Political Obligation*, (A,F,G)

SPENCER. *The Man Versus the State*

MAINE. *Popular Government*

MAITLAND. *Justice and Police*

W. WILSON. *Congressional Government*

KROPOTKIN. *Anarchism*

BOSANQUET. *The Philosophical Theory of the State*

BRYCE. "The Nature of Sovereignty," in *Studies in History and Jurisprudence*

SANTAYANA. *Reason in Society*, CH 3

CHESTERTON. *The Napoleon of Notting Hill*

——. *The Man Who Was Thursday*

FRANCE. *Penguin Island*

MORLEY. *Notes on Politics and History*

PARETO. *The Mind and Society*, VOL IV, CH 12

LASKI. *Authority in the Modern State*

STEFFENS. *Autobiography*

STURZO. *The Inner Laws of Society*

F. G. WILSON. *The Elements of Modern Politics*

B. RUSSELL. *Proposed Roads to Freedom*, CH 5

——. *Power*

MARITAIN. *Scholasticism and Politics*, CH III-IV

SIMON. *Nature and Functions of Authority*

A. J. CARLYLE. *Political Liberty*

BARKER. *Reflections on Government*

FERRERO. *The Principles of Power*

MACIVER. *The Web of Government*

Chapter 32: HABIT

INTRODUCTION

THE familiar word "habit" has a tremendous range of meaning. Some of its meanings in technical discourse are so divergent from one another—as well as from the popular understanding of the term—that it is difficult to find a common thread of derivation whereby to pass from one meaning to another.

We can eliminate at once the use of the word to designate apparel, as when we speak of a "riding habit." Yet even this sense contains a root of meaning which cannot be dismissed. Augustine points out that "the term 'habit' is derived from the verb 'to have'" and Aristotle, considering the meanings of 'to have,' includes the sense in which a man may be said "to have a coat or tunic" along with the sense in which a man may be said to have a habit—"a piece of knowledge or a virtue." Just as clothes are something a person *has* or *possesses* in a manner more or less fitting to the body, so habits in the psychological sense are qualities which a person has or possesses, and they too can be judged for their fitness.

This understanding of habit is conveyed in the ancient remark which has become a common expression—that "habit is second nature." Habit is not *original* nature, but something added thereto as clothes are added to the body. But unlike clothes, which are added externally and merely by contact, habits as second nature are nature itself transformed or developed. In the words of an ancient poet, whom Aristotle quotes with approval, "habit's but long practice, and this becomes men's nature in the end."

Not all, as we shall see, would grant that practice is essential to habit. Nevertheless the word "practice" suggests one notion that is common to all theories of acquired habit, namely, that habit is a *retained effect*—the result of something done or experienced. Within this common understanding, there are opposite views. According to one view, the acquisition of habits depends on activity. According to another, habits are modifications, passively, not actively, acquired.

The word "habit" is also used in a sense diametrically opposite to the meanings so far considered. It is the sense in which Aristotle, in the *History of Animals*, discusses the habits of animals, and differentiates species according to the differences in their habits. Here the word "habit" is used to signify not an acquired pattern of behavior, but an innate predisposition to act or react in a certain way. The difference between acquired habits and "the habits to which there is an innate tendency," James tells us, is marked by the fact that the latter generally "are called instincts."

The opposition between these two meanings of "habit" is clear. On the one hand, habits represent what, in the case of living things at least, is added by nurture to nature—the results of experience, training, or activity. On the other hand, habits which are identical with instincts belong to original nature itself—part of the native endowment of the animal. Is there any common thread of meaning in the notions of acquired and innate habit which may explain the use of the word in such opposite senses?

The familiar statement that a person does what he is in the habit of doing indicates that a habit is a tendency to a particular sort of behavior. Knowledge of a person's habits enables us to predict what he is likely to do in any situation which elicits habitual conduct on his part. So, too, an animal's behavior in a particular situation may be predicted from a knowledge of its instincts. Instinct and habit—or innate and acquired habits—seem to have this common character, that they are tendencies to behavior of a specific or determinate sort. They are definitely not random behavior. In the one case, the tendency is preformed, a part of the inherited nature of the organism. In the other, the tendency is somehow a product of experience and learning. In neither case does "habit" refer to mere capacity for action, unformed and indeterminate, nor does it refer to the action, but rather to the tendency to act.

THE MODIFIABILITY OF instincts by experience indicates another and more dynamic connection between innate and acquired habits. William James conceives innately determined behavior as if it were a plastic material out of which new patterns of conduct can be formed. The process of animal learning he thinks can be generally described as the replacement of instincts by habits. "Most instincts," he writes, "are implanted for the sake of giving rise to habits, and this purpose once accomplished, the instincts themselves, as such, have no *raison d'être* in the psychical economy, and consequently fade away."

Some years before the Russian physiologists Bechterev and Pavlov experimentally studied the conditioning of reflexes, James described animal learning in terms of the substitution of new for old responses to stimuli which had previously called forth an instinctive reaction, or in terms of the attachment of instinctive responses to new stimuli. "The actions we call instinctive," James writes, "all conform to the general reflex type" and "are called forth by determinate sensory stimuli." For example, a predatory animal, instinctively responsive to various perceptible signs of the whereabouts of its prey, may learn to hunt for its food in a particular locality, at a particular time, and in a particular way. Or, to take the example James gives, "if a child, in his first attempts to pat a dog, gets snapped at or bitten, so that the impulse of fear is strongly aroused, it may be that for years to come no dog will excite in him the impulse to fondle again." Similarly, an animal which has no instinctive fear of man may acquire an habitual tendency to flee at man's approach, as the result of experiences in which the appearance of man is associated with instinctively recognized signs of danger.

In the classification of animals, from Aristotle on, the instincts peculiar to each species have been used in their differentiation. In addition, the degree to which the instincts of an animal are either relatively inflexible at one extreme or easily modifiable at the other has been thought to indicate that animal's rank in the scale of intelligence. The higher animals seem to have a greater capacity to form habits and to be capable, therefore, of modifying their instinctive patterns of behavior as the result of experience. In consequence, their behavior is both more adaptive and more variable than that of animals which always follow the lines of action laid down by instinct.

Species whose instincts are largely unmodifiable are at a disadvantage in a changing environment or in one to which they are not innately adapted. In the struggle for existence, Darwin observes, it is the organism that "varies ever so little, either in habits or structure" which "gains an advantage over some other inhabitant of the same country." Though for the most part instincts seem to be directed toward the animal's survival, intelligence, or the power of modifying instincts by learning, may sometimes be needed to save the animal from his own instincts.

If the lower animals are most dependent on their instincts and least able to modify them, that would seem to indicate a kind of opposition between instinct and intelligence. Darwin quotes Cuvier to the effect that "instinct and intelligence stand in an inverse ratio to each other," but he himself does not wholly accept this view. He thinks that the behavior of beavers, for example, or of certain classes of insects, shows that "a high degree of intelligence is certainly compatible with complex instincts." Yet he admits that "it is not improbable that there is a certain amount of interference between the development of free intelligence and of instinct."

On this subject of instinct in relation to intelligence or reason, James seems to take a less equivocal position. According to him, "man possesses all the impulses that [animals] have, and a great many more besides." After enumerating what he considers to be the instinctive tendencies of the human species, he concludes by saying that "no other mammal, not even the monkey, shows so large an array." But since James also thinks that man has the keenest intelligence and may even be the only reasoning animal, he cannot believe that there is any "material antagonism between instinct and reason." On the contrary, a high development of the faculties of memory, of associating ideas, and of making inferences implies not the absence of instinct, but the modifiability of instinct by experience and learning. "Though the animal richest in reason might be also the animal richest in instinctive impulses too," James writes, "he would never seem the fatal automaton which a *merely* instinctive animal would be."

The opposite position is taken by those who, like Cuvier, hold that the more adequate an animal's instinctive equipment is for its survival, the less it needs free intelligence for adaptive purposes, and the less important is the role of learning and habit formation. Some writers, like Aquinas, go further than this and maintain that in the case of man, the power of reason as an instrument of learning and of solving life's problems supplants instinct almost entirely, or needs to be supplemented by instinctive impulses of an extremely rudimentary sort—hardly more complex than simple reflexes.

What other animals do by instinct man does by reason. "Brute animals," Aquinas writes, "do not act at the command of reason," but "if they are left to themselves, such animals act from natural instinct." Since in his opinion habits can be formed only by acts which involve reason as a factor, he does not think that, strictly speaking, habits are to be found in brutes. But, he adds, to the extent that man's reason may influence brutes "by a sort of conditioning to do things in this or that way, so in this sense to a certain extent we can admit the existence of habits in brute animals."

THE MODIFICATION of instincts in the course of individual life raises a question about their modifiability from generation to generation. The question has obvious significance for the theory of evolution.

It is thought by some that an animal's instincts represent the past experience of the race. In a passage quoted by James, Herbert Spencer, for example, maintains that "reflex actions and instincts . . . . result from the registration of experience continued for numberless generations." Freud appears to hold much the same opinion. "All organic instincts are conservative," he writes. They are "historically acquired, and are directed towards regressions, towards reinstate-

ment of something earlier." Indeed, he claims that the instincts of living things revert back *beyond* ancestral history to the inorganic. They go back to "an ancient starting point, which the living being left long ago." They are an "imprint" left upon the development of the organism by "the evolution of our earth and its relation to the sun."

James, on the other hand, claims that there is "perhaps not one single unequivocal item of positive proof" in favor of the view that "adaptive changes are inherited." He thinks the variability of instincts from generation to generation must be accounted for by some other means than the inheritance of acquired characteristics, according to which the habits *acquired* by earlier generations gradually become, through hereditary transmission, the *innate* habits of later generations.

The question of their origin aside, what is the structure of instincts? In the chapter on EMOTION, where this matter is considered, instinctive behavior is described as having three components. It involves, first, an innate ability to recognize certain objects; second, an emotional reaction to them which includes an impulse to act in a certain way; and, third, the ability to execute that impulse without benefit of learning.

James covers two of these three points when he defines an instinct as "the faculty of acting in such a way as to produce certain ends, without foresight of the ends, and without previous education in the performance"; and he touches on the remaining one when he declares that "instinctive reactions and emotional expressions shade imperceptibly into each other. Every object that excites an instinct," he goes on to say, "excites an emotion as well," but emotions "fall short of instincts in that the emotional reaction usually terminates in the subject's own body, whilst the instinctive reaction is apt to go further and enter into practical relations with the exciting object."

In the discussion of instincts from Aristotle to Freud, the emphasis on one or another of these components has varied from time to time. Mediaeval psychologists, if we take Aquinas as an example, seem to stress the cognitive aspect. He speaks of the sheep running away "when it sees the wolf, not because of its color or shape, but as a natural enemy." The point which he thinks notable here is not the fact that the sheep runs away, but rather the fact that without any previous experience of wolves, the sheep recognizes the wolf as dangerous. "The sheep, seeing the wolf, judges it a thing to be shunned . . . not from deliberation, but from natural instinct." This instinctive power of recognizing what is to the animal's advantage or peril Aquinas calls "the estimative power" and assigns it, along with memory and imagination, to the sensitive faculty.

Later writers stress the emotional and conative aspects of instinct—feeling and impulse. James, for example, indicates this emphasis when he says that "every instinct is an impulse"; and Freud makes desire central rather than perception or action. An instinct, he says, may be described as a stimulus, but it would be more exact to speak of "a stimulus of instinctual origin" as a "need." The instincts are the basic cravings or needs, and these instinctual needs are the primary unconscious determinants of behavior and thought.

What Freud calls "instinctual needs" seem to be the counterpart of what, in an earlier phase of the tradition, are called "natural desires." These two notions are far from being strictly interchangeable, but they do have a certain similarity in their reference to desires which are not conscious or acquired through experience. This matter is further discussed in the chapter on DESIRE.

IF WE TURN NOW to the consideration of habit as something acquired by the individual, we find two major issues. The first of these has already been mentioned in connection with the conception of habit as a *retained effect*.

According to William James, the capacity for habit formation is a general property of nature, found in inanimate matter as well as in living things. "The moment one tries to define what habit is," he writes, "one is led to the fundamental properties of matter." He regards the laws of nature, for example, as "nothing but the immutable habits which the different elementary sorts of matter follow in their actions and reactions upon each other. In the organic world, however, the habits are more variable than this."

James attributes this universal capacity for habit formation to what he calls the "plasticity" of matter, which consists in "the possession of a structure weak enough to yield to an influence, but strong enough not to yield all at once. Each relatively stable phase of equilibrium in such a structure is marked by what we may call a new set of habits." He cites as examples of habit formation in inorganic matter such things as the magnetizing of an iron bar, the setting of plaster, scratches on a polished surface or creases in a piece of cloth. The matter in each of these cases is not only plastic and yielding, but retentive through its inertia. "When the structure has yielded," he writes, "the same inertia becomes the condition of its comparative permanence in the new form, and of the new habits the body then manifests."

The habits of living things or of the human mind are to be regarded only as special cases of nature's general plasticity and retentiveness. James does not fail to observe the difference between the magnetized bar, the scratched surface, or the creased cloth, and the habits of a trained animal or a skilled workman. The latter are acquired by activity—by practicing the same act repeatedly. Furthermore, they are not merely passive relics of a past impression, but are themselves tendencies to action. They erupt into action almost spontaneously when the occasion for performance arises.

It may be questioned whether the word "habit" should be used so broadly. Unlike James, most writers restrict its application to living things, and even there they limit habit formation to the sphere of learning. If the capacity to learn from experience is not a property of plant life, then plants cannot form habits. The same may be said of certain species of animals whose activity is entirely and inflexibly instinctive. Habits are possessed only by those organisms—animals or men —whose future conduct can be determined by their own past behavior. Aquinas, as we have seen, goes further than this, and limits habit formation in a strict sense to man alone.

This leads at once to the second issue. For those who believe that man is not specifically different from all other animals, man's habits and his habit formation require no special distinction or analysis. They hold that human intelligence differs from animal intelligence only in degree, not in kind. No other factors, they think, are present in human learning than those which operate when animals somehow profit from experience or acquire new modes of behavior. In the great books there is to be found, however, a very special theory of habit which is part of the doctrine that man is specifically different from all other animals in that he alone is rational and has free will.

The issue about man's nature is discussed in other chapters (ANIMAL, EVOLUTION, MAN, MIND). Here we must examine the consequences for the theory of habit of these opposing views. Do animals and men form habits *in the same sense* of that term? The use of the word is not at stake, for "habit" may be used in a different sense for the acquired dispositions of animals. Those who hold that brute animals and men do not have habits in the same sense acknowledge that men may have, in addition to their specifically human habits, the sort of modified instincts or conditioned reflexes which are typical of animal habit formation. Furthermore, it is recognized that human and animal habits are alike in certain respects. Both are acquired by activity and both are tendencies to activity of a determinate sort.

The question, therefore, is simply this: Does one conception of habit apply to men and animals, or does human nature require a special conception applicable to man alone? To clarify this issue, it is necessary to summarize the analysis of human habits which Aristotle and Aquinas develop more fully than other writers, even than those who share their view of the rationality and freedom of man.

THAT ARISTOTLE and Aquinas should be the authors of an elaborate theory of human habits becomes intelligible in terms of two facts.

In the first place, they consider habit in the context of moral theory. For them the virtues, moral or intellectual, are habits, and so necessarily are the opposite vices. Virtues are good habits, vices bad habits; hence, good or bad, human habits must be so formed and constituted that they can have the moral quality connoted by virtue or vice. Since virtue is praiseworthy and vice blameworthy only if their possessor is responsible, human habit is conceived as arising from freely chosen acts.

In the second place, their understanding of habit is affected by their psychological doctrine

of faculties, and especially by their analysis of the powers and activities which they think belong peculiarly to man. This in turn gives a metaphysical meaning to habit, for they treat human powers and human acts as special cases of potentiality and actualization.

Aquinas bases much of his discussion of habit on Aristotle's definition of it as "a disposition whereby that which is disposed is disposed well or ill, and this, either in regard to itself or in regard to another." In calling a habit a disposition, Aristotle goes on to say that all "dispositions are not necessarily habits," for while dispositions are unstable or ephemeral, habits "are permanent" or at least "difficult to alter."

For a disposition to be a habit, certain other conditions must be present, according to Aquinas. "That which is disposed should be distinct from that to which it is disposed," he writes, and hence "should be related to it as potentiality is to act." If there is a being which lacks all potentiality, he points out, "we can find no room in such a thing for habit . . . as is clearly the case in God."

It is also necessary that "that which is in a state of potentiality in regard to something else be capable of determination in several ways and to various things." If there were a potentiality which could be actualized in one way and one way only, then such a power of operation could not be determined by habits. Some of man's powers seem to be of this sort. His faculty of sensation, for example, functions perfectly when the sense organs have normally matured. A man does not learn to *see* colors or to *hear* tones, and so the simple use of his senses—apart from aesthetic perceptions and trained discriminations—does not lead to sensory habits. "The exterior apprehensive powers, as sight, hearing, and the like," Aquinas maintains, "are not susceptive of habits but are ordained to their fixed acts, according to the disposition of their nature."

In contrast, man's faculty of thinking and knowing can be improved or perfected by activity and exercise. The words "improved" and "perfected" are misleading if they are thought to exclude bad habits, for a bad habit is no less a habit than a good one. The definition of habit, Aquinas points out, includes dispositions which "dispose the subject well or ill to its form or to its operation." Hence when we say that a power of operation is "improved" or "perfected" by being exercised, we must mean only that after a number of particular acts, the individual has a *more determinate* capacity for definite operation than he had before.

A man may have at birth the mere capacity for knowing grammar or geometry, but after he has learned these subjects he has the habit of such knowledge. This, according to Aristotle and Aquinas, means that his original capacity has been rendered more determinate in its activity. It would be so even if he had learned errors, that is, even if the intellectual habits he had formed disposed his mind in a manner which would be called "ill" rather than "well."

The difference between a man who has learned grammar and one who has not is a difference in their capacity for a certain intellectual performance, a difference resulting from the intellectual work which has been done by the man who has learned grammar. That difference is an intellectual habit. The man who has not learned grammar has the same undeveloped capacity for knowing grammar with which he was born. The man who has learned grammar has had his native capacity for grammatical knowledge developed. That developed capacity is a habit of knowledge or skill which manifests itself in the way in which he writes and speaks. But even when he is not actually exercising his grammatical skill, the fact that he has formed this particular habit means that he will be able, whenever the occasion arises, to do correctly with speed and facility what the man who does not have the habit cannot do readily or easily if he can do it at all.

It may be helpful to illustrate the same points by reference to a bodily habit, such as a gymnastic or athletic skill which, being an art, is a habit not of body alone, but of mind as well. If two men are born with normal bodies equally capable of certain muscular coordinations, they stand in the same relation to performing on the tennis court. Both are equally able to learn the game. But when one of them has learned to play, his acquired skill consists in the trained capacity for the required acts or motions. The other man may be able to perform all these acts or go through all these motions, but not with the same facility and grace, or as pleasantly, as the man whose mastery of the game lies in a habit formed by much practice in doing what is required. As the habit gradually grows, awkwardness is overcome, speed increases, and pleasure in performance replaces pain or difficulty.

Clearly, then, the habit exists even when it is not in operation. It may even develop during periods of inactivity. As William James remarks, there is a sense in which "we learn to swim during the winter and to skate during the summer" when we are not actually engaging in these sports. This would seem to be inconsistent with the general insight, common to all observers, that habits are strengthened by exercise and weakened or broken by disuse or by the performance of contrary acts. But James explains that his point, stated less paradoxically, means only that during periods of rest the effects of prior activity seem to consolidate and build up a habit.

The dynamism of habit formation and habitual activity is summarized, in the language of Aristotle and Aquinas, by the statement that "habit is a kind of medium between mere power and mere act." On the one hand, a habit is like a power or capacity, for though it is an improvement on native ability, it is still only an ability to perform certain acts; it is *not* the actual performance of them. On the other hand, habit is like operation or activity, for it represents an actualization or development of capacity, even as a particular operation is an actualization of the power to act. That is why habit is sometimes called a second grade of potentiality (compared to natural capacity as first potentiality) and also "a first grade of actuality" (compared to operation as complete act).

ACCORDING TO THE theory of specifically human habits, habits are situated only in man's powers of reason and will. Habits are formed in the other powers only to the extent that they are subject to direction by his reason and will. Specifically human habits can be formed only in that area of activity in which men are free to act or not to act; and, when they act, free to act this way or that. Habit, the product of freedom, is not thought of as abolishing freedom. However difficult it may be to exert a free choice against a strong habit, even the strongest habit is not conceived as unbreakable; and if it is breakable, it must permit action contrary to itself. Habitual behavior only seems to lack freedom because a man does habitually, without conscious attention to details, what he would be forced to do by conscious choice at every step if he lacked the habit.

In the theory under consideration habits are classified according to the faculty which they determine or perfect, on the ground that "every power which may be variously directed to act needs a habit whereby it is well disposed to its act." Consequently there are intellectual habits, or habits of thinking and knowing; and appetitive habits, or habits of desire which involve the emotions and the will, and usually entail specific types of conduct. Within a single faculty, such as the intellect, habits are further differentiated by reference to their objects or to the end to which their characteristic operation is directed. For example, the habit of knowing which consists in a science like geometry and the habit of artistic performance such as skill in grammar both belong to the intellect, but they are distinct habits according to their objects or ends.

All of these distinctions have moral as well as psychological significance. They are used in formulating the criteria of *good* and *bad* habits which are more appropriately discussed in the chapter on VIRTUE AND VICE. But here one further psychological distinction deserves comment. Some of man's acquired habits are regarded as natural in a special sense—not in the sense in which instincts are called "natural" or "innate" habits. The distinction is drawn from the supposition that certain habits develop in *all* men because, since human nature is the same for all, men will inevitably form these habits if they act at all. This word "natural" here applied to a habit simply means that it is common to all having the same nature.

For example, the understanding of the law of contradiction—that *the same thing cannot be affirmed and denied at the same time*—and other simple axioms of theoretic knowledge are said to be possessed by the human mind as a matter of natural habit. If a man thinks at all he will come to know these truths. "It is owing to the very nature of the intellectual soul," Aquinas writes, "that man, having once grasped what is

a whole and what is a part, should at once perceive that every whole is larger than its part."

The sense in which Aquinas says that "*the understanding of first principles* is called a natural habit" applies to the first principles of the practical reason as well as to the axioms of theoretic knowledge. Just as no man who makes theoretic judgments about the true and the false can be, in his opinion, without habitual knowledge of the principle of contradiction, so he thinks no man who makes practical judgments about good and evil can be without habitual knowledge of the natural moral law, the first principle of which is that *the good is to be sought and evil avoided*. "Since the precepts of the natural law are sometimes considered by reason actually," Aquinas writes, "while sometimes they are in the reason only habitually, in this way the natural law may be called a habit."

In a different phase of the tradition Hume regards it as an inevitable tendency of the human mind to interpret any repeated sequence of events in terms of cause and effect. If one thing has preceded another a certain number of times in our experience, we are likely to infer that if the first occurs, the second will follow. The principle which determines us "to form such a conclusion" is, Hume says, "Custom or Habit." All our inferences from experience are "effects of custom, not of reasoning"; and since the habit of inferring a future connection between things which have been customarily conjoined in the past is, in his opinion, universally present in human nature, Hume refers to it as "a species of natural instinct which no reasoning or process of thought and understanding is able either to produce or prevent."

Even Kant's synthetic judgments *a priori* have a certain similarity to the thing called "natural habit." They comprise judgments the mind will make because of its own nature or, in Kant's terms, its transcendental structure. Though *a priori*, the judgment itself is not innate, for it arises only when actual experience provides its subject matter. So, too, the natural habit of first principles, of which Aquinas speaks, is not innate, but a result of experience.

THERE IS STILL ONE other traditional meaning of the phrase "natural habit." It occurs in

Christian theology. Habits are there distinguished according as they are acquired by man's own efforts or are a gift of God's grace, which adds to or elevates human nature. The former are natural, the latter supernatural.

In the sphere of supernatural habits the theologian makes a distinction between grace itself and the special habits which accompany grace. Aquinas, for example, writes that "just as the natural light of reason is something different from the acquired virtues, which are ordained to this natural light, so also the light of grace, which is a participation of the divine nature, is something different from the infused virtues which are derived from and are ordained to this light." These "infused virtues," like the natural virtues, are good habits—principles of operation, determining acts of thought or desire. They are either the specifically theological virtues of faith, hope, and charity, or the supernatural counterparts of the acquired intellectual and moral virtues—the habits which are called "the infused virtues" and "the moral and intellectual gifts."

Grace, taken in itself rather than in its consequences, is not an *operative* habit, that is, it is not a habit of performing certain acts. Nevertheless, regarded as something added to and perfecting nature, it is considered under the aspect of habit. But rather than "a habit whereby power is inclined to an act," Aquinas includes it among those habits by which "the nature is well or ill disposed to something, and chiefly when such a disposition has become a sort of nature." Through the habit of grace, man's nature is elevated by becoming "a partaker . . . of the divine nature."

To distinguish this kind of habit from those in the operative order, it is sometimes called an "entitative habit"—a habit of the very *being* of man's personality. On the purely natural plane, health may be thought of in the same way as a habit which is entitative rather than operative. It is a habit not of thought, desire, or conduct, but of man's physical being.

THE WORD "CUSTOM" is sometimes a synonym for "habit" and sometimes a variant with special connotations. What a man does habitually is customary for him to do. So far as the single individual is concerned, there seems to be no difference between habit and custom. But we usually think of customs in terms of the group or community rather than the individual. As indicated in the chapter on CUSTOM AND CONVENTION, the prevailing modes of behavior in a society and its widely shared beliefs represent common habits of thought and action on the part of its members. Apart from the habits of individuals social customs have no existence whatsoever. But social customs and individual habits cannot be equated because, with respect to any customary practice or opinion, there may be non-conforming individuals —men of divergent habit. The prevalent or predominant customs are the habits of the majority.

No society endures for long or functions peacefully unless common habits generate the ties of custom. To perpetuate itself, the state necessarily attempts to mould the habits of each growing generation—by every means of education, by tradition, by law. So important is the stability of custom in the life of society, according to Montaigne, that it is "very unjust . . . to subject public and established customs and institutions to the weakness and instability of a private and particular fancy." He doubts "whether any so manifest benefit can accrue from the alteration of a law received, let it be what it will, as there is danger and inconvenience in altering it." His extreme caution with regard to changing the law comes from a preference for the stability of settled customs and from the recognition that "government is a structure composed of diverse parts and members joined and united together, with so strict connection, that it is impossible to stir so much as one brick or stone, but the whole body will be sensible of it."

Without habits of action, at least, neither the individual nor society can avoid chaos. Habits bind day to day in a continuity which would be lost if the recurring problems of conduct or thought had to be solved anew each time they arose. Without habits life would become unbearably burdensome; it would bog down under the weight of making decisions. Without habits men could not live with themselves, much less with one another. Habits are, as William James remarks, "the fly-wheel of society."

OUTLINE OF TOPICS

REFERENCES

To find the passages cited, use the numbers in heavy type, which are the volume and page numbers of the passages referred to. For example, in **4** HOMER: *Iliad*, BK II [265–283] **12d**, the number **4** is the number of the volume in the set; the number **12d** indicates that the passage is in section d of page 12.

PAGE SECTIONS: When the text is printed in one column, the letters a and b refer to the upper and lower halves of the page. For example, in **53** JAMES: *Psychology*, 116a–119b, the passage begins in the upper half of page 116 and ends in the lower half of page 119. When the text is printed in two columns, the letters a and b refer to the upper and lower halves of the left-hand side of the page, the letters c and d to the upper and lower halves of the right-hand side of the page. For example, in **7** PLATO: *Symposium*, 163b–164c, the passage begins in the lower half of the left-hand side of page 163 and ends in the upper half of the right-hand side of page 164.

AUTHOR'S DIVISIONS: One or more of the main divisions of a work (such as PART, BK, CH, SECT) are sometimes included in the reference; line numbers, in brackets, are given in certain cases; *e.g.*, *Iliad*, BK II [265–283] **12d**.

BIBLE REFERENCES: The references are to book, chapter, and verse. When the King James and Douay versions differ in title of books or in the numbering of chapters or verses, the King James version is cited first and the Douay, indicated by a (D), follows; *e.g.*, OLD TESTAMENT: *Nehemiah*, 7:45—(D) *II Esdras*, 7:46.

SYMBOLS: The abbreviation "esp" calls the reader's attention to one or more especially relevant parts of a whole reference; "passim" signifies that the topic is discussed intermittently rather than continuously in the work or passage cited.

For additional information concerning the style of the references, see the Explanation of Reference Style; for general guidance in the use of *The Great Ideas*, consult the Preface.

1. Diverse conceptions of habit: as second nature, perfection of power, retained modification of matter

7 PLATO: *Republic*, BK III, 330a
8 ARISTOTLE: *Categories*, CH 8 [8ᵇ26–9ᵃ13] 13d-14a / *Physics*, BK VII, CH 3 [246ᵃ10–248ᵃ6] 329c-330d / *Metaphysics*, BK V, CH 20 544a / *Soul*, BK II, CH 5 [417ᵃ21–418ᵃ6] 647d-648d
9 ARISTOTLE: *Ethics*, BK II, CH I [1103ᵃ14–ᵇ2] 348b,d-349a; BK VII, CH 10 [1152ᵃ28–33] 403b / *Politics*, BK VII, CH 13 [1332ᵃ39–ᵇ10] 537a-b / *Rhetoric*, BK I, CH II [1370ᵃ5–8] 613b
18 AUGUSTINE: *Confessions*, BK VIII, par 10 55c-d / *Christian Doctrine*, BK I, CH 24, 630d-631a
19 AQUINAS: *Summa Theologica*, PART I, Q 18, A 2, REP 2 105c-106b; Q 87, A 2 466c-467b
20 AQUINAS: *Summa Theologica*, PART I-II, Q 49 1a-6a; Q 94, A I 221a-d
25 MONTAIGNE: *Essays*, 489c-d
27 SHAKESPEARE: *Hamlet*, ACT III, SC IV [160–170] 56b
33 PASCAL: *Pensées*, 93 190a
35 LOCKE: *Human Understanding*, BK II, CH XXXIII, SECT 6 249a-b

35 HUME: *Human Understanding*, SECT V, DIV 36, 464d
43 MILL: *Liberty*, 269c-d
46 HEGEL: *Philosophy of Right*, PART III, par 151 57a
49 DARWIN: *Origin of Species*, 119b-d
53 JAMES: *Psychology*, 68a-83b esp 68a-69b, 73b-74a, 78b-79a

1*a*. Habit in relation to potency and act

8 ARISTOTLE: *Physics*, BK VII, CH 3 [246ᵃ10–248ᵃ8] 329c-330d; BK VIII, CH 4 [255ᵃ30–ᵇ23] 340a-c / *Metaphysics*, BK IX, CH 1–2 570b,d-572a; CH 5 573a-c / *Soul*, BK II, CH I [412ᵃ22–28] 642b; CH 5 [417ᵃ21–418ᵃ6] 647d-648d; BK III, CH 4 [429ᵇ5–23] 661d-662a / *Sense and the Sensible*, CH 4 [441ᵇ16–24] 679b
9 ARISTOTLE: *Ethics*, BK II, CH I [1103ᵃ14–ᵇ2] 348b,d-349a
19 AQUINAS: *Summa Theologica*, PART I, Q 14, A I, REP I 75d-76c; Q 18, A 2, REP 2 105c-106b; Q 79, AA 6–7 419b-421c; A 10, ANS 423d-424d; A 12 425c-426b; Q 87, A 2, ANS 466c-467b; Q 89, A 6, REP 3 478b-d
20 AQUINAS: *Summa Theologica*, PART I-II, QQ 49–56 1a-35a passim; Q 71, A 4, ANS and REP 3 108b-109a; Q 94, A I, REP I 221a-d

1b. Habit in relation to the plasticity of matter

20 AQUINAS: *Summa Theologica*, PART I–II, Q 50, A I, ANS 6a-7b; A 6, ANS and REP I 11a-12a

53 JAMES: *Psychology*, 68a-71a; 423a-424a passim; 429a-430a

54 FREUD: *Beyond the Pleasure Principle*, 651d-652c

2. The kinds of habit: the distinction of habit from disposition and other qualities

8 ARISTOTLE: *Categories*, CH 8 [8^{b}26–9^{a}13] 13d-14a; CH 15 21c-d / *Physics*, BK VII, CH 3 [246^a 10–248^{a}6] 329c-330d / *Metaphysics*, BK I, CH I [981^{b}2–5] 499d; BK V, CH 19–20 543d-544a; BK IX, CH 1–2 570b,d-572a; CH 5 573a-c

9 ARISTOTLE: *Ethics*, BK II, CH I [1103^{a}14–^{b}2] 348b,d-349a

20 AQUINAS: *Summa Theologica*, PART I–II, Q 49, AA 1–3 1b-5a; Q 54 22d-25d; Q 71, A 4, ANS and REP 3 108b-109a; Q 74, A 4, REP 3 131a-d; PART III, Q 7, A 13, REP 2 755c-756c; Q 9, A 3, REP 2 765b-766b

2a. Differentiation of habits according to origin and function: innate and acquired, entitative and operative habits

8 ARISTOTLE: *Metaphysics*, BK IX, CH 5 [1047^{b}31–34] 573a

20 AQUINAS: *Summa Theologica*, PART I–II, Q 49, A 2, ANS 2b-4a; A 3, ANS and REP 2 4b-5a; Q 50, AA 1–2 6a-8a; A 6 11a-12a; Q 51 12a-15d; Q 54, A I, ANS 22d-23d; A 2, ANS 23d-24c; A 3 24c-25b; Q 55, A 2 27a-d; Q 82, A I 168a-d; Q 110, AA 3–4 350a-351d

23 HOBBES: *Leviathan*, PART I, 54a; 66c-d; 68b

28 HARVEY: *On Animal Generation*, 428a-c

35 HUME: *Human Understanding*, SECT IX, DIV 83–85 487c-488c

42 KANT: *Practical Reason*, 303d-304a

43 MILL: *Utilitarianism*, 459b-461c

49 DARWIN: *Origin of Species*, 68b-69c esp 69a; 119a-d / *Descent of Man*, 304b,d [fn 5]; 310b

53 JAMES: *Psychology*, 68a

54 FREUD: *General Introduction*, 591d-592b; 594d-595b / *War and Death*, 758a-759c

2b. Differentiation of habits according to the capacity habituated or to the object of the habit's activity

7 PLATO: *Theaetetus*, 518a-b

8 ARISTOTLE: *Physics*, BK VII, CH 3 [246^{a}10–248^{a}6] 329c-330d

9 ARISTOTLE: *Ethics*, BK I, CH 13 [1102^{a}26–1103^{a}10] 347d-348d; BK VI, CH 12 [1144^{a}1–11] 393c-d / *Politics*, BK VII, CH 14 [1333^{a}16-36] 538a-b; CH 15 [1334^{b}8-28] 539b-d

20 AQUINAS: *Summa Theologica*, PART I–II, Q 50 6a-12a; Q 54, AA 1–2 22d-24c; A 3, REP 1,3 24c-25b; A 4, ANS 25b-d; PART II–II, Q 24, A 5, ANS 492b-493d

28 HARVEY: *On Animal Generation*, 333a-b

3. The instincts or innate habits of animals and men

7 PLATO: *Republic*, BK II, 320b-c

8 ARISTOTLE: *Categories*, CH 8 [9^{a}13–28] 14b / *Metaphysics*, BK IX, CH 5 [1047^{b}31–34] 573a

9 ARISTOTLE: *History of Animals*, BK I, CH I [487^{a}11–488^{b}29] 7d-9d; BK VIII, CH I 114b,d-115b esp [588^{b}23–589^{a}10] 115b; CH 12 [596^{b}20–28] 122d / *Politics*, BK VII, CH 13 [1332^{a}39–^{b}10] 537a-b

10 GALEN: *Natural Faculties*, BK I, CH 12, 173a-c

12 LUCRETIUS: *Nature of Things*, BK III [741–747] 39c-d

19 AQUINAS: *Summa Theologica*, PART I, Q 18, A 3, ANS 106b-107c; Q 59, A 3, ANS 308b-309a; Q 83, A I, ANS 436d-438a; PART I–II, Q 40, A 3 794c-795a; Q 46, A 4, REP 2 815b-d

20 AQUINAS: *Summa Theologica*, PART I–II, Q 50, A 3 8b-9a

26 SHAKESPEARE: *Henry V*, ACT I, SC II [187–204] 535d-536a

28 HARVEY: *On Animal Generation*, 428a-c

35 HUME: *Human Understanding*, SECT IX, DIV 85 488c

38 MONTESQUIEU: *Spirit of Laws*, BK I, 2b-d

38 ROUSSEAU: *Inequality*, 334d-336a

40 GIBBON: *Decline and Fall*, 409d-410a

49 DARWIN: *Origin of Species*, 119a-135a,c esp 119a-121a, 134d-135a,c / *Descent of Man*, 287d-291c esp 287d-288d; 308a-312d

51 TOLSTOY: *War and Peace*, BK VII, 278a-287a passim; BK XI, 499c-500c

53 JAMES: *Psychology*, 8a-17b esp 12b; 47b-52a esp 49b-50a; 68a; 700a-737a esp 700a-703a

54 FREUD: *Instincts* 412a-421a,c esp 412b-415b / *Unconscious*, 439d / *General Introduction*, 615b-616c / *Beyond the Pleasure Principle* 639a-663d esp 651d-653a / *Ego and Id*, 708d-709b / *Civilization and Its Discontents*, 789d-791d esp 790a-d, 791b-d / *New Introductory Lectures*, 846a-853b esp 846a-847b, 851a-d

3a. Instinctual needs or drives

6 HERODOTUS: *History*, BK II, 62d-63a; 67b-c; BK III, 111d-112c

7 PLATO: *Symposium*, 157b-159b; 165c-166b

8 ARISTOTLE: *Metaphysics*, BK I, CH I [980^{a}22–28] 499a

9 ARISTOTLE: *History of Animals*, BK V, CH 8 [542^{a}17–^{b}1] 68d-69a; BK VI, CH 18 [571^{b}6–573^{a}30] 97b-99a; BK VII, CH I [581^{a}21–^{b}22] 107a-b; BK VIII, CH 12 [596^{b}20-28] 122d / *Generation of Animals*, BK III, CH I [749^{b}1–750^{a}11] 290d-291b; CH 2 [753^{a}7–17] 294a-b / *Ethics*, BK III, CH 11 [1118^{b}8–18] 365a-b; BK VII, CH 6 [1149^{b}24–1150^{a}8] 400b-c

10 GALEN: *Natural Faculties*, BK I, CH 12, 173a-c

12 LUCRETIUS: *Nature of Things*, BK IV [1037–1057] 57d

12 EPICTETUS: *Discourses*, BK I, CH 23 128c-d

(3. *The instincts or innate habits of animals and men. 3a. Instinctual needs or drives.*)

19 AQUINAS: *Summa Theologica*, PART I-II, Q 12, A 5, ANS and REP 3 672a-c; Q 13, A 2, REP 2-3 673c-674c; Q 16, A 2, REP 2 684d-685b; Q 17, A 2, REP 3 687d-688b; Q 41, A 1, REP 3 798b-d

21 DANTE: *Divine Comedy*, PURGATORY, XVIII [19-75] 80a-c

22 CHAUCER: *Manciple's Tale* [17,104-144] 490a-b

23 HOBBES: *Leviathan*, PART I, 61a-d; 84c-86b; PART II, 141a-b

25 MONTAIGNE: *Essays*, 184a-b; 424d-425c; 512a-b

28 HARVEY: *On Animal Generation*, 339b; 346a-347d; 349a-350a; 361c-362a; 402a-d; 460d-461a; 476b-477b

30 BACON: *Advancement of Learning*, 72c-73a

31 DESCARTES: *Meditations*, VI, 99d-103a

31 SPINOZA: *Ethics*, PART III, PROP 4-9 398d-399c

35 LOCKE: *Civil Government*, CH VII, SECT 78-80 42b-43a / *Human Understanding*, BK I, CH II, SECT 3 104b-d

35 HUME: *Human Understanding*, SECT V, DIV 38, 466b; DIV 45 469c; SECT IX, DIV 85 488c; SECT XII, DIV 118 504c-d

38 ROUSSEAU: *Inequality*, 342c-346d passim

43 MILL: *Utilitarianism*, 469b-470c

46 HEGEL: *Philosophy of History*, INTRO, 164b-c

48 MELVILLE: *Moby Dick*, 286b-288a

49 DARWIN: *Origin of Species*, 122d-131b / *Descent of Man*, 298a-c; 304a-314b esp 304b-305a, 308a-310a, 311a-312d; 371c-372c; 456b-457c; 583a

51 TOLSTOY: *War and Peace*, EPILOGUE I, 665a-d

53 JAMES: *Psychology*, 198b-199a; 700a-704a; 712b-737a esp 736b-737a [fn 1]

54 FREUD: *Narcissism*, 400c-402c esp 401a-c / *General Introduction*, 569c-593b esp 574a-d, 590a-593b; 615b-616c; 618d-619a / *Beyond the Pleasure Principle* 639a-663d esp 651d-663c / *Group Psychology*, 669a-b; 673b-c; 684d-686c esp 685a-b / *Ego and Id*, 708c-712c esp 708d-709b, 711c-712a; 714c-717a,c esp 717c / *Civilization and Its Discontents*, 787a-788d esp 787a-c; 789b-791d / *New Introductory Lectures*, 837b-d; 846b-852c esp 851a-d; 883b-c

3b. **The innate sense of the beneficial and harmful: the estimative power**

6 HERODOTUS: *History*, BK II, 63b-c

9 ARISTOTLE: *History of Animals*, BK VIII, CH 12 [596b20-28] 122d; BK IX, CH 5-6 136d-138b

17 PLOTINUS: *Fourth Ennead*, TR IV, CH 20 167d-168b

19 AQUINAS: *Summa Theologica*, PART I, Q 19, A 10, ANS 117d-118b; Q 59, A 3, ANS 308b-309a; Q 76, A 5, REP 4 394c-396a; Q 78, A 4, ANS and REP 4-5 411d-413d; Q 81, A 2, REP 2 429c-430c; A 3, ANS and REP 2 430c-431d; Q 83, A 1, ANS 436d-438a; Q 96, A 1, ANS and REP 4 510b-511b

22 CHAUCER: *Nun's Priest's Tale* [15,279-287] 457b

25 MONTAIGNE: *Essays*, 286d-287b

28 HARVEY: *On Animal Generation*, 456d-457a

31 DESCARTES: *Meditations*, VI, 100a

35 LOCKE: *Civil Government*, CH VII, SECT 79-80 42c-43a / *Human Understanding*, BK I, CH II, SECT 3 104b-d; BK II, CH X, SECT 3 141c-d; CH XI, SECT 5 144d-145a; SECT 11 145d-146a

38 ROUSSEAU: *Inequality*, 337d-338a

48 MELVILLE: *Moby Dick*, 144a-b; 146b-148a

49 DARWIN: *Origin of Species*, 121a; 122c / *Descent of Man*, 287d-288a; 290c-291a; 292b-c

51 TOLSTOY: *War and Peace*, BK III, 111a-c; 129a-c

53 JAMES: *Psychology*, 8a; 13a; 708a-709a; 720b-725a passim; 729b

54 FREUD: *General Introduction*, 607d-609c; 612c-614a esp 613d-614a; 623b-c / *Beyond the Pleasure Principle*, 640d-641a / *Inhibitions, Symptoms, and Anxiety*, 720a-721c esp 721a; 737b-738a; 751a-752b / *New Introductory Lectures*, 845a-846a

3c. **Instinct in relation to reason**

8 ARISTOTLE: *Physics*, BK II, CH 8 [199a20-33] 276c

9 ARISTOTLE: *History of Animals*, BK IX, CH 7 [612b18-613a16] 138b-d / *Politics*, BK VII, CH 13 [1332a39-b10] 537a-b; CH 15 [1334b7-28] 539b-d

12 AURELIUS: *Meditations*, BK III, SECT 16 262d-263a,c

17 PLOTINUS: *Fourth Ennead*, TR IV, CH 20-21 167d-168c

19 AQUINAS: *Summa Theologica*, PART I, Q 18, A 3, ANS 106b-107c; Q 59, A 3, ANS 308b-309a; Q 76, A 5, REP 4 394c-396a; Q 78, A 4, ANS and REP 4-5 411d-413d; Q 83, A 1, ANS 436d-438a; Q 96, A 1, REP 4 510b-511b; PART I-II, Q 12, A 5, ANS and REP 3 672a-c; Q 17, A 2, REP 3 687d-688b

20 AQUINAS: *Summa Theologica*, PART I-II, Q 50, A 3 8b-9a

25 MONTAIGNE: *Essays*, 216b-219b

28 HARVEY: *On Animal Generation*, 428a-c

30 BACON: *Novum Organum*, BK I, APH 108 128d

31 DESCARTES: *Discourse*, PART V, 59d-60b / *Objections and Replies*, 156a-d

31 SPINOZA: *Ethics*, PART III, PROP 9, SCHOL 399c

33 PASCAL: *Pensées*, 339-344 233a-b / *Vacuum*, 357a-b

35 HUME: *Human Understanding*, SECT V, DIV 38, 466b; DIV 45 469c; SECT IX, DIV 85 488c; SECT XII, DIV 118-119 504c-505b

38 ROUSSEAU: *Social Contract*, BK I, 393b-c

40 GIBBON: *Decline and Fall*, 409d-410a

42 KANT: *Fund. Prin. Metaphysic of Morals*, 256d-257a / *Practical Reason*, 316c-317a / *Judgement*, 602b,d [fn 1]

43 MILL: *Utilitarianism*, 465a-b

46 HEGEL: *Philosophy of History*, INTRO, 164b-c; 171b-c; PART IV, 361c-d

(4. *Habit formation. 4b. The growth and decay of habits: ways of strengthening and breaking habits.*)

12 EPICTETUS: *Discourses*, BK I, CH 27 132b-133b; BK II, CH 18 161a-162b; BK III, CH 12 187b-188b

12 AURELIUS: *Meditations*, BK V, SECT 16 271c-d

17 PLOTINUS: *Sixth Ennead*, TR III, CH 20, 293a

20 AQUINAS: *Summa Theologica*, PART I-II, QQ 52-53 15d-22d; Q 54, A 4, REP 1,3 25b-d

25 MONTAIGNE: *Essays*, 64a-b; 390b-c; 391c-393b; 395b-396d; 525d-527a

30 BACON: *Advancement of Learning*, 69a; 69d-70a; 79b-c; 80a-b

31 DESCARTES: *Discourse*, PART III, 48b-49d

33 PASCAL: *Pensées*, 6 173a

35 LOCKE: *Human Understanding*, BK II, CH XXI, SECT 71 197b-198a

43 MILL: *Utilitarianism*, 464a-d

44 BOSWELL: *Johnson*, 259a

49 DARWIN: *Descent of Man*, 309c

53 JAMES: *Psychology*, 79b-83b; 332a

5. The analysis of specifically human habits

8 ARISTOTLE: *Physics*, BK VII, CH 3 [246^{a}10–248^{a}6] 329c-330d

9 ARISTOTLE: *Ethics*, BK II, CH 1–6 348b,d-352d passim

20 AQUINAS: *Summa Theologica*, PART I-II, QQ 49–54 1a-25d

31 DESCARTES: *Rules*, I 1a-2a

53 JAMES: *Psychology*, 73b-83b

5a. Habits of body: manual arts and the skills of play

7 PLATO: *Protagoras*, 46c / *Republic*, BK III, 334d-335b; BK VII, 391d / *Theaetetus*, 518a-b / *Laws*, BK VII, 717b-d

8 ARISTOTLE: *Physics*, BK VII, CH 3 [246^{a}10–^{b}19] 329c-330a / *Heavens*, BK II, CH 12 [292^{a}14–^{b}18] 383d-384b / *Metaphysics*, BK V, CH 20 [1022^{b}10–13] 544a

9 ARISTOTLE: *Ethics*, BK II, CH 1 [1103^{a}33–35] 348d; [1103^{b}6–13] 349a / *Politics*, BK IV, CH 1 [1288^{b}10–20] 487a-b; BK VII, CH 15 [1334^{b}7–28] 539b-d; CH 17 [1336^{a}3–22] 541a-b; BK VIII, CH 4 544a-c

10 HIPPOCRATES: *Articulations*, par 52 109b-110a; par 55, 111c; par 58 112b-113a / *Aphorisms*, SECT II, par 49–50 133d

12 EPICTETUS: *Discourses*, BK III, CH 15, 190a-c

13 VIRGIL: *Aeneid*, BK IX [590–620] 295a-b

14 PLUTARCH: *Lycurgus*, 40d-42a / *Coriolanus*, 175b / *Philopoemen*, 293d-294a / *Demosthenes*, 693c; 695b

17 PLOTINUS: *Third Ennead*, TR II, CH 8, 87a-b

20 AQUINAS: *Summa Theologica*, PART I-II, Q 49, A 2, REP 1,3 2b-4a; A 3, REP 3 4b-5a; A 4, ANS 5a-6a; Q 50, A 1 6a-7b; A 3, REP 2 8b-9a; Q 52, A 1, ANS 15d-18a; A 2, ANS 18a-19a; Q 54, A 1, ANS 22d-23d

24 RABELAIS: *Gargantua and Pantagruel*, BK I, 28a-29b

25 MONTAIGNE: *Essays*, 43d; 66c-67a; 73c; 316b-c

30 BACON: *Advancement of Learning*, 53d-54a

36 SWIFT: *Gulliver*, PART IV, 166b-167a

38 ROUSSEAU: *Inequality*, 335a-b

39 SMITH: *Wealth of Nations*, BK I, 53a; BK V, 337d-338a

40 GIBBON: *Decline and Fall*, 5a-b

42 KANT: *Judgement*, 586a-b

46 HEGEL: *Philosophy of Right*, PART I, par 52, 25c / *Philosophy of History*, PART II, 267b-268b

49 DARWIN: *Descent of Man*, 269b-271a; 278c-d

50 MARX: *Capital*, 164b-167a; 170c-171a; 237d-240c

53 JAMES: *Psychology*, 73b-78b esp 75a; 332a; 774a

5b. Habits of appetite and will: the moral virtues as good habits

8 ARISTOTLE: *Physics*, BK VII, CH 3 [246^{b}20–247^{a}19] 330a-b

9 ARISTOTLE: *History of Animals*, BK VII, CH 1 [581^{b}11–22] 107b / *Ethics*, BK II, CH 1–6 348b,d-352d; BK VII, CH 5 [1148^{b}15–1149^{a}4] 399a-c; CH 10 [1152^{a}28–33] 403b / *Politics*, BK VII, CH 15 [1334^{b}8–28] 539b-d

12 EPICTETUS: *Discourses*, BK III, CH 3 178d-180a; CH 8 184b-c; BK IV, CH 1 213a-223d

14 PLUTARCH: *Cato the Younger*, 637b-c

18 AUGUSTINE: *Confessions*, BK VIII, par 10 55c-d; par 20–21 58c-59a

20 AQUINAS: *Summa Theologica*, PART I-II, Q 49, A 1, REP 3 1b-2b; A 2, REP 3 2b-4a; Q 50, A 3 8b-9a; A 5 10b-d; Q 56, A 4 32b-33c; A 6 34b-35a; QQ 58–61 41a-59d; Q 94, A 1, REP 1 221a-d

27 SHAKESPEARE: *Hamlet*, ACT III, SC IV [160–170] 56b

30 BACON: *Advancement of Learning*, 69d-70a; 78d-81c esp 79a

35 LOCKE: *Human Understanding*, BK II, CH XXI, SECT 71 197b-198a

42 KANT: *Practical Reason*, 357c-360d / *Pref. Metaphysical Elements of Ethics*, 368d; 378a-b / *Judgement*, 521b-523c; 604d-606d esp 606a-d

43 MILL: *Utilitarianism*, 445d-446a; 463d-465b

44 BOSWELL: *Johnson*, 386a

46 HEGEL: *Philosophy of History*, INTRO, 171b-c

49 DARWIN: *Descent of Man*, 304a-305c esp 304b,d [fn 5]; 310c-319a esp 311c-d, 318a-319a; 321b-322d; 593a-b

53 JAMES: *Psychology*, 80a-83b; 798b-808a passim, esp 799a-b

54 FREUD: *War and Death*, 757c-759d

5c. The natural habits of reason: innate predispositions of the mind

8 ARISTOTLE: *Metaphysics*, BK I, CH 1 [980^{a}22–28] 499a; BK IV, CH 3 [1005^{b}15–34] 524d-525a; BK XI, CH 5 [1061^{b}34–1062^{a}5] 590a-b

9 ARISTOTLE: *Ethics*, BK VI, CH 11 [1143^{a}25-^{b}13] 392d-393a / *Rhetoric*, BK I, CH 1 [1355^{a}14-17] 594b

12 EPICTETUS: *Discourses*, BK I, CH 22 127c-128c; BK II, CH 11 150a-151b

12 AURELIUS: *Meditations*, BK IV, SECT 4 264a

17 PLOTINUS: *First Ennead*, TR III, CH 1-3 10a-11a; TR VIII, CH 9, 31c

19 AQUINAS: *Summa Theologica*, PART I, Q 16, A 6, REP 1 98b-d; Q 18, A 3, ANS 106b-107c; Q 79, AA 12-13 425c-427a; PART I-II, Q 1, A 4, REP 2 612a-613a; A 5, ANS 613a-614a

20 AQUINAS: *Summa Theologica*, PART I-II, Q 51, A 1, ANS and REP 1-2 12b-13c; Q 53, A 1, ANS 19d-21a; Q 94, A 1 221a-d; PART III, Q 9, A 1, ANS 763b-764c

21 DANTE: *Divine Comedy*, PURGATORY, XVI [73-81] 77c-d; XVIII [19-21] 80a; [49-66] 80b-c

23 HOBBES: *Leviathan*, PART I, 54a; 60a-b; 86b-d

30 BACON: *Advancement of Learning*, 59c-d; 60c-61c / *Novum Organum*, BK I, APH 48 110d-111a

31 DESCARTES: *Rules*, I, 1a-b; IV, 5c-d; VIII, 13c-d / *Discourse*, PART I, 41b; PART V, 54c / *Objections and Replies*, 224b,d

31 SPINOZA: *Ethics*, PART IV, PROP 19 429d

33 PASCAL: *Pensées*, I, 171a; 81 186b / *Geometrical Demonstration*, 440b

35 LOCKE: *Civil Government*, CH II, SECT 5-8 26a-27a / *Human Understanding*, BK I 95b,d-121a,c passim

35 HUME: *Human Understanding*, SECT V, DIV 38, 466b; DIV 45 469c; SECT XII, DIV 118 504c-d

42 KANT: *Pure Reason*, 20a; 48a-c; 58c-59b; 66d-72c esp 67c-69c; 109b-c; 157d; 229b-c; 234c / *Judgement*, 562a-564c; 604d-606d esp 606a-d

43 FEDERALIST: NUMBER 31, 103c-d

43 MILL: *Utilitarianism*, 445d-446a; 465a-b; 469b-470c

53 JAMES: *Psychology*, 851a-890a esp 851a-852a, 879b-882a, 889a-b

5d. The acquired habits of mind: the intellectual virtues

7 PLATO: *Theaetetus*, 518b; 542a-c

8 ARISTOTLE: *Physics*, BK VII, CH 3 [247^{b}1-248^a 9] 330b-d; BK VIII, CH 4 [255^{a}30-^{b}23] 340a-c / *Metaphysics*, BK IX, CH 5 [1047^{b}31-34] 573a; CH 8 [1049^{b}32-1050^{a}3] 575c-d / *Soul*, BK II, CH 5 [417^{a}21-418^{a}6] 647d-648d / *Memory and Reminiscence*, CH 2 [451^{b}10-452^{b}6] 693a-694b

9 ARISTOTLE: *Ethics*, BK VI 387a-394d / *Politics*, BK VII, CH 15 [1334^{b}8-28] 539b-d

12 EPICTETUS: *Discourses*, BK III, CH 3 178d-180a; CH 8 184b-c; BK IV, CH 1, 216c-223d

12 AURELIUS: *Meditations*, BK III, SECT 4 260b-261a; BK V, SECT 16 271c-d

19 AQUINAS: *Summa Theologica*, PART I, Q 14, A 1, REP 1-2 75d-76c; Q 79, AA 6-7 419b-421c; A 10, ANS 423d-424d; Q 86, A 2, ANS 462a-463a; Q 87, A 2, REP 2-3 466c-467b

20 AQUINAS: *Summa Theologica*, PART I-II, Q 49, A 1, REP 3 1b-2b; A 2, REP 3 2b-4a; Q 50, A 3,

REP 3 8b-9a; A 4 9a-10b; Q 51, A 3 14b-15a; Q 52, A 1, ANS 15d-18a; A 2, ANS 18a-19a; Q 53, A 1, ANS and REP 2-3 19d-21a; A 3, ANS and REP 3 21d-22d; Q 54, A 4, REP 3 25b-d; QQ 57-58 35a-45c; Q 64, A 3 68b-69b

23 HOBBES: *Leviathan*, PART I, 54a; 60a-b; 66c-68c

30 BACON: *Advancement of Learning*, 26a-27a

31 DESCARTES: *Rules*, I 1a-2a / *Discourse*, PART I, 41b,d

31 SPINOZA: *Ethics*, PART IV, PROP 25-28 430d-431c; PART V, PROP 10, SCHOL 455a-456a

35 LOCKE: *Human Understanding*, BK II, CH IX, SECT 8-10 139b-140b; CH XXXIII, SECT 5-18 248d-251c passim; BK IV, CH I, SECT 8-9 308b-309b

35 HUME: *Human Understanding*, SECT V, DIV 35-38 464c-466c; DIV 40, 467c; DIV 44 468d-469c; SECT VII, DIV 59-61 476b-478a passim; SECT IX, DIV 83-84 487c-488b

38 ROUSSEAU: *Inequality*, 347a-b

42 KANT: *Pure Reason*, 223a-d

44 BOSWELL: *Johnson*, 135c-136a

46 HEGEL: *Philosophy of Right*, ADDITIONS, 97 132c-133a

49 DARWIN: *Descent of Man*, 320b-321a passim; 593a

53 JAMES: *Psychology*, 83b; 295b-298a esp 296b; 331b-336a; 361a-380a passim; 427b-430a; 433a-434a esp 434a; 502a-507a esp 504a; 520a-526b esp 520b, 524a-525a; 555a-557b passim; 852b-853a; 860b-862a

5e. Supernatural habits

5e(1) Grace as an entitative habit of the person

20 AQUINAS: *Summa Theologica*, PART I-II, Q 50, A 2, ANS 7c-8a; Q 51, A 4 15a-d; Q 82, A 1 168a-d; Q 110 347d-351d

5e(2) The infused virtues and the supernatural gifts

OLD TESTAMENT: *I Kings*, 3:5-15; 4:29-34—(D) *III Kings*, 3:5-15; 4:29-34 / *I Chronicles*, 22:12 —(D) *I Paralipomenon*, 22:12 / *II Chronicles*, 1:7-12—(D) *II Paralipomenon*, 1:7-12 / *Job*, 32:8 / *Psalms*, 119:34-40,73,125,130,144,169—(D) *Psalms*, 118:34-40,73,125,130,144,169 / *Proverbs*, 2 esp 2:6 / *Ecclesiastes*, 2:26 / *Isaiah*, 11:2-5—(D) *Isaias*, 11:2-5 / *Daniel*, 1 esp 1:17; 2:20-23

APOCRYPHA: *Wisdom of Solomon*, 3:9; 7:7,22; 8:7,21; 9—(D) OT, *Book of Wisdom*, 3:9; 7:7,22; 8:7,21; 9 / *Ecclesiasticus*, 1:1,5,10; 11:15; 15:5; 24:24-28; 43:33; 50:29; 51:17—(D) OT, *Ecclesiasticus*, 1:1,5,10; 11:15; 15:5; 24:34-38; 43:37; 50:31; 51:22-23

NEW TESTAMENT: *Matthew*, 6:33 / *Acts*, 2:1-21 / *I Corinthians*, 1:30; 2; 12:4-11 / *Ephesians*, 1:16-18; 4:17-5:21 / *Philippians*, 3:9 / *James*, 1:5-7,17; 3:13-18 / *II Peter*, 1:1-10

(5e. Supernatural'habits. 5e(2) The infused virtues and the supernatural gifts.)

20 AQUINAS: *Summa Theologica*, PART I–II, Q 51,
A 4 15a-d; Q 55, A 4, ANS and REP 6 28c-29d;
Q 63, AA 3–4 65a-66c; Q 68 87c-96c esp A 3 90d-
91b; Q 100, A 12, ANS and REP 3 264d-265d; Q
110, A 3, ANS and REP 3 350a-d; A 4, REP 1
350d-351d; PART II–II, QQ 8–9 416d-426c; Q
19 465a-474d; Q 45 598c-603c

23 HOBBES: *Leviathan*, PART I, 57c; PART III,
176d-177b; PART IV, 270c-d

5e(3) The theological virtues

OLD TESTAMENT: *Psalms*, 22; 25; 71—(D) *Psalms*,
21; 24; 70 / *Proverbs*, 3:1-26 / *Isaiah*, 40:31—
(D) *Isaias*, 40:31 / *Jeremiah*, 39:18—(D) *Jeremias*, 39:18

APOCRYPHA: *Wisdom of Solomon*, 3:9—(D) OT,
Book of Wisdom, 3:9 / *Ecclesiasticus*, 2:6-9;
13:14—(D) OT, *Ecclesiasticus*, 2:6-10; 13:18

NEW TESTAMENT: *Matthew*, 9:20-22,27-30;
15:22-28; 17:14-21 esp 17:19-21; 19:16-23 esp
19:21—(D) *Matthew*, 9:20-22,27-30; 15:22-
28; 17:14-20 esp 17:18-20; 19:16-23 esp 19:21
/ *Mark*, 9:17-27 esp 9:23-24—(D) *Mark*,
9:16-26 esp 9:22-23 / *Luke*, 17:5-6 / *John*,
14:21; 20:26-29 / *Romans*, 1:5,16-17; 3:20-5:9;
8:24-25; 10 / *I Corinthians*, 13 / *Galatians*, 5:5-6
/ *Ephesians*, 2:1-10 / *Colossians*, 1:1-8 / *I Thessalonians*, 5:8 / *Hebrews*, 6; 11 / *James*, 2:14-26
/ *II Peter*, 1:5-8 / *I John* / *II John* / *III John*

18 AUGUSTINE: *City of God*, BK X, CH 3 300b-
301a; BK XXI, CH 16 573b-574a

20 AQUINAS: *Summa Theologica*, PART I–II, Q 51,
A 4 15a-d; Q 58, A 3, REP 3 43b-44a; Q 62 59c-
63a; Q 63, A 3 65a-d; Q 64, A 4 69b-70a; Q 67,
AA 3–6 83b-87c; Q 110, A 3, REP 1 350a-d; A 4,
ANS 350d-351d; PART II–II, Q 23 482c-489c

21 DANTE: *Divine Comedy*, PARADISE, XXIV [1]-
XXVI [81] 142d-146c

23 HOBBES: *Leviathan*, PART II, 149c-d; PART III,
241c-242a

30 BACON: *Advancement of Learning*, 2c-4c

32 MILTON: *Paradise Lost*, BK XII [576-605] 331b-
332a

6. The force of habit in human life

OLD TESTAMENT: *Job*, 20:11-13 / *Proverbs*, 22:6 /
Jeremiah, 13:23—(D) *Jeremias*, 13:23

6 HERODOTUS: *History*, BK I, 35c-d; BK III, 97d-
98a; BK IV, 137a-138c

7 PLATO: *Laws*, BK VII, 716a-b; 717d-718d

8 ARISTOTLE: *Metaphysics*, BK II, CH 3 [994^b31-
995^a6] 513c

9 ARISTOTLE: *Ethics*, BK II, CH 1–6 348b,d-352d
passim, esp CH 1 [1103^b22-25] 349b; BK VII,
CH 5 [1148^b15-1149^a4] 399a-c; CH 10 [1152^a28-
33] 403b / *Rhetoric*, BK I, CH 10 [1368^b28-
1369^b27] 612a-613a esp [1369^a1-7] 612a-b,
[1369^b6-8] 612d, [1369^b16-19] 612d-613a

12 LUCRETIUS: *Nature of Things*, BK III [307-322]
34a-b

18 AUGUSTINE: *Confessions*, BK VII, par 23 50b-c;
BK VIII, par 18 57d-58a; par 25-26 60a-b /
Christian Doctrine, BK I, CH 24 630c-631a

20 AQUINAS: *Summa Theologica*, PART I–II, Q 49,
AA 3–4 4b-6a

23 MACHIAVELLI: *Prince*, CH XXV, 35d

25 MONTAIGNE: *Essays*, 16c-d; 42b-43d; 63d-
64b; 307c-308a; 316b-c; 390b-c; 391c-393b;
395b-396d; 489b-490c; 524b-527a

28 HARVEY: *Motion of the Heart*, 285b-c

31 DESCARTES: *Discourse*, PART III, 48b-49d

33 PASCAL: *Pensées*, 6 173a

35 HUME: *Human Understanding*, SECT V, DIV 35-
36 464c-465c; DIV 44-45, 469b-c

38 ROUSSEAU: *Inequality*, 347a-b

40 GIBBON: *Decline and Fall*, 464d

41 GIBBON: *Decline and Fall*, 125a

43 FEDERALIST: NUMBER 27, 95c-d

43 MILL: *Representative Government*, 370c-d /
Utilitarianism, 464a-d

44 BOSWELL: *Johnson*, 259a

49 DARWIN: *Descent of Man*, 308b; 317b-d

51 TOLSTOY: *War and Peace*, BK III, 150c; BK VI,
244a-b; BK VIII, 303a-305b; BK XI, 486a; BK
XII, 556d-557a; BK XIV, 609d; BK XV, 639c

53 JAMES: *Psychology*, 73b-83b

54 FREUD: *Beyond the Pleasure Principle*, 643d-
646a esp 645b-646a

6a. The automatic or unconscious functioning of habits

8 ARISTOTLE: *Categories*, CH 8 [8^b26-9^a13] 13d-
14a

9 ARISTOTLE: *Ethics*, BK VII, CH 10 [1152^a28-
33] 403b / *Rhetoric*, BK I, CH 11 [1370^a5-8]
613b

20 AQUINAS: *Summa Theologica*, PART I–II, Q 49,
A 2 2b-4a; Q 109, A 8, ANS 344d-346a

25 MONTAIGNE: *Essays*, 307c-308a; 316b-c

35 LOCKE: *Human Understanding*, BK II, CH IX,
SECT 8-10 139b-140b passim

43 MILL: *Utilitarianism*, 464a-b

49 DARWIN: *Origin of Species*, 119b

53 JAMES: *Psychology*, 3b; 73b-78b; 93a; 295b-
298a esp 296b; 774a; 788a-789a esp 788b-
789a; 790b-791a; 810a-b

54 FREUD: *General Introduction*, 455b

6b. The contribution of habit to the perfection of character and mind

OLD TESTAMENT: *Proverbs*, 22:6 / *Jeremiah*, 13:23
—(D) *Jeremias*, 13:23

APOCRYPHA: *Ecclesiasticus*, 30:8—(D) OT, *Ecclesiasticus*, 30:8

5 EURIPIDES: *Suppliants* [857-917] 266a-b

6 THUCYDIDES: *Peloponnesian War*, BK II, 396d-
397a

7 PLATO: *Republic*, BK III, 330a-331c; 333b-d;
BK VII, 389d-390b; 391c-d / *Timaeus*, 474d-
475d / *Theaetetus*, 518b / *Laws*, BK II, 653a-c

8 ARISTOTLE: *Categories*, CH 10 [13^a16-31] 18d
/ *Physics*, BK VII, CH 3 [246^a10-248^a6] 329c-
330d

CROSS-REFERENCES

For: Terms of fundamental relevance to the conception of habit, *see* BEING 7c–7c(3); MATTER 2a; MIND 2b; NATURE 2c.

The psychological analysis of the faculties or powers in which habits are situated, *see* ANIMAL 1a–1a(3); LIFE 3; MAN 4–4d; SOUL 2c–2c(3); VIRTUE AND VICE 2a.

Other discussions of instinct, *see* ANIMAL 1d; DESIRE 3a; EMOTION 1c; EVOLUTION 3b; SENSE 3d(3).

Consideration of the factors involved in the formation or breaking of habits, *see* EDUCATION 3–6; LAW 6d; VIRTUE AND VICE 4–4d(4).

The role of habit in the theory of virtue, *see* VIRTUE AND VICE 1e; for other discussions of the intellectual virtues, *see* ART 1; MIND 4c, 4e–4f; PRUDENCE 1–2c; SCIENCE 1a(1); VIRTUE AND VICE 2a, 2a(2); WISDOM 2a; for other discussions of the moral virtues, *see* COURAGE 1, 4; JUSTICE 1c–1d; TEMPERANCE 1–1b; VIRTUE AND VICE 2a–2a(1), 3b; for other discussions of the theological virtues, *see* KNOWLEDGE 6c(5); LOVE 5b–5b(2); MIND 5c; RELIGION 1a; VIRTUE AND VICE 2b, 8d–8d(3); and for other discussions of the infused virtues and the supernatural gifts, *see* MIND 4f, 5c; VIRTUE AND VICE 8e.

Matters relevant to grace as an entitative habit, *see* GOD 7d; MAN 9b(2); NATURE 6b; SIN 3c, 4d, 7; VIRTUE AND VICE 8b; WILL 7e(2).

Other considerations of the natural habits of the mind, *see* JUDGMENT 8a; KNOWLEDGE 6c(2)–6c(4); LAW 4a; MIND 4d(2)–4d(3); PRINCIPLE 2b(2), 3a(1), 4; VIRTUE AND VICE 4a.

The relation of habit to freedom, *see* WILL 3a(2).

The relation of habit to custom and law, *see* CUSTOM AND CONVENTION 2, 6b; LAW 5f, 6d.

ADDITIONAL READINGS

Listed below are works not included in *Great Books of the Western World*, but relevant to the idea and topics with which this chapter deals. These works are divided into two groups:

I. Works by authors represented in this collection.
II. Works by authors not represented in this collection.

For the date, place, and other facts concerning the publication of the works cited, consult the Bibliography of Additional Readings which follows the last chapter of *The Great Ideas*.

I.

AQUINAS. *Quaestiones Disputatae, De Veritate*, Q 16
DESCARTES. *The Passions of the Soul*, XVI, XLIV, L
HUME. *A Treatise of Human Nature*, BK I, PART III, SECT VIII–IX, XIV; BK II, PART III, SECT V
C. R. DARWIN. *A Posthumous Essay on Instinct*
——. *The Expression of Emotions in Man and Animals*

II.

SENECA. "On the Diseases of the Soul," in *Moral Letters*
SUÁREZ. *Disputationes Metaphysicae*, XXXIX, XLII (2–5), XLIII–XLIV, XLVI (3), LIII
MALEBRANCHE. *De la recherche de la vérité*, BK II (1), CH 5
LEIBNITZ. *New Essays Concerning Human Understanding*, BK II, CH 22 (10)

HARTLEY. *Observations on Man, His Frame, His Duty and His Expectations*, VOL I, PROPOSITION 21
CONDILLAC. *Traité des animaux*, PART II, CH 5
VOLTAIRE. "Instinct," in *A Philosophical Dictionary*
T. REID. *Essays on the Active Powers of the Human Mind*, III, PART I, CH 2–3
BENTHAM. *An Introduction to the Principles of Morals and Legislation*, CH 11
MAINE DE BIRAN. *The Influence of Habit on the Faculty of Thinking*
D. STEWART. *Outlines of Moral Philosophy*, PART I, CH 10
——. *Elements of the Philosophy of the Human Mind*, PART II, CH 5
SCHOPENHAUER. *The World as Will and Idea*, VOL III, SUP, CH 27
J. MILL. *Analysis of the Phenomena of the Human Mind*, CH III
RAVAISSON-MOLLIEN. *De l'habitude*

E. HARTMANN. *Philosophy of the Unconscious*, (A) III; (B) I

HERING. *Memory*

S. BUTLER. *Life and Habit*

RADESTOCK. *Habit and Its Importance in Education*

ROMANES. *Mental Evolution in Animals*, CH 11–18

C. S. PEIRCE. *Collected Papers*, VOL III, par 154–164, 359–403; VOL VI, par 259–263

H. R. MARSHALL. *Instinct and Reason*

BERGSON. *Creative Evolution*, CH 2

WOODWORTH. *Psychological Issues*, CH 9

C. L. MORGAN. *Habit and Instinct*

——. *Instinct and Experience*

JUNG. *Instinct and the Unconscious*

RIVERS. *Instinct and the Unconscious*

B. RUSSELL. *The Analysis of Mind*, LECT 2

DEWEY. *Human Nature and Conduct*, PART I–II

PAVLOV. *Conditioned Reflexes*

VANN. *Morals Makyth Man*

THORNDIKE. *Man on His Works*

Chapter 33: HAPPINESS

INTRODUCTION

THE great questions about happiness are concerned with its definition and its attainability. In what does happiness consist? Is it the same for all men, or do different men seek different things in the name of happiness? Can happiness be achieved on earth, or only hereafter? And if the pursuit of happiness is not a futile quest, by what means or steps should it be undertaken?

On all these questions, the great books set forth the fundamental inquiries and speculations, as well as the controversies to which they have given rise, in the tradition of western thought. There seems to be no question that men want happiness. "Man wishes to be happy," Pascal writes, "and only wishes to be happy, and cannot wish not to be so." To the question, what moves desire? Locke thinks only one answer is possible: "happiness, and that alone."

But this fact, even if it goes undisputed, does not settle the issue whether men are right in governing their lives with a view to being or becoming happy. There is therefore one further question. *Should* men make happiness their goal and direct their acts accordingly?

According to Kant, "the principle of *private happiness*" is "the direct opposite of the principle of morality." He understands happiness to consist in "the satisfaction of all our desires: *extensive*, in regard to their multiplicity; *intensive*, in regard to their degree; *protensive*, in regard to their duration." What Kant calls the "pragmatic" rule of life, which aims at happiness, "tells us what we have to do, if we wish to become possessed of happiness."

Unlike the moral law, it is a hypothetical, not a categorical, imperative. Furthermore, Kant points out that such a pragmatic or utilitarian ethics (which is for him the same as an "ethics of happiness") cannot help being empirical, "for it is only by experience," he says, "that I can learn either what inclinations exist which desire satisfaction, or what are the natural means of satisfying them." Such empirical knowledge "is available for each individual in his own way." Hence there can be no universal solution in terms of desire of the problem of how to be happy. To reduce moral philosophy to "a theory of happiness" must result, therefore, in giving up the search for ethical principles which are both universal and *a priori*.

In sharp opposition to the pragmatic rule, Kant sets the "moral or ethical law," the motive of which is not simply to be happy, but rather to be *worthy* of happiness. In addition to being a categorical imperative which imposes an absolute obligation upon us, this law, he says, "takes no account of our desires or the means of satisfying them." Rather it "dictates how we ought to act in order to deserve happiness." It is drawn from pure reason, not from experience, and therefore has the universality of an *a priori* principle, without which, in Kant's opinion, a genuine science of ethics—or metaphysic of morals—is impossible.

With the idea of moral worth—that which alone deserves happiness—taken away, "happiness alone is," according to Kant, "far from being the complete good. Reason does not approve of it (however much inclination may desire it) except as united with desert. On the other hand," Kant admits, "morality alone and, with it, mere *desert*, is likewise far from being the complete good." These two things must be united to constitute the true *summum bonum* which, according to Kant, means both the *supreme* and the *complete* good. The man "who conducts himself in a manner not unworthy of happiness, must be able to hope for the possession of happiness."

But even if happiness combined with moral

worth does constitute the supreme good, Kant still refuses to admit that happiness, as a practical objective, can function as a moral principle. Though a man can hope to be happy only if under the moral law he does his duty, he should not do his duty with the hope of thereby becoming happy. "A disposition," he writes, "which should require the prospect of happiness as its necessary condition, would not be moral, and hence also would not be worthy of complete happiness." The moral law commands the performance of duty *unconditionally*. Happiness should be a consequence, but it cannot be a condition, of moral action.

In other words, happiness fails for Kant to impose any moral obligation or to provide a standard of right and wrong in human conduct. No more than pleasure can happiness be used as a first principle in ethics, if morality must avoid all calculations of utility or expediency whereby things are done or left undone for the sake of happiness, or any other end to be enjoyed.

THIS ISSUE BETWEEN an ethics of duty and an ethics of happiness, as well as the conflict it involves between law and desire as sources of morality, are considered, from other points of view, in the chapters on DESIRE and DUTY, and again in GOOD AND EVIL where the problem of the *summum bonum* is raised. In this chapter, we shall be concerned with happiness as an ethical principle, and therefore with the problems to be faced by those who, in one way or another, accept happiness as the supreme good and the end of life. They may see no reason to reject moral principles which work through desire rather than duty. They may find nothing repugnant in appealing to happiness as the ultimate end which justifies the means and determines the order of all other goods. But they cannot make happiness the first principle of ethics without having to face many questions concerning the nature of happiness and its relation to virtue.

Discussion begins rather than ends with the fact that happiness is what all men desire. Once they have asserted that fact, once they have made happiness the most fundamental of all ethical terms, writers like Aristotle or Locke, Aquinas or Mill, cannot escape the question

whether *all* who seek happiness look for it or find it in the *same* things.

Holding that a definite conception of happiness cannot be formulated, Kant thinks that happiness fails even as a pragmatic principle of conduct. "The notion of happiness is so indefinite," he writes, "that although every man wishes to attain it, yet he never can say definitely and consistently what it is that he really wishes." He cannot "determine with certainty what would make him truly happy; because to do so he would need to be omniscient." If this is true of the individual, how various must be the notions of happiness which prevail among men in general.

Locke plainly asserts what is here implied, namely, the fact that "everyone does not place his happiness in the same thing, or choose the same way to it." But admitting this fact does not prevent Locke from inquiring how "in matters of happiness and misery ... men come often to prefer the worse to the better; and to choose that which, by their own confession, has made them miserable." Even though he declares that "the same thing is not good to every man alike," Locke thinks it is possible to account "for the misery that men often bring on themselves" by explaining how the individual may make errors in judgment—"how things come to be represented to our desires under deceitful appearances ... by the judgment pronouncing wrongly concerning them."

But this applies to the individual only. Locke does not think it is possible to show that when two men differ in their notions of happiness, one is right and the other wrong. "Though all men's desires tend to happiness, yet they are not moved by the same object. Men may choose different things, and yet all choose right." He does not quarrel with the theologians who, on the basis of divine revelation, describe the eternal happiness in the life hereafter which is to be enjoyed *alike* by all who are saved. But revelation is one thing, and reason another.

With respect to temporal happiness on earth, reason cannot achieve a definition of the end that has the certainty of faith concerning salvation. Hence Locke quarrels with "the philosophers of old" who, in his opinion, vainly sought to define the *summum bonum* or happiness in such a way that all men would agree on what happiness is; or, if they failed to, some would be in error and misled in their pursuit of happiness.

It may be wondered, therefore, what Locke means by saying that there is a science of what man ought to do "as a rational and voluntary agent for the attainment of . . . happiness." He describes ethics as the science of the "rules and measures of human actions, which lead to happiness" and he places "morality amongst the sciences capable of demonstration, wherein . . . from self-evident propositions, by necessary consequences, as incontestable as those in mathematics, the measures of right and wrong might be made out, to any one that will apply himself with the same indifferency and attention to the one, as he does to the other of these sciences."

THE ANCIENT philosophers with whom Locke disagrees insist that a science of ethics depends on a first principle which is self-evident in the same way to all men. Happiness is not that principle if the content of happiness is what each man thinks it to be; for if no universally applicable definition of happiness can be given —if when men differ in their conception of what constitutes happiness, one man may be as right as another—then the fact that all men agree upon giving the name "happiness" to what they ultimately want amounts to no more than a nominal agreement. Such nominal agreement, in the opinion of Aristotle and Aquinas, does not suffice to establish a science of ethics, with rules for the pursuit of happiness which shall apply universally to all men.

On their view, what is truly human happiness must be the same for all men. The reason, in the words of Aquinas, is that "all men agree in their specific nature." It is in terms of their specific or common nature that happiness can be objectively defined. Happiness so conceived is a common end for all, "since nature tends to one thing only."

It may be granted that there are in fact many different opinions about what constitutes happiness, but it cannot be admitted that all are equally sound without admitting a complete relativism in moral matters. That men do *in fact* seek different things under the name of happiness does not, according to Aristotle and Aquinas, alter the truth that the happiness they

should seek must be something appropriate to the humanity which is common to them all, rather than something determined by their individually differing needs or temperaments. If it were the latter, then Aristotle and Aquinas would admit that questions about what men should do to achieve happiness would be answerable only by individual opinion or personal preference, not by scientific analysis or demonstration.

With the exception of Locke and perhaps to a less extent Mill, those who think that a science of ethics can be founded on happiness as the first principle tend to maintain that there can be only one right conception of human happiness. They regard other notions as misconceptions which may appear to be, but are not really the *summum bonum*. The various definitions of happiness which men have given thus present the problem of the real and the apparent good, the significance of which is considered in the chapter on GOOD AND EVIL.

IN THE EVERYDAY discourse of men there seems to be a core of agreement about the meaning of the words "happy" and "happiness." This common understanding has been used by philosophers like Aristotle and Mill to test the adequacy of any definition of happiness.

When a man says "I feel happy" he is saying that he feels pleased or satisfied—that he has what he wants. When men contrast tragedy and happiness, they have in mind the quality a life takes from its end. A tragedy on the stage, in fiction, or in life is popularly characterized as "a story without a happy ending." This expresses the general sense that happiness is the quality of a life which comes out well on the whole despite difficulties and vicissitudes along the way. Only ultimate defeat or frustration is tragic.

There appears to be some conflict here between *feeling* happy at a given moment and *being* happy for a lifetime, that is, living happily. It may be necessary to choose between having a good time and leading a good life. Nevertheless, in both uses of the word "happy" there is the connotation of satisfaction. When men say that what they want is happiness, they imply that, having it, they would ask for nothing more. If they are asked why they want to be happy, they find it difficult to give any reason except "for its own sake." They can think of nothing beyond happiness for which happiness serves as a means or a preparation. This aspect of ultimacy or finality appears without qualification in the sense of happiness as belonging to a whole life. There is quiescence, too, in the momentary feeling of happiness, but precisely because it does not last, it leaves another and another such moment to be desired.

Observing these facts, Aristotle takes the word "happiness" from popular discourse and gives it the technical significance of ultimate good, last end, or *summum bonum.* "The chief good," he writes, "is evidently something final. . . . Now we call that which is in itself worthy of pursuit more final than that which is worthy of pursuit for the sake of something else, and that which is never desirable for the sake of something else more final than the things that are desirable both in themselves and for the sake of that other thing. Therefore, we call final without qualification that which is always desirable in itself and never for the sake of something else. Such a thing happiness, above all else, is held to be; for this we choose always for itself and never for the sake of something else."

The ultimacy of happiness can also be expressed in terms of its completeness or sufficiency. It would not be true that happiness is desired for its own sake and everything else for the sake of happiness, if the happy man wanted something more. The most obvious mark of the happy man, according to Aristotle, is that he wants for nothing. The happy life leaves nothing to be desired. It is this insight which Boethius later expresses in an oft-repeated characterization of happiness as "a life made perfect by the possession in aggregate of all good things." So conceived, happiness is not a particular good itself, but the sum of goods. "If happiness were to be counted as one good among others," Aristotle argues, "it would clearly be made more desirable by the addition of even the least of goods." But then there would be something left for the happy man to desire, and happiness would not be "something final and self-sufficient and the end of action."

Like Aristotle, Mill appeals to the common sense of mankind for the ultimacy of happiness.

"The utilitarian doctrine," he writes, "is that happiness is desirable, and the only thing desirable as an end; all other things being only desirable as means." No reason can or need be given why this is so, "except that each person, so far as he believes it to be attainable, desires his own happiness." This is enough to prove that happiness is *a* good. To show that it is *the* good, it is "necessary to show, not only that people desire happiness, but that they never desire anything else."

Here Mill's answer, like Aristotle's, presupposes the rightness of the prevailing sense that when a man is happy, he has everything he desires. Many things, Mill admits, may be desired for their own sake, but if the possession of any one of these leaves something else to be desired, then it is desired only as a part of happiness. Happiness is "a concrete whole, and these are some of its parts. . . . Whatever is desired otherwise than as a means to some end beyond itself, and ultimately to happiness, is desired as itself a part of happiness, and is not desired for itself until it has become so."

THERE ARE OTHER conceptions of happiness. It is not always approached in terms of means and ends, utility and enjoyment or satisfaction. Plato, for example, identifies happiness with spiritual well-being—a harmony in the soul, an inner peace which results from the proper order of all the soul's parts.

Early in the *Republic,* Socrates is challenged to show that the just man will be happier than the unjust man, even if in all externals he seems to be at a disadvantage. He cannot answer this question until he prepares Glaucon for the insight that justice is "concerned not with the outward man, but with the inward." He can then explain that "the just man does not permit the several elements within him to interfere with one another. . . . He sets in order his own inner life, and is his own master and his own law, and is at peace with himself."

In the same spirit Plotinus asks us to think of "two wise men, one of them possessing all that is supposed to be naturally welcome, while the other meets only with the very reverse." He wants to know whether we would "assert that they have an equal happiness." His own answer is that we should, "if they are equally wise . . . [even] though the one be favored in body and in all else that does not help towards wisdom." We are likely to misconceive happiness, Plotinus thinks, if we consider the happy man in terms of our own feebleness. "We count alarming and grave what his felicity takes lightly; he would be neither wise nor in the state of happiness if he had not quitted all trifling with such things."

According to Plotinus, "Plato rightly taught that he who is to be wise and to possess happiness draws his good from the Supreme, fixing his gaze on That, becoming like to That, living by That . . . All else he will attend to only as he might change his residence, not in expectation of any increase in his settled felicity, but simply in a reasonable attention to the differing conditions surrounding him as he lives here or there." If he "meets some turn of fortune that he would not have chosen, there is not the slightest lessening of his happiness for that." Like Plato, Plotinus holds that nothing external can separate a virtuous man from happiness—that no one can injure a man except himself.

The opposite view is more frequently held. In his argument with Callicles in the *Gorgias*, Socrates meets with the proposition that it is better to injure others than to be injured by them. This can be refuted, he thinks, only if Callicles can be made to understand that the unjust or vicious man is miserable in himself, regardless of his external gains. The fundamental principle, he says, is that "the happy are made happy by the possession of justice and temperance and the miserable miserable by the possession of vice." Happiness is one with justice because justice or virtue in general is "the health and beauty and well-being of the soul."

This association of happiness with health—the one a harmony in the soul as the other is a harmony in the body—appears also in Freud's consideration of human well-being. For Freud, the ideal of health, not merely bodily health but the health of the whole man, seems to identify happiness with peace of mind. "Anyone who is born with a specially unfavorable instinctual constitution," he writes, "and whose libido-components do not go through the transformation and modification necessary for suc-

cessful achievement in later life, will find it hard to obtain happiness." The opposite of happiness is not tragedy but neurosis. In contrast to the neurotic, the happy man has found a way to master his inner conflicts and to become well-adjusted to his environment.

The theory of happiness as mental health or spiritual peace may be another way of seeing the self-sufficiency of happiness, in which all striving comes to rest because all desires are fulfilled or quieted. The suggestion of this point is found in the fact that the theologians conceive beatitude, or supernatural happiness, in both ways. For them it is both an ultimate end which satisfies all desires and also a state of peace or heavenly rest.

"The ultimate good," Augustine writes, "is that for the sake of which other things are to be desired, while it is to be desired for its own sake"; and, he adds, it is that by which the good "is finished, so that it becomes complete"—all-satisfying. But what is this "final blessedness, the ultimate consummation, the unending end"? It is peace. "Indeed," Augustine says, "we are said to be blessed when we have such peace as can be enjoyed in this life; but such blessedness is mere misery compared to that final felicity," which can be described as "either peace in eternal life or eternal life in peace."

THERE MAY BE differences of another kind among those who regard happiness as their ultimate end. Some men identify happiness with the possession of one particular type of good—wealth or health, pleasure or power, knowledge or virtue, honor or friendship—or, if they do not make one or another of these things the only component of happiness, they make it supreme. The question of which is chief among the various goods that constitute the happy life is the problem of the order of goods, to which we shall return presently. But the identification of happiness with some one good, to the exclusion or neglect of the others, seems to violate the meaning of happiness on which there is such general agreement. Happiness cannot be that which leaves nothing to be desired if any good —anything which is in any way desirable—is overlooked.

But it may be said that the miser desires nothing but gold, and considers himself happy when he possesses a hoard. That he may consider himself happy cannot be denied. Yet this does not prevent the moralist from considering him deluded and in reality among the unhappiest of men. The difference between such illusory happiness and the reality seems to depend on the distinction between conscious and natural desire. According to that distinction, considered in the chapter on DESIRE, the miser may have all that he consciously desires, but lack many of the things toward which his nature tends and which are therefore objects of natural desire. He may be the unhappiest of men if, with all the wealth in the world, yet self-deprived of friends or knowledge, virtue or even health, his exclusive interest in one type of good leads to the frustration of many other desires. He may not consciously recognize these, but they nevertheless represent needs of his nature demanding fulfillment.

As suggested in the chapter on DESIRE, the relation of natural law to natural desire may provide the beginning, at least, of an answer to Kant's objection to the ethics of happiness on the ground that its principles lack universality or the element of obligation. The natural moral law may command obedience at the same time that it directs men to happiness as the satisfaction of all desires which represent the innate tendencies of man's nature. The theory of natural desire thus also has a bearing on the issue whether the content of happiness must really be the same for all men, regardless of how it may appear to them.

Even if men do not identify happiness with one type of good, but see it as the possession of every sort of good, can there be a reasonable difference of opinion concerning the types of good which must be included or the order in which these several goods should be sought? A negative answer seems to be required by the view that real as opposed to apparent goods are the objects of natural desire.

Aquinas, for example, admits that "*happy is the man who has all he desires*, or *whose every wish is fulfilled*, is a good and adequate definition" only "if it be understood in a certain way." It is "an inadequate definition if understood in another. For if we understand it simply of all that man desires by his natural appetite, then it is true that he who has all that he desires

is happy; since nothing satisfies man's natural desire, except the perfect good which is Happiness. But if we understand it of those things that man desires according to the apprehension of reason," Aquinas continues, then "it does not belong to Happiness to have certain things that man desires; rather does it belong to unhappiness, in so far as the possession of such things hinders a man from having all that he desires naturally." For this reason, Aquinas points out, when Augustine approved the statement that "*happy is he who has all he desires*," he added the words "provided he *desires nothing amiss*."

As men have the same complex nature, so they have the same set of natural desires. As they have the same natural desires, so the real goods which can fulfill their needs comprise the same variety for all. As different natural desires represent different parts of human nature —lower and higher—so the several kinds of good are not equally good. And, according to Aquinas, if the natural object of the human will "is the universal good," it follows that "naught can satisfy man's will save the universal good." This, he holds, "is to be found, not in any created thing, but in God alone."

We shall return later to the theologian's conception of perfect happiness as consisting in the vision of God in the life hereafter. The happiness of this earthly life (which the philosopher considers) may be imperfect by comparison, but such temporal felicity as men can attain is no less determined by natural desire. If a man's undue craving for one type of good can interfere with his possession of another sort of good, then the various goods must be ordered according to their worth; and this order, since it reflects natural desire, must be the same for all men. In such terms Aristotle seems to think it possible to argue that the reality of happiness can be defined by reference to human nature and that the rules for achieving happiness can have a certain universality—despite the fact that the rules must be applied by individuals differently to the circumstances of their own lives. No particular good should be sought excessively or out of proportion to others, for the penalty of having too much of one good thing is deprivation or disorder with respect to other goods.

THE RELATION OF happiness to particular goods raises a whole series of questions, each peculiar to the type of good under consideration. Of these, the most insistent problems concern pleasure, knowledge, virtue, and the goods of fortune.

With regard to pleasure, the difficulty seems to arise from two meanings of the term which are more fully discussed in the chapter on PLEASURE AND PAIN. In one of these meanings pleasure is an object of desire, and in the other it is the feeling of satisfaction which accompanies the possession of objects desired. It is in the latter meaning that pleasure can be identified with happiness or, at least, be regarded as its correlate, for if happiness consists in the possession of all good things it is also the sum total of attainable satisfactions or pleasures. Where pleasure means satisfaction, pain means frustration, not the sensed pain of injured flesh. Happiness, Locke can therefore say, "is the utmost pleasure we are capable of"; and Mill can define it as "an existence exempt as far as possible from pain, and as rich as possible in enjoyments." Nor does Aristotle object to saying that the happy life "is also in itself pleasant."

But unlike Locke and Mill, Aristotle raises the question whether all pleasures are good, and all pains evil. Sensuous pleasure as an object often conflicts with other objects of desire. And if "pleasure" means satisfaction, there can be conflict among pleasures, for the satisfaction of one desire may lead to the frustration of another. At this point Aristotle finds it necessary to introduce the principle of virtue. The virtuous man is one who finds pleasure "in the things that are by nature pleasant." The virtuous man takes pleasure *only* in the right things, and is willing to suffer pain for the right end. If pleasures, or desires and their satisfaction, can be better or worse, there must be a choice among them for the sake of happiness. Mill makes this choice depend on a discrimination between lower and higher pleasures, not on virtue. He regards virtue merely as one of the parts of happiness, in no way different from the others. But Aristotle seems to think that virtue is the principal means to happiness because it regulates the choices which must be rightly made in order to obtain all good things; hence his definition of happiness as "activity in accordance with virtue."

This definition raises difficulties of still another order. As the chapter on VIRTUE AND VICE indicates, there are for Aristotle two kinds of virtue, moral and intellectual, the one concerned with desire and social conduct, the other with thought and knowledge. There are also two modes of life, sometimes called the active and the contemplative, differing as a life devoted to political activity or practical tasks differs from a life occupied largely with theoretic problems in the pursuit of truth or in the consideration of what is known. Are there two kinds of happiness then, belonging respectively to the political and the speculative life? Is one a better kind of happiness than another? Does the practical sort of happiness require intellectual as well as moral virtue? Does the speculative sort require both also?

In trying to answer these questions, and generally in shaping his definition of happiness, Aristotle considers the role of the goods of fortune, such things as health, wealth, auspicious birth, native endowments of body or mind, and length of life. These gifts condition virtuous activity or may present problems which virtue is needed to solve. But to the extent that having or not having them is a matter of fortune, they are not within a man's control—to get, keep, or give up. If they are indispensable, happiness is precarious, or even unattainable by those who are unfortunate. In addition, if the goods of fortune are indispensable, the definition of happiness must itself be qualified. More is required for happiness than activity in accordance with virtue.

"Should we not say," Aristotle asks, "that he is happy who is active in accordance with complete virtue and is sufficiently equipped with external goods, not for some chance period but throughout a complete life? Or must we add 'and who is destined to live thus and die as befits his life'? . . . If so, we shall call happy those among living men in whom these conditions are, and are to be, fulfilled—but happy *men*."

THE CONSIDERATION of the goods of fortune has led to diverse views about the attainability of happiness in this life. For one thing, they may act as an obstacle to happiness. Pierre Bezùkhov in *War and Peace* learned, during his period of captivity, that "man is created for happiness; that happiness lies in himself, in the satisfaction of his natural human cravings; that all unhappiness arises not from privation but from superfluity."

The vicissitudes of fortune seem to be what Solon has in mind when, as reported by Herodotus, he tells Croesus, the king of Lydia, that he will not call him happy "until I hear that thou has closed thy life happily . . . for oftentimes God gives men a gleam of happiness, and then plunges them into ruin." For this reason, in judging of happiness, as "in every matter, it behoves us to mark well the end."

Even if it is possible to call a man happy while he is alive—on the ground that virtue, which is within his power, may be able to withstand anything but the most outrageous fortune—it is still necessary to define happiness by reference to a complete life. Children cannot be called happy, Aristotle holds, because their characters have not yet matured and their lives are still too far from completion. To call them happy, or to call happy men of any age who still may suffer great misfortune, is merely to voice the hopes we have for them. "The most prosperous," Aristotle writes, "may fall into great misfortunes in old age, as is told of Priam in the Trojan cycle; and one who has experienced such chances and has ended wretchedly no one calls happy."

Among the goods of fortune which seem to have a bearing on the attainment of happiness, those which constitute the *individual* nature of a human being at birth—physical traits, temperament, degree of intelligence—may be unalterable in the course of life. If certain inherited conditions either limit the capacity for happiness or make it completely unattainable, then happiness, which is defined as the end of man, is not the *summum bonum* for all, or not for all in the same way.

In the Aristotelian view, for example, women cannot be happy to the same degree or in the same manner as men; and natural slaves, like beasts, have no capacity for happiness at all, though they may participate in the happiness of the masters they serve. The theory is that through serving him, the slave gives the master the leisure necessary for the political or speculative life open to those of auspicious birth. Even as the man who is a slave belongs wholly to another man, so the highest good of his life lies in his contribution to the happiness of that other.

The question whether happiness can be achieved by all normal human beings or only by those gifted with very special talents, depends for its answer in part on the conception of happiness itself. Like Aristotle, Spinoza places happiness in intellectual activity of so high an order that the happy man is almost godlike; and, at the very end of his *Ethics*, he finds it necessary to say that the way to happiness "must indeed be difficult since it is so seldom discovered." Nevertheless, "true peace of soul" can be found by the rare individual. "All noble things are as difficult as they are rare." In contrast, a statement like Tawney's—that "if a man has important work to do, and enough leisure and income to enable him to do it properly, he is in possession of as much happiness as is good for any of the children of Adam"—seems to make happiness available to more than the gifted few.

Whether happiness is attainable by all men, even on Tawney's definition, may also depend on the economic system and the political constitution, to the extent that they determine whether all men will be granted the opportunity and the leisure to use whatever talents they have for leading a decent human life. There seems to be a profound connection between conceiving happiness in such a way that all normal men are capable of it and insisting that all normal men deserve political status and economic liberty. Mill, for example, differs from Aristotle on both scores.

DIFFERING FROM the position of both Aristotle and Mill is the view that happiness is an illusory goal—that the besetting ills of human life as well as the frailty of men lead inevitably to tragedy. The great tragic poems and the great tragedies of history may, of course, be read as if they dealt with the exceptional case, but another interpretation is possible. Here writ large in the life of the hero, the great or famous man, is the tragic pattern of human life which is the lot of all men.

Sophocles seems to be saying this, when he writes in *Oedipus at Colonus:* "Not to be born is, past all prizing, best; but, when a man hath seen the light, this is next best by far, that with all speed he should go thither, whence he hath come. For when he hath seen youth go by, with its light follies, what troublous affliction is strange to his lot, what suffering is not therein? —envy, factions, strife, battles, and slaughters; and, last of all, age claims him for her own— age, dispraised, infirm, unsociable, unfriended, with whom all woe of woe abides."

Death is sometimes regarded as the symbol of tragic frustration. Sometimes it is not death, but the fear of death which overshadows life, so that for Montaigne, learning how to face death well seems indispensable to living well. "The very felicity of life itself," he writes, "which depends upon the tranquility and contentment of a well-descended spirit, and the resolution and assurance of a well-ordered soul, ought never to be attributed to any man till he has first been seen to play the last, and, doubtless, the hardest act of his part. There may be disguise and dissimulation in all the rest ... but, in this scene of death, there is no more counterfeiting: we must speak out plain and discover what there is of good and clean in the bottom of the pot."

So, too, for Lucretius, what happiness men can have depends on their being rid of the fear of death through knowing the causes of things. But neither death nor the fear of death may be the crucial flaw. It may be the temporal character of life itself.

It is said that happiness consists in the possession of all good things. It is said that happiness is the quality of a whole life, not the feeling of satisfaction for a moment. If this is so, then Solon's remark to Croesus can be given another meaning, namely, that happiness is not something actually enjoyed by a man at any moment of his life. Man can come to possess all good things only in the succession of his days, not simultaneously; and so happiness is never actually achieved but is always in the process of being achieved. When that process is completed, the man is dead, his life is done.

It may still be true that to live well or virtuously—with the help of fortune—is to live happily, but so long as life goes on, happiness is pursued rather than enjoyed. On earth and in time, man does not seem able to come to rest in any final satisfaction, with all his desires quieted at once and forever by that vision of perfection which would deserve Faust's "Stay, thou art so fair!"

As ALREADY INTIMATED, the problem of human happiness takes on another dimension when it is treated by the Christian theologians. Any happiness which men can have on earth and in time is, according to Augustine, "rather the solace of our misery than the positive enjoyment of felicity.

"Our very righteousness," he goes on to say, "though true in so far as it has respect to the true good, is yet in this life of such a kind that it consists rather in the remission of sins than in the perfecting of virtues. . . . For as reason, though subjected to God, is yet 'pressed down by the corruptible body,' so long as it is in this mortal condition, it has not perfect authority over vice. . . . For though it exercises authority, the vices do not submit without a struggle. For however well one maintains the conflict, and however thoroughly he has subdued these enemies, there steals in some evil thing, which, if it do not find ready expression in act, slips out by the lips, or insinuates itself into the thought; and therefore his peace is not full so long as he is at war with his vices."

Accepting the definition of happiness as the possession of all good things and the satisfaction of all desires, the theologians compare the successive accumulation of finite goods with the unchanging enjoyment of an infinite good. An endless prolongation of the days of our mortal life would not increase the chances of becoming perfectly happy, because time and change permit no rest, no finality. Earthly happiness is therefore intrinsically imperfect.

Perfect happiness belongs to the eternal life of the immortal soul, completely at rest in the beatific vision, for in the vision of God the soul is united to the infinite good by knowledge and love. In the divine presence and glory all the natural desires of the human spirit are simultaneously satisfied—the intellect's search for truth and the will's yearning for the good. "That final peace to which all our righteousness has reference, and for the sake of which it is maintained," Augustine describes as "the felicity of a life which is done with bondage"—to vice or conflict, to time and change. In contrast, the best human life on earth is miserable with frustrations and an ennui that human nature cannot escape.

The doctrine of immortality is obviously presupposed in the theological consideration of happiness. For Kant immortality is a necessary condition of the soul's infinite progress toward the moral perfection, the holiness, which alone deserves perfect happiness. But for theologians like Augustine and Aquinas, neither change nor progress play any part in immortal life. On the contrary, the immortal soul finds its salvation in eternal rest. The difference between motion and rest, between time and eternity, belongs to the very essence of the theologian's distinction between imperfect happiness on earth and perfect happiness hereafter.

These matters, of relevance to the theory of happiness, are discussed in the chapters on ETERNITY and IMMORTALITY; and in the chapter on SIN we find another religious dogma, that of original sin, which has an obvious bearing on earthly happiness as well as on eternal salvation. Fallen human nature, according to Christian teaching, is incompetent to achieve even the natural end of imperfect temporal happiness without God's help. Milton expounds this doctrine of indispensable grace in *Paradise Lost*, in words which God the Father addresses to His Son:

Man shall not quite be lost, but sav'd who will,
Yet not of will in him, but grace in me
Freely voutsaft; once more I will renew
His lapsed powers, though forfeit and enthrall'd
By sin to foul exorbitant desires;
Upheld by me, yet once more he shall stand
On even ground against his mortal foe,
By me upheld, that he may know how frail
His fall'n condition is, and to me owe
All his deliv'rance, and to none but me.

God's grace is needed for men to lead a good life on earth as well as for eternal blessedness. On earth, man's efforts to be virtuous require the reinforcement of supernatural gifts—faith, hope, and charity, and the infused moral virtues. The beatific vision in Heaven totally exceeds the natural powers of the soul and comes with the gift of added supernatural light. It seems, in short, that there is no purely natural happiness according to the strict tenets of Christian doctrine.

Aquinas employs the conception of eternal beatitude not only to measure the imperfection of earthly life, but also to insist that temporal happiness is happiness at all only to the extent that it is a remote participation of true and perfect happiness. It cannot be said of temporal happiness that it "excludes every evil and fulfills every desire. In this life every evil cannot be excluded. For this present life is subject to many unavoidable evils: to ignorance on the part of the intellect; to inordinate affection on the part of the appetite; and to many penalties on the part of the body. . . . Likewise," Aquinas continues, "neither can the desire for good be satiated in this life. For man naturally desires the good which he has to be abiding. Now the goods of the present life pass away, since life itself passes away. . . . Wherefore it is impossible to have true happiness in this life."

If perfect happiness consists in "the vision of the Divine Essence, which men cannot obtain in this life," then, according to Aquinas, only the earthly life which somehow partakes of God has a measure of happiness in it. Earthly happiness, imperfect because of its temporal and bodily conditions, consists in a life devoted to God—a kind of inchoate participation here and now of the beatific vision hereafter. On earth there can be only a beginning "in respect of that operation whereby man is united to God. . . . In the present life, in as far as we fall short of the unity and continuity of that operation, so do we fall short of perfect happiness. Nevertheless it is a participation of happiness; and so much the greater, as the operation can be more continuous and more one. Consequently the active life which is busy with many things, has less of happiness than the contemplative life, which is busied with one thing, *i.e.*, the contemplation of truth."

When the theologians consider the modes of life on earth in terms of the fundamental distinction between the secular and the religious, or the active and the contemplative, they seem to admit the possibility of imperfect happiness in either mode. In either, a devout Christian dedicates every act to the glory of God, and through such dedication embraces the divine in the passing moments of his earthly pilgrimage.

OUTLINE OF TOPICS

REFERENCES

To find the passages cited, use the numbers in heavy type, which are the volume and page numbers of the passages referred to. For example, in **4** HOMER: *Iliad*, BK II [265–283] 12d, the number **4** is the number of the volume in the set; the number **12d** indicates that the passage is in section d of page 12.

PAGE SECTIONS: When the text is printed in one column, the letters **a** and **b** refer to the upper and lower halves of the page. For example, in **53** JAMES: *Psychology*, 116a–119b, the passage begins in the upper half of page 116 and ends in the lower half of page 119. When the text is printed in two columns, the letters **a** and **b** refer to the upper and lower halves of the left-hand side of the page, the letters **c** and **d** to the upper and lower halves of the right-hand side of the page. For example, in **7** PLATO: *Symposium*, 163b–164c, the passage begins in the lower half of the left-hand side of page 163 and ends in the upper half of the right-hand side of page 164.

AUTHOR'S DIVISIONS: One or more of the main divisions of a work (such as PART, BK, CH, SECT) are sometimes included in the reference; line numbers, in brackets, are given in certain cases; *e.g.*, *Iliad*, BK II [265–283] 12d.

BIBLE REFERENCES: The references are to book, chapter, and verse. When the King James and Douay versions differ in title of books or in the numbering of chapters or verses, the King James version is cited first and the Douay, indicated by a (D), follows; *e.g.*, OLD TESTAMENT: *Nehemiah*, 7:45—(D) II *Esdras*, 7:46.

SYMBOLS: The abbreviation "esp" calls the reader's attention to one or more especially relevant parts of a whole reference; "passim" signifies that the topic is discussed intermittently rather than continuously in the work or passage cited.

For additional information concerning the style of the references, see the Explanation of Reference Style; for general guidance in the use of *The Great Ideas*, consult the Preface.

1. The desire for happiness: its naturalness and universality

7 PLATO: *Euthydemus*, 69a / *Symposium*, 164c-d
9 ARISTOTLE: *Ethics*, BK I, CH 4 [1095^{a}13–29] 340b-c; CH 7 [1097^{a}24–^{b}22] 342c-343a; BK X, CH 6 [1176^{a}30–^{b}8] 430d-431a / *Politics*, BK VII, CH 13 [1331^{b}39–1332^{a}4] 536c / *Rhetoric*, BK I, CH 5 [1360^{b}4–13] 600d-601a; CH 6 [1362^{b}10–12] 603b
11 NICOMACHUS: *Arithmetic*, BK I, 811d
12 EPICTETUS: *Discourses*, BK III, CH 24, 203c-204c
18 AUGUSTINE: *Confessions*, BK X, par 31–34 79c-80c / *City of God*, BK X, CH I, 298b,d; BK XIX, CH 12 517b-519a
19 AQUINAS: *Summa Theologica*, PART I, Q 2, A I, REP I 10d-11d; Q 12, A I, ANS 50c-51c; A 8, REP 4 57b-58b; Q 19, A 3, ANS 110b-111c; Q 26, A 2, ANS and REP 2 150c-151a; Q 62, A I, ANS 317d-318c; Q 63, A 3 327b-328b; Q 82, A I 431d-432c; Q 83, A I, REP 5 436d-438a; A 2, ANS 438a-d; PART I–II, Q I, AA 4–8 612a-615c; Q 2, A 2, REP 3 616d-617b; Q 3, A 6, REP 2 627b-628a; Q 5, A I, ANS 636d-637c; A 4, ANS and REP 2 639a-640b; A 8 642d-643d
20 AQUINAS: *Summa Theologica*, PART I–II, Q 63, A I 63a-64a; Q 84, A 4, ANS 176d-178a; PART II–II, Q 29, A 2 531a-d

21 DANTE: *Divine Comedy*, PURGATORY, XVII [127–129] 79d; XVIII [19–33] 80a
23 HOBBES: *Leviathan*, PART I, 76c-d
25 MONTAIGNE: *Essays*, 6d-7a; 149b-d
31 SPINOZA: *Ethics*, PART IV, PROP 19–21 429d-430b
33 PASCAL: *Pensées*, 169 203a; 425 243b-244b; 437 251a / *Geometrical Demonstration*, 440b
35 LOCKE: *Human Understanding*, BK I, CH II, SECT 3, 104c; BK II, CH XXI, SECT 42–73 188c-199c passim, esp SECT 42 188c, SECT 51 191b-c, SECT 55–56 192c-193b, SECT 64 195a-b, SECT 70 197a-b
42 KANT: *Pure Reason*, 235a-b / *Fund. Prin. Metaphysic of Morals*, 258d-259a; 261c; 266b-c; 267b-d / *Practical Reason*, 300a-d; 306a / *Pref. Metaphysical Elements of Ethics*, 369c-370d / *Judgement*, 478a-479a; 584d-585c; 588b [fn 2]
43 MILL: *Utilitarianism*, 461c-464d
46 HEGEL: *Philosophy of Right*, PART II, par 123 44a-b; ADDITIONS, 78 128c-d
47 GOETHE: *Faust*, PART I [1544–1706] 37b-41a; PART II [11,559–594] 281b-282a
48 MELVILLE: *Moby Dick*, 123a
49 DARWIN: *Descent of Man*, 316d-317a; 592d
51 TOLSTOY: *War and Peace*, BK XIII, 577a-578b; BK XIV, 605b-d; BK XV, 630c-631c
52 DOSTOEVSKY: *Brothers Karamazov*, BK V, 127b-137c passim
54 FREUD: *Civilization and Its Discontents*, 772a

2b. The content of a happy life: the parts or constituents of happiness

5 AESCHYLUS: *Agamemnon* [351–474] 55d–57b

5 SOPHOCLES: *Antigone* [1155–1171] 140d–141a

5 EURIPIDES: *Ion* [585–647] 287d–288b / *Bacchantes* [878–911] 347b–c

6 HERODOTUS: *History*, BK I, 6c–8a

7 PLATO: *Euthydemus*, 69a–71a; 74b–76b / *Gorgias*, 267c–270a; 275b–276b / *Republic*, BK I, 295d–297b; BK V, 364c–365d / *Timaeus*, 475d–476b / *Laws*, BK I, 643c; BK II, 656d–658d; BK V, 688c–690c; 694a–d; BK VIII, 737c–d; BK IX, 751c

9 ARISTOTLE: *Ethics*, BK I, CH 4 [1095^{a}13–27] 340b; CH 5 340d–341b; CH 8 [1099^{a}31]–CH 9 [1100^{a}9] 344d–345c esp CH 9 [1099^{b}25–31] 345b; BK IX, CH 9 423a–424b passim / *Politics*, BK III, CH 9 [1280^{a}31–34] 477d–478a; BK VII, CH 13 [1331^{b}24–1332^{a}27] 536b–537a / *Rhetoric*, BK I, CH 5 600d–602d; CH 9 [1367^{b}33–35] 610d

12 LUCRETIUS: *Nature of Things*, BK II [1–61] 15a–d; BK V [1–54] 61a–d; BK VI [1–42] 80a–d

12 EPICTETUS: *Discourses*, BK IV, CH 4 225a–228a; CH 6–7 230b–235a

12 AURELIUS: *Meditations*, BK III, SECT 12 262b–c; BK V, SECT 8 269d–270b; BK VIII, SECT I 285a–b; BK IX, SECT 2 291c–d; BK X, SECT 6 297a–b; BK XII, SECT 3 307b–d

14 PLUTARCH: *Solon*, 66b–d; 74c–75c / *Poplicola-Solon* 86a–87d / *Demosthenes*, 691b,d

17 PLOTINUS: *First Ennead*, TR V 19b–21a / *Second Ennead*, TR IX, CH 9, 70d–71a; CH 15 74d–75b

18 AUGUSTINE: *Confessions*, BK VI, par 9–10 37c–38b; par 18–20 40d–41c; BK X, par 33–34 79d–80c / *City of God*, BK IV, CH 21 198d–199d; BK VIII, CH 8 270a–d; BK XIX, CH 1–4 507a–513c; BK XXII, CH 24 609a–612a

19 AQUINAS: *Summa Theologica*, PART I, Q 18, A 2, REP 2 105c–106b; Q 26, A 4 151c–152a,c; PART I–II, Q 1, A 5, REP 1 613a–614a; A 7 614c–615a; Q 2 615c–622b; Q 4 629c–636c

22 CHAUCER: *Knight's Tale* [1251–1267] 180b / *Wife of Bath's Prologue* [5583–6410] 256a–269b

23 HOBBES: *Leviathan*, PART I, 76c–d

24 RABELAIS: *Gargantua and Pantagruel*, BK I, 60c–66b esp 65c–66b; BK III, 133b–140b

25 MONTAIGNE: *Essays*, 70d–72a; 107a–112d; 126b–131a; 231d–238d; 279d–281a; 312c–314b; 459c–462a; 471a–472a; 478c–479c; 486b–497b

29 CERVANTES: *Don Quixote*, PART II, 379d–380a

30 BACON: *Advancement of Learning*, 71d–72c

31 SPINOZA: *Ethics*, PART IV, PROP 18, SCHOL–PROP 28 429a–431c; APPENDIX, IV 447b–c

33 PASCAL: *Pensées*, 164–172 202b–203b; 174 204a

35 LOCKE: *Human Understanding*, BK II, CH XXI, SECT 55–56 192c–193b

37 FIELDING: *Tom Jones*, 311b–312a; 403a–405d esp 403c–d, 404b

38 MONTESQUIEU: *Spirit of Laws*, BK XIV, 104c–105a

39 SMITH: *Wealth of Nations*, BK V, 336c–d; 343b–c

40 GIBBON: *Decline and Fall*, 572a–c; 644d

41 GIBBON: *Decline and Fall*, 297c–298a

42 KANT: *Pure Reason*, 236b–237c / *Fund. Prin. Metaphysic of Morals*, 256a–257c; 258d–259a; 266a–c; 267b–d / *Practical Reason*, 345a–c / *Pref. Metaphysical Elements of Ethics*, 370b–d / *Judgement*, 584d–586a

43 MILL: *Utilitarianism*, 448a–453a passim; 461c–464d

44 BOSWELL: *Johnson*, 123b; 203b–c; 214b; 350d–351b; 505c

46 HEGEL: *Philosophy of Right*, INTRO, par 20 17a; ADDITIONS, 15 118d

47 GOETHE: *Faust* esp PART I [354–521] 11a–15a, [602–784] 16b–20b, [1064–1125] 26b–28a, [1544–1571] 37b–38a, [1660–1706] 40a–41a, [1765–1775] 42b, [3217–3281] 79a–80a, PART II [9356–9573] 227a–232a, [9695–9944] 235a–241b, [11,441–452] 278b

48 MELVILLE: *Moby Dick*, 308a–b

51 TOLSTOY: *War and Peace*, BK V, 194a–198b passim; 215b–218b; BK VI, 235a–238a; BK VII, 275a; BK XIII, 577a–578b; BK XIV, 605b–d; BK XV, 630c–634a

52 DOSTOEVSKY: *Brothers Karamazov*, BK II, 25d–27d; 37c–38a; BK V, 127b–137c passim, esp 135d–136b

53 JAMES: *Psychology*, 199b–204b passim, esp 199b–202a

54 FREUD: *Civilization and Its Discontents*, 771a–779a esp 772a–776b, 777a–b

2b(1) The contribution of the goods of fortune to happiness: wealth, health, longevity

OLD TESTAMENT: *Exodus*, 20:17 / *Deuteronomy*, 11:13–17 / *Psalms*, 34:9–10; 91; 112:1–3; 128; 144:11–15—(D) *Psalms*, 33:10–11; 90; 111:1–3; 127; 143:11–15 / *Proverbs*, 10:27; 15:16–17; 16:8 / *Ecclesiastes*, 2:4–11; 4:5–8; 5–6 esp 5:9–17—(D) *Ecclesiastes*, 2:4–11; 4:5–8; 5–6 esp 5:8–16

APOCRYPHA: *Ecclesiasticus*, 30:14–17—(D) OT, *Ecclesiasticus*, 30:14–17

NEW TESTAMENT: *Matthew*, 19:16–30 / *Philippians*, 4:10–23 / *I Timothy*, 6 / *Hebrews*, 13:5

5 AESCHYLUS: *Persians* [155–172] 16d–17a

5 SOPHOCLES: *Oedipus at Colonus* [1211–1248] 125b–c

5 EURIPIDES: *Suppliants* [1080–1113] 267d–268a / *Trojan Women* [466–510] 274a–b / *Electra* [420–431] 331a / *Phoenician Maidens* [552–558] 382d / *Cyclops* [316–346] 443b

5 ARISTOPHANES: *Birds* [592–610] 550a–c / *Plutus* 629a–642d esp [415–618] 633d–636d

6 HERODOTUS: *History*, BK I, 7b–8a; BK VII, 224d–225a

7 PLATO: *Euthydemus*, 69a–71a; 74b–76b / *Republic*, BK I, 295d–297b; BK III, 325b–c; BK III–IV, 341c–343b; BK V, 364c–365d / *Critias*, 485b–c / *Laws*, BK V, 690a–c; 694a–d; BK IX, 751c / *Seventh Letter*, 805d–806a

(*2b. The content of a happy life: the parts or constituents of happiness. 2b(1) The contribution of the goods of fortune to happiness: wealth, health, longevity.*)

9 ARISTOTLE: *Ethics*, BK I, CH 4 [1095ª13–27] 340b; CH 5 [1096ª5–10] 341a-b; CH 7 [1098ª18–19] 343c; CH 8 [1099ª31–ᵇ8] 344d-345a; CH 10–11 345c-347a; BK VII, CH 13 [1153ᵇ14–24] 405a; BK X, CH 8 [1178ᵇ33–1179ª16] 433c-d / *Politics*, BK VII, CH 1 527a-d esp [1323ᵇ22–29] 527c-d; CH 13 [1331ᵇ39–1332ª27] 536c-537a / *Rhetoric*, BK I, CH 5 [1360ᵇ14–30] 601a-b; [1361ᵇ27–35] 602b-c

12 LUCRETIUS: *Nature of Things*, BK II [1–61] 15a-d; BK III [59–78] 30d-31a; [1076–1094] 44a,c; BK V [1113–1135] 75c-d

12 EPICTETUS: *Discourses*, BK IV, CH 6 230b-232c

14 PLUTARCH: *Solon*, 74c-75c / *Aemilius Paulus*, 224d-225c; 229a-c / *Marcus Cato*, 285c-d / *Pyrrhus*, 320c-321a / *Caius Marius*, 353d-354a,c / *Demosthenes*, 691b,d

15 TACITUS: *Annals*, BK VI, 91c; BK XIV, 154a-c

17 PLOTINUS: *First Ennead*, TR V 19b-21a

18 AUGUSTINE: *City of God*, BK VIII, CH 8, 270a-b; BK XIX, CH 3, 510a-c; CH 13–14 519a-520d

19 AQUINAS: *Summa Theologica*, PART I, Q 26, A 4, ANS and REP 2 151c-152a,c; PART I–II, Q I, A 7, ANS 614c-615a; Q 2, AA 1–5 615d-619c esp A 4, ANS 618a-d; Q 4, AA 5–7 632c-636a; Q 5, A 4, ANS 639a-640b; Q 12, A 3, REP 1 670d-671b

21 DANTE: *Divine Comedy*, HELL, VII [25–96] 9d-10c; PURGATORY, XV [40–81] 75d-76a

22 CHAUCER: *Prologue of Man of Law's Tale* [4519–4546] 235b-236a / *Tale of Melibeus*, par 49–50 422a-423a / *Parson's Tale*, par 28, 515a

24 RABELAIS: *Gargantua and Pantagruel*, BK III, 133b-140b; BK IV, 234a-235a

25 MONTAIGNE: *Essays*, 33b-36a; 108c-110c; 122a-124d; 126b-129d; 368d

26 SHAKESPEARE: *As You Like It*, ACT II, SC I [1–20] 603c-d

27 SHAKESPEARE: *Hamlet*, ACT III, SC II [68–79] 49c-d / *Othello*, ACT I, SC III [199–220] 211a-b / *Sonnets*, CXLVI 608c

30 BACON: *Advancement of Learning*, 86b-c

31 DESCARTES: *Discourse*, PART VI, 61a-d

36 SWIFT: *Gulliver*, PART III, 124a-129a

37 FIELDING: *Tom Jones*, BK 2; 263c-d; 283a-b

38 ROUSSEAU: *Inequality*, 350c; 363a-366d

42 KANT: *Fund. Prin. Metaphysic of Morals*, 256a-b / *Practical Reason*, 330d-331a / *Pref. Metaphysical Elements of Ethics*, 370b-d

43 MILL: *Utilitarianism*, 451d-452b; 462c-463b

44 BOSWELL: *Johnson*, 102d-103a; 124d-125d; 349a-c; 403a; 491b; 492b-c; 494b; 498d-499a

51 TOLSTOY: *War and Peace*, BK V, 194c-d; BK X, 430a-b; BK XI, 514b-d; BK XIII, 577a-578b; BK XIV, 605b-d; BK XV, 630c-631a

52 DOSTOEVSKY: *Brothers Karamazov*, BK VI, 164b-d

53 JAMES: *Psychology*, 189a-b

54 FREUD: *Civilization and Its Discontents*, 777a-779a

2*b*(2) Pleasure and happiness

OLD TESTAMENT: *Proverbs*, 13:19; 21:17; 23:20–21,29–35 / *Ecclesiastes*, 2:1–2; 3:12–13,22; 5:18–20; 8:15—(D) *Ecclesiastes*, 2:1–2; 3:12–13,22; 5:18–19; 8:15 / *Isaiah*, 22:12–13—(D) *Isaias*, 22:12–13

APOCRYPHA: *Wisdom of Solomon*, 2:1–9—(D) OT, *Book of Wisdom*, 2:1–9

NEW TESTAMENT: *Luke*, 12:16–21 / *II Peter*, 2:12–14

5 SOPHOCLES: *Antigone* [1155–1171] 140d-141a

5 EURIPIDES: *Alcestis* [773–802] 243d-244a / *Cyclops* [163–174] 441d

7 PLATO: *Protagoras*, 57d-62d / *Gorgias*, 275b-284d / *Republic*, BK IX, 421a-427b / *Philebus* 609a-639a,c esp 635c-639a,c / *Laws*, BK I, 646a; BK V, 689c-690c; BK VII, 715c-716a / *Seventh Letter*, 801b-c

8 ARISTOTLE: *Metaphysics*, BK XII, CH 7 [1072ᵇ14–24] 602d-603a

9 ARISTOTLE: *Ethics*, BK I, CH 5 [1095ᵇ13–22] 340d; CH 8 [1099ª7–30] 344c-d; BK VII, CH 11–14 403c-406a,c esp CH 13 [1153ᵇ8–1154ª6] 404d-405b; BK IX, CH 9 423a-424b; BK X, CH 1–5 426a-430d passim; CH 6 [1176ᵇ8]–CH 7 [1178ª8] 431a-432c esp CH 7 [1177ª24–28] 431d-432a / *Politics*, BK VIII, CH 3 [1337ᵇ27–1338ª9] 543a-b; CH 5 [1339ᵇ32–40] 545b-c / *Rhetoric*, BK I, CH 5 [1360ᵇ14–18] 601a

12 LUCRETIUS: *Nature of Things*, BK II [1–36] 15a-c; BK III [1003–1010] 43a; BK V [1412–1435] 79b-d

14 PLUTARCH: *Demetrius*, 747b

17 PLOTINUS: *First Ennead*, TR IV, CH 1–2 12b-13c; CH 6–7 15a-16a; CH 12 17d; TR V, CH 4 19c; CH 8–9 20c-d / *Second Ennead*, TR IX, CH 15 74d-75b

18 AUGUSTINE: *City of God*, BK VIII, CH 8 270a-d

19 AQUINAS: *Summa Theologica*, PART I, Q 26, A 4, ANS and REP 2 151c-152a,c; PART I–II, Q I, A 6, REP 1 614a-c; A 7, ANS 614c-615a; Q 2, A 6 619d-620d; Q 3, A 4, ANS 625a-626b; Q 4, AA 1–2 629d-631a; Q 5, A 8 642d-643d; Q 34, AA 3 770c-771c; Q 35, A 5 775d-777a

20 AQUINAS: *Summa Theologica*, PART I–II, Q 84, A 4, ANS 176d-178a; PART II–II, Q 28 527b-530a; Q 180, A 7 614d-616a; PART III SUPPL, Q 81, A 4, REP 4 966d-967d; Q 90, A 3 1014d-1016a; Q 95, A 5, ANS 1048a-1049d

21 DANTE: *Divine Comedy*, PURGATORY, XVII [127–139] 79d; XIX [1–69] 81c-82a; XXX–XXXI 99b-102b

22 CHAUCER: *Prologue* [331–360] 165a

24 RABELAIS: *Gargantua and Pantagruel*, BK I, 60c-66b esp 65c-66b

25 MONTAIGNE: *Essays*, 28a-d; 70d-72a; 110c-112a; 235c-236a; 394a-395b; 406a-408b; 431c-432d; 527b-528a; 538a-543a,c
26 SHAKESPEARE: *Love's Labour's Lost*, ACT I, SC I [1–162] 254a-256a
29 CERVANTES: *Don Quixote*, PART I, 193b
30 BACON: *Advancement of Learning*, 71d-72a
33 PASCAL: *Pensées*, 139-143 196b-200a
35 LOCKE: *Human Understanding*, BK II, CH VII, SECT 2 131c-d; SECT 5 132c; CH XXI, SECT 42–47 188c-190b passim, esp SECT 42–43 188c-d; SECT 55–56 192c-193b passim
40 GIBBON: *Decline and Fall*, 192b
41 GIBBON: *Decline and Fall*, 234c-d
42 KANT: *Fund. Prin. Metaphysic of Morals*, 256c-257c; 258d-259a / *Practical Reason*, 298c-300d esp 298c-d / *Judgement*, 478b-d
43 MILL: *Utilitarianism*, 447b-455a esp 448a; 461c-464d
44 BOSWELL: *Johnson*, 378a-b
46 HEGEL: *Philosophy of Right*, ADDITIONS, 15 118d
47 GOETHE: *Faust*, PART I [1741–1775] 41b-42b
48 MELVILLE: *Moby Dick*, 94a
51 TOLSTOY: *War and Peace*, BK VI, 259d-260a; BK VIII, 334d-335a; BK XIII, 577a-578b; BK XIV, 605b-d; BK XV, 630c-631c
52 DOSTOEVSKY: *Brothers Karamazov*, BK III 46a-82a,c esp 54b-58a; BK IV, 88d; BK XII, 370b-d
54 FREUD: *General Introduction*, 599b-d / *Civilization and Its Discontents*, 772a-774c esp 772a-c

2b(3) Virtue in relation to happiness

OLD TESTAMENT: *Exodus*, 15:26; 20:12 / *Psalms*, 1; 34:11-22; 106:3; 112; 119; 128—(D) *Psalms*, 1; 33:12-23; 105:3; 111; 118; 127 / *Proverbs*, 3:13-26,33; 10:6-7; 10:27-11:11; 16:8,20,32; 28:14,16,20; 29:18; 31:10-31 / *Ecclesiastes*, 7:16-17—(D) *Ecclesiastes*, 7:17-18 / *Ezekiel*, 18:5-9—(D) *Ezechiel*, 18:5-9
APOCRYPHA: *Ecclesiasticus*, 14:1-10; 25:1-12—(D) OT, *Ecclesiasticus*, 14:1-10; 25:1-16
NEW TESTAMENT: *Romans*, 4:6-8 / *I Timothy*, 6
7 PLATO: *Euthydemus*, 69a-71a; 74b-76b / *Phaedrus*, 128d-129c / *Gorgias*, 262a-270a; 275b-284d / *Republic*, BK I, 295d-297b; 304a-c; BK I–II, 306b-315c; BK IX, 418d-421a; BK X, 436c-437c; 439b-d / *Timaeus*, 475d-476b / *Critias*, 485b-c / *Theaetetus*, 528c-531a / *Laws*, BK II, 656c-658c; BK V, 688c-690c esp 690b-c / *Seventh Letter*, 806b-c
9 ARISTOTLE: *Ethics*, BK I, CH 5 [1095^{b}26–1096^{a}4] 341a; CH 7-13 342c-348d passim, esp CH 8 344a-345a; BK VI, CH 12 393b-394a passim, esp [1144^{a}1–6] 393c; BK X, CH 6 [1176^{a}30–^{b}8] 430d-431a; CH 6 [1177^{a}1]–CH 8 [1179^{a}32] 431c-434a / *Politics*, BK IV, CH 11 [1295^{a}35–38] 495c; BK VII, CH I 527a-d esp [1323^{b}21–1324^{a}4] 527c-d; CH 8 [1328^{a}37–^{b}2] 532d; CH 9 [1328^{b}33–1329^{a}2] 533b; [1329^{a}18–24] 533c; CH 13 [1332^{a}8–27] 536d-537a; CH 15 [1334^{a}12–^{b}7] 539a-b / *Rhetoric*, BK I, CH 5 [1360^{b}14–27] 601a

12 EPICTETUS: *Discourses*, BK I, CH 3 108b-c; BK III, CH 24 203c-210a; BK IV, CH I 213a-223d
12 AURELIUS: *Meditations*, BK III, SECT 12 262b-c; BK V, SECT 34–36 273c-d; BK VI, SECT 16 275b-d; BK VII, SECT 28 281d; SECT 68 284c-d
14 PLUTARCH: *Numa Pompilius*, 60a-b / *Aristides*, 265c-d / *Demosthenes*, 691b,d
17 PLOTINUS: *Second Ennead*, TR IX, CH 15 74d-75b
18 AUGUSTINE: *City of God*, BK VIII, CH 8 270a-d; BK IX, CH 4 287a-288b; BK XIX, CH 1-4 507a-513c
19 AQUINAS: *Summa Theologica*, PART I, Q 26, A 1, REP 2 150b-c; PART I–II, Q 2, A 2, REP 1 616d-617b; A 4, ANS 618a-d; A 7 620d-621c; Q 4, A 4 631d-632c; Q 5, A 4, ANS 639a-640b; A 7, ANS 642a-d
24 RABELAIS: *Gargantua and Pantagruel*, BK I, 65c-66b
25 MONTAIGNE: *Essays*, 28a-d; 70d-72a; 146b-c; 389d-390a
29 CERVANTES: *Don Quixote*, PART II, 222b-c
30 BACON: *Advancement of Learning*, 71d-72a
31 SPINOZA: *Ethics*, PART IV, PROP 18, SCHOL-PROP 28 429a-431c; PART V, PROP 42 463b-d
35 LOCKE: *Human Understanding*, BK II, CH XXI, SECT 72 198a-c
36 STERNE: *Tristram Shandy*, 538a-539a
37 FIELDING: *Tom Jones*, 316a-c
39 SMITH: *Wealth of Nations*, BK V, 336c-d
42 KANT: *Fund. Prin. Metaphysic of Morals*, 282d-283d / *Practical Reason*, 306d-307a; 338c-348b esp 339a-b, 340c-342a, 344c-347d / *Pref. Metaphysical Elements of Ethics*, 366a-b; 374a-c
43 MILL: *Utilitarianism*, 452b-455a; 461d-464d
51 TOLSTOY: *War and Peace*, BK V, 214c-216d
52 DOSTOEVSKY: *Brothers Karamazov*, BK II, 26a-27d; BK VI 146b,d-170d esp 164a-165a, 167b-168c; EPILOGUE, 411b-412d
54 FREUD: *Civilization and Its Discontents*, 793a-794a / *New Introductory Lectures*, 878a-b

2b(4) The role of honor in happiness

4 HOMER: *Iliad*, BK IX [307–429] 60b-61c; BK XII [290–328] 85b-c
5 AESCHYLUS: *Seven Against Thebes* [683–684] 34c
5 EURIPIDES: *Andromache* [768–789] 321d / *Hecuba* [299–331] 355b-c
6 HERODOTUS: *History*, BK I, 6c-7b; BK IX, 304a
6 THUCYDIDES: *Peloponnesian War*, BK II, 397d-398d
7 PLATO: *Euthydemus*, 69a-b / *Republic*, BK II, 310c-315c passim; BK IX, 421a-422b / *Seventh Letter*, 805d-806a
9 ARISTOTLE: *Ethics*, BK I, CH 5 [1095^{b}22-31] 340d-341a / *Politics*, BK VII, CH 13 [1332^{a}8-27] 536d-537a; CH 14 [1333^{a}30–^{b}25] 538a-c; CH 15 [1334^{a}12–^{b}8] 539a-b / *Rhetoric*, BK I, CH 5 [1360^{b}19-27] 601a

48 MELVILLE: *Moby Dick*, 36b-39b

51 TOLSTOY: *War and Peace*, BK III, 116c-117a; 122b-c; BK V, 214c-215b; BK XI, 525c-526b; BK XV, 642c-643b

52 DOSTOEVSKY: *Brothers Karamazov*, BK II, 27c-d; BK VI, 158b-159a; 167b-168c; 169c-170b

54 FREUD: *Civilization and Its Discontents*, 774d-775a; 782d-783b; 792a-d

2b(6) The effect of political power or status on happiness

6 HERODOTUS: *History*, BK I, 6c-8a

7 PLATO: *Euthydemus*, 75c-76b / *Gorgias*, 262a-270a esp 262a-265c / *Republic*, BK I, 304a-c; BK II, 311a-313a; BK IX, 416a-421a esp 418d-421a; BK X, 439b-440c

9 ARISTOTLE: *Ethics*, BK X, CH 7-8 431d-434a passim, esp CH 7 [1177^{b}4-25]432a-c, CH 8 [1178^{b}33-1179^{a}15] 433c-d / *Politics*, BK VII, CH 2-3 528a-530a; CH 14 [1333^{a}17]-CH 15 [1334^{b}8] 538a-539b

12 LUCRETIUS: *Nature of Things*, BK II [37-61] 15c-d; BK III [59-78] 30d-31a; [995-1002] 42d-43a; BK V [1117-1135] 75d

12 EPICTETUS: *Discourses*, BK IV, CH 4-6 225a-232c; CH 9-10 237d-240d

14 PLUTARCH: *Numa Pompilius*, 51c-52b / *Solon*, 74c-75c / *Pyrrhus*, 320c-321a / *Nicias*, 425b-c / *Crassus* 438b,d-455a,c / *Demosthenes*, 701a-702a

15 TACITUS: *Annals*, BK XIV, 154a-c

17 PLOTINUS: *First Ennead*, TR V, CH 10 20d-21a

18 AUGUSTINE: *City of God*, BK V, CH 24-26 227d-230a,c; BK XIX, CH 5-7 513d-515c; CH 19 523b-d

19 AQUINAS: *Summa Theologica*, PART I, Q 26, A 4, ANS 151c-152a,c; PART I-II, Q 2, A 4 618a-d

20 AQUINAS: *Summa Theologica*, PART I-II, Q 66, A 5, REP 1-2 79b-80c

21 DANTE: *Divine Comedy*, HELL, XII [100-139] 17b-d; PURGATORY, XI [73-117] 69c-70a; PARADISE, VI 113c-115a

23 HOBBES: *Leviathan*, PART I, 76c-d

25 MONTAIGNE: *Essays*, 107a-112d; 126b-131a; 382b-383d; 400b-d; 443d-446a; 486b-489b; 538d-540b

26 SHAKESPEARE: *3rd Henry VI*, ACT II, SC V [1-54] 81d-82a / *Richard II*, ACT IV, SC I [162-334] 343b-345a / *2nd Henry IV*, ACT III, SC I [4-31] 482d-483a / *Henry V*, ACT IV, SC I [247-301] 554a-c

29 CERVANTES: *Don Quixote*, PART I, 193a-b; PART II, 368c-d

38 ROUSSEAU: *Inequality*, 326b-327a; 362b-d; 364a-b / *Political Economy*, 372b-377b esp 373c-374a

40 GIBBON: *Decline and Fall*, 157b-d; 572a-c

41 GIBBON: *Decline and Fall*, 194a-d; 297c-298a

43 MILL: *Representative Government*, 382b / *Utilitarianism*, 462c-463b passim

46 HEGEL: *Philosophy of History*, INTRO, 167b-c

51 TOLSTOY: *War and Peace*, BK V, 215d-216d

54 FREUD: *Civilization and Its Discontents*, 799c

2b(7) The function of knowledge and wisdom in the happy life: the place of speculative activity and contemplation

OLD TESTAMENT: *I Kings*, 10:1-10—(D) *III Kings*, 10:1-10 / *II Chronicles*, 9:1-9—(D) *II Paralipomenon*, 9:1-9 / *Proverbs*, 1-4; 8-9; 16:16; 17:16; 19:8; 20:15; 22:17-18; 24:13-14 / *Ecclesiastes*, 1:13-18; 2:12-26; 6:8,11; 7:11-12,16-19; 9:13-18—(D) *Ecclesiastes*, 1:13-18; 2:12-26; 6:8,11; 7:12-13,17-20; 9:13-18

APOCRYPHA: *Wisdom of Solomon*, 6-11—(D) OT, *Book of Wisdom*, 6-11 / *Ecclesiasticus*, 4:11-19; 6:18-37; 14:19-15:8; 24:13-21; 37:24—(D) OT, *Ecclesiasticus*, 4:12-22; 6:18-37; 14:20-15:8; 24:17-29; 37:27

5 SOPHOCLES: *Antigone* [1348-1353] 142d

5 EURIPIDES: *Medea* [292-305] 214c-d

5 ARISTOPHANES: *Clouds* 488a-506d

7 PLATO: *Charmides*, 12a-13c / *Lysis*, 16c-18a / *Euthydemus*, 69a-71a; 74b-76b / *Symposium*, 167a-d / *Meno*, 183d-184c / *Apology* 200a-212a,c / *Phaedo* 220a-251d / *Republic*, BK VI, 380d-381a; BK VII 388a-401d / *Timaeus*, 475d-476b / *Theaetetus*, 528c-531a / *Statesman*, 587d-588c / *Philebus* 609a-639a,c esp 635c-639a,c / *Laws*, BK V, 688c / *Seventh Letter*, 806b-c; 808c-809a

8 ARISTOTLE: *Metaphysics*, BK I, CH 1-2 499a-501c; BK XII, CH 7 [1072^{b}14-29] 602d-603a

9 ARISTOTLE: *Ethics*, BK I, CH 7 [1097^{b}22-1098^{a}19] 343a-c; BK VI, CH 12 393b-394a esp [1143^{b}17-1144^{a}6] 393b-c; BK X, CH 7-8 431d-434a / *Politics*, BK VII, CH 2 [1324^{a}23-35] 528b

11 NICOMACHUS: *Arithmetic*, BK I, 811d

12 LUCRETIUS: *Nature of Things*, BK II [1-61] 15a-d; BK V [1-54] 61a-d; [1113-1135] 75c-d; BK VI [1-42] 80a-d

12 EPICTETUS: *Discourses*, BK I, CH 29 134d-138a; BK III, CH 10 185d-187a; CH 15 190a-191a; CH 22 195a-201a; BK IV, CH 4 225a-228a; CH 6 230b-232c

12 AURELIUS: *Meditations*, BK III, SECT 6 261a-c; SECT 9 261d; SECT 12 262b-c; BK IV, SECT 16 264d; BK V, SECT 9 270b-c; BK VI, SECT 12 274c; BK X, SECT 12 298c-d

13 VIRGIL: *Georgics*, II [490-493] 65b

14 PLUTARCH: *Pericles*, 121a-122b / *Caius Marius*, 353d-354a,c

15 TACITUS: *Annals*, BK XIV, 154a-c

17 PLOTINUS: *First Ennead*, TR IV 12b-19b esp CH 3-4 13c-14c, CH 9-10 16c-17c; TR V, CH 10 20d-21a / *Sixth Ennead*, TR VII, CH 34-35 338b-339c; TR IX, CH 9-11 358d-360d

18 AUGUSTINE: *Confessions*, BK V, PAR 7-9 28c-29b / *City of God*, BK VIII, CH 8 270a-d; BK X, CH 2 299d-300a; BK XIX, CH 1-3 507a-511a; CH 14 520a-d; CH 19 523b-d

(2*b*. *The content of a happy life: the parts or constituents of happiness.* 2*b*(7) *The function of knowledge and wisdom in the happy life: the place of speculative activity and contemplation.*)

19 AQUINAS: *Summa Theologica*, PART I, Q 26 150a-152a,c passim, esp A 2 150c-151a; PART I–II, Q I, A 6, REP I–2 614a-c; Q 3, AA 3–8 624b-629c; Q 5, A 4, ANS 639a-640b; Q 35, A 5 775d-777a

20 AQUINAS: *Summa Theologica*, PART I–II, Q 66, A 5 esp REP 2 79b-80c; PART II–II, Q 180 607d-616d; Q 182 620b-624d

21 DANTE: *Divine Comedy*, HELL, IV [106–147] 6c-7a; PURGATORY, XXX–XXXI 99b-102b

22 CHAUCER: *Prologue* [285–308] 164a-b

23 HOBBES: *Leviathan*, PART I, 63a; 65a-b; 76c

25 MONTAIGNE: *Essays*, 6d-7a; 28a-29c; 70d-72a; 231d-238d; 399d-401a; 502c-504c; 508a-512a; 541d-543a,c

26 SHAKESPEARE: *Love's Labour's Lost*, ACT I, SC I [1–162] 254a-256a

27 SHAKESPEARE: *Pericles*, ACT III, SC II [26–42] 434d-435a

29 CERVANTES: *Don Quixote*, PART I, 145d-146a

30 BACON: *Advancement of Learning*, 18a-b; 27c-d; 71a-c

31 DESCARTES: *Rules*, I, 1d / *Discourse*, PART I, 41d-42a; PART III, 49d-50b / *Meditations*, III, 88d-89a

31 SPINOZA: *Ethics*, PART IV, PROP 26–28 431a-c; APPENDIX, IV 447b-c; XXXII 450c-d; PART V, PROP 31–33 459d-460c; PROP 37 461c

32 MILTON: *Il Penseroso* 21a-25a

33 PASCAL: *Pensées*, 73–74 185a-b

35 LOCKE: *Human Understanding*, BK II, CH XXI, SECT 44 188d-189b; SECT 55–56 192c-193b passim

38 ROUSSEAU: *Inequality*, 345a / *Political Economy*, 373c-374a

40 GIBBON: *Decline and Fall*, 645c-d

42 KANT: *Fund. Prin. Metaphysic of Morals*, 256c-257d; 267b-d

43 MILL: *Utilitarianism*, 448d-449c; 451c-452a

44 BOSWELL: *Johnson*, 118a; 299b-d

46 HEGEL: *Philosophy of Right*, INTRO, par 20 17a; ADDITIONS, 15 118d

47 GOETHE: *Faust*, PART I [354–521] 11a-15a; [3217–3246] 79a-b

48 MELVILLE: *Moby Dick*, 255a

54 FREUD: *Civilization and Its Discontents*, 773b-774c

3. **The argument concerning happiness as a first principle of morality: the conflicting claims of duty and happiness**

9 ARISTOTLE: *Ethics*, BK I 339a-348d passim, esp CH 4 340b-d, CH 7 342c-344a, CH 12 347a-b

12 EPICTETUS: *Discourses*, BK I, CH 22 127c-128c; BK II, CH 11 150a-151b; CH 19 162c-164b; BK

III, CH 2 177c-178d; CH 10 185d-187a; CH 14 189c-190a; CH 24 203c-210a

12 AURELIUS: *Meditations*, BK II, SECT 11–12 258a-c; BK III, SECT 6 261a-c; BK VII, SECT 55 283b-c; BK VIII, SECT I 285a-b; SECT 32 287d-288a; SECT 39 288c; BK IX, SECT I 291a-c; SECT 7 292b

18 AUGUSTINE: *City of God*, BK IX, CH 4–5 287a-289a; BK XIV, CH 8–9 381c-385b

19 AQUINAS: *Summa Theologica*, PART I–II, Q I 609a-615c passim; Q 5, A 8 642d-643d

20 AQUINAS: *Summa Theologica*, PART I–II, Q 90, A 2, ANS 206b-207a; Q 91, A 4, ANS 210c-211c; Q 94, A 2, ANS 221d-223a

23 HOBBES: *Leviathan*, PART I, 76c-d

24 RABELAIS: *Gargantua and Pantagruel*, BK I, 65c-66b

30 BACON: *Advancement of Learning*, 71d-72b

33 PASCAL: *Provincial Letters*, 62b-68b

35 LOCKE: *Human Understanding*, BK I, CH II, SECT 3, 104c; BK II, CH XXI, SECT 42–73 188c-199c passim

39 SMITH: *Wealth of Nations*, BK V, 336c-d

42 KANT: *Pure Reason*, 235a-b; 236b-239a / *Fund. Prin. Metaphysic of Morals* 253a-287d esp 256a-257d, 258a-259a, 261c-264a, 266a-b, 267b-d, 274d-275b, 282b-283d, 286a-c / *Practical Reason* 291a-361d esp 304d-307d, 325a-327d, 330c-331a, 338c-355d / *Pref. Metaphysical Elements of Ethics*, 365b-366d; 367c; 369c-373b / *Intro. Metaphysic of Morals*, 387b-388c; 389a-390a,c / *Judgement*, 478a-479a; 584d-587a; 588b [fn 2]; 591b-592c; 595a-c; 596c-597d; 604d-606d esp 604d-605c, 605d-606b [fn 2]

43 MILL: *Utilitarianism* 445a-476a,c

46 HEGEL: *Philosophy of Right*, PART II, par 124 44b-d; par 134–135 47b-d; PART III, par 155 57c; par 261 83a-d; ADDITIONS, 76–81 128a-129a; 85–87 129b-d

49 DARWIN: *Descent of Man*, 316a-317a; 592d

52 DOSTOEVSKY: *Brothers Karamazov*, BK V, 127b-137c passim

54 FREUD: *Origin and Development of Psycho-Analysis*, 20c-d / *Civilization and Its Discontents*, 772a-b; 800c-801b

4. **The pursuit of happiness**

6 HERODOTUS: *History*, BK I, 6c-8a; BK II, 77a-b; BK III, 98b-99a

9 ARISTOTLE: *Ethics*, BK I, CH 10 345c-346c

11 NICOMACHUS: *Arithmetic*, BK I, 811d

12 LUCRETIUS: *Nature of Things*, BK III [1076–1094] 44a,c

12 EPICTETUS: *Discourses*, BK III, CH 24 203c-210a

14 PLUTARCH: *Solon*, 66b-d; 74c-75b / *Caius Marius*, 353d-354a,c

17 PLOTINUS: *First Ennead*, TR IV 12b-19b / *Third Ennead*, TR II, CH 4–5 84c-85c

18 AUGUSTINE: *Confessions*, BK X, par 29–34 78d-80c

4a. Man's capacity for happiness: differences in human nature with respect to happiness

4b. The attainability of happiness: the fear of death and the tragic view of human life

(4. *The pursuit of happiness. 4b. The attainabil-*
ity of happiness: the fear of death and the
tragic view of human life.)

18 AUGUSTINE: *City of God*, BK VIII, CH 8 270a-d;
BK XIX, CH 4-8 511a-516a; BK XXII, CH 22-24
606d-612a

19 AQUINAS: *Summa Theologica*, PART I-II, Q 5
636d-643d

21 DANTE: *Divine Comedy*, PARADISE, XI [1-12]
122a

22 CHAUCER: *Troilus and Cressida*, BK I, STANZA
31-35 5a-b; BK III, STANZA 117-120 69b-70a;
BK IV, STANZA 72-74 98a; BK V, STANZA 262-
263 154b / *Knight's Tale* [1303-1324] 181b;
[2837-2852] 206b-207a / *Merchant's Tale*
[9927-9954] 332a-b / *Monk's Tale* 434a-448b

23 HOBBES: *Leviathan*, PART I, 65a-b; 76c-d;
79b-d; PART II, 163d-164a

25 MONTAIGNE: *Essays*, 6d-10a; 26d-36b; 70d-
72a; 115b-119d; 124c-125a; 149b-d; 231d-
233c; 312c-314b; 326b-327b; 339a-d; 402c-
403c; 478c-479c; 509b-512a; 528c-529b;
541b-c

26 SHAKESPEARE: *Richard II*, ACT III, SC II [144-
185]337a-b; ACT IV, SC I [162-318] 343b-344d;
ACT V, SC V [1-41] 349d-350a

27 SHAKESPEARE: *Hamlet*, ACT I, SC II [129-137]
32d-33a; SC IV [13-38] 36a-b; ACT II, SC II
[303-322] 43d; ACT III, SC I [56-157] 47c-48c
/ *Measure for Measure*, ACT III, SC I [1-43]
186d-187a / *Timon of Athens*, ACT IV, SC I
409c-d; ACT IV, SC III-ACT V, SC I 410c-419b /
Henry VIII, ACT III, SC II [350-372] 572c-d

30 BACON: *Advancement of Learning*, 26a-c;
70b-d; 73d-74a

31 SPINOZA: *Ethics*, PART IV, PROP 67 444d-445a;
PART V, PROP 42 463b-d

32 MILTON: *Paradise Lost*, BK II [496-505] 122a;
BK X [782-844] 291b-292b

33 PASCAL: *Pensées*, 109-110 193b-194a; 126-147
195b-201a; 156-157 201b-202a; 164-183 202b-
204b; 199 210b; 386 239a

35 LOCKE: *Human Understanding*, BK II, CH VII,
SECT 5 132c; CH XXI, SECT 45 189b-d

36 STERNE: *Tristram Shandy*, 383a-384a; 388a-
399b; 459a-460a

37 FIELDING: *Tom Jones*, 283a-b

38 ROUSSEAU: *Inequality*, 338b-c; 363a-366d passim, esp 363a-b, 366b-d

42 KANT: *Fund. Prin. Metaphysic of Morals*,
256d-257d; 258b; 267b-d / *Practical Reason*,
345a-347a / *Judgement*, 584d-586a

43 MILL: *Utilitarianism*, 450c-453a

44 BOSWELL: *Johnson*, 95c-d; 102d-103b; 104b;
254b-c; 312b; 350d-351b; 362c-363a; 376c-
377a; 540b-542a

46 HEGEL: *Philosophy of History*, INTRO, 162a-
170b; PART I, 245b-d; PART III, 285a-b

47 GOETHE: *Faust* esp PART I [354-517] 11a-
14b, [614-736] 17a-19b, [1064-1125] 26b-28a,
[1544-1571] 37b-38a, [1583-1638] 38b-39b,

[1699-1706] 41a, [1765-1815] 42b-43a, [3217-
3250] 79a-b, PART II [9695-9944] 235a-241b,
[11,433-452] 278a-b, [11,559-586] 281b-282a,
[11,934-12,111] 290b-294b

48 MELVILLE: *Moby Dick* esp 175b-176a, 313b-
314a, 316a-b, 319a-b, 341b-342a, 357a, 360b-
361a

51 TOLSTOY: *War and Peace*, BK II, 80d-81a; BK
III, 117d; BK VI, 235a-238a; 262d-263a; BK
VII, 294b-296a; BK VIII, 303a-305b; BK IX,
357d-358b; 373b-374d; BK XII, 560a-562a;
BK XIII, 577a-578b; BK XIV, 605b-d; BK XV,
630c-631c; EPILOGUE I, 659c-d; 671c-672a

52 DOSTOEVSKY: *Brothers Karamazov*, BK II, 25d-
27d; BK III, 53b-54b; BK V, 121d-127b; 127b-
137c passim; BK XI, 345a-c

54 FREUD: *Civilization and Its Discontents*, 771a-
802a,c esp 772b-c, 776b-777c, 778d-779a,
788d-789b, 793d-794a, 796b-c, 799c-800a

5. The social aspects of happiness: the doctrine
of the common good

7 PLATO: *Euthydemus*, 75c-76b / *Republic*, BK
IV, 342a-d; BK V, 365c; BK VII, 390b-391b /
Statesman, 599c-603d

9 ARISTOTLE: *Ethics*, BK I, CH 1-2 339a-d; BK V,
CH I [1129^{b}11-1130^{a}13] 377a-c / *Politics*, BK III,
CH 9 [1280^{a}31-34] 477d-478a; BK IV, CH II
[1295^{a}25-^{b}1] 495b-c; BK VII, CH 1-3 527a-
530a; CH 13-15 536b-539d

12 EPICTETUS: *Discourses*, BK I, CH 19 125b-126c;
BK II, CH 10 148c-150a

12 AURELIUS: *Meditations*, BK II, SECT 3 257a-b;
BK III, SECT 4 260b-261a; BK IV, SECT 4 264a;
BK V, SECT I 268b,d; SECT 6 269b-d; SECT 16
271c-d; SECT 22 272b; BK VI, SECT 14 274d-
275a; SECT 45 278c; SECT 54 279c; BK VII,
SECT 44-46 282b-c; BK VIII, SECT 12 286b-c;
SECT 23 287b; BK IX, SECT I 291a-c; SECT 23
293c; SECT 42 295c-296a,c; BK X, SECT 6-7
297a-c; SECT 20 299b

18 AUGUSTINE: *City of God*, BK XIX, CH 1-8
507a-516a; CH 12-17 517b-523a; CH 26 528d-
529a

19 AQUINAS: *Summa Theologica*, PART I, Q 21, A
I, ANS and REP 1,3 124b-125b; Q 60, A 5, ANS
313b-314c; Q 92, A 1, REP 3 488d-489d; Q 96,
A 4 512b-513c; PART I-II, Q I, A 5, ANS 613a-
614a; A 7 614c-615a; Q 19, A 10, ANS 710b-
711d; Q 21, A 3 718d-719c; A 4, REP 3 719d-
720a,c

20 AQUINAS: *Summa Theologica*, PART I-II, Q 59,
AA 4-5 48c-49d; Q 60, A 2 50d-51b; Q 90, A 2
206b-207a; A 3, ANS and REP 3 207a-c; A 4,
ANS 207d-208b; Q 91, A 6, REP 3 212c-213c;
Q 92, A 1, ANS and REP 1,3-4 213c-214c; Q 93,
A 1, REP 1 215b,d-216c; Q 94, A 2, ANS 221d-
223a; A 3, REP I 223a-c; Q 95, A 4, ANS 229b-
230c; Q 96, A 3, ANS and REP 3 232b-233a; A 4,
ANS 233a-d; A 6, ANS 235a-d; Q 97, A 1, ANS
and REP 3 236a-d; A 2, ANS and REP 2 236d-
237b; A 4 238b-239b; Q 98, A 1, ANS 239b-

240c; Q 99, A 3, ANS 247a-248a; Q 100, A 2, ANS 252b-253a; A 8, ANS and REP 3 259d-261a; A 11, REP 3 263c-264d; Q 105, A 1, REP 3 307d-309d; A 2, ANS and REP 1,4 309d-316a; A 3, ANS and REP 5 316a-318b; PART II–II, Q 39, A 2, REP 3 575b-576b; Q 187, A 3, REP 1,3 666a-669b; PART III SUPPL, Q 96, A 6, REP 11 1058a-1061b; A 7, REP 3 1061b-1062a

23 HOBBES: *Leviathan*, PART I, 84c-86b

30 BACON: *Advancement of Learning*, 69d-76a esp 71b-c, 72b-c

31 SPINOZA: *Ethics*, PART IV, PROP 18, SCHOL 429a-d

35 LOCKE: *Human Understanding*, BK I, CH II, SECT 6 105b-c

36 SWIFT: *Gulliver*, PART IV, 180b-184a

38 ROUSSEAU: *Inequality*, 323a-328a,c; 333b-c; 342c-343b; 351c-352a; 363a-366d / *Political Economy*, 372b-377b / *Social Contract*, BK II, 400c-401a; 401d

42 KANT: *Pure Reason*, 114b-d / *Pref. Metaphysical Elements of Ethics*, 369c-373b / *Science of Right*, 438d-439a

43 FEDERALIST: NUMBER 45, 147c-148a

43 MILL: *Utilitarianism*, 453a-454a; 460a-461c; 461d; 475a-476a

44 BOSWELL: *Johnson*, 211b-c

49 DARWIN: *Descent of Man*, 316a-317a; 592d

52 DOSTOEVSKY: *Brothers Karamazov*, BK V, 127b-137c passim

54 FREUD: *Civilization and Its Discontents*, 799a-802a,c esp 799c-800a

5a. The happiness of the individual in relation to the happiness or good of other men

5 SOPHOCLES: *Ajax* [263–281] 145c

6 HERODOTUS: *History*, BK III, 99a

7 PLATO: *Gorgias*, 262a-270c; 284a-285a

9 ARISTOTLE: *Ethics*, BK IX, CH 6 [1167^{b}5–15] 420d-421a; CH 8 [1168^{b}28–1169^{a}11] 422b-d; CH 9 423a-424b; CH 11 425a-d

12 LUCRETIUS: *Nature of Things*, BK II [1–13] 15a

12 EPICTETUS: *Discourses*, BK I, CH 19 125b-126c; BK II, CH 5 142c-144a; CH 10 148c-150a

12 AURELIUS: *Meditations*, BK III, SECT 4 260b-261a; BK V, SECT 6 269b-d; BK VI, SECT 14 274d-275a; BK VIII, SECT 12 286b-c; SECT 56 290c; BK IX, SECT 1 291a-c; SECT 23 293c; SECT 42 295c-296a,c; BK X, SECT 6 297a-b

18 AUGUSTINE: *Confessions*, BK IV, par 7–14 20d-23a / *City of God*, BK XIX, CH 8 515c-516a; CH 12–14 517b-520d

19 AQUINAS: *Summa Theologica*, PART I–II, Q 1, A 5, ANS 613a-614a; A 7 614c-615a; Q 4, A 8 636a-c; Q 32, AA 5–6 762a-763c

20 AQUINAS: *Summa Theologica*, PART I–II, Q 94, A 2, ANS 221d-223a; PART II–II, Q 17, A 3 458c-459a; Q 26 510b-520d passim; Q 39, A 2, REP 3 575b-576b; PART III SUPPL, Q 71 900d-917b; Q 94 1040d-1042c; Q 96, A 7, REP 3 1061b-1062a

21 DANTE: *Divine Comedy*, PURGATORY, XV [40–81] 75d-76a; XVI [91–138] 77d-78b

35 LOCKE: *Toleration*, 15d-16a

37 FIELDING: *Tom Jones*, 291d-292a; 305d; 330b-c

38 MONTESQUIEU: *Spirit of Laws*, BK XXIV, 203a

38 ROUSSEAU: *Inequality*, 343d-345c; 363a-366d esp 363b-364a

42 KANT: *Fund. Prin. Metaphysic of Morals*, 272d-273a / *Practical Reason*, 304b-305c / *Pref. Metaphysical Elements of Ethics*, 369c-373b esp 372a-b; 373d; 375d-376b

43 MILL: *Utilitarianism*, 450b; 452b-454a; 460a-461c; 461d; 463a-b; 469b-470c

44 BOSWELL: *Johnson*, 221d-224a

46 HEGEL: *Philosophy of Right*, PART II, par 125–126 44d-45b; par 134 47b; PART III, par 155 57c; par 182–183 64a; par 189 65d-66a; par 192 66b-c; par 249 78c; ADDITIONS, 116 135c-d; 127 137b

47 GOETHE: *Faust*, PART II [11,559–572] 281b

49 DARWIN: *Descent of Man*, 310a-319a esp 312a-313a, 314b-315d, 316c-317c; 592d

51 TOLSTOY: *War and Peace*, BK III, 116c-117a; 127d-128d; BK V, 197b-c; 214c-216d; BK X 430a-b; EPILOGUE I, 670d-671c

52 DOSTOEVSKY: *Brothers Karamazov*, BK II, 25d-27d; 37c-38a; BK V, 121d-127b; BK VI, 154d-159a; 165b-167b

5b. The happiness of the individual in relation to the welfare of the state: happiness in relation to government and diverse forms of government

OLD TESTAMENT: *Proverbs*, 11:10–11

5 AESCHYLUS: *Seven Against Thebes* 27a-39a,c esp [1011–1084] 38b-39a,c

5 SOPHOCLES: *Antigone* 131a-142d esp [162–210] 132c-d / *Philoctetes* 182a-195a,c

5 EURIPIDES: *Phoenician Maidens* [834–1018] 385c-387b; [1582–1684] 391d-392d / *Iphigenia at Aulis* 425a-439d esp [1255–1275] 436c, [1368–1401] 437c-d

6 HERODOTUS: *History*, BK I, 6c-7a

6 THUCYDIDES: *Peloponnesian War*, BK II, 397d-398c; 402b-c; BK VI, 511c-d

7 PLATO: *Crito* 213a-219a,c esp 216d-219a,c / *Republic*, BK I, 302c-306a; BK II, 311b-c; BK IV, 342a-d; BK V, 364c-365d; BK VI, 379b-380b; BK VII, 390b-391b; 401a-b; BK IX, 416a-421a esp 418d-421a / *Laws*, BK V, 692c-693a; BK VI, 707c-708a; BK IX, 754a-b / *Seventh Letter*, 814b-c

9 ARISTOTLE: *Ethics*, BK I, CH 2 [1094^{b}8–10] 339c-d / *Politics*, BK I, CH 1 [1252^{a}1–6] 445a; BK II, CH 5 [1264^{b}16–25] 459d-460a; BK III, CH 6 [1278^{b}15–29] 475d-476a; BK VII, CH 1–3 527a-530a; CH 8 [1328^{a}35–^{b}2] 532c-d; CH 9 [1328^{b}33–1329^{a}2] 533b; [1329^{a}21–24] 533c; CH 13–14 536b-538d; BK VIII, CH 1 [1337^{a}28–30] 542b

(5. The social aspects of happiness: the doctrine of the common good. 5b. The happiness of the individual in relation to the welfare of the state: happiness in relation to government and diverse forms of government.)

12 EPICTETUS: *Discourses*, BK I, CH 19 125b-126c; BK II, CH 10 148c-150a; BK III, CH 22 195a-201a

12 AURELIUS: *Meditations*, BK III, SECT 4 260b-261a; BK V, SECT 16 271c-d; SECT 22 272b; BK VI, SECT 54 279c; BK VII, SECT 5 280a-b; BK XI, SECT 21 305d-306a

14 PLUTARCH: *Lycurgus* 32a-48d esp 44d-45c, 48b-c / *Numa Pompilius*, 51c-52b; 59d-60b / *Poplicola-Solon* 86a-87d esp 87a-b / *Nicias*, 425b-c / *Demosthenes*, 691b,d; 699c-700a

15 TACITUS: *Histories*, BK II, 226d-228a

18 AUGUSTINE: *City of God*, BK XIX, CH 17 522b-523a; CH 26 528d-529a

19 AQUINAS: *Summa Theologica*, PART I, Q 60, A 5, ANS 313b-314c; Q 96, A 4 512d-513c; PART I–II, Q 19, A 10, ANS 710b-711d; Q 21, A 3 718d-719c; A 4, REP 3 719d-720a,c

20 AQUINAS: *Summa Theologica*, PART I–II, Q 90, A 2 206b-207a; A 3, REP 3 207a-c; Q 92, A 1, ANS and REP 1,3–4 213c-214c; Q 94, A 2, ANS 221d-223a; Q 95, A 4, ANS 229b-230c; Q 96, A 3, ANS and REP 3 232b-233a; A 4, ANS 233a-d; A 6, ANS 235a-d; Q 97, A 4 238b-239b; Q 98, A 1, ANS 239b-240c; Q 99, A 3, ANS 247a-248a; Q 100, A 2, ANS 252b-253a; A 8, ANS and REP 3 259d-261a; A 11, REP 3 263c-264d; Q 105, A 2, ANS and REP 1,4 309d-316a; A 3, ANS and REP 5 316a-318b; Q 111, A 5, REP 1 355d-356c; PART III SUPPL, Q 96, A 6, REP 11 1058a-1061b

23 HOBBES: *Leviathan*, PART I, 84c-86b; PART II, 99a; 104b-d; 105c-d; 112b-c; 153a

25 MONTAIGNE: *Essays*, 381a-388c; 480b-482b; 486b-489b; 490c-491d

27 SHAKESPEARE: *Coriolanus*, ACT I, SC I [67-167] 352a-353a

30 BACON: *Advancement of Learning*, 74b-76a

31 SPINOZA: *Ethics*, PART IV, PROP 37, SCHOL 2 435b-436a

32 MILTON: *Samson Agonistes* [843-902] 358a-359a

35 LOCKE: *Toleration*, 16d-17b / *Civil Government*, CH VI, SECT 57 36d-37b; CH IX 53c-54d; CH XI 55b-58b passim; CH XV, SECT 171 65a-b

36 SWIFT: *Gulliver*, PART III, 112a-115b esp 112a-113a

38 MONTESQUIEU: *Spirit of Laws*, BK IV, 16c; BK V, 19a-c; 26c; BK VI, 38a-b

38 ROUSSEAU: *Inequality*, 323a-328a,c; 359a-b / *Political Economy*, 368c; 372b-377b esp 374a-d / *Social Contract*, BK I, 393b-c; BK III, 415d; 417c-418a; 421d

39 SMITH: *Wealth of Nations*, BK V, 350d-351a

40 GIBBON: *Decline and Fall*, 31d-34a,c passim, esp 32c-33a

41 GIBBON: *Decline and Fall*, 176c; 320d-321a

42 KANT: *Pure Reason*, 114b-d / *Science of Right*, 438d-439a

43 DECLARATION OF INDEPENDENCE: [7-15] 1a-b

43 CONSTITUTION OF THE U.S.: PREAMBLE 11a,c

43 FEDERALIST: NUMBER 14, 62a-d; NUMBER 45, 147c-148a

43 MILL: *Representative Government*, 337b; 338b-c / *Utilitarianism*, 460a-461c

44 BOSWELL: *Johnson*, 221d-224a; 304c; 393a-c

46 HEGEL: *Philosophy of Right*, PART III, par 205 68d; par 261 83a-d; par 294 98b-d; par 325 107d; par 337 109d-110a; ADDITIONS, 116-117 135c-136a; 127 137b; 154-156 142a-b; 158 142d / *Philosophy of History*, INTRO, 164b; 192c-193a; PART I, 213b; PART III, 285a-b

51 TOLSTOY: *War and Peace*, BK VI, 238c-243d; 260a-262a; BK XI, 475b-476c; 480a-482b; 505a-511b esp 509d-510a; 514b-515a; BK XII, 537b-538a; BK XIII, 577b-c; BK XV, 634a-635a

54 FREUD: *Civilization and Its Discontents*, 799c-801a / *New Introductory Lectures*, 852d-853b

6. The happiness of men in relation to the gods or the after-life

4 HOMER: *Iliad*, BK XV [47-77] 104c-d; BK XVI [843-861] 121c-d

5 AESCHYLUS: *Agamemnon* [351-474] 55d-57b / *Eumenides* 81a-91d

5 SOPHOCLES: *Oedipus the King* [1186-1221] 110b-c; [1524-1530] 113c / *Antigone* [582-624] 136b-c; [1348-1353] 142d / *Trachiniae* [121-140] 171b / *Philoctetes* [1314-1347] 193d-194a

5 EURIPIDES: *Helen* [1687-1692] 314c / *Andromache* [91-102] 316a; [1284-1288] 326c / *Bacchantes* [878-911] 347b-c / *Hecuba* [952-961] 360d-361a / *Iphigenia at Aulis* [16-33] 425b

6 HERODOTUS: *History*, BK I, 6c-10a esp 6c-8a, 9c-10a; 20b-21a; BK II, 77a-b; BK III, 98b-99a

7 PLATO: *Apology*, 211c-d / *Phaedo*, 223a-225c; 249c-250b / *Republic*, BK VII, 401a-b; BK X, 437c-438c / *Laws*, BK II, 658c-d; BK V, 689c

9 ARISTOTLE: *Ethics*, BK I, CH 10-11 345c-347a; BK VII, CH 14 [1154^{b}20-30] 406c; BK X, CH 7 431d-432c esp [1177^{b}16-1178^{a}8] 432b-c; CH 8 [1178^{b}8-32] 433b-c

12 LUCRETIUS: *Nature of Things*, BK I [62-135] 1d-2d; BK III [1-93] 30a-31b; [978-1023] 42d-43b; BK V [1161-1240] 76b-77b; BK VI [43-79] 80d-81b

12 EPICTETUS: *Discourses*, BK IV, CH 1 213a-223d

12 AURELIUS: *Meditations*, BK II, SECT 11 258a-b

13 VIRGIL: *Aeneid*, BK VI [264-678] 218a-229a; [724-751] 230b-231a

15 TACITUS: *Annals*, BK VI, 91b-d / *Histories*, BK I, 190a

18 AUGUSTINE: *Confessions*, BK VI, par 26 42d-43a

7. The distinction between temporal and eternal happiness

18 AUGUSTINE: *City of God*, BK X, CH 18 310b-d; BK XIX, CH 4-11 511a-517b

19 AQUINAS: *Summa Theologica*, PART I–II, QQ
2–5 615c-643d passim

22 CHAUCER: *Merchant's Tale* [9511–9558] 325b-
326a

23 HOBBES: *Leviathan*, PART I, 65a-b

38 ROUSSEAU: *Social Contract*, BK IV, 437d-438b

39 SMITH: *Wealth of Nations*, BK V, 336c-d

52 DOSTOEVSKY: *Brothers Karamazov*, BK V, 127b-
137c passim

7a. The effects of original sin: the indispensability of divine grace for the attainment of natural happiness

OLD TESTAMENT: *Genesis*, 3:14–24

NEW TESTAMENT: *Romans*, 5:14–21 / *I Corinthians*, 15:21–22

18 AUGUSTINE: *Confessions*, BK X, par 33–34 79d-
80c / *City of God*, BK IX, CH 14–17 293a-295c;
BK X, CH 2–3 299d-301a; CH 22–32 312a-
322a,c; BK XIV, CH 1 376b,d-377a; BK XXI,
CH 15–16 572c-574a; BK XXII, CH 22–24 606d-
612a / *Christian Doctrine*, BK I, CH 15 628b-c

20 AQUINAS: *Summa Theologica*, PART I–II, Q 85
178b-184a; Q 91, A 6 212c-213c; Q 109, A 2
339c-340b; AA 7–8 344a-346a

21 DANTE: *Divine Comedy*, PURGATORY, XXVIII
[91]–XXIX [36] 97a-98a; PARADISE, VII 115a-
116c

22 CHAUCER: *Second Nun's Tale* [15,788–822]
467a-b / *Parson's Tale*, par 1–15 495a-506b

23 HOBBES: *Leviathan*, PART III, 195d-196a

32 MILTON: *Paradise Lost*, BK III [56–415] 136b-
144b esp [130–134] 138a, [227–238] 140b; BK
XI [1–44] 299a-300a; BK XI [334]–BK XII [649]
306b-333a

33 PASCAL: *Pensées*, 425–430 243b-247b; 447 253a

37 FIELDING: *Tom Jones*, 38d

52 DOSTOEVSKY: *Brothers Karamazov*, BK V, 121d-
127b esp 125d-126b; BK VI, 168a-c

7b. The imperfection of temporal happiness: its failure to satisfy natural desire

18 AUGUSTINE: *Confessions*, BK IV, par 7–19 20d-
24b; BK VIII, par 17 57d; BK IX, par 23–26
68a-d / *City of God*, BK VIII, CH 8 270a-d; BK
IX, CH 14–15 293a-294a; BK XII, CH 1 342b,d-
343c; BK XIX, CH 4–10 511a-516d; CH 20 523d-
524a; CH 27 529a-d / *Christian Doctrine*, BK I,
CH 4 625b-c; CH 38 635c-d

19 AQUINAS: *Summa Theologica*, PART I–II, Q 2,
A 1, REP 3 615d-616c; A 3 617b-618a; A 8 621c-
622b; Q 3, A 2, REP 4 623a-624b; AA 6–8 627b-
629c; Q 5, A 1, REP 2 636d-637c; A 3 638b-
639a; A 4, ANS 639a-640b; A 5 esp REP 3 640b-
641a

20 AQUINAS: *Summa Theologica*, PART I–II, Q 66,
A 5, REP 2 79b-80c

21 DANTE: *Divine Comedy*, PARADISE, XI [1–12]
122a

22 CHAUCER: *Knight's Tale* [1303–1324] 181b /
Nun's Priest's Tale [15,210–215] 456b

23 HOBBES: *Leviathan*, PART I, 65a-b; 76c-d

25 MONTAIGNE: *Essays*, 99b-100a

29 CERVANTES: *Don Quixote*, PART II, 366d-367a

32 MILTON: *Paradise Lost*, BK II [496–505] 122a

33 PASCAL: *Pensées*, 106 193b; 109–110 193b-
194a; 126–147 195b-201a; 156–157 201b-202a;
164–183 202b-204b; 184–241 205a-217b; 389
239b; 425–555 243b-270a passim

35 LOCKE: *Human Understanding*, BK II, CH VII,
SECT 5 132c; CH XXI, SECT 45 189b-d; SECT
61–62 194b-d; SECT 72 198a-c

35 HUME: *Human Understanding*, SECT XI, DIV
107, 499d-500a

38 ROUSSEAU: *Inequality*, 366c-d

42 KANT: *Practical Reason*, 346b-347b

44 BOSWELL: *Johnson*, 256d; 401a-b

47 GOETHE: *Faust*, PART I [1544–1571] 37b-38a

51 TOLSTOY: *War and Peace*, BK V, 216d-218b;
BK VI, 273c-274a,c; BK XI, 525c-526b; BK XII,
560a-562a; EPILOGUE I, 650b; 659c-d; 671c-
672a

52 DOSTOEVSKY: *Brothers Karamazov*, BK V, 127b-
137c passim; BK VI, 153d-167b

7c. Eternal beatitude: the perfection of human happiness

18 AUGUSTINE: *Confessions*, BK I, par 31 8d-9a;
BK IX, par 23–26 68a-d; BK XIII, par 50–52
124c-d / *City of God*, BK VII, CH 31 261d-262a;
BK IX, CH 15 293a-294a; BK X, CH 1–3 298b,d-
301a; CH 18 310b-d; CH 22 312a-b; CH 32
319d-322a,c; BK XI, CH 12 329b-c; BK XII, CH I
342b,d-343c; BK XIII, CH 20 370c-371a; BK
XIX, CH 4 511a-513c; CH 10–11 516c-517b; CH
13 519a-520a; CH 20 523d-524a; CH 27 529a-d;
BK XXI, CH 15 572c-573b; BK XXII 586b,d-
618d esp CH 1 586b,d-587b, CH 3 588a-b, CH
29–30 614b-618d / *Christian Doctrine*, BK I,
CH 4 625b-c; CH 15 628b-c; CH 32–33 633c-
634b

19 AQUINAS: *Summa Theologica*, PART I, Q 12, A
1, ANS 50c-51c; Q 18, A 2, REP 2 105c-106b; Q
26 150a-152a,c; Q 62 317c-325b; Q 66, A 3,
ANS 347b-348d; Q 73, A 2, REP 3 371b-d; Q 75,
A 7, REP 1 384d-385c; Q 82, A 2, ANS 432d-
433c; PART I–II, Q 2, A 8 621c-622b; Q 3, A 8
628d-629c; QQ 4–5 629c-643d; Q 19, A 10, REP
1 710b-711d

20 AQUINAS: *Summa Theologica*, PART I–II, Q 55,
A 2, REP 3 27a-d; Q 62 59d-63a; Q 63, A 3, ANS
and REP 2 65a-d; Q 67 81b-87c; Q 68, AA 2–6
89c-94c; Q 69 96c-101c; Q 109 338a-347d;
PART II–II, Q 2, AA 3–8 392a-398b; Q 17, AA
2–3 457a-459a; Q 26, A 13 519a-520d; PART
III SUPPL, Q 75, A 1 935b-937a; QQ 82–85
968a-992a; QQ 92–96 1025b-1066a

21 DANTE: *Divine Comedy*, PURGATORY, XV [40–
81] 75d-76a; PARADISE, III [43–90] 109d-110b;
XIV [1–66] 126d-127c; XXI [1–102] 138b-139b;
XXII [1–75] 139d-140c; XXVI [1–69] 145d-146c;
XXVIII [1–114] 148d-150a

22 CHAUCER: *Merchant's Tale* [9511–9558] 325b-
326a

44 BOSWELL: *Johnson*, 192d-193a

52 DOSTOEVSKY: *Brothers Karamazov*, BK II, 22b-23c; BK XI, 341d-342c

53 JAMES: *Psychology*, 199b

7c(3) The misery of the damned

OLD TESTAMENT: *Job*, 20:4-29 / *Psalms*, 9:16-17; 21:8-12; 116:3—(D) *Psalms*, 9:17-18; 20:9-13; 114:3 / *Isaiah*, 5:14-15; 14:4-23; 26:10; 66:24—(D) *Isaias*, 5:14-15; 14:4-23; 26:10; 66:24 / *Ezekiel*, 31:10-18—(D) *Ezechiel*, 31:10-18 / *Daniel*, 12:2

APOCRYPHA: *Judith*, 16:17—(D) OT, *Judith*, 16:20-21 / *Wisdom of Solomon*, 4:16-5:23 passim—(D) OT, *Book of Wisdom*, 4:16-5:24 passim / *Ecclesiasticus*, 7:17; 21:9-10—(D) OT, *Ecclesiasticus*, 7:19; 21:10-11

NEW TESTAMENT: *Matthew*, 8:12; 13:41-42,49-50; 18:6-9; 25:41-46 / *Mark*, 9:42-48—(D) *Mark*, 9:41-47 / *Luke*, 16:19-26 / *Romans*, 2:5-9 / *II Thessalonians*, 1:7-9 / *Jude*, 5-7 / *Revelation* passim, esp 14:9-11, 17:1-20:15—(D) *Apocalypse* passim, esp 14:9-11, 17:1-20:15

18 AUGUSTINE: *City of God*, BK XI, CH 33 341a-d; BK XIII, CH 2 360b-361a; CH 12 365d-366a; CH 14-16 366b-367d; BK XIII, CH 24-BK XIV, CH 1, 376a,c-377a; BK XIV, CH 15 388d-390a; BK XV, CH 1 397b,d-398c; BK XIX, CH 13 519a-520a; CH 28 529d-530a,c; BK XX, CH 6 534a-535a; CH 14-15 542d-544b; BK XXI 560a-586a,c esp CH 1-3 560a-562a, CH 9-10 568d-570b, CH 13 571c-572a, CH 17 574a-b, CH 23 576c-577b / *Christian Doctrine*, BK I, CH 20-21 629b

19 AQUINAS: *Summa Theologica*, PART I, Q 10, A 3, REP 2 42c-43b; Q 21, A 4, REP 1 126c-127c

20 AQUINAS: *Summa Theologica*, PART I-II, Q 87, AA 3-5 187b-189c; PART III SUPPL, Q 70, A 3 897d-900d; Q 86 992b-996a,c; Q 87, A 1, REP 4 997b-998c; Q 90, A 3 1014d-1016a; Q 94 1040d-1042c; QQ 97-99 1066a-1085a,c

21 DANTE: *Divine Comedy*, HELL 1a-52d esp III [1-18] 4a-b, [82-129] 5a-b, VI [100-115] 9c, VII [100-130] 10c-d, XI 15a-16b, XIV [16-72] 19c-20b, XXVII [55-136] 40a-41b, XXXIII [91-148] 50c-51a; PARADISE, VII [64-93] 115d-116a; XV [10-12] 128c

22 CHAUCER: *Friar's Tale* [7216-7234] 283b-284a / *Summoner's Prologue* 284b-285a / *Parson's Tale*, par 10 498b-502a

23 HOBBES: *Leviathan*, PART III, 195b-d

24 RABELAIS: *Gargantua and Pantagruel*, BK II, 119b-122a

26 SHAKESPEARE: *Richard III*, ACT I, SC IV [42-63] 115a-b

29 CERVANTES: *Don Quixote*, PART II, 418c-419a

31 DESCARTES: *Objections and Replies*, 226d-227a

32 MILTON: *Paradise Lost*, BK I-II 93a-134a; BK VI [867-877] 215a-b

35 LOCKE: *Human Understanding*, BK II, CH XXI, SECT 62 194c-d; SECT 72 198a-c

40 GIBBON: *Decline and Fall*, 188d-189a

41 GIBBON: *Decline and Fall*, 234a-c

52 DOSTOEVSKY: *Brothers Karamazov*, BK V, 127c-d; BK VI, 169c-170b; BK VII, 185a-c

7d. The beatitude of God

OLD TESTAMENT: *Exodus*, 33:18-20 / *I Chronicles*, 29:11-13—(D) *I Paralipomenon*, 29:11-13 / *Psalms*, 8; 19; 24; 104:1; 113:4; 138; 145—(D) *Psalms*, 8; 18; 23; 103:1; 112:4; 137; 144 / *Isaiah*, 6:1-4—(D) *Isaias*, 6:1-4

NEW TESTAMENT: *Mark*, 8:38 / *John*, 8:54 / *I Peter*, 4:11 / *II Peter*, 1:16-18 / *Revelation*, 5:9-14—(D) *Apocalypse*, 5:9-14

18 AUGUSTINE: *Confessions*, BK XIII, par 4 111c; par 53 124d-125a,c / *City of God*, BK VIII, CH 6 268d-269c; BK XII, CH 17 353a-354a; BK XXII, CH 29 614b-616d

19 AQUINAS: *Summa Theologica*, PART I, Q 26 150a-152a,c; Q 62, A 4, ANS 320b-321b; Q 63, A 3 327b-328b; Q 65, A 2, ANS 340b-341b; Q 73, A 2, REP 3 371b-d; PART I-II, Q 2, A 2, REP 2 616d-617b; Q 3, A 1, REP 1 622c-623a; A 2, REP 1,4 623a-624b; A 8, REP 2 628d-629c; Q 5, A 3, REP 2 638b-639a; A 7, ANS and REP 2 642a-d

20 AQUINAS: *Summa Theologica*, PART III, Q 19, A 3 819c-820c; Q 26, A 1, REP 2 845b-846a; PART III SUPPL, Q 71, A 8, REP 1 909d-910d; Q 92, A 1, REP 5 1025c-1032b

21 DANTE: *Divine Comedy*, PARADISE, I [1-9] 106a; XXXIII [46-145] 156d-157d

31 SPINOZA: *Ethics*, PART V, PROP 17 456c-d; PROP 35-36 460d-461c

32 MILTON: *Upon the Circumcision* 12b-13a / *Paradise Lost*, BK III [56-415] 136b-144b

42 KANT: *Practical Reason*, 347d-348b / *Judgement*, 594d [fn 1]

CROSS-REFERENCES

For: Matters most relevant to the general theory of happiness, *see* GOOD AND EVIL 3a, 5a; PLEASURE AND PAIN 6-6b, 6d.

Particular goods or virtues which are related to happiness, *see* COURAGE 5; HONOR 2b; KNOWLEDGE 8b(4); LOVE 3a; PRUDENCE 2a; TEMPERANCE 3; VIRTUE AND VICE 1d; WEALTH 10a; WISDOM 2c; and for the discussion of means and ends in the order of goods, *see* GOOD AND EVIL 4b, 5b-5c.

Other treatments of the conflict between an ethics of happiness and an ethics of duty, *see* DUTY 2; PLEASURE AND PAIN 8b; PRINCIPLE 4-4b.

For: The bearing of natural desire on the pursuit of happiness, *see* Desire 2a, 3a, 7b; Love 5a–5a(1); Will 7d.

The relation of happiness to death and the fear of death, *see* Immortality 1; Life and Death 8a–8c.

Other considerations of individual happiness in relation to the state or the common good, *see* Good and Evil 5d; State 2f.

Basic notions involved in the Christian doctrine of supernatural happiness or eternal beatitude, *see* Eternity 4d; God 6c(4), 7d, 7g; Immortality 5e–5g; Love 5a(2); Punishment 5d, 5e(1); Sin 3c–3d, 4d, 6d, 7; Virtue and Vice 8b, 8e; Will 7e–7e(2).

Another discussion of the beatitude of God, *see* God 4h.

ADDITIONAL READINGS

Listed below are works not included in *Great Books of the Western World*, but relevant to the idea and topics with which this chapter deals. These works are divided into two groups:

I. Works by authors represented in this collection.
II. Works by authors not represented in this collection.

For the date, place, and other facts concerning the publication of the works cited, consult the Bibliography of Additional Readings which follows the last chapter of *The Great Ideas*.

I.

Plutarch. "Of the Tranquillity of the Mind," "Whether Vice is Sufficient to Render a Man Unhappy," in *Moralia*

Augustine. *The Happy Life*

Aquinas. *Summa Contra Gentiles*, bk i, ch 100–102; bk iii, ch 17–63

Dante. *Convivio (The Banquet)*, fourth treatise, ch 12

———. *On World-Government or De Monarchia*, bk iii, ch 16

Hume. *An Inquiry Concerning the Principles of Morals*

A. Smith. *The Theory of Moral Sentiments*, part vi

Kant. *Lectures on Ethics*

Dostoevsky. *Notes from Underground*

———. *The Idiot*

II.

Cicero. *De Finibus (On the Supreme Good)*

———. *Tusculan Disputations*, v

Seneca. *De Beata Vita (On the Happy Life)*

Sextus Empiricus. *Against the Ethicists*

———. *Outlines of Pyrrhonism*, bk iii, ch 21–32

Pomerius. *The Contemplative Life*

Boethius. *The Consolation of Philosophy*, bk iii

Abailard. *Ethics (Scito Teipsum)*

Maimonides. *The Guide for the Perplexed*, part iii, ch 8–9

Nicolas of Cusa. *The Vision of God*

Teresa of Jesus. *The Way of Perfection*

Suárez. *Disputationes Metaphysicae*, xxx (11, 14)

John of the Cross. *Ascent of Mount Carmel*

S. Johnson. *History of Rasselas*

Hutcheson. *A System of Moral Philosophy*

Voltaire. *Candide*

Paley. *Moral Philosophy*, bk i, ch 6

T. Reid. *Essays on the Active Powers of the Human Mind*, iii, part iii, ch 1–4

Bentham. *An Introduction to the Principles of Morals and Legislation*, ch 1

Wordsworth. *The Prelude*

Schopenhauer. *The World as Will and Idea*, vol i, bk iv; vol iii, sup, ch 45–50

Leopardi. *Essays, Dialogues, and Thoughts*

Whewell. *The Elements of Morality*, bk ii, ch 25

Kierkegaard. *Philosophical Fragments*

———. *Concluding Unscientific Postscript*

Lotze. *Microcosmos*, bk viii, ch 2

Flaubert. *Madame Bovary*

Emerson. *The Conduct of Life*

H. Sidgwick. *The Methods of Ethics*, bk ii, ch 1–6; bk iii, ch 14; bk iv

Ibsen. *A Doll's House*

Nietzsche. *Beyond Good and Evil*

———. *The Will to Power*

Hauptmann. *The Weavers*

Chekhov. *Three Sisters*

Mann. *Buddenbrooks*

Dewey and Tufts. *Ethics*, part ii, ch 14–15

Moore. *Principia Ethica*, ch 2–3

———. *Ethics*, ch 1–2

Unamuno. *The Tragic Sense of Life*

B. Russell. *What I Believe*, ch 4–5

———. *Skeptical Essays*, viii

A. E. Taylor. *The Faith of a Moralist*, series i (9)

Kirk. *The Vision of God*

Santayana. *Some Turns of Thought in Modern Philosophy*, ch 4

Maritain. *Scholasticism and Politics*, ch vii

Adler. *A Dialectic of Morals*

Lubac. *Surnaturel*

O'Connor. *The Eternal Quest*

Chapter 34: HISTORY

INTRODUCTION

IN our language the term *History*," Hegel observes, "unites the objective with the subjective side. . . . It comprehends not less what has *happened* than the *narration* of what has happened. This union of the two meanings we must regard as of a higher order than mere outward accident; we must suppose historical narrations to have appeared contemporaneously with historical deeds and events."

Our daily speech confirms Hegel's observation that "history" refers to that which has happened as well as to the record of it. We speak of the history of a people or a nation, or of the great events and epochs of history; and we also call a history the book which gives a narrative account of these matters.

It is as if we used the word "physics" to name both the object of study and the science of that object; whereas normally we tend to use "physics" for the science and refer to its subject matter as the physical world. We do not say that matter in motion is physics, but that it is the object of physics, one of the things a physicist studies. We might similarly have adopted the convention of using "history" in a restricted sense to signify a kind of knowledge or a kind of writing, and then called the phenomena written about or studied "historical" but not "history."

That, however, is not the prevailing usage. The word "history" seems to have at least four distinct meanings. It refers to a kind of knowledge. It refers to a type of literature. It means an actual sequence of events in time, which constitutes a process of irreversible change. This can be *either* change in the structure of the world or any part of nature, *or* change in human affairs, in society or civilization.

Historical knowledge and historical writing can be about natural history or human history. In his classification of the kinds of knowledge, Francis Bacon makes this distinction when he divides history into "natural, civil, ecclesiastical, and literary." Whereas the last three deal with human things, the first is concerned with the non-human part of the natural world. At the same time, this natural history is not, in Bacon's judgment, the same thing as "natural philosophy," or what we would now call "natural science."

In this set of great books, natural history, even cosmic history, makes its appearance in works which we ordinarily classify as science or philosophy; for example, Darwin's *Origin of Species*, Lucretius' *On the Nature of Things*, or Plato's *Timaeus*. The great books of history deal with man and society, not nature or the universe. For the most part this is true also of the great philosophies of history. They, too, are primarily concerned with human civilization, not the physical world.

IN ITS ORIGINAL Greek root, the word "history" means research, and implies the act of judging the evidences in order to separate fact from fiction. The opening line of Herodotus is sometimes translated not "these are the histories of Herodotus of Halicarnassus," but "these are the researches . . ."

The word "research" can, of course, mean any sort of inquiry—into what is the case as well as into what has happened. The title of one of Aristotle's biological works, the *History of Animals*, suggests that it is concerned with researches about animals. The book does not deal with natural history; it is not a history of animals in the sense of giving the stages of their development in the course of time. The redundancy of "historical research" can therefore be excused on the ground that it is necessary to distinguish between two kinds of inquiry or research—scientific and historical.

711

Originally, research set the historian apart from the poet and the maker of myths or legends. They told stories, too; but only the historian restricted himself to telling a story based on the facts ascertained by inquiry or research. Herodotus deserves the title "father of history" for having originated a style of writing which differs from poetry in this extraordinary respect. He tries to win the reader's belief not by the plausibility of his narrative, but rather by giving the reader some indication of the sources of information and the reliability of the evidence on which the narrative is based.

The poet tries to tell a likely story, but the historian tries to make credible statements about particular past events. He makes an explicit effort to weigh the evidence himself or, as Herodotus so frequently does, to submit conflicting testimony to the reader's own judgment. "Such is the account which the Persians give of these matters," he writes, "but the Phoenicians vary from the Persian statements"; or "this much I know from information given me by the Delphians; the remainder of the story the Milesians add"; or "that these were the real facts I learnt at Memphis from the priests of Vulcan"; or "such is the truth of this matter; I have also heard another account which I do not at all believe"; or again, "thus far I have spoken of Egypt from my own observation, relating what I myself saw, the ideas that I formed, and the results of my own researches. What follows rests on accounts given me by the Egyptians, which I shall now repeat, adding thereto some particulars which fell under my own notice."

Herodotus seems quite conscious of the difference between himself and Homer, especially on those matters treated by the poet which fall within his purview as an historian. The Trojan War lies in the background of the conflict with which Herodotus is directly concerned—the Persian invasion of Greece—for the Persians "trace to the attack upon Troy their ancient enmity towards the Greeks."

Herodotus does not doubt that the siege of Troy took place as Homer relates, but he learns from the Egyptians a legend about the landing of Paris and Helen on Egyptian soil and the detention of Helen by Proteus, king of Memphis. "Such is the tale told me by the priests concerning the arrival of Helen at the court of Proteus. It seems to me that Homer was acquainted with this story, and while discarding it, because he thought it less adapted for epic poetry than the version which he followed, showed that it was not unknown to him."

Herodotus cites passages in the *Iliad* and the *Odyssey* to corroborate this point. He is willing to use the Homeric poems as one source of information, but not without checking them against conflicting accounts. "I made inquiry," he writes, "whether the story which the Greeks tell about Troy is a fable or not." When he comes to the conclusion that Helen was never within the walls of the city to which the Greeks laid siege for ten years, he tells the reader his reasons for thinking so. Homer, however, when he narrates Helen's actions during the siege, does not bother to establish the facts of the matter or to give the reader contrary versions of what took place. That is not the poet's task, as Herodotus recognizes. It belongs to the historian, not the poet. The story which may have greater probability in fact may not be the better story for the poet.

SINCE HE IS BOTH an investigator and a storyteller, the historian stands comparison with the scientist in one respect and with the poet in another. The special character of history as a kind of knowledge distinct from science or philosophy seems clear from its object—the singular or unique events of the past. The scientist or philosopher is not concerned with what has happened, but with the nature of things. Particular events may serve as evidences for him, but his conclusions go beyond statements of particular fact to generalizations about the way things are or happen at any time and place. In contrast, the historian's research begins and ends with particulars. He uses particulars directly observed by himself or testified to by others as the basis for circumstantial inference to matters which cannot be established by direct evidence. The method of investigation developed by the early historians may be the precursor of scientific method, but the kind of evidence and the mode of argument which we find in Hippocrates or Plato indicate the divergence of the scientist and philosopher from the procedure of the historian.

The contrast between history and science—or what for the purpose of comparison may be the same, philosophy—is formulated in Aristotle's statement concerning poetry, that it is "more philosophical than history, because poetry tends to express the universal, history the particular." History deals with what has actually happened, whereas poetry, like philosophy, may be concerned with whatever is or can be.

One comparison leads to another. Unlike poetry, history and science are alike in that they both attempt to prove what they say. But in distinction from science or philosophy, history resembles poetry, especially the great epic and dramatic poems, in being narrative literature. The historian and the poet both tell stories.

If the poet and the historian—including, of course, a biographer like Plutarch—are also moralists, they are moralists in the same way. Their works do not contain expositions of ethical or political doctrine, but rather concrete exemplifications of theories concerning the conduct of human life and social practices. That fact explains why much of the content of the great historical books is cited in other chapters dealing with moral and political, even psychological, topics. But in this chapter we are concerned with history itself rather than with the particulars of history. We are concerned with the methods and aims of history as a kind of knowledge and literature; and we are concerned with the historical process as a whole, the consideration of which belongs to the philosophy of history.

THE AIMS AND methods of writing history are discussed by the historian himself, as well as by the philosopher. Philosophers like Hobbes, Bacon, or Descartes consider history largely from the point of view of the kind of knowledge it is and the contribution it makes to the whole of human learning. Historians like Herodotus, Thucydides, Tacitus, and Gibbon state more specifically the objectives of their work, the standards of reliability or authenticity by which they determine what is fact, and the principles of interpretation by which they select the most important facts, ordering them according to some hypothesis concerning the meaning of the events reported.

Herodotus writes, he tells us, "in the hope of preserving from decay the remembrance of what men have done, and of preventing the great and wonderful actions of the Greeks and the barbarians from losing their due meed of glory." Thucydides proceeds in the belief that the war between the Peloponnesians and the Athenians "was the greatest movement yet known in history, not only of the Hellenes, but of a large part of the barbarian world—I had almost said of mankind." Not very different is the declaration of Tacitus: "My purpose is not to relate at length every motion, but only such as were conspicuous for excellence or notorious for infamy. This I regard as history's highest function, to let no worthy action be uncommemorated, and to hold out the reprobation of posterity as a terror to evil words and deeds."

But though there seems to be a striking similarity in the purpose of these historians, Tacitus alone of the three avows a moral purpose. Furthermore, each of the three is conscious of the individual way in which he has put his intention into effect. Thucydides, for example, seems to have Herodotus in mind when he fears that "the absence of romance in my history will detract somewhat from its interest; but if it be judged useful by those inquirers who desire an exact knowledge of the past. . . . I shall be content." Like Thucydides, Tacitus is an historian of contemporary events and he fears comparison with the historian of antiquity who can "enchain and refresh a reader's mind" with "descriptions of countries, the various incidents of battle, glorious deaths of great generals." His own work may be instructive, he thinks, but it may also give very little pleasure because he has "to present in succession the merciless biddings of a tyrant, incessant prosecutions, faithless friendships, the ruin of innocence, the same causes issuing in the same results, and [he is] everywhere confronted with a wearisome monotony in [his] subject-matter."

As we have already noted, Herodotus seems satisfied to let the reader decide between conflicting accounts. Only occasionally does he indicate which is more likely in his own judgment. Thucydides claims that he has made a greater effort to determine the facts. "I did not even trust my own impressions," he writes; the narrative "rests partly on what I saw myself, partly on what others saw for me, the accuracy of the report being always tried by the most severe and detailed tests possible. My conclusions have cost me some labor from the want of coincidence between the accounts of the same occurrences by different eye-witnesses." But he thinks that his conclusions "may safely be relied on," undisturbed "either by the lays of a poet displaying the exaggeration of his craft, or by the compositions of the chroniclers which are attractive at truth's expense."

The historians are aware of the difficulty of combining truth-telling with storytelling. Most men, Thucydides remarks, are unwilling to take enough pains "in the investigation of truth, accepting readily the first story that comes to hand." The difficulty, according to Tacitus, is the obscurity of the greatest events, "so that some take for granted any hearsay, whatever its source, others turn truth into falsehood, and both errors find encouragement with posterity."

Reviewing the enormous scope of his work, Gibbon at the very end concludes that "the historian may applaud the importance and variety of his subject; but, while he is conscious of his own imperfections, he must often accuse the deficiency of his materials." Because of the scarcity of authentic memorials, he tells us in another place, the historian finds it hard "to preserve a clear and unbroken thread of narration. Surrounded with imperfect fragments, always concise, often obscure, and sometimes contradictory, he is reduced to collect, to compare, and to conjecture; and though he ought never to place his conjectures in the rank of facts, yet the knowledge of human nature, and of the sure operation of its fierce and unrestrained passions, might, on some occasions, supply the want of historical materials."

Clearly, the historians have different criteria of relevance in determining the selection and rejection of materials and different principles of interpretation in assigning the causes which explain what happened. These differences are reflected in the way each historian constructs from the facts a grand story, conceives the line of its plot and the characterization of its chief actors. Herodotus, for example, has been compared with Homer as writing in an epic manner; Thucydides, with the dramatic writers of

tragedy. Even if they all agreed on the ascertainment of fact, the great historians would differ from one another as the great poets do; each has a style and a vision as personal and poetic as Homer or Virgil, Melville or Tolstoy.

ONLY ONE OF THE great books is, by title and design, devoted entirely to the philosophy of history—to the formulation of a theory which embraces the whole of man's career on earth. This is Hegel's *Philosophy of History*. Augustine's *City of God* presents an equally comprehensive vision, but a comparison of the two suggests that they differ from one another as philosophy from theology.

The point of this comparison is not that God and His providence are omitted from the philosopher's view. On the contrary, Hegel regards the history of the world as a "process of development and the realization of Spirit—this is the true theodicy, the justification of God in History. Only this insight can reconcile Spirit with the History of the World—*viz.*, that what has happened and is happening every day is not only not 'without God' but is essentially His Work."

The difference is rather to be found in the ultimate source of insight concerning human development and destiny. Augustine sees everything in the light of God's revelation of His plan in Holy Writ; Hegel and other philosophers of history from Vico to Toynbee seek and sometimes claim to find in the records of history itself the laws which govern and the pattern which inheres in the procession of events from the beginning to the end of human time.

For Augustine, the great epochs of history are defined religiously. They are stages in the development of the city of God on earth, not the city of man. Man is viewed as dwelling on earth under four distinct dispensations from God: (1) in Paradise before the Fall; (2) in the world after expulsion from Eden and before the Promise and the Law were given to the Jews; (3) under the Law and before the coming of Christ; (4) between the first and second coming under the dispensation of grace.

Augustine sometimes makes other divisions of history, but they are always primarily religious. For example, he divides all of time into seven ages, corresponding to the seven days of creation. "The first age, as the first day, extends from Adam to the deluge; the second from the deluge to Abraham. ... From Abraham to the advent of Christ there are, as the evangelist Matthew calculates, three periods, in each of which are fourteen generations—one period from Abraham to David, a second from David to the captivity, a third from the captivity to the birth of Christ in the flesh. There are thus five ages in all. The sixth is now passing, and cannot be measured by any number of generations. ... After this period God shall rest as on the seventh day, when He shall give us (who shall be the seventh day) rest in Himself. ... The seventh shall be our Sabbath, which shall be brought to a close, not by an evening, but by the Lord's day, as an eighth and eternal day, consecrated by the resurrection of Christ, and prefiguring the eternal repose not only of the spirit, but also of the body ... This is what shall be in the end without end."

This same projection of history—in all essentials, at least—is laid before Adam by the archangel Michael in Milton's *Paradise Lost*, just before Adam leaves the Garden of Eden.

Unlike the four major dispensations of which Augustine and Milton speak, Hegel's four stages of the world are epochs in the development of Spirit as manifested in the State. They are secularly defined as the Oriental, the Greek, the Roman, and the German world and are seen as a "progress of the consciousness of Freedom." The "various grades in the consciousness of Freedom," Hegel writes, "supply us with the natural division of universal History. ... The Orientals have not attained the knowledge that Spirit—Man *as such*—is free; and because they do not know this, they are not free. They only know that *one is free* ... that *one* is therefore only a Despot; not a *free man*. The consciousness of Freedom first arose among the Greeks, and therefore they were free; but they, and the Romans likewise, knew only that *some* are free—not man as such. ... The Greeks, therefore, had slaves and their whole life and the maintenance of their splendid liberty, was implicated with the institution of slavery. ... The German nations, under the influence of

Christianity, were the first to attain the consciousness that man, as man, is free."

With the complete emancipation of man in the German-Christian world, history is consummated for Hegel. "The grand principle of being is realized," he declares; "consequently the end of days is fully come." Another sign of the finality of the German-Christian world seems to be its reconciliation of Church and State: "European history is the exhibition of the growth of each of these principles severally ... then of an antithesis on the part of both ... lastly, of the harmonizing of the antithesis." In the German-Christian world, the secular and the religious modes of life are ultimately harmonized, fused in a single order of "rational Freedom."

APART FROM THE opposition between the philosophical and theological approaches, here represented by Hegel and Augustine, there seem to be two main issues in the general theory of human history. The first concerns the pattern of change; the second, the character of the causes at work.

The pattern most familiar because of its prevalence in modern speculations is that of progress or evolution. The progress may be conceived as a dialectical motion in the realm of Spirit, contrasted by Hegel with the realm of Matter or Nature, according as "the essence of Matter is Gravity ... and the essence of Spirit is Freedom." But it may also be thought to occur, as in the dialectical materialism of Marx and Engels, through the resolution of conflicting material or economic forces.

"The whole history of mankind," Engels writes in his preface to the *Communist Manifesto*, "since the dissolution of primitive tribal society, holding land in common ownership, has been a history of class struggles, contests between exploiting and exploited, ruling and oppressed classes; the history of these class struggles forms a series of evolutions in which, now-a-days, a stage has been reached where the exploited and oppressed class, the proletariat, cannot attain its emancipation from the sway of the exploiting and ruling class, the bourgeoisie, without, at the same time, and once for all, emancipating society at large from all exploitation, oppression, class-distinction and class-struggle." The four great economic systems—the systems of slave labor, feudal serfdom, industrial capitalism, and the communistic or classless society—are thus seen as the stages of progress toward an ultimate perfection in which history comes to rest because it has at last fully realized its controlling tendency.

The pattern of progress may be conceived not as a dialectical motion involving conflict and synthesis, but rather, as by Kant, in terms of an increasing actualization of the potentialities for good in human life. Giving the name of *culture* to "the production in a rational being of an aptitude for any ends whatever of his own choosing," Kant declares, "it is only culture that can be the ultimate end which we have cause to attribute to nature in respect of the human race." The progressive realization of culture consists in "the liberation of the will from the despotism of desires whereby, in our attachment to certain natural things, we are rendered incapable of exercising a choice of our own." In these terms history moves toward a perfection which can never be fully achieved on earth, for man's "own nature is not so constituted as to rest or be satisfied in any possession or enjoyment whatever."

As conceived by the evolutionist, progress may or may not attain its limit, but in either case its manifestation in human history appears to be analogous to as well as an extension of the line of development along which the world or all of living nature has gradually advanced.

THESE VIEWS ARE given further discussion in the chapters on EVOLUTION, PROGRESS, and WORLD. Whether or not the same pattern of change obtains in the historical order of nature as in the history of man and society, is a question to be answered by those who deny as well as by those who affirm progress. There is cyclical change in nature, the same pattern of birth, growth, decay, and death repeating itself generation after generation. That history too repeats itself with the rise and decline of cities and civilizations, seems to be the ancient view. It reappears in our day with Spengler and, somewhat qualified by the possibility of progress, with Toynbee.

"The cities which were formerly great," Herodotus observes, "have most of them become insignificant; and such as are at present powerful were weak in olden time. I shall, therefore, discourse equally of both, convinced that prosperity never continues long in one stay." Lucretius finds the cyclical pattern both in the succession of worlds and in the succession of civilizations. The myth of the golden age of Kronos and the earth-bound age of Zeus, which Plato tells in the *Statesman*, also applies both to nature and society.

According to the myth, "there is a time when God himself guides and helps to roll the world in its course; and there is a time, on the completion of a certain cycle, when he lets go, and the world being a living creature, and having originally received intelligence from its author and creator, turns about and by an inherent necessity revolves in the opposite direction." Thus the history of the world runs through "infinite cycles of years," and one age succeeds another in an endless round.

There is still a third view which sees history as neither cyclical nor simply progressive. Virgil reverses the order of the Platonic myth by placing the golden age in the future. It dawns with Rome, where, in the words of the 4th *Eclogue*, "the majestic roll of circling centuries begins anew: Justice returns, returns old Saturn's reign, with a new breed of men sent down from heaven . . . and the iron shall cease, the golden race arise."

Rome for Virgil is not only the beginning of the golden age; it is also the consummation of history. In the *Aeneid* Jupiter himself declares that he has given the Romans "dominion without end"—that he has ordained for them "neither period nor boundary of empire." The "gowned race of Rome" shall be "the lords of the world"; then "war shall cease, and the iron ages soften." Thus, Jupiter says, "is it willed," and so "a day will come in the lapse of cycles." The perpetuity of Rome seems to leave little room for any further essential progress and no chance for another cycle of decay and regeneration.

The Christian dogma of the fall of man from grace and his return through divine mediation to grace and salvation seems to give history a pattern that is partly Platonic in the sequence which makes the loss of a golden age the occasion for striving to regain it. But it also seems to be Virgilian in part. The epochal transitions of history happen only once. The coming of Christ is an absolutely singular event, after which there is no essential progress in man's condition until the Last Judgment at the end of the world.

COMMON TO THESE diverse conceptions of the pattern of history is the problem concerning the causes which are at work as history unfolds. Whatever the factors, they will operate in the future as they have in past, unless the millenium is already upon us or about to dawn. From the knowledge of their own past or from their dim perception of divine providence, men derive a sense of the future; but they look forward to that future differently according as some part of it will stem from choices freely made, or according as all of it is inexorably determined by causes beyond their control.

The basic alternatives of fate and freedom, of necessity and contingency, God's will and man's choice, are considered in the chapters on CHANCE, FATE, and NECESSITY AND CONTINGENCY. Sometimes the issue is resolved in the same way for the course of nature and the course of history: necessity reigns in both; as there is contingency in the events of nature, so there is freedom in the acts of history. Sometimes the processes of nature and history are distinguished: the motions of matter are governed by inviolable laws; whereas the motions of men are directed by laws which leave them free to work out a destiny which is determined by, rather than determines, the human spirit.

Those who do not deny freedom entirely in the realm of history seldom give it unlimited scope. What men can do is conditioned from below by the operation of material forces, and from above by what Hegel calls "God's purpose with the world." The vast "arras-web of Universal History" is woven by the interaction between God's will (the Absolute Idea) and human purposes or interests, which Hegel calls "the complex of human passions."

History for him is "the union of Freedom and Necessity," where "the latent abstract process of Spirit is regarded as Necessity, while that which exhibits itself in the conscious will of men, as their interest, belongs to the domain of freedom." But this freedom which coheres

with necessity seems to belong more to the human race as a whole than to individual men. The individual man is tossed aside if he tries to obstruct the path of history. He is powerless to change its course.

Not even great men can make or determine history. They are great only because, sensing the next phase of the historical process, they identify themselves with the wave of the future and conform their purposes to the march of events—the dialectical development of the Absolute Idea. A few men thus become "world-historical individuals" because their own "particular aims involve those large issues which are the will of the World-Spirit." They have "an insight into the requirements of the time —what was ripe for development . . . the very Truth for their age, for their world; the species next in order, so to speak, and which was already formed in the womb of time."

Like Hegel and unlike the ancient historians, Tolstoy also regards the leadership of great men as illusory. To believe in the efficacy of heroes or great men, he thinks, is to commit the fallacy of the man "who, watching the movements of a herd of cattle and paying no attention to the varying quality of the pasturage in different parts of the field, or to the driving of the herdsman, attributes the direction the herd takes to the animal which happens to be at its head."

Great men are only celebrated puppets, pushed ahead on the moving front of history. The motion of history derives its force and direction from the individual acts of the innumerable nameless men who comprise the human mass. The act of the individual counts little. The mass motion is a complex resultant of slight impulses tending in many directions. But however slight the impulse each man gives, his contribution to history is a free act, conditioned only by the circumstances under which he makes a choice and by the divine providence which grants him the freedom to choose. Like "every human action," history, according to Tolstoy, thus "appears to us as a certain combination of freedom and inevitability."

DIFFERENT FROM speculations on a grand scale concerning the whole historical process is that type of philosophizing about history which considers its place in education—the light it affords to the mind, and the lessons it teaches for the guidance of conduct.

Montaigne, for example, makes the reading of history and biography the window through which a man looks out upon the world. "This great world," he writes, "is the mirror wherein we are to behold ourselves, to be able to know ourselves as we ought to do in the true bias." Only against the large scene history reveals and amidst the variety of human nature it exhibits can a man truly know himself and his own time. In a similar vein, Gibbon declares that "the experience of history exalts and enlarges the horizon of our intellectual view." Hegel, on the other hand, insists that "what experience and history teach is that peoples and governments never have learned anything from history, or acted on principles deduced from it.

On the practical side, political writers like Machiavelli, Montesquieu, and the Federalists use history to exemplify or confirm their generalizations. They agree with Thucydides that "an exact knowledge of the past is an aid to the interpretation of the future, which in the course of human things must resemble if it does not reflect it." Most men, adds Tacitus, "learn wisdom from the fortunes of others."

It is on these grounds that the great books of history belong with treatises on morals and politics and in the company of philosophical and theological speculations concerning the nature and destiny of man. Liberal education needs the particular as well as the universal, and these are combined in the great historical narratives. Apart from their utility, they have the originality of conception, the poetic quality, the imaginative scope which rank them with the great creations of the human mind.

OUTLINE OF TOPICS

REFERENCES

To find the passages cited, use the numbers in heavy type, which are the volume and page numbers of the passages referred to. For example, in **4** Homer: *Iliad*, bk ii [265–283] 12d, the number **4** is the number of the volume in the set; the number 12d indicates that the passage is in section d of page 12.

Page Sections: When the text is printed in one column, the letters a and b refer to the upper and lower halves of the page. For example, in **53** James: *Psychology*, 116a-119b, the passage begins in the upper half of page 116 and ends in the lower half of page 119. When the text is printed in two columns, the letters a and b refer to the upper and lower halves of the left-hand side of the page, the letters c and d to the upper and lower halves of the right-hand side of the page. For example, in **7** Plato: *Symposium*, 163b-164c, the passage begins in the lower half of the left-hand side of page 163 and ends in the upper half of the right-hand side of page 164.

Author's Divisions: One or more of the main divisions of a work (such as part, bk, ch, sect) are sometimes included in the reference; line numbers, in brackets, are given in certain cases; *e.g., Iliad*, bk ii [265–283] 12d.

Bible References: The references are to book, chapter, and verse. When the King James and Douay versions differ in title of books or in the numbering of chapters or verses, the King James version is cited first and the Douay, indicated by a (D), follows; *e.g.,* Old Testament: *Nehemiah*, 7:45—(D) *II Esdras*, 7:46.

Symbols: The abbreviation "esp" calls the reader's attention to one or more especially relevant parts of a whole reference; "passim" signifies that the topic is discussed intermittently rather than continuously in the work or passage cited.

For additional information concerning the style of the references, see the Explanation of Reference Style; for general guidance in the use of *The Great Ideas*, consult the Preface.

1. History as knowledge and as literature: its kinds and divisions; its distinction from poetry, myth, philosophy, and science

6 Herodotus: *History*, bk ii, 71a-73b esp 72a-b; 75b; bk iv, 127a-b; bk vii, 242c-d
6 Thucydides: *Peloponnesian War*, bk i, 354a-d
7 Plato: *Cratylus*, 112b / *Republic*, bk ii, 323d-324a / *Timaeus*, 447a / *Critias*, 479d / *Laws*, bk iii 663d-677a
9 Aristotle: *Poetics*, ch 9 [1451ª36–ᵇ32] 686a-c; ch 23 695a-c
14 Plutarch: *Theseus*, 1a-c / *Romulus* 15a-30a,c passim, esp 15a-18d / *Themistocles*, 102a,c / *Pericles*, 128d-129a / *Timoleon*, 195a-b / *Cimon*, 390b-d / *Alexander*, 540b,d-541a / *Dion*, 794c-795a
15 Tacitus: *Annals*, bk iii, 60d; bk iv, 71d-72b; bk xi, 107c; bk xiii, 133b / *Histories*, bk ii, 228a-b
18 Augustine: *Christian Doctrine*, bk ii, ch 27–28 650a-d
23 Hobbes: *Leviathan*, part i, 67b-c; 71c-d
25 Montaigne: *Essays*, 24a-c; 41c-42a; 199a-200d; 305d-306a; 347c-350d; 457a-b
26 Shakespeare: *Richard III*, act iii, sc i [72–88] 123c-d / *Henry V*, prologue 532b,d

28 Harvey: *On Animal Generation*, 473b
29 Cervantes: *Don Quixote*, part ii, 213b-c
30 Bacon: *Advancement of Learning*, 32d-39a esp 32d-33a, 38c-39a / *Novum Organum*, bk i, aph 87, 123b
31 Descartes: *Rules*, iii, 3b-d / *Discourse*, part i, 43a-b
33 Pascal: *Pensées*, 628 287a / *Vacuum*, 355a-356a
35 Locke: *Human Understanding*, bk iv, ch xvi, sect 7–11 368d-370a
35 Hume: *Human Understanding*, sect viii, div 65, 479b-c; sect xii, div 132, 509c
37 Fielding: *Tom Jones*, 19a-20a; 49b-50c
40 Gibbon: *Decline and Fall*, 88a-d; 97c-98d passim; 211a; 398b; 471c-d
41 Gibbon: *Decline and Fall*, 337c
44 Boswell: *Johnson*, 203a-b; 258d-259a; 353b-c
46 Hegel: *Philosophy of Right*, intro, par 3, 10a-11c; part iii, par 355, 112d / *Philosophy of History*, intro, 153a-158a; 182d-183d; 193d-194a; part i, 230c-231b; 248c; part iii, 285d-286a
51 Tolstoy: *War and Peace*, bk x, 430d-431a; bk xi, 469a-470c; bk xiii, 563a-b; epilogue ii 675a-696d passim
53 James: *Psychology*, 863b [fn 2]

2. The light and lesson of history: its role in the education of the mind and in the guidance of human conduct

OLD TESTAMENT: *Deuteronomy*, 6:20–25; 7:6–11,17–19; 8; 16:1–12; 29 / *Joshua*, 24:1–27—(*D*) *Josue*, 24:1–27 / *I Samuel*, 12:6–25—(*D*) *I Kings*, 12:6–25 / *Ezra*, 4:7–23—(*D*) *I Esdras*, 4:7–23 / *Nehemiah*, 9—(*D*) *II Esdras*, 9 / *Psalms*, 44:1–3; 78; 81; 105–106; 136 esp 136:10–24—(*D*) *Psalms*, 43:1–4; 77; 80; 104–105; 135 esp 135:10–24 / *Ecclesiastes*, 1:11; 2:16 / *Isaiah*, 46:8–11—(*D*) *Isaias*, 46:8–11 / *Jeremiah*, 2:1–9—(*D*) *Jeremias*, 2:1–9 / *Ezekiel*, 20:1–44—(*D*) *Ezechiel*, 20:1–44
APOCRYPHA: *Wisdom of Solomon*, 2:2–4—(*D*) OT, *Book of Wisdom*, 2:2–4
NEW TESTAMENT: *II Peter*, 2 / *Jude*

4 HOMER: *Iliad*, BK IX [485–605] 62a–63b
6 HERODOTUS: *History*, BK I, 2b; BK V, 175b; BK VIII, 273b-c; BK IX, 309d-310a
6 THUCYDIDES: *Peloponnesian War*, BK I, 354b-c; 379c-d
7 PLATO: *Timaeus*, 452b / *Statesman*, 587d / *Philebus*, 612a / *Laws*, BK III 663d-677a esp 667a-b; BK XII, 788a
8 ARISTOTLE: *Sophistical Refutations*, CH 34 [183^{b}16–184^{b}8] 253a-d / *Metaphysics*, BK I, CH 3–10 501c-511d esp CH 3 [983^{b}1–7] 501c-d, CH 10 511c-d; BK II, CH I [993^{a}30–^{b}19] 511b,d-512a; BK III 513b,d-522a,c passim, esp CH I [995^{a}23–^{b}4] 513b,d; BK XII, CH I[1069^{a}25–29] 598b; CH 8 [1074^{b}1–14] 604d-605a / *Soul*, BK I 631a-641d passim, esp CH 2 [403^{b}20–23] 633a
9 ARISTOTLE: *Ethics*, BK X, CH 9 [1181^{b}12–24] 436c / *Politics*, BK VII, CH 10 [1329^{a}40–^{b}35] 533d-534b / *Rhetoric*, BK I, CH 4 [1360^{a}30–37] 600d; BK II, CH 20 [1393^{a}25–^{b}3] 641a
12 AURELIUS: *Meditations*, BK VI, SECT 46 278c-d; BK VII, SECT I 279b; SECT 49 282d; BK IX, SECT 28 293d-294a; BK X, SECT 27 299d; BK XI, SECT 26 306b
14 PLUTARCH: *Pericles*, 121a-122b / *Timoleon*, 195a-b; 201b-202c / *Nicias*, 423a-c / *Alexander*, 540b,d-541a / *Cato the Younger*, 634a-c / *Demetrius*, 726a-d
15 TACITUS: *Annals*, BK III, 58b-d; 60d; BK IV, 71d-72b / *Histories*, BK I, 189d-190a; BK II, 255b-c
18 AUGUSTINE: *Confessions*, BK II, par I 9a; BK X, par 3–6 72a-73a; BK XI, par I 89b-c / *City of God*, BK I, CH 8–9 133a-135a; BK IV, CH 33–34 206c-207a,c; BK V, CH 25 228b-c; BK XI, CH 18 331b-332a; BK XV, CH 21 415b-416a; BK XVII 449a-472a,c esp CH 3 450c-451c; BK XXII, CH 30, 618a-b / *Christian Doctrine*, BK II, CH 28 650a-d; CH 39 654c-655b
20 AQUINAS: *Summa Theologica*, PART I–II, Q 97, A I, ANS 236a-d
21 DANTE: *Divine Comedy*, PARADISE, VI [31–111] 113d-114d; XI [43–139] 122c-123c; XII [22–126] 123a-125a; XV [88]–XVI [154] 129b-132a; XVII [103–142] 133b-c

22 CHAUCER: *Monk's Tale* 434a-448b
23 MACHIAVELLI: *Prince*, CH VI, 8c-d; CH XIV–XV, 22a-b; CH XVIII 25a-26a
23 HOBBES: *Leviathan*, PART I, 53c-54a
24 RABELAIS: *Gargantua and Pantagruel*, BK I, 58a-59d
25 MONTAIGNE: *Essays*, 24a-c; 41b-42a; 68b-69d; 198c-200d; 455d-456b
26 SHAKESPEARE: *2nd Henry IV*, ACT III, SC I [45–96] 483b-d
29 CERVANTES: *Don Quixote*, PART I, 23c-d; 32c-33a
30 BACON: *Advancement of Learning*, 4c-6c; 32d-34b; 85a-c / *Novum Organum*, BK I, APH 98 126d-127b
31 DESCARTES: *Discourse*, PART I, 43a-b
32 MILTON: *Areopagitica*, 384b-386b
33 PASCAL: *Pensées*, 619–641 284b-290a / *Vacuum*, 355a-358b
35 LOCKE: *Civil Government*, CH VIII, SECT 100–112 47c-51b passim, esp SECT 103 48b-c / *Human Understanding*, BK IV, CH XVI, SECT II 369d-370a
35 HUME: *Human Understanding*, SECT VIII, DIV 65, 479b-c
38 ROUSSEAU: *Social Contract*, BK III, 420a-c; BK IV, 428a-435a
39 SMITH: *Wealth of Nations*, BK V, 334c-343d
40 GIBBON: *Decline and Fall*, 33c; 211a; 632a-b
41 GIBBON: *Decline and Fall*, 13d; 194a-d; 311a-312b; 326d-328a,c
42 KANT: *Pure Reason*, 5a-8d; 248d-250a,c / *Fund. Prin. Metaphysic of Morals*, 266d [fn 2] / *Practical Reason*, 357c-d
43 FEDERALIST: NUMBER I, 30b; NUMBER 5, 37b-c; NUMBER 6, 39a; NUMBER 17, 70a-d; NUMBER 18–20 71a-78b; NUMBER 30, 102b; NUMBER 70, 211b-d
43 MILL: *Utilitarianism*, 456a-b
44 BOSWELL: *Johnson*, xiia-c; 3c-4c; 116b; 258d-259a; 314c-315b; 347c-d; 458d
46 HEGEL: *Philosophy of History*, INTRO, 155b-156a; 157b-c; 168d-169d; 174d-175d; 178a-184b; PART I, 230c-231b; PART IV, 368d-369a,c
47 GOETHE: *Faust*, PART I [570–585] 16a
50 MARX: *Capital*, 7b-d
50 MARX-ENGELS: *Communist Manifesto*, 415a-425b
52 DOSTOEVSKY: *Brothers Karamazov*, BK X, 291b-d

3. The writing of history: research and narration

APOCRYPHA: *II Maccabees*, 2:22–31—(*D*) OT, *II Machabees*, 2:23–32
6 HERODOTUS: *History*, BK I 1a-48a,c passim, esp 1a,c, 2b, 4d-5a, 23a-b; BK II, 68b-d; 75b; BK VII, 242c-d
6 THUCYDIDES: *Peloponnesian War*, BK I, 349a-355a passim; 373c; BK V, 489a-b
9 ARISTOTLE: *Rhetoric*, BK III, CH 9 [1409^{a}23–34] 660d; CH 16 670c-672a

3a. The determination and choice of fact: the classification of historical data

3b. The explanation or interpretation of historic fact: the historian's treatment of causes

54 Freud: *Civilization and Its Discontents*, 801d-802a,c

4a(2) Material forces in history: economic, physical, and geographic factors

6 Herodotus: *History*, BK II, 50a-56c esp 51b-d; BK III, 114b-c; BK VII, 237b-c; BK IX, 314a,c

6 Thucydides: *Peloponnesian War*, BK I, 349b-d; 350d; 352a-d; 372c-d

7 Plato: *Timaeus*, 444d-445b / *Statesman*, 587b-589c / *Laws*, BK III, 663d-666d; BK IV, 677a-678c

38 Montesquieu: *Spirit of Laws*, BK I, 3c-d; BK VIII, 56b-57c; BK XIV 102b,d-108d; BK XVII–XVIII, 122a-129c; BK XXI 153a-173d

39 Smith: *Wealth of Nations*, BK I, 3a-6d; 8b-10b; 34a-b; 71a-d; BK III, 173b-d; 177c-179a; BK IV, 189c-191a; 243b,d-246d; BK V, 305b 309a,c

40 Gibbon: *Decline and Fall*, 89b-d; 90c-d; 236c-237a

41 Gibbon: *Decline and Fall*, 220b-225a passim, esp 224b; 338b-c; 355c-d; 427b-428a

43 Mill: *Representative Government*, 327b,d-332d passim, esp 331b-332d

46 Hegel: *Philosophy of Right*, PART III, par 346 111b / *Philosophy of History*, INTRO, 190b-201a,c esp 190b-d, 194a-195c, 199d-201a,c; 203a-b; PART I, 236d-237a; 243d-244c; 248c-d; PART II, 259d-260a; PART III, 286b

49 Darwin: *Descent of Man*, 323a-328c passim, esp 323a-b

50 Marx: *Capital*, 6d-7d; 10b-11d; 25c-d; 35b-36c; 86c; 181d [fn 3]; 187a-c; 239b-241a; 377c-378d

50 Marx-Engels: *Communist Manifesto* 415a-434d esp 416c-d, 419b,d, 421d-422a, 427a-b, 428b-d

54 Freud: *New Introductory Lectures*, 834c; 882c-883b; 884c

4a(3) World history as the development of Spirit: the stages of the dialectic of history

46 Hegel: *Philosophy of Right*, PART III, par 279, 94b-d; par 340–360 110b-114a,c; ADDITIONS, 153 141d / *Philosophy of History*, INTRO, 156c-162a; 163a-165b; 166b-c; 169d-171b; 176b-c; 177d-190b; 203a-206a,c; PART IV, 368d-369a,c

4a(4) The role of the individual in history: the great man, hero, or leader

9 Aristotle: *Politics*, BK I, CH 2 [1253^{a}29–31] 446d

13 Virgil: *Aeneid*, BK VI [756–892] 231a-235a; BK VIII [608–731] 275a-278b

14 Plutarch: *Theseus* 1a-15a,c esp 9a-d / *Romulus* 15a-30a,c / *Lycurgus* 32a-48d esp 47a-48c / *Numa Pompilius* 49a-61d esp 59c-60b / *Solon* 64b,d-77a,c / *Pericles* 121a-141a,c esp 129c-130b, 140c-141a,c / *Timoleon* 195a-213d

esp 212c-213d / *Flamininus*, 307d-308a / *Lysander*, 358b-d / *Pompey* 499a-538a,c / *Caesar* 577a-604d / *Antony* 748a-779d esp 750a-b / *Marcus Brutus* 802b,d-824a,c

15 Tacitus: *Annals*, BK II, 44d-45a

23 Machiavelli: *Prince*, CH VI 8c-10a; CH XX, 30d; CH XXV-XXVI, 35c-37d

24 Rabelais: *Gargantua and Pantagruel*, BK IV, 267c-270b

32 Milton: *Lord Gen. Cromwell* 69a-b

38 Montesquieu: *Spirit of Laws*, BK X, 65d-68a

38 Rousseau: *Inequality*, 362a-b / *Political Economy*, 373c-374a / *Social Contract*, BK II, 400c-402a

40 Gibbon: *Decline and Fall*, 633d-634a,c

41 Gibbon: *Decline and Fall*, 220b; 251d-253a,c; 327d-328a,c; 492a

43 Federalist: NUMBER 72, 217d-218a

43 Mill: *Representative Government*, 332a-c

46 Hegel: *Philosophy of Right*, PART I, par 93 36a-b; par 102 39a-b; par 124 44b-d; PART III, par 167 60b; par 318 105b; par 344 111a; par 348 111d; par 350 112a; ADDITIONS, 58 125c; 186 149b / *Philosophy of History*, INTRO, 162a-170b; 184b-d; PART I, 241d-242b; PART II, 259b-c; 273a; 275d-276a; 280b-281a; 281d-282d; 283c-d; PART III, 298a-b; 300a-301c; PART IV, 360b-c; 361d-362a; 366b

47 Goethe: *Faust*, PART I [570–580] 16a

48 Melville: *Moby Dick*, 107a-b

51 Tolstoy: *War and Peace* passim, esp BK I, 8d-10d, BK III, 143a-c, 162b-164a,c, BK IX, 342a-344b, BK X, 389a-391c, 405a-b, 430b-432c, 447c-448c, 465c-467a, BK XI, 469a-470c, 497c-499c, 507a, BK XIII, 563a-575a, BK XIV, 610d-611c, BK XV, 619c-621b, EPILOGUE I, 645a-650c, EPILOGUE II 675a-696d passim

54 Freud: *Civilization and Its Discontents*, 800a-b / *New Introductory Lectures*, 834b-c

4b. The laws and patterns of historical change: cycles, progress, evolution

6 Herodotus: *History*, BK I, 2b

6 Thucydides: *Peloponnesian War*, BK I, 349a-352a

7 Plato: *Republic*, BK VIII, 403a-d / *Timaeus*, 444d-445b / *Statesman*, 587b-589c / *Laws*, BK III, 663d-666d

8 Aristotle: *Physics*, BK IV, CH 14 [223^{b}24–30] 303c-d / *Metaphysics*, BK XII, CH 8 [1074^{b}11–13] 605a

12 Lucretius: *Nature of Things*, BK II [1105-1174] 29a-30a,c; BK V [65–109] 62a-c; [170–194] 63b-c; [772–1457] 71a-80a,c

12 Aurelius: *Meditations*, BK II, SECT 14 258d; BK VI, SECT 46 278c-d; BK VII, SECT I 279b; SECT 49 282d; BK IX, SECT 28 293d-294a; BK X, SECT 27 299d

13 Virgil: *Eclogues*, IV 14a-15b / *Aeneid*, BK VIII [306–336] 267b-268a

14 Plutarch: *Sulla*, 372a-c

(4. *The philosophy of history. 4b. The laws and patterns of historical change: cycles, progress, evolution.*)

15 TACITUS: *Annals*, BK III, 51b-52b; 58b-d

18 AUGUSTINE: *City of God*, BK X, CH 14 307c-308a; BK XI, CH 18 331d-332a; BK XV-XVIII 397b,d-507a,c; BK XXII, CH 30, 618c-d

20 AQUINAS: *Summa Theologica*, PART I-II, Q 97, A 1, ANS 236a-d

21 DANTE: *Divine Comedy*, HELL, VII [67-96] 10b-c; XIV [94-120] 20c-d

25 MONTAIGNE: *Essays*, 439c-440b; 443a-b; 465a-c

26 SHAKESPEARE: *2nd Henry IV*, ACT III, SC I [45-91] 483b-c / *Julius Caesar*, ACT IV, SC III [218-224] 590d

36 SWIFT: *Gulliver*, PART II, 79a-80a; PART III, 121a-b

40 GIBBON: *Decline and Fall*, 544d-545d; 632a-634a,c

41 GIBBON: *Decline and Fall*, 62c-d; 349a

42 KANT: *Judgement*, 584d-587a

43 MILL: *Liberty*, 300d-301c

46 HEGEL: *Philosophy of Right*, PART III, par 340 110b-c; par 344 111a; par 347 111b-c; par 354-360 112c-114a,c / *Philosophy of History*, INTRO, 161a-c; 174d-175c; 178a-179c; 187a-c; 203b-206a,c; PART I, 235d-236a; 258b-d; PART II, 259c-d; 282d-284a,c; PART III, 286c-287a; 308a-b; PART IV, 315b-317d; 342d-343a

49 DARWIN: *Descent of Man*, 323a; 327a-330a,c esp 327b

50 MARX: *Capital*, 10b-11d; 377c-378d

50 MARX-ENGELS: *Communist Manifesto*, 416c-d

51 TOLSTOY: *War and Peace*, BK XI, 469a-472b; EPILOGUE I, 645a-650c; EPILOGUE II 675a-696d

54 FREUD: *Beyond the Pleasure Principle*, 651d-652d / *Civilization and Its Discontents*, 781a-789b esp 785c; 799a-802a,c / *New Introductory Lectures*, 834c; 882c-883a; 883c

4c. **The spirit of the time as conditioning the politics and culture of a period**

33 PASCAL: *Pensées*, 354 234b

38 ROUSSEAU: *Inequality*, 362a-d

46 HEGEL: *Philosophy of Right*, PREF, 6c-7a; INTRO, par 3 10a-12c; PART III, par 218 72c-d / *Philosophy of History*, INTRO, 173a-175c; 177c-178a; 182d-183a; 185a-186d; 187d-189a; PART I, 211a-219d esp 219c-d; 219d-235c esp 220b-221a, 222a-223a, 233b-235c; 247b-257c; PART II, 259d-260c; 263d-281b; PART III, 286c-298a

47 GOETHE: *Faust*, PART I [570-580] 16a

51 TOLSTOY: *War and Peace*, EPILOGUE I, 645a-646c

52 DOSTOEVSKY: *Brothers Karamazov*, BK XI, 345a-c

5. **The theology of history**

5a. **The relation of the gods or God to human history: the dispensations of providence**

OLD TESTAMENT: *Genesis*, 3; 6-9 passim; 16-17; 21:1-24; 22:1-18 esp 22:15-18; 28:11-16; 35:9-13; 45:1-13; 46:1-4 / *Exodus*, 3-20 passim; 23:20-33 / *Deuteronomy*, 4:1-40; 7-11 passim; 29 / *Joshua*, 6:1-20; 10; 24:1-25—(D) *Josue*, 6:1-20; 10; 24:1-25 / *I Samuel*, 12:6-25—(D) *I Kings*, 12:6-25 / *Nehemiah*, 9:1-10:29—(D) *II Esdras*, 9:1-10:29 / *Psalms*, 44:1-3; 78; 81; 105-106; 136 esp 136:10-24 —(D) *Psalms*, 43:1-4; 77; 80; 104-105; 135 esp 135:10-24 / *Jeremiah*, 43:8-13; 44:30; 46—(D) *Jeremias*, 43:8-13; 44:30; 46

APOCRYPHA: *Judith* passim, esp 5-6, 8-16—(D) OT, *Judith* passim, esp 5-6, 8-16

NEW TESTAMENT: *Romans*, 1-11 / *I Corinthians*, 15:19-55 / *Galatians*, 3-4 / *II Thessalonians*, 1:7-2:14 / *Hebrews* passim / *II Peter*, 3:3-13 / *Revelation*—(D) *Apocalypse*

5 AESCHYLUS: *Persians* 15a-26d esp [737-908] 23a-24d / *Prometheus Bound* 40a-51d esp [436-502] 44c-45a

6 HERODOTUS: *History*, BK I, 21d-22a; BK VI, 204b-c; BK VII, 214d-220b esp 218b-220b; 237a-b; 238d-239a; 250b-d; BK VIII, 273b-c; BK IX, 309d-310a

7 PLATO: *Protagoras*, 44a-45a / *Symposium*, 157b-159b / *Republic*, BK VI, 378a-b / *Critias* 478a-485d / *Statesman*, 587a-589c / *Laws*, BK IV, 679a-b; 682d-683d; BK X, 765d-768d

12 EPICTETUS: *Discourses*, BK III, CH 22 195a-201a; BK IV, CH 1 213a-223d; CH 3 224b-d; CH 7 232c-235a

12 AURELIUS: *Meditations*, BK II, SECT 11 258a-b; BK III, SECT 11 262a-b; BK VI, SECT 44 278b-c

13 VIRGIL: *Aeneid* 103a-379a

14 PLUTARCH: *Romulus*, 18d; 28b-29c / *Numa Pompilius*, 50d-51c / *Camillus*, 107b-d / *Coriolanus*, 188d-192b / *Sulla* 372a-c / *Demosthenes*, 698a-699a / *Marcus Brutus*, 822a-b

15 TACITUS: *Histories*, BK I, 189b-190a

18 AUGUSTINE: *Confessions*, BK XIII, par 49-51 124a-d / *City of God*, BK I, PREF 129a-d; CH 36 149c-d; BK II, CH 2-3 150c-151c; BK IV, CH 33-34 206c-207a,c; BK V, CH 11-26 216c-230a,c; BK X, CH 14 307c-308a; BK XI, CH 1 322b,d-323a; CH 18 331d-332a; BK XII, CH 21 357a-b; BK XV, CH 1 397b,d-398c; CH 21-22 415b-416c; BK XVII, CH 1-3 449a-451c; BK XVIII, CH 1-2 472b,d-473d; BK XXII, CH 30, 618c-d

19 AQUINAS: *Summa Theologica*, PART I, Q 73, A 1, REP 1 370a-371a

20 AQUINAS: *Summa Theologica*, PART I–II, Q 98, A 6 244c-245b; Q 106, AA 3–4 323a-325c; PART II–II, Q I, A 7 385c-387a; PART III, Q I, AA 5–6 707a-709c

21 DANTE: *Divine Comedy*, HELL, II [13–27] 2d; VII [61–96] 10b-c; PURGATORY, XVI [52–129] 77b-78a; XXIX 97d-99b; XXXII [37]–XXXIII [78] 102d-105a; PARADISE, VI [I–III] 113c-114d; VIII [91–148] 117d-118c; XI [28–39] 122b; XII [37–45] 124a; XVIII [52]–XX [148] 134a-138b passim; XXX [124]–XXXII [138] 153a-156a

23 MACHIAVELLI: *Prince*, CH XXVI, 36b-37a

25 MONTAIGNE: *Essays*, 306a-d

26 SHAKESPEARE: *Richard III* 105a-148a,c esp ACT V, SC III 143b-147d

30 BACON: *Advancement of Learning*, 19b-d; 35b; 37c-38a / *Novum Organum*, BK I, APH 93 125d-126a

31 SPINOZA: *Ethics*, PART I, APPENDIX 369b-372d

32 MILTON: *Paradise Lost* 93a-333a esp BK I [I–26] 93b-94a, BK III [80–134] 137a-138a, BK V [224–245] 180a-b, [519–543] 186b-187a, BK VI [169–188] 200a, BK VII [139–173] 220a-221a, BK X [I–21] 274b-275a, [616–640] 288a-b, [720–844] 290a-292b, BK XI [334]–BK XII [605] 306b-332a / *Samson Agonistes* [60–67] 340b-341a; [300–325] 346a-b; [373–419] 347b-348b; [667–709] 354a-355a

33 PASCAL: *Pensées*, 611–613 282b-283a; 619–736 284b-317b esp 655 292b, 699 302b

40 GIBBON: *Decline and Fall*, 292d-293b

46 HEGEL: *Philosophy of Right*, PART III, par 343 110d-111a / *Philosophy of History*, INTRO, 156c-160b; PART III, 303c-309d; PART IV, 321b-d; 368d-369a,c

48 MELVILLE: *Moby Dick*, 85a

51 TOLSTOY: *War and Peace*, BK IX, 343b-c; EPILOGUE II, 675a-677b; 680b-c; 684b-d

5b. The city of God and the city of man; church and state

OLD TESTAMENT: *Psalms*, 2; 46:4; 48:1,8; 72:8–11; 87:3; 101:8; 127:1—(D) *Psalms*, 2; 45:5; 47:1,9; 71:8-11; 86:3; 100:8; 126:1 / *Isaiah*, 60:14—(D) *Isaias*, 60:14 / *Daniel*, 2:44; 4:3,34; 7:14—(D) *Daniel*, 2:44; 3:100; 4:31; 7:14

APOCRYPHA: *Wisdom of Solomon*, 6:2–4—(D) OT, *Book of Wisdom*, 6:3–5

NEW TESTAMENT: *Matthew*, 6:33; 17:24-27; 22:15–22–(D) *Matthew*, 6:33; 17:23–26; 22:15–22 / *Mark*, 12:13-17 / *Luke*, 12:31; 20:21–26 / *John*, 18:33–37 / *Acts*, 5:29 / *Romans*, 13:1–8 / *I Corinthians*, 15:24–25 / *Ephesians*, 2:19 / *Colossians*, 1:12–13 / *I Timothy*, 2:1–3 / *Titus*, 3:1 / *I Peter*, 2:13–17

12 EPICTETUS: *Discourses*, BK II, CH 5, 143d-144a; CH 14, 155a-b

12 AURELIUS: *Meditations*, BK III, SECT 11 262a-b; BK IV, SECT 23 265c

18 AUGUSTINE: *City of God*, BK I, PREF 129a-d; CH 35 149b-c; BK IV, CH 33–34 206c-207a,c; BK V, CH 15–16 220d-221b; CH 25 228b-c; BK XI, CH I 322b,d-323a; BK XIV, CH 28–BK XV, CH 5 397a-400c; BK XV, CH 21–22 415b-416c; BK XVII, CH I–3 449a-451c; BK XVIII, CH I–2 472b,d-473d; BK XIX, CH 5 513d-514b; CH 11 516d-517b; CH 14 520a-d; CH 17 522b-523a; CH 19–26 523b-529a / *Christian Doctrine*, BK I, CH 10 627b

21 DANTE: *Divine Comedy*, HELL, II [20–30] 2d-3a; XIV [94–120] 20c-d; XXXIV [61–68] 51d-52a; PURGATORY, VI [91–96] 61d; XIII [91–96] 72d; XVI [52–132] 77b-78b; XXIX 97d-99b; XXXII [37]–XXXIII [78] 102d-105a; PARADISE, VI [I–III] 113c-114d; XVIII [52]–XX [148] 134a-138b passim; XXX [124]–XXXII [138] 153a-156a

23 HOBBES: *Leviathan*, PART II, 151a-c; 160a-c; PART III, 177c-180a; 191b-204a; 240a-c; PART III–IV, 245c-249b; PART IV, 266a-c; 275a-278d

32 MILTON: *Paradise Lost*, BK XII [485–551] 329b-331a

38 ROUSSEAU: *Social Contract*, BK IV, 435a-439c esp 437c-438c

42 KANT: *Science of Right*, 442c-d; 444a-c / *Judgement*, 509d-510a

46 HEGEL: *Philosophy of History*, INTRO, 175c-177d; 205d-206a,c; PART I, 245d-247b; PART III, 308b-c; 311b-d; PART IV, 315d; 316a-d; 331b-342a; 348a-369a,c

52 DOSTOEVSKY: *Brothers Karamazov*, BK II, 28d-32c

CROSS-REFERENCES

For: The general consideration of history as a kind of knowledge, *see* KNOWLEDGE 5a(5); MEMORY
AND IMAGINATION 3d; TIME 6e; and for other comparisons of history with poetry, science,
and philosophy, *see* NATURE 4c; PHILOSOPHY 1d; POETRY 5b; SCIENCE 2b.

The educational significance of history or of historical examples, *see* EDUCATION 4d; VIRTUE
AND VICE 4d(4).

Other discussions of the logic or method of historical research, *see* LOGIC 4c; REASONING 6d.

The theory of historical causation, *see* CAUSE 8; and for the factors of chance and fate, freedom and necessity, *see* CHANCE 6b; FATE 6; LIBERTY 6a; NECESSITY AND CONTINGENCY
5f; PROGRESS 1a; WILL 7b.

The idea of progress in the philosophy of history, *see* EVOLUTION 7c; PROGRESS 1–1c; and for
a cyclical theory of history, *see* LABOR 1a; MAN 9a; PROGRESS 1c.

Other discussions of a materialist philosophy of history, *see* DIALECTIC 2d; LABOR 7c–7c(3);
MATTER 6; OPPOSITION 5b; PROGRESS 1a; WAR AND PEACE 2c; WEALTH 11.

Other considerations of history as a dialectical process in the development of Spirit, *see*
DIALECTIC 2d–2d(2); LIBERTY 6a; MIND 10f–10f(2); PROGRESS 4b.

The role of the great man or hero in history, *see* HONOR 5d.

The historian or philosopher of history as a prophet, *see* FATE 6.

Other expressions of historical relativism, *see* CUSTOM AND CONVENTION 9–9b; RELATION
6–6c; UNIVERSAL AND PARTICULAR 7–7c.

Divine providence in relation to the events of history and to the issue of necessity and freedom in history, *see* FATE 4; GOD 7b; LIBERTY 5a–5b; WILL 7b.

Other discussions of the city of God and the city of man, or of the issue of church and state,
see RELIGION 4; STATE 2g.

ADDITIONAL READINGS

Listed below are works not included in *Great Books of the Western World*, but relevant to the
idea and topics with which this chapter deals. These works are divided into two groups:

I. Works by authors represented in this collection.
II. Works by authors not represented in this collection.

For the date, place, and other facts concerning the publication of the works cited, consult
the Bibliography of Additional Readings which follows the last chapter of *The Great Ideas*.

I.

MONTESQUIEU. *Considerations on the Causes of the
Grandeur and Decadence of the Romans*

GIBBON. *An Essay on the Study of Literature*, LXXVIII–
LXXXII

KANT. *The Idea of a Universal History on a Cosmo-
Political Plan*

HEGEL. *The Philosophy of Mind*, SECT II, SUB-SECT C
(CC, γ)

J. S. MILL. *A System of Logic*, BK VI, CH 10–11

W. JAMES. "Great Men and Their Environment,"
in *The Will to Believe*

II.

POLYBIUS. *Histories*, VOL II, BK XII (XVII–XXVIII)

LUCIAN. *The Way to Write History*

BODIN. *Method for the Easy Comprehension of
History*

BOSSUET. *Discours sur l'histoire universelle*

VICO. *The New Science*

VOLTAIRE. "History," in *A Philosophical Dictionary*
———. *The Philosophy of History*

HERDER. *Outlines of a Philosophy of the History of
Man*

CONDORCET. *Outlines of an Historical View of the
Progress of the Human Mind*

SCHELLING. *The Ages of the World*

SCHOPENHAUER. *The World as Will and Idea*, VOL III,
SUP, CH 38

GUIZOT. *General History of Civilization in Europe*,
LECT I–II

MACAULAY. "History," in *Miscellaneous Essays*

F. SCHLEGEL. *The Philosophy of History*

Chapter 35: HONOR

INTRODUCTION

THE notions of honor and fame are sometimes used as if their meanings were interchangeable, and sometimes as if each had a distinct connotation. In the tradition of the great books, both usages will be found. It is seldom just a matter of words. The authors who see no difference between a man's honor and his fame are opposed on fundamental issues of morality to those who think the standards of honor are independent of the causes of fame. This opposition will usually extend to psychological issues concerning human motivation and to political issues concerning power and justice. It entails contrary views of the role of rewards and punishments in the life of the individual and of society.

Praise and blame seem to be common elements in the significance of fame and honor. The meaning of honor seems to involve in addition the notion of worth or dignity. But whether a man is virtuous or not, whether he *deserves* the good opinion of his fellow men, does not seem to be the indispensable condition on which his fame or infamy rests. Nor does his good or ill repute in the community necessarily signify that he is a man of honor or an honorable man.

The connection and distinction of these terms would therefore appear to be the initial problem of this chapter. Any solution of the problem must consider the relation of the individual to the community, and the standards by which the individual is appraised—by himself and his fellow men. Honor and fame both seem to imply public approval, but the question is whether both presuppose the same causes or the same occasions for social esteem.

"The manifestation of the value we set on one another," writes Hobbes, "is that which is commonly called Honoring and Dishonoring. To value a man at a high rate, is to *honor* him;

at a low rate, is to *dishonor* him. But high and low, in this case, is to be understood by comparison to the rate that each man setteth on himself." Does Hobbes mean that the value a man sets on himself is the true standard of his worth? Apparently not. Let men, he says, "rate themselves at the highest value they can; yet their true value is no more than it is esteemed by others." What, then, is the measure of such esteem? "The *value*, or worth of a man," answers Hobbes, "is as of all other things, his price; that is to say, so much as would be given for the use of his power; and therefore, is not absolute but a thing dependent on the need and judgment of another."

Here, then, honor is not what a man has in himself, but what he receives from others. Honor is paid him. He may think himself dishonored if others do not pay him the respect which accords with his self-respect, but their evaluation of him is somehow independent of the standard by which he measures himself. It depends on the relation in which he stands to them, in terms of his power and their need. Virtue and duty—considerations of good and evil, right and wrong—do not enter into this conception of honor. The distinction between honor and fame tends to disappear when honor reflects the opinion of the community, based on the political utility rather than the moral worth of a man.

THERE IS ANOTHER conception of honor which not only separates it from fame, but also makes it independent of public approbation. This is not an unfamiliar meaning of the term. The man who says "on my honor" or "my word of honor" may not be an honest man, but if he is, he pledges himself by these expressions to fulfill a promise or to live up to certain expectations. He is saying that he needs no external check or sanction. A man who had to be compelled by threat or force to honor his obligations would not be acting from a sense of honor.

"It is not for outward show that the soul is to play its part," Montaigne writes, "but for ourselves within, where no eyes can pierce but our own; there she defends us from the fear of death, of pain, of shame itself; there she arms us against the loss of our children, friends, and fortunes; and when opportunity presents itself, she leads us on to the hazards of war: 'Not for any profit, but for the honor of honesty itself.'"

A sense of honor thus seems to function like a sense of duty. Both reflect the light of conscience. Both operate through an inner determination of the will to do what reason judges to be right in the particular case. If there is a difference between them, it is not so much in their effects as in their causes.

Duty usually involves obligations to others, but a man's sense of honor may lead him to act in a certain way though the good of no other is involved. To maintain his self-respect he must respect a standard of conduct which he has set for himself. Accordingly, a man can be ashamed of himself for doing or thinking what neither injures anyone else nor ever comes to the notice of others. A sense of shame—the reflex of his sense of honor—torments him for having fallen short of his own ideal, for being disloyal to his own conceptions of what is good or right; and his shame may be even more intense in proportion as the standard he has violated is not one shared by others, but is his own measure of what a man should be or do.

Dmitri Karamazov exhibits these mixed feelings of honor and shame when he declares at the preliminary legal investigation: "You have to deal with a man of honor, a man of the highest honor; above all—don't lose sight of it—a man who's done a lot of nasty things, but has always been, and still is, honorable at bottom, in his inner being. . . . That's just what's made me wretched all my life, that I yearned to be honorable, that I was, so to say, a martyr to a sense of honor, seeking for it with a lantern, with the lantern of Diogenes, and yet all my life I've been doing filthy things."

The sense of honor and the sense of duty differ in still another respect. Duty presupposes law. The essence of law is its universality. A sense of duty, therefore, leads a man to do what is expected of him, but not of him alone, for he is no different from others in relation to what the law commands. In contrast, a sense of honor presupposes *self-consciousness* of virtue in the individual. It binds him in conscience to live up to the image of his own character, insofar as it has lineaments which seem admirable to him.

Without some self-respect, a man can have no sense of honor. In the great tragic poems, the hero who dishonors himself in his own eyes dies spiritually with the loss of his self-respect. To live on in the flesh thereafter would be almost a worse fate than the physical demise which usually symbolizes the tragic ending.

THE SENSE IN WHICH a man can honor or dishonor himself is closely akin to the sense in which he can be honored or dishonored by others. Both involve a recognition of virtue or its violation. But they differ in this: that a man's personal honor is an internal consequence of virtue and inseparable from it, whereas public honor bestowed upon a man is an external reward of virtue. It is not always won by those who deserve it. When it is, "it is given to a man," as Aquinas points out, "on account of some excellence in him, and is a sign and testimony of the excellence that is in the person honored."

There can be no separation between what a community considers honorable and what it considers virtuous or excellent in mind or character. But it does not necessarily follow that the man who is actually virtuous will always receive the honor which is due him. Public honor can be misplaced——either undeservedly given or unjustly withheld. The virtuous should be prepared for this, in the judgment of Aquinas, since honor is not "the reward for which the virtuous work, but they receive honor from men by way of reward, *as from those who have nothing greater to offer.*" Happiness, he goes on to say, is the "true reward . . . for which the virtuous work; for if they worked for honor, it would no longer be virtue, but ambition."

Tolstoy, however, deplores the injustice of the honor given Napoleon and the dishonor in which Kutuzov was held. "Napoleon," he writes, "that most insignificant tool of history who never anywhere, even in exile, showed human dignity—Napoleon is the object of adulation and enthusiasm; he is *grand*. But Kutuzov—the man who from the beginning to the end of his activity in 1812, never once swerving by word or deed from Borodino to Vilna, presented an example exceptional in history of self-sacrifice and a present consciousness of the future importance of what was happening—Kutuzov seems to them something indefinite and pitiful, and when speaking of him and of the year 1812 they always seem a little ashamed."

Kutuzov later received some measure of honor when he was presented with the rarely awarded Order of St. George. But what is perhaps a much higher honor came to him after his death when Tolstoy enshrined him as one of the heroes of *War and Peace*. Sometimes the virtuous or truly honorable man, living in a bad society, goes without honor in his own time to be honored only by posterity. He may even be dishonored by a society which has contempt for virtue. Sometimes a man of indifferent character and achievement, or even one who is actually base and ignoble, wins honor through cleverly simulating the possession of admirable traits.

It seems appropriate to consider the proportion between a man's intrinsic worth and the honor he receives. The distribution of honors raises questions of justice—in fact, it is thought to be one of the chief problems of distributive justice. For those who hold that honor and fame are utterly distinct in principle, this is the clear mark of their difference. Justice does not require that fame be proportionate to virtue. Though there is a sense in which fame may not be deserved, the qualities in a person which justify fame are of a different order from those which honor should reward. Fame belongs to the great, the outstanding, the exceptional, without regard to virtue or vice. Infamy is fame no less than good repute. The great scoundrel can be as famous as the great hero. Existing in the reputation a man has regardless of his character or accomplishments, fame does not

tarnish, as honor does, when it is unmerited. But for the same reason, fame is often lost as fortuitously as it is acquired. "Fame has no stability," Aquinas observes; "it is easily ruined by false report. And if it sometimes endures, this is by accident."

THE DISTINCTION between honor and fame is not acknowledged by those who ignore merit as a condition of praise. Machiavelli, for example, places fame—or, as he sometimes calls it, glory—in that triad of worldly goods which men want without limit and without relation to justice. If the aim of life is to get ahead in the world, money, fame, and power are the chief marks of success. A man is deemed no less successful if he acquires power by usurping it, or gains it by foul means rather than fair; so, too, if he becomes famous through chicanery or deception and counterfeits whatever form of greatness men are prone to praise.

Along with riches, fame, says Machiavelli, is "the end which every man has before him." This men seek to obtain by various methods: "one with caution, another with haste; one by force, another by skill; one by patience, another by its opposite; and each one succeeds in reaching the goal by a different method." Some methods, he admits in another place, "may gain empire, but not glory," such as "to slay fellow-citizens, to deceive friends, to be without faith, without mercy, without religion." Nevertheless, he declares: "Let a prince have the credit of conquering and holding a state, the means will always be considered honest, and he will be praised by everybody."

Because fame seems to be morally neutral, it replaces honor in the discussions of those who measure men in terms of success instead of virtue, duty, or happiness. Because it is morally neutral, it is the term used by those who wish to judge, not men, but the impression they make. What counts is the magnitude of that impression, not its correspondence with reality.

To be famous is to be widely, not necessarily well, spoken of by one's fellow men, now or hereafter. The man who stands above the herd, whose outlines are clear and whose deeds are memorable, takes his place among the famous of his time or of all times. Plutarch the moralist certainly does not regard the men whose lives he writes as paragons of virtue. On the contrary, he plainly indicates that many of them are examples of extraordinary depravity. But Plutarch the biographer treats them all as famous. He takes that as a matter of historic fact, not of moral judgment. Good or bad, they were acknowledged to be great men, leaders, figures of eminent proportions, engaged in momentous exploits. They were not all victorious. Few if any were successful in all that they attempted or were able to preserve what successes they achieved. But each ventured beyond the pale of ordinary men; and each succeeded at least in becoming a symbol of great deeds, a monument in human memory.

The opposite of fame is anonymity. In Dante's moral universe, only the Trimmers on the rim of Hell are totally anonymous; neither good nor bad, they lack name and fame. Because they "lived without infamy and without praise," Hell will not receive them, "for the damned would have some boast of them." To them alone no fame can be allowed. Honor and glory belong only to the blessed, but the damned in the pits of Hell, by the record they left for men to revile, are as well remembered, and hence as famous, as the saints in Heaven.

THAT MEN NORMALLY desire the esteem of their fellow men seems to be undisputed. "He must be of a strange and unusual constitution," Locke writes, "who can content himself to live in constant disgrace and disrepute with his own particular society. Solitude many men have sought, and been reconciled to; but nobody that has the least thought or sense of a man about him, can live in society under the constant dislike and ill opinion of his familiars, and those he converses with. This is a burden too heavy for human sufferance."

A society of misanthropes, despising each other, is as unthinkable as an economy of misers. The social nature of man requires sympathy and fellow feeling, love and friendship, and all of these involve some measure of approval based on knowledge or understanding. According to one theory, the highest type of friendship springs from mutual admiration, the respect which men have for one another. The old saying that "there is honor among thieves" suggests that even among bad men there is a

desire to hold the approbation of those who share a common life. With this in mind apparently, William James describes fame and honor as a man's "image in the eyes of his own 'set,' which exalts or condemns him as he conforms or not to certain requirements that may not be made of one in another walk of life."

Though Pascal regards "the pursuit of glory" as "the greatest baseness of man," he must admit that "it is also the greatest mark of his excellence; for whatever possessions he may have on earth, whatever health and essential comfort, he is not satisfied if he has not the esteem of men. He values human reason so highly that, whatever advantages he may have on earth, he is not content if he is not also ranked highly in the judgment of man. . . . Those who most despise men, and put them on a level with brutes, yet wish to be admired and believed by men, and contradict themselves by their own feelings."

But is this universal wish for the esteem of others a desire for honor or a desire for fame? Does it make any difference to our conception of happiness whether we say that men cannot be happy without honor or that they cannot be happy unless they are famous?

Even those who do not distinguish between honor and fame are led by these questions to discriminate between fame and infamy. As we have already noted, fame and infamy are alike, since both involve the notoriety enjoyed by the outstanding, the exceptional, the great, whether good or bad. If what men desire is simply to be known by others, and to have a kind of immortality through living on in the memory of later generations, then evil will serve as well as good repute. All that matters is the size of the reputation, and its vitality. But if the desire is for approbation or praise, good opinion alone will satisfy, and then the question becomes whether the object is fame or honor. Which does Iago have in mind when he says, "Good name in man and woman, dear my Lord, is the immediate jewel of their souls"?

Opposite answers seem to be determined by opposite views of human nature and human happiness. Those who, like Plato, think that virtue is an indispensable ingredient of happiness, include honor among the "good things" which the virtuous man will seek in the right way. Possession of good things by itself is not sufficient, Socrates says in the *Euthydemus*. A man must also use them and use them well, for "the wrong use of a thing is far worse than the non-use." Applied to honor, this would seem to mean that the virtuous man will not seek praise for the wrong reasons—either for that which is not praiseworthy in himself or from others whose lack of virtue disqualifies them from giving praise with honesty. The virtuous man will not seek fame or be unhappy lacking it, for fame, like pleasure or wealth, can be enjoyed by bad men as well as good and be sought for wrong as well as right reasons or in the wrong as well as the right way. Virtue, according to the moralists, protects a man from the seductions of money, fame, and power— the things for which men undisciplined by virtue seem to have an inordinate desire.

In the theory of virtue, honor, unlike fame, belongs only to the good and is always a good object, worthy of pursuit. Honor is, in fact, the object of two virtues which Aristotle defines in the *Ethics*. One of these virtues he calls "ambition," and the Greek name for the other, which is literally rendered by "high-mindedness," is sometimes translated by the English word "magnanimity" and sometimes by "pride." The Christian connotation of "pride" makes it a difficult word to use as the name for a virtue, but it can nevertheless be so used when it is understood to mean a justifiable degree of self-respect—not conceit but a middle-ground between undue self-esteem and inordinate self-deprecation. When the Aristotelian names for these two vices are translated in English by "vanity" and "humility," it is again necessary to point out that "humility" must be understood, not in its Christian significance as meaning the virtue of the truly religious man, but rather as signifying an exaggerated meekness or pusillanimity.

The difference between pride and ambition lies in the magnitude of the other virtues they accompany and the scale of honor with which they are concerned. Both are concerned with honor, which Aristotle calls "the greatest of external goods." In both cases, "honor is the prize of virtue, and it is to the good that it is rendered." The proud man is one "who, being truly worthy of great things, also thinks himself worthy of them; for he who does so beyond his deserts is a fool, but no virtuous man is foolish or silly." The proud man will be pleased "only by honors that are great and that are conferred by good men . . . Honor from casual people and on trifling grounds, he will utterly despise, since it is not this that he deserves."

Humility and vanity are, according to Aristotle, the vices of defect and excess which occur when a man fails to be proud. The unduly humble man, underestimating his worth, does not seek the honor he deserves. The vain man, at the other extreme, overestimates himself and wants honor out of proportion to his qualities. Honor, like any other external good, "may be desired more than is right, or less, or from the right sources and in the right way. We blame both the over-ambitious man as aiming at honor more than is right and from the wrong sources, and the unambitious man as not willing to be honored even for noble reasons."

However words are used, the point seems to be clear. It is possible for men to desire honor more than they should and less. It is also possible for honor to be rightly desired. Honor desired to excess or in the wrong way may be called "fame," even as the excessive desire for honor is sometimes regarded as the vice of ambition or an aspect of the sin of pride. The word "pride" seems to have both a good and a bad connotation. But the point remains that the difference between these two meanings of "pride," like the difference between honor and fame, is understood by moralists in terms of virtue, and it is discounted by those who reject the relevance of virtue.

THOUGH HONOR MAY be regarded as inseparable from virtue in moral theory, certain political philosophers make its separation from virtue the principle of a type of government.

In Plato's *Republic*, monarchy and aristocracy are defined in terms of the virtue of the rulers—either of the one wise man or of the excellent few. Government by the few is oligarchy rather than aristocracy when wealth rather than virtue is the principle of their selection. Plato sees the possibility of an intermediate between these two which occurs as a kind of transitional form when aristocracy tends to degenerate into oligarchy. He calls that intermediate "timocracy" and describes it as "a mixture of good and evil" in which the ruler is "a lover of power and a lover of honor, claiming to be a ruler, not because he is eloquent, or on any ground of that sort, but because he is a soldier and has performed feats of arms." In such a state, he claims, "one thing, and one thing only, is predominantly seen—the spirit of contention and ambition; and these are due to the prevalence of the passionate or spirited element." In a timocracy, in other words, honor is divorced from virtue and wisdom and becomes the only qualification for public office.

With Montesquieu, the situation is quite reversed. For him, virtue is absolutely requisite in popular government or democracy, and to a less extent in that other form of republic which he calls "aristocracy." As virtue is necessary in a republic, so is honor in a monarchy. "Honor —that is, the prejudice of every person and rank—supplies the place of political virtue. A monarchical government supposes pre-eminences and ranks, as likewise a noble descent. Since it is the nature of honor to aspire to preferments and titles, it properly placed in this government."

Though Montesquieu and Plato differ in their classification of the forms of government, they seem to agree that honor divorced from virtue is a counterfeit. Honor identified with ranks and titles, honor which moves individuals to serve the public good in order to promote their own interests, Montesquieu admits is a false honor, "but even this false honor is as useful to the public as true honor could possibly be to private persons." Considering the laws of education characteristic of monarchical governments, Montesquieu points out that it is not in colleges or academies, but in the world itself, which is the school of honor, that the subjects of monarchy are chiefly trained. "Here the actions of men are judged, not as virtuous, but as shining; not as just, but as great; not as reasonable, but extraordinary."

HEROISM IS DISCUSSED in the chapter on COURAGE, and the role of the hero—the leader or great man—in the chapter on HISTORY. Here we are concerned with the hero in the esteem of his fellow men, the symbol of human greatness and the object of human admiration.

Honor, fame, and glory combine in various proportions to constitute the heroic figures of classical antiquity: honor, to the extent that none is without some virtue and each possesses certain virtues at least to a remarkable degree; fame, because they are the great among men, outstanding and well-known, godlike in their pre-eminence; and glory, almost in the theological sense, inasmuch as the heroes celebrated by Homer and Virgil are beloved by the gods.

It is not accidental that the central figure in the Greek tragedies is called a "hero," since in the ancient view the tragic character must necessarily belong to a great man, a man of noble proportions, one who is "better than the ordinary man," says Aristotle. If he also has some fault or flaw, it is a consequence of strength misused, not a mark of individual weakness. Such weakness as he has is the common frailty of man.

In the modern world heroism and the heroic are more difficult to identify or define. We tend to substitute the notion of genius in considering the exceptionally gifted among men. Glory is dimly recognized and honor takes second place to fame. That portion of modern poetry which deals in heroes—as, for example, the tragedies and historical plays of Shakespeare—borrows them from, or models them on, legendary figures. The great modern novels, counterparts of the epic poems of antiquity, portray exceptional men and women without idealizing them to heroic stature. One of these novels, Tolstoy's *War and Peace*, seeks to deflate the fame of great men. They do not deserve even their reputation for great deeds, much less the honor owed the truly great.

"If we assume as historians do that great men lead humanity to the attainment of certain ends ... then it is impossible," Tolstoy declares, "to explain the facts of history without introducing the conceptions of *chance* and *genius*." But in Tolstoy's opinion "the words *chance* and *genius* do not denote any really existing thing and therefore cannot be defined." We can dispense with these meaningless words, he thinks, if we are willing to renounce "our claim to discern a purpose immediately intelligible to us" and admit "the ultimate purpose to be beyond our ken." Then "not only shall we have no need to see exceptional ability in Napoleon and Alexander, but we shall be unable to consider them to be anything but like ordinary men, and we shall not be obliged to have recourse to *chance* for an explanation of those small events which made these people what they were, but it will be clear that all those small events were inevitable."

This view of history, with its emphasis on impersonal forces, finds another expression in Marxist theory. The machine and the proletariat mass are the heroes of history, or of the revolution. Yet the modern period is not without an opposite strain of thought. Machiavelli calls for a great man, a hero, to become the "liberator" of Italy, "who shall yet heal her wounds and put an end to the ravaging and plundering of Lombardy, to the swindling and taxing of the kingdom and of Tuscany, and cleanse those sores that for long have festered." His maxims for the prince may be read, not merely as advice for getting and holding power, but as preparing for an heroic effort in which the prince's power and fame will be used for liberty. The great man has the historic mission of a pioneer, not the role of a puppet.

Even in the Renaissance, however, Machiavelli is answered by Montaigne, who prizes moderation too much to praise heroism more than a little. Comparing Socrates and Alexander, Montaigne places all of the latter's actions under the maxim, "Subdue the world," whereas Socrates, he says, acts on the principle that it is wise "to carry on human life conformably with its natural condition." To Montaigne, "the virtue of the soul does not consist in flying high, but in walking orderly; its grandeur does not exercise itself in grandeur, but in mediocrity."

The mediaeval Christian conception of heroism centers on the practice of heroic virtue, by which the theologian defines sanctity. In the calendar of saints, there is every type of spiritual excellence, but all alike—martyrs, virgins, confessors, doctors—are regarded as having, with God's grace, superhuman strength. The saints not only perform acts of exemplary perfection; they are godlike men in their exemption from the frailties of human flesh.

The heroes of antiquity also wear an aspect of divinity, but, like Achilles, each has a weakness in his armor. Moreover, the heroes of the *Iliad*, the *Odyssey*, and the *Aeneid* are men of overweening pride. They are relentlessly jealous of their honor. They strive not so much for victory as for the due meed of honor which is its fruit. Nothing grieves them so much as to have their deeds go unrequited by abundant praise. In the contribution made by this love of praise to the growth of the Roman empire, Augustine sees the providential working of God. In order that that empire "might overcome the grievous evils which existed among other nations," he writes, God "purposely granted it to such men as, for the sake of honor, and praise, and glory, consulted well for their country, in whose glory they sought their own, and whose safety they did not hesitate to prefer to their own, suppressing the desire of wealth and many other vices for this one vice, namely, the love of praise."

To Augustine, however, this glory found in human praise is far removed from the true glory. It is, in fact, a sin. "So hostile is this vice to pious faith," he writes, "if the love of glory be greater in the heart than the fear or love of God, that the Lord said, 'How can ye believe, who look for glory from one another, and do not seek the glory which is from God alone?'"

The Christian hero, consequently, seeks not his own glory, but the glory of God, and in contrast to the pagan hero, he is great, not in pride, but in humility. His model is seen in the Apostles, who, according to Augustine, "amidst maledictions and reproaches, and most grievous persecutions and cruel punishments, were not deterred from the preaching of human salvation. And when . . . great glory followed them in the church of Christ, they did not rest in that as in the end of their virtue, but referred that glory itself to the glory of God . . . For their Master had taught them not to seek to be good for the sake of human glory, saying, 'Take heed that ye do not your righteousness before men to be seen of them' . . . but 'Let your works shine before men, that they may see your good deeds, and glorify your Father who is in heaven.'"

The word "glory" in its theological connotation thus has a meaning distinct from, and even opposed to, the sense in which it is sometimes used as a synonym for "fame." In the liturgy of the church, the psalms and hymns (especially those of the doxology which sing the *gloria Patri* and the *gloria in excelsis Deo*) render unto God the homage which is due His infinite goodness, the reflexive splendor of which is the divine glory. As in the strict moral sense honor on the human plane is due to virtue alone, so in a strict theological sense glory belongs only to God.

Strictly, God's glory cannot be increased by human recognition. Yet every act of religious devotion is said to redound to the greater glory of God and to diffuse His glory among creatures through the divinity they acquire when they love God and are beloved by Him. God is "all fullness in Himself and the height of all perfection"; nevertheless, Montaigne writes, "His name may be augmented and increased by the blessing and praise we attribute to His exterior works."

According to Dante, "the glory of Him who moves everything penetrates through the universe, and is resplendent in one part more and in another less." In his journey through Paradise, he beholds the saints whom God loves especially, each with a distinct degree of glory according to the proximity with which he approaches the presence of God. Their halos and aureoles, in the imagery of Christian art, are the symbols of the glory in which they are bathed as in reflected light.

OUTLINE OF TOPICS

REFERENCES

To find the passages cited, use the numbers in heavy type, which are the volume and page numbers of the passages referred to. For example, in 4 HOMER: *Iliad*, BK II [265-283] 12d, the number 4 is the number of the volume in the set; the number 12d indicates that the passage is in section d of page 12.

PAGE SECTIONS: When the text is printed in one column, the letters a and b refer to the upper and lower halves of the page. For example, in 53 JAMES: *Psychology*, 116a-119b, the passage begins in the upper half of page 116 and ends in the lower half of page 119. When the text is printed in two columns, the letters a and b refer to the upper and lower halves of the left-hand side of the page, the letters c and d to the upper and lower halves of the right-hand side of the page. For example, in 7 PLATO: *Symposium*, 163b-164c, the passage begins in the lower half of the left-hand side of page 163 and ends in the upper half of the right-hand side of page 164.

AUTHOR'S DIVISIONS: One or more of the main divisions of a work (such as PART, BK, CH, SECT) are sometimes included in the reference; line numbers, in brackets, are given in certain cases; *e.g., Iliad*, BK II [265-283] 12d.

BIBLE REFERENCES: The references are to book, chapter, and verse. When the King James and Douay versions differ in title of books or in the numbering of chapters or verses, the King James version is cited first and the Douay, indicated by a (D), follows; *e.g.*, OLD TESTAMENT: *Nehemiah*, 7:45—(D) II *Esdras*, 7:46.

SYMBOLS: The abbreviation "esp" calls the reader's attention to one or more especially relevant parts of a whole reference; "passim" signifies that the topic is discussed intermittently rather than continuously in the work or passage cited.

For additional information concerning the style of the references, see the Explanation of Reference Style; for general guidance in the use of *The Great Ideas*, consult the Preface.

1. The relation of honor and fame: praise and reputation

4 HOMER: *Iliad*, BK I 3a-9a,c
5 EURIPIDES: *Andromache* [319-332] 318a; [693-705] 321a-b / *Hecuba* [251-257] 355a; [623-628] 358a / *Heracles Mad* [140-205] 366b-d
6 THUCYDIDES: *Peloponnesian War*, BK II, 395d-396a
7 PLATO: *Protagoras*, 52a-b / *Laws*, BK XII, 788d-789a
8 ARISTOTLE: *Topics*, BK II, CH 11 [115^{b}29-35] 162a,c; BK VI, CH 8 [146^{b}20-24] 200c
9 ARISTOTLE: *Ethics*, BK I, CH 5 [1095^{b}22-30] 340d-341a; BK IV, CH 3-4 370b-372d; BK VIII, CH 8 [1159^{a}13-26] 411b / *Rhetoric*, BK I, CH 9 608c-611c
12 AURELIUS: *Meditations*, BK VI, SECT 16 275b-d; SECT 51 279b-c; BK IX, SECT 30 294b-c
13 VIRGIL: *Aeneid*, BK I [441-493] 115a-116b
14 PLUTARCH: *Marcellus-Pelopidas*, 262d / *Aristides*, 265c-d / *Marcus Cato*, 282a / *Agis*, 648b,d-649a / *Demetrius*, 737b-d
15 TACITUS: *Annals*, BK IV, 73b-d
18 AUGUSTINE: *Confessions*, BK IV, par 21-23 24c-25a / *City of God*, BK V, CH 12-20 216d-226a
19 AQUINAS: *Summa Theologica*, PART I-II, Q 2, AA 2-3 616d-618a

22 CHAUCER: *Troilus and Cressida*, BK II, STANZA 25-27 24b-25a; STANZA 53-55 28b; STANZA 100-115 34b-36b; STANZA 162-163 42b-43a; BK III, STANZA 22-25 57b; STANZA 36-50 59a-61a / *Knight's Tale* [3041-3056] 210a
23 MACHIAVELLI: *Prince*, CH VIII, 13b-c
23 HOBBES: *Leviathan*, PART I, 71d-76b esp 73b-c, 76b; PART II, 146d
25 MONTAIGNE: *Essays*, 126b-127c; 300c-307a; 390a-391c; 411a-d; 445c-446a; 450c-453c; 462b-c; 494b-d; 496c-d
26 SHAKESPEARE: *Love's Labour's Lost*, ACT IV, SC I [1-40] 264b-d / *Richard II*, ACT I, SC I [165-185] 322b-c
27 SHAKESPEARE: *Troilus and Cressida*, ACT III, SC III [38-241] 122d-125a / *Othello*, ACT II, SC III [262-277] 219d; ACT III, SC III [155-161] 223d / *Cymbeline*, ACT III, SC IV 466d-468d / *Henry VIII*, ACT III, SC II [350-458] 572c-573d / *Sonnets*, LXIX-LXX 596d-597a; CXXI 604d
29 CERVANTES: *Don Quixote*, PART II, 203a-b; 222b-c; 227d-228d
30 BACON: *Advancement of Learning*, 91d-92b
31 SPINOZA: *Ethics*, PART III, PROP 29 405b; PROP 53, COROL 413a; PART IV, PROP 58, SCHOL 441d-442a
32 MILTON: *Samson Agonistes* [960-996] 360b-361a

33 PASCAL: *Pensées*, 147-159 200b-202a; 333 232b; 400-401 240b-241a; 404 241a

36 SWIFT: *Gulliver*, PART III, 119a-121b

37 FIELDING: *Tom Jones*, 223d-224b

38 MONTESQUIEU: *Spirit of Laws*, BK III, 11c-12a; BK IV, 13b,d-15a

38 ROUSSEAU: *Inequality*, 360a-362d passim, esp 362b-d / *Social Contract*, BK IV, 434b-435a

44 BOSWELL: *Johnson*, 412b-d

49 DARWIN: *Descent of Man*, 310c-d; 312a-313a passim

51 TOLSTOY: *War and Peace*, BK III, 146d-147c; BK IV, 170d-171c; BK V, 204a-b; 214d-215a; BK VI, 241c-242b; 247a-c; 250c; BK VIII, 304c; BK XV, 619c-621b

52 DOSTOEVSKY: *Brothers Karamazov*, BK X, 273a-d

53 JAMES: *Psychology*, 189b-191a

2. Honor and fame in the life of the individual

2a. The sense of honor and of shame: loyalty to the good

4 HOMER: *Iliad*, BK I [1-510] 3a-8b; BK III 19a-23d; BK IV [326-418] 27b-28a; BK V [520-532] 35c; BK VI [312-358] 43b-d; [440-465] 44c-d; BK IX 57a-64a,c esp [96-114] 58a-b, [307-429] 60b-61c, [606-619] 63b; BK XII [290-328] 85b-c; BK XXII [99-130] 156b-c; [289-305] 158b

5 SOPHOCLES: *Ajax* [430-480] 146d-147b / *Philoctetes* 182a-195a,c esp [50-122] 182d-183b

5 EURIPIDES: *Hippolytus* [373-430] 228b-d / *Heracleidae* [1-11] 248a; [484-596] 252c-253b / *Suppliants* [857-917] 266a-b / *Helen* [838-854] 306b-c / *Hecuba* [342-383] 355d-356a / *Heracles Mad* [275-311] 367c-d / *Phoenician Maidens* [991-1018] 387a-b

6 HERODOTUS: *History*, BK VI, 187b-188d; BK VII, 225d-226b; 238a-c; 255b-259a; BK IX, 304d-305c

7 PLATO: *Symposium*, 152b-d; 154d-155a / *Apology*, 205d-206a / *Laws*, BK I, 651a-652a; BK V, 686d-688a; BK VII, 730d-731d; BK XII, 788d-789a / *Seventh Letter*, 802c-803a

9 ARISTOTLE: *Ethics*, BK IV, CH 3-4 370b-372d; CH 9 375d-376a,c; BK X, CH 9 [1179^{b}4-1180^{a}11] 434b-d / *Rhetoric*, BK II, CH 6 629d-631c

12 EPICTETUS: *Discourses*, BK I, CH 5 110b-c

13 VIRGIL: *Aeneid*, BK IV [1-30] 167a-b; BK X [656-688] 320a-321a

14 PLUTARCH: *Aristides*, 264a-d

15 TACITUS: *Annals*, BK I, 11a-b; BK III, 58a; BK VI, 92c; BK XVI, 180d-183a; 183d-184a / *Histories*, BK IV, 266d; 267b-268a; 289d-290a

18 AUGUSTINE: *Confessions*, BK II, par 9 10d-11a; par 16-17 12c-13a; BK VIII, par 18-30 57d-61c / *City of God*, BK V, CH 12 216d-219b

22 CHAUCER: *Troilus and Cressida*, BK II, STANZA 53-59 28b-29a; STANZA 100-115 34b-36b;

STANZA 162-163 42b-43a; BK III, STANZA 22-25 57b; STANZA 36-50 59a-61a / *Prologue* [43-78] 159b-160a / *Knight's Tale* [859-1004] 174a-176b; [3041-3056] 210a / *Franklin's Tale* [11,667-928] 361b-366a / *Physician's Tale* 366a-371a esp [12,137-191] 369b-370b

24 RABELAIS: *Gargantua and Pantagruel*, BK I, 65c-d

25 MONTAIGNE: *Essays*, 13d-14c; 16a-d; 174d-176a; 300c-307a; 386a-388c

26 SHAKESPEARE: *Richard II*, ACT I, SC I [165-185] 322b-c / *2nd Henry IV*, ACT IV, SC V [21-47] 494c-d / *Much Ado About Nothing*, ACT IV, SC I 520b-523d / *Henry V*, ACT IV, SC VII [124]-SC VIII [77] 560a-561b

27 SHAKESPEARE: *Hamlet*, ACT IV, SC IV [53-66] 59b-c / *Troilus and Cressida*, ACT II, SC II 113c-115d / *Measure for Measure*, ACT II, SC IV [87-187] 185c-186c; ACT III, SC I [133-176] 188b-c / *Antony and Cleopatra*, ACT II, SC VII, [61-90] 326a-c / *Cymbeline*, ACT I, SC I [55-169] 450a-451c / *Winter's Tale*, ACT III, SC II [92-117] 502b-c

29 CERVANTES: *Don Quixote*, PART I 32c-34d; 57d-58a; 81b-84c; 123a-b; 147b-d; PART II, 203a-b; 222c; 227d-228d; 254d-255a; 290a-d

31 SPINOZA: *Ethics*, PART IV, PROP 58, SCHOL 441d-442a

33 PASCAL: *Pensées*, 630 287b

37 FIELDING: *Tom Jones*, 36a-38b esp 38a-b; 146b-147a

46 HEGEL: *Philosophy of Right*, PART I, par 69, 30c-d; PART III, par 207 69b-c; par 244 77c; par 253 79a-c; ADDITIONS, 130 137c-d; 149 140d-141a / *Philosophy of History*, PART I, 214d-215a; PART IV, 320c; 334b-c

49 DARWIN: *Descent of Man*, 310d-314b esp 310d, 312a-313a; 322b-c

51 TOLSTOY: *War and Peace*, BK II, 102b-d; BK IV, 173d-179a esp 177d-178a; BK VII, 281a-d; 291a-292b; 301b-302d; BK VIII, 321d-323b; 333b-334c; 336b-337d; BK IX, 365d-366a; BK XI, 527b-528b; EPILOGUE I, 650d-652a

52 DOSTOEVSKY: *Brothers Karamazov*, BK II, 41a-b; BK III, 54b-58a; BK VI, 153d-157b; BK IX, 245a-b; 260a-263a

53 JAMES: *Psychology*, 190a-191a; 207a-208a

2b. Honor as an object of desire and as a factor in virtue and happiness

OLD TESTAMENT: *Esther*, 5:9-14 / *Proverbs*, 25:6-7

APOCRYPHA: *Ecclesiasticus*, 7:4—(D) OT, *Ecclesiasticus*, 7:4 / *I Maccabees*, 3:14; 9:10—(D) OT, *I Machabees*, 3:14; 9:10

4 HOMER: *Iliad*, BK I [1-510] 3a-8b; BK IX 57a-64a,c esp [96-114] 58a-b, [307-429] 60b-61c, [606-619] 63b; BK XII [290-328] 85b-c / *Odyssey*, BK I [267-305] 185d-186a

5 AESCHYLUS: *Seven Against Thebes* [683-684] 34c

5 SOPHOCLES: *Philoctetes* [50-122] 182d-183b; [1314-1347] 193d-194a

(2. *Honor and fame in the life of the individual.*
2b. *Honor as an object of desire and as a factor in virtue and happiness.*)

5 EURIPIDES: *Rhesus* [756-761] 209d / *Hippolytus* [373-430] 228b-d / *Andromache* [768-801] 321d-322a / *Hecuba* [299-331] 355b-c / *Heracles Mad* [275-311] 367c-d

6 HERODOTUS: *History*, BK I, 6c-7b; BK III, 118a-c; 122a-d; 123c-d; BK VI, 205a-b; BK VII, 215c-216b; 243d-245a; 255c-d; BK VIII, 264c; 282c-283a; BK IX, 304a

6 THUCYDIDES: *Peloponnesian War*, BK I, 370a-c; BK II, 397d-398d; BK V, 486a-d

7 PLATO: *Euthydemus*, 69a-b / *Symposium*, 154d-155a / *Apology*, 205d-206a / *Republic*, BK II, 310c-315c; BK V, 370b-c; BK VIII, 404d-405a; BK IX, 421a-422b / *Laws*, BK I, 651a-652a; BK V, 686d-688a; BK XII, 788d-789a / *Seventh Letter*, 805c-806a; 807d-808a; 810d-811a; 814b-c

8 ARISTOTLE: *Topics*, BK VI, CH 8 [146^{b}20-24] 200c

9 ARISTOTLE: *Ethics*, BK I, CH 5 [1095^{b}22-30] 340d-341a; CH 10 [1100^{a}10-31] 345c-d; BK II, CH 7 [1107^{b}22-1108^{a}1] 353b-c; BK III, CH 10 [1117^{b}24-36] 364b-c; BK IV, CH 3-4 370b-372d; CH 7 [1127^{b}9-22] 374d-375a; BK VII, CH 4 398a-399a; BK VIII, CH 8 [1159^{a}13-26] 411b; BK IX, CH 8 [1168^{a}28-34] 421d-422a; BK X, CH 9 [1179^{b}4-1180^{a}11] 434b-d / *Politics*, BK VII, CH 13 [1332^{a}9-29] 536d-537a; CH 14 [1333^{a}30-^{b}10] 538a-b / *Rhetoric*, BK I, CH 5 [1360^{b}4-1361^{b}2] 600d-602a esp [1361^{a}25-^{b}2] 601d-602a; CH 6 [1362^{b}10-28] 603b-c esp [1362^{b}20-23] 603c; CH 11 [1371^{a}7-17] 614c

12 LUCRETIUS: *Nature of Things*, BK III [59-86] 30d-31b; BK V [1105-1135] 75c-d

12 EPICTETUS: *Discourses*, BK I, CH 21 127b-c; BK IV, CH 6, 230b-c

12 AURELIUS: *Meditations*, BK II, SECT 11-12 258a-c; BK IV, SECT 33 266c-d; BK VI, SECT 51 279b-c; BK VIII, SECT I 285a-b

13 VIRGIL: *Aeneid*, BK I [441-493] 115a-116b; BK VI [886-892] 234b-235a; BK VIII [608-731] 275a-278b; BK X [276-286] 309b-310a; [656-688] 320a-321a; BK XI [376-444] 338b-340a

14 PLUTARCH: *Theseus*, 2c-3b / *Themistocles*, 89a-90b; 95d-96a / *Alcibiades* 155b,d-174d / *Alcibiades-Coriolanus*, 194b-195a,c / *Aristides*, 264a-b; 265c-d / *Marcus Cato*, 282a / *Flamininus* 302b,d-313a,c / *Lysander*, 354b,d / *Sulla*, 369a-d / *Lysander-Sulla*, 387d-388a / *Pompey* 499a-538a,c / *Alexander* 540b,d-576d esp 542a-d / *Caesar*, 599b-d / *Agis*, 648b,d-649b / *Cicero* 704a-723d esp 706b-c, 717a-b

15 TACITUS: *Annals*, BK IV, 73b-d; BK VI, 92c-d; BK XI, 101c-102a; BK XIV, 154a-b; BK XV, 162c-163a / *Histories*, BK I, 195a-b; BK II, 226d-228a; BK IV, 267b-d

18 AUGUSTINE: *Confessions*, BK II, par 13, 11d;

BK X, par 59-64 86b-87d / *City of God*, BK V, CH 12-16 216d-221b; BK VIII, CH 8, 270a-b

19 AQUINAS: *Summa Theologica*, PART I, Q 26, A 4, ANS 151c-152a,c; PART I-II, Q 2, AA 2-3 616d-618a; Q 4, A 8, REP I 636a-c

20 AQUINAS: *Summa Theologica*, PART I-II, Q 60, A 5, ANS 53a-54d; PART II-II, Q 25, A I, REP 2 501b-502a; Q 185, A I, ANS and REP 1-2 639c-641c; PART III SUPPL, Q 96, A 7, REP 3 1061b-1062a

21 DANTE: *Divine Comedy*, HELL, III [22-69] 4b-d; IV 5c-7a; VI [76-93] 9a-b; XIII [31-78] 18b-c; XVI [1-90] 22c-23b; XXIV [43-60] 35a-b; XXXII [1]-XXXIII [9] 47c-49c; PURGATORY, XI [73-117] 69c-70a; PARADISE, I [13-36] 106a-b; VI [112-126] 114d-115a; IX [37-63] 119a

22 CHAUCER: *Troilus and Cressida*, BK II, STANZA 53-55 28b; STANZA 100-115 34b-36b; STANZA 162-163 42b-43a; BK III, STANZA 22-25 57b; STANZA 36-50 59a-61a

24 RABELAIS: *Gargantua and Pantagruel*, BK I, 65c-d

25 MONTAIGNE: *Essays*, 110d-111a; 112a-d; 125a-c; 300c-307a; 462b-c; 495d-496d

26 SHAKESPEARE: *Titus Andronicus*, ACT V, SC III [35-64] 196d-197a / *Love's Labour's Lost*, ACT IV, SC I [1-40] 264b-d / *Richard II*, ACT I, SC I [165-185] 322b-c; ACT IV, SC I [162-334] 343d-345a / *1st Henry IV*, ACT I, SC I [78-90] 435b; SC III [160-208] 439b-d; ACT III, SC II [129-161] 454b-c; ACT V, SC I [127-144] 462a-b; SC IV [59-101] 464d-465b / *Henry V*, ACT IV, SC I [261-301] 554a-c; SC III [18-67] 555d-556b; SC V 558a-b / *Julius Caesar*, ACT I, SC II [84-96] 570b

27 SHAKESPEARE: *Troilus and Cressida*, ACT II, SC II 113c-115d; ACT V, SC III [23-28] 137b / *Othello*, ACT II, SC III [262-270] 219d; ACT III, SC III [154-161] 223d / *Coriolanus*, ACT I, SC III [1-50] 355b-d / *Sonnets*, XXV 590a

29 CERVANTES: *Don Quixote* esp PART I, 32c-33a, 57d-58a, 147b-d, PART II, 222b-c, 227c-228d

31 DESCARTES: *Discourse*, PART VI, 65c-d; 66d-67a,c

31 SPINOZA: *Ethics*, PART III, PROP 53 413a; PROP 55, SCHOL 413b-d; PART IV, PROP 52 439d-440a

32 MILTON: *Lycidas* [64-84] 29a-b

33 PASCAL: *Pensées*, 100 191a-192b; 158-164 202a-b; 400-401 240b-241a; 404 241a

35 LOCKE: *Human Understanding*, 90c-d; BK II, CH XXVIII, SECT 10-12 230b-231c

37 FIELDING: *Tom Jones*, 146c-147a; 223d-224b; 273b; 313d-314d

38 ROUSSEAU: *Inequality*, 360a-362d esp 360c-361a, 362b-d

39 SMITH: *Wealth of Nations*, BK I, 44d-45c; BK IV, 269d-271a

40 GIBBON: *Decline and Fall*, 3a

41 GIBBON: *Decline and Fall*, 176c; 194c; 494b,d-495a

42 KANT: *Fund. Prin. Metaphysic of Morals*, 256a-b; 258b-c

43 FEDERALIST: NUMBER 57, 177b-c; NUMBER 72, 217a-c

43 MILL: *Utilitarianism*, 448d-449c

44 BOSWELL: *Johnson*, 128b; 163d [fn 4]; 479a-d; 498c-499a

46 HEGEL: *Philosophy of Right*, PART II, par 124 44b-d; PART III, par 207 69b-c; par 253 79a-c

48 MELVILLE: *Moby Dick*, 45b-46a

49 DARWIN: *Descent of Man*, 310c-d; 312a-317b esp 312c-313b; 322a-c; 592d

51 TOLSTOY: *War and Peace*, BK I, 15d-16a; BK III, 146d-147c; BK IV, 177d-178a; BK V, 214c-215a; BK IX, 365d-366a; 370c-372a; BK XIV, 590d-604b

53 JAMES: *Psychology*, 189b-191a; 198b-199b; 203a-204b; 207a-b; 208b

2c. Honor as due self-esteem: magnanimity or proper pride

4 HOMER: *Iliad*, BK XII [290–328] 85b-c

5 AESCHYLUS: *Agamemnon* [914–957] 61d-62b

6 THUCYDIDES: *Peloponnesian War*, BK VI, 513a-d

7 PLATO: *Apology*, 208c-209b / *Laws*, BK V, 686d-689c

9 ARISTOTLE: *Ethics*, BK II, CH 7 [1107^{b}22–1108^{a}1] 353b-c; BK IV, CH 2-4 368d-372d esp CH 2 [1122^{b}19–24] 369c; CH 7 [1127^{b}9–33] 374d-375a

12 EPICTETUS: *Discourses*, BK I, CH 19, 125c-d

12 AURELIUS: *Meditations*, BK VI, SECT 16 275b-d

14 PLUTARCH: *Marcus Cato*, 283b-d / *Cicero*, 706b-c; 713b-c / *Demosthenes-Cicero*, 724c-d

15 TACITUS: *Annals*, BK IV, 73c-d

18 AUGUSTINE: *Confessions*, BK X, par 59–65 86b-88b / *City of God*, BK XIV, CH 13 387c-388c

20 AQUINAS: *Summa Theologica*, PART I-II, Q 60, A 5, ANS 53a-54d; Q 66, A 4, REP 3 78c-79b

21 DANTE: *Divine Comedy*, PURGATORY, XI [46–120] 69b-70a

25 MONTAIGNE: *Essays*, 180c-181d; 307a-320b passim, esp 307a-c; 322b-323b; 408b-409c; 456c-d

27 SHAKESPEARE: *Troilus and Cressida*, ACT II, SC II-III 113c-118c / *Coriolanus* 351a-392a,c esp ACT I, SC IX 359c-360c, ACT II, SC II [71–164] 364d-366a, SC III [44–162] 366b-367d, ACT III, SC II [39–145] 374a-375a, ACT IV, SC VII [28–59] 384c-d

29 CERVANTES: *Don Quixote*, PART I, 40b-c; 57d-58a; 123a-b; 177a-b; PART II, 203a-b

32 MILTON: *Paradise Lost*, BK VIII [561–594] 244b-245a

33 PASCAL: *Pensées*, 100 191a-192b; 147–159 200b-202a / *Vacuum*, 361a

38 MONTESQUIEU: *Spirit of Laws*, BK IV, 13b,d-15a

38 ROUSSEAU: *Inequality*, 362b-d

42 KANT: *Practical Reason*, 321b-329a esp 325a-327d / *Pref. Metaphysical Elements of Ethics*, 376b-c

43 FEDERALIST: NUMBER 70, 212a

43 MILL: *Utilitarianism*, 448d-449c

44 BOSWELL: *Johnson*, xiid-xiiia; 16d-17a; 73a-b; 116b-117c; 383c-d

46 HEGEL: *Philosophy of History*, PART II, 267c-268b

51 TOLSTOY: *War and Peace*, BK II, 72d-74a; 102b-d; BK III, 133b-c; BK IV, 173d-179a esp 177d-178a; BK VII, 291a-292b; 301b-302d; BK VIII, 321d-322d; 335b-337d; 338b-339c esp 339b-c; BK IX, 365d-366a; BK X, 442c-443b; BK XI, 498b-d; 527b-528b; BK XIII, 569d-570a

52 DOSTOEVSKY: *Brothers Karamazov*, BK IV, 104b-109a,c; BK V, 110c-111c

53 JAMES: *Psychology*, 211a-212a

54 FREUD: *Narcissism*, 407b-409c passim / *Ego and Id*, 707c

2d. Honor or fame as a mode of immortality

OLD TESTAMENT: *Psalms*, 72:17—(D) *Psalms*, 71:17 / *Proverbs*, 10:7 / *Ecclesiastes*, 2:16

APOCRYPHA: *Wisdom of Solomon*, 4:1–2; 8:9–13 —(D) OT, *Book of Wisdom*, 4:1–2; 8:9–13 / *Ecclesiasticus*, 37:26; 39:9–11; 44:8–15; 46:11–12—(D) OT, *Ecclesiasticus*, 37:29; 39:12–15; 44:8–15; 46:13–15 / *I Maccabees*, 3:1–7—(D) OT, *I Machabees*, 3:1–7 / *II Maccabees*, 6:21–31—(D) OT, *II Machabees*, 6:21–31

4 HOMER: *Iliad*, BK IX [307–429] 60b-61c; BK XII [290–328] 85b-c; BK XXII [289–305] 158b / *Odyssey*, BK XXIV [191–202] 319a

5 AESCHYLUS: *Seven Against Thebes* [683–684] 34c

5 SOPHOCLES: *Philoctetes* [1408–1444] 194d-195a,c

6 THUCYDIDES: *Peloponnesian War*, BK II, 398a-c

7 PLATO: *Symposium*, 166b-167a

9 ARISTOTLE: *Ethics*, BK I, CH 10 [1100^{a}10–31] 345c-d / *Politics*, BK V, CH 10 [1312^{a}23–39] 514d

12 EPICTETUS: *Discourses*, BK I, CH 19, 126b

12 AURELIUS: *Meditations*, BK III, SECT 10 261d-262a; BK IV, SECT 3, 263d; SECT 19 265a; SECT 33 266c-d; SECT 35 266d; SECT 48 267d-268a; BK VI, SECT 18 275d; BK VII, SECT 6 280b; SECT 34 282a; BK VIII, SECT 21 287a; SECT 44 289a; BK IX, SECT 30 294b-c; BK X, SECT 34 301a

13 VIRGIL: *Aeneid*, BK I [450–465] 115b

14 PLUTARCH: *Pericles*, 125b

15 TACITUS: *Histories*, BK I, 195b

21 DANTE: *Divine Comedy*, HELL, III [22–69] 4b-d; IV 5c-7a; VI [76–93] 9a-b; XIII [31–78] 18b-c; XVI [1–90] 22c-23b; XXXII [1]–XXXIII [9] 47c-49c; PURGATORY, XI [73–117] 69c-70a; PARADISE, IX [37–63] 119a

23 HOBBES: *Leviathan*, PART I, 77a-b

24 RABELAIS: *Gargantua and Pantagruel*, BK II, 81a-d

25 MONTAIGNE: *Essays*, 112d-113a; 267a-b; 301b-c; 304d-306a

27 SHAKESPEARE: *Sonnets*, LV 594c-d; LXV 596a-b; LXXXI 598c-d

12 AURELIUS: *Meditations*, BK IV, SECT 3, 263d

13 VIRGIL: *Aeneid*, BK I [142–156] 107a; [450–465] 115b

14 PLUTARCH: *Themistocles*, 95b-c; 97b-d / *Camillus*, 117a-c / *Fabius* 141a-154a,c esp 149b-c / *Alcibiades* 155b,d-174d esp 161d-162b, 165c-d / *Coriolanus*, 177b-179c / *Timoleon*, 212c-213d / *Aemilius Paulus*, 226c-229c / *Pelopidas*, 245a-d / *Marcellus*, 256b-d / *Aristides*, 265c-266b / *Flamininus*, 309a-b; 310b / *Sertorius*, 464a-c / *Pompey*, 499a-b / *Caesar*, 598d-601a / *Cato the Younger*, 624a-625b; 637a-c / *Cicero*, 712d-713b / *Demetrius*, 737b-d

15 TACITUS: *Annals*, BK II, 33c; 41c-d; 43c-44a; BK III, 45a-46b; 60d; BK IV, 73b-d; BK XIV, 153d-155a

18 AUGUSTINE: *City of God*, BK V, CH 12, 218b-c; CH 15 220d-221a; CH 17–18 221b-224b

19 AQUINAS: *Summa Theologica*, PART I–II, Q 2, A 2 616d-617b

21 DANTE: *Divine Comedy*, HELL, IV [64–147] 6a-7a; PURGATORY, VIII [121–139] 65c-d; XI [73–117] 69c-70a; PARADISE, XVI [16–154] 130a-132a; XVII [46–142] 132c-133c

23 MACHIAVELLI: *Prince*, CH XVIII, 25d-26a

23 HOBBES: *Leviathan*, PART I, 73b-c; 75a-b

25 MONTAIGNE: *Essays*, 181d-183a; 445c-446a

26 SHAKESPEARE: *Julius Caesar*, ACT I, SC I [37–65] 568d-569a; ACT V, SC V 595a-596a,c esp [68–81] 596a,c

27 SHAKESPEARE: *Troilus and Cressida*, ACT III, SC III [175–233] 124b-125a / *Coriolanus* 351a-392a,c esp ACT I, SC IX 359c-360c, ACT II, SC I [134–247] 362b-363c, SC II–III 364a-369a / *Timon of Athens*, ACT III, SC V 406d-408a

29 CERVANTES: *Don Quixote*, PART I, 65c-68b

30 BACON: *Advancement of Learning*, 20b-c

32 MILTON: *Areopagitica*, 383a

33 PASCAL: *Pensées*, 337 232b-233a

36 SWIFT: *Gulliver*, PART I, 28b; PART III, 119a-121b

37 FIELDING: *Tom Jones*, 54d-55a; 313d-314d

38 ROUSSEAU: *Inequality*, 360a-362d passim, esp 360b-c / *Political Economy*, 374d-375b / *Social Contract*, BK IV, 434a

40 GIBBON: *Decline and Fall*,' 28b-29b; 92a; 219d-220a; 298b; 381b-d

41 GIBBON: *Decline and Fall*, 318b-319b

42 KANT: *Judgement*, 504a-b

43 FEDERALIST: NUMBER 57, 177a-c

43 MILL: *Liberty*, 278c-279a; 298b-299a

44 BOSWELL: *Johnson*, xia; 8a-c; 383c; 479a-d; 498c-499a

46 HEGEL: *Philosophy of Right*, PART III, par 348 111d / *Philosophy of History*, INTRO, 167a-168a; PART II, 262a-c; 272c-273a; 280b-281a

47 GOETHE: *Faust*, PART I [1011–1021] 25b-26a

48 MELVILLE: *Moby Dick*, 79a-82b; 84b-85a

51 TOLSTOY: *War and Peace*, BK IV, 171c-173d; BK VIII, 338c-d; BK XIII, 578b; 582a-584b; BK XV, 619c-621b; 629b-c

3b. The conditions of honor or fame and the causes of dishonor or infamy

OLD TESTAMENT: *Joshua*, 6:27—(D) *Josue*, 6:27 / *Judges*, 5 / *I Samuel*, 18:6-8—(D) *I Kings*, 18:6-8 / *I Kings*, 10—(D) *III Kings*, 10 / *I Chronicles*, 29:12—(D) *I Paralipomenon*, 29:12 / *II Chronicles*, 9:1-28—(D) *II Paralipomenon*, 9:1-28 / *Proverbs*, 3:16; 4:8,18; 8:18; 14:28; 31:23,25,28-31 / *Ecclesiastes*, 1:11; 2:16; 7:1 —(D) *Ecclesiastes*, 1:11; 2:16; 7:2 / *Isaiah*, 14:20—(D) *Isaias*, 14:20 / *Jeremiah*, 9:23-24 —(D) *Jeremias*, 9:23-24

APOCRYPHA: *Judith*, 8:8—(D) OT, *Judith*, 8:8 / *Wisdom of Solomon*, 3:16-17; 4:1-8; 8:9-10— (D) OT, *Book of Wisdom*, 3:16-17; 4:1-8; 8:9-10 / *Ecclesiasticus*, 1:19; 10:5; 10:19-11:2; 37:26; 44:1-15—(D) OT, *Ecclesiasticus*, 1:24; 10:5; 10:23-11:2; 37:29; 44:1-15 / *I Maccabees*, 2:50-51—(D) OT, *I Machabees*, 2:50-51

NEW TESTAMENT: *Acts*, 21:26-40 / *Romans*, 14:15-18 / *II Corinthians*, 10:8-18; 11:16-30 / *I Thessalonians*, 1:6-10

4 HOMER: *Iliad*, BK I 3a-9a,c; BK III 19a-23d; BK VI [312–358] 43b-d; [503–529] 45b-d; BK IX 57a-64a,c esp [307–429] 60b-61c; BK X [102–130] 66a-b; BK XII [290–328] 85b-c; BK XXII [99–130] 156b-c; [289–305] 158b

5 AESCHYLUS: *Seven Against Thebes* [1011–1084] 38b-39a,c

5 SOPHOCLES: *Oedipus the King* 99a-113a,c esp [31–57] 99b-d, [463–511] 103c-d, [1187–1221] 110b-c / *Antigone* [163–210] 132c-d; [441–525] 134d-135c / *Ajax* 143a-155a,c esp [430–480] 146d-147b, [1047–1421] 152a-155a,c

5 EURIPIDES: *Rhesus* [149–203] 204c-205a / *Suppliants* [857–917] 266a-b / *Hecuba* [251–257] 355a; [299–331] 355b-c

6 HERODOTUS: *History*, BK II, 70c-d; 76a-b; 85b-86b; BK III, 93c; BK IV, 134d-135b; BK V, 160d-161a; 168d-169a; BK VI, 206d-207a; BK VII, 231d; 233d-234b; 248d; 257a; 257c; BK IX, 303c-304a; 305a-c

6 THUCYDIDES: *Peloponnesian War*, BK I, 350b; BK II, 395d-396a; 398d-399a; 402c-d; 403c-404a; BK III, 427a-c; BK VI, 513a-d

7 PLATO: *Laches*, 27b-d; 31a-c / *Symposium*, 152d-153b; 154d-155a / *Apology*, 205d-206a / *Republic*, BK I, 296c-d; BK V, 366c-367b; 370b-c; BK VIII, 405d-406a; BK IX, 422a / *Laws*, BK III, 673d

8 ARISTOTLE: *Topics*, BK II, CH 11 [115^{b}22–35] 161d-162a,c

9 ARISTOTLE: *Ethics*, BK IV, CH 3–4 370b-372d / *Politics*, BK V, CH 10 [1312^{a}23–39] 514d / *Rhetoric*, BK I, CH 5 [1361^{a}27–34] 601d; CH 9 608c-611c; BK II, CH 11 [1388^{a}28–^{b}28] 635b-636a

12 LUCRETIUS: *Nature of Things*, BK V [1105–1135] 75c-d

12 AURELIUS: *Meditations*, BK IV, SECT 3, 263d; BK VII, SECT 34 282a

(3. *The social realization of honor and fame.* 3b. *The conditions of honor or fame and the causes of dishonor or infamy.*)

13 VIRGIL: *Aeneid*, BK I [441–493] 115a-116b; [561–568] 118b; BK IX [590–620] 295a-b

14 PLUTARCH: *Camillus*, 117a-c / *Fabius* 141a-154a,c esp 149b-c / *Alcibiades* 155b,d-174d esp 172b / *Alcibiades-Coriolanus*, 194a-195a,c / *Aemilius Paulus*, 224d-229c / *Pelopidas*, 243c-244b / *Marcellus-Pelopidas*, 262d / *Aristides*, 264a-d; 265c-d / *Cimon*, 392d-393b / *Nicias*, 425c-d / *Agesilaus*, 497a-b / *Pompey*, 509d-510a / *Caesar*, 598d-601a / *Phocion*, 604b,d-605d / *Cato the Younger*, 637a-c / *Agis*, 648b,d-649b / *Cleomenes*, 659d-660a / *Cicero*, 712d-713b / *Demetrius*, 737b-d / *Dion*, 784a-b

15 TACITUS: *Annals*, BK I, 16d-17a; BK II, 33c; 41c-d; BK III, 60d-61a; BK IV, 72d-73d; BK XI, 101c-102a; BK XV, 169a / *Histories*, BK II, 226d-228a; BK III, 248b-c; 259c-260a; BK IV, 289d-290a

18 AUGUSTINE: *City of God*, BK V, CH 12–20 216d-226a passim

19 AQUINAS: *Summa Theologica*, PART I–II, Q 2, AA 2–3 616d-618a

20 AQUINAS: *Summa Theologica*, PART I–II, Q 73, A 10, ANS 128a-d; PART II–II, Q 25, A 1, REP 2 501b-502a; Q 43 585a-592d

21 DANTE: *Divine Comedy*, HELL, III [22–69] 4b-d; VI [76–93] 9a-b; VII [1–66] 9c-10b; XIII [31–78] 18b-c; XVI [1–90] 22c-23b; XXIV [43–60] 35a-b; XXXII [1]–XXXIII [9] 47c-49c; PURGATORY, VIII [121–139] 65c-d; XI [73–117] 69c-70a; PARADISE, XVI [16–154] 130a-132a; XVII [46–142] 132c-133c

22 CHAUCER: *Parson's Tale*, par 10, 500a

23 MACHIAVELLI: *Prince*, CH VIII 12d-14c esp 13b-c; CH XIV–XIX 21b-30a; CH XX, 30d; CH XXI 31d-33a

23 HOBBES: *Leviathan*, PART I, 74c-75b; PART II, 146d; PART IV, 261c

25 MONTAIGNE: *Essays*, 7a-d; 103c-104d; 112d-113d; 126b-127c; 130b-d; 302b-306a; 314c-316a; 390c-391c; 445a-446a; 450c-453c; 495d-496d

26 SHAKESPEARE: *2nd Henry VI*, ACT I, SC II 36b-37c / *Richard II*, ACT V, SC II [1–40] 346b-d / *Henry V*, ACT IV, SC I [247–301] 554a-c

27 SHAKESPEARE: *Hamlet*, ACT IV, SC IV [46–66] 59b-c / *Troilus and Cressida*, ACT II, SC II 113c-115d; ACT III, SC III [74–233] 123b-125a / *Coriolanus*, ACT II, SC I [220–275] 363b-364a; ACT III, SC II–III 373c-377a; ACT IV, SC VII [27–57] 384c-d / *Henry VIII*, ACT III, SC II [350–458] 572c-573d / *Sonnets*, XXV 590a

29 CERVANTES: *Don Quixote*, PART II, 227a-228d; 303a-c

30 BACON: *Advancement of Learning*, 83c; 92a-b

32 MILTON: *Lycidas* [64–84] 29a-b / *Paradise Lost*, BK II [430–456] 120b-121a / *Samson Agonistes* [960–996] 360b-361a

33 PASCAL: *Pensées*, 319–324 229b-230b; 337 232b-233a

36 SWIFT: *Gulliver*, PART I, 15b-16b; PART III, 119a-121b

37 FIELDING: *Tom Jones*, 9a-d; 38b; 146c-147a; 223d-224b; 308a-310a; 313d-314d

38 ROUSSEAU: *Inequality*, 360a-362d esp 362b-d / *Political Economy*, 372d; 374d-375b / *Social Contract*, BK IV, 434b-435a

39 SMITH: *Wealth of Nations*, BK V, 354c-d

40 GIBBON: *Decline and Fall*, 2a; 3a; 92a; 435a-436b

41 GIBBON: *Decline and Fall*, 27c-29a; 31b,d-32c; 68a-b; 71b,d; 176c-d; 209d; 494b,d-495d; 504c-505c

43 FEDERALIST: NUMBER 68, 206b-c

43 MILL: *Utilitarianism*, 452c-453a

44 BOSWELL: *Johnson*, 62b-c; 124d-125d; 140b-141a; 160b; 189d-190b; 194c-195a; 197c; 198b-d; 250d-251a; 256d; 299a-b; 412b-d; 479a-d; 498c-499a

46 HEGEL: *Philosophy of Right*, PART III, par 244 77c

47 GOETHE: *Faust*, PART I [3734–3763] 91a-b

48 MELVILLE: *Moby Dick*, 79a-82b; 84b-85a

51 TOLSTOY: *War and Peace*, BK IV, 170d-171c; 173d-179a esp 177d-178a; BK V, 204a-205b; 228b-234a; BK VI, 247a-c; 250c; BK VIII, 304c; 338c-d; BK XIII, 582a-584b; BK XIV, 610c-611c; BK XV, 619c-621b

54 FREUD: *Civilization and Its Discontents*, 767a

4. Honor in the political community and in government

4a. Honor as a principle in the organization of the state: timocracy and monarchy

4 HOMER: *Iliad*, BK XII [290–328] 85b-c

7 PLATO: *Symposium*, 152b-d / *Republic*, BK VIII, 402b-405c

9 ARISTOTLE: *Politics*, BK V, CH 10 [1310^{b}40–1311^{a}7] 513b; BK VII, CH 2 [1324^{b}2–1325^{a}7] 528c-529a

14 PLUTARCH: *Themistocles*, 99b-c / *Lysander-Sulla*, 387d-388a

18 AUGUSTINE: *City of God*, BK V, CH 12, 218d-219b

23 HOBBES: *Leviathan*, PART I, 74b-c

25 MONTAIGNE: *Essays*, 181d-182c

26 SHAKESPEARE: *Richard II*, ACT IV, SC I [162–334] 343b-345a; ACT V, SC II [1–40] 346b-d

27 SHAKESPEARE: *Coriolanus*, ACT III, SC I [142–161] 370d-371a

36 SWIFT: *Gulliver*, PART III, 120a

38 MONTESQUIEU: *Spirit of Laws*, BK III, 11c-12b; BK IV, 13b,d-15a; BK V, 32d; BK VIII, 53b-c

38 ROUSSEAU: *Inequality*, 326b-327a; 360a-362d passim, esp 360a-361a / *Political Economy*, 375a-b

40 GIBBON: *Decline and Fall*, 630b

41 GIBBON: *Decline and Fall*, 81c-d; 317b-318b

46 HEGEL: *Philosophy of Right*, PART III, par 273, 91c-d / *Philosophy of History*, PART II, 262a-c; PART IV, 334b-c

51 TOLSTOY: *War and Peace*, BK VI, 241c-242b

4b. The scale of honor in the organization of the state: the just distribution of honors

NEW TESTAMENT: *Romans*, 13:7

4 HOMER: *Iliad*, BK I [1–510] 3a-8b; BK IX 57a-64a,c; BK XII [290–328] 85b-c

5 AESCHYLUS: *Seven Against Thebes* [1011–1084] 38b-39a,c

5 SOPHOCLES: *Antigone* [162–210] 132c-d / *Ajax* 143a-155a,c esp [430–480] 146d-147b, [1047–1421] 152a-155a,c

5 EURIPIDES: *Hecuba* [299–331] 355b-c

6 HERODOTUS: *History*, BK II, 85a; BK VI, 194d-195b

6 THUCYDIDES: *Peloponnesian War*, BK II, 395d-399a; BK III, 427a-c; BK VIII, 587a-b

7 PLATO: *Republic*, BK I, 305d-306b; BK V, 366d-367a / *Laws*, BK III, 673d-674b; BK IV, 683b-c; BK V, 686d-688a; BK VI, 699d-700b

9 ARISTOTLE: *Ethics*, BK V, CH 2 [1130^{b}30–34] 378b; CH 3 [1131^{a}24–29] 378d; CH 6 [1134^{b}1–7] 382b; BK VIII, CH 14 [1163^{b}5–13] 416a,c / *Politics*, BK I, CH 12 [1259^{b}5–8] 454a; BK II, CH 7 [1266^{b}36–1267^{a}2] 462c; [1267^{a}37–41] 463b; CH 9 [1270^{b}18–25] 466d-467a; CH 11 [1273^{a}32–^{b}7] 469d-470a; BK III, CH 5 [1278^{a}35–39] 475c; CH 10 [1281^{a}29–34] 479a; CH 13 481b-483a; BK V, CH 2 [1302^{a}16]–CH 3 [1302^{b}20] 503b-504a; CH 4 [1304^{a}17–38] 505d-506a; CH 8 [1308^{a}8–11] 510a; [1308^{b}10–17] 510d; [1309^{a}13–15] 511b; CH 12 [1316^{b}21–24] 519d; BK VII, CH 14 [1332^{b}42–1333^{a}16] 537d-538a / *Athenian Constitution*, CH 12, par 1 557b-c

14 PLUTARCH: *Pompey*, 505a-c / *Cato the Younger*, 636d-637c

15 TACITUS: *Annals*, BK XI, 105d-107b

18 AUGUSTINE: *City of God*, BK V, CH 12, 218b-c

23 MACHIAVELLI: *Prince*, CH XXI, 32d-33a

23 HOBBES: *Leviathan*, PART I, 73b-c; 74b-c; 75b-76b; PART II, 103c-d; 104b; 146d; 156c

25 MONTAIGNE: *Essays*, 181d-183a

32 MILTON: *Paradise Lost*, BK II [430–456] 120b-121a / *Areopagitica*, 383a

33 PASCAL: *Pensées*, 305 228a

36 SWIFT: *Gulliver*, PART I, 15b-16b; 28a-b; PART III, 119a-121b

38 MONTESQUIEU: *Spirit of Laws*, BK III, 11c-12b; BK V, 23c-25c; 31a-b; BK XI, 71d-72a

38 ROUSSEAU: *Inequality*, 326b-327a; 358b-c; 360a-362d passim, esp 360b,d [fn 1] / *Social Contract*, BK III, 408c-d

40 GIBBON: *Decline and Fall*, 17a-b; 240c-244c esp 240c-241b, 244b-c; 245d-247a passim; 501c

41 GIBBON: *Decline and Fall*, 39d; 81c-d; 317b-318b

42 KANT: *Science of Right*, 444c-445a

43 ARTICLES OF CONFEDERATION: VI [87–93] 6b

43 CONSTITUTION OF THE U.S.: ARTICLE I, SECT 9 [289–295] 14a

43 FEDERALIST: NUMBER 84, 252a

44 BOSWELL: *Johnson*, 141a; 197c

46 HEGEL: *Philosophy of Right*, PART III, par 206 68d-69b; par 319, 106b-c / *Philosophy of History*, PART I, 222a-224a

47 GOETHE: *Faust*, PART II [10,849–976] 264a-267a

48 MELVILLE: *Moby Dick*, 108a-112a

51 TOLSTOY: *War and Peace*, BK III, 131c-135c; BK V, 206b-c; 228b-234a; BK VI, 241c-242b; 250c

4c. Honor as a political technique: the uses of praise, prestige, public opinion

4 HOMER: *Iliad*, BK X [60–71] 65d

5 EURIPIDES: *Hecuba* [251–257] 355a; [299–331] 355b-c

6 THUCYDIDES: *Peloponnesian War*, BK II, 395d-399a; BK III, 427a-c

7 PLATO: *Republic*, BK I, 305d-306b; BK VI, 377a-379c / *Laws*, BK VII, 730d-731d

9 ARISTOTLE: *Politics*, BK I, CH 12 [1259^{b}5–8] 454a; BK II, CH 11 [1273^{a}32–^{b}7] 469d-470a; BK III, CH 5 [1278^{a}35–39] 475c; BK V, CH 8 [1308^{b}10–20] 510d; CH 11 [1315^{a}4–24] 517d-518a; BK VII, CH 2 [1324^{b}10–23] 528c-d / *Rhetoric*, BK I, CH 9 608c-611c

13 VIRGIL: *Aeneid*, BK I [142–156] 107a; [450–465] 115b

14 PLUTARCH: *Lycurgus*, 45c-46b / *Alcibiades*, 165c-d / *Caesar*, 598d-599b / *Cleomenes*, 659d-660a

15 TACITUS: *Histories*, BK I, 209d-210b

23 MACHIAVELLI: *Prince*, CH XXI, 32d-33a; CH XXII, 33c

23 HOBBES: *Leviathan*, PART II, 146d; 156c

25 MONTAIGNE: *Essays*, 181d-183a; 306a-d

27 SHAKESPEARE: *Troilus and Cressida*, ACT III, SC III [38–241] 122d-125a

36 SWIFT: *Gulliver*, PART I, 15b-16b; PART III, 119a-121b

38 MONTESQUIEU: *Spirit of Laws*, BK III, 11c-12b

38 ROUSSEAU: *Inequality*, 358b-c; 360a-362d passim, esp 360a-b / *Political Economy*, 375a-b

39 SMITH: *Wealth of Nations*, BK IV, 269d-270d

40 GIBBON: *Decline and Fall*, 4d; 644d

41 GIBBON: *Decline and Fall*, 81c-d; 317b-318b

43 FEDERALIST: NUMBER 57, 177b-c; NUMBER 68, 206b-c; NUMBER 72, 217a-c

44 BOSWELL: *Johnson*, 124d; 127b-c; 141a

46 HEGEL: *Philosophy of Right*, PART III, par 318 105b; ADDITIONS, 186 149b

47 GOETHE: *Faust*, PART II [10,849–976] 264a-267a

51 TOLSTOY: *War and Peace*, BK IV, 170d-173d; BK V, 204c-205b; 228c-d; 230b; 232a-233b; BK VI, 241c-242b; BK IX, 366d-367b

5. Honor, fame, and the heroic

4 HOMER: *Iliad* 3a-179d

6 HERODOTUS: *History*, BK II, 70c-d; BK IX, 293c-294c

6 THUCYDIDES: *Peloponnesian War*, BK II, 395d-399a

7 PLATO: *Cratylus*, 92c-93a / *Republic*, BK V, 366d-367a

9 ARISTOTLE: *Ethics*, BK IV, CH 3-4 370b-372d

14 PLUTARCH: *Theseus* 1a-15a,c esp 2c-3b

21 DANTE: *Divine Comedy*, HELL, III [22-69] 4b-d; IV 5c-7a

23 HOBBES: *Leviathan*, PART I, 77c-d

25 MONTAIGNE: *Essays*, 181d-183a

32 MILTON: *Samson Agonistes* 339a-378a esp [23-67] 340a-341a, [164-175] 343a-b, [340-372] 347a-b, [521-540] 351a-b, [667-709] 354a-355a, [1065-1300] 362b-368a, [1334-1362] 368b-369a

38 ROUSSEAU: *Political Economy*, 373c-374a

41 GIBBON: *Decline and Fall*, 31b,d-32c

51 TOLSTOY: *War and Peace*, BK II, 89b-d; BK III, 131c-135c; 146d-147c; 150a-164a,c; BK VI, 250c; BK IX, 344b-346a; 366d-367b; BK X, 442c-443b; BK XV, 619c-621b

53 JAMES: *Psychology*, 826a-827a

5a. Honor as a motivation of heroism

4 HOMER: *Iliad*, BK I 3a-9a,c; BK III [139-160] 20c; BK V [520-532] 35c; BK VI [440-465] 44c-d; BK VIII [130-156] 52c; BK IX 57a-64a,c; BK XII [290-328] 85b-c; BK XXII [99-130] 156b-c; [289-305] 158b

5 SOPHOCLES: *Ajax* [430-480] 146d-147b

5 EURIPIDES: *Heracleidae* [1-11] 248a; [484-596] 252c-253b / *Suppliants* [857-917] 266a-b / *Hecuba* [343-383] 355d-356a; [482-603] 357a-358a / *Heracles Mad* [275-311] 367c-d / *Phoenician Maidens* [991-1030] 387a-b

5 ARISTOPHANES: *Knights* [565-598] 477a-c

6 HERODOTUS: *History*, BK VII, 226b-c; 234a-b; 255c-d; BK IX, 291c-292a

6 THUCYDIDES: *Peloponnesian War*, BK II, 395d-399a esp 397d-398c; 402c-404a; BK V, 484a-c; BK VII, 556b-d

7 PLATO: *Symposium*, 152b-d; 166b-167a / *Apology*, 205d-206a / *Republic*, BK V, 366c-367b / *Laws*, BK I, 651a-652a

9 ARISTOTLE: *Ethics*, BK III, CH 6-9 361a-364b; BK IV, CH 3 370b-372b passim, esp [1123^{b}31-33] 370d, [1124^{b}7-9] 371b-c / *Politics*, BK V, CH 10 [1312^{a}24-39] 514d

13 VIRGIL: *Aeneid*, BK I [441-493] 115a-116b; BK X [276-286] 309b-310a; BK XI [376-444] 338b-340a; BK XII [650-696] 371b-372b

14 PLUTARCH: *Theseus*, 2c-9a esp 3a-b, 3d / *Romulus-Theseus*, 30a-b / *Poplicola*, 83b-84a / *Coriolanus*, 175d-176b / *Pelopidas*, 238b-239c / *Flamininus*, 302b / *Alexander* 540b,d-576d esp 542a-d, 553b-c / *Caesar*, 583b-585d; 599b-d / *Cato the Younger* 620a-648a,c

15 TACITUS: *Annals*, BK III, 49d; BK XVI, 180d-183a; 183d-184a / *Histories*, BK I, 195a-b; BK II, 226d-228a; BK III, 248b-c; 256b-c

18 AUGUSTINE: *City of God*, BK V, CH 12 216d-219b

22 CHAUCER: *Troilus and Cressida*, BK I, STANZA 68-70 10a / *Knight's Tale* [859-1029] 174a-177a

26 SHAKESPEARE: *1st Henry IV*, ACT I, SC III [194-208] 439d / *Henry V*, ACT IV, SC III [16-67] 555d-556b / *Julius Caesar*, ACT I, SC II [84-96] 570b; ACT V, SC V [68-81] 596a,c

27 SHAKESPEARE: *Troilus and Cressida*, ACT II, SC II 113c-115d

29 CERVANTES: *Don Quixote* esp PART I, 82c-d, 122d-123a, 147b-c, 190d-191d, PART II, 203a-b, 227b-d, 256a-d, 280b-c

33 PASCAL: *Pensées*, 800 328a

38 ROUSSEAU: *Social Contract*, BK IV, 437d-438c

40 GIBBON: *Decline and Fall*, 3a-b; 92a-b; 93d-94b; 217d-220d esp 219c-220d; 370b-d; 376a-c

41 GIBBON: *Decline and Fall*, 324c-325a

42 KANT: *Practical Reason*, 326b-327d

43 MILL: *Utilitarianism*, 452c-453a

46 HEGEL: *Philosophy of Right*, ADDITIONS, 189 149d / *Philosophy of History*, INTRO, 166b-168a; 184b-d; PART IV, 341a-c

48 MELVILLE: *Moby Dick*, 45b-46a

49 DARWIN: *Descent of Man*, 322c

51 TOLSTOY: *War and Peace*, BK I, 21d-22b; BK II, 77c-81b; 89b-d; 97c-106d; BK III, 146d-147c; 150a-164a,c; BK IX, 366d-367b; 369a-372a; BK XI, 527b-528b; BK XIII, 569d-570a; BK XIV, 590d-604b passim, esp 603a-604b; BK XV, 618b-619d; EPILOGUE I, 673d-674a,c

52 DOSTOEVSKY: *Brothers Karamazov*, BK X, 273a-d; EPILOGUE, 408a-c

54 FREUD: *War and Death*, 765a-b

5b. Hero-worship: the exaltation of leaders

4 HOMER: *Iliad*, BK XII [290-328] 85b-c

5 ARISTOPHANES: *Frogs* [1008-1098] 576b-577c

6 HERODOTUS: *History*, BK V, 168d-169a; 183d-184a; BK VI, 192c; BK VII, 235b-c

6 THUCYDIDES: *Peloponnesian War*, BK II, 395d-398a; BK V, 485b-c

7 PLATO: *Republic*, BK III, 340a-b; BK V, 366c-367b; BK VII, 401b

9 ARISTOTLE: *Politics*, BK VII, CH 14 [1332^{b}17-27] 537b-c

13 VIRGIL: *Aeneid*, BK I [267-290] 110a-111a; BK VI [756-892] 231a-235a; BK VIII [608-731] 275a-278b

14 PLUTARCH: *Theseus*, 14c-15a,c / *Romulus*, 28a-30a,c / *Themistocles*, 99b-c / *Pericles*, 140c-141a,c / *Aemilius Paulus*, 226c-230d / *Lysander*, 361d-362a / *Demetrius*, 729d-731a; 734b-735a

15 TACITUS: *Annals*, BK IV, 73b-d / *Histories*, BK I, 198c-d

24 RABELAIS: *Gargantua and Pantagruel*, BK IV 267c-270b

25 Montaigne: *Essays*, 103c-104d; 126b-128d; 145d-146d; 362a-365a; 390c-391c; 452d-453b
26 Shakespeare: *Richard II*, ACT V, SC II [1–40] 346b-d / *King John*, ACT I 376a-379c / *Julius Caesar*, ACT I, SC I [37–65] 568d-569a; SC II [90–161] 570b-571a; ACT V, SC V [68–75] 596a,c
27 Shakespeare: *Antony and Cleopatra*, ACT V, SC II [82–100] 347a-b
29 Cervantes: *Don Quixote*, PART I, 1a-8c; 32c-33a; 41a-c; 82c-d; PART II, 254d-255a
32 Milton: *Lord Gen. Fairfax* 68b-69a / *Lord Gen. Cromwell* 69a-b
38 Rousseau: *Political Economy*, 373c-d
40 Gibbon: *Decline and Fall*, 12b-c; 28b-d; 92a; 263a; 298b; 471c-d; 627a-d
41 Gibbon: *Decline and Fall*, 131b; 209d; 415d-416c; 536c-d
43 Mill: *Liberty*, 298d-299a
48 Melville: *Moby Dick*, 107a-b
51 Tolstoy: *War and Peace*, BK I, 9c-10d; BK II, 97c-101c; BK III, 135c-137c; 140c-142d; 159b-161b; 162b-164a,c; BK IV, 170d-173d; BK V, 230b-234a; BK VI, 238c-243d esp 242c-243c; 260a-262a; BK IX, 344b-346a; 354a-355c; 366d-367b; 382a-388a,c; BK X, 405a-406c; 444a-445d; BK XI, 518c-d; BK XIII, 578b; 582a-584b; BK XIV, 600d; 610c-611c; BK XV, 619c-621b; EPILOGUE I, 647b-649d; 673d-674a,c
53 James: *Psychology*, 826b-827a
54 Freud: *Group Psychology*, 669a-c; 674b-675b; 676b-c; 683c-684a; 686b-689d; 691d-693a / *War and Death*, 762c

5c. The occasions of heroism in war and peace

4 Homer: *Iliad* 3a-179d esp BK IV [220–418] 26b-28a, BK V [520–532] 35c, BK X [203–253] 67a-c, BK XII [290–328] 85b-c / *Odyssey*, BK I [267–305] 185d-186a
5 Euripides: *Rhesus* [149–263] 204c-205c / *Heracles Mad* [140–205] 366b-d / *Phoenician Maidens* [991–1018] 387a-b
6 Herodotus: *History*, BK II, 69a-b; BK III, 101c-d; 122a-123d; BK IV, 134d-135b; BK VI, 187b-188d; BK VII, 233d-234b; 238a-c; 248d; 255a-257d; BK IX, 291c-292a; 303c-304a
6 Thucydides: *Peloponnesian War*, BK II, 395d-399a; BK IV, 457b-c; BK V, 484c-485c; 502b-c
7 Plato: *Apology*, 205d-206a
9 Aristotle: *Ethics*, BK III, CH 6–9 361a-364b; BK IV, CH 3 370b-372b passim / *Politics*, BK VII, CH 2 [1324^b10–23] 528c-d
13 Virgil: *Aeneid*, BK IX [168–449] 283b-291a
14 Plutarch: *Theseus* 1a-15a,c / *Poplicola*, 83b-84a / *Coriolanus*, 174b,d-179c / *Aemilius Paulus*, 219d-229c / *Marcellus* 246b,d-261a,c / *Alexander* 540b,d-576d / *Cato the Younger* 620a-648a,c / *Demosthenes*, 695d-703b / *Cicero*, 712d-713b
15 Tacitus: *Annals*, BK I, 11a-b; BK III, 49d; BK VI, 92c; BK XVI, 180d-183a; 183d-184a / *Histories*, BK I, 200b-c; BK II, 226d-228a; BK III, 246b-c; 248b-c; 249b; 256a-c

20 Aquinas: *Summa Theologica*, PART III SUPPL, Q 96, AA 5–7 1055c-1062a; AA 11–12 1063d-1065b
21 Dante: *Divine Comedy*, HELL, XXVI 38a-39c
22 Chaucer: *Troilus and Cressida*, BK II, STANZA 25–29 24b-25b; STANZA 88–92 33a-b; BK V, STANZA 258 154a / *Prologue* [43–78] 159b-160a / *Knight's Tale* 174a-211a esp [859–1004] 174a-176b
23 Machiavelli: *Prince*, CH XXVI 36b-37d
23 Hobbes: *Leviathan*, PART I, 73b-76b
24 Rabelais: *Gargantua and Pantagruel*, BK I, 32c-35a; 42a-44a; 50c-52d
25 Montaigne: *Essays*, 302b-303a; 340a-343b passim; 362a-365a; 390c-391c
26 Shakespeare: *Henry V*, ACT III, SC I 543d-544b; ACT IV, SC III [16–67] 555d-556b
27 Shakespeare: *Troilus and Cressida*, ACT II, SC II 113c-115d / *Coriolanus*, ACT I, SC I [256–280] 354b-c; ACT II, SC I [130–178] 362b-c; SC III [86–128] 366d-367b / *Timon of Athens*, ACT III, SC V 406d-408a
29 Cervantes: *Don Quixote* esp PART I, 147b-d, PART II, 203a-b, 280b-c
32 Milton: *Lord Gen. Fairfax* 68b-69a
38 Rousseau: *Social Contract*, BK IV, 437d-438c
40 Gibbon: *Decline and Fall*, 217d-220d esp 219c-220d; 240b-247a passim; 369d-376c esp 370a-c, 375b-c; 644d-645c
41 Gibbon: *Decline and Fall*, 19d-20a; 357c-359c; 415d-416c; 534b-536d passim; 549c-550c
46 Hegel: *Philosophy of History*, PART I, 241d-242b; 247a; PART II, 262c-363a; 274a-275a; 281d-282d; PART III, 298a-b
51 Tolstoy: *War and Peace*, BK II, 77c-81b; 89b-d; 97c-106d; BK III, 146d-147c; 150a-164a,c; BK VI, 250c; BK IX, 366d-367b; 369a-372a; BK XIV, 590d-604b

5d. The estimation of the role of the hero in history

13 Virgil: *Aeneid*, BK VI [756–892] 231a-235a; BK VIII [608–731] 275a-278b
14 Plutarch: *Theseus* 1a-15a,c esp 9a-d / *Romulus* 15a-30a,c / *Lycurgus* 32a-48d esp 47a-48c / *Numa Pompilius* 49a-61d esp 59c-60b / *Pericles* 121a-141a,c esp 129c-130b, 140c-141a,c / *Timoleon* 195a-213d esp 212c-213d / *Flamininus*, 307d-308a / *Pompey* 499a-538a,c / *Caesar* 577a-604d / *Antony* 748a-779d esp 750a-b / *Marcus Brutus* 802b,d-824a,c
23 Machiavelli: *Prince*, CH VI, 9a-b; CH XX, 30d; CH XXV-XXVI, 35a-37a
24 Rabelais: *Gargantua and Pantagruel*, BK IV, 267c-268a
25 Montaigne: *Essays*, 362a-365a
38 Montesquieu: *Spirit of Laws*, BK X, 65d-68a
38 Rousseau: *Inequality*, 362a-b; 364a-b / *Political Economy*, 373c-374a / *Social Contract*, BK II, 400c-402a
40 Gibbon: *Decline and Fall*, 633d-634a,c

(5. Honor, fame, and the heroic. 5d. The estimation of the role of the hero in history.)

41 GIBBON: *Decline and Fall*, 220b; 251d-252a

43 FEDERALIST: NUMBER 72, 217d-218a

43 MILL: *Liberty*, 298d-299a

46 HEGEL: *Philosophy of Right*, PART I, par 93 36a-b; PART II, par 124 44b-d; PART III, par 318 105b; par 344 111a; par 348 111d; par 350 112a; ADDITIONS, 58 125c; 186 149b / *Philosophy of History*, INTRO, 162a-170b; 184b-d; PART I, 241d-242b; PART II, 259b-c; 273a; 274a-275a; 275d-276a; 280b-281a; 281d-282d; 283c-d; PART III, 298a-b; 300a-301c; PART IV, 360b-c; 361d-362a; 366b

47 GOETHE: *Faust*, PART I [570-580] 16a

48 MELVILLE: *Moby Dick*, 107a-b

51 TOLSTOY: *War and Peace* passim, esp BK I, 8d-10d, BK III, 143a-c, 162b-164a,c, BK IX, 342a-344b, 350d-355c, BK X, 389a-391c, 405a-b, 430b-432c, 447c-448c, 465c-467a, BK XI, 469a-470c, 497c-499c, 507a, BK XIII, 563a-575a, BK XIV, 610d-611c, BK XV, 619d-621b, EPILOGUE I, 645a-650c, EPILOGUE II 675a-696d passim

53 JAMES: *Psychology*, 826b-827a

54 FREUD: *Civilization and Its Discontents*, 800a-b / *New Introductory Lectures*, 884b-c

6. The idea of glory: its distinction from honor and fame

NEW TESTAMENT: *John*, 5:44

18 AUGUSTINE: *City of God*, BK V, CH 12, 218b-c; CH 14 220a-d; CH 17-19 221b-225b

19 AQUINAS: *Summa Theologica*, PART I-II, Q 2, A 2, REP 2 616c-617b; A 3, ANS and REP 1-2 617b-618a; Q 4, A 8, REP 1 636a-c

20 AQUINAS: *Summa Theologica*, PART III SUPPL, Q 90, A 2 1013d-1014d; Q 96, A 7, REP 3 1061b-1062a

21 DANTE: *Divine Comedy*, PARADISE, I [1-9] 106a; VII [1-9] 115a-b; XIV [1-66] 126d-127c

25 MONTAIGNE: *Essays*, 300c-d

29 CERVANTES: *Don Quixote*, PART II, 227d-228d

33 PASCAL: *Pensées*, 793 326b-327a

38 ROUSSEAU: *Social Contract*, BK IV, 437d-438c

42 KANT: *Practical Reason*, 347d-348b

53 JAMES: *Psychology*, 203a-204b

6a. The glory of God: the signs and the praise of the divine glory

OLD TESTAMENT: *Exodus*, 15:1-21 / *II Samuel*, 6; 22—(D) *II Kings*, 6; 22 / *I Kings*, 8—(D) *III Kings*, 8 / *I Chronicles*, 16:7-36; 17:16-27; 29:10-19—(D) *I Paralipomenon*, 16:7-36; 17:16-27; 29:10-19 / *Psalms* passim, esp 8, 18-19, 24, 29-30, 33-34, 47, 57, 66, 68, 81, 92-93, 95-96, 111, 117, 134-136, 138, 145-150—(D) *Psalms* passim, esp 8, 17-18, 23, 28-29, 32-33, 46, 56, 65, 67, 80, 91-92, 94-95, 110, 116, 133-135, 137, 144-150 / *Isaiah*, 6:1-6 esp 6:3; 12:1-6; 25-26; 42 esp 42:8-12—(D) *Isaias*, 6:1-6 esp 6:3; 12:1-6; 25-26; 42 esp 42:8-12

APOCRYPHA: *Tobit*, 8:15-17; 12:6-7; 13—(D) OT, *Tobias*, 8:16-19; 12:6-7; 13 / *Judith*, 16:1-18—(D) OT, *Judith*, 16:1-22 / *Rest of Esther*, 13:8-18—(D) OT, *Esther*, 13:8-18 / *Ecclesiasticus*, 18; 39:12-35; 42:15-43:33; 51:1-12—(D) OT, *Ecclesiasticus*, 18; 39:16-41; 42:15-43:37; 51:1-17 / *Song of Three Children*, 28-68—(D) OT, *Daniel*, 3:51-90 / *I Maccabees*, 4:24—(D) OT, *I Machabees*, 4:24

NEW TESTAMENT: *Matthew*, 5:13-16 / *Luke*, 1:46-55,68-79; 2:8-14 / *John*, 8:54 / *I Peter*, 4:11 / *II Peter*, 1:16-19 / *Revelation*, 5:9-14; 7:9-17; 11:16-18; 21-22—(D) *Apocalypse*, 5:9-14; 7:9-17; 11:16-18; 21-22

18 AUGUSTINE: *Confessions*, BK I, par 1 1a-b; par 4 2a; par 31 8d-9a; BK II, par 13, 11d; BK V, par 1 27a-b; BK VII, par 19 49c-d; par 23 50b-c; BK IX, par 1 61c-d; par 34 70c-d; BK X, par 38 81a / *City of God*, BK V, CH 14 220a-d; CH 17 221b-222a; BK VIII, CH 6 268d-269c; BK XI, CH 29 339a-b; BK XII, CH 4-5 344b-345b; BK XXII, CH 29 614b-616d

19 AQUINAS: *Summa Theologica*, PART I, Q 26, A 4, ANS 151c-152a,c; Q 44, A 4 241a-d; Q 65, A 2 340b-341b; Q 70, A 2, ANS 364b-365a; PART I-II, Q 2, A 2, REP 2 616c-617b; A 3, REP 1 617b-618a

20 AQUINAS: *Summa Theologica*, PART II-II, Q 25, A I, REP 2 501b-502a; Q 31, A I, REP 1 536d-537c; PART III, Q 19, A 3 819c-820c; Q 25 839c-845a; PART III SUPPL, QQ 90-92 1012a-1037c passim

21 DANTE: *Divine Comedy*, PURGATORY, XI [1-30] 68d-69a; PARADISE, I [1-9] 106a; VII [1-9] 115a-b; XIII [1-30] 125b-c; XXVII [1-9] 147b; XXXIII [49-145] 156d-157d

23 HOBBES: *Leviathan*, PART II, 161b-163d; PART IV, 261c-d

25 MONTAIGNE: *Essays*, 300c-d

31 SPINOZA: *Ethics*, PART V, PROP 36, SCHOL 461b-c

32 MILTON: *On Time* 12a-b / *Upon the Circumcision* 12b-13a / *At a Solemn Musick* 13a-b / *Paradise Lost*, BK III [56-415] 136b-144b esp [80-134] 137a-138a; BK V [136-208] 178a-179b; BK VII [565-640] 229b-231a / *Samson Agonistes* 339a-378a esp [23-67] 340a-341a, [164-175] 343a-b, [340-375] 347a-b, [667-709] 354a-355a, [1130-1155] 364a-b, [1262-1286] 367a-b, [1570-1758] 374a-378a

33 PASCAL: *Pensées*, 233, 216a

42 KANT: *Practical Reason*, 347d-348b / *Judgement*, 594d [fn 1]

47 GOETHE: *Faust*, PROLOGUE [243-270] 7a-b

6b. The reflected glory of the angels and saints

OLD TESTAMENT: *Exodus*, 34:29-35 / *Psalms*, 84:11; 85:8-9—(D) *Psalms*, 83:12; 84:9-10 / *Isaiah*, 60—(D) *Isaias*, 60

APOCRYPHA: *Ecclesiasticus*, 44-50—(D) OT, *Ecclesiasticus*, 44-50

CROSS-REFERENCES

For: Honor or fame in relation to virtue, duty, and happiness, *see* DUTY 4–4b; HAPPINESS 2b(4); VIRTUE AND VICE 4d(2), 6d.

The sense in which pride is a vice and humility a virtue, *see* SIN 4c; VIRTUE AND VICE 8f.

Fame as a mode of immortality, *see* IMMORTALITY 6b.

Mutual respect or honor as a condition of friendship, *see* LOVE 2b(3); VIRTUE AND VICE 6e.

The political significance of honor, *see* GOVERNMENT 2a; JUSTICE 9e; STATE 9c.

The rhetorical uses of praise or honor, *see* RHETORIC 4a.

Other discussions of heroism and the heroic, *see* COURAGE 5; TEMPERANCE 6a; and for the conception of the tragic or epic hero, *see* POETRY 7b.

Various estimations of the role of heroes, leaders, and great men in history, *see* HISTORY 4a(4).

The theological significance of glory, *see* GOD 4h; HAPPINESS 7c(2), 7d; IMMORTALITY 5f.

ADDITIONAL READINGS

Listed below are works not included in *Great Books of the Western World*, but relevant to the idea and topics with which this chapter deals. These works are divided into two groups:

    I. Works by authors represented in this collection.
    II. Works by authors not represented in this collection.

For the date, place, and other facts concerning the publication of the works cited, consult the Bibliography of Additional Readings which follows the last chapter of *The Great Ideas*.

I.

CHAUCER. *The House of Fame*
——. *The Legend of Good Women*
F. BACON. "Of Praise," "Of Vainglory," "Of Honor and Reputation," in *Essays*
HOBBES. *The Elements of Law, Natural and Politic*, PART I, CH 8
HUME. *A Treatise of Human Nature*, BK II, PART I
A. SMITH. *The Theory of Moral Sentiments*, PART I, SECT III, CH 2–3

II.

THEOPHRASTUS. *The Characters*
BENEDICT OF NURSIA. *The Rule*

BOETHIUS. *The Consolation of Philosophy*, BK II
Beowulf
Song of Roland
CHRÉTIEN DE TROYES. *Arthurian Romances*
Völsung Saga
FRANCIS OF ASSISI. *The Rules*
JACOBUS DE VORAGINE. *The Golden Legend*
Njalssaga
LULL. *The Book of the Ordre of Chyvalry*
FROISSART. *Chronicles*
DIAZ DE GAMEZ. *The Unconquered Knight*
MALORY. *Le morte d'Arthur*
ARIOSTO. *Orlando Furioso*
CASTIGLIONE. *The Book of the Courtier*
ELYOT. *The Governour*

Chapter 36: HYPOTHESIS

INTRODUCTION

A COMPARISON of their Greek and Latin roots shows that the English words "hypothesis" and "supposition" are synonymous. To hypothesize or to suppose is *to place under*— to make one thing the basis of another in the process of thought.

The word "hypothesis" is today often popularly misapplied to mean a guess or hunch. The sleuth in a detective story speaks of having an hypothesis about who committed the crime. The popular notion of what it means to suppose something, or to entertain a supposition, more accurately reflects the meaning of hypothesis in logic, mathematics, and scientific or philosophical method.

A supposition is generally understood to be something taken for granted, something assumed for the purpose of drawing implications or making inferences. What is supposed is not known to be true; it may be true or false. When we make a supposition, our first concern is to see what follows from it, and only then to consider its truth in the light of its consequences. We cannot reverse this order, when we employ suppositions, and ask first about their truth.

The word "if" expresses the essence of supposing. The word "then" or the phrase "it follows that" introduces the consequences for the consideration of which we make the supposition. We are not interested in the "if" for its own sake, but for the sake of what it may lead to. In any statement of the "if ... then ..." sort, it is the if-clause which formulates the supposition or the hypothesis; the other part of the statement, the then-clause, formulates the consequences or implications. The whole complex statement, which makes an *if* the logical basis for a *then*, is not an hypothesis. Rather it is what is traditionally called in logic a hypothetical proposition.

THERE IS ONE USE of the word "hypothesis" in mathematics which seems at odds with the foregoing summary. In Euclid's *Elements*, for example, an hypothesis is that which is given, not as the basis from which the conclusion is drawn or proved, but as a condition of solving the geometric problem under consideration. Let us take Proposition 6 of Book I. It reads: "*If* in a triangle two angles be equal to one another, *then* the sides which subtend the equal angles will also be equal to one another." In the demonstration of this theorem, a triangle having two equal angles is regarded as *given* or *granted*. That figure or geometrical condition is a fact obtained by *hypothesis*. It is the fact stated in the hypothesis, or the if-clause, of the theorem.

If the geometrical reality of that fact itself is questioned, the answer would have to be obtained by a prior proof that such a figure, conforming to the definition of an isosceles triangle, can be constructed by the use of no other instruments than a straight edge and a compass. The construction is not made, however, as part of the proof of Theorem 6, any more than is the demonstration of an antecedent theorem, which may have to be used in the proof of Theorem 6. In the proof of Theorem 6, the first line, beginning with the word "let," declares that the constructibility of the figure is to be taken for granted as a matter of hypothesis.

The whole problem of Theorem 6 is to prove that the then-clause follows from the if-clause. Euclid appears to accomplish this by introducing other propositions—drawn from his axioms, definitions, postulates, or theorems previously demonstrated—which establish this connection and so certify the conclusion as following from the hypothesis. Two points about this procedure should be noted.

First, the conclusion does not follow from

the hypothesis directly, for if that were so, the "if-then" proposition would be self-evident and would need no proof. The mind which sees immediately that the sides opposite to the equal angles in an isosceles triangle are necessarily equal does not need any demonstration of the connection between equal angles and equal sides. The Euclidean demonstration consists in making this connection, which is not *immediately* evident, *mediately* evident; that is, evident through the mediation of other propositions. It is not the hypothesis alone which proves the conclusion, but the hypothesis in the company of other propositions which serve to take the mind step by step from the hypothesis granted to the conclusion implied.

Second, the proposition with the truth of which the reasoning seems to end is not the proposition to be proved. The Q.E.D. at the end of a Euclidean demonstration does not apply to the last proposition in the line of proof, but to the theorem itself, for that is the proposition to be proved. The last proposition in the reasoning is merely the consequent which, according to the theorem, is proposed as following from the hypothesis. When he is able to verify the proposed connection between the hypothesis and its conclusion or consequent, Euclid says Q.E.D. to the theorem as a whole— *the whole if-then statement.*

The process of proof seems to be the same when the theorem is stated categorically rather than hypothetically. For example, Theorem 6 might have been stated, as other Euclidean theorems are, in the following manner: "The sides subtended by equal angles in a triangle are also equal to one another." This variation in mode of statement raises a question, not about the meaning of "by hypothesis" in Euclidean proof, but about the difference between hypothetical and categorical propositions, which we will consider later.

THE EUCLIDEAN USE of a given (that is, a constructible) figure as an hypothesis does not seem to be a method of making a supposition in order to discover its implications. Nor does it seem to be a way of testing the truth of an hypothesis by reference to its consequences. Both of these aspects of hypothetical reasoning do appear, however, in Plato's dialogues.

In the *Meno*, for example, Socrates proposes, at a certain turn in the conversation about virtue and knowledge, that he and Meno entertain the hypothesis that virtue *is* knowledge. Socrates immediately inquires about the consequences. "If virtue is knowledge," he asks, "will it be taught?" Since Meno already understands that knowledge is teachable, he answers the question affirmatively. The utility of advancing the hypothesis that virtue is knowledge gradually appears in the next phase of the dialogue, wherein it is discovered that virtue is not teachable at all, or at least not in the way in which the arts and sciences are teachable. The discovery throws some doubt on the truth of the hypothesis that virtue is knowledge; at least it does not seem to be knowledge in the same sense as science or art.

This mode of reasoning exemplifies the use of an hypothesis to test its truth in terms of its consequences. The underlying logical principle is that the denial of the consequences requires a denial of the antecedent hypothesis, just as an affirmation of the antecedent would require an affirmation of the consequent. Nothing follows logically from a denial of the hypothesis, or from an affirmation of its consequences.

This example from the *Meno* also illustrates the difference between Euclid's and Plato's use of hypotheses. Socrates is not here trying to prove that *if* virtue is knowledge, *then* virtue is teachable. The validity of the foregoing if-then statement is already understood in terms of the fact that *knowledge is teachable.* With the if-then statement accepted as valid, Socrates uses it for the purpose of ascertaining whether or in what sense virtue is knowledge. It is not the hypothetical or if-then statement which is proved, but the hypothesis—the antecedent in that statement—which is tested.

The same general method of employing hypotheses and testing them is found in the empirical sciences. In medical practice, the physician, according to Hippocrates, "must be able to form a judgment from having made himself acquainted with all the symptoms, and estimating their powers in comparison with one another"; he should then "cultivate prognosis," since "he will manage the cure best who has foreseen what is to happen from the present state of matters."

The preliminary diagnosis states an hypothesis (what the disease may be) and the prognosis foresees a set of consequences (what is likely to happen if the diagnosis is correct). Observation of the course of the symptoms and the patient's changing condition will either confirm or invalidate the prognosis. Confirmation leaves the diagnosis a lucky guess, but fails to prove it. If the disease does not run the predicted course, however, the diagnosis on which the prognosis was based can be dismissed as a false hypothesis.

WHEN AN HYPOTHESIS takes the form of a prediction of what should happen if the hypothesis is true, the failure of the consequences to occur refutes the hypothesis. Though discussions of scientific method frequently speak of "prediction and verification," it would seem as though prediction can only lead to the refutation of an hypothesis rather than to its verification. An hypothesis is overthrown when its prediction fails, but it is not verified when its prediction comes true. To think that it can be verified in this way is to commit the logical fallacy of arguing from the truth of a conclusion to the truth of its premises. How, then, do empirical scientists prove an hypothesis to be true? What do they mean by prediction and verification in relation to the use of hypothesis?

There seem to be two possible ways in which an hypothesis can be proved by empirical or experimental research. One way can be used when we know that the consequences implied follow *only* from the truth of the hypothesis. Should the consequences implied be impossible *unless* the supposed condition exists, then the confirmation of the prediction verifies the hypothesis.

The other possible method of verification has come to be called "the method of multiple working hypotheses." The validity of this method depends on our knowing that the several hypotheses being entertained *exhaust* all the relevant possibilities. Each hypothesis generates a prediction; and if upon investigation the observed facts negate every prediction except one, then that one remaining hypothesis is verified. If negative instances have eliminated the false hypotheses, the hypothesis remaining must be true, on the condition, of course, that it is the *only* possibility which is left.

Both of these methods seem to be valid only if a prerequisite condition is fulfilled. To verify one of a series of multiple hypotheses through the elimination of the others, the scientist must know that the hypotheses enumerated are truly *exhaustive*. In the verification of a single hypothesis by the confirmation of its prediction, the scientist must know that the observed consequences can follow from no other supposition. Since such knowledge is often unavailable, probability rather than complete proof results from the testing of hypotheses by observation or experiment.

In his *Treatise on the Vacuum*, Pascal offers a summary of the logical situation by distinguishing the true, the false, and the doubtful or probable hypothesis. "Sometimes its negation brings a conclusion of obvious absurdity, and then the hypothesis is true and invariable. Or else one deduces an obvious error from its affirmation, and then the hypothesis is held to be false. And when one has not been able to find any mistake either in its negation or its affirmation, then the hypothesis remains doubtful, so that, in order that the hypothesis may be demonstrable, it is not enough that all the phenomena result from it, but rather it is necessary, if there ensues something contrary to a single one of the expected phenomena, that this suffice to establish its falsity."

BOTH THE USE of hypotheses and the method of verifying them vary from science to science, according as the character of the science happens to be purely empirical (*e.g.*, the work of Hippocrates, Darwin, Freud), or experimental (*e.g.*, the work of Harvey and Faraday), or a combination of experimentation with mathematical reasoning (*e.g.*, the work of Galileo, Newton, Fourier). Not all scientific work is directed or controlled by hypotheses, but in the absence of well-formulated hypotheses, the research can hardly be better than exploration.

A well-constructed experiment, especially what Bacon calls an *experimentum crucis*, derives its demonstrative character from the hypothetical reasoning which formulates the problem to be solved. The value of such a crucial experiment appears in Bacon's reasoning about the rise and fall of the tides. "If it be found," he writes, "that during the ebb the surface of the waters at sea is more curved and round, from the waters rising in the middle, and sinking at the sides or coast, and if, during a flood, it be more even and level, from the waters returning to their former position, then assuredly, by this decisive instance, the raising of them by a magnetic force can be admitted; if otherwise, it must be entirely rejected."

In the field of mathematical physics, and particularly in astronomy, the meaning of hypothesis is both enlarged and altered. So far we have considered hypotheses which are single propositions implying certain consequences. But in mathematical physics, a whole theory—a complex system of propositions—comes to be regarded as a single hypothesis.

In his preface to the work of Copernicus, Osiander says that the task of the astronomer is "to use painstaking and skilled observation in gathering together the history of the celestial movements; and then—since he cannot by any line of reasoning reach the true causes of these movements—to think up or construct whatever causes or hypotheses he pleases, such that, by the assumption of these causes, those same movements can be calculated from the principles of geometry, for the past and for the future too." The elaborate system constructed by Copernicus and the system constructed by Ptolemy which Copernicus hopes to replace are sometimes called "the Copernican hypothesis" and "the Ptolemaic hypothesis"; and sometimes these two theories are referred to as "the heliocentric hypothesis" and "the geocentric hypothesis."

A whole theory, regarded as an hypothesis, must be tested in a different way from a single proposition whose implication generates a prediction. As rival hypotheses, one theory may be superior to another in internal consistency or in mathematical simplicity and elegance. Kepler is thus able to argue against Ptolemy by appealing to criteria which Ptolemy accepts, pointing out that Ptolemy himself wishes "to construct hypotheses which are as simple as possible, if that can be done. And so if anyone constructs simpler hypotheses than he—understanding simplicity geometrically—he, on the contrary, will not defend his composite hypotheses."

But even if the Copernican hypothesis is superior on the grounds of being geometrically simpler, it must meet another test. As indicated in the chapter on ASTRONOMY, mathematical theories about physical phenomena must be more than ideal constructions of possible universes. They must try to account for this one real world and are therefore subject to the test of their applicability to reality. However elegant it may be mathematically, an hypothesis —when considered from the point of view of physics—is satisfactory only if it accounts for the phenomena it was invented to explain. In the words of Simplicius, it must "save the appearances."

An hypothesis can therefore be tested for its application to reality by the way in which it fits the observed facts. "In those sciences where mathematical demonstrations are applied to natural phenomena," Galileo writes, "the principles" which are "the foundations of the entire superstructure" must be "established by well-chosen experiments." By such means Galileo chooses between the hypothesis that the uniform acceleration of a freely falling body is proportional to the units of space traversed and the hypothesis that it is proportional to the units of time elapsed.

To borrow Plato's expression in the *Timaeus*, the mathematical consistency of a theory makes it "a likely story." The theoretical integrity of the hypothesis makes it credible. But when competing credible hypotheses exist, each saving the relevant appearances equally well, which is to be believed? The fact that one of them, as in the case of the Copernican-Ptolemaic controversy, is mathematically superior cannot decide the question, since the question is, Which is true of reality?

Sometimes a single fact, such as the phenomenon of the Foucault pendulum, may exercise a decisive influence, if one of the two competing theories finds that fact congenial and the other leaves it inexplicable. Sometimes, as appears in the discussion of the Copernican hypothesis in the chapter on ASTRONOMY, of two hypotheses which are equally satisfactory so far as purely astronomical phenomena are concerned, one may have the additional virtue of covering other fields of phenomena which that hypothesis was not originally designed to explain.

As interpreted by Kepler and as developed in Newton's theory of universal gravitation, the Copernican hypothesis brings the terrestrial phenomena of the tides and of falling bodies under the same set of laws which applies to the celestial motions. The hypothesis then has the amazing quality of consilience—a bringing together under one formulation of phenomena not previously thought to be related. This seems to be what Huygens has in mind when he considers the degree of probability that is attainable through experimental research." We have "scarcely less than complete proof," he writes, when "things which have been demonstrated by the principles assumed, correspond perfectly to the phenomena which experiment has brought under observation; and further, principally, when one can imagine and foresee new phenomena which ought to follow from the hypotheses which one employs, and when one finds that therein the fact corresponds to our prevision."

Then, in common parlance, we say that it is no longer a theory, but has become a fact. Yet the question remains whether the empirical tests which eliminate the less satisfactory hypothesis can ever make the more satisfactory hypothesis more than a likely story.

IN THE *Mathematical Principles of Natural Philosophy*, Newton says, "I have not been able to discover the cause of those properties of gravity from phenomena, and I frame no hypotheses; for whatever is not deduced from the phenomena is to be called an hypothesis; and hypotheses, whether metaphysical or physical, whether of occult qualities or mechanical, have no place in experimental philosophy." The context of this passage, and of a similar statement at the end of the *Optics*, as well as the association in Newton's mind of hypotheses with occult qualities, substantial forms, and hidden causes, seems to indicate a special meaning of "hypothesis."

Newton criticizes the vortices in the physics of Descartes on the ground that it is unnecessary to appeal to occult or unobservable *entities* in order to explain natural phenomena. The Cartesian vortices, like the substantial forms of Aristotle, are, for Newton, hypotheses in a very special sense. They are *hypothetical entities*. They are not inferred from the phenomena. Although treated as if they were realities underlying the phenomena, they are, as Gilbert says of the *primum mobile*, a "fiction, something not comprehensible by any reasoning and evidenced by no visible star, but purely a product of imagination and mathematical hypothesis."

There is almost a play on words in this identification of hypotheses with imaginary entities to which reality is attributed; for in their Greek and Latin roots, the words "hypothesis" and "hypostasis," "supposition" and "substance," are closely related. The first word in each of these pairs refers to a *proposition* which underlies reasoning, the second to a *reality* which underlies observable qualities or phenomena. To make hypotheses, in the sense in which Newton excludes them from experimental philosophy, is to *hypostatize* or to *reify*, that is, to make a thing out of, or to give reality to, a fiction or construction of the mind.

It has seemed to some critics that, no less than the Cartesian vortices, the ether in Newton's theory of light is an hypothesis in precisely this sense—an imaginary entity. For many centuries, the atoms and molecules postulated to explain chemical combinations and changes were attacked as fictions and defended as useful hypotheses. On the one hand, there is an issue concerning the theoretic usefulness of such constructions; on the other, a question concerning their counterparts in reality.

It is sometimes thought that fictions are useful for purposes of explanation even when their unreality is admitted. Rousseau, for example, explicitly denies any historical reality to the idea of man living in a state of nature prior to the formation of society by the social contract. In this matter, he says, we can lay "facts aside, as they do not affect the question." These related notions—the state of nature and the social contract—are "rather calculated to explain the nature of things, than to ascertain their actual origin; just like the hypotheses which our physicists daily form respecting the formation of the world."

Similarly Lavoisier posits the existence of "caloric" for its explanatory value. "It is difficult," he writes, "to comprehend these phenomena, without admitting them as the effects of a real and material substance, or very subtle fluid, which, insinuating itself between the particles of bodies, separates them from each other; and, even allowing the existence of this fluid to be hypothetical, we shall see in the sequel, that it explains the phenomena of nature in a very satisfactory manner."

ONE OTHER MEANING of hypothesis remains to be considered. It is the sense in which postulates or assumptions are distinguished from axioms in the foundations of a science. In Euclid's geometry, as in Descartes', both sorts of principles appear. The axioms or common notions are those propositions which are immediately seen to be true without proof. The postulates or assumptions are hypotheses in the sense that their truth is taken for granted without proof.

Both sorts of propositions serve as principles or starting points for the demonstration of theorems, or the conclusions of the science. Both are principles of demonstration in that they are used to demonstrate other propositions without themselves being demonstrated. But axioms are traditionally regarded as intrinsically indemonstrable, whereas hypotheses—postulates or assumptions—may not be indemonstrable. They are simply asserted without demonstration.

The possibility of demonstrating an hypothesis gives it the character of a provisional assumption. In the *Discourse on Method*, Descartes refers to certain matters assumed in his *Dioptrics* and *Meteors*, and expresses his concern lest the reader should take "offence because I call them hypotheses and do not appear to care about their proof." He goes on to say: "I have not named them hypotheses with any other object than that it may be known that while I consider myself able to deduce them from the primary truths which I explained above, yet I particularly desired not to do so, in order that certain persons may not for this reason take occasion to build up some extravagant philosophical system on what they take to be my principles."

The distinction between axioms and postulates or hypotheses raises two issues. The first concerns the genuineness of the distinction itself. Axioms, self-evident propositions, or what William James calls "necessary truths," have been denied entirely or dismissed as tautologies. The only principles of science must then be

hypotheses—assumptions voluntarily made or conventionally agreed upon. This issue is more fully discussed in the chapter on PRINCIPLE. The other issue presupposes the reality of the distinction, but is concerned with different applications of it in the analysis of science.

Aristotle, for example, defines scientific knowledge in terms of three elements, one of which consists of the primary premises upon which demonstrations rest. The principles of a particular science may be axioms in the strict sense of being self-evident truths and hence absolutely indemonstrable; or they may be provisional assumptions which, though not proved in this science, can nevertheless be proved by a higher science, as in "the application of geometrical demonstrations to theorems in mechanics or optics, or of arithmetical demonstrations to those of harmonics." The latter are not axioms because they are demonstrable; yet in a particular science they may play the role of axioms insofar as they are used, without being demonstrated, to demonstrate other propositions.

Reasoning which rests either on axioms or on demonstrable principles Aristotle calls *scientific*, but reasoning which rests only on hypotheses he regards as *dialectical*. Reasoning results in scientific demonstration, according to Aristotle, "when the premises from which the reasoning starts are true and primary, or are such that our knowledge of them has originally come through premises which are primary and true." In contrast, reasoning is dialectical "if it reasons from opinions that are generally accepted," and, Aristotle explains, "those opinions are 'generally accepted' which are accepted by everyone or by the majority or by the philosophers—*i.e.*, by all, or by a majority, or by the most notable and illustrious of them." In another place, he adds one important qualification. In defining a dialectical proposition as one that is "held by all men or by most men or by the philosophers," he adds: "provided it be not contrary to the general opinion; for a man would assent to the view of the philosophers, only if it were not contrary to the opinions of most men."

For Aristotle, dialectical reasoning or argument moves entirely within the sphere of opinion. Even an opinion generally accepted, not only by the philosophers but also by most men, remains an opinion. The best opinions are probabilities—propositions which are not self-evident and which cannot be proved. They are not merely *provisional* assumptions. Resting on assumptions which cannot ever be more than probable, the conclusions of dialectical reasoning are also never more than probable. Since they lack the certain foundation which axioms give, they cannot have the certitude of science.

Plato, on the other hand, seems to think that the mathematical sciences are hypothetical in their foundation, and that only in the science of dialectic, which he considers the highest science, does the mind rise from mere hypotheses to the ultimate principles of knowledge. "The students of geometry, arithmetic, and the kindred sciences," Socrates says in the *Republic*, "assume the odd and the even, and the figures and the three kinds of angle and the like in their several branches of science; these are their hypotheses, which they and everybody are supposed to know, and therefore they do not deign to give an account of them either to themselves or others." There is a higher sort of knowledge, he goes on, "which reason herself attains by the power of dialectic, using the hypotheses not as first principles, but only as hypotheses—that is to say, as steps and points of departure into a world which is above hypotheses, in order that she may soar beyond them to first principles."

The issue between Plato and Aristotle may be only verbal—a difference in the use of such words as "science" and "dialectic." Whether it is verbal or real is considered in the chapters on DIALECTIC and METAPHYSICS. In any case, the issue throws light on the difference between an hypothesis as a merely provisional assumption, susceptible to proof by higher principles, and an hypothesis as a probability taken for granted for the purposes of argument, which is itself incapable of being proved.

FINALLY WE COME to the meaning of "hypothetical" in the analysis of propositions and syllogisms. The distinction between the categorical and the hypothetical proposition or syllogism, briefly touched on in Aristotle's *Organon*, is developed in the tradition of logic which begins with that book.

In his work on *Interpretation* he distinguishes between simple and compound propositions. The compound proposition consists of several simple propositions in some logical relation to one another. In the tradition of logical analysis, three basic types of relation have been defined as constituting three different kinds of compound proposition. One type of relation is the *conjunctive*; it is signified by the word "and." Another is the *disjunctive*; it is signified by the words "either . . . or . . ." The third type is the *hypothetical* and is signified by the words "if . . . then . . ."

To take an example we have already used, "virtue is knowledge" and "virtue is teachable" are simple propositions. In contrast, the statement, "*if* virtue is knowledge, *then* virtue is teachable," is a compound proposition, hypothetical in form. If the proposition were stated in the sentence, "*either* virtue is knowledge *or* it is not teachable," it would be disjunctive in form; if stated in the sentence "virtue is knowledge *and* virtue is teachable," it would be conjunctive in form. In each of these three cases, the compound proposition consists of the two simple propositions with which we began, though in each case they appear to be differently related.

Whereas Aristotle divides propositions into simple and compound, Kant divides all judgments into the categorical, the hypothetical, and the disjunctive. In the categorical judgment, he says, "we consider two concepts"; in the hypothetical, "two judgements"; in the disjunctive, "several judgements in their relation to one another." As an example of the hypothetical proposition, he offers the statement, "If perfect justice exists, the obstinately wicked are punished." As an example of the disjunctive judgment, "we may say . . . [that] the world exists either by blind chance, or by internal necessity, or by an external cause." Each of these three alternatives, Kant points out, "occupies a part of the sphere of all possible knowledge with regard to the existence of the world, while all together occupy the whole sphere." The hypothetical judgment does no more than state "the relation of two propositions . . . Whether both these propositions are true remains unsettled. It is only the consequence," Kant says, "which is laid down by this judgement."

In the *Prior Analytics*, Aristotle distinguishes between the categorical and the hypothetical syllogism. The following reasoning is categorical in form: "Knowledge is teachable, virtue is knowledge; therefore, virtue is teachable." The following reasoning is hypothetical in form:"*If* virtue is knowledge, it is teachable; *but* virtue is knowledge; *therefore* it is teachable"; or "*If* virtue is knowledge, it is teachable; *but* virtue is not teachable; *therefore* it is not knowledge."

The basic issue with respect to the distinction between categorical and hypothetical syllogisms is whether the latter are always reducible to the former. One thing seems to be clear. The rules for the hypothetical syllogism formally parallel the rules for the categorical syllogism. In hypothetical reasoning, the consequent must be affirmed if the antecedent is affirmed; the antecedent must be denied if the consequent is denied. In categorical reasoning, the affirmation of the premises requires an affirmation of the conclusion, and a denial of the conclusion requires a denial of the premises.

With respect to the distinction between the categorical and hypothetical proposition, there is also an issue whether propositions stated in one form can always be converted into propositions having the other form of statement. In modern mathematical logic, for example, general propositions, such as "All men are mortal," are sometimes expressed in hypothetical form:

"If anything is a man, it is mortal." Logicians like Bertrand Russell think that the hypothetical form is more exact because it explicitly refrains from suggesting that men exist; it merely states that if the class 'man' should have any existent members, they will also belong to the class 'mortal.'

Apart from the question whether a universal proposition should or should not be interpreted as asserting the existence of anything, there seems to be a formal difference between the categorical and hypothetical proposition. This is manifest only when the hypothetical is truly a compound proposition, not when it is the statement of a simple proposition in hypothetical form, as, for example, the simple proposition "All men are mortal," is stated in hypothetical form by "If anything is a man, it is mortal." Because it is truly a compound proposition, and not merely the hypothetical statement of a general proposition, the proposition, "If virtue is knowledge, then virtue is teachable," cannot be restated in the form of a simple categorical proposition.

A simple proposition, whether stated categorically or hypothetically, may be the conclusion of either a categorical or a hypothetical syllogism. But the hypothetical statement which is really a compound proposition can never be the conclusion of any sort of syllogism, though it may be one of the premises in hypothetical reasoning.

OUTLINE OF TOPICS

REFERENCES

To find the passages cited, use the numbers in heavy type, which are the volume and page numbers of the passages referred to. For example, in 4 HOMER: *Iliad*, BK II [265–283] 12d, the number 4 is the number of the volume in the set; the number 12d indicates that the passage is in section d of page 12.

PAGE SECTIONS: When the text is printed in one column, the letters a and b refer to the upper and lower halves of the page. For example, in 53 JAMES: *Psychology*, 116a–119b, the passage begins in the upper half of page 116 and ends in the lower half of page 119. When the text is printed in two columns, the letters a and b refer to the upper and lower halves of the left-hand side of the page, the letters c and d to the upper and lower halves of the right-hand side of the page. For example, in 7 PLATO: *Symposium*, 163b–164c, the passage begins in the lower half of the left-hand side of page 163 and ends in the upper half of the right-hand side of page 164.

AUTHOR'S DIVISIONS: One or more of the main divisions of a work (such as PART, BK, CH, SECT) are sometimes included in the reference; line numbers, in brackets, are given in certain cases; *e.g., Iliad*, BK II [265–283] 12d.

BIBLE REFERENCES: The references are to book, chapter, and verse. When the King James and Douay versions differ in title of books or in the numbering of chapters or verses, the King James version is cited first and the Douay, indicated by a (D), follows; *e.g.,* OLD TESTAMENT: *Nehemiah*, 7:45—(D) II *Esdras*, 7:46.

SYMBOLS: The abbreviation "esp" calls the reader's attention to one or more especially relevant parts of a whole reference; "passim" signifies that the topic is discussed intermittently rather than continuously in the work or passage cited.

For additional information concerning the style of the references, see the Explanation of Reference Style; for general guidance in the use of *The Great Ideas*, consult the Preface.

1. The use of hypotheses in the process of dialectic

7 PLATO: *Charmides*, 9d–10a / *Protagoras*, 49a / *Meno*, 183b–190a,c / *Phaedo*, 242b–243c / *Republic*, BK IV, 350d–351b; BK VI, 383d–388a esp 386d–388a; BK VII, 397a–398c / *Timaeus*, 462b–c / *Parmenides*, 491a–511d / *Sophist*, 570a–d

8 ARISTOTLE: *Prior Analytics*, BK I, CH I [24^{a}21–^{b}16] 39a–c / *Posterior Analytics*, BK I, CH 6 [75^{a}18–28] 103a–b / *Topics* 143a–223a,c esp BK I, CH I–3 143a–144b, CH 10–11 147b–148c, CH 14 149a–d, BK VIII 211a–223a,c

12 EPICTETUS: *Discourses*, BK I, CH 7 112b–113d

42 KANT: *Pure Reason*, 227a–230c esp 227d–228b / *Science of Right*, 457a–b / *Judgement*, 603b–c

2. Hypothetical reasoning and hypothetical constructions in philosophy

7 PLATO: *Meno*, 183b–190a,c / *Phaedo*, 242b–243c / *Republic*, BK VI, 386d–388a; BK VII, 397a–398c / *Parmenides*, 491a–511d

8 ARISTOTLE: *Posterior Analytics*, BK I, CH 2 [72^{a}19–21] 98d; BK II, CH 6 125d–126b / *Heavens*, BK I, CH 12 [281^{b}3–25] 373a–b / *Metaphysics*, BK IV, CH 3 [1005^{b}5–17] 524c–d

19 AQUINAS: *Summa Theologica*, PART I–II, Q 14, A 6, ANS 680c–681a

25 MONTAIGNE: *Essays*, 258d–259a

31 DESCARTES: *Rules*, XII, 23a–c / *Discourse*, PART II–III, 44c–50b passim; PART VI, 66a–b / *Meditations*, 72b,d; I–II, 75a–78a / *Objections and Replies*, 123d–124c

35 LOCKE: *Civil Government*, CH I, SECT I 25a–c / *Human Understanding*, BK II, CH I, SECT 10 123b–d; CH XIII, SECT 19–20 152c–d; CH XXIII, SECT I–2 204a–c

35 HUME: *Human Understanding*, SECT XI, DIV 107 499c–500b

38 ROUSSEAU: *Inequality*, 329a–331d passim, esp 329d–330b; 333d–334a; 348a,c

42 KANT: *Pure Reason*, 7a–d; 176d–177b; 186d–187a; 194b–200c; 227a–230c; 232c–233d / *Science of Right*, 457a–b / *Judgement*, 603b–c

46 HEGEL: *Philosophy of History*, INTRO, 156d–158a

53 JAMES: *Psychology*, 84a–119b passim; 221a–238b; 820b–827a; 880b–886a esp 884b–886a

3. The foundations of mathematics: postulates, assumptions

7 PLATO: *Meno*, 183b–c / *Republic*, BK VI, 386d–388a; BK VII, 397c–d

8 ARISTOTLE: *Posterior Analytics*, BK I, CH I [71^{a}1–16] 97a–b; CH 2 [72^{a}19–24] 98d; CH 10 104d–105d; CH 12 [77^{a}36–^{b}15] 106c–d; BK II, CH 9 [93^{b}21–25] 128a–b / *Physics*, BK I, CH 2 [185^{a}1–3] 259c–d / *Heavens*, BK III, CH 4 [302^{b}27–31] 394a / *Metaphysics*, BK XI, CH 3

(3. *The foundations of mathematics: postulates, assumptions.*)

[1061ª29–ᵇ4] 589c; BK XIII, CH 2 [1077ᵇ11]–CH 3 [1078ª31] 609a-d

9 ARISTOTLE: *Ethics*, BK VII, CH 8 [1151ª15–19] 402a

11 EUCLID: *Elements*, BK I, POSTULATES–COMMON NOTIONS 2a

11 ARCHIMEDES: *Sphere and Cylinder*, BK I, ASSUMPTIONS 404b / *Spirals*, 484b / *Quadrature of the Parabola*, 527a-b

31 DESCARTES: *Rules*, II, 2d-3b / *Meditations*, 73a / *Geometry*, BK II, 304a-305a; 316a-b

33 PASCAL: *Pensées*, 1–5 171a-173a / *Vacuum*, 365b-366a / *Geometrical Demonstration*, 430b-439b passim; 442a-443b

34 NEWTON: *Principles*, 1a-b

34 HUYGENS: *Light*, PREF, 551b-552a

35 LOCKE: *Human Understanding*, BK IV, CH XII, SECT 1–7 358c-360c passim

42 KANT: *Pure Reason*, 17d-18d; 24c-25b; 46a-c; 110a; 211c-218d esp 217a-c / *Practical Reason*, 302d-303b; 312c-d; 330d-331a / *Pref. Metaphysical Elements of Ethics*, 376c-d / *Judgement*, 551a-553c

43 FEDERALIST: NUMBER 31, 103c-104a

43 MILL: *Utilitarianism*, 445b-c

45 FOURIER: *Theory of Heat*, 175b

52 DOSTOEVSKY: *Brothers Karamazov*, BK V, 120d-121b

53 JAMES: *Psychology*, 869a-870a; 874a-878a

4. The role of hypotheses in science

7 PLATO: *Meno*, 183b-c / *Republic*, BK VI, 386d-388a / *Timaeus*, 447a-d

8 ARISTOTLE: *Meteorology*, BK I, CH 7 [344ª5–9] 450b / *Metaphysics*, BK XII, CH 6 [1071ᵇ12]–CH 7 [1072ª22] 601b-602b; CH 8 603b-605a

10 HIPPOCRATES: *Prognostics*, par 1 19a-b; par 25 26a,c

16 COPERNICUS: *Revolutions of the Heavenly Spheres*, 505a-506a

19 AQUINAS: *Summa Theologica*, PART I, Q 32, A 1, REP 2 175d-178a; PART I–II, Q 14, A 6, ANS 680c-681a

30 BACON: *Novum Organum*, BK I, APH 105–106 128b-c

31 DESCARTES: *Rules*, XII, 23a-c / *Discourse*, PART VI, 66a-b

33 PASCAL: *Vacuum*, 368b-370a

34 NEWTON: *Principles*, BK III, RULE I 270a; RULE IV 271b; GENERAL SCHOL, 371b-372a / *Optics*, BK III, 543a-b

35 LOCKE: *Human Understanding*, BK IV, CH III, SECT 16 317a-c; CH XII, SECT 12–13 362a-d

36 SWIFT: *Gulliver*, PART III, 118a-119a

42 KANT: *Pure Reason*, 7a-d / *Judgement*, 603b-c

45 LAVOISIER: *Elements of Chemistry*, PREF, 2a-b; 6d-7a; PART I, 23b-c

45 FOURIER: *Theory of Heat*, 184a

45 FARADAY: *Researches in Electricity*, 467a-b; 607a,c; 851a-c

49 DARWIN: *Origin of Species*, 239c / *Descent of Man*, 590a

51 TOLSTOY: *War and Peace*, BK XIII, 563a-b

53 JAMES: *Psychology*, 324b; 862a-866a, 882a-884b

54 FREUD: *Interpretation of Dreams*, 351c / *Narcissim*, 400d-401a / *Beyond the Pleasure Principle*, 661c-662b

4a. Theories, provisional assumptions, fictions, reifications

7 PLATO: *Meno*, 183b-c / *Republic*, BK VI, 386d-388a; BK VII, 397c-d / *Timaeus*, 447d-450c / *Laws*, BK VII, 730a-c

8 ARISTOTLE: *Posterior Analytics*, BK I, CH 10 [76ᵇ22–77ª4] 105c-d / *Heavens*, BK I, CH 12 [281ᵇ3–25] 373a-b; BK II, CH 5 379b-c / *Metaphysics*, BK VI, CH 1 [1025ᵇ1–13] 547b; BK XI, CH 7 [1064ª4–9] 592b; BK XII, CH 6 [1071ᵇ12]–CH 7 [1072ª22] 601b-602b; CH 8 603b-605a

11 ARCHIMEDES: *Equilibrium of Planes*, BK I, POSTULATES 502a-b / *Floating Bodies*, BK I, POSTULATE 1 538a; POSTULATE 2 541b

16 PTOLEMY: *Almagest*, BK III, 83a; 86b-87a; BK IX, 270b-273a; 291a-292a; BK XIII, 429a-b

16 COPERNICUS: *Revolutions of the Heavenly Spheres*, BK I, 513b-514b; BK III, 628b-629a; BK IV, 675b-678a; BK V, 740a-b; 784b-785b

16 KEPLER: *Epitome*, BK IV, 863b-872b; 890b-892a; 929a-b; 932a-933a; BK V, 964b; 966a-967a; 984b-985b; 991a-994b / *Harmonies o the World*, 1023b-1080b

19 AQUINAS: *Summa Theologica*, PART I, Q 32, A 1, REP 2 175d-178a

25 MONTAIGNE: *Essays*, 258d-259a

28 GILBERT: *Loadstone*, BK VI, 108b-110b

28 GALILEO: *Two New Sciences*, SECOND DAY, 179c-d; THIRD DAY, 200a-d; 203d-205b; FOURTH DAY, 240d-241c

28 HARVEY: *Circulation of the Blood*, 316a-318b passim, esp 316a-b / *On Animal Generation*, 383d

30 BACON: *Novum Organum*, BK I, APH 66 114d-115c; BK II, APH 36, 165d-166b; APH 46, 178c

31 DESCARTES: *Rules*, XII, 23a-c

33 PASCAL: *Pensées*, 72, 182b / *Vacuum*, 367a-370a

34 NEWTON: *Principles*, BK II, HYPOTHESIS 259a; BK III, HYPOTHESIS I 285a; HYPOTHESIS II 331b; GENERAL SCHOL, 371b-372a / *Optics*, BK I, 379a; BK III, 516a-544a esp 520a-522b, 525b-530b

34 HUYGENS: *Light*, CH I, 557b-560b

35 LOCKE: *Human Understanding*, BK IV, CH III, SECT 16 317a-c; CH XII, SECT 13 362c-d

36 SWIFT: *Gulliver*, PART III, 118a-119a

42 KANT: *Pure Reason*, 227d-228b / *Science of Right*, 457a-b / *Judgement*, 603b-c

43 MILL: *Utilitarianism*, 445b-c

45 LAVOISIER: *Elements of Chemistry*, PART I, 9a-10b

45 FARADAY: *Researches in Electricity*, 273a-277a; 758a-759c; 777d-778c; 830b-832c; 850b,d-855a,c esp 850b,d-851c

(4. *The role of hypotheses in science.* 4d. *The task of verification: the plurality of hypotheses.*)

54 FREUD: *Narcissism*, 401a / *General Introduction*, 502d-503c / *New Introductory Lectures*, 815a-b; 818c-819b

5. Hypothetical propositions and syllogisms: the distinction between the hypothetical and the categorical

8 ARISTOTLE: *Prior Analytics*, BK I, CH I [24ª21–ᵇ16] 39a-c; CH 23 [40ᵇ23–29] 57b-c; [41ª21–41]

58a-b; CH 29 62d-63d; CH 44 68d-69b; BK II, CH 11-14 81b-84b / *Posterior Analytics*, BK II, CH 6 125d-126b

19 AQUINAS: *Summa Theologica*, PART I, Q 14, A 13, REP 2 86d-88c; Q 19, A 8, REP 1,3 116a-d

42 KANT: *Pure Reason*, 39c-41c esp 40d-41c; 51d-52a; 110d-111c esp 111b; 129c-d; 179c-180c; 193a-200c esp 194b-d; 232c-233c / *Fund. Prin. Metaphysic of Morals*, 265c-267a esp 266a-c / *Practical Reason*, 297a-298a

CROSS-REFERENCES

For: The distinction between axioms and postulates, assumptions, and hypotheses, *see* JUDGMENT 8a; PRINCIPLE 2b(2), 3c-3c(3); TRUTH 4c, 7a.

Other discussions of the use of hypotheses in dialectic and philosophy, *see* DIALECTIC 2a(2); LOGIC 4d; PHILOSOPHY 3b-3c; and for the distinction between scientific and dialectical reasoning, *see* PRINCIPLE 3c(2); REASONING 5b-5c.

Other discussions of postulates in mathematics, *see* LOGIC 4a; MATHEMATICS 3a; and for other treatments of hypothetical judgments and hypothetical reasoning, *see* JUDGMENT 6d; REASONING 2b.

The employment and verification of hypotheses in empirical science, *see* ASTRONOMY 2b; EXPERIENCE 5a-5c; LOGIC 4b; MECHANICS 2b; PHYSICS 4b-4d; SCIENCE 4e, 5e.

ADDITIONAL READINGS

Listed below are works not included in *Great Books of the Western World*, but relevant to the idea and topics with which this chapter deals. These works are divided into two groups:

I. Works by authors represented in this collection.
II. Works by authors not represented in this collection.

For the date, place, and other facts concerning the publication of the works cited, consult the Bibliography of Additional Readings which follows the last chapter of *The Great Ideas*.

I.

DESCARTES. *The Principles of Philosophy*, PART III, 43–47
HOBBES. *Concerning Body*, PART IV, CH 26
SPINOZA. *Correspondence*, VI, XIII
KANT. *Introduction to Logic*, X
J. S. MILL. *A System of Logic*, BK III, CH 14

II.

ARNAULD. *Logic or the Art of Thinking*, PART II
BOYLE. *Reflections upon the Hypothesis of Alkali and Acidum*
T. REID. *Essays on the Intellectual Powers of Man*, I, CH 3
BROWN. *Lectures on the Philosophy of the Human Mind*, VOL I, pp 220–241
HERSCHEL. *A Preliminary Discourse on the Study of Natural Philosophy*, par 202, 208, 210, 216
COMTE. *The Positive Philosophy*, BK III, CH I
WHEWELL. *The Philosophy of the Inductive Sciences*, VOL II, BK XIII
——. *On the Philosophy of Discovery*, APPENDIX H

BERNARD. *Introduction to Experimental Medicine*, PART I, CH 2
TYNDALL. *Scientific Use of the Imagination*
JEVONS. *The Principles of Science*, CH 23
BRADLEY. *The Principles of Logic*, BK I, CH 2
BOSANQUET. *Logic*, VOL II, CH 5
C. S. PEIRCE. *Collected Papers*, VOL II, par 619–644, 669–693, 755–791; VOL VI, par 7–34
VENN. *Principles of Empirical or Inductive Logic*, CH 16
POINCARÉ. *Science and Hypothesis*, PART IV, CH 9–10
MACH. *Erkenntnis und Irrtum* (Die Hypothese)
DUHEM. *La théorie physique, son objet—sa structure*
PARETO. *The Mind and Society*, VOL I, CH 4–5
N. R. CAMPBELL. *Physics; the Elements*, CH 6
——. *What Is Science?*, CH 5
BOHR. *Atomic Theory and the Description of Nature*
NORTHROP. *Science and First Principles*
EINSTEIN. *On the Method of Theoretical Physics*
FISHER. *The Design of Experiments*
DEWEY. *Logic, the Theory of Inquiry*, CH 7

Chapter 37: IDEA

INTRODUCTION

As the topical analysis or outline in each chapter indicates, the great ideas are not simple objects of thought. Each of the great ideas seems to have a complex interior structure—an order of parts involving related meanings and diverse positions which, when they are opposed to one another, determine the basic issues in that area of thought.

The great ideas are also the conceptions by which we think about things. They are the terms in which we state fundamental problems; they are the notions we employ in defining issues and discussing them. They represent the principal content of our thought. They are *what* we think as well as what we think *about*.

If, in addition to its objects and content, we wish to think about thought itself—its acts or processes—we shall find in the tradition of the great books a number of related terms which indicate the scope of such inquiry. Some of them are: idea, judgment, understanding, and reasoning; perception, memory, and imagination; sense and mind. Here we are concerned with one of these—the idea IDEA. It is probably the most elementary of all these related terms, for according to different conceptions of the nature and origin of ideas, the analysis of thought and knowledge will vary. Different positions will be taken concerning the faculties by which men know, the acts and processes of thinking, and the limits of human understanding.

Does THE WORD "idea," when it is used in the technical discourse of metaphysics or psychology, signify that which is known or understood? Does it signify, not the object of thought, but the thought itself? Or both? Certainly in popular speech the word is used both ways, for men speak of understanding an idea and note differences in their understanding of the same

idea; and they also say that they have different ideas about the same thing, meaning that they understand the same thing differently.

The word "idea" has many other oppositions of meaning in its tremendous range of ambiguity. It is sometimes used exclusively for the eternal types in the divine mind or the intelligible forms that exist apart from material things which are their copies; sometimes for concepts in the human mind, abstracted from sense-experience; sometimes for the seeds of understanding which belong innately to the intellect and so do not need to be derived from sense. Sometimes "idea" means a sensation or a perception as well as an abstract thought, and then its connotation extends to almost every type of mental content; sometimes it is denied that there are any abstract or general ideas; and sometimes "idea" has the extremely restricted meaning of an image which is the memory of a sense-impression.

Kant vigorously protests against what he thinks is a needless abuse of the term *idea*. "I beg those who really have philosophy at heart," he writes, "to exert themselves to preserve to the expression *idea* its original signification." There is, he insists, "no want of words to denominate adequately every mode of representation without encroaching upon terms which are proper to others."

Kant proposes a "graduated list" of such terms. He begins with *perception*, which he divides into *sensation* and *cognition*, according as it is subjective or objective. A cognition, he then goes on, "is either an *intuition* or a *conception*," according as it has either an immediate or a mediate relation to its object. Dividing conceptions into the *empirical* and the *pure*, Kant finally reaches the term *idea* as one sub-division of pure conceptions. If the pure conception "has its origin in the understanding alone, and is not the conception of a pure sensuous image," it is a *notio* or notion; and "a conception formed from notions, which transcends the possibility of experience, is an *idea*, or a conception of reason."

According to Kant, anyone "who has accustomed himself to these distinctions," will find it "quite intolerable to hear the representation of the color red called an idea." Tolerable or intolerable, the word "idea" has been used quite persistently with the very meaning that Kant abominates, as well as with a variety of others. The reader of the great books must be prepared for all these shifts in meaning and, with them, shifts in doctrine; for according to these differences in meaning, there are different analyses of the nature or being of ideas, different accounts of their origin or their coming to be in the human mind, and different classifications of ideas. These three questions—what ideas are, how ideas are obtained, and of what sorts they are—are so connected that the answer given to one of them tends to circumscribe the answers which can be given to the other two.

THE UNITY OF EACH chapter in this guide to the great books depends on some continuity of meaning in its central term, some common thread of meaning, however thin or tenuous, which unites and makes intelligible the discussions of various authors about the same thing. Without this, they would not move in the same universe of discourse at all. Nor could they even disagree with one another, if the words they used were utterly equivocal, as for example the word "pen" is equivocal when it designates a writing instrument and an enclosure for pigs.

The extraordinary ambiguity of the word "idea" as it is used in the great books puts this principle to the test. Are Plato and Hume talking about the same thing *at all*, when the one discusses ideas as the only intelligible reality and the other treats ideas as the images derived through memory from the original impressions of sense-experience? Is there any common ground between Aristotle and Berkeley—between the identification of human ideas with abstract or general conceptions, quite distinct from the perceptions or images of sense, and the

identification of ideas with particular perceptions, accompanied by a denial of abstract or general notions?

Do writers like Locke or William James, for whom ideas of sensation and abstract ideas (or percepts and concepts) belong to the one faculty of understanding or to the single stream of consciousness, communicate with writers like Plotinus, Descartes, and Spinoza, for whom ideas belong to the intellect or to the thinking being, separate from matter and from sensations which are only bodily reactions? Or with writers like Aristotle and Aquinas, for whom there is a sharp distinction between the faculties of sense and intellect? Can Aristotle and Aquinas in turn explain the origin of concepts or intelligible species by reference to the intellect's power of abstracting them from experience or sensible species, and still carry on discussion with Plato, Augustine, and Descartes, who regard the intellect as in some way innately endowed with ideas, with the principles or seeds of understanding?

The foregoing is by no means an exhaustive inventory. It fails, for example, to ask about the sense in which the theologians speak of ideas in the mind of God and of the illumination of the angelic or the human intellect by ideas divinely infused. (What is the common thread of meaning between such discourse and that concerned with the formation of abstract concepts or with the revival of sense-impressions in images?) It fails also to question the meaning of idea in Kant's tripartite analysis of the faculties of intuition, judgment, and reasoning; or in Hegel's ultimate synthesis of all nature and history in the dialectical life of the Absolute Idea. (What do these meanings of "idea" have in common with the sense in which Freud distinguishes between conscious and unconscious ideas?)

The inventory is also incomplete in that it does not indicate the many divergent routes taken by authors who seem to share a common starting point. Even those who, on certain points, seem to talk the same language, appear to have no basis for communication on other points in the theory of ideas. But the questions which have been asked suffice for the purpose at hand. However great the ambiguity of "idea," it does not reach that limit of equivocation which would destroy the universe of discourse. There is a slender thread of meaning which ties all the elements of the tradition together—not in a unity of truth or agreement, but in an intelligible joining of issues.

This unity can be seen in two ways. It appears first in the fact that any consideration of ideas—whether as objects or contents of the mind—involves a theory of knowledge. This much is common to all meanings of "idea."

Those, like Plato and Berkeley, for whom ideas constitute a realm of intelligible or sensible being, make knowledge of reality consist in the apprehension or understanding of ideas. Those, like Aristotle and James, for whom ideas have no being except as perceptions or thoughts, make them the instruments whereby reality is known. On either view, knowledge involves a relationship between a knower and a known, or between a knowing faculty and a knowable entity; but on one view ideas are the reality which is known, and on the other they are the representations by which is known a reality that does not include ideas among its constituents. These two views do not exhaust the possibilities.

Ideas are sometimes regarded both as objects of knowledge and as representations of reality. Some writers (as, for example, Plato) distinguish two orders of reality—the sensible and the intelligible—and two modes of apprehension—sensing and understanding; and they use the word "idea" for both the intelligible object and the understanding of it. Locke, begging the reader's pardon for his frequent use of the word "idea," says that it is the term "which serves best to stand for whatsoever is the object of the understanding when a man thinks." But Locke also distinguishes between knowledge of real existences through ideas "that the mind has of things as they are in themselves," and knowledge of the relations among our own ideas, which the mind "gets from their comparison with one another." For Hume, too, ideas as well as impressions are involved in our knowledge of matters of fact, but relations between ideas may also be objects of knowledge, as in "the sciences of geometry, algebra, and arithmetic."

This double use of "idea" is sometimes accompanied, as in Aquinas, by an explicit ac-

knowledgement and ordering of the two senses. For Aquinas, concepts are primarily the means of knowledge, not the objects of knowledge. A concept, Aquinas writes, "is not *what* is actually understood, but *that by which* the intellect understands"—that by which something else is known. Secondarily, however, concepts become *that which* we know when we reflexively turn our attention to the contents of our own mind. Using the phrase "intelligible species" to signify concepts, Aquinas explains that "since the intellect reflects upon itself, by such reflection it understands not only its own act of intelligence but also the species by which it understands. Thus the intelligible species is that which is understood secondarily; but that which is primarily understood is the object, of which the species is the likeness."

It is possible, therefore, to have ideas about things or ideas about ideas. In the vocabulary of this analysis by Aquinas, the ideas or concepts whereby real things are understood are sometimes called the "first intentions" of the mind. The ideas whereby we understand these ideas or first intentions are called the mind's "second intentions." An idea is always a mental intention, an awareness or representation, never an independent reality for the mind to know.

Locke's differentiation between ideas of sensation and ideas of reflection seems to parallel the mediaeval distinction between first and second intentions; but whereas second intentions are ideas engaged in a reflexive understanding of ideas as objects to be understood, Locke's ideas of reflection comprise "the perception of the operations of our own mind within us, as it is employed about the ideas it has got." A closer parallel, perhaps, is to be found in Locke's distinction between our knowledge of reality or of real existences and our knowledge of the relations existing between our own ideas.

THE SECOND WAY of seeing a connection among meanings of "idea" depends on recognizing what is common to contrary views.

The word "pen" is utterly equivocal, as we have noted, when it names a writing instrument and an animal enclosure. Hence men cannot contradict one another no matter what opposite things they may say about *pens* in one sense and *pens* in the other. The two meanings of "pen" are not even connected by being opposed to one another. But all the meanings of "idea" do seem to be connected by opposition at least, so that writers who use the word in its different senses and have different theories of idea cannot avoid facing the issues raised by their conflicting analyses.

The root of this opposition lies in the positive and negative views of the relation of ideas to sensations—or, more generally, to sense and the sensible. Though there are different analyses of sensation, one or both of two points seems to be agreed upon: that sensations are particular perceptions and that sensations result from the impingement of physical stimuli upon the sense organs of a living body.

Berkeley insists upon the first point while emphatically denying the second. Ideas or sensations are always particulars; but, he says, "the various sensations or ideas imprinted on the sense, however blended or combined together (that is, whatever objects they compose), cannot exist otherwise than in a mind perceiving them," and their cause is neither physical matter nor the perceiving mind, but "some other will or spirit that produces them." Others, like Lucretius and Hobbes, who regard sensations as particular perceptions, do not use the word "idea," as Berkeley does, for perceptions of external origin, but restrict it to inner productions of the mind itself in its acts of memory or imagination.

The various theories of idea thus range from those which identify an idea with a sensation or perception or with the derivatives of sensation, to those which deny the identity or even any relationship between ideas and sensations or images of sense.

THE FIRST POSITION is taken by writers who conceive mind or understanding, in men or animals, as the only faculty of knowledge. It performs all the functions of knowing and thinking. It is sensitive as well as reflective. It perceives and remembers as well as imagines and reasons.

Within this group of writers there are differences. Berkeley, for example, thinks "the ob-

jects of human knowledge" include "either ideas actually imprinted on the senses; or else such as are perceived by attending to the passions and operations of the mind; or lastly ideas formed by the help of memory and imagination—either compounding, dividing, or barely representing those originally perceived in the aforesaid ways." Hume, on the other hand, divides "all the perceptions of the mind into two classes or species, which are distinguished by their different degrees of force or vivacity. The less forcible and lively are commonly denominated *Thoughts* or *Ideas*. The other species want a name in our language and in most others . . . Let us, therefore, use a little freedom and call them *Impressions*." By this term, Hume explains, "I mean all our more lively perceptions, when we hear, or see, or feel, or love, or hate, or desire, or will."

Another use of terms is represented by Locke, who distinguishes between ideas of sensation and reflection, simple and complex ideas, particular and general ideas, and uses the word "idea" both for the original elements of sense-experience and for all the derivatives produced by the mind's activity in reworking these given materials, whether by acts of memory, imaginative construction, or abstraction. Still another variation is to be found in William James. Despite the authority of Locke, he thinks that the word " 'idea' has not domesticated itself in the language so as to cover bodily sensations." Accordingly, he restricts the word "idea" to concepts, and never uses it for sensations or perceptions. Nevertheless, like Locke, he does not think that the development of concept from percept needs the activity of a special faculty. Both concept and percept belong to the single "stream of thought" and are "states of consciousness."

THE SECOND POSITION is taken by writers who in one way or another distinguish between sense and intellect and regard them as quite separate faculties of knowing. The one is supposed to perform the functions of perception, imagination, and memory; the other, the functions of thought—conception, judgment, and reasoning, or if not these, then acts of intellectual vision or intuition. Here, too, there are differences within the group.

Just as the extreme version of the first position is taken by those who identify ideas with perceptions, so here the opposite extreme consists in the denial of any connection between ideas and all the elements of sense-experience. The ideas in the divine mind, or the ideas infused by God into the angelic intellects, have no origin in experience, nor any need for the perceptions, memories, or images of sense. They are not abstract ideas, that is, they are not concepts abstracted from sense-materials.

"Our intellect," Aquinas writes, "abstracts the intelligible species from the individuating principles"—the material conditions of sense and imagination. "But the intelligible species in the divine intellect," he continues, "is immaterial, not by abstraction, but of itself." The divine ideas, Aquinas quotes Augustine as saying, "are certain original forms or permanent and immutable models of things which are contained in the divine intelligence." Following Augustine's statement that "each thing was created by God according to the idea proper to it," Aquinas restricts the word "idea" to the "exemplars existing in the divine mind" and to the species of things with which God informs the angelic intellects. He uses the word "concept" where others speak of "ideas" in the human mind.

Descartes, on the other hand, endows the human mind with ideas—not concepts abstracted from and dependent on sense, but intuitive apprehensions which, since they cannot be drawn in any way from sense-experience, must be an innate property of the human mind. He does not, however, always use the word "idea" in this strict sense. Some ideas, he says, "appear to be innate, some adventitious, and others to be formed or invented by myself." The ideas called "adventitious" are those which seem to come from the outside, as when "I hear some sound, or see the sun, or feel heat." Those which we form or invent ourselves are "constructions of the imagination." Only innate ideas, in Descartes' view, are truly ideas in the sense of being the elements of certain knowledge and the sources of intellectual intuition. "By intuition," he says, "I understand, not the fluctuating testimony of the senses, nor the misleading judgment that proceeds from the blundering constructions of the imagination,"

but "the undoubting conception of an unclouded and attentive mind" which "springs from the light of reason alone."

As mind and body are separate substances for Descartes—mind being conceived by him as a *res cogitans* or thinking substance, quite separate from a *res extensa* or the extended matter of a bodily substance—so ideas and sensations are independent in origin and function. Like infused ideas in the angelic intellect, innate ideas in the human mind are not abstract, for they are not abstracted. But unlike the angelic intellect, the human mind, even when it employs innate ideas, is discursive or cogitative. It is never conceived as entirely free from the activities of judgment and reasoning, even when its power is also supposed to be intuitive—that is, able to apprehend intelligible objects without analysis or without recourse to the representations of sense.

The doctrine of innate ideas does not always go as far as this in separating intellectual knowledge—or knowledge by means of ideas—from sense-experience. In the theories of Plato and Augustine, for example, sense-experience serves to awaken the understanding to apprehend the intelligible objects for the intuition of which it is innately equipped.

"To learn those things which do not come into us as images by the senses," Augustine writes, "but which we know within ourselves without images ... is in reality only to take things that the memory already contains scattered and unarranged ... and by thinking bring them together." Moreover, the memory contains, not only "images impressed upon it by the senses of the body, but also the notions of the very things themselves, which notions we never received by any avenue of the body."

This process of learning by remembering appears to be similar to the process which Plato also calls "recollection" or "reminiscence." In the *Meno* Socrates demonstrates that a slave-boy, who thinks he knows no geometry, can be led simply by questioning to discover that he knew all the while the solution of a geometric problem. "There have always been true thoughts in him," Socrates tells Meno, thoughts "which only needed to be awakened into knowledge by putting questions to him." Hence "his soul must always have possessed this knowledge."

Learning, according to this doctrine of innate ideas, must therefore be described as an attempt "to recollect," not "what you do not know," but "rather what you do not remember."

Learning by recollection or reminiscence seems to be a process in which latent ideas (whether they are retained by the soul from a previous life or are part of the soul's endowment at its creation) become active either through the questioning of a teacher or through being awakened by the perceptions of the bodily senses. Though such bodily stimulation of thought implies a functional connection between body and soul, nevertheless both Plato and Augustine hold that ideas are independent in origin. They are not derived from sense, though their appearance may be occasioned by events in the world of sense.

ONE OTHER VIEW still remains to be considered. It denies that ideas are innate in the human mind at the same time that it distinguishes between the intellect and the senses as separate faculties of knowing. Having to explain whence the intellect gets its ideas, writers like Aristotle and Aquinas attribute to the human intellect an abstractive power by which it draws "the intelligible species" from sensory images, which Aquinas calls "phantasms."

The concepts by which "our intellect understands material things," we obtain "by abstracting the form from the individual matter which is represented by the phantasms." Through the universal concept thus abstracted, we are able, Aquinas holds, "to consider the nature of the species apart from its individual principles." It should be added here that abstractions are not vehicles of intuitive apprehension. Conception, which is the first act of the mind, yields knowledge only when concepts are used in subsequent acts of judgment and reasoning.

Abstract or universal concepts are as different from the ideas which belong to intellects separate from bodies—the divine or angelic intellects—as they are different from the particular perceptions or images of sense. They occupy an intermediate position between the two, just as, according to Aquinas, "the human intellect holds a middle place" between angelic intelligence and corporeal sense. On the one hand, the human intellect is for Aquinas an incorporeal power; on the other hand, it functions only in cooperation with the corporeal powers of sense and imagination. So the concepts which the human intellect forms, being universal, are immaterial; but they are also dependent, in origin and function, on the materials of sense. Not only are universal concepts abstracted from the phantasms, but for the intellect to understand physical things, "it must of necessity," Aquinas writes, "turn to the phantasms in order to perceive the universal nature existing in the individual."

This theory of abstract ideas seems not far removed from the position of Locke, who distinguishes between particular and general ideas (which he calls "abstract") or that of William James, who distinguishes between universal concepts and sense-perceptions. Yet on one question the difference between them is radical, namely, whether particular sensations and universal ideas belong to the same faculty of mind or to the quite distinct faculties of sense and intellect.

This difference seems to have considerable bearing on the way in which these writers explain the process of abstraction or generalization, with consequences for certain subtleties, acknowledged or ignored, in the analysis of the grades of abstraction. Nevertheless, the resemblance between the positions of Locke and Aquinas, or those of William James and Aristotle, each affirming in his own way that the mind contains nothing not rooted in the senses, serves to mediate between the more extreme positions.

THE DISPUTE ABOUT innate ideas and the controversy over abstract ideas are issues in psychology inseparable from fundamental differences concerning the nature and operation of the faculty or faculties of knowing. There are other issues which concern the being or the truth of ideas. Here the first question is not whether ideas are objects of knowledge, but whether the existence of ideas is real or mental —outside the mind or in it.

One aspect of this controversy is considered in the chapter on FORM, viz., the argument between Aristotle and Plato about the being of the Ideas or Forms apart from both matter and mind. It is in the context of this argument that the traditional epithet "realism" gets one of its meanings, when it signifies the view that ideas or universals have an independent reality of their own. The various opponents of this view are not called "idealists." If they deny any existence to universal ideas outside the mind, they are usually called "conceptualists"; if they deny the presence of universals even in the mind, they are called "nominalists." These doctrines are more fully discussed in the chapters on SAME AND OTHER, UNIVERSAL AND PARTICULAR.

The controversy about the being of ideas has another phase that has already been noted in this chapter; and it is in this connection that the epithet "idealism" gets one of its traditional meanings. The doctrine is not that ideas have real existence outside the mind. On the contrary, it is that the only realities are mental—either minds or the ideas in them.

Berkeley's famous proposition—*esse est percipi*, to be is to be perceived—seems intended to permit only one exception. The perceiving mind has being without being perceived, but nothing else has. Everything else which exists is an idea, a being of and in the mind. According to this doctrine (which takes different forms in Berkeley and in Hegel, for example), the phrase "idea of" is meaningless. Nothing exists of which an idea can be a representation. There is no meaning to the distinction between thing and idea. The real and the ideal are identical.

Plato is sometimes called an "idealist" but not in this sense. He has never been interpreted as completely denying reality to the changing material things which imitate or copy the eternal ideas, the immutable archetypes or Forms. Applied to Plato or to Plotinus, "idealism" seems to signify the superior reality of ideal (as opposed to material or physical) existence. Just as "idealism" has these widely divergent meanings, so does "realism" when it designates, on the one hand, those who attribute independent reality to ideas and, on the other hand, those who affirm the existence of an order of real existences independent of the ideas which represent them in the mind.

Writers who distinguish between things and ideas, or between the order of reality and the mind's conception of it, face the problem of differentiating between these two modes of being. To say that ideas or concepts exist only in the mind is not to say that they do not exist at all, but only that they do not exist in the same way as things outside the mind.

Does an entity in its real existence apart from knowledge have the same character that it has when, as an object known, it somehow belongs to the knowing mind? Is there a kind of neutral essence which can assume both modes of existence—real existence, independent of mind, and ideal existence, or existence in the mind, as an object conceived or known? Is an idea or concept in the mind nothing but the real thing objectified, or transformed into an object of knowledge; or is the real thing, the thing in itself, utterly different from the objects of experience or knowledge—neither knowable nor capable of representation by concepts?

These questions, relevant to the consideration of ideas as representations of reality, are, of course, also relevant to problems considered in the chapters on BEING, EXPERIENCE, and KNOWLEDGE. The issues indicated are there discussed.

Intimately connected with them are questions about the truth of ideas. Can ideas or concepts be true or false in the sense in which truth and falsity are attributed to propositions or judgments? Under what conditions is an idea true? In what does its truth consist, and what are the signs or marks of its truth? These matters are discussed in the chapter on TRUTH. Here it is sufficient to point out that the traditional distinction between adequate and inadequate ideas, and the comparison of clear and distinct with obscure and confused ideas, are used to determine the criteria of truth. It may be the truth of a concept taken by itself or of the judgment into which several concepts enter. To the extent that ideas are regarded as representative, their truth (or the truth of the judgments they form) seems to consist in some mode of agreement or correspondence with the reality they represent, or, as Spinoza says, its *ideatum*.

Within the conceptual or mental order itself, there is a further distinction between ideas which do not perform a representative function and those which do. The former are treated as fantasies, fictions, or chimeras; the latter are called, by contrast, "real ideas," or ideas having some reference to reality. The question of the reality of ideas takes precedence over the question of their truth, at least for those who regard the division into true and false as applicable only to representations. Yet the criteria of the distinction between the real and the imaginary are difficult to separate from the criteria of true and false. The separation is made most readily by those who use "idea" to mean memory image. They can test the reality of an idea by tracing it back to the impression from which it originated.

Another sort of test is applied by those who measure the reality of abstract ideas by their fidelity to the sense-perceptions from which they were abstracted. Still another criterion, proposed by William James, is that of freedom from contradiction. An idea has truth and its object has reality if it "remains uncontradicted." The idea of a winged horse illustrates the point.

"If I merely dream of a horse with wings," James writes, "my horse interferes with nothing else and has not to be contradicted. . . . But if with this horse I make an inroad into the world otherwise known, and say, for example, 'That is my old mare Maggie, having grown a pair of wings where she stands in her stall,' the whole case is altered; for now the horse and place are identified with a horse and place otherwise known, and what is known of the latter objects is incompatible with what is perceived with the former."

THE CONSIDERATION of ideas or concepts belongs to logic as well as to psychology and metaphysics. The logician sometimes deals with concepts directly and with the judgments into which they enter; sometimes he deals with them only as they find verbal expression in terms and propositions.

The distinction between concepts and judgments (or between terms and propositions) is discussed in the chapter on JUDGMENT. There also we see that the classification of judgments or propositions depends in part on the acceptance or rejection of the notions of subject and predicate in the analysis of concepts or terms; and, if they are accepted, on the way in which

terms are distinguished both as subjects and as predicates.

This in turn depends upon certain traditional divisions which are applicable to terms, if not always to concepts, such as the familiar distinctions between concrete and abstract, and particular and universal, terms. When the concept, which is sometimes called the "mental word," is regarded as by its very nature abstract and universal, these distinctions are applicable only to the physical words which are terms. Concrete and particular terms are then treated as verbal expressions of sense-perceptions or images; abstract and universal terms, as verbal expressions of ideas or concepts. But when ideas are identified with sense-perceptions or images, and abstract concepts are denied, the existence of general names in ordinary discourse suffices for the distinction between particular and universal terms, even though the latter do not express any actual content of the mind.

Unlike the foregoing, other divisions of terms, as, for example, the distinction between the univocal and the analogical, or between species and genera, do not occur throughout the tradition of logic. They tend to be characteristic of the logic of Aristotle and its mediaeval development. Of these two distinctions, that between univocal and analogical terms or concepts appears explicitly, so far as this set of great books is concerned, only in the *Summa Theologica*. Nevertheless, Aquinas does have some background for his special theory of analogical terms in Aristotle's treatment of univocal and equivocal names, and in his separation of terms which predicate a sameness in species or genus from those which predicate a sameness by analogy. The analysis of these distinctions is undertaken in the chapters on SAME AND OTHER and SIGN AND SYMBOL.

Other writers, in dealing with universal terms, recognize that they have different degrees of generality. They sometimes formulate this as an order of more and less inclusive classes. Sometimes they refer to the intension and extension, or connotation and denotation, of terms. The more general terms have a less restricted connotation and hence represent more extensive or inclusive classes. The more specific terms have a more determinate meaning and so also have a narrower denotation and represent less inclusive classes. What seems to be peculiar to Aristotle's analysis of species and genera is the setting of upper and lower limits to the hierarchy of universal terms, with a small number of irreducible categories (or *summa genera*) under which all species fall, and, at the other extreme, with a finite number of lowest (or *infimae*) species which are incapable of subsuming other species.

The terms which fall under the lowest species must either be particulars or accidental classes. Those which seem to be predicable of the categories themselves, such as *being* or *one*, cannot be genera. These are the terms which Aristotle's mediaeval followers call "transcendental" and "analogical." Using the word "transcendental" in a different sense, Kant enumerates a set of concepts which bear some resemblance to Aristotle's *summa genera*, but which he treats as transcendental categories.

The difference among concepts with respect to generality is of interest to the psychologist as well as the logician, for it raises the problem of whether the more or the less general takes precedence in the order of learning. The order and relation of ideas is even more the common ground of both logic and psychology. Both, for example, deal with the position and sequence of terms or concepts in reasoning, though the logician aims to *prescribe* the forms which reasoning must take in order to be valid, whereas the psychologist tries to *describe* the steps by which thinking actually goes on.

Only the logician, however, is concerned with the way in which terms are ordered to one another as positive and negative, or as contraries; just as from Aristotle to Freud, only the psychologist deals with the association of ideas in the stream of thought by relationships of contiguity and succession, similarity and difference. According as the logical connection of ideas or their psychological association is made the primary fact, radically divergent interpretations are given of the nature of mind, the life of reason, and the process of thought.

OUTLINE OF TOPICS

REFERENCES

To find the passages cited, use the numbers in heavy type, which are the volume and page numbers of the passages referred to. For example, in 4 HOMER: *Iliad*, BK II [265–283] 12d, the number 4 is the number of the volume in the set; the number 12d indicates that the passage is in section d of page 12.

PAGE SECTIONS: When the text is printed in one column, the letters a and b refer to the upper and lower halves of the page. For example, in 53 JAMES: *Psychology*, 116a-119b, the passage begins in the upper half of page 116 and ends in the lower half of page 119. When the text is printed in two columns, the letters a and b refer to the upper and lower halves of the left-hand side of the page, the letters c and d to the upper and lower halves of the right-hand side of the page. For example, in 7 PLATO: *Symposium*, 163b-164c, the passage begins in the lower half of the left-hand side of page 163 and ends in the upper half of the right-hand side of page 164.

AUTHOR'S DIVISIONS: One or more of the main divisions of a work (such as PART, BK, CH, SECT) are sometimes included in the reference; line numbers, in brackets, are given in certain cases; *e.g., Iliad*, BK II [265–283] 12d.

BIBLE REFERENCES: The references are to book, chapter, and verse. When the King James and Douay versions differ in title of books or in the numbering of chapters or verses, the King James version is cited first and the Douay, indicated by a (D), follows; *e.g.,* OLD TESTAMENT: *Nehemiah*, 7:45—(D) II *Esdras*, 7:46.

SYMBOLS: The abbreviation "esp" calls the reader's attention to one or more especially relevant parts of a whole reference; "passim" signifies that the topic is discussed intermittently rather than continuously in the work or passage cited.

For additional information concerning the style of the references, see the Explanation of Reference Style; for general guidance in the use of *The Great Ideas*, consult the Preface.

1. Doctrines of idea

1a. Ideas, or relations between ideas, as objects of thought or knowledge: the ideas as eternal forms

7 PLATO: *Cratylus*, 113c-114a,c / *Phaedrus*, 125a-126d / *Symposium*, 167a-d / *Euthyphro*, 193a-c / *Phaedo*, 224a-c; 228d-230c; 231c-232a; 242b-243c / *Republic*, BK III, 333b-334b; BK V, 368c-373c; BK VI, 383d-388a; BK VII, 392b-393b; 397a-398c / *Timaeus*, 455c-458b / *Parmenides* 486a-511d / *Theaetetus*, 534d-536a / *Sophist*, 571a-574c / *Statesman*, 595a-c / *Philebus*, 610d-613a / *Seventh Letter*, 809c-810d

17 PLOTINUS: *Third Ennead*, TR IX, CH 1 136a-d / *Fifth Ennead*, TR V, CH 1-2 228b-229d; TR IX, CH 6-9 249a-250b / *Sixth Ennead*, TR II, CH 21 279b-280a

18 AUGUSTINE: *Confessions*, BK X, par 16-38 75b-81a passim / *City of God*, BK VIII, CH 6-7 268d-269d; BK XII, CH 7 346c-d

19 AQUINAS: *Summa Theologica*, PART I, Q 84, AA 1-2 440d-443c; A 4, ANS 444d-446b; AA 5-7 446c-450b; Q 85, A 1, ANS and REP 1-2 451c-453c; A 2, ANS 453d-455b; A 3, REP 1,4 455b-457a; A 8, ANS 460b-461b; Q 86, A 4, REP 2 463d-464d; Q 87, A 1, ANS 465a-466c; Q 88, A 1, ANS 469a-471c; A 2, ANS 471c-472c

30 BACON: *Advancement of Learning*, 43d-44c

31 DESCARTES: *Meditations*, 71d-72a; III, 82d-83a; VI, 96d-97a / *Objections and Replies*, 121a-c; DEF II–III 130a-b; AXIOM V–VI 131d-132a; 137d; 157b-158a; 212c-213a

35 LOCKE: *Human Understanding*, INTRO, SECT 8 95c-d; BK II, CH VIII, SECT 8 134b-c; CH IX, SECT I 138b-c; CH XXI, SECT 5 179c-d; BK III, CH V, SECT 12 266d-267a; SECT 14 267b-c; BK IV, CH I, SECT I–CH IV, SECT 12 307a-326d passim, esp CH II, SECT 1-7 309b-311a, SECT 15 312d-313a, CH III, SECT 31 323c-d; CH IV, SECT 18 328d-329a; CH VI, SECT 13 335c-d; SECT 16 336d; CH VII, SECT 1-7 337a-338c esp SECT 2 337a; CH XI, SECT 13-14 357d-358c; CH XVII, SECT 2 371d-372b; SECT 8 377b-d

35 BERKELEY: *Human Knowledge* 404a-444d passim, esp INTRO, SECT 21-25 411b-412a,c, SECT I 413a-b, SECT 18 416b-c, SECT 23 417b-c, SECT 86-91 429c-431a, SECT 135-142 440a-441c

35 HUME: *Human Understanding*, SECT IV, DIV 20 458b

42 KANT: *Pure Reason*, 16a-c esp 16b; 113b-115c esp 113c-d; 173b-174a esp 173b-d / *Practical Reason*, 352c-353a / *Judgement*, 551a-552c

46 HEGEL: *Philosophy of Right*, PART II, par 140, 53a-b

53 JAMES: *Psychology*, 300a-301a; 307a

(1. *Doctrines of idea.*)

1b. Ideas or conceptions as that by which the mind thinks or knows

8 ARISTOTLE: *Interpretation*, CH 1 [16ᵃ4–8] 25a / *Soul*, BK III, CH 4 661b-662c

19 AQUINAS: *Summa Theologica*, PART I, Q 12, A 2 51c-52c; AA 9–10 58b-59d; Q 13, A I, ANS 62c-63c; A 5, ANS 66b-67d; Q 14, A I, ANS and REP 3 75d-76c; A 2, ANS and REP 2–3 76d-77d; A 4, ANS 78b-79a; A 5 esp REP 2–3 79a-80a; A 6, REP I 80a-81c; A 8, ANS 82c-83b; A 12, ANS 85d-86d; Q 16, A 2 95c-96b; Q 17, A 3, ANS 102d-103c; Q 27, A I, ANS and REP 2–3 153b-154b; A 2, ANS and REP 2 154c-155b; Q 32, AA 2–3 178a-180b; Q 34, A I 185b-187b; QQ 55–58 288d-306b; Q 82, A 3, ANS 433c-434c; Q 84 440b-451b; Q 85, A 2 453d-455b; A 4 457a-d; A 8, REP 3 460b-461b; Q 86, A I, ANS 461c-462a; A 2, ANS and REP 2–4 462a-463a; Q 87, A I 465a-466c; Q 88, A I, REP 2 469a-471c; Q 89, A 2, ANS and REP 2 475a-d; A 6, ANS and REP 2 478b-d

31 DESCARTES: *Meditations*, 71d-72a; III, 82d-83a / *Objections and Replies*, 108b-109d; 121a-c; DEF II–III 130a-b; AXIOM V–VI 131d-132a; 137d; 157b-158a; 212c-213a

31 SPINOZA: *Ethics*, PART II, DEF 3 373b

35 LOCKE: *Human Understanding*, BK IV, CH IV, SECT 3 324b-c

42 KANT: *Pure Reason*, 15b-c; 22a,c; 30b-c; 31a-d; 38-39c; 41c-42a; 53b-54b; 58c-59b; 85d-93c; 109d-113b esp 112d-113b; 115b-c; 130b-c; 197a-b

53 JAMES: *Psychology*, 300a-314b esp 300a-301b, 302b-303a, 307a, 313-314a

1c. Ideas as the data of sense-experience or their residues

12 LUCRETIUS: *Nature of Things*, BK IV [722–817] 53d-54d

18 AUGUSTINE: *City of God*, BK VIII, CH 7 269c-d

23 HOBBES: *Leviathan*, PART I, 49a; 52c; 54b-c; PART IV, 261a; 262a-b

31 DESCARTES: *Objections and Replies*, 137d

31 SPINOZA: *Ethics*, PART II, PROP 48, SCHOL 391b-c; PROP 49, SCHOL, 392a-c

35 LOCKE: *Human Understanding*, BK I, CH I, SECT 15 98d-99a; BK II, CH I, SECT 1–8 121a-123a; SECT 17 125c-d; CH I, SECT 20–CH IV, SECT I 126d-129c; CH IV, SECT 6–CH V 131a-b; CH VII–IX 131c-141a passim, esp CH IX, SECT I–7 138b-139b, SECT 15 141a; CH XII, SECT 1–2 147b-d passim; SECT 8 148c-d; CH XIII, SECT 2 149a; CH XIV, SECT 31 161d-162a; CH XX, SECT 1–2 176b-c; SECT 15 177d; CH XXIII, SECT 1 204a-b; SECT 3 204c-d; SECT 7 205d-206a; SECT 9 206b-c; SECT 15 208c-d; SECT 29–30 211d-212b; SECT 32–37 212c-214b passim; CH XXXII, SECT 14–16 245c-246b; BK III, CH I, SECT 5 252b-c; CH IV, SECT 7–15 260d-263b esp SECT 11–15 261d-263b; CH VI, SECT 46–47

281d-282b; CH XI, SECT 21–23 304d-305b; BK IV, CH II, SECT 11–13 311c-312b; CH III, SECT 23 320a-c; CH IV, SECT 4 324c

35 BERKELEY: *Human Knowledge*, SECT I 413a-b; SECT 18 416b-c; SECT 29–33 418c-419a; SECT 36 419c-d; SECT 88–91 430a-431a

35 HUME: *Human Understanding*, SECT II 455b-457b; SECT VII, DIV 49 471c-d; DIV 61 477c-478a

36 STERNE: *Tristram Shandy*, 234b-236b

42 KANT: *Pure Reason*, 45b-46a esp 45d-46a; 48b-c; 54b-55a; 101b-102a esp 102a; 115b-c / *Fund. Prin. Metaphysic of Morals*, 282b-c

54 FREUD: *Unconscious*, 442b-443a / *Ego and Id*, 700a-701a; 701d

1d. Ideas as the pure concepts of reason: regulative principles

42 KANT: *Pure Reason*, 15c-16a; 37b-39c; 108a-209d esp 108a-109c, 113b-115c, 117b-119a, 129c-131c, 158a-159d, 166c-171a, 173b-174a, 187a-c, 193b-d, 200d-202a, 203b-d, 209b-d; 237b; 239a-240b / *Practical Reason*, 310d-311d; 329a-d; 343a; 349b-355a esp 349b-350c / *Intro. Metaphysic of Morals*, 390b / *Judgement*, 461a-462d; 464c-467a; 489b-c; 504d-505a; 506a-511a esp 509d-510a; 528c-530c; 542b-544c; 570b-572c; 581a-582c; 596c-598b; 604a-b

1e. Ideas in the order of supra-human intelligence or spirit: the eternal exemplars and archetypes; the modes of the divine mind

12 LUCRETIUS: *Nature of Things*, BK V [181–200] 63b-c

17 PLOTINUS: *First Ennead*, TR III, CH 1–2 10a-d; TR VI, CH 2–3 21d-23a; CH 9, 26a / *Third Ennead*, TR IX, CH 1, 136a-c / *Fourth Ennead*, TR IV, CH 13 164d-165b / *Fifth Ennead* 208a-251d passim, esp TR III 215c-226c, TR V–VII 228b-239b, TR VIII, CH 7 242d-243c, TR IX 246c-251d / *Sixth Ennead*, TR II, CH 21 279b-280a; TR VII, CH 2–17 322b-331a

18 AUGUSTINE: *Confessions*, BK I, par 9, 3a; BK XII, par 38 108d-109a / *City of God*, BK VIII, CH 3–4 266a-267c; BK XI, CH 10, 328c-d; BK XII, CH 17–18 353a-354d / *Christian Doctrine*, BK II, CH 38 654b-c

19 AQUINAS: *Summa Theologica*, PART I, Q 14, PREAMBLE 75c-d; A 4, ANS 78b-79a; A 5 79a-80a; A 6 esp REP 3 80a-81c; A 8, ANS 82c-83b; A 11, REP 1–2 84c-85c; A 14, ANS and REP 2 88d-89b; Q 15 91b-94a; Q 16, A I, ANS and REP 2 94b-95c; Q 18, A 4 107d-108c; QQ 22–24 127c-143c passim; Q 34, A 3, REP 4 188b-189a; Q 44, A 3 240b-241a; Q 47, A I, REP 2 256a-257b; QQ 55–56 288d-294d; Q 58 300b-306b passim; Q 74, A 3, REP 5 375a-377a,c; Q 84, A 2, ANS and REP 3 442b-443c; A 3, REP I 443d-444d; AA 4–5 444d-447c; Q 85, A 4, ANS 457a-d; Q 87, A I, ANS and REP 2–3 465a-466c; Q 89, A 3, ANS

and REP 1,3 475d-476c; Q 105, A 3, ANS 540c-541b; Q 106, A 1, ANS and REP 1 545d-546d; Q 107 549b-552b; Q 108, A 1, ANS and REP 2 552c-553c; Q 115, A 2, ANS 587c-588c

20 AQUINAS: *Summa Theologica*, PART I-II, Q 61, A 5, ANS 58b-59d; PART III, Q 9, A 3, ANS 765b-766b

21 DANTE: *Divine Comedy*, PARADISE, XIII [52-87] 126a-b

30 BACON: *Novum Organum*, BK I, APH 23 108c; APH 124 133c-d; BK II, APH 15 149a

31 DESCARTES: *Objections and Replies*, 137d

31 SPINOZA: *Ethics*, PART I, PROP 17, SCHOL 362c-363c passim; PART II, PROP 3, DEMONST 374a-b; PROP 4-5 374c-d; PROP 9 376a-c; PROP 19-20 382b-d

32 MILTON: *Paradise Lost*, BK II [146-151] 114b; BK V [469-505] 185b-186a

35 LOCKE: *Human Understanding*, BK III, CH VI, SECT 3 268d; CH XI, SECT 23 305a-b

35 BERKELEY: *Human Knowledge*, SECT 29-33 418c-419a esp SECT 33 419a; SECT 70-71 426d-427a; SECT 75-76 427c-428a; SECT 81 428c-d

42 KANT: *Pure Reason*, 113c-118a; 173b-174a esp 173b-c / *Judgement*, 551a-552c; 575b-577a; 580c-d

46 HEGEL: *Philosophy of History*, INTRO, 169d-170b

1*f*. Idea as the unity of determinate existence and concept: the Absolute Idea

46 HEGEL: *Philosophy of Right*, PREF, 6a-7a; INTRO, par 1-2 9a-10a; par 31-32 19c-20b; PART III, par 279, 93b-c; par 345 111b; par 352-353 112b-c; par 360 113d-114a,c; ADDITIONS, 2 115d; 19 119c-d / *Philosophy of History*, INTRO, 156c-162a esp 156d-157b, 158c, 160b-162a; 163a-165b esp 165a-b; 166b-c; 169d-171b; 176b-c; 182d

2. The origin or derivation of ideas in the human mind

2*a*. The infusion of ideas: divine illumination

18 AUGUSTINE: *Confessions*, BK IV, par 25 25c; BK VII, par 8, 45d; par 16 48c-49a; par 23 50b-c; BK XIII, par 19 115c-d / *City of God*, BK VIII, CH 7 269c-d; CH 9 270d-271a; BK X, CH 2 299d-300a; BK XI, CH 24-25 335c-336d; CH 27, 337d

19 AQUINAS: *Summa Theologica*, PART I, Q 84, A 4 444d-446b; Q 89, A 1, REP 3 473b-475a; A 2, REP 2 475a-d; A 4, ANS 476c-477a; A 7, ANS 478d-479c

20 AQUINAS: *Summa Theologica*, PART III, Q 9, A 3 765b-766b; A 4, REP 2-3 766b-767b; PART III SUPPL, Q 92, A 1, ANS 1025c-1032b

31 DESCARTES: *Meditations*, VI, 99a-b

35 BERKELEY: *Human Knowledge*, SECT 26-33 418a-419a; SECT 57 423d-424a; SECT 67 426a-b

42 KANT: *Pure Reason*, 113b-c

2*b*. The innate endowment or retention of ideas: the activation of the mind's native content or structure by sense, by memory, or by experience

7 PLATO: *Phaedrus*, 124a-126c esp 126a-c / *Meno*, 179d-183a; 188d-189a / *Phaedo*, 228a-230d / *Theaetetus*, 515d-517b

8 ARISTOTLE: *Posterior Analytics*, BK I, CH 1 97a-d; BK II, CH 19 [99^{b}20-33] 136a-b / *Metaphysics*, BK I, CH 9 [992^{b}24-993^{a}11] 511a-c

12 EPICTETUS: *Discourses*, BK I, CH 22 127c-128c; BK II, CH 11 150a-151b

17 PLOTINUS: *First Ennead*, TR II, CH 4, 8b-c / *Fourth Ennead*, TR III, CH 25, 155b; TR IV, CH 5 160d-161b / *Fifth Ennead*, TR III, CH 2, 216b

18 AUGUSTINE: *Confessions*, BK X, par 15-19 75a-76b; par 26-38 78a-81a / *City of God*, BK VIII, CH 6, 269b-c

19 AQUINAS: *Summa Theologica*, PART I, Q 55, A 2 289d-290d; A 3, REP 1 291a-d; Q 57, A 1, REP 3 295a-d; Q 84, A 3 443d-444d; A 4, ANS 444d-446b; A 6, ANS 447c-449a; Q 89, A 1, REP 3 473b-475a; Q 117, A 1, ANS and REP 4 595d-597c

28 HARVEY: *On Animal Generation*, 333d-335a esp 334c-d

30 BACON: *Advancement of Learning*, 1b-c

31 DESCARTES: *Rules*, IV, 5c-d; 6d; VIII, 13c-d / *Discourse*, PART IV, 53b; PART V, 54c / *Meditations*, II 77d-81d; III, 83b; 88c-d; VI, 96d-97a; 99a-c / *Objections and Replies*, 120c-d; 140c; 215b-c; 224b,d

35 LOCKE: *Human Understanding*, 90d-91b; BK I, CH I, SECT 1 95b,d-96a; SECT 15 98d-99a; SECT 23-24 101b-102b; CH II, SECT 12 107b-d; CH III 112c-121a,c passim, esp SECT 21 118b-119a; BK II, CH I, SECT 1 121a-b; SECT 6 122b-c; SECT 9 123a; SECT 17 125c-d; CH IX, SECT 6 139a; CH XI, SECT 16 147a

35 HUME: *Human Understanding*, SECT II, DIV 17, 457b,d [fn 1]

42 KANT: *Pure Reason*, 14a-108a,c esp 14a-b, 22a,c, 23a-34c, 41c-42b, 48d-51d, 53b-55a, 58d-59a, 61a-62c, 66d-93c; 113b-115a / *Practical Reason*, 352c-353a / *Judgement*, 551a-589c

53 JAMES: *Psychology*, 851a-890a esp 851b-852a, 856a-b, 859a-860b, 867a-868b, 879b, 889a

54 FREUD: *General Introduction*, 512b-513b esp 512b; 526c-d; 532b; 599a-b / *Group Psychology*, 688d-689a; 689b [fn 1] / *Ego and Id*, 707c-708b esp 708b

2*c*. The acquirement of ideas by perception or intuition: simple ideas or forms as direct objects of the understanding

7 PLATO: *Phaedo*, 224a-c / *Republic*, BK VI, 383d-388a; BK VII, 392b-393c / *Timaeus*, 457c-458a / *Parmenides*, 487d-488a / *Theaetetus*, 535b-d

18 AUGUSTINE: *City of God*, BK VIII, CH 6, 269b-c; BK XII, CH 7 346c-d

(*2. The origin or derivation of ideas in the human mind. 2c. The acquirement of ideas by perception or intuition: simple ideas or forms as direct objects of the understanding.*)

19 Aquinas: *Summa Theologica*, PART I, Q 84, A I, ANS and REP I 440d-442a; A 2, ANS 442b-443c; A 4, ANS and REP I-2 444d-446b; AA 5-7 446c-450b

31 Descartes: *Rules*, III, 4a-b / *Meditations*, VI, 99a-c

31 Spinoza: *Ethics*, PART II, PROP 14-23 380c-383c

35 Locke: *Human Understanding*, BK I, CH I, SECT 15 98d-99a; CH III, SECT 21 118b-119a; BK II, CH I-IX 121a-141b passim, esp CH I, SECT I-8 121a-123a, SECT 17 125c-d, CH I, SECT 20-CH IV, SECT I 126d-129c, CH IV, SECT 6-CH V 131a-b, CH IX, SECT I-7 138b-139b, SECT 15 141a; CH XI, SECT 17-CH XII, SECT 2 147a-d; CH XII, SECT 8 148c-d; CH XIII, SECT 2 149a; CH XIV, SECT 2 155b-c; SECT 31 161d-162a; CH XV, SECT 9 164b-d; CH XVI, SECT I 165c-d; CH XVII, SECT 22-CH XVIII, SECT I 173d-174a; CH XVIII, SECT 6 174c-d; CH XX, SECT I-2 176b-c; SECT 15 177d; CH XXI, SECT 75 200b-d; CH XXIII, SECT I 204a-b; SECT 3 204c-d; SECT 5 205a-b; SECT 7 205d-206a; SECT 9 206b-c; SECT 15 208c-d; SECT 29-30 211d-212b; SECT 32-37 212c-214b passim; CH XXV, SECT 9 216d; SECT II 217a; CH XXX, SECT 2 238b-c; CH XXXI, SECT 2 239b-d; CH XXXII, SECT 14-16 245c-246b; BK III, CH I, SECT 5 252b-c; CH IV 260a-263c passim, esp SECT II-15 261d-263b; CH V, SECT 2 263d-264a; CH VI, SECT 46-47 281d-282b; CH XI, SECT 21-23 304d-305b; BK IV, CH II, SECT II-13 311c-312b; CH III, SECT 23 320a-c; CH IV, SECT 4 324c; CH XVIII, SECT 3 381b-c

35 Berkeley: *Human Knowledge*, SECT I 413a-b; SECT 18 416b-c; SECT 25-33 417d-419a passim; SECT 36 419c-d; SECT 88-91 430a-431a passim

35 Hume: *Human Understanding*, SECT II 455b-457b; SECT VII, DIV 49 471c-d; DIV 61 477c-478a

36 Sterne: *Tristram Shandy*, 318b-319a

42 Kant: *Pure Reason*, 14a-b; 23a-33d esp 25b-c, 27c, 28d-29d, 32a-c; 34a-c; 41c-42a; 45b-46a; 53b-55a; 66d-72c esp 69c-72c; 85d-93c; 99a-107b; 131a-c; 186d-187a / *Judgement*, 465a-c; 528c-530c; 570c-572b

45 Lavoisier: *Elements of Chemistry*, PREF, 1c-d

53 James: *Psychology*, 502a-505b esp 502a

2d. **Reflection as a source of ideas: the mind's consideration of its own acts or content**

8 Aristotle: *Soul*, BK III, CH 4 [429^{b}26-430^{a}9] 662b-c

12 Epictetus: *Discourses*, BK I, CH I 105a-106c; CH 17 122d-124a; CH 20 126c-127b

18 Augustine: *Confessions*, BK X, par 12-31 74b-79d

19 Aquinas: *Summa Theologica*, PART I, Q 12, A 9, REP 2 58b-59a; Q 28, A 4, REP 2 160c-161d; Q 85, A 2 453d-455b; Q 87, A 3 467b-468a

31 Descartes: *Meditations*, VI, 96d-97a

35 Locke: *Human Understanding*, BK II, CH I, SECT I-8 121a-123a; SECT 17 125c-d; SECT 24 127b-c; CH III, SECT I, 128d; CH VI-VII 131b-133b; CH IX, SECT I-2 138b-c; CH XI, SECT 14, 146d; CH XII, SECT I-2 147b-d; SECT 8 148c-d; CH XIV, SECT 2-6 155b-156c; SECT 31 161d-162a; CH XVII, SECT 22 173d-174a; CH XVIII, SECT 6 174c-d; CH XX, SECT I-2 176b-c; SECT 15 177d; CH XXI, SECT 4 178d-179c; SECT 75 200b-d; CH XXIII, SECT I 204a-b; SECT 5 205a-b; SECT 15 208c-d; SECT 29-30 211d-212b; SECT 32-37 212c-214b passim; CH XXV, SECT 9 216d; SECT II 217a; BK III, CH I, SECT 5 252b-c; CH V, SECT 2 263d-264a; BK IV, CH III, SECT 23 320a-c

35 Berkeley: *Human Knowledge*, SECT I 413a-b

35 Hume: *Human Understanding*, SECT II, DIV 14 456b

42 Kant: *Pure Reason*, 15c-16c; 55a-56c; 99a-107b; 121a-123b

46 Hegel: *Philosophy of Right*, PART II, par 138 48c-d; ADDITIONS, 89 129d-130a

53 James: *Psychology*, 121a-b; 122b-126a passim, esp 122b-124b

2e. **The genesis of ideas by the recollection of sense-impressions: the images of sense**

18 Augustine: *Confessions*, BK X, par 8-18 73b-76a

23 Hobbes: *Leviathan*, PART I, 49a-d; PART IV, 258b-c; 262a-b

30 Bacon: *Novum Organum*, BK II, APH 26 156a-157a

31 Descartes: *Rules*, XII, 19a-20d

31 Spinoza: *Ethics*, PART II, PROP 17-18 380d-382b; PROP 40, SCHOL 2 388a-b; PROP 49, SCHOL, 391d-392c

35 Locke: *Human Understanding*, BK I, CH III, SECT 21 118b-119a; BK II, CH X 141b-143d passim, esp SECT 2 141b-c, SECT 7 142c-d; BK IV, CH II, SECT 14 312b-d

35 Hume: *Human Understanding*, SECT II 455b-457b; SECT VII, DIV 49 471c-d; DIV 61 477c-478a

38 Rousseau: *Inequality*, 341d-342a

42 Kant: *Pure Reason*, 54b-55a

53 James: *Psychology*, 480a-501b esp 480a-b

54 Freud: *Interpretation of Dreams*, 351c-352d esp 351d-352a; 363c-364b; 367b-c; 384c-385c esp 385b-c / *Unconscious*, 442d-443a / *General Introduction*, 518c-d / *Ego and Id*, 700a-701d

2f. **The production of ideas by the reworking of the materials of sense: the imaginative construction of concepts or the formation of complex from simple ideas**

12 Lucretius: *Nature of Things*, BK IV [722-748] 53d-54a

18 AUGUSTINE: *Confessions*, BK X, par 14 74d-75a

19 AQUINAS: *Summa Theologica*, PART I, Q 12, A 9, REP 2 58b-59a

23 HOBBES: *Leviathan*, PART I, 50d

31 DESCARTES: *Meditations*, I, 76a-b; III, 83b / *Objections and Replies*, 210d

32 MILTON: *Paradise Lost*, BK V [95-128] 177b-178a

35 LOCKE: *Human Understanding*, BK II, CH I, SECT 5 122a-b; SECT 24 127b-c; CH II, SECT 1-2 127d-128b; CH VII, SECT 10 133a-b; CH XI, SECT 6-7 145a-b; CH XII-XXVII 147b-233d passim, esp CH XIII, SECT 1 148d-149a, SECT 4-6 149b-d, SECT 27 154c-d, CH XIV, SECT 27-31 160d-162a, CH XV, SECT 2-3 162c-d, SECT 9 164b-d, CH XVI, SECT 1-2 165c-d, SECT 5 166b-c, SECT 8 167c, CH XVII, SECT 3 168b, SECT 5 168d-169a, SECT 22 173d-174a, CH XXI, SECT 75 200b-d, CH XXII, SECT 2 201a-b, SECT 9 202c-203a, CH XXV, SECT 9 216d, SECT 11 217a, CH XXVIII, SECT 14 231d-232a, SECT 18 232d-233b; CH XXX, SECT 3-5 238c-239b; CH XXXI, SECT 3-14 240a-243c passim; CH XXXII, SECT 12 245b-c; SECT 17-18 246b-247a; SECT 22-25 247c-248a passim; BK III, CH II, SECT 3 253c; CH IV, SECT 12-14 262b-263a; CH IV, SECT 17-CH V, SECT 16 263c-268b; CH VI, SECT 11 271b-d; SECT 26-51 274d-283a passim; CH XI, SECT 15 303b-c; SECT 18 304a-b; BK IV, CH IV, SECT 5-8 324d-325c; SECT 11-12 326b-d

35 BERKELEY: *Human Knowledge*, INTRO, SECT 10 406d-407b; SECT 1 413a-b; SECT 28 418b-c

35 HUME: *Human Understanding*, SECT II, DIV 13-14 455d-456b; SECT III, DIV 18 457c-d; SECT V, DIV 39, 466c-d; DIV 40, 467b; SECT VII, DIV 49, 471d

38 ROUSSEAU: *Inequality*, 338a; 341d-342a

42 KANT: *Pure Reason*, 5d-6b; 31c-d; 45d-46a; 65d-108a,c esp 66d-91d, 101b-107b; 193a-195a; 211d-216c / *Judgement*, 493c-495a,c

53 JAMES: *Psychology*, 104a-106b; 149b-153b esp 150a, 153a-b; 179b-181a esp 181b [fn 1]; 362a-363b; 480a-481a

54 FREUD: *Interpretation of Dreams*, 270c-271a

2g. The abstraction of ideas from sense-experience: the concept as the first act of the mind; the grades of abstraction

8 ARISTOTLE: *Posterior Analytics*, BK II, CH 19 [99ᵇ20-100ᵇ4] 136a-d / *Physics*, BK II, CH 2 [193ᵇ22-194ᵃ11] 270a-c / *Metaphysics*, BK I, CH I [980ᵃ28-981ᵇ13] 499a-500a; BK IV, CH 4 [1006ᵃ12-ᵇ12] 525b-d; BK VI, CH I [1025ᵇ28-1026ᵃ6] 547d-548a; BK VII, CH 10 [1035ᵇ35-1036ᵃ12] 559b-c; BK XI, CH 3 [1061ᵃ29-ᵇ12] 589c-d; BK XIII, CH 2 [1077ᵇ1]-CH 3 [1078ᵇ5] 608d-610a / *Soul*, BK I, CH I [403ᵃ2-16] 632a-b; BK III, CH 4 [429ᵇ10-23] 661d-662a; CH 7 [431ᵃ14-ᵇ19] 663d-664b; CH 8 664b-d / *Memory and Reminiscence*, CH I [449ᵇ30-450ᵃ25] 690c-691a

19 AQUINAS: *Summa Theologica*, PART I, Q I, A I, REP 2 3b-4a; Q 12, A 13, ANS 61c-62b; Q 14, A II, REP I 84c-85c; Q 40, A 3, ANS 215c-216d; Q 54, A 4, ANS and REP 2 287b-288a; Q 55, A 2 289d-290d; Q 57, A I, REP 3 295a-d; Q 75, A 2, REP 3 379c-380c; A 3, REP 2 380c-381b; A 5, ANS 382a-383b; Q 76, A 2, REP 4 388c-391a; Q 79, AA 3-4 416a-418c; A 5, REP 2 418c-419b; Q 84, A 2, ANS 442b-443c; A 6 447c-449a; Q 85, AA 1-3 451c-457a; AA 5-6 457d-459c; A 8 460b-461b; Q 89, A I, REP 3 473b-475a; A 4, ANS and REP I 476c-477a; A 7, ANS 478d-479c; Q 117, A I 595d-597c; PART I-II, Q 29, A 6, ANS and REP 1,3 748b-749a

20 AQUINAS: *Summa Theologica*, PART III, Q 9, A 4 766b-767b; PART III SUPPL, Q 92, A I, ANS 1025c-1032b

28 HARVEY: *Circulation of the Blood*, 305a / *On Animal Generation*, 332a-335c

31 DESCARTES: *Rules*, XIV, 29b-30d / *Discourse*, PART IV, 53b / *Objections and Replies*, 215b-c; 216d-217d

31 SPINOZA: *Ethics*, PART II, PROP 40, SCHOL 2 388a-b

35 LOCKE: *Human Understanding*, BK I, CH I, SECT 15 98d-99a; BK II, CH XI, SECT 9-11 145b-146a; CH XII, SECT I, 147b-c; CH XXXII, SECT 6-8 244b-d; BK III, CH III, SECT 6-9 255c-256c; CH VI, SECT 32-33 277c-278c; BK IV, CH VII, SECT 9 338d-339b; CH IX, SECT I 349a

35 BERKELEY: *Human Knowledge*, INTRO 405a-412a,c esp SECT 6-19 405d-410c; SECT 5 414a-b; SECT 97-100 431d-432c; SECT 118-120 436b-d; SECT 143 441c-d

35 HUME: *Human Understanding*, SECT XII, DIV 122 505c-d; DIV 124-125 506a-507a esp DIV 125, 507b [fn 1]

38 ROUSSEAU: *Inequality*, 341b-342b

42 KANT: *Pure Reason*, 23a-24a; 45d-46a; 115b-c; 193a-195a

49 DARWIN: *Descent of Man*, 296c-297b passim

53 JAMES: *Psychology*, 305a-312a passim; 329a-331b esp 331b

54 FREUD: *Unconscious*, 442b-443d

2h. The derivation of transcendental ideas from the three syllogisms of reason

42 KANT: *Pure Reason*, 109d-120c esp 110d-111c

3. The division of ideas according to their objective reference

3a. Ideas about things distinguished from ideas about ideas: the distinction between first and second intentions

19 AQUINAS: *Summa Theologica*, PART I, Q 12, A 9, REP 2 58b-59a; Q 14, A 6, REP I 80a-81c; A 13, REP 2-3 86d-88c; Q 15, A 2, ANS and REP 2 92a-93b; Q 29, A I, REP 3 162a-163b; Q 30, A 4, ANS 170c-171b; Q 66, A 2, ANS and REP 2 345d-347b; Q 84, A I, REP I 440d-442a; Q 85, A 2 453d-455b

(3. The division of ideas according to their objective reference. 3a. Ideas about things distinguished from ideas about ideas: the distinction between first and second intentions.)

23 HOBBES: *Leviathan*, PART IV, 270a

24 RABELAIS: *Gargantua and Pantagruel*, BK II, 79c; BK III, 150a

35 LOCKE: *Human Understanding*, BK III, CH II 252d-254c passim; CH IV, SECT 2 260b; CH V, SECT 12 266d-267a; SECT 14 267b-c; CH VI, SECT 19, 273b; SECT 48-50 282b-d; CH XI, SECT 10 302b; SECT 24 305b-d

42 KANT: *Pure Reason*, 15d-16c esp 16c; 55a-56c; 99a-101b; 121a-123b

46 HEGEL: *Philosophy of History*, INTRO, 156d-158a

53 JAMES: *Psychology*, 300b

3b. Adequate and inadequate ideas: clear and distinct ideas as compared with obscure and confused ideas

8 ARISTOTLE: *Physics*, BK I, CH I 259a-b

19 AQUINAS: *Summa Theologica*, PART I, Q 12, A 6, ANS and REP 3 55b-56a; Q 13 62b-75b; Q 14, A 6 80a-81c; A 12, REP 2 85d-86d; Q 55, A 3 291a-d; Q 85, A 3 455b-457a; A 4, REP 3 457a-d; A 8, ANS 460b-461b; Q 89, A 1, ANS 473b-475a; A 2, ANS and REP 2 475a-d; A 3, ANS and REP 2,4 475d-476c; A 4, ANS and REP 2 476c-477a; Q 94, A 1, REP 3 501d-503a; Q 117, A 1, REP 4 595d-597c

20 AQUINAS: *Summa Theologica*, PART III, Q 10, A 2, REP 3 768b-769c; PART III SUPPL, Q 92, A 1, REP 2 1025c-1032b

28 HARVEY: *On Animal Generation*, 332a-333d

30 BACON: *Novum Organum*, BK I, APH 14-17 107d-108a

31 DESCARTES: *Discourse*, PART IV, 51b-52a / *Meditations*, 73d-74a; III, 82a-d; 85b-86b; VI, 99a-c / *Objections and Replies*, POSTULATE V-VI 131b-c

31 SPINOZA: *Ethics*, PART II, DEF 4 373b; PROP 34-36 385d-386b; PROP 38 386c-d; PROP 40-43 387a-389b; PART III, DEF 1-3 395d-396a; PROP I 396a-c; PROP 3 398b-c; PART IV, APPENDIX, II 447b; PART V, PROP 3-4 453a-d

35 LOCKE: *Human Understanding*, 91d-92c; BK I, CH III, SECT 19 117c-d; BK II, CH XIII, SECT 17-20 152a-d; CH XVI, SECT 3-4 165d-166b; CH XVII, SECT 7-8 169b-170a; SECT 12-21 170d-173d passim, esp SECT 15 171b-172a; CH XXV, SECT 8 216b-c; CH XXVIII, SECT 19 233b-c; CH XXIX 233d-238a; CH XXXI 239b-243c passim; CH XXXII, SECT 18, 246d-247a; BK III, CH VI, SECT 37 279b; SECT 40 280a-b; SECT 43-51 280c-283a; CH X, SECT 2-4 291d-292c; CH XI, SECT 24 305b-d; BK IV, CH II, SECT 15 312d-313a; CH III, SECT 26 321b-c; CH XII, SECT 14 362d-363a

35 BERKELEY: *Human Knowledge*, SECT 30 418c; SECT 33 419a; SECT 36 419c-d

35 HUME: *Human Understanding*, SECT VII, DIV 48-49 470d-471d; SECT XII, DIV 125 506d-507a

42 KANT: *Pure Reason*, 1a-4a,c; 30b-31a; 125b [fn 1]; 193a-b / *Judgement*, 603c-d

53 JAMES: *Psychology*, 311b-312b [fn 1]; 480b-484a

3c. Real and fantastic or fictional ideas: negations and chimeras

12 LUCRETIUS: *Nature of Things*, BK IV [722-748] 53d-54a

19 AQUINAS: *Summa Theologica*, PART I, Q 12, A 9, REP 2 58b-59a; Q 17, A 2, REP 2 102a-d

23 HOBBES: *Leviathan*, PART I, 50d; 57b-c; PART IV, 258b-d; 261a; 262a-c

30 BACON: *Novum Organum*, BK I, APH 60 112c-113a

31 DESCARTES: *Meditations*, I, 76a-77c; III, 83b / *Objections and Replies*, 210d

35 LOCKE: *Human Understanding*, BK II, CH VIII, SECT 1-6 133b-134a; CH XVII, SECT 12-21 170d-173d esp SECT 15 171b-172a; CH XXX 238a-239b; BK III, CH I, SECT 4 252a; BK IV, CH IV, SECT 1-12 323d-326d passim; CH V, SECT 7-8 330b-d

35 BERKELEY: *Human Knowledge*, SECT 29-30 418c; SECT 33-34 419a-c; SECT 36 419c-d; SECT 82-84 428d-429c; SECT 86-91 429c-431a

42 KANT: *Pure Reason*, 62d-63a; 174d-175b; 193a-c

53 JAMES: *Psychology*, 300b; 639a-644a esp 640a-641b, 642b [fn 2], 643b [fn 1]; 646b-655a; 659a-660b

54 FREUD: *Interpretation of Dreams*, 158a-d; 270c-271a / *General Introduction*, 597b-598a

4. The logic of ideas

4a. The verbal expression of ideas or concepts: terms

7 PLATO: *Cratylus* 85a-114a,c / *Phaedrus*, 138c-140c / *Sophist*, 575d-577b / *Seventh Letter*, 809c-810d

8 ARISTOTLE: *Categories* 5a-21d / *Prior Analytics*, BK I, CH I [24^{b}16-18] 39c; CH 35 66c-d

18 AUGUSTINE: *Confessions*, BK XIII, par 36 120c-d

19 AQUINAS: *Summa Theologica*, PART I, Q 34, A 1, ANS 185b-187b; Q 85, A 2, REP 3 453d-455b; Q 107, A 1, ANS 549b-550b

23 HOBBES: *Leviathan*, PART I, 54c-58a; PART IV, 270a

30 BACON: *Advancement of Learning*, 57d-58a; 60b-c; 61b-c; 62c-d / *Novum Organum*, BK I, APH 14 107d-108a; APH 59 112b-c

31 DESCARTES: *Rules*, XIII, 26b-c / *Objections and Replies*, 137a

31 SPINOZA: *Ethics*, PART II, PROP 49, SCHOL, 392a-c

33 PASCAL: *Pensées*, 392 239b-240a

35 LOCKE: *Human Understanding*, BK II, CH XXII
200d-204a passim, esp SECT 3-10 201b-203c;
CH XXXII, SECT 7-8 244c-d; BK III 251b,d-
306d passim, esp CH I-VIII 251b,d-285a, CH XI
300a-306d; BK IV, CH V, SECT 4 329b-d; CH
VI, SECT 1-3 331b-d

35 BERKELEY: *Human Knowledge*, INTRO, SECT
11-12 407b-408b; SECT 15 409a-b; SECT 18-19
410a-c

38 ROUSSEAU: *Inequality*, 340a-342c

45 LAVOISIER: *Elements of Chemistry*, PREF, 1b-c

49 DARWIN: *Origin of Species*, 40c-d

53 JAMES: *Psychology*, 127b-128a; 153b-154a;
158a-159b; 181b-183a; 332b-334a

54 FREUD: *Beyond the Pleasure Principle*, 662a-b

4b. The classification of terms: problems in the use of different kinds of terms

4b(1) Concrete and abstract terms

8 ARISTOTLE: *Prior Analytics*, BK I, CH 34 66b-c

19 AQUINAS: *Summa Theologica*, PART I, Q 3, A
3, REP 1 16a-d; Q 13, A 1, REP 2 62c-63c; A 9,
ANS 71b-72c; Q 32, A 2 178a-179b; Q 39, AA
4-5 205c-208c; Q 54, A 1, REP 2 285a-d

23 HOBBES: *Leviathan*, PART I, 57a

35 LOCKE: *Human Understanding*, BK III, CH VIII
284b-285a

38 ROUSSEAU: *Inequality*, 341b-c

53 JAMES: *Psychology*, 305a-308b esp 308b-309b
[fn 1-3]; 689a

54 FREUD: *General Introduction*, 516b-c

4b(2) Particular and universal terms

8 ARISTOTLE: *Categories*, CH 2 [1ᵃ20-ᵇ9] 5b-c;
CH 5 [2ᵃ11-3ᵇ23] 6a-8a / *Interpretation*, CH 7
[17ᵃ37-40] 26d / *Metaphysics*, BK VII, CH 10
[1035ᵇ28-32] 559b; CH 11 [1037ᵃ5-9] 560c

17 PLOTINUS: *Fifth Ennead*, TR IX, CH 12 251a

19 AQUINAS: *Summa Theologica*, PART I, Q 13, A
9 71b-72c; Q 29, A 1 162a-163b; A 4, ANS and
REP 4 165c-167a; Q 30, A 4 170c-171b; Q 33, A
3, REP 1 182c-183c; Q 36, A 1, ANS 191a-192a;
Q 40, A 3, ANS 215c-216d; Q 55, A 3, REP 3
291a-d; Q 57, A 2, REP 3 295d-297a; Q 76,
A 2, REP 3 388c-391a; Q 85, A 2, REP 2 453d-
455b; A 3, REP 1,4 455b-457a; Q 86, A 2, REP 4
462a-463a; PART I-II, Q 30, A 4, REP 2 751c-
752b

20 AQUINAS: *Summa Theologica*, PART III, Q 7, A
13, REP 3 755c-756c; Q 10, A 3, REP 2 769d-
771b

23 HOBBES: *Leviathan*, PART I, 55b-c

31 SPINOZA: *Ethics*, PART II, PROP 40, SCHOL 1
387b-388a

35 LOCKE: *Human Understanding*, BK I, CH I,
SECT 15 98d-99a; BK II, CH XI, SECT 8-11 145b-
146a; CH XVI, SECT 1 165c-d; BK III, CH I,
SECT 3 251d-252a; CH III 254d-260a; CH VI,
SECT 1 268b-c; SECT 32-33 277c-278c; BK IV,
CH III, SECT 31 323c-d; CH VII, SECT 9 338d-
339b

35 BERKELEY: *Human Knowledge*, INTRO, SECT
11-12 407b-408b; SECT 15-16 409a-d; SECT 18-
19 410a-c; SECT 122 437b-c

38 ROUSSEAU: *Inequality*, 341b-342b

53 JAMES: *Psychology*, 307a-312a

4b(3) Specific and generic terms: *infimae species* and *summa genera*

8 ARISTOTLE: *Categories*, CH 3-9 5d-16d / *Prior
Analytics*, BK I, CH 27 [43ᵃ25-44] 60c-d /
Posterior Analytics, BK I, CH 19-22 111c-115b /
Topics, BK I, CH 9 147a-b; CH 15 [107ᵃ3-11]
151a; BK IV, CH 1 [120ᵇ36-121ᵃ9] 168d-169a;
CH 2 [122ᵃ3-19] 170a-b; CH 4 [124ᵇ15-22] 173c;
CH 4 [125ᵃ5]-CH 5 [125ᵇ19] 173d-174d; CH 6
[128ᵃ13-29] 177d-178a; BK V, CH 3 [132ᵃ10-23]
182d-183a; CH 4 [132ᵇ35-133ᵃ11] 184a; BK VI,
CH 5 196b-d; BK VII, CH 1 [152ᵃ38-39] 207b /
Sophistical Refutations, CH 22 245a-246c /
Physics, BK I, CH 2 [185ᵃ20-ᵇ4] 260a-b; BK III,
CH 1 [200ᵇ32-201ᵃ3] 278b; BK IV, CH 3 [210ᵃ
17-19] 289a; BK VII, CH 4 330d-333a esp
[249ᵃ8-ᵇ26] 332a-333a / *Heavens*, BK IV, CH 4
[312ᵃ12-17] 403d / *Generation and Corruption*,
BK I, CH 3 413c-416c / *Metaphysics*, BK III, CH
1 [995ᵇ27-31] 514b; CH 3 517a-518a; BK V,
CH 3 [1014ᵇ3-13] 534d; CH 7 [1017ᵃ24-31]
537d-538a; CH 8 538b-c; CH 13-15 541b-543a;
CH 19-21 543d-544b; CH 25 [1023ᵇ22-25]
545c; CH 28 [1024ᵇ10-16] 546c; BK VII, CH 3
[1029ᵃ11-26] 551c-d; CH 12-13 561b-563a; BK
VIII, CH 6 569d-570d; BK IX, CH 1 [1045ᵇ27-
33] 570b; BK XI, CH 1 [1059ᵇ21-1060ᵃ1] 587d-
588a; BK XIV, CH 1 [1088ᵃ23-ᵇ4] 620c-d; CH 2
[1089ᵃ6-1090ᵃ3] 621b-622c / *Soul*, BK I, CH 1
[402ᵃ23-25] 631b-c; CH 5 [410ᵃ12-23] 640a-b

9 ARISTOTLE: *Parts of Animals*, BK I, CH 3 [642ᵇ
20-643ᵃ28] 166a-d

18 AUGUSTINE: *Christian Doctrine*, BK III, CH 34,
670c-671a

19 AQUINAS: *Summa Theologica*, PART I, Q 3, A
4, REP 1 16d-17c; A 5 17c-18b; A 6, REP 2 18c-
19a; Q 5, A 3, REP 1 25a-d; A 6, REP 1 27c-28b;
Q 11, A 1, REP 1 46d-47d; Q 12, A 9, REP 2 58b-
59a; Q 13, A 7, ANS 68d-70d; Q 15, A 3, REP 4
93b-94a; Q 28, A 1, ANS and REP 1-2 157c-
158d; A 2 158d-160a; Q 29, A 2, REP 4 163b-
164b; Q 30, A 4, ANS and REP 3 170c-171b; Q
50, A 2, REP 1 270a-272a; Q 66, A 2, REP 2
345d-347b; Q 76, A 3, REP 4 391a-393a; A 6,
REP 1-2 396a-d; Q 77, A 4, REP 1 403a-d; Q 85,
A 3, ANS and REP 4 455b-457a; A 4, ANS
457a-d; A 5, REP 3 457d-458d; Q 88, A 2,
REP 4 471c-472c; PART I-II, Q 18, A 7, REP 3
698c-699c; Q 35, A 8, ANS and REP 3 779c-
780c

20 AQUINAS: *Summa Theologica*, PART I-II, Q 49,
A 1 1b-2b; Q 61, A 1, REP 1 54d-55c; PART III
SUPPL, Q 92, A 1, ANS 1025c-1032b

23 HOBBES: *Leviathan*, PART I, 55b-c

30 BACON: *Novum Organum*, BK II, APH 28 158d-
159a

(4b. The classification of terms: problems in the use of different kinds of terms. 4b(3) Specific and generic terms: infimae species *and* summa genera.*)*

35 LOCKE: *Human Understanding,* BK III, CH III, SECT 8-9 256a-c; CH IV, SECT 16 263b-c; CH VI, SECT 11-12 271b-272b; SECT 32-33 277c-278c; SECT 36-41 279a-280b

38 ROUSSEAU: *Inequality,* 341b-342b

42 KANT: *Pure Reason,* 42b-43b; 193a-200c

49 DARWIN: *Origin of Species,* 30d-31b; 64a; 207a-208a esp 207d; 210b-211b; 238b-c; 241d-242a / *Descent of Man,* 332b-c; 347a-b

53 JAMES: *Psychology,* 345a-b; 870b-871a

4b(4) Univocal and analogical terms

8 ARISTOTLE: *Categories,* CH I 5a-b / *Topics,* BK I, CH 15 [107ª3-18] 151a-b; BK VI, CH 10 [148ª 23-25] 202b; [148ª38-b4] 202c; BK VIII, CH 3 [158b8-159ª2] 215b-c / *Sophistical Refutations,* CH I [165ª6-12] 227b-c; CH 33 [182b13-21] 251d / *Physics,* BK I, CH 2 [185ª20]-CH 3 [187ª 10] 260a-262a; BK VII, CH 4 [249ª3-24] 331d-332b / *Metaphysics,* BK IV, CH 2 [1003ª33-b15] 522b-c; BK VII, CH 4 [1030ª32-b3] 553a-b; BK XI, CH 3 [1060b34-1061ª10] 589a-b; BK XII, CH 4-5 599d-601a

19 AQUINAS: *Summa Theologica,* PART I, Q 3, A 6, REP I 18c-19a; Q 13, AA 5-6 66b-68c; A 10 72c-73c; Q 16, A 6, ANS 98b-d; Q 29, A 4, REP 4 165c-167a; Q 32, A I, REP 2 175d-178a

20 AQUINAS: *Summa Theologica,* PART I-II, Q 61, A I, REP I 54d-55c; PART III, Q 60, A I, ANS and REP 3 847b-848a

23 HOBBES: *Leviathan,* PART I, 57d-58a

30 BACON: *Advancement of Learning,* 60b-c / *Novum Organum,* BK I, APH 43 109d-110a; APH 59-60 112b-113a

31 SPINOZA: *Ethics,* PART II, PROP 40, SCHOL 1-2 387b-388b

35 LOCKE: *Human Understanding,* BK II, CH IV, SECT 5, 131a; CH XIII, SECT 18 152a-c; CH XXIX, SECT 6-12 234d-236c; BK III, CH VI, SECT 28 276a-b; SECT 47-51 282a-283a; CH IX 285a-291c

35 HUME: *Human Understanding,* SECT VIII, DIV 62-63 478b-d

36 STERNE: *Tristram Shandy,* 307b-308b

42 KANT: *Judgement,* 547b-548c; 602b-603a

53 JAMES: *Psychology,* 549b-550a; 689a-b

4c. The correlation, opposition, and order of terms

7 PLATO: *Protagoras,* 49a-50b / *Phaedo,* 226d-227a; 242d-245c / *Republic,* BK IV, 350c-353d esp 351b-352b; BK VII, 392b-393b / *Sophist,* 573b-574a

8 ARISTOTLE: *Categories,* CH 5 [3b24-31] 8a; CH 6 [5b11-6ª18] 10a-c; CH 7 11a-13d; CH 8 [10b11-25] 15d; CH 10-15 16d-21d / *Prior Analytics,* BK I, CH 46 70b-71d / *Topics,* BK II, CH 7-8

158b-160a; BK IV, CH 3 [123b1-124ª10] 171d-172c; CH 4 [124ª35-b34] 173a-d; [125ª5-b14] 173d-174c; BK V, CH 6 187a-188c; BK VI, CH 8 200b-201a; CH 9 [147ª23-148ª9] 201b-202a; CH 12 [149b4-23] 203d-204a / *Physics,* BK III, CH I [201ª4-8] 278c / *Metaphysics,* BK IV, CH 2 [1004ª9-17] 523a-b; [1004b27-1005ª2] 523d-524a; BK V, CH 10 539a-c; CH 15 542a-543a; BK IX, CH I [1046ª29-36] 571b; CH 2 [1046b 7-15] 571c-d; BK X, CH 3 [1054b23]-CH 10 [1059ª15] 581c-586d; BK XI, CH 3 [1061ª18-28] 589b-c; BK XII, CH 10 [1075b20-24] 606c

19 AQUINAS: *Summa Theologica,* PART I, Q 13, A 7 68d-70d; Q 16, AA 3-4 96b-97c; Q 17, A I, ANS 100d-101d; A 4, ANS 103c-104b; Q 28 157c-161d passim; Q 32, A 2, ANS 178a-179b; Q 33, A 4, REP 1-3 183c-185a; QQ 40-41 213a-224a passim; Q 48, A I, ANS and REP I 259b-260c; A 3, REP 3 261b-262a; Q 49, A 3, ANS and REP I 266d-268a,c; Q 103, A 3, REP 2 530a-c; A 8, REP 3 533d-534b; PART I-II, Q 18, A 8, REP I 699d-700b; Q 29, A 2, REP I 745c-746b; Q 35, A 4, ANS and REP 2 774d-775d; Q 36, A I, ANS 780c-781b; Q 46, A I, REP 2 813b-814a

20 AQUINAS: *Summa Theologica,* PART I-II, Q 64, A 3, REP 3 68b-69b; Q 67, A 3, ANS 83b-84d; Q 71, A 6, REP I 110b-111b; Q 72, A 6 116b-117a; PART II-II, Q 21, A 3, REP 2-3 479c-480b

23 HOBBES: *Leviathan,* PART I, 57b-c; 58a-c

24 RABELAIS: *Gargantua and Pantagruel,* BK I, 12d-13b

53 JAMES: *Psychology,* 869a-872b; 878a-879b

5. Ideas or concepts in the process of thought

5a. Concept and judgment: the division of terms as subjects and predicates; kinds of subjects and predicates

8 ARISTOTLE: *Categories,* CH 2-3 5b-d; CH 5 [2ª11-3b24] 6a-8a / *Interpretation* 25a-36d / *Prior Analytics,* BK I, CH 27 [43ª25-44] 60c-d / *Posterior Analytics,* BK I, CH 4 100a-101b; CH 19 [81b23-30] 111d / *Topics,* BK I, CH 4-9 144b-147b / *Physics,* BK I, CH 3 [186ª22-187ª10] 261b-262a; CH 6 [189ª28-33] 264d

18 AUGUSTINE: *Confessions,* BK IV, par 28-29 26a-b

19 AQUINAS: *Summa Theologica,* PART I, Q 2, A I, ANS 10d-11d; Q 3, A 4, REP 2 16d-17c; Q 13, A 12 74c-75b; Q 16, A 2 95c-96b; Q 58, A 2 301b-d; A 4 302d-303c; Q 76, A 3, ANS 391a-393a; Q 85, A 2, REP 3 453d-455b; AA 5-6 457d-459c; A 8, ANS 460b-461b

23 HOBBES: *Leviathan,* PART IV, 270a-c

31 DESCARTES: *Rules,* XII, 22a-b / *Meditations,* III, 83a / *Objections and Replies,* DEF IX 130d

42 KANT: *Pure Reason,* 39a-44c; 51d-52b; 59c-66d esp 63d-64a; 180c-182b / *Judgement,* 480d-482b; 562a-d; 572b-575b

53 JAMES: *Psychology,* 144a-b; 178a-179a; 313a-b; 638b; 861b; 870b-873a

(6. The being and truth of ideas. 6a. The distinction between real and intentional existence, between thing and idea: ideas as symbols, or intentions of the mind.)

19 AQUINAS: *Summa Theologica*, PART I, Q 2, A I, REP 2 10d-11d; Q 3, A 4, REP 2 16d-17c; Q 5, A 2, ANS 24b-25a; Q II, A I esp REP 3 46d-47d; A 3, REP 2 49a-c; Q 12, A 2 51c-52c; Q 13, A I, ANS 62c-63c; A 3, ANS and REP 3 64d-65c; A 4 65c-66b; A 7, ANS and REP 2,4-6 68d-70d; A 9, ANS and REP 2 71b-72c; A II, ANS 73c-74b; A 12 74c-75b; Q 14, A I, ANS and REP 3 75d-76c; A 2, ANS and REP 2-3 76d-77d; A 6, REP I 80a-81c; A 8, ANS 82c-83b; A 9, ANS 83b-d; A 13, REP 2-3 86d-88c; Q 15, A I, ANS and REP 1,3 91b-92a; A 3, REP 4 93b-94a; Q 16, A 2 95c-96b; A 7, REP 2 99a-d; Q 17, A 3, ANS 102d-103c; Q 18, A 4 107d-108c; Q 19, A 3, REP 6 110b-111c; Q 27, A I, ANS and REP 2 153b-154b; A 2, ANS and REP 2 154c-155b; A 3, ANS 155c-156a; A 4, ANS and REP 2 156b-d; Q 28 157c-161d passim; Q 29, A I, REP 3 162a-163b; Q 30, A I, REP 4 167a-168a; A 4 170c-171b; Q 32, AA 2-3 178a-180b; Q 34, A I 185b-187b; A 3, ANS 188b-189a; Q 37, A I, ANS 197c-199a; Q 50, A 2, ANS 270a-272a; QQ 55-58 288d-306b passim; Q 66, A 2, REP 2 345d-347b; Q 67, A 3, ANS 351b-352a; Q 74, A 3, REP 5 375a-377a,c; Q 76, A 3, REP 4 391a-393a; A 6, REP 2 396a-d; Q 78, A 3, ANS 410a-411d; A 4, ANS and REP 2 411d-413d; Q 79, A 4, REP 4 417a-418c; Q 82, A 3, ANS 433c-434c; Q 84 440b-451b; Q 85, A 2 453d-455b; A 3, REP 1,4 455b-457a; A 4 457a-d; A 5, REP 3 457d-458d; A 8, REP 3 460b-461b; Q 86, A I, ANS 461c-462a; Q 87, A I 465a-466c; Q 88, A I, REP 2 469a-471c; A 2, REP 4 471c-472c; Q 89, A 2, ANS and REP 2 475a-d; A 3, ANS and REP 1,3 475d-476c; A 5, ANS 477a-478b; PART I-II, Q 5, A 6, REP 2 641a-642a; Q 6, A 6, ANS and REP 2 649a-650a; Q 8, A I, ANS and REP 3 655b-656a; Q 12, A 3, REP 2-3 670d-671b; Q 17, A 4, ANS 688d-689c; Q 22, A 2, ANS and REP 3 721c-722c; Q 28, A I, REP 3 740b-741a

20 AQUINAS: *Summa Theologica*, PART I-II, Q 93, A I, REP 2 215b,d-216c; PART III, Q 2, A 5, REP 2 715a-716b; PART III SUPPL, Q 82, A 3, ANS and REP 2 971a-972d

23 HOBBES: *Leviathan*, PART I, 53c; PART III, 172a-d; PART IV, 262a-d; 270a-c

26 SHAKESPEARE: *Richard II*, ACT V, SC V [1-41] 349d-350a

29 CERVANTES: *Don Quixote* esp PART I, 1a-8c, 18d-22a, PART II, 285a-288c

31 DESCARTES: *Meditations*, 71d-72a; III, 83b-86a; V, 93a-94a / *Objections and Replies*, 108b-109d; 121a-c; DEF I-IV 130a-b; AXIOM V-VI 131d-132a; 157b-158a; 212c-213a

31 SPINOZA: *Ethics*, PART I, APPENDIX 369b-372d esp 371c-372c; PART II, PROP 5-9 374c-376c

35 LOCKE: *Human Understanding*, BK II, CH VIII 133b-138b passim, esp SECT 8 134b-c; CH

XXII, SECT 2 201a-b; CH XXX, SECT 2 238b-c; CH XXXI, SECT 2 239b-d; CH XXXII, SECT 8 244d; SECT 14-18 245c-247a; BK III, CH III, SECT 12-20 257b-260a; CH IV, SECT 2 260b; CH V, SECT 12 266d-267a; CH VI 268b-283a passim; BK IV, CH II, SECT 14 312b-d; CH IX, SECT I 349a; CH XI, SECT 4-9 355b-357a

35 BERKELEY: *Human Knowledge*, SECT 1-96 413a-431d esp SECT 1-24 413a-417d, SECT 29-44 418c-421a, SECT 48-49 422a-b, SECT 82-84 428d-429c, SECT 86-91 429c-431a

35 HUME: *Human Understanding*, SECT V, DIV 44 468d-469c; SECT XII, DIV 117-123 504a-506a

42 KANT: *Pure Reason*, 23a-33d; 85d-93c; 95a-d; 97a-b; 117b-118a; 200c-209d; 211c-212a / *Practical Reason*, 295b-d / *Judgement*, 528c-d; 551a-553c; 604a-b

44 BOSWELL: *Johnson*, 134c-d

46 HEGEL: *Philosophy of Right*, PREF, 6a-7a / *Philosophy of History*, INTRO, 153a-c; 158a-160b; 188d-189a; PART I, 219d-220a; 236a-c; 257c-d; PART IV, 354b; 364b-c

48 MELVILLE: *Moby Dick*, 385b

50 MARX: *Capital*, 11b-c

53 JAMES: *Psychology*, 128a-b; 142a-b; 176a-184a passim, esp 176a-b, 178a-181a; 191b-192a; 299a-302a esp 302b [fn I]; 307a-311a esp 311b-312b [fn I]; 639a-645b esp 640a; 659a-b; 852a; 865a-866a; 868b; 878a-882a esp 880b-882a; 889a-890a

54 FREUD: *General Introduction*, 467d; 597d-598a

6b. The nature and being of ideas in relation to the nature and being of the mind

7 PLATO: *Cratylus*, 113c-114a,c / *Phaedrus*, 125a-b / *Republic*, BK V, 369a-373c; BK VI, 383d-388a / *Timaeus*, 457b-458a / *Parmenides*, 486a-491d / *Sophist*, 567a-569a

8 ARISTOTLE: *Soul*, BK III, CH 4 661b-662c

12 LUCRETIUS: *Nature of Things*, BK IV [722-817] 53d-54d

18 AUGUSTINE: *Confessions*, BK X, par 16-38 75b-81a / *City of God*, BK VIII, CH 6, 269b-c / *Christian Doctrine*, BK III, CH 38, 654c

19 AQUINAS: *Summa Theologica*, PART I, Q 15, A I esp REP I 91b-92a; Q 16, A 7, REP 2 99a-d; Q 29, A 2, REP 4 163b-164b; Q 76, A 2, REP 3 388c-391a; Q 79, A 3, ANS 416a-417a; Q 84, A I, ANS 440d-442a; QQ 85-89 451b-480c passim; Q 110, A I, REP 3 564c-565d

23 HOBBES: *Leviathan*, PART I, 49a

30 BACON: *Advancement of Learning*, 43d-44c

31 DESCARTES: *Objections and Replies*, 162b; 212c-213a

31 SPINOZA: *Ethics*, PART II, DEF 3 373b; PROP II, DEMONST 377b; PROP 49, SCHOL, 392a-c

35 LOCKE: *Human Understanding*, BK I, CH I, SECT 15 98d-99a; BK II, CH VIII 133b-138b passim; CH XXII, SECT 2 201a-b; CH XXX 238a-239b passim, esp SECT 2-3 238b-d; CH XXXI, SECT 2 239b-d; CH XXXII, SECT 14-16 245c-246b; BK III, CH V 263d-268a; CH VI, SECT 26-

51 274d-283a passim; ʙᴋ ɪᴠ, ᴄʜ ɪᴠ, sᴇᴄᴛ 4–5 324c-d; sᴇᴄᴛ 11–12 326b-d; ᴄʜ xɪ, sᴇᴄᴛ 4–9 355b-357a

35 Bᴇʀᴋᴇʟᴇʏ: *Human Knowledge* 404a-444d esp sᴇᴄᴛ 2–4 413b-414a, sᴇᴄᴛ 25–33 417d-419a, sᴇᴄᴛ 48–49 422a-b, sᴇᴄᴛ 86–91 429c-431a

42 Kᴀɴᴛ: *Pure Reason*, 14c-15c; 34a-35b; 113c-118a; 173b-174a; 179c-182b / *Fund. Prin. Metaphysic of Morals*, 281c-282d; 285a-287d / *Judgement*, 461a-462d; 542b-544c; 551a-552c; 604a-b

46 Hᴇɢᴇʟ: *Philosophy of Right*, ᴘʀᴇꜰ, 6a-7a / *Philosophy of History*, ɪɴᴛʀᴏ, 165a-b

50 Mᴀʀx: *Capital*, 11b-c

53 Jᴀᴍᴇs: *Psychology*, 104a-115a passim, esp 105b-106b, 110a-b, 113a-115a; 149b-154a esp 151b-153b; 325a-327a esp 326a-b [fn 1]; 394a-b

54 Fʀᴇᴜᴅ: *Unconscious*, 430d-432c esp 431c-432c; 442b-443a

6c. The agreement between an idea and its object: the criterion of adequacy in correspondence

31 Dᴇsᴄᴀʀᴛᴇs: *Meditations*, ɪɪɪ, 83a; 84a-85a; ᴠɪ, 99a-c / *Objections and Replies*, 108b-109d; 121a-c; ᴅᴇꜰ ɪ–ɪɪɪ 130a-b; ᴀxɪᴏᴍ ᴠ–ᴠɪ 131d-132a; 153a-c; 157b-158a

31 Sᴘɪɴᴏᴢᴀ: *Ethics*, ᴘᴀʀᴛ ɪ, ᴀxɪᴏᴍ 6 355d; ᴘᴀʀᴛ ɪɪ, ᴅᴇꜰ 1–4 373a-b; ᴘʀᴏᴘ 24–40 383c-388b; ᴘʀᴏᴘ 43 388c-389b; ᴘᴀʀᴛ ɪᴠ, ᴘʀᴏᴘ ɪ 424c-425a

35 Lᴏᴄᴋᴇ: *Human Understanding*, ʙᴋ ɪɪ, ᴄʜ ᴠɪɪɪ 133b-138b passim, esp sᴇᴄᴛ 2 133c, sᴇᴄᴛ 7 134b, sᴇᴄᴛ 15 135c; ᴄʜ xxɪɪɪ, sᴇᴄᴛ 8–11 206a-207a passim; sᴇᴄᴛ 37, 214a-b; ᴄʜ xxx-xxxɪ 238a-243c; ᴄʜ xxxɪɪ, sᴇᴄᴛ 8 244d; sᴇᴄᴛ 13–18 245c-247a passim; ʙᴋ ɪɪɪ, ᴄʜ ᴠɪ, sᴇᴄᴛ 9 270d-271a; sᴇᴄᴛ 28–31 276a-277c passim; sᴇᴄᴛ 37 279b; sᴇᴄᴛ 40 280a-b; sᴇᴄᴛ 46–47 281c-282b; ᴄʜ xɪ, sᴇᴄᴛ 24 305b-d; ʙᴋ ɪᴠ, ᴄʜ ɪᴠ, sᴇᴄᴛ 1–12 323d-326d esp sᴇᴄᴛ 3 324b-c

35 Hᴜᴍᴇ: *Human Understanding*, sᴇᴄᴛ ᴠ, ᴅɪᴠ 44 468d-469c esp 469b-c

42 Kᴀɴᴛ: *Pure Reason*, 36b-37a; 77b-d; 85d-88a esp 86b-87c; 91d-93c

45 Lᴀᴠᴏɪsɪᴇʀ: *Elements of Chemistry*, ᴘʀᴇꜰ, 1b-c

48 Mᴇʟᴠɪʟʟᴇ: *Moby Dick*, 231a

53 Jᴀᴍᴇs: *Psychology*, 141a-142a; 301b-302a; 307a-b; 480b-484a

54 Fʀᴇᴜᴅ: *Unconscious*, 430b-c

6d. Clarity and distinctness in ideas as criteria of their truth

31 Dᴇsᴄᴀʀᴛᴇs: *Meditations*, 73d-74a; ɪɪɪ, 82a-d; 85b-86d; ɪᴠ, 89a-b; ᴠ 93a-96a esp 93a-94a; ᴠɪ, 99a-c / *Objections and Replies*, 120a-c; ᴘᴏsᴛᴜʟᴀᴛᴇ ᴠɪ–ᴠɪɪ 131c; 210b-c; 237c-238b

31 Sᴘɪɴᴏᴢᴀ: *Ethics*, ᴘᴀʀᴛ ɪɪ, ᴅᴇꜰ 4 373b; ᴘʀᴏᴘ 24–40 383c-388b; ᴘᴀʀᴛ ᴠ, ᴘʀᴏᴘ 4, ᴄᴏʀᴏʟ and sᴄʜᴏʟ 453b-d

35 Lᴏᴄᴋᴇ: *Human Understanding*, 91d-92c; ʙᴋ ɪɪ, ᴄʜ xɪɪɪ, sᴇᴄᴛ 11 150d-151b; ᴄʜ xxɪɪɪ, sᴇᴄᴛ 32, 212d; ᴄʜ xxɪx 233d-238a

35 Bᴇʀᴋᴇʟᴇʏ: *Human Knowledge*, sᴇᴄᴛ 30 418c; sᴇᴄᴛ 33 419a; sᴇᴄᴛ 36 419c-d

35 Hᴜᴍᴇ: *Human Understanding*, sᴇᴄᴛ xɪɪ, ᴅɪᴠ 125 506d-507a

6e. The criterion of genesis: the test of an idea's truth or meaning by reference to its origin

12 Lᴜᴄʀᴇᴛɪᴜs: *Nature of Things*, ʙᴋ ɪ [690–700] 9c; ʙᴋ ɪᴠ [469–521] 50b-51a

23 Hᴏʙʙᴇs: *Leviathan*, ᴘᴀʀᴛ ɪ, 49a; 54b-c

30 Bᴀᴄᴏɴ: *Advancement of Learning*, 16a; 43d-44c; 57d-58b

31 Dᴇsᴄᴀʀᴛᴇs: *Meditations*, ᴠɪ, 99a-c

35 Lᴏᴄᴋᴇ: *Human Understanding*, ʙᴋ ɪɪ, ᴄʜ xxx, sᴇᴄᴛ 2 238b-c; ʙᴋ ɪᴠ, ᴄʜ ɪᴠ, sᴇᴄᴛ 4 324c

35 Bᴇʀᴋᴇʟᴇʏ: *Human Knowledge*, sᴇᴄᴛ 29–30 418c; sᴇᴄᴛ 33 419a; sᴇᴄᴛ 36 419c-d; sᴇᴄᴛ 82–84 428d-429c; sᴇᴄᴛ 86–91 429c-431a

35 Hᴜᴍᴇ: *Human Understanding*, sᴇᴄᴛ 11 455b-457b; sᴇᴄᴛ ᴠɪɪ, ᴅɪᴠ 49 471c-d

50 Mᴀʀx-Eɴɢᴇʟs: *Communist Manifesto*, 427a-b; 428b-d

6f. The truth and falsity of simple apprehensions, sensations, or conceptions: contrasted with the truth and falsity of judgments or assertions

7 Pʟᴀᴛᴏ: *Cratylus*, 85a-86b; 107c-108b / *Republic*, ʙᴋ ᴠɪɪ, 392b-393b / *Sophist*, 575d-577b

8 Aʀɪsᴛᴏᴛʟᴇ: *Categories*, ᴄʜ 4 [2^a4–10] 6a / *Interpretation*, ᴄʜ 1 [16^a9–18] 25a-b / *Metaphysics*, ʙᴋ ɪᴠ, ᴄʜ 5 [1010^b14–29] 530b-c; ʙᴋ ᴠ, ᴄʜ 29 [1024^b27–38] 546d-547a; ʙᴋ ᴠɪ, ᴄʜ 4 [1027^b18–28] 550a,c; ʙᴋ ɪx, ᴄʜ 10 577c-578a,c; ʙᴋ xɪɪɪ, ᴄʜ 3 [1078^a14–32] 609c-d / *Soul*, ʙᴋ ɪɪ, ᴄʜ 6 [418^a6–18] 648d-649a; ʙᴋ ɪɪɪ, ᴄʜ 3 [427^b6–15] 659d-660a; [428^a5–429^a2] 660b-661a; ᴄʜ 6 662d-663c

12 Lᴜᴄʀᴇᴛɪᴜs: *Nature of Things*, ʙᴋ ɪᴠ [324–521] 48c-51a esp [469–521] 50b-51a

19 Aǫᴜɪɴᴀs: *Summa Theologica*, ᴘᴀʀᴛ ɪ, ǫ 16, ᴀ 2 95c-96b; ǫ 17, ᴀᴀ 2–3 102a-103c; ǫ 58, ᴀ 4, ᴀɴs 302d-303c; ǫ 85, ᴀ 1, ʀᴇᴘ 1 451c-453c; ᴀ 6 458d-459c; ǫ 89, ᴀ 5, ᴀɴs 477a-478b; ǫ 94, ᴀ 4 505a-506a

23 Hᴏʙʙᴇs: *Leviathan*, ᴘᴀʀᴛ ɪ, 56b

30 Bᴀᴄᴏɴ: *Advancement of Learning*, 57d-58b / *Novum Organum*, ʙᴋ ɪ, ᴀᴘʜ 14 107d-108a

31 Dᴇsᴄᴀʀᴛᴇs: *Rules*, xɪɪ 18b-25a passim / *Discourse*, ᴘᴀʀᴛ ɪᴠ, 52a / *Meditations*, ɪɪɪ, 83a; ɪᴠ 89a-93a / *Objections and Replies*, 123d-125c; 157b-158a; 215d-216c; 229d-230d

31 Sᴘɪɴᴏᴢᴀ: *Ethics*, ᴘᴀʀᴛ ɪɪ, ᴘʀᴏᴘ 32–35 385c-386b; ᴘʀᴏᴘ 49, sᴄʜᴏʟ, 392a-d

35 Lᴏᴄᴋᴇ: *Human Understanding*, ʙᴋ ɪɪ, ᴄʜ xxxɪɪ 243c-248b; ʙᴋ ɪɪɪ, ᴄʜ ᴠɪɪ, sᴇᴄᴛ 1 283a-b; ʙᴋ ɪᴠ, ᴄʜ ᴠ 329a-331b; ᴄʜ ᴠɪ, sᴇᴄᴛ 16 336d

42 Kᴀɴᴛ: *Pure Reason*, 36b-37d; 64d-65c; 108a-d; 179c-180c; 193a-b; 211c-218d / *Judgement*, 570b-571c

53 Jᴀᴍᴇs: *Psychology*, 299a-314b passim; 638b; 640b; 668a-671a

CROSS-REFERENCES

For: The theory of Ideas as eternal forms existing apart from mind and matter, *see* CHANGE 15a; ETERNITY 4c; FORM 1a, 2a–2b; UNIVERSAL AND PARTICULAR 2a.

The theory of ideas as universal conceptions abstracted from the materials of sense, *see* FORM 3a–3b; MEMORY AND IMAGINATION 5b, 6c(1); SENSE 5a; UNIVERSAL AND PARTICULAR 2b, 4c–4d; and for abstraction in relation to generalization and induction, *see* EXPERIENCE 2b; INDUCTION 1a, 3.

The theory of ideas as sense impressions or sense images, *see* MEMORY AND IMAGINATION 1a, 5a; SENSE 1d, 5a.

The doctrine of innate ideas and the related theory of reminiscence and intuitive knowledge, *see* KNOWLEDGE 6c(3); MEMORY AND IMAGINATION 3a; MIND 4d(2).

The theory of the transcendental concepts or ideas as constitutive or regulative principles, *see* FORM 1c, 3a; KNOWLEDGE 6b(4), 6c(4); MIND 4d(3); PRINCIPLE 2b(3); and for the dialectical employment of the ideas of pure reason, *see* DIALECTIC 2c(2).

The theory of the Absolute Idea, *see* HISTORY 4a(3); MIND 10f–10f(2).

The theory of the divine ideas as eternal exemplars, or of the ideas infused into angelic intellects, *see* ANGEL 3d; FORM 2b; GOD 5f; KNOWLEDGE 7a–7b; MIND 10e, 10g; UNIVERSAL AND PARTICULAR 4b.

The issue concerning the distinction of, and the relation between, sense and intellect, *see* BEING 8a–8b; KNOWLEDGE 6a(1), 6b–6b(4); MEMORY AND IMAGINATION 5b, 6b, 6d; MIND 1–1g(3); SENSE 1a–1b, 4a, 5c.

Another discussion of the distinction between first and second intentions, and of the related distinction between first and second impositions, *see* SIGN AND SYMBOL 2a–2b.

Other discussions of adequate and inadequate, or clear and distinct ideas, *see* KNOWLEDGE 6d(3); OPINION 3b; TRUTH 1a; and for other considerations of mental fictions or chimeras, *see* BEING 7d(5); MEMORY AND IMAGINATION 5a.

The consideration of the expression of ideas in words or terms, *see* LANGUAGE 1a, 7; SIGN AND SYMBOL 1f; for the distinction of concrete and abstract terms, *see* SIGN AND SYMBOL 2e; for the distinction of particular and universal terms, *see* SIGN AND SYMBOL 2d; UNIVERSAL AND PARTICULAR 5c; for the distinction of species and genera, *see* RELATION 5a(4); SAME AND OTHER 3a(1); UNIVERSAL AND PARTICULAR 5b; and for the distinction between univocal, equivocal, and analogical terms, *see* RELATION 1d; SAME AND OTHER 3b, 4c; SIGN AND SYMBOL 3d.

The treatment of the definition of terms as the expression or analysis of concepts, *see* DEFINITION 1, 1b.

The correlation and opposition of concepts or terms, *see* OPPOSITION 1a–1b; RELATION 1c, 4e.

The role played by concepts in the acts of judgment and reasoning, or for terms in relation to propositions and syllogisms, *see* JUDGMENT 5b–5c; REASONING 2a(1).

Other discussions of the association of ideas, *see* MEMORY AND IMAGINATION 2c; MIND 1g(1); RELATION 4f.

The metaphysical problem of the being of ideas, and for the theory of intentional existence, *see* BEING 7d–7d(5); SIGN AND SYMBOL 1b; UNIVERSAL AND PARTICULAR 2c.

Another consideration of the truth or reality of ideas, *see* TRUTH 3b(1).

ADDITIONAL READINGS

Listed below are works not included in *Great Books of the Western World*, but relevant to the idea and topics with which this chapter deals. These works are divided into two groups:

I. Works by authors represented in this collection.
II. Works by authors not represented in this collection.

For the date, place, and other facts concerning the publication of the works cited, consult the Bibliography of Additional Readings which follows the last chapter of *The Great Ideas*.

I.

AQUINAS. *On the Trinity of Boethius*, QQ 5–6
——. *Quaestiones Disputatae, De Veritate*, Q 3
——. *De Natura Verbi Intellectus*
DESCARTES. *The Principles of Philosophy*, PART I, 9–10, 45–47
SPINOZA. *Of the Improvement of the Understanding*
HUME. *A Treatise of Human Nature*, BK I, PART I
BERKELEY. *Siris*
KANT. *Prolegomena to Any Future Metaphysic*, par 39, 56
HEGEL. *The Phenomenology of Mind*
——. *Science of Logic*, VOL II, SECT I, CH I; SECT III, CH I(C), 3
——. *Logic*, CH 9
J. S. MILL. *A System of Logic*, BK IV, CH 2
W. JAMES. *Some Problems of Philosophy*, CH 4–6

II.

CICERO. *Academics*
PHILO JUDAEUS. *On the Creation of the World (De Opificio Mundi)*, par 16
PORPHYRY. *Introduction to Aristotle's Predicaments*
BOETHIUS. *In Isagogem Porphyrii Commenta*
ERIGENA. *De Divisione Naturae*, BK III
JOHN OF SALISBURY. *Metalogicon*, BK II, CH 17
BONAVENTURA. *On the Reduction of the Arts to Theology*
DUNS SCOTUS. *Opus Oxoniense*, BK I, DIST 35 (I)
CAJETAN. *De Nominum Analogia*
——. *De Conceptu Entis*
SUÁREZ. *Disputationes Metaphysicae*, XXV
JOHN OF SAINT THOMAS. *Cursus Philosophicus Thomisticus, Ars Logica*, PART II, QQ 3–5, 23
ARNAULD. *Logic or the Art of Thinking*, PART I
MALEBRANCHE. *De la recherche de la vérité*, BK III (II), CH 1–8
——. *Dialogues on Metaphysics and Religion*, III
LEIBNITZ. *What Is "Idea"?*
——. *Discourse on Metaphysics*, XXIV–XXIX
——. *Philosophical Works*, CH 3 (*Thoughts on Knowledge, Truth and Ideas*)

LEIBNITZ. *New Essays Concerning Human Understanding*, BK I; BK II, CH 1–8, 12, 30–33
VOLTAIRE. "Idea," in *A Philosophical Dictionary*
T. REID. *Essays on the Intellectual Powers of Man*, IV–V
J. G. FICHTE. *The Science of Knowledge*
COLERIDGE. *Biographia Literaria*, CH 5–8
SCHOPENHAUER. *The World as Will and Idea*, VOL I, BK I, III; VOL II, SUP, CH 14; VOL III, SUP, CH 29
J. MILL. *Analysis of the Phenomena of the Human Mind*, CH 2–3, 6, 9
W. HAMILTON. *Lectures on Metaphysics and Logic*, VOL I (34–36); VOL II (7–12)
WHEWELL. *The Philosophy of the Inductive Sciences*, VOL I, BK I, CH 7
SIGWART. *Logic*, PART I, CH I; PART II, CH I; PART III, CH 1–2
LOTZE. *Microcosmos*, BK II, CH 3
——. *Logic*, BK I, CH I
C. S. PEIRCE. *Collected Papers*, VOL V, par 388–410
VENN. *Principles of Empirical or Inductive Logic*, CH 7
RIBOT. *The Evolution of General Ideas*
ROYCE. *The World and the Individual*, SERIES I(7)
CROCE. *Logic as the Science of Pure Concept*
TITCHENER. *Lectures on the Experimental Psychology of the Thought-Processes*
CASSIRER. *Substance and Function*, PART I, CH I
HUSSERL. *Logische Untersuchungen*
——. *Ideas: General Introduction to Pure Phenomenology*
BRADLEY. *The Principles of Logic*, BK II, PART II, CH I
——. *Collected Essays*, VOL I(12)
——. *Essays on Truth and Reality*, CH 3
DEWEY. *Essays in Experimental Logic*, VII–VIII
——. *The Quest for Certainty*, CH 5–6
WHITEHEAD. *Science and the Modern World*, CH 10
——. *Process and Reality*, PART I
MARITAIN. *Réflexions sur l'intelligence et sur la vie propre*, CH I
——. *An Introduction to Logic*, CH I
——. *The Degrees of Knowledge*, CH 2
BLONDEL. *La pensée*

Chapter 38: IMMORTALITY

INTRODUCTION

THE mortality of man defines by contrast the immortality which some men hope for, some men fear, some men scoff at, but no man ever fails sooner or later to consider. The life of man, like that of other animals, moves through a normal span of years between birth and death. Legend tells of certain heroes upon whom the immortal gods bestowed immortal life, gracing them with an aspect of their own divinity. Jewish and Christian faith holds that Adam, with all his posterity, would never have suffered disease or death if he had refrained from sin. But according to the theologians, the imperishability of the bodily frame of man in a state of grace is a preternatural condition. Except, then, for the miraculous or the supernatural, death follows birth and life, that which comes to be passes away, all things of flesh and blood perish.

The proposition "All men are mortal" has been repeated during centuries of lessons in logic. Its truth has never been seriously challenged even by those who have criticized the syllogism which reaches the conclusion that since he is a man, Socrates is mortal. But throughout the same period, the great books of poetry and religion, of philosophy and theology, have recorded the qualifications which men have placed upon this truth.

Man dies in the flesh to be reborn in the spirit. Man, composite of soul and body, perishes as do all things which are subject to dissolution; but the soul itself, a simple spiritual substance, is immortal, living on after its union with the body is dissolved. The immortal soul is sometimes conceived as having many incarnations, inhabiting now this body, now that, in an endless pilgrimage through endless time; and sometimes, as in the Christian faith, each soul has only one embodiment on earth. It is specially created by God to inform the body of a human being. It is destined to be his immortal spirit in a future which belongs to eternity rather than to time.

Except for the form it takes in the doctrine of reincarnation, or the transmigration of souls, the idea of immortality is usually attended by conceptions of an after-life in another world—the life of the shades in the Elysian Fields or in Hades, the life of the blessed in Heaven or of the damned in Hell. The after-life is never merely a continuation of the life begun on earth. The other world is not just an abode for the disembodied soul. It is a place of judgment, of rewards and punishments, in which the soul realizes the good, or pays the penalty for the evil, toward which its earthly career inclined. The connection of immortality with rewards and punishments appears even in the theory of reincarnation, for as the soul passes from one embodiment to another, it enjoys or suffers the consequences befitting its previous existence.

STATED AS A speculative problem, the question of immortality is traditionally formulated as a question about the soul or the spirit of man: whether it exists by itself either before or after its conjunction with a human body; and if so, in what manner it subsists. For those who affirm the soul's separate existence, there seems to be no question about its everlasting endurance, either without beginning at all or from the moment of its creation. But the manner of the soul's subsistence leads to speculation concerning an after-life or an other-life in a world of spirits, or in realms as far apart as Heaven and Hell.

We shall presently consider to what extent such speculations have been submitted to argument and to what extent they have been matters of religious belief. But in both these modes of consideration, the theme of immortality is never merely a matter of speculative interest, never merely a question of spiritual substances and their subsistence. It is always a problem for the moralist.

Is this earthly life and its brief temporal span enough for the aspirations of the human spirit, and for its striving toward a perfection of knowledge, of love, and of repose? If external sanctions are needed to support the voice of conscience, are earthly rewards and punishments—either humanly dispensed, or capriciously distributed by chance or fortune—sufficient sanction for the moral law? Can perfect justice be done unless there is a divine law and a divine judge, a judge who can see beyond the acts of men into their hearts, from whose judgment no one escapes, and whose rewards and punishments are supernaturally established states of blessedness and misery for the soul?

Whether or not God, freedom, and immortality are, as Kant suggests, the three great objects of speculative thought, they do seem to form the basic triad of religious beliefs. In the religions of the west, these beliefs take various forms, but the belief in immortality is seldom if ever found separate from belief in a supernatural order, in gods or a God to whom man owes certain duties and before whom man stands to be judged as a responsible moral agent who was free to obey or disobey the divine commands. But, this fact admitted, the question remains whether the principles of morality can be adequately stated, or made effective in the regulation of human conduct, without a religious foundation, or at least without reference to God and immortality.

On this the moralists disagree. The argument in Plato's *Gorgias*, for example, about whether it is better to do or suffer injustice, ends with a myth which tells of the soul standing naked before its divine judge after a man's death, showing no marks of the evil the individual has suffered during his life, but only of the evil he has done. The reader who thinks the myth is necessary to complete the argument concerning justice and punishment, takes one position on the question. He adopts the view that without the judgment of souls in an after-life justice cannot be done.

The preoccupation with immortality in a great many of Plato's dialogues is not always based upon moral considerations. It appears as frequently in discussions of the relation between the soul and the objects of its knowledge. If, to be proper objects of knowledge, the Ideas must be eternal, the soul which knows them must also be immortal. But when the discussion of immortality involves a comparison of this life and the life to come, it usually turns on considerations of goodness rather than of knowledge and truth. For Kant, if not for Plato, immortality is almost entirely a moral matter; and where the Platonic myth deals with just rewards and punishments in an after-life, the Kantian argument is concerned with the achievement of moral perfection.

In his *Critique of Practical Reason*, Kant affirms immortality, along with the existence of God and the freedom of the will, as necessary practical postulates—indispensable conditions of the moral life. "The perfect accordance of the will with the moral law," Kant writes, "is *holiness*, a perfection of which no rational being of the sensible world is capable at any moment of his existence ... It can only be found in a progress *in infinitum* towards that perfect accordance ... It is necessary to assume such a practical progress as the real object of our will." The realization of happiness, or the *summum bonum*, Kant concludes, "is only possible practically on the supposition of the immortality of the soul."

The opposite view appears to be taken in Aristotle's *Ethics* and Mill's *Utilitarianism*. The *summum bonum* is a temporal happiness, a perfection attainable on earth and by purely natural means. In those passages in which Aristotle defines happiness in terms of contemplative activity, he also speaks of it as a godlike life and therefore one which has a touch of immortality. Man is able to lead such a life, he writes, only "in so far as something divine is present in him." To lead the life of reason, which is divine in comparison with any other mode of human life, we must, he says, "so far as we can, make ourselves immortal, and strain every nerve to live in accordance with the best thing in us."

But to be immortal in this way seems to mean the possession of a godlike quality in this life rather than the promise of a life hereafter.

Aristotle demands only "a complete term of life" as a necessary condition for "the complete happiness of man." He passes lightly over the question whether "the dead share in any good or evil." So far as he considers a *blessedness* which the gods can add to human happiness, it does not belong to an after-life, but consists rather in the good fortune which the gods grant to some men and which increases and secures their happiness beyond that which is attainable by virtue alone.

The moral issue concerning immortality is more explicitly faced by Mill in his examination of the need for religious or supernatural sanctions. While he does not admit their indispensability, neither does he deny their utility. "There is evidently no reason," he declares, "why all these motives for observance should not attach themselves to the utilitarian morality, as completely and as powerfully as to any other." Yet he himself stresses "the possibility of giving to the service of humanity, even without the aid of belief in a Providence, both the psychological power and the social efficacy of a religion."

Mill does not go as far as Lucretius in regarding the belief in immortality, with the attendant possibility of everlasting torment for the soul, as itself an immoral doctrine. For Lucretius it is a nightmare which haunts the waking hours of men, filling them with false fears and putting future pains in the way of present pleasures. He dedicates his poem to "driving headlong forth that dread of Acheron, troubling as it does the life of man from its inmost depths and overspreading all things with the blackness of death, allowing no pleasure to be pure and unalloyed."

Where others see in man's fear of death his natural desire for immortality, Lucretius thinks it is the dread of immortality which causes man's fear of death. "We have nothing to fear after death," he says, if death is the end. "He who exists not, cannot become miserable."

In the great poems of antiquity we find the imagery and detail of the pagan conception of the life hereafter. Both Odysseus and Aeneas visit the underworld. They see the shades of the departed heroes; all that is visible to the bodily eye are shimmering wraiths. They talk with the departed, listen to their memories, or hear them speak prophetically of the future. From Anchises, his dead father, Aeneas learns his destiny; and Odysseus hears in Hades what has befallen his companions at Troy and his family at home during his years of wandering.

Yet there is a striking difference between Virgil's poem and Homer's with respect to the after-life. The division which Virgil makes between Elysium and Tartarus corresponds much more closely than anything in Homer—or for that matter in the other Greek poets—to the Christian distinction between Heaven and Hell. Though Elysium and Tartarus both belong to the underworld, one is the abode of the blessed, the other a place of torment for sinners.

In the sixth book of the *Aeneid*, the Sibyl explains the topography of the underworld to Aeneas. There is a place "where splits the road in twain," she says:

The right leads to the giant walls of Dis,
Our way to Elysium; but the left wreaks doom
On sinners, and to guilty Tartarus sends.

Tartarus, the abode of the condemned, is surrounded by "a fierce torrent of billowy fire," and is filled with the noise of punishment. Elysium, on the other hand, is

The happy region and green pleasaunces
Of the blest woodlands, the abode of joy.
An ampler ether with purpureal light
Clothes here the plain; another sun than ours,
And other stars they know.

Its inhabitants, in sharp contrast with the unfortunates in Tartarus, seem to pass their time in peace and pleasure.

Homer makes no such sharp division between the realm of the blessed and the realm of the condemned. Plutarch speaks of "the isles of the blessed celebrated by Homer," but the reference cannot be substantiated. In one passage in the *Iliad* Menelaus is promised that he will be taken "to the Elysian plain, which is at the end of the world. There fair-haired Rhadamanthus reigns, and men lead an easier life than anywhere else in the world, for in Elysium there falls not rain, nor hail, nor snow." But even this seems to describe a different life rather than an after-life.

So far as the underworld is described on the occasion of Odysseus' descent "into the house of Hades and dread Prosperine," we are told that the Theban prophet Teiresias alone has his "reason still unshaken." All "the other ghosts flit about aimlessly." The shades of good men and bad alike languish in the domain of darkness. Tityus, Tantalus, and Sisyphus are subjected to special punishments for their grievous sins and transgressions, but all the shades—even of those men whom the gods loved and honored —seem to be in a state of misery. Though they are not all beset with torments and agonies, none seems to be overcome with joy or to have reached contentment.

Those whom the gods love do not join the deities on Mount Olympus. When they enter the somber realm of Pluto—the deity of the underworld—they, like all the other shades whom Charon ferries across the river Styx, are more remote from the gods than are mortal men on earth. The only exception perhaps is Heracles, whom Odysseus meets in Hades, or rather "his phantom only, for he is feasting ever with the immortal gods, and has lovely Hebe to wife."

The general attitude of all who dwell in the underworld is summed up by Achilles when he tells Odysseus: "Say not a word in death's favor; I would rather be a paid servant in a poor man's house and be above ground than king of kings among the dead." And the mother of Odysseus describes the condition of the dead "in the abode of darkness" as one in which "the sinews no longer hold the flesh and bones together; these perish in the fierceness of consuming fire as soon as life has left the body, and the soul flits away as though it were a dream."

Among other ancient peoples such as the Egyptians, the Babylonians, and the Persians, Herodotus found other views of immortality than those which prevailed in Greece. He reports, for example, the doctrine of transmigration or reincarnation—a doctrine which also appears in the myth of Er at the end of Plato's *Republic* and is alluded to elsewhere in the Platonic dialogues. "The Egyptians," Herodotus writes, "were the first to broach the opinion that the soul of man is immortal, and that, when the body dies, it enters into the form of an animal which is born at the moment, thence passing on from one animal into another, until it has circled through the forms of all creatures which tenant the earth, the water, and the air, after which it enters again into a human frame and is born anew."

Herodotus, however, seems more interested in the effect of such beliefs on the practices of the living, especially their funeral rites and other devotions, than he is with the truth of conflicting theories of immortality.

"The doctrine of a future state," according to Gibbon, "was scarcely considered among the devout polytheists of Greece and Rome as a fundamental article of faith." Before the time of Christ, "the description of the infernal regions had been abandoned to the fancy of painters and of poets, who peopled them with so many phantoms and monsters who dispensed their rewards and punishments with so little equity, that a solemn truth, the most congenial to the human heart, was oppressed and disgraced by the absurd mixture of the wildest fictions." Lacking an acceptable or satisfying belief, yet inclined to believe in, as men are inclined to hope for, a better life, the pagan world, Gibbon thinks, could not long resist the appeal of Christian teaching. "When the promise of eternal happiness was proposed to mankind on condition of adopting the faith, and of observing the precepts of the Gospel, it is no wonder," he declares, "that so advantageous an offer should have been accepted by great numbers of every religion, of every rank, and of every province in the Roman empire."

THE ARGUMENTS for personal immortality which Christian theologians draw from the nature of the human soul do not differ essentially from the proofs offered by philosophers without recourse to religious faith. This applies to arguments advanced before Christianity by Plato and Plotinus as well as to those developed by philosophers like Descartes and Locke who belong to the Christian community. The exclusively theological aspects of the Christian doctrine of immortality are those matters which, since they are beyond the reach of reason, belong to faith alone.

The doctrine that the individual soul is created and that it has a unique affiliation with one human body, is not capable of being proved or defended by reason against the quite opposite theory that the soul has always existed and inhabits any number of bodies in the course of many reincarnations. The existence of Hell, Purgatory, and Heaven as supernatural states of the soul; the time, place, and manner of the Last Judgment; the resurrection of the body and the difference between the bodies reunited with the souls of the blessed and the damned; the joy of eternal happiness and the misery of eternal damnation—these dogmas of Christian orthodoxy go far beyond all merely philosophical attempts to prove the soul's immortality or to consider its life apart from the body.

The great theologians undertake to do more than expound these articles of faith. Reason asks questions which the man of faith must try to answer, defending his faith, not by proof, but by overcoming doubts, by answering objections, by making dogmas intelligible. Yet the great theologians admit an irreducible core of mystery. The joy of the soul united to God in the beatific vision surpasses temporal understanding. The mysteries of Hell are perhaps even greater.

The deprivation of God's love and exclusion from His presence constitute a spiritual misery comparable to the beatitude of beholding God and being within the circle of the divine light. One is an infinite anguish of frustration and loss; the other, an infinite rest of peace and fulfillment. But the theologians also teach that the damned suffer the pains of sense in Hell, as well as the pains of deprivation. "That hell, which also is called a lake of fire and brimstone," Augustine says, "will be material fire and will torment the bodies of the damned." When hell-fire and the expiatory punishments of Purgatory are not merely symbols for the imagination, they raise extraordinarily difficult questions, as both Augustine and Aquinas admit.

Dante asks us to read the descriptions he gives of Hell, Purgatory, and Paradise in the Divine Comedy in a strictly literal sense as well as in several symbolic meanings, such as the moral and the allegorical. But he explains in his own commentary on the poem that the literal meaning also involves symbolism, insofar as the things that the words refer to when taken in their literal sense are themselves the symbols of other things. In any case the poet may be more successful than the theologian in making intelligible through symbol and metaphor what

in its literal significance is strictly unimaginable. The imagery of darkness, sultriness, noise, and heaviness, which grows more intense as the descent proceeds in the Inferno, does more than the anguished outcries of the damned to convey the reality of Hell.

The metaphors of music and agility express the harmony of Heaven. But it is especially the symbolism of light which captures the invisible in terms of vision, except perhaps when it reaches a climax in the blinding effulgence at the end of the Paradiso. As Dante moves upward in the realm of love, where courtesy prevails in every speech and charity suffuses every will, he sees the mystic rose of Heaven entirely through reflected light. The saints, and especially those glorious spirits who instruct his progress, become pale mirrors of the ineffable vision which they themselves behold.

Milton too pictures Heaven and Hell, but in Paradise Lost the destiny of the immortal soul remains a prophecy, a consequence of the earthly immortality which Adam lost. Except for the Prologue, Hell and Heaven are offstage in Goethe's Faust, though they are the main implications of the wager Faust makes with Mephistopheles, which puts his immortal soul in the balance.

THE PHILOSOPHICAL issue concerning immortality cannot be separated from issues concerning the existence and nature of man's soul. The various arguments for immortality seem to rest not merely on the reality of the distinction between soul and body, but more precisely on the immateriality of the soul. Lucretius, for example, does not deny the existence of soul, nor does he fail to differentiate the soul from the body wherein it is located. The soul, according to Lucretius, like everything else in the universe, consists of atoms. They differ from those of the body by their roundness, smoothness, and mobility. They are "much smaller than those of which our body and flesh are formed; they are also much fewer in number and are disseminated merely in scanty number through the frame."

On this view of the soul as material in nature and as constituted of many quite separable parts, the soul is necessarily as perishable as the rest of the body. "When the body has been shattered by the mastering might of time," Lucretius writes, "and the frame has drooped with its forces dulled . . . it naturally follows then that the whole nature of the soul is dissolved, like smoke, into the high air; since we see it is begotten along with the body and grows up along with it and . . . breaks down at the same time worn out with age."

It should be observed, however, that it is not the materiality of the soul, but rather its divisibility into parts, which accounts for its mortality. The atoms after all are material, but since as the ultimate units of matter they are simple bodies and so are absolutely indivisible, they cannot perish. Only the simple is imperishable.

The *imperishability of the simple* (*i.e.*, of that which has no parts) occurs as a premise in one of the great arguments for the immortality of the soul. In Plato's *Phaedo*, which formulates this argument as immortality is discussed in the prison cell where Socrates awaits his execution, two assumptions seem to be made: first, that the soul is the principle of life in animate bodies, for, as Socrates says, "whatever the soul possesses, to that she comes bearing life"; and second, that as an immaterial being, the soul must be simple, for only bodies are "composite" and "changing."

From the first of these assumptions, the argument proceeds in terms of what it means for bodies to be alive or dead. Socrates argues from examples. "If any one asks you," he says, "what that is, of which the inherence makes the body hot, you will reply not heat . . . but fire. . . . Or if any one asks you why a body is diseased, you will not say from disease, but from fever." So if any one asks, "what is that of which the inherence will render the body alive?" the answer is not life but "the soul." As the principle of life itself, the soul "will never receive the opposite of what she brings," namely, death. Therefore the soul is immortal.

On the second assumption, the endless duration of the soul follows from its simplicity as an immaterial and immutable being. "The compound or composite," Socrates says, "may be supposed to be naturally capable, as of being compounded, so also of being dissolved; but that which is uncompounded, and that only, must be, if anything is, indissoluble." When the soul leaves the body, for which it has been both motor and pilot, the body ceases to be alive and perishes in the manner of material things; the soul lives on, freed from temporary bondage to the body, its prison house. It "departs to the invisible world—to the divine and immortal and rational."

The argument from simplicity, as repeated in Moses Mendelssohn's *Phädon*, is criticized by Kant. Admitting that a truly "simple being cannot cease to exist," Kant contends that the *knowable* soul—which is for him the empirical ego or consciousness—may have intensive, though it lacks extensive, quantity. It would therefore be capable of diminution in reality; and so it "can become less and less through an infinite series of smaller degrees."

With regard to the soul as an immaterial and simple substance (*i.e.*, the transcendental ego), Kant is willing to affirm that immortality necessarily belongs to such a nature. But he denies that we can have any knowledge of the soul except as a phenomenon of experience. There can be no valid theoretic argument for immortality precisely because there can be no scientific knowledge of the nature of transcendental objects—beings beyond all possible experience. What Kant calls "the paralogisms of rational psychology" are offered to show the dialectical futility of proofs or disproofs of immortality, in the same way that "the cosmological antinomies" attempt to expose the untenability of arguments for or against the infinity of time and space, the infinite divisibility of matter, the existence of a free will and of God.

Without deciding whether Kant's theory of experience and knowledge is true, this much we can learn from him about the issue of immortality. Those philosophers who, like Descartes and Locke, think they have grounds for affirming the existence of the soul (or mind or spirit) as an immaterial substance, also have grounds for affirming its immortality. Those who, like Lucretius and Hobbes, think they have grounds for denying the existence of anything except material particles, also have grounds for denying either the existence of the soul or its having a permanence not possessed by other material wholes. And those who, like Hume, think there are no grounds for affirming the existence of any kind of enduring substance, material or spiritual—even to the point of doubting personal identity from moment to moment—can admit no grounds for affirming a substantial, much less an immortal, soul.

ONE OTHER POSITION remains to be considered. Though it does not fall outside the foregoing alternatives, Aristotle's theory represents an important variation on one of them. As against Hume or Kant, Aristotle holds that substances exist and are knowable. The sensible, material things of experience are such substances. But, according to Aristotle, these substances are not *exclusively* material. They are composed of two principles, matter and form, neither of which is a substance capable of existing by itself. As the exposition of this theory (in the chapters on FORM and MATTER) tries to make plain, form and matter exist only in union with one another. It is the composite substance resulting from their union which exists in and of itself.

The form which enters into the composition of a substance can be called its "substantial form." In relation to the matter with which it is united, the substantial form is the actualization of the potentiality in matter to exist as a substance of a certain kind. Not all substances are of the same kind. Some are alive; some inanimate and inert. In the case of living substances, the substantial form, according to Aristotle, confers upon matter not only the act of existing as a substance, but also the act of being alive. Because it thus differs from the form of an inanimate substance, Aristotle gives a special name to the substantial form of a living thing. Because the word "soul" has long been used to designate "the principle of life in living things," Aristotle feels justified in using it as the name for the substantial forms of plants and animals as well as men.

This theory and its principal opposite (which regards the human soul as a complete substance, not a substantial form) are more fully discussed in the chapter on SOUL. Here we are concerned only with the consequences of Aristotle's theory for human immortality. If, as he seems to hold, substantial forms exist only insofar as they exist in the substances of which they are the forms, then when a composite substance perishes through the decomposition of its matter and form, the form perishes also. Souls—the substantial forms of living things—would seem to be no exception. "The soul," Aristotle writes, "is inseparable from its body, or at any rate certain parts of it are (if it has parts)—for the actuality of some of them is nothing but the actualities of their bodily parts. Yet some may be separable because they are not the actualities of any body at all."

The exception which Aristotle seems to have in mind is that part of the human soul which is the intellect. It differs from other powers of the soul, he suggests, as the eternal from the perishable. "It alone," he says, "is capable of existence in isolation from all other psychic powers." He argues that "in so far as the realities it knows" —or at least some of them—"are capable of being separated from their matter, so is it also with the power of the mind."

What is the significance, for the immortality of the human soul, of the supposed ability of the intellect to act independently of the body? Aristotle answers in terms of the principle that "if there is any way of acting or being acted upon proper to soul, soul will be capable of separate existence; if there is none, its separate existence is impossible." If we consider nutrition, sensation, and emotion, there seems to be, he admits, "no case in which the soul can act or be acted upon without involving the body." The one possible exception may be thinking, but Aristotle adds at once that "if this too proves to be a form of imagination or to be impossible without imagination, it too requires a body as a condition of its existence."

Later, when he is discussing the power of thought, Aristotle flatly insists that "the soul never thinks without an image" and that "no one can learn or understand anything in the absence of sense," for "when the mind is actively aware of anything it is necessarily aware of it along with an image." According to his own principles it would seem to follow that since thinking proves "to be impossible without imagination, it too requires a body as a condition of its existence." Hence the intellect is not separable from matter, nor is the human soul, of which the intellect is the highest power.

Nevertheless, Aristotle declares, in a passage which has become famous, that mind as the active power of thinking "is separable, impassible, unmixed"; and with this declaration of the intellect's separability from matter, he seems to affirm immortality, at least for the intellectual part of the soul. "When mind is set free from its present conditions," he writes, "it appears as just what it is and nothing more: this alone is immortal and eternal."

THE PASSAGES QUOTED have been subject to conflicting interpretations. The Arabic commentators on Aristotle, notably Averroes, find in them no basis for the immortality of the individual human soul. The texts, according to their view, support the theory of a *single* active intellect which exists apart from the minds of individual men—almost a divine principle in the universe which, acting on the rational souls of individual men, enables them to think and understand. Aquinas argues against them to the opposite conclusion.

Against the Averroists Aquinas contends that if the individual man, Socrates, can be said to think, then whatever powers are required for thinking must belong to his individual nature. The powers required for thinking are, according to Aquinas, twofold: an active intellect, able to abstract the intelligible forms of things from their material representation in sensory images; and a possible or potential intellect, capable of receiving these forms when separated from matter by the act of abstraction.

The theory of knowledge and thought which this involves is discussed in the chapters on FORM, IDEA, MIND, and UNIVERSAL AND PARTICULAR. Here we are concerned only with the point which Aquinas makes, that since thinking involves universal notions, and since forms can be universal only apart from matter, the intellect which abstracts and receives abstractions must itself be immaterial. The intellectual powers do not operate through a bodily organ, as the power of nutrition operates through the alimentary system or the power of vision through the eye. The brain, in other words, is not the organ of understanding or thought, but rather, along with the external sense-organs, it is the material organ of perception, memory, and imagination.

The argument for the immortality of the human soul then proceeds on the premise that that which can *act* apart from matter can also

exist apart from matter. "The intellectual principle which we call the mind or the intellect has an operation *per se* apart from the body. Now only that which subsists can have an operation *per se*, for nothing can operate but what is actual; wherefore a thing operates according as it is." Hence Aquinas concludes that "the human soul, which is called the intellect or mind, is something incorporeal and subsistent." The attribution of subsistence to the human soul means that although it is the substantial form of the human body, it is also capable of existing in and of itself as if it were a simple substance.

Unlike angels, which as spiritual substances are by their very nature *separate* forms, not forms of matter, human souls are substantial forms which, having a certain degree of immateriality, are also to that degree separable from matter. But the reverse is also true. To the extent that the soul's powers, such as sensation and imagination, require corporeal organs, the soul is inseparable from the body. Since, furthermore, Aquinas agrees with Aristotle that every act of understanding or thought involves imagination, he faces the difficulty of explaining how the soul can function in any way when separated from the body after death.

"To solve this difficulty," he says, "we must consider that as nothing acts except as it is actual, the mode of action in every agent follows from its mode of existence. Now the soul has one mode of being when in the body, and another when apart from it. . . . The soul, therefore, when united to the body, has consistently with that mode of existence, a mode of understanding by turning to corporeal images, which are in corporeal organs; but when it is separated from the body, it has a mode of understanding by turning to simply intelligible objects, as is proper to other separate substances." Nevertheless, Aquinas adds, it is not natural for the soul to understand in the latter way, for it is not by nature a separate substance. Therefore, "to be separated from the body is not in accordance with its nature."

THIS LAST POINT has both philosophical and theological significance. Philosophically, it may be easier to prove the immortality of the soul if one starts, as the Platonists do, with the proposition that the soul is a purely spiritual principle or substance which does not depend upon the body. But then, according to Aquinas, you prove the immortality of the soul at the expense of destroying the unity of man, for if the soul is a substance rather than a form, the individual man, composed of body and soul, consists of two distinct substances.

Theologically, Christian faith believes in the resurrection of the body after the Last Judgment and the end of the world, as well as in the soul's separate existence immediately after death. From the point of view of a theologian like Aquinas, a philosophical proof of immortality must corroborate both of these dogmas. In his judgment a proof which rests upon the proposition that the soul has a nature akin to that of an angel (i.e., a purely spiritual substance), makes the Christian dogma of the resurrected body unintelligible or even abhorrent.

If the immortal soul were a complete and separate substance, it would have no need for its body in the life hereafter. It has that need only if its nature is that of a substantial form, partly immersed in matter and partly separate therefrom. Then, because of these two aspects of its nature, it can be said, not only that "the human soul retains its proper existence when separated from the body," but also that it has "an aptitude and a natural inclination to be united to the body."

The incompleteness of the soul without the body and, even more, the dependence of man's mind upon his bodily senses and imagination raise, as we have seen, the difficult problem of how the soul exists and operates when separated from the body by death and before it is re-united to a resurrected body. It may even raise the question whether the reasoning of Aquinas constitutes a valid philosophical argument for the actual existence of the soul in separation from the body, or merely suggests the possibility of such existence. But the facts which create these difficulties are the very facts to which Aquinas appeals in his Treatise on the Resurrection, in order to explain the basis in nature for the miraculous re-union of the body with the soul.

THE ARGUMENTS FOR and against immortality so far considered are couched in the form of proofs or disproofs which aim at certainty. All except one are, moreover, theoretical or speculative in the sense that they proceed in terms of observations, assumptions, and inferences about the nature of things—about atoms and substances, matter and form, extension and thought, inert bodies and living organisms. The one exception, already mentioned, is Kant's practical argument based on the moral necessity of an immortal life.

There is still another argument, both speculative and practical in character, which does not aim at certainty nor take the form of a proof. It is the proposal of a wager concerning the equally unknown alternatives of oblivion after death and eternal life. Supposing no rational evidence to favor the truth of either alternative, Pascal weighs the probability of gain and loss which is consequent upon living according to each hypothesis. The probability, he thinks, vastly preponderates on the side of those who choose to forego the worldly life because, to take the chance of gaining the whole world during the short term of earthly life, they would risk the loss of eternal happiness for their immortal souls.

Locke engages in the same type of calculation. "When infinite happiness is put into one scale, against infinite misery in the other; if the worst that comes to the pious man, if he mistakes, be the best that the wicked can attain to, if he be right, who," Locke asks, "can without madness run the venture? Who in his wits would choose to come within the possibility of infinite misery; which if he miss, there is yet nothing to be got by that hazard? Whereas, on the other side, the sober man ventures nothing against infinite happiness to be got, if his expectation comes to pass." If, wagering on immortal life, "the good man be right, he is eternally happy"; but "if he mistakes"—if death ends all—"he is not miserable, he feels nothing."

ALL THESE THEORIES, including Kant's postulate and the wager proposed by Pascal and Locke, are clearly concerned with arguing for personal immortality or individual survival. Among those who deny the survival of the individual human spirit, some—Hegel and Spinoza, for example—conceive an impersonal type of immortality.

For Hegel it is Spirit itself which is immortal. "The successive phases of Spirit that animate the Nations in a necessitated gradation," he writes, "are themselves only steps in the development of the one Universal Spirit, which through them elevates and completes itself to a self-comprehending totality." In considering the history of the world, he regards everything as the manifestation of Spirit; and because of this, even when we traverse the past, we have, he says, "only to do with what is *present*; for philosophy, as occupying itself with the True, has to do with the *eternally present*. Nothing in the past is lost for it, for the Idea is ever present; Spirit is immortal; with it there is no past, no future, but an essential now. This necessarily implies that the present form of Spirit comprehends within it all earlier steps. . . . The grades which Spirit seems to have left behind it, it still possesses in the depths of its present."

What Spirit is for Hegel, Nature is for Spinoza. Spinoza, however, conceives a kind of immortality for the individual man, which is achieved through his participation in the eternity of Nature. The body of the individual man, according to Spinoza, belongs to the infinite matter of Nature. It is "a certain mode of extension actually existing." The individual human mind is similarly "a part of the infinite intellect of God." In one sense, both the body and the mind are temporal things which, like all other finite modes of God or Nature, have a fixed and limited duration. Furthermore, the personal memories and thoughts of the individual man depend on the co-existence of his mind and body. "The mind can imagine nothing, nor can it recollect anything that is past," Spinoza writes, "except while the body exists."

But Spinoza also maintains that "only in so far as it involves the actual existence of the body, can the mind be said to possess duration, and its existence be limited by a fixed time." Of every individual thing—whether it is a finite mind or a finite body—there exists in the infinite and eternal essence of God a conception or idea. "To conceive things under the form of eternity," Spinoza writes, "is to conceive them in so far as they are conceived through the essence of God." Because he holds that the human mind can have adequate knowledge of God, he holds that the mind can conceive "it-

self and its body under the form of eternity." Hence through knowing God, or the eternal truth about temporal things, the mind participates in eternity.

Imagination and memory may belong to time, but not the intellect, which is capable of knowing God. To explain why we feel "that we are eternal," Spinoza points out that "the mind is no less sensible of those things which it conceives through intelligence than of those which it remembers." Although we cannot *imagine* or *remember* that "we existed before the body," we can *know intellectually* something about mind and body which belongs to eternity; because, in addition to conceiving them as "existing with relation to a fixed time and place," we can conceive them as "contained in God" and as following "from the necessity of the divine nature." Since it "pertains to the nature of the mind to conceive the essence of the body under the form of eternity," Spinoza concludes that "the human mind cannot be absolutely destroyed with the body, but something of it remains which is eternal."

Such immortality is, in a way, enjoyed in this life, for it is a present participation in eternity through the mind's knowledge of God. There is also the impersonal immortality which men enjoy through contemplating the perpetuation of the species, or more particularly the persistence of an image of themselves in their offspring. In the *Symposium*, Socrates reports a conversation with Diotima in which she explains to him that in procreation "the mortal nature is seeking as far as is possible to be everlasting and immortal." Men hope that offspring "will preserve their memory and give them the blessedness and immortality which they desire in the future." But if procreation through the pregnancy of the body is a way of achieving immortality, artistic creation through a kind of pregnancy in the soul, Diotima argues, is even more so. "Who, when he thinks of Homer and Hesiod and other great poets," she asks, "would not rather have their children than ordinary ones? Who would not emulate them in the creation of children such as theirs, which have preserved their memory and given them everlasting glory?"

One need think "only of the ambition of men" and what they will do "for the sake of leaving behind them a name which shall be eternal," to realize how deeply "they are stirred by the love of an immortality of fame." Even deeper, according to Diotima, is their love of the good, or more precisely, their desire for "the everlasting possession of the good" which leads all men necessarily to "desire immortality together with the good."

Whether it is to be attained through the perpetuation of the species, through survival in the memory of mankind, through knowledge of God, or through the subsistence of the soul, the desire for immortality seems to express

man's dread of disappearance into utter nothingness. Yet, facing death, Socrates faces the alternatives with equanimity. "Either death," he declares, "is a state of nothingness and utter unconsciousness, or, as men say, there is a change and migration of the soul from this world to another." Either it is like a dreamless and undisturbed sleep or it opens a new world to which the good man can look forward with hope. On either alternative we can be of good cheer, he tells his friends, if we believe that "no evil can happen to a good man, either in life or after death."

OUTLINE OF TOPICS

REFERENCES

To find the passages cited, use the numbers in heavy type, which are the volume and page numbers of the passages referred to. For example, in 4 HOMER: *Iliad*, BK II [265–283] 12d, the number 4 is the number of the volume in the set; the number 12d indicates that the passage is in section d of page 12.

PAGE SECTIONS: When the text is printed in one column, the letters a and b refer to the upper and lower halves of the page. For example, in 53 JAMES: *Psychology*, 116a-119b, the passage begins in the upper half of page 116 and ends in the lower half of page 119. When the text is printed in two columns, the letters a and b refer to the upper and lower halves of the left-hand side of the page, the letters c and d to the upper and lower halves of the right-hand side of the page. For example, in 7 PLATO: *Symposium*, 163b-164c, the passage begins in the lower half of the left-hand side of page 163 and ends in the upper half of the right-hand side of page 164.

AUTHOR'S DIVISIONS: One or more of the main divisions of a work (such as PART, BK, CH, SECT) are sometimes included in the reference; line numbers, in brackets, are given in certain cases; *e.g.*, *Iliad*, BK II [265–283] 12d.

BIBLE REFERENCES: The references are to book, chapter, and verse. When the King James and Douay versions differ in title of books or in the numbering of chapters or verses, the King James version is cited first and the Douay, indicated by a (*D*), follows; *e.g.*, OLD TESTAMENT: *Nehemiah*, 7:45—(*D*) *II Esdras*, 7:46.

SYMBOLS: The abbreviation "esp" calls the reader's attention to one or more especially relevant parts of a whole reference; "passim" signifies that the topic is discussed intermittently rather than continuously in the work or passage cited.

For additional information concerning the style of the references, see the Explanation of Reference Style; for general guidance in the use of *The Great Ideas*, consult the Preface.

1. The desire for immortality: the fear of death

OLD TESTAMENT: *II Samuel*, 22:5-7—(*D*) *II Kings*, 22:5-7 / *Job*, 14; 30:23-24 / *Psalms*, 6 esp 6:4-5; 13 esp 13:3; 16 esp 16:10; 18:4-6; 49:6-12; 55 esp 55:4-8; 89:47-48; 116:1-9—(*D*) *Psalms*, 6 esp 6:5-6; 12 esp 12:4; 15 esp 15:10; 17:5-7; 48:7-13; 54 esp 54:5-9; 88:48-49; 114 / *Ecclesiastes*, 8:8 / *Isaiah*, 38:10-19—(*D*) *Isaias*, 38:10-19

APOCRYPHA: *II Maccabees*, 6:18-7:42 esp 7:9—(*D*) OT, *II Machabees*, 6:18-7:42 esp 7:9

NEW TESTAMENT: *Matthew*, 10:28; 19:16-30 / *Mark*, 10:17-31 / *Luke*, 10:25-37 / *Acts*, 7:54-60—(*D*) *Acts*, 7:54-59 / *Romans*, 2:5-8 esp 2:7 / *I Corinthians*, 15 / *II Corinthians*, 1:9-10; 4:9-18; 5:1-9 / *I Thessalonians*, 4:13-17—(*D*) *I Thessalonians*, 4:12-17 / *I Timothy*, 6:11-19 esp 6:12, 6:19 / *II Timothy*, 4:6-8 / *Hebrews*, 2:14-15

4 HOMER: *Iliad*, BK XII [309-328] 85b-c / *Odyssey*, BK V [203-224] 210a-b

5 SOPHOCLES: *Oedipus at Colonus* [1579-1779] 128c-130a,c

7 PLATO: *Symposium*, 165b-167a / *Apology*, 211b-212a,c / *Phaedo*, 230d-235a / *Republic*, BK I, 297a-b; BK III, 324c-325b; BK VI, 374a-d / *Laws*, BK V, 687a-b

9 ARISTOTLE: *Ethics*, BK X, CH 7 [1177^{b}26-1178^{a}1] 432c

12 LUCRETIUS: *Nature of Things*, BK I [102-126] 2b-c; BK III [31-93] 30b-31b; [830-1094] 40c-44a,c

12 EPICTETUS: *Discourses*, BK I, CH 9, 115b-d; BK II, CH 1, 139b

12 AURELIUS: *Meditations*, BK II, SECT 11-12 258a-c; BK III, SECT 3 260b; BK IV, SECT 48 267d-268a; SECT 50 268c; BK VIII, SECT 25 287b-c; SECT 58 290d; BK IX, SECT 3 291d-292a

14 PLUTARCH: *Aristides*, 265d

17 PLOTINUS: *First Ennead*, TR IV, CH 16, 19a; TR VI, CH 6, 24a-b; TR VII, CH 3 26d-27a

18 AUGUSTINE: *Confessions*, BK IV, par 11 21d-22a; par 14 22d-23a; BK VI, par 18-19 40d-41b; BK IX, par 23-29 68a-69c / *City of God*, BK I, CH 22, 143b; BK IX, CH 14-15 293a-294a; BK XIII, CH 4 361d-362a; BK XIX, CH 4-10 511a-516d; BK XXII, CH 23 608c-609a

19 AQUINAS: *Summa Theologica*, PART I, Q 75, A 6, ANS 383c-384c

20 AQUINAS: *Summa Theologica*, PART I-II, Q 85, A 6 182d-184a

22 CHAUCER: *Second Nun's Tale* [15,788-801] 467a

25 MONTAIGNE: *Essays*, 33d-36b; 99b-100a; 211a-b; 267a-c; 402c-403c

(1. *The desire for immortality: the fear of death.*)

27 SHAKESPEARE: *Hamlet*, ACT III, SC I [56–88] 47c-d / *Measure for Measure*, ACT III, SC I [116–136] 188a-b

29 CERVANTES: *Don Quixote*, PART II, 366d-367a

30 BACON: *Advancement of Learning*, 28a-c

31 SPINOZA: *Ethics*, PART V, PROP 23 458b-d; PROP 32 460b; PROP 38–39 461d-462c

32 MILTON: *Paradise Lost*, BK X [770–844] 291a-292b

33 PASCAL: *Pensées*, 166,168–169 203a; 210 211b; 239 217a

36 SWIFT: *Gulliver*, PART III, 124a-129a

37 FIELDING: *Tom Jones*, 86c-d

40 GIBBON: *Decline and Fall*, 186a; 219c-220d; 327d-328a; 376a-c

41 GIBBON: *Decline and Fall*, 238c

42 KANT: *Judgement*, 600c-d

44 BOSWELL: *Johnson*, 174b; 238b; 347a-c; 394a-c; 399d-400a; 573a-574a

51 TOLSTOY: *War and Peace*, BK V, 200c-d; 217c-218b; BK XII, 560a-562d

52 DOSTOEVSKY: *Brothers Karamazov*, BK II, 26a-27d passim; BK VI, 148d-150d

53 JAMES: *Psychology*, 224a-225a; 653a

54 FREUD: *War and Death*, 763c-764b

2. The knowledge of immortality: arguments for and against personal survival

7 PLATO: *Phaedrus*, 124b-c / *Meno*, 179d-183a / *Apology*, 211b-212a,c / *Phaedo* 220a-251d / *Republic*, BK X, 434d-436a / *Laws*, BK XII, 793c-d

8 ARISTOTLE: *Metaphysics*, BK XII, CH 3 [1070^{a}24–30] 599c / *Soul*, BK I, CH I [403^{a}2–15] 632a-b; CH 2 [405^{a}29–34] 634d; BK II, CH I [413^{a}3–9] 643a; CH 2 [413^{b}24–29] 643d-644a; BK III, CH 4 [429^{a}19–^{b}4] 661c-d; CH 5 662c-d; CH 7 [431^{a}15] 663d; CH 8 [432^{a}5–10] 664c

9 ARISTOTLE: *Generation of Animals*, BK II, CH 3 [736^{b}15–737^{a}12] 277b-d

12 LUCRETIUS: *Nature of Things*, BK III [323–1023] 34b-43b

12 EPICTETUS: *Discourses*, BK III, CH 24, 203d

12 AURELIUS: *Meditations*, BK II, SECT 14 258d; SECT 17 259b-d; BK IV, SECT 21 265b-c; BK V, SECT 13 271b; BK VII, SECT 50 283a; BK VIII, SECT 37 288c; BK X, SECT 7 297b-c; BK XII, SECT 5 307d-308a; SECT 14 308c

17 PLOTINUS: *Fourth Ennead*, TR I 139a-b; TR IV, CH 15 165c-d; TR VII 191c-200c

18 AUGUSTINE: *City of God*, BK X, CH 31 319b-d; BK XIII, CH 2 360b-361a

19 AQUINAS: *Summa Theologica*, PART I, Q 61, A 2, REP 3 315c-316a; Q 75, A 2 379c-380c; A 6 383c-384c; Q 76, A 1 385d-388c; A 3, REP 1–2 391a-393a; PART I–II, Q 22, A 1, REP 3 720d-721c

20 AQUINAS: *Summa Theologica*, PART I–II, Q 85, A 6 182d-184a

21 DANTE: *Divine Comedy*, PURGATORY, XXV [1–108] 91b-92c; PARADISE, VII [64–84] 115d-116a; [121–148] 116b-c

23 HOBBES: *Leviathan*, PART III, 192c-193c; PART IV, 250c-251b; 253b-254a; 269d-270d

25 MONTAIGNE: *Essays*, 250a; 264b-269b

30 BACON: *Advancement of Learning*, 27d-28c

31 DESCARTES: *Discourse*, PART IV, 51d-52a; PART V, 60b-c / *Meditations*, 69a-71a,c passim; 73a-c / *Objections and Replies*, 127c-d; DEF X 130d; PROP IV 133c

31 SPINOZA: *Ethics*, PART V, PROP 21–40 458a-462d esp PROP 21–23 458a-d, PROP 38 461d-462a, PROP 40 462c-d

32 MILTON: *Paradise Lost*, BK X [782–844] 291b-292b

33 PASCAL: *Pensées*, 556, 271b

35 BERKELEY: *Human Knowledge*, SECT 141 441a-b

40 GIBBON: *Decline and Fall*, 186a-187b passim

42 KANT: *Pure Reason*, 120c-129c esp 124d-128a; 203d-204c; 218d-223d esp 219b-d; 234c-240b esp 234c-235c, 237d-238a / *Practical Reason*, 291a-292a / *Judgement*, 600c-d; 610a-b

44 BOSWELL: *Johnson*, 57d-58a

51 TOLSTOY: *War and Peace*, BK II, 77d-78b; 97a-c

53 JAMES: *Psychology*, 224b-225a

3. Belief in immortality

5 EURIPIDES: *Helen* [1009–1016] 307d

6 HERODOTUS: *History*, BK II, 75b; BK IV, 140c-141a

7 PLATO: *Apology*, 211b-212a,c / *Seventh Letter*, 806a

12 AURELIUS: *Meditations*, BK III, SECT 3 260b

13 VIRGIL: *Georgics*, IV [219–227] 89b

14 PLUTARCH: *Romulus*, 29a-b

17 PLOTINUS: *Fourth Ennead*, TR VII, CH 15 200c

18 AUGUSTINE: *Confessions*, BK VI, par 26 42d-43a

22 CHAUCER: *Second Nun's Tale* [15,787–800] 467a

24 RABELAIS: *Gargantua and Pantagruel*, BK IV, 269a-b

26 SHAKESPEARE: *Romeo and Juliet*, ACT V, SC I [17–21] 314d / *2nd Henry IV*, ACT II, SC II [109–114] 477a

27 SHAKESPEARE: *Hamlet*, ACT I, SC IV [60–68] 36c / *Cymbeline*, ACT V, SC IV [152–194] 482d-483a

29 CERVANTES: *Don Quixote*, PART II, 366d-367a

31 DESCARTES: *Meditations*, 69d

32 MILTON: *On Time* 12a-b / *Lycidas* [165–181] 31b

33 PASCAL: *Pensées*, 556 270b-272a

35 LOCKE: *Human Understanding*, BK IV, CH III, SECT 6, 314c

38 MONTESQUIEU: *Spirit of Laws*, BK XXIV, 205c-206c

40 GIBBON: *Decline and Fall*, 186c-187b

41 GIBBON: *Decline and Fall*, 135a

42 KANT: *Pure Reason,* 242a-d / *Judgement,* 604d-606d

44 BOSWELL: *Johnson,* 256d

46 HEGEL: *Philosophy of History,* PART I, 255c-256b

48 MELVILLE: *Moby Dick,* 27a-28a

49 DARWIN: *Descent of Man,* 593c

51 TOLSTOY: *War and Peace,* BK V, 200c-d; 217c-218b; BK VII, 295b-c; BK XII, 560a-562d; BK XV, 615a-616a

52 DOSTOEVSKY: *Brothers Karamazov,* BK II, 33c-34b; 40b-c; BK III, 68b-c; BK XI, 312b-d

54 FREUD: *Interpretation of Dreams,* 296d [fn 2] / *War and Death,* 763c-764c

3a. The postulation of immortality: practical grounds for belief in immortality

17 PLOTINUS: *Fourth Ennead,* TR VII, CH 15 200c

25 MONTAIGNE: *Essays,* 210d-212a; 267a-268a

33 PASCAL: *Pensées,* 184-241 205a-217b passim; 556, 271b

35 LOCKE: *Human Understanding,* BK II, CH XXI, SECT 72 198a-c

40 GIBBON: *Decline and Fall,* 186a-b

42 KANT: *Pure Reason,* 15c-16c; 120b [fn 1]; 127a-128a; 234c-236a; 240b-243c / *Practical Reason,* 291a-292a; 338c-352c esp 344a-c, 348b-349b / *Judgement,* 599d-600d; 603b-607c esp 606d-607c

44 BOSWELL: *Johnson,* 394c

48 MELVILLE: *Moby Dick,* 347a

53 JAMES: *Psychology,* 224a-225a; 653a

3b. The revelation of immortality: immortality as an article of religious faith

OLD TESTAMENT: *II Samuel,* 14:14—(D) *II Kings,* 14:14 / *Job,* 14:14; 19:25-29; 21; 30:23-24 / *Psalms,* 16 esp 16:10; 37 esp 37:26-40; 49 esp 49:15; 116:1-9—(D) *Psalms,* 15 esp 15:10; 36 esp 36:26-40; 48:2-21 esp 48:16; 114 / *Proverbs,* 10:2; 11:4,19; 12:28; 13:14; 14:27; 18:21 / *Ecclesiastes,* 12:7 / *Isaiah,* 25:8; 38:10-19—(D) *Isaias,* 25:8; 38:10-19 / *Ezekiel,* 37:1-14—(D) *Ezechiel,* 37:1-14 / *Daniel,* 12:1-3 / *Hosea,* 13:14—(D) *Osee,* 13:14

APOCRYPHA: *Tobit,* 4:10—(D) OT, *Tobias,* 4:11 / *Wisdom of Solomon,* 2:23; 3:1-10; 5:15-16—(D) OT, *Book of Wisdom,* 2:23; 3:1-10; 5:16-17 / *Baruch,* 2:17—(D) OT, *Baruch,* 2:17 / *II Maccabees,* 6:18-7:42 esp 6:23, 6:26, 7:9-10, 7:14, 7:36; 12:39-45 esp 12:43-45—(D) OT, *II Machabees,* 6:18-7:42 esp 6:23, 6:26, 7:9-10, 7:14, 7:36; 12:39-46 esp 12:43-46

NEW TESTAMENT: *Matthew,* 5:1-12; 10:28; 25 esp 25:31-46 / *Mark,* 9:42-48; 10:28-30—(D) *Mark,* 9:41-47; 10:28-30 / *Luke,* 10:25-37; 16:19-31 / *John,* 3:14-17; 4:9-14 esp 4:13-14; 4:35-36; 5:21-29; 6:34-59; 8:51; 10:25-30 esp 10:28; 11:1-44; 12:24-25; 17:2-3 / *Acts,* 13:48 / *Romans,* 2:5-8 esp 2:7; 6:1-11; 8:9-11 / *I Corinthians,* 15 / *II Corinthians,* 1:9-10; 4:9-18 / *Galatians,* 6:7-8 / *Ephesians,* 2:1-10 /

I Thessalonians, 4:13-18—(D) *I Thessalonians,* 4:12-17 / *I Timothy,* 6:11-19 esp 6:12, 6:19 / *II Timothy,* 1:10 / *Hebrews,* 2:9,14-16 / *I Peter,* 1:3-5 esp 1:4 / *I John,* 2:15-25 esp 2:17, 2:25 / *Revelation* passim, esp 21—(D) *Apocalypse* passim, esp 21

18 AUGUSTINE: *Confessions,* BK VI, par 18-19 40d-41b; BK IX, par 11 64c-d; par 29 69b-c; BK XIII, par 50-53 124c-125a,c / *City of God,* BK XIII, CH 4 361d-362a

19 AQUINAS: *Summa Theologica,* PART I, Q 75, A 6, REP 1 383c-384c; Q 97, A 1 513c-514c

20 AQUINAS: *Summa Theologica,* PART I-II, Q 85, AA 5-6 181d-184a

21 DANTE: *Divine Comedy,* PARADISE, XXV [40-96] 144c-145b

22 CHAUCER: *Second Nun's Tale* [15,788-800] 467a

23 HOBBES: *Leviathan,* PART III, 191b-193c; PART IV, 250c-251b; 253b-254a

25 MONTAIGNE: *Essays,* 248c-250b; 267a-268a

30 BACON: *New Atlantis,* 203a-c

31 DESCARTES: *Meditations,* 69b-d

32 MILTON: *Lycidas* [165-181] 31b

33 PASCAL: *Pensées,* 556 270b-272a; 560 272b

35 LOCKE: *Human Understanding,* BK IV, CH III, SECT 6, 314c

37 FIELDING: *Tom Jones,* 379c-380a

40 GIBBON: *Decline and Fall,* 186c-187b

52 DOSTOEVSKY: *Brothers Karamazov,* BK II, 26a-27d passim

4. The moral significance of immortality: rewards and sanctions

OLD TESTAMENT: *Psalms,* 49—(D) *Psalms,* 48 / *Proverbs,* 10:2; 11:4,19; 14:32; 21:16

APOCRYPHA: *Tobit,* 4:8-11—(D) OT, *Tobias,* 4:9-12 / *Wisdom of Solomon,* 1:12-6:20—(D) OT, *Book of Wisdom,* 1:12-6:21 / *II Maccabees,* 7 passim, esp 7:17-18, 7:30-37—(D) OT, *II Machabees,* 7 passim, esp 7:17-18, 7:30-37

NEW TESTAMENT: *Matthew,* 5:1-12,22,29-30; 18:7-9; 19:16-30; 25:31-46 / *Mark,* 9:43-48; 10:17-31; 16:16—(D) *Mark,* 9:42-47; 10:17-31; 16:16 / *Luke,* 10:25-37; 14:7-14; 16:19-31; 18:18-30 / *Romans,* 2:1-11 / *Galatians,* 6:7-8 / *II Thessalonians,* 2:10-12—(D) *II Thessalonians,* 2:10-11 / *II Timothy,* 4:8 / *Hebrews,* 10:26-31 / *II Peter,* 2

4 HOMER: *Odyssey,* BK XI [568-600] 248d-249a

5 EURIPIDES: *Helen* [1009-1016] 307d

7 PLATO: *Euthydemus,* 74c / *Phaedrus,* 124a-126c / *Meno,* 179d-180b / *Apology,* 211a-212a,c / *Phaedo,* 230d-234c; 246d-250b / *Gorgias,* 292b-294d / *Republic,* BK I, 297a-b; BK II, 313b-314d; BK X, 436c-441a,c / *Timaeus,* 452d-453b / *Laws,* BK IX, 757a; BK X, 768b-d; BK XII, 793c-d / *Seventh Letter,* 806a

9 ARISTOTLE: *Ethics,* BK I, CH 10-11 345c-347a; BK X, CH 7 [1177^{b}26-1178^{a}1] 432c

(4. *The moral significance of immortality: rewards and sanctions.*)

12 LUCRETIUS: *Nature of Things*, BK III [31–93] 30b-31b; [830–1094] 40c-44a,c

13 VIRGIL: *Aeneid*, BK VI [637–678] 228a-229a; [724–751] 230b-231a

14 PLUTARCH: *Romulus*, 29a-b

17 PLOTINUS: *Third Ennead*, TR II, CH 13 88d-89b; TR III, CH 4 94c-95c / *Fourth Ennead*, TR III, CH 24 154b-d

18 AUGUSTINE: *Confessions*, BK VI, par 26 42d-43a

19 AQUINAS: *Summa Theologica*, PART I, Q 97, A I 513c-514c; A 4 515d-516d; PART I–II, QQ 1–5 609a-643d

21 DANTE: *Divine Comedy* esp HELL, III [1–18] 4a-b, [82–129] 5a-b, VII [100–130] 10c-d, XI 15a-16b, XXVII [55–136] 40a-41b, XXVIII [139–142] 43a, PURGATORY, III [118–145] 57a-c, V [85–129] 59d-60c, IX 65d-67b, XVII [82–139] 79b-d, XXX–XXXI 99b-102b, PARADISE, VII [19–120] 115b-116b, XIX [22–148] 135b-136c

22 CHAUCER: *Friar's Tale* 278a-284a / *Summoner's Prologue* 284b-285a / *Monk's Tale* 434a-448b / *Parson's Tale*, par 10 498b-502a

25 MONTAIGNE: *Essays*, 206d-207a; 210d-212a; 248c-250b esp 250a; 264b-269b; 311a-b

26 SHAKESPEARE: *Richard III*, ACT I, SC IV [42–63] 115a-b

27 SHAKESPEARE: *Hamlet*, ACT I, SC V [9–22] 37a

31 DESCARTES: *Discourse*, PART V, 60b-c / *Meditations*, 69b

31 SPINOZA: *Ethics*, PART V, PROP 41, SCHOL 463a-b

32 MILTON: *Comus* [1–17] 33a-b / *Paradise Lost*, BK X [782–844] 291b-292b

33 PASCAL: *Pensées*, 184–241 205a-217b passim

35 LOCKE: *Toleration*, 15d-16a / *Human Understanding*, BK II, CH XXI, SECT 62 194c-d; SECT 72 198a-c

35 HUME: *Human Understanding*, SECT XI, DIV 108–109 500b-501a

38 MONTESQUIEU: *Spirit of Laws*, BK XXIV, 205c-206c

38 ROUSSEAU: *Inequality*, 366c-d / *Social Contract*, BK IV, 437d-438c

39 SMITH: *Wealth of Nations*, BK V, 336c-d

40 GIBBON: *Decline and Fall*, 187b-c; 198d-199a; 219c-d

41 GIBBON: *Decline and Fall*, 233c-234c passim

42 KANT: *Fund. Prin. Metaphysic of Morals*, 264b [fn 1] / *Practical Reason*, 306b-307a; 344a-c

43 MILL: *Liberty*, 290c-d

44 BOSWELL: *Johnson*, 256d; 363a-b

48 MELVILLE: *Moby Dick*, 341b-342b

51 TOLSTOY: *War and Peace*, BK V, 200c-d; BK VI, 273c-274a

52 DOSTOEVSKY: *Brothers Karamazov*, BK II, 33c-34b; 40b-c; BK XI, 312b-d; 345a-c

53 JAMES: *Psychology*, 225a

5. Conceptions of the after-life

4 HOMER: *Iliad*, BK XX [54–74] 142d-143a; BK XXIII [54–107] 161d-162b / *Odyssey*, BK X [487–574] 241a-242a,c; BK XI 243a-249d; BK XXIV [1–202] 317a-319a

5 EURIPIDES: *Alcestis* 237a-247a,c / *Helen* [1009–1016] 307d

5 ARISTOPHANES: *Frogs* 564a-582a,c

6 HERODOTUS: *History*, BK II, 75b; BK IV, 140c-141a

7 PLATO: *Phaedrus*, 124b-126a / *Apology*, 211a-212a,c / *Republic*, BK II, 313b-314d; BK III, 324c-325b; BK X, 437c-441a,c / *Laws*, BK V, 687a; BK X, 767c-768c

9 ARISTOTLE: *Ethics*, BK I, CH 10 [1100ª10–31] 345c-d; CH 11 346c-347a

12 EPICTETUS: *Discourses*, BK III, CH 13 188b-189c

12 AURELIUS: *Meditations*, BK VII, SECT 50 283a

13 VIRGIL: *Georgics*, IV [219–227] 89b; [467–485] 96a-b / *Aeneid*, BK VI 211a-235a

18 AUGUSTINE: *City of God*, BK XIX–XXII 507a-618d

20 AQUINAS: *Summa Theologica*, PART III SUPPL, QQ 69–99 885a-1085a,c

21 DANTE: *Divine Comedy*

22 CHAUCER: *Second Nun's Tale* [15,788–822] 467a-b

23 HOBBES: *Leviathan*, PART III, 191b-198a

25 MONTAIGNE: *Essays*, 248c-250b; 264b-269b

29 CERVANTES: *Don Quixote*, PART II, 366d-367a

31 DESCARTES: *Meditations*, III, 88d-89a / *Objections and Replies*, 226d-227a

32 MILTON: *Paradise Lost*, BK X [782–844] 291b-292b

38 MONTESQUIEU: *Spirit of Laws*, BK XXIV, 205c-206c

40 GIBBON: *Decline and Fall*, 94a; 186c-d; 187b-188a

41 GIBBON: *Decline and Fall*, 233c-234d

44 BOSWELL: *Johnson*, 363a-b

48 MELVILLE: *Moby Dick*, 134b

51 TOLSTOY: *War and Peace*, BK XII, 560a-562d; BK XV, 615a-616a

52 DOSTOEVSKY: *Brothers Karamazov*, BK XI, 341c-345c passim

5*a*. The transmigration of souls: reincarnation

4 HOMER: *Odyssey*, BK XI [298–304] 246a

6 HERODOTUS: *History*, BK II, 75b

7 PLATO: *Phaedrus*, 125b-126a / *Meno*, 179d-183a / *Phaedo*, 226c-234c; 246d-250b / *Republic*, BK X, 437c-441a,c / *Timaeus*, 452d-453b; 476a-477a,c / *Laws*, BK X, 767c-768c

8 ARISTOTLE: *Soul*, BK I, CH 3 [406ª30–ᵇ5] 635d

12 LUCRETIUS: *Nature of Things*, BK III [670–783] 38d-40a

12 AURELIUS: *Meditations*, BK IV, SECT 21 265b-c

13 VIRGIL: *Georgics*, IV [219–227] 89b / *Aeneid*, BK VI [710–751] 230a-231a

14 PLUTARCH: *Romulus*, 28a-29b

17 PLOTINUS: *First Ennead*, TR I, CH II 5b-c /
Third Ennead, TR II, CH 13 88d-89b; TR III,
CH 4, 95b-c; TR IV, CH 2–3 97d-98c; CH 6 99b-
100b / *Fourth Ennead*, TR III, CH 8, 145d; CH 9,
146d; CH 13–15 149b-150c; CH 24 154b-d; CH
27, 156d; TR VII, CH 14 200b-c; TR VIII, CH 3–5
202a-203d / *Sixth Ennead*, TR IV, CH 14–16
304a-305c

18 AUGUSTINE: *City of God*, BK X, CH 30 318b-
319b; BK XII, CH 20 355b-357a; BK XXII, CH
27–28 613b-614a

20 AQUINAS: *Summa Theologica*, PART III SUPPL,
Q 77, A I, ANS 943a-944d; Q 79, A I, ANS 951b-
953b

21 DANTE: *Divine Comedy*, PARADISE, IV [49–63]
111b

25 MONTAIGNE: *Essays*, 206b-207a; 249b-250a;
264b-265c; 268a-269a

35 LOCKE: *Human Understanding*, BK II, CH
XXVII, SECT 6 220c-d; SECT 14 223d-224b;
SECT 27 227d-228a

38 MONTESQUIEU: *Spirit of Laws*, BK XXIV,
207a-c

41 GIBBON: *Decline and Fall*, 135a; 226b

46 HEGEL: *Philosophy of History*, INTRO, 187a-b;
PART I, 255c-256b

47 GOETHE: *Faust*, PART I [737–807] 19b-21a

48 MELVILLE: *Moby Dick*, 316b

51 TOLSTOY: *War and Peace*, BK VII, 295b-c

54 FREUD: *War and Death*, 764b

5b. The state of the soul apart from the body

4 HOMER: *Iliad*, BK XXII [361–366] 159a; BK
XXIII [54–107] 161d-162b / *Odyssey*, BK XI
243a-249d; BK XXIV [1–203] 317a-319a

5 EURIPIDES: *Helen* [1009–1016] 307d

7 PLATO: *Phaedrus*, 124c-126c / *Phaedo*, 223a-
226c; 230d-234c; 246d-247b / *Gorgias*, 292b-
294d / *Republic*, BK X, 437c-441a,c / *Laws*,
BK XII, 793c-d

12 AURELIUS: *Meditations*, BK IV, SECT 21 265b-c;
BK VII, SECT 50 283a

13 VIRGIL: *Georgics*, IV [471–477] 96b

14 PLUTARCH: *Romulus*, 29a-b

17 PLOTINUS: *Fourth Ennead*, TR I 139a-b; TR III,
CH 13 149b-d; CH 18 151b-c; CH 24–25 154b-
155c; CH 27 156c-d; TR IV, CH I 159a-d

18 AUGUSTINE: *City of God*, BK XI, CH 23 334c-
335c; BK XIII, CH 2 360b-361a; CH 16 367a-d

19 AQUINAS: *Summa Theologica*, PART I, Q 29,
A I, REP 5 162a-163b; Q 77, A 8 406b-407a;
Q 89 473a-480c; Q 117, A 4 599b-d; Q 118, A 3
603b-604b

20 AQUINAS: *Summa Theologica*, PART I–II, Q 67,
AA 1–2 81c-83b; PART III SUPPL, Q 70 893c-
900d; Q 93, A I 1037d-1039a

21 DANTE: *Divine Comedy*, PURGATORY, XXV
[67–108] 92a-c

23 HOBBES: *Leviathan*, PART IV, 270c-271b

24 RABELAIS: *Gargantua and Pantagruel*, BK III,
150d-151c

25 MONTAIGNE: *Essays*, 248c-250a

31 SPINOZA: *Ethics*, PART V, PROP 38–40 461d-
462d

41 GIBBON: *Decline and Fall*, 233d

44 BOSWELL: *Johnson*, 192d-193c; 224b

48 MELVILLE: *Moby Dick*, 28a

5c. The judgment of souls

OLD TESTAMENT: *Job*, 19:29; 21 / *Psalms*, 49:6–9;
50 esp 50:4, 50:6, 50:21–22; 96:10–13—(D)
Psalms, 48:7–11; 49 esp 49:4, 49:6, 49:21–22;
95:10–13 / *Proverbs*, 22:22–23 / *Ecclesiastes*,
3:16–17; 11:9–10; 12:14 / *Isaiah*, 11:1–9 esp
11:3–5; 24:21–22; 34; 66—(D) *Isaias*, 11:1–9
esp 11:3–5; 24:21–22; 34; 66 / *Daniel*, 12 / *Joel*

APOCRYPHA: *Judith*, 16:17—(D) OT, *Judith*,
16:20–21 / *II Maccabees*, 7:31–36—(D) OT,
II Machabees, 7:31–36

NEW TESTAMENT: *Matthew*, 3:7–12 esp 3:10,
3:12; 7:1–2; 10:14–15; 11:20–24; 12:34–37;
13:18–50 esp 13:30, 13:39–43, 13:49–50; 24–
25 / *John*, 12:48 / *Acts*, 17:31 / *Romans*, 2 /
II Timothy, 4:1 / *Hebrews*, 9:27 / *I Peter*, 4:5–6
/ *II Peter*, 2:9; 3:7–13 / *I John*, 4:17 / *Jude*,
14–15 / *Revelation*, 20:9–15—(D) *Apocalypse*,
20:8–15

4 HOMER: *Odyssey*, BK XI [568–571] 248d

5 AESCHYLUS: *Suppliant Maidens* [228–231] 3d

5 EURIPIDES: *Helen* [1013–1016] 307d

7 PLATO: *Phaedrus*, 125b-126a / *Phaedo*, 249c-
250a / *Gorgias*, 292b-294d / *Republic*, BK X,
437c-438c / *Laws*, BK XII, 793c-d / *Seventh
Letter*, 806a

13 VIRGIL: *Aeneid*, BK VI [426–439] 222b; [548–
569] 225b-226a

17 PLOTINUS: *Fourth Ennead*, TR III, CH 24 154b-d

18 AUGUSTINE: *City of God*, BK XX 530a-560a,c;
BK XXI, CH 11–27 570b-586a,c passim

20 AQUINAS: *Summa Theologica*, PART III SUPPL,
QQ 87–90 997a-1016a

21 DANTE: *Divine Comedy*, HELL, III [70–136] 4d-
5b; V [1–24] 7a-b; VI [94–115] 9b-c; XIII [85–
108] 18d-19a; XX [1–39] 28b-d; XXVII [55–136]
40a-41b; XXIX [103–120] 44a-b; PURGATORY,
IX 65d-67b; PARADISE, XIX [100–148] 136a-c

22 CHAUCER: *Parson's Tale*, par 10 498b-502a

25 MONTAIGNE: *Essays*, 250a; 265b-c

27 SHAKESPEARE: *Macbeth*, ACT II, SC III [1–23]
292b

32 MILTON: *Christs Nativity* [149–164] 5a-b / *Paradise Lost*, BK III [315–338] 142a-b; BK XI [45–
83] 300a-301a; BK XII [451–465] 329a; [537–
551] 331a

35 LOCKE: *Toleration*, 17b

40 GIBBON: *Decline and Fall*, 187c; 188d-189a

41 GIBBON: *Decline and Fall*, 233c-234b

44 BOSWELL: *Johnson*, 514d-515a; 573c-574a

5d. The process of purification: the state of Purgatory

OLD TESTAMENT: *Isaiah*, 4:4—(D) *Isaias*, 4:4

APOCRYPHA: *II Maccabees*, 12:43–46—(D) OT,
II Machabees, 12:43–46

(5. *Conceptions of the after-life.* 5d. *The process of purification: the state of Purgatory.*)

NEW TESTAMENT: *Matthew*, 12:32 / *I Corinthians*, 3:11-15

7 PLATO: *Cratylus*, 95a-c / *Phaedo*, 224a-225c; 232d-234c; 246d-250b / *Gorgias*, 292b-294d / *Republic*, BK X, 437c-438c

13 VIRGIL: *Aeneid*, BK VI [264-751] 218a-231a

14 PLUTARCH: *Romulus*, 28a-29b

17 PLOTINUS: *First Ennead*, TR I, CH II 5b-c / *Third Ennead*, TR IV, CH 6 99b-100b / *Fourth Ennead*, TR III, CH 27, 156d

18 AUGUSTINE: *City of God*, BK X, CH 30 318b-319b; BK XX, CH 25 554c-555a; BK XXI, CH 13 571c-572a; CH 24 577b-579d

20 AQUINAS: *Summa Theologica*, PART III SUPPL, Q 69, A 2, ANS and REP 2 886c-887d; A 7, ANS and REP 6 891d-893c; Q 71, A 6 908b-909c; Q 97, A 1, REP 2 1066b-d

21 DANTE: *Divine Comedy*, PURGATORY 53a-105d esp I-II 53a-55d, IX 65d-67b, X [106-139] 68c-d, XIII [34-93] 72b-d, XVII [82-139] 79b-d, XIX [97-126] 82c-d, XXI [34-72] 85b-d, XXIII [1-75] 88b-89a, XXVII 94c-96a, XXX-XXXI 99b-102b

23 HOBBES: *Leviathan*, PART III, 244b-c; PART IV, 251b-c; 255b-258b; 271a-b

27 SHAKESPEARE: *Hamlet*, ACT I, SC V [9-22] 37a

41 GIBBON: *Decline and Fall*, 234b; 520c

44 BOSWELL: *Johnson*, 173d; 193a-b

52 DOSTOEVSKY: *Brothers Karamazov*, BK XI, 341c-345c passim

5e. The state of the damned: Hell

OLD TESTAMENT: *Deuteronomy*, 32:22 / *Job*, 26:6 / *Psalms*, 9:16-17; 116:3—(D) *Psalms*, 9:17-18; 114:3 / *Proverbs*, 7:27; 15:11,24; 27:20 / *Ecclesiastes*, 6:6 / *Isaiah*, 5:14-15; 14:4-23; 26:10; 33:10-14; 66:24—(D) *Isaias*, 5:14-15; 14:4-23; 26:10; 33:10-14; 66:24 / *Ezekiel*, 31:10-18—(D) *Ezechiel*, 31:10-18

APOCRYPHA: *Judith*, 16:17—(D) OT, *Judith*, 16:20-21 / *Wisdom of Solomon*, 4:16-5:14 esp 4:19—(D) OT, *Book of Wisdom*, 4:16-5:15 esp 4:19 / *Ecclesiasticus*, 7:17; 18:24; 21:9-10—(D) OT, *Ecclesiasticus*, 7:19; 18:24; 21:10-11 / *Baruch*, 2:17—(D) OT, *Baruch*, 2:17

NEW TESTAMENT: *Matthew*, 3:7-12; 5:22,29; 8:12; 10:28; 11:20-24; 13:41-42,49-50; 18:7-9; 25:31-46 esp 25:41, 25:46 / *Mark*, 3:29; 9:43-50—(D) *Mark*, 3:29; 9:42-49 / *Luke*, 12:5; 16:19-26 / *John*, 15:6 / *II Thessalonians*, 1:7-9 / *Hebrews*, 10:26-31 / *Jude*, 6-7 / *Revelation* passim, esp 9, 12, 17, 19-20—(D) *Apocalypse* passim, esp 9, 12, 17, 19-20

4 HOMER: *Odyssey*, BK XI 243a-249d esp [487-489] 247d, [568-600] 248d-249a

5 ARISTOPHANES: *Frogs* [143-159] 565d-566a

7 PLATO: *Phaedo*, 249c-250a / *Republic*, BK X, 437c-438c / *Laws*, BK IX, 757a; BK X, 767c-768c

12 LUCRETIUS: *Nature of Things*, BK III [978-1023] 42d-43b

13 VIRGIL: *Aeneid*, BK VI [548-627] 225b-227b; [735-747] 230b-231a

18 AUGUSTINE: *City of God*, BK XI, CH 33 341a-d; BK XIII, CH 2 360b-361a; CH 12 365d-366a; CH 14-15 366b-d; BK XIII, CH 23-BK XIV, CH I 372a-377a; BK XIV, CH 15 388d-390a; BK XV, CH I 397b,d-398c; BK XIX, CH 13 519a-520a; CH 28 529d-530a,c; BK XX, CH 15 543d-544b; BK XXI, 560a-586a,c / *Christian Doctrine*, BK I, CH 20-21 629b

19 AQUINAS: *Summa Theologica*, PART I, Q 10, A 3, REP 2 42c-43b

20 AQUINAS: *Summa Theologica*, PART III SUPPL, Q 69 885a-893c; Q 70, A 3 897d-900d; Q 86 992b-996a,c; Q 87, A 1, REP 4 997b-998c; Q 90, A 3 1014d-1016a; QQ 97-99 1066a-1085a,c

21 DANTE: *Divine Comedy*, HELL 1a-52d esp III [1-18] 4a-b, [82-129] 5a-b, VI [100-111] 9c, VII [100-130] 10c-d, XI 15a-16b, XIV [16-72] 19c-20b, XXVII [55-136] 40a-41b, XXVIII [139-142] 43a, XXXIII [91-150] 50c-51a; PARADISE, VII [64-84] 115d-116a; XV [10-12] 128c

22 CHAUCER: *Friar's Tale* 278a-284a / *Summoner's Prologue* 284b-285a / *Parson's Tale*, par 10, 499b-502a

23 HOBBES: *Leviathan*, PART III, 193d-195d; PART IV, 250c-251b; 254a-255b; 271a-b

24 RABELAIS: *Gargantua and Pantagruel*, BK II, 119b-122a

25 MONTAIGNE: *Essays*, 266c

26 SHAKESPEARE: *Richard III*, ACT I, SC IV [42-63] 115a-b

29 CERVANTES: *Don Quixote*, PART II, 418c-419a

31 DESCARTES: *Objections and Replies*, 227a

32 MILTON: *Paradise Lost*, BK I-II 93a-134a esp BK I [44-270] 94b-99a, BK II [521-628] 122b-125a; BK VI [867-877] 215a-b

35 LOCKE: *Human Understanding*, BK II, CH XXI, SECT 62 194c-d; SECT 72 198a-c

40 GIBBON: *Decline and Fall*, 188d-189a

41 GIBBON: *Decline and Fall*, 149c-150c passim; 234a-c

44 BOSWELL: *Johnson*, 363a-b

48 MELVILLE: *Moby Dick*, 347a

52 DOSTOEVSKY: *Brothers Karamazov*, BK I, 10c-d; BK V, 127c-d; BK VI, 169c-170b; BK XI, 341c-345c

5f. The state of the blessed: Heaven

OLD TESTAMENT: *Psalms*, 16 esp 16:10; 36 36:8-9; 37; 84; 149—(D) *Psalms*, 15 esp 15:10; 35 esp 35:9-10; 36; 83; 149 / *Isaiah*, 65:8-25—(D) *Isaias*, 65:8-25 / *Daniel*, 7:18

APOCRYPHA: *Wisdom of Solomon*, 1:15; 3:1-9,13-15; 4:7-5:5; 5:15-16—(D) OT, *Book of Wisdom*, 1:15; 3:1-9,13-15; 4:7-5:5; 5:16-17

NEW TESTAMENT: *Matthew*, 5:1-12,19-20; 6:19-21,33; 7:21-23; 13:43; 19:21; 25:31-46 esp 25:34, 25:46 / *Luke*, 16:19-26 / *John*, 6:38-40; 8:51; 10:24-30; 11:23-27; 16:20-24; 17:1-3

5g. The resurrection of the body

6. Doctrines of impersonal survival

6a. Immortality through offspring: the perpetuation of the species

(6. *Doctrines of impersonal survival.* 6a. *Immortality through offspring: the perpetuation of the species.*)

28 HARVEY: *On Animal Generation*, 364a; 384b; 390c-391c

30 BACON: *Advancement of Learning*, 29a-b; 72c-73a

46 HEGEL: *Philosophy of Right*, PART III, par 173 61a-b / *Philosophy of History*, INTRO, 189b-c; PART I, 212b-c; 246d-247a

48 MELVILLE: *Moby Dick*, 340b-341a

54 FREUD: *Narcissism*, 401b; 406c / *General Introduction*, 616a-b / *Beyond the Pleasure Principle*, 653b-c; 655b-656a

6b. Enduring fame: survival in the memory

OLD TESTAMENT: *Proverbs*, 10:7 / *Ecclesiastes*, 9:5
APOCRYPHA: *Judith*, 16:20-25—(D) OT, *Judith*, 16:24-31 / *Wisdom of Solomon*, 4:1-6; 8:9-13 —(D) OT, *Book of Wisdom*, 4:1-6; 8:9-13 / *Ecclesiasticus*, 37:26; 39:1-11; 40:19; 44:8-15; 46:11-12—(D) OT, *Ecclesiasticus*, 37:29; 39:1-15; 40:19; 44:8-15; 46:13-15 / *I Maccabees*, 3:1-7—(D) OT, *I Machabees*, 3:1-7 / *II Maccabees*, 6:21-31—(D) OT, *II Machabees*, 6:21-31

4 HOMER: *Iliad*, BK IX [410-429] 61b-c; BK XII [309-328] 85b-c; BK XXII [299-305] 158b / *Odyssey*, BK XXIV [191-202] 319a

5 SOPHOCLES: *Philoctetes* [1408-1444] 194d-195a,c

6 HERODOTUS: *History*, BK I, 1a-b

6 THUCYDIDES: *Peloponnesian War*, BK II, 398a-c

7 PLATO: *Symposium*, 165b-167a / *Laws*, BK IV, 685b-c

9 ARISTOTLE: *Politics*, BK V, CH 10 [1312ᵃ23-39] 514d

12 LUCRETIUS: *Nature of Things*, BK I [121-124] 2c

12 AURELIUS: *Meditations*, BK III, SECT 10 261d-262a; BK IV, SECT 19 265a; SECT 33 266c-d; BK VI, SECT 18 275d; BK VII, SECT 6 280b; BK VIII, SECT 44 289a; BK IX, SECT 30 294b-c

13 VIRGIL: *Aeneid*, BK I [453-463] 115b; [606-610] 119b; BK IV [321-322] 175b

14 PLUTARCH: *Pericles*, 125b

15 TACITUS: *Histories*, BK I, 195a-b

21 DANTE: *Divine Comedy*, HELL, IV 5c-7a; XVI [1-90] 22c-23b; PURGATORY, XI [73-117] 69c-70a; PARADISE, IX [37-63] 119a

23 HOBBES: *Leviathan*, PART I, 77a-b

24 RABELAIS: *Gargantua and Pantagruel*, BK II, 81a-d

25 MONTAIGNE: *Essays*, 112d-113a; 267a-c; 301b-c; 304d-306a

27 SHAKESPEARE: *Sonnets*, LV 594c-d; LXV 596a-b; LXXXI 598c-d

28 HARVEY: *Circulation of the Blood*, 312c-d

29 CERVANTES: *Don Quixote*, PART II, 226d-228d

30 BACON: *Advancement of Learning*, 27d-28c; 29a-b; 36a-c; 72c-73a

32 MILTON: *On Shakespear. 1630* 16a

33 PASCAL: *Pensées*, 148 201a

36 STERNE: *Tristram Shandy*, 535a-536a

37 FIELDING: *Tom Jones*, 273b; 274d

40 GIBBON: *Decline and Fall*, 94a-b; 219d

41 GIBBON: *Decline and Fall*, 494b,d-495a

42 KANT: *Science of Right*, 428b-429a

44 BOSWELL: *Johnson*, 57d-58a; 163d [fn 4]

46 HEGEL: *Philosophy of Right*, PART III, par 348 111d / *Philosophy of History*, INTRO, 153b-c; PART I, 212b-c; 254d-255d; PART II, 262c-263a; 274a-275a; 278d-279a; 281d-282d

47 GOETHE: *Faust*, PRELUDE [59-74] 2b-3a; PART II [9981-9982] 243a

6c. Participation in the eternity of truth, ideas, or love

17 PLOTINUS: *Sixth Ennead*, TR VII, CH 34-36 338b-339d

31 SPINOZA: *Ethics*, PART V, PROP 21-42 458a-463d

46 HEGEL: *Philosophy of History*, INTRO, 156d-168c esp 156d-157b, 168b-c; 190a-b; 203c-206a,c

CROSS-REFERENCES

For: Other discussions of man's attitude toward mutability and death, *see* CHANGE 12b; HAPPINESS 4b; LIFE AND DEATH 8c; TIME 7.

The basic terms and propositions involved in arguments for or against the immortality of the soul, *see* BEING 7b(1)–7b(4); ETERNITY 4a; FORM 2d; MAN 3a–3a(2), 3c; MATTER 2d; MIND 1b, 2a, 2d–2e; SOUL 3a–3d, 4b; and for the contrast between souls and angels with respect to their mode of being, *see* ANGEL 4; ETERNITY 4a; FORM 2d; MAN 3b; SOUL 4d(2).

Other discussions of immortality as a postulate of the practical reason, *see* METAPHYSICS 2d; NECESSITY AND CONTINGENCY 4b.

Another statement of the doctrine of reincarnation or the transmigration of souls, *see* SOUL 4d(1).

Articles of religious belief bearing on immortality, such as predestination, the Last Judgment, and the resurrection of the body, *see* GOD 7f–7h; HAPPINESS 7c; SOUL 4d(3).

The relevance of the doctrine of innate ideas to immortality, *see* IDEA 2b; KNOWLEDGE 6c(3); MEMORY AND IMAGINATION 3a; MIND 4d(2).

The relevance to immortality of the theory of mind or intellect as an incorporeal power, *see* MAN 3a(2); MATTER 4d; MIND 2a; SOUL 3b.

The state of the soul separated from the body, *see* KNOWLEDGE 7c; SOUL 4d.

The moral significance of immortality in relation to divine rewards and punishments, *see* GOD 5i; PUNISHMENT 5d.

Other discussions of the underworld, or of Hell, Purgatory, and Heaven, *see* ETERNITY 4d; HAPPINESS 7c–7c(3); PUNISHMENT 5e–5e(2); SIN 6d–6e.

The immortality of enduring fame, *see* HONOR 2d.

ADDITIONAL READINGS

Listed below are works not included in *Great Books of the Western World*, but relevant to the idea and topics with which this chapter deals. These works are divided into two groups:

I. Works by authors represented in this collection.
II. Works by authors not represented in this collection.

For the date, place, and other facts concerning the publication of the works cited, consult the Bibliography of Additional Readings which follows the last chapter of *The Great Ideas*.

I.

AUGUSTINE. *On the Immortality of the Soul*
AQUINAS. *Summa Contra Gentiles*, BK IV, CH 79–95
——. *Quaestiones Disputatae, De Anima*, A 14
DANTE. *Convivio (The Banquet)*, SECOND TREATISE, CH 9 (4–6)
F. BACON. "Of Death," in *Essays*
HUME. *Of the Immortality of the Soul*
——. *Of Suicide*
J. S. MILL. "Theism," PART III, in *Three Essays on Religion*
W. JAMES. *Human Immortality*

II.

EPICURUS. *Letter to Menoeceus*
CICERO. *De Republica (The Republic)*, VI
——. *Tusculan Disputations*, I
——. *De Senectute (Of Old Age)*
OVID. *Metamorphoses*
SENECA. *De Consolatione ad Marciam (On Consolation to Marcia)*
GREGORY OF NYSSA. *On the Soul and the Resurrection*
PROCLUS. *The Elements of Theology*, PROPOSITIONS 104–105, 208–210
SAADIA GAON. *The Book of Beliefs and Opinions*, TREATISE VI, VIII
BONAVENTURA. *Breviloquium*, PART VII
R. BACON. *Opus Majus*, PART VII
ALBO. *The Book of Principles (Sefer ha-Ikkarim)*, BK IV, CH 29–41
NICOLAS OF CUSA. *The Vision of God*
POMPONAZZI. *On the Immortality of the Soul*
VAUGHAN. *The Retreate*
KING. *The Exequy*
BROWNE. *Hydriotaphia*
H. MORE. *The Immortality of the Soul*

Chapter 39: INDUCTION

INTRODUCTION

AS the list of Additional Readings indicates, the theory of induction falls within the province of logic and is part of the logician's concern with the methods of inference or reasoning employed in the sciences. The great controversies about induction seem to be of relatively recent origin in the history of logic, beginning perhaps with the argument between William Whewell and J. S. Mill over the contributions of reason and experience to the inductive process. Later in the nineteenth century and in our own time, writers like Johnson and Keynes, Russell and Nicod, who present different formulations of inductive inference, call attention to the unsolved problems with which any theory is left. They underline the assumptions that seem to be unavoidable in any statement of the formal conditions which validate the so-called "inductive leap"—the jump from observed particulars to general truths, truths having a wider generality than the particular evidences from which they are drawn or on which they are based.

The problem of induction, in anyone's version of it, is the problem of generalization. This may involve psychological questions about how the mind generalizes from experience. But however they are answered, the basic logical questions remain substantially unaltered. By what criteria is valid distinguished from fallacious induction? Can induction be secured from error by rules of inference? Is induction indispensable in the development of scientific knowledge, or is there, as Whewell, for example, suggests, a sharp distinction between the inductive and the deductive sciences?

What is the relation of induction to deduction? Is it the relation of a method of discovery to a method of demonstration or proof? Is it a relation between two modes of reasoning, both of which can be formulated as processes of proof? Is there both an inductive and a deductive type of syllogism, or is induction the very opposite of all forms of reasoning and proof?

It is with these last questions that the discussion of induction begins in the great books, especially in Aristotle's *Organon* and Bacon's *Novum Organum*, but also in the writings of Descartes and Locke, and in observations on scientific method by Newton, Harvey, and Pascal. Though many of the controversies and problems which become central in the nineteenth century do not appear explicitly in the earlier tradition, they are anticipated by the fundamental distinctions and issues which can be found in the earlier writers.

Bacon's dissatisfaction with Aristotle, for example, leads him to formulate specific rules for induction. Going further in the same general direction, Mill later develops his elaborate theory of inductive inference. We move in the opposite direction if we are guided by Aristotle's distinction between scientific and dialectical induction and by his way of setting induction off as the very opposite of reasoning. The question then arises whether Bacon and Mill are treating induction in all or in only one of several quite distinct senses.

As THE CHAPTER on LOGIC indicates, the names of Aristotle and Bacon are sometimes used as the symbols of opposed tendencies in logic. The one is supposed to represent an almost exclusive emphasis on deduction, the other the primacy and importance of induction. An opposition between Aristotle and Bacon is also implied in the current use of such phrases as "inductive logic" and "deductive logic." These phrases are sometimes used to suggest that the inductive or the deductive process can be favored to the exclusion, or at least the subordination, of the other. Such understanding of the matter usually includes the popular notion that induction is always reasoning from particulars to universals and deduction always reasoning from universals to particulars.

But none of these things seems to be true, or at least not without serious qualification. Neither Aristotle nor Bacon emphasizes deduction or induction to the exclusion of the other. On the contrary, both appear to insist on the absolute priority of induction, since, according to them, it provides deductive reasoning with its ultimate premises. Far from conflicting, induction and deduction complement each other. "The consilience of the results of both these processes," Mill writes, "each corroborating and verifying the other, is requisite to give to any general proposition the kind and degree of evidence which constitutes scientific proof."

Until principles are established, the deduction of their implications or consequences cannot begin. Unless principles, once they are obtained, are then used in the proof of other truths, or are otherwise rationally employed, the purpose of inductive generalization is not fully realized. In this understanding of the relationship between induction and reasoning, Aristotle and Bacon do not seem to disagree, nor does either of them conceive induction as a process of *reasoning* from particulars to universals.

There is no question that the direction of induction is from particulars; but in the precise sense in which induction precedes deduction— the sense in which both Bacon and Aristotle regard it as the source of axioms—they do not think it is a process of reasoning or a form of proof. As for deduction, it is questionable, at least for Aristotle, whether its direction can be described as from the universal to the particular.

Aristotle seldom uses the word "deduction" as the name for that phase of thought which is complementary to induction. He speaks rather of demonstration. Demonstration takes place through the various forms of reasoning which he calls "syllogisms." As the chapter on REASONING explains, these are collections of premises each of which yields a conclusion by valid inference. In the most perfect forms of reasoning, the conclusion is as universal as its premises, and though there are syllogisms in which a par-

ticular proposition can be demonstrated from a universal and a particular premise, it is seldom the case that from exclusively universal premises a particular conclusion can be validly drawn. The statement that deduction is reasoning from universals to particulars certainly does not seem to fit Aristotle's theory of the syllogism, and even less his conception of scientific demonstration, the aim of which is to prove universal, not particular, propositions.

"WE LEARN EITHER by induction or by demonstration," Aristotle writes in the *Prior Analytics*. "Demonstration develops from universals, induction from particulars." In the *Posterior Analytics* he says that the ultimate premises of demonstration must be primary or basic truths. A basic truth is an immediate proposition—what is sometimes called a "first principle" or an "axiom." Since in his view "an immediate proposition is one which has no other proposition prior to it," the basic premises cannot be demonstrated.

Whence come these primary premises which are indispensable to demonstration but which demonstration cannot establish? Aristotle's answer is that "we know the primary premises by induction." In another place he says, "it is by intuition that we obtain the primary premises."

The word "intuition" indicates an essential characteristic of the sort of induction which, because it is not itself a form of reasoning, can be prior to all reasoning and *must be*, in order to supply the premises from which reasoning proceeds. Reasoning is discursive. It is a process involving steps. One proposition is drawn from another by the mediation of a third. Intuition, in contrast, is immediate. Like an act of seeing, it apprehends its object at once and directly. When Aristotle speaks of induction as a kind of intuition, he implies, therefore, that it consists in the immediate grasp of a universal truth. The proposition thus held he calls "immediate" precisely because it can be known intuitively and in no other way. Intuitive induction, as opposed to what may be called "inductive reasoning," consists in seeing the universal in the particular. When what is seen is expressed in the form of a proposition, the universal implicit in the known particulars is made explicit.

Induction and intuition are, however, not identical for Aristotle. In one passage in the *Prior Analytics* he considers syllogistic induction, which can hardly be called "intuitive." And in the *Ethics*, where he discusses intuitive reason, he distinguishes between two sorts of primary truth that can be known by intuition.

"Intuitive reason," he writes, "is concerned with the ultimates in both directions; for both the first terms and the last are objects of intuitive reason and not of argument, and the intuitive reason which is presupposed by demonstrations grasps the unchangeable and first terms, while the intuitive reason involved in practical reasoning grasps the last and variable fact, *i.e.*, the minor premise. For these variable facts are the starting-points for the apprehension of the end, since the universals are reached from the particulars; of these therefore we must have perception, and this perception is intuitive reason."

This applies to theoretic as well as practical knowledge. By intuitive reason, it seems, we grasp both the universal principles or axioms and the particular facts of sense-perception. As perception is intuition on the part of the sensitive faculty, so induction is an intuitive use of the intellect (though Aristotle attributes both to "intuitive reason").

These two forms of intuition are functionally related. The induction of universal truths from particulars is impossible without sense-perception, "for it is sense-perception alone which is able to grasp the particulars." But, according to Aristotle, a single isolated perception does not give rise to an intuitive induction. Repeated perceptions of things of a certain sort—particulars of a certain class—are formed by memory into what he calls "an experience." Because the experience refers, not to a single individual, but to a class of similar individuals, it provides the material for the mind's intuitive act of induction.

This theory of the role of experience in induction is more fully discussed in the chapter on EXPERIENCE. For our present purposes, the main point is that the universal, lying implicitly in the experience, is ready, as it were, to be extracted therefrom and made explicit. "Though the act of sense-perception is of the particular, its content is universal," Aristotle writes. With the help of memory and experience, induction makes the latent universal manifest.

BACON'S CRITICISM of the logic of Aristotle seems to rest on two counts: first, he complains of Aristotle's over-emphasis on syllogisms, whether they are used dialectically or demonstratively; and second, he charges Aristotle with a superficial understanding of induction. One of the chief efforts of the *Novum Organum* is to correct the latter mistake.

"There are and can exist," says Bacon, "but two ways of investigating and discovering truth. The one hurries on rapidly from the senses and particulars to the most general axioms, and from them, as principles, and from their supposed indisputable truth, deduces the intermediate axioms. This is the way now in use. The other constructs its axioms from the senses and particulars, by ascending continually and gradually, until it finally arrives at the most general axioms, which is the true but unattempted way."

Where Aristotle proposes that only the primary truths or first principles be established by induction, while all the others (which Bacon calls "intermediate axioms") are to be derived from them by demonstration, Bacon urges a method of induction which shall mount gradually from the least general to the most universal propositions. We should not "suffer the understanding to jump and fly from particulars to remote and most general axioms." We should "proceed by a true scale and successive steps, without interruption or breach, from particulars to the lesser axioms, thence to the intermediate (rising one above the other), and lastly, to the most general."

According to this theory, induction can intuitively draw more general from less general truths, as well as the least general truths from the particulars of perception. It might seem at first as if there were no place for deduction in the development of science. But Bacon divides the study of nature into two phases: "the first regards the eliciting or creating of axioms from experiments, the second the deducing or deriving of new experiments from axioms." Here too there seems to be a crucial difference between Bacon and Aristotle. This difference is indicated by Bacon's emphasis upon *experiments* both as the source of inductive generalization and also as that which is ultimately derived by deduction from axioms.

The difference between *experience* (which Aristotle makes the source of induction) and *experiment* is more than verbal. "The axioms now in use," Bacon contends, "are derived from a scanty handful, as it were, of experience, and a few particulars of frequent occurrence." There has been too little attention given to negative instances, that is, of cases which seem to run counter to the generalization being formed. "In establishing any true axiom," Bacon insists, "the negative instance is the most powerful."

The chapter on EXPERIENCE dwells on the difference between ordinary experience and planned experiments. Where Aristotle seems to be satisfied with the ordinary experience which arises from the perceptions of men in the course of daily life, Bacon thinks it does not suffice. Because it is haphazard, it fails to collect the variety of instances, both positive and negative, upon which genuine and solid inductions can be founded. Unusual and special experiences must be sought out, and the effort must be made to invent experiences which do not arise spontaneously. For this, experiment—or the production of experiences—is necessary. Bacon thinks we must, "by every kind of experiment, elicit the discovery of causes and true axioms."

Two CONSEQUENCES FOLLOW from the several differences we have noted between Aristotle's and Bacon's theories of induction.

In the first place, Aristotle does not seem to think that induction can be methodically prescribed by logical rules. It is a natural act of intelligence to draw universals from experience. Though men may differ in the readiness of their native wit, the induction of the primary truths, which are the axioms or first principles of science, does not require special genius nor can it be improved or rendered more certain by following rules. Precisely because it is intuitive rather than discursive, induction, unlike reasoning, cannot be regulated by rules of inference such as those which govern the syllogism.

Without disagreeing that it is intuitive rather than argumentative, Bacon seems to think that induction requires the practice of the most detailed and precise method. Not only must the various ascending stages of induction be regulated by observance of an order of generality, but the making of experiments and the collection and arrangement of particulars, "forming tables and coordinations of instances," must be governed by a complex set of rules. The twenty-seven tables of instances, set forth in the second book of the *Novum Organum*, constitute the heart of Bacon's method of induction. This new method "of discovering the sciences," he observes, "levels men's wits and leaves but little of their superiority, since it achieves everything by the most certain rules."

In the second place, since genuine induction depends for Bacon upon ample experiments, it belongs primarily to the method of the experimental sciences—the physical or natural sciences in which experimentation is possible. Though the first principles or axioms of arithmetic and geometry may be learned by induction, the method of gradual ascent from experiments through intermediate generalizations does not apply to mathematics. Here we may have the beginning of the notion that only the experimental sciences are primarily inductive, whereas other sciences, like mathematics, are primarily deductive.

But such a division of the sciences does not accord with Aristotle's theory of induction. He thinks mathematics and metaphysics require induction for their foundation no less than physics and in no different way; if anything, induction is of the greatest importance for metaphysics, because all its principles are indemonstrable, whereas some of the principles needed in mathematics and physics can be demonstrated in metaphysics. Yet no science is peculiarly inductive, just as none stands in a special relation to experience. All depend equally upon experience for the induction of the primary truths on which their demonstrations rest.

Descartes seems to fall somewhere between Aristotle and Bacon. He regards arithmetic and geometry as more certain than the physical sciences, because mathematics is largely developed by deduction, whereas the study of nature depends upon induction from experiments. In this lies the superiority of mathematics. "While our inferences from experience are frequently fallacious," Descartes writes, "deduction, or the pure illation of one thing from another . . . cannot be erroneous when performed by an understanding that is in the least degree rational."

Nevertheless, Descartes does not exclude induction as the source of the axioms of mathematics or, for that matter, of metaphysics; he only excludes the kind of induction which depends upon experiments. Such axioms as *when equals are taken from equals the remainders are equal* or *the whole is greater than any of its parts* are products of induction, as may be seen, he points out, from the fact that a child can be taught these general truths only "by showing him examples in particular cases." Similarly, the metaphysical truth in the proposition *I think; therefore, I exist* cannot be learned by deduction or syllogistic reasoning. The axiom that *to think is to exist* has to be learned by induction "from the experience of the individual—that unless he exists he cannot think. For our mind is so constituted by nature that general propositions are formed out of the knowledge of particulars."

FROM THE FOREGOING we can gather that different theories of induction may be, in large part, theories about different kinds of induction. Common to induction of every sort is the motion of the mind from particulars, apprehended by sense, to general propositions or universal notions. But the character of the induction, or its conditions and method, may differ according to the precise character of its source: (1) whether it arises from ordinary sense-experience or from planned experiments; and (2) whether it is based upon a single experiment or upon an enumeration of instances. There remains the most radical distinction in type of induction: (3) whether it is intuitive or discursive—accomplished by an act of immediate insight or by a process of reasoning from premises to a conclusion.

These three divisions cross one another to some extent. Descartes, for example, seems to regard the complete enumeration of a series of connected facts as a way of drawing a general conclusion about their connection. That he has inductive reasoning rather than intuitive induction in mind, we learn from his statement

that "by adequate enumeration or induction is meant that method by which we attain surer conclusions than by any other type of proof, with the exception of simple intuition."

Pascal seems to be making the same point when he says that "in all matters whose proof is by experiment and not by demonstration, no universal assertion can be made except by the general enumeration of all the parts and all the different cases." Bacon, on the other hand, always thinks of induction as intuitive generalization, and therefore maintains that "induction which proceeds by simple enumeration is puerile, leads to uncertain conclusions, and is exposed to danger from one contradictory instance."

The elaborate procedure which Bacon proposes for collating instances stresses, not completeness of enumeration, but an examination of their relation to one another and, in the light thereof, an interpretation of their significance. Mill's four or five methods of induction bear a close resemblance to Bacon's more numerous tables of instances; but Mill's methods are attempts to formulate the rules of inference for inductive reasoning, whereas Bacon's rules are rules, not of reasoning, but of tabulating the particulars from which intuitive generalizations can be formed.

On Mill's view of induction, it may be questioned whether induction from an exhaustive enumeration is induction at all, for it seems to result in a *summary* of the facts enumerated rather than a *generalization* from particulars. Where there is no inductive leap, there is no induction. Where the inductive leap does occur, however, it seems easier to understand it as an intuitive act—a seeing of the universal in the particular—rather than as a process of reasoning. Each of Mill's methods requires a rule of inference which is itself a universal proposition. His critics have asked, Whence come these universal propositions about the relations of cause and effect or about the order and uniformity of nature? They point out that he cannot answer that these propositions are themselves conclusions of inductive reasoning without begging the question.

SUCH CRITICISM of inductive reasoning does not seem to apply to Aristotle's conception of it, for with him it is not, as with Mill, distinct in form from the syllogism. It is simply a distinct type of syllogism, which consists in reasoning from effect to cause rather than from cause to effect. Nor does the observation that an inductive inference cannot be more than probable apply to what Aristotle means by an inductive syllogism.

The certainty or probability of non-syllogistic induction depends on the source of the inference—whether it derives from a single specially constructed experiment or from an enumeration of particular instances, with or without a statistical calculation based on their frequency. The conception of a perfect experiment implies that the operation of a universal law can be exhibited in a single case. It is almost as if the controlling aim of the experiment were to make the universal manifest in the particular.

Newton's experiments on reflection and refraction seem to be of this sort. From them certain laws of optics are directly induced, even as, according to Aristotle and Descartes, the axioms of mathematics or metaphysics can be directly induced from simple experiences, available to a child or familiar to all men. Yet Newton does not think that the inductive establishment of such laws is as certain as demonstration.

The analytic method, he writes, "consists in making experiments and observations and in drawing general conclusions from them by induction. And although the arguing from experiments and observations by induction be no demonstration of general conclusions; yet it is the best way of arguing which the nature of things admits of, and may be looked upon as so much stronger, by how much the induction is more general. If no exception occur from phenomena, the conclusion may be pronounced generally; but if at any time afterwards any exception shall occur from experiments, it may then begin to be pronounced with such exceptions as occur."

Because it must depend on inductive generalizations from experience which, in his view, can never be certain, Locke doubts that physics can ever become a science. "I deny not," he writes, "that a man, accustomed to rational and regular experiments, shall be able to see further into the nature of bodies and guess righter at their yet unknown properties, than one that is a stranger to them; but yet, as I have said, this is but judgment and opinion, not knowledge and certainty. This way of *getting and improving our knowledge in substances only by experience and history*, which is all that the weakness of our faculties in this state of mediocrity . . . can attain to, makes me suspect," Locke concludes, "that *natural philosophy is not capable of being made a science*."

Hume offers two reasons for the inconclusiveness and uncertainty which he thinks qualify all our generalizations or inductions from experience. The first calls attention to the fact that, unlike mathematical reasoning, inferences from experience in the realm of physical matters depend on the number of cases observed. "The conclusions which [reason] draws from considering one circle," he says, "are the same it would form upon surveying all the circles in the universe. But no man, having seen only one body move, after being impelled by another, could infer that every other body will move after a like impulse."

The principle "which determines him to form such a conclusion" is, according to Hume, "Custom or Habit"; and precisely because inductive generalization is an effect of custom rather than of reasoning in the strict sense, the strength of the induction—or the force of custom—varies with the number of cases from which it arises. "After the constant conjunction of two objects—heat and flame, for instance, weight and solidity—we are determined by custom alone to expect the one from the appearance of the other. This hypothesis," Hume maintains, "seems . . . the only one which explains the difficulty, why we draw, from a thousand instances, an inference which we are not able to draw from one instance, that is in no respect different from them. Reason is incapable of any such variation."

Since *all* the relevant cases can never be exhaustively observed, the inference from a customary conjunction must always remain uncertain, no matter how high a probability it derives from the multiplication of like instances. To this first point, concerning the dependence of the probability of generalizations from experience upon the frequency of the observed instances, Hume adds a second point about the similarity of the cases under observation. Analogy, he says, "leads us to expect from any cause the same events, which we have observed to result from similar causes. Where the causes are entirely similar, the analogy is perfect, and the inference drawn from it is regarded as certain and conclusive. ... But where the objects have not so exact a similarity, the analogy is less perfect, and the inference is less conclusive; though still it has some force, in proportion to the degree of similarity and resemblance." The absence of perfect similarity is Hume's second reason for the inconclusiveness or uncertainty of inductive generalizations.

The contrary supposition—that one case can be perfectly representative of an infinite number of similar cases—may explain why Aristotle seems to think that induction is able to produce the primary truths or principles of science with a certitude which gives certainty to all the demonstrations founded on these axioms. Another explanation of Aristotle's view may be found in his distinction between scientific and dialectical induction. He regards the former as based on the kind of common experience which, unlike even the best experiment, admits of no exceptions. In contrast, dialectical induction, or the still weaker form of induction which he calls "rhetorical," is based on an enumeration of cases (which may not be complete) or upon a single example (which provides no safeguard against possible exceptions).

In its dialectical form, the inductive argument proceeds from a number of particulars

taken for granted. Aristotle offers this example of dialectical induction: "Supposing the skilled pilot is the most effective, and likewise the skilled charioteer, then, in general, the skilled man is the best at his particular task." In its rhetorical form, no more than a single example may be used, as when the orator generalizes that honesty is the best policy from the story of a particular individual who was finally rewarded for his virtue.

In both forms, the inductive generalization is at best probable; and it is more or less probable according to the soundness of the suppositions or the examples from which it originates —to be tested only by extending the enumeration of particulars. But if an induction is merely probable in the first place, it can only be made more probable, it can never be made certain, by multiplying cases or by increasing their variety.

Aristotle's theory of dialectical induction thus seems to have a bearing on the probability of induction from limited experiments (or from a single experiment whose perfection is not assured) and of induction from the frequency or variety of observed instances. The other point to be noted is that Bacon's basic rule of gradual ascent from particular cases through less general to more general propositions seems to be relevant to dialectical induction, but not, on Aristotle's view, to that kind of induction which produces the axioms or principles of science.

OUTLINE OF TOPICS

REFERENCES

To find the passages cited, use the numbers in heavy type, which are the volume and page numbers of the passages referred to. For example, in 4 HOMER: *Iliad*, BK II [265-283] 12d, the number 4 is the number of the volume in the set; the number 12d indicates that the passage is in section d of page 12.

PAGE SECTIONS: When the text is printed in one column, the letters a and b refer to the upper and lower halves of the page. For example, in 53 JAMES: *Psychology*, 116a-119b, the passage begins in the upper half of page 116 and ends in the lower half of page 119. When the text is printed in two columns, the letters a and b refer to the upper and lower halves of the left-hand side of the page, the letters c and d to the upper and lower halves of the right-hand side of the page. For example, in 7 PLATO: *Symposium*, 163b-164c, the passage begins in the lower half of the left-hand side of page 163 and ends in the upper half of the right-hand side of page 164.

AUTHOR'S DIVISIONS: One or more of the main divisions of a work (such as PART, BK, CH, SECT) are sometimes included in the reference; line numbers, in brackets, are given in certain cases; *e.g.*, *Iliad*, BK II [265-283] 12d.

BIBLE REFERENCES: The references are to book, chapter, and verse. When the King James and Douay versions differ in title of books or in the numbering of chapters or verses, the King James version is cited first and the Douay, indicated by a (*D*), follows; *e.g.*, OLD TESTAMENT: *Nehemiah*, 7:45—(*D*) II *Esdras*, 7:46.

SYMBOLS: The abbreviation "esp" calls the reader's attention to one or more especially relevant parts of a whole reference; "passim" signifies that the topic is discussed intermittently rather than continuously in the work or passage cited.

For additional information concerning the style of the references, see the Explanation of Reference Style; for general guidance in the use of *The Great Ideas*, consult the Preface.

1. The theory of induction: generalization from particulars

1a. Induction and intuition: their relation to reasoning or demonstration

8 ARISTOTLE: *Posterior Analytics*, BK I, CH 3 [72^{b}18-24] 99b-c; CH 23 [84^{b}31-85^{a}1] 115d-116a; CH 31 [87^{b}39-88^{a}17] 120a-c; CH 33 [88^{b}30-89^{a}1] 121b-c; BK II, CH 2 [90^{a}24-30] 123b-c; CH 19 136a-137a,c / *Topics*, BK I, CH 12 148d; BK VIII, CH I [155^{b}35-156^{a}7] 211d-212a; [156^{b}10-18] 212c-d / *Metaphysics*, BK I, CH 9 [992^{b}24-993^{a}1] 511a-b

9 ARISTOTLE: *Ethics*, BK I, CH 7 [1098^{a}34-^{b}3] 343d; BK VI, CH 3 388b-c; CH 6 389d; CH 8 [1142^{a}23-31] 391b-c; CH II 392c-393b esp [1143^{a}32-^{b}6] 392d-393a / *Rhetoric*, BK II, CH 20 [1393^{a}25-26] 641a

28 HARVEY: *On Animal Generation*, 332a-335c esp 333d-334d

30 BACON: *Advancement of Learning*, 43d-44c; 59c; 61d; 96d-97a / *Novum Organum*, 105a-195d esp BK I, APH II-26 107d-108d, APH 69 116a-b, APH 105 128b-c, BK II, APH I-19 137a-140d, APH 15-16 149a-b, APH 20-22 150d-153c, APH 52 194c-195d

31 DESCARTES: *Rules*, III 3b-5a esp 4a-b; VII, 10c-12a; IX 14d-15d; XI, 17b-d / *Objections and Replies*, 123a-b; 167c-d

31 SPINOZA: *Ethics*, PART II, PROP 40, SCHOL 2 388a-b

33 PASCAL: *Pensées*, 1-5 171a-173a

35 HUME: *Human Understanding*, SECT I, DIV 2 451b-c; DIV 9 454c-455a; SECT IV, DIV 26 460b-c

1b. Inductive reasoning: the issue concerning inductive and deductive proof

8 ARISTOTLE: *Prior Analytics*, BK II, CH 23 90a-c / *Posterior Analytics*, BK I, CH I [71^{a}1-11] 97a; CH 3 [72^{b}25-33] 99c; CH 18 111b-c; BK II, CH 7 [92^{a}34-^{b}1] 126b / *Topics*, BK I, CH 18 [108^{b}7-12] 152d / *Physics*, BK VIII, CH I [252^{a}23-25] 336a

9 ARISTOTLE: *Ethics*, BK I, CH 4 [1095^{a}30-^{b}8] 340c; CH 7 [1098^{a}35-^{b}3] 343d; BK VI, CH 3 388b-c / *Rhetoric*, BK I, CH 2 [1356^{b}5-18] 596a-b

28 GALILEO: *Two New Sciences*, FOURTH DAY, 252a-b

28 HARVEY: *Motion of the Heart*, 280c

30 BACON: *Advancement of Learning*, 42a-c; 57b-58b; 61d; 96d-97a / *Novum Organum* 105a-195d esp BK I, APH II-26 107d-108d, APH 69 116a-b, APH 103-106 127d-128c, BK II, APH 10-52 140c-195d

31 DESCARTES: *Rules*, II, 2d-3a; VII, 10c-12a; XI 17b-18b; XII, 24a-b / *Discourse*, PART VI, 61d-62c / *Objections and Replies*, 167c-d

34 Newton: *Principles*, bk iii, rule iv 271b / *Optics*, bk iii, 543a-b

35 Locke: *Human Understanding*, bk iv, ch xii, sect 10 361b-c

35 Hume: *Human Understanding*, sect iv, div 26 460b-c; sect ix, div 82 487b-c; sect xii, div 131-132 508d-509d passim

42 Kant: *Pure Reason*, 45b-46a

43 Mill: *Utilitarianism*, 445a-447b passim; 475b,d [fn 1] passim

45 Faraday: *Researches in Electricity*, 659a

51 Tolstoy: *War and Peace*, epilogue ii, 690b

53 James: *Psychology*, 674a-675b esp 675b

2. The conditions or sources of induction: memory, experience, experiment

8 Aristotle: *Prior Analytics*, bk i, ch 30 [46ª 18–28] 64a; bk ii, ch 23 [68ᵇ15–29] 90b-c / *Posterior Analytics*, bk i, ch 1 [71ª1–8] 97a; ch 3 [72ᵇ25–33] 99c; ch 18 111b-c; ch 31 [87ᵇ39–88ª17] 120a-c; bk ii, ch 2 [90ª24–30] 123b-c; ch 7 [92ª34–ᵇ1] 126b; ch 19 [99ᵇ20–100ᵇ5] 136a-d / *Topics*, bk i, ch 12 148d; ch 18 [108ᵇ7–12] 152d; bk ii, ch 7 [113ª31–33] 158d; bk viii, ch 1 [155ᵇ35–156ª7] 211d-212a; [156ᵇ10–18] 212c-d / *Physics*, bk i, ch 1 259a-b; ch 8 [191ª24–34] 267a-b / *Heavens*, bk iii, ch 7 [306ª6–18] 397b-c / *Generation and Corruption*, bk i, ch 2 [316ª5–8] 411c / *Metaphysics*, bk i, ch 1 499a-500b; ch 9 [992ᵇ24–993ª1] 511a-b

9 Aristotle: *Ethics*, bk i, ch 4 [1095ª30–ᵇ8] 340c; ch 7 [1098ª34–ᵇ8] 343d-344a; bk vi, ch 8 [1142ª12–19] 391b; ch 11 [1143ª32–ᵇ6] 392d-393a / *Rhetoric*, bk ii, ch 20 [1393ª22–1394ª8] 640d-641d

20 Aquinas: *Summa Theologica*, part i-ii, q 51, a 1, ans 12b-13c

28 Gilbert: *Loadstone*, pref, 1a-c

28 Galileo: *Two New Sciences*, third day, 200a-b; 207d-208a

28 Harvey: *Motion of the Heart*, 267b,d-268d; 285c-d / *Circulation of the Blood*, 322d-323d; 324c-d / *On Animal Generation*, 331b-335c; 383d; 473a

30 Bacon: *Advancement of Learning*, 16a; 34b; 57b-d; 59c / *Novum Organum*, bk i, aph 17 108a; aph 19 108b; aph 22 108c; aph 25 108d; aph 69 116a-b; aph 104-105 128a-c; bk ii, aph 11-15 140d-149a

31 Descartes: *Rules*, ii, 2d-3a; vii, 10c-12a / *Discourse*, part vi, 61d-62c / *Objections and Replies*, 167c-d

31 Spinoza: *Ethics*, part ii, prop 40, schol 1-2 387b-388b

33 Pascal: *Vacuum*, 358a-b

34 Newton: *Principles*, bk iii, rule iii-iv 270b-271b / *Optics*, bk iii, 543a-b

35 Berkeley: *Human Knowledge*, sect 107 433d-434a

35 Hume: *Human Understanding*, sect iii, div 19, 458a

42 Kant: *Pure Reason*, 5a-13d; 45b-46a; 66d-93c / *Judgement*, 562d-563b

45 Faraday: *Researches in Electricity*, 659a

46 Hegel: *Philosophy of History*, part iv, 361a-b

54 Freud: *Instincts*, 412a

3. The products of induction: definitions, axioms, principles, laws

8 Aristotle: *Prior Analytics*, bk ii, ch 23 90a-c / *Posterior Analytics*, bk i, ch 3 [72ᵇ25–30] 99c; ch 18 111b-c; ch 31 [87ᵇ39–88ª17] 120a-c; bk ii, ch 2 [90ª24–30] 123b-c; ch 7 [92ª34–ᵇ1] 126b; ch 19 136a-137a,c / *Topics*, bk i, ch 12 148d; ch 18 [108ᵇ7–12] 152d; bk viii, ch 1 [155ᵇ35–156ª7] 211d-212a; [156ᵇ10–18] 212c-d / *Generation and Corruption*, bk i, ch 2 [316ª 5–8] 411c

9 Aristotle: *Ethics*, bk i, ch 4 [1095ª30–ᵇ8] 340c; ch 7 [1098ª34–ᵇ3] 343d; bk vi, ch 3 [1139ᵇ25–34] 388c; ch 6 389d; ch 11 [1143ª25–ᵇ13] 392d-393a

19 Aquinas: *Summa Theologica*, part i, q 79, a 12, ans 425c-426b

28 Gilbert: *Loadstone*, pref, 1a-c

28 Galileo: *Two New Sciences*, third day, 200a-b; 207d-208a

28 Harvey: *On Animal Generation*, 333d-335a esp 334c-d

30 Bacon: *Advancement of Learning*, 34b; 57b-d; 96d-97a / *Novum Organum*, bk i, aph 17-25 108a-d; aph 103-106 127d-128c; bk ii, aph 1-10 137a-140d

31 Descartes: *Objections and Replies*, 123a-b; 167c-d

34 Newton: *Principles*, bk iii, rule iii-iv 270b-271b / *Optics*, bk iii, 543a-b

35 Locke: *Human Understanding*, bk i, ch iii, sect 25 120c-d

35 Berkeley: *Human Knowledge*, sect 107 433d-434a

35 Hume: *Human Understanding*, sect i, div 2 451b-c; div 9 454c-455a; sect iv, div 26 460b-c

42 Kant: *Pure Reason*, 5a-13d; 66d-93c; 110a

43 Mill: *Utilitarianism*, 475b,d [fn 1]

46 Hegel: *Philosophy of History*, part iv, 361a-b

51 Tolstoy: *War and Peace*, epilogue ii, 690b

54 Freud: *Instincts*, 412a-b

4. The use of induction in argument

4a. Dialectical induction: securing assumptions for disputation

8 Aristotle: *Topics*, bk i, ch 12 148d; ch 18 [108ᵇ7–12] 152d; bk viii, ch 1 [155ᵇ16–156ª7] 211b-212a; [156ᵇ10–18] 212c-d; ch 2 [157ª19–38] 213b-d; ch 8 [160ª35–ᵇ1] 217d; ch 14 [164ª 12–17] 222d

9 Aristotle: *Rhetoric*, bk i, ch 2 [1356ª36–ᵇ26] 596a-b

(4. *The use of induction in argument.*)

4b. Rhetorical induction: inference from example in the process of persuasion

8 ARISTOTLE: *Prior Analytics*, BK II, CH 24 90c-91a / *Topics*, BK VIII, CH 1 [156^{b}10–18] 212c-d; CH 8 [160^{a}35–^{b}1] 217d / *Metaphysics*, BK II, CH 3 [995^{a}6–8] 513c

9 ARISTOTLE: *Rhetoric*, BK I, CH 2 [1356^{a}36–1358^{a}3] 596a-597d; CH 9 [1368^{a}29–31] 611b-c; BK II, CH 20 640d-641d; CH 23 [1398^{a}32–^{b}18] 646d-647a; CH 25 [1403^{a}5–9] 652d; BK III, CH 17 [1417^{b}35–1418^{a}3] 672b

30 BACON: *Advancement of Learning*, 58c-59a

42 KANT: *Pref. Metaphysical Elements of Ethics*, 376c-d

5. The role of induction in the development of science: the methods of experimental and enumerative induction

8 ARISTOTLE: *Prior Analytics*, BK II, CH 23 90a-c / *Posterior Analytics*, BK I, CH 3 [72^{b}25–33] 99c; CH 18 111b-c; BK II, CH 19 136a-137a,c / *Physics*, BK I, CH 2 [185^{a}13–14] 259d; BK V, CH 1 [224^{b}28–30] 304d; BK VIII, CH 1 [252^{a}23–^{b}5] 336a-b / *Generation and Corruption*, BK I, CH 2 [316^{a}5–14] 411c-d / *Metaphysics*, BK I, CH 9 [992^{b}30–993^{a}1] 511b; BK VI, CH 1 [1025^{b}1–16] 547b; BK XI, CH 7 [1064^{a}4–9] 592b; BK XIII, CH 4 [1078^{b}28–30] 610b

9 ARISTOTLE: *Generation of Animals*, BK V, CH 8 [788^{b}10–21] 330c / *Ethics*, BK I, CH 4 [1095^{a}30–^{b}8] 340c; CH 7 [1098^{a}34–^{b}3] 343d; BK VI, CH 3 388b-c

10 GALEN: *Natural Faculties*, BK III, CH 1–2 199a-200a esp 199c-d

28 GILBERT: *Loadstone*, PREF, 1a-c

28 GALILEO: *Two New Sciences*, THIRD DAY, 200a-b; 207d-208a

28 HARVEY: *Motion of the Heart*, 280c; 285c-d / *Circulation of the Blood*, 324c-d / *On Animal Generation*, 332a-335c esp 334c-d; 383d; 473a

30 BACON: *Advancement of Learning*, 16a; 34b; 42a-c; 56b-58c; 96d-97a / *Novum Organum* 105a-195d esp BK I, APH 11–26 107d-108d, APH 69 116a-b, APH 104–106 128a-c, BK II, APH 1–10 137a-140d, APH 15–16 149a-b, APH 20–21 150d-153b, APH 52 194c-195d

31 DESCARTES: *Rules*, II, 2d-3a; VII 10b-12a / *Discourse*, PART VI, 61d-62c / *Objections and Replies*, 167c-d

33 PASCAL: *Vacuum*, 358a-b / *Arithmetical Triangle*, 451b-452a; 458b-459b; 464a-466a

34 NEWTON: *Principles*, BK III, RULE III–IV 270b-271b; GENERAL SCHOL, 371b-372a / *Optics*, BK III, 543a-b

35 BERKELEY: *Human Knowledge*, SECT 107 433d-434a

35 HUME: *Human Understanding*, SECT I, DIV 9 454c-455a; SECT III, DIV 19, 458a; SECT IV, DIV 26 460b-c

42 KANT: *Pure Reason*, 5a-13d; 45b-46a; 72c-85d esp 72c-74b, 82a-b / *Intro. Metaphysic of Morals*, 387a-b / *Judgement*, 562d-563b

43 MILL: *Utilitarianism*, 445d-446b; 475b,d [fn 1]

45 FARADAY: *Researches in Electricity*, 659a

51 TOLSTOY: *War and Peace*, EPILOGUE II, 690b

53 JAMES: *Psychology*, 385a-b; 677b; 862a-865a

54 FREUD: *Instincts*, 412a-b

CROSS-REFERENCES

For: Other discussions of induction as an intuitive act of generalization, see JUDGMENT 8a; KNOWLEDGE 6c(2); PRINCIPLE 3a(1), 3a(3)–3b; REASONING 5b(1); SCIENCE 5d.

Other treatments of inductive reasoning and its relation to deductive reasoning, see REASONING 4c, 6c; SCIENCE 5d; and for parallel distinctions in modes of argument, see EXPERIENCE 2d; REASONING 5b(3), 5b(5).

Discussions dealing with the sources or conditions of induction, generalization, or abstraction, see EXPERIENCE 2b; IDEA 2g; MEMORY AND IMAGINATION 3c, 6c(1); SENSE 5b; UNIVERSAL AND PARTICULAR 4c.

Induction as the source of principles, axioms, or scientific laws, see PRINCIPLE 3b; SCIENCE 4d; UNIVERSAL AND PARTICULAR 4f.

Other treatments of dialectical and rhetorical induction, see DIALECTIC 2b, 3b; RHETORIC 4c(1); and for their contrast with dialectical and rhetorical reasoning, see DIALECTIC 3c; REASONING 5c–5d; RHETORIC 4c(2).

The role of induction in the experimental sciences, see EXPERIENCE 5a; REASONING 6c; SCIENCE 4d, 5d.

ADDITIONAL READINGS

Listed below are works not included in *Great Books of the Western World*, but relevant to the idea and topics with which this chapter deals. These works are divided into two groups:

I. Works by authors represented in this collection.
II. Works by authors not represented in this collection.

For the date, place, and other facts concerning the publication of the works cited, consult the Bibliography of Additional Readings which follows the last chapter of *The Great Ideas*.

I.

J. S. MILL. *A System of Logic,* BK III–IV

II.

PHILODEMUS. *On Methods of Inference*
JOHN OF SAINT THOMAS. *Cursus Philosophicus Thomisticus, Ars Logica,* PART I, BK III, CH 2; Q 8 (2); PART II, Q 5
WHATELY. *Elements of Logic,* BK IV, CH I
GRATRY. *Logic,* PART IV
WHEWELL. *The Philosophy of the Inductive Sciences,* VOL II, BK XI, CH 1–6; BK XIII
——. *On the Philosophy of Discovery*
SIGWART. *Logic,* PART III, CH 5
JEVONS. *The Principles of Science,* CH 7, 11; BK IV, esp CH 22
LOTZE. *Logic,* BK I, CH 3 (A)
BRADLEY. *The Principles of Logic,* BK II, PART II, CH 3
C. S. PEIRCE. *Collected Papers,* VOL II, par 619–644, 669–693, 755–791
VENN. *Principles of Empirical or Inductive Logic,* CH 5–15, 17, 24

PEARSON. *The Grammar of Science,* CH 3
BOSANQUET. *Logic,* VOL II, CH 3–5
——. *Science and Philosophy,* 4
J. C. WILSON. *Statement and Inference,* PART IV
POINCARÉ. *Science and Method,* BK II, CH 3–4
CASSIRER. *Substance and Function,* PART II, CH 5
N. R. CAMPBELL. *Physics; the Elements,* CH 4
W. E. JOHNSON. *Logic,* PART II, CH 8–11; PART III, CH 2
J. M. KEYNES. *A Treatise on Probability,* PART III
NICOD. "The Logical Problem of Induction," in *Foundations of Geometry and Induction*
MISES. *Probability, Statistics, and Truth*
M. R. COHEN. *Reason and Nature,* BK I, CH 3(3)
JEFFREYS. *Scientific Inference*
MEYERSON. *Du cheminement de la pensée*
DEWEY. *Logic, the Theory of Inquiry,* CH 21
B. RUSSELL. *The Problems of Philosophy,* CH 6
——. *Introduction to Mathematical Philosophy,* CH 3
——. *Human Knowledge, Its Scope and Limits,* PART V, CH 7; PART VI, CH 2–3

Chapter 40: INFINITY

INTRODUCTION

ONE of the persistent questions concerning infinity is whether we can know or comprehend it. Another is whether the infinite exists, and if so, to what kind of thing infinity belongs. It is not surprising, therefore, that the discussion of infinity often borders on the unintelligible.

The idea of infinity, like the idea of eternity, lacks the support of the imagination or of sense-experience. The fact that the infinite cannot be perceived or imagined seems sufficient to lead Hobbes and Berkeley to deny its reality. "Whatsoever we imagine is *finite*," writes Hobbes. "Therefore there is no idea, or conception of anything we call *infinite*. . . . When we say anything is infinite, we signify only that we are not able to conceive the ends and bounds of the thing named, having no conception of the thing, but of our own inability."

On similar grounds Berkeley rejects the possibility of infinite division. "If I cannot perceive innumerable parts in any infinite extension," he writes, "it is certain that they are not contained in it: but it is evident, that I cannot distinguish innumerable parts in any particular line, surface, or solid, which I either perceive by sense, or figure to myself in my mind; wherefore I conclude that they are not contained in it."

But for most of the great writers on the subject, the impossibility of representing infinity and eternity to the imagination does not render them inconceivable or meaningless. Yet it does account for the difficulty of grasping their meaning, a difficulty further increased by the fact that, whatever their meaning, *infinity* and *eternity* are indefinable. To define the infinite would be to limit—even in thought—the unlimited.

The notion of infinity involves greater perplexities than that of eternity. The meaning of eternity is weighted with the mystery of God, the world, and time. All these affect the conception of infinity; but for the infinite there are also the mysteries of number and of space, of matter and motion. In the sphere of quantity, or of things subject to quantity, infinity is itself the source of mystery, or at least the root of difficulty in analysis. It is the central term in the discussion of the continuous and the indivisible, the nature of series and of limits.

As INDICATED in the chapter on ETERNITY, that idea in each of its applications seems to have one or the other of two meanings—(1) the meaning in which it signifies infinite time, time without beginning or end, and (2) the meaning in which it signifies the timelessness or immutability of being. Both meanings are negative, so far as our understanding is concerned. Yet what is signified by the second is in itself something positive, at least in the opinion of those who think that to be exempt from change entails having every perfection or being lacking in nothing.

This split in meaning also occurs in the idea of infinity. As applied to being, the term *infinite* signifies something positive, even though our understanding of what is signified remains negative or, at best, analogical. An infinite being is one which lacks no attribute that can belong to a being. This is the positive condition of absolute perfection. The infinite here still means the unlimited, but that which is unlimited in being has no defect. To lack deficiencies is to be perfect.

It is in this sense that Spinoza defines God as "Being absolutely infinite, that is to say, substance consisting of infinite attributes, each one of which expresses eternal and infinite essence." Like Spinoza, Aquinas maintains that "besides God nothing can be infinite." But he distinguishes the absolute or positive sense in which God alone is infinite from the sense of the word in which it can be said that "things other than God can be relatively infinite, but not absolutely infinite." This other meaning, according to Aquinas, is not only relative but negative, for it connotes "something imperfect." It signifies indeterminacy or lack of perfection in being.

What Aquinas calls the relative or potential infinite, he attributes to matter and to quantities—to bodies, to the magnitudes of space and time, and to number. This sense of "infinite" corresponds to that meaning of "eternal," according to which time consists of an endless series of moments, each having a predecessor, each a successor, no matter how far one counts them back into the past or ahead into the future.

But in the field of quantities other than time, the meanings of infinite and eternal part company. There is, of course, some parallelism between infinite space and infinite time, insofar as an infinite extension is one which does not begin at any point or end at any; but the consideration of space and number leads to an aspect of infinity which has no parallel in the consideration of eternity.

"In sizes or numbers," Pascal writes, "nature has set before man two marvelous infinities. . . . For, from the fact that they can always be increased, it follows absolutely that they can always be decreased. . . . If we can multiply a number up to 100,000 times, say, we can also take a hundred thousandth part of it by dividing it by the same number we multiply it with, and thus every term of increase will become a term of division by changing the integer into a fraction. So that infinite increase includes necessarily infinite division." As endless addition produces the infinitely large, so endless division produces the infinitesimal or the infinitely small.

A trillion trillion is a finite number, because the addition of a single unit creates a larger number. The fact that the addition of another unit produces a different number indicates that a trillion trillion has a determinate size, which is the same as saying that it is a finite number. An infinite number cannot be increased by addition, for it is constituted—in thought at least—as a number larger than the sum of any two finite numbers; which is another way of saying that it is approached by carrying on the process of addition endlessly. The size of an infinite number is therefore indeterminate.

What Galileo points out about two infinite quantities seems to hold for an infinite and a finite quantity. He asks us to consider the totality of all integers (which is infinite) and the totality of their squares (which is also infinite). On the one hand, there appear to be as many squares as there are integers; on the other hand, the totality of integers includes all the squares. Precisely because "the number of squares is not less than the totality of all numbers, nor the latter *greater than* the former," Galileo insists that "the attributes 'equal,' 'greater,' and 'less' are not applicable to infinite, but only to finite quantities." Nor does the sense in which one finite quantity can be greater or less than another—that is, by a determinate difference between them—apply in the comparison of a finite and an infinite quantity. The latter, being indeterminately large, is indeterminately larger than any finite quantity.

These remarks apply to the infinitely small as well. The infinitesimal is immeasurably small or indeterminately less than any finite fraction, no matter how small, because its own size is indeterminate. The finite fraction, itself a product of division, can be divided again, but if an infinitesimal quantity were capable of further division, it would permit a smaller, and since that smaller quantity would be a determinate fraction of itself, the infinitesimal would have to be determinate in size. Since that is not so, the infinitesimal must be conceived as the indivisible or as the limit approached by carrying on division endlessly.

"Because the hypothesis of indivisibles seems somewhat harsh," Newton proposes an analysis in terms of what he calls "nascent and evanescent quantities," or quantities just *beginning* to be more than nothing or just at the point at which they *vanish* into nothing. "As there is a limit which the velocity at the end of a motion may attain, but not exceed . . . there is a like limit in all quantities and proportions that begin or cease to be." Newton warns his reader, therefore, that if he "should happen to mention quantities as least, or evanescent, or ultimate," the reader is "not to suppose that quantities of any determinate magnitude are meant, but such as are conceived to be always diminished without end."

Later, speaking of quantities which are "variable and indetermined, and increasing or decreasing, as it were, by a continual motion or flux," he adds: "Take care not to look upon finite quantities as such." The method of fluxions provides an infinitesimal calculus on the hypothesis of limits rather than of indivisibles.

THROUGH ALL THESE conceptions of infinity—metaphysical, mathematical, and physical—run the paired notions of the unlimited and of limits approached but not attained. The finite is neither unlimited nor does it insensibly approach a limit. There are also the opposite notions of the perfect and the indeterminate. The finite is neither, for it is determinate without being a totality or complete.

Though they have a common thread of meaning, and though each raises similar difficulties for the understanding, the conception of infinity in being or power, and the conception of infinite (or infinitesimal) quantity require separate consideration. The same questions may be asked of each, questions about the existence of the infinite and about our knowledge of it, but the same answers will not be given in each case. There are those who deny the existence of an actually infinite body or an actually infinite number, yet affirm the infinite existence of God. There are those who declare the infinity of matter to be intrinsically unintelligible, but maintain that God, Who is infinite, is intrinsically the most intelligible object. They add, of course, that the infinite being of God cannot be comprehended by our finite intellects.

On each of these points, an opposite view has been taken, but the dispute concerning the infinity of God involves issues other than those which occur in the controversy over the infinite divisibility of matter or the infinity of space and time. It seems advisable, therefore, to deal separately with the problems of infinity as they arise with respect to different objects or occur in different subject matters.

THE CONCEPTION of God, in the words of Anselm, as a being "than which a greater cannot be conceived"—or, in the words of Kant, as an *ens realissimum*, a most real being—expresses the plenitude of the divine nature and existence. The mediaeval thesis, defended by Descartes, that God's essence and existence are identical, implies that neither is contracted or determined by the other. The still earlier notion of Aristotle, repeated by Aquinas, that God is pure actuality, carries with it the attributes of completeness or perfection, which are the positive aspects of immutability or incapacity for change. Spinoza's definition of substance as that which exists, not only in itself, but through itself and by its very nature, entails the autonomy or utter independence of the divine being.

These are so many different ways of stating that God is an infinite being. Both Aquinas and Spinoza make infinity the basis for proving that there can be only one God. When Spinoza argues that "a plurality of substances possessing the same nature is absurd," he has in mind the identification of infinite substance with God. "If many gods existed," Aquinas writes, "they would necessarily differ from each other. Something would therefore belong to one, which did not belong to another. And if this were a privation, one of them would not be absolutely perfect; but if it were a perfection, one of them would be without it. So it is impossible for many gods to exist"—that is, of course, if infinity is a property of the divine nature. Aquinas makes this condition clear when he goes on to say that "the ancient philosophers, constrained as it were by the truth, when they asserted an infinite principle, asserted likewise that there was only one such principle."

But while it is impossible for there to be two infinities of being, it is not impossible for there to be two, or more, infinite quantities. One explanation of this difference seems to be the actuality or existence of an infinite being, in contrast to the conceptual character of the infinite objects of mathematics, which are sometimes called "potential infinites" because they are conceived as in an endless process of becoming, or as approaching a limit that is never reached.

When the physical existence of infinite quantities is asserted, as, for example, a universe of infinite extent or an infinite number of atoms, the uniqueness of these actual totalities seems to follow. Two infinite worlds cannot co-exist, though the one world can be infinite in several distinct respects—in space or duration, or in the number of its constituents—even as the infinity of God, according to Spinoza, involves "infinite attributes, each one of which expresses eternal and infinite essence."

Spinoza's argument against two actual infinities seems to find confirmation in the position taken by Aquinas that God's omnipotence does not include the power to create an infinite world. God's infinity, as we have already noted, follows from the identity of God's essence and existence. Since a created being has existence added to its essence, Aquinas asserts that "it is against the nature of a created thing to be absolutely infinite. Therefore," he continues, "as God, although He has infinite power, cannot make a thing to be not made (for this would imply that two contradictories are true at the same time), so likewise He cannot make anything to be absolutely infinite."

On this view, an infinite world cannot co-exist with an infinite God, if, in their separate existence, one is dependent on the other, as creature upon creator. The infinity of the world or of nature, in Spinoza's conception, is not separate from the infinity of God, but consists in the infinity of two of God's attributes—extension and thought.

In our time there has arisen the conception of a finite God—a God who, while the most perfect being, yet is not without capacity for growth or change, a God who is eternal without being immutable. This conception, which in the light of traditional theology appears to be as self-contradictory as *round square*, has arisen in response to the difficulties certain critics have found in the traditional doctrine of an infinite being. They point to the difficulty of understanding how finite beings can exist separate from, yet in addition to, an infinite being; they also cite difficulties in the notions of infinite knowledge, infinite power, and infinite goodness.

The infinity of the divine omniscience extends to the possible as well as to the actual. But the possible includes things which are in-

compatible with one another, things which, in the language of Leibnitz, are not *compossible*. The *incompossible* would thus seem to be embraced in the infinite scope of divine thought or knowledge. In the view of one theologian, Nicolas of Cusa, the mystery of God's infinity is best expressed by affirming that in God all contradictions are somehow reconciled.

The infinity of God's power, or the divine omnipotence, also raises questions about the possible and the impossible. Is nothing impossible to God or must it be said that there are certain things which not even God can do, such as reverse the order of time or create a world which shall be as infinite and perfect as himself? In the assertion that God cannot do the impossible, Aquinas sees no limitation on God's power. The impossible, he writes, does not "come under the divine omnipotence, not because of any defect in the power of God, but because it has not the nature of a feasible or possible thing." For this reason, he claims, "it is better to say that such things cannot be done, than that God cannot do them." The inability to do the *undoable* constitutes no violation of infinite power, even as the lack of nothing does not deprive infinite being of anything.

The infinite goodness of God is sometimes set against the fact of evil, or the existence of imperfections, in the created world. This aspect of the problem of evil, like that which concerns man's freedom to obey or disobey the divine will, cannot be separated from the fundamental mystery of God's infinity—in power and knowledge as well as in goodness. The problem is considered in the chapter on GOOD AND EVIL. The point there mentioned, that evil is essentially non-being or deprivation of being, leads to one solution of the problem. It accepts the finitude, and consequently the imperfection, of creatures as a necessary consequence of God's infinity. The best of all possible worlds cannot be infinitely good.

TO MAN ALONE, among all admittedly finite things, has infinity been attributed and even made a distinctive mark of his nature. Does this introduce a new meaning of infinity, neither quantitative nor divine?

It has seldom if ever been questioned that man is finite in being and power. The limits of human capacity for knowledge or achievement are a perennial theme in man's study of man. Yet it is precisely with regard to *capacity* that certain writers have intimated man's infinity.

Pascal, for example, finds the apparent contradictions in human nature intelligible only when man is understood as yearning for or impelled toward the infinite. "We burn with desire," he says, "to find solid ground and an ultimate sure foundation whereon to build a tower reaching to the Infinite. But our whole groundwork cracks and the earth opens to abysses." In this fact lies both the grandeur and the misery of man. He aspires to the infinite, yet he is a finite being dissatisfied with his own finitude and frustrated by it.

It is sometimes said that the touch of infinity in man—with the suggestion that it is a touch of madness—consists in his wanting to be God. Those who regard such desire as abnormal or perverse interpret it as a misdirection of man's natural desire to know God face to face and to be filled with the love of God in the divine presence. But, according to the theory of natural desire, the tendency of each nature is somehow proportionate to its capacity. If man's restless search for knowledge and happiness can be quieted only by the possession of the infinite truth and goodness which is God, then man's intellect and will must somehow be as infinite in nature as they are in tendency. Yet that is not an unqualified infinity, for the same theologians who teach that man naturally seeks God also hold that man's finite intellect cannot *comprehend* the infinite being of God as God knows Himself. Nor do they think that man's capacity for knowing and loving God can be fulfilled except in the beatific vision, which is a supernatural gift rather than a natural achievement.

These and related matters are discussed in the chapters on DESIRE and KNOWLEDGE. The great books speak of other objects than God as objects of man's infinite desire. The appetite for money, for pleasure, or for power seems to be an infinite craving which no finite quantity of these goods ever satisfies. Two comments are made upon this fact, which is so amply evidenced in the human record. One is that man's infinite lust for worldly goods expresses even as it conceals his natural desire for a truly infinite good. The other is that these worldly goods are

seductive objects precisely because they are infinite.

Here the word "infinite" is used, not in the sense which signifies perfection, but in the quantitative sense which has the meaning of indetermination. Plato's division, in the *Philebus*, of goods into the finite and the infinite separates measured and definite goods from those which need some limitation in quantity. Socrates exemplifies the distinction by reference to the fact that "into the hotter and the colder there enters a more and a less" and since "there is never any end of them . . . they must also be infinite." In contrast, "when definite quantity is once admitted, there can be no longer a 'hotter' or a 'colder.'" Such things, he says, "which do not admit of more or less" belong "in the class of the limited or finite."

Following the line of this example, Socrates later distinguishes between infinite and finite pleasures, or pleasures without limit and those which have some intrinsic measure. "Pleasures which are in excess," he says, "have no measure, but those which are not in excess have measure; the great, the excessive . . . we shall be right in referring to the class of the infinite, and of the more and less," and "the others we shall refer to the class which has measure." The fact that the goodness of wealth or of certain pleasures is indeterminate or indefinite makes it necessary to determine or measure the amount of wealth it is good to possess, or the quantity of such pleasure it is good to enjoy.

As in the case of desire, so the human intellect is also said to be infinite in the sense of reaching to an indefinite quantity. On the theory which he holds that the intellect knows by means of universal concepts, Aquinas attributes to the human mind "an infinite power; for it apprehends the universal, which can extend itself to an infinitude of singular things." Each universal signifies what is common to an indefinitely large class of particular instances.

There is still another sense in which the intellect is said to be infinite, namely, by reason of its having the potentiality to apprehend *all* knowable things. But this is a relative infinity, as is the corresponding infinity of prime matter, which is conceived as the potentiality for taking on all forms. In both cases, the infinite is qualified by a restriction—on the kind of things knowable to the intellect and the type of forms receivable in matter. The infinity of prime matter—matter totally devoid of form—is also comparable to the infinity of God in a contrast of extreme opposites: the absolute indeterminacy of pure potentiality on the one hand, the absolute perfection of pure actuality on the other.

THE INFINITY OF matter involves different considerations when the problem concerns, not prime matter, but material things—bodies. The question is twofold. Can there be a body of infinite magnitude? Is there an infinite number of bodies? To both questions Aristotle gives the negative answer, while Spinoza seems to answer the first, and Lucretius the second, affirmatively.

Spinoza's affirmation may be qualified, of course, by his conception of infinite body as an attribute of God. But there is no qualification on Lucretius' assertion that "the first-beginnings of things are infinite," unless it is his statement that "the first-beginnings of things have different shapes, but the number of shapes is finite." It is only the number of atoms which is infinite, not their variety.

Aristotle presents many arguments against the existence of an infinite body or an infinite number of things, all of which ultimately rest on his distinction between an actual and a potential infinite. It is not that infinity in magnitude or multitude is impossible—for he affirms the infinity of time and he insists upon the infinite divisibility of matter—but rather that if an infinite body existed its infinity would have to be actual. Its actuality would necessarily involve certain determinations, especially those of dimension and place, which would be inconsistent with the indeterminacy of the infinite. Similarly, a multitude of co-existing things—unlike the moments of time which do not co-exist—cannot be infinite, because their co-existence implies that they can be actually numbered, whereas their infinity implies that they are numberless.

The potential infinite, Aristotle writes, "exhibits itself in different ways—in time, in the generations of man, and in the division of magnitudes. For generally," he says, "the infinite has this mode of existence: one thing is always

being taken after another, and each thing that is taken is always finite, but always different." When this takes place in the division of spatial magnitudes, "what is taken persists, while in the succession of times and of men, it takes place by the passing away of these in such a way that the source of supply never gives out."

The opposition between Lucretius and Aristotle with regard to the divisibility of matter is discussed in the chapter on ELEMENT. The notions of infinity and continuity are differently employed on the two sides of the argument. Where Aristotle makes the continuity of matter the condition of its infinite divisibility, Lucretius makes the atom's continuity—its solidity or lack of void—the cause of its indivisibility. Where Aristotle asserts that at any moment there can be only a finite number of particles in the world because the partition of matter cannot be infinitely carried out short of infinite time, Lucretius, on the contrary, thinks that the division of matter into smaller and smaller parts finds an end in the atomic particles; and yet he also asserts an infinite number of atoms.

To contain an infinite number of atoms, an infinite space is required, according to Lucretius. This presents no greater difficulty for him than an infinite time. Aristotle, on the other hand, differentiates between space and time with respect to infinity. Time can be potentially infinite by way of addition because "each part that is taken passes in succession out of existence." But though space may be infinitely divisible, it cannot be infinitely extended, for all its parts, unlike those of time, must co-exist. It would therefore have to be an *actually*, rather than a *potentially*, infinite quantity, and this Aristotle thinks is impossible.

These and other conflicting views concerning the infinity of space and time appear in Kant's statement of the first cosmological antinomy. His intention is not to resolve the issues, but to show that they cannot be resolved by proof or argument. To do this, Kant sets up what seems to him to be equally strong—or equally inconclusive—arguments for and against the infinity of space and time.

Suppose it be granted, Kant argues on the one hand, that "the world has no beginning in time." Then it would follow that "up to every given moment in time, an eternity must have elapsed, and therewith passed away an infinite series of successive conditions or states of things in the world." But since "the infinity of a series consists in the fact that it can never be completed by means of a successive synthesis," it also "follows that an infinite series already elapsed is impossible, and that consequently a beginning of the world is a necessary condition of its existence."

On the other hand, Kant argues with what he thinks is equal force, "let it be granted that [the world] has a beginning. A beginning," he explains, "is an existence which is preceded by a time in which the thing does not exist." Then, Kant continues, "on the above supposition, it follows that there must have been a time in which the world did not exist, that is, a void time. But in a void time, the origination of a thing is impossible; because no part of any such time contains a distinctive condition of being in preference to that of non-being. ... Consequently, many series of things may have a beginning in the world, but the world itself cannot have a beginning, and is, therefore, in relation to past time, infinite."

With regard to the infinity or finitude of space, Kant proceeds similarly. If we suppose space to be infinite, then "the world must be an infinite given total of co-existent things." But in order to "cogitate the world, which fills all spaces, as a whole, the successive synthesis of the parts of an infinite world must be looked upon as completed; that is to say, an infinite time must be regarded as having elapsed in the enumeration of all co-existing things." This, Kant argues, "is impossible," and therefore "an infinite aggregate of actual things cannot be considered as a given whole." Hence it follows that "the world is, as regards extension in space, *not infinite*, but enclosed in limits."

If, however, we suppose "that the world is finite and limited in space, it follows," according to Kant, "that it must exist in a void space, which is not limited. We should, therefore, meet not only with a relation of things *in space*, but also a relation of things *to space*." But the "relation of the world to a void space is merely a relation to *no object*" and "such a relation, and consequently the limitation of the world by void space, is nothing." It follows, therefore, Kant concludes, that "the world, as regards space, is not limited; that is, it is infinite in regard to extension."

The way in which these opposite arguments nullify each other reveals more than our inability to prove or disprove the infinity of space and time. It shows, in Kant's theory of human knowledge, that we are "not entitled to make any assertion at all respecting the whole object of experience—the world of sense."

ONE OTHER PROBLEM of infinity in the sphere of physics receives its initial formulation in one of the great books—in the part of the *Dialogues Concerning the Two New Sciences* where Galileo discusses the uniform acceleration of a freely falling body. The body which is said to accumulate equal increments of velocity in equal intervals of time is also said to start "from infinite slowness, *i.e.*, from rest." One of the persons in the dialogue challenges this, saying that "as the instant of starting is more and more nearly approached, the body moves so slowly that, if it kept on moving at this rate, it would not traverse a mile in an hour, or in a day, or in a year, or in a thousand years; indeed, it would not traverse a span in an even greater time; a phenomenon which baffles the imagination, while our senses show us that a heavy falling body suddenly acquires great speed."

What our senses *seem* to show us is corrected by an experiment which refines the observation. But this still leaves a purely analytical question. Against the statement that the "velocity can be increased or diminished without limit," Simplicio points out in the dialogue that "if the number of degrees of greater and greater slowness is limitless, they will never be all exhausted," and therefore the body will never come to rest when it is slowing down or be able to start to move when it is at rest.

"This would happen," Salviati answers, "if the moving body were to maintain its speed for any length of time at each degree of velocity, but it merely passes each point without delaying more than an instant, and since each time interval, however small, may be divided into an infinite number of instants, these will always be sufficient to correspond to the infinite degrees of diminished velocity."

The problem of the infinitesimal velocity provides another illustration of the difference between infinity in the physical and the mathematical orders. Unlike parallel lines in Euclidean geometry, which are lines that remain equidistant from one another when both are prolonged to infinity, an asymptote is a straight line which a curved line continuously approaches but never meets, even when both are infinitely extended. The distance between the curve and its asymptote diminishes to smaller and smaller intervals, but no matter how small they become, the two lines never coincide. The diminishing intervals between the curve and its asymptote are like the diminishing degrees of velocity in a body starting from or coming to rest. But we know that the body does begin or cease to move, and so there is the mysterious jumping of the gap between rest and motion in the physical order, whereas in the mathematical order the limiting point can be forever approached and never reached.

THERE IS ONE other context in which infinity is discussed in the great books.

The logicians treat certain terms and judgments as infinite. Aristotle, for example, regards the negative term—such as *not-man* or *not-white*—as indefinite. The indefiniteness of its signification may be seen when such terms are used as subjects of discourse. What is being talked about? The answer must be given, in part at least, in positive terms: *not-man* represents the *whole universe* leaving man out, or the *totality of everything* except man. Thus, in its positive signification, the negative term has a kind of infinity—the infinite totality of subjects diminished by one, the one that is negated.

In his classification of judgments, Kant makes a threefold division of judgments according to quality: the affirmative, the negative, and the infinite. The infinite judgment involves a negative in its construction, but when that negative is given an affirmative interpretation, the infinite significance of the proposition becomes apparent. An example will make this clear.

The proposition *this animal is-not white* is negative; it simply denies a certain quality of a certain thing. But the proposition *this animal is not-white* is infinite, for it affirms the negated term, and so places the subject in the infinite class or totality which includes everything except white things. (The position of the hyphen serves to indicate whether the statement shall be construed negatively or affirmatively *and* infinitely.)

The problems of definition and demonstration are differently solved by logicians according to the way in which they propose to avoid infinite regressions in analysis or reasoning. There would be no end to the process of defining if every term had to be defined before it could be used in the definition of another term. There would be no beginning to the process of proof if, before a proposition could be used as a premise to demonstrate some conclusion, it had itself to be demonstrated as a conclusion from prior premises.

In his essay *On Geometrical Demonstration*, Pascal refers to the proposal of a plan for defining and proving everything. "Certainly this method would be beautiful," he says, "but it is absolutely impossible; for it is evident that the first terms we wished to define would presuppose others for their explication, and that similarly the first propositions we wished to prove would suppose others that preceded them, and it is thus clear we should never arrive at the first propositions."

The chapter on DEFINITION considers the character and choice of the indefinable terms by which an infinite regression is avoided in the elucidation of meanings. The chapters on INDUCTION and PRINCIPLE consider the various sorts of primary propositions—axioms, postulates, assumptions—by which a similar regression is avoided in the process of proof. The chapter on CAUSE deals with the problem of an infinite regression in causes and effects. Here it is appropriate to consider the difference between an infinite series of reasons and an infinite series of causes.

To the extent that both are truly series—the succession of one thing after another—neither seems to be impossible, *given infinite time*. Those who deny the possibility of an infinite number of causes distinguish between essential and accidental causes, that is, between causes which must co-exist with their effects and causes which can precede their effects, and cease to be before their effects occur. If there were an infinite time, there could be an infinite series of accidental causes. But it may be questioned whether, even granted an infinite time, the relation between the premises and conclusion of reasoning permits an infinite regression. If the truth of a conclusion cannot be known until the truth of its premises is known, then the pursuit of truth may be vitiated by a search *ad infinitum*.

OUTLINE OF TOPICS

REFERENCES

To find the passages cited, use the numbers in heavy type, which are the volume and page numbers of the passages referred to. For example, in 4 HOMER: *Iliad*, BK II [265–283] 12d, the number 4 is the number of the volume in the set; the number 12d indicates that the passage is in section d of page 12.

PAGE SECTIONS: When the text is printed in one column, the letters a and b refer to the upper and lower halves of the page. For example, in 53 JAMES: *Psychology*, 116a–119b, the passage begins in the upper half of page 116 and ends in the lower half of page 119. When the text is printed in two columns, the letters a and b refer to the upper and lower halves of the left-hand side of the page, the letters c and d to the upper and lower halves of the right-hand side of the page. For example, in 7 PLATO: *Symposium*, 163b–164c, the passage begins in the lower half of the left-hand side of page 163 and ends in the upper half of the right-hand side of page 164.

AUTHOR'S DIVISIONS: One or more of the main divisions of a work (such as PART, BK, CH, SECT) are sometimes included in the reference; line numbers, in brackets, are given in certain cases; *e.g., Iliad*, BK II [265–283] 12d.

BIBLE REFERENCES: The references are to book, chapter, and verse. When the King James and Douay versions differ in title of books or in the numbering of chapters or verses, the King James version is cited first and the Douay, indicated by a (D), follows; *e.g.,* OLD TESTAMENT: *Nehemiah*, 7:45—(D) *II Esdras*, 7:46.

SYMBOLS: The abbreviation "esp" calls the reader's attention to one or more especially relevant parts of a whole reference; "passim" signifies that the topic is discussed intermittently rather than continuously in the work or passage cited.

For additional information concerning the style of the references, see the Explanation of Reference Style; for general guidance in the use of *The Great Ideas*, consult the Preface.

1. The general theory of infinity

8 ARISTOTLE: *Physics*, BK III, CH 4–8 280c–286d
12 LUCRETIUS: *Nature of Things*, BK I [951–1113] 12d–14d
17 PLOTINUS: *Sixth Ennead*, TR VI, CH 2 311b-c; CH 17–18, 319d–320d
19 AQUINAS: *Summa Theologica*, PART I, Q 7 31a–34c
20 AQUINAS: *Summa Theologica*, PART III SUPPL, Q 92, A 1, REP 6,12 1025c–1032b
28 GALILEO: *Two New Sciences*, FIRST DAY, 139c–153a passim, esp 144b–145a
30 BACON: *Novum Organum*, BK I, APH 48 110d–111a
31 DESCARTES: *Meditations*, III, 86b / *Objections and Replies*, 112a-c; 123c-d
31 SPINOZA: *Ethics*, PART I, DEF 2 355a; DEF 6 355b; DEF 8 355c; PROP 7–8 356c–357d
33 PASCAL: *Pensées*, 72 181a–184b; 231–233, 213b–214a / *Geometrical Demonstration*, 434b–439b
34 NEWTON: *Principles*, BK I, LEMMA I–II and SCHOL 25a–32a
35 LOCKE: *Human Understanding*, BK II, CH XVI, SECT 8–CH XVII, SECT 22 167c–174a
35 BERKELEY: *Human Knowledge*, SECT 123–132 437c–439c

35 HUME: *Human Understanding*, SECT XII, DIV 124–125 506a–507a
42 KANT: *Pure Reason*, 24d; 26d; 130b–149d esp 130b–133c, 136a–137a [thesis]; 156b–157d
46 HEGEL: *Philosophy of Right*, ADDITIONS, 17 119a
51 TOLSTOY: *War and Peace*, EPILOGUE II, 693c–694d

1a. The definite and indefinite: the measured and the indeterminate

7 PLATO: *Parmenides*, 505c–506d; 510c–511a / *Philebus* 609a–639a,c esp 615c–617d
8 ARISTOTLE: *Prior Analytics*, BK I, CH 13 [32^{b}4–23] 48b-d / *Metaphysics*, BK I, CH 5 [986^{a}12–^{b}2] 504b-c; CH 6 [987^{b}19–988^{a}16] 505d–506b; CH 8 [989^{a}30–^{b}21] 507c-d; BK V, CH 30 547a-d; BK VII, CH 10 [1036^{a}2–9] 559b-c; BK IX, CH 7 [1049^{a}19–^{b}1] 574d–575a; BK XIII, CH 10 [1087^{a}10–25] 619c
9 ARISTOTLE: *Ethics*, BK II, CH 6 [1106^{b}28–35] 352b-c
11 NICOMACHUS: *Arithmetic*, BK I, 811d–812a; 826d–827a
16 KEPLER: *Harmonies of the World*, 1078a-b
17 PLOTINUS: *First Ennead*, TR VIII, CH 3 28a-c / *Second Ennead*, TR IV, CH 13–16 55b–57c / *Sixth Ennead*, TR VI, CH 18, 320c-d

(1. *The general theory of infinity.* 1a. *The definite and indefinite: the measured and the indeterminate.*)

18 AUGUSTINE: *Confessions*, BK V, par 20 32d-33a / *City of God*, BK XII, CH 18 354b-d

19 AQUINAS: *Summa Theologica*, PART I, Q 48, A 1, REP 4 259b-260c; PART I–II, Q 1, A 4 612a-613a; Q 7, A 2, REP 2 652d-653c

31 DESCARTES: *Objections and Replies*, 112a-b

42 KANT: *Pure Reason*, 158a-159d; 196c-197a

46 HEGEL: *Philosophy of Right*, ADDITIONS, 6 117a-b

1b. **The infinite in being and quantity: the actual and potential infinite; the formal and the material infinite**

7 PLATO: *Parmenides*, 495c-497c / *Sophist*, 571d-573b

8 ARISTOTLE: *Physics*, BK I, CH 2 [185ª28–b4] 260a-b; [185b17-19] 260c; BK III, CH 4–8 280c-286d / *Generation and Corruption*, BK I, CH 3 [318ª13-24] 414c-d / *Metaphysics*, BK I, CH 5 [987ª13-19] 505b; BK IX, CH 6 [1048b9-17] 574a; BK XI, CH 10 [1066ª35-b22] 594d-595b; BK XII, CH 7 [1073ª3-13] 603a-b

11 NICOMACHUS: *Arithmetic*, BK I, 812a

17 PLOTINUS: *Sixth Ennead*, TR VI, CH 17, 319d-320a

18 AUGUSTINE: *Confessions*, BK VII, par 20–21 49d-50a

19 AQUINAS: *Summa Theologica*, PART I, Q 7 31a-34c; Q 12, A 1, REP 2 50c-51c; Q 14, A 1, ANS 75d-76c; Q 50, A 2, REP 4 270a-272a; Q 54, A 2, ANS 285d-286c; PART I–II, Q 1, A 4, REP 2 612a-613a; Q 2, A 6, ANS 619d-620d

20 AQUINAS: *Summa Theologica*, PART III, Q 7, A 12, REP 1 754c-755c; Q 10, A 3, REP 1–2 769d-771b; PART III SUPPL, Q 92, A 1, REP 12 1025c-1032b

28 GALILEO: *Two New Sciences*, FIRST DAY, 145b-146c; 150d-151c

31 DESCARTES: *Meditations*, III, 86a-88d / *Objections and Replies*, 112b; DEF VIII 130d

31 SPINOZA: *Ethics*, PART I, DEF 3,6 355b; PROP 8, DEMONST and SCHOL 1 356d; PROP 9 357d; PROP 10, SCHOL 358a-b; PROP 13–14 359c-360a; PROP 15, SCHOL–PROP 16 360b-362a; PROP 21–23 364a-365a; PROP 28, DEMONST 365d-366a

33 PASCAL: *Pensées*, 121 195a / *Geometrical Demonstration*, 434b-439b

34 NEWTON: *Principles*, BK III, GENERAL SCHOL, 370a-371a

35 LOCKE: *Human Understanding*, BK II, CH XIII, SECT 4–6 149b-d; CH XIV, SECT 26–27 160c-161a; SECT 30 161c-d; CH XV, SECT 2–4 162c-163b; CH XVI, SECT 8 167c; CH XVII 167d-174a passim, esp SECT 7 169b-c; CH XXIX, SECT 16 237b-238a

35 BERKELEY: *Human Knowledge*, SECT 123–132 437c-439c

35 HUME: *Human Understanding*, SECT XII, DIV 124, 506b

42 KANT: *Pure Reason*, 124d-125b; 130b-133c; 135a-137a,c; 160b-163a / *Judgement*, 498b-501b

46 HEGEL: *Philosophy of Right*, INTRO, par 22 17c-d; PART I, par 104—PART II, par 105 39b-40a; ADDITIONS, 17 119a / *Philosophy of History*, INTRO, 156d-160b; 165a-b

53 JAMES: *Psychology*, 668a-669a

2. **Infinity in the logical order**

2a. **The infinity of negative and indefinite terms**

7 PLATO: *Sophist*, 571d-573c / *Philebus*, 615c-616c

8 ARISTOTLE: *Interpretation*, CH 2 [16ª30–33] 25c; CH 3 [16b11-16] 25d; CH 10 [19b5-11] 29d / *Prior Analytics*, BK I, CH 46 70b-71d

42 KANT: *Pure Reason*, 158a-159d

2b. **The distinction between negative and infinite judgments**

8 ARISTOTLE: *Categories*, CH 10 [12b6-15] 17d-18a / *Interpretation*, CH 5 [17ª8-9] 26b; CH 6 26c-d; CH 10 29d-31c / *Prior Analytics*, BK I, CH 3 [25b19-26] 40c; CH 46 70b-71d

35 LOCKE: *Human Understanding*, BK III, CH VII, SECT 1 283a-b

42 KANT: *Pure Reason*, 40a-c; 210c-d

46 HEGEL: *Philosophy of Right*, PART I, par 53 25c-d

2c. **Infinite regression in analysis and reasoning**

7 PLATO: *Parmenides*, 489a-d / *Theaetetus*, 542a-544a esp 543d-544a

8 ARISTOTLE: *Posterior Analytics*, BK I, CH 3 99b-100a; CH 19–23 111c-116a / *Physics*, BK I, CH 4 [187b7-14] 262d; CH 6 [189ª11-19] 264c / *Metaphysics*, BK IV, CH 3 [1005b15-34] 524d-525a; CH 4 [1006ª5-12] 525a-b; CH 6 [1011ª3-14] 530d; BK XI, CH 6 [1063b7-12] 531d / *Soul*, BK I, CH 3 [407ª22-30] 636d-637a

9 ARISTOTLE: *Ethics*, BK I, CH 2 [1094ª18-22] 339b; BK III, CH 3 [1112b33-1113ª3] 358d-359a

12 EPICTETUS: *Discourses*, BK I, CH 17, 122d-123a; BK II, CH 20, 164c-d

19 AQUINAS: *Summa Theologica*, PART I, Q 36, A 3, REP 4 194c-195d; PART I–II, Q 1, A 4, REP 2 612a-613a

20 AQUINAS: *Summa Theologica*, PART I–II, Q 94, A 2, ANS 221d-223a

25 MONTAIGNE: *Essays*, 292c-d

30 BACON: *Novum Organum*, BK I, APH 48 110d-111a

31 DESCARTES: *Objections and Replies*, 111a-d; 213c-d; 224b,d

33 PASCAL: *Geometrical Demonstration*, 431b-434a / *Arithmetical Triangle*, 451b-452a; 458b-459b; 464a-466a

35 LOCKE: *Human Understanding*, BK II, CH XXI, SECT 23 183b-d; SECT 25 184a-b; BK III, CH IV, SECT 5 260c

42 KANT: *Pure Reason*, 111d-112d; 115d-119a; 135a-173a esp 158a-159d

53 JAMES: *Psychology*, 321b [fn 1]; 525a-526b

3. The infinite in quantity

3a. Number: the infinite of division and addition

7 PLATO: *Parmenides*, 495d-497b

8 ARISTOTLE: *Physics*, BK III, CH 4 [203^{b}22–24] 281c; [204^{a}7–8] 282a; CH 5 [204^{b}6–9] 282c; CH 6 [206^{a}15] 284b; [206^{b}3–207^{a}14] 284d-285c; CH 7 [207^{a}32–^{b}14] 285d-286a / *Metaphysics*, BK XI, CH 10 [1066^{b}23–26] 595b

11 EUCLID: *Elements*, BK IX, PROP 20 183b-184a

11 ARCHIMEDES: *Sand-Reckoner* 520a-526b passim

11 NICOMACHUS: *Arithmetic*, BK I, 812a; BK II, 829b

17 PLOTINUS: *Sixth Ennead*, TR VI, CH 2 311b-c; CH 17, 319d-320a

18 AUGUSTINE: *City of God*, BK XII, CH 18 354b-d

19 AQUINAS: *Summa Theologica*, PART I, Q 7, A 3, REP 3 32c-33c; A 4 33d-34c; PART I–II, Q 1, A 4, REP 2 612a-613a

20 AQUINAS: *Summa Theologica*, PART III, Q 7, A 12, REP 1 754c-755c; Q 10, A 3, REP 2 769d-771b

28 GALILEO: *Two New Sciences*, FIRST DAY, 144b-145a

31 DESCARTES: *Objections and Replies*, 112b

33 PASCAL: *Pensées*, 121 195a; 233, 213b-214a / *Geometrical Demonstration*, 434b-439b

35 LOCKE: *Human Understanding*, BK II, CH XIV, SECT 30 161c-d; CH XVI, SECT 8 167c; CH XVII 167d-174a passim, esp SECT 9 170a-b; CH XXIX, SECT 16, 237b-d

35 BERKELEY: *Human Knowledge*, SECT 127 438c-d

42 KANT: *Pure Reason*, 136a-b / *Judgement*, 498b-d; 499d-500a

3b. The infinite divisibility of continuous quantities: the infinitesimal; the method of exhaustion and the theory of limits

8 ARISTOTLE: *Physics*, BK III, CH 1 [200^{b}15–19] 278a; CH 4 [203^{b}15–18] 281c; CH 6 [206^{a}8–^{b}33] 284b-285b; CH 7 285d-286c passim; BK V, CH 3 [227^{a}21–34] 308a-b; BK VI, CH 1–2 312b,d-315d; CH 10 [240^{b}8–241^{a}26] 324c-325b / *Heavens*, BK I, CH 1 [268^{a}6–11] 359a; CH 5 [271^{b}8–12] 362d / *Generation and Corruption*, BK I, CH 2 [317^{a}3–13] 412d-413a / *Metaphysics*, BK III, CH 4 [1001^{b}7–19] 520b-c; BK V, CH 13 [1020^{a}9–14] 541b; [1020^{a}26–33] 541c

11 EUCLID: *Elements*, BK V, DEFINITIONS, 4 81a; BK X, PROP 1 191b-192a; BK XII, PROP 2 339a-340b; PROP 5 345b-346b; PROP 10–12 351b-359a; PROP 18 367a-368b

11 ARCHIMEDES: *Sphere and Cylinder*, BK I, ASSUMPTIONS, 5 404b; PROP 13–14 411a-414a; PROP 33–34 424b-427a; PROP 42 431b-432b; PROP 44 433a-b / *Measurement of a Circle* 447a-451b passim / *Conoids and Spheroids*, PROP 4 459a-460b; PROP 21–22 470a-471b; PROP 25–30 473a-479b / *Spirals*, 484b; PROP 18–20 492b-495b; PROP 24–27 496b-500a / *Equilibrium of Planes*, BK I, PROP 6–7 503b-504b; PROP 9 505a-b; PROP 13 507a-508b; BK II, PROP 4 512b-513a / *Quadrature of the Parabola* 527a-537b esp 527a-b, PROP 16 533b-534a, PROP 24 537a-b / *Method* 569a-592a

11 NICOMACHUS: *Arithmetic*, BK I, 811d-812a

16 KEPLER: *Epitome*, BK V, 973a-975a; 979b-983b passim

19 AQUINAS: *Summa Theologica*, PART I, Q 7, A 3, REP 3 32c-33c; Q 53, A 1, ANS and REP 1 280d-282a; A 2, ANS and REP 1 282a-283b

20 AQUINAS: *Summa Theologica*, PART III SUPPL, Q 84, A 3, CONTRARY 985d-989b

28 GALILEO: *Two New Sciences*, FIRST DAY, 139c-153a passim; SECOND DAY, 193b-194d; THIRD DAY, 201a-202a; 205b-d; 224b-c

31 DESCARTES: *Objections and Replies*, 112b

31 SPINOZA: *Ethics*, PART I, PROP 15, SCHOL, 361b-c

33 PASCAL: *Equilibrium of Liquids*, 395a-b / *Geometrical Demonstration*, 434b-439b

34 NEWTON: *Principles*, BK I, LEMMA 1–11 and SCHOL 25a-32a esp LEMMA 1 25a, LEMMA 11, SCHOL 30b-32a; PROP 73, SCHOL 133b-134a; BK II, LEMMA 2 and SCHOL 168a-170a / *Optics*, BK III, 542b-543a

35 LOCKE: *Human Understanding*, BK II, CH XV, SECT 9 164b-d; CH XVI, SECT 4 166a-b; CH XVII, SECT 12 170d; SECT 18 172c-d; CH XXIX, SECT 16 237b-238a

35 BERKELEY: *Human Knowledge*, SECT 98 432a; SECT 123–132 437c-439c

35 HUME: *Human Understanding*, SECT XII, DIV 124 506a-c

42 KANT: *Pure Reason*, 70c-d; 161d-163a

45 FOURIER: *Theory of Heat* 169a-251b passim, esp 172b, 177a

51 TOLSTOY: *War and Peace*, BK XI, 469a-d; EPILOGUE II, 695b-c

3c. The infinity of asymptotes and parallels

11 EUCLID: *Elements*, BK I, DEFINITIONS, 23 2a; POSTULATES, 5 2a

11 APOLLONIUS: *Conics*, BK II, PROP 14–15 691b-692b; PROP 17 693b-694a

31 DESCARTES: *Geometry*, BK II, 306b-307a

34 NEWTON: *Principles*, BK I, LEMMA 18, SCHOL 57a-b; LEMMA 22, 65b; PROP 27, SCHOL 69b-70a

52 DOSTOEVSKY: *Brothers Karamazov*, BK V, 120d-121c

(3. *The infinite in quantity.*)

3d. The infinite extent of space

8 ARISTOTLE: *Physics*, BK III, CH 5 [205ª10–206ª8] 283b-284b; BK IV, CH 5 [212ᵇ11–21] 292a / *Heavens*, BK I, CH 5–7 362c-367b / *Metaphysics*, BK XI, CH 10 [1066ᵇ22–1067ª38] 595b-596a

12 LUCRETIUS: *Nature of Things*, BK I [951–1113] 12d-14d esp [951–1007] 12d-13b; BK II [89–94] 16a-b; [294–307] 18d-19a; [1048–1066] 28b-c

18 AUGUSTINE: *City of God*, BK XI, CH 5 324d-325c

19 AQUINAS: *Summa Theologica*, PART I, Q 23, A 7, ANS 138d-140a; Q 46, A 1, REP 8 250a-252d; Q 66, A 4, REP 5 348d-349d

23 HOBBES: *Leviathan*, PART I, 54b-c; PART II, 162b-c; PART IV, 271b

30 BACON: *Novum Organum*, BK I, APH 48 110d-111a

31 DESCARTES: *Objections and Replies*, 112b

33 PASCAL: *Pensées*, 121 195a; 205–206 211a / *Geometrical Demonstration*, 434b-439b passim

34 NEWTON: *Principles*, DEFINITIONS, SCHOL, 8b-11a / *Optics*, BK III, 542b-543a

35 LOCKE: *Human Understanding*, BK II, CH XIII, SECT 4 149b; SECT 21 152d-153b; CH XIV, SECT 26 160c-d; CH XV 162b-165c passim; CH XVI, SECT 8 167c; CH XVII 167d-174a passim, esp SECT 3–4 168b-d, SECT 11 170c

35 BERKELEY: *Human Knowledge*, SECT 117 436a

42 KANT: *Pure Reason*, 24c-d; 28d-29c; 135a-137a,c; 152a-d; 160b-163a / *Judgement*, 501a-b

51 TOLSTOY: *War and Peace*, EPILOGUE II, 693c-694a

53 JAMES: *Psychology*, 631a

3e. The infinite duration of time and motion

7 PLATO: *Phaedrus*, 124b-c / *Timaeus*, 450c-451a; 460c-d

8 ARISTOTLE: *Topics*, BK I, CH 11 [104ᵇ13–18] 148a-b / *Physics*, BK III, CH 7 [207ᵇ21–27] 286b; CH 8 [208ª20–23] 286d; BK IV, CH 13 [222ª29–32] 302b; BK VI, CH 2 [233ª13–ᵇ16] 315a-c; CH 10 [241ª26–ᵇ20] 325b-d; BK VIII, CH 1–2 334a-337b; CH 6 344b-346b passim; BK IV, CH 8–9 348b-353b / *Heavens*, BK I, CH 2 [269ᵇ2–10] 360c-d; CH 3 [270ᵇ1–24] 361c-362a; BK I, CH 9 [279ª12]–BK II, CH 1 [284ᵇ6] 370b-376a passim; BK II, CH 6 379c-380c / *Generation and Corruption*, BK II, CH 10–11 437d-441a,c / *Meteorology*, BK I, CH 14 [353ª15–19] 459c / *Metaphysics*, BK IX, CH 8 [1050ᵇ20–28] 576c-d; BK XI, CH 10 [1067ª33–38] 596a; BK XII, CH 6 [1071ᵇ3]–CH 7 [1072ᵇ14] 601b-602d; CH 7 [1073ª5–11] 603b; CH 8 [1073ª24–34] 603c

9 ARISTOTLE: *Motion of Animals*, CH 6 [700ᵇ29–701ª7] 236a-b

12 LUCRETIUS: *Nature of Things*, BK I [215–264] 3d-4b; [483–634] 7a-8d; [988–1051] 13b-14a; BK II [80–141] 16a-d; [294–307] 18d-19a; [569–580] 22b; [1048–1066] 28b-c; [1105–1147]

29a-c; BK V [170–194] 63b-c; [376–379] 66a; [416–431] 66c-d; [1204–1217] 76d-77a

12 AURELIUS: *Meditations*, BK V, SECT 13 271b; SECT 23 272b; BK VI, SECT 15 275a-b; BK IX, SECT 28 293d-294a; BK X, SECT 7 297b-c; SECT 27 299d

16 PTOLEMY: *Almagest*, BK XIII, 429a-b

16 KEPLER: *Epitome*, BK IV, 888b-891a

17 PLOTINUS: *Second Ennead*, TR I, CH 1–5 35a-37c / *Third Ennead*, TR VII 119b-129a passim / *Fourth Ennead*, TR IV, CH 8 161d-162d

18 AUGUSTINE: *Confessions*, BK VII, par 21 49d-50a; BK XI, par 12–17 92b-93c; par 40 98d-99a / *City of God*, BK XI, CH 4–6 324a-325d; BK XII, CH 12–20 349b-357a

19 AQUINAS: *Summa Theologica*, PART I, Q 10, A 2, REP 2 41d-42c; A 4, ANS 43b-44b; A 5, ANS 44b-45c; Q 14, A 12, ANS 85d-86d; Q 46 250a-255d; Q 61, A 2 315c-316a; Q 66, A 4 348d-349d; Q 75, A 1, REP 1 378b-379c

20 AQUINAS: *Summa Theologica*, PART III SUPPL, Q 77, A 2, ANS and REP 1 945a-946b; Q 91, A 2 1017c-1020c

21 DANTE: *Divine Comedy*, PARADISE, I [73–81] 107a

23 HOBBES: *Leviathan*, PART I, 50a

25 MONTAIGNE: *Essays*, 293d-294a

28 GALILEO: *Two New Sciences*, FOURTH DAY, 245b-d

30 BACON: *Novum Organum*, BK I, APH 48 110d-111a; BK II, APH 35, 163a-b; APH 48, 186b-d

31 DESCARTES: *Rules*, XIII, 27b-c

33 PASCAL: *Pensées*, 121 195a; 205–206 211a; 231–232 213b / *Geometrical Demonstration*, 434b-439b passim

34 NEWTON: *Principles*, DEF III 5b; DEFINITIONS, SCHOL, 8b; LAW I 14a / *Optics*, BK III, 540a-541b

35 LOCKE: *Human Understanding*, BK II, CH XIV, SECT 26–31 160c-162a; CH XV, SECT 3–5 162d-163c; SECT 11–12 165a-c; CH XVI, SECT 8 167c; CH XVII 167d-174a passim, esp SECT 5 168d-169a, SECT 10 170b-c, SECT 16 172a-b; CH XXIX, SECT 15 237a; SECT 16, 237d-238a

36 STERNE: *Tristram Shandy*, 292a-293b

42 KANT: *Pure Reason*, 26d; 27b-c; 130b-133c; 135a-137a,c; 152c; 160b-161d

51 TOLSTOY: *War and Peace*, EPILOGUE II, 693c-694a

53 JAMES: *Psychology*, 882a

4. The infinity of matter

4a. The infinite quantity or extent of matter: the problem of an actually infinite body

8 ARISTOTLE: *Physics*, BK I, CH 4 [187ᵇ14–22] 262d; BK III, CH 4 [203ᵇ15–29] 281c-d; CH 5 [204ª35–206ª8] 282b-284b / *Heavens*, BK I, CH 5–7 362c-367b / *Metaphysics*, BK XII, CH 7 [1073ª3–13] 603a-b

4b. The infinite divisibility of matter: the issue concerning atoms

4c. The infinite potentiality of matter: the conception of prime or formless matter

5. Infinity in the world

5a. The infinite number of things and the infinite number of kinds

5b. The number of causes

6. The finite and the infinite in the nature of man

6a. The infinity of desire and will: the limits of human capacity

OLD TESTAMENT: *Psalms*, 42; 63—(D) *Psalms*, 41; 62 / *Proverbs*, 27:20 / *Ecclesiastes*, 4:7–8; 5:10–12; 6:7—(D) *Ecclesiastes*, 4:7–8; 5:9–11; 6:7 / *Isaiah*, 14:12–14—(D) *Isaias*, 14:12–14 / *Habakkuk*, 2:5—(D) *Habacuc*, 2:5

APOCRYPHA: *Ecclesiasticus*, 10:9; 11:10; 14:9; 23:16–17; 31:1–11—(D) OT, *Ecclesiaticus*, 10:10; 11:10; 14:9; 23:21–24; 31:1–11 / *Baruch*, 3:16–19—(D) OT, *Baruch*, 3:16–19

NEW TESTAMENT: *John*, 4:13–14 / *I Timothy*, 6:10

5 EURIPIDES: *Phoenician Maidens* [499–525] 382b-c

5 ARISTOPHANES: *Plutus* [143–197] 630d-631b

7 PLATO: *Gorgias*, 275d-277b / *Republic*, BK VIII, 412a / *Philebus* 609a-639a,c / *Laws*, BK VIII, 733b-d; BK IX, 751b-d

8 ARISTOTLE: *Metaphysics*, BK II, CH 2 [994^{b}9–16] 512d-513a

9 ARISTOTLE: *Ethics*, BK I, CH 2 [1094^{a}18–22] 339b; BK III, CH 12 [1119^{b}6–12] 366c / *Politics*, BK I, CH 8 [1256^{b}26]–CH 9 [1258^{a}18] 450c-452b; BK II, CH 7 [1267^{a}42–^{b}5] 463b

12 LUCRETIUS: *Nature of Things*, BK III [59–93] 30d-31b; [931–977] 42a-c; [1003–1010] 43a; [1076–1084] 44a; BK IV [1097–1120] 58c-d; BK V [1405–1435] 79b-d; BK VI [1–34] 80a-c

12 EPICTETUS: *Discourses*, BK III, CH 9 184c-185d; BK IV, CH 4–5 225a-230b; CH 9 237d-238d

14 PLUTARCH: *Pyrrhus*, 319b-321a / *Caius Marius*, 353d-354a,c / *Pompey*, 525a-b; 533a-c / *Caesar*, 599b-c / *Cicero*, 706b-c

18 AUGUSTINE: *Confessions*, BK I, par 1–6 1a-2c; par 19 5d; BK II, par 2–4 9b-d; BK IV, par 15–19 23a-24b; BK VI, par 26 42d-43a; BK XI, par 1–4 89b-90b; BK XII, par 10 101c

19 AQUINAS: *Summa Theologica*, PART I, Q 63, A 3 327b-328b; PART I–II, Q I, A 4 612a-613a; Q 2, A 1, REP 3 615d-616c; Q 30, A 4 751c-752b

20 AQUINAS: *Summa Theologica*, PART II–II, Q 27, A 6 524c-525c; Q 28, A 3 528d-529c

22 CHAUCER: *Troilus and Cressida*, BK I, STANZA 58–66 8b-9b / *Wife of Bath's Prologue* [5953–5960] 262a

23 HOBBES: *Leviathan*, PART I, 76c-d

25 MONTAIGNE: *Essays*, 123d; 149b-d; 224d-225a; 350d-354b; 429a-b; 489b-c; 503b-d

26 SHAKESPEARE: *Julius Caesar*, ACT II, SC I [10–34] 574c-d; ACT III, SC II 583c-586c

27 SHAKESPEARE: *Troilus and Cressida*, ACT I, SC III [109–124] 109b; ACT III, SC II [65–107] 120d-121b / *Macbeth*, ACT I, SC V 288a-d; SC VII 289b-290b

31 DESCARTES: *Meditations*, IV 89a-93a passim, esp 90b-91b

33 PASCAL: *Pensées*, 109 193b-194a; 125–183 195b-204b; 425 243b-244b

35 LOCKE: *Human Understanding*, BK II, CH XXI, SECT 45 189b-d

36 STERNE: *Tristram Shandy*, 236b-238a

39 SMITH: *Wealth of Nations*, BK I, 71b-d

42 KANT: *Fund. Prin. Metaphysic of Morals*, 256c-257c / *Practical Reason*, 298d-300a / *Judgement*, 584d-585c; 586d-587a

43 MILL: *Utilitarianism*, 462c-463a

46 HEGEL: *Philosophy of Right*, INTRO, par 5–10 13a-15a; par 13–14 15c-16a; par 22–27 17c-18d; PART I, par 35 21a-b; PART II, par 105 40a; ADDITIONS, 6 117a-b; 11 118a; 17 119a; 22 120c-d; 26 121a-b; 118 136a-b

47 GOETHE: *Faust* esp PART I [3217–3250] 79a-b, PART II [11,239–258] 273b-274a

50 MARX: *Capital*, 62a-b; 71d-72c; 292c-295a

51 TOLSTOY: *War and Peace*, EPILOGUE I, 671d-672a; EPILOGUE II, 692c-694d

54 FREUD: *Civilization and Its Discontents*, 800d-801a

6b. The infinity of the intellect: man's knowledge of the infinite

OLD TESTAMENT: *Exodus*, 33:12–33 / *Job*, 11:7–9; 26:14; 28; 36:26; 38–41 / *Proverbs*, 20:24; 25:3 / *Ecclesiastes*, 3:11; 8:17; 11:5

APOCRYPHA: *Wisdom of Solomon*, 9:13–16—(D) OT, *Book of Wisdom*, 9:13–16 / *Ecclesiasticus*, 1:2; 18:4–7—(D) OT, *Ecclesiasticus*, 1:2; 18:2–6

NEW TESTAMENT: *John*, 1:18 / *Romans*, 11:33–34 / *I Corinthians*, 2:16 / *I Timothy*, 6:15–16

7 PLATO: *Philebus*, 610d-613a

8 ARISTOTLE: *Physics*, BK I, CH 4 [187^{b}7–14] 262d; CH 6 [189^{a}11–19] 264c; BK III, CH 6 [207^{a}21–31] 285c-d / *Metaphysics*, BK II, CH 2 [994^{b}17–30] 513a-b; BK III, CH 4 [999^{a}24–29] 518a; BK XII, CH 7 [1072^{b}14–29] 602d-603a; BK XIII, CH 10 [1087^{a}10–25] 619c / *Soul*, BK I, CH 3 [407^{a}22–30] 636d-637a; BK III, CH 4 [429^{a}19–28] 661c; CH 5 [430^{a}10–17] 662c

9 ARISTOTLE: *Rhetoric*, BK I, CH 2 [1356^{b}28–35] 596b-c

11 NICOMACHUS: *Arithmetic*, BK I, 812a

16 KEPLER: *Harmonies of the World*, 1080a

17 PLOTINUS: *Sixth Ennead*, TR VI, CH 3, 312a-b

18 AUGUSTINE: *Confessions*, BK V, par 20 32d-33a; BK VII, par 20–21 49d-50a; BK XII, par 3–6 99d-100c

19 AQUINAS: *Summa Theologica*, PART I, Q I, A I 3b-4a; Q 7, A 2, REP 2 31d-32c; QQ 12–13 50b-75b; Q 14, A I, ANS 75d-76c; A 12 85d-86d; Q 28, A 4, REP 2 160c-161d; Q 32, A I 175d-178a; Q 54, A 2, ANS 285d-286c; Q 79, A 2, ANS 414d-416a; Q 86, A 2 462a-463a; Q 87, A 3, REP 2 467b-468a; Q 88, A I, ANS 469a-471c; A 3 472c-473a; Q 91, A 3, REP 2 486b-487d; Q 94, A I, ANS 501d-503a; PART I–II, Q 2, A 6,

7. The infinity of God

7a. The infinite being or essence of God

(7. *The infinity of God.*)

7b. The infinite power of God

OLD TESTAMENT: *Genesis*, 18:14 / *Exodus*, 15:18 / *Deuteronomy*, 10:14; 32:39 / *I Samuel*, 2:6-8 —(D) *I Kings*, 2:6-8 / *Job*, 12:14-15; 38-41 / *Psalms*, 62:11; 114; 148—(D) *Psalms*, 61:12; 113:1-8; 148 / *Isaiah*, 40:22-31; 44:24-46:13 —(D) *Isaias*, 40:22-31; 44:24-46:12 / *Jeremiah*, 32:27—(D) *Jeremias*, 32:27 / *Daniel*, 4:34-35 —(D) *Daniel*, 4:31-32

APOCRYPHA: *Judith*, 16:13-17—(D) OT, *Judith*, 16:15-21 / *Rest of Esther*, 13:9-11—(D) OT, *Esther*, 13:9-11 / *Wisdom of Solomon*, 11:17-26; 12:12-18—(D) OT, *Book of Wisdom*, 11:18-27; 12:12-18 / *Ecclesiasticus*, 18:1-7—(D) OT, *Ecclesiasticus*, 18:1-6 / *II Maccabees*, 8:18— (D) OT, *II Machabees*, 8:18

NEW TESTAMENT: *Matthew*, 3:9; 19:26 / *Mark*, 10:27 / *Luke*, 1:37 / *Revelation*, 19:6—(D) *Apocalypse*, 19:6

8 ARISTOTLE: *Metaphysics*, BK XII, CH 7 [1073ª3-11] 603a-b

17 PLOTINUS: *Fifth Ennead*, TR V, CH 10 233b-c

18 AUGUSTINE: *Confessions*, BK I, par 12 4a; BK V, par 20 32d-33a; BK VII, par 6-7 44d-45d / *City of God*, BK V, CH 10 215c-216c; BK VII, CH 30 261b-d; BK XIV, CH 27 396c-397a; BK XXI, CH 5-8 563d-568d

19 AQUINAS: *Summa Theologica*, PART I, Q 25, AA 2-3 144c-147a; Q 45, A 5, REP 3 245c-247a; Q 65, A 3, REP 3 341c-342b; Q 92, A 2, REP 2 489d-490c; PART I-II, Q 1, A 4, REP 1 612a-613a

20 AQUINAS: *Summa Theologica*, PART I-II, Q 113, A 9 368d-369c; PART II-II, Q 23, A 2, REP 3 483d-484d; PART III, Q 10, A 3, REP 3 769d-771b

31 DESCARTES: *Meditations*, III, 86a / *Objections and Replies*, 229c-d

31 SPINOZA: *Ethics*, PART I, DEF 3-6 355b; DEF 8 355c; PROP 1-8 355d-357d; PROP 11-17 358b-363c; PROP 20-25 363d-365b; PROP 32-35 367a-369a; APPENDIX 369b-372d; PART II, PROP 3 374a-c

32 MILTON: *Paradise Lost*, BK II [119-225] 113b-116a; BK III [372-415] 143b-144b / *Samson Agonistes* [300-329] 346a-b

33 PASCAL: *Pensées*, 654 292b

34 NEWTON: *Principles*, BK III, GENERAL SCHOL, 370a

35 LOCKE: *Human Understanding*, BK II, CH XV, SECT 12 165b-c; CH XVII, SECT 1 167d-168a; CH XXIII, SECT 34-35 213a-c passim; BK III, CH VI, SECT 11-12 271b-272b passim

35 BERKELEY: *Human Knowledge*, SECT 152 443c-d

36 STERNE: *Tristram Shandy*, 334a-b

37 FIELDING: *Tom Jones*, 186c-d

42 KANT: *Pure Reason*, 180b-c; 181b; 192c-d; 201b-c / *Practical Reason*, 352a-c / *Judgement*, 502d-503a; 504b-d; 592a-c; 600d-601c

46 HEGEL: *Philosophy of History*, INTRO, 156d-160b

51 TOLSTOY: *War and Peace*, EPILOGUE II, 684b-d

7c. God's infinite goodness and love

OLD TESTAMENT: *Isaiah*, 43:1-4; 46:3-4; 49:14-15; 63:8-9—(D) *Isaias*, 43:1-4; 46:3-4; 49:14-15; 63:8-9 / *Jeremiah*, 31 esp 31:3— (D) *Jeremias*, 31 esp 31:3

APOCRYPHA: *Wisdom of Solomon*, 11:23-26; 16:20-29—(D) OT, *Book of Wisdom*, 11:24-27; 16:20-29

NEW TESTAMENT: *Matthew*, 19:16-17 / *John*, 3:16; 13:31-17:26 / *Romans*, 8:35-39 / *Galatians*, 2:20 / *Ephesians*, 3:14-21 / *I John*, 3:1

17 PLOTINUS: *Fifth Ennead*, TR V, CH 10-11 233b-234a

18 AUGUSTINE: *Confessions*, BK V, par 20 32d-33a; BK XIII, par 2-5 111a-d / *City of God*, BK XI, CH 10 327d-328d; BK XII, CH 1-3 342b,d-344b

19 AQUINAS: *Summa Theologica*, PART I, Q 2, A 3, REP 1 12c-14a; Q 4, A 1 20d-21b; Q 6, AA 1-3 28b-30b; Q 11, A 3, ANS 49a-c; Q 54, A 2, ANS 285d-286c; PART I-II, Q 1, A 4, REP 1 612a-613a; Q 5, A 2, REP 3 637c-638a

20 AQUINAS: *Summa Theologica*, PART I-II, Q 64, A 4, REP 3 69b-70a; PART II-II, Q 23, A 2, REP 3 483d-484d; PART III, Q 1, A 1 701d-703a

21 DANTE: *Divine Comedy*, PURGATORY, XV [40-81] 75d-76a; PARADISE, XXIX [127-145] 151c-d

31 DESCARTES: *Objections and Replies*, 229c-d

31 SPINOZA: *Ethics*, PART V, PROP 35-36 460d-461c

32 MILTON: *Paradise Lost*, BK VII [139-173] 220a-221a

33 PASCAL: *Pensées*, 580 276b

35 LOCKE: *Human Understanding*, BK II, CH XVII, SECT 1 167d-168a; BK III, CH VI, SECT 11-12 271b-272b passim

37 FIELDING: *Tom Jones*, 186c-d

42 KANT: *Fund. Prin. Metaphysic of Morals*, 263a-b / *Practical Reason*, 325d-326a; 345a-c; 351b-352c / *Judgement*, 592a-c

44 BOSWELL: *Johnson*, 539d-540a

52 DOSTOEVSKY: *Brothers Karamazov*, BK II, 24a-c

7d. God's infinite knowledge

OLD TESTAMENT: *I Samuel*, 2:3—(D) *I Kings*, 2:3 / *Job*, 11:5-11; 34:21-25; 36:4; 37:16 / *Psalms*, 94:7-12; 100:5; 117:2; 119:142,160; 139; 146:6; 147:5—(D) *Psalms*, 93:7-12; 99:5; 116:2; 118:142,160; 138; 145:6-7; 146:5 / *Proverbs*, 15:3,11 / *Isaiah*, 29:15-16; 40:28— (D) *Isaias*, 29:15-16; 40:28

APOCRYPHA: *Rest of Esther*, 13:12—(D) OT, *Esther*, 13:12 / *Ecclesiasticus*, 15:18-19; 16:17-20; 17:15,17,19-20; 23:18-20; 39:19-21; 42:18-21—(D) OT, *Ecclesiasticus*, 15:19-20; 16:16-20; 17:13-17; 23:25-29; 39:24-25; 42:18-22 / *Susanna*, 42-43—(D) OT, *Daniel*, 13:42-43

CROSS-REFERENCES

For: The distinction between the potential and actual infinite, and the infinite of division and addition, *see* Quantity 7.

The issue concerning the existence of atoms or the infinite divisibility of matter, *see* Element 5b; One and Many 3a(3).

Other discussions of the infinity of space, time, and motion, *see* Astronomy 8c(1); Change 13; Eternity 2; Space 3a; Time 2b; World 4a; and for the conception of eternity as infinite time, *see* Eternity 1; Time 2.

The problem of an infinite regression in causes, *see* Cause 1b, 7b; Change 14; Principle 1b; and for the related problem of infinite regression in definition and reasoning, *see* Definition 1c; Principle 3a(3); Reasoning 5b(1).

The treatment of the infinite and the infinitesimal in mathematics, *see* Mathematics 4d; Quantity 2, 3a, 3c, 4c, 7.

The special logical sense in which judgments are called "infinite," *see* Judgment 6b.

The conception of the human intellect and of prime matter as having comparable types of infinity, *see* Mind 2b.

Another discussion of the finite and the infinite in relation to human nature, *see* Man 10d, 13.

The special consideration of infinity in relation to human desire, *see* Desire 7–7a(3); and for the special consideration of the limits of human knowledge, *see* Knowledge 5a–5a(6).

The problem of our knowledge of the infinite, *see* Knowledge 5a(4).

The infinity of God, and of God's knowledge, power, and goodness, *see* Being 7b(4); God 4e–4f, 5c, 5f; Good and Evil 2; Knowledge 7a; Liberty 5d; Mind 10f; Nature 1b; Truth 2d; Will 4b; World 3a.

ADDITIONAL READINGS

Listed below are works not included in *Great Books of the Western World*, but relevant to the idea and topics with which this chapter deals. These works are divided into two groups:

I. Works by authors represented in this collection.

II. Works by authors not represented in this collection.

For the date, place, and other facts concerning the publication of the works cited, consult the Bibliography of Additional Readings which follows the last chapter of *The Great Ideas*.

I.

DESCARTES. *The Principles of Philosophy*, PART I, 26–27

SPINOZA. *Correspondence*, XII

NEWTON. *The Method of Fluxions and Infinite Series*

BERKELEY. *The Analyst*
——. *A Defence of Free Thinking in Mathematics*

HUME. *A Treatise of Human Nature*, BK I, PART II, SECT I–II

KANT. *De Mundi Sensibilis (Inaugural Dissertation)*
——. *Prolegomena to Any Future Metaphysic*, par 50–54

HEGEL. *Science of Logic*, VOL I, BK I, SECT I, CH 2 (B,C); SECT II, CH 2 (C)

W. JAMES. *Some Problems of Philosophy*, CH 10–11

II.

PROCLUS. *The Elements of Theology*, (J)

ANSELM OF CANTERBURY. *Monologium*
——. *Proslogium*

MAIMONIDES. *The Guide for the Perplexed*, PART I, CH 73

DUNS SCOTUS. *Opus Oxoniense*, BK I, DIST 13
——. *Reportata Parisiensia*

CRESCAS. *Or Adonai*, PROPOSITIONS 1–3

NICOLAS OF CUSA. *De Docta Ignorantia*

BRUNO. *De l'infinito, universo e mondi*
——. *De Immenso et Innumerabilibus*

DONNE. *Lovers Infinitenesse*

SUÁREZ. *Disputationes Metaphysicae*, XXVIII, XXX (2), XXXV (3), XLI (5)

LEIBNITZ. *New Essays Concerning Human Understanding*, BK II, CH 17
——. *Correspondence with Clarke*

VOLTAIRE. "Infinity," in *A Philosophical Dictionary*
——. *The Ignorant Philosopher*, CH 18

BOLZANO. *Paradoxien des Unendlichen*

WHEWELL. *On the Philosophy of Discovery*, CH 26

STALLO. *Concepts and Theories of Modern Physics*, CH 13

BRADLEY. *The Principles of Logic*, Terminal Essays, VI

FULLERTON. *The Conception of the Infinite, and the Solution of the Mathematical Antinomies*

BOSANQUET. *Logic*, VOL I, CH 4

C. S. PEIRCE. *Collected Papers*, VOL VI, par 112–126

COUTURAT. *De l'infini mathématique*

CANTOR. *Contributions to the Founding of the Theory of Transfinite Numbers*

ROYCE. *The World and the Individual*, SERIES I; Supplementary Essay (4)

PEANO. *Formulaire de mathématique*

E. W. HOBSON. *The Theory of Functions of a Real Variable and the Theory of Fourier's Series*

POINCARÉ. *Science and Method*, BK II, CH 3

WHITEHEAD and RUSSELL. *Principia Mathematica*, PART III, SECT C; PART V, SECT E

B. RUSSELL. *Principles of Mathematics*, CH 13, 17, 23, 37–43
——. *Our Knowledge of the External World*, V–VII
——. *Introduction to Mathematical Philosophy*, CH 3, 9, 13

SITTER. *Kosmos* (The Expanding Universe)

WEYL. *The Open World*, LECT III

Chapter 41: JUDGMENT

INTRODUCTION

THE word "judgment" has a range of meanings which includes three principal variants referring to (1) *a quality of the mind*, (2) *a faculty of the mind*, and (3) *an act of the mind*. Of these three meanings, it is the third which is extensively considered in this chapter; and it is this meaning of "judgment" which many writers use the word "proposition" to express. They sometimes substitute the one word entirely for the other; sometimes they use both words, not as strict synonyms, but to express distinct yet closely related aspects of the same fundamental phenomenon.

The sense in which judgment is *a quality of the mind* is the sense in which we ordinarily speak of a person as having sound judgment or poor judgment. "We credit the same people," Aristotle says, "with possessing judgment and having reached years of reason and with having practical wisdom and understanding." To be "a man of understanding and of good or sympathetic judgment," he continues, is to be "able to judge about the things with which practical wisdom is concerned."

The capacity to judge well concerning what is to be done is often connected with the capacity to deliberate about the advantages and disadvantages or other circumstances relevant to the action in question. It may or may not be accompanied by a capacity to resolve thought into action, to carry into execution the decision which judgment has formed. These three qualities of mind—deliberateness, judgment, and decisiveness—are conceived by Aristotle and Aquinas as belonging together as parts of the intellectual virtue they call "prudence" or "practical wisdom." The qualities may occur separately, but the prudent man will possess all three.

This meaning of "judgment" is reserved for discussion in the chapter on PRUDENCE; and in the chapter on LAW will be found the consider-

ation of the judgment which a court renders—the judgment which is the decision of a judge when he applies the law to the particular case. In the legal sense of a judicial decision, judgment reflects not so much the quality of the judge's mind as his duty and authority to dispose of the case and to have his decision executed by the appropriate officers of the law. The legal significance of judgment is not primarily psychological or logical; and, just as the moral consideration of judgment falls under prudence, the legal consideration is also more appropriately developed in the context of other ideas.

We are left with the meanings which belong to psychology, logic, and the theory of knowledge. The sense in which "judgment" designates *a faculty or function of the mind*—a distinct sphere of mental operation—is much more special than the sense in which "judgment" or "proposition" signifies *a particular act of the mind* in the process of knowing or in the verbal expression of that process. Many authors discuss the kinds of judgment which the mind makes, and the kinds of propositions it forms and asserts or denies, but only a few—notably Locke and Kant—use the word "judgment" to name a mental faculty.

Locke, for example, says that "the mind has two faculties conversant about truth and falsehood." One is the faculty of knowing; the other of judging. "The faculty which God has given man to supply the want of clear and certain knowledge, in cases where that cannot be had, is *judgment*: whereby the mind takes its ideas to agree and disagree, or, which is the same, any proposition to be true or false, without perceiving a demonstrative evidence in the proofs." The way in which Locke distinguishes between knowing and judging and the fact that he relates this distinction to the difference between certainty and probability suggest the parallel distinction between knowledge and opinion. The faculty of judgment for Locke is the equivalent of what other writers treat as the forming of opinions.

Kant also makes judgment a faculty. Along with understanding and reason, judgment is one of the three faculties of cognition. It has a distinct function of its own and is coordinate with the other two. As the laws of nature are the work of the understanding in the sphere of speculative reason; as the rules of the moral law are the work of the reason in the practical sphere, wherein it is related to the faculty of desire; so the purposiveness of nature comes under the faculty of judgment which operates in relation to the faculty of pleasure and pain.

Kant divides all the faculties of the soul into "three which cannot be any further derived from one common ground: the *faculty of knowledge*, the *feeling of pleasure and pain* and the *faculty of desire*." He sees each of the three cognitive functions (of understanding, judgment, and reason) as standing in a peculiar relation to these three primary faculties. The faculty of judgment functions with respect to pleasure and pain, which is connected with the faculty of desire. Yet the aesthetic judgment of beauty and the theological judgment of purposiveness in nature are of a speculative rather than a practical character. Because of these two related facts, Kant holds that "the judgement in the order of our cognitive faculties, forms a mediating link between Understanding and Reason."

Kant, perhaps more than any other thinker, makes judgment—both as a faculty and as an act—one of the central terms in his philosophy. It is pivotal in each of the three critiques, but it is the *Critique of Judgement* which serves to connect the *Critique of Pure Reason* and the *Critique of Practical Reason*. "The Understanding legislates *a priori* for nature as an object of sense—for theoretical knowledge of it in a possible experience. Reason legislates *a priori* for freedom and its peculiar causality; as the supersensible in the subject, for an unconditioned practical knowledge. The realm of the natural concept under one legislation, and that of the concept of freedom under the other, are entirely removed from all mutual influence which

they might have upon one another (each according to its fundamental laws) by the great gulf that separates the supersensible from phenomena." It is the judgment, according to Kant, which "furnishes the mediating concept between the concept of nature and that of freedom."

KANT'S THEORY of the faculties of understanding, judgment, and reason is so complex a doctrine that it cannot be readily compared with other analyses of the capacities or functions of mind. His threefold division bears a superficial —perhaps only a verbal—resemblance to Aquinas' division of mental acts into conception, judgment, and reasoning.

According to Aquinas, judgment is the second of the three acts of a single cognitive faculty variously called "mind" or "intellect" or "reason." This faculty, he writes, "first apprehends something about a thing, such as its essence, and this is its first and proper object; and then it understands the properties, accidents, and various dispositions affecting the essence. Thus it necessarily relates one thing with another by composition or division; and from one composition and division it necessarily proceeds to another, and this is *reasoning*."

The first act of the mind is conception, *i.e.*, the simple apprehension of the essence and properties of a thing. Judgment, the second act, unites or separates concepts by affirming or denying one of another. As in the Kantian analysis, judgment is a kind of mediating link; for after the judgment is formed by what Aquinas calls the "composition or division" of concepts, it in turn serves as the unit of the mind's third act, which is reasoning. Reasoning is the process of going from judgment to judgment.

The act of judgment is that act of the mind, and the only act, which can have the quality of truth or falsity. "Truth," Aquinas writes, "resides in the intellect composing and dividing"; for when the intellect "judges that a thing corresponds to the form which it apprehends about that thing, then it first knows and expresses truth. . . . In every proposition," the mind "either applies to, or removes from, the thing signified by the subject some form signified by the predicate." Moreover, the judgment involves assertion or denial as the concept does not. Whatever truth there is implicitly in concepts must be explicated in judgments and the truth of the conclusion in reasoning depends upon the truth of the judgments which are the premises. The judgment, therefore, is the basic unit of knowledge.

On this last point Kant seems to be in agreement with earlier writers. It is possible, therefore, to compare Kant's classification of judgments or propositions with the classifications of Aristotle, Descartes, or Locke. But it is necessary, first, to consider the relation between judgment and proposition. After that we can examine the difference between theoretic and practical judgments. With respect to the theoretic judgment (or proposition), we shall be able to state opposite views of the nature of the judgment and diverse views of the formal structure of judgments, their material content, their relation to one another and to the whole process of knowing.

THE SENTENCE "all men are mortal" can be interpreted as expressing a judgment or a proposition. From certain points of view, the choice of interpretation makes no difference; for example, it does not matter whether, in a consideration of "all men are mortal" and "some men are not mortal," the comparison is expressed in terms of universal and particular, affirmative and negative, judgments *or* propositions, or whether it is said that these are contradictory judgments *or* contradictory propositions. The basic problems of logic seem to be conceived in the same way by writers like Aristotle and Locke, who tend to use "proposition" in place of "judgment," and by writers like Aquinas, Descartes, and Kant, who tend to use both words with some difference in meaning.

What is the difference? It is sometimes understood as a difference between an act of the mind, asserting or denying, and the subject matter being asserted or denied. The proposition is that which may be either asserted or denied; or in the third alternative stressed by Descartes, the mind may suspend judgment and merely entertain the proposition. It may decline to judge it true or false, and so refuse to assert or deny it. The fact that the proposition is itself either affirmative or negative does not signify its assertion or denial by a judgment of the mind, for an affirmative proposition can be denied and a negative can be affirmed.

Judgment adds to the proposition in question the mind's decision with respect to its truth or falsity. That decision may be right or wrong. A proposition which is in fact true may be denied. The truth of the proposition is unaffected by the falsity of the judgment, or if the mind suspends judgment on a proposition which is true, the truth of the proposition has failed to elicit a judgment. This seems to confirm the separation between the proposition and the judgment.

Sometimes the difference between the judgment and the proposition is found in the difference between the mind's act of "composing" or "dividing" concepts and the formulation of that act in words. On this view, the proposition is related to the judgment as the term to the concept, as the physical to the mental word, as language to thought. In consequence, there is no separation for either the judgment or the proposition between that which can be asserted or denied and the assertion or denial of it. The affirmative judgment *is* an assertion, the negative a denial; and the same holds for the affirmative and the negative proposition.

But on either theory of the difference, it is thought necessary to distinguish between the sentence and the proposition, especially when the proposition is also regarded as a verbal formulation—a statement of thought in words. This is particularly important in a logical treatise like Aristotle's, which analyzes *terms*, *propositions*, and *syllogisms* rather than *concepts*, *judgments*, and *reasonings*.

In both the *Categories*, which deals with terms, and the treatise *On Interpretation*, which deals with propositions, Aristotle differentiates between a grammatical and a logical handling of the units of language. His distinction, for example, between simple and composite expressions (words and phrases on the one hand, and sentences on the other) is related to, but it is not identical with, his distinction between terms and propositions. Not every simple expression can be used as a term. For example, prepositions and conjunctions cannot be used as terms, as nouns and verbs can be. Nor can every sentence be used as a proposition.

"A sentence is a significant portion of speech,"

Aristotle writes, "some parts of which have an independent meaning, that is to say, as an utterance, though not as the expression of any positive judgment. . . . Every sentence has meaning," he goes on, "by convention. Yet every sentence is not a proposition; only such are propositions as have in them truth or falsity. Thus a prayer is a sentence, but is neither true nor false. Let us therefore dismiss all other types of sentence but the proposition, for this last concerns our present inquiry, whereas the investigation of the others belongs rather to the study of rhetoric or of poetry."

It seems possible to relate the two separate distinctions we have been considering—that between sentence and proposition and that between proposition and judgment. As the proposition can be regarded as a sentence logically (rather than grammatically) construed, so it can also be regarded as the linguistic expression of a judgment of the mind. The proposition thus appears to be a kind of middle ground between language and thought, for when a sentence is used for the purpose of stating a proposition it can also express a judgment. When a judgment is expressed in words, the verbal statement is also a proposition. The proposition is thus the logical aspect of a sentence and the verbal aspect of a judgment. A similar consideration of terms in relation to words and concepts occurs in the chapter on IDEA.

WHAT IS PERHAPS the most fundamental division in the sphere of judgments—the separation of the practical from the theoretic or speculative—can be initially explained by reference to the forms of language. Aristotle's remark about sentences and propositions tends to identify propositions with declarative sentences. Sentences in the subjunctive mood state prayers or wishes, not propositions. An interrogative sentence asks a question to which the answers may be propositions, or they may be hopes and desires. The imperative sentence issues a command to act in a certain way, whether the command is a direction for others or a decision for one's self. This last type of sentence represents the practical mood of thought as well as speech —thought concerned with actions to be done or not done, rather than with what does or does not exist.

The imperative sentence is not the only kind of practical statement. It is merely the most terse and emphatic. It is also the expression of that type of practical judgment which most immediately precedes action itself, or the execution of a command. There are other sentences which, because they are apparently declarative in form, conceal their imperative mood. Yet upon examination their essentially practical rather than theoretic significance can be discovered.

Sentences which contain the words "ought" or "should" are of this sort, e.g., "Men ought to seek the truth," "You should work for peace," "I ought to make this clear." By omitting "should" or "ought," these sentences can be changed into the strictly declarative mood of theoretic propositions, e.g., "Men do seek the truth," "You will work for peace," "I shall make this clear." They can also be made plainly imperative, e.g., "Seek the truth," etc. The chief difference between the blunt form of the imperative and its indicative expression using "ought" or "should" is that the latter indicates the person to whom the command is addressed.

The contrast in significance between a declarative and an imperative statement does, therefore, convey the distinction between a theoretic and a practical proposition or judgment. Kant's further division of practical judgments into the hypothetical and the categorical simply differentiates commands or "oughts" which involve no preamble from those which propose that action be taken to achieve a certain end, or which base a direction to employ this or that means on the supposition that a certain end is desired or sought. Examples of hypothetical or conditional imperatives would be such judgments as "If you want to be happy, seek the truth" or "Seek the truth in order to be happy."

The distinction between theoretic and practical judgments is currently made in terms of the contrast between statements of fact and statements of value or, as in judicial procedure, between statements of fact and rules of law. A rule of law has the form of a general practical statement, usually a conditional rather than a categorical imperative; whereas the decision of a court applying the rule to a case is a particular practical judgment.

Beginning with Francis Bacon, the distinction between the theoretic and the practical is also made in terms of the difference between the pure sciences and their applications in technology. Technical judgments, prescribing the way to make something or produce a certain effect, are traditionally associated, under the head of the practical, with moral judgments concerning the good to be sought and the ways of seeking it. Both are prescriptive of conduct rather than descriptive of existence or nature in the manner of theoretical statements.

Thinkers like Aristotle, Aquinas, and Kant, who divide science or philosophy into the theoretical disciplines (e.g., physics, mathematics, metaphysics) and the practical or moral disciplines (e.g., ethics, economics, politics), place the discussion of the difference between theoretical and practical judgments in the context of other distinctions; as, for example, between the speculative and the practical reason, or between theoretic and practical knowledge; or in the context of considering the kinds of truth appropriate to each, and the modes of inference or demonstration in each. These related distinctions and considerations are treated in the chapters on KNOWLEDGE, MIND, REASONING, and TRUTH.

For the most part, however, the great books in the tradition of logic itself do not give an analysis of practical judgments or reasoning in any way comparable to their treatment of the theoretic forms of thought and statement. The logical problems concerning propositions or judgments, now to be considered, apply only to the theoretic forms.

TWO BASIC ISSUES in the theory of propositions or judgments have their origin in the tradition of the great books, but for their explicit and full development other works must be consulted—the special treatises on logic, of relatively recent date, listed in the Additional Readings. One of these two issues has already been briefly commented on, but for the full implications of the distinction between propositions and judgments one must go to such writers as Hegel, Bradley, Bosanquet, Cook Wilson, W. E. Johnson, and John Dewey, who make this distinction the crux of a controversy over the scope of formal logic.

The other basic issue lies in the opposition between what has come to be called "subject-predicate logic" and "relational logic." Here one side is fully represented by the Organon of Aristotle and by the later books which adopt the Aristotelian logic of predication. The other logical theory is intimated but not fully developed by such writers as Locke, Hume, Kant, and William James who, though they sometimes employ the subject-predicate formulation, tend to construct the unit of knowledge—the proposition or judgment—as a relation between ideas or concepts.

The fact that Kant places substance and accident under the category of relation can be taken as exemplifying this tendency, as can Locke's emphasis on the connection of, and agreement or disagreement between, our ideas. Nevertheless, these are at most intimations of the theory that the proposition is a relation of two or more terms, not the application of a predicate to a subject. As indicated in the chapter on LOGIC, the relational theory does not receive an adequate exposition until the modern development of symbolic or mathematical logic, beginning with the writings of Boole, Jevons, and Venn, and culminating in such works as the Principia Mathematica of Russell and Whitehead.

In the Aristotelian logic, simple propositions consist of a subject and a predicate—what is being talked about and what is said of it. The copula "is" is the sign of predication; it also signifies an affirmation of the unity of subject and predicate. For example, in "Socrates is a man" the predicate man is applied to the subject Socrates, and the unity of being Socrates and being a man is affirmed. All the terms of discourse can be classified according to their character as subjects and predicates; so, too, can propositions be classified by reference to the type of subject-term and the type of predicate-term which comprise them. The formal structure not only of the proposition, but also of the syllogism, is determined by the order of subjects and predicates. "When one term is predicated of another," Aristotle writes, "any term which is predicable of the predicate will also be predicable of its subject."

According to the theory of the proposition as a relation of terms or of classes, predication represents merely one type of relationship—the membership of an individual in a class, or the inclusion of one class in another. There are many other types of relation which, it is held, cannot be reduced to class-membership or class-inclusion; as, for example, the relationship stated by the proposition "John hit James," or the proposition "January comes before February." Propositions can be classified according to the number of terms involved in a single relationship, or by reference to the type of relation which organizes them, whether it is symmetrical or asymmetrical, transitive or intransitive, reflexive or irreflexive. In this theory it is the character of the relationship, not the character of the terms, which is the fundamental element in logical analysis, and this determines the formal structure of inference as well as of propositions.

It has been claimed for each of these logical theories that it is the more general analysis and that it is able to reduce the formulations of the opposite theory to its own terms or subsume them as a special case. Certainly it is verbally possible to convert all predications into statements of relationship, or all relational statements into subject-predicate propositions. But this by itself does not seem to resolve the issue to the satisfaction of either theory; each side contends that such reductions violate its fundamental principles. Stated in its most drastic form, the unresolved question is whether there is one logic or two—or perhaps more.

WITHIN THE tradition of Aristotelian logic, there are divergent schemes for classifying propositions or judgments. So far as the great books are concerned, this can be best illustrated by mentioning Kant's departures in analysis.

Aristotle distinguishes between simple and composite propositions, the former consisting of a single subject and predicate, the latter "compounded of several propositions." For example, since the two predicates in the proposition "This man is good and a shoemaker" do not form a unity, the sentence expresses a conjunction of two simple propositions: "This man is good" and "This man is a shoemaker." Other types of compound propositions are the hypothetical and the disjunctive, e.g., "If Socrates is a man, Socrates is mortal," and "Either all men

are mortal or no men are mortal." Kant treats these distinctions under the head of *relation*. He calls the proposition which is a "relation of the predicate to the subject, categorical" and he regards the hypothetical or disjunctive judgment (based on relations of cause and effect or of the parts of a whole) as concerned with propositions "in relation to each other."

Aristotle classifies simple propositions by reference to their quantity and quality. In regard to quantity he distinguishes between the universal (e.g., "All men are mortal") and the particular (e.g., "Some men are mortal"). To these he adds the indefinite proposition which leaves the quantity (*all* or *some*) undetermined. Under the head of quantity, Kant makes a threefold division according to unity, plurality, and totality. He adds the singular proposition "Socrates is mortal" to Aristotle's particular and universal. The difference between the singular on the one hand, and the particular and the universal on the other, seems to be represented in Aristotle's thought by the distinction between propositions about an individual subject and propositions about a universal subject.

The quality of categorical propositions, according to Aristotle, is either affirmative (i.e., positive) or negative, e.g., "All men are mortal" and "Some men are *not* mortal." To these two Kant adds a third type of judgment under the head of *quality*—the infinite judgment which affirms a negative predicate of a subject, e.g., "The soul is non-mortal." Though Aristotle recognizes the special character of a term like "non-mortal," since it is both negative and indefinite, he does not seem to think that the use of such terms affects the quality of a proposition.

Finally, Aristotle divides propositions according to whether they are simple assertions of fact or are assertions qualified by the notions of necessity or contingency (i.e., possibility). Every proposition, he says, "states that something either is or must be or may be the attribute of something else." The distinction between the necessary and contingent modes of statement has come to be called a difference in "modality," and statements which have one or another modality are called "modal propositions."

It is sometimes thought that the Aristotelian classification treats only necessary and contingent propositions, with their several opposites, as modal propositions, and separates the simple or pure assertion from them as non-modal. In contrast to this, Kant makes a threefold division of judgments under the head of modality: the "problematical" (*i.e.*, the possible, what *may be*), the "assertoric" (*i.e.*, the existent, what *is*), and the "apodictic" (*i.e.*, the necessary, what *must be*).

THE CLASSIFICATION of the types of judgment or proposition is usually preliminary in logical analysis to a consideration of their order and connection.

The formal pattern of what is traditionally called "the square of opposition" is determined by the quality and quantity of the simple propositions which are therein related as contradictory, contrary, and sub-contrary. Two propositions are contradictory if they are opposite in both quality and quantity (*e.g.*, "All men are mortal" is contradicted by "Some men are not mortal"). Two universal propositions are contrary if one is affirmative and the other negative (*e.g.*, "All men are mortal" is contrary to "No men are mortal"); and an affirmative and a negative particular proposition are related as sub-contraries (*e.g.*, "Some men are mortal" and "Some men are not mortal"). The significance of these three basic relationships for the truth and falsity of the opposed propositions is discussed in the chapter on OPPOSITION; and in the chapter on NECESSITY AND CONTINGENCY the special problems of opposition among modal propositions are examined.

Other than their opposition, the only formal relationship of propositions or judgments occurs in the structure of inference or reasoning. According to the traditional analysis, the implication of one proposition by another—insofar as that is determined by the form of each—is immediate inference. In contrast, the pattern of *mediated* inference or reasoning always involves at least three propositions, ordered not only with respect to the sequence from premises to conclusion, but also by the relation of the premises to one another. These matters are discussed in the chapter on REASONING.

With respect to their origin, status, or import, judgments or propositions are subject to

further distinctions in type. The certainty or probability with which propositions are asserted or judgments are made is connected by some writers with the distinction between knowledge and opinion, by others with the difference between science and dialectic, and by others with the difference between knowing the relation of ideas and knowing matters of fact or real existence. Propositions which express certain knowledge are, furthermore, divided by some analysts into those which are axiomatic, self-evident, or immediate and those which are known only by mediated inference, reasoning, or demonstration, not by intuition or induction. The former are also sometimes called "principles," the latter "conclusions."

Locke's distinction between "trifling" and "instructive" propositions, like Kant's distinction between "analytic" and "synthetic" judgments, is made in the general context of an examination of how we learn or know.

Trifling propositions, according to Locke, "are universal propositions which, though they be certainly true, yet they add no light to our understanding; bring no increase to our knowledge." All "purely identical propositions" are of this sort—propositions such as "body is body" or "a vacuum is a vacuum." Such propositions "teach nothing but what every one who is capable of discourse knows without being told, *viz.*, that the same term is the same term, and the same idea the same idea." They are all instances of the law of identity; or, as Locke expresses it, they are all "equivalent to this proposition, *viz.*, *what is*, *is*." If the trifling proposition, the analytical judgment, or what in our day is called a "tautology," goes beyond the statement of an identity between subject and predicate, it goes no further than the explication of a definition. It predicates, Locke says, "a part of the definition of the word defined," as, for example, in the proposition "Lead is a metal."

Analytical or explicative judgments, Kant says in the *Prolegomena*, "express nothing in the predicate but what has already been actually thought in the concept of the subject . . . When I say, 'all bodies are extended,' I have not amplified in the least my concept of body, but have only analyzed it . . . On the contrary, this judgment, 'All bodies have weight,' contains in its predicate something not actually thought in the general concept of body; it amplifies my knowledge, by adding something to my concept, and must therefore be called synthetical."

For Locke not all axioms or self-evident propositions are trifling or tautological, for some go beyond statements of identity or the explication of definitions, as, for example, that the whole is greater than the part. Nor are they all useless. Some which Locke distinguishes from the rest by calling them "maxims," are of use, he maintains, "in the ordinary methods of teaching sciences as far as they are advanced, but of little or none in advancing them further. They are of use in disputes, for the silencing of obstinate wranglers, and bringing those contests to some conclusion."

For Kant there is a further division of judgments into the *a posteriori* and the *a priori*, according as their truth is or is not grounded in the data of experience. The former are empirical in origin, the latter transcendental, that is, they have a foundation which transcends experience. These two types of judgment express two corresponding types of knowledge—*a priori* knowledge by which Kant understands "not such as is independent of this or that kind of experience, but such as is absolutely so of *all* experience. Opposed to this is empirical knowledge, or that which is possible only *a posteriori*, that is, through experience."

In Kant's view, there is no problem about the truth of analytic judgments, for these have an *a priori* foundation in the principle of contradiction. (The contradictory of an analytic judgment is always self-contradictory.) Nor do synthetic judgments which are empirical or *a posteriori* raise any special difficulties. The central question in the theory of knowledge concerns the possibility and validity of synthetic judgments *a priori*.

"If I go out of and beyond the conception A, in order to recognize another, B, as connected with it, what foundation have I to rest on," Kant asks, "whereby to render the synthesis possible? I have here no longer the advantage of looking out in the sphere of experience for what I want. Let us take, for example, the proposition, 'everything that happens has a cause.' In the conception of *something that hap-*

pens, I indeed think an existence which a certain time antecedes, and from this I can derive analytical judgments. But the conception of a cause lies quite outside the above conception, and indicates something entirely different from 'that which happens,' and is consequently not contained in that conception. How then am I able to assert concerning the general conception—'that which happens'—something entirely different from that conception, and to recognize the conception of cause although not contained in it, yet as belonging to it, and even necessarily? What is here the unknown X, upon which the understanding rests when it believes it has found, outside the conception A, a foreign predicate B, which it nevertheless considers to be connected with it?" It is the discovery and solution of this problem which Kant believes to be the signal contribution of his transcendental logic of the judgment.

It may be wondered whether this problem can be stated in terms other than those peculiar to Kant's analytical vocabulary. Other writers admit that propositions which are particular and contingent have "existential import." Their truth concerns real existences, and so whether they are true or not can and must be learned from experience. These are like Kant's synthetic judgments *a posteriori*. Universal and necessary propositions, on the other hand, are sometimes interpreted as having no existential significance. Instead of being read as asserting that anything exists, they are taken simply as statements of the relation between our own ideas. These, for Locke and Hume, are like Kant's *a priori* analytic judgments.

What remains is to discover a parallel for Kant's synthetic judgments *a priori*. In terms other than Kant's, the most likely parallel seems to be the universal and necessary proposition conceived as a statement about reality rather than about relations in the realm of our own concepts. When universal propositions are so interpreted, two questions arise. How do we establish that the subjects of such propositions really exist? What is the ultimate ground for the truth of such propositions, the unlimited universality of which outruns experience? In these two questions we find a problem which is at least analogous to Kant's problem of the possibility of synthetic judgments *a priori*.

OUTLINE OF TOPICS

REFERENCES

To find the passages cited, use the numbers in heavy type, which are the volume and page numbers of the passages referred to. For example, in 4 HOMER: *Iliad*, BK II [265–283] 12d, the number 4 is the number of the volume in the set; the number 12d indicates that the passage is in section d of page 12.

PAGE SECTIONS: When the text is printed in one column, the letters a and b refer to the upper and lower halves of the page. For example, in 53 JAMES: *Psychology*, 116a-119b, the passage begins in the upper half of page 116 and ends in the lower half of page 119. When the text is printed in two columns, the letters a and b refer to the upper and lower halves of the left-hand side of the page, the letters c and d to the upper and lower halves of the right-hand side of the page. For example, in 7 PLATO: *Symposium*, 163b-164c, the passage begins in the lower half of the left-hand side of page 163 and ends in the upper half of the right-hand side of page 164.

AUTHOR'S DIVISIONS: One or more of the main divisions of a work (such as PART, BK, CH, SECT) are sometimes included in the reference; line numbers, in brackets, are given in certain cases; *e.g.*, *Iliad*, BK II [265–283] 12d.

BIBLE REFERENCES: The references are to book, chapter, and verse. When the King James and Douay versions differ in title of books or in the numbering of chapters or verses, the King James version is cited first and the Douay, indicated by a (*D*), follows; *e.g.*, OLD TESTAMENT: *Nehemiah*, 7:45—(*D*) *II Esdras*, 7:46.

SYMBOLS: The abbreviation "esp" calls the reader's attention to one or more especially relevant parts of a whole reference; "passim" signifies that the topic is discussed intermittently rather than continuously in the work or passage cited.

For additional information concerning the style of the references, see the Explanation of Reference Style; for general guidance in the use of *The Great Ideas*, consult the Preface.

---

1. **Judgment as an act or faculty of the mind: its contrast with the act of conception or with the faculties of understanding and reason**

   8 ARISTOTLE: *Categories*, CH 4 [2ᵃ4–10] 6a / *Interpretation*, CH I [16ᵃ9–18] 25a-b / *Metaphysics*, BK VI, CH 4 [1027ᵇ18–28] 550a,c; BK IX, CH 10 577c-578a,c / *Soul*, BK III, CH 6 662d-663c

   18 AUGUSTINE: *Confessions*, BK VII, par 23 50b-c; BK X, par 10 73d-74a / *City of God*, BK VIII, CH 6, 269b-c

   19 AQUINAS: *Summa Theologica*, PART I, Q 3, A 4, REP 2 16d-17c; Q 13, A 12, ANS 74c-75b; Q 14, A 14 88d-89b; Q 16, A 2 95c-96b; Q 17, A 3 102d-103c; Q 58, A 2, ANS 301b-d; A 4, ANS 302d-303c; Q 85, A 5, ANS and REP 3 457d-458d; A 6 458d-459c

   20 AQUINAS: *Summa Theologica*, PART II-II, Q I, A 2 381a-c

   23 HOBBES: *Leviathan*, PART I, 66c-67a

   30 BACON: *Advancement of Learning*, 59c-61d esp 59c-60a; 64a-b

   31 DESCARTES: *Rules*, XII, 21d-22a / *Meditations*, II, 81a; IV 89a-93a esp 89c-90a / *Objections and Replies*, 124b-c; 141a; 215d-216c

   31 SPINOZA: *Ethics*, PART II, PROP 48–49 391a-394d

   35 LOCKE: *Human Understanding*, BK II, CH XX-, SECT 5 179c-d; BK IV, CH V, SECT 5–6 329dI 330b; CH XIV 364b-365a

   42 KANT: *Pure Reason*, 16d-19a; 34a-45b esp 39a-c, 41c-42c; 51d-52b; 59c-64a esp 60a-c; 64d-66d; 99a-101b; 108a-112d esp 110d-111c; 166c-171a; 193a-200c; 240b-243c / *Fund. Prin. Metaphysic of Morals*, 282b-c / *Judgement*, 461a-475d esp 465c-467d, 474b-475d; 550a-551a,c; 558a; 572b-575b

   53 JAMES: *Psychology*, 178a-179a; 213b-214a; 313b; 638a-b; 859a; 861b

2. **The division of judgments in terms of the distinction between the theoretic and the practical**

   8 ARISTOTLE: *Heavens*, BK III, CH 7 [306ᵃ14–18] 397b-c / *Metaphysics*, BK I, CH I 499a-500b; BK IV, CH 4 [1008ᵇ2–32] 527d-528b / *Soul*, BK III, CH 7 [431ᵇ2–12] 664a-b; CH 9 [432ᵇ26–433ᵃ9] 665c

   9 ARISTOTLE: *Ethics*, BK I, CH 3 339d-340b; CH 7 [1098ᵃ25–35] 343d; BK II, CH 2 [1103ᵇ26–1104ᵃ9] 349b-c; BK VI, CH 2 [1139ᵃ21–31] 387d-388a; CH 5 [1140ᵇ11–19] 389b-c; CH 8 [1142ᵃ13–19] 391b

   19 AQUINAS: *Summa Theologica*, PART I, Q 14, A 16 90b-91b; Q 79, AA 11–13 424d-427a; PART I-II, Q 13, A 6, REP 2 676c-677b

20 AQUINAS: *Summa Theologica*, PART I–II, Q 57, A 5, REP 3 39a-40a; Q 90, A 1, REP 2 205b-206b; A 2, REP 3 206b-207a; Q 94, A 4, ANS 223d-224d; PART III, Q 11, A 1, REP 3 772b-773a; Q 13, A 1, REP 3 780a-781b

31 DESCARTES: *Discourse*, PART I, 44a-c / *Objections and Replies*, 126a-b; 237b-c; 243c-d

35 LOCKE: *Human Understanding*, BK I, CH II, SECT 1 103d-104a

42 KANT: *Pure Reason*, 190c-191a / *Fund. Prin. Metaphysic of Morals*, 260d-261b; 271a-c / *Practical Reason*, 297a-c; 300d [fn 1]; 310a-b; 319c-321b; 329a-330c esp 329a-d; 343a-d / *Judgement*, 461a-475d esp 463a-467a, 474b-475d

43 MILL: *Utilitarianism*, 445c-d

46 HEGEL: *Philosophy of Right*, PREF, 5c-6a; PART III, par 227 74b-d

53 JAMES: *Psychology*, 186a

3. The analysis of practical or moral judgments: judgments of good and evil, means and ends; categorical and hypothetical imperatives

8 ARISTOTLE: *Topics*, BK III, CH 1–4 162a-166b / *Metaphysics*, BK I, CH 1 499a-500b; BK IV, CH 4 [1008^{b}2–32] 527d-528b

9 ARISTOTLE: *Ethics*, BK I, CH 3 339d-340b; BK II, CH 2 [1103^{b}27–1104^{a}9] 349b-c passim; BK VI, CH 2 [1139^{a}21–31] 387d-388a; CH 5 [1140^{b}11–19] 389b-c; CH 8 [1142^{a}13–19] 391b; CH 10–11 392b-393b; BK VII, CH 3 396c-398a / *Politics*, BK III, CH 11 [1281^{b}39–1282^{a}23] 479d-480a / *Rhetoric*, BK I, CH 7 604c-607d

17 PLOTINUS: *Third Ennead*, TR VI, CH 1 106b-107a

18 AUGUSTINE: *Confessions*, BK III, par 13 16c-d; BK VII, par 23 50b-c / *City of God*, BK VIII, CH 8 270a-d; BK XIX, CH 1–14 507a-520d / *Christian Doctrine*, BK III, CH 10, 661d-662a

19 AQUINAS: *Summa Theologica*, PART I, Q 59, A 3, ANS and REP 1 308b-309a; Q 79, AA 11–13 424d-427a; Q 83, A 1, ANS 436d-438a; A 2, ANS and REP 1 438a-d; A 3, ANS and REP 2 438d-439c; PART I–II, Q 17, A 1 686d-687c

20 AQUINAS: *Summa Theologica*, PART I–II, Q 57, A 6, ANS and REP 2–3 40a-41a

22 CHAUCER: *Tale of Melibeus* 401a-432a esp par 7–13 402b-405a, par 17–36 407b-417b, par 59–78 427a-432a

23 HOBBES: *Leviathan*, PART I, 53a-54a; 60d; 61d-62a; 65b-c; 66c-67d; 68b-c; 96a; PART II, 149b-c

25 MONTAIGNE: *Essays*, 51a-55d esp 52c-53c; 136b-139b; 520b-522a

27 SHAKESPEARE: *Troilus and Cressida*, ACT II, SC II 113c-115d

30 BACON: *Advancement of Learning*, 86c-95b

31 DESCARTES: *Discourse*, PART III, 49a-b / *Objections and Replies*, 126a-b

33 PASCAL: *Pensées*, 4 172b; 98 190b; 375–385 237b-239a; 456–457 254a; 505 261a-b

35 LOCKE: *Human Understanding*, BK II, CH XXI, SECT 59–70 193d-197b passim

35 HUME: *Human Understanding*, SECT V, DIV 36, 465a-d [fn 1]

42 KANT: *Pure Reason*, 114d-115a; 190c-d; 236d-237a / *Fund. Prin. Metaphysic of Morals*, 260a-261d; 266a-267d; 268c-271a; 272a-b / *Practical Reason*, 318c-321b esp 320c-321b; 327d-329a; 357c-360d / *Pref. Metaphysical Elements of Ethics*, 367c; 368d; 369b-c; 373d; 377c-d / *Intro. Metaphysic of Morals*, 386b-d; 387b; 387d-388a; 390b,d-391c; 392b-393a / *Science of Right*, 397b-398a; 416b-417b / *Judgement*, 477b-c; 557d [fn 2]; 586a-b; 595a-d; 596c-598b; 605d-606b [fn 2]

43 FEDERALIST: NUMBER 1, 29d

43 MILL: *Liberty*, 275a-278c passim, esp 276b-277b; 287b-c / *Utilitarianism*, 446d-447a; 455c-457b passim; 461c-462a

46 HEGEL: *Philosophy of Right*, PART II, par 140 49b-54a; PART III, par 191–192 66b-c / *Philosophy of History*, INTRO, 165a-166b; PART IV, 362d

53 JAMES: *Psychology*, 202b; 794a-798b; 886b-888a

54 FREUD: *Civilization and Its Discontents*, 792b-c; 801d

4. The distinction between the aesthetic and the teleological judgment

42 KANT: *Judgement*, 471b-473a; 476a-483d; 485b-489a; 492b-493b; 513b-516b; 516d-517c; 528b-c; 548c-549d; 550c-551a,c; 558a-b; 559c-560c; 562a-564c; 567c-570a; 572b-578a

5. The nature of theoretic judgments

5a. The linguistic expression of judgments: sentences and propositions

7 PLATO: *Cratylus*, 85d-86b; 109a-b / *Sophist*, 574d-577b

8 ARISTOTLE: *Interpretation*, CH 4–5 26a-c / *Prior Analytics*, BK I, CH 1 [24^{a}16–^{b}15] 39a-c / *Posterior Analytics*, BK I, CH 2 [72^{a}7–14] 98c

19 AQUINAS: *Summa Theologica*, PART I, Q 13, A 12 74c-75b; Q 85, A 2, REP 3 453d-455b

20 AQUINAS: *Summa Theologica*, PART II–II, Q 1, A 2 381a-c

23 HOBBES: *Leviathan*, PART I, 56b; 60a; PART IV, 270a-c

33 PASCAL: *Geometrical Demonstration*, 433a-b

35 LOCKE: *Human Understanding*, BK II, CH XXXIII, SECT 19 251c-d; BK III, CH VII, SECT 1 283a-b; BK IV, CH V 329a-331b passim; CH VI, SECT 1–3 331b-d

38 ROUSSEAU: *Inequality*, 341b-342c

53 JAMES: *Psychology*, 144a-b

5b. The judgment as a predication: the classification of subjects and predicates

8 ARISTOTLE: *Categories*, CH 2–3 5b-d; CH 5 [2^{a}11–3^{b}24] 6a-8a / *Interpretation*, CH 4–8 26a-28a; CH 11 31c-32c / *Prior Analytics*, BK I, CH 27 [43^{a}25–44] 60c-d / *Posterior Analytics*, BK I, CH 4 100a-101b; CH 18–22 111b-115b / *Topics*,

19 AQUINAS: *Summa Theologica*, PART I, Q 14,
A 7, ANS 81d-82b; Q 58, A 3 301d-302d; A 4,
ANS 302d-303c; Q 79, AA 8-9 421c-423d; Q 85,
A 5, ANS 457d-458d
23 HOBBES: *Leviathan*, PART I, 58a-c; 60a
30 BACON: *Advancement of Learning*, 59c-60a
31 DESCARTES: *Rules*, XIV, 28b-c
35 LOCKE: *Human Understanding*, BK IV, CH II,
SECT 2-8 309d-311a; CH XV, SECT 1 365a-c;
CH XVII, SECT 4, 373a-375a passim; SECT 15-
17 378d-379c
42 KANT: *Pure Reason*, 110d-112d; 115d-119a /
Practical Reason, 329a-d
53 JAMES: *Psychology*, 313b; 666b-674b esp 667b-
668a, 672b; 868b-879b esp 870b-873a, 878a

8. The differentiation of judgments according to origin, ground, or import

8a. Self-evident and demonstrable propositions: immediate and mediated, intuitive and reasoned judgments

8 ARISTOTLE: *Posterior Analytics*, BK I, CH I
97a-d; CH 3 99b-100a; CH 15 109a-b; CH 19-22
111c-115b; CH 23 [84^{b}19-85^{a}1] 115c-116a; CH
31 [88^{a}5-17] 120b-c; BK II, CH 9 128a-b; CH 19
136a-137a,c
9 ARISTOTLE: *Ethics*, BK VI, CH 3 [1139^{b}25-34]
388c; CH 6 389d; CH 8 [1142^{a}25-29] 391b-c;
CH 11 [1143^{a}32-^{b}5] 392d-393a / *Rhetoric*, BK I,
CH 2 [1356^{b}26-27] 596b
19 AQUINAS: *Summa Theologica*, PART I, Q 2, A
1 10d-11d; Q 14, A 1, REP 2 75d-76c; A 7,
ANS 81d-82b; Q 17, A 3, REP 2 102d-103c;
Q 79, A 12, ANS 425c-426b; Q 84, A 3, REP 3
443d-444d; Q 85, A 6, ANS 458d-459c; Q 117,
A 1 595d-597c; PART I-II, Q 1, A 4, REP 2 612a-
613a
20 AQUINAS: *Summa Theologica*, PART I-II, Q 57,
A 2 36a-37b; Q 94, A 2, ANS 221d-223a; A 4,
ANS 223d-224d; PART I-II, Q 1, A 4, ANS 382c-
383b; Q 8, A 1, REP 2 417a-d
25 MONTAIGNE: *Essays*, 259d-261a; 272a-d
30 BACON: *Advancement of Learning*, 59c-d;
97a
31 DESCARTES: *Rules*, III, 4a-d; XII, 20d-25a /
Objections and Replies, 123a-b; 125a-b
33 PASCAL: *Pensées*, I 171a-172a
35 LOCKE: *Human Understanding*, BK I, CH I,
SECT 15-16 98d-99c; SECT 18 99d-100b; SECT
23 101b-102a; CH II, SECT 1 103d-104a; SECT 4
104d-105a; CH III, SECT 23 119b-120a; BK IV,
CH I, SECT 9 308c-309b passim, esp 309b; CH
II 309b-313a; CH III, SECT 2-4 313a-c; CH VII,
SECT 1-11 337a-342d passim; CH IX, SECT 2-3
349a-c; CH XV, SECT 1 365a-c; CH XVII, SECT
2-3 371d-372b; SECT 14-17 378c-379c
42 KANT: *Pure Reason*, 39a-c; 99a-c; 110d-111c;
211c-218d / *Judgement*, 542d-543a
43 FEDERALIST: NUMBER 31, 103c-d; NUMBER
83, 244b-c
43 MILL: *Utilitarianism*, 446a-447a

8b. Analytic and synthetic judgments: trifling and instructive propositions

35 LOCKE: *Human Understanding*, BK IV, CH V,
SECT 6, 330b; CH VIII 345a-348d
42 KANT: *Pure Reason*, 16d-19a; 31a-d; 64d-66d;
179c-182b / *Practical Reason*, 339a; 351c /
Science of Right, 405b-c / *Judgement*, 516b-d
53 JAMES: *Psychology*, 879b-880b [fn 2]

8c. A priori and a posteriori, non-existential and existential judgments: the problem of a priori synthetic judgments

35 LOCKE: *Human Understanding*, BK I, CH I,
SECT 15-16 98d-99c; SECT 23 101b-102a; BK
IV, CH I, SECT 1-7 307a-308a; CH III, SECT
7-21 315b-319c; CH IX, SECT 1 349a; CH
XI, SECT 13-14 357d-358c; CH XVII, SECT 2,
371d
35 HUME: *Human Understanding*, SECT IV 458a-
463d passim, esp DIV 20-21 458a-c, DIV 30,
462a; SECT V, DIV 34-38, 464b-466c; SECT X,
DIV 89 490b-c; SECT XII, DIV 131-132 508d-
509d passim
42 KANT: *Pure Reason*, 5a-8b; 14a-108a,c esp 14a-
20c, 23a-24a, 25b-26b, 27b-28b, 29d-33d,
35b-36a, 41c-42b, 46a-48d, 57d-59b, 64b-
66d, 85d-88a; 108b-d; 110a-113b; 134c-d;
146a; 179c-182b; 192a-b; 211c-218d; 224a-
227a / *Fund. Prin. Metaphysic of Morals*,
268b-d; 280a-b; 283b / *Practical Reason*,
309b-d; 329d-330c; 351c / *Pref. Metaphysical
Elements of Ethics*, 367d-368a / *Science of
Right*, 405b-407a esp 405b-d / *Judgement*,
467a-475d; 570b-572d; 603a-b
43 MILL: *Utilitarianism*, 445d-446d
46 HEGEL: *Philosophy of History*, INTRO, 156d-
158a; 182d-183c
53 JAMES: *Psychology*, 639a-641a esp 640b;
659a-660a; 851a-890a esp 851a-852a, 859a-
861b, 867a-869a, 879b, 880b-881a, 884b-
885a, 889b-890a; 897a-b

8d. The division of judgments into the determinant and the reflective: judgments as constitutive or as regulative

42 KANT: *Pure Reason*, 72c-74b; 193a-200c esp
193c-d, 194b-c; 201d-202a; 206a-207b /
Judgement, 461a-475d esp 471b-474b; 550a-
551a,c; 558a; 559a-560c; 562a-d; 564a-c;
567b-568c; 570b-572c; 577b; 584d-585a;
588c; 597b-599b; 601d

9. Degrees of assent: certainty and probability

8 ARISTOTLE: *Interpretation*, CH 9 28a-29d /
Topics, BK V, CH 3 [131^{b}19-30] 182b-c /
Metaphysics, BK XII, CH 8 [1074^{a}14-16] 604c
9 ARISTOTLE: *Ethics*, BK I, CH 3 [1094^{b}11-28]
339d-340a; CH 7 [1098^{a}25-35] 343d; BK II,
CH 2 [1103^{b}27-1104^{a}9] 349b-c / *Rhetoric*, BK I,
CH 2 [1357^{a}23-^{b}24] 596d-597c; BK II, CH 25
[1402^{b}13-1403^{a}1] 652b-d

(9. Degrees of assent: certainty and probability.)

16 Copernicus: *Revolutions of the Heavenly Spheres*, 505a-506a

19 Aquinas: *Summa Theologica*, PART I, Q 14, A 13 86d-88c; Q 57, A 3, ANS 297b-298a; Q 58, A 7, REP 3 305c-306b; Q 86, A 4, ANS 463d-464d; PART I-II, Q 17, A 6, ANS 690b-d

20 Aquinas: *Summa Theologica*, PART I-II, Q 51, A 3 14b-15a; Q 67, A 3, ANS 83b-84d; PART II-II, Q 1, AA 4-5 382c-384b; Q 4, A 8 409a-d; Q 9, A 1, ANS and REP 1 423c-424b; A 2, ANS 424b-425a; Q 18, A 4 464c-465a; PART III, Q 7, A 3, REP 3 747b-748a

23 Hobbes: *Leviathan*, PART I, 65b-c

25 Montaigne: *Essays*, 240c-242a; 272a-d; 292a-d; 499c-d

31 Descartes: *Rules*, I-II 1a-3b; XII, 23a-c / *Discourse*, PART IV, 53c-d; PART VI, 63c-64d / *Meditations*, 74a,c; IV, 92c-93a / *Objections and Replies*, 125b-126b

35 Locke: *Human Understanding*, INTRO, SECT 2-6 93b-95a; BK IV, CH VI 331b-336d passim, esp SECT 13 335c-d; CH XI, SECT 3 355a-b; SECT 8-12 356b-357d; CH XIV-XVI 364b-371c; CH XVII, SECT 2 371d-372b; SECT 14-17 378c-379c; CH XIX, SECT I 384c-d

35 Hume: *Human Understanding*, SECT VI 469d-470d; SECT X, DIV 86-91 488d-491c passim, esp DIV 87 489b-d

38 Rousseau: *Inequality*, 348a,c

42 Kant: *Pure Reason*, 194b-c; 228c-d; 240b-243c / *Judgement*, 600d-604b passim

43 Mill: *Liberty*, 275a-277b

53 James: *Psychology*, 636a-638b; 659a-660b

54 Freud: *General Introduction*, 463d / *Beyond the Pleasure Principle*, 661c-662a / *New Introductory Lectures*, 818c-819b

10. The truth and falsity of judgments

7 Plato: *Euthydemus*, 71c-74a / *Cratylus*, 85d-86d; 109a-b / *Theaetetus*, 541a-544a / *Sophist*, 561d-577b esp 575a-577b

8 Aristotle: *Categories*, CH 4 [2^{a}4-10] 6a; CH 5 [4^{a}10-^{b}19] 8b-9a / *Interpretation*, CH 1 [16^{a}9-

18] 25a-b; CH 4-14 26a-36d passim, esp CH 4 [17^{a}1-4] 26b, CH 7 26d-27d, CH 9 28a-29d, CH 14 35c-36d / *Metaphysics*, BK IV, CH 7 [1011^{b}25-29] 531c; [1012^{a}1-17] 531d-532a; CH 8 [1012^{a}29-^{b}22] 532b-d; BK VI, CH 4 550a,c; BK IX, CH 10 [1051^{a}34-^{b}18] 577c-d / *Soul*, BK III, CH 3 [427^{b}15-25] 660a; CH 6 662d-663c

9 Aristotle: *Ethics*, BK II, CH 7 [1107^{a}27-32] 352d-353a; BK VI, CH 2 [1139^{a}21-31] 387d-388a; CH 3 [1139^{b}14-18] 388b

12 Lucretius: *Nature of Things*, BK IV [353-521] 48d-51a esp [469-521] 50b-51a

18 Augustine: *City of God*, BK VIII, CH 6, 269b-c / *Christian Doctrine*, BK II, CH 31-34 651d-653b

19 Aquinas: *Summa Theologica*, PART I, Q 3, A 4, REP 2 16d-17c; Q 13, A 12 74c-75b; Q 14, A 15, REP 3 89b-90b; Q 16, A 2 95c-96b; A 7, ANS and REP 4 99a-d; A 8, REP 3-4 99d-100d; Q 17, AA 3-4 102d-104b; Q 58, A 4, REP 2 302d-303c; A 5 303c-304c; Q 85, A 1, REP 1 451c-453c; A 5, REP 3 457d-458d; A 6 458d-459c; Q 94, A 4 505a-506a

20 Aquinas: *Summa Theologica*, PART I-II, Q 57, A 5, REP 3 39a-40a

23 Hobbes: *Leviathan*, PART I, 56b; 57c; 59a-60a; 65b-c

25 Montaigne: *Essays*, 240c-242a; 259d-261a; 271b-272c; 292a-d

31 Descartes: *Rules*, XII 18b-25a passim / *Discourse*, PART IV, 52a / *Meditations*, III, 83a; 85c; IV 89a-93a esp 90b-91b / *Objections and Replies*, 124b-c; 125b-126b; DEF IX 130d; 141a; 156d-158a; 168b-d; 215d-216c; 229d-230d

31 Spinoza: *Ethics*, PART II, PROP 49 391c-394d

35 Locke: *Human Understanding*, BK II, CH XXXII 243c-248b passim, esp SECT 1-3 243c-244a, SECT 19-26 247a-248b; BK III, CH VII, SECT 1 283a-b; BK IV, CH V 329a-331b; CH VI, SECT 3 331c-d; SECT 16 336d

42 Kant: *Pure Reason*, 99a-100a; 108a-d; 193a-c; 240b-243c

53 James: *Psychology*, 460a-469b esp 462b-465a, 468b-469a; 508a; 638a-b; 879a-881b

CROSS-REFERENCES

For: The comparison of judgment with other acts of the mind, *see* IDEA 2g, 5a; KNOWLEDGE 6b(4); REASONING 1; and for the relation of judgment to other faculties of the mind, *see* MIND 1e-1e(3).

Discussions relevant to the distinction between theoretic and practical judgments, *see* KNOWLEDGE 6e(1); PHILOSOPHY 2a; PRUDENCE 2a; REASONING 5e-5e(1); THEOLOGY 4d; TRUTH 2c; WISDOM 1b.

Other considerations of practical or moral judgments, and of judgment in relation to prudence, *see* GOOD AND EVIL 5b-5c; KNOWLEDGE 6e(2); PRUDENCE 5a; and for the theory of the categorical imperative, *see* DUTY 5; NECESSITY AND CONTINGENCY 5a(2).

Other treatments of language in relation to thought, *see* IDEA 4a; LANGUAGE 7.

For: The theory of predication and the analysis of subjects and predicates, *see* IDEA 5a; UNIVERSAL AND PARTICULAR 5C.

The relational theory of propositions, *see* RELATION 4b.

Other discussions bearing on the quantity, quality, and modality of propositions, *see* INFINITY 2b; NECESSITY AND CONTINGENCY 4e(1); UNIVERSAL AND PARTICULAR 5c–5d; and for other considerations of the distinction between the categorical and the hypothetical in judgment and reasoning, *see* HYPOTHESIS 5; REASONING 2b.

Another treatment of the square of opposition, *see* OPPOSITION 1d(1)–1d(2).

The relation of judgments to one another in immediate inference or in reasoning, *see* REASONING 4a; RELATION 4b.

The distinction between self-evident and demonstrable judgments, *see* INDUCTION 3; KNOWLEDGE 6c(2); PRINCIPLE 2b(2); and for other treatments of the *a priori* and the *a posteriori*, *see* EXPERIENCE 2d; KNOWLEDGE 6c(4); REASONING 5b(3).

A discussion relevant to the distinction between existential and non-existential judgments, *see* KNOWLEDGE 6a(3).

The problem of the truth and falsity of judgments, or their certainty and probability, *see* KNOWLEDGE 6d(1)–6d(2); OPINION 3a–3b; TRUTH 2e, 3b(2)–3c, 7a.

Another consideration of the aesthetic judgment, *see* BEAUTY 5; UNIVERSAL AND PARTICULAR 7c.

ADDITIONAL READINGS

Listed below are works not included in *Great Books of the Western World,* but relevant to the idea and topics with which this chapter deals. These works are divided into two groups:

I. Works by authors represented in this collection.
II. Works by authors not represented in this collection.

For the date, place, and other facts concerning the publication of the works cited, consult the Bibliography of Additional Readings which follows the last chapter of *The Great Ideas.*

I.

AQUINAS. *De Propositionibus Modalibus*
HOBBES. *Concerning Body,* PART I, CH 3
KANT. *Prolegomena to Any Future Metaphysic,* par 2–3
HEGEL. *Science of Logic,* VOL II, SECT I, CH 2
J. S. MILL. *A System of Logic,* BK I, CH 4–6

II.

CICERO. *Academics,* II (xlvii)
SEXTUS EMPIRICUS. *Against the Logicians*
JOHN OF SALISBURY. *Metalogicon*
SUÁREZ. *Disputationes Metaphysicae,* VIII–IX
JOHN OF SAINT THOMAS. *Cursus Philosophicus Thomisticus, Ars Logica,* PART I, QQ 5–7
ARNAULD. *Logic or the Art of Thinking,* PART II
LEIBNITZ. *New Essays Concerning Human Understanding,* BK IV, CH 5
T. REID. *Essays on the Intellectual Powers of Man,* VI
W. HAMILTON. *Lectures on Metaphysics and Logic,* VOL II (13–14)
BOOLE. *An Investigation of the Laws of Thought,* CH 21
J. H. NEWMAN. *An Essay in Aid of a Grammar of Assent*

SIGWART. *Logic,* PART I–II
JEVONS. *Pure Logic,* CH 2, 7, 10, 12
———. *Studies in Deductive Logic,* CH 3–6
LOTZE. *Logic,* BK I, CH 2
———. *Outlines of Logic,* I, CH 2
BRADLEY. *The Principles of Logic,* BK I; Terminal Essays, II–III, VI
J. N. KEYNES. *Studies and Exercises in Formal Logic,* PART II
BOSANQUET. *Logic,* VOL I, CH 1–9
VENN. *Symbolic Logic,* CH 6–8
———. *Principles of Empirical or Inductive Logic,* CH 8–10
J. C. WILSON. *Statement and Inference,* PART II
WHITEHEAD and RUSSELL. *Principia Mathematica,* PART I, SECT C, D; PART II, SECT B, C, D, E; PART IV–V
ROYCE. *The Principles of Logic*
W. E. JOHNSON. *Logic,* PART I, CH 1–5, 9–10
MARITAIN. *An Introduction to Logic,* CH 2
WHITEHEAD. *Process and Reality,* PART II, CH 9
DEWEY et al. *Studies in Logical Theory,* I–IV
DEWEY. *Essays in Experimental Logic,* II–VI, XII–XIV
———. *Reconstruction in Philosophy,* CH 6
———. *Logic, the Theory of Inquiry,* CH 6–14
M. R. COHEN. *A Preface to Logic,* II–III

Chapter 42: JUSTICE

INTRODUCTION

THE discussion of justice is the central theme in two dialogues of Plato—the *Republic* and the *Gorgias*. The dispute between Socrates and Thrasymachus in the one and between Socrates and Callicles in the other is of such universal scope and fundamental character that it recurs again and again in the great books with little change except in the personalities and vocabularies of the disputants.

It is a conflict of such polar opposites that all other differences of opinion about justice became arguable only after one or the other of the two extreme positions is abandoned. It is the conflict between the exponents of might and the exponents of right—between those who think that might *makes* right and that justice *is* expediency, and those who think that power can be wrongly as well as rightly exercised and that justice, the measure of men and states, cannot be measured by utility.

Though Plato gives us the first full-fashioned statement of this issue, he does not fashion it out of whole cloth. The issue runs through the fabric of Greek life and thought in the age of the imperialistic city-states which played the game of power politics culminating in the Peloponnesian War. In his history of that war, Thucydides highlights the Melian episode by dramatically constructing a conversation between the Athenian envoys and the representatives of Melos, a little island colony of Sparta which had refused to knuckle under to Athenian aggression.

Recognizing the superior force of the aggressors, the Melians enter the conference with a sense of its futility, for, as they point out, if they insist upon their rights and refuse to submit, they can expect nothing from these negotiations except war and, in the end, slavery. The Athenians reply with a frankness that is seldom found in the diplomatic exchanges of our own day, though in their real contentions the conferences which have preceded or followed the world wars of our century repeat what happened, if not what was said, at Melos.

The Athenians tell the Melians that they will not waste time with specious pretences "either of how we have a right to our empire . . . or are now attacking you because of a wrong you have done us." Why make a long speech, they say, which would not be believed? Instead they come directly to the point and put the matter simply or, as we now say, realistically. "You know as well as we do," they tell the Melians, "that right, as the world goes, is only in question between equals in power, whereas the stronger do whatever they can and the weaker suffer whatever they must." There is nothing left for the Melians except an appeal to expediency. "You debar us from talking about justice and invite us to obey your interest," they reply to the Athenians, before trying to persuade them that their policy will end in disaster for Athens.

The language of Thrasymachus in the *Republic* resembles that of the Athenian envoys. "I proclaim," he says, "that justice is nothing else than the interest of the stronger. . . . The different forms of government make laws democratical, aristocratical, tyrannical, with a view to their several interests; and these laws, which are made by them for their own interests, are the justice which they deliver to their subjects, and him who transgresses them they punish as a breaker of the law, and unjust. And this is what I mean when I say that in all states there is the same principle of justice which is the interest of the government; and as the government must be supposed to have power, the only reasonable conclusion is that everywhere there is one principle of justice which is the interest of the stronger."

The thesis seems to have two applications. For the stronger, it means that they have the right, as far as they have the might, to exact from the weaker whatever serves their interests. Their laws or demands cannot be unjust. They cannot do injustice. They can only fail to exert sufficient might to hold on to the power which can secure them, not from the charge of injustice, but from reprisals by those whom they have oppressed or injured.

The thesis also means, for the weaker, that they can only do injustice but not suffer it. Injustice on their part consists in disobeying the law of their rulers. Hence for them, too, justice is expediency, only now in the sense that they are likely to suffer if they try to follow their own interests rather than the interests of the stronger.

This thesis appears to be repeated in somewhat different language by Hobbes and Spinoza. To men living in a purely natural condition, the notions of justice and injustice do not apply. They apply only to men living in civil society. "Where there is no Commonwealth," Hobbes writes, "there is nothing unjust. So that the nature of justice consists in the keeping of valid covenants; but the validity of covenants begins not but with the constitution of a civil power sufficient to compel men to keep them." The breach of civil laws or covenants "may be called injustice, and the observance of them justice."

It is Spinoza's opinion that "everything has by nature as much right as it has power to exist and operate." It follows, therefore, that "in a natural state there is nothing which can be called just or unjust, but only in a civil state." Here as before justice consists in obedience, injustice in disobedience, to whatever laws the state has the power to enforce, the laws themselves being formulated not by reference to justice, but to the interests of the state which must seek its own preservation and has the right to do so, so long as it has the power.

THOSE WHO TAKE the opposite view agree that justice is political in the sense that the state, in organization and operation, is a work of justice. Wisdom is the virtue of the rulers in the *Republic*, but justice is the organizing principle of Plato's ideal state.

Aristotle maintains that man is a political animal, whereas other animals are merely gregarious. He cites the fact that man alone has a power of speech able to communicate opinions about the expedient and the just. "Justice is the bond of men in states, for the administration of justice, which is the determination of what is just, is the principle of order in political society." Aristotle describes man "when separated from law and justice" as the worst of animals. Augustine describes the state without justice as "no better than a band of robber thieves."

Those who agree that political institutions involve justice are confronted by these alternatives: *either* the principle of justice is antecedent to the state, its constitution, covenants, and laws, *or* the determination of what is just and unjust is entirely relative to the constitution of a state, dependent upon its power, and consequent to its laws.

When the second alternative is chosen, the proposition that justice is political is seriously qualified. It is *merely* political. There is no natural justice, no justice apart from man-made laws, nothing that is just or unjust in the very nature of the case and without reference to civil institutions. On this theory, only the individual who is subject to government can be judged just or unjust. The government itself cannot be so judged, nor can its constitution, its laws, or its acts; for, since these determine what is just and unjust, they cannot themselves be judged for their justice.

The opposite answer conceives political justice as a determination of natural justice. "Political justice," Aristotle remarks, "is partly natural and partly conventional or legal." The fact that there is a sense in which just action on the part of a citizen consists in law-abiding conduct, does not exclude another sense in which the laws themselves can be called just or unjust, not only the laws, but the constitution of the state itself. Though the justice of civil laws is partly relative to the constitution under which they are made and administered, there are some enactments which, since they violate natural justice, cannot be justified under any constitution. The constitution, moreover, cannot be regarded as the ultimate standard of justice by those who compare the justice of different forms of government or diverse constitutions. On their view, the ultimate measure of justice in all human institutions and acts, as well as in the characters of men, is not itself a man-made standard, but rather a natural principle of justice, holding for all men at all times everywhere.

THE ISSUE JOINED BY these two theories of justice extends by implication into many related matters. The opposition, for example, between those who affirm the reality of natural law as the source of legality in all civil regulations and those who derive the legality of positive laws from the will of the sovereign alone, is considered in the chapter on LAW, but its parallelism with the issue of natural and conventional justice should be noted here.

Those who deny natural justice and natural law also tend to deny natural rights, which, unlike civil rights, are not conferred on the individual by the state, but are inherent in his human personality. They are, according to the Declaration of Independence, "unalienable" in the sense that the state cannot rescind them. What the state does not create, it cannot destroy. If a government transgresses natural rights, it negates its own reason for being, since it is "to secure these rights [that] governments are instituted among men."

Those who deny natural rights, among which the right to liberty is usually included, do not have a standard for judging when governments violate the rights and invade the liberties of men. When men are thought to have no rights except those granted by their rulers, the absolute power which the rulers exercise cannot be criticized as tyrannical or despotic.

Considering the situation of men in what he calls "a state of perfect freedom"—apart from government and civil institutions—Locke says of this state of nature that it "has a law of nature to govern it, which obliges everyone; and reason, which is that law, teaches all mankind who will but consult it, that, being all equal and independent, no one ought to harm another in his life, health, liberty, or possessions. . . . Everyone, as he is bound to preserve himself, and not quit his station willfully, so, by the like reason, when his own preservation comes not in competition, ought he, as much as he can, to preserve the rest of mankind, and not, unless it be to do justice on an offender, take away or

impair the life, or what tends to the preservation of the life, the liberty, health, limb, or goods of another." Since this law of nature, and its implied principle of just dealing between men, is not abolished when men associate in the common life of a civil society, natural justice and natural rights remain, according to Locke and others, to limit the powers of government and to measure the justice of its laws.

The principle of natural justice is sometimes not accompanied by a doctrine of natural law and natural rights, as for example in Greek thought. Their connection first seems to occur in Roman jurisprudence and mediaeval theory. Not all the opponents of natural justice avoid the use of the words "natural law" and "natural rights." Using these words in a different sense, Hobbes, for example, speaks of men living under natural law in a state of nature, which is "a condition of war of every one against every one," and "in such condition every man has a right to everything, even to another's body." Only when men *abandon* this unlimited right in order to form a commonwealth, do they acquire in recompense certain civil rights or, as Hobbes says, "proprieties." Then, and only then, can there be any meaning to justice, conceived according to the ancient maxim which Hobbes accepts, that justice is "the constant will to render to each man what is his due."

Both Spinoza and Hume make the same point. Where there is no recognized title to property, or *legally established* right, there can be no justice—no respecting of what is a man's own or giving him what belongs to him. The difference between Locke and these others seems to lie in his conception of *property* as the natural right which a man has to the preservation of his life, liberty, and estate. There can be justice, therefore, between men in a state of nature, for even then each has some property that the others are bound to respect.

THE MEANING of natural justice can be examined apart from these different interpretations of the so-called "state of nature." Those who, like Aristotle and Aquinas, do not conceive the origin of political society as a transition from the "state of nature" do, nevertheless, appeal to a principle of natural justice. For Aquinas, this principle seems to be an integral part of the natural law. Sometimes the statement of the first precept of the natural law is "Seek the good; avoid evil." Sometimes it is "Do good to others, injure no one, and render to every man his own." In this second formulation, the natural law seems to be identical with the precept of justice. The essential content of this precept seems to be present—separate from any doctrine of natural law—in Aristotle's analysis of the nature of justice both as a virtue and as a quality of human acts.

"The just," Aristotle says, "is the lawful and the fair." What he means by the word "lawful" in this context does not seem to be simply the law-abiding, in the sense of conforming to the actual laws of a particular society. He thinks of law as aiming "at the common advantage. . . . We call those acts just," he writes, "that tend to produce and preserve happiness and its components for the political society." Lawful (or just) actions thus are those which are for the common good or the good of others; unlawful (or unjust) actions, those which do injury to others or despoil the society.

It is in this sense of justice that both Plato and Aristotle lay down the primary criterion for differentiating between good and bad governments. Those which are lawful and serve the common good are just; those which are lawless and serve the private interests of the rulers are unjust. This meaning of justice applies as readily to all citizens—to all members of a society—as it does to those who have the special duties or occupy the special offices of government.

Whether it is stated in terms of the good of other individuals or in terms of the common good of a community (domestic or political), this understanding of justice seems to consider the actions of a man as they affect the well-being, not of himself, but of others. "Justice, alone of the virtues," says Aristotle, "is thought to be 'another's good,' because it is related to our neighbor." Concerned with what is due another, justice involves the element of duty or obligation. "To each one," Aquinas writes, "is due what is his own," and "it evidently pertains to justice," he adds, "that a man give another his due." That is why "justice alone, of all the virtues, implies the notion of duty." Doing good to others or not injuring them, when

undertaken as a matter of strict justice, goes no further than to discharge the debt which each man owes every other.

In consequence, a difference of opinion arises concerning the adequacy of justice to establish the peace and harmony of a society. Some writers, like Kant, seem to think that if perfect justice obtained, a multitude of individual wills would be perfectly harmonized in free action. Others, like Aquinas, think justice necessary but insufficient precisely because it is a matter of duty and debt. "Peace," he writes, "is the *work of justice* indirectly, in so far as justice removes the obstacles to peace; but it is the *work of charity* directly, since charity, according to its very nature, causes peace; for love is *a unitive force*." The bonds of love and friendship unite men where justice merely governs their interaction. What men do for one another out of the generosity of love far exceeds the commands of justice. That is why mercy and charity are called upon to qualify justice or even to set it aside. "Earthly power," Portia declares in the *Merchant of Venice*, "doth then show likest God's when mercy seasons justice."

THE PRECEPT "to render unto others what is their due" is read in a different light when the other aspect of justice is considered. When the just is conceived as the fair, the fairness which is due ourselves or others applies, not to benefit and injury generally, but to the exchange and distribution of goods or burdens. What is the principle of a fair exchange or a fair distribution? Aristotle's answer to this question is in terms of equality.

In the transactions of commerce, fairness seems to require the exchange of things equivalent in value. The rule of an eye for an eye, a tooth for a tooth, is another expression of the principle of equality as the criterion of a fair penalty or a just compensation. If honors or rewards are to be distributed, equals should in fairness be treated equally, and those who are unequal in merit should receive unequal shares. For all to share alike is not a just distribution of deserts if all do not deserve alike. "Awards should be 'according to merit,'" Aristotle writes. He claims that "all men agree" with this, "though they do not all specify the same sort of merit, but democrats identify it with the status of freeman, supporters of oligarchy with wealth or with noble birth, and supporters of aristocracy with excellence." The unequal treatment of unequals, however, still derives its fairness from the principle of equality, for there is an equivalence of ratios in the proportion of giving more to the more deserving and less to the less.

Aristotle employs the distinction between these modes of equality—arithmetic and geometric, or simple and proportional, equality—to define the difference between fairness in exchange and fairness in distribution. The one is the type of justice which is traditionally called "commutative," "corrective," or "remedial," the other "distributive."

The type of justice "which plays a rectifying part in transactions between man and man," Aristotle further divides into two kinds. "Of transactions," he writes, "(1) some are voluntary and (2) others involuntary—voluntary such transactions as sale, purchase, loan for consumption, pledging, loan for use, depositing, letting . . . while of the involuntary (a) some are clandestine, such as theft, adultery, poisoning, procuring, enticement of slaves, assassination, false witness, and (b) others are violent, such as assault, imprisonment, murder, robbery with violence, mutilation, abuse, insult." The sphere which Aristotle assigns to commutative or corrective justice thus appears to cover both criminal acts and civil injuries. But, as applied to civil injuries, the principle of fairness in exchange usually involves a payment for damages, restitution, or compensation in kind; whereas the principle of commutative justice as applied to criminal wrongdoing usually calls for a punishment somehow equalized in severity to the gravity of the offense. This last is the principle of the *lex talionis*—an eye for an eye, a life for a life. The problems of justice which it raises are considered in the chapter on PUNISHMENT.

JUSTICE IS SOMETIMES divided into economic and political according as, on the one hand, fairness or equalization concerns the kind of goods which originate with the expenditure of labor, or as, on the other hand, it involves the status of men in the state. The difference between these two modes of justice seems to be largely

dependent upon the kind of transaction to which the principle of justice is applied. The forms of justice—the two modes of equality or fairness—appear to remain the same. The special problems of economic justice are more fully examined in the chapters on LABOR and WEALTH, as the special problems of political justice are treated in greater detail in all the chapters dealing with the state, government, and the several forms of government. Here we shall consider only the generalities, and especially those which touch the main issues in the theory of justice.

Though Karl Marx does not engage in the controversy over natural justice, he seems to take the side which looks upon justice as a universal standard that does not derive from, but rather measures, human institutions. Something like 'from each according to his ability, to each according to his needs'—or, in another variant of the maxim, 'to each according to his deserts'—seems to be for Marx the maxim of a just economy, stated without argument as if a principle self-evident in the very nature of the case. So, too, in his consideration of the exploitation of labor in its various historic forms—chattel slavery, feudal serfdom or agrarian peonage, and what he calls "wage slavery" under industrial capitalism—Marx assumes that a clear and unquestionable principle of justice is being violated when the goods produced by the labor of one man enrich another disproportionately to that other's contribution or desert. Such basic words in *Capital* as "expropriation," "exploitation," and "unearned increment" seem never to be simply terms of description, but of evaluation. Each implies a specific injustice.

The labor theory of value, the origin of which he attributes to Adam Smith, Marx conceives as solving a problem in justice which Aristotle stated but did not solve. He refers to the chapter in the book on justice in Aristotle's *Ethics*, in which Aristotle discusses money as a medium to facilitate the exchange of commodities. Money permits so many units of one commodity to be equated with so many units of another. But the problem is how to determine equivalents in the exchange of unlike things, apparently incommensurable in value. How can the value of a house be commensurated with the value of a bed, so that an equality in value can be set up between a house and a certain number of beds? Abstracting entirely from considerations of supply and demand, the determination of a just exchange or a fair price requires an equation of comparable quantities.

Aristotle tells us, Marx points out, why he found the problem insoluble. "It was the absence of any concept of value. What is that equal something, that common substance, which admits of the value of beds being expressed by a house? Such a thing, in truth, cannot exist, says Aristotle. And why not? Compared with beds, the house does represent something equal to them, in so far as it represents what is really equal, both in the beds and the house. And that is—human labor. ... The brilliancy of Aristotle's genius is shown by this alone, that he discovered, in the expression of the value of commodities, a relation of equality. The peculiar conditions of the society in which he lived alone prevented him from discovering what, 'in truth,' was at the bottom of this equality."

We cannot help noting the character of the labor theory of value as an analysis not only of justice in exchange, but also of just compensation to labor for its productivity. The principle of justice here employed seems to be the same as that underlying the mediaeval condemnation of interest as unjust or usurious, or the later effort to discriminate between just and unjust interest rates. The principle even seems to be implicitly involved in Adam Smith's distinction between real or natural price and the market price which fluctuates with variations in supply and demand.

When the economic problem is one of distribution rather than exchange, another standard of fairness—the proportional equality of distributive justice—becomes relevant.

The assumption of a primitive possession of all things in common, especially land and its resources, is the background against which such thinkers as Aquinas and Hobbes, Locke and Rousseau, Montesquieu and Hegel, Adam Smith and Karl Marx consider the origin or justification of private property. Insofar as the question is one of justification, rather than of actual historic origin, the division of common holdings into privately held shares is a matter of justice in distribution. In the opinion of many, a just

distribution would recognize that labor alone entitles a man to claim possession of the raw materials improved by his work and of the finished products of that work.

The other face of the problem assumes an existing inequitable distribution. It is then asked how this can be rectified by some method of redistributing wealth more justly; or it is proposed that the whole system of private property be reformed in the direction of public ownership of the means of production, as the basis for a just distribution of the fruits of human productivity.

THE CONNECTION which has become evident between justice and both liberty and equality does not imply that these three basic notions are simply coordinate with one another. On the contrary, equality seems to be the root of justice, at least insofar as it is identified with fairness in exchange or distribution; and justice in turn seems to be the foundation, not the consequence of liberty.

The condemnation of slavery confirms this observation. If slavery were not unjust, the slave would have no right to be free. The injustice of treating a man as a chattel ultimately rests on the equality between him and his master as human beings. His right to the same liberty which his master enjoys stems from that equality. The justice of equal treatment for equals recognizes that right and sets him free. Aristotle's theory of natural slavery is based on a supposition of natural inequality which is thought to justify the enslavement of some men and the freedom of others. Whenever slavery is justified or a criminal is justly imprisoned, neither the slave nor the criminal is regarded as deprived of any liberty to which he has a right.

It would seem to follow that if a man is justly treated, he has all the liberty which he deserves. From the opposite angle, Mill argues that a man is entitled to all the liberty that he can use justly, that is, use without injuring his fellow man or the common good. More liberty than this would be license. When one man encroaches on the rights of others, or inflicts on them "any loss or damage not justified by his own rights," he is overstepping the bounds of liberty and is, according to Mill, a fit object "of moral reprobation, and, in grave cases, of moral retribution and punishment."

The various relations of liberty to justice, and of both to law, are considered in the chapters on LIBERTY and LAW. All the writers who make the distinction between government by law and government by men fundamental in their political theory also plainly express a preference for the former on grounds both of justice and liberty.

Absolute government, which violates the equality of men, unjustly subjects them, even when it does not through tyranny enslave them. The benevolence of the despot ruling for the common good has one aspect of justice, but there are other aspects of political justice which can be achieved, as Mill points out, only if "despotism consents not to be despotism . . . and allows the general business of government to go on as if the people really governed themselves." The greater justice of constitutional government consists in its granting to men who deserve the equal freedom of equals, the equality of citizenship—an equality under the law which levels those citizens who happen to hold public office with those in private life.

The major controversy over the several forms of constitutional government turns on a third point of justice. The defenders of democracy and oligarchy each contend that equalities or inequalities in birth or wealth justify a broader or a narrower franchise. It is Mill again who insists that nothing less than universal suffrage provides a just distribution of the political status of citizenship, and that "it is a personal injustice to withhold from anyone, unless for the prevention of greater evils, the ordinary privilege of having his voice reckoned in the disposal of affairs in which he has the same interest as other people."

Of the three points of justice which seem to be involved in the comparison of forms of government, only the first (concerned with whether political power is exercised for the common good or the ruler's private interests) is not recognizable as a matter of distributive justice. Yet even here the requirement that the ruler should treat the ruled as ends rather than as means derives from a fundamental equality between ruler and ruled. The injustice of tyranny lies in a violation of this equality.

ONE MEANING of justice remains to be considered. It is related to all the foregoing considerations of economic and political justice, of just constitutions, just laws, and just acts. It is that meaning of justice in which a man is said to be just—to possess a just will, to be just in character, to have the virtue of justice. Here difference in theory reflects the difference between those moralists for whom virtue is the basic conception, and those who, like Kant, emphasize duty or who, like Mill, reduce the propensity for justice to a moral sentiment. But even among those who treat justice as a virtue, there seems to be a profound difference in analysis.

For Aristotle, the virtue of justice, like other moral virtues, is a habit of conduct. It differs from courage and temperance in that it is a habit of action, not of the passions. It is not a rationally moderated tendency of the emotions with regard to things pleasant and painful. It is that settled inclination of the will "in virtue of which the just man is said to be a doer, by choice, of that which is just, and one who will distribute either between himself and another or between two others not so as to give more of what is desirable to himself and less to his neighbor (and conversely with what is harmful), but so as to give what is equal in accordance with proportion."

Another difference between justice and the other moral virtues is that courageous and temperate acts are performed only by courageous and temperate men, whereas an act which is outwardly just can be done by an unjust man as well as by a just one.

Fair dealing in the exchange or distribution of goods, determined by objective relations of equality, is the substance of justice as a special virtue; but there is in addition what Aristotle calls "general" as opposed to "special" justice. Aristotle calls the general virtue of justice "complete virtue," because "he who possesses it can exercise his virtue not only in himself but towards his neighbor also." It embraces all the moral virtues insofar as their acts are directed to the good of others.

"Justice in this sense," he goes on to say, "is not a part of virtue, but virtue entire"; whereas special justice—the justice of distributions and exchanges—is merely a part of moral virtue, merely one particular virtue. Yet special justice, no less than general justice, is a social virtue. The difference between the way each directs actions toward the good of others seems to be like the difference between the lawful and the fair, or the difference between the common good of society as a whole and the good of other individuals.

The thoroughly social conception of justice in Aristotle may have some parallel in the meaning of justice in Plato's *Gorgias* (where the question is whether it is better to suffer than to do injustice), but the definition of justice as a virtue in the *Republic* does not express or develop the social reference. In the state as in the soul, justice is a fitting disposition or harmonious order—of the several classes of men in the state, of the several virtues in the soul. The just state is not described as acting justly toward other states, nor is the just man pictured as a doer of good deeds. Rather the picture of the soul in which justice resides is one of interior peace or spiritual health—the well-being of happiness.

"Justice," Socrates declares, is concerned "not with the outward man, but with the inward, which is the true self and concernment of man: for the just man does not permit the several elements within him to interfere with one another, or any of them to do the work of others—he sets in order his own inner life, and is his own master and his own law, and at peace with himself." His is "one entirely temperate and perfectly adjusted nature."

This conception of justice bears a certain resemblance to what the Christian theologians mean by "original justice." The perfect disposition of Adam's soul in a state of supernatural grace consisted, according to Aquinas, in "his reason being subject to God, the lower powers to reason, and the body to the soul—the first subjection being the cause of both the second and the third, since while reason was subject to God, the lower powers remained subject to reason." The justice of man's obedience to God seems to be inseparable from the injustice internal to his own members.

The way in which justice is discussed in the *Gorgias* may similarly be inseparable from the way it is defined in the *Republic*. Certainly Callicles will never understand why it is always better to suffer injustice than to do it, unless Socrates succeeds in explaining to him that the man who is wronged suffers injury in body or in external things, while the man who does wrong injures his own soul by destroying what, to Socrates, is its greatest good—that equable temper from which all fitting actions flow.

OUTLINE OF TOPICS

REFERENCES

To find the passages cited, use the numbers in heavy type, which are the volume and page numbers of the passages referred to. For example, in 4 HOMER: *Iliad*, BK II [265-283] 12d, the number 4 is the number of the volume in the set; the number 12d indicates that the passage is in section d of page 12.

PAGE SECTIONS: When the text is printed in one column, the letters a and b refer to the upper and lower halves of the page. For example, in 53 JAMES: *Psychology*, 116a-119b, the passage begins in the upper half of page 116 and ends in the lower half of page 119. When the text is printed in two columns, the letters a and b refer to the upper and lower halves of the left-hand side of the page, the letters c and d to the upper and lower halves of the right-hand side of the page. For example, in 7 PLATO: *Symposium*, 163b-164c, the passage begins in the lower half of the left-hand side of page 163 and ends in the upper half of the right-hand side of page 164.

AUTHOR'S DIVISIONS: One or more of the main divisions of a work (such as PART, BK, CH, SECT) are sometimes included in the reference; line numbers, in brackets, are given in certain cases; *e.g.*, *Iliad*, BK II [265-283] 12d.

BIBLE REFERENCES: The references are to book, chapter, and verse. When the King James and Douay versions differ in title of books or in the numbering of chapters or verses, the King James version is cited first and the Douay, indicated by a (D), follows; *e.g.*, OLD TESTAMENT: *Nehemiah*, 7:45—(D) *II Esdras*, 7:46.

SYMBOLS: The abbreviation "esp" calls the reader's attention to one or more especially relevant parts of a whole reference; "passim" signifies that the topic is discussed intermittently rather than continuously in the work or passage cited.

For additional information concerning the style of the references, see the Explanation of Reference Style; for general guidance in the use of *The Great Ideas*, consult the Preface.

1. Diverse conceptions of justice

1a. Justice as the interest of the stronger or conformity to the will of the sovereign

5 SOPHOCLES: *Antigone* [631-765] 136c-137d / *Ajax* [1047-1393] 152a-155a,c

6 THUCYDIDES: *Peloponnesian War*, BK V, 504c-508a,c

7 PLATO: *Gorgias*, 271b-275d / *Republic*, BK I-II, 300b-315c / *Laws*, BK IV, 681d-682c; BK X, 760c

9 ARISTOTLE: *Politics*, BK I, CH 6 [1255^{a}3-20] 448c-d; BK III, CH 13 [1283^{b}23-26] 481d; BK VI, CH 3 [1318^{b}1-5] 521d-522a; BK VII, CH 2 [1324^{b}22-41] 528d-529a

14 PLUTARCH: *Theseus*, 2c-d / *Camillus*, 108b-c / *Alexander*, 566a-b

18 AUGUSTINE: *City of God*, BK XIX, CH 21 524a-525a

23 HOBBES: *Leviathan*, PART I, 86b; 91a-b; PART II, 99b; 101a-102c; 103a; 124d-125a; 130c; 132a; 140b; 149b-c; 157b

25 MONTAIGNE: *Essays*, 281a-282a; 519c-520b

31 SPINOZA: *Ethics*, PART IV, PROP 37, SCHOL 2 435b-436a

33 PASCAL: *Pensées*, 291-338 225a-233a; 878 345a-b

35 LOCKE: *Civil Government*, CH II, SECT 13

28a-b; CH III 28d-29d; CH VII, SECT 90-94 44d-46c; CH XVI 65d-70c passim / *Human Understanding*, BK I, CH II, SECT 5 105a-b

38 ROUSSEAU: *Inequality*, 333c-d; 347b-d; 353c-355d passim; 361c-362a / *Political Economy*, 368d-369b / *Social Contract*, BK I, 388d-389a; 393b-c

46 HEGEL: *Philosophy of Right*, PART III, par 219 72d-73a; par 258, 81c-82d [fn I]; ADDITIONS, 155 142a-b / *Philosophy of History*, INTRO, 171c-172b; PART I, 207b-c; PART II, 277d-278a; PART III, 299a-c; PART IV, 327d-330b esp 328c-d, 330b; 344a-c

47 GOETHE: *Faust*, PART II [11,171-188] 272a-b

48 MELVILLE: *Moby Dick*, 292a-297a

50 MARX-ENGELS: *Communist Manifesto*, 428b-d

51 TOLSTOY: *War and Peace*, BK XII, 547a-549d esp 547c; EPILOGUE I, 647b-649d

54 FREUD: *Civilization and Its Discontents*, 780b-d

1b. Justice as harmony or right order in the soul: original justice

7 PLATO: *Cratylus*, 99d-100c / *Gorgias*, 282c-285a esp 282c-283a / *Republic*, BK I, 309b-310b; BK IV, 346a-355a; BK IX, 425c-427b / *Statesman*, 586d-589c / *Laws*, BK IV, 681b-d; BK IX, 748b-c

(1. *Diverse conceptions of justice.* 1*b. Justice as harmony or right order in the soul: original justice.*)

9 ARISTOTLE: *Ethics*, BK V, CH 11 [1138^{b}5–13] 387a,c

13 VIRGIL: *Eclogues*, IV 14a–15b

17 PLOTINUS: *Third Ennead*, TR VI, CH 2, 107a–c

18 AUGUSTINE: *City of God*, BK XIV, CH 10–11 385b–387a; CH 19 391c–392a; CH 26, 395d

19 AQUINAS: *Summa Theologica*, PART I, QQ 95–96 506b–513c; Q 100 520d–522b

20 AQUINAS: *Summa Theologica*, PART I–II, QQ 81–83 162d–174b; Q 85, A 1, ANS 178b–179b; Q 91, A 6, ANS 212c–213c; Q 100, A 2, REP 2 252b–253a; Q 113, A 1, ANS and REP 1 360d–361d

32 MILTON: *Paradise Lost*, BK IV [288–294] 158b; BK XII [63–110] 320b–321b

1*c.* **Justice as a moral virtue directing activity in relation to others and to the community: the distinction between the just man and the just act**

7 PLATO: *Crito*, 216d–219a,c / *Republic*, BK IV 342a–356a esp 348d–350a

8 ARISTOTLE: *Topics*, BK I, CH 15 [106^{a}2–8] 149d; BK III, CH 1 [116^{b}11–13] 163a; BK IV, CH 2 [121^{b}24–30] 169d; BK VI, CH 5 [143^{a}15–19] 196c–d; CH 7 [145^{b}34–146^{a}3] 199d

9 ARISTOTLE: *Ethics*, BK V, CH 1 [1129^{b}25–1130^{a}13] 377b–c; CH 5 [1133^{b}16–23] 381b–c; [1133^{b}30–1134^{a}15] 381c–d; CH 8–9 383a–385c; BK VI, CH 12 [1144^{a}11–20] 393d; BK X, CH 8 [1178^{a}8–22] 432d / *Politics*, BK III, CH 12 [1282^{b}15–22] 480c; CH 13 [1283^{a}37–40] 481c; BK VII, CH 2 [1324^{b}32–40] 528d–529a / *Rhetoric*, BK I, CH 6 [1362^{b}10–28] 603b–c; CH 9 [1366^{a}33–1367^{a}22] 608d–609d

12 AURELIUS: *Meditations*, BK III, SECT 4 260b–261a; SECT 6 261a–c; BK IV, SECT 10 264c; BK V, SECT 6 269b–d; SECT 34 273c; BK VI, SECT 2 274a; SECT 22–23 276a–b; SECT 26 276b–c; BK VII, SECT 44 282b–c; BK VIII, SECT 32 287d–288a; BK IX, SECT 1 291a–c; BK X, SECT 11 298b–c; BK XI, SECT 10 303b–c

14 PLUTARCH: *Aristides*, 265c–d / *Agesilaus*, 491a–b / *Cato the Younger*, 636d–637c

18 AUGUSTINE: *Confessions*, BK III, par 13–15 16c–17b / *City of God*, BK II, CH 21 161b–162d; BK XIX, CH 21 524a–525a

19 AQUINAS: *Summa Theologica*, PART I, Q 21, A 1 124b–125b

20 AQUINAS: *Summa Theologica*, PART I–II, Q 59, AA 4–5 48c–49d; Q 60, AA 2–3 50d–52b; Q 99, A 5, REP 1 249a–250a; Q 100, A 2, REP 2 252b–253a; A 3, REP 3 253a–d; A 12 264d–265d; Q 113, A 1 360d–361d

23 HOBBES: *Leviathan*, PART I, 92c–93c; 96a–b

46 HEGEL: *Philosophy of History*, PART II, 272a–b

51 TOLSTOY: *War and Peace*, BK V, 214c–216d

1*d.* **Justice as the whole of virtue and as a particular virtue: the distinction between the lawful and the fair**

7 PLATO: *Meno*, 178c–179a / *Republic*, BK IV, 349a–350a / *Laws*, BK I, 642d–643b

8 ARISTOTLE: *Topics*, BK VI, CH 13 [150^{a}1–15] 204c

9 ARISTOTLE: *Ethics*, BK V, CH 1 [1129^{a}31]–CH 2 [1131^{a}9] 376d–378c / *Politics*, BK III, CH 13 [1283^{a}37–40] 481c / *Rhetoric*, BK I, CH 9 [1366^{a}33–1367^{a}22] 608d–609d

12 AURELIUS: *Meditations*, BK XI, SECT 10 303b–c

20 AQUINAS: *Summa Theologica*, PART I–II, Q 55, A 4, REP 4 28c–29d; Q 57, A 3, REP 2 37b–38a; Q 60, A 3 51c–52b; Q 66, A 4 78c–79b; Q 99, A 5, REP 1 249a–250a; Q 100, A 2, REP 2 252b–253a; A 12, ANS 264d–265d; Q 113, A 1, ANS and REP 2 360d–361d

25 MONTAIGNE: *Essays*, 301d–302b

42 KANT: *Pref. Metaphysical Elements of Ethics*, 368c–d; 377a–d

43 MILL: *Utilitarianism*, 468b–469b

1*e.* **Justice as an act of will or duty fulfilling obligations to the common good: the harmonious action of individual wills under a universal law of freedom**

42 KANT: *Pure Reason*, 114d–115a / *Pref. Metaphysical Elements of Ethics*, 366d–367a; 368b–369a; 371b–372a / *Intro. Metaphysic of Morals* 383a–394a,c esp 383a–d, 386b–387a,c, 389a–390a,c, 391a–c, 392d–393c / *Science of Right*, 397a–402a,c esp 397c–399c; 435a–b; 438d–439a

46 HEGEL: *Philosophy of Right*, INTRO, par 29 19a–b; PART III, par 219 72d–73a; par 261 83a–d; par 278 92c–93a; ADDITIONS, 177 147d / *Philosophy of History*, INTRO, 199b–c; PART I, 207b–c; PART II, 272a–d; PART IV, 333c–d; 363c–d; 365b–c

53 JAMES: *Psychology*, 886b–888a

1*f.* **Justice as a custom or moral sentiment based on considerations of utility**

7 PLATO: *Republic*, BK II, 310c–315c / *Theaetetus*, 528b–c; 531a–b

25 MONTAIGNE: *Essays*, 46b–47c; 281a–283c

33 PASCAL: *Pensées*, 309 228b; 312 229a

35 LOCKE: *Human Understanding*, BK I, CH II, SECT 2 104a–b

43 MILL: *Liberty*, 300d–301a / *Utilitarianism*, 464d–476a,c esp 476a,c

2. **The precepts of justice: doing good, harming no one, rendering to each his own, treating equals equally**

OLD TESTAMENT: *Exodus*, 20:1–17; 21:1–23:9 / *Leviticus*, 19:9–18,32–37 / *Deuteronomy*, 5:6–21; 15:7–18; 16:18–20; 19:11–21; 20:10–12; 21:15–17; 22:1–4,13–29; 23:15–16,24–25; 24:6,10–22; 25:1–3,13–16 / *I Kings*, 3:16–28 —(D) *III Kings*, 3:16–28 / *Proverbs*, 3:27–30;

20:22; 24:23–25,29; 25:21 / *Isaiah*, 1:10–20 esp 1:16–17; 56:1–2—(D) *Isaias*, 1:10–20 esp 1:16–17; 56:1–2 / *Jeremiah*, 5:21–29 esp 5:26–28—(D) *Jeremias*, 5:21–29 esp 5:26–28 / *Ezekiel*, 45:9–11—(D) *Ezechiel*, 45:9–11 / *Hosea*, 4:1–3—(D) *Osee*, 4:1–3 / *Amos*, 5:7–27 / *Micah*, 6:8—(D) *Micheas*, 6:8 / *Zechariah*, 7:8–14—(D) *Zacharias*, 7:8–14 / *Malachi*, 2:9—(D) *Malachias*, 2:9

NEW TESTAMENT: *Matthew*, 5:38–48; 19:16–24 / *Luke*, 6:27–38; 18:18–27 / *Romans*, 12:17–21; 15:1–2 / *II Corinthians*, 8:9–15

5 AESCHYLUS: *Suppliant Maidens* [338–394] 5a-d / *Eumenides* [544–565] 87a

5 SOPHOCLES: *Oedipus the King* [863–910] 107b-c / *Ajax* [1047–1421] 152a-155a,c

5 EURIPIDES: *Suppliants* [286–380] 260d-261c; [513–584] 262d-263c / *Helen* [865–1031] 306c-308a / *Hecuba* [239–331] 354d-355c / *Phoenician Maidens* [528–585] 382c-383a

5 ARISTOPHANES: *Acharnians* [676–718] 463a-c / *Wasps* [725–726] 516d

6 HERODOTUS: *History*, BK VI, 201d-202c

7 PLATO: *Crito*, 216a-d / *Republic*, BK I, 297b-300b; BK IV, 349a-350a

9 ARISTOTLE: *Ethics*, BK V, CH 1 [1129^{b}19–24] 377a; CH 5 [1133^{b}30–1134^{a}14] 381c-d; CH 11 [1138^{a}4–13] 386b-c / *Rhetoric*, BK I, CH 9 [1366^{a}33–^{b}11] 608d-609a

12 EPICTETUS: *Discourses*, BK II, CH 16, 158c-d; CH 22 167d-170a; BK IV, CH 1, 220c-223d

12 AURELIUS: *Meditations*, BK II, SECT 1 256b,d; BK IV, SECT 10 264c; BK V, SECT 6 269b-d; BK VII, SECT 44 282b-c

20 AQUINAS: *Summa Theologica*, PART I–II, Q 92, A 2 214d-215a,c; Q 94, A 2 221d-223a; Q 99, A 4 248a-d; QQ 104–105 304a-321a

22 CHAUCER: *Troilus and Cressida*, BK II, STANZA 50 28a / *Reeve's Tale* 225a-232a esp [4311–4322] 231b-232a / *Tale of Melibeus*, par 30–31, 413b-414a

23 HOBBES: *Leviathan*, PART I, 86d-87b; 91b; PART II, 155b-c

27 SHAKESPEARE: *Hamlet*, ACT II, SC II [552–558] 46a / *Troilus and Cressida*, ACT II, SC II [163–188] 115b-c / *Macbeth*, ACT I, SC VII [1–28] 289b-c

29 CERVANTES: *Don Quixote*, PART I, 145d; PART II, 332d-333b

33 PASCAL: *Pensées*, 878–879 345a-b

35 LOCKE: *Civil Government*, CH II, SECT 5–6 26a-c

36 SWIFT: *Gulliver*, PART IV, 165b-166a

36 STERNE: *Tristram Shandy*, 257a-263a

38 MONTESQUIEU: *Spirit of Laws*, BK I, 1c-d

42 KANT: *Fund. Prin. Metaphysic of Morals*, 264b [fn 1] / *Pref. Metaphysical Elements of Ethics*, 375d-376b / *Science of Right*, 400b,d-401b

43 MILL: *Liberty*, 302d-303a / *Representative Government*, 414a-b / *Utilitarianism*, 464d-476a,c passim

46 HEGEL: *Philosophy of Right*, PART I, par 36 21b-c; par 49 24c-25a; par 85 35a-b; ADDITIONS, 29 121c

51 TOLSTOY: *War and Peace*, BK V, 202d; 214c-216d; BK VIII, 304c-305a

52 DOSTOEVSKY: *Brothers Karamazov*, BK III, 73a; BK V, 123c-127b; BK VI, 166c-167a; 168c-d

53 JAMES: *Psychology*, 211a-b; 886b-888a

54 FREUD: *Group Psychology*, 686a-b

3. The duties of justice compared with the generosity of love and friendship

OLD TESTAMENT: *Exodus*, 23:4–5 / *Leviticus*, 19:17–18 / *Deuteronomy*, 13:6–11; 21:18–21 / *Judges*, 11:28–40 / *Proverbs*, 20:22; 24:29; 25:21 / *Zechariah*, 13:3—(D) *Zacharias*, 13:3

NEW TESTAMENT: *Matthew*, 5:38–48 / *Luke*, 6:27–38 / *Romans*, 12:17–21 / *I Peter*, 3:8–18

6 HERODOTUS: *History*, BK II, 83d-84a

8 ARISTOTLE: *Topics*, BK III, CH 1 [116^{a}31–39] 162d; CH 2 [118^{a}1–7] 164d

9 ARISTOTLE: *Ethics*, BK IV, CH 6 373d-374b passim; BK VIII, CH 1 [1155^{a}22–28] 406d; CH 7 [1158^{b}12–1159^{a}13] 410c-411a; CH 9 411d-412c; CH 11 413b-d; CH 12 [1162^{a}29–33] 414d; CH 13 [1162^{b}17–1163^{a}23] 415b-d; BK IX, CH 2 417c-418b; CH 6 420c-421a esp [1167^{b}5–15] 420d-421a

12 AURELIUS: *Meditations*, BK III, SECT 11 262a-b

13 VIRGIL: *Aeneid*, BK IV [333–387] 176a-177b

14 PLUTARCH: *Marcus Cato*, 278d-279c / *Agesilaus*, 482b-c; 486c / *Marcus Brutus*, 816c-d

19 AQUINAS: *Summa Theologica*, PART I, Q 23, A 5, REP 3 135d-137d

20 AQUINAS: *Summa Theologica*, PART I–II, Q 66, A 4, REP 1 78c-79b; Q 114, A 4 373a-d; PART II–II, Q 23, A 3, REP 1 485a-d; Q 29, A 3 531d-532c; Q 31, A 1, REP 3 536d-537c

21 DANTE: *Divine Comedy*, PURGATORY, XV [85–114] 76b-c

22 CHAUCER: *Franklin's Tale* [11,830–928] 364b-366a

25 MONTAIGNE: *Essays*, 86a-d; 467b-470a

29 CERVANTES: *Don Quixote*, PART I, 71b-c; 108c-109b; 177a-b; PART II, 332d-333b

30 BACON: *Advancement of Learning*, 24b

37 FIELDING: *Tom Jones*, 27b-30a

38 ROUSSEAU: *Political Economy*, 373a-b

41 GIBBON: *Decline and Fall*, 233c

42 KANT: *Fund. Prin. Metaphysic of Morals*, 259a / *Pref. Metaphysical Elements of Ethics*, 368c-d; 371b-372a; 375d-376b

43 MILL: *Utilitarianism*, 466c-467a; 468b-469b; 474b-c

44 BOSWELL: *Johnson*, 392b-c

46 HEGEL: *Philosophy of Right*, ADDITIONS, 23 120d

51 TOLSTOY: *War and Peace*, BK VI, 271d; BK XII, 548d-549c; EPILOGUE I, 655b-c

4. The comparison of justice and expediency: the choice between doing and suffering injustice; the relation of justice to happiness

OLD TESTAMENT: *Leviticus*, 19:17-18 / *Proverbs*, 20:22; 24:29; 25:21

APOCRYPHA: *Susanna*—(D) OT, *Daniel*, 13

NEW TESTAMENT: *Matthew*, 5:38-48 / *Luke*, 6:27-38 / *Romans*, 12:17-21 / *I Corinthians*, 4:10-14; 6:1-11 / *I Peter*, 2:19-21; 3:8-18

5 AESCHYLUS: *Prometheus Bound* [944-1093] 50b-51d / *Eumenides* [490-565] 86b-87a

5 SOPHOCLES: *Antigone* [631-765] 136c-137d

5 EURIPIDES: *Medea* 212a-224a,c / *Alcestis* 237a-247a,c / *Helen* [998-1031] 307d-308a / *Hecuba* [239-331] 354d-355c / *Iphigenia at Aulis* 425a-439d

5 ARISTOPHANES: *Clouds* [886-1104] 499b-502a

6 HERODOTUS: *History*, BK III, 105c-d; BK VII, 218a-b; 238c

6 THUCYDIDES: *Peloponnesian War*, BK V, 504d-508a passim

7 PLATO: *Apology*, 206d / *Crito* 213a-219a,c / *Gorgias*, 263d-267c / *Republic* 295a-441a,c esp BK I-II, 300b-315a, BK X, 436c-437c / *Laws*, BK II, 656d-658b; BK IX, 746a-747c

8 ARISTOTLE: *Topics*, BK VI, CH 3 [141ª15-18] 194b / *Sophistical Refutations*, CH 25 [180ᵇ21-32] 249a

9 ARISTOTLE: *Ethics*, BK V, CH 8-9 383a-385c esp CH 9 [1136ª10-ᵇ14] 384a-d; CH 11 386b-387a,c esp [1138ª28-ᵇ4] 386d-387a / *Politics*, BK I, CH 2 [1253ª14-15] 446c; BK V, CH 8 [1308ª2-17] 510a-b / *Rhetoric*, BK I, CH 7 [1364ᵇ21-24] 606c; BK II, CH 23 [1397ª19-22] 645b

12 EPICTETUS: *Discourses*, BK I, CH 22 127c-128c; BK II, CH 10, 149c-150a; BK III, CH 18 192a-c; BK IV, CH 1, 222c-223d; CH 5 228a-230b

12 AURELIUS: *Meditations*, BK IV, SECT 10 264c; BK VII, SECT 36 282b

14 PLUTARCH: *Themistocles*, 96c-d / *Camillus*, 106b-107a / *Aristides*, 265c-d; 274d-275a / *Pyrrhus*, 319b-d / *Lysander*, 357a-b / *Sertorius*, 468b-469a / *Agesilaus*, 490d-491b / *Cato the Younger*, 636d-637c / *Dion*, 784d-785a / *Marcus Brutus*, 816c-d

18 AUGUSTINE: *City of God*, BK XII, CH 3 343d-344b / *Christian Doctrine*, BK I, CH 36 634d-635b

22 CHAUCER: *Tale of Melibeus*, par 30-31, 413b-414a

23 HOBBES: *Leviathan*, PART I, 86b; 91b-92b; 95d; PART II, 140b

25 MONTAIGNE: *Essays*, 301d-302b; 519a-c

26 SHAKESPEARE: *2nd Henry VI*, ACT III, SC I [223-237] 49c / *King John*, ACT II, SC I [561-598] 385c-386a

36 SWIFT: *Gulliver*, PART I, 37a-b

38 ROUSSEAU: *Social Contract*, BK I, 387b

43 MILL: *Utilitarianism*, 464d-476a,c esp 473c-476a,c

44 BOSWELL: *Johnson*, 261c-d

51 TOLSTOY: *War and Peace*, BK I, 9c-10d; 40b-41a; BK III, 123d-124a; BK V, 216b-d; BK VIII, 304d-305a; BK XIV, 598d-599a; EPILOGUE I, 656d-657a

5. Justice and equality: the kinds of justice in relation to the measure and modes of equality and inequality

5 EURIPIDES: *Phoenician Maidens* [528-558] 382c-d

6 THUCYDIDES: *Peloponnesian War*, BK V, 505b

7 PLATO: *Republic*, BK VIII, 411d-413a / *Laws*, BK VI, 699d-700b

8 ARISTOTLE: *Topics*, BK VI, CH 5 [143ª15-19] 196c-d; CH 7 [145ᵇ33-146ª3] 199d

9 ARISTOTLE: *Ethics*, BK V, CH 2 [1130ᵇ30-34] 378b; CH 3-5 378c-381d; CH 6 [1134ª25-ᵇ17] 382a-c; CH 9 [1136ᵇ15-1137ª4] 384d-385a; BK VIII, CH 7 [1158ᵇ12-33] 410c-d; CH 11 413b-d / *Politics*, BK I, CH 12-13 453d-455a,c; BK II, CH 2 [1261ª23-ᵇ6] 456a-b; CH 7 461d-463c; BK III, CH 9 477c-478d esp [1280ª8-31] 477c-d; CH 12-13 480c-483a; CH 16 [1287ª10-23] 485c; BK IV, CH 4 [1291ᵇ30-1292ª7] 491a-b; BK V, CH I [1301ª25-ᵇ4] 502b-c; [1301ᵇ29-1302ª8] 503a-b; CH 8 [1308ª2-17] 510a-b; CH 9 [1310ª25-36] 512c; BK VI, CH 2 520d-521b esp [1317ª40-ᵇ16] 520d, [1318ª4-10] 521b; CH 3 521c-522a; BK VII, CH 14 537b-538d esp [1332ᵇ13-41] 537b-d / *Athenian Constitution*, CH 12 557b-558a

12 AURELIUS: *Meditations*, BK I, SECT 14 254b-c

14 PLUTARCH: *Poplicola-Solon*, 87a

19 AQUINAS: *Summa Theologica*, PART I, Q 21, A I, ANS and REP 3 124b-125b; Q 65, A 2, REP 3 340b-341b

20 AQUINAS: *Summa Theologica*, PART I-II, Q 60, A 3, ANS 51c-52b; Q 64, A 2 67d-68b; Q 114, A I, ANS 370c-371c

23 HOBBES: *Leviathan*, PART I, 93b-c; 94b-95c; PART II, 156b-157a

24 RABELAIS: *Gargantua and Pantagruel*, BK III, 134b-c

35 LOCKE: *Civil Government*, CH II 25d-28c; CH VI, SECT 54 36c; CH VII, SECT 90-94 44d-46c

38 MONTESQUIEU: *Spirit of Laws*, BK VIII, 52a-b; BK XI, 71d; BK XIII, 96a-b

38 ROUSSEAU: *Inequality*, 333a-d; 359c-d; 360b,d [fn I]; 361c-362a; 362d-363a,c / *Social Contract*, BK II, 397a-398a; 405b-c

39 SMITH: *Wealth of Nations*, BK IV, 284d

40 GIBBON: *Decline and Fall*, 617c-d

42 KANT: *Science of Right*, 401b-c; 419c-420a; 431a-432c; 433c-d; 435c-437c esp 436d

43 DECLARATION OF INDEPENDENCE: [7-15] 1a-b

43 ARTICLES OF CONFEDERATION: IV [17-36] 5b-c

43 CONSTITUTION OF THE U.S.: ARTICLE IV, SECT 2 [519-521] 16a; AMENDMENTS, XIII, SECT I-XIV, SECT I 18c-d; XV 19b; XIX 19d

43 FEDERALIST: NUMBER 80, 236a-b

43 MILL: *Representative Government*, 370a-389b passim / *Utilitarianism*, 460a-461a; 467a-b; 472d-473a; 474d-476a

46 HEGEL: *Philosophy of Right*, PART I, par 49 24c-25a; PART III, par 200 67c-68a; par 209 69d; ADDITIONS, 29 121c; 177 147d / *Philosophy of History*, PART IV, 362d-363a

50 MARX: *Capital*, 25a-d

52 DOSTOEVSKY: *Brothers Karamazov*, BK IV, 104b-107a

54 FREUD: *Group Psychology*, 685d-686c / *Civilization and Its Discontents*, 787d-788b [fn 3]

6. Justice and liberty: the theory of human rights

5 AESCHYLUS: *Suppliant Maidens* 1a-14a,c

5 SOPHOCLES: *Antigone* [441-525] 134d-135c; [891-943] 138d-139a / *Ajax* [1047-1421] 152a-155a,c

5 EURIPIDES: *Suppliants* [513-565] 262d-263b / *Bacchantes* [878-911] 347b-c / *Phoenician Maidens* [1625-1682] 392b-d / *Orestes* [491-604] 399a-400a

7 PLATO: *Republic*, BK VIII, 411d-413a / *Laws*, BK IV, 682a-683d

8 ARISTOTLE: *Sophistical Refutations*, CH 12 [173ᵃ7-31] 238b-c

9 ARISTOTLE: *Ethics*, BK V, CH 6 [1134ᵃ24-ᵇ17] 382a-c / *Politics*, BK V, CH 9 [1310ᵃ25-36] 512c; BK VI, CH 2 520d-521b esp [1317ᵃ40-ᵇ16] 520d / *Rhetoric*, BK I, CH 10 [1368ᵇ7-10] 611d; CH 13 [1373ᵇ1-17] 617c-d

12 AURELIUS: *Meditations*, BK I, SECT 14 254b-c; BK IV, SECT 4 264a; BK VII, SECT 55 283b-c

15 TACITUS: *Histories*, BK IV, 271b

18 AUGUSTINE: *Confessions*, BK III, par 15 17a-b / *City of God*, BK IV, CH 4 190d; BK XIX, CH 21 524a-525a

20 AQUINAS: *Summa Theologica*, PART I-II, Q 94, A 2, ANS 221d-223a

23 HOBBES: *Leviathan*, PART II, 112d-117b

29 CERVANTES: *Don Quixote*, PART I, 71b-c; 108c-109b; 177a-b

30 BACON: *Advancement of Learning*, 20c-d

31 SPINOZA: *Ethics*, PART IV, APPENDIX, VIII 447d

35 LOCKE: *Civil Government* 25a-81d

38 MONTESQUIEU: *Spirit of Laws*, BK I, 1a-3a; BK VI, 34b-c

38 ROUSSEAU: *Inequality*, 356b-358d; 361c-362a / *Political Economy*, 370b-d / *Social Contract*, BK I 387b,d-394d esp 388d-390d, 393b-394d; BK II, 398b-399a

39 SMITH: *Wealth of Nations*, BK I, 61b; BK II, 140b; BK IV, 228a

41 GIBBON: *Decline and Fall*, 237c

42 KANT: *Pure Reason*, 113b-115a; 222b-c / *Science of Right*, 400b,d-402a; 421c-422d / *Judgement*, 586a-587a

43 DECLARATION OF INDEPENDENCE: [7-28] 1a-b

43 CONSTITUTION OF THE U.S.: AMENDMENTS, I-IX 17a-18a; XIII, SECT I-XIV, SECT I 18c-d

43 FEDERALIST: NUMBER 51, 164a-165a; NUMBER 84, 251a-253d

43 MILL: *Liberty* 267a-323a,c esp 271c-273b / *Utilitarianism*, 464d-476a,c

46 HEGEL: *Philosophy of Right*, PART I, par 44 23c; PART III, par 230 75c; par 261 83a-d; ADDITIONS, 81 128d-129a / *Philosophy of History*, INTRO, 199b-c; PART IV, 345a-b; 362d-363a; 364a-365c

48 MELVILLE: *Moby Dick*, 292a-297a

50 MARX: *Capital*, 83d-84a

54 FREUD: *Civilization and Its Discontents*, 780c-781a

6a. The relation of natural rights to natural law and natural justice

5 SOPHOCLES: *Antigone* [441-525] 134d-135c

9 ARISTOTLE: *Rhetoric*, BK I, CH 13 [1373ᵇ1-17] 617c-d

12 AURELIUS: *Meditations*, BK IV, SECT 4 264a; BK VII, SECT 55 283b-c

18 AUGUSTINE: *City of God*, BK XIX, CH 21 524a-525a

19 AQUINAS: *Summa Theologica*, PART I, Q 96, A 1 510b-511b; A 4 512d-513c

20 AQUINAS: *Summa Theologica*, PART I-II, Q 91, A 2 208d-209d; Q 94, A 2, ANS 221d-223a; Q 95, A 2 227c-228c; A 4 229b-230c

23 HOBBES: *Leviathan*, PART I, 86c-87d; PART II, 131a-c; 138c

27 SHAKESPEARE: *Troilus and Cressida*, ACT II, SC II [163-188] 115b-c

30 BACON: *Advancement of Learning*, 94d-95b

31 SPINOZA: *Ethics*, PART IV, PROP 37, SCHOL 2 435b-436a; APPENDIX, VIII 447d

32 MILTON: *Samson Agonistes* [888-902] 359a

35 LOCKE: *Civil Government*, CH II-IX 25d-54d passim; CH XI, SECT 135-137 55d-57b; CH XV, SECT 171-172 65a-c

38 MONTESQUIEU: *Spirit of Laws*, BK I, 1c-d

38 ROUSSEAU: *Inequality*, 330a-331b; 333c-d; 342c-347d

39 SMITH: *Wealth of Nations*, BK I, 61b; BK II, 140b

41 GIBBON: *Decline and Fall*, 86d-87a

42 KANT: *Intro. Metaphysic of Morals*, 392b / *Science of Right*, 397a-b; 400b,d-402a; 421c-422d; 429a-c; 430a-432c; 434a; 435a-457b esp 436c, 437c-d, 447b-450b, 451c-d

43 DECLARATION OF INDEPENDENCE: [1-28] 1a-b

43 MILL: *Liberty*, 272d-273b

46 HEGEL: *Philosophy of History*, INTRO, 171c-172b

6b. The relation between natural and positive rights, innate and acquired rights, private and public rights: their correlative duties

5 AESCHYLUS: *Suppliant Maidens* 1a-14a,c

5 SOPHOCLES: *Antigone* [441-525] 134d-135c; [891-943] 138d-139a / *Ajax* [1047-1421] 152a-155a,c

(6. Justice and liberty: the theory of human rights.
6b. The relation between natural and posi-
tive rights, innate and acquired rights,
private and public rights: their correlative
duties.)

5 EURIPIDES: *Suppliants* [513–565] 262d-263b
/ *Bacchantes* [878–911] 347b-c / *Phoenician*
Maidens [1625–1682] 392b-d / *Orestes* [491–
604] 399a-400a

7 PLATO: *Laws*, BK IV, 682a-683d

8 ARISTOTLE: *Sophistical Refutations*, CH 12
[173ª7–31] 238b-c

9 ARISTOTLE: *Rhetoric*, BK I, CH 10 [1368ᵇ7–10]
611d; CH 13 [1373ᵇ1–17] 617c-d

18 AUGUSTINE: *Confessions*, BK III, par 13–15
16c-17b; par 17 17d-18a / *City of God*, BK XIX,
CH 17 522b-523a

20 AQUINAS: *Summa Theologica*, PART I–II, Q
100, A 1 251b-252a

23 HOBBES: *Leviathan*, PART II, 113c-116c; 131a-c;
136d-137b; 138c; 151a-c

25 MONTAIGNE: *Essays*, 281a-283c; 519a-520b

27 SHAKESPEARE: *King Lear*, ACT I, SC II [1–22]
247d-248a

30 BACON: *Advancement of Learning*, 100d

31 SPINOZA: *Ethics*, PART IV, PROP 37, SCHOL 2
435b-436a

35 LOCKE: *Civil Government*, CH II 25d-28c
passim; CH IV, SECT 21 29d; CH V, SECT 45
34d-35a; CH VI, SECT 56–63 36d-38c; CH VII,
SECT 87–89 44a-d; SECT 91 45a-c; CH VIII,
SECT 95–99 46c-47c; CH IX 53c-54d; CH XI
55b-58b / *Human Understanding*, BK I, CH II,
SECT 13 107d-108c

38 MONTESQUIEU: *Spirit of Laws*, BK I, 1a-3a;
BK VIII, 52a-b; BK XXVI, 215b-216c; 217b;
221c-d

38 ROUSSEAU: *Inequality*, 333a-d; 342c-347d;
362d-363a,c / *Political Economy*, 370b-d /
Social Contract, BK I, 393b-c; BK II, 396d-
398b; 399b-c

41 GIBBON: *Decline and Fall*, 82b-83c; 86d-89b
passim; 404a

42 KANT: *Intro. Metaphysic of Morals*, 392b /
Science of Right 397a-458a,c esp 401b-402a,c,
410d-415d, 418c-422d, 429a-433c, 435c-436b,
436d

43 DECLARATION OF INDEPENDENCE: [1–28]
1a-b

44 BOSWELL: *Johnson*, 221d-224a

46 HEGEL: *Philosophy of Right*, PART I, par 38
21d; par 40 21d-22c; PART III, par 155 57c;
par 210–228 69d-75b esp par 210–211 69d-70c,
par 217 72b-c; ADDITIONS, I 115a-d

6c. **The inalienability of natural rights: their**
violation by tyranny and despotism

15 TACITUS: *Histories*, BK IV, 271b

20 AQUINAS: *Summa Theologica*, PART I–II, Q 94,
AA 5–6 224d-226b; Q 96, A 6 235a-d; Q 97
235d-239b

23 HOBBES: *Leviathan*, PART I, 87c-d; 90a-b;
94b-d; PART II, 115a-116a; 142b-c

35 LOCKE: *Toleration*, 20d-21a / *Civil Govern-*
ment, CH II, SECT 10–11 27b-d; CH III, SECT
16–19 28d-29c; CH IV 29d-30b; CH VII, SECT
87–94 44a-46c; CH IX, SECT 131 54d; CH XI,
SECT 135–140 55d-58a; CH XIV, SECT 168
64b-c; CH XV, SECT 171–172 65a-c; CH XVI–
XIX 65d-81d

38 MONTESQUIEU: *Spirit of Laws*, BK XV, 109a-
110a

38 ROUSSEAU: *Social Contract*, BK I, 388a-c; 389a-
390d; BK II, 396d-398b

39 SMITH: *Wealth of Nations*, BK I, 61b

40 GIBBON: *Decline and Fall*, 33c-34a,c

42 KANT: *Science of Right*, 401b-402a; 421c-422d;
445c-446a; 451d-452a; 454d-455c

43 DECLARATION OF INDEPENDENCE: 1a-3b

43 CONSTITUTION OF THE U.S.: AMENDMENTS, IX
17d-18a

43 FEDERALIST: NUMBER 28, 97c; NUMBER 84,
251d-252a

43 MILL: *Liberty*, 270d; 316b-d

44 BOSWELL: *Johnson*, 363c-364a

46 HEGEL: *Philosophy of Right*, PART I, par 57
26b-27a; par 66 29a-c / *Philosophy of History*,
PART III, 310d-311a

6d. **Justice as the basis for the distinction be-**
tween liberty and license

6 THUCYDIDES: *Peloponnesian War*, BK II, 396c-d

7 PLATO: *Laws*, BK III, 674d-676c

9 ARISTOTLE: *Politics*, BK V, CH 9 [1310ª25–36]
512c; BK VI, CH 4 [1318ᵇ33–1319ª4] 522b-c;
[1319ᵇ27–32] 523b

12 EPICTETUS: *Discourses*, BK I, CH 12, 119a-b

15 TACITUS: *Annals*, BK III, 57b-58d

20 AQUINAS: *Summa Theologica*, PART II–II, Q
183, A 4, ANS 627d-628d

23 HOBBES: *Leviathan*, PART II, 114c-115b

27 SHAKESPEARE: *Measure for Measure*, ACT I,
SC III 177b-d

32 MILTON: *Sonnets*, XII 65a-b / *Areopagitica*
381a-412b

35 LOCKE: *Civil Government*, CH II, SECT 4–6
25d-26c

38 MONTESQUIEU: *Spirit of Laws*, BK III, 10a;
BK VIII, 51a-52c; BK XI, 69a-c

38 ROUSSEAU: *Inequality*, 324a-b / *Social Con-*
tract, BK I, 393b-c

40 GIBBON: *Decline and Fall*, 622d-623c; 653a

43 MILL: *Liberty*, 271c-273b; 302d-323a,c passim

46 HEGEL: *Philosophy of Right*, PART III, par 319
105b-106c / *Philosophy of History*, PART IV,
342b-d

6e. **Justice and natural rights as the source of**
civil liberty

19 AQUINAS: *Summa Theologica*, PART I, Q 96,
A 4 512d-513c

23 HOBBES: *Leviathan*, PART II, 138c

7. Domestic justice: the problems of right and duty in the family

(7. Domestic justice: the problems of right and duty in the family.)

50 MARX: *Capital*, 241a-d

51 TOLSTOY: *War and Peace*, BK I, 38d-41a; 45b-47b; EPILOGUE I, 654a-662a

52 DOSTOEVSKY: *Brothers Karamazov*, BK I, 1a-11a; BK II, 34d-36b; BK XII, 370b-371c; 395a-398a

54 FREUD: *New Introductory Lectures*, 876c

'8. Economic justice: justice in production, distribution, and exchange

OLD TESTAMENT: *Exodus*, 20:15,17 / *Leviticus*, 19:11,35–36; 25:35–37 / *Deuteronomy*, 5:19,21; 24:10–15; 25:13–16; 27:17 / *II Samuel*, 12:1–6—(D) *II Kings*, 12:1–6 / *I Kings*, 21—(D) *III Kings*, 21 / *II Kings*, 5:20–27—(D) *IV Kings*, 5:20–27 / *Nehemiah*, 5:1–12—(D) *II Esdras*, 5:1–12 / *Job*, 24 / *Proverbs*, 1:10–19; 6:30–31; 11:1; 14:31; 16:11; 20:10; 21:6–7; 22:16,22–23; 23:10–11; 28:8,24; 30:8–9 / *Isaiah*, 3:14–15; 10:1–2—(D) *Isaias*, 3:14–15; 10:1–2 / *Jeremiah*, 17:11—(D) *Jeremias*, 17:11 / *Ezekiel*, 22:12–13,25–29; 45:9–12—(D) *Ezechiel*, 22:12–13,25–29; 45:9–12 / *Amos*, 2:6–7; 5:11–12; 8:1–7 esp 8:4–6 / *Micah*, 6:9–12—(D) *Micheas*, 6:9–12 / *Zechariah*, 5:3 —(D) *Zacharias*, 5:3

APOCRYPHA: *Ecclesiasticus*, 5:8,14; 20:25; 26:29; 27:2; 29:19; 34:18–22—(D) OT, *Ecclesiasticus*, 5:10,16–17; 20:27; 26:28; 27:2; 29:25; 34:21–27

NEW TESTAMENT: *Matthew*, 19:18 / *Mark*, 10:19 / *Luke*, 3:12–13; 18:20 / *Acts*, 2:44–47; 4:31–5:11 / *Romans*, 13:9 / *I Corinthians*, 6:10 / *Ephesians*, 4:28 / *II Thessalonians*, 3:10

5 EURIPIDES: *Helen* [903–908] 306d-307a / *Phoenician Maidens* [528–567] 382c-d

5 ARISTOPHANES: *Plutus* 629a-642d esp [76–111] 630a-b

6 HERODOTUS: *History*, BK II, 87a-b; BK VI, 201d-202c; BK VII, 245b

7 PLATO: *Republic*, BK I, 297a-c; BK II, 316a-319b; BK III–IV, 340c-343a; BK V, 364c-365d / *Laws*, BK V 686d-697a passim; BK VIII, 738c-743a / *Seventh Letter*, 814b-c

9 ARISTOTLE: *Ethics*, BK V, CH 2 [1130ᵃ13–ᵇ17] 377c-378a; BK VIII, CH 13–14 414d-416d passim / *Politics*, BK I, CH 3–11 446d-453d passim; BK II, CH 5 458a-460a; CH 7 461d-463c; BK V, CH 1 [1301ᵃ25–ᵇ2] 502b-c / *Athenian Constitution*, CH 12 557b-558a

12 AURELIUS: *Meditations*, BK VIII, SECT 33 288a

14 PLUTARCH: *Lycurgus*, 36a-37b / *Solon*, 68d-70c / *Poplicola-Solon*, 87a

19 AQUINAS: *Summa Theologica*, PART I, Q 21, A 1 124b-125b; Q 98, A 1, REP 3 516d-517c

21 DANTE: *Divine Comedy*, HELL, XI 15a-16b passim

22 CHAUCER: *Tale of Melibeus*, par 49–51 422a-424a

23 HOBBES: *Leviathan*, PART I, 93b-c; PART II, 124d-126a; 156c-157a

24 RABELAIS: *Gargantua and Pantagruel*, BK III, 133b-134d

25 MONTAIGNE: *Essays*, 42a-b

27 SHAKESPEARE: *Coriolanus*, ACT I, SC I 351a-354d

30 BACON: *Advancement of Learning*, 86b-c

33 PASCAL: *Provincial Letters*, 91a-94a

35 LOCKE: *Civil Government*, CH V 30b-36a passim

36 SWIFT: *Gulliver*, PART IV, 154b-155b

38 MONTESQUIEU: *Spirit of Laws*, BK V, 19a-d; 23a-25a; 29c; BK XIII 96a-102a,c; BK XVIII, 128b; BK XX, 146b-d; BK XXIII, 199b-200a,c

38 ROUSSEAU: *Inequality*, 348b; 354a-355b; 360b-361a; 365b-366a / *Political Economy*, 377b-385a,c / *Social Contract*, BK III, 415b-417c

39 SMITH: *Wealth of Nations*, BK I, 20b-23b passim, esp 21a-c; 27b-37b esp 33c; BK V, 309a-311c

40 GIBBON: *Decline and Fall*, 22c

41 GIBBON: *Decline and Fall*, 86d-87c

42 KANT: *Science of Right*, 443b-d; 446a-b

43 CONSTITUTION OF THE U.S.: ARTICLE I, SECT 2 [17–29] 11b; SECT 9 [273–275] 13d; ARTICLE VI [578–582] 16d; AMENDMENTS, V [645–648] 17c; VII 17d; XIV, SECT 1 [748–750] 18d; SECT 4 19a; XVI 19b

43 FEDERALIST: NUMBER 73, 218d-219b; NUMBER 79, 233c-d

43 MILL: *Liberty*, 322c-d / *Representative Government*, 335a-b; 366c-367a / *Utilitarianism*, 470c-471b passim; 472d-473c

44 BOSWELL: *Johnson*, 125b-c

46 HEGEL: *Philosophy of Right*, PART I, par 49 24c-25a; PART III, par 241 76d-77a; ADDITIONS, 29 121c; 148 140c-d / *Philosophy of History*, PART IV, 353b-c

48 MELVILLE: *Moby Dick*, 292a-297a

50 MARX: *Capital* 1a-383d esp 19c-25d, 37d-38b [fn 5], 42b-47a, 79a-84a,c, 89a-94a, 112c-113c, 150a-151a,c, 161b-162d, 261d-262a, 264a-275c, 280c-286a, 327b, 354b-c, 377c-378d

50 MARX-ENGELS: *Communist Manifesto* 415a-434d esp 420b-423a, 425d-426d, 428d-429c, 434c-d

51 TOLSTOY: *War and Peace*, BK V, 197b-c; 211a-213a

52 DOSTOEVSKY: *Brothers Karamazov*, BK VI, 165b-166a

54 FREUD: *Civilization and Its Discontents*, 787d-788a

8a. Private and public property: the just distribution of economic goods

OLD TESTAMENT: *Exodus*, 20:15,17 / *Leviticus*, 19:11 / *Deuteronomy*, 5:19,21; 27:17 / *II Samuel*, 12:1–6—(D) *II Kings*, 12:1–6 / *I Kings*, 21 —(D) *III Kings*, 21 / *Job*, 24 / *Proverbs*, 6:30–

31; 21:6-7; 23:10; 24; 30:8-9 / *Jeremiah*, 17:11—(D) *Jeremias*, 17:11

NEW TESTAMENT: *Matthew*, 19:18 / *Mark*, 10:19 / *Luke*, 3:12-13; 18:20 / *Acts*, 2:44-47; 4:31-5:11 / *Romans*, 13:9 / *Ephesians*, 4:28

5 EURIPIDES: *Phoenician Maidens* [528-567] 382c-d

5 ARISTOPHANES: *Ecclesiazusae* 615a-628d esp [554-1111] 621b-628a / *Plutus* 629a-642d

7 PLATO: *Republic*, BK III, 341c-d; BK V, 364c-365d / *Laws*, BK V 686d-697a passim; BK VIII, 738c-742a / *Seventh Letter*, 814b-c

9 ARISTOTLE: *Ethics*, BK V, CH 4 [1131^{b}27-33] 379b-c; CH 9 [1136^{b}15-1137^{a}4] 384d-385a; BK VIII, CH 9 411d-412c; CH 13-14 414d-416d passim / *Politics*, BK II, CH 1 [1260^{b}36-1261^{a}7] 455b,d; CH 3 [1261^{b}16-38] 456c-d; CH 5 458a-460a; CH 6 [1265^{a}28-^{b}17] 460c-461a; CH 7 461d-463c; BK III, CH 10 [1281^{a}11-28] 478d-479a; BK V, CH 8 [1308^{b}10-1309^{a}32] 510d-511c; CH 9 [1309^{b}18-1310^{a}12] 511d-512b; BK VI, CH 4 [1319^{a}6-19] 522c-d; BK VII, CH 9 [1329^{a}18-26] 533c; CH 10 [1329^{b}35-1330^{a}3] 534b-c / *Athenian Constitution*, CH 12 557b-558a

14 PLUTARCH: *Lycurgus*, 36a-b / *Solon*, 68d-70c / *Poplicola-Solon*, 87a / *Agis* 648b,d-656d / *Tiberius Gracchus*, 674c-681a,c

15 TACITUS: *Annals*, BK II, 31a-b; 32b-d / *Histories*, BK II, 236d-237a; BK IV, 286c-287a

19 AQUINAS: *Summa Theologica*, PART I, Q 98, A I, REP 3 516d-517c

20 AQUINAS: *Summa Theologica*, PART I-II, Q 94, A 5, REP 3 224d-225d; Q 105, A 2, ANS and REP 1-6 309d-316a; PART II-II, Q 32, AA 5-6 544a-546b

23 HOBBES: *Leviathan*, PART I, 94d-95a; PART II, 124d-125d; 156b-157a

27 SHAKESPEARE: *King Lear*, ACT III, SC IV [26-36] 264c; ACT IV, SC I [66-73] 270a-b

29 CERVANTES: *Don Quixote*, PART II, 391b-d

31 SPINOZA: *Ethics*, PART IV, APPENDIX, XVII 448d

33 PASCAL: *Provincial Letters*, 91a-94a; 97b-98b

35 LOCKE: *Civil Government*, CH V 30b-36a

36 SWIFT: *Gulliver*, PART IV, 154b-155b

36 STERNE: *Tristram Shandy*, 310a-311b

38 MONTESQUIEU: *Spirit of Laws*, BK V, 19a-21d passim; 23a-25a; 29c; BK XXVI, 221c-222b

38 ROUSSEAU: *Inequality*, 353a; 360b-361a; 362d-363a,c / *Political Economy*, 375b-d; 377b-385a,c / *Social Contract*, BK III, 415b-417c

39 SMITH: *Wealth of Nations*, BK I, 27b-37b esp 33c; 52b-62a esp 52b-c; BK IV, 225d-228a; 239c-240a; BK V, 309a-311c

40 GIBBON: *Decline and Fall*, 22b-c; 127a-c; 251d-255d passim; 501b-502b

41 GIBBON: *Decline and Fall*, 86d-89d

42 KANT: *Science of Right*, 403a-410d; 411c-415d; 422b,d-425b; 426b-428a; 431a-432c; 441d-443d; 446a-b

43 CONSTITUTION OF THE U.S.: AMENDMENTS, V 17b-c; XIV, SECT 1 18d

43 FEDERALIST: NUMBER 35-36 112a-117d passim; NUMBER 73, 218d-219b; NUMBER 79, 233c-d

43 MILL: *Liberty*, 309a-c; 322c-d / *Representative Government*, 335a-b; 366c-367a / *Utilitarianism*, 467b; 472d-473a

44 BOSWELL: *Johnson*, 125b-c

46 HEGEL: *Philosophy of Right*, PART I, par 46 23d-24a; par 49 24c-25a; par 64 28c-d; par 68 29d-30a; PART III, par 237 76c; par 241 76d-77a; par 244-245 77c-d; ADDITIONS, 27 121b; 29 121c; 145 140b; 148-149 140c-141a / *Philosophy of History*, PART II, 275b-276a; 277b-c; PART III, 287d-288b; 289a-b; PART IV, 353b-c

48 MELVILLE: *Moby Dick*, 292a-297a

50 MARX: *Capital*, 34d-35c; 61c-62b; 89a-b; 174d-175c; 218d-219a; 286a-296a esp 288b-d, 292-295d; 302d-383d esp 303b-305a, 308d-309b, 317c-321b, 325d-326a, 354a-355d, 369c-371c, 377c-378d, 383d

50 MARX-ENGELS: *Communist Manifesto*, 425c-427b; 428d-429a

51 TOLSTOY: *War and Peace*, BK V, 197b-c; BK X, 414c-416c

54 FREUD: *Civilization and Its Discontents*, 787d-788b

8b. Fair wages and prices: the just exchange of goods and services

OLD TESTAMENT: *Leviticus*, 19:11,13,35-36; 25:35-37 / *Deuteronomy*, 24:10-15; 25:13-16 / *I Kings*, 21—(D) *III Kings*, 21 / *II Kings*, 5:20-27—(D) *IV Kings*, 5:20-27 / *Nehemiah*, 5:1-12—(D) *II Esdras*, 5:1-12 / *Proverbs*, 6:30-31; 11:1; 16:11; 20:10; 22:22-23; 28:8 / *Jeremiah*, 22:13—(D) *Jeremias*, 22:13 / *Ezekiel*, 22:12-13; 45:9-12—(D) *Ezechiel*, 22:12-13; 45:9-12 / *Amos*, 8:4-6 / *Micah*, 6:9-12—(D) *Micheas*, 6:9-12

APOCRYPHA: *Tobit*, 4:14—(D) OT, *Tobias*, 4:15 / *Ecclesiasticus*, 26:29; 27:2; 34:20-22—(D) OT, *Ecclesiasticus*, 26:28; 27:2; 34:24-27

NEW TESTAMENT: *Matthew*, 10:10 / *Luke*, 10:7 / *I Timothy*, 5:18 / *II Timothy*, 2:6

6 HERODOTUS: *History*, BK IV, 158b-c

7 PLATO: *Laws*, BK VIII, 740d-743a; BK XI, 772d-775d esp 775a

9 ARISTOTLE: *Ethics*, BK V, CH 4 [1132^{b}11]-CH 5 [1133^{b}29] 380b-381c; BK VIII, CH 9 411d-412c; CH 13-14 414d-416d passim; BK IX, CH 1 416b,d-417c / *Politics*, BK I, CH 9-10 450d-452d

18 AUGUSTINE: *Confessions*, BK V, par 22 33b-c

20 AQUINAS: *Summa Theologica*, PART I-II, Q 95, A 4, ANS 229b-230c; Q 105, A 2, ANS and REP 3-6 309d-316a

21 DANTE: *Divine Comedy*, HELL, XI 15a-16b passim

23 HOBBES: *Leviathan*, PART II, 126a

25 MONTAIGNE: *Essays*, 42a-b

(8. *Economic justice: justice in production, distribution, and exchange.* 8b. *Fair wages and prices: the just exchange of goods and services.*)

27 SHAKESPEARE: *Coriolanus*, ACT I, SC I [1–167] 351a-353a

30 BACON: *Advancement of Learning*, 30c-d

36 SWIFT: *Gulliver*, PART IV, 154b-155b

38 MONTESQUIEU: *Spirit of Laws*, BK XVIII, 128b; BK XX, 146b-d

38 ROUSSEAU: *Inequality*, 353b; 365d

39 SMITH: *Wealth of Nations*, BK I, 13a-16a; 20b-23b esp 20c, 21c; 27b-37b esp 33c; 42a-62a passim, esp 52b-c, 56b-57a, 61c-d; 106c-107a; BK IV, 225d-228a

40 GIBBON: *Decline and Fall*, 22c

42 KANT: *Science of Right*, 424b-425a; 446a-b

43 CONSTITUTION OF THE U.S.: AMENDMENTS, VII 17d

43 MILL: *Liberty*, 309a-c; 322c-d / *Representative Government*, 366d-367a / *Utilitarianism*, 467b; 470c-d; 472d-473a

46 HEGEL: *Philosophy of Right*, PART III, par 236 76a-c; ADDITIONS, 145 140b / *Philosophy of History*, PART IV, 353b-c

48 MELVILLE: *Moby Dick*, 292a-297a

50 MARX: *Capital*, 13a-50a esp 13d-18a, 19d-20b, 24c-25d, 27a-c, 31b-33b, 37c-39c, 42b-44c; 69a-84a,c esp 74c-78a, 79c-84a; 89d-102b passim, esp 93b-96a, 100a-101a; 171a-c; 256b-260c esp 258b-c; 264a-275c; 296c-298a; 305c-307c; 324a-327b esp 327b; 366a-368a

50 MARX-ENGELS: *Communist Manifesto*, 423c-d; 425d-427b

51 TOLSTOY: *War and Peace*, BK XIII, 572d-573b

8c. Justice in the organization of production

50 MARX: *Capital*, 33d-36c esp 34d-35a; 37d-38b [fn 5]; 85a-263d esp 111c-115c, 160d-164a, 171d-180d, 192d-209a, 215a-217b, 226d-227d, 261c-262a; 279d-286a esp 285c-286a; 311c-321b; 354a-355d; 377c-378d

50 MARX-ENGELS: *Communist Manifesto*, 419d-425b esp 421a-422c; 426a-427b

8c(1) Economic exploitation: chattel slavery and wage slavery

9 ARISTOTLE: *Ethics*, BK V, CH 6 [1134^{b}7–17] 382b-c; BK VIII, CH II [1161^{a}30–^{b}10] 413c-d / *Politics*, BK I, CH 3–7 446d-449c; CH 11 [1259^{a}18]–CH 13 [1260^{b}7] 453c-455a; BK III, CH 6 [1278^{b}32–37] 476a-b / *Athenian Constitution*, CH 2 553a-c

14 PLUTARCH: *Lycurgus*, 46c-47a / *Marcus Cato*, 278d-279c

20 AQUINAS: *Summa Theologica*, PART I–II, Q 105, A 4, ANS and REP 1–4 318b-321a

32 MILTON: *Samson Agonistes* [1–51] 339b-340b

36 SWIFT: *Gulliver*, PART IV, 154b-155a

38 ROUSSEAU: *Inequality*, 352a; 353c-355b; 365b-366a

39 SMITH: *Wealth of Nations*, BK I, 28a-d; 61c-d; 109d-110d; BK III, 165b-170c; BK IV, 253c-254a; 287c-d

40 GIBBON: *Decline and Fall*, 144b

41 GIBBON: *Decline and Fall*, 45b

42 KANT: *Science of Right*, 421c-422d; 445c-446a

43 CONSTITUTION OF THE U.S.: ARTICLE I, SECT 9 [260–266] 13d; ARTICLE IV, SECT 2 [529–535] 16b; AMENDMENTS, XIII 18c

43 MILL: *Representative Government*, 339d-340c

44 BOSWELL: *Johnson*, 363c-364a

46 HEGEL: *Philosophy of History*, PART IV, 335b-336c

50 MARX: *Capital* 1a-383d esp 102b-105c, 112c-115c, 127c-131a, 150a-c, 176a-178d, 193a-209a, 264a-275c, 282d-286a, 296c-301b, 354a-355d, 366a-368b, 376c-377a, 379a-383d

50 MARX-ENGELS: *Communist Manifesto*, 420c-d; 422c-423a; 424b-425a; 426b-428a

51 TOLSTOY: *War and Peace*, BK V, 211a-213a

52 DOSTOEVSKY: *Brothers Karamazov*, BK VI, 165b-c

8c(2) Profit and unearned increment

14 PLUTARCH: *Marcus Cato*, 287c-d

39 SMITH: *Wealth of Nations*, BK I, 20b-23b passim, esp 21a-c; 27b-28a; 109d-110d

46 HEGEL: *Philosophy of Right*, PART III, par 243 77b-c

50 MARX: *Capital*, 71d-72c; 85a-263d esp 92c-94a, 100a-101b, 104b-105c, 112c, 154d-156d, 198c-199b, 254c-255a, 263c-d; 267b; 267d-275c passim, esp 271b-c; 286a-301b passim, esp 288b-289c, 295a-d, 301a-b; 327b

8d. Justice and the use of money: usury and interest rates

OLD TESTAMENT: *Exodus*, 22:25 / *Leviticus*, 25:35–37 / *Deuteronomy*, 23:19–20; 24:10–13 / *Nehemiah*, 5—(D) *II Esdras*, 5 / *Psalms*, 15:5 —(D) *Psalms*, 14:5 / *Proverbs*, 28:8 / *Jeremiah*, 15:10—(D) *Jeremias*, 15:10 / *Ezekiel*, 18:4–21 esp 18:8, 18:13, 18:17; 22:12—(D) *Ezechiel*, 18:4–21 esp 18:8, 18:13, 18:17; 22:12

7 PLATO: *Republic*, BK VIII, 408c-d / *Laws*, BK V, 694c-d; BK XI, 775c-d

9 ARISTOTLE: *Ethics*, BK V, CH 2 [1130^{a}13–^{b}8] 377c-378a; CH 5 [1133^{a}5–^{b}29] 380d-381c; BK IX, CH 2 [1164^{b}30–1165^{a}11] 417d-418a / *Politics*, BK I, CH 9–10 450d-452d esp CH 10 [1258^{a}38–^{b}8] 452d / *Athenian Constitution*, CH 12, par 4 557d-558a

14 PLUTARCH: *Marcus Cato*, 287c-d / *Lucullus*, 409b-d

15 TACITUS: *Annals*, BK VI, 90a-c

20 AQUINAS: *Summa Theologica*, PART I–II, Q 105, A 2, REP 4 309d-316a

21 DANTE: *Divine Comedy*, HELL, XI [91–111] 16a-b; XVII [31–75] 24a-c

24 RABELAIS: *Gargantua and Pantagruel*, BK III, 133b-140b

(9. Political justice: justice in government. 9b. Justice as the moral principle of political organization: the bond of men in states.)

20 AQUINAS: *Summa Theologica*, PART I–II, Q 100, A 2, ANS 252b-253a; Q 105, A 2, ANS 309d-316a

21 DANTE: *Divine Comedy*, PARADISE, XVIII [52]–XX [148] 134a-138b

23 HOBBES: *Leviathan*, PART I, 91a-92b

27 SHAKESPEARE: *Troilus and Cressida*, ACT I, SC III [98–124] 109a-b

31 SPINOZA: *Ethics*, PART IV, APPENDIX, XV–XVI 448c-d

35 LOCKE: *Toleration*, 3a / *Civil Government*, CH II, SECT 13 28a-b; CH VII, SECT 90–94 44d-46c; CH XI, SECT 135–139 55d-58a; CH XIX, SECT 219 75b-c / *Human Understanding*, BK I, CH II, SECT 2 104a-b

38 ROUSSEAU: *Political Economy*, 369a-b / *Social Contract*, BK II, 396d-398b

43 FEDERALIST: NUMBER 51, 164c-d

43 MILL: *Liberty*, 302d-303a / *Representative Government*, 422b / *Utilitarianism*, 460a-461c; 464d-476a,c passim, esp 470a-471b, 473d-474b

46 HEGEL: *Philosophy of Right*, ADDITIONS, 141 139c; 155 142a-b; 160 142d-143a / *Philosophy of History*, PART II, 272a-d; PART IV, 321a; 334b-c

54 FREUD: *Group Psychology*, 685c-686c / *Civilization and Its Discontents*, 780b-781a

9c. The criteria of justice in various forms of government and diverse constitutions

6 HERODOTUS: *History*, BK II, 107c-108c

6 THUCYDIDES: *Peloponnesian War*, BK III, 396c-d

7 PLATO: *Republic*, BK VIII, 401d-416a / *Statesman*, 598b-604b / *Laws*, BK III, 670c-671a; 672c-676c; BK IV, 681d-682c

9 ARISTOTLE: *Ethics*, BK V, CH 3 [1131^{a}24–29] 378d; CH 7 [1134^{b}36–1135^{b}4] 382a-383c; BK VIII, CH II 413b-d / *Politics*, BK III, CH 6 475d-476c esp [1279^{a}17–22] 476c; CH 9–13 477c-483a; CH 15–17 484b-487a; BK IV, CH I [1289^{a}13–20] 488a; BK V, CH I [1301^{a}25–39] 502b-c; CH 9 [1310^{a}25–36] 512c; BK VI, CH 2 520d-521b esp [1317^{a}40–^{b}16] 520d, [1318^{a}4–10] 521b; CH 3 521c-522a; BK VII, CH 14 537b-538d esp [1333^{b}13–1334^{a}10] 538b-d

14 PLUTARCH: *Lycurgus*, 46c

20 AQUINAS: *Summa Theologica*, PART I–II, Q 95, A 4, ANS 229b-230c; Q 100, A 2, ANS 252b-253a; Q 105, A 1 307d-309d

38 MONTESQUIEU: *Spirit of Laws*, BK III, 12b-13c; BK VI, 33a-35a

38 ROUSSEAU: *Political Economy*, 369a-d / *Social Contract*, BK II, 405a-406a

40 GIBBON: *Decline and Fall*, 616d-617d passim

41 GIBBON: *Decline and Fall*, 94c-95c; 403b; 575d-577b

42 KANT: *Science of Right*, 450a-d

43 MILL: *Representative Government*, 343b-344d; 350b-355b

46 HEGEL: *Philosophy of History*, PART II, 271d-272d

50 MARX-ENGELS: *Communist Manifesto*, 428d-429c

9d. The relation of ruler and ruled: the justice of the prince or statesman and of the subject or citizen

OLD TESTAMENT: *Exodus*, 22:28 / *I Samuel*, 8:10-20—(D) *I Kings*, 8:10-20 / *II Samuel*, 23:3—(D) *II Kings*, 23:3 / *II Chronicles*, 1:7-12—(D) *II Paralipomenon*, 1:7-12 / *Proverbs*, 16:12; 17:7; 20:28; 24:21; 28:15-16; 29:14 / *Ecclesiastes*, 10:20 / *Isaiah*, 3:14—(D) *Isaias*, 3:14

NEW TESTAMENT: *Matthew*, 22:16-22 / *Acts*, 23:5 / *Romans*, 13:1-7 / *Titus*, 3:1

5 AESCHYLUS: *Suppliant Maidens* [365–401] 5c-6a

5 SOPHOCLES: *Antigone* [162–210] 132c-d; [631–765] 136c-137d

5 EURIPIDES: *Suppliants* [342–358] 261b-c / *Helen* [1627–1641] 313c-d

6 HERODOTUS: *History*, BK II, 84b-c; BK III, 107c-d; 120b-c; BK VII, 223c-d; 245b

7 PLATO: *Republic*, BK I, 301b-306b; BK IV, 346a-350a / *Laws*, BK I, 642d-643b; BK III, 670c-671a; 672c-676c; BK IV, 681b-682c; BK VIII, 733d-734a / *Seventh Letter*, 806d-807b; 814b-c

9 ARISTOTLE: *Ethics*, BK V, CH I [1130^{a}1–5] 377b; CH 6 [1134^{a}25–^{b}17] 382a-c; CH II [1138^{a}4–13] 386b-c; [1138^{b}5–13] 387a,c; BK VIII, CH II 413b-d / *Politics*, BK I, CH 12–13 453d-455a,c; BK III, CH 4 [1277^{b}16–20] 474d; CH 6 475d-476c esp [1278^{b}30–1279^{a}22] 476a-c; CH 10 478d-479a; CH 13 481b-483a; BK VII, CH 14 [1332^{b}13–1333^{a}16] 537b-538a

12 EPICTETUS: *Discourses*, BK III, CH 7 182b-184a

12 AURELIUS: *Meditations*, BK VI, SECT 30 276d-277a

13 VIRGIL: *Aeneid*, BK VI [847–853] 233b-234a

14 PLUTARCH: *Lycurgus*, 48a / *Numa Pompilius*, 59d-60b / *Lycurgus-Numa*, 61b,d-62c / *Aristides* 262b,d-276a,c esp 263d-266b, 273d-275c / *Agesilaus*, 490d-491b; 494a-c / *Agesilaus-Pompey*, 539a / *Alexander*, 566a-b / *Phocion*, 604b,d-605d / *Cato the Younger* 620a-648a,c esp 636d-637c / *Demetrius*, 742c-743b / *Dion*, 784d-785a; 798b-d

15 TACITUS: *Histories*, BK IV, 290a-d

18 AUGUSTINE: *City of God*, BK XIV, CH 28 397a-d; BK XIX, CH 15–16 521a-522a; CH 21 524a-525a

19 AQUINAS: *Summa Theologica*, PART I, Q 96 510a-513c

20 AQUINAS: *Summa Theologica*, PART I–II, Q 105, AA 1–3 307d-318b

9e. The just distribution of honors, ranks, offices, suffrage

51 TOLSTOY: *War and Peace*, BK IX, 346a-355c; BK X, 442c-443b; BK XII, 547a-551c; BK XIV, 589a-c

54 FREUD: *War and Death*, 755a-757d esp 757b-c; 761a-c

9g. The tempering of political justice by clemency: amnesty, asylum, and pardon

OLD TESTAMENT: *Numbers*, 35:6,11–15,28–33 / *Deuteronomy*, 4:41–43; 19:1–13 / *Joshua*, 21— (D) *Josue*, 21

5 ARISTOPHANES: *Frogs* [686–705] 572a-b

6 HERODOTUS: *History*, BK I, 20b-d; 36b-c; BK II, 71b-72a; BK VI, 212a-c; BK VII, 251a-b

6 THUCYDIDES: *Peloponnesian War*, BK III, 424d-429a; 433d-434a; BK IV, 451d

12 EPICTETUS: *Discourses*, BK IV, CH 5 228a-230b

13 VIRGIL: *Aeneid*, BK XI [100–111] 330b-331a

14 PLUTARCH: *Lycurgus*, 37b-c / *Solon*, 68a / *Aristides*, 275c / *Agesilaus*, 494a-c / *Pompey*, 503a-d / *Caesar*, 599a-b / *Dion*, 798b-d

15 TACITUS: *Annals*, BK II, 39b-c; BK III, 59d; BK XII, 113d-114a; BK XIV, 151d-152c / *Histories*, BK I, 208b-c

18 AUGUSTINE: *City of God*, BK I, CH 1–7 129d-133a; BK IX, CH 5 288b-289a

21 DANTE: *Divine Comedy*, PURGATORY, X [70–93] 68a-b; XV [85–114] 76b-c

22 CHAUCER: *Tale of Melibeus*, par 77–78, 431a-432a / *Parson's Tale*, par 68 533b-534a

23 HOBBES: *Leviathan*, PART I, 94a

25 MONTAIGNE: *Essays*, 3a-5a; 51a-53c

26 SHAKESPEARE: *Merchant of Venice*, ACT IV, SC I [182–205] 427c-d / *1st Henry IV*, ACT V, SC V 466a-d / *Henry V*, ACT II, SC II [39–83] 539c-540a

27 SHAKESPEARE: *Measure for Measure*, ACT II, SC II [25–162] 182b-183d / *Cymbeline*, ACT V, SC V [286–422] 486c-488d

29 CERVANTES: *Don Quixote*, PART I, 71b-d; 108c-109b; 177a-b; PART II, 332d-333b

30 BACON: *New Atlantis*, 205a

35 LOCKE: *Civil Government*, CH XIV, SECT 159 62b-c

38 MONTESQUIEU: *Spirit of Laws*, BK VI, 36a-b; 43c-d; BK XXV, 209b-d; BK XXIX, 264b-c

40 GIBBON: *Decline and Fall*, 176a; 302d; 449d-451a

42 KANT: *Science of Right*, 449c

43 CONSTITUTION OF THE U.S.: ARTICLE II, SECT 2 [417–420] 15a

43 FEDERALIST: NUMBER 69, 208c-d; NUMBER 74, 221d-222d

44 BOSWELL: *Johnson*, 335c; 344a-b

46 HEGEL: *Philosophy of Right*, PART III, par 282 95d-96a; ADDITIONS, 74 127d-128a; 173 146d

51 TOLSTOY: *War and Peace*, BK V, 230b-232a; BK XII, 548d-549b

52 DOSTOEVSKY: *Brothers Karamazov*, BK XII, 398a-d

10. Justice and law

4 HOMER: *Iliad*, BK XVIII [497–508] 135b

7 PLATO: *Gorgias*, 261b-d / *Republic*, BK II, 311b-c / *Laws*, BK IV, 681b-683d; BK IX 743a-757d

9 ARISTOTLE: *Ethics*, BK V, CH I [1129^{b}12–24] 377a; CH 6 [1134^{a}25–^{b}8] 382a-b; CH 7 382c-383a / *Politics*, BK III, CH 16 [1287^{a}10–^{b}25] 485c-486b / *Rhetoric*, BK I, CH I [1354^{a}16–1355^{a}3] 593b-594a

13 VIRGIL: *Aeneid*, BK I [507–508] 117a; BK VI [847–853] 233b-234a

14 PLUTARCH: *Lycurgus-Numa* 61b,d-64a,c / *Solon*, 66a-b

18 AUGUSTINE: *Confessions*, BK III, par 13–17 16c-18a / *City of God*, BK II, CH 21 161b-162d; BK XIX, CH 21 524a-525a; CH 24 528b-c / *Christian Doctrine*, BK IV, CH 18 686d-687d

19 AQUINAS: *Summa Theologica*, PART I, Q 21, A 2 125c-d

20 AQUINAS: *Summa Theologica*, PART I-II, Q 91, A 5, ANS 211c-212c; Q 94, A 4 223d-224d; Q 95, AA 1–3 226b-229b esp A 1, REP 2–3 226c-227c; Q 100, A 2, ANS 252b-253a

23 HOBBES: *Leviathan*, PART I, 86b; PART II, 131a-c; 157b

33 PASCAL: *Pensées*, 291–338 225a-233a

35 LOCKE: *Civil Government*, CH IX 53c-54d; CH XVIII 71a-73c passim

38 MONTESQUIEU: *Spirit of Laws*, BK I, 1c-d; BK XXVI 214b,d-225a,c passim

38 ROUSSEAU: *Political Economy*, 370b-371c / *Social Contract*, BK II, 399b-400c

41 GIBBON: *Decline and Fall*, 96a-d

42 KANT: *Intro. Metaphysic of Morals*, 392a / *Science of Right*, 400b-d; 432c-433a

43 FEDERALIST: NUMBER 10, 50d-51b

43 MILL: *Utilitarianism*, 465c-466b; 467c-468a

46 HEGEL: *Philosophy of Right*, PART III, par 212–213 70d-71a; par 215 71c-d

51 TOLSTOY: *War and Peace*, BK XII, 553a

10a. The measure of justice in laws made by the state: natural and constitutional standards

5 EURIPIDES: *Bacchantes* [878–911] 347b-c

6 THUCYDIDES: *Peloponnesian War*, BK II, 396c-d

7 PLATO: *Protagoras*, 52b / *Gorgias*, 271b-274c / *Republic*, BK II, 316a-319b esp 318a; BK IV, 349a-350a / *Statesman*, 598b-604b / *Laws*, BK IV, 680c-683b; BK IX, 747c; BK X, 760c

8 ARISTOTLE: *Sophistical Refutations*, CH 12 [173^{a}7–19] 238b-c

9 ARISTOTLE: *Ethics*, BK V, CH I [1129^{b}12–24] 377a; CH 7 382c-383a; CH 9 [1136^{b}32–35] 385a; CH 11 [1138^{a}4–13] 386b-c / *Politics*, BK I, CH 6 [1255^{a}3–^{b}4] 448c-449a; BK III, CH 11 [1282^{b}1–14] 480b-c; CH 16 [1287^{a}28–^{b}5] 485d-

(10. *Justice and law. 10a. The measure of justice in laws made by the state: natural and constitutional standards.*)

486a; BK IV, CH I [1289ᵃ13-20] 488a / *Rhetoric*, BK I, CH 10 [1368ᵇ7-10] 611d; CH 13 [1373ᵇ1-17] 617c-d; CH 15 [1375ᵃ25-ᵇ25] 619d-620b; [1376ᵃ33-ᵇ31] 621a-c

12 AURELIUS: *Meditations*, BK IV, SECT 4 264a

18 AUGUSTINE: *Confessions*, BK III, par 15 17a-b; par 17 17d-18a / *City of God*, BK II, CH 21 161b-162d; BK XIX, CH 21 524a-525a; CH 24 528b-c / *Christian Doctrine*, BK IV, CH 18 686d-687d

20 AQUINAS: *Summa Theologica*, PART I-II, Q 91, A 3 209d-210c; Q 93, A 3 217b-218a; Q 94, A 4 223d-224d; Q 95, A 2 227c-228c; Q 96, A 4, ANS 233a-d

23 HOBBES: *Leviathan*, PART I, 91a-b; PART II, 113d; 116a-b; 131a-c; 132a-b; 134b-135b; 156b-c; 157b

25 MONTAIGNE: *Essays*, 47c-48a; 281a-283c; 384b-c; 519a-520b

30 BACON: *Advancement of Learning*, 94d-95b

32 MILTON: *Samson Agonistes* [888-902] 359a

33 PASCAL: *Pensées*, 291-338 225a-233a; 878-879 345a-b

35 LOCKE: *Toleration*, 11b-12c / *Civil Government*, CH II, SECT 12 27d-28a; CH IX 53c-54d; CH XI 55b-58b; CH XVIII 71a-73c passim; CH XIX, SECT 221-222 75d-76c; SECT 240-242 81b-d

38 MONTESQUIEU: *Spirit of Laws*, BK I, 1c-d; 3c-d; BK VI, 39b; BK VIII, 54b; BK XII, 85c-86d; BK XIX, 136a; 138a-c; BK XXVI 214b,d-225a,c passim, esp 214b,d; BK XXIX, 262a; 265d

38 ROUSSEAU: *Political Economy*, 369c-d; 370b-d / *Social Contract*, BK II, 397b-c; 399b-400c; 405a-406a; BK IV, 426b-d

39 SMITH: *Wealth of Nations*, BK I, 61b; BK II, 140b; BK IV, 228a; 232b; 284d; BK V, 397a-c

40 GIBBON: *Decline and Fall*, 525d-526c; 617a-d

41 GIBBON: *Decline and Fall*, 76d-77b; 89d-94b passim; 403b

42 KANT: *Pure Reason*, 114b-d / *Science of Right*, 429a-c; 434a; 435a-436a; 450d-452a

43 DECLARATION OF INDEPENDENCE: 1a-3b

43 CONSTITUTION OF THE U.S.: PREAMBLE 11a,c; ARTICLE I, SECT 8-10 13a-14b; ARTICLE VI [583-590] 16d; AMENDMENTS, I-X 17a-18a

43 FEDERALIST: NUMBER 33, 108b-c; NUMBER 44, 145c-147a; NUMBER 78, 230d-232d; NUMBER 81, 237d-238b

43 MILL: *Liberty*, 302d-323a,c passim / *Utilitarianism*, 465d-466b; 467c-d

44 BOSWELL: *Johnson*, 203d-204a; 205b; 363c-364a

46 HEGEL: *Philosophy of Right*, PART III, par 212-213 70d-71a; ADDITIONS, 134 138b-c / *Philosophy of History*, PART IV, 364b

10b. **The legality of unjust laws: the extent of obedience required of the just man in the unjust society**

5 SOPHOCLES: *Antigone* 131a-142d esp [43-99] 131c-132a, [441-496] 134d-135b, [631-765] 136c-137d, [891-943] 138d-139a

5 EURIPIDES: *Phoenician Maidens* [1625-1670] 392b-d

7 PLATO: *Apology* 200a-212a,c / *Crito* 213a-219a,c / *Republic*, BK VI, 379d-380b / *Laws*, BK VI, 706b-c / *Seventh Letter*, 800c-d

9 ARISTOTLE: *Politics*, BK III, CH 11 [1282ᵇ1-14] 480b-c; CH 13 [1284ᵃ3-37] 482a-c / *Rhetoric*, BK I, CH 13 [1373ᵇ1-12] 617c-d; CH 15 [1375ᵃ25-ᵇ25] 619d-620b; [1376ᵇ5-28] 621b-c

15 TACITUS: *Annals*, BK XV, 172c-173c; BK XVI, 180d-184a,c

18 AUGUSTINE: *Confessions*, BK III, par 17 17d-18a / *City of God*, BK XIX, CH 17 522b-523a

20 AQUINAS: *Summa Theologica*, PART I-II, Q 92, A I, REP 4 213c-214c; Q 93, A 3, REP 2 217b-218a; Q 94, A 6, REP 3 225d-226b; Q 95, A 2 227c-228c; A 4 229b-230c; Q 96, A 4, ANS and REP 2-3 233a-d; Q 97, A 2 236d-237b; PART II-II, Q 42, A 2, REP 3 584b-d

23 HOBBES: *Leviathan*, PART II, 102b-c; 104b-d; 112b-d; 113d-114b; 115a-116a; 134b-135b; 157b; PART III, 238b-c

25 MONTAIGNE: *Essays*, 7a-d; 47a-51a; 319a-b; 381a-388c esp 383c-d, 384d-385a, 388a-c; 463a-465c; 480b-482b; 504c-506a; 519a-520b

32 MILTON: *Samson Agonistes* [888-902] 359a

33 PASCAL: *Provincial Letters*, 114b / *Pensées*, 326 231a

35 LOCKE: *Toleration*, 16d-17b / *Civil Government*, CH XIII, SECT 155 60d-61a; CH XIV, SECT 168 64b-c; CH XVI-XIX 65d-81d

38 ROUSSEAU: *Inequality*, 366b-d / *Political Economy*, 369c-d / *Social Contract*, BK I, 388d-389a; BK IV, 426b-d

39 SMITH: *Wealth of Nations*, BK V, 397a-c

42 KANT: *Science of Right*, 439a-441d; 451d-452a

43 DECLARATION OF INDEPENDENCE: 1a-3b passim

43 FEDERALIST: NUMBER 16, 68b-c; NUMBER 28, 97c-d; NUMBER 33, 108b-109a; NUMBER 78, 230d-232d

43 MILL: *Utilitarianism*, 465d-466b

51 TOLSTOY: *War and Peace*, BK VI, 244d-245d; EPILOGUE I, 668a-669c; 670d-671a

10c. **The justice of punishment for unjust acts: the distinction between retribution and vengeance**

OLD TESTAMENT: *Genesis*, 9:6 / *Exodus*, 21:12-29 esp 21:23-25 / *Leviticus*, 24:16-21 / *Deuteronomy*, 19:11-13,21

NEW TESTAMENT: *Romans*, 13:2-4

5 AESCHYLUS: *Choephoroe* 70a-80d esp [306-314] 73a-b, [400-404] 74a / *Eumenides* 81a-91d esp [490-565] 86b-87a

5 SOPHOCLES: *Electra* 156a-169a,c

5 EURIPIDES: *Medea* 212a-224a,c esp [764–819] 218d-219b / *Electra* 327a-339a,c esp [907–1100] 335b-337a / *Orestes* [470–629] 398d-400b

6 HERODOTUS: *History*, BK III, 99c-100a; BK VII, 237d-239a; BK VIII, 278c-279a; BK IX, 306c-307a

6 THUCYDIDES: *Peloponnesian War*, BK III, 424d-429a; 429c-434c; BK VII, 556d-557a

7 PLATO: *Protagoras*, 45b-d / *Euthyphro*, 194c-d / *Republic*, BK IX, 426d / *Laws*, BK IX, 743a-d; 746a-748d; BK X, 769d-770c

9 ARISTOTLE: *Ethics*, BK III, CH 5 [1113^{b}21–1114^{a}2] 359d-360a; BK V, CH 4 379b-380b esp [1132^{a}3–30] 379c-380a; CH 5 [1132^{b}21–29] 380b-c; CH 11 [1138^{a}7–10] 386b; [1138^{a}20–23] 386c; BK X, CH 9 [1180^{a}5–13] 434d / *Rhetoric*, BK I, CH 10 [1369^{b}12–14] 612d

14 PLUTARCH: *Theseus*, 4a-b / *Solon*, 70d; 71b

18 AUGUSTINE: *City of God*, BK XII, CH 3, 344b; BK XIV, CH 15 388d-390a; BK XIX, CH 13 519a-520a; CH 15 521a-c; BK XXI, CH 11–12 570b-571c

19 AQUINAS: *Summa Theologica*, PART I, Q 19, A 9, ANS 116d-117d; Q 21, A 4, REP 3 126c-127c; Q 49, A 2, ANS 266a-c

20 AQUINAS: *Summa Theologica*, PART I-II, Q 87 185c-192d; Q 95, A 1 226c-227c; Q 105, A 2, ANS and REP 9-12 309d-316a; Q 108, A 3, REP 2 334a-336b; PART II-II, Q 25, A 6, REP 2 504d-505d; PART III SUPPL, Q 89, A 6, ANS and REP 1 1009d-1010c; A 7 1010d-1011b; A 8, ANS 1011b-1012a; Q 99 1078b-1085a,c

21 DANTE: *Divine Comedy*, PURGATORY, XIX [70–145] 82b-83a

22 CHAUCER: *Tale of Melibeus* 401a-432a esp par 55, 426b, par 63–65 428a-b

23 HOBBES: *Leviathan*, PART I, 94a; PART II, 145a-d; 147b-c; 157d-158a

25 MONTAIGNE: *Essays*, 23b-24a

26 SHAKESPEARE: *Titus Andronicus*, ACT IV, SC III–IV 189d-192b / *Merchant of Venice*, ACT IV, SC I 425c-430b / *2nd Henry IV*, ACT V, SC II [73–145] 498d-499b / *Henry V*, ACT II, SC II 539a-541a

27 SHAKESPEARE: *Measure for Measure* 174a-204d

29 CERVANTES: *Don Quixote*, PART I, 68b-73a

31 SPINOZA: *Ethics*, PART IV, PROP 51, SCHOL 439d; PROP 63, SCHOL 444a

35 LOCKE: *Civil Government*, CH II, SECT 7–12 26c-28a

36 SWIFT: *Gulliver*, PART I, 28a-b

37 FIELDING: *Tom Jones*, 27b-30a; 399c-d

38 MONTESQUIEU: *Spirit of Laws*, BK VI, 37d-43c; BK XI, 85c-86d; BK XIX, 138c

38 ROUSSEAU: *Inequality*, 351b-d; 360b,d [fn 1] / *Political Economy*, 371a-c / *Social Contract*, BK II, 398b-399a; 406c

40 GIBBON: *Decline and Fall*, 175d-176a; 617b-d

41 GIBBON: *Decline and Fall*, 91a-93c passim

42 KANT: *Practical Reason*, 306b-c / *Intro. Metaphysic of Morals*, 391d-394a,c / *Science of Right*, 400b-d; 446a-449c esp 446b-447c, 448b-d; 450a

43 CONSTITUTION OF THE U.S.: ARTICLE III, SECT 2 [493]–SECT 3 [511] 15d-16a; ARTICLE IV, SECT 2 [522–528] 16a-b; AMENDMENTS, V–VI 17b-d; VIII 17d; XIII 18c

43 MILL: *Liberty*, 272b-d; 302d-312a passim, esp 304c-305b; 312a-323a,c passim / *Utilitarianism*, 467d-468c; 469c-470d; 471d-472d; 474b-d

46 HEGEL: *Philosophy of Right*, PART I, par 96 36c-37a; par 99–100 37b-38a; par 103 39b; PART III, par 218 72c-d; par 220 73a-b; par 319, 106a; ADDITIONS, 60 125d; 62–65 126a-c; 74 127d-128a; 138 139a-b; 173 146d / *Philosophy of History*, PART I, 214d-216a

52 DOSTOEVSKY: *Brothers Karamazov*, BK II, 30b-32a; BK V, 123c-124a; BK XII, 384c-d; 398b-d

10d. The correction of legal justice: equity in the application of human law

6 HERODOTUS: *History*, BK I, 32b-c; BK VI, 211d-212a

7 PLATO: *Laws*, BK IX, 754a-d; BK XI, 777d-778b; BK XII, 785c-786a

8 ARISTOTLE: *Topics*, BK VI, CH 3 [141^{a}15–18] 194b

9 ARISTOTLE: *Ethics*, BK V, CH 10 385c-386b / *Politics*, BK III, CH 15 [1286^{a}10–37] 484b-d; CH 16 [1287^{a}23–28] 485d; [1287^{b}15–25] 486a-b / *Rhetoric*, BK I, CH 13 [1374^{a}17–^{b}24] 618c-619a; CH 15 [1375^{a}25–^{b}25] 619d-620b; [1376^{b}19–21] 621b-c

14 PLUTARCH: *Fabius*, 150c-151a / *Agesilaus*, 494a-c / *Agesilaus-Pompey*, 539a

20 AQUINAS: *Summa Theologica*, PART I-II, Q 96, A 6 235a-d; Q 97, A 4 238b-239b; Q 100, A 8, ANS and REP 1 259d-261a

23 HOBBES: *Leviathan*, PART I, 94d; PART II, 132d; 134b-135d; 136b; 142a-144d; 156b-c

25 MONTAIGNE: *Essays*, 50b-51a; 519a-c

26 SHAKESPEARE: *Merchant of Venice*, ACT IV, SC I 425c-430b

27 SHAKESPEARE: *Timon of Athens*, ACT III, SC V 406d-408a

29 CERVANTES: *Don Quixote*, PART I, 68b-73a; PART II, 333a-b; 340d-343a; 353b-356d; 361a-d

30 BACON: *Advancement of Learning*, 94d-95a

35 LOCKE: *Civil Government*, CH XIV 62b-64c

36 SWIFT: *Gulliver*, PART IV, 152b-154a

37 FIELDING: *Tom Jones*, 8c-10c; 12b-c

38 MONTESQUIEU: *Spirit of Laws*, BK VI, 35d-36a; 39b; 40a-b; 42a-c; BK XII, 85c-86d

38 ROUSSEAU: *Social Contract*, BK II, 397a-d

41 GIBBON: *Decline and Fall*, 73d-74b; 77d-78a; 91b-c

42 KANT: *Science of Right*, 399c-400a

43 FEDERALIST: NUMBER 78, 232c-d; NUMBER 80, 237a-b; NUMBER 83, 248d-249a

46 HEGEL: *Philosophy of Right*, PART III, par 223–229 73c-75b

11. Divine justice: the relation of God or the gods to man

11a. The divine government of man: the justice and mercy of God or the gods

OLD TESTAMENT: *Genesis*, 3; 6:5–8:22 esp 8:20–22; 18:20–19:29 / *Exodus*, 20 / *Leviticus*, 26 / *Numbers*, 13–14 esp 14:11–20; 25 / *Deuteronomy*, 32 / *II Samuel*, 24—(D) *II Kings*, 24 / *II Chronicles*, 6; 12—(D) *II Paralipomenon*, 6; 12 / *Nehemiah*, 9:5–38—(D) *II Esdras*, 9:5–38 / *Job*; *Psalms*, 5–7; 28; 37; 59–60; 73; 76; 81; 83; 89:14; 146—(D) *Psalms*, 5–7; 27; 36; 58–59; 72; 75; 80; 88:15; 145 / *Proverbs*, 14:32 / *Ecclesiastes*, 12:14 / *Isaiah*, 1; 30–31; 42 esp 42:1–7; 45:21–25; 59—(D) *Isaias*, 1; 30–31; 42 esp 42:1–7; 45:21–26; 59 / *Jeremiah*, 15; 24; 29–31; 34 —(D) *Jeremias*, 15; 24; 29–31; 34 / *Lamentations* / *Ezekiel*, 11; 14; 18; 33–34—(D) *Ezechiel*, 11; 14; 18; 33–34 / *Daniel*, 4:4–37 —(D) *Daniel*, 4 / *Joel*, 3 / *Amos* / *Obadiah* —(D) *Abdias* / *Jonah*—(D) *Jonas* / *Micah*, 1–3—(D) *Micheas*, 1–3 / *Nahum* / *Malachi*, 3–4—(D) *Malachias*, 3–4

APOCRYPHA: *Tobit*, 3—(D) OT, *Tobias*, 3 / *Wisdom of Solomon*, 1–6 passim; 12—(D) OT, *Book of Wisdom*, 1–6 passim; 12 / *Ecclesiasticus*, 16; 35—(D) OT, *Ecclesiasticus*, 16; 35 / *II Maccabees*, 6:12–17—(D) OT, *II Machabees*, 6:12–17

NEW TESTAMENT: *Matthew*, 5:22,29–30; 11:20–24; 12:36–37; 13:24–30,36–43; 18:7–9,11–14; 19:16–20:16; 23 / *Mark*, 9:43–48; 10:17–31; 16:16—(D) *Mark*, 9:42–47; 10:17–31; 16:16 / *Luke*, 1:46–55; 6:36–38; 7:36–50; 10:25–28; 14:7–14; 15; 16:19–26; 18:1–8; 23:34,39–43 / *John*, 5:30; 8:1–11 / *Romans*, 1:16–2:16; 6:28 / *Galatians*, 6:7–8 / *Ephesians*, 2 / *II Thessalonians*, 2:10–12—(D) *II Thessalonians*, 2:10–11 / *II Timothy*, 4:8–9—(D) *II Timothy*, 4:8 / *Hebrews*, 10:26–31 / *I Peter*, 3:18 / *II Peter*, 2 / *I John*, 1:9 / *Jude* / *Revelation* passim, esp 17–20—(D) *Apocalypse* passim, esp 17–20

4 HOMER: *Iliad*, BK XXIV [513–551] 176d-177a / *Odyssey*, BK I [11–95] 183a-184a

5 AESCHYLUS: *Suppliant Maidens* [1–175] 1a-3a / *Prometheus Bound* 40a-51d / *Agamemnon* [636–781] 58d-60b; [1560–1566] 68c / *Choephoroe* [772–780] 77c / *Eumenides* 81a-91d

5 SOPHOCLES: *Antigone* [279–289] 133c / *Ajax* 143a-155a,c esp [430–459] 146d-147a, [748–783] 149c-d / *Electra* [173–179] 157c / *Trachiniae* [1264–1278] 181c / *Philoctetes* [446–452] 186a

5 EURIPIDES: *Suppliants* [598–617] 263c-d / *Helen* [191–305] 300a-d; [711–721] 304d-305a / *Hecuba* [1023–1033] 361c-d / *Heracles Mad* [772–816] 371c-d

5 ARISTOPHANES: *Plutus* [86–92] 630a

6 HERODOTUS: *History*, BK I, 20b-22a; BK II, 77a-b; BK IV, 159d; BK VI, 199c-d; 201d-202c;

203a-b; 212c-213a; BK VII, 237d-239a; BK VIII, 278d-279a; 283d; BK IX, 308a-c

6 THUCYDIDES: *Peloponnesian War*, BK V, 506b-c; BK VII, 560a-b

7 PLATO: *Republic*, BK X, 437c-441a,c / *Theaetetus*, 530b-531a / *Laws*, BK IV, 682d-683b; BK IX, 757a; BK X 757d-771b / *Seventh Letter*, 806a

13 VIRGIL: *Aeneid*, BK I [8–33] 103a-104a; [223–296] 109a-111a; BK XII [791–843] 375a-376b

14 PLUTARCH: *Romulus*, 26b-27a / *Camillus*, 108b-c / *Aristides*, 265c-d / *Phocion*, 605b-d / *Cato the Younger*, 639d-640a / *Dion*, 784d-785a

15 TACITUS: *Histories*, BK IV, 284b-c

17 PLOTINUS: *Third Ennead*, TR II, CH 13 88d-89b

18 AUGUSTINE: *Confessions*, BK I, par 4 2a; BK II, par 15 12b-c; BK III, par 13–15 16c-17b; par 17 17d-18a; BK V, par 1–2 27a-c; BK VII, par 5 44c-d; BK IX, par 34–36 70c-71a / *City of God*, BK I, CH 21 142d-143a; BK V, CH 9–11 213b-216d; CH 15–16 220d-221b; CH 21 226a-c; BK XI, CH 23 334c-335c; BK XII, CH 3 343d-344b; BK XIII, CH 1–8 360a-363c; CH 12–16 365d-367d; CH 21 371a-c; BK XIV, CH 1 376b,d-377a; CH 15 388d-390a; BK XV, CH 24–25 418d-419b; BK XVI, CH 4 425b-426a; BK XIX, CH 11–17 516d-523a; CH 21 524a-525a; BK XX, CH 1 530a-531a; BK XXI, CH 11–12 570b-571c / *Christian Doctrine*, BK I, CH 15 628b-c; CH 32 633c-d; BK II, CH 23 648a-c

19 AQUINAS: *Summa Theologica*, PART I, Q 19, A 6, ANS and REP 1 113c-114d; A 9, ANS 116d-117d; Q 21 124b-127c; Q 22, A 2, REP 4 128d-130d; Q 65, A 2, REP 3 340b-341b; Q 96, A 3, REP 3 512a-c; Q 103, A 5, REP 2–3 531b-532b; A 8, REP 1 533d-534b; Q 105, A 6, REP 2 543b-544a; PART I-II, Q 5, A 7 642a-d; Q 21, A 4 719d-720a,c; Q 39, A 2, REP 3 790d-791b; Q 47, A 1, REP 1 819c-820b

20 AQUINAS: *Summa Theologica*, PART I-II, Q 72, A 5 115a-116b; Q 73, A 9, REP 3 126d-128a; A 10, REP 2 128a-d; Q 79, AA 3–4 158a-159c; Q 81, A 2, REP 1 164d-165c; Q 87 185c-192d; Q 91, AA 4–6 210c-213c; Q 94, A 5, REP 2 224d-225d; QQ 98–108 239b-337d; PART II-II, Q 19, A 1, REP 2 465a-d; Q 24, A 12 499c-500d; PART III SUPPL, QQ 97–99 1066a-1085a,c

21 DANTE: *Divine Comedy* esp HELL, II [1]–III [18] 2c-4b, XI 15a-16b, PURGATORY, III [103–145] 57a-c, VI [25–48] 61a-b, XVI [52–81] 77b-c, XVIII [40–75] 80b-c, XIX [115–126] 82d, XXX–XXXI 99b-102b, PARADISE, III [1]–V [87] 109b-113a, VII [19–120] 115b-116b, XVIII [52]–XX [148] 134a-138b, XXXII [37–84] 155a-c

22 CHAUCER: *Tale of Melibeus*, par 77–78, 431a-432a / *Parson's Tale* 495a-550a esp par 10 498b-502a, par 56 527b-528b, par 68 533b-534a

23 HOBBES: *Leviathan*, PART I, 88c-89a; PART II, 160c-161a; 163d-164a; PART III, 197d-198a; 240c-d; 245b-c; PART IV, 254a-b; 276d-277a

11*b*. Man's debt to God or the gods: the religious acts of piety and worship

CROSS-REFERENCES

For: Matters relevant to the conception of justice as a virtue and as it relates to the other virtues and to happiness, *see* COURAGE 4; GOOD AND EVIL 3e; HAPPINESS 5-5b; TEMPERANCE 1a; VIRTUE AND VICE 2a(1), 3b; WILL 8c; and for the theological doctrine of original justice, *see* SIN 3a.

The relation of justice and duty, *see* DUTY 7; WILL 8e.

The comparison of justice with love and friendship, *see* LOVE 3c, 4b.

Other considerations of natural rights and civil liberties, *see* LAW 4e, 7c; LIBERTY 1e-1g; SLAVERY 3d; TYRANNY 5a.

Problems of economic justice, *see* DEMOCRACY 4a(2); LABOR 7a-7b, 7c(2), 7d-7f; LIBERTY 2d; SLAVERY 4a-4c, 5a-5b; WEALTH 5e, 6d(2), 10d.

Problems of justice in government and law, *see* ARISTOCRACY 1a-1b; CONSTITUTION 5a; DEMOCRACY 4a-4a(1), 4b; HONOR 4b; LAW 5c, 6c; LIBERTY 1f; MONARCHY 1a(2), 4e(3), 5a-5b; OLIGARCHY 4, 5a; SLAVERY 5a-5b, 6d; STATE 3e; TYRANNY 1a-1b, 4b, 6; and for the special problem of the distinction between justice and equity, *see* LAW 5h; UNIVERSAL AND PARTICULAR 6c.

Justice in the relation of states to one another and in the issues of war and peace, *see* LAW 4g; STATE 9c; WAR AND PEACE 3a-3b, 11b.

The issue concerning the justice of punishment as a political instrument, *see* LAW 6e(3); PUNISHMENT 1b, 2, 4c-4d.

The justice of divine punishment and the relation of God's mercy to God's justice, *see* GOD 5i; PUNISHMENT 5e; SIN 6a-6b.

The justice involved in man's debt to God, *see* DUTY 11; GOD 3d; RELIGION 2.

ADDITIONAL READINGS

Listed below are works not included in *Great Books of the Western World*, but relevant to the idea and topics with which this chapter deals. These works are divided into two groups:

I. Works by authors represented in this collection.
II. Works by authors not represented in this collection.

For the date, place, and other facts concerning the publication of the works cited, consult the Bibliography of Additional Readings, which follows the last chapter of *The Great Ideas*.

I.

PLUTARCH. "Delays in Divine Justice," in *Moralia*
AQUINAS. *Summa Theologica*, PART II-II, QQ 57–80, 108–113, 120–122
DANTE. *On World-Government or De Monarchia*, BK I, CH 11; BK II, CH 6
F. BACON. "Of Usury," in *Essays*
SPINOZA. *Tractatus Politicus (Political Treatise)*, CH 2
HUME. *A Treatise of Human Nature*, BK III, PART II, SECT I–VI
FIELDING. *Amelia*
A. SMITH. *The Theory of Moral Sentiments*, PART II
———. *Lectures on Justice, Police, Revenue and Arms*
KANT. *Lectures on Ethics*, pp 191–253
HEGEL. *The Philosophy of Mind*, SECT II, SUB-SECT C, (BB, b, c)
DOSTOEVSKY. *The House of the Dead*
TOLSTOY. *Resurrection*

II.

CICERO. *De Finibus (On the Supreme Good)*
———. *De Officiis (On Duties)*, II (ix)
SENECA. *De Beneficiis (On Benefits)*
SAADIA GAON. *The Book of Beliefs and Opinions*, TREATISE IV–V, IX
Njalssaga
LANGLAND. *Piers Plowman*
SOTO. *Libri Decem de Justitia et Jure*
SPENSER. *The Faerie Queene*, BK V
HOOKER. *Of the Laws of Ecclesiastical Polity*
GROTIUS. *The Rights of War and Peace*
H. MORE. *An Account of Virtue (Enchiridion Ethicum)*, BK II
LEIBNITZ. *Philosophical Works*, CH 8 (*On the Notions of Right and Justice*)
VOLTAIRE. *Essay on Toleration*
———. "Equality," "Justice," "Rights," "Toleration," in *A Philosophical Dictionary*

VOLTAIRE. *The Ignorant Philosopher*, CH 32
BENTHAM. *Defence of Usury*
PAINE. *Rights of Man*
GODWIN. *An Enquiry Concerning Political Justice*
LIEBER. *Manual of Political Ethics*
WHEWELL. *The Elements of Morality*, BK II, CH 21–22; BK IV
PROUDHON. *De la justice dans la révolution et dans l'église*
BAKUNIN. *God and the State*
H. SIDGWICK. *The Methods of Ethics*, BK III, CH 5
GEORGE. *Progress and Poverty*
T. H. HUXLEY. *Methods and Results*, VIII
T. H. GREEN. *The Principles of Political Obligation*, (H,I,0)
O. W. HOLMES JR. *The Common Law*
RITCHIE. *Natural Rights*
ZOLA. *Letter to M. Félix Faure (J'accuse)*
WILLOUGHBY. *Social Justice*
VECCHIO. *The Formal Bases of Law*
CROCE. *The Philosophy of the Practical*
G. DICKINSON. *Justice and Liberty*
STAMMLER. *The Theory of Justice*
KAFKA. *The Trial*
HOBHOUSE. *The Elements of Social Justice*
HOCKING. *Present Status of the Philosophy of Law and of Rights*
J. DICKINSON. *Administrative Justice and the Supremacy of Law in the United States*
BERDYAYEV. *Christianity and the Class War*
M. R. COHEN. *Reason and Nature*, BK III, CH 4
TAWNEY. *The Acquisitive Society*
———. *Equality*
MOUNIER. *A Personalist Manifesto*
MICHEL. *Christian Social Reconstruction*
MARITAIN. *Ransoming the Time*, CH 1
———. *The Rights of Man and Natural Law*
KELSEN. *Society and Nature*

Chapter 43: KNOWLEDGE

INTRODUCTION

KNOWLEDGE, like being, is a term of comprehensive scope. Its comprehensiveness is, in a way, correlative with that of being. The only thing which cannot be an object of knowledge or opinion, which cannot be thought about in any way except negatively, is that which has no being of any sort—in short, *nothing*. Not all things may be knowable to us, but even the skeptic who severely limits or completely doubts man's power to know is usually willing to admit that things beyond man's knowledge are in themselves knowable. Everyone except Berkeley would agree that the surfaces of bodies which we cannot see are not, for that reason, in themselves invisible.

The consideration of knowledge extends, therefore, to all things knowable, to all kinds of knowers, to all the modes of knowledge, and all the methods of knowing. So extensive an array of topics exceeds the possibility of treatment in a single chapter and requires this chapter to be related to many others.

The Cross-References which follow the References indicate the other chapters which deal with particulars we cannot consider here. For example, the nature of history, science, philosophy, and theology, and their distinction from one another, are treated in the chapters devoted to those subjects. So, too, the chapters on metaphysics, mathematics, physics, mechanics, and medicine deal with the characteristics and relations of these special sciences. The psychological factors in knowing—the faculties of sense and mind, of memory and imagination, the nature of experience and reasoning—also have their own chapters. Still other chapters deal with the logical elements of knowledge, such as idea and judgment, definition, hypothesis, principle, induction, and reasoning, logic and dialectic.

THE PROGRAM which Locke sets himself in his *Essay Concerning Human Understanding* is often taken to include the basic questions about knowledge. His purpose, he tells us, is "to inquire into the original, certainty, and extent of human knowledge, together with the grounds and degrees of belief, opinion, and assent." Two other matters, not explicitly mentioned by Locke in his opening pages, assume central importance in the fourth book of his essay. One is the question about the nature of knowledge itself. The other concerns the kinds of knowledge.

It may be thought that certain questions are prior to these and all others. Is knowledge possible? Can we know anything? The man the skeptic challenges is one who thinks that knowledge is attainable and who may even claim to possess knowledge of some sort. But the issue between the skeptic and his adversaries cannot be simply formulated. Its formulation depends in part upon the meaning given knowledge and the various things with which it is sometimes contrasted, such as belief and opinion, or ignorance and error. It also depends in part on the meaning of truth and probability. It would seem, therefore, that some consideration of the nature of knowledge should precede the examination of the claims concerning knowledge which provoke skeptical denials.

The theory of knowledge is a field of many disputes. Most of the major varieties of doctrine or analysis are represented in the tradition of the great books. But the fact that knowledge involves a relationship between a knower and a known seems to go unquestioned. William James expresses this insight, perhaps more dogmatically than some would allow, in the statement that knowledge "is a thoroughgoing dualism. It supposes two elements, mind knowing and thing known . . . Neither gets out of itself or into the other, neither in any way *is* the other, neither *makes* the other. They just stand face to face in a common world, and one simply knows, or is known unto, its counterpart." This remains true even when attention is turned to the special case of knowledge about knowledge or the knower knowing himself. The mind's examination of itself simply makes the mind an object to be known as well as a knower.

This suggests a second point about the nature of knowledge which seems to be undisputed. If knowledge relates a knower to a known, then what is somehow possessed when a person claims to have knowledge, is the object known. It does not seem possible for anyone to say that he knows something without meaning that he *has* that thing *in mind*. "Some sort of signal," James writes, "must be given by the thing to the mind's brain, or the knowing will not occur—we find as a matter of fact that the mere *existence* of a thing outside the brain is not a sufficient cause for our knowing it: it must strike the brain in some way, as well as be there, to be known." What is not in any way present to or represented in the mind is not known in any of the various senses of the word "know." What the mind cannot reach to and somehow grasp cannot be known. The words which are common synonyms for knowing—"apprehending" and "comprehending"—convey this sense that knowledge somehow takes hold of and surrounds its object.

That knowledge is a kind of possession occasions the comparisons which have been made between knowledge and love. The ancients observed that likeness and union are involved in both. Plato, for example, suggests in the *Symposium* that both the knower and the lover strive to become one with their object. "Love is also a philosopher," Diotima tells Socrates, and, as "a lover of wisdom," the philosopher is also a lover.

With regard to some objects, love and knowledge are almost inseparable. To know them is to love them. But this does not hold for all objects, nor does the inseparability of knowledge and love in certain cases prevent their analytical distinction in all. Like is known by like, but unlikes attract each other. Furthermore, according to one theory of knowledge, expounded by Aquinas, the knower is satisfied to possess an image of the thing to be known. This image

provides the likeness through which knowledge occurs; and thus, Aquinas writes, "the idea of the thing understood is in the one who understands." The lover, on the other hand, is "inclined to the thing itself, as existing in itself." He seeks to be united with it directly. The nobility or baseness of the object known does not affect the knower as the character of the object loved affects the lover. This understanding of the difference between knowledge and love leads Aquinas to say that "to love God is better than to know God; but, on the contrary, to know corporeal things is better than to love them."

The principle of likeness between knower and known does not go undisputed. On the contrary, the opposite views here form one of the basic issues about the nature of knowledge. The issue is whether the thing known is actually present to the knower, existing in the mind or consciousness exactly as it exists in itself; or whether the thing is represented in the mind by a likeness of itself, through which the mind knows it. In this view, the mode of existence of the thing outside the mind is different from the way in which its representative exists in the mind.

Berkeley, at one extreme, identifies being and being known. "As to what is said of the absolute existence of unthinking things without any relation to their being perceived, that seems perfectly unintelligible," he writes. "Their *esse* is *percipi*, nor is it possible they should have any existence, out of the minds or thinking things which perceive them."

At the other extreme are those like Kant for whom the thing in itself is unknowable precisely because there can be no resemblance between the phenomenal order of objects represented under the conditions of experience and the noumenal order of the unconditioned. "All conceptions of things in themselves," he writes, "must be referred to intuitions, and with us men these can never be other than sensible, and hence can never enable us to know objects as things in themselves but only as appearances. . . . The unconditioned," he adds, "can never be found in this chain of appearances."

In between these extremes there are those who agree that things exist apart from being known without ceasing to be knowable, but who nevertheless differ with respect to whether the thing exists in reality in the same way that it exists in the mind. The several forms of idealism and realism, distinguished in the chapter on IDEA, mark the range of traditional differences in the discussion of this difficult problem.

FOR ANY THEORY of what knowledge is there is a distinction between knowledge and ignorance —between having or not having something in mind. Nor does anyone confuse ignorance and error. The mind in error claims to know that of which, in fact, it is ignorant. This, as Socrates points out in the Meno, makes it easier to teach a person aware of his ignorance than a person in error; for the latter, supposing himself to know, resists the teacher. Hence getting a person to acknowledge ignorance is often the indispensable first step in teaching.

But though the difference between knowledge and ignorance and that between ignorance and error seems to be commonly understood, it does not follow that everybody similarly agrees upon the difference between knowledge and error. This much is agreed, that to know is to possess the truth about something, whereas to err is to be deceived by falsity mistaken for truth. The disagreement of the philosophers begins, however, when the meaning of truth and falsity is examined.

Truth is one thing for those who insist upon some similarity between the thing known and that by which it is known or represented in the mind. It is another for those who think that knowledge can be gained without the mediation of images or representations. In the first case, truth will consist in some kind of correspondence between what the mind thinks or understands and the reality it tries to know. In the other, truth will be equivalent to consistency among the mind's own ideas.

The examination of this fundamental disagreement is reserved for the chapter on TRUTH. Here the identification of knowing with having the truth calls for the consideration of another distinction, first made by Plato. In his language, as in that of Aristotle and others, it is the difference between knowledge and opinion. Sometimes, as with Locke, a similar distinction is made in terms of knowledge and judgment; sometimes it is made in terms of knowledge and belief; sometimes in terms of adequate and inadequate, or certain and probable, knowledge.

The difference between these opposites, unlike that between knowledge and error, is not a matter of truth and falsity. There is such a thing as "right opinion," according to Socrates, and it is "not less useful than knowledge." Considering the truth so far as it affects action, Socrates claims that the man with right opinion "will be just as good a guide if he thinks the truth, as he who knows the truth." The difference between right opinion and knowledge is here expressed by the contrast between the words "thinks" and "knows." It does not consist in the truth of the conclusion, but in the way that conclusion has been reached or is held by the mind.

The trouble with right opinion as compared with knowledge, Socrates explains, is that it lacks stability and permanence. Right opinions are useful "while they abide with us ... but they run away out of the human soul and do not remain long, and therefore they are not of much value until they are fastened by the tie of the cause"—or, in other words, until they are fixed in the mind by the reasons on which they are grounded. "When they are bound," Socrates declares, "they have the nature of knowledge and ... they are abiding."

At this point in his conversation with Meno, Socrates makes the unusual confession that "there are not many things which I profess to know, but this is most certainly one of them," namely, that "knowledge differs from true opinion." It may be that Socrates claims to know so little because he regards knowledge as involving so much more than simply having the truth, as the man of right opinion has it. In addition to having the truth, knowledge consists in seeing the reason why it is true.

This criterion can be interpreted to mean that a proposition which is neither self-evident nor demonstrated expresses opinion rather than knowledge. Even when it happens to be true, the opinion is qualified by some degree of doubt or some estimate of probability and counterprobability. In contrast, when the mind has adequate grounds for its judgment, when it knows that it knows and why, it has the certainty of knowledge.

For some writers, such as Plato, certitude is as inseparable from knowledge as truth is. To speak of "a false knowledge as well as a true" seems to him impossible; and "uncertain knowledge" is as self-contradictory a phrase as "false knowledge."

Others use the word "knowledge" more loosely to cover both adequate and inadequate knowledge, the probable as well as the certain. They make a distinction within the sphere of knowledge that is equivalent to the distinction between knowledge and opinion.

Spinoza, for example, distinguishes three kinds of knowledge. He groups the perception of individual things through the bodily senses, which he calls "knowledge from vague experience," with knowledge "from signs" which depends on ideas formed by the memory and imagination. "These two ways of looking at things," he writes, "I shall hereafter call knowledge of the first kind—opinion or imagination." In contrast, that which is derived "from our possessing common notions and adequate ideas of the properties of things," he calls "reason and knowledge of the second kind."

The third kind, which he calls "intuitive science," is that sort of knowing which "advances from an adequate idea of certain attributes of God to the adequate knowledge of the essence of things." Knowledge of the second and third kinds, he maintains, "is necessarily true." That there can be falsity in the first kind, and only there, indicates that it is not genuinely knowledge at all, but what other writers would insist upon calling "opinion."

The several meanings of the word "belief" are determined by these distinctions. Sometimes belief is associated with opinion, sometimes with knowledge, and sometimes it is regarded as an intermediate state of mind. But in any of these meanings belief stands in contrast to make-believe, and this contrast has a bearing on knowledge and opinion as well. To know or to opine puts the mind in some relation to the real or actual rather than the merely possible, and subjects it to the criteria of truth and falsity. The fanciful or imaginary belongs to the realm of the possible (or even the impossible) and the mind in imagining is fancy-free—free from the restraints and restrictions of truth and reality.

SKEPTICISM in its most extreme form takes the position that there is nothing true or false. But even those who, like Montaigne, deny certitude with respect to everything except matters of religious faith, do not go this far.

In his *Apology for Raimond de Sebonde* he concedes that if opinions are weighed as more or less probable, their truth or falsity is implied —at least as being the limit which an increasing probability or improbability approaches. Referring to ancient skeptics of the Academic school, he comments on the fact that they acknowledged "some things to be more likely than others"—as, for example, that snow is white rather than black. The more extreme skeptics, the Pyrrhonians, he points out, were bolder and also more consistent. They refused to incline toward one proposition more than toward another, for to do so, Montaigne declares, is to recognize "some more apparent truth in this than in that." How can men "suffer themselves," he asks, "to incline to and be swayed by probability, if they know not the truth itself? How should they know the similitude of that whereof they do not know the essence?"

In this respect Montaigne's own skepticism tends to be of the more moderate variety, since, in the realm of action at least, he would admit the need for judgments of probability. But in all other respects, he takes a firm skeptical stand that nothing is self-evident, nothing has been proved. The contradictory of everything has been asserted or argued by someone. "Men can have no principles," he writes, "if not revealed to them by the Divinity; of all the rest, the beginning, the middle, and the end are nothing but dream and vapor.... Every human presupposition and every declaration has as much authority, one as another. . . . The persuasion of certainty is a certain testimony of folly and extreme uncertainty."

The skeptical extreme is represented in the great books only through references to it for the purpose of refutation. Aristotle in the *Metaphysics*, for example, reports the position of those who say that all propositions are true or that all propositions are false, and who therefore deny the principle of contradiction and with it the distinction between true and false. But if all propositions are true, then the proposition "Some propositions are false" is also true; if all propositions are false, the proposition "All propositions are false" is also false. The skeptic may reply, of course, that he is not checked by arguments which try to make him contradict himself, for he does not mind contradicting himself. To this there is only one answer, which is not to argue with the skeptic any further.

From the skeptic's point of view his position is irrefutable so long as he does not allow himself to accept any of the standards by which refutation can be effected. From his opponent's point of view complete skepticism is self-refuting because if the skeptic says anything definite at all, he appears to have some knowledge or at least to hold one opinion in preference to another. His only choice is to remain silent. If he insists upon making statements in defiance of self-contradiction, his opponent can do nothing but walk away.

"It may seem a very extravagant attempt of the skeptics to destroy *reason* by argument and ratiocination," Hume writes, "yet this is the grand scope of all their enquiries and disputes." He has in mind the excessive skepticism, or *Pyrrhonism*, from which he tries to distinguish a mitigated and beneficial form of skepticism. Referring to Berkeley's arguments against the independent reality of matter or bodies, Hume says their effect is skeptical, despite Berkeley's professed intention to the contrary. That his arguments are skeptical "appears from this, *that they admit of no answer and produce no conviction*. Their only effect is to cause that momentary amazement and irresolution and confusion, which is the result of skepticism."

Here and elsewhere, as in his comment on Descartes' skeptical method of doubting everything which can be doubted, Hume does not seem to think that excessive skepticism is refutable or even false. But it is impractical. "The great subverter of *Pyrrhonism* or the excessive principles of skepticism," he says, "is action, and employment, and the occupations of life." Extreme skepticism becomes untenable in thought the moment thought must face the choices of life and take some responsibility for action.

There is, however, "a more *mitigated* skepticism or *academical* philosophy which may be both durable and useful." This, according to Hume, consists in becoming "sensible of the strange infirmities of human understanding," and consequently in "the limitation of our enquiries to such subjects as are best adapted to the narrow capacity of human understanding."

His own view of the extent and certainty of human knowledge seems to him to exemplify such mitigated skepticism in operation. The only objects with respect to which demonstration is possible are quantity and number. Mathematics has the certitude of knowledge, but it deals only with relations between ideas, not with what Hume calls "matters of fact and existence." Such matters "are evidently incapable of demonstration." This is the sphere of "moral certainty," which is not a genuine certainty, but only a degree of probability *sufficient for action*. Probabilities are the best that experimental reasoning or inquiry about matters of fact can achieve. If probability is characteristic of opinion rather than knowledge, then we can have nothing better than opinion concerning real existences.

THE DIAMETRICAL opposite to the extreme of skepticism would have to be a dogmatism which placed no objects beyond the reach of human knowledge, which made no distinction between degrees of knowability and admitted equal certitude in all matters. Like excessive skepticism this extreme is not a position actually held in the great books. All the great thinkers who have considered the problem of human knowledge have set limits to man's capacity for knowledge. They have placed certain objects beyond man's power to apprehend at all, or have distinguished between those which he can apprehend in some inadequate fashion, but cannot comprehend. They have indicated other objects concerning which his grasp is adequate and certain.

They all adopt a "mitigated skepticism"—to use Hume's phrase—if this can be taken to mean avoiding the extremes of saying that nothing is knowable at all and that everything is equally knowable. But they differ in the criteria they employ to set the limits of knowledge and to distinguish between the areas of certainty and probability. Consequently they differ in their determination of the knowability of certain types of objects, such as God or the infinite, substance or cause, matter or spirit, the real or the ideal, the self or the thing in itself.

For example, Plato and Aristotle agree that knowledge must be separated from opinion and even appeal to certain common principles in making that separation; but they do not define the scope of knowledge in the same way, as is indicated by their disagreement about the knowability of sensible things. Nor do Descartes and Locke, Bacon and Spinoza, Hume and Kant agree about the knowability of God or of the soul or about the conditions any object must meet in order to be knowable. All alike proceed from a desire to be critical. Each criticizes what other men have proposed as knowledge and each proposes a new method by which the pursuit of knowledge will be safeguarded from illusory hopes or endless controversy.

In this last respect the moderns depart most radically from their mediaeval and ancient predecessors. At all times men have been interested in examining knowledge itself as well as in exercising their powers to know. But in the earlier phase of the tradition knowledge about knowledge does not seem to take precedence over all other inquiries or to be prerequisite to them. On the contrary, the ancients proceed as if the study of knowledge necessarily presupposed the existence of knowledge. With them the examination takes place because the mind is essentially reflexive rather than for reasons of self-criticism. But beginning with Descartes' *Discourse on the Method*, in which a method of universal doubt is proposed to clear the ground before the foundations of the sciences can be laid, the consideration of knowing is put before any attempt to know.

Sometimes, as with Descartes and Bacon, the emphasis is upon a new method which will at last establish knowledge on a firm footing or advance learning. Sometimes, as with Locke and Hume, attention is given first of all to the faculty of understanding itself.

"If we can find out," says Locke, "how far the understanding can extend its views, how far it has faculties to attain certainty, and in what cases it can only judge and guess, we may learn to content ourselves with what is attainable by us in this state. . . . When we know our own strength, we shall the better know what to undertake with hopes of success; and when we have well surveyed the powers of our own minds, and made some estimate of what we may expect from them, we shall not be inclined either to sit still, and not set our thoughts to work at all, in despair of knowing anything; nor, on the other side, question everything, and disclaim all knowledge, because some things are not to be understood."

Hume also proposes that a study of human understanding precede everything else, to "show from an exact analysis of its powers and capacity" what subjects it is or is not fitted to investigate. "There is a truth and falsehood in all propositions on this subject which lie not beyond the compass of human understanding." No one can doubt that a science of the mind—or knowledge about knowing—is possible unless he entertains "such a skepticism as is entirely subversive of all speculations, and even action."

Disagreeing with the principles of Locke and Hume, as well as with their conclusions, Kant does approve the priority they give to the question of the possibility of knowing certain objects. To proceed otherwise, as Kant charges most other philosophers with doing, is dogmatism. The use of the word "critique" in the title of Kant's three major works signifies his intention to construct a critical philosophy which does not presume that "it is possible to achieve anything in metaphysic without a previous criticism of pure reason." He does not object to what he calls "the dogmatical procedure of reason" in the development of science, but only after reason's self-criticism has determined just how far reason can go. For Kant, as for Bacon, dogmatism and skepticism are the opposite excesses which only a critical method can avoid.

THESE TWO different approaches to the theory of knowledge seem to result in different conclusions concerning the nature and scope of human knowledge. Those who begin with the established sciences and merely inquire into their foundations and methods, appear to end with unqualified confidence in man's ability to know. Those who make the inquiry into the foundations and methods of science a necessary preparation for the development of the sciences, tend for the most part to set narrower boundaries to the area of valid knowledge. The two approaches also affect the way in which the various kinds of knowledge are distinguished and compared.

There are two sorts of comparison involved

in the classification of kinds of knowledge. One is a comparison of human knowledge with divine, or with angelic knowledge and the knowledge of brute animals. The other is a comparison of the parts or modes of human knowledge according to such criteria as the objects to be known, the faculties engaged in the process of knowing, and the manner of their operation. Though made separately, those two comparisons are seldom independent of one another. As the nature of man is conceived in relation to other beings, superior or inferior to himself, his faculties will be rated accordingly, and his power as a knower will suggest the methods or means available to him for knowing.

Aquinas, for example, attributes to man the kind of knowledge appropriate to his station in the hierarchy of beings. Man is superior to the brutes because he has a faculty of reason in addition to the faculties of sense and imagination which he shares with them. Man is inferior to purely spiritual beings—the angels and God—because, since he is corporeal, his intellect cannot function independently of his bodily senses and imagination. Unlike the angels and God, he is not a purely intellectual being.

Accordingly, the essential characteristics of human knowledge are, first, that it is always both sensitive and intellectual, never merely sense-perception as with the brutes or pure intellectual intuition as with the angels; second, that its appropriate object is the physical world of sensible, material things, with respect to which the senses enable man to know the existence of individuals, while the intellect apprehends their universal natures; and, finally, that the way in which the human mind knows the natures of things is abstractive and discursive, for the intellect draws its concepts from sense and imagination and proceeds therefrom by means of judgment and reasoning.

This analysis denies innate ideas. It denies man's power to apprehend ideas intuitively or to use them intuitively in the apprehension of things. It can find no place for a distinction between a priori and a posteriori knowledge, since sense-perception and rational activity contribute elements to every act of knowing. It affirms that knowledge is primarily of real existence, not of the relations between ideas; but it does not limit human knowledge to the changing temporal things of the material universe. Though these are the objects man is able to know with greatest adequacy, he can also know something of the existence and nature of immaterial and eternal beings.

Yet, according to Aquinas, even when man's knowledge rises above the realm of experienceable things, it is obtained by the same natural processes and involves the cooperation of the senses with reason. The theologian does, however, distinguish sharply between knowledge gained through man's own efforts and knowledge received through divine revelation. In addition to all knowledge acquired by the natural exercise of his faculties, man may be elevated by the supernatural gift of knowledge—the wisdom of a faith surpassing reason.

The foregoing summary illustrates, in the case of one great doctrine, the connection between an analysis of the kinds of knowledge and a theory of the nature and faculties of man in relation to all other things. There is no point in this analysis which is not disputed by someone —by Plato or Augustine, Descartes, Spinoza, or Locke, by Hume, Kant, or William James. There are many points on which others agree— not only Aristotle and Bacon, but even Augustine, Descartes, and Locke.

These agreements or disagreements about the kinds of knowledge, or the scope of human knowledge, its faculties, and its methods, seldom occur or are intelligible except in the wider context of agreements and disagreements in theology and metaphysics, psychology and logic. Hence most of the matters considered under the heading "kinds of knowledge" receive special consideration in other chapters. The Cross-References should enable the reader to examine the presuppositions or context of the materials assembled here.

THE CULT OF IGNORANCE receives little or no attention in the tradition of the great books. Even those who, like Rousseau, glorify the innocence of the primitives, or who satirize the folly so often admixed with human wisdom and the foibles attending the advance of learning, do not seriously question the ancient saying that all men by nature desire to know. Nor is it generally doubted that knowledge is good; that its possession contributes to the happiness of men and the welfare of the state; that its pursuit by the individual and its dissemination in a society should be facilitated by education, by the support and freedom of scholars and scientists, and by every device which can assist men in communicating what they know to one another.

But knowledge is not valued by all for the same reason. That knowledge is useful to the productive artist, to the statesman, to the legislator, and to the individual in the conduct of his life, seems to be assumed in discussions of the applications of science in the various arts, in the consideration of statecraft, and in the analysis of virtue. In this last connection, the problem is not whether knowledge is morally useful, but whether knowledge of good and evil is identical with virtue so that sin and vice result from error or ignorance.

If there is a negative opinion here, it consists in saying that knowledge is not enough. To know is not to do. Something more than knowledge is required for acting well.

The more radical dispute about the value of knowledge concerns the goodness of knowledge for its own sake, without any regard to its technical or moral utility. Is the contemplation of the truth an ultimate end, or does the goodness of knowledge always consist in its power to effect results in the mastery of nature and the guidance of conduct? The utility of knowledge is seldom denied by those who make speculative wisdom and theoretic science good in themselves, even the highest goods, quite apart from any use to which they may be put. The contrary position, however, does not admit the special value of contemplation or the separation of truth from utility. To those who say that "the contemplation of truth is more dignified and exalted than any utility or extent of effects," Francis Bacon replies that "truth and utility are perfectly identical, and the effects are more of value as pledges of truth than from the benefit they confer on men."

How knowledge and action are related is one question; how knowledge itself is divided into the speculative and practical is quite another. Bacon, for example, insists upon the necessity of distinguishing the speculative and practical branches of natural philosophy—concerned with "the search after causes and the production of effects." Unlike Aristotle and Kant he does not use the word "practical" for the kind of knowledge which is contained in such sciences as ethics or politics, but only for the applied sciences or technology. Ethics and politics fall under what he calls "civil philosophy."

Despite these differences in language, the way in which Bacon divides the whole sphere of knowledge closely resembles Aristotle's tripartite classification of the sciences as theoretic, productive (or technical), and practical (or moral); and, no less, a similar threefold division by Kant. But Kant and Aristotle (and, it should be added, Aquinas) give a more elaborate analysis of these three types of knowledge, especially with regard to the principles appropriate to each, the nature of the judgments and reasoning by which they are developed, and the character and criteria of their truth.

OUTLINE OF TOPICS

REFERENCES

To find the passages cited, use the numbers in heavy type, which are the volume and page numbers of the passages referred to. For example, in 4 HOMER: *Iliad*, BK II [265–283] 12d, the number 4 is the number of the volume in the set; the number 12d indicates that the passage is in section d of page 12.

PAGE SECTIONS: When the text is printed in one column, the letters a and b refer to the upper and lower halves of the page. For example, in 53 JAMES: *Psychology*, 116a–119b, the passage begins in the upper half of page 116 and ends in the lower half of page 119. When the text is printed in two columns, the letters a and b refer to the upper and lower halves of the left-hand side of the page, the letters c and d to the upper and lower halves of the right-hand side of the page. For example, in 7 PLATO: *Symposium*, 163b–164c, the passage begins in the lower half of the left-hand side of page 163 and ends in the upper half of the right-hand side of page 164.

AUTHOR'S DIVISIONS: One or more of the main divisions of a work (such as PART, BK, CH, SECT) are sometimes included in the reference; line numbers, in brackets, are given in certain cases; *e.g.*, *Iliad*, BK II [265–283] 12d.

BIBLE REFERENCES: The references are to book, chapter, and verse. When the King James and Douay versions differ in title of books or in the numbering of chapters or verses, the King James version is cited first and the Douay, indicated by a (D), follows; *e.g.*, OLD TESTAMENT: *Nehemiah*, 7:45—(D) II *Esdras*, 7:46.

SYMBOLS: The abbreviation "esp" calls the reader's attention to one or more especially relevant parts of a whole reference; "passim" signifies that the topic is discussed intermittently rather than continuously in the work or passage cited.

For additional information concerning the style of the references, see the Explanation of Reference Style; for general guidance in the use of *The Great Ideas*, consult the Preface.

1. The nature of knowledge: the relation between knower and known; the issue concerning the representative or intentional character of knowledge

7 PLATO: *Cratylus*, 113c–114a,c / *Phaedrus*, 124c–126c esp 126a–c / *Meno*, 179d–183a esp 180a–b, 182c–183a; 188d–189b / *Phaedo*, 228a–230d; 231b–232b / *Republic*, BK III, 333b–d; BK V, 371b–373c; BK VI–VII, 383d–398c esp BK VII, 397a–398c / *Timaeus*, 476b / *Theaetetus*, 515d–517b; 521d–522b; 538d–541a / *Seventh Letter*, 809c–810d

8 ARISTOTLE: *Categories*, CH 7 [6ᵇ1–6] 11a; [7ᵇ22–8ᵃ12] 12c–13a; CH 8 [11ᵃ20–39] 16b–c / *Interpretation*, CH 1 [16ᵃ4–9] 25a / *Topics*, BK IV, CH 1 [121ᵃ1–6] 168d; CH 4 [124ᵇ15–19] 173c; [124ᵇ27–34] 173c–d; BK VI, CH 5 [143ᵃ9–12] 196c; CH 6 [145ᵃ12–18] 198d; CH 8 [146ᵃ37–ᵇ9] 200b–c; CH 12 [149ᵇ3–23] 203d–204a / *Physics*, BK VII, CH 3 [247ᵇ1–248ᵃ6] 330b–d / *Metaphysics*, BK V, CH 15 [1021ᵃ27–ᵇ3] 542c–d; BK IX, CH 6 [1048ᵇ18–34] 574a–c; BK X, CH 1 [1053ᵃ32–ᵇ3] 580a; BK XII, CH 7 [1072ᵇ14–29] 602d–603a; CH 9 605a–d; BK XIII, CH 10 [1087ᵃ10–25] 619c / *Soul*, BK I, CH 5 [409ᵇ18–411ᵃ7] 639c–641a; BK II, CH 2 [414ᵃ4–14] 644a–b; CH 5 [416ᵇ32–417ᵃ2] 647b;

[417ᵃ17–21] 647d; [418ᵃ2–6] 648c–d; BK III, CH 2 [425ᵇ17–26] 657d–658a; CH 3 [427ᵃ16–ᵇ6] 659c–d; CH 4 661b–662c; CH 5 [430ᵃ14–16] 662c; [430ᵃ20–22] 662d; CH 7 [431ᵃ1–8] 663c; CH 8 664b–d / *Memory and Reminiscence*, CH 1 [450ᵃ25–451ᵃ19] 691a–692b

9 ARISTOTLE: *Ethics*, BK VI, CH 1 [1139ᵃ6–11] 387c

12 LUCRETIUS: *Nature of Things*, BK IV [26–109] 44b–45c; [722–817] 53d–54d

17 PLOTINUS: *First Ennead*, TR I, CH 7 3d–4a / *Third Ennead*, TR VIII, CH 6, 132a; CH 8, 132d–133b; CH 9, 134a–b / *Fifth Ennead*, TR I, CH 4, 210b–c; TR III, CH 4–5 217b–218c; CH 10–13 221b–224b; TR V, CH 1–2 228b–229d; TR IX, CH 7 249b–c / *Sixth Ennead*, TR VII, CH 36–41 339c–342c

18 AUGUSTINE: *Confessions*, BK X, par 11–38 74a–81a esp par 17 75c–d, par 19 76a–b, par 22–24 76d–77c, par 27–28 78b–d / *City of God*, BK VIII, CH 6, 269b / *Christian Doctrine*, BK II, CH 38, 654c

19 AQUINAS: *Summa Theologica*, PART I, Q 3, A 3, REP 1 16a–d; Q 5, A 4, REP 1 25d–26c; Q 8, A 3, REP 3 36b–37c; Q 12, A 1, REP 4 50c–51c; A 2 51c–52c; A 4, ANS and REP 1 53b–54c; AA 9–10 58b–59d; Q 13, A 7, ANS and REP 6 68d–70d; Q 14, A 1, ANS and REP 3 75d–76c; A 2 76d–77d;

2. Man's natural desire and power to know

(2. Man's natural desire and power to know.)

39 SMITH: *Wealth of Nations*, BK V, 335b-c

44 BOSWELL: *Johnson*, 130b; 151d

46 HEGEL: *Philosophy of History*, INTRO, 157b-158a

47 GOETHE: *Faust*, PART I [354-517] 11a-14b; [522-601] 15a-16b; [1765-1784] 42b

48 MELVILLE: *Moby Dick*, 4b-5a

53 JAMES: *Psychology*, 522b-525a esp 524b-525a; 711b-712b; 729a-730a; 851b-852a

54 FREUD: *Origin and Development of Psycho-Analysis*, 16b

3. Principles of knowledge

7 PLATO: *Phaedo*, 228a-230c / *Republic*, BK III, 333b-d; BK IV, 350d-351b; BK VI-VII, 383d-398c / *Theaetetus*, 544d-547c / *Seventh Letter*, 809c-810d

8 ARISTOTLE: *Posterior Analytics*, BK II, CH 19 136a-137a,c / *Physics*, BK I, CH 1 259a-b; CH 5 [188^{b}26-189^{a}9] 264b-c / *Metaphysics*, BK I, CH 1 499a-500b; BK V, CH 1 [1013^{a}14-23] 533b; CH 6 [1016^{b}18-25] 537b / *Soul*, BK II, CH 2 [413^{a}11-13] 643a

9 ARISTOTLE: *Ethics*, BK VI, CH 3 [1139^{b}25-34] 388c; CH 6 389d

12 LUCRETIUS: *Nature of Things*, BK I [690-700] 9c; BK IV [469-521] 50b-51a

18 AUGUSTINE: *Confessions*, BK I, PAR 1 1a-b; BK IV, PAR 25 25c; BK V, PAR 4 27d-28a; BK X, PAR 65 87d-88a; BK XIII, PAR 46 123a-c / *City of God*, BK VIII, CH 4-7 266d-269d; CH 9-10 270d-271d; BK X, CH 2 299d-300a; BK XI, CH 7 326a-c; CH 24-25 335c-336d; CH 27-29 337b-339b; BK XIX, CH 18 523a-b / *Christian Doctrine*, BK I, CH 37-40 635b-636a,c; BK II, CH 7 638d-639c; BK III, CH 37, 674a-d

19 AQUINAS: *Summa Theologica*, PART I, Q 2, A 1, ANS and REP 1,3 10d-11d; Q 15 91b-94a passim, esp A 3, ANS 93b-94a; Q 18, A 2, ANS 105c-106b; Q 84, AA 4-6 444d-449a; Q 85, A 3 455b-457a; Q 88, A 3, REP 1 472c-473a; Q 105, A 3 540c-541b; PART I-II, Q I, A 4, REP 2 612a-613a; A 5, ANS 613a-614a

20 AQUINAS: *Summa Theologica*, PART I-II, Q 50, A 3, REP 3 8b-9a; Q 51, A 1, ANS 12b-13c; PART III, Q 11, A 6, REP 3 775d-776b

21 DANTE: *Divine Comedy*, PURGATORY, XVIII [49-60] 80b-c; PARADISE, IV [28-48] 111a

25 MONTAIGNE: *Essays*, 285c-286a

28 HARVEY: *On Animal Generation*, 332a-335c esp 333d-334d

30 BACON: *Advancement of Learning*, 39d-40a; 58b / *Novum Organum*, BK I, APH 14 107d-108a; APH 39-40 109c

31 DESCARTES: *Rules*, I 1a-2a; IV, 5c-d; 6d; VI, 8d-9a; VIII, 13c-d / *Discourse*, PART IV 51b-54b / *Meditations*, II 77d-81d / *Objections and Replies*, 224b,d

31 SPINOZA: *Ethics*, PART II, PROP 37-40 386b-388b

35 LOCKE: *Human Understanding*, BK I, CH III, SECT 23, 120a; BK II, CH I 121a-127d passim, esp SECT 1-8 121a-123a, SECT 22-25 127a-d; CH VII, SECT 10 133a-b; CH IX, SECT 15-CH X, SECT 2 141a-c; CH X, SECT 8 142d-143a; CH XII 147b-148d; CH XIV, SECT 2 155b-c; CH XVII, SECT 22-CH XVIII, SECT 1 173d-174a; CH XVIII, SECT 6 174c-d; CH XXII, SECT 9 202c-203a; CH XXV, SECT 9 216d; SECT 11 217a; BK III, CH I, SECT 5 252b-c; CH XI, SECT 23 305a-b; BK IV, CH I, SECT 9-CH II, SECT 1 308c-309d; CH II, SECT 7-8 310d-311a; CH III, SECT 1-2 313a; CH VII 337a-344d esp SECT 1 337a, SECT 10-11, 339b-340a; CH XII, SECT 1-6 358c-360a; SECT 15 363a-b

35 BERKELEY: *Human Knowledge*, INTRO, SECT 4 405c-d; SECT 25 412a,c; SECT 1-2 413a-b; SECT 25-33 417c-419a; SECT 89 430b-c

35 HUME: *Human Understanding*, SECT II 455b-457b esp DIV 13-14 455d-456b; SECT VII, DIV 49 471c-d; DIV 61, 477c

38 ROUSSEAU: *Inequality*, 338c-339b

42 KANT: *Pure Reason*, 34a-35b; 66d-72c esp 67d-68a / *Practical Reason*, 343a / *Judgement*, 492c-d; 517d [fn 2]; 550a-551a,c; 562a-d; 570b-572b; 577b; 578a-d

46 HEGEL: *Philosophy of Right*, INTRO, PAR 2 9b-10a

53 JAMES: *Psychology*, 213b-214a; 299a-300a; 315a-319a esp 317b-318a; 360a; 453a-459b esp 453b-454a, 455a-457a; 859a-860b

54 FREUD: *Ego and Id*, 700a-701d

4. Knowledge in relation to other states of mind

4a. Knowledge and truth: the differentiation of knowledge, error, and ignorance

7 PLATO: *Symposium*, 163b / *Meno*, 179b-183a esp 180d, 181d, 182c-d; 188c-189b / *Apology*, 201d-202d / *Gorgias*, 256b / *Republic*, BK V, 368c-373c; BK VI-VII, 383d-398c / *Timaeus*, 447b-d; 450b-c; 457c-d / *Parmenides*, 490b-d / *Theaetetus*, 535c-536a; 542a-544a / *Sophist*, 557c-558b / *Laws*, BK IX, 748a

8 ARISTOTLE: *Prior Analytics*, BK II, CH 21 87d-89b / *Posterior Analytics*, BK I, CH 6 [75^{a}12-18] 103a; CH 16-18 109b-111c / *Topics*, BK VI, CH 9 [147^{a}16-21] 201a-b; [147^{b}26-148^{a}9] 201d-202a; CH 14 [151^{a}32-^{b}3] 206b-c / *Metaphysics*, BK II, CH 1 511b,d-512b; BK IV, CH 7 [1011^{b}25-29] 531c; [1012^{a}1-17] 531d-532a; BK V, CH 29 [1024^{b}27-38] 546d-547a; BK VI, CH 4 550a,c; BK IX, CH 10 577c-578a,c; BK XII, CH 10 [1075^{b}20-24] 606c / *Soul*, BK III, CH 3 [427^{a}16-^{b}6] 659c-d

9 ARISTOTLE: *Ethics*, BK VI, CH 9 [1142^{b}7-12] 391d / *Rhetoric*, BK I, CH 1 [1355^{a}21-39] 594c-d

11 ARCHIMEDES: *Sphere and Cylinder*, BK I, 403b

12 LUCRETIUS: *Nature of Things*, BK IV [469-521] 50b-51a

4b. Knowledge, belief, and opinion: their relation or distinction

**(4. Knowledge in relation to other states of mind.
4b. Knowledge, belief, and opinion: their
relation or distinction.)**

364b-366c esp CH XV, SECT 1–3 365a-d; CH XVI,
SECT 14 371b-c; CH XVII, SECT 2 371d-372b;
SECT 14–24 378c-380d passim; CH XVIII–XIX
380d-388d

35 HUME: *Human Understanding*, SECT IV 458a-
463d passim, esp DIV 20–21 458a-c, DIV 30
461d-462b; SECT VI, 469d [fn 1]

36 SWIFT: *Gulliver*, PART IV, 165a-b

39 SMITH: *Wealth of Nations*, BK V, 335d-336a

42 KANT: *Pure Reason*, 2a-4a,c; 228c-d; 240b-
243c / *Judgement*, 601d-607c esp 601d-602a,
603a-b, 603d-604b, 604d-606d

43 MILL: *Liberty*, 274b-293b passim

46 HEGEL: *Philosophy of Right*, PREF 1a-7d pas-
sim; INTRO, par 1 9a; PART II, par 132, 46b-c;
PART III, par 147 55d-56a; par 316 104c; ADDI-
TIONS, 1 115a-d

52 DOSTOEVSKY: *Brothers Karamazov*, BK I, 11a-b

53 JAMES: *Psychology*, 636a-638b passim

54 FREUD: *Beyond the Pleasure Principle*, 661c-
662a / *New Introductory Lectures*, 881d-882b

**4c. The distinction between knowledge and
fancy or imagination**

7 PLATO: *Ion*, 142a-148a,c / *Republic*, BK VI-
VII, 383d-389c; BK X, 427c-431d esp 430b-
431b / *Sophist*, 577a-b / *Laws*, BK IV, 684b-c
/ *Seventh Letter*, 809b-810b

8 ARISTOTLE: *Soul*, BK III, CH 3 659c-661b

14 PLUTARCH: *Coriolanus*, 191d-192b

18 AUGUSTINE: *Confessions*, BK III, par 10–11 15b-
16a

19 AQUINAS: *Summa Theologica*, PART I, Q 12,
A 3, ANS and REP 3 52c-53b; A 11, REP 1 59d-
60d; A 13, ANS and REP 2 61c-62b; Q 17, A 2,
REP 2 102a-d; Q 54, A 5 288a-d; Q 57, A 1,
REP 2 295a-d; Q 78, A 4, ANS 411d-413d; Q 84,
A 2, REP 1 442b-443c; A 6, REP 1–2 447c-449a;
A 7, REP 2 449b-450b; A 8, REP 2 450b-451b;
Q 93, A 6, REP 4 496b-498a; PART I–II, Q 17,
A 7, REP 3 690d-692a

20 AQUINAS: *Summa Theologica*, PART III SUPPL,
Q 70, A 2, REP 3 896a-897d

21 DANTE: *Divine Comedy*, PURGATORY, XVII
[13–45] 78c-79a

28 HARVEY: *On Animal Generation*, 335a-c

29 CERVANTES: *Don Quixote*, PART I, 189d-
193c; PART II, 205a-209d; 273c-278a; 326c-
331a

30 BACON: *Advancement of Learning*, 32d; 33c-d;
38d-39b; 55a-d / *Novum Organum*, BK I, APH
15 108a; APH 60 112c-113a / *New Atlantis*, 203a

31 DESCARTES: *Rules*, III, 4a-b; VIII, 13a; 14b;
XIV, 29b-31c / *Discourse*, PART IV, 53b; 54a-b
/ *Meditations*, I, 75d-76c; II, 79a-81d; III,
82d-86a; VI 96b-103d passim, esp 96b-d /
Objections and Replies, 122c-d; 136d-137a;
212a; 218c-d; 219b-c

31 SPINOZA: *Ethics*, PART II, PROP 17, COROL 381a;
PROP 17, SCHOL–PROP 18 381b-382b; PROP 26
384a-b; PROP 40, SCHOL 1 387b-388a; PROP 44
389b-390a; PROP 49, SCHOL 391d-394d passim;
PART V, PROP 34 460c-d

32 MILTON: *Paradise Lost*, BK V [95–128] 177b-
178a; BK VIII [179–197] 236a-b

33 PASCAL: *Pensées*, 82–86 186b-189a

35 LOCKE: *Human Understanding*, BK II, CH XXX
238a-239b; BK IV, CH IV, SECT 1–12 323d-
326d passim, esp SECT 1–3 323d-324c; SECT 18
328d-329a; CH V, SECT 7–8 330b-d

35 BERKELEY: *Human Knowledge*, SECT 29–30
418c; SECT 33 419a; SECT 36 419c-d; SECT 82
428d-429a; SECT 84 429b-c; SECT 86 429c-d

35 HUME: *Human Understanding*, SECT V, DIV
39–40 466c-467c

40 GIBBON: *Decline and Fall*, 345c

42 KANT: *Pure Reason*, 173b-174a / *Judgement*,
528c-529c; 532b-d; 575b-c

46 HEGEL: *Philosophy of History*, PART I, 220c-
221a

53 JAMES: *Psychology*, 639a-641a; 646b-655a;
659a-660b

4d. Knowledge and love

7 PLATO: *Phaedrus*, 126a-129d / *Symposium*,
164d-165b; 167a-d

17 PLOTINUS: *First Ennead*, TR III, CH 2 10d /
Third Ennead, TR V, CH 3, 102a-b; CH 7, 104a-c
/ *Sixth Ennead*, TR VII, CH 34–35 338b-339c

18 AUGUSTINE: *Confessions*, BK I, par 1–6 1a-2c;
BK X, par 33–35 79d-80c; par 38 81a; BK XI,
par 3 89d-90a / *City of God*, BK VIII, CH 4–5,
267c-268b; CH 8–10 270a-271d; BK X, CH 3
300b-301a; BK XI, CH 7 326a-c; CH 25–29
336b-339b; BK XIV, CH 28 397a-d / *Christian
Doctrine*, BK I, CH 36–40 634d-636a,c; BK II,
CH 7 638d-639c; CH 38, 654c; CH 41–42
656a-d

19 AQUINAS: *Summa Theologica*, PART I, Q 1, A 6,
REP 3 6b-7a; A 8, REP 2 7c-8d; Q 8, A 3, REP 3
36b-37c; Q 12, A 6, ANS 55b-56a; A 7, REP 1
56a-57b; Q 14, A 15, REP 1 89b-90b; Q 16, A 1,
ANS 94b-95c; A 4 esp ANS and REP 1–2 97a-c;
Q 23, A 4 135a-d; Q 27, AA 3–5 155c-157c; Q 28,
A 4, ANS 160c-161d; Q 30, A 2, REP 2 168a-
169b; Q 35, A 2, ANS 189d-190d; Q 36, A 2,
ANS and REP 4–5 192a-194c; Q 37 197c-200c;
Q 59, A 2 307c-308b; Q 60, A 1, REP 3 310b-
311a; A 2 311a-d; A 3, ANS and REP 3 311d-
312b; A 5, REP 5 313b-314c; Q 64, A 1, ANS
334a-335c; Q 78, A 1, ANS and REP 3 407b-
409a; Q 82, A 3, ANS and REP 3 433c-434c; Q
87, A 1, REP 1 465a-466c; Q 93, AA 7–8 498a-
500c; PART I–II, Q 1, A 8 615a-c; Q 3, A 4 625a-
626b; Q 22, A 2, ANS 721c-722c; Q 27, A 2
737d-738c; Q 28, A 1 esp REP 3 740b-741a;
A 2, ANS and REP 2 741a-742a; A 3, ANS and
REP 1 742a-d; A 4, REP 2 742d-743c

20 AQUINAS: *Summa Theologica*, PART I–II, Q 50,
A 5, REP 1 10b-d; Q 66, A 6, REP 1 80c-81b;

Q 86, A 1, REP 2 184a-d; PART II–II, Q 23, A 6, REP 1 487a-d; Q 27, A 4 523c-524a

21 DANTE: *Divine Comedy*, PURGATORY, XVII [1–75] 78c-79b; PARADISE, IV [115]–V [12] 111d-112b; XXVI [25–36] 146a; XXVIII [88–114] 149c-150a

26 SHAKESPEARE: *Love's Labour's Lost*, ACT IV, SC III [289–365] 271c-272a

31 DESCARTES: *Objections and Replies*, 227b-c

31 SPINOZA: *Ethics*, PART II, AXIOM 3 373d; PROP 48–49 391a-394d; PART V, PROP 24–33 458d-460c; PROP 34, COROL 460d; PROP 35–37 460d-461c; PROP 42 463b-d

33 PASCAL: *Geometrical Demonstration*, 440a

5. The extent or limits of human knowledge

5a. The knowable, the unknowable, and the unknown: the knowability of certain objects

7 PLATO: *Meno*, 179d-183a esp 180a / *Parmenides*, 489d-491a; 492a-504c esp 495b-c, 504c; 507c-d; 509d-510b esp 510b; 511c-d / *Theaetetus*, 544c-547c / *Sophist*, 560a-b

8 ARISTOTLE: *Interpretation*, CH 3 [16^{b}19–26] 25d-26a / *Physics*, BK II, CH 4 [197^{a}5–7] 273a / *Metaphysics*, BK I, CH 2 [982^{a}30–^{b}3] 500c-d; BK VI, CH 2 548c-549c; BK VII, CH 10 [1036^a 9–12] 559c; CH 15 563c-564c

9 ARISTOTLE: *Parts of Animals*, BK I, CH 5 [644^b 21–645^{a}5] 168c-d

12 EPICTETUS: *Discourses*, BK II, CH 20 164c-166c

17 PLOTINUS: *Fifth Ennead*, TR III 215d-226c esp CH 13 223d-224b

18 AUGUSTINE: *Confessions*, BK I, par 1–6 1a-2c / *City of God*, BK XI, CH 2 323a-c; BK XII, CH 7 346c-d; BK XXI, CH 5 563d-564d

19 AQUINAS: *Summa Theologica*, PART I, Q 3, A 4, REP 2 16d-17c; Q 5, A 2, ANS 24b-25a; Q 12, A 1 50c-51c; Q 14, A 3, ANS 77d-78b; A 10, ANS and REP 4 83d-84c; Q 16, A 3 96b-d; Q 50, A 2, ANS 270a-272a; Q 55, A 1, REP 2 289a-d; Q 57, A 3, ANS 297b-298a; Q 79, A 3 416a-417a; Q 84, A 2, ANS 442b-443c; Q 87 464d-468d passim

20 AQUINAS: *Summa Theologica*, PART III, Q 10, A 3 769d-771b; PART III SUPPL, Q 92, A 1 1025c-1032b

21 DANTE: *Divine Comedy*, HELL, VII [61–96] 10b-c; PURGATORY, III [16–45] 56a-b; PARADISE, XIX [22–99] 135b-136a; XXI [73–102] 139a-b

25 MONTAIGNE: *Essays*, 80b-82b; 98b-99a; 238c-239c; 246a-261c passim; 271b-273a; 291b-294b; 439c-440a

27 SHAKESPEARE: *Hamlet*, ACT III, SC I [56–88] 47c-d

28 HARVEY: *On Animal Generation*, 363d-364a; 389b; 492c

30 BACON: *Advancement of Learning*, 2c-4c; 96d-97b / *Novum Organum*, BK I, APH 1 107a

31 DESCARTES: *Rules*, II 2a-3b; VIII, 12a-14a; XII, 22b-c / *Meditations*, IV, 90a-b / *Objections and Replies*, 112a-d; 215a-b

31 SPINOZA: *Ethics*, PART I, PROP 30 366c-d; APPENDIX 369b-372d; PART II, AXIOM 5 373d

32 MILTON: *Paradise Lost*, BK V [544–576] 187a-b; BK VII [109–130] 219b-220a; BK VIII [114–130] 234b-235a; [179–214] 236a-b / *Samson Agonistes* [60–67] 340b-341a

33 PASCAL: *Pensées*, 72 181a-184b; 263 221a-b

35 LOCKE: *Human Understanding*, INTRO, SECT 3–7 93d-95c; BK II, CH I, SECT 1–8 121a-123a; SECT 24 127b-c; CH II, SECT 3 128b-c; CH VII, SECT 10 133a-b; CH XIV, SECT 26 160c-d; CH XV, SECT 11 165a-b; CH XXII, SECT 9 202c-203a; CH XXIII 204a-214b passim; CH XXXI, SECT 6–13 240d-243b; CH XXXII, SECT 24 247c-d; BK III, CH III, SECT 15–18 258b-259c; CH VI 268b-283a passim; BK IV, CH III 313a-323d; CH VI, SECT 4–16 331d-336d passim; CH VIII, SECT 9 347d-348a; CH X, SECT 19 354a-c; CH XII, SECT 7–13 360b-362d; CH XV, SECT 12 370b-371a; CH XVII, SECT 9–10 377d-378a; SECT 23 380b-c; CH XVIII, SECT 7 383b

35 BERKELEY: *Human Knowledge*, INTRO, SECT 2–3 405b-c; SECT 81 428c-d; SECT 89 430b-c

35 HUME: *Human Understanding*, SECT I, DIV 7–10 453c-455b; SECT IV, DIV 26 460b-c; SECT VIII, DIV 62, 478c; SECT IX, DIV 84, 488b [fn 1]; SECT XII 503c-509d

40 GIBBON: *Decline and Fall*, 159a-c; 308c-d

42 KANT: *Pure Reason*, 1a-4a,c; 19d-20c; 117b-118a; 120c-121a; 175b [fn 1]; 215d-216c; 224a-c / *Fund. Prin. Metaphysic of Morals*, 281c-282d; 285a-287d / *Practical Reason*, 292a-c; 296a-d; 309b; 337a-c; 354d-355d / *Judgement*, 465a-c; 564a-c; 599d-600d; 604a-b

47 GOETHE: *Faust*, PART I [672–675] 18a; PART II [11,441–452] 278b

48 MELVILLE: *Moby Dick*, 366a-b

53 JAMES: *Psychology*, 116a-119b esp 117b, 119b; 122b; 223b-224a; 656b-657a; 822b

54 FREUD: *Interpretation of Dreams*, 383b-c

5a(1) God as an object of knowledge

OLD TESTAMENT: *Exodus*, 33:12–23 / *Deuteronomy*, 34:10 / *I Chronicles*, 28:9—(D) *I Paralipomenon*, 28:9 / *Job*, 11:7–9; 26:14; 36:26; 38:1–42:6 / *Psalms*, 19:1–4; 46:10; 83:18; 100:3 —(D) *Psalms*, 18:1–5; 45:11; 82:19; 99:3 / *Proverbs*, 2:5 / *Ecclesiastes*, 3:11; 8:16-17; 11:5 / *Isaiah*, 11:9; 49:22–26; 60:16—(D) *Isaias*, 11:9; 49:22–26; 60:16 / *Jeremiah*, 24:7; 31:34 —(D) *Jeremias*, 24:7; 31:34 / *Ezekiel*, 6:9-10,13–14; 28:22–26—(D) *Ezechiel*, 6:9-10,13-14; 28:22–26 / *Hosea*, 2:20; 6:2–3,6—(D) *Osee*, 2:20; 6:3,6

APOCRYPHA: *Wisdom of Solomon*, 8:1–4; 9:13-16; 13:1–9—(D) OT, *Book of Wisdom*, 8:1–4; 9:13-16; 13:1–9 / *II Maccabees*, 7:28—(D) OT, *II Machabees*, 7:28

(5a. The knowable, the unknowable, and the unknown: the knowability of certain objects. 5a(1) God as an object of knowledge.)

5a(2) Matter and the immaterial as objects of knowledge

31 DESCARTES: *Meditations*, 74a,c; I–II 75a-81d esp II, 81b-c / *Objections and Replies*, 120b-c; 122c; POSTULATE II 131a; 152b,d-155d

33 PASCAL: *Pensées*, 72, 184a-b

35 LOCKE: *Human Understanding*, BK II, CH XV, SECT II 165a-b; CH XXIII 204a-214b passim, esp SECT 5 205a-b, SECT 15 208c-d, SECT 29 211d-212a; BK III, CH VI, SECT 11–12 271b-272b; CH XI, SECT 23 305a-b; BK IV, CH III, SECT 6 313c-315b; SECT 9–17 315c-317c passim, esp SECT 17 317c; SECT 23–27 320a-322a; CH VI, SECT 14 335d-336b; CH X, SECT 19 354a-c; CH XI, SECT 12 357c-d; CH XVI, SECT 12 370b-371a

35 BERKELEY: *Human Knowledge*, SECT 16–20 416a-417a; SECT 25–27 417d-418b; SECT 86–89 429c-430c esp SECT 89 430b-c; SECT 135–148 440a-442d

35 HUME: *Human Understanding*, SECT XII, DIV 123 506a

39 SMITH: *Wealth of Nations*, BK V, 336b-c

42 KANT: *Pure Reason*, 186b-d / *Practical Reason*, 319c-321b / *Judgement*, 603a-d

5a(3) Cause and substance as objects of knowledge

8 ARISTOTLE: *Physics*, BK II, CH 4 [196^{b}5–7] 273a / *Metaphysics*, BK I, CH 2 [983^{a}5–10] 501b; BK III, CH 2 [996^{a}18–^{b}26] 514d-515b; CH 4 [999^{a}24–29] 518a; CH 6 [1003^{a}5–17] 521d-522a,c; BK VII, CH 15 563c-564c; BK XI, CH 2 [1060^{b}20–23] 588d; BK XII, CH 10 618c-619a,c

9 ARISTOTLE: *Generation of Animals*, BK II, CH 6 [742^{b}17–35] 283d-284a

12 LUCRETIUS: *Nature of Things*, BK V [526–533] 67d-68a; BK VI [703–711] 89c-d

16 COPERNICUS: *Revolutions of the Heavenly Spheres*, 505a-506a

17 PLOTINUS: *Sixth Ennead*, TR VIII, CH 11 348b-c

19 AQUINAS: *Summa Theologica*, PART I, Q 12, A 8, ANS 57b-58b; Q 19, A 5, REP 2 112d-113c; Q 29, A I, REP 1,3 162a-163b; Q 56, A I, REP 2 292a-d; Q 57, A 3, ANS 297b-298a; Q 77, A I, REP 7 399c-401b; Q 84, A 7, ANS 449b-450b; Q 86, A I, ANS 461c-462a

20 AQUINAS: *Summa Theologica*, PART I–II, Q 49, A 2, REP 3 2b-4a

21 DANTE: *Divine Comedy*, PURGATORY, III [24–45] 56a-b; XVIII [49–60] 80b-c

23 HOBBES: *Leviathan*, PART I, 78a-80c; PART IV, 271c-272c

25 MONTAIGNE: *Essays*, 271b-272c; 497d-498a

30 BACON: *Advancement of Learning*, 45a-46a / *Novum Organum*, BK II, APH 2 137b-c / *New Atlantis*, 210d

31 DESCARTES: *Meditations*, IV, 90a-b / *Objections and Replies*, 108a-112a; 209c-210b; 211b-c; 215a-b

31 SPINOZA: *Ethics*, PART I, DEF 3–4 355b; AXIOM 4 355d; PROP 8, SCHOL 2 356d-357d; PROP 10 358a-b; APPENDIX 369b-372d; PART IV, PREF, 422b,d-423b

33 PASCAL: *Pensées*, 184–241 205a-217b passim, esp 233–241 213b-217b

34 NEWTON: *Principles*, BK III, GENERAL SCHOL, 371b-372a

35 LOCKE: *Human Understanding*, BK I, CH III, SECT 19 117c-d; BK II, CH XIII, SECT 17–20 152a-d; CH XXI, SECT 1–6 178b-180a; CH XXIII 204a-214b passim, esp SECT 2 204b-c, SECT 5 205a-b, SECT 15 208c-d, SECT 28–29 211b-212a; CH XXV, SECT II–CH XXVI, SECT 2 217a-d; CH XXXI, SECT 6–13 240d-243b; CH XXXII, SECT 24 247c-d; BK III, CH III, SECT 15–18 258b-259c; CH VI 268b-283a passim, esp SECT 7–10 270b-271b; CH IX, SECT 11–17 287d-290a; CH XI, SECT 19–25 304b-306c esp SECT 22 305a; BK IV, CH III, SECT 9–17 315c-317c; SECT 24–29 320c-323a esp SECT 29 322c-323a; CH IV, SECT 12 326c-d; CH VI, SECT 4–16 331d-336d; CH VIII, SECT 9 347d-348a; CH XII, SECT 9–12 360d-362c; CH XVI, SECT 12, 370b-c

35 BERKELEY: *Human Knowledge*, SECT 101–102 432c-433a

35 HUME: *Human Understanding*, SECT III, DIV 18–SECT VIII, DIV 74 457c-484c passim; SECT XI, DIV 105 498d-499a; DIV 115 503b-c; SECT XII, DIV 127 507b-c

42 KANT: *Pure Reason*, 15a-b; 17c-d; 46d-47c; 57c-d; 58d-59b; 63d-64a; 76c-83b esp 81b-83b; 86c-d; 95a-d; 99a-100d esp 100c-d; 110b; 133a; 140b,d-145c; 171a-172c; 214b,d [fn 1] / *Fund. Prin. Metaphysic of Morals*, 267d-268a; 285c-286a / *Practical Reason*, 294c-295d; 302a-d; 313b-314d / *Judgement*, 550a-551a,c; 556b-c; 557c-558b; 564a-c; 574a-b; 584c-d; 611d-613a,c

45 FOURIER: *Theory of Heat*, 169a

51 TOLSTOY: *War and Peace*, BK XIII, 563a-b; EPILOGUE I, 646c-647b passim; 650b-c; EPILOGUE II, 693c; 694d-695c

53 JAMES: *Psychology*, 89b-90a; 885b-886a

5a(4) The infinite and the individual as objects of knowledge

7 PLATO: *Philebus*, 610d-617d

8 ARISTOTLE: *Categories*, CH 5 [2^{b}6–37] 6c-7a / *Posterior Analytics*, BK I, CH 31 120a-c / *Physics*, BK I, CH 4 [187^{b}7–14] 262d; CH 5 [189^{a}5–7] 264b-c; CH 6 [189^{a}11–19] 264c; BK III, CH 6 [207^{a}21–31] 285c-d; BK VII, CH 3 [247^{b}3–7] 330b / *Metaphysics*, BK II, CH 2 [994^{b}17–30] 513a-b; BK III, CH 4 [999^{a}24–29] 518a; CH 6 [1003^{a}5–17] 521d-522a,c; BK VII, CH 10 [1036^{a}2–7] 559b-c; CH 15 563c-564c; BK XI, CH 2 [1060^{b}20–23] 588d; BK XIII, CH 10 618c-619a,c

9 ARISTOTLE: *Rhetoric*, BK I, CH 2 [1356^{b}28–35] 596b-c

11 NICOMACHUS: *Arithmetic*, BK I, 812a

17 PLOTINUS: *Sixth Ennead*, TR VI, CH 3 311c-312b

18 AUGUSTINE: *Confessions*, BK VII, par 20–21 49d-50a; BK XII, par 3–6 99d-100c

(5a. *The knowable, the unknowable, and the unknown: the knowability of certain objects. 5a(4) The infinite and the individual as objects of knowledge.*)

19 AQUINAS: *Summa Theologica*, PART I, Q 3, A 3, ANS 16a-d; Q 12, A 1, REP 2 50c-51c; A 7, ANS 56a-57b; A 8, REP 4 57b-58b; Q 14, AA 11-12 84c-86d; Q 15, A 3, REP 4 93b-94a; Q 22, A 2, ANS and REP 1 128d-130d; Q 29, A 1, REP 1 162a-163b; A 2, REP 3 163b-164b; Q 30, A 4 170c-171b; Q 32 175d-180d; Q 56, A 1, REP 2 292a-d; Q 57, A 2 295d-297a; Q 84, A 7, ANS and REP 1 449b-450b; Q 86, AA 1-3 461c-463d; Q 89, A 4, ANS 476c-477a; PART I-II, Q 14, A 6, REP 3 680c-681a

20 AQUINAS: *Summa Theologica*, PART III, Q 10, A 3 769d-771b; Q 11, A 1, REP 3 772b-773a; Q 12, A 1, REP 3 776c-777b; PART III SUPPL, Q 92, A 1, REP 12 1025c-1032b

23 HOBBES: *Leviathan*, PART I, 54b-c; PART IV, 262b

28 HARVEY: *On Animal Generation*, 332a-333b

31 DESCARTES: *Meditations*, III, 86a-d; 88c-89a / *Objections and Replies*, 112a-d; 121d-122b; 169a; 211c-d; 212c-213a; 213d-214a

31 SPINOZA: *Ethics*, PART II, PROP 10, SCHOL 376d-377a; PROP 30-31 385a-c

33 PASCAL: *Pensées*, 72 181a-184b; 233 213b-216a / *Geometrical Demonstration*, 435a-b

35 LOCKE: *Human Understanding*, BK II, CH XIII, SECT 4 149b; CH XIV, SECT 26-31 160c-162a passim; CH XV, SECT 2-3 162c-d; SECT 12 165b-c; CH XVI, SECT 8 167c; CH XVII 167d-174a esp SECT 15 171b-172a; CH XXIII, SECT 31 212b-c; SECT 33-34 212d-213b; CH XXIX, SECT 15-16 237a-238a

35 BERKELEY: *Human Knowledge*, INTRO, SECT 2 405b

46 HEGEL: *Philosophy of History*, PART II, 278a-b

47 GOETHE: *Faust*, PART I [1810-1815] 43a

51 TOLSTOY: *War and Peace*, BK XV, 631a-c; EPILOGUE II, 693c-694d

53 JAMES: *Psychology*, 312a; 631a

5a(5) The past and the future as objects of knowledge

OLD TESTAMENT: *Proverbs*, 27:1 / *Ecclesiastes*, 6:12; 8:6-7; 9:11-12; 11:2,6—(D) *Ecclesiastes*, 7:1; 8:6-7; 9:11-12; 11:2,6

APOCRYPHA: *Wisdom of Solomon*, 8:8—(D) OT, *Book of Wisdom*, 8:8

NEW TESTAMENT: *James*, 4:13-14—(D) *James*, 4:13-15

5 AESCHYLUS: *Suppliant Maidens* [86-103] 2a-b

5 SOPHOCLES: *Oedipus the King* [463-512] 103c-d; [1524-1530] 113c / *Ajax* [1419-1421] 155c

5 EURIPIDES: *Medea* [1415-1419] 224c / *Alcestis* [1159-1163] 247c / *Helen* [1688-1692] 314c / *Andromache* [1284-1288] 326c / *Bacchantes* [1388-1392] 352a,c

6 THUCYDIDES: *Peloponnesian War*, BK I, 349b; 354a-c

7 PLATO: *Critias*, 479d / *Theaetetus*, 531a-532a

8 ARISTOTLE: *Interpretation*, CH 9 28a-29d / *Memory and Reminiscence*, CH 1 [449^{b}3-29] 690a-c

9 ARISTOTLE: *Rhetoric*, BK II, CH 19 [1392^{b}14-1393^{a}8] 640b-c

10 HIPPOCRATES: *Prognostics*, par 1 19a-b / *Epidemics*, BK III, SECT III, par 16 59b-c

13 VIRGIL: *Aeneid*, BK VI [713-755] 230a-231a

14 PLUTARCH: *Theseus*, 1a-b / *Pericles*, 129a

15 TACITUS: *Annals*, BK IV, 79b

18 AUGUSTINE: *Confessions*, BK X, par 23-24 77a-c; BK XI, par 17-41 93b-99b / *Christian Doctrine*, BK II, CH 30 651c-d

19 AQUINAS: *Summa Theologica*, PART I, Q 14, A 13 86d-88c; A 15, REP 3 89b-90b; Q 57, A 3 297b-298a; Q 78, A 4, ANS and REP 5 411d-413d; Q 79, A 6, ANS and REP 2 419b-420d; Q 86, A 4 463d-464d; Q 89, A 3, REP 3 475d-476c; A 7, REP 3 478d-479c

20 AQUINAS: *Summa Theologica*, PART III, Q 12, A 1, REP 3 776c-777b

22 CHAUCER: *Troilus and Cressida*, BK IV, STANZA 56 95b-96a; STANZA 136-154 106a-108b

23 HOBBES: *Leviathan*, PART I, 53c-54a; 65b-c

25 MONTAIGNE: *Essays*, 41c-d; 439c-440a

30 BACON: *Advancement of Learning*, 13d-14a; 54c-55a

31 DESCARTES: *Objections and Replies*, 259a-b

31 SPINOZA: *Ethics*, PART IV, PROP 62, SCHOL 443c-d; PROP 66, DEMONST 444c

35 LOCKE: *Human Understanding*, BK II, CH XV, SECT 12 165b-c; BK IV, CH XI, SECT 11 357b-c

35 BERKELEY: *Human Knowledge*, SECT 44 420d-421a; SECT 105 433b-c

35 HUME: *Human Understanding*, SECT VI 469d-470d

38 ROUSSEAU: *Inequality*, 348a,c / *Social Contract*, BK IV, 428a

40 GIBBON: *Decline and Fall*, 88a-c; 96b,d; 413b-d

42 KANT: *Pure Reason*, 234d / *Judgement*, 579d-580a; 583d-584c

44 BOSWELL: *Johnson*, 277c

46 HEGEL: *Philosophy of History*, INTRO, 155b-c; 181b-d; 190a-b

47 GOETHE: *Faust*, PART I [570-585] 16a; PART II [8591-8603] 209b

48 MELVILLE: *Moby Dick*, 366b

49 DARWIN: *Origin of Species*, 42a; 59d-60a; 166a,c; 231d-233b esp 233a-b; 242b-243c / *Descent of Man*, 287d

51 TOLSTOY: *War and Peace*, BK XIII, 584d-585b; EPILOGUE II, 685a

53 JAMES: *Psychology*, 852b

54 FREUD: *Interpretation of Dreams*, 387a,c

5a(6) The self and the thing in itself as objects of knowledge

8 ARISTOTLE: *Soul*, BK III, CH 6 [430^{b}21-26] 663b

12 EPICTETUS: *Discourses*, BK I, CH 27, 133a-b

12 AURELIUS: *Meditations*, BK XI, SECT 1, 302a

17 PLOTINUS: *Third Ennead*, TR IX, CH 3, 137c-d / *Fourth Ennead*, TR IV, CH 2 159d-160b / *Fifth Ennead*, TR III, CH 1-8 215d-220d

18 AUGUSTINE: *Confessions*, BK X, par 7 73a; par 21-25 76c-77d; par 41 81c-d / *City of God*, BK XI, CH 26 336d-337b

19 AQUINAS: *Summa Theologica*, PART I, Q 14, A 2, REP 1,3 76d-77d; Q 56, A 1 292a-d; Q 78, A 4, REP 2 411d-413d; Q 87 464d-468d; Q 88, A 1, REP 1 469a-471c; A 2, REP 3 471c-472c; Q 89, A 2, ANS 475a-d

23 HOBBES: *Leviathan*, INTRO, 47b-d

29 CERVANTES: *Don Quixote*, PART II, 332b

30 BACON: *Advancement of Learning*, 88c-89b

31 DESCARTES: *Meditations*, II 77d-81d esp 81b-c / *Objections and Replies*, POSTULATE II 131a; 209d-210a; 215b-c

31 SPINOZA: *Ethics*, PART II, PROP 19-30 382b-383c

35 LOCKE: *Human Understanding*, BK IV, CH IX, SECT 2-3 349a-c

38 ROUSSEAU: *Inequality*, 362c

42 KANT: *Pure Reason*, 1a-4a,c esp 1b-d; 7d-8b; 9a-10b; 12c-d [fn 1]; 32a-c; 49c-50c; 51b-c; 55a-56c; 120c-129c; 200c-204c / *Fund. Prin. Metaphysic of Morals*, 281c-282d; 285a-287d esp 285c-286a / *Practical Reason*, 292a-293b; 307d-310c; 311d-314d; 327d-329a; 331c-337a,c; 337a-c / *Judgement*, 465a-c; 497a-498b; 574b-577a; 594d [fn 1]; 599d-600d

46 HEGEL: *Philosophy of Right*, PART I, par 35 21a-b; par 44 23c; ADDITIONS, 22 120c-d / *Philosophy of History*, PART I, 257d-258a

48 MELVILLE: *Moby Dick*, 370b-371b

51 TOLSTOY: *War and Peace*, EPILOGUE II, 688b-c

53 JAMES: *Psychology*, 121a-125b; 177b-178a; 191a-197a esp 196a-197a; 213a-238b esp 213b-217a, 223b-224a, 227b-228b, 232b-233b; 471b-472b

54 FREUD: *Unconscious*, 428a-430c esp 429c-430c / *Civilization and Its Discontents*, 767d-768d

5b. The distinction between what is more knowable in itself and what is more knowable to us

8 ARISTOTLE: *Prior Analytics*, BK II, CH 23 [68^{b}30-36] 90c / *Posterior Analytics*, BK I, CH 2 [71^{b}28-72^{a}6] 98b-c / *Topics*, BK VI, CH 4 [141^{a}26-142^{a}22] 194c-195c; BK VIII, CH 1 [155^{b}35-156^{a}7] 211d-212a / *Physics*, BK I, CH 1 259a-b; CH 5 [188^{b}26-189^{a}9] 264b-c; CH 7 [189^{b}30-33] 265b-c / *Generation and Corruption*, BK I, CH 3 [318^{b}13-319^{a}2] 415b-d / *Metaphysics*, BK II, CH 1 [993^{a}30-^{b}11] 511b,d; BK VII, CH 3 [1029^{a}35-^{b}12] 552a / *Soul*, BK II, CH 2 [413^{a}11-19] 643a-b

9 ARISTOTLE: *Ethics*, BK I, CH 4 [1095^{b}1-4] 340c

19 AQUINAS: *Summa Theologica*, PART I, Q 1, A 5, REP 1-2 5c-6a; A 9 8d-9c; Q 2, A 1, ANS 10d-11d; A 2, ANS and REP 2-3 11d-12c; Q 3, A 3, REP 1 16a-d; Q 10, A 1, ANS and REP 1 40d-41d;

Q 12, A 1, ANS and REP 2 50c-51c; AA 7-8 56a-58b; Q 13 62b-75b passim; Q 50, A 2, ANS 270a-272a; Q 85, A 3 455b-457a; A 8 460b-461b; Q 88, A 1, REP 3-4 469a-471c

28 HARVEY: *On Animal Generation*, 332a-c

31 DESCARTES: *Discourse*, PART IV 51b-54b / *Meditations*, 69b-d; II 77d-81d passim; IV, 89b; V 93a-96a / *Objections and Replies*, POSTULATE II 131a

31 SPINOZA: *Ethics*, PART II, PROP 47, 390c-d

42 KANT: *Judgement*, 601d

5c. Dogmatism, skepticism, and the critical attitude with respect to the extent, certainty, and finality of human knowledge

7 PLATO: *Euthydemus* 65a-84a,c / *Cratylus*, 86b-d / *Meno*, 179b-180b / *Apology*, 203a / *Phaedo*, 236c-238a / *Timaeus*, 447b-d / *Theaetetus*, 521d-526b

8 ARISTOTLE: *Prior Analytics*, BK I, CH 13 [32^{b}4-23] 48b-d / *Posterior Analytics*, BK I, CH 1 [71^{a}26]-CH 2 [72^{b}4] 97c-99a; CH 6 102b-103c; CH 33 121b-122a,c / *Heavens*, BK II, CH 5 [287^{b}29-288^{a}3] 379b-c / *Generation and Corruption*, BK I, CH 2 [316^{a}5-14] 411c-d / *Metaphysics*, BK IV, CH 5-6 528c-531c; BK X, CH 1 [1053^{a}31-^{b}3] 580a; CH 6 [1057^{a}7-11] 584b; BK XI, CH 6 [1062^{b}12-1063^{b}14] 590d-592a

9 ARISTOTLE: *Ethics*, BK I, CH 3 [1094^{b}11-27] 339d-340a; CH 7 [1098^{a}20-^{b}2] 343c-d; BK II, CH 2 [1103^{b}26-1104^{a}9] 349b-c; BK VI, CH 3 388b-c

12 LUCRETIUS: *Nature of Things*, BK IV [469-521] 50b-51a

12 EPICTETUS: *Discourses*, BK II, CH 17 158d-161a; CH 20 164c-166c; BK III, CH 2, 177c-178b; CH 21 193d-195a

18 AUGUSTINE: *Confessions*, BK V, par 19 32b-c / *City of God*, BK XIX, CH 18 523a-b

19 AQUINAS: *Summa Theologica*, PART I, Q 1, A 1 3b-4a; A 5, ANS and REP 1 5c-6a; Q 84, A 1, ANS 440d-442a; Q 85, A 2, ANS 453d-455b; Q 86, AA 1-3 461c-463d; Q 87, A 1 465a-466c; Q 88, A 1 469a-471c

20 AQUINAS: *Summa Theologica*, PART I-II, Q 64, AA 3-4 68b-70a; PART II-II, Q 4, A 8 409a-d

23 HOBBES: *Leviathan*, PART I, 65c; PART IV, 267a-b

24 RABELAIS: *Gargantua and Pantagruel*, BK III, 197b-200a

25 MONTAIGNE: *Essays*, 80b-82b; 208a-294b esp 240c-246a, 253c-254a, 257d-264a, 269d-279c, 285c-294b; 308c-d; 318a-319b; 439c-440a; 497b-502c; 516b-524a

28 GILBERT: *Loadstone*, PREF, 1c-2a

28 HARVEY: *Motion of the Heart*, 267b,d-268d / *On Animal Generation*, 411c-d

30 BACON: *Advancement of Learning*, 13a-c; 15a-17b esp 15d-16b; 47d-48d; 57d-58b / *Novum Organum*, PREF 105a-106d; BK I, APH 37 109b-c; APH 67 115d-116a; APH 75 118b-d; APH 95 126b-c; APH 126 134b

(5. *The extent or limits of human knowledge. 5c. Dogmatism, skepticism, and the critical attitude with respect to the extent, certainty, and finality of human knowledge.*)

31 DESCARTES: *Rules*, IV, 5a-d / *Discourse*, PART II 44c-48b / *Meditations*, 72b,d; I 75a-77c; III, 83b-84a / *Objections and Replies*, 168b-d; 272a-c

31 SPINOZA: *Ethics*, PART II, DEF 4 373b; PROP 37–47 386b-391a

33 PASCAL: *Pensées*, 381–385 238b-239a; 432 248a; 434–435 248a-251a / *Vacuum*, 355a-358b

35 LOCKE: *Human Understanding*, INTRO 93a-95d esp SECT 4–7 94a-95c; BK I, CH III, SECT 24 120a-c; BK II, CH II, SECT 3 128b-c; CH XV, SECT 11 165a-b; CH XXIII, SECT 12–13 207a-208b; SECT 36 213c-d; BK III, CH VI, SECT 1–9 268b-271a esp SECT 9 270d-271a; BK IV, CH III, SECT 22–30 319c-323c esp SECT 22 319c-320a; CH VI, SECT 4–16 331d-336d passim; CH X, SECT 19 354a-c; CH XII, SECT 9–13 360d-362d; CH XIV, SECT 1–2 364b-c; CH XVII, SECT 9–10 377d-378a

35 BERKELEY: *Human Knowledge*, INTRO, SECT 3–4 405b-d; SECT 17 409d-410a; SECT 86–88 429c-430b; SECT 101–102 432c-433a; SECT 133 439c-440a

35 HUME: *Human Understanding*, SECT I, DIV 7–10 453c-455b; SECT IV, DIV 20–21 458a-c; DIV 26 460b-c; SECT IV, DIV 28–SECT V, DIV 38 460d-466c passim; SECT VII, DIV 60, 477a; SECT XII 503c-509d esp DIV 129–130 508a-d

42 KANT: *Pure Reason*, 1a-4a,c; 15c-16c; 19a-22a,c; 101d-102a; 129c-130a; 133c-134d; 146a-149d; 157d; 187c-188b; 193a-b; 196b-197c; 218d-227a esp 221c-222b; 248d-250a,c / *Fund. Prin. Metaphysic of Morals*, 253c-d; 277d-279d / *Practical Reason*, 292d-293b; 295b-d; 311d-313d; 320c-321b; 331a-332d; 335b-c; 336d-337a,c / *Judgement*, 492c-d; 567c-568a

43 FEDERALIST: NUMBER 31, 103d-104a; NUMBER 37, 119b-120b

43 MILL: *Liberty*, 274b-293b

44 BOSWELL: *Johnson*, 121c-d; 126a-b

46 HEGEL: *Philosophy of Right*, PREF, 7a; INTRO, par 31 19c-20a

47 GOETHE: *Faust*, PART I [656–675] 17b-18a; [1064–1067] 26b; [1810–1815] 43a; [1868–2050] 44b-48b esp [1948–1963] 46a-b, [1968–1979] 46b-47a, [2011–2022] 47b-48a; [4343–4362] 107a-b

48 MELVILLE: *Moby Dick*, 78a-b; 250b; 257a; 276a-b

49 DARWIN: *Descent of Man*, 253d

51 TOLSTOY: *War and Peace*, BK V, 195a

53 JAMES: *Psychology*, 881b

54 FREUD: *New Introductory Lectures*, 828b-c; 873d-884d passim, esp 874d-875a, 878d-880b, 883d-884a

5d. **The method of universal doubt as prerequisite to knowledge: God's goodness as the assurance of the veracity of our faculties**

31 DESCARTES: *Rules*, II 2a-3b / *Discourse* 41a-67a,c esp PART II 44c-48b, PART IV 51b-54b / *Meditations*, 72b,d; I 75a-77c; III, 82b-d; IV, 89b-c; V, 95b-96a / *Objections and Replies*, 119c; 123a-d; 124b-125b; POSTULATE VII 131c; 134b-c; 142c; 143c; 162a; 167a-c; 206a-c; 207b; 215c-d; 226d-227a; 229c-d; 237b-238b; 239a-240a; 242c-244c; 245c

35 LOCKE: *Human Understanding*, BK II, CH XXVII, SECT 13 223b-d; BK IV, CH IX, SECT 3 349b-c

35 BERKELEY: *Human Knowledge*, INTRO, SECT 3 405b-c

35 HUME: *Human Understanding*, SECT XII, DIV 116, 503d-504a; DIV 120 505b; DIV 129–130 508a-d

53 JAMES: *Psychology*, 881b

5e. **Knowledge about knowledge as the source of criteria for evaluating claims to knowledge**

35 LOCKE: *Human Understanding*, 87d; INTRO 93a-95d esp SECT 4–7 94a-95c; BK IV, CH III, SECT 22 319c-320a

35 BERKELEY: *Human Knowledge*, INTRO, SECT 4 405c-d; SECT 17 409d-410a

35 HUME: *Human Understanding*, SECT I, DIV 7–10 453c-455b; SECT II, DIV 17 457a-b; SECT VII, DIV 49–53 471c-474b esp DIV 49 471c-d

42 KANT: *Pure Reason*, 1a-12d esp 1b-d, 8c-9a; 55a-56c; 99a-101b; 121a-123b / *Practical Reason*, 292d-293b; 294a-b; 307d-310c; 331a-332d

6. **The kinds of knowledge**

6a. **The classification of knowledge according to diversity of objects**

6a(1) Being and becoming, the intelligible and the sensible, the necessary and the contingent, the eternal and the temporal, the immaterial and the material as objects of knowledge

7 PLATO: *Cratylus*, 86b-d; 113c-114a,c / *Phaedrus*, 125a-126c / *Symposium*, 167a-d / *Phaedo*, 223d-232d esp 223d-225a, 228b-232d / *Republic*, BK III, 333b-334b; BK V, 368c-373c esp 372a-373b; BK VI-VII, 383d-398c / *Timaeus*, 447b-d; 457b-458a / *Theaetetus*, 521d-522b; 534d-536b / *Sophist*, 565a-569a esp 568a-569a / *Statesman*, 595a-c / *Philebus*, 610d-613a; 633a-635a esp 634b-635a / *Seventh Letter*, 809c-810d

8 ARISTOTLE: *Categories*, CH 5 [4^{a}10–^{b}19] 8b-9a / *Prior Analytics*, BK I, CH 13 [32^{b}4–23] 48b-d / *Posterior Analytics*, BK I, CH 2 [71^{b}8–16] 97d-98a; CH 4 [73^{a}21–^{b}30] 100a-101a; CH 6–8

102b-104b; CH 30 119d; CH 33 121b-122a,c /
Physics, BK II, CH 2 270a-271a; CH 7 [198ᵃ22–
31] 275b-c / *Heavens*, BK III, CH 1 [298ᵇ13–
24] 390a-b; CH 7 [306ᵃ10–12] 397b / *Metaphysics*, BK I, CH 5 [986ᵇ25–987ᵃ1] 504d-505a;
CH 6 [987ᵃ29–ᵇ18] 505b-d; CH 8 [989ᵇ21–990ᵃ
8] 507d-508a; BK II, CH 1 511b,d-512b; CH 3
[995ᵃ15–20] 513d; BK III, CH 4 [999ᵃ24–ᵇ4]
518a-b; BK IV, CH 5-6 528c-531c; BK VI, CH 1
547b,d-548c; BK VII, CH 15 [1039ᵇ31–1040ᵃ8]
563d-564a; BK IX, CH 10 577c-578a,c; BK X,
CH 1 [1053ᵃ31–ᵇ3] 580a; CH 6 [1057ᵃ7–11]
584b; BK XI, CH 2 588a-589a; CH 6 [1062ᵇ12–
1063ᵇ14] 590d-592a; CH 7 [1063ᵇ36]–CH 8
[1065ᵃ6] 592b-593b; BK XII, CH 1 [1069ᵃ30–ᵇ2]
598b-c / *Soul*, BK I, CH 1 [403ᵃ25–ᵇ19] 632b-d
/ *Memory and Reminiscence*, CH 1 [449ᵇ30–
450ᵃ10] 690c-d

   9 ARISTOTLE: *Parts of Animals*, BK I, CH 5 [644ᵇ
21–645ᵃ5] 168c-d / *Ethics*, BK VI, CH 1 [1139ᵃ
3–13] 387b-d; CH 3 [1139ᵇ19–25] 388b-c /
Rhetoric, BK I, CH 2 [1357ᵃ14–ᵇ21] 596d-597c

 11 NICOMACHUS: *Arithmetic*, BK I, 811a-812a

 14 PLUTARCH: *Marcellus*, 252b-e

 17 PLOTINUS: *Fifth Ennead*, TR V, CH 1, 228c-
229c; TR IX, CH 7 249b-c / *Sixth Ennead*,
TR VII, CH 36 339c-d

 18 AUGUSTINE: *Confessions*, BK V, par 3-5 27c-
28c; BK VI, par 6 36c-d; BK VII, par 23 50b-c;
BK X, par 8-11 73b-74b; BK XII, par 5 100a-b
/ *City of God*, BK VIII, CH 6 268d-269c;
CH 10 271a-d; BK XIX, CH 18 523a-b / *Chris-
tian Doctrine*, BK I, CH 8 626c-627a; BK II,
CH 27-39 650a-655b esp CH 27 650a

 19 AQUINAS: *Summa Theologica*, PART I, Q I, A 1,
REP 2 3b-4a; A 9 8d-9c; Q 2, AA 1-2 10d-12c;
Q 5, A 2, ANS 24b-25a; Q 10, A 1, ANS 40d-41d;
Q 12, A 4, ANS and REP 3 53b-54c; AA 8-10 57b-
59d; Q 13, A 12, REP 3 74c-75b; Q 14, A 13,
ANS and REP 3 86d-88c; Q 16, A 1, REP 2
94b-95c; Q 54, A 4, ANS and REP 2 287b-288a;
QQ 56-57 291d-300b; Q 79, A 9 422b-423d;
QQ 84-88 440b-473a

 20 AQUINAS: *Summa Theologica*, PART I-II, Q 66,
A 5 79b-80c; Q 84, A 1, REP 3 174b-175a; Q 93,
A 2 216c-217b; Q 94, A 4, ANS 223d-224d;
PART II-II, Q 9, A 2 424b-425a

 23 HOBBES: *Leviathan*, PART I, 49d

 25 MONTAIGNE: *Essays*, 291b-294b

 30 BACON: *Advancement of Learning*, 40a-c; 41b-
42a; 43d-44c

 31 DESCARTES: *Rules*, II 2a-3b; XII, 21b-c / *Discourse*, PART IV, 53b / *Meditations*, II 77d-81d
esp 81b-c; V 93a-96a passim / *Objections and
Replies*, 122b-c; POSTULATE II 131a; 218c-d;
219b-c

 31 SPINOZA: *Ethics*, PART I, DEF 8 355c; PROP 7
356c; PROP 8, SCHOL 2 356d-357d; PART II,
PROP 10, SCHOL 376d-377a; PROP 24-45
383c-390b

 33 PASCAL: *Pensées*, 72, 184a-b

 35 LOCKE: *Human Understanding*, BK II, CH
XXIII, SECT 5 205a-b; SECT 15-37 208c-214b;
BK IV, CH III, SECT 9-17 315c-317c passim,
esp SECT 17 317c; SECT 23-27 320a-322a passim; CH VI, SECT 5-16 332b-336d passim; CH
XI, SECT 1-12 354c-357d passim, esp SECT 12
357c-d; CH XVI, SECT 12 370b-371a

 35 BERKELEY: *Human Knowledge*, SECT 25-27
417d-418b; SECT 135-142 440a-441c; SECT 148
442b-d

 39 SMITH: *Wealth of Nations*, BK V, 336b-c

 42 KANT: *Pure Reason*, 16a-b; 113c-115a / *Judgement*, 551a-552c

 48 MELVILLE: *Moby Dick*, 120a-b

 51 TOLSTOY: *War and Peace*, BK IX, 365a-b

6a(2) Knowledge of natures or kinds distin- guished from knowledge of individuals

   8 ARISTOTLE: *Posterior Analytics*, BK I, CH 24
116b-118a; CH 31 120a-c; BK II, CH 19 [100ᵃ14–
ᵇ3] 136d / *Physics*, BK I, CH 5 [188ᵇ26–189ᵃ9]
264b-c / *Metaphysics*, BK I, CH 1 [980ᵇ25–981ᵇ
13] 499b-500a; BK III, CH 4 [999ᵃ24–ᵇ4]
518a-b; CH 6 [1003ᵃ5–17] 521d-522a,c; BK VII,
CH 10 [1035ᵇ35–1036ᵃ8] 559b-c; CH 15 563c-
564c; BK XI, CH 2 [1060ᵇ20–23] 588d; BK XIII,
CH 10 618c-619a,c

   9 ARISTOTLE: *Ethics*, BK VI, CH 6 389d; CH 7
[1141ᵃ20–34] 390a-b; [1141ᵇ14–20] 390c-d; CH
11 [1143ᵃ32–ᵇ5] 392d-393a; BK X, CH 9 [1180ᵇ
13–23] 435b-c / *Rhetoric*, BK I, CH 2 [1356ᵇ
28–35] 596b-c

 19 AQUINAS: *Summa Theologica*, PART I, Q I, A 2,
REP 2 4a-c; Q 12, A 8, REP 4 57b-58b; Q 14,
A 11 84c-85c; A 12, ANS 85d-86d; Q 15, A 3,
REP 4 93b-94a; Q 22, A 2, ANS 128d-130d; Q
29, A 1, REP 1 162a-163b; A 2, REP 3 163b-
164b; Q 30, A 4 170c-171b; Q 55, A 1, REP 3
289a-d; A 3, REP 2 291a-d; Q 56, A 1, REP 2
292a-d; Q 57, A 2 295d-297a; Q 59, A 1, REP 1
306c-307b; Q 75, A 5, ANS 382a-383b; Q 76,
A 2, REP 4 388c-391a; Q 79, A 5, REP 2 418c-
419b; A 6, ANS and REP 2 419b-420d; Q 84,
A 7, ANS and REP 1 449b-450b; Q 85, A 1
451c-453c; A 2, REP 2 453d-455b; A 3 455b-
457a; Q 86, A 1 461c-462a; AA 3-4 463b-464d;
Q 89, A 4 476c-477a

 20 AQUINAS: *Summa Theologica*, PART III, Q 11,
A 1, REP 3 772b-773a

 30 BACON: *Novum Organum*, BK II, APH 1-9
137a-140c

 31 DESCARTES: *Objections and Replies*, 167c-d

 31 SPINOZA: *Ethics*, PART II, PROP 37-39 386b-
387a; PROP 44, COROL 2-PROP 46 390a-c

 35 LOCKE: *Human Understanding*, BK II, CH
XXXII, SECT 6-8 244b-d; BK III, CH III, SECT
7-9 255d-256c; CH VI, SECT 32-33 277c-278c;
BK IV, CH IV, SECT 5-8 324d-325c; CH VII,
SECT 9 338d-339b

 35 HUME: *Human Understanding*, SECT XII, DIV
132 509a-d

(6a. The classification of knowledge according to diversity of objects. 6a(2) Knowledge of natures or kinds distinguished from knowledge of individuals.)

42 KANT: *Pure Reason*, 211c-218d / *Judgement*, 572a-b; 572d-574b

53 JAMES: *Psychology*, 305a-312a esp 309a-312a

6a(3) Knowledge of matters of fact or real existence distinguished from knowledge of our ideas or of the relations between them

19 AQUINAS: *Summa Theologica*, PART I, Q 84, A I, REP I 440d-442a; Q 85, A 2 453d-455b

23 HOBBES: *Leviathan*, PART I, 60a-b; 65c; 71c-d

35 LOCKE: *Human Understanding*, BK I, CH I, SECT 15–16 98d-99c; SECT 23 101b-102a; BK III, CH V, SECT 12 266d-267a; SECT 14 267b-c; CH VI, SECT 43–51 280c-283a esp SECT 43 280c-d; BK IV, CH I, SECT 1–7 307a-308a; CH II 309b-313a passim, esp SECT 14 312b-d; CH III, 313a-323d esp SECT 29 322c-323a; CH IV, SECT 1–12 323d-326d passim; SECT 18 328d-329a; CH V, SECT 6–8 330a-d; CH VI, SECT 13 335c-d; SECT 16 336d; CH IX 349a-c; CH XI 354c-358c esp SECT 13–14 357d-358c; CH XII, SECT 6–13 360a-362d; CH XVII, SECT 8 377b-d

35 BERKELEY: *Human Knowledge*, SECT 18–20 416b-417a; SECT 23 417b-c

35 HUME: *Human Understanding*, SECT IV 458a-463d esp DIV 20–21 458a-c, DIV 30 461d-462b; SECT V, DIV 34–38, 464b-466c; SECT IX 487b-488c esp DIV 82 487b-c; SECT XII, DIV 131–132 508d-509d

46 HEGEL: *Philosophy of Right*, PREF, 5c-6a / *Philosophy of History*, PART IV, 354b

53 JAMES: *Psychology*, 157b-161a esp 158b-159b; 301b-304b passim; 453a-b; 867a-890a esp 868b-869a, 879b-882a, 886a, 889a-b

6a(4) Knowledge in relation to the distinction between the phenomenal and the noumenal, the sensible and supra-sensible

42 KANT: *Pure Reason*, 25c-26a; 27b-33d; 37b-d; 53b-59b; 93c-99a esp 94b-95a, 96a-97b, 97d-98c; 101b-108a,c esp 106b-107b; 117b-118a; 120c-121d; 153a-157d; 164a-165c; 172c-173a; 193a-b; 224a-230c / *Fund. Prin. Metaphysic of Morals*, 253a-d; 264d; 281c-282d; 285a-287d / *Practical Reason*, 291a-296d esp 292a-293b; 307d-314d esp 307d-308b, 310d-311d; 319c-321b; 328a-329a; 331a-332d; 337a-c; 340a-342d esp 340c-341c; 349b-355d / *Intro. Metaphysic of Morals*, 383c-d; 390b / *Judgement*, 465a-c; 474b-475d esp 474d [fn I]; 497a-498b; 500c-d; 501d-502a; 506d-507a; 510b-c; 530a; 541a-542a; 543a; 543c-544c; 564a-c; 570b-572b; 574b-577a; 578d-579a; 581a-b; 584c-d; 587d-588a; 596c-598b; 599d-600d; 603a-b; 603d-606d esp 603d-604b, 606a-d

53 JAMES: *Psychology*, 233a-234b

6b. The classification of knowledge according to the faculties involved in knowing

7 PLATO: *Phaedo*, 224a-232d esp 224a-225a, 228b-232d / *Republic*, BK VI–VII, 383d-398c; BK X, 431c-d

8 ARISTOTLE: *Posterior Analytics*, BK II, CH 19 [99ᵇ34–100ᵇ3] 136b-d / *Topics*, BK IV, CH 4 [125ᵃ25–33] 174b / *Physics*, BK I, CH 5 [188ᵇ 26–189ᵃ9] 264b-c / *Metaphysics*, BK I, CH I [980ᵃ28–982ᵃI] 499a-500b; BK III, CH 4 [999ᵃ 24–ᵇ5] 518a-b / *Soul*, BK II, CH 5 [417ᵇ17–28] 648b-c

17 PLOTINUS: *First Ennead*, TR I, CH 7 3d-4a / *Fourth Ennead*, TR IV, CH 13 164d-165b; TR VI, CH 2 189d-190b / *Fifth Ennead*, TR III, CH 2–3 216b-217b; TR V, CH I, 228c-229c; CH 7 231d-232b; TR IX, CH 7 249b-c / *Sixth Ennead*, TR III, CH 18, 291a-b

18 AUGUSTINE: *Confessions*, BK III, par 10–11 15b-16a; BK X, par 8–38 73b-81a / *City of God*, BK VIII, CH 6–7 268d-269d; BK XI, CH 2–3 323a-d; BK XIX, CH 18 523a-b / *Christian Doctrine*, BK I, CH 12 627c-d; BK II, CH 27–39 650a-655b esp CH 27 650a; BK IV, CH 5, 677b-c

19 AQUINAS: *Summa Theologica*, PART I, Q 12, A 3 52c-53b; A 4, ANS and REP 3 53b-54c; Q 14, A I, ANS 75d-76c; A 2, REP I 76d-77d; Q 18, A 2, ANS and REP I 105c-106b; A 3, ANS 106b-107c; Q 85, A I, ANS 451c-453c

20 AQUINAS: *Summa Theologica*, PART I–II, Q 50, A 3, REP 3 8b-9a; PART II–II, Q 8, A I, ANS 417a-d

23 HOBBES: *Leviathan*, PART I, 60a-b; 71c-d

30 BACON: *Advancement of Learning*, 32d; 55b-d

31 DESCARTES: *Rules*, XIV, 29b-31c / *Meditations*, VI 96b-103d passim / *Objections and Replies*, 119d-120c; 124d-125a; POSTULATE I–II 130d-131a; AXIOM V 131d-132a; 136d-137a; 157c-d; 162d-165d; 211d-212a; 217c-d; 218c-d; 219b-c; 228c-229c; 229d-230c

31 SPINOZA: *Ethics*, PART II, PROP 10 376c-377a; PROP 40, SCHOL 2–PROP 44 388a-390a

35 LOCKE: *Human Understanding*, BK IV, CH II 309b-313a passim, esp SECT 14 312b-d; CH III, SECT 2–5 313a-c; CH IX, SECT 2 349a; CH XI, SECT 13–14 357d-358c

35 BERKELEY: *Human Knowledge*, INTRO, SECT I 405a-b; SECT 18 416b-c; SECT 27 418a-b

46 HEGEL: *Philosophy of Right*, PART III, par 227 74b-d

53 JAMES: *Psychology*, 144b-145a; 157b-167b esp 157b-161a, 167b; 450a-451b; 453a-457a esp 453b, 455a

6b(1) Sensitive knowledge: sense-perception as knowledge; judgments of perception and judgments of experience

7 PLATO: *Phaedo*, 224a-225a; 231c-232a / *Republic*, BK VI–VII, 383d-398c esp BK VI, 386d-387a, 387d-388a, BK VII, 389b, 392c-393a / *Timaeus*, 447b / *Theaetetus*, 517b-536a esp 521d-526d, 533a-536a

8 ARISTOTLE: *Posterior Analytics*, BK II, CH 19 [99^{b}20–100^{b}5] 136a-d / *Topics*, BK II, CH 8 [114^{a}18–26] 159d-160a / *Physics*, BK I, CH 5 [188^{b}26–189^{a}9] 264b-c / *Heavens*, BK III, CH 7 [306^{a}1–18] 397b-c / *Metaphysics*, BK I, CH 1 [980^{a}20–^{b}24] 499a; [981^{b}10–13] 499d-500a; BK IV, CH 5 [1009^{b}1–17] 528d-529a; [1010^{b}1–1011^{a}2] 530a-c; BK XI, CH 6 [1062^{b}34–1063^{a}9] 591a-b; CH 7 [1064^{a}4–9] 592b / *Soul*, BK II, CH 5 647b-648d; BK III, CH 2 657d-659c

9 ARISTOTLE: *Generation of Animals*, BK I, CH 23 [731^{a}30–^{b}5] 271c-d / *Ethics*, BK I, CH 7 [1098^{b}35–^{b}8] 343d-344a; BK II, CH 9 [1109^{b}20–23] 355c; BK VI, CH 8 [1142^{a}12–31] 391b-c; BK VII, CH 3 [1147^{a}25–^{b}19] 397c-398a

10 HIPPOCRATES: *Surgery*, par 1 70b

12 LUCRETIUS: *Nature of Things*, BK IV [379–521] 49a-51a

12 EPICTETUS: *Discourses*, BK I, CH 6, 110c-111c

14 PLUTARCH: *Marcellus*, 252b-c

17 PLOTINUS: *First Ennead*, TR I, CH 6–7 3c-4a / *Fourth Ennead*, TR III, CH 23 153d-154b; CH 26, 155c; TR IV, CH 23–25 169c-171b; TR VI, CH 1–2 189b-190b / *Fifth Ennead*, TR V, CH 1, 228c-229c; TR IX, CH 7 249b-c / *Sixth Ennead*, TR III, CH 18, 291a-b

18 AUGUSTINE: *Confessions*, BK III, par 10–11 15b-16a; BK IV, par 15–17 23a-c; BK X, par 8–11 73b-74b / *Christian Doctrine*, BK II, CH 27–30 650a-651d

19 AQUINAS: *Summa Theologica*, PART I, Q 5, A 4, REP 1 25d-26c; Q 12, A 4, ANS and REP 3 53b-54c; Q 14, A 1, ANS 75d-76c; A 2, ANS and REP 1 76d-77d; A 6, REP 1 80a-81c; A 11, ANS and REP 1–2 84c-85c; A 12, ANS 85d-86d; Q 16, A 2 95c-96b; Q 17, A 2 102a-d; A 3, ANS 102d-103c; Q 18, A 2, ANS and REP 1 105c-106b; A 3, ANS 106b-107c; Q 54, A 5 288a-d; Q 57, A 1, REP 2 295a-d; A 2, ANS 295d-297a; Q 59, A 1, REP 1 306c-307b; Q 75, A 3, ANS and REP 2 380c-381b; A 5, ANS 382a-383b; Q 76, A 2, REP 4 388c-391a; Q 77, A 5, REP 3 403d-404c; Q 78, A 1, ANS 407b-409a; AA 3–4 410a-413d; Q 79, A 3, ANS and REP 1–2 416a-417a; A 6, ANS and REP 1–2 419b-420d; Q 84, A 1, ANS and REP 2 440d-442a; A 2, ANS 442b-443c; A 4, ANS and REP 2 444d-446b; A 6 447c-449a; Q 85, A 1, ANS and REP 1,3 451c-453c; A 2 453d-455b; A 3, ANS 455b-457a; A 6, ANS 458d-459c; Q 86, A 1, ANS and REP 2,4 461c-462a; A 3 463b-d; Q 87, A 3, REP 3 467b-468a

20 AQUINAS: *Summa Theologica*, PART III SUPPL, Q 82, AA 3–4 971a-974c

21 DANTE: *Divine Comedy*, PARADISE, IV [28–48] 111a

23 HOBBES: *Leviathan*, PART I, 49a-d

25 MONTAIGNE: *Essays*, 285c-286a

28 HARVEY: *On Animal Generation*, 332a-335c

30 BACON: *Novum Organum*, BK I, APH 41 109c-d; APH 50 111b; BK II, APH 40 170c-173d

31 DESCARTES: *Discourse*, PART IV, 53b / *Meditations*, I 75a-77c passim; II, 80c-81d; III, 83d-84a; VI 96b-103d passim / *Objections and Replies*, 119d-120c; 124d-125a; POSTULATE I–III 130d-131a; AXIOM V 131d-132a; 162d-165d; 211a-b; 211d-212a; 228c-230c; 231a-b

31 SPINOZA: *Ethics*, PART II, AXIOM 4–5 373d; PROP 11–13 377b-378c; POSTULATE 5 380b; PROP 14–17 380c-381d; PROP 19 382b-c; PROP 22–29 383b-385a

34 NEWTON: *Principles*, BK III, RULE III 270b-271a

35 LOCKE: *Human Understanding*, BK II, CH IX, SECT 8–10 139b-140b; BK III, CH VI, SECT 9 270d-271a; BK IV, CH II, SECT 14 312b-d; CH III, SECT 14 316b-d; SECT 21 319c; CH XI 354c-358c

35 BERKELEY: *Human Knowledge*, INTRO, SECT I 405a-b; SECT 18 416b-c; SECT 25–33 417d-419a passim; SECT 135–142 440a-441c

42 KANT: *Pure Reason*, 108a-d

46 HEGEL: *Philosophy of Right*, PART III, par 227 74b-d

53 JAMES: *Psychology*, 450a-471a esp 453a-459b, 469a-b, 470b-471a; 502a-525a passim, esp 503a-505b, 508a; 564a-b

6b(2) Memory as knowledge

8 ARISTOTLE: *Topics*, BK II, CH 4 [111^{b}24–31] 156d-157a; BK IV, CH 4 [125^{b}4–14] 174c / *Metaphysics*, BK I, CH 1 [980^{a}28–981^{a}1] 499a-b / *Memory and Reminiscence*, CH 1 [449^{b}1]–CH 2 [452^{a}13] 690a-693d

17 PLOTINUS: *Fourth Ennead*, TR III, CH 25–TR IV, CH 9 154d-163a passim; TR VI, CH 3 190b-191c

18 AUGUSTINE: *Confessions*, BK X, par 12–38 74b-81a / *Christian Doctrine*, BK II, CH 9 640c-d; BK IV, CH 5, 677b-c

19 AQUINAS: *Summa Theologica*, PART I, Q 54 A 5 288a-d; Q 78, A 4, ANS and REP 5 411d-413d; Q 79, AA 6–7 419b-421c; Q 89, A 6, REP 1 478b-d

20 AQUINAS: *Summa Theologica*, PART I–II, Q 51, A 3 14b-15a; PART III SUPPL, Q 70, A 2, REP 4 896a-897d

21 DANTE: *Divine Comedy*, PARADISE, V [34–42] 112c

23 HOBBES: *Leviathan*, PART I, 50b-c; 53a-54a

30 BACON: *Advancement of Learning*, 32d

31 DESCARTES: *Rules*, III, 4c-d; VII, 10b-c; XI 17b-18b; XII 18b-25a passim / *Meditations*, V, 95d-96a / *Objections and Replies*, 125a-b

31 SPINOZA: *Ethics*, PART II, PROP 18, SCHOL 382a-b

35 LOCKE: *Human Understanding*, BK I, CH III, SECT 21 118b-119a; BK II, CH X, SECT 2 141b-c; BK IV, CH I, SECT 8–9 308b-309b; CH XI, SECT 11 357b-c; CH XVI, SECT 1–2 366d-367a

53 JAMES: *Psychology*, 145a; 421a-422a passim; 424b-427a; 450a-451b

(6b. The classification of knowledge according to the faculties involved in knowing. 6b(2) Memory as knowledge.)

54 FREUD: *Unconscious*, 428d / *General Introduction*, 484c-486a

6b(3) Rational or intellectual knowledge

7 PLATO: *Phaedrus*, 125a-b / *Phaedo*, 224a-232d esp 224a-225a, 228b-232d / *Republic*, BK VI-VII, 383d-398c esp BK VI, 387a-388a, BK VII, 389b, 393a-c / *Theaetetus*, 534d-536a / *Laws*, BK X, 765b

8 ARISTOTLE: *Physics*, BK VII, CH 3 [247^{b}1-248^{a}9] 330b-d / *Metaphysics*, BK I, CH 1 [980^{b}25-982^{a}1] 499b-500b

9 ARISTOTLE: *Ethics*, BK VI, CH 1 [1139^{a}6-11] 387c; CH 3-7 388b-390d

12 LUCRETIUS: *Nature of Things*, BK IV [469-521] 50b-51a

14 PLUTARCH: *Numa Pompilius*, 53b-c / *Marcellus*, 252b-c

17 PLOTINUS: *Fourth Ennead*, TR IV, CH 1 159a-d; TR VI, CH 2 189d-190b / *Fifth Ennead*, TR V, CH 1, 228c-229c; TR IX, CH 7 249b-c / *Sixth Ennead*, TR III, CH 18, 291a-b

18 AUGUSTINE: *Confessions*, BK X, par 10 73d-74a; par 16-19 75b-76b; par 30 79b-c; par 36 80c-d / *Christian Doctrine*, BK II, CH 31-38 651d-654c

19 AQUINAS: *Summa Theologica*, PART I, Q 14, A 1, ANS 75d-76c; A 2, ANS and REP 1 76d-77d; A 11, ANS and REP 1-2 84c-85c; A 12, ANS 85d-86d; Q 16, A 2 95c-96b; Q 17, A 3 102d-103c; Q 18, A 2, ANS and REP 1 105c-106b; A 3, ANS 106b-107c; Q 54 284d-288d passim; Q 57, A 1, REP 2 295a-d; A 2, ANS 295d-297a; Q 59, A 1, REP 1 306c-307b; Q 78, A 1, ANS 407b-409a; A 4, ANS and REP 4-6 411d-413d; Q 79 413d-427a; QQ 84-89 440b-480c

20 AQUINAS: *Summa Theologica*, PART I-II, QQ 57-58 35a-45c

23 HOBBES: *Leviathan*, PART I, 58a-61a; 65c-d; 71c; PART II, 163a; PART IV, 267a-c

30 BACON: *Advancement of Learning*, 32d

31 DESCARTES: *Meditations*, II 77d-81d passim; VI 96b-103d passim / *Objections and Replies*, 119d-120c; 124d-125a; DEF I-II 130a-b; AXIOM V 131d-132a; 162d-165d; 228c-230c

31 SPINOZA: *Ethics*, PART II, PROP 37-40 386b-388b; PROP 44, COROL 2-PROP 46 390a-c; PART V, PROP 29 459b-d

35 LOCKE: *Human Understanding*, BK IV, CH II, SECT 1-8 309b-311a; CH III, SECT 2-4 313a-c; CH IX, SECT 2 349a; CH XI, SECT 13-14 357d-358c

35 BERKELEY: *Human Knowledge*, INTRO, SECT 1 405a-b; SECT 89 430b-c

46 HEGEL: *Philosophy of Right*, PART III, par 227 74b-d

53 JAMES: *Psychology*, 299a-314b esp 302b-304b, 313b-314a

6b(4) Knowledge in relation to the faculties of understanding, judgment, and reason; and to the work of intuition, imagination, and understanding

42 KANT: *Pure Reason*, 23a-110d esp 25b-c, 27c, 28d-29d, 32a-c, 34a-c, 37b-39c, 41c-45b, 48c-d, 52c-55a, 57d-59b, 65d-66d, 94b-95a, 99a-101b, 109d-110d; 130b-c; 166c-171a; 193a-195a / *Fund. Prin. Metaphysic of Morals*, 282b-c / *Intro. Metaphysic of Morals*, 385a-c / *Judgement*, 461a-476c; 493c-495a,c; 518a-d; 542b-543c; 570b-572b

53 JAMES: *Psychology*, 232b-235a

6c. The classification of knowledge according to the methods or means of knowing

6c(1) Vision, contemplation, or intuitive knowledge distinguished from discursive knowledge

7 PLATO: *Phaedrus*, 125a-126c / *Symposium*, 150c-151a; 167a-d / *Phaedo*, 224a-225a / *Republic*, BK VI-VII, 386d-389c / *Seventh Letter*, 809c-810d

8 ARISTOTLE: *Metaphysics*, BK VII, CH 10 [1036^{a}1-8] 559b-c; BK XII, CH 7 [1072^{b}13-29] 602d-603a; CH 9 [1075^{a}5-11] 605c-d

9 ARISTOTLE: *Ethics*, BK X, CH 8 [1178^{b}20-32] 433b-c

16 KEPLER: *Harmonies of the World*, 1083b-1084b

17 PLOTINUS: *Fourth Ennead*, TR III, CH 18 151b-c; TR IV, CH 1 159a-d / *Fifth Ennead*, TR III, CH 3 216c-217b; TR V, CH 1-2 228b-229d passim; CH 7 231d-232b

18 AUGUSTINE: *Confessions*, BK IX, par 23-25 68a-c; BK XII, par 16 102d-103a / *City of God*, BK IX, CH 16, 294a-b; CH 22 296d-297a; BK XI, CH 2 323a-c; CH 7 326a-c; CH 21 333a-d; CH 29 339a-b; BK XVI, CH 6 426c-427a; BK XXII, CH 29, 614b-d

19 AQUINAS: *Summa Theologica*, PART I, Q 12 50b-62b esp A 10 59a-d; Q 14, A 1, REP 2 75d-76c; A 7 81d-82b; A 9, ANS 83b-d; A 12, REP 1-2 85d-86d; A 13, ANS and REP 3 86d-88c; A 14 88d-89b; A 15, REP 2-3 89b-90b; Q 16, A 5, REP 1 97c-98b; Q 19, A 5, ANS 112d-113c; Q 34, A 1, REP 2 185b-187b; Q 46, A 2, REP 3 253a-255a; Q 57, A 1, REP 2 295a-d; A 3, ANS and REP 2 297b-298a; Q 58 300b-306b esp A 4 302d-303c; Q 59, A 1, REP 1 306c-307b; Q 60, A 2, ANS 311a-d; Q 78, A 4, REP 6 411d-413d; Q 79, A 4, ANS 417a-418c; A 8 421c-422b; Q 85, A 5 457d-458d; Q 86, A 2, ANS 462a-463a; A 4, ANS 463d-464d; PART I-II, Q 14, A 1, REP 2 677b-678a

20 AQUINAS: *Summa Theologica*, PART II-II, Q 8 416d-423b; Q 9, A 1, REP 1 423c-424b; Q 180, AA 3-6 609c-614d; PART III, Q 11, AA 3-4 773d-775a; PART III SUPPL, Q 92, A 3 1034b-1037c

21 DANTE: *Divine Comedy*, PARADISE, II [37–45] 108a; XXX [1–123] 151d-153a; XXXIII [46–145] 156c-157d

30 BACON: *Novum Organum*, BK II, APH 15 149a

32 MILTON: *Paradise Lost*, BK V [469–505] 185b-186a

33 PASCAL: *Pensées*, 1–5 171a-173a; 277–288 222b-224b

35 LOCKE: *Human Understanding*, BK IV, CH IX, SECT 2–3 349a-c

42 KANT: *Pure Reason*, 33a-d; 52c-53b / *Practical Reason*, 320c-321b; 337a-c; 350c-351b / *Judgement*, 572d-574b

46 HEGEL: *Philosophy of History*, PART IV, 349b-350a

48 MELVILLE: *Moby Dick*, 276a-b

54 FREUD: *New Introductory Lectures*, 874a-875a

6c(2) The distinction between immediate and mediated judgments: induction and reasoning, principles and conclusions

8 ARISTOTLE: *Posterior Analytics*, BK I, CH 1–3 97a-100a; CH 15 109a-b; CH 22 [83^{b}32–84^{b}2] 114c-115b; CH 23 [84^{b}19–85^{a}1] 115c-116a; CH 31 [88^{a}5–17] 120b-c; CH 33 [88^{b}30–89^{a}1] 121b-c; [89^{a}17–22] 121d; BK II, CH 9 128a-b; CH 13 [97^{b}31–39] 133c; CH 19 136a-137a,c / *Topics*, BK I, CH 12 148d / *Physics*, BK VIII, CH 1 [252^{a}19–^{b}5] 335d-336b / *Metaphysics*, BK II, CH 2 [994^{b}16–27] 513a-b; BK III, CH 2 [997^{a}25–32] 515d-516a; BK IV, CH 3 [1005^{b}5]–CH 4 [1006^{a}12] 524c-525b; CH 6 [1011^{a}3–14] 530d; BK VII, CH 17 [1041^{b}9–11] 565d; BK IX, CH 10 [1051^{b}18–1052^{a}4] 577d-578a,c; BK XI, CH 1 [1059^{a}29–34] 587b; CH 6 [1063^{b}7–12] 591d; CH 7 [1064^{a}4–9] 592b

9 ARISTOTLE: *Ethics*, BK I, CH 7 [1098^{a}35–^{b}4] 343d; BK VI, CH 3 [1139^{b}25–34] 388c; CH 6–7 389d-390d; CH 8 [1142^{a}23–31] 391b-c; CH 11 [1143^{a}32–^{b}5] 392d-393a

19 AQUINAS: *Summa Theologica*, PART I, Q 1, AA 7–8 7a-8d; Q 2, AA 1–2 10d-12c; Q 12, A 8, ANS 57b-58b; Q 14, A 1, REP 2 75d-76c; A 7, ANS and REP 2–3 81d-82b; Q 17, A 3, REP 2 102d-103c; Q 19, A 5, ANS 112d-113c; Q 58, A 3, ANS and REP 2 301d-302d; A 4, ANS 302d-303c; Q 60, A 2, ANS 311a-d; Q 79, A 8, ANS 421c-422b; A 12, ANS 425c-426b; Q 85, A 6, ANS 458d-459c; Q 87, A 1, REP 1 465a-466c; PART I–II, Q 1, A 4, REP 2 612a-613a; A 5, ANS 613a-614a

20 AQUINAS: *Summa Theologica*, PART I–II, Q 57, A 2 36a-37b; Q 94, A 2, ANS 221d-223a; PART II–II, Q 8, A 1, REP 2 417a-d

23 HOBBES: *Leviathan*, PART I, 58d-59a; 65c-d; 71c

30 BACON: *Advancement of Learning*, 59c; 61d; 96d-97a / *Novum Organum*, PREF 105a-106d; BK I 107a-136a,c esp APH 11–26 107d-108d, APH 69 116a-b, APH 103–106 127d-128c; BK II, APH 5, 139a; APH 10 140c-d

31 DESCARTES: *Rules*, II, 2d-3a; III, 4a-d; VII, 10c-12a; IX, 14d; XI 17b-18b; XII–XIV, 20d-28b / *Discourse*, PART VI, 62a-b / *Objections and Replies*, 123a-b; 125a-b; 224b,d

31 SPINOZA: *Ethics*, PART II, PROP 40, SCHOL 2–PROP 42 388a-c; PROP 47, SCHOL 390c-391a; PART V, PROP 28 459b

33 PASCAL: *Pensées*, 1–5 171a-173a

35 LOCKE: *Human Understanding*, BK I, CH II, SECT 1 103d-104a; SECT 4 104d-105a; CH III, SECT 23 119b-120a; BK IV, CH I, SECT 9–CH III, SECT 4, 309b-313c; CH VII, SECT 1–11 337a-342d passim; CH IX, SECT 2–3 349a-c; CH XV, SECT 1 365a-c; SECT 3 365d; CH XVII, SECT 2–3 371d-372b; SECT 14–17 378c-379c

42 KANT: *Pure Reason*, 39a-c; 66d-72c esp 67d-68a; 99a-b; 109d-111c; 211c-218d / *Judgement*, 542d-543a

43 FEDERALIST: NUMBER 31, 103c-104a; NUMBER 83, 244b-c

43 MILL: *Utilitarianism*, 461c

46 HEGEL: *Philosophy of Right*, PREF, 1a-c

53 JAMES: *Psychology*, 144a-b; 167b; 453a-457a esp 453b-454a, 456a

6c(3) The doctrine of knowledge as reminiscence: the distinction between innate and acquired knowledge

7 PLATO: *Phaedrus*, 124a-126c / *Meno*, 179d-183a; 188d-189a / *Phaedo*, 228a-230d / *Theaetetus*, 515d-517b

8 ARISTOTLE: *Posterior Analytics*, BK I, CH I [71^{a}26–^{b}9] 97c-d; BK II, CH 19 [99^{b}20–33] 136a-b / *Metaphysics*, BK I, CH 9 [992^{b}24–993^{a}11] 511a-c

10 GALEN: *Natural Faculties*, BK I, CH 12, 173a-b

12 EPICTETUS: *Discourses*, BK II, CH 11 150a-151b

17 PLOTINUS: *First Ennead*, TR II, CH 4, 8b-c / *Fourth Ennead*, TR III, CH 25 154d-155c; TR IV, CH 5 160d-161b

18 AUGUSTINE: *Confessions*, BK X, par 10 73d-74a; par 16–19 75b-76b; par 26–38 78a-81a / *City of God*, BK VIII, CH 6, 269b-c / *Christian Doctrine*, BK I, CH 9 627a

19 AQUINAS: *Summa Theologica*, PART I, Q 54, A 4, ANS and REP 1 287b-288a; Q 55, A 2 289d-290d; Q 57, A 1, REP 3 295a-d; Q 58, A 1 300c-301a; Q 60, A 1, REP 3 310b-311a; A 2, ANS 311a-d; Q 84, A 3 443d-444d; A 4, ANS 444d-446b; A 6, ANS 447c-449a; Q 89, A 1, REP 3 473b-475a; Q 117, A 1, ANS 595d-597c

25 MONTAIGNE: *Essays*, 264d-265b

28 HARVEY: *On Animal Generation*, 333d-334d

30 BACON: *Advancement of Learning*, 1b-c

31 DESCARTES: *Rules*, IV, 5c-d; 6d; VI, 8d-9a; VIII, 13c-d / *Discourse*, PART V, 54c; PART VI, 62a / *Meditations*, II 77d-81d esp 81a-d; III, 83b; 88c-d; VI, 96d-97a / *Objections and Replies*, 120c-d; 140b-c; 215b-c; 224b,d-225a

31 SPINOZA: *Ethics*, PART V, PROP 23, SCHOL 458c-d

30 BACON: *Advancement of Learning*, 2c-4c; 17b-c; 19b-c; 39d-40a; 41b-d; 54c-55d; 95d-101d / *Novum Organum*, BK I, APH 65 114b-c; APH 89 124a-d

31 DESCARTES: *Rules*, III, 4d-5a / *Discourse*, PART I, 43c / *Meditations*, 69a-71a,c; III, 88d-89a / *Objections and Replies*, 125c-126b; 168b-169a; 232b; 284d

32 MILTON: *Paradise Lost*, BK III [1-55] 135b-136b; BK VII [109-130] 219b-220a; BK XII [552-587] 331a-332a

33 PASCAL: *Provincial Letters*, 27a; 147b; 163a-166b passim / *Pensées*, 184-229 205a-213b; 233, 214a-b; 245 218b; 248 219a; 265-290 221b-225a; 425-427 243b-244b; 561-567 272b-273b; 585-588 277a-b / *Geometrical Demonstration*, 440a-b

35 LOCKE: *Human Understanding*, BK III, CH IX, SECT 23 291b-c; BK IV, CH VII, SECT 11, 340b-c; CH XVI, SECT 14 371b-c; CH XVII, SECT 23–CH XVIII, SECT 11 380b-384b; CH XIX, SECT 4 385a-b; SECT 14 387d-388a

35 HUME: *Human Understanding*, SECT VII, DIV 55, 474d-475a; SECT X, DIV 86 488d-489b; DIV 101 497a-b; SECT XII, DIV 132, 509c

37 FIELDING: *Tom Jones*, 182a-c; 379c-380a

40 GIBBON: *Decline and Fall*, 189b-190d passim, esp 190c-d; 307d-309d

42 KANT: *Practical Reason*, 346b-347a; 349b-351a / *Judgement*, 579a; 588d-589c; 604d-606d esp 606a-d; 607d-609b

43 MILL: *Utilitarianism*, 455a-c

44 BOSWELL: *Johnson*, 394a-b; 395a-b

46 HEGEL: *Philosophy of History*, PART IV, 349d

47 GOETHE: *Faust*, PART I [386-481] 11b-14a; PART II [11,441-458] 278b

51 TOLSTOY: *War and Peace*, BK V, 196b-197b; BK VI, 248d-249a; BK XV, 630d-631c

52 DOSTOEVSKY: *Brothers Karamazov*, BK I, 11a-b; BK VI, 168b-c; BK VII, 177b-180a; BK XI, 338a-b; BK XII, 396d-397a

54 FREUD: *New Introductory Lectures*, 874a-d; 877d-879d passim, esp 879c-d

6d. The classification of knowledge according to the degrees of assent

6d(1) The distinction between certain and probable knowledge

8 ARISTOTLE: *Interpretation*, CH 9 28a-29d / *Prior Analytics*, BK I, CH 13 [32^{b}4-23] 48b-d; BK II, CH 25 91a-b / *Posterior Analytics*, BK I, CH 2 97d-99a esp [72^{a}25-^{b}4] 98d-99a; CH 33 [89^{a}4-10] 121c / *Topics*, BK I, CH I [100^{a}25-^{b}23] 143a-b; BK V, CH 3 [131^{b}19-30] 182b-c / *Meteorology*, BK I, CH 7 [344^{a}5-7] 450b / *Metaphysics*, BK IV, CH 3 [1005^{b}8-34] 524c-525a; BK VI, CH I [1025^{b}1-16] 547b; BK XI, CH 7 [1064^{a}4-9] 592b; BK XII, CH 8 [1074^{a}14-16] 604c

9 ARISTOTLE: *Ethics*, BK VI, CH 3 [1139^{b}14-34] 388b-c; BK VII, CH 3 [1146^{b}23-30] 396d-397a

/ *Rhetoric*, BK I, CH I [1355^{a}14-17] 594b; CH 2 [1357^{a}23-^{b}24] 596d-597c; BK II, CH 25 [1402^{b}13-1403^{a}17] 652b-653a

16 COPERNICUS: *Revolutions of the Heavenly Spheres*, 505a-506a

18 AUGUSTINE: *City of God*, BK VIII, CH 3 266a-d

19 AQUINAS: *Summa Theologica*, PART I, Q I, A 8, ANS and REP 2 7c-8d; Q 14, A 3, ANS 77d-78b; A 13 86d-88c; Q 32, A I, REP 2 175d-178a; Q 47, A I, REP 3 256a-257b; Q 57, A 3, ANS 297b-298a; Q 58, A 7, REP 3 305c-306b; Q 79, A 9, REP 3-4 422b-423d; Q 82, A 2, ANS 432d-433c; Q 84, A I, ANS 440d-442a; Q 85, A 6, ANS 458d-459c; Q 86, A 4, ANS 463d-464d

20 AQUINAS: *Summa Theologica*, PART I-II, Q 51, A 3 14b-15a; Q 57, A 2, REP 3 36a-37b; Q 94, A 4, ANS 223d-224d; PART II-II, Q I, AA 4-5 382c-384b; Q 4, A 8 409a-d

23 HOBBES: *Leviathan*, PART I, 60c-61a; 65b-c

25 MONTAIGNE: *Essays*, 240c-241b; 271b-273b; 292a-d; 499c-d

30 BACON: *Novum Organum*, BK II, APH 33 161b-d

31 DESCARTES: *Rules*, I-II 1a-3b; XII, 22a-b; 23a-c / *Discourse*, PART I, 43d; PART II, 47a-48a; PART III, 49d-51a; PART IV, 51b-52a; 53c-d; PART VI, 63d / *Meditations*, I-II 75a-81d; III, 81d-82d; V, 95b-96a / *Objections and Replies*, 119d-120c; 123b; 124b-125b; POSTULATE I-III 130d-131a; POSTULATE VI-VII 131c; 168b-d; 260d-261a

31 SPINOZA: *Ethics*, PART I, PROP 11, SCHOL 358d-359b; PART II, PROP 24-45 383c-390b esp PROP 43, SCHOL 388d-389b; PROP 49, SCHOL 391d-394d; PART III, PROP 17, SCHOL 401d-402a

33 PASCAL: *Provincial Letters*, 27a-44a / *Pensées*, 233-241 213b-217b

35 LOCKE: *Human Understanding*, INTRO 93a-95d passim; BK IV, CH III, SECT 14 316b-d; SECT 24-29 320c-323a esp SECT 29 322c-323a; CH IV 323d-329a passim, esp SECT 6-8 325a-c, SECT 18 328d-329a; CH VI 331b-336d; CH IX, SECT I 349a; CH XI, SECT 9-12 356d-357d; CH XII, SECT 6-14 360a-363a passim; CH XIV, SECT I-CH XVI, SECT 3 364b-367c; CH XVII, SECT 2 371d-372b; SECT 14-17 378c-379c

35 HUME: *Human Understanding*, SECT IV, DIV 20-21 458a-c; DIV 30, 462a; SECT VI, 469d [fn 1]

36 SWIFT: *Gulliver*, PART IV, 165a-b

38 ROUSSEAU: *Inequality*, 348a,c

39 SMITH: *Wealth of Nations*, BK V, 335d-336a

42 KANT: *Pure Reason*, 1a-4a,c; 194b-c; 211c-218d; 228c-d; 230c-233d; 240b-243c / *Practical Reason*, 330d-331a / *Judgement*, 601d; 603a-b

43 MILL: *Liberty*, 274b-293b passim

46 HEGEL: *Philosophy of Right*, PART II, par 140, 50b-c; ADDITIONS, I 115a-d; 91, 131b-c

54 FREUD: *General Introduction*, 463d

(6d. The classification of knowledge according to the degrees of assent.)

6d(2) The types of certainty and the degrees of probability

8 ARISTOTLE: *Prior Analytics*, BK II, CH 25 91a-b
9 ARISTOTLE: *Ethics*, BK I, CH 3 [1094^{b}12–28] 339d-340a; CH 7 [1098^{a}25–35] 343d; BK II, CH 2 [1104^{a}1–9] 349b-c; BK III, CH 3 [1112^{a}30–^{b}12] 358b-c
19 AQUINAS: *Summa Theologica*, PART I, Q 1, A 5, ANS and REP 1 5c-6a; Q 54, A 5 288a-d
20 AQUINAS: *Summa Theologica*, PART II–II, Q 4, A 8 409a-d; Q 8, A 8 422c-423b; Q 9, A 1 423c-424b; A 2, ANS 424b-425a; Q 18, A 4, ANS 464c-465a; PART III, Q 7, A 3, REP 3 747b-748a
23 HOBBES: *Leviathan*, PART I, 53c-54a
25 MONTAIGNE: *Essays*, 240c-241b
30 BACON: *Novum Organum*, BK I, APH 126 134b
31 DESCARTES: *Rules*, III, 4a-5a / *Discourse*, PART II, 45a; PART III, 48b-51a / *Objections and Replies*, 124d-125a; 126a-b; 206c-207a; 226d; 243c-d
33 PASCAL: *Provincial Letters*, 102a-108a / *Pensées*, 907–924 349a-352a passim
35 LOCKE: *Human Understanding*, BK IV, CH II 309b-313a passim, esp SECT 1 309b-d, SECT 6-7 310c-311a, SECT 14 312b-d; CH XI, SECT 3 355a-b; CH XV–XVI 365a-371c; CH XVII, SECT 14-17 378c-379c; CH XIX, SECT 1 384c-d
35 HUME: *Human Understanding*, SECT VI 469d-470d; SECT IX, DIV 82 487b-c; SECT X, DIV 86–91 488d-491c passim, esp DIV 87 489b-d
38 ROUSSEAU: *Inequality*, 348a,c / *Social Contract*, BK III, 408a-b
42 KANT: *Pure Reason*, 5a-b; 66d-72c esp 67d-68a; 202b-203c; 240b-243c / *Intro. Metaphysic of Morals*, 387a-d / *Judgement*, 542d-543a; 600d-603d
43 FEDERALIST: NUMBER 31, 103c-104a
54 FREUD: *General Introduction*, 463d / *Beyond the Pleasure Principle*, 661c-662b / *New Introductory Lectures*, 818c-d

6d(3) The distinction between adequate and inadequate, or perfect and imperfect knowledge

18 AUGUSTINE: *City of God*, BK XIX, CH 18 523a-b
19 AQUINAS: *Summa Theologica*, PART I, Q 12, AA 7–8 56a-58b; A 12 60d-61c; Q 14, A 3 77d-78b; A 5, ANS 79a-80a; A 6 80a-81c; Q 17, A 4, ANS 103c-104b; Q 56, A 3, REP 1-2 294a-d; Q 57, A 5, REP 2 299b-300b; Q 84, A 2, ANS 442b-443c; A 7, ANS and REP 1 449b-450b; Q 85, A 3 455b-457a; A 7 459c-460b; A 8, REP 1 460b-461b; Q 89, A 1, ANS 473b-475a; A 2 475a-d; A 3, ANS and REP 2,4 475d-476c; A 4, ANS and REP 2 476c-477a; Q 117, A 1, REP 4 595d-597c; PART I–II, Q 27, A 2, REP 2 737d-738c
20 AQUINAS: *Summa Theologica*, PART I–II, Q 67,

A 3, ANS 83b-84d; PART III, Q 9, A 3, REP 2 765b-766b; Q 10 767b-772a
28 HARVEY: *On Animal Generation*, 333b
31 DESCARTES: *Rules*, II–III 2a-5a / *Objections and Replies*, 127b-c; POSTULATE VI–VII 131c; 152d-153c
31 SPINOZA: *Ethics*, PART II, DEF 4 373b; PROP II, COROL 377b-c; PROP 24-43 383c-389b; PART IV, PROP 64 444b
35 LOCKE: *Human Understanding*, BK II, CH XXXI 239b-243c passim, esp SECT 6 240d-241d, SECT 13 243a-b; BK III, CH VI, SECT 30–31 276d-277c; SECT 37 279b; SECT 40 280a-b; SECT 43-47 280c-282b passim
42 KANT: *Pure Reason*, 2b-4a,c; 125b[fn 1];193a-c; 240b-243c esp 240d-241a / *Judgement*, 498b-499c; 603a-b
53 JAMES: *Psychology*, 318b-319a; 668a-671a esp 669a-b; 676a-677a
54 FREUD: *General Introduction*, 560c-561b

6e. The classification of knowledge according to the end or aim of the knowing

6e(1) The distinction between theoretic and practical knowledge: knowing for the sake of knowledge and for the sake of action or production

7 PLATO: *Charmides*, 7d-8a / *Republic*, BK VII, 391d-394d esp 393c, 394b-c / *Statesman*, 581a / *Laws*, BK VII, 728b-729a
8 ARISTOTLE: *Topics*, BK VI, CH 6 [145^{a}12–18] 198d / *Heavens*, BK III, CH 7 [306^{a}14–18] 397b-c / *Metaphysics*, BK I, CH 1-2 499a-501c esp CH 2 [982^{a}30–^{b}27] 500c-501a; BK II, CH 1 [993^{b}20–23] 512a; BK IV, CH 4 [1008^{b}2–32] 527d-528b; BK VI, CH 1 [1025^{b}18–28] 547d; BK XI, CH 7 [1064^{a}10–19] 592b-c; BK XII, CH 9 [1074^{b}35–1075^{a}2] 605c / *Soul*, BK I, CH 3 [407^{a}22–30] 636d-637a; BK III, CH 7 663c-664b; CH 9 [432^{b}26–433^{a}9] 665c
9 ARISTOTLE: *Ethics*, BK I, CH 3 339d-340b; CH 7 [1098^{a}25–35] 343d; BK II, CH 2 [1103^{b}26–1104^{a}9] 349b-c; CH 4 350d-351b esp [1105^{b}12–18] 351a-b; BK III, CH 3 [1112^{a}30–^{b}12] 358b-c; BK VI, CH 2 [1139^{a}21–^{b}14] 387d-388b; CH 5 389a-c; CH 7 390a-d; CH 8 [1142^{a}13–19] 391b; CH 12 [1143^{b}17–1144^{a}5] 393b-c
12 EPICTETUS: *Discourses*, BK I, CH 26 131b-132b; BK III, CH 6 181d-182b
14 PLUTARCH: *Marcellus*, 252a-255a
16 PTOLEMY: *Almagest*, BK I, 5a
18 AUGUSTINE: *City of God*, BK VIII, CH 4 266d-267c
19 AQUINAS: *Summa Theologica*, PART I, Q I, A 4 5a-b; A 5, ANS 5c-6a; Q 14, A 1, REP 2 75d-76c; A 16 90b-91b; Q 15, A 3 93b-94a; Q 34, A 3 188b-189a; Q 79, A 9, ANS 422b-423d; AA 11–13 424d-427a; Q 84, A 8, ANS 450b-451b; Q 86, A 1, REP 2 461c-462a; A 3, CONTRARY 463b-d; PART I–II, Q 1, A 6, REP 2 614a-c; Q 3, A 5 626b-627a; Q 7, A 2 652d-653c

20 AQUINAS: *Summa Theologica*, PART I–II, Q 56, A 3, ANS 31a-32b; Q 57, A 5, REP 3 39a-40a; A 6, ANS and REP 2–3 40a-41a; Q 94, A 4, ANS 223d-224d; PART II–II, Q 8, A 3 418c-419a; Q 9, A 3 425b-d; Q 45, A 3 600c-601a; Q 179, A 2, ANS 607a-c; PART III, Q 11, A 1, REP 3 772b-773a; Q 13, A 1, REP 3 780a-781b

21 DANTE: *Divine Comedy*, PARADISE, X [109-114] 121b-c; XIII [37–111] 125d-126c

23 HOBBES: *Leviathan*, PART I, 60a-61a; PART IV, 267a-b

25 MONTAIGNE: *Essays*, 55d-62a esp 56b-57b; 63d-77d passim, esp 69d-72a; 327b-d; 520b-522a

30 BACON: *Advancement of Learning*, 16d-17a; 42a-c; 46c-47c; 55b-d; 65d-66a; 69c; 86b-c / *Novum Organum*, BK I, APH 3 107b; APH 66 114d-115c; BK II, APH 1–9 137a-140c

31 DESCARTES: *Rules*, I 1a-2a / *Discourse*, PART I, 44a-c; PART III, 48b-49b; PART VI, 60d-61c; 66d-67a / *Objections and Replies*, 126a-b; 162d; 206c-207a; 237b-c; 243c-d

33 PASCAL: *Provincial Letters*, 102a-108a

35 LOCKE: *Human Understanding*, INTRO, SECT 5–6 94b-95a; BK I, CH II, SECT 1 103d-104a; SECT 3–4 104b-105a; BK IV, CH XI, SECT 8 356b-d; CH XXI 394d-395a,c

35 BERKELEY: *Human Knowledge*, INTRO, SECT 2 405b; SECT 119-122 436c-437c passim; SECT 131 439b-c

35 HUME: *Human Understanding*, SECT 1 451a-455b esp DIV 1–5 451a-453b; SECT VIII, DIV 65, 479b-c; SECT XI, DIV 104 498b-c

42 KANT: *Pure Reason*, 5a-13d; 190c-191a; 234c-235a / *Fund. Prin. Metaphysic of Morals*, 253a-d; 260d-261b; 266a-d; 271a-c; 283d-284d / *Practical Reason*, 291a-297c; 300d [fn 1]; 307d-314d esp 310a-b; 329a-330c / *Intro. Metaphysic of Morals*, 388a-d; 390b,d-391a / *Judgement*, 461a-475d esp 463a-467a, 474b-475d; 515b-c; 523d-524a; 578a-b

43 FEDERALIST: NUMBER 31, 103c-104a

43 MILL: *Representative Government*, 341d-342d; 346d-347a / *Utilitarianism*, 445c-d

46 HEGEL: *Philosophy of Right*, PART III, par 227, 74b-c; ADDITIONS, 1 115a-d / *Philosophy of History*, PART IV, 360d-361a

51 TOLSTOY: *War and Peace*, BK IX, 361d-365c

53 JAMES: *Psychology*, 656b

6e(2) The types of practical knowledge: the use of knowledge in production and in the direction of conduct; technical and moral knowledge

7 PLATO: *Charmides*, 5c-6d / *Lysis*, 16c-18b / *Euthydemus*, 70b-c; 74b-c / *Statesman*, 580d-582a / *Laws*, BK I, 649c-d

8 ARISTOTLE: *Topics*, BK VI, CH 6 [145ª12-18] 198d

9 ARISTOTLE: *Ethics*, BK I, CH 1–2 339a-d; BK II, CH 4 350d-351b; BK VI, CH 2 [1139ª32-b5] 388a; CH 4–5 388d-389c

19 AQUINAS: *Summa Theologica*, PART I, Q 21, A 2, ANS 125c-d; Q 65, A 2, REP 3 340b-341b; PART I–II, Q 34, A 1, REP 3 768c-769d

20 AQUINAS: *Summa Theologica*, PART I–II, Q 57, AA 3–6 37b-41a; Q 58, A 2, REP 1 42a-43a; A 5, REP 2 44d-45c; Q 65, A 1, REP 4 70b-72a; Q 93, A 1, ANS 215b,d-216c; Q 97, A 2, REP 1 236d-237b

31 DESCARTES: *Discourse*, PART VI, 60d-61c

42 KANT: *Pure Reason*, 149d-150a; 234c-235a / *Fund. Prin. Metaphysic of Morals*, 253a-255d esp 253a-254b; 260d-261b; 264b-d; 266b-d; 271a-d; 283d-287d / *Practical Reason*, 305d-307d; 314d-321b esp 318c-321b; 329a-330c; 354d-355d; 357c-360d / *Pref. Metaphysical Elements of Ethics*, 367c / *Intro. Metaphysic of Morals*, 383a-d; 387b; 388a-d; 390b,d-391a / *Judgement*, 463a-467a; 515b-c; 523d-524a; 596c-598b

54 FREUD: *Psycho-Analytic Therapy*, 127a,c

7. Comparison of human with other kinds of knowledge

7a. Human and divine knowledge

OLD TESTAMENT: *Genesis*, 3:1-7,22 / *I Samuel*, 16:7—(D) *I Kings*, 16:7 / *Job*, 11:1-12; 12:16-17; 28:12-25; 38-41 / *Psalms*, 92:5-6; 94:11; 139—(D) *Psalms*, 91:6-7; 93:11; 138 / *Proverbs*, 20:24 / *Ecclesiastes*, 3:10-11; 8:16-17; 11:1-6 / *Isaiah*, 40:12-31 esp 40:28; 44:24-25; 55:8-9 —(D) *Isaias*, 40:12-31 esp 40:28; 44:24-25; 55:8-9 / *Jeremiah*, 10:7-8,12-15; 51:15-18— (D) *Jeremias*, 10:7-8,12-15; 51:15-18

APOCRYPHA: *Wisdom of Solomon*, 9:13-17—(D) OT, *Book of Wisdom*, 9:13-17 / *Ecclesiasticus*, 1:1-10; 23:18-20; 24:24-29; 42:17-22—(D) OT, *Ecclesiasticus*, 1:1-10; 23:25-29; 24:35-39; 42:17-23

NEW TESTAMENT: *Romans*, 11:33-36 / *I Corinthians*, 1:17-2:16; 3:18-21

5 AESCHYLUS: *Suppliant Maidens* [86-103] 2a-b / *Prometheus Bound* [526-554] 45b-c

5 EURIPIDES: *Iphigenia Among the Tauri* [570-575] 416a / *Bacchantes* [386-433] 343a-b

7 PLATO: *Phaedrus*, 125a-126c / *Apology*, 203a / *Parmenides*, 489d-490d

8 ARISTOTLE: *Metaphysics*, BK I, CH 2 [982ᵇ28-983ª11] 501a-b; BK XII, CH 7 [1072ᵇ14-29] 602d-603a; CH 9 605a-d

9 ARISTOTLE: *Ethics*, BK X, CH 8 [1178ᵇ20-23] 433b-c

12 EPICTETUS: *Discourses*, BK I, CH 3 108b-c; CH 12, 119d-120a; CH 14 120d-121c; BK IV, CH 11, 240d-241a

17 PLOTINUS: *Fifth Ennead*, TR III, CH 2-4 216b-217d

18 AUGUSTINE: *Confessions*, BK V, par 5 28b-c; BK XI, par 6 90c-d; par 41 99a-b; BK XIII, par 46 123a-c / *City of God*, BK IX, CH 22 296d-297a; BK XI, CH 10, 328c-d; CH 21 333a-d; BK XII, CH 18 354b-d; BK XXII, CH 29, 614b-d

(7. Comparison of human with other kinds of knowledge. 7a. Human and divine knowledge.)

/ *Christian Doctrine*, BK I, CH 8–10 626c–627b; CH 12–14 627c–628b

19 AQUINAS: *Summa Theologica*, PART I, Q 1, A 2 4a–c; A 4 5a–b; A 5, ANS 5c–6a; A 6 6b–7a; A 8, REP 2 7c–8d; Q 3, A 1, REP 1 14b–15b; A 6, REP 1 18c–19a; Q 8, A 3, ANS and REP 2–4 36b–37c; Q 12, A 1, REP 1 50c–51c; A 4 53b–54c; AA 7–8 56a–58b; Q 14 75c–91b; Q 16 94b–100d passim; Q 18, AA 3–4 106b–108c; QQ 22–24 127c–143c passim; Q 27, AA 1–2 153b–155b; Q 28, A 4, REP 1–2 160c–161d; Q 34 185a–189a passim; Q 44, A 3 240b–241a; Q 46, A 2, REP 3 253a–255a; Q 55, A 1, ANS and REP 3 289a–d; A 3, ANS 291a–d; Q 57, A 1, ANS 295a–d; A 2, ANS 295d–297a; A 3, ANS and REP 1 297b–298a; A 4, ANS 298a–299a; Q 62, A 9, ANS 324a–325b; Q 79, A 1, ANS 414a–d; A 2, ANS 414d–416a; A 4, ANS and REP 1,5 417a–418c; A 10, REP 2 423d–424d; Q 84, A 2, ANS and REP 3 442b–443c; Q 85, A 4, ANS 457a–d; A 5, ANS 457d–458d; Q 86, A 2, REP 1 462a–463a; A 4, ANS 463d–464d; Q 87, A 1, ANS 465a–466c; A 3, ANS 467b–468a; Q 89, A 1, ANS 473b–475a; A 4, ANS 476c–477a; Q 93, A 4, ANS 494c–495b; PART I–II, Q 2, A 3, ANS 617b–618a; Q 3, A 8, REP 2 628d–629c; Q 14, A 1, REP 2 677b–678a

20 AQUINAS: *Summa Theologica*, PART I–II, Q 91, A 3, REP 1 209d–210c; Q 110, A 2, REP 2 349a–d; A 4, ANS 350d–351d; PART II–II, Q 45, A 6, REP 1–2 602b–603c; Q 180, A 8, REP 3 616a–d; PART III, Q 9, A 1 763b–764c; A 4, ANS 766b–767b; Q 10 767b–772a; Q 13, A 1, REP 2–3 780a–781b; Q 15, A 3 789d–790c; A 10, ANS 795b–796a; PART III SUPPL, Q 92, A 3 1034b–1037c

21 DANTE: *Divine Comedy*, PARADISE, IV [124–132] 112a; XIX [22–66] 135b–d; XXI [73–102] 139a–b; XXVI [103–108] 146d–147a

22 CHAUCER: *Troilus and Cressida*, BK IV, STANZA 136–154 106a–108b

23 HOBBES: *Leviathan*, PART II, 162c

25 MONTAIGNE: *Essays*, 213a–b; 238c–239c

30 BACON: *Advancement of Learning*, 17b–c; 98d–99b / *Novum Organum*, BK I, APH 23 108c; BK II, APH 15 149a

31 DESCARTES: *Objections and Replies*, 152d–153c

31 SPINOZA: *Ethics*, PART I, PROP 17, SCHOL 362c–363c

32 MILTON: *Paradise Lost*, BK III [654–735] 149b–151b; BK VII [109–130] 219b–220a; BK VIII [66–197] 233b–236b; [412–418] 241a / *Samson Agonistes* [60–62] 340b–341a

33 PASCAL: *Pensées*, 793, 326b

35 LOCKE: *Human Understanding*, BK II, CH I, SECT 10, 123b; CH X, SECT 9 143a–c; CH XV, SECT 12 165b–c; CH XXIII, SECT 34 213a–b; BK III, CH VI, SECT 3 268d; SECT 11–12 271b–272b; BK IV, CH X, SECT 5–6 350a–c

42 KANT: *Pure Reason*, 33a–d; 52c–53b / *Practical Reason*, 344a–c; 350c–351b / *Judgement*, 572d–574b; 579a

47 GOETHE: *Faust*, PART I [1765–1784] 42b

53 JAMES: *Psychology*, 669a–b

7b. Human and angelic knowledge

18 AUGUSTINE: *Confessions*, BK XII, par 12, 102a; par 16 102d–103a; par 20 103c–d; par 23 104b–c / *City of God*, BK VIII, CH 25 283b–c; BK IX, CH 21–22 296b–297a; BK XI, CH 29 339a–b; BK XVI, CH 6 426c–427a; BK XXII, CH 1 586b,d–587b; CH 29, 614b–d

19 AQUINAS: *Summa Theologica*, PART I, Q 12, A 4 53b–54c; A 10, ANS and REP 2 59a–d; QQ 54–58 284d–306b passim; Q 59, A 1, REP 1 306c–307b; Q 60, A 2, ANS 311a–d; Q 64, A 1, REP 2 334a–335c; Q 79, A 8, ANS and REP 3 421c–422b; A 10, ANS 423d–424d; Q 84, A 2, ANS and REP 3 442b–443c; A 3, REP 1 443d–444d; A 7, ANS 449b–450b; Q 85, A 1, ANS 451c–453c; A 5, ANS 457d–458d; Q 87, A 1, ANS and REP 2–3 465a–466c; A 3, ANS 467b–468a; Q 89, A 3, ANS and REP 1,3 475d–476c; A 4, ANS 476c–477a; QQ 106–107 545c–552b passim; Q 108, A 1, ANS 552c–553c; Q 117, A 2 597c–598c

20 AQUINAS: *Summa Theologica*, PART I–II, Q 51, A 1, ANS 12b–13c; PART III, Q 9, A 3, ANS 765b–766b; A 4, ANS 766b–767b; Q 11, A 3, REP 3 773d–774c; A 4 774c–775a; A 6, ANS and REP 1 775d–776b; Q 12, A 4 779a–d

21 DANTE: *Divine Comedy*, PARADISE, XIX [22–66] 135b–d; XXIX [70–81] 151a

30 BACON: *Novum Organum*, BK II, APH 15 149a

32 MILTON: *Paradise Lost*, BK III [654–735] 149b–151b; BK V [388–505] 183b–186a esp [404–413] 184a, [469–490] 185b–186a; [544–576] 187a–b; BK VI [316–353] 203a–204a; BK VIII [66–75] 233b

33 PASCAL: *Pensées*, 285 224a; 793, 326b

35 LOCKE: *Human Understanding*, BK II, CH X, SECT 9 143a–c; CH XXIII, SECT 36 213c–d; BK III, CH VI, SECT 3 268d; CH XI, SECT 23 305a–b; BK IV, CH III, SECT 6, 315a–b; SECT 23 320a–c; CH XVII, SECT 14 378c–d

35 BERKELEY: *Human Knowledge*, SECT 81 428c–d

36 STERNE: *Tristram Shandy*, 318b; 394a

42 KANT: *Fund. Prin. Metaphysic of Morals*, 285a–287d / *Practical Reason*, 354d–355d / *Judgement*, 572d–574b

7c. Knowledge in this life compared with knowledge in the state of innocence and knowledge hereafter

OLD TESTAMENT: *Genesis*, 2:19–20; 3:1–22 esp 3:5, 3:22

NEW TESTAMENT: *I Corinthians*, 13:12

7 PLATO: *Phaedrus*, 124b–126d / *Meno*, 179d–180b / *Phaedo*, 228a–230c

17 PLOTINUS: *Fourth Ennead*, TR IV, CH 1–5 159a–161b

18 AUGUSTINE: *Confessions*, BK IX, par 23–25 68a-c; BK X, par 7 73a; BK XIII, par 18, 115c / *City of God*, BK XXII, CH 29 614b-616d / *Christian Doctrine*, BK I, CH 37–38 635b-d; BK II, CH 7 638d-639c

19 AQUINAS: *Summa Theologica*, PART I, Q I, A 9, REP 3 8d-9c; Q 12 50b-62b esp AA 11–13 59d-62b; Q 62, A I, ANS 317d-318c; Q 84, A 5 446c-447c; Q 88, A I, ANS 469a-471c; Q 89 473a-480c; Q 94 501c-506a; Q 101 522c-523d

20 AQUINAS: *Summa Theologica*, PART I-II, Q 67, AA 2–3 82c-84d; Q 69, A 2, REP 3 97b-98c; PART II-II, Q 180, A 5 611d-613a; PART III, Q 11, A I, REP 2 772b-773a; A 2, ANS and REP 1–2 773a-d; PART III SUPPL, Q 72, A I, REP I 917c-919a; Q 82, A 3, REP 4 971a-972d; Q 92, A I, REP 3,5,13,15 1025c-1032b; A 2, ANS 1032b-1034b

21 DANTE: *Divine Comedy*, HELL, X [94–108] 14c-d; PURGATORY, III [16–45] 56a-b; PARA-DISE, XV [37–69] 128d-129a; XIX [22–66] 135b-d; XX [130–148] 138a-b; XXI [73–102] 139a-b; XXVI [91–108] 146d-147a; XXX [1–123] 151d-153a

31 DESCARTES: *Meditations*, III, 88d-89a

33 PASCAL: *Pensées*, 242, 218a; 425–427 243b-244b

46 HEGEL: *Philosophy of Right*, ADDITIONS, 90 130b-d

52 DOSTOEVSKY: *Brothers Karamazov*, BK VI, 168a-c

7d. The knowledge of men and brutes

5 EURIPIDES: *Trojan Women* [669–672] 275d

7 PLATO: *Laches*, 35b-36a / *Republic*, BK II, 320b-c

8 ARISTOTLE: *Metaphysics*, BK I, CH I [980^{b}25–27] 499b / *Soul*, BK III, CH 3 [427^{b}7–14] 659d-660a; [428^{a}20–24] 660c; CH 10 [433^{a}8–13] 665d

9 ARISTOTLE: *History of Animals*, BK I, CH I [488^{b}24–27] 9d; BK VIII, CH I [588^{a}18–^{b}4] 114b,d / *Generation of Animals*, BK I, CH 23 [731^{a}30–^{b}5] 271c-d / *Ethics*, BK VII, CH 3 [1147^{b}2–5] 397d

10 GALEN: *Natural Faculties*, BK I, CH 12, 173a-c

12 EPICTETUS: *Discourses*, BK I, CH 6, 110c-111c; CH 9, 114c-d; CH 28, 134b; BK II, CH 8, 146a-c; BK IV, CH 7, 233a

12 AURELIUS: *Meditations*, BK III, SECT 16 262d-263a,c; BK VI, SECT 23 276b; BK IX, SECT 9 292b-d

19 AQUINAS: *Summa Theologica*, PART I, Q 18, A 2, ANS and REP I 105c-106b; Q 78, A 4, ANS and REP 4–6 411d-413d; Q 79, A 6, REP I 419b-420d; A 8, REP 3 421c-422b; Q 84, A 2, REP I 442b-443c

23 HOBBES: *Leviathan*, PART I, 52b; 53a-b; 53d-54a; 63a; 79b-c; PART II, 100a-c; PART IV, 267b

25 MONTAIGNE: *Essays*, 215a-223b

30 BACON: *Novum Organum*, BK I, APH 73 117d-118a; BK II, APH 40, 173c-d

31 DESCARTES: *Discourse*, PART V, 59c-60b / *Objections and Replies*, 156a-d

32 MILTON: *Paradise Lost*, BK VII [506–516] 228a; BK VIII [369–451] 240a-242a; BK IX [549–566] 259b

33 PASCAL: *Vacuum*, 357a-358a

35 LOCKE: *Human Understanding*, BK II, CH IX, SECT 12–15 140c-141a; CH XI, SECT 4–11 144d-146a; CH XXVII, SECT 8 221a-222a; BK III, CH VI, SECT 12, 272b

35 BERKELEY: *Human Knowledge*, INTRO, SECT 11 407b-408a

35 HUME: *Human Understanding*, SECT IX 487b-488c; SECT XII, DIV 118, 504c

38 MONTESQUIEU: *Spirit of Laws*, BK I, 1d-2a

38 ROUSSEAU: *Inequality*, 338a

42 KANT: *Pure Reason*, 164a-165c / *Practical Reason*, 316c-317a / *Pref. Metaphysical Elements of Ethics*, 372a-b / *Judgement*, 479a-c; 584d-585c; 602b,d [fn 1]

48 MELVILLE: *Moby Dick*, 244a-245b

49 DARWIN: *Descent of Man*, 288d-289a; 290c-298c passim, esp 292a-293a, 294d-295a

53 JAMES: *Psychology*, 678b-686b; 704a-b

8. The use and value of knowledge

8a. The technical use of knowledge in the sphere of production: the applications of science in art

OLD TESTAMENT: *Genesis*, 5:22 / *Exodus*, 31:1–11; 35:30–36:8

5 AESCHYLUS: *Prometheus Bound* [442–506] 44c-45a

7 PLATO: *Lysis*, 16c-18b / *Protagoras*, 43b-45a / *Euthydemus*, 70a-c / *Ion* 142a-148a,c / *Gorgias*, 261a-262a / *Republic*, BK VII, 392a-b; 394b-d / *Statesman*, 580d-581a / *Philebus*, 633a-634b / *Laws*, BK IV, 684c-685a

8 ARISTOTLE: *Posterior Analytics*, BK II, CH 19 [100^{a}6–9] 136c / *Physics*, BK II, CH 2 [194^{a}21–^{b}13] 270c-271a / *Metaphysics*, BK I, CH I 499a-500b; BK VII, CH 7 [1032^{a}25–1033^{a}4] 555b-556a; CH 9 [1034^{a}21–32] 557c; BK IX, CH 2 571c-572a; CH 5 [1047^{b}31–1048^{a}10] 573a-b; BK XI, CH 7 [1064^{a}10–14] 592b-c / *Sense and the Sensible*, CH I [436^{a}16–^{b}2] 673b / *Youth, Life, and Breathing*, CH 27 [480^{b}21–31] 726d

9 ARISTOTLE: *Ethics*, BK I, CH I 339a-b; CH 7 [1098^{a}28–32] 343d; BK II, CH 4 [1105^{a}17–^{b}4] 350d-351a; BK VI, CH 4 388d-389a

10 HIPPOCRATES: *Ancient Medicine* 1a-9a,c esp par 1–4 1a-2c, par 14 5a-c, par 20–22 7b-8d / *Prognostics*, par I 19a-b; par 25 26a,c / *Epidemics*, BK III, SECT III, par 16 59b-c / *Surgery*, par I 70b / *Articulations*, par 58, 112d / *The Law*, par 4 144d

10 GALEN: *Natural Faculties*, BK II, CH 9, 195c-196a

(8. The use and value of knowledge. 8a. The technical use of knowledge in the sphere of production: the applications of science in art.)

11 NICOMACHUS: *Arithmetic*, BK I, 812d-813a

12 LUCRETIUS: *Nature of Things*, BK V [1241-1457] 77b-80a,c passim

12 EPICTETUS: *Discourses*, BK II, CH 17, 158d-159b

13 VIRGIL: *Georgics* 37a-99a passim, esp II [475-515] 65a-66a

14 PLUTARCH: *Marcellus*, 252a-255a

19 AQUINAS: *Summa Theologica*, PART I, Q 14, A 8 82c-83b; Q 16, A 1, ANS 94b-95c; Q 17, A 1, ANS 100d-101d; Q 19, A 4, REP 4 111c-112c

20 AQUINAS: *Summa Theologica*, PART I-II, Q 57, A 3, ANS and REP 1,3 37b-38a; A 4 esp ANS and REP 2 38a-39a; A 5, REP 3 39a-40a; Q 95, A 2, ANS 227c-228c

22 CHAUCER: *Troilus and Cressida*, BK I, STANZA 153 21a

23 HOBBES: *Leviathan*, PART I, 60a-b; 73b; PART IV, 267a-b

25 MONTAIGNE: *Essays*, 450d-451a; 523c-524b

28 GILBERT: *Loadstone*, BK V, 100c-101c

28 GALILEO: *Two New Sciences*, FIRST DAY, 154c-155b; 160d-161a; SECOND DAY, 191b-193b

28 HARVEY: *Motion of the Heart*, 289d; 291d-292a / *Circulation of the Blood*, 305a-d

29 CERVANTES: *Don Quixote*, PART I, 145c-d

30 BACON: *Advancement of Learning*, 5b-c; 48d-49b; 50c-51d; 74b-c / *Novum Organum*, BK I, APH 3 107b; APH 11 107d; APH 81 120b-c; APH 85 121d-122d; APH 129 134d-135d; BK II, APH 4 137d-138b; APH 44-52 175d-195d passim / *New Atlantis* 199a-214d esp 210d-214d

31 DESCARTES: *Discourse*, PART VI, 61b-d; 66d-67a

33 PASCAL: *Equilibrium of Liquids*, 392b-393a

34 NEWTON: *Principles*, 1a-b; COROL II 15a-16b

35 LOCKE: *Human Understanding*, BK IV, CH XII, SECT 11-12 361c-362c

35 HUME: *Human Understanding*, SECT I, DIV 5 452d-453b

36 SWIFT: *Gulliver*, PART III, 97b; 106a-112a

39 SMITH: *Wealth of Nations*, BK I, 5b-6a

40 GIBBON: *Decline and Fall*, 633c; 661c-663c

42 KANT: *Pure Reason*, 60a-c / *Fund. Prin. Metaphysic of Morals*, 266d-267a / *Practical Reason*, 300d [fn 1] / *Intro. Metaphysic of Morals*, 388d / *Judgement*, 463a-464c; 523d-524a; 526a-527b

43 MILL: *Representative Government*, 369a

45 LAVOISIER: *Elements of Chemistry*, PART I, 45c-d

45 FOURIER: *Theory of Heat*, 170a; 184a; 213b

45 FARADAY: *Researches in Electricity*, 433a-440a,c

46 HEGEL: *Philosophy of History*, PART I, 218d-219a

49 DARWIN: *Origin of Species*, 19c-d

50 MARX: *Capital*, 167a-171c passim, esp 170a-171a; 176d-178d; 180d-189b esp 188b-189b; 239b-241a; 299b-d

51 TOLSTOY: *War and Peace*, BK IX, 361d-365c; BK X, 424a-c; 425b-426a; 441b-c; 456a-457c; EPILOGUE II, 685a

54 FREUD: *Psycho-Analytic Therapy*, 123a-125a esp 123b, 125a / *Civilization and Its Discontents*, 777a-c; 778b-d

8b. The moral use of knowledge and the moral value of knowledge

8b(1) The knowledge of good and evil: the relation of knowledge to virtue and sin

OLD TESTAMENT: *Genesis*, 2:9,16-17; 3:1-7,22 / *Job*, 28:28 / *Psalms*, 37:30; 82:4-5—(D) *Psalms*, 36:30; 81:4-5 / *Proverbs*, 1:1-23; 2:1-20; 7-8 esp 8:8, 8:20; 10:8,31; 11:12; 14:9,16-18,22,29; 15:21; 19:8; 24:1-14; 28:7; 29:8 / *Ecclesiastes*, 2:26

APOCRYPHA: *Wisdom of Solomon*, 1:1-7; 6:12-20; 8:5-7; 9:9-10:14; 14:22-27—(D) OT, *Book of Wisdom*, 1:1-7; 6:13-20; 8:5-7; 9:9-10:14; 14:22-27 / *Ecclesiasticus*, 17:7; 19:22-24; 50:28-29—(D) OT, *Ecclesiasticus*, 17:6; 19:19-21; 50:30-31

NEW TESTAMENT: *Luke*, 23:34 / *John*, 3:17-21 / *Romans*, 2:17-23; 7 esp 7:15-25; 16:19 / *Philippians*, 1:9-11 / *Colossians*, 1:9-11 / *Titus*, 1:16 / *Hebrews*, 5:14 / *James*, 4:17 / *II Peter*, 1:1-11

5 EURIPIDES: *Hippolytus* [373-387] 228b-c

6 THUCYDIDES: *Peloponnesian War*, BK II, 397b-c; 402d-403b

7 PLATO: *Charmides*, 7b-c; 12a-13c / *Laches*, 31a-b; 33a-37a / *Protagoras*, 40b-41a; 56b; 57d-64d / *Euthydemus*, 69a-71a; 74b-76b / *Meno* 174a-190a,c esp 177d-178b, 183b-190a,c / *Phaedo*, 225d-226c; 230d-234c / *Gorgias*, 256d-259c; 280c-281b / *Republic*, BK I, 301d-302c; 306c-308a; BK II, 314d-315a; BK III, 333b-d; 337b-d; BK IV, 354d-355a; BK VI-VII, 383d-401d; BK X, 439b-441a,c / *Theaetetus*, 530b-531a / *Laws*, BK I, 643c-d; 645b-652d; BK III, 670b; BK V, 689d-690c; 696c-697a; BK VII, 724c-728a; BK IX, 748a-b; 754a-b; BK XII, 788d-789a; 792c-d; 795c-d / *Seventh Letter*, 801b; 806b-c; 809c-810d esp 810c-d

8 ARISTOTLE: *Prior Analytics*, BK II, CH 25 [69ᵃ20-28] 91a / *Topics*, BK II, CH 9 [114ᵇ9-13] 160b; BK III, CH 6 [120ᵃ26-31] 168a; BK IV, CH 2 [121ᵇ24-122ᵃ2] 169d-170a; CH 3 [124ᵃ10-14] 172d; BK V, CH 7 [137ᵃ13-17] 189b / *Metaphysics*, BK III, CH 2 [996ᵃ21-ᵇ13] 514d-515a

9 ARISTOTLE: *Ethics*, BK I, CH 1-3 339a-340b; CH 4 [1095ᵃ30-ᵇ12] 340c-d; CH 6 [1096ᵇ32-1097ᵃ14] 342b-c; BK II, CH 2 [1103ᵇ26-1104ᵃ9] 349b-c; CH 4 350d-351b esp [1105ᵇ1-4] 351a, [1105ᵇ13-18] 351a-b; CH 6 [1106ᵇ36-1107ᵃ3] 352c; BK III, CH 1 [1110ᵇ17-35] 356b-c; BK V, CH 8 [1135ᵇ9-1136ᵃ9] 383c-384a; BK VI, CH 5

389a-c; CH 8 [1141^{b}33-1142^{a}19] 391a-b; CH
9-10 391c-392c; CH 12-13 393b-394d; BK VII,
CH 2-3 395c-398a; BK X, CH 9 [1179^{b}4-1180^a
13] 434b-d / *Rhetoric*, BK I, CH 10 [1368^{b}7-13]
611d; CH 13 [1373^{b}27-39] 618a

12 EPICTETUS: *Discourses*, BK I, CH 5 110b-c; CH
11 116d-118d; CH 26-28 131b-134d; BK II, CH
11 150a-151b; CH 22 167d-170a; CH 26 174c-d;
BK III, CH 10 185d-187a; BK IV, CH I 213a-223d

12 AURELIUS: *Meditations*, BK II, SECT I 256b,d;
BK III, SECT 12 262b-c; SECT 16 262d-263a,c;
BK VII, SECT 22 281b; SECT 26 281c; SECT 62-
63 283d-284a; BK VIII, SECT 14 286c; BK IX,
SECT 42 295c-296a,c; BK XII, SECT 12 308b-c

14 PLUTARCH: *Pericles*, 121a-122a / *Timoleon*,
197c-198a / *Agesilaus*, 490d-491b / *Alexander*,
543b-544a

17 PLOTINUS: *First Ennead*, TR II, CH 6-7 9a-10a;
TR III, CH 6-TR IV, CH 3 11d-14a

18 AUGUSTINE: *Confessions*, BK X, par 54-57
85a-86a; BK XIII, par 46 123a-c / *City of God*,
BK VIII, CH 3 266a-d; CH 10 271a-d; BK IX,
CH 20 296a-b; BK XI, CH 28 338a-d; BK XVIII,
CH 40 495a-b; BK XIX, CH 20, 524a / *Christian
Doctrine*, BK I, CH 36-37 634d-635c; CH 40
636a,c; BK II, CH 9 640c-d; CH 38 654b-c

19 AQUINAS: *Summa Theologica*, PART I, Q I, A 6,
REP 3 6b-7a; Q 14, A 10 83d-84c; Q 15, A 3, REP
1 93b-94a; Q 18, A 4, REP 4 107d-108c; Q 22, A
1 127d-128d; A 3, REP 3 130d-131c; Q 54, A 5
288a-d; Q 59, A 3, ANS 308b-309a; Q 79, AA
11-13 424d-427a; PART I-II, Q I, A 6, REP 3
614a-c; Q 2, A I, REP I 615d-616c; Q 19, AA
3-6 704c-708a

20 AQUINAS: *Summa Theologica*, PART I-II, Q 51,
AA 2-3 13c-15a; Q 58, A 2 42a-43a; Q 76 140d-
144d; PART II-II, Q 18, A 4, ANS 464c-465a; Q
45, AA 3-5 600c-602b; PART III SUPPL, Q 87
997a-1000c

21 DANTE: *Divine Comedy*, HELL, III [1-18] 4a-b;
XXVI [49-142] 38c-39c; PURGATORY, III [16-
45] 56a-b; X [112-139] 68c-d; XXXII [37-60]
102d-103a; PARADISE, XIX [22-66] 135b-d;
XXVI [25-45] 146a-b

23 HOBBES: *Leviathan*, PART I, 95d-96b; PART II,
112a-b

25 MONTAIGNE: *Essays*, 208a; 213a-216c; 218c-
219a; 232b-242d; 478c-480c; 502c-504c; 508a-
512a

26 SHAKESPEARE: *Merchant of Venice*, ACT I, SC
II [11-24] 408b-c

27 SHAKESPEARE: *Measure for Measure*, ACT II,
SC IV [2-17] 184d

30 BACON: *Advancement of Learning*, 17d-18a;
26c-27a; 79c-80a

31 DESCARTES: *Discourse*, PART I, 43c; PART III,
49d-50b

31 SPINOZA: *Ethics*, PART IV, PREF 422b,d-424a;
DEF 1-2 424a; PROP 8 426b-c; PROP 14-17
428a-d; PROP 24 430d; PROP 26-27 431a-c;
PROP 35-73 433b-447a; PART V, PROP 1-20
452d-458a; PROP 42 463b-d

32 MILTON: *Paradise Lost*, BK VII [519-549] 228b-
229a; BK VIII [316-337] 239a-b; BK IX [677-
779] 262a-264a; BK XI [84-98] 301a / *Areopagitica*, 389a-396a passim, esp 390b-391a, 394b-
395a

33 PASCAL: *Pensées*, 67 180b; 381-385 238b-239a;
425-427 243b-244b; 460 254b

34 NEWTON: *Optics*, BK III, 543b-544a

35 LOCKE: *Human Understanding*, INTRO, SECT
5-6 94b-95a; BK II, CH XXI, SECT 35 186b-d;
SECT 62 194c-d

35 BERKELEY: *Human Knowledge*, SECT 100
432b-c

35 HUME: *Human Understanding*, SECT I, DIV I
451a-b; DIV 3-5 451d-453b passim

37 FIELDING: *Tom Jones*, 182a-c

38 ROUSSEAU: *Inequality*, 343b-345c esp 345a-c

42 KANT: *Pure Reason*, 164a-165c / *Fund. Prin.
Metaphysic of Morals*, 260d-261d; 265b; 282b-
283d / *Practical Reason*, 318b-319b; 326b-
327a / *Pref. Metaphysical Elements of Ethics*,
365b [fn 1]; 368b-369a / *Intro. Metaphysic of
Morals*, 388d

43 MILL: *Utilitarianism*, 445a-447b passim; 448d-
450a

44 BOSWELL: *Johnson*, 151b-c

46 HEGEL: *Philosophy of Right*, PART II, par 139-
140 48d-54a; ADDITIONS, 74 127d-128a; 90
130b-d / *Philosophy of History*, INTRO, 168b-d;
PART II, 279c-d; 280b-281b; PART III, 304d-
305b

51 TOLSTOY: *War and Peace*, BK V, 194b-195a;
214c-215b; BK XII, 537c-538a

52 DOSTOEVSKY: *Brothers Karamazov*, BK IV,
83c-84a; BK V, 122b-125a; 127b-137c; BK XI,
335c-336b; 342d-345c; BK XII, 396d-397a

53 JAMES: *Psychology*, 806a-807a

54 FREUD: *General Introduction*, 560c-d; 625a-b

8b(2) Knowledge as a condition of voluntariness in conduct

7 PLATO: *Laws*, BK V, 689d-690c; BK IX, 746a-
748c

9 ARISTOTLE: *Ethics*, BK III, CH I [1110^{b}17-1111^a
23] 356b-357a; CH 2 [1111^{b}6-9] 357b; BK V,
CH 8 383a-384a esp [1135^{a}22-^{b}2] 383b /
Rhetoric, BK I, CH 10 [1368^{b}7-13] 611d; CH 13
[1373^{b}27-37] 618a

10 GALEN: *Natural Faculties*, BK I, CH 12,
173b-c

12 AURELIUS: *Meditations*, BK II, SECT I 256b,d;
SECT 10 257d-258a; BK VII, SECT 22 281b;
SECT 26 281c; SECT 62-63 283d-284a; BK VIII,
SECT 14 286c; BK IX, SECT 42 295c-296a,c;
BK XII, SECT 12 308b-c

17 PLOTINUS: *Sixth Ennead*, TR VIII, CH 1-4
342d-344d

19 AQUINAS: *Summa Theologica*, PART I, Q 18, A
3, ANS 106b-107c; Q 47, A I, REP I 256a-257b;
Q 82, A I, ANS and REP 1,3 431d-432c; Q 84,
A 8, CONTRARY 450b-451b; Q 105, A 4, REP
2-3 541c-542a; PART I-II, Q I, A 6, REP 3

(8b. The moral use of knowledge and the moral value of knowledge. 8b(2) Knowledge as a condition of voluntariness in conduct.)

614a-c; Q 6, AA 1–2 644d-646c; A 8 650d-651c; Q 7, A 2, ANS 652d-653c; Q 19, A 6 707a-708a; Q 20, A 2, REP 3 712d-713c

20 AQUINAS: *Summa Theologica*, PART I–II, Q 76, A 2, ANS 141d-142c

23 HOBBES: *Leviathan*, PART I, 61a-b; 64b-c

27 SHAKESPEARE: *Hamlet*, ACT V, SC II [37–255] 68b-70c

31 DESCARTES: *Objections and Replies*, 228c

35 LOCKE: *Human Understanding*, BK II, CH XXI, SECT 5, 179c; SECT 7–13 180a-181b esp SECT 13 181b; SECT 69 196d-197a

38 ROUSSEAU: *Inequality*, 337d-338a

42 KANT: *Pure Reason*, 149d-150a; 164a-165c; 169c-170a / *Practical Reason*, 333a-334b / *Intro. Metaphysic of Morals*, 386b-d

46 HEGEL: *Philosophy of Right*, PART II, par 117 42c-d; par 139 48d-49b; PART III, par 142–143 55a; ADDITIONS, 90 130b-d

53 JAMES: *Psychology*, 767b-768a

8b(3) Knowledge in relation to prudence and continence

7 PLATO: *Protagoras*, 59c-d

9 ARISTOTLE: *Ethics*, BK I, CH 3 [1094^{b}29–1095^{a}12] 340a-b; CH 13 [1102^{b}13–28] 348a-b; BK VI, CH 5–13 389a-394d; BK VII, CH 1 [1145^{b}8]–CH 2 [1146^{a}8] 395b-396a; CH 3 396c-398a

14 PLUTARCH: *Timoleon*, 197c-198a

18 AUGUSTINE: *City of God*, BK XIX, CH 4, 512a

19 AQUINAS: *Summa Theologica*, PART I, Q 1, A 6, ANS 6b-7a; Q 22, A 1 127d-128d

20 AQUINAS: *Summa Theologica*, PART I–II, Q 56, A 3, ANS 31a-32b; Q 57, AA 4–6 38a-41a; Q 58, A 3 43b-44a; A 5, ANS 44d-45c; Q 77, AA 2–3 145d-148b; PART II–II, Q 181, A 2 617d-618c; PART III, Q 11, A 1, REP 3 772b-773a

21 DANTE: *Divine Comedy*, PARADISE, X [109–114] 121b-c; XIII [37–111] 125d-126c

23 HOBBES: *Leviathan*, PART I, 60a-61a; 84c-d; PART IV, 267a-b

25 MONTAIGNE: *Essays*, 60c-61c; 327b-d; 520c-d

31 SPINOZA: *Ethics*, PART IV, PROP 14–17 428a-d

32 MILTON: *Areopagitica*, 389b-391a

42 KANT: *Judgement*, 586a-587a

8b(4) The possession or pursuit of knowledge as a good or satisfaction: its relation to pleasure and pain; its contribution to happiness

OLD TESTAMENT: *I Kings*, 10:1–8—(D) *III Kings*, 10:1–8 / *II Chronicles*, 9:1–7,22–23—(D) *II Paralipomenon*, 9:1–7,22–23 / *Job*, 28:12–20 / *Proverbs*, 1:24–33; 3:13–20; 10:1; 14:24; 16:16; 19:2,8; 20:15; 23:23–25; 24:13–14 / *Ecclesiastes*, 1:13–18; 2:12–21; 6:8; 7:11–13; 9:13–18

APOCRYPHA: *Ecclesiasticus*, 6:18–37; 21:21; 25:5, 10; 37:24; 51:13–28—(D) OT, *Ecclesiasticus*, 6:18–37; 21:24; 25:7,13; 37:27; 51:18–36

NEW TESTAMENT: *I Corinthians*, 8:1; 13:2

5 AESCHYLUS: *Agamemnon* [160–183] 53d-54a

5 SOPHOCLES: *Antigone* [1348–1353] 142d

7 PLATO: *Charmides*, 12a-13c / *Protagoras*, 59a-64d / *Euthydemus*, 69a-71a; 74b-76b / *Phaedrus*, 125a-126c / *Symposium*, 167a-d / *Meno*, 183d-184c / *Republic*, BK I, 295d-296c; BK II, 310c-d; 323c-d; BK VI, 374a-375a; BK IX, 421a-425b / *Timaeus*, 475d-476b / *Philebus*, 609a-639a,c / *Laws*, BK II, 655a-656a; 660a-662a; BK III, 669b-670c; BK V, 688c; BK VII, 728b-d / *Seventh Letter*, 801b; 808c-809a

8 ARISTOTLE: *Heavens*, BK II, CH 12 [291^{b}24–29] 383b-c / *Metaphysics*, BK I, CH 1–2 499a-501c; BK XII, CH 7 [1072^{b}14–29] 602d-603a / *Soul*, BK I, CH 1 [402^{a}1–6] 631a

9 ARISTOTLE: *Parts of Animals*, BK I, CH 5 [644^{b}22–645^{a}26] 168c-169a / *Ethics*, BK I, CH 8 [1098^{b}12–29] 344a-b passim; BK III, CH 10 [1117^{b}28–32] 364b; BK VI, CH 12 [1143^{b}17–1144^{a}6] 393b-c; BK VII, CH 12 [1152^{b}33–1153^{a}2] 404a; [1153^{a}21–24] 404c; BK X, CH 3 [1173^{b}15–18] 427d-428a; CH 4–5 428b-430d passim; CH 7–8 431d-434a / *Politics*, BK VIII, CH 3 [1338^{a}4–13] 543b; CH 5 [1339^{a}27–32] 544d; [1339^{b}17–20] 545a / *Rhetoric*, BK I, CH 11 [1371^{a}30–34] 614d; [1371^{b}4–10] 615a; [1371^{b}26–28] 615b / *Poetics*, CH 4 [1448^{b}5–20] 682c-d

12 LUCRETIUS: *Nature of Things*, BK I [62–145] 1d-2d; [921–950] 12b-c; BK II [1–61] 15a-d; BK III [1053–1075] 43c-d; BK IV [1–25] 44a-b; BK V [1–54] 61a-d; [1113–1135] 75c-d; BK VI [1–42] 80a-d

12 EPICTETUS: *Discourses*, BK II, CH 1 138b,d-140c; BK III, CH 2 177c-178d; CH 10 185d-187a; CH 15 190a-191a; CH 22 195a-201a; CH 23, 202c-203b; BK IV, CH 4 225a-228a; CH 6 230b-232c

12 AURELIUS: *Meditations*, BK III, SECT 6 261a-c; SECT 9 261d; BK IV, SECT 16 264d; BK V, SECT 9 270b-c; BK VI, SECT 12 274c; BK X, SECT 12 298c-d

13 VIRGIL: *Georgics*, II [490–493] 65b

14 PLUTARCH: *Pericles*, 121a-122a; 122d-123c / *Alexander*, 543b-544a

17 PLOTINUS: *First Ennead*, TR II, CH 6 9a-c; TR IV 12b-19b esp CH 3–4, 13d-14b, CH 9, 16d-17a, CH 15 18c-d

18 AUGUSTINE: *Confessions*, BK I, par 19–27 5d-7d; BK III, par 7–8 14c-15a; BK V, par 7–9 28c-29b; BK VI, par 26 42d-43a; BK IX, par 23–25 68a-c; BK X, par 33–34 79d-80c; par 54–57 85a-86a; BK XI, par 2–5 89c-90c / *City of God*, BK VIII, CH 8 270a-d / *Christian Doctrine*, BK II, CH 7 638d-639c

19 AQUINAS: *Summa Theologica*, PART I, Q 1, A 1 3b-4a; A 4 5a-b; A 5, ANS and REP 1 5c-6a; Q 5, A 4, REP 1 25d-26c; Q 12, A 1, ANS 50c-51c; A 5, ANS and REP 3 54c-55b; A 6, ANS 55b-56a; A 7,

8c. The political use of knowledge: the knowledge requisite for the statesman, legislator, or citizen

CROSS-REFERENCES

For: The differences between human and other kinds of knowledge, *see* ANGEL 3d; ANIMAL 1a(1)–1a(2); GOD 5f; INFINITY 7d; MIND 4e–4f; WISDOM 1d.

    Other discussions bearing on the nature of human knowledge, its relation to truth, error, and ignorance, and its distinction from opinion, belief, and fancy, *see* MEMORY AND IMAGINATION 6a; ONE AND MANY 4f; OPINION 1, 3–4b; PRINCIPLE 3c(2); SAME AND OTHER 4a; TRUTH 2e, 3d; WILL 3b(1); and for the elements, causes, or principles of knowledge, *see* DEFINITION 5; EXPERIENCE 3; FORM 3, 4; IDEA 1a–1c; INDUCTION 3; JUDGMENT 8–8d; PRINCIPLE 2–2b(3); REASONING 5a–5b(5); WILL 3b(1).

    Other considerations of the limits of human knowledge and of the knowability of certain objects, *see* ANGEL 2b; BEING 8a–8c, 8e; CAUSE 5d; EXPERIENCE 4a; FORM 3b; GOD 6–6b; INFINITY 6b; MAN 2a; MATTER 4a; ONE AND MANY 4e; OPINION 3c; PRINCIPLE 5; SCIENCE 4e; SOUL 1d; THEOLOGY 3c; TIME 6e–6f; TRUTH 7a; UNIVERSAL AND PARTICULAR 4e.

    Matters relevant to the classification of the kinds of knowledge by reference to its objects, *see* BEING 8a–8b; FORM 3–3a; IDEA 1a; MIND 1a(1); NATURE 4a–4c; NECESSITY AND CONTINGENCY 4a; RELATION 4d; RELIGION 1a; SENSE 4a–4b; UNIVERSAL AND PARTICULAR 4a.

    Matters relevant to the classification of the kinds of knowledge by reference to the faculties involved, *see* MEMORY AND IMAGINATION 3, 6a; MIND 1a(1); SENSE 4a–4b.

    Matters relevant to the classification of the kinds of knowledge by reference to the methods or means of knowing, *see* EXPERIENCE 2d; GOD 6c–6c(4); INDUCTION 1a; JUDGMENT 8a; MEMORY AND IMAGINATION 3a; OPINION 4a; REASONING 1b; RELIGION 6g; THEOLOGY 2; WISDOM 1c; and for methodology in general and the methods of the particular sciences, *see* ASTRONOMY 2a–2c; HISTORY 3a; LOGIC 4–4f; MATHEMATICS 3–3d; MECHANICS 2–2c; METAPHYSICS 2c; PHILOSOPHY 3–3c; PHYSICS 4–4d; SCIENCE 5–5e; THEOLOGY 4c.

For: Matters relevant to the classification of the kinds of knowledge by reference to the degrees of assent, *see* JUDGMENT 9; OPINION 3–3b; TRUTH 2e.

Other discussions of the distinction between theoretic and practical knowledge, *see* JUDGMENT 2; PHILOSOPHY 2a; PRUDENCE 2a; REASONING 5e–5e(1); THEOLOGY 4d; TRUTH 2c; WISDOM 1b.

The basic divisions of theoretic knowledge, *see* ASTRONOMY 4; DIALECTIC 4; HISTORY 1; MATHEMATICS 1a; METAPHYSICS 3b–3c; NATURE 4b; PHILOSOPHY 2b; PHYSICS 1a, 2; SCIENCE 1a(2), 1c, 2a; THEOLOGY 3a, 4a; TRUTH 4c; and for the problem of the hierarchy of the sciences and the definition of the highest form of human knowledge, *see* DIALECTIC 4; METAPHYSICS 1; THEOLOGY 4a; WISDOM 1a.

The basic divisions of practical knowledge, *see* ART 6c; PHILOSOPHY 2c; PRUDENCE 6a–6b; SCIENCE 3a–3b; WEALTH 9.

The moral or political value of knowledge, *see* CITIZEN 6; GOOD AND EVIL 6a–6c; HAPPINESS 2b(7); PHILOSOPHY 4a–4c; PLEASURE AND PAIN 4c, 4c(2); PRUDENCE 2c; SCIENCE 1b(2); STATE 8c–8d; VIRTUE AND VICE 1a; WILL 3a(1); WISDOM 2b.

The technical use of knowledge and the applications of science to production, *see* ART 6c; MEDICINE 2a; PHYSICS 5; SCIENCE 1b(1), 3b; WEALTH 3a.

The general problem of the dissemination and communication of knowledge, *see* EDUCATION 5b; LANGUAGE 1b; LIBERTY 2a; OPINION 5b.

The development of human knowledge, the advancement of learning, or progress in science and philosophy, *see* ART 12; PHILOSOPHY 7; PROGRESS 6a–6e; SCIENCE 6a–6b; TRUTH 6.

ADDITIONAL READINGS

Listed below are works not included in *Great Books of the Western World*, but relevant to the idea and topics with which this chapter deals. These works are divided into two groups:

I. Works by authors represented in this collection.
II. Works by authors not represented in this collection.

For the date, place, and other facts concerning the publication of the works cited, consult the Bibliography of Additional Readings which follows the last chapter of *The Great Ideas*.

I.

AUGUSTINE. *Answer to Skeptics*
——. *On the Profit of Believing*
——. *On Faith in Things Unseen*
AQUINAS. *On the Trinity of Boethius*, QQ 5–6
——. *Summa Contra Gentiles*, BK I, CH 48–71
——. *Quaestiones Disputatae, De Veritate*
SPINOZA. *Of the Improvement of the Understanding*
BERKELEY. *Three Dialogues Between Hylas and Philonous*
HUME. *A Treatise of Human Nature*, BK I, PART IV, SECT I–IV
KANT. *Prolegomena to Any Future Metaphysic*
——. *Metaphysical Foundations of Natural Science*
——. *Introduction to Logic*, V–VI, IX–X
HEGEL. *The Phenomenology of Mind*, VIII
——. *Logic*, CH 3–5
FARADAY. *Observations on the Education of the Judgment*
J. S. MILL. *An Examination of Sir William Hamilton's Philosophy*, CH 2–3

W. JAMES. *The Will to Believe*
——. *The Meaning of Truth*, CH 1–2, 4

II.

SEXTUS EMPIRICUS. *Outlines of Pyrrhonism*, BK I–II
SAADIA GAON. *The Book of Beliefs and Opinions*, INTRODUCTORY TREATISE
ANSELM OF CANTERBURY. *Dialogue on Truth*
MAIMONIDES. *The Guide for the Perplexed*, PART III, CH 20–21
ALBERTUS MAGNUS. *On the Intellect and the Intelligible*
MATTHEW OF AQUASPARTA. *Ten Disputed Questions on Knowledge*, QQ I–II
DUNS SCOTUS. *Oxford Commentary*, BK I, DIST 3, Q 4
PETRARCH. *On His Own Ignorance*
ALBO. *The Book of Principles (Sefer ha-Ikkarim)*, BK IV, CH I
SUÁREZ. *Disputationes Metaphysicae*, I (6) VIII–IX, XIII (6), XX (I), XXII (I), XXIII (7–8), XXX (11–12), XXXV (4)

Chapter 44: LABOR

INTRODUCTION

MEN have dreamed of a golden age in the past when the world was young and everything needed for the support of life existed in profusion. Earth, Lucretius writes, "first spontaneously of herself produced for mortals goodly corn-crops and joyous vineyards; of herself gave sweet fruits and glad pastures; which now-a-days scarce attain any size even when furthered by our labor; we exhaust the oxen and the strength of the husbandmen; we wear out our iron, scarcely fed after all by the tilled fields; so niggardly are they of their produce and after so much labor do they let it grow." When the aged plowman "compares present times with times past," Lucretius adds, "he praises the fortunes of his sire" living in the time of earth's plenty.

This ancient myth of a golden age has sometimes taken the form, as with Rousseau, of an idealization of primitive society, uncorrupted by civilization, in which an easy, almost effortless, existence corresponded to the simplicity of man's needs. Rousseau pictures a situation in which "the produce of the earth furnished [man] with all he needed, and instinct told him how to use it," so that "singing and dancing, the true offspring of love and leisure, became the amusement, or rather the occupation of men and women assembled together with nothing else to do."

In our own day, industrial utopias have been projected into a future made free from toil by the adequacy of machines or the efficiency of atomic energy. Long before the industrial era, Aristotle envisioned, as a supposition contrary to fact, a society built upon labor-saving machines. "If every instrument could accomplish its own work," he writes, if it could obey or anticipate commands, if "the shuttle would weave . . . without a hand to guide it, the chief workmen would not want servants, nor masters slaves."

In all these conceptions of a better life, labor is eliminated or reduced. The implication seems to be that the labor required for the maintenance of all historic societies is an affliction, a drudgery, a crushing burden which deforms the lives of many, if not all. The pains of toil do not belong to human life by any necessity of human nature, but rather through the accident of external circumstances which might be other than they are. "Work became indispensable," according to Rousseau, only when "property was introduced," and then "vast forests became smiling fields, which man had to water with the sweat of his brow." It was the result of "some fatal accident, which, for the public good, should never have happened." Man might have realized his nature more surely and richly if, like the lilies of the field, he neither toiled nor spun.

The contrary view would maintain that work is not a curse but a blessing, filling man's hours usefully, turning to service energies which would otherwise be wasted or misspent in idleness or mischief. The sinfulness of sloth implies the virtue of work. The principle of activity, according to Hegel, whereby "the workman has to perform for his subsistence," gives man a dignity which "consists in his depending entirely on his diligence, conduct, and intelligence for the supply of his wants. In direct contravention of this principle" are "pauperism, laziness, inactivity."

It is even suggested that useful occupations save men from a boredom they fear more than the pain of labor, as evidenced by the variety of amusements and diversions they invent or frantically pursue to occupy themselves when work is finished. The satisfactions of labor are as peculiarly human as its burdens. Not merely to keep alive, but to keep his self-respect, man is obliged to work.

"In the morning when thou risest unwilling," the emperor Marcus Aurelius tells himself, "let this thought be present—I am rising to the work of a human being. Why, then, am I dissatisfied if I am going to do the things for which I exist and for which I was brought into the world? Or have I been made for this, to lie in the bed-clothes and keep myself warm? But this is more pleasant. Dost thou exist, then, to take thy pleasure, and not at all for action and exertion?"

The perspectives of theology give still another view of labor. It is not an accidental misfortune which men may some day be able to correct. But neither is it a blessing nor the thing for which man was created. When the golden age of Saturn came to an end, and Jupiter replaced him on the throne of heaven, then, as Virgil tells the story, labor was first introduced into the world. "Before Jove

Fields knew no taming hand of husbandmen;
To mark the plain or mete with boundary-line—
Even this was impious; for the common stock
They gathered, and the earth of her own will
All things more freely, no man bidding, bore.
He to black serpents gave their venom-bane,
And bade the wolf go prowl, and ocean toss;
Shook from the leaves their honey, put fire away,
And curved the random rivers running wine,
That use by gradual dint of thought on thought
Might forge the various arts, with furrow's help
The corn-blade win, and strike out hidden fire
From the flint's heart.

Here, while labor may in some sense be a punishment, or at least a fall from the golden age, it still does result in benefits. "The divers arts arose" from Jove's "whetting the minds of men with care on care, nor suffering realm of his in drowsy sloth to stagnate." But although "toil conquered all," it is still "remorseless toil."

According to Christian doctrine, labor is an inevitable consequence of man's fall from grace, a punishment for Adam's disobedience like disease and death. In the earthly paradise of Eden, the children of Adam would have lived without labor or servitude of any sort. But when Adam sinned, the Lord God said unto him: "Cursed is the ground for thy sake; in toil shalt thou eat of it all the days of thy life . . . In the sweat of thy face, shalt thou eat bread, till thou return into the ground."

That work should be painful belongs to its very essence. Otherwise it would not serve as a penalty or a penance. But, in the Christian as in the Virgilian view, labor also contributes to such happiness as man can enjoy on earth. The distinction between temporal and eternal happiness is a distinction between a life of work on earth and the activity of contemplation in Heaven. This does not mean the elimination of leisure and enjoyment from earthly life, but it does make labor their antecedent and indispensable condition. It also means that even in his highest activities—in the development of his arts and sciences—man must be perpetually at work. His achievement of truth or beauty is never so perfect and lasting that he can rest in it.

IN THESE DIVERSE conceptions of the relation of labor to human life, work seems to have several different meanings. It always involves activity or exertion. Its clearest opposite is sleep. But other things are also opposed to work—play or amusement, leisure, idleness. When leisure is not identified with idleness, it involves activity no less than work. So, too, many of the forms of play require intense exertion of body or mind. The difference, therefore, must lie in the nature or purpose of the activity.

Aristotle suggests what the difference is when he puts play, work, and leisure in an ordered relationship to one another. Nature, he writes, "requires that we should be able, not only to work well, but to use leisure well." Leisure is "the first principle of all action" and so "leisure is better than work and is its end." As play and with it rest (i.e., sleep) are for the sake of work, so work in turn is for the sake of leisure.

The characteristics of work as the middle term here seem to be, first, that work is activity directed to an end beyond itself and, second, that it is productive of the necessities which sustain life rather than of the goods by which life is perfected. The political or speculative activity which Aristotle considers the proper occupation of leisure is intrinsically good or enjoyable. For participation in such activities leisure—in the sense of time free from labor—is required; but since the good life cannot be lived unless life itself is sustained, labor also is a prerequisite.

Work is thus defined by wealth as its immediate end—the production of the external, economic, or consumable goods which support life. Though play has the immediately enjoyable character of an activity performed for its own sake, Aristotle subordinates it to work, assigning to it the same utility which rest has. Both refresh men from the fatigues of labor and re-create the energies needed for work. "Amusement," he writes, "is needed more amid serious occupations than at other times, for he who is hard at work has need for relaxation, and amusement gives relaxation."

The economic sense which connects work and labor with wealth seems to be the primary but not the only sense in which these terms are used in the great books. There is the more general sense of human work as any productive activity in which men exercise some art or skill. The familiar distinction between skilled and unskilled labor may be only a distinction in degree if there is truth in the theory that some degree of skill—some rudimentary art at least —is required for the performance of the simplest tasks of hand and eye.

Kinds of work, according to this theory, can be differentiated by reference to the type of art involved. The ancient distinction between the servile and the liberal arts also divides workers into those who manipulate and transform physical materials and those who employ the symbols of poetry, music, or science to produce things for the mind. This distinction between manual and mental work, based on the character of the work itself, is not to be identified with the distinction between slave and free labor. The latter is based on the status of the worker. Even in the slave economies of the ancient world, some freemen were artisans, farmers, or sailors, and some slaves were philosophers. Nor is mental as opposed to manual work necessarily directed to the production of the goods of the mind. The white-collar workers of an industrial economy, employed with the symbols of finance, accounting, or management, do mental work which has its ultimate end in the production or exchange of material goods.

THERE ARE STILL other traditional distinctions among kinds of work and types of workers, all of which cannot be put together into a single scheme of classification without much overlapping. Some distinctions, like that between hand-work and machine-labor or between healthful and unhealthful occupations, turn on the characteristics of the work itself. Some depend on the social conditions under which the work is done or on the relationship between the individual worker and other men. The work to be done may be accomplished by an individual working alone, or by the cooperative labor of many; and, in the latter case, the social organization of the laboring group may involve the ranking of men according to the functions they perform.

Here we get the division into the mastercraftsmen, who plan and superintend, and all grades of helpers who execute their directions. One meaning of the word "menial" as applied to work signifies the inferior tasks in the hierarchy of functions; but it is also used to express society's opinion of those who perform certain tasks, such as that of the domestic servant. The distinction between what is menial and what is dignified work varies, of course, from society to society.

The characterization of labor as productive or non-productive, and of work as useful or wasteful, is based on strictly economic criteria and on considerations of social welfare. The sense in which work cannot be divorced from the production of some extrinsic effect is not violated by the conception of non-productive labor as work which in no way increases the wealth of nations.

"There is one sort of labor which adds to the subject upon which it is bestowed; there is another which has no such effect. The former," writes Adam Smith, "may be called productive; the latter, unproductive labor . . . The labor of some of the most respectable orders in society is. . . unproductive of any value . . . The sovereign, for example, with all the officers both of justice and war who serve under him, the whole army and navy, are unproductive laborers . . . Like the declamation of the actor, the harangue of the orator, or the tune of the musician, the work of all of them perishes in the very instant of its production."

The standard by which Marx judges the usefulness of labor also implies the economic notion of a commodity. "Nothing can have value," he says, "without being an object of utility. If the thing is useless, so is the labor contained in it." But Marx also adds a criterion of social utility. "Whoever directly satisfies his own wants with the produce of his labor, creates, indeed, use-values, but not commodities. In order to produce the latter, he must not only produce use-values, but use-values for others, social use-values." It is by this last criterion that Marx criticizes the capitalist economy for its "most outrageous squandering of labor power" in superfluous or socially useless production.

THE PRINCIPLE OF the division of labor does not depend upon any particular classification of work or workers according to type. Nor does it belong to one system of economy rather than another. But the ancients, concerned as they were with its bearing on the origin and development of the state, saw the division of labor as primarily of political significance; whereas the moderns are more concerned with its economic causes and consequences.

Thucydides compares the poverty and crude life of the early Hellenic tribes with the wealth, the power, and the civilization of Athens, Sparta, Corinth, and other city-states at the opening of the Peloponnesian War. The difference is not to be accounted for in terms of the invention of new tools, but rather in terms of the greater efficiency in production which is obtained by a division of labor. This is both an effect and a cause of the enlargement of the community, and its increasing population. The greater the number of men associated in a common life, the greater the number of specialized tasks which can be assigned to different members of the community.

This observation is formulated by Plato and Aristotle in their accounts of the origin of the state. The advantages which the state confers upon its members are in part won by the division of labor in which they participate.

The isolated family, Aristotle remarks, is barely able to supply the "everyday wants" of its members. The tribe or village, which is an association of families, can achieve a little more than bare subsistence; but not until several tribes unite to form a city does a truly self-sufficing community come into existence, and one with an adequate division of labor. Some men, if not all, can then acquire the leisure to engage in the arts and sciences and politics—the

pursuits of civilization which have their material basis in sufficient wealth.

The effect of the division of labor on the social structure of the state seems to be generally agreed upon by all observers, ancient and modern. Men are divided into social classes according to the kind of work they do—not only by reference to the type of economically productive labor, but also in terms of the distinction between labor and leisure, or between economic and other functions in society.

All do not agree, however, that such class distinctions are as beneficial to society as the increase of wealth or opulence which the division of labor affords. They not only threaten the unity and peace of the society, but tend to degrade the condition of labor by reducing the individual worker to a cog in the machine. The division of labor frequently restricts him to a slight and insignificant task, repetitively performed, and so makes it impossible for him to develop his skill or to enjoy any pride of workmanship. From a purely economic point of view, Adam Smith advocates the greatest intensification of the division of labor. Each more minute sub-division of tasks augments efficiency in production. But from the human point of view, he sees that this method of maximizing wealth by dividing men into functional groups—one man, one task—leads to the mental impoverishment of the men, who require a multiplicity of functions for their development.

"In the progress of the division of labor," Smith writes, "the employment of the far greater part of those who live by labor . . . comes to be confined to a few very simple operations, frequently one or two . . . The man whose whole life is spent in performing a few simple operations . . . has no occasion to exert his understanding or to exercise his invention . . . He naturally loses, therefore, the habit of such exertion, and generally becomes as stupid and ignorant as it is possible for a human creature to become." The situation seems even worse to Marx. The industrial system, revolutionizing the mode of work, "converts the laborer into a crippled monstrosity, by forcing his detailed dexterity at the expense of a world of productive capabilities and instincts." It makes the individual worker "the automatic motor of a fractional operation."

THE GREAT ISSUES concerning labor seem to be moral and political rather than economic. The consideration of the division of labor from the point of view of efficiency in production remains purely economic only when it is abstracted from any concern about the effect upon the laborer. The analysis of factors affecting the productivity of labor ceases to be merely economic when the hours, conditions, and organization of work are viewed in terms of the working men.

The determination of wages by the buying and selling of labor (or, as Marx insists, of labor-power) as a commodity subject to market conditions of supply and demand; the difference between real and nominal wages as determined by the level of wages in relation to the price of other commodities; the so-called "iron law of wages" according to which wages cannot be reduced below the minimum of bare subsistence for the laborer and his family—these are matters which the economist may deal with in a descriptive or historical manner, calculating rates and ratios without regard to questions of justice. But in terms of such formulations questions of justice are raised and become the great issues concerning the rights of workmen to the fruits of their labor, to the security of full employment and other forms of protection, to collective bargaining, to a voice in the management of industry or business.

Stated in this way, the issues seem to be peculiarly modern. These are the problems of a capitalist economy, to which the partisans of capital and of labor propose different solutions. Yet the principles of justice to which the parties in conflict appeal seem to be no less applicable to earlier conflicts in other economic systems—between master and slave or between feudal lord and serf. All the institutional differences among these three economies should not, according to Karl Marx, conceal from us the profound analogy which obtains in the relation between owners and workers, whether the workers are chattel slaves, peons bound to the land, or industrial proletarians selling their labor-power.

"Wherever a part of society possesses a monopoly of the means of production," he writes, "the laborer, free or not free, must add to the working time necessary for his own maintenance an extra working time in order to produce the means of subsistence for the owners of the means of production, whether this proprietor be the Athenian gentleman, Etruscan theocrat, civis Romanus, Norman baron, American slave-owner, Wallachian Boyard, modern landlord or capitalist."

Marx undertakes to explain how the surface difference between slave labor and wage labor conceals the analogy. "In slave labor, even that part of the working-day in which the slave is only replacing the value of his own means of existence, in which, therefore, he works for himself alone, appears as labor for his master. All the slave's labor appears as unpaid labor. In wage-labor, on the contrary, even surplus labor, or unpaid labor, appears as paid. There the property-relation conceals the labor of the slave for himself; here the money-relation conceals the unrequited labor of the wage laborer."

Two phrases here—"unpaid labor" and "unrequited labor"—indicate that Marx is thinking in terms of justice. Elsewhere he calls the industrial proletariat "wage-slaves" to emphasize the presence in an apparently free economy of the same unjust exploitation which the word "slave" connotes when it refers to the use of men as chattel. The essential similarity in all forms of economic exploitation—which makes all forms of economic slavery essentially similar—is seen by Marx in terms of the production of a surplus value by the laborer; that is, he produces a greater value in commodities than he needs to support his own subsistence. This surplus value, when appropriated by the owner of the materials and the tools on and with which the propertyless laborer works, becomes an unearned increment, or, in other words, an unjust profit from the work of another man.

The controversy over the theory of surplus value in Marx's *Capital* can be separated from the controversy over the revolutionary program of the *Communist Manifesto*. But neither can be separated from issues of justice. It is questionable whether those economists join issue with Marx who criticize his analysis in terms of the facts or conclusions of economics as a purely descriptive science, and who put aside all considerations of the fair and the equitable. Yet those facts or conclusions, especially with regard to the operation of the capitalist economy, become relevant in the dispute as to whether capitalist profits are intrinsically unjust, because they are incapable of accruing except from the exploitation of labor.

Those who dispute this matter seldom deny that chattel slavery is unjust. On that there may be conflicting opinions, as indicated in the chapter on SLAVERY, but they are not germane to the present issue. Nor do the opponents seem to argue their case in terms of a different theory of what is just and unjust. They themselves appeal to the common principle of fairness in exchange and distribution to defend the rights of the owners of capital to a profit in return for their own prior labor in accumulating capital stock, as well as for the risks they take when they invest their reserves in productive enterprises. The problem, therefore, seems to narrow down to such questions as whether laborers are exploited when they receive in wages less than the full value their work creates; whether capitalist profits are entirely reaped from the surplus value which is the differential between what labor creates and what labor receives; or whether, if profit is not identical with surplus value, it always contains a marginal element of unearned increment derived from the exploitation of labor.

THE NOTION OF VALUE—the value of commodities and the value of labor itself—is obviously of central importance. As indicated in the chapter on JUSTICE, the formulae of equality, which determine fair exchanges or distributions, require some measure of equivalents in value. What determines the intrinsic value of a commodity according to which it can be compared with another commodity, without reference to the price of each in the market place? Adam Smith's answer to this question is *labor*. It is the answer given before him by Locke, and after him by Marx.

"Equal quantities of labor, at all times and places," Smith declares, "may be said to be of equal value to the laborer. In his ordinary state of health, strength and spirits; in the ordinary degree of his skill and dexterity, he must always lay down the same portion of his ease, his liberty, and his happiness. The price which he pays must always be the same, whatever may be the quantity of goods which he receives in return for it. Of these, indeed, it may sometimes purchase a greater and sometimes a smaller quantity; but it is their value which varies, not that of the labor which purchases them." From this Adam Smith concludes that "labor alone, therefore, never varying in its own value, is alone the ultimate and real standard by which the value of all commodities can at all times and places be estimated and compared. It is their real price; money is their nominal price only."

This labor theory of value raises the further question of the value of labor itself. What determines its natural or real price, as opposed to its market or nominal price? On this Marx and Smith appear to part company, which may account for their further divergence when Marx declares that "the real value of labor is the cost of its production, not the average price it can command in the market"; and then goes on to explain how a surplus value is derived by the capitalist who pays for labor-power on a basis of the cost of producing and sustaining the laborer, but uses his labor-power to produce a real value in commodities which exceeds the real price of labor itself.

Smith, on the other hand, holds that "the whole produce of labor belongs to the laborer" only "in that original state of things, which precedes both the appropriation of land and the accumulation of stock." When "land becomes private property," the landlord "makes the first deduction" in the form of *rent*; and the capitalist, or the person who invests some part of his stock accumulation, "makes a second deduction" in the form of *profit*. After rent and profit are taken, the laborer's *wage* represents what is left of "the whole produce of labor."

Yet Smith also says of the landlords that "as soon as the land of any country has all become private property," they, "like all other men, love to reap where they never sowed." The implication of unearned increment in this remark suggests that Smith is neither disinclined to mix moral judgment with economic description, nor at variance with Marx on the principle of economic justice. That Smith regards profit as the price properly paid for the use of capital and that he does not see reaping without sowing as an essential element in profit-making may perhaps be read as a challenge to Marx's development of the labor theory of value into a theory of surplus value and unearned increment.

IT IS POSSIBLE, of course, that the difference in the conclusions of Smith and Marx from a common premise can be explained by the different directions their analyses take. It may not represent a direct opposition on a point of fact. The proposition that value derives from labor seems to yield a number of theoretical consequences.

Locke, for example, holding that it is labor which "puts the difference of value on everything," makes this the basis for the right to private property, certainly in its original appropriation from the common domain which is God's gift to mankind. "Though the earth and all inferior creatures be common to all men, yet every man has a property in his own person. The labor of his body and the work of his hands we may say are properly his. Whatsoever, then, he removes out of the state that nature hath provided and left it in, he hath mixed his labor with, and joined to it something that is his own, and thereby makes it his property."

This view seems to be shared by Rousseau. "It is impossible to conceive," he says, "how property can come from anything but manual labor; for what else can a man add to things which he does not originally create, so as to make them his own property?" In the same vein, Smith declares that "the property which every man has in his own labor, as it is the original foundation of all other property, so it is the most sacred and inviolable."

What further conclusions follow from this justification of private property as a right founded upon labor? How is the original right to property extended into a right of inheritance? How does this conception of the origin of property bear on the Marxist conception of the origin of the proletariat—the propertyless workers who have nothing but their labor-power to sell? Denying the charge that communists desire to abolish "the right of personally acquiring property as the fruit of a man's own labor," Marx and Engels make the countercharge that the development of industrial capitalism "has to a great extent already destroyed it and is still destroying it daily." They propose public ownership of the means of production to protect the property rights of labor;

they seek to abolish only "the bourgeois form of private property" which, in their view, is a use of property to exploit labor.

The rights of labor seem to be central in any formulation of the problem of a just distribution of wealth. But when other rights are taken into consideration, the problem of economic justice becomes more complex; and different solutions result from differences in emphasis. Even with regard to one group of solutions, J. S. Mill observes that "some communists consider it unjust that the produce of the labor of the community should be shared on any other principle than that of exact equality; others think it just that those should receive most whose wants are greatest." To weigh the merits of competing solutions, as well as to reach an adequate statement of the problem, the discussion of labor must be connected with the discussion of related considerations in the chapters on JUSTICE, REVOLUTION, and WEALTH.

THERE ARE ISSUES of justice concerning labor other than the strictly economic problem of distribution. In the ancient world, for example, not only chattel slaves but also free artisans were frequently regarded as incapable of participation in political life. Only men of independent wealth had enough leisure for the activities of citizenship which, in the Greek city-states, was almost a full-time occupation. This, according to Aristotle, is one reason for the disfranchisement of the laboring classes who must devote a great part of their energy to earning a living and who have neither the time nor training for liberal pursuits. "Since leisure is necessary both for the development of virtue and the performance of political duties," citizens, he maintains, cannot "lead the life of mechanics or tradesmen."

Against this oligarchical view (which also involves the notion that wealth deserves special political privileges), the Greek democrats take the position that all free men should be citizens on an equal footing, regardless of the amount of their property or their conditions of labor and leisure. But the oligarchical principle still tends to prevail among republicans in the 18th century. Kant, for example, holds that citizenship "presupposes the independence or self-sufficiency of the individual citizen among the people." On this basis he excludes from the suffrage, as only "passive" citizens, "the apprentice of a merchant or tradesman, a servant who is not in the employ of the state, a minor (*naturaliter vel civiliter*), all women, and, generally, everyone who is compelled to maintain himself not according to his own industry, but as it is arranged by others (the state excepted)." They are "without civil personality, and their existence is only, as it were, incidentally included in the state."

The preference shown by the writers of *The Federalist* for a republican as opposed to a democratic form of government—or representative government as opposed to direct democracy—rests partly on their fear of the political incompetence, as well as the factional interests, of wage earners and day-laborers. While expressing "disapprobation" of poll taxes, they still defend the right of the government to exact them, in the belief that "there may exist certain critical and tempestuous conjunctures of the State, in which a poll-tax may become an inestimable resource." Yet such a tax would seem to be primarily a device for disfranchising working-

men of no property and small income, and in the opinion of a later day it is so regarded.

The democratic revolution does not begin until the middle of the 19th century. But even then, Mill, who advocates universal suffrage, argues for the disqualification of paupers or those on the dole, without raising the question whether the right to work—to avoid poverty and involuntary indigence—is not a democratic right inseparable from the right to citizenship. It is "required by first principles," Mill writes, "that the receipt of parish relief should be a peremptory disqualification for the franchise. He who cannot by his labor suffice for his own support has no claim to the privilege of helping himself to the money of others. By becoming dependent on the remaining members of the community for actual subsistence, he abdicates his claim to equal rights with them in other respects."

The historic connection of democracy with a movement toward political justice for the laboring classes seems to suggest that political democracy must be accompanied by economic democracy in order to attain its full realization.

OUTLINE OF TOPICS

REFERENCES

To find the passages cited, use the numbers in heavy type, which are the volume and page numbers of the passages referred to. For example, in 4 HOMER: *Iliad*, BK II [265-283] 12d, the number 4 is the number of the volume in the set; the number 12d indicates that the passage is in section d of page 12.

PAGE SECTIONS: When the text is printed in one column, the letters a and b refer to the upper and lower halves of the page. For example, in 53 JAMES: *Psychology*, 116a-119b, the passage begins in the upper half of page 116 and ends in the lower half of page 119. When the text is printed in two columns, the letters a and b refer to the upper and lower halves of the left-hand side of the page, the letters c and d to the upper and lower halves of the right-hand side of the page. For example, in 7 PLATO: *Symposium*, 163b-164c, the passage begins in the lower half of the left-hand side of page 163 and ends in the upper half of the right-hand side of page 164.

AUTHOR'S DIVISIONS: One or more of the main divisions of a work (such as PART, BK, CH, SECT) are sometimes included in the reference; line numbers, in brackets, are given in certain cases; *e.g.*, *Iliad*, BK II [265-283] 12d.

BIBLE REFERENCES: The references are to book, chapter, and verse. When the King James and Douay versions differ in title of books or in the numbering of chapters or verses, the King James version is cited first and the Douay, indicated by a (*D*), follows; *e.g.*, OLD TESTAMENT: *Nehemiah*, 7:45—(*D*) *II Esdras*, 7:46.

SYMBOLS: The abbreviation "esp" calls the reader's attention to one or more especially relevant parts of a whole reference; "passim" signifies that the topic is discussed intermittently rather than continuously in the work or passage cited.

For additional information concerning the style of the references, see the Explanation of Reference Style; for general guidance in the use of *The Great Ideas*, consult the Preface.

1. Labor in human life

1a. The curse of labor: myths of a golden age and the decay of the world

OLD TESTAMENT: *Genesis*, 3:17-19,23 / *Psalms*, 90:10—(*D*) *Psalms*, 89:10 / *Ecclesiastes*, 1:3-2:11; 2:17-24; 3:9-13; 4:4-8; 5:15-16; 6:7—(*D*) *Ecclesiastes*, 1:3-2:11; 2:17-24; 3:9-13; 4:4-8; 5:14-16; 6:7 / *Jeremiah*, 20:18—(*D*) *Jeremias*, 20:18

APOCRYPHA: *Ecclesiasticus*, 7:15; 31:3-4; 40:1—(*D*) OT, *Ecclesiasticus*, 7:16; 31:3-4; 40:1

NEW TESTAMENT: *II Thessalonians*, 3:7-12

7 PLATO: *Statesman*, 588a-589c / *Laws*, BK III, 664a-665c; BK IV, 681b-c

9 ARISTOTLE: *Politics*, BK I, CH 4 [1253ᵇ33-40] 447b-c

12 LUCRETIUS: *Nature of Things*, BK II [1105-1174] 29a-30a,c; BK V [195-217] 63c-d

13 VIRGIL: *Eclogues*, IV [16-47] 14b-15a / *Georgics*, I [118-159] 40a-41b / *Aeneid*, BK VIII [306-336] 267a-268a

18 AUGUSTINE: *City of God*, BK XIV, CH 10 385b-d

21 DANTE: *Divine Comedy*, PURGATORY, XXII [130-154] 87d-88a; XXVIII [91-96] 97a

27 SHAKESPEARE: *Tempest*, ACT II, SC I [143-168] 532d-533a

29 CERVANTES: *Don Quixote*, PART I, 27b-28a

32 MILTON: *Paradise Lost*, BK X [1046-1104] 297a-298b; BK XI [84-98] 301a; [162-180] 302b-303a; [251-262] 304b-305a

38 ROUSSEAU: *Inequality*, 348b,d-353b; 362b-c

46 HEGEL: *Philosophy of Right*, ADDITIONS, 125 137a

48 MELVILLE: *Moby Dick*, 316a-b; 355b-356a

50 MARX: *Capital*, 199c-200a esp 199d [fn 4]

51 TOLSTOY: *War and Peace*, BK VII, 275a

1b. Labor, leisure, and happiness: the servile, political, and contemplative life

OLD TESTAMENT: *Proverbs*, 6:6-11; 13:4; 15:19; 18:9; 19:15,24; 20:4; 21:25-26; 24:30-34; 26:13-16; 28:19

APOCRYPHA: *Ecclesiasticus*, 11:11-14; 38:24-34—(*D*) OT, *Ecclesiasticus*, 11:11-14; 38:25-39

NEW TESTAMENT: *Luke*, 10:38-42

5 ARISTOPHANES: *Plutus* [415-618] 633d-636d

6 HERODOTUS: *History*, BK II, 86b; BK V, 161a

7 PLATO: *Protagoras*, 43b-d / *Republic*, BK VII, 390b-391b / *Critias*, 479d / *Statesman*, 581b-c / *Laws*, BK VII, 710c; 722d-723c; BK VIII, 740d-741a

8 ARISTOTLE: *Metaphysics*, BK I, CH 1 [981ᵇ13-24] 500a; CH 2 [982ᵇ11-28] 500d-501a

9 ARISTOTLE: *Ethics*, BK X, CH 6-7 430d-432c / *Politics*, BK I, CH 4 [1253ᵇ33-40] 447b-c; CH 5

1c. The pain of labor and the expiation of sin: the disciplinary and penal use of labor

1d. The social necessity of labor and the moral obligation to work

50 MARX: *Capital*, 16a; 18d; 113c-114a; 251c-d; 253a; 254c-255a; 292d; 307c

50 MARX-ENGELS: *Communist Manifesto*, 426b

2b. The process of work: the relations of art, hand, machine, and matter

7 PLATO: *Republic*, BK II, 319a-c / *Statesman*, 591d-593d; 596a-b; 596d / *Philebus*, 633a-c

8 ARISTOTLE: *Soul*, BK III, CH 8 [432^{a}1] 664c

9 ARISTOTLE: *Ethics*, BK II, CH I 348b,d-349b / *Politics*, BK I, CH 4 447b-c

18 AUGUSTINE: *Christian Doctrine*, BK II, CH 30 651c-d

19 AQUINAS: *Summa Theologica*, PART I, Q 91, A 3, REP 2 486b-487d

20 AQUINAS: *Summa Theologica*, PART I-II, Q 85, A 6, ANS 182d-184a; PART II-II, Q 187, A 3, ANS and REP I 666a-669b

23 HOBBES: *Leviathan*, PART I, 73b

28 HARVEY: *On Animal Generation*, 407c

35 LOCKE: *Civil Government*, CH V, SECT 42-43 34a-c

38 ROUSSEAU: *Inequality*, 352a-d

39 SMITH: *Wealth of Nations*, BK I, 4d-5a; 54d-55a

46 HEGEL: *Philosophy of Right*, PART I, par 68 29d-30a; PART III, par 196 67a; ADDITIONS, 126 137a-b

49 DARWIN: *Descent of Man*, 278c-d

50 MARX: *Capital*, 16d-17a; 31a-b; 85a-88d; 180d-188c esp 184b, 188b-c; 197a-198a; 251a-c

51 TOLSTOY: *War and Peace*, BK XIII, 576b-577a

54 FREUD: *Civilization and Its Discontents*, 778b-c

3. The kinds of work and the relationship of different types of workers

3a. The differentiation of work according to the human talent or ability required: skilled and unskilled labor; manual and mental work

7 PLATO: *Republic*, BK II, 316c-320c / *Timaeus*, 442b / *Statesman*, 581c-582a

8 ARISTOTLE: *Metaphysics*, BK I, CH I [981^{a}31-^{b}7] 499d

9 ARISTOTLE: *Politics*, BK I, CH 7 [1255^{b}20-37] 449b-c; CH II [1258^{b}35-39] 453b; BK VIII, CH 4 [1339^{a}6-10] 544c

12 LUCRETIUS: *Nature of Things*, BK V [1350-1360] 78c-d

14 PLUTARCH: *Marcellus*, 252a-255a esp 253d

19 AQUINAS: *Summa Theologica*, PART I, Q 91, A 3, REP 2-3 486b-487d

20 AQUINAS: *Summa Theologica*, PART II-II, Q 187, A 3 666a-669b

21 DANTE: *Divine Comedy*, PARADISE, VIII [115-148] 118b-c

25 MONTAIGNE: *Essays*, 60a-c; 110c-112a; 156d-158a,c; 460a-461a

30 BACON: *Advancement of Learning*, 6c-d

36 SWIFT: *Gulliver*, PART I, 29b-31a; PART IV, 158b; 164b

39 SMITH: *Wealth of Nations*, BK I, 42d-43c; 54c-55a; 56b-57b

40 GIBBON: *Decline and Fall*, 597a-598a

42 KANT: *Judgement*, 524a-b; 586a-587a

43 MILL: *Representative Government*, 366d-367a; 385b-d

46 HEGEL: *Philosophy of Right*, PART I, par 68 29d-30a; PART III, par 200 67c-68a; par 204 68c-d; ADDITIONS, 44 123c; 126 137a-b

49 DARWIN: *Descent of Man*, 324b

50 MARX: *Capital*, 17b-18a; 95c-96a esp 95d-96b [fn 2]; 165d-166b; 170c-171b; 176d-178a; 186b-d; 212a-c; 251b-d

3b. The differentiation of work according to the social status of the worker: servile and free, menial and honorable work

6 HERODOTUS: *History*, BK II, 84d-85b

7 PLATO: *Laws*, BK VII, 722d-723c; BK VIII, 740d-741a; BK XI, 774a-775a

8 ARISTOTLE: *Metaphysics*, BK I, CH I [981^{a}31-^{b}7] 499d

9 ARISTOTLE: *Politics*, BK I, CH 7 [1255^{b}20-27] 449b-c; CH II [1258^{b}35-39] 453b; CH 13 [1260^{a}33-^{b}2] 455a; BK III, CH 4 [1277^{a}30-^{b}6] 474b-c; BK IV, CH 4 [1290^{b}37-1291^{a}19] 490a-b; BK VI, CH 4 [1319^{a}20-27] 522d; BK VII, CH 8-9 532c-533d; BK VIII, CH 2 [1337^{b}3-23] 542c-d / *Rhetoric*, BK I, CH 9 [1367^{a}28-32] 610a

14 PLUTARCH: *Lycurgus*, 44d-45b / *Solon*, 64d-65b / *Pericles*, 121a-122b / *Demetrius*, 733b-c

25 MONTAIGNE: *Essays*, 110c-112a; 459c-462a

26 SHAKESPEARE: *2nd Henry VI*, ACT IV, SC II 57d-59d

35 LOCKE: *Civil Government*, CH IV, SECT 23 30a-b; CH VII, SECT 85 43c-d

37 FIELDING: *Tom Jones*, 134a-b; 256b-c

38 ROUSSEAU: *Social Contract*, BK IV, 428c-d

39 SMITH: *Wealth of Nations*, BK I, 42b-d; 44c-45c; 56b-58b; BK III, 164c-d; 169c-171c

42 KANT: *Judgement*, 524a-b

46 HEGEL: *Philosophy of Right*, ADDITIONS, 44 123c

50 MARX-ENGELS: *Communist Manifesto*, 420d

52 DOSTOEVSKY: *Brothers Karamazov*, BK VI, 165b-167b

3c. The classification of occupations by reference to bodily and mental concomitants of the work: healthy and unhealthy occupations; pleasant and unpleasant tasks

9 ARISTOTLE: *Politics*, BK I, CH II [1258^{b}35-39] 453b; BK VIII, CH 2 542b-d; CH 4 [1339^{a}6-10] 544c

14 PLUTARCH: *Pompey*, 512c-d

25 MONTAIGNE: *Essays*, 110c-112a; 459c-462a passim

38 ROUSSEAU: *Inequality*, 365b-c

(3. *The kinds of work and the relationship of different types of workers. 3c. The classification of occupations by reference to bodily and mental concomitants of the work: healthy and unhealthy occupations; pleasant and unpleasant tasks.*)

39 SMITH: *Wealth of Nations*, BK I, 42b-d; 54d-55a; BK III, 164a; BK V, 340c-343d

42 KANT: *Judgement*, 524a-b

50 MARX: *Capital*, 85c-d; 117c-130c passim; 166b-c; 176d-178a; 194b-195c; 200a-204c passim, esp 204a-c; 206b-209a; 227d-231b

53 JAMES: *Psychology*, 79b

3d. **Types of work distinguished by reference to the manner in which the work is done: solitary and group work; the relation of master-craftsmen and helpers**

7 PLATO: *Statesman*, 581c-582a

8 ARISTOTLE: *Metaphysics*, BK I, CH I [981^{a}31–^{b}7] 499d

9 ARISTOTLE: *Politics*, BK III, CH 4 [1277^{a}30–^{b}6] 474b-c

39 SMITH: *Wealth of Nations*, BK I, 3d-5b; 35c-36a; 50a-c; 51b-53b; 109a

43 MILL: *Representative Government*, 385b-d

50 MARX: *Capital*, 157a-164a esp 158d-159d, 160d-162a; 165d-166b; 170c-171b; 186b-188c; 251b-c

3e. **Types of work distinguished by reference to their effect on the increase of wealth: productive and non-productive labor**

38 ROUSSEAU: *Inequality*, 365b-366b

39 SMITH: *Wealth of Nations*, BK II, 142d-151c esp 142d-143c; BK IV, 288c-292a; 294b-296a

50 MARX: *Capital*, 16b-17a; 17c; 86d-87d esp 87b [fn 2]; 96a-97a; 219a-d; 251a-252a; 290d-292a

3f. **The differentiation of work in terms of its relation to the common welfare: socially useful and wasteful or superfluous work**

7 PLATO: *Republic*, BK II, 318b-d

9 ARISTOTLE: *Politics*, BK IV, CH 4 [1290^{b}37–1291^{a}33] 490a-c; BK VII, CH 8–9 532c-533d

12 AURELIUS: *Meditations*, BK VII, SECT 5 280a-b

14 PLUTARCH: *Lycurgus*, 36c-d / *Marcellus*, 255d-256b / *Demetrius*, 733b-c

20 AQUINAS: *Summa Theologica*, PART II–II, Q 187, A 3, REP 3 666a-669b

21 DANTE: *Divine Comedy*, HELL, XI [91–111] 16a-b

38 ROUSSEAU: *Inequality*, 365b-366b / *Social Contract*, BK IV, 428c-d

39 SMITH: *Wealth of Nations*, BK II, 142d-151c esp 142d-143c

49 DARWIN: *Descent of Man*, 324b

50 MARX: *Capital*, 16a-18d esp 16a, 18d; 31a-32c esp 32a-c; 34d-35c; 48b-d; 174a-b; 261d-262a

4. **The division of labor**

7 PLATO: *Charmides*, 5d; 12a-b / *Republic*, BK II, 316a-319c; BK IV, 349a-350a / *Timaeus*, 442b-c; 445c-d / *Critias*, 480a-481b / *Laws*, BK VIII, 740d-741a

9 ARISTOTLE: *Politics*, BK IV, CH 4 [1290^{b}20–1291^{b}29] 489d-491a; BK VII, CH 8–9 532c-533d

18 AUGUSTINE: *City of God*, BK VII, CH 4, 246d

20 AQUINAS: *Summa Theologica*, PART II–II, Q 187, A 3, REP I 666a-669b

21 DANTE: *Divine Comedy*, PARADISE, VIII [115–148] 118b-c

30 BACON: *New Atlantis*, 210d-214d

35 LOCKE: *Civil Government*, CH V, SECT 42–43 34a-c

38 ROUSSEAU: *Inequality*, 352a-353c

39 SMITH: *Wealth of Nations*, BK I, 3a-10b; BK II, 117a-d

42 KANT: *Fund. Prin. Metaphysic of Morals*, 253c-d

43 MILL: *Representative Government*, 420a-b

46 HEGEL: *Philosophy of Right*, PART III, par 198–208 67b-69c; par 243 77b-c

49 DARWIN: *Descent of Man*, 278d

50 MARX: *Capital*, 164a-180d esp 164a-165c, 171d-176a, 178d-179c

4a. **The economic causes and effects of the division of labor: its relation to the exchange, production, and distribution of goods and services; its bearing on opulence**

7 PLATO: *Republic*, BK II, 316c-319a

35 LOCKE: *Civil Government*, CH V, SECT 42–43 34a-c

36 SWIFT: *Gulliver*, PART IV, 154b-155b

38 MONTESQUIEU: *Spirit of Laws*, BK XXIII, 191a-c

38 ROUSSEAU: *Inequality*, 352a-353c; 365b-366b

39 SMITH: *Wealth of Nations*, BK I, 3a-10c; BK II, 117a-d; BK III, 163a-c; BK IV, 191a

40 GIBBON: *Decline and Fall*, 21c-23b; 655d-656a

42 KANT: *Fund. Prin. Metaphysic of Morals*, 253c

46 HEGEL: *Philosophy of Right*, PART III, par 198–199 67b-c / *Philosophy of History*, PART I, 250a-c

50 MARX: *Capital*, 16c-d; 17b-c; 31a-37c esp 32a-c, 34c-35a; 48b-50b; 80b-81a; 164a-165b; 167a-170b; 171c-175c; 176a-d; 178a-180d esp 178c-179c; 218c-219b; 251a-255a passim; 377c-378a

4b. **The social consequences of the division of labor: the development of classes**

6 HERODOTUS: *History*, BK II, 84d-85b; BK VI, 196c

7 PLATO: *Republic*, BK II–IV, 316c-356a / *Laws*, BK VIII, 740d-741a

9 ARISTOTLE: *Politics*, BK I, CH 4 447b-c; BK II, CH 5 [1264^{a}1–^{b}25] 459a-460a; CH 8 [1268^{a}16–^{b}4] 464a-b; BK III, CH 5 [1277^{b}33–1278^{a}25]

475a-c; BK IV, CH 4 [1290^{b}21–1291^{b}29] 489d-
491a; BK VI, CH I [1317^{a}17–29] 520b-c; BK VII,
CH 8–10 532c-534d

26 SHAKESPEARE: *2nd Henry VI*, ACT IV, SC II
57d-59d

36 SWIFT: *Gulliver*, PART IV, 154b-155b; 158a-b

38 MONTESQUIEU: *Spirit of Laws*, BK XV, 111c

38 ROUSSEAU: *Inequality*, 353a-355b; 365b-366a

39 SMITH: *Wealth of Nations*, BK I, 7d-8b; 55d-
56a; 109d-110d; BK III, 169c-170b; BK V,
301a-309a,c passim, esp 303d-304a

40 GIBBON: *Decline and Fall*, 89d; 498c-d;
501b-c; 655d-656a

42 KANT: *Judgement*, 586a-587a

43 FEDERALIST: NUMBER 35, 113b-114a; NUMBER
36, 114c-115a

43 MILL: *Representative Government*, 369b-370a

44 BOSWELL: *Johnson*, 127b-c; 140b-141a

46 HEGEL: *Philosophy of Right*, PART III, par 198–
208 67b-69c; par 243 77b-c; ADDITIONS, 128–
129 137b-c / *Philosophy of History*, PART I,
222a-d; 250a-c; PART II, 275b-276a; PART IV,
335a-336c

50 MARX: *Capital*, 16c-d; 165c-166a; 170c-176a
esp 170c-172c, 174c-175c; 179a-c; 186b-d;
205c-206c; 218c-219d; 239d-240c; 261d-262a;
317c-319a

50 MARX-ENGELS: *Communist Manifesto*, 422b-
424c esp 422c-d

52 DOSTOEVSKY: *Brothers Karamazov*, BK VI,
165b-167b

54 FREUD: *New Introductory Lectures*, 882c-d

4c. The moral aspects of the division of labor: the acquisition of the virtue of art; the attenuation of art by insignificant tasks

13 VIRGIL: *Georgics*, I [118–159] 40a-41b

20 AQUINAS: *Summa Theologica*, PART II–II,
Q 187, A 3, REP I 666a-669b

38 ROUSSEAU: *Inequality*, 352a; 353b-d

39 SMITH: *Wealth of Nations*, BK I, 7d-8a; 54c-
55a; 109d-110d; BK IV, 291a-c; BK V, 340d-
342a

42 KANT: *Fund. Prin. Metaphysic of Morals*,
253c-d / *Judgement*, 524a-b

50 MARX: *Capital*, 164b-c; 165a-166c; 170c-171a;
173b; 176a-178d; 205c-208a; 226d-231b;
249a-250c; 319d-320a

50 MARX-ENGELS: *Communist Manifesto*, 422c-d

5. The organization of production: the position of labor in different economies

38 ROUSSEAU: *Inequality*, 365b-366a

39 SMITH: *Wealth of Nations*, INTRO, 1d-2a,c;
BK I, 50a-c; 109a

50 MARX: *Capital*, 33b-36c esp 36c-d [fn 2];
79c-81a esp 79d-80b [fn 4]; 80b-c; 104b-105a;
113c-115c esp 113c-d; 149a-150c; 157a-164a
esp 158d-160d, 162d-164a; 171d-176a; 266c;
267c; 283c-d; 354c-355d; 377c-378d

50 MARX-ENGELS: *Communist Manifesto*, 420a-d;
425b-429c esp 426b-c, 429b-c

5a. Domestic or chattel slavery in a slave economy

OLD TESTAMENT: *Exodus*, 1:8–14; 21:1–12,16,20–
21,26–27,32 / *Leviticus*, 25:44–55 / *Deuteronomy*, 15:12–18; 23:15–16; 24:14–15

APOCRYPHA: *Ecclesiasticus*, 33:24–31—(D) OT,
Ecclesiasticus, 33:25–33

NEW TESTAMENT: *Colossians*, 3:22–4:1 / *Titus*,
2:9–11 / *Philemon*

4 HOMER: *Odyssey*, BK XIV [55–71] 260d; BK XV
[351–379] 269c-d

5 ARISTOPHANES: *Plutus* [507–526] 635a-b

7 PLATO: *Laws*, BK VI, 709a-710a

9 ARISTOTLE: *Politics*, BK I, CH 2 [1252^{a}26–^{b}13]
445c-d; CH 3–7 446d-449c passim; CH 13
454a-455a,c passim; BK II, CH 9 [1269^{a}33–^{b}12]
465c-d; BK VII, CH 10 [1330^{a}25–34] 534d /
Rhetoric, BK I, CH 5 [1361^{a}12–14] 601c

14 PLUTARCH: *Marcus Cato*, 278d-279a; 287b-d
/ *Crassus*, 439a-c

20 AQUINAS: *Summa Theologica*, PART I–II, Q
105, A 4, ANS and REP 1–4 318b-321a

23 HOBBES: *Leviathan*, PART II, 110b-111a; PART
IV, 261d-262a

38 MONTESQUIEU: *Spirit of Laws*, BK XIII, 96d-
97b; BK XV, 109a-d; 111d-112c; BK XVI, 116a

39 SMITH: *Wealth of Nations*, BK III, 167a-d; BK
IV, 239c-240a; 253c-254a

40 GIBBON: *Decline and Fall*, 16c-17d; 144b;
498b-500b passim, esp 500a-b; 620a-c

41 GIBBON: *Decline and Fall*, 81d-82b

43 CONSTITUTION OF THE U.S.: ARTICLE I, SECT
9 [260–266] 13d; ARTICLE IV, SECT 2 [529–535]
16b; AMENDMENTS, XIII 18c

43 FEDERALIST: NUMBER 42, 137b-c; NUMBER
54, 170b-d

43 MILL: *Representative Government*, 339d-340c

44 BOSWELL: *Johnson*, 363b-364c

46 HEGEL: *Philosophy of Right*, PART I, par 66
29a-c

50 MARX: *Capital*, 95a-b [fn 1]; 113c-114a; 128d-
129a; 266c; 267c; 283c-d; 354c-355d

52 DOSTOEVSKY: *Brothers Karamazov*, BK VI,
165b-167b

5b. Serfdom or agrarian peonage in a feudal economy

38 MONTESQUIEU: *Spirit of Laws*, BK XIII, 96d-
97b

39 SMITH: *Wealth of Nations*, BK III, 165b-170c
esp 167a-170c; 175d-179a

40 GIBBON: *Decline and Fall*, 144b-c; 628c-d

41 GIBBON: *Decline and Fall*, 404c-d; 452d-
453a,c

43 MILL: *Representative Government*, 351d-352b

46 HEGEL: *Philosophy of Right*, PART I, par 66
29a-c / *Philosophy of History*, PART IV, 335a-
336c; 352a

50 MARX: *Capital*, 34b; 79d-80b [fn 4]; 114a-
115c; 266c; 354c-355d; 355d-364a passim

50 MARX-ENGELS: *Communist Manifesto*, 420a-d

(5. *The organization of production: the position of labor in different economies. 5b. Serfdom or agrarian peonage in a feudal economy.*)

51 TOLSTOY: *War and Peace*, BK V, 211a-213a; BK VI, 235a; BK X, 410c-411a; EPILOGUE I, 654a-655c

52 DOSTOEVSKY: *Brothers Karamazov*, BK VI, 165b-166a

5c. The wage earner or industrial proletariat in a capitalist economy

38 ROUSSEAU: *Inequality*, 365d-366a

39 SMITH: *Wealth of Nations*, BK I, 20b-21c; 27b-37b passim; 42a-62a passim

42 KANT: *Science of Right*, 436d-437c

43 MILL: *Liberty*, 309b-c / *Representative Government*, 345c-346a; 366d-367b; 369b-370a / *Utilitarianism*, 473b-c

46 HEGEL: *Philosophy of Right*, PART III, par 251–256 78d-80a

50 MARX: *Capital*, 79a-256a esp 82d-84a,c, 88d-89b, 104b-105c, 112c, 115c-131a, 150a-c, 161b-162d, 176a-178d, 192d-250c, 254c-255a; 261d-262a; 279a-383d esp 280c-286a, 287b-290c, 303b-305a, 311c-353a,c, 354c-355d, 364a-368b, 377a-378b

50 MARX-ENGELS: *Communist Manifesto*, 422c-423a; 424b-c; 426b-428a

52 DOSTOEVSKY: *Brothers Karamazov*, BK VI, 165b-c

5d. The condition of the worker in a socialist economy

43 MILL: *Liberty*, 309b-c

50 MARX: *Capital*, 34d-35c

50 MARX-ENGELS: *Communist Manifesto*, 425b-429c esp 426b, 429b-c

6. The wages of labor: kinds of wage payments

39 SMITH: *Wealth of Nations*, BK I, 27b-37b; 42a-62a

43 MILL: *Liberty*, 309b-c / *Representative Government*, 366d-367a / *Utilitarianism*, 472d-473a

50 MARX: *Capital*, 82d-83c; 264a-278a,c

6a. Labor as a commodity: the labor market

23 HOBBES: *Leviathan*, PART II, 124c

36 SWIFT: *Gulliver*, PART IV, 154b-155b

38 ROUSSEAU: *Inequality*, 365d-366a

39 SMITH: *Wealth of Nations*, BK I, 13a-16d; 20b-21c; 27b-37b esp 28a-d, 29b-33c; 42a-62a; 107b; BK IV, 243b,d-244a; BK V, 380b,d

42 KANT: *Science of Right*, 424b-425a

43 MILL: *Liberty*, 319b-d

50 MARX: *Capital*, 79a-84a,c; 91a-95a passim, esp 93b-94a; 112c-113c; 211a-219d esp 211a-c, 216a-d; 302d-317c esp 303b-305a, 315c-317c; 379a-383d esp 381b, 382c-383d

50 MARX-ENGELS: *Communist Manifesto*, 422c-423a

6b. The iron law of wages: the subsistence level and the minimum wage

39 SMITH: *Wealth of Nations*, BK I, 28d-29a; 41b; BK V, 383b-384c

50 MARX: *Capital*, 81a-82c; 256b

50 MARX-ENGELS: *Communist Manifesto*, 422c-d; 424d-425a; 426b

6c. The distinction between real and nominal wages: variable factors affecting wage levels

39 SMITH: *Wealth of Nations*, BK I, 13a-20b esp 14b-d; 23c-27b passim; 27b-37b esp 28a-32b; 39d-40b; 42a-62a; 82d-83a; 87b-c; BK II, 123b-124a; BK IV, 265a-d; BK V, 380b,d-382a,c; 383b-387b; 391b-392a

50 MARX: *Capital*, 171a-c; 223a esp 223b [fn I]; 256b-260c esp 258b-c; 267d-268c; 302d-307c; 315c-316c

50 MARX-ENGELS: *Communist Manifesto*, 422c-d; 423c; 425a-b

6d. The natural wages of labor and the labor theory of value

35 LOCKE: *Civil Government*, CH V 30b-36a

38 ROUSSEAU: *Inequality*, 353a-b

39 SMITH: *Wealth of Nations*, BK I, 13a-14d; 16a; 20b-21c; 27b-28a

42 KANT: *Science of Right*, 424b-425a

50 MARX: *Capital*, 13a-25d esp 14c-16a, 24c-25d; 32c-33b; 35d-36a [fn I]; 36a-b [fn I]; 78c-d; 93b-96a; 100a-101c; 112c-113b; 264a-267d esp 265a-266a

7. Economic and political justice to the laborer

7a. Fair wages, hours, and working conditions: labor legislation

OLD TESTAMENT: *Exodus*, 12:16; 20:9-10; 21:1-12,16,20,26-27,32; 31:14-17 / *Leviticus*, 16:29; 19:13; 23:3-8,21,25,27-36; 25:1-12,39-55 / *Numbers*, 28:16-18,25-26; 29:1,7,12,35 / *Deuteronomy*, 5:12-15; 15:12-18; 16:8; 23:15-16; 24:14-15 / *Jeremiah*, 17:22,24; 22:13—(D) *Jeremias*, 17:22,24; 22:13

APOCRYPHA: *Tobit*, 4:14—(D) OT, *Tobias*, 4:15 / *Ecclesiasticus*, 7:20-21; 33:24-31; 34:20-22 —(D) OT, *Ecclesiasticus*, 7:22-23; 33:25-33; 34:24-27

NEW TESTAMENT: *Matthew*, 10:10; 20:8 / *Luke*, 3:14; 10:7 / *Ephesians*, 6:5-9 / *I Timothy*, 5:18 / *II Timothy*, 2:6

7 PLATO: *Laws*, BK VIII, 741b-d

9 ARISTOTLE: *Ethics*, BK IX, CH I 416b,d-417c

20 AQUINAS: *Summa Theologica*, PART I-II, Q 105, A 2, REP 6 309d-316a

30 BACON: *Advancement of Learning*, 30c-d

36 SWIFT: *Gulliver*, PART IV, 154b-155b

38 MONTESQUIEU: *Spirit of Laws*, BK XV, 111b-c

38 ROUSSEAU: *Inequality*, 353b; 365b-d

39 SMITH: *Wealth of Nations*, BK I, 13a-14d; 20b-

23b esp 20b-21c; 27b-37b esp 28a-29b, 33c-35b; 42a-62a passim, esp 52b-c, 56b-57a, 58b-61d; 106c-107a; BK IV, 200c-201a; 287b-c
42 KANT: *Science of Right*, 424b-425a
43 MILL: *Liberty*, 309b-c; 310c-d / *Representative Government*, 345c-346a; 366d-367b / *Utilitarianism*, 467b; 472d-473c
46 HEGEL: *Philosophy of Right*, PART III, par 236 76a-c; ADDITIONS, 145 140b
50 MARX: *Capital*, 81a-84a,c; 102b-156d esp 104b-105c, 112c-113c, 127c-146c, 150a-c, 156c-d; 192d-209a passim, esp 193a-194b; 226a-248d esp 236c-242a; 256b-275c passim, esp 261c-262a, 263c-d, 266a-267c; 296b-307c passim, esp 296c-298a, 305c-307c; 366a-368a
50 MARX-ENGELS: *Communist Manifesto*, 422c-423a; 423c-d

7b. The right to property: the ownership of the means of production

7 PLATO: *Republic*, BK III-IV, 341c-342d / *Laws*, BK V, 692d-693a; 695a-696b
9 ARISTOTLE: *Politics*, BK II, CH 5 458a-460a
14 PLUTARCH: *Lycurgus*, 36a-37b / *Tiberius Gracchus*, 674c-681a,c esp 675b-d
35 LOCKE: *Civil Government*, CH V 30b-36a
38 ROUSSEAU: *Inequality*, 339c-d; 353a / *Social Contract*, BK I, 394a
39 SMITH: *Wealth of Nations*, BK III, 165b-170c; BK IV, 239c-240a; 243b,d-244a
41 GIBBON: *Decline and Fall*, 86d-87a
42 KANT: *Science of Right*, 404a; 409d-410d; 414c-415c; 426b-428a; 431a-432a; 441d-443b
43 MILL: *Representative Government*, 366d
46 HEGEL: *Philosophy of Right*, PART I, par 52 25a-c; par 67-69 29c-31a; ADDITIONS, 32 121d-122a
48 MELVILLE: *Moby Dick*, 295a-297a
50 MARX: *Capital*, 88d-89b; 113c-d; 149a-151a,c passim, esp 150b-c; 160d-162d; 173c-174a; 280c-283d passim, esp 282b-c; 288b-290c; 319c-d; 354a-364a esp 354a-355d, 359c-361d; 369c-370b; 377c-378d
50 MARX-ENGELS: *Communist Manifesto*, 424c; 425c-427b esp 426a-b; 428d-429c
54 FREUD: *Civilization and Its Discontents*, 787d-788b passim, esp 787d-788b [fn 3]

7c. The consequences of economic inequality or oppression: the class war

7c(1) The economic determination of antagonistic social classes: slaves *vs.* freemen; laboring *vs.* leisure classes; propertyless *vs.* propertied classes

5 EURIPIDES: *Suppliants* [228-245] 260b-c
5 ARISTOPHANES: *Plutus* [507-526] 635a-b
6 HERODOTUS: *History*, BK VI, 203a-b; BK VII, 243b-c
6 THUCYDIDES: *Peloponnesian War*, BK III, 423a-c; 427d-428a; 428c-d; 434c-438c; BK

IV, 458d-459c; 463a-465c; BK V, 482d-483a; 502d-504b; BK VI, 520a-d; 524d-525d; 533a-c; BK VIII 564a-593a,c passim, esp 568d-569a, 575c-576c, 577b-d; 579c-583c, 584b-585a, 585d-586b, 587a-590c
7 PLATO: *Republic*, BK IV, 343c-d; BK VIII, 405c-416a
9 ARISTOTLE: *Politics*, BK II, CH 6 [1265^{b}6-12] 461a; CH 7 461d-463c; CH 9 [1269^{a}33-^{b}12] 465c-d; BK III, CH 10 [1281^{a}11-29] 478d-479a; CH 15 [1286^{b}8-22] 484d-485a; BK IV, CH 4 [1291^{b}2-11] 490d; CH 6 [1293^{a}12-34] 492d-493a; CH 11-12 495b-497b; BK V, CH 3 [1303^{b}5-8] 505a; CH 4 [1304^{b}1-6] 506a; CH 5 [1304^{b}18]-CH 6 [1305^{b}22] 506b-507c; CH 7 [1306^{b}22-1307^{a}2] 508c-d; CH 9 [1310^{a}19-25] 512c; CH 10 [1310^{b}9-15] 512d-513a; CH 12 [1316^{a}39-^{b}22] 519c-d; BK VI, CH 3 521c-522a; CH 7 524c-525b / *Athenian Constitution*, CH 2-6 553a-555c esp CH 5 554d-555a
14 PLUTARCH: *Lycurgus*, 36a-37c / *Solon*, 68d-71c / *Camillus*, 117c-121a,c / *Coriolanus*, 176b-184c / *Agis* 648b,d-656d / *Tiberius Gracchus*, 674c-681a,c
15 TACITUS: *Annals*, BK VI, 97b / *Histories*, BK II, 224d-225a
23 MACHIAVELLI: *Prince*, CH IX, 14c-d
26 SHAKESPEARE: *2nd Henry VI*, ACT IV, SC II 57d-59d
27 SHAKESPEARE: *Coriolanus*, ACT I, SC I [1-167] 351a-353a
36 SWIFT: *Gulliver*, PART IV, 154b-155b
38 MONTESQUIEU: *Spirit of Laws*, BK XI, 77b-83c
38 ROUSSEAU: *Inequality*, 355a-356a / *Political Economy*, 375b-d; 381c-382b / *Social Contract*, BK IV, 429c-d
39 SMITH: *Wealth of Nations*, BK I, 28a-d; 55d-56a; 109d-110d; BK III, 169c-170b; BK IV, 239c-240c; 243b,d-244a; BK V, 309a-311c
40 GIBBON: *Decline and Fall*, 126d-127c; 144a-d; 501b-502c
43 FEDERALIST: NUMBER 10, 50b-51b; NUMBER 35, 113b-114a; NUMBER 36, 114c-115a; NUMBER 60, 185b-186a
43 MILL: *Representative Government*, 345c-346a; 366d-367b; 369b-370a / *Utilitarianism*, 473b-c
46 HEGEL: *Philosophy of Right*, PART III, par 244 77c; ADDITIONS, 149 140d-141a / *Philosophy of History*, INTRO, 193b-c; PART I, 250a-c; PART II, 263c-d; 275b-276a; PART III, 287d-288b; 295d-297b; PART IV, 335a-336c; 356c-357a
50 MARX: *Capital*, 6d-9c; 63b-c; 111c-146c esp 113c, 130a-131a, 134c-d, 141b-c, 145a; 209c-215a esp 209c, 214a-215a; 262a; 282d-286a; 354a-364a; 378d
50 MARX-ENGELS: *Communist Manifesto*, 415b-416d esp 416c-d; 419b,d-425b esp 419b,d-420a, 421a, 422c-425b; 428c-d; 429c-430d; 432d-433a; 434a-d
52 DOSTOEVSKY: *Brothers Karamazov*, BK VI, 165b-c
54 FREUD: *New Introductory Lectures*, 882b-884d

(7c. *The consequences of economic inequality or oppression: the class war.*)

7c(2) The organization of workmen and the formation of trade unions to protect labor's rights and interests

39 SMITH: *Wealth of Nations*, BK I, 28a-d; 51a-56b; 61c-d

43 MILL: *Liberty*, 309b-c / *Representative Government*, 345d-346a; 366d-367b

50 MARX: *Capital*, 121c-122b; 137b-138c; 146a-c; 317b-c; 367c-368b

50 MARX-ENGELS: *Communist Manifesto*, 415a-416c; 423b-d; 425b-c

7c(3) The proletariat as a revolutionary class: its revolutionary aims

50 MARX: *Capital*, 9c; 294b-295a esp 295a; 377c-378d esp 378d-379b [fn 2]

50 MARX-ENGELS: *Communist Manifesto*, 415b-417a,c esp 416b-d; 422c; 424a-d; 425b-434d esp 425b-c, 428d-430a, 434c-d

7d. The underprivileged condition of workers: the exclusion of slaves from citizenship; the disfranchisement of the laboring classes

5 ARISTOPHANES: *Frogs* [686–705] 572a-b

6 HERODOTUS: *History*, BK III, 107d-108a

7 PLATO: *Republic*, BK VIII, 405c-407a / *Laws*, BK VIII, 740d-741a

9 ARISTOTLE: *Politics*, BK II, CH 7 [1267^{b}14–19] 463b-c; CH 8 [1268^{a}16–33] 464a-b; BK III, CH 1 [1275^{a}5–10] 471d; CH 4 [1277^{a}30–^{b}6] 474b-c; CH 5 [1277^{b}33–1278^{a}34] 475a-c; BK IV, CH 6 [1292^{b}22–1293^{a}10] 492b-c; BK VI, CH 4 522a-523b; CH 7 [1321^{a}27–32] 525a; BK VII, CH 8 [1328^a–35–38] 532c; CH 9 533a-d; CH 10 [1330^{a}25–34] 534d / *Athenian Constitution*, CH 2–5 553a-555a

38 MONTESQUIEU: *Spirit of Laws*, BK XV, 114c-115b

38 ROUSSEAU: *Social Contract*, BK III, 412b-c; BK IV, 429c-d

39 SMITH: *Wealth of Nations*, BK I, 27b-37b

40 GIBBON: *Decline and Fall*, 17a-b; 144b

41 GIBBON: *Decline and Fall*, 73b; 81d-82b; 404c-d; 452d

42 KANT: *Science of Right*, 436d-437c

43 CONSTITUTION OF THE U.S.: AMENDMENTS, XIII, SECT I–XIV, SECT I 18c-d; XV 19b

43 FEDERALIST: NUMBER 54, 170b-171b passim

43 MILL: *Representative Government*, 339d-340c; 345c-346a; 351d-352b; 383d-387d passim; 394a-395c passim / *Utilitarianism*, 473b-c

50 MARX: *Capital*, 137b-141b passim, esp 138b, 140a-b; 283d-286a; 316d-317c; 364a-368b esp 367c-368b

50 MARX-ENGELS: *Communist Manifesto*, 424c-425a; 428a

7e. The problem of poverty and pauperism: unemployment and the right to work

7 PLATO: *Laws*, BK V, 695a-c; BK XI, 783b

9 ARISTOTLE: *Politics*, BK VI, CH 5 [1320^{a}17–^{b}13] 523d-524b

14 PLUTARCH: *Lycurgus*, 36a-37b / *Lycurgus-Numa*, 62b-c / *Pericles*, 127a-128a / *Lucullus*, 409b-d

23 HOBBES: *Leviathan*, PART II, 157a

36 SWIFT: *Gulliver*, PART IV, 154b-155b

38 MONTESQUIEU: *Spirit of Laws*, BK XX, 147a; BK XXIII, 190a-b; 191b-c; 199b-200a,c

38 ROUSSEAU: *Inequality*, 365c-366a / *Political Economy*, 375b-d / *Social Contract*, BK III, 415b-d

39 SMITH: *Wealth of Nations*, BK I, 27b-37b esp 28a-d, 30b-31b; 58c-62a; BK IV, 239c-240a

40 GIBBON: *Decline and Fall*, 501c-d; 658c

43 MILL: *Liberty*, 322c-d / *Representative Government*, 383d-384a

44 BOSWELL: *Johnson*, 428b

46 HEGEL: *Philosophy of Right*, PART III, par 230 75c; par 241–245 76d-77d; par 254 79c; ADDITIONS, 148–149 140c-141a

50 MARX: *Capital*, 209c-225d passim, esp 211a-c, 215d-217c; 302d-366a esp 303d-305a, 311c-325c, 354b-355b, 358a-d, 364a-c

50 MARX-ENGELS: *Communist Manifesto*, 424d-425a

7f. The relation of economic to political freedom: economic democracy

9 ARISTOTLE: *Politics*, BK III, CH 9 477c-478d; BK IV, CH 4 [1291^{b}30–38] 491a-b; CH 6 492b-493a; CH 11 [1295^{b}2–1296^{b}2] 495c-496c; BK V, CH 5 [1305^{a}29–34] 507a; BK VI, CH 4 [1318^{b}6–1319^{b}2] 522a-523a; BK VII, CH 9 533a-d

14 PLUTARCH: *Solon*, 68d-70d / *Poplicola-Solon*, 87a / *Tiberius Gracchus* 671b,d-681a,c esp 675b-d / *Caius Gracchus* 681b,d-689a,c

38 MONTESQUIEU: *Spirit of Laws*, BK V, 19d-21d; BK VII, 44d-45b; BK XIII, 99b-100c; BK XV, 114c-115b

38 ROUSSEAU: *Inequality*, 353c-355b passim; 355d-356a / *Social Contract*, BK II, 405b-c esp 405b [fn 1]; BK III, 422c-d

39 SMITH: *Wealth of Nations*, BK I, 51a-62a passim, esp 52b-c, 61b; 109d-110d; BK IV, 287c-288c

40 GIBBON: *Decline and Fall*, 144b

41 GIBBON: *Decline and Fall*, 73b; 452d-453a,c

42 KANT: *Science of Right*, 436d-437c

43 FEDERALIST: NUMBER 10, 50b-51d; NUMBER 35, 113b-114a

43 MILL: *Liberty*, 309a-c / *Representative Government*, 369b-370a; 382c-d

46 HEGEL: *Philosophy of Right*, PART III, par 243 77b-c; ADDITIONS, 44 123c; 145 140b / *Philosophy of History*, PART III, 287d-288b; PART IV, 352a; 364d

50 MARX-ENGELS: *Communist Manifesto*, 426b-c; 428d-429c esp 429b-c

8. Historical observations on the condition of labor

6 HERODOTUS: *History*, BK II, 84d-85b; BK VI, 196c

9 ARISTOTLE: *Politics*, BK II, CH 9 [1269^a33-^b7] 465c

13 VIRGIL: *Georgics*, I [118-159] 40a-41b

14 PLUTARCH: *Lycurgus*, 36a-37c / *Solon*, 72d / *Pericles*, 127a-129b / *Marcus Cato*, 278d-279a; 287b-d / *Crassus*, 439a-c

15 TACITUS: *Annals*, BK XIV, 151d-152c

20 AQUINAS: *Summa Theologica*, PART I-II, Q 105, A 4, ANS and REP 1-4 318b-321a

25 MONTAIGNE: *Essays*, 411a-d

30 BACON: *Advancement of Learning*, 30c-d

38 ROUSSEAU: *Inequality*, 348b,d-353b / *Social Contract*, BK IV, 428d; 429d

39 SMITH: *Wealth of Nations*, BK I, 27b-37b esp 27b-28a, 29d-33c; 42a-62a passim, esp 50a-53a, 56b-58b, 59a-62a; 88c-d; BK III, 165b-173b; 175d-179a; BK IV, 200c-201a; 239c-240a; 287b-c

40 GIBBON: *Decline and Fall*, 16c-17d; 113c; 144b-c; 498b-501c passim

41 GIBBON: *Decline and Fall*, 404c-d; 452d-453a,c

46 HEGEL: *Philosophy of Right*, ADDITIONS, 149 140d-141a

48 MELVILLE: *Moby Dick*, 295a-297a

50 MARX: *Capital*, 63b-c; 113c-115c; 127c-146c; 162d-163c; 333c-377a esp 355d-368b

50 MARX-ENGELS: *Communist Manifesto*, 415a-425b passim, esp 415b-416c, 419b,d, 424d-425a; 429c-433d

52 DOSTOEVSKY: *Brothers Karamazov*, BK VI, 165b-c

CROSS-REFERENCES

ADDITIONAL READINGS

Listed below are works not included in *Great Books of the Western World*, but relevant to the idea and topics with which this chapter deals. These works are divided into two groups:

I. Works by authors represented in this collection.
II. Works by authors not represented in this collection.

For the date, place, and other facts concerning the publication of the works cited, consult the Bibliography of Additional Readings which follows the last chapter of *The Great Ideas*.

I.

AUGUSTINE. *Of the Work of Monks*
HEGEL. *The Phenomenology of Mind*, IV (A)
MARX. *The Poverty of Philosophy*, CH 2 (2,5)
J. S. MILL. *Principles of Political Economy*, BK I, CH 1–3, 7–8, 10; BK II, CH 11–14; BK III, CH 6; BK IV, CH 7
——. "The Claims of Labor," in VOL II, *Dissertations and Discussions*
ENGELS. *The Condition of the Working Classes in England*
——. *Herr Eugen Dühring's Revolution in Science*, PART II
TOLSTOY. "On Labor and Luxury," in *What Then Must We Do?*

II.

HESIOD. *Works and Days*
LANGLAND. *Piers Plowman*
T. MORE. *Utopia*
PARACELSUS. *The Miners' Sickness and Other Miners' Diseases*
DEKKER. *The Shoemaker's Holiday*
RAMAZZINI. *De Morbis Artificum (The Diseases of Workers)*
FRANKLIN. *Poor Richard's Almanack*
FOURIER. *Social Destinies*
SOUTHEY. *Essays, Moral and Political*, IV
RICARDO. *The Principles of Political Economy and Taxation*, esp CH 1, 5, 16
MALTHUS. *An Essay on Population*
——. *Principles of Political Economy*, esp BK I, CH 1–2, 4; BK II, CH I, SECT 10
SKIDMORE. *The Rights of Man to Property!*
T. CARLYLE. *Sartor Resartus*
HESS. *Sozialistische Aufsätze*
PROUDHON. *The Philosophy of Misery*
KIERKEGAARD. *Christian Discourses*, PART IV (2)
THOREAU. *Walden*, CH 1
RUSKIN. *Time and Tide*
——. *Munera Pulveris*
——. *Fors Clavigera*
GEORGE. *Progress and Poverty*
STEVENSON. "An Apology for Idlers," in *Virginibus Puerisque*
JEVONS. *The State in Relation to Labour*
ZOLA. *Germinal*
SMILES. *Life and Labor*
NIETZSCHE. *The Dawn of Day*, APH 173
——. *The Joyful Wisdom*, APH 42, 329, 348

NIETZSCHE. *Beyond Good and Evil*, CH III (58)
——. *The Genealogy of Morals*, III (18)
A. MARSHALL. *Principles of Economics*, esp BK IV, CH 6, 9; BK VI, CH 3–5
LEO XIII. *Rerum Novarum* (Encyclical on the Condition of Labor)
DURKHEIM. *The Division of Labor in Society*
BÜCHER. *Arbeit und Rhythmus*
S. and B. WEBB. *Industrial Democracy*, esp PART II–III
GROOS. *The Play of Men*
——. *The Play of Animals*
KROPOTKIN. *The Conquest of Bread*
——. *Fields, Factories and Workshops*
SINCLAIR. *The Jungle*
PÉGUY. *Basic Verities* (The Honor of Work)
NEXÖ. *Pelle the Conqueror*
SOREL. *Reflexions on Violence*, CH 7
TROELTSCH. *The Social Teaching of the Christian Churches*
BRADLEY. *Essays on Truth and Reality*, CH 3
J. A. HOBSON. *The Evolution of Modern Capitalism*
——. *Work and Wealth*
T. VEBLEN. *The Theory of the Leisure Class*
——. *The Instinct of Workmanship, and the State of the Industrial Arts*
HAMSUN. *Growth of the Soil*
MICHELS. *Economia e felicità*
TAWNEY. *The Acquisitive Society*
BRIEFS. *The Proletariat, a Challenge to Western Civilization*
DE MAN. *Joy in Work*
BEVERIDGE. *Unemployment*
PIUS XI. *Quadragesimo Anno* (Encyclical on the Reconstruction of the Social Order)
BERLE and MEANS. *The Modern Corporation and Private Property*
E. CHAMBERLIN. *The Theory of Monopolistic Competition*
DUNKMANN. *Soziologie der Arbeit*
B. RUSSELL. *Proposed Roads to Freedom*, CH 4
——. *Freedom Versus Organization*
A. R. BURNS. *The Decline of Competition*
BORNE and HENRY. *A Philosophy of Work*
GILL. *Work and Leisure*
——. *Work and Property*
SIMON. *Trois leçons sur le travail*
STEINBECK. *The Grapes of Wrath*
MARITAIN. *Freedom in the Modern World*, APPENDIX I
——. *Scholasticism and Politics*, CH VII
J. M. CLARK. *Alternative to Serfdom*

Chapter 45: LANGUAGE

INTRODUCTION

THE liberal arts of grammar, rhetoric, and logic are all concerned with language. Each of these disciplines establishes its own rules for the use of language, each by reference to a special standard of excellence or correctness which measures language as an instrument of thought or communication. Together these three arts regulate discourse as a whole. Their relation to one another represents the relation of the various aspects of discourse—the emotional, the social, and the intellectual.

The tradition of the great books is the tradition of the liberal arts. Their greatness consists not only in the magnitude of the ideas or problems with which they deal, but also in their formal excellence as products of liberal art. Some of the great books are expositions of logic or rhetoric. None is a treatise on grammar. But they all plainly exemplify, even where they do not expound, the special refinements of the arts of language; and many of them, especially the works of science, philosophy, and theology, and even some of the poetical works, deal explicitly with the difficulties of discourse, and the devices that have been used to overcome them. Language is their instrument, and they are consciously critical in its use.

One of the great books—Augustine's treatise *On Christian Doctrine*—is directly and explicitly concerned with grammar in the broad sense of the art of reading. Addressed to "earnest students of the word," it attempts to "lay down rules for interpretation," and, in so doing, it is compared by Augustine to "one who teaches reading, that is, shows others how to read for themselves." It is not reading in general, however, but the reading of one book—the Bible—with which Augustine is concerned. We shall return later to this special problem of interpreting the word of God, or language which is thought to be inspired.

In our day, there is a lively interest in the problems of language. This is partly because of the development of historical and comparative studies of the various human languages, and the scientific formulation of what is common to all languages in origin, structure, and change. But it also results in part from the claims of a discipline popularly called "semantics" to have discovered the properties of language as a medium of expression, and especially to have discovered its limitations. The claims of semantics often go so far as to find in the misuse of language the origin of many human ills. The novelty of semantics is supposed to lie both in the diagnosis and in the remedies proposed.

Of these two sources of current interest in language, the second calls attention to the vitality of the liberal arts, of which semantics is a contemporary formulation. It might almost be said that there is nothing new about semantics except the name. Hobbes, Bacon, and Locke, for example, deal explicitly with the abuses of language and the treachery of words. Each makes recommendations for the correction of these faults. Plato and Aristotle, Augustine and Aquinas, Berkeley and Hume, are similarly concerned with ambiguity in speech, with the multiple senses in which discourse of every sort can be interpreted, and with the methods by which men can approximate precision in the use of language.

The other interest in language is also represented in the great books. Though the science of linguistics and the history of languages are researches of recent origin, speculation about the origin of language and, in that context, consideration of the natural and conventional aspects of language extend throughout the tradition. At all times the discussion of the nature of man and society considers language as one of the principal characteristics of the specifically human world or compares the language of men with the speech of brutes.

In addition there is the broad philosophical inquiry into the nature of signs and symbols in general. This is not limited to the problem of how written or spoken words get their meaning. The general question calls for an examination of every type of signifying and every sort of symbol, verbal and non-verbal, natural and artificial, human and divine. Though these matters are closely related to the problems of language and may therefore be touched upon here, their main treatment is reserved for the chapter on SIGN AND SYMBOL.

THE TREATMENT of language seems to have a different tenor in ancient and modern times. The philosophers of antiquity appreciate the need to safeguard discourse from the aberrations of speech. Plato and Aristotle usually preface their discussion of a subject with an examination of the relevant words in current use. Discovering the variety of meanings attached to common words, they take pains to enumerate the various senses of a word, and to put these meanings in some order. They pursue definitions or construct them to control the ambiguity that is latent in the language anyone must use to express or communicate ideas. But they do not expect to remove ambiguity entirely. They tend to accept the fact that the same word will have to be used in a number of senses; and they discriminate between the occasions when it is desirable to be precise about a word's meaning and those times when the purpose of discourse is better served by permitting a word to carry a whole range of meanings. They see no special difficulty in abstract as opposed to concrete words, or in general names as distinguished from the proper names which designate individuals, or in words which refer to purely intelligible objects like ideas rather than to the objects of sense-experience.

The mood of the ancients, which also prevails for the most part among the philosophers and theologians of the Middle Ages, seems to express a certain tolerance of the imperfections of language. If men do not think clearly, if they do not reason cogently or argue honestly, the fault is primarily the result of the misuse of their faculties, not of the betrayal of their in-

tentions by the intractable character of language as an instrument. Even when men misunderstand one another, the inadequacy of language as a medium of communication is not solely responsible for the failure of minds to meet through the interchange of words. With greater effort, with a more assiduous application of the liberal arts, men can succeed even if language works against them.

Some things are inexpressible in human speech even as they are incapable of being fully grasped by human thought. "My vision," Dante says when he reaches the mystic rose of Paradise, "was greater than our speech." Such knowledge as we can have of "the highest matters and the first principles of things" Plato thinks "does not admit of exposition like other branches of knowledge." In his *Seventh Letter*, he even goes so far as to say that "no man of intelligence will venture to express his philosophical views in language."

With these exceptions the ancients seem to adopt a mood of tolerance towards language. This does not imply an underestimation of the difficulties of using language well. It simply does not make of language an insidious enemy of clarity and truth. The deficiencies of language are like the weaknesses of the flesh. As man can in large part overcome them through the discipline of the moral virtues, so through the discipline of the liberal arts—by skill in grammar, rhetoric, and logic—he can make language express almost as much truth as he can acquire, and communicate it almost as clearly as he can think it. Men need not succumb to the tyranny of words if they will make the requisite effort to master language to serve their purpose.

But the liberal arts do not guarantee purity of purpose. Obscurantism, obfuscation, deception, and falsification are sometimes the aim. Men try to persuade others at all costs, or to win the argument regardless of where the truth lies. They try to confuse their opponents or mislead their audience. The use of language for such ends requires as much skill as its employment in the service of truth. If such use is a misuse, then language is equally available for use or misuse.

It is an ancient saying that only the competent in grammar can make grammatical errors intentionally. So, as Plato recognizes, the difference between the sophist and the philosopher is not one of skill but of purpose. When he criticizes the trickery of sophistical argument, he also acknowledges the cleverness with which the sophists juggle words and propound absurdities under the cover of superficially significant speech. The sophistical fallacies which Aristotle enumerates are seldom accidental errors. Far from being the result of the impediments which language places in the way of thought, they are in large measure artfully contrived equivocations. They are ways of using language against logic. According to Aristotle, they represent "foul fighting in disputation" and are resorted to only by "those who are resolved to win at all costs."

IN THE MODERN treatment of language there is more of an imputation that words cause men unwittingly to deceive themselves as often as they enable one man intentionally to deceive another. Men are duped or tricked by the tendency of words to counterfeit a reality which does not exist. This, in the view of Hobbes or Locke, Berkeley or Hume, is particularly true of general or universal names—or words that signify nothing which can be perceived or imagined.

We cannot imagine anything infinite, says Hobbes. Hence a word like "infinite" is a form of absurd speech "taken upon credit (without any signification at all) from deceived philosophers and deceived, or deceiving, Schoolmen." In addition to the deceptions of ordinary ambiguity and of metaphorical speech, Hobbes pays particular attention to the absurd, insignificant, or nonsensical use of words "whereby we conceive nothing but the sound"; he gives as examples, not merely "round quadrangle," but "infused virtue," "free will," and "immaterial substance."

In the light of the examples, this theory of insignificant or meaningless speech explains what Hobbes means when he says that "words are wise men's counters, they do but reckon by them; but they are the money of fools." It also indicates how Hobbes uses the susceptibility of men to self-deception through language as a way of explaining the errors—he calls them "absurdities"—into which his predecessors have fallen. What is novel here is not that he disagrees with

earlier thinkers on points of psychology and metaphysics or theology, but that he reduces what might be supposed to be an issue between true and false opinions to a difference between significant and absurd speech. His opponents might reply that unless his own views about matter and mind are true, his semantic criticism of them does not hold. They have been seduced by language into talking nonsense only if Hobbes is right in his metaphysics and psychology.

The criticism of arguments which seem to rely on metaphors is not peculiarly modern. In his attack on the Platonic theory of ideas, Aristotle dismisses the statement that the Forms "are patterns and other things share in them" as a use of "empty words and poetical metaphors." But Hobbes carries this method of criticism much further. He frequently rests his case against other philosophers entirely on the ground that they are talking nonsense. Though he himself catches the imagination, almost as often as Plato does, by his skillfully wrought metaphors, he would insist that what he says can always be rendered literally, whereas the metaphors of others conceal the insignificance of their speech.

Bacon provides another illustration of the modern attitude which ascribes a diabolical character to language. "There arises from a bad and unapt formation of words," he writes, "a wonderful obstruction to the mind. Nor can the definitions and explanations with which learned men are wont to guard and protect themselves in some instances afford a complete remedy—words still manifestly force the understanding, throw everything into confusion, and lead mankind into vain and innumerable controversies and fallacies." He goes on to say that "the idols imposed upon the understanding by words are of two kinds. They are either names of things which have no existence ... or they are names of actual objects, but confused, badly defined, and hastily or irregularly abstracted from things."

Here, as in the case of Hobbes, a theory of reality and of the way in which the mind draws its ideas from experience seems to underlie the charge that language tangles the mind in a web of words, so that it deals with words rather than with things. In the same spirit, though not from the same premises, Locke tells his reader why he found it necessary to include in his *Essay Concerning Human Understanding* the long third book on language, which examines in detail the imperfections as well as the abuses of words, and the remedies therefor.

"Vague and insignificant forms of speech, and abuse of language," he says, "have so long passed for mysteries of science; and hard or misapplied words with little or no meaning have, by prescription, such a right to be mistaken for deep learning and height of speculation, that it will not be easy to persuade either those who speak, or those who hear them, that they are but the covers of ignorance, and hinderance of true knowledge. . . . So few are apt to think they deceive, or are deceived in the use of words or that the language of the sect they are of has any faults in it."

Without judging the fundamental issues involved concerning the nature of things and of man and his mind, one point seems to be clear. According as men hold different conceptions of the relation of language to thought (and in consequence assume different attitudes toward the imperfections or misuse of language), they inevitably take opposite sides on these issues. Whether the discipline of language is called semantics or the liberal arts, the standards by which one man criticizes the language of another seem to depend upon what he holds to be true.

The present work on the great ideas aims, in part, to record the agreements and disagreements among the great minds of the western tradition. It also records how those minds have used the same word in different senses or have used quite distinct words for the same thing. It could not do either unless it did both. This indicates the basic relationship between language and thought which the great books exemplify, even when they do not explicitly make it the basis of their discussion of the relation between language and thought.

THE IDEAL OF A perfect and universal language seems to arise in modern times from dissatisfaction with the inadequacy of ordinary language for the analytical refinement and precision of mathematics or science. As Descartes holds up the method of mathematics as the procedure to be followed in all other inquiries and subject matters, so his conception of a "universal mathe-

sis" calls for a language which shall be the perfect instrument of analysis and demonstration.

It is sometimes supposed that the symbolism of mathematics is itself that perfect language. Lavoisier quotes Condillac to the effect that algebra, "in the most simple, most exact, and best manner, is at the same time a language and an analytical method." Of the analytical equations "which Descartes was the first to introduce into the study of curves and surfaces," Fourier remarks that "they extend to all general phenomena. There cannot be a language more universal and more simple, more free from errors and obscurities, that is to say, more worthy to express the invariable relations of natural things. . . . Its chief attribute is clearness; it has no marks to express confused notions. . . . It follows the same course in the study of all phenomena; it interprets them by the same language."

This praise of mathematical symbolism indicates that one feature of the ideal is an exact correspondence between words and ideas. "Like three impressions of the same seal," Lavoisier says, "the word ought to produce the idea, and the idea to be a picture of the fact." If there were a perfect one-to-one correspondence between physical symbols and mental concepts, there would never be any failures of communication. Men would be able to understand each other as well as if they could see directly into each other's minds. Though they still used external signs as a medium of communication, they would approximate the immediate communication which the theologians attribute to angels. In addition, the process of thinking itself, quite apart from communication, could be perfectly regulated by the rules of grammar — the rules for manipulating symbols.

In the sense in which Lavoisier says that "the art of reasoning is nothing more than a language well arranged," the rules of thought might be reduced to the rules of syntax if there were a perfect language. If the symbols of mathematics lack the universality to express every sort of concept, then it may be necessary, as Leibnitz proposes, to construct a "universal characteristic" which would make possible a symbolic calculus for the performance of all the operations of thought. This conception seems to contain the principle and the motivation for the various logistical schemes which accompany the modern development of symbolic or mathematical logic, from Boole and Venn to Peano, Couturat, Russell, and Whitehead. The hopes to be realized by an algebra of logic find expression in Jevons' plan for a logical abacus which, like an adding machine or comptometer, would be a thinking machine able to solve all problems that can be put in suitable terms.

IS THE IDEAL of a perfect and universal language a genuine hope or a utopian dream? Not all modern scientists seem to agree with Lavoisier's point that the improvement of a science and the improvement of its language are inseparable. Faraday, for example, apologizing for the invention of new words to name electrical phenomena, says that he is "fully aware that names are one thing and science another." The utopian character of the ideal seems to be implied in Swift's satirization of a universal language. On his voyage to the cloud-land of the scientists in Laputa, Gulliver learns of a project which is being considered by the professors of language. "Since words are only names for things, it would be more convenient for all men to carry about them such things as were necessary to express the particular business they are to discourse on." The substitution of things for words would thus provide a "universal language to be understood in all civilized nations."

In the ancient world the imperfection of ordinary speech gives rise, not to the conception of a perfect language which man should try to construct, but to the consideration of the distinction between a hypothetical natural language and the existing conventional languages actually in use. If there were a natural language, it would not only be the same for all men everywhere, but its words would also be perfect images or imitations of things. That human language is conventional rather than natural may be seen not only in the plurality of tongues, but also in the fact that existing languages embody contradictory principles of symbolization.

This fact, Plato suggests in the *Cratylus*, indicates that human language does not originate as a gift from the gods, for if the gods had given men the names they use, signs would be perfectly and consistently adapted to things signified. The hypothesis of a natural or god-given language is not proposed as an ideal to inspire

men to try to invent a perfect language for themselves. It functions rather as a norm for the criticism of man-made language and for discovering the natural elements common to all conventional languages.

Like human society, human language seems to be partly natural, partly conventional. As there are certain political principles, such as that of natural justice, common to all societies despite the diversity of their customs and institutions, so all conventional languages have certain common characteristics of structure which indicate their natural basis in the physical and mental constitution of man. In the tradition of the liberal arts, the search for a universal grammar, applicable to all conventional languages, represents not the hope to create a universal or perfect language, but the conviction that all languages have a common, natural basis.

THE HYPOTHESIS of a natural language takes another form and has another implication in the Judaeo-Christian tradition, where it is discussed in the light of certain portions of revelation. Yet it retains the same fundamental relevance to the problem of the origin and characteristics of the many conventional languages which now exist.

Genesis relates how, after God formed every beast of the field and every fowl of the air, He "brought them to Adam to see what he would call them; and whatsoever Adam called every living creature, that was the name thereof." The names which Adam devised constituted a natural language, at least insofar as, according to Augustine's interpretation, it is the one "common language of the race" both before the flood and for some time after. But there is the further question whether the names which Adam gave to things were their rightful or proper names—whether they were natural signs in the sense of true representations of the natures of the things signified.

Hobbes suggests one answer when he says that "the first author of speech was God himself, who instructed Adam how to name such creatures as he presented to his sight"; Augustine suggests another answer by identifying the original language of man with Hebrew, and by affirming the continuity of the Hebrew spoken after Babel with the language all men spoke before the confusion of tongues.

At the time when men began to build "a tower whose top may reach unto heaven," Genesis tells us that "the whole earth was of one language and one speech. . . . And the Lord said, Behold, the people is one, and they have all one language; and this they begin to do; and now nothing will be restrained from them, which they have imagined to do. Go to, let us go down, and there confound their language, that they may not understand one another's speech."

This, according to Hobbes, means that the language "gotten and augmented by Adam and his posterity, was again lost at the tower of Babel, when by the hand of God every man was stricken for his rebellion, with an oblivion of his former language." If the further implication is that the lost language was unlike any of the conventional languages in the historical record, then it may be supposed to have been that natural form of speech in which each thing is named according to its nature. The modern ideal of a perfect and universal language may even be looked upon as an impious wish to achieve what God took away from men at Babel.

THE PROBLEM of the origin of human language is not an easy one for the theologian. It is more difficult still for those who speculate about it in purely naturalistic terms. Rousseau tries to expose some of the perplexities in such speculations.

If speech did not become a social necessity until men passed from isolation in a state of nature to living together in society, how, he asks, could societies have been formed before languages had been invented? "If men need speech to learn to think," he remarks, "they must have stood in much greater need of the art of thinking, to be able to invent that of speaking." The development of languages already in existence, or the way in which the child learns to speak through living in an environment where speech exists, "by no means explains how languages were originally formed."

Rousseau imagines a primitive condition in which men uttered instinctive cries "to implore assistance in case of danger, or relief in case of suffering"; he supposes that to such cries, men may have added gestures to signify visible and movable objects, and imitative sounds to signify audible ones. Such methods of expression being insufficient to convey ideas about absent or future things, men had at last to invent "the articulate sounds of the voice" and to institute these as conventional signs. But, as he observes, "such an institution could only be made by common consent . . . itself still more difficult to conceive, since such a common agreement must have had motives, and speech, therefore, seems to have been highly necessary in order to establish the use of it."

The problem of the origin of human language is not only connected with the problem of the origin of human society, but also with the problem of the origin of man himself. The faculty of articulate speech does not, according to Darwin, "offer any insuperable objection to the belief that man has been developed from some lower form." Though the habitual use of articulate language is peculiar to man, "he uses, in common with the lower animals, inarticulate cries to express his meaning, aided by gestures and the movements of the muscles of the face." The songs of birds and the speech of parrots show that animals can learn to make and repeat certain definite sounds, and even to connect words with things. It seems to Darwin quite credible that man's articulate language "owes its origin to the imitation and modification of various natural sounds, the voices of other animals, and man's own instinctive cries, aided by signs and gestures."

SUCH AN ACCOUNT of the origin of human speech is not credible, however, to those who disagree with Darwin's statement that "the lower animals differ from man solely in his almost infinitely larger power of associating together the most diversified sounds and ideas." Those who hold that human rationality differs in kind, rather than degree, from animal intelligence tend to find a corresponding difference in kind between human language and the sounds of brutes. Aristotle, for example, says that man is the only animal whom nature "has endowed with the gift of speech. Mere vocalization is only an indication of pleasure and pain and is therefore found in other animals," but men alone have the power to discuss the expedient and the just, and this fact distinguishes human association from the companionship of gregarious animals.

Human speech is, for Descartes, one of the two criteria by which we can "recognize the difference that exists between men and brutes. For it is a very remarkable fact that there are none so depraved and stupid, without even excepting idiots, that they cannot arrange different words together, forming of them a statement by which they can make known their thoughts; while, on the other hand, there is no other animal . . . which can do the same. It is not the want of organs that brings this to pass, for it is evident that magpies and parrots can utter words just like ourselves, and yet they cannot speak as we do, that is, so as to give evidence that they think of what they say. . . . This does not merely show that the brutes have less reason than men, but that they have none at all."

The difference between men and other animals is more fully discussed in the chapter on MAN. Here we are concerned with opposite opinions on that subject only in relation to opposite views of human language and its origin. When, as in Descartes' view, human language is distinguished by syntax and grammar or, as in Locke's, by man's special power to use sounds "as signs of internal conceptions, and to make them stand as marks for ideas within his own mind," the origin of human speech does not seem explicable in evolutionary terms.

THE RELATION OF grammar to the other liberal arts and to the various uses of language is considered in the chapters on LOGIC, POETRY, and RHETORIC. Isolated from these others, grammar is primarily concerned with the distinction of the parts of speech, such as noun and verb, or particle and adjective.

"By a noun," says Aristotle, "we mean a sound significant by convention, which has no reference to time, and of which no part is significant apart from the rest." In contrast to the noun, the verb is defined by Aristotle as the sort of word which, "in addition to its proper meaning, carries with it the notion of time. . . . Moreover," he continues, "a verb is always a sign of something said of something else." The grammatical function of nouns and verbs is, in Locke's opinion, more generally

recognized and better defined than that of particles, prepositions, and conjunctions. Such words, Locke writes, "show what connexion, restriction, distinction, opposition, emphasis, etc. [a man] gives to each respective *part* of his discourse. . . . He who would show the right use of particles, and what significancy and force they have, must take a little more pains, enter into his own thoughts, and observe nicely the several postures of his mind in discoursing."

Grammar is also concerned with the difference between words (or phrases) and sentences, or, in Aristotle's terms, between simple and composite expressions; and with the rules of syntax which govern the order and agreement of words according to their function as parts of speech. By reference to these rules the grammarian critizes the misuse of language and classifies a great variety of common errors.

One test of whether grammar is a universal art applicable to all languages—not just a set of rules for using a particular conventional language correctly—is the naturalness of its theoretical distinctions. Does Aristotle's distinction between noun and verb, for example, respond to something natural in all discourse, or is it peculiar to the Greek or to the Indo-European languages?

THERE IS A MEANING of language which includes more than the speech of men and brutes. From Hippocrates on, the physician regards the symptoms of disease as if they were a connected system of signs, a language for which his diagnostic art provides a grammar of interpretation. This is particularly true in the psychological realm where, in the psychoanalysis of the neuroses and especially in Freud's interpretation of dreams, both symptom and dream-symbol are treated as an elaborate language. That language serves to express the unconscious thoughts and desires which cannot be expressed in the ordinary language of social intercourse over which consciousness exercises some control.

These medical examples represent a conception of language according to which the whole of nature is a book to be read by the scientist. He penetrates the mysteries of nature by learning the grammar of natural signs. To know the relation of natural things as cause and effect or whole and part is to discover nature's syntax. According to another conception, expressed by Galileo, the book of nature "is written in mathematical language, its symbols being triangles, circles, and other geometrical figures, without whose help it is impossible to comprehend a single word of it."

The book of nature may also be read as the language of God. Prophecy or divination is such a reading of dreams or of other events as omens and portents which bespeak the divine purpose. When he reaches the highest heaven Dante finds in the vision of the Trinity, "bound up with love in one volume, that which is dispersed in leaves through the universe." Berkeley goes further than this. All of the ideas which man gets by sense-perception are words in a divine vocabulary. The uniform appearances of nature "may not unfitly be styled the Language of its Author, whereby He discovers His attributes to our view and directs us how to act for the convenience and felicity of life."

God speaks to man in still another way. Within the Judaeo-Christian tradition at least, God is believed to have revealed himself to man through the vehicle of human language. Written by men under divine inspiration, Sacred Scripture is the word of God. Because it is at once human and divine, this language is the most difficult for man to interpret.

The art of interpreting the Bible involves the most elaborate theory of signs, and of the types and levels of meaning. It involves special rules of reading. The development of this theory and these rules by Augustine and Aquinas, Maimonides and Spinoza, Hobbes and Pascal, has deepened the liberal arts and enlarged the scope of man's understanding of other languages—his own or nature's. Since the heart of this larger consideration of language lies in the analysis of meaning and the modes of signification, the discussion of the symbolism of nature and the word of God belongs to the chapter on SIGN AND SYMBOL; and, in its theological aspects, to the chapters on PROPHECY and RELIGION.

THE DISCUSSION of language, as we have seen, cannot be separated from the consideration of human nature and human society. Because He "designed man for a sociable creature," God, according to Locke, "made him not only with an inclination, and under a necessity to have fellowship with those of his own kind, but furnished him also with language, which was to be the great instrument and common tie of society."

It is not merely that the fellowship of men depends upon speech. According to Locke, men cannot enjoy "the comfort and advantage of society . . . without the communication of thoughts." The fact that "man had by nature his organs so fashioned as to be fit to frame articulate sounds . . . was not enough to produce language"—at least not human language, "for parrots, and several other birds, can be taught to make articulate sounds distinct enough," and yet, Locke writes, they are "by no means capable of language. Besides articulate sounds, therefore, it was further necessary," he insists, that the sounds men formed should be the instrument whereby "the thoughts of men's minds [are] conveyed from one to another."

Rousseau, on the other hand, seems to think that under the primitive circumstances surrounding the origin of both society and language, the association of men "would not require a language much more refined than that of rooks or monkeys, who associate together for much the same purpose. Inarticulate cries, plenty of gestures and some imitative sounds, must have been for a long time the universal language," he writes; "and by the addition, in every country, of some conventional articulate sounds . . . particular languages were produced; but these were rude and imperfect, and nearly such as are now to be found among some savage nations."

The plurality of conventional, historic languages seems to parallel the plurality of the nations or societies into which mankind is divided. But underlying the diversity of tongues there is also a unity which implies the possibility of mankind's unification. To the extent that language expresses thought, diverse languages are but different mediums for the same thing. "All men [may] not have the same speech sounds," Aristotle declares, "but the mental experiences, which these directly symbolize, are the same for all."

The human community conceived in terms of the communication of thought extends as far as the bounds of such communication among men. It is not limited by political boundaries. It overcomes by translation the barriers set up by a diversity of tongues. It includes the living and the dead and extends to those as yet unborn. In this sense, human civilization can be described as the civilization of the dialogue, and the tradition of the great books can be conceived as the great conversation in which all men can participate. The extent of this conversation measures the range of western thought. The vocabulary of its language is the stock of ideas with which each individual can begin to think for himself when he turns from dialogue to soliloquy; for, as Plato observes, "thought and speech are the same, with this exception, that what is called thought is the unuttered conversation of the soul with itself."

OUTLINE OF TOPICS

REFERENCES

To find the passages cited, use the numbers in heavy type, which are the volume and page numbers of the passages referred to. For example, in 4 HOMER: *Iliad*, BK II [265–283] 12d, the number 4 is the number of the volume in the set; the number 12d indicates that the passage is in section d of page 12.

PAGE SECTIONS: When the text is printed in one column, the letters a and b refer to the upper and lower halves of the page. For example, in 53 JAMES: *Psychology*, 116a–119b, the passage begins in the upper half of page 116 and ends in the lower half of page 119. When the text is printed in two columns, the letters a and b refer to the upper and lower halves of the left-hand side of the page, the letters c and d to the upper and lower halves of the right-hand side of the page. For example, in 7 PLATO: *Symposium*, 163b–164c, the passage begins in the lower half of the left-hand side of page 163 and ends in the upper half of the right-hand side of page 164.

AUTHOR'S DIVISIONS: One or more of the main divisions of a work (such as PART, BK, CH, SECT) are sometimes included in the reference; line numbers, in brackets, are given in certain cases; *e.g.*, *Iliad*, BK II [265–283] 12d.

BIBLE REFERENCES: The references are to book, chapter, and verse. When the King James and Douay versions differ in title of books or in the numbering of chapters or verses, the King James version is cited first and the Douay, indicated by a (*D*), follows; *e.g.*, OLD TESTAMENT: *Nehemiah*, 7:45—(*D*) *II Esdras*, 7:46.

SYMBOLS: The abbreviation "esp" calls the reader's attention to one or more especially relevant parts of a whole reference; "passim" signifies that the topic is discussed intermittently rather than continuously in the work or passage cited.

For additional information concerning the style of the references, see the Explanation of Reference Style; for general guidance in the use of *The Great Ideas*, consult the Preface.

1. The nature and functions of language: the speech of men and brutes

OLD TESTAMENT: *Genesis*, 11:1–9
APOCRYPHA: *Ecclesiasticus*, 4:24—(*D*) OT, *Ecclesiasticus*, 4:29
NEW TESTAMENT: *I Corinthians*, 14 / *Ephesians*, 4:29
6 HERODOTUS: *History*, BK II, 61a-b
7 PLATO: *Cratylus* 85a–114a,c / *Theaetetus*, 547c-d / *Sophist*, 575d–577b / *Seventh Letter*, 809c-810d
8 ARISTOTLE: *Categories*, CH 6 [4^{b}32–36] 9b / *Interpretation*, CH 1 [16^{a}4–8] 25a / *Soul*, BK II, CH 8 [420^{b}5–421^{a}6] 651d-652c
9 ARISTOTLE: *History of Animals*, BK I, CH I [488^{a}33–^{b}3] 9b-c; BK IV, CH 9 62a-63c / *Parts of Animals*, BK II, CH 16 [659^{b}28]–CH 17 [660^{b}3] 186d-187c / *Politics*, BK I, CH 2 [1253^{a}7–18] 446b-c / *Rhetoric*, BK III, CH 2 [1404^{b}1–3] 654c; CH 10 [1410^{b}9–28] 662c-d / *Poetics*, CH 6 [1450^{b}10–15] 685a; CH 19 [1456^{a}33–^{b}8] 691d-692a
12 LUCRETIUS: *Nature of Things*, BK V [1028–1090] 74c-75b
14 PLUTARCH: *Demosthenes*, 692a
17 PLOTINUS: *First Ennead*, TR II, CH 3, 8a / *Fourth Ennead*, TR III, CH 18 151b-c

18 AUGUSTINE: *Confessions*, BK X, par 19 76a-b / *Christian Doctrine*, BK I, CH 13 627d; BK II, CH 3 637c-d
19 AQUINAS: *Summa Theologica*, PART I, Q 13, A I, ANS 62c-63c; Q 34, A I, ANS 185b-187b; Q 107, A I, REP 1–3 549b-550b
20 AQUINAS: *Summa Theologica*, PART III, Q 60, A 6, ANS 851b-852b
21 DANTE: *Divine Comedy*, PARADISE, XXVI [124–138] 147a-b
23 HOBBES: *Leviathan*, PART I, 54c-55b; PART II, 100b; PART IV, 270a
25 MONTAIGNE: *Essays*, 215b-216b; 218a-c; 300c; 323c-324b
26 SHAKESPEARE: *Richard II*, ACT I, SC III [154–173] 325b
30 BACON: *Advancement of Learning*, 62c-63a / *Novum Organum*, BK I, APH 14 107d-108a
31 DESCARTES: *Discourse*, PART V, 59c-60b
32 MILTON: *Paradise Lost*, BK VIII [369–451] 240a-242a; BK IX [549–612] 259b-260b
33 PASCAL: *Pensées*, 45 178b; 912 349b
35 LOCKE: *Human Understanding*, BK II, CH XI, SECT 8–11 145b-146a; CH XVIII, SECT 7 174d-175a; CH XXII, SECT 5 201d; CH XXVII, SECT 8 221a-222a; CH XXVIII, SECT 2 228c-229a; CH XXXII, SECT 7–8 244c-d; BK III, CH I 251b,d-252d; CH II 252d-254c passim; CH III,

5b. Insignificant speech: meaninglessness, absurdity

6. The improvement of speech: the ideal of a perfect language

7. Grammar and logic: the formulation and statement of knowledge

8. Grammar and rhetoric: the effective use of language in teaching and persuasion

9. The language of poetry

10. **The language of things and events: the book of nature; the symbolism of dreams; prophetic signs**

(10. *The language of things and events: the book of nature; the symbolism of dreams; prophetic signs.*)

14 PLUTARCH: *Theseus*, 8d-9a; 14d-15a,c / *Numa Pompilius*, 52b-c; 56d-57b / *Pericles*, 123c-124a / *Alcibiades*, 174a-d / *Timoleon*, 198c-d / *Pelopidas*, 239d-240c / *Marcellus*, 259c-260c / *Pyrrhus*, 329c-d / *Sulla*, 371d-372c / *Cimon*, 398d-399b / *Lucullus*, 411a-b / *Nicias*, 429d-430b / *Eumenes*, 473a-b / *Alexander*, 548d-549a / *Dion*, 789b-790a

15 TACITUS: *Annals*, BK I, 9a-b; BK II, 26c-27a; 27b; BK IV, 79b; BK VI, 95d-96a; BK XI, 101b; 103a-b; BK XII, 112d-113a; 119b; 124b; BK XIII, 141a-b; BK XIV, 147a-b; 149b-c; BK XV, 159b-c; 168d-169a / *Histories*, BK I, 189d-190a; 195b-c; 206a; BK II, 228a-b; 235a-c; BK III, 256d-257a; BK IV, 293a-294a

16 KEPLER: *Epitome*, BK IV, 853b-854a / *Harmonies of the World*, 1080b-1085b passim

18 AUGUSTINE: *Confessions*, BK I, par 13 4b-c; BK III, par 19–20 18b-19a; BK XIII, par 6–48 112a-124a passim / *City of God*, BK I, PREF 129a-d; CH 36 149c-d; BK II, CH 2–3 150c-151c; BK IV, CH 33–34 206c-207a,c; BK V, CH I 207d-208c; CH 11–26 216c-230a,c; BK X, CH 5 301b-302a; CH 8 303a-d; CH 12–20 306d-311c; BK XI, CH 18 331d-332a; CH 24–28 335c-338d; BK XV, CH I 397b,d-398c; CH 21–22 415b-416c; BK XVI, CH 25 438a-b; BK XVII, CH 1–3 449a-451c; BK XVIII, CH 1–2 472b,d-473d; BK XXII, CH 30, 618c-d / *Christian Doctrine*, BK I, CH 2 624d-625a; BK II, CH 1–3 636b,d-637d esp CH I, 637a; BK IV, CH 21, 690d-691b

19 AQUINAS: *Summa Theologica*, PART I, Q 57, A 4, ANS 298a-299a; Q 104, A 4, ANS and REP I 538a-c

20 AQUINAS: *Summa Theologica*, PART III, Q 12, A 3, REP 2 778b-779a; QQ 60–65 847a-884a,c esp Q 60, A 2, ANS and REP I 848a-d, A 4, REP I 849c-850b

21 DANTE: *Divine Comedy*, HELL, XXIV [1–21] 34d; XXXIII [1–90] 49c-50c; PURGATORY, IX [13–69] 66a-c; XIX [1–69] 81c-82a

22 CHAUCER: *Troilus and Cressida*, BK V, STANZA 52–55 127a-b; STANZA 177–185 143b-144b; STANZA 207–217 147a-148b; STANZA 245 152a / *Nun's Priest's Tale* [14,898–15,162] 451a-455b

23 HOBBES: *Leviathan*, PART I, 53c-d; 80b-c; 81d-82b

24 RABELAIS: *Gargantua and Pantagruel*, BK III, 146a-147d; 148d-150d; 154a-156c; 159d-163c; 166a-169d; 175c-178a; 215c-218a

25 MONTAIGNE: *Essays*, 69b-d; 212a-c; 215a-216b; 218a-c

26 SHAKESPEARE: *2nd Henry VI*, ACT I, SC II [17–40] 36c-d / *3rd Henry VI*, ACT V, SC VI [44–79] 103c-104a / *Richard III*, ACT I, SC IV [1–83] 114d-115c / *Romeo and Juliet*, ACT I, SC IV [49–103] 291a-c / *Richard II*, ACT II, SC IV

[7–24] 334c-d / *Midsummer-Night's Dream*, ACT II, SC II [145–156] 360b-c / *1st Henry IV*, ACT III, SC I [1–63] 450a-d / *2nd Henry IV*, ACT I, SC I [60–103] 468d-469b / *Julius Caesar*, ACT I, SC III [1–78] 572c-573b; ACT II, SC II [71–90] 578d-579a; ACT V, SC I [71–92] 592d-593a / *As You Like It*, ACT II, SC I [3–20] 603c-d

27 SHAKESPEARE: *Hamlet*, ACT I, SC I [64–125] 30b-31a / *King Lear*, ACT I, SC II [112–164] 249a-b / *Macbeth*, ACT V, SC I 306b-307a / *Cymbeline*, ACT V, SC IV [30–151] 481c-482c; SC V [426–465] 488b-d

28 GALILEO: *Two New Sciences*, THIRD DAY, 200a-b

28 HARVEY: *On Animal Generation*, 331b-332a

29 CERVANTES: *Don Quixote*, PART II, 381a-b

30 BACON: *Advancement of Learning*, 54c-55a

31 DESCARTES: *Discourse*, PART I, 44a-c

31 SPINOZA: *Ethics*, PART I, PROP 25, COROL 365b; PART II, DEF I 373a

32 MILTON: *Paradise Lost*, BK V [28–128] 176a-178a; BK V [308]–BK VIII [653] 182a-246b esp BK VIII [283–499] 238b-243a; BK XI [193]–BK XII [649] 303b-333a / *Areopagitica*, 389a-b

33 PASCAL: *Pensées*, 173 203b-204a; 643–646 290b-291b esp 643 290b-291a; 652–657 292a-293a; 670 295a-b; 675 296b-297a; 693–736 301b-317b; 803–856 328b-341b

34 NEWTON: *Principles*, BK III, GENERAL SCHOL, 369a-371a / *Optics*, BK III, 528b-529a

35 BERKELEY: *Human Knowledge*, SECT 44 420d-421a; SECT 65–66 425d-426a; SECT 108–109 434a-b; SECT 146–154 442a-444b passim, esp SECT 148 442b-d

37 FIELDING: *Tom Jones*, 162b-163a

40 GIBBON: *Decline and Fall*, 294a-296b; 547a-b; 571a

41 GIBBON: *Decline and Fall*, 398b-399b

46 HEGEL: *Philosophy of History*, PART II, 263d-265c

47 GOETHE: *Faust*, PART I [430–481] 12b-14a

48 MELVILLE: *Moby Dick*, 1a-3a; 115b-117a; 120a-b; 135a-136a; 138b-145a; 204a-205a; 231a; 331a-332a

51 TOLSTOY: *War and Peace*, BK V, 198b-203a; BK VI, 248d-250a; 259c-d; BK VII, 298d-299b; 300c-301b; 302c-d; BK VIII, 340d-341a,c; BK IX, 377d-379a; BK X, 428a-429a; BK XI, 481b-482a; BK XII, 546a-d; 561b-562a; BK XIV, 608a-b; EPILOGUE I, 673d-674a,c

52 DOSTOEVSKY: *Brothers Karamazov*, BK II, 36b-c; BK VI, 147c-148a; BK VII, 189a-191a,c

54 FREUD: *Origin and Development of Psycho-Analysis*, 11b-12d passim / *Hysteria*, 57a-59d / *Interpretation of Dreams*, 137d-138d; 173a-174d; 178a-205c esp 178b-179c, 194b-d, 197b-198d; 230b-231c; 252c-340a esp 252c-253a, 264c-272c, 282a-285b, 332a-333b / *Unconscious*, 440c-442b / *General Introduction*, 467a-b; 489c-494d esp 492d-493c; 504d-

519d esp 505b-506c, 513d-518d / *New Introductory Lectures*, 808d-810d; 812d-817a esp
813c-814a, 814d-816b

11. Immediate communication: the speech of angels and the gift of tongues

OLD TESTAMENT: *Numbers*, 11:16-17,24-30
NEW TESTAMENT: *Mark*, 16:17 / *Acts*, 2:1-21;
10:44-47; 19:5-6 / *I Corinthians*, 12-14 esp 14
17 PLOTINUS: *Fourth Ennead*, TR III, CH 18 151b-c
18 AUGUSTINE: *City of God*, BK XVI, CH 6 426c-
427a
19 AQUINAS: *Summa Theologica*, PART I, QQ
106-107 545c-552b
20 AQUINAS: *Summa Theologica*, PART I-II, Q 51,
A 4, ANS 15a-d
21 DANTE: *Divine Comedy*, PARADISE, IV [1-21]
110d; VII [1-24] 115a-c; XI [13-27] 122a-b;
XV [1-90] 128b-129b; XXIII [70-139] 142a-c;
XXVI [82-108] 146c-147a; XXIX [1-12] 150b
30 BACON: *Advancement of Learning*, 55a-b /
New Atlantis, 203c
35 LOCKE: *Human Understanding*, BK II, CH
XXIII, SECT 36 213c-d
40 GIBBON: *Decline and Fall*, 189b
53 JAMES: *Psychology*, 846a-847b esp 846b-847b
[fn 3]
54 FREUD: *New Introductory Lectures*, 820c-829d
esp 820d-821a, 822b-823d, 829a-c

12. The language of God or the gods: the deliverances of the oracles; the inspiration, revelation, and interpretation of Sacred Scripture

OLD TESTAMENT: *Genesis*, 1 / *Exodus*, 4:11-12;
24:12; 31:18; 32:15-16; 34:1 / *Numbers*, 12:6-
8; 22:20-38 / *Deuteronomy*, 4:2; 8:3; 9:10;
18:18-22; 29:29; 30:11-14 / *Job*, 38-42 /
Psalms, 12:6; 33:6,9; 119:105,130—(D) *Psalms*,
11:7; 32:6,9; 118:105,130 / *Proverbs*, 30:5-6 /
Isaiah, 28:9-13; 34:16; 40:8; 51:15-16; 55:8-
11; 59:21—(D) *Isaias*, 28:9-13; 34:16; 40:8;
51:15-16; 55:8-11; 59:21 / *Jeremiah*, 1:7-9;
5:14; 13:1-11; 15:16; 18:1-6; 23:28-32; 24;
36:1-4—(D) *Jeremias*, 1:7-9; 5:14; 13:1-11;
15:16; 18:1-6; 23:28-32; 24; 36:1-4 / *Ezekiel*,
2:7-3:11—(D) *Ezechiel*, 2:7-3:11 / *Daniel*,
2:20-22,28-29,47; 5:5-28 / *Joel*, 2:28-29
APOCRYPHA: *Wisdom of Solomon*, 16:26—(D)
OT, *Book of Wisdom*, 16:26 / *Ecclesiasticus*,
1:5; 39:16-17; 42:15,19; 43:26—(D) OT, *Ecclesiasticus*, 1:5; 39:16-17; 42:15,19; 43:28 /
I Maccabees, 12:9—(D) OT, *I Machabees*, 12:9
NEW TESTAMENT: *Matthew*, 4:4; 10:19-20; 11:25;
13:1-53; 15:10-20; 16:16-17; 19:3-9; 21:33-
45; 22:29 / *Mark*, 2:23-28; 4:3-34; 10:2-9;
12:24; 14:49 / *Luke*, 1:70; 2:25-26; 8:4-15;
10:21; 11:28; 20:37-38; 21:33; 24:27,32,44-
45 / *John*, 5:38-39,46-47; 10:1-14,35; 12:47-
50; 14:24; 16:25-29 / *Acts*, 2:17-18; 17:11 /
Romans, 1:20; 10:8; 15:4; 16:25-27 / *I Corinthians*, 2:7-16; 14:26-39 / *II Corinthians*,

3:2-7; 12:1-7 / *Galatians*, 1:11-12 / *Ephesians*,
3:2-5 / *II Timothy*, 3:14-17 / *Hebrews*, 1:1-3;
4:12 / *I Peter*, 1:10-13,23-25; 2:5-8 / *II Peter*,
1:19-21; 3:5,15-16 / *I John*, 2:20,27
4 HOMER: *Iliad*, BK I [59-67] 3d; BK II [1-34]
10a-b / *Odyssey*, BK XIV [321-336] 263b-c;
BK XIX [291-307] 292b
5 AESCHYLUS: *Seven Against Thebes* [742-777]
35b-c / *Prometheus Bound* [640-682] 46d-
47b / *Choephoroe* [269-305] 72d-73a; [1021-
1076] 80a-d / *Eumenides* [1-33] 81a-b
5 SOPHOCLES: *Oedipus the King* 99a-113a,c /
Oedipus at Colonus [386-419] 117d-118a /
Trachiniae [155-177] 171c; [821-830] 177b
5 EURIPIDES: *Iphigenia Among the Tauri* [1234-
1283] 422b-c / *Iphigenia at Aulis* [872-883]
433a
5 ARISTOPHANES: *Knights* [108-233] 471b-472d;
[941-1099] 481d-483d / *Peace* [1017-1126]
537c-539a / *Birds* [959-991] 554c-555a /
Lysistrata [762-780] 593a-b / *Plutus* [1-78]
629a-630a
6 HERODOTUS: *History*, BK I, 4d; 10a-c; 11b-d;
14a-15c; 20a-b; 21b-22a; 38a-b; 39c-d; BK
II, 60d-61b; 70d-71a; 77a-b; 80c; 81d-82b;
83b-c; BK III, 101d-102b; 103b-d; BK IV,
126d-127a; 153b-d; BK V, 160a-b; 175b-c;
178a-180a; 183d-184a; BK VI, 189a-b; 191d-
192b; 194d-195b; 197d-198a; 199d-201a; 201d-
202c; 211b-d; 212d-213a,c; BK VII, 234d;
239c-240d; 241c-242a; 246b-c; 248b-c; 250b;
255c-d; BK VIII, 263b-c; 268b-d; 269c-270a;
273b-c; 276d-277a; 281a; 284d-285b; BK IX,
295d-296c; 302b-c; 308a-c
6 THUCYDIDES: *Peloponnesian War*, BK I, 355b-
c; 378a-b; 380a-d; BK II, 392a-b; 401a-b;
415d-416c; BK III, 442c-443a; BK V, 489a-b
7 PLATO: *Ion* 142a-148a,c esp 142d-145c /
Apology, 201d-203a / *Timaeus*, 467b-c
13 VIRGIL: *Aeneid*, BK II [108-136] 127a-b; BK
III [84-191] 149b-152a; BK VI [42-101] 212a-
213b; BK VII [81-106] 238a-239a
14 PLUTARCH: *Aristides*, 268a-d / *Cimon*, 392b-c
15 TACITUS: *Annals*, BK II, 37a-b / *Histories*, BK
II, 235a-c
18 AUGUSTINE: *Confessions*, BK III, par 9 15a-b;
BK VI, par 6-8 36c-37c; BK XI-XIII 89b-125a,c
/ *City of God*, BK XI, CH 3 323d; BK XV, CH
26-27, 419d-421d; BK XVI, CH 2, 423c-d; CH 6
426c-427a; BK XVII, CH 3 450c-451c; BK XVIII,
CH 23 483d-485a; CH 42-44 496d-498c; CH
46-47 500a-501b; BK XX 530a-560a,c esp CH
21, 549d, CH 28-29 556c-557c / *Christian
Doctrine* 621a-698a,c
19 AQUINAS: *Summa Theologica*, PART I, Q 1,
AA 9-10 8d-10c; Q 3, A 1, REP 1-5 14b-15b;
Q 34 185a-189a
20 AQUINAS: *Summa Theologica*, PART I-II, QQ
101-103 265d-304a; PART II-II, Q 1 380a-
390d; PART III, QQ 60-65 847a-884a,c
21 DANTE: *Divine Comedy*, PARADISE, IV [22-48]
110d-111a; XIX [40-66] 135c-d; XXIV [52-114]

(12. *The language of God or the gods: the deliverances of the oracles; the inspiration, revelation, and interpretation of Sacred Scripture.*)

143b-d; xxv [67–102] 145a-b; xxvi [1–69] 145d-146c

23 HOBBES: *Leviathan*, PART I, 70c-71a; 81d-82a; PART II, 160b-c; PART III, 165a-167b; 171a-172a; 176d-177b; 181a-186c; 215b-216b; 241a-242a; 246c; PART IV, 247a-258b

25 MONTAIGNE: *Essays*, 284d

27 SHAKESPEARE: *Cymbeline*, ACT V, SC IV [91–122] 482a-b; SC V [426–485] 488b-d

30 BACON: *Advancement of Learning*, 2c-4c; 97c-100b / *New Atlantis*, 202d-203c

31 DESCARTES: *Objections and Replies*, 123d-124a; 227a-228a

32 MILTON: *Paradise Lost*, BK V [544–576] 187a-b

33 PASCAL: *Provincial Letters*, 78b-80b; 163a-

164b / *Pensées*, 570–588 273b-277b passim; 642–736 290b-317b; 775 323b-324a; 803–856 328b-341b

35 LOCKE: *Toleration*, 5a-b; 21c-22d / *Human Understanding*, BK III, CH IX, SECT 9 286d-287b; SECT 23 291b-c; CH X, SECT 12 294b-c

35 BERKELEY: *Human Knowledge*, SECT 44 420d-421a; SECT 65–66 425d-426a

38 ROUSSEAU: *Social Contract*, 401c-402a

40 GIBBON: *Decline and Fall*, 186d-188a passim

41 GIBBON: *Decline and Fall*, 230c-232c

43 FEDERALIST: NUMBER 37, 120a-b

43 MILL: *Liberty*, 290a-291d passim / *Utilitarianism*, 455b

46 HEGEL: *Philosophy of History*, PART III, 308c-309d

47 GOETHE: *Faust*, PART I [1220–1237] 30a-b

48 MELVILLE: *Moby Dick*, 30a-36b

52 DOSTOEVSKY: *Brothers Karamazov*, BK V, 127b-137c

CROSS-REFERENCES

For: The other major discussion of language in terms of the variety of signs and the modes of signification, *see* SIGN AND SYMBOL.

Other considerations of language as an instrument of thought, *see* IDEA 4a; JUDGMENT 5a; LOGIC 3a; MATHEMATICS 3d; RHETORIC 1b, 2c-2d; SIGN AND SYMBOL 1d, 4b, 4e.

The distinction of the natural and the conventional as applied to language, *see* CUSTOM AND CONVENTION 1; SIGN AND SYMBOL 1b, 1d, 1f.

The general discussion of the liberal arts of grammar, rhetoric, and logic, *see* ART 6b; and for the relation of grammar to these other arts, *see* LOGIC 3a; RHETORIC 1b, 3c.

Another analysis of the imperfections of language, and for the remedies proposed by semantics, *see* SIGN AND SYMBOL 3a, 4c.

The language of poetry, *see* POETRY 8b.

The language of symptoms in medicine, of dreams in psychoanalysis, and of omens and portents in prophecy and divination, *see* MEDICINE 3c; MEMORY AND IMAGINATION 8d–8e; PROPHECY 3b–3c; SIGN AND SYMBOL 4e, 5b, 6a–6c.

The language of God or the gods in Sacred Scripture or oracular utterances, and for the problem of interpreting the divine word, *see* GOD 6c(1); PROPHECY 3a–3d; RELIGION 1b(1); SIGN AND SYMBOL 5e; THEOLOGY 4b.

ADDITIONAL READINGS

Listed below are works not included in *Great Books of the Western World*, but relevant to the idea and topics with which this chapter deals. These works are divided into two groups:

I. Works by authors represented in this collection.
II. Works by authors not represented in this collection.

For the date, place, and other facts concerning the publication of the works cited, consult the Bibliography of Additional Readings which follows the last chapter of *The Great Ideas*.

I.

DANTE. *De Vulgari Eloquentia*
———. *Convivio (The Banquet)*, FIRST TREATISE, CH 5–7, 9–13

HOBBES. *The Elements of Law, Natural and Politic*, PART I, CH 13

MILTON. *Grammar*

SPINOZA. *Tractatus Theologico-Politicus (Theological-Political Treatise)*, CH 7–13

LOCKE. *Conduct of the Understanding*

ROUSSEAU. *Essai sur l'origine des langues*

A. SMITH. *A Dissertation on the Origin of Languages*

J. S. MILL. *A System of Logic*, BK I; BK IV, CH 3–6

II.

EPICURUS. *Letter to Herodotus*

QUINTILIAN. *Institutio Oratoria (Institutes of Oratory)*, BK I–III

JOHN OF SALISBURY. *Metalogicon*, BK I

MAIMONIDES. *The Guide for the Perplexed*, PART I; PART II, CH 30; PART III, CH 1–7

R. BACON. *Opus Majus*, PART III

SUÁREZ. *Disputationes Metaphysicae*, XXX (13), XLI (3)

JOHN OF SAINT THOMAS. *Cursus Philosophicus Thomisticus, Ars Logica*, PART I, QQ 1–3

ARNAULD and LANCELOT. *A General and Rational Grammar Containing the Principles of the Art of Speaking*

ARNAULD. *Logic or the Art of Thinking*, PART I, CH 15; PART II, CH 1–2

LEIBNITZ. *New Essays Concerning Human Understanding*, BK III

J. HARRIS. *Hermes, or A Philosophical Inquiry Concerning Universal Grammar*

BURKE. *A Philosophical Enquiry into the Origin of Our Ideas of the Sublime and Beautiful*, PART V

VOLTAIRE. "Languages," in *A Philosophical Dictionary*

CONDILLAC. *La langue des calculs*

——. *Logique*, PART II

BLAIR. *Lectures on Rhetoric and Belles Lettres*, XI–XIV

TOOKE. *The Diversions of Purley*

D. STEWART. *Elements of the Philosophy of the Human Mind*, PART II, CH I

A. JOHNSON. *A Treatise on Language*

J. MILL. *Analysis of the Phenomena of the Human Mind*, CH 4

EMERSON. *Nature*

GRIMM. *Über den Ursprung der Sprache*

TRENCH. *On the Study of Words*

COMTE. *System of Positive Polity*, VOL II, *Social Statics*, CH 4

BOOLE. *An Investigation of the Laws of Thought*

LOTZE. *Microcosmos*, BK V, CH 3

RENAN. *De l'origine du langage*

MULLER. *The Languages of the Seat of War in the East. With a Survey of the Three Families of Language, Semitic, Arian, and Turanian*

——. *Comparative Mythology*

——. *The Science of Language*

SCHLEICHER. *Darwinism Tested by the Science of Language*

FARRAR. *Chapters on Language*

WEDGWOOD. *On the Origin of Language*

E. HARTMANN. *The Philosophy of the Unconscious*, (B) VI

WHITNEY. *Oriental and Linguistic Studies*

JEVONS. *On the Mechanical Performance of Logical Inference*

——. *The Principles of Science*, CH 6 (17–18)

SAYCE. *Introduction to the Science of Language*

VENN. *Symbolic Logic*

——. *Principles of Empirical or Inductive Logic*, CH 6, 22

BRADLEY. *Appearance and Reality*, BK I, CH 2

BRÉAL. *Semantics*

A. SIDGWICK. *The Use of Words in Reasoning*

CROCE. *Aesthetic as Science of Expression*

COUTURAT and LEAU. *Histoire de la langue universelle*

DILTHEY. *Das Erlebnis und die Dichtung*

WHITEHEAD and RUSSELL. *Principia Mathematica*, INTRO

SHAW. *Pygmalion*

PARETO. *The Mind and Society*, VOL I, CH 1–2

SAPIR. *Language*

VENDRYÈS. *Language*

OGDEN and RICHARDS. *The Meaning of Meaning*, CH 1, 9–10

H. DELACROIX. *Le langage et la pensée*

JESPERSEN. *Language*

——. *The Philosophy of Grammar*

CASSIRER. *Philosophie der symbolischen Formen*, VOL I, *Die Sprache*

——. *Language and Myth*

DEWEY. *Experience and Nature*, CH 5

HEAD. *Aphasia and Kindred Disorders of Speech*

WHITEHEAD. *An Introduction to Mathematics*, CH 5

——. *Process and Reality*, PART I, CH 1 (5)

BÜHLER. *Sprachtheorie*

R. A. WILSON. *The Miraculous Birth of Language*

RICHARDS. *Interpretation in Teaching*

JOYCE. *Finnegans Wake*

URBAN. *Language and Reality*

AYER. *Thinking and Meaning*

CARNAP. *The Logical Syntax of Language*

——. *Introduction to Semantics*

——. *Meaning and Necessity*

B. RUSSELL. *An Inquiry into Meaning and Truth*, CH 1–6, 13–15, 25

——. *Human Knowledge, Its Scope and Limits*, PART II

Chapter 46: LAW

INTRODUCTION

THE notion of law is associated with a diversity of subject matters, and its meaning undergoes many variations as the discussion shifts from one context to another. The most radical difference separates the way in which natural scientists use the term *law* from the way in which it is used in the arts and in morals or politics.

We ordinarily think of law as a rule—a command or a prohibition—which should be obeyed and can be disobeyed. Both alternatives are usually present. Though the duty or obligation which a law creates is one of obedience, there would be no moral significance to discharging this duty if the law could not be violated. But the laws of nature which the scientist tries to discover do not have this characteristic. They are inviolable. The so-called law of gravitation, for example, or Newton's three laws of motion, cannot be disobeyed. Scientists may disagree about the truth of any formulation of a natural law, but if the formulation is valid, then the general rule of behavior is supposed to obtain without exception; and if exceptions are found, they are not interpreted as instances of disobedience, but rather as cases to which the law does not apply.

The rules of an art may be violated, either unwittingly or intentionally. For example, grammatical errors can be made by those ignorant of the rules or by those who wish to disregard them. The so-called "law of contradiction" in the art of logic seems to be like the rules of grammar or of any other art. Men certainly contradict themselves in spite of the rule which places the penalty of error on those who make contradictory statements.

But according to another conception of the law of contradiction, which belongs to the science of metaphysics rather than to the art of logic, nothing can both be and not be at the same time in the same respect. This law of being, like the laws of motion, is regarded as inviolable by those who think it true. In this it has the aspect of a scientific or natural law. The law of contradiction, conceived as a rule of logic, may also be natural in the sense of *not being man-made*. In the opinion of certain philosophers, man does not invent either the metaphysical rule which all existences *must* observe or the logical rule which the human mind *should* always obey. He discovers both.

There still remains that other class of rules to which the word "law" is most commonly applied. These are rules of moral action or social conduct which, like rules of art, are essentially violable. "Laws, in their most general signification," Montesquieu writes, "are the necessary relations arising from the nature of things. In this sense all beings have their laws." But he points out that law operates differently in the realm of physical nature and in the realm of intelligent beings like man. The latter, he says, "does not conform to [its laws] so exactly as the physical world. This is because, on the one hand, particular intelligent beings are of a finite nature, and consequently liable to error; and on the other, their nature requires them to be free agents." Hence, even the laws "of their own instituting, they frequently infringe."

The profound division between laws of nature and laws of human conduct thus seems to involve two points: (1) the former may apply to all things, the latter are addressed to man alone; (2) the former, being inviolable, state the necessities of behavior, the latter, precisely because they are violable, imply freedom in those to whom they are addressed.

These two kinds of law have this much in common. Both the laws of nature discovered by the scientist and the rules of conduct instituted by the legislator are general rather than particular. Their generality has been made, in the tradition of jurisprudence, the basis for differentiating rules of law from particular decisions or decrees. On theological grounds, however, the two kinds of law can be said to have a more significant characteristic in common.

Aquinas conceives the laws of nature which the scientist discovers as laws implanted in the very nature of things at their creation by God. The laws which God implants in human nature do not differ in their eternal origin in the divine intellect and will, or in their manifestation of the divine government of the world. They differ only in that it is part of man's nature to be free and therefore able to disobey even the rules of his own nature. Thus both sorts of law are directions of behavior. Only if the laws which science discovers are not attributed to God, will they seem to be merely descriptive rather than prescriptive.

In this chapter we shall be primarily concerned with law as a direction of human conduct or, as Kant would say, law in the sphere of freedom. But within the one meaning of law which concerns us here, there are still many important distinctions of type. The division of law into divine and human, natural and positive, private and public, moral and political—to name only some of the traditional distinctions —determines the outlines of the diverse philosophies of law which the great books contain, and underlies the great issues concerning the origin, the properties, and the authority of law.

DIFFERENT WRITERS use different criteria to set up their classification of the kinds of law. It is nevertheless possible to perceive certain parallels in analysis and classification. The opposite of natural law is sometimes called "human law," "positive law," or "written law," sometimes "civil law" or "municipal law." Sometimes, as with Kant, for whom the analysis of law derives from an analysis of rights, the differentiation between natural and positive right is also expressed in terms of innate and acquired right, public and private right.

Thus, for Kant, "natural right rests upon pure rational principles *a priori*; positive or statutory right is what proceeds from the will of a legislator. . . . Innate right is that right which belongs to everyone by nature, independent of all juridical acts of experience. Acquired right is that right which is founded upon such juridical acts." From natural or innate right develops "the system of those laws which require no external promulgation" and which therefore belong to the sphere of private right. Positive or civil rights are the acquired rights of men living in a state of civil society under "the system of those laws which require public promulgation" and which therefore belong to the sphere of public right. The source of differentiation here seems threefold: whether the right is inherent in human nature or acquired from the state; whether men are viewed as living in a state of nature or as living in a civil society; whether the laws do or do not need to be publicly promulgated.

The distinction between the state of nature and the state of civil society is used by many other writers in differentiating between natural and positive (or civil) law, *e.g.*, by Hobbes, Spinoza, Locke, Montesquieu, Rousseau. They also recognize that the law which governs men living in a state of nature is natural in the sense of being instinctive, or a rule of conduct which man's reason is innately competent to prescribe; whereas the civil law originates with specific acts of legislation by a political power, vested in a sovereign person, in a representative assembly, or in the whole body of the people.

Dividing all laws into two kinds—"laws of nature and laws of the land"—Hegel holds that "the laws of nature are simply what they are and are valid as they are." In contrast, positive law is "valid in a particular state, and this legal authority is the guiding principle for the knowledge of right in this positive form, *i.e.*, for the science of positive law." Our manner of knowing their content further distinguishes between these two kinds of law. "To know the law of nature," Hegel explains, "we must learn to know nature, since its laws are rigid, and it is only our ideas about them that can be false. . . . Knowledge of the laws of the land is in one way similar, but in another way not. These laws too we learn to know just as they exist . . . But the difference in the case of laws of the land is that they arouse the spirit of reflection, and their diversity at once draws attention to the fact that they are not absolute."

This leads us to the heart of the distinction. The law of the land, or civil law, is "something posited, something originated by men." It is positive law in the sense that it must be *posited* (*i.e.*, officially instituted) in order to exist. The civil law is not something *discovered* by examining man's nature. It is *made*, and must be externally promulgated so that those who are subject to it can learn its provisions. Anyone who will inquire can learn the natural law for himself; or he can be helped to discover it by a teacher who instructs him in this matter as he would instruct him in geometry, not as a lawyer informs clients concerning the prevailing laws of the state.

AQUINAS BOTH subtracts from and adds to this analysis of the difference between natural and positive law. On the one hand, he does not appeal to the condition of man in a state of nature as contrasted with civil society. On the other hand, he finds the chief difference between the natural and the positive law in their originating sources. The one is made by God, the other by man. "The natural law," Aquinas writes, "is nothing else than the rational creature's participation in the eternal law." It is God's eternal law with respect to man as that is received and exists in human nature. It exists in man as the first principle of his practical reason and includes all the precepts which can be discovered by reasoning therefrom.

Hence, for Aquinas as for Locke, the law of nature is not only the law of reason but the law of nature's God. But Aquinas distinguishes between the law of nature generally, or the eternal law, and the natural law in man. The latter is a *moral* law, both in the sense that it is a law governing free acts, and also in the sense that it directs man with regard to good and evil in the sphere of his private life, not merely with regard to the political common good.

Natural and positive law are alike in the very respects in which they differ. Both share in the nature of law which, according to Aquinas, "is nothing else than an ordinance of reason for the common good, made by him who has care of the community, and promulgated." Each has a maker, God or man; each proceeds in a certain way from the reason and will of its maker; each must be promulgated, though not in the same manner; and each is concerned with a common good—human happiness or the welfare of the state.

The further additions which Aquinas makes consist of distinctions with respect to divine and human law. With respect to the divine law he distinguishes between God's eternal ordinances and His positive commandments. The eternal part of the divine law, as we have seen, is that which, at the moment of creation, "God imprints on the whole of nature" to instill in each created species "the principles of its proper actions." "If man were ordained to no other end than that which is proportionate to his natural faculties," Aquinas writes, "there would be no need for man to have any further direction . . . besides the natural law and the human law which is derived from it." But "man is ordained to the end of eternal happiness"; and since salvation is a supernatural end which exceeds man's power to achieve without God's help, "it was necessary that . . . man should be directed to this end by a law given by God."

God gave such a body of law to man, not at creation, but at a certain moment in history. He did not implant it in his nature but promulgated it, in the manner appropriate to positive law, through verbal declaration—through His revealed word in the Old and the New Testaments, *e.g.*, the Ten Commandments and the two precepts of charity.

The human law Aquinas divides "into the *law of nations* [or the *ius gentium*] and *civil law*." The civil law is that which is instituted by a community for its own members. With regard to the *ius gentium* Aquinas follows the tradition of the Roman jurists. What he has in mind in using this term should, therefore, not be confused with what later writers, such as Grotius, treat as the *ius inter gentes* or international law. Yet applicable to both the law of nations and international law is the question whether such law belongs more properly to the sphere of natural or to the sphere of positive law.

International law concerns the relations between autonomous states which, as Hegel points out, are "in a state of nature in relation to one another," since "the sovereignty of a state is the principle of its relations to others." Laws cannot be applied to sovereign states with the coercive force of positive law. "It follows," says

Hegel, "that if states disagree and their particular wills cannot be harmonized, the matter can only be settled by war." His statement that international law "does not go beyond an ought-to-be" separates it from positive law. On similar grounds Aquinas separates the *ius gentium* from positive law. He recognizes, as will presently appear, that it does not result from legislative enactment. Furthermore, he points out that it is discovered by reason and derives its rules by way of deduction from natural law. The law of nations is, therefore, not positively instituted.

That the law of nations lacks some of the properties of civil law does not make it, for Aquinas, less essentially a body of law; but for Hegel it falls short of the essence of law, which consists in a determinate and universal rule of right posited by a sovereign will. The great legal positivists of the 19th century, such as Austin, go further and deny that anything is truly law except the positive enactments of a government which has the power to enforce its ordinances. The laws of nature are laws only in a metaphorical sense.

The Greeks also appear to regard law as primarily a creation of the state. Aristotle conceives political justice as "part natural, part legal—natural, that which everywhere has the same force and does not exist by people's thinking this or that; legal, that which is originally indifferent, but when it has been laid down is not indifferent." This tends to identify the legal aspect of justice with the conventional. The threefold division of law into civil law, law of nations, and natural law is not Greek but Roman in origin.

Yet the Greeks do not hold that all law is of human institution or merely a matter of local convention. The fundamental opposition between the divine law and the man-made law of the state occurs frequently in the Greek tragedies, and with particular force in the *Antigone* of Sophocles. In burying her brother, Antigone violates the king's edict, but, in her view, not to have done so would have been to violate the "unwritten statutes of heaven" which, she declares, are "not of today or yesterday, but from all time, and no man knows when they were first put forth. Not through dread of any human pride," she says, "could I answer to the gods for breaking *these*."

Aristotle cites this passage from Sophocles when, in his *Rhetoric*, he advises the forensic orator (or trial lawyer) "to appeal to the universal law, and insist on its greater equity and justice," *if* "the written law tells against our case." Under such circumstances, he thinks it is wise to "urge that the principles of equity are permanent and changeless, and that the universal law does not change either, for it is the law of nature, whereas written laws often do change." Under the opposite circumstances, that is, when "the written law supports our case," he prescribes an opposite course—to cite the laws of the state and to urge that they be upheld.

Though Aristotle here speaks of "the law of nature," he seems to have in mind the notion of "a universal law," or a body of law that is *common* to all peoples. For the most part, he speaks of natural justice rather than natural law. Whether or not the two notions are equivalent, his principle of natural justice stands in the same relation to political enactments as, for later writers, the natural law stands to the positive law. Plato's conception of law as "a disposition of reason" which orders things according to their natures, even more explicitly recognizes that law neither depends upon nor derives its authority from the power of the state. The phrase "natural law" may be infrequent in the Greek books, but its meaning is not unrepresented in Greek thought.

OTHER DISTINCTIONS in kinds of law—written and unwritten, statutory and customary, constitutional law and the various particular bodies of law, such as the law of contracts, of crimes, or of torts—are for the most part subdivisions of positive law. The one exception, perhaps, is the unwritten law, which, when not identified with customary law, stands for the natural law or the law of reason. With respect to these parts of law, the chief problems concern constitutions and customs. The difference between a constitution as law and all other laws obtaining in a state is considered in the chapter on CONSTITUTION; and the legal force of custom, both in itself and also in relation to legislative enactments, is discussed in the chapter on CUSTOM.

Here our major concern is with positive law as a whole, with its properties and defects, but above all with its relation to natural law. Some of the properties of positive law are agreed upon even by those who sharply disagree concerning its relation to natural law.

It is generally agreed, for example, that a rule of positive law cannot be made by *any* man, but only by him who exercises the legislative authority and has the power to enforce the rule. Agreement also prevails concerning the mutability of positive law, though not all would go as far as Montaigne in holding that "there is nothing more subject to perpetual agitation than the laws." Yet it is generally recognized that the content of positive law continually undergoes change with the nullification or amendment of old rules and the addition of new ones, and that positive regulations on any particular matter may vary from state to state.

No less common is the understanding of the indispensability of courts and judges. "Laws are a dead letter without courts to expound and define their true meaning and operation," Hamilton writes. Though rules of law, in distinction from decrees, are formulated to cover an indefinite number of like cases, the cases to which they must be applied by the judicial process are far from uniform. Courts and judges have the task of deciding whether the facts of the particular case bring that case under the specific provisions of the law. This is the field of judicial discretion and the battleground of litigants and lawyers.

The propensities of men of law, on the bench and at the bar, to protract and complicate the procedures of a trial, to multiply and divide the issues, to separate themselves from laymen by a heavy curtain of language, have been satirically noted in the great diatribes against the legal profession, from Aristophanes to Chaucer, Rabelais, Montaigne, and Swift.

Rabelais, for example, has Pantagruel undertake to arbitrate in the litigation between "Lord Kissbreech, plaintiff of one side, and . . . Lord Suckfist, defendant of the other, whose controversy was so high and difficult in law that the court of parliament could make nothing of it." Pantagruel conducts the proceedings in an unusual style. When the counsellors and attorneys "delivered into his hands the bags wherein were the writs and pancarts concerning that suit, which for bulk and weight were almost enough to load four great couillard

or stoned asses, Pantagruel said unto them, Are the two lords, between whom this debate and process is, yet living?" Upon being told they are alive, "to what a devil, then, said he, serve so many paltry heaps and bundles of papers and copies which you give me? Is it not better to hear their controversy from their own mouths, whilst they are face to face before us, than to read these vile fopperies, which are nothing but trumperies, deceits, diabolical cozenages of Cepola, pernicious slights and subversions of equity."

Furthermore, Pantagruel continues, "seeing the laws are excerpted out of the middle of moral and natural philosophy, how should these fools have understood it, that have, by G—, studied less in philosophy than my mule? In respect of human learning, and the knowledge of antiquities and history, they are truly laden with these faculties as a toad is with feathers. And yet of all this the laws are so full, that without it they cannot be understood. . . . Therefore, if you will that I make any meddling in this process, first, cause all these papers to be burned; secondly, make the two gentlemen come personally before me, and, afterwards, when I shall have heard them, I will tell you my opinion freely, without any feignedness or dissimulation whatsoever." The trial which Pantagruel then conducts, in which the two lords are forced to plead without benefit of counsel, is a choice and proper piece of litigation.

THE PROBLEMS of casuistry, with which Pascal deals at length in his *Provincial Letters*, are sometimes thought of as peculiar to the canon law, but casuistry, in the sense of distinguishing cases and examining them in relation to general rules, necessarily occurs in the judicial application of any body of law. The most difficult cases are those which may fall under the letter of a law but seem to be inconsistent with its spirit. The reverse also happens; cases fall outside the letter of the law but the purpose of the law seems to cover them. All such cases indicate an unavoidable defect in rules of law.

The defect is unavoidable, Aristotle says. Law aims at universality "but about some things it is not possible to make a universal statement which shall be correct." To remedy this defect, the intention of the lawmaker should be consulted. The particular case should be treated as he would have treated it if he had had it in mind when he framed the general rule. Such handling of the difficult case is what Aristotle means by the equitable—"a correction of the law where it is defective owing to its universality."

The law which equity is called upon to correct may be a just rule, but that does not prevent its being unjustly applied. Equity prevents the injustice of misapplication by dispensing justice in the particular case according to the spirit, not the letter, of the law. It is a kind of justice, Aristotle says; "not legal justice but a correction of legal justice . . . not better than absolute justice but better than the error which arises from the absoluteness of the rule."

Those who share Aristotle's theory of equity acknowledge a standard of justice by which not only the law's application, but also the law itself, is to be measured. In his terms, natural justice provides this standard. The justice of laws made by the state is not only relative to the constitution of the state, but since the constitution itself can be more or less just, there is a standard of justice prior to and independent of the state—in this sense, *natural*.

Essentially the same point is made by those who, like Montesquieu and Locke, appeal to the natural law, both as a measure of constitutions and as a criterion for distinguishing good from bad law. "Before laws were made," Montesquieu writes, "there were relations of possible justice. To say that there is nothing just or unjust but what is commanded or forbidden by positive laws, is the same as saying that before the describing of a circle all the radii were not equal."

The law of nature, according to Locke, does not apply only to the conduct of men living in a state of nature. The law of nature which Locke describes as a rule "of common reason and equity which is that measure God has set to the actions of men for their mutual security," is not abolished when men enter into civil society. "The obligations of the law of nature cease not in society, but only in many cases are drawn closer, and have by human laws known penalties annexed to them, to enforce their observation. Thus the law of nature stands as an eternal rule

to all men, legislators as well as others." The rules of positive law, writes Locke, must "be conformable to the law of nature, *i.e.*, to the will of God, of which that is the declaration." The municipal laws of any particular state "are only so far right as they are founded on the law of nature, by which they are to be regulated and interpreted."

THE POSITION of Locke and Aquinas makes natural law the source as well as the standard of positive law. As a source, natural law gives rise to positive law in a way which, for Aquinas at least, differentiates it from the law of nations or the *ius gentium*.

"Something may be derived from the natural law in two ways," he writes. "First, as a conclusion from premises; secondly, by way of determination of certain generalities. The first way," he explains, "is like to that by which, in sciences, demonstrated conclusions are drawn from the principles; while the second mode is likened to that whereby, in the arts, general forms are particularized as to details: thus the craftsman needs to determine the general form of a house to some particular shape." Now "to the law of nations belong those things which are derived from the law of nature, as conclusions from premises, *e.g.*, just buyings and sellings, and the like, without which men cannot live together, which is a point of the law of nature, since man is by nature a social animal. . . . But those things which are derived from the law of nature by way of particular determination, belong to the civil law, according as each state decides on what is best for itself."

Aquinas exemplifies the determinations of positive law by pointing out that "the law of nature has it that the evildoer should be punished; but that he be punished in this way or that, is a determination of the law of nature," which the positive law must institute. He might also have used as an example the fact that the universal prohibition of killing is a conclusion from the principle of natural law that "*one should do harm to no man*," whereas the various kinds and degrees of murder are differently defined in different countries according to the determination of the natural law made by the positive law of homicide in each country.

The rules of positive law cannot be arrived at deductively. They do not follow necessarily from principles. They are only determinations which particularize the precepts of natural law in a manner which fits the contingent circumstances of a particular society. Whatever is made determinate by positive law is something which the natural law leaves indeterminate because no point of justice or right is involved. Other determinations could have been made. An element of choice is involved in the making of positive laws. In addition to being formulated by the reason, they must be posited by the will of whoever has the authority to make laws.

Rules of positive law are the work of reason to the extent that reason is called upon to propose various *possible* determinations of the natural law, *e.g.*, one or another definition of murder in the first degree, one or another definition of the penalty for it. Since a definite rule of positive law cannot be instituted until a choice is made among the alternative possibilities, the positive law cannot be solely the work of reason. Choice, according to Aquinas, is always an act of the will.

Though he recognizes the role of choice, and hence of the will, in the enactment of positive law, Aquinas does not go to the other extreme of making the will the sole arbiter of what is law. The legality of the state's ordinances does not depend entirely on their being posited by the will of a sovereign authority. If a positive regulation is not derived from the natural law, it cannot be a just rule. Quoting Augustine's remark that "a law which is not just is a law in name only," Aquinas goes on to say: "Every human law has just so much of the nature of law as it is derived from the law of nature. But if in any point it departs from the law of nature, it is no longer a law but a perversion of law."

An ordinance which had no other foundation than the will of a sovereign prince or government might have the coercive force of law, but it would lack the moral authority of law. It would bind men, not through conscience, but only through their fear of punishment for disobedience. "That force and tyranny may be an element in law," writes Hegel, "is accidental to law, and has nothing to do with its nature."

A COMPLETELY opposite view is taken by those who deny natural law or principles of innate right and natural justice. There is, in addition, a theory of natural law which leads to an opposite view of the legal and the just, though the opposition in this case is qualified to some extent.

According to Hobbes, "civil and natural law are not different kinds, but different parts of law." The law of nature and the civil law, he says, "contain each other and are of equal extent." But he also says that "the laws of nature . . . are not properly laws, but qualities that dispose men to peace and to obedience."

Before the formation of a commonwealth, by the contract or covenant whereby men transfer the rights and liberties which they possess in a state of nature, the natural law directs men, first, to preserve their lives in the war "of every man against every man"; and second, to seek the security of peace by leaving the natural state of war to join with their fellow men in the order of a civil society. The nineteen precepts of natural law which Hobbes enumerates seem to set forth reason's recognition of the advantages of civil society over the state of nature and also reason's understanding of the conditions indispensable to a firm foundation of the commonwealth.

These rules of reason "are the laws of nature, dictating peace, for a means of the conservation of men in multitudes, and which only concern the doctrine of civil society." But until the commonwealth exists, the laws of nature bind in conscience only, and they are therefore not effective in achieving their end, which is security. "When a commonwealth is settled, then they are actually laws and not before; as being then the commands of the commonwealth, and therefore also civil laws. For it is the sovereign power which obliges men to obey them."

The distinction between natural and civil law then becomes a distinction between unwritten and written rules; but the test of whether any rule is actually a law is the same, namely, whether it is adopted and enforced by the sovereign. "All laws, written and unwritten, have their authority and force from the will of the commonwealth," Hobbes writes.

The difference between the Hobbesian theory and that of Locke or Aquinas reveals itself in its consequences. Under what circumstances can a subject or citizen refuse obedience to the laws of the state? On the ground that they are unjust or tyrannical? By the criterion that they violate precepts of natural law or the positive commandments of God? Is the individual bound in conscience to obey every command of the civil law, because the civil law includes the natural law, interprets it, and gives it the authority and force of law; and because the natural law itself commands obedience to the civil law once a commonwealth has been instituted? Or, on the contrary, is an individual in conscience free to disobey those positive enactments which lack the authority of law because they are not in conformity to the natural law or the divine law?

To QUESTIONS OF THIS sort, and to the whole problem of the right of rebellion, different answers seem to be given in terms of different views of the nature of law, the sources of its authority, and its sanctions.

At one extreme there is the doctrine that rebellion is never justified, that the security of peace, which the maintenance of law and order provides, is always better than the anarchy and war which result from rebellion. Hobbes, for example, holds that "nothing the sovereign representative can do to a subject, on what pretence soever, can properly be called injustice, or injury." The rebel would, therefore, always be a criminal, a man who takes the law into his own hands, and uses force to gain his ends. A man may be justified in using force, according to Hobbes, only to repel force used against him, and then only in defense of his life. So much the law of nature permits or requires. But it does not permit or require him to decide which laws enacted by his sovereign he shall obey or disobey.

At the other extreme there is the doctrine of civil disobedience as expounded by Thoreau and, of course, Gandhi. Unjust laws, or laws which violate a man's conscience, may have the force of the state behind them. But they exert no authority over him. The just man is called upon to break them and to submit gladly to the consequences of breaking them, by suffering whatever penalties may be attached to their breach. It is not enough for the individual citizen to satisfy his conscience by criticizing the government and joining with like-minded fellow citizens in an effort to get unjust laws abolished or reformed. He is obliged in conscience not to await help from others or to be patient in the use of gradual means. He is obliged to act alone and at once—by disobeying the unjust law.

Kant seems to go this far when he interprets the precept "Do wrong to no one" as meaning "Do no wrong to anyone, even if thou shouldst be under the necessity, in observing this duty, to cease from all connection with others and to avoid all society." But he qualifies this somewhat by the precept: "Enter, if wrong cannot be avoided, into a society with others in which everyone may have *secured* to him what is his own."

Another sort of qualification limits disobedience, rebellion, or secession from society—even when the individual conscience recoils from the injustice or illegality of a civil ordinance. The principle, as stated by Aquinas, seems to be that the common good may, under certain circumstances, be better served by acquiescence than by disobedience. Unless what the law commands involves a transgression of God's commandments, an unjust law may be obeyed "in order to avoid scandal or disturbance."

Even with regard to reforming law by legal means Aquinas recommends that the disadvantages resulting from the change of law be weighed against the advantages. The effectiveness of law depends upon the habits of obedience it forms and upon the customary behavior it establishes. "Consequently," Aquinas says, "when a law is changed, the binding power of law is diminished, in so far as custom is abolished." This harm to the common welfare may, of course, be compensated either by "the benefit conferred by the new enactment" or by the fact that "the existing law is clearly unjust, or its observance extremely harmful."

Locke states the principle somewhat differently. So long as due process of law is available to remedy unjust ordinances or illegal acts, the individual is not justified in disobedience, for such action would "unhinge and overturn all polities, and, instead of government and order, leave nothing but anarchy and confusion." Nor is it effective for the individual to act alone in using force to resist tyranny or injustice. But if these illegal acts have extended to the majority of the people "and they are persuaded in their consciences, that their laws, and with them their estates, liberties, and lives are in danger, and perhaps, their religion too, how they will be hindered from resisting illegal force used against them, I cannot tell. This is an inconvenience, I confess, that attends all governments." There is no alternative then but rebellion—"properly a state of war wherein the appeal lies only to heaven."

As the foregoing discussion indicates, the basic issues in the philosophy of law are inseparable from questions about justice and liberty, the rights of the individual and the authority of the state, the powers of government, and the fundamental alternatives of crime and punishment, war and peace. These matters are considered in the chapters appropriate to the terms mentioned above. More particular consequences of the theory of law, especially natural law, are found in such chapters as REVOLUTION, SLAVERY, and TYRANNY, CITIZEN, CONSTITUTION, and WEALTH.

OUTLINE OF TOPICS

REFERENCES

To find the passages cited, use the numbers in heavy type, which are the volume and page numbers of the passages referred to. For example, in 4 HOMER: *Iliad*, BK II [265-283] 12d, the number 4 is the number of the volume in the set; the number 12d indicates that the passage is in section d of page 12.

PAGE SECTIONS: When the text is printed in one column, the letters a and b refer to the upper and lower halves of the page. For example, in 53 JAMES: *Psychology*, 116a-119b, the passage begins in the upper half of page 116 and ends in the lower half of page 119. When the text is printed in two columns, the letters a and b refer to the upper and lower halves of the left-hand side of the page, the letters c and d to the upper and lower halves of the right-hand side of the page. For example, in 7 PLATO: *Symposium*, 163b-164c, the passage begins in the lower half of the left-hand side of page 163 and ends in the upper half of the right-hand side of page 164.

AUTHOR'S DIVISIONS: One or more of the main divisions of a work (such as PART, BK, CH, SECT) are sometimes included in the reference; line numbers, in brackets, are given in certain cases; *e.g.*, *Iliad*, BK II [265-283] 12d.

BIBLE REFERENCES: The references are to book, chapter, and verse. When the King James and Douay versions differ in title of books or in the numbering of chapters or verses, the King James version is cited first and the Douay, indicated by a (D), follows; *e.g.*, OLD TESTAMENT: *Nehemiah*, 7:45—(D) II *Esdras*, 7:46.

SYMBOLS: The abbreviation "esp" calls the reader's attention to one or more especially relevant parts of a whole reference; "passim" signifies that the topic is discussed intermittently rather than continuously in the work or passage cited.

For additional information concerning the style of the references, see the Explanation of Reference Style; for general guidance in the use of *The Great Ideas*, consult the Preface.

1. The definition of law

7 PLATO: *Statesman*, 599c-601b / *Laws*, BK I, 650a-b; BK IV, 681b-c; BK IX, 743a-b; 754a-b; 757a

9 ARISTOTLE: *Ethics*, BK V, CH 1 [1129^{b}14-19] 377a; BK X, CH 9 [1180^{a}14-24] 434d-435a / *Politics*, BK III, CH 16 [1287^{a}28-32] 485d; [1287^{b}3-5] 486a; BK VII, CH 4 [1326^{a}29-32] 530b-c

12 AURELIUS: *Meditations*, BK XI, SECT 1 302a-b

20 AQUINAS: *Summa Theologica*, PART I-II, Q 90 205a-208b esp A 4, ANS 207d-208b

23 HOBBES: *Leviathan*, PART II, 130b-c; 131a-c; 149c; 157b

35 LOCKE: *Civil Government*, CH VI, SECT 57 36d-37b; CH IX, SECT 124 53d-54a; CH XI 55b-58b

38 MONTESQUIEU: *Spirit of Laws*, BK I, 1a-2b; 3c

38 ROUSSEAU: *Inequality*, 330b-d / *Political Economy*, 370b-d / *Social Contract*, BK II, 399b-400c esp 399c-d

42 KANT: *Pure Reason*, 110c / *Fund. Prin. Metaphysic of Morals*, 266c-d / *Pref. Metaphysical Elements of Ethics*, 367b-c / *Intro. Metaphysic of Morals* 383a-394a,c esp 392b / *Science of Right*, 397a-399c

43 FEDERALIST: NUMBER 33, 108d-109a; NUMBER 62, 191b

44 BOSWELL: *Johnson*, 203d-204a

46 HEGEL: *Philosophy of Right*, PREF, 4a-b; INTRO, par 3 10a-12c; ADDITIONS, 1 115a-d

1a. The end of law: peace, order, and the common good

7 PLATO: *Republic*, BK I, 301b-304a; BK II, 311b-c; BK V, 363b-365d; BK IX, 425c-427b esp 426c-d / *Theaetetus*, 531a-b / *Statesman*, 599c-601b / *Laws*, BK I-III 640a-677a esp BK I, 643a-644a, 650a-b, BK III, 669b-d, 676b-c; BK IV, 677d; 681b-682c; BK VI, 706b-c; BK IX, 747d; 754a-b; 757a; BK XII, 795c-796b / *Seventh Letter*, 804b-c

9 ARISTOTLE: *Ethics*, BK V, CH 1 [1129^{b}14-19] 377a; CH 6 [1134^{a}29-32] 382a / *Politics*, BK III, CH 16 [1287^{a}18-^{b}35] 485c-486c; BK VII, CH 4 [1326^{a}29-32] 530b-c

14 PLUTARCH: *Solon*, 72b

18 AUGUSTINE: *City of God*, BK XIX, CH 17 522b-523a

20 AQUINAS: *Summa Theologica*, PART I-II, Q 90, A 2 206b-207a; A 3, ANS and REP 3 207a-c; Q 91, A 1, REP 3 208b-d; A 5, ANS 211c-212c; A 6, REP 3 212c-213c; Q 92, A 1, ANS and REP 1,3-4 213c-214c; Q 93, A 1, REP 1 215b,d-216c; A 4, CONTRARY 218b-d; Q 94, A 2, ANS 221d-223a; A 3, REP 1 223a-c; Q 95, A 1 226c-227c;

A 3 228c-229b; A 4, ANS 229b-230c; Q 96, AA 2–3 231c-233a; A 4, ANS 233a-d; A 6, ANS 235a-d; Q 97, A 1, ANS and REP 3 236a-d; A 2, ANS and REP 2 236d-237b; A 4 238b-239b; Q 98, A 1, ANS 239b-240c; Q 99, A 1, ANS and REP 1–2 245c-246b; A 2, ANS 246b-247a; A 3, ANS 247a-248a; Q 100, A 2, ANS 252b-253a; A 8, ANS 259d-261a; A 9, CONTRARY 261b-262b; A 11, REP 3 263c-264d; Q 105, A 2, ANS and REP 1,4 309d-316a; Q 107, A 1, ANS 325c-327b; A 2, ANS 327b-329a

21 DANTE: *Divine Comedy*, PURGATORY, XVI [85–102] 77d

23 HOBBES: *Leviathan*, PART II, 103a; 131b-c; 157b-c

30 BACON: *Advancement of Learning*, 20c-d

31 SPINOZA: *Ethics*, PART IV, PROP 37, SCHOL 2 435b-436a

35 LOCKE: *Toleration*, 8c; 11b; 15c; 16a-17b passim / *Civil Government*, CH I, SECT 3 25d; CH VI, SECT 57 36d-37b; CH IX 53c-54d; CH XI 55b-58b; CH XV, SECT 171 65a-b; CH XIX, SECT 219 75b-c

36 STERNE: *Tristram Shandy*, 262a

38 MONTESQUIEU: *Spirit of Laws*, BK I, 2c-3d passim

38 ROUSSEAU: *Inequality*, 353d-355b esp 354d-355a; 359c-d / *Political Economy*, 370b-d; 375b-c / *Social Contract*, BK II, 399b-c

40 GIBBON: *Decline and Fall*, 617a

42 KANT: *Pure Reason*, 114b-115a / *Fund. Prin. Metaphysic of Morals*, 259c-261d esp 259c-d; 272a-b; 274a-277b / *Pref. Metaphysical Elements of Ethics*, 373d / *Science of Right*, 398c-399c; 408c-409c; 412c-414a

44 BOSWELL: *Johnson*, 204b-c; 219d-220a

46 HEGEL: *Philosophy of Right*, PART III, par 299 99c-100b; ADDITIONS, 135 138c / *Philosophy of History*, INTRO, 170c-171c; PART II, 271d-272a

54 FREUD: *Civilization and Its Discontents*, 780b-d

1b. Law in relation to reason or will

7 PLATO: *Gorgias*, 271c-272b / *Republic*, BK I, 301c-302c / *Laws*, BK I, 650a-b; BK III, 669b-670c; BK IV, 679c-680d; 681b-682c; 685d; BK IX, 754a-b; BK XII, 792c-d

9 ARISTOTLE: *Ethics*, BK X, CH 9 [1180^{a}14–24] 434d-435a / *Politics*, BK I, CH 2 [1253^{a}31–37] 446d; BK III, CH 16 485b-486c esp [1287^{a}19–32] 485c-d; BK VI, CH 3 521c-522a

12 AURELIUS: *Meditations*, BK IV, SECT 4 264a

19 AQUINAS: *Summa Theologica*, PART I, Q 21, A 2, REP 1 125c-d

20 AQUINAS: *Summa Theologica*, PART I–II, Q 90, A 1 205b-206b; A 3 207a-c; Q 95, A 1 226c-227c

23 HOBBES: *Leviathan*, PART I, 86b-87a; 96b; PART II, 127b; 131d-132b; 133a; 160b-c; PART IV, 272c

35 LOCKE: *Civil Government*, CH II, SECT 6–8 26b-27a; CH VI, SECT 57–63 36d-38c; CH XI 55b-58b passim; CH XIII, SECT 151 59d-60a; CH XIX, SECT 212 74a-b

36 STERNE: *Tristram Shandy*, 266a-b

38 MONTESQUIEU: *Spirit of Laws*, BK I, 1a; 3c

38 ROUSSEAU: *Political Economy*, 368d-371a / *Social Contract*, BK II, 395b-d; 399b-400c; BK III, 419c-420a

42 KANT: *Fund. Prin. Metaphysic of Morals*, 264b-d; 273d-274a / *Practical Reason*, 309d / *Intro. Metaphysic of Morals*, 390b; 393a / *Science of Right*, 435a; 448b-d; 450a-b / *Judgement*, 596c-598b

43 FEDERALIST: NUMBER 78, 230d-232a

46 HEGEL: *Philosophy of Right*, INTRO, par 4 12d-13a / *Philosophy of History*, INTRO, 170c-171c; PART IV, 328a; 364d-365a

50 MARX-ENGELS: *Communist Manifesto*, 427a-b

1c. The authority and power needed for making law

9 ARISTOTLE: *Ethics*, BK X, CH 9 [1180^{a}14–24] 434d-435a / *Politics*, BK III, CH 16 485b-486c; BK VI, CH 3 521c-522a

14 PLUTARCH: *Lycurgus* 32a-48d esp 34b-d, 47a-c / *Numa Pompilius*, 52b-c / *Solon* 64b,d-77a,c

20 AQUINAS: *Summa Theologica*, PART I–II, Q 90, A 3 207a-c; Q 92, A 2, REP 3 214d-215a,c; Q 95, A 1 226c-227c

23 MACHIAVELLI: *Prince*, CH XII, 18a

23 HOBBES: *Leviathan*, PART II, 100c-101a; 123a-b; 130b-132a; 137b-138b; 157b; 160c-161a; PART III, 171a-172a; 201a-b; 231d-234d

29 CERVANTES: *Don Quixote*, PART I, 147a; PART II, 362b

31 DESCARTES: *Discourse*, PART VI, 61a

35 LOCKE: *Civil Government*, CH VII, SECT 87–88 44a-c; CH IX 53c-54d; CH XI 55b-58b; CH XIII, SECT 149 59b-d; CH XIX, SECT 212 74a-b / *Human Understanding*, BK I, CH II, SECT 5–6 105a-c; SECT 12–13 107b-108c; BK II, CH XXVIII, SECT 5–12 229c-231c passim, esp SECT 6 229d

38 ROUSSEAU: *Political Economy*, 369a / *Social Contract*, BK II, 399d-400a; 400c-402a; BK III, 420a-421c

42 KANT: *Intro. Metaphysic of Morals*, 393c / *Science of Right*, 398b-c; 399c; 405d-406c; 412c-414c; 435c-436c; 438b-c

43 DECLARATION OF INDEPENDENCE: [43–47] 2a

43 FEDERALIST: NUMBER 33, 107b-108a; 108d-109a; NUMBER 44, 145c-146d; NUMBER 78, 230d-232a

46 HEGEL: *Philosophy of Right*, PART I, par 94 36b; PART III, par 212 70d-71a / *Philosophy of History*, PART I, 207b-c

51 TOLSTOY: *War and Peace*, EPILOGUE II, 680d-684a

1d. The promulgation of law: the need and the manner of its declaration

OLD TESTAMENT: *Deuteronomy*, 27:1-8 / *Joshua*, 8:30-35—(D) *Josue*, 8:30-35

NEW TESTAMENT: *Romans*, 2:14-15

3a(2) The distinction between the eternal law and the positive commandments of God

3b. The divine positive law: the difference between the law revealed in the Old and the New Testament

3b(1) Law in the Old Testament: the moral, the judicial, and the ceremonial precepts of the Old Law

(*3b. The divine positive law: the difference between the law revealed in the Old and the New Testament. 3b(1) Law in the Old Testament: the moral, the judicial, and the ceremonial precepts of the Old Law.*)

33 PASCAL: *Pensées*, 619–620 284b-286a
40 GIBBON: *Decline and Fall*, 180b-182c passim; 208a-c
43 MILL: *Utilitarianism*, 467c
46 HEGEL: *Philosophy of History*, PART I, 246c-247a

3b(2) Law in the New Testament: the law of love and grace; ceremonial precepts of the New Law

NEW TESTAMENT: *Matthew*, 5–7 esp 5:17–20; 16:18–19; 18:18; 22:34–40; 28:19 / *Mark*, 12:28–34 / *Luke*, 6:20–49; 10:25–37; 16:16–17; 22:15–20 / *John*, 3:1–8; 6 esp 6:47–58; 13:31–17:26; 20:21–23—(D) *John*, 3:1–8; 6 esp 6:47–59; 13:31–17:26; 20:21–23 / *Acts*, 2:37–42; 8:14–17,26–40; 10:34–48; 13:2–4,38–39; 15:22–29; 19:1–7; 21:20–25 / *Romans* esp 3–13 / *I Corinthians*, 11:23–34; 13 / *Galatians* esp 3–6 / *Colossians* / *I Timothy*, 4:14 / *Hebrews*, 7–10 / *James*, 5:14–15 / *I Peter*, 4:8–11 / *I John* / *II John*
18 AUGUSTINE: *City of God*, BK X, CH 25 313c-314c; BK XX, CH 4 532b-c / *Christian Doctrine*, BK I, CH 22–30 629b-633b; CH 35 634c-d; BK III, CH 10 661c-662a
20 AQUINAS: *Summa Theologica*, PART I-II, Q 91, A 5 211c-212c; Q 98, A 4, ANS 242b-243c; Q 101, A 2, ANS 267a-268a; A 4, REP 2 269a-270b; Q 102, A 1, REP 1 270c-271b; A 4, REP 2–4 276d-283c; A 5, REP 3 283c-292c; Q 103, A 3, ANS 300d-302a; QQ 106–108 321a-337d; PART II-II, Q 16, A 1, REP 2 454c-455c
22 CHAUCER: *Parson's Tale*, par 31 517b-518b; par 68 533b-534a
23 HOBBES: *Leviathan*, PART III, 180c-d; 206c-207a; 218a-219d; 240d; PART IV, 257c-258a
30 BACON: *Advancement of Learning*, 81a; 100d
32 MILTON: *Paradise Lost*, BK XII [285–314] 325b-326a; [576–605] 331b-332a
33 PASCAL: *Pensées*, 672 296a
42 KANT: *Fund. Prin. Metaphysic of Morals*, 259a / *Practical Reason*, 327c-d
43 MILL: *Liberty*, 286b-287a
51 TOLSTOY: *War and Peace*, BK XI, 525c-526b
52 DOSTOEVSKY: *Brothers Karamazov*, BK V, 121d-137c esp 121d-122b, 126c-127b; BK VI, 150a-c; 166c-170a

4. The natural law

4a. The law of reason or the moral law: the order and habit of its principles

12 AURELIUS: *Meditations*, BK III, SECT 11 262a-b; BK IV, SECT 4 264a; BK VII, SECT 55 283b-c; BK XI, SECT 1 302a-b

18 AUGUSTINE: *Confessions*, BK II, par 9, 10d
19 AQUINAS: *Summa Theologica*, PART I, Q 79, A 12 425c-426b
20 AQUINAS: *Summa Theologica*, PART I-II, Q 58, AA 4–5 44a-45c; Q 63, A 1 63a-64a; Q 90, A 1 205b-206b; Q 91, A 2 208d-209d; A 5, REP 3 211c-212c; A 6 212c-213c; Q 94 220d-226b
23 HOBBES: *Leviathan*, PART I, 86b-87a; 91a-96b esp 96b; PART II, 132c-d; 133b
25 MONTAIGNE: *Essays*, 23b-c; 184a-b; 520c-d
30 BACON: *Advancement of Learning*, 96a-c
31 SPINOZA: *Ethics*, PART IV, PROP 18, SCHOL 429a-d; PROP 31–35 432a-434a; PROP 37, SCHOL 2 435b-436a
35 LOCKE: *Civil Government*, CH II 25d-28c esp SECT 6–11 26b-27d; CH VI, SECT 56–63 36d-38c; CH IX, SECT 124 53d-54a / *Human Understanding*, 90d; BK I, CH II, SECT 5–6 105a-c passim; SECT 13, 108b-c
38 ROUSSEAU: *Social Contract*, BK II, 399b
42 KANT: *Pure Reason*, 235a-b; 236d-237a / *Fund. Prin. Metaphysic of Morals*, 253d-254d; 259c-261d; 264b-265a; 268d [fn 2]; 271c-d; 282b-287b / *Practical Reason*, 306d-310b; 314d-321b; 360d-361d / *Intro. Metaphysic of Morals*, 386b-387a,c; 388b-c; 390b
46 HEGEL: *Philosophy of Right*, PART II, par 140, 52a-53a; PART III, par 213 71a; ADDITIONS, 1 115a-d / *Philosophy of History*, INTRO, 170d-171a

4b. The law of men living in a state of nature

7 PLATO: *Republic*, BK II, 311b-312d
23 HOBBES: *Leviathan*, PART I, 84c-87b; PART II, 99a-b
30 BACON: *Advancement of Learning*, 20c-d
35 LOCKE: *Civil Government*, CH II-III 25d-29d; CH IX 53c-54d
38 MONTESQUIEU: *Spirit of Laws*, BK I, 2b-d
38 ROUSSEAU: *Inequality*, 330a-331b; 333b-d; 342c-348a esp 343b-345c / *Social Contract*, BK I, 389d-390a
41 GIBBON: *Decline and Fall*, 237c
42 KANT: *Pure Reason*, 222b-c / *Science of Right*, 402c; 433c-436c
46 HEGEL: *Philosophy of Right*, PART I, par 93 36a-b / *Philosophy of History*, INTRO, 171c-172b

4c. The *a priori* principles of innate or abstract right: universal law in the order of freedom; the objectification of the will

42 KANT: *Pure Reason*, 110c; 114b-115a / *Intro. Metaphysic of Morals*, 390b; 392b / *Science of Right*, 400b,d-402a; 412c-414c; 416b-417b; 429a-c; 435a-436b
43 MILL: *Utilitarianism*, 446a-d; 458d-459d
46 HEGEL: *Philosophy of Right*, INTRO, par 4–30 12d-19c esp par 4 12d-13a, par 15 16a-b, par 22 17c-d, par 27–30 18d-19c; par 33 20b-d; PART I 21a-39d esp par 36 21b-c, par 94 36b; PART II, par 106–114 40a-42b; par 133 47a; par 135

47b-d; PART III, par 142–157 55a-57d esp par 149 56b; par 209 69d; ADDITIONS, I 115a-d; 46 123d-124a; 84 129b; 86 129c; 94 132b; 131 137d / *Philosophy of History*, INTRO, 170c-171c; PART IV, 362b-d; 364c-d

4d. The natural law as underlying the precepts of virtue: its relation to the moral precepts of divine law

OLD TESTAMENT: *Exodus*, 20:1–17 / *Deuteronomy*, 5:6–21 / *Jeremiah*, 31:33—(D) *Jeremias*, 31:33

NEW TESTAMENT: *Romans*, 1:18–32; 2:11–16; 3

18 AUGUSTINE: *Confessions*, BK II, par 9, 10d; BK III, par 13–15 16c-17b; par 17 17d-18a

19 AQUINAS: *Summa Theologica*, PART I–II, Q 19, A 4 705b-c; A 6, ANS and REP 2 707a-708a

20 AQUINAS: *Summa Theologica*, PART I–II, Q 51, A 1, ANS 12b-13c; Q 91, A 4, ANS and REP I 210c-211c; Q 94, A 3 223a-c; A 5 224d-225d; Q 98, AA 5–6 243c-245b; Q 99, A 2 246b-247a; A 4, REP 2 248a-d; A 5, ANS 249a-250a; Q 100 251a-265d; PART III, Q 61, A 3, REP 2 856c-857c

23 HOBBES: *Leviathan*, PART I, 91a-96b esp 95d-96b; PART II, 131a-b; 136d-137a; PART III, 216c-217a; 240d-241a

30 BACON: *Advancement of Learning*, 96a-c; 100d

31 SPINOZA: *Ethics*, PART IV, PROP 18, SCHOL 429a-d

35 LOCKE: *Civil Government*, CH II, SECT 4–6 25d-26c / *Human Understanding*, BK I, CH II, SECT 5–6 105a-c passim

38 MONTESQUIEU: *Spirit of Laws*, BK I, 1c-d

38 ROUSSEAU: *Inequality*, 343b-345c; 366c-d

42 KANT: *Fund. Prin. Metaphysic of Morals*, 275b / *Practical Reason*, 317b-318c; 327c-d

46 HEGEL: *Philosophy of History*, PART IV, 361c-d

52 DOSTOEVSKY: *Brothers Karamazov*, BK II, 33c-34b

4e. The relation of natural law to natural rights and natural justice

5 SOPHOCLES: *Antigone* [441–525] 134d-135c

9 ARISTOTLE: *Politics*, BK I, CH 5 447d-448c / *Rhetoric*, BK I, CH 13 [1373ᵇ1–17] 617c-d

12 AURELIUS: *Meditations*, BK IV, SECT 4 264a; BK VII, SECT 55 283b-c

18 AUGUSTINE: *City of God*, BK XIX, CH 21 524a-525a

19 AQUINAS: *Summa Theologica*, PART I, Q 96, A I 510b-511b; A 4 512d-513c

20 AQUINAS: *Summa Theologica*, PART I–II, Q 91, A 2 208d-209d; Q 94, A 2, ANS 221d-223a; Q 95, A 2 227c-228c; A 4 229b-230c

23 HOBBES: *Leviathan*, PART I, 86c-d; PART II, 131a-c; 138c

27 SHAKESPEARE: *Troilus and Cressida*, ACT II, SC II [163–188] 115b-c

30 BACON: *Advancement of Learning*, 94d-95b

31 SPINOZA: *Ethics*, PART IV, PROP 37, SCHOL 2 435b-436a; APPENDIX, VIII 447d

32 MILTON: *Samson Agonistes* [888–902] 359a

35 LOCKE: *Civil Government*, CH II–IX 25d-54d passim; CH XI, SECT 135–137 55d-57b; CH XV, SECT 171–172 65a-c

37 FIELDING: *Tom Jones*, 53b-d

38 ROUSSEAU: *Inequality*, 330a-331b

39 SMITH: *Wealth of Nations*, BK I, 61b; BK II, 140b

41 GIBBON: *Decline and Fall*, 86d-87a

42 KANT: *Intro. Metaphysic of Morals*, 392b / *Science of Right*, 397a-b; 421c-422d; 429a-c; 430a-432c; 434a; 435a-457b esp 436c, 437c-d, 447b-450b, 451c-d

43 DECLARATION OF INDEPENDENCE: [1–28] 1a-b

43 MILL: *Liberty*, 272d-273b

46 HEGEL: *Philosophy of History*, INTRO, 171c-172b

4f. The relation of natural law to civil or municipal law: the state of nature and the regulations of the civil state

5 SOPHOCLES: *Antigone* [450–460] 135a

9 ARISTOTLE: *Ethics*, BK V, CH 7 [1134ᵇ18–1135ª4] 382c-d / *Rhetoric*, BK I, CH 13 [1373ᵇ1–18] 617c-d; CH 15 [1375ª26–ᵇ8] 619d-620a; [1376ª33–ᵇ31] 621a-c

18 AUGUSTINE: *Confessions*, BK III, par 15 17a-b; par 17 17d-18a / *City of God*, BK I, CH 21 142d-143a; BK XIX, CH 12 517b-519a; CH 21 524a-525a; CH 24 528b-c

20 AQUINAS: *Summa Theologica*, PART I–II, Q 91, A 3 209d-210c; Q 94, AA 4–6 223d-226b passim; Q 95, A 2 227c-228c; A 4, ANS 229b-230c; Q 99, A 3, REP 2 247a-248a

23 HOBBES: *Leviathan*, PART I, 84c-87b; 91a-96b passim; PART II, 99a-b; 103a; 115b-c; 124d-125a; 131a-c; 132c-d; 134b-135b; 138c; 142a-c; 156b-c; PART IV, 273c-d

24 RABELAIS: *Gargantua and Pantagruel*, BK II, 87a

25 MONTAIGNE: *Essays*, 281a-282a; 516c-517a; 519a-520b

31 SPINOZA: *Ethics*, PART IV, PROP 37, SCHOL 2 435b-436a

32 MILTON: *Samson Agonistes* [888–902] 359a

35 LOCKE: *Civil Government*, CH II, SECT 7–13 26c-28b; CH VII, SECT 89 44d; CH IX 53c-54d; CH XI 55b-58b; CH XIII, SECT 149 59b-d; CH XIV, SECT 159 62b-c; SECT 168 64b-c; CH XV, SECT 171 65a-b

38 MONTESQUIEU: *Spirit of Laws*, BK I, 1c-d; BK VIII, 52a; BK XVI, 119d; BK XXVI, 215b-218a; 219d-221c

38 ROUSSEAU: *Inequality*, 333b-c; 353d-355b; 361c-362a / *Political Economy*, 369a-b; 370d / *Social Contract*, BK I, 393b-394d; BK II, 397a; 399b-c; 405d-406a

39 SMITH: *Wealth of Nations*, BK I, 52b-c; 61b; BK IV, 228a; BK V, 397a-c

41 GIBBON: *Decline and Fall*, 82b; 86d-89b esp 86d-87d

(4. *The natural law. 4f. The relation of natural law to civil or municipal law: the state of nature and the regulations of the civil state.*)

42 KANT: *Pure Reason*, 222b-c / *Science of Right*, 397a-b; 402c; 405d-406c; 426b-429a; 430a-432c; 433c-434d; 435c-436b

43 FEDERALIST: NUMBER 43, 143b-c

43 MILL: *Utilitarianism*, 470d-471b

44 BOSWELL: *Johnson*, 120b-c; 275d

46 HEGEL: *Philosophy of Right*, PART III, par 214 71a-c; par 217 72b-c; ADDITIONS, 1 115a-d / *Philosophy of History*, INTRO, 186a-c; PART I, 207b-c; 208b-d; PART IV, 361c-d

4g. The relation of natural law to the law of nations and to international law: sovereign states and the state of nature

12 AURELIUS: *Meditations*, BK IV, SECT 4 264a

14 PLUTARCH: *Camillus*, 108b-109a

20 AQUINAS: *Summa Theologica*, PART I-II, Q 94, A 4 223d-224d; Q 95, A 2, ANS 227c-228c; A 4 229b-230c

23 HOBBES: *Leviathan*, PART I, 86a; PART II, 114b-c; 159c

24 RABELAIS: *Gargantua and Pantagruel*, BK I, 13a-b

35 LOCKE: *Civil Government*, CH II, SECT 9 27a-b; SECT 14 28b-c; CH III, SECT 19 29b-c; CH XII, SECT 145-146 58d-59a

38 MONTESQUIEU: *Spirit of Laws*, BK I, 2d-3b; BK X, 61b,d-63d; BK XXIV, 201b-c; BK XXVI, 223c-224a

38 ROUSSEAU: *Inequality*, 355b-c / *Political Economy*, 369a-b / *Social Contract*, BK I, 389d-390d

41 GIBBON: *Decline and Fall*, 604c [n 107]

42 KANT: *Science of Right*, 435a-b; 452a-455c esp 452a-d; 456b-457a

43 FEDERALIST: NUMBER 64, 197d-198a; NUMBER 75, 223b-c

46 HEGEL: *Philosophy of Right*, PART III, par 338 110a-b / *Philosophy of History*, PART IV, 361c-d

4h. The precepts of the natural law and the condition of the state of nature with respect to slavery and property

9 ARISTOTLE: *Politics*, BK I, CH 5-6 447d-449b

12 EPICTETUS: *Discourses*, BK I, CH 13 120b-c

18 AUGUSTINE: *City of God*, BK XIX, CH 15 521a-c

19 AQUINAS: *Summa Theologica*, PART I, Q 92, A 1, REP 2 488d-489d; Q 96, A 4 512d-513c

20 AQUINAS: *Summa Theologica*, PART I-II, Q 94, A 5, REP 3 224d-225d

22 CHAUCER: *Parson's Tale*, par 65-67, 531a-532a

23 HOBBES: *Leviathan*, PART I, 85d; 86b; 91a-b; 94b-c; PART II, 103a; 124d-125c

35 LOCKE: *Civil Government*, CH IV-V 29d-36a; CH VII, SECT 85 43c-d; SECT 87 44a-b; CH IX 53c-54d passim; CH XI, SECT 138-140 57b-58a; CH XV, SECT 171-173 65a-c; CH XVI, SECT 183 67d-68b

38 MONTESQUIEU: *Spirit of Laws*, BK XV, 109b-110a; 110d-111b; BK XXVI, 216a-217b

38 ROUSSEAU: *Inequality*, 333b-d; 348b,d; 353a; 353d-355b; 356c-357a; 357c-358b / *Political Economy*, 368a / *Social Contract*, BK I, 388a-c; 389a-390d; 393c-394d

39 SMITH: *Wealth of Nations*, BK I, 52b-c; BK IV, 228a; BK V, 309a-311c

41 GIBBON: *Decline and Fall*, 86d-87b

42 KANT: *Science of Right*, 401b-402a; 413d-414a; 421c-422d; 445c-446a; 454a-455a

43 DECLARATION OF INDEPENDENCE: [7-10] 1a

46 HEGEL: *Philosophy of Right*, PART I, par 49 24c-25a

50 MARX-ENGELS: *Communist Manifesto*, 427b

5. The human or positive law: the sanction of coercive force

7 PLATO: *Crito* 213a-219a,c esp 216b-219a,c / *Republic*, BK IV, 344a-345d / *Statesman*, 599c-604b / *Laws*, BK IV, 684b-686c

9 ARISTOTLE: *Ethics*, BK X, CH 9 [1179^{a}35-1180^{b}28] 434a-435c / *Politics*, BK III, CH 15 [1286^{b}28-41] 485b / *Athenian Constitution*, CH 12, par 4 557d-558a

18 AUGUSTINE: *City of God*, BK XIX, CH 17, 522d-523a

20 AQUINAS: *Summa Theologica*, PART I-II, Q 90, A 1 205b-206b; A 3, REP 2 207a-c; QQ 95-97 226b-239b

23 MACHIAVELLI: *Prince*, CH XII, 18a

23 HOBBES: *Leviathan*, PART II, 103a; 113c; 130b-138d

29 CERVANTES: *Don Quixote*, PART II, 362b

30 BACON: *Advancement of Learning*, 94d-95b

35 LOCKE: *Toleration*, 3a; 3c-4a / *Civil Government*, CH IX 53c-54d passim; CH XIX, SECT 219 75b-c / *Human Understanding*, BK I, CH II, SECT 5 105a-b; BK II, CH XXVIII, SECT 6 229d; SECT 9-13 230b-231c esp SECT 9 230b

38 MONTESQUIEU: *Spirit of Laws*, BK I, 3c

38 ROUSSEAU: *Inequality*, 345d / *Political Economy*, 371a-c / *Social Contract*, BK II, 399b-400c; BK IV, 426b-d

41 GIBBON: *Decline and Fall*, 71b,d-96d

42 KANT: *Intro. Metaphysic of Morals*, 392b / *Science of Right*, 439a-b

43 FEDERALIST: NUMBER 15, 65a-d; NUMBER 16 66c-68d passim, esp 67d-68a; NUMBER 21, 78b-d; NUMBER 28, 96c; NUMBER 33, 108d

43 MILL: *Utilitarianism*, 467d-468c passim

46 HEGEL: *Philosophy of Right*, PART III, par 211-228 70a-75b; ADDITIONS, 131 137d / *Philosophy of History*, PART III, 290a-b; PART IV, 364d-365a

5a. The difference between laws and decrees

7 PLATO: *Laws*, BK IX, 745c-746a

9 ARISTOTLE: *Politics*, BK IV, CH 4 [1292^{a}4-37] 491b-d

20 AQUINAS: *Summa Theologica*, PART I-II, Q 96, A 1, REP 1 230c-231c

35 LOCKE: *Civil Government*, CH IX, SECT 131 54d; CH XI, SECT 136-137 56c-57b

38 MONTESQUIEU: *Spirit of Laws*, BK II, 6b; BK VI, 33a-34d; BK XXIX, 268c

38 ROUSSEAU: *Social Contract*, BK II, 395b-d; 397b-c; 399c-400a

41 GIBBON: *Decline and Fall*, 73d-74b

42 KANT: *Science of Right*, 438a-b

43 FEDERALIST: NUMBER 64, 197a-c

46 HEGEL: *Philosophy of Right*, PART III, par 299 99c-100b / *Philosophy of History*, PART I, 207b-c

5*b*. The kinds or divisions of positive law

7 PLATO: *Laws*, BK III, 674b

9 ARISTOTLE: *Ethics*, BK V, CH 2 [1130^{b}30–1131^{a}9] 378b-c / *Politics*, BK IV, CH 1 [1289^{a}13–25] 488a-b

14 PLUTARCH: *Lycurgus*, 38c

20 AQUINAS: *Summa Theologica*, PART I–II, Q 95, A 4 229b-230c; Q 100, A 2, ANS 252b-253a

23 HOBBES: *Leviathan*, PART II, 136b-137b; 138b-c

38 MONTESQUIEU: *Spirit of Laws*, BK XXVI, 221c-223b passim

38 ROUSSEAU: *Social Contract*, BK II, 406a-d

41 GIBBON: *Decline and Fall*, 96a

43 FEDERALIST: NUMBER 53, 167d-168b; NUMBER 81, 241c-d; NUMBER 84, 252a-b

46 HEGEL: *Philosophy of Right*, PART I, par 40 21d-22c; PART III, par 211 70a-c

5*c*. The justice of positive law: the standards of natural law and constitutionality

5 SOPHOCLES: *Antigone* [450–460] 135a

5 EURIPIDES: *Bacchantes* [878–911] 347b-c

6 THUCYDIDES: *Peloponnesian War*, BK II, 396c-d

7 PLATO: *Protagoras*, 52b / *Gorgias*, 271b-272b; 273d-274c / *Statesman*, 598b-604b / *Laws*, BK IV, 680c-683b; BK IX, 747c; BK X, 760c

8 ARISTOTLE: *Sophistical Refutations*, CH 12 [173^{a}7–19] 238b-c

9 ARISTOTLE: *Ethics*, BK V, CH 1 [1129^{b}12–24] 377a; CH 7 382c-383a; CH 9 [1136^{b}32–35] 385a; CH 11 [1138^{a}4–13] 386b-c / *Politics*, BK I, CH 6 [1255^{a}3–^{b}4] 448c-449a; BK III, CH 11 [1282^{b}1–14] 480b-c; CH 16 [1287^{a}28–^{b}5] 485d-486a; BK IV, CH 1 [1289^{a}13–25] 488a-b / *Rhetoric*, BK I, CH 10 [1368^{b}7–10] 611d; CH 13 [1373^{b}1–17] 617c-d; CH 15 [1375^{a}25–^{b}25] 619d-620b; [1376^{a}33–^{b}31] 621a-c

12 AURELIUS: *Meditations*, BK IV, SECT 4 264a

18 AUGUSTINE: *Confessions*, BK III, par 15 17a-b; par 17 17d-18a / *City of God*, BK II, CH 21 161b-162d; BK XIX, CH 21 524a-525a; CH 24 528b-c / *Christian Doctrine*, BK IV, CH 18 686d-687d

20 AQUINAS: *Summa Theologica*, PART I–II, Q 91, A 3 209d-210c; Q 93, A 3 217b-218a; Q 95, A 2 227c-228c; Q 96, A 4, ANS 233a-d

23 HOBBES: *Leviathan*, PART I, 91a-b; PART II, 131a-c; 132a-b; 134b-135b; 156b-c; 157b-c

25 MONTAIGNE: *Essays*, 47c-48a; 281a-282a; 384b-c; 519a-520b

30 BACON: *Advancement of Learning*, 94d-95b

32 MILTON: *Samson Agonistes* [888–902] 359a

33 PASCAL: *Pensées*, 291–338 225a-233a; 878–879 345a-b

35 LOCKE: *Civil Government*, CH II, SECT 12 27d-28a; CH IX 53c-54d; CH XI 55b-58b; CH XVIII 71a-73c passim; CH XIX, SECT 221–222 75d-76c; SECT 240–242 81b-d

38 MONTESQUIEU: *Spirit of Laws*, BK I, 1c-d; 3c-d; BK VI, 39b; BK VIII, 54b; BK XII, 85c-86d; BK XIX, 136a; 138a-c; BK XXVI, 214b,d-225a passim, esp 214b,d-215a; BK XXIX, 262a-b; 265d

38 ROUSSEAU: *Political Economy*, 369c-d; 370d / *Social Contract*, BK II, 399b-400a; 405a-406a; BK IV, 426b-d

39 SMITH: *Wealth of Nations*, BK I, 61b; BK II, 140b; BK IV, 228a; 284d; BK V, 397a-b

40 GIBBON: *Decline and Fall*, 525d-526c; 617b-d

41 GIBBON: *Decline and Fall*, 76d-77b; 89d-94b passim; 403b-404d

42 KANT: *Pure Reason*, 114b-d / *Science of Right*, 429a-c; 434a; 435a-436a; 450d-451c

43 DECLARATION OF INDEPENDENCE: 1a-3b

43 CONSTITUTION OF THE U.S.: PREAMBLE 11a,c; ARTICLE I, SECT 8–10 13a-14b; ARTICLE VI [583–590] 16d; AMENDMENTS, I–X 17a-18a

43 FEDERALIST: NUMBER 33, 108b-109b; NUMBER 44, 145c-147a; NUMBER 78, 230d-232d passim; NUMBER 81, 237d-238b

43 MILL: *Liberty*, 302d-323a,c passim / *Utilitarianism*, 465d-466b; 467c-d

44 BOSWELL: *Johnson*, 203d-204a; 205b-c; 363c-364a

46 HEGEL: *Philosophy of Right*, PART III, par 212–213 70d-71a / *Philosophy of History*, PART IV, 364b

5*d*. The origins of positive law in the legislative process: the function of the legislator

7 PLATO: *Republic*, BK I, 301c-302b; BK IV, 344a-346a / *Theaetetus*, 531a-b / *Statesman*, 599c-600d / *Laws*, BK III, 666b-c; BK IV, 679c-680d; 684b-686c; BK VI, 705d-706c; BK IX, 745c-746a; 754a-d; BK XI, 782a-b / *Seventh Letter*, 807a-b

9 ARISTOTLE: *Ethics*, BK VI, CH 8 [1141^{b}23–33] 390d-391a; BK X, CH 9 434a-436a,c / *Politics*, BK III, CH 11 [1282^{b}1–14] 480b-c; BK IV, CH 14 498b-499c / *Rhetoric*, BK I, CH 1 [1354^{a}13–1355^{a}3] 593b-594a

12 LUCRETIUS: *Nature of Things*, BK V [1143–1160] 76a-b

14 PLUTARCH: *Lycurgus* 32a-48d / *Solon* 64b,d-77a,c

15 TACITUS: *Annals*, BK III, 51a-52a

(5. *The human or positive law: the sanction of coercive force. 5d. The origins of positive law in the legislative process: the function of the legislator.*)

20 AQUINAS: *Summa Theologica*, PART I–II, Q 90, A 4 207d-208b; Q 95, A 1 226c-227c; A 4, ANS 229b-230c

23 HOBBES: *Leviathan*, PART II, 103a; 123b-d; 130d-131a; 131d-132a; 133d-134a; 151c-152a; PART IV, 273d

29 CERVANTES: *Don Quixote*, PART II, 363d-364a

30 BACON: *Advancement of Learning*, 94d-95a

31 DESCARTES: *Discourse*, PART II, 44d-45a

35 LOCKE: *Toleration*, 11b; 16a-c / *Civil Government*, CH VII, SECT 88–89 44c-d; CH IX, SECT 127–CH X, SECT 132 54a-55b; CH XI, SECT 134 55b-d; CH XI, SECT 141–CH XII, SECT 143 58a-d; CH XIII, SECT 150 59d; CH XIX, SECT 212–217 74a-75a

36 SWIFT: *Gulliver*, PART II, 73a-74b

38 MONTESQUIEU: *Spirit of Laws*, BK II, 6b; BK VI, 33a-35c; BK XI, 69d; 71a-72b passim; BK XXIX 262a-269a,c

38 ROUSSEAU: *Inequality*, 324c-d / *Political Economy*, 368c-369a / *Social Contract*, BK II, 399b-402a; BK III, 419c-423a

40 GIBBON: *Decline and Fall*, 27d-28a; 154a-b; 616d-617a; 624b-c

41 GIBBON: *Decline and Fall*, 71d-75b esp 72a, 73b-c; 79d-80b; 93b-c; 108a-c

42 KANT: *Intro. Metaphysic of Morals*, 393c / *Science of Right*, 397a-b; 436b-c; 438b-c; 451d-452a

43 DECLARATION OF INDEPENDENCE: [29–47] 1b-2a; [62–64] [78–79] 2b

43 CONSTITUTION OF THE U.S.: ARTICLE I, SECT 1–9 11a-14a

43 FEDERALIST: NUMBER 33, 107b-108c; NUMBER 38, 121b-124a; NUMBER 40, 130c-132a; NUMBER 44, 145c-146d; NUMBER 53, 168b-169b

43 MILL: *Representative Government*, 356b-362c

44 BOSWELL: *Johnson*, 255d

46 HEGEL: *Philosophy of Right*, PART III, par 298 99c / *Philosophy of History*, PART II, 271d-273a; PART III, 290a-b; PART IV, 364d-365d

5e. The mutability or variability of positive law: the maintenance or change of laws

OLD TESTAMENT: *Esther*, 1:19 / *Daniel*, 6 esp 6:8, 6:15

6 HERODOTUS: *History*, BK I, 6c; BK III, 108c

6 THUCYDIDES: *Peloponnesian War*, BK III, 425a-c; 438a-b

7 PLATO: *Republic*, BK IV, 344b-345d; BK VIII, 403a-404a / *Statesman*, 598b-604b / *Laws*, BK IV, 679c-680d; BK VI, 705d-706c; 707a-b; BK VII, 717d-718c; BK VIII, 740c-d

9 ARISTOTLE: *Ethics*, BK V, CH 7 [1134^{b}18–1135^{a}4] 382c-d / *Politics*, BK II, CH 8 [1268^{b}23–1269^{a}28] 464d-465b; BK V, CH 9 [1310^{a}12–19] 512b-c / *Rhetoric*, BK I, CH 15 [1375^{a}25–^{b}25] 619d-620b

14 PLUTARCH: *Lycurgus*, 38c; 47a-48a / *Lycurgus-Numa*, 63d-64a,c / *Solon*, 69c-d / *Agesilaus*, 494a-c / *Agesilaus-Pompey*, 539a

15 TACITUS: *Annals*, BK I, 21b-c; BK III, 51a-52a; 57d-58b; BK XI, 106d; BK XIV, 151d-152c

20 AQUINAS: *Summa Theologica*, PART I–II, Q 97 235d-239b

23 HOBBES: *Leviathan*, PART I, 78b-c; PART II, 116a-b; 157c-d

25 MONTAIGNE: *Essays*, 47a-51a; 131b-132a; 281a-c; 318c-319b; 462c-465c; 504c-506a; 516c-517a

35 LOCKE: *Civil Government*, CH XIII, SECT 157–158 61c-62b; CH XIX, SECT 223 76c-d

38 MONTESQUIEU: *Spirit of Laws*, BK XI, 77d; BK XIV, 102b; 104c; BK XVIII, 126d; BK XIX, 135d-136a; BK XXIX, 268d

38 ROUSSEAU: *Inequality*, 324d / *Social Contract*, BK II, 405d-406b; BK III, 419c-420a

39 SMITH: *Wealth of Nations*, BK III, 166a

41 GIBBON: *Decline and Fall*, 78b-81c passim, esp 80d-81b; 96b-c

42 KANT: *Science of Right*, 441b-c; 450d-452a

43 DECLARATION OF INDEPENDENCE: [76–77] 2b

43 CONSTITUTION OF THE U.S.: ARTICLE V 16c

43 FEDERALIST: NUMBER 37, 118d-119b; NUMBER 39, 127d-128b; NUMBER 40 128b-132a; NUMBER 43, 143a-b; NUMBER 49–50 159b-162c; NUMBER 53, 167d-168b; NUMBER 62, 190d-191c; NUMBER 64, 197a-c; NUMBER 73, 220a-b; NUMBER 81, 239a-b; NUMBER 85, 257a-259a

43 MILL: *Representative Government*, 359a-d; 360c

44 BOSWELL: *Johnson*, 203d-205a; 205d; 276a-b; 277b

46 HEGEL: *Philosophy of Right*, INTRO, par 3, 11c-d; PART III, par 216 71d-72a; ADDITIONS, 176 147c-d

47 GOETHE: *Faust*, PART I [1972–1979] 46b-47a

50 MARX-ENGELS: *Communist Manifesto*, 427a-b

51 TOLSTOY: *War and Peace*, BK VI, 238c-243d; BK VIII, 308d

5f. The relation of positive law to custom

5 EURIPIDES: *Bacchantes* [877–911] 347b-c / *Hecuba* [798–805] 359d

6 HERODOTUS: *History*, BK III, 97d-98a

7 PLATO: *Symposium*, 154a-c / *Republic*, BK IV, 344b-d; BK VII, 401c-d / *Statesman*, 600a-b / *Laws*, BK III, 666b-c; BK IV, 678d-679a; BK VII, 713c-716b; 718b-c; 730d-731b; BK VIII, 736c-737a

8 ARISTOTLE: *Metaphysics*, BK II, CH 3 [995^{a}4–6] 513c

9 ARISTOTLE: *Ethics*, BK V, CH 7 382c-383a / *Politics*, BK II, CH 8 [1268^{b}23–1269^{a}28] 464d-465b; BK III, CH 16 [1287^{b}5–7] 486a; BK V, CH 8 [1307^{b}30–38] 509d-510a; CH 9 [1310^{a}12–19] 512b-c

14 PLUTARCH: *Lycurgus* 32a-48d esp 38b-d / *Lycurgus-Numa*, 63d-64a / *Themistocles*, 99b-c

15 TACITUS: *Annals*, BK XII, 111b-c; BK XIV, 151d-152c

5g. The application of positive law to cases: the casuistry of the judicial process; the conduct of a trial; the administration of justice

6b. The exemption of the sovereign person from the coercive force of law

6c. The force of tyrannical, unjust, or bad laws: the right of rebellion or disobedience

6d. The educative function of law in relation to virtue and vice: the efficacy of law as limited by virtue in the individual citizen

(6. Law and the individual. 6d. The educative function of law in relation to virtue and vice: the efficacy of law as limited by virtue in the individual citizen.)

15 TACITUS: *Annals*, BK III, 57b-58d

20 AQUINAS: *Summa Theologica*, PART I-II, Q 92 213c-215a,c; Q 95, A 1 226c-227c; Q 96, AA 2-3 231c-233a; Q 98, A 6, ANS 244c-245b; Q 100 251a-265d

21 DANTE: *Divine Comedy*, PURGATORY, XVI [85-105] 77d

23 HOBBES: *Leviathan*, PART II, 131a-b; 140b-141b; 149b-c; 153a-155c

25 MONTAIGNE: *Essays*, 131b-132a

27 SHAKESPEARE: *Measure for Measure*, ACT I, SC III [19-39] 177c; ACT II, SC I [225-270] 181a-c; ACT V, SC I [318-324] 202b

30 BACON: *Advancement of Learning*, 78d-81c

32 MILTON: *Paradise Lost*, BK XII [285-306] 325b-326a / *Areopagitica*, 383a-395b

35 LOCKE: *Toleration*, 8c; 14a / *Human Understanding*, BK II, CH XXVIII, SECT 9-13 230b-231c

37 FIELDING: *Tom Jones*, 267b-268b

38 MONTESQUIEU: *Spirit of Laws*, BK IV, 13b,d-17b; BK V, 18b,d-23a; BK VII, 44d-45c; 47c-50c; BK XII, 86b; 87c-88a; BK XIV, 104a-108d passim; BK XVI, 119d; BK XIX, 138c-142a

38 ROUSSEAU: *Inequality*, 345d; 359d / *Political Economy*, 372a-377b esp 372a-373a, 375d-377a / *Social Contract*, BK I, 393b-c; BK II, 400d-401a; BK IV, 434b-435a

40 GIBBON: *Decline and Fall*, 100c-101b; 291d

41 GIBBON: *Decline and Fall*, 93d-94a

42 KANT: *Pref. Metaphysical Elements of Ethics*, 367b-c; 373b-c / *Intro. Metaphysic of Morals*, 383a-b / *Science of Right*, 448d-449c

43 CONSTITUTION OF THE U.S.: AMENDMENTS, XVIII 19c-d; XXI 20c

43 FEDERALIST: NUMBER 12, 58b-c

43 MILL: *Liberty*, 272d-273d; 302d-312a passim, esp 306b-307a; 315d-316b / *Representative Government*, 336c-337b / *Utilitarianism*, 467b-468a

44 BOSWELL: *Johnson*, 222d-223b; 301c-d

46 HEGEL: *Philosophy of Right*, PART III, par 150 56c-57a; par 153 57c / *Philosophy of History*, INTRO, 166b; PART IV, 333c-d

49 DARWIN: *Descent of Man*, 328c-d

52 DOSTOEVSKY: *Brothers Karamazov*, BK II, 30d-32a

54 FREUD: *War and Death*, 758c-d

6e. The breach of law: crime and punishment

6e(1) The nature and causes of crime

6 THUCYDIDES: *Peloponnesian War*, BK II, 400d-401a; BK III, 436d-438b

7 PLATO: *Laws*, BK II, 654c-d; BK V, 690d-691b; BK IX, 743c; 746a-750a; BK X, 758b-

760c; BK XI 771b-784b passim; BK XII, 784b-786b; 791c-d

9 ARISTOTLE: *Ethics*, BK V, CH 2 [1130^{b}30-1131^{a}9] 378b-c; CH 11 [1138^{a}4-13] 386b-c / *Politics*, BK II, CH 7 461d-463c esp [1267^{a}2-16] 462c-d; BK IV, CH 11 [1295^{b}3-12] 495c / *Rhetoric*, BK I, CH 10-14 611c-619d

18 AUGUSTINE: *Christian Doctrine*, BK III, CH 10, 662a

23 HOBBES: *Leviathan*, PART II, 139c-144d

25 MONTAIGNE: *Essays*, 23b-c; 334b-335a

31 SPINOZA: *Ethics*, PART IV, PROP 37, SCHOL 2 435b-436a

35 LOCKE: *Civil Government*, CH II, SECT 6-13 26b-28b

37 FIELDING: *Tom Jones*, 271c-273a,c

38 MONTESQUIEU: *Spirit of Laws*, BK XII, 85c-86d

38 ROUSSEAU: *Inequality*, 364d

39 SMITH: *Wealth of Nations*, BK V, 309a-c; 397a-c

40 GIBBON: *Decline and Fall*, 35a; 175c

41 GIBBON: *Decline and Fall*, 92c; 93c

42 KANT: *Intro. Metaphysic of Morals*, 391d-392a / *Science of Right*, 446a-b

46 HEGEL: *Philosophy of Right*, PART I, par 95-102 36b-39b; PART III, par 218 72c-d; par 319, 106a

50 MARX: *Capital*, 364a-c

52 DOSTOEVSKY: *Brothers Karamazov*, BK II, 33c-34b

54 FREUD: *Ego and Id*, 714a-b

6e(2) The prevention of crime

5 AESCHYLUS: *Eumenides* [490-565] 86b-87a

5 SOPHOCLES: *Electra* [1501-1507] 169a,c

5 EURIPIDES: *Orestes* [491-525] 399a-b

5 ARISTOPHANES: *Clouds* [1303-1464] 504b-506c

6 HERODOTUS: *History*, BK II, 87a-b; BK V, 164c

6 THUCYDIDES: *Peloponnesian War*, BK II, 400d-401a; BK III, 424d-429a

7 PLATO: *Protagoras*, 45b-d / *Gorgias*, 267c-270c / *Republic*, BK II, 321d-322d / *Laws*, BK V, 688d-689a; 690d-691b; BK IX, 743a-c; 757a; BK X, 769d-770c; BK XI, 782a-b; BK XII, 786a

9 ARISTOTLE: *Ethics*, BK III, CH 5 [1113^{b}21-1114^{a}2] 359d-360a; BK X, CH 9 [1179^{a}33-1180^{a}32] 434a-435a / *Politics*, BK II, CH 7 461d-463c esp [1267^{a}2-16] 462c-d / *Rhetoric*, BK I, CH 12 [1372^{a}23-27] 615d-616a; CH 14 [1375^{a}1-7] 619b-c

15 TACITUS: *Annals*, BK III, 61c-d; BK XIV, 151d-152c; BK XV, 162c-d

18 AUGUSTINE: *City of God*, BK XIX, CH 16 521d-522a

20 AQUINAS: *Summa Theologica*, PART I-II, Q 87, A 3, REP 2 187b-188b; Q 105, A 2, REP 9 309d-316a

22 CHAUCER: *Tale of Melibeus*, par 40 418b-419a

23 HOBBES: *Leviathan*, PART I, 94a; PART II, 140a; 141b; 143d; 145a; 145d; 147a-b; 157d-158a

6e(3) The punishment of crime

7. Law and the state

7a. The distinction between government by men and government by laws: the nature of constitutional or political law

5 AESCHYLUS: *Eumenides* [681–710] 88b-c

5 SOPHOCLES: *Oedipus at Colonus* [907–931] 122d-123a

5 EURIPIDES: *Suppliants* [399–462] 261d-262b

5 ARISTOPHANES: *Wasps* [463–507] 512d-513c

6 HERODOTUS: *History*, BK III, 107c-d; BK VII, 233a-d

6 THUCYDIDES: *Peloponnesian War*, BK I, 368c-d; BK II, 396b-c

7 PLATO: *Statesman*, 598b-604b / *Laws*, BK III, 667c-d; BK IV, 681b-682c; BK IX, 754a-b / *Seventh Letter*, 805d; 807a-b

9 ARISTOTLE: *Ethics*, BK V, CH 6 [1134^{a}25–^{b}8] 382a-b; BK X, CH 9 [1180^{a}14–24] 434d-435a / *Politics*, BK I, CH 1 [1252^{a}6–16] 445a-b; CH 5 [1254^{a}34–^{b}9] 448a; CH 7 [1255^{b}15–20] 449b; CH 12 453d-454a; BK II, CH 10 [1272^{a}35–^{b}11] 468d-469a; BK III, CH 10 [1281^{a}29–38] 479a; CH 11 [1282^{b}1–14] 480b-c; CH 15 [1285^{b}34]–CH 17 [1288^{a}5] 484b-486c; BK IV, CH 4 [1292^{a}4–37] 491b-d; CH 6 492b-493a; CH 8 [1293^{b}22–27] 493c; CH 10 [1295^{a}9–23] 495a-b

14 PLUTARCH: *Cato the Younger*, 635a-b; 638b-639a

15 TACITUS: *Annals*, BK II, 36b; BK III, 51b-c; 61c-62a

20 AQUINAS: *Summa Theologica*, PART I–II, Q 90, A 3 207a-c; Q 95, A 1, REP 2 226c-227c

23 HOBBES: *Leviathan*, PART II, 149d-150a; PART IV, 273a-c

27 SHAKESPEARE: *Henry VIII*, ACT I, SC II [91–101] 553d

35 LOCKE: *Civil Government* 25a-81d esp CH IV, SECT 21 29d, CH VI, SECT 57 36d-37b, CH VII, SECT 87–94 44a-46c, CH XI, SECT 137 56d-57b, CH XVIII, SECT 199–202 71a-72a

38 MONTESQUIEU: *Spirit of Laws*, BK II, 4a; 7c-9a,c; BK III, 12a-13c; BK VI, 33a-35a; BK XIX, 137c-d

38 ROUSSEAU: *Inequality*, 323d-324a; 358b; 361c-362a / *Social Contract*, BK II, 400a

41 GIBBON: *Decline and Fall*, 96d

42 KANT: *Pure Reason*, 114b-d / *Science of Right*, 401c; 436c-d; 451b-c / *Judgement*, 586c

43 DECLARATION OF INDEPENDENCE: 1a-3b passim

43 CONSTITUTION OF THE U.S.: ARTICLE VI [583–599] 16d

43 FEDERALIST: NUMBER 33 107b-109b passim; NUMBER 44, 146d-147a; NUMBER 53, 167d-168b

43 MILL: *Representative Government*, 340a-c

46 HEGEL: *Philosophy of Right*, PART III, par 260–271 82a-89c; par 349 111d-112a; ADDITIONS, 171 146b-c / *Philosophy of History*, INTRO, 198b-199c; PART I, 213b; PART II, 271d; PART III, 303a-b; PART IV, 329b-c; 342b-c

54 FREUD: *Civilization and Its Discontents*, 780b-d

7b. The supremacy of law as the principle of political freedom

5 EURIPIDES: *Suppliants* [429–441] 262a-b

6 THUCYDIDES: *Peloponnesian War*, BK II, 396c-d; BK III, 438a-b

7 PLATO: *Laws*, BK III, 672d-674d

9 ARISTOTLE: *Politics*, BK III, CH 17 [1288^{a}11–14] 486d; BK IV, CH 4 [1292^{a}4–37] 491b-d; BK V, CH 9 [1310^{a}25–36] 512c / *Athenian Constitution*, CH 45 573d-574a

12 AURELIUS: *Meditations*, BK I, SECT 14 254b-c

35 LOCKE: *Civil Government*, CH IV, SECT 21 29d; CH VI, SECT 57–60 36d-38a; CH IX, SECT 124–131 53d-54d; CH XI, SECT 136–139 56c-58a; CH XVIII, SECT 202 71d-72a; SECT 206 72c

38 MONTESQUIEU: *Spirit of Laws*, BK VI, 34c-d; BK XI, 69a-b; BK XII, 85a-c; BK XV, 109c; 112c-d; BK XXVI, 223c-d

38 ROUSSEAU: *Inequality*, 353d-355b esp 354d-355a / *Political Economy*, 370b-d; 375b-c / *Social Contract*, BK I, 393b-c

39 SMITH: *Wealth of Nations*, BK V, 314d-315a,c

42 KANT: *Science of Right*, 398c-399c; 436c-d

43 DECLARATION OF INDEPENDENCE: [1–47] 1a-2a passim; [72–79] 2b

43 CONSTITUTION OF THE U.S.: PREAMBLE 11a,c; AMENDMENTS, V–VII 17b-d; XIII, SECT 1–XIV, SECT 1 18c-d

43 FEDERALIST: NUMBER 1, 30a-c; NUMBER 9, 47b-c; NUMBER 53, 167d-168b; NUMBER 57, 177d-178a; NUMBER 84, 251b-253d

43 MILL: *Liberty* 267a-323a,c passim, esp 267b,d-274a / *Representative Government*, 339d-340c

46 HEGEL: *Philosophy of Right*, PART III, par 208 69c; par 265 84b; par 286 96c-97a; ADDITIONS, 129 137c; 135 138c / *Philosophy of History*, INTRO, 170c-171c; 180c-d; PART I, 230a-c; PART II, 271d-272d; PART IV, 321a; 342b-d; 345a-b; 364b-c

7c. The priority of natural to civil law: the inviolability or inalienability of natural rights

5 SOPHOCLES: *Antigone* [450–460] 135a

9 ARISTOTLE: *Rhetoric*, BK I, CH 13 [1373^{b}1–17] 617c-d; CH 15 [1375^{a}25–^{b}13] 619d-620a; [1376^{a}33–^{b}31] 621a-c

18 AUGUSTINE: *City of God*, BK II, CH 21 161b-162d; BK XIX, CH 21 524a-525a

20 AQUINAS: *Summa Theologica*, PART I–II, Q 94, AA 4–6 223d-226b; Q 95, A 2 227c-228c

23 HOBBES: *Leviathan*, PART I, 86c-87d; 90a-b; 94b-95a; PART II, 115b-116a; 131a-c; 134c; 138c; 142b-c; 153c; PART IV, 273c-d

25 MONTAIGNE: *Essays*, 519a-520b

30 BACON: *Advancement of Learning*, 94d-95b

35 LOCKE: *Toleration*, 20d-21a / *Civil Government*, CH II, SECT 10–12 27b-28a; CH III, SECT 16–19 28d-29c; CH IV, SECT 21 29d; CH VII, SECT 87–94 44a-46c; CH IX 53c-54d; CH XI, SECT 135–140 55d-58a; CH XIV, SECT 168 64b-c; CH XVI–XIX 65d-81d passim

38 MONTESQUIEU: *Spirit of Laws*, BK I, 1c-d; 2b-d; BK XV, 109b-110a; 111a-b; BK XXVI, 215b-217c

38 ROUSSEAU: *Inequality*, 357c-358b / *Social Contract*, BK I, 393d-394d; BK II, 397a-b; 399b-c

39 SMITH: *Wealth of Nations*, BK I, 52b-c; 61b; BK II, 140b; BK IV, 228a

42 KANT: *Science of Right*, 408d-409c; 426b-429b esp 426b-c; 434a; 436a-b; 456b-457a

43 DECLARATION OF INDEPENDENCE: 1a-3b esp [1-28] 1a-b

43 CONSTITUTION OF THE U.S.: AMENDMENTS, IX 17d-18a

43 FEDERALIST: NUMBER 28, 97c; NUMBER 43, 143b-c

43 MILL: *Utilitarianism*, 465d-466b

44 BOSWELL: *Johnson*, 363c-364a

46 HEGEL: *Philosophy of Right*, PART I, par 66 29a-c; PART II, par 127 45b-c; PART III, par 323-324 107a-d; ADDITIONS, 43 123c / *Philosophy of History*, PART IV, 362d-363a; 364d-365a

7*d*. Tyranny and treason or sedition as illegal acts: the use of force without authority

6 THUCYDIDES: *Peloponnesian War*, BK III, 432b-c

7 PLATO: *Laws*, BK IX, 744c-d

9 ARISTOTLE: *Politics*, BK III, CH 10 [1281ᵃ19-28] 478d-479a; BK V, CH 10 [1313ᵃ8-18] 515c-d; BK VII, CH 2 [1324ᵇ23-41] 528d-529a

14 PLUTARCH: *Poplicola*, 77a-80d; 81d / *Timoleon*, 196c-197b / *Lysander-Sulla*, 387b,d-388c

15 TACITUS: *Annals*, BK II, 36b

20 AQUINAS: *Summa Theologica*, PART I-II, Q 92, A 1, REP 4 213c-214c; Q 93, A 3, REP 2 217b-218a; Q 95, A 4, ANS 229b-230c; Q 96, A 4, ANS and REP 2 233a-d; PART II-II, Q 42, A 2 584b-d

23 HOBBES: *Leviathan*, PART II, 101a-102c; 114d-115a; 115d-116a; 121b-122b; 144a; 147c; 150c-151a; 152b-c; 153c; PART IV, 273a-c

26 SHAKESPEARE: *Henry V*, ACT II, SC II [102-144] 540b-c

33 PASCAL: *Pensées*, 298 227a; 325-326 230b-231a; 332 232a-b

35 LOCKE: *Civil Government*, CH XI, SECT 136-140 56c-58a; CH XIII, SECT 155 60d-61a; CH XVII-XIX 70c-81d

38 ROUSSEAU: *Inequality*, 361c-362a / *Social Contract*, BK I, 388d-389a; BK III, 419a-c

40 GIBBON: *Decline and Fall*, 251d; 525d-526c

41 GIBBON: *Decline and Fall*, 92d-93c

42 KANT: *Science of Right*, 439a-441d

43 DECLARATION OF INDEPENDENCE: 1a-3b esp [25-30] 1b

43 ARTICLES OF CONFEDERATION: IV [37-44] 5d; V [74-81] 6a

43 CONSTITUTION OF THE U.S.: ARTICLE II, SECT 4 15c; ARTICLE III, SECT 3 15d-16a

43 FEDERALIST: NUMBER 16, 68b-c; NUMBER 43, 140c-d; NUMBER 65 198a-200c passim; NUMBER 74, 222b-d

43 MILL: *Liberty*, 274b,d [fn 1]

46 HEGEL: *Philosophy of Right*, PART III, par 278 92c-93a / *Philosophy of History*, PART IV, 328b

51 TOLSTOY: *War and Peace*, BK I, 8d-10d; BK XI, 505a-511b; EPILOGUE I, 668a-669d

7*e*. The need for administrative discretion in matters undetermined by law: the royal prerogative

7 PLATO: *Statesman*, 600a-b / *Laws*, BK VI, 705d-706c

9 ARISTOTLE: *Ethics*, BK V, CH 10 385c-386b passim, esp [1137ᵇ26-31] 386a / *Politics*, BK III, CH 16 [1287ᵃ24-28] 485d; [1287ᵇ15-25] 486a-b / *Athenian Constitution*, CH 9 556c-d / *Rhetoric*, BK I, CH 1 [1354ᵇ4-7] 593c

20 AQUINAS: *Summa Theologica*, PART I-II, Q 95, A 1, REP 3 226c-227c; Q 96, A 6, REP 3 235a-d; Q 97, A 4 238b-239b

23 HOBBES: *Leviathan*, PART II, 103c

30 BACON: *Advancement of Learning*, 94d-95a

35 LOCKE: *Civil Government*, CH XII, SECT 147 59a-b; CH XIV 62b-64c

41 GIBBON: *Decline and Fall*, 73d-75b

42 KANT: *Science of Right*, 448a-b

46 HEGEL: *Philosophy of Right*, PART III, par 214 71a-c; ADDITIONS, 134 138b-c

7*f*. The juridical conception of the person: the legal personality of the state and other corporations

23 HOBBES: *Leviathan*, PART I, 96c-98a,c; PART II, 100c-102c; 104a-b; 117b-119a; 119d-120c; 122b-124b esp 122b-c; 130b-d; 132a-b; 151c-152a

38 ROUSSEAU: *Political Economy*, 368d-369a / *Social Contract*, BK I, 392a; 393a; BK II, 396d-397a; BK III, 408b-409a; 412c

42 KANT: *Science of Right*, 429b; 438b; 454a-c

46 HEGEL: *Philosophy of Right*, PART I, par 46 23d-24a; PART III, par 279, 93c; ADDITIONS, 191 150a-c / *Philosophy of History*, PART III, 285b-d; 302d-303c

8. Historical observations on the development of law and on the diversity of legal systems or institutions

NEW TESTAMENT: *Romans*, 3:1-5:21 / *Galatians*, 3:1-5:14

6 HERODOTUS: *History*, BK I, 6c; 14a-c; BK II, 77d-78b; 87a-b; BK III, 96a-b

7 PLATO: *Critias*, 484c-485d / *Laws*, BK III, 664b-670a esp 666b-c, 668a; 674d-676b

9 ARISTOTLE: *Politics*, BK II, CH 7-12 461d-471d passim / *Athenian Constitution* 553a-584a,c passim, esp CH 27, par 3-5 565b-c, CH 63-69 581d-584a,c

12 LUCRETIUS: *Nature of Things*, BK V [1136-1160] 76a-b

14 PLUTARCH: *Romulus*, 26a-b / *Lycurgus* 32a-48d passim / *Numa Pompilius* 49a-61d passim / *Lycurgus-Numa* 61b,d-64a,c / *Solon* 64b,d-77a,c / *Poplicola*, 81b-82a / *Poplicola-Solon*, 86d-87b

CROSS-REFERENCES

For: Other discussions bearing on the kinds of law, see CONSTITUTION 2b; GOD 7c; JUSTICE 1e, 10a; LIBERTY 1b, 3c; LOVE 5b(1); NATURE 2b; NECESSITY AND CONTINGENCY 5c; PRINCIPLE 4, 4b; PUNISHMENT 4c; STATE 3b(2)–3c; VIRTUE AND VICE 4d(3); WAR AND PEACE 1; WILL 5a(4); WORLD 1c; and for the comparable distinctions in the sphere of rights, see JUSTICE 6–6b.

The relation of law to liberty, justice, and peace, see DEMOCRACY 4a; JUSTICE 10–10c; LIBERTY 1d, 1g; MONARCHY 4e(1); TYRANNY 5a; WAR AND PEACE 11a, 11c; and for the distinction between government by law and government by men, see CONSTITUTION 1; MONARCHY 1a(1); TYRANNY 5–5b.

The relation of law to duty, virtue, and sin, see DUTY 3, 5; EDUCATION 4c; SIN 1; VIRTUE AND VICE 4d(3); WILL 8d.

The conception of the common good as an end of government and law, see GOOD AND EVIL 5d; GOVERNMENT 1c; HAPPINESS 5–5b; LIBERTY 1e; STATE 2f.

Other discussions of the making of law, see GOVERNMENT 3c–3c(2); PRUDENCE 6b.

The factors of authority and power in lawmaking, see GOVERNMENT 1d; TYRANNY 1a; and for law in relation to sovereignty, see GOVERNMENT 1a; LIBERTY 1b; TYRANNY 5c; WAR AND PEACE 11d.

Other discussions of the application of laws to particular cases, see GOVERNMENT 3d–3d(2); OPINION 6b; PRUDENCE 6b; and for the problem of equity in the application of law, see JUSTICE 10d; UNIVERSAL AND PARTICULAR 6c.

The relation of law to custom and habit, see CUSTOM AND CONVENTION 6b; HABIT 7.

The consideration of punishment for the breach of human and divine law, see GOD 5i; JUSTICE 10c; PUNISHMENT 4–4d, 5a–5e(2); SIN 6–6e.

Other discussions of the use of lawless force, and of the right of rebellion or civil disobedience, see JUSTICE 10b; REVOLUTION 6a–6b.

ADDITIONAL READINGS

Listed below are works not included in *Great Books of the Western World*, but relevant to the idea and topics with which this chapter deals. These works are divided into two groups:

I. Works by authors represented in this collection.
II. Works by authors not represented in this collection.

For the date, place, and other facts concerning the publication of the works cited, consult the Bibliography of Additional Readings which follows the last chapter of *The Great Ideas*.

I.

AUGUSTINE. *On the Spirit and the Letter*
AQUINAS. *Summa Contra Gentiles*, BK III, CH 111–121, 128–130
——. *Quaestiones Disputatae, De Veritate*, Q 16
——. *The Two Precepts of Charity and the Ten Commandments*
F. BACON. *The Maxims of the Law*
HOBBES. *Philosophical Rudiments Concerning Government and Society*, CH 2–4
——. *The Elements of Law, Natural and Politic*
——. *A Dialogue Between a Philosopher and a Student of the Common Laws of England*
SPINOZA. *Tractatus Theologico-Politicus (Theological-Political Treatise)*, CH 4, 12

HUME. *A Treatise of Human Nature*, BK III, PART II, SECT XI
——. *Of the Original Contract*
A. SMITH. *Lectures on Justice, Police, Revenue and Arms*
KANT. *Lectures on Ethics*, pp 47–70
HEGEL. *The Philosophy of Mind*, SECT II, SUB-SECT A,C (CC,a,β)
FREUD. *Totem and Taboo*

II.

CICERO. *De Republica (The Republic)*, III
——. *De Legibus (The Laws)*
QUINTILIAN. *Institutio Oratoria (Institutes of Oratory)*, BK V; BK VII, CH 5–7, 10
GAIUS. *Commentaries*
Talmud

Chapter 47: LIBERTY

INTRODUCTION

LIBERTY and law, liberty and justice, liberty and equality—the familiar connection of these terms breeds neglect of the meaning they confer upon one another through association. A few simple questions may help to restore the significance of these relationships. Are men free when their actions are regulated by law or coercion? Does liberty consist in doing whatever one pleases or whatever one has the power to do, or is one required by justice to abstain from injury to others? Do considerations of justice draw the line between liberty and license? Can there be liberty apart from equality and perhaps also fraternity?

Other questions immediately suggest themselves. Does not the rule of law secure liberty to the governed? Is not slavery the condition of those who are ruled tyrannically or lawlessly? Does it make a difference to freedom whether the law or the constitution is just? Or is that indifferent because government itself is the impediment to liberty? Does liberty increase as the scope of government dwindles and reach fullness only with anarchy or when men live in a state of nature?

Yet are not some forms of government said to be fitting and some uncongenial to free men? Do all men have a right to freedom, or only some? Are some men by nature free and some slave? Does such a differentiation imply both equality and inequality in human nature with, as a consequence, equality and inequality in status or treatment? What implications for law, justice, and equality has the distinction between free societies and dependent or subject communities?

As Tolstoy points out, the variety of questions which can be asked about liberty indicates the variety of subject matters or sciences in which the problems of freedom are differently raised. "What is sin, the conception of which arises from the consciousness of man's freedom? That is a question for theology ... What is man's responsibility to society, the conception of which results from the conception of freedom? That is a question for jurisprudence ... What is conscience and the perception of right and wrong in actions that follow from the consciousness of freedom? That is a question for ethics ... How should the past life of nations and of humanity be regarded—as the result of the free, or as the result of the constrained, activity of man? That is a question for history."

The great traditional issues of liberty seem to be stated by these questions. From the fact that most, perhaps all, of these questions elicit opposite answers from the great books, it might be supposed that there are as many basic issues as there are questions of this sort. But the answers to certain questions presuppose answers to others. Furthermore, the meaning of liberty or freedom or independence is not the same throughout the questions we have considered. Answers which appear to be inconsistent may not be so when the meanings involved in their formulation are distinguished. We must, therefore, find the roots of the several distinct doctrines of liberty in order to separate real issues from verbal conflicts.

THE HISTORIANS report the age-old struggle on the part of men and of states for liberty or independence. History as a development of the spirit does not begin, according to Hegel, until this struggle first appears. "The History of the world," he writes, "is none other than the progress of the consciousness of Freedom," which does not reach its climax until freedom is universally achieved. But though freedom is its product, history, in Hegel's view, is not a work of freedom, but "involves an absolute necessity." Each stage of its development occurs inevitably.

Other historians see man as free to work out his destiny, and look upon the great crises of civilization as turning points at which free men, that is, men having free will, exercise a free choice for better or for worse. "Whether we speak of the migration of the peoples and the incursions of the barbarians, or of the decrees of Napoleon III, or of someone's action an hour ago in choosing one direction out of several for his walk, we are unconscious of any contradiction," Tolstoy declares, between freedom and necessity. "Our conception of the degree of freedom," he goes on to say, "often varies according to differences in the point of view from which we regard the event, but every human action appears to us as a certain combination of freedom and inevitability. In every action we examine we see a certain measure of freedom and a certain measure of inevitability. And always the more freedom we see in any action the less inevitability do we perceive, and the more inevitability the less freedom."

Accordingly, neither necessity which flows from the laws of matter or of spirit, nor overhanging and indomitable fate determines the direction of events. If the theologians say that nothing happens which God does not foresee, they also say that divine providence leaves the world full of contingencies and man a free agent to operate among them. "Though there is for God a certain order of all causes," it does not follow, Augustine says, that nothing depends "on the free exercise of our own wills, for our wills themselves are included in that order of causes which is certain to God, and is embraced by His foreknowledge, for human wills are also causes of human actions."

These matters are further discussed in the chapters on FATE, HISTORY, and NECESSITY AND CONTINGENCY. The mention of them here suggests another meaning of liberty—that of free choice or free will—and with it issues other than those involved in the relation of the individual to the state or to his fellow men. Yet the metaphysical questions about liberty and necessity, or freedom and causality, and the theological questions about man's freedom under God, are not without bearing on the political problems of man's freedom in society, or his rights and powers. The fundamental doctrines of civil liberty certainly seem to differ according to the conception of natural freedom on which they are based. Freedom may be natural in the sense that free will is a part of human nature; or in the sense that freedom is a birthright, an innate and inalienable right. It may be natural in the sense in which freedom in a state of nature is distinguished from political liberty, or liberty under civil law and government.

THE EFFORT TO clarify meanings requires us to look at the three words which we have used as if they were interchangeable—"liberty," "freedom," and "independence." For the most part, "liberty" and "freedom" are synonyms. Both words are used in English versions of the great books. Though authors or translators sometimes prefer one, sometimes the other, their preference does not seem to reflect a variation in meaning.

In English the word "freedom" has a little greater range in that it permits the formation of the adjective "free." It is also adapted to speaking of freedom *from* certain restraints or undesirable conditions, as well as of freedom *to* act in accordance with desire or to exercise certain privileges. In consequence, the word "freedom" is more frequently employed in the discussion of free will. Though the traditional enumeration of civil liberties may use the phrasing "liberty of conscience or worship" as frequently as "freedom of conscience or worship," "freedom of speech" is more usual, and "freedom from fear or want or economic dependence" does not seem to have an alternative phrasing.

The word "independence" has special connotations which make it equivalent to only part of the meaning of "freedom" or "liberty." Negatively, independence is a freedom from limitation or from being subject to determination by another. Positively, independence implies self-sufficiency and adequate power. When we speak of a man of independent means, we refer not only to his freedom from want or economic dependence on others, but also to his having sufficient wealth to suit his tastes or purposes. A moment's reflection will show that this is a relative matter. It is doubtful whether absolute economic independence is possible for men or even for nations.

The real question here seems to be a metaphysical one. Can any finite thing be absolutely independent? The traditional answer is No. As appears in the chapter on INFINITY, only a being infinite in perfection and power—only the Supreme One of Plotinus, the uncreated God of Aquinas, or the self-caused God of Spinoza—has complete independence. God has the freedom of autonomy which cannot belong to finite things. There is, however, another sense of divine freedom which Aquinas affirms and both Plotinus and Spinoza deny. That is freedom of choice.

"God does not act from freedom of will," Spinoza writes; yet God alone acts as a free cause, for God alone "exists from the necessity of his own nature and is determined to action by himself alone." The divine freedom consists in God's self-determination which, for Spinoza, does not exclude necessity. The opposite view is most clearly expressed in the Christian doctrine of creation. The created world does not follow necessarily from the divine nature. "Since the goodness of God is perfect," Aquinas writes, "and can exist without other things, inasmuch as no perfection can accrue to Him from them, it follows that for Him to will things other than Himself is not absolutely necessary." This issue of freedom or necessity with regard to God's will and action is more fully discussed in the chapters on WILL and WORLD.

The metaphysical identification of independence with infinity does not carry over into the sphere of political freedom. Yet in one respect there is an analogy. The autonomous is that which is a law unto itself. It admits no superior authority. When in the tradition of political thought states are called "free and independent," their autonomy or sovereignty means that by virtue of which, in the words of the Declaration of Independence, "they have full power to levy war, conclude peace, contract alliances, establish commerce, and to do all other acts and things which independent states may of right do."

Free and independent states do not have infinite power. There is always the possibility of their being subjugated by another state and reduced to the condition of a dependency. But though their power is not infinite, they acknowledge no superior. To be a sovereign is to accept commands from no one.

Since autonomy or sovereignty is incompatible with living under human law or government, the independence of sovereign princes or states must be an anarchic freedom—a freedom from law and government. This seems to be the view of Hobbes, Locke, Kant, and Hegel, all of whom refer to the anarchy of independent states or sovereign princes to explain what they mean by the "state of nature." Sovereigns are, in the words of Kant, "like lawless savages."

Applying this conception to individual men, Hobbes and Locke define natural as opposed to civil liberty in terms of man's independence in a state of nature. In a state of nature man had a limited independence, since each man might be coerced by a superior force; but it was an absolute independence in the sense that he was subject to no human government or man-made law.

THE NATURAL FREEDOM of man, according to Hobbes, is not free will. Since "every act of man's will, and every desire and inclination, proceed from some cause, and that from another cause, in a continual chain (whose first link is in the hand of God, the first of all causes), they proceed from *necessity*." Liberty is not of the will, but of the man, consisting in this: "that he finds no stop in doing what he has the will, desire, or inclination to do." The proper application of the word "free" is to bodies in motion, and the liberty it signifies when so applied is merely "the absence of external impediments."

The natural right of every man is "the liberty each man has to use his own power . . . for the preservation of his own nature, that is to say, of his own life . . . and consequently of doing anything which in his own judgment and reason he shall conceive to be the aptest means thereunto." This liberty or natural right belongs to man only in a state of nature. When men leave the state of nature and enter the commonwealth, they surrender this natural liberty in exchange for a civil liberty which, according to Hobbes, consists in nothing more than their freedom to do what the law of the state does not prohibit, or to omit doing what the law does not command.

Locke agrees that man's natural liberty is not the freedom of his will in choosing, but the freedom to do what he wills without constraint or impediment. He differs from Hobbes, however, in his conception of natural liberty because he differs in his conception of the state of nature.

For Hobbes the state of nature is a state of war; the notions of right and wrong, justice and injustice, can have no place in it. "Where there is no common power, there is no law; where no law, no injustice." The liberty which sovereign states now have is the same as "that which every man should have if there were no civil laws, nor commonwealth at all. And the effects of it also are the same. For as amongst masterless men, there is perpetual war of every man against his neighbor . . . so in states and commonwealths not dependent on one another, every commonwealth has an absolute liberty to do what it shall judge . . . most conducing to its benefit."

For Locke the state of nature is not a state of war, but a natural as opposed to a civil society, that is, a society in which men live together under natural rather than under civil law. Men who live in this condition are "in a state of perfect freedom to order their actions and dispose of their possessions as they think fit, within the bounds of the law of nature." This is a limited, not an absolute freedom; or, as Locke says, "though this be a state of liberty, yet it is not a state of license." The line between liberty and license is drawn by the precepts of the natural law. The difference, then, between natural and civil liberty lies in this. Natural liberty consists in being "free from any superior power on earth," or not being "under the will or legislative authority of man." Only the rules of natural law limit freedom of action. Civil liberty, or liberty under civil law, consists in being "under no other legislative power but that established by consent." It is a freedom for the individual to follow his own will in all matters not prescribed by the law of the state.

IN THE ARGUMENTS for and against free will, one view regards free will as incompatible with the principle of causality, natural necessity, or God's omnipotence; the other conceives free choice as falling within the order of nature or causality and under God's providence. We shall not consider these alternatives in this chapter, since this issue is reserved for the chapter on WILL.

Yet one thing is clear for the present consideration of political liberty. If the statement that men are born free means that it is a property of their rational natures to possess a free will, then they do not lose their innate freedom when they live in civil society. Government may interfere with a man's actions, but it cannot coerce his will. Government can go no further than to regulate the expression of man's freedom in external actions.

Nor is the range of free will limited by law. As indicated in the chapter on LAW, any law—moral or civil, natural or positive—which directs human conduct can be violated. It leaves man free to disobey it and take the consequences. But if the rule is good or just, then the act which transgresses it must have the opposite quality. The freedom of a free will is therefore morally indifferent. It can be exercised to do either good or evil. We use our freedom properly, says Augustine, when we act virtuously; we misuse it when we choose to act viciously. "The will," he writes, "is then truly free, when it is not the slave of vices and sins."

Those who conceive the natural moral law as stating the precepts of virtue or the commands of duty and who, in addition, regard every concrete act which proceeds from a free choice of the will as either good or bad—never indifferent—find that the distinction between liberty and license applies to every free act. The meaning of this distinction is the same as that between freedom properly used and freedom misused. Furthermore, since there is no good act which is not prescribed by the moral law, the whole of liberty, as opposed to license, consists in doing what that moral law commands.

These considerations affect the problem of political liberty, especially on the question whether the spheres of law and liberty are separate, or even opposed. One view, as we have seen, is that the area of civil liberty lies outside the realm of acts regulated by law. To break the law may be criminal license, but to obey it is not to be free. The sphere of liberty increases as the scope or stringency of law diminishes.

The opposite view does not regard freedom as freedom *from* law. "Freedom," Hegel maintains, "is nothing but the recognition and adoption of such universal substantial objects as Right and Law." All that matters in the relation between liberty and law is whether the law is just and whether a man is virtuous. If the law is just, then it does not *compel* a just man to do what he would not *freely* elect to do even if the law did not exist. Only the criminal is coerced or restrained by good laws. To say that such impediment to action destroys freedom would be to deny the distinction between liberty and license.

Nevertheless, liberty can be abridged by law. That is precisely the problem of the good man living under unjust laws. If, as Montesquieu says, "liberty can consist only in the power of doing what we ought to will, and in not being constrained to do what we ought not to will," then governments and laws interfere with liberty when they command or prohibit acts contrary to the free choice of a good man.

The conception of freedom as the condition of those who are rightly governed—who are commanded to do only what they would do anyway—seems to be analogically present in Spinoza's theory of human bondage and human freedom. It is there accompanied by a denial of the will's freedom of choice.

According to Spinoza human action is causally determined by one of two factors in man's nature—the passions or reason. When man is governed by his passions, he is in "bondage, for a man under their control is not his own master, but is mastered by fortune, in whose power he is, so that he is often forced to follow the worse, although he sees the better before him." When man is governed by reason he is free, for he "does the will of no one but himself, and does those things only which he knows are of greatest importance in life, and which he therefore desires above all things." The man who acts under the influence of the passions acts in terms of inadequate ideas and in the shadow of error or ignorance. When reason rules, man acts with adequate knowledge and in the light of truth.

So, too, in the theory of Augustine and Aquinas, the virtuous man is morally or spiritually free because human reason has triumphed in its conflict with the passions to influence the free judgment of his will. The rule of reason does not annul the will's freedom. Nor is the will less free when it is moved by the promptings of the passions. "A passion," writes Aquinas, "cannot draw or move the will directly." It does so indirectly, as, for example, "when those who are in some kind of passion do not easily turn their imagination away from the object of their affections." But though the will is not altered in its freedom by whether reason or emotion dominates, the situation is not the same with the human person as a whole. The theologians see him as a moral agent and a spiritual being who gains or loses freedom according as the will submits to the guidance of reason or follows the passions.

On the supernatural level, the theologians teach that God's grace assists reason to conform human acts to the divine law, but also that grace does not abolish free choice on the part of the will. "The first freedom of the will," Augustine says, "which man received when he was created upright, consisted in an ability not to sin, but also in an ability to sin." So long as man lives on earth, he remains free to sin. But supernatural grace, added to nature, raises man to a higher level of spiritual freedom than he can ever achieve by the discipline of the acquired virtues.

Still higher is the ultimate freedom of beatitude itself. Augustine calls this "the last freedom of will" which, by the gift of God, leaves man "not able to sin." It is worth noting that this ultimate liberty consists in freedom from choice or the need to choose, not in freedom from love or law. Man cannot be more free than when he succeeds, with God's help, in submitting himself through love to the rule of God.

THE POLITICAL significance of these moral and theological doctrines of freedom would seem to be that man *can be* as free in civil society as in a state of nature. Whether in fact he *is* depends upon the justice of the laws which govern him, not upon their number or the matters with which they deal. He is, of course, not free to do whatever he pleases regardless of the well-being of other men or the welfare of the community, but that, in the moral conception of liberty, is not a loss of freedom. He loses freedom in society only when he is mistreated or misgoverned—when, being the equal of other men, he is not treated as their equal; or when, being capable of ruling himself, he is denied a voice in his own government.

The meaning of tyranny and slavery seems to confirm this conception of political liberty. To be a slave is not merely to be ruled by another; it consists in being subject to the mastery of another, *i.e.*, to be ruled as a means to that other's good and without any voice in one's own government. This implies, in contrast, that to be ruled as a free man is to be ruled for one's own good and with some degree of participation in the government under which one lives.

According to Aristotle's doctrine of the natural slave—examined in the chapter on SLAVERY—some men do not have the nature of free men, and so should not be governed as free men. Men who are by nature slaves are not unjustly treated when they are enslaved. "It is better for them as for all inferiors," Aristotle maintains, "that they should be under the rule of a master." Though they do not in fact have the liberty of free men, they are not deprived thereby of any freedom which properly belongs to them, any more than a man who is justly imprisoned is deprived of a freedom which is no longer his by right.

The root of this distinction between free men and slaves by nature lies in the supposition of a natural inequality. The principle of equality is also relevant to the injustice of tyranny and the difference between absolute and constitutional government. In the *Republic* Plato compares the tyrant to an owner of slaves. "The only difference," he writes, "is that the tyrant has more slaves" and enforces "the harshest and bitterest form of slavery." The tyrannical ruler enslaves those who are his equals by nature and who should be ruled as free men. Throughout the whole tradition of political thought the name of tyranny signifies the abolition of liberty. But absolute or despotic government is not uniformly regarded as the enemy of liberty.

The issue concerning the legitimacy or justice of absolute government is examined in the chapters on MONARCHY and TYRANNY. But we can take it as generally agreed that the subjects of a despot, unlike the citizens of a republic, do not enjoy any measure of self-government. To the extent that political liberty consists in some degree of self-government, the subjects of absolute rule lack the sort of freedom possessed by citizens under constitutional government. For this reason the supremacy of law is frequently said to be the basic principle of political liberty.

"Wherever law ends, tyranny begins," Locke writes. In going beyond the law, a ruler goes beyond the grant of authority vested in him by the consent of the people, which alone makes man "subject to the laws of any government." Furthermore, law for Locke is itself a principle of freedom. "In its true notion," he writes, it "is not so much the limitation as the direction of a free and intelligent agent to his proper interest, and prescribes no farther than is for the general good of those under that law. Could they be happier without it, the law, as a useless thing, would of itself vanish, and that ill deserves the name of confinement which hedges us in only from bogs and precipices. So that however it may be mistaken, the end of law is not to abolish or restrain, but to preserve and enlarge freedom."

A constitution gives the ruled the status of citizenship and a share in their own government. It may also give them legal means with which to defend their liberties when officers of government invade their rights in violation of the constitution. According to Montesquieu, for whom political liberty exists only under government by law, never under despotism or the rule of men, the freedom of government itself demands "from the very nature of things that power should be a check to power." This is accomplished by a separation of powers. A system of checks and balances limits the power of each branch of the government and permits the law of the constitution to be applied by one department against another when its officials usurp powers not granted by the constitution or otherwise act unconstitutionally.

Yet, unlike tyranny, absolute government has been defended. The ancients raise the question whether, if a truly superior or almost godlike man existed, it would not be proper for him to govern his inferiors in an absolute manner. "Mankind will not say that such a one is to be expelled and exiled," Aristotle writes; "on the other hand, he ought not to be a subject— that would be as if mankind should claim to rule over Zeus, dividing his offices among them. The only alternative," he concludes, "is that all should joyfully obey such a ruler, according to what seems to be the order of nature, and that men like him should be kings in their state for life." Those subject to his government would be free only in the sense that they would be ruled for their own good, perhaps better than they could rule themselves. But they would lose that portion of political freedom which consists in self-government. Faced with this alternative to constitutional government —which Aristotle describes as the government of free men and equals—what should be the choice of men who are by nature free?

THE ANCIENT ANSWER is not decisively in one direction. There are many passages in both Plato and Aristotle in which the absolute rule of a wise king (superior to his subjects as a father is to children, or a god to men) seems to be pictured as the political ideal. The fact that free men would be no freer than children in a well administered household does not seem to Plato and Aristotle to be a flaw in the picture. They do not seem to hold that the fullness of liberty is the primary measure of the goodness of government.

On the contrary, justice is more important. As Aristotle suggests, it would be unjust for the superior man to be treated as an equal and given the status of one self-governing citizen among others. But he also points out that "democratic states have instituted ostracism" as a means of dealing with such superior men. "Equality is above all things their aim, and therefore they ostracized and banished from the city for a time those who seemed to predominate too much." Because it saves the superior man from injustice and leaves the rest free to practice self-government, "the argument for ostracism," Aristotle claims, "is based upon a kind of political justice," in that it preserves the balance within the state, and perhaps also because it leaves men free to practice self-government among themselves.

Since the eighteenth century, a strong tend-ency in the opposite direction appears in the political thought of Locke, Montesquieu, Rousseau, Kant, the American constitutionalists, and J. S. Mill. Self-government is regarded as the essence of good government. It is certainly the mark of what the eighteenth century writers call "free government." Men who are born to be free, it is thought, cannot be satisfied with less civil liberty than this.

"Freedom," says Kant, "is independence of the compulsory will of another; and in so far as it can co-exist with the freedom of all according to a universal law, it is the one sole, original inborn right belonging to every man in virtue of his humanity. There is, indeed, an innate equality belonging to every man which consists in his right to be independent of being bound by others to anything more than that to which he may also reciprocally bind them." The fundamental equality of men thus appears to be founded in their equal right to freedom; and that, for Kant at least, rests on the freedom of will with which all men are born. The criterion of the good society is the realization of freedom.

Kant's conception of human society as a realm of ends, in which no free person should be degraded to the ignominy of being a means, expresses one aspect of political freedom. The other is found in his principle of the harmonization of individual wills which results in the freedom of each being consistent with the freedom of all. In institutional terms, republican government, founded on popular sovereignty and with a system of representation, is the political ideal precisely because it gives its citizens the dignity of free men and enables them to realize their freedom in self-government.

Citizenship, according to Kant, has three inseparable attributes: "1. constitutional freedom, as the right of every citizen to have to obey no other law than that to which he has given his consent or approval; 2. civil equality, as the right of the citizen to recognize no one as a superior among the people in relation to himself, except in so far as such a one is as subject to *his* moral power to impose obligations, as that other has power to impose obligations upon him; and 3. political independence, as the right to owe his existence and continuance in society not to the arbitrary will of another, but to his own rights and powers as a member of the commonwealth, and, consequently, the possession of a civil personality, which cannot be represented by any other than himself."

Kant leans heavily on Rousseau's conclusions with regard to political liberty. Rousseau, however, approaches the problem of freedom somewhat differently. "Man is born free," he begins, "and everywhere he is in chains." He next considers two questions. What makes government legitimate, "since no man has a natural authority over his fellow, and force creates no right"? Answering this first question in terms of a convention freely entered into, Rousseau then poses the second problem—how to form an association "in which each, while uniting himself with all, may still obey himself alone, and remain as free as before." This, he says, is "the fundamental problem of which the *Social Contract* provides the solution."

The solution involves more than republican government, popular sovereignty, and a participation of the individual through voting and representation. It introduces the conception of the general will, through which alone the freedom of each individual is to be ultimately preserved. Like Kant's universal law of freedom, the general will ordains what each man would freely will for himself if he adequately conceived the conditions of his freedom. "In fact," says Rousseau, "each individual, as a man, may have a particular will contrary or dissimilar to the general will which he has as a citizen. His particular interest may speak to him quite differently from the common interest." Nevertheless, under conditions of majority rule, the members of the minority remain free even though they appear to be ruled against their particular wills.

When a measure is submitted to the people, the question is "whether it is in conformity with the general will, which is their will. Each man, in giving his vote, states his opinion on that point; and the general will is found by counting votes. When, therefore, the opinion that is contrary to my own prevails, this proves neither more nor less than that I was mistaken, and that what I thought to be the general will was not so. If my particular opinion had carried the day, I should have achieved the opposite of what was my will; and it is in that case

that I should not have been free. This presupposes, indeed, that all the qualities of the general will still reside in the majority; when they cease to do so, whatever side a man may take, liberty is no longer possible."

J. S. MILL SEES THE same problem from the opposite side. Constitutional government and representative institutions are indispensable conditions of political liberty. Where Aristotle regards democracy as the type of constitution most favorable to freedom because it gives the equality of citizenship to all *free-born* men, Mill argues for universal suffrage to give equal freedom to *all* men, for all are born equal. But neither representative government nor democratic suffrage is sufficient to guarantee the liberty of the individual and his freedom of thought or action.

Such phrases as "self-government" and "the power of the people over themselves" are deceptive. "The 'people' who excercise the power," Mill writes, "are not always the same people with those over whom it is exercised; and the 'self-government' spoken of is not the government of each by himself, but of each by all the rest. The will of the people, moreover, practically means the will of the most numerous or the most active part of the people; the majority, or those who succeed in making themselves accepted as the majority."

To safeguard individual liberty from the tyranny of the majority, Mill proposes a single criterion for social control over the individual, whether by the physical force of law or the moral force of public opinion. "The sole end for which mankind are warranted, individually or collectively, in interfering with the liberty of action of any of their number, is self-protection. ... The only part of the conduct of anyone, for which he is amenable to society, is that which concerns others. In the part which merely concerns himself, his independence is, of right, absolute. Over himself, over his own body and mind, the individual is sovereign."

Mill's conception of individual liberty at first appears to be negative—to be freedom *from* externally imposed regulations or coercions. Liberty increases as the sphere of government diminishes; and, for the sake of liberty, that government governs best which governs least, or governs no more than is necessary for the public safety. "There is a sphere of action," Mill writes, "in which society, as distinguished from the individual, has, if any, only an indirect interest; comprehending all that portion of a person's life and conduct which affects only himself, or if it also affects others, only with their free, voluntary, and undeceived consent and participation. When I say only himself," Mill continues, "I mean directly and in the first instance; for whatever affects himself, may affect others through himself. . . . This, then, is the appropriate region of human liberty."

But it is the positive aspect of freedom from governmental interference or social pressures on which Mill wishes to place emphasis. Freedom *from* government or social coercion is freedom *for* the maximum development of individuality—freedom to be as different from all others as one's personal inclinations, talents, and tastes dispose one and enable one to be.

"It is desirable," Mill writes, "that in things which do not primarily concern others, individuality should assert itself." Liberty is undervalued as long as the free development of individuality is not regarded as one of the principal ingredients of human happiness and indispensable to the welfare of society. "The only freedom which deserves the name," Mill thinks, "is that of pursuing our own good in our own way, so long as we do not attempt to deprive others of theirs, or impede their efforts to obtain it"; for, "in proportion to the development of his individuality, each person becomes more valuable to himself, and is therefore capable of being more valuable to others. There is a greater fullness of life about his own existence, and when there is more life in the units there is more in the mass which is composed of them."

Mill's praise of liberty as an ultimate good, both for the individual and for the state, finds a clearly antiphonal voice in the tradition of the great books. Plato, in the *Republic*, advocates political regulation of the arts, where Mill, even more than Milton before him, argues against censorship or any control of the avenues of human expression. But the most striking opposition to Mill occurs in those passages in which Socrates deprecates the spirit of democracy because of its insatiable desire for freedom. That spirit, Socrates says, creates a city "full of freedom and frankness, in which a man may do and say what he likes . . . Where such freedom exists, the individual is clearly able to order for himself his own life as he pleases."

The democratic state is described by Socrates as approaching anarchy through relaxation of the laws or through utter lawlessness. Under such circumstances there will be the greatest variety of individual differences. It will seem "the fairest of states, being like an embroidered robe which is spangled with every sort of flower." But it is a state in which liberty has been allowed to grow without limit at the expense of justice and order. It is "full of variety and disorder, and dispensing a sort of equality to equals and unequals alike."

OUTLINE OF TOPICS

REFERENCES

To find the passages cited, use the numbers in heavy type, which are the volume and page numbers of the passages referred to. For example, in **4** HOMER: *Iliad*, BK II [265–283] **12d**, the number **4** is the number of the volume in the set; the number **12d** indicates that the passage is in section d of page 12.

PAGE SECTIONS: When the text is printed in one column, the letters a and b refer to the upper and lower halves of the page. For example, in **53** JAMES: *Psychology*, 116a–119b, the passage begins in the upper half of page 116 and ends in the lower half of page 119. When the text is printed in two columns, the letters a and b refer to the upper and lower halves of the left-hand side of the page, the letters c and d to the upper and lower halves of the right-hand side of the page. For example, in **7** PLATO: *Symposium*, 163b–164c, the passage begins in the lower half of the left-hand side of page 163 and ends in the upper half of the right-hand side of page 164.

AUTHOR'S DIVISIONS: One or more of the main divisions of a work (such as PART, BK, CH, SECT) are sometimes included in the reference; line numbers, in brackets, are given in certain cases; *e.g.*, *Iliad*, BK II [265–283] **12d**.

BIBLE REFERENCES: The references are to book, chapter, and verse. When the King James and Douay versions differ in title of books or in the numbering of chapters or verses, the King James version is cited first and the Douay, indicated by a (*D*), follows; *e.g.*, OLD TESTAMENT: *Nehemiah*, 7:45–(*D*) II *Esdras*, 7:46.

SYMBOLS: The abbreviation "esp" calls the reader's attention to one or more especially relevant parts of a whole reference; "passim" signifies that the topic is discussed intermittently rather than continuously in the work or passage cited.

For additional information concerning the style of the references, see the Explanation of Reference Style; for general guidance in the use of *The Great Ideas*, consult the Preface.

1. Natural freedom and political liberty

1a. The birthright of freedom

18 AUGUSTINE: *City of God*, BK XIX, CH 15 521a-c

19 AQUINAS: *Summa Theologica*, PART I, Q 96, A 4 512d-513c

20 AQUINAS: *Summa Theologica*, PART I–II, Q 94, A 5, REP 3 224d-225d

26 SHAKESPEARE: *Julius Caesar*, ACT I, SC II [90–99] 570b

32 MILTON: *Paradise Lost*, BK XII [63–110] 320b-321b

35 LOCKE: *Civil Government*, CH VI 36a-42a

37 FIELDING: *Tom Jones*, 53b-d

38 MONTESQUIEU: *Spirit of Laws*, BK XV, 109b-d

38 ROUSSEAU: *Inequality*, 357c-d / *Social Contract*, BK I, 387c-390d passim

42 KANT: *Science of Right*, 401b-402a; 420d-421a; 421c-d

43 DECLARATION OF INDEPENDENCE: [1–15] 1a-b

44 BOSWELL: *Johnson*, 363c-364a

46 HEGEL: *Philosophy of Right*, PART I, par 57 26b-27a; par 66 29a-c; ADDITIONS, 36 122b-c / *Philosophy of History*, INTRO, 171c-172b

1b. The independence of men and the autonomy of sovereigns in a state of nature or anarchy

15 TACITUS: *Histories*, BK IV, 271a-b

23 HOBBES: *Leviathan*, PART I, 84c-87b; PART II, 99b-c; 113d-115a; 159c

30 BACON: *Advancement of Learning*, 20c-d

31 SPINOZA: *Ethics*, PART IV, PROP 37, SCHOL 2 435b-436a

35 LOCKE: *Civil Government*, CH II–VI 25d-42a passim, esp CH II, SECT 14 28b-c; CH VII, SECT 87 44a-b; CH IX, SECT 123 53c-d; SECT 128 54b-c; CH XI, SECT 136–137 56c-57b; CH XII, SECT 145 58d-59a; CH XIX, SECT 211 73d-74a

38 MONTESQUIEU: *Spirit of Laws*, BK I, 2b-d; BK VIII, 52a; BK XXVI, 221c-d

38 ROUSSEAU: *Inequality*, 342c-345c; 352a; 353c-355b passim; 356c-357a / *Political Economy*, 369a-b; 374a-b / *Social Contract*, BK I, 393b-c; BK II, 398a-b; BK III, 419a-b

41 GIBBON: *Decline and Fall*, 237c-d

42 KANT: *Pure Reason*, 222b-c / *Science of Right*, 402c; 408c-d; 433c-434d; 435c-436a; 452a-d

46 HEGEL: *Philosophy of Right*, PART III, par 194 66c-d; par 333–334 109b-c / *Philosophy of History*, INTRO, 171c-172b; PART IV, 317d-318a

54 FREUD: *Civilization and Its Discontents*, 780d

(1. *Natural freedom and political liberty.*)

1c. The relation of liberty to free will: the conceptions of liberty as freedom from interference and freedom for personal development

23 HOBBES: *Leviathan*, PART I, 59b; 86c-d; PART II, 112d-113d

24 RABELAIS: *Gargantua and Pantagruel*, BK I, 65c-66b

32 MILTON: *Paradise Lost*, BK II [246-257] 116b / *Areopagitica*, 394b-395b; 408a-b

35 LOCKE: *Civil Government*, CH IV, SECT 21 29d; CH VI, SECT 57-63 36d-38c / *Human Understanding*, BK II, CH XXI, SECT 7-27 180a-184c passim; SECT 57 193b-c; SECT 73 198c-199c

35 HUME: *Human Understanding*, SECT VIII, DIV 73 483c-484a

38 MONTESQUIEU: *Spirit of Laws*, BK XI, 69a-b; BK XII, 85a; BK XXVI, 223c

38 ROUSSEAU: *Political Economy*, 370b-d / *Social Contract*, BK I, 393a-c; BK IV, 426c-d

42 KANT: *Intro. Metaphysic of Morals*, 386d-387a,c

43 MILL: *Liberty*, 272d-273b; 293b-323a,c passim, esp 312b-c

44 BOSWELL: *Johnson*, 161a-b

46 HEGEL: *Philosophy of Right*, PART III, par 121 43d; par 260 82a-83a; par 299 99c-100b; ADDITIONS, 117 135d-136a; 155-156 142a-b; 158 142d; 177 147d

50 MARX: *Capital*, 237a

1d. The supremacy of law as a condition of political liberty

5 EURIPIDES: *Suppliants* [429-441] 262a-b

6 HERODOTUS: *History*, BK VII, 233c-d

6 THUCYDIDES: *Peloponnesian War*, BK II, 396c-d; BK III, 436d-438b esp 438a-b

9 ARISTOTLE: *Ethics*, BK V, CH 6 [1134^{a}24-^{b}17] 382a-c passim / *Politics*, BK III, CH 6 [1279^{a}8-22] 476b-c; BK IV, CH 4 [1292^{a}4-37] 491b-d; BK V, CH 9 [1310^{a}25-36] 512c

12 AURELIUS: *Meditations*, BK I, SECT 14 254b-c

31 SPINOZA: *Ethics*, PART IV, PROP 73, DEMONST 446c

35 LOCKE: *Civil Government*, CH IV, SECT 21 29d; CH VI, SECT 56-63 36d-38c; CH IX, SECT 124-131 53d-54d; CH XI, SECT 135-139 55d-58a; CH XVIII, SECT 202 71d-72a; SECT 206 72c

38 MONTESQUIEU: *Spirit of Laws*, BK VI, 34d; BK XI, 69a-b; BK XII, 85a-c; BK XV, 109a-b; BK XXVI, 223c

38 ROUSSEAU: *Inequality*, 323d-324a; 355a-b; 356b-c / *Political Economy*, 370b-371c; 375b-c / *Social Contract*, BK I, 393b-c

39 SMITH: *Wealth of Nations*, BK V, 308b-c; 314d-315a,c

41 GIBBON: *Decline and Fall*, 96c-d; 161c-162a

42 KANT: *Pure Reason*, 114b-d / *Science of Right*, 398c-399c; 401c-402a; 436c-d / *Judgement*, 586c

43 DECLARATION OF INDEPENDENCE: [1-47] 1a-2a passim; [72-79] 2b

43 CONSTITUTION OF THE U.S.: PREAMBLE 11a,c; AMENDMENTS, V-VII 17b-d; XIV, SECT 1 18d

43 FEDERALIST: NUMBER 1, 30a-c; NUMBER 37, 118d-119b; NUMBER 53, 167d-168b; NUMBER 57, 177d-178a

43 MILL: *Liberty*, 267b,d-274a / *Representative Government*, 339d-340c

46 HEGEL: *Philosophy of Right*, PART I, par 93 36a-b; PART III, par 194 66c-d; par 208 69c; par 265 84b; par 286 96c-97a; ADDITIONS, 129 137c; 135 138c / *Philosophy of History*, INTRO, 170c-172b; 173a-175c; 180c-181a; PART II, 271d-272d; PART IV, 321a; 342b-d; 345a-b; 364b-c

1e. The restriction of freedom by justice: the distinction between liberty and license

6 THUCYDIDES: *Peloponnesian War*, BK II, 396c-d; BK III, 436d-438b

7 PLATO: *Republic*, BK II, 314d-315d; BK IV, 349a-d / *Laws*, BK III, 674c-676c

9 ARISTOTLE: *Politics*, BK V, CH 9 [1310^{a}25-36] 512c; BK VI, CH 4 [1318^{b}38-1319^{a}5] 522c; [1319^{b}27-32] 523b

12 EPICTETUS: *Discourses*, BK I, CH 12, 119a-c

14 PLUTARCH: *Lycurgus*, 44d-45b

15 TACITUS: *Annals*, BK III, 57b-58d

19 AQUINAS: *Summa Theologica*, PART I, Q 96, A 4 512d-513c

23 HOBBES: *Leviathan*, PART I, 86c-87b; PART II, 113b-116b; 138c

27 SHAKESPEARE: *Measure for Measure*, ACT I, SC II [120-134] 176b-c; SC III [7-54] 177b-d

31 SPINOZA: *Ethics*, PART IV, PROP 37, SCHOL 2, 435b-d; PROP 73, DEMONST 446c

32 MILTON: *Sonnets*, XII 65a-b / *Areopagitica*, 384a-386a

35 LOCKE: *Toleration*, 12c-13b; 17c-18c / *Civil Government*, CH II, SECT 4-6 25d-26c

38 MONTESQUIEU: *Spirit of Laws*, BK III, 10a; BK VIII, 51a-52c; BK XI, 68b,d-69c; BK XII, 92b-c

38 ROUSSEAU: *Inequality*, 324a-b / *Social Contract*, BK I, 393b-c; BK II, 396d-398b

39 SMITH: *Wealth of Nations*, BK II, 140b

40 GIBBON: *Decline and Fall*, 622d-623c; 653a

42 KANT: *Science of Right*, 398c-399c

43 MILL: *Liberty*, 271c-d; 297a-b; 302d-323a,c passim

44 BOSWELL: *Johnson*, 422c

46 HEGEL: *Philosophy of Right*, INTRO, par 29 19a-b; PART III, par 319 105b-106c; ADDITIONS, 127 137b; 145 140b / *Philosophy of History*, PART IV, 321a; 328b; 342b-d

54 FREUD: *Civilization and Its Discontents*, 780c-781a

1f. The freedom of equals under government: the equality of citizenship

5 EURIPIDES: *Suppliants* [399-462] 261d-262b

6 HERODOTUS: *History*, BK III, 107c-108d; BK VII, 232d-233d; 238c

2. The issues of civil liberty

2a. Freedom of thought and expression: the problem of censorship

(2. *The issues of civil liberty. 2a. Freedom of thought and expression: the problem of censorship.*)

5 SOPHOCLES: *Antigone* [499–511] 135b-c; [683–700] 137a

5 ARISTOPHANES: *Acharnians* [366–384] 459c-d; [497–508] 460d-461a

6 HERODOTUS: *History*, BK V, 172d-173b; BK VI, 189c; BK VII, 217a

6 THUCYDIDES: *Peloponnesian War*, BK II, 397b-c; BK III, 427a-c; BK VIII, 580b-c

7 PLATO: *Protagoras*, 43b-c / *Apology* 200a-212a,c / *Gorgias*, 259d / *Republic*, BK II–III, 320c-334b; BK IV, 344b-d; BK X, 427c-434c esp 432d-434c / *Statesman*, 601c-602c / *Laws*, BK II, 653a-658b esp 654d-656b; BK III, 675c-676b; BK VII, 719d-721a; 727c-728b; BK VIII, 732c; BK XI, 782d-783b

12 AURELIUS: *Meditations*, BK I, SECT 6 253b; SECT 14 254b-c

14 PLUTARCH: *Solon*, 76a / *Timoleon*, 212b-c / *Cato the Younger*, 632d; 636b-d

15 TACITUS: *Annals*, BK I, 21b-22d; BK III, 56d-57b; BK IV, 67c; 72b-73a; BK VI, 87c-88d; BK XIV, 152d-153c; BK XVI, 180d-183a / *Histories*, BK I, 189a-b

18 AUGUSTINE: *City of God*, BK II, CH 9 154a-c; CH 12 155c-d; CH 14 156c-157c; BK VIII, CH 13 273b-d

23 HOBBES: *Leviathan*, PART II, 102d-103a; 150c-151a; PART IV, 273c-d; 274c-d

25 MONTAIGNE: *Essays*, 260b; 270c-d; 408b-410c

29 CERVANTES: *Don Quixote*, PART I, 13b-16c; 117d-119d; 185b-188c

30 BACON: *Advancement of Learning*, 7b-c

31 DESCARTES: *Discourse*, PART VI, 60d-61a

32 MILTON: *Areopagitica* 381a-412b esp 384b-389a, 398a-b

35 LOCKE: *Human Understanding*, BK IV, CH III, SECT 20 319b-c; CH XVI, SECT 4 367c-368b

35 HUME: *Human Understanding*, SECT XI, DIV 102–104 497b-498c; DIV 114 503a-b

36 SWIFT: *Gulliver*, PART II, 75b

38 MONTESQUIEU: *Spirit of Laws*, BK V, 32c-33a,c; BK XII, 89b-90c; BK XIX, 146a,c

38 ROUSSEAU: *Social Contract*, BK IV, 425d

40 GIBBON: *Decline and Fall*, 148a; 355b-d; 668d-671b passim, esp 669b

41 GIBBON: *Decline and Fall*, 300a-b

42 KANT: *Pure Reason*, 220b-221b; 223a-c / *Science of Right*, 425c-426a

43 CONSTITUTION OF THE U.S.: AMENDMENTS, I 17a

43 FEDERALIST: NUMBER 84, 253a-b

43 MILL: *Liberty*, 272d-293b; 297b-298b / *Representative Government*, 341a-c; 361b-362c; 418c

44 BOSWELL: *Johnson*, 29a-b; 86a-b; 161a-b; 221d-224a; 300c-301a esp 301a-d [fn 1]; 313d-316d; 512c-d

46 HEGEL: *Philosophy of Right*, PART III, par 270,

88c-89b; par 319 105b-106c; ADDITIONS, 184–185 149a / *Philosophy of History*, PART I, 210d; 213d-214a; PART II, 272c-d; 279d-280b

54 FREUD: *Psycho-Analytic Therapy*, 125d-127a,c / *War and Death*, 757b-c / *New Introductory Lectures*, 879b-880b; 883d

2b. Liberty of conscience and religious freedom

OLD TESTAMENT: *II Kings*, 10:18–28; 11:18; 23—(D) *IV Kings*, 10:18–28; 11:18; 23 / *Ezra*, 1; 6–7—(D) *I Esdras*, 1; 6-7 / *Nehemiah*, 2:1–9—(D) *II Esdras*, 2:1–9 / *Daniel*, 3; 6—(D) *Daniel*, 3:1–23,91–97; 6

APOCRYPHA: *Rest of Esther*, 16—(D) OT, *Esther*, 16 / *I Maccabees*, 1–2—(D) OT, *I Machabees*, 1–2 / *II Maccabees*, 6–8—(D) OT, *II Machabees*, 6–8

NEW TESTAMENT: *Matthew*, 5:11–12; 10:16–23; 23:34–38; 24:9; 26:59-66 / *Mark*, 13:9–13; 14:42-65 / *Luke*, 11:47–51; 21:12–18; 22:66–71 / *John*, 5:16–18; 7:1; 15:18–16:3 / *Acts*, 4:1–22; 5:17–18,25–42; 6:9–14; 7:54–8:3; 9:1–5,23–24; 12:1–6,18–20; 13:27–29,50; 14:5; 16:19–40; 17:5–14; 18:12–16; 28:17–29 / *Romans*, 8:35–36 / *I Corinthians*, 4:9–13; 15:9 / *II Corinthians*, 1:5–8; 11:24–26; 12:9–10 / *Galatians*, 1:8–9,13–24; 2:1–5; 4:29; 5:10–12; 6:12 / *Philippians*, 1:28–30 / *I Thessalonians*, 2:14–16 / *II Thessalonians*, 1:3–5 / *II Timothy*, 3:10–12 / *Titus*, 3:10–11 / *Hebrews*, 11:35–38

5 SOPHOCLES: *Antigone* 131a-142d

6 HERODOTUS: *History*, BK IV, 137a-c; 138a-c

7 PLATO: *Apology*, 204d-205c / *Laws*, BK X, 769d-771b

15 TACITUS: *Annals*, BK I, 21c-d; BK II, 44b-c; BK XV, 168a-c

18 AUGUSTINE: *City of God*, BK XIX, CH 17 522b-523a

20 AQUINAS: *Summa Theologica*, PART II–II, Q 10, AA 7–12 431b-437d; Q 11, AA 3–4 440b-442b; Q 12, A 2 443b-444b

22 CHAUCER: *Second Nun's Tale* [15,826–16,021] 467b-471b

23 HOBBES: *Leviathan*, PART II, 149b-c; PART IV, 273c-d

25 MONTAIGNE: *Essays*, 116d-117c; 208b-c; 324c-326b

30 BACON: *New Atlantis*, 209a-b

32 MILTON: *New Forcers of Conscience* 68a-b / *Lord Gen. Cromwell* 69a-b / *Samson Agonistes* [1334–1379] 368b-369b / *Areopagitica* 381a-412b esp 386a-b, 388a-b, 397a-b, 402a-b, 404b, 411a-b

35 LOCKE: *Toleration* 1a-22d esp 2d-3a, 18c-20c / *Human Understanding*, BK IV, CH XVI, SECT 4 367c-368b

36 STERNE: *Tristram Shandy*, 257a-258a

38 MONTESQUIEU: *Spirit of Laws*, BK XIX, 144c-145a; BK XXV, 211d-213d; BK XXVI, 218d-219a

38 ROUSSEAU: *Social Contract*, BK IV, 438d-439c

39 SMITH: *Wealth of Nations*, BK V, 344a-b; 345b-346c; 347d-348a

40 GIBBON: *Decline and Fall*, 12a-14a; 206b,d-232b *passim*, esp 211a-b; 290d-291c; 324b; 349a-c; 464b-d; 601d-603b

41 GIBBON: *Decline and Fall*, 227b-d; 285d; 333b-335a,c esp 335a,c; 480d-481a

42 KANT: *Science of Right*, 433b-c; 444a-c

43 ARTICLES OF CONFEDERATION: III 5b

43 CONSTITUTION OF THE U.S.: ARTICLE VI [591-599] 16d; AMENDMENTS, I 17a

43 FEDERALIST: NUMBER I, 30a; NUMBER 51, 164b-c

43 MILL: *Liberty*, 270c-271a; 272d-274a; 276d-287b; 290a-292a; 307d-309a; 311a-312a / *Representative Government*, 341a-c; 437d-438b

44 BOSWELL: *Johnson*, 221d-224a; 421d; 436d-438b; 512c-d

46 HEGEL: *Philosophy of Right*, PART I, par 66 29a-c; PART III, par 270 84d-89c; ADDITIONS, 67 126d / *Philosophy of History*, INTRO, 193a-b; PART IV, 350d-351a; 353c-d

48 MELVILLE: *Moby Dick*, 60b-65a

50 MARX-ENGELS: *Communist Manifesto*, 428b-c

52 DOSTOEVSKY: *Brothers Karamazov*, BK V, 127b-137c *passim*

2c. Freedom in the sphere of economic enterprise: free trade; freedom from governmental restrictions

35 LOCKE: *Civil Government*, CH V 30b-36a *passim*

38 MONTESQUIEU: *Spirit of Laws*, BK XX, 148d-149a; 149c-d

39 SMITH: *Wealth of Nations*, BK I, 42a,c; 51a-62a *passim*; BK II, 142d; BK IV 182a-300d *passim*, esp 194a-c, 287c-288c, 291d-294a, 300a-c; BK V, 397a-c

42 KANT: *Science of Right*, 441d-443b

43 MILL: *Liberty*, 312c-315c / *Representative Government*, 348c-349a

46 HEGEL: *Philosophy of Right*, PART III, par 179 62b-c; par 235-236 76a-c; ADDITIONS, 145 140b / *Philosophy of History*, PART II, 277b-c; PART IV, 345a-b; 364d

50 MARX: *Capital*, 79c-81a; 83d-84a,c; 127c-146c *passim*, esp 130c-131a, 135d-138c, 141a-c, 144a-146c; 194a-b; 236c-248d *passim*, esp 241a-242a, 243d-244a; 277d-278a,c; 316d-317c; 367c-368b

50 MARX-ENGELS: *Communist Manifesto*, 420d; 421d-422a; 426c

51 TOLSTOY: *War and Peace*, BK XIII, 573a-b

2d. Economic dependence as a limitation of civil liberty: economic slavery or subjection

9 ARISTOTLE: *Politics*, BK III, CH 5 [1277^{b}34-1278^{a}39] 475a-c; BK VII, CH 9 [1328^{b}34-1329^{a}1] 533b

14 PLUTARCH: *Poplicola-Solon*, 87a

35 LOCKE: *Civil Government*, CH VII, SECT 85 43c-d

38 MONTESQUIEU: *Spirit of Laws*, BK V, 20d-21d; BK XIII, 99b-100c

---

38 ROUSSEAU: *Political Economy*, 381a-b / *Social Contract*, BK II, 405a-c

40 GIBBON: *Decline and Fall*, 144b

41 GIBBON: *Decline and Fall*, 73b

42 KANT: *Science of Right*, 436d-437c

43 FEDERALIST: NUMBER 10, 50b-51d; NUMBER 79, 233c

43 MILL: *Representative Government*, 339d-340c; 382c-d

46 HEGEL: *Philosophy of Right*, PART III, par 243 77b-c; ADDITIONS, 145 140b / *Philosophy of History*, PART IV, 352a

50 MARX: *Capital*, 138b; 366c-368b esp 367c-368b

50 MARX-ENGELS: *Communist Manifesto*, 420b-d; 424c; 426b-d; 428c-429c; 434c-d

3. Moral or spiritual freedom

3a. Human bondage, or the dominance of the passions

OLD TESTAMENT: *Genesis*, 4:1-16; 6:5,12; 8:20-22 / *Numbers*, 11:4-35—(D) *Numbers*, 11:4-34 / *II Samuel*, 11; 13—(D) *II Kings*, 11; 13 / *Proverbs*, 5:22-23

APOCRYPHA: *Ecclesiasticus*, 18:30-31; 23:5-6; 31:1-7,29-30—(D) OT, *Ecclesiasticus*, 18:30-31; 23:6; 31:1-7,39-40

NEW TESTAMENT: *Matthew*, 26:41 / *Mark*, 14:38 / *John*, 8:31-36 / *Acts*, 8:18-23 / *Romans*, 1:18-32; 5:12-6:23; 7:8-8:21 / *Galatians*, 4:1-10; 5:1,13-26 / *Philippians*, 3:18-19 / *I Timothy*, 6:9-10 / *Titus*, 3:3 / *James*, 1:12-16; 4:1-7 / *I Peter*, 2:11 / *II Peter*, 2 esp 2:19-20 / *I John*, 2:15-17

7 PLATO: *Phaedrus*, 120b-c; 128a-129c / *Phaedo*, 224d; 232a-234c / *Gorgias*, 275d-280d / *Republic*, BK I, 296b-c; BK IV, 347d-348d; BK VIII-IX, 411d-427b / *Laws*, BK III, 669b-d / *Seventh Letter*, 801b-c; 814b

9 ARISTOTLE: *Ethics*, BK III, CH 12 [1119^{a}35-^{b}18] 366a,c / *Politics*, BK III, CH 16 [1287^{a}28-32] 485d

12 LUCRETIUS: *Nature of Things*, BK III [59-93] 30d-31b; BK V [1113-1135] 75c-d

12 EPICTETUS: *Discourses*, BK I, CH 1 105a-106c; CH 4, 109c-d; BK II, CH 18 161a-162b; BK III, CH 15, 190d; CH 22 195a-201a; BK IV, CH 1 213a-223d

12 AURELIUS: *Meditations*, BK II, SECT 10 257d-258a

17 PLOTINUS: *Third Ennead*, TR I, CH 10 82b / *Sixth Ennead*, TR IV, CH 15, 304c-d

18 AUGUSTINE: *Confessions*, BK VI, par 18-26 40d-43a; BK VII, par 27 51d-52c; BK VIII, par 10-11 55c-56b / *City of God*, BK IV, CH 3 190a-c; BK XIV, CH 11, 385d-386b; CH 15 388d-390a; BK XIX, CH 15 521a-c / *Christian Doctrine*, BK I, CH 24 630c-631a

19 AQUINAS: *Summa Theologica*, PART I, Q 89, A 2, REP 1 475a-d; PART I-II, Q 9, A 2 658d-659c; Q 10, A 3 664d-665c

(3. Moral or spiritual freedom. 3a. Human bondage, or the dominance of the passions.)

20 AQUINAS: *Summa Theologica*, PART I–II, Q 72, A 2, REP 4 112b-113a; Q 73, A 5 123a-d; Q 77 144d-152a esp A 2 145d-147c

21 DANTE: *Divine Comedy*, HELL, V [25–45] 7b-c

22 CHAUCER: *Manciple's Tale* [17,130–144] 490b

25 MONTAIGNE: *Essays*, 165c-166a; 232b-c; 488b-489b

27 SHAKESPEARE: *Hamlet*, ACT III, SC II [61–79] 49c-d / *Othello*, ACT IV, SC I 229d-233a / *Antony and Cleopatra*, ACT III, SC XIII [111–116] 335d-336a; [195–201] 336d-337a / *Winter's Tale*, ACT II, SC III [1–192] 498c-500d

30 BACON: *Advancement of Learning*, 66c-d; 78a-d

31 SPINOZA: *Ethics*, PART III, PROP 2, SCHOL, 397c-d; PART IV, PREF–PROP 18 422b,d-429d

32 MILTON: *Paradise Lost*, BK VIII [561–594] 244b-245a; BK XII [79–110] 321a-b

35 LOCKE: *Human Understanding*, BK II, CH XXI, SECT 12 180d-181a; SECT 54 192b-c; SECT 69 196d-197a

36 STERNE: *Tristram Shandy*, 239b

38 ROUSSEAU: *Social Contract*, BK I, 393c

46 HEGEL: *Philosophy of History*, PART I, 233b-c; PART IV, 348d-349b

52 DOSTOEVSKY: *Brothers Karamazov*, BK VI, 164b-d

54 FREUD: *War and Death*, 760d-761a

3b. Human freedom or the rule of reason: freedom through knowledge of the truth

NEW TESTAMENT: *John*, 8:31–59 / *II Corinthians*, 3:17 / *James*, 1 esp 1:25

7 PLATO: *Lysis*, 16c-18b / *Phaedrus*, 120b-c; 128a-129c / *Phaedo*, 230d-234c / *Republic*, BK IV, 347d-348d; BK IX, 425c-427b / *Theaetetus*, 528c-531a / *Laws*, BK I, 650a-b; BK III, 669b-d; BK IX, 754a-b

8 ARISTOTLE: *Topics*, BK V, CH I [129^{a}10–16] 179a

9 ARISTOTLE: *Ethics*, BK I, CH 13 [1102^{b}13–1103^{a}3] 348a-c; BK III, CH 12 [1119^{a}35–^{b}18] 366a,c / *Politics*, BK I, CH 5 [1254^{a}33–^{b}26] 448a-b; CH 13 [1260^{a}4–15] 454c; BK III, CH 16 [1287^{a}28–32] 485d

12 LUCRETIUS: *Nature of Things*, BK II [1–61] 15a-d; BK V [1117–1120] 75d

12 EPICTETUS: *Discourses*, BK I, CH 12 118d-120b; BK II, CH 1–2, 139c-141c; CH 18 161a-162b; BK III, CH 7 182b-184a; CH 15, 190d; CH 22 195a-201a; BK IV, CH 1 213a-223d; CH 7 232c-235a

12 AURELIUS: *Meditations*, BK II, SECT 5 257b-c; SECT 16–17 259a-d; BK III, SECT 6 261a-c; BK IV, SECT 24 265c-d; BK V, SECT 9 270b-c; SECT 26 272c; BK VII, SECT 55 283b-c; SECT 68–69 284c-d; BK XI, SECT 18, 305b

14 PLUTARCH: *Cato the Younger*, 646b-648a

17 PLOTINUS: *Third Ennead*, TR I, CH 10 82b / *Sixth Ennead*, TR VIII, CH 3 344a-b

18 AUGUSTINE: *Christian Doctrine*, BK I, CH 24 630c-631a; CH 34 634b-c; BK III, CH 5–9 659d-661c

19 AQUINAS: *Summa Theologica*, PART I, Q 81, A 3 430c-431d; Q 83, A 1, REP 1 436d-438a; Q 95, A 2 507c-508a; PART I–II, Q 24, A 1 727b-d

20 AQUINAS: *Summa Theologica*, PART I–II, Q 50, A 3 8b-9a; Q 56, A 4 32b-33c; Q 57, A 3, REP 3 37b-38a; Q 59, AA 2–3 46c-48c; PART II–II, Q 183, A 4, ANS and REP 1 627d-628d

21 DANTE: *Divine Comedy*, PURGATORY, XVIII [19–75] 80a-c

23 HOBBES: *Leviathan*, PART I, 58c-d

24 RABELAIS: *Gargantua and Pantagruel*, BK I, 65c-66b

25 MONTAIGNE: *Essays*, 70a-c; 184b-d; 204d-205b

27 SHAKESPEARE: *Hamlet*, ACT III, SC II [61–79] 49c-d / *Othello*, ACT I, SC III [322–337] 212b-c

30 BACON: *Advancement of Learning*, 71d-72b; 78a-d

31 SPINOZA: *Ethics*, PART IV, PROP 67–73 444d-447a; PART V 451a-463d esp PROP 3–4 453a-d, PROP 20, SCHOL 457b-458a, PROP 42 463b-d

32 MILTON: *Sonnets*, XII 65a-b / *Paradise Lost*, BK XII [79–110] 321a-b / *Areopagitica*, 404a-b; 409b-410a

35 LOCKE: *Civil Government*, CH VI, SECT 56–63 36d-38c passim / *Human Understanding*, BK II, CH XXI, SECT 46–54 189d-192c; SECT 69 196d-197a

38 ROUSSEAU: *Social Contract*, BK I, 393c

41 GIBBON: *Decline and Fall*, 300b

42 KANT: *Fund. Prin. Metaphysic of Morals*, 282b-283d / *Practical Reason*, 296a-d / *Pref. Metaphysical Elements of Ethics*, 378c

44 BOSWELL: *Johnson*, 92b-c

46 HEGEL: *Philosophy of History*, INTRO, 160c-161c; PART II, 279d-280b; PART IV, 315a; 348d-349b; 350a-b; 361b-c

54 FREUD: *Psycho-Analytic Therapy*, 126a-127a,c / *General Introduction*, 625a-d / *Ego and Id*, 702c-d; 715c-716a / *New Introductory Lectures*, 838c-839b

3c. Virtue as the discipline of free choice: freedom as the determination of the will by the moral law of practical reason

9 ARISTOTLE: *Ethics*, BK II, CH 6 [1106^{b}36–1107^{a}6] 352c; BK III, CH 1–2 355b,d-358a

18 AUGUSTINE: *City of God*, BK IV, CH 3, 190c; BK XIV, CH 11, 386b; BK XIX, CH 20 523c-524a; BK XXII, CH 30, 617c-618a

19 AQUINAS: *Summa Theologica*, PART I, Q 83, A 2, ANS and REP 3 438a-d

20 AQUINAS: *Summa Theologica*, PART II–II, Q 183, A 4, ANS 627d-628d

21 DANTE: *Divine Comedy*, PURGATORY, XVIII [19–75] 80a-c; XXVII 94c-96a esp [139–142] 96a; PARADISE, XXXI [73–90] 154a

32 MILTON: *Areopagitica*, 391a-392a; 394b-395b

42 KANT: *Fund. Prin. Metaphysic of Morals*, 275b / *Practical Reason*, 302a-d; 307d-314d; 331a-b; 332a-334b; 342a-c / *Pref. Metaphysical Elements of Ethics*, 367d-368a; 378a-b / *Intro. Metaphysic of Morals*, 386b-387a,c; 390b,d-391a / *Science of Right*, 420d-421a / *Judgement*, 571c-572a

46 HEGEL: *Philosophy of Right*, INTRO, par 29 19a-b; PART II, par 105-114 40a-42b; PART III, par 149 56b; ADDITIONS, 95 132b / *Philosophy of History*, INTRO, 171a-c; PART IV, 328a; 362d-363a

52 DOSTOEVSKY: *Brothers Karamazov*, BK VI, 164a-165b

3d. Freedom from conflict and freedom for individuality as conditions of happiness

6 THUCYDIDES: *Peloponnesian War*, BK II,398a-c

7 PLATO: *Lysis*, 16c-18a / *Gorgias*, 275d-276b / *Republic*, BK I, 295d-296c

9 ARISTOTLE: *Politics*, BK III, CH 9 [1280^{a}32-34] 477d-478a

12 LUCRETIUS:*Nature of Things*, BK V [1-54]61a-d

12 EPICTETUS: *Discourses*, BK I, CH I 105a-106c; CH 4 108d-110a; CH 12 118d-120b; CH 18 124a-125a; BK II, CH 1-2 138b,d-141c; BK III, CH 22 195a-201a; CH 24 203c-210a; BK IV, CH 1-2 213a-224b; CH 4 225a-228a; CH 6-7 230b-235a

12 AURELIUS: *Meditations*, BK X, SECT 12 298c-d

18 AUGUSTINE: *Confessions*, BK VIII, par 10-30 55c-61c / *City of God*, BK XIX, CH 20 523d-524a; BK XXII, CH 30, 617c-618a

20 AQUINAS: *Summa Theologica*, PART II-II, Q 182, A I, REP 2 620b-621d

22 CHAUCER:*Manciple's Tale*[17,109-123] 490a-b

24 RABELAIS: *Gargantua and Pantagruel*, BK I, 65c-66b

25 MONTAIGNE: *Essays*, 109a; 318a-319b; 469a-470a; 486b-489b

29 CERVANTES: *Don Quixote*, PART II, 379d-380a

35 LOCKE: *Human Understanding*, BK II, CH XXI, SECT 52-53 191d-192b

42 KANT: *Pref. Metaphysical Elements of Ethics*, 378c-379a

43 MILL: *Liberty*, 269b-c; 272d-274a; 293b-302c / *Utilitarianism*, 451d-452a

46 HEGEL: *Philosophy of Right*, ADDITIONS, 118 136a-b; 158 142d / *Philosophy of History*, PART II, 276a-d; PART IV, 320c-321a; 364d

51 TOLSTOY: *War and Peace*, BK V, 221b-d; BK XIII, 577a-578b; BK XIV, 605b-d; BK XV, 630c-631a

53 JAMES: *Psychology*, 199b-202a

54 FREUD: *Origin and Development of Psycho-Analysis*, 9a-b; 20a-d / *General Introduction*, 593c; 623d-625d; 633d-634d; 635c

4. The metaphysics of freedom

19 AQUINAS: *Summa Theologica*, PART I, Q 19, A 3 110b-111c; A 8 116a-d; A 10 117d-118b; Q 22, A 2, REP 4 128d-130d; A 4 131c-132b; Q 59, A 3 308b-309a; Q 83 436c-440b; PART I-II, Q 6,

A I, REP 3 644d-646a; Q 10 662d-666a,c; Q 13, A 6 676c-677b; Q 17 686b,d-693d esp A 6 690b-d; Q 21, A 4, REP 2 719d-720a,c

31 SPINOZA: *Ethics*, PART I, DEF 7 355b; PROP 17 362b-363c; PROP 32-33 367a-369a; APPENDIX 369b-372d; PART II, PROP 48-49 391a-394d; PART III, 395a-d; DEF 1-3 395d-396a; PROP 1-3 396a-398c; PART IV, PREF 422b,d-424a; DEF 8 424b-c; PROP 23 430c-d; PROP 66-73 444c-447a; PART V 451a-463d esp PREF 451a-452c, PROP 40-42 462c-463d

42 KANT: *Pure Reason*, 133a; 140b,d-143a; 164a-172c esp 169c-170a, 170c-171a; 190c-d; 234c-235a / *Fund. Prin. Metaphysic of Morals*, 264d-265a; 279b,d-287d / *Practical Reason*, 291a-293c esp 292a-293b; 296a-d; 307d-314d esp 309d, 310b-311d; 331c-337a,c; 340a-342d; 351b-352c / *Intro. Metaphysic of Morals*, 390b,d-391a / *Judgement*, 463a-467a; 571c-572a; 587d-588a; 606d-607c; 609b-610a

46 HEGEL: *Philosophy of Right*, PART II, par 139 48d-49b / *Philosophy of History* 153a-369a,c esp INTRO, 156d-190b, 203a-206a,c, PART IV, 368d-369a,c

51 TOLSTOY: *War and Peace*, EPILOGUE II, 688a-696d

4a. The relation of human liberty to chance and contingency

7 PLATO: *Republic*, BK X, 439b-441a,c / *Laws*, BK IV, 679a-b

9 ARISTOTLE: *Ethics*, BK III, CH 3 [1112^{a}18-^{b}12] 358a-c

12 LUCRETIUS: *Nature of Things*, BK II [251-293] 18b-d

15 TACITUS: *Annals*, BK III, 49c; BK IV, 69a-b; BK VI, 91b-d

17 PLOTINUS: *Third Ennead*, TR I, CH 8-10 81d-82b

18 AUGUSTINE: *City of God*, BK V, CH 9 213b-215c

19 AQUINAS: *Summa Theologica*, PART I, Q 82, A 2 432d-433c; Q 83, A I 436d-438a; Q 116, A I 592d-593d

21 DANTE: *Divine Comedy*, PARADISE, XVII [13-42] 132b-c

23 MACHIAVELLI: *Prince*, CH XXV, 35a-b

42 KANT: *Intro. Metaphysic of Morals*, 392d-393c

46 HEGEL: *Philosophy of Right*, INTRO, par 15 16a-b; PART III, par 206 68d-69b; ADDITIONS, 12 118a-c / *Philosophy of History*, PART IV, 368d-369a,c

48 MELVILLE: *Moby Dick*, 158b-159a

4b. The opposites of freedom: causality or necessity, nature, and law

8 ARISTOTLE: *Metaphysics*, BK IX, CH 5 [1047^{b}35-1048^{a}24] 573b-c

9 ARISTOTLE: *Ethics*, BK III, CH 3 [1112^{a}18-^{b}12] 358a-c

12 LUCRETIUS: *Nature of Things*, BK II [251-260] 18b

(4. The metaphysics of freedom. 4b. The opposites of freedom: causality or necessity, nature, and law.)

15 TACITUS: *Annals*, BK IV, 69a-b; BK VI, 91b-d
17 PLOTINUS: *Third Ennead*, TR I, CH 4 79d-80a; CH 8–10 81d-82b
18 AUGUSTINE: *City of God*, BK V, CH 9–10 213b-216c
19 AQUINAS: *Summa Theologica*, PART I, Q 19, AA 3–9 110b-117d passim; Q 41, A 2 218c-219d; Q 47, A 1, REP 1 256a-257b; Q 59, A 3 308b-309a; Q 62, A 8, REP 2 323c-324a; Q 83, A 1 436d-438a; Q 103, A 1, REP 1,3 528b-529a; Q 115, A 6, ANS 591d-592d; PART I–II, Q 10 662d-666a,c; Q 13, A 6 676c-677b
20 AQUINAS: *Summa Theologica*, PART I–II, Q 50, A 3 8b-9a; Q 71, A 4, ANS and REP 3 108b-109a
21 DANTE: *Divine Comedy*, HELL, VII [61–96] 10b-c; PURGATORY, XVI [52–114] 77b-78a
22 CHAUCER: *Troilus and Cressida*, BK IV, STANZA 138–154 106b-108b / *Nun's Priest's Tale* [15,236–256] 456b-457a
23 HOBBES: *Leviathan*, PART II, 113b-c; PART III, 165c
25 MONTAIGNE: *Essays*, 216c-219a
31 SPINOZA: *Ethics*, PART I, DEF 7 355b; PROP 17, SCHOL 362c-363c; APPENDIX 369b-372d
32 MILTON: *Paradise Lost*, BK III [80–134] 137a-138a
35 LOCKE: *Human Understanding*, BK II, CH XXI, SECT 7–27 180a-184c
35 HUME: *Human Understanding*, SECT VIII 478b-487a
38 ROUSSEAU: *Inequality*, 337d-338a
42 KANT: *Pure Reason*, 133a; 140b,d-143a; 164a-171a; 234c-235a / *Fund. Prin. Metaphysic of Morals*, 264d-265a; 279b,d-287d esp 283d-285a / *Practical Reason*, 292a-293b; 296a-d; 301d-302d; 307d-314d esp 310b-311d; 331c-337a,c / *Intro. Metaphysic of Morals*, 386b-387a,c; 390b / *Judgement*, 463a-467a; 571c-572a; 587a-588a; 607c; 609b-610a
44 BOSWELL: *Johnson*, 392d-393a; 549c
46 HEGEL: *Philosophy of Right*, PART II, par 139 48d-49b; PART III, par 186–187 64d-65c; ADDITIONS, 90 130b-d / *Philosophy of History*, INTRO, 160c-161c; 171b; 186b-c; PART I, 236a-c
48 MELVILLE: *Moby Dick*, 158b-159a; 209b; 237a
50 MARX: *Capital*, 7b-c; 42a
51 TOLSTOY: *War and Peace*, BK VIII, 303d-304b; BK IX, 342a-344b; BK X, 389a-391c; BK XI, 469a-472b; BK XIII, 563a-564c; BK XIV, 588a-590c; EPILOGUE I, 645a-650c; EPILOGUE II, 688a-696d
53 JAMES: *Psychology*, 84a-94b passim, esp 87b-90b; 291a-295b esp 291a-b; 823a-826a esp 825b-826b [fn 2]
54 FREUD: *Origin and Development of Psycho-Analysis*, 13c / *General Introduction*, 454b-c; 462d; 486d

5. The theology of freedom

5a. Man's freedom in relation to fate or to the will of God

OLD TESTAMENT: *Genesis*, 3; 4:5–7 / *Exodus*, 4:21; 7–14 esp 7:3, 10:1, 14:17 / *Deuteronomy*, 11:26–28; 30 esp 30:15, 30:19–20 / *Joshua*, 11:19–20; 24:14–24—(D) *Josue*, 11:19–20; 24:14–24 / *I Kings*, 8:57–58—(D) *III Kings*, 8:5~–58 / *Job*, 3:23; 12:14–25; 34:29 / *Psalms*, 119:36; 139:15–16; 141:4—(D) *Psalms*, 118:36; 138:15–16; 140:4 / *Proverbs*, 21:1 / *Ecclesiastes*, 3:14–15 / *Isaiah*, 14:24–27; 63:17; 64:8—(D) *Isaias*, 14:24–27; 63:17; 64:8 / *Malachi*, 4:6—(D) *Malachias*, 4:6
APOCRYPHA: *Rest of Esther*, 13:8–18—(D) OT, *Esther*, 13:8–18 / *Wisdom of Solomon*, 7:16—(D) OT, *Book of Wisdom*, 7:16 / *Ecclesiasticus*, 15:11–20—(D) OT, *Ecclesiasticus*, 15:11–21
NEW TESTAMENT: *Matthew*, 20:1–16; 23:37; 26:39 / *John*, 6:44,64–65,70–71; 10:26–29; 12:37–40; 13:18–27—(D) *John*, 6:44,65–66,71–72; 10:26–29; 12:37–40; 13:18–27 / *Acts*, 4:27–28; 7:51–53; 13:48; 17:24–27 esp 17:26 / *Romans*, 8:28–9:24; 11:1–10 / *I Corinthians*, 7:21–23; 9:16–23; 12 / *Ephesians*, 1:3–12; 2:8–10; 4:7–14 / *Philippians*, 2:13 / *II Thessalonians*, 2:11–14—(D) *II Thessalonians*, 2:10–13 / *II Timothy*, 1:9 / *James*, 4:13–15
4 HOMER: *Iliad*, BK VI [342–358] 43c-d; BK XIX [74–94] 137d-138a; BK XXIV [507–551] 176c-177a / *Odyssey*, BK XVIII [117–150] 285b-c
5 SOPHOCLES: *Oedipus the King* 99a-113a,c esp [1297–1415] 111b-112b / *Oedipus at Colonus* 114a-130a,c esp [258–291] 116c-d, [960–999] 123b-c / *Philoctetes* [169–200] 183d-184a; [1316–1347] 193d-194a
5 EURIPIDES: *Helen* [711–721] 304d-305a / *Electra* [1168–1359] 337d-339a,c / *Heracles Mad* [1255–1357] 376a-d
6 HERODOTUS: *History*, BK I, 7b-8c; 20a-22a; BK II, 77a-b; BK III, 98b-99a; BK VII, 218b-220b; BK IX, 291b-c
7 PLATO: *Republic*, BK X, 439b-441a,c / *Laws*, BK I, 650a-b; BK IV, 679a-b; BK X, 765d-769c esp 767c-768b
8 ARISTOTLE: *Metaphysics*, BK XII, CH 10 [1075ᵃ 12–24] 605d-606a
12 EPICTETUS: *Discourses*, BK I, CH 12 118d-120b; BK II, CH 8, 147b; BK III, CH 22, 197c-198b; CH 24, 209c-210a; BK IV, CH 1, 218d-219c; CH 3, 224d; CH 7, 233d
12 AURELIUS: *Meditations*, BK III, SECT 11 262a-b; BK VI, SECT 42–46 278a-d; BK X, SECT 5 296d
13 VIRGIL: *Aeneid*, BK III [492–505] 160b-161a; BK IV [333–361] 176a-177a
14 PLUTARCH: *Coriolanus*, 188d-189c / *Sulla*, 370c-371b
15 TACITUS: *Annals*, BK IV, 69a; BK VI, 91b-d
17 PLOTINUS: *Third Ennead*, TR II–III 82c-97b passim
18 AUGUSTINE: *Confessions*, BK II, par 14 12a-b / *City of God*, BK V, CH 9–10 213b-216c

19 AQUINAS: *Summa Theologica*, PART I, Q 19, A 8 116a-d; Q 22, A 2, REP 4–5 128d-130d; QQ 23–24 132b-143c; Q 83, A 1, REP 2–4 436d-438a; Q 103, A 5 esp REP 3 531b-532b; AA 7–8 533b-534b; Q 105, AA 3–5 540c-543b; Q 116 592d-595c; PART I–II, Q 6, A 1, REP 3 644d-646a; A 4, REP 1 647b-648a; Q 9, A 6 662a-d; Q 10, A 4 665d-666a,c; Q 21, A 4, REP 2 719d-720a,c

21 DANTE: *Divine Comedy*, HELL, VII [61–96] 10b-c; PURGATORY, XVI [52–114] 77b-78a; XVIII [1–75] 79d-80c; PARADISE, I [94–142] 107b-d; III [64–90] 110a-b; XVII [13–45] 132b-c

22 CHAUCER: *Troilus and Cressida*, BK IV, STANZA 138–154 106b-108b

23 MACHIAVELLI: *Prince*, CH XXV, 35a-b

23 HOBBES: *Leviathan*, PART II, 113b-c; PART IV, 272b-c

25 MONTAIGNE: *Essays*, 515a; 520b-d

27 SHAKESPEARE: *Hamlet*, ACT III, SC II [220–223] 51b / *King Lear*, ACT I, SC II [128–164] 249a-b

29 CERVANTES: *Don Quixote*, PART II, 408c

31 DESCARTES: *Objections and Replies*, 141b

31 SPINOZA: *Ethics*, PART I, APPENDIX 369b-372d

32 MILTON: *Paradise Lost*, BK III [80–134] 137a-138a; BK V [224–245] 180a-b; [506–543] 186a-187a; BK VI [169–188] 200a; BK VII [139–173] 220a-221a; BK IX [342–375] 254b-255b; BK X [615–640] 287b-288b / *Samson Agonistes* [667–709] 354a-355a / *Areopagitica*, 394b-395b

35 LOCKE: *Civil Government*, CH II, SECT 6 26b-c

41 GIBBON: *Decline and Fall*, 230b

42 KANT: *Practical Reason*, 334a-335c

44 BOSWELL: *Johnson*, 549c

46 HEGEL: *Philosophy of History*, INTRO, 161d-162a

48 MELVILLE: *Moby Dick*, 159a; 396b; 409b-410b

51 TOLSTOY: *War and Peace*, BK XI, 481d; BK XII, 553b; EPILOGUE I, 650b-c; EPILOGUE II, 675a-677b; 680b-c; 684b-d

54 FREUD: *Interpretation of Dreams*, 246c-247d / *General Introduction*, 582a-b

5b. Man's freedom and God's knowledge

OLD TESTAMENT: *Psalms*, 139:15–16—(D) *Psalms*, 138:15–16

APOCRYPHA: *Ecclesiasticus*, 42:19—(D) OT, *Ecclesiasticus*, 42:19 / *Susanna*, 13:42–43—(D) OT, *Daniel*, 13:42–43

NEW TESTAMENT: *Acts*, 2:23 / *Romans*, 8:28–30 / *Ephesians*, 1:4–12 / *I Peter*, 1:2,19–20

12 AURELIUS: *Meditations*, BK VI, SECT 44 278b-c

18 AUGUSTINE: *City of God*, BK V, CH 9–10 213b-216c; BK XXII, CH 1, 587a-b

19 AQUINAS: *Summa Theologica*, PART I, Q 14, A 13 86d-88c; Q 22, A 2, REP 4 128d-130d; QQ 23–24 132b-143c; Q 86, A 4, ANS 463d-464d; PART I–II, Q 40, A 3, REP 1 794c-795a

21 DANTE: *Divine Comedy*, PARADISE, XVII [13–42] 132b-c

22 CHAUCER: *Troilus and Cressida*, BK IV, STANZA

138–154 106b-108b / *Nun's Priest's Tale* [15,236–256] 456b-457a

23 HOBBES: *Leviathan*, PART IV, 271b

25 MONTAIGNE: *Essays*, 342a

32 MILTON: *Paradise Lost*, BK III [80–134] 137a-138a; BK V [224–245] 180a-b; BK X [1–62] 274b-275b

41 GIBBON: *Decline and Fall*, 230b

44 BOSWELL: *Johnson*, 173c; 392d-393a

5c. Man's freedom and God's grace: the freedom of the children of God

OLD TESTAMENT: *Proverbs*, 1:20–33

NEW TESTAMENT: *John*, 1:1–18 esp 1:12–13; 6:44,65–66; 8:31–36 / *Acts*, 13:14–52; 15:1–11 / *Romans* passim, esp 3:1–8:21, 11:1–10 / *I Corinthians*, 6:11–12; 7:21–23; 8:9–13; 9:1–5,19–21; 10:23–29 / *II Corinthians*, 3:17; 6:1–2 / *Galatians*, 2:4; 4:1–5:4; 5:13,18,22–24 / *Ephesians*, 1:3–12; 2:4–22 / *Philippians*, 2:12–13 / *Colossians*, 1:12–13 / *Titus*, 2:11–14; 3:3–7 / *James*, 1:25; 2:10–12 / *I Peter*, 2:15–16 / *Revelation*, 3:20—(D) *Apocalypse*, 3:20

18 AUGUSTINE: *Confessions*, BK IX, par 1 61c-d / *City of God*, BK X, CH 32 319d-322a,c; BK XXII, CH 1, 587a-b; CH 30, 617c-618a

19 AQUINAS: *Summa Theologica*, PART I, Q 23, A 3, REP 3 134b-135a; AA 5–6 135d-138c; A 8 140a-141a; Q 62, A 3, REP 2 319c-320b; A 4, ANS 320b-321b; Q 83, A 2, CONTRARY 438a-d; Q 95, A 1, REP 3,5 506b-507c; PART I–II, Q 5, A 5, REP 1 640b-641a; Q 9, A 6, REP 3 662a-d

20 AQUINAS: *Summa Theologica*, PART I–II, Q 108, A 1, ANS and REP 2 331a-332b; Q 109, A 2 339c-340b; Q 111, A 2 352d-353d; Q 113, A 3 362c-363c; A 5 364b-365a; PART II–II, Q 183, A 4, REP 1 627d-628d

21 DANTE: *Divine Comedy*, PURGATORY, I [1–84] 53a-54a; XXVII 94c-96a esp [139–142] 96a; PARADISE, III [64–90] 110a-b; VII [64–84] 115d-116a; XXI [52–75] 138d-139a

31 DESCARTES: *Meditations*, IV, 91a-b

31 SPINOZA: *Ethics*, BK IV, PROP 68, SCHOL, 445a-b

32 MILTON: *Paradise Lost*, BK II [1024–1033] 133b; BK III [56–415] 136b-144b esp [130–134] 138a, [227–238] 140b; BK XI [1–21] 299a-b; [251–262] 304b-305a

33 PASCAL: *Provincial Letters*, 154b-159a

42 KANT: *Pure Reason*, 238b

46 HEGEL: *Philosophy of Right*, PART II, par 140, 50a / *Philosophy of History*, PART III, 310d-311a

5d. The divine freedom: the independence or autonomy of infinite being; divine choice

OLD TESTAMENT: *Exodus*, 33:19 / *Psalms*, 135:6 —(D) *Psalms*, 134:6 / *Isaiah*, 14:24–25; 46:9–13—(D) *Isaias*, 14:24–25; 46:9–12 / *Jeremiah*, 4:28—(D) *Jeremias*, 4:28 / *Daniel*, 4:4–37—(D) *Daniel*, 4

NEW TESTAMENT: *Matthew*, 20:1–16 / *John*, 5:21 / *Romans*, 8:28–9:26 esp 9:15–18 / *I Corinthians*, 12:7–18 / *Ephesians*, 1:9–11 / *Philippians*, 2:12–13 / *II Timothy*, 1:8–10 / *James*, 1:18

(5. *The theology of freedom. 5d. The divine freedom: the independence or autonomy of infinite being; divine choice.*)

4 HOMER: *Odyssey*, BK XIV [441–445] 264c

5 AESCHYLUS: *Agamemnon* [1017–1034] 63a

8 ARISTOTLE: *Metaphysics*, BK V, CH 5 [1015^{b}9–16] 536a; BK XII, CH 6–7 601b-603b; CH 10 [1075^{a}12–16] 605d

12 EPICTETUS: *Discourses*, BK III, CH 13, 188c-d; BK IV, CH 6, 230c-d

17 PLOTINUS: *Sixth Ennead*, TR VIII 342d-353d

18 AUGUSTINE: *Confessions*, BK VII, par 6–7 44d-45d; BK XII, par 18, 103a-b; BK XIII, par 5 111d; par 12 113b-d; par 19 115c-d / *City of God*, BK V, CH 10 215c-216c; BK XII, CH 17 353a-354a; BK XXI, CH 7–8 565d-568d; BK XXII, CH 2 587b-588a; CH 30, 617d-618a

19 AQUINAS: *Summa Theologica*, PART I, Q 7, AA 1–2 31a-32c; Q 9, A 1 38c-39c; Q 19, AA 3–5 110b-113c; A 10 117d-118b; Q 22, A 3, REP 3 130d-131c; Q 23, A 5, REP 3 135d-137d; A 6, REP 3 137d-138c; Q 25, A 2 144c-145b; AA 5–6 147d-150a; Q 46, A 1, REP 9–10 250a-252d; Q 47, A 1, REP 1 256a-257b; Q 61, A 2, REP 1 315c-316a; Q 104, A 3 537b-d; Q 105, A 1, REP 2 538d-539c

20 AQUINAS: *Summa Theologica*, PART I-II, Q 93, A 4, REP 1 218b-d; PART III, Q 21, A 1, ANS 823d-824d; PART III SUPPL, Q 91, A 1, REP 2 1016b-1017c

23 HOBBES: *Leviathan*, PART II, 113b-c

30 BACON: *Advancement of Learning*, 38a

31 DESCARTES: *Objections and Replies*, 228a-c

31 SPINOZA: *Ethics*, PART I, DEF 6–7 355b; PROP 17 362b-363c; PROP 32–35 367a-369a; APPENDIX 369b-372d

32 MILTON: *Paradise Lost*, BK VII [139–173] 220a-221a / *Samson Agonistes* [300–329] 346a-b

33 PASCAL: *Pensées*, 654 292b

35 LOCKE: *Human Understanding*, BK II, CH XXI, SECT 50–51 191b-c

35 BERKELEY: *Human Knowledge*, SECT 57 423d-424a; SECT 106 433c-d

42 KANT: *Fund. Prin. Metaphysic of Morals*, 265b-c esp 265b,d [fn 1] / *Practical Reason*, 321b-c; 324d-325a; 325d; 328b; 342c / *Intro. Metaphysic of Morals*, 393c

46 HEGEL: *Philosophy of History*, INTRO, 160c-161a

51 TOLSTOY: *War and Peace*, EPILOGUE II, 684c-d

6. Liberty in history

6a. **The historical significance of freedom: stages in the realization of freedom; the beginning and end of the historical process**

6 HERODOTUS: *History*, BK I, 23a-b; 38b-c; BK V, 175b; BK VI, 207b-208c; BK VII, 233a-b; 238b-c

6 THUCYDIDES: *Peloponnesian War*, BK I, 353c-d

7 PLATO: *Laws*, BK III 663d-677a

15 TACITUS: *Annals*, BK III, 51b-c

20 AQUINAS: *Summa Theologica*, PART I-II, Q 108, A 1 331a-332b

40 GIBBON: *Decline and Fall*, 24c; 32c-34a,c esp 33c-d; 51c; 90d-91a; 475a; 521c-523a,c esp 522d-523a; 523d-524a

41 GIBBON: *Decline and Fall*, 161c-162a; 202a-d; 300a-b; 452d-453a,c

43 MILL: *Liberty*, 267d-268b; 271d-272a / *Representative Government*, 339a-341d; 346a-c / *Utilitarianism*, 475d

46 HEGEL: *Philosophy of Right*, INTRO, par 4, 12d; PART I, par 57 26b-27a; PART III, par 340–360 110b-114a,c; ADDITIONS, 36 122b-c / *Philosophy of History* 153a-369a,c esp INTRO, 156d-190b, 203a-206a,c, PART I, 207a-209a, 219d-221a, 230a-c, 235d-236c, 245d-246c, 251c, 257a-258a, PART II, 259a-260c, 263d-267a, 268b-274a, PART III, 286c-287a, 303c-307b, 310d-311d, PART IV, 315a, 319b-321c, 331d-333d, 348a-c, 350a-c, 360c-365c, 368d-369a,c

50 MARX: *Capital*, 35b-c

6b. **The struggle for civil liberty and economic freedom: the overthrow of tyrants, despots, and oppressors**

OLD TESTAMENT: *I Kings*, 12:1–25—(D) *III Kings*, 12:1–25 / *II Kings*, 9:1–10:11; 11; 21:18–26—(D) *IV Kings*, 9:1–10:11; 11; 21:18–26 / *II Chronicles*, 10—(D) *II Paralipomenon*, 10

6 HERODOTUS: *History*, BK III, 120b-c; BK IV, 124a-d; BK V, 167a-b; 171c-175b; 177d-180a; BK VI, 193b-c; 201a-b; 208d-209b; BK VII, 243b-c

6 THUCYDIDES: *Peloponnesian War*, BK I, 353c; BK VI, 523c-524d; BK VIII 564a-593a,c esp 582a-583c, 585d-586b, 587a-589a, 590a-c

7 PLATO: *Seventh Letter*, 813d-814d

9 ARISTOTLE: *Politics*, BK V, CH 10 512d-515d / *Athenian Constitution*, CH 5 554d-555a; CH 13–20 558b-562b; CH 33–41 568b-572a passim

14 PLUTARCH: *Solon* 64b,d-77a,c / *Poplicola* 77a-86a,c / *Poplicola-Solon* 86a-87d / *Coriolanus* 174b,d-193a,c / *Timoleon* 195a-213d esp 206d / *Pelopidas* 232a-246a,c / *Caesar*, 600a-604d / *Cato the Younger* 620a-648a,c esp 643a-644b / *Agis* 648b,d-656d / *Tiberius Gracchus* 671b,d-681a,c esp 678b-d / *Caius Gracchus* 681b,d-689a,c / *Demetrius*, 728b-729d / *Antony*, 752a-755c / *Marcus Brutus* 802b,d-824a,c / *Aratus* 826a-846a,c

15 TACITUS: *Annals*, BK XI, 104a-c; BK XII, 112a-113b; 115d-116b; 117a; BK XV, 169a-176b / *Histories*, BK I, 195a-201c esp 197a-c

26 SHAKESPEARE: *2nd Henry VI*, ACT IV, SC II–X 57d-64d / *Richard III*, ACT V, SC III [237–270] 146b-c / *Julius Caesar* 568a-596a,c esp ACT I, SC III [72–130] 573b-d, ACT III, SC I 580b-583c

27 SHAKESPEARE: *Coriolanus* 351a-392a,c

32 MILTON: *Lord Gen. Fairfax* 68b-69a / *Lord Gen. Cromwell* 69a-b

CROSS-REFERENCES

For: The problem of the freedom of the will, *see* WILL 5-6c, 8a; and for the relation of political liberty to free will, *see* WILL 5a(2), 7a.

The freedom of men in a state of nature or anarchy, and for the independence of sovereign states, *see* GOVERNMENT 1a; NATURE 2b; STATE 3c, 9d; WAR AND PEACE 1.

Matters relevant to political liberty or the freedom of the individual as a member of society, *see* CITIZEN 2b; CONSTITUTION 1, 2b, 7b; DEMOCRACY 4a, 4b, 5c; GOVERNMENT 1h; JUSTICE 6, 6c-6e; LAW 7b-7c; MONARCHY 1a(1), 4d-5b; SLAVERY 6-6d; TYRANNY 5-5c; and for the relation of economic to political liberty, *see* DEMOCRACY 4a(2); LABOR 7f; SLAVERY 5-5b; WEALTH 9d.

Other discussions of freedom of thought or expression, *see* ART 10b; EDUCATION 8c; KNOWLEDGE 9b; OPINION 5a-5b; POETRY 9b; PROGRESS 6e; TRUTH 8d; and for other discussions of liberty of conscience and freedom of worship, *see* RELIGION 6c(1)-6e; THEOLOGY 4e.

The moral or psychological freedom in the relation of reason and emotion, *see* DESIRE 5-6c; EMOTION 4-4b(2); MIND 9d; SLAVERY 7; TYRANNY 5d.

The metaphysical consideration of liberty and matters related thereto, *see* CAUSE 3; FATE 3; NATURE 2f; NECESSITY AND CONTINGENCY 5a, 5a(3), 5f; WILL 5a(3), 5c, 8a.

The theological consideration of liberty, *see* FATE 4; GOD 4e, 5f-5g, 7b, 7d, 7f; SIN 6a, 7; WILL 4b, 7c-7e(2).

For: The issue of freedom and necessity in the philosophy of history, *see* FATE 6; HISTORY 4a(1), 4a(3); WILL 7b; and for the history of man's struggle for civil liberty and economic freedom, *see* CITIZEN 9; LABOR 7c–7c(3); REVOLUTION 5a–5c, 6a, 7; TYRANNY 8.

ADDITIONAL READINGS

Listed below are works not included in *Great Books of the Western World*, but relevant to the idea and topics with which this chapter deals. These works are divided into two groups:

I. Works by authors represented in this collection.
II. Works by authors not represented in this collection.

For the date, place, and other facts concerning the publication of the works cited, consult the Bibliography of Additional Readings which follows the last chapter of *The Great Ideas*.

I.

DANTE. *On World-Government or De Monarchia,* BK I, CH 12

MACHIAVELLI. *The Discourses*

MILTON. *The Readie and Easie Way to Establish a Free Commonwealth*

SPINOZA. *Tractatus Theologico-Politicus (Theological-Political Treatise),* CH 20

LOCKE. *Four Letters on Toleration in Religion,* II–IV

HEGEL. *The Phenomenology of Mind,* IV(B)

DOSTOEVSKY. *The House of the Dead*

II.

LUTHER. *A Treatise on Christian Liberty*

CALVIN. *Institutes of the Christian Religion,* BK IV

SUÁREZ. *Disputationes Metaphysicae,* XI (3), XIX, XXX (16), XXXV (5)

DEFOE. *The Shortest Way with the Dissenters*

LEIBNITZ. *New Essays Concerning Human Understanding,* BK II, CH 21

FRANKLIN. *Dissertation on Liberty and Necessity, Pleasure and Pain*

VOLTAIRE. *Essay on Toleration*

——. "Liberty," "Liberty of Opinion," "Liberty of the Press," "Toleration," in *A Philosophical Dictionary*

T. REID. *Essays on the Active Powers of the Human Mind,* IV

PAINE. *Rights of Man*

BURKE. *Reflections on the Revolution in France*

GODWIN. *An Enquiry Concerning Political Justice,* BK II, CH 4–6

SCHILLER. *William Tell*

SCHELLING. *Of Human Freedom*

SCHOPENHAUER. *The World as Will and Idea,* VOL I, BK IV

SHELLEY. *Prometheus Unbound*

BYRON. *Sonnet on Chillon*

——. *The Isles of Greece*

BENTHAM. *On the Liberty of the Press*

EMERSON. "Self-Reliance," in *Essays,* I

J. H. NEWMAN. "Private Judgment," in VOL II, *Essays and Sketches*

THOREAU. *Civil Disobedience*

WHITMAN. *Leaves of Grass*

LOTZE. *Microcosmos,* BK I, CH 1 (4)

BURCKHARDT. *Force and Freedom*

J. F. STEPHEN. *Liberty, Equality, Fraternity*

ACTON. *Essays on Freedom and Power,* CH 2–4, 9

BRADLEY. *Ethical Studies,* I

ARNOLD. "Democracy," "Equality," in *Mixed Essays*

T. H. GREEN. *The Principles of Political Obligation,* (H, I)

——. *Prolegomena to Ethics,* BK I, CH 3

SPENCER. *The Man Versus the State*

R. BROWNING. *Why I Am a Liberal*

LECKY. *Democracy and Liberty*

BOSANQUET. *The Philosophical Theory of the State*

GIDE. *The Immoralist*

SANTAYANA. *Reason in Society,* CH 6

PÉGUY. *Basic Verities* (Freedom)

BURY. *A History of Freedom of Thought*

BURGESS. *Reconciliation of Government with Liberty*

GARRIGOU-LAGRANGE. *God, His Existence and Nature,* PART II, CH 4

DUGUIT. *Souveraineté et liberté*

B. RUSSELL. *Skeptical Essays,* XII–XIV

LASKI. *Liberty in the Modern State*

WHITEHEAD. *Adventures of Ideas,* CH 4–5

GORKY. *Forty Years—the Life of Clim Samghin*

DEWEY. "The Idea of Freedom," in *Outlines of a Critical Theory of Ethics*

——. *The Study of Ethics,* CH 8

——. *Characters and Events,* VOL II, BK III (14)

——. *Experience and Education,* CH 5–6

——. *Freedom and Culture*

CROCE. *History as the Story of Liberty*

——. "The Roots of Liberty," in *Freedom, Its Meaning*

KOESTLER. *Darkness at Noon*

MARITAIN. "A Philosophy of Freedom," in *Freedom in the Modern World*

——. *Scholasticism and Politics,* CH V

BECKER. *New Liberties for Old*

A. J. CARLYLE. *Political Liberty*

BARKER. *Reflections on Government,* CH 1–2

MALINOWSKI. *Freedom and Civilization*

BERDYAEV. *Freedom and the Spirit*

——. *Slavery and Freedom*

HOCKING. *Freedom of the Press*

SIMON. *Community of the Free,* CH 1

Chapter 48: LIFE AND DEATH

INTRODUCTION

MEN have divided the totality of things in various ways. The three most fundamental divisions rest on the distinction between the natural and the supernatural, between the material and the spiritual, and between the lifeless and the living.

The same kind of basic question is raised by each of these divisions, and given opposite answers in the tradition of the great books. The question is not always formulated in the same way. It may be a question about the existence of the supernatural order or of incorporeal beings. It may be a problem of whether the terms of the division represent a real duality or merely different aspects of one and the same whole. Are God and nature one or are they radically distinct? Is spirituality merely one expression of bodily existence, or are there two worlds, a world of bodies and a world of spirits?

These issues are considered in the chapters on GOD, NATURE, ANGEL, and MATTER, as well as in the chapter on BEING. The issue raised by the third great division is one of the central topics in this chapter. That issue concerns the difference between the living and the non-living. There is no question here about whether, in the order of nature, living things exist. The fact of life is not denied, at least not as a matter of observation. On the surface there certainly appears to be a striking difference between the living tree and the stone, or between the animal which a moment ago was alive and is now dead.

But how this difference is to be understood is the question. Does it signify an absolute break, a discontinuity, between the world of living bodies and the domain of inanimate things? Or is the continuity of nature preserved across the line which divides inorganic and organic matter? Is the difference between the non-living and the living (or the living and the dead) one of kind or of degree?

Those who answer that it is a difference in kind usually formulate a definition of life which draws a sharp line, on one side of which are the things that have the indispensable properties of life, while on the other side are things totally lacking in these properties. The critical point here turns on whether vitality is present in some degree or totally absent. The definition of life may not always be the same. It may not always, for example, postulate the soul as the principle in all living things, or involve the same conception of soul in relation to living organisms. But when life is defined as an essential characteristic of some natures, the definition implies the existence of natures which are totally lacking in the properties essential to life. It also implies the impossibility of intermediate links between the lowest form of life and the most complex of the inorganic substances.

The opposite answer that there is only a difference in degree between the inanimate and the animate, affirms the continuity of nature across the gap between things which appear lifeless and those which seem to be alive. All bodies have the same fundamental properties, though not in the same magnitude. But here there is a further question. It can be asked whether those properties are the powers or functions commonly associated with the appearance of being alive, such as growth, reproduction, sensitivity, desire, locomotion; or whether they are the mechanical properties of matter in motion—properties which vary only with the degrees of complexity in the organization of matter.

According to the doctrine which is sometimes called "animism" and sometimes "panpsychism," everything is alive, every body is be-souled, though at the lower end of the scale the signs of vitality remain hidden from ordinary observation. Although this theory is usually attributed to a primitive view of nature, it appears in a subtle form in certain philosophical developments which make soul or mind a principle as universal as matter. "There is one common substance," says Marcus Aurelius, "though it is distributed among countless bodies which have their several qualities. There is one soul, though it is distributed among infinite natures and individual circumscriptions."

The doctrine which in modern times is called "mechanism" conceives the continuity of nature in terms of the universality of purely mechanical principles. It reduces all phenomena to the interaction of moving parts or particles. No new principle is needed to explain the phenomena of life. The laws of physics and chemistry suffice. Biophysics and biochemistry simply deal with the mechanics of more complex material systems. The apparent differences in function between "living" and "non-living" things represent the same functions. They are altered only in *appearance* by the more complex organization of the matter which is called "living."

THE CONTROVERSY over mechanistic principles in the analysis of life arose with great explicitness in the latter part of the nineteenth century and continues to our own day. The chief opponents of the mechanists are those who at one time called themselves "vitalists" to signify their insistence upon an essential difference between vital and mechanical phenomena. The work of Jacques Loeb can be taken to represent the mechanistic side of this controversy; the writings of Bergson, Haldane, Whitehead, the vitalist position.

Those who regard the realm of living things as a distinct domain in nature also think that the study of living things has special concepts, principles, and methods as different from those of physics and chemistry as the objects studied are distinct.

Biology is a science of ancient origin. The Hippocratic collection of writings on health and disease, the extensive biological researches of Aristotle, the work of Galen, represent more than a bare beginning of the science. The ancient classification of vital functions establishes

the terms of biological analysis. Ideas which have come to seem obvious because of traditional acceptance were once great discoveries; for example, that all living bodies nourish themselves, grow, and reproduce; that these are the minimal, not the maximal, functions of organic matter; that there is a regular cycle of growth and decay in the normal life span which is itself different for different types of organisms; that in the dynamic equilibrium between the living organism and its physical environment, the organism actively maintains itself through a certain balance of exchanges in the biological economy, of which breathing is a prime example.

The great books of biological science from Aristotle to Harvey seem to be of one mind on the point that living matter possesses distinctive powers and performs functions which are not present *in any degree* in the realm of the inert or inorganic. For the most part they reflect the theory that the living body possesses a soul which is the principle of its vitality and the source of the vital powers embodied in its various organs.

In ancient and mediaeval theory, the soul is not conceived as belonging peculiarly to man; it is not identified with mind or with the intellectual faculties. The word "animal" derives from the Latin name for soul—the principle of animation. It is true that Galen distinguishes between what he calls the "natural" and the "psychic" faculties. The latter for him are the powers of sensitivity, desire, and locomotion. Yet his analysis of the vegetative powers of nutrition, growth, and reproduction which are common to plants and animals squares with Aristotle's conception of the vegetative soul.

"What has soul in it," Aristotle writes, "differs from what has not, in that the former displays life. Now this word has more than one sense. . . . Living, that is, may mean thinking or perception or local movement and rest, or movement in the sense of nutrition, decay, and growth. Hence we think of plants also as living, for they are observed to possess in themselves an originative power through which they increase and decrease in all spatial directions. This power of self-nutrition . . . is the originative power, the possession of which leads us to speak of things as *living*."

IN THE GREAT BOOKS the opposite position with respect to the living and non-living seems to appear for the first time with Descartes. It might be supposed that Lucretius, since he denies the soul as an immaterial principle, would also tend to reject anything except a difference in degree between animate and inanimate bodies. But this is not the case. According to Lucretius living things are not merely more complex combinations of atoms and void. Their constitution includes a special type of soul-atom, whose round, smooth shape and speed of movement through all parts of the living body accounts for the powers and activities which are peculiar to that body. Lucretius is recognized as a materialist and a mechanist, yet he sharply separates living from non-living bodies and appeals to a special principle—the soul-atom—to explain this difference in kind.

As appears in the chapters on MIND and SOUL, Descartes is at variance not only with Lucretius but also with Aristotle, Galen, and Plotinus in his conception of the soul and of life. The soul is not a body or composed of bodies. Neither, in his opinion, is it an immaterial principle conjoined with organic matter to constitute the living body. It is itself an immaterial substance, quite separate from the human body to which it is allied.

Descartes tells us how he passed from "a description of inanimate bodies and plants . . . to that of animals, and particularly to that of men." He asks us to consider the supposition that "God formed the body of man altogether like one of ours . . . without making use of any matter other than that which I have described and without at first placing in it a rational soul or any other thing which might serve as a vegetative or sensitive soul." He then goes on to say that "examining the functions which might in accordance with this supposition exist in this body, I found precisely all those which might exist in us without our having the power of thought, and consequently without our soul— that is to say, this part of us, distinct from the body, of which it has been said that its nature is to think."

The mechanistic implications of his supposition are explicitly developed by Descartes in his consideration of Harvey's discovery of the motions of the heart and blood. These movements, he says, follow "as necessarily from the very disposition of the organs . . . as does that of a clock from the power, the situation, and the form, of its counterpoise and of its wheels." In these motions, as well as in the actions of the nerves, brain, and muscles, it is not necessary to suppose any other cause than those operating according "to the laws of Mechanics which are identical with those of nature."

This will not seem strange, Descartes adds, to those who know "how many different automata or moving machines can be made by the industry of man, without employing in so doing more than a very few parts in comparison with the great multitude of bones, muscles, nerves, arteries, veins or other parts that are found in the body of each animal. From this aspect, the body is regarded as a machine, which, having been made by the hands of God, is incomparably better arranged, and possesses in itself movements which are much more admirable, than any of those which can be invented by man." Only the functions of reason, only the acts of thinking—not those of living—operate under other than the mechanical laws of corporeal nature. Whether living or not, all bodies without reason or a rational soul are automata or machines. Whatever they do can be explained as a kind of clockwork—by the disposition and interaction of their parts.

ANOTHER SOURCE and another version of the view that the continuity of nature is uninterrupted, comes from the theory of evolution. Darwin himself, in his brief consideration of the origin of life, deals mainly with the alternative hypotheses of the divine creation of a *single* original form or of *several* primitive forms from which the whole of the plant and animal kingdoms has developed by the natural steps of evolution. He rejects the division of the animate world into more than the two great kingdoms of plant and animal life, and holds that man differs from other animals only in degree, not in kind.

As indicated in the chapters on ANIMAL and EVOLUTION, Darwin questions the discontinuity between plants and animals. He refers to the intermediate forms which seem to belong to both kingdoms. He suggests the possibility that the lowest forms of animal life may have developed by natural evolutionary descent from plant organisms. But he does not *seriously* consider the hypothesis of an evolutionary transition from inorganic matter to living organisms. Here, on the contrary, he seems to recognize a difference in kind. "The most humble organism," he writes, "is something much higher than the inorganic dust under our feet; and no one with an unbiased mind can study any living creature, however humble, without being struck with enthusiasm at its marvellous structure and properties." He questions the notion that living organisms might have originated from inorganic matter by spontaneous generation. "Science has not as yet proved the truth of this belief," he says, "whatever the future may reveal."

Nevertheless, with the extension of Darwin's theory of the origin of species into a doctrine of cosmic evolution, what James calls "the evolutionary afflatus" leads writers like Tyndall and Spencer to "talk as if mind grew out of body in a continuous way. . . . So strong a postulate is continuity," James writes, that the evolutionists try to "leap over the breach" between inorganic matter and consciousness.

"In a general theory of evolution," he explains, "the inorganic comes first, then the lowest forms of animal and vegetable life, then forms of life that possess mentality, and finally those like ourselves that possess it in a high degree. . . . We are dealing all the time with matter and its aggregations and separations; and although our treatment must perforce be hypothetical, this does not prevent it from being *continuous*. The point which as evolutionists we are bound to hold fast is that all the new forms of being that make their appearance are nothing more than results of the redistribution of the original and unchanging materials. The self-same atoms which, chaotically dispersed, made the nebula, now, jammed and temporarily caught in peculiar position, form our brains; and the 'evolution' of the brains, if understood, would be simply the account of how the atoms came to be so caught and jammed. In this story no new *natures*, no factors not present at the beginning, are introduced at any later stage."

James is here presenting a theory which he himself rejects. He recognizes the strength of the "postulate of continuity" in the theories of Spencer, Tyndall, and other evolutionists, but he thinks the evident "contrasts between living and inanimate performances" favor the division of nature into two realms. Yet he also seems to regard some degree of intelligence or mentality as an accompaniment of life. Hence his criterion of the difference in kind "between an intelligent and a mechanical performance"—namely, purposiveness or "the pursuance of future ends and the choice of means"—also serves as the mark of distinction between the animate and the inanimate.

IT IS WORTH remarking that this criterion is one of the tests Descartes proposes for differentiating man from all the rest of nature, man alone having reason or thought. It is also worth noting that in associating different degrees of mentality or consciousness with life at all levels of development, James himself affirms a continuity in the realm of all living things. He therefore does not go as far in the direction of discontinuity as do those in the tradition of the great books who find an essential difference between the inanimate and the living, between plant and animal, and between brute and human life.

The issues raised by these last two distinctions are further considered in the chapters on ANIMAL, MAN, and MIND. Here we are concerned only with the fact that those who find genuine differences in kind in the world of animate things also tend to distinguish between the living and the non-living by reference to the most generic properties of corporeal life, that is, the powers or functions shared by plants, animals, and men. The question of origins does not seem to be relevant to the problem of differences. Aquinas, for example, does not seem to regard the hypothesis of the spontaneous generation of living organisms from putrefying organic matter as inconsistent with his assertion that the vegetative functions of plants and animals are not performed—*in any degree*—by inanimate bodies.

When Aristotle says of natural bodies that "some have life in them, others not; and by life we mean self-nutrition and growth," he is aware that the word "growth" occurs in the description of a certain type of change in inanimate bodies. Other than living things increase in size. To avoid an equivocal use of the word "growth," he assigns three distinguishing characteristics to the quantitative change or increase in living things: "(1) Any and every part of the growing magnitude is made bigger, (2) by the accession of something, and (3) in such a way that the growing thing is preserved and persists."

To exemplify this difference, Galen compares the growth of an organism with the expansion of a dried bladder when children blow air into it. The expanding bladder seems to grow, but not as it did when it was a part of a living animal and when the growth of the whole involved the growth of each part. "In these doings of the children," Galen writes, "the more the interior cavity of the bladder increases in size, the thinner, necessarily, does its substance become. But, if the children were able to bring nourishment to this thin part, then they would make the bladder big in the same way that Nature does. ... To be distended in all directions belongs only to bodies whose growth is directed by Nature; for those which are distended by us undergo this distension in one direction but grow less in the others; it is impossible to find a body which will remain entire and not be torn through whilst we stretch it in the three dimensions. Thus Nature alone has the power to expand a body in all directions so that it remains unruptured and preserves completely its previous form."

Modern biologists sometimes compare the growth of crystals in solution with living growth and reproduction. Or, making the point that "other systems in dynamic equilibrium show in essence all the properties of living things," they say that "it is almost impossible to distinguish a candle flame from a living organism." Aristotle considers the latter comparison and rejects it. He observes that "the growth of fire goes on without limit so long as there is a supply of fuel"; but no amount of nutriment can increase the size of living things without limit. "There is a limit or ratio which determines their size and increase, and the limit and ratio are marks of the soul, but not of fire."

The flame is a lively thing, but to say that it is alive, that it grows or dies, is in Aristotle's view a poetic metaphor, not a scientific statement. "When I have plucked the rose," Othello says, "I cannot give it vital growth again, it

needs must wither." But to the candle burning beside Desdemona's bed, he says: "If I quench thee, thou flaming minister, I can again thy former light restore." The flame is lit or extinguished by motions from without; but the birth and death, the nourishing and growth of the living thing is self-movement.

According to Aristotle and Aquinas self-movement is the essential mark of being alive. "All things are said to be alive," Aquinas writes, "which determine themselves to movement or operation of any kind; whereas those things which cannot by their own nature do so, cannot be called living except by a similitude." He further defines the meaning of self-movement by distinguishing between the *transitive* action of one inert body upon another and the *immanent* activity of a living thing, whereby the agent itself is perfected. Growing, sensing, and understanding are immanent actions because they are activities which affect the growing, sensing, or understanding thing. The result of such actions *remains in the agent*. In contrast, heating is a transitive action. In heating, one thing acts upon another, and the hot thing loses its own heat in the process.

As vital operations differ thus from the actions of inanimate bodies, so do vital powers differ from the capacities of inert matter, through which bodies can act upon or react to other bodies. The power of self-movement (or immanent activity) enables living things alone to change from a less perfect to a more perfect state of being, as measured by the thing's nature, rather than simply to change from contrary to contrary, as a body changes when it moves locally from this place to that, or alters from hot to cold, or cold to hot.

FOR THE THEOLOGIAN, there is an additional aspect to the problem of defining life. If the realm of corporeal substances is divided into inert and living bodies, what is to be said about incorporeal substances (*i.e.*, the angels) and about God? It is easier to think of the angels as *not being* than to conceive them as *not being alive*. More than "infinite" or "omnipotent" or "eternal," "the ever-living God" is the phrase which, in the language of religious worship, expresses positively the divine nature. But the fundamental activities which distinguish living from non-living bodies (such as nutrition, growth, reproduction) are essentially corporeal in nature. So, too, are sensing and locomotion. What common meaning of life, then, can apply to material and spiritual beings?

Aquinas answers by saying that "since a thing is said to live in so far as it operates of itself and not as moved by another, the more perfectly this power is found in anything, the more perfect is the life of that thing." By this criterion, plants are less perfectly alive than animals, in whom self-movement is found to a higher degree because of their sensitive faculties; and among animals, there are grades of life according to degrees of sensitivity, and according to the possession of mobility, a power which certain animals seem to lack. In both the higher animals and in man, there is purposive behavior, but man alone, through his intellect and will, can freely determine his own ends and choose the means to them; hence these faculties give human life an even greater degree of self-movement.

But the action of the human intellect is not perfectly self-determined, for it depends in part upon external causes. Wherefore Aquinas concludes that life in the highest degree belongs properly to God—"that being whose act of understanding is its very nature and which, in what it naturally possesses, is not determined by another." He quotes Aristotle's remark that the perfection of God's life is proportionate to the perfection of the divine intellect, which is purely actual and eternally in act. And he goes on to remark that, in the sense in which understanding is movement, and that which understands itself moves itself, "Plato also taught that God moves Himself."

Nourishment, growth, and reproduction are indispensable features of corporeal life precisely because corporeal things are perishable. They need "reproduction to preserve the species," Aquinas writes, "and nourishment to preserve the individual." Hence the higher powers of life, such as sensing and understanding, are never found in corporeal things apart from the vegetative powers. This does not hold, however, for spiritual beings which are by nature imperishable. Spiritual life is essentially immortal life.

Subject to the ravages of time, corporeal life at every moment betrays its mortality—in its need for sleep, in the enfeeblement of its pow-

ers, in disease, decay, or degeneration. Death is the correlative of life for those who sharply divide the living from the non-living. Rocks may crumble into dust, bodies may disintegrate, and atoms explode—but they do not die. Death is a change which only living matter undergoes.

The transition from life to death accentuates the mystery of life. The notion of spontaneous generation aside, life always seems to come from life. Whether by cell division or by germination, the living thing that is generated comes from the living substance of another thing. But when a living thing dies, it crosses the gap between the living and the non-living. As the organic matter of the corpse decomposes, nothing is left but the familiar inorganic elements and compounds. This seems to be a change more radical than generation or birth. All the metaphysical problems of form and substance, of matter and the soul, of continuity and discontinuity in nature, which appear in the analysis of life, become more intense in the understanding of death.

As APPEARS in the chapter on IMMORTALITY, the living are preoccupied with death, not predominantly with analyzing it, but with facing and fearing it, struggling against or embracing it. Death, as the great poems reveal, is the object of soliloquy in moments of greatest introspection or self-appraisal. To die well, Montaigne points out, requires greater moral stamina than to live well. For him the essence of the philosophical temper, as for others the meaning of heroism or martyrdom, consists in facing death with an equanimity which reflects the highest qualities of a well-resolved life.

Montaigne devotes a long essay to the subject that "to philosophise is to learn to die," and begins it by quoting Cicero's statement that "to study philosophy is nothing but to prepare one's self to die." Socrates then is the prototype of the philosopher, for in conversation with his friends in prison while awaiting death, he tells them that "the true votary of philosophy . . . is always pursuing death, and dying." He tries to prove to them, by his actions as well as by his words, that "the real philosopher has reason to be of good cheer when he is about to die."

Not only death but the dead exercise a profound effect upon the living. The historians describe the various forms which the ceremonials of death take in every society. Whether the rituals are secular or sacred, they are among the most significant customs of any culture, for they reveal the value placed upon life and the conception of life's meaning and man's destiny. No deeper differences exist among the great religions than those which appear in the practices or sacraments in preparation for death and in the services for the dead.

The moral, social, and religious aspects of death appear to be peculiarly human. Yet on the biological level, the same fundamental instincts and emotions seem to prevail in animals and men. The struggle to remain alive may be presumed to occur in plants. But it is not there as plainly discernible as in the specific patterns of behavior manifested by the animal instinct of self-preservation. Almost in proportion to the degree of vitality, the instinct of self-preservation operates with a strength and pertinacity as vigorous as the love for life and arouses as an emotional corollary an equally devouring fear of death.

The instinct of self-preservation is the life instinct. Directed toward the related ends of maintaining and increasing life are the reproductive impulses and the erotic instincts. But, according to Freud, there is in all living matter a more primitive instinct than these, and one which aims in the opposite direction. That is the death instinct—the impulse of the living to return to lifelessness.

"It would be contrary to the conservative nature of instinct," Freud writes, "if the goal of life were a state never hitherto reached. It must rather be an ancient starting point, which the living being left long ago, and to which it harks back again. . . . If we may assume as an experience admitting of no exception that everything dies from causes within itself, and returns to the inorganic, we can only say 'The goal of all life is death.' "

The death instinct, according to Freud, originates with life itself. "At one time or another, by some operation of force which completely baffles conjecture, the properties of life were awakened in lifeless matter. . . . The tension then aroused in the previously inanimate matter strove to attain an equilibrium; the first instinct was present, that to return to lifelessness." The death instinct acts against the tendency of

the erotic instincts, "which are always trying to collect living substances together into ever larger unities. . . . The cooperation and opposition of these two forces produce the phenomena of life to which death puts an end."

Freud's hypothesis of the death instinct has a bearing on the impulse to commit suicide and on the question whether it is natural or perverse for men to choose this escape from the tensions and difficulties of life. The psychological problem here, especially with regard to the unconscious forms of the suicidal impulse, is not the same as the moral problem. The question whether animals other than men ever commit suicide, like the question whether the killing of one animal by another can be called "murder," indicates the difference between psychological description and moral judgment.

FOR THE MORALIST the condemnation of suicide seems to rest on the same grounds as the condemnation of murder. With Kant, for example, it represents the same type of violation of the universal moral law. The categorical imperative requires us to act always as if the maxim of our individual action could be universalized as a rule for all men to follow. But, in the case of suicide as in the case of murder, the maxim of the action cannot be universalized without accomplishing a result which no one intends. Furthermore, suicide is not consistent with the idea of the human person as an end in itself. The man, says Kant, who destroys himself "in order to escape from painful circumstances uses a person merely as a means to maintain a tolerable condition up to the end of life."

Suicide is also condemned by the theologians as a contravention of the divine as well as of the natural law. Men are God's handiwork and, therefore, as Locke puts it, "they are His property . . . made to last during His, not one another's, pleasure." Under the natural law, a man is not at liberty to destroy himself, nor consequently is he at liberty to sell himself into slavery. Everyone "is bound to preserve himself and not quit his station willfully." If, furthermore, there is an after-life of rewards and punishments, suicide is no escape. "Death so snatched," Adam tells Eve in *Paradise Lost*, "will not exempt us from the pain we are by doom to pay."

There is similar reasoning in pagan antiquity. Suicide is an act of violence and, says Plotinus, "if there be a period allotted to all by fate, to anticipate the hour could not be a happy act. . . . If everyone is to hold in the other world a standing determined by the state in which he quitted this, there must be no withdrawal as long as there is any hope of progress." A Christian would add that to relinquish hope as long as life persists is the sin of despair.

But the pagan tradition also speaks with an opposite voice. For the Stoics, suicide does not seem to be as reprehensible as murder. To those who complain of life's pains and the fetters of the body, Epictetus says, "The door is open." In a doctrine in which all things that affect only the body are indifferent to the soul's well-being, death too is indifferent. "Death is the harbor for all; this is the place of refuge; as soon as you choose, you may be out of the house."

OUTLINE OF TOPICS

REFERENCES

To find the passages cited, use the numbers in heavy type, which are the volume and page numbers of the passages referred to. For example, in 4 HOMER: *Iliad*, BK II [265–283] 12d, the number 4 is the number of the volume in the set; the number 12d indicates that the passage is in section d of page 12.

PAGE SECTIONS: When the text is printed in one column, the letters a and b refer to the upper and lower halves of the page. For example, in 53 JAMES: *Psychology*, 116a–119b, the passage begins in the upper half of page 116 and ends in the lower half of page 119. When the text is printed in two columns, the letters a and b refer to the upper and lower halves of the left-hand side of the page, the letters c and d to the upper and lower halves of the right-hand side of the page. For example, in 7 PLATO: *Symposium*, 163b–164c, the passage begins in the lower half of the left-hand side of page 163 and ends in the upper half of the right-hand side of page 164.

AUTHOR'S DIVISIONS: One or more of the main divisions of a work (such as PART, BK, CH, SECT) are sometimes included in the reference; line numbers, in brackets, are given in certain cases; *e.g.*, *Iliad*, BK II [265–283] 12d.

BIBLE REFERENCES: The references are to book, chapter, and verse. When the King James and Douay versions differ in title of books or in the numbering of chapters or verses, the King James version is cited first and the Douay, indicated by a (*D*), follows; *e.g.*, OLD TESTAMENT: *Nehemiah*, 7:45—(*D*) II *Esdras* 7:46.

SYMBOLS: The abbreviation "esp" calls the reader's attention to one or more especially relevant parts of a whole reference; "passim" signifies that the topic is discussed intermittently rather than continuously in the work or passage cited.

For additional information concerning the style of the references, see the Explanation of Reference Style; for general guidance in the use of *The Great Ideas*, consult the Preface.

1. The nature and cause of life: the soul as the principle of life in organic bodies

OLD TESTAMENT: *Genesis*, 1:20–27; 2:7 / *Job*, 12:9–10

7 PLATO: *Cratylus*, 93c / *Phaedrus*, 124b-d / *Phaedo*, 223c-d; 225b; 244–246c / *Gorgias*, 275d-277b passim / *Laws*, BK X, 763a-764a

8 ARISTOTLE: *Topics*, BK VI, CH 10 [148^{a}23–37] 202b-c / *Metaphysics*, BK V, CH 4 [1014^{b}22–26] 535a; CH 8 [1017^{b}10–17] 538b; BK VII, CH 10 [1035^{b}14–28] 559a-b; BK IX, CH 6 [1048^{b}18–34] 574a-c; BK XII, CH 7 [1072^{b}14–29] 602d-603a; BK XIII, CH 2 [1077^{a}20–23] 608c / *Soul*, BK I 631a-641d passim; BK II, CH 1–4 642a-647b; BK III, CH 12–13 667a-668d / *Youth, Life, and Breathing*, CH 1–4 714a-716b; CH 14 720d-721a

9 ARISTOTLE: *Parts of Animals*, BK I, CH 1 [640^{b}30–641^{a}33] 163c-164b / *Generation of Animals*, BK I, CH 19 [726^{b}15–29] 266d-267a; BK II, CH 1 [731^{b}29–33] 272a-b; [734^{b}20–735^{a}9] 275b-d; CH 3 [737^{a}18–34] 278a-b; CH 5 [741^{a}6–31] 282a-b; BK III, CH 11 [762^{a}18–^{b}22] 303b-d

10 GALEN: *Natural Faculties*, BK I, CH 1 167a-b; BK II, CH 3, 185a-b

12 LUCRETIUS: *Nature of Things*, BK II [865–1022] 26a-28a; BK III [94–416] 31b-35c; BK V [783–825] 71b-d

17 PLOTINUS: *First Ennead*, TR I 1a-6b passim / *Second Ennead*, TR III, CH 12–13 46c-47b / *Third Ennead*, TR VI, CH 3, 108b; TR VIII, CH 8, 133a-b / *Fourth Ennead*, TR III, CH 8, 146c-d; CH 9, 147b-c; CH 19 151d-152b; CH 23, 153d; TR IV, CH 29 173b-174b; TR V, CH 7, 188b-c; TR VII, CH 2–5 192a-194a; CH 14 200b-c / *Fifth Ennead*, TR I, CH 2, 208c-209a / *Sixth Ennead*, TR IV, CH 1 297b-d; CH 4–6 299a-300b; CH 16, 305a; TR V, CH 12 310b-d

18 AUGUSTINE: *City of God*, BK XII, CH 25 358b-359a; BK XIII, CH 2 360b-361a; BK XXII, CH 24, 609c-610a / *Christian Doctrine*, BK I, CH 8 626c-627a

19 AQUINAS: *Summa Theologica*, PART I, Q 3, A 1, ANS 14b-15b; Q 4, A 2, REP 3 21b-22b; Q 10, A 1, REP 2 40d-41d; Q 18 104b-108c; Q 27, A 2, ANS 154c-155b; Q 51, A 1, REP 3 275b-276b; A 3 277a-278c; Q 69, A 2 361c-362c; Q 70, A 3, ANS and REP 2–5 365b-367a; QQ 71–72 367a-369d; QQ 75–76 378a-399b passim; Q 97, A 3, ANS 515a-d; QQ 118–119 600a-608d passim

20 AQUINAS: *Summa Theologica*, PART I-II, Q 56, A 1, REP 1 30a-c; PART II-II, Q 23, A 2, REP 2 483d-484d; PART III, Q 2, A 5 715a-716b; Q 5, A 3 737d-739a

1. The nature and cause of life: the soul as the principle of life in organic bodies.)

21 DANTE: *Divine Comedy*, PURGATORY, XVIII [49–54] 80b-c; XXV [19–108] 91c-92c; PARADISE, II [127–148] 109a-b; VII [121–148] 116b-c

23 HOBBES: *Leviathan*, INTRO, 47a-b; PART I, 65a; PART III, 173d; 176d; PART IV, 251a

24 RABELAIS: *Gargantua and Pantagruel*, BK III, 138a-b

28 HARVEY: *Motion of the Heart*, 285d-286a; 296a-d / *Circulation of the Blood*, 316a-318b; 325d-326d / *On Animal Generation*, 384d-390b passim; 431b-434a esp 433c-d; 488d-496d

31 DESCARTES: *Objections and Replies*, 156a-d; 207a; 226b

35 LOCKE: *Human Understanding*, BK II, CH XXVII, SECT 3–5 219d-220c passim; BK III, CH X, SECT 22, 297d

36 STERNE: *Tristram Shandy*, 191b-192b

42 KANT: *Judgement*, 555a-558b

46 HEGEL: *Philosophy of Right*, PART I, par 47 24a-b; ADDITIONS, 28 121b; 161 143a-b

47 GOETHE: *Faust*, PART II [6819–7004] 167a-171b; [7851–7864] 191b

48 MELVILLE: *Moby Dick*, 27b-28a; 344b-345a

49 DARWIN: *Origin of Species*, 145b-c

51 TOLSTOY: *War and Peace*, BK XII, 561b-d; BK XIV, 608a-b

53 JAMES: *Psychology*, 140a

54 FREUD: *Beyond the Pleasure Principle*, 652d; 654c-656d esp 655c-656a; 659d-660b / *Ego and Id*, 708d-709a / *New Introductory Lectures*, 851c

2. Continuity or discontinuity between living and non-living things: comparison of vital powers and activities with the potentialities and motions of inert bodies

8 ARISTOTLE: *Physics*, BK IV, CH 5 [213^{a}4–9] 292c; BK V, CH 3 [227^{a}10–17] 307d-308a; BK VII, CH 2 [244^{b}1–245^{a}12] 328b-d; BK VIII, CH I [250^{b}11–14] 334a; CH 4 338d-340d; CH 6 [259^{a}20–^{b}31] 345a-d / *Heavens*, BK II, CH 2 [284^{a}30–285^{a}1] 376c / *Meteorology*, BK IV, CH 1–3 482b,d-486a / *Metaphysics*, BK V, CH 4 [1014^{b}17–26] 534d-535a; BK VII, CH 16 [1040^{b}5–16] 564c / *Soul*, BK I, CH 5 [411^{a}7–23] 641a-b; BK II, CH 1 642a-643a; CH 4 645b-647b; CH 12 656a-d / *Longevity*, CH 2–3 710b-711b

9 ARISTOTLE: *History of Animals*, BK VIII, CH I [588^{b}4–10] 114d-115a / *Parts of Animals*, BK IV, CH 5 [681^{a}12–15] 211d / *Motion of Animals*, CH 1 [698^{a}15–21] 233b; CH 4 [700^{a}5–27] 235b-c; CH 6 235d-236b; CH 7 [701^{b}1]–CH 8 [702^{b}12] 236d-238a / *Generation of Animals*, BK I, CH 23 [731^{a}30–^{b}8] 271c-d; BK II, CH 4 [740^{a}13–18] 281a; BK III, CH 11 [761^{b}25–763^{b}15] 302d-304d

10 GALEN: *Natural Faculties*, BK I, CH 7 170c-171a; BK II, CH 3, 186c-d

12 LUCRETIUS: *Nature of Things*, BK I [215–264] 3d-4b; BK II [865–930] 26a-d

12 AURELIUS: *Meditations*, BK IX, SECT 9 292b-d

19 AQUINAS: *Summa Theologica*, PART I, Q 3, A 1, ANS 14b-15b; Q 18, A I 104c-105c; A 4 107d-108c; Q 27, A 2, ANS and REP I 154c-155b; Q 51, A 3 277a-278c; Q 69, A 2, REP I 361c-362c; Q 70, A 3 365b-367a; Q 78, A 1, ANS and REP 3 407b-409a; A 3, ANS 410a-411d; Q 118, A 1, ANS 600a-601c; PART I-II, Q 17, A 9, REP 2 692d-693d

23 HOBBES: *Leviathan*, INTRO, 47a-b

27 SHAKESPEARE: *Othello*, ACT V, SC II [7–15] 239a

28 GILBERT: *Loadstone*, BK III, 67b-d

28 HARVEY: *On Animal Generation*, 384a-b; 457a

30 BACON: *Novum Organum*, BK II, APH 27, 157b-158a; APH 40, 171a-d; APH 48 179d-188b

31 DESCARTES: *Discourse*, PART V, 59a-d

33 PASCAL: *Pensées*, 75 185b-186a / *Great Experiment*, 382b-383a / *Weight of Air*, 425a

35 LOCKE: *Human Understanding*, BK II, CH XXVI, SECT 2, 217c; CH XXVII, SECT 3–5 219d-220c passim; BK III, CH VI, SECT 12 271d-272b; BK IV, CH III, SECT 25 321a-b; CH XVI, SECT 12, 370c-371a

38 ROUSSEAU: *Inequality*, 337d-338a

42 KANT: *Judgement*, 555a-558b; 578d-582c esp 579d-580a, 582b-c; 602b,d [fn 1]

43 FEDERALIST: NUMBER 37, 119c

45 FARADAY: *Researches in Electricity*, 836d

49 DARWIN: *Descent of Man*, 341c-d

51 TOLSTOY: *War and Peace*, BK X, 449b-c

53 JAMES: *Psychology*, 4a-6b; 68a-71b passim, esp 68a-b; 85a-b; 95b-96a

54 FREUD: *Unconscious*, 429c-d / *Beyond the Pleasure Principle*, 651d-652d; 661b-c / *New Introductory Lectures*, 849d; 851c

3. The modes or grades of corporeal life: the classification and order of the various vital powers or functions

OLD TESTAMENT: *Genesis*, 1:11–12,20–31 / *Psalms*, 8 esp 8:4–8—(D) *Psalms*, 8 esp 8:5–9 / *Ecclesiastes*, 3:18–22

7 PLATO: *Phaedrus*, 124c-128d passim / *Symposium*, 165c-166b / *Republic*, BK IV, 350c-353d / *Timaeus*, 466a-c; 469d-470a

8 ARISTOTLE: *Physics*, BK II, CH 8 [199^{a}20–^{b}13] 276c-d / *Heavens*, BK II, CH 12 383b-384c / *Generation and Corruption*, BK I, CH 5 417b-420b / *Meteorology*, BK IV, CH 2 [379^{b}10–25] 483d-484a / *Metaphysics*, BK I, CH 1 [980^{a}22–^{b}27] 499a-b; BK IX, CH 2 571c-572a; CH 5 573a-c / *Soul* 631a-668d esp BK I, CH 5 [410^{b}16–411^{a}2] 640d-641a, BK II, CH 2–3 643a-645b, BK III, CH 12–13 667a-668d / *Sense and the Sensible* 673a-689a,c / *Memory and Reminiscence* 690a-695d / *Sleep* 696a-701d / *Youth, Life, and Breathing* 714a-726d

9 ARISTOTLE: *History of Animals*, BK VIII, CH I 114b,d-115b / *Parts of Animals*, BK I, CH I

[641^{b}5–10] 164b-c; BK II, CH 10 [655^{b}28–656^{a}14] 181d-182b; BK IV, CH 5 [681^{a}12–15] 211d; CH 10 [686^{b}23–687^{a}1] 218b-c / *Motion of Animals*, CH 6–11 235d-239d esp CH 10 238c-239a / *Gait of Animals*, CH 4 244a-245a / *Generation of Animals*, BK I, CH 23 [731^{a}24–^{b}8] 271c-d; BK II, CH 3 [736^{a}25–^{b}29] 276d-277c; CH 4 [740^{b}25]–CH 5 [741^{a}31] 281d-282b; BK III, CH 7 [757^{b}14–30] 298c-d; CH 11 [761^{a}12–^{b}23] 302b-d / *Ethics*, BK I, CH 7 [1097^{b}33–1098^{a}7] 343b; CH 13 [1102^{a}33–1103^{a}3] 347d-348c / *Politics*, BK VII, CH 13 [1332^{a}39–^{b}8] 537a-b

10 GALEN: *Natural Faculties* 167a-215d esp BK I, CH 1 167a-b, CH 5–8 169b-171a

12 LUCRETIUS: *Nature of Things*, BK III [258–322] 33b-34b

12 EPICTETUS: *Discourses*, BK I, CH 6, 111a-c; BK II, CH 8, 146a-b

12 AURELIUS: *Meditations*, BK III, SECT 16 262d-263a,c; BK V, SECT 16 271c-d; BK VIII, SECT 7 286a; BK IX, SECT 9 292b-d

16 KEPLER: *Epitome*, BK IV, 854b-856a

17 PLOTINUS: *First Ennead*, TR I, CH 1–7 1a-4a passim; CH 11 5b-c; TR IV, CH 3, 13d / *Fourth Ennead*, TR III, CH 19 151d-152b; CH 23 153d-154b; TR IV, CH 28 172a-173b; TR VII, CH 14 200b-c; TR IX, CH 3 206a-b / *Fifth Ennead*, TR II, CH 2 215a-c

18 AUGUSTINE: *City of God*, BK VII, CH 23, 256b-c; CH 29 261a-b; BK XIX, CH 13, 519a / *Christian Doctrine*, BK I, CH 8 626c-627a

19 AQUINAS: *Summa Theologica*, PART I, Q 3, A 1, REP 2 14b-15b; Q 18, AA 1–3 104c-107c; Q 27, A 2, ANS 154c-155b; Q 45, A 5, REP 1 245c-247a; Q 51, A 3 277a-278c; Q 69, A 2 361c-362c; Q 70, A 3 365b-367a; QQ 71–72 367a-369d; Q 75, A 1, ANS 378b-379c; A 6, REP 1 383c-384c; Q 76, A 5, REP 3-4 394c-396a; QQ 77–83 399b-440b; Q 98 516c-519a; QQ 118–119 600a-608d; PART I-II, Q 17, AA 8–9 692a-693d

20 AQUINAS: *Summa Theologica*, PART I-II, Q 110, A 4, REP 3 350d-351d; PART III, Q 7, A 9, ANS 751d-752c

21 DANTE: *Divine Comedy*, PURGATORY, XXV [37–84] 91d-92b; PARADISE, VII [121–148] 116b-c

24 RABELAIS: *Gargantua and Pantagruel*, BK III, 137b-c; 138a-139b; 192d

28 HARVEY: *On Animal Generation*, 369d-370b; 384d-390b passim; 397b-398c; 441a-443b; 444c-445c; 447a-b; 456b-458a esp 457a-d

30 BACON: *Novum Organum*, BK II, APH 30 159c-d; APH 48, 186d

31 DESCARTES: *Discourse*, PART V, 56a-b; 59a-60c / *Objections and Replies*, 156a-d; 207a; 244b-c

31 SPINOZA: *Ethics*, PART III, PROP 57, SCHOL 415b

32 MILTON: *Paradise Lost*, BK V [469–490] 185b-186a; BK VII [307–338] 223b-224b; [387–550] 225b-229a

33 PASCAL: *Pensées*, 75 185b-186a; 339–344 233a-b

35 LOCKE: *Human Understanding*, BK II, CH IX, SECT 11–15 140b-141a; CH XXVII, SECT 4–6 220a-d; BK III, CH VI, SECT 12 271d-272b; BK IV, CH XVI, SECT 12, 370c-371a

38 ROUSSEAU: *Inequality*, 337d-338a

42 KANT: *Pure Reason*, 199c-200c / *Judgement*, 578d-580a; 583b-c; 602b,d [fn 1]

45 FARADAY: *Researches in Electricity*, 836d

49 DARWIN: *Origin of Species*, 3a-b; 47c-49c; 60b-61d; 64a-d; 71a-d; 241b-c / *Descent of Man*, 331b-c

53 JAMES: *Psychology*, 4a-7a; 68b-73b esp 68b, 71a; 95b; 699a

54 FREUD: *Narcissism*, 401a-d / *Instincts*, 415b / *Beyond the Pleasure Principle*, 647a-648a; 648b-c; 651d-654b; 654d-657d esp 656a, 657b-c; 659d-661c / *Ego and Id*, 708d-709b; 711c-712a / *New Introductory Lectures*, 851a-c

3*a*. Continuity or discontinuity between plants and animals: comparison of plant and animal nutrition, respiration, growth, and reproduction

7 PLATO: *Republic*, BK VIII, 403b-d / *Timaeus*, 469d-470a

8 ARISTOTLE: *Topics*, BK VI, CH 10 [148^{a}23–38] 202b-c / *Physics*, BK II, CH 8 [199^{a}20–^{b}13] 276c-d / *Heavens*, BK II, CH 12 [292^{b}1–11] 384a / *Soul*, BK I, CH 5 [410^{b}16–411^{a}2] 640d-641a; BK II, CH 2 [413^{a}20–^{b}4] 643b-c; CH 4 [415^{b}28–416^{a}5] 646a-b / *Sleep*, CH 1 696a-697c

9 ARISTOTLE: *History of Animals*, BK IV, CH 6 [531^{b}8–9] 58b; BK V, CH 1 [539^{a}15–26] 65b-d; CH 11 [543^{b}23–31] 70c; BK VIII, CH 1 [588^{b}4–589^{a}2] 114d-115b / *Parts of Animals*, BK II, CH 3 [650^{a}1–37] 174c-175a; CH 10 [655^{b}27–656^{a}8] 181b-182a; BK IV, CH 4 [677^{b}36–678^{a}15] 207d-208a; CH 5 [681^{a}10–^{b}9] 211c-212b; CH 6 [682^{a}26–28] 213d; CH 10 [686^{b}23–687^{a}1] 218b-c / *Gait of Animals*, CH 4 [705^{a}26–^{b}9] 244a-b / *Generation of Animals*, BK I, CH 1 [715^{b}17–716^{a}2] 255d-256a; CH 23 271b-d; BK II, CH 1 [732^{a}12–24] 272c; [735^{a}13–26] 275d-276a; CH 3 [736^{a}24–^{b}14] 276d-277b; CH 4 [740^{a}24]–CH 5 [741^{a}32] 281b-282b; BK III, CH 2 [752^{a}10–23] 293a-b; CH 5 [755^{b}6–13] 296c-d; CH 7 [757^{b}14–30] 298c-d; CH 11 302b-304d; BK V, CH 1 [778^{b}30–779^{a}4] 321a-b / *Ethics*, BK I, CH 13 [1102^{a}34–^{b}4] 347d / *Politics*, BK I, CH 2 [1252^{a}26–31] 445c

10 GALEN: *Natural Faculties*, BK I, CH 1 167a-b

12 LUCRETIUS: *Nature of Things*, BK II [700–710] 23d-24a; BK V [783–820] 71b-d

12 EPICTETUS: *Discourses*, BK II, CH 8, 146a-b

19 AQUINAS: *Summa Theologica*, PART I, Q 18, A 1, ANS and REP 2 104c-105c; A 2, REP 1 105c-106b; A 3, ANS and REP 3 106b-107c; Q 69, A 2, REP 1 361c-362c; Q 72, A 1, REP 1,5 368b-369d; Q 118, A 1 esp REP 2 600a-601c; Q 119 604c-608d

24 RABELAIS: *Gargantua and Pantagruel*, BK III, 143a-144c

(3. *The modes or grades of corporeal life: the classification and order of the various vital powers or functions. 3a. Continuity or discontinuity between plants and animals: comparison of plant and animal nutrition, respiration, growth, and reproduction.*)

28 HARVEY: *Motion of the Heart*, 278b; 299b-c / *Circulation of the Blood*, 327d-328a / *On Animal Generation*, 368a-b; 369d-370b; 372b; 384c-d; 397c-398c; 428c-429a; 442b-c; 449a-b; 457c-d; 461b-d; 468b-469b; 471b-c

30 BACON: *Novum Organum*, BK II, APH 27, 158a-b

35 LOCKE: *Human Understanding*, BK II, CH IX, SECT 11-15 140b-141a passim; BK III, CH VI, SECT 12 271d-272b

42 KANT: *Judgement*, 579d-580a; 582b-c

43 FEDERALIST: NUMBER 37, 119c

45 LAVOISIER: *Elements of Chemistry*, PART II, 57b-c

49 DARWIN: *Origin of Species*, 47c-49c passim, esp 49a-c; 115b; 241b-c / *Descent of Man*, 372b-c

53 JAMES: *Psychology*, 8a

3b. **The grades of animal life: types and degrees of mobility and sensitivity; analogies of structure and function**

OLD TESTAMENT: *Genesis*, 1:20-25

8 ARISTOTLE: *Posterior Analytics*, BK II, CH 14 [98ᵃ20-23] 134a / *Soul*, BK II, CH 2 [413ᵇ4-10] 643c; [414ᵃ1-3] 644a; BK III, CH 11 [433ᵇ31-434ᵃ9] 666d; CH 12-13 667a-668d / *Sense and the Sensible*, CH 1 [436ᵇ12-437ᵃ17] 673c-674a; CH 5 [443ᵇ17-445ᵃ4] 681c-682d / *Youth, Life, and Breathing* 714a-726d passim

9 ARISTOTLE: *History of Animals* 7a-158d esp BK I, CH 1-6 7a-13a, BK II, CH 1 19b,d-23d, BK IV, CH 8 59d-62a, BK V, CH 1 65a-66a, BK VIII, CH 1 114b,d-115b / *Parts of Animals* 161a-229d passim, esp BK I, CH 4 167d-168c, CH 5 [645ᵇ1-646ᵃ5] 169b-d / *Gait of Animals* 243a-252a,c / *Generation of Animals* 255a-331a,c esp BK I, CH 1-19 255a-268a, BK II, CH 1 272a-276a, BK III 290a-304d, BK IV, CH 4-6 311c-317d, BK V 320a-331a,c

10 GALEN: *Natural Faculties*, BK III, CH 2 199d-200a

12 AURELIUS: *Meditations*, BK III, SECT 16 262d-263a,c

19 AQUINAS: *Summa Theologica*, PART I, Q 18, A 2, REP 1 105c-106b; A 3, ANS 106b-107c; Q 50, A 4, REP 1 273b-274b; QQ 71-72 367a-369d; Q 76, A 5, REP 3 394c-396a; Q 78, A 1, ANS and REP 4 407b-409a

28 HARVEY: *Motion of the Heart*, 274b-d; 277b-278d; 280c-283a; 299b-302c / *On Animal Generation*, 336b-d; 338a-496d esp 449a-454c, 463d-464a, 470c-472c

30 BACON: *Novum Organum*, BK II, APH 27, 158a; APH 30 159c-d

35 LOCKE: *Human Understanding*, BK II, CH IX SECT 11-15 140b-141a; BK III, CH VI, SECT 12 271d-272b

35 HUME: *Human Understanding*, SECT IX, DIV 82 487b-c

42 KANT: *Judgement*, 578d-580a esp 579b-c; 602b,d [fn 1]

48 MELVILLE: *Moby Dick*, 273a-274a; 279a-b

49 DARWIN: *Origin of Species*, 75b-78c; 82d-94c; 112b-113c; 207a-229a,c esp 228c-229a,c; 238b-239a / *Descent of Man*, 255a-265d; 271a-275c; 278c-284b; 300a-b; 331a-341d esp 332a-c, 337a-341d; 348b-c; 402b-c

53 JAMES: *Psychology*, 13a-14b; 19b-42b passim, esp 40a, 41b; 51a-52a; 705b-706b

54 FREUD: *Beyond the Pleasure Principle*, 651d-654b esp 653b, 654a / *Civilization and Its Discontents*, 768d-769a

4. **The biological economy: the environment of the organism; the interdependence of plants and animals**

OLD TESTAMENT: *Genesis*, 1:11-13,20-31

6 HERODOTUS: *History*, BK II, 63b-c; 64b-c; BK III, 112d-113b

7 PLATO: *Republic*, BK VI, 377c-d / *Timaeus*, 469d-470a

8 ARISTOTLE: *Physics*, BK II, CH 2 [194ᵇ13] 271a / *Meteorology*, BK IV, CH 1 482b,d-483c / *Longevity* 710a-713a,c

9 ARISTOTLE: *History of Animals*, BK I, CH 1 [487ᵃ14-ᵇ5] 8a-b; BK V, CH 11 [543ᵇ19-31] 70b-c; CH 22 [553ᵇ20-23] 80c; CH 31 [557ᵃ4-32] 83d-84a; BK VI, CH 17 [570ᵇ29-571ᵃ2] 96d; BK VIII, CH 2-29 115c-132d esp CH 2-13 115c-125b, CH 18-20 127b-129b, CH 28-29 131c-132d; BK IX, CH 1 [608ᵇ19]-CH 2 [610ᵇ 19] 134a-136b; CH 31 [618ᵇ9-13] 144a-b; CH 32 [619ᵃ27-31] 144d-145a; CH 37 [622ᵃ8-15] 147c / *Parts of Animals*, BK IV, CH 8 [684ᵃ1-14] 215b; CH 12 [693ᵃ10-24] 225a / *Gait of Animals*, CH 15 [713ᵃ3]-CH 18 [714ᵇ8] 250d-252a / *Generation of Animals*, BK III, CH 10 [760ᵃ27-ᵇ28] 301b-d

10 HIPPOCRATES: *Airs, Waters, Places* 9a-19a,c esp par 1-2 9a-c

10 GALEN: *Natural Faculties*, BK II, CH 8-9 191b-199a,c

12 LUCRETIUS: *Nature of Things*, BK III [784-787] 40b; BK V [837-877] 72a-c; [925-1010] 73b-74b

17 PLOTINUS: *Fourth Ennead*, TR IV, CH 32, 175d-176a

19 AQUINAS: *Summa Theologica*, PART I, Q 69, A 2 361c-362c; QQ 71-72 367a-369d; Q 118, A 1, REP 3 600a-601c

28 GALILEO: *Two New Sciences*, FIRST DAY, 160c-d; SECOND DAY, 187d-188c

28 HARVEY: *On Animal Generation*, 453c

33 PASCAL: *Equilibrium of Liquids*, 401a-403a / *Weight of Air*, 415a-b

36 STERNE: *Tristram Shandy*, 224a-b; 295b-296b

(5. *Normal vitality and its impairment by disease, degeneration, and enfeeblement with age. 5a. The nature and causes of health.*)

30 BACON: *Advancement of Learning*, 72b
32 MILTON: *Areopagitica*, 407b
36 STERNE: *Tristram Shandy*, 412a-417a
38 ROUSSEAU: *Inequality*, 335a-b; 336b-337a
39 SMITH: *Wealth of Nations*, BK IV, 293d-294b
40 GIBBON: *Decline and Fall*, 87d-88a
42 KANT: *Pref. Metaphysical Elements of Ethics*, 368d-369a / *Judgement*, 509c-d
44 BOSWELL: *Johnson*, 171d-172a
49 DARWIN: *Descent of Man*, 324d; 356d-357c
51 TOLSTOY: *War and Peace*, BK I, 52d
54 FREUD: *General Introduction*, 635b-c

5b. The restorative function of rest or sleep

5 SOPHOCLES: *Philoctetes* [821-832] 189c
8 ARISTOTLE: *Sleep* 696a-701d esp CH 2 [455^{b}13-28] 698b-c
9 ARISTOTLE: *Parts of Animals*, BK II, CH 7 [653^{a}11-20] 178b-c / *Ethics*, BK I, CH 13 [1102^{a}34-^{b}13] 347d-348a
10 HIPPOCRATES: *Prognostics*, par 10 21c
12 LUCRETIUS: *Nature of Things*, BK IV [907-961] 56a-d
26 SHAKESPEARE: *Midsummer-Night's Dream*, ACT III, SC II [431-436] 367c / *2nd Henry IV*, ACT III, SC I [1-31] 482d-483a / *Henry V*, ACT IV, SC I [270-301] 554b-c
27 SHAKESPEARE: *King Lear*, ACT IV, SC IV [1-20] 272b-c / *Macbeth*, ACT II, SC II [35-43] 291c-d / *Henry VIII*, ACT V, SC I [1-5] 578a / *Sonnets*, XXVII 590c
29 CERVANTES: *Don Quixote*, PART II, 413b
36 STERNE: *Tristram Shandy*, 348b-349b
38 ROUSSEAU: *Inequality*, 337c
39 SMITH: *Wealth of Nations*, BK I, 35a-b
44 BOSWELL: *Johnson*, 352b-c
47 GOETHE: *Faust*, PART II [4613-4727] 115a-117b
48 MELVILLE: *Moby Dick*, 91b
50 MARX: *Capital*, 112b; 128a-b
51 TOLSTOY: *War and Peace*, BK III, 144d-146d; BK XII, 554b-d; BK XIII, 584c
54 FREUD: *General Introduction*, 478c-d; 617b-c

5c. The nature and causes of disease

OLD TESTAMENT: *Leviticus*, 26:16 / *Numbers*, 12:10-15; 16:46-50 / *Deuteronomy*, 28:21-22,27-28,35,58-62 / *II Kings*, 5:27—(D) *IV Kings*, 5:27 / *I Chronicles*, 21:14-15—(D) *I Paralipomenon*, 21:14-15 / *II Chronicles*, 26:18-21—(D) *II Paralipomenon*, 26:18-21 / *Job*, 2:7 / *Psalms*, 107:17-20—(D) *Psalms*, 106:17-20
APOCRYPHA: *Ecclesiasticus*, 37:29-31—(D) OT, *Ecclesiasticus*, 37:32-34 / *II Maccabees*, 3:27-29—(D) OT, *II Machabees*, 3:27-29
NEW TESTAMENT: *Matthew*, 9:32-33; 17:14-18 / *I Corinthians*, 11:25-30

6 HERODOTUS: *History*, BK I, 32c-d; 38a-b; BK II, 64c-d; BK III, 96c; BK IV, 135c-d; 157a
6 THUCYDIDES: *Peloponnesian War*, BK II, 399b-401b
7 PLATO: *Symposium*, 155d-157a esp 156d / *Republic*, BK III, 334b-337a; BK IV, 345b-c; 355b-c; BK X, 435a-c / *Timaeus*, 472a-474b
8 ARISTOTLE: *Physics*, BK VII, CH 3 [246^{a}10-^{b}19] 329c-330a / *Meteorology*, BK IV, CH 7 [384^{a}25-34] 488c
9 ARISTOTLE: *History of Animals*, BK III, CH 11 [518^{b}2-4] 43a; CH 15 [519^{b}15-20] 44c; CH 19 [521^{a}10-32] 46a-b; BK VII, CH 1 [581^{b}22-582^{a}4] 107b-c; CH 12 114c; BK VIII, CH 18-27 127b-131b passim; CH 29 132c-d / *Parts of Animals*, BK II, CH 5 [651^{a}37-^{b}18] 176c; CH 7 [653^{b}1-7] 178d-179a; BK III, CH 7 [670^{b}5-11] 199a; BK IV, CH 2 [677^{a}5-^{b}1] 206d-207b / *Generation of Animals*, BK IV, CH 7 317d-318b; BK V, CH 4 [784^{a}31-^{b}35] 326b-d / *Ethics*, BK II, CH 2 [1104^{a}10-19] 349c; BK V, CH 1 [1129^{a}12-25] 376b-c; CH 11 [1138^{a}29-32] 386d; BK VII, CH 8 [1150^{b}29-35] 401c-d
10 HIPPOCRATES: *Ancient Medicine*, par 1 1a-b; par 3 1d-2b; par 6 2d-3a; par 9-11 3b-4b; par 13-22 4c-8d / *Airs, Waters, Places*, par 1-10 9a-14a; par 22 17b-18a / *Regimen in Acute Diseases*, par 9-10 29d-30d; APPENDIX, par 1 35c-d; par 3 35d-36a; par 5-6 36b-37a; par 17 40d-41a / *Epidemics*, BK I, SECT I, par 1 44a-b; SECT II, par 7-8 47a-c; BK III, SECT III, par 1-2 56d-57a; par 15 59b / *Surgery*, par 20 73d / *Fractures*, par 31, 87a / *Articulations*, par 12 96a-b; par 58, 113a / *Aphorisms*, SECT II, par 51 133d; SECT III, par 1-19 134a-d; SECT V, par 16-24 138b-c / *Fistulae*, par 1 150a / *Hemorrhoids*, par 1 152b / *Sacred Disease* 154a-160d esp 155d-156a, 160b-d
10 GALEN: *Natural Faculties*, BK II, CH 8-9 191b-199a,c passim; BK III, CH 12 208b-209b esp 208d
12 LUCRETIUS: *Nature of Things*, BK III [459-614] 36a-38a; BK VI [769-829] 90c-91b; [1090-1286] 94d-97a,c
17 PLOTINUS: *Second Ennead*, TR IX, CH 14 74b-d
20 AQUINAS: *Summa Theologica*, PART I-II, Q 71, A 1, REP 3 105d-106c; Q 72, A 5, ANS 115a-116b; Q 77, A 3, ANS 147c-148b; Q 88, A 1, ANS 193a-194b
23 HOBBES: *Leviathan*, PART II, 151b-c
25 MONTAIGNE: *Essays*, 330b-c; 367b-368a; 369d-370a; 371c-d; 528c-529b
28 HARVEY: *Motion of the Heart*, 296a-d / *Circulation of the Blood*, 305a-d; 316c-d; 321d-322a / *On Animal Generation*, 386d-387a; 407a; 423b; 433a-c; 455d-456a; 493a-b
30 BACON: *Advancement of Learning*, 52b-d
31 DESCARTES: *Discourse*, PART VI, 61c
32 MILTON: *Paradise Lost*, BK XI [477-548] 309b-311a
36 SWIFT: *Gulliver*, PART IV, 155b-157a; 161b-162a

6. The life span and the life cycle

6a. The life span of plants and animals, and of different species of plants and animals

6b. The human life span

6c. The biological characteristics of the stages of life

8. The concern of the living with life and death

8*a*. The love of life: the instinct of self-preservation; the life instinct

OLD TESTAMENT: *Genesis*, 3:22–24 / *Job*, 2:4 / *Psalms*, 21:4; 34:12–14; 49:6–12; 91:16—(*D*) *Psalms*, 20:5; 33:13–15; 48:7–13; 90:16 / *Ecclesiastes*, 9:4–6

NEW TESTAMENT: *Matthew*, 19:16–30 / *Mark*, 10:17–31 / *Luke*, 10:25–37 / *John*, 12:25; 15:13 / *I Timothy*, 6:17–19 / *I Peter*, 3:10–11

5 EURIPIDES: *Hippolytus* [189–197] 226c-d / *Alcestis* 237a-247a,c esp [629–746] 242c-243c / *Iphigenia at Aulis* [1211–1252] 436a-c

6 HERODOTUS: *History*, BK IV, 140d-141a; BK VI, 191a-b; BK VII, 224d-225a; BK IX, 296c-297a

6 THUCYDIDES: *Peloponnesian War*, BK VII, 559b-d

9 ARISTOTLE: *Ethics*, BK IX, CH 9 [1170ª13–b8] 423d-424b; BK X, CH 4 [1175ª10–22] 429c / *Rhetoric*, BK II, CH 13 [1389b32–35] 637b

12 LUCRETIUS: *Nature of Things*, BK III 30a-44a,c passim

12 AURELIUS: *Meditations*, BK II, SECT 11 258a-b

15 TACITUS: *Histories*, BK V, 301d

18 AUGUSTINE: *Confessions*, BK IV, par 11 21d-22a; BK VIII, par 18 57d-58a; par 25 60a / *City of God*, BK XIX, CH 4, 513a

19 AQUINAS: *Summa Theologica*, PART I, Q 75, A 6, ANS 383c-384c

22 CHAUCER: *Nun's Priest's Tale* [15,282–287] 457b

23 HOBBES: *Leviathan*, PART I, 86c; 90a; PART II, 115d; 142b-c; 155b-c

25 MONTAIGNE: *Essays*, 31d-32c; 184a; 267b-c; 339a-d; 511d-512a

26 SHAKESPEARE: *1st Henry IV*, ACT V, SC IV [111–132] 465c

27 SHAKESPEARE: *Othello*, ACT I, SC III [306–369] 212b-d / *King Lear*, ACT V, SC III [184–186] 281b

30 BACON: *Advancement of Learning*, 51b-c; 72c-73a

31 SPINOZA: *Ethics*, PART IV, PROP 18, SCHOL-PROP 25 429a-431a

33 PASCAL: *Pensées*, 156–157 201b-202a

35 LOCKE: *Civil Government*, CH II, SECT 6–8 26b-27a; CH III, SECT 16–18 28d-29b

36 SWIFT: *Gulliver*, PART III, 124a-129a

36 STERNE: *Tristram Shandy*, 238a-239b; 459a-460a

37 FIELDING: *Tom Jones*, 250b-d

38 MONTESQUIEU: *Spirit of Laws*, BK I, 2b

38 ROUSSEAU: *Inequality*, 330d-331b; 337c; 342d-343a; 343c

42 KANT: *Fund. Prin. Metaphysic of Morals*, 258b

46 HEGEL: *Philosophy of Right*, PART II, par 127 45b-c; ADDITIONS, 81 128d-129a

47 GOETHE: *Faust*, PART I [602–807] 16b-21a; [1544–1626] 37b-39a; PART II [8909–9126] 216b-221b

48 MELVILLE: *Moby Dick*, 144a; 344b-345a

49 DARWIN: *Descent of Man*, 311a-b

51 TOLSTOY: *War and Peace*, BK III, 159d-160a; BK VI, 262d-263a; BK X, 439b-440a; 457a-c; 461d-464a; BK XI, 527a-b; BK XII, 549c-551c; 558a-562d; EPILOGUE I, 665a-d

52 DOSTOEVSKY: *Brothers Karamazov*, BK V, 118b-119a; BK VI, 149c-150d

53 JAMES: *Psychology*, 92a-b; 198b; 208a-209b; 700b; 709b

54 FREUD: *Narcissism*, 399b / *Instincts*, 414d-415b / *General Introduction*, 591d-592c; 607d-608a; 615b-616b; 623b-c / *Beyond the Pleasure Principle*, 651d-662b esp 653a-d, 657c-659a, 659d-661c; 663c / *Ego and Id*, 708d-712a passim, esp 708d-709b, 711c; 717c / *Civilization and Its Discontents*, 790a-b; 791a-d / *New Introductory Lectures*, 846b-c; 851c-d

8*b*. The desire for death: the death instinct; the problem of suicide

OLD TESTAMENT: *I Samuel*, 31:4–6—(*D*) *I Kings*, 31:4–6 / *II Samuel*, 17:23—(*D*) *II Kings*, 17:23 / *I Chronicles*, 10:1–6—(*D*) *I Paralipomenon*, 10:1–6 / *Job*, 3 esp 3:13–22; 6:8–13; 7:13–16,21; 10:1,18–22; 14:13–14; 16:22–17:1; 17:13–16—(*D*) *Job*, 3 esp 3:13–22; 6:8–13; 7:13–16,21; 10:1,18–22; 14:13–14; 16:23–17:1; 17:13–16 / *Proverbs*, 8:36; 11:19; 21:6 / *Ecclesiastes*, 4:2–3; 6:3–5; 7:1–4—(*D*) *Ecclesiastes*, 4:2–3; 6:3–5; 7:2–5 / *Isaiah*, 28:14–18—(*D*) *Isaias*, 28:14–18 / *Jeremiah*, 8:3; 20:14–18—(*D*) *Jeremias*, 8:3; 20:14–18 / *Jonah*, 4—(*D*) *Jonas*, 4

APOCRYPHA: *Tobit*, 4:2—(*D*) OT, *Tobias*, 4:1 / *Wisdom of Solomon*, 1:12–16; 2:23–24—(*D*) OT, *Book of Wisdom*, 1:12–16; 2:23–25 / *Ecclesiasticus*, 23:14; 30:17; 41:2–3—(*D*) OT, *Ecclesiasticus*, 23:18–19; 30:17; 41:3–5

NEW TESTAMENT: *John*, 11:16 / *Acts*, 20:24 / *Philippians*, 1:20–24 / *Revelation*, 9:6—(*D*) *Apocalypse*, 9:6

5 SOPHOCLES: *Oedipus the King* [1297–1415] 111b-112b / *Oedipus at Colonus* [1211–1248] 125b-c / *Antigone* [1261–1353] 141d-142d / *Ajax* [394–865] 146c-150c / *Electra* [804–822] 162c-d / *Trachiniae* [871–1278] 177d-181a,c / *Philoctetes* [779–809] 189a-b

5 EURIPIDES: *Rhesus* [756–761] 209d / *Trojan Women* [622–683] 275b-d / *Helen* [252–305] 300c-d / *Hecuba* [218–582] 354d-357d / *Heracles Mad* [1088–1393] 374b-377b

6 HERODOTUS: *History*, BK I, 9d-10a; 47c-d; BK II, 62d-63a; BK V, 160c-d; BK VI, 199c-d; BK VII, 224d-225a; 245d; BK IX, 303c-304a

7 PLATO: *Phaedo*, 222a-225c / *Laws*, BK IX, 753b

9 ARISTOTLE: *Ethics*, BK V, CH 11 [1138ª4–13] 386b-c; BK IX, CH 4 [1166b11–13] 419d

12 LUCRETIUS: *Nature of Things*, BK III [31–93] 30b-31b

12 EPICTETUS: *Discourses*, BK I, CH 9 114c-116b; CH 24 129a-d

8c. The contemplation and fear of death: the attitude of the hero, the philosopher, the martyr

(8. *The concern of the living with life and death.*
8c. The contemplation and fear of death:
the attitude of the hero, the philosopher,
the martyr.)

44 BOSWELL: *Johnson*, 93d-94b; 102b; 167a;
169d; 174b-c; 238b; 347a-c; 394a-c; 399d-
400a; 573b-574a

46 HEGEL: *Philosophy of History*, INTRO, 197c-
d; PART I, 245b-d; 255a-257a; PART IV,
339b-d

47 GOETHE: *Faust*, PART I [1544-1626] 37b-39a;
PART II [8909-9126] 216b-221b; [11,384-401]
277a-b

48 MELVILLE: *Moby Dick*, 27a-28a; 168a-169b;
209b; 238a; 316a-b; 318b; 331a-332a; 351a-b

49 DARWIN: *Descent of Man*, 311a-b

51 TOLSTOY: *War and Peace*, BK I, 34b-c; 37d-
47b; BK II, 77c-81b; 97a-106d; BK III, 146d-
147c; BK IV, 179b-180d; BK V, 194c-d;
200c-d; 216d-218b; 226d-227a; BK VII,
288b-c; BK VIII, 311a-313a; BK IX, 369a-
372a; BK X, 416c-417b; 433d-434a; 439b-
440a; 457a-c; 461d-464a; BK XI, 481a-482a;
BK XII, 549c-551c; 558a-562d; BK XIII, 569d-
570a; BK XIV, 607c-608d; BK XV, 614a-618b;
636c-637c

52 DOSTOEVSKY: *Brothers Karamazov*, BK II, 26a;
BK V, 118b-119a; BK VI, 148d-150d esp 149c-
150d

54 FREUD: *Interpretation of Dreams*, 243a-c / *Ego
and Id*, 716c-717a,c / *Inhibitions, Symptoms,
and Anxiety*, 735d-736b / *War and Death*,
761c-766d

8d. The ceremonials of death: the rites of burial in war and peace

OLD TESTAMENT: *Genesis*, 23; 49:1-50:13 /
Leviticus, 19:28; 21:1-5 / *Deuteronomy*, 14:1-
2; 33 / *II Samuel*, 1:17-27; 3:31-36—(D)
II Kings, 1:17-27; 3:31-36 / *II Chronicles*,
16:13-14—(D) *II Paralipomenon*, 16:13-14 /
Isaiah, 3:16-26; 15:1-4—(D) *Isaias*, 3:16-26;
15:1-4 / *Jeremiah*, 16:6—(D) *Jeremias*, 16:6
/ *Ezekiel*, 7:18; 24:16-23—(D) *Ezechiel*, 7:18;
24:16-23 / *Amos*, 8:10

APOCRYPHA: *Ecclesiasticus*, 22:11-12; 38:16-23
—(D) OT, *Ecclesiasticus*, 22:10-13; 38:16-22

NEW TESTAMENT: *Matthew*, 8:21-22; 27:57-60
/ *Mark*, 15:43-16:1 / *Luke*, 23:50-24:1 /
John, 19:38-42 / *James*, 5:14-15

4 HOMER: *Iliad*, BK XI [446-455] 76d-77a; BK
XIX [198-237] 139a-b; BK XXII [247-272]
157d-158a; BK XXIII-XXIV 161a-179d / *Odyssey*, BK XI [51-80] 243c-d; BK XXIV [1-190]
317a-319a

5 AESCHYLUS: *Seven Against Thebes* [1011-1084]
38b-39a,c

5 SOPHOCLES: *Oedipus at Colonus* [1579-1779]
128c-130a,c / *Antigone* 131a-142d / *Ajax*
[1040-1421] 152a-155a,c / *Electra* [404-471]
159b-d / *Trachiniae* [1191-1278] 180b-181a,c

5 EURIPIDES: *Suppliants* 258a-269a,c / *Trojan
Women* [1123-1255] 279c-280c / *Phoenician
Maidens* [1625-1670] 392b-d

6 HERODOTUS: *History*, BK I, 38a-b; BK II, 65c-
66c; BK III, 94b-c; BK IV, 128c-d; 136a-d;
157c; BK V, 160d-161a; BK VI, 196b-c; BK VII,
235b-c; BK IX, 293a; 305a-c; 306b-c

6 THUCYDIDES: *Peloponnesian War*, BK II, 395c-
399a; 400c-d

7 PLATO: *Republic*, BK V, 367b / *Laws*, BK XII,
793a-794a

13 VIRGIL: *Georgics*, IV [451-558] 95b-99a /
Aeneid, BK III [60-68] 148b-149a; BK IV [474-
705] 180a-186b; BK VI [212-235] 216b-217b;
[295-383] 219a-221a; BK IX [207-223] 284b-
285a; BK X [898-908] 327a; BK XI [182-212]
333a-b

14 PLUTARCH: *Lycurgus*, 46a-b / *Numa Pompilius*, 55b-c / *Poplicola*, 80d; 86a,c / *Coriolanus*, 192c-d / *Pelopidas*, 245a-d / *Pompey*,
537d-538a,c / *Alexander*, 574c-575a / *Cato
the Younger*, 623c-624a / *Demetrius*, 747c-d /
Marcus Brutus, 810b-d

15 TACITUS: *Annals*, BK I, 3c-4a; BK III, 45d-
46a; BK XVI, 177b-c

18 AUGUSTINE: *City of God*, BK I, CH 12-13 137a-
138b; BK VIII, CH 26-27 283c-285d

20 AQUINAS: *Summa Theologica*, PART III, Q 65,
A 1, ANS 879c-881d; A 2, ANS and REP 5 881d-
882c; A 3, ANS 882d-883d; PART III SUPPL, Q
71 900d-917b

22 CHAUCER: *Knight's Tale* [859-1004] 174a-176b

25 MONTAIGNE: *Essays*, 5a-10a; 32b-c; 36a-b;
405a-c; 473d-477b; 483b-484a

26 SHAKESPEARE: *1st Henry IV*, ACT V, SC IV
[77-101] 465a-b / *Julius Caesar*, ACT V, SC V
[76-81] 596c

27 SHAKESPEARE: *Hamlet*, ACT V, SC I [1-35]
64c-d; [241-266] 66d-67a / *Cymbeline*, ACT IV,
SC II [186-290] 475a-476b

29 CERVANTES: *Don Quixote*, PART II, 427d-
429d

32 MILTON: *Epitaph on the Marchioness of Win-
chester* 14a-15b / *On Shakespear. 1630* 16a /
On the University Carrier 16b / *Another on the
Same* 17a-b / *Lycidas* 27b-32a / *Death of a
Fair Infant* 57a-59a esp [1-21] 57a-b / *Sonnets*,
XIV-XV 66a-b; XIX 67b-68a

37 FIELDING: *Tom Jones*, 34d

40 GIBBON: *Decline and Fall*, 263a; 381a-d;
513b; 568d-569a

44 BOSWELL: *Johnson*, 193a-b

46 HEGEL: *Philosophy of History*, INTRO, 197c-d;
PART I, 211d-212c; 252a-c; 255a-257a

48 MELVILLE: *Moby Dick*, 25b-28a; 350b-354b

51 TOLSTOY: *War and Peace*, BK I, 38b; 43b-44b;
BK XI, 512a-b; BK XII, 549d-551c; BK XV,
624d-625b

52 DOSTOEVSKY: *Brothers Karamazov*, BK VII,
171a-c

54 FREUD: *General Introduction*, 510b-c / *War
and Death*, 762a-b

CROSS-REFERENCES

For: The doctrine of soul as the principle of life, *see* ANIMAL 1a, 1e; SOUL 1b.

The general issue concerning continuity or hierarchy in nature, *see* ANIMAL 1b–1c, 2c; EVOLUTION 4a, 4c, 7b; MAN 1–1c, 8b–8c; NATURE 3b; WORLD 6b.

The contrast between the powers and activities of living and non-living bodies, *see* ANIMAL 4a; CHANGE 6c, 8a–8b, 9a–9b, 10a–10b; and for other discussions of the distinctive powers of plant, animal, and human life, *see* ANIMAL 1a(1)–1a(4), 1c–1c(2), 8d; MAN 1–1c, 4a–4c; SOUL 2c–2c(3).

The anatomical and physiological considerations relevant to the analysis of vital powers and operations, *see* ANIMAL 3–3d, 4b–4c, 5a–5g, 6a–7, 8b–8c(4).

Discussions of animal sensitivity and intelligence, *see* ANIMAL 1a(1), 1c(2); MAN 1c; MEMORY AND IMAGINATION 1; MIND 3a–3b; SENSE 2b–2c.

Other considerations of health and disease, *see* MEDICINE 4, 5a–5d.

A discussion of the human life cycle, *see* MAN 6c.

Other discussions of man's attitude toward death, *see* HAPPINESS 4b; IMMORTALITY 1; and for matters relevant to the special problem of the life and death instincts, *see* ANIMAL 1d; DESIRE 3a; HABIT 3a.

Another discussion of sleeping and waking, *see* ANIMAL 1a(5).

Another discussion of the relation between the living organism and its environment, *see* ANIMAL 11b.

ADDITIONAL READINGS

Listed below are works not included in *Great Books of the Western World*, but relevant to the idea and topics with which this chapter deals. These works are divided into two groups:

I. Works by authors represented in this collection.
II. Works by authors not represented in this collection.

For the date, place, and other facts concerning the publication of the works cited, consult the Bibliography of Additional Readings which follows the last chapter of *The Great Ideas*.

I.

DANTE. *Convivio (The Banquet)*, SECOND TREATISE, CH 8

F. BACON. "Of Death," "Of Youth and Age," in *Essays*

GOETHE. *William Meister*

HEGEL. *The Phenomenology of Mind*, V, A (2)

——. *Science of Logic*, VOL II, SECT III, CH I

DOSTOEVSKY. *The House of the Dead*

TOLSTOY. *Three Deaths*

——. *Memoirs of a Madman*

——. *The Death of Ivan Ilyitch*

II.

EPICURUS. *Letter to Menoeceus*

CICERO. *Tusculan Disputations*, I

——. *De Senectute (Of Old Age)*

SUÁREZ. *Disputationes Metaphysicae*, XXX (14)

CALDERÓN. *Life Is a Dream*

KING. *The Exequy*

BROWNE. *Hydriotaphia*

GRAY. *Elegy Written in a Country Church-Yard*

VOLTAIRE. "Life," in *A Philosophical Dictionary*

E. DARWIN. *The Loves of the Plants*

BICHAT. *General Anatomy, Applied to Physiology and Medicine*

BRYANT. *Thanatopsis*

SHELLEY. *Adonais*

HAZLITT. *Table Talk*, XXXIII

LAMB. "New Year's Eve," in *Essays of Elia*

COMTE. *The Positive Philosophy*, BK V

SCHWANN. *Microscopical Researches into the Accordance in the Structure and Growth of Animals and Plants*

WHEWELL. *The Philosophy of the Inductive Sciences*, VOL I, BK IX

R. BROWNING. *The Bishop Orders His Tomb at Saint Praxed's*

EMERSON. *Threnody*

SCHOPENHAUER. *The World as Will and Idea*, VOL III, SUP, CH 42

——. *On the Doctrine of the Indestructibility of Our True Nature by Death*

——. "On Suicide," in *Studies in Pessimism*

LOTZE. *Microcosmos*, BK I

Virchow. *Cellular Pathology*

Bernard. *Introduction to Experimental Medicine*

Stevenson. "Æs Triplex," in *Virginibus Puerisque*

T. H. Huxley. *Methods and Results*, III

Weismann. "Life and Death," in vol I, *Essays upon Heredity and Kindred Biological Problems*

Tennyson. *Crossing the Bar*

Frazer. *The Golden Bough*, PART III; PART V, CH 13; PART VI, CH 7

Hertwig. *The Cell*

Pearson. *The Chances of Death*

Andreyev. *Lazarus*

Driesch. *The Science and Philosophy of the Organism*

Loeb. *The Mechanistic Conception of Life*

Joyce. *Dubliners*, esp "The Dead"

Osler. *A Way of Life*

Unamuno. *Mist*

D. W. Thompson. *On Growth and Form*

Bergson. *Creative Evolution*

Bergson. *Mind-Energy*, CH I

Uexküll. *Theoretical Biology*

J. S. Haldane and J. G. Priestley. *Respiration*

Pearl. *The Biology of Death*

Lillie. *Protoplasmic Action and Nervous Action*

Santayana. *Scepticism and Animal Faith*, CH 23

Dewey. *Experience and Nature*, CH 7

Jung. *Spirit and Life*

G. N. Lewis. *The Anatomy of Science*, ESSAY VIII

Henderson. *Blood*

J. S. Haldane. *Mechanism, Life and Personality*

——. *The Sciences and Philosophy*, LECT I–VI

Woodger. *Biological Principles*

Cannon. *The Wisdom of the Body*

Goldstein. *The Organism*

Whitehead. *Modes of Thought*, LECT VIII

Sherrington. *The Integrative Action of the Nervous System*

——. *Man on His Nature*

Schrödinger. *What Is Life?*

Chapter 49: LOGIC

INTRODUCTION

IN this set of great books, the *Organon* of Aristotle, the *Novum Organum* of Bacon, Descartes' *Discourse on Method* and his *Rules for the Direction of the Mind*, and Kant's *Critique of Pure Reason* indicate or discuss the nature, scope and divisions of the discipline which has come to be called "logic." Though of all the works mentioned the *Organon* is perhaps the most extensive treatment of the subject, Aristotle does not use the word "logic" to name the science or art of which he seems to be the inventor—certainly the first systematic expounder—in the tradition of western thought.

Here as elsewhere Aristotle is indebted to his predecessors for providing him with materials to develop or criticize: to the sophists for the construction of arguments, for the formulation of methods of disputation, and for the discovery of fallacies; to Plato for the theory of classification and definition, for the root notion of the syllogism and a conception of proof or demonstration, for the general outlines of an intellectual method to which Plato gives the name "dialectic."

As indicated in the chapter on DIALECTIC, Aristotle uses Plato's name for the whole method of the mind in the pursuit of truth, in order to designate just one part of his method, the part concerned with probability rather than truth. Yet in the Roman and mediaeval tradition, the words "logic" and "dialectic" come to be used interchangeably. This is exemplified by the Stoic division of the sciences into physics, ethics, and logic *or* dialectic, and by the mediaeval enumeration of the liberal arts of the *trivium* as grammar, rhetoric, and logic *or* dialectic. So used, these names designate the whole range of discussion to be found in Aristotle's *Organon*.

In their opposition to Aristotelian or what they sometimes call "scholastic" logic, modern inventors of new methods, like Bacon or Descartes, tend to restrict the meaning of logic. For them logic is little more than the doctrine of the syllogism. And this they judge to be no part of genuinely fruitful method, or they hold it to be of use mainly as a critical instrument in disputation rather than discovery. Their identification of logic with dialectic (like their association of both with rhetoric) seems to have an intentionally invidious significance.

But with Kant, who was influenced by the scholasticism of Christian Wolff, "logic" is generally restored as the name for the whole range of materials in Aristotle's *Organon*, of which dialectic again becomes a part. In his own *Introduction to Logic*, Kant speaks of Aristotle as "the father of Logic." Though "logic has not gained much in extent since Aristotle's time," he says, "there are two amongst more recent philosophers who have again brought general logic into vogue, Leibnitz and Wolff." Since their day, and certainly since Kant's, as may be seen from the titles listed under Additional Readings, "logic" prevails as the name for treatises which discuss, in whole or part, the matters treated in Aristotle's *Organon*.

"Logic" is also used in modern times as the name for an inquiry or study which bears little resemblance to the discipline expounded in Aristotle's *Organon*. What is called "modern logic" to distinguish it from the traditional Aristotelian or scholastic logic, is purely a science, and in no sense an organon, methodology, instrument, or art. It does not restrict itself to stating the laws of thought or formulating the rules of inference. In the words of Josiah Royce, it is "the science of order" and it is applicable to the order of things as well as the order of thought. So conceived, the science of logic is sometimes regarded as having the kind of generality which is traditionally assigned to metaphysics; as, for example, by Bertrand Russell in his essay, "Logic as the Essence of Philosophy."

But it is mathematics rather than metaphysics with which logic is identified by its modern exponents. "Logistic or mathematical logic," writes Russell, "is mathematical in two different senses: it is itself a branch of mathematics, and it is the logic which is specially applicable to other more traditional branches of mathematics." Since Boole's *Laws of Thought*, which, according to Russell, initiates the modern development of mathematical logic, "logic has become more mathematical and mathematics has become more logical. The consequence," he says, "is that it has now become wholly impossible to draw a line between the two; in fact, the two are one."

ARISTOTLE's *Organon* stands to the tradition of logic as Euclid's *Elements* stands to the tradition of geometry. In both cases the work of later minds may alter considerably the structure and content of the discipline. In both cases there are modern departures from the earlier tradition. As in the one case we have Descartes' analytical geometry and the various non-Euclidean geometries, so in the other we have Kant's transcendental logic and the various non-Aristotelian logics.

But all these innovations, even when they might be described as anti-Aristotelian rather than simply as non-Aristotelian, bear the marks of their traditional origin. Kant, for example, takes pains everywhere to indicate the parallelism between the formulations of his transcendental logic and those of Aristotle's logic. Even the various systems of relational and mathematical logic usually attempt to show that the Aristotelian logic of subject and predicate, of particular and universal propositions, and of syllogisms can be treated as a special case under their own formulations. The proposals of Bacon or Mill with respect to induction and the method of Descartes, though accompanied in each case by a critique of the syllogism, are less radical departures, for they do not apparently reject Aristotle's basic doctrines of predication and proof.

Many of these issues in logical theory are dealt with in other chapters, *e.g.*, in DIALECTIC, IN-DUCTION, and HYPOTHESIS, in IDEA, JUDGMENT, and REASONING. Here we are principally concerned with the conception of logic itself, not with the detailed content of the science as much as with its character as an art or science, its relation to other arts and sciences, its major divisions, and its leading principles. Though such considerations are more explicitly treated by Kant than by Aristotle, the formative influence of the *Organon* warrants examining it first.

THE PARTS OF LOGIC, as Aristotle conceives them, seem to be indicated by the subject matter of the various books which comprise the collection of writings assembled under the title of *Organon*. That title has a bearing on the question whether logic is a science or an art and on its difference from other sciences and arts. The word "organon" has the meaning of instrument or method. That in turn suggests something to be used as rules of art are used—as directions to be followed to produce a certain result.

Aristotle's own differentiation of the speculative sciences, the practical sciences, and the arts throws light on this view of logic as an art. "The end of theoretical knowledge," he writes, "is truth, while that of practical knowledge is action." In other words, the theoretical, or speculative, sciences differ from the practical sciences in that they are knowledge for its own sake as opposed to knowledge for an ulterior end. According as the ulterior end is the production or "making" of something, as distinct from human action or conduct, art is distinct from the other practical sciences. "Making and acting are different," Aristotle says; "the reasoned state of capacity to act is different from the reasoned state of capacity to make. Hence, too, they are not included one in the other; for neither is acting making nor is making acting." Logic, then, if it is an art, will be concerned with the "making" of something, with producing a work or an effect.

The way in which Aristotle himself refers to the *Organon* seems to confirm this view. He regards it as a preparation for work in the theoretic sciences. "Due to a want of training in logic," he writes, some men attempt to discuss the criteria of truth in mathematics or physics at the same time that they are considering the subject matter of these sciences. "They should know these things already when they come to a special study, and not be inquiring into them while they are listening to lectures on it." Logic, in Aristotle's view, trains the mind in the ways of science. Its productive goal as an art is the making of science itself. For this reason, in the mediaeval period, logic comes to be called a "speculative art" or, with grammar and rhetoric, a liberal art.

"Even in speculative matters," Aquinas says, "there is something by way of work, e.g., the making of a syllogism, or of a fitting speech, or the work of counting or measuring. Hence whatever habits are ordained to such works of the speculative reason are, by a kind of comparison, called arts indeed, but *liberal* arts, in order to distinguish them from those arts that are ordained to works done by the body. . . . On the other hand, those sciences which are not ordained to any such work are called sciences absolutely and not arts."

But though it may not be a science, *absolutely speaking*, because it is an instrument of intellectual work, logic, in addition to being an art, may also have some of the characteristics of a science. If it is a science, what is the object of its knowledge?

Aristotle's division of the speculative sciences, which he seems to present as exhaustive, leaves no place for logic. "There are three kinds of theoretical sciences," he writes, "physics, mathematics, theology" or metaphysics, as the last came to be called. Each of these sciences, furthermore, seems to have a distinctive subject matter which is some aspect of reality, such as change, or quantity, or being. But insofar as logic is concerned with the study of terms, propositions, and syllogisms, it deals with elements common to all sciences.

This suggests that whereas reality is the object of the other sciences, the object of logic as a science is science itself, or more generally the whole of discourse. It considers the elements or patterns of discourse in a formal manner; that is, it considers them apart from their reference to reality or their real significance as the terms, propositions, and syllogisms of particular subject matters or sciences. Because it separates the forms which discursive thought takes from the matter or content it may have, logic is traditionally called a "formal science."

WHERE ARISTOTLE makes his object the elements of discourse (or thought expressed in language), later logicians treat the formal aspect of thought itself. They deal with concepts, judgments, and reasoning instead of with terms, propositions, and syllogisms. This difference results in a definition of logic as the science of thought; the basic formulations of logic are the laws of thought. Thus, for example, Kant says that logic "treats of nothing but the mere forms of thought." Its limits "are definitely fixed by the fact that it is a science which has nothing to do but fully to exhibit and strictly to prove all formal rules of thought."

The logical principles of identity, excluded middle, and contradiction, as well as the principles of inference, are said to be "laws of thought." James proposes as the most "fundamental principle of inference" what he calls the "axiom of skipped intermediaries," which states that *"skipping intermediary terms leaves relations the same."* That "equals of equals are equal" is a special application of this principle in the sphere of quantities. Because it applies to all subject matters equally, James regards the principle as "on the whole the broadest and deepest law of man's thought."

In either conception of logic as a formal science, questions arise concerning the relation of logic to other sciences. For Aristotle the question is about logic and metaphysics, because both seem to have an unrestricted scope. Metaphysics considers the being of *everything* which is; logic, the formal components of discourse about *anything*. Aristotle says of philosophy in relation to dialectic, that both "embrace all things" but that "dialectic is merely critical where philosophy claims to know." The same comparison could apply to metaphysics and logic. Both "embrace all things" but not from the same point of view.

Aristotle also asks whether it belongs to metaphysics as well as to logic to inquire "into the truths which are called axioms"—especially those which are the first principles of all knowledge or demonstration, not merely the foundations of knowledge about some limited subject matter. "Since these truths clearly hold good for all things *qua* being," the science which studies being *qua* being (*i.e.*, metaphysics) must be concerned with them. It also belongs to metaphysics as well as to logic "to inquire into the principles of the syllogism."

The principles of identity, excluded middle, and contradiction belong to both sciences—to the one as the most universal truths about existence, to the other as the basic rules of discourse or the laws of thought. This sharing of a common ground does not seem to Aristotle to violate their separateness; but Bacon charges him with having "corrupted natural philosophy by logic." Of Aristotle's physics, he says that it is built of "mere logical terms," and, Bacon adds, Aristotle "remodelled the same subject in his metaphysics under a more imposing title."

Whereas Aristotle considers the relation of logic to metaphysics, Kant considers its relation to psychology. Both logic and psychology are concerned with thinking and knowing. Distinguishing between pure and applied logic, Kant says that pure logic "has nothing to do with empirical principles and borrows nothing from psychology." Applied logic depends on psychology. In fact, says Kant in his *Introduction to Logic*, it is "a psychology in which we consider what is the usual process in our thought, not what is the right one." Applied logic ought not to be called logic at all, for "logic is the science of the right use of the understanding and the reason generally, not subjectively, that is, not according to empirical (psychological) principles, as to how the understanding actually thinks, but objectively, that is, according to *a priori* principles, as to how it ought to think."

James also insists upon the distinction between psychology and logic. He even uses Kant's terms in calling logic an *a priori* and psychology an empirical science. What the psychologist calls "laws of thought," such as the laws of the association of ideas, describe the actual flow of thought and connections which depend upon similarity and succession. The laws of logic, in contrast, state reason's perception of the rational structure of thought itself and the relations which must obtain if thought is to be rational.

RETURNING NOW to the indication of the parts of logic which may be found in the structure of the *Organon*, we can see two orders in the books. The first three books—the *Categories, On Interpretation*, and the *Prior Analytics*—deal with terms, propositions, and syllogisms: with the

classification of terms and their relation to one another; with the classification of propositions and their opposition to one another; with the analysis of the various types of syllogisms and the formulation of the rules of valid inference. Terms are the elements of propositions; terms and propositions are the elements of the syllogism. This seems to determine the order of the first three books.

The first three books as a whole stand in a certain order to the remaining books. Taking the latter as a group, their differentiation from what precedes them seems to lie in the fact that they deal with terms, propositions, and syllogisms, not abstracted from all considerations of knowledge and truth about reality, but rather with primary emphasis upon the logic of actual knowledge, or on the processes of knowing and arguing about what is true or probable. In the traditional development of Aristotelian logic, this division between the first three and the remaining books of the *Organon* is sometimes characterized as a distinction between *formal* and *material* logic.

In the *Posterior Analytics* and the *Topics* Aristotle considers the discovery and establishment of either the true or the probable. He distinguishes between induction and syllogism (or reasoning) as modes of learning and arguing. The later division of logic into deductive and inductive—sometimes confused with the distinction between formal and material logic—does not seem to correspond to the difference between the *Prior* and the *Posterior Analytics*. In the *Advancement of Learning*, for example, Bacon divides the art of judgment, "which treats of the nature of proof or demonstration," into that which concludes by induction and that which concludes by syllogism; whereas Aristotle appears to treat induction as that upon which syllogistic demonstration depends for its primary and indemonstrable premises.

The distinction between truth and probability, or between knowledge and opinion, does not affect the formal character of either induction or syllogism. A syllogism may be scientific (*i.e.*, demonstratively certain) or dialectical (*i.e.*, merely probable) according to the character of its premises. In either case its formal structure remains the same. Similarly, the difference between scientific and dialectical induction appears only in its result, *i.e.*, whether it is knowledge or opinion. The *Posterior Analytics* and the *Topics* consider the employment of both syllogism and induction. The *Posterior Analytics* treats them in relation to the development and structure of scientific knowledge. The *Topics* discusses them in relation to the dialectical procedures of argument and discovery.

The last book of the *Organon*, which is concerned with exposing the fallacies in sophistical proofs or refutations, serves to protect both scientific and dialectical reasoning from such sophistry. Unlike the philosopher or the dialectician, the sophist does not aim at the truth. Sophistry misuses the weapons of logic—the same weapons used by the scientist or dialectician—to produce a counterfeit of wisdom or, as Aristotle says, "a wisdom which exists only in semblance." Though the dialectician cannot claim to know, he does, nevertheless, deal with opinions critically and respects the canons of logic as much as the philosopher.

The art of logic seems to have three main employments. To its use by the scientist and the dialectician, Aristotle adds its utilization by the orator for the purposes of persuasion. The rhetorician and the dialectician are most closely allied because both deal with probabilities and disputable matters concerning which opposite conclusions can be drawn. "As in dialectic, there is induction on the one hand and syllogism. . . on the other, so it is in rhetoric." Aristotle says that "the enthymeme is a rhetorical syllogism, and the example a rhetorical induction."

The foregoing suggests that a certain order obtains between two of the three arts traditionally called the *trivium*. The elements and principles of logic are, in a sense, prior to the rules of rhetoric. The art of rhetoric depends on and uses logic. The third art, that of grammar, seems to serve both logic and rhetoric. It serves the logician in his task of forming terms and propositions out of words, phrases, and sentences. It serves the rhetorician in his effort to make a forceful use of language. This conception of the uses of grammar appears in Aristotle's *Rhetoric* in his consideration of style, and in the opening books of the *Organon* in his discussion of univocal and equivocal names, the parts of speech, simple and composite expressions, and the different types of sentences.

KANT SEEMS TO diverge from Aristotle both with regard to the unity of logic and with regard to the nature and relation of its parts. Formal or elementary logic, Kant thinks, is not the same as an organon of the sciences. He explains, in his *Introduction to Logic*, that an organon gives instruction as to "how some particular branch of knowledge is to be attained. . . . An organon of the sciences is therefore not a mere logic, since it presupposes the accurate knowledge of the objects and sources of the sciences. . . . Logic, on the contrary, being the general propaedeutic of every use of the understanding and of the reason, cannot meddle with the sciences and anticipate their matter." Conceding that it may be called an organon so far as it serves, "not for the *enlargement*, but only for the *criticism* and *correction* of our knowledge," Kant insists that "logic is not a general art of discovery, nor an organon of truth; it is not an algebra by the help of which hidden truths may be discovered."

Aristotle, according to Kant, treats the whole of his logic as an organon, dividing it into an analytical and a dialectical part. As Kant sees it, the dialectical part arises from a misuse of the analytical part. This occurs, he says in the *Critique of Pure Reason*, when general or elementary logic (*i.e.*, the analytic part) "which is meant to be a mere canon of criticism, is employed as if it were an organon, for the real production of at least the semblance of objective assertions. . . . This general logic," says Kant, "which assumes the semblance of an organon, is called dialectic."

Kant here seems to identify dialectic with what Aristotle calls sophistry. He says of dialectic that "different as are the significations in which the ancients use this name of a science or art, it is easy to gather from its actual employment that with them it was nothing but a logic of semblance. It was a sophistic art of giving to one's ignorance, nay, to one's intentional casuistry, the outward appearance of truth, by imitating the accurate method which logic always requires." When logic is treated as an organon, it "is always an illusive logic, that is, dialectical. For as logic teaches nothing with regard to the contents of knowledge . . . any attempt at using it as an organon in order to extend and enlarge our knowledge, at least in appearance, can end in nothing but mere talk, by asserting with a certain plausibility anything one likes, or, if one likes, denying it."

Yet Kant himself retains Analytic and Dialectic as the major divisions of his own transcendental logic, explaining that he employs the title of dialectic, not for the misuse of logic, but rather to signify that portion of logic which is the critique of "dialectical semblance" or sophistry. General or ordinary logic takes no account of the content of knowledge and applies to all objects universally because "it treats of the form of thought in general." Transcendental logic does not entirely ignore the content of knowledge, but only the content of that knowledge which is empirical in origin. If there are transcendental or *a priori* concepts which do not originate from experience, then there can be a science which treats "of that knowledge which belongs to the pure understanding, and by which we may think objects entirely *a priori*."

That is the science Kant calls *"transcendental Logic."* It deals, he writes, "with the laws of the understanding and reason in so far only as they refer *a priori* to objects." That part of it "which teaches the elements of the pure knowledge of the understanding, and the principles without which no object can be thought, is the transcendental Analytic." The second part of it is the transcendental Dialectic—"a critique of the understanding and reason with regard to their hyperphysical employment, in order thus to lay bare the false semblance of its groundless pretensions . . . serving as a protection of the pure understanding against all sophistical illusions."

THE ISSUE between Kant and Aristotle cannot be understood if it is read simply as a dispute about the nature and divisions of logic. Their diverse views of logic must be seen against the larger background of their philosophical differences with regard to the nature of the mind, the nature of reality, the origin of knowledge, and the character of its objects. Controversies about logic (and even within logic, about this or that theory of judgment or reasoning) usually reflect fundamental issues in psychology and metaphysics. The attack made by some modern logicians, for example, against the subject-predicate logic of Aristotle cannot be separated from their rejection of his doctrine of substance and

accident in physics and metaphysics; even as their own relational logic represents a different view of the structure of reality or the constituents of experience.

On the other hand, the criticism of Aristotelian logic by Bacon and Descartes seems to be motivated primarily by considerations of method. They do not have a different logic to propose, as do Kant and later symbolic or mathematical logicians. Rather for them logic itself—by which they mean Aristotle's logic and particularly his doctrine of the syllogism—appears useless for the purposes of enlarging knowledge, discovering new truths, and developing the sciences. Where Kant criticizes Aristotle for regarding logic as an organon or method for acquiring knowledge, Bacon and Descartes complain that logic does not serve that purpose at all, and therefore a *novum organum*—not a new logic, but a new method—is needed.

"The present system of logic is useless for the discovery of the sciences," Bacon writes. It "rather assists in confirming and rendering inveterate the errors founded on vulgar notions than in searching after truth, and is therefore more hurtful than useful." The syllogism, for example, "is unequal to the subtlety of nature. . . . Our only hope is in genuine induction." Induction is the key to an art of discovery, and the rules of induction the heart of a fruitful method of inquiry.

The relation of induction to demonstration in Aristotle's logic, and the difference between Aristotle's and Bacon's theories of induction, are discussed in the chapter on that subject. In Bacon's view, the *Novum Organum* departs radically from the old *Organon*. The new can be substituted for the old in its entirety. It may be asked, he says, "whether we talk of perfecting natural philosophy alone according to our method, or the other sciences also, such as logic, ethics, politics." His answer is that "as common logic, which regulates matters by syllogisms, is applied not only to natural, but also to every other science, so our inductive method likewise comprehends them all."

Demonstration is opposed not only to induction, but to discovery. Accordingly, logic conceived as concerned only with the rules of demonstration is opposed to other methods which aim at directing scientific inquiry and research.

The basic contrast is between criticism and construction, or between examining what is offered as knowledge for its validity and developing techniques for adding new knowledge to old. In his *Two New Sciences* Galileo says that logic "teaches us how to test the conclusiveness of any argument or demonstration already discovered and completed" but not "to discover correct arguments and demonstrations." It does not, "as regards stimulation to discovery, compare with the power of sharp distinction which belongs to geometry."

In the same vein Descartes says of logic that "the syllogisms and the great part of the other teaching serve better in explaining to others those things that one knows . . . than in learning what is new. . . . This made me feel that some other method must be found." The four rules of the method he then states, which codify the steps he himself has taken to make discoveries in geometry and physics, seem to him a general procedure for insuring the advancement of all fields of learning.

As his *Rules for the Direction of the Mind* indicates, Descartes' method does not omit the intuition of principles and the deduction of conclusions therefrom—the apparent equivalents of induction and demonstration in Aristotle's *Organon*. But he explains why he has "omitted all the precepts of the dialecticians" even though he is himself concerned with improving "our power of deducing one truth from another." Their style of argument, he says, "contributes nothing at all to the discovery of the truth. . . . Its only possible use is to serve to explain at times more easily to others the truths we have already ascertained; hence it should be transferred from Philosophy to Rhetoric."

Furthermore, the forms of the traditional syllogism do not seem able to accommodate the connections in mathematical reasoning or the structure of mathematical proof. "Everyone will perceive in mathematical demonstrations," Locke writes, "that the knowledge gained thereby, comes shortest and clearest without syllogisms." Locke identifies logic with the doctrine of the syllogism and, even more explicitly than Descartes, rejects it as an aid to reasoning.

THE QUESTION whether logic is itself a methodology, or includes rules for the discovery as well as the demonstration of truth, is answered in terms of broader and narrower conceptions of the science or art. Those who regard the rules of logic as primarily a canon of criticism, which test the validity of intellectual work, look elsewhere for a method whose rules are productive rather than critical. The question then usually arises whether there is one methodology applicable to *all* fields of inquiry, or as many distinct methods as there are different disciplines or subject matters.

The difference between the traditional Aristotelian and the modern mathematical logic suggests that there may be a plurality of logics. The attempts made by the exponents of each to subsume the other as a special case do not seem to be entirely successful. Though Aristotelian logic appears to give a satisfactory account of the forms of judgment and reasoning in certain types of discourse, it cannot, in the opinion of symbolic logicians, be applied to mathematics. "Mathematics consists of deductions, and yet," according to Bertrand Russell, "the orthodox accounts of deduction are largely or wholly inapplicable to existing mathematics." Symbolic logic, on the other hand, may succeed in formulating the relational structure of modern mathematics, but it does not, in the opinion of its critics, hold for metaphysics—at least not the sort of metaphysics which treats relation as a category subordinate to substance.

The difference between the kind of thinking that men do in science and in law suggests another type of diversity among logics. The practical or moral judgment seems to involve a special type of predicate. What Aristotle calls the "practical syllogism" and what Aquinas describes as the process of "determination"— quite distinct from deduction—by which positive laws are derived from natural law, seem to call for a logic of practical thinking, quite distinct from the logic of all the theoretic sciences.

Using the word "logic" in its broadest sense, we must ask whether there is one logic common to all the sciences; or a logic which fits mathematics but not physics or metaphysics, a logic appropriate to speculative philosophy but not to experimental or empirical research, a logic peculiar to the nature of the practical or moral sciences, such as ethics and politics, or to the work of jurisprudence.

There is evidence in the great books that sciences as different as mathematics and physics, or as metaphysics and politics, differ in their methods of discovery and demonstration. This may mean that they differ in their logics as well. Yet it also appears to be the case that the principle of contradiction applies in all, that fallacious inference is detected by the same criteria in all, and to this extent all share a common logic. Where alternative methods have been proposed within a single major field—notably in the case of philosophy—this may reflect different conceptions of philosophy itself rather than alternative routes to the same end.

Because of their relevance to the basic issues about logic (and especially those concerning its scope and unity), the rules of methodology in general and the various methods proposed for particular disciplines are included in this chapter. They are also considered, of course, in chapters devoted to the special disciplines or subject matters, *e.g.*, ASTRONOMY, HISTORY, MATHEMATICS, METAPHYSICS, PHYSICS, THEOLOGY; and in the chapters on SCIENCE and PHILOSOPHY. What is distinctive about each of these methods is discussed in those chapters in relation to the type of knowledge or inquiry which seems to require a method of its own.

OUTLINE OF TOPICS

REFERENCES

To find the passages cited, use the numbers in heavy type, which are the volume and page numbers of the passages referred to. For example, in 4 HOMER: *Iliad*, BK II [265–283] 12d, the number 4 is the number of the volume in the set; the number 12d indicates that the passage is in section d of page 12.

PAGE SECTIONS: When the text is printed in one column, the letters a and b refer to the upper and lower halves of the page. For example, in 53 JAMES: *Psychology*, 116a-119b, the passage begins in the upper half of page 116 and ends in the lower half of page 119. When the text is printed in two columns, the letters a and b refer to the upper and lower halves of the left-hand side of the page, the letters c and d to the upper and lower halves of the right-hand side of the page. For example, in 7 PLATO: *Symposium*, 163b-164c, the passage begins in the lower half of the left-hand side of page 163 and ends in the upper half of the right-hand side of page 164.

AUTHOR'S DIVISIONS: One or more of the main divisions of a work (such as PART, BK, CH, SECT) are sometimes included in the reference; line numbers, in brackets, are given in certain cases; *e.g.*, *Iliad*, BK II [265–283] 12d.

BIBLE REFERENCES: The references are to book, chapter, and verse. When the King James and Douay versions differ in title of books or in the numbering of chapters or verses, the King James version is cited first and the Douay, indicated by a (*D*), follows; *e.g.*, OLD TESTAMENT: *Nehemiah*, 7:45—(*D*) *II Esdras*, 7:46.

SYMBOLS: The abbreviation "esp" calls the reader's attention to one or more especially relevant parts of a whole reference; "passim" signifies that the topic is discussed intermittently rather than continuously in the work or passage cited.

For additional information concerning the style of the references, see the Explanation of Reference Style; for general guidance in the use of *The Great Ideas*, consult the Preface.

1. Logic as a science: its scope and subject matter compared with psychology and metaphysics

7 PLATO: *Republic*, BK VII, 397a-398c / *Sophist*, 571a-c / *Philebus*, 634b-635a

8 ARISTOTLE: *Prior Analytics*, BK I, CH I [24ª10–11] 39a / *Metaphysics*, BK III, CH I [995ᵇ6–10] 514a; CH 2 [996ᵇ26-997ª15] 515b-d; BK IV, CH 2 [1004ᵇ15–26] 523d; CH 3–8 524b-532d; BK V, CH 7 [1017ª22–28] 537d-538a; BK XI, CH I [1059ª23–26] 587a; CH 4–6 589d-592b

9 ARISTOTLE: *Rhetoric*, BK I, CH I [1354ª1–11] 593a; CH 2 [1358ª2–35] 597d-598b

12 EPICTETUS: *Discourses*, BK I, CH 7 112b-113d; CH 17 122d-124a

17 PLOTINUS: *First Ennead*, TR III, CH 4 11a-c

18 AUGUSTINE: *City of God*, BK VIII, CH 4 266d-267c; CH 7 269c-d / *Christian Doctrine*, BK II, CH 31 651d-652b

20 AQUINAS: *Summa Theologica*, PART I-II, Q 57, A 3, REP 3 37b-38a; A 6, REP 3 40a-41a; Q 94, A 2, ANS 221d-223a

23 HOBBES: *Leviathan*, PART I, 58a-b; 72a-d

28 GALILEO: *Two New Sciences*, SECOND DAY, 190b-c

30 BACON: *Advancement of Learning*, 55b-61d esp 56c-58c, 59c-60c

31 DESCARTES: *Rules*, II, 2c-3b / *Discourse*, PART II, 46c-d

33 PASCAL: *Geometrical Demonstration* 430a-446b esp 445a-446b

35 LOCKE: *Human Understanding*, BK IV, CH XXI 394d-395a,c

35 BERKELEY: *Human Knowledge*, INTRO, SECT 6 405d-406a

39 SMITH: *Wealth of Nations*, BK V, 335d-336a

42 KANT: *Pure Reason*, 5a-6d; 34a-37d; 59c; 210b-c / *Fund. Prin. Metaphysic of Morals*, 253a-c; 254c-d / *Judgement*, 463a; 492c-d

46 HEGEL: *Philosophy of History*, INTRO, 182d

53 JAMES: *Psychology*, 524a; 867a; 872b-874a; 878a; 880b; 889a-b

1*a*. The axioms of logic: the laws of thought; the principles of reasoning

7 PLATO: *Euthydemus*, 72d-73b / *Republic*, BK IV, 350d-351b

8 ARISTOTLE: *Categories*, CH 3 [1ᵇ10–16] 5c-d; CH 10 [13ᵇ1–35] 19a-c / *Prior Analytics*, BK I, CH 1–3 39a-40c / *Posterior Analytics*, BK I, CH 1-2 97a-99a; CH 11 105d-106b / *Metaphysics*, BK III, CH I [995ᵇ6–10] 514a; CH 2 [996ᵇ26–997ª15] 515b-d; BK IV, CH 3–8 524b-532d; BK XI, CH I [1059ª23–26] 587a; CH 4–6 589d-592b

PART I, 43b; PART VI, 66d / *Objections and Replies*, 290c-d
31 SPINOZA: *Ethics*, PART II, PROP 47, SCHOL 390c-391a
33 PASCAL: *Pensées*, 22-23 175b; 392 239b-240a
35 LOCKE: *Human Understanding*, BK II, CH XXXIII, SECT 19 251c-d; BK III, CH III, SECT 10, 256d-257a; CH VII 283a-284b esp SECT 2 283b-c; BK IV, CH IV, SECT 17 328d; CH V, SECT 1-3 329a-b; CH VI, SECT 1-3 331b-d
35 BERKELEY: *Human Knowledge*, INTRO, SECT 19 410c; SECT 52 422d-423a
38 ROUSSEAU: *Inequality*, 339d-342c
42 KANT: *Pure Reason*, 1a-4a,c
45 LAVOISIER: *Elements of Chemistry*, PREF, 1a-c; 4a-5d; 7c
46 HEGEL: *Philosophy of History*, INTRO, 182b-c
49 DARWIN: *Origin of Species*, 40c-d
51 TOLSTOY: *War and Peace*, EPILOGUE I, 672a-b
53 JAMES: *Psychology*, 144a-b

3b. The relation of logic and rhetoric

5 ARISTOPHANES: *Clouds* 488a-506d esp [882–1112] 499b-502b
7 PLATO: *Phaedrus*, 131b-141a,c / *Gorgias* 252a-294d / *Philebus*, 633a-635a esp 634b-635a
8 ARISTOTLE: *Interpretation*, CH 4 [17ᵃ1-7] 26b
9 ARISTOTLE: *Ethics*, BK I, CH 3 [1094ᵇ19-27] 339d-340a / *Rhetoric*, BK I, CH 1-2 593a-598b; CH 4 [1359ᵇ1-18] 599d; BK II, CH 22-26 643c-653a,c
10 GALEN: *Natural Faculties*, BK I, CH 16, 180d-181a
18 AUGUSTINE: *Christian Doctrine*, BK II, CH 36-37 653d-654b; BK IV, CH 4 676d-677a
23 HOBBES: *Leviathan*, PART I, 55a-b; 60d; 67c; 72a-d; PART II, 127d; 128d
30 BACON: *Advancement of Learning*, 31a-d; 58c-59a; 64a-b; 66c-67c
31 DESCARTES: *Rules*, II, 2c; X, 16d-17a esp 17a / *Discourse*, PART II, 46c-d
33 PASCAL: *Pensées*, 22-23 175b
35 LOCKE: *Human Understanding*, BK III, CH X, SECT 34 299d-300a

4. Methodology: rules for the conduct of the mind in the processes of thinking, learning, inquiring, knowing

7 PLATO: *Euthydemus* 65a-84a,c / *Parmenides*, 491a-c / *Philebus*, 610d-613a
8 ARISTOTLE: *Prior Analytics*, BK I, CH 30 63d-64b / *Topics*, BK I, CH 14 149a-d; BK VIII, CH 14 221d-223a,c / *Metaphysics*, BK II, CH 3 513c-d; BK V, CH 1 [1013ᵃ1-3] 533a
9 ARISTOTLE: *Parts of Animals*, BK I, CH 1 161a-165d / *Ethics*, BK I, CH 3 [1094ᵇ12-27] 339d-340a; BK II, CH 2 [1104ᵃ14-15] 349c; BK VI, CH 3 [1139ᵇ24-34] 388c; CH 11 392c-393b esp [1143ᵃ31-ᵇ6] 392d-393a
12 EPICTETUS: *Discourses*, BK II, CH 12 151b-152c; CH 25 174b-c
17 PLOTINUS: *First Ennead*, TR III, CH 4 11a-c

23 HOBBES: *Leviathan*, PART I, 55a-56d; 58d-61a
25 MONTAIGNE: *Essays*, 63d-66b; 240c-242a; 270a-271c; 446d-450a; 453c-454d
28 GALILEO: *Two New Sciences*, SECOND DAY, 190b-c
28 HARVEY: *On Animal Generation*, 331a-337a
30 BACON: *Advancement of Learning*, 11a-17c esp 14c-15a, 16b-c; 33d-34b; 43d-44c; 47d-49b; 55b-61d esp 57d-58b; 64a-66a; 96d-97a / *Novum Organum*, PREF 105a-106d; BK I 107a-136a,c esp APH 11-26 107d-108d, APH 39-69 109c-116b, APH 103-106 127d-128c; BK II, APH 27-32 157b-161b esp APH 32 161a-b
31 DESCARTES: *Rules* 1a-40a,c esp III-VI, 4a-9b; VII 10b-12a, X, 16d-17a, XII-XIII, 24d-27d, XIV, 28b-29b / *Discourse* 41a-67a,c esp PART I, 41d-42b, PART II, 45b-c, 46c-48b, PART III, 50b-51a, PART IV, 52a / *Objections and Replies*, 237b-c; 267a-277a,c
33 PASCAL: *Pensées*, 1-5 171a-173a / *Geometrical Demonstration* 430a-446b passim
35 LOCKE: *Human Understanding*, INTRO, SECT 4-7 94a-95c; BK I, CH III, SECT 24-26 120a-121a,c; BK II, CH I, SECT 10 123b-d; CH XI, SECT 15 146d-147a; BK III, CH X, SECT 34 299d-300a; BK IV, CH III, SECT 22 319c-320a; SECT 30 323a-c; CH IV, SECT 17 328d; CH VII, SECT 11, 340c-341a; CH XII 358c-363b passim, esp SECT 7 360b-c, SECT 14 362d-363a; CH XVII, SECT 19-22 379d-380b
35 BERKELEY: *Human Knowledge*, INTRO, SECT 21-25 411b-412a,c
35 HUME: *Human Understanding*, SECT II, DIV 17 457a-b; SECT VII, DIV 49 471c-d; SECT VIII, DIV 75, 484c; SECT XII, DIV 116, 503d-504a; DIV 132 509a-d
42 KANT: *Pure Reason*, 1a-4a,c esp 1b-d, 3c-d; 101b-d; 133c-134d; 179d-182b; 218d-227a; 248d-250a,c / *Fund. Prin. Metaphysic of Morals*, 253a-b / *Practical Reason*, 293c-294b; 336d-337a,c / *Pref. Metaphysical Elements of Ethics*, 376c-d / *Judgement*, 551a-552c; 575b-c
43 MILL: *Liberty*, 276c-d; 283d-284d
51 TOLSTOY: *War and Peace*, EPILOGUE II, 690a-b

4a. Mathematical analysis and reasoning: the search for a universal method

7 PLATO: *Republic*, BK VI, 386d-387d / *Theaetetus*, 514b-515d
8 ARISTOTLE: *Prior Analytics*, BK I, CH 41 [49ᵇ32-50ᵃ3] 68c / *Posterior Analytics*, BK I, CH 7 103c-d; CH 10 104d-105d / *Topics*, BK VI, CH 4 [141ᵇ3-22] 194d-195a; BK VII, CH 3 [153ᵃ6-11] 208a-b / *Physics*, BK II, CH 9 [200ᵃ15-29] 277c-d / *Metaphysics*, BK II, CH 3 513c-d; BK III, CH 2 [996ᵃ22-36] 514d-515a; BK VI, CH 1 [1026ᵃ7-32] 548a-c; BK VII, CH 10 [1036ᵃ2-13] 559b-c; BK IX, CH 9 [1051ᵃ22-34] 577b-c; BK XI, CH 3 [1061ᵃ29-ᵇ3] 589c; CH 4 589d-590a; BK XIII, CH 2 [1077ᵇ1]-CH 3 [1078ᵃ32] 608d-609d

(4. *Methodology: rules for the conduct of the mind in the processes of thinking, learning, inquiring, knowing. 4a. Mathematical analysis and reasoning: the search for a universal method.*)

9 ARISTOTLE: *Ethics*, BK III, CH 3 [1112^{b}20–24] 358d; BK VII, CH 8 [1151^{a}15–19] 402a

11 ARCHIMEDES: *Method* 569a-592a esp 569b-570a

11 NICOMACHUS: *Arithmetic*, BK II, 831d-841c

16 KEPLER: *Harmonies of the World*, 1012b-1014b

19 AQUINAS: *Summa Theologica*, PART I, Q 85, A 8, REP 2 460b-461b

23 HOBBES: *Leviathan*, PART I, 56b; 58a-c; 59b-c

28 GALILEO: *Two New Sciences*, SECOND DAY, 190b-c

30 BACON: *Advancement of Learning*, 65b / *Novum Organum*, BK I, APH 59 112b-c

31 DESCARTES: *Rules* 1a-40a,c esp II 2a-3b, IV, 5c-7d, VI 8a-10a, XII, 24d-25a, XIV-XVI 28a-35c, XVIII-XXI 36b-40a,c / *Discourse*, PART I, 43b-c; PART II, 46c-48b; PART III, 50d / *Objections and Replies*, 128a-129a; 130a-133a,c / *Geometry* 295a-353b esp BK I, 295a-298b, BK II, 304a-306a, 316a-317a, BK III, 331b, 353a

33 PASCAL: *Pensées*, 1–5 171a-173a / *Geometrical Demonstration*, 430a-434a; 442a-446b / *Arithmetical Triangle*, 451b-452a; 458b-459b; 464a-466a

34 NEWTON: *Principles*, 1a-b; BK I, LEMMA I-II and SCHOL 25a-32a esp LEMMA II, SCHOL, 31a-32a; PROP 31, SCHOL 79a-81a; BK II, LEMMA 2 168a-169b; BK III, LEMMA 5 338b-339a

35 LOCKE: *Human Understanding*, BK II, CH XVI, SECT 4 166a-b; BK IV, CH I, SECT 9 308c-309b; CH II, SECT 9-10 311b-c; CH III, SECT 18-20 317d-319c; SECT 30 323a-c; CH IV, SECT 6-9 325a-326b; CH VII, SECT 11, 340c-341a; CH XII, SECT 1-8 358c-360c passim; SECT 14-15 362d-363b; CH XVII, SECT 11 378b

35 BERKELEY: *Human Knowledge*, INTRO, SECT 12 408a-b; SECT 19 410c; SECT 15-16 415d-416a; SECT 118-132 436b-439c passim

35 HUME: *Human Understanding*, SECT IV, DIV 20 458a-b; SECT VII, DIV 48 470d-471c; SECT XII, DIV 131 508d-509a

36 SWIFT: *Gulliver*, PART III, 109b-111a; 118b-119a

42 KANT: *Pure Reason*, 5a-13d; 15c-16c; 17d-19a; 46a-b; 68a-69c; 211c-212a; 215d-217a; 217c-218d / *Practical Reason*, 302d-303b; 330d-331a / *Science of Right*, 399a-b / *Judgement*, 497a-498d esp 498b-d; 551a-553c

43 MILL: *Liberty*, 283d-284a

45 LAVOISIER: *Elements of Chemistry*, PREF, 2b

45 FOURIER: *Theory of Heat*, 172a-173b; 249a-251b

51 TOLSTOY: *War and Peace*, BK XI, 469a-d; EPILOGUE II, 694d-695c

53 JAMES: *Psychology*, 175a-176a; 870a; 874a-878a

4b. The heuristic principles of research in experimental and empirical science

8 ARISTOTLE: *Heavens*, BK III, CH 7 [306^{a}1–18] 397b-c / *Generation and Corruption*, BK I, CH 2 [316^{a}5-14] 411c-d / *Meteorology*, BK I, CH 7 [344^{a}5-9] 450b

9 ARISTOTLE: *History of Animals*, BK I, CH 6 [491^{a}5-26] 12c-13a / *Parts of Animals*, BK I, CH I 161a-165d esp [642^{a}14–^{b}4] 165b-d / *Generation of Animals*, BK III, CH 10 [760^{b}28-33 301d-302a

10 HIPPOCRATES: *Ancient Medicine*, par 1-8 1a-3b; par 20 7b-d

10 GALEN: *Natural Faculties*, BK I, CH 13 173d-177a

16 COPERNICUS: *Revolutions of the Heavenly Spheres*, 505a-506a; 507a-508a

16 KEPLER: *Epitome*, BK IV, 888b-890a; 907b-908b

18 AUGUSTINE: *Confessions*, BK V, par 3-6 27c-28c esp par 6 28c

19 AQUINAS: *Summa Theologica*, PART I, Q 32, A I, REP 2 175d-178a

25 MONTAIGNE: *Essays*, 377a-d

28 GILBERT: *Loadstone*, PREF, 1a-2a; BK I, 6a-7a esp 6d-7a; BK II, 27b-c

28 GALILEO: *Two New Sciences*, FIRST DAY, 131a-138b; 148c-149c; 157b-177a,c passim; THIRD DAY, 200a-d; 202d-203a; 207d-208c; 236d-237a

28 HARVEY: *Motion of the Heart*, 285c-d / *Circulation of the Blood*, 322d-323d; 324c-d / *On Animal Generation*, 331a-337a esp 331b-333d, 335c-336c

30 BACON: *Advancement of Learning*, 13d-14b; 15d; 34b; 42a-c; 56c-59c; 64d-65a / *Novum Organum* 105a-195d esp PREF 105a-106d, BK I, APH 1-26 107a-108d, APH 50 111b, APH 70 116b-117a, APH 95 126b-c, APH 104-106 128a-c, BK II, APH 1-9 137a-140c, APH 52 194c-195d / *New Atlantis*, 210d-214d

31 DESCARTES: *Discourse*, PART VI 60d-67a,c esp 61d-62c, 66a-b / *Meditations*, IV, 90a-b / *Objections and Replies*, 215a-b

33 PASCAL: *Vacuum*, 355a-358b; 365b-371a passim / *Great Experiment* 382a-389b

34 NEWTON: *Principles*, 1a-2a; BK III, RULES 270a-271b; GENERAL SCHOL, 371b-372a / *Optics*, BK I, 379a; BK III, 542a; 543a-b

34 HUYGENS: *Light*, PREF, 551b-552a; CH I, 553a-554a

35 LOCKE: *Human Understanding*, BK IV, CH VI, SECT 13 335c-d; CH XII, SECT 9-13 360d-362d

35 HUME: *Human Understanding*, SECT III, DIV 19, 458a; SECT IV, DIV 23-27 459a-460d; SECT IX, DIV 82 487b-c

42 KANT: *Pure Reason*, 5a-13d esp 5c-6c; 210b-c; 215d-216d

45 LAVOISIER: *Elements of Chemistry*, PREF, 1c-2b; 6d-7a,c; PART I, 17a; 23c; PART III, 87b-c

45 FOURIER: *Theory of Heat*, 169a-174a; 175b; 181b; 184a

45 FARADAY: *Researches in Electricity*, 440b,d; 467a-b; 659a; 774d-775a

50 MARX: *Capital*, 6c

51 TOLSTOY: *War and Peace*, EPILOGUE II, 690a-b; 694d-696d

53 JAMES: *Psychology*, 3b-4a; 120a-129b passim; 348a-359a esp 351a-352a; 385a-b; 677b; 862a-865b; 882a-886a passim, esp 883a-884a

54 FREUD: *Narcissism*, 400d-401a / *Instincts*, 412a-b / *General Introduction*, 463d; 483d-485a esp 484d-485a / *Beyond the Pleasure Principle*, 661c-662b / *New Introductory Lectures*, 815a-b; 818c-819b; 874a-c; 879c; 881b-c

4c. The criteria of evidence and inference in historical inquiry

6 HERODOTUS: *History*, BK I, 17b-c; BK II, 49a-56b passim; 59a; 69b-d; 71a-73b; 76d; BK III, 89c-d; 99b-c; BK V, 168b-c; BK VII, 254c-d; BK VIII, 281d-282b

6 THUCYDIDES: *Peloponnesian War*, BK I, 353d-354b; BK II, 391c-d; BK VI, 523c-524d passim; BK VIII, 586b-d

14 PLUTARCH: *Romulus* 15a-30a,c passim, esp 15a-18d / *Numa Pompilius*, 49a-b / *Themistocles*, 102a,c / *Aristides*, 262b,d-263c / *Nicias*, 423a-c

15 TACITUS: *Annals*, BK III, 49c-d; BK IV, 66b-d

40 GIBBON: *Decline and Fall*, 96b,d; 232c; 296a

46 HEGEL: *Philosophy of History*, INTRO, 153a-158a; 180c-183d; PART III, 285d-286a

51 TOLSTOY: *War and Peace*, BK XIII, 563a-b; EPILOGUE II 675a-696d

54 FREUD: *General Introduction*, 450d-451a

4d. The diverse methods of speculative philosophy: the role of intuition, analysis, dialectic, genetic or transcendental criticism

7 PLATO: *Protagoras*, 50d-52d; 57a-c / *Euthydemus* 65a-84a,c / *Phaedrus* 115a-141a,c esp 131b-141a,c / *Meno*, 179d-183a / *Republic*, BK VI-VII, 383d-398c / *Parmenides*, 491a-c / *Theaetetus*, 514b-515d; 525d-526b / *Sophist* 551a-579d esp 552b-561d, 571a-c / *Statesman* 580a-608d esp 595a-d / *Philebus* 609a-639a,c esp 609a-617d / *Seventh Letter*, 809c-810d

8 ARISTOTLE: *Posterior Analytics* 97a-137a,c / *Topics*, BK I, CH 1 [100ª25–b21] 143a-b; BK VIII, CH 1 [155b1–16] 211a-b; CH 14 [163b8–16] 222a / *Sophistical Refutations*, CH 16 [175ª1–12] 241a / *Physics*, BK I, CH 1 259a-b; CH 2 [184b25–185ª19] 259c-260a; BK II, CH 7–9 275b-278a,c / *Heavens*, BK II, CH 13 [294b6–14] 386a; BK III, CH 7 [306ª1–18] 397b-c / *Generation and Corruption*, BK I, CH 2 [316ª5–14] 411c-d / *Metaphysics*, BK I, CH 3 [983ª 24–b6] 501c-d; CH 9 [992b18–993ª2] 511a-b; BK II, CH 1 [993ª30–b19] 511b,d-512a; CH 3 513c-d; BK III, CH 1 [995ª23–b4] 513b,d; BK IV, CH 2 522b-524b esp [1004ª25–31] 523b-c; CH 4 [1005b35–1006ª28] 525a-c; CH 7 [1012ª

17–24] 532a-b; CH 8 [1012ª29–b8] 532b-c; BK VI, CH 1 547b,d-548c; BK VII, CH 3 [1029ª 34–b12] 552a; CH 17 [1041ª6–b11] 565a-d; BK VIII, CH 4 [1044ª33–b20] 569a-b; BK IX, CH 6 [1048ª35–b9] 573d-574a; BK X, CH 1 [1052b1–15] 578d-579a; BK XI, CH 3 589a-d; CH 5 590a-d; CH 6 [1063ª13–16] 591b; CH 7 [1063b36–1064ª9] 592b; BK XIII, CH 1 [1076ª 10–16] 607a; CH 3 [1077b17–1078ª31] 609a-d / *Soul*, BK I, CH 1 [402ª1]–CH 2 [403b23] 631a-633a; BK II, CH 2 [413ª11–19] 643a-b; CH 3 [414b20]–CH 4 [415ª22] 644d-645c

9 ARISTOTLE: *Ethics*, BK VI, CH 3 388b-c; CH 6 389d; CH 8 [1142ª13–19] 391b; CH 11 392c-393b esp [1143ª31–b6] 392d-393a

17 PLOTINUS: *First Ennead*, TR III, CH 4–6 11a-12b / *Sixth Ennead*, TR II, CH 4 270c-271a

18 AUGUSTINE: *City of God*, BK VIII, CH 2–8 265b-270d passim

19 AQUINAS: *Summa Theologica*, PART I, Q 1, A 2, ANS and REP 1 4a-c; Q 2, A 2 11d-12c; Q 32, A 1, REP 2 175d-178a; PART I-II, Q 18 693b,d-703a passim

23 HOBBES: *Leviathan*, PART I, 56b-d; 60a-b; 65c-d; PART IV, 267a-c; 269b-c

24 RABELAIS: *Gargantua and Pantagruel*, BK II, 101b-106a

30 BACON: *Advancement of Learning*, 16b-c; 42a-c; 56c-59c; 61d

31 DESCARTES: *Rules*, II–XIV, 2d-33b / *Discourse*, PART II, 46c-47b; PART IV 51b-54b / *Meditations*, 69a-71a,c; 72b,d; I 75a-77c; III, 82a-d / *Objections and Replies*, 119c-120c; 126a-b; 128a-129a; POSTULATE I–VII 130d-131c; 167c; 206c-207a; 237b-238b; 244a-b; 245d-246a; 267a-277a,c

31 SPINOZA: *Ethics*, PART II, PROP 10, SCHOL 376d-377a

33 PASCAL: *Geometrical Demonstration*, 430a-434a; 442a-443b

35 LOCKE: *Human Understanding*, 87d; INTRO 93a-95d; BK I, CH III, SECT 24–25 120a-d

35 BERKELEY: *Human Knowledge*, INTRO, SECT 21–25 411b-412a,c

35 HUME: *Human Understanding*, SECT I, DIV 2 451b-c; DIV 7–9 453c-455a; SECT II, DIV 17 457a-b; SECT XII, DIV 116, 503d-504a; DIV 130 508c-d

38 ROUSSEAU: *Inequality*, 339d; 341b-342b; 362a-d passim

42 KANT: *Pure Reason*, 1a-13d; 16a-c; 109d-112d; 115d-116a; 119a-b; 133c-134d; 184b-c; 185b-c; 193a-200c esp 193d-194b, 199a-c; 215d-216d; 218d-227a; 248d-250a,c / *Fund. Prin. Metaphysic of Morals*, 253a-c; 254b-c; 263b-d; 264b-d esp 264d; 271a-c; 283d-284d / *Practical Reason*, 293c-294b esp 293d [fn 3]; 297a-c; 329d-330c; 335b-c; 336d-337a,c; 358a / *Pref. Metaphysical Elements of Ethics*, 365a-366a; 376c-d / *Intro. Metaphysic of Morals*, 387a-388d / *Judgement*, 570b-572d

43 FEDERALIST: NUMBER 31, 103c-104a

(4. *Methodology: rules for the conduct of the mind in the processes of thinking, learning, inquiring, knowing. 4d. The diverse methods of speculative philosophy: the role of intuition, analysis, dialectic, genetic or transcendental criticism.*)

43 MILL: *Liberty*, 287b-288c / *Utilitarianism*, 445a-447b

46 HEGEL: *Philosophy of Right*, PREF, 1a-c; INTRO, par 2, 9d-10a; ADDITIONS, 3 116a / *Philosophy of History*, INTRO, 156c-158a

51 TOLSTOY: *War and Peace*, EPILOGUE II, 690a-b

53 JAMES: *Psychology*, 674a-675b esp 675b; 687a

54 FREUD: *Beyond the Pleasure Principle*, 661c-662b / *New Introductory Lectures*, 874c-875b esp 875a

4e. The logic of practical thinking: the methods of ethics, politics, and jurisprudence

5 ARISTOPHANES: *Wasps* [799–1002] 517c-519d

9 ARISTOTLE: *Motion of Animals*, CH 7 [701ᵃ5–39] 236b-d / *Ethics*, BK I, CH 3 [1094ᵇ12–27] 339d-340a; CH 4 [1095ᵃ30–ᵇ8] 340c; CH 7 [1098ᵃ25–ᵇ8] 343d-344a; BK II, CH 2 349b-350a esp [1103ᵇ27–1104ᵃ9] 349b-c; CH 7 [1107ᵃ27–32] 352d-353a; BK III, CH 3 358a-359a; BK V, CH 10 [1137ᵇ12–31] 385d-386a; BK VI, CH 1 [1138ᵇ16–34] 387a-b; CH 5 389a-c passim; CH 8–9 390d-392b; CH 11 392c-393b esp [1143ᵃ31–ᵇ6] 392d-393a; BK VII, CH 2–3 395c-398a; CH 8 [1151ᵃ15–19] 402a / *Politics*, BK I, CH 1 [1252ᵃ18–24] 445b

19 AQUINAS: *Summa Theologica*, PART I, Q 19, A 5, ANS 112d-113c; A 7, ANS 114d-115d; Q 81, A 3, ANS and REP 2 430c-431d; Q 83, A 1, ANS 436d-438a; Q 86, A 1, REP 2 461c-462a; PART I-II, QQ 13–15 672d-684a; Q 44, A 2 808b-d

20 AQUINAS: *Summa Theologica*, PART I-II, Q 76, A 1, ANS 141a-c; Q 77, A 2, REP 4 145d-147c; Q 95, A 2 227c-228c; A 4 229b-230c

23 HOBBES: *Leviathan*, PART I, 53a-54a; 58a-b; 60b-61a; 66c-68a; 78a-d; PART II, 112d; 129a-b; 158c-d

26 SHAKESPEARE: *Merchant of Venice*, ACT II, SC VII [1–75] 416a-417a; SC IX [19–72] 417d-418b; ACT III, SC II [73–139] 420d-421b

30 BACON: *Advancement of Learning*, 57d-58b; 79c-80a; 81d-82a; 94d-95b

31 DESCARTES: *Discourse*, PART III, 48b-50b / *Objections and Replies*, 126a-b

33 PASCAL: *Provincial Letters*, 27a-80b; 90a-127a

35 LOCKE: *Human Understanding*, BK I, CH II, SECT 1 103d-104a; SECT 4 104d-105a; BK III, CH XI, SECT 15–18 303b-304b; BK IV, CH III, SECT 18–20 317d-319c; CH IV, SECT 7–10 325b-326b; CH XII, SECT 8 360c

35 HUME: *Human Understanding*, SECT I, DIV 1–5 451a-453b passim; DIV 9, 454d-455a; SECT XII, DIV 131–132 508d-509d passim, esp DIV 132, 509c-d

41 GIBBON: *Decline and Fall*, 75d-81c passim, esp 76d-78b

42 KANT: *Pure Reason*, 60a-c; 149d-150a / *Fund. Prin. Metaphysic of Morals*, 253a-254d; 264b-d; 266b-c; 271a-c; 283d-284d / *Practical Reason*, 291a-297c; 306d-307a; 307d-309b; 309d-310b; 319c-321b; 329a-331a / *Pref. Metaphysical Elements of Ethics* 365a-379d / *Intro. Metaphysic of Morals*, 388a-d; 390b; 393a / *Science of Right*, 397a-b; 398a-399c; 413d-414a; 416b-417a

43 FEDERALIST: NUMBER 31, 103c-104a; NUMBER 85, 258d

43 MILL: *Liberty*, 284b-d / *Utilitarianism*, 445a-447b; 456a-457b

46 HEGEL: *Philosophy of Right*, INTRO, par 3 10a-12c; PART III, par 222–223 73b-d; par 225 73d-74a; par 229 75b; ADDITIONS, 140 139b-c

50 MARX: *Capital*, 6a-d; 10a-11d; 301d [fn 3]

50 MARX-ENGELS: *Communist Manifesto*, 430c-433d passim, esp 431a-c

51 TOLSTOY: *War and Peace*, EPILOGUE II, 680d-681a; 683d-684a; 690a-b

53 JAMES: *Psychology*, 887a-888a

4f. Theological argument: the roles of faith, reason, and authority

18 AUGUSTINE: *Confessions*, BK I, par 1 1a-b; BK XII, par 32–36 107a-108c; par 41–43 110a-d; BK XIII, par 36 120c-d / *City of God*, BK VIII, CH 4–12 266d-273a / *Christian Doctrine*, BK I, CH 37 635b-c; BK II, CH 31 651d-652b; BK III, CH 28 668a

19 AQUINAS: *Summa Theologica*, PART I, Q 1 3a-10c; Q 2, A 2 11d-12c; Q 12, A 12 60d-61c; Q 19, A 5, REP 2 112d-113c; Q 32, A 1 175d-178a; A 4 180b-d; Q 46, A 2 253a-255a; Q 68, A 1, ANS 354a-355c; Q 102, A 1, ANS and REP 4 523d-525a; Q 113, A 7, REP 1 580b-581a

20 AQUINAS: *Summa Theologica*, PART I-II, Q 102, A 2 271b-272a; PART II-II, Q 1, A 5, REP 2 383b-384b; Q 2, A 10 399b-400b; PART III SUPPL, Q 75, A 3, REP 2 938a-939d

21 DANTE: *Divine Comedy*, PARADISE, XXIV 142d-144b

23 HOBBES: *Leviathan*, PART I, 66a-c; 83b; PART II, 137b-c; 149c-d; 160b-c; 163a-b; PART III, 165a-c; 167a-b; 241c-242a

25 MONTAIGNE: *Essays*, 98b-99a; 208b-209c; 212a-213a; 292c-294b

29 CERVANTES: *Don Quixote*, PART I, 122b-c

30 BACON: *Advancement of Learning*, 12c-13c; 17b-c; 39d-40a; 41b-d; 95d-101b

31 DESCARTES: *Discourse*, PART I, 43c / *Meditations*, 69a-72d

32 MILTON: *Paradise Lost*, BK XII [552–587] 331a-332a

33 PASCAL: *Provincial Letters*, 163a-166a / *Pensées*, 242–253 217b-220a; 265–290 221b-225a; 557–567 272b-273b; 862–866 342b-343b; 903 348a / *Vacuum*, 355b-356b

35 LOCKE: *Human Understanding*, BK IV, CH XVII, SECT 24 380c-d; CH XVIII 380d-384b passim; CH XIX, SECT 14 387d-388a

35 HUME: *Human Understanding*, SECT XI 497b-

CROSS-REFERENCES

For: Logic as a science in relation to other sciences, *see* DIALECTIC 4; METAPHYSICS 3c; PHILOSOPHY 3d.

The conception of the liberal arts and their place in education, *see* ART 4, 6b; EDUCATION 5b; MATHEMATICS 1b.

The conception of logic or dialectic as an art, in itself and in relation to other arts, *see* DIALECTIC 1, 2a(2)–2b; LANGUAGE 7; MATHEMATICS 1a; RHETORIC 1b.

Other discussions of the laws of thought and the rules of inference, *see* JUDGMENT 7a–7b; OPPOSITION 1d(1)–1d(2); PRINCIPLE 1c, 3a(3); REASONING 2–2c, 4a; and for the examination of logical fallacies, *see* REASONING 3a–3c; TRUTH 3d(2)–3d(3).

Particular problems in the art or science of logic, *see* DEFINITION 1, 2a–2e, 4–5; HYPOTHESIS 5; IDEA 4b–4c; INDUCTION 1–1b, 4–4a, 5; JUDGMENT 6–6d, 8–8d; OPPOSITION 1a–1c(2); REASONING 4d–4f, 5b–5e(3); SAME AND OTHER 3a(1)–3b.

Matters bearing on the distinction between inductive and deductive logic, *see* INDUCTION 1b; REASONING 4b–4c, 5b(3); SCIENCE 5d; and for discussions relevant to the principles of transcendental logic, *see* DIALECTIC 2c–2c(2), 3c; IDEA 1d, 5c; JUDGMENT 4, 8d; MEMORY AND IMAGINATION 1a; METAPHYSICS 2c, 4b; OPPOSITION 1e; PRINCIPLE 2b(3); QUALITY 1; QUANTITY 1; RELATION 4c.

The special problem of the difference between a logic of predication and a relational logic, *see* IDEA 5a; JUDGMENT 5b–5c; RELATION 4b.

The methodology of the particular sciences, *see* ASTRONOMY 2a–2c; HISTORY 3a; MATHEMATICS 3–3d; MECHANICS 2–2c; METAPHYSICS 2c; PHILOSOPHY 3–3c; SCIENCE 5–5e; THEOLOGY 4c.

Other statements of the attack on sophistry or logic-chopping, *see* DIALECTIC 6; METAPHYSICS 4a; SCIENCE 7b; THEOLOGY 5.

ADDITIONAL READINGS

Listed below are works not included in *Great Books of the Western World*, but relevant to the idea and topics with which this chapter deals. These works are divided into two groups:

I. Works by authors represented in this collection.
II. Works by authors not represented in this collection.

For the date, place, and other facts concerning the publication of the works cited, consult the Bibliography of Additional Readings which follows the last chapter of *The Great Ideas*.

I.

AQUINAS. *De Fallaciis*
HOBBES. *Concerning Body*, PART I, CH 6
SPINOZA. *Of the Improvement of the Understanding*
LOCKE. *Conduct of the Understanding*
KANT. *Introduction to Logic*, I–II
HEGEL. *Science of Logic*
J. S. MILL. *A System of Logic*
——. *An Examination of Sir William Hamilton's Philosophy*, CH 20–23

II.

SEXTUS EMPIRICUS. *Against the Logicians*
PORPHYRY. *Introduction to Aristotle's Predicaments*
BOETHIUS. *In Isagogem Porphyri Commenta*
ABAILARD. *Dialectica*
MAIMONIDES. *Treatise on Logic*
JOHN OF SALISBURY. *Metalogicon*
GILBERT DE LA PORRÉE. *Liber de Sex Principiis*
SUÁREZ. *Disputationes Metaphysicae*, LIV
JOHN OF SAINT THOMAS. *Cursus Philosophicus Thomisticus, Ars Logica*, PROLOGUS; PART II, Q I–2
ARNAULD. *Logic or the Art of Thinking*, PART IV
MALEBRANCHE. *De la recherche de la vérité*, BK VI
LEIBNITZ. *New Essays Concerning Human Understanding*, BK IV, CH 2
EULER. *Letters to a German Princess*
COLERIDGE. *Treatise on Method*
SCHOPENHAUER. *The World as Will and Idea*, VOL II, SUP, CH 9
WHATELY. *Elements of Logic*
W. HAMILTON. *Lectures on Metaphysics and Logic*, VOL II (I–4)
DE MORGAN. *Formal Logic*
BOOLE. *Mathematical Analysis of Logic*
——. *An Investigation of the Laws of Thought*
SIGWART. *Logic*

LOTZE. *Logic*, BK I, INTRO, (10–13)
JEVONS. *Pure Logic*
——. *The Principles of Science*
——. *Studies in Deductive Logic*
BRADLEY. *The Principles of Logic*
BOSANQUET. *Logic*
C. S. PEIRCE. *Collected Papers*, VOL II, par 1–218; VOL III, par 154–251, 359–403; VOL IV, par 80–152; VOL VI, par 102–163, 185–237
VENN. *Symbolic Logic*
——. *Principles of Empirical or Inductive Logic*
BRUNETIÈRE. *An Apology for Rhetoric*
FRAZER. *The Golden Bough*, PART I, CH 3
LEWIS CARROLL. *Alice's Adventures in Wonderland*
——. *Through the Looking-Glass and What Alice Found There*
——. *Symbolic Logic*
COUTURAT. *The Algebra of Logic*
POINCARÉ. *Science and Method*, BK II, CH 3–5
WHITEHEAD and RUSSELL. *Principia Mathematica*, (Introductions to first and second editions)
B. RUSSELL. *Principles of Mathematics*, CH 2
——. *Our Knowledge of the External World*, II
——. *Mysticism and Logic*, CH I
——. *Introduction to Mathematical Philosophy*, CH 18
W. E. JOHNSON. *Logic*
WITTGENSTEIN. *Tractatus Logico-Philosophicus*
MARITAIN. *An Introduction to Logic*
BRIDGMAN. *The Logic of Modern Physics*
GILSON. *The Unity of Philosophical Experience*, CH I
SANTAYANA. *The Realm of Truth*, CH 3
DEWEY. *Essays in Experimental Logic*
——. *Reconstruction in Philosophy*, CH 6
——. *The Quest for Certainty*, CH 9
——. *Logic, the Theory of Inquiry*, PART I
WEISS. *Reality*, BK I, CH 7
BLANSHARD. *The Nature of Thought*
M. R. COHEN. *A Preface to Logic*, esp I, IX
DEWEY and BENTLEY. *Knowing and the Known*

Chapter 50: LOVE

INTRODUCTION

HERE, as in the chapters on GOD and MAN, almost all the great books are represented except those in mathematics and the physical sciences. Even those exceptions do not limit the sphere of love. As the theologian understands it, love is not limited to things divine and human, nor to those creatures less than man which have conscious desires. Natural love, Aquinas writes, is not only "in all the soul's powers, but also in all the parts of the body, and universally in all things: because, as Dionysius says, 'Beauty and goodness are beloved by all things.' "

Love is everywhere in the universe—in all things which have their being from the bounty and generosity of God's creative love and which in return obey the law of love in seeking God or in whatever they do to magnify God's glory. Love sometimes even takes the place of other gods in the government of nature. Though he thinks the motions of the world are without direction from the gods, Lucretius opens his poem On the Nature of Things with an invocation to Venus, "the life-giver"—without whom nothing "comes forth into the bright coasts of life, nor waxes glad nor lovely."

Nor is it only the poet who speaks metaphorically of love as the creative force which engenders things and renews them, or as the power which draws all things together into a unity of peace, preserving nature itself against the disruptive forces of war and hate. The imagery of love appears even in the language of science. The description of magnetic attraction and repulsion borrows some of its fundamental terms from the vocabulary of the passions; Gilbert, for example, refers to "the love of the iron for the loadstone."

On the other hand, the impulses of love are often compared with the pull of magnetism. But such metaphors or comparisons are seldom intended to conceal the ambiguity of the word "love" when it is used as a term of universal application. "Romeo wants Juliet as the filings want the magnet," writes William James, "and if no obstacles intervene he moves toward her by as straight a line as they. But Romeo and Juliet, if a wall be built between them, do not remain idiotically pressing their faces against its opposite sides"—like iron filings separated from the magnet by a card.

THE LOVE BETWEEN man and woman makes all the great poems contemporaneous with each other and with ourselves. There is a sense in which each great love affair is unique—a world in itself, incomparable, unconditioned by space and time. That, at least, is the way it feels to the romantic lovers, but even to the dispassionate observer there seems to be a world of difference between the relationship of Paris and Helen in the Iliad and that of Prince Andrew and Natasha in War and Peace, or Troilus and Cressida, Tom Jones and Sophia, Don Quixote and Dulcinea, Jason and Medea, Aeneas and Dido, Othello and Desdemona, Dante and Beatrice, Hippolytus and Phaedra, Faust and Margaret, Henry V and Catherine, Paola and Francesca, Samson and Delilah, Antony and Cleopatra, Admetus and Alcestis, Orlando and Rosalind, Haemon and Antigone, Odysseus and Penelope, and Adam and Eve.

The analyst can make distinctions here. He can classify these loves as the conjugal and the illicit, the normal and the perverse, the sexual and the idyllic, the infantile and the adult, the romantic and the Christian. He can, in addition, group all these loves together despite their apparent variety and set them apart from still other categories of love: the friendships between human beings without regard to gender; the familial ties—parental, filial, fraternal; the love of a man for himself, for his fellow men, for his country, for God. All these other loves are, no less than the love between man and woman, the materials of great poetry even as they are omnipresent in every human life.

The friendship of Achilles and Patroclus dominates the action of the *Iliad* even more, perhaps, than the passion of Paris for Helen. The love of Hamlet for his father and, in another mood, for his mother overshadows his evanescent tenderness for Ophelia. Prince Hal and Falstaff, Don Quixote and Sancho Panza, Pantagruel and Panurge seem to be bound more closely by companionship than any of them is ever tied by Cupid's knot. The love of Cordelia for Lear surpasses, though it does not defeat, the lusts of Goneril and Regan. The vision of Rome effaces the image of Dido from the heart of Aeneas. Brutus lays down his life for Rome as readily as Antony gives up his life for Cleopatra.

Richard III, aware that he "wants love's majesty," implies that he cannot love anyone because he is unable to love himself. Why should "I love myself," he asks, "for any good that I myself have done unto myself"? This element of self-love which, in varying degrees, prompts the actions of Achilles, Odysseus, Oedipus, Macbeth, Faust, and Captain Ahab, finds its prototype in the almost infinite *amour-propre* of Lucifer in *Paradise Lost*. This self-love, which in its extreme form the psychoanalyst calls "narcissism," competes with every other love in human life. Sometimes it qualifies these other loves; when, for example, it enters into Pierre Bezúkhov's meditations about freeing his serfs and turns his sentiment of brotherly love into a piece of sentimentality which is never confirmed by action.

Yet self-love, like sexual love, can be overcome by the love which is charity toward or compassion for others. True self-love, according to Locke, necessarily leads to love of neighbor; and, in Dante's view of the hierarchy of love, men ascend from loving their neighbors as themselves to loving God. Through the love he bears Virgil and Beatrice for the goodness they represent, Dante mounts to the highest heaven where he is given the Good itself to love.

The panorama of human love is not confined to the great works of poetry or fiction. The same drama, with the same types of plot and character, the same lines of action, the same complications and catastrophes, appears in the great works of history and biography. The stories of love told by Herodotus, Thucydides, Plutarch, Tacitus, and Gibbon run the same gamut of the passions, the affections, the tender feeling and the sacrificial devotion, in the attachments of the great figures of history.

Here the loves of a few men move the lives of many. History itself seems to turn in one direction rather than another with the turning of an emperor's heart. Historic institutions seem to draw their strength from the ardor of a single patriot's zeal; and the invincible sacrifices of the martyrs, whether to the cause of church or state, seem to perpetuate with love what neither might of arms nor skill of mind could long sustain. History's blackest as well as brightest pages tell of the lengths to which men have gone for their love's sake, and as often as not the story of the inner turbulence lies half untold between the lines which relate the consequences in acts of violence or heroism.

STILL OTHER OF THE great books deal with love's exhibition of its power. A few of the early dialogues of Plato discuss love and friendship, but more of them dramatically set forth the love his disciples bear Socrates, and Socrates' love of wisdom and the truth. Montaigne can be skeptical and detached in all matters. He can suspend judgment about everything and moderate every feeling by the balance of its opposite, except in the one case of his friendship with Etienne de la Boetie where love asserts its claims above dispute and doubt. The princely examples with which Machiavelli documents his manual of worldly success are lovers of riches, fame, and power—that triad of seducers which alienates the affections of men for truth, beauty, and goodness.

The whole of Pascal's meditations, insofar as they are addressed to himself, seems to express one thought, itself a feeling. "The heart has its reasons, which the reason does not know. We feel it in a thousand things. I say that the heart naturally loves the Universal Being, and also itself, according as it gives itself to them; and it hardens itself against one or the other at its will. You have rejected the one, and kept the other. Is it by reason that you love yourself?"

In the *Confessions* of Augustine, a man who finally resolved the conflict of his loves lets his memory dwell on the torment of their disorder, in order to repent each particular sin against the love of God. "What was it that I delighted in," he writes, "but to love, and be beloved? but I kept not the measure of love, of mind to mind, friendship's bright boundary; but out of the muddy concupiscence of the flesh, and the bubblings of youth, mists fumed up which beclouded and overcast my heart, that I could not discern the clear brightness of love, from the fog of lustfulness."

Augustine shows us the myriad forms of concupiscence and avarice in the lusting of the flesh and of the eyes, and in the self-love which is pride of person. In no other book except perhaps the Bible are so many loves arrayed against one another. Here, in the life of one man, as tempestuous in passion as he was strong of will, their war and peace produce his bondage and his freedom, his anguish and his serenity.

In the Bible, the history of mankind itself is told in terms of love, or rather the multiplicity of loves. Every love is here—of God and Mammon, perverse and pure, the idolatry and vanity of love misplaced, every unnatural lust, every ecstasy of the spirit, every tie of friendship and fraternity, and all the hates which love engenders.

THESE BOOKS of poetry and history, of meditation, confession, and revelation, teach us the facts of love even when they do not go beyond that to definition and doctrine. Before we turn to the theory of love as it is expounded by the philosophers and theologians, or to the psychological analysis of love, we may find it useful to summarize the facts of which any theory must take account. And on the level of the facts we also meet the inescapable problems which underlie the theoretical issues formed by conflicting analyses.

First and foremost seems to be the fact of the plurality of loves. There are many different kinds of love—different in object, different in tendency and expression—and as they occur in the individual life, they raise the problem of unity and order. Does one love swallow up or subordinate all the others? Can more than one love rule the heart? Is there a hierarchy of

loves which can harmonize all their diversity? These are the questions with which the most comprehensive theories of love find it necessary to begin.

Plato's ladder of love in the *Symposium* has different loves for its rungs. Diotima, whom Socrates describes as his "instructress in the art of love," tells him that if a youth begins by loving a visibly beautiful form, "he will soon of himself perceive that the beauty of one form is akin to the beauty of another," and, therefore, "how foolish would he be not to recognize that the beauty in every form is one and the same." He will then "abate his violent love of the one," and will pass from being "a lover of beautiful forms" to the realization that "the beauty of the mind is more honorable than the beauty of the outward form." Thence he will be led to love "the beauty of laws and institutions . . . and after laws and institutions, he will go on to the sciences, that he may see their beauty." As Diotima summarizes it, the true order of love "begins with the beauties of earth and mounts upwards . . . from fair forms to fair practices, and from fair practices to fair notions, until from fair notions [we] arrive at the notion of absolute beauty."

Aristotle classifies different kinds of love in his analysis of the types of friendship. Since the lovable consists of "the good, pleasant, or useful," he writes, "there are three kinds of friendship, equal in number to the things that are lovable; for with respect to each there is a mutual and recognized love, and those who love each other wish well to each other in that respect in which they love one another." Later in the *Ethics* he also considers the relation of self-love to all love of others, and asks "whether a man should love himself most, or someone else."

Aquinas distinguishes between love in the sphere of the passions and love as an act of will. The former he assigns to what he calls the "concupiscible faculty" of the sensitive appetite; the latter, to the "rational or intellectual appetite." The other basic distinction which Aquinas makes is that between love as a natural tendency and as a supernatural habit. Natural love is that "whereby things seek what is suitable to them according to their nature." When love exceeds the inclinations of nature, it does so by "some habitual form superadded to the natural power," and this habit of love is the virtue of charity.

Freud's theory places the origin of love in the sexual instincts, and so for him the many varieties of love are simply the forms which love takes as the libido fixes upon various objects. "The nucleus of what we mean by love," he writes, "naturally consists . . . in sexual love with sexual union as its aim. We do not separate from this," he goes on to say, "on the one hand, self-love, and on the other, love for parents and children, friendship and love for humanity in general, and also devotion to concrete objects and to abstract ideas . . . All these tendencies are an expression of the same instinctive activities." They differ from sexual love only because "they are diverted from its aim or are prevented from reaching it, though they always preserve enough of their original nature to keep their identity recognizable." Sexual love undergoes these transformations according as it is repressed or sublimated, infantile or adult in its pattern, degraded to the level of brutal sexuality or humanized by inhibitions and mixed with tenderness.

All of these classifications and distinctions belong to the theory of human love. But the fact of love's diversity extends the theory of love to other creatures and to God. In the tradition of biology from Aristotle to Darwin, the mating of animals and the care of their young is thought to exhibit an emotion of love which is either sharply contrasted with or regarded as the root of human love. Darwin, for example, maintains, "it is certain that associated animals have a feeling of love for each other, which is not felt by non-social adult animals."

At the opposite pole, the theologians identify God with love and see in God's love for Himself and for His creatures the principle not only of creation, and of providence and salvation, but also the measure of all other loves by which created things, and men especially, turn toward or away from God. "Beloved, let us love one another," St. John writes, "for love is of God; and everyone that loveth is born of God, and knoweth God. He that loveth not knoweth not God; for God is love. In this was manifested the love of God toward us, because that God sent his only begotten Son into the world, that we might live through him. Herein is love, not that we loved God, but that he loved us . . . And we have known and believed the love that God hath to us. God is love; and he that dwelleth in love dwelleth in God, and God in him."

In the moral universe of the *Divine Comedy*, heaven is the realm of love, "pure light," Beatrice says, "light intellectual full of love love of true good full of joy, joy which transcends every sweetness." There courtesy prevails among the blessed, and charity alone of the theological virtues remains. The beatitude of those who see God dispenses with faith and hope, but the vision of God is inseparable from the fruition of love. "The Good which is the object of the will," Dante writes, "is all collected in it; and outside of it, that is defective which is perfect there." Desire and will are "revolved, like a wheel which is moved evenly, by the Love which moves the sun and the other stars." Hell is made by the absence of God's love—the punishment of those who on earth loved other things more than God.

THERE IS A second fact about love to which poetry and history bear testimony. Love frequently turns into its opposite, hate. Sometimes there is love and hate of the same object; sometimes love inspires hate, as it occasions jealousy, of the things which threaten it. Anger and fear, too, follow in the wake of love. Love seems to be the primal passion, generating all the others according to the oppositions of pleasure and pain and by relations of cause and effect. Yet not all the analysts of love as a passion seem to agree upon this point, or at least they do not give the fact the same weight in their theories.

Hobbes, for example, gives primacy to fear, and Spinoza to desire, joy, and sorrow. Spinoza defines love as "joy with the accompanying idea of an external cause," and he defines hatred similarly in terms of sorrow. Nevertheless, Spinoza, like Aquinas and Freud, deals more extensively with love and hate than with any of the other passions. He, like them, observes how their fundamental opposition runs through the whole emotional life of man. But he does not, like Aquinas, regard love as the root of all the other passions. Treating the combination of love and hate toward the same object as a mere "vacillation of the mind," he does not, like Freud, develop an elaborate theory of emotional ambivalence which tries to explain why the deepest affections of men are usually mixtures of love and hate.

A THIRD FACT which appears in almost every one of the great love stories points to another aspect of love's contrariness. There seems to be no happiness more perfect than that which love confirms. But there is also no misery more profound, no depth of despair greater, than that into which lovers are plunged when they are bereft, disappointed, unrequited. Can the pleasures of love be had without its pains? Is it better to have loved and suffered than never to have loved at all? Is it wiser not to love than to love not wisely but too well? Is the world well lost for love?

These questions paraphrase the soliloquies of lovers in the great tragedies and comedies of love. For every praise of love there is, in Shakespearian speech or sonnet, an answering complaint. "All creatures in the world through love exist, and lacking love, lack all that may persist." But "thou blind fool, love, what does thou to mine eyes, that they behold and see not what they see?" "The greater castle of the world is lost," says Antony to Cleopatra; "we have kissed away kingdoms and provinces." But in Romeo's words to Juliet, "My bounty is as boundless as the sea, my love as deep; the more I give to thee, the more I have, for both are infinite."

Love is all opposites—the only reality, the great illusion; the giver of life and its consumer; the benign goddess whose benefactions men beseech, and—to such as Hippolytus or Dido—the dread Cyprian who wreaks havoc and devastation. She is a divinity to be feared when not propitiated, her potions are poison, her darts are shafts of destruction. Love is itself an object of love and hate. Men fall in love with love and fight against it. *Omnia vincit amor*, Virgil writes—"love conquers all."

In the dispassionate language of the moralist, the question is simply whether love is good or bad, a component of happiness or an obstacle thereto. How the question is answered depends upon the kind of love in question. The love which consists in the best type of friendship seems indispensable to the happy life and, more than that, to the fabric of any society, domestic or political.

Such love, Aristotle writes, "is a virtue or implies virtue, and is besides most necessary with a view to living. For without friends no one would choose to live though he had all other goods. . . . Friendship seems too to hold states together, and lawgivers care more for it than for justice." When it is founded on virtue, it goes further than justice, for it binds men together through benevolence and generosity. "When men are friends," Aristotle says, "they have no need of justice."

But Aristotle does not forget that there are other types of friendship, based on utility or pleasure-seeking rather than upon the mutual admiration of virtuous men. Here, as in the case of other passions, the love may be good or bad. It is virtuous only when it is moderated by reason and restrained from violating the true order of goods, in conformity to which man's various loves should themselves be ordered.

When the love in question is the passion of the sexual instinct, some moralists think that temperance is an inadequate restraint. Neither reason nor law is adequate to the task of subduing—or, as Freud would say, of domesticating—the beast. To the question Socrates asks, whether life is harder towards the end, the old man Cephalus replies in the words of Sophocles, when he was asked how love suits with age, "I feel as if I had escaped from a mad and furious master."

In the most passionate diatribe against love's passion, Lucretius condemns the sensual pleasures which are so embittered with pain. Venus should be entirely shunned, for once her darts have wounded men, "the sore gains strength and festers by feeding, and day by day the madness grows, and the misery becomes heavier. . . . This is the one thing, whereof the more and more we have, the more does our heart burn with the cursed desire. . . . When the gathering desire is sated, the old frenzy is back upon them . . . nor can they discover what device may conquer their disease; in such deep doubt they waste beneath their secret wound . . . These ills are found in love that is true and fully prosperous; but when love is crossed and hopeless, there are ills which you might detect with closed eyes, ills without number; so that it is better to be on the watch beforehand, even as I have taught you, and to beware that you are not entrapped. For to avoid being drawn into the meshes of love, is not so hard a task as when caught amid the toils to issue out and break through the strong bonds of Venus."

In the doctrines of most moralists, however, the sexual passion calls for no special treatment different from other appetites and passions. Because it is more complex in its manifestations, perhaps, and more imperious in its urges, more effort on the part of reason may be required to regulate it, to direct or restrain it. Yet no special principles of virtue or duty apply to sexual love. Even the religious vow of chastity is matched by the vow of poverty. The love of money is as serious a deflection from loving God as the lust of the flesh.

WHAT IS COMMON to all these matters is discussed in the chapters on DUTY, EMOTION, VIRTUE, and SIN. But here one more fact remains to be considered—the last fact about love which the poets and the historians seem to lay before the moralists and theologians.

When greed violates the precepts of justice, or gluttony those of temperance, the vice or sin appears to have no redeeming features. These are weaknesses of character incompatible with heroic stature. But many of the great heroes of literature are otherwise noble men or women who have, for love's sake, deserted their duty or transgressed the rules of God and man, acknowledging their claims and yet choosing to risk the condemnation of society even to the point of banishment, or to put their immortal souls in peril. The fact seems to be that only love retains some honor when it defies morality; not that moralists excuse the illicit act, but that in the opinion of mankind, as evidenced by its poetry at least, love has some privileged status. Its waywardness and even its madness are extenuated.

The poets suggest the reason for this. Unlike the other passions which man shares with the animals, characteristically human love is a thing of the spirit as well as the body. A man is piggish when he is a glutton, a jackal when he is craven, but when his emotional excess in the sphere of love lifts him to acts of devotion and sacrifice, he is incomparably human. That is why the great lovers, as the poets depict them, seem admirable in spite of their transgressions. They almost seem to be justified—poetically, at least, if not morally—in acting as if love exempted them from ordinary laws; as if their love could be a law unto itself. "Who shall give a lover any law?" Arcite asks in Chaucer's Knight's Tale. "Love is a greater law," he says, "than man has ever given to earthly man."

To a psychologist like Freud, the conflict between the erotic impulses and morality is the central conflict in the psychic life of the individual and between the individual and society. There seems to be no happy resolution unless each is somehow accommodated to the other. At one extreme of repression, "the claims of our civilization," according to Freud, "make life too hard for the greater part of humanity, and so further the aversion to reality and the origin of neuroses"; the individual suffers neurotic disorders which result from the failure of the repressed energies to find outlets acceptable to the moral censor. At the other extreme of expression, the erotic instinct "would break all bounds and the laboriously erected structure of civilization would be swept away." Integration would seem to be achieved in the individual personality and society would seem to prosper only when sexuality is transformed into those types of love which reinforce laws and duties with emotional loyalty to moral ideals and invest ideal objects with their energies, creating the highest goods of civilization.

To the theologian, the conflict between love and morality remains insoluble—not in principle, but in practice—until love itself supplants all other rules of conduct. The "good man," according to Augustine, is not he "who knows what is good, but who loves it. Is it not then obvious," he goes on to say, "that we love in ourselves the very love wherewith we love whatever we love? For there is also a love wherewith we love that which we ought not to love; and this love is hated by him who loves that wherewith he loves what ought to be loved. For it is quite possible for both to exist in one man. And this co-existence is good for a man, to the end that this love which conduces to our living well may grow, and the other, which leads us to evil may decrease, until our whole life be perfectly healed and transmuted into good." Only a better love, a love that is wholly virtuous and right, has the power requisite to overcome love's errors. With this perfect love goes only one rule, Augustine says: *Dilige, et quod vis fac*—"love, and do what you will."

This perfect love, which alone deserves to be a law unto itself, is more than fallen human nature can come by without God's grace. It is, according to Christian theology, the supernatural virtue of charity whereby men participate in God's love of Himself and His creatures—loving God with their whole heart and soul and mind, and their neighbors as themselves. On these two precepts of charity, according to the teaching of Christ, "depends the whole law and the prophets."

The questions which Aquinas considers in his treatise on charity indicate that the theological resolution of the conflict between love and morality is, in essence, the resolution of a conflict between diverse loves, a resolution accomplished by the perfection of love itself. Concerning the objects and order of charity, he asks, for example, "whether we should love charity out of charity," "whether irrational creatures also ought to be loved out of charity," "whether a man ought to love his body out of charity," "whether we ought to love sinners out of charity," "whether charity requires that we should love our enemies," "whether God ought to be loved more than our neighbors," "whether, out of charity, man is bound to love God more than himself," "whether, out of charity, man ought to love himself more than his neighbor," "whether a man ought to love his neighbor more than his own body," "whether we ought to love one neighbor more than another," "whether we ought to love those who are better more than those who are more closely united to us," "whether a man ought, out of charity, to love his children more than his father," "whether a man ought to love his wife more than his father and mother," "whether a man ought to love his benefactor more than one he has benefited."

THE DIVERSITY of love seems to be both the basic fact and the basic problem for the psychologist, the moralist, the theologian. The ancient languages have three distinct words for the main types of love: *eros, philia, agape* in Greek; *amor, amicitia* (or *dilectio*), and *caritas* in Latin. Because English has no such distinct words, it seems necessary to use such phrases as "sexual love," "love of friendship," and "love of charity" in order to indicate plainly that love is common to all three, and to distinguish the three meanings. Yet we must observe what Augustine points out, namely, that the Scriptures "make no distinction between *amor, dilectio,* and *caritas,*" and that in the Bible "*amor* is used in a good connection."

The problem of the kinds of love seems further to be complicated by the need to differentiate and relate love and desire. Some writers use the words "love" and "desire" interchangeably, as does Lucretius who, in speaking of the pleasures of Venus, says that "Cupid [*i.e.*, desire] is the Latin name of love." Some, like Spinoza, use the word "desire" as the more general word and "love" to name a special mode of desire. Still others use "love" as the more general word and "desire" to signify an aspect of love. "Love," Aquinas writes, "is naturally the first act of the will and appetite; for which reason all the other appetitive movements presuppose love, as their root and origin. For nobody desires anything nor rejoices in anything, except as a good that is loved."

One thing seems to be clear, namely, that both love and desire belong to the appetitive faculty—to the sphere of the emotions and the will rather than to the sphere of perception and knowledge. When a distinction is made between desire and love as two states of appetite, it seems to be based on their difference in tendency. As indicated in the chapter of DESIRE, the tendency of desire is acquisitive. The object of desire is a good to be possessed, and the drive of desire continues until, with possession, it is satisfied. Love equated with desire does not differ from any other hunger.

But there seems to be another tendency which impels one not to possess the object loved, but to benefit it. The lover wishes the well-being of the beloved, and reflexively wishes himself well through being united with the object of his love. Where desire devoid of love is selfish in the sense of one's seeking goods or pleasures for oneself without any regard for the good of the other, be it thing or person, love seeks to give rather than to get, or to get only as the result of giving. Whereas nothing short of physical possession satisfies desire, love can be satisfied in the contemplation of its object's beauty or goodness. It has more affinity with knowledge than with action, though it goes beyond knowledge in its wish to act for the good of the beloved, as well as in its wish to be loved in return.

Those who distinguish love and desire in such terms usually repeat the distinction in differentiating kinds of love. The difference between sexual love and the love which is pure friendship, for example, is said to rest on the predominance of selfish desires in the one and the predominance of altruistic motives in the other. Sexual love is sometimes called the "love of desire" to signify that it is a love born of desire; whereas in friendship love is thought to precede desire and to determine its wishes.

In contrast to the love of desire, the love of friendship makes few demands. "In true friendship, wherein I am perfect," Montaigne declares, "I more give myself to my friend, than I endeavor to attract him to me. I am not only better pleased in doing him service than if he conferred a benefit upon me, but, moreover, had rather he should do himself good than me, and he most obliges me when he does so; and if absence be either more pleasant or convenient for him, 'tis also more acceptable to me than his presence."

These two loves appear in most of the great analyses of love, though under different names: concupiscent love and fraternal love; the friendship base on pleasure or utility and the friendship based on virtue; animal and human love; sexuality and tenderness. Sometimes they

are assigned to different faculties: the love of desire to the sensitive appetite or the sphere of instinct and emotion; the love of friendship to the will or faculty of intellectual desire, capable of what Spinoza calls the *amor intellectualis Dei*—"the intellectual love of God." Sometimes the two kinds of love are thought able to exist in complete separation from one another as well as in varying degrees of mixture, as in romantic and conjugal love; and sometimes the erotic or sexual component is thought to be present to some degree in all love. Though he asserts this, Freud does not hold the converse, that sexuality is always accompanied by the tenderness which characterizes human love. The opposite positions here seem to be correlated with opposed views of the relation of man to other animals, or with opposed theories of human nature, especially in regard to the relation of instinct and reason, the senses and the intellect, the emotions and the will.

As suggested above, romantic love is usually conceived as involving both possessive and altruistic motives, the latter magnified by what its critics regard as an exaggerated idealization of the beloved. The theological virtue of charity, on the other hand, is purely a love of friendship, its purity made perfect by its supernatural foundation. One of the great issues here is whether the romantic is compatible with the Christian conception of love, whether the adoration accorded a beloved human being does not amount to deification—as much a violation of the precepts of charity as the pride of unbounded self-love. Which view is taken affects the conception of conjugal love and the relation of love in courtship to love in marriage. These matters and, in general, the forms of love in the domestic community are discussed in the chapter on FAMILY.

OUTLINE OF TOPICS

REFERENCES

To find the passages cited, use the numbers in heavy type, which are the volume and page numbers of the passages referred to. For example, in 4 HOMER: *Iliad*, BK II [265–283] 12d, the number 4 is the number of the volume in the set; the number 12d indicates that the passage is in section d of page 12.

PAGE SECTIONS: When the text is printed in one column, the letters a and b refer to the upper and lower halves of the page. For example, in 53 JAMES: *Psychology*, 116a–119b, the passage begins in the upper half of page 116 and ends in the lower half of page 119. When the text is printed in two columns, the letters a and b refer to the upper and lower halves of the left-hand side of the page, the letters c and d to the upper and lower halves of the right-hand side of the page. For example, in 7 PLATO: *Symposium*, 163b–164c, the passage begins in the lower half of the left-hand side of page 163 and ends in the upper half of the right-hand side of page 164.

AUTHOR'S DIVISIONS: One or more of the main divisions of a work (such as PART, BK, CH, SECT) are sometimes included in the reference; line numbers, in brackets, are given in certain cases; e.g., *Iliad*, BK II [265–283] 12d.

BIBLE REFERENCES: The references are to book, chapter, and verse. When the King James and Douay versions differ in title of books or in the numbering of chapters or verses, the King James version is cited first and the Douay, indicated by a (D), follows; e.g., OLD TESTAMENT: *Nehemiah*, 7:45—(D) II Esdras, 7:46.

SYMBOLS: The abbreviation "esp" calls the reader's attention to one or more especially relevant parts of a whole reference; "passim" signifies that the topic is discussed intermittently rather than continuously in the work or passage cited.

For additional information concerning the style of the references, see the Explanation of Reference Style; for general guidance in the use of *The Great Ideas*, consult the Preface.

1. The nature of love

1a. Conceptions of love and hate: as passions and as acts of will

APOCRYPHA: *Wisdom of Solomon*, 6:17–18—(D) OT, *Book of Wisdom*, 6:18–19

NEW TESTAMENT: *I John*, 4:7–8,16,18

7 PLATO: *Lysis* 14a–25a,c / *Cratylus*, 103b-d / *Phaedrus*, 115a–129d / *Symposium* 149a–173a,c / *Laws*, BK VIII, 736b-c

9 ARISTOTLE: *Ethics*, BK II, CH 5 [1105^{b}20–23] 351b; BK IV, CH 6 [1126^{b}20–25] 373d; BK VIII, CH 1 406b,d–407a esp [1155^{a}32–^{b}15] 406d–407a; CH 3 [1156^{a}31–^{b}5] 408a; CH 5 [1157^{b}28–33] 409c; CH 6 [1158^{a}10–17] 409d–410a; BK IX, CH 5 [1166^{b}33–1167^{a}3] 420b; CH 7 [1168^{a}19–21] 421d; CH 10 [1171^{a}11–12] 424d / *Politics*, BK VII, CH 7 [1327^{b}40–1328^{a}17] 532a-b / *Rhetoric*, BK II, CH 4 626c–628b

17 PLOTINUS: *First Ennead*, TR III, CH 1–3 10a–11a; TR VI, CH 5 23b–24a / *Third Ennead*, TR V 100c–106b / *Sixth Ennead*, TR V, CH 10, 309a-b; TR VII, CH 33 337d–338b; TR IX, CH 9, 359b-c

18 AUGUSTINE: *City of God*, BK XIV, CH 7 380c–381c / *Christian Doctrine*, BK III, CH 10, 662a

19 AQUINAS: *Summa Theologica*, PART I, Q 20, A 1, ANS and REP 1 120a–121b; Q 27, A 3, ANS

and REP 3 155c–156a; A 4, ANS and REP 2 156b-d; Q 37, A 1, ANS and REP 2 197c–199a; Q 60, AA 1–2 310b–311d; Q 82, A 5, REP 1 435c–436c; PART I–II, Q 23, A 4 726a–727a; Q 25, A 2 731b–732a; Q 26 733d–737a; Q 28, A 1, ANS and REP 1–2 740b–741a; Q 29 744d–749a

20 AQUINAS: *Summa Theologica*, PART I–II, Q 62, A 3, ANS and REP 3 61c–62b; PART II–II, Q 23, A 2, ANS 483d–484d

21 DANTE: *Divine Comedy*, PURGATORY, XVII [82]–XVIII [75] 79b–80c; PARADISE, XXVI [1–81] 145d–146c

22 CHAUCER: *Troilus and Cressida*, BK III, STANZA 1–7 54b–55b; STANZA 250–253 87a-b

23 HOBBES: *Leviathan*, PART I, 61c; 63a

25 MONTAIGNE: *Essays*, 424d

31 SPINOZA: *Ethics*, PART II, AXIOM 3 373d; PART III, PROP 13, SCHOL 400d; PROP 38–49 408a–411b; THE AFFECTS, DEF 6–7 417b-d; PART IV, APPENDIX, XIX–XX 449a

35 LOCKE: *Human Understanding*, BK II, CH XX, SECT 4–5 176d–177a

36 STERNE: *Tristram Shandy*, 453a–456a; 502a-b; 523b–526b

37 FIELDING: *Tom Jones*, 9b-c

38 ROUSSEAU: *Inequality*, 343d–345d

42 KANT: *Fund. Prin. Metaphysic of Morals*, 259a / *Intro. Metaphysic of Morals*, 385c–386d

(1. *The nature of love.* 1c. *The distinction between love and desire: the generous and acquisitive aims.*)

21 DANTE: *Divine Comedy*, PURGATORY, XV [40–81] 75d-76a; XVII [82]–XVIII [75] 79b-80c
23 HOBBES: *Leviathan*, PART I, 61c; 63a
25 MONTAIGNE: *Essays*, 83d-84a; 398c-399d
31 SPINOZA: *Ethics*, PART IV, APPENDIX, I–II 447a-b
32 MILTON: *Paradise Lost*, BK VIII [500–617] 243a-245b
35 LOCKE: *Human Understanding*, BK II, CH XX, SECT 4–6 176d-177b
37 FIELDING: *Tom Jones*, 346c-d
38 ROUSSEAU: *Inequality*, 345c-346b
51 TOLSTOY: *War and Peace*, BK XI, 525c-526b
53 JAMES: *Psychology*, 204b-209b passim
54 FREUD: *Narcissism*, 404d-406b; 409b-411a,c / *Instincts*, 420a-421a / *General Introduction*, 581b; 617c-618a / *Group Psychology*, 673b-674a; 679a-b; 681c-682b; 693a-694c / *Civilization and Its Discontents*, 783b-c / *New Introductory Lectures*, 847d-848a

1d. **The objects of love: the good, the true, the beautiful; God, man, things**

OLD TESTAMENT: *Genesis*, 29:17–18 / *Song of Solomon*—(D) *Canticle of Canticles* / *Zechariah*, 8:19—(D) *Zacharias*, 8:19
APOCRYPHA: *Wisdom of Solomon*, 8:1–3—(D) OT, *Book of Wisdom*, 8:1–3 / *Ecclesiasticus*, 4:11–19; 9:8; 36:22—(D) OT, *Ecclesiasticus*, 4:12–22; 9:8–9; 36:24
NEW TESTAMENT: *Matthew*, 10:37 / *Luke*, 14:26 / *Romans*, 12:9 / *Colossians*, 3:1–2 / *I Timothy*, 6:10–11 / *I John*, 2:15–16; 4:20–21
4 HOMER: *Iliad*, BK III [121–160] 20b-c; BK XIV [193–221] 100a-b
5 EURIPIDES: *Andromache* [205–208] 317a
6 HERODOTUS: *History*, BK V, 168d-169a; BK VI, 196d-197b
7 PLATO: *Lysis*, 18d-24d / *Phaedrus*, 120a-c; 126b-129d / *Symposium*, 161d-167d / *Euthyphro*, 194b / *Phaedo*, 225c / *Republic*, BK I, 296d-297a; BK V–VI, 368c-375b; BK VI, 376d / *Laws*, BK V, 687b; BK VIII, 735b-738c
8 ARISTOTLE: *Posterior Analytics*, BK I, CH 2 [72ᵃ25–30] 98d / *Metaphysics*, BK XII, CH 7 [1072ᵃ23–ᵇ4] 602b-c
9 ARISTOTLE: *Ethics*, BK VIII, CH 2–4 407a-409b; BK IX, CH 3 418c-419a passim, esp [1165ᵇ13–17] 418d; CH 5 [1167ᵃ3–6] 420b; CH 7 421a-d esp [1167ᵇ34–1168ᵃ18] 421b-c; CH 8 421d-423a passim; CH 9 [1170ᵃ13–ᵇ19] 423d-424b; CH 12 425d-426a,c; BK X, CH 4 [1175ᵃ10–22] 429c / *Rhetoric*, BK I, CH 11 [1371ᵇ12–25] 615a-b; BK II, CH 4 626c-628b; CH 12 [1389ᵃ12–15] 636b; CH 13 [1389ᵇ32–34] 637b; [1390ᵃ14–17] 637c
12 LUCRETIUS: *Nature of Things*, BK III [59–78] 30d-31a
12 EPICTETUS: *Discourses*, BK II, CH 22 167d-170a

17 PLOTINUS: *First Ennead*, TR III, CH 1–3 10a-11a; TR VI 21a-26a / *Third Ennead*, TR V 100c-106b / *Fifth Ennead*, TR V, CH 12, 234a-c / *Sixth Ennead*, TR V, CH 10, 309a-b; TR VII, CH 33 337d-338b; TR IX, CH 9, 359b-c
18 AUGUSTINE: *Confessions*, BK III, par 1 13b-c; BK IV, par 7–20 20d-24c; BK VIII, par 10–30 55c-61c passim; BK X, par 38–70 81a-89b / *City of God*, BK XII, CH 8–9 346d-348b; BK XIV, CH 7 380c-381c; BK XV, CH 22 416a-c; BK XIX, CH 10–17 516c-523a / *Christian Doctrine*, BK I, CH 3–5 625b-626a; CH 9–10 627a-b; CH 22–29 629b-632c; CH 35 634c-d; CH 38 635c-d; CH 40 636a,c
19 AQUINAS: *Summa Theologica*, PART I, Q 20, A 1, ANS and REP 3 120a-121b; Q 60, AA 3–5 311d-314c; PART I–II, Q I, A 8 615a-c; Q 2, A I, REP 3 615d-616c; Q 23, A 4 726a-727a; Q 27 737a-740a; Q 29, A I 745a-c; AA 4–5 747a-748b; Q 32, A 5, ANS 762a-d
20 AQUINAS: *Summa Theologica*, PART I–II, Q 62, A 3, ANS and REP 3 61c-62b; Q 66, A 6, REP I 80c-81b; Q 67, A 6 87a-c; Q 110, A I, ANS and REP I 347d-349a; PART II–II, Q 23, A 4, ANS 485d-486b; A 6, REP I 487a-d; Q 24, A I, ANS and REP I 489d-490b; QQ 25–27 501a-527b passim
21 DANTE: *Divine Comedy*, PURGATORY, XV [40–81] 75d-76a; XVI [85–102] 77d; XVII [82]–XVIII [75] 79b-80c; PARADISE, I [97–142] 107b-d; IV [115]–V [12] 111d-112b; VI [112–126] 114d-115a; XXVI [1–81] 145d-146c
22 CHAUCER: *Prologue* [285–308] 164a-b
23 HOBBES: *Leviathan*, PART I, 61c-62a; 76c-77b
25 MONTAIGNE: *Essays*, 84b-85a; 191c-192d
26 SHAKESPEARE: *Romeo and Juliet*, ACT I, SC I [214–244] 287d-288a; SC V [43–55] 292b; ACT II, SC II [1–32] 294b-c
29 CERVANTES: *Don Quixote*, PART II, 381c-382a
30 BACON: *Advancement of Learning*, 80b-81a
31 SPINOZA: *Ethics*, PART III, PROP 56, DEMONST 414a-c; PART V, PROP 15–16 456c; PROP 18 456d; PROP 33 460c
32 MILTON: *Paradise Lost*, BK VIII [500–560] 243a-244a / *Samson Agonistes* [1003–1007] 361b
33 PASCAL: *Pensées*, 81 186b; 100 191a-192b; 323 230a-b
35 LOCKE: *Human Understanding*, BK II, CH XX, SECT 4–5 176d-177a; BK IV, CH XIX, SECT I 384c-d
37 FIELDING: *Tom Jones*, 15b-c; 17b-c; 50d-51a; 130b-c; 198d-199a
38 ROUSSEAU: *Inequality*, 345d-346a; 347b-c
42 KANT: *Practical Reason*, 326a-327a / *Judgement*, 476a-483d; 585d-586a
47 GOETHE: *Faust*, PART II [8516–8523] 207b; [9192–9944] 223b-241b
51 TOLSTOY: *War and Peace*, BK I, 5d-6b; BK III, 113a-115a; BK VI, 249d-250a; BK XI, 525c-526b; BK XII, 555b-c; 560a-561c; BK XIV, 608a-b; EPILOGUE I, 659a; 660b-c

52 Dostoevsky: *Brothers Karamazov*, BK II, 26d-27d; BK III, 53d-54b; BK IV, 83c-84a; BK V, 121d-122d passim; BK VI, 167b-168c

53 James: *Psychology*, 204b-211a

54 Freud: *Instincts*, 418d-420b esp 420a-b / *Group Psychology*, 673b-c / *Civilization and Its Discontents*, 775b-c; 783a-b

1e. The intensity and power of love: its increase or decrease; its constructive or destructive force

OLD TESTAMENT: *II Samuel*, 11–12—(D) *II Kings*, 11–12 / *Proverbs*, 5:3–14; 6:23–29; 23:26–28 / *Ecclesiastes*, 7:26—(D) *Ecclesiastes*, 7:27 / *Song of Solomon*, 8:6–7—(D) *Canticle of Canticles*, 8:6–7

4 Homer: *Iliad*, BK XVIII [1–126] 130a-131c; BK XIX [276–368] 139d-140c; BK XXII [21–98] 155b-156a; [405–515] 159c-160d

5 Aeschylus: *Choephoroe* [585–651] 75d-76b

5 Sophocles: *Antigone* [781–805] 138a / *Trachiniae* 170a-181a,c esp [427–530] 173d-174d

5 Euripides: *Medea* [627–642] 217c / *Hippolytus* 225a-236d esp [1–57] 225a-c, [1268–1282] 235b-c / *Suppliants* [990–1071] 267a-c / *Trojan Women* [895–1059] 277c-279a / *Andromache* [274–308] 317d / *Iphigenia at Aulis* [543–589] 429d-430a

5 Aristophanes: *Birds* [685–707] 551b-d / *Lysistrata* 583a-599a,c

6 Herodotus: *History*, BK IX, 311b-312d

6 Thucydides: *Peloponnesian War*, BK VI, 523c-524c

7 Plato: *Phaedrus*, 124a-129d / *Symposium* 149a-173a,c esp 152b-167d / *Republic*, BK V, 361b-c; BK IX, 417a-418a / *Laws*, BK VIII, 736b

9 Aristotle: *Politics*, BK VII, CH 7 [1327^{b}40–1328^{a}17] 532a-b / *Rhetoric*, BK II, CH 12 [1389^{b}3–5] 636d; CH 13 [1389^{b}22–24] 637a

12 Lucretius: *Nature of Things*, BK I [1–41] 1a-c; BK IV [1037–1208] 57d-60a

13 Virgil: *Eclogues*, II [56–73] esp [68] 7b-8a; x 32a-34a esp [69] 34a / *Georgics*, IV [452–527] 95b-98a / *Aeneid*, BK I [657–756] 121a-123b; BK IV 167a-186b

17 Plotinus: *Fourth Ennead*, TR IV, CH 40 180b-c

18 Augustine: *Confessions*, BK III, par 1 13b-c; BK IV, par 7–14 20d-23a; BK VI, par 18–26 40d-43a; BK VIII, par 10–30 55c-61c passim; BK X, par 38–70 81a-89b

19 Aquinas: *Summa Theologica*, PART I, Q 20, A 1, REP 3 120a-121b; Q 98, A 2, ANS and REP 3 517d-519a; PART I–II, Q 25, A 2 731b-732a; Q 26, A 2, REP 1–2 734d-735c; Q 28 740a-744d esp A 6 744b-d; Q 29, AA 2–3 745c-747a

20 Aquinas: *Summa Theologica*, PART II–II, QQ 31–33 536d-558d

21 Dante: *Divine Comedy*, HELL, V 7a-8b; XII [31–48] 16d; PURGATORY, VIII [67–84] 65a; XV [40–81] 75d-76a; XVII [82]-XVIII [75] 79b-

80c; XXIV [49–63] 90a-b; PARADISE, I [97–142] 107b-d; XXX–XXXIII 151d-157d

22 Chaucer: *Troilus and Cressida*, BK I, STANZA 1–8 1a-2a; STANZA 31–37 5a-6a; STANZA 58–67 8b-9b; STANZA 143–144 19b-20a; BK III, STANZA 1–7 54b-55b; STANZA 142–254 73a-87b / *Knight's Tale* [1152–1186] 179a-b / *Reeve's Prologue* [3853–3896] 224a-b

25 Montaigne: *Essays*, 6a-b; 39a-40a; 410a-c; 414d-416c; 431c-432d

26 Shakespeare: *Comedy of Errors*, ACT V, SC I [68–86] 165d-166a / *Two Gentlemen of Verona*, ACT II, SC IV [126–142] 237c-d; SC VI 239a-c / *Love's Labour's Lost*, ACT III, SC I [175–207] 264a-b; ACT IV, SC III [290–365] 271c-272a / *Romeo and Juliet*, ACT II 293c-300d / *Midsummer-Night's Dream* 352a-375d esp ACT I, SC I [226–251] 354d-355a / *Merchant of Venice*, ACT II, SC VI [1–19] 415b-c / *Much Ado About Nothing*, ACT II, SC I [379–405] 511a; SC III 511d-514b; ACT III, SC I [104–116] 515c / *As You Like It*, ACT III, SC II [420–425] 613c

27 Shakespeare: *Twelfth Night* 1a-28d esp ACT II, SC IV [82–127] 11b-d, ACT III, SC I [161–176] 15d / *Troilus and Cressida*, ACT III, SC I [106–146] 119c-120a; SC II [8–30] 120b-c; [87–90] 121a; ACT IV, SC IV [11–50] 128b-c; ACT V, SC II [154–181] 136c-d / *Othello* 205a-243a,c / *King Lear*, ACT V, SC III [257–273] 282b / *Antony and Cleopatra* 311a-350d / *Cymbeline*, ACT III, SC IV 466d-468d / *Sonnets*, XVII–CLIV 588d-609d passim

29 Cervantes: *Don Quixote*, PART I, 79d-80a; 120b-137d; PART II, 381c

31 Spinoza: *Ethics*, PART IV, PROP 44 437c-438a

32 Milton: *Paradise Lost*, BK IX [990–1189] 269a-273a / *Samson Agonistes* [999–1060] 361b-362b

36 Sterne: *Tristram Shandy*, 453a-456a

37 Fielding: *Tom Jones*, 14c-d; 30a-32a; 68d; 167c-169c; 237b-c; 334b-d

38 Rousseau: *Inequality*, 345c-346b

44 Boswell: *Johnson*, 169d-170b

46 Hegel: *Philosophy of History*, PART IV, 323b-c

47 Goethe: *Faust*, PART I [3025–3072] 73b-74b; [4460–4612] 111b-114b; PART II [8339–8487] 203a-206b; [9192–9944] 223b-241b

48 Melville: *Moby Dick*, 370b-371a

51 Tolstoy: *War and Peace*, BK II, 70d; BK III, 116c-117a; 141b-d; 159b-161b; BK IV, 184c; 185b; BK VI, 235a-238c; 262b-271c; BK VIII, 316b-c; 327c-d; 340c-341a,c; BK IX, 377b-c; BK XI, 525c-527a; BK XII, 541d-542b; 557b-c; 560a-561c; BK XIV, 608a-b; BK XV, 616a-618b esp 617a-b

52 Dostoevsky: *Brothers Karamazov*, BK II, 26a-27d; BK VI, 167b-168c; BK VIII, 200c-201c

54 Freud: *Beyond the Pleasure Principle*, 657c-d / *Group Psychology*, 678a-c / *Ego and Id*, 708d-712a passim, esp 708d-709a, 711c / *Civilization and Its Discontents*, 791a-d

9 ARISTOTLE: *History of Animals*, BK VI, CH 18 [571^{b}5-10] 97b-c

12 LUCRETIUS: *Nature of Things*, BK IV [1037–1120] 57d-58d; [1192–1208] 59d-60a; BK V [962–965] 73c

13 VIRGIL: *Aeneid*, BK I [657–756] 121a-123b

15 TACITUS: *Annals*, BK IV, 64b-c; BK XI, 103b-c; 107b-108c; BK XIII, 137b-c

17 PLOTINUS: *Third Ennead*, TR V, CH 1-2 100c-102a

18 AUGUSTINE: *Confessions*, BK I, par 25-26 7a-c; BK II, par 1-8 9a-10d; BK III, par 1-5 13b-14b; BK IV, par 2 19d; BK VI, par 18-26 40d-43a / *City of God*, BK XII, CH 8 346d-347b; BK XIV, CH 16-18 390a-391c; CH 26 395d-396c; BK XV, CH 22-23 416a-418c / *Christian Doctrine*, BK III, CH 10 661c-662a; CH 18-21 664d-666b

19 AQUINAS: *Summa Theologica*, PART I, Q 98, A 2, ANS and REP 3 517d-519a; PART I-II, QQ 26-28 733d-744d

20 AQUINAS: *Summa Theologica*, PART II-II, Q 15, A 3 453c-454c; Q 46, A 3 604d-605a,c; PART III, Q 65, A I, REP 5 879c-881d

21 DANTE: *Divine Comedy*, HELL, V 7a-8b; XI [76–90] 16a; PURGATORY, VIII [67–84] 65a; XVII [127–139] 79d; XIX [1–69] 81c-82a; XXV [109]–XXVI [148] 92c-94c; PARADISE, VIII–IX 116d-120a esp IX [103–108] 119d

22 CHAUCER: *Troilus and Cressida*, BK III, STANZA 172–219 77a-83a / *Miller's Tale* 212b-223b / *Reeve's Tale* 225a-232a / *Squire's Tale* [10,813–943] 347a-349a / *Physician's Tale* 366a-371a / *Manciple's Tale* [17,088–103] 490a / *Parson's Tale*, par 19 507b-508b; par 74–86 535b-544a

23 HOBBES: *Leviathan*, PART I, 63a

24 RABELAIS: *Gargantua and Pantagruel*, BK II, 106a-107c; BK III, 164d-166a; 188d-193c

25 MONTAIGNE: *Essays*, 6a-b; 36c-40a; 83d-85a; 297d-299c; 398c-399c; 406a-434d

26 SHAKESPEARE: *Titus Andronicus* 170a-198d esp ACT II 176a-181d

27 SHAKESPEARE: *Hamlet*, ACT I, SC V [40–91] 37b-d; ACT III, SC IV [40–96] 55a-c / *Troilus and Cressida* 103a-141a,c esp ACT IV, SC I [51–79] 126b-c, SC V [13–63] 130a-c, ACT V, SC II 134c-137a / *Measure for Measure* 174a-204d esp ACT II, SC I [234–257] 181a-b, SC II [162–187] 183d-184a / *Othello*, ACT I, SC III [306–388] 212b-213a / *King Lear*, ACT IV, SC VI [109–135] 274c-d; ACT V, SC I 277d-278d / *Pericles*, ACT I, PROLOGUE–SC I 421b-423c; ACT IV, SC V–VI 441a-443b / *Sonnets*, CXXIX 606a

31 SPINOZA: *Ethics*, PART III, PROP 35 406d-407b; THE AFFECTS, DEF 48 421b-d; PART IV, APPENDIX, XIX 449a

32 MILTON: *Paradise Lost*, BK V [443–450] 185a; BK VIII [500–643] 243a-246a; BK IX [990–1133] 269a-272a esp [1004–1098] 269a-271a / *Samson Agonistes* [373–419] 347b-348b; [766–842] 356b-358a

33 PASCAL: *Pensées*, 402–403 241a; 451–461 253b-255a

36 STERNE: *Tristram Shandy*, 513a-516a; 521a-b; 525a-526a; 554b-556a

37 FIELDING: *Tom Jones*, 9b-c; 58b-59b; 130b-c; 138b-d; 289b-290b; 321b-322a; 352d-353a

38 MONTESQUIEU: *Spirit of Laws*, BK XIV, 103c-104a; BK XVI, 118a-b; 119a-b; 119d

38 ROUSSEAU: *Inequality*, 345d-346b; 348d

40 GIBBON: *Decline and Fall*, 92c-d; 649d-650c

44 BOSWELL: *Johnson*, 301c-d

46 HEGEL: *Philosophy of Right*, PART III, par 162 58b-d

47 GOETHE: *Faust*, PART I [2605–2677] 63b-65a

49 DARWIN: *Descent of Man*, 371c-372c

51 TOLSTOY: *War and Peace*, BK I, 15b-16a; BK II, 76a-b; 86b-87b; BK III, 111a-118d esp 113d-115a; 122b-c; BK V, 201a-c; 204a-206c passim; BK VIII, 318a-341a,c; BK XI, 476c-480a

52 DOSTOEVSKY: *Brothers Karamazov*, BK II, 20a-b; 39a-40a; BK III 46a-82a,c esp 53c-54b

54 FREUD: *"Wild" Psycho-Analysis*, 128d-129a / *Narcissism* 399a-411a,c esp 404d-406c, 409b-410d / *Instincts*, 418c-421a,c esp 420b-c / *General Introduction*, 569c-585a esp 569d-570a, 574c-d, 580a-581b; 615b-618a esp 616d-618a / *Group Psychology*, 673b-674a; 681c-683d; 693a-695b / *Civilization and Its Discontents*, 782a-b,d [fn 1]; 783c; 784a-785a esp 785a-b [fn 1] / *New Introductory Lectures*, 854a-863d esp 862b-863c

2a(1) The sexual instinct: its relation to other instincts

7 PLATO: *Symposium*, 157b-159b; 165b-c / *Timaeus*, 476c-d / *Laws*, BK IV, 685a-c; BK VI, 712b

9 ARISTOTLE: *History of Animals*, BK V, CH 8 [542^{a}17–^{b}4] 68d-69a; BK VI, CH 18–BK VII, CH 2 97b-108c passim, esp BK VI, CH 18 97b-99c, BK VII, CH I 106b,d-108a / *Generation of Animals*, BK IV, CH I [764^{b}4–7] 305c / *Rhetoric*, BK II, CH 7 [1385^{a}21–25] 631d

12 LUCRETIUS: *Nature of Things*, BK IV [1037–1057] 57d

22 CHAUCER: *Wife of Bath's Prologue* [5697–5744] 258a-b

25 MONTAIGNE: *Essays*, 414d-416c; 424d-425b

28 HARVEY: *On Animal Generation*, 346a-347d; 349a-350a; 402a-d; 405c-406a; 476c-477a

36 STERNE: *Tristram Shandy*, 555a-556a

38 ROUSSEAU: *Inequality*, 345d-346d

49 DARWIN: *Descent of Man*, 287d

53 JAMES: *Psychology*, 734b-735b

54 FREUD: *Narcissism*, 401a-402c / *Instincts*, 414d-418c esp 414d-415d / *General Introduction*, 574a-576a esp 574a; 580a-d; 587d-588b; 590a-593b; 615b-616b; 618d-619a / *Beyond the Pleasure Principle*, 651d-662b esp 653b-d, 654c-d, 657c-659a, 662b,d [fn 1] / *Ego and Id*, 708d-709c; 710c-712a / *Civilization and Its Discontents*, 789c-790c / *New Introductory Lectures*, 846a-851d esp 847b-d, 849c-850c, 851b-c

(2a. Lustful, sexual, or selfish love: concupiscent love.)

2a(2) Infantile sexuality: polymorphous perversity

54 FREUD: *Origin and Development of Psycho-Analysis,* 15a-18a esp 15d-16c / *Hysteria,* 113d-114b / *Sexual Enlightenment of Children,* 119d-120b / *General Introduction,* 530d-531d; 572d-576d; 578b-585a esp 578c-580d / *Group Psychology,* 693a-b / *New Introductory Lectures,* 847c-848d; 855d-861c

2a(3) Object-fixations, identifications, and transferences: sublimation

12 LUCRETIUS: *Nature of Things,* BK IV [1058–1072] 57d-58a
14 PLUTARCH: *Solon,* 66b-d
25 MONTAIGNE: *Essays,* 10b-11b; 191c-192d; 398c-399d
26 SHAKESPEARE: *3rd Henry VI,* ACT III, SC II [123–195] 87c-88a
31 SPINOZA: *Ethics,* PART III, PROP 13–17 400c-402a; PART IV, PROP 6 426a; PROP 44, SCHOL 437d-438a
38 ROUSSEAU: *Inequality,* 345d-346a
53 JAMES: *Psychology,* 734b-735b
54 FREUD: *Origin and Development of Psycho-Analysis,* 16b-20d esp 17b-c, 19a-c, 20a-d / *Narcissism* 399a-411a,c esp 399d-400b, 404d-406c, 409d-410d / *Instincts,* 414b / *General Introduction,* 551a-589c passim, esp 574c-d, 581b-c, 583c-d, 587d-588a, 589a-b; 594d-597b; 599d-600d; 616d-622c; 627b-630d; 634b-d / *Beyond the Pleasure Principle,* 644d-645d / *Group Psychology,* 678d-681a; 681b,d [fn 4]; 685c-686a; 691c-692a; 693a-694b / *Ego and Id,* 703c-706c esp 704d-705c; 711b-c; 712b-c / *New Introductory Lectures,* 832b-834b esp 832d-833b; 847a-849b; 856a-863d esp 856b-d, 862d-863c

2a(4) The perversion, degradation, or pathology of love: infantile and adult love

OLD TESTAMENT: *Genesis,* 19:4-13; 38:6-10 / *Exodus,* 22:19 / *Leviticus,* 18; 20:13-16 / *Deuteronomy,* 27:21 / *Judges,* 19:22-30
NEW TESTAMENT: *Romans,* 1:24-27
7 PLATO: *Symposium,* 170b-171c / *Laws,* BK I, 645d-646a; BK VIII, 735d-736a
9 ARISTOTLE: *Ethics,* BK VII, CH 5 399a-d passim
13 VIRGIL: *Eclogues,* VI [45–60] 20a-b / *Aeneid,* BK VI [23–30] 211b
18 AUGUSTINE: *Confessions,* BK III, par 1 13b-c
21 DANTE: *Divine Comedy,* HELL, XV-XVI 21a-23d; PURGATORY, XXVI [25–87] 93b-d
25 MONTAIGNE: *Essays,* 36c-40a; 84b-85a; 225a; 427b-d
27 SHAKESPEARE: *Pericles* 421a-448a,c esp ACT I, PROLOGUE-SC I 421b-423c
28 HARVEY: *On Animal Generation,* 349b-c

31 SPINOZA: *Ethics,* PART IV, PROP 44, SCHOL 437d-438a
32 MILTON: *Paradise Lost,* BK II [629–870] 125a-130a
36 SWIFT: *Gulliver,* PART IV, 163b
38 MONTESQUIEU: *Spirit of Laws,* BK XII, 87c-88a; BK XVI, 117d; BK XXVI, 219d-221c
41 GIBBON: *Decline and Fall,* 93d-94c; 169a
42 KANT: *Science of Right,* 419b [fn 1]
47 GOETHE: *Faust,* PART II [11,676–843] 284a-288a
51 TOLSTOY: *War and Peace,* BK I, 24a-25a; BK IV, 177c-d; BK VI, 271c-d; BK VII, 292b-296a; BK VIII, 305b-307d; 322c; BK IX, 355c-d; 357a-b; 357d-358b; BK XI, 520a-d
52 DOSTOEVSKY: *Brothers Karamazov,* BK I, 4a-d; BK II, 39a-40a; BK III 46a-82a,c esp 53c-54b, 58d-59b, 69d-70c; BK IV, 95b-100c; BK VIII, 200c-201c; BK X, 282b-283c; BK XI, 324a-b; BK XII, 366a-368c
53 JAMES: *Psychology,* 735a-b; 802b; 804a-805b
54 FREUD: *Origin and Development of Psycho-Analysis,* 14b-15a; 16d-17a; 18a-b / *Hysteria,* 84a-86c; 90d-96a; 97d-106c esp 97d-99d; 111a-118a,c esp 111b-115a / *Narcissism,* 409c-410d / *Instincts,* 415d-418c / *General Introduction,* 547b-549d esp 548d-549a; 569c-573a; 577a-578c; 583d-591d; 593d-599b; 604c-606a; 611a-d; 619b-622b esp 620d-622a / *Beyond the Pleasure Principle,* 659b-d / *Group Psychology,* 680c-d / *Inhibitions, Symptoms, and Anxiety,* 718b-d; 724a-728b esp 725d-726c, 728a-b; 733c-735a / *Civilization and Its Discontents,* 789d-790c / *New Introductory Lectures,* 847c-850c; 859c-d; 861c-862a

2b. Friendly, tender, or altruistic love: fraternal love

OLD TESTAMENT: *Leviticus,* 19:17-18,33-34 / *Deuteronomy,* 10:18-19 / *I Samuel,* 18:1-4; 19:1-7; 20; 23:15-18—(D) *I Kings,* 18:1-4; 19:1-7; 20; 23:15-18 / *II Samuel,* 1—(D) *II Kings,* 1 / *Psalms,* 133—(D) *Psalms,* 132 / *Proverbs,* 17:17-18; 18:19,24; 27:6
APOCRYPHA: *Ecclesiasticus,* 6:1,13-17; 7:18-19; 9:10; 25:1; 27:16-21; 29:10,15; 37:1-2,6; 40:23-24—(D) OT, *Ecclesiasticus,* 6:1,13-17; 7:20-21; 9:14-15; 25:1-2; 27:17-24; 29:13,19; 37:1-2,6; 40:23-24
NEW TESTAMENT: *Matthew,* 5:21-26; 19:19; 22:39 / *Mark,* 12:31 / *Luke,* 10:27 / *John,* 15:13 / *Romans,* 13:9 / *Galatians,* 5:14 / *Colossians,* 4:7-18 / *I Thessalonians,* 4:9-10 / *II Timothy,* 4:9-22 / *James,* 2:8 / *I Peter,* 3:8 / *II Peter,* 1:5-7 / *I John,* 3:11-17
4 HOMER: *Iliad,* BK IV [153–183] 25c-d; BK VI [212–236] 42b-c; BK XVI 112a-121d; BK XVIII 130a-136d; BK XIX [276–368] 139d-140c; BK XXIII [1–261] 161a-163d / *Odyssey,* BK VIII [581–586] 228c
5 SOPHOCLES: *Ajax* [666–683] 148d-149a

5 EURIPIDES: *Iphigenia Among the Tauri* [578–616] 416a-b; [674–715] 416d-417b

7 PLATO: *Lysis* 14a-25a,c / *Protagoras*, 52b / *Phaedrus*, 124a-129d esp 128d-129c / *Symposium*, 153b-155c / *Laws*, BK VIII, 735c-738c

9 ARISTOTLE: *Ethics*, BK VIII–IX 406b,d-426a,c / *Rhetoric*, BK II, CH 4 626c-628b

12 EPICTETUS: *Discourses*, BK II, CH 22 167d-170a

13 VIRGIL: *Aeneid*, BK IX [168–449] 283b-291a

14 PLUTARCH: *Alcibiades*, 156c-158b / *Pelopidas*, 233b-d

18 AUGUSTINE: *Confessions*, BK IV, par 7–14 20d-23a; BK VI, par 11–26 38b-43a passim / *City of God*, BK XIX, CH 7–8 515a-516a

20 AQUINAS: *Summa Theologica*, PART II–II, QQ 23–33 482c-558d passim

21 DANTE: *Divine Comedy*, HELL, II 2c-4a; XV 21a-22c; PURGATORY, XIII [1]–XV [81] 71d-76a; XVII [82–139] 79b-d; XXI [1]–XXII [129] 85a-87d; XXX–XXXI 99b-102b

22 CHAUCER: *Knight's Tale* 174a-211a esp [1092–1186] 178a-179b, [1574–1627] 186a-b

25 MONTAIGNE: *Essays*, 82b-88d; 396a-398c passim; 446d-448c; 472a-473b

26 SHAKESPEARE: *3rd Henry VI*, ACT V, SC VI [61–93] 103d-104a / *Richard II*, ACT II, SC III [46–49] 333a-b / *Merchant of Venice*, ACT I, SC I [119–160] 407c-408a; ACT III, SC II [223–330] 422b-423b / *As You Like It*, ACT II, SC VII [174–200] 609a-b; ACT IV, SC III [120–133] 620c-d

27 SHAKESPEARE: *Hamlet*, ACT I, SC III [62–65] 35a; ACT III, SC II [57–95] 49c-d; [206–225] 51b; [360–389] 52d-53a / *Troilus and Cressida*, ACT II, SC III [110–111] 116d / *Othello*, ACT III, SC III [142–144] 223c / *Antony and Cleopatra*, ACT V, SC I [13–48] 345b-c / *Coriolanus*, ACT IV, SC IV [12–22] 379b / *Timon of Athens*, ACT I, SC II [91–107] 398a-b / *Henry VIII*, ACT II, SC I [126–131] 559b-c / *Sonnets*, I–CXVI 586a-604a

29 CERVANTES: *Don Quixote*, PART II, 428b-c

31 SPINOZA: *Ethics*, PART IV, PROP 18, SCHOL 429a-d; PROP 29–40 431d-437a; PROP 73 446c-447a

35 LOCKE: *Human Understanding*, BK II, CH XX, SECT 5 176d-177a

42 KANT: *Fund. Prin. Metaphysic of Morals*, 259a; 262a-d / *Practical Reason*, 326a-b / *Pref. Metaphysical Elements of Ethics*, 375d-376b

44 BOSWELL: *Johnson*, 101a-c; 199a

46 HEGEL: *Philosophy of Right*, ADDITIONS, 101 133b / *Philosophy of History*, PART IV, 341a-c

48 MELVILLE: *Moby Dick*, 36b-39b; 381a

51 TOLSTOY: *War and Peace*, BK I, 15a-b; 28c-31a; 49a; 51d; 56b; BK II, 69a-c; 95d-96c; BK III, 127d-128d; 135c-137c; 140c-142d; BK IV, 167c-d; 183d-186c; 188a-190c; BK V, 220b-c; 222d-223a; BK VI, 262b-c; 266c-267c; 271a-b; BK VIII, 303b-d; 305d-306a; 311a-b; 327a-333a; 334d-341a,c passim; BK X, 465a-c; BK XI, 502b-503a; BK XII, 557b-c; BK XIV,

597a-598a; 600d; BK XV, 617b-618a; 625c-626d; 631c-633a

52 DOSTOEVSKY: *Brothers Karamazov*, BK VII, 180a-189a; BK X, 281b-297d; EPILOGUE, 408a-412d

54 FREUD: *Group Psychology*, 673b-c; 681d-682b; 693b-694b / *Civilization and Its Discontents*, 783a-c

2b(1) The relation between love and friendship

5 SOPHOCLES: *Ajax* [666–683] 148d-149a

7 PLATO: *Lysis* 14a-25a,c / *Phaedrus*, 115a-118c / *Laws*, BK VIII, 736a-c

8 ARISTOTLE: *Prior Analytics*, BK II, CH 22 [68ª25–ᵇ7] 89d-90a

9 ARISTOTLE: *Ethics*, BK IV, CH 6 [1126ᵇ20–25] 373d; BK VIII, CH 2–3 407a-408c; CH 5 [1157ᵇ28–37] 409c-d; CH 8 411b-d; BK IX, CH 4–5 419a-420c passim; CH 10 [1171ª11–15] 424d-425a; CH 12 425d-426a,c / *Politics*, BK VII, CH 7 [1327ᵇ40–1328ª17] 532a-b

12 EPICTETUS: *Discourses*, BK II, CH 22 167d-170a

18 AUGUSTINE: *Confessions*, BK IV, par 7–14 20d-23a

19 AQUINAS: *Summa Theologica*, PART I, Q 20, A 2, REP 3 121b-122a; Q 60, A 3, ANS 311d-312b; PART I–II, Q 26, A 4 736b-737a; Q 27, A 3 738c-739c; Q 28, A 1 740b-741a; A 2, ANS 741a-742a; A 3, ANS and REP 2–3 742a-d; A 4 742d-743c; Q 29, A 3, REP 2 746b-747a

20 AQUINAS: *Summa Theologica*, PART I–II, Q 65, A 5, ANS 74c-75a; Q 66, A 6, REP 2 80c-81b; PART II–II, Q 19, A 6 469a-d; Q 23, A 1 482d-483d

25 MONTAIGNE: *Essays*, 82b-88d esp 83d-85a; 410a-413a; 472b-473b

37 FIELDING: *Tom Jones*, 291d-292a

42 KANT: *Pref. Metaphysical Elements of Ethics*, 375d-376b

44 BOSWELL: *Johnson*, 257b; 392b-c

51 TOLSTOY: *War and Peace*, BK VIII, 339d-341a,c; BK IX, 373c-374a; BK XII, 555a-c; BK XV, 617b-d

54 FREUD: *Group Psychology*, 693d-694b / *Civilization and Its Discontents*, 783b-c

2b(2) Self-love in relation to the love of others

OLD TESTAMENT: *Leviticus*, 19:18,33–34

APOCRYPHA: *Ecclesiasticus*, 14:5-7—(D) OT, *Ecclesiasticus*, 14:5-7

NEW TESTAMENT: *Matthew*, 5:38-47; 19:19; 22:39 / *Mark*, 12:31 / *Luke*, 6:27-35; 10:27 / *Romans*, 13:9 / *Galatians*, 5:14 / *James*, 2:8

5 EURIPIDES: *Alcestis* [614–740] 242c-243c

7 PLATO: *Laws*, BK V, 689b

9 ARISTOTLE: *Ethics*, BK VIII, CH 7 [1158ᵇ29–1159ª12] 410d-411a; CH 12 [1161ᵇ16–33] 414a-b; BK IX, CH 4 419a-420a; CH 8–9 421d-424b esp CH 9 [1170ª14–ᵇ19] 423d-424b; CH 12 [1171ᵇ33–1172ª2] 425d / *Politics*, BK II, CH 5 [1263ª40–ᵇ4] 458c / *Rhetoric*, BK I, CH 11 [1371ᵇ12–25] 615a-b

(2b. Friendly, tender, or altruistic love: fraternal love. 2b(2) Self-love in relation to the love of others.)

12 Epictetus: Discourses, bk i, ch 19 125b-126c; bk ii, ch 17 158d-161a

18 Augustine: Confessions, bk iv, par 7–14 20d-23a; bk x, par 58–64 86a-87d / City of God, bk xiv, ch 28 397a-d / Christian Doctrine, bk i, ch 22–27 629b-631d; ch 35 634c-d

19 Aquinas: Summa Theologica, part i, q 20, a 1, rep 3 120a-121b; a 2, rep 1 121b-122a; q 60, aa 3–5 311d-314c; q 63, a 2 326c-327b; part i–ii, q 27, a 3 738c-739c; q 28, a 1 740b-741a; a 2, ans 741a-742a; a 3, ans and rep 3 742a-d; a 4, ans and rep 1–2 742d-743c; q 29, a 3, rep 2 746b-747a; a 4 747a-c; q 32, aa 5–6 762a-763c; q 40, a 7 797a-c

20 Aquinas: Summa Theologica, part i–ii, q 62, a 4, ans and rep 3 62b-63a; q 66, a 6, rep 2–3 80c-81b; q 73, a 1, rep 3 119c-120c; q 77, a 4 148b-149a; q 84, a 2 175b-176a; part ii–ii, q 23, a 1 482d-483d; q 25, aa 4–5 503c-504c; a 7 506a-d; a 12 509c-510b; q 26, aa 3–13 511d-520d

21 Dante: Divine Comedy, purgatory, xvii [82–139] 79b-d

23 Hobbes: Leviathan, part i, 83c; part ii, 104d

25 Montaigne: Essays, 486b-489b

26 Shakespeare: 3rd Henry VI, act v, sc vi [80–84] 104a / Richard III, act v, sc iii [177–206] 145c-d

27 Shakespeare: Twelfth Night, act i, sc v [97–104] 5b

31 Spinoza: Ethics, part iv, prop 46 438c-d; prop 48–49 439a-b

33 Pascal: Pensées, 100 191a-192b; 455–457 253b-254a; 471–477 256a-257a; 492 259b

35 Locke: Civil Government, ch ii, sect 5 26a-b

36 Swift: Gulliver, part ii, 70b

37 Fielding: Tom Jones, 58d-59a; 167c-170a esp 169d-170a; 291d-292a; 305d; 330b-c; 354c-d

38 Rousseau: Inequality, 330d-331b; 343d-345c

42 Kant: Fund. Prin. Metaphysic of Morals, 262a-d; 268d-270a / Practical Reason, 297a-314d esp 298a-300a, 304d-307d; 321b-327d esp 325a-327d / Pref. Metaphysical Elements of Ethics, 376b-c

43 Federalist: number 70, 212a

43 Mill: Representative Government, 367d-368a / Utilitarianism, 451b-c; 453a-c

44 Boswell: Johnson, 169d-170b; 310d-311a

46 Hegel: Philosophy of Right, additions, 101 133b / Philosophy of History, intro, 172b-d

49 Darwin: Descent of Man, 308d-309a; 310a-d; 316d-317a

51 Tolstoy: War and Peace, bk i, 31a-32a; bk iii, 146d-147c; 159d-160a; bk vi, 254b-c; 267d-268c; bk viii, 323b-324b; bk ix, 354a-355c; bk xii, 545b-547a; bk xv, 617b-d; epilogue i, 651d-652a; 656d-657a

53 James: Psychology, 204b-211a

54 Freud: Narcissism 399a-411a,c esp 404d-406c, 409b-411a,c / General Introduction, 528d; 616c-618a esp 617c-618a / Group Psychology, 677d-678c / War and Death, 758c-d

2b(3) The types of friendship: friendships based on utility, pleasure, or virtue

Old Testament: Proverbs, 14:20; 17:17–18

Apocrypha: Ecclesiasticus, 6:1–17; 9:10; 12:8–9; 37:1–9; 40:24—(D) OT, Ecclesiasticus, 6:1–17; 9:14–15; 12:8–9; 37:1–11; 40:24

5 Euripides: Rhesus [319–478] 206a-207b / Heracles Mad [55–59] 365c-d; [1214–1228] 375c / Orestes [356–806] 397b-402c / Iphigenia at Aulis [334–401] 427d-428b

6 Thucydides: Peloponnesian War, bk ii, 397b-c

7 Plato: Lysis 14a-25a,c / Symposium, 153b-155c / Gorgias, 285d-286b / Republic, bk i, 299b-c / Seventh Letter, 805b-c

9 Aristotle: Ethics, bk viii, ch 2–8 407a-411d; ch 13–14 414d-416d; bk ix, ch 1 416b,d-417c passim; ch 5 [1167a10–20] 420b-c; ch 9 [1169b22–1170a12] 423b-d; ch 10 424c-425a passim, esp [1170b23–31] 424c; ch 11 425a-d esp [1171a20–33] 425a-b; ch 12 [1172a2–8] 425d-426a; bk x, ch 3 [1173b32–1174a1] 428a-b / Rhetoric, bk i, ch 5 [1361b35–40] 602c; bk ii, ch 4 [1380b34–1381b38] 626d-627d; ch 12 [1389a35–b3] 636d

12 Epictetus: Discourses, bk ii, ch 22 167d-170a; bk iii, ch 16 191a-d; bk iv, ch 2 223d-224b

18 Augustine: Confessions, bk ii, par 16–17 12c-13a; bk iv, par 12–14 22a-23a; par 21–23 24c-25a

19 Aquinas: Summa Theologica, part i–ii, q 4, a 8, ans 636a-c; q 26, a 4, rep 3 736b-737a; q 27, a 3 738c-739c; q 31, a 6, rep 3 756d-757c

20 Aquinas: Summa Theologica, part ii–ii, q 23, a 1, rep 3 482d-483d; a 3, rep 1 485a-d; a 5, ans and rep 3 486b-487a

22 Chaucer: Tale of Melibeus, par 20–21, 409a-b

23 Machiavelli: Prince, ch xvii, 24a-b

23 Hobbes: Leviathan, part i, 77b-c

25 Montaigne: Essays, 82b-88d

26 Shakespeare: Two Gentlemen of Verona, act ii, sc vi 239a-c; act iv, sc i 245b-246b / Richard II, act v, sc i [55–70] 345d / Midsummer-Night's Dream, act iii, sc ii [192–219] 364d-365a / 2nd Henry IV, act v, sc v 501b-502c / Julius Caesar, act iv, sc ii [10–27] 587d / As You Like It, act ii, sc vii [174–190] 609a-b

27 Shakespeare: Hamlet, act iii, sc ii [57–99] 49c-50a; [206–225] 51b; [360–389] 52d-53a / Troilus and Cressida, act ii, sc iii [110–111] 116d / Timon of Athens 393a-420d esp act i, sc ii 397a-400a, act iv, sc i 409c-d, sc iii [464–543] 415d-416d

2b(4) Patterns of love and friendship in the family

VIII, 314b; 316b-c; 318a-340c; BK IX, 367c-369a; 373c-374a; 377b-d; 379a-381d; BK X, 417c-421c; 439d; 443c-444a; BK XI, 520d-521b; 522c-527b; BK XII, 539c-545a; 555d-556a; BK XV, 635a-644a,c; EPILOGUE I, 652b-654a

53 JAMES: *Psychology*, 190a

54 FREUD: *Narcissism*, 410c-d / *Group Psychology*, 682a-683a; 694c-695d / *Civilization and Its Discontents*, 768a

2d. Conjugal love: its sexual, fraternal, and romantic components

OLD TESTAMENT: *Genesis*, 2:23-24; 24:67; 29:28-30 / *I Samuel*, 1:1-8—(D) *I Kings*, 1:1-8 / *II Samuel*, 11; 13:1-20—(D) *II Kings*, 11; 13:1-20 / *Proverbs*, 5; 6:20-7:27 / *Ecclesiastes*, 9:9 / *Song of Solomon*—(D) *Canticle of Canticles*

APOCRYPHA: *Tobit*, 6:10-17—(D) OT, *Tobias*, 6:11-22 / *Ecclesiasticus*, 7:19,26; 25:1; 40:23 —(D) OT, *Ecclesiasticus*, 7:21,28; 25:1-2; 40:23

NEW TESTAMENT: *Matthew*, 19:4-6 / *Mark*, 10:6-9 / *I Corinthians*, 7:1-15,32-34 / *Ephesians*, 5:22-33 / *Colossians*, 3:18-19 / *I Peter*, 3:1-7

4 HOMER: *Iliad*, BK XIV [153-360] 99d-101d / *Odyssey*, BK XXIII [152-365] 313d-316a; BK XXIV [191-202] 319a

5 AESCHYLUS: *Agamemnon* [681-781] 59b-60b / *Choephoroe* [585-651] 75d-76b; [892-930] 78d-79b

5 SOPHOCLES: *Trachiniae* 170a-181a,c

5 EURIPIDES: *Medea* 212a-224a,c esp [446-662] 215d-217c / *Hippolytus* 225a-236d esp [373-481] 228b-229b / *Alcestis* 237a-247a,c esp [152-198] 238c-239a, [329-368] 240a-b / *Suppliants* [990-1071] 267a-c / *Trojan Women* [634-683] 275c-d / *Helen* 298a-314a,c / *Andromache* 315a-326a,c esp [147-308] 316c-317d / *Electra* [988-1122] 336a-337b

5 ARISTOPHANES: *Lysistrata* 583a-599a,c / *Thesmophoriazusae* 600a-614d esp [383-532] 604d-606a

6 HERODOTUS: *History*, BK VI, 197a-c; BK IX, 311b-312d

7 PLATO: *Symposium*, 152d-153a / *Republic*, BK V, 361b-363b

9 ARISTOTLE: *Ethics*, BK VIII, CH 12 [1162ª15-28] 414c-d

12 LUCRETIUS: *Nature of Things*, BK IV [1192-1287] 59d-61a,c

13 VIRGIL: *Georgics*, IV [452-527] 95b-98a / *Aeneid*, BK II [730-794] 144b-146b; BK IV [1-361] 167a-177a

14 PLUTARCH: *Lycurgus*, 39d-40b / *Lycurgus-Numa*, 62d-63c / *Solon*, 71d-72a / *Demetrius*, 731a-b / *Antony*, 756c-779d / *Marcus Brutus*, 807b-d; 811c-d

15 TACITUS: *Annals*, BK IV, 64b-c; BK XI, 107b-110a; BK XII, 121c

17 PLOTINUS: *Third Ennead*, TR V, CH I 100c-101c

18 AUGUSTINE: *Confessions*, BK II, par 2-8 9b-10d; BK IV, par 2 19d; BK VI, par 21-25 41c-42d; BK IX, par 19-22 67a-d / *City of God*, BK XIV, CH 16-26 390a-396c; BK XV, CH 16 411b-c / *Christian Doctrine*, BK III, CH 12 663a-c; CH 18-21 664d-666b

19 AQUINAS: *Summa Theologica*, PART I, Q 92 A 2, ANS 489d-490c; Q 98, A 2, ANS and REP 3 517d-519a; PART I-II, Q 28, A 4, ANS 742d-743c

20 AQUIANS: *Summa Theologica*, PART I-II, Q 105, A 4, ANS 318b-321a; PART II-II, Q 26, A 11 518b-519a; PART III, Q 6, A 1, REP 3 740b-741b

21 DANTE: *Divine Comedy*, PURGATORY, VIII [67-84] 65a; XXV [109-139] 92c-d

22 CHAUCER: *Miller's Tale* 212b-223b / *Wife of Bath's Prologue* [5583-6410] 256a-269b / *Tale of Wife of Bath* 270a-277a / *Clerk's Tale* 296a-318a / *Merchant's Tale* 319a-338a / *Franklin's Tale* [11,041-125] 351b-352b / *Manciple's Tale* [17,088-103] 490a / *Parson's Tale*, par 79-80 541a-542a

23 HOBBES: *Leviathan*, PART II, 155b-c; PART IV, 272d

24 RABELAIS: *Gargantua and Pantagruel*, BK I, 8c-d; BK II, 73b-74b; 106a-108d; 109c-126d; BK III, 144d-146a; 148d-150d; 154a-156c; 159d-163c; 166a-169d; 186d-188c; 196b-d; 197b-198b

25 MONTAIGNE: *Essays*, 37c-39c; 84a-b; 89d-90c; 306d-307a; 358b-362a; 406a-434d esp 410a-413a; 472a-473a

26 SHAKESPEARE: *1st Henry VI*, ACT V, SC III [80-195] 28a-29b; SC V [48-78] 31d-32a / *Comedy of Errors*, ACT II, SC I 152a-153b; SC II [112-148] 154c-d; ACT III, SC II [1-70] 157c-158b; ACT V, SC I [38-122] 165c-166b / *Two Gentlemen of Verona*, ACT I, SC II [1-34] 230d-231b / *Richard II*, ACT V, SC I [71-102] 345d-346b / *Henry V*, ACT V, SC II [98-306] 564b-566a / *Julius Caesar*, ACT II, SC I [261-309] 577b-c / *As You Like It*, ACT IV, SC I [115-157] 618a-c; ACT V, SC IV [114-156] 625a-b

27 SHAKESPEARE: *Hamlet*, ACT I, SC II [137-159] 33a; SC III [5-51] 34c-d; SC V [34-91] 37b-d; ACT III, SC I [120-157] 48b-c / *Merry Wives of Windsor* 73a-102d / *Othello* 205a-243a,c esp ACT IV, SC III 235d-237a, ACT V, SC II 238d-243a,c / *Cymbeline* 449a-488d esp ACT II, SC V 463a-c, ACT III, SC IV 466d-468d, ACT V, SC V [25-68] 483c-484a, [129-227] 484d-485d / *Tempest*, ACT IV, SC I [1-133] 542b-543a

29 CERVANTES: *Don Quixote*, PART I, 120b-137d; PART II, 261c-262a; 270c-271a

31 SPINOZA: *Ethics*, PART IV, APPENDIX, XIX-XX 449a

32 MILTON: *Paradise Lost*, BK IV [440-504] 162a-163b; [736-775] 168b-169a; BK V [443-450] 185a; BK VIII [39-65] 233a-b; [491-520] 243a-b; BK IX [226-269] 252a-253a; [952-959] 268a; BK X [888-908] 293b-294a

36 STERNE: *Tristram Shandy*, 193b-194a; 522a-523a

(2. The kinds of love. 2d. Conjugal love: its sexual, fraternal, and romantic components.)

37 FIELDING: *Tom Jones*, 2b-c; 14b-16b; 17a-b; 30a-32a; 118d; 124a-125b; 130b-c; 167c-168d; 230a-231c; 283b-c; 289b-291a; 321b-322a; 332a-333a; 349b-350b; 352d-353a; 360b-d; 405a,c

38 ROUSSEAU: *Inequality*, 364d-365b

40 GIBBON: *Decline and Fall*, 92c-93a; 649c-652a

42 KANT: *Science of Right*, 419a-420b

44 BOSWELL: *Johnson*, 22a; 57a; 64a; 107a; 160b; 194a; 291a; 294d-295a

46 HEGEL: *Philosophy of Right*, PART III, par 158 58a; par 161–168 58b-60c; ADDITIONS, 101–108 133b-134c

47 GOETHE: *Faust*, PART I [4243–4250] 104a; PART II [9356–9944] 227a-241b

51 TOLSTOY: *War and Peace*, BK I, 3a-c; BK III, 122b-c; BK IV, 177a-179d; BK VI, 245d-249d; 269c-d; BK VII, 287a-291a passim; 301b-302d; BK VIII, 311a-313a; EPILOGUE I, 660d-661b; 669d-672a

52 DOSTOEVSKY: *Brothers Karamazov*, BK I, 4a-5b; BK II, 21b-24d; 39a

53 JAMES: *Psychology*, 735a-b

54 FREUD: *Narcissism*, 404d-406b / *Group Psychology*, 694b-695a / *New Introductory Lectures*, 862d-863c

3. The morality of love

3a. Friendship and love in relation to virtue and happiness

5 SOPHOCLES: *Ajax* [666–683] 148d-149a

5 EURIPIDES: *Suppliants* [955–1164] 266d-268c / *Iphigenia at Aulis* [543–589] 429d-430a

7 PLATO: *Lysis*, 19d-24b / *Symposium*, 152d-155c; 164c-167d / *Republic*, BK I, 299b-c; 308b-309b; BK III, 333b-334b; BK IX, 417b-418a / *Critias*, 485c-d / *Seventh Letter*, 804c; 805b-c

8 ARISTOTLE: *Topics*, BK III, CH 1 [116ᵃ31–39] 162d; [116ᵇ36–117ᵃ4] 163c; CH 2 [118ᵃ1–7] 164d; CH 3 [118ᵇ5–9] 165c

9 ARISTOTLE: *Ethics*, BK I, CH 11 346c-347a; BK IV, CH 6 373d-374b passim; BK VIII, CH 1 [1155ᵃ1–32] 406b,d; CH 2 [1155ᵇ16–26] 407a-b; CH 3 [1156ᵇ6–32] 408a-c; CH 4–5 408c-409d; CH 6 [1158ᵃ22–28] 410a-b; CH 7 [1158ᵇ29–1159ᵃ12] 410d-411a; CH 8 411b-d esp [1159ᵇ2–10] 411c; CH 13 414d-415d passim; BK IX, CH 1 [1164ᵃ33–ᵇ6] 417b; CH 3 418c-419a passim; CH 4 419a-420a; CH 6 [1167ᵇ5–15] 420d-421a; CH 8–12 421d-426a,c / *Rhetoric*, BK I, CH 5 [1360ᵇ19–30] 601a-b; [1361ᵇ35–40] 602c; BK II, CH 4 [1381ᵃ36–ᵇ9] 627b-c

12 LUCRETIUS: *Nature of Things*, BK IV [1058–1191] 57d-59d

12 EPICTETUS: *Discourses*, BK II, CH 22 167d-170a; BK III, CH 16 191a-d; BK IV, CH 2 223d-224b

12 AURELIUS: *Meditations*, BK XI, SECT 9 303b

14 PLUTARCH: *Alcibiades*, 156c-158b / *Pelopidas*, 233b-d / *Cato the Younger*, 623a-b

18 AUGUSTINE: *Confessions*, BK III, par 1 13b-c; BK IV, par 7–14 20d-23a; BK VI, par 11–26 38b-43a passim / *City of God*, BK XIX, CH 3, 510d; CH 5–9 513d-516c; CH 13–14 519a-520d / *Christian Doctrine*, BK I, CH 27–30 631d-633b

19 AQUINAS: *Summa Theologica*, PART I, Q 60, A 4, REP 3 312c-313b; PART I–II, Q 4, A 8 636a-c; Q 27, A 1 737b-d

20 AQUINAS: *Summa Theologica*, PART II–II, Q 23, AA 3–8 485a-489c; Q 31, A 1, REP 3 536d-537c

21 DANTE: *Divine Comedy*, HELL, XI [13–90] 15b-16a; PURGATORY, XV [40–81] 75d-76a; XVII [82]–XVIII [75] 79b-80c

22 CHAUCER: *Troilus and Cressida*, BK II, STANZA 111–112 36a; STANZA 119–128 37a-38a; BK III, STANZA 241–247 86a-b; STANZA 254–258 87b-88a

23 MACHIAVELLI: *Prince*, CH XVII, 24b

24 RABELAIS: *Gargantua and Pantagruel*, BK I, 65c-66b

25 MONTAIGNE: *Essays*, 82b-88d; 396a-398c passim; 431c-432d; 478b-c

26 SHAKESPEARE: *Love's Labour's Lost*, ACT IV, SC III 268b-272c / *Richard II*, ACT II, SC III [46–49] 333a-b / *Midsummer-Night's Dream*, ACT I, SC I [67–78] 353a-b

27 SHAKESPEARE: *Hamlet*, ACT III, SC II [57–99] 49c-50a / *Othello*, ACT IV, SC II [47–64] 233c-d / *King Lear*, ACT V, SC III [1–26] 279a-b / *Timon of Athens* 393a-420d esp ACT I, SC II [91–107] 398a-b, ACT III, SC II [71–94] 404c-d, SC III [27–42] 405b, ACT IV, SC I 409c-d, SC III [249–305] 413c-414a / *Sonnets*, XXV 590a; CXXXVII–CLII 607a-609c

31 SPINOZA: *Ethics*, PART IV, PROP 46 438c-d; PROP 70–73 445c-447a; APPENDIX, IX 448a; XX 449a

33 PASCAL: *Pensées*, 211 211b

36 SWIFT: *Gulliver*, PART IV, 165b-166a

37 FIELDING: *Tom Jones*, 17a-b

38 ROUSSEAU: *Inequality*, 343d-345c / *Political Economy*, 373c-374a

43 MILL: *Representative Government*, 367d-368a

44 BOSWELL: *Johnson*, 83b-c; 107a; 423c-d; 490a

46 HEGEL: *Philosophy of Right*, ADDITIONS, 101 133b

47 GOETHE: *Faust*, PART I [3125–3136] 76a-b; [3374–3413] 82b-83a; PART II [9356–9573] 227a-232a

48 MELVILLE: *Moby Dick*, 36b-39b

49 DARWIN: *Descent of Man*, 312a-314b; 317c-d; 592d-593a

51 TOLSTOY: *War and Peace*, BK I, 15b-16a; BK III, 116c-117a; 122b-c; 127d-128d; BK IV, 183d-186c; BK V, 201a-c; BK VI, 266c-267c; BK VIII, 311a-313a; 327a-329c; 340c-341a,c;

(4. *The social or political force of love, sympathy, or friendship.* *4a. Love between equals and unequals, like and unlike: the fraternity of citizenship.*)

52 DOSTOEVSKY: *Brothers Karamazov*, BK VI, 165b-170b

54 FREUD: *Group Psychology*, 674b-675a; 676c-d; 687d; 691d-692a

4b. **The dependence of the state on friendship and patriotism: comparison of love and justice in relation to the common good**

4 HOMER: *Iliad*, BK XII [230-250] 84c-d

5 SOPHOCLES: *Antigone* [162-210] 132c-d / *Philoctetes* 182a-195a,c

5 EURIPIDES: *Phoenician Maidens* [929-1018] 386b-387b

6 HERODOTUS: *History*, BK IV, 142c; BK VII, 225d-226b; 239a-c; 258b-d; BK VIII, 273d

6 THUCYDIDES: *Peloponnesian War*, BK II, 397d-398c; 402b-404a; BK III, 419a

7 PLATO: *Republic*, BK I, 308b-309b / *Laws*, BK V, 692b-c; 694d / *Seventh Letter*, 804b-c

9 ARISTOTLE: *Ethics*, BK VIII, CH 1 [1155^{a}22-28] 406d; CH 9-12 411d-414d; BK IX, CH 6 420c-421a; CH 8 421d-423a esp [1169^{a}6-32] 422c-423a / *Politics*, BK II, CH 3-4 456c-458a esp CH 4 [1262^{a}40-^{b}23] 457c-d; BK III, CH 9 [1280^{b}33-1281^{a}4] 478c; BK IV, CH 11 495b-496d

12 LUCRETIUS: *Nature of Things*, BK V [1011-1027] 74b-c

14 PLUTARCH: *Lycurgus* 32a-48d / *Pelopidas*, 233b-d / *Sertorius*, 467d-469a / *Dion*, 784d-785a; 798b-d

18 AUGUSTINE: *City of God*, BK XIX, CH 21-24 524a-528c

19 AQUINAS: *Summa Theologica*, PART I, Q 60, A 5, ANS 313b-314c

20 AQUINAS: *Summa Theologica*, PART I-II, Q 99, A 1, REP 2 245c-246b; A 2, ANS 246b-247a; PART II-II, Q 26, A 3, ANS 511d-512c; A 8, ANS and REP 3 516a-517a; QQ 37-42 570c-584d; Q 45, A 6 602b-603c

25 MONTAIGNE: *Essays*, 84b-85a; 382b-383d; 471a-c

26 SHAKESPEARE: *Richard II*, ACT I, SC III [275-309] 326c-d; ACT II, SC I [40-68] 328a-b

27 SHAKESPEARE: *Coriolanus*, ACT V, SC III [94-171] 388a-d

31 SPINOZA: *Ethics*, PART IV, PROP 18, SCHOL 429a-d; APPENDIX, IX-XVII 448a-d

32 MILTON: *Samson Agonistes* [843-870] 358a-b

38 MONTESQUIEU: *Spirit of Laws*, xxiia-d; BK IV, 15d-16a; BK V, 18d-19c

38 ROUSSEAU: *Inequality*, 323b-d; 325a-b / *Political Economy*, 372b-377b esp 373c-374a / *Social Contract*, BK IV, 437b-438c

42 KANT: *Fund. Prin. Metaphysic of Morals*, 269d / *Pref. Metaphysical Elements of Ethics*, 375d-376b

43 FEDERALIST: NUMBER 2, 31c-d; NUMBER 14, 62a-b; NUMBER 27, 95c-d; NUMBER 45, 148b-d; NUMBER 62, 189b-c; 191b-c

43 MILL: *Representative Government*, 343a; 424c-425d; 428b-c

44 BOSWELL: *Johnson*, 253c

46 HEGEL: *Philosophy of Right*, PART III, par 267-269 84b-d / *Philosophy of History*, PART II, 283c-d; PART III, 298c-d

51 TOLSTOY: *War and Peace*, BK V, 214c-216d; BK XI, 474a-b; 475b-476c; BK XII, 537b-538a

4c. **The brotherhood of man and the world community**

OLD TESTAMENT: *Genesis*, 4:1-15 / *Exodus*, 12:48-49; 22:21; 23:9 / *Leviticus*, 19:17-18,33-34; 24:22 / *Deuteronomy*, 10:18-19 / *I Kings*, 8:41-43—(D) *III Kings*, 8:41-43 / *Psalms*, 22:27-31; 68:29-35; 103:19-22; 133:1; 145:11-13—(D) *Psalms*, 21:28-32; 67:30-36; 102:19-22; 132:1; 144:11-13 / *Isaiah*, 2:1-4—(D) *Isaias*, 2:1-4 / *Jeremiah*, 16:19-21—(D) *Jeremias*, 16:19-21 / *Ezekiel*, 37:26-28—(D) *Ezechiel*, 37:26-28 / *Micah*, 4:1-4—(D) *Micheas*, 4:1-4 / *Malachi*, 2:10—(D) *Malachias*, 2:10

APOCRYPHA: *Ecclesiasticus*, 25:1—(D) OT, *Ecclesiasticus*, 25:1-2

NEW TESTAMENT: *Matthew*, 12:46-50; 19:19; 22:39; 23:8-9; 25:34-40 / *Mark*, 12:31-33 / *Luke*, 10:27 / *John*, 1:12; 13:34-35; 15:9-17; 17:26; 18:36 / *Acts*, 17:22-34 esp 17:24-26 / *Romans*, 8:14-19; 12; 13:8-10; 14:10 / *Galatians*, 5:13-14 / *Ephesians*, 2:13-22; 4:1-16 esp 4:13-16; 4:32; 5:1-2 / *Philippians*, 2:1-2 / *Colossians*, 3:9-17 esp 3:11 / *I Thessalonians*, 4:9-10 / *Hebrews*, 13:1-3 / *James*, 2:8 / *I Peter*, 1:22; 3:8 / *I John*, 2:9-11; 3:2,10-18; 4:7-5:2 / *II John*, 5

4 HOMER: *Odyssey*, BK VI [207] 216b; BK VII [181] 220a; BK XIV [55-56] 260d

6 HERODOTUS: *History*, BK I, 20b-d; 31d-32a; BK IV, 137a-138c; BK VI, 189c

9 ARISTOTLE: *Politics*, BK I, CH 2 [1252^{b}6-8] 445d

12 EPICTETUS: *Discourses*, BK I, CH 9 114c-116b; CH 13 120b-c; BK II, CH 10 148c-150a; CH 20, 164d-165c; BK III, CH 11 187a-b; CH 22, 199c-d; CH 24 203c-210a

12 AURELIUS: *Meditations*, BK III, SECT 4 260b-261a; SECT 11 262a-b; BK IV, SECT 3-4 263b-264a; BK VI, SECT 44 278b-c; BK XI, SECT 9 303b; SECT 13 303d

13 VIRGIL: *Aeneid*, BK I [254-296] 110a-111a; BK VI [845-853] 233b-234a

18 AUGUSTINE: *City of God*, BK XII, CH 21-22 357a-c; CH 27, 359d; BK XIX, CH 7 515a-c; CH 17, 522d

20 AQUINAS: *Summa Theologica*, PART II-II, Q 26, AA 6-8 514a-517a; Q 184, A 2, REP 3 629d-630d

22 CHAUCER: *Parson's Tale*, par 31 517b-518b

25 MONTAIGNE: *Essays*, 471a-c

27 SHAKESPEARE: *Timon of Athens*, ACT IV, SC I 409c-d

30 BACON: *Advancement of Learning*, 31d-32a

31 SPINOZA: *Ethics*, PART IV, APPENDIX, IX–XVII 448a-d

38 MONTESQUIEU: *Spirit of Laws*, BK XXIV, 206c

38 ROUSSEAU: *Inequality*, 355b-c / *Political Economy*, 369a-b; 373c / *Social Contract*, BK IV, 437c-d

42 KANT: *Science of Right*, 449c-458a,c esp 455c-456a, 457a-458a,c / *Judgement*, 586a-587a

43 MILL: *Representative Government*, 424c-428a passim, esp 426a-b / *Utilitarianism*, 451b-c

44 BOSWELL: *Johnson*, 392b-c

46 HEGEL: *Philosophy of History*, PART I, 224a

49 DARWIN: *Descent of Man*, 317c-d; 318d

50 MARX-ENGELS: *Communist Manifesto*, 428a-b

51 TOLSTOY: *War and Peace*, BK II, 69a-c; BK V, 198b-203a passim, esp 199b-200d, 202d; 217a; BK VI, 244d-245d; BK IX, 375d; BK X, 466b-c; BK XII, 548d-549c esp 549b; 555b-c; BK XIII, 575d-577a; BK XV, 625c-626d; 632b-c

52 DOSTOEVSKY: *Brothers Karamazov*, BK I, 13c-d; BK V, 121d-122d; BK VI, 164b-170b esp 166c-167b

54 FREUD: *Group Psychology*, 674c-d; 691d-692a / *War and Death*, 755a-761c esp 755b-757c, 761a-c / *Civilization and Its Discontents*, 783a-b; 785d-788d esp 786a-c, 788b-c

5. Divine love

5*a*. God as the primary object of love

OLD TESTAMENT: *Deuteronomy*, 6:4–9

NEW TESTAMENT: *Matthew*, 6:33 / *Luke*, 12:31

12 EPICTETUS: *Discourses*, BK II, CH 16, 158b-d; BK III, CH 24 203c-210a; BK IV, CH 12, 243c

18 AUGUSTINE: *Confessions*, BK I, par 1 1a-b; BK IV, par 7–20 20d-24c; BK VII, par 22 50a; BK VIII, par 10–30 55c-61c passim; BK IX, par 23–25 68a-c; BK X, par 8–11 73b-74b; par 38 81a; BK XII, par 10 101c; par 23 104b-c / *City of God*, BK X, CH 18 310b-d; BK XII, CH 8–9 346d-348b; BK XIV, CH 7, 380c-d; BK XV, CH 22, 416c / *Christian Doctrine*, BK I, CH 3–4 625b-c; CH 9–10 627a-b; CH 22–23 629b-630c; BK III, CH 10, 662a

19 AQUINAS: *Summa Theologica*, PART I, Q 12, A 1, ANS 50c-51c; A 8, REP 4 57b-58b; Q 60, A 5 313b-314c; PART I–II, Q 1, A 8 615a-c; Q 2, A 1, REP 3 615d-616c; A 8 621c-622b; Q 4, A 8, ANS and REP 3 636a-c

20 AQUINAS: *Summa Theologica*, PART I–II, Q 109, A 3 340c-341b; PART II–II, Q 24, A 2, REP 2 490b-d; Q 25, A 12 509c-510b; Q 26, AA 2–3 511a-512c; Q 27, A 3 522c-523b; A 8 526c-527b

21 DANTE: *Divine Comedy*, PURGATORY, XV [40–81] 75d-76a; XVII [82]–XVIII [75] 79b-80c; XXX–XXXI 99b-102b; PARADISE, I [97–142] 107b-d; IV [115]–V [12] 111d-112b; XXVI [1–81] 145d-146c

30 BACON: *Advancement of Learning*, 80b-81a

31 DESCARTES: *Meditations*, III, 88c-89a

31 SPINOZA: *Ethics*, PART IV, APPENDIX, IV 447b-c; PART V, PROP 15–16 456c; PROP 18 456d; PROP 32–33 460b-c

42 KANT: *Practical Reason*, 325a-327d / *Judgement*, 504b-505a; 611a-c

51 TOLSTOY: *War and Peace*, BK IX, 373b-377b passim; BK XI, 525c-526b; BK XII, 560a-561c

52 DOSTOEVSKY: *Brothers Karamazov*, BK V, 127b-137c passim

5*a*(1) Man's love of God in this life: respect for the moral law

OLD TESTAMENT: *Exodus*, 20:5–6 / *Deuteronomy*, 5:9–10; 6; 7:9–11; 10:12; 11:1,13,22; 13:3; 19:9; 30:6,15–20 / *Joshua*, 22:1–6; 23:11—(D) *Josue*, 22:1–6; 23:11 / *Psalms* passim, esp 18:1, 31:23, 97:10, 116:1, 119:132, 122:6, 145:20—(D) *Psalms* passim, esp 17:2, 30:24, 96:10, 114:1, 118:132, 121:6, 144:20 / *Ecclesiastes*, 12:13 / *Isaiah*, 29:8–9—(D) *Isaias*, 29:8–9 / *Jeremiah*, 2:2—(D) *Jeremias*, 2:2

APOCRYPHA: *Tobit*, 13:12–14—(D) OT, *Tobias*, 13:16–18 / *Ecclesiasticus*, 2; 7:30; 10:19; 13:14; 25:11–12; 34:16; 47:8—(D) OT, *Ecclesiasticus*, 2; 7:32; 10:23; 13:18; 25:14–16; 34:19; 47:9–10

NEW TESTAMENT: *Matthew*, 22:36–38 / *Mark*, 12:30–32 / *Luke*, 10:25–28 / *John*, 14:15,21,23–24 / *Acts*, 20:22–24; 21:7–15 / *Romans*, 5:5; 8:28 / *I Corinthians*, 8:1–3 / *Ephesians*, 3:14–21 / *II Thessalonians*, 3:5 / *James*, 1:12; 2:5 / *I Peter*, 1:7–8 / *I John*, 2:5,12–17; 4:19–5:3 / *II John*, 6

12 EPICTETUS: *Discourses*, BK I, CH 16 121d-122d; BK II, CH 16, 158b-d; BK III, CH 24 203c-210a; BK IV, CH 12, 243c

18 AUGUSTINE: *Confessions*, BK III, par 15–16 17a-d; BK IV, par 14–19 22d-24b; BK VII, par 23–24 50b-51a; BK VIII, par 10–30 55c-61c passim; BK IX, par 1 61c-d; BK X, par 8 73b-c; par 38–70 81a-89b / *City of God*, BK X, CH 1 298b,d-299d; CH 3 300b-301a; BK XII, CH 20 355b-357a; BK XIV, CH 28 397a-d; BK XV, CH 22 416a-c; BK XIX, CH 20 523d-524a; BK XXI, CH 15–16 572c-574a / *Christian Doctrine*, BK I, CH 15–16 628b-d; CH 22–23 629b-630c; CH 26–27 631b-d; CH 29–30 632a-633b; CH 33 633d-634b; CH 35–37 634c-635c; BK II, CH 38, 654c

19 AQUINAS: *Summa Theologica*, PART I, Q 62, A 9, REP 1 324a-325b; Q 82, A 3, ANS and REP 3 433c-434c; PART I–II, Q 27, A 2, REP 2 737d-738c; Q 28, A 5 743c-744b; Q 35, A 5, REP 1 775d-777a

20 AQUINAS: *Summa Theologica*, PART I–II, Q 65, A 5, ANS and REP 1,3 74c-75a; Q 67, A 5 85d-86d; Q 73, A 1, REP 3 119c-120c; Q 110, A 1 347d-349a; Q 114, A 8 376a-d; PART II–II, Q 23, A 1, REP 1 482d-483d; Q 24, A 2, REP 2 490b-d; AA 4–12 491d-500d; Q 27 520d-527b esp A 4 523c-524a; Q 34 558d-562d; Q 184, AA 1–3 629a-632c

(5a. *God as the primary object of love.* 5a(1)
*Man's love of God in this life: respect for
the moral law.*)

21 DANTE: *Divine Comedy*, PURGATORY, XV [40–
81] 75d-76a; XXX–XXXI 99b-102b; PARADISE,
III [91–108] 110b-c; XI 122a-123c; XXVI [1–81]
145d-146c

22 CHAUCER: *Troilus and Cressida*, BK V, STANZA
263–267 154b-155a / *Parson's Tale*, par 31
517b-518b

23 HOBBES: *Leviathan*, PART III, 240d

30 BACON: *Advancement of Learning*, 80b-81a

31 DESCARTES: *Meditations*, III, 88d-89a

31 SPINOZA: *Ethics*, PART IV, APPENDIX, IV
447b-c; PART V, PROP 15–16 456c

32 MILTON: *Sonnets*, XIV 66a / *Paradise Lost*, BK
V [153–208] 178b-179b

33 PASCAL: *Provincial Letters*, 78b-80b / *Pensées*,
430 245a-247b; 463–492 255a-259b; 544 266a;
556 270b-272a

42 KANT: *Practical Reason*, 321b-329a esp 326b-
327a / *Pref. Metaphysical Elements of Ethics*,
370a-b; 375a-b / *Judgement*, 504b-505a;
509a-c; 593a-d; 611a-c

46 HEGEL: *Philosophy of History*, PART III, 307b-
308a

51 TOLSTOY: *War and Peace*, BK XI, 525c-526b;
BK XII, 560a-561c; BK XIV, 608a-b

52 DOSTOEVSKY: *Brothers Karamazov*, BK V,
127b-137c passim

5a(2) Beatitude as the fruition of love

18 AUGUSTINE: *Confessions*, BK IX, par 23–25
68a-c / *City of God*, BK XXII, CH 29–30 614b-
618d / *Christian Doctrine*, BK I, CH 15 628b-c;
CH 32–33 633c-634b; CH 38 635c-d

19 AQUINAS: *Summa Theologica*, PART I, Q 62,
AA 7–8 322d-324a; A 9, REP I 324a-325b; PART
I–II, Q 2, A 8 621c-622b; Q 4, AA 1–3 629d-
631d; A 8 esp REP 3 636a-c; Q 5, A 4 639a-640b

20 AQUINAS: *Summa Theologica*, PART I–II, Q 65,
A 5, ANS and REP 1,3 74c-75a; Q 67, A 6 87a-c;
Q 114, A 4 373a-d; A 8 376a-d; PART II–II, Q
23, A 1, REP 1 482d-483d; Q 24, A 6, REP 1
493d-494b; A 7, REP 1 494b-495b; A 8, ANS
and REP 1 495b-496a; A 9, ANS and REP 3
496a-d; A 11, ANS 498b-499c; Q 25, A 10
508b-d; Q 26, A 13 519d-520d; Q 28, A 3
528d-529c; Q 184, A 2, ANS and REP 1–2 629d-
630d; PART III SUPPL, Q 90, A 3 1014d-1016a;
Q 93 1037c-1040c esp A 3 1039d-1040c; QQ
95–96 1042c-1066a

21 DANTE: *Divine Comedy*, PURGATORY, XV [40–
81] 75d-76a; PARADISE 106a-157d esp III
[34–90] 109d-110b, IV [115]–V [12] 111d-112b,
XXI [19–102] 138c-139b, XXII [61–69] 140b,
XXVI [1–81] 145d-146c, XXVIII 148d-150b,
XXX [34–45] 152a-b, XXXIII 156b-157d

31 SPINOZA: *Ethics*, PART IV, APPENDIX, IV
447b-c; PART V, PROP 21–42 458a-463d esp
PROP 32–37 460b-461c, PROP 42 463b-d

32 MILTON: *Sonnets*, XIV 66a

42 KANT: *Practical Reason*, 346b-347c

5b. Charity, or supernatural love, compared with natural love

NEW TESTAMENT: *I Corinthians*, 13

18 AUGUSTINE: *Confessions*, BK VII, par 23–24
50b-51a; BK VIII, par 10–30 55c-61c passim;
BK X, par 38–70 81a-89b; BK XIII, par 8
112b-c / *City of God*, BK XV, CH 22 416a-c /
Christian Doctrine, BK III, CH 10, 662a

19 AQUINAS: *Summa Theologica*, PART I, Q 8,
A 3, ANS and REP 4 36b-37c; Q 60 310a-314c
esp A 1, REP 3 310b-311a, A 5, ANS and REP
4–5 313b-314c; Q 62, A 2, REP 1 318d-319c;
A 7 322d-323b; Q 63, A 1, REP 3 325c-326c;
PART I–II, Q 26, A 1, ANS and REP 3 734a-d;
A 2, ANS 734d-735c; A 3, ANS and REP 4 735c-
736b; Q 29, A 1, ANS and REP 3 745a-c; AA 4–5
747a-748b

20 AQUINAS: *Summa Theologica*, PART I–II, Q 62,
A 3, ANS and REP 3 61c-62b; Q 65, A 5, REP 1
74c-75a; Q 109, A 3 340c-341b; Q 110, A 1
347d-349a; PART II–II, Q 24, AA 2–3 490b-
491d; A 10 496d-498a; Q 25, AA 7–8 506a-
507c; Q 26, A 3, ANS 511d-512c; A 5 513b-d;
A 6, ANS 514a-d; AA 8–11 516a-519a; Q 31, A 3
538b-539c; Q 32, A 9 548c-549b

21 DANTE: *Divine Comedy*, PURGATORY, XV [40–
81] 75d-76a; XXX–XXXI 99b-102b; PARADISE,
IV [115]–V [12] 111d-112b; VIII–IX 116d-120a

23 HOBBES: *Leviathan*, PART III, 240d

30 BACON: *Advancement of Learning*, 2c-4c;
80b-81a

32 MILTON: *Paradise Lost*, BK XII [576–605]
331b-332a

33 PASCAL: *Pensées*, 793 326b-327a

37 FIELDING: *Tom Jones*, 26a-27a

44 BOSWELL: *Johnson*, 392b-c

51 TOLSTOY: *War and Peace*, BK I, 50a; BK III,
128c-d; BK V, 214c-218b; BK X, 465a-c; BK
XI, 525c-526b; BK XII, 560a-561c; BK XV, 617d

52 DOSTOEVSKY: *Brothers Karamazov*, BK V,
121d-122d passim

54 FREUD: *Group Psychology*, 691d-692a /
Civilization and Its Discontents, 786a-d

5b(1) The precepts of charity: the law of love

OLD TESTAMENT: *Leviticus*, 19:17-18,33-34 /
Deuteronomy, 6:5; 10:12,18-19; 11:1,13,22;
13:3-4; 19:9; 24:19-22; 30:6,16 / *Proverbs*,
10:12; 25:21-22

APOCRYPHA: *Wisdom of Solomon*, 3:9; 6:17-18—
(D) OT, *Book of Wisdom*, 3:9; 6:18-19 /
Ecclesiasticus, 4:1-10; 13:14; 28:1-8; 29—(D)
OT, *Ecclesiasticus*, 4:1-11; 13:18; 28:1-11; 29

NEW TESTAMENT: *Matthew*, 5:20-26,38-48;
19:19; 22:34-40 / *Mark*, 12:28-34 / *Luke*,
6:27-38; 10:25-37 / *John*, 13:34-17:26 passim
/ *Romans*, 8:35-39; 12:9-21; 13:8-10 / *Corinthians*, 8:1-3; 13; 16:14 / *II Corinthians*, 2:4-
11; 6; 8:7-8 / *Galatians*, 5 / *Ephesians*, 1:4;

5b(2) The theological virtue of charity: its relation to the other virtues

5c. God's love of Himself and of creatures

(5. *Divine love. 5c. God's love of Himself and of creatures.*)

19 AQUINAS: *Summa Theologica*, PART I, Q 3, A 1, REP 1 14b-15b; Q 6, A 4 30b-d; Q 19, A 2, ANS and REP 2-4 109c-110b; A 4, ANS and REP 1 111c-112c; Q 20 119d-124a; Q 27, AA 3-4 155c-156d; Q 37 197c-200c; Q 74, A 3, REP 3-4 375a-377a,c; Q 82, A 5, REP 1 435c-436c; Q 93, A 4, ANS 494c-495b; PART I-II, Q 28, A 3, CONTRARY 742a-d; A 4, CONTRARY 742d-743c

20 AQUINAS: *Summa Theologica*, PART I-II, Q 65, A 5, ANS and REP 3 74c-75a; QQ 109-114 338a-378a,c esp Q 110, A 1 347d-349a, A 4, ANS 350d-351d; PART II-II, Q 23, AA 1-2 482d-484d; Q 24, AA 2-3 490b-491d; A 8, ANS 495b-496a; A 12 499c-500d; Q 184, A 2, ANS 629d-630d

21 DANTE: *Divine Comedy*, HELL, I [37-40] 1b-c; PURGATORY, III [103-145] 57a-c; X [22-45] 67c-d; XI [1-30] 68d-69a; XV [40-81] 75d-76a; XXVIII [91-96] 97a; PARADISE, III [34-90] 109d-110b; VII [1-120] 115a-116b; X [1-27]

120b-c; XIII [52-87] 126a-b; XIX [86-90] 135d-136a; XXVI [1-66] 145d-146c; XXVII [97-120] 148b-c; XXIX [13-48] 150b-d; [127-145] 151c-d; XXXII [139]-XXXIII [145] 156a-157d

22 CHAUCER: *Troilus and Cressida*, BK III, STANZA 1-7 54b-55b; STANZA 250-253 87a-b; BK V, STANZA 263-267 154b-155a / *Tale of Melibeus*, par 78 431b-432a

31 DESCARTES: *Objections and Replies*, 229c

31 SPINOZA: *Ethics*, PART V, PROP 17, COROL 456d; PROP 19 457a; PROP 35-36 460d-461c

32 MILTON: *Paradise Lost*, BK III [56-343] 136b-143a; BK IV [411-439] 161b-162a

35 BERKELEY: *Human Knowledge*, INTRO, SECT 3 405b-c; SECT 154 444a-b

37 FIELDING: *Tom Jones*, 186c-d

42 KANT: *Judgement*, 592a-c

48 MELVILLE: *Moby Dick*, 381a

51 TOLSTOY: *War and Peace*, BK VI, 271d-272b; BK IX, 373b-377b passim

52 DOSTOEVSKY: *Brothers Karamazov*, BK II, 24a-c; BK V, 127b-137c passim; BK VI, 153a-d; BK VII, 189a-191a,c passim

CROSS-REFERENCES

For: The basic psychological terms in the analysis of love, *see* DESIRE 3c; EMOTION 1, 2-2c; PLEASURE AND PAIN 7a; and for the comparison of love and knowledge, *see* KNOWLEDGE 4d.

Other discussions of the objects of love, *see* BEAUTY 3; DESIRE 1, 2b; GOOD AND EVIL 1a, 3c; TRUTH 8e; WILL 7d.

Other considerations of the sexual instincts, sexual love, and their normal or abnormal development, *see* DESIRE 4b-4d; EMOTION 1c, 3c-3c(3); HABIT 3-3a; PLEASURE AND PAIN 4b, 7b, 8b-8c; TEMPERANCE 2, 6a-6b.

Other considerations of conjugal love and its components, *see* FAMILY 7a.

For the moral problems raised by love, *see* DUTY 8; JUSTICE 3; OPPOSITION 4d; PLEASURE AND PAIN 8b; SIN 2b; TEMPERANCE 6a-6b; VIRTUE AND VICE 6e.

The role of friendship in the life of the individual, the family, and the state, *see* FAMILY 7c; HAPPINESS 2b(5); STATE 3e; VIRTUE AND VICE 6e; and for other discussions of the brotherhood of man and the world community, *see* CITIZEN 8; MAN 11b; STATE 10f; WAR AND PEACE 11d.

Man's love of God, or charity, as a theological virtue, *see* DESIRE 7b; VIRTUE AND VICE 8d(3), 8f; WILL 7d; and for the fruition of this love in eternal beatitude, *see* HAPPINESS 7c-7c(2); IMMORTALITY 5f.

God's love of Himself and of His creatures, *see* GOD 5h; GOOD AND EVIL 2a.

ADDITIONAL READINGS

Listed below are works not included in *Great Books of the Western World*, but relevant to the idea and topics with which this chapter deals. These works are divided into two groups:

I. Works by authors represented in this collection.
II. Works by authors not represented in this collection.

For the date, place, and other facts concerning the publication of the works cited, consult the Bibliography of Additional Readings, which follows the last chapter of *The Great Ideas*.

I.

PLUTARCH. "Of Envy and Hatred," "How to Know a Flatterer from a Friend," "Of Brotherly Love," "Of Love," "Five Tragical Histories of Love," in *Moralia*
AUGUSTINE. *Of Continence*
——. *Of Marriage and Concupiscence*
AQUINAS. *Quaestiones Disputatae, De Caritate*
——. *Summa Theologica*, PART II-II, QQ 106-107, 114-119, 151-154
——. *The Two Precepts of Charity and the Ten Commandments*
DANTE. *La Vita Nuova* (*The New Life*)
——. *Convivio* (*The Banquet*)
F. BACON. "Of Love," "Of Friendship," "Of Followers and Friends," in *Essays*
PASCAL. *Discours sur les passions de l'amour*
HUME. *A Treatise of Human Nature*, BK II, PART II
A. SMITH. *The Theory of Moral Sentiments*
ROUSSEAU. *Eloisa* (*La nouvelle Héloïse*)
GOETHE. *Sorrows of Young Werther*
——. *Elective Affinities*
TOLSTOY. *The Law of Love and the Law of Violence*
——. *Anna Karenina*
——. *On Life*
FREUD. *Three Contributions to the Theory of Sex*
——. *"Civilized" Sexual Morality and Modern Nervousness*
——. *Contributions to the Psychology of Love*

II.

CATULLUS. *The Poems*
CICERO. *Laelius de Amicitia* (*Of Friendship*)
OVID. *Amores*
——. *The Art of Love*
Amis and Amilon
Song of Roland
PETRUS ALPHONSI. *Disciplina Clericalis*, FABLES I-II (*Concerning the Complete Friend*)
BERNARD OF CLAIRVAUX. *On the Love of God*, CH 7
ABAILARD. *Letters*
WILLIAM OF SAINT-THIERRY. *De Natura et Dignitate Amoris*
Aucassin and Nicolette
CHRÉTIEN DE TROYES. *Arthurian Romances*
ANDRÉ LE CHAPELAIN. *The Art of Courtly Love*
Tristan and Iseult

The Romance of the Rose
FRANCIS OF ASSISI. *The Little Flowers of St. Francis of Assisi*, CH 21-22
PETRARCH. *Sonnets*
——. *The Triumph of Love*
BOCCACCIO. *Il Filocolo*
——. *Decameron*
Sir Gawain and the Green Knight
GOWER. *Confessio Amantis*
ALBO. *The Book of Principles* (*Sefer ha-Ikkarim*), BK III, CH 35
THOMAS À KEMPIS. *The Imitation of Christ*, BK II; BK III, CH 5-10
VILLON. *The Debate of the Heart and Body of Villon*
Valentine and Orson
G. PICO DELLA MIRANDOLA. *A Platonick Discourse upon Love*
EBREO. *The Philosophy of Love*
ARIOSTO. *Orlando Furioso*
CASTIGLIONE. *The Book of the Courtier*
MICHELANGELO. *Sonnets*
R. EDWARDS. *Damon and Pithias*
P. SIDNEY. *Astrophel and Stella*
JOHN OF THE CROSS. *The Living Flame of Love*
DONNE. *Songs and Sonnets*
SPENSER. *The Faerie Queene*, BK IV
——. *Epithalamion*
——. *An Hymne of Heavenly Love*
SUÁREZ. *Disputationes Metaphysicae*, XXX (16), XLVII (14)
BURTON. *The Anatomy of Melancholy*, PART III, SECT I-III
TIRSO DE MOLINA. *The Love Rogue*
CORNEILLE. *La Place Royale*
CAREW. *A Rapture*
CRASHAW. *The Flaming Heart*
MARVELL. *To His Coy Mistress*
J. TAYLOR. "The Marriage-Ring," in *Twenty-Five Sermons*
——. *A Discourse of the Nature, Offices and Measures of Friendship*
MOLIÈRE. *Le misanthrope* (*The Man-Hater*)
MALEBRANCHE. *De la recherche de la vérité*, BK IV, CH 5-13
RACINE. *Andromaque*
——. *Phèdre*
LA FAYETTE. *The Princess of Cleves*
DRYDEN. *All for Love*
CONGREVE. *The Way of the World*

RICHARDSON. *Pamela*

HURD. *Letters on Chivalry and Romance*

VOLTAIRE. "Charity," "Friendship," "Love," "Love of God," "Love (Socratic Love)," in *A Philosophical Dictionary*

F. SCHLEGEL. *Lucinde*

SCHLEIERMACHER. *Soliloquies*

SCHOPENHAUER. *The World as Will and Idea*, VOL III, SUP, CH 44

BYRON. *Don Juan*

MANZONI. *The Betrothed*

STENDHAL. *On Love*

——. *The Red and the Black*

——. *The Charterhouse of Parma*

EMERSON. "Love," in *Essays*, I

BALZAC. *At the Sign of the Cat and Racket*

——. *Cousin Bette*

C. BRONTË. *Jane Eyre*

E. J. BRONTË. *Wuthering Heights*

KIERKEGAARD. *Either/Or*

——. *Stages on Life's Way*

——. *Works of Love*

E. B. BROWNING. *Sonnets from the Portuguese*

HAWTHORNE. *The Blithedale Romance*

FLAUBERT. *Madame Bovary*

MICHELET. *L'amour*

TURGENEV. *Liza*

MEREDITH. *Modern Love*

E. HARTMANN. *Philosophy of the Unconscious*, (C) XIII (3)

PATMORE. *Mystical Poems of Nuptial Love*

H. SIDGWICK. *The Methods of Ethics*, BK I, CH 7; BK III, CH 4

ROSSETTI. *The House of Life*

L. STEPHEN. *The Science of Ethics*

STEVENSON. *Virginibus Puerisque*

C. S. PEIRCE. *Collected Papers*, VOL VI, par 287–317

FRAZER. *The Golden Bough*, PART I, CH 11–12

CHEKHOV. *The Sea-Gull*

ROSTAND. *Cyrano de Bergerac*

BRADLEY. *Ethical Studies*, VII

——. *Aphorisms*

——. *Collected Essays*, VOL I (3)

GOURMONT. *The Natural Philosophy of Love*

SHAW. *Man and Superman*

SANTAYANA. *Interpretations of Poetry and Religion*, CH 5

——. *Reason in Society*, CH I, 7

GIDE. *Strait Is the Gate*

SYNGE. *Deirdre of the Sorrows*

ELLIS. *Studies in the Psychology of Sex*

J. R. HARRIS. *Boanerges*

SCHELER. *Wesen und Formen der Sympathie*

D. H. LAWRENCE. *Women in Love*

NYGREN. *Agape and Eros*

PROUST. *Remembrance of Things Past*

C. S. LEWIS. *The Allegory of Love*

ROUGEMONT. *Love in the Western World*

XIRAU. *Amor y mundo*

D'ARCY. *The Mind and Heart of Love*